The **R&A**

# GOLFER'S HANDBOOK 2014

EDITOR RENTON LAIDLAW

The R&A is golf's world rules and developement body and organiser of The Open Championship. It operates with the concent of more than 130 national and international, amateur and professional organisations, from over 120 countries and on behalf of an estimated 30 million golfers in Europe, Africa, Asia-Pacific and The Americas (outside the USA and Mexico). The United States Golf Association (USGA) is the game's governing body in the United States and Mexico.

hamlyn

An Hachette UK Company
www.hachette.co.uk

The R&A Golfer's Handbook first published 1899

This edition published 2014 by Hamlyn, a division of

Octopus Publishing Group Ltd
Endeavour House
189 Shaftesbury Avenue
London
WC2H 8JY
www.octopusbooks.co.uk

The right of Renton Laidlaw to be identified as the
editor of this work has been asserted by him in accordance
with the Copyright, Designs and Patents Act 1988.

ISBN: 978-0-600-62910-8

A CIP catalogue record for this book is available from the
British Library

10 9 8 7 6 5 4 3 2 1

**Correspondence**
Letters on editorial matters should be addressed to:
The Editor, The R&A Golfer's Handbook, Octopus Publishing Group, Endeavour House,
Shaftesbury Avenue, London WC2H 8JY.

**Note**
Whilst every care has been taken in compiling the information contained in this book, the
Publishers, Editor and Sponsors accept no responsibility for any errors or ommissions.

Designed and typeset by Penrose Typography, Maidstone, Kent

Printed and bound in the UK by William Clowes

# Contents

# Australian businessman Sandy Dawson proud to be Captain of The Royal and Ancient Golf Club

© GSR Photographic

Sandy Dawson, who has taken over from Frenchman Pierre Bechmann as Captain of The Royal and Ancient Golf Club of St Andrews, is only the second Captain in the history of the club, founded in 1754, to come from Australia. Viscount Bruce of Melbourne served in that capacity in 1954.

As Captain, Mr Dawson will represent the R&A. and support its work in encouraging golf around the world. In his ambassadorial role he will attend all R&A Championships and International Matches throughout his year of office.

Born in 1943, Mr Dawson, a former Australian Universities' champion, is a member of the Royal Sydney Golf Club where he was captain from 1988 to 1993. He has been Club President since 2010 and he currently plays off 4.

A former managing director and CEO of Arnott's, one of the largest food companies in the Asia-Pacific Region, Mr Dawson was also chairman of United Distillers (Australia) and a director of Allied Mills, Goodman Fielder and the Darling Harbour Authority.

Married to Jane, he has three children and nine grandchildren and has been a member of The Royal and Ancient Golf Club of St Andrews since 1974.

# Updating the Rules to cope with modern TV technology

## Peter Dawson on the importance of fairness in golf

One of the ongoing issues in the modern game which will continue to be addressed going forward is the subject of television evidence at the top level of competition. Golf is a rare beast in as much as it's the only sport where the audience watching at home on TV could influence the outcome of an event by reporting a Rules violation.

It is sometimes the case that observations which couldn't be made with the naked eye can now be detected by high definition cameras showing replays in hyper slow motion. Let's be clear, the Rules of Golf never contemplated this kind of scrutiny.

That's why, at the start of 2014, we clarified the impact of TV evidence on the ball at rest being moved through the introduction of new Decision 18/4. This concerns an example where a player observes a slight motion of the ball but believes it has only oscillated and not left its original position. The player plays the ball as it lies. Later, if TV evidence shows the ball did move, but the movement was only discernible through the use of sophisticated technology, there is no penalty. However, if the movement was evident to the naked eye, then a penalty would apply for causing the ball to move and failing to replace it as required by the Rules. This new Decision clarifies that the Definition of 'moved' does not contemplate movements of the ball that can only be seen through the use of high definition TV.

It is doubtful whether this is the last word on the subject of television evidence and our Rules of Golf Committee at The R&A is busy weighing up an appropriate response to the wider issue. It can be argued the highest profile golfers are the ones most disadvantaged by the glare of the cameras simply because they are on TV more often. Of course, that profile works both ways because the élite tend to be followed by large crowds, can enjoy favourable bounces off spectators and rarely lose a ball.

In my view, the harshest penalty arose when a player signed for a score and TV evidence later brought to light a breach, which he had no way of knowing, and which led to disqualification. Thankfully, that outcome was changed two years ago (through the introduction of Decision 33–7/4.5): a player can still be penalised after the player has signed the card but no longer must be disqualified.

I feel we need to ensure there's a balance drawn between what actually happened and what a player could reasonably expect to know had happened. The range of options regarding how to proceed is broad. It stretches from, on the one hand, not allowing TV evidence at all, or, on the other, to simply go with the facts as they are subsequently presented. The answer probably lies somewhere in between those positions.

R&A Chief Executive Peter Dawson.

Still on the Rules, it was important to deal with the issue of anchoring. While the process wasn't exactly straightforward, it was important to know that various professional tours will implement the ban on anchoring from January 1, 2016 and the worldwide game will continue to be played under the same Rules. Inevitably, there was a debate over what was a polarising issue, especially in the USA. What was critical, though, was that the game of golf remained on an even keel.

Otherwise, we continue to monitor the hitting distance on tour where I believe we have the issue well surrounded. Interestingly, in 2013, driving distances were down. On the PGA Tour last year the average distance of the player who drove furthest, Luke List, was 306.3 yards. This was a drop from Bubba Watson's leading average of 315.5 yards in 2012. And the falls in distance were not just recorded among the biggest hitters. The golfer who finished 100th on the driving distance list in 2013 averaged 287.1 yards compared to 289.4 in 2012.

Perhaps one development we need to keep a watchful eye on is the length of the driver shaft. The average length of many new driver shafts is now 46 inches and the maximum is 48. I think if people began to master those two extra inches we would want to have a close look at the impact on clubhead speed and distance struck.

As Chief Executive of The R&A, I'm conscious of treading a fine line between sound commercial

practice and running a golf organisation. Firstly, I make no apology for The R&A being a more business-like organisation today than it once was. We use the money we make for the benefit of the game of golf, not for the pockets of shareholders. Having said that, you can go too far in a commercial sense and we still want to present our championships in as clean a manner as possible. Right now, the balance is about right. If we didn't generate the income, we couldn't carry out much of the good work we do and it would be difficult to uphold many of our principles.

There was a school of thought that ticket prices had an adverse impact on attendances at last year's staging of The Open at Muirfield. We commissioned a considerable amount of research into this subject and if you compare The Open with other sporting events of a similar stature, there's no doubt our ticket prices are where they should be. Except for the Ryder Cup, compared to other golf events in

## The R&A appoint new Far East ambassador

Liang Wen-Chong has been appointed an R&A Working for Golf ambassador with the role of fostering the game in China and making those who play the game more conversant with the Rules. He's seen here with Degang Wan, the Chinese Consul in Edinburgh, The R&A's David Rickman, Executive Director – Rules and Equipment Standards (left) and Duncan Weir, Executive Director – Working for Golf. Padraig Harrington and Suzann Pettersen are also ambassadors.

the UK, they are a good deal more expensive, but The Open is the only one which features all of the world's top male players.

Perhaps the tendency for spectators to spend a longer period at The Open has reduced, at least in part because of the spiralling cost of accommodation. In the end, crowd figures were slightly disappointing at Muirfield and we are aware of the views on ticket prices. It's true we also stopped the concession for seniors, in line with other top sporting events. We are at Hoylake this summer and the previous occasion we were there in 2006, for the first time since 1967, both the weather and the crowds were exceptional. So, let's see how all of that settles down.

In terms of fine-tuning the courses that stage The Open, we've put enhancements in place at all of them to ensure the test today remains relevant. We want to do the minimum required to accomplish that goal without affecting the amateur golfer's experience of these great links. On the Old Course, the issue we examined was precision of approach play where you could miss greens and still have a very flat putt. So there's been some rippling and shading on that count. The big change was on the 11th green which will give us more left-hand pin positions for The Open in 2015. This prompted a 'how dare you' response from some when the truth is that the Old Course is constantly changing. We found an aerial photograph taken by the RAF of the golf course in the 1940s and the changes between then and now are remarkable.

## Digital revolution

Certainly, as far as the staging of the championship at Muirfield was concerned, the introduction of a wireless mesh to enable spectators to access digital content was revolutionary. For the first time in the grandstands and the tented villages, spectators with smartphones enjoyed the opportunity to see what was happening elsewhere on the course as well as savouring the live experience. Although this innovation went largely unreported, it was a significant upgrade of the golf viewing experience.

We were also very pleased at Muirfield to present a fast running links for the first time in a while. The way Phil Mickelson came through over the back nine on Sunday to lift The Claret Jug was stunning. In the end Phil won quite easily, though there was plenty of drama along the way.

Phil and Rory McIlroy, of course, are the only golfers of late to have won more than one major championship. It could be argued going into this year's championships that the fields are now so deep almost anyone could win. In 2014, far more golfers are capable of winning than in, say, the era dominated by Jack Nicklaus. The players are coached more effectively, they are more athletic and their equipment is better fitted. On top of all that, the rank and file work harder. The golfer ranked 50th in the world rolls up his sleeves further today than his predecessors.

## 19 different winners

But is it a good thing or bad for the game when the jam is spread around so evenly? Up to and including the US PGA won by Jason Dufner in 2013, the most recent 21 mens major titles were won by 19 golfers. Compare this scenario to the Grand Slam tournaments in tennis, where the contrast could hardly be starker – Rafael Nadal with eight wins, Novak Djokovic with five, Roger Federer with five and Andy Murray with two left room only for Juan Martin del Potro as the sole winner of a single élite title during this same five year stretch.

For golf, there are elements of both good and bad attached to this pattern. It's positive that many people have a chance to win but perhaps less so when it's harder for stars to emerge more consistently than they do. Do I think it would be good for the narrative of golf if around half-a-dozen or so golfers won more often? Yes, I do believe that.

All of which makes Tiger Woods' dominance of the game between 1999 and 2008, when he won 14 major titles, the more truly astonishing. Perhaps only now do we start to appreciate the scale of what Tiger accomplished in a sport which is tougher to dominate – each week it pits you against 155 rivals – than any other.

Finally, I felt one of the most important actions undertaken by The R&A in 2013 was the appointment of Liang Wen-Chong as a Working for Golf Ambassador with a remit to support the development of the game and a greater understanding of the Rules in China. The first Chinese golfer to tee up in The Open, he will help us to ensure the expansion of the game in Asia proceeds in tandem with an appreciation for the game's Rules, etiquette and values.

# Men's Amateur Champions 2013

Garrick Porteous (ENG)
Amateur Champion

Ashley Chesters (ENG)
European Amateur Champion

Chang-woo Lee (KOR)
Asia–Pacific Amateur Champion

Matt Fitzpatrick (ENG)
United States Amateur Champion

# Women's Amateur Champions 2013

© LGU

Georgia Hall (ENG)
British Amateur Champion

© EGA

Emily Kristine Pedersen (DEN)
European Amateur Champion

© USGA

Emma Talley (USA)
United States Amateur Champion

# America wins back the Walker Cup

*America's Walker Cup team putted better than the Great Britain and Ireland side and scored a decisive win to avenge their defeat two years earlier.*

# Europe's historic Solheim Cup victory

*Europe's Solheim Cup side captained by Liselotte Neumann blew away their American opposition to win for the first time on US soil.*

# Swede Henrik Stenson's half year fireworks guarantee him top spot

## Renton Laidlaw chooses 12 who shone brilliantly in 2013

Half-way through last year, not long after The Open Championship at Muirfield, I was already contemplating that my Golfer of the Year could be Phil Mickelson.

Putting aside all the headline-making nonsense of whether an Open should or should not be played at an all-male club to concentrate on what really mattered – the golf – Mickelson produced an awesome performance that swept an annoying monkey off his back

He proved that after 19 fruitless attempts to win the Claret Jug he had broken the code. He had learned how to play links golf winning the Scottish Open at Castle Stuart and then gloriously The Open.

And then along came Henrik Stenson who had chased Mickelson home both weeks and went on to top the money lists on both sides of the Atlantic. Truly majestic.

If you were happy for Mickelson winning a major he never thought he could, you were delighted for Stenson who, in winning the FedEx Cup and the Race to Dubai, recouped all he had lost in an unhappy investment with convicted fraudster Allen Stanford.

Stenson rose Lazarus-like from a deep slump, from 230th in the World Rankings into the top three in a wondrous last five months of the year with golf of such high quality that it resembled Tiger Woods when he was at his most impressive several years ago.

Stenson's driving (mostly with a strong 3-wood) was long and straight; his short game immaculate and he holed out with a calmness and precision that was far removed from the more volatile Stenson of a few years ago.

The Swede was so focussed, so disciplined, so confident that he deservedly earns my Player of the Year award from Mickelson. There is much to admire about the friendly always approachable Swede and his total professionalism.

Like Mickelson he is a wonderful ambassador for the game as is Justin Rose, the slim Englishman who played some of his best, most controlled golf at Merion to win the US Open and in the process left Mickelson to ponder just what he has to do to win his own national title – he has been a gut-wrenching second six times.

*Henrik Stenson won the FedEx Cup and topped the money list in America. He also won the Race to Dubai and the DP World Championship on the European Tour.*

© Getty Images

The dignified way Rose handled his first major success showed how well he had been taught by his late father. He was a polite but determined competitor on the course and a perfect gentleman off it. He completed his American triumph with a superbly struck Hogan-like long iron to the last green. It was a fitting climax.

Earlier in the year, stylish Adam Scott laid to rest the disappointment of letting a four shot lead with four to play slip to lose the 2012 Open to Ernie Els with an historic and far from easy victory at Augusta.

Scott won in a play-off against former winner Angel Cabrera. It was an emotional moment since so many of his fellow Australians (notably Greg Norman) had failed to earn a Green Jacket and a place in the Champions' Locker room when in a position to do so

Scott was a hero when he played in and won the Australian Masters later in the year. Golf fans showed their appreciation by wearing something green on the second day as a tribute to his achievement.

We all cope with pressure in different ways. American Jason Dufner's *modus operandi* is to remain Faldo-like in the zone limiting any sign of emotion until the job is done. And what a job he made of winning the US PGA Championship – an event he had spectacularly thrown away just two years earlier. He produced some of the best golf of his life while being pressured by that man Stenson.

*Caroline Hedwall from Sweden made history when becoming the first player from either side to score five points out of five in the Solheim Cup ... and she holed the winning putt.*

Last year there were three first time major title-holders but my roll of honour includes one multi-major winner whom we have come to expect in the top half dozen – Tiger Woods. Maybe he is not so fearsome a competitor as he once was, maybe he will not equal or pass Jack Nicklaus' major tally but he still knows how to win.

He won five titles on the PGA Tour and earned for himself the Tour's Player of the Year award for a remarkable 11th time. He still draws the crowds wherever he is playing around the world. His presence at a tournament is always electric.

I have not yet mentioned the stars of the women's scene but two golfers in particular are stand-outs – record-equalling Inbee Park, who won the first three majors of the year in 2013, and Lydia Ko, who retained her No 1 spot in amateur golf for a third year before turning pro.

Park's performance in matching Babe Zaharias' 1950 record (when there were only three majors) was amazing. She won the Kraft Nabisco, the Wegman's LPGA in a play-off with Catriona Matthew and the US Women's Open for a second time before she came to St Andrews and, under immense pressure and emotional tiredness, lost her swing and her incredible putting touch.

A no-nonsense competitor who just gets on with the job, Inbee loves the game and it will be interesting to see how she fares this year when another talented young Korean, Lydia Ko, joins her on Tour.

Fifteen-year-old Ko has been given permission to join the Tour ahead of the age regulations –

something that an under-age Inbee was refused when she asked for the same concession a few years ago. To turn down Ko would have been churlish since she had not only won the Canadian Open on the LPGA Tour in 2012 but successfully defended it last year.

At the Evian Masters, Ko was second to another of my top 12 selections, Norway's Suzann Pettersen. That event, although now considered a major, was reduced to 54-holes so who knows what might have happened if there had been a final day. There was delight, however, that the Scandinavian, one of The R&A's Working for Golf ambassadors, won another major after a gap of five years.

Another lady making my top 12 is the incredibly-courageous Stacy Lewis who spent eight years in a back brace suffering from scoliosis. She won the Ricoh Women's British Open at St Andrews – fittingly perhaps for someone who has a deep love affair with the Old Course.

She won in style finishing with two birdies. At the 17th she drilled a 5-iron to four feet and holed the putt and after driving into the Valley of Sin she chipped and putted from 25 feet to win by two.

Before leaving the women I must include Caroline Hedwall of Sweden who became the first player, European or American, to score five points out of five in the Solheim Cup. The Europeans were undoubtedly the team of the year as all of them – from "baby" Charley Hull to the most experienced Catriona Matthew – combined brilliantly under the captaincy of Liselotte Neumann to shock the maybe over-confident home side to score a first win on US soil.

In amateur golf, England's Matthew Fitzpatrick had a wonderful run in mid summer. He was leading amateur in The Open, runner up in the English Amateur Championship and then became the first English winner for over 100 years of the US Amateur where, for the first time in history, no Americans made it through to the last four.

At the famous Country Club at Brookline where Francis Ouimet famously beat Ted Ray and Harry Vardon in the 1912 US Open, Fitzpatrick even had his young brother as his caddie.

Which leaves me with just one more to complete my dozen and I have chosen 20-year-old Jordan Spieth who began his rookie year in 810th spot in the World Rankings and ended up in the top 25 having won one event, finishing second three times in other tournaments, amassing $3.9 million in prize-money and making his début in the Presidents Cup. You could not make it up.

Spieth pipped Peter Uihlein, Europe's Sir Henry Cotton Rookie of the Year, for 12th spot. Uihlein finished the season after one win, two seconds and five more top 10's.

# A year of drama, glory and four great winners in men's majors

## James Corrigan on Scott, Rose, Mickelson and Dufner

Has any golfing season witnessed so many rubicons being crossed on the pathway to major glory? If 2013 reminded us of one truth in this ancient game it was that fulfillment is worth the wait.

Three of the four winners were first-timers and, of course, the career breakthrough always comes replete with its back story of a childhood fantasy. But there was something about the tales of this quartet which transcended the usual "dream comes true" narrative. And perhaps the man winning his fifth major best summed up these lessons of perseverance shining through.

At Muirfield, Phil Mickelson became just the 15th golfer to have won at least three of the four professional majors. In truth, few expected the hat-trick to arrive in Scotland. On his 20th effort, the 42-year-old finally cracked the links code after being bemused by its intricacies for so long.

And because of his history with seaside golf and because of what this meant to his standing in the game – as he joined Severiano Ballesteros and Byron Nelson on the major roll call with five – it seemed perfectly legitimate to ask if The Open has ever witnessed a better final back nine than Mickelson's 32. The left-hander birdied four of the last six and on that brutal stretch this was frankly ridiculous.

While everyone else had been cowed into caution by Muirfield's glorious menace, the game's gunslinger took it on – and stood proudly, in every sense of the expression. Having also won at Castle Stuart the week before, Mickelson became the first to complete the Scottish Open–Open double. What made his performance seem all the more remarkable was that the previous month he had watched yet another US Open slip from his grasp as he was overhauled by Justin Rose. It was his sixth runner-up placing in his national championship and it clearly hurt.

Indeed, his wife Amy outlined how miserable he was in the wake of Merion. "He couldn't get out of bed for two days," she said. But showing the same determination which saw him learn to cope with a debilitating arthritic condition, Mickelson looked forwards and set his sights on amending his Open void.

"You have to be resilient in this game, and you have to use the setbacks as a motivation rather than let them beat you," Mickelson said. "You have to come back strong, and these last couple of weeks, I've played some of the best golf of my career." Not to mention the gutsiest.

Adam Scott became the first Australian to win the Masters Tournament Green Jacket after a play-off against former winner Angel Cabrera.

"Phil's done that his whole career," said his coach, Butch Harmon. "He just gets up off the mat time and time again. It's funny, he didn't really believe he could win an Open. But I told him he's the most creative player I've ever seen and because of the nature of links golf and the vision it requires, there was no reason why he shouldn't. He embraced links golf and took it to heart."

For Mickelson's ever-swelling fan club all roads lead to the US Open at Pinehurst next June to see if he can become only the sixth player to win the career Grand Slam. "Hopefully that will happen," Amy said. "I think it will."

Rose is far too nice a chap to wish sporting heartbreak on anyone, particularly a fellow pro of such generosity as Mickelson, who famously applauded the Englishman as he rolled in putt after putt to win a critical point in the Sunday singles at the 2012 Ryder Cup. Yet Rose will be intent on denying Mickelson at the US Open again – and anyone else who intends to take his title. Put simply, Rose has seen too much in his already fabled career to give up the garlands meekly.

© Getty Images

*Jason Dufner made no mistake this time when winning the US PGA Championship title two years after having let his lead slip in the same event and losing to Keegan Bradley in a play-off.*

It has long been entered in golf's folklore about the skinny 17-year-old amateur who pitched in on the 18th at Birkdale to finish fourth in the 1998 Open. Then he turned pro and proceeded to miss his fist 21 cuts. Fast forward 15 years and there Rose was, a man, winning at Merion. It was a victory Rose dedicated to his father, Ken, who died from leukaemia in 2002. There was also a tribute to Adam Scott, the friend who reaffirmed that golf always presents its heroes another chance.

Scott's redemption was so much more than personal despite his blow-out in The Open at Lytham nine months before when he had been four ahead with four to play. It says much about what it meant to his country that in his moment of glory Scott was minded to shout: "C'mon Aussie".

As he stretched his arms out wide, Scott's playing partner and countryman Marc Leishman cele-

brated with as much gusto as if he had won and not finished fourth. Jason Day was also leaping up and down, despite leading with three to go and eventually coming third. But then, this was the title they desired above all others. Australians had won each of the other majors, but had watched eight of their men finish runner-up at Augusta.

Greg Norman is Georgia's most famous bridesmaid, having three times filled that damnable position, most notoriously when losing a six-shot lead to Nick Faldo in 1996. The sports folk Down Under had long since blamed the fates. Norman had always taken his Augusta agony with class, but on that Sunday night, as he watched the finale in his Florida living room, it became too much.

Scott had just holed his 20-footer for birdie on the final hole of regulation play when that remarkable Argentinian Angel Cabrera struck his incredible approach to three feet to force the play-off. "When Angel played that shot, I went to my knees," Norman said. "My son almost had to pick me up. I sent a text out to hundreds of people saying, 'No! The golfing gods can't be that mean to Australia'."

## Magnificent job

And so embarked the sudden-death shoot-out which was hailed as "the best Masters play-off in history". After Cabrera came within centimetres of chipping in on the first extra hole – making Norman's knees hit Axminster again – Scott summoned the wherewithal to birdie the next and so ignite a million barbies. "C'mon Aussie", indeed.

"That shows you the amount of emotion he had within. Adam knew he had a huge responsibility, not just to himself, but to his family and his country," Norman said. "He did a magnificent job of regrouping in a very short time. That's the beauty of golf. It's such a passive game for five hours, and then all of a sudden, it's like a volcano erupting."

There was no danger of Dufner erupting when he won the US PGA at Oak Hill. The American happens to be the most laidback sportsman in existence. But beneath that ultra-calm exterior a heart beat so quickly as he made a mockery of all those taunts which greeted his play-off loss to Keegan Bradley in the same major two years before. Dufner, a supposed journeyman, had been five clear with four holes remaining, before Bradley, the rookie, struck back. "He'll never win," they said.

Never say never, in golf. Adam and Australia didn't, neither did Justin, Phil or Jason. When the golfing gets tough, the tough get golfing.

# Mickelson learns how to putt Open Championship greens

John Huggan salutes success at last for left-hander Phil

It was, alongside his famous frustration at the sharp end of his own national championship – six US Open runner-up finishes and counting – something of a mystery. Why did Phil Mickelson, clearly the second-best American golfer of the Tiger Woods generation, have such a poor record in the world's oldest and most important championship?

"Poor," in fact, hardly does justice to Mickelson's long history of futility in the cradle of the game that has been his working life.

When he arrived at Muirfield for what would be his nineteenth Open Championship, golf's greatest-ever left-hander could "boast" only two top-three finishes in his previous 19 visits to British shores. On four occasions he had missed the halfway cut; eight times he had ended up 30th or lower. So what was it about golf by the seaside that so befuddled this obviously gifted shot-maker?

Talking just after his opening round in the Scottish Open at Castle Stuart – an event he would go on to win – in the week prior to the 142nd Open, Mickelson admitted to being "surprised and unfulfilled" by his perplexing paucity of success on UK soil. But, tellingly, he also identified the solution to his perennial woes. "For the last eight or nine years, I haven't had a problem getting the ball on the ground and playing the course effectively," he continued. "Where I have struggled is on the greens; I have not putted well. Actually, for the last four or five years, I haven't putted well at all, certainly not as well as I have this year. On fescue greens the ball will wobble if you don't put a pure strike on it. But if you roll it great it will hold its line and you can make them. I think I have that worked out; that is evident here at Castle Stuart. I have putted well on these fescue greens."

Those words, of course, were to prove more than prophetic. Seven days after claiming his first regular European Tour title in the picturesque Scottish Highlands, Mickelson showed that the spectacular touch and artistry he displayed en route to beating South African Branden Grace in a sudden-death play-off had not deserted him. Indeed, his play over Sunday's back nine was something of a tour de force.

Mickelson and his caddie Jim "Bones" McKay are such a good friends that he is like a member of the family.

While everyone else in contention struggled mightily in the deteriorating conditions, the 43-year-old Californian made four birdies in the last six holes to win by three shots from Sweden's Henrik Stenson. It was a magnificent example of controlled and intelligent play on a hard and fast-running course, rounded off by one last birdie – courtesy of a perfectly-weighted 15-foot putt – on Muirfield's famously elusive 18th green.

"I felt a tremendous satisfaction for Phil," says his swing coach, Butch Harmon, "because I knew The Open was the one event he never thought he had the game to win. I knew he did and I kept harping on at him to do it. And to do it the way he did; to go out and dominate and take the tournament away from everybody was just incredible."

That it was. But it was also, despite Mickelson's insistence that the previous problem was poor putting, a victory over his naturally attacking instincts. Until recently, the San Diego native was loyal and true to his inherently risk-taking character, both on and off the course.

"I tend to be aggressive in investments," he explains. "I like to play hard. When Amy and I go on trips or spend time with the kids, we do just that. We love to go skiing. And we were just in Montana, where we went white water rafting. I've tried archery and trap shooting. I've done a bungee-jump. But I think I'll leave sky diving until my kids are out of college. So yes, I'd say my approach to life pretty closely mirrors my attitude on the course. I enjoy life and I love new challenges."

*Phil Mickelson finally won The Open at Muirfield at his 19th attempt. The only surprise was it had taken him so long to win it.*

© Getty Images

Such an approach might be fine on a course like Augusta National – where Mickelson has won the Masters three times – but when the sea breeze is blowing and the turf is unpredictable and bouncy such a philosophy is likely to lead to trouble more than triumph.

Harmon tells a story that hints strongly at the real reason why his star pupil took so long to "figure out" links golf. Warming up before a tournament round and employing the easy, controlled swing he uses when hitting six-irons, the now five-time major champion was "killing" the ball with his driver.

"It was beautiful to watch," says Harmon. At the end of the session and as his charge left to tee-up alongside the long-hitting Dustin Johnson, Harmon

told Mickelson not to get involved in a driving contest with his playing partner. "Keep using that same swing," he said. "Aw Butch," came the reply. "I think we both know that isn't going to happen."

Mickelson's long-standing caddie, Jim "Bones" McKay, is another who has long tried to rein in his adventure-seeking boss. Once a year, McKay is allowed what the pair call a "veto" where the caddie gets to choose the next shot. Once, in New Orleans, Mickelson drove through a fairway and wanted to skip the next shot off the water and onto the green. Bones vetoed that one. Which was a good decision; having laid-up short of the pond, Mickelson made par.

On the other hand, during the 2002 Open at Muirfield, Mickelson was in a bunker left of the 14th fairway. The lie was really awkward and he was on his knees with a 6-iron in his hands. Bones wanted to veto but was told it was "only good in the United States." In the end, Mickelson had to make a 15-foot putt for double bogey. These are tales Mickelson does not deny – "I should listen to Bones more than I do" – for he has a history of taking his own sweet time to arrive at decisions those around him have long advocated.

## No comparison

Sometimes he doesn't even listen to himself. As far back as 2004, Mickelson was asked about his rivalry with the 14-time major champion, Woods. "The reality is, even if I play at the top of my game for the rest of my career and achieve all my goals – let's say win 50 tournaments and ten majors – I still won't get to where Tiger is now," he said. "So I won't compare myself with him. It makes no sense."

Nor did his record in The Open. Now, however, all is clear, much to Mickelson's delight. In the days following his victory at Muirfield, Mickelson bombarded Harmon with a series of text messages. All had the same playful theme: "I don't know if you heard, but I just won the (British) Open." Clearly, the fifth major win of his already impressive career had an unprecedented effect on the boy who was born to play golf.

"When I was a kid, I never wanted to leave the course," says Mickelson. Which is true. On his first-ever 18-hole round with his father, the young Phil refused to play the last hole, "because then everything will be over."

And now, almost four decades later, they might be just getting started.

*Mickelson only had one thing on his mind when he holed the winning putt – the Claret Jug.*

# Honorary Royal and Ancient Membership
## for Sir Michael Bonallack

© The R&A

Sir Michael Bonallack, OBE, former Captain and Secretary of the Royal and Ancient Golf Club of St Andrews, has become the 16th Honorary Member of the Club.

Frenchman Pierre Bechmann, the 2012–2013 Captain of the Club, presided over the unveiling of a specially commissioned portrait of Sir Michael which now hangs in the clubhouse's Big Room.

"I am extremely proud to be named an Honorary Member. I feel priviledged to have been involved with the Club for so much of my life. The Club and St Andrews are incredibly dear to me and I thank all the Past Captains and members for their support and friendship over the years. It has been an honour to serve the Club."

Born in 1934, Sir Michael had a distinguished playing career winning the Amateur Championship five times, the English Amateur title five times and the English Amateur Stroke Play title four times.

He played in nine Walker Cups and was Captain of the GB&I team on two occasions. He was twice leading amateur in The Open. A member of the Royal and Ancient Golf Club since 1960, he was appointed Secretary in 1983 in succession to the late Keith Mackenzie. He was knighted in 1998, a year before he retired after 16 years as Secretary. He was Captain of the Club in 1999–2000.

The other honorary members are His Royal Highness The Duke of Edinburgh, His Royal Highness The Duke of York, His Royal Highness The Duke of Kent, the Honourable George W H Bush, former Open Champions Kel Nagle and Peter Thomson, CBE, Jack Nicklaus, Arnold Palmer and Gary Player, Tom Watson, Lee Trevino, Roberto de Vicenzo and Tony Jacklin, CBE, along with John Jacobs, OBE, and Peter Alliss.

# Stenson shows consistent streak of a champion – now for a major

## Renton Laidlaw applauds the record breaking Swede

Few would have begrudged the likeable Swedish golfer Henrik Stenson his success in 2013. Few would have dreamed that his bounce back from languishing outside the top 200 in the world would be so dramatic that he is challenging for Tiger's No 1 spot.

The two-time Ryder Cup star, who lost a reputed seven million sum when he signed up with and invested a large slice of his earnings with Sir Allen Stanford, who is serving a 100 year jail sentence for master-minding a fraudulent Ponzi scheme, would bounce back so effectively, so Tiger-like in his prime. This really was a case of that old cliché "when the going gets tough the tough get going" proving 100 per cent accurate in Stenson's case.

After becoming the first man to win the highly complicated end of season points gathering FedEx Cup on the PGA Tour and finishing No 1 on the European Tour's Race to Dubai, Stenson's next piece of golfing magic must be to win a major. His CV demands it.

He has the game. He has the determination. He has the temperament to do so. Finishing a creditable runner-up to Phil Mickelson at The Open at Muirfield and third in the US PGA Championship to Jason Dufner this year was further evidence of what he is capable of. He had earlier finished tied third in the 2008 Open and fourth in the US PGA in the same year. He drives the ball long – very long – and straight (with a 3-wood) and around the greens and on them he displays a delicate touch.

Amazingly, in a 12 tournament run that began in Scotland in July and ended in Dubai, he averaged earnings of one million pounds per event.

He yearns to be the first Swedish man to win a major. Would you bet against him achieving that in the next year or so? I don't think so. This Swede is in a different class on and off the course … and, yes, good guys do sometimes win.

Luke Donald, a former No 1 on both sides of the Atlantic, enthused that the Swede resembled Tiger in his peak.

"Henrik's ball striking has been as good as I have ever seen from anyone, probably as good as Tiger in his prime. It's not as if he is draining putts from everywhere."

Stenson's caddie concurred and described the Swede's 5-iron from 173 yards to a foot on the 12th at Jumeirah as the best iron shot he had ever seen.

© The R&A

*English caddie Gareth Lord shared in Henrik Stenson success last year … and now drives a Ferrari.*

Whether he is nervous or not is, in a way, immaterial.

The fact is he never shows it now although there were times in the past when he could "boil over"! When he hit his 3-wood second to tap in distance at the last to win the Race to Dubai and the DP World title he wandered up the imaginatively designed (by Greg Norman) final hole with the relaxed air of a holidaymaker taking a leisurely stroll in the evening air before dinner.

Of course it helped that he had blitzed the field and had a five shot lead (later to become a six shot winning margin) over Ian Poulter – a near neighbour in Lake Nona as was another challenger, US Open Champion Justin Rose – on that windy afternoon in Dubai where Stenson lived for ten years.

Doing the double – finishing No 1 money earner on both sides of the Atlantic – drained him mentally and physically but he is confident that he will challenge as strongly this year as he did in 2013. That's just what the normally quiet-mannered yet steely competitor with an understated sense of humour would say.

## A team effort

Onwards and upwards after all is the motto of the 35 year old who, with the help of his team – coach Peter Cowen, caddie Gareth Lord (who now lives in Monaco and drives a Ferrari) his team leader Torsten Hansson, a former military man and physiotherapist Cornel Driessen – has achieved what many of his fellow professionals strive for. It was typical he would stress the importance of his backroom men. "I could not have done what I have done without them," was his classy comment in Dubai.

While Tiger Woods won five tournaments during the year and was named the PGA Tour's Player of the Year, I suspect he would be quick to agree that for the last six months of 2013 the best player not only in America but in the world was Stenson.

If there is a slight worry it is that there is a history of a dramatic tailing off in the performances of former Race to Dubai winners such as Lee Westwood, Luke Donald and Rory McIlroy who found it tough to continue playing to such a high standard the following season.

This, however, is the nature of the game – highs and lows irrespective of how good you are. Even Jack and Tiger are no exceptions and Stenson, after all, has rebounded from two slumps that were much deeper than he would have liked.

His victory in the 2012 South African Open, his first win for five years, was probably the inspiration he needed but what he has achieved with his team is the result of good old fashioned hard work and an inner belief that he could do it.

Though there are no guarantees, strength of mind and body could earn Stenson a first major in 2014; it would be a fitting accomplishment.

After a well-earned break (with plenty of time to think how best to invest his new-found riches), Stenson's main goals in 2014 are to make it to No 1 in the world officially and win his first major not just for himself and his family but for Sweden.

The Scandinavian major winners have until now all plied their trade on the LPGA Tour. Henrik Stenson is ready to put that right.

## Henrik Stenson – his 2013 season from July

| Tournament | Position | Rounds | Score |
|---|---|---|---|
| Scottish Open | 3 | 70-64-66-73—273 | −15 |
| Open Championship* | 2 | 70-74-70-70—284 | E |
| WGC–Bridgestone Invitational* | T2 | 65-70-67-70—272 | −8 |
| PGA Championship* | 3 | 68-66-69-70—273 | −7 |
| FedEx – The Barclays | T43 | 65-73-75-71—284 | E |
| FedEx – Deutsche Bank | 1 | 67-63-66-66—262 | −22 |
| FedEx – BMW Championship | T33 | 72-70-67-74—283 | −1 |
| FedEx – Tour Championship | 1 | 64-66-69-68—267 | −13 |
| Final Series – BMW Masters | T34 | 72-74-79-65—290 | +2 |
| Final Series – WGC–HSBC* | T31 | 74-76-67-65—282 | −6 |
| Final Series – Turkish Airlines | T 7 | 64-68-69-69—270 | −18 |
| Final Series – DP World | 1 | 68-64-67-64—263 | −25 |

Season in USA:
Played 18    Made cut 16    Earned $6,388,230    FedEx Bonus $10,000,000

Season in Europe:
Played 17    Made cut 17    Earned €4,103,708

*WGC and Majors appear on both Tours

# Winning the US Open title was just reward for Justin

## Derek Lawrenson writes on gentlemanly Rose's rise to fame

There are some sporting deeds that resonate so strongly they persuade you to hitch your wagon to the fate of the protagonist and follow their fortunes to the end.

So it was in the summer of 1998, two young men in their late teens pulled off feats so stirring they earned themselves a multitude of admirers who revelled in the good times but also kept the faith when fortune was less kind.

One was 18-year-old footballer Michael Owen, who slalomed his way through the Argentina defence to score the goal of that year's World Cup. The other was 17-year-old Justin Rose, who holed his third shot to the final hole of The Open at Royal Birkdale to finish joint fourth as an amateur, and provoke from Sir Michael Bonallack, then Secretary of the Royal and Ancient Golf Club, an immortal comment: "That was the loudest roar I have ever heard in my life."

Fast forward 15 summers to 2013, and two more landmark occasions. Owen announced the completion of his journey following a rollercoaster career plagued with hamstring injuries but dotted with more than enough good times to make supporters of the various clubs he played for glad they watched him perform.

And then there was Rose, who completed something of a journey of his own following a career to that point marked like Owen's by marvellous highs but also shocking lows. On a sublime afternoon at magical Merion, the museum of the American game where so many of the greats like Bobby Jones, Lee Trevino and Ben Hogan had left their mark, Rose found himself standing in the middle of the 18th fairway and facing the shot he had waited all his life to play.

It was at this point that all those people who had been with him from the start and were now watching on televisions around the world collectively held their breath. Rose had shown on many occasions that he was a man of considerable guts, bouncing back from any number of setbacks. But now the United States Open, one of the game's four most prized trophies, was within his grasp. Pull off this shot and he would surely hold on to win from the

Justin Rose played beautifully at Merion to become the first Englishman in 43 years to win the US Open. Tony Jacklin was the winner in 1970.

© Getty Images

eternal US Open bridesmaid Phil Mickelson and the plucky Australian, Jason Day.

What if he didn't, though? Would there be any way back if it all went horribly wrong this time, following all the years of preparation and hard work? Other disappointments could be put down to the experience of learning what it takes to win. Now that he knew he was ready, what if he still couldn't deliver?

The stakes, then, were as high as they could possibly be. It is no exaggeration to say this, more than any other stroke he would ever play, would determine his place in the game's ultimate pecking order. Events leading up to it had been encouraging. The 17th and the 18th were the two hardest finishing holes imaginable, but Rose had played a beautiful long iron to walk off the 17th hole with a par three, and had striped his drive down the last.

Just to complete the picture, a few short paces away was Hogan's plaque, commemorating the stupendous one iron he played on his way to winning the 1950 US Open. "This is it, then", said Rose, inwardly. "Time to show you can stand here and play the shot that wins you a major championship."

Justin Rose dedicated his victory to his late father Ken who had been his guiding light until his death at the age of 57 in 2002.

Given these momentous circumstances, it is hard to believe there was a stroke played in 2013 that rivalled the one Rose pulled off. Granted, it was a four iron compared to the one iron Hogan had to play. But it is not lapsing into modern hyperbole to suggest it was a better shot than even Hogan played; better than the shot that became the most widely admired and most famous golf photograph of all time. Yes, that's how good it was.

So pure, indeed, it was something of a travesty when the blow that never left the flag for a second kept on rolling and finished in the first cut of rough, some 25ft from the hole. At least it was an easy shot left for a player of Rose's calibre, and particularly after what he had just faced. Played deftly with a three wood, he coaxed the ball next to the hole to leave the sort of putt we all feel we could hole to win a major.

It wasn't quite in the bag, given that Day and Mickelson were coming up behind. But it left them needing the miracle that didn't materialise and Rose in that blissful condition of knowing he had successfully accomplished his end of the bargain, which is all that any player can ever ask.

When the putt had been holed, Rose raised his eyes to the heavens and lifted up his arms. All those of us familiar with his life's work didn't need any explanation. He was thinking of his father Ken, his guiding light who had so tragically lost his life to cancer in 2002 at the far too young age of 57.

## Sad Friday afternoons

Rose has always been a credit to him and his mother Annie, both before and after Ken's death. I always think a measure of a golfer as a man is how they react on the debilitating days. Rose was just 18 with all those expectations from Birkdale heaped upon his shoulders when he turned professional and promptly began with 21 missed halfway cuts in a row. I've lost count of how many of those sad Friday afternoons I was present at, as he spoke to the media about his latest failure. Not once did he shirk his responsibilities, nor rail against the questions that were all couched inevitably in the same negative tone.

That's why this was one of those victories that transcended the golfing audience to appeal to anyone with an interest in the drama of the human experience. This was one of those wins that leave you feeling, yes, here was a man who earned his due.

A win earned the hard way, in other words. Forged from the misery of all those missed halfway cuts came a gradual progression that led to regular tour wins on both sides of the Atlantic before the dramatic transfusion of self-belief that followed his win over Phil Mickelson in the Ryder Cup singles matches, perhaps the most miraculous of all the miracles on that blessed Sunday at Medinah.

What of the future, after becoming the first English golfer for 43 years to win the US Open? At 33, his shot of a lifetime on the 18th at Merion carries with it the promise that similarly prodigious blows lie in his future, leading to more major championships. That, however, is for another day.

For now, after such a long and at times agonising journey, it's surely enough to wallow in this one, and the fulfilment of a dream that took shape amidst the sacred golfing acreage of the Southport coastline, in the unforgettable summer of 1998.

# Magnificent Europe! Solheim Cup team score historic win

## Lewine Mair congratulates Liselotte Neumann's heroines

Pat Bradley, aunt to Keegan Bradley and a winner of all but one of the LPGA's majors in 1986, was an avid spectator at the Colorado Golf Club for the 2013 Solheim Cup where Europe won for a first time on US soil, with the score a record 18–10. The 62-year-old Bradley marvelled at the performance of the modern Europeans but what struck her still more was the extent to which both teams' striking had improved across the match's 23-year-history.

"In my day," she said, "you couldn't have compared our striking with the men's. We didn't begin to be in their league. These girls, though, are bigger, stronger and different. I never thought there would come a day when I would be saying this, but they're hitting masculine shots and doing virtually everything that Keegan and his friends can do. It's great to see."

Bradley's was quite a statement and one which went hand-in-hand with what turned out to be a rather more hotly contested match than the scoreline would suggest. The Europeans won four and a half of the eight foursomes and six of the eight fourballs over the first two days to embark on the Sunday singles with a 10½–5½ lead. In other words, they needed no more than 3½ points from the 12 matches to tie the match and make off with the Solheim Cup for the second time in a row.

But the history of Solheim, Ryder, Walker and Curtis Cups is such that the Europeans knew not to take anything for granted.

Again, the Americans were able to draw on positive memories from the match of 1996 at St Pierre. That was the occasion when spectators poured into the venue from all over the UK in expectation of a European victory, only for the Americans to win all but one of the singles and claim the spoils.

In Colorado, there were times when the Americans were ahead in as many as seven of the last 12 matches, only for their fight-back to be more than somewhat doused as the 17-year-old Charley Hull reeled off five birdies in 12 holes to defeat Paula Creamer. It was one of those performances which gave the rest of the team that extra shot of confidence they needed to get the job done.

*Teenage rookie Charley Hull shot five birdies in 12 holes to beat experienced Paula Creamer and then asked for her autograph.*

© Getty Images

Carlota Ciganda defeated Morgan Pressel by 4/2 in Match No. 4 and, after not too much more to-ing and fro-ing, it fell to Caroline Hedwall to claim the point which ensured that the visitors could not lose. Then, fittingly, it fell to Catriona Matthew to nail the extra half point – she was playing Gerina Piller – needed for victory.

Everyone had trusted Matthew to hole her all-important six-footer on the home green and her putt was never in doubt. In every sense, Matthew is an out-and-out star. At 42, she improves every year, with officials in Scottish golf saying at a winter meeting that they just wished that the rest of Scotland's golfing taskforce could match the intelligent way she goes about her business.

"On the fitness side of things, she does everything she needs to do to be able to take on the up-and-coming younger players," said the Scottish fitness guru.

Hedwall, for her part, did what no player had ever done before in winning five points out of five, with the shot she will remember the longest, the four-and-a-half footer it took to defeat Michelle Wie on the home green. "It was an unbelievable feeling," said the Swede, before admitting that she had carried on shaking long after the putt had dropped. It was well over a month later that she reported, delightedly, of the longer-term after-effects. Apparently, on those days when she is able to linger in that happy state between sleeping and waking, she finds herself re-living that 18th green experience. "I can't," expanded the 24-year-old, "picture the ball going in because that was something I never saw. I took my last look at it when it was about three or four inches from the hole and I knew, then, that it couldn't go anywhere else."

"If you look at the video," she continued, "you will see that I'm actually raising a celebratory fist before it disappeared."

## McGinley congratulations

Europe's clean sweep of the Saturday fourballs could not have done more to pave the way for Sunday's excitement. Karine Icher's moment of moments came when she made a 45-footer from the back of the home green for her and Beatriz Recari to defeat Cristie Kerr and Morgan Pressel. It had been half dark at the time but the US Captain, Meg Mallon, suggested, ruefully, that Icher's

ball had looked positively luminous to her as it headed inexorably for the hole.

Paul McGinley, the 2014 European Ryder Cup captain, was one of the first to pass on his congratulations to the European side. He thought they had played magnificently and that the result would help to take the LET forward in much the same way as the men's first victory on American soil – in 1987 at Muirfield Village – had given such a boost to their circuit and its finances.

McGinley, though, was altogether less impressed with some of the on-course manners. At a time when he and Tom Watson had been discussing how they wanted the match of '14 to stand out for passion and electricity combined with integrity, he did not mind saying that he disapproved of the way certain Americans would walk to the next tee before their opponents had finished putting.

Yet the over-riding memories of the Solheim of '13 were magnificent, with one moment to tickle everyone's fancy coming when Hull, after beating Creamer, asked that celebrated performer to sign her ball for a friend at home. The 27-year-old Creamer managed a smile but, a month or so later, she laughingly admitted to what she had really thought. "I don't mind saying I was a bit taken aback," chuckled the American. "It was kind of funny. It made me realise that I'm the veteran now."

---

# Concentration and consistency the keys to Ko's success

Over the years, we have seen plenty of Lydia Kos in the world of tennis – Martina Hingis and Jennifer Capriati to name but two. Those precociously-gifted youngsters not only made the more senior tennis players look bad but old. A devastating combination!

The 16-year-old Ko, who in October successfully petitioned the LPGA to allow her to tee up on their Tour ahead of the usual determining age of 18, comes across a little differently. She has always gone very quietly about her winning ways and afforded her elders nothing but respect. At the time of writing, the Korean-born New Zealander, who started golf at five when the family moved to New Zealand, had four professional titles under her belt – two LPGA Tour titles in the Canadian Opens of 2012 and 2013, along with the 2012 NSW Open and the 2013 Handa New Zealand Women's Open. Had she been a professional, she would have pocketed around $1.5 million.

Another point which Mike Whan, the CEO of the LPGA, would have considered when he was looking into Ko's request was her consistency. In 25 starts among the professionals across 2011 and 2012, she never missed a cut and when, last September, she headed back to her New Zealand school after finishing second in the 2013 Evian, she was as well-placed as fifth in the World Rankings.

Ko, who turned professional in 2014, is plenty long off the tee and endlessly straight. Again her course management, like her concentration, is in the same league as the wiliest of major champions.

# Unflappable Inbee stakes a claim to be 2013 Golfer of the Year

## Henry Currie full of praise for American-based Korean star

Swede Henrik Stenson, who topped the money list on both sides of the Atlantic, and Tiger Woods, a five time winner on the PGA Tour, have every right to consider that they deserve 2013 Player of the Year honours but arguably there is a third even better qualified candidate laying claim to the honour – South Korea's Inbee Park.

The LPGA Rolex Player of the Year was a six-time winner in 2013 and those victories included three major wins – the Kraft Nabisco Championship, the Wegman's LPGA Championship and the US Women's Open for a second time. And not only that, she won them in a row!

Only two other players in LPGA history – Mickey Wright in 1961 and Pat Bradley in 1986 – have won three majors in one season and only the late, great Babe Zaharias ever won three in a row back in 1950 when there were only three majors on the calendar.

By any stretch of the imagination what the 25-year-old American-based Korean did on the golf course was not only outstanding, it was incredible.

Her aim was never to win all the majors in one season – only Bobby Jones did that in 1930 – but just to win them all once in her career and that leaves the Ricoh Women's British Open and the Evian Championship as the two she will have to target in the next couple of years.

Going for a fourth successive win in the British event last August was just beyond her. The pressure was too great and in the end she was glad her Grand Slam bid that had so dominated her thinking for so many weeks leading up to St Andrews, was all over.

"Winning a Grand Slam takes so much hard work. It is a lot to do. I gave it a try at St Andrews and lost but it was a great experience and I consider myself a very lucky person."

Most golfers yearn to win one major in their careers but winning three in a row left her fellow golfers full of admiration and disbelief.

Angela Stanford summed up Park's amazing feat best of all when she told reporters: "I thought the only player who could do what Inbee has done was Annika Sörenstam. It is so impressive to win three

in a row. I don't know how she does it but, obviously, she is a great putter, hits the ball straight off the tee and keeps her emotions in check.

*Inbee Park was 32 under par when winning the first three majors on the LPGA circuit.*

I K Kim, who was second to her at the US Women's Open, pin-pointed another plus: "She is happy with not just her golf but also her life. She has her family and friends for support and it works for her."

She started playing golf when she was 10 and credits her father Gun Gyu Park as being the most influential person in her career. Another who has helped her greatly is her swing coach Gi Hyeob Nam, a former Korean PGA Tour player who just happens to be her fiancé.

Of course, her success on the LPGA Tour is not surprising because she had an impressive amateur career after moving to America. She won nine events on the American Junior Golf Association circuit and was a five time Rolex Junior All-American. In 2002, the year she won US Girls' Junior

Championship, she was Rolex Junior Player of the Year.

Just 5ft 6in in height, Inbee, a fluent English speaker, has those putting gurus on Tour marvelling at the simple way she handles that part of the game.

David Orr, who coaches Justin Rose, says that when she approaches an important putt she is not thinking what the putt means in monetary terms. It is just a putt. He insists you are not born a good putter, you have to learn that skill and she has.

## Great tempo

Dave Stockton, who is putting coach to many players on Tour, likes her approach. "Putting is a mental exercise, very different from the rest of the game. The key to her success is that whatever she is doing she is not getting ahead of herself and not letting the moment overwhelm her."

Fellow Korean So Yeon Ryu pinpoints another reason why Park has been so successful "It's her tempo. It's great and always consistent."

Inbee may not be as demonstrative as some of her colleagues on Tour but Dottie Pepper likens her to Fred Couples in the way she channels her personality to her game. Trying to make her more extrovert, she claims, would only be detrimental for her golf.

Brittany Lincicome is also full of praise for Park's achievements: "I cannot imagine playing on the Korean Tour and having to learn the Korean language and adjust to the Korean culture. Inbee has done really well here in America. I have played junior golf with her and she was phenomenal then. It's just great to see her step up and do so well as a professional."

As for Park, who never dreamed she would equal a record set in 1950, she says she feels pressure off the course like anybody else but when on it, with just the ball and the club to think about, it makes makes her calm. That's why when she felt pressure on the course at St Andrews while trying to win her fourth major it was unusual.

"I have never experienced such pressure but I will never forget this season unless of course I win four in a row some time in the future," she said.

Although she started well making six birdies in her first ten holes at the Ricoh, she hit a poor tee shot at the 12th and was never a threat after that finishing tied 42nd with amateur superstar Lydia Ko, who has now turned professional.

Ironically perhaps the most disappointing and surprising aspect of her failure at St Andrews was the fact that she lost her way on the huge double greens. Unusual because she has the reputation of having one of the purest putting strokes in the business.

## Bamboozled

"The St Andrews greens were tough to judge," said Park. "One minute they were quick and one minute they were slow."

"I know I have a long way to go. I'm still in the learning process but in 2013 I feel I have taken a step towards achieving what Yani Tseng, Annika Sörenstam and Lorena Ochoa have in their careers."

I'm sure Stenson and Woods would readily agree that Inbee Park should be up there on the podium with them sharing the congratulations for what was for all of them a great year.

## Inbee Park's six wins on the LPGA Tour

| | | | |
|---|---|---|---|
| Honda LPGA Thailand | 67-71-71-67—276 | (−12) | $225,000 |
| Kraft Nabisco | 70-67-67-69—273 | (−19) | $300,000 |
| North Texas LPGA | 67-70-67-67—271 | (−13) | $195.000 |
| Wegman's LPGA | 72-68-68-75—283 | (−5) | $337,500 |
| Walmart NW Arkansas | 69-65-67—201 | (−12) | $300,000 |
| US Women's Open | 67-68-71-74—280 | (−8) | $585,000 |
| Total | | (−69) | $1,934,500 |

She finished tied 42nd in the Ricoh Women's British Open and 57th in the Evian Championship.

Season earnings:
Wins 6        Top 10's 11        Prize-money $2,456,619

Career earnings:
Wins 9        Top 10's 48        Prize-money $7,724,343

# The golf match that captures the imagination of the world

## Mike Aitken on only the second Ryder Cup in Scotland

Although it wasn't officially known as the Ryder Cup in 1921, golf's first ever match between the professionals of Great Britain and the USA took place at Gleneagles over the King's Course when the players on both sides were as much enchanted by the spirit of international competition as the breathtaking views of the Ochil Hills and Ben Vorlich.

This year, the match returns to Perthshire for only the second official staging of the biennial contest in Scotland. As might be expected, the home of golf can reflect on a substantial contribution made to the match over the years. No fewer than 20 Scottish players won 94 points between 1927 and 2012 while six Scottish captains led the team in nine of those matches. The first official venue in 1927, Worcester Country Club in Massachusetts, was designed by Dornoch's Donald Ross.

Heavens, four Scots (Fred McLeod, Jock Hutchison, Harry Hampton and Clarence Hackney) even played for the USA at Gleneagles and another brace, Tommy Armour and Bobby Cruickshank, represented the Stars and Stripes in 1926 at Wentworth in another match deemed an unofficial friendly.

When it came to hosting the Ryder Cup, however, the Scots enjoyed slimmer pickings. Until this autumn, 15 of the biennial matches held on the European side of the Atlantic over the past 87 years were contested in England with Scotland, Spain, Wales and Ireland putting on but one apiece.

It was St Andrews' Hutchison, then the US PGA champion, who is credited with the idea of holding the duel at Gleneagles in 1921, though Sylvanus P Jermain, who helped establish Inverness Golf Club in Ohio, is thought to have come up with the original concept of a contest between golfers from the old and new worlds. According to Dave Shedloski, the Ohio based golf writer, a story from the *Toledo News-Bee* in 1931 quotes George Sargent, then president of the PGA of America, recalling: "The credit for the idea (of the Ryder Cup) should go to Sylvanus P Jermain of Toledo, who made the suggestion back in 1921, the year after the US Open was staged at Inverness. I remember he suggested the scheme to me, and I tried to put it across without success."

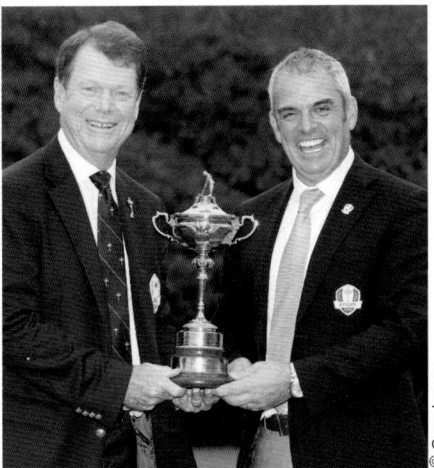

© Getty Images

*The Captains of the 2014 teams with the Cup.*

Ed Hodge, in *Jewel in the Glen*, a comprehensive account of golf and the Ryder Cup at Gleneagles, also gives credit in the book to James Harnett, a New Yorker who worked for *Golf Illustrated*, driving the idea forward with a campaign in the magazine to fund the transatlantic travelling expenses of a ten man team to Scotland. In 1921 The Open was staged in late June at St Andrews with the lucrative *Glasgow Herald* tournament taking place at Gleneagles earlier in the month. This happy coincidence enabled the leading golfers from Britain and America to also take part in an 'International Challenge Match' on June 6.

The sweeping terrain of the King's and the Queen's were laid out by James Braid years before the hotel itself was opened. Between 1918 and 1924 these courses earned a reputation as among the most beautiful in a country long renowned as the home of golf. With the hotel still under construction, however, Hodge reveals that the American team were housed in five railway carriages at Auchterarder station without so much as the convenience of running water.

If life off the course for the players was spartan, golf on the King's was spectacular and drew favourable comparisons from the Americans with Pine Valley. Britain's old guard, spearheaded by the great triumvirate of Braid, J H Taylor and Harry Vardon, who collectively won The Open 16 times between them, savoured home advantage and saw off the young pups from America by 9–3.

More than half a century after that low-key trial run at Gleneagles, until now the only staging of the Ryder Cup itself at the home of golf took place during a chilly September of 1973 when Bernard Hunt, who passed away last year at the age of 83, led the side from Great Britain and Ireland and Jackie Burke brought an American team to Muirfield in East Lothian showcasing the formidable talents of Jack Nicklaus, Arnold Palmer and Lee Trevino. It was the first time in 46 years the match had been held in Scotland.

Of course, this was the era of relentless American dominance when both teams were searching for a formula which might make the outcome of the contest slightly less one-sided. In Gullane, eligibility for the home side was broadened from Britain to Britain and Ireland (it wasn't until six years later the Europeans were included) and the format was tweaked with a session of foursomes and fourballs played on each of the first two days rather than the all-foursomes, all-fourballs formula which had gone before.

The teams in 1973 were made up of 12-a-side with four sessions of foursomes and fourballs as well as two rounds of singles on the final day. The home side consisted of Brian Barnes and Bernard Gallacher from Scotland, Ireland's Christy O'Connor and Eddie Polland, Brian Huggett from Wales and England's Tony Jacklin, Neil Coles, Peter Oosterhuis, Maurice Bembridge, Peter Butler, Clive Clark and John Garner, who didn't play. Along with Nicklaus, Palmer and Trevino, the US team included Billy Casper, Tom Weiskopf, Gay Brewer, J C Snead, Homero Blancas, Dave Hill and Chi Chi Rodriguez.

In foursomes and fourballs, Hunt's men proved equal to the task. On the opening morning of foursomes, Barnes and Gallacher were sent out first and duly dispatched Trevino and Casper by one hole. O'Connor and Coles saw off Weiskopf and Snead 3 and 2, Jacklin and Oosterhuis halved with Rodriguez and Lou Graham and only the might of Nicklaus and Palmer prevailed by 6 and 5 over Bembridge and Butler.

The afternoon session of fourballs was just as competitive. Barnes and Gallacher thrashed the Masters champions Tommy Aaron and Brewer 5 and 4, Bembridge and Huggett famously claimed the scalp of Nicklaus and Palmer by 3 and 1, Jacklin and Oosterhuis saw off Weiskopf and Casper by the same margin (they went out in a stunning better ball of 28) and only Trevino and Blancas stopped the rot for the Americans with a 2 and 1 win over O'Connor and Coles. At the end of the first day, GB&I led 5½–2½.

Perhaps the turning point in this match took place away from the links rather than on it when, as The Scotsman's Norman Mair observed, a Scot with as much stomach for the fight against the Americans as any golfer (he was Europe's captain three times in 1991,1993 and 1995) was laid low by food poisoning. Gallacher had gone to bed knowing he and Barnes were again detailed to lead the charge. However, when Bernard woke in a sweat feeling dizzy and chilled, his wife, Lesley, called for a doctor at 4.30am and food poisoning was diagnosed. Gallacher phoned Hunt at 6am to pass on the bad news.

Breaking up the only partnership from the opening day which collected full points proved catastrophic for GB&I. When Gallacher walked off the 14th green, it was his seventh win in 11 matches against the Americans. Left out of the foursomes and fourballs to recuperate, Gallacher was still under the weather when the singles took place the following day – he had only managed to consume a

*It was not called the Ryder Cup then but the first match between America and Great Britain was at Gleneagles in 1921. The hotel was not finished and the American team included some Scots who had become naturalised Americans*

bowl of soup since illness struck – and lost to both Weiskopf and Brewer.

In the meantime, Hunt knocked on Butler's bedroom door before 7am and told the Englishman he was on the tee at 8.30. While Butler could hardly be faulted for his efforts – he aced the 16th with a 3 iron, no less – the foursomes partnership with Barnes was less well oiled than the Scottish combination and Nicklaus and Weiskopf won by one hole. Although Oosterhuis and Jacklin held the fort against Palmer and Hill and Bembridge and Huggett demolished Rodriguez and Graham, Trevino and Casper's win over Coles and O'Connor ensured the US deficit didn't widen.

Still trailing by three points, the Americans held a crisis team meeting after lunch when Burke, who had been a losing playing captain at Lindrick in 1957, decided to abandon plans to rest Palmer. The American icon, in the company of Snead, duly spearheaded the charge in the afternoon. The visitors went on to secure three of the four fourball ties with Trevino holing a three-footer for a half in the last match to ensure the sides were level going into the final day.

The Americans won the first three singles of the morning session and, by the time Jacklin stopped the rot with a win over Aaron, the damage was done. Trailing by three points going into the afternoon, GB&I were boosted by Huggett's win over Blancas but only Jacklin and Oosterhuis, who claimed Palmer's scalp with a 4 and 2 success, interrupted America's serene progress to a 19–13 victory. As usual, the Americans had found another gear when it was required and Edward Heath, the Prime Minister, presented Samuel Ryder's trophy to Burke.

What the contests of 1921 and 1973 both had in common, of course, was a low key atmosphere compared to the razzamatazz and commercialism of the modern day matches. The showdown at Gleneagles in September of this year is due to be fought in front of a global TV audience of no less than 600 million with an economic benefit to the country estimated by Shona Robison, Scotland's sports minister, at £100 million. Of course, it wasn't until Europe, under the captaincy of Tony Jacklin, started beating the USA at the Belfry in 1985 that the event turned a profit. As recently as 1981, the match at Walton Heath posted a loss of £50,000, and it took until 1987, at Muirfield Village, for the match to sell out in America. Now, it's established as one of the greatest sporting shows on earth.

If there's an element of symmetry attached to the Ryder Cup at Gleneagles in 2014 because the story effectively started here in 1921, it's also fitting Scotland's most notable contributor to the match with 23½ should live nearby. When the BBC conducted a poll during the 2006 match at the K Club to identify Europe's greatest ever Ryder Cup player, Colin Montgomerie received 49 per cent of the vote and came out well ahead of Seve Ballesteros and Nick Faldo. Today, perhaps, it would be possible to predict a different outcome because Ian Poulter is shaping up as one of the most effective players the match has ever produced, with a higher winning average, 80 per cent, than even America's leading light, Palmer.

Just as Seve was never greater than in partnership with José Maria Olazábal – the pair won 12 points out of 15 together, and prompted the observation from the late Dai Davies, The Guardian's golf writer, "no-one was ever able to work out who was holding whose hand" – Montgomerie was also often at his best in tandem with Bernhard Langer. If Seve played the game like a man possessed, compensating for missed fairways and greens by hitting stunning recovery shots, Monty brought a clockwork certainty to his work off the tee and a conviction to his putting which might have won him

*Set in the Perthshire hills Gleneagles is one of the most beautiful and challenging courses and only the second Scottish venue to be host to the Ryder Cup. Muirfield in 1973 was the other one.*

three or four majors had he only been able to hole out as effectively in the most prized strokeplay competitions as he did in the Ryder Cup. For all his close shaves in the majors, fate decreed the Ryder Cup would be the arena in which Montgomerie overshadowed his peers.

Not that Monty, who was also a winning captain at Celtic Manor in 2010, is the only candidate for the honorary title of Scotland's Mr Ryder Cup. Between 1969 and 1995, Gallacher was involved in every match as either a player or a captain. Most notably, he was in charge of a famous victory at

Oak Hill in 1995. Similarly, Sam Torrance played in every Ryder Cup between 1981 and 1995 (where he holed the winning putt against Andy North) before captaining Europe's victory in 2002. Barnes, with ten and a half points, and Sandy Lyle, with eight, are among the country's other Ryder Cup notables.

In 1921, the *Perthshire Advertiser* insisted: "Gleneagles has captured the imagination of the world of golf." In 2014, the Ryder Cup comes full circle and that homecoming boast will resonate around the globe again.

*The European team produced a wonderful last day recovery to beat the Americans in the 2012 Ryder Cup at Medinah.*

# The champion from Jersey who became a golfing colossus

## John Hopkins on Harry Vardon, winner of six Opens

To every question there is usually an answer. So what is the answer to two particular questions: Could Harry Vardon have won more Opens after 1914 when he captured his sixth and last, the one that we are celebrating this year? And good as he was, how would he compare to the best golfers of today, one hundred years later?

One person we know not to ask is the man himself. Some people like talking about themselves. Vardon did not. Despite appearances to the contrary, he was not a confident man. He had never enjoyed the full approbation of his father during his upbringing and as a result he was always seeking his father's approval. Usually he didn't get it.

Whereas most fathers do their best to build up their offspring's confidence, Vardon's seemed to do the opposite. After Harry had won his third Open, you might have thought his father would have been really proud. Instead he said: "Harry may win the tournaments but it's Tom who plays the golf."

One story illustrates how modest and quiet Vardon was. He and James Braid were having dinner in a restaurant in Piccadilly with their golf bags resting on a nearby chair. A young man at an adjoining table was talking rather loudly about golf to his two female companions. Seeing the two golf bags he took a club out of one of them, waggled it knowingly and remarked there was something wrong with its balance. Vardon gazed at him. Braid smiled indulgently. Neither spoke a word.

Vardon was born on 9th May 1870, so in 1914, when The Open was held at Prestwick in June, he had just passed his 44th birthday. These days 44 is nothing. Look at Miguel Angel Jiménez and his performances in his forties. Remember how Tom Watson nearly won The Open when he was 59? But one hundred years ago 44 was nearer two thirds of a man's lifespan than one half. Furthermore, when he was only 33, Vardon contracted tuberculosis, a very dangerous illness in those days, and had to recuperate in hospital in Norfolk. He regained his form but his health was never the same.

What happens when you age? You remain able to hit the ball as solidly and accurately as ever but the shots that require the most delicacy, ones you may

*But for illness, Harry Vardon might have won more than six Open Championships.*

© Getty Images

have been able to play with extreme deftness in days gone by, become harder and harder. The putts you once holed with abandon now torture you.

There was no doubting Vardon's ability. He won three Open championships with the rubber-cored ball and three with the gutty ball. "In the days of the solid gutty ball, the brassie was an immensely important club and Vardon was the master of it," Bernard Darwin, the noted golf writer and golf correspondent of *The Times*, wrote. "At his peak he was a model of fitness" Darwin observed. "Andrew Kirkcaldy used to call him The Greyhound. About five foot 10 or 11 inches in height, very fit and lithe, with a bearing both gallant and gay, he looked the model of an athlete who could have played anything."

Nine months or so before his triumph at Prestwick, Vardon had been beaten in the famous playoff for the 1913 US Open won by American Francis Ouimet, an amateur. Vardon's ball striking at The Country Club in Brookline, Boston, was superb, as always, but his putting was frail.

"Vardon's putting is the most uncertain factor in this championship" said a correspondent in one paper reporting from the event. After reading this, Vardon said: "You know, I can putt an awful lot worse than I am now." In the fourth round, Vardon's score was 79 and he was convinced that he stood no chance. "It is my wretched putting which has broken me down again" he said. Apart from the early years when he had a Woods-like ability to sink putts, Vardon struggled on the greens. The older he got the more he struggled as Hogan and many others would years later.

With this frailty in a department of the game that he had to face on almost every green of every round he played, it is hard to imagine that Vardon could have won more Opens, even though six years later, by now 50, he led the 1920 US Open by four strokes with seven holes to play before bad weather and his bad putting got him. Six Opens is a record, a phenomenal achievement, one unmatched in golf.

How good was he, this son of a Jerseyman father and a French mother, the fourth of five sons and three daughters who was christened Henry William? How would he fare on today's courses against today's stars?

Darwin once wrote that Vardon loved golf more than anything and wanted to "touch golf and be around it constantly." David Normoyle, the writer and historian, has written: "I imagine Vardon would have embraced all the growth, change, modernity and excitement that has come from golf through the years... He was a hard man from a difficult background who suffered through illness and travelled the world because of golf. He was a professional in the clearest sense, which is why the European Tour honours him with their logo and the PGA Tour honours him with their scoring trophy. He was an innovator in his time with his swing, his grip and his style, the predecessor to the life-long competitiveness of Watson, the athleticism of Woods, the grace of Snead, the dominance of Nicklaus, the physical resilience of Hogan, the attractiveness and business acumen of Palmer. In all of these modern heroes are strains of one man: Harry Vardon."

To compare a member of the Great Triumvirate of a century ago with a modern player is a good subject for discussion but one about which it is impossible to reach a conclusion. All we can do is pay attention to what his peers said.

Here's Andrew Kirkcaldy, a fellow professional, on Vardon: "If twenty of the best professional golfers were asked to write down the names of the four greatest golfers, they would put down Vardon, [J H] Taylor, [James] Braid and [Sandy] Herd. If these four were asked to name the greatest among them, all save Vardon would put a cross against his name."

Here's J H Taylor, another of The Great Triumvirate: "My solemn and considered judgement is that Harry Vardon is the finest and most finished golfer the game has ever produced. This judgement I give after watching every player over some fifty years..."

Here's Francis Ouimet after winning the 1913 US Open: "I consider Harry Vardon the greatest golfer I have ever seen."

And here's Darwin: "I once ... asked the late Mr Leslie Balfour Melville how he compared Vardon with the famous young Tommy Morris, who had died in 1895. He thought for a moment and then gave me the right answer: 'I can't imagine anyone playing better than Tommy did.' So I will only say in my turn that in the conditions of his time I cannot possibly imagine a greater golfer than Harry Vardon. Only those who were playing with him or watching him at his zenith can fully realise how he truly did bestride the world of golf like a Colossus."

## Harry Vardon's record six Open wins

Harry Vardon, the only man to have won six Opens, won three of them at Prestwick, two at Royal St George's one and one at Muirfield.

He, James Braid and J H Taylor – The Great Triumvirate – won 17 Opens in a 21-year period beginning in 1894.

Vardon, in addition to his six wins, was second four times and third twice between 1894 and 1914. In that time, despite his tuberculosis, he was out of the top 10 only twice.

| Year | Course | Score | Entry | Prize Fund £ |
|------|--------|-------|-------|--------------|
| 1896 | Muirfield* | 83-78-78-77—316 | 64 | 100 |
| 1898 | Prestwick | 79-75-77-76—307 | 78 | 100 |
| 1899 | Royal St George's | 76-76-81-77—310 | 98 | 100 |
| 1903 | Prestwick | 73-77-72-78—300 | 127 | 125 |
| 1911 | Royal St George's | 74-74-75-80—303 | 226 | 135 |
| 1914 | Prestwick | 73-77-78-78—306 | 194 | 135 |

*After 36-hole play off with J H Taylor

# What started as a simple idea is now of vital global importance

## Alistair Tait on the benefits of the world rankings

The year 2004 was a seminal moment for the world of amateur golf. It helped create the most comprehensive system of ranking top flight amateurs ever devised.

The World Amateur Golf Ranking (WAGR) can be traced back to the 2004 season, in particular the 2004 Amateur Championship at St Andrews. A pretty strong field assembled at the Home of Golf, but not quite as strong as it should have been. Andrew Martin was the reigning Australian Amateur Champion that year. Needless to say, he submitted his entry form for the Amateur Championship with high hopes of becoming the second Australian to win the game's most prestigious amateur championship. He never got the chance.

Martin didn't play at St Andrews because his handicap wasn't low enough. He was balloted out of the 288-man field. His handicap of scratch wasn't even close to making the field. That caused a lot of soul searching at The R&A's headquarters in St Andrews.

"It was a watershed moment," The R&A's Chief Executive Peter Dawson admitted. "It clearly wasn't acceptable for the Australian national champion not to be playing in the Amateur Championship."

The R&A had long realised that the diverse handicap systems in operation around the world didn't always guarantee that the truly best players got into the Amateur Championship. "Having handicaps as a criteria of entry wasn't ideal because of the various handicapping systems around the world," Dawson said. "You could have someone in Australia playing off a handicap of scratch who was clearly better than someone in another country playing off plus 2, yet that Australian couldn't get into our Amateur Championship. It wasn't a very satisfactory system of entry criteria."

Step forward David Moir with the solution. Former Scottish Golf Union president Moir was employed at The R&A in the entries department at the time. He had been devising a ranking system to replace the SGU's Order of Merit. "I told Peter about my project and he asked me to look at devising a rankings system that The R&A could use as the basis of entries to the Amateur Championship in future.

"The Andrew Martin situation was clearly inequitable," Moir said. "There were too many handicapping systems across the world, and that made entries based on handicaps not very reliable. It didn't always produce the best possible field, and you want the best players in the Amateur Championship."

Moir spent two years devising and testing his ranking system. By 2007 he had come up with a system he and The R&A felt would guarantee the best possible field for the Amateur Championship, as well as identify the world's élite amateurs.

Moir was a one-man band back in 2007. In those days only male amateurs were ranked. WAGR began with just over 800 tournaments deemed counting events. The system works on tournaments ranked on strength of field and players ranked on the basis of their average performance in those events over a rolling cycle of the previous 52 weeks.

Andy McDonald started working in the rankings department in 2008. Like Moir, he was a one-man operation then. Not now. Women's rankings were launched in 2011. The USGA became joint administrator in 2011. WAGR has grown to the point where McDonald, The R&A's World Amateur Golf Ranking Manager, leads a six-person team dealing with ranking amateur players on a week-to-week basis.

"When I think back to those days I wonder how I managed to get through it," McDonald said. "The ranking has grown to the point where we will cover probably between 4,500–4,700 tournaments in 2013 with nearly 10,000 players in the men's and women's rankings. When I started five years ago there were 833 men's ranking tournaments. This year there are over 2,900 men's events." As of October 2013, there were 6,237 men ranked and 3,163 women. England's Matthew Fitzpatrick headed the men's WAGR table while New Zealand's Lydia Ko topped the women's rankings. Both celebrated the 2013 as winner's of the Mark H McCormack Medal as the world's leading male and female amateurs in 2013.

This year's Walker Cup was representative of how the WAGR table reflects the strength of world

© Getty Images

*New Zealand's Korean-born Lydia Ko was world amateur No 1 three years in a row before turning professional. She won the Canadian Open on the LPGA Tour twice as an amateur.*

amateur golf. Five of the world's top 10 played in the match at the National Golf Links in Southampton, New York, including the number one, two and three players in the world in Fitzpatrick, Michael Kim and Cory Whitsett. Five of the WAGR top 10 were in action, 12 of the top 20 and 15 of the world top 30. Only four of the 20 players were outside the world top 50.

McDonald does not see many more tournaments being added to the WAGR system at present, but is cognisant of what golf in the 2016 Olympic Games might do for growth of the game around the world. "If there is a big increase in tournaments due to new nations coming on board, then that's something we will have to discuss," McDonald said. "At present we can handle things, but we would have to look at the system should the number of amateur tournaments around the world grow."

Of course no system is perfect, especially when you have to rank players around the world that might never play against each other. "It was hard to devise a system that takes account of players competing in different regions around the world, but I think WAGR does that," Moir said. "We've proved it is possible to build a ranking that is based on the strength of fields and how players do against each other in those fields

against players in other tournaments with different strength fields."

Anomalies do crop up from time to time, though. Last year's Women's World Amateur Team Championship was a case in point. It came as no surprise that Ko was the leading individual in Turkey. However, Korea took the team title, the Espirito Santo Trophy, even though the three Korean players did not feature that prominently on the WAGR table.

"No system is every going to be perfect," Dawson said. "However, I think on the whole the system David Moir came up with and has evolved to this day provides a pretty accurate picture of the strength of amateur golf. I think the fact that the world's two governing bodies endorse and jointly administer the ranking gives it international credence."

The Andrew Martin situation wouldn't crop up nowadays. The R&A uses the WAGR table exclusively to determine spots in the Amateur Championship. The USGA exempts the top 50 players on the WAGR table into the US Amateur Championship. Other events around the world also use the WAGR table to determine entries. The Lytham Trophy, one of the world's most prestigious amateur tournaments, began using WAGR for the first time for the 2013 tournament. The Ladies' European Tour exempts the top 25 straight into its Final Qualifying School.

"I never envisaged the ranking I created becoming this big," Moir said. "I'm not sure what I envisioned back in 2004 — I didn't really have time to think — but its growth has been phenomenal. I'm very proud of what I've created. It's my greatest achievement in over 40 years of working in amateur golf."

Future Australian Amateur champions say amen to that.

*This graph shows how many countries are represented in the amateur world rankings now*

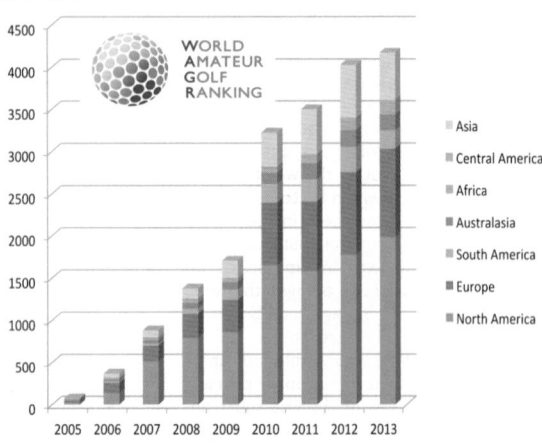

WORLD AMATEUR GOLF RANKING

Asia
Central America
Africa
Australasia
South America
Europe
North America

# A sporting success story spanning over 40 years

## Bill Elliott on how the European Tour has grown

Forty-three years ago the PGA European Tour was born. The mission statement – if indeed they had such curious things back then – was straightforward enough: grow.

Viewed now, no-one can argue that they have not achieved their target. Indeed, inspected how you like, analysed whichever way you desire, the expansion of the European Tour since those early birth pangs has been prodigious. Arguably, but not much, theirs has been the sporting success story of the second half of the 20th century.

Until 1971 and the emergence of John Jacobs as Tournament Director-General of the new organisation, professional tournaments had been handled by the Professional Golfers' Association. Jacob's brief was to establish a proper circuit, good enough, strong enough and wealthy enough to offer full-time opportunities to those golfers who did not wish to spend most of their days in and around a club shop.

The template, of course, was the already strongly established PGA Tour in the United States. In many ways, this remains the case today. Hardly surprising when one considers that close to half the world's golfers are American or that the sale of balls alone in the state of Florida exceeds the total sale of golf equipment throughout Europe. The American circuit is many things but big is the most relevant adjective, rich would be another.

Not that the European Tour is small or poor. These things remain relative but while the Americans have the advantage of a land mass and a common language, the European Tour bosses must tussle with the rest of the world, a web of languages and cultures and, inevitably, expectations.

This expansion around the world was not, naturally, in Jacobs' mind when he took up residence in a cramped office somewhere in the depths of the The Oval cricket ground in south London all those years ago. Survival was his immediate desire. To assist him in this quest he engaged the services of a young Scottish bank manager called Ken Schofield. It turned out to be a smart move.

Schofield was a restlessly ambitious and enthusiastic man. He was also occasionally pugnacious and eternally sociable. His hobby was sport, any sport. He collected and remembered sporting facts and

figures. His knowledge of games and his determination to establish the new golf tour meant that in 1975 he succeeded Jacobs who retreated back to teaching and coaching and, in 1979 and 1981, captaining Ryder Cup teams.

By then another young man, George O'Grady had been attracted to The Oval office from his job

*Ken Schofield (left) was handpicked by first tournament director John Jacobs to take over the running and expansion of the European Tour and when he retired George O'Grady who had worked with him took over.*

in The City. This move turned out to be another pivotal moment for the fledgling tour. Swiftly Schofield and O'Grady formed a partnership that was to survive the ups and downs of the next four decades. No other sport has enjoyed such longevity of tenure.

Apart, the two men seemed unlikely companions but once together and united in their passion for the game they brought a mixed menu of skills that was to drive the tour forward. Schofield's gung-ho enthusiasm meant he was naturally adept at battering down doors, meanwhile O'Grady proved excellent at hanging them back on their hinges and, if necessary, calming everyone down.

When Schofield finally stepped down as chief executive in 2004 O'Grady was the natural successor. By then Schofield had broken through doors so that his players could more easily gain entry to the three majors in America and the PGA Tour itself. He had also taken the tour outside Europe, a barnstorming foreign campaign based on the emergence in the 1980s of a platoon of outstanding players.

Napoleon said that what a great general needed more than anything else was luck. To this we may add timing and thirty-four years ago Schofield enjoyed both with the emergence of Europe's own Generation X in Seve Ballesteros, Nick Faldo, Sandy Lyle, Bernhard Langer and Ian Woosnam.

"When Seve, Faldo and the rest came along we found ourselves in a strong position," says O'Grady. "They were at the top of the rankings, everyone wanted to see them play and for us they represented a fantastic negotiating tool for expansion. If I were to give the Tour marks out of ten with regard to its health I'd presently give it seven and a half, maybe eight but back in the mid-eighties when those players were at the top of their game and then Volvo came on board to support not just a tournament but the whole Tour I'd give it 10 out of 10."

As Seve and his pals swaggered their way to a kind of global dominance both in achievement and personality, the Tour bosses seized their opportunity. Not everybody saw their strategy at the time as the sharp side of smart. As a consequence of this divergence of opinion, the Tour was lampooned in certain quarters as the term European began to embrace not just the UK and Ireland, not only Spain and France, Italy, Scandinavia, Portugal and the rest but also South Africa, chunks of the Far East, Australia and New Zealand. Soon the Middle East was added.

## Most prescient

This sudden expansion made the Tour a sitting target for those determined to giggle at such apparently preposterous geographic moves. Viewed now, however, this ambition not only to move the goalposts but also to alter the shape of the pitch may be seen as probably the most prescient move by any significant sporting body in the last half-century.

Along the way we have lost tournaments in the heartland of the UK. In this modern, confused world, the big companies want serious exposure elsewhere. The money goees where the emerging markets exist and, for now, that is east of everything familiar.

Schofield's campaign for greater access to America's riches for his players has meant too many star names setting up camp on the other side of the Atlantic once they have honed their skills on the European Tour. It is, of course, their choice as self-employed men but it continues to be a frustration for those trying to expand further outside America.

The last several years have been difficult. The implosion of the financial world and the rolling recession has hurt everyone. It is not, however, all bad. A new, long-distance contract with the Golf Channel and thus their partner NBC means the Tour has a bedrock of global exposure that could only have been lusted after before. The 2013 Scottish Open, for example, was the first full-blown European Tour event to be broadcast in its entirety to an American audience by NBC. It will not be the last.

## World circuit

Meanwhile the big names dip in and out of here and there and while there is not yet an official World Tour there most obviously is a World Circuit. The PGA Tour's Tim Finchem has said: "I think at some point in time men's professional golf will become integrated globally. What form it takes, whether it's a total integration, whether it's a FIFA type I don't know. But there's movement. I would see that continuing towards integration. We're not going to play a ton of tournaments over there (outside America) so it shouldn't be a problem. George (O'Grady) knows that. We're talking to him constantly about what our plan should be. My guess is it will result in us doing even more together."

While we wait to see how this pans out, the European Tour continues to roll on and should grow even stronger. It has come a long way since those early, stumbling steps and much has been achieved. There is never any room for complacency but for now there is much more that should be applauded and appreciated.

This applause is likely to be led by men like Mark Roe. A touring professional for 21 years and now a TV analyst with Sky as well as a board member of the Tour, Roe knows better than most just how much the Tour has changed. "The first tournament I played was in Cannes in 1985. I had to lug my own practice balls over with me and then when I got off the plane I looked for other players to share a taxi to the hotel.

"It was the same when I got to the course. First thing to do was to look up who you were drawn with and ask if they fancied sharing taxis back and forth. Then you'd join a queue in the clubhouse to buy a sandwich while the members looked at you in that funny way. That first year I earned £6,456 and just managed to keep my card. Then I won £26,000 for the season and finished 38th on the old Order of Merit. Finishing 38th last year in the Race to Dubai earned around £750,000.

"Ken Schofield and now George O'Grady have done a fantastic job to this point. No-one is looking for a taxi share any more. There are courtesy cars and players' lounges and our own agronomy team so that courses are presented brilliantly. It helps create an atmosphere of excellence that you now see reflected in play. It's why I am incredibly proud of of the European Tour and what it has achieved and how it has evolved."

Roe is not alone in feeling this way. No-one could have foreseen the phenomenal growth of the Tour but then no-one could have foreseen the modern world and a planet more connected than ever before and quite possibly more confused as well.

Fact is that the global village is here and the European Tour is indeed a vibrant, small part of this new world. It is a long time since the Tour began the week after the United States Masters with the Portuguese Open before ending in early September.

Back then computers were confined to NASA and a few scientists. Back then private jets were objects of desire not the preferred mode of travel for successful golfers. Back then the editor of this book used to help this journalist light an early morning fire to combat the cold of a Madrid Open in April, the Media Centre a small, chilly room on the first floor of the Puerta de Hierro clubhouse, the players' scores written by hand and hauled up to us via a piece of string tied to a wicker basket.

Yes, indeed, an awful lot of people can take pride in what has happened since those early, happy days.

## Join the European Tour (not the navy) to see the world!

The European Tour is truly global. When former Executive Director Ken Schofield shrewdly pointed out that the European Tour was defined by its members and not by its geographical position that was the green light for the Tour to expand and develop perhaps to an even greater extent than was first imagined.

Just how wide Schofield saw his new "playing field" can best be judged by the fact that European Tour events have been played in South America, Australia, South Africa, Asia and that of course means China where the game is likely to grow dramatically over the next few years.

In more recent times Australia, whose golfers have been part of the backbone of the Tour since the start, have preferred to go it more or less on their own – the limited international "flavour" to their events coming from China, Asia and imported Americans rather than Europe but offsetting this is an expansion of European ties with the Sunshine circuit in South Africa.

Just to underline how international the Tour, second only to the PGA Tour in America is, can be judged from the number of countries that have provided winners – 35 to be exact.

Seve Ballesteros won 50 titles on the European Tour.

© The R&A

The figures in brackets show the number of wins per country: Argentina (30), Australia (111), Austria (5), Belgium (3), Brazil (1), Canada (3), Chile (1), China (2), Chinese Taipei (2). Denmark (27), England (282). Fiji (13) Finland (3), France (30), Germany (64) India (9), Ireland (48), Italy (19), Japan (1), Netherlands (7), New Zealand (25) Northern Ireland (49), Portugal (2), Scotland (132), Singapore (1), South Africa (117), South Korea (6), Spain (166), Sweden (95), Switzerland (1), Thailand (8), Trinidad and Tobago (2), United States of America (133), Wales (46) and Zimbabwe (29).

The late Severiano Ballesteros with 50 wins leads the list of players who have won most titles on the Tour since its inception. His total was eight more than second placed Bernhard Langer, 17 more than third placed Colin Montgomerie and 16 more than six-time major winner Sir Nick Faldo.

# The Claret Jug – golf's most coveted prize

Arguably the most famous sporting trophy in the world and easily the most readily recognised, the Golf Champion Trophy, more commonly known as the Claret Jug, is the trophy awarded annually to the winner of The Open Championship.

Hallmarked 1873, the first winner to be presented with it was Tom Kidd. However, the name of 1872 winner, Tom Morris Jr, was the first to be engraved on the Claret Jug. He won the Championship for a fourth time in that year but, as the trophy was not ready for presentation, he was given a gold medal instead.

The rule stipulating that the winner would retain the trophy after three wins in a row was removed when the Championship resumed in 1872. If it had remained, the Championship would now be on its fifth trophy, as Jamie Anderson, Bob Ferguson and Peter Thomson all succeeded in achieving a hat-trick of victories.

In 1927, The Royal and Ancient Golf Club's Championship Committee decided to retain the Claret Jug for safe-keeping, with future winners being presented with a replica.

Every winner, from Walter Hagan in 1928 to the present, has received this replica, which they keep until the following Open as Champion Golfer of the Year. The original remains on permanent display in The Royal and Ancient Clubhouse.

Most people witnessing the presentation ceremony will be unaware of a mini-drama that takes place immediately after the winning shot is played when the engraver, Garry Harvey, has a mere 8–12 minutes in which to add the winner's name, the year, the venue and the winning score. It started when Roberto de Vicencio returned the jug without his name on it. After a few years, The R&A decided that it would be a good idea for the jug to be engraved on site right after the final putt. Alexander Harvey, Garry's father, undertook that duty for 33 years.

The first time Garry engraved the trophy was when Todd Hamilton won it at Royal Troon in 2004.

A talented and successful golfer, Garry won the British Boys Championship at Moortown, Leeds, in 1972 when he engraved the trophy himself (surely a unique event?) having been runner-up the year before to Howard Clark. Turning professional in 1976, Garry held a European Tour card until 1986 when he won the Kenya Open.

*Photos courtesy of The British Golf Museum*

# Five time Open champion Peter Thomson – the golfing pioneer

## Peter Stone charts the Australian's global legacy

Modesty, despite his grand achievements in the world of golf, both on and off the golf course, has always been Peter Thomson's constant companion. Yes, he was, and still is for that matter, forever confident but quietly so unlike others who've reached similar lofty heights.

Indeed, Thomson was very much an amateur at heart in a professional game that, these days, has almost obscenely huge purses which, sadly, are matched by the egos of many who pocket the fat cheques.

Back in 1993, fellow Australian Greg Norman proposed a world tour of golf with 10 tournaments. He had the financial backing of media baron Rupert Murdoch and his international News Corporation and the verbal support of many of the leading players but Norman has always believed the PGA Tour and its Commissioner Tim Finchem nobbled his idea.

Norman says in his book, *The Way of the Shark*, "(the players) changed their minds. 'If the PGA Tour is not involved, I won't play,' said one. 'I like the concept because it's the free enterprise system at work,' said another. 'But I'm not going to turn my back on the PGA Tour'."

Then, lo and behold, the PGA Tour – and Finchem – created its series of World Golf Championships with three tournaments coming onto the scene in 1999 and, although there have been different sponsors they remain as the WGC–Accenture Match Play Championship, the WGC–Cadillac Championship and the WGC–Bridgestone Championship. A fourth – the WGC–HSBC Champions – began in 2009.

Since then, Norman has been forever aggrieved.

In truth, it was P W Thomson who saw golf as a global game, not one that was confined to the magnificent links courses of Britain and Ireland, nor the European courses and certainly not in the United States where Arnold Palmer with his raw appeal had so popularised the game of golf in the mid to late 1950s.

Just recently, and a few days after I'd been asked to write this article, I woke before the birds and turned the television onto a sports channel that was showing a re-run of an archival documentary

Peter Thomson, winner of five Opens, was a global player long before golfers travelled the world as they do today.

© Getty Images

on The Big Three – Palmer, Jack Nicklaus and Gary Player – who had their tours around the globe playing exhibitions arranged by their manager, the late Mark McCormack.

Indeed, the claim was made it was The Big Three who globalised golf. What nonsense. When I first became the senior golf correspondent of a metropolitan newspaper in Australia in 1969 – at the *Melbourne Age* – Thomson was the golf columnist, and he took me under his wing.

We spoke often, sometimes over a convivial drop of the deadener when the day was done, Thomson, or Five-Times as we called him because of his five Open Championship victories (1954-55-56-58-65), talked of his pioneering days in the Far East and his trips to southern Africa with fondness and a sense of achievement.

He'd had the chance to make The Big Three The Big Four for McCormack asked him to join his troupe of travellers but he politely declined, and continued to do things his way – as he has always done.

His view was it was necessary to have a healthy circuit outside the US because there were too many golfers to have just one circuit in the world. It is true Thomson never embraced America, nor did Americans embrace him but he did play full-time on its tour in 1953-54 and, in 1956, he played eight events winning the Texas Invitational.

In the 1950s, Thomson's name was instantly recogniseable everywhere golf was played save for

*Peter Thomson won the Open five times and still had time to do his journalistic duties and send his news reports back to Australia.*

the US of A where folk didn't know, or didn't want to know, there was a big wide world outside their own country. It is an attitude that still prevails in some quarters.

He did, of course, go to the States in 1985 to plunder the US Seniors Tour, winning nine times, and one wonders what might have been had he actually made that country his home away from home during his prime.

It was instead the Far East – or Asia as we now call it – that beckoned Thomson. His first overseas trip was to Manila for the Philippine Open as a 20-year-old soon after he had turned professional. The godfather of Australian golf – the late Norman Von Nida – had arranged Thomson an invitation and they travelled together via Singapore.

"It was my first taste of the exotic east," Thomson says. "It was fascinating because you're not accustomed to it and the people involved and the environment and, for a young boy on his first overseas trip, an entirely new scene and very attractive."

One can totally understand that. He grew up in the poor inner-west suburb of Brunswick in Melbourne where tough – and rough – men were born and, while Thomson was never the latter, he was always the former with a love of golf and a humanitarian view on life.

In that Philippine Open he finished fifth, and received the extraordinary sum of 750 pounds. That year, South African Bobby Locke at Troon won his second of four Open Championships at Royal Troon and his purse was just 300 pounds.

"It was massive, and it set me on my tracks," Thomson said. After the Philippines, I went to South Africa to accept an invitation to tour southern Africa with the two of us showing off in exhibition games and that again multiplied my bank account and sent me further on track."

Sponsors put up the cash, and there was no appearance money involved. Thomson, through the years, has been a vocal opponent of appearance fees and says: "I can honestly say I never accepted money before I played. I learned that with my brief entry to the United States field, discovering they had strong rules against appearance fees. The sponsors agreed as a group to outlaw it. Every one should be equal."

Thomson did go to the Far East in the late 1950s, as the winner of four Open Championships at the time, to play the local champion for cash put up by sponsors.

"I guess you could say I went to exhibit myself. There were 500 or so people watching and I said to local officials: "Can you imagine what it would be like if we had a whole contingent of golfers to watch – Australians, the rest of Asia and the players from the United Kingdom?" Thomson says.

"If you come and play, we'll make it happen," the various golfing officials said.

And, with that, Thomson became the universally recognised founding father of Asian golf. Tournaments in eight countries – Japan, Korea, Taiwan, Hong Kong, Thailand, India, Indonesia and the Philippines – were co-ordinated into a single circuit in February–March, months when the northern hemisphere was waking up after winter.

It was the early 1960s.

A committee was formed with representatives from each country with Thomson on board to give the players perspective. Thomson was the guiding light while an expatriate Welshman Kim Hall who was a member of the Royal Hong Kong GC (the "Royal" has since been dropped after the Chinese reclaimed the territory in 1997) was his right-hand man.

Thomson urged the Asians that they needed to televise the tournaments. They were ambivalent to the idea, happy enough that there would be a few spectators on the ground but Thomson was persuasive. In another calling, he surely could have been a diplomat.

Airline travel was coordinated to limit costs and the good players were earning around six thousand pounds if they played well. That sounds miniscule by today's standards but it was a fortune back in the 1960s in a region where wages were low and the cost of living was equally so.

The foreign players who ventured into those parts were happy enough, save for the courses that were being played. Thomson says: "The greens were an indigenous grass and it was a battle to get them cut. The ball had to be struck hard but putting on lousy greens is a real lesson I can tell you.

"But you were playing golf. Turn your back on it and you weren't playing golf. It was very important for every one of us who aspired to make a living to learn how to do it in Asia. It was a training ground for many of them including myself. It's a fact that you keep learning if you're astute enough."

Mind you, when Thomson played in the US in the 1950s he wasn't exactly enamoured by some courses. In Indianapolis they played one inside the racetrack, in San Antonio for the Texas Open they played off rubber mats on the tee and the Los Angeles Open was played on a public course.

In November in 2013, the Indian Open celebrated its 50th anniversary at the Delhi GC. Thomson won the first Indian Open, one of three, with that inaugural victory. He was invited back to join the party but declined, having already accepted to attend the centenary New Zealand PGA championship, a tournament he won nine times. He sent a video message of congratulations.

Asked now, about whether he felt he was the founding father of Asian golf, now embraced by the European Tour with co-sanctioned events, he said, modestly as always, "That's for others to judge."

He did admit though – (Development of an Asian circuit) would have come anyway, but it may have taken 10 or so years more."

Through his illustrious career of more than 100 tournament victories, Thomson won the national titles of 10 different countries, more than any other golfer, and if anyone is entitled to refer to himself as the pioneer of global golf, he is. He doesn't. He's too modest for that. His has been a love and passion for golf like few others.

## Peter Thomson's Open record second to none

Peter Thomson's Open record is quite remarkable. He first came and played in the Championship in 1951 when, for the only time, The Open was played at Royal Portrush. He came sixth that year behind Max Faulkner but that was only the start of an incredible run which saw him finish in the top two for the next seven years.

In 1952 he finished second to Bobby Locke at Royal Lytham and St Annes and was again runner up the following year to Ben Hogan at Carnoustie. In 1954 he won the first of his five Opens at Royal Birkdale, followed that up by successfully defending the following year at St Andrews before completing a hat trick of wins in 1956 at Royal Liverpool. He was second again to Bobby Locke in 1957 before winning for a fourth time in 1958.

His run of 2-2-1-1-1-2-1 in the most prestigious Championship in the world was truly a golden period for him between 1952 and 1958. It was all achieved with quiet modesty.

Most people consider that his fifth Open triumph in 1965, again at Royal Birkdale, was his greatest because of the number of top Americans in the field. In the final round he played with the defending champion "Champagne" Tony Lema who was later killed in an aeroplane accident.

© Getty Images

Twenty years later, after a failed bid to make it into the Australian parliament, Thomson joined the Senior Tour in America and proved he had lost none of his competitive edge by taking nine titles in one season. It is hardly surprising that a man who has done so much for golf over the years is an Honorary Member of the Royal and Ancient Golf Club of St Andrews.

# Americans gain revenge for their Walker Cup defeat in Aberdeen

## Renton Laidlaw on a disappointing visit to Long Island

After England's Matthew Fitzpatrick won the US Amateur Championship, for the first time in the event's history stretching back to the 1890's, there was a glimmer of hope that the Great Britain and Ireland Walker Cup team might just pull off another rare win on US soil.

It was not to be. Instead, over the famous National Golf Links on Long Island which played host to the first Walker Cup in 1922, they lost 17–9. It was America's biggest winning margin since their 18–6 victory at Quaker Ridge in New York State in 1997.

The victory, by an arguably very strong American side determined to avenge their defeat at Royal Aberdeen two years earlier, meant that they now lead 7–6 as far as the last 13 matches are concerned. Of course, overall the Americans have won 35, lost eight and drawn one at Five Farms in 1965.

The fact was that the Americans adapted better to the fast greens on the Charles Blair Macdonald course than the Europeans who found that putting surfaces running at 11ft 8 ins were tantalisingly difficult to handle.

Nigel Edwards, the Welshman who led Great Britain and Ireland to success in 2011, said when it was all over: "We are all bitterly disappointed. We did not do the simple things well. We didn't hole enough putts, we missed greens with wedge approach shots which is always very costly especially when you short-side yourself in the process

"The lads played their hearts out. It's not that they didn't try. It's just that having had so much success in recent years it is – well disappointing but we shall learn from the experience."

Although the Great Britain and Ireland players won four foursomes to the Americans' three with one drawn, they were well beaten in the singles winning only four and drawing one of the 18 games.

On the brighter side, it was a good week for the 19-year-old World No 1 Fitzpatrick who won two foursomes in partnership with 27-year-old Neil Raymond and then, having lost by 3 and 1 in the Saturday singles to Michael Weaver, best him 3 and 2 when they met again on Sunday.

When it was all over the American captain, Jim Holtgrieve, who had been given the chance to captain the side for a second time, said: "I wanted to win but I also wanted to do something good for golf and victory here was to me truly good for golf."

Well, for American golf anyway.

The 45th match will be played in 2015 at Royal Lytham and St Annes on September 12 and 13.

## It was a family affair when Fitzpatrick won the US Amateur

© Getty Images

Matthew Fitzpatrick, who won three out of four points for Great Britain and Ireland in the Walker Cup, had his young brother Alex caddying for him when he won the US Amateur Championship – the first Englishman to do so in over 100 years. Incidentally, when Alejandro Larrazabal won the Amateur title at Royal Porthcawl in 2002, his caddie was his young brother Pablo, now a European Tour professional

# Back to Royal Liverpool where mighty champions are bred

## Mike Aitken writes about a course steeped in history

Although The Open will be held at Royal Liverpool for a dozenth occasion in July, the Merseyside links is preparing to play host to the world's greatest players for just the fourth championship there in more than half-a-century. Since Peter Thomson lifted the Claret Jug in 1956 – taking home the modest remuneration of £1,000 for his trouble – only Roberto de Vicenzo in 1967 and Tiger Woods in 2006 have embraced glory at Hoylake.

It was Bernard Darwin who once famously described Hoylake as "blown upon by mighty winds, breeder of mighty champions." Alas, between de Vicenzo's triumphant moment during the summer of love and Woods' successful defence of the title eight years ago, a generation of champions were conspicuous only by their absence from the Wirral.

Bobby Jones, Walter Hagen, J.H. Taylor and Fred Daly are among the past thoroughbred winners of the Claret Jug on a links which originally shared land with a racecourse. Yet for 39 years not even a footnote was added to the story of a great seaside course which Peter Dawson, the Chief Executive of The R&A, believes is "steeped" in history.

For it was here the first Amateur championship was held in 1885 and in 1897 became only the second English club (Royal St George's was the first)

to lure The Open south from Scotland. The oldest major was staged here ten times in 70 years before the modern demands of event infrastructure, created by ever increasing spectator numbers, caused a hiatus after the Argentine won in 1967.

The inaugural golf match between Scotland and England was also contested at Hoylake in 1902 and in 1921 the first encounter between the USA and Great Britain and Ireland – the forerunner of the Walker Cup – went to Royal Liverpool. When the club celebrates its 150th anniversary in 2019, the Walker Cup proper will be held there for the first time since 1983.

In many respects it was appropriate that Woods, the best player of recent times, should win Hoylake's comeback presentation of The Open and enable the links to emerge from the shadows of abstraction in front of huge crowds of 230,000, a record for the championship in England. This was a massive leap from the 30,000 who paid to watch in 1967.

Perhaps there were many who feared Hoylake might never return to the championship rota. Indeed, that might have been the case had the club, with the support of The R&A, not been able to purchase a parcel of land beside the eighth hole from a former preparatory school which accommodated

The first Amateur Championship was held at the Royal Liverpool club in 1885 and it was the venue of the first Great Britain and Ireland v America match before the Walker Cup was instituted.

*John Ball, along with Harold Hilton, was one of the early members who put the club on he map. He won the Amateur Championship eight times and in 1890 won both the Amateur and Open titles matched only by Bobby Jones in 1930.*

both corporate hospitality facilities and the BBC's outside broadcast unit.

Given Royal Liverpool's place at the beating heart of English golf – only Westward Ho! has been around longer – it was little wonder the sense of bemusement felt by Dawson before the 2006 Open when he took a telephone call from "a very senior" American professional who wanted to know if the links was new. "He will remain nameless," smiled the Chief Executive, "but clearly we were away too long."

If Woods' winning score of 18 under par on a fast, running links said as much about the conditions in 2006 as Tiger's own tactical brilliance, the lay-out

at Hoylake can still be regarded as one of the two or three toughest seaside courses. Demanding holes pepper the links which require long, accurate drives and those who get out of position are likely to be punished. In 2012, when the Ricoh Women's British Open featured gales blowing up to 60 mph, Jiyai Shin's winning score was an impressive 279. However, she was the only player in the élite field to finish in the red figures which denote scores below par, nine strokes clear of her nearest rival.

In 2013, Ewan Ferguson became the first Scot in a decade to win the Boys' Championship at Hoylake with a 10 and 9 win over Germany's Michael Himmer. It was the most one sided final since Sandy Lyle lost by a similar margin in 1974, also at Royal Liverpool.

Donald Steel, the architect who oversaw the changes for 2006, insisted he just "re-arranged the furniture." Nevertheless, even Steel conceded the decision to open the batting with what was previously the 17th, meant Hoylake now confronts the game's best players with "as stout an opening hole as any on the Open rota." The old first, now the third, with out of bounds on the right, is also as fierce as ever. After once sending five balls out of play here, Jamie Anderson, the winner of three Opens, rued: "My God, it's like playing up a spout…"

Change has been gradual at Hoylake rather than violent with the links showing a modest increase in length this year of under 100 yards to 7,350 yards compared to The Open in 2006. Since Woods' victory, 13 bunkers have been removed leaving 82 in total; five holes have new swales around the greens to punish errant shots with more varied hazards; and the green on "Royal" (the members' 17th and the opening championship hole) was redesigned in 2010. It's now 40 yards long with tricky run-off areas on either side. A testing start awaits.

## Quality winners of 11 previous Opens at Hoylake

| Year | Winner | Score | Entry | Prize Money £ |
| --- | --- | --- | --- | --- |
| 1897 | Harold Hilton (Royal Liverpool) (am) | 314 | 86 | 100 |
| 1902 | Sandy Herd (Huddersfield) | 307 | 112 | 125 |
| 1907 | Arnaud Massey (France) | 312 | 193 | 125 |
| 1913 | J H Taylor (Mid-Surrey) | 304 | 269 | 135 |
| 1924 | Walter Hagen (USA) | 301 | 277 | 225 |
| 1930 | Bobby Jones (USA) (am) | 291 | 296 | 400 |
| 1937 | Alf Padgham (Sundridge Park) | 287 | 286 | 500 |
| 1947 | Fred Daly (Balmoral | 293 | 263 | 1,000 |
| 1956 | Peter Thomson (Australia) | 286 | 360 | 3,750 |
| 1967 | Roberto de Vicenzo (Argentina) | 278 | 326 | 15,000 |
| 2006 | Tiger Woods (USA) | 270 | 2,434 | 2,750,000 |

# How profits from The Open are wisely used to aid golf

As a result of the commercial success of The Open Championship Duncan Weir, Executive Director of The R&A in charge of the successful Working for Golf project, has a budget of several million pounds each year to fund a varied number of projects guaranteed to benefit the game.

Using the 135 affiliated organisations around the world The R&A invests in key areas affecting the playing and development of golf worldwide.

Because The R&A administers the Rules of Golf worldwide except in America and Mexico which comes under the jurisdiction of the USGA, Rules Schools are regularly held most recently in Brazil, Argentina, Laos and Singapore. In addition David Rickman, Executive Director – Rules and Equipment Standards, has inaugurated an online Rules Academy. It can be found on the internet at www.randa.org/rules academy

Top professionals are sent to coach golfers in countries where golf is a comparatively new sport but which is growing quickly in popularity. Most recently The R&A sent out coaches to Estonia, China, Hungary, Iran, Jordan, Lithuania and Abu Dhabi where Dunhill Links champion David Howell was involved.

Of course, sometimes The R&A representatives do not need to travel as far. Bill Murray, a former member of the European Tour, has coached in Jamaica, France, Colombia, Uganda, Italy, France

and Germany but, most recently, was involved in Scotland coaching youngsters in Shetland, Skye and the Outer Hebrides.

The R&A have an extensive equipment testing programme supervised by Steve Otto Director – Research and Testing, whose team examines thousands of items each year. With the assistance of major manufacturers, The R&A also provides sets of golf clubs to areas of the world where they are in short supply.

Since 2001, The R&A has delivered greenkeeping machinery to courses in need of help. Over 40 countries have benefitted including Fiji, Kenya and Romania. The greenkeeping staff shown below were delighted with their new mowers provided under the scheme.

Of course, The R&A support amateur golf tournaments around the world and are actively involved supporting university and student golf throughout the year... including help in financing the Palmer Cup, the annual match between students from America and Europe.

Steve Isaac's Golf Course Management Depart-ment provides a global information resource to help raise awareness of the economic, environmental and social benefits a well-managed course can deliver. Information can be found at the www.randa.org/golfcoursemanagement site.

© The R&A

# Jiménez makes European Tour history – again

© Asian Tour

When Spanish veteran star Miguel Angel Jiménez claimed a record-equalling fourth Hong Kong Open victory last year by defeating Thailand's Prom Meesawat and Stuart Manley of Wales at the first-hole of a sudden-death play-off, he was writing another chapter of European Tour history.

Jimenez, who turned 50 in January, rolled in a 15-foot birdie putt to win and, at the age of 49 years and 337 days, became the oldest winner on the European Tour and the second oldest on the Asian Tour.

He already held the oldest European winner record set when he won the Hong Kong event in 2012. He also won in 2005 and 2008.

After securing his 20th career victory – 13 of them since turning 40 – Jiménez said: "Winning in a play-off is always harder because you need to play the extra holes carefully. It's always tough against two guys at the top of their game."

The popular champion closed with a four-under-par 66 for a 12-under-par 268 aggregate, which was matched by Prom, who charged home in 65, thanks to two glorious eagles. Then Manley forced his way into the play-off with a stunning chip-in birdie on the 18th green during regulation play.

Jiménez, who was recently named as the playing captain for the EurAsia Cup, credited his experience of the event and the course for sealing his place in the winner's circle once more. It was his 618th European Tour event.

Only Hsieh Yung-yo had won four Hong Kong Opens previously in 1963, 1964, 1975 and 1977. Jiménez missed a large part of the 2013 season when recovering from an injury he received while skiing.

# Championship dates

| | The Masters | US Open | The Open | US PGA Championship |
|---|---|---|---|---|
| 2014 | **April 10–13**<br>Augusta National,<br>Augusta, GA | **June 12–15**<br>Pinehurst Resort<br>(Course No 2), NC | **July 17–20**<br>Royal Liverpool,<br>Hoylake, Merseyside | **August 7–10**<br>Valhalla GC, Louisville, KY |
| 2015 | **April 9–12**<br>Augusta National,<br>Augusta, GA | **June 18–21**<br>Chambers Bay,<br>University Place, WA | **July 16–19**<br>St Andrews, Fife | **August 13–16**<br>Whistling Straits GC (Straits<br>Course), Kohler, WI |
| 2016 | **April 7–10**<br>Augusta National,<br>Augusta, GA | **June 16–19**<br>Oakmont CC, PA | **July 14–17**<br>Royal Troon, Ayrshire | **July 28–31**<br>Baltusrol GC (Lower Course),<br>Springfield, NJ |
| 2017 | **April 6–9**<br>Augusta National,<br>Augusta, GA | **June 15–18**<br>Erin Hills, Erin, WI | **July 20–23**<br>Venue TBA | **August 10–13**<br>Quail Hollow GC, Charlotte,<br>NC |

## Ryder Cup
**2014** Gleneagles Hotel, Perthshire, Scotland Sept 26–28
**2016** Hazeltine National GC, Chaska, MN
**2018** Le Golf National, Versailles, France
**2020** Whistling Straits, Kohler, WI

## Solheim Cup
**2015** St Leon-Rot GC, Frankfurt, Germany Sept 18–20
**2017** Des Moines G&CC, IA

## Presidents Cup
(USA v Rest of the World except Europe)
**2015** South Korea – Jack Nicklaus GC

## Curtis Cup
**2014** St Louis CC, MO                                      June 6–8
**2016** Dun Laoghaire GC, Ireland                  June 10–12

---

## R&A Contacts
Peter Dawson, Chief Executive

### Business Affairs
Michael Tate, Executive Director – Business Affairs
Robin Bell, Marketing Director        Malcolm Booth, Communications Director
Angus Farquhar, Commercial Director

### Championships
Johnnie Cole-Hamilton, Executive Director – Championships.
Rhodri Price, Director – Championship Operations
Michael Wells, Director – Championship Staging
Euan Mordaunt, Director – Amateur Events

### Finance
John Murray, Executive Director – Finance

### Rules and Equipment Standards
David Rickman, Executive Director – Rules and Equipment Standards
Grant Moir, Director – Rules        Steve Otto, Director – Research and Testing

### Working for Golf
Duncan Weir, Executive Director – Working for Golf
Angela Howe, Museum and Heritage Director        Steve Isaac, Director Golf Course Management
Dominic Wall, Director – Asia/Pacific

Up-to-date news of The R&A and its activities can be found at www.RandA.org
The R&A can be contacted on: Tel 01334 460000   Fax 01334 460001

# R&A championship dates, 2014–2016

|  | 2014 | 2015 | 2016 |
|---|---|---|---|
| **The Open Championship** | July 17–20<br>Royal Liverpool | July 16–19<br>St Andrews | July 14–17<br>Royal Troon |
| **The Open Championship Final Qualifying (local)** | July 1<br>Glasgow – Gailes Links<br>Hillside<br>Royal Cinque Ports<br>Woburn | June 30<br>Glasgow – Gailes Links<br>Hillside<br>Royal Cinque Ports<br>Woburn | June 28<br>Glasgow – Gailes Links<br>Hillside<br>Royal Cinque Ports<br>Woburn |
| **The Senior Open Championship** | July 24–27<br>Royal Porthcawl | July 23–26<br>Venue TBA | July 21–24<br>Venue TBA |
| **The Amateur Championship** | June 16–21<br>Royal Portrush<br>Portstewart | June 15–20<br>Carnoustie<br>Panmure | June 13–18<br>Royal Porthcawl<br>Pyle & Kenfig |
| **The Seniors Amateur Championship** | August 6–8<br>Ganton | August 5–7<br>Royal County Down | August 3–5<br>Formby |
| **The Junior Open Championship** | July 14–16<br>West Lancashire | – | July 11–13<br>Kilmarnock (Barassie) |
| **The Boys' Amateur Championship** | August 12–17<br>Prestwick<br>Dundonald Links | August 11–16<br>Royal Birkdale<br>Southport & Ainsdale | August 9–14<br>Muirfield<br>The Renaissance |
| **The Boys' Home Internationals** | August 5–7<br>Western Gailes | August 4–6<br>Conwy (Caernarvonshire) | August 2–4<br>Ballyliffen – Glashedy Links |
| **The Jacques Léglise Trophy** | August 29–30<br>Sweden | August 28–29<br>Royal Dornoch | August 26–27<br>Prince's |
| **The Walker Cup** | – | September 12–13<br>Royal Lytham & St Annes | – |
| **The St Andrews Trophy** | August 29–30<br>Sweden | – | August 26–27<br>Prince's |
| **The World Amateur Team Championships (Espirito Santo Trophy)** | September 3–6<br>Karuizawa, Japan | – | September 14–17<br>Mexico |
| **The World Amateur Team Championships (Eisenhower Trophy)** | September 10–13<br>Karuizawa, Japan | – | September 21–24<br>Mexico |

Other fixtures and tour schedules
can be found on pages 494–500

# Abbreviations

| | | | | | | | |
|---|---|---|---|---|---|---|---|
| AFG | Afghanistan | HKG | Hong Kong | PAR | Paraguay |
| ALB | Albania | HUN | Hungary | PER | Peru |
| ALG | Algeria | INA | Indonesia | PHI | Philippines |
| ARG | Argentina | IND | India | PNG | Papua New Guinea |
| AUS | Australia | IOM | Isle of Man | POL | Poland |
| AUT | Austria | IRI | Iran | POR | Portugal |
| BAH | Bahamas | IRL | Ireland | PUR | Puerto Rico |
| BAN | Bangladesh | ISL | Iceland | QAT | Qatar |
| BAR | Barbados | ISR | Israel | ROM | Romania |
| BDI | Burundi | ISV | US Virgin Islands | RSA | South Africa |
| BEL | Belgium | ITA | Italy | RUS | Russia |
| BER | Bermuda | JAM | Jamaica | SAM | Samoa |
| BHU | Bhutan | JOR | Jordan | SCO | Scotland |
| BOL | Bolivia | JPN | Japan | SIN | Singapore |
| BOT | Botswana | KAZ | Kazakhstan | SKA | St Kitts & Nevis |
| BRA | Brazil | KEN | Kenya | SLO | Slovenia |
| BRN | Bahrain | KGZ | Kyrgyzstan | SOL | Solomon Islands |
| BUL | Bulgaria | KOR | Korea (South) | SRB | Serbia |
| CAM | Cambodia | KSA | Saudi Arabia | SRI | Sri Lanka |
| CAN | Canada | KUW | Kuwait | SUI | Switzerland |
| CAY | Cayman Islands | LAO | Laos | SVK | Slovakia |
| CHI | Chile | LAT | Latvia | SWE | Sweden |
| CHN | China | LBA | Libya | SWZ | Swaziland |
| CIV | Côte d'Ivoire | LBN | Lebanon | TAN | Tanzania |
| COK | Cook Islands | LCA | Saint Lucia | TCI | Turks and Caicos |
| COL | Colombia | LTU | Lithuania | | Islands |
| CRC | Costa Rica | LUX | Luxembourg | THA | Thailand |
| CRO | Croatia | MAC | Macau | TPE | Taiwan |
| CYP | Cyprus | MAW | Malawi | | (Chinese Taipei) |
| CZE | Czech Republic | MAR | Morocco | TRI | Trinidad and Tobago |
| DEN | Denmark | MAS | Malaysia | TUN | Tunisia |
| DOM | Dominican Rep. | MEX | Mexico | TUR | Turkey |
| ECU | Ecuador | MGL | Mongolia | UAE | United Arab |
| EGY | Egypt | MON | Monaco | | Emirates |
| ENG | England | MYA | Myanmar | UGA | Uganda |
| ESA | El Salvador | NAM | Namibia | UKR | Ukraine |
| ESP | Spain | NCA | Nicaragua | URU | Uruguay |
| EST | Estonia | NED | Netherlands | USA | United States |
| FIJ | Fiji | NEP | Nepal | VAN | Vanuatu |
| FIN | Finland | NIG | Niger | VEN | Venezuela |
| FRA | France | NIR | Northern Ireland | VIE | Vietnam |
| GER | Germany | NGR | Nigeria | WAL | Wales |
| GRE | Greece | NOR | Norway | ZAM | Zambia |
| GUA | Guatemala | NZL | New Zealand | ZIM | Zimbabwe |
| GUM | Guam | PAK | Pakistan | | |
| HON | Honduras | PAN | Panama | | |

GB&I    Great Britain and Ireland

| | | | | | | | |
|---|---|---|---|---|---|---|---|
| (am) | Amateur | (M) | Match play | Jr | Junior |
| (D) | Defending champion | (S) | Stroke play | Sr | Senior |

Where available, total course yardage and the par for a course are displayed in square brackets, i.e. [6686–70]

* indicates winner after play-off

# New qualifying system for The Open

John Senden, Rhein Gibson and Bryden Macpherson qualified for this year's Open Championship at Hoylake through the first event in the new Open Qualifying Series.

The three Australians secured the three places on offer at the Emirates Australian Open at Royal Sydney to join winner Rory McIlroy and runner-up Adam Scott in the field for golf's oldest and most international major championship.

The new series will take in 14 events in nine countries on five continents as players on the world's leading Tours bid to qualify for The Open at Royal Liverpool from 13–20 July.

The 42-year-old Senden from Brisbane, who shot a closing 66 to finish third in the Championship,will make his eighth appearance in The Open with his best finish coming at Royal Lytham and St Annes in 20012 where he tied 34th behind Ernie Els.

Gibson and Macpherson finished two shots back on nine-under-par for the championship. Gibson will be making his début in a major. The 29-year-old from New South Wales is currently ranked 998th in the Official World Golf Ranking and experienced links golf when he played in the Amateur Championship at Royal Lytham and St Annes in 2007 and Turnberry in 2008.

Macpherson matched Gibson's final round to take his place in The Open for a second time. The 23-year-old from Melbourne won the 2011 Amateur Championship at Hillside. He played in The Open that year at Royal St George's and the 2012 Masters Tournament.

The R&A introduced the new Open Qualifying Series to further enhance the global appeal of The Open and improve the qualifying process for the players. In addition to the qualifying procedure in Australia The new Open Qualifying Series will offer the following additional qualification places:

South Africa – The Joburg Open – three places to the leading three players (not otherwise exempt) who finish in the top 10 and ties.

Thailand – The Open Qualifying Series – four places to the leading four players.

Japan – The Mizuno Open – four places to the leading four players (not otherwise exempt) who finish in the top 12 and ties.

Ireland – The Irish Open – three places to the leading three players (not otherwise exempt) who finish in the top 10 and ties.

France – Alstom Open de France – three places to the leading three players (not otherwise exempt) who finish in the top 10 and ties.

Scotland – Aberdeen Asset Management Scottish Open – three places to the leading three players (not otherwise exempt) who finish in the top 10 and ties.

USA – AT&T National – four places to the leading four players (not otherwise exempt) who finish in the top 12 and ties.

USA – The Greenbrier Classic – four places to the leading four players (not otherwise exempt) who finish in the top 12 and ties.

USA – John Deere Classic – one place to the leading player (not otherwise exempt) who finishes in the top five and ties. This one place is available because of the logisitics involved traveling to Hoylake at short notice.

Final Qualifying – Gailes Links, Hillside, Royal Cinque Ports and Woburn 12 places (three from each event).

Any player who has qualified through The Open Qualifying Series is deemed an exempt player. In the event that that player subsequently fulfils other exemption categories those places will be made available to the highest ranked players on the World Golf Rankings after the close of entries.

The Open delivers an annual economic benefit of up to £100 million to its host region, while the Championship's commercial success supports the development of the game worldwide.

# PART I

# The Major Championships

# After 22 years of trying Mickelson is a glorious winner of The Open

It was entirely fitting the best round of Phil Mickelson's life, a bewitching 66 over Muirfield's magical links in the final round of The Open which featured shot-making and putting of the highest order, should not only inscribe the golfer's name on the Claret Jug for the first time but also write a fresh chapter in the game's history.

If winning The Open Championship was not reward enough for a player who grew up thousands of miles from East Lothian in California and took decades to master the shots required to thrive on the British linksland, Mickelson's victory in Gullane also meant he followed in the elite footsteps of Ernie Els, Sir Nick Faldo, twice, Tom Watson, Lee Trevino, Jack Nicklaus, Gary Player and Henry Cotton as a Muirfield champion in the modern era.

Moreover, his success in The Open, after major triumphs at the Masters and US PGA championships, meant Mickelson joined Arnold Palmer, Tom Watson, Sam Snead Byron Nelson, Lee Trevino and Ray Floyd in the illustrious group of players who have won three different major titles.

And with five major triumphs on his CV – three wins at Augusta as well as The Open Championship and the US PGA – Mickelson is now ranked beside Nelson, Severiano Ballesteros, James Braid, J H Taylor and Peter Thomson on the list of nine all time great champions.

Bearing in mind he's finished runner up in the US Open on a record six occasions, it isn't entirely out of the question, before he puts his clubs away, that Mickelson could join Gene Sarazen, Ben Hogan, Player, Nicklaus and Tiger Woods in the elite band of golfers who have won the career Grand Slam.

The first left-hander golfer to win The Open since Sir Bob Charles half-a-century earlier at Lytham in 1963, Mickelson, 43, also became the oldest Open champion since Roberto de Vicenzo, 44, lifted the Claret Jug at Hoylake in 1967. His triumph over the fairest links continued a recent trend of experience counting for more than youth in The Open. After Darren Clarke, 42, at St George's and Els, 42, at Lytham, Mickelson was the third consecutive champion golfer in his 40s.

Just as Nicklaus once proved his mettle on the links at Muirfield in 1966, often using a 1 iron off the tee to avoid the rough, so Mickelson found a way to navigate the inhospitable seaside terrain of East Lothian with a 3 wood which married power and accuracy. Although the left-hander left the driver out of his bag altogether, he was still able to reach the green of the par 5 17th, all 575 yards, in two mighty blows on Sunday afternoon, thereby setting up the birdie which all but sealed his spectacular victory.

Mickelson's two putt birdie on the 17th came after he'd made a heroic par 3 on the short 16th. Having found the green with a fine iron shot, he looked on in horror as his ball caught a slope and ran off the front of the putting surface. Mickelson's chip and putt for par was as crucial as both of the birdie putts he would go on to make on 17 and 18.

"Phil's round was incredible," observed Nicklaus. "After his bad break on 16 (where his tee shot rolled back off the green), to then get up and down showed a lot of guts. And the two great shots at 17 (to set up a birdie) ended the tournament."

When Mickelson first teed up in The Open as a swashbuckling amateur at Birkdale in 1991, carding 67 in the second round and completing 72 holes, few observers would have been taken aback to learn how the southpaw would go on to win the championship as a professional. The more surprising news might have been it would take the American all of 22 years to unlock the ancient secrets of the links.

This was due, in part, to the fact that, at the start of his career, Mickelson had looked so much at ease over Portmarnock when he played in the Walker Cup. "Well, I did enjoy links golf when I first played at the Walker Cup in 1991 at Portmarnock," he recalled. "It was a wonderful test and I played well. But the conditions and the penalty for missed shots in The Open Championship are much more severe than we played then. And it took me a while to figure it out, I would say. It's been the last eight or nine years I've started to play it more effectively. Yet it is so different from what I grew up playing. I always wondered if I would develop the skills needed to win this championship."

Perhaps it was that question mark against his gifts as a links golfer which persuaded Mickelson to physically hold onto the Claret Jug throughout his champion's press conference, as if he might wake from a reverie and discover it all had been a dream. The reality, though, was he played with the conviction of a champion, and the grip on his game was as secure as his hold on the trophy.

Having finished third at Troon in 2004 and runner-up over Sandwich in 2011, there were positive signs for Mickelson to draw on when he teed up in heatwave conditions at Muirfield. Moreover, his victory the previous week in the Scottish Open, where he was able to hone the lower ball flight required to craft the shots required to succeed on a links, was significant. "I don't think people realised how important winning the Scottish Open at Castle Stuart was," noted his coach Butch Harmon. "It isn't as difficult a course as Muirfield but the environment is the same. You have to control your ball, watch how it bounces and control every other part of your game. That was a special win going to The Open."

True, a negative spin could have been applied to the play-off victory over Branden Grace in Inverness, since many professionals find the emotional cost of victory too draining to perform at the highest level in successive weeks. Indeed, the last golfer to win the week before becoming Open champion was Lee Trevino at Birkdale in 1971 when he secured the Canadian Open. Mickelson, however, already knew how to pull off the trick since he'd won the Bellsouth in Atlanta the week before his Masters win in 2006.

Playing with a winning combination of daring and judgement, Mickelson cradled his first Open at the 20th time of asking, to prove the adage that even old dogs can learn new tricks. The only golfer to negotiate 72 holes of an exacting Muirfield test in a score which bettered par, his three under total of 281, three strokes clear of the rising Henrik Stenson and four ahead of Ian Poulter, Lee Westwood and Adam Scott, was a remarkable accomplishment.

> "I was not trying to force birdies, just hit good shots and made a bunch of putts."
>
> *Mickelson on his closing winning 66*

Subscribing to the old theory that champions drive for show and putt for dough, Mickelson identified a reliable putting stroke as his greatest strength in compiling an extraordinary inward half of 32 in that closing 66. He used his putter just 26 times on Sunday.

"The wow factor just kind of happened," he said. "It wasn't like I set out thinking I need to make birdies or I was trying to force birdies. I was just trying to hit good shots. And I made a bunch of putts. It's as good as I ever putted in my career. Links greens have actually been the reason why I have not been in contention very often here. More so than some of the ball striking. But I putted these greens phenomenally well."

Mickelson's sense of contentment after the final round, mark you, was in stark contrast with his demeanour on Thursday when the course set-up angered the American, even though he signed for a respectable opening salvo of 69. "The organisers should let go of their ego and set the course up the way the best players can win," he rapped. It was an ungracious outburst which the player soon regretted and publicly acknowledged 24 hours later had been unfair.

In a championship where age is no deterrent, the story of the opening day celebrated experience. Zach Johnson, 37, a former Masters' champion, led the way on 66, closely followed by a packed leaderboard which included former winners Mark O'Meara, 56, Tom Lehman, 54, and Todd Hamilton, 47. As O'Meara had quipped: "One for the old farts…"

Flying the flag for the younger generation was Jordan Speith, 19, who opened with a tidy knock of 69. The first teenager to win on the US PGA Tour since Ralph Guldahl at the 1931 Santa Monica Open, the winner of the John Deere Classic had previous experience of links golf when he played for the USA in the Walker Cup match at Royal Aberdeen.

Less content with his youthful lot was Rory McIlroy, the two time major winner who came into the championship at odds with his game and duly posted a dishevelled eight over par score of 79. Whatever was ailing the 24-year-old Ulsterman, it wasn't a lack of candour. "I made stupid mental errors," he reported. "I let shots get away from me – too many loose shots. Sometimes I feel like I'm walking around out there a bit unconscious. I've got to try to think a bit more. I'm trying to concentrate. I can't really fathom it. It's so brain dead."

A day later, and a missed cut in spite of a slightly improved round of 75, left McIlroy better equipped to put the experience in perspective. He said he had a clear picture in his mind of what was required. He'd decided to get the head down and play his way out of bother.

It was left to another "old codger", Miguel Angel Jiménez, 49, to make his mark in the second round with 71 for the halfway lead on 139, three under par. Blessed with a relaxed attitude to the game and the ability to enjoy a glass of Rioja and a fine cigar, the Spaniard confessed: "I tell you I love what I'm doing. I play golf. I do this for a living and I've kept doing the same thing for 25 years. I don't know what's going to happen tomorrow but I'm going to hit some balls now and then have a nice cigar."

Tiger Woods was on 140 thanks to a second round of 71 and well positioned. Striking some glorious iron shots and putting well, the world No 1 performed with enough gusto over the opening 36 holes to suggest his five year drought without a major – his last notable victory was at the US Open in 2008 – could end sooner rather than later.

Mickelson, though, was underwhelmed by his performance on Friday, shooting 74, and it was helpful that his coach, Harmon, was on site to assist with a productive session on Saturday morning which would eventually enable the American to rip through the field on Sunday afternoon.

In the third round, it was another forty-something golfer, Westwood, who was in the spotlight thanks to a round of 70 which handed the Englishman a two shot lead going into the final day. He putted beautifully and had clearly benefited from a lesson given by Ian Baker-Finch in Florida. Now resident in the sunshine state, Westwood said of the baking temperatures in East Lothian: "Little did I know when I moved to Florida that I was acclimatising for The Open in Scotland...."

Martin Laird, the Scot who plies his trade on the US PGA Tour, was entitled to see nothing but blue skies when he walked onto the third tee on Saturday afternoon. He was one under for the opening two holes, two under for the championship, and just a stroke behind the leader, Jiménez, who was on the first. Then, as he reached for a 2 iron he would whack into the right rough, Laird was tossed into a black storm of muddled decision making and poor execution. By the time he included two penalty drops, the Scot had taken a calamitous 9 and his Open chances were over. Proving it never rains but it pours, even when the sun is shining, Laird was also penalised a stroke on the tenth for slightly moving his ball to identify it in the rough. Laird signed for 81.

The Scot wasn't the only golfer in trouble with the officials on Saturday. Hideki Matsuyama was penalised a stroke for slow play on the 17th. It was an infraction which meant the Japanese golfer would eventually finish sixth in the championship rather than celebrate a share of third place.

As for the final day, the silver medal awarded to the leading amateur golfer went to Matthew Fitzpatrick, an 18-year-old slip of an English boy who looked even younger than his tender years and was mistaken on the range earlier in the week for Tiger Woods' ball carrier. Paired with Fred Couples over the closing round, the teenager signed off with 72 for 294 and will now follow in Luke Donald's footsteps by attending Northwestern University in Chicago. Fitzpatrick won the US Amateur title a few weeks later – the first Englishman to win since Harold Hilton in 1911.

> Tiger's conservative game plan back-fired and his chance of a first major win since 2008 was history

In pursuit of the Claret Jug, Mickelson trailed Westwood by five strokes when the final round got underway before a sublime 66, one of the great rounds in championship history, proved too good for the Englishman who finished with an untidy 75, four shots adrift of the winning mark.

If Woods had seemed a likelier winner before a ball was struck on Sunday, his conservative game plan was hindered by a poor day with the putter – he began by missing a three foot putt for par on the first. Thereafter, the winner of 14 majors was a shadow of his former self when the heat was on. His closing score of 74 was sufficient only for a share of sixth.

Like Mickelson, Stenson had played at Castle Stuart and the links experience served him well as he finished off with 70 and matched the par of 284 for 72 holes. While that wasn't quite good enough to become the first Swedish winner of a major, it left the 37-year-old from Gothenburg believing his chance will come, particularly as he enjoyed such a searing end of the season.

With a hot new putter fashioning a remarkable run of six 3s in seven holes between the seventh and the 13th, Poulter gave a shot of adrenalin to the final day's play. His closing 67 for 285 was exceptional and might have run Mickelson even closer had the Englishman not stalled over the closing four holes.

And Mickelson, who emulated Justin Leonard's feat at The Open in 1997 and Faldo at the Masters in 1996 by overcoming a five shot deficit to win by three, finished off with a spree of four birdies in the last six holes. Harmon recalled describing Greg Norman's 64 in 1993 at Sandwich as the best he'd ever seen. "Phil rivals it," he volunteered.

At the end of a week in which the membership policy of the Honourable Company of Edinburgh Golfers had been the subject of widespread debate, the criteria applied to Open winners at Muirfield remained unapologetically exclusive. Only A-list champions need apply.

Mike Aitken

| First Round | Second Round | Third Round | Fourth Round |
|---|---|---|---|
| −5 Zach Johnson | −3 Miguel Angel Jiménez | −3 Lee Westwood | −3 Phil Mickelson |
| −4 Rafael Cabrera-Bello | −2 Dustin Johnson | −1 Hunter Mahan | = Henrik Stenson |
| −4 Mark O'Meara | −2 Tiger Woods | −1 Tiger Woods | +1 Ian Poulter |
| −3 Brandt Snedeker | −2 Lee Westwood | = Adam Scott | +1 Adam Scott |
| −3 Miguel Angel Jiménez | −2 Henrik Stenson | +1 Ryan Moore | +1 Lee Westwood |
| −3 Dustin Johnson | −1 Martin Laird | +1 Zach Johnson | +2 Hideki Matsuyama |
| −3 Tom Lehman | −1 Rafael Cabrera–Bello | +1 Henrik Stenson | +2 Tiger Woods |
| −3 Shiv Kapur | −1 Zach Johnson | +1 Angel Cabrera | +2 Zach Johnson |
| −2 Phil Mickelson | −1 Angel Cabrera | +2 Phil Mickelson | +3 Francesco Molinari |
| −2 Tiger Woods | = Ryan Moore | +2 Francesco Molinari | +3 Hunter Mahan |

# The Open Championship (142nd) *Muirfield, East Lothian, Scotland* July 18–21

[7192–71]

Total Prize Money: £5,250,000. Entries: 2,500. 14 Regional Qualifying Courses: Abridge, Bruntsfield Links, Buckinghamshire, Clitheroe, East Sussex National. Hankley Common, Little Aston, Luffenham Heath, Mere, Moortown, Northumberland, Remedy Oak, The Island, The London

## International Final Qualifying:

**Africa** (Royal Johannesburg & Kensington)
March 5–6

| | |
|---|---|
| Justin Harding (RSA) | 66-64—130 |
| Eduardo de la Riva (ESP) | 67-66—133 |
| Darryn Lloyd (RSA) | 66-69—135 |

**America** (Gleneagles, Dallas, TX) March 5–6

| | |
|---|---|
| Josh Teater (USA) | 64-69—133 |
| Johnson Wagner (USA) | 68-66—134 |
| Camilo Villegas (COL) | 68-66—134 |
| Scott Brown (USA) | 71-64—135 |
| Brian Davis (ENG) | 66-69—135 |
| Robert Karlsson (SWE) | 67-69—136 |
| Luke Guthrie (USA) | 65-71—136 |
| Bud Cauley (USA) | 70-66—136 |

**Asia** (Amata Spring, Thailand) Feb 28 & March 1

| | |
|---|---|
| Kiradech Aphibarnrat (THA) | 68-63—131 |
| Hideki Matsuyama (JPN) (am) | 66-69—135 |
| Daisuke Maruyama (JPN) | 71-65—136 |
| Ashun Wu (CHN) | 68-68—136 |

**Australasia** (Kingston Heath) Jan 29–30

| | |
|---|---|
| Mark Brown (NZL) | 72-62—134 |
| Steven Jeffress (AUS) | 68-67—135 |
| Stephen Dartnall (AUS) | 67-69—136 |

**Europe** (Sunningdale, England) June 24

| | |
|---|---|
| Brooks Koepka (USA) | 69-65—134 |
| Oliver Fisher (ENG) | 70-65—135 |
| Alvaro Quiros (ESP) | 70-66—136 |
| Grégory Bourdy (FRA) | 68-68—136 |
| Richard McEvoy (ENG) | 71-65—136 |
| Gareth Maybin (NIR) | 67-69—136 |
| Niclas Fasth (SWE) | 68-69—137 |
| Scott Jamieson (SCO) | 71-66—137 |
| Estanislao Goya (ARG) | 68-70—138 |

## Local Final Qualifying:

**Dunbar**

| | |
|---|---|
| Grant Forrest (Craigielaw) (am) | 67-65—132 |
| Shiv Kapur (IND) | 69-64—133 |
| John Wade (AUS) | 70-63—133 |

**Gullane No 1**

| | |
|---|---|
| Ben Stow (Rushmore) (am) | 72-68—140 |
| Oscar Floren (SWE) | 72-69—141 |
| Matthew Fitzpatrick (Hallamshire) (am) | 69-72—141 |

**North Berwick**

| | |
|---|---|
| Jimmy Mullen (Royal North Devon) (am) | 68-68—136 |
| Gareth Wright (West Linton) | 69-68—137 |
| George Murray (unattached) | 73-64—137 |

**The Musselburgh**

| | |
|---|---|
| Steven Tiley (unattached) | 64-69—133 |
| Lloyd Saltman (Archerfield Links) | 68-68—136 |
| Tyrrell Hatton (Harleyford) | 69-67—136 |

## 2013 Open Championship – rulings

There were 234 rulings at the 2013 Open, which compares with 339 in 2012 at Lytham where a large number of rulings were given due to casual water on the course caused by the very wet summer. The majority of the rulings given at Muirfield were relatively simple such as unplayable ball (18 rulings), identifying ball (17), interference from movable obstructions such as cables (20) and relief from immovable obstructions such as sprinkler heads (29), which underlines the importance of knowing the basics. There were, however, incidents which represent a selection of some of the more unusual or perhaps unfortunate rulings that occurred during the Championship and these are outlined on the following pages.

142nd Open Championship *continued*

The final field of 156 players included eight amateurs. 84 players (two amateurs) qualified for the last two rounds with scores of 150 or less.

| | | | |
|---|---|---|---|
| 1 | Phil Mickelson (USA) | 69-74-72-66—281 | £945,000 |
| 2 | Henrik Stenson (SWE) | 70-70-74-70—284 | 545,000 |
| 3 | Ian Poulter (ENG) | 72-71-75-67—285 | 280,666 |
| | Adam Scott (AUS) | 71-72-70-72—285 | 280,666 |
| | Lee Westwood (ENG) | 72-68-70-75—285 | 280,666 |
| 6 | Hideki Matsuyama (JPN) | 71-73-72-70—286 | 163,333 |
| | Zach Johnson (USA) | 66-75-73-72—286 | 163,333 |
| | Tiger Woods (USA) | 69-71-72-74—286 | 163,333 |
| 9 | Francesco Molinari (ITA) | 69-74-72-72—287 | 115,000 |
| | Hunter Mahan (USA) | 72-72-68-75—287 | 115,000 |
| 11 | Brandt Snedeker (USA) | 68-79-69-72—288 | 93,500 |
| | Angel Cabrera (ARG) | 69-72-73-74—288 | 93,500 |
| 13 | Justin Leonard (USA) | 74-70-74-71—289 | 79,500 |
| | Miguel Angel Jiménez (ESP) | 68-71-77-73—289 | 79,500 |
| 15 | Eduardo de la Riva (ESP) | 73-73-75-69—290 | 63,916 |
| | Harris English (USA) | 74-71-75-70—290 | 63,916 |
| | Charl Schwartzel (RSA) | 75-68-76-71—290 | 63,916 |
| | Danny Willett (ENG) | 75-72-72-71—290 | 63,916 |
| | Matt Kuchar (USA) | 74-73-72-71—290 | 63,916 |
| | Keegan Bradley (USA) | 75-74-70-71—290 | 63,916 |
| 21 | Stephen Gallacher (SCO) | 76-70-76-69—291 | 47,300 |
| | Darren Clarke (NIR) | 72-71-76-72—291 | 47,300 |
| | Richard Sterne (RSA) | 75-75-68-73—291 | 47,300 |
| | Rafael Cabrera-Bello (ESP) | 67-74-76-74—291 | 47,300 |
| | Sergio García (ESP) | 75-73-68-75—291 | 47,300 |
| 26 | Jason Dufner (USA) | 72-77-76-67—292 | 37,350 |
| | Stewart Cink (USA) | 72-75-76-69—292 | 37,350 |
| | Jonas Blixt (SWE) | 72-78-73-69—292 | 37,350 |
| | Steven Tiley (ENG) | 72-75-73-72—292 | 37,350 |
| | Paul Lawrie (SCO) | 81-69-70-72—292 | 37,350 |
| | Ernie Els (RSA) | 74-74-70-74—292 | 37,350 |
| 32 | Oliver Fisher (ENG) | 70-78-77-68—293 | 25,750 |
| | Shane Lowry (IRL) | 74-74-75-70—293 | 25,750 |
| | Fred Couples (USA) | 75-74-73-71—293 | 25,750 |
| | Y E Yang (KOR) | 78-70-73-72—293 | 25,750 |
| | Thongchai Jaidee (THA) | 79-71-71-72—293 | 25,750 |
| | Bubba Watson (USA) | 70-73-77-73—293 | 25,750 |
| | Bud Cauley (USA) | 74-75-71-73—293 | 25,750 |
| | Martin Kaymer (GER) | 72-74-72-75—293 | 25,750 |
| | Dustin Johnson (USA) | 68-72-76-77—293 | 25,750 |
| | Jason Day (AUS) | 73-71-72-77—293 | 25,750 |
| | Jamie Donaldson (WAL) | 74-71-71-77—293 | 25,750 |
| | Ryan Moore (USA) | 72-70-72-79—293 | 25,750 |
| 44 | Bo van Pelt (USA) | 76-73-77-68—294 | 17,694 |
| | Tim Clark (RSA) | 72-76-76-70—294 | 17,694 |
| | Martin Laird (SCO) | 70-71-81-72—294 | 17,694 |
| | Fredrik Jacobson (SWE) | 72-75-75-72—294 | 17,694 |
| | Matthew Fitzpatrick (ENG) (am) | 73-76-73-72—294 | Silver Medal |
| | Geoff Ogilvy (AUS) | 75-75-72-72—294 | 17,694 |
| | Mark Brown (NZL) | 77-73-72-72—294 | 17,694 |
| | K J Choi (KOR) | 76-74-71-73—294 | 17,694 |
| | Jordan Spieth (USA) | 69-74-76-75—294 | 17,694 |
| | Shingo Katayama (JPN) | 73-77-69-75—294 | 17,694 |
| 54 | Padraig Harrington (IRL) | 73-75-77-70—295 | 13,575 |
| | Marcus Fraser (AUS) | 73-74-76-72—295 | 13,575 |
| | Gonzalo Fernandez-Castano (ESP) | 70-79-73-73—295 | 13,575 |
| | Carl Pettersson (SWE) | 74-76-70-75—295 | 13,575 |
| 58 | Mark O'Meara (USA) | 67-78-77-74—296 | 13,050 |

| 58T | Richie Ramsay (SCO) | 76-74-72-74—296 | 13,050 |
| | Boo Weekley (USA) | 74-76-71-75—296 | 13,050 |
| | Tom Lehman (USA) | 68-77-75-76—296 | 13,050 |
| | Graeme McDowell (NIR) | 75-71-73-77—296 | 13,050 |
| | Johnson Wagner (USA) | 73-72-73-78—296 | 13,050 |
| 64 | Ben Curtis (USA) | 74-71-80-72—297 | 12,400 |
| | Chris Wood (ENG) | 75-75-75-72—297 | 12,400 |
| | Branden Grace (RSA) | 74-71-77-75—297 | 12,400 |
| | Webb Simpson (USA) | 73-70-77-77—297 | 12,400 |
| | Bernd Wiesberger (AUT) | 71-74-75-77—297 | 12,400 |
| | Grégory Bourdy (FRA) | 76-70-74-77—297 | 12,400 |
| | Ken Duke (USA) | 70-77-73-77—297 | 12,400 |
| 71 | Gareth Wright (WAL) | 71-78-75-74—298 | 11,950 |
| | George Coetzee (RSA) | 76-71-75-76—298 | 11,950 |
| 73 | Shiv Kapur (IND) | 68-77-83-71—299 | 11,550 |
| | K T Kim (KOR) | 73-76-77-73—299 | 11,550 |
| | Russell Henley (USA) | 78-71-75-75—299 | 11,550 |
| | Jimmy Mullen (ENG) (am) | 71-78-75-75—299 | |
| | Todd Hamilton (USA) | 69-81-70-79—299 | 11,550 |
| | Thomas Bjørn (DEN) | 73-74-72-80—299 | 11,550 |
| 79 | Kevin Streelman (USA) | 74-71-82-73—300 | 11,100 |
| | Mikko Ilonen (FIN) | 72-78-76-74—300 | 11,100 |
| | Peter Senior (AUS) | 74-76-73-77—300 | 11,100 |
| 82 | Josh Teater (USA) | 72-77-75-77—301 | 10,900 |
| 83 | Graham Delaet (CAN) | 76-72-76-79—303 | 10,800 |
| 84 | Sandy Lyle (SCO) | 76-72-80-79—307 | 10,700 |

*The following players missed the cut:*

| 85 | Oscar Floren (SWE) | 74-77—151 | 3,700 |
| | Marc Leishman (AUS) | 76-75—151 | 3,700 |
| | Alvaro Quiros (ESP) | 77-74—151 | 3,700 |
| | Kyle Stanley (USA) | 82-69—151 | 3,700 |
| | Michael Thompson (USA) | 72-79—151 | 3,700 |
| | Bill Haas (USA) | 77-74—151 | 3,700 |
| | Marcel Siem (GER) | 75-76—151 | 3,700 |
| | George Murray (SCO) | 76-75—151 | 3,700 |
| | Thomas Aiken (RSA) | 71-80—151 | 3,700 |
| | Jimmy Walker (USA) | 72-79—151 | 3,700 |
| | Nicolas Colsaerts (BEL) | 75-76—151 | 3,700 |
| | Camilo Villegas (COL) | 72-79—151 | 3,700 |
| 97 | Niclas Fasth (SWE) | 77-75—152 | 3,000 |
| | Jim Furyk (USA) | 78-74—152 | 3,000 |
| | Luke Donald (ENG) | 80-72—152 | 3,000 |
| | Hiroyuki Fujita (JPN) | 78-74—152 | 3,000 |
| | Justin Harding (RSA) | 78-74—152 | 3,000 |
| | Steve Dartnall (AUS) | 80-72—152 | 3,000 |
| | Marc Warren (SCO) | 72-80—152 | 3,000 |
| | Justin Rose (ENG) | 75-77—152 | 3,000 |
| | Nick Watney (USA) | 75-77—152 | 3,000 |
| | Mark Calcavecchia (USA) | 72-80—152 | 3,000 |
| | Hyung-Sung Kim (KOR) | 76-76—152 | 3,000 |
| 108 | Toru Taniguchi (JPN) | 78-75—153 | 3,000 |
| | D A Points (USA) | 78-75—153 | 3,000 |
| | Ben Stow (ENG) (am) | 76-77—153 | |
| | A-Shun Wu (CHN) | 76-77—153 | 3,000 |
| | Robert Garrigus (USA) | 78-75—153 | 3,000 |
| | John Senden (AUS) | 77-76—153 | 3,000 |
| | Garrick Porteous (ENG) (am) | 76-77—153 | |
| | Tom Watson (USA) | 75-78—153 | 3,000 |
| 116 | Vijay Singh (FIJ) | 77-77—154 | 3,000 |
| | Thorbjorn Olesen (DEN) | 78-76—154 | 3,000 |
| | Rickie Fowler (USA) | 78-76—154 | 3,000 |

| 116T | Gareth Maybin (IRL) | 78-76—154 | 3,000 |
| | Robert Karlsson (SWE) | 77-77—154 | 3,000 |
| | Scott Stallings (USA) | 76-78—154 | 3,000 |
| | David Lynn (ENG) | 79-75—154 | 3,000 |
| | Billy Horschel (USA) | 74-80—154 | 3,000 |
| | Rory McIlroy (NIR) | 79-75—154 | 3,000 |
| | John Huh (USA) | 74-80—154 | 3,000 |
| 126 | Kenichi Kuboya (JPN) | 76-79—155 | 2,500 |
| | Darryn Lloyd (RSA) | 79-76—155 | 2,500 |
| | David Duval (USA) | 76-79—155 | 2,500 |
| | Richard McEvoy (ENG) | 73-82—155 | 2,500 |
| | Steven Jeffress (AUS) | 76-79—155 | 2,500 |
| | John Wade (AUS) | 74-81—155 | 2,500 |
| 132 | Lucas Glover (USA) | 80-76—156 | 2,500 |
| | Thaworn Wiratchant (THA) | 79-77—156 | 2,500 |
| | Brett Rumford (AUS) | 79-77—156 | 2,500 |
| | Scott Jamieson (SCO) | 80-76—156 | 2,500 |
| | Lloyd Saltman (SCO) | 79-77—156 | 2,500 |
| | Brooks Koepka (USA) | 76-80—156 | 2,500 |
| | Tano Goya (ARG) | 75-81—156 | 2,500 |
| | Brendan Jones (AUS) | 78-78—156 | 2,500 |
| 140 | Steven Fox (USA) (am) | 78-79—157 | |
| | Matteo Manassero (ITA) | 76-81—157 | 2,500 |
| | Daisuke Maruyama (JPN) | 78-79—157 | 2,500 |
| | Kiradech Aphibarnrat (THA) | 72-85—157 | 2,500 |
| | Brian Davis (ENG) | 80-77—157 | 2,500 |
| | Nick Faldo (ENG) | 79-78—157 | 2,500 |
| 146 | Luke Guthrie (USA) | 78-80—158 | 2,500 |
| 147 | Grant Forrest (SCO) (am) | 73-86—159 | |
| | Makoto Inoue (JPN) | 83-76—159 | 2,500 |
| 149 | Scott Brown (zzz) | 79-81—160 | 2,500 |
| 150 | Rhys Pugh (WAL) (am) | 84-77—161 | |
| | Satoshi Kodaira (JPN) | 80-81—161 | 2,500 |

### 142nd Open Championship *continued*

| | | | |
|---|---|---|---|
| 151T | Tyrrell Hatton (ENG) (am) | 82-79—161 | |
| 153 | Scott Piercy (USA) | 74-88—162 | 2,500 |

| | | |
|---|---|---|
| Alexander Noren (SWE) | 83 | WD |
| Peter Hanson (SWE) | | WD |
| Louis Oosthuizen (RSA) | | WD |

## 2012 Open Championship *Royal Lytham & St Annes*    July 19–22    [7086–70]

Total Prize Money: £5 million. Entries: 2,012. 14 Regional Qualifying Courses: Abridge, Berwick-upon-Tweed (Goswick), Bruntsfield Links, Buckinghamshire, Clitheroe, Coventry, East Sussex National, Ferndown, Hankley Common, Lindrick, Mere, Moortown, Royal Dublin and The London. Final field: 156 (2 amateurs) of whom 83 (no amateurs) made the half-way cut with scores of 143 or less.

| | | | | | | | | | |
|---|---|---|---|---|---|---|---|---|---|
| 1 | Ernie Els (RSA) | 67-70-68-68—273 | £900,000 | | 9T | Thorbjørn Olesen (DEN) | 69-66-71-74—280 | 79,600 |
| 2 | Adam Scott (AUS) | 64-67-68-75—274 | 520,000 | | | Zach Johnson (USA) | 65-74-66-75—280 | 79,600 |
| 3 | Tiger Woods (USA) | 67-67-70-73—277 | 297,500 | | 19 | Hunter Mahan (USA) | 70-71-70-70—281 | 50,750 |
| | Brandt Snedeker (USA) | 66-64-73-74—277 | 297,500 | | | Steven Alker (NZL) | 69-69-72-71—281 | 50,750 |
| 5 | Luke Donald (ENG) | 70-68-71-69—278 | 195,000 | | | Louis Oosthuizen (RSA) | 72-68-68-73—281 | 50,750 |
| | Graeme McDowell (NIR) | 67-69-67-75—278 | 195,000 | | | Bill Haas (USA) | 71-68-68-74—281 | 50,750 |
| 7 | Nicolas Colsaerts (BEL) | 65-77-72-65—279 | 142,500 | | 23 | Carl Pettersson (SWE) | 71-68-73-70—282 | 38,438 |
| | Thomas Aiken (RSA) | 68-68-71-72—279 | 142,500 | | | Simon Dyson (ENG) | 72-67-73-70—282 | 38,438 |
| 9 | Geoff Ogilvy (AUS) | 72-68-73-67—280 | 79,600 | | | Steve Stricker (USA) | 67-71-73-71—282 | 38,438 |
| | Miguel Angel Jiménez (ESP) | 71-69-73-67—280 | 79,600 | | | Peter Hanson (SWE) | 67-72-72-71—282 | 38,438 |
| | | | | | | Matthew Baldwin (ENG) | 69-73-69-71—282 | 38,438 |
| | Ian Poulter (ENG) | 71-69-73-67—280 | 79,600 | | | James Morrison (ENG) | 68-70-72-72—282 | 38,438 |
| | Alexander Noren (SWE) | 71-71-69-69—280 | 79,600 | | | Nick Watney (USA) | 71-70-69-72—282 | 38,438 |
| | Vijay Singh (FIJ) | 70-72-68-70—280 | 79,600 | | | Bubba Watson (USA) | 67-73-68-74—282 | 38,438 |
| | Dustin Johnson (USA) | 73-68-68-71—280 | 79,600 | | 31 | Rickie Fowler (USA) | 71-72-70-70—283 | 30,167 |
| | Matt Kuchar (USA) | 69-67-72-72—280 | 79,600 | | | Anirban Lahiri (IND) | 68-72-70-73—283 | 30,167 |
| | Mark Calcavecchia (USA) | 71-68-69-72—280 | 79,600 | | | Jason Dufner (USA) | 70-66-73-74—283 | 30,167 |

**Other players who made the cut:** John Senden (AUS), Jim Furyk (USA), Gary Woodland (USA), Paul Lawrie (SCO), Keegan 284; Richard Sterne (RSA), K J Choi (KOR), Troy Matteson (USA), Francesco Molinari (ITA), Padraig Harrington (IRL), Kyle Stanley (USA) 285; Ross Fisher (ENG), Bob Estes (USA), Pablo Larrazabal (ESP), Lee Westwood (ENG), Rafa Echenique (ARG), Joost Luiten (NED), Justin Hicks (USA), Greg Chalmers (AUS), Simon Khan (ENG) 286; Fredrik Jacobson (SWE), Yoshinori Fujomoto (JPN), Gonzalo Fernandez-Castaño (ESP), Greg Owen (ENG), Harris English (USA), Thomas Bjørn (DEN) 287; Rory McIlroy (NIR), Ted Potter Jr (USA), Jamie Donaldson (WAL), Dale Whitnell (ENG) 288; Charles Howell III (USA), Lee Slattery (ENG), Retief Goosen (RSA), S M Bae (KOR), Garth Mulroy (RSA) 289; Jeev Milkha Singh (IND), Aaron Baddeley (AUS), Adilson Da Silva (BRA) 290; Martin Laird (SCO), Chad Campbell (USA), Juvic Pagunsan (PHI), Brendan Jones (AUS), Toshinori Muro (JPN) 291; Tom Watson (USA), Warren Bennett (ENG), Jaidee Thongchai (THA), Branden Grace (RSA) 292; John Daly (USA), Rafael Cabrera-Bello (ESP) 294; Andres Romero (ARG) 298

## 2011 Open Championship *Royal St George's*    July 14–17    [7204–70]

Total Prize Money: £5 million. Entries: 1,955. 16 Regional Qualifying Courses: Abridge, Berwick-upon-Tweed (Goswick), Bruntsfield Links, Buckinghamshire, Clitheroe, Coventry, East Sussex National, Enville, Ferndown, Gog Magog, Hankley Common, Lindrick, Mere, Pannal, Royal Dublin and The London. Final field: 156 (2 amateurs) of whom 71 (2 amateurs) made the half-way cut with scores of 146 or less.

| | | | | | | | | | |
|---|---|---|---|---|---|---|---|---|---|
| 1 | Darren Clarke (NIR) | 68-68-69-70—275 | £900,000 | | 15T | Y E Yang (KOR) | 71-69-73-72—285 | 67,428 |
| 2 | Dustin Johnson (USA) | 70-68-68-72—278 | 427,500 | | 22 | Anders Hansen (DEN) | 69-69-72-76—286 | 44,666 |
| | Phil Mickelson (USA) | 70-69-71-68—278 | 427,500 | | | Tom Lehman (USA) | 71-67-73-75—286 | 44,666 |
| 4 | Thomas Bjørn (DEN) | 65-72-71-71—279 | 260,000 | | | Tom Watson (USA) | 72-70-72-72—286 | 44,666 |
| 5 | Chad Campbell (USA) | 69-68-74-69—280 | 181,666 | | 25 | Miguel Angel Jiménez (ESP) | 66-71-72-78—287 | 39,000 |
| | Rickie Fowler (USA) | 70-70-68-72—280 | 181,666 | | | Rory McIlroy (NIR) | 71-69-74-73—287 | 39,000 |
| | Anthony Kim (USA) | 72-68-70-70—280 | 181,666 | | | Adam Scott (AUS) | 69-70-73-75—287 | 39,000 |
| 8 | Raphaël Jacquelin (FRA) | 74-67-71-69—281 | 130,000 | | 28 | Charles Howell III (USA) | 71-70-73-74—288 | 35,350 |
| 9 | Simon Dyson (ENG) | 68-72-72-70—282 | 104,333 | | | Ryan Moore (USA) | 69-74-76-69—288 | 35,350 |
| | Sergio García (ESP) | 70-70-74-68—282 | 104,333 | | 30 | Stewart Cink (USA) | 70-71-77-71—289 | 28,642 |
| | Davis Love III (USA) | 70-68-72-72—282 | 104,333 | | | Jason Day (AUS) | 71-70-76-72—289 | 28,642 |
| 12 | Lucas Glover (USA) | 66-70-73-74—283 | 78,333 | | | Pablo Larrazábal (ESP) | 68-70-76-75—289 | 28,642 |
| | Kaymer (GER) | 68-69-73-73—283 | 78,333 | | | Tom Lewis (ENG) (am) | 65-74-76-74—289 | Silver |
| | Steve Stricker (USA) | 69-71-72-71—283 | 78,333 | | | | | Medal |
| 15 | George Coetzee (RSA) | 69-69-72-74—284 | 75,521 | | | | | |
| | Richard Green (AUS) | 70-71-73-71—285 | 67,428 | | | Seung-yul Noh (KOR) | 69-72-75-73—289 | 28,642 |
| | Fredrik Jacobson (SWE) | 70-70-73-72—285 | 67,428 | | | Ryan Palmer (USA) | 68-71-72-78—289 | 28,642 |
| | Zach Johnson (USA) | 72-68-71-74—285 | 67,428 | | | Bubba Watson (USA) | 69-72-74-74—289 | 28,642 |
| | Charl Schwartzel (RSA) | 71-67-75-72—285 | 67,428 | | | Gary Woodland (USA) | 75-68-74-72—289 | 28,642 |
| | Webb Simpson (USA) | 66-74-72-73—285 | 67,428 | | | | | |

**Other players who made the cut:** Gary Boyd (ENG), Yuta Ikeda (JPN), Trevor Immelman (RSA), Simon Khan (ENG), Jeff Overton (USA), Robert Rock (ENG) 290; K J Choi (KOR), Spencer Levin (USA), Justin Rose (ENG), Kyle Stanley (USA) 291; Robert Allenby (AUS), Grégory Bourdy (FRA), Floris De Vries (NED), Jim Furyk (USA), Richard McEvoy (ENG), Peter Uihlein (USA) (am) 292; Paul Casey (ENG), Louis Oosthuizen (RSA), Rory Sabbatini (RSA) 293; Fredrik Andersson Hed (SWE), Ricky Barnes (USA), Stephen Gallacher (SCO), Bill Haas (USA), Grégory Havret (FRA), Bo Van Pelt (USA) 294; Joost Luiten (NED), Matthew Millar (AUS), Mark Wilson (USA) 296; Paul Lawrie (SCO), Edoardo Molinari (ITA) 297; Henrik Stenson (SWE) 298; Harrison Frazar (USA) 299; Kenneth Ferrie (ENG) 301; Jung-gon Hwang (KOR) 304

## 2010 Open Championship Old Course, St Andrews July 15–18 [7305–72]

Total Prize Money: £4.8 million. Entries: 2,500. 16 Regional Qualifying Courses: Abridge, Berwick upon Tweed (Goswick), Clitheroe, County Louth, Coventry, East Sussex National, Effingham, Enville, Ferndown, Gog Magog, Lindrick, Mere, Musselburgh, Old Fold Manor, Pannal, The London. Final field: 156 (7 amateurs) of whom 77 (1 amateur) made the halfway cut with scores of 146 or less.

| | | | |
|---|---|---|---|
| 1 Louis Oosthuizen (RSA) | 65-67-69-71—272 £1,011,840 | 14T Dustin Johnson (USA) | 69-72-69-74—284 68,076 |
| 2 Lee Westwood (ENG) | 67-71-71-70—279 595,200 | Robert Karlsson (SWE) | 69-71-72-72—284 68,076 |
| 3 Paul Casey (ENG) | 69-69-67-75—280 305,536 | Tom Lehman (USA) | 71-68-75-70—284 68,076 |
| Rory McIlroy (NIR) | 63-80-69-68—280 305,536 | Charl Schwartzel (RSA) | 71-75-68-70—284 68,076 |
| Henrik Stenson (SWE) | 68-74-67-71—280 305,536 | 23 Stephen Gallacher (SCO) | 71-73-70-71—285 49,996 |
| 6 Retief Goosen (RSA) | 69-70-72-70—281 208,320 | Trevor Immelman (RSA) | 68-74-75-68—285 49,996 |
| 7 Martin Kaymer (GER) | 69-71-68-74—282 144,336 | Graeme McDowell (NIR) | 71-68-76-70—285 49,996 |
| Sean O'Hair (USA) | 67-72-72-71—282 144,336 | Tiger Woods (USA) | 67-73-73-72—285 49,996 |
| Robert Rock (ENG) | 68-78-67-69—282 144,336 | 27 Robert Allenby (AUS) | 69-75-71-71—286 37,200 |
| Nick Watney (USA) | 67-73-71-71—282 144,336 | Alejandro Cañizares (ESP) | 67-71-71-77—286 37,200 |
| 11 Luke Donald (ENG) | 73-72-69-69—283 97,216 | Bradley Dredge (WAL) | 66-76-74-70—286 37,200 |
| Jeff Overton (USA) | 73-69-72-69—283 97,216 | Ryo Ishikawa (JPN) | 68-73-75-70—286 37,200 |
| Alvaro Quiros (ESP) | 72-70-74-67—283 97,216 | Miguel Angel Jiménez (ESP) | 72-67-74-73—286 37,200 |
| 14 Rickie Fowler (USA) | 79-67-71-67—284 68,076 | Matt Kuchar (USA) | 72-74-71-69—286 37,200 |
| Sergio García (ESP) | 71-71-70-72—284 68,076 | Edoardo Molinari (ITA) | 69-76-73-68—286 37,200 |
| Ignacio Garrido (ESP) | 69-71-73-71—284 68,076 | Kevin Na (USA) | 70-74-70-72—286 37,200 |
| J B Holmes (USA) | 70-72-70-72—284 68,076 | Adam Scott (AUS) | 72-70-72-72—286 37,200 |
| Jin Jeong (KOR) (am) | 68-70-74-72—284 Silver Medal | Marcel Siem (GER) | 67-75-74-70—286 37,200 |

**Other players who made the cut:** Thomas Aiken (RSA), Woody Austin (USA), Grégory Bourdy (FRA), Bart Bryant (USA), Ariel Canete (ARG), David Duval (USA), Ross Fisher (ENG), Simon Khan (ENG), Graeme Storm (ENG), Camilo Villegas (COL), Mike Weir (CAN), Jay Williamson (USA) 296; Stuart Appleby (AUS), Michael Campbell (NZL), David Frost (RSA), Sergio García (ESP), Zach Johnson (USA), Doug Labelle II (USA), Anthony Wall (ENG) 297; Richard Finch (ENG), Tom Gillis (USA), Peter Hanson (SWE), Colin Montgomerie (SCO), Kevin Stadler (USA), Scott Verplank (USA) 298; Søren Hansen (DEN), Wen Chong Liang (CHN), Jonathan Lomas (ENG) 299; Jean-Baptiste Gonnet (FRA), David Horsey (ENG), Lee Westwood (ENG) 300; Brendan Jones (AUS), Pablo Larrazabal (ESP), Jose-Filipe Lima (POR), Jeff Overton (USA), Craig Parry (AUS), John Rollins (USA), Justin Rose (ENG), Martin Wiegele (AUT) 301; Nick Dougherty (ENG), Lucas Glover (USA) 302; Martin Kaymer (GER) 303; Philip Archer (ENG) 304; Sean O'Hair (USA) 306; Chih Bing Lam (SIN) 311

## Only 13 players made the cut in all four majors

Six players from the USA, four Europeans, two Australians and a Korean made the cut in all of the 2013 men's majors.

| Name | Masters | US Open | Open | US PGA | Par | Prize money $ |
|---|---|---|---|---|---|---|
| Adam Scott (AUS) | 1 | 45 | 3 | 5 | +2 | 1,435,819 |
| Phil Mickelson (USA) | 54 | 2 | 1 | 72 | +21 | 1,420,291 |
| Jason Dufner (USA) | 20 | 4 | 32 | 1 | +4 | 1,230,353 |
| Henrik Stenson (SWE) | 18 | 21 | 2 | 3 | +4 | 1,033,222 |
| Jason Day (AUS) | 3 | 2 | 32 | 8 | +2 | 968,382 |
| Lee Westwood (ENG) | 8 | 15 | 3 | 33 | +10 | 543,403 |
| Tiger Woods (USA) | 4 | 32 | 6 | 40 | +14 | 441,569 |
| Brandt Snedeker (USA) | 6 | 17 | 11 | 66 | +19 | 359,843 |
| Matt Kuchar (USA) | 8 | 28 | 15 | 22 | +15 | 301,528 |
| Dustin Johnson (USA) | 13 | 55 | 32 | 8 | +22 | 270,023 |
| Sergio García (ESP) | 8 | 45 | 21 | 61 | +27 | 227,462 |
| Martin Kaymer (GER) | 35 | 59 | 32 | 33 | +34 | 90,851 |
| K J Choi (KOR) | 46 | 44 | 47 | 32 | +33 | 74,444 |

## 2009 Open Championship Turnberry July 16–19 [7173–70]

Total Prize Money: £4.26 million. Entries: 2,418. 16 Regional Qualifying Courses: Abridge, Alwoodley, Berwick-upon-Tweed (Goswick), Coventry, Effingham, Enville, Ferndown, Gog Magog, Lindrick, Mere, Musselburgh, Old Fold Manor, Pleasington, Rochester & Cobham Park, Royal Ashdown Forest, Royal Dublin. Final qualifying courses: Glasgow Gailes, Kilmarnock (Barassie), Western Gailes. Final field: 156 (2 amateurs) of whom 73 (1 amateur) made the half-way cut with scores of 144 or less.

| | | | | | | | |
|---|---|---|---|---|---|---|---|
| 1 | Stewart Cink (USA)* | 66-72-71-69—278 | £750,000 | 13T | Jeff Overton (USA) | 70-69-76-67—282 | 50,900 |
| 2 | Tom Watson (USA) | 65-70-71-72—278 | 450,000 | | Andres Romero (ARG) | 68-74-73-67—282 | 50,900 |
| *Cink won after a four-hole play-off | | | | | Justin Rose (ENG) | 69-72-71-70—282 | 50,900 |
| 3 | Lee Westwood (ENG) | 68-70-70-71—279 | 255,000 | | Henrik Stenson (SWE) | 71-70-71-70—282 | 50,900 |
| | Chris Wood (ENG) | 70-70-72-67—279 | 255,000 | | Camilo Villegas (COL) | 66-73-73-70—282 | 50,900 |
| 5 | Luke Donald (ENG) | 71-72-70-67—280 | 157,000 | | Boo Weekley (USA) | 67-72-72-71—282 | 50,900 |
| | Mathew Goggin (AUS) | 66-72-69-73—280 | 157,000 | 24 | Angel Cabrera (ARG) | 69-70-72-72—283 | 36,333 |
| | Retief Goosen (RSA) | 67-70-71-72—280 | 157,000 | | Peter Hanson (SWE) | 70-71-72-70—283 | 36,333 |
| 8 | Thomas Aiken (RSA) | 71-72-69-69—281 | 90,400 | | Oliver Wilson (ENG) | 72-70-71-70—283 | 36,333 |
| | Ernie Els (RSA) | 69-72-72-68—281 | 90,400 | 27 | Mark Calcavecchia (USA) | 67-69-77-71—284 | 29,357 |
| | Søren Hansen (DEN) | 68-72-74-67—281 | 90,400 | | John Daly (USA) | 68-72-72-72—284 | 29,357 |
| | Richard S Johnson (SWE) | 70-72-69-70—281 | 90,400 | | James Kingston (RSA) | 67-71-74-72—284 | 29,357 |
| | Justin Leonard (USA) | 70-70-73-68—281 | 90,400 | | Søren Kjeldsen (DEN) | 68-76-71-69—284 | 29,357 |
| 13 | Ross Fisher (ENG) | 69-68-70-75—282 | 50,900 | | Kenichi Kuboya (JPN) | 65-72-75-72—284 | 29,357 |
| | Thongchai Jaidee (THA) | 69-72-69-72—282 | 50,900 | | Davis Love III (USA) | 69-73-73-69—284 | 29,357 |
| | Miguel Angel Jiménez (ESP) | 64-73-76-69—282 | 50,900 | | Nick Watney (USA) | 71-72-71-70—284 | 29,357 |
| | Matteo Manassero (ITA) (am) | 71-70-72-69—282 | Silver Medal | 34 | Jim Furyk (USA) | 67-72-70-76—285 | 23,500 |
| | | | | | Martin Kaymer (GER) | 69-70-74-72—285 | 23,500 |
| | Francesco Molinari (ITA) | 71-70-71-70—282 | 50,900 | | Graeme McDowell (NIR) | 68-73-71-73—285 | 23,500 |
| | | | | | Richard Sterne (RSA) | 67-73-75-70—285 | 23,500 |

**Other players who made the cut:** Nick Dougherty (ENG), Sergio García (ESP), Thomas Levet (FRA), Steve Marino (USA), Vijay Singh (FIJ) 286; Branden Grace (RSA), Paul McGinley (IRL), Bryce Molder (USA), Anthony Wall (ENG) 287; Paul Casey (ENG), Gonzalo Fernandez-Castaño (ESP), Zach Johnson (USA), Paul Lawrie (SCO), Rory McIlroy (NIR) 288; Robert Allenby (AUS), Darren Clarke (NIR), Johan Edfors (SWE), David Howell (ENG), Billy Mayfair (USA), Kenny Perry (USA), Graeme Storm (ENG), Steve Stricker (USA) 289; Paul Broadhurst (ENG), David Drysdale (SCO), Tom Lehman (USA), Kevin Sutherland (USA) 290; Ryuji Imada (JPN) 291; Fredrik Andersson Hed (SWE), Stuart Appleby (AUS), Padraig Harrington (IRL), Sean O'Hair (USA) 292; J B Holmes (USA) 293; Fredrik Jacobson (SWE), Mark O'Meara (USA) 295; Paul Goydos (USA) 303; Daniel Gaunt (AUS) 304

## 2013 Open Championship – rulings

### Hideki Matsuyama – slow play penalty

Pace of play has become a hot topic for discussion over the last few years and the Rules of Golf allow the Committee to deal with this by establishing a pace of play policy (Note 2 to Rule 6-7). As with most organisations that run professional and top level amateur events, The R&A implements such a policy and this is used at The Open and all other R&A Championships. Each hole is given a time limit and if a group is behind the accumulated time allowed and more than their initial starting gap behind the group in front they are considered out of position and put 'on the clock'. If a group is 'on the clock' the first player to play a tee shot, approach shot or putt has 50 seconds to play and the other players in the group have 40 seconds to play. The group are taken 'off the clock' when they are either back in position with the group in front or back on their time schedule.

During the third round of the Open Championship, Hideki Matsuyama's group was put on the clock on the 15th hole as they were 15 minutes over the scheduled time and 5 minutes out of position on the group ahead. Matsuyama's first bad time was recorded on his first putt on the 15th at 1 minute 12 seconds. It was made clear to the player at this point that he had a bad time and that a further bad time would result in a one stroke penalty.

Matsuyama was then given a second bad time for his second shot to the 17th hole. Given his tee shot had gone in to the crowd and considering the difficulty of the shot, Matsuyama was given additional time to deal with the crowd and to go forward to assess his shot. The timing for the shot therefore only started when the player had returned to his ball; however he then took a further 2 minutes 12 seconds to play the shot. That second bad time resulted in a one shot penalty being applied to Matsuyama's score on the 17th hole which became 6.

## 2008 Open Championship Royal Birkdale July 17–20 [7173–70]

Total Prize Money: £4.26 million. Entries: 2,418. 16 Regional Qualifying Courses: Abridge, Alwoodley, Berwick-upon-Tweed (Goswick), Coventry, Effingham, Enville, Ferndown, Gog Magog, Lindrick, Mere, Musselburgh, Old Fold Manor, Pleasington, Rochester & Cobham Park, Royal Ashdown Forest, Royal Dublin. Final qualifying courses: Hillside, Southport & Ainsdale, West Lancashire. Final field: 156 (5 amateurs) of whom 83 (2 amateurs) made the half-way cut with scores of 149 or less.

| | | | | | | | | |
|---|---|---|---|---|---|---|---|---|
| 1 | Padraig Harrington (IRL) | 74-68-72-69—283 | £750,000 | 19T | Grégory Havret (FRA) | 71-75-77-71—294 | 37,770 |
| 2 | Ian Poulter (ENG) | 72-71-75-69—287 | 450,000 | | Trevor Immelman (RSA) | 74-74-73-73—294 | 37,770 |
| 3 | Greg Norman (AUS) | 70-70-72-77—289 | 255,000 | | Fredrik Jacobson (SWE) | 71-72-79-72—294 | 37,770 |
| | Henrik Stenson (SWE) | 76-72-70-71—289 | 255,000 | | Davis Love III (USA) | 75-74-70-75—294 | 37,770 |
| 5 | Jim Furyk (USA) | 71-71-77-71—290 | 180,000 | | Graeme McDowell (NIR) | 69-73-80-72—294 | 37,770 |
| | Chris Wood (ENG) (am) | 75-70-73-72—290 | Silver | | Rocco Mediate (USA) | 69-73-76-76—294 | 37,770 |
| | | | Medal | | Phil Mickelson (USA) | 79-68-76-71—294 | 37,770 |
| 7 | Robert Allenby (AUS) | 69-73-76-74—292 | 96,944 | | Alexander Noren (SWE) | 72-70-75-77—294 | 37,770 |
| | Stephen Ames (CAN) | 73-70-78-71—292 | 96,944 | | Thomas Sherreard | 77-69-76-72—294 | |
| | Paul Casey (ENG) | 78-71-73-70—292 | 96,944 | | (ENG) (am) | | |
| | Ben Curtis (USA) | 78-69-70-75—292 | 96,944 | | Jean Van de Velde (FRA) | 73-71-80-70—294 | 37,770 |
| | Ernie Els (RSA) | 80-69-74-69—292 | 96,944 | | Simon Wakefield (ENG) | 71-74-70-79—294 | 37,770 |
| | David Howell (ENG) | 76-71-78-67—292 | 96,944 | | Paul Waring (ENG) | 73-74-76-71—294 | 37,770 |
| | Robert Karlsson (SWE) | 75-73-75-69—292 | 96,944 | 32 | Retief Goosen (RSA) | 71-75-73-76—295 | 25,035 |
| | Anthony Kim (USA) | 72-74-71-75—292 | 96,944 | | Richard Green (AUS) | 76-72-76-71—295 | 25,035 |
| | Steve Stricker (USA) | 77-71-71-73—292 | 96,944 | | Todd Hamilton (USA) | 74-74-72-75—295 | 25,035 |
| 16 | K J Choi (KOR) | 72-67-75-79—293 | 53,166 | | Tom Lehman (USA) | 74-73-73-75—295 | 25,035 |
| | Justin Leonard (USA) | 77-70-73-73—293 | 53,166 | | Nick O'Hern (AUS) | 74-75-74-72—295 | 25,035 |
| | Adam Scott (AUS) | 70-74-77-72—293 | 53,166 | | Andres Romero (ARG) | 77-72-74-72—295 | 25,035 |
| 19 | Anders Hansen (DEN) | 78-68-74-74—294 | 37,770 | | Heath Slocum (USA) | 73-76-74-72—295 | 25,035 |

**Other players who made the cut:** Thomas Aiken (RSA), Woody Austin (USA), Grégory Bourdy (FRA), Bart Bryant (USA), Ariel Canete (ARG), David Duval (USA), Ross Fisher (ENG), Simon Khan (ENG), Graeme Storm (ENG), Camilo Villegas (COL), Mike Weir (CAN), Jay Williamson (USA) 296; Stuart Appleby (AUS), Michael Campbell (NZL), David Frost (RSA), Sergio Garcia (ESP), Zach Johnson (USA), Doug Labelle II (USA), Anthony Wall (ENG) 297; Richard Finch (ENG), Tom Gillis (USA), Peter Hanson (SWE), Colin Montgomerie (SCO), Kevin Stadler (USA), Scott Verplank (USA) 298; Søren Hansen (DEN), Wen Chong Liang (CHN), Jonathan Lomas (ENG) 299; Jean-Baptiste Gonnet (FRA), David Horsey (ENG), Lee Westwood (ENG) 300; Brendan Jones (AUS), Pablo Larrazabal (ESP), Jose-Filipe Lima (POR), Jeff Overton (USA), Craig Parry (AUS), John Rollins (USA), Justin Rose (ENG), Martin Wiegele (AUT) 301; Nick Dougherty (ENG), Lucas Glover (USA) 302; Martin Kaymer (GER) 303; Philip Archer (ENG) 304; Sean O'Hair (USA) 306; Chih Bing Lam (SIN) 311

## 2007 Open Championship Carnoustie July 19–22 [7421–71]

Total Prize Money: £4.2 million. Entries: 2,443. 16 Regional Qualifying Courses: Ashridge, Effingham, Enville, Gog Magog, Minchinhampton, Musselburgh, Notts, Old Fold Manor, Pannal, Pleasington, Prestbury, Rochester & Cobham Park, Royal Ashdown Forest, Royal Dublin, Silloth-on-Solway, Trentham. Final qualifying courses: Downfield, Monifieth, Montrose, Panmure. Final field: 156 (6 amateurs) of whom 70 (1 amateur) made the half-way cut with scores of 146 or less.

| | | | | | | | | |
|---|---|---|---|---|---|---|---|---|
| 1 | Padraig Harrington (IRL)* | 69-73-68-67—277 | £750,000 | 20T | Zach Johnson (USA) | 73-73-68-70—284 | 42,000 |
| 2 | Sergio García (ESP) | 65-71-68-73—277 | 450,000 | | Pat Perez (USA) | 73-70-71-70—284 | 42,000 |
| | *Four-hole play-off – Harrington 3-3-4-5; García 5-3-4-4 | | | 23 | Jonathan Byrd (USA) | 73-72-70-70—285 | 35,562 |
| 3 | Andres Romero (ARG) | 71-70-70-67—278 | 290,000 | | Mark Calcavecchia | 74-70-72-69—285 | 35,562 |
| 4 | Ernie Els (RSA) | 72-70-68-69—279 | 200,000 | | (USA) | | |
| | Richard Green (AUS) | 72-73-70-64—279 | 200,000 | | Chris DiMarco (USA) | 74-70-66-75—285 | 35,562 |
| 6 | Stewart Cink (USA) | 69-73-68-70—280 | 145,500 | | Retief Goosen (RSA) | 70-71-73-71—285 | 35,562 |
| | Hunter Mahan (USA) | 73-73-69-65—280 | 145,500 | 27 | Paul Casey (ENG) | 72-73-69-72—286 | 28,178 |
| 8 | K J Choi (KOR) | 69-69-72-71—281 | 94,750 | | Lucas Glover (USA) | 71-72-70-73—286 | 28,178 |
| | Ben Curtis (USA) | 72-74-70-65—281 | 94,750 | | J J Henry (USA) | 70-71-71-74—286 | 28,178 |
| | Steve Stricker (USA) | 71-72-64-74—281 | 94,750 | | Rodney Pampling (AUS) | 70-72-72-72—286 | 28,178 |
| | Mike Weir (CAN) | 71-68-72-70—281 | 94,750 | | Ian Poulter (ENG) | 73-73-70-70—286 | 28,178 |
| 12 | Markus Brier (AUT) | 68-75-70-69—282 | 58,571 | | Adam Scott (AUS) | 73-70-72-71—286 | 28,178 |
| | Paul Broadhurst ENG) | 71-71-68-72—282 | 58,571 | | Vijay Singh (FIJ) | 72-71-68-75—286 | 28,178 |
| | Telle Edberg (SWE) | 72-73-67-70—282 | 58,571 | 34 | Angel Cabrera (ARG) | 68-73-72-74—287 | 24,000 |
| | Jim Furyk (USA) | 70-70-71-71—282 | 58,571 | 35 | Niclas Fasth (SWE) | 75-69-73-71—288 | 20,107 |
| | Miguel Angel Jiménez | 69-70-72-71—282 | 58,571 | | Mark Foster (ENG) | 76-70-73-69—288 | 20,107 |
| | (ESP) | | | | Charley Hoffman (USA) | 75-69-72-72—288 | 20,107 |
| | Justin Rose (ENG) | 75-70-67-70—282 | 58,571 | | Shaun Micheel (USA) | 70-76-70-72—288 | 20,107 |
| | Tiger Woods (USA) | 69-74-69-70—282 | 58,571 | | Nick Watney (USA) | 72-71-70-75—288 | 20,107 |
| 19 | Paul McGinley (IRL) | 67-75-68-73—283 | 46,000 | | Boo Weekley (USA) | 68-72-75-73—288 | 20,107 |
| 20 | Rich Beem (USA) | 70-73-69-72—284 | 42,000 | | Lee Westwood (ENG) | 71-70-73-74—288 | 20,107 |

## 2007 Open Championship *continued*

**Other players who made the cut:** Nick Dougherty (ENG), Rory McIlroy (NIR) (am) (Silver Medal), Ryan Moore (USA) 289; Ross Bain (SCO), Arron Oberholser (USA), Carl Pettersson (SWE), John Senden (AUS) 290; Jerry Kelly (USA), Won Joon Lee (KOR) 291; Tom Lehman (USA), Kevin Stadler (USA) 293; Thomas Bjørn (DEN), Grégory Bourdy (FRA), Brian Davis (ENG), David Howell (ENG) 294; Michael Campbell (NZL), Anders Hansen (DEN), Scott Verplank (USA) 295; Trevor Immelman (RSA), Mark O'Meara (USA), Toru Taniguchi (JPN) 296; John Bevan (ENG), Luke Donald (ENG) 297; Raphaël Jacquelin (FRA), Sandy Lyle (SCO) 298; Alastair Forsyth (SCO), Sean O'Hair (USA) 299; Fredrik Andersson Hed (SWE), Peter Hanson (SWE) 300

## 2006 Open Championship *Royal Liverpool, Hoylake* July 20–23 [7528–72]

Total Prize Money: £3,898,000. Entries: 2,434. 16 Regional Qualifying Courses: Ashridge, County Louth, Effingham, Little Aston, Minchinhampton, Musselburgh, Notts, Old Fold Manor, Orsett, Pannal, Pleasington, Prestbury, Rochester & Cobham Park, Royal Ashdown Forest, Silloth-on-Solway, Trentham. Final qualifying courses: Conwy, Formby, Wallasey, West Lancashire. Final field: 156 (4 amateurs) of whom 71 (2 amateurs) made the half-way cut on 143 or less.

| | | | | | | |
|---|---|---|---|---|---|---|
| 1 | Tiger Woods (USA) | 67-65-71-67—270 | £720,000 | 16T | Brett Rumford (AUS) | 68-71-72-71—282  45,000 |
| 2 | Chris DiMarco (USA) | 70-65-69-68—272 | 430,000 | 22 | Mark Hensby (AUS) | 68-72-74-69—283  35,375 |
| 3 | Ernie Els (RSA) | 68-65-71-71—275 | 275,000 | | Phil Mickelson (USA) | 69-71-73-70—283  35,375 |
| 4 | Jim Furyk (USA) | 68-71-66-71—276 | 210,000 | | Greg Owen (ENG) | 67-73-68-75—283  35,375 |
| 5 | Sergio García (ESP) | 68-71-65-73—277 | 159,500 | | Charl Schwartzel (RSA) | 74-66-72-71—283  35,375 |
| | Hideto Tanihara (JPN) | 72-68-66-71—277 | 159,500 | 26 | Paul Broadhurst (ENG) | 71-71-73-69—284  29,100 |
| 7 | Angel Cabrera (ARG) | 71-68-66-73—278 | 128,000 | | Jerry Kelly (USA) | 72-67-69-76—284  29,100 |
| 8 | Carl Pettersson (SWE) | 68-72-70-69—279 | 95,333 | | Hunter Mahan (USA) | 73-70-68-73—284  29,100 |
| | Andres Romero (ARG) | 70-70-68-71—279 | 95,333 | | Rory Sabbatini (RSA) | 69-70-73-72—284  29,100 |
| | Adam Scott (AUS) | 68-69-70-72—279 | 95,333 | | Lee Slattery (ENG) | 69-72-71-72—284  29,100 |
| 11 | Ben Crane (USA) | 68-71-71-70—280 | 69,333 | 31 | Simon Khan (ENG) | 70-72-68-75—285  24,500 |
| | S K Ho (KOR) | 68-73-69-70—280 | 69,333 | | Scott Verplank (USA) | 70-73-67-75—285  24,500 |
| | Anthony Wall (ENG) | 67-73-71-69—280 | 69,333 | | Lee Westwood (ENG) | 69-72-75-69—285  24,500 |
| 14 | Retief Goosen (RSA) | 70-66-72-73—281 | 56,500 | | Thaworn Wiratchant (THA) | 71-68-74-72—285  35,591 |
| | Sean O'Hair (USA) | 69-73-72-67—281 | 56,500 | 35 | Michael Campbell (NZL) | 70-71-75-70—286  19,625 |
| 16 | Robert Allenby (AUS) | 69-70-69-74—282 | 45,000 | | Luke Donald (ENG) | 74-68-73-71—286  19,625 |
| | Mikko Ilonen (FIN) | 68-69-73-72—282 | 45,000 | | Marcus Fraser (AUS) | 68-71-72-75—286  19,625 |
| | Peter Lonard (AUS) | 71-69-68-74—282 | 45,000 | | Robert Karlsson (SWE) | 70-71-71-74—286  19,625 |
| | Geoff Ogilvy (AUS) | 71-69-70-72—282 | 45,000 | | Rod Pampling (AUS) | 69-71-74-72—286  19,625 |
| | Robert Rock (ENG) | 69-69-73-71—282 | 45,000 | | John Senden (AUS) | 70-73-73-70—286  19,625 |

# 2013 Open Championship – rulings

## Graeme McDowell – ball interfering with play

Many viewers of the TV coverage of The Open on Friday witnessed Graeme McDowell on the 4th green move his ball-marker as it was interfering with the line of putt of Tiger Woods. McDowell then replaced his ball and putted out from this spot.

It therefore appeared that McDowell had putted out from a wrong place (in breach of Rule 20-7). However, what was not shown on camera was the fact that Tiger Woods had asked McDowell to mark his ball and move the ball-marker to the side as it was interfering with his first putt. When Tiger's first putt finished short of the hole, it was still his turn to play. But now McDowell's ball-marker, in its moved position, was interfering with Tiger's next putt.

Woods asked McDowell to replace it back to his original spot so he could putt out. McDowell did this and was filmed doing so. He actually returned the ball-marker to its original position and eventually replaced the ball and putted out from the correct place.

If a player considers that another ball might interfere with his play, he may have it lifted (Rule 22-2). Before lifting the ball, McDowell was required to mark its position. The Note to Rule 20-1 clarifies that the position of the ball to be lifted should be marked by placing a ball-marker, a small coin or other similar object immediately behind the ball. If the ball-marker interferes with the play of another player, it should be placed one or more clubhead-lengths to the side.

When moving a ball or ball-marker to the side to prevent it from interfering with another player's stance or stroke, the player may measure from the side of the ball or ball-marker. In order to accurately replace the ball on the spot from which it was lifted, the steps used to move the ball or ball-marker to the side should be reversed.

**Other players who made the cut:** Stephen Ames (CAN), Thomas Bjørn (DEN), Mark Calcavecchia (USA), Miguel Angel Jiménez (ESP), Brandt Jobe (USA), Søren Kjeldsen (DEN), Jeff Sluman (USA) 287; John Bickerton (ENG), Simon Dyson (ENG), Gonzalo Fernandez Castano (ESP), Andrew Marshall (ENG), Henrik Stenson (SWE), Marius Thorp (NOR) (am) (Silver Medal), Tom Watson (USA), Simon Wakefield (ENG) 288; Tim Clark (RSA), David Duval (USA), Keiichiro Fukabori (JPN), José-María Olazábal (ESP), Mike Weir (CAN) 289; Andrew Buckle (AUS), Graeme McDowell (NIR) 290; Mark O'Meara (USA), Marco Ruiz (PAR) 291; Chad Campbell (USA) 292; Fred Funk (USA), Vaughn Taylor (USA) 294; Todd Hamilton (USA), Edoardo Molinari (ITA) (am) 295; Bart Bryant (USA) 296; Paul Casey (ENG) 298

## 2005 Open Championship  *St Andrews (Old Course)*  June 14–17 [7279–72]

Total Prize Money: £3,854,900. Entries: 2,499 (record). 16 Regional Qualifying Courses: Alwoodley, Ashridge, Hadley Wood, Hindhead, The Island, Little Aston, Minchinhampton, Notts, Orsett, Pleasington, Prestbury, Renfrew, Rochester & Final qualifying courses: Ladybank, Leven, Lundin, Scotscraig. Cobham Park, Royal Ashdown Forest, Silloth-on-Solway, Trentham. Final Field: 156 (7 amateurs), of whom 80 (4 amateurs) made the half-way cut on 145 or less.

| | | | | | | | | |
|---|---|---|---|---|---|---|---|---|
| 1 | Tiger Woods (USA) | 66-67-71-70—274 | £720,000 | 15T | Lloyd Saltman (SCO) (am) | 73-71-68-71—283 | Silver |
| 2 | Colin Montgomerie (SCO) | 71-66-70-72—279 | 430,000 | | | | Medal |
| 3 | Fred Couples (USA) | 68-71-73-68—280 | 242,500 | 23 | Bart Bryant (USA) | 69-70-71-74—284 | 32,500 |
| | José-María Olazábal (ESP) | 68-70-68-74—280 | 242,500 | | Tim Clark (RSA) | 71-69-70-74—284 | 32,500 |
| 5 | Michael Campbell (NZL) | 69-72-68-72—281 | 122,167 | | Scott Drummond (SCO) | 74-71-69-70—284 | 32,500 |
| | Sergio García (ESP) | 70-69-69-73—281 | 122,167 | | Brad Faxon (USA) | 72-66-70-76—284 | 32,500 |
| | Retief Goosen (RSA) | 68-73-66-74—281 | 122,167 | | Nicholas Flanagan (AUS) | 73-71-69-71—284 | 32,500 |
| | Bernhard Langer (GER) | 71-69-70-71—281 | 122,167 | | Tom Lehman (USA) | 75-69-70-70—284 | 32,500 |
| | Geoff Ogilvy (AUS) | 71-74-67-69—281 | 122,167 | | Eric Ramsay (SCO) (am) | 68-74-74-68—284 | |
| | Vijay Singh (FIJ) | 69-69-71-72—281 | 122,167 | | Tadahiro Takayama (JPN) | 72-72-70-70—284 | 32,500 |
| 11 | Nick Faldo (ENG) | 74-69-70-69—282 | 66,750 | | Scott Verplank (USA) | 68-70-72-74—284 | 32,500 |
| | Graeme McDowell (NIR) | 69-72-74-67—282 | 66,750 | 32 | Richard Green (AUS) | 72-68-72-73—285 | 26,500 |
| | Kenny Perry (USA) | 71-71-68-72—282 | 66,750 | | Sandy Lyle (SCO) | 74-67-69-75—285 | 26,500 |
| | Ian Poulter (ENG) | 70-72-71-69—282 | 66,750 | 34 | Simon Dyson (ENG) | 70-71-72-73—286 | 22,000 |
| 15 | Darren Clarke (NIR) | 73-70-67-73—283 | 46,286 | | Ernie Els (RSA) | 74-67-75-70—286 | 22,000 |
| | John Daly (USA) | 71-69-70-73—283 | 46,286 | | Peter Hanson (SWE) | 72-72-71-71—286 | 22,000 |
| | David Frost (RSA) | 77-65-72-69—283 | 46,286 | | Thomas Levet (FRA) | 69-71-75-71—286 | 22,000 |
| | Mark Hensby (AUS) | 67-77-69-70—283 | 46,286 | | Joe Ogilvie (USA) | 74-70-73-69—286 | 22,000 |
| | Trevor Immelman (RSA) | 68-70-73-72—283 | 46,286 | | Adam Scott (AUS) | 70-71-70-75—286 | 22,000 |
| | Sean O'Hair (USA) | 73-70-70-73—283 | 46,286 | | Henrik Stenson (SWE) | 74-67-73-72—286 | 22,000 |
| | Nick O'Hern (AUS) | 73-69-71-70—283 | 46,286 | | | | |

**Other players who made the cut:** Stuart Appleby (AUS), K J Choi (KOR), Hiroyuki Fujita (JPN), Søren Hansen (DEN), Tim Herron (USA), Simon Khan (ENG), Maarten Lafeber (NED), Paul McGinley (IRL), Bob Tway (USA), Tom Watson (USA), Steve Webster (ENG) 287; Robert Allenby (AUS), Luke Donald (ENG), Fredrik Jacobson (SWE), Thongchai Jaidee (THA), Miguel Angel Jiménez (ESP), Paul Lawrie (SCO), Justin Leonard (USA), Bo Van Pelt (USA) 288; John Bickerton (ENG), Mark Calcavecchia (USA), Phil Mickelson (USA), Edoardo Molinari (ITA) (am), Greg Norman (AUS), Tino Schuster (GER) 289; Peter Lonard (AUS) 290; Chris DiMarco (USA), Pat Perez (USA), Chris Riley (USA), Robert Rock (ENG), David Smail (NZL), Duffy Waldorf (USA) 291; Patrik Sjöland (SWE) 292; Scott Gutschewski (USA), S K Ho (KOR), Ted Purdy (USA) 293; Steve Flesch (USA), 294; Rodney Pampling (AUS), Graeme Storm (ENG) 296; Matthew Richardson (ENG) (am) 297

# 2013 Open Championship – rulings

## Martin Laird – identifying ball

Martin Laird had a tough day at the office during his third round at The Open. On the third hole he fell foul of the thick Muirfield rough and had to take two unplayable drops, each under penalty of one stroke resulting in a quintuple bogey 9.

Just seven holes later he once again found himself in the thick rough. A ball spotter found a ball but as Laird was unable to see his identification mark he announced to the spotter that he was going to identify the ball. He then marked and lifted it just far enough to see that it was his. A player is entitled to mark his ball and lift it to check if it is his ball, however, he must also announce that he is going to do so to either his marker or fellow-competitor (in stroke play), or his opponent (in match play) or a referee, and give them the opportunity to observe the marking and identifying process (Rule 12-2). Unfortunately, Laird's announcement to the spotter did not meet the requirements of the Rule and he was assessed a one stroke penalty under Rule 12-2. He finally signed for a round of 81 which took him out of contention for the Championship.

## 2004 Open Championship *Royal Troon* July 15–18                    [7175–71]

Total Prize Money: £4,064,000. Entries: 2221 Regional Qualifying Courses: Alwoodley, Ashridge, Co.Louth, Hadley Wood, Hindhead, Little Aston, Minchinhampton, Notts, Orsett, Pleasington, Prestbury, Renfrew, Rochester & Cobham Park, Royal Ashdown Forest, Silloth-on-Solway, Trentham. Final qualifying courses: Glasgow (Gailes), Irvine, Turnberry Kintyre, Western Gailes. Final Field: 156 (5 amateurs), of whom 73 (1 amateur) made the half-way cut on 145 or less.

| | | | | |
|---|---|---|---|---|
| 1 | Todd Hamilton (USA)* | 71-67-67-69—274 | £720,000 | |
| 2 | Ernie Els (RSA) | 69-69-68-68—274 | 430,000 | |
| *Four-hole play-off: Hamilton 4-4-3-4; Els 4-4-4-4* | | | | |
| 3 | Phil Mickelson (USA) | 73-66-68-68—275 | 275,000 | |
| 4 | Lee Westwood (ENG) | 72-71-68-67—278 | 210,000 | |
| 5 | Thomas Levet (FRA) | 66-70-71-72—279 | 159,500 | |
| | Davis Love III (USA) | 72-69-71-67—279 | 159,500 | |
| 7 | Retief Goosen (RSA) | 69-70-68-73—280 | 117,500 | |
| | Scott Verplank (USA) | 69-70-70-71—280 | 117,500 | |
| 9 | Mike Weir (CAN) | 71-68-71-71—281 | 89,500 | |
| | Tiger Woods (USA) | 70-71-68-72—281 | 89,500 | |
| 11 | Mark Calcavecchia (USA) | 72-73-69-68—282 | 69,333 | |
| | Darren Clarke (NIR) | 69-72-73-68—282 | 69,333 | |
| | Skip Kendall (USA) | 69-66-75-72—282 | 69,333 | |
| 14 | Stewart Fink (USA) | 72-71-71-69—283 | 56,500 | |
| | Barry Lane (ENG) | 69-68-71-75—283 | 56,500 | |
| 16 | K J Choi (KOR) | 68-69-74-73—284 | 47,000 | |
| | Joakim Haeggman (SWE) | 69-73-72-70—284 | 47,000 | |
| | Justin Leonard (USA) | 70-72-71-71—284 | 47,000 | |
| | Kenny Perry (USA) | 69-70-73-72—284 | 47,000 | |
| 20 | Michael Campbell (NZL) | 67-71-74-73—285 | 38,100 | |
| 20T | Paul Casey (ENG) | 66-77-70-72—285 | 38,100 | |
| | Bob Estes (USA) | 73-72-69-71—285 | 38,100 | |
| | Gary Evans (ENG) | 68-73-73-71—285 | 38,100 | |
| | Vijay Singh (FIJ) | 68-70-76-71—285 | 38,100 | |
| 25 | Colin Montgomerie (SCO) | 69-69-72-76—286 | 32,250 | |
| | Ian Poulter (ENG) | 71-72-71-72—286 | 32,250 | |
| 27 | Takashi Kamiyama (JPN) | 70-73-71-73—287 | 29,000 | |
| | Rodney Pampling (AUS) | 72-68-74-73—287 | 29,000 | |
| | Jyoti Randhawa (IND) | 73-72-70-72—287 | 29,000 | |
| 30 | Kelichiro Fukabori (JPN) | 73-71-70-74—288 | 24,500 | |
| | Shigeki Maruyama (JPN) | 71-72-74-71—288 | 24,500 | |
| | Mark O'Meara (USA) | 71-74-68-75—288 | 24,500 | |
| | Nick Price (ZIM) | 71-71-69-77—288 | 24,500 | |
| | David Toms (USA) | 71-71-74-72—288 | 24,500 | |
| | Bo Van Pelt (USA) | 72-71-71-74—288 | 24,500 | |
| 36 | Stuart Appleby (AUS) | 71-70-73-75—289 | 18,750 | |
| | Kim Felton (AUS) | 73-67-72-77—289 | 18,750 | |
| | Tetsuji Hiratsuka (JPN) | 70-74-70-75—289 | 18,750 | |
| | Steve Lowery (USA) | 69-73-75-72—289 | 18,750 | |
| | Hunter Mahan (USA) | 74-69-71-75—289 | 18,750 | |
| | Tjaart Van Der Walt (RSA) | 70-73-72-74—289 | 18,750 | |

**Other players who made the cut:** Kenneth Ferrie (ENG), Charles Howell III (USA), Trevor Immelman (RSA), Andrew Oldcorn (SCO), Adam Scott (AUS) 290; Paul Bradshaw (ENG), Alastair Forsyth (SCO), Mathias Grönberg (SWE), Migel Angel Jiménez (ESP), Jerry Kelly (USA), Shaun Micheel (USA), Sean Whiffin (ENG) 291; Steve Flesch (USA), Ignacio Garrido (ESP), Rafaël Jacquelin (FRA) 292; James Kingston (RSA), Paul McGinley (IRL), Carl Pettersson (SWE) 293; Paul Broadhurst (ENG), Gary Emerson (ENG), Brad Faxon (USA) 294; Chris DiMarco (USA), Mark Foster (ENG), Stuart Wilson (SCO) (am) (Silver Medal) 296; Mårten Olander (SWE), Rory Sabbatini (RSA) 297; Martin Erlandsson (SWE), Paul Wesselingh (ENG) 298; Bob Tway (USA) 299; Rich Beem (USA), Christian Cévaër (FRA) 300; Sandy Lyle (SCO) 303

# 2013 Open Championship – rulings

### Thomas Björn – ball strikes TV camera

Thomas Björn had a smashing start to his first round of The 2013 Open Championship, when he found the rough with his tee shot. In playing his second from the rough, he managed to hit the ball into a TV camera, breaking its screen.

TV cameras positioned on the course are outside agencies so when a player's ball in motion is deflected or stopped by any outside agency, it is a rub of the green and there is no penalty. The ball is then played as it lies (Rule 19-1).

A "rub of the green" is the term used to describe this deflection by an outside agency and it can produce some random results. For example, Luke Donald's third shot at the 9th hole during the first round benefitted from a rub of the green when the Englishman's pulled approach shot first hit the top of the boundary wall before hitting the hospitality complex situated beyond the boundary and ricocheting back in bounds to the front of the green, allowing him to get up and down for a regulation par 5.

Björn, was not so fortunate in that he eventually finished with a double-bogey six for his opening hole but steadied to complete the round on two over. The TV camera, however, was rendered out of order!

### Charl Schwarzel – club damaged other than in the normal course of play

The frustrations of the Muirfield rough also got to Charl Schwartzel at the 15th hole of his first round. After a string of bogeys, a miss-hit shot out of the rough at the 15th was the last straw for Schwartzel and he threw his club to the ground in frustration. The club broke in two on hitting the firm ground and so Schwartzel had to complete the round without his 8 iron.

As the club was not broken in the normal course of play the player was no longer entitled to use it or to replace the broken club (Rule 4-3b). The penalty for using such a damaged club would be disqualification (Rule 4-3).

# Open Championship History

## The Belt

| Date | | Winner | Score | Venue | Entrants | Prize money £ |
|------|---|--------|-------|-------|----------|---------------|
| 1860 | Oct 17 | W Park, Musselburgh | 174 | Prestwick | 8 | — |
| 1861 | Sept 26 | T Morris Sr, Prestwick | 163 | Prestwick | 12 | — |
| 1862 | Sept 11 | T Morris Sr, Prestwick | 163 | Prestwick | 6 | — |
| 1863 | Sept 18 | W Park, Musselburgh | 168 | Prestwick | 14 | 10 |
| 1864 | Sept 16 | T Morris Sr, Prestwick | 167 | Prestwick | 6 | 15 |
| 1865 | Sept 14 | A Strath, St Andrews | 162 | Prestwick | 10 | 20 |
| 1866 | Sept 13 | W Park, Musselburgh | 169 | Prestwick | 12 | 11 |
| 1867 | Sept 26 | T Morris Sr, St Andrews | 170 | Prestwick | 10 | 16 |
| 1868 | Sept 23 | T Morris Jr, St Andrews | 154 | Prestwick | 12 | 12 |
| 1869 | Sept 16 | T Morris Jr, St Andrews | 157 | Prestwick | 14 | 12 |
| 1870 | Sept 15 | T Morris Jr, St Andrews | 149 | Prestwick | 17 | 12 |

Having won it three times in succession, the Belt became the property of Young Tom Morris and the Championship was held in abeyance for a year. In 1872 the Claret Jug was, and still is, offered for annual competition but it was not available to present at the time to Tom Morris Jr in 1872.

## The Claret Jug

| Date | | Winner | Score | Venue | Entrants | Prize money £ |
|------|---|--------|-------|-------|----------|---------------|
| 1872 | Sept 13 | T Morris Jr, St Andrews | 166 | Prestwick | 8 | 20 |
| 1873 | Oct 4 | T Kidd, St Andrews | 179 | St Andrews | 26 | 20 |
| 1874 | April 10 | M Park, Musselburgh | 159 | Musselburgh | 32 | 29 |
| 1875 | Sept 10 | W Park, Musselburgh | 166 | Prestwick | 18 | 20 |
| 1876 | Sept 30 | B Martin, St Andrews | 176 | St Andrews | 34 | 27 |
| *(D Strath tied but refused to play off)* | | | | | | |
| 1877 | April 6 | J Anderson, St Andrews | 160 | Musselburgh | 24 | 20 |
| 1878 | Oct 4 | J Anderson, St Andrews | 157 | Prestwick | 26 | 20 |
| 1879 | Sept 27 | J Anderson, St Andrews | 169 | St Andrews | 46 | 45 |
| 1880 | April 9 | B Ferguson, Musselburgh | 162 | Musselburgh | 30 | † |
| 1881 | Oct 14 | B Ferguson, Musselburgh | 170 | Prestwick | 22 | 21 |
| 1882 | Sept 30 | B Ferguson, Musselburgh | 171 | St Andrews | 40 | 45 |
| 1883 | Nov 16 | W Fernie*, Dumfries | 158 | Musselburgh | 41 | 20 |
| *After a play-off with B Ferguson, Musselburgh: Fernie 158; Ferguson 159* | | | | | | |
| 1884 | Oct 3 | J Simpson, Carnoustie | 160 | Prestwick | 30 | 23 |
| 1885 | Oct 3 | B Martin, St Andrews | 171 | St Andrews | 51 | 34 |
| 1886 | Nov 5 | D Brown, Musselburgh | 157 | Musselburgh | 46 | 20 |
| 1887 | Sept 16 | W Park Jr, Musselburgh | 161 | Prestwick | 36 | 20 |
| 1888 | Oct 6 | J Burns, Warwick | 171 | St Andrews | 53 | 24 |
| 1889 | Nov 8 | W Park Jr*, Musselburgh | 155 | Musselburgh | 42 | 22 |
| *After a play-off with A Kirkaldy: Park Jr 158; Kirkaldy 163* | | | | | | |
| 1890 | Sept 11 | J Ball, Royal Liverpool (am) | 164 | Prestwick | 40 | 29.50 |
| 1891 | Oct 6 | H Kirkaldy, St Andrews | 166 | St Andrews | 82 | 30.50 |

*After 1891 the competition was extended to 72 holes and for the first time entry money was imposed*

| Date | | Winner | Score | Venue | Entrants | Prize money £ |
|------|---|--------|-------|-------|----------|---------------|
| 1892 | Sept 22–23 | H Hilton, Royal Liverpool (am) | 305 | Muirfield | 66 | 100 |
| 1893 | Aug 31–Sept 1 | W Auchterlonie, St Andrews | 322 | Prestwick | 72 | 100 |
| 1894 | June 11–12 | J Taylor, Winchester | 326 | Royal St George's | 94 | 100 |
| 1895 | June 12–13 | J Taylor, Winchester | 322 | St Andrews | 73 | 100 |
| 1896 | June 10–11 | H Vardon*, Ganton | 316 | Muirfield | 64 | 100 |
| *After a 36-hole play-off with JH Taylor: Vardon 157; Taylor 161* | | | | | | |
| 1897 | May 19–20 | H Hilton, Royal Liverpool (am) | 314 | Royal Liverpool | 86 | 100 |
| 1898 | June 8–9 | H Vardon, Ganton | 307 | Prestwick | 78 | 100 |
| 1899 | June 7–8 | H Vardon, Ganton | 310 | Royal St George's | 98 | 100 |
| 1900 | June 6–7 | J Taylor, Mid-Surrey | 309 | St Andrews | 81 | 125 |
| 1901 | June 5–6 | J Braid, Romford | 309 | Muirfield | 101 | 125 |
| 1902 | June 4–5 | A Herd, Huddersfield | 307 | Royal Liverpool | 112 | 125 |
| 1903 | June 10–11 | H Vardon, Totteridge | 300 | Prestwick | 127 | 125 |

† prize money not known

## Open Championship Claret Jug winners history *continued*

| Date | Winner | Score | Venue | Entrants | Qualifiers | Prize-money £ |
|---|---|---|---|---|---|---|
| 1904 June 8–10 | J White, Sunningdale | 296 | Royal St George's | 144 | | 125 |
| 1905 June 7–9 | J Braid, Walton Heath | 318 | St Andrews | 152 | | 125 |
| 1906 June 13–15 | J Braid, Walton Heath | 300 | Muirfield | 183 | | 125 |
| 1907 June 20–21 | A Massy, La Boulie | 312 | Royal Liverpool | 193 | | 125 |
| 1908 June 18–19 | J Braid, Walton Heath | 291 | Prestwick | 180 | | 125 |
| 1909 June 10–11 | J Taylor, Mid-Surrey | 295 | Royal Cinque Ports | 204 | | 125 |
| 1910 June 22–24 | J Braid, Walton Heath | 299 | St Andrews | 210 | | 135 |
| 1911 June 26–29 | H Vardon*, Totteridge | 303 | Royal St George's | 226 | | 135 |

*After a play-off with A Massy. The play-off was over 36 holes, but Massy picked up at the 35th before holing out. He had taken 148 for 34 holes, and when Vardon holed out at the 35th hole his score was 143*

| Date | Winner | Score | Venue | Entrants | Qualifiers | Prize-money £ |
|---|---|---|---|---|---|---|
| 1912 June 24–25 | E Ray, Oxhey | 295 | Muirfield | 215 | | 135 |
| 1913 June 23–24 | J Taylor, Mid-Surrey | 304 | Royal Liverpool | 269 | | 135 |
| 1914 June 18–19 | H Vardon, Totteridge | 306 | Prestwick | 194 | | 135 |
| 1915–19 *No Championship* | | | | | | |
| 1920 June 30–July 1 | G Duncan, Hanger Hill | 303 | Royal Cinque Ports | 190 | 81 | 225 |
| 1921 June 23–25 | J Hutchison*, Glenview, Chicago | 296 | St Andrews | 158 | 85 | 225 |

*After a play-off with R Wethered (am): Hutchison 150; Wethered 159*

| Date | Winner | Score | Venue | Entrants | Qualifiers | Prize-money £ |
|---|---|---|---|---|---|---|
| 1922 June 22–23 | W Hagen, Detroit, USA | 300 | Royal St George's | 225 | 80 | 225 |
| 1923 June 14–15 | A Havers, Coombe Hill | 295 | Troon | 222 | 88 | 225 |
| 1924 June 26–27 | W Hagen, Detroit, USA | 301 | Royal Liverpool | 277 | 86 | 225 |
| 1925 June 25–26 | J Barnes, USA | 300 | Prestwick | 200 | 83 | 225 |
| 1926 June 23–25 | R Jones, USA (am) | 291 | Royal Lytham & St Annes | 293 | 117 | 225 |
| 1927 July 13–15 | R Jones, USA (am) | 285 | St Andrews | 207 | 108 | 275 |
| 1928 May 9–11 | W Hagen, USA | 292 | Royal St George's | 271 | 113 | 275 |
| 1929 May 8–10 | W Hagen, USA | 292 | Muirfield | 242 | 109 | 275 |
| 1930 June 18–20 | R Jones, USA (am) | 291 | Royal Liverpool | 296 | 112 | 400 |
| 1931 June 3–5 | T Armour, USA | 296 | Carnoustie | 215 | 109 | 500 |
| 1932 June 8–10 | G Sarazen, USA | 283 | Sandwich, Prince's | 224 | 110 | 500 |
| 1933 July 5–7 | D Shute*, USA | 292 | St Andrews | 287 | 117 | 500 |

*After a play-off with C Wood, USA: Shute 149; Wood 154*

| Date | Winner | Score | Venue | Entrants | Qualifiers | Prize-money £ |
|---|---|---|---|---|---|---|
| 1934 June 27–29 | T Cotton, Waterloo, Belgium | 283 | Royal St George's | 312 | 101 | 500 |
| 1935 June 26–28 | A Perry, Leatherhead | 283 | Muirfield | 264 | 109 | 500 |
| 1936 June 25–27 | A Padgham, Sundridge Park | 287 | Royal Liverpool | 286 | 107 | 500 |
| 1937 July 7–9 | T Cotton, Ashridge | 290 | Carnoustie | 258 | 141 | 500 |
| 1938 July 6–8 | R Whitcombe, Parkstone | 295 | Royal St George's | 268 | 120 | 500 |
| 1939 July 5–7 | R Burton, Sale | 290 | St Andrews | 254 | 129 | 500 |
| 1940–45 *No Championship* | | | | | | |
| 1946 July 3–5 | S Snead, USA | 290 | St Andrews | 225 | 100 | 1,000 |
| 1947 July 2–4 | F Daly, Balmoral | 293 | Royal Liverpool | 263 | 100 | 1,000 |
| 1948 June 30–July 2 | T Cotton, Royal Mid-Surrey | 284 | Muirfield | 272 | 97 | 1,000 |
| 1949 July 6–8 | A Locke*, RSA | 283 | Royal St George's | 224 | 96 | 1,500 |

*After a play-off with H Bradshaw: Locke 135; Bradshaw 147*

| Date | Winner | Score | Venue | Entrants | Qualifiers | Prize-money £ |
|---|---|---|---|---|---|---|
| 1950 July 5–7 | A Locke, RSA | 279 | Troon | 262 | 93 | 1,500 |
| 1951 July 4–6 | M Faulkner, England | 285 | Royal Portrush | 180 | 98 | 1,700 |
| 1952 July 9–11 | A Locke, RSA | 287 | Royal Lytham & St Annes | 275 | 96 | 1,700 |
| 1953 July 8–10 | B Hogan, USA | 282 | Carnoustie | 196 | 91 | 2,500 |
| 1954 July 7–9 | P Thomson, Australia | 283 | Royal Birkdale | 349 | 97 | 3,500 |
| 1955 July 6–8 | P Thomson, Australia | 281 | St Andrews | 301 | 94 | 3,750 |
| 1956 July 4–6 | P Thomson, Australia | 286 | Royal Liverpool | 360 | 96 | 3,750 |
| 1957 July 3–5 | A Locke, RSA | 279 | St Andrews | 282 | 96 | 3,750 |
| 1958 July 2–4 | P Thomson*, Australia | 278 | Royal Lytham & St Annes | 362 | 96 | 4,850 |

*After a play-off with D Thomas: Thomson 139; Thomas 143*

| Date | Winner | Score | Venue | Entrants | Qualifiers | Prize-money £ |
|---|---|---|---|---|---|---|
| 1959 July 1–3 | G Player, RSA | 284 | Muirfield | 285 | 90 | 5,000 |
| 1960 July 6–8 | K Nagle, Australia | 278 | St Andrews | 410 | 74 | 7,000 |
| 1961 July 12–14 | A Palmer, USA | 284 | Royal Birkdale | 364 | 101 | 8,500 |
| 1962 July 11–13 | A Palmer, USA | 276 | Troon | 379 | 119 | 8,500 |
| 1963 July 10–12 | R Charles*, New Zealand | 277 | Royal Lytham & St Annes | 261 | 119 | 8,500 |

*After a play-off with P Rodgers, USA: Charles 140; Rodgers 148*

| Date | Winner | Score | Venue | Entrants | Qualifiers | Prize-money £ |
|---|---|---|---|---|---|---|
| 1964 July 8–10 | T Lema, USA | 279 | St Andrews | 327 | 119 | 8,500 |
| 1965 July 7–9 | P Thomson, Australia | 285 | Royal Birkdale | 372 | 130 | 10,000 |
| 1966 July 6–9 | J Nicklaus, USA | 282 | Muirfield | 310 | 130 | 15,000 |
| 1967 July 12–15 | R De Vicenzo, Argentina | 278 | Royal Liverpool | 326 | 130 | 15,000 |
| 1968 July 10–13 | G Player, RSA | 289 | Carnoustie | 309 | 130 | 20,000 |
| 1969 July 9–12 | A Jacklin, England | 280 | Royal Lytham & St Annes | 424 | 129 | 30,334 |

| Date | Winner | Score | Venue | Entrants | Qualifiers | Prize-money £ |
|------|--------|-------|-------|----------|------------|---------------|
| 1970 July 8–11 | J Nicklaus*, USA | 283 | St Andrews | 468 | 134 | 40,000 |
| *After a play-off with Doug Sanders, USA: Nicklaus 72; Sanders 73* | | | | | | |
| 1971 July 7–10 | L Trevino, USA | 278 | Royal Birkdale | 528 | 150 | 45,000 |
| 1972 July 12–15 | L Trevino, USA | 278 | Muirfield | 570 | 150 | 50,000 |
| 1973 July 11–14 | T Weiskopf, USA | 276 | Troon | 569 | 150 | 50,000 |
| 1974 July 10–13 | G Player, RSA | 282 | Royal Lytham & St Annes | 679 | 150 | 50,000 |
| 1975 July 9–12 | T Watson*, USA | 279 | Carnoustie | 629 | 150 | 50,000 |
| *After a play-off with J Newton (AUS): Watson 71; Newton 72* | | | | | | |
| 1976 July 7–10 | J Miller, USA | 279 | Royal Birkdale | 719 | 150 | 75,000 |
| 1977 July 6–9 | T Watson, USA | 268 | Turnberry | 730 | 150 | 100,000 |
| 1978 July 12–15 | J Nicklaus, USA | 281 | St Andrews | 788 | 150 | 125,000 |
| 1979 July 18–21 | S Ballesteros, Spain | 283 | Royal Lytham & St Annes | 885 | 150 | 155,000 |
| 1980 July 17–20 | T Watson, USA | 271 | Muirfield | 994 | 151 | 200,000 |
| 1981 July 16–19 | B Rogers, USA | 276 | Royal St George's | 971 | 153 | 200,000 |
| 1982 July 15–18 | T Watson, USA | 284 | Royal Troon | 1,121 | 150 | 250,000 |
| 1983 July 14–17 | T Watson, USA | 275 | Royal Birkdale | 1,107 | 151 | 310,000 |
| 1984 July 19–22 | S Ballesteros, Spain | 276 | St Andrews | 1,413 | 156 | 445,000 |
| 1985 July 18–21 | A Lyle, Scotland | 282 | Royal St George's | 1,361 | 149 | 530,000 |
| 1986 July 17–20 | G Norman, Australia | 280 | Turnberry | 1,347 | 152 | 634,000 |
| 1987 July 16–19 | N Faldo, England | 279 | Muirfield | 1,407 | 153 | 650,000 |
| 1988 July 14–18 | S Ballesteros, Spain | 273 | Royal Lytham & St Annes | 1,393 | 153 | 700,000 |
| 1989 July 20–23 | M Calcavecchia*, USA | 275 | Royal Troon | 1,481 | 156 | 750,000 |
| *Four-hole play-off (1st, 2nd, 17th and 18th): Calcavecchia 4-3-3-3, W Grady (AUS) 4-4-4-4, G Norman (AUS) 3-4-4-X* | | | | | | |
| 1990 July 19–22 | N Faldo, England | 270 | St Andrews | 1,707 | 152 | 825,000 |
| 1991 July 18–21 | I Baker-Finch, Australia | 272 | Royal Birkdale | 1,496 | 156 | 900,000 |
| 1992 July 16–19 | N Faldo, England | 272 | Muirfield | 1,666 | 156 | 950,000 |
| 1993 July 15–18 | G Norman, Australia | 267 | Royal St George's | 1,827 | 156 | 1,000,000 |
| 1994 July 14–17 | N Price, Zimbabwe | 268 | Turnberry | 1,701 | 156 | 1,100,000 |
| 1995 July 20–23 | J Daly*, USA | 282 | St Andrews | 1,836 | 159 | 1,250,000 |
| *Four-hole play-off (1st, 2nd, 17th and 18th): Daly 4-3-4-4, C Rocca (ITA) 5-4-7-3* | | | | | | |
| 1996 July 18–21 | T Lehman, USA | 271 | Royal Lytham & St Annes | 1,918 | 156 | 1,400,000 |
| 1997 July 17–20 | J Leonard, USA | 272 | Royal Troon | 2,133 | 156 | 1,586,300 |
| 1998 July 16–19 | M O'Meara*, USA | 280 | Royal Birkdale | 2,336 | 152 | 1,800,000 |
| *Four-hole play-off (15th–18th): O'Meara 4-4-5-4, B Watts (AUS) 5-4-5-5* | | | | | | |
| 1999 July 15–18 | P Lawrie*, Scotland | 290 | Carnoustie | 2,222 | 156 | 2,000,000 |
| *Four-hole play-off: Lawrie 5-4-3-3, J Leonard (USA), J Van de Velde (FRA) 5-4-4-5* | | | | | | |
| 2000 July 20–23 | T Woods, USA | 269 | St Andrews | 2,477 | 156 | 2,750,000 |
| 2001 July 19–22 | D Duval, USA | 274 | Royal Lytham & St Annes | 2,255 | 156 | 3,300,000 |
| 2002 July 18–21 | E Els*, RSA | 278 | Muirfield | 2,260 | 156 | 3,800,000 |
| *Four hole play-off: Els 4-3-5-4–16, T Levet (FRA) 4-2-5-5, S Appleby (AUS) 4-4-4-5, S Elkington (AUS) 5-3-4-5. Sudden death: Els 4, Levet 5* | | | | | | |
| 2003 July 17–20 | B Curtis, USA | 283 | Royal St George's | 2,152 | 156 | 3,898,000 |
| 2004 July 15–18 | T Hamilton*, USA | 274 | Royal Troon | 2,221 | 156 | 4,064,000 |
| *Four-hole play-off: Hamilton 4-4-3-4, Els (RSA) 4-4-4-4* | | | | | | |
| 2005 July 14–17 | T Woods, USA | 274 | St Andrews | 2,499 | 156 | 4,000,000 |
| 2006 July 20–23 | T Woods, USA | 270 | Royal Liverpool | 2,434 | 156 | 4,000,000 |
| 2007 July 19–22 | P Harrington, Ireland* | 277 | Carnoustie | 2,443 | 156 | 4,200,000 |
| *Four-hole play-off: Harrington 3-3-4-5, S Garcia (ESP) 5-3-4-4* | | | | | | |
| 2008 July 17–20 | P Harrington, Ireland | 283 | Royal Birkdale | 2,418 | 156 | 4,260,000 |
| 2009 July 16–19 | S Cink*, USA | 278 | Turnberry | 2,418 | 156 | 4,260,000 |
| *Four-hole play-off: Cink 4-3-4-3, T Watson (USA) 5-3-7-5* | | | | | | |
| 2010 July 15–18 | L Oosthuizen, RSA | 272 | St Andrews | 2,500 | 156 | 4,800,000 |
| 2011 July 14–17 | D Clarke, Northern Ireland | 275 | Royal St George's | 1,995 | 156 | 5,000,000 |
| 2012 July 19–22 | E Els, RSA | 273 | Royal Lytham & St Annes | 2,012 | 156 | 5,000,000 |
| 2013 July 18–21 | P Mickelson, USA | 281 | Muirfield | 2,500 | 156 | 5,250,000 |

# The Open Silver Medal winners 1949–2013

The Open Championship's Silver Medal was first presented in 1949 to the leading amateur who plays all four rounds. In the early years, American Frank Stranahan was top amateur five out seven years from 1947 but won only four silver medals because he was leading amateur in 1947 before the medals were awarded.

Among those who had or still have silver medals in their trophy cabinets are Ireland's Joe Carr who was twice lowest amateur, England's Michael Bonallack, who took the medal on three occasions, Scotland's Ronnie Shade, England's Peter McEvoy, another double winner, Spain's José María Olazábal, Northern Ireland's Rory McIlroy, Jin Jeong, the only Asian winner of the medal and American Tiger Woods.

Today, in addition to the leading amateur receiving the silver medal, any amateur who makes all four rounds of the Championship earns a bronze medal. No medals have been awarded on 17 occasions since 1949 when no amateurs managed to complete 72 holes. Since 1946 the four leading amateurs who missed out on medals were:

    1946   K Bell (ENG), St Andrews
    1947   Frank Stranahan (USA), Royal Liverpool
    1948   Mario Gonzalez (BRA), E Kingsley (USA), Muirfield

| Year | Name | Venue | Final Position | Final Score |
|------|------|-------|----------------|-------------|
| 1949 | Frank Stranahan (USA) | Royal St George's | 13 | 290 |
| 1950 | Frank Stranahan (USA) | Troon | 9 | 286 |
| 1951 | Frank Stranahan (USA) | Royal Portrush | 12 | 295 |
| 1952 | J W Jones (ENG) | Royal Lytham & St Annes | 27 | 304 |
| 1953 | Frank Stranahan (USA) | Carnoustie | 2 | 286 |
| 1954 | Peter Toogood (AUS) | Royal Birkdale | 15 | 291 |
| 1955 | Joe Conrad (USA) | St Andrews | 22 | 293 |
| 1956 | Joe Carr (IRL) | Hoylake | 36 | 306 |
| 1957 | W D Smith (SCO) | St Andrews | 5 | 286 |
| 1958 | Joe Carr (IRL) | Royal Lytham & St Annes | 37 | 298 |
| 1959 | Reid Jack (SCO) | Muirfield | 5 | 288 |
| 1960 | Guy Wolstenholme (ENG) | St Andrews | 6 | 283 |
| 1961 | Ronald White (ENG) | Royal Birkdale | 38 | 306 |
| 1962 | Charles Green (SCO) | Troon | 37 | 308 |
| 1965 | Michael Burgess (ENG) | Royal Birkdale | 29 | 299 |
| 1966 | Ronnie Shade (SCO) | Muirfield | 16 | 293 |
| 1968 | Michael Bonallack (ENG) | Carnoustie | 21 | 300 |
| 1969 | Peter Tupling (ENG) | Royal Lytham & St Annes | 28 | 294 |
| 1970 | Steve Melnyk (USA) | St Andrews | 41 | 298 |
| 1971 | Michael Bonallack (ENG) | Royal Birkdale | 22 | 291 |
| 1973 | Danny Edwards (USA) | Troon | 39 | 296 |
| 1978 | Peter McEvoy (ENG) | Carnoustie | 39 | 293 |
| 1979 | Peter McEvoy (ENG) | Royal Lytham & St Annes | 17 | 294 |
| 1980 | Jay Sigel (USA) | Muirfield | 38 | 291 |
| 1981 | Hal Sutton (USA) | Royal St George's | 47 | 295 |
| 1982 | Malcolm Lewis (ENG) | Royal Troon | 42 | 300 |
| 1985 | José-María Olazábal (ESP) | Royal St George's | 24 | 289 |
| 1987 | Paul Mayo (IRL) | Muirfield | 57 | 297 |
| 1988 | Paul Broadhurst (ENG) | Royal Lytham & St Annes | 57 | 296 |
| 1989 | Russell Claydon (ENG) | Royal Troon | 69 | 293 |
| 1991 | Jim Payne (ENG) | Royal Birkdale | 38 | 284 |
| 1992 | Daren Lee (ENG) | Muirfield | 68 | 293 |
| 1993 | Iain Pyman (ENG) | Royal St George's | 27 | 281 |
| 1994 | Warren Bennett (ENG) | Turnberry | 70 | 286 |
| 1995 | Steve Webster (ENG) | St Andrews | 24 | 289 |
| 1996 | Tiger Woods (USA) | Royal Lytham & St Annes | 21 | 281 |
| 1997 | Barclay Howard (SCO) | Royal Troon | 59 | 293 |
| 1998 | Justin Rose (ENG) | Royal Birkdale | 4 | 282 |
| 2001 | David Dixon (ENG) | Royal Lytham & St Annes | 30 | 285 |
| 2004 | Stuart Wilson (SCO) | Royal Troon | 63 | 296 |
| 2005 | Lloyd Saltman (SCO) | St Andrews | 15 | 283 |
| 2006 | Marius Thorp (NOR) | Hoylake | 48 | 288 |
| 2007 | Rory McIlroy (NIR) | Carnoustie | 42 | 289 |
| 2008 | Chris Wood (ENG) | Royal Birkdale | 5 | 290 |
| 2009 | Matteo Manassero (ITA) | Turnberry | 13 | 282 |
| 2010 | Jin Jeong (KOR) | St Andrews | 14 | 284 |
| 2011 | Tom Lewis (ENG) | Royal St George's | 30 | 289 |
| 2013 | Matthew Fitzpatrick (ENG) | Muirfield | 44 | 294 |

# Justin Rose's perfect thank-you to his late Dad with memorable US Open win

Although British winners of major championships were hardly an endangered species in recent years – Rory McIlroy, Graeme McDowell, Darren Clarke and Paul Lawrie had all triumphed since 1999 – the arrival at Merion of the first English champion since Sir Nick Faldo signed off at the Masters in 1996 was an overdue cause for celebration.

Following in the footsteps of Tony Jacklin, who won the US Open at Hazeltine in 1970, Justin Rose succeeded in America's national championship thanks to an outstanding display of ball striking, shrewd course management and nerveless self-assurance under intense pressure. Courtesy of a closing round of 70 for 281, one over par, Rose even thwarted local hero Phil Mickelson who finished two shots shy of the winning mark and finished runner-up for the sixth time since 1999.

Rose's command of technique and desire was never better illustrated than on the 72nd hole. Believing he needed a par to win on one of the toughest closing holes in golf, Rose struck his drive within a foot or two of the plaque in the middle of the 18th fairway which commemorates Ben Hogan's famous 1-iron in 1950. Rose drew a 4-iron out of his bag and even the peerless Hogan might have been impressed by a swing of such exquisite execution the ball soared high and true, never leaving the middle of the green.

Under the level of scrutiny which separates champions from also-rans, Rose had unleashed one of the shots of the year. Perhaps not since Faldo himself rifled a 3-iron to the 18th green at Muirfield at The Open in 1992 had an Englishman struck a more telling long iron in the majors. Reflecting on the moment, Rose recalled: "I've seen that Hogan photograph a million times. I just stood over the shot and said to myself: 'This is my time'. I wanted to do myself justice and put a good enough swing on it that even Ben Hogan might have thought it a decent shot, too."

It was a career changing blow which deserved a better fate than to run 20 feet past the stick, trickle off the back of the green and settle in a trim cut of rough. Rather than risk a wedge he might have thinned or fluffed, Rose opted to putt with a fairway wood and left the ball no more than an inch or two from the cup. "He finished like a true champion," admired Jacklin. "It takes a lot of courage to win a major championship. You have to stay in the moment, which sounds very easy, but when the stakes are high, it's very hard."

After tapping in, Rose knew it would now take something exceptional to force a play-off and he raised his head in thanks to the heavens. On Father's Day, it was entirely fitting Justin should remember his late father, Ken, who did more than anyone to nurture the golfer's career before cancer ended his life prematurely at the age of 57 in 2002.

It was a moment of such keen emotion and poignancy, one wondered how Rose would have coped if Mickelson had been able to force a play-off. As it turned out, however, the left-hander missed the fairway on 18 and made bogey. "I'd texted my mother late on Saturday night and said: 'Let's do it for Dad tomorrow'," Rose recalled. "And she just simply texted me back that would be fantastic. I did get hold of her after my round and we both were in floods of tears speaking to each other. She misses him immensely. I miss him immensely. And I thought today was just a fitting time in which I could honour him by looking up. Even if Phil had finished birdie, birdie, I felt like I had done what I could out there. I'd put into practice a lot of the lessons he'd taught me. And I conducted myself in a way he would be proud of, win or lose. That's what the day was about for me."

On a course where a minor error resulted in bogey and big mistakes proved even costlier (in the final round Tiger Woods ran up eight at the second hole), Rose took his punishment when he got out of position and didn't fall into the trap of playing too aggressively. It was a key component of his victory that over four days the Englishman kept a double bogey off his card.

If his momentum from three birdies in four holes on Sunday was halted by a three-putt bogey on the 11th, Rose gave himself room to breathe over the closing stretch of treacherous holes by making successive birdies on the 12th and 13th. When a rain shower forced Rose to slip on a waterproof jacket, he gave a shot back on the 14th after finding a greenside bunker. Thereafter, though, Rose was unflinching. "I kind of knew no-one was going to play the last five perfectly," recalled the third British winner of the US Open in four years. "So if you were coming into the last five holes on two or three over par already, you were going to have a hard time closing out the tournament."

If patience was a significant asset on Sunday afternoon in Ardmore, Pennsylvania, it was no disadvantage either on Thursday morning when thunderstorms interrupted play for over four hours over two weather delays. No one played with more authority in the first round than Mickelson who grabbed the lead with a superb 67 which made light of the fact he'd flown home to Rancho Santa Fe in California to attend his daughter Amanda's school graduation on Wednesday evening. After arriving back in Philadelphia around 3:30 on Thursday morning, Mickelson acquitted himself well on a few hours of sleep. The southpaw, mark you, was quick to remind everyone that on a course made soft by rain and with little wind, only the easiest part of the challenge was accomplished.

One of ten golfers who carded 71 in the opening round, Rose took an important step forward on Friday, shooting 69 and keeping Mickelson and Billy Horschel, who led the way at the halfway mark, in his sights. "That's the job of the first two rounds, to get yourself in striking distance, and Saturday is an important day to hang around and give yourself a chance on Sunday," Rose volunteered. "You can't get ahead of yourself. On this kind of golf course you don't know what to expect. So I don't think you're safe until you've carded your score here. You could be four or five under going into the last few holes and you don't know how the round is going to pan out. So you have to stay focused."

> "You can't get ahead of yourself. On this kind of course you do not know what to expect."
>
> *Justin Rose assesses Merion*

One of the stories of the week was the performance of amateur golfer Michael Kim, 19, who filled tenth spot on the leaderboard on Saturday evening after posting 71 for the 54 hole total of four over par. It would have been an even more notable effort had he not finished with three bogeys, but then the teenager wasn't alone in that respect. (On Sunday Kim finished with 76 for 290, good enough for 17th place and the honour of low amateur.)

Going into the final day, Mickelson led the way, just as he had done at Winged Foot in 2006. One shot adrift were Hunter Mahan, Charl Schwartzel and Steve Stricker while Rose, Luke Donald and Horschel were the other golfers well placed to mount a charge.

To describe the final day's unfolding action as a championship in flux would be a considerable understatement. The top of the leaderboard changed no fewer than 19 times before Rose made his sublime move at the last. Those who reckoned the United States Golf Association had over-egged the pudding with regard to location of pin positions and density of rough on an already tricky lay-out, however, could not point to the make-up of the leaderboard at Merion as proof of a glorified lottery.

Pursued by Mickelson, Jason Day, Mahan and others, Rose led a cast of leading men in the fourth round just about as far from the profile of random contenders as could be imagined. Jason Dufner also revived the art of making birdies – six in a closing round of 67 – only to lash the ball out of bounds on the 15th. And on the 17th, a 213 yard par 3, Shawn Stefani aced the hole with a 4-iron which missed the green, rebounded off a hill and found the cup.

It was the first ever hole-in-one at Merion in a US Open and another memorable scene in the gripping last act of a compelling championship. Afterwards, as Rose joined the company of Hogan, Bobby Jones and Lee Trevino among Merion's notables, the winner recalled talking to a local caddie who told him the course was equal parts drama, comedy and tragedy – "like a good theatrical play". In that context, Rose was surely a deserving leading man.

Mike Aitken

| First Round | Second Round | Third Round | Fourth Round |
|---|---|---|---|
| −3 Phil Mickelson | −1 Phil Mickelson | −1 Phil Mickelson | +1 Justin Rose |
| −2 Luke Donald | −1 Billy Horschel | = Charl Schwartzel | +3 Phil Mickelson |
| −2 Matthew Goggin | = Luke Donald | = Hunter Mahan | +3 Jason Day |
| −1 Nicolas Colsaerts | = Steve Stricker | = Steve Stricker | +5 Jason Dufner |
| −1 Russell Knox | = Justin Rose | +1 Justin Rose | +5 Ernie Els |
| = Charl Schwartzel | = Ian Poulter | +1 Luke Donald | +5 Hunter Mahan |
| = Jason Day | = Cheng Tsung Pan | +1 Billy Horschel | +5 Billy Horschel |
| = Rickie Fowler | +1 John Senden | +2 Jason Day | |
| = John Senden | +1 Nicolas Colsaerts | +3 Rickie Fowler | |
| = Lee Westwood | +1 Charley Hoffman | +4 Michael Kim | |

# 113th US Open Championship   *Merion GC, Ardmore, PA*   [6996–70]

Prize Money: $8 million. Entries 9,860   June 13–16

*Players are of American nationality unless stated*

## Final Qualifying

### Walton Heath, Surrey, UK

| | |
|---|---|
| Suimon Khan (ENG) | 67-60—137 |
| Jaco Van Zyle (RSA) | 71-67—138 |
| Paul Casey (ENG) | 74-64—138 |
| Morten Ørum Madsen (DEN) | 67-72—139 |
| Peter Hedblom (SWE) | 67-73—140 |
| Eddie Pepperell (ENG) | 70-70—140 |
| Marcus Fraser (AUS) | 71-69—140 |
| John Parry (ENG) | 66-65—141 |
| David Howell (ENG) | 68-73—141 |
| José Maria Olazábal (ESP) | 68-73—141 |
| Estanislao Goya (ARG) | 69-72—141 |
| Chris Doak (SCO) | 71-70—141 |

### Ibaraki, Japan

| | |
|---|---|
| Hideki Matsuyama | 67-65—132 |
| Jung-Gon Hwang (KOR) | 68-68—136 |
| Yui Ueda | 65-72—137 |
| Yoshinobu Tsukada | 72-66—138 |
| Hiroyuki Fujita | 68-70—13 |

### Newport Beach, CA

| | |
|---|---|
| Bio Kim (KOR) | 62-71—133 |
| Steven Alker (NZL) | 69-68—137 |
| Roger Tambellini | 69-68—137 |
| Cory McElyea | 69-69—138 |
| Max Homa (am) | 66-72—138 |

### St Louis, MO

| | |
|---|---|
| Jay Don Blake | 71-68—139 |
| Mackenzie Hughes (CAN) | 72-70—142 |

### Bull Ground, GA

| | |
|---|---|
| Ryan Nelson | 68-65—133 |
| Michael Kim (am) | 67-66—133 |
| Grayson Murray (am) | 69-66—135 |

### Cle Elum, WA

| | |
|---|---|
| WQil Collins, Wil | 70-68—138 |
| Cheng-Tsung Pan (TPE) (am) | 69-70—139 |

### Memphis, TN

| | |
|---|---|
| Kevin Sutherland | 66-67—133 |
| Shawn Stefani | 68-66—134 |
| Jerry Kelly | 67-67—134 |
| Morgan Hoffman | 69-68—137 |
| Joe Ogilvie | 69-68—137 |
| Scott Langley | 71-67—138 |
| Brandon Crick | 70-68—138 |
| Alistair Presnell (AUS) | 71-68—139 |
| Andrew Svoboda | 66-73—139 |

### Bradenton, FL

| | |
|---|---|
| Kevin Phelan (IRL) (am) | 65-70—135 |
| John Hahn | 65-71—136 |
| John Nieporte | 71-66—137 |

### Rockville, MD

| | |
|---|---|
| Russell Knox (SCO) | 65-67—132 |
| Randall Hutchison | 65-67—132 |
| Adam Hadwin (CAN) | 65-67—132 |
| Ryan Sullivan | 61-73—134 |
| Matt Harmon | 70-65—135 |
| Cliff Kresge | 66-69—135 |
| Mathew Goggin (AUS) | 65-70—135 |
| Matt Bettencourt | 70-66—136 |

### Dallas, TX

| | |
|---|---|
| Matt Weibring | 70-64—134 |
| Edward Loar | 70-64—134 |
| Jordan Spieth | 67-67—134 |
| Zack Fischer | 67-68—135 |

### Springfield, OH

| | |
|---|---|
| Brian Stuard | 65-64—129 |
| Brandon Brown | 70-65—135 |

### Columbus, OH

| | |
|---|---|
| Charley Hoffman | 65-68—133 |
| David Hearn | 69-65—134 |
| Nicholas Thompson | 68-66—134 |
| Robert Karlsson (SWE) | 66-68—134 |
| Josh Teater | 63-71—134 |
| David Lingmerth (SWE) | 70-65—135 |
| Brandt Jobe | 68-67—135 |
| Brendan Steele | 67-68—135 |
| Ted Potter Jr | 69-67—136 |
| Aaron Baddeley (AUS) | 67-69—136 |
| Lukas Guthrie | 67-69—136 |
| Rory Sabbatini (RSA) | 66-70—136 |
| Justin Hicks | 66-70—136 |
| Sang Moon Bae (KOR) | 64-72—136 |
| Douglas Labelle II | 64-72—136 |

### Purchase, NY

| | |
|---|---|
| Jesse Smith | 70-67—137 |
| Gavin Hall (am) | 70-67—137 |
| Geoffrey Sisk | 68-69—137 |
| Jim Herman | 70-68—138 |

US Open Championship *continued*

Final Field: 155 (10 amateurs), of whom 74 (including 4 amateurs) made the cut on 145 or less.

| | | | |
|---|---|---|---|
| 1 | Justin Rose (ENG) | 71-69-71-70—281 | $1,440,000 |
| 2 | Jason Day (AUS) | 70-74-68-71—283 | 696,104 |
| | Phil Mickelson | 67-72-70-74—283 | 696,104 |
| 4 | Jason Dufner | 74-71-73-67—285 | 291,406 |
| | Ernie Els (RSA) | 71-72-73-69—285 | 291,406 |
| | Billy Horschel | 72-67-72-74—285 | 291,406 |
| | Hunter Mahan | 72-69-69-75—285 | 291,406 |
| 8 | Luke Donald (ENG) | 68-72-71-75—286 | 210,006 |
| | Steve Stricker | 71-69-70-76—286 | 210,006 |
| 10 | Hideki Matsuyama (JPN) | 71-75-74-67—287 | 168,530 |
| | Nicolas Colsaerts (BEL) | 69-72-74-72—287 | 168,530 |
| | Gonzalo Fernandez-Castano (ESP) | 71-72-72-72—287 | 168,530 |
| | Rickie Fowler | 70-76-67-74—287 | 168,530 |
| 14 | Charl Schwartzel (RSA) | 70-71-69-78—288 | 144,444 |
| 15 | Lee Westwood (ENG) | 70-77-69-73—289 | 132,453 |
| | John Senden (AUS) | 70-71-74-74—289 | 132.453 |
| 17 | John Huh (KOR) | 71-73-75-71—290 | 115,591 |
| | Brandt Snedeker | 74-74-70-72—290 | 115,591 |
| | David Lingmerth (SWE) | 74-71-71-74—290 | 115,591 |
| | Michael Kim (am) | 73-70-71-76—290 | |
| 21 | Martin Laird (SCO) | 74-73-76-68—291 | 86,579 |
| | David Hearn (CAN) | 78-69-73-71—291 | 86,579 |
| | Padraig Harrington (IRL) | 73-71-75-72—291 | 86,579 |
| | Mathew Goggin (AUS) | 68-74-76-73—291 | 86,579 |
| | Bo Van Pelt | 73-71-72-75—291 | 86,579 |
| | Ian Poulter (ENG) | 71-71-73-76—291 | 86,579 |
| | Henrik Stenson (SWE) | 74-68-73-76—291 | 86,579 |
| 28 | Mike Weir (CAN) | 72-76-75-69—292 | 60,183 |
| | John Parry (ENG) | 76-71-72-73—292 | 60,183 |
| | Matt Kuchar | 74-73-72-73—292 | 60,183 |
| | Morten Ørum Madsen (DEN) | 74-74-70-74—292 | 60,183 |
| 32 | Kevin Chappell | 72-76-74-71—293 | 42,246 |
| | Geoff Ogilvy (AUS) | 74-70-77-72—293 | 42,246 |
| | Webb Simpson | 71-75-75-72—293 | 42,246 |
| | K J Choi (KOR) | 70-76-75-72—293 | 42,246 |
| | Tiger Woods | 73-70-76-74—293 | 42,246 |
| | Jamie Donaldson (WAL) | 73-73-73-74—293 | 42,246 |
| | Edward Loar | 73-71-73-76—293 | 42,246 |
| | Bubba Watson | 71-76-70-76—293 | 42,246 |
| | Paul Lawrie (SCO) | 76-71-69-77—293 | 42,246 |
| 41 | Carl Pettersson (SWE) | 72-75-74-73—294 | 37,324 |
| | Scott Langley | 75-70-75-74—294 | 37,324 |
| | Rory McIlroy (NIR) | 73-70-75-76—294 | 37,324 |
| | Jerry Kelly | 70-73-75-76—294 | 37,324 |
| 45 | Steven Alker (NZL) | 73-75-72-95—295 | 28,961 |
| | Russell Knox (SCO) | 69-75-77-74—295 | 28,961 |
| | Sergio García (ESP) | 73-73-75-74—295 | 28,961 |
| | Bio Kim (KOR) | 72-75-73-75—295 | 28,961 |
| | Adam Scott (AUS) | 72-75-73-75—295 | 28,961 |
| | Cheng Tsung Pan (TPE) (am) | 72-72-75-76—295 | |
| | Charley Hoffman | 71-73-72-79—295 | 28,961 |
| | Paul Casey (ENG) | 73-72-71-79—295 | 28,961 |
| 53 | Scott Stallings | 71-76-76-73—296 | 23,446 |
| | Matt Bettencourt | 72-71-76-77—296 | 23,446 |
| 55 | Dustin Johnson | 71-77-75-74—297 | 22,561 |
| 56 | Josh Teater | 74-74-74-76—298 | 21,485 |
| | Nicholas Thompson | 72-76-74-76—298 | 21,485 |
| | George Coetzee (RSA) | 71-73-77-77—298 | 21,485 |

| 59 | Shawn Stefani | 72-73-85-69—299 | 20,111 |
|---|---|---|---|
| | Martin Kaymer (GER) | 76-72-77-74—299 | 20,111 |
| | Marcel Siem (GER) | 73-71-77-78—299 | 20,111 |
| 62 | Kevin Phelan (IRL) (am) | 71-77-78-74—300 | |
| | Matt Weibring | 75-73-76-76—300 | 19,406 |
| 64 | Michael Weaver (am) | 74-74-78-75—301 | |
| 65 | Peter Hedblom (SWE) | 70-78-79-75—302 | 18,926 |
| | David Howell (ENG) | 77-71-77-77—302 | 18,926 |
| 67 | Kevin Sutherland | 73-74-84-72—303 | 17,965 |
| | John Peterson | 73-75-78-77—303 | 17,965 |
| | Jim Herman | 76-72-76-79—303 | 17,965 |
| | Alistair Presnell (AUS) | 73-75-76-79—303 | 17,965 |
| 71 | Robert Karlsson (SWE) | 74-72-86-73—305 | 17,165 |
| 72 | Simon Khan (ENG) | 74-74-82-76—306 | 16,844 |
| 73 | Kyle Stanley | 71-74-85-78—308 | 16,523 |

*The following players missed the half-way cut:*

| 74 | Justin Hicks | 76-73—149 |
|---|---|---|
| | Chris Williams (am) | 75-74—149 |
| | Michael Thompson | 71-78—149 |
| | Cliff Kresge | 75-74—149 |
| | Tim Clark (RSA) | 70-79—149 |
| | Peter Hanson (SWE) | 74-75—149 |
| | Aaron Baddeley (AUS) | 75-74—149 |
| | Rory Sabbatini (RSA) | 77-72—149 |
| | Matteo Manassero (ITA) | 75-74—149 |
| | Fredrik Jacobson (SWE) | 73-76—149 |
| | Doug LaBelle II | 75-74—149 |
| 85 | Brian Stuard | 75-75—150 |
| | Morgan Hoffmann | 76-74—150 |
| | Casey Wittenberg | 79-71—150 |
| | Kevin Streelman | 72-78—150 |
| | Steven Fox (am) | 76-74—150 |
| | Stewart Cink | 72-78—150 |
| | Hiroyuki Fujita (JPN) | 76-74—150 |
| | Ted Potter Jr | 76-74—150 |
| | Jaco Van Zyl (RSA) | 73-77—150 |
| | Chris Doak (SCO) | 73-77—150 |
| 95 | Zach Johnson | 74-77—151 |
| | D A Points | 77-74—151 |
| | Sang-Moon Bae (KOR) | 77-74—151 |
| | Gavin Hall (am) | 74-77—151 |
| | Max Homa (am) | 73-78—151 |
| | Nick Watney | 73-78—151 |
| | Bill Haas | 77-74—151 |
| | Boo Weekley | 75-76—151 |
| | Andrew Svoboda | 81-70—151 |

| 95T | Ryan Nelson | 73-78—151 |
|---|---|---|
| 105 | Brendan Steele | 76-76—152 |
| | David Toms | 75-77—152 |
| | Marcus Fraser (AUS) | 79-73—152 |
| | Francesco Molinari (ITA) | 78-74—152 |
| | Luke Guthrie | 73-79—152 |
| | Brandon Brown | 75-77—152 |
| | Keegan Bradley | 77-75—152 |
| | Y E.Yang (KOR) | 77-75—152 |
| 113 | Marc Leishman | 78-75—153 |
| | Graeme McDowell (NIR) | 76-77—153 |
| | Thongchai Jaidee (THA) | 79-74—153 |
| | Branden Grace (RSA) | 70-83—153 |
| | Jordan Spieth | 77-76—153 |
| | Jung-Gon Hwang (KOR) | 75-78—153 |
| | Ryan Yip (CAN) | 76-77—153 |
| | Mackenzie Hughes (CAN) | 75-78—153 |
| | Geoffrey Sisk | 78-75—153 |
| | Randall Hutchison | 74-79—153 |
| | John Hahn | 75-78—153 |
| 124 | Estanislao Goya (ARG) | 71-83—154 |
| | Scott Piercy | 78-76—154 |
| | Eddie Pepperell (ENG) | 77-77—154 |
| | Jesse Smith | 73-81—154 |
| | Jay Don Blake | 74-80—154 |
| | Michael Campbell (NZL) | 76-78—154 |

| 124T | Brandt Jobe | 74-80—154 |
|---|---|---|
| | Ryan Palmer | 75-79—154 |
| 132 | Darren Clarke (NIR) | 80-75—155 |
| | Angel Cabrera (ARG) | 74-81—155 |
| | Rikard Karlberg (SWE) | 78-77—155 |
| | Wil Collins | 76-79—155 |
| | Harold Varner, III | 76-79—155 |
| 137 | José Maria Olazábal (ESP) | 75-81—156 |
| | Jim Furyk | 77-79—156 |
| | Joe Ogilvie | 75-81—156 |
| | Lucas Glover | 74-82—156 |
| | Ryan Moore | 79-77—156 |
| 142 | Russell Henley | 77-80—157 |
| | Adam Hadwin (CAN) | 81-76—157 |
| 144 | Thorbjørn Olesen (DEN) | 79-79—158 |
| | Yoshinobu Tsukada (JPN) | 78-80—158 |
| | Zack Fischer | 82-76—158 |
| 147 | Matt Harmon | 78-81—159 |
| 147 | Brandon Crick | 81-78—159 |
| 148 | Roger Tambellini | 80-80—160 |
| | Cory McElyea (am) | 81-79—160 |
| 150 | Yui Ueda (JPN) | 78-83—161 |
| 151 | John Nieporte | 78-84—162 |
| 152 | Ryan Sullivan | 81-82—163 |
| 153 | Grayson Murray (am) | 83-81—164 |
| | Louis Oosthuizen (RSA) | 75 WD |
| | Robert Garrigus | 80 WD |

## Did you know?

The First US Open, played at the Newport Country Club, Rhode Island, USA on 4 October 1895, was won by 21-year-old Englishman Horace Rawlins (1874–1940) who was victorious by two shots over Willie Dunn.

## 2012 US Open *Olympic Club, San Fransisco, CA*   June 14–17    [7170–70]

Prize money: $8 million. Entries: 9,006

| | | | | | | | | |
|---|---|---|---|---|---|---|---|---|
| 1 | Webb Simpson | 72-73-68-68—281 | $1,440,000 | 15T | Fredrik Jacobson (SWE) | 72-71-68-75—286 | 118,969 |
| 2 | Michael Thompson | 66-75-74-67—282 | 695,216 | 21 | Nick Watney | 69-75-73-70—287 | 86,348 |
| | Graeme McDowell | 69-72-68-73—282 | 695,216 | | Jordan Spieth (am) | 74-74-69-70—287 | 86,348 |
| | (NIR) | | | | Raphael Jacquelin (FRA) | 72-71-73-71—287 | 86,348 |
| 4 | David Toms | 69-70-76-68—283 | 276,841 | | Justin Rose (ENG) | 69-75-71-72—287 | 86,348 |
| | Padraig Harrington | 74-70-71-68—283 | 276,841 | | Tiger Woods | 69-70-75-73—287 | 86,348 |
| | (IRL) | | | | Blake Adams | 72-70-70-75—287 | 86,348 |
| | John Peterson | 71-70-72-70—283 | 276,841 | 27 | Matt Kuchar | 70-73-71-74—288 | 68,943 |
| | Jason Dufner | 72-71-70-70—283 | 276,841 | | Nicholas Colsaerts | 72-69-71-76—288 | 68,943 |
| | Jim Furyk | 70-69-70-74—283 | 276,841 | | (BEL) | | |
| 9 | Ernie Els (RSA) | 75-69-68-72—284 | 200,280 | 29 | Davis Love III | 73-74-73-69—289 | 53,168 |
| 10 | Casey Wittenberg | 71-77-67-70—285 | 163,594 | | Alistair Presnell (AUS) | 70-74-75-70—289 | 53,168 |
| | Retief Goosen (RSA) | 75-70-69-71—285 | 163,594 | | Morgan Hoffmann | 72-74-73-70—289 | 53,168 |
| | Kevin Chappell | 74-71-68-72—285 | 163,594 | | Francesco Molinari | 71-76-72-70—289 | 53,168 |
| | John Senden (AUS) | 72-73-68-72—285 | 163,594 | | (ITA) | | |
| | Lee Westwood (ENG) | 73-72-67-73—285 | 163,594 | | Robert Karlsson (SWE) | 70-75-72-72—289 | 53,168 |
| 15 | K J Choi (KOR) | 73-70-74-69—286 | 118,969 | | Kevin Na | 74-71-71-73—289 | 53,168 |
| | Steve Stricker | 76-68-73-69—286 | 118,969 | | Scott Langley | 76-70-70-73—289 | 53,168 |
| | Adam Scott (AUS) | 76-70-70-70—286 | 118,969 | | Charlie Wi (KOR) | 74-70-71-74—289 | 53,168 |
| | Aaron Watkins | 72-71-72-71—286 | 118,969 | | Beau Hossler (am) | 70-73-70-76—289 | 53,168 |
| | Martin Kaymer (GER) | 74-71-69-72—286 | 118,969 | | | | |

**Other players who made the cut:** Charl Schwartzel (RSA), Hunter Mahan, Sergio García 290; Zach Johnson, Patrick Cantlay (am), Rickie Fowler, Ian Poulter (ENG), Alex Cejka (GER) 291; Matteo Manassero (ITA), Bob Estes, Angel Cabrera (ARG), Steve LeBrun, Hunter Hamrick 292; Simon Dyson (ENG), Jesse Mueller, Nicholas Thompson, Hiroyuki Fujita (JPN), Branden Grace (RSA) 293; J B Park (KOR), Michael Allen, Jeff Curl, Jonathan Byrd 294; Bo Van Pelt, Jason Day (AUS), Matthew Baldwin (ENG), Kevin Streelman, Darron Stiles 295; Marc Warren (SCO), Phil Mickelson 296; Kyung-Tae Kim (KOR) 297; Stephen Ames (CAN), Keegan Bradley 298; Rod Pampling (AUS) 299; Jason Bohn 301; Joe Ogilvie 303

## 2011 US Open *Congressional CC, Bethesda, MD*   June 16–19    [7574–71]

Prize money: $7.5 million. Entries: 8,300

| | | | | | | | | |
|---|---|---|---|---|---|---|---|---|
| 1 | Rory McIlroy (NIR) | 65-66-68-69—268 | $1,440,000 | 19T | Steve Stricker | 75-69-69-70—283 | 105,905 |
| 2 | Jason Day (AUS) | 71-72-65-68—276 | 865,000 | 21 | Ryan Palmer | 69-72-73-70—284 | 97,242 |
| 3 | Kevin Chappell | 76-67-69-66—278 | 364,241 | | Patrick Cantlay (am) | 75-67-70-72—284 | |
| | Robert Garrigus | 70-70-68-70—278 | 364,241 | 23 | Robert Rock (ENG) | 70-71-76-68—285 | 76,455 |
| | Lee Westwood (ENG) | 75-68-65-70—278 | 364,241 | | Gary Woodland | 73-71-73-68—285 | 76,455 |
| | Y E Yang (KOR) | 68-69-70-71—278 | 364,241 | | Retief Goosen (RSA) | 73-73-71-68—285 | 76,455 |
| 7 | Peter Hanson (SWE) | 72-71-69-70—279 | 228,416 | | Dustin Johnson | 75-71-69-70—285 | 76,455 |
| | Sergio García (ESP) | 69-71-69-70—279 | 228,416 | | Bill Haas | 73-73-68-71—285 | 76,455 |
| 9 | Charl Schwartzel (RSA) | 68-74-72-66—280 | 192,962 | | Brandt Jobe | 71-70-70-74—285 | 76,455 |
| | Louis Oosthuizen (RSA) | 69-73-71-67—280 | 192,962 | | Henrik Stenson (SWE) | 70-72-69-74—285 | 76,455 |
| 11 | Brandt Snedeker | 70-70-72-69—281 | 163,083 | 30 | Ryo Ishikawa (JPN) | 74-70-74-68—286 | 50,436 |
| | Davis Love III | 70-71-70-70—281 | 163,083 | | Gregory Havret (FRA) | 77-69-71-69—286 | 50,436 |
| | Heath Slocum | 71-70-70-70—281 | 163,083 | | Seung-yul Noh (KOR) | 72-70-73-71—286 | 50,436 |
| 14 | Graeme McDowell | 70-74-69-69—282 | 129,517 | | Rory Sabbatini (RSA) | 72-73-70-71—286 | 50,436 |
| | (NIR) | | | | John Senden (AUS) | 70-72-72-72—286 | 50,436 |
| | Webb Simpson | 75-71-66-70—282 | 129,517 | | Do-Hoon Kim (KOR) | 73-71-70-72—286 | 50,436 |
| | Matt Kuchar | 72-68-69-73—282 | 129,517 | | Harrison Frazar | 72-73-68-73—286 | 50,436 |
| | Fredrik Jacobson (SWE) | 74-69-66-73—282 | 129,517 | | Zach Johnson | 71-69-72-74—286 | 50,436 |
| | Bo Van Pelt | 76-67-68-71—282 | 129,517 | | Kyung-tae Kim (KOR) | 69-72-69-76—286 | 50,436 |
| 19 | Johan Edfors (SWE) | 70-72-74-67—283 | 105,905 | | | | |

**Other players who made the cut:** Adam Hadwin (CAN), Martin Kaymer (GER), Sunghoon Kang (KOR) 287; Sang-Moon Bae (KOR), Lucas Glover, Russell Henley (am) 288; Charley Hoffman, Luke Donald (ENG), Michael Putnam, Chez Reavie, Robert Karlsson (SWE), Padraig Harrington (IRL) 289; Scott Piercy, Alexander Noren (SWE), Marc Leishman (AUS) 290; J J Henry, Anthony Kim (KOR), Phil Mickelson, Matteo Manassero (ITA), Edoardo Molinari (ITA), Alvaro Quiros (ESP) 291; Todd Hamilton, Justin Hicks, Marcel Siem (GER) 292; Bubba Watson, Brian Gay, Jeff Overton, William Cauley 293; Kevin Streelman 295; Alexandre Rocha (BRA), Christo Greyling (RSA), Kenichi Kuboya (JPN) 297; Wes Heffernan (CAN) 303; Brad Benjamin (am) 305

## 2010 US Open Pebble Beach, CA June 17–20 [7260–71]

Prize money: $7.5 million. Entries: 9,052

| | | | | | | | |
|---|---|---|---|---|---|---|---|
| 1 | Graeme McDowell (NIR) | 71-68-71-74—284 | $1,350,000 | 22T | Padraig Harrington (IRL) | 73-73-74-73—293 | 83,634 |
| 2 | Grégory Havret (FRA) | 73-71-69-72—285 | 810,000 | | John Malinger | 77-72-70-74—293 | 83,634 |
| 3 | Ernie Els (RSA) | 73-68-72-73—286 | 480,687 | | Shaun Micheel | 69-77-75-72—293 | 83,634 |
| 4 | Phil Mickelson | 75-66-73-73—287 | 303,119 | 27 | Ricky Barnes | 72-76-74-72—294 | 67,195 |
| | Tiger Woods | 74-72-66-75—287 | 303,119 | | Robert Karlsson (SWE) | 75-72-74-73—294 | 67,195 |
| 6 | Matt Kuchar | 74-72-74-68—288 | 228,255 | 29 | Robert Allenby (AUS) | 74-74-73-74—295 | 54,871 |
| | Davis Love III | 75-74-68-71—288 | 228,255 | | Stuart Appleby (AUS) | 73-76-76-70—295 | 54,871 |
| 8 | Alex Cejka (GER) | 70-72-74-73—289 | 177,534 | | Henrik Stenson (SWE) | 77-70-74-74—295 | 54,871 |
| | Dustin Johnson | 71-70-66-82—289 | 177,534 | | Tom Watson | 78-71-70-76—295 | 54,871 |
| | Martin Kaymer (GER) | 74-71-72-72—289 | 177,534 | 33 | Brendon De Jonge (ZIM) | 69-73-77-77—296 | 44,472 |
| | Brandt Snedeker | 75-74-69-71—289 | 177,534 | | Jason Dufner | 72-73-79-72—296 | 44,472 |
| 12 | Tim Clark (RSA) | 72-72-72-74—290 | 143,714 | | Ryo Ishikawa (JPN) | 70-71-75-80—296 | 44,472 |
| | Sean O'Hair | 76-71-70-73—290 | 143,714 | | Søren Kjeldsen (DEN) | 72-71-75-78—296 | 44,472 |
| 14 | Ben Curtis | 78-70-75-68—291 | 127,779 | | Ryan Moore | 75-73-75-73—296 | 44,472 |
| | Justin Leonard | 72-73-73-73—291 | 127,779 | | Kenny Perry | 72-77-73-74—296 | 44,472 |
| 16 | Jim Furyk | 72-75-74-71—292 | 108,458 | | David Toms | 71-75-76-74—296 | 44,472 |
| | Peter Hanson (SWE) | 73-76-74-69—292 | 108,458 | 40 | Paul Casey (ENG) | 69-73-77-78—297 | 34,722 |
| | Russell Henley (am) | 73-74-72-73—292 | | | Stewart Cink | 76-73-71-77—297 | 34,722 |
| | Scott Langley (am) | 75-69-77-71—292 | | | Bobby Gates | 75-74-71-77—297 | 34,722 |
| | Charl Schwartzel (RSA) | 74-71-74-73—292 | 108,458 | | Ross McGowan (ENG) | 72-73-78-74—297 | 34,722 |
| | Lee Westwood (ENG) | 74-71-76-71—292 | 108,458 | | Noh Seung-yul (KOR) | 74-72-76-75—297 | 34,722 |
| 22 | Angel Cabrera (ARG) | 75-72-74-72—293 | 83,634 | | Vijay Singh (FIJ) | 74-72-75-76—297 | 34,722 |
| | Sergio García (ESP) | 73-76-73-71—293 | 83,634 | | Bo Van Pelt | 72-75-82-68—297 | 34,722 |

**Other players who made the cut:** Jason Allred, Rafael Cabrera Bello (ESP), K J Choi (KOR), Luke Donald (ENG), Jason Gore, Jim Herman, Thongchai Jaidee (THA), Edoardo Molinari (ITA), Ian Poulter (ENG), Chris Stroud, Scott Verplank (298; Hiroyuki Fujita (JPN), Lucas Glover, Retief Goosen (RSA), Yuta Ikeda (JPN), Steve Stricker 299; Eric Axley, Jerry Kelly, Steve Marino, Gareth Maybin (NIR), Toru Taniguchi (JPN), Steve Wheatcroft 300; Erick Justesen 301; Matt Bettencourt, David Duval, Fred Funk, Camilo Villegas (COL) 302; Rhys Davies (WAL), Kent Jones 303; Nick Watney 305; Craig Barlow, Zach Johnson, Matthew Richardson (ENG) 306; Ty Tryon, Mike Weir (CAN) 307; Pablo Martin (ESP), Jason Preeo 311

## 2009 US Open Bethpage, Farmingdale, NY June 18–21 [7426–70]

Prize money: $7.5 million. Entries: 9,086

| | | | | | | | |
|---|---|---|---|---|---|---|---|
| 1 | Lucas Glover | 69-64-70-73—276 | $1,350,000 | 23 | Sean O'Hair | 69-69-71-76—285 | 76,422 |
| 2 | Ricky Barnes | 67-65-70-76—278 | 559,830 | | Steve Stricker | 73-66-72-74—285 | 76,422 |
| | David Duval | 67-70-70-71—278 | 559,830 | | Lee Westwood (ENG) | 72-66-74-73—285 | 76,422 |
| | Phil Mickelson | 69-70-69-70—278 | 559,830 | | Oliver Wilson (ENG) | 70-70-71-74—285 | 76,422 |
| 5 | Ross Fisher (ENG) | 70-68-69-72—279 | 289,146 | 27 | Stewart Cink | 73-69-70-74—286 | 56,041 |
| 6 | Søren Hansen (DEN) | 70-71-70-69—280 | 233,350 | | Johan Edfors (SWE) | 70-74-68-74—286 | 56,041 |
| | Hunter Mahan | 72-68-68-72—280 | 233,350 | | J B Holmes | 73-67-73-73—286 | 56,041 |
| | Tiger Woods | 74-69-68-69—280 | 233,350 | | Francesco Molinari (ITA) | 71-70-74-71—286 | 56,041 |
| 9 | Henrik Stenson (SWE) | 73-70-70-68—281 | 194,794 | | Vijay Singh (FIJ) | 72-72-73-69—286 | 56,041 |
| 10 | Stephen Ames (CAN) | 74-66-70-72—282 | 154,600 | | Azuma Yano (JPN) | 72-65-77-72—286 | 56,041 |
| | Matt Bettencourt | 75-67-71-69—282 | 154,600 | 33 | Jim Furyk | 72-69-74-72—287 | 47,404 |
| | Sergio García (ESP) | 70-70-72-70—282 | 154,600 | | Kevin Sutherland | 71-73-73-70—287 | 47,404 |
| | Rory McIlroy (NIR) | 72-70-72-68—282 | 154,600 | | Camilo Villegas (COL) | 71-71-72-73—287 | 47,404 |
| | Ryan Moore | 70-69-72-71—282 | 154,600 | 36 | Todd Hamilton | 67-71-71-79—288 | 42,935 |
| | Mike Weir (CAN) | 64-70-74-74—282 | 154,600 | | Carl Pettersson (SWE) | 75-68-73-72—288 | 42,395 |
| 16 | Retief Goosen (RSA) | 73-68-68-74—283 | 122,128 | | Adam Scott (AUS) | 69-71-73-75—288 | 42,395 |
| | Anthony Kim | 71-71-71-70—283 | 122,128 | | Nick Taylor (am) | 73-65-75-75—288 | |
| 18 | Peter Hanson (SWE) | 66-71-73-74—284 | 100,308 | 40 | Tim Clark (RSA) | 73-71-74-71—289 | 38,492 |
| | Graeme McDowell (NIR) | 69-72-69-74—284 | 100,308 | | Dustin Johnson | 72-69-76-72—289 | 38,492 |
| | Ian Poulter (ENG) | 70-74-73-67—284 | 100,308 | | Billy Mayfair | 73-70-72-74—289 | 38,492 |
| | Michael Sim (AUS) | 71-70-71-72—284 | 100,308 | | Drew Weaver (am) | 69-72-74-74—289 | |
| | Bubba Watson | 72-70-67-75—284 | 100,308 | 44 | Kenny Perry | 71-72-75-72—290 | 35,536 |

**Other players who made the cut:** Thomas Levet (FRA), John Mallinger 291; K J Choi (KOR), Tom Lehman, Rocco Mediate, Geoff Ogilvy (AUS), Andres Romero (ARG), Gary Woodland 292; Kyle Stanley (am) 293; Angel Cabrera (ARG), Jean-François Lucquin (FRA), Andrew McLardy (RSA) 294; Ben Curtis, 296; Jeff Brehaut 297, Trevor Murphy 297; Fred Funk 301

## 2008 US Open  *Torrey Pines, La Jolla, CA*  June 12–15                    [7643–71]

Prize money: $7.5 million. Entries: 8,390

| | | | | | | | | |
|---|---|---|---|---|---|---|---|---|
| 1 | Tiger Woods* | 72-68-70-73—283 | $1,350,000 | 18T | Mike Weir (CAN) | 73-74-69-74—290 | 87,230 |
| 2 | Rocco Mediate | 69-71-72-71—283 | 810,000 | 26 | Anthony Kim | 74-75-70-72—291 | 61,252 |
| *Tiger Woods won at the 19th hole of the extra round* | | | | | Adam Scott (AUS) | 73-73-75-70—291 | 61,252 |
| 3 | Lee Westwood (ENG) | 70-71-70-73—284 | 491,995 | | Boo Weekley | 73-76-70-72—291 | 61,252 |
| 4 | Robert Karlsson (SWE) | 70-75-75-71—286 | 307,303 | 29 | Aaron Baddeley (AUS) | 74-73-71-74—292 | 48,482 |
| | D J Trahan | 72-69-73-72--286 | 307,303 | | Bart Bryant | 75-70-78-69—292 | 48,482 |
| 6 | Miguel Angel Jiménez | 75-66-74-72—287 | 220,686 | | Jeff Quinney | 79-70-70-73—292 | 48,482 |
| | (ESP) | | | | Patrick Sheehan | 71-74-74-73—292 | 48,482 |
| | John Merrick | 73-72-71-71—287 | 220,686 | | Steve Stricker | 73-76-71-72—292 | 48,482 |
| | Carl Pettersson (SWE) | 71-71-77-68—287 | 220,686 | | Michael Thompson | 74-73-73-72—292 | |
| 9 | Eric Axley | 69-79-71-69—288 | 160,769 | | (am) | | |
| | Geoff Ogilvy (AUS) | 69-72-72-74—288 | 160,769 | | Scott Verplank | 72-72-74-74—292 | 48,482 |
| | Heath Slocum | 75-74-74-65—288 | 160,769 | 36 | Stuart Appleby (AUS) | 69-70-79-75—293 | 35,709 |
| | Brandt Snedeker | 76-73-68-71—288 | 160,769 | | Daniel Chopra (SWE) | 73-75-75-70—293 | 35,709 |
| | Camilo Villegas (COL) | 73-71-71-73—288 | 160,769 | | Robert Dinwiddie | 73-71-75-74—293 | 35,709 |
| 14 | Stewart Cink | 72-73-77-67—289 | 122,159 | | (ENG) | | |
| | Ernie Els (RSA) | 70-72-74-73—289 | 122,159 | | Jim Furyk | 74-71-73-75—293 | 35,709 |
| | Retief Goosen (RSA) | 76-69-77-67—289 | 122,159 | | Todd Hamilton | 74-74-73-72—293 | 35,709 |
| | Rod Pampling (AUS) | 74-70-75-70—289 | 122,159 | | Padraig Harrington (IRL) | 78-67-77-71—293 | 35,709 |
| 18 | Robert Allenby (AUS) | 70-72-73-75—290 | 87,230 | | Justin Leonard | 75-72-75-71—293 | 35,709 |
| | Chad Campbell | 77-72-71-70—290 | 87,230 | | Jonathan Mills | 72-75-75-71—293 | 35,709 |
| | Sergio García (ESP) | 76-70-70-74—290 | 87,230 | | Joe Ogilvie | 71-76-73-73—293 | 35,709 |
| | Ryuji Imada (JPN) | 74-75-70-71—290 | 87,230 | | Pat Perez | 75-73-75-70—293 | 35,709 |
| | Brandt Jobe | 73-75-69-73—290 | 87,230 | | Andres Romero (ARG) | 71-73-77-72—293 | 35,709 |
| | Hunter Mahan | 72-74-69-75—290 | 87,230 | | Oliver Wilson (ENG) | 72-71-74-76—293 | 35,709 |
| | Phil Mickelson | 71-75-76-68—290 | 87,230 | | | | |

**Other players who made the cut:** Tim Clark (RSA), Dustin Johnson, Matt Kuchar, Jarrod Lyle (AUS), John Rollins 294; Ben Crane, Søren Hansen (DEN), Martin Kaymer (GER), Davis Love III, Kevin Streelman 295; Stephen Ames (CAN), Rory Sabbatini (RSA) 296; Alastair Forsyth (SCO), Rickie Fowler (am), Brett Quigley, David Toms, Nick Watney 297; Paul Casey (ENG), Trevor Immelman (RSA), John Malinger, Vijay Singh (FIJ) 298; Derek Fathauer (am), D A Points 299; Woody Austin, Andrew Dresser, Andrew Svoboda 300; Justin Hicks, Ian Leggatt (CAN), Jesper Parnevik (SWE) 301; Ross McGowan (ENG) 303; Rich Beem, Chris Kirk 304, Luke Donald (ENG) WD

## 2007 US Open  *Oakmont, PA*  June 14–17                    [7230–70]

Prize money: $6.8 million. Entries: 8,544

| | | | | | | | | |
|---|---|---|---|---|---|---|---|---|
| 1 | Angel Cabrera (ARG) | 69-71-76-69—285 | $1,260,000 | 20T | Mike Weir (CAN) | 74-72-73-75—294 | 86,200 |
| 2 | Jim Furyk | 71-75-70-70—286 | 611,336 | 23 | Ken Duke | 74-75-73-73—295 | 71,905 |
| | Tiger Woods | 71-74-69-72—286 | 611,336 | | Nick O'Hern (AUS) | 76-74-71-74—295 | 71,905 |
| 4 | Niclas Fasth (SWE) | 71-71-75-70—287 | 325,923 | | Brandt Snedeker | 71-73-77-74—295 | 71,905 |
| 5 | David Toms | 72-72-73-72—289 | 248,948 | 26 | Stuart Appleby (AUS) | 74-72-71-79—296 | 57,026 |
| | Bubba Watson | 70-71-74-74—289 | 248,948 | | J J Henry | 71-78-75-72—296 | 57,026 |
| 7 | Nick Dougherty (ENG) | 68-77-74-71—290 | 194,245 | | Camilo Villegas (COL) | 73-77-75-71—296 | 57,026 |
| | Jerry Kelly | 74-71-73-72—290 | 194,245 | | Boo Weekley | 72-75-77-72—296 | 57,026 |
| | Scott Verplank | 73-71-74-72—290 | 194,245 | 30 | D J Brigman | 74-74-74-75—297 | 45,313 |
| 10 | Stephen Ames (CAN) | 73-69-73-76—291 | 154,093 | | Fred Funk | 71-78-74-74—297 | 45,313 |
| | Paul Casey (ENG) | 77-66-72-76—291 | 154,093 | | Peter Hanson (SWE) | 71-74-78-74—297 | 45,313 |
| | Justin Rose (ENG) | 71-71-73-76—291 | 154,093 | | Pablo Martin (ESP) | 71-76-77-73—297 | 45,313 |
| 13 | Aaron Baddeley (AUS) | 72-70-70-80—292 | 124,706 | | Graeme McDowell | 73-72-75-77—297 | 45,313 |
| | Lee Janzen | 73-73-73-73—292 | 124,706 | | (NIR) | | |
| | Hunter Mahan | 73-74-72-73—292 | 124,706 | | Charl Schwartzel (RSA) | 75-73-73-76—297 | 45,313 |
| | Steve Stricker | 75-73-68-76—292 | 124,706 | 36 | Mathew Goggin (AUS) | 77-73-74-74—298 | 37,159 |
| 17 | Jeff Brehaut | 73-75-70-75—293 | 102,536 | | Shingo Katayama (JPN) | 72-74-79-73—298 | 37,159 |
| | Jim Clark (RSA) | 72-76-71-74—293 | 102,536 | | Jeev Milkha Singh (IND) | 75-75-73-75—298 | 37,159 |
| | Carl Pettersson (SWE) | 72-72-75-74—293 | 102,536 | | Tom Pernice | 72-72-75-79—298 | 37,159 |
| 20 | Anthony Kim | 74-73-80-67—294 | 86,200 | | Ian Poulter (ENG) | 72-77-72-77—298 | 37,159 |
| | Vijay Singh (FIJ) | 71-77-70-76—294 | 86,200 | | Lee Westwood (ENG) | 72-75-79-72—298 | 37,159 |

**Other players who made the cut:** Kenneth Ferrie (ENG), Geoff Ogilvy (AUS), John Rollins 299; Olin Browne, Ben Curtis, Chris DiMarco, Marcus Fraser (AUS), Zach Johnson, José-María Olazábal (ESP) 300; Ernie Els (RSA), Charles Howell III, Rory Sabbatini (RSA), Dean Wilson 301; Anders Hansen (DEN), Michael Putnam 302; Chad Campbell 303; Michael Campbell (NZL), Bob Estes, Harrison Frazar, Kevin Sutherland 304; Jason Dufner 305; George McNeill 306

## 2006 US Open Winged Foot, Mamaroneck, NY June 15–18 [7264–70]

Prize money: $6.25 million. Entries: 8,584

| | | | | | | | | |
|---|---|---|---|---|---|---|---|---|
| 1 | Geoff Ogilvy (AUS) | 71-70-72-72—285 | $,1225,000 | 16T | Arron Oberholser | 75-68-74-74—291 | 99,417 |
| 2 | Jim Furyk | 70-72-74-70—286 | 501,249 | 21 | Peter Hedblom (SWE) | 72-74-71-75—292 | 74,252 |
| | Phil Mickelson | 70-73-69-74—286 | 501,249 | | Trevor Immelman (RSA) | 76-71-70-75—292 | 74,252 |
| | Colin Montgomerie (SCO) | 69-71-75-71—286 | 501,249 | | José-María Olazábal (ESP) | 75-73-73-71—292 | 74,252 |
| 5 | Padraig Harrington (IRL) | 73-69-74-71—287 | 255,642 | | Tom Pernice Jr | 79-70-72-71—292 | 74,252 |
| | | | | | Adam Scott (AUS) | 72-76-70-74—292 | 74,252 |
| 6 | Kenneth Ferrie (ENG) | 71-70-71-76—288 | 183,255 | 26 | Craig Barlow | 72-75-72-74—293 | 52,314 |
| | Nick O'Hern (AUS) | 75-70-74-69—288 | 183,255 | | Angel Cabrera (ARG) | 74-73-74-72—293 | 52,314 |
| | Vijay Singh (FIJ) | 71-74-70-73—288 | 183,255 | | Ernie Els (RSA) | 74-73-74-72—293 | 52,314 |
| | Jeff Sluman | 74-73-72-69—288 | 183,255 | | Sean O'Hair | 76-72-74-71—293 | 52,314 |
| | Steve Stricker | 70-69-76-73—288 | 183,255 | | Ted Purdy | 78-71-71-73—293 | 52,314 |
| | Mike Weir (CAN) | 71-74-71-72—288 | 183,255 | | Henrik Stenson (SWE) | 75-71-73-74—293 | 52,314 |
| 12 | Luke Donald (ENG) | 78-69-70-72—289 | 131,670 | 32 | Woody Austin | 72-76-72-74—294 | 41,912 |
| | Ryuji Imada (JPN) | 76-73-69-71—289 | 131,670 | | Bart Bryant | 72-72-73-77—294 | 41,912 |
| | Ian Poulter (ENG) | 74-71-70-74—289 | 131,670 | | Scott Hend (AUS) | 72-72-75-75—294 | 41,912 |
| 15 | Paul Casey (ENG) | 77-72-72-69—290 | 116,735 | | Steve Jones | 74-74-71-75—294 | 41,912 |
| 16 | Robert Allenby (AUS) | 73-74-72-72—291 | 99,417 | | Rodney Pampling (AUS) | 73-75-75-71—294 | 41,912 |
| | David Duval | 77-68-75-71—291 | 99,417 | 37 | Stewart Cink | 75-71-77-72—295 | 36,647 |
| | David Howell (ENG) | 70-78-74-69—291 | 99,417 | | Jay Haas | 75-72-74-74—295 | 36,647 |
| | Miguel Angel Jiménez (ESP) | 70-75-74-72—291 | 99,417 | | Charles Howell III | 77-71-73-74—295 | 36,647 |

**Other players who made the cut:** Tommy Armour III, Chad Collins, John Cook, Jason Dufner, Fred Funk, Stephen Gangluff (CAN), Bo Van Pelt, Lee Williams 296; Phillip Archer (ENG), Thomas Bjørn (DEN), Fred Couples, Charley Hoffman, J B Holmes, Kent Jones, Graeme McDowell (NIR), Charl Schwartzel (RSA) 297; Darren Clarke (NIR) 298; Ben Curtis 299; Kenny Perry 301; Skip Kendal, Jeev Milkha Singh (IND), Camilo Villegas (COL) 302; Ben Crane 303; Tim Herron 305

## 2005 US Open Pinehurst No.2, NC June 16–19 [7214–70]

Prize money: $6.25 million. Entries: 9,048

| | | | | | | | | |
|---|---|---|---|---|---|---|---|---|
| 1 | Michael Campbell (NZL) | 71-69-71-69—280 | $1,170,000 | 15T | Peter Jacobsen | 72-73-69-75—289 | 88,120 |
| | | | | | David Toms | 70-72-70-77—289 | 88,120 |
| 2 | Tiger Woods | 70-71-72-69—282 | 700,000 | 23 | Olin Browne | 67-71-72-80—290 | 59,633 |
| 3 | Tim Clark (RSA) | 76-69-70-70—285 | 320,039 | | Paul Claxton | 72-72-72-74—290 | 59,633 |
| | Sergio García (ESP) | 71-69-75-70—285 | 320,039 | | Fred Funk | 73-71-76-70—290 | 59,633 |
| | Mark Hensby (AUS) | 71-68-72-74—285 | 320,039 | | Justin Leonard | 76-71-70-73—290 | 59,633 |
| 6 | Davis Love III | 77-70-70-69—286 | 187,813 | | Kenny Perry | 75-70-71-74—290 | 59,633 |
| | Rocco Mediate | 67-74-74-71—286 | 187,813 | 28 | Stephen Allan (AUS) | 72-69-73-77—291 | 44,486 |
| | Vijay Singh (FIJ) | 70-70-74-72—286 | 187,813 | | Matt Every (am) | 75-73-73-70—291 | 44,486 |
| 9 | Arron Oberholser | 76-67-71-73—287 | 150,834 | | Jim Furyk | 71-70-75-75—291 | 44,486 |
| | Nick Price (ZIM) | 72-71-72-72—287 | 150,834 | | Geoff Ogilvy (AUS) | 72-74-71-74—291 | 44,486 |
| 11 | Bob Estes | 70-73-75-70—288 | 123,857 | | Adam Scott (AUS) | 70-71-74-76—291 | 44,486 |
| | Retief Goosen (RSA) | 68-70-69-81—288 | 123,857 | 33 | Angel Cabrera (ARG) | 71-73-73-75—292 | 35,759 |
| | Peter Hedblom (SWE) | 77-66-70-75—288 | 123,857 | | Steve Elkington (AUS) | 74-69-79-70—292 | 35,759 |
| | Corey Pavin | 73-72-70-73—288 | 123,857 | | Tim Herron | 74-73-70-75—292 | 35,759 |
| 15 | K J Choi (KOR) | 69-70-74-76—289 | 88,120 | | Brandt Jobe | 68-73-79-72—292 | 35,759 |
| | Stewart Cink | 73-74-73-69—289 | 88,120 | | Bernhard Langer (GER) | 74-73-71-74—292 | 35,759 |
| | John Cook | 71-76-70-72—289 | 88,120 | | Shigeki Maruyama (JPN) | 71-74-72-75—292 | 35,759 |
| | Fred Couples | 71-74-74-70—289 | 88,120 | | Phil Mickelson | 69-77-72-74—292 | 35,759 |
| | Ernie Els (RSA) | 71-76-72-70—289 | 88,120 | | Ted Purdy | 73-71-73-75—292 | 35,759 |
| | Ryuji Imada (JPN) | 77-68-73-71—289 | 88,120 | | Lee Westwood (ENG) | 68-72-73-79—292 | 35,759 |

**Other players who made the cut:** Chad Campbell, Peter Lonard (AUS), Paul McGinley (IRL), Colin Montgomerie (SCO), Tom Pernice, Rob Rashell, Mike Weir (CAN) 293; Jason Gore, J L Lewis, Nick O'Hern (AUS) 294; Thomas Bjørn (DEN), Nick Dougherty (ENG), Richard Green (AUS), Søren Kjeldsen (DEN), Thomas Levet (FRA) 295; Tommy Armour III, Luke Donald (ENG), Keiichiro Fukabori (JPN), J J Henry, Lee Janzen, Steve Jones, Frank Lickliter, Jonathan Lomas (ENG), Ryan Moore (am), Ian Poulter (ENG) 296; Michael Allen, Steve Flesch, Bill Glasson, John Mallinger 297; Stephen Ames (TRI), D J Brigman, J Hayes, Rory Sabbatini (RSA) 298; John Daly, Charles Howell III, Omar Uresti, 299; Jeff Maggert, Bob Tway 300; Graeme McDowell (NIR), Chris Nallen 301; Craig Barlow 303; Jerry Kelly 305

## 2004 US Open Shinnecock Hills, Southampton, NY June 17–20                    [6996–70]

Prize money: $6.25 million. Entries: 8,726

| | | | | | | | | |
|---|---|---|---|---|---|---|---|---|
| 1 | Retief Goosen (RSA) | 70-66-69-71—276 | $1,125,000 | | 20T | David Toms | 73-72-70-76—291 | 80,644 |
| 2 | Phil Mickelson | 68-66-73-71—278 | 675,000 | | | Kirk Triplett | 71-70-73-77—291 | 80,644 |
| 3 | Jeff Maggert | 68-67-74-72—281 | 424,604 | | 24 | Daniel Chopra (SWE) | 73-68-76-75—292 | 63,328 |
| 4 | Shigeki Maruyama (JPN) | 66-68-74-76—284 | 267,756 | | | Lee Janzen | 72-70-71-79—292 | 63,328 |
| | | | | | | Tim Petrovic | 69-75-72-76—292 | 63,328 |
| | Mike Weir (CAN) | 69-70-71-74—284 | 267,756 | | | Nick Price (ZIM) | 73-70-72-77—292 | 63,328 |
| 6 | Fred Funk | 70-66-72-77—285 | 212,444 | | 28 | Shaun Micheel | 71-72-70-80—293 | 51,774 |
| 7 | Robert Allenby (AUS) | 70-72-74-70—286 | 183,828 | | | Vijay Singh (FIJ) | 68-70-77-78—293 | 51,774 |
| | Steve Flesch | 68-74-70-74—286 | 183,828 | | 30 | Ben Curtis | 68-75-72-79—294 | 46,089 |
| 9 | Stephen Ames (TRI) | 74-66-73-74—287 | 145,282 | | 31 | K J Choi (KOR) | 76-68-76-75—295 | 41,759 |
| | Ernie Els (RSA) | 70-67-70-80—287 | 145,282 | | | Padraig Harrington (IRL) | 73-71-76-75—295 | 41,759 |
| | Chris DiMarco | 71-71-70-75—287 | 145,282 | | | Peter Lonard (AUS) | 71-73-77-74—295 | 41,759 |
| | Jay Haas | 66-74-76-71—287 | 145,282 | | | David Roesch | 68-73-74-80—295 | 41,759 |
| 13 | Tim Clark (RSA) | 73-70-66-79—288 | 119,770 | | | Bo Van Pelt | 69-73-73-80—295 | 41,759 |
| | Tim Herron | 75-66-73-74—288 | 119,770 | | 36 | Charles Howell III | 75-70-68-83—296 | 36,813 |
| | Spencer Levin (am) | 69-73-71-75—288 | | | | Hidemichi Tanaka (JPN) | 70-74-73-79—296 | 36,813 |
| 16 | Angel Cabrera (ARG) | 66-71-77-75—289 | 109,410 | | | Lee Westwood (ENG) | 73-71-73-79—296 | 36,813 |
| 17 | Skip Kendall | 68-75-74-73—290 | 98,477 | | | Casey Wittenberg (am) | 71-71-75-79—296 | |
| | Corey Pavin | 67-71-73-79—290 | 98,477 | | | | | |
| | Tiger Woods | 72-69-73-76—290 | 98,477 | | | | | |
| 20 | Mark Calcavecchia | 71-71-74-75—291 | 80,644 | | | | | |
| | Sergio García (ESP) | 72-68-71-80—291 | 80,644 | | | | | |

**Other players who made the cut:** Bill Haas (am), Jerry Kelly, Stephen Leaney (AUS), Spike McRoy, Joe Ogilvie, Pat Perez, Geoffrey Sisk, Scott Verplank 297; Kristopher Cox, Jim Furyk, Zachary Johnson, Chris Riley, John Rollins 298; Dudley Hart, Scott Hoch 299; Tom Carter, Trevor Immelman (RSA) 300; Joakim Haeggman (SWE), Tom Kite, Phillip Price (WAL) 302; Alex Cejka (GER), Craig Parry (AUS) 303; Cliff Kresge, Chez Reavie (am) 304; J J Henry 306; Kevin Stadler 307; Billy Mayfair 310

# US Open Championship History

| Year | Winner | Runner-up | Venue | Score |
|---|---|---|---|---|
| 1894 | W Dunn | W Campbell | St Andrews, NY | 2 holes |

*After 1894 decided by stroke-play. From 1895–1897. 36-holes From 1898 72-holes*

| Year | Winner | Venue | Score | | Year | Winner | Venue | Score |
|---|---|---|---|---|---|---|---|---|
| 1895 | H J Rawlins | Newport | 173 | | 1913 | F Ouimet* (am) | Brookline, MA | 304 |
| 1896 | J Foulis | Southampton | 152 | | *After a play-off: Ouimet 72, H Vardon 77, T Ray 78 | | | |
| 1897 | J Lloyd | Wheaton, IL | 162 | | 1914 | W Hagen | Midlothian | 297 |
| 1898 | F Herd | South Hamilton, MA | 328 | | 1915 | J Travers (am) | Baltusrol | 290 |
| 1899 | W Smith | Baltimore | 315 | | 1916 | C Evans (am) | Minneapolis | 286 |
| 1900 | H Vardon (ENG) | Wheaton, IL | 313 | | 1917-18 | No Championship | | |
| 1901 | W Anderson* | Myopia, MA | 315 | | 1919 | W Hagen* | Braeburn | 301 |
| *After a play-off: Anderson 85, A Smith 86 | | | | | *After a play-off: Hagen 77, M Brady 78 | | | |
| 1902 | L Auchterlonie | Garden City | 305 | | 1920 | E Ray (ENG) | Inverness | 295 |
| 1903 | W Anderson* | Baltusrol | 307 | | 1921 | J Barnes | Washington | 289 |
| *After a play-off: Anderson 82, D Brown 84 | | | | | 1922 | G Sarazen | Glencoe | 288 |
| 1904 | W Anderson | Glenview | 304 | | 1923 | R Jones Jr* (am) | Inwood, NY | 295 |
| 1905 | W Anderson | Myopia, MA | 335 | | *After a play-off: Jones 76, R Cruikshank 78 | | | |
| 1906 | A Smith | Onwentsia | 291 | | 1924 | C Walker | Oakland Hills | 297 |
| 1907 | A Ross | Chestnut Hill, PA | 302 | | 1925 | W MacFarlane* | Worcester | 291 |
| 1908 | F McLeod* | Myopia, MA | 322 | | *After a play-off: MacFarlane 147, R Jones Jr 148 | | | |
| *After a play-off: McLeod 77, W Smith 83 | | | | | 1926 | R Jones Jr* (am) | Scioto | 293 |
| 1909 | G Sargent | Englewood, NJ | 290 | | 1927 | T Armour* | Oakmont | 301 |
| 1910 | A Smith* | Philadelphia | 289 | | *After a play-off: Armour 76, H Cooper 79 | | | |
| *After a play-off: Smith 71, J McDermott 75, M Smith 77 | | | | | 1928 | J Farrell* | Olympia Fields | 294 |
| 1911 | J McDermott* | Wheaton, IL | 307 | | *After a play-off: Farrell 143, R Jones Jr (am) 144 | | | |
| *After a play-off with M Brady and G Simpson: McDermott 80, Brady 82, Simpson 85 | | | | | 1929 | R Jones Jr* (am) | Winged Foot, NY | 294 |
| | | | | | *After a play-off: Jones 141, A Espinosa 164 | | | |
| 1912 | J McDermott | Buffalo, NY | 294 | | 1930 | R Jones Jr (am) | Interlachen | 287 |

| Year | Winner | Venue | Score | Year | Winner | Venue | Score |
|------|--------|-------|-------|------|--------|-------|-------|
| 1931 | B Burke* | Inverness | 292 | 1973 | J Miller | Oakmont, PA | 279 |
| *After a play-off: Burke 149-148, G von Elm 149-149 | | | | 1974 | H Irwin | Winged Foot, NY | 287 |
| 1932 | G Sarazen | Fresh Meadow | 286 | 1975 | L Graham* | Medinah, IL | 287 |
| 1933 | J Goodman (am) | North Shore | 287 | *After a play-off: Graham 71, J Mahaffey 73 | | | |
| 1934 | O Dutra | Merion | 293 | 1976 | J Pate | Atlanta, GA | 277 |
| 1935 | S Parks | Oakmont | 299 | 1977 | H Green | Southern Hills, Tulsa | 278 |
| 1936 | T Manero | Springfield | 282 | 1978 | A North | Cherry Hills | 285 |
| 1937 | R Guldahl | Oakland Hills | 281 | 1979 | H Irwin | Inverness, OH | 284 |
| 1938 | R Guldahl | Cherry Hills | 284 | 1980 | J Nicklaus | Baltusrol | 272 |
| 1939 | B Nelson* | Philadelphia | 284 | 1981 | D Graham (AUS) | Merion, PA | 273 |
| *After a play-off: Nelson 138, C Wood 141, D Shute 76 | | | | 1982 | T Watson | Pebble Beach | 282 |
| 1940 | W Lawson Little* | Canterbury, OH | 287 | 1983 | L Nelson | Oakmont, PA | 280 |
| *After a play-off: Little 70, G Sarazen 73 | | | | 1984 | F Zoeller* | Winged Foot | 276 |
| 1941 | C Wood | Fort Worth, TX | 284 | *After a play-off: Zoeller 67, G Norman 75 | | | |
| 1942–45 | No Championship | | | 1985 | A North | Oakland Hills, MI | 279 |
| 1946 | L Mangrum* | Canterbury | 284 | 1986 | R Floyd | Shinnecock Hills, NY | 279 |
| *After a play-off: Mangrum 144, B Nelson 145, V Ghezzi 145 | | | | 1987 | S Simpson | Olympic, San Francisco | 277 |
| 1947 | L Worsham* | St Louis | 282 | 1988 | C Strange* | Brookline, MA | 278 |
| *After a play-off: Worsham 69, S Snead 70 | | | | *After a play-off: Strange 71, N Faldo 75 | | | |
| 1948 | B Hogan | Los Angeles | 276 | 1989 | C Strange | Rochester, NY | 278 |
| 1949 | Dr C Middlecoff | Medinah, IL | 286 | 1990 | H Irwin* | Medinah | 280 |
| 1950 | B Hogan* | Merion, PA | 287 | *After a play-off: Irwin 74, M Donald 74 (Irwin won sudden death | | | |
| *After a play-off: Hogan 69, L Mangrum 73, D Fazio 75 | | | | play-off 3 to 4 at first extra hole) | | | |
| 1951 | B Hogan | Oakland Hills, MI | 287 | 1991 | P Stewart* | Hazeltine, MN | 282 |
| 1952 | J Boros | Dallas, TX | 281 | *After a play-off: Stewart 75, S Simpson 77 | | | |
| 1953 | B Hogan | Oakmont | 283 | 1992 | T Kite | Pebble Beach, FL | 285 |
| 1954 | E Furgol | Baltusrol | 284 | 1993 | L Janzen | Baltusrol | 272 |
| 1955 | J Fleck* | San Francisco | 287 | 1994 | E Els* (RSA) | Oakmont, PA | 279 |
| *After a play-off: Fleck 69, B Hogan 72 | | | | *After a play-off: Els 74, L Roberts 74, C Montgomerie 78 (Els won | | | |
| 1956 | Dr C Middlecoff | Rochester, NY | 281 | sudden death playoff: Els 4,4, Roberts 4,5) | | | |
| 1957 | D Mayer* | Inverness | 282 | 1995 | C Pavin | Shinnecock Hills, NY | 280 |
| *After a play-off: Mayer 72, C Middlecoff 79 | | | | 1996 | S Jones | Oakland Hills, MI | 278 |
| 1958 | T Bolt | Tulsa, OK | 283 | 1997 | E Els (RSA) | Congressional, Bethesda, MD | 276 |
| 1959 | W Casper | Winged Foot, NY | 282 | 1998 | L Janzen | Olympic, San Francisco, CA | 280 |
| 1960 | A Palmer | Denver, CO | 280 | 1999 | P Stewart | Pinehurst No. 2, NC | 279 |
| 1961 | G Littler | Birmingham, MI | 281 | 2000 | T Woods | Pebble Beach, CA | 272 |
| 1962 | J Nicklaus* | Oakmont | 283 | 2001 | R Goosen* (RSA) | Southern Hills CC, OK | 276 |
| *After a play-off: Nicklaus 71, A Palmer 74 | | | | *After a play-off: Goosen 70, M Brooks 72 | | | |
| 1963 | J Boros* | Brookline, MA | 293 | 2002 | T Woods | Farmingdale, NY | 277 |
| *After a play-off: Boros 70, J Cupit 73, A Palmer 76 | | | | 2003 | J Furyk | Olympia Fields, IL | 272 |
| 1964 | K Venturi | Washington | 278 | 2004 | R Goosen (RSA) | Shinnecock Hills, NY | 276 |
| 1965 | G Player* (RSA) | St Louis, MO | 282 | 2005 | M Campbell (NZL) | Pinehurst No.2, NC | 280 |
| *After a play-off: Player 71, K Nagle 74 | | | | 2006 | G Ogilvy (AUS) | Winged Foot, NY | 285 |
| 1966 | W Casper* | San Francisco | 278 | 2007 | A Cabrera (ARG) | Oakmont, PA | 285 |
| *After a play-off: Casper 69, A Palmer 73 | | | | 2008 | T Woods* | Torrey Pines, CA | 283 |
| 1967 | J Nicklaus | Baltusrol | 275 | *Beat R Mediate at 19th hole of extra round | | | |
| 1968 | L Trevino | Rochester, NY | 275 | 2009 | L Glover | Farmingdale, NY | 276 |
| 1969 | O Moody | Houston, TX | 281 | 2010 | G McDowell (NIR) | Pebble Beach, CA | 284 |
| 1970 | A Jacklin (ENG) | Hazeltine, MN | 281 | 2011 | R McIlroy (NIR) | Congressional, Bethesda, MD | 268 |
| 1971 | L Trevino | Merion, PA | 280 | 2012 | W Simpson | Olympic, San Francisco, CA | 281 |
| *After a play-off: Trevino 68, J Nicklaus 71 | | | | 2013 | J Rose (ENG) | Merion GC, Ardmore, PA | 281 |
| 1972 | J Nicklaus | Pebble Beach | 290 | | | | |

# Month by month in 2013

Paul McGinley becomes Ireland's first Ryder Cup captain. Rory McIlroy signs for Nike, but immediately misses the cut in Abu Dhabi, as does Tiger Woods after a two-stroke penalty for an incorrect drop. Jamie Donaldson lifts the title, while Woods is a winner a week later at Torrey Pines and Chris Wood eagles the last to triumph in Qatar.

# Adam Scott ends 76 years of Aussie heartbreak with victory at Augusta

As stories of redemption go, this one delivered a plot twist which allowed the champion to finally recognise his own true identity as a major winner. Just nine months after enduring an epic collapse in The Open at Royal Lytham, Adam Scott came from behind to win The Masters thanks to a dramatic play-off victory over past champion Angel Cabrera.

The pain of dropping shots on each of the four closing holes at Lytham was replaced by a sense of euphoria at Augusta as Scott followed a 20 foot birdie on the 72nd hole with another long putt for victory on the second hole of a compelling sudden death play-off. These strokes of genius marked both a notable personal triumph for Scott and a sense of national pride Down Under where Australia celebrated its first Masters' success in 76 attempts.

Scott had been runner-up at the Masters before, just like his compatriots Jason Day, Jack Newton, Bruce Crampton, Jim Ferrier and the luckless Greg Norman, who filled second place on no fewer than three occasions. This time, though, Australians dominated the tournament as never before with Scott claiming the Green Jacket on nine under par while Day – who led with three holes to play – finished third and Marc Leishman was fourth.

Although the scars of losing to Ernie Els in the oldest major could have been fatal to his major dreams, Scott used the experience as a positive reminder that he was resilient enough to win one of the game's most prestigious titles. "Everything I said after The Open is how I felt, and I meant it," he recalled. "It did give me more belief that I could win a major. It proved to me, in fact, that I could. It was up to myself now; you know you can do it. The time, there's not a better time…"

It was that sense of seizing the moment which embraced Scott on the 72nd hole as he lined up a similar putt to the one he recalled watching Mark O'Meara hole to win The Masters in 1998. "I was really pumped and felt like this was my chance," he added. "And I took it."

Maybe the 32-year-old recalled the words he wrote as a teenager in his school yearbook: "If all else fails, birdie the last." Normally guarded about showing his feelings, once he'd holed that putt the emotion poured out of Scott like lava erupting from a volcano. "For a split second," he admitted, "I thought I'd won." The tournament, however, as he knew, was far from over. Cabrera, 43, standing in the middle of the 18th fairway, had looked by far the calmest contender for much of the afternoon. Apart from a course management error on the par 5 13th, when he dumped his second shot in Rae's Creek, the veteran Argentine was very much in control.

Able to call on his past experience as a Masters winner and US Open champion, perhaps, in the end, only fate derailed Cabrera's attempt to win a third major title. He could easily have made birdie on the 17th and, in spite of Scott's heroics with the broomhandle putter, he struck one of the shots of the day on the home hole to convert a tap-in birdie to force a play-off.

When the play-off got underway, Cabrera could hardly believe his chip from the front of the 18th green skimmed over the hole rather than falling into the cup. And before Scott made his timely birdie putt on the second extra hole, thanks to a shrewd read from caddie Steve Williams, the Argentine's right-to-left breaking putt ,which stopped half an inch from the hole, would surely have dropped in drier conditions. "But that's golf," rued the runner-up, who was quick to embrace Scott after playing a key role in arguably the most compelling play-off in Masters history. "Golf gives and takes. Sometimes you make those putts, sometimes you just miss them. I wasn't lucky, but I was very much in this play-off."

In truth, the last hour or so of this championship added the excitement and brilliance which had been conspicuous mainly by its absence during a sodden afternoon when the patrons who stayed dry by holding their Masters' umbrellas aloft found few reasons to drop their brollies and applaud. There was no shortage of wayward drives, errant approach shots and missed putts until Scott and Cabrera took centre stage.

Conditions were more benign when the tournament began on Thursday, Scott opening with a canny 69 while Sergio García took a share of the lead with Leishman on six under par. The Spaniard putted with more assurance than he'd done for some time at Augusta and added sparkle to a leaderboard which also included notables such as Dustin Johnson on five under and Fred Couples on 68.

By Friday, Augusta National was far more challenging, offering almost as great a test of patience as the US Open rather than the spectacle which usually defines this annual rite of spring. Although Aussie rules would take hold by Sunday, much of the attention in the second round centred on a brace of high profile rules violations.

Tiger Woods didn't enjoy much luck on the 15th hole when his approach shot struck the flag stick and rebounded back into the water. Choosing not to go to the drop zone, the world No 1 went back to where he originally played the shot. Instead of dropping by his divot, however, he deliberately went back two yards and acknowledged as much in an interview afterwards. When the rules violation emerged, Tiger had already signed for an incorrect score and looked likely to be disqualified. Instead, he was penalised two strokes under Rule 33-7 which states that a player need not be disqualified because of "facts he did not know and could not reasonably have discovered prior to returning his scorecard." This interpretation of the revised rule divided opinion.

At the tender age of 14, many observers were concerned Guan Tianlang was a soft target for a one stroke penalty imposed for slow play bearing in mind no golfer had been called to account for slow play in an event run by the US PGA Tour since Glen Day in 1995. (Gregory Bourdy was also disciplined for tardiness at the US PGA championship in 2010.) However, referee John Paramor later revealed Guan had been warned four times about how long he took to execute shots before eventually being taken to task on the 17th. Happily, the penalty didn't prevent the gifted Chinese schoolboy from making the cut and going on to finish as the low amateur and winner of the Silver Cup on 12 over par.

> "My heart was about to stop, thinking is this it?"
>
> *Scott's comment after Cabrera's chip shot for a birdie nearly went in at the first play-off hole*

By Saturday afternoon, the focus was back on the golf. Cabrera, who seems to borrow Harry Potter's cloak of invisibility between the majors, followed up the 31 he shot on the back nine on Friday afternoon with another round of 69. Scott matched that score as did Brandt Snedeker while Day stumbled over the closing holes and posted 73.

On Sunday, the Australian responded bravely to the set-back with a birdie-eagle start to his round and was in pole position when he came to the 16th tee. Once again, however, Day faltered in sight of the finishing line and had to settle for third. While Snedeker engaged reverse with a closing 75 and dropped to a share of sixth, Thorbjørn Olesen, the impressive young Dane, overcame the setback of an opening 78 to twice card 68 over the weekend and earn an invitation to return in 2014.

Years ago, when playing mostly on the European Tour, one of Scott's sponsors arranged for some golf writers to play a few holes with the young man in St Andrews. I was among that group and Scott's picture perfect swing was even more impressive up close than it is from the other side of the ropes – compact, rhythmic and powerful. Put it this way: you didn't need a particularly shrewd eye for technique to appreciate that here was a golfer whose shot-making skills were honed to thrive in the arena of major championships.

Scott's destiny as a major winner may have taken longer to fulfil than many expected – he made his début at The Open as long ago as 2000 and finished in the top ten at The Masters on his first appearance at Augusta in 2002 – yet the Australian never lost faith in his own ability. The fourth golfer in the space of 20 months to win a major with an anchored putting stroke, the amiable Scott also benefited from the harder edge brought to his game by caddie Williams.

Although he'd taken plenty of knocks along the way, Scott's game proved robust enough to handle the slings and arrows of outrageous fortune. And when destiny came calling again at Augusta, the golfer was unflinching.

Mike Aitken

| First Round | Second Round | Third Round | Fourth Round |
|---|---|---|---|
| −6 Sergio García | −6 Jason Day | −7 Brandt Snedeker | −9 Adam Scott |
| −6 Marc Leishman | −5 Fred Couples | −7 Angel Cabrera | −9 Angel Cabrera |
| −5 Dustin Johnson | −5 Marc Leishman | −6 Adam Scott | −7 Jason Day |
| −4 David Lynn | −4 Angel Cabrera | −5 Marc Leishman | −5 Tiger Woods |
| −4 Rickie Fowler | −4 Jim Furyk | −5 Jason Day | −5 Marc Leishman |
| −4 Gonzalo Fdez-Castano | −4 Brandt Snedeker | −4 Matt Kuchar | −4 Thorbjørn Olesen |
| −4 Trevor Immelman | −3 Adam Scott | −3 Tiger Woods | −4 Brandt Snedeker |
| −4 Fred Couples | −3 Justin Rose | −3 Tim Clark | −3 Sergio García |
| −4 Matt Kuchar | −3 Lee Westwood | −2 Rickie Fowler | −3 Matt Kuchar |
| −3 Jim Furyk | −3 David Lynn | −2 Steve Stricker | −3 Lee Westwood |

## The 77th Masters Tournament   Augusta National GC, GA   April 11–14   [7435–72]

Prize money: $8m. Final field of 93 players (six amateurs) of whom 61 (including one amateurs) made the half-way cut on 148 or less.

*Players are of American nationality unless stated.*

| | | | |
|---|---|---|---|
| 1 | Adam Scott (AUS)* | 69-72-69-69—279 | $1,440,000 |
| 2 | Angel Cabrera (ARG) | 71-69-69-70—279 | 864,000 |

*\*Scott won at the second extra hole*

| | | | |
|---|---|---|---|
| 3 | Jason Day (AUS) | 70-68-73-70—281 | 544,000 |
| 4 | Tiger Woods | 70-73-70-70—283 | 352,000 |
| | Marc Leishman (AUS) | 66-73-72-72—283 | 352,000 |
| 6 | Thorbjørn Olesen (DEN) | 78-70-68-68—284 | 278,000 |
| | Brandt Snedeker | 70-70-69-75—284 | 278,000 |
| 8 | Sergio García (ESP) | 66-76-73-70—285 | 232,000 |
| | Lee Westwood (ENG) | 70-71-73-71—285 | 232,000 |
| | Matt Kuchar | 68-75-69-73—285 | 232,000 |
| 11 | John Huh (KOR) | 70-77-71-68—286 | 192,000 |
| | Tim Clark (RSA) | 70-76-67-73—286 | 192,000 |
| 13 | David Toms | 70-74-76-67—287 | 145,600 |
| | Ernie Els (RSA) | 71-74-73-69—287 | 145,600 |
| | Dustin Johnson | 67-76-74-70—287 | 145,600 |
| | Fred Couples | 68-71-77-71—287 | 145,600 |
| | Nick Watney | 78-69-68-72—287 | 145,600 |
| 18 | Henrik Stenson (SWE) | 75-71-73-69—288 | 116,000 |
| | Branden Grace (RSA) | 78-70-71-69—288 | 116,000 |
| 20 | Bill Haas | 71-72-74-72—289 | 89,920 |
| | Jason Dufner | 72-69-75-73—289 | 89,920 |
| | Gonzalo Fernandez-Castano (ESP) | 68-74-73-74—289 | 89,920 |
| | Bo Van Pelt | 71-74-70-74—289 | 89,920 |
| | Steve Stricker | 73-70-71-75—289 | 89,920 |
| 25 | Michael Thompson | 73-71-79-67—290 | 56,040 |
| | Rory McIlroy (NIR) | 72-70-79-69—290 | 56,040 |
| | Richard Sterne (RSA) | 73-72-75-70—290 | 56,040 |
| | Stewart Cink | 75-71-73-71—290 | 56,040 |
| | Luke Donald (ENG) | 71-72-75-72—290 | 56,040 |
| | Charl Schwartzel (RSA) | 71-71-75-73—290 | 56,040 |
| | Fredrik Jacobson (SWE) | 72-73-72-73—290 | 56,040 |
| | Justin Rose (ENG) | 70-71-75-74—290 | 56,040 |
| | Jim Furyk | 69-71-74-76—290 | 56,040 |
| | Bernhard Langer (GER) | 71-71-72-76—290 | 56,040 |
| 35 | Martin Kaymer (GER) | 72-75-74-70—291 | 41,200 |
| | John Senden (AUS) | 72-70-75-74—291 | 41,200 |
| | Zach Johnson | 69-76-71-75—291 | 41,200 |
| 38 | Ryan Moore | 71-72-81-68—292 | 32,000 |
| | Ryo Ishikawa (JPN) | 71-77-76-68—292 | 32,000 |
| | Paul Lawrie (SCO) | 76-70-75-71—292 | 32,000 |
| | Vijay Singh (FIJ) | 72-74-74-72—292 | 32,000 |
| | Brian Gay | 72-74-74-72—292 | 32,000 |
| | DA Points | 72-75-72-73—292 | 32,000 |
| | Robert Garrigus | 76-71-72-73—292 | 32,000 |
| | Rickie Fowler | 68-76-70-78—292 | 32,000 |
| 46 | Thomas Björn (DEN) | 73-73-76-71—293 | 23,307 |
| | David Lynn (ENG) | 68-73-80-72—293 | 23,307 |
| | KJ Choi (KOR) | 70-71-77-75—293 | 23,307 |
| 49 | Lucas Glover | 74-74-73-73—294 | 20,800 |
| 50 | Peter Hanson (SWE) | 72-75-76-72—295 | 19,480 |
| | Trevor Immelman (RSA) | 68-75-78-74—295 | 19,480 |
| | José Maria Olazábal (ESP) | 74-72-74-75—295 | 19,480 |
| | Bubba Watson | 75-73-70-77—295 | 19,480 |
| 54 | Keegan Bradley | 73-73-82-69—297 | 18,320 |
| | Sandy Lyle (SCO) | 73-72-81-71—297 | 18,320 |

| 54T | Phil Mickelson | 71-76-77-73—297 | 18,320 |
| | Scott Piercy | 75-69-78-75—297 | 18,320 |
| 58 | Tianlang Guan (CHN) (am) | 73-75-77-75—300 | |
| 59 | Kevin Na | 70-76-74-81—301 | 17,920 |
| 60 | John Peterson | 71-77-74-80—302 | 17,670 |
| 61 | Carl Pettersson (SWE) | 76-70-77-81—304 | 17,600 |

*The following players missed the half-way cut. Each professional player received $10,000:*

| 62 | George Coetzee (RSA) | 75-74—149 |
| | Jamie Donaldson (WAL) | 74-75—149 |
| | Martin Laird (SCO) | 76-73—149 |
| | Matteo Manassero (ITA) | 75-74—149 |
| | Graeme McDowell (NIR) | 73-76—149 |
| | Larry Mize | 73-76—149 |
| | Ted Potter Jr | 76-73—149 |
| | Webb Simpson | 73-76—149 |
| | YE Yang (KOR) | 72-77—149 |
| 71 | Louis Oosthuizen (RSA) | 74-76—150 |
| 72 | Nicolas Colsaerts (BEL) | 74-77—151 |
| | Ben Curtis | 76-75—151 |
| | John Merrick | 74-77—151 |
| | Mark O'Meara | 74-77—151 |
| | Ian Poulter (ENG) | 76-75—151 |
| | Mike Weir (CAN) | 72-79—151 |
| 78 | TJ Vogel (am) | 77-75—152 |
| | Michael Weaver (am) | 78-74—152 |
| | Thaworn Wiratchant (THA) | 79-73—152 |
| 81 | Padraig Harrington (IRL) | 78-75—153 |
| | Russell Henley | 72-81—153 |
| 81T | Kevin Streelman | 76-77—153 |
| 84 | Francesco Molinari (ITA) | 74-81—155 |
| | Nathan T Smith (am) | 77-78—155 |
| 86 | Steven Fox (am) | 7-681—157 |
| | Tom Watson Tom | 79-78—157 |
| 88 | Hunter Mahan | 76-82—158 |
| | Craig Stadler | 79-79—158 |
| | Ian Woosnam (WAL) | 80-78—158 |
| 91 | Alan Dunbar (am) (NIR) | 83-77—160 |
| 92 | Ben Crenshaw | 80-84—164 |
| | Hiroyuki Fujita (JPN) | 79-85—164 |

## 2012 Masters April 5–8 [7435–72]

Prize money: $8 million. Field of 95 players (five amateurs) of whom 62 (including three amateurs) made the half-way

| 1 | Bubba Watson* | 69-71-70-68—278 | $1,440,000 |
| 2 | Louis Oosthuizen (RSA) | 68-72-69-69—278 | 864,000 |

*Watson beat Oosthuizen at the second play-off hole – Watson 4,4; Oosthuizen 4,5*

| 3 | Lee Westwood (ENG) | 67-73-72-68—280 | 384,000 |
| | Matt Kuchar | 71-70-70-69—280 | 384,000 |
| | Peter Hanson (SWE) | 68-74-65-73—280 | 384,000 |
| | Phil Mickelson | 74-68-66-72—280 | 384,000 |
| 7 | Ian Poulter (ENG) | 72-72-70-69—283 | 268,000 |
| 8 | Adam Scott (AUS) | 75-70-73-66—284 | 232,000 |
| | Justin Rose (ENG) | 72-72-72-68—284 | 232,000 |
| | Padraig Harrington (IRL) | 71-73-68-72—284 | 232,000 |
| 11 | Jim Furyk | 70-73-72-70—285 | 200,000 |
| 12 | Kevin Na | 71-75-72-68—286 | 156,000 |
| | Graeme McDowell (NIR) | 75-72-71-68—286 | 156,000 |
| | Sergio García (ESP) | 72-68-75-71—286 | 156,000 |
| | Fred Couples | 72-67-75-72—286 | 156,000 |
| | Hunter Mahan | 72-72-68-74—286 | 156,000 |
| 17 | Bo Van Pelt | 73-75-75-64—287 | 124,000 |
| | Ben Crane | 69-73-72-73—287 | 124,000 |
| 19 | Geoff Ogilvy (AUS) | 74-72-71-71—288 | 96,960 |
| | Charles Howell III | 72-70-74-72—288 | 96,960 |
| | Brandt Snedeker | 72-75-68-73—288 | 96,960 |
| | Fredrik Jacobson (SWE) | 76-68-70-74—288 | 96,960 |
| | Francesco Molinari (ITA) | 69-75-70-74—288 | 96,960 |
| 24 | Anders Hansen (DEN) | 76-72-73-68—289 | 70,400 |
| | Jason Dufner | 69-70-75-75—289 | 70,400 |
| | Paul Lawrie (SCO) | 69-72-72-76—289 | 70,400 |
| 27 | Keegan Bradley | 71-77-73-69—290 | 56,800 |
| | Rickie Fowler | 74-74-72-70—290 | 56,800 |
| | Vijay Singh (FIJ) | 70-72-76-72—290 | 56,800 |
| | Scott Stallings | 70-77-70-73—290 | 56,800 |
| | Jonathan Byrd | 72-71-72-75—290 | 56,800 |
| 32 | Luke Donald (ENG) | 75-73-75-68—291 | 45,280 |
| 32T | Angel Cabrera (ARG) | 71-78-71-71—291 | 45,280 |
| | Zach Johnson | 70-74-75-72—291 | 45,280 |
| | Nick Watney | 71-71-72-77—291 | 45,280 |
| | Sean O'Hair | 73-70-71-77—291 | 45,280 |
| 37 | Thomas Björn (DEN) | 73-76-74-69—292 | 37,600 |
| | Bill Haas | 72-74-76-70—292 | 37,600 |
| | Sang-Moon Bae (KOR) | 75-71-69-77—292 | 37,600 |
| 40 | Aaron Baddeley (AUS) | 71-71-77-74—293 | 32,000 |
| | Tiger Woods | 72-75-72-74—293 | 32,000 |
| | Rory McIlroy (NIR) | 71-69-77-76—293 | 32,000 |
| | Henrik Stenson (SWE) | 71-71-70-81—293 | 32,000 |
| 44 | Martin Kaymer (GER) | 72-75-75-72—294 | 26,400 |
| | Kevin Chappell | 71-76-71-76—294 | 26,400 |
| | Webb Simpson | 72-74-70-78—294 | 26,400 |
| 47 | Patrick Cantlay (am) | 71-78-74-72—295 | |
| | Ross Fisher (ENG) | 71-77-73-74—295 | 22,560 |
| | Steve Stricker | 71-77-72-75—295 | 22,560 |
| 50 | Stewart Cink | 71-75-81-69—296 | 19,960 |
| | Robert Karlsson (SWE) | 74-74-77-71—296 | 19,960 |
| | Charl Schwartzel (RSA) | 72-75-75-74—296 | 19,960 |
| | David Toms | 73-73-75-75—296 | 19,960 |
| 54 | Scott Verplank | 73-75-74-77—297 | 18,880 |
| | Hideki Matsuyama (JPN) (am) | 71-74-72-80—297 | |
| 56 | Miguel Angel Jiménez (ESP) | 69-72-76-81—298 | 18,560 |
| 57 | Edoardo Molinari (ITA) | 75-74-76-74—299 | 18,240 |
| | Martin Laird (SCO) | 76-72-74-77—299 | 18,240 |
| | Y E Yang (KOR) | 73-70-75-81—299 | 18,240 |
| 60 | Trevor Immelman (RSA) | 78-71-76-76—301 | 17,920 |
| 61 | Gonzalo Fernandez-Castano (ESP) | 74-75-76-77—302 | 17,760 |
| 62 | Kelly Kraft (am) | 74-75-77-80—306 | |

## 2011 Masters April 7–10 [7435–72]

Prize money: $7.5 million. Field of 93 players (six amateurs) of whom 49 (including one amateur) made the half-way cut.

| | | | | | | | | |
|---|---|---|---|---|---|---|---|---|
| 1 | Charl Schwartzel (RSA) | 69-71-68-66—274 | $1,444,000 | 27 | Charley Hoffman | 74-69-72-72—287 | | 54,400 |
| 2 | Jason Day (AUS) | 72-64-72-68—276 | 704,000 | | Miguel Angel Jiménez | 71-73-70-73—287 | | 54,400 |
| | Adam Scott (AUS) | 72-70-67-67—276 | 704,000 | | (ESP) | | | |
| 4 | Luke Donald (ENG) | 72-68-69-69—278 | 330,667 | | Robert Karlsson (SWE) | 72-70-74-71—287 | | 54,400 |
| | Geoff Ogilvy (AUS) | 69-69-73-67—278 | 330,667 | | Matt Kuchar | 68-75-69-75—287 | | 54,400 |
| | Tiger Woods | 71-66-74-67—278 | 330,667 | | Hideki Matsuyama (JPN) | 72-73-68-74—287 | | |
| 7 | Angel Cabrera (ARG) | 71-70-67-71—279 | 268,000 | | (am) | | | |
| 8 | K J Choi (KOR) | 67-70-71-72—280 | 240,000 | | Phil Mickelson | 70-72-71-74—287 | | 54,400 |
| | Bo Van Pelt | 73-69-68-70—280 | 240,000 | | Ian Poulter (ENG) | 74-69-71-73—287 | | 54,400 |
| 10 | Ryan Palmer | 71-72-69-70—282 | 216,000 | | Alvaro Quiros (ESP) | 65-73-75-74—287 | | 54,400 |
| 11 | Edoardo Molinari (ITA) | 74-70-69-70—283 | 176,000 | 35 | Alex Cejka (GER) | 72-71-75-70—288 | | 43,200 |
| | Justin Rose (ENG) | 73-71-71-68—283 | 176,000 | | Sergio García (ESP) | 69-71-75-73—288 | | 43,200 |
| | Steve Stricker | 72-70-71-70—283 | 176,000 | | Ryan Moore | 70-73-72-73—288 | | 43,200 |
| | Lee Westwood (ENG) | 72-67-74-70—283 | 176,000 | 38 | Paul Casey (ENG) | 70-72-76-71—289 | | 36,600 |
| 15 | Fred Couples | 71-68-72-73—284 | 128,000 | | Rickie Fowler | 70-69-76-74—289 | | 36,600 |
| | Ross Fisher (ENG) | 69-71-71-73—284 | 128,000 | | Dustin Johnson | 74-68-73-74—289 | | 36,600 |
| | Trevor Immelman (RSA) | 69-73-73-69—284 | 128,000 | | Bubba Watson | 73-71-67-78—289 | | 36,600 |
| | Rory McIlroy (NIR) | 65-69-70-80—284 | 128,000 | 42 | Bill Haas | 74-70-74-72—290 | | 32,000 |
| | Brandt Snedeker | 69-71-74-70—284 | 128,000 | | Steve Marino | 74-71-72-73—290 | | 32,000 |
| 20 | Ricky Barnes | 68-71-75-71—285 | 93,200 | 44 | Kyung-tae Kim (KOR) | 70-75-78-68—291 | | 28,800 |
| | Ryo Ishikawa (JPN) | 71-71-73-70—285 | 93,200 | | Jeff Overton | 73-72-72-74—291 | | 28,800 |
| | Martin Laird (SCO) | 74-69-69-73—285 | 93,200 | 46 | Nick Watney | 72-72-75-73—292 | | 26,400 |
| | Y E Yang (KOR) | 67-72-73-73—285 | 93,200 | 47 | Aaron Baddeley (AUS) | 75-70-74-74—293 | | 24,000 |
| 24 | Jim Furyk | 72-68-74-72—286 | 70,400 | | Ernie Els (RSA) | 75-70-76-72—293 | | 24,000 |
| | David Toms | 72-69-73-72—286 | 70,400 | 49 | Camilo Villegas (COL) | 70-75-73-76—294 | | 21,920 |
| | Gary Woodland | 69-73-74-70—286 | 70,400 | | | | | |

## 2010 Masters April 8–11 [7435–72]

Prize money: $7.5 million. Field of 96 players (six amateurs) of whom 48 (including one amateur) made the half-way cut.

| | | | | | | | | |
|---|---|---|---|---|---|---|---|---|
| 1 | Phil Mickelson | 67-71-67-67—272 | $1,350,000 | 24T | Matt Kuchar | 70-73-74-71—288 | | 69,000 |
| 2 | Lee Westwood (ENG) | 67-69-68-71—275 | 810,000 | 26 | Bill Haas) | 72-70-71-76—289 | | 57,750 |
| 3 | Anthony Kim | 68-70-73-65—276 | 510,000 | | Geoff Ogilvy (AUS) | 74-72-69-74—289 | | 57,750 |
| 4 | K J Choi (KOR) | 67-71-70-69—277 | 330,000 | | Kenny Perry | 72-71-72-74—289 | | 57,750 |
| | Tiger Woods | 68-70-70-69—277 | 330,000 | 29 | Yuta Ikeda (JPN) | 70-77-72-71—290 | | 53,250 |
| 6 | Fred Couples | 66-75-68-70—279 | 270,000 | 30 | Jason Dufner | 75-72-75-69—291 | | 45,563 |
| 7 | Nick Watney | 68-76-71-65—280 | 251,250 | | Søren Kjeldsen (DEN) | 70-71-75-75—291 | | 45,563 |
| 8 | Hunter Mahan | 71-71-68-71—281 | 225,000 | | Francesco Molinari (ITA) | 70-74-75-72—291 | | 45,563 |
| | Y E Yang (KOR) | 67-72-72-70—281 | 225,000 | | Sean O'Hair | 72-71-72-76—291 | | 45,563 |
| 10 | Ricky Barnes | 68-70-72-73—283 | 195,000 | | Charl Schwartzel (RSA) | 69-76-72-74—291 | | 45,563 |
| | Ian Poulter (ENG) | 68-68-74-73—283 | 195,000 | | Steve Stricker | 73-73-74-71—291 | | 45,563 |
| 12 | Miguel Angel Jiménez | 72-75-72-66—285 | 165,000 | 36 | Lucas Glover | 76-71-71-74—292 | | 38,625 |
| | (ESP) | | | | Matteo Manassero (ITA) | 71-76-73-72—292 | | |
| | Jerry Kelly | 72-74-67-72—285 | 165,000 | | (am) | | | |
| 14 | Trevor Immelman (RSA) | 69-73-72-72—286 | 131,250 | 38 | Steve Flesch | 75-71-70-78—294 | | 34,500 |
| | Steve Marino | 71-73-69-73—286 | 131,250 | | Retief Goosen (RSA) | 74-71-76-73—294 | | 34,500 |
| | Ryan Moore | 72-73-73-68—286 | 131,250 | | Dustin Johnson | 71-72-76-75—294 | | 34,500 |
| | David Toms | 69-75-71-71—286 | 131,250 | | Camilo Villegas (COL) | 74-72-71-77—294 | | 34,500 |
| 18 | Angel Cabrera (ARG) | 73-74-69-71—287 | 94,500 | 42 | Zach Johnson | 70-74-76-75—295 | | 30,750 |
| | Ernie Els (RSA) | 71-73-75-68—287 | 94,500 | 43 | Robert Karlsson (SWE) | 71-72-77-76—296 | | 28,500 |
| | Adam Scott (AUS) | 69-75-72-71—287 | 94,500 | | Mike Weir (CAN) | 71-72-76-77—296 | | 28,500 |
| | Heath Slocum | 72-73-70-72—287 | 94,500 | | Robert Allenby (AUS) | 72-75-78-73—298 | | 24,750 |
| | Scott Verplank | 73-73-73-68—287 | 94,500 | | Chad Campbell | 79-68-80-71—298 | | 24,750 |
| | Tom Watson | 67-74-73-73—287 | 94,500 | | Sergio García (ESP) | 74-70-76-78—298 | | 24,750 |
| 24 | Ben Crane | 71-75-74-68—288 | 69,000 | 48 | Nathan Green (AUS) | 72-75-80-75—302 | | 21,750 |

## 2009 Masters April 9–12           [7445–72]

Prize money: $7 million. Field of 96 players (five amateurs) of whom 50 (no amateurs) made the half-way cut.

| | | | |
|---|---|---|---|
| 1 | Angel Cabrera (ARG)* | 68-68-69-71—276 | $1,350,000 |
| 2 | Kenny Perry | 68-67-70-71—276 | 660,000 |
| | Chad Campbell | 65-70-72-69—276 | 660,000 |
| *Cabrera won at the second extra hole – Cabrera 4,4; Campbell 5,–; Perry 4,5 | | | |
| 4 | Shingo Katayama (JPN) | 67-73-70-68—278 | 360,000 |
| 5 | Phil Mickelson | 73-68-71-67—279 | 300,000 |
| 6 | Steve Flesch | 71-74-68-67—280 | 242,813 |
| | John Merrick | 68-74-72-66—280 | 242,813 |
| | Steve Stricker | 72-69-68-71—280 | 242,813 |
| | Tiger Woods | 70-72-70-68—280 | 242,813 |
| 10 | Jim Furyk | 66-74-68-73—281 | 187,500 |
| | Hunter Mahan | 66-75-71-69—281 | 187,500 |
| | Sean O'Hair | 68-76-68-69—281 | 187,500 |
| 13 | Tim Clark (RSA) | 68-71-72-71—282 | 150,000 |
| | Camilo Villegas (COL) | 73-69-71-69—282 | 150,000 |
| 15 | Todd Hamilton | 68-70-72-73—283 | 131,250 |
| | Geoff Ogilvy (AUS) | 71-70-73-69—283 | 131,250 |
| 17 | Aaron Baddeley (AUS) | 68-74-73-69—284 | 116,250 |
| | Graeme Mcdowell (NIR) | 69-73-73-69—284 | 116,250 |
| 19 | Nick Watney | 70-71-71-73—285 | 105,000 |
| 20 | Stephen Ames (CAN) | 73-68-71-74—286 | 71,400 |
| | Paul Casey (ENG) | 72-72-73-69—286 | 71,400 |
| | Ryuji Imada (JPN) | 73-72-72-69—286 | 71,400 |
| | Trevor Immelman (RSA) | 71-71-72-69—286 | 71,400 |
| | Anthony Kim | 75-65-72-74—286 | 71,400 |
| | Sandy Lyle (SCO) | 72-70-73-71—286 | 71,400 |
| 20T | Rory McIlroy (NIR) | 72-73-71-70—286 | 71,400 |
| | Ian Poulter (ENG) | 71-73-68-74—286 | 71,400 |
| | Justin Rose (ENG) | 74-70-71-71—286 | 71,400 |
| | Rory Sabbatini (RSA) | 73-67-70-76—286 | 71,400 |
| 30 | Stuart Appleby (AUS) | 72-73-71-71—287 | 46,575 |
| | Ross Fisher (ENG) | 69-76-73-69—287 | 46,575 |
| | Dustin Johnson | 72-70-72-73—287 | 46,575 |
| | Larry Mize | 67-76-72-72—287 | 46,575 |
| | Vijay Singh (FIJ) | 71-70-72-74—287 | 46,575 |
| 35 | Ben Curtis | 73-71-74-70—288 | 38,625 |
| | Ken Duke | 71-72-73-72—288 | 38,625 |
| | Padraig Harrington (IRL) | 69-73-73-73—288 | 38,625 |
| 38 | Luke Donald (ENG) | 73-72-72-72—289 | 33,000 |
| | Sergio García (ESP) | 73-67-75-74—289 | 33,000 |
| | Henrik Stenson (SWE) | 71-70-75-73—289 | 33,000 |
| 42 | Bubba Watson | 72-72-73-73—290 | 29,250 |
| 43 | Lee Westwood (ENG) | 70-72-70-79—291 | 27,250 |
| 44 | Dudley Hart | 72-72-73-75—292 | 27,250 |
| 45 | D J Trahan | 72-73-72-76—293 | 27,250 |
| 46 | Miguel Angel Jiménez (ESP) | 70-73-78-73—294 | 21,850 |
| | Kevin Sutherland | 69-76-77-72—294 | 21,850 |
| | Mike Weir (CAN) | 68-75-79-72—294 | 21,850 |
| 49 | Andres Romero (ARG) | 69-75-77-76—297 | 19,200 |
| 50 | Rocco Mediate | 73-70-78-77—298 | 19,200 |

## 2008 Masters April 10–13           [7445–72]

Prize money: $7.4 million. Field of 93 players (three amateurs) of whom 45 (no amateurs) made the half-way cut.

| | | | |
|---|---|---|---|
| 1 | Trevor Immelman (RSA) | 68-68-69-75—280 | $1,350,000 |
| 2 | Tiger Woods | 72-71-68-72—283 | 810,000 |
| 3 | Stewart Cink | 72-69-71-72—284 | 435,000 |
| | Brandt Snedeker | 69-68-70-77—284 | 435,000 |
| 5 | Steve Flesch | 72-67-69-78—286 | 273,750 |
| | Padraig Harrington (IRL) | 74-71-69-72—286 | 273,750 |
| | Phil Mickelson | 71-68-75-72—286 | 273,750 |
| 8 | Miguel Angel Jiménez (ESP) | 77-70-72-68—287 | 217,500 |
| | Robert Karlsson (SWE) | 70-73-71-73—287 | 217,500 |
| | Andres Romero (ARG) | 72-72-70-73—287 | 217,500 |
| 11 | Paul Casey (ENG) | 71-69-69-79—288 | 172,500 |
| | Nick Watney | 75-70-72-71—288 | 172,500 |
| | Lee Westwood (ENG) | 69-73-73-73—288 | 172,500 |
| 14 | Stuart Appleby (AUS) | 76-70-72-71—289 | 135,000 |
| | Sean O'Hair | 72-71-71-75—289 | 135,000 |
| | Vijay Singh (FIJ) | 72-71-72-74—289 | 135,000 |
| 17 | Retief Goosen (RSA) | 71-71-72-76—290 | 112,500 |
| | Henrik Stenson (SWE) | 74-72-72-72—290 | 112,500 |
| | Mike Weir (CAN) | 73-68-75-74—290 | 112,500 |
| 20 | Brian Bateman | 69-76-74-74—291 | 84,300 |
| | Zach Johnson | 70-76-68-77—291 | 84,300 |
| | Justin Leonard | 72-74-72-73—291 | 84,300 |
| 20T | Bubba Watson | 74-71-73-73—291 | 84,300 |
| | Boo Weekley | 72-74-68-77—291 | 84,300 |
| 25 | Stephen Ames (CAN) | 70-70-77-75—292 | 54,844 |
| | Angel Cabrera (ARG) | 73-72-73-74—292 | 54,844 |
| | J B Holmes | 73-70-73-76—292 | 54,844 |
| | Arron Oberholser | 71-70-74-77—292 | 54,844 |
| | Ian Poulter (ENG) | 70-69-75-78—292 | 54,844 |
| | Adam Scott (AUS) | 75-71-70-76—292 | 54,844 |
| | Jeev Milkha Singh (IND) | 71-74-72-75—292 | 54,844 |
| | Richard Sterne (RSA) | 73-72-73-74—292 | 54,844 |
| 33 | Nick Dougherty (ENG) | 74-69-74-76—293 | 42,375 |
| | Jim Furyk | 70-73-73-77—293 | 42,375 |
| | Heath Slocum | 71-76-77-69—293 | 42,375 |
| 36 | Todd Hamilton | 74-73-75-73—295 | 36,875 |
| | Justin Rose (ENG) | 68-78-73-76—295 | 36,875 |
| | Johnson Wagner | 72-74-74-75—295 | 36,875 |
| 39 | Niclas Fasth (SWE) | 75-70-76-75—296 | 33,000 |
| | Geoff Ogilvy (AUS) | 75-71-76-74—296 | 33,000 |
| 41 | K J Choi (KOR) | 72-75-78-73—298 | 30,750 |
| 42 | Robert Allenby (AUS) | 72-74-72-81—299 | 28,500 |
| | David Toms | 73-74-72-80—299 | 28,500 |
| 44 | Ian Woonam (WAL) | 75-71-76-78—300 | 26,250 |
| 45 | Sandy Lyle (SCO) | 72-75-78-77—302 | 24,750 |

---

## Adam's win at Augusta was top for Australians

Not surprisingly, Adam Scott's Masters victory – the first by an Australian at Augusta – was voted the Australian PGA Tour's number one moment of 2013. In a compilation of the year's top 10 moments Scott's feat beat Phil Mickelson's Open win, Justin Rose's US Open triumph and Jason Dufner's PGA victory.

## 2007 Masters April 5–8 [7445–72]

Prize money: $7.4 million. Field of 96 players, of whom 60 (no amateurs) made the half-way cut.

| | | | | | | | | |
|---|---|---|---|---|---|---|---|---|
| 1 | Zach Johnson | 71-73-76-69—289 | $1,305,000 | 30T | Robert Karlsson (SWE) | 77-73-79-72—301 | 43,085 |
| 2 | Retief Goosen (RSA) | 76-76-70-69—291 | 541,333 | | Scott Verplank | 73-77-76-75—301 | 43,085 |
| | Rory Sabbatini (RSA) | 73-76-73-69—291 | 541,333 | | Lee Westwood (ENG) | 79-73-72-77—301 | 43,085 |
| | Tiger Woods | 73-74-72-72—291 | 541,333 | | Dean Wilson | 75-72-76-78—301 | 43,085 |
| 5 | Jerry Kelly | 75-69-78-70—292 | 275,500 | | Yong-Eun Yang (KOR) | 75-74-78-74—301 | 43,085 |
| | Justin Rose (ENG) | 69-75-75-73—292 | 275,500 | 37 | Angel Cabrera (ARG) | 77-75-79-71—302 | 31,900 |
| 7 | Stuart Appleby (AUS) | 75-70-73-75—293 | 233,812 | | J J Henry | 71-78-77-76—302 | 31,900 |
| | Padraig Harrington (IRL) | 77-68-75-73—293 | 233,812 | | Tim Herron | 72-75-83-72—302 | 31,900 |
| 9 | David Toms | 70-78-74-72—294 | 210,250 | | Rod Pampling (AUS) | 77-75-74-76—302 | 31,900 |
| 10 | Paul Casey (ENG) | 79-68-77-71—295 | 181,250 | | Jeev Milkha Singh (IND) | 72-75-76-79—302 | 31,900 |
| | Luke Donald (ENG) | 73-74-75-73—295 | 181,250 | | Brett Wetterich | 69-73-83-77—302 | 31,900 |
| | Vaughn Taylor | 71-72-77-75—295 | 181,250 | 43 | Sandy Lyle (SCO) | 79-73-80-71—303 | 26,825 |
| 13 | Tim Clark (RSA) | 71-71-80-74—296 | 135,937 | 44 | Bradley Dredge (WAL) | 75-70-76-83—304 | 22,533 |
| | Jim Furyk | 75-71-76-74—296 | 135,937 | | David Howell (ENG) | 70-75-82-77—304 | 22,533 |
| | Ian Poulter (ENG) | 75-75-76-70—296 | 135,937 | | Miguel Angel Jiménez | 79-73-76-76—304 | 22,533 |
| | Vijay Singh (FIJ) | 73-71-79-73—296 | 135,937 | | (ESP) | | |
| 17 | Stewart Cink | 77-75-75-70—297 | 108,750 | | Shingo Katayama (JPN) | 79-72-80-73—304 | 22,533 |
| | Tom Pernice Jr | 75-72-79-71—297 | 108,750 | | José-María Olazábal | 74-75-78-77—304 | 22,533 |
| | Henrik Stenson (SWE) | 72-76-77-72—297 | 108,750 | | (ESP) | | |
| 20 | Mark Calcavecchia | 76-71-78-73—298 | 84,462 | 49 | Jeff Sluman | 76-75-79-75—305 | 18,560 |
| | Lucas Glover | 74-71-79-74—298 | 84,462 | | Craig Stadler | 74-73-79-79—305 | 18,560 |
| | John Rollins | 77-74-76-71—298 | 84,462 | 51 | Brett Quigley | 76-76-79-75—306 | 17,835 |
| | Mike Weir (CAN) | 75-72-80-71—298 | 84,462 | 52 | Aaron Baddeley (AUS) | 79-72-76-80—307 | 17,255 |
| 24 | Stephen Ames (CAN) | 76-74-77-72—299 | 63,000 | | Carl Pettersson (SWE) | 76-76-79-76—307 | 17,255 |
| | Phil Mickelson | 76-73-73-77—299 | 63,000 | 54 | Rich Beem | 71-81-75-81—308 | 16,820 |
| | Geoff Ogilvy (AUS) | 75-70-81-73—299 | 63,000 | 55 | Ben Crenshaw | 76-74-84-75—309 | 16,530 |
| 27 | K J Choi (KOR) | 75-75-74-76—300 | 53,650 | | Niclas Fasth (SWE) | 77-75-77-80—309 | 16,530 |
| | Davis Love III | 72-77-77-74—300 | 53,650 | | Trevor Immelman (RSA) | 74-77-81-77—309 | 16,530 |
| | Adam Scott (AUS) | 74-78-76-72—300 | 53,650 | 58 | Arron Oberholser | 74-76-84-76—310 | 16,240 |
| 30 | Fred Couples | 75-74-78-74—301 | 43,085 | 59 | Billy Mayfair | 76-75-83-77—311 | 16,095 |
| | Charles Howell III | 75-77-75-74—301 | 43,085 | 60 | Fuzzy Zoeller | 74-78-79-82—313 | 15,950 |

## 2006 Masters April 6–9 [7445–72]

Prize money: $7 million. Field of 90 players, of whom 47 (no amateurs) made the half-way cut.

| | | | | | | | | |
|---|---|---|---|---|---|---|---|---|
| 1 | Phil Mickelson | 70-72-70-69—281 | $1,260,000 | 22T | Jim Furyk | 73-75-68-75—291 | 67,200 |
| 2 | Tim Clark (RSA) | 70-72-72-69—283 | 758,000 | | Mark Hensby (AUS) | 80-67-70-74—291 | 67,200 |
| 3 | Chad Campbell | 71-67-75-71—284 | 315,700 | | Davis Love III | 74-71-74-72—291 | 67,200 |
| | Fred Couples | 71-70-72-71—284 | 315,700 | 27 | Ernie Els (RSA) | 71-71-74-76—292 | 49,700 |
| | Retief Goosen (RSA) | 70-73-72-69—284 | 315,700 | | Padraig Harrington (IRL) | 73-70-75-74—292 | 49,700 |
| | José-María Olazábal | 76-71-71-66—284 | 315,700 | | Shingo Katayama (JPN) | 75-70-73-74—292 | 49,700 |
| | (ESP) | | | | Carl Pettersson (SWE) | 72-74-73-73—292 | 49,700 |
| | Tiger Woods | 72-71-71-70—284 | 315,700 | | Adam Scott (AUS) | 72-74-75-71—292 | 49,700 |
| 8 | Angel Cabrera (ARG) | 73-74-70-68—285 | 210,000 | 32 | Thomas Bjørn (DEN) | 73-75-76-69—293 | 40,512 |
| | Vijay Singh (FIJ) | 67-74-73-71—285 | 210,000 | | Brandt Jobe | 72-76-77-68—293 | 40,512 |
| 10 | Stewart Cink | 72-73-71-70—286 | 189,000 | | Zach Johnson | 74-72-77-70—293 | 40,512 |
| 11 | Stephen Ames (CAN) | 74-70-70-73—287 | 161,000 | | Ted Purdy | 72-76-74-71—293 | 40,512 |
| | Miguel Angel Jiménez | 72-74-69-72—287 | 161,000 | 36 | Tim Herron | 76-71-71-76—294 | 34,416 |
| | (ESP) | | | | Rocco Mediate | 68-73-73-80—294 | 34,416 |
| | Mike Weir (CAN) | 71-73-73-70—287 | 161,000 | | Rory Sabbatini (RSA) | 76-70-74-74—294 | 34,416 |
| 14 | Billy Mayfair | 71-72-73-72—288 | 129,500 | 39 | Jason Bohn | 73-71-77-74—295 | 30,100 |
| | Arron Oberholser | 69-75-73-71—288 | 129,500 | | Ben Curtis | 71-74-77-73—295 | 30,100 |
| 16 | Geoff Ogilvy (AUS) | 70-75-73-71—289 | 112,000 | | Justin Leonard | 75-70-79-71—295 | 30,100 |
| | Rod Pampling (AUS) | 72-73-72-72—289 | 112,000 | 42 | Rich Beem | 71-73-73-79—296 | 25,900 |
| | Scott Verplank | 74-70-74-71—289 | 112,000 | | Luke Donald (ENG) | 74-72-76-74—296 | 25,900 |
| 19 | Stuart Appleby (AUS) | 71-75-73-71—290 | 91,000 | | Larry Mize | 75-72-77-72—296 | 25,900 |
| | David Howell (ENG) | 71-71-76-72—290 | 91,000 | 45 | Olin Browne | 74-69-80-74—297 | 23,100 |
| | Nick O'Hern (AUS) | 71-72-76-71—290 | 91,000 | 46 | Sergio García (ESP) | 72-74-79-73—298 | 21,700 |
| 22 | Robert Allenby (AUS) | 73-73-74-71—291 | 67,200 | 47 | Ben Crenshaw | 71-72-78-79—300 | 20,300 |
| | Darren Clarke (NIR) | 72-70-72-77—291 | 67,200 | | | | |

## 2005 Masters April 7–10 [7290–72]

Prize money: $7 million. Field of 93 players, of whom 50 (including two amateurs) made the half-way cut.

| | | | | | | | | |
|---|---|---|---|---|---|---|---|---|
| 1 | Tiger Woods* | 74-66-65-71—276 | $1,260,000 | 25T | Joe Ogilvie | 74-73-73-70—290 | 61,600 | |
| 2 | Chris DiMarco | 67-67-74-68—276 | 756,000 | | Craig Parry (AUS) | 72-75-69-74—290 | 61,600 | |
| *Play-off: Woods 3, DiMarco 4* | | | | 28 | Jim Furyk | 76-67-74-74—291 | 53,900 | |
| 3 | Luke Donald (ENG) | 68-77-69-69—283 | 406,000 | 29 | Steve Flesch | 76-70-70-76—292 | 50,750 | |
| | Retief Goosen (RSA) | 71-75-70-67—283 | 406,000 | | Kenny Perry | 76-68-71-77—292 | 50,750 | |
| 5 | Mark Hensby (AUS) | 69-73-70-72—284 | 237,300 | 31 | Miguel Angel Jiménez | 74-74-73-72—293 | 46,550 | |
| | Trevor Immelman (RSA) | 73-73-65-73—284 | 237,300 | | (ESP) | | | |
| | Rodney Pampling (AUS) | 73-71-70-70—284 | 237,300 | | Mark O'Meara | 72-74-72-75—293 | 46,550 | |
| | Vijay Singh (FIJ) | 68-73-71-72—284 | 237,300 | 33 | K J Choi (KOR) | 73-72-76-73—294 | 39,620 | |
| | Mike Weir (CAN) | 74-71-68-71—284 | 237,300 | | Shingo Katayama (JPN) | 72-74-73-75—294 | 39,620 | |
| 10 | Phil Mickelson | 70-72-69-74—285 | 189,000 | | Luke List (am) | 77-69-78-70—294 | | |
| 11 | Tim Herron | 76-68-70-72—286 | 168,000 | | Ian Poulter (ENG) | 72-74-72-76—294 | 39,620 | |
| | David Howell (ENG) | 72-69-76-69—286 | 168,000 | | Adam Scott (AUS) | 71-76-72-75—294 | 39,620 | |
| 13 | Tom Lehman | 74-74-70-69—287 | 135,333 | | Casey Wittenberg | 72-72-74-76—294 | 39,620 | |
| | Justin Leonard | 75-71-70-71—287 | 135,333 | 39 | Tim Clark (RSA) | 74-74-72-75—295 | 32,200 | |
| | Thomas Levet (FRA) | 71-75-68-73—287 | 135,333 | | Fred Couples | 75-71-77-72—295 | 32,200 | |
| | Ryan Moore (am) | 71-71-75-70—287 | | | Todd Hamilton | 77-70-71-77—295 | 32,200 | |
| 17 | Chad Campbell | 73-73-67-75—288 | 112,000 | | Ryan Palmer | 70-74-74-77—295 | 32,200 | |
| | Darren Clarke (NIR) | 72-76-69-71—288 | 112,000 | 43 | Stuart Appleby (AUS) | 69-76-72-79—296 | 28,000 | |
| | Kirk Triplett | 75-68-72-73—288 | 112,000 | | Jonathan Kaye | 72-74-76-74—296 | 28,000 | |
| 20 | Stewart Cink | 72-72-74-71—289 | 84,840 | 45 | Stephen Ames (CAN) | 73-74-75-75—297 | 25,200 | |
| | Jerry Kelly | 75-70-73-71—289 | 84,840 | | Nick O'Hern (AUS) | 72-72-76-77—297 | 25,200 | |
| | Bernhard Langer (GER) | 74-74-70-71—289 | 84,840 | 47 | Ernie Els (RSA) | 75-73-78-72—298 | 23,100 | |
| | Jeff Maggert | 74-74-72-69—289 | 84,840 | 48 | Jay Haas | 76-71-76-78—301 | 21,700 | |
| | Scott Verplank | 72-75-69-73—289 | 84,840 | 49 | Chris Riley | 71-77-78-78—304 | 20,300 | |
| 25 | Thomas Bjørn (DEN) | 71-67-71-81—290 | 61,600 | 50 | Craig Stadler | 75-73-79-79—306 | 19,180 | |

## 2004 Masters April 8–11 [7290–72]

Prize money: $6 million. Field of 93, of whom 44 (including two amateurs) made the half-way cut.

| | | | | | | | | |
|---|---|---|---|---|---|---|---|---|
| 1 | Phil Mickelson | 72-69-69-69—279 | $1,170,000 | 22T | Shaun Micheel | 72-76-72-70—290 | 70,200 | |
| 2 | Ernie Els (RSA) | 70-72-71-67—280 | 702,000 | | Justin Rose (ENG) | 67-71-81-71—290 | 70,200 | |
| 3 | K J Choi (KOR) | 71-70-72-69—282 | 442,000 | | Tiger Woods | 75-69-75-71—290 | 70,200 | |
| 4 | Sergio García (ESP) | 72-72-75-66—285 | 286,000 | 26 | Alex Cejka (GER) | 70-70-78-73—291 | 57,200 | |
| | Bernhard Langer (GER) | 71-73-69-72—285 | 286,000 | 27 | Mark O'Meara | 73-70-75-74—292 | 51,025 | |
| 6 | Paul Casey (ENG) | 75-69-68-74—286 | 189,893 | | Bob Tway | 75-71-74-72—292 | 51,025 | |
| | Fred Couples | 73-69-74-70—286 | 189,893 | 29 | Scott Verplank | 74-71-76-72—293 | 48,100 | |
| | Chris DiMarco | 69-73-68-76—286 | 189,893 | 30 | José María Olazábal | 71-69-79-75—294 | 46,150 | |
| | Davis Love III | 75-67-74-70—286 | 189,893 | | (ESP) | | | |
| | Nick Price (ZIM) | 72-73-71-70—286 | 189,893 | 31 | Bob Estes | 76-72-73-74—295 | 41,275 | |
| | Vijay Singh (FIJ) | 75-73-69-69—286 | 189,893 | | Brad Faxon | 72-76-76-71—295 | 41,275 | |
| | Kirk Triplett | 71-74-69-72—286 | 189,893 | | Jerry Kelly | 74-72-73-76—295 | 41,275 | |
| 13 | Retief Goosen (RSA) | 75-73-70-70—288 | 125,667 | | Ian Poulter (ENG) | 75-73-74-73—295 | 41,275 | |
| | Padraig Harrington (IRL) | 74-74-68-72—288 | 125,667 | 35 | Justin Leonard | 76-72-72-76—296 | 35,913 | |
| | Charles Howell III | 71-71-76-70—288 | 125,667 | | Phillip Price (WAL) | 71-76-73-76—296 | 35,913 | |
| | Casey Wittenberg (am) | 76-72-71-69—288 | | 37 | Paul Lawrie (SCO) | 77-70-73-77—297 | 32,663 | |
| 17 | Stewart Cink | 74-73-69-73—289 | 97,500 | | Sandy Lyle (SCO) | 72-74-75-76—297 | 32,663 | |
| | Steve Flesch | 76-67-77-69—289 | 97,500 | 39 | Eduardo Romero (ARG) | 74-73-74-77—298 | 30,550 | |
| | Jay Haas | 69-75-72-73—289 | 97,500 | 40 | Todd Hamilton | 77-71-76-75—299 | 29,250 | |
| | Fredrik Jacobson (SWE) | 74-74-67-74—289 | 97,500 | 41 | Tim Petrovic | 72-75-75-78—300 | 27,950 | |
| | Stephen Leaney (AUS) | 76-71-73-69—289 | 97,500 | | Brandt Snedeker (am) | 73-75-75-77—300 | | |
| 22 | Stuart Appleby (AUS) | 73-74-73-70—290 | 70,200 | 43 | Jeff Sluman | 73-70-82-77—302 | 26,650 | |
| | | | | 44 | Chris Riley | 70-78-78-78—304 | 25,350 | |

# The Masters History (players are American unless stated)

| Date | Winner | Score | Date | Winner | Score |
|---|---|---|---|---|---|
| 1934 Mar 22–25 | H Smith | 284 | 1978 Apr 6–9 | G Player (RSA) | 277 |
| 1935 Apr 4–8 | G Sarazen* | 282 | 1979 Apr 12–15 | F Zoeller* | 280 |
| *After a play-off: Sarazen 144, C Wood 149* | | | *After a play-off: Zoeller 4,3; T Watson 4,4;* | | |
| 1936 Apr 2–6 | H Smith | 285 | E Sneed 4,4 | | |
| 1937 Apr 1–4 | B Nelson | 283 | 1980 Apr 10–13 | S Ballesteros (ESP) | 275 |
| 1938 Apr 1–4 | H Picard | 285 | 1981 Apr 9–12 | T Watson | 280 |
| 1939 Mar 30–Apr 2 | R Guldahl | 279 | 1982 Apr 8–11 | C Stadler* | 284 |
| 1940 Apr 4–7 | J Demaret | 280 | *After a play-off with Dan Pohl: Stadler 4, Pohl 5* | | |
| 1941 Apr 3–6 | C Wood | 280 | 1983 Apr 7–11 | S Ballesteros (ESP) | 280 |
| 1942 Apr 9–12 | B Nelson* | 280 | 1984 Apr 12–15 | B Crenshaw | 277 |
| *After a play-off: Nelson 69, B Hogan 70* | | | 1985 Apr 11–14 | B Langer (GER) | 282 |
| 1946 Apr 4–7 | H Keiser | 282 | 1986 Apr 10–13 | J Nicklaus | 279 |
| 1947 Apr 3–6 | J Demaret | 281 | 1987 Apr 9–12 | L Mize* | 285 |
| 1948 Apr 8–11 | C Harmon | 279 | *After a play-off; Mize 4,3, G Norman 4,4,* | | |
| 1949 Apr 7–10 | S Snead | 283 | S Ballesteros 5 | | |
| 1950 Apr 6–9 | J Demaret | 282 | 1988 Apr 7–10 | A Lyle (SCO) | 281 |
| 1951 Apr 5–8 | B Hogan | 280 | 1989 Apr 6–9 | N Faldo (ENG)* | 283 |
| 1952 Apr 3–6 | S Snead | 286 | *After a play-off: Faldo 5,3, S Hoch 5,4* | | |
| 1953 Apr 9–12 | B Hogan | 274 | 1990 Apr 5–8 | N Faldo (ENG)* | 278 |
| 1954 Apr 8–12 | S Snead* | 289 | *After a play-off: Faldo 4,4; R Floyd 4,5* | | |
| *After a play-off: Snead 69, B Hogan 70* | | | 1991 Apr 11–14 | I Woosnam (WAL) | 277 |
| 1955 Apr 7–10 | C Middlecoff | 279 | 1992 Apr 9–12 | F Couples | 275 |
| 1956 Apr 5–8 | J Burke | 289 | 1993 Apr 8–11 | B Langer (GER) | 277 |
| 1957 Apr 4–7 | D Ford | 283 | 1994 Apr 7–10 | JM Olazábal (ESP) | 279 |
| 1958 Apr 3–6 | A Palmer | 284 | 1995 Apr 6–9 | B Crenshaw | 274 |
| 1959 Apr 2–5 | A Wall | 284 | 1996 Apr 11–14 | N Faldo (ENG) | 276 |
| 1960 Apr 7–10 | A Palmer | 282 | 1997 Apr 10–13 | T Woods | 270 |
| 1961 Apr 6–10 | G Player (RSA) | 280 | 1998 Apr 9–12 | M O'Meara | 279 |
| 1962 Apr 5–9 | A Palmer* | 280 | 1999 Apr 8–11 | JM Olazábal (ESP) | 280 |
| *After a play-off: Palmer 68, G Player 71,* | | | 2000 Apr 6–9 | V Singh (FIJ) | 278 |
| D Finsterwald 77 | | | 2001 Apr 5–8 | T Woods | 272 |
| 1963 Apr 4–10 | J Nicklaus | 286 | 2002 Apr 11–14 | T Woods | 276 |
| 1964 Apr 9–12 | A Palmer | 276 | 2003 Apr 10–13 | M Weir (CAN)* | 281 |
| 1965 Apr 8–11 | J Nicklaus | 271 | *After a play-off: Weir 4, L Mattiace 6* | | |
| 1966 Apr 7–11 | J Nicklaus* | 288 | 2004 Apr 8–11 | P Mickelson | 279 |
| *After a play-off: Nicklaus 70, T Jacobs 72,* | | | 2005 Apr 7–10 | T Woods* | 276 |
| G Brewer Jr 78 | | | *After a play-off: Woods 3, C DiMarco 4* | | |
| 1967 Apr 6–9 | G Brewer | 280 | 2006 Apr 6–9 | P Mickelson | 281 |
| 1968 Apr 11–14 | R Goalby | 277 | 2007 Apr 5–8 | Z Johnson | 289 |
| 1969 Apr 10–13 | G Archer | 281 | 2008 Apr 10–13 | T Immelman (RSA) | 280 |
| 1970 Apr 9–13 | W Casper* | 279 | 2009 Apr 9–12 | A Cabrera (ARG) | 276 |
| *After a play-off: Casper 69, G Littler 74* | | | *After a play-off with Kenny Perry and Chad* | | |
| 1971 Apr 8–11 | C Coody | 279 | Campbell | | |
| 1972 Apr 6–9 | J Nicklaus | 286 | 2010 Apr 8–11 | P Mickelson | 272 |
| 1973 Apr 5–9 | T Aaron | 283 | 2011 Apr 7–10 | C Schwartzel (RSA) | 274 |
| 1974 Apr 11–14 | G Player (RSA) | 278 | 2012 Apr 5–8 | B Watson* | 278 |
| 1975 Apr 10–13 | J Nicklaus | 276 | *After a play-off: Watson 4,4; Oosthuizen (RSA) 4,5* | | |
| 1976 Apr 8–11 | R Floyd | 271 | 2013 Apr 11–14 | A Scott (AUS)* | 279 |
| 1977 Apr 7–10 | T Watson | 276 | *After a play-off with Angel Cabrera (ARG)* | | |

# Cool, calm Dufner joins majors élite with a truly polished display at Oak Hill

On a testing course, lined by thick rough, which rewarded accurate shot-making and required a cool head, no one struck the ball with more precision or kept a stronger grip on their emotions at Oak Hill than Jason Dufner. Two years after he surrendered a five stroke advantage over the closing holes of the season's final major at Atlanta Athletic Club before losing a play-off, Dufner finally placed his hands on the Wanamaker Trophy thanks to an unflappable display of ball striking which routed the competition at the US PGA Championship.

True, he faltered over the closing two holes, carding a brace of bogeys, but by then Dufner was in such a commanding position he was still able to sign for a closing round of 68 and a ten under par total of 270, two shots clear of fellow American Jim Furyk and three ahead of Sweden's Henrik Stenson. Moreover, Dufner secured a spot in the record books by delivering a winning score which was four strokes lower than the mark set by Jack Nicklaus at the 1980 PGA, the previous low tally in the half-dozen majors staged over the classic lay-out designed by Donald Ross.

That was largely thanks to the wet weather conditions which softened the course on Friday and allowed the champion to match the low score in the history of major championship golf, 63. Indeed, had he holed a 12 footer on the final hole in the second round, Dufner would have become the first golfer ever to post 62 in the majors. Without the defence of firm and fast greens, Oak Hill lowered its guard.

Given that perhaps the least reliable part of Dufner's game is usually his work with the short stick from inside five feet under pressure, the medium paced greens probably worked in his favour as it allowed his talent for finding fairways with the driver and gift for hitting wedge shots to the flag to prove decisive. His approach to the 16th for example which landed just past the hole and spun back to within a few inches of the cup was exceptional.

Like Inbee Park in the women's game, Dufner, 36, plays with the kind of insouciance which makes rivals wonder if he has a pulse. Round faced with unkempt hair trying to escape from his baseball cap, few would describe the American as athletic. He has a rare gift for concealing his emotions, however, and good-naturedly played along with the 'Dufnering' fad which went viral on social media after the laid back golfer was snapped during a visit to a primary school in a slumped pose against a classroom wall, with an almost stupefied look on his face.

Distinguished on the course by a trademark waggle which involves an idiosyncratic cocking of the wrists before he pulls the trigger on his backswing, Dufner was the 19th different winner of a major in the last 21 stagings. It was another measure of the strength-in-depth of the game over the past five years, as well as the lack of a truly dominant figure, that 15 of those successes, including Dufner's, have been earned by first time major winners. The only multiple winners of the glittering prizes during this period were Phil Mickelson, Ernie Els and Rory McIlroy.

Not that Dufner, 36, remotely resembled a rookie champion during the final round in Rochester, New York, when he played with such authority the rest of the field were given little or no encouragement. Carrying responsibility like a man accustomed to bearing anchors, he found fairways with metronomic consistency for 16 holes. Not only that, between the 2nd and the 16th he conjured up no fewer than ten single putt greens. For those unfamiliar with the nuances and challenges of championship golf, this might not have looked overtly thrilling: in truth, seasoned observers knew this closing round of golf was every bit as exceptional as the brilliant denouements constructed earlier in the season by Adam Scott at Augusta, Justin Rose at Merion and Phil Mickelson at Muirfield.

"I come across as a pretty cool customer, I guess," Dufner conceded, "but there are definitely some nerves out there, especially when you're trying to win a major championship. I felt good after I made that putt on the first hole and would say I was pretty flatlined for most of the day after that. For me to be competitive on this type of golf course, I felt like I had to have a great week of ball striking and I was able to do it. I hit a lot of fairways. If I did miss the fairways, I wasn't in the thick, thick stuff, so I could manage to get it up by the greens. When I did hit the fairways, I hit a ton of greens, and that was the difference for me. For me, golf is a little bit more boring [than other sports]. It's pretty matter of fact. I hit it in the fairway or I don't; I hit the green or I didn't. Usually I'm struggling with the putter, so there's not too much to get excited about with that!"

As is often the case when so much attention surrounds Tiger Woods, Mickelson, McIlroy and other marquee golfers before a ball is struck in the most prestigious events, Dufner came into the final major of 2013 more or less under the radar. And it's fair to say his opening 68, which positioned the American three strokes behind the early benchmark set by Adam Scott and Furyk, didn't turbo-charge his profile.

The Masters' champion was the man who caught the eye on Thursday, making five consecutive birdies over the front nine and reaching the turn in 30. Scott found the inward half more testing and eventually carded 65, the same score as Furyk, who returned to contention after missing cuts at both The Open and the US Open. After lapping the field the previous week at Firestone, Woods struggled on the big stage. He lost control of his opening round over the closing holes when he ran up two 6s, including a double bogey on the ninth, for 71. The world number one was never a factor thereafter, failing to better par each day in a four round total of 284.

There was no escaping Dufner on Friday, mark you, when he set a course record of 63 – the 26th time the low score in major golf had been posted. (For the record, there have been a dozen 63s in the US PGA, eight in The Open, four in The US Open and two at the Masters.) For someone who often resembles a fellow awakening from 40 winks, Dufner had drifted off for much of 2013, finishing no higher in any event than fourth at the US Open, which was largely down to a freewheeling 67 on Sunday at Merion.

> "I come across as a pretty cool customer but there are nerves out there when you are trying for a major."
>
> *Jason Dufner*

Here, though, Dufner was eagle-eyed from the moment he holed out for 2 on the par 4 second hole from 105 yards. After reaching the turn in 31, he kept up the good work with another birdie at the 16th and a brace of sterling pars on the home holes to lower Ben Hogan's longstanding share of the course record. "Obviously the rain which softened the golf course made it scoreable," he reflected. "But to join history and shoot 63 in a major is pretty unbelievable."

As often happens to golfers who shoot low, it can be tricky to play half-as-well the next day. As Oak Hill's greens found a little fire following a soggy surrender in the second round, Dufner gave up the two shot lead he held at the halfway mark and went into the last day trailing Furyk by a stroke after carding 71. Without a magic wand to wave as he'd done on Friday, Dufner was happy enough, after a sluggish start when he made 6 from the water on the fifth, to grind out eight pars and a birdie after the turn.

Forty-three-year-old Furyk moved into pole position thanks to a tidy 68 where the highlight was a birdie on the 17th which felt almost as good as an eagle: the veteran struck a hybrid which flew 244 yards onto the green before holing a 20 foot putt for 3. McIlroy was one of the other notables to match that feat on the penultimate hole as he signalled a return to form. The defending champion shot 67 and 70 over the week-end for a total of three under par and a share of eighth.

With a swing as flat as his nervous system – some might say it was Hoganesque – Dufner drew level with Furyk during the final round on the fourth green and was one ahead when he birdied the 8th. By the turn, after Furyk dropped a shot on the ninth, he was two strokes clear. Perhaps he most important stroke Dufner made in the final round, however, was the three foot putt he holed for par on the first. The grip on Dufner's putter, incidentally, resembles an elephant's trunk. It's not the kind of grip used by a confident putter.

Although Furyk continued to play par golf until the closing holes, the former US Open champion was unable to pressurise the leader. "But I didn't lose the golf tournament," he insisted. "I was just beaten by someone who played better."

Had he birdied the 14th rather than taken bogey from a poor lie in a divot Stenson, arguably the form player of the second half of the season, might have edged closer to becoming the first Swede to win a men's major. As it was, his challenge for the PGA faded in the wake of that unfortunate set-back and he had to settle for third place after finishing runner-up to Mickelson at The Open.

The spoils at Oak Hill went to Dufner, although, as expected, you would never have known from the look on his face.

Mike Aitken

| First round | Second round | Third round | Fourth round |
|---|---|---|---|
| −5 Jim Furyk | −9 Jason Dufner | −9 Jim Furyk | −10 Jason Dufner |
| −5 Adam Scott | −7 Jim Furyk | −8 Jason Dufner | −8 Jim Furyk |
| −4 David Hearn | −7 Adam Scott | −7 Henrik Stenson | −7 Henrik Stenson |
| −4 Lee Westwood | −7 Matt Kuchar | −6 Jonas Blixt | −6 Jonas Blixt |
| −3 Robert Garrigus | −6 Henrik Stenson | −5 Steve Stricker | −5 Adam Scott |
| −3 Paul Casey | −6 Justin Rose | −5 Adam Scott | −5 Scott Piercy |
| −3 Matt Kuchar | −5 Steve Stricker | −3 Rory McIlroy | −4 David Toms |
| −3 Marcus Fraser | −5 Robert Garrigus | −3 Lee Westwood | −3 Zach Johnson |
| −3 Scott Piercy | −4 Martin Kaymer | −2 Dustin Johnson | −3 Rory McIlroy |
| −3 Jason Day | −4 Webb Simpson | −2 Kevin Streelman | −3 Jason Day |

## US PGA Championship (95th)   *Oak Hill CC, Rochester, NY*   August 8–11   [7163–70]

Prize money: $8 million. Final field of 156 players, of whom 75 made the half-way cut on 143 or less.

*Players are of American nationality unless stated*

| | | | |
|---|---|---|---|
| 1 | Jason Dufner | 68-63-71-68—270 | $1,445,000 |
| 2 | Jim Furyk | 65-68-68-71—272 | 865,000 |
| 3 | Henrik Stenson (SWE) | 68-66-69-70—273 | 545,000 |
| 4 | Jonas Blixt (SWE) | 68-70-66-70—274 | 385,000 |
| 5 | Scott Piercy | 67-71-72-65—275 | 304,000 |
| | Adam Scott (AUS) | 65-68-72-70—275 | 304,000 |
| 7 | David Toms | 71-69-69-67—276 | 259,000 |
| 8 | Jason Day (AUS) | 67-71-72-67—277 | 206,250 |
| | Zach Johnson | 69-70-70-68—277 | 206,250 |
| | Dustin Johnson | 72-71-65-69—277 | 206,250 |
| | Rory McIlroy (NIR) | 69-71-67-70—277 | 206,250 |
| 12 | Graeme McDowell (NIR) | 70-69-73-66—278 | 132,785 |
| | Boo Weekley | 72-69-70-67—278 | 132,785 |
| | Marc Leishman (AUS) | 70-70-70-68—278 | 132,785 |
| | Roberto Castro | 68-69-71-70—278 | 132,785 |
| | Marc Warren (SCO) | 74-67-68-69—278 | 132,785 |
| | Kevin Streelman | 70-72-66-70—278 | 132,785 |
| | Steve Stricker | 68-67-70-73—278 | 132,785 |
| 19 | Keegan Bradley | 69-72-72-66—279 | 93,166 |
| | Hideki Matsuyama (JPN) | 72-68-73-66—279 | 93,166 |
| | Rickie Fowler | 70-68-72-69—279 | 93,166 |
| 22 | Michael Thompson | 72-67-72-69—280 | 75,000 |
| | Matt Kuchar | 67-66-76-71—280 | 75,000 |
| | David Lynn (ENG) | 69-69-71-71—280 | 75,000 |
| 25 | Kiradech Aphibarnrat (THA) | 68-71-71-71—281 | 58,750 |
| | Robert Garrigus | 67-68-74-72—281 | 58,750 |
| | Webb Simpson | 72-64-73-72—281 | 58,750 |
| | Bill Haas | 68-70-71-72—281 | 58,750 |
| 29 | Miguel Angel Jiménez (ESP) | 68-72-75-67—282 | 48,500 |
| | Rafael Cabrera-Bello (ESP) | 68-75-69-70—282 | 48,500 |
| | Scott Jamieson (SCO) | 69-72-70-71—282 | 48,500 |
| | Ryo Ishikawa (JPN) | 69-71-70-72—282 | 48,500 |
| 33 | Peter Hanson (SWE) | 72-69-74-68—283 | 38,571 |
| | Martin Kaymer (GER) | 68-68-78-69—283 | 38,571 |
| | Paul Casey (ENG) | 67-72-74-70—283 | 38,571 |
| | Brendon de Jonge (ZIM) | 71-71-71-70—283 | 38,571 |
| | Justin Rose (ENG) | 68-66-77-72—283 | 38,571 |
| | Francesco Molinari (ITA) | 72-68-70-73—283 | 38,571 |
| | Lee Westwood (ENG) | 66-73-68-76—283 | 38,571 |
| 40 | Matt Jones (AUS) | 72-71-73-68—284 | 28,000 |
| | Thorbjørn Olesen (DEN) | 71-70-74-69—284 | 28,000 |
| | J J Henry | 71-71-73-69—284 | 28,000 |
| | Danny Willett (ENG) | 73-70-72-69—284 | 28,000 |
| | D A Points | 73-70-72-69—284 | 28,000 |
| | Tiger Woods | 71-70-73-70—284 | 28,000 |
| | Charley Hoffman | 69-67-73-75—284 | 28,000 |
| 47 | Thongchai Jaidee (THA) | 70-71-75-69—285 | 18,875 |
| | John Merrick | 75-68-73-69—285 | 18,875 |
| | Ryan Palmer | 73-70-71-71—285 | 18,875 |
| | Josh Teater | 71-71-71-72—285 | 18,875 |
| | David Hearn (CAN) | 66-76-71-72—285 | 18,875 |
| | K J Choi (KOR) | 76-65-71-73—285 | 18,875 |
| | Marcus Fraser (AUS) | 67-69-75-74—285 | 18,875 |
| | Luke Guthrie | 71-71-69-74—285 | 18,875 |
| 55 | Scott Stallings | 73-70-73-70—286 | 16,900 |
| | Ryan Moore | 69-71-73-73—286 | 16,900 |
| 57 | Hunter Mahan | 70-68-78-71—287 | 16,300 |

US PGA Championship *continued*

| | | | |
|---|---|---|---|
| 57T | Shane Lowry (IRL) | 71-70-75-71—287 | 16,300 |
| | Chris Kirk | 71-69-73-74—287 | 16,300 |
| | Ken Duke | 75-68-70-74—287 | 16,300 |
| 61 | Stephen Gallacher (SCO) | 75-68-76-69—288 | 15,700 |
| | Ian Poulter (ENG) | 70-71-77-70—288 | 15,700 |
| | Tommy Gainey | 69-74-73-72—288 | 15,700 |
| | Harris English | 74-69-72-73—288 | 15,700 |
| | Sergio García (ESP) | 69-68-75-76—288 | 15,700 |
| 66 | Ben Curtis | 73-70-74-72—289 | 15,350 |
| | Brandt Snedeker | 70-73-70-76—289 | 15,350 |
| 68 | Tim Clark (RSA) | 69-71-75-75—290 | 15,150 |
| | Vijay Singh (FIJ) | 70-72-73-75—290 | 15,150 |
| 70 | John Senden (AUS) | 72-70-73-76—291 | 14,950 |
| | Brooks Koepka | 71-72-71-77—291 | 14,950 |
| 72 | Phil Mickelson | 71-71-78-72—292 | 14,750 |
| | Matteo Manassero (ITA) | 72-69-74-77—292 | 14,750 |
| 74 | Gary Woodland | 73-70-80-70—293 | 14,600 |
| 75 | Darren Clarke (NIR) | 69-73-74-80—296 | 14,500 |

*The following players missed the half-way cut:*

| | | | | | | | | |
|---|---|---|---|---|---|---|---|---|
| 76 | Charles Howell III | 71-73—144 | 96T | Charlie Beljan | 71-75—146 | 124T | Jaco Van Zyl (RSA) | 74-76—150 |
| | Joost Luiten (NED) | 71-73—144 | | Ernie Els (RSA) | 74-72—146 | 132 | Danny Balin | 73-78—151 |
| | Nicolas Colsaerts (BEL) | 71-73—144 | | Richard Sterne (RSA) | 72-74—146 | | Kyle Stanley | 73-78—151 |
| | Bubba Watson | 70-74—144 | | Y E Yang (KOR) | 72-74—146 | | Kevin Chappell | 79-72—151 |
| | Sang-Moon Bae (KOR) | 75-69—144 | | Stewart Cink | 75-71—146 | | Rob Labritz | 78-73—151 |
| | Woody Austin | 69-75—144 | | Jason Kokrak | 74-72—146 | | Bob Gaus | 74-77—151 |
| | Martin Laird (SCO) | 71-73—144 | 107 | Brett Rumford (AUS) | 70-77—147 | | Thomas Bjørn (DEN) | 70-81—151 |
| | Chris Stroud | 71-73—144 | | Kevin Stadler | 74-73—147 | 139 | Paul McGinley (IRL) | 78-74—152 |
| | Charl Schwartzel (RSA) | 71-73—144 | | Richie Ramsay (SCO) | 72-75—147 | | Lucas Glover | 76-76—152 |
| | Paul Lawrie (SCO) | 72-72—144 | | Hiroyuki Fujita (JPN) | 71-76—147 | | Mike Small | 76-76—152 |
| | Davis Love III | 74-70—144 | | Billy Horschel | 69-78—147 | | Shaun Micheel | 76-76—152 |
| | Branden Grace (RSA) | 71-73—144 | | Scott Brown | 73-74—147 | 143 | Freddie Jacobson (SWE) | 76-77—153 |
| 88 | Jimmy Walker | 71-74—145 | | Padraig Harrington (IRL) | 76-71—147 | | Mark Sheftic | 75-78—153 |
| | Luke Donald (ENG) | 71-74—145 | | Brian Gay | 73-74—147 | | Stuart Smith | 78-75—153 |
| | Mikko Ilonen (FIN) | 73-72—145 | | Peter Uihlein | 77-70—147 | 146 | Kirk Hanefeld | 76-78—154 |
| | David Muttitt (ENG) | 75-70—145 | 116 | Derek Ernst | 72-76—148 | 147 | Bob Sowards | 73-82—155 |
| | Marcel Siem (GER) | 73-72—145 | | Kohki Idoki (JPN) | 72-76—148 | 148 | Jeff Martin | 78-78—156 |
| | Rich Beem | 71-74—145 | | Geoff Ogilvy (AUS) | 74-74—148 | | Rod Perry | 78-78—156 |
| | David Lingmerth (SWE) | 74-71—145 | | Jordan Spieth | 74-74—148 | | Sonny Skinner | 76-80—156 |
| | Bernd Wiesberger (AUT) | 70-75—145 | | Matt Every | 71-77—148 | 151 | Mark Brown | 77-82—159 |
| 96 | John Huh | 72-74—146 | | Jeff Sorenson | 73-75—148 | 152 | Chip Sullivan | 84-76—160 |
| | Russell Henley | 76-70—146 | 122 | Alex Noren (SWE) | 76-73—149 | 153 | Lee Rhind | 81-82—163 |
| | Gonzalo Fernandez-Castano (ESP) | 74-72—146 | | J C Anderson | 73-76—149 | | Angel Cabrera (ARG) | NC |
| | Carl Pettersson (SWE) | 74-72—146 | 124 | Tom Watson | 73-77—150 | | Bo Van Pelt | WD |
| | Graham DeLaet (CAN) | 70-76—146 | | Nick Watney | 76-74—150 | | Jamie Donaldson (WAL) | WD |
| | | | | George Coetzee (RSA) | 74-76—150 | | | |
| | | | | Chris Wood (ENG) | 75-75—150 | | | |
| | | | | Pablo Larrazabal (ESP) | 76-74—150 | | | |
| | | | | David McNabb | 74-76—150 | | | |
| | | | | Ryan Polzin | 73-77—150 | | | |

---

## Twenty-nine states

Since its inauguration in 1916 the US PGA Championship has been played in 29 of the 50 states of the USA. Topping the list is New York (where the first championship was held) with 12 championships, closely followed by Oklahoma with 11 and Pennsylvania with nine.

# 2012 US PGA Championship Kiaawah Island Resort (Ocean), Kiawah Island, SC   August 9–12

[7676–72]

Prize money: $8 million. Final field of 156, of whom 72 made the half-way cut.

| | | | | | | | | |
|---|---|---|---|---|---|---|---|---|
| 1 | Rory McIlroy (NIR) | 67-75-67-66—275 | $1,445,000 | 21T | Louis Oosthuizen (RSA) | 70-79-70-69—288 | 72,666 |
| 2 | David Lynn (ENG) | 73-74-68-68—283 | 865,000 | | Robert Garrigus | 74-73-74-67—288 | 72,666 |
| 3 | Justin Rose (ENG) | 69-79-70-66—284 | 384,500 | | Pat Perez | 69-76-71-72—288 | 72,666 |
| | Keegan Bradley | 68-77-71-68—284 | 384,500 | | Seung-Yul Noh (KOR) | 74-75-74-65—288 | 72,666 |
| | Ian Poulter (ENG) | 70-71-74-69—284 | 384,500 | | Jimmy Walker | 73-75-67-73—288 | 72,666 |
| | Carl Pettersson (SWE) | 66-74-72-72—284 | 384,500 | 27 | Thorbjørn Olesen | 75-74-71-69—289 | 51,900 |
| 7 | Blake Adams | 71-72-75-67—285 | 226,000 | | (DEN) | | |
| | Jamie Donaldson (WAL) | 69-73-73-70—285 | 226,000 | | Miguel Angel Jiménez | 69-77-72-71—289 | 51,900 |
| | Peter Hanson (SWE) | 69-75-70-71—285 | 226,000 | | (ESP) | | |
| | Steve Stricker | 74-73-67-71—285 | 226,000 | | Jason Dufner | 74-76-68-71—289 | 51,900 |
| 11 | Ben Curtis | 69-77-73-67—286 | 143,285 | | Marc Leishman (AUS) | 74-72-71-72—289 | 51,900 |
| | Bubba Watson | 73-75-70-68—286 | 143,285 | | Trevor Immelman (RSA) | 71-72-70-76—289 | 51,900 |
| | Tim Clark (RSA) | 71-73-73-69—286 | 143,285 | 32 | John Senden (AUS) | 73-74-72-71—290 | 42,625 |
| | Geoff Ogilvy (AUS) | 68-78-70-70—286 | 143,285 | | Greg Chalmers (AUS) | 70-76-72-72—290 | 42,625 |
| | Graeme McDowell | 68-76-71-71—286 | 143,285 | | Bill Haas | 75-73-69-73—290 | 42,625 |
| | (NIR) | | | | Luke Donald (ENG) | 74-76-74-66—290 | 42,625 |
| | Tiger Woods | 69-71-74-72—286 | 143,285 | 36 | Fredrik Jacobson (SWE) | 71-75-73-72—291 | 34,750 |
| | Adam Scott (AUS) | 68-75-70-73—286 | 143,285 | | Rich Beem | 72-76-72-71—291 | 34,750 |
| 18 | John Daly | 68-77-73-69—287 | 99,666 | | Phil Mickelson | 73-71-73-74—291 | 34,750 |
| | Padraig Harrington (IRL) | 70-76-69-72—287 | 99,666 | | Y E Yang (KOR) | 73-74-74-70—291 | 34,750 |
| | Bo Van Pelt | 73-73-67-74—287 | 99,666 | | Marcel Siem (GER) | 72-73-71-75—291 | 34,750 |
| 21 | Joost Luiten (NED) | 68-76-75-69—288 | 72,666 | | Vijay Singh (FIJ) | 71-69-74-77—291 | 34,750 |

**Other players who made the cut:** J J Henry, Jim Furyk, Aaron Baddeley (AUS), Gary Woodland, David Toms, Martin Laird (SCO) 292; Paul Lawrie (SCO), Ernie Els (RSA), Dustin Johnson, Thomas Björn (DEN), Retief Goosen (RSA), Scott Piercy 293; Francesco Molinari (ITA), Sang Moon Bae (KOR), Darren Clarke (NIR), Brendon de Jonge (ZIM), K J Choi (KOR) 294; Charl Schwartzel (RSA), Ryo Ishikawa (JPN) 295; K T Kim (KOR) 296; Gonzalo Fernandez-Castano (ESP), Chez Reavie, Ken Duke, George McNeill 297; Alex Noren (SWE), Marcus Fraser (AUS) 298; Toru Taniguchi (JPN), John Huh 299; Zach Johnson 300; Matt Every 304; Cameron Tringale 306

---

# 2011 US PGA Championship Atlanta Athletic Club, Johns Creek, GA   August 12–15   [7467–70]

Prize money: $8 million. Field of 156, of whom 75 made the half-way cut.

| | | | | | | | | |
|---|---|---|---|---|---|---|---|---|
| 1 | Keegan Bradley* | 71-64-69-68—272 | $1,445,000 | 19T | Hunter Mahan | 72-72-66-70—280 | 81,214 |
| 2 | Jason Dufner | 70-65-68-69—272 | 865,000 | | John Senden (AUS) | 68-68-72-72—280 | 81,214 |
| *Bradley beat Dufner in three hole play-off | | | | | Brendan Steele | 69-68-66-77—280 | 81,214 |
| 3 | Anders Hansen (DEN) | 68-69-70-66—273 | 545,000 | 26 | Charles Howell III | 72-68-73-68—281 | 51,062 |
| 4 | Robert Karlsson (SWE) | 70-71-67-67—275 | 331,000 | | Robert Allenby (AUS) | 72-70-71-68—281 | 51,062 |
| | David Toms | 72-71-65-67—275 | 331,000 | | Jerry Kelly | 65-73-74-69—281 | 51,062 |
| | Scott Verplank | 67-69-69-70—275 | 331,000 | | Bubba Watson | 74-68-70-69—281 | 51,062 |
| 7 | Adam Scott (AUS) | 69-69-70-68—276 | 259,000 | | Mark Wilson | 69-71-71-70—281 | 51,062 |
| 8 | Lee Westwood (ENG) | 71-68-70-68—277 | 224,500 | | Scott Piercy | 71-68-71-71—281 | 51,062 |
| | Luke Donald (ENG) | 70-71-68-68—277 | 224,500 | | Brendon de Jonge | 68-72-69-72—281 | 51,062 |
| 10 | Kevin Na | 72-69-70-67—278 | 188,000 | | (RSA) | | |
| | D A Points | 69-67-71-71—278 | 188,000 | | Spencer Levin | 71-70-68-72—281 | 51,062 |
| 12 | Trevor Immelman (RSA) | 69-71-71-68—279 | 132,786 | 34 | Chris Kirk | 72-72-69-69—282 | 40,000 |
| | Gary Woodland | 70-71-70-68—279 | 132,786 | | Francesco Molinari (ITA) | 72-71-67-72—282 | 40,000 |
| | Sergio García (ESP) | 72-69-69-69—279 | 132,786 | | Alexander Noren (SWE) | 70-72-68-72—282 | 40,000 |
| | Bill Haas | 68-73-69-69—279 | 132,786 | 37 | Matteo Manassero (ITA) | 68-74-71-70—283 | 36,250 |
| | Nick Watney (AUS) | 70-71-68-70—279 | 132,786 | | Ben Crane | 71-72-66-74—283 | 36,250 |
| | Charl Schwartzel (RSA) | 71-71-66-71—279 | 132,786 | 39 | Johan Edfors (SWE) | 71-70-73-70—284 | 30,250 |
| | Steve Stricker | 63-74-69-73—279 | 132,786 | | Harrison Frazar | 72-69-72-71—284 | 30,250 |
| 19 | Brian Davis (ENG) | 69-73-69-69—280 | 81,214 | | Ian Poulter (ENG) | 74-68-70-72—284 | 30,250 |
| | Phil Mickelson | 71-70-69-70—280 | 81,214 | | K J Choi (KOR) | 70-73-69-72—284 | 30,250 |
| | Ryan Palmer | 71-70-69-70—280 | 81,214 | | Bill Lunde | 71-71-69-73—284 | 30,250 |
| | Matt Kuchar | 71-71-68-70—280 | 81,214 | | Jim Furyk | 71-65-73-75—284 | 30,250 |

**Other players who made the cut:** Pablo Larrazabal (ESP), Ross Fisher (ENG), Seung-yul Noh (KOR), Andres Romero (ARG), Yuta Ikeda (JPN), Brandt Jobe 285; Rickie Fowler, John Rollins, Jhonattan Vegas (COL), Johnson Wagner, Simon Dyson (ENG) 286; Ryan Moore, Ricky Barnes, Bryce Molder 287; Michael Bradley, Zach Johnson, K T Kim (KOR) 288; Robert Garrigus, Kevin Streelman 290; Sean O'Hair, Peter Hanson (SWE), Padraig Harrington (IRL), Rory McIlroy (NIR), Miguel Angel Jiménez (ESP) 291; Edoardo Molinari (ITA), Y E Yang (KOR), Mike Small 292; Paul Casey (ENG), Davis Love III 294; Shaun Micheel, Rory Sabbatini (RSA) 295

## 2010 US PGA Championship Whistling Straits, Kohler, WI    August 12–15    [7507–72]

Prize money: $7.5 million. Field of 156, of whom 72 made the half-way cut.

| | | | | | | | | |
|---|---|---|---|---|---|---|---|---|
| 1 | Martin Kaymer (GER)* | 72-68-67-70—277 | $1,350,000 | | 24 | Jim Furyk | 70-68-70-77—285 | 58,600 |
| 2 | Bubba Watson | 68-71-70-68—277 | 810,000 | | | J B Holmes | 72-66-77-70—285 | 58,600 |
| *Kaymer won after a 3-hole play-off: Kaymer 4-2-5; Watson | | | | | | Simon Khan (ENG) | 69-70-71-75—285 | 58,600 |
| 3-3-6 | | | | | | Carl Pettersson (SWE) | 71-70-71-73—285 | 58,600 |
| 3 | Zach Johnson | 69-70-69-70—278 | 435,000 | | 28 | David Horsey (ENG) | 71-70-72-73—286 | 46,700 |
| | Rory McIlroy (NIR) | 71-68-67-72—278 | 435,000 | | | Troy Matteson | 72-72-70-72—286 | 46,700 |
| 5 | Dustin Johnson | 71-68-67-73—279 | 206,410 | | | Noh Seung-yui (KOR) | 68-71-72-75—286 | 46,700 |
| | Jason Dufner | 73-66-69-71—279 | 206,410 | | | Bo Van Pelt | 73-67-72-74—286 | 46,700 |
| | Steve Elkington (AUS) | 71-70-67-71—279 | 206,410 | | | Tiger Woods | 71-70-72-73—286 | 46,700 |
| 8 | Liang Wen-chong (CHN) | 72-71-64-73—280 | 210,000 | | 33 | Gonzalo Fernandez- | 70-73-73-71—287 | 37,133 |
| | Camilo Villegas (COL) | 71-71-70-68—280 | 210,000 | | | Castaño (ESP) | | |
| 10 | Jason Day (AUS) | 69-72-66-74—281 | 175,800 | | | Edoardo Molinari (ITA) | 71-72-70-74—287 | 37,133 |
| | Matt Kuchar | 67-69-73-72—281 | 175,800 | | | Francesco Molinari (ITA) | 68-73-71-75—287 | 37,133 |
| 12 | Paul Casey (ENG) | 72-71-70-69—282 | 138,050 | | | Ryan Palmer | 71-68-75-73—287 | 37,133 |
| | Simon Dyson (ENG) | 71-71-68-72—282 | 138,050 | | | Heath Slocum | 73-72-68-74—287 | 37,133 |
| | Phil Mickelson | 73-69-73-67—282 | 138,050 | | | David Toms | 74-71-67-75—287 | 37,133 |
| | Bryce Molder | 72-67-70-73—282 | 138,050 | | 39 | K J Choi (KOR) | 74-69-71-74—288 | 25,933 |
| 16 | Robert Karlsson (SWE) | 71-71-71-70—283 | 110,050 | | | Tim Clark (RSA) | 72-71-70-75—288 | 25,933 |
| | D A Points | 70-72-70-71—283 | 110,050 | | | Ben Crane | 73-68-73-74—288 | 25,933 |
| 18 | Stewart Cink | 77-68-66-73—284 | 84,733 | | | Brian Davis (ENG) | 71-72-69-76—288 | 25,933 |
| | Ernie Els (RSA) | 68-74-69-73—284 | 84,733 | | | Justin Leonard | 73-69-73-73—288 | 25,933 |
| | Stephen Gallacher | 71-69-72-72—284 | 84,733 | | | Hunter Mahan | 74-71-68-75—288 | 25,933 |
| | (SCO) | | | | | Adam Scott (AUS) | 72-73-71-72—288 | 25,933 |
| | Charl Schwartzel (RSA) | 73-69-72-70—284 | 84,733 | | | Vijay Singh (FIJ) | 73-66-73-76—288 | 25,933 |
| | Steve Stricker | 72-72-68-72—284 | 84,733 | | | Brandt Snedeker | 75-70-67-76—288 | 25,933 |
| | Nick Watney | 69-68-66-81—284 | 84,733 | | | | | |

**Other players who made the cut:** Darren Clarke (NIR), Brendon de Jonge (ZIM), Charles Howell III, Kim Kyung-tae (KOR), Martin Laird (SCO), Marc Leishman (AUS), Shaun Micheel 289; Retief Goosen (RSA), Tom Lehman, Davis Love III 290; Grégory Bourdy (FRA), Rickie Fowler, Peter Hanson (SWE), Kevin Na (KOR) 291; Fredrik Andersson Hed (SWE), Chad Campbell, Rhys Davies (WAL) 292; Brian Gay, Ryan Moore 293; D J Trahan 294; Stuart Appleby (AUS), Rob Labritz 295; Ross McGowan (ENG) 297; Jeff Overton 298; Ian Poulter (ENG) WD

## Tiger Woods longest as world No 1

Tiger Woods has been 662 weeks as World No. 1 in the professional golf rankings – easily leading the table of players who have filled the top spot.

Sixteen players (including Woods) have been World No 1 in the 24 year history of the rankings. Eight have been from Europe, four from America and one each from Zimbabwe, Fiji, South Africa and Australia

The list is: Tiger Woods (USA) 662 weeks; Bernard Langer (GER) three weeks; Severiano Ballesteros (ESP) 61 weeks; Greg Norman (AUS) 331 weeks; Sir Nick Faldo (ENG) 97 weeks; Ian Woosnam (WAL) 50 weeks; Fred Couples (USA) 16 weeks; Nick Price (ZIM) 44 weeks; Tom Lehman (USA) one week; Ernie Els (RSA) nine weeks; David Duval (USA) 15 weeks; Vijay Singh (FIJ) 32 weeks; Martin Kaymer (GER) eight weeks; Lee Westwood (ENG) 22 weeks; Luke Donald (ENG) 56 weeks; Rory McIlroy (NIR) 39 weeks.

## 2009 US PGA Championship  Hazeltine, Chaska, MN    August 13–16    [7674–72]

Prize money: $7.5 million. Field of 156, of whom 80 made the half-way cut.

| | | | | | | | | |
|---|---|---|---|---|---|---|---|---|
| 1 | Yong-Eun Yang (KOR) | 73-70-67-70—280 | $1,350,000 | 24T | Ben Curtis | 73-72-73-73—291 | 53,112 |
| 2 | Tiger Woods | 67-70-71-75—283 | 810,000 | | Brendan Jones (AUS) | 71-70-73-77—291 | 53,112 |
| 3 | Rory McIlroy (NIR) | 71-73-71-70—285 | 435,000 | | Scott McCarron | 75-72-71-73—291 | 53,112 |
| | Lee Westwood (ENG) | 70-72-73-70—285 | 435,000 | | Alvaro Quiros (ESP) | 69-76-69-77—291 | 53,112 |
| 5 | Lucas Glover | 71-70-71-74—286 | 300,000 | | John Rollins | 73-73-68-77—291 | 53,112 |
| 6 | Ernie Els (RSA) | 75-68-70-74—287 | 233,125 | 32 | Gonzalo Fernandez- | 70-77-73-72—292 | 40,387 |
| | Martin Kaymer (GER) | 73-70-71-73—287 | 233,125 | | Castaño (ESP) | | |
| | Søren Kjeldsen (DEN) | 70-73-70-74—287 | 233,125 | | Steve Flesch | 74-73-69-76—292 | 40,387 |
| | Henrik Stenson (SWE) | 73-71-68-75—287 | 233,125 | | Jeff Overton | 72-74-75-71—292 | 40,387 |
| 10 | Padraig Harrington (IRL) | 68-73-69-78—288 | 150,633 | | Kevin Sutherland | 73-72-74-73—292 | 40,387 |
| | Dustin Johnson | 72-73-73-70—288 | 150,633 | 36 | Woody Austin | 73-73-73-74—293 | 31,735 |
| | Zach Johnson | 74-73-70-71—288 | 150,633 | | Fred Couples | 74-74-73-72—293 | 31,735 |
| | Graeme McDowell | 70-75-71-72—288 | 150,633 | | Søren Hansen (DEN) | 72-76-74-71—293 | 31,735 |
| | (NIR) | | | | Thongchai Jaidee (THA) | 70-76-73-74—293 | 31,735 |
| | John Merrick | 72-72-74-70—288 | 150,633 | | Miguel Angel Jiménez | 75-73-71-74—293 | 31,735 |
| | Francesco Molinari (ITA) | 74-73-69-72—288 | 150,633 | | (ESP) | | |
| 16 | Tim Clark (RSA) | 76-68-71-74—289 | 106,566 | | David Toms | 69-75-72-77—293 | 31,735 |
| | Hunter Mahan | 69-75-74-71—289 | 106,566 | | Boo Weekley | 74-74-71-74—293 | 31,735 |
| | Vijay Singh (FIJ) | 69-72-75-73—289 | 106,566 | 43 | Rich Beem | 71-76-75-72—294 | 21,112 |
| 19 | Michael Allen | 74-71-72-73—290 | 81,760 | | Chad Campbell | 74-73-73-74—294 | 21,112 |
| | Ross Fisher (ENG) | 73-68-73-76—290 | 81,760 | | Ben Crane | 70-75-72-77—294 | 21,112 |
| | Corey Pavin | 73-71-71-75—290 | 81,760 | | Luke Donald (ENG) | 71-77-73-73—294 | 21,112 |
| | Ian Poulter (ENG) | 72-70-76-72—290 | 81,760 | | Kevin Na | 73-75-71-75—294 | 21,112 |
| | Oliver Wilson (ENG) | 74-72-72-72—290 | 81,760 | | Geoff Ogilvy (AUS) | 71-73-78-72—294 | 21,112 |
| 24 | Robert Allenby (AUS) | 69-75-75-72—291 | 53,112 | | Kenny Perry | 74-70-78-72—294 | 21,112 |
| | Stephen Ames (CAN) | 74-71-70-76—291 | 53,112 | | Charl Schwartzel (RSA) | 76-70-72-76—294 | 21,112 |
| | K J Choi (KOR) | 73-72-73-73—291 | 53,112 | | | | |

**Other players who made the cut:** Retief Goosen (RSA), Anthony Kim, Thomas Levet (FRA), Michael Sim (AUS), Camilo Villegas (COL), 295; Hiroyuki Fujita (JPN), Ryo Ishikawa (JPN), Bob Tway, Charlie Wi (KOR) 296; Richard Green (AUS), Tom Lehman, John Mallinger 297; Angel Cabrera (ARG), Jim Furyk, Nathan Green (AUS), J J Henry 298; Stewart Cink, Paul Goydos, Justin Leonard, Rory Sabbatini (RSA), Jeev Milkha Singh (IND), David Smail (NZL) 299; Phil Mickelson 300; Greg Bisconti 301; Sean O'Hair 302; Bob Estes, Grant Sturgeon, Chris Wood (ENG) 303; Alastair Forsyth (SCO) 305; Richard Sterne (RSA) Rtd

## 2008 US PGA Championship  Oakland Hills (South Course), Bloomfield, MI  August 7–10  [7131–70]

Prize money: $7.5 million. Field of 156, of whom 73 made the half-way cut.

| | | | | | | | | |
|---|---|---|---|---|---|---|---|---|
| 1 | Padraig Harrington | 71-74-66-66—277 | $1,350,000 | 20T | Boo Weekley | 72-71-79-66—288 | 78.900 |
| | (IRL) | | | 24 | Mark Brown (NZL) | 77-69-74-69—289 | 57,000 |
| 2 | Ben Curtis | 73-67-68-71—279 | 660.000 | | Retief Goosen (RSA) | 72-74-69-74—289 | 57,000 |
| | Sergio García (ESP) | 69-73-69-68—279 | 660.000 | | Fredrik Jacobson (SWE) | 75-71-70-73—289 | 57,000 |
| 4 | Henrik Stenson (SWE) | 71-70-68-72—281 | 330.000 | | Brandt Snedeker | 71-71-74-73—289 | 57,000 |
| | Camilo Villegas (COL) | 74-72-67-68—281 | 330.000 | | Nicholas Thompson | 71-72-73-73—289 | 57,000 |
| 6 | Steve Flesch | 73-70-70-69—282 | 270.000 | 29 | Jim Furyk | 71-77-70-72—290 | 47.550 |
| 7 | Phil Mickelson | 70-73-71-70—284 | 231,250 | | J B Holmes | 71-68-70-81—290 | 47.550 |
| | Andres Romero (ARG) | 69-78-65-72—284 | 231,250 | 31 | Robert Allenby (AUS) | 76-72-72-71—291 | 38.825 |
| 9 | Alastair Forsyth (SCO) | 73-72-70-70—285 | 176.725 | | Chris DiMarco | 75-72-72-72—291 | 38.825 |
| | Justin Rose (ENG) | 73-67-74-71—285 | 176.725 | | Ernie Els (RSA) | 71-75-70-75—291 | 38.825 |
| | Jeev Milkha Singh (IND) | 68-74-70-73—285 | 176.725 | | Paul Goydos | 74-69-73-75—291 | 38.825 |
| | Charlie Wi | 70-70-71-74—285 | 176.725 | | Geoff Ogilvy (AUS) | 73-74-74-70—291 | 38.825 |
| 13 | Aaron Baddeley (AUS) | 71-71-71-73—286 | 137,250 | | Sean O'Hair | 69-73-76-73—291 | 38.825 |
| | Ken Duke | 69-73-73-71—286 | 137,250 | | Ian Poulter (ENG) | 74-71-73-73—291 | 38.825 |
| 15 | Stuart Appleby (AUS) | 76-70-69-72—287 | 107.060 | | D J Trahan | 72-71-76-72—291 | 38.825 |
| | Paul Casey (ENG) | 72-74-72-69—287 | 107.060 | 39 | Steve Elkington (AUS) | 71-73-73-75—292 | 30.200 |
| | Graeme McDowell | 74-72-68-73—287 | 107.060 | | Rory Sabbatini (RSA) | 72-73-73-74—292 | 30.200 |
| | (NIR) | | | | Steve Stricker | 71-75-77-69—292 | 30.200 |
| | Prayad Marksaeng | 76-70-68-73—287 | 107.060 | 42 | Briny Baird | 71-72-73-77—293 | 24,500 |
| | (THA) | | | | Michael Campbell | 73-71-75-74—293 | 24,500 |
| | David Toms | 72-69-72-74—287 | 107.060 | | (NZL) | | |
| 20 | Angel Cabrera (ARG) | 70-72-72-74—288 | 78.900 | | Tom Lehman | 74-70-75-74—293 | 24,500 |
| | Brian Gay | 70-74-72-72—288 | 78.900 | | John Senden (AUS) | 76-72-72-73—293 | 24,500 |
| | Robert Karlsson (SWE) | 68-77-71-72—288 | 78.900 | | Mike Weir (CAN) | 73-75-71-74—293 | 24,500 |

## 2008 US PGA Championship *continued*

**Other players who made the cut:** Michael Allen, Charles Howell III, Billy Mayfair, Carl Petterson (SWE), Dean Wilson 294; Peter Hanson (SWE), John Merrick, Charl Schwartzel (RSA) 295; Tim Clark (RSA), Anthony Kim, James Kingston (RSA) 296; Justin Leonard, Pat Perez 297; John Malinger, Steve Marino, Chez Reavie 298; Paul Azinger, Mark Calcavecchia, Niclas Fasth (SWE), Corey Pavin, Kevin Sutherland 299; Hiroyuki Fujita (JPN), Peter Lonard (AUS) 300; Bubba Watson 301; Richard Green (AUS), 303; Rocco Mediate 304; Louis Oosthuizen (RSA) 306

---

# 2007 US PGA Championship *Southern Hills, Tulsa, OK*  August 9–12                [7131–70]

Prize money: $7 million. Field of 156, of whom 72 made the half-way cut.

| | | | | | | | | |
|---|---|---|---|---|---|---|---|---|
| 1 | Tiger Woods | | 71-63-69-69—272 | $1,260,000 | 23T | Peter Hanson (SWE) | 72-71-69-73—285 | 51,000 |
| 2 | Woody Austin | | 68-70-69-67—274 | 756,000 | | Kenny Perry | 72-72-71-70—285 | 51,000 |
| 3 | Ernie Els (RSA) | | 72-68-69-66—275 | 476,000 | | Ian Poulter (ENG) | 71-73-70-71—285 | 51,000 |
| 4 | Arron Oberholser | | 68-72-70-69—279 | 308,000 | | Heath Slocum | 72-70-72-71—285 | 51,000 |
| | John Senden (AUS) | | 69-70-69-71—279 | 308,000 | | Steve Stricker | 77-68-69-71—285 | 51,000 |
| 6 | Simon Dyson (ENG) | | 73-71-72-64—280 | 227,500 | | Camilo Villegas (COL) | 69-71-74-71—285 | 51,000 |
| | Trevor Immelman (RSA) | | 75-70-66-69—280 | 227,500 | 32 | Brad Bryant | 74-70-72-70—286 | 34,750 |
| | Geoff Ogilvy (AUS) | | 69-68-74-69—280 | 227,500 | | Stewart Cink | 72-70-72-72—286 | 34,750 |
| 9 | Kevin Sutherland | | 73-69-68-71—281 | 170,333 | | John Daly | 67-73-73-73—286 | 34,750 |
| | Scott Verplank | | 70-66-74-71—281 | 170,333 | | Luke Donald (ENG) | 72-71-70-73—286 | 34,750 |
| | Boo Weekley | | 76-69-65-71—281 | 170,333 | | Shaun Micheel | 73-71-70-72—286 | 34,750 |
| 12 | Stephen Ames (CAN) | | 68-69-69-76—282 | 119,833 | | Phil Mickelson | 73-69-75-69—286 | 34,750 |
| | Stuart Appleby (AUS) | | 73-68-72-69—282 | 119,833 | | Lee Westwood (ENG) | 69-74-75-68—286 | 34,750 |
| | K J Choi (KOR) | | 71-71-68-72—282 | 119,833 | | Brett Wetterich | 74-71-70-71—286 | 34,750 |
| | Anders Hansen (DEN) | | 71-71-71-69—282 | 119,833 | 40 | Paul Casey (ENG) | 72-70-74-71—287 | 27,350 |
| | Justin Rose (ENG) | | 70-73-70-69—282 | 119,833 | | Richard Green (AUS) | 72-73-70-72—287 | 27,350 |
| | Adam Scott (AUS) | | 72-68-70-72—282 | 119,833 | 42 | Darren Clarke (NIR) | 77-66-71-74—288 | 20,850 |
| 18 | Ken Duke | | 73-71-69-71—284 | 81,600 | | Niclas Fasth (SWE) | 71-68-79-70—288 | 20,850 |
| | Joe Durant | | 71-73-70-70—284 | 81,600 | | Padraig Harrington (IRL) | 69-73-72-74—288 | 20,850 |
| | Hunter Mahan | | 71-73-72-68—284 | 81,600 | | Charles Howell III | 75-70-72-71—288 | 20,850 |
| | Pat Perez | | 70-69-77-68—284 | 81,600 | | Colin Montgomerie (SCO) | 72-73-73-70—288 | 20,850 |
| | Brandt Snedeker | | 74-71-69-70—284 | 81,600 | | Sean O'Hair | 70-72-70-76—288 | 20,850 |
| 23 | Steve Flesch | | 72-73-68-72—285 | 51,000 | | Rod Pampling (AUS) | 70-74-72-72—288 | 20,850 |
| | Retief Goosen (RSA) | | 70-71-74-70—285 | 51,000 | | David Toms | 71-74-71-72—288 | 20,850 |
| | Nathan Green (AUS) | | 75-68-67-75—285 | 51,000 | | | | |

---

**Other players who made the cut:** Brian Bateman, Lucas Glover, Frank Lickliter II, Shingo Katayama (JPN), Anthony Kim, Nick O'Hern, Bob Tway 289; Chad Campbell, Robert Karlsson (SWE), Will MacKenzie 290; Billy Mayfair, Paul McGinley (IRL) 291; Thomas Bjørn (DEN), Corey Pavin, Brett Quigley, Graeme Storm (ENG) 293; Todd Hamilton, Tim Herron, Troy Matteson 294; Tom Lehman, Mike Small 296; Ryan Benzel 297; Sergio García (ESP) DQ

**Links** – originating from the from the Scottish word *lynkis* (ridges, hummocks). Originally applied to rough, open, typically treeless and gorse-covered low-lying land on the east coast of the Lowlands. From the Middle Ages such land was decreed common land and used for sports that included bowls, archery and golf.

*Dictionary of Golfing Terms*

## 2006 US PGA Championship Medinah, II August 16–20    [7561–72]

Prize money: $6.5 million. Field of 156, of whom 70 made the half-way cut.

| | | | | | | | |
|---|---|---|---|---|---|---|---|
| 1 | Tiger Woods | 69-68-65-68—270 | $1,224,000 | 24 | Chad Campbell | 71-72-75-66—284 | 53,100 |
| 2 | Shaun Micheel | 69-70-67-69—275 | 734,400 | | Stewart Cink | 68-74-73-69—284 | 53,100 |
| 3 | Luke Donald (ENG) | 68-68-66-74—276 | 353,600 | | Tim Clark (RSA) | 70-69-75-70—284 | 53,100 |
| | Sergio García (ESP) | 69-70-67-70—276 | 353,600 | | Steve Flesch | 72-71-69-72—284 | 53,100 |
| | Adam Scott (AUS) | 71-69-69-67—276 | 353,600 | | Anders Hansen (DEN) | 72-71-70-71—284 | 53,100 |
| 6 | Mike Weir (CAN) | 72-67-65-73—277 | 244,800 | 29 | Jim Furyk | 70-72-69-74—285 | 41,100 |
| 7 | K J Choi (KOR) | 73-67-67-71—278 | 207,787 | | Robert Karlsson (SWE) | 71-73-69-72—285 | 41,100 |
| | Steve Stricker | 72-67-70-69—278 | 207,787 | | Heath Slocum | 73-70-72-70—285 | 41,100 |
| 9 | Ryan Moore | 71-72-67-69—279 | 165,000 | | Lee Westwood (ENG) | 69-72-71-73—285 | 41,100 |
| | Geoff Ogilvy (AUS) | 69-68-68-74—279 | 165,000 | | Dean Wilson | 74-70-74-67—285 | 41,100 |
| | Ian Poulter (ENG) | 70-70-68-71—279 | 165,000 | 34 | Retief Goosen (RSA) | 70-73-68-75—286 | 34,500 |
| 12 | Chris DiMarco | 71-70-67-72—280 | 134,500 | | Trevor Immelman (RSA) | 73-71-70-72—286 | 34,500 |
| | Sean O'Hair | 72-70-70-68—280 | 134,500 | | Davis Love III | 68-69-73-76—286 | 34,500 |
| 14 | Tim Herron | 69-67-72-73—281 | 115,000 | 37 | Richard Green (AUS) | 73-69-73-72—287 | 29,250 |
| | Henrik Stenson (SWE) | 68-68-73-72—281 | 115,000 | | J B Holmes | 71-70-68-78—287 | 29,250 |
| 16 | Woody Austin | 71-69-69-73—282 | 94,000 | | Graeme McDowell | 75-68-72-72—287 | 29,250 |
| | Ernie Els (RSA) | 71-70-72-69—282 | 94,000 | | (NIR) | | |
| | Phil Mickelson | 69-71-68-74—282 | 94,000 | | Billy Mayfair | 69-69-73-76—287 | 29,250 |
| | David Toms | 71-67-71-73—282 | 94,000 | 41 | Billy Andrade | 67-69-78-74—288 | 23,080 |
| 20 | Robert Allenby (AUS) | 68-74-71-70—283 | 71,250 | | Daniel Chopra (SWE) | 72-67-76-73—288 | 23,080 |
| | Jonathan Byrd | 69-72-74-68—283 | 71,250 | | J J Henry | 68-73-73-74—288 | 23,080 |
| | Harrison Fraser | 69-72-69-73—283 | 71,250 | | Chris Riley | 66-72-73-77—288 | 23,080 |
| | Fred Funk | 69-69-74-71—283 | 71,250 | | Justin Rose (ENG) | 73-70-70-75—288 | 23,080 |

**Other players who made the cut:** Olin Browne, Lucas Glover 289; Jerry Kelly 290; Rich Beem, Nathan Green (AUS), Ryan Palmer, Corey Pavin, Kenny Perry, Joey Sindelar 291; Stephen Ames (CAN), Stuart Appleby (AUS), Aaron Baddeley (AUS), José-María Olazábal (ESP), Hideto Tanihara (JPN) 292; Ben Curtis, Steve Lowery 293; Jason Gore, Jeff Maggert, Charles Warren 295; Miguel Angel Jiménez (ESP), Bob Tway 296; David Howell (ENG) 297; Jay Haas, Don Yrene 300; Jim Kane 301

## 2005 US PGA Championship Baltusrol, NJ August 11–15    [7392–70]

Prize money: $6.25 million. Field of 156, of whom 79 made the half-way cut.

| | | | | | | | |
|---|---|---|---|---|---|---|---|
| 1 | Phil Mickelson | 67-65-72-72—276 | $1,700,00 | 23T | Shingo Katayama (JPN) | 71-66-74-72—283 | 56,400 |
| 2 | Thomas Bjørn (DEN) | 71-71-63-72—277 | 572,000 | | Paul McGinley (IRL) | 72-70-72-69—283 | 564,00 |
| | Steve Elkington (AUS) | 68-70-68-71—277 | 572,000 | | Tom Pernice Jr | 69-73-69-72—283 | 56,400 |
| 4 | Davis Love III | 68-68-68-74—278 | 286,000 | | Kenny Perry | 69-70-70-74—283 | 56,400 |
| | Tiger Woods | 75-69-66-68—278 | 286,000 | 28 | Chad Campbell | 71-71-70-72—284 | 41,500 |
| 6 | Michael Campbell | 73-68-69-69—279 | 201,500 | | Stewart Cink | 71-72-66-75—284 | 41,500 |
| | (NZL) | | | | Bob Estes | 71-72-73-68—284 | 41,500 |
| | Retief Goosen (RSA) | 68-70-69-72—279 | 201,500 | | Arron Oberholser | 74-68-69-73—284 | 41,500 |
| | Geoff Ogilvy (AUS) | 69-69-72-69—279 | 201,500 | | Jesper Parnevik (SWE) | 68-69-72-75—284 | 41,500 |
| | Pat Perez | 68-71-67-73—279 | 201,500 | | Vaughn Taylor | 75-69-71-69—284 | 41,500 |
| 10 | Steve Flesch | 70-71-69-70—280 | 131,800 | 34 | Jason Bohn | 71-68-68-78—285 | 31,917 |
| | Dudley Hart | 70-73-66-71—280 | 131,800 | | Ben Curtis | 67-73-67-78—285 | 31,917 |
| | Ted Purdy | 69-75-70-66—280 | 131,800 | | Jim Furyk | 72-71-70-72—285 | 31,917 |
| | Vijay Singh (FIJ) | 70-67-69-74—280 | 131,800 | | Fredrik Jacobson (SWE) | 72-69-73-71—285 | 31,917 |
| | David Toms | 71-72-69-68—280 | 131,800 | | Jerry Kelly | 70-65-74-76—285 | 31,917 |
| 15 | Stuart Appleby (AUS) | 67-70-69-75—281 | 102,500 | | Scott Verplank | 71-72-71-71—285 | 31,917 |
| | Charles Howell III | 70-71-68-72—281 | 102,500 | 40 | K J Choi (KOR) | 71-70-73-72—286 | 22,300 |
| 17 | Tim Clark (RSA) | 71-73-70-68—282 | 82,500 | | Ben Crane | 68-76-72-70—286 | 22,300 |
| | Trevor Immelman (RSA) | 67-72-72-71—282 | 82,500 | | Miguel Angel Jiménez | 72-72-69-73—286 | 22,300 |
| | Jack Johnson | 70-70-73-69—282 | 82,500 | | (ESP) | | |
| | Joe Ogilvie | 74-68-69-71—282 | 82,500 | | John Rollins | 68-71-73-74—286 | 22,300 |
| | Bo Van Pelt | 70-70-68-74—282 | 82,500 | | Steve Schneiter (CAN) | 72-72-69-73—286 | 22,300 |
| | Lee Westwood (ENG) | 68-68-71-75—282 | 82,500 | | Adam Scott (AUS) | 74-69-72-71—286 | 22,300 |
| 23 | Sergio García (ESP) | 72-70-71-70—283 | 56,400 | | Patrick Sheehan | 73-71-71-71—286 | 22,300 |

**Other players who made the cut:** Fred Funk, Todd Hamilton, Bernhard Langer (GER), JL Lewis, José María Olazábal (ESP), Greg Owen (ENG), Ryan Palmer, Ian Poulter (ENG), Heath Slocum, Henrik Stenson (SWE), Mike Wier (CAN) 287; Paul Casey (ENG), Carlos Franco (PAR), Peter Hanson (SWE), Mark Hensby (AUS), Scott McCarron, Sean O'Hair, Steve Webster (ENG) 288; Woody Austin, Luke Donald (ENG), Ron Philo Jr, Chris Riley 289; Mark Calcavecchia, Fred Couples 290; Stephen Ames (CAN), Joe Durant 291; John Daly, Rory Sabbatini (RSA) 292; Mike Small 295; Kevin Sutherland 296; Darrell Kestner 299; Hal Sutton 300

## 2004 US PGA Championship Whistling Straits, Kohler, WI  August 12–15   [7514–72]

Prize money: $6.25 million. Field of 155, of whom 73 made the half-way cut.

| | | | |
|---|---|---|---|
| 1 | Vijay Singh (FIJ)* | 67-68-69-76—280 | $1,125,000 |
| 2 | Justin Leonard | 66-69-70-75—280 | 550,000 |
| | Chris DiMarco | 68-70-71-71—280 | 550,000 |

*Three hole play-off: Singh 3-3-4; Leonard 4-3-4; DiMarco 4-3-4

| | | | |
|---|---|---|---|
| 4 | Ernie Els (RSA) | 66-70-72-73—281 | 267,500 |
| | Chris Riley | 69-70-69-73—281 | 267,500 |
| 6 | K J Choi (KOR) | 68-71-73-70—282 | 196,000 |
| | Paul McGinley (IRL) | 69-74-70-69—282 | 196,000 |
| | Phil Mickelson | 69-72-67-74—282 | 196,000 |
| 9 | Robert Allenby (AUS) | 71-70-72-70—283 | 152,000 |
| | Stephen Ames (CAN) | 68-71-69-75—283 | 152,000 |
| | Ben Crane | 70-74-69-70—283 | 152,000 |
| | Adam Scott (AUS) | 71-71-69-72—283 | 152,000 |
| 13 | Darren Clarke (NIR) | 65-71-72-76—284 | 110,250 |
| | Brian Davis (ENG) | 66-70-74-74—284 | 110,250 |
| | Brad Faxon | 71-71-70-72—284 | 110,250 |
| | Arron Oberholser | 73-71-70-70—284 | 110,250 |
| 17 | Stuart Appleby (AUS) | 68-75-72-70—285 | 76,857 |
| | Stewart Cink | 73-70-70-72—285 | 76,857 |
| | Matt Gogel | 71-71-69-74—285 | 76,857 |
| | Fredrik Jacobson (SWE) | 72-70-70-73—285 | 76,857 |
| | Jean-François Remesy (FRA) | 72-71-70-72—285 | 76,857 |
| | Loren Roberts | 68-72-70-75—285 | 76,857 |

| | | | |
|---|---|---|---|
| 17T | David Toms | 72-72-69-72—285 | 76,857 |
| 24 | Tom Byrum | 72-73-71-70—286 | 46,714 |
| | Chad Campbell | 73-70-71-72—286 | 46,714 |
| | Luke Donald (ENG) | 67-73-71-75—286 | 46,714 |
| | JL Lewis | 73-69-72-72—286 | 46,714 |
| | Shaun Micheel | 77-68-70-71—286 | 46,714 |
| | Geoff Ogilvy (AUS) | 68-73-71-74—286 | 46,714 |
| | Tiger Woods | 75-69-69-73—286 | 46,714 |
| 31 | Carlos Daniel Franco (PAR) | 69-75-72-71—287 | 34,250 |
| | Charles Howell III | 70-71-72-74—287 | 34,250 |
| | Miguel Angel Jiménez (ESP) | 76-65-75-71—287 | 34,250 |
| | Nick O'Hern (AUS) | 73-71-68-75—287 | 34,250 |
| | Chip Sullivan | 72-71-73-71—287 | 34,250 |
| | Bo Van Pelt | 74-71-70-72—287 | 34,250 |
| 37 | Briny Baird | 67-69-75-77—288 | 24,687 |
| | Steve Flesch | 73-72-67-76—288 | 24,687 |
| | Jay Haas | 68-72-71-77—288 | 24,687 |
| | Todd Hamilton | 72-73-75-68—288 | 24,687 |
| | Trevor Immelman (RSA) | 75-69-72-72—288 | 24,687 |
| | Zach Johnson | 75-70-69-74—288 | 24,687 |
| | Ian Poulter (ENG) | 73-72-70-73—288 | 24,687 |
| | Brett Quigley | 74-69-73-72—288 | 24,687 |

**Other players who made the cut:** Tommy Armour III, Niclas Fasth (SWE), Padraig Harrington (IRL), David Howell (ENG) 289; Michael Campbell (NZL), Nick Faldo (ENG), Joe Ogilvie, Patrick Sheehan, Duffy Waldorf 290; Carl Pettersson (SWE) 291; Paul Azinger, S K Ho (KOR), Rod Pampling (AUS), Craig Parry (AUS), Eduardo Romero (ARG), Hidemichi Tanaka (JPN), Bob Tway 292; Woody Austin, Shingo Katayama (JPN), Jeff Sluman, Scott Verplank 293; Scott Drummond (SCO), Bernhard Langer (GER) 294; Robert Gamez, Mark Hensby (AUS) 296; Colin Montgomerie (SCO) 297; Roy Biancalana 299; Jeff Coston 301; Skip Kendall 304

## Play-off history

Jason Dufner's victory was fitting compensation for his narrow defeat just two years ago when he was defeated by Keegan Bradley at the first extra play-off hole. Since the Championship's inauguration in 1916 there have been 17 other play-offs:

Match Play

1923   Gene Sarazen defeated Walter Hagen, 1-up, 38 holes

1934   Paul Runyan defeated Craig Wood, 1-up, 38 holes

1937   Denny Shute defeated Harold "Jug" McSpaden, 1-up, 37 holes

1939   Henry Picard defeated Byron Nelson, 1-up, 37 holes

1941   Vic Ghezzi defeated Byron Nelson, 1-up, 38 holes

Changed to Stroke Play in 1958

1961   Jerry Barber defeated Don January, 67 to 68, in an 18-hole playoff

1967   Don January defeated Don Massengale, 69 to 71, in an 18-hole playoff

1977   Lanny Wadkins defeated Gene Littler at the third extra hole

1978   John Mahaffey defeated Jerry Pate and Tom Watson at the second extra hole

1979   David Graham defeated Ben Crenshaw at the the third extra hole

1987   Larry Nelson defeated Lanny Wadkins at the first extra hole

1993   Paul Azinger defeated Greg Norman at the second extra hole

1995   Steve Elkington defeated Colin Montgomerie at the first extra hole

1996   Mark Brooks defeated Kenny Perry at the first extra hole

2000   Tiger Woods defeated Bob May in the first three-hole aggregate score play-off in major and PGA Championship history

2004   Vijay Singh defeated Chris DiMarco and Justin Leonard in a three-hole aggregate score play-off

2010   Martin Kaymer defeated Bubba Watson in a three-hole aggregate score play-off

# US PGA Championship History

| Date | Winner | Runner-up | Venue | By |
|------|--------|-----------|-------|-----|
| 1916 Oct 8–14 | J Barnes | J Hutchison | Siwanoy, NY | 1 hole |
| 1919 Sept 15–20 | J Barnes | F McLeod | Engineers' Club, NY | 6 and 5 |
| 1920 Aug 17–21 | J Hutchison | D Edgar | Flossmoor, IL | 1 hole |
| 1921 Sept 26–Oct 1 | W Hagen | J Barnes | Inwood Club, NY | 3 and 2 |
| 1922 Aug 12–18 | G Sarazen | E French | Oakmont, PA | 4 and 3 |
| 1923 Sept 23–29 | G Sarazen | W Hagen | Pelham, NY | 38th hole |
| 1924 Sept 15–20 | W Hagen | J Barnes | French Lick, IN | 2 holes |
| 1925 Sept 21–26 | W Hagen | W Mehlhorn | Olympic Fields, IL | 6 and 4 |
| 1926 Sept 20–25 | W Hagen | L Diegel | Salisbury, NY | 4 and 3 |
| 1927 Oct 31–Nov 5 | W Hagen | J Turnesa | Dallas, TX | 1 hole |
| 1928 Oct 1–6 | L Diegel | A Espinosa | Five Farms, MD | 6 and 5 |
| 1929 Dec 2–7 | L Diegel | J Farrell | Hill Crest, CA | 6 and 4 |
| 1930 Sept 8–13 | T Armour | G Sarazen | Fresh Meadows, NY | 1 hole |
| 1931 Sept 7–14 | T Creavy | D Shute | Wannamoisett, RI | 2 and 1 |
| 1932 Aug 31–Sept 4 | O Dutra | F Walsh | St Paul, MN | 4 and 3 |
| 1933 Aug 8–13 | G Sarazen | W Goggin | Milwaukee, WI | 5 and 4 |
| 1934 July 24–29 | P Runyan | C Wood | Buffalo, NY | 38th hole |
| 1935 Oct 18–23 | J Revolta | T Armour | Oklahoma City, OK | 5 and 4 |
| 1936 Nov 17–22 | D Shute | J Thomson | Pinehurst, NC | 3 and 2 |
| 1937 May 26–30 | D Shute | H McSpaden | Pittsburgh, PA | 37th hole |
| 1938 July 10–16 | P Runyan | S Snead | Shawnee, PA | 8 and 7 |
| 1939 July 9–15 | H Picard | B Nelson | Pomonok, NY | 37th hole |
| 1940 Aug 26–Sept 2 | B Nelson | S Snead | Hershey, PA | 1 hole |
| 1941 July 7–13 | V Ghezzie | B Nelson | Denver, CO | 38th hole |
| 1942 May 23–31 | S Snead | J Turnesa | Atlantic City, NJ | 2 and 1 |
| 1943 No Championship | | | | |
| 1944 Aug 14–20 | B Hamilton | B Nelson | Spokane, WA | 1 hole |
| 1945 July 9–15 | B Nelson | S Byrd | Dayton, OH | 4 and 3 |
| 1946 Aug 19–25 | B Hogan | E Oliver | Portland, OR | 6 and 4 |
| 1947 June 18–24 | J Ferrier | C Harbert | Detroit, MI | 2 and 1 |
| 1948 May 19–25 | B Hogan | M Turnesa | Norwood Hills, MO | 7 and 6 |
| 1949 May 25–31 | S Snead | J Palmer | Richmond, VA | 3 and 2 |
| 1950 June 21–27 | C Harper | H Williams | Scioto, OH | 4 and 3 |
| 1951 June 27–July 3 | S Snead | W Burkemo | Oakmont, PA | 7 and 6 |
| 1952 June 18–25 | J Turnesa | C Harbert | Louisville, KY | 1 hole |
| 1953 July 1–7 | W Burkemo | F Lorza | Birmingham, MI | 2 and 1 |
| 1954 July 21–27 | C Harbert | W Burkemo | St Paul, MN | 4 and 3 |
| 1955 July 20–26 | D Ford | C Middlecoff | Meadowbrook, MI | 4 and 3 |
| 1956 July 20–24 | J Burke | T Kroll | Canton, MA | 3 and 2 |
| 1957 July 17–21 | L Hebert | D Finsterwald | Dayton, OH | 3 and 1 |

*Changed to stroke play in 1958*

| Date | Winner | Venue | Score | Date | Winner | Venue | Score |
|------|--------|-------|-------|------|--------|-------|-------|
| 1958 July 17–20 | D Finsterwald | Llanerch, PA | 276 | 1977 Aug 11–14 | L Wadkins* | Pebble Beach, CA | 287 |
| 1959 July 30–Aug 2 | B Rosburg | Minneapolis, MN | 277 | *After a play-off: Wadkins 4-4-3; G Littler 4-4-4 | | | |
| | | | | 1978 Aug 3–6 | J Mahaffey* | Oakmont, PA | 276 |
| 1960 July 21–24 | J Hebert | Firestone, Akron, OH | 281 | *After a play-off: Mahaffey 4-3; J Pate 4,4; T Watson 4-4 | | | |
| 1961 July 27–31 | J Barber* | Olympia Fields, IL | 277 | 1979 Aug 2–5 | D Graham (AUS)* | Oakland Hills, MI | 272 |
| *After a play-off: Barber 67, D January 68 | | | | | | | |
| | | | | *After a play-off: Graham 4-4-2; B Crenshaw 4-4-4 | | | |
| 1962 July 19–22 | G Player (RSA) | Aronimink, PA | 278 | 1980 Aug 7–10 | J Nicklaus | Oak Hill, NY | 274 |
| 1963 July 18–21 | J Nicklaus | Dallas, TX | 279 | 1981 Aug 6–9 | L Nelson | Atlanta, GA | 273 |
| 1964 July 16–19 | B Nichols | Columbus, OH | 271 | 1982 Aug 5–8 | R Floyd | Southern Hills, OK | 272 |
| 1965 July 18–21 | D Marr | Laurel Valley, PA | 280 | 1983 Aug 4–7 | H Sutton | Pacific Palisades, CA | 274 |
| 1966 July 21–24 | A Geiberger | Firestone, Akron, OH | 280 | 1984 Aug 16–19 | L Trevino | Shoal Creek, AL | 273 |
| 1967 July 20–24 | D January* | Columbine, CO | 281 | 1985 Aug 8–11 | H Green | Cherry Hills, Denver, CO | 278 |
| *After a play-off: January 69, D Massengale 71 | | | | | | | |
| 1968 July 18–21 | J Boros | Pecan Valley, TX | 281 | 1986 Aug 7–10 | R Tway | Inverness, Toledo, OH | 276 |
| 1969 Aug 14–17 | R Floyd | Dayton, OH | 276 | 1987 Aug 6–9 | L Nelson* | PGA National, FL | 287 |
| 1970 Aug 13–16 | D Stockton | Southern Hills, OK | 279 | *After a play-off: Nelson 4, L Wadkins 5 | | | |
| 1971 Feb 25–28 | J Nicklaus | PGA National, FL | 281 | 1988 Aug 11–14 | J Sluman | Oaktree, OK | 272 |
| 1972 Aug 3–6 | G Player (RSA) | Oakland Hills, MI | 281 | 1989 Aug 10–13 | P Stewart | Kemper Lakes, IL | 276 |
| 1973 Aug 9–12 | J Nicklaus | Canterbury, OH | 277 | 1990 Aug 9–12 | W Grady (AUS) | Shoal Creek, AL | 282 |
| 1974 Aug 8–11 | L Trevino | Tanglewood, NC | 276 | 1991 Aug 8–11 | J Daly | Crooked Stick, IN | 276 |
| 1975 Aug 7–10 | J Nicklaus | Firestone, Akron, OH | 276 | 1992 Aug 13–16 | N Price (ZIM) | Bellerive, MS | 278 |
| 1976 Aug 12–16 | D Stockton | Congressional, MD | 281 | | | | |

## US PGA Championship history *continued*

| Winner | | Venue | Score | Date |
|---|---|---|---|---|
| 1993 Aug 12–15 | P Azinger* | Inverness, Toledo, OH | 272 | |
| *After a play-off: Azinger 4-4, G Norman 4-5* | | | | |
| 1994 Aug 11–14 | N Price (ZIM) | Southern Hills, OK | 269 | |
| 1995 Aug 10–13 | S Elkington (AUS)* | Riviera, LA | 267 | |
| *After a play-off: Elkington 3, C Montgomerie 4* | | | | |
| 1996 Aug 8–11 | M Brooks* | Valhalla, Louisville, KY | 277 | |
| *After a play-off against Kenny Perry: Brooks 4, Perry 5* | | | | |
| 1997 Aug 14–17 | D Love III | Winged Foot, NY | 269 | |
| 1998 Aug 13–16 | V Singh (FIJ) | Sahalee, Seattle, WA | 271 | |
| 1999 Aug 12–15 | T Woods | Medinah, IL | 277 | |
| 2000 Aug 17–20 | T Woods* | Valhalla, Louisville, KY | 270 | |
| *After a play-off: Woods 3,4,5, B May 4,4,5* | | | | |
| 2001 Aug 16–19 | D Toms | Atlanta Athletic Club, GA | 265 | |
| 2002 Aug 15–18 | R Beem | Hazeltine National, MN | 278 | |

| Winner | | Venue | Score | Date |
|---|---|---|---|---|
| 2003 Aug 14–17 | S Micheel | Oak Hill, NY | 276 | |
| 2004 Aug 12–15 | V Singh (FIJ)* | Whistling Straits, WI | 280 | |
| *After a play-off: Singh 3,3,4, C DiMarco 4,3,4, J Leonard 4,3,4* | | | | |
| 2005 Aug 11–15 | P Mickelson | Baltusrol, NJ | 276 | |
| 2006 Aug 16–20 | T Woods | Medinah, IL | 270 | |
| 2007 Aug 9–12 | T Woods | Southern Hills, OK | 272 | |
| 2008 Aug 7–10 | P Harrington | Oakland Hills, MI | 277 | |
| 2009 Aug 14–16 | Y E Yang | Hazeltine, Chaska, MN | 280 | |
| 2010 Aug 12–15 | M Kaymer* | Whistling Straits, WI | 277 | |
| *After a play-off: Kaymer 4,2,5, B Watson 3,3,6* | | | | |
| 2011 Aug 11–14 | K Bradley* | Atlanta Athletic Club, GA | 272 | |
| *After a play-off: Bradley 3,3,4, J Dufner 4,4,3* | | | | |
| 2012 Aug 9–12 | R McIlroy | Kiawah Island, SC | 275 | |
| 2013 Aug 8–11 | J Dufner | Oak Hill, NY | 270 | |

## How Oak Hill played during the US PGA Championship

The two toughest holes in the 2013 US PGA Championship were the last two – par 4's that played well over their rating in the Championship. Even Jason Dufner, the winner, was four over for these two holes. Oak Hill's two par 5's were the easiest. During the week the field scored 11 eagles, 1,295 birdies. 5,023 pars, 1,689 bogeys 224 double bogeys and there were 33 scores worse than that 13 of them at the par 4 fifth.

| Hole | Rank | Yards | Par | Average |
|---|---|---|---|---|
| 1 | 7 | 460 yds | 4 | 4.20 |
| 2 | 11 | 401 yds | 4 | 4.02 |
| 3 | 9 | 214 yds | 3 | 3.16 |
| 4 | 18 | 570 yds | 5 | 4.78 |
| 5 | 5 | 428 yds | 4 | 4.22 |
| 6 | 14 | 175 yds | 3 | 3.00 |
| 7 | 3 | 461 yds | 4 | 4.32 |
| 8 | 13 | 428 yds | 4 | 4.01 |
| 9 | 8 | 452 yds | 4 | 4.19 |
| 10 | 10 | 429 yds | 4 | 4.07 |
| 11 | 6 | 226 yds | 3 | 3.21 |
| 12 | 15 | 372 yds | 4 | 3.95 |
| 13 | 17 | 598 yds | 5 | 4.89 |
| 14 | 16 | 323 yds | 4 | 3.89 |
| 15 | 4 | 181 yds | 3 | 3.25 |
| 16 | 12 | 439 yds | 4 | 4.01 |
| 17 | 1 | 509 yds | 4 | 4.41 |
| 18 | 2 | 497 yds | 4 | 4.34 |
| Total | | 7,163 yds | 70 | 71.99 |

# Men's Grand Slam Titles

Jack Nicklaus

Tiger Woods

Walter Hagen

The modern Grand Slam comprises four events – the British and US Open Championships, the US PGA Championship and The Masters Tournament at Augusta.

|  | Open | US Open | Masters | US PGA | Total Titles |
|---|---|---|---|---|---|
| Jack Nicklaus (USA) | 3 | 4 | 6 | 5 | 18 |
| Tiger Woods (USA) | 3 | 3 | 4 | 4 | 14 |
| Walter Hagen (USA) | 4 | 2 | 0 | 5 | 11 |
| Ben Hogan (USA) | 1 | 4 | 2 | 2 | 9 |
| Gary Player (RSA) | 3 | 1 | 3 | 2 | 9 |
| Tom Watson (USA) | 5 | 1 | 2 | 0 | 8 |
| Arnold Palmer (USA) | 2 | 1 | 4 | 0 | 7 |
| Gene Sarazen (USA) | 1 | 2 | 1 | 3 | 7 |
| Sam Snead (USA) | 1 | 0 | 3 | 3 | 7 |
| Lee Trevino (USA) | 2 | 2 | 0 | 2 | 6 |
| Nick Faldo (ENG) | 3 | 0 | 3 | 0 | 6 |

The original Grand Slam comprised the British and US Open Championships and the British and US Amateur Championships.

|  | Open | US Open | Amateur | US Amateur | Total Titles |
|---|---|---|---|---|---|
| Bobby Jones (USA) | 3 | 4 | 1 | 5 | 13 |
| John Ball (ENG) | 1 | 0 | 8 | 0 | 9 |
| Harold Hilton (ENG) | 2 | 0 | 4 | 1 | 7 |
| Harry Vardon (ENG) | 6 | 1 | 0 | 0 | 7 |

Note: Tiger Woods won three consecutive US Amateur Championships in 1994, 1995 and 1996. Only Bobby Jones has won all four recognised Grand Slam events in the same year – 1930.

# How the holes played at The Open Championship

The three par 5's at Muirfield were the easiest holes on the course. The toughest hole was the eighth and the easiest the ninth. During the Championship the players scored 38 eagles – 35 of them on the par 5's – 1,134 birdies, 4,972 pars, 2,041 bogeys, 322 double bogeys and there were 56 scores higher than that during the week.

| Hole | Rank | Yards | Par | Average |
|------|------|-------|-----|---------|
| 1 | 9 | 447 yds | 4 | 4.31 |
| 2 | 15 | 364 yds | 4 | 4.01 |
| 3 | 13 | 377 yds | 4 | 4.06 |
| 4 | 2 | 226 yds | 3 | 3.39 |
| 5 | 17 | 559 yds | 5 | 4.78 |
| 6 | 3 | 461 yds | 4 | 4.39 |
| 7 | 11 | 184 yds | 3 | 3.10 |
| 8 | 1 | 441 yds | 4 | 4.40 |
| 9 | 18 | 554 yds | 5 | 4.71 |
| 10 | 6 | 469 yds | 4 | 4.37 |
| 11 | 12 | 387 yds | 4 | 4.07 |
| 12 | 14 | 379 yds | 4 | 4.06 |
| 13 | 10 | 190 yds | 3 | 3.28 |
| 14 | 5 | 475 yds | 4 | 4.38 |
| 15 | 6 | 448 yds | 4 | 4.37 |
| 16 | 8 | 186 yds | 3 | 3.36 |
| 17 | 16 | 575 yds | 5 | 4.97 |
| 18 | 4 | 470 yds | 4 | 4.38 |
| Total | | 7,192 yds | 71 | 74.47 |

# How Augusta played during the 2013 Masters

During the Masters the field scored 35 eagles, 967 birdies, 3,249 pars, 1,145 bogeys 129 double bogeys and there were 19 hole scores recorded which were higher than that – 15 of them on the back nine. Par was 72 and the average score 73.41. The toughest hole was the short fourth and the easiest the par 5 15th. The par 5's at Augusta were the four easiest holes on the course.

| Hole | Rank | Yards | Par | Average |
|------|------|-------|-----|---------|
| 1 | 2 | 445 yds | 4 | 4.29 |
| 2 | 16 | 575 yds | 5 | 4.71 |
| 3 | 14 | 350 yds | 4 | 4.00 |
| 4 | 1 | 240 yds | 3 | 3.38 |
| 5 | 5 | 455 yds | 4 | 4.22 |
| 6 | 10 | 180 yds | 3 | 3.10 |
| 7 | 4 | 450 yds | 4 | 4.24 |
| 8 | 17 | 570 yds | 5 | 4.67 |
| 9 | 11 | 460 yds | 4 | 4.10 |
| 10 | 8 | 495 yds | 4 | 4.20 |
| 11 | 3 | 505 yds | 4 | 4.27 |
| 12 | 7 | 155yds | 3 | 3.21 |
| 13 | 15 | 510 yds | 5 | 4.75 |
| 14 | 12 | 440 yds | 4 | 4.10 |
| 15 | 18 | 530 yds | 5 | 4.63 |
| 16 | 13 | 170 yds | 3 | 3.05 |
| 17 | 6 | 440 yds | 4 | 4.22 |
| 18 | 9 | 465 yds | 4 | 4.18 |
| Total | | 7,435 yds | 72 | 73.41 |

# Stacey Lewis inspired by the Old Course finishes strongly to take the British title

**Trailing Na Yeon Choi by three shots with six holes left to play at an enthralling staging of the Ricoh Women's British Open in St Andrews, Stacey Lewis won her second major reeling off three exquisite birdies in the last five holes of her final round to post a 72 and an eight under par winning total of 280.**

Eventually finishing two shots clear of Choi and her South Korean compatriot Hee Young Park, the 28-year-old American brought to a halt, or at least interrupted, the Asian dominance of women's championship golf which had lasted for ten consecutive majors. Savouring her first elite triumph since the Kraft Nabisco in 2011, Lewis made no secret either of her affection for the Home of Golf or how she was smitten by the Old Course.

"I guess it suits me," she said of St Andrews. "I felt so comfortable here. I felt like it was meant to be. When I came here for the Curtis Cup, instantly, I fell in love with the Old Course. I think it's more the history [of the place] than anything, just knowing all the great champions who have played here.  Golf started here. I mean, it's amazing to even think about it. I love this golf course more than I think any other links I've played."

In her final tournament as an amateur, Lewis had laid down a marker for her professional career in the summer of 2008 when she became the first, and, so far, only golfer, to claim all five points in the USA's 13–7 demolition of Great Britain and Ireland over the Old Course.

Lewis caught the eye that week in St Andrews with her composed demeanour and impressive shot-making, even grabbing the winning point with a 3 and 2 victory over Liz Bennett in the singles.

Fast forward five years and the player ranked second in the Rolex World Rankings had just walked onto the 72nd green in St Andrews after splitting the 18th fairway with a fine drive and, appropriately for a woman who grew  up in Houston but has an affinity for the Old Course, used the Texas wedge to putt some 25 feet past the hole from around 40 yards.

Eyeing up the long putt for birdie, Lewis' mind drifted back to the Curtis Cup. "I remembered one of my matches and the pin was in a similar place," she recalled. "I remembered having a putt back up the hill and leaving it short. Because you see the swale on the other side, you think it's downhill when it's actually back up the hill. So I had a little bit of knowledge there. The whole right half of the green doesn't break as much as you think. It's kind of a visual thing and I knew what that putt did. The hardest part was just getting it to the hole. Right off the face, it looked good, and it was pretty cool when it went in."

Although she wasn't to know it at the time, Lewis' previous birdie on the Road Hole proved to be the decisive strike in a closing flourish which secured the second major title of her career. In the fabled history of the 17th on the Old Course – think, for example, of Seve Ballesteros' six iron from the rough unhinging Tom Watson at The Open in 1984 – Lewis' five iron from 170 yards, which soared low into the Fife sky before drawing into the green and finishing a couple of feet from the cup, simply added more lustre to the legend of the hole.

She knew the shot was special even before her head came up, feeling the vibration through the shaft of the club into her hands. "I hit the perfect golf shot," confided Lewis. "I mean, I saw the shot in my head, but to actually pull it off, when it counts: a shot like that doesn't happen very often. So I knew after I hit it close, I knew I had to make the putt. Somehow that putt was going to go in, because the shot was so good."

From the age of 11, Lewis wore back braces for 18 hours a day to help overcome scoliosis and correct the curvature in her spine. Eventually she underwent surgery which placed a titanium rod and screws in her back. The success of that procedure was evident in how this courageous young woman was able to play 36 holes on the final day in St Andrews and not feel so much as a twinge in her spine.

If the performance of the world No 2 was the only story in town on Sunday, it helped that the American had come into the Auld Grey Toun under the radar, so intense was the spotlight for most of the week on the hopes of Inbee Park becoming the first player, male or female, to win four consecutive professional majors in the same season. The global attention surrounding Park was sufficiently enthusiastic that her feats were described as not only a once in a lifetime opportunity for her but also for women's golf.

After ten holes of the first round, it seemed as if the remarkable South Korean was ready and willing to carry on where she left off in the three previous majors and march into history. At the top of the leaderboard on six under par after holing a five foot putt for birdie on the tenth green, it came as a jolt on the back nine to discover not even Park's hot putter could compensate for the issues caused by wayward driving. She dropped four shots, two bogeys and a double, between the 11th and the 17th before a birdie on the last enabled her to sign for 69, just three shots off the lead shared by Morgan Pressel and Camilla Lennarth.

> "I fell in love with the Old Course. It's knowing all the great champions played here."
>
> Stacey Lewis

Perhaps, understandably overwhelmed by the weight of expectancy and the caprice of links golf, Park was never again a factor in the winning of this championship. She posted further sores of 73, 74 and 78 to finish well down the field. Even her magnificent putting stroke deserted her in the final round when she four-putted the first green and needed her short stick to make 40 putts.

It was a humbling experience for the World No 1 who doubted if a similar opportunity would come along again any time soon. "I've done something amazing this season," she reflected, "winning three in a row. I don't know if I can do that again. That's going to be really tough. It might take a long time to beat that record. Obviously this week playing under all the pressure, that's one thing that I've learned about. You know, to go for four majors in a row and have everybody watching me, that felt a little bit weird. I even get to do an interview when I shoot six over par! But I think I'll always remember this moment. You know not many people get to experience something like this. I was the lucky one."

When the wind picked up during Friday's second round, no one dealt with the conditions more astutely than Choi, the winner of the US Women's Open in 2012.

She posted a five under score of 67 to build one stroke advantage over Japan's Miki Saiki, who shot the low round of the day with 66. What made Choi's performance notable was that she pieced her round together in the afternoon when the breeze was gusting around 30mph. Earlier in the week, she'd walked the course backwards from the 18th green to the first tee with a local St Andrews caddie and felt the preparation helped her to see the lines.

On Saturday, the wind blew stronger and only nine players completed their rounds before play was suspended for the day at 12.30. When the players returned early on Sunday to complete the third round, conditions were less taxing and Pressel, thanks to a 20 foot birdie putt on the last, shot 71 to lead by one shot over Lewis who forced her way back into contention with 69 as Choi ran up 74 to drop back. Scotland's Catriona Matthew also made a move thanks to a birdie, eagle finish for 68. Holing her approach shot from 67 yards on the last for two drew one of the biggest roars of the week for the North Berwick golfer.

Alas, Matthew's surge didn't last and she needed ten shots more in the afternoon for 78 and a level par total of 288, good enough only for a share of 11th place. The best score of the afternoon came from Cristie Kerr, who carded 69, while Natalie Gulbis' 70 took her into the top ten.

At the summit of the leaderboard, Lewis was the only player who finished in the first eight to match par. Even the champion, though, had to grind for victory during a roller-coaster final round when she matched five birdies with five bogeys. The American got off to a difficult start, dropping shots at the second and fourth holes before producing that blazing birdie, birdie denouement to follow Lorena Ochoa as a worthy winner of the Women's British Open in St Andrews.

Mike Aitken

| First Round | Second Round | Third Round | Fourth Round |
|---|---|---|---|
| −6 Morgan Pressel | −10 Na-Yeon Choi | −9 Morgan Pressel | −8 Stacy Lewis |
| −5 Stacy Lewis | −9 Miki Saiki | −8 Stacy Lewis | −6 Na-Yeon Choi |
| −5 Eun-Hee Ji | −8 Morgan Pressel | −7 Suzann Pettersen | −6 Hee-Young Park |
| −5 Sydney Michaels | −7 Suzann Pettersen | −7 Hee-Young Park | −5 Suzann Pettersen |
| −5 Ryann O'Toole | −7 Jee-Young Lee | −7 Miki Saiki | −5 Morgan Pressel |
| −5 Na-Yeon Choi | −7 Nicole Castrale | −7 Na-Yeon Choi | −3 Lizette Salas |
| −5 Nicole Castrale | −6 Mikaela Parmlid | −6 Catriona Matthew | −2 Mamiko Higa |
| −4 Catriona Matthew | −5 Stacy Lewis | −6 Meena Lee | −2 Miki Saiki |
| −4 Paula Creamer | −5 Angela Stanford | −5 Mamiko Higa | −1 Natalie Gulbis |
| −4 Georgia Hall | −5 Hee-Young Park | −4 Paula Creamer | −1 Nicole Castrale |

## Ricoh Women's British Open Championship

*St Andrews (Old Course)*    Aug 1–4    [6672–72]

Prize money: €1,920,130. Final field of 144 (6 amateurs), of whom 69 (3 amateurs) made the half-way cut on 145 or under.

**Final Qualifying at Kingsbarns Golf Links:**

| | | |
|---|---|---|
| 65 Xiyu Lin (CHN) | 68T Gabriella Cowley (ENG) | 68T Sahra Hassan (WAL) |
| 66 Emily Taylor (ENG) | (am) | 69 Louise Larsson (SWE) |
| Malene Jorgensen (DEN) | Daniela Holmqvist (SWE) | Tania Elosequi (ESP) |
| 67 Marta Silva (ESP) | Laura Diaz (USA) | Carly Booth (SCO) |
| Sydnee Michaels (USA) | Dori Carter (USA) | Camilla Lennarth (SWE) |
| 68 Amy Boulden (WAL) (am) | Margherita Rigon (ITA) | |

| | | | |
|---|---|---|---|
| 1 | Stacy Lewis (USA) | 67-72-69-72—280 | €302,982 |
| 2 | Hee Young Park (KOR) | 70-69-70-73—282 | 161,437 |
|  | Na Yeon Choi (KOR) | 67-67-75-73—282 | 161,437 |
| 4 | Suzann Pettersen (NOR) | 70-67-72-74—283 | 94,495 |
|  | Morgan Pressel (USA) | 66-70-71-76—283 | 94,495 |
| 6 | Lizette Salas (USA) | 68-72-72-73—285 | 74,203 |
| 7 | Mamiko Higa (JPN) | 70-69-72-75—286 | 63,759 |
|  | Miki Saiki (JPN) | 69-66-74-77—286 | 63,759 |
| 9 | Natalie Gulbis (USA) | 71-72-74-70—287 | 52,420 |
|  | Nicole Castrale (USA) | 67-70-76-74—287 | 52,420 |
| 11 | Meena Lee (KOR) | 71-69-70-78—288 | 38,235 |
|  | Anna Nordqvist (SWE) | 70-74-72-72—288 | 38,235 |
|  | Catriona Matthew (SCO) | 68-74-68-78—288 | 38,235 |
|  | Pernilla Lindberg (SWE) | 68-73-73-74—288 | 38,235 |
|  | Paula Creamer (USA) | 68-72-72-76—288 | 38,235 |
| 16 | Cristie Kerr (USA) | 71-74-75-69—289 | 29,840 |
| 17 | Xi Yu Lin (CHN) | 72-68-73-77—290 | 25,861 |
|  | Ayako Uehara (JPN) | 69-74-70-77—290 | 25,861 |
|  | Jenny Shin (KOR) | 69-71-74-76—290 | 25,861 |
|  | Angela Stanford (USA) | 69-70-76-75—290 | 25,861 |
|  | So Yeon Ryu (KOR) | 69-70-73-78—290 | 25,861 |
| 22 | Karine Icher (FRA) | 70-74-75-72—291 | 21,750 |
|  | Katherine Hull-Kirk (AUS) | 69-73-75-74—291 | 21,750 |
|  | Mariajo Uribe (COL) | 69-73-72-77—291 | 21,750 |
| 25 | Jessica Korda (USA) | 72-71-73-76—292 | 16,710 |
|  | Candie Kung (TPE) | 72-70-73-77—292 | 16,710 |
|  | Sun Young Yoo (KOR) | 71-71-72-78—292 | 16,710 |
|  | Lee-Anne Pace (RSA) | 70-71-72-79—292 | 16,710 |
|  | Shanshan Feng (CHN) | 69-76-76-71—292 | 16,710 |
|  | Hee-Kyung Seo (KOR) | 69-76-76-71—292 | 16,710 |
|  | Sandra Gal (GER) | 69-74-75-74—292 | 16,710 |
|  | Malene Jorgensen (DEN) | 69-74-75-74—292 | 16,710 |
|  | Dori Carter (USA) | 68-72-72-80—292 | 16,710 |
|  | Eun Hee Ji (KOR) | 67-75-72-78—292 | 16,710 |
|  | Ryann O'Toole (USA) | 67-73-73-79—292 | 16,710 |
| 36 | Gerina Piller (USA) | 74-69-77-73—293 | 12,433 |
|  | Jiyai Shin (KOR) | 71-72-77-73—293 | 12,433 |
|  | Holly Clyburn (ENG) | 70-73-75-75—293 | 12,433 |
|  | Jee Young Lee (KOR) | 70-67-77-79—293 | 12,433 |
|  | Marianne Skarpnord (NOR) | 69-74-75-75—293 | 12,433 |
|  | Mikaela Parmlid (SWE) | 69-69-75-80—293 | 12,433 |
| 42 | Lydia Ko (NZL) (am) | 69-76-75-74—294 | |
|  | Florentyna Parker (ENG) | 69-74-76-75—294 | 10,411 |
|  | Inbee Park (KOR) | 69-73-74-78—294 | 10,411 |
|  | Danielle Kang (USA) | 68-75-75-76—294 | 10,411 |
|  | Georgia Hall (ENG) (am) | 68-75-74-77—294 | |
| 47 | Christel Boeljon (NED) | 72-71-77-75—295 | 8,594 |

Ricoh Women's British Open Championship *continued*

| 47T | Minea Blomqvist (FIN) | 71-74-76-74—295 | 8,594 |
|---|---|---|---|
| | Se Ri Pak (KOR) | 71-73-75-76—295 | 8,594 |
| | Ashleigh Simon (RSA) | 71-72-75-77—295 | 8,594 |
| | I K Kim (KOR) | 70-73-75-77—295 | 8,594 |
| 52 | Moriya Jutanugarn (THA) | 72-73-79-72—296 | 6,564 |
| | Mi Jung Hur (KOR) | 72-72-78-74—296 | 6,564 |
| | Brittany Lincicome (USA) | 70-73-81-72—296 | 6,564 |
| | Sydnee Michaels (USA) | 67-75-79-75—296 | 6,564 |
| 56 | Michelle Wie (USA) | 74-70-78-75—297 | 5,172 |
| | Dewi Claire Schreefel (NED) | 73-71-80-73—297 | 5,172 |
| | Celine Boutier (FRA) (am) | 72-72-81-72—297 | |
| 59 | Mika Miyazato (JPN) | 74-71-80-74—299 | 4,575 |
| | Lindsey Wright (AUS) | 70-74-79-76—299 | 4,575 |
| | Linda Wessberg (SWE) | 70-73-78-78—299 | 4,575 |
| 62 | Line Vedel (NOR) | 72-71-80-77—300 | 4,177 |
| 63 | Gwladys Nocera (FRA) | 74-71-78-78—301 | 3,879 |
| | Liz Young (ENG) | 68-75-77-81—301 | 3,879 |
| 65 | Rikako Morita (JPN) | 70-75-86-71—302 | 3,580 |
| 66 | Thidapa Suwannapura (THA) | 71-74-83-75—303 | 3,282 |
| | Emily Taylor (ENG) | 70-74-82-77—303 | 3,282 |
| 68 | Sarah Kemp (AUS) | 73-71-78-86—308 | 2,065 |
| | Moira Dunn (USA) | 71-74-81-82—308 | 2,065 |

*The following players missed the cut:*

| | | | | | | |
|---|---|---|---|---|---|---|
| 70 | Yani Tseng (TPE) | 72-74—146 | | 104T | Karrie Webb (AUS) | 74-76—150 |
| | Belen Mozo (ESP) | 72-74—146 | | | Beth Allen (USA) | 74-76—150 |
| | Nontaya Srisawang (THA) | 71-75—146 | | | Austin Ernst (USA) | 74-76—150 |
| | Brittany Lang (USA) | 70-76—146 | | | Marta Silva Zamora (ESP) | 74-76—150 |
| | Katie Burnett (USA) | 69-77—146 | | | Juli Inkster (USA) | 73-77—150 |
| | Caroline Hedwall (SWE) | 69-77—146 | | | Kristy McPherson (USA) | 73-77—150 |
| 76 | Amy Yang (KOR) | 76-71—147 | | | Haeji Kang (KOR) | 73-77—150 |
| | Jennifer Rosales (PHI) | 73-74—147 | | | Katie Futcher (USA) | 72-78—150 |
| | Jacqui Concolino (USA) | 71-76—147 | | | Jeong Jang (KOR) | 72-78—150 |
| | Jane Park (USA) | 71-76—147 | | | Mina Harigae (USA) | 71-79—150 |
| | Alison Walshe (USA) | 71-76—147 | | | Amy Boulden (WAL) (am) | 70-80—150 |
| | Ji Young Oh (KOR) | 69-78—147 | | 119 | Carly Booth (SCO) | 78-73—151 |
| | Mi Jeong Jeon (KOR) | 67-80—147 | | | Nicole Hage (USA) | 75-76—151 |
| 83 | Charley Hull (ENG) | 76-72—148 | | | Nikki Campbell (AUS) | 75-76—151 |
| | Lisa McCloskey (USA) | 76-72—148 | | | Sarah-Jane Smith (AUS) | 75-76—151 |
| | Giulia Sergas (ITA) | 76-72—148 | | | Momoko Ueda (JPN) | 75-76—151 |
| | Mo Martin (USA) | 75-73—148 | | | Jennifer Johnson (USA) | 74-77—151 |
| | Margherita Rigon (ITA) | 73-75—148 | | | Stacey Keating (AUS) | 74-77—151 |
| | Azahara Muñoz (ESP) | 73-75—148 | | | Paolo Moreno (COL) | 72-79—151 |
| | Laura Davies (ENG) | 72-76—148 | | | Laura Diaz (USA) | 71-80—151 |
| | Julieta Granada (PAR) | 71-77—148 | | 128 | Lexi Thompson (USA) | 75-77—152 |
| | Irene Cho (USA) | 71-77—148 | | | Whitney Hagen (AUS) | 75-77—152 |
| | Chella Choi (KOR) | 71-77—148 | | | Christina Kim (USA) | 75-77—152 |
| | Ai Miyazato (JPN) | 69-79—148 | | | Amelia Lewis (USA) | 74-78—152 |
| | Camilla Lennarth (SWE) | 66-82—148 | | | Mindy Kim (KOR) | 73-79—152 |
| 95 | Jodi Ewart (ENG) | 76-73—149 | | 133 | Felicity Johnson (ENG) | 76-77—153 |
| | Il Hee Lee (KOR) | 76-73—149 | | | Chie Arimura (JPN) | 75-78—153 |
| | Louise Larsson (SWE) | 74-75—149 | | 135 | Beatriz Recari (ESP) | 78-76—154 |
| | Klara Spilkova (CZE) | 73-76—149 | | | Becky Morgan (WAL) | 76-78—154 |
| | Pornanong Phatlum (THA) | 72-77—149 | | | Tania Elosegui (ESP) | 75-79—154 |
| | Sophie Gustafson (SWE) | 72-77—149 | | | Sahra Hassan (WAL) | 74-80—154 |
| | Trish Johnson (ENG) | 72-77—149 | | 139 | Carlota Ciganda (ESP) | 74-81—155 |
| | Cindy Lacrosse (USA) | 72-77—149 | | | Helen Alfredsson (SWE) | 73-82—155 |
| | Daniela Holmqvist (SWE) | 71-78—149 | | | Veronica Zorzi (ITA) | 73-82—155 |
| 104 | Caroline Masson (GER) | 76-74—150 | | 142 | Gabriella Cowley (ENG) (am) | 75-81—156 |
| | Bree Arthur (AUS) | 75-75—150 | | 143 | Vicky Hurst (USA) | 77-82—159 |
| | Sakura Yokomine (JPN) | 74-76—150 | | | Sarah-Jane Boyd (ENG) (am) | 77-82—159 |
| | Karen Stupples (ENG) | 74-76—150 | | | | |

## 2012 Ricoh Women's British Open   Royal Liverpool   [6490–72]

Prize money: €1.920 million

| | | | | | | | | |
|---|---|---|---|---|---|---|---|---|
| I | Jiyai Shin (KOR) | 71-64-71-73—279 | €331,936 | 17T | Vicky Hurst (USA) | 71-72-79-75—297 | 28,338 |
| 2 | Inbee Park (KOR) | 72-68-72-76—288 | 208,079 | 23 | Lydia Hall (WAL) | 71-75-75-77—298 | 23,780 |
| 3 | Paula Creamer (USA) | 73-72-72-72—289 | 145,655 | | Juli Inkster (USA) | 79-69-72-78—298 | 23,780 |
| 4 | Mika Miyazato (JPN) | 71-70-72-77—290 | 113,948 | | Angela Stanford (USA) | 72-72-74-80—298 | 23,780 |
| 5 | So Yeon Ryu (KOR) | 70-74-71-76—291 | 87,195 | 26 | Hee-Kyung Seo (KOR) | 72-73-75-79—299 | 19,941 |
| | Karrie Webb (AUS) | 71-70-68-82—291 | 87,195 | | Amy Yang (KOR) | 73-72-75-79—299 | 19,941 |
| 7 | Julieta Granada (PAR) | 74-71-74-74—293 | 73,323 | | Beatriz Recari (ESP) | 72-77-73-77—299 | 19,941 |
| 8 | Stacy Lewis (USA) | 74-70-76-74—294 | 63,415 | | Holly Clyburn (ENG) (am) | 72-73-74-80—299 | |
| | Katie Futcher (USA) | 71-71-73-79—294 | 63,415 | | Yani Tseng (TPE) | 72-72-76-79—299 | 19,941 |
| 10 | In Kyung Kim (KOR) | 75-72-73-75—295 | 49,873 | | Yuki Ichinose (JPN) | 72-72-72-83—299 | 19,941 |
| | Chella Choi (KOR) | 72-73-72-78—295 | 49,873 | | Ai Miyazato (JPN) | 71-72-73-83—299 | 19,941 |
| | Catriona Matthew (SCO) | 76-73-71-75—295 | 49,873 | 33 | Bronte Law (ENG) (am) | 75-71-77-77—300 | |
| 13 | Na Yeon Choi (KOR) | 73-73-75-75—296 | 36,785 | | Karine Icher (FRA) | 75-72-76-77—300 | 16,596 |
| | Cindy Lacrosse (USA) | 73-75-72-76—296 | 36,785 | | Hee Young Park (KOR) | 78-71-76-75—300 | 16,596 |
| | Michelle Wie (USA) | 75-70-72-79—296 | 36,785 | | Line Vedel (NOR) | 80-69-74-77—300 | 16,596 |
| | Cristie Kerr (USA) | 72-73-74-77—296 | 36,785 | | Katherine Hull (AUS) | 72-72-77-79—300 | 16,596 |
| 17 | Carlota Ciganda (ESP) | 76-71-77-73—297 | 28,338 | 38 | Candie Kung (TPE) | 73-76-75-77—301 | 15,358 |
| | Lindsey Wright (AUS) | 76-72-75-74—297 | 28,338 | 39 | Jane Park (USA) | 74-72-78-78—302 | 14,119 |
| | Lexi Thompson (USA) | 74-75-76-72—297 | 28,338 | | Hee-Won Han (KOR) | 72-75-74-81—302 | 14,119 |
| | Jenny Shin (KOR) | 75-68-71-83—297 | 28,338 | | Erina Hara (JPN) | 75-73-77-77—302 | 14,119 |
| | Lydia Ko (NZL) (am) | 72-71-76-78—297 | | | Lee-Anne Pace (RSA) | 76-73-77-76—302 | 14,119 |

**Other players who made the cut:** Amy Hung (TPE), Morgan Pressel (USA), Carin Koch (SWE), Sarah-Jane Smith (USA) 303; Dewi Claire Schreefel (NED), Becky Morgan (WAL), Sun Young Yoo (KOR) 74-75-75-80—304, Stephanie Na (AUS), Haeji Kang (TPE), Jing Yan (CHN) (am) 304; Sydnee Michaels (USA), Eun Hee Ji (TPE) 305; Florentyna Parker (ENG) 306; Trish Johnson (ENG) 309; Mo Martin (USA) 312

## 2011 Ricoh Women's British Open   Carnoustie Links   [6490–72]

Prize money: €1.8 million

| | | | | | | | | |
|---|---|---|---|---|---|---|---|---|
| I | Yani Tseng (TPE) | 71-66-66-69—272 | €272,365 | 22 | Karen Stupples (ENG) | 74-68-72-71—285 | 18,394 |
| 2 | Brittany Lang (USA) | 70-70-69-67—276 | 170,736 | | Hee-Kyung Seo (KOR) | 72-71-71-71—285 | 18,394 |
| 3 | Sophie Gustafson (SWE) | 68-71-70-68—277 | 119,515 | | Karrie Webb (AUS) | 70-71-72-72—285 | 18,394 |
| 4 | Amy Yang (KOR) | 68-70-73-67—278 | 93,498 | | Rachel Jennings (ENG) | 71-73-69-72—285 | 18,394 |
| 5 | Catriona Matthew (SCO) | 70-69-68-72—279 | 71,546 | | Momoko Ueda (JPN) | 69-71-72-73—285 | 18,394 |
| | Caroline Masson (GER) | 68-65-68-78—279 | 71,546 | | Angela Stanford (USA) | 68-72-72-73—285 | 18,394 |
| 7 | Sun Young Yoo (KOR) | 71-70-69-70—280 | 52,236 | 28 | Michelle Wie (USA) | 74-68-72-72—286 | 15,752 |
| | Anna Nordqvist (SWE) | 70-71-69-70—280 | 52,236 | | Vicky Hurst (USA) | 70-71-71-74—286 | 15,752 |
| | Na Yeon Choi (KOR) | 69-67-72-72—280 | 52,236 | 30 | Amy Hung (TPE) | 69-72-78-68—287 | 13,444 |
| | Inbee Park (KOR) | 70-64-73-73—280 | 52,236 | | Haeji Kang (KOR) | 75-70-73-69—287 | 13,444 |
| 11 | Stacy Lewis (USA) | 74-68-71-68—281 | 39,025 | | Beth Allen (USA) | 71-70-75-71—287 | 13,444 |
| | Dewi Claire Schreefel (NED) | 70-66-74-71—281 | 39,025 | | Tiffany Joh (USA) | 71-69-75-72—287 | 13,444 |
| | | | | | Caroline Hedwall (SWE) | 69-69-76-73—287 | 13,444 |
| 13 | Maria Hjörth (SWE) | 72-69-73-68—282 | 34,147 | | Brittany Lincicome (USA) | 67-71-76-73—287 | 13,444 |
| 14 | Katie Futcher (USA) | 71-74-74-64—283 | 25,964 | | Shanshan Feng (CHN) | 70-75-67-75—287 | 13,444 |
| | Cristie Kerr (USA) | 72-69-74-68—283 | 25,964 | 37 | Melissa Reid (ENG) | 75-70-73-70—288 | 10,772 |
| | Candie Kung (TPE) | 72-73-69-69—283 | 25,964 | | Eun Hee Ji (KOR) | 70-71-75-72—288 | 10,772 |
| | Song-Hee Kim (KOR) | 69-72-71-71—283 | 25,964 | | Suzann Pettersen (NOR) | 76-66-73-73—288 | 10,772 |
| | Sun Ju Ahn (KOR) | 71-71-70-71—283 | 25,964 | | Meena Lee (KOR) | 65-69-80-74—288 | 10,772 |
| | Mika Miyazato (JPN) | 69-69-72-73—283 | 25,964 | | Linda Wessberg (SWE) | 73-66-75-74—288 | 10,772 |
| | Se Ri Pak (KOR) | 72-64-73-74—283 | 25,964 | | In Kyung Kim (KOR) | 71-72-71-74—288 | 10,772 |
| 21 | Jiyai Shin (KOR) | 75-66-72-71—284 | 21,138 | | | | |

**Other players who made the cut:** Hiromi Mogi (JPN), Hee Won Han (KOR), Lorie Kane (CAN), Hee Young Park (KOR), Kristy McPherson (USA), Paula Creamer (USA) 289; Azahara Muñoz Guijarro (ESP), Danielle Kang (USA) (am), Morgan Pressel (USA), Pat Hurst (USA), Cindy LaCrosse (USA) 290; Christel Boeljon (NED), Janice Moodie (SCO), Sandra Gal (GER), Chella Choi (KOR), Amanda Blumenherst (USA) 291; Miki Saiki (JPN), Kylie Walker (SCO), Holly Aitchison (ENG), Julieta Granada (PAR), Sophie Giquel-Bettan (FRA) 292; Virginie Lagoutte-Clement (FRA), Jaclyn Sweeney (USA) 295; Georgina Simpson (ENG) 297; Sophie Popov (GER) (am) 299; Jimin Kang (KOR) RTD

## 2010 Ricoh Women's British Open    Royal Birkdale    [6463–72]

Prize money: €2.5 million

| | | | | | | | | |
|---|---|---|---|---|---|---|---|---|
| 1 | Yani Tseng (TPE) | 68-68-68-73—277 | €313,530 | 21T | Paula Creamer (USA) | 74-74-70-72—290 | 22,032 |
| 2 | Katherine Hull (AUS) | 68-74-66-70—278 | 196,541 | | Juli Inkster (USA) | 71-70-76-73—290 | 22,032 |
| 3 | Na Yeon Choi (KOR) | 74-70-69-68—281 | 122,604 | | Jeong Jang (KOR) | 74-73-74-69—290 | 22,032 |
| | In-Kyung Kim (KOR) | 70-72-68-71—281 | 122,604 | | Lee-Anne Pace (RSA) | 74-72-71-73—290 | 22,032 |
| 5 | Cristie Kerr (USA) | 73-67-72-70—282 | 77,992 | 27 | Caroline Hedwall (SWE) | 74-75-72-70—291 | |
| | Hee-Kyung Seo (KOR) | 73-69-70-70—282 | 77,992 | | (am) | | |
| | Amy Yang (KOR) | 69-71-74-68—282 | 77,992 | | Karine Icher (FRA) | 74-72-70-75—291 | 18,484 |
| 8 | Morgan Pressel (USA) | 77-71-65-71—284 | 62,707 | | Jimin Kang (KOR) | 74-73-74-70—291 | 18,484 |
| 9 | Christina Kim (USA) | 74-68-70-74—286 | 47,544 | | Mindy Kim (KOR) | 72-75-73-71—291 | 18,484 |
| | Brittany Lincicome (USA) | 69-71-71-75—286 | 47,544 | 31 | Anne-Lise Caudal (FRA) | 69-73-75-75—292 | 14,292 |
| | Ai Miyazato (JPN) | 76-70-73-67—286 | 47,544 | | Katie Futcher (USA) | 74-74-72-72—292 | 14,292 |
| | Inbee Park (KOR) | 72-71-77-66—286 | 47,544 | | M J Hur (KOR) | 74-68-75-75—292 | 14,292 |
| | Momoko Ueda (JPN) | 72-70-70-74—286 | 47,544 | | Vicky Hurst (USA) | 77-71-74-70—292 | 14,292 |
| 14 | Maria Hernandez (ESP) | 73-70-73-71—287 | 33,224 | | Haeji Kang (KOR) | 75-74-72-71—292 | 14,292 |
| | Suzann Pettersen (NOR) | 73-68-71-75—287 | 33,224 | | Mi Hyun Kim (KOR) | 72-77-73-70—292 | 14,292 |
| | Jiyai Shin (KOR) | 71-71-72-73—287 | 33,224 | | Stacy Lewis (USA) | 71-74-75-72—292 | 14,292 |
| 17 | Gwladys Nocera (FRA) | 71-75-72-70—288 | 28,779 | | Ji Young Oh (KOR) | 79-69-75-69—292 | 14,292 |
| | Michelle Wie (USA) | 70-76-71-71—288 | 28,779 | | Melissa Reid (ENG) | 77-71-74-70—292 | 14,292 |
| 19 | Song-Hee Kim (KOR) | 75-73-71-70—289 | 25,971 | | Sakura Yokomine (JPN) | 74-71-75-72—292 | 14,292 |
| | Azahara Muñoz (ESP) | 74-71-72-72—289 | 25,971 | | Sun Young Yoo (KOR) | 69-72-78-73—292 | 14,292 |
| 21 | Chie Arimura (JPN) | 77-68-70-75—290 | 22,032 | | Henrietta Zuel (ENG) | 74-73-73-72—292 | 14,292 |
| | Becky Brewerton (WAL) | 73-73-71-73—290 | 22,032 | | | | |

**Other players who made the cut:** Sophie Gustafson (SWE), Amy Hung (TPE), Brittany Lang (USA), Meena Lee (KOR), Stacy Prammanasudh (USA), Ashleigh Simon (RSA), Karrie Webb (AUS) 293; Irene Cho (KOR), Moira Dunn (USA), Angela Stanford (USA), Sherri Steinhauer (USA), Kristin Tamulis (USA) 294; Carin Koch (SWE), Janice Moodie (SCO), Hee Young Park (KOR), Florentyna Parker (ENG), Sarah-Jane Smith (AUS), Iben Tinning (DEN), Wendy Ward (USA) 295; Seon Hwa Lee (KOR), Jee Young Lee (KOR) 296; Sarah Lee (KOR), Anja Monke (GER), Alena Sharp (CAN) 297; Stacy Bregman (RSA), Eunjang Yi (KOR) 298; Laura Davies (ENG), Meaghan Francella (USA), Anna Nordqvist (SWE), Mariajo Uribe (COL) 299; Shanshan Feng (CHN), Giulia Sergas (ITA) 300; Jennifer Rosales (PHI) 302

## 2009 Ricoh Women's British Open    Royal Lytham & St Annes    [6492–72]

Prize money: €1.5 million

| | | | | | | | | |
|---|---|---|---|---|---|---|---|---|
| 1 | Catriona Matthew (SCO) | 74-67-71-73—285 | €235,036 | 20T | Angela Stanford (USA) | 70-76-74-74—294 | 17,890 |
| 2 | Karrie Webb (AUS) | 77-71-72-68—288 | 147,336 | | Yani Tseng (TPE) | 74-70-78-72—294 | 17,890 |
| 3 | Paula Creamer (USA) | 74-74-70-71—289 | 76,825 | 24 | Inbee Park (KOR) | 76-72-76-71—295 | 16,137 |
| | Hee-Won Han (KOR) | 77-73-69-70—289 | 76,825 | 25 | Jeong Jang (KOR) | 79-73-72-72—296 | 15,172 |
| | Christina Kim (USA) | 73-71-71-74—289 | 76,825 | | Shinobu Moromizato | 74-73-71-78—296 | 15,172 |
| | Ai Miyazato (JPN) | 75-71-70-73—289 | 76,825 | | (JPN) | | |
| 7 | Kristy McPherson (USA) | 74-74-72-70—290 | 51,918 | 27 | Jade Schaeffer (FRA) | 79-71-75-72—297 | 14,383 |
| 8 | Na Yeon Choi (KOR) | 80-71-70-70—291 | 42,797 | 28 | Katie Futcher (USA) | 75-77-70-76—298 | 12,839 |
| | Cristie Kerr (USA) | 76-71-75-69—291 | 42,797 | | Vicky Hurst (USA) | 74-75-77-72—298 | 12,839 |
| | Jiyai Shin (KOR) | 77-71-68-75—291 | 42,797 | | Brittany Lincicome (USA) | 77-73-79-69—298 | 12,839 |
| 11 | Maria Hjörth (SWE) | 72-76-73-71—292 | 28,590 | | Teresa Lu (TPE) | 75-76-77-70—298 | 12,839 |
| | Song-ee Kim (KOR) | 70-73-74-75—292 | 28,590 | | Lorena Ochoa (MEX) | 75-77-72-74—298 | 12,839 |
| | Mika Miyazato (JPN) | 76-72-69-75—292 | 28,590 | 33 | Yuri Fudoh (JPN) | 80-73-70-76—299 | 10,524 |
| | Hee Young Park (KOR) | 71-75-73-73—292 | 28,590 | | Sandra Gal (GER) | 69-80-75-75—299 | 10,524 |
| | Giulia Sergas (ITA) | 74-67-78-73—292 | 28,590 | | Sophie Gustafson (SWE) | 74-71-82-72—299 | 10,524 |
| | Michelle Wie (USA) | 73-76-74-69—292 | 28,590 | | Brittany Lang (USA) | 81-70-71-77—299 | 10,524 |
| 17 | Kyeong Bae (KOR) | 73-71-74-75—293 | 21,048 | | Yuko Mitsuka (JPN) | 71-71-79-78—299 | 10,524 |
| | Jane Park (USA) | 74-72-72-75—293 | 21,048 | | Becky Morgan (WAL) | 80-71-72-76—299 | 10,524 |
| | Michelle Redman (USA) | 75-75-73-70—293 | 21,048 | | Sun-Young Yoo (KOR) | 79-73-75-72—299 | 10,524 |
| 20 | In-Kyung Kim (KOR) | 81-70-70-73—294 | 17,890 | 40 | Allison Hanna (USA) | 76-76-73-75—300 | 8,945 |
| | Se-Ri Pak (KOR) | 76-71-73-74—294 | 17,890 | | Katherine Hull (AUS) | 75-77-77-71—300 | 8,945 |

**Other players who made the cut:** Martina Eberl (GER), Meena Lee (KOR), Morgan Pressel (USA), Marianne Skarpnord (NOR) 301; Carmen Alonso (ESP), Il Mi Chung (KOR), Laura Davies (ENG), Mi-Jung Hur (JPN), Ursula Wikstrom (FIN) 302; Irene Cho (KOR), Samantha Head (ENG), Sarah Lee (KOR), Anna Nordqvist (SWE) 303; Jin Young Pak (KOR), Louise Stahle (SWE), Momoko Ueda (JPN) 304; Christel Boeljom (NED), Eunjang Yi (KOR) 305; Anne-Lise Caudal (FRA), Young Kim (KOR), Emma Zackrisson (SWE) 306; Lee-Anne Pace (RSA), Reilley Rankin (USA) 307; Kristin Tamulis (USA) 308; Vikki Laing (SCO) 309; Laura Diaz (USA), Shanshan Feng (CHN), Stacy Prammanasudh (USA) 310; Karin Sjodin (SWE) Rtd; Eun Hee Ji (KOR) DQ

## 2008 Ricoh Women's British Open   *Sunningdale*   [6408–72]

Prize money: £1.55 million

| | | | | | | | | |
|---|---|---|---|---|---|---|---|---|
| 1 | Jiyai Shin (KOR) | 66-68-70-66—270 | €202,336 | | 21T | Kristy McPherson (USA) | 67-75-74-65—281 | 15,175 |
| 2 | Ya-Ni Tseng (TPE) | 70-69-68-66—273 | 126.460 | | 24 | Meredith Duncan (USA) | 71-73-71-67—282 | 11,786 |
| 3 | Eun Hee Ji (KOR) | 68-70-69-67—274 | 79.037 | | | Sophie Gustafson (SWE) | 69-69-74-70—282 | 11,786 |
| | Yuri Fudoh (JPN) | 66-68-69-71—274 | 79.037 | | | Mi Hyun Kim (KOR) | 70-70-67-75—282 | 11,786 |
| 5 | Ai Miyazato (JPN) | 68-69-68-70—275 | 56.907 | | | Eun-A Lin (KOR) | 74-71-72-65—282 | 11,786 |
| 6 | Cristie Kerr (USA) | 71-65-70-70—276 | 49.319 | | | Jane Park (USA) | 69-70-73-70—282 | 11,786 |
| 7 | Lorena Ochoa (MEX) | 69-68-71-69—277 | 42.464 | | | Suzann Pettersen (NOR) | 70-70-71-71—282 | 11,786 |
| | Momoko Ueda (JPN) | 66-72-70-69—277 | 42.464 | | | Stacy Prammanasudh (USA) | 66-74-72-70—282 | 11,786 |
| 9 | Paula Creamer (USA) | 72-69-70-67—278 | 30.603 | | | Annika Sörenstam (SWE) | 72-72-70-68—282 | 11,786 |
| | Natalie Gulbis (USA) | 69-68-70-71—278 | 30.603 | | | Karen Stupples (ENG) | 67-73-72-70—282 | 11,786 |
| | Hee Won Han (KOR) | 71-69-71-67—278 | 30.603 | | | Sakura Yokomine (JPN) | 71-72-69-70—282 | 11,786 |
| | In-Kyung Kim (KOR) | 71-68-72-67—278 | 30.603 | | 34 | Laura Diaz (USA) | 66-72-75-70—283 | 9,010 |
| | Karrie Webb (AUS) | 72-69-69-68—278 | 30.603 | | | Anja Monke (GER) | 73-67-70-73—283 | 9,010 |
| 14 | Juli Inkster (USA) | 65-70-71-73—279 | 21.709 | | | Angela Park (BRA) | 71-74-71-37—283 | 9,010 |
| | Seon Hwa Lee (KOR) | 71-68-70-70—279 | 21.709 | | | Bo Bae Song (KOR) | 68-68-74-73—283 | 9,010 |
| | Hee Young Park (KOR) | 69-71-69-70—279 | 21.709 | | 38 | Ji-Hee Lee (KOR) | 68-75-68-73—284 | 7,745 |
| 17 | Shi Hyun Ahn (KOR) | 68-72-71-69—280 | 17.625 | | | Leta Lindley (USA) | 71-71-72-70—284 | 7,745 |
| | Minea Blomqvist (FIN) | 68-73-72-67—280 | 17.625 | | | Paula Marti (ESP) | 68-72-72-72—284 | 7,745 |
| | Jee Yound Lee (KOR) | 71-72-71-66—280 | 17.625 | | | Catriona Matthew (SCO) | 68-75-72-69—284 | 7,745 |
| | Ji Young Oh (KOR) | 66-73-71-70—280 | 17.625 | | | | | |
| 21 | Nicole Castrale (USA) | 69-72-72-68—281 | 15,175 | | | | | |
| | Na Yeon Choi (KOR) | 69-71-68-73—281 | 15,175 | | | | | |

**Other players who made the cut:** Candie Kung (TPE), Anna Nordqvist (SWE) (am), Reilley Rankin (USA) 285; Lora Fairclough (ENG), Janice Moodie (SCO), Sun Young Yoo (KOR) 286; Hye Jung Choi (KOR), Jin Joo Hong (KOR), Katherine Hull (AUS), Jill McGill (USA), Joanne Mills (AUS), Gloria Park (KOR), Karin Sjodin (SWE), Lotta Wahlin (SWE) 287; Helen Alfredsson (SWE), Il-Mi Chung (KOR), Rebecca Hudson (ENG) 288; Jimin Kang (KOR), Teresa Lu (TPE), Becky Morgan (WAL), Kris Camulis (USA), Wendy Ward (USA) 289; Erica Blasberg (USA), Christina Kim (USA), Gwladys Nocera (FRA), Marianne Skarpnord (NOR), Sherri Steinhauer (USA) 290; Tania Elosegui (ESP), Johanna Head (ENG), Rachel Hetherington (AUS), Maria Hjörth (SWE), Trish Johnson (ENG) 291; Becky Brewerton (WAL) 292; Moira Dunn (USA), Maria Jose Uribe (COL) (am) 294; Laura Davies (ENG) 295; Mhairi McKay (SCO) 296

## 2007 Ricoh Women's British Open   *St Andrews Old Course*   [6638–73]

Prize money: £2.5 million

| | | | | | | | | |
|---|---|---|---|---|---|---|---|---|
| 1 | Lorena Ochoa (MEX) | 67-73-73-74—287 | £160.000 | | 16T | Melissa Reid (ENG) (am) | 73-75-76-72—296 | |
| 2 | Maria Hjörth (SWE) | 75-73-72-71—291 | 85,000 | | | Annika Sörenstam (SWE) | 72-71-77-76—296 | 14.041 |
| | Jee Young Lee (KOR) | 72-73-75-71—291 | 85,000 | | 23 | Beth Bader (USA) | 73-77-75-72—297 | 11.060 |
| 4 | Reilley Rankin (USA) | 73-74-74-71—292 | 55,000 | | | Natalia Gulbis (USA) | 73-76-76-72—297 | 11.060 |
| 5 | Eun Hee Ji (KOR) | 73-71-77-72—293 | 42,000 | | | Alena Sharp (CAN) | 77-70-79-71—297 | 11.060 |
| | Se Ri Pak (KOR) | 73-73-75-72—293 | 42,000 | | | Sherri Steinhauer (USA) | 72-71-80-74—297 | 11.060 |
| 7 | Paula Creamer (USA) | 73-75-74-72—294 | 30,500 | | | Wendy Ward (USA) | 71-70-80-76—297 | 11.060 |
| | Catriona Matthew (SCO) | 73-68-80-73—294 | 30,500 | | 28 | Jimin Kang (KOR) | 77-72-75-75—299 | 9,100 |
| | Miki Saiki (JPN) | 76-70-81-67—294 | 30,500 | | | Sarah Lee (KOR) | 72-76-79-72—299 | 9,100 |
| | Linda Wessberg (SWE) | 74-73-72-75—294 | 30,500 | | | Suzann Pettersen (NOR) | 74-76-78-71—299 | 9,100 |
| 11 | Yuri Fudoh (JPN) | 74-69-81-71—295 | 20,300 | | | Ji-Yai Shin (KOR) | 76-74-77-72—299 | 9,100 |
| | Brittany Lincicome (USA) | 71-76-75-73—295 | 20,300 | | | Karrie Webb (AUS) | 77-73-74-75—299 | 9,100 |
| | Mhairi McKay (SCO) | 75-74-79-67—295 | 20,300 | | 33 | Louise Friberg (SWE) | 69-76-80-75—300 | 7,062 |
| | Na On Min (KOR) | 72-75-75-73—295 | 20,300 | | | Sophie Gustafson (SWE) | 73-72-81-74—300 | 7,062 |
| | Inbee Park (KOR) | 69-79-76-71—295 | 20,300 | | | Kim Hall (USA) | 74-74-79-73—300 | 7,062 |
| 16 | Becky Brewerton (WAL) | 74-75-74-73—296 | 14.041 | | | Juli Inkster (USA) | 79-68-82-71—300 | 7,062 |
| | Karine Icher (FRA) | 72-71-77-76—296 | 14.041 | | | Trish Johnson (ENG) | 75-75-77-73—300 | 7,062 |
| | Virginie Lagoutte-Clement (FRA) | 72-73-78-73—296 | 14.041 | | | Cristie Kerr (USA) | 77-71-79-73—300 | 7,062 |
| | Gloria Park (KOR) | 74-75-76-71—296 | 14.041 | | | Candie Kung (TPE) | 72-74-79-75—300 | 7,062 |
| | Stacy Prammanasudh (USA) | 74-76-72-74—296 | 14.041 | | | Meena Lee (KOR) | 71-76-79-74—300 | 7,062 |
| | | | | | | Gwladys Nocera (FRA) | 78-72-75-75—300 | 7,062 |

**Other players who made the cut:** Rebecca Hudson (ENG), In-Kyung Kim (KOR), Michele Redman (USA), Kerry Smith (ENG) (am), Karen Stupples (ENG), Lotta Wahlin (SWE) 301; Hye Yong Choi (KOR) (am), Catrin Nilsmark (SWE) 303; Dina Ammaccapane (USA), Rachel Bell (ENG), Beth Daniel (USA), Grace Park (KOR), Sally Watson (SCO) (am) 304; Rachel Hetherington (AUS), Bélen Mozo (ESP) (am), Momoko Ueda (JPN) 305; Lisa Hall (ENG), Jin Joo Hong (KOR), Christina Kim (USA), Ai Miyazato (JPN), Anna Nordquist (SWE) (am), Iben Tinning (DEN) 306; Joanne Mills (AUS) 308; Diana D'Alessio (USA), Martina Eberl (GER) 309; Nicole Castrale (USA) 310; Meg Mallon (USA) 311; Naomi Edwards (ENG) (am) 312

## 2006 Weetabix Women's British Open   Royal Lytham & St Annes   [6308–72]

Prize money: £1.05 million

| | | | | | | | | |
|---|---|---|---|---|---|---|---|---|
| 1 | Sherri Steinhauer (USA) | 73-70-66-72—281 | £160,000 | 22T | Jee Young Lee (KOR) | 72-77-69-74—292 | 11,500 |
| 2 | Sophie Gustafson (SWE) | 76-67-69-72—284 | 85,000 | 25 | Shi Hyun Ahn (KOR) | 75-73-69-76—293 | 10,600 |
| | Cristie Kerr (USA) | 71-76-66-71—284 | 85,000 | 26 | Jackie Gallagher-Smith | 77-74-71-72—294 | 9,460 |
| 4 | Juli Inkster (USA) | 66-72-74-73—285 | 50,000 | | (USA) | | |
| | Lorena Ochoa (MEX) | 74-73-65-73—285 | 50,000 | | Tracy Hanson (USA) | 74-77-70-73—294 | 9,460 |
| 6 | Beth Daniel (USA) | 73-70-71-72—286 | 37,000 | | Jeong Jang (KOR) | 78-73-68-75—294 | 9,460 |
| | Lorie Kane (CAN) | 73-69-74-70—286 | 37,000 | | Michelle Wie (USA) | 74-74-72-74—294 | 9,460 |
| 8 | Julieta Granada (PAR) | 71-73-70-73—287 | 32,000 | | Young-A Yang (KOR) | 72-75-68-79—294 | 9,460 |
| 9 | Ai Miyazato (JPN) | 71-75-75-67—288 | 29,000 | 31 | Nicole Castrale (USA) | 73-75-71-76—295 | 7,810 |
| 10 | Hee Won Han (KOR) | 80-71-69-70—290 | 21,250 | | Anja Monke (GER) | 75-76-70-74—295 | 7,810 |
| | Karine Icher (FRA) | 72-73-71-74—290 | 21,250 | | Liselotte Neumann | 76-72-70-77—295 | 7,810 |
| | Joo Mi Kim (KOR) | 73-73-73-71—290 | 21,250 | | (SWE) | | |
| | Candie Kung (TPE) | 72-70-71-77—290 | 21,250 | | Annika Sörenstam | 72-71-73-79—295 | 7,810 |
| | Nina Reis (SWE) | 70-76-69-75—290 | 21,250 | | (SWE) | | |
| | Karen Stupples (ENG) | 73-69-70-78—290 | 21,250 | | Lindsey Wright (USA) | 71-71-74-79—295 | 7,810 |
| 16 | Il-Mi Chung (KOR) | 72-71-75-73—291 | 14,041 | 36 | Becky Brewerton (WAL) | 76-73-73-74—296 | 6,375 |
| | Laura Davies (ENG) | 72-72-73-74—291 | 14,041 | | Vicki Goetze-Ackerman | 75-72-71-78—296 | 6,375 |
| | Natalie Gulbis (USA) | 72-74-67-78—291 | 14,041 | | (USA) | | |
| | Gwladys Nocera (FRA) | 70-73-71-77—291 | 14,041 | | Young Jo (KOR) | 80-70-74-72—296 | 6,375 |
| | Sukura Yokomine (JPN) | 72-73-75-71—291 | 14,041 | | Angela Stanford (USA) | 76-69-80-71—296 | 6,375 |
| | Heather Young (USA) | 72-74-70-75—291 | 14,041 | | Sun Young Yoo (KOR) | 76-74-71-75—296 | 6,375 |
| 22 | Kyeong Bae (KOR) | 73-73-75-71—292 | 11,500 | | Veronica Zorzi (ITA) | 74-76-78-68—296 | 6,375 |
| | Paula Creamer (USA) | 72-71-73-76—292 | 11,500 | | | | |

**Other players who made the cut:** Yuri Fudoh (JPN), Nikki Garrett (AUS), Patricia Meunier-Lebouc (FRA) 297; Chieko Amanuma (JPN), Silvia Cavalleri (ITA), Maria Hjörth (SWE), Christina Kim (USA), Sarah Lee (KOR) 298; Marisa Baena (COL), Rita Hakkarainen (FIN), Allison Hanna (USA), Teresa Lu (TPE), Joanne Morley (ENG), Lee Ann Walker-Cooper (USA) 299; Brittany Lincicome (USA), Becky Morgan (WAL), Morgan Pressel (USA), Kris Tamulis (USA) 300; Amy Yang (KOR) (am) 301; Lynnette Brooky (NZL), Seon Hwa Lee (KOR), Elisa Serramia (ESP), Ursula Wikstrom (FIN) 302; Laura Diaz (USA) 303; Marta Prieto (ESP) 304; Helena Alterby (SWE), Wendy Ward (USA) 305; Rachel Hetherington (AUS) 306; Bélen Mozo (ESP) (am) 307; Iben Tinning (DEN) 311

## 2005 Weetabix Women's British Open   Royal Birkdale, Southport, Lancashire   [6463–72]

Prize money: £1.05 million

| | | | | | | | | |
|---|---|---|---|---|---|---|---|---|
| 1 | Jeong Jang (KOR) | 68-66-69-69—272 | £160.000 | 21 | Catriona Matthew (SCO) | 73-72-72-67—284 | 13,500 |
| 2 | Sophie Gustafson (SWE) | 69-73-67-67—276 | 100,000 | 22 | Brandie Burton (USA) | 74-75-71-65—285 | 117,67 |
| 3 | Young Kim (KOR) | 74-68-67-69—278 | 70,000 | | Cecilia Ekelundh (SWE) | 77-69-71-68—285 | 11,767 |
| | Michelle Wie (USA) (am) | 75-67-67-69—278 | | | Candie Kung (TAI) | 76-71-67-71—285 | 11,767 |
| 5 | Cristie Kerr (USA) | 73-66-69-71—279 | 46,333 | | Nicole Perrot (CHI) | 70-72-69-74—285 | 11,767 |
| | Liselotte Neumann | 71-70-68-70—279 | 46,333 | | Sophie Sandolo (ITA) | 71-73-73-68—285 | 11,767 |
| | (SWE) | | | | Linda Wessberg (SWE) | 72-71-73-69—285 | 11,767 |
| | Annika Sörenstam (SWE) | 73-69-66-71—279 | 46,333 | 28 | Shi Hyun Ahn (KOR) | 78-68-67-73—286 | 9,283 |
| 8 | Natalie Gulbis (USA) | 76-70-68-66—280 | 33,500 | | Becky Brewerton (WAL) | 75-71-65-75—286 | 9,283 |
| | Grace Park (KOR) | 77-68-67-68—280 | 33,500 | | Laura Davies (ENG) | 76-70-66-74—286 | 9,283 |
| | Louise Stahle (SWE) (am) | 73-65-73-69—280 | | | Christina Kim (USA) | 79-70-71-66—286 | 9,283 |
| 11 | Ai Miyazato (JPN) | 72-73-69-67—281 | 25,250 | | Anja Monke (GER) | 73-73-70-70—286 | 9,283 |
| | Michele Redman (USA) | 75-71-67-68—281 | 25,250 | | Miriam Nagl (GER) | 74-75-69-68—286 | 9,283 |
| | Karen Stupples (ENG) | 74-71-65-71—281 | 25,250 | 34 | Heather Bowie (USA) | 74-69-72-72—287 | 7,530 |
| | Karrie Webb (AUS) | 75-66-69-71—281 | 25,250 | | Marty Hart (USA) | 79-70-71-67—287 | 7,530 |
| 15 | Paula Creamer (USA) | 75-69-65-73—282 | 17,300 | | Rebecca Hudson (ENG) | 78-70-71-68—287 | 7,530 |
| | Yuri Fudoh (JPN) | 75-69-68-70—282 | 17,300 | | Emilee Klein (USA) | 71-73-70-73—287 | 7,530 |
| | Juli Inkster (USA) | 74-68-68-72—282 | 17,300 | | Jill McGill (USA) | 76-70-72-69—287 | 7,530 |
| | Carin Koch (SWE) | 76-68-66-72—282 | 17,300 | 39 | Minea Blomquist (SWE) | 78-68-72-70—288 | 6,500 |
| | Becky Morgan (WAL) | 79-66-67-70—282 | 17,300 | | Wendy Doolan (AUS) | 77-72-67-72—288 | 6,500 |
| 20 | Pat Hurst (USA) | 75-65-70-73—283 | 14,250 | | Sherri Steinhauer (USA) | 74-73-70-71—288 | 6,500 |

**Other players who made the cut:** Helen Alfredsson (SWE), Michelle Ellis (AUS), Riikka Hakkarainen (FIN), Rachel Hetherington (AUS), Riko Higashio (JPN), Amanda Moltke-Leth (DEN), Gwladys Nocera (FRA), Kim Saiki (USA), Iben Tinning (DEN), Kris Tschetter (USA) 289; Carlota Ciganda (ESP) (am), Moira Dunn (USA), Kris Lindstrom (USA), Kimberley Williams (USA) 290; Catherine Cartwright (USA), Beth Daniel (USA) 291; Young Jo (KOR), Lorie Kane (CAN), Aree Song (KOR), Bo Bae Song (KOR) 292; Judith Van Hagen (NED), Shani Waugh (AUS) 293; Laura Diaz (USA), Sung Ah Yim (KOR) 294; Amy Hung (TAI), Paula Marti (ESP) 295; Siew-Ai Lim (MAS), Yu Ping Lin (TAI) 296; Karen Lunn (AUS) 301

## 2004 Weetabix Women's British Open  Sunningdale (Old Course)  [6392–72]

Prize money: £1.05 million

| | | | | | | | | |
|---|---|---|---|---|---|---|---|---|
| 1 | Karen Stupples (ENG) | 65-70-70-64—269 | £160,000 | 21T | Se Ri Pak (KOR) | 73-70-69-69—281 | 12,250 |
| 2 | Rachel Teske (AUS) | 70-69-65-70—274 | 100,000 | 23 | Jeong Jang (KOR) | 70-68-73-71—282 | 11,250 |
| 3 | Heather Bowie (USA) | 70-69-65-71—275 | 70,000 | | Aree Song (KOR) | 72-70-70-70—282 | 11,250 |
| 4 | Lorena Ochoa (MEX) | 69-71-66-70—276 | 55,000 | 25 | Juli Inkster (USA) | 71-75-69-68—283 | 10,200 |
| 5 | Beth Daniel (USA) | 69-69-71-68—277 | 39,667 | | Seol-An Jeon (KOR) | 69-69-70-75—283 | 10,200 |
| | Michele Redman (USA) | 70-71-70-66—277 | 39,667 | | Toshimi Kimura (JPN) | 70-75-68-70—283 | 10,200 |
| | Guilia Sergas (ITA) | 72-71-67-67—277 | 39,667 | 28 | Alison Nicholas (ENG) | 75-71-70-69—285 | 9,450 |
| 8 | Minea Blomqvist (FIN) | 68-78-62-70—278 | 29,000 | 29 | Candie Kung (TPE) | 73-69-71-73—286 | 8,925 |
| | Laura Davies (ENG) | 70-69-69-70—278 | 29,000 | | Catriona Matthew | 68-74-68-76—286 | 8,925 |
| | Jung Yeon Lee (KOR) | 67-72-70-69—278 | 29,000 | | (SCO) | | |
| 11 | Pat Hurst (USA) | 72-72-66-69—279 | 23,000 | 31 | Wendy Doolan (AUS) | 71-72-74-70—287 | 7,950 |
| | Cristie Kerr (USA) | 69-73-63-74—279 | 23,000 | | Natascha Fink (AUT) | 74-70-70-73—287 | 7,950 |
| 13 | Laura Diaz (USA) | 70-69-70-71—280 | 15,906 | | Gloria Park (KOR) | 72-73-75-67—287 | 7,950 |
| | Natalie Gulbis (USA) | 68-71-70-71—280 | 15,906 | | Kirsty Taylor (ENG) | 72-74-72-69—287 | 7,950 |
| | Hee Won Han (KOR) | 72-68-70-70—280 | 15,906 | 35 | Soo-Yun Kang (KOR) | 71-74-74-69—288 | 7,000 |
| | Christina Kim (USA) | 73-68-68-71—280 | 15,906 | | Becky Morgan (WAL) | 72-74-69-73—288 | 7,000 |
| | Carin Koch (SWE) | 70-70-70-70—280 | 15,906 | | Jennifer Rosales (PHI) | 75-70-70-73—288 | 7,000 |
| | Paula Marti (ESP) | 73-66-68-73—280 | 15,906 | 38 | Denise Killeen (USA) | 72-72-70-75—289 | 6,125 |
| | Grace Park (KOR) | 71-70-69-70—280 | 15,906 | | Jill McGill (USA) | 71-72-71-75—289 | 6,125 |
| | Annika Sörenstam (SWE) | 68-71-70-71—280 | 15,906 | | Patricia Meunier-Lebouc (FRA) | 70-75-71-73—289 | 6,125 |
| 21 | Michelle Estill (USA) | 70-72-68-71—281 | 12,250 | | Nadina Taylor (AUS) | 69-74-72-74—289 | 6,125 |

**Other players who made the cut:** Hiromi Mogi (JPN), Shiho Ohyama (JPN), Ana B Sanchez (ESP), Louise Stahle (SWE) (am), Sherri Steinhauer (USA) 290; Bettina Hauert (GER), Angela Jerman (USA), Pamela Kerrigan 291; Ashli Bunch (USA), Audra Burks (USA), Johanna Head (ENG), Katherine Hull (AUS), Kelli Kuehne (USA), Gwladys Nocera (FRA) 292; Lynnette Brooky (NZL), A J Eathorne (CAN), Wendy Ward (USA) 293; Emilee Klein (USA) 294; Helen Alfredsson (SWE), Hsiao Chuan Lu (CHN), Betsy King (USA), Janice Moodie (SCO) 295; Raquel Carriedo (ESP), Ana Larraneta (ESP) 296; Vicki Goetze-Ackerman (USA), Laurette Maritz (RSA) 297; Samantha Head (ENG) 298; Maria Hjörth (SWE) 305

# Women's British Open History

| Year | Winner | Country | Venue | Score |
|---|---|---|---|---|
| 1976 | J Lee Smith | England | Fulford | 299 |
| 1977 | V Saunders | England | Lindrick | 306 |
| 1978 | J Melville | England | Foxhills | 310 |
| 1979 | A Sheard | South Africa | Southport and Ainsdale | 301 |
| 1980 | D Massey | USA | Wentworth (East) | 294 |
| 1981 | D Massey | USA | Northumberland | 295 |
| 1982 | M Figueras-Dotti | Spain | Royal Birkdale | 296 |
| 1983 | Not played | | | |
| 1984 | A Okamoto | Japan | Woburn | 289 |
| 1985 | B King | USA | Moor Park | 300 |
| 1986 | L Davies | England | Royal Birkdale | 283 |
| 1987 | A Nicholas | England | St Mellion | 296 |
| 1988 | C Dibnah* | Australia | Lindrick | 296 |

*Won play-off after a tie with S Little

| | | | | |
|---|---|---|---|---|
| 1989 | J Geddes | USA | Ferndown | 274 |
| 1990 | H Alfredsson* | Sweden | Woburn | 288 |

*Beat J Hill at the fourth exyta hole

| | | | | |
|---|---|---|---|---|
| 1991 | P Grice-Whittaker | England | Woburn | 284 |
| 1992 | P Sheehan | USA | Woburn | 207 |

Reduced to 54 holes by rain

| | | | | |
|---|---|---|---|---|
| 1993 | K Lunn | Australia | Woburn | 275 |
| 1994 | L Neumann | Sweden | Woburn | 280 |
| 1995 | K Webb | Australia | Woburn | 278 |
| 1996 | E Klein | USA | Woburn | 277 |
| 1997 | K Webb | Australia | Sunningdale | 269 |
| 1998 | S Steinhauer | USA | Royal Lytham & St Annes | 292 |
| 1999 | S Steinhauer | USA | Woburn | 283 |
| 2000 | S Gustafson | Sweden | Royal Birkdale | 282 |

Women's British Open History *continued*

| Year | Winner | Country | Venue | Score |
|------|--------|---------|-------|-------|
| 2001 | S R Pak | Korea | Sunningdale | 277 |
| 2002 | K Webb | Australia | Turnberry | 273 |
| 2003 | A Sörenstam | Sweden | Royal Lytham & St Annes | 278 |
| 2004 | Karen Stupples | England | Sunningdale (Old Course) | 269 |
| 2005 | Jeong Jang | Korea | Royal Birkdale | 272 |
| 2006 | Sherri Steinhauer | USA | Royal Lytham & St Annes | 281 |
| 2007 | Lorena Ochoa | Mexico | St Andrews Old Course | 287 |
| 2008 | Ji-Yai Shin | Korea | Sunningdale | 270 |
| 2009 | Catriona Matthew | Scotland | Royal Lytham & St Annes | 285 |
| 2010 | Yani Tseng | Chinese Tapei | Royal Birkdale | 277 |
| 2011 | Yani Tseng | Chinese Tapei | Carnoustie Links | 272 |
| 2012 | Jiyai Shin | Korea | Royal Liverpool | 279 |
| 2013 | Stacy Lewis | USA | St Andrews Old Course | 280 |

## Seventeen made the cut in all five women's majors

With her three victories, Korean golfer Inbee Park made $1,241,999 from the five women's majors in 2013. This was nearly $700,000 more than Ricoh British Women's Open winner Stacy Lewis the next most financially successful golfer in the majors.

Only Inbee Park finished collectively under par for the majors finishing 14 under par. American Angela Stanford was level par with China's Shanshan Feng one over, Anna Nordquist and Na Yeon Choi two over and Stacy Lewis and Catriona Matthew next best at three over.

| Name | Kraft | LPGA | US Open | Ricoh | Evian | Earnings |
|------|-------|------|---------|-------|-------|----------|
| Inbee Park (KOR) | 1 | 1 | 1 | 42T | 67T | $1,241,999 |
| Stacy Lewis (USA) | 32T | 28T | 42T | 1 | 6T | $561,972 |
| I K Kim (KOR) | 55T | 22T | 2 | 47T | 19T | $425,303 |
| Catriona Matthew (SCO) | 7T | 2 | 15T | 11T | 64T | $360,535 |
| Na Yeon Choi (KOR) | 32T | 9T | 17T | 2T | 44T | $318,532 |
| Morgan Pressel (USA) | 57T | 3T | 20T | 4T | 31T | $317,123 |
| Angela Stanford (USA) | 19T | 28T | 4T | 17T | 6T | $312,852 |
| Paula Creamer (USA) | 13T | 58T | 4T | 11T | 19T | $245,734 |
| Shanshan Feng (CHN) | 25T | 9T | 9T | 25T | 11T | $223,612 |
| Anna Nordqvist (SWE) | 7T | 12T | 11T | 11T | 44T | $211,678 |
| Jessica Korda (USA) | 25T | 49T | 7T | 25T | 37T | $158,844 |
| Ayako Uehara (JPN) | 19T | 44T | 36T | 17T | 27T | $110,282 |
| Mariajo Uribe (COL) | 32T | 53T | 17T | 22T | 67T | $101,351 |
| Jenny Shin (KOR) | 55T | 22T | 54T | 17T | 31T | $93,780 |
| Mika Miyazato (JPN) | 63T | 22T | 31T | 59T | 19T | $90,645 |
| Eur-Hee Ji (KOR) | 48T | 22T | 61T | 35T | 37T | $77,824 |
| Lydia Ko (NZL) (am) | 25T | 17T | 36T | 42T | 2 | |

# Unflappable Inbee wins a third major to match the record of Babe and Ben

It was a measure of the unflappable Inbee Park's extraordinary accomplishment in winning the first three women's majors of 2013 that the only other golfer to pull off this feat in the history of the game was the incomparable wonder girl, Babe Zaharias, who won all three major championships staged in 1950. Ben Hogan, incidentally, was the last male to win the first three majors in 1953.

Utterly in control, again, in the US Women's Open held at Sebonack Golf Club on Long Island, New York, Park followed up her major victories at the Kraft Nabisco and the LPGA Championship with another master class in how to remain composed under pressure. Matching the achievements of Mickey Wright in 1961 and Pat Bradley in 1968 as only the fourth woman to win three majors in a single season, the South Korean posted the eight-under-par total of 280 to win her fourth major title by four shots from her compatriot I K Kim.

On a testing lay-out where only three golfers out of 156 completed 72 holes in the red figures which denote scores under par (So Yeon Ryu, the 2011 US Women's Open champion, was the third musketeer on one under), Park played with the same insouciant sense of control which had distinguished her game for the past two seasons. Her reward was a cheque for $585,000 and an entry in the record books.

During a spell of dominance every bit as impressive as the runs at the summit of the game enjoyed by her No 1 Rolex Ranking predecessors Annika Sörenstam, Lorena Ochoa and Yani Tseng, Park's victory in Southampton was also her third consecutive tournament win on the LPGA – the first golfer to win three-in-a-row since Ochoa in 2008.

It was, fittingly, Babe Didrikson Zaharias who once posed the rhetorical question: "I don't see any point in playing the game if you don't win, do you?" Perhaps the mantra had filtered into Park's mind during the 2012 and 2013 seasons as she dismantled the opposition with barely a flicker of emotion. Over a run of 24 consecutive tournaments, Park won eight times and was runner-up on five other occasions. In other words, she finished in the first two in more than half of the events she entered.

How did she do it? She doesn't resemble either the Babe or the Hawk in the slightest and has a swing which might best be described as her own. Not particularly long off the tee, Park averages around 247 yards with the driver and is middling for accuracy. She hits plenty of greens, though, and putts like a demon. While Park, 24, isn't as powerful as Tseng at her best or as compelling a shot maker as either Ochoa or Sörenstam, it's debatable if any female golfer ever brought a cooler temperament to the course. "I think I have a heartbeat," volunteered Karrie Webb, the Australian with seven major titles on her CV. "I don't know if Inbee has one."

As the ice maiden of golf, treating the old imposters of triumph and disaster with the same nonchalance once exalted by Rudyard Kipling, Park is particularly effective with the putter in hand. In fact, if you needed a golfer, man or woman, to hole a putt from ten feet for your life, it would be tough to think of anyone more reliable on the greens than the South Korean, who is second to none at relaxing her arms and shoulders.

According to Dave Stockton, one of golf's foremost experts on the putting stroke, there's a clear link between Park's mental strength and her gift for holing out. "Mentally, she is in a league of her own out there," observed the former US Ryder Cup captain. "What I love is her total lack of being affected by where she stands. She's very calm, very composed and it serves her well. The rhythm with her stroke and throughout the whole swing [is a constant]. Most of the time in a US Open you see others losing that. But she withstood it really, really well. I think it's because of that demeanour. No shot is more important than the last one or a future one. She doesn't change her routine depending on the pressure."

Explaining her Zen-like state under the cosh, Park said: "Believe it or not, I was very calm out there. It was weird. I didn't feel much pressure when I was on the golf course. I was nervous last night, but on the golf course, somehow, I felt very calm."

Seeking her sixth win in 13 starts in 2013 as well as her second US Open title, Park lived up to her billing as championship favourite when she posted 67, five under, to trail the early leader, Ha-Neul Kim, by a stroke at the end of the first round.

While events set up by the United States Golf Association are hardly renowned as festivals of low scoring, the likely arrival of strong winds on Long Island persuaded the organisers to present a gentler test than usual. As it turned out, the weather was more benign than the forecast and the world's best women golfers took advantage.

"The USGA was a little generous with us," acknowledged Park, previously the champion at Interlachen in 2008. "A lot of tees were moved up. So instead of hitting 5 irons, we were hitting 9 irons, and that made the course much easier. I was actually able to go for some pins and give myself a lot of opportunities. I made a lot of putts and didn't leave much out there."

As for Kim, on her US Open début, she took the lead with a birdie on the 17th and pieced together an impressive 66 which was bogey free. All six of her birdies were tap-ins, which confirmed how well she executed her wedge shots and mid-irons.

The weather was less kind on Friday when the breeze finally kicked in and a band of fog brought play to a halt earlier than planned. As was to be expected, reality kicked in for Ha-Neul Kim, who shot 77, while Park took control of the tournament at the halfway mark on nine under thanks to a crisply executed 68.

> "I made a lot of putts. I didn't leave much out there."
>
> *Inbee's summing up of her round*

I K Kim moved into contention with 69 and England's Jodi Ewart Shadoff also clambered up the leaderboard by adding 69 to her opening 70. The former English Amateur champion from North Yorkshire, who also featured at the Kraft Nabisco, reckoned assured ball striking was the key to her advance as she attempted to match the success of her compatriot, Justin Rose, at the US Open.

Once the 41 golfers who had not finished on Friday completed their rounds on Saturday morning after the fog lifted, there was still a testing wind to challenge the players as the third round got underway. By now, the championship was back on more familiar USGA territory with par a score to be coveted. Park knew as much and, in the process of starting with eight consecutive pars, looked more or less unassailable. By the time she'd signed for 71 – the leader was the only golfer to break par on Saturday – the world No 1 led by four shots.

The combination of breezy conditions overhead and tricky pin positions meant that opportunities for the rest of the field to take a run at Park and Kim were limited. If the leader was a model of calm, there was a question mark against Jessica Korda's temperament when she fired her caddie after taking 40 blows to reach the turn. The 20-year-old invited her boyfriend, a pro on the Web.com tour, to carry the bag on the back nine, shot 36, and finished the day in a tie for sixth.

According to Brittany Lincicome, Park was playing a different course from the rest of the field. "She's on a roll, there's nothing you can do," said the American who trailed the 54 hole leader by 11 strokes. In fact, Park wasn't infallible, making three consecutive bogeys after the turn before bouncing back with three birdies in the closing five holes.

On Sunday she again made mistakes at the sixth and seventh holes as well as the 14th and 15th but consecutive birdies at the ninth and tenth meant she was able to stay in her comfort zone and card 74. Again, no one could find the shift into top gear which might have unsettled the leader. After threatening with a birdie at the second, Kim made three bogeys before the turn and held onto the runner-up spot with 74.

"Like Yani, Annika and Lorena [before me], they did what they did because they were experienced and had been in that position so many times they didn't feel that much pressure, at least not as much as other players would feel," reflected the champion. "I think I'm taking like one step towards them. I know I have a long way to go to match them."

Not so many steps, mark you, to prevent her from becoming the most dominant golfer of 2013.

Mike Aitken

| First Round | Second Round | Third Round | Fourth Round |
|---|---|---|---|
| –6 Ha-Neul Kim | –9 Inbee Park | –10 Inbee Park | –8 Inbee Park |
| –5 Inbee Park | –7 I K Kim | –6 I K Kim | –4 I K Kim |
| –4 Anna Nordqvist | –5 Jodi Ewart Shadoff | –3 Jodi Ewart Shadoff | –1 So Yeon Ryu |
| –4 I K Kim | –4 Lizette Salas | –1 Angela Stanford | +1 Paula Creamer |
| –4 Lizette Salas | –3 Angela Stanford | –1 So Yeon Ryu | +1 Jodi Ewart Shadoff |
| –4 Caroline Hedwall | –3 Jessica Korda | +1 Paula Creamer | +1 Angela Stanford |
| –3 Maud-Aimee Leblanc | –2 So Yeon Ryu | +1 Jessica Korda | +2 Brittany Lang |
| –3 Paz Echeverria | –2 Karine Icher | +2 Cristie Kerr | +2 Jessica Korda |
| –2 Catriona Matthew | –2 Anna Nordqvist | +2 Brittany Lang | +3 Shanshan Feng |
| –2 Jessica Korda | –1 Caroline Hedwall | +2 Ai Miyazato | +3 Brittany Lincicome |

# US Women's Open Championship (68th)   June 27–30

*Sebonack GC, Southampton, NY*   [6821–72]

Prize Money: $3,250,000. Entries 1,420. Field 155 (24 amateurs) of whom 67 (including six amateurs) made the cut on 150 or less

*Players are of American nationality unless stated*

| | | | |
|---|---|---|---|
| 1 | Inbee Park (KOR) | 67-68-71-74—280 | $585,000 |
| 2 | I K Kim (KOR) | 68-69-73-74—284 | 350,000 |
| 3 | So Yeon Ryu (KOR) | 73-69-73-72—287 | 217,958 |
| 4 | Paula Creamer | 72-73-72-72—289 | 127,972 |
| | Angela Stanford | 73-68-74-74—289 | 127,972 |
| | Jodi Ewart Shadoff (EMG) | 70-69-74-76—289 | 127,972 |
| 7 | Brittany Lang | 76-69-73-72—290 | 94,357 |
| | Jessica Korda | 70-71-76-73—290 | 94,357 |
| 9 | Shanshan Feng (CHN) | 71-75-75-70—291 | 79,711 |
| | Brittany Lincicome | 72-72-74-73—291 | 79,711 |
| 11 | Anna Nordqvist (SWE) | 68-74-77-73—292 | 69,432 |
| | Ai Miyazato (JPN) | 76-70-72-74—292 | 69,432 |
| 13 | Lexi Thompson | 75-69-76-73—293 | 61,477 |
| | Karrie Webb (AUS) | 73-73-73-74—293 | 61,477 |
| 15 | Catriona Matthew (SCO) | 70-75-74-75—294 | 54,755 |
| | Lindy Duncan | 71-73-75-75—294 | 54,755 |
| 17 | Mariajo Uribe (COL) | 70-76-76-73—295 | 47,784 |
| | Haeji Kang (KOR) | 71-73-77-74—295 | 47,784 |
| | Na Yeon Choi (KOR) | 71-77-72-75—295 | 47,784 |
| 20 | Morgan Pressel | 73-74-75-74—296 | 37,920 |
| | Jennifer Rosales (PHI) | 70-76-76-74—296 | 37,920 |
| | Lizette Salas | 68-72-82-74—296 | 37,920 |
| | Karine Icher (FRA) | 70-72-77-77—296 | 37,920 |
| | Cristie Kerr | 72-72-74-78—296 | 37,920 |
| | Casie Cathrea (am) | 75-73-79-70—297 | |
| 25 | Hee Kyung Seo (KOR) | 75-74-75-73—297 | 27,548 |
| | Chella Choi (KOR) | 73-75-76-73—297 | 27,548 |
| | Julieta Granada (PAR) | 74-76-73-74—297 | 27,548 |
| | Mi Jung Hur (KOR) | 75-71-75-76—297 | 27,548 |
| | Ha-Neul Kim (KOR) | 66-77-78-76—297 | 27,548 |
| 31 | Meena Lee (KOR) | 71-79-77-71—298 | 21,434 |
| | Gerina Piller | 73-76-76-73—298 | 21,434 |
| | Christina Kim | 75-75-74-74—298 | 21,434 |
| | Mika Miyazato (JPN) | 72-77-74-75—298 | 21,434 |
| | Caroline Hedwall (SWE) | 68-75-79-76—298 | 21,434 |
| 36 | Lydia Ko (NZL) (am) | 72-76-79-72—299 | |
| | Dewi Claire Schreefel (NED) | 76-71-77-75—299 | 18,263 |
| | Ayako Uehara (JPN) | 75-75-73-76—299 | 18,263 |
| | Soo-Jin Yang (KOR) | 72-72-79-76—299 | 18,263 |
| | Thidapa Suwannapura (THA) | 75-74-73-77—299 | 18,263 |
| | Kristy McPherson | 74-75-72-78—299 | 18,263 |
| 42 | Jane Park | 73-76-76-75—300 | 15,430 |
| | Mo Martin | 74-74-77-75—300 | 15,430 |
| | Ryann O'Toole | 72-73-78-77—300 | 15,430 |
| | Stacy Lewis | 71-76-75-78—300 | 15,430 |
| 46 | Pornanong Phatlum (THA) | 71-77-76-77—301 | 13,544 |
| | Sarah Jane Smith (AUS) | 71-76-76-78—301 | 13,544 |
| 48 | Austin Ernst | 75-74-82-71—302 | 12,287 |
| | Azahara Muñoz (ESP) | 73-74-73-82—302 | 12,287 |
| 50 | Doris Chen (am) | 74-74-79-76—303 | |
| | Laura Diaz | 76-74-76-77—303 | 10,715 |
| | Amy Yang (KOR) | 74-72-78-79—303 | 10,715 |
| | Maude-Aimee Leblanc (CAN) | 69-77-77-80—303 | 10,715 |
| 54 | Yueer Cindy Feng (CHN) (am) | 72-77-79-76—304 | |
| | Jenny Shin (KOR) | 78-71-78-77—304 | 9,693 |

US Women's Open Championship *continued*

| | | | |
|---|---|---|---|
| 54T | Caroline Masson (GER) | 71-74-81-78—304 | 9,693 |
| 57 | Carlota Ciganda (ESP) | 76-72-82-75—305 | 9,211 |
| | Amy Meier | 74-72-82-77—305 | 9,211 |
| 59 | Brooke Mackenzie Henderson (CAN) (am) | 71-76-83-77—307 | |
| | Caroline Westrup (SWE) | 74-76-78-79—307 | 8,875 |
| 61 | Eun-Hee Ji (KOR) | 73-77-83-75—308 | 8,574 |
| | Natalie Gulbis | 70-78-76-84—308 | 8,574 |
| 63 | Cindy Lacrosse | 74-74-82-79—309 | 8,313 |
| 64 | Nelly Korda (am) | 73-77-79-81—310 | |
| | Moira Dunn | 78-72-77-83—310 | 8,089 |
| | Becky Morgan (WAL) | 75-73-79-83—310 | 8,089 |
| 67 | Danah Bordner | 73-74-82-83—312 | 7,890 |

*The following players missed the cut:*

| | | | | | | | | |
|---|---|---|---|---|---|---|---|---|
| 68 | Christel Boeljon (NED) | 77-74—151 | 99 | Annie Park (am) | 79-75—154 | 129 | Hannah Suh (am) | 80-79—159 |
| | Alison Walshe, | 77-74—151 | | Giulia Sergas (ITA) | 79-75—154 | | Macarena Silva (CHI) | 79-80—159 |
| | Sun Young Yoo, (KOR) | 77-74—151 | | Jamie Hullett | 78-76—154 | | Alexandra Kaui (am) | 78-81—159 |
| | Sandra Gal (GER) | 76-75—151 | | Chie Arimura (JPN) | 76-78—154 | | Se Ri Pak (KOR) | 78-81—159 |
| | Yani Tseng (TPE) | 76-75—151 | | Ilhee Lee (KOR) | 76-78—154 | 133 | Aimee Cho (KOR) | 81-79—160 |
| | Char Young Kim (KOR) | 75-76—151 | | Suzann Pettersen (NOR) | 76-78—154 | | Mariel Galdiano (am) | 80-80—160 |
| | Kris Tamulis | 75-76—151 | | Jiyai Shin (KOR) | 76-78—154 | | Taylore Karle | 78-82—160 |
| | Rachel Rohanna (am) | 74-77—151 | | Karen Stupples (ENG) | 75-79—154 | 136 | Shannon Aubert (FRA) (am) | 81-80—161 |
| | Lindsey Wright, (AUS) | 73-78—151 | 107 | Birdie Kim (KOR) | 78-77—155 | | Chelsea Harris | 81-80—161 |
| | Juli Inkster | 72-79—151 | | Irene Cho | 77-78—155 | | Amelia Lewis | 78-83—161 |
| | Je-Yoon Yang (KOR) | 70-81—151 | | Gabriella Then (am) | 77-78—155 | 139 | Erica Herr (am) | 77-85—162 |
| | Paz Echeverria (CHI) | 69-82—151 | | Tiffany Lua | 76-79—155 | 140 | Kelli Bowers (am) | 84-79—163 |
| 80 | Beatriz Recari (ESP) | 81-71—152 | | Miki Saiki (JPN) | 75-80—155 | | Janice Moodie (SCO) | 84-79—163 |
| | Vicky Hurst | 79-73—152 | | Brooke Pancake | 74-81—155 | | Mikayla Harmon (am) | 79-84—163 |
| | Katie Futcher | 78-74—152 | 113 | Hee-Won Han (KOR) | 80-76—156 | | Catherine Matranga | 78=85—163 |
| | Megan Grehan | 78-74—152 | | Carly Booth (SCO) | 78-78—156 | 144 | Sally Watson (SCO) | 82-82—164 |
| | Lorie Kane (CAN) | 77-75—152 | | Belen Mozo (ESP) | 78-78—156 | 145 | Kendra Little | 77-88—165 |
| | Pernilla Lindberg (SWE) | 76-76—152 | | Stephanie Sherlock (CAN) | 78-78—156 | | Elena Robles | 77-88—165 |
| | Nicole Jeray | 75-77—152 | | P K Kongkraphan (THA) | 76-80—156 | 147 | Alice Kim (am) | 89-77—166 |
| | Christi Cano | 74-78—152 | | Tiffany Joh | 75-81—156 | | Tiffany Tavee | 85-81—166 |
| | Emily Tubert (am) | 74-78—152 | | Danielle Kang | 74-82—156 | 149 | Christine Song | 78-89—167 |
| | Momoko Ueda (JPN) | 73-79—152 | 120 | Katy Harris | 78-79—157 | 150 | Karinn Dickinson (am) | 86-82—168 |
| 90 | Ji Young Oh (KOR) | 79-74—153 | | Mariah Stackhouse (am) | 78-79—157 | 151 | Elizabeth Schultz (am) | 78-91—169 |
| | Nicole Castrale | 78-75—153 | | Jessica Shepley, (CAN) | 77-80—157 | 152 | Isabelle Beisiegel (CAN) | 84-86—170 |
| | Sophie Gustafson (SWE) | 78-75—153 | | Nicole Zhang, (CAN) (am) | 77-80—157 | | Yoon-Kyung Heo (KOR) | 79 WD |
| | Sydnee Michaels | 78-75—153 | | Jennifer Johnson | 76-81—157 | | Candie Kung (TPE) | 79 WD |
| | Mina Harigae | 77-76—153 | | Stacey Keating (AUS) | 76-81—157 | | Michelle Wie | 80 WD |
| | Hee Young Park (KOR) | 76-77—153 | 126 | Felicity Johnson (ENG) | 83-75—158 | | | |
| | Katherine Hull-Kirk (AUS) | 73-80—153 | | Emily Childs | 77-81—158 | | | |
| | Caroline Powers (am) | 73-80—153 | | Kirby Dreher (CAN) | 77-81—158 | | | |
| | Kyung Kim (am) | 71-82—153 | | | | | | |

# Month by month in 2013

Matt Kuchar takes the first WGC crown of the season, beating holder Hunter Mahan in the final of the Accenture Match Play after world top two Rory McIlroy and Tiger Woods both make first round exits – McIlroy to fellow Irishman Shane Lowry and Woods to former Presidents Cup partner Charles Howell.

## 2012 US Women's Open Championship Blackwolf Run, Kohler, WI [6984–72]

Prize money: $3.25 million

| | | | | | | | | |
|---|---|---|---|---|---|---|---|---|
| 1 | Na Yeon Choi (KOR) | 71-72-65-73—281 | $585,000 | 21 | Yeon-Ju Jung (KOR) | 74-72-80-69—295 | 33,799 |
| 2 | Amy Yang (KOR) | 73-72-69-71—285 | 350,000 | | Diana Luna (ITA) | 76-72-76-71—295 | 33,799 |
| 3 | Sandra Gal (GER) | 71-70-74-74—289 | 218,840 | | Brittany Lang | 73-74-77-71—295 | 33,799 |
| 4 | Ilhee Lee (KOR) | 72-71-77-70—290 | 128,487 | | Jennie Lee | 70-74-79-72—295 | 33,799 |
| 4 | Shanshan Feng (CHN) | 74-74-71-71—290 | 128,487 | | Numa Gulyanamitta (THA) | 73-76-73-73—295 | 33,799 |
| | Giulia Sergas (ITA) | 74-71-73-72—290 | 128,487 | | Jimin Kang (KOR) | 72-72-78-73—295 | 33,799 |
| 7 | Paula Creamer | 73-73-71-74—291 | 94,736 | | Azahara Muñoz (ESP) | 73-73-73-76—295 | 33,799 |
| | Mika Miyazato (JPN) | 71-71-73-76—291 | 94,736 | 28 | Anna Nordqvist (SWE) | 72-74-79-71—296 | 23,604 |
| 9 | Se Ri Pak (KOR) | 72-73-76-71—292 | 72,596 | | Mina Harigae | 77-71-75-73—296 | 23,604 |
| | Nicole Castrale | 73-70-74-75—292 | 72,596 | | Pornanong Phatlum (THA) | 76-69-76-75—296 | 23,604 |
| | Inbee Park (KOR) | 71-70-76-75—292 | 72,596 | | Ai Miyazato (JPN) | 70-74-75-77—296 | 23,604 |
| | Cristie Kerr | 69-71-77-75—292 | 72,596 | 32 | Sun Young Yoo (KOR) | 76-72-81-68—297 | 20,880 |
| | Suzann Pettersen (NOR) | 71-68-78-75—292 | 72,596 | | Jin Young Pak (KOR) | 73-72-80-72—297 | 20,880 |
| 14 | Cindy Lacrosse | 73-74-74-72—293 | 55,161 | | Lizette Salas | 69-73-75-80—297 | 20,880 |
| | Danielle Kang | 78-70-71-74—293 | 55,161 | 35 | Jenny Shin (KOR) | 76-71-76-75—298 | 18,653 |
| | So Yeon Ryu (KOR) | 74-71-74-74—293 | 55,161 | | Jennifer Johnson | 76-70-76-76—298 | 18,653 |
| | Lexi Thompson | 70-73-72-78—293 | 55,161 | | Beatriz Recari (ESP) | 70-75-76-77—298 | 18,653 |
| 18 | Hee Kyung Seo (KOR) | 72-73-80-69—294 | 45,263 | | Michelle Wie | 74-66-78-80—298 | 18,653 |
| | Brittany Lincicome | 69-80-74-71—294 | 45,263 | | | | |
| | Vicky Hurst | 71-70-75-78—294 | 45,263 | | | | |

**Other players who made the cut:** Carlota Ciganda (ESP), Heather Bowie Young, Lydia Ko (NZL) (am), Katie Futcher, Jeong Jang (KOR), Jessica Korda, Sakura Yokomine (JPN) 300; Emma Talley (am), Jennifer Song, Stacy Lewis, Alison Walshe 301; Karrie Webb (AUS), Gerina Piller, Yani Tseng (TPE), Melissa Reid (ENG) 302; Angela Stanford, Meena Lee (KOR) 303; Sophie Gustafson (SWE) 304; Dewi Claire Schreefel (NED), Angela Oh, Katherine Hull (AUS) 305; Ji-Hee Lee (KOR), Alison Lee (am), Kristy McPherson 306; Lorie Kane (CAN) 307; Paige Mackenzie 309; Sue Kim (KOR) 313

## 2011 US Women's Open Championship Colorado Springs, CO [7047–71]

Prize money: $3.25 million

| | | | | | | | | |
|---|---|---|---|---|---|---|---|---|
| 1 | So Yeon Ryu (KOR)* | 74-69-69-69—281 | $585,000 | 21T | Meena Lee (KOR) | 75-71-72-73—291 | 36,374 |
| 2 | Hee Kyung Seo (KOR) | 72-73-68-68—281 | 350,000 | | Morgan Pressel | 75-72-71-73—291 | 36,374 |
| *So Yeon Ryu won at the third extra hole | | | | | Leta Lindley | 73-71-72-75—291 | 36,374 |
| 3 | Cristie Kerr | 71-72-69-71—283 | 215,493 | 25 | Mi-Jeong Jeon (KOR) | 72-73-76-71—292 | 30,122 |
| 4 | Angela Stanford | 72-70-70-72—284 | 150,166 | | Sun Young Yoo (KOR) | 74-68-77-73—292 | 30,122 |
| 5 | Mika Miyazato (JPN) | 70-67-76-72—285 | 121,591 | 27 | Brittany Lincicome | 75-74-74-70—293 | 24,042 |
| 6 | Karrie Webb (AUS) | 70-73-72-71—286 | 98,128 | | Sakura Yokomine (JPN) | 72-74-77-70—293 | 24,042 |
| | Ai Miyazato (JPN) | 70-68-76-72—286 | 98,128 | | Beatriz Recari (ESP) | 76-72-72-73—293 | 24,042 |
| | Inbee Park (KOR) | 71-73-70-72—286 | 98,128 | | Alison Walshe | 74-73-73-73—293 | 24,042 |
| 9 | Ryann O'Toole | 69-72-75-71—287 | 81,915 | | Eun-Hee Ji (KOR) | 73-69-74-77—293 | 24,042 |
| 10 | Jiyai Shin (KOR) | 73-72-73-70—288 | 70,996 | 32 | Natalie Gulbis | 73-75-74-72—294 | 21,189 |
| | Amy Yang (KOR) | 75-69-73-71—288 | 70,996 | | Moriya Jutanugarn (THA) (am) | 76-69-76-73—294 | |
| | I K Kim (KOR) | 70-69-76-73—288 | 70,996 | 34 | Shinobu Moromizato (JPN) | 76-72-74-73—295 | 18,370 |
| 13 | Chella Choi (KOR) | 71-76-70-72—289 | 60,780 | | Mina Harigae | 75-74-72-74—295 | 18,370 |
| | Candie Kung (TPE) | 76-69-71-73—289 | 60,780 | | Sandra Gal (GER) | 77-72-72-74—295 | 18,370 |
| 15 | Karen Stupples (ENG) | 72-77-73-68—290 | 48,658 | | Maria Hjörth (SWE) | 70-78-73-74—295 | 18,370 |
| | Suzann Pettersen (NOR) | 71-75-72-72—290 | 48,658 | | Stacy Lewis | 68-73-79-75—295 | 18,370 |
| | Junthima Gulyanamitta (THA) | 73-76-68-73—290 | 48,658 | | Jessica Korda | 73-75-72-75—295 | 18,370 |
| | Yani Tseng (TPE) | 73-73-71-73—290 | 48,658 | | Song-Hee Kim (KOR) | 73-73-74-75—295 | 18,370 |
| | Lizette Salas | 69-73-73-75—290 | 48,658 | | Wendy Ward | 73-69-74-79—295 | 18,370 |
| | Paula Creamer | 72-70-73-75—290 | 48,658 | | | | |
| 21 | Catriona Matthew (SCO) | 76-70-74-71—291 | 36,374 | | | | |

**Other players who made the cut:** Shanshan Feng (CHN), Karin Sjodin (SWE), Meaghan Francella 296; Vicky Hurst, Hee Young Park (KOR), Azahara Muñoz (ESP), Jennifer Johnson, Se Ri Pak(KOR) 297; Brittany Lang, Jin Young Pak (KOR), Soo-Jin Yang (KOR), Sue Kim (CAN), Lindsey Wright (AUS) 298; Michelle Wie, Danah Bordner, Lee-Anne Pace (RSA), Mariajo Uribe (COL) 299; Yoo Kyeong Kim, Lindy Duncan (am), Victoria Tanco (ARG) (am), Jean Chua (MAS) 300; Amy Anderson (am) 301; Anya Sarai Alvarez, Shin-Ae Ahn (KOR), Haru Nomura (JPN), Becky Morgan (WAL), 302; Danielle Kang (am) 303; Paola Moreno (COL) 304; Sherri Steinhauer 305; Gwladys Nocera (FRA) 307; Bo-Mee Lee (KOR) WD

## 2010 US Women's Open Championship *Oakmont, PA*    [6613–71]

Prize money: $3.25 million

| | | | | | | | | |
|---|---|---|---|---|---|---|---|---|
| 1 | Paula Creamer | 72-70-70-69—281 | $585,000 | 19T | Jeong Jang (KOR) | 73-72-74-75—294 | 39,285 |
| 2 | Na Yeon Choi (KOR) | 75-72-72-66—285 | 284,468 | | Kristy McPherson | 72-78-74-70—294 | 39,285 |
| | Suzann Pettersn (NOR) | 73-71-72-69—285 | 284,468 | | Azahara Muñoz (ESP) | 75-74-71-74—294 | 39,285 |
| 4 | In-Kyung Kim (KOR) | 74-71-73-68—286 | 152,565 | | Angela Sanford | 73-72-74-75—294 | 39,285 |
| 5 | Jiyai Shin | 76-71-72-68—287 | 110,481 | 25 | Jee Young Lee (KOR) | 72-76-76-71—295 | 29,625 |
| | Brittany Lang | 69-74-75-69—287 | 110,481 | | Brittany Lincicome | 73-78-71-73—295 | 29,625 |
| | Amy Yang (KOR) | 70-75-71-71—287 | 110,481 | | So Yeon Ryu (KOR) | 74-74-76-71—295 | 29,625 |
| 8 | Inbee Park (KOR) | 70-78-73-68—289 | 87,202 | 28 | Chie Arimura (JPN) | 74-72-76-74—296 | 24,096 |
| | Christine Kim | 72-72-72-73—289 | 87,202 | | Maria Hjörth (SWE) | 73-72-75-76—296 | 24,096 |
| 10 | Alexis Thompson | 73-74-70-73—290 | 72,131 | | Candie Kung (TPE) | 76-72-79-69—296 | 24,096 |
| | Saura Yokomine (JPN) | 71-71-76-72—290 | 72,131 | 31 | Ashli Bunch | 78-74-75-70—297 | 21,529 |
| | Yani Tseng (TPE) | 73-76-73-68—290 | 72,131 | | M J Hur (KOR) | 70-81-74-72—297 | 21,529 |
| 13 | Song-Hee Kim (KOR) | 72-76-78-65—291 | 63,524 | | Ai Miyazato (JPN) | 73-74-80-70—297 | 21,529 |
| 14 | Natalie Gulbis | 73-73-72-74—292 | 56,659 | 34 | Meaghan Francella | 75-72-77-74—298 | 18,980 |
| | Stacy Lewis | 75-70-75-72—292 | 56,659 | | Jeong Eun Lee (KOR) | 72-78-73-75—298 | 18,980 |
| | Wendy Ward | 72-73-70-77—292 | 56,659 | | Mhairi McKay (SCO) | 71-78-76-73—298 | 18,980 |
| 17 | Cristie Kerr | 72-71-75-75—293 | 49,365 | | Shinobu Moromizato (JPN) | 72-77-77-72—298 | 18,980 |
| | Karrie Webb (AUS) | 74-72-73-74—293 | 49,365 | | Morgan Pressel | 74-75-75-74—298 | 18,980 |
| 19 | Shi Hyun Ahn (KOR) | 72-77-73-72—294 | 39,285 | | | | |
| | Sophie Gustafson (SWE) | 72-72-74-76—294 | 39,285 | | | | |

**Other players who made the cut:** Eun-Hee Ji (KOR). Karen Stupples (ENG) 299; Maria Hernandez (ESP), Katherine Hull (AUS), Vicky Hurst, Jennifer Johnson (am), Hee Young Park (KOR), Jennifer Rosales (PHI), Heather Young 300; Alena Sharp (CAN), Louise Stahle (SWE), Lindsay Wright (AUS) 301; Sandra Gal (GER) 302; Naon Min (KOR), Sherri Steinhauer 303; Allison Fouch 304; Paige Mackenzie, Anna Rawson (AUS), Christine Wong (CAN) (am) 305; Tamie Durdin (AUS), Libby Smith, Jennifer Song 307; Chella Choi (KOR) 308; Lisa McCloskey (am), Heekyung Seo (KOR) 309; Danielle Kang (am) 310; Meredith Duncan, Kelli Shean (RSA) (am) 312; Sarah Kemp (AUS) 313; Tiffany Lim (am) 320

## 2009 US Women's Open Championship *Interlachen CC, Edina, MN*    [6789–73]

Prize money: $3.1 million

| | | | | | | | | |
|---|---|---|---|---|---|---|---|---|
| 1 | Eun-Hee Ji (KOR) | 71-72-70-71—284 | $585,000 | 17T | Akiko Fukushima (JPN) | 76-72-72-72—292 | 42,724 |
| 2 | Candie Kung (TPE) | 71-77-68-69—285 | 350,000 | | Anna Grzebien | 73-77-69-73—292 | 42,724 |
| 3 | Cristie Kerr | 69-70-72-75—286 | 183,568 | | Jimin Kang (KOR) | 76-71-74-71—292 | 42,724 |
| | In-Kyung Kim (KOR) | 72-72-72-70—286 | 183,568 | | Teresa Lu (TPE) | 76-69-70-77—292 | 42,724 |
| 5 | Brittany Lincicome | 72-72-73-70—287 | 122,415 | | Jean Reynolds | 69-72-74-77—292 | 42,724 |
| 6 | Paula Creamer | 72-68-79-69—288 | 99,126 | | Lindsey Wright (AUS) | 74-70-77-71—292 | 42,724 |
| | Ai Miyazato (JPN) | 74-74-71-69—288 | 99,126 | 26 | He Yong Choi (KOR) | 77-74-74-68—293 | 27,420 |
| | Suzann Pettersen (NOR) | 74-71-72-71—288 | 99,126 | | Juli Inkster | 78-73-72-70—293 | 27,420 |
| 9 | Kyeong Bae (KOR) | 75-73-69-72—289 | 76,711 | | Jessica Korda (am) | 72-77-75-69—293 | |
| | Na Yeon Choi (KOR) | 68-74-76-71—289 | 76,711 | | Alison Lee (am) | 74-76-70-73—293 | |
| | Hee Young Park (KOR) | 70-74-72-73—289 | 76,711 | | Anna Nordqvist (SWE) | 71-75-75-72—293 | 27,420 |
| 12 | Song-Hee Kim (KOR) | 74-69-75-72—290 | 66,769 | | Lorena Ochoa (MEX) | 69-79-73-72—293 | 27,420 |
| 13 | Sun Ju Ahn (KOR) | 75-71-72-73—291 | 59,428 | | Inbee Park (KOR) | 75-71-77-70—293 | 27,420 |
| | Morgan Pressel | 74-75-69-73—291 | 59,428 | 33 | Sun Young Yoo (KOR) | 72-74-72-76—294 | 22,603 |
| | Jiyai Shin (KOR) | 72-75-76-68—291 | 59,428 | 34 | Louise Friberg (SWE) | 75-72-73-75—295 | 20,702 |
| | Jennifer Song (am) | 72-74-73-72—291 | | | Maria Hernandez (ESP) | 74-72-77-72—295 | 20,702 |
| 17 | Nicole Castrale | 74-71-74-73—292 | 42,724 | | Kristy McPherson | 71-74-77-73—295 | 20,702 |
| | Laura Davies (ENG) | 72-75-73-72—292 | 42,724 | | Alexis Thompson (am) | 71-73-78-73—295 | |
| | Meaghan Francella | 73-72-74-73—292 | 42,724 | | Karrie Webb (AUS) | 75-72-74-74—295 | 20,702 |
| | | | | | Amy Yang (KOR) | 75-71-75-74—295 | 20,702 |

**Other players who made the cut:** Misun Cho (KOR), Sandra Gal (GER), Young Kim (KOR), Brittany Lang, Azahara Muñoz (ESP) (am), Ji Young Oh (KOR), Michele Redman, Momoko Ueda (JPN) 296; Shanshan Feng (CHN), Stacy Lewis, Hee-Kyung Seo (KOR), Maria Jose Uribe (COL) 297; Amanda Blumenherst, Hye Jung Choi (KOR), Christina Kim, Giulia Sergas (ITA), Karen Stupples (ENG) 298; Yuri Fudoh (JPN), Haeji Kang (KOR), Mika Miyazato (JPN), Stacy Prammanasudh 299; Cindy Lacrosse, Ji Hee Lee (KOR), Meena Lee (KOR), Becky Morgan (WAL) 300; Allison Fouch, Allie White (am) 301; Karine Icher (FRA), Mina Harigae, Jennie Lee 304; Candace Schepperle (am) 306; Carolina Llano (COL) 307; Lisa Ferrero 312

## 2008 US Women's Open Championship *Interlachen CC, Edina, MN* [6789–73]

Prize money: $3.1 million

| | | | | | | | | |
|---|---|---|---|---|---|---|---|---|
| 1 | Inbee Park (KOR) | 72-69-71-71—283 | $585,000 | 19T | Jessica Korda (CZE) | 72-78-75-69—294 | | |
| 2 | Helen Alfredsson (SWE) | 70-71-71-75—287 | 350,000 | | (am) | | | |
| 3 | In-Kyung Kim (KOR) | 71-73-69-75—288 | 162,487 | | Candy Kung (TPE) | 72-70-79-73—294 | 43,376 | |
| | Stacy Lewis | 73-70-67-78—288 | 162,487 | | Jiyai Shin (KOR) | 69-74-79-72—294 | 43,376 | |
| | Angela Park (BRA) | 73-67-75-73—288 | 162,487 | 24 | Pat Hurst | 67-78-77-73—295 | 35,276 | |
| 6 | Nicole Castrale | 74-70-74-71—289 | 94,117 | | Song-Hee Kim (KOR) | 68-76-75-76—295 | 35,276 | |
| | Paula Creamer | 70-72-69-78—289 | 94,117 | | Annika Sörenstam | 75-70-72-78—295 | 35,276 | |
| | Mi Hyun Kim (KOR) | 72-72-70-75—289 | 94,117 | | (SWE) | | | |
| | Giulia Sergas (ITA) | 73-74-72-70—289 | 94,117 | 27 | Minea Blomqvist (FIN) | 72-69-76-79—296 | 28,210 | |
| 10 | Teresa Lu (TPE) | 71-72-73-74—290 | 75,734 | | Laura Diaz | 77-70-73-76—296 | 28,210 | |
| | Maria Jose Uribe | 69-74-72-75—290 | | | Seon Hwa Lee (KOR) | 75-70-73-78—296 | 28,210 | |
| | (COL) (am) | | | | Ai Miyazato (JPN) | 71-72-76-77—296 | 28,210 | |
| 12 | Stacy Prammanasudh | 75-72-71-73—291 | 71,002 | 31 | Sun-Ju Ahn (KOR) | 76-71-78-72—297 | 21,567 | |
| 13 | Cristie Kerr | 72-70-75-75—292 | 60,878 | | Young Kim (KOR) | 74-71-71-81—297 | 21,567 | |
| | Jee Young Lee (KOR) | 71-75-74-72—292 | 60,878 | | Brittany Lang | 71-75-74-77—297 | 21,567 | |
| | Suzann Pettersen | 77-71-73-71—292 | 60,878 | | Lorena Ochoa (MEX) | 73-74-76-74—297 | 21,567 | |
| | (NOR) | | | | Ji Young Oh (KOR) | 67-76-76-78—297 | 21,567 | |
| | Momoko Ueda (JPN) | 72-71-73-76—292 | 60,878 | | Karen Stupples (ENG) | 74-73-75-75—297 | 21,567 | |
| 17 | Catriona Matthew | 70-77-73-73—293 | 51,380 | | Alison Walshe (am) | 73-74-73-77—297 | | |
| | (SCO) | | | 38 | Amanda Blumenherst | 72-78-71-77—298 | | |
| | Morgan Pressel | 74-74-72-73—293 | 51,380 | | (am) | | | |
| 19 | Na Yeon Choi (KOR) | 76-71-71-76—294 | 43,376 | | Jennifer Rosales (PHI) | 74-72-77-75—298 | 18,690 | |
| | Jeong Jang (KOR) | 73-69-74-78—294 | 43,376 | | Sherri Steinhauer | 75-75-71-77—298 | 18,690 | |
| | | | | | Karrie Webb (AUS) | 75-75-72-76—298 | 18,690 | |

**Other players who made the cut:** Rachel Hetherington (AUS), Katherine Hull (AUS), Eun-Hee Ji (KOR), Ma On Min (KOR), Paola Moreno (COL) (am), Jane Park, Reilley Rankin, Yani Tseng (TPE), Lindsey Wright (AUS); Maria Hjörth (SWE), Sakura Yokomine (JPN) 300; Louise Friberg (SWE), Christina Kim, Leta Lindley, Sherri Turner 301; Linda Wessberg (SWE) 302; Marcy Hart, Brittany Lincicome, Meg Mallon, Karin Sjodin (SWE), Angela Stanford, Whitney Wade 303; Shi Hyun Ahn (KOR), Na Ri Kim (KOR), Sydnee Michaels (am), Janice Moodie (SCO) 304; Jimin Kang (KOR) 305; Kim Hall 306; Michele Redman 307; Il Mi Chung (KOR), Hee-Won Han (KOR), Tiffany Lua (am) 308; Meena Lee (KOR) 311

## 2007 US Women's Open Championship *Southern Pines, SC* [6664–71]

Prize money: $3.1 million

| | | | | | | | | |
|---|---|---|---|---|---|---|---|---|
| 1 | Cristie Kerr | 71-72-66-70—279 | $560,000 | 25T | Il Mi Chung (KOR) | 73-72-74-72—291 | 24,767 | |
| 2 | Lorena Ochoa (MEX) | 71-71-68-71—281 | 271,022 | | Katherine Hull (AUS) | 72-74-71-74—291 | 24,767 | |
| | Angela Park (BRA) | 68-69-74-70—281 | 271,022 | | Mi-Jeong Jeon (KOR) | 76-72-73-70—291 | 24,767 | |
| 4 | Se Ri Pak (KOR) | 74-72-68-68—282 | 130,549 | | Young Kim (KOR) | 75-71-72-73—291 | 24,767 | |
| | Inbee Park (KOR) | 69-73-71-69—282 | 130,549 | | Seon Hwa Lee (KOR) | 72-73-71-75—291 | 24,767 | |
| 6 | Ji-Yai Shin (KOR) | 70-69-71-74—284 | 103,581 | | Sherri Steinhauer | 75-72-72-72—291 | 24,767 | |
| 7 | Jee Young Lee (KOR) | 72-71-71-71—285 | 93,031 | 32 | Laura Davies (ENG) | 72-75-72-73—292 | 19,754 | |
| 8 | Jeong Jang (KOR) | 72-71-70-73—286 | 82,464 | | Moire Dunn | 73-71-74-74—292 | 19,754 | |
| | Mi Hyun Kim (KOR) | 71-75-70-70—286 | 82,464 | | Annika Sörenstam | 70-77-72-73—292 | 19,754 | |
| 10 | Kyeong Bae (KOR) | 74-71-72-70—287 | 66,177 | | (SWE) | | | |
| | Julieta Granada (PAR) | 70-69-75-73—287 | 66,177 | 35 | Nicole Castrale | 75-73-70-75—293 | 17,648 | |
| | Ai Miyazato (JPN) | 73-73-72-69—287 | 66,177 | | Natalie Gulbis | 74-72-74-73—293 | 17,648 | |
| | Morgan Pressel | 71-70-69-77—287 | 66,177 | | Charlotte Mayorkas | 70-73-78-72—293 | 17,648 | |
| 14 | Joo Mi Kim (KOR) | 70-73-70-75—288 | 55,032 | | Kris Tamulis | 72-71-74-76—293 | 17,648 | |
| | Brittany Lincicome | 71-74-71-72—288 | 55,032 | 39 | Shi Hyun Ahn (KOR) | 70-72-76-76—294 | 14,954 | |
| 16 | Paula Creamer | 72-74-71-72—289 | 44,219 | | Erica Blasberg | 74-69-75-76—294 | 14,954 | |
| | Amy Hung (TPE) | 70-69-75-75—289 | 44,219 | | Laura Diaz | 74-72-73-75—294 | 14,954 | |
| | Jimin Kang (KOR) | 73-73-73-70—289 | 44,219 | | Jennie Lee (am) | 71-74-75-74—294 | | |
| | Birdie Kim (KOR) | 73-70-71-75—289 | 44,219 | | Janice Moodie (SCO) | 71-76-74-73—294 | 14,954 | |
| | Catriona Matthew | 75-67-74-73—289 | 44,219 | | Becky Morgan (WAL) | 75-72-73-74—294 | 14,954 | |
| | (SCO) | | | | Jennifer Song (am) | 72-73-73-76—294 | | |
| | Angela Stanford | 72-71-73-73—289 | 44,219 | 46 | Diana D'Alessio | 73-70-77-75—295 | 12,268 | |
| 22 | Dina Ammaccapane | 75-72-70-73—290 | 33,878 | | Wendy Doolan (AUS) | 73-70-75-77—295 | 12,268 | |
| | Shiho Ohyama (JPN) | 69-73-73-75—290 | 33,878 | | Meena Lee (KOR) | 71-74-75-75—295 | 12,268 | |
| | Sakura Yokomine (JPN) | 72-71-74-73—290 | 33,878 | | Sherri Turner | 73-74-73-75—295 | 12,268 | |
| 25 | Hye Jung Choi (KOR) | 77-68-70-76—291 | 24,767 | | | | | |

**Other players who made the cut:** Amanda Blumenherst (am), Jimin Jeong (KOR), Song-Hee Kim (KOR), Su A Kim (KOR), Leta Lindley, Teresa Lu (TPE), Amy Yang (KOR), Sung Ah Yim (KOR) 296; Katie Futcher, Candie Kung (TPE), Jane Park 297; Pat Hurst, In-Kyung Kim (KOR) 298; Allison Fouch, Karin Sjodin (SWE) 300; Aree Song (KOR) 301; Mina Harigae (am), Karine Icher (FRA) 305

## 2006 US Women's Open Championship Newport CC, Newport, RI   [6564–71]

Prize money: $3.1 million

| | | | | | | | | |
|---|---|---|---|---|---|---|---|---|
| 1 | Annika Sörenstam (SWE)* | 69-71-73-71—284 | $560,000 | 20T | Kristina Tucker (SWE) | 72-74-74-76—296 | 41,654 |
| 2 | Pat Hurst | 69-71-75-69—284 | 335,000 | 24 | Amy Hung (TPE) | 76-72-77-72—297 | 32,873 |
| *Play off: 18 holes: Sörenstam 70, Hurst 74* | | | | | Lorie Kane (CAN) | 73-72-75-77—297 | 32,873 |
| 3 | Se Ri Pak (KOR) | 69-74-74-69—286 | 156,038 | | Sherri Steinhauer | 72-75-72-78—297 | 32,873 |
| | Stacy Prammanasudh | 72-71-71-72—286 | 156,038 | | Shani Waugh (AUS) | 77-72-73-75—297 | 32,873 |
| | Michelle Wie | 70-72-71-73—286 | 156,038 | 28 | Tracy Hanson | 75-71-78-74—298 | 22,529 |
| 6 | Juli Inkster | 73-70-71-73—287 | 103,575 | | Jeong Jang (KOR) | 72-71-75-80—298 | 22,529 |
| 7 | Brittany Lincicome | 72-72-69-78—291 | 93,026 | | Cristie Kerr | 73-74-75-76—298 | 22,529 |
| 10 | Amanda Blumenherst (am) | 70-77-73-73—293 | | | Carin Koch (SWE) | 74-73-73-78—298 | 22,529 |
| | Sophie Gustafson (SWE) | 72-72-71-78—293 | 66,174 | | Candie Kung (TPE) | 74-70-77-77—298 | 22,529 |
| | | | | | Ai Miyazato (JPN) | 74-75-70-79—298 | 22,529 |
| | Young Kim (KOR) | 75-69-75-74—293 | 66,174 | | Becky Morgan (WAL) | 70-74-77-77—298 | 22,529 |
| | Jee Young Lee (KOR) | 71-75-70-77—293 | 66,174 | | Suzann Pettersen (NOR) | 73-74-75-76—298 | 22,529 |
| | Patricia Meunier-Lebouc (FRA) | 72-73-73-75—293 | 66,174 | | Morgan Pressel | 76-74-75-73—298 | 22,529 |
| | Jane Park (am) | 69-73-75-76—293 | | 37 | Dawn Coe-Jones (CAN) | 74-75-73-77—299 | 17,647 |
| 16 | Paula Creamer | 71-72-76-75—294 | 53,577 | | Karrie Webb (AUS) | 73-76-74-76—299 | 17,647 |
| | Natalie Gulbis | 76-71-74-73—294 | 53,577 | | Lindsey Wright (AUS) | 74-73-76-76—299 | 17,647 |
| | Sherri Turner | 72-74-76-72—294 | 53,577 | | Heather Young | 76-71-77-75—299 | 17,647 |
| 19 | Catriona Matthew (SCO) | 74-76-72-73—295 | 48,007 | 41 | Maria Hjörth (SWE) | 74-75-73-78—300 | 14,954 |
| 20 | Lorena Ochoa (MEX) | 71-73-77-75—296 | 41,654 | | Mi Hyun Kim (KOR) | 75-72-75-78—300 | 14,954 |
| | Gloria Park (KOR) | 70-78-76-72—296 | 41,654 | | Yu Ping Lin (TPE) | 76-74-75-75—300 | 14,954 |
| | Karen Stupples (ENG) | 78-72-70-76—296 | 41,654 | | Aree Song (KOR) | 77-72-79-72—300 | 14,954 |
| | | | | | Wendy Ward | 77-73-77-73—300 | 14,954 |

**Other players who made the cut:** Yuri Fudoh (JPN), Julieta Granada (PAR), Nancy Scranton 301; Dana Dormann, Seon Hwa Lee (KOR), Siew-Ai Lin (MAS), Alena Sharp (CAN), Karin Sjodin (SWE), Angela Stanford 302; Moira Dunn, Karine Icher (FRA) 303; Nicole Castrale, Silvia Cavalleri (ITA), Rosie Jones, Ashley Knoll (am), Diana Luna (MON) 304; Beth Bader 305; Dana Ammaccapane 306; Denise Munzlinger, Sung Ah Yin (KOR) 307; Kimberly Kim (am), Kim Saiki 309; Lynnette Brooky (NZL) 311

## 2005 US Women's Open Championship Cherry Hill, CO   [6749–71]

Prize money: $1.5 million

| | | | | | | | | |
|---|---|---|---|---|---|---|---|---|
| 1 | Birdie Kim (KOR) | 74-72-69-72—287 | $560,000 | 23T | Sarah Huarte | 74-76-73-73—296 | 34,556 |
| 2 | Brittany Lang (am) | 69-77-72-71—289 | | | Gloria Park (KOR) | 74-75-74-73—296 | 34,556 |
| | Morgan Pressel (am) | 71-73-70-75—289 | | | Nicole Perrot (CHI) | 70-70-78-78—296 | 34,556 |
| 4 | Natalie Gulbis | 70-75-74-71—290 | 272,723 | | Jennifer Rosales (PHI) | 72-76-73-75—296 | 34,556 |
| | Lorie Kane (CAN) | 74-71-76-69—290 | 272,723 | | Annika Sörenstam (SWE) | 71-75-73-77—296 | 34,556 |
| 6 | Karine Icher (FRA) | 69-75-75-72—291 | 116,310 | | Michelle Wie (am) | 69-73-72-82—296 | |
| | Young Jo (KOR) | 74-71-70-76—291 | 116,310 | 31 | Rachel Hetherington (AUS) | 74-69-76-78—297 | 23,479 |
| | Candie Kung (TPE) | 73-73-71-74—291 | 116,310 | | Mi Hyun Kim (KOR) | 72-73-76-76—297 | 23,479 |
| | Lorena Ochoa (MEX) | 74-68-77-72—291 | 116,310 | | Brittany Lincicome | 74-74-78-71—297 | 23,479 |
| 10 | Cristie Kerr | 74-71-72-75—292 | 80,523 | | Catriona Matthew (SCO) | 73-72-75-77—297 | 23,479 |
| | Angela Stanford | 69-74-73-76—292 | 80,523 | | Karrie Webb (AUS) | 76-73-73-75—297 | 23,479 |
| | Karen Stupples (ENG) | 75-70-69-78—292 | 80,523 | 36 | Kim Saiki | 74-73-74-77—298 | 20,386 |
| 13 | Tina Barrett | 73-74-71-75—293 | 61,402 | | Wendy Ward | 74-74-75-75—298 | 20,386 |
| | Heather Bowie | 77-73-69-74—293 | 61,402 | 38 | Il Mi Chung (KOR) | 75-71-76-77—299 | 17,939 |
| | Jamie Hullett | 75-72-70-76—293 | 61,402 | | Johanna Head (ENG) | 74-73-75-77—299 | 17,939 |
| | Soo Yun Kang (KOR) | 74-74-74-71—293 | 61,402 | | Juli Inkster | 77-71-75-76—299 | 17,939 |
| | Paige MacKenzie (am) | 75-75-69-74—293 | | | Young Kim (KOR) | 73-73-70-83—299 | 17,939 |
| | Meg Mallon | 71-75-74-73—293 | 61,402 | | Sarah Lee (KOR) | 79-70-75-75—299 | 17,939 |
| 19 | Paula Creamer | 74-69-72-79—294 | 47,480 | | Amanda McCurdy (am) | 75-75-71-78—299 | |
| | Rosie Jones | 73-72-74-75—294 | 47,480 | | Aree Song (KOR) | 77-70-72-80—299 | 17,939 |
| | Leta Lindley | 73-76-73-72—294 | 47,480 | | | | |
| | Liselotte Neumann (SWE) | 70-75-73-76—294 | 47,480 | | | | |
| 23 | Helen Alfredsson (SWE) | 72-73-74-77—296 | 34,556 | | | | |
| | Laura Diaz | 75-73-72-76—296 | 34,556 | | | | |

**Other players who made the cut:** Se Ri Pak (KOR), Nancy Scranton 300; Beth Bader, Dorothy Delasin (PHI), Hee Won Han (KOR), 301; Arnie Cochran (am), Jeong Janh (KOR) 302; Katie Allison, Eva Dahllof (SWE), Stephanie Louden, Grace Park (KOR), Suzann Pettersen (NOR), Kris Tschetter 303; Katie Futcher, Sophie Gustafson (SWE), Kaori Higo (JPN), Carri Wood 304; Candy Hannemann (BRA) 307; Jean Bartholomew 309.

## 2004 US Women's Open Championship The Orchards, South Hadley, MA    [6473–71]

Prize money: $3.1 million

| | | | | | | | | |
|---|---|---|---|---|---|---|---|---|
| 1 | Meg Mallon | 73-69-67-65—274 | $560,000 | 20T | Kate Golden | 74-71-72-71—288 | 38,660 |
| 2 | Annika Sörenstam (SWE) | 71-68-70-67—276 | 335,000 | | Johanna Head (ENG) | 76-69-70-73—288 | 38,660 |
| | | | | | Rosie Jones | 74-72-72-70—288 | 38,660 |
| 3 | Kelly Robbins | 74-67-68-69—278 | 208,863 | | Young Kim (KOR) | 71-73-76-68—288 | 38,660 |
| 4 | Jennifer Rosales (PHI) | 70-67-69-75—281 | 145,547 | | Kim Saiki | 70-68-74-76—288 | 38,660 |
| 5 | Candie Kung (TPE) | 70-68-74-70—282 | 111,173 | | Liselotte Neumann | 72-72-72-72—288 | 38,660 |
| | Michele Redman | 70-72-73-67—282 | 111,173 | | (SWE) | | |
| 7 | Moira Dunn | 73-67-72-71—283 | 86,744 | 27 | Beth Daniel | 69-74-71-75—289 | 29,195 |
| | Pat Hurst | 70-71-71-71—283 | 86,744 | | Cristie Kerr | 73-71-74-71—289 | 29,195 |
| | Jeong Jang (KOR) | 72-74-71-66—283 | 86,744 | 29 | Shi Hyun Ahn (KOR) | 73-71-72-74—290 | 24,533 |
| 10 | Michelle Ellis (Aus) | 70-69-72-73—284 | 68,813 | | Lorie Kane (CAN) | 75-70-72-73—290 | 24,533 |
| | Carin Koch (SWE) | 72-67-75-70—284 | 68,813 | | Deb Richard | 71-73-72-74—290 | 24,533 |
| | Rachel Teske (AUS) | 71-69-70-74—284 | 68,813 | 32 | Allison Hanna | 71-75-74-71—291 | 20,539 |
| 13 | Paula Creamer (am) | 72-69-72-72—285 | | | Becky Morgan (WAL) | 71-74-73-73—291 | 20,539 |
| | Patricia Meunier– | 67-75-74-69—285 | 60,602 | | Se Ri Pak (KOR) | 70-76-71-74—291 | 20,539 |
| | Labouc (FRA) | | | | Sherri Steinhauer | 74-71-73-73—291 | 20,539 |
| | Michelle Wie (am) | 71-70-71-73—285 | | | Karen Stupples (ENG) | 71-72-77-71—291 | 20,539 |
| 16 | Mi Hyun Kim (KOR) | 76-68-71-71—286 | 54,052 | 37 | Jenna Daniels | 76-71-72-73—292 | 16,897 |
| | Suzann Pettersen | 74-72-71-69—286 | 54,052 | | AJ Easthorne (CAN) | 73-72-75-72—292 | 16,897 |
| | (NOR) | | | | Natalie Gulbis | 73-71-75-73—292 | 16,897 |
| | Karrie Webb (AUS) | 72-71-71-72—286 | 54,052 | | Jamie Hullett | 72-74-74-72—292 | 16,897 |
| 19 | Catriona Matthew | 73-71-72-71—287 | 48,432 | | Christina Kim | 74-71-76-71—292 | 16,897 |
| | (SCO) | | | | Jill McGill | 71-75-71-75—292 | 16,897 |
| 20 | Dawn Coe-Jones (CAN) | 71-73-72-72—288 | 38,660 | | Gloria Park (KOR) | 76-71-73-72—292 | 16,897 |

**Other players who made the cut:** Donna Andrews, Laura Diaz, Jennifer Greggain, Ji-Hee Lee, Mhairi McKay (SCO), Lorena Ochoa (MEX) 293; Jennie Lee (am) 294; Katherine Hull 295; Tina Barrett, Catherine Cartwright, Hee-Won Han (KOR) 296; Brittany Lincicome (am) 297; Loraine Lambert, Aree Song (KOR) 298; Liz Earley, Allison Finney, Juli Inkster 299; Mee Lee (KOR), Seol-An Jeon (KOR), Courtney Swaim 300; Hilary Lunke, Grace Park (KOR) 301; Li Ying Ye (CHN) 304.

# US Women's Open History

| Year | Winner | Runner-up | Venue | Score |
|---|---|---|---|---|
| 1946 | P Berg | B Jamieson | Spokane | 5 and 4 |

*Changed to strokeplay*

| Year | Winner | Venue | Score |
|---|---|---|---|
| 1947 | B Jamieson | Greensboro | 300 |
| 1948 | B Zaharias | Atlantic City | 300 |
| 1949 | L Suggs | Maryland | 291 |
| 1950 | B Zaharias | Wichita | 291 |
| 1951 | B Rawls | Atlanta | 294 |
| 1952 | L Suggs | Bala, PA | 284 |
| 1953 | B Rawls* | Rochester, NY | 302 |
| *After a play-off with J Pung 71-77* | | | |
| 1954 | B Zaharias | Peabody, MA | 291 |
| 1955 | F Crocker | Wichita | 299 |
| 1956 | K Cornelius* | Duluth | 302 |
| *After a play-off with B McIntire (am) 75-82* | | | |
| 1957 | B Rawls | Mamaroneck | 299 |
| 1958 | M Wright | Bloomfield Hills, MI | 290 |
| 1959 | M Wright | Pittsburgh, PA | 287 |
| 1960 | B Rawls | Worchester, MA | 292 |
| 1961 | M Wright | Springfield, NJ | 293 |
| 1962 | M Lindstrom | Myrtle Beach | 301 |
| 1963 | M Mills | Kenwood | 289 |
| 1964 | M Wright* | San Diego | 290 |
| *After a play-off with R Jessen 70-72* | | | |

US Women's Open History *continued*

| Year | Winner | Venue | Score |
|------|--------|-------|-------|
| 1965 | C Mann | Northfield, NJ | 290 |
| 1966 | S Spuzich | Hazeltine National, MN | 297 |
| 1967 | C Lacoste (FRA) (am) | Hot Springs, VA | 294 |
| 1968 | S Berning | Moselem Springs, PA | 289 |
| 1969 | D Caponi | Scenic-Hills | 294 |
| 1970 | D Caponi | Muskogee, OK | 287 |
| 1971 | J Gunderson-Carner | Erie, PA | 288 |
| 1972 | S Berning | Mamaroneck, NY | 299 |
| 1973 | S Berning | Rochester, NY | 290 |
| 1974 | S Haynie | La Grange, IL | 295 |
| 1975 | S Palmer | Northfield, NJ | 295 |
| 1976 | J Carner* | Springfield, PA | 292 |

*After a play-off: Carner 76, S Palmer 78*

| Year | Winner | Venue | Score |
|------|--------|-------|-------|
| 1977 | H Stacy | Hazeltine, MN | 292 |
| 1978 | H Stacy | Indianapolis | 299 |
| 1979 | J Britz | Brooklawn, CN | 284 |
| 1980 | A Alcott | Richland, TN | 280 |
| 1981 | P Bradley | La Grange, IL | 279 |
| 1982 | J Alex | Del Paso, Sacramento, CA | 283 |
| 1983 | J Stephenson (AUS) | Broken Arrow, OK | 290 |
| 1984 | H Stacy | Salem, MA | 290 |
| 1985 | K Baker | Baltusrol, NJ | 280 |
| 1986 | J Geddes* | NCR | 287 |

*After a play-off with Sally Little*

| Year | Winner | Venue | Score |
|------|--------|-------|-------|
| 1987 | L Davies (ENG)* | Plainfield | 285 |

*After a play-off: Davies 71, A Okamoto 73, J Carner 74*

| Year | Winner | Venue | Score |
|------|--------|-------|-------|
| 1988 | L Neumann (SWE) | Baltimore | 277 |
| 1989 | B King | Indianwood, MI | 278 |
| 1990 | B King | Atlanta Athletic Club, GA | 284 |
| 1991 | M Mallon | Colonial, TX | 283 |
| 1992 | P Sheehan* | Oakmont, PA | 280 |

*After a play-off: Sheehan 72, J Inkster 74*

| Year | Winner | Venue | Score |
|------|--------|-------|-------|
| 1993 | L Merton | Crooked Stick | 280 |
| 1994 | P Sheehan | Indianwood, MI | 277 |
| 1995 | A Sörenstam (SWE) | The Broadmore, CO | 278 |
| 1996 | A Sörenstam (SWE) | Pine Needles Lodge, NC | 272 |
| 1997 | A Nicholas (ENG) | Pumpkin Ridge, OR | 274 |
| 1998 | SR Pak (KOR)* | Blackwolf Run, WI | 290 |

*After a play-off: Pak 5,3; J Chausiriporn (am) 5,4*

| Year | Winner | Venue | Score |
|------|--------|-------|-------|
| 1999 | J Inkster | Old Waverley, West Point, MS | 272 |
| 2000 | K Webb (AUS) | Merit Club, Libertyville, IL | 282 |
| 2001 | K Webb (AUS) | Pine Needles Lodge & GC, NC | 273 |
| 2002 | J Inkster | Prairie Dunes, KS | 276 |
| 2003 | H Lunke* | Pumpkin Ridge GC, OR | 283 |

*After a play-off: Lunke 70, A Stanford 71, K Robins 73*

| Year | Winner | Venue | Score |
|------|--------|-------|-------|
| 2004 | M Mallon | The Orchards, S Hadley, MA | 274 |
| 2005 | B Kim (KOR) | Cherry Hills CC, CO | 287 |
| 2006 | A Sörenstam (SWE)* | Newport CC, RI | 284 |

*After a play-off: Sörenstam 70, P Hurst 74*

| Year | Winner | Venue | Score |
|------|--------|-------|-------|
| 2007 | C Kerr | Southern Pines, NC | 279 |
| 2008 | I Park (KOR) | Interlachen, MN | 283 |
| 2009 | E-H Ji (KOR) | Saucon Valley, PA | 284 |
| 2010 | P Creamer | Oakmont, PA | 281 |
| 2011 | S Y Ryu (KOR)* | The Broadmoor, CO | 281 |

*Beat H K Seo (KOR) at the third extra hole*

| Year | Winner | Venue | Score |
|------|--------|-------|-------|
| 2012 | N Y Choi (KOR) | Blackwolf Run, Kohler, WI | 281 |
| 2013 | I Park (KOR) | Sebonack GC, Southampton, NY | 280 |

## The 59th LPGA Championship

# Inbee Park wins again but Scotland's Catriona Matthew gave her a fright

Hard on the heels of winning the Kraft Nabisco, Inbee Park secured the third major title of her career and her fourth victory of 2013 with a dogged play-off triumph over Catriona Matthew in the Wegmans LPGA. Although the South Korean ran up three bogeys in her closing five holes, she showed the mettle of a champion to bounce back and force a decisive birdie at the third hole of a sudden death play-off at Locust Hill country club in Pittsford, New York.

In an event disrupted by wet weather, Park and Matthew played 39 holes of golf during a gripping final day's play. The Rolex Rankings world No 1 was in a strong position after 54 holes on eight under par while the Scot was seven strokes adrift and appeared to have little chance of thwarting Park's ambition to become only the seventh woman to win the first two majors of the season and the first since Annika Sörenstam in 2005.

While not quite as far off the pace as her compatriot, Paul Lawrie, when the Aberdonian made up a ten shot disadvantage on Jean Van de Velde during the final round of The Open Championship at Carnoustie in 1999, the North Berwick golfer nevertheless shot a flawless closing 68 to take advantage of the faltering Park's struggles off the tee.

After scrambling for 75 and posting the same five under par total as Matthew, Park dug deep and somehow rediscovered the knack of finding fairways in the play-off. After twice matching the pars crafted by the Scot, this superb putter holed an 18 footer for birdie at the third extra hole to maintain the remarkable run of success savoured by Asian golfers, who had annexed no fewer than nine consecutive major titles since the LPGA in 2011.

Perhaps Park's resilience shouldn't have come as much of a surprise. Her form since finishing in the top ten at the LPGA Championship in 2012 had been blistering. In 26 events, she'd earned 13 top ten finishes, six victories and nearly $3.3 million in prize money. The 24-year-old's remarkable level of consistency, consequently, elevated her to No 1 in the world.

"I felt I ran a marathon," she said, "and I'm just happy that we got it done. This golf course was so tough and fair at the same time, and I really enjoyed playing. You had to be perfect on every shot. I didn't know that I was going to be able to do it – I was hitting the ball everywhere in the final round. It just made my day so much tougher. Putting my name on the Wegmans LPGA championship trophy means so much to me. I'm getting a lot closer to the goals I set for my golf career."

At 43, whatever Matthews conceded to Park in terms of zest, she more than matched in seasoned determination. The winner of the Ricoh Women's British Open at Lytham in 2009, the Scot has also been runner-up in the Kraft Nabisco three times and was fourth at the US Women's Open in 2001. A mother of two daughters and a member of the LPGA since 1995, few have played as well for as long in the majors with as little fanfare as the accountancy graduate.

"The last time I saw the scoreboard, Inbee had a solid lead, so I was quite surprised when I looked again on the 18th and discovered two putts would get me in a play-off," Matthew recalled. "When I started the last round I probably didn't realise I could win. So to play well and get into the play-off was pretty good. Obviously when you get into it [and lose], it's disappointing. Looking back I think it was great to have a chance. I've been out here for 19 years now, so these are the big tournaments. They're certainly the ones you're trying to win. My youngest one keeps telling me not to come home unless I get a trophy. So I'm getting closer. She's a hard task master…"

No one played more aggressively in the final round than Suzann Pettersen, who signed for 65 and narrowly missed out on a spot in the play-off. Having putted poorly in earlier rounds, Pettersen made an adjustment to her stance during a practice session between the third and fourth rounds on Sunday and was rewarded with a share of third spot alongside Morgan Pressel, the leader at the halfway mark, who dropped back to four under with a closing 75.

It said much about the resilience of the players, not to mention the dedication of the ground crew staff, that the championship finished more or less on schedule after heavy rain and bolts of lightning in the Rochester area prevented any play on Thursday. The course was saturated by two and a half inches of rain over a 24 hour period and was still sodden on Friday when the first round eventually got under-way.

Chella Choi made the fastest start, carding six birdies in her opening ten holes before signing for 67. The key to the South Korean's success was keeping the ball in play off the tee: finding 14 fairways in regulation figures gaving her a platform to attack. In continuously wet conditions, she dropped a shot on the back nine but only missed three greens and built a one stroke advantage over Pressel and Jiyai Shin.

> "The last time I saw the leaderboard, Inbee had a solid lead then I had two putts to tie."
>
> *Catriona Matthew*

Like most champions, Park began steadily on level par. The world No 1 might have been closer to the lead had she not ran up a double bogey on the home hole after finding herself between clubs and making the wrong selection. "It wasn't a bad start," she surmised, " and I have three more rounds to play good."

Park was as good as her word on Saturday, firing a four under round of 68 and moving to within a shot of the lead held, going into the final day, by Pressel. The area where her game most improved from the previous day lay in ball striking. Starting at the tenth, she hit her 9 iron approach close to the flag and enjoyed a tap-in from a couple of feet for birdie. That lifted her spirits and for a spell Park almost made the game look easy. "If you hit the ball straight the game is easier," she acknowledged. "But, no, it's never easy."

Pressel, without a win in five years, would have concurred with that assertion, alright, as this was the first time she'd so much as held the lead at the halfway mark of an event since the same tournament in 2008. Encouraged by three birdies in her opening six holes, Pressel eventually signed for 70 and a total of six under par. The youngest female winner of a major title at 18 in 2007 was hoping the memory of that early success would stand her in good stead. "I've been through a lot since then," she cautioned. " A lot has happened in golf and life, but that being said, I've done it before. So I just need to go out there and remember that I can do it."

Pressel acquitted herself pretty well on Sunday morning, shooting 71 in the third round, and keeping in touch with Park, who followed Saturday's 68 with another four under par round to grab the lead. Matthew, meanwhile, who was typically diligent on Friday and Saturday, returning successive scores of 71, before appearing to fall out of the frame with a 73.

In championship golf, of course, it pays to expect the unexpected. In the final round, thanks to birdies at the second and ninth holes, the Scot reached the turn in 33 and found herself in contention for a second major title after further birdies at the 12th and 17th holes. As important as the birdies she made were the bogeys Matthew avoided. After making two in the first round, three in the second and four in the third, the former Women's British Open champion enjoyed a glimpse of glory by keeping her fourth round card bogey free. The fact she only took 26 putts didn't hurt either.

Park is one of the steadiest players in women's golf and most of the cognoscenti would have closed the book on her after she birdied the fifth to reach nine under par. Unusually for the South Korean, though, she lost control of line and length with the driver and spilled strokes at the sixth and eighth. Even more surprising were her struggles on the home stretch where she made four 5s, including three bogeys, over the closing five holes.

Having missed eight fairways and spurned a sizeable lead, it took courage for Park to re-focus when she returned to face Matthew in the sudden death play-off. "Nothing seemed to be working," she said. "So I really cleared my head, and looked at the fairway. Then I just smashed it."

After Park and Matthew traded pars over the first two extra holes, it was the Scot who missed the short grass at the third attempt and effectively handed the initiative to the South Korean who finished in style by holing a long birdie putt. "It was almost a miracle that I won," said the champion. "But I tried not to give up and that really paid off."

Mike Aitken

| First Round | Second Round | Third Round | Fourth Round |
|---|---|---|---|
| –5 Chella Choi | –6 Morgan Pressel | –8 Inbee Park | –5 Inbee Park |
| –4 Jiyai Shin | –4 Inbee Park | –7 Morgan Pressel | –5 Catriona Matthew |
| –4 Morgan Pressel | –4 Chella Choi | –6 Jiyai Shin | –4 Suzann Pettersen |
| –3 Brittany Lincicome | –3 Sarah Jane Smith | –4 Sun Young Yoo | –4 Morgan Pressel |
| –2 Jessica Korda | –3 Amy Yang | –4 Na Yeon Choi | –3 Amy Yang |
| –2 Se Ri Pak | –3 Jiyai Shin | –3 Chella Choi | –3 Chella Choi |
| –1 Laura Davies | –2 Sun Young Yoo | –2 Kristy McPherson | –3 Sun Young Yoo |
| –1 Catriona Matthew | –2 Na Yeon Cho | –1 Catriona Matthew | –3 Jiyai Shin |
| –1 Lexi Thomson | –2 Catriona Matthew | –1 Michelle Wie | |
| –1 Amy Yang | –2 Angela Stanford | | |

# Wegmans LPGA Championship   *Locust Hill, Pittsford, NY*   June 3–9   [6534–72]

Prize Money: $2.5 million. Field of 146 players, of whom 76 made the half-way cut on 150 or less.

*Players are of American nationality unless stated*

| | | | |
|---|---|---|---|
| 1 | Inbee Park (KOR)* | 72-68-68-75—283 | $337,500 |
| 2 | Catriona Matthew (SCO) | 71-71-73-68—283 | 206,304 |

*Park won at the third extra hole*

| | | | |
|---|---|---|---|
| 3 | Suzann Pettersen (NOR) | 72-73-74-65—284 | 132,716 |
| | Morgan Pressel | 68-70-71-75—284 | 132,716 |
| 5 | Jiyai Shin (KOR) | 68-73-69-75—285 | 72,288 |
| | Chella Choi (KOR) | 67-73-73-72—285 | 72,288 |
| | Amy Yang (KOR) | 71-70-74-70—285 | 72,288 |
| | Sun Young Yoo (KOR) | 73-69-70-73—285 | 72,288 |
| 9 | Michelle Wie | 76-68-71-71—286 | 46,121 |
| | Shanshan Feng (CHN) | 74-70-72-70—286 | 46,121 |
| | Na Yeon Choi (KOR) | 72-70-70-74—286 | 46,121 |
| 12 | Caroline Masson (GER) | 74-69-71-73—287 | 37,122 |
| | Anna Nordqvist (SWE) | 71-74-73-69—287 | 37,122 |
| | Cristie Kerr | 75-72-70-70—287 | 37,122 |
| 15 | Ai Miyazato (JPN) | 74-75-66-73—288 | 31,851 |
| | Kristy McPherson | 73-72-69-74—288 | 31,851 |
| 17 | Lydia Ko (NZL) (am) | 77-70-73-69—289 | |
| | Brittany Lincicome | 69-73-77-70—289 | 29,367 |
| 19 | Beatriz Recari (ESP) | 74-71-73-72—290 | 26,957 |
| 19 | Jennifer Rosales (PHI) | 76-71-70-73—290 | 26,957 |
| | Yani Tseng (TPE) | 72-74-71-73—290 | 26,957 |
| 22 | Eun-Hee Ji (KOR) | 72-72-74-73—291 | 22,873 |
| | Jenny Shin (KOR) | 78-70-70-73—291 | 22,873 |
| | Danielle Kang | 75-72-72-72—291 | 22,873 |
| | Mina Harigae | 75-74-73-69—291 | 22,873 |
| | I K Kim (KOR) | 75-74-73-69—291 | 22,873 |
| | Mika Miyazato (JPN) | 77-71-71-72—291 | 22,873 |
| 28 | Lexi Thompson | 71-73-75-73—292 | 18,478 |
| | Se Ri Pak (KOR) | 70-74-76-72—292 | 18,478 |
| | Angela Stanford | 71-71-75-75—292 | 18,478 |
| | Stacy Lewis | 74-72-76-70—292 | 18,478 |
| | Pernilla Lindberg (SWE) | 73-71-71-77—292 | 18,478 |
| 33 | Haeji Kang (KOR) | 73-74-71-75—293 | 15,389 |
| | Chie Arimura (JPN) | 71-72-73-77—293 | 15,389 |
| | Danah Bordner | 73-71-73-76—293 | 15,389 |
| | Karrie Webb (AUS) | 76-72-75-70—293 | 15,389 |
| 37 | Ji Young Oh (KOR) | 75-72-71-76—294 | 12,296 |
| | Mi Jung Hur (KOR) | 71-74-76-73—294 | 12,296 |
| | Moira Dunn | 75-71-75-73—294 | 12,296 |
| | Carlota Ciganda (ESP) | 75-71-71-77—294 | 12,296 |
| | Paige Mackenzie | 76-74-71-73—294 | 12,296 |
| | Mo Martin | 77-73-71-73—294 | 12,296 |
| | Caroline Hedwall (SWE) | 77-71-70-76—294 | 12,296 |
| 44 | Candie Kung (TPE) | 75-75-71-74—295 | 9,623 |
| | Pornanong Phatlum (THA) | 72-74-73-76—295 | 9,623 |
| | Vicky Hurst | 73-72-77-73—295 | 9,623 |
| | Giulia Sergas (ITA) | 76-72-73-74—295 | 9,623 |
| | Ayako Uehara (JPN) | 76-73-73-73—295 | 9,623 |
| 49 | Jessica Korda | 70-74-76-76—296 | 8,414 |
| | Lisa Ferrero | 78-71-71-76—296 | 8,414 |
| 51 | Hee Young Park (KOR) | 75-71-75-76—297 | 7,794 |
| | Paola Moreno | 74-74-73-76—297 | 7,794 |
| 53 | Sarah Jane Smith | 72-69-76-81—298 | 7,003 |
| | Ilhee Lee (KOR) | 71-74-74-79—298 | 7,003 |
| | Laura Diaz | 75-73-73-77—298 | 7,003 |
| | Mariajo Uribe (COL) | 76-74-74-74—298 | 7,003 |

## LPGA Championship *continued*

| | | | |
|---|---|---|---|
| 53T | Nicole Castrale | 73-72-77-76—298 | 7,003 |
| 58 | Paula Creamer | 76-71-76-76—299 | 5,987 |
| | Lorie Kane (CAN) | 74-74-74-77—299 | 5,987 |
| | Belen Mozo (ESP) | 77-71-74-77—299 | 5,987 |
| | Breanna Elliott (AUS) | 75-74-77-73—299 | 5,987 |
| 62 | Jacqui Concolino | 78-70-77-75—300 | 5,478 |
| | Lisa McCloskey | 74-72-76-78—300 | 5,478 |
| 64 | Marcy Hart | 78-71-75-78—302 | 5,026 |
| | Laura Davies (ENG) | 71-73-80-78—302 | 5,026 |
| | Melissa Reid (ENG) | 76-74-76-76—302 | 5,026 |
| | Moriya Jutanugarn (THA) | 74-74-72-82—302 | 5,026 |
| | Jane Park | 74-74-78-76—302 | 5,026 |
| | Mi Hyang Lee (KOR) | 75-71-78-78—302 | 5,026 |
| 70 | Alison Walshe | 75-74-77-77—303 | 4,631 |
| 71 | Amelia Lewis | 74-74-78-78—304 | 4,519 |
| 72 | Brittany Lang | 75-71-80-79—305 | 4,405 |
| | Sue Kim (CAN) | 75-74-81-75—305 | 4,405 |
| | Tiffany Joh | 77-72-78-78—305 | 4,405 |
| 75 | Kathleen Ekey | 76-74-79-78—307 | 4,292 |
| 76 | Lauren Doughtie | 75-75-81-80—311 | 4,240 |

*The following players missed the cut:*

| | | | | | | | | |
|---|---|---|---|---|---|---|---|---|
| 77 | Jeong Jang (KOR) | 72-78—150 WDC | 96T | Sandra Gal (GER) | 79-74—153 | 123T | Amanda Blumenherst | 80-76—156 |
| 78 | Becky Morgan (WAL) | 74-77—151 | | Momoko Ueda (JPN) | 79-74—153 | | Reilley Rankin | 75-81—156 |
| | Stephanie Sherlock (CAN) | 77-74—151 | | Hee Kyung Seo (KOR) | 74-79—153 | | Jin Young Pak (KOR) | 79-77—156 |
| | Silvia Cavalleri (ITA) | 77-74—151 | | Thidapa Suwannapura (THA) | 79-74—153 | | Juli Inkster | 78-78—156 |
| | Kayla Mortellaro | 77-74—151 | | Amy Hung (TPE) | 75-78—153 | 130 | Sue Ginter | 81-76—157 |
| | Jennie Lee | 73-78—151 | | Dori Carter | 79-74—153 | | Meaghan Francella | 82-75—157 |
| | Jennifer Johnson | 75-76—151 | 107 | Sarah Kemp (AUS) | 80-74—154 | 132 | Cindy LaCrosse | 80-78—158 |
| | Jennifer Song | 77-74—151 | | Karine Icher (FRA) | 78-76—154 | | Wendy Ward | 80-78—158 |
| | Christina Kim | 74-77—151 | | Sandra Changkija | 74-80—154 | 134 | Nicole Jeray | 78-81—159 |
| | Paz Echeverria (CHI) | 75-76—151 | | Pat Hurst | 79-75—154 | | Eunjung Yi (KOR) | 79-80—159 |
| | Lizette Salas | 75-76—151 | | Katie Futcher | 76-78—154 | 136 | Mindy Kim | 81-79—160 |
| 88 | Austin Ernst | 78-74—152 | | Felicity Johnson (ENG) | 74-80—154 | | Julia Boland (AUS) | 83-77—160 |
| | Dewi Claire Schreefel (NED) | 77-75—152 | 113 | Christel Boeljon (NED) | 78-77—155 | 138 | Stefanie Ferguson | 82-80—162 |
| | Heather Bowie Young | 77-75—152 | | Meena Lee (KOR) | 76-79—155 | 139 | Sara-Maude Juneau (CAN) | 82-81—163 |
| | Jane Rah | 76-76—152 | | Julieta Granada (PAR) | 80-75—155 | 140 | Jean Bartholomew | 81-87—168 |
| | Jill McGill | 76-76—152 | | Katie M Burnett | 78-77—155 | | Irene Cho | 76-76 WDC |
| | Jodi Ewart Shadoff (ENG) | 78-74—152 | | Gerina Piller | 79-76—155 | | Sophie Gustafson (SWE) | 77-77 WDC |
| | Natalie Gulbis | 78-74—152 | | Nicole Smith | 75-80—155 | | Karen Stupples (ENG) | 79-79 DQC |
| | Lindsey Wright (AUS) | 77-75—152 | | Lisa Grimes | 74-81—155 | | Hee-Won Han (KOR) | 80-80 WDC |
| 96 | Seon Hwa Lee (KOR) | 78-75—153 | | Mitsuki Katahira (JPN) | 81-74—155 | | Stacy Prammanasudh (THA) | 81-81 WDC |
| | Maria Hjörth (SWE) | 76-77—153 | | Kris Tamulis | 81-74—155 | | Veronica Felibert (VEN) | 84-84 WDC |
| | So Yeon Ryu (KOR) | 76-77—153 | | Sydnee Michaels | 81-74—155 | | | |
| | Ryann O'Toole | 80-73—153 | 123 | Rebecca Lee-Bentham (CAN) | 81-75—156 | | | |
| | Azahara Muñoz (ESP) | 79-74—153 | | Alena Sharp (CAN) | 79-77—156 | | | |
| | Katherine Hull-Kirk (AUS) | 76-77—153 | | Daniela Iacobelli | 79-77—156 | | | |

---

## Ten states

Since its inauguration in 1955, the LPGA Championship has been played in just 10 of the 50 states of the USA. Topping the list is Ohio where the championship was held from 1978 to 1989, closely followed by Maryland (1975–76, 1990–93, 2005–09) and Delaware (1995–2004).

## 2012 Wegmans LPGA Championship Locust Hill, Pitsford, NY [6534–72]

Prize money: $2.5 million

| | | | | | | | | |
|---|---|---|---|---|---|---|---|---|
| 1 | Shanshan Feng (CHN) | 72-73-70-67—282 | $375,000 | 23T | Christel Boeljon (NED) | 74-74-73-70—291 | 25,597 |
| 2 | Eun-Hee Ji (KOR) | 75-68-69-72—284 | 158,443 | | Brittany Lincicome | 76-73-73-70—292 | 22,872 |
| | Suzann Pettersen (NOR) | 71-72-71-70—284 | 158,443 | 25 | I K Kim (KOR) | 73-73-73-73—292 | 22,872 |
| | Stacy Lewis | 72-72-70-70—284 | 158,443 | | Lizette Salas | 74-70-73-75—292 | 22,872 |
| | Mika Miyazato (JPN) | 70-72-73-69—284 | 158,443 | | So Yeon Ryu (KOR) | 73-70-74-75—292 | 22,872 |
| 6 | Karrie Webb (AUS) | 74-71-68-72—285 | 73,285 | 29 | Candie Kung (TPE) | 71-77-75-70—293 | 20,655 |
| | Ai Miyazato (JPN) | 70-74-73-68—285 | 73,285 | 30 | Sophie Gustafson (SWE) | 73-72-74-75—294 | 18,015 |
| | Gerina Piller | 74-71-72-68—285 | 73,285 | | Mo Martin | 71-77-77-69—294 | 18,015 |
| 9 | Paula Creamer | 70-72-73-71—286 | 51,742 | | Mi Jung Hur (KOR) | 74-69-77-74—294 | 18,015 |
| | Giulia Sergas (ITA) | 69-76-69-72—286 | 51,742 | | Mariajo Uribe (COL) | 74-76-71-73—294 | 18,015 |
| | Inbee Park (KOR) | 72-70-72-72—286 | 51,742 | | Sydnee Michaels | 72-71-72-79—294 | 18,015 |
| 12 | Cristie Kerr | 70-76-70-71—287 | 42,956 | | Lexi Thompson | 74-72-74-74—294 | 18,015 |
| | Sandra Gal (GER) | 71-71-75-70—287 | 42,956 | 36 | Catriona Matthew (SCO) | 75-72-76-72—295 | 13,263 |
| 14 | Hee Young Park (KOR) | 77-70-73-68—288 | 39,028 | | Sarah Jane Smith (AUS) | 75-72-77-71—295 | 13,263 |
| 15 | Jeong Jang (KOR) | 70-74-71-74—289 | 33,960 | | Alison Walshe | 73-77-73-72—295 | 13,263 |
| | Karin Sjodin (SWE) | 75-69-73-72—289 | 33,960 | | Chella Choi (KOR) | 75-74-74-72—295 | 13,263 |
| | Sun Young Yoo (KOR) | 72-72-71-74—289 | 33,960 | | Pornanong Phatlum (THA) | 75-74-72-74—295 | 13,263 |
| | Mina Harigae | 74-72-74-69—289 | 33,960 | | Ryann O'Toole | 69-76-75-75—295 | 13,263 |
| 19 | Nicole Castrale | 76-74-70-70—290 | 28,638 | | Jodi Ewart (ENG) | 75-72-72-76—295 | 13,263 |
| | Se Ri Pak (KOR) | 70-71-76-73—290 | 28,638 | | Haru Nomura (JPN) | 74-77-70-74—295 | 13,263 |
| | Jenny Shin (KOR) | 71-75-71-73—290 | 28,638 | | Maude-Aimee Leblanc | 72-73-75-75—295 | 13,263 |
| | Jennifer Johnson | 73-71-71-75—290 | 28,638 | | (CAN) | | |
| 23 | Marcy Hart | 72-75-73-71—291 | 25,597 | | | | |

**Other players who made the cut:** Karine Icher (FRA), Leta Lindley, Morgan Pressel, Ji Young Oh (KOR), Hee-Won Han (KOR), Beatriz Recari (ESP) 296; Katherine Hull (AUS), Becky Morgan (WAL), Haeji Kang (KOR) 297; Karen Stupples (ENG), Katie Futcher, Amelia Lewis, Jessica Korda 299; Anna Nordqvist (SWE) 300; Amy Hung (TPE), Yani Tseng (TPE), Belen Mozo (ESP) 301; Alena Sharp (CAN), Kris Tamulis, Brittany Lang, Pat Hurst, Dewi Claire Schreefel (NED) 302; Jennifer Rosales (PHI), Ilhee Lee (KOR), Meaghan Francella 303; Taylor Coutu 304; Stephanie Louden, Grace Park (KOR); 305; Na Yeon Choi DQ

---

## 2011 Wegmans LPGA Championship Locust Hill, Pitsford, NY [6534–72]

Prize money: $2.5 million

| | | | | | | | | |
|---|---|---|---|---|---|---|---|---|
| 1 | Yani Tseng (TPE) | 66-70-67-66—269 | $375,000 | 20T | Paige Mackenzie | 72-73-70-71—286 | 26,795 |
| 2 | Morgan Pressel | 69-69-70-71—279 | 228,695 | | Karrie Webb (AUS) | 74-69-71-72—286 | 26,795 |
| 3 | Suzann Pettersen (NOR) | 72-72-69-67—280 | 132,512 | | Candie Kung (TPE) | 71-71-71-73—286 | 26,795 |
| | Paula Creamer | 67-72-72-69—280 | 132,512 | 25 | Hee-Won Han (KOR) | 71-72-74-70—287 | 22,162 |
| | Cristie Kerr | 72-72-67-69—280 | 132,512 | | Anna Nordqvist (SWE) | 73-70-74-70—287 | 22,162 |
| 6 | Meena Lee (KOR) | 68-73-70-71—282 | 77,630 | | Jimin Kang (KOR) | 71-70-73-73—287 | 22,162 |
| | Stacy Lewis | 69-72-70-71—282 | 77,630 | | Pornanong Phatlum (THA) | 71-72-71-73—287 | 22,162 |
| 8 | Maria Hjörth (SWE) | 71-71-70-71—283 | 53,840 | | Tiffany Joh | 71-70-72-74—287 | 22,162 |
| | Pat Hurst | 70-67-75-71—283 | 53,840 | 30 | Jennifer Song (KOR) | 72-72-72-72—288 | 18,531 |
| | Mika Miyazato (JPN) | 72-72-68-71—283 | 53,840 | | Reilley Rankin | 73-68-74-73—288 | 18,531 |
| | Azahara Muñoz (ESP) | 70-71-71-71—283 | 53,840 | | Angela Stanford | 68-72-74-74—288 | 18,531 |
| 12 | Amy Yang (KOR) | 70-69-74-71—284 | 42,445 | | Momoko Ueda (JPN) | 72-69-71-76—288 | 18,531 |
| | I K Kim (KOR) | 73-70-69-72—284 | 42,445 | 34 | Karen Stupples (ENG) | 72-74-78-65—289 | 14,232 |
| 14 | Amy Hung (TPE) | 69-73-73-70—285 | 33,765 | | M J Hur (KOR) | 70-75-76-68—289 | 14,232 |
| | Heather Bowie Young | 72-70-73-70—285 | 33,765 | | Jiyai Shin (KOR) | 75-71-73-70—289 | 14,232 |
| | Inbee Park (KOR) | 73-69-71-72—285 | 33,765 | | Se Ri Pak (KOR) | 78-68-72-71—289 | 14,232 |
| | Katie Futcher | 75-68-69-73—285 | 33,765 | | Juli Inkster | 74-70-73-72—289 | 14,232 |
| | Hee Young Park (KOR) | 69-69-72-75—285 | 33,765 | | Catriona Matthew (SCO) | 73-69-75-72—289 | 14,232 |
| | Cindy LaCrosse | 70-69-69-77—285 | 33,765 | | Michele Redman | 73-70-73-73—289 | 14,232 |
| 20 | Brittany Lincicome | 74-72-71-69—286 | 26,795 | | Yoo Kyeong Kim (KOR) | 72-72-71-74—289 | 14,232 |
| | Sun Young Yoo (KOR) | 73-72-72-69—286 | 26,795 | | Hee Kyung Seo (KOR) | 71-73-71-74—289 | 14,232 |

**Other players who made the cut:** Taylor Leon, Eun-Hee Ji (KOR), Mindy Kim (KOR), Mi Hyun Kim (KOR), Na Yeon Choi (KOR), Jennifer Johnson, Karin Sjodin (SWE) 290; Shanshan Feng (CHN), Kristy McPherson, Sarah Jane Smith, Julieta Granada (PAR), Sarah Kemp (AUS), Beatriz Recari (ESP), Danielle Kang (am) 291; Becky Morgan (WAL), Christel Boeljon (NED), Sophie Gustafson (SWE), Ryann O'Toole, Leta Lindley, Dewi Claire Schreefel (NED), Lorie Kane (CAN), Laura Davies (ENG), Jeehae Lee (KOR), Stacy Prammanasudh, Katherine Hull (AUS) 292; Jennie Lee, Jenny Shin (KOR), Natalie Gulbis, Minea Blomqvist (FIN) 293; Kyeong Bae (KOR), Michelle Wie, Haeji Kang (KOR) 294; Sherri Steinhauer, Silvia Cavalleri (ITA) 295; Grace Park (KOR) 296; Diana D'Alessio 301

## 2010 Wegmans LPGA Championship Locust Hill, Pitsford, NY                    [6506–72]
Prize money: $2.25 million

| | | | | | | | | |
|---|---|---|---|---|---|---|---|---|
| 1 | Cristie Kerr | 68-66-69-66—269 | $337,500 | 19T | Michelle Wie | 72-74-73-70—289 | 24,800 |
| 2 | Song-Hee Kim (KOR) | 72-71-69-69—281 | 207,790 | 25 | Natalie Gulbis | 72-75-71-72—290 | 18,669 |
| 3 | Ai Miyazato (JPN) | 76-71-70-66—283 | 133,672 | | Sophie Gustafson (SWE) | 73-75-72-70—290 | 18,669 |
| | Jiyai Shin (KOR) | 72-70-70-71—283 | 133,672 | | Jeong Jang (KOR) | 71-73-75-71—290 | 18,669 |
| 5 | In-Kyung Kim (KOR) | 72-70-72-70—284 | 85,323 | | Christina Kim | 70-76-70-74—290 | 18,669 |
| | Karriev Webb (AUS) | 72-72-69-71—284 | 85,323 | | Anna Nordqvist (SWE) | 73-72-73-72—290 | 18,669 |
| 7 | Meaghann Francella | 73-71-70-71—285 | 54,323 | | Angela Stanford | 74-74-74-68—290 | 18,669 |
| | Jimin Kang (KOR) | 74-67-70-74—285 | 54,323 | | Sakura Yokomine (JPN) | 71-72-73-74—290 | 18,669 |
| | Inbee Park (KOR) | 69-70-75-71—285 | 54,323 | | Sun Young Yoo (KOR) | 72-75-71-72—290 | 18,669 |
| | Morgan Pressel | 72-76-68-69—285 | 54,323 | | Heather Bowie Young | 70-77-74-69—290 | 18,669 |
| 11 | Azahara Muñoz (ESP) | 72-69-70-75—286 | 41,238 | 34 | Shi Hyun Ahn (KOR) | 74-71-72-74—291 | 13,182 |
| | Suzann Pettersen (NOR) | 74-72-69-71—286 | 41,238 | | Chie Arimura (JPN) | 73-72-73-73—291 | 13,182 |
| 13 | Mika Miyazato (JPN) | 69-70-72-76—287 | 37,314 | | Katherine Hull (AUS) | 74-73-76-68—291 | 13,182 |
| 14 | Stacy Lewis | 68-74-73-73—288 | 31,398 | | Amy Hung (TPE) | 72-76-73-70—291 | 13,182 |
| | Brittany Lincicome | 71-69-75-73—288 | 31,398 | | M J Hur (KOR) | 72-73-73-73—291 | 13,182 |
| | Sarah Jane Smith | 74-71-69-74—288 | 31,398 | | Haeji Kang (KOR) | 73-73-73-72—291 | 13,182 |
| | Lindsey Wright (AUS) | 69-74-72-73—288 | 31,398 | | Catriona Matthew (SCO) | 74-71-69-77—291 | 13,182 |
| | Amy Yang (KOR) | 73-67-76-72—288 | 31,398 | | Jennifer Rosales (PHI) | 73-74-72-72—291 | 13,182 |
| 19 | Meena Lee (KOR) | 71-76-74-68—289 | 24,800 | 42 | Helen Alfredsson (SWE) | 75-73-69-75—292 | 10,079 |
| | Seon Hwa Lee (KOR) | 68-74-73-74—289 | 24,800 | | Paula Creamer | 71-72-74-75—292 | 10,079 |
| | Na On Min (KOR) | 74-67-74-74—289 | 24,800 | | Mi Hyun Kim (KOR) | 75-73-75-69—292 | 10,079 |
| | Karin Sjodin (SWE) | 74-73-74-68—289 | 24,800 | | Brittany Lang | 75-71-71-75—292 | 10,079 |
| | Yani Tseng (TPE) | 75-71-70-73—289 | 24,800 | | Michele Redman | 74-67-79-72—292 | 10,079 |

**Other players who made the cut:** Chelia Choi (KOR), Laura Davies (ENG), Hee-Won Han (KOR), Yoo Kyeong Kim (KOR), Janice Moodie (SCO), Paola Moreno (COL), Alena Sharp (CAN) 293; Shanshan Feng (CHN), Vicky Hurst, Soo-Yun Kang (KOR), Sherri Steinhauer, Gloria Park (KOR) 294; Irene Cho, Mina Harigae, Teresa Lu (TPE) 295; Silvia Cavalleri (ITA), Juli Inkster 296; Louise Friberg (SWE), Lorie Kane (CAN), Stacy Prammanasudh 297; Louise Stahle (SWE), Mariajo Uribe (COL), Wendy Ward, Leah Wigger 298; Amanda Blumenherst 299; Candie Kung (TPE) 301; Giulia Sergas (ITA) 306

## Multiple winners

Since its inauguration in 1955, there have been 13 multiple winners of the LPGA Championship:

| | |
|---|---|
| Mickey Wright (USA) | 1958, 1960, 1961, 1963 |
| Kathy Whitworth (USA) | 1967, 1971, 1975 |
| Nancy Lopez (USA) | 1978, 1985, 1989 |
| Patty Sheehan (USA) | 1983, 1984, 1993 |
| Annika Sörenstam (SWE) | 2003, 2004, 2005 |
| Se Ri Pak (KOR) | 1998, 2002, 2006 |
| Betsy Rawls (USA) | 1959, 1969 |
| Mary Mills (USA) | 1964, 1973 |
| Sandra Haynie (USA) | 1965, 1974 |
| Donna Caponi (USA) | 1979, 1981 |
| Laura Davies (ENG) | 1994, 1996 |
| Juli Inkster (USA) | 1999, 2000 |
| Yani Tseng (TPE) | 2008, 2011 |

For the first decade of the championship, players from the USA won every title. They almost achieved a perfect ten for the next decade with only Canadian Sandra Post spoiling their record in 1968. US players maintained their dominance for the next two decades with seven and nine victories with England's Laura Davies spoiling their perfect ten in 1994, the first of her two LPGA victories.

During the following decade (1995–2004), the US victory tally fell to four with Europe coming a close second with Laura Davies' second title in 1996 and Swede Annika Sörenstam's two victories in 2003 and 2004 on her way to a record-breaking three in a row.

Thus far, in the first eight years of the current decade, Asia tops the list with four victories, Europe has three and the US takes the remaining slot.

## 2009 McDonald's LPGA Championship Bulle Rock, Havre de Grace, MD [6641–72]

Prize money: $2 million

| | | | | | | | | |
|---|---|---|---|---|---|---|---|---|
| 1 | Anna Nordqvist (SWE) | 66-70-69-68—273 | $300,000 | 23T | Eun-Hee Ji (KOR) | 74-69-73-71—287 | 18,105 |
| 2 | Lindsey Wright (AUS) | 70-68-69-70—277 | 182,950 | | Mindy Kim | 74-69-72-72—287 | 18,105 |
| 3 | Jiyai Shin (KOR) | 73-68-69-68—278 | 132,717 | | Paige Mackenzie | 68-77-69-73—287 | 18,105 |
| 4 | Kyeong Bae (KOR) | 70-69-72-68—279 | 102,668 | | Lorena Ochoa (MEX) | 72-69-73-73—287 | 18,105 |
| 5 | Nicole Castrale | 65-72-74-69—280 | 68,947 | | Yani Tseng (TPE) | 73-71-69-74—287 | 18,105 |
| | Kirsty McPherson | 70-70-70-70—280 | 68,947 | | Michelle Wie | 70-74-73-70—287 | 18,105 |
| | Angela Stanford | 70-71-70-69—280 | 68,947 | 31 | Beth Bader | 73-73-74-68—288 | 13,146 |
| 8 | Na Yeon Choi (KOR) | 68-71-70-72—281 | 49,582 | | Heather Bowie Young | 75-70-70-73—288 | 13,146 |
| 9 | Song Hee Kim (KOR) | 73-72-68-69—282 | 39,440 | | Soo-Yun Kang (KOR) | 73-71-72-72—288 | 13,146 |
| | Stacy Lewis | 68-72-71-71—282 | 39,440 | | Cristie Kerr | 76-70-70-72—288 | 13,146 |
| | Jin Young Pak | 69-71-69-73—282 | 39,440 | | Na Ri Kim (KOR) | 71-73-72-72—288 | 13,146 |
| | Amy Yang (KOR) | 68-74-70-70—282 | 39,440 | | Young Kim (KOR) | 72-74-71-71—288 | 13,146 |
| 13 | Brandie Burton | 73-71-72-67—283 | 32,853 | | Michele Redman | 72-73-72-71—288 | 13,146 |
| 14 | Irene Cho (KOR) | 72-75-65-72—284 | 29,949 | | Ashleigh Simon (RSA) | 68-74-74-72—288 | 13,146 |
| | Inbee Park (KOR) | 70-72-73-69—284 | 29,949 | 39 | Brittany Lang | 72-72-72-73—289 | 10,016 |
| 16 | Shi Hyun Ahn (KOR) | 73-70-72-70—285 | 25,041 | | Seon Hwa Lee (KOR) | 74-71-76-68—289 | 10,016 |
| | Paula Creamer | 74-70-71-70—285 | 25,041 | | Mika Miyazato (JPN) | 72-74-70-73—289 | 10,016 |
| | Sophie Gustafsson (SWE) | 69-74-70-72—285 | 25,041 | | Janice Moodie (SCO) | 74-73-70-72—289 | 10,016 |
| | Katherine Hull (AUS) | 69-69-76-71—285 | 25,041 | | Ji Young Oh (KOR) | 73-74-71-71—289 | 10,016 |
| | In-Kyung Kim (KOR) | 72-74-68-71—285 | 25,041 | 44 | Minea Blomqvist (FIN) | 73-69-70-78—290 | 8,213 |
| 21 | Natalie Gulbis | 72-75-69-70—286 | 21,836 | | Anna Grzebien | 74-73-69-74—290 | 8,213 |
| | Hee-Won Han (KOR) | 70-69-73-74—286 | 21,836 | | M J Hur (KOR) | 71-72-74-73—290 | 8,213 |
| 23 | Allison Hanna-Williams | 72-74-69-72—287 | 18,105 | | Juli Inkster | 73-71-73-73—290 | 8,213 |
| | Maria Hjörth (SWE) | 71-75-72-69—287 | 18,105 | | Kris Tschetter | 70-72-73-75—290 | 8,213 |

**Other players who made the cut:** Sandra Gal (GER), Stacy Prammanasudh, Karrie Webb (AUS), Sun Young Yoo (KOR) 291; Chella Choi (KOR), Moira Dunn, Johanna Mundy (ENG), Eunjung Yi (KOR) 292; Helen Alfredsson (SWE), Il Mi Chung (KOR), Wendy Doolan (AUS), Candie Kung (TPE), Taylor Leon, Karin Sjodin (SWE), Aree Song (KOR), Monoko Ueda (JPN) 293; Marty Hart, Jee Young Lee (KOR), Becky Morgan (WAL), Se Ri Pak (KOR) 294; Katie Futcher, Carin Koch (SWE) 295; Meaghan Francella, Jamie Hullett, Teresa Lu (TPE) 296; Karine Icher (FRA) 297; Julieta Granada (PAR) 298; Marisa Baena (COL) 299; Jackie Gallagher-Smith 303

## 2008 McDonald's LPGA Championship Bulle Rock, Havre de Grace, MD [6596–72]

Prize money: $2 million

| | | | | | | | | |
|---|---|---|---|---|---|---|---|---|
| 1 | Yani Tseng (TPE)* | 73-70-65-68—276 | $300000 | 18T | Jeong Jang (KOR) | 72-72-68-70—282 | 21,929 |
| 2 | Maria Hjörth (SWE) | 68-72-65-71—276 | 180180 | | Brittany Lang | 70-67-71-74—282 | 21,929 |
| *Tseng won at the fourth extra hole | | | | | Jee Young Lee (KOR) | 70-69-65-78—282 | 21,929 |
| 3 | Lorena Ochoa (MEX) | 69-65-72-71—277 | 115911 | | Jill McGill | 72-70-72-68—282 | 21,929 |
| | Annika Sörenstam (SWE) | 70-68-68-71—277 | 115911 | | Lindsey Wright (AUS) | 67-68-73-74—282 | 21,929 |
| 5 | Laura Diaz | 71-68-69-70—278 | 81,385 | 25 | Jimin Kang (KOR) | 72-68-70-73—283 | 17,806 |
| 6 | Shi Hyun Ahn (KOR) | 73-69-69-69—280 | 53,763 | | Kristy McPherson | 73-70-72-68—283 | 17,806 |
| | Irene Cho (KOR) | 72-68-69-71—280 | 53,763 | | Angela Stanford | 72-71-67-73—283 | 17,806 |
| | Kelli Kuehne | 69-70-71-70—280 | 53,763 | | Momoko Ueda (JPN) | 72-67-71-73—283 | 17,806 |
| | Morgan Pressel | 73-69-70-68—280 | 53,673 | 29 | H J Choi (KOR) | 69-74-71-70—284 | 14,896 |
| 10 | Nicole Castrale | 68-72-71-70—281 | 31,938 | | Eun-Hee Ji (KOR) | 72-70-72-70—284 | 14,896 |
| | Paula Creamer | 71-70-71-69—281 | 31,938 | | Liselotte Neumann | 70-72-71-71—284 | 14,896 |
| | Jimin Jeong (KOR) | 73-68-69-71—281 | 31,938 | | (SWE) | | |
| | Cristie Kerr | 71-70-71-69—281 | 31,938 | | Ji Young Oh (KOR) | 69-68-72-75—284 | 14,896 |
| | Mi Hyun Kim (KOR) | 72-70-71-68—281 | 31,938 | | Karrie Webb (AUS) | 71-71-69-73—284 | 14,896 |
| | Candie Kung (TPE) | 70-72-70-69—281 | 31,938 | 34 | Louise Friberg (SWE) | 70-73-73-69—285 | 11,887 |
| | Seon Hwa Lee (KOR) | 73-71-70-67—281 | 31,938 | | Sophie Gituel (FRA) | 70-72-72-71—285 | 11,887 |
| | Giulia Sergas (ITA) | 71-71-69-70—281 | 31,938 | | Young Kim (KOR) | 69-73-69-74—285 | 11,887 |
| 18 | Marisa Baena (COL) | 68-70-81-73—282 | 21,929 | | Brittany Lincicome | 75-68-70-72—285 | 11,887 |
| | Na Yeon Choi (KOR) | 75-67-69-71—282 | 21,929 | | Jane Park | 72-69-70-74—285 | 11,887 |

**Other players who made the cut:** Kyeong Bae (KOR), Karine Icher (FRA), Rachel Hetherington (AUS), Su A Kim (KOR), Carolina Llano (COL), Se Ri Pak (KOR), Inbee Park (KOR), Stacy Prammanasudh, Jennifer Rosales (PHI), Sherri Steinhauer 287; Wendy Doolan (AUS), Sandra Gal (GER) 288; Silvia Cavelleri (ITA), Shanshan Feng (CHN), Candy Hannemann (BRA), Jin Joo Hong (KOR), Michele Redman, Nancy Scranton, Karen Stupples (ENG) 289; Julieta Granada (PAR), Leta Lindley, Becky Lucidi, Mhairi McKay (SCO), Linda Wessberg (SWE) 290; Angela Park (BRA), 291; Charlotte Mayorkas, Young-A Yang (KOR) 292; Moira Dunn, Tracy Hanson, Soo-Yun Kang (KOR), Alena Sharp (CAN) 293; Meaghan Francella, Sun Young Yoo (KOR) 294; Danielle Downey 295; Jamie Hullett 297; Allison Fouch 299

## 2007 McDonald's LPGA Championship Bulle Rock, Havre de Grace, MD          [6596–72]
Prize money: $2 million

| | | | | | | | | |
|---|---|---|---|---|---|---|---|---|
| 1 | Suzann Pettersen (NOR) | 69-67-71-67—274 | $300,000 | 21T | Juli Inkster | 73-73-73-66—285 | 20,585 |
| 2 | Karrie Webb (AUS) | 68-69-71-67—275 | 179,038 | | In-Kyung Kim (KOR) | 73-70-71-71—285 | 20,585 |
| 3 | Ma On Min (KOR) | 71-70-65-70—276 | 129,880 | 25 | Wendy Doolan (AUS) | 76-70-70-70—286 | 17,350 |
| 4 | Lindsey Wright (AUS) | 71-70-71-66—278 | 100,473 | | Pat Hurst | 69-75-76-66—286 | 17,350 |
| 5 | Angela Park (BRA) | 67-73-68-71—279 | 80,869 | | Jeong Jang (KOR) | 73-71-71-71—286 | 17,350 |
| 6 | Paula Creamer | 71-68-73-68—280 | 53,422 | | Birdie Kim (KOR) | 67-71-73-75—286 | 17,350 |
| | Sophie Gustafson (SWE) | 70-71-71-68—280 | 53,422 | | Kim Saiki-Maloney | 67-73-70-76—286 | 17,350 |
| | Brittany Lincicome | 69-69-73-69—280 | 53,422 | 30 | Laura Davies (ENG) | 68-75-71-73—287 | 14,801 |
| | Lorena Ochoa (MEX) | 71-71-69-69—280 | 53,422 | | Leta Lindley | 76-69-72-70—287 | 14,801 |
| 10 | Nicole Castrale | 70-73-68-70—281 | 35,730 | | Teresa Lu (TPE) | 70-72-72-73—287 | 14,801 |
| | Jee Young Lee (KOR) | 71-72-68-70—281 | 35,730 | 33 | Maria Hjörth (SWE) | 69-75-74-70—288 | 13,069 |
| | Sarah Lee (KOR) | 71-69-72-69—281 | 35,730 | | Se Ri Pak (KOR) | 73-70-74-71—288 | 13,069 |
| | Catriona Matthew (SCO) | 71-69-74-67—281 | 35,730 | | Angela Stanford | 73-71-72-72—288 | 13,069 |
| 14 | Morgan Pressel | 68-71-70-73—282 | 30,192 | 36 | Kate Golden | 74-73-74-68—289 | 11,096 |
| 15 | Mi Hyun Kim (KOR) | 70-73-71-69—283 | 26,925 | | Jimin Kang (KOR) | 73-72-74-70—289 | 11,096 |
| | Stacy Prammanasudh | 68-74-71-70—283 | 26,925 | | Seon Hwa Lee (KOR) | 71-74-71-73—289 | 11,096 |
| | Annika Sörenstam (SWE) | 70-69-73-71—283 | 26,925 | | Nancy Scranton | 73-73-74-69—289 | 11,096 |
| 18 | Cristie Kerr | 75-70-73-66—284 | 23,396 | | Giulia Sergas (ITA) | 69-74-74-72—289 | 11,096 |
| | Siew-Ai Lim (MAS) | 72-69-70-73—284 | 23,396 | 41 | Irene Cho | 72-72-76-70—290 | 9,037 |
| | Mhairi McKay (SCO) | 71-69-74-70—284 | 23,396 | | Johanna Head (ENG) | 75-72-75-68—290 | 9,037 |
| 21 | Shi Hyun Ahn (KOR) | 71-73-71-70—285 | 20,585 | | Becky Morgan (WAL) | 73-72-75-70—290 | 9,037 |
| | Meaghan Francella | 72-75-68-70—285 | 20,585 | | Reilley Rankin | 71-71-74-74—290 | 9,037 |

**Other players who made the cut:** Kyeong Bae (KOR), Dorothy Delasin, Kimberly Hall, Marcy Hart, Joo Mi Kim (KOR), Mena Lee (KOR), Ji-Young Oh (KOR), Gloria Park (KOR), Michele Redman, Linda Wessberg, Jeong Jang (KOR), Teresa Lu (TPE), Charlotte Mayorkas, Sherri Steinhauer 292; Rachel Hetherington (AUS), Karin Sjodin (SWE), Heather Young 293; Silvia Cavalleri (ITA), Katherine Hull (AUS), Lorie Kane (CAN), Yu Ping Lin (TPE), In-Bee Park (KOE), Young-A Yang (KOR) 294; Liselotte Neumann (SWE) 295; Maria Baena (COL), Il Mi Chung (KOR), Moira Dunn, Jackie Gallagher-Smith, Brittany Lang 296; Virada Nirapathpongporn (THA), Jane Park 297; Erica Blasberg, Eva Dahllof (SWE), Karen Davies, Vicki Goetze-Ackerman, Sung Ah Yim (KOR) 298; Laura Diaz 299; Meredith Duncan, Patricia Meunier-Lebouc (FRA) 299; Michelle Wie 309

## 2006 McDonald's LPGA Championship Bulle Rock, Havre de Grace, MD          [6596–72]
Prize money: $1.8 million

| | | | | | | | | |
|---|---|---|---|---|---|---|---|---|
| 1 | Se Ri Pak (KOR)* | 71-69-71-69—280 | $270,000 | 25T | Hee-Won Han (KOR) | 68-73-75-71—287 | 16,207 |
| 2 | Karrie Webb (AUS) | 70-70-72-68—280 | 163,998 | | Heather Young | 71-75-70-71—287 | 16,207 |
| | *Play-off: 1st extra hole: Pak 3, Webb 4 | | | 29 | Il-Ne Chung (KOR) | 71-72-75-70—288 | 13,558 |
| 3 | Mi Hyun Kim (KOR) | 68-71-71-71—281 | 105,501 | | Liselotte Neumann (SWE) | 69-74-75-70—288 | 13,558 |
| | Ai Miyazato (JPN) | 68-72-69-72—281 | 105,501 | | Nancy Scranton | 73-73-73-69—288 | 13,558 |
| 5 | Shi Hyun Ahn (KOR) | 69-70-71-72—282 | 57,464 | | Angela Stanford | 70-76-72-70—288 | 13,558 |
| 9 | Young Kim (KOR) | 69-72-73-69—283 | 34,174 | | Kris Tamulis | 73-71-75-69—288 | 13,558 |
| | Lorena Ochoa (MEX) | 68-72-71-72—283 | 34,174 | 34 | Marisa Baena (COL) | 72-72-74-71—289 | 11,044 |
| | Reilley Rankin | 68-73-74-68—283 | 34,174 | | Nicole Castrale | 64-75-74-76—289 | 11,044 |
| | Annika Sörenstam (SWE) | 71-69-75-68—283 | 34,174 | | Rachel Hetherington (AUS) | 70-72-74-73—289 | 11,044 |
| | Sung Ah Yim (KOR) | 72-68-74-69—283 | 34,174 | | Juli Inkster | 70-74-73-72—289 | 11,044 |
| 14 | Jee Young Lee (KOR) | 70-71-70-73—284 | 26,847 | | Nina Reis (SWE) | 70-73-73-73—289 | 11,044 |
| | Meena Lee (KOR) | 71-72-69-72—284 | 26,847 | 39 | Beth Daniel | 71-71-73-75—290 | 8,979 |
| 16 | Silvia Cavalleri (ITA) | 69-71-72-73—285 | 22,896 | | Allison Hanna | 74-69-78-69—290 | 8,979 |
| | Seon Hwa Lee (KOR) | 67-74-75-69—285 | 22,896 | | Maria Hjörth (SWE) | 68-77-73-72—290 | 89,79 |
| | Sherri Steinhauer | 70-71-71-73—285 | 22,896 | | Nicole Perrot (CHI) | 70-71-76-73—290 | 8,979 |
| | Wendy Ward | 69-74-70-72—285 | 22,896 | | Michele Redman | 73-72-72-73—290 | 8,979 |
| 20 | Yuri Fudoh (JPN) | 69-74-71-72—286 | 19,215 | 44 | Julieta Grenada (PAR) | 71-73-71-76—291 | 7,363 |
| | Natalie Gulbis | 72-73-72-69—286 | 19,215 | | Sophie Gustafson (SWE) | 72-72-75-72—291 | 7,363 |
| | Young Jo (KOR) | 72-72-70-72—286 | 19,215 | | Candie Kung (TPE) | 68-78-71-74—291 | 7,363 |
| | Suzann Pettersen (NOR) | 70-72-74-70—286 | 19,215 | | Yu Ping Lin (TPE) | 74-72-72-73—291 | 7,363 |
| | Lindsey Wright (AUS) | 72-73-68-73—286 | 19,215 | | Jessica Reese-Quayle | 73-73-72-73—291 | 7,363 |
| 25 | Minea Blomqvist (FIN) | 71-71-70-75—287 | 16,207 | | | | |
| | Laura Diaz | 71-74-72-70—287 | 16,207 | | | | |

**Other players who made the cut:** Paula Creamer, Rosie Jones, Carin Koch, Brittany Lincicome, Kim Saiki 292; Michelle Ellis (AUS), Jill McGill, Miriam Nagl (GER), Mikaela Parmlid (SWE) 293; Jackie Gallagher-Smith, Jeong Jang (KOR), Teresa Lu (TPE) 294; Christina Kim, Siew-Ai Lim (MAS), Gloria Park (KOR), Karin Sjodin (SWE) 295; Laura Davies (ENG), Wendy Doolan (AUS), Birdie Kim (KOR), Sarah Lee (KOR) 296; Ashli Bunch, Dorothy Delasin, Morgan Pressel, Karen Stupples (ENG) 297; Kristi Albers 299; Moira Dunn 300; Jamie Fischer, Becky Iverson 302

## 2005 McDonald's LPGA Championship Bulle Rock, Havre de Grace, MD    [6486–72]

Prize money: $1.8 million

| | | | |
|---|---|---|---|
| 1 | Annika Sörenstam (SWE) | 68-67-69-73—277 | $270,000 |
| 2 | Michelle Wie (am) | 69-71-71-69—280 | |
| 3 | Paula Creamer | 68-73-74-67—282 | 140,517 |
| | Laura Davies (ENG) | 67-70-74-71—282 | 140,517 |
| 5 | Natalie Gulbis | 67-71-73-73—284 | 82,486 |
| | Lorena Ochoa (MEX) | 72-72-68-72—284 | 82,486 |
| 7 | Moira Dunn | 71-68-72-74—285 | 43,993 |
| | Pat Hurst | 72-73-71-69—285 | 43,993 |
| | Mi Hyun Kim (KOR) | 69-75-74-67—285 | 43,993 |
| | Young Kim (KOR) | 73-68-68-76—285 | 43,993 |
| | Carin Koch (SWE) | 74-70-69-72—285 | 43,993 |
| | Gloria Park (KOR) | 71-71-72-71—285 | 43,993 |
| 13 | Juli Inkster | 75-71-71-69—286 | 29,309 |
| | Jeong Jang (KOR) | 71-71-69-75—286 | 29,309 |
| | Candie Kung (TAI) | 72-73-73-68—286 | 29,309 |
| 16 | Marisa Baena (COL) | 70-69-73-75—287 | 23,899 |
| | Jennifer Rosales (PHI) | 71-73-69-74—287 | 23,899 |
| | Angela Stanford | 69-73-73-72—287 | 23,899 |
| | Lindsey Wright (AUS) | 71-72-72-72—287 | 23,899 |
| 20 | Beth Bader | 72-72-72-72—288 | 19,797 |
| | Heather Bowie | 72-71-71-74—288 | 19,797 |
| 20T | Laura Diaz | 67-72-76-73—288 | 19,797 |
| | Meena Lee (KOR) | 70-71-72-75—288 | 19,797 |
| | Karrie Webb (AUS) | 74-75-72-67—288 | 19,797 |
| 25 | Shi Hyun Ahn (KOR) | 78-71-72-68—289 | 16,096 |
| | Kirsti Albers | 70-72-73-74—289 | 16,096 |
| | Il Mi Chung (KOR) | 71-68-79-71—289 | 16,096 |
| | Hee-Won Han (KOR) | 73-74-72-70—289 | 16,096 |
| | Leta Lindley | 72-72-75-70—289 | 16,096 |
| | Karen Stupples (ENG) | 72-71-71-75—289 | 16,096 |
| 31 | Rosie Jones | 72-69-74-75—290 | 13,733 |
| | Liselotte Neumann (SWE) | 70-71-74-75—290 | 13,733 |
| 33 | Jamie Hullett | 70-75-71-75—291 | 11,225 |
| | Jimin Kang (KOR) | 73-74-72-72—291 | 11,225 |
| | Cristie Kerr | 74-72-67-78—291 | 11,225 |
| | Christina Kim | 73-72-78-68—291 | 11,225 |
| | Brittany Lincicome | 72-72-75-72—291 | 11,225 |
| | Meg Mallon | 74-69-76-72—291 | 11,225 |
| | Janice Moodie (SCO) | 73-72-74-72—291 | 11,225 |
| | Stacy Prammanasudh | 72-76-72-71—291 | 11,225 |

**Other players who made the cut:** Birdie Kim (KOR) 292; Rachel Hetherington (AUS), Hilary Lunke, Paula Marti (ESP), Joanne Morley (ENG) 293; Johanna Head (ENG), Lorie Kane (CAN), Aree Song (KOR) 294; Heather Daly-Donofrio, Catriona Matthew (SCO), Suzann Pettersen (NOR), Michele Redman, Kim Saiki 295; Dawn Coe-Jones (CAN), Beth Daniel, Wendy Doolan (AUS), Yu Ping Lin (TAI), Stephanie Louden, Jill McGill, Nicole Perrot (CHI), Nancy Scranton, Sung Ah Yim (KOR) 296; Tina Barrett, Patricia Baxter-Johnson, Tina Fischer (GER), Laurel Kean, Emilee Klein, Bernadette Luse, Sae-Hee Son (KOR), Kris Tschetter 297; Maria Hjörth (SWE) 298; Katie Allison, Catherine Cartwright, A J Eathorne (CAN), Katherine Hull (AUS), Reilley Rankin 299; Laurie Rinker, Nadina Taylor (AUS) 300; Candy Hannemann (BRA) 302; Barb Mucha 305.

## 2004 McDonald's LPGA Championship Du Pont CC, DE    [6408–71]

Prize money: $1.6 million

| | | | |
|---|---|---|---|
| 1 | Annika Sörenstam (SWE) | 68-67-64-72—271 | $240,000 |
| 2 | Shi Hyun Ahn (KOR) | 69-70-69-66—274 | 144,780 |
| 3 | Grace Park (KOR) | 68-70-70-68—276 | 105,028 |
| 4 | Gloria Park (KOR) | 67-72-68-71—278 | 73,322 |
| | Angela Stanford | 69-71-67-71—278 | 73,322 |
| 6 | Juli Inkster | 70-66-70-73—279 | 49,145 |
| | Christina Kim | 74-69-64-72—279 | 49,145 |
| 8 | Wendy Doolan (AUS) | 73-70-65-72—280 | 35,538 |
| | Soo-Yun Kang | 69-68-71-72—280 | 35,538 |
| | Lorena Ochoa (MEX) | 71-67-67-75—280 | 35,538 |
| 11 | Carin Koch (SWE) | 69-71-68-73—281 | 28,734 |
| | Reilley Rankin | 70-67-71-73—281 | 28,734 |
| 13 | Pat Hurst | 69-69-75-69—282 | 24,466 |
| | Mhairi McKay (SCO) | 72-69-72-69—282 | 24,466 |
| | Jennifer Rosales (PHI) | 66-70-74-72—282 | 24,466 |
| 16 | Meg Mallon | 69-73-70-71—283 | 21,718 |
| 17 | Kristi Albers | 70-74-69-71—284 | 18,654 |
| | Dawn Coe-Jones (CAN) | 72-72-70-70—284 | 18,654 |
| | Michelle Ellis (AUS) | 72-70-69-73—284 | 18,654 |
| | Cristie Kerr | 69-73-71-71—284 | 18,654 |
| 17T | Betsy King | 76-70-70-68—284 | 18,654 |
| | Se Ri Pak (KOR) | 69-73-70-72—284 | 18,654 |
| 23 | Tina Barrett | 75-71-68-71—285 | 14,596 |
| | Jeong Jang (KOR) | 71-71-71-72—285 | 14,596 |
| | Siew-Ai Lim (MAS) | 72-70-71-72—285 | 14,596 |
| | Stacy Prammanasudh | 73-71-69-72—285 | 14,596 |
| | Kim Saiki | 69-72-72-72—285 | 14,596 |
| | Sherri Steinhauer | 69-72-74-70—285 | 14,596 |
| | Chiharu Yamaguchi (JPN) | 67-73-70-75—285 | 14,596 |
| 30 | Moira Dunn | 68-74-72-72—286 | 10,631 |
| | Mi-Hyun Kim (KOR) | 72-70-74-70—286 | 10,631 |
| | Young Kim (KOR) | 70-73-74-69—286 | 10,631 |
| | Patricia Meunier-Lebouc (FRA) | 71-70-76-69—286 | 10,631 |
| | Janice Moodie (SCO) | 72-71-73-70—286 | 10,631 |
| | Aree Song (KOR) | 71-72-69-74—286 | 10,631 |
| | Charlotta Sörenstam (SWE) | 74-70-70-72—286 | 10,631 |
| | Karen Stupples (ENG) | 67-73-73-73—286 | 10,631 |
| | Wendy Ward | 72-72-71-71—286 | 10,631 |

**Other players who made the cut:** Beth Daniel, Stephanie Louden (AUS), Karrie Webb (AUS) 287; Jean Bartholomew, Ashli Bunch, Laura Davies (ENG), Becky Iverson, Becky Morgan (WAL), Deb Richard, Karen Pearce (AUS) 289; Heather Daly-Donofrio, Hee-Won Han (KOR), Lorie Kane (CAN), Yu Ping Lin (TPE), Kelly Robbins, Giulia Sergas (ITA), Rachel Teske (AUS) 290; Pat Bradley, Diana D'Alessio, Kate Golden, Jamie Hullett, Emilee Klein 291; Helen Alfredsson (SWE), Natalie Gulbis, Catriona Matthew (SCO) 292; Amy Fruhwirth, Tammy Green, Seol-An Jeon (KOR), Angela Jerman, Candie Kung (TPE), Soo Young Moon (KOR) 293; Isabelle Beisiegel (CAN), Vicki Goetz-Ackerman, Jill McGill, Dotty Pepper 294; Jenna Daniels, Sophie Gustafson (SWE), Kim Williams 295; Candy Hannemann (BRA) 296; Jackie Gallagher-Smith 297; Heather Bowie 299.

# LPGA Championship History

The Championship was known simply as the LPGA Championship from its inauguration in 1955 until 1987. It was sponsored by Mazda from 1988 until 1993 when the sponsorship was taken over by McDonald's. The tournament has been sponsored by Wegmans since 2010. Only in the first year was it decided by match-play when Beverly Hanson beat Louise Suggs in the final.

| | | | | | | | |
|---|---|---|---|---|---|---|---|
| 1955 | B Hanson | Orchard Ridge, IN | 4 and 3 | 1989 | N Lopez | Kings Island, OH | 274 |
| 1956 | M Hagge* | Forest Lake, MI | 291 | 1990 | B Daniel | Bethesda, MD | 280 |
| *After a play-off with P Berg | | | | 1991 | M Mallon | Bethesda, MD | 274 |
| 1957 | L Suggs | Churchill Valley, PA | 285 | 1992 | B King | Bethesda, MD | 267 |
| 1958 | M Wright | Churchill Valley, PA | 288 | 1993 | P Sheehan | Bethesda, MD | 275 |
| 1959 | B Rawls | Churchill Valley, PA | 288 | 1994 | L Davies (ENG) | Wilmington, DE | 275 |
| 1960 | M Wright | French Lick, IN | 292 | 1995 | K Robbins | Wilmington, DE | 274 |
| 1961 | M Wright | Stardust, NV | 287 | 1996 | L Davies (ENG) | Wilmington, DE | 213 |
| 1962 | J Kimball | Stardust, NV | 282 | *Reduced to 54 holes – bad weather* | | | |
| 1963 | M Wright | Stardust, NV | 294 | 1997 | C Johnson | Wilmington, DE | 281 |
| 1964 | M Mills | Stardust, NV | 278 | 1998 | Se Ri Pak (KOR) | Wilmington, DE | 273 |
| 1965 | S Haynie | Stardust, NV | 279 | 1999 | J Inkster | Wilmington, DE | 268 |
| 1966 | G Ehret | Stardust, NV | 282 | 2000 | J Inkster* | Wilmington, DE | 281 |
| 1967 | K Whitworth | Pleasant Valley, MA | 284 | *Beat S Croce (ITA) at the second extra hole* | | | |
| 1968 | S Post* | Pleasant Valley, MA | 294 | 2001 | K Webb (AUS) | Wilmington, DE | 270 |
| *After a play-off with K Whitworth* | | | | 2002 | Se Ri Pak (KOR) | Wilmington, DE | 279 |
| 1969 | B Rawls | Concord, NY | 293 | 2003 | A Sörenstam | Wilmington, DE | 271 |
| 1970 | S Englehorn* | Pleasant Valley, MA | 285 | | (SWE)* | | |
| *After a play-off with K Whitworth* | | | | *Beat G Park (KOR) at the first extra hole* | | | |
| 1971 | K Whitworth | Pleasant Valley, MA | 288 | 2004 | A Sörenstam | Wilmington, DE | 271 |
| 1972 | K Ahern | Pleasant Valley, MA | 293 | | (SWE) | | |
| 1973 | M Mills | Pleasant Valley, MA | 288 | 2005 | A Sörenstam | Bulle Rock, MD | 277 |
| 1974 | S Haynie | Pleasant Valley, MA | 288 | | (SWE) | | |
| 1975 | K Whitworth | Pine Ridge, MD | 288 | 2006 | Se Ri Pak (KOR)* | Bulle Rock, MD | 280 |
| 1976 | B Burfeindt | Pine Ridge, MD | 287 | *Beat K Webb (AUS) at first extra hole* | | | |
| 1977 | C Higuchi (JPN) | Bay Tree, SC | 279 | 2007 | S Pettersen | Bulle Rock, MD | 274 |
| 1978 | N Lopez | Kings Island, OH | 275 | | (NOR) | | |
| 1979 | D Caponi | Kings Island, OH | 279 | 2008 | Y Tseng (TPE)* | Bulle Rock, MD | 278 |
| 1980 | S Little (SA) | Kings Island, OH | 285 | *Beat M Hjörth (SWE) at the fourth extra hole* | | | |
| 1981 | D Caponi | Kings Island, OH | 280 | 2009 | A Nordqvist | Bulle Rock, MD | 273 |
| 1982 | J Stephenson (AUS) | Kings Island, OH | 279 | | (SWE) | | |
| 1983 | P Sheehan | Kings Island, OH | 279 | 2010 | C Kerr | Locust Hill, Pitsford, NY | 269 |
| 1984 | P Sheehan | Kings Island, OH | 272 | 2011 | Y Tseng (TPE) | Locust Hill, Pitsford, NY | 269 |
| 1985 | N Lopez | Kings Island, OH | 273 | 2012 | S Feng (CHN) | Locust Hill, Pitsford, NY | 282 |
| 1986 | P Bradley | Kings Island, OH | 277 | 2013 | I Park (KOR)* | Locust Hill, Pitsford, NY | 283 |
| 1987 | J Geddes | Kings Island, OH | 275 | *Beat C Matthew (SCO) at third extra hole* | | | |
| 1988 | S Turner | Kings Island, OH | 281 | | | | |

## Major streak: Asia's nine-in-a-row

**2011:** Wegmans LPGA Championship – Yani Tseng; US Women's Open – Na Yeon Ryu; Ricoh Women's British Open – Yani Tseng

**2012:** Kraft Nabisco Championship – Sun Young Yoo; Wegmans LPGA Championship – Shanshan Feng; US Women's Open – Na Yeon Choi; Ricoh Women's British Open – Jiyai Shin

**2013:** Kraft Nabisco Championship – Inbee Park; Wegman's LPGA Championship – Inbee Park

# Inbee Park races to victory at Palm Springs as Asians continue to dominate majors

Just as Hubert Green wryly observed at Turnberry in 1977 how he won the championship he was playing in – the American had finished a distant ten shots behind Jack Nicklaus after Tom Watson won the 'Duel in the Sun' – it was left to So Yeon Ryu, runner-up to Inbee Park at Mission Hills in California, to remark that the winner of the season's first women's major was playing a different game from the rest of the field. "She looks like she played another golf course," Ryu admitted.

While Park's margin of victory over Ryu on the Dinah Shore tournament course was a relatively trim four shots, the gap was only so narrow because Ryu played beautifully on Sunday afternoon and carded 65, the low round of the week. Her freewheeling parting shot of seven under par, for an 11 under total, created the illusion of competition when the truth was Park won the Kraft Nabisco Championship in a canter. If Ryu, in the end, didn't quite need a telescope to keep her compatriot within range at the top of the leaderboard, the outcome of this championship was, so to speak, a walk in the park.

Of course, there is no tougher trick to pull off in golf than make such a difficult game on a demanding lay-out look like child's play. Blessed with a smooth putting touch and a consistent knack of finding fairways and greens, however, Park won the second major of her career thanks to an unrivalled gift for holing out.

According to Stacy Lewis, the World No 1 going into the tournament, Park is all but unbeatable when her putter is hot. "I played with her at the Evian last year when she had, I think, 22 or 23 putts in the final round. When she rolls it, you can't beat her. She's the best putter on tour. The course here was a little softer than normal, so I think that was to her advantage."

Ryu was just as complimentary about her friend's assured putting stroke which, incidentally, converted no fewer than 20 birdie opportunities during the championship. "Actually, she really likes to gamble, so when I practice with her she always wants to play for ten bucks a hole or whatever," smiled Ryu. "She always makes the hardest par putts, the eight foot par putts, the 16 foot par putts. I can't win ten bucks [from her]. She always wins 50 bucks. She always takes my money, so she buys me dinner or lunch. Anyway, the important thing is she just looks so easy [on the greens], and putting is so easy for her. Her tempo is always consistent."

## Operating under the radar

Park, 24, won her first major, the US Women's Open at Interlachen in 2008, and felt her second elite title was overdue. In 2012, she won twice on tour, posted six runner-up finishes and led the LPGA money list as well as winning the Vare Trophy for low scoring average. Her form after winning the Evian Masters in France was outstanding. She finished in the top three at her next four events and won the LPGA Malaysia in October. When she returned to competition in February of 2013, she duly won the LPGA Thailand. With the benefit of hindsight, Park was one of the form horses coming into the Kraft Nabisco.

Rounds of 70, 67, 67 and 69 for the 15 under par total of 273 earned the South Korean a winner's cheque for $300,000. Her victory not only boosted her own standing but also further underlined the dominance of Asian players in the women's game. It was the third consecutive major won by a South Korean golfer and the fifth success in the last seven stagings of the top events.

Asked if winning a second major title was particularly significant in terms of building a platform for the rest of her career, Park replied: "Of course. I only had one major in my seven year career until now. I hadn't won one for a while. I had a good year last year, but I definitely needed to show a little more good play. Maybe winning a couple more majors now would be nice...."

One of the most consistent competitors in women's golf, Park's knack of operating under the radar was evident even during the first round of the championship when few remarked on her steady opening salvo of 70. Instead, the attention settled on the early pace set by Norway's Suzann Pettersen, South Korea's Na Yeon Choi and England's Jodi Ewart Shadoff who all moved to the top of the leaderboard thanks to scores of 68.

The 25-year-old from Northallerton in Yorkshire might have led on her own but for a late dropped shot on the 16th hole. Recently married to Sarasota TV sports presenter Adam Shadoff (she was formerly

Jody Ewart), the golfer lives in Florida and has spent the past three years playing on the LPGA. A former English Amateur champion who showed a smooth touch with the belly putter in Rancho Mirage, the British player was phlegmatic about the proposed ban on anchoring. "If they decide to ban it, it wouldn't be a big issue for me," she said. "I'd have to spend a couple months really working out with a short putter, but it wouldn't be a huge deal."

Ewart Shadoff proved her first round was no fluke by consolidating her spot on the leaderboard with level par on Friday but the spotlight switched to Park when she reeled off six birdes and gave just one shot back to move into pole position. On a warm, breezy afternoon, it was Park's dominance on the greens which was telling.

> "Putting is so easy for her. Her tempo is always consistent."
>
> So Yeon Ryu
> on winner Park

"Obviously, I putted really good out there – especially on the back nine," she said. "The wind picked up, so it was tough. On the last four holes I made all pars and I'm really happy with that. We were playing about a club and a half of breeze. I'm just happy I have a chance on the weekend and that I could win. I've played this golf course about eight years of my career and never really had a chance before on the weekend so I'm happy to be in the mix."

Park put her foot to the accelerator on Saturday when she added another five birdies to her tally and kept a bogey off her card. A poker faced golfer who is regarded as something of a quiet assassin by her contemporaries, the South Korean took issue, though, with the suggestion that she doesn't feel pressure. Park said she felt the demands of winning and losing as much as the next player but didn't show how she was feeling through her facial expressions.

The closest golfer to Park after 54 holes was Lizette Salas, a native of southern California who enjoyed an element of local support as she carded 69 to keep the leader within three shots. She said the backing of her friends and family helped her to remain calm. "I'm playing in my backyard, so I can't ask for more than that," she said.

Sadly for Salas, nerves got the better of her on Sunday when she struck her opening drive into the rough, fluffed her second shot and hit her third short of the green. As the challenger collapsed with a double bogey, Park extended her lead to six strokes thanks to an apparently effortless drive, approach and 20 foot putt for birdie.

From that moment, the championship was effectively over as a contest. Park enjoyed sufficient leeway to drop three shots, including a visit to the water, yet still shoot 69 and come up just a little shy of Dottie Pepper's tournament record low score. A brace of Scandinavians, Pettersen and Caroline Hedwall, shared third place while Scotland's Catriona Mathew's closing 68 was sufficient for a share of seventh spot in the company of Ewart Shadoff.

Mike Aitken

| First Round | Second Round | Third Round | Fourth Round |
|---|---|---|---|
| −4 Jodi Ewart Shadoff | −7 Inbee Park | −12 Inbee Park | −15 Inbee Park |
| −4 Suzann Pettersen | −6 Lizette Salas | −9 Lizette Salas | −11 So Yeon Ryu |
| −4 Na Yeon Choi | −5 Caroline Hedwall | −6 Angela Stanford | −9 Caroline Hedwall |
| −3 Amy Yang | −5 Giulia Sergas | −6 Karrie Webb | −9 Suzann Petterssen |
| −3 Anna Nordqvist | −4 Pornanong Phatlum | −6 Suzann Pettersen | −6 Karrie Webb |
| −2 Jane Park | −4 Hee Young Park | −6 Karine Icher | −6 Haeji Kang |
| −2 Jacqui Concolino | −4 Jodi Ewart Shadoff | −6 Jessica Korda | −5 Catriona Matthew |
| −2 Angela Stanford | −3 Se Ri Pak | −6 Pornanong Phatlum | −5 Jodi Ewart Shadoff |
| −2 Jiyai Shin | −3 Jiyai Shin | −5 Paula Creamer | −5 Giulia Sergas |
| −2 Lizette Salas | −3 Haeji Kang | −5 Caroline Hedwall | −5 Anna Nordqvist |

## Kraft Nabisco Championship *Rancho Mirage, CA* April 4–7 [6738–72]

Prize money: $2m. Final field of 111 players (including eight amateurs), of whom 73 (including five amateurs) made the half-way cut on 149 or less. *(Players are of American nationality unless stated)*

| | | | |
|---|---|---|---|
| 1 | Inbee Park (KOR) | 70-67-67-69—273 | $300,000 |
| 2 | So Yeon Ryu (KOR) | 73-71-68-65—277 | 187,073 |
| 3 | Suzann Pettersen (NOR) | 68-75-67-69—279 | 120,345 |
| | Caroline Hedwall (SWE) | 71-68-72-68—279 | 120,345 |
| 5 | Haeji Kang (TPE) | 72-69-73-68—282 | 76,816 |
| | Karrie Webb (AUS) | 72-71-67-72—282 | 76,816 |
| 7 | Giulia Sergas (ITA) | 70-69-76-68—283 | 44,980 |
| | Jiyai Shin (KOR) | 70-71-71-71—283 | 44,980 |
| | Hee Young Park (KOR) | 70-70-72-71—283 | 44,980 |
| | Jodi Ewart Shadoff (ENG) | 68-72-74-69—283 | 44,980 |
| | Anna Nordqvist (SWE) | 69-72-72-70—283 | 44,980 |
| | Catriona Matthew (SCO) | 72-73-70-68—283 | 44,980 |
| 13 | Caroline Masson (GER) | 70-73-71-70—284 | 29,156 |
| | Moriya Jutanugarn (THA) | 70-72-72-70—284 | 29,156 |
| | Jennifer Johnson | 72-71-73-68—284 | 29,156 |
| | Paula Creamer | 74-68-69-73—284 | 29,156 |
| | Pornanong Phatlum (THA) | 71-69-70-74—284 | 29,156 |
| | Hee Kyung Seo (KOR) | 72-70-71-71—284 | 29,156 |
| 19 | Se Ri Pak (KOR) | 72-69-75-69—285 | 22,328 |
| | Angela Stanford | 70-74-66-75—285 | 22,328 |
| | Karine Icher (FRA) | 72-70-68-75—285 | 22,328 |
| | Ayako Uehara (JPN) | 72-72-70-71—285 | 22,328 |
| | Jane Park | 70-73-73-69—285 | 22,328 |
| | Cristie Kerr | 71-71-72-71—285 | 22,328 |
| 25 | Lydia Ko (NZL) (am) | 72-74-71-69—286 | |
| | Beatriz Recari (ESP) | 75-70-71-70—286 | 17,787 |
| | Jacqui Concolino | 70-73-73-70—286 | 17,787 |
| | Alison Walshe | 71-74-72-69—286 | 17,787 |
| | Jessica Korda | 70-72-68-76—286 | 17,787 |
| | Shanshan Feng (CHN) | 78-71-70-67—286 | 17,787 |
| | Lizette Salas | 70-68-69-79—286 | 17,787 |
| 32 | Sarah Jane Smith (AUS) | 72-72-69-74—287 | 13,178 |
| | Jee Young Lee (KOR) | 76-70-72-69—287 | 13,178 |
| | Mariajo Uribe (COL) | 72-76-69-70—287 | 13,178 |
| | Chella Choi (COR) | 75-72-69-71—287 | 13,178 |
| | Stacy Lewis | 73-71-71-72—287 | 13,178 |
| | Mina Harigae | 72-74-71-70—287 | 13,178 |
| | Natalie Gulbis | 74-72-72-69—287 | 13,178 |
| | Na Yeon Choi (KOR) | 68-75-72-72—287 | 13,178 |
| | Amy Yang (KOR) | 69-73-73-72—287 | 13,178 |
| 41 | Belen Mozo (ESP) | 74-72-69-73—288 | 9,645 |
| | Michelle Wie | 72-70-73-73—288 | 9,645 |
| | Julieta Granada (PAR) | 77-69-73-69—288 | 9,645 |
| | Gerina Piller | 73-71-73-71—288 | 9,645 |
| | Christel Boeljon (NED) | 74-73-71-70—288 | 9,645 |
| | Momoko Ueda (JPN) | 74-71-71-72—288 | 9,645 |
| 47 | Stephanie Meadow (NIR) (am) | 73-73-71-72—289 | |
| 48 | Eun-Hee Ji (KOR) | 73-71-72-74—290 | 8,091 |
| | Lexi Thompson | 76-72-71-71—290 | 8,091 |
| | Yani Tseng (TPE) | 72-75-69-74—290 | 8,091 |
| | Ashlan Ramsey (am) | 71-75-73-71—290 | |
| 52 | Karin Sjodin (SWE) | 72-74-73-73—292 | 7,204 |
| | Ha-Neul Kim (KOR) | 73-75-73-71—292 | 7,204 |
| | Morgan Pressel | 72-75-72-73—292 | 7,204 |
| 55 | Vicky Hurst | 75-74-71-73—293 | 6,248 |
| | Ai Miyazato (JPN) | 74-68-75-76—293 | 6,248 |
| | Jenny Shin (KOR) | 75-74-71-73—293 | 6,248 |

## Kraft Nabisco Championship *continued*

| 55T | Angel Yin (am) | 73-75-74-71—293 | |
| | Pernilla Lindberg (SWE) | 72-75-74-72—293 | 6,248 |
| | Karen Stupples (ENG) | 73-72-75-73—293 | 6,248 |
| | IK Kim (KOR) | 75-73-74-71—293 | 6,248 |
| 62 | Hee-Won Han (KOR) | 74-75-73-72—294 | 5,530 |
| 63 | Sophie Gustafson (SWE) | 74-72-74-75—295 | 5,156 |
| | Paige Mackenzie | 72-75-76-72—295 | 5,156 |
| | Mika Miyazato (JPN) | 76-72-76-71—295 | 5,156 |
| 66 | Carlota Ciganda (ESP) | 76-72-70-78—296 | 4,865 |
| | Mo Martin | 78-71-71-76—296 | 4,865 |
| 68 | Cindy LaCrosse | 72-73-74-78—297 | 4,712 |
| 69 | Maria Hjorth (SWE) | 75-74-75-74—298 | 4,507 |
| | Meena Lee (KOR) | 76-72-75-75—298 | 4,507 |
| | Candie Kung (TPE) | 75-72-77-74—298 | 4,507 |
| 72 | Camilla Hedberg (ESP) (am) | 72-72-79-78—301 | |
| 73 | Lindsey Wright (AUS) | 74-75-76-79—304 | 4,301 |

*The following players missed the cut:*

| 74 | Chie Arimura (JPN) | 75-75—150 | | 93 | Pat Hurst | 74-78—152 |
| | Stacy Prammanasudh | 74-76—150 | | | Dewi Claire Schreefel (NED) | 72-80—152 |
| | Austin Ernst | 74-76—150 | | | Mindy Kim | 76-76—152 |
| | Seon Hwa Lee (KOR) | 74-76—150 | | | Sandra Gal (GER) | 78-74—152 |
| | Jennie Lee | 77-73—150 | | | Helen Alfredsson (SWE) | 75-77—152 |
| | Jennifer Song | 74-76—150 | | 98 | Becky Morgan (WAL) | 75-78—153 |
| | Azahara Muñoz (ESP) | 76-74—150 | | | Katie Futcher | 76-77—153 |
| | Veronica Felibert (VEN) | 73-77—150 | | | Mi Jung Hur (KOR) | 81-72—153 |
| | Lindy Duncan (am) | 81-69—150 | | | Jimin Kang (KOR) | 76-77—153 |
| | Danielle Kang | 74-76—150 | | | Sun Young Yoo (KOR) | 77-76—153 |
| | Sydnee Michaels | 78-72—150 | | 103 | Georgia Hall (ENG) | 79-75—154 |
| 85 | Doris Chen (am) | 74-77—151 | | 104 | Katherine Hull-Kirk (AUS) | 82-74—156 |
| | Louise Friberg (SWE) | 71-80—151 | | 105 | Ilhee Lee (KOR) | 76-81—157 |
| | Brittany Lincicome | 77-74—151 | | | Amanda Blumenherst | 79-78—157 |
| | Brittany Lang | 80-71—151 | | 107 | Ji Young Oh (KOR) | 74-84—158 |
| | Juli Inkster | 77-74—151 | | 108 | Amy Alcott | 81-80—161 |
| | Thidapa Suwannapura (THA) | 79-72—151 | | 109 | Isabelle Lendl (am) | 84-89—173 |
| | Yoon-Kyung Heo (KOR) | 77-74—151 | | | Jeong Jang (KOR) | 80–WD |
| | Nicole Castrale | 79-72—151 | | | Eunjung Yi (KOR) | 81–WD |

## What is the answer?

**Q:** Are "Gimmies" allowed?

**A:** There is no mention of "Gimmies" in the Rules of Golf which states the game consists of playing a ball from the teeing ground into a hole by successive strokes. While it is possible to concede a stroke, (a "gimmie") to your opponent in match play it is not possible to do so in a stroke play competition. In stroke play, failure to hole out and complete the hole before playing a stroke from the next tee leads to disqualification.

## 2012 Kraft Nabisco Championship [6702–72]

Prize money: $2 million

| | | | | | | | | |
|---|---|---|---|---|---|---|---|---|
| 1 | Sun Young Yoo (KOR) | 69-69-72-69—279 | $300,000 | 15T | Azahara Muñoz (ESP) | 73-72-67-72—284 | 26,184 |
| 2 | I K Kim (KOR) | 70-70-70-69—279 | 182,538 | 20 | Paula Creamer | 69-73-71-72—285 | 22,586 |
| *Yoo won at the first extra hole – Sun Young Yoo 4; I K Kim 5 | | | | | Katherine Hull (AUS) | 69-73-69-74—285 | 22,586 |
| 3 | Yani Tseng (TPE) | 68-68-71-73—280 | 132,418 | 22 | Cristie Kerr | 71-70-72-73—286 | 20,587 |
| 4 | Karin Sjodin (SWE) | 72-67-68-74—281 | 77,202 | | Shanshan Feng (CHN) | 72-70-73-71—286 | 20,587 |
| | Amy Yang (KOR) | 66-74-72-69—281 | 77,202 | | Ariya Jutanugarn (THA) (am) | 71-73-71-71—286 | |
| | Stacy Lewis | 74-71-70-66—281 | 77,202 | | Lexi Thompson | 72-72-68-74—286 | 20,587 |
| | Hee Kyung Seo (KOR) | 69-72-69-71—281 | 77,202 | 26 | Brittany Lang | 74-74-69-70—287 | 16,401 |
| 8 | Natalie Gulbis | 76-71-70-65—282 | 44,806 | | Inbee Park (KOR) | 71-74-68-74—287 | 16,401 |
| | Se Ri Pak (KOR) | 70-69-72-71—282 | 44,806 | | Hee Young Park (KOR) | 72-71-70-74—287 | 16,401 |
| | Na Yeon Choi (KOR) | 72-67-71-72—282 | 44,806 | | Anna Nordqvist (SWE) | 74-74-67-72—287 | 16,401 |
| 11 | Ha-Neul Kim (KOR) | 71-71-70-71—283 | 34,003 | | Jiyai Shin (KOR) | 72-71-70-74—287 | 16,401 |
| | Angela Stanford | 72-71-70-70—283 | 34,003 | | Beatriz Recari (ESP) | 72-76-70-69—287 | 16,401 |
| | Eun-Hee Ji (KOR) | 71-69-70-73—283 | 34,003 | | Cindy LaCrosse | 73-71-70-73—287 | 16,401 |
| | Vicky Hurst | 70-70-71-72—283 | 34,003 | | Jodi Ewart ( (DEN)ENG) | 69-73-73-72—287 | 16,401 |
| 15 | Catriona Matthew (SCO) | 74-70-70-70—284 | 26,184 | | Jennifer Johnson | 72-71-73-71—287 | 16,401 |
| | Suzann Pettersen (NOR) | 72-74-66-72—284 | 26,184 | 35 | Karine Icher (FRA) | 73-73-67-75—288 | 12,792 |
| | Karrie Webb (AUS) | 71-72-71-70—284 | 26,184 | | Julieta Granada (PAR) | 70-75-73-70—288 | 12,792 |
| | Haeji Kang (KOR) | 69-68-72-75—284 | 26,184 | | Mi Jung Hur (KOR) | 73-70-75-70—288 | 12,792 |

**Other players who made the cut:** Kris Tamulis, Maria Hjörth (SWE), Sandra Gal (GER), Mina Harigae, Charley Hull (ENG) (am) 289; Heather Bowie Young, Pat Hurst, Lindsey Wright (AUS) 290; Morgan Pressel, Lizette Salas, Ji-Hee Lee (KOR) 291; Hee-Won Han (KOR), Candie Kung, Becky Morgan (WAL), Seon Hwa Lee (KOR), Chella Choi (KOR), Caroline Masson (GER), Austin Ernst (am) 292; Wendy Ward, Ai Miyazato (JPN), Pornanong Phatlum (THA), Jennifer Song, Diana Luna (ITA), Melissa Reid (ENG), Caroline Hedwall (SWE), So Yeon Ryu (KOR), Christel Boeljon (NED), Jaye Marie Green (am) 293; Katie Futcher, Sarah Kemp (AUS), Momoko Ueda (JPN), Dewi Claire Schreefel (NED) 294; Reilley Rankin, Mo Martin, Amanda Blumenherst, Cydney Clanton, Yukari Baba (JPN) 295; Alena Sharp (CAN), Christina Kim, Karen Stupples (ENG) 73-72-75-76—296; Leta Lindley 298; Nicole Castrale, Lorie Kane (CAN) 299; Kyeong Bae (KOR) 301; Ji Young Oh (KOR) 303

## 2011 Kraft Nabisco Championship [6238–72]

Prize money: $2 million

| | | | | | | | | |
|---|---|---|---|---|---|---|---|---|
| 1 | Stacy Lewis | 66-69-71-69—275 | $300,000 | 19T | Maria Hjorth (SWE) | 75-70-72-73—290 | 21,992 |
| 2 | Yani Tseng (TPE) | 70-68-66-74—278 | 184,255 | | Amy Yang (KOR) | 70-69-76-75—290 | 21,992 |
| 3 | Katie Futcher | 70-71-74-69—284 | 106,763 | | Jimin Kang (KOR) | 72-69-72-77—290 | 21,992 |
| | Angela Stanford | 72-72-67-73—284 | 106,763 | 25 | Meaghan Francella | 75-71-73-72—291 | 18,562 |
| | Morgan Pressel | 70-69-69-76—284 | 106,763 | | Ariya Jutanugarn (THA) | 74-73-71-73—291 | |
| 6 | Michelle Wie | 74-67-69-75—285 | 68,093 | | (am) | | |
| 7 | Julieta Granada (PAR) | 72-70-75-69—286 | 50,608 | | Alena Sharp (CAN) | 71-73-73-74—291 | 18,562 |
| | Chie Arimura (JPN) | 68-73-71-74—286 | 50,608 | | Eun-Hee Ji (KOR) | 75-71-69-76—291 | 18,562 |
| | Mika Miyazato (JPN) | 67-75-70-74—286 | 50,608 | 29 | Inbee Park (KOR) | 76-72-71-73—292 | 16,166 |
| 10 | In-Kyung Kim (KOR) | 75-67-75-70—287 | 37,997 | | Jiyai Shin (KOR) | 73-72-74-73—292 | 16,166 |
| | Anna Nordqvist (SWE) | 69-74-73-71—287 | 37,997 | | Leta Lindley | 72-71-75-74—292 | 16,166 |
| | Se Ri Pak (KOR) | 73-71-71-72—287 | 37,997 | | Karen Stupples (ENG) | 71-72-71-78—292 | 16,166 |
| 13 | Karrie Webb (AUS) | 69-74-74-71—288 | 32,079 | 33 | Song-Hee Kim (KOR) | 74-74-76-72—293 | 12,698 |
| | Brittany Lincicome | 66-72-74-76—288 | 32,079 | | Ai Miyazato (JPN) | 71-75-73-74—293 | 12,698 |
| 15 | Christel Boeljon (NED) | 74-73-71-71—289 | 27,035 | | Melissa Reid (ENG) | 71-75-73-74—293 | 12,698 |
| | Juli Inkster | 73-73-71-72—289 | 27,035 | | Hee Kyung Seo (KOR) | 76-71-72-74—293 | 12,698 |
| | Sandra Gal (GER) | 67-74-75-73—289 | 27,035 | | Momoko Ueda (JPN) | 70-76-73-74—293 | 12,698 |
| | Sophie Gustafson (SWE) | 72-68-74-75—289 | 27,035 | | Becky Morgan (WAL) | 72-73-73-75—293 | 12,698 |
| 19 | Stacy Prammanasudh | 71-75-73-71—290 | 21,992 | | Wendy Ward | 70-71-77-75—293 | 12,698 |
| | Suzann Pettersen (NOR) | 75-71-72-72—290 | 21,992 | | Mi Hyun Kim (KOR) | 70-75-69-79—293 | 12,698 |
| | Paula Creamer | 73-74-70-73—290 | 21,992 | | | | |

**Other players who made the cut:** Karine Icher (FRA), Amanda Blumenherst, Kristy McPherson, So Yeon Ryu (KOR), Vicky Hurst, Jane Park 294; Laura Diaz, Mariajo Uribe (COL), Na Yeon Choi (KOR), Natalie Gulbis, Seon Hwa Lee (KOR) 295; Azahara Muñoz (ESP), Lindsey Wright (AUS), Maria Hernandez (ESP) 296; Shanshan Feng (CHN), Reilley Rankin 297; Shi Hyun Ahn (KOR), Laura Davies (ENG), Paige Mackenzie, Brittany Lang, Gwladys Nocera (FRA) 298; Candie Kung (TPE), Kyeong Bae (KOR), Stephanie Sherlock (CAN), Sun Young Yoo (KOR) 299; Nicole Castrale, Mindy Kim (KOR), Shiho Oyama (JPN) 300; Katherine Hull (AUS) 301; Hee Young Park (KOR), Lee-Anne Pace (RSA) 302; Pornanong Phatlum (THA) 304; Sarah Jane Smith 305; Yukari Baba (JPN) 307; Eunjung Yi (KOR) 309

## 2010 Kraft Nabisco Championship

[6702–72]

Prize money: $2 million

| | | | |
|---|---|---|---|
| 1 | Yani Tseng (TPE) | 69-71-67-68—275 | $300,000 |
| 2 | Suzann Pettersen (NOR) | 67-73-67-69—276 | 183,814 |
| 3 | Song-Hee Kim (KOR) | 69-68-72-70—279 | 133,344 |
| 4 | Lorena Ochoa (MEX) | 68-70-71-73—282 | 103,152 |
| 5 | Cristie Kerr | 71-67-74-72—284 | 64,408 |
| | Jiyai Shin (KOR) | 72-72-69-71—284 | 64,408 |
| | Karen Stupples (ENG) | 69-69-68-78—284 | 64,408 |
| | Karrie Webb (AUS) | 69-70-72-73—284 | 64,408 |
| 9 | Chie Arimura (JPN) | 73-72-68-72—285 | 44,784 |
| 10 | Sophie Gusatafson (SWE) | 70-73-70-73—286 | 35,544 |
| | Brittany Lang | 72-71-69-74—286 | 35,544 |
| | Anna Nordqvist (SWE) | 74-72-69-71—286 | 35,544 |
| | Grace Park (KOR) | 71-74-68-73—286 | 35,544 |
| | Inbee Park (KOR) | 73-74-70-69—286 | 35,544 |
| 15 | Catriona Matthew (SCO) | 73-74-67-73—287 | 26,971 |
| | Se Ri Pak (KOR) | 79-71-67-70—287 | 26,971 |
| | Hee Young Park (KOR) | 73-71-70-73—287 | 26,971 |
| | Angela Stanford | 78-68-69-72—287 | 26,971 |
| 19 | Stacy Lewis | 71-68-75-74—288 | 23,549 |
| | Morgan Pressel | 71-72-72-73—288 | 23,549 |
| 21 | Brittany Lincicome | 70-74-72-73—289 | 21,939 |
| | Hee Kyung Seo (KOR) | 72-73-76-68—289 | 21,939 |
| | Jennifer Song (KOR) (am) | 71-71-76-71—289 | |
| 24 | Katherine Hull (AUS) | 72-71-72-75—290 | 20,329 |
| | Gwladys Nocera (FRA) | 75-70-71-74—290 | 20,329 |
| | Alexis Thompson (am) | 74-72-73-71—290 | |
| 27 | Na Yeon Choi (KOR) | 74-73-72-72—291 | 17,151 |
| | Jimin Kang (KOR) | 72-74-72-73—291 | 17,151 |
| | Na On Min (KOR) | 69-75-71-76—291 | 17,151 |
| | Momoko Ueda (JPN) | 72-78-68-73—291 | 17,151 |
| | Michelle Wie | 71-71-71-78—291 | 17,151 |
| | Amy Yang (KOR) | 71-71-71-78—291 | 17,151 |
| | Sakura Yokomina (JPN) | 70-71-72-78—291 | 17,151 |
| 34 | Heather Bowie Young | 76-74-72-70—292 | 13,183 |
| | Sandra Gal (GER) | 72-70-80-70—292 | 13,183 |
| | Hee-Won Han (KOR) | 71-76-72-73—292 | 13,183 |
| | Paige Mackenzie | 75-74-70-73—292 | 13,183 |
| | Kirsty McPherson | 72-72-78-70—292 | 13,183 |
| | Melissa Reid (ENG) | 73-75-71-73—292 | 13,183 |

**Other players who made the cut:** Mi-Jeong Jeon (KOR), Jee Young Lee (KOR), Mika Miyazato (JPN), Shinobu Moromizato (JPN) 293; Vicky Hurst, In-Kyung Ki, (KOR), Teresa Lu (TPE), Jane Park 294; Laura Davies (ENG), Katie Futcher, Pat Hurst, Jeong Jang (KOR), Haeji Kang (KOR), Sarah Lee (KOR), Stacy Prammanasudh, Michele Redman 295; Shi Hyun Ahn (KOR), Hye Jung Choi (KOR), Karine Icher (FRA), Mi Hyun Kim (KOR), Meena Lee (KOR), Seon Hwa Lee (KOR), Giulia Sergas (ITA), Alena Sharp (CAN) 296; Louise Friberg (SWE), Carin Koch (SWE), So Yeon Ryu (KOR) 297; Jessica Korda (am), Sherri Steinhauer 298; Candie Kung (TPE), Yuko Mitsuka (JPN), Eunjung Yi (KOR) 299; Becky Brewerton (WAL), Allison Fouch, Jennifer Rosales (PHI) 300; Julieta Granada (PAR), Eun-Hee Ji (KOR) 301; Ilmi Chung (KOR), Becky Morgan (WAL) 303; Jennifer Johnson (am) 305

## 2009 Kraft Nabisco Championship

[6673–72]

Prize money: $2 million

| | | | |
|---|---|---|---|
| 1 | Brittany Lincicome | 66-74-70-69—279 | $300,000 |
| 2 | Cristie Kerr | 71-68-70-71—280 | 161,853 |
| | Kristy McPherson | 68-70-70-72—280 | 161,853 |
| 4 | Lindsey Wright (AUS) | 70-71-71-70—282 | 105,281 |
| 5 | Meaghan Francella | 72-73-69-69—283 | 77,036 |
| | Suzann Pettersen (NOR) | 71-72-74-66—283 | 77,036 |
| 7 | Christina Kim | 69-69-75-72—285 | 58,034 |
| 8 | Katherine Hull (AUS) | 69-74-71-72—286 | 44,167 |
| | Pat Hurst | 71-71-73-71—286 | 44,167 |
| | Jimin Kang (KOR) | 71-70-71-74—286 | 44,167 |
| | Karrie Webb (AUS) | 73-72-72-69—286 | 44,167 |
| 12 | Helen Alfredsson (SWE) | 72-70-72-73—287 | 31,841 |
| | Lorena Ochoa (MEX) | 73-73-72-69—287 | 31,841 |
| | Michele Redman | 72-73-72-70—287 | 31,841 |
| | Angela Stanford | 67-75-74-71—287 | 31,841 |
| | Sun Young Yoo (KOR) | 70-78-73-66—287 | 31,841 |
| 17 | Paula Creamer | 70-72-77-69—288 | 25,542 |
| | Brittany Lang | 67-80-71-70—288 | 25,542 |
| | Yani Tseng (TPE) | 69-75-75-69—288 | 25,542 |
| 20 | Jee Young Lee (KOR) | 69-80-72-68—289 | 23,624 |
| 21 | Tiffany Joh (am) | 71-75-73-71—290 | |
| | Song-Hee Kim (KOR) | 69-78-72-71—290 | 22,392 |
| | Jiyai Shin (KOR) | 72-76-71-71—290 | 22,392 |
| | Alexis Thompson (am) | 72-72-77-69—290 | |
| 25 | Nicole Castrale | 71-75-73-72—291 | 20,372 |
| | Allison Fouch | 76-73-69-73—291 | 20,372 |
| | Sakura Yokomine (JPN) | 72-73-74-72—291 | 20,372 |
| 28 | Hee-Won Han (KOR) | 75-73-72-72—292 | 18,540 |
| | In-Kyung Kim (KOR) | 70-73-75-74—292 | 18,540 |
| 30 | Young Kim (KOR) | 76-71-75-71—293 | 15,835 |
| | Candie Kung (TPE) | 72-73-74-74—293 | 15,835 |
| | Seon Hwa Lee (KOR) | 74-77-69-73—293 | 15,835 |
| | Janice Moodie (SCO) | 75-73-74-71—293 | 15,835 |
| | Jane Park | 74-76-68-75—293 | 15,835 |
| | Momoko Ueda (JPN) | 76-72-75-70—293 | 15,835 |
| 36 | Yuri Fudoh (JPN) | 71-76-73-74—294 | 12,891 |
| | Eun-Hee Ji (KOR) | 75-72-76-71—294 | 12,891 |
| | Ji Young Oh (KOR) | 67-78-78-71—294 | 12,891 |
| | Wendy Ward | 75-72-74-73—294 | 12,891 |

**Other players who made the cut:** Na Yeon Choi (KOR), Joo Mi Kim (KOR), Azahara Muñoz (ESP) (am), Se Ri Pak (KOR), Morgan Pressel, Alena Sharp (CAN) 295; Hye Jung Choi (KOR), Natalie Gulbis 296; Mi Hyun Kim (KOR), Gwladys Nocera (FRA), Angela Park (BRA), Jennifer Rosales (PHI), Giulia Sergas (ITA) 297; Soo-Yun Kang (KOR), Teresa Lu (TPE), Hee Young Park (KOR) 298; Shi Hyun Ahn (KOR), Moira Dunn, Rachel Hetherington (AUS), Inbee Park (KOR) 299; Laura Diaz, Ji-Hee Lee (KOR), Becky Morgan (WAL) 301; Il Mi Chung (KOR) 302; Sophie Gustafson (SWE), Stacy Lewis, Heather Young 303; Diana D'Alessio, Michelle Wie 304; Ai Miyazato (JPN) 305; Silvia Cavalleri (ITA) 306

## 2008 Kraft Nabisco Championship [6673–72]

Prize money: $2 million

| | | | | | | | | |
|---|---|---|---|---|---|---|---|---|
| 1 | Lorena Ochoa (MEX) | 68-71-71-67—277 | $300,000 | | 21T | Paula Creamer | 71-74-73-74—292 | 19,506 |
| 2 | Suzann Pettersen (NOR) | 74-75-65-68—282 | 160,369 | | | Cristie Kerr | 74-72-66-80—292 | 19,506 |
| | Annika Sörenstam (SWE) | 71-70-73-68—282 | 160,369 | | | Candie Kung (TPE) | 73-74-75-70—292 | 19,506 |
| 4 | Maria Hjörth (SWE) | 70-70-72-71—283 | 104,317 | | | Brittany Lang | 75-70-72-75—292 | 19,506 |
| 5 | Seon Hwa Lee (KOR) | 73-71-68-72—284 | 83,963 | | | Jee Young Lee (KOR) | 73-71-75-73—292 | 19,506 |
| 6 | Na Yeon Choi (KOR) | 74-72-69-70—285 | 58,859 | | | Angela Park (BRA) | 77-71-73-71—292 | 19,506 |
| | Hee-Won Han (KOR) | 72-69-70-74—285 | 58,859 | | | Michele Redman | 71-72-76-73—292 | 19,506 |
| | Mi Hyun Kim (KOR) | 70-70-76-69—285 | 58,859 | | | Yani Tseng (TPE) | 72-71-75-74—292 | 19,506 |
| 9 | Inbee Park (KOR) | 73-70-70-73—286 | 45,289 | | 30 | Amanda Blumenhurst (am) | 73-73-73-74—293 | |
| 10 | Se Ri Pak (KOR) | 72-70-73-72—287 | 39,692 | | 31 | Heather Daly-Donofrio | 75-71-73-75—294 | 14,190 |
| | Heather Young | 69-70-74-74—287 | 39,692 | | | Rachel Hetherington (AUS) | 76-69-74-75—294 | 14,190 |
| 12 | Karen Stupples (ENG) | 67-75-74-72—288 | 35,621 | | | Jeong Jang (KOR) | 73-73-74-74—294 | 14,190 |
| 13 | Natalie Gulbis | 69-74-73-73—289 | 32,364 | | | Ai Miyazato (JPN) | 68-74-77-75—294 | 14,190 |
| | Karrie Webb (AUS) | 76-70-69-74—289 | 32,364 | | | Ji-Young Oh (KOR) | 77-72-71-74—294 | 14,190 |
| 15 | Diana D'Alessio | 74-69-72-75—290 | 27,275 | | | Shiho Oyama (JPN) | 72-72-76-74—294 | 14,190 |
| | Meg Mallon | 73-73-72-72—290 | 27,275 | | | Ji-Yai Shin (KOR) | 73-71-76-74—294 | 14,190 |
| | Liselotte Neumann (SWE) | 70-72-71-77—290 | 27,275 | | 38 | Katherine Hull (AUS) | 76-70-74-75—295 | 11,271 |
| | Angela Stanford | 75-73-71-71—290 | 27,275 | | | Hee Young Park (KOR) | 75-72-74-75—295 | 11,271 |
| 19 | Janice Moodie (SCO) | 73-73-74-71—291 | 23,815 | | | Morgan Pressel | 71-74-75-75—295 | 11,271 |
| | Sakura Yokomini (JPN) | 76-73-72-70—291 | 23,815 | | | Giulia Sergas ITA) | 74-75-77-69—295 | 11,271 |
| 21 | Helen Alfredsson (SWE) | 75-72-73-72—292 | 19,506 | | | | | |

**Other players who made the cut:** Shi Hyun Ahn (KOR), H J Choi (KOR), Sophie Gustafson (SWE), Mhairi McKay (SCO), Lindsey Wright (AUS), 296; Beth Bader, Marisa Baena (COL), Minea Blomqvist (FIN), Momoko Ueda (JPN), 297; Silvia Cavalleri (ITA), Russy Gulyanamitta (THA), Soo-Yun Kang (KOR), Becky Morgan (WAL), 298; Laura Davies (ENG), Pat Hurst, Reilley Rankin, 299; Il Mi Chung (KOR), Juli Inkster, Teresa Lu (TPE), Maria Jose Uribe (am), Wendy Ward, 300; Moira Dunn, Julieta Granada (PAR), Carin Koch (SWE), Meena Lee (KOR), Sarah Lee (KOR), 301; Mallory Blackwelder (am), Alena Sharp (CAN), 302; Meaghan Francella, 303; Sung Ah Yim (KOR), 312

## 2007 Kraft Nabisco Championship [6673–72]

Prize money: $1.8 million

| | | | | | | | | |
|---|---|---|---|---|---|---|---|---|
| 1 | Morgan Pressel | 74-72-70-69—285 | $300,000 | | 20T | Laura Davies (ENG) | 74-73-73-73—293 | 22,881 |
| 2 | Brittany Lincicome | 72-71-71-72—286 | 140,945 | | | Cristie Kerr | 75-73-72-73—293 | 22,881 |
| | Catriona Matthew (SCO) | 70-73-72-71—286 | 140,945 | | | Sherri Steinhauer | 71-78-70-74—293 | 22,881 |
| | Suzann Pettersen (NOR) | 72-69-71-74—286 | 140,945 | | | Karrie Webb (AUS) | 70-77-73-73—293 | 22,881 |
| 5 | Shi Hyun Ahn (KOR) | 68-73-74-72—287 | 69,688 | | 24 | Juli Inkster | 75-75-72-72—294 | 20,451 |
| | Meaghan Francella | 72-72-69-74—287 | 69,688 | | | Christina Kim | 72-77-71-74—294 | 20,451 |
| | Stacy Lewis (am) | 71-73-73-70—287 | | | 26 | Jimin Kang (KOR) | 76-73-73-73—295 | 19,337 |
| | Stacy Prammanasudh | 76-70-70-71—287 | 69,688 | | 27 | Nicole Castrale | 76-71-74-75—296 | 17,565 |
| 9 | Maria Hjörth (SWE) | 70-73-72-73—288 | 50,114 | | | Julieta Granada (PAR) | 74-77-72-73—296 | 17,565 |
| 10 | Lorena Ochoa (MEX) | 69-71-77-72—289 | 41,340 | | | Angela Park (BRA) | 73-74-75-74—296 | 17,565 |
| | Se Ri Pak (KOR) | 72-70-70-77—289 | 41,340 | | | Lindsey Wright (AUS) | 74-69-77-76—296 | 17,565 |
| | Angela Stanford | 72-75-73-69—289 | 41,340 | | 31 | Laura Diaz | 73-79-71-74—297 | 14,116 |
| 13 | Jee Young Lee (KOR) | 70-77-71-72—290 | 34,321 | | | Young Jo (KOR) | 74-76-72-75—297 | 14,116 |
| | Sarah Lee (KOR) | 72-74-70-74—290 | 34,321 | | | Mi Hyun Kim (KOR) | 74-72-74-77—297 | 14,116 |
| 15 | Paula Creamer | 73-67-73-78—291 | 28,651 | | | Leta Lindley | 73-75-73-76—297 | 14,116 |
| | Brittany Lang | 71-73-75-72—291 | 28,651 | | | Hee-Young Park (KOR) | 73-74-77-73—297 | 14,116 |
| | Ai Miyazato (JPN) | 76-73-69-73—291 | 28,651 | | | Annika Sörenstam (SWE) | 75-76-71-75—297 | 14,116 |
| | Ji-Yai Shin (KOR) | 76-72-71-72—291 | 28,651 | | | Heather Young | 74-75-76-72—297 | 14,116 |
| 19 | Moira Dunn | 76-73-72-71—292 | 25,108 | | 38 | Helen Alfredsson (SWE) | 78-69-74-77—298 | 10,782 |

**Other players who made the cut:** Sophie Gustafson (SWE), Kim Saiki-Maloney, Sakura Yokomine (JPN) 299; Wendy Doolan, Shiho Oyama (JPN), Gloria Park (KOR) 300; Tina Barrett, Hee-Won Han (KOR), Young Kim (KOR), Becky Morgan (WAL) 301; Karine Icher (FRA), Jeong Jang (KOR), Reilley Rankin, Veronica Zorzi (ITA) 302; Diana D'Alessio, Soo-Yun Kang (KOR), Aree Song (KOR) 303; Carin Koch (SWE). Candie Kung (TPE), Liselotte Neumann (SWE), Nicole Perrot (CHI) 304; Mi-Jeong Jeon (KOR) 305; Tracy Hanson, Taylor Leon (am), Michele Redman 306; Esther Choe (am); Joo Mi Kim (KOR), Grace Park (KOR) 307; Jin Joo Hong (KOR) 310; Meg Mallon 311

## 2006 Kraft Nabisco Championship [6569–72]

Prize money: $1.8 million

| | | | |
|---|---|---|---|
| 1 | Karrie Webb* (AUS) | 70-68-76-65—279 | $270,000 |
| 2 | Lorena Ochoa (MEX) | 62-71-74-72—279 | 168,226 |
| *Webb won sudden death play-off:: Webb 5, Ochoa 6 | | | |
| 3 | Natalie Gulbis | 73-71-68-68—280 | 108,222 |
| | Michelle Wie | 66-71-73-70—280 | 108,222 |
| 5 | Juli Inkster | 69-73-74-68—284 | 75,985 |
| 6 | Hee-Won Han (KOR) | 75-72-68-71—286 | 57,104 |
| | Annika Sörenstam (SWE) | 71-72-73-70—286 | 57,104 |
| 8 | Shi Hyun Ahn (KOR) | 70-71-71-75—287 | 41,293 |
| | Helen Alfredsson (SWE) | 70-72-72-73—287 | 41,293 |
| | Brittany Lang | 70-74-72-71—287 | 41,293 |
| 11 | Stacy Prammanasudh | 67-73-76-72—288 | 33,388 |
| | Michele Redman | 72-72-72-72—288 | 33,388 |
| 13 | Beth Daniel | 72-72-72-73—289 | 29,289 |
| | Morgan Pressel | 69-76-70-74—289 | 29,289 |
| 15 | Yuri Fudoh (JPN) | 75-73-69-73—290 | 26,710 |
| | Angela Park (am) | 68-73-75-74—290 | |
| 17 | Pat Hurst | 73-73-73-72—291 | 24,592 |
| | Karen Stupples (ENG) | 69-74-72-76—291 | 24,592 |
| 19 | Tina Barrett | 72-75-74-71—292 | 21,221 |
| | Jeong Jang (KOR) | 71-75-76-70—292 | 21,221 |
| | Young Kim (KOR) | 74-73-70-75—292 | 21,221 |
| | Seon Hwa Lee (KOR) | 69-69-74-80—292 | 21,221 |
| 19T | Veronica Zorzi (ITA) | 74-72-75-71—292 | 21,221 |
| 24 | Paula Creamer | 69-71-79-74—293 | 1,7610 |
| | Dorothy Delasin | 72-72-74-75—293 | 17,610 |
| | Karine Icher (FRA) | 73-73-77-70—293 | 17,610 |
| | Carin Koch (SWE) | 70-72-76-75—293 | 17,610 |
| | Candie King (TAI) | 72-75-72-74—293 | 17,610 |
| 29 | Young Jo (KOR) | 72-73-75-74—294 | 14,199 |
| | Meena Lee (KOR) | 72-76-72-74—294 | 14,199 |
| | Patricia Meunier-Lebouc (FRA) | 77-67-77-73—294 | 14,199 |
| | Ai Miyazato (JPN) | 70-77-72-75—294 | 14,199 |
| | Becky Morgan (WAL) | 76-70-75-73—294 | 14,199 |
| | Jennifer Rosales (PHI) | 72-76-73-73—294 | 14,199 |
| 35 | Il Mi Chung (KOR) | 72-77-73-73—295 | 11,329 |
| | Cristie Kerr | 71-76-75-73—295 | 11,329 |
| | Grace Park (KOR) | 74-72-78-71—295 | 11,329 |
| | Sherri Steinhauer | 72-77-75-71—295 | 11,329 |
| | Wendy Ward | 71-75-76-73—295 | 11,329 |
| 40 | Suzann Pettersen (NOR) | 75-72-75-74—296 | 9,763 |
| | Aree Song (KOR) | 74-76-72-74—296 | 9,763 |
| 42 | Marisa Baena (COL) | 75-72-71-79—297 | 8,842 |
| | Mi Hyun Kim (KOR) | 75-74-75-73—297 | 8,842 |
| | Rachel Hetherington (AUS) | 74-75-76-72—297 | 8,842 |

**Other players who made the cut:** Kyeong Bae (KOR), Jimin Kang (KOR), Birdie Kim (KOR), Sarah Lee (KOR), Janice Moodie (SCO), Liselotte Neumann (SWE), Se Ri Pak (KOR) 298; Johanna Head (ENG), Christine Kim, Gwladys Nocera (FRA), Kim Saiki 299; Jee Young Lee (KOR), Sung Ah Yim (KOR) 300; Lorie Kane (CAN), Soo Young Moon (KOR), Reilley Rankin 301; Brandie Burton 302; Maru Martinez (am), In-Bee Park (am) 304; Joo Mi Kim (KOR) 305; Nicole Perrot (CHI) 306; Katherine Hull (AUS), Meg Mallon 307; Kate Golden, Sydnee Michaels (am) 308; A J Eathorne (CAN) 314

## 2005 Kraft Nabisco Championship [6460–72]

Prize money: $1.8 million

| | | | |
|---|---|---|---|
| 1 | Annika Sörenstam (SWE) | 70-69-66-68—273 | $270,000 |
| 2 | Rosie Jones | 69-70-71-71—281 | 166,003 |
| 3 | Laura Diaz | 75-69-71-68—283 | 106,791 |
| | Cristie Kerr | 72-70-70-71—283 | 1067,91 |
| 5 | Mi Hyun Kim (KOR) | 69-71-72-72—284 | 68,165 |
| | Grace Park (KOR) | 73-68-76-67—284 | 68,165 |
| 7 | Juli Inkster | 70-74-72-69—285 | 51,350 |
| 8 | Lorie Kane (CAN) | 71-76-69-70—286 | 44,988 |
| 9 | Beth Daniel | 74-72-69-72—287 | 34,591 |
| | Dorothy Delasin (PHI) | 71-72-73-71—287 | 34,591 |
| | Wendy Doolan (AUS) | 74-69-73-71—287 | 34,591 |
| | Candie Kung (TPE) | 72-73-71-71—287 | 34,591 |
| | Reilley Rankin | 73-68-74-72—287 | 34,591 |
| 14 | Brandie Burton | 72-71-72-73—288 | 27,175 |
| | Kim Saiki | 74-71-70-73—288 | 27,175 |
| | Michelle Wie (am) | 70-74-73-71—288 | |
| 17 | Natalie Gulbis | 73-71-72-73—289 | 24,267 |
| | Hee-Won Han (KOR) | 76-71-69-73—289 | 24,267 |
| 19 | Shi Hyun Ahn (KOR) | 77-76-71-66—290 | 2,1692 |
| | Paula Creamer | 74-72-72-72—290 | 21,692 |
| | Young Kim (KOR) | 76-70-70-74—290 | 21,692 |
| | Morgan Pressel (am) | 70-73-72-75—290 | |
| 23 | Laura Davies (ENG) | 73-71-71-77—292 | 19,086 |
| | Pat Hurst | 71-74-74-73—292 | 19,086 |
| | Sherri Steinhauer | 71-72-75-74—292 | 19,086 |
| | Karen Stupples (ENG) | 69-80-70-73—292 | 19,086 |
| 27 | Dawn Coe-Jones (CAN) | 74-73-74-72—293 | 16,723 |
| | Jeong Jang (KOR) | 74-74-71-71—293 | 16,723 |
| | Se Ri Pak (KOR) | 77-70-70-76—293 | 16,723 |
| 30 | Michelle Estill | 71-79-71-73—294 | 14,565 |
| | Julieta Granada (PAR) (am) | 75-71-70-78—294 | |
| | Carin Koch (SWE) | 70-73-75-76—294 | 14,565 |
| | Jill McGill | 73-72-77-72—294 | 14,565 |
| | Stacy Prammanasudh | 75-74-74-71—294 | 14,565 |
| 35 | Helen Alfredsson (SWE) | 76-72-74-73—295 | 12,383 |
| | Leta Lindley | 74-77-73-71—295 | 12,383 |
| | Lorena Ochoa (MEX) | 76-75-73-71—295 | 12,383 |
| | Jennifer Rosales (PHI) | 71-79-74-71—295 | 12,383 |
| 39 | Tina Barrett | 73-77-71-75—296 | 10,288 |
| | Yuri Fudoh (JPN) | 75-75-75-71—296 | 10,288 |
| | Rachel Hetherington (AUS) | 77-73-72-74—296 | 10,288 |
| | Christina Kim | 76-71-73-76—296 | 10,288 |
| | Janice Moodie (SCO) | 74-77-74-71—296 | 10,288 |

**Other players who made the cut:** Joo Mi Kim (KOR), Catriona Matthew (SCO), Ai Miyazato (JPN), Gloria Park (KOR), Charlotta Sörenstam (SWE), Karrie Webb (AUS) 297; Heather Bowie, Tina Fischer (GER), Meg Mallon, Jane Park (am), Wendy Ward 298; Liselotte Neumann (SWE), Giulia Sergas (ITA), Bo Bae Song (KOR) 299; Katherine Hull (AUS), Kelli Kuehne, Michele Redman, Angela Stanford 300; Donna Andrews, Betsy King 301; Trish Johnson (ENG), Aree Song (KOR) 302; Sophie Gustafson (SWE), Emilee Klein 303; Stephanie Arricau (FRA), Hilary Lunke 304; Heather Daly-Donofrio, Candy Hannemann (BRA) 305; Nancy Scranton 306; Catrin Nilsmark (SWE) 310; Jamie Hullett 311; Laurel Kean 316

## 2004 Nabisco Dinah Shore [6673–72]

Prize money: $1.6 million

| | | | | | | | | |
|---|---|---|---|---|---|---|---|---|
| 1 | Grace Park (KOR) | 72-69-67-69—277 | $240,000 | 23 | Jeong Jang (KOR) | 76-71-70-72—289 | 17,203 |
| 2 | Aree Song (KOR) | 66-73-69-70—278 | 146,826 | 24 | Brandie Burton | 70-76-71-73—290 | 15,944 |
| 3 | Karrie Webb (AUS) | 68-71-71-69—279 | 106,512 | | Tammie Green | 71-78-71-70—290 | 15,944 |
| 4 | Michelle Wie (am) | 69-72-69-71—281 | | | Jane Park (am) | 71-74-73-72—290 | |
| 5 | Cristie Kerr | 71-71-71-69—282 | 74,358 | | Dottie Pepper | 68-70-74-78—290 | 15,944 |
| | Catriona Matthew (SCO) | 67-75-70-70—282 | 74,358 | 28 | Danielle Ammaccapane | 75-77-73-66—291 | 13,682 |
| 7 | Mi-Hyun Kim (KOR) | 71-70-71-71—283 | 54,261 | | Donna Andrews | 70-74-73-74—291 | 13,682 |
| 8 | Rosie Jones | 67-73-71-73—284 | 36,737 | | Tina Barrett | 75-70-73-73—291 | 13,682 |
| | Christina Kim | 72-72-70-70—284 | 36,737 | | Juli Inkster | 74-74-73-70—291 | 13,682 |
| | Candie Kung (TPE) | 69-75-71-69—284 | 36,737 | | Wendy Ward | 72-74-70-75—291 | 13,682 |
| | Jung Yeon Lee (KOR) | 69-69-71-75—284 | 36,737 | 33 | Vicki Goetze-Ackerman | 73-79-71-69—292 | 11,897 |
| | Lorena Ochoa (MEX) | 67-76-74-67—284 | 36,737 | | Kelly Robbins | 69-74-78-71—292 | 11,897 |
| 13 | Hee-Won Han (KOR) | 72-71-71-71—285 | 26,420 | 35 | Dorothy Delasin (PHI) | 76-71-71-75—293 | 10,306 |
| | Stacy Prammanasudh | 71-71-69-74—285 | 26,420 | | Pat Hurst | 72-76-69-76—293 | 10,306 |
| | Annika Sörenstam (SWE) | 71-76-69-69—285 | 26,420 | | Lorie Kane (CAN) | 72-74-76-71—293 | 10,306 |
| 16 | Laura Davies (ENG) | 71-77-70-68—286 | 20,633 | | Rachel Teske (AUS) | 75-71-71-76—293 | 10,306 |
| | Wendy Doolan (AUS) | 70-69-72-75—286 | 20,633 | | Iben Tinning (DEN) | 70-75-77-71—293 | 10,306 |
| | Young Kim (KOR) | 74-72-67-73—286 | 20,633 | 40 | Helen Alfredsson (SWE) | 75-72-71-76—294 | 8,541 |
| | Carin Koch (SWE) | 70-72-71-73—286 | 20,633 | | Beth Daniel | 72-74-74-74—294 | 8,541 |
| | Se Ri Pak (KOR) | 72-73-72-69—286 | 20,633 | | Kate Golden | 73-78-74-69—294 | 85,41 |
| | Karen Stupples (ENG) | 70-76-68-72—286 | 20,633 | | Elizabeth Janangelo (am) | 71-78-70-75—294 | |
| 22 | Michele Redman | 73-73-70-71—287 | 17,846 | | Emilee Klein | 71-73-76-74—294 | 8,541 |

**Other players who made the cut:** Beth Bauer, Paula Creamer (am), Jill McGill 295; Sophie Gustafson (SWE), Stephanie Louden, Meg Mallon, Sherri Steinhauer 296; Michelle Ellis (AUS), Laurel Kean, Becky Morgan (WAL) 297; Jackie Gallagher-Smith, Ji-Hee Lee (KOR), Charlotta Sörenstam (SWE) 298; Moira Dunn, Natalie Gulbis, Betsy King, Jennifer Rosales (PHI) 300; Marisa Baena (COL), Heather Bowie, Heather Daly-Donofrio, Soo-Yun Kang (KOR), Miho Koga (JPN), Yu Ping Lin (TPE), Janice Moodie (SCO) 301; Hilary Lunke 302; JoAnne Carner, Dawn Coe-Jones, Joanne Mills (AUS) 303; Mhairi McKay (SCO), Shani Waugh (AUS) 304; Mardi Lunn (AUS) 305; Kelli Kuehne 306; Amy Alcott 308; Nancy Lopez WD

# Kraft Nabisco History

This event was inaugurated in 1972 as the Colgate Dinah Shore and continued to be sponsored by Colgate until 1981. Nabisco took over the sponsorship in 1982; and the Nabisco Dinah Shore was designated a Major Championship in 1983. The Championship became the Kraft Nabisco in 2005. Mission Hills CC, Rancho Mirage, California, is the event's permanent venue.

| Year | Winner | Score | Year | Winner | Score |
|---|---|---|---|---|---|
| 1972 | J Blalock | 213 | 1992 | D Mochrie* | 279 |
| 1973 | M Wright | 284 | *After a play-off with J Inkster | | |
| 1974 | J Prentice* | 289 | 1993 | H Alfredsson (SWE) | 284 |
| *After a play-off with J Blalock and S Haynie | | | 1994 | D Andrews | 276 |
| 1975 | S Palmer | 283 | 1995 | N Bowen | 285 |
| 1976 | J Rankin | 285 | 1996 | P Sheehan | 281 |
| 1977 | K Whitworth | 289 | 1997 | B King | 276 |
| 1978 | S Post* | 283 | 1998 | P Hurst | 281 |
| *After a play-off with P Pulz | | | 1999 | D Pepper | 269 |
| 1979 | S Post* | 276 | 2000 | K Webb (AUS) | 274 |
| *After a play-off with N Lopez | | | 2001 | A Sörenstam (SWE) | 281 |
| 1980 | D Caponi | 275 | 2002 | A Sörenstam (SWE) | 280 |
| 1981 | N Lopez | 277 | 2003 | P Meunier-Lebouc (FRA) | 281 |
| 1982 | S Little | 278 | 2004 | G Park (KOR) | 277 |
| 1983 | A Alcott | 282 | 2005 | A Sörenstam (SWE) | 273 |
| 1984 | J Inkster* | 280 | 2006 | K Webb (AUS)* | 279 |
| *After a play-off with P Bradley | | | *After a play-off with L Ochoa (MEX) | | |
| 1985 | A Miller | 278 | 2007 | M Pressel | 285 |
| 1986 | P Bradley | 280 | 2008 | L Ochoa (MEX) | 277 |
| 1987 | B King* | 283 | 2009 | B Lincicombe | 279 |
| *After a play-off with P Sheehan | | | 2010 | Y Tseng (TPE) | 275 |
| 1988 | A Alcott | 274 | 2011 | S Lewis | 275 |
| 1989 | J Inkster | 279 | 2012 | S Y Yoo (KOR)* | 279 |
| 1990 | B King | 283 | *After a play-off with I K Kim (KOR) | | |
| 1991 | A Alcott | 273 | 2013 | I Park (KOR) | 273 |

## The Evian Championship

# Norway's Suzann Pettersen wins major after six year wait

More than six years since she won her first major title, the LPGA Championship at Bulle Rock in Maryland, it was little wonder Suzann Pettersen gave her caddie, Brian Dilley, a smile of blessed relief on the final green at the Evian resort club when her closest rival, Lydia Ko, narrowly failed to chip in for birdie.

It meant the Norwegian golfer enjoyed the comfort of knowing she could take three putts from the middle of the green and still win the inaugural staging of the Evian Championship after it was upgraded to become the fifth major in women's golf. Even though her lag putt was a little undercooked, Pettersen holed out smoothly from five feet for par and won her second major by two shots from the 16-year-old amateur prodigy.

Pettersen's ten under par total of 203 in the weather-shortened event was sufficient to bank the winner's cheque for €366,393 and end a run of near misses in the game's most prized tournaments which saw her finish second at the Kraft Nabisco in 2008 and 2010, second at the US Women's Open in 2010 and second in the LPGA Championship in 2012.

Having won the Safeway Classic prior to the Evian, Pettersen came to France in arguably the best form of her life. She had been a key figure in Europe's victory over the USA in the Solheim Cup and could also reflect on a streak of noteworthy performances which numbered four top three finishes in five consecutive events.

"It was such a great month, five weeks for me, starting off with the Solheim," Pettersen recalled. "I mean, the feelings during the Solheim never really get old. We had a fantastic team. It was kind of a great kick start for what became probably the month of my career, I would probably say so."

At 32, Pettersen has been around the summit of the women's game long enough to understand the slings and arrows of an unforgiving game. Once renowned for the shortness of her fuse, the Scandinavian is more comfortable in her own skin these days.

"Well, a lot of people have tried to tell me this for years," she said. "I guess you can only take action when you first realise it [for yourself]. It's a maturing process, I think. I'm just in a very good, happy spot in life right now. I have nothing to worry about. Everyone around me is very supportive. My family are all great. I must say, I feel like I've come to this age where I'm too old to be around [the game] and not be happy. I know you guys didn't see me smile that much in the past, but you've probably seen a few more now."

It was the 19th win of the European's career, her fourth of 2013, and lifted her to second in the Rolex Rankings. According to Judy Rankin, the former professional and insightful broadcaster, Pettersen's combination of power, physique and intelligence makes her "everything you want from a female athlete."

Unsurprisingly, this sporting Valkyrie chose not to lay up on the testing final hole even with the edge of a two stroke advantage. "I was so in-between laying up or not," she acknowledged. "It was chicken to lay up. Brian, my caddie, said, if Lydia lays up, we lay up. I'm like, Okay. She has a wood in her hand. She's going to go for it. For me, it was almost the perfect shot. I could just hit a little fade with my hybrid. The 18th has definitely become a very tough hole. This is what they want, for us to question what we're going to do. Even when you have a two shot lead, it did not feel easy."

Unfortunately for the sponsors, the players and the organisers even before the tournament began, the weather in Evian-Les-Bains on the shore of Lac Leman was sodden – four inches of rain fell – and further precipitation on Thursday meant the first round was suspended.

Once it became clear the long range weather forecast offered little respite from the downpours, it was decided to trim the tournament to 54 holes with the cut made at 70 and ties rather than lowering the cut number and attempting to play 36 holes on Sunday.

With a purse of €2,496,170, the Evian is the most lucrative tournament in women's golf and there was understandable disappointment when that decision was made. It was the first time a women's major had been shortened since the LPGA Championship of 1996 won by Laura Davies and applied a minor gloss to the new major.

An R&A Working for Golf Ambassador since 2011, Pettersen laid down a marker on Friday when the first round eventually got underway in sunny, pleasant conditions. Playing for a fifth consecutive week, the Norwegian overcame any feelings of fatigue and reckoned she was invariably at her best during a spell of regular competition before signing for 66, one stroke behind Mika Miyazato, the early leader.

Always a fine striker of the ball, it was again evident how much more confident a putter Pettersen became in 2013. "My ball striking is my bread and butter," she agreed, "and it's always easy to spend time working on that. But really I've just tried to be disciplined enough to put in the time and the effort to get my putting up to a level where I feel it's good enough. Now the ball drops in the hole a bit more often. Pays off on the scorecard…"

Certainly, it was Miyazato's hot putter which made the difference during the opening round as she used the short stick just 25 times during a splendid opening salvo of 65. Apart from holing out well, the leader found plenty of greens in regulation. Her approach play was sterling and she only once, from 25 feet, made a lengthy putt.

> "My putting is up to a level where I feel it's good enough."
>
> *Suzann Pettersen*

The 23-year-old from Japan was almost as impressive in the second round when she compiled a battling 69 to retain the lead on eight under. It was a stalwart effort bearing in mind how poorly she began with a brace of bogeys over the opening holes. To her credit, Miyazato remained steadfast, bouncing back with birdies on the sixth and seventh holes. "Pretty nice comeback," she smiled.

Pettersen was also short of her best but managed her game well enough to remain in contention. She felt the pin positions were challenging but made enough birdie putts and par saving putts to sign for seven under and earn a spot in the final group on Sunday. It was also significant to hear how pragmatic the golfer felt about issues over which she had no control. "I've been very laid back," she said. "I understand we're in a difficult position. It's not ideal for either the championship or for the players or the Tour in general to cut down on major rounds. So we do the best we can."

The story of the second round was Ko's sparkling 67 which featured four birdies and gave nothing away to par. The teenager's only regret was that she didn't make more of the opportunities created by her approach work. As to the decision to play 54 holes rather than 72, Ko reckoned the tournament's major status meant the organisers should have trimmed the cut to 50 players and attempted to fit in four rounds. "It's hard not playing 72 holes for a major," she reasoned.

More rain fell overnight and the organisers opted to cover the greens with tarpaulins to keep them playable on Sunday. Although the start was delayed by 90 minutes, the third round unfolded in relatively fair conditions. Miyazato, with a closing 79, was undone by another poor start which included an 8 on the seventh hole while Pettersen was quick to put her foot on the accelerator with birdies at the second and third holes before dropping a shot at the seventh.

Ko, who was striving to become the youngest winner of a major, got back on level terms at that point only to drop back on the eighth when Pettersen regained the lead. The Norwegian never surrendered her advantage thereafter thanks to dogged scrambling.

Two strokes in front by the time she reached the closing hole, Pettersen was glad the Kiwi took on the 18th green with a metal wood and, for her, eliminated the option of playing safe. "No guts," she reasoned, "no glory."

Mike Aitken

| First Round | Second Round | Third Round |
|---|---|---|
| −6 Mika Miyazato | −8 Mika Miyazato | −10 Suzann Pettersen |
| −5 Suzann Pettersen | −7 Suzann Pettersen | −8 Lydia Ko |
| −5 Sandra Gal | −7 Lydia Ko | −6 Lexi Thomson |
| −5 Se Ri Pak | −6 Stacey Lewis | −5 Se Ri Pak |
| −4 Christina Kim | −5 Chella Choi | −5 So Yeon Ryu |
| −3 Karrie Webb | −5 So Yeon Ryu | −4 Angela Stanford |
| −3 Michelle Wie | −5 Se Ri Pak | −4 Chella Choi |
| −3 Lydia Ko | −4 I K Kim | −4 Stacy Lewis |
| −3 Lindsey Wright | −4 Beatriz Recari | −3 Jennifer Johnson |
| −3 Danah Bordner | −4 Lindsey Wright | −3 Beatriz Recari |

## The Evian Championship Evian Masters GC, Evian-les-Bains, France    Sep 12–15
[6428–71]

Prize money: €2,496,170. Final field of 120 players (including one amateur), of whom 77 (including one amateur) made the cut on 70 or less.

| | | | |
|---|---|---|---|
| 1 | Suzann Pettersen (NOR) | 66-69-68—203 | €366,393 |
| 2 | Lydia Ko (NZL) (am) | 68-67-70—205 | |
| 3 | Lexi Thompson (USA) | 72-67-68—207 | 223,963 |
| 4 | So Yeon Ryu (KOR) | 71-66-71—208 | 144,065 |
| | Se Ri Pak (KOR) | 66-71-71—208 | 144,065 |
| 6 | Chella Choi (KOR) | 70-67-72—209 | 84,408 |
| | Angela Stanford (USA) | 69-71-69—209 | 84,408 |
| | Stacy Lewis (USA) | 69-67-73—209 | 84,408 |
| 9 | Jennifer Johnson (USA) | 70-70-70—210 | 57,633 |
| | Beatriz Recari (ESP) | 69-69-72—210 | 57,633 |
| 11 | Rebecca Lee-Bentham (CAN) | 75-66-70—211 | 44,693 |
| | Shanshan Feng (CHN) | 70-72-69—211 | 44,693 |
| | Lizette Salas (USA) | 70-71-70—211 | 44,693 |
| | Il Hee Lee (KOR) | 70-71-70—211 | 44,693 |
| 15 | Ai Miyazato (JPN) | 75-68-69—212 | 34,697 |
| | Cindy Lacrosse (USA) | 73-70-69—212 | 34,697 |
| | Katherine Hull-Kirk (AUS) | 71-71-70—212 | 34,697 |
| | Karrie Webb (AUS) | 68-72-72—212 | 34,697 |
| 19 | Caroline Hedwall (SWE) | 74-68-71—213 | 26,777 |
| | Mi Hyang Lee (KOR) | 73-70-70—213 | 26,777 |
| | Hee Young Park (KOR) | 72-74-67—213 | 26,777 |
| | Azahara Muñoz (ESP) | 70-71-72—213 | 26,777 |
| | Paula Creamer (USA) | 70-69-74—213 | 26,777 |
| | I K Kim (KOR) | 69-69-75—213 | 26,777 |
| | Sandra Gal (GER) | 66-74-73—213 | 26,777 |
| | Mika Miyazato (JPN) | 65-69-79—213 | 26,777 |
| 27 | Mina Harigae (USA) | 71-73-70—214 | 21,275 |
| | Holly Clyburn (ENG) | 71-70-73—214 | 21,275 |
| | Momoko Ueda (JPN) | 70-70-74—214 | 21,275 |
| | Ayako Uehara (JPN) | 69-73-72—214 | 21,275 |
| 31 | Danielle Kang (USA) | 72-73-70—215 | 17,436 |
| | Jenny Shin (KOR) | 71-73-71—215 | 17,436 |
| | Meena Lee (KOR) | 71-72-72—215 | 17,436 |
| | Morgan Pressel (USA) | 70-72-73—215 | 17,436 |
| | Hee-Won Han (KOR) | 69-72-74—215 | 17,436 |
| | Christina Kim (USA) | 67-73-75—215 | 17,436 |
| 37 | Jessica Korda (USA) | 75-70-71—216 | 13,343 |
| | Belen Mozo (ESP) | 75-70-71—216 | 13,343 |
| | Juli Inkster (USA) | 74-68-74—216 | 13,343 |
| | Eun Hee Ji (KOR) | 72-74-70—216 | 13,343 |
| | Sydnee Michaels (USA) | 71-72-73—216 | 13,343 |
| | Caroline Masson (GER) | 70-72-74—216 | 13,343 |
| | Michelle Wie (USA) | 68-72-76—216 | 13,343 |
| 44 | Jodi Ewart Shadoff (ENG) | 77-68-72—217 | 9,886 |
| | Brittany Lincicome (USA) | 75-71-71—217 | 9,886 |
| | Anna Nordqvist (SWE) | 74-68-75—217 | 9,886 |
| | Jiyai Shin (KOR) | 73-71-73—217 | 9,886 |
| | Haeji Kang (KOR) | 72-72-73—217 | 9,886 |
| | Vicky Hurst (USA) | 71-68-78—217 | 9,886 |
| | Ji Young Oh (KOR) | 69-74-74—217 | 9,886 |
| | Na Yeon Choi (KOR) | 69-73-75—217 | 9,886 |
| 52 | Carlota Ciganda (ESP) | 78-68-72—218 | 7,840 |
| | Natalie Gulbis (USA) | 75-69-74—218 | 7,840 |
| | Candie Kung (TPE) | 73-73-72—218 | 7,840 |
| | Pornanong Phatlum (THA) | 72-71-75—218 | 7,840 |

| | | | |
|---|---|---|---|
| 52T | Lindsey Wright (AUS) | 68-70-80—218 | 7,840 |
| 57 | Thidapa Suwannapura (THA) | 76-70-73—219 | 6,427 |
| | Paige Mackenzie (USA) | 75-71-73—219 | 6,427 |
| | Brittany Lang (USA) | 74-71-74—219 | 6,427 |
| | Mo Martin (USA) | 73-72-74—219 | 6,427 |
| | Kris Tamulis (USA) | 73-71-75—219 | 6,427 |
| | Julieta Granada (PAR) | 73-71-75—219 | 6,427 |
| | Lee-Anne Pace (RSA) | 69-74-76—219 | 6,427 |
| 64 | Catriona Matthew (SCO) | 73-73-74—220 | 5,642 |
| | Pernilla Lindberg (SWE) | 72-73-75—220 | 5,642 |
| | Hee-Kyung Seo (KOR) | 70-76-74—220 | 5,642 |
| 67 | Jane Park (USA) | 75-70-76—221 | 5,056 |
| | Gwladys Nocera (FRA) | 74-72-75—221 | 5,056 |
| | Inbee Park (KOR) | 74-71-76—221 | 5,056 |
| | Giulia Sergas (ITA) | 73-70-78—221 | 5,056 |
| | Amy Yang (KOR) | 72-73-76—221 | 5,056 |
| | Gerina Piller (USA) | 72-72-77—221 | 5,056 |
| | Mariajo Uribe (COL) | 70-76-75—221 | 5,056 |
| 74 | Amanda Blumenherst (USA) | 75-71-76—222 | 4,714 |
| 75 | Lisa McCloskey (USA) | 70-76-77—223 | 4,665 |
| 76 | Danah Bordner (USA) | 69-73-82—224 | 4,592 |
| 77 | Sarah Kemp (AUS) | 73-72-81—226 | 4,543 |

*The following players missed the cut:*

| | | | | | | |
|---|---|---|---|---|---|---|
| 78 | Sandra Changkija (USA) | 78-69—147 | | 95T | Charley Hull (ENG) | 74-75—149 |
| | Moriya Jutanugarn (THA) | 77-70—147 | | 101 | Joanna Klatten (FRA) | 76-74—150 |
| | Jennifer Song (USA) | 76-71—147 | | | Kristy McPherson (USA) | 74-76—150 |
| | Sun Young Yoo (KOR) | 75-72—147 | | | Karine Icher (FRA) | 73-77—150 |
| | Moira Dunn (USA) | 74-73—147 | | | Paolo Moreno (COL) | 73-77—150 |
| | Laura Davies (ENG) | 74-73—147 | | | Sarah-Jane Smith (AUS) | 72-78—150 |
| | Alison Walshe (USA) | 73-74—147 | | | Heather Bowie Young (USA) | 72-78—150 |
| | Mi Jung Hur (TPE) | 71-76—147 | | 107 | Cheyenne Woods (USA) | 80-71—151 |
| | Helen Alfredsson (SWE) | 71-76—147 | | | Ryann O'Toole (USA) | 78-73—151 |
| | Marianne Skarpnord (NOR) | 71-76—147 | | | Katie Burnett (USA) | 76-75—151 |
| 88 | Cristie Kerr (USA) | 76-72—148 | | | Dewi Claire Schreefel (NED) | 75-76—151 |
| | Jennifer Rosales (PHI) | 76-72—148 | | | Dori Carter (USA) | 74-77—151 |
| | Irene Cho (USA) | 75-73—148 | | | Austin Ernst (USA) | 71-80—151 |
| | Katie Futcher (USA) | 74-74—148 | | 113 | Becky Morgan (WAL) | 76-76—152 |
| | Christel Boeljon (NED) | 74-74—148 | | | Mindy Kim (TPE) | 75-77—152 |
| | Kathlyn Ekey (USA) | 73-75—148 | | 115 | Melissa Reid (ENG) | 80-75—155 |
| | Sophie Gustafson (SWE) | 71-77—148 | | | Laura Diaz (USA) | 79-76—155 |
| 95 | Xi Yu Lin (CHN) | 77-72—149 | | 117 | Brooke Pancake (USA) | 77-79—156 |
| | Amelia Lewis (USA) | 77-72—149 | | 118 | Rebecca Artis (AUS) | 80-77—157 |
| | Jacqui Concolino (USA) | 75-74—149 | | | Jee Young Lee (KOR) | RTD |
| | Ann-Kathrin Lindner (GER) | 75-74—149 | | | Jeong Jang (KOR) | RTD |
| | Yani Tseng (TPE) | 75-74—149 | | | | |

## Sweden's Helen Alfredsson calls it a day

It seemed a good place for her to call time on her tournament career. The 48-year-old chose the Evian tournament, which she won three times, to bow out saying "I don't like travelling any more" then adding: "It's time to get a real job."

The often fiery-tempered Alfredsson won seven times on the LPGA Tour including the first major of the year – the Nabisco Dinah Shore event – in 1993 a year after winning the Ladies' British Open.

The Swede played in seven Solheim Cup matches and captained the side in 1973. In addition to winning titles in America she won in Europe, Australia and Japan.

She will miss the camaraderie of the Tour but is hoping to study sports psychology and concentrate on raising money for research into Alzheimer's Disease, which claimed her mother.

Reflecting on her career she said: "It was fun when we were in Japan. We used to have a party bus and a non-party bus which showed up an hour later!"

# du Maurier Classic History

The du Maurier Classic was inaugurated in 1973 and designated a Major Championship in 1979.
It was discontinued after 2000 and was replaced as a major on the US LPGA schedule by the Weetabix Women's
British Open.

*Players are of American nationality unless stated*

| | | | |
|---|---|---|---|
| 1973 | J Bourassa* | Montreal GC, Montreal | 214 |
| *After a play-off with S Haynie and J Rankin* | | | |
| 1974 | CJ Callison | Candiac GC, Montreal | 208 |
| 1975 | J Carner* | St George's CC, Toronto | 214 |
| *After a play-off with C Mann* | | | |
| 1976 | D Caponi* | Cedar Brae G&CC, Toronto | 212 |
| *After a play-off with J Rankin* | | | |
| 1977 | J Rankin | Lachute G&CC, Montreal | 214 |
| 1978 | J Carner | St George's CC, Toronto | 278 |
| 1979 | A Alcott | Richelieu Valley CC, Montreal | 285 |
| 1980 | P Bradley | St George's CC, Toronto | 277 |
| 1981 | J Stephenson (AUS) | Summerlea CC, Dorian, Quebec | 278 |
| 1982 | S Haynie | St George's CC, Toronto | 280 |
| 1983 | H Stacy | Beaconsfield CC, Montreal | 277 |
| 1984 | J Inkster | St George's CC, Toronto | 279 |
| 1985 | P Bradley | Beaconsfield CC, Montreal | 278 |
| 1986 | P Bradley* | Board of Trade CC, Toronto | 276 |
| *After a play-off with A Okamoto* | | | |
| 1987 | J Rosenthal | Islesmere GC, Laval, Quebec | 272 |
| 1988 | S Little (RSA) | Vancouver GC, Coquitlam, BC | 279 |
| 1989 | T Green | Beaconsfield GC, Montreal | 279 |
| 1990 | C Johnston | Westmount G&CC, Kitchener, Ontario | 276 |
| 1991 | N Scranton | Vancouver GC, Coquitlam, BC | 279 |
| 1992 | S Steinhauer | St Charles CC, Winnipeg, Manitoba | 277 |
| 1993 | B Burton* | London H&CC, Ontario | 277 |
| *After a play-off with B King* | | | |
| 1994 | M Nause | Ottawa Hunt Club, Ontario | 279 |
| 1995 | J Lidback | Beaconsfield CC, Montreal | 280 |
| 1996 | L Davies (ENG) | Edmonton CC, Edmonton, Alberta | 277 |
| 1997 | C Walker | Glen Abbey GC, Toronto | 278 |
| 1998 | B Burton | Essex G&CC, Ontario | 270 |
| 1999 | K Webb (AUS) | Priddis Greens G&CC, Calgary, Alberta | 277 |
| 2000 | M Mallon | Royal Ottawa GC, Aylmer, Quebec | 282 |

## Month by month in 2013

Tiger Woods is back to world number one after victories at the WGC
Cadillac Championship and, for the eighth time in his career, the Arnold
Palmer Invitational. There is a change of the top of the women's game
too with Stacy Lewis ending Yani Tseng's 25-month reign after winning
the HSBC Champions·

# Women's Grand Slam Titles

*Patty Berg*

*Mickey Wright*

*Louise Suggs*

| | British Open[1] | US Open[2] | LPGA[3] | Kraft Nabisco[4] | du Maurier[5] | Title-holders[6] | Western[7] | Evian[8] | Total Titles |
|---|---|---|---|---|---|---|---|---|---|
| Patty Berg (USA) | 0 | 1 | 0 | — | — | 7 | 7 | — | 15 |
| Mickey Wright (USA) | 0 | 4 | 4 | — | — | 2 | 3 | — | 13 |
| Louise Suggs (USA) | 0 | 2 | 1 | — | — | 4 | 4 | — | 11 |
| Annika Sörenstam (SWE) | 1 | 3 | 3 | 3 | 0 | — | — | — | 10 |
| 'Babe' Zaharias (USA) | 0 | 3 | — | — | — | 3 | 4 | — | 10 |
| Karrie Webb (AUS) | 3 | 2 | 1 | 2 | 1 | — | — | — | 9 |
| Betsy Rawls (USA) | 0 | 4 | 2 | — | — | 0 | 2 | — | 8 |
| Juli Inkster (USA) | 0 | 2 | 2 | 2 | 1 | — | — | — | 7 |

[1] The Ricoh Women's British Open was designated a major on the LPGA Tour in 2001
[2] The US Open became an LPGA major in 1950
[3] The Wegmans LPGA Championship was designated a major in 1955
[4] The Kraft Nabisco event was designated a major in 1983
[5] The du Maurier event was designated a major in 1979 but discontinued after 2000
[6] The Titleholders Championship was a major from 1937–1966 and in 1972
[7] The Western event was a major from 1937 to 1967
[8] The Evian event was designated a major in 2013

Super Career Grand Slam: Only Karrie Webb has won five of the qualifying majors – the Women's British Open, the US Open, the LPGA Championship, the Kraft Nabisco and du Maurier. She completed her Super Grand Slam in 2002.

Career Grand Slam: Only Louise Suggs (1957), Mickey Wright (1962), Pat Bradley (1986), Julie Inkster (1999), Karrie Webb (2001) and Annika Sörenstam (2003) have won all the designated majors at the time they were playing.

Grand Slam: Only Babe Zaharias in 1950 (three majors) and Sandra Haynie (USA) in 1964 (two majors) have won all the majors available that season. Inbee Park won the first three of the five majors in 2013.

Note: Glenna Collett Vare (USA) won six US Amateurs between 1922 and 1935 including three in a row in 1928, 1929 and 1930. Jo Anne Carner (USA) won five US Amateurs between 1957 and 1968. Julie Inkster won three US Amateurs in 1980, 1981 and 1982.

# Peter Uihlein named Sir Henry Cotton Rookie of the Year

American Peter Uihlein won the Sir Henry Cotton Rookie of the Year award following his hugely successful first season on The European Tour, in which he won his maiden title and finished 14th in The Race to Dubai.

The 24-year-old is the first player from America to win the prestigious award, and follows in the footsteps of golfing legends such as Sir Nick Faldo (1977), Sandy Lyle (1978), José María Olazábal (1986), Colin Montgomerie (1988) and more recently Sergio Garcia (1999), Ian Poulter (2000), Paul Casey (2001), Martin Kaymer (2007) and Matteo Manassero (2010).

Having turned professional in December 2011 following a glittering amateur career, Uihlein secured a European Challenge Tour card for 2013 and made a promising start. He also received several invitations for European Tour events, and took advantage of the opportunities to notch up top ten finishes in the Tshwane Open and the Open de España early in the season.

His season-changing victory came in May, at the Madeira Islands Open, through which he earned full European Tour playing rights and meant his schedule changed dramatically for the rest of the year. He continued to show he could deal with the step up, finishing tied tenth in both the BMW International Open and the Aberdeen Asset Management Scottish Open, before a fine spell in the second half of the campaign.

In August the Floridian was denied a second title by a barnstorming finish from Grégory Bourdy in the ISPS Handa Wales Open where he finished second and he maintained that superb form at the Alfred Dunhill Links Championship, where he came within a whisker of recording the first 59 in European Tour history at Kingsbarns in the second round.

The 12 under par 60 helped him tie for the lead after 72 holes, but he was thwarted by David Howell at the second hole of a sudden-death play-off. In his next appearance on the European Tour, Uihlein tied for fifth in the BMW Masters presented by SRE Group, the first event in the inaugural Final Series.

The Oklahoma State University graduate was thrilled to be the 49th recipient of the award, which was launched in 1960.

"It's an honour to win the Sir Henry Cotton Rookie of the Year award," said Uihlein, who reached world amateur number one 2010. "I wasn't expecting it, but it's been a great year and I'm very pleased. I think I'm the first non-European to win it, so that's a great honour. Any time you're the first of anything, it's neat.

"The win in Madeira was great and I had a lot of top tens. I played well all week in Madeira and handled myself well in the wind, and it was nice to get the job done. The win opened a few doors for me and I was able to play at Wentworth (the BMW PGA Championship) the following week.

"I was supposed to start the year on the Challenge Tour, but instead I was 11th in The Race to Dubai heading into the final event, so it wasn't what I'd planned on but obviously it's fantastic the way it has worked out."

Before joining the paid ranks, Uihlein won the 2010 US Amateur Championship, and won four points from four matches in the 2009 Walker Cup. George O'Grady, Chief Executive of The European Tour, said: "We heartily congratulate Peter on an outstanding season, during which he has thrilled golf fans and challenged for several titles. He is a worthy winner of the Sir Henry Cotton Rookie of the Year.

"His incredible 60 at Kingsbarns, which ended with his eagle putt for a 59 missing by a fraction, will go down as one of the finest displays on The European Tour.

"Peter enjoyed a wonderful career as an amateur and it is so pleasing to see him fulfilling his potential at the game's highest level. We wish him every success for the future."

# PART II

# Men's Professional Tournaments

# World Golf Rankings 2013

Among many notable gains in the 2013 World Rankings top 50 were Henrik Stenson who advanced from 115th position in 2012 to occupy the third spot and Jordan Spieth who only turned professional in 2012 yet was placed in 22nd position. Others to make significant improvements were Kevin Streelman and Billy Horschel.

| Ranking | Name | | Country | Points Average | Total Points | No. of Events | 2011/2012 Pts Lost | 2013 Pts Gained |
|---|---|---|---|---|---|---|---|---|
| 1 | Tiger Woods | (3) | USA | 11.69 | 479.49 | 41 | −350.08 | +488.25 |
| 2 | Adam Scott | (5) | AUS | 9.60 | 393.43 | 41 | −243.02 | +375.74 |
| 3 | Henrik Stenson | (53) | SWE | 9.16 | 476.20 | 52 | −117.14 | +484.60 |
| 4 | Justin Rose | (4) | ENG | 7.16 | 372.50 | 52 | −301.43 | +339.05 |
| 5 | Phil Mickelson | (17) | USA | 7.06 | 345.92 | 49 | −240.46 | +356.52 |
| 6 | Rory McIlroy | (1) | NIR | 6.50 | 318.44 | 49 | −462.67 | +159.81 |
| 7 | Matt Kuchar | (21) | USA | 6.15 | 319.93 | 52 | −245.86 | +339.45 |
| 8 | Steve Stricker | (18) | USA | 5.72 | 228.94 | 40 | −192.80 | +231.13 |
| 9 | Zach Johnson | (25) | USA | 5.45 | 283.23 | 52 | −183.64 | +254.53 |
| 10 | Sergio García | (16) | ESP | 5.31 | 265.30 | 50 | −207.52 | +240.82 |
| 11 | Jason Day | (37) | AUS | 5.29 | 232.65 | 44 | −153.87 | +259.45 |
| 12 | Ian Poulter | (12) | ENG | 5.24 | 256.68 | 49 | −193.95 | +195.73 |
| 13 | Brandt Snedeker | (10) | USA | 5.18 | 253.89 | 49 | −259.79 | +241.62 |
| 14 | Graeme McDowell | (15) | NIR | 5.01 | 260.31 | 52 | −226.31 | +233.35 |
| 15 | Jason Dufner | (9) | USA | 4.98 | 258.83 | 52 | −229.07 | +218.06 |
| 16 | Dustin Johnson | (23) | USA | 4.80 | 230.55 | 48 | −197.11 | +218.44 |
| 17 | Luke Donald | (2) | ENG | 4.76 | 233.48 | 49 | −360.90 | +154.64 |
| 18 | Charl Schwartzel | (14) | RSA | 4.74 | 246.50 | 52 | −212.93 | +206.78 |
| 19 | Jim Furyk | (27) | USA | 4.55 | 218.20 | 48 | −165.32 | +184.42 |
| 20 | Keegan Bradley | (13) | USA | 4.31 | 224.18 | 52 | −231.88 | +198.42 |
| 21 | Webb Simpson | (11) | USA | 4.30 | 219.10 | 51 | −238.86 | +201.59 |
| 22 | Jordan Spieth | (809) | USA | 4.15 | 166.06 | 40 | −27.52 | +188.46 |
| 23 | Hideki Matsuyama | (127) | JPN | 3.88 | 155.03 | 40 | −54.11 | +157.47 |
| 24 | Thomas Björn | (45) | DEN | 3.76 | 191.95 | 51 | −112.53 | +185.92 |
| 25 | Lee Westwood | (7) | ENG | 3.69 | 191.88 | 52 | −276.56 | +154.91 |
| 26 | Jamie Donaldson | (47) | WAL | 3.66 | 179.34 | 49 | −109.82 | +176.75 |
| 27 | Ernie Els | (24) | RSA | 3.55 | 184.37 | 52 | −185.13 | +147.38 |
| 28 | Bubba Watson | (8) | USA | 3.45 | 162.32 | 47 | −218.38 | +121.27 |
| 29 | Bill Haas | (35) | USA | 3.35 | 174.21 | 52 | −169.88 | +180.66 |
| 30 | Nick Watney | (20) | USA | 3.26 | 169.72 | 52 | −188.72 | +123.07 |
| 31 | Hunter Mahan | (26) | USA | 3.23 | 168.15 | 52 | −202.69 | +170.32 |
| 32 | Victor Dubuisson | (132) | FRA | 3.22 | 132.20 | 41 | −47.56 | +130.20 |
| 33 | Ryan Moore | (40) | USA | 3.16 | 160.96 | 51 | −109.43 | +137.81 |
| 34 | Louis Oosthuizen | (6) | RSA | 2.96 | 154.07 | 52 | −249.53 | +82.89 |
| 35 | Gonzalo Fdez-Castano | (33) | ESP | 2.95 | 153.59 | 52 | −120.24 | +141.36 |
| 36 | Graham Delaet | (177) | CAN | 2.86 | 148.60 | 52 | −48.65 | +157.01 |
| 37 | Miguel Angel Jiménez | (54) | ESP | 2.79 | 130.96 | 47 | −89.88 | +108.41 |
| 38 | Francesco Molinari | (30) | ITA | 2.77 | 144.20 | 52 | −141.63 | +109.59 |
| 39 | Martin Kaymer | (28) | GER | 2.71 | 140.82 | 52 | −164.66 | +115.51 |
| 40 | Rickie Fowler | (31) | USA | 2.66 | 133.13 | 50 | −160.00 | +121.28 |
| 41 | Billy Horschel | (312) | USA | 2.63 | 136.58 | 52 | −57.88 | +166.56 |
| 42 | Jonas Blixt | (72) | SWE | 2.62 | 136.44 | 52 | −77.92 | +125.73 |
| 43 | Matteo Manassero | (44) | ITA | 2.60 | 135.32 | 52 | −116.82 | +117.91 |
| 44 | Kevin Streelman | (225) | USA | 2.58 | 134.42 | 52 | −73.66 | +166.62 |
| 45 | David Lynn | (46) | ENG | 2.58 | 134.13 | 52 | −102.89 | +121.87 |
| 46 | Thongchai Jaidee | (117) | THA | 2.57 | 133.67 | 52 | −82.94 | +122.79 |
| 47 | Jimmy Walker | (120) | USA | 2.48 | 128.87 | 52 | −78.54 | +136.33 |
| 48 | Peter Hanson | (19) | SWE | 2.40 | 120.12 | 50 | −187.10 | +66.74 |
| 49 | Joost Luiten | (108) | NED | 2.35 | 120.09 | 51 | −78.38 | +121.92 |
| 50 | Branden Grace | (34) | RSA | 2.34 | 121.77 | 52 | −139.88 | +97.27 |

*Ranking in brackets indicates position at end of 2012 season*

# European Tour Race to Dubai 2013

www.europeantour.com

## Final Order of Merit (Top 110 keep their cards for the 2014 season)

| # | Name | Amount | # | Name | Amount |
|---|------|--------|---|------|--------|
| 1 | Henrik Stenson (SWE) | €4,103,796 | 61 | Søren Kjeldsen (DEN) | 532,750 |
| 2 | Ian Poulter (ENG) | 3,172,729 | 62 | Daanny Willett (ENG) | 531,447 |
| 3 | Justin Rose (ENG) | 2,665,376 | 63 | Paul Lawrie (SCO) | 513,307 |
| 4 | Graeme McDowell (NIR) | 2,420,306 | 64 | Justin Walters (RSA) | 512,158 |
| 5 | Jamie Donaldson (WAL) | 2,181,113 | 65 | Ricardo Santos (POR) | 499,756 |
| 6 | Victor Dubuisson (FRA) | 2,031,675 | 66 | Ricardo Gonzalez (ARG) | 499,651 |
| 7 | Gonzalo Fernandez-Castaño (ESP) | 1,767,156 | 67 | Steve Webster (ENG) | 498,979 |
| 8 | Richard Sterne (RSA) | 1,687,014 | 68 | Padraig Harrington (IRL) | 464,326 |
| 9 | Thongchai Jaidee (THA) | 1,585,521 | 69 | Paul Waring (ENG) | 459,862 |
| 10 | Thomas Björn (DEN) | 1,546,736 | 70 | Richie Ramsay (SCO) | 459,252 |
| 11 | Matteo Manassero (ITA) | 1,414,471 | 71 | Grégory Havret (FRA) | 425,240 |
| 12 | Joost Luiten (NED) | 1,411,910 | 72 | Simon Dyson (ENG) | 417,332 |
| 13 | Francesco Molinari (ITA) | 1,367,566 | 73 | Maximilian Kieffer (GER) | 416,910 |
| 14 | Peter Uihlein (USA) | 1,360,268 | 74 | Robert-Jan Derksen (NED) | 411,959 |
| 15 | Lee Westwood (ENG) | 1,299,694 | 75 | Graeme Storm (ENG) | 401,264 |
| 16 | Sergio García (ESP) | 1,280,581 | 76 | Eddie Pepperell (ENG) | 389,766 |
| 17 | Brett Rumford (AUS) | 1,277,022 | 77 | John Parry (ENG) | 388,415 |
| 18 | Branden Grace (RSA) | 1,224,192 | 78 | Liang Wen-Chong (CHN) | 382,265 |
| 19 | Stephen Gallacher (SCO) | 1,173,315 | 79 | Jb Hansen (DEN) | 375,037 |
| 20 | Ernie Els (RSA) | 1,166,712 | 80 | David Drysdale (SCO) | 364,721 |
| 21 | David Howell (ENG) | 1,158,049 | 81 | Morten Ørum Madsen (DEN) | 357,417 |
| 22 | Miguel Angel Jiménez (ESP) | 1,157,142 | 82 | Damien McGrane (IRL) | 342,165 |
| 23 | Mikko Ilonen (FIN) | 1,065,066 | 83 | Anders Hansen (DEN) | 339,944 |
| 24 | Martin Kaymer (GER) | 1,042,037 | 84 | Romain Wattel (FRA) | 332,032 |
| 25 | Grégory Bourdy (FRA) | 1,011,375 | 85 | Robert Rock (ENG) | 330,345 |
| 26 | Tommy Fleetwood (ENG) | 1,007,872 | 86 | Jaco Van Zyl (RSA) | 325,974 |
| 27 | Charl Schwartzel (RSA) | 1,006,692 | 87 | Matthew Baldwin (ENG) | 324,141 |
| 28 | Bernd Wiesberger (AUT) | 998,332 | 88 | Peter Whiteford (SCO) | 324,128 |
| 29 | Chris Wood (ENG) | 998,281 | 89 | Emiliano Grillo (ARG) | 324,124 |
| 30 | Paul Casey (ENG) | 969,422 | 90 | Hennie Otto (RSA) | 323,563 |
| 31 | Scott Jamieson (SCO) | 966,321 | 91 | Eduardo Molinari (ITA) | 319,760 |
| 32 | Thorbjørn Olesen (DEN) | 963,876 | 92 | Michael Hoey (NIR) | 318,960 |
| 33 | Marc Warren (SCO) | 925,854 | 93 | Jin Jeong Jin (KOR) | 308,336 |
| 34 | Pablo Larrazábal (ESP) | 908,224 | 94 | Tom Lewis (ENG) | 303,354 |
| 35 | Rory McIlroy (NIR) | 862,177 | 95 | Gareth Maybin (NIR) | 300,962 |
| 36 | Shane Lowry (IRL) | 834,043 | 96 | Jorge Campillo (ESP) | 299,672 |
| 37 | Raphaël Jacquelin (FRA) | 801,531 | 97 | Seve Benson (ENG) | 297,959 |
| 38 | Nicolas Colsaerts (BEL) | 799,098 | 98 | Andy Sullivan (ENG) | 279,999 |
| 39 | Kiradech Aphibarnrat (THA) | 797,868 | 99 | Lee Slattery (ENG) | 277,013 |
| 40 | Ross Fisher (ENG) | 767,933 | 100 | Mark Foster (ENG) | 275,872 |
| 41 | Rafa Cabrera-Bello (ESP) | 767,904 | 101 | Chris Doak (SCO) | 261,507 |
| 42 | Julien Quesne (FRA) | 749,928 | 102 | Gaganjeet Bhullar (IND) | 259,804 |
| 43 | Luke Donald (ENG) | 745,154 | 103 | Kristoffer Broberg (SWE) | 258,105 |
| 44 | Thomas Aiken (RSA) | 739,773 | 104 | Alvaro Quiros (ESP) | 256,761 |
| 45 | Marcus Fraser (AUS) | 738,938 | 105 | Matthew Nixon (ENG) | 252,179 |
| 46 | Jonas Blixt (SWE) | 728,760 | 106 | Magnus A Carlsson (SWE) | 251,434 |
| 47 | Louis Oosthuizen (RSA) | 727,152 | 107 | Dawie Van Der Walt (RSA) | 249,550 |
| 48 | Darren Fichardt (RSA) | 722,287 | 108 | Richard Bland (ENG) | 247,733 |
| 49 | Peter Hanson (SWE) | 704,835 | 109 | Alexander Levy (FRA) | 240,540 |
| 50 | Felipe Aguilar (CHI) | 703,070 | 110 | Peter Lawrie (IRL) | 233,630 |
| 51 | Alejandro Cañizares (ESP) | 694,467 | 111 | James Kingston (RSA) | 225,150 |
| 52 | David Lynn (ENG) | 685,808 | 112 | Richard Green (AUS) | 218,463 |
| 53 | Marcel Siem (GER) | 674,890 | 113 | Brooks Koepka (USA) | 217,762 |
| 54 | George Coetzee (RSA) | 667,215 | 114 | Mark Tullo (CHI) | 216,165 |
| 55 | Simon Khan (ENG) | 647,807 | 115 | David Higgins (IRL) | 215,356 |
| 56 | Alex Noren (SWE) | 612,104 | 116 | Alexandre Kaleka (FRA) | 209,866 |
| 57 | David Horsey (ENG) | 594,034 | 117 | Lorenzo Gagli (ITA) | 209,227 |
| 58 | Eduardo de la Riva (ESP) | 593,361 | 118 | Oliver Fisher (ENG) | 207,538 |
| 59 | Craig Lee (SCO) | 581,828 | 119 | Andreas Hartø (DEN) | 199,447 |
| 60 | Garth Mulroy (RSA) | 579,076 | 120 | Scott Henry (SCO) | 197,601 |

# Career Money List (at end of 2013 season)

## Ernie retains top place

Ernie Els retained his place at the top of the table with places two to six also unchanged. English players occupied 23 places in the top 100 followed by Scotland and Spain with nine and South Africa and Sweden on eight apiece.

| | | | | | | |
|---|---|---|---|---|---|---|
| 1 | Ernie Els (RSA) | €29,467,156 | 51 | Paul Broadhurst (ENG) | 6,840,372 |
| 2 | Lee Westwood (ENG) | 29,291,837 | 52 | Peter O'Malley (AUS) | 6,791,533 |
| 3 | Colin Montgomerie (SCO) | 24,477,508 | 53 | Ignacio Garrido (ESP) | 6,661,032 |
| 4 | Padraig Harrington (IRL) | 23,801,121 | 54 | Grégory Havret (FRA) | 6,337,771 |
| 5 | Retief Goosen (RSA) | 21,840,422 | 55 | Richard Sterne (RSA) | 6,168,552 |
| 6 | Miguel Angel Jiménez (ESP) | 21,127,730 | 56 | Ricardo Gonzalez (ARG) | 6,159,823 |
| 7 | Ian Poulter (ENG) | 21,005,384 | 57 | Jamie Donaldson (WAL) | 6,092,280 |
| 8 | Darren Clarke (NIR) | 20,113,062 | 58 | Nick Dougherty (ENG) | 6,039,710 |
| 9 | Sergio Garcia (ESP) | 18,433,688 | 59 | Brett Rumford (AUS) | 5,926,724 |
| 10 | Thomas Björn (DEN) | 17,855,975 | 60 | Simon Khan (ENG) | 5,906,910 |
| 11 | Rory McIlroy (NIR) | 16,788,123 | 61 | Gary Orr (SCO) | 5,861,541 |
| 12 | Graeme McDowell (NIR) | 16,299,851 | 62 | Jeev Milkha Singh (IND) | 5,834,098 |
| 13 | Luke Donald (ENG) | 15,848,567 | 63 | Oliver Wilson (ENG) | 5,826,646 |
| 14 | Paul Casey (ENG) | 15,627,394 | 64 | Andrew Coltart (SCO) | 5,733,959 |
| 15 | Henrik Stenson (SWE) | 15,595,171 | 65 | Alex Noren (SWE) | 5,686,782 |
| 16 | Martin Kaymer (GER) | 15,401,995 | 66 | Sam Torrance (SCO) | 5,491,084 |
| 17 | Angel Cabrera (ARG) | 14,732,659 | 67 | Marcel Siem (GER) | 5,309,281 |
| 18 | Vijay Singh (FIJ) | 14,143,414 | 68 | John Bickerton (ENG) | 5,307,064 |
| 19 | Justin Rose (ENG) | 13,883,889 | 69 | Robert-Jan Derksen (NED) | 5,301,288 |
| 20 | Bernhard Langer (GER) | 12,724,888 | 70 | Peter Hedblom (SWE) | 5,188,070 |
| 21 | José María Olazábal (ESP) | 12,249,314 | 71 | Graeme Storm (ENG) | 5,162,980 |
| 22 | David Howell (ENG) | 12,229,427 | 72 | Grégory Bourdy (FRA) | 5,161,035 |
| 23 | Peter Hanson (SWE) | 12,083,967 | 73 | Alastair Forsyth (SCO) | 5,119,287 |
| 24 | Charl Schwartzel (RSA) | 12,064,118 | 74 | Johan Edfors (SWE) | 5,107,847 |
| 25 | Paul Lawrie (SCO) | 11,919,128 | 75 | Peter Lawrie (IRL) | 5,097,986 |
| 26 | Michael Campbell (NZL) | 11,892,642 | 76 | Marcus Fraser (AUS) | 4,914,089 |
| 27 | Anders Hansen (DEN) | 11,693,389 | 77 | Maarten Lafeber (NED) | 4,823,748 |
| 28 | Francesco Molinari (ITA) | 11,322,747 | 78 | Fredrik Andersson Hed (SWE) | 4,793,456 |
| 29 | Paul McGinley (IRL) | 11,207,370 | 79 | Matteo Manassero (ITA) | 4,759,427 |
| 30 | Søren Kjeldsen (DEN) | 10,159,326 | 80 | Jarmo Sandelin (SWE) | 4,693,972 |
| 31 | Niclas Fasth (SWE) | 10,130,730 | 81 | Nicolas Colsaerts (BEL) | 4,631,480 |
| 32 | Louis Oosthuizen (RSA) | 9,859,371 | 82 | José Manuel Lara (ESP) | 4,623,061 |
| 33 | Ian Woosnam (WAL) | 9,607,799 | 83 | Mark James (ENG) | 4,597,602 |
| 34 | Simon Dyson (ENG) | 9,568,024 | 84 | Pablo Larrazábal (ESP) | 4,537,958 |
| 35 | Raphaël Jacquelin (FRA) | 9,525,752 | 85 | Damien McGrane (IRL) | 4,509,123 |
| 36 | Ross Fisher (ENG) | 9,054,620 | 86 | Joakim Haeggman (SWE) | 4,487,376 |
| 37 | Richard Green (AUS) | 8,921,023 | 87 | James Kingston (RSA) | 4,479,008 |
| 38 | Soren Hansen (DEN) | 8,769,159 | 88 | Joost Luiten (NED) | 4,371,414 |
| 39 | Gonzalo Fernandez-Castaño (ESP) | 8,522,787 | 89 | Robert Rock (ENG) | 4,370,456 |
| 40 | David Lynn (ENG) | 8,198,645 | 90 | Stephen Dodd (WAL) | 4,291,734 |
| 41 | Sir Nick Faldo (ENG) | 8,004,560 | 91 | Brian Davis (ENG) | 4,278,849 |
| 42 | Thomas Levet (FRA) | 7,893,113 | 92 | Mikko Ilonen (FIN) | 4,275,801 |
| 43 | Stephen Gallacher (SCO) | 7,614,934 | 93 | Rafa Cabrera-Bello (ESP) | 4,188,681 |
| 44 | Thongchai Jaidee (THA) | 7,522,581 | 94 | Markus Brier (AUT) | 4,068,686 |
| 45 | Bradley Dredge (WAL) | 7,509,587 | 95 | Branden Grace (RSA) | 3,994,239 |
| 46 | Phillip Price (WAL) | 7,306,744 | 96 | Jean-François Remesy (FRA) | 3,961,735 |
| 47 | Steve Webster (ENG) | 7,107,947 | 97 | Marc Warren (SCO) | 3,944,964 |
| 48 | Anthony Wall (ENG) | 7,099,129 | 98 | Thomas Aiken (RSA) | 3,889,971 |
| 49 | Barry Lane (ENG) | 6,975,306 | 99 | Sandy Lyle (SCO) | 3,840,158 |
| 50 | Alvaro Quiros (ESP) | 6,862,480 | 100 | Mark Foster (ENG) | 3,839,359 |

# Tour Statistics (Genworth Statistics)

## Stroke Average

| Pos | Name | Total Rounds | Stroke Avg. | Pos | Name | Total Rounds | Stroke Avg. |
|---|---|---|---|---|---|---|---|
| 1 | Charl Schwartzel (RSA) | 41 | 69.63 | 6 | Justin Rose (ENG) | 46 | 70.00 |
| 2 | Henrik Stenson (SWE) | 60 | 69.72 | 7 | Richard Sterne (RSA) | 70 | 70.04 |
| 3 | Ross Fisher (ENG) | 65 | 69.83 | 8 | Berry Henson (USA) | 15 | 70.13 |
| 4 | Jin Jeong (KOR) | 12 | 69.92 | 9 | Victor Dubuisson (FRA) | 63 | 70.13 |
| 5 | Joost Luiten (NED) | 83 | 69.92 | 10 | Adilson da Silva (BRA) | 25 | 70.16 |

## Driving accuracy

| Pos | Name | Rounds | % |
|---|---|---|---|
| 1 | Adilson da Silva (BRA) | 24 | 81.4 |
| 2 | Simon Wakefield (ENG) | 83 | 80.9 |
| 3 | Mohd Siddikur (BAN) | 12 | 73.1 |
| 4 | Richie Ramsay (SCO) | 72 | 71.9 |
| 5 | Grégory Bourdy (FRA) | 95 | 71.8 |
| 6 | Phillip Price (WAL) | 59 | 71.8 |
| 7 | Felipe Aguilar (CHI) | 84 | 71.5 |

## Putts per round

| Pos | Name | Rounds | Putts per Round |
|---|---|---|---|
| 1 | Brett Rumford (AUS) | 83 | 27.9 |
| 2 | Darren Fichardt (RSA) | 72 | 28.1 |
| 3 | Mohd Siddikur (BAN) | 12 | 28.4 |
| 4 | Fredrik Andersson Hed (SWE) | 65 | 28.5 |
| 5 | Christian Cévaër (FRA) | 59 | 28.6 |
| 6 | Marcus Fraser (AUS) | 72 | 28.6 |
| 7 | Thaworn Wiratchant (THA) | 16 | 28.6 |

## Driving distance

| Pos | Name | Rounds | Avg. yards |
|---|---|---|---|
| 1 | Brooks Koepka (USA) | 35 | 318.2 |
| 2 | Scott Hend (AUS) | 33 | 316.5 |
| 3 | Alvaro Quiros (ESP) | 58 | 309.5 |
| 4 | Nicolas Colsaerts (BEL) | 51 | 308.7 |
| 5 | Charl Schwartzel (RSA) | 39 | 307.8 |
| 6 | Scott Henry (SCO) | 82 | 306.4 |
| 7 | Peter Uihlein (USA) | 71 | 305.5 |

## Average one putts per round

| Pos | Name | Rounds | One putts Average |
|---|---|---|---|
| 1 | Oliver Bekker (RSA) | 16 | 55.31 |
| 2 | Edoardo Molinari (ITA) | 35 | 51.66 |
| 3 | Mohd Siddikur (BAN) | 12 | 51.5 |
| 4 | Bradley Dredge (WAL) | 12 | 47.5 |
| 5 | Jbe Kruger (RSA) | 60 | 46.32 |
| 6 | Thaworn Wiratchant (THA) | 16 | 44.56 |
| 7 | Ross McGowan (ENG) | 13 | 43.62 |

## Greens in regulation

| Pos | Name | Rounds | % |
|---|---|---|---|
| 1 | Soren Hansen (RSA) | 66 | 76.8 |
| 2 | Magnus A Carlsson (SWE) | 76 | 76.6 |
| 3 | Adilson Da Silva (BRA) | 24 | 76.4 |
| 4 | Emiliano Grillo (ARG) | 77 | 76.3 |
| 5 | Ross Fisher (ENG) | 62 | 75.8 |
| 6 | Paul Casey (ENG) | 86 | 75.6 |
| 7 | Henrik Stenson (SWE) | 60 | 75.3 |

## Sand saves

| Pos | Name | Rounds | % |
|---|---|---|---|
| 1 | Gaganjeet Bhullar (IND) | 30 | 85.7 |
| 2 | José Manuel Lara (ESP) | 62 | 83.7 |
| 3 | Adilson Da Silva (BRA) | 24 | 75.0 |
| 4 | Peter Hanson (SWE) | 42 | 70.7 |
| 5 | Mark Tullo (CHI) | 72 | 67.9 |
| 6 | Matteo Manassero (ITA) | 86 | 67.4 |
| 7 | Ricardo Santos (POR) | 86 | 67.3 |

## Putts per greens in regulation

| Pos | Name | Rounds | Putts per GIR |
|---|---|---|---|
| 1 | Seuk-Hyun Baek (KOR) | 13 | 1.701 |
| 2 | Darren Fichardt (RSA) | 72 | 1.440 |
| 3 | Garth Mulroy (RSA) | 74 | 1.719 |
| 4 | Mikko Ilonen (FIN) | 78 | 1.729 |
| 5 | Brett Rumford (AUS) | 83 | 1.730 |
| 6 | Alex Noren (SWE) | 60 | 1.736 |
| 7 | Fredrik Andersson Hed (SWE) | 65 | 1.741 |

## Scrambles (where player makes par after missing GIR)

| Pos | Name | Rounds | % |
|---|---|---|---|
| 1 | Robert-Jan Derksen (RSA) | 79 | 63.5 |
| 2 | Berry Henson (USA) | 15 | 63.3 |
| 3 | Jamie Donaldson (WAL) | 72 | 63.3 |
| 4 | Mohd Siddikur (BAN) | 12 | 63.0 |
| 5 | David Horsey (ENG) | 84 | 62.4 |
| 6 | Marcus Fraser (AUS) | 72 | 61.6 |
| 7 | Peter Hanson (SWE) | 42 | 61.3 |

# PGA European Tour statistics 2013

## Thirty-three holes-in-one

Keith Horne (RSA) – Alfred Dunhill C/ship (hole 12, rounds 1 and 2)
Magnus A Carlsson (SWE) – Alfred Dunhill C/ship
Bryce Easton (RSA) – Joburg Open
Vaughn Groenewald (RSA) – Joburg Open
Scott Henry (SCO) – Tshwane Open
Liang Wen-chong (CHN) – Avantha Masters
Emiliano Grillo (ARG) – Trophée Hassan II
Jamie Donaldson (WAL) – Masters Tournament
Tetsuji Hiratsuka (JPN) – Ballantine's C/ship
Magnus A Carlsson (SWE) – Ballantine's Cship
Mark Tullo (CHI) – Madeira Islands Open
Jason Levermore (ENG) – BMW PGA C/ship
Andy Sullivan (ENG) – BMW PGA C/ship
Andrew Dodt (AUS) – Nordea Masters (round 2, hole 11; round 4, hole 16)
José Maria Olazábal (ESP) – Nordea Masters
Simon Thornton (IRL) – Najeti Hotels et Golfs Open

Shawn Stefani (USA) – Open Championship
Damian Mooney (NIR) – Irish Open
Matteo Manassero (ITA) – Aberdeen Asset Management Scottish Open
Jarmo Sandelin (SWE) – M2M Russian Open
Tim Clark (RSA) – PGA Championship
Scott Hend (AUS) – Johnnie Walker C/ship
Richard Finch (ENG) – Johnnie Walker C/ship
Ricardo Santos (POR) – ISPS Handa Wales Open
Richard Finch (ENG) – Omega European Masters
Soren Hansen (DEN) – Omega European Masters
Hennie Otto (RSA) – Open D'Italia Lindt
Miguel Angel Jiménez (ESP) – Portugal Masters
David McKenzie (AUS) – ISPS HANDA Perth International
Rohan Blizard (AUS) – ISPS HANDA Perth International
Jamie Donaldson (WAL) – Turkish Airlines Open

## Twenty-one course records

65 (–7)†    Ballantine's Championship – Thongchai Jaidee (THA)
63 (–9)†    Volvo China Open – Mikko Ilonen (FIN)
63 (–9)†    Nordea Masters – Mikko Ilonen (FIN)
63 (–9)†    Nordea Masters – Peter Whiteford (SCO)
64 (–8)    Irish Open – Scott Henry (SCO)
61 (–9)    WGC–Bridgestone Invitational – Tiger Woods (USA)
63 (–7)    US PGA Championship – Jason Dufner (USA)
63 (–9)†    Johnnie Walker Championship – Paul Waring (ENG)
61 (–10)†    Omega European Masters – Craig Lee (SCO)
63 (–7)†    KLM Open – Simon Dyson (ENG)
63 (–7)†    KLM Open – Jorge Campillo (ESP)
66 (–6)    70 Open D'Italia Lindt – Romain Wattel (FRA)
66 (–6)†    70 Open D'Italia Lindt – Scott Hend (AUS)
60 (–12)†    Alfred Dunhill Links Championship (Kingsbarns) – Peter Uihlein (USA)
64 (–8)†    Alfred Dunhill Links Championship (Carnoustie) – Thomas Levet (FRA)
62 (–10)†    Alfred Dunhill Links Championship (St Andrews) – Paul Casey (ENG)
64 (–8)†    Alfred Dunhill Championship (Carnoustie) – Shane Lowry (IRL)
60 (–11)    Portugal Masters – Scott Jamieson (SCO)
65 (–7)†    ISPS HANDA Perth International – Brett Rumford (AUS)
62 (–10)    WGC–HSBC Champions – Martin Kaymer (GER)
62 (–10)    Turkish Airlines Open – Raphael Jaequlin (FRA)
† equals existing record

## Five multiple winners

Brett Rumford (AUS) – Ballantine's Championship; Volvo China Open
Phil Mickelson (USA) – Aberdeen Asset Management Scottish Open; 142nd Open Championship

Tiger Woods (USA) – WGC–Cadillac Championship; WGC–Bridgestone Invitational
Joost Luiten (NED) – Lyoness Open; KLM Open
Graeme McDowell (NIR) – Volvo World Match Play Championship; Alstom Open de France

## Five high finishes by winner

71 (–1)    Stephen Gallacher (SCO) – Omega Dubai Desert Classic
71 (–1)    Darren Fichardt (RSA) – Africa Open
71 (–1)    Raphael Jacquelin (FRA) – Open de España

71 (–1)    Joost Luiten (NED) – Lyoness Open
71 (–1)    Tiger Woods (USA) – WGC–Cadillac Championship

# PGA European Tour statistics 2013

### Twelve first-time winners

Scott Jamieson (SCO) – Nelson Mandela C/ship
Chris Wood (ENG) – Qatar Masters
Matt Kuchar (USA) – WGC–Accenture MP
Dawie Van Der Walt (RSA) – Tshwane Open
Kiradech Aphibarnrat (THA) – Maybank Open
Peter Uihlein (USA) – Madeira Islands

Simon Thornton (IRL) – Najeti Hotels Open
Jason Dufner (USA) – US PGA Championship
Tommy Fleetwood (ENG) – J. Walker C\ship
Jin Jeong (KOR) – ISPS HANDA Perth Int.
Dustin Johnson (USA) – WGC–HSBC Champs
Victor Dubuisson (FRA) – Turkish Airlines Open

### Most top ten finishes

8 Felipe Aguilar (CHI)
8 Peter Uihlein (USA)
8 Pablo Larrazabal (ESP)
8 Thomas Björn (DEN)
7 Joost Luiten (NED)
7 Julien Quesne (FRA)
7 Thongchai Jaidee (THA)

7 Martin Kaymer (GER)
6 Richard Sterne (RSA)
6 Nicolas Colsaerts (BEL)
6 David Howell (ENG)
6 Shane Lowry (IRL)
6 Stephen Gallacher (SCO)
6 Brett Rumford (AUS)

6 Gonzalo Fdez Castano (ESP)
6 Victor Dubuisson (FRA)
6 Jamie Donaldson (WAL)
6 Henrik Stenson (SWE)
6 Bernd Wiesberger (AUT)
6 Ross Fisher (ENG)

# Top money earners on the European Tour 1972–2013

### (European Tour members only)

| | | | | | |
|---|---|---|---|---|---|
| 1972 | Bob Charles (NZL) | €25,953 | 2000 | Lee Westwood (ENG) | €3,125,147 |
| 1975 | Dale Hayes (RSA) | €28,710 | 2005 | Colin Montgomerie (SCO) | €2,794,223 |
| 1980 | Greg Norman (AUS) | €104,761 | 2010 | Martin Kaymer (GER) | €4,461,011 |
| 1985 | Sandy Lyle (SCO) | €356,595 | 2011 | Luke Donald (ENG) | €4,216,226 |
| 1990 | Ian Woosnam (WAL) | €1,033,169 | 2012 | Rory McIlroy (NIR) | €5,519,118 |
| 1995 | Colin Montgomerie (SCO) | €1,454,205 | 2013 | Henrik Stenson (SWE) | €4,103,796 |

# Williams is new European Tour chairman

David Williams, who has a wide commercial experience in both private and public business, has taken over from Neil Coles, who retired last year, as Chairman of the European Tour.

Williams has had senior management roles over the past 35 years in the Whitbread Group PLC, Diageo PLC, Pepsico Restaurants Inc, Mothercare PLC and the Royal London Mutual Insurance Group Ltd.

Before joining the Tour he was Chair of the Operating Partners at Duke Street Capital. He has an MSc in Management from the London Business School where he was a Governor.

His appointment met all the objectives of the nomination committee – proven business leadership, an interest in golf and an ability to deal with the diverse sporting business and political issues faced by the Tour.

David Williams said: "To follow in the footsteps of someone who has been such a figurehead as Neil Coles is a tremendous honour"

Welcoming the appointment George O'Grady CBE, Chief Executive of the European Tour, said : "I look forward to working with David as we face our challenges on the European and global fronts."

In his role as a member of the Players' committee and as Ryder Cup captain, Paul McGinley spoke of his own appreciation of the tireless work done for over 38 years by Neil Coles.

"Everyone has the utmost respect for what Neil has achieved both on and off the golf course. We all wish him well in his retirement."

# European Tour top 20

MC Missed cut     Rtd Retired     WD Withdrew

| | Nelson Mandela C/ship | Alfred Dunhill C/ship | Volvo Golf Champions | Abu Dhabi Championship | Qatar Masters | Dubai Desert Clasic | Joburg Open | Africa Open | WGC–Accenture C/ship | Tshwane Open | WGC–Cadillac C/ship | Avantha Masters | Maybank Malaysian Open | Trophée Hassan II | The Masters |
|---|---|---|---|---|---|---|---|---|---|---|---|---|---|---|---|
| 1 Henrik Stenson (SWE) | — | — | 22 | 23 | 16 | 26 | — | — | 33 | — | — | — | — | — | 18 |
| 2 Ian Poulter (ENG) | — | — | — | — | — | — | — | — | 4 | — | 28 | — | — | — | MC |
| 3 Justin Rose (ENG) | — | — | — | 2 | 16 | — | — | — | 17 | — | 8 | — | — | — | 25 |
| 4 Graeme McDowell (NIR) | — | — | — | — | — | — | — | — | 5 | — | 3 | — | — | — | MC |
| 5 Jamie Donaldson (WAL) | — | — | 16 | 1 | — | 37 | — | — | 33 | — | 63 | — | — | — | MC |
| 6 Victor Dubuisson (FRA) | — | — | — | MC | 9 | MC | — | — | — | — | — | 9 | 4 | — | — |
| 7 Gonzalo Fernandez-Castaño (ESP) | — | — | 20 | 9 | 16 | — | — | — | 9 | — | 43 | — | — | — | 20 |
| 8 Richard Sterne (RSA) | MC | 7 | — | — | — | 2 | 1 | — | 17 | — | 12 | — | — | — | 25 |
| 9 Thongchai Jaidee (THA) | — | — | 3 | 9 | 9 | 64 | — | — | 33 | — | — | 43 | 33 | — | — |
| 10 Thomas Björn (DEN) | — | — | 9 | 52 | 59 | MC | — | — | 33 | — | — | — | — | — | 46 |
| 11 Matteo Manassero (ITA) | — | — | 9 | 23 | 22 | 12 | — | — | 33 | — | 23 | — | 17 | — | MC |
| 12 Joost Luiten (NED) | — | — | — | 6 | — | MC | — | 49 | — | 27 | — | MC | — | 15 | — |
| 13 Francesco Molinari (ITA) | — | — | 9 | MC | — | — | — | — | 33 | — | 28 | — | — | 15 | MC |
| 14 Peter Uihlein (USA) | MC | 55 | — | — | — | — | 19 | — | — | 4 | — | — | — | — | — |
| 15 Lee Westwood (ENG) | — | — | — | — | — | 5 | — | — | 33 | — | 25 | — | — | — | 8 |
| 16 Sergio García (ESP) | — | — | — | 2 | 17 | — | — | — | 17 | — | 3 | — | — | — | 8 |
| 17 Brett Rumford (AUS) | — | — | MC | 22 | MC | — | 12 | — | — | — | — | 71 | — | MC | — |
| 18 Branden Grace (RSA) | 39 | 12 | 7 | 5 | 6 | — | MC | — | 33 | — | 49 | — | — | — | 18 |
| 19 Stephen Gallacher (SCO) | — | — | MC | 59 | — | 1 | — | — | 33 | — | 53 | — | 22 | 38 | — |
| 20 Ernie Els (RSA) | — | — | 18 | 39 | 73 | — | — | — | 33 | — | 28 | — | — | — | 13 |

# 2013 performances at a glance

— Did not play     * Involved in play-off

| Open de España | Ballantine's C/ship | Volvo China Open | Volvo World MP C/ship | Madeira Islands Open | BMW PGA Championship | Nordea Masters | Lyoness Open | Najeti Hotels et Golfs Open | US Open Championship | BMW International Open | The Irish Open | Open de France | Scottish Open | 142nd Open Championship | Russian Open | WGC–Bridgestone Inv. | US PGA Championship | Johnnie Walker C/ship | Wales Open | Omega European Masters | KLM Open | Italian Open | Dunhill Links C/ship | Portugal Masters | Perth International | BMW Masters | WGC–HSBC Champions | Turkish Airlines Open | DP World Tour C/ship |
|---|---|---|---|---|---|---|---|---|---|---|---|---|---|---|---|---|---|---|---|---|---|---|---|---|---|---|---|---|---|
| — | — | — | 17 | — | — | — | — | 21 | 10 | — | — | 3 | 2 | — | 2 | 3 | — | — | — | — | — | — | — | — | — | 34 | 31 | 7 | 1 |
| — | — | — | 17 | — | MC | — | — | — | 21 | — | — | 25 | — | 3 | 19 | 61 | — | — | — | — | — | — | — | — | — | 15 | 2 | 5 | 2 |
| — | — | — | — | 50 | — | — | — | 1 | — | — | — | — | MC | — | 17 | 33 | — | — | — | — | — | — | — | — | — | — | 5 | 3 | 10 |
| — | — | — | 1 | — | MC | — | — | — | MC | — | MC | 1 | — | 58 | — | 40 | 12 | — | — | — | — | — | — | — | — | 53 | 3 | — | 17 |
| — | — | — | 17 | — | 37 | 11 | — | — | 32 | — | 10 | 6 | — | 32 | — | 17 | Rtd | — | — | MC | — | — | 26 | 6 | — | — | 8 | 2 | 8 |
| 61 | MC | 3 | — | — | MC | — | — | — | — | 53 | MC | 18 | 17 | — | — | — | — | WD | 3 | — | — | — | 17 | — | — | 44 | — | 1 | 3 |
| 44 | — | — | — | — | 62 | — | — | — | — | — | 38 | — | 54 | — | 38 | MC | — | 8 | 49 | — | 38 | — | 57 | — | 1 | 39 | — | — | 37 |
| — | — | — | 9 | — | 57 | — | — | — | — | 22 | 2 | 31 | 21 | — | 9 | MC | — | — | 13 | — | — | 50 | — | — | — | 31 | 39 | 36 | 14 |
| — | 6 | — | 2 | — | 40 | — | — | — | MC | 41 | — | MC | 66 | 32 | — | — | 47 | 17 | 26 | 9 | — | MC | MC | — | — | 2 | 46 | 29 | 47 |
| — | MC | 8 | — | — | 40 | 4 | 2 | — | — | 2 | 18 | 8 | MC | 43 | — | — | MC | MC | 58 | 1* | — | — | — | 57 | — | 5 | 39 | 18 | 21 |
| 16 | — | — | — | — | 1 | 4 | — | MC | 22 | — | 25 | 57 | MC | — | 53 | 72 | — | — | 34 | 26 | 42 | — | MC | — | — | — | 21 | 44 | 21 |
| 21 | — | 8 | — | MC | 11 | 1 | — | — | 10 | 2 | 49 | — | — | — | MC | — | 4 | 44 | 1* | — | 24 | 51 | — | Rtd | — | — | — | 18 | 4 |
| MC | — | — | 5 | — | 9 | 21 | — | MC | — | 32 | 18 | 42 | 9 | — | 44 | 33 | 42 | MC | MC | — | 16 | — | 17 | — | — | 2 | 21 | 25 | 13 |
| 8 | 65 | — | — | 1 | 12 | 21 | — | — | — | 10 | 32 | MC | 10 | — | — | MC | MC | 2 | MC | — | — | 2* | — | — | — | 5 | 55 | 57 | 51 |
| — | — | — | — | 9 | — | — | — | 15 | — | — | — | 3 | — | 40 | 33 | — | — | — | — | — | — | — | — | — | — | 24 | 55 | 29 | 5 |
| 12 | — | — | — | — | 19 | — | — | 45 | 7 | — | — | — | 21 | — | 40 | 61 | — | — | — | — | — | — | — | — | — | — | 4 | — | — |
| — | 1* | 1 | 9 | — | 62 | — | — | — | 35 | 22 | MC | — | MC | — | 63 | MC | 6 | 8 | 15 | — | MC | — | 6 | 15 | — | — | 76 | 72 | 47 |
| — | — | 33 | 3 | — | 24 | — | — | — | MC | — | — | — | 2 | 64 | — | 65 | MC | — | MC | — | MC | — | 59 | — | 43 | 61 | 39 | 29 | 52 |
| — | 6 | 24 | 17 | — | MC | — | — | — | — | 47 | 8 | MC | 21 | — | 44 | 61 | 2 | Rtd | 9 | — | MC | 3 | — | — | — | 53 | 63 | 25 | 34 |
| — | — | — | — | 6 | — | — | — | 4 | 1 | — | — | MC | 26 | — | 48 | MC | — | — | — | — | 17 | — | — | 11 | — | — | — | — | — |

# 2013 European Tour
(in chronological order)
For past results see earlier editions of *The R&A Golfer's Handbook*

## 2012

**Nelson Mandela Championship**   *Royal Durban GC, Durban, RSA*   Dec 6–9   [5594–65]

| | | | |
|---|---|---|---|
| 1 | Scott Jamieson (SCO)* | 66-57—123 | €118,875 |
| 2 | Eduardo de la Riva (ESP) | 62-61—123 | 69,075 |
| | Steve Webster (ENG) | 63-60—123 | 69,075 |

*\*Jamieson won at the second extra hole*

**Alfred Dunhill Championship**   *Leopard Creek CC, Malelene, RSA*   Dec 13–16   [7326–72]

| | | | |
|---|---|---|---|
| 1 | Charl Schwartzel (RSA) | 67-64-64-69—264 | €237,750 |
| 2 | Kristoffer Broberg (SWE) | 70-69-67-70—276 | 172,500 |
| 3 | Grégory Bourdy (FRA) | 66-65-74-72—277 | 73,125 |
| | Scott Jamieson (SCO) | 70-68-71-68—277 | 73,125 |
| | Garth Mulroy (RSA) | 71-68-70-68—277 | 73,125 |
| | Andy Sullivan (ENG) | 73-71-64-69—277 | 73,125 |

## 2013

**Volvo Golf Champions**   *Durban CC, Durban, RSA*   Jan 10–13   [7372–72]

| | | | |
|---|---|---|---|
| 1 | Louis Oosthuizen (RSA) | 68-64-74-66—272 | €350,000 |
| 2 | Scott Jamieson (SCO) | 69-64-68-72—273 | 226,300 |
| 3 | Thongchai Jaidee (THA) | 65-68-73-68—274 | 131,300 |

**Abu Dhabi HSBC Golf Championship**   *Abu Dhabi, UAE*   Jan 17–20   [7600–72]

| | | | |
|---|---|---|---|
| 1 | Jamie Donaldson (WAL) | 67-70-69-68—274 | €336,726 |
| 2 | Thorbjørn Olesen (DEN) | 68-69-69-69—275 | 175,479 |
| | Justin Rose (ENG) | 67-69-68-71—275 | 175,479 |

**Commercialbank Qatar Masters**   *Doha GC, Doha, Qatar*   Jan 23–26   [7400–72]

| | | | |
|---|---|---|---|
| 1 | Chris Wood (ENG) | 67-70-64-69—270 | €310,917 |
| 2 | George Coetzee (RSA) | 69-67-70-65—271 | 162,029 |
| | Sergio García (ESP) | 69-66-70-66—271 | 162,029 |

**Omega Dubai Desert Classic**   *Emirates, Dubai, UAE*   Jan 31–Feb 3   [7316–72]

| | | | |
|---|---|---|---|
| 1 | Stephen Gallacher (SCO) | 63-70-62-71—266 | €309,233 |
| 2 | Richard Sterne (RSA | 62-70-66-71—269 | 206,153 |
| 3 | Felipe Aguilar (CHI) | 68-68-66-69—271 | 104,460 |
| | Thorbjørn Olesen (DEN) | 67-66-67-71—271 | 104,460 |

**Joburg Open**   *Royal Johannesburg and Kensington, RSA*   Feb 7–10   [East 7658–72, West 7203–71]

| | | | |
|---|---|---|---|
| 1 | Richard Sterne (RSA) | 63-65-68-64—260 | €206,050 |
| 2 | Charl Schwartzel (RSA) | 68-65-68-66—267 | 149,500 |
| 3 | Felipe Aguilar (CHI) | 67-66-68-67—268 | 69,160 |
| | George Coetzee (RSA) | 67-64-70-67—268 | 69,160 |
| | Ricardo Santos (POR) | 70-65-69-64—268 | 69,160 |

**Africa Open**   *East London, Eastern Cape, RSA*   Feb 14–17   [6632–72]

| | | | |
|---|---|---|---|
| 1 | Darren Fichardt (RSA) | 69-67-65-71—272 | €158,500 |
| 2 | Grégory Bourdy (FRA) | 70-67-67-70—274 | 92,100 |
| | Jaco van Zyle (RSA) | 66-67-68-73—274 | 92,100 |

## WGC – Accenture Match Play Championship  Dove Mountain, Marana, AZ, USA
Feb 20–23  [7791–72]

Winner:  Matt Kuchar (USA)  €1,148,809
Runner-up: Hunter Mahan (USA)  670,138
Third place: Jason Day (AUS)  471,011
Full details of this event can be found on page 206

## Tshwane Open  Copperleaf Golf & Country Estate, Centurion, RSA   Feb 28–Mar 3   [7791–72]
| | | | |
|---|---|---|---|
| 1 | Dawie van der Walt (RSA) | 68-65-67-67—267 | €237,750 |
| 2 | Darren Fichardt (RSA) | 65-71-64-69—269 | 172,500 |
| 3 | Louis de Jager (RSA) | 71-65-65-69—270 | 103,800 |

## WGC – Cadillac Championship  Doral, Orlando, FL, USA  Mar 7–10   [7334–72]
| | | | |
|---|---|---|---|
| 1 | Tiger Woods (USA) | 66-65-67-71—269 | €1,139,523 |
| 2 | Steve Stricker (USA) | 67-67-69-68—271 | 668,520 |
| 3 | Sergio García (ESP) | 66-72-67-69—274 | 317,167 |
| | Graeme McDowell (NIR) | 66-67-69-72—274 | 317,167 |
| | Phil Mickelson (USA) | 67-67-69-71—274 | 317,167 |
| | Adam Scott (AUS) | 72-70-68-64—274 | 317,167 |
Full details of this event can be found on page 207

## Avantha Masters  Jaypee Greens Golf & Spa Resort, Delhi, India  Mar 14–17   [7347–72]
| | | | |
|---|---|---|---|
| 1 | Thomas Aiken (RSA) | 67-69-62-67—265 | €300,000 |
| 2 | Gaganjeet Bhullar (IND) | 68-69-67-64—268 | 200,000 |
| 3 | Wen-chong Liang (CHN) | 66-66-69-69—270 | 112,680 |

## Maybank Malaysian Open  Kuala Lumpur, Malaysia  Mar 21–24   [6967–72]
| | | | |
|---|---|---|---|
| 1 | Kiradech Aphibarnrat (THA) | 65-68-70—203 | €350,411 |
| 2 | Edoardo Molinari (ITA) | 66-71-67—204 | 233,604 |
| 3 | Anders Hansen (DEN) | 66-73-66—205 | 131,615 |
Reduced to three rounds due to bad weather

## Trophée Hassan II  Golf du Palais Royal, Agadir, Morocco  Mar 28–31   [6951–72]
| | | | |
|---|---|---|---|
| 1 | Marcel Siem (GER) | 64-68-69-70—271 | €250,000 |
| 2 | David Horsey (ENG) | 68-67-70-69—274 | 130,280 |
| | Mikko Ilonen (FIN) | 69-66-70-69—274 | 130,280 |

## The MASTERS TOURNAMENT  Augusta National, GA, USA  April 11–14   [7435–72]
| | | | |
|---|---|---|---|
| 1 | Adam Scott (AUS)* | 69-72-69-69—279 | €1,104,379 |
| 2 | Angel Cabrera (ARG) | 71-69-69-70—279 | 662,628 |
*Scott won at the second extra hole
| 3 | Jason Day (AUS) | 70-68-73-70—281 | 417,210 |
Full details of this event can be found on page 82

## Open de España  Parador de El Saler, Valencia, Spain  April 18–21   [7052–72]
| | | | |
|---|---|---|---|
| 1 | Raphaël Jacquelin (FRA)* | 73-66-73-71—283 | €250,000 |
| 2 | Felipe Aguilar (CHI) | 68-71-74-70—283 | 130,280 |
| | Maximilian Kieffer (GER) | 75-68-69-71—283 | 130,280 |
*Jacquelin won at the ninth extra hole

## Ballantine's Championship   Blackstone GC, Incheon, South Korea   April 25–28   [7281–72]

| | | | |
|---|---|---|---|
| 1 | Brett Rumford (AUS)* | 73-67-69-68—277 | €367,500 |
| 2 | Marcus Fraser (AUS) | 70-70-69-68—277 | 191,516 |
| | Peter Whiteford (SCO) | 70-69-69-69—277 | 191,516 |

*Rumford won at the first extra hole

## Volvo China Open   Binhai Lake GC, Tianjin, China   May 2–5   [7378–72]

| | | | |
|---|---|---|---|
| 1 | Brett Rumford (AUS) | 68-67-69-68—272 | €407,906 |
| 2 | Mikko Ilonen (FIN) | 69-63-73-71—276 | 271,938 |
| 3 | ictor Dubuisson (FRA) | 71-72-66-68—277 | 153,210 |

## Volvo World Match Play Championship   Thracian Cliffs Golf & Beach Resort, Kavarna, Bulgaria
May 16–19   [7291–72]

**Semi-Finals:**
Thongchai Jaidee (THA) beat Thomas Aiken (RSA)  3 and 2      Winner: €499,999
Graeme McDowell (NIR) beat Branden Grace (RSA)  3 and 2      Runner-up: €333,333
**Final:**                                                   3rd: €168,900
Graeme McDowell beat Thongchai Jaidee  2 and 1

## Madeira Islands Open – Portugal – BPI   Santo da Serra, Madeira, Portugal   May 16–19
[6826–72]

| | | | |
|---|---|---|---|
| 1 | Peter Uihlein (USA) | 72-64-69-68—273 | €100,000 |
| 2 | Morten Ørum Madsen (DEN) | 72-69-676-7—275 | 52,110 |
| | Mark Tullo (CHI) | 67-69-68-71—275 | 52,110 |

## BMW PGA Championship   Wentworth Club, Surrey, England   May 23–26   [7302–72]

| | | | |
|---|---|---|---|
| 1 | Matteo Manassero (ITA) | 69-71-69-69—278 | €791,660 |
| 2 | Simon Khan (ENG) | 69-72-71-66—278 | 412,560 |
| | Marc Warren (SCO) | 69-70-70-69—278 | 412,560 |
| 4 | Alejandro Cañizares (ESP) | 69-70-68-72—279 | 219,450 |
| | Miguel Angel Jiménez (ESP) | 76-69-67-67—279 | 219,450 |
| 6 | Ernie Els (RSA) | 72-69-72-67—280 | 142,500 |
| | James Kingston (RSA) | 66-77-69-68—280 | 142,500 |
| | Eddie Pepperell (ENG) | 71-69-71-69—280 | 142,500 |
| 9 | Francesco Molinari (ITA) | 70-68-73-70—281 | 96,267 |
| | Richie Ramsay (SCO) | 71-75-66-69—281 | 96,267 |
| | Lee Westwood (ENG) | 70-71-67-73—281 | 96,267 |
| 12 | Grégory Bourdy (FRA) | 71-73-70-68—282 | 70,436 |
| | Niclas Fasth (SWE) | 70-71-72-69—282 | 70,436 |
| | Mikko Ilonen (FIN) | 67-76-70-69—282 | 70,436 |
| | Pablo Larrazábal (ESP) | 71-73-67-71—282 | 70,436 |
| | Shane Lowry (IRL) | 70-71-69-72—282 | 70,436 |
| | Peter Uihlein (USA) | 72-73-68-69—282 | 70,436 |
| | Bernd Wiesberger (AUT) | 73-71-70-68—282 | 70,436 |
| 19 | Richard Bland (ENG) | 71-71-69-72—283 | 55,385 |
| | David Drysdale (SCO) | 71-73-69-70—283 | 55,385 |
| | Sergio García (ESP) | 72-71-68-72—283 | 55,385 |
| | Grégory Havret (FRA) | 70-71-71-71—283 | 55,385 |
| | Edoardo Molinari (ITA) | 71-71-69-72—283 | 55,385 |
| 24 | George Coetzee (RSA) | 69-70-75-70—284 | 45,838 |
| | Nicolas Colsaerts (BEL) | 72-70-73-69—284 | 45,838 |
| | Tommy Fleetwood (ENG) | 71-74-68-71—284 | 45,838 |
| | Mark Foster (ENG) | 70-69-72-73—284 | 45,838 |
| | Branden Grace (RSA) | 71-73-71-69—284 | 45,838 |
| | Raphaël Jacquelin (FRA) | 71-71-73-69—284 | 45,838 |
| | Phillip Price (WAL) | 73-69-70-72—284 | 45,838 |
| | Fabrizio Zanotti (PAR) | 71-75-70-68—284 | 45,838 |

| 32 | Darren Clarke (NIR) | 74-70-72-69—285 | 36,860 |
|---|---|---|---|
| | Ross Fisher (ENG) | 72-73-68-72—285 | 36,860 |
| | Alexander Noren (SWE) | 74-71-71-69—285 | 36,860 |
| | Alvaro Quiros (ESP) | 70-73-69-73—285 | 36,860 |
| | Danny Willett (ENG) | 73-72-73-67—285 | 36,860 |
| 37 | Jamie Donaldson (WAL) | 71-75-73-67—286 | 32,775 |
| | Anders Hansen (DEN) | 70-74-73-69—286 | 32,775 |
| | Lee Slattery (ENG) | 71-71-69-75—286 | 32,775 |
| 40 | Thomas Björn (DEN) | 69-74-75-69—287 | 28,975 |
| | Chris Doak (SCO) | 74-71-72-70—287 | 28,975 |
| | Thongchai Jaidee (THA) | 74-71-72-70—287 | 28,975 |
| | Marcel Siem (GER) | 75-71-71-70—287 | 28,975 |
| | Graeme Storm (ENG) | 73-71-69-74—287 | 28,975 |
| 45 | Oliver Fisher (ENG) | 70-75-73-70—288 | 24,225 |
| | Søren Kjeldsen (DEN) | 74-72-70-72—288 | 24,225 |
| | Colin Montgomerie (SCO) | 71-75-72-70—288 | 24,225 |
| | Garth Mulroy (RSA) | 74-71-72-71—288 | 24,225 |
| | Jaco van Zyl (RSA) | 75-69-73-71—288 | 24,225 |
| 50 | Martin Kaymer (GER) | 70-74-73-72—289 | 18,525 |
| | Jber Kruger (RSA) | 71-74-72-72—289 | 18,525 |
| | Thomas Levet (FRA) | 71-75-70-73—289 | 18,525 |
| | Wen-Chong Liang (CHN) | 75-68-72-74—289 | 18,525 |
| | Paul McGinley (IRL) | 71-75-70-73—289 | 18,525 |
| | Justin Rose (ENG) | 72-74-69-74—289 | 18,525 |
| | Ricardo Santos (POR) | 73-72-76-68—289 | 18,525 |
| 57 | Peter Lawrie (IRL) | 74-72-72-72—290 | 14,488 |
| | Richard Sterne (RSA) | 71-74-71-74—290 | 14,488 |
| 59 | Gary Lockerbie (ENG) | 71-74-73-73—291 | 13,300 |
| | Damien McGrane (IRL) | 72-73-72-74—291 | 13,300 |
| | Jarmo Sandelin (SWE) | 76-69-74-72—291 | 13,300 |
| 62 | Gonzalo Fernandez-Castaño (ESP) | 68-75-74-75—292 | 11,638 |
| | Greig Hutcheon (SCO) | 72-74-67-79—292 | 11,638 |
| | Brett Rumford (AUS) | 75-71-72-74—292 | 11,638 |
| | Alessandro Tadini (ITA) | 73-71-74-74—292 | 11,638 |
| 66 | Jason Levermore (ENG) | 72-70-73-78—293 | 10,450 |
| 67 | Andrew Dodt (AUS) | 75-71-73-75—294 | 9,975 |
| 68 | Julien Quesne (FRA) | 71-75-78-71—295 | 9,500 |
| 69 | Robert Coles (ENG) | 75-71-75-75—296 | 8,273 |
| | Scott Drummond (SCO) | 70-75-75-76—296 | 8,273 |
| | José María Olazábal (ESP) | 75-71-78-72—296 | 8,273 |

77 players missed the cut

## Nordea Masters  *Bro Hof Slott, Stockholm, Sweden*  May 30–June 2  [7607–72]

| 1 | Mikko Ilonen (FIN) | 70-63-65-69—267 | €250,000 |
|---|---|---|---|
| 2 | Jonas Blixt (SWE) | 70-66-66-68—270 | 166,660 |
| 3 | Bernd Wiesberger (AUT) | 69-72-64-66—271 | 93,900 |

## Lyoness Open  *Diamond CC, Atzenbrugg, Austria*  June 6–9  [7386–72]

| 1 | Joost Luiten (NED) | 65-68-67-71—271 | €166,660 |
|---|---|---|---|
| 2 | Thomas Björn (DEN) | 71-70-64-68—273 | 111,110 |
| 3 | Wen-chong Liang (CHN) | 67-72-69-66—274 | 56,300 |
| | Romain Wattel (FRA) | 68-68-69-69—274 | 56,300 |

## 112th US OPEN CHAMPIONSHIP  *Ardmore, Pennsylvania, USA*  June 13–16  [6996–70]

| 1 | Justin Rose (ENG) | 71-69-71-70—281 | €1,101,397 |
|---|---|---|---|
| 2 | Jason Day (AUS) | 70-74-68-71—283 | 532,422 |
| | Phil Mickelson (USA) | 67-72-70-74—283 | 532,422 |

Full details of this event can be found on page 71

## Najeti Hotels et Golfs Open  Aa St Omer GC, St Omer, France   June 13–16   [6799–71]

| | | | |
|---|---|---|---|
| 1 | Simon Thornton (IRL)* | 74-70-65-70—279 | €83,330 |
| 2 | Tjaart Van der Walt (RSA) | 67-71-71-70—279 | 55,550 |

*Thornton won at the first extra hole
| | | | |
|---|---|---|---|
| 3 | Seve Benson (ENG) | 75-65-70-70—280 | 31,300 |

## BMW International Open  Golfclub München Eichenried, Germany   June 20–23   [7157–72]

| | | | |
|---|---|---|---|
| 1 | Ernie Els (RSA) | 63-69-69-69—270 | €333,330 |
| 2 | Thomas Björn (DEN) | 68-69-65-69—271 | 222,220 |
| 3 | Alexander Levy (FRA) | 65-68-68-71—272 | 125,200 |

## The Irish Open  Carton House GC, Maynooth, Co. Kildare, RoI   June 27–30   [7301–72]

| | | | |
|---|---|---|---|
| 1 | Paul Casey (ENG) | 68-72-67-67—274 | €333,330 |
| 2 | Joost Luiten (NED) | 67-70-66-74—277 | 173,710 |
| | Robert Rock (ENG) | 69-66-71-71—277 | 173,710 |

## Alstom Open de France  Le Golf National, Paris, France   July 4–7   [7347–71]

| | | | |
|---|---|---|---|
| 1 | Graeme McDowell (NIR) | 69-69-70-67—275 | €500,000 |
| 2 | Richard Sterne (RSA) | 68-69-71-71—279 | 333,330 |
| 3 | Eduardo de la Riva (ESP) | 72-67-72-69—280 | 168,900 |
| | Graeme Storm (ENG) | 70-68-73-69—280 | 168,900 |

## Aberdeen Asset Management Scottish Open  Castle Stuart, Inverness, Scotland
July 11–14   [7193–72]

| | | | |
|---|---|---|---|
| 1 | Phil Mickelson (USA)* | 66-70-66-69—271 | €579,080 |
| 2 | Branden Grace (RSA) | 71-65-66-69—271 | 386,049 |

*Mickelson won at the first extra hole
| | | | |
|---|---|---|---|
| 3 | J B Hansen (DEN) | 68-65-69-71—273 | 195,613 |
| | Henrik Stenson (SWE) | 70-64-66-73—273 | 195,613 |

## The 142nd OPEN CHAMPIONSHIP  Muirfield, East Lothian, Scotland   July 18–21   [7192–71]

| | | | |
|---|---|---|---|
| 1 | Phil Mickelson (USA) | 69-74-72-66—281 | €1,097,570 |
| 2 | Henrik Stenson (SWE) | 70-70-74-70—284 | 632,900 |
| 3 | Ian Poulter (ENG) | 72-71-75-67—285 | 436,174 |
| | Adam Scott (AUS) | 71-72-70-72—285 | 436,174 |
| | Lee Westwood (ENG) | 72-68-70-75—285 | 436,174 |

Full details of this events can be found on page 54

## M2M Russian Open  Tseleevo Golf & Polo Club, Moscow Region, Russia   July 25–28   [7491–72]

| | | | |
|---|---|---|---|
| 1 | Michael Hoey (NIR) | 70-67-65-70—272 | €166,660 |
| 2 | Alexandre Kaleka (FRA) | 70-67-71-68—276 | 86,855 |
| | Matthew Nixon (ENG) | 69-70-68-69—276 | 86,855 |

## WGC – Bridgestone Invitational  Firestone CC, Akron, OH, USA   Aug 1–4   [7400–70]

| | | | |
|---|---|---|---|
| 1 | Tiger Woods (USA) | 66-61-68-70—265 | €1,139,341 |
| 2 | Keegan Bradley (USA) | 66-68-71-67—272 | 525,996 |
| | Henrik Stenson (SWE) | 65-70-67-70—272 | 525,996 |

Full details of this event can be found on page 208

## US PGA CHAMPIONSHIP  Oak Hill CC, Rochester, New York, USA  Aug 8–11  [7163–70]

| | | | |
|---|---|---|---|
| 1 | Jason Dufner (USA) | 68-63-71-68—270 | €1,084,021 |
| 2 | Jim Furyk (USA) | 65-68-68-71—272 | 648,912 |
| 3 | Henrik Stenson (SWE) | 68-66-69-70—273 | 408,852 |

Full details of this event can be found on page 91

## Johnnie Walker Championship  Gleneagles Hotel, Perthshire, Scotland  Aug 22–25  [7060–72]

| | | | |
|---|---|---|---|
| 1 | Tommy Fleetwood (ENG)* | 68-65-67-70—270 | €272,273 |
| 2 | Stephen Gallacher (SCO) | 71-68-64-67—270 | 141,889 |
| | Ricardo Gonzalez (ARG) | 65-65-70-70—270 | 141,889 |

*Fleetwood won at the first extra hole

## ISPS Handa Wales Open  The Celtic Manor Resort, Newport, Wales  Aug 29–Sep 1  [7352–71]

| | | | |
|---|---|---|---|
| 1 | Grégory Bourdy (FRA) | 67-72-70-67—276 | €348,660 |
| 2 | Peter Uihlein (YSA) | 69-70-67-72—278 | 232,440 |
| 3 | Søren Kjeldsen (DEN) | 69-74-70-66—279 | 130,957 |

## Omega European Masters  Crans-sur-Sierre, Switzerland since 1939  Sep 5–8  [6881–71]

| | | | |
|---|---|---|---|
| 1 | Thomas Björn (DEN)* | 66-66-67-65—264 | €366,660 |
| 2 | Craig Lee (SCO) | 71-65-61-67—264 | 244,440 |

*Björn won at the first extra hole

| | | | |
|---|---|---|---|
| 3 | Victor Dubuisson (FRA) | 68-65-66-66—265 | 137,720 |

## KLM Open  Kennemer G&CC, Zandvoort, The Netherlands  Sep 12–15  [6626–70]

| | | | |
|---|---|---|---|
| 1 | Joost Luiten (NED)* | 69-65-66-68—268 | €300,000 |
| 2 | Miguel Angele Jiménez (ESP) | 64-67-70-67—268 | 200,000 |

*Luiten won at the first extra hole

| | | | |
|---|---|---|---|
| 3 | Simon Dyson (ENG) | 69-63-71-68—271 | 85,500 |
| | Ross Fisher (ENG) | 69-68-68-66—271 | 85,500 |
| | Grégory Havret (FRA) | 67-70-68-66—271 | 85,500 |
| | Damien McGrane (IRL) | 65-70-67-69—271 | 85,500 |

## 70th Open d'Italia Lindt  Golf Club Torino, Turin, Italy  Sep 19–22  [7208–72]

| | | | |
|---|---|---|---|
| 1 | Julien Quesne (FRA) | 70-68-71-67—276 | €250,000 |
| 2 | David Higgins (IRL) | 67-69-73-68—277 | 130,280 |
| | Steve Webster (ENG) | 67-69-73-68—277 | 130,280 |

## Alfred Dunhill Links Championship  St Andrews Old course, Kingsbarns and Carnoustie, Scotland

Sep 26–29                    St Andrews [7279–72], Kingbarns [7150–72], Carnoustie [7412–72]

| | | | |
|---|---|---|---|
| 1 | David Howell (ENG) | 67-68-63-67—265 | €589,562 |
| 2 | Peter Uihlein (USA) | 71-60-65-69—265 | 393,039 |

*Howell won at the second extra hole

| | | | |
|---|---|---|---|
| 3 | Tom Lewis (ENG) | 64-65-73-64—266 | 199,154 |
| | Shane Lowry (IRL) | 68-66-64-68—266 | 199,154 |

## Seve Trophy by Golf+  Saint-Nom-La-Bretèche, Paris, France  Oct 3–6  [6983–71]

Continent of Europe 15, Great Britain & Ireland 13

Full details of this event can be found on page 227

## Portugal Masters  *Oceânico Victoria, Vilamoura, Portugal*    Oct 10–13    [7157–71]

| | | | |
|---|---|---|---|
| 1 | David Lynn (ENG) | 65-65-73-63—266 | €333,330 |
| 2 | Justin Walters (RSA) | 69-63-69-66—267 | 222,220 |
| 3 | Stephen Gallacher (SCO) | 70-67-65-66—268 | 103,333 |
| | Paul Waring (ENG) | 67-63-67-71—268 | 103,333 |
| | Bernd Wiesberger (AUT) | 66-65-70-67—268 | 103,333 |

## Perth International  *Lake Karrinyup CC, Perth, Western Australia*    Oct 17–20    [7143–72]

| | | | |
|---|---|---|---|
| 1 | Jeong Jin (KOR)* | 68-72-69-69—278 | €245,438 |
| 2 | Fisher Ross (ENG) | 72-67-71-68—278 | 163,626 |

*Jin won at the first extra hole

| | | | |
|---|---|---|---|
| 3 | Ninyette Brody (AUS) | 72-69-67-72—280 | 76,087 |
| | Papadatos Dimitrios (AUS) | 69-71-72-68—280 | 76,087 |
| | Willett Danny (ENG) | 72-71-68-69—280 | 76,087 |

## BMW Masters  *Lake Malaren GC, Shanghai, China*    Oct 24–27    [7607–72]

| | | | |
|---|---|---|---|
| 1 | Gonzalo Fernandez-Castaño (ESP) | 71-71-67-68—277 | € 851,346 |
| 2 | Thongchai Thongchai (THA) | 70-70-72-66—278 | 445,158 |
| | Francesco Molinari (ITA) | 72-71-71-64—278 | 445,158 |

## WGC – HSBC Champions  *Sheshan International GC, Shanghai, China*    Oct 31–Nov 3
[7266–72]

| | | | |
|---|---|---|---|
| 1 | Dustin Johnson (USA) | 69-63-66-66—264 | €1,012,146 |
| 2 | Ian Poulter (ENG) | 71-67-63-66—267 | 614,517 |
| 3 | Graeme McDowell (NIR) | 69-69-64-66—268 | 347,021 |

Full details of this event can be found on page 210

## Turkish Airlines Open  *The Montgomerie Maxx Royal, Antalya, Turkey*    Nov 7–10    [7093–72]

| | | | |
|---|---|---|---|
| 1 | Victor Dubuisson (FRA) | 67-65-63-69—264 | €848,930 |
| 2 | Jamie Donaldson (WAL) | 68-67-68-63—266 | 567,603 |
| 3 | Justin Rose (ENG) | 70-66-67-65—268 | 287,567 |
| | Tiger Woods (USA) | 70-63-68-67—268 | 287,567 |

## DP World Tour Championship, Dubai  *Jumeirah Golf Estates, Dubai, UAE*    Nov 14–17
[7675–72]

| | | | |
|---|---|---|---|
| 1 | Henrik Stenson (SWE) | 68-64-67-64—263 | €985,476 |
| 2 | Ian Poulter (ENG) | 69-68-66-66—269 | 657,009 |
| 3 | Victor Dubuisson (FRA) | 70-66-64-71—271 | 384,345 |
| 4 | Joost Luiten (NED) | 73-68-65-66—272 | 295,650 |
| 5 | Luke Donald (ENG) | 73-66-67-67—273 | 200,106 |
| | Rory McIlroy (NIR) | 71-676-8-67—273 | 200,106 |
| | Lee Westwood (ENG) | 70-70-65-68—273 | 200,106 |
| 8 | Donaldson (WAL) | 68-72-67-67—274 | 153,738 |
| | Jamie Jiménez Miguel Angel (ESP) | 72-66-66-70—274 | 153,738 |
| 10 | Peter Hanson (SWE) | 70-68-70-67—275 | 130,086 |
| | Justin Rose (ENG) | 70-67-68-70—275 | 130,086 |
| 12 | Jonas Blixt (SWE) | 72-65-71-68—276 | 118,260 |
| 13 | Francesco Molinari (ITA) | 70-68-70-69—277 | 112,347 |
| 14 | Rafa Cabrera-Bello (ESP) | 68-71-68-71—278 | 100,521 |
| | Alejandro Cañizares (ESP) | 66-67-70-75—278 | 100,521 |
| | Richard Sterne (RSA) | 70-70-70-68—278 | 100,521 |
| 17 | Graeme McDowell (NIR) | 72-68-68-71—279 | 85,739 |
| | Thorbjørn Olesen (DEN) | 69-70-71-69—279 | 85,739 |
| 19 | Mikko Ilonen (FIN) | 72-68-69-71—280 | 73,913 |
| | Martin Kaymer (GER) | 70-69-72-69—280 | 73,913 |
| 21 | Thomas Björn (DEN) | 71-74-69-67—281 | 65,043 |

| 21T | Grégory Bourdy (FRA) | 76-70-66-69—281 | 65,043 |
|---|---|---|---|
| | Darren Fichardt (RSA) | 71-71-67-72—281 | 65,043 |
| | Marcus Fraser (AUS) | 67-69-72-73—281 | 65,043 |
| | Matteo Manassero (ITA) | 71-72-68-70—281 | 65,043 |
| 26 | Ross Fisher (ENG) | 75-64-72-71—282 | 57,947 |
| | Scott Jamieson (SCO) | 73-70-70-69—282 | 57,947 |
| | Pablo Larrazábal (ESP) | 72-66-72-72—282 | 57,947 |
| 29 | Kiradech Aphibarnrat (THA) | 67-70-70-76—283 | 52,626 |
| | David Horsey (ENG) | 72-72-68-71—283 | 52,626 |
| | Chris Wood (ENG) | 73-66-71-73—283 | 52,626 |
| 32 | George Coetzee (RSA) | 74-67-69-74—284 | 48,191 |
| | Louis Oosthuizen (RSA) | 73-70-71-70—284 | 48,191 |
| 34 | Stephen Gallacher (SCO) | 77-71-71-66—285 | 44,348 |
| | David Howell (ENG) | 75-66-70-74—285 | 44,348 |
| | Bernd Wiesberger (AUT) | 72-73-66-74—285 | 44,348 |
| 37 | Gonzalo Fernandez-Castaño (ESP) | 71-74-67-74—286 | 41,391 |
| | Tommy Fleetwood (ENG) | 72-76-70-68—286 | 41,391 |
| 39 | Simon Khan (ENG) | 72-72-74-69—287 | 38,435 |
| | Shane Lowry (IRL) | 71-71-74-71—287 | 38,435 |
| | Marcel Siem (GER) | 75-67-70-75—287 | 38,435 |
| 42 | Nicolas Colsaerts (BEL) | 71-75-71-71—288 | 35,478 |
| | David Lynn (ENG) | 71-72-73-72—288 | 35,478 |
| 44 | Eduardo de la Riva (ESP) | 71-71-72-75—289 | 32,522 |
| | Raphaël Jacquelin (FRA) | 77-66-72-74—289 | 32,522 |
| | Craig Lee (SCO) | 73-70-71-75—289 | 32,522 |
| 47 | Felipe Aguilar (CHI) | 79-66-73-72—290 | 28,382 |
| | Thongchai Jaidee (THA) | 69-70-74-77—290 | 28,382 |
| | Julien Quesne (FRA) | 74-73-69-74—290 | 28,382 |
| | Brett Rumford (AUS) | 71-72-74-73—290 | 28,382 |
| 51 | Peter Uihlein (USA) | 72-72-76-71—291 | 25,426 |
| 52 | Branden Grace (RSA) | 76-70-71-75—292 | 23,652 |
| | Marc Warren (SCO) | 74-71-73-74—292 | 23,652 |
| 54 | Paul Casey (ENG) | 75-68-73-77—293 | 21,878 |
| 55 | Thomas Aiken (RSA) | 76-74-73-74—297 | 20,696 |
| 56 | Garth Mulroy (RSA) | 76-75-74-78—303 | 19,513 |

## ISPS Handa World Cup of Golf   Royal Melbourne GC, Victoria, Australia   Nov 21–24
[6985–72]

| 1 | Australia | 143-138-134-136—551 |
|---|---|---|
| 2 | USA | 137-137-142-145—561 |
| 3 | Denmark | 137-140-147-139—563 |
| | Japan | 143-138-141-141—563 |

Full details can be found on page 231

# 2014

## South African Open Championship   Glendower GC, Ekurhuleni, Gauteng, RSA   Nov 21–24
[6899–72]

| 1 | Morten Ørum Madsen (DEN) | 67-66-69-67—269 | €174,350 |
|---|---|---|---|
| 2 | Jbe Kruger (RSA) | 65-70-71-65—271 | 101,310 |
| | Hennie Otto (RSA) | 72-66-65-68—271 | 101,310 |

## Alfred Dunhill Championship   Leopard Creek CC ,Malelane, RSA   Jan Nov 28–Dec 1
[7287–72]

| 1 | Charl Schwartzel (RSA) | 68-68-67-68—271 | €237,750 |
|---|---|---|---|
| 2 | Richard Finch (ENG) | 68-70-67-70—275 | 172,500 |
| 3 | Simon Dyson (ENG) | 72-69-70-67—278 | 79,800 |
| | Ross Fisher (ENG) | 72-65-72-69—278 | 79,800 |
| | Romain Wattel (FRA) | 70-69-68-71—278 | 79,800 |

## Nedbank Golf Challenge   Gary Player CC, Sun City, RSA   Dec 5–8   [7831–72]

| 1 | Thomas Björn (DEN) | 67-70-66-65—268 | €795,338 |
|---|---|---|---|
| 2 | Jamie Donaldson | 67-66-67-70—270 | 414,478 |
|   | Sergio García (ESP) | 66-73-66-65—270 | 414,478 |

## Hong Kong Open   Hong Kong GC, Fanling, Hong Kong   Dec 5–8   [6699–70]

| 1 | Miguel Angel Jiménez (ESP)* | 70-67-65-66—268 | €159,063 |
|---|---|---|---|
| 2 | Stuart Manley (WAL) | 67-67-66-68—268 | 82,894 |
|   | Prom Meesawat (THA) | 66-70-67-65—268 | 82,894 |

*Jiménez won at the first extra hole

## The Nelson Mandela Championship   Mount Edgecombe CC, Durban, RSA   Dec 11–14
[6612–70]

| 1 | Dawie Van Der Walt (RSA) | 67-62-66—195 | €158,500 |
|---|---|---|---|
| 2 | Matthew Baldwin (ENG) | 67-62-68—197 | 92,100 |
|   | Jorge Campillo (ESP) | 70-59-68—197 | 92,100 |

---

## Two trophies for the European Tour

The European Tour won two trophies at the inaugural Sport 360 Middle East Golf Awards, created to recognise the rapidly growing achievements of the golf industry in the region.

The DP World Tour Championship, Dubai, won Best Professional Tournament of the Year, while Nick Tarratt, European Tour Dubai Director, received the final award of the evening for Best Business Personality of the Year, in conjunction with golf course designer Peter Harradine, for their contribution to golf in the Middle East for more than 20 years.

---

## Gallacher earns Lifetime Achievement Award

Bernard Gallacher OBE was honoured with a Lifetime Achievement at the 2014 Scottish Golf Awards.

The 64-year-old Scot – eight-time Ryder Cup player and victorious captain in 1995 – suffered a cardiac arrest before giving an after-dinner speech at the Marcliffe Hotel in Aberdeen in August last year and spent almost a week in intensive care.

Now he is heavily involved in leading a campaign for the defibrillator machine that saved his life at the Marcliffe to be made widely available at golf courses throughout Britain.

All proceeds from the 'Long Putt Challenge' at the Scottish Golf Awards evening went towards Gallacher's fundraising efforts, with the new Scottish Golf Charitable Trust also benefitting.

"I'm delighted to be accepting a Scottish Golf Lifetime Achievement Award in such a special year for golf in the country," said Gallacher, who will join Colin Montgomerie, Paul Lawrie, Sam Torrance and 2013 recipient Sandy Lyle in the nation's Hall of Fame.

"I enjoyed my playing career, as an amateur and a professional, but it's probably my contribution to the Ryder Cup for which I'm best remembered. It was a privilege to captain three teams.

"I played in the first Ryder Cup in Scotland in 1973 at Muirfield and, like all golf fans, I'm looking forward to it coming back for what will be a fantastic contest at Gleneagles."

Remarkably, Gallacher was involved in every Ryder Cup team between 1969 and 1995 – either as a player, assistant or captain.

One of the most highly respected of all Scottish golfers, he was Tony Jacklin's assistant from 1985 to 1989, toasting a first-ever European victory over the Americans at The Belfry in 1985 and on US soil for the first time two years later.

Emulating another Bathgate Golf Club stalwart, Eric Brown, Gallacher was appointed team captain at Kiawah Island in 1991 and then at The Belfry two years later, before victory duly came at Oak Hill.

Gallacher, whose nephew Stephen is Scotland's No 1 professional, scored 22 professional wins, finishing in the top 10 on the European Tour Order of Merit five times between 1972 and 1982. In his amateur days, he was a Scotland international and won the 1967 Scottish Stroke Play Championship.

# European Tour Qualifying School

## Five former Tour winners earn their cards for 2014

Five former winners won their cards for the 2014 season at the six-round Final Stage of the European Tour's Qualifying School at the PGA Catalunya Resort, near Girona, Spain.

Sweden's Mikael Lundberg and Patrick Sjoland, England's James Morrison, Estanislao Goya of Argentina and Scotland's Alastair Forsyth did well enough to finish in the top 27 with scores of nine-under-par or better. Forsyth made it on the mark.

Of the 27 successful players ten will be playing the European Tour for the first time but among those who missed out were former Tour winners Oliver Fisher from England and Welshman Bradley Dredge along with Former Ryder Cupper Oliver Wilson.

Winner of the Final Stage Qualifying was Spain's Carlos del Moral who has earned his European ticket in this way three times previously. His winning total of 26-under-par 402 gave Del Moral a five shot advantage over the field at the end.

A total of 968 players – one short of the record- took part in the qualifying stages and the 27 golfers who earned cards came for 15 difference countries around the world.

Adrien Saddier from France was the youngest of three 21-year-old who were successful while Swede Patrik Sjoland at 42 was the oldest

| | | |
|---|---|---|
| 1 | Carlos del Moral (ESP) | 67-71-69-63-65-67—402 |
| 2 | Fabrizio Zanotti (PAR) | 66-70-67-68-68-68—407 |
| 3 | Marco Crespi (ITA) | 71-70-67-68-67-70—413 |
| 4 | Gary Stal (FRA) | 71-68-69-68-68-70—414 |
| 5 | Mikael Lundberg (SWE) | 69-68-70-71-66-71—415 |
| | Adrien Saddier (FRA) | 71-66-69-71-67-71—415 |
| | John Hahn (USA) | 66-66-73-68-71-71—415 |
| 8 | Connor Arendell (USA) | 72-70-71-65-70-68—416 |
| | Wade Ormsby (AUS) | 69-67-70-69-70-71—416 |
| | Stuart Manley (WAL) | 68-71-67-69-69-72—416 |
| | James Morrison (ENG) | 72-67-63-70-71-73—416 |
| 12 | James Heath (ENG) | 69-71-70-69-69-69—417 |
| | Simon Wakefield (ENG) | 69-68-67-69-75-69—417 |
| | Jens Dantorp (SWE) | 66-68-68-72-73-70—417 |
| | Brinson Paolini (USA) | 70-71-68-64-72-72—417 |
| | Patrik Sjöland (SWE) | 66-72-67-67-73-72—417 |
| 17 | Kevin Phelan (IRL) | 73-67-68-71-70-69—418 |
| | Andreas Hartø (DEN) | 67-70-69-72-69-71—418 |
| | Daniel Brooks (ENG) | 65-71-69-66-76-71—418 |
| | Thomas Pieters (BEL) | 64-73-72-68-68-73—418 |
| | Lucas Bjerregaard (DEN) | 65-70-69-72-73—418 |
| 22 | Jason Knutzon (USA) | 70-69-71-69-69-71—419 |
| | Mikko Korhonen (FIN) | 69-71-68-70-70-71—419 |
| | Estanislao Goya (ARG) | 66-70-67-73-72-71—419 |
| | Jack Doherty (SCO) | 68-70-66-71-73-71—419 |
| | Adam Gee (ENG) | 66-70-71-69-69-74—419 |
| 22T | Alastair Forsyth (SCO) | 65-70-70-69-71-74—419 |
| 28 | Tjaart van der Walt (RSA) | 72-69-68-71-69-71—420 |
| 29 | Espen Kofstad (NOR) | 70-68-67-72-71-72—420 |
| | Edouard Espana (FRA) | 62-74-69-67-74-74—420 |
| 31 | Berry Henson (USA) | 71-70-70-68-73-69—421 |
| | Cyril Bouniol (FRA) | 73-70-71-66-71-70—421 |
| | Jason Barnes (ENG) | 66-72-72-69-72-70—421 |
| | Andrew McArthur (SCO) | 66-73-70-73-68-71—421 |
| | Oliver Wilson (ENG) | 69-67-74-68-71-72—421 |
| | Oscar Stark (SWE) | 66-71-67-71-72-74—421 |
| 37 | Hugo Leon (CHI) | 68-70-70-72-71-71—422 |
| | Doug McGuigan (SCO) | 71-68-71-70-70-72—422 |
| | Rikard Karlberg (SWE) | 66-77-72-65-69-73—422 |
| 40 | Oliver Fisher (ENG) | 72-69-72-67-73-70—423 |
| | Mathias Grönberg (SWE) | 75-67-73-66-71-71—423 |
| | Chris Hanson (ENG) | 66-77-71-66-70-73—423 |
| | Chris Paisley (ENG) | 67-70-70-70-71-75—423 |
| 44 | Bradley Dredge (WAL) | 68-71-70-68-74-73—424 |
| | Daniel Im (USA) | 70-73-72-64-71-74—424 |
| | Niccolo Quintarelli (ITA) | 68-74-71-62-74-75—424 |
| | Fredrik Andersson Hed (SWE) | 69-68-71-69-73-76—424 |
| 48 | Andrew Marshall (ENG) | 71-70-69-70-72-73—425 |
| | Richard Finch (ENG) | 64-71-70-72-75-73—425 |
| | Maarten Lafeber (NED) | 71-68-67-71-72-76—425 |

# European Senior Tour 2013

www.europeantour.com

## Order of Merit (Top 30 earn full Tour card for 2014)

| | | | | | | |
|---|---|---|---|---|---|---|
| 1 | Paul Wesselingh (ENG) | €311,644 | | 50 | John Gould (ENG) | 32,736 |
| 2 | Steen Tinning (DEN) | 206,087 | | 51 | Mark James (ENG) | 32,371 |
| 3 | Simon P Brown (ENG) | 181,493 | | 52 | Hendrik Buhrmann (RSA) | 32,233 |
| 4 | Miguel Angel Martin (ESP) | 181,349 | | 53 | Terry Price (AUS) | 31,661 |
| 5 | Peter Fowler (AUS) | 174,994 | | 54 | Steve Van Vuuren (RSA) | 26,678 |
| 6 | Philip Golding (ENG) | 152,166 | | 55 | Gordon J Brand (ENG) | 25,564 |
| 7 | Andrew Oldcorn (SCO) | 147,017 | | 56 | Wraith Grant (ENG) | 25,558 |
| 8 | Santiago Luna (ESP) | 136,201 | | 57 | John Harrison (ENG) | 23,622 |
| 9 | Angel Franco (PAR) | 123,620 | | 58 | Anders Forsbrand (SWE) | 20,259 |
| 10 | David J Russell (ENG) | 123,320 | | 59 | Steve Cipa (ENG) | 19,720 |
| 11 | Colin Montgomerie (SCO) | 115,366 | | 60 | José Rivero (ESP) | 19,063 |
| 12 | Carl Mason (ENG) | 107,294 | | 61 | Andrew Murray (ENG) | 18,898 |
| 13 | Ian Woosnam (WAL) | 98,721 | | 62 | Gerry Norquist (USA) | 17,937 |
| 14 | Gordon Brand Jr (SCO) | 90,618 | | 63 | Tony Johnstone (ZIM) | 16,340 |
| 15 | Bob Cameron (ENG) | 86,030 | | 64 | Jean Laforce (CAN) | 15,911 |
| 16 | Gary Wolstenholme (ENG) | 84,828 | | 65 | Costantino Rocca (ITA) | 14,139 |
| 17 | Barry Lane (ENG) | 83,099 | | 66 | Tim Elliott (AUS) | 12,860 |
| 18 | Paul Eales (ENG) | 78,865 | | 67 | Stephen Bennett (ENG) | 12,815 |
| 19 | Mike Harwood (AUS) | 76,898 | | 68 | Angel Fernandez (CHI) | 11,959 |
| 20 | Pedro Linhart (ESP) | 76,407 | | 69 | Gary Emerson (ENG) | 11,134 |
| 21 | Mike Cunning (USA) | 76,202 | | 70 | Glenn Ralph (ENG) | 10,940 |
| 22 | Nick Job (ENG) | 68,874 | | 71 | Paul Curry (ENG) | 10,495 |
| 23 | Ross Drummond (SCO) | 67,791 | | 72 | Domingo Hospital (ESP) | 10,411 |
| 24 | Greg Turner (NZL) | 66,025 | | 73 | Roger Sabarros (FRA) | 8,572 |
| 25 | Gordon Manson (AUT) | 64,254 | | 74 | Stephen McAllister (SCO) | 8,570 |
| 26 | Tim Thelen (USA) | 63,256 | | 75 | Eamonn Darcy (IRL) | 8,153 |
| 27 | Des Smyth (IRL) | 59,853 | | 76 | David James (SCO) | 7,394 |
| 28 | José Manuel Carriles (ESP) | 58,598 | | 77 | Graham Banister (AUS) | 7,338 |
| 29 | Denis O'Sullivan (IRL) | 58,476 | | 78 | Noel Ratcliffe (AUS) | 6,902 |
| 30 | Boonchu Ruangkit (THA) | 55,851 | | 79 | André Bossert (SUI) | 5,987 |
| | | | | 80 | Mark Belsham (ENG) | 5,959 |
| 31 | Chris Williams (ENG) | 55,688 | | 81 | Manuel Piñero (ESP) | 5,889 |
| 32 | Kevin Spurgeon (ENG) | 53,272 | | 82 | Denis Durnian (ENG) | 4,895 |
| 33 | Katsuyoshi Tomori (JPN) | 50,614 | | 83 | John Lindberg (SWE) | 4,397 |
| 34 | Rick Gibson (CAN) | 49,359 | | 84 | Alan Saddington (SCO) | 4,207 |
| 35 | Andrew Sherborne (ENG) | 47,823 | | 85 | Roger Roper (ENG) | 3,783 |
| 36 | Jamie Spence (ENG) | 45,720 | | 86 | Graeme Bell (ENG) | 3,701 |
| 37 | Marc Farry (FRA) | 45,210 | | 87 | Paul Way (ENG) | 3,609 |
| 38 | Peter Mitchell (ENG) | 45,178 | | 88 | Mark Wharton (ENG) | 2,656 |
| 39 | Phil Jonas (CAN) | 44,491 | | 89 | Peter Dahlberg (SWE) | 2,593 |
| 40 | Bill Longmuir (SCO) | 41,092 | | 90 | Mitch Kierstenson (ENG) | 2,251 |
| 41 | Juan Quiros (ESP) | 40,689 | | 91 | Maurice Bembridge (ENG) | 2,121 |
| 42 | Sam Torrance (SCO) | 39,596 | | 92 | Jean Pierre Sallat (FRA) | 1,987 |
| 43 | Jerry Bruner (USA) | 39,142 | | 93 | Antonio Garrido (ESP) | 1,815 |
| 44 | George Ryall (ENG) | 38,583 | | 94 | Charlie Bolling (USA) | 1,694 |
| 45 | Luis Carbonetti (ARG) | 38,161 | | 95 | James Murphy (ENG) | 1,481 |
| 46 | Robert Thompson (USA) | 36,291 | | 96 | Bill Hardwick (CAN) | 1,287 |
| 47 | Philip Walton (IRL) | 36,125 | | 97 | Mus Deboub (ALG) | 1,094 |
| 48 | Massy Kuramoto (JPN) | 35,455 | | 98 | Stephen McNally (ENG) | 1,044 |
| 49 | Mike McLean (ENG) | 35,349 | | 99 | Barrie Stevens (ENG) | 401 |

# Career Money List

| | | | | | | |
|---|---|---|---|---|---|---|
| 1 | Carl Mason (ENG) | €2,510,859 | 51 | Andrew Oldcorn (SCO) | 596,225 |
| 2 | Nick Job (ENG) | 1,567,825 | 52 | Boonchu Ruangkit (THA) | 591,260 |
| 3 | Sam Torrance (SCO) | 1,536,589 | 53 | Alan Tapie (USA) | 590,860 |
| 4 | Tommy Horton (ENG) | 1,527,506 | 54 | Costantino Rocca (ITA) | 587,106 |
| 5 | Noel Ratcliffe (AUS) | 1,378,441 | 55 | Gordon Brand Jr (SCO) | 582,138 |
| 6 | Bill Longmuir (SCO) | 1,374,566 | 56 | David Frost (RSA) | 574,069 |
| 7 | Jerry Bruner (USA) | 1,334,727 | 57 | Stewart Ginn (AUS) | 572,687 |
| 8 | Denis O'Sullivan (IRL) | 1,312,856 | 58 | Kevin Spurgeon (ENG) | 567,833 |
| 9 | Tom Watson (USA) | 1,297,899 | 59 | Mark James (ENG) | 567,075 |
| 10 | Bob Cameron (ENG) | 1,229,154 | 60 | Bobby Lincoln (RSA) | 550,944 |
| 11 | Jim Rhodes (ENG) | 1,209,266 | 61 | Gary Wolstenholme (ENG) | 540,979 |
| 12 | Des Smyth (IRL) | 1,127,878 | 62 | John Grace (USA) | 539,694 |
| 13 | John Chillas (SCO) | 1,109,058 | 63 | Peter Mitchell (ENG) | 536,161 |
| 14 | Seiji Ebihara (JPN) | 1,056,140 | 64 | Pete Oakley (USA) | 528,177 |
| 15 | Bernhard Langer (GER) | 1,038,603 | 65 | Martin Gray (SCO) | 528,014 |
| 16 | Delroy Cambridge (JAM) | 1,029,204 | 66 | David Merriman (AUS) | 513,819 |
| 17 | Terry Gale (AUS) | 1,026,697 | 67 | David Huish (SCO) | 512,325 |
| 18 | David J Russell (ENG) | 1,022,889 | 68 | Katsuyoshi Tomori (JPN) | 507,951 |
| 19 | Juan Quiros (ESP) | 1,007,629 | 69 | Mike Harwood (AUS) | 506,260 |
| 20 | Luis Carbonetti (ARG) | 979,539 | 70 | Ray Carrasco (USA) | 505,330 |
| 21 | Denis Durnian (ENG) | 976,324 | 71 | Paul Wesselingh (ENG) | 503,307 |
| 22 | Gordon J Brand (ENG) | 971,559 | 72 | Peter Senior (AUS) | 498,137 |
| 23 | David Good (AUS) | 945,648 | 73 | Bobby Verwey (RSA) | 496,778 |
| 24 | Ian Woosnam (WAL) | 934,099 | 74 | Glenn Ralph (ENG) | 485,998 |
| 25 | Neil Coles (ENG) | 928,968 | 75 | Brian Waites (ENG) | 482,280 |
| 26 | Eduardo Romero (ARG) | 899,045 | 76 | Tom Lehman (USA) | 481,048 |
| 27 | Giuseppe Cali (ITA) | 854,579 | 77 | Alberto Croce (ITA) | 469,904 |
| 28 | Malcolm Gregson (ENG) | 833,972 | 78 | Liam Higgins (IRL) | 469,088 |
| 29 | Peter Fowler (AUS) | 794,552 | 79 | Bob Lendzion (USA) | 462,937 |
| 30 | Maurice Bembridge (ENG) | 787,661 | 80 | Michael Allen (USA) | 460,498 |
| 31 | José Rivero (ESP) | 780,430 | 81 | Bob Shearer (AUS) | 459,657 |
| 32 | Angel Franco (PAR) | 760,671 | 82 | Mike Miller (SCO) | 455,395 |
| 33 | Barry Lane (ENG) | 749,803 | 83 | Ian Mosey (ENG) | 443,469 |
| 34 | Simon Owen (NZL) | 747,697 | 84 | Fred Couples (USA) | 442,409 |
| 35 | Ross Drummond (SCO) | 747,471 | 85 | Tom Kite (USA) | 442,363 |
| 36 | Horacio Carbonetti (ARG) | 741,396 | 86 | Christy O'Connor Jr (IRL) | 424,118 |
| 37 | Roger Chapman (ENG) | 737,375 | 87 | Mike Cunning (USA) | 420,530 |
| 38 | Loren Roberts (USA) | 734,526 | 88 | Bill Hardwick (CAN) | 419,564 |
| 39 | Bob Charles (NZL) | 721,172 | 89 | Gery Watine (FRA) | 416,791 |
| 40 | Eamonn Darcy (IRL) | 702,786 | 90 | Paul Leonard (NIR) | 414,918 |
| 41 | Guillermo Encina (CHI) | 682,238 | 91 | Russ Cochran (USA) | 403,335 |
| 42 | John Bland (RSA) | 674,808 | 92 | Marc Farry (FRA) | 396,032 |
| 43 | David Creamer (ENG) | 664,695 | 93 | Tim Thelen (USA) | 395,138 |
| 44 | Eddie Polland (NIR) | 651,591 | 94 | Bertus Smit (RSA) | 391,294 |
| 45 | Jay Haas (USA) | 647,941 | 95 | Bernard Gallacher (SCO) | 390,919 |
| 46 | Chris Williams (ENG) | 639,446 | 96 | Priscillo Diniz (BRA) | 388,580 |
| 47 | Brian Huggett (WAL) | 638,783 | 97 | Gary Player (RSA) | 386,948 |
| 48 | Tony Johnstone (ZIM) | 627,789 | 98 | David Jones (IRL) | 374,369 |
| 49 | Antonio Garrido (ESP) | 614,268 | 99 | John Fourie (RSA) | 371,197 |
| 50 | Ian Stanley (AUS) | 607,584 | 100 | Corey Pavin (USA) | 370,632 |

# Tour Results

| | | | | |
|---|---|---|---|---|
| May 23–26 | **US Senior PGA Championship** | St Louis, Missouri, USA | | |
| | 1 Kohki Idoki (JPN) | 71-69-68-65—273 | | |
| | 2 Kenny Perry (USA) | 69-66-68-72—275 | | |
| | Jay Haas (USA) | 66-72-67-70—275 | | |
| June 6–9 | ISPS Handa PGA Seniors Championship | Mottram St Andrew, Cheshire, England | Paul Wesselingh (ENG) | 272 (–20) |
| June 14–16 | Speedy Services Wales Senior Open | Royal Porthcawl GC, Bridgend, Wales | Philip Golding (ENG) | 211 (–2) |
| July 5–7 | Bad Ragaz PGA Sen. Open | Bad Ragaz, Switzerland | Paul Wesselingh (ENG)* | 201 (–9) |
| | *Beat Kevin Spurgeon (ENG) at the third extra hole | | | |
| July 11–14 | **US Senior Open** | Omaha, NE, USA | | |
| | 1 Kenny Perry (USA) | 67-73-64-63—267 | | |
| | 2 Fred Funk (USA) | 67-70-67-68—272 | | |
| | 3 Rocco Mediate (USA) | 68-67-72-66—273 | | |
| | Corey Pavin (USA) | 69-73-64-67—273 | | |
| July 25–28 | **The Senior Open** | Royal Birkdale, Southport, England | | |
| | 1 Mark Wiebe (USA)* | 70-65-70-66—271 | | |
| | 2 Bernhard Langer (GER) | 68-67-66-70—271 | | |
| | *Wiebe won at the fifth extra hole | | | |
| | 3 Corey Pavin (USA) | 69-71-69-65—274 | | |
| | Peter Senior (AUS) | 68-71-69-66—274 | | |
| | David Frost (RSA) | 68-68-68-70—274 | | |
| Aug 2–4 | Berenberg Masters | Cologne, Germany | Steen Tinning (DEN) | 207 (–9) |
| Aug 16–18 | Scottish Senior Open | St. Andrews, Scotland | Santiago Luna (ESP) | 211 (–5) |
| Aug 30– Sep 1 | Travis Perkins plc Senior Masters | Fairmont St Andrews, Fife, Scotland | Colin Montgomerie (SCO) | 206 (–10) |
| Sep 6–8 | WINSTONgolf Senior Open | Vorbeck, Germany | Gordon Brand Jr (SCO) | 204 (–12) |
| Sep 13–15 | Russian Open Golf Championship (Senior) | Moscow, Russia | Simon P Brown (ENG) | 204 (–12) |
| Sep 20–22 | French Riviera Masters | Provence, France | Peter Fowler (AUS) | 205 (–11) |
| Oct 4–6 | English Senior Open | Darlington, England | Steen Tinning (DEN) | 199 (–17) |
| Oct 11–13 | Dutch Senior Open | Amsterdam, Netherlands | Simon P Brown (ENG) | 143 (–3) |
| | *Reduced to two rounds due to flooding* | | | |
| Nov 15–17 | Fubon Senior Open | Miramar G&CC, Taiwan | Paul Wesselingh (ENG) | 207 (–9) |
| Dec 13–15 | MCB Tour Championship | Constance Belle Mare Plage, Mauritius | Paul Wesselingh (ENG) | 202 (–14) |

## Senior Tour Records 2013

| | | | |
|---|---|---|---|
| **Low 9 holes** | 29 (–7) | Andrew Oldcorn | WINSTONgolf Senior Open |
| **Low 18 holes** | 61 (–11) | Andrew Oldcorn | WINSTONgolf Senior Open |
| **Largest winning margin** | 6 shots | Colin Montgomerie | Travis Perkins plc Senior Masters |
| **Largest 18 hole lead** | 2 shots | Greg Turner | Berenberg Masters |
| **Largest 36 hole lead** | 4 shots | Andrew Oldcorn | French Riviera Masters |
| **Low finish by a winner** | 64 (–9) | Paul Wesselingh | ISPS HANDA PGA Seniors Championship |
| | 64 (–6) | Paul Wesselingh | Bad Ragaz PGA Seniors Open |
| **High finish by a winner** | 71 (–2) | Simon Brown | Dutch Senior Open |
| | 71 (–1) | Santiago Luna | SSE Scottish Senior Open |

# Senior Tour Records 2013

**First time winners**

| | |
|---|---|
| Kouki Idoki | US Senior PGA Championship presented by KitchenAid |
| Philip Golding | Speedy Services Wales Senior Open |
| Mark Wiebe | The Senior Open Championship presented by Rolex |
| Steen Tinning | Berenberg Masters |
| Santiago Luna | SSE Scottish Senior Open |
| Colin Montgomerie | Travis Perkins plc Senior Masters |
| Simon Brown | Russian Open Golf Championship (Senior) |

**Course records**

| | | |
|---|---|---|
| Andrew Oldcorn | 61 (–11) | WINSTONgolf Senior Open |
| Steen Tinning | 63 (–9) | English Senior Open |
| Nick Job | 72 (–1) | Dutch Senior Open |
| Simon Brown | 72 (–1)* | Dutch Senior Open |
| Marc Farry | 72 (–1)* | Dutch Senior Open |

**Multiple winners**

| | |
|---|---|
| Paul Wesselingh | ISPS Handa PGA Seniors Championship |
| | Bad Ragaz PGA Senior Open |
| | Fubon Senior Open |
| | MCB Tour Championship |
| Steen Tinning | Berenberg Masters |
| | English Senior Open |
| Simon P Brown | Russian Open Golf Championship (Senior) |
| | Dutch Senior Open |

| **Most top 10 finishes** | | **Most top 5 finishes** | |
|---|---|---|---|
| Miguel Angel Martin | 8 | Steen Tinning | 5 |
| Paul Wesslingh | 8 | Paul Wesselingh | 5 |
| Andrew Oldcorn | 7 | Philip Golding | 4 |
| Philip Golding | 7 | Miguel Angel Martin | 4 |
| Steen Tinning | 6 | Andrew Oldcorn | 4 |
| Ian Woosnam | 5 | Paul Eales | 4 |
| Angel Franco | 5 | Carl Mason | 3 |
| Barry Lane | 4 | Peter Fowler | 3 |
| Peter Fowler | 4 | Ian Woosnam | 3 |
| Santiago Luna | 4 | Santiago Luna | 3 |
| David J Russell | 4 | David J Russell | 3 |
| Chris Williams | 4 | Bernhard Langer | 2 |
| Bob Cameron | 4 | Barry Lane | 2 |
| Paul Eales | 4 | Angel Franco | 2 |
| Mike Cunning | 3 | Colin Montgomerie | 2 |
| Gary Wolstenholme | 3 | Greg Turner | 2 |
| Jose Manuel Carriles | 3 | Simon Brown | 2 |
| Gordon Manson | 3 | Ross Drummond | 2 |
| Simon Brown | 3 | Bob Cameron | 2 |
| Tim Thelen | 3 | | |
| Phil Jonas | 3 | | |

**Holes-in-one**

| | | |
|---|---|---|
| Pedro Linhart | Round 2, Hole 3 | Bad Ragaz PGA Seniors Open |
| Jean Laforce | Round 3, Hole 14 | Bad Ragaz PGA Seniors Open |
| Gordon J Brand | Round 1, Hole 11 | WINSTONgolf Senior Open |
| Mike McLean | Round 3, Hole 3 | English Senior Open |
| Lin Te-ming | Round 2, Hole 17 | Fubon Senior Open |
| Denis O'Sullivan | Round 3, Hole 7 | Fubon Senior Open |

*equals existing record

# European Challenge Tour 2013

www.europeantour.com

## Final Order of Merit (top 20 earn card for PGA European Tour)

| | | | | | | |
|---|---|---|---|---|---|---|
| 1 | Andrea Pavan (ITA) | €147,811 | 51 | Jason Barnes (ENG) | 31,636 |
| 2 | José-Filipe Lima (POR) | 123,697 | 52 | Daniel Vancsik (ARG) | 28,658 |
| 3 | Brooks Koepka (USA) | 119,423 | 53 | Damian Ulrich (SUI) | 28,484 |
| 4 | Shiv Kapur (IND) | 118,323 | 54 | George Murray (SCO) | 28,163 |
| 5 | Johan Carlsson (SWE) | 113,066 | 55 | Christophe Brazillier (FRA) | 26,102 |
| 6 | Daan Huizing (NED) | 104,870 | 56 | Scott Arnold (AUS) | 25,743 |
| 7 | Adrian Otaegui (ESP) | 104,811 | 57 | Alvaro Velasco (ESP) | 25,738 |
| 8 | Roope Kakko (FIN) | 100,293 | 58 | Andrea Rota (ITA) | 25,724 |
| 9 | Sihwan Kim (KOR) | 95,708 | 59 | Sam Hutsby (ENG) | 25,018 |
| 10 | Tyrrell Hatton (ENG) | 92,114 | 60 | Raymond Russell (SCO) | 24,108 |
| 11 | Victor Riu (FRA) | 87,297 | 61 | Gary Stal (FRA) | 23,676 |
| 12 | Robert Dinwiddie (ENG) | 86,489 | 62 | Mark F Haastrup (DEN) | 23,632 |
| 13 | François Calmels (FRA) | 85,534 | 63 | Pedro Oriol (ESP) | 22,805 |
| 14 | Nacho Elvira (ESP) | 82,785 | 64 | Filippo Bergamaschi (ITA) | 22,663 |
| 15 | Jamie McLeary (SCO) | 78,676 | 65 | Carlos Aguilar (ESP) | 22,159 |
| 16 | Sam Walker (ENG) | 76,106 | 66 | Jerome Lando Casanova (FRA) | 21,643 |
| 17 | Daniel Im (USA) | 75,870 | 67 | Luke Goddard (ENG) | 21,181 |
| 18 | Marco Crespi (ITA) | 74,921 | 68 | Andrew Johnston (ENG) | 20,975 |
| 19 | Stuart Manley (WAL) | 71,996 | 69 | Pontus Widegren (SWE) | 20,201 |
| 20 | Duncan Stewart (SCO) | 70,227 | 70 | Paul Maddy (ENG) | 19,966 |
| 21 | Jens Dantorp (SWE) | 67,342 | 71 | Gareth Shaw (NIR) | 19,832 |
| 22 | Edouard Dubois (FRA) | 66,491 | 72 | Tapio Pulkkanen (FIN) | 19,662 |
| 23 | Rhys Davies (WAL) | 66,229 | 73 | Luis Claverie (ESP) | 19,533 |
| 24 | Jordi Garcia Pinto (ESP) | 65,611 | 74 | Nicolo Ravano (ITA) | 19,219 |
| 25 | Byeong-Hun An (KOR) | 64,396 | 75 | Roland Steiner (AUT) | 18,762 |
| 26 | Andrew McArthur (SCO) | 62,628 | 76 | James Heath (ENG) | 18,586 |
| 27 | Jens Fahrbring (SWE) | 59,175 | 77 | Chan Kim (USA) | 17,557 |
| 28 | Phillip Archer (ENG) | 58,734 | 78 | Charles-Edouard Russo (FRA) | 17,079 |
| 29 | Brinson Paolini (USA) | 58,563 | 79 | Benjamin Hebert (FRA) | 17,022 |
| 30 | Agustin Domingo (ESP) | 58,289 | 80 | Guillaume Cambis (FRA) | 16,680 |
| 31 | Tim Sluiter (NED) | 56,612 | 81 | Brandon Stone (RSA) | 16,601 |
| 32 | Dylan Frittelli (RSA) | 52,659 | 82 | Dodge Kemmer (USA) | 15,341 |
| 33 | Daniel Gaunt (AUS) | 52,323 | 83 | Ross McGowan (ENG) | 14,603 |
| 34 | Lucas Bjerregaard (DEN) | 51,546 | 84 | Max Glauert (GER) | 14,484 |
| 35 | Jamie Elson (ENG) | 51,167 | 85 | Markus Brier (AUT) | 14,170 |
| 36 | Steven Tiley (ENG) | 50,692 | 86 | Florian Praegant (AUT) | 13,890 |
| 37 | Bernd Ritthammer (GER) | 49,097 | 87 | Chris Hanson (ENG) | 13,756 |
| 38 | Jeppe Huldahl (DEN) | 47,597 | 88 | Eirik Tage Johansen (NOR) | 12,307 |
| 39 | Lloyd Kennedy (ENG) | 46,263 | 89 | Edouard Espana (FRA) | 11,351 |
| 40 | Wil Besseling (NED) | 45,508 | 90 | Adrien Bernadet (FRA) | 11,309 |
| 41 | Adam Gee (ENG) | 45,104 | 91 | Sebastian Garcia Rodriguez (ESP) | 11,235 |
| 42 | Oliver Wilson (ENG) | 44,824 | 92 | Wallace Booth (SCO) | 11,188 |
| 43 | Niklas Lemke (SWE) | 44,679 | 93 | Baptiste Chapellan (FRA) | 10,851 |
| 44 | Julien Guerrier (FRA) | 41,747 | 94 | Paul Dwyer (ENG) | 10,692 |
| 45 | Thomas Nørret (DEN) | 40,890 | 95 | Lloyd Saltman (SCO) | 10,230 |
| 46 | Terry Pilkadaris (AUS) | 35,667 | 96 | Adrien Saddier (FRA) | 9,911 |
| 47 | Pelle Edberg (SWE) | 35,541 | 97 | Niccolo Quintarelli (ITA) | 9,737 |
| 48 | Matt Ford (ENG) | 35,093 | 98 | Matt Haines (ENG) | 9,634 |
| 49 | Knut Borsheim (NOR) | 34,990 | 99 | Domenico Geminiani (ITA) | 9,576 |
| 50 | Daniel Brooks (ENG) | 34,089 | 100 | Tom Murray (ENG) | 9,524 |

# Results

| | | | | |
|---|---|---|---|---|
| Jan 31–Feb 3 | Gujarat Kensville Chall. | Ahmedabad, India | Shiv Kapur (IND) | 274 (–14) |
| Feb 14–17 | Barclays Kenya Open | Karen CC, Nairobi, Kenya | Jordi Garcia Pinto (ESP) | 272 (–12) |
| Apr 24–27 | Challenge de Madrid | Madrid, Spain | François Calmels (FRA) | 271 (–17) |
| May 2–5 | Montecchia Golf Open | Padova, Italy | Brooks Koepka (USA) | 261 (–23) |
| May 16–19 | Madeira Islands Open | Santo da Serra, Portugal | Peter Uihlein (USA) | 273 (–15) |
| May 23–26 | Telenet Trophy | Lasne, Belgium | Daniel Gaunt (AUS)* | 273 (–11) |
| | *Beat Wil Besseling (NED) at the first extra hole | | | |
| May 30–June 2 | Fred Olsen Challenge de España | La Gomera, Canary Is., Spain | Brooks Koepka (USA) | 260 (–24) |
| June 6–9 | D+D Real Czech Challenge Open | Drítec, Czech Republic | François Calmels (FRA) | 266 (–22) |
| June 13–16 | Najeti Hotels et Golfs Open | St Omer, Lumbres, France | Simon Thornton (IRL)* | 279 (–5) |
| | *Beat Tjaart Van der Walt (RSA) in play-off | | | |
| June 20–23 | Scottish Hydro Challenge | Aviemore, Scotland | Brooks Koepka (USA) | 266 (–18) |
| June 27–30 | Kärnten Golf Open | Längsee, Austria | Dylan Fritelli (RSA) | 267 (–17) |
| July 4–7 | Bad Griesbach Challenge Tour | Bad Griesbach, Germany | Andrea Pavan (ITA) | 269 (–19) |
| July 11–14 | Swiss Challenge | Lucerne, Switzerland | Victor Riu (FRA) | 265 (–19) |
| July 18–21 | Mugello Tuscany Open | Scarperia, Florence, Italy | Marco Crespi (ITA) | 267 (–17) |
| July 25–28 | Le Vaudreuil Golf Chall. | Le Vaudreuil, France | Brinson Paolini (USA) | 203 (–19) |
| Aug 1–4 | Finnish Challenge | Hyvinkää, Finland | Stuart Manley (WAL) | 267 (–21) |
| Aug 8–11 | Norwegian Challenge | Finstadjordet, Oslo, Norway | Jens Fahrbring (SWE) | 269 (–19) |
| Aug 21–24 | Rolex Trophy | Geneva, Switzerland | Jens Dantorp (SWE) | 270 (–18) |
| Aug 29–Sep 1 | Northern Ireland Open Challenge | Galgorm Castle GC, Ballymena, County Antrim | Daan Huizing (NED) | 271 (–13) |
| Sep 5–8 | Open Blue Green Côtes d'Armor Bretagne | Pléneuf, France | Andrea Pavan (ITA) | 269 (–11) |
| Sep 12–15 | Kharkov Superior Cup | Kharkov, Ukraine | Daan Huizing (NED) | 273 (–15) |
| Sep 19–22 | Kazakhstan Open | Almaty, Kazakhstan | Johan Carlsson (SWE) | 270 (–18) |
| Oct 17–20 | The Foshan Open | Foshan City, China | Nacho Elvira (ESP) | 274 (–14) |
| Oct 24–27 | National Bank of Oman Golf Classic | Muscat, Oman | Roope Kakko (FIN) | 274 (–14) |
| Oct 31–Nov 3 | Challenge Tour Grand Final | Dubai, UAE | Shiv Kapur (IND) | 272 (–16) |

## Challenge Tour Records 2013

| | | | |
|---|---|---|---|
| Low 9 holes | 28 (–8) | Knut Borsheim (NOR) | Mugello Tuscany Open |
| Low 18 holes | 61 (–11) | Dan Huizing (NED) | Le Vaudreuil Golf Challenge |
| Low first 36 holes | 127 (–15) | Knut Borsheim (NOR) | Mugello Tuscany Open |
| Low final 36 holes | 128 (–16) | Jens Fahrbring (SWE) | Norwegian Challenge |
| | 128 (–14) | Brooks Koepka (USA) | Montecchia Golf Open |
| Largest winning margin | 10 shots | Brooks Koepka (USA) | Fred Olsen Challenge de España |

**Multiple winners**

| | |
|---|---|
| Brooks Koepka (USA) | Montecchia Golf Open; Fred Olsen Challenge de España; Scottish Hydro Challenge |
| Andrea Pavan (ITA) | Bad Griesbach Challenge Tour; Open Blue Green Cotes d'Armor Bretagne |
| François Calmels (FRA) | Challenge de Madrid; D+D Real Czech Challenge Open |
| Daan Huizing (NED) | Northern Ireland Open Challenge; Kharkov Superior Cup |
| Shiv Kapur (IND) | Gujarat Kensville Challenge; Challenge Tour Grand Final |

# US PGA Tour 2013

*Players are of US nationality unless stated*                          www.pgatour.com

## Final Ranking

The top 125 on the money list retained their cards for the 2013–14 season. The top 40 earned a spot at The Masters.

| | | | | | | | | | |
|---|---|---|---|---|---|---|---|---|---|
| 1 | Tiger Woods | $8,553,439 | 44 | Bubba Watson | 1,759,276 | 91 | Mark Wilson | 913,730 |
| 2 | Henrik Stenson (SWE) | 6,388,230 | 45 | Martin Laird (SCO) | 1,755,393 | 92 | Brian Harman | 909,759 |
| 3 | Matt Kuchar | 5,616,808 | 46 | David Lingmerth (SWE) | 1,748,109 | 93 | Geoff Ogilvy (AUS) | 892,920 |
| 4 | Phil Mickelson | 5,495,793 | 47 | Chris Kirk | 1,728,616 | 94 | Martin Kaymer (GER) | 882,937 |
| 5 | Brandt Snedeker | 5,318,087 | 48 | Matt Jones (AUS) | 1,724,707 | 95 | D H Lee (KOR) | 882,793 |
| 6 | Adam Scott (AUS) | 4,892,611 | 49 | Ian Poulter (ENG) | 1,723,463 | 96 | Morgan Hoffmann | 871,003 |
| 7 | Steve Stricker | 4,440,532 | 50 | Ken Duke | 1,722,583 | 97 | William McGirt | 867,384 |
| 8 | Justin Rose (ENG) | 4,146,148 | 51 | Sang-Moon Bae (KOR) | 1,714,640 | 98 | James Hahn | 853,507 |
| 9 | Zach Johnson | 4,044,509 | 52 | Michael Thompson | 1,707,637 | 99 | Jerry Kelly | 832,407 |
| 10 | Jordan Spieth | 3,879,820 | 53 | David Lynn (ENG) | 1,633,253 | 100 | Ted Potter Jr | 829,770 |
| 11 | Keegan Bradley | 3,636,813 | 54 | Scott Stallings | 1,622,627 | 101 | James Driscoll | 821,101 |
| 12 | Jason Day (AUS) | 3,625,030 | 55 | Chris Stroud | 1,602,122 | 102 | Bryce Molder | 816,922 |
| 13 | Billy Horschel | 3,501,703 | 56 | Kevin Chappell | 1,589,839 | 103 | Martin Flores | 805,597 |
| 14 | Bill Haas | 3,475,563 | 57 | Charley Hoffman | 1,582,423 | 104 | Johnson Wagner | 801,955 |
| 15 | Jim Furyk | 3,204,779 | 58 | John Huh | 1,529,482 | 105 | Ben Crane | 796,947 |
| 16 | Jason Dufner | 3,132,268 | 59 | Ryan Palmer | 1,521,592 | 106 | Bob Estes | 769,717 |
| 17 | Kevin Streelman | 3,088,284 | 60 | Marc Leishman | 1,491,359 | 107 | J J Henry | 761,861 |
| 18 | Hunter Mahan | 3,036,164 | 61 | Ryan Moore | 1,490,265 | 108 | Lucas Glover | 747,812 |
| 19 | Dustin Johnson | 2,963,214 | 62 | Kyle Stanley | 1,462,943 | 109 | Jason Bohn | 739,030 |
| 20 | Webb Simpson | 2,957,582 | 63 | Brian Gay | 1,426,017 | 110 | Carl Pettersson (SWE) | 738,143 |
| 21 | Graham DeLaet (CAN) | 2,834,900 | 64 | Tim Clark (RSA) | 1,355,952 | 111 | Justin Hicks | 732,742 |
| 22 | Boo Weekley | 2,786,662 | 65 | Josh Teater | 1,332,652 | 112 | Jeff Overton | 721,723 |
| 23 | D A Points | 2,658,887 | 66 | Derek Ernst | 1,330,856 | 113 | Aaron Baddeley (AUS) | 721,024 |
| 24 | Nick Watney | 2,477,639 | 67 | Rory Sabbatini (RSA) | 1,327,822 | 114 | Nicolas Colsaerts (BEL) | 720,164 |
| 25 | Charl Schwartzel (RSA) | 2,256,723 | 68 | Kevin Stadler | 1,281,177 | 115 | Andres Romero (ARG) | 718,507 |
| 26 | Sergio García (ESP) | 2,251,139 | 69 | Daniel Summerhays | 1,277,886 | 116 | Padraig Harrington (IRL) | 711,244 |
| 27 | Harris English | 2,201,167 | 70 | Jason Kokrak | 1,267,525 | 117 | Camilo Villegas (COL) | 709,677 |
| 28 | Graeme McDowell (NIR) | 2,174,595 | 71 | Freddie Jacobson (SWE) | 1,236,722 | 118 | Steven Bowditch (AUS) | 697,775 |
| 29 | Roberto Castro | 2,154,898 | 72 | Brian Davis (ENG) | 1,221,524 | 119 | Justin Leonard | 694,139 |
| 30 | Jimmy Walker | 2,117,570 | 73 | Matt Every | 1,188,867 | 120 | John Senden (AUS) | 667,027 |
| 31 | Lee Westwood (ENG) | 2,081,731 | 74 | Ernie Els (RSA) | 1,173,761 | 121 | Charlie Wi (KOR) | 656,672 |
| 32 | Jonas Blixt (SWE) | 2,027,517 | 75 | David Hearn (CAN) | 1,171,515 | 122 | Erik Compton | 651,660 |
| 33 | Russell Henley | 2,008,026 | 76 | John Rollins | 1,164,049 | 123 | David Toms | 646,161 |
| 34 | John Merrick | 1,969,478 | 77 | Robert Garrigus | 1,132,355 | 124 | Greg Chalmers (AUS) | 632,283 |
| 35 | Patrick Reed | 1,961,519 | 78 | Stewart Cink | 1,052,712 | 125 | Peter Hanson (SWE) | 610,178 |
| 36 | Luke Donald (ENG) | 1,930,646 | 79 | Brian Stuard | 1,032,028 | | | |
| 37 | Gary Woodland | 1,915,732 | 80 | Jeff Maggert | 1,022,331 | 126 | Chez Reavie | 590,925 |
| 38 | Charles Howell III | 1,877,389 | 81 | Scott Brown | 1,012,142 | 127 | Scott Langley | 590,684 |
| 39 | Scott Piercy | 1,830,084 | 82 | Brendan Steele | 1,004,161 | 128 | Gonzalo Fernandez-Castano (ESP) | 589,653 |
| 40 | Rickie Fowler | 1,816,742 | 83 | Luke Guthrie | 991,902 | | | |
| | | | 84 | Pat Perez | 974,800 | 129 | Fabian Gomez (ARG) | 586,942 |
| 41 | Rory McIlroy (NIR) | 1,802,443 | 85 | K J Choi (KOR) | 973,751 | 130 | Woody Austin | 568,800 |
| 42 | Brendon de Jonge (RSA) | 1,795,244 | 86 | Cameron Tringale | 971,209 | | | |
| 43 | Angel Cabrera (ARG) | 1,791,183 | 87 | Nicholas Thompson | 959,434 | | | |
| | | | 88 | Bo Van Pelt | 956,629 | | | |
| | | | 89 | Richard Lee | 920,836 | | | |
| | | | 90 | Charlie Beljan | 916,229 | | | |

# Career Money List (at end of 2013 season)

| | | | | | | |
|---|---|---|---|---|---|---|
| 1 | Tiger Woods | $109,504,139 | | 51 | Jeff Sluman | 18,165,266 |
| 2 | Phil Mickelson | 73,140,492 | | 52 | Steve Flesch | 18,107,004 |
| 3 | Vijay Singh (FIJ) | 67,587,095 | | 53 | John Rollins | 17,808,284 |
| 4 | Jim Furyk | 55,924,238 | | 54 | Ben Crane | 17,776,774 |
| 5 | Ernie Els (RSA) | 45,945,170 | | 55 | Brad Faxon | 17,769,249 |
| 6 | Davis Love III | 42,511,946 | | 56 | Bill Haas | 17,574,956 |
| 7 | Steve Stricker | 39,520,093 | | 57 | Brian Gay | 17,189,998 |
| 8 | David Toms | 39,511,939 | | 58 | Sean O'Hair | 16,973,027 |
| 9 | Adam Scott (AUS) | 33,199,065 | | 59 | Jonathan Byrd | 16,914,303 |
| 10 | Sergio García (ESP) | 32,833,713 | | 60 | Rocco Mediate | 16,792,617 |
| 11 | Justin Leonard | 32,555,538 | | 61 | Woody Austin | 16,259,534 |
| 12 | Stewart Cink | 31,889,707 | | 62 | Aaron Baddeley (AUS) | 16,034,935 |
| 13 | Kenny Perry | 31,850,152 | | 63 | Corey Pavin | 16,021,370 |
| 14 | Luke Donald (ENG) | 30,791,079 | | 64 | John Senden (AUS) | 16,011,164 |
| 15 | Zach Johnson | 30,321,802 | | 65 | Lee Janzen | 15,933,193 |
| 16 | K J Choi (KOR) | 28,347,605 | | 66 | Bob Tway | 15,785,815 |
| 17 | Retief Goosen (RSA) | 27,841,344 | | 67 | Lee Westwood (ENG) | 15,726,139 |
| 18 | Scott Verplank | 27,463,847 | | 68 | Lucas Glover | 15,722,797 |
| 19 | Stuart Appleby (AUS) | 27,296,190 | | 69 | Kevin Sutherland | 15,658,171 |
| 20 | Mike Weir (CAN) | 27,016,460 | | 70 | Jason Dufner | 15,578,277 |
| 21 | Rory Sabbatini (RSA) | 26,792,660 | | 71 | Camilo Villegas (COL) | 15,559,825 |
| 22 | Geoff Ogilvy (AUS) | 26,631,077 | | 72 | Steve Elkington | 15,505,418 |
| 23 | Robert Allenby (AUS) | 26,613,093 | | 73 | Ryan Moore | 15,467,978 |
| 24 | Matt Kuchar | 26,416,027 | | 74 | Jesper Parnevik (SWE) | 15,314,382 |
| 25 | Charles Howell III | 25,625,971 | | 75 | Hal Sutton | 15,267,685 |
| 26 | Justin Rose (ENG) | 25,277,765 | | 76 | Heath Slocum | 15,215,556 |
| 27 | Hunter Mahan | 24,759,057 | | 77 | Rory McIlroy (NIR) | 15,160,003 |
| 28 | Jerry Kelly | 24,677,570 | | 78 | Loren Roberts | 15,154,767 |
| 29 | Mark Calcavecchia | 24,147,827 | | 79 | Steve Lowery | 15,121,961 |
| 30 | Chris DiMarco | 22,650,073 | | 80 | Webb Simpson | 15,002,789 |
| 31 | Fred Couples | 22,494,714 | | 81 | John Huston | 14,967,146 |
| 32 | Padraig Harrington (IRL) | 22,357,058 | | 82 | Tom Pernice Jr | 14,950,594 |
| 33 | Chad Campbell | 21,791,877 | | 83 | Henrik Stenson (SWE) | 14,512,285 |
| 34 | Tom Lehman | 21,495,878 | | 84 | Greg Norman (AUS) | 14,484,458 |
| 35 | Brandt Snedeker | 21,416,311 | | 85 | Paul Azinger | 14,467,496 |
| 36 | Bob Estes | 21,380,179 | | 86 | Jay Haas | 14,440,317 |
| 37 | Nick Watney | 21,209,914 | | 87 | Ian Poulter (ENG) | 14,344,097 |
| 38 | Fred Funk | 21,097,907 | | 88 | Freddie Jacobson (SWE) | 14,313,825 |
| 39 | Tim Clark (RSA) | 20,737,477 | | 89 | Ryan Palmer | 14,256,514 |
| 40 | Nick Price (ZIM) | 20,576,104 | | 90 | Mark O'Meara | 14,189,882 |
| 41 | Billy Mayfair | 20,212,093 | | 91 | Pat Perez | 14,167,574 |
| 42 | Dustin Johnson | 19,907,913 | | 92 | Kirk Triplett | 14,096,656 |
| 43 | Carl Pettersson (SWE) | 19,878,666 | | 93 | Mark Wilson | 13,895,879 |
| 44 | Stephen Ames (CAN) | 19,569,404 | | 94 | Jason Day (AUS) | 13,828,356 |
| 45 | Jeff Maggert | 19,004,409 | | 95 | Joe Durant | 13,812,426 |
| 46 | David Duval | 18,852,383 | | 96 | Shigeki Maruyama (JPN) | 13,809,170 |
| 47 | Bo Van Pelt | 18,848,667 | | 97 | Rod Pampling (AUS) | 13,710,763 |
| 48 | Bubba Watson | 18,718,918 | | 98 | J J Henry | 13,553,776 |
| 49 | Tim Herron | 18,568,711 | | 99 | Kevin Na | 13,264,601 |
| 50 | Scott Hoch | 18,530,156 | | 100 | Ben Curtis | 13,082,685 |

# 2013 Tour Statistics

## Driving accuracy
(Percentage of fairways hit in regulation)

| Pos | Name | Rds | % |
| --- | --- | --- | --- |
| 1 | Jerry Kelly | 75 | 71.81 |
| 2 | Mark Wilson | 56 | 70.74 |
| 3 | Steve Stricker | 51 | 70.65 |
| 4 | Jim Furyk | 80 | 70.47 |
| 5 | Tim Clark | 64 | 70.31 |
| 6 | Chez Reavie | 72 | 70.29 |
| 7 | Henrik Stenson | 65 | 70.09 |
| 8 | Zach Johnson | 84 | 69.68 |
| 9 | Justin Hicks | 79 | 69.61 |
| 10 | Ken Duke | 87 | 69.28 |

## Greens in regulation

| Pos | Name | Rds | % |
| --- | --- | --- | --- |
| 1 | Henrik Stenson (SWE) | 65 | 71.96 |
| 2 | Steve Stricker | 51 | 71.16 |
| 3 | Graham DeLaet (CAN) | 94 | 70.51 |
| 4 | Ricky Barnes | 74 | 70.48 |
| 5 | Bubba Watson | 76 | 69.41 |
| 6 | Boo Weekley | 100 | 69.39 |
| 7 | Vijay Singh (FIJ) | 61 | 69.13 |
| 8 | Kevin Stadler | 83 | 68.92 |
| 9 | Justin Rose (ENG) | 62 | 68.89 |
| 10 | Brendon de Jonge (ZIM) | 110 | 68.84 |

## Driving distance (Average yards per drive)

| Pos | Name | Rds | Yds |
| --- | --- | --- | --- |
| 1 | Phil Mickelson | 78 | 450 |
| 2 | Kyle Stanley | 71 | 428 |
| 3 | Ian Poulter (ENG) | 59 | 426 |
| 4 | Graham DeLaet (CAN) | 94 | 420 |
| 5 | Charlie Beljan | 62 | 418 |
| 6 | Carl Pettersson (SWE) | 82 | 416 |
| 7 | Stewart Cink | 71 | 415 |
| 8 | Gary Woodland | 94 | 411 |
| 9 | Dustin Johnson | 71 | 410 |
| 10 | Scott Piercy | 78 | 409 |

## Putting averages (Average per round)

| Pos | Name | Rds | Avg |
| --- | --- | --- | --- |
| 1 | Phil Mickelson | 78 | 1.718 |
| 2 | David Hearn (CAN) | 88 | 1.724 |
| 3 | Aaron Baddeley (AUS) | 68 | 1.727 |
| 4 | Greg Chalmers (AUS) | 77 | 1.731 |
| | Bryce Molder | 82 | 1.731 |
| | Steve Stricker | 51 | 1.731 |
| 7 | Chris Kirk | 89 | 1.733 |
| | Charlie Wi (KOR) | 75 | 1.733 |
| 9 | Brandt Snedeker | 79 | 1.734 |
| | Jordan Spieth | 82 | 1.734 |

## Sand saves

| Pos | Name | Rds | % |
| --- | --- | --- | --- |
| 1 | K.J. Choi | 85 | 67.18 |
| 2 | Steven Bowditch (AUS) | 67 | 64.91 |
| 3 | Matt Kuchar | 93 | 64.90 |
| 4 | Lee Williams | 62 | 63.64 |
| 5 | Casey Wittenberg | 72 | 63.30 |

| Pos | Name | Rds | % |
| --- | --- | --- | --- |
| 6 | Ben Crane | 62 | 63.11 |
| 7 | Tom Gillis | 69 | 62.61 |
| 8 | Kevin Chappell | 80 | 61.74 |
| 9 | Stuart Appleby (AUS) | 88 | 61.72 |
| 10 | Cameron Tringale | 80 | 61.47 |

## Scoring averages

| Pos | Name | Rds | Avg |
| --- | --- | --- | --- |
| 1 | Steve Stricker | 51 | 68.945 |
| 2 | Tiger Woods | 61 | 68.985 |
| 3 | Justin Rose (ENG) | 62 | 69.266 |
| 4 | Henrik Stenson (SWE) | 65 | 69.287 |
| 5 | Adam Scott (AUS) | 61 | 69.341 |
| 6 | Sergio García (ESP) | 65 | 69.583 |
| 7 | Matt Kuchar | 93 | 69.589 |
| 8 | Charl Schwartzel (RSA) | 69 | 69.687 |
| 9 | Jordan Spieth | 82 | 69.698 |
| 10 | Keegan Bradley | 88 | 69.752 |

| Pos | Name | Rds | Avg |
| --- | --- | --- | --- |
| 11 | Jason Day (AUS) | 86 | 69.763 |
| 12 | Phil Mickelson | 78 | 69.773 |
| 13 | Webb Simpson | 92 | 69.811 |
| 14 | Brandt Snedeker | 79 | 69.822 |
| 15 | Luke Donald (ENG) | 60 | 69.836 |
| 16 | Jim Furyk | 80 | 69.859 |
| 17 | Jason Dufner | 78 | 69.944 |
| 18 | Bill Haas | 85 | 70.052 |
| 19 | Zach Johnson | 84 | 70.103 |
| 20 | Freddie Jacobson (SWE) | 63 | 70.108 |

# Jim Furyk joins the élite 59 club

Ryder Cup star Jim Furyk kept his nerve to become the sixth person on the PGA Tour in America to shoot a 59. He made his score on the second day of the BMW Championship at the Conway Farms Country Club in Lake Forest, Illinois, but did not go on to win the event. Zach Johnson beat him by three over four rounds.

Furyk began on the back nine and helped by six birdies and an eagle was 11-under-par through 13 holes and rounded it all off with three foot birdie at his last hole. He never missed a fairway, hit all but one green in regulation and needed only 23 putts.

Al Geiberger was the first to shoot a 59 in the second round of the Danny Thomas Memphis Classic which he went on to win. The special six – five Americans and one Australian are:

| 1977 | Al Geiberger | Danny Thomas Memphis Classic | −13 | 1st |
| 1991 | Chip Beck | Las Vegas Invitational | −13 | 3rd |
| 1999 | David Duval | Bob Hope Chrysler Classic | −13 | 1st |
| 2010 | Paul Goydos | John Deere Classic | −12 | 2nd |
| 2010 | Stuart Appleby | Greenbrier Classic | −11 | 1st |
| 2013 | Jim Furyk | BMW Championship | −12 | 3rd |

# New China Golf Tour planned

The China Golf Association has joined up with the PGA Tour and event promoter China Olympic Sports Industry to established a new professional golf tour in China that begins with 12 tournaments being played throughout the country this year.

PGA Tour China is also open to professionals outside of China. Fields are expected to be between 120 and 156 players and purses will be in the $200,000 range per tournament. Plans are to increase the number of events after the first year.

"We are very pleased to announce the establishment of PGA Tour China, which builds upon our longstanding relationship with the China Golf Association," PGA Tour Commissioner Tim Finchem said. "As with the structure of NEC Series–PGA Tour Latinoamérica and PGA Tour Canada, PGA Tour China will provide open competition on a quality tour for élite players from China and other countries and the opportunity to advance to the world stage. Also similar to those two Tours, we plan to provide access to the Web.com Tour for the season's top players."

The initial schedule and further details, such as specifics on Web.com Tour qualifying, were to be announced at a later date.

"We have seen great advancement of Chinese élite golfer development in the last few years, and the creation of this Tour is the next positive step forward for this sport in China," Zhang Xiaoning, Secretary General of the China Golf Association, said. "This will raise the level of golf in China even further and prepare players from China to participate in the Olympics and other significant global competitions."

The PGA Tour will be involved in all aspects of the Tour's operations and work with COSI, a division of the China Sports Industry Group, on bringing sponsors to the Tour. COSI has extensive knowledge and experience in promoting global-quality events.

"We are excited to be a part of this major milestone for golf in China," said Sun Liping, President of COSI. "This is the start of a Tour that will continue to grow within China in the short- and long-term."

The Tour has multiple existing broadcast partners in China and a digital partnership with SINA Corporation. A retail licensing agreement has established nearly 40 PGA Tour-branded stores in China, with more planned. Additionally, earlier this year, the Tour and Bose Corporation announced a sponsorship agreement for category rights in China, marking the first official corporate sponsorship the Tour has made specific to China.

# US PGA Tour top 20

MC  Missed cut        — Did not play

Players are of US nationality unless stated otherwise

| | Hyundai Tournament | Sony Open | Humana Challenge | Farmers Insurance Open | Phoenix Open | AT&T Pebble Beach | Northern Trust Open | WGC-Accenture C/ship | The Honda Classic | WGC-Cadillac C/ship | Puerto Rico Open | Tampa Bay Championship | Arnold Palmer Invitational | Shell Houston Open | Valero Texas Open |
|---|---|---|---|---|---|---|---|---|---|---|---|---|---|---|---|
| 1 Tiger Woods | — | — | — | 1 | — | — | — | T33 | T37 | 1 | — | — | 1 | — | — |
| 2 Henrik Stenson (SWE) | — | — | — | — | — | — | — | T33 | MC | — | T39 | — | T8 | T2 | — |
| 3 Matt Kuchar | T9 | T5 | T16 | — | — | — | T38 | 1 | — | T35 | — | T14 | — | — | T22 |
| 4 Phil Mickelson | — | — | T37 | T51 | 1 | T60 | T21 | — | — | T3 | — | — | MC | T16 | — |
| 5 Brandt Snedeker | 3 | — | T23 | T2 | 2 | 1 | — | — | — | — | — | — | MC | MC | — |
| 6 Adam Scott (AUS) | — | — | — | — | — | — | T10 | T33 | — | T3 | — | T30 | — | — | — |
| 7 Steve Stricker | 2 | — | — | — | — | — | — | T5 | — | 2 | — | — | — | T38 | — |
| 8 Justin Rose (ENG) | — | — | — | — | — | — | — | T17 | T4 | T8 | — | — | 2 | — | — |
| 9 Zach Johnson | T18 | MC | T23 | — | — | — | MC | T33 | — | T47 | — | MC | T34 | — | — |
| 10 Jordan Spieth | — | — | — | MC | — | T22 | — | — | — | — | T2 | T7 | — | T50 | MC |
| 11 Keegan Bradley | T4 | T49 | — | MC | T24 | — | T16 | T33 | T4 | 7 | — | — | T3 | T10 | — |
| 12 Jason Day (AUS) | — | — | — | T9 | T57 | 6 | — | 3 | — | T33 | — | T43 | T45 | — | — |
| 13 Billy Horschel | — | T54 | T10 | T39 | T11 | T28 | — | — | T46 | — | — | T56 | 75 | T2 | T3 |
| 14 Bill Haas | T23 | — | MC | T9 | T6 | — | T3 | T33 | — | T43 | — | — | T8 | T10 | — |
| 15 Jim Furyk | — | — | — | — | — | T30 | T13 | T17 | — | T35 | — | T7 | T65 | — | T3 |
| 16 Jason Dufner | T18 | — | — | MC | — | — | — | T33 | T51 | T12 | — | T21 | — | MC | — |
| 17 Kevin Streelman | — | T26 | T10 | — | MC | T40 | T27 | — | T41 | — | MC | 1 | T21 | — | — |
| 18 Hunter Mahan | T26 | — | — | T15 | T16 | T16 | T8 | 2 | — | T25 | — | — | T21 | MC | — |
| 19 Dustin Johnson | 1 | WD | — | T51 | — | MC | MC | T33 | T46 | T12 | — | — | — | T4 | — |
| 20 Webb Simpson | T11 | T20 | MC | — | — | T26 | T6 | T5 | — | T20 | — | T17 | MC | — | — |

# 2013 performances at a glance

\* Involved in play-off    WD Withdrew

| | The Masters | RBC Heritage | Zurich Classic | Wells Fargo C/ship | The Players C/ship | Byron Nelson C/ship | Crowne Plaza Invitational | Memorial Tournament | Fedex St Jude Classic | US Open Championship | Travelers Championship | AT&T National | Greenbrier Classic | John Deere Classic | Sanderson Farms C/ship | The Open Championship | RBC Canadian Open | WGC– Bridgestone Inv. | Reno-Tahoe Open | US PGA Championship | Wyndham Championship | The Barclays | Deutsche Bank C/ship | BMW Championship | Tour Championship |
|---|---|---|---|---|---|---|---|---|---|---|---|---|---|---|---|---|---|---|---|---|---|---|---|---|---|
| | T4 | — | — | — | I | — | — | T65 | — | T32 | — | — | — | — | — | T6 | — | I | — | T40 | — | T2 | T65 | T11 | T22 |
| | T18 | — | — | MC | T5 | — | T35 | T41 | — | T21 | — | — | — | — | — | 2 | — | T2 | — | 3 | — | T43 | I | T33 | I |
| | T8 | T35 | — | — | T48 | T33 | 2 | I | — | T28 | — | — | — | — | — | T15 | T2 | T27 | — | T22 | — | T19 | T4 | T24 | T26 |
| | T54 | — | — | 3 | MC | — | — | — | 2 | T2 | — | — | MC | — | — | I | — | T21 | — | T72 | — | T6 | T41 | T33 | T12 |
| | T6 | T59 | — | — | T8 | — | — | MC | MC | T17 | — | T8 | — | — | — | T11 | I | T33 | — | T66 | MC | MC | T47 | T8 | T20 |
| | I* | — | — | — | T19 | — | — | T13 | — | T45 | — | T57 | — | — | — | T3 | — | T14 | — | T5 | — | I | T53 | T28 | T14 |
| | T20 | — | — | T37 | — | — | — | — | T8 | — | — | — | T10 | — | — | — | 13 | — | — | T12 | — | — | 2 | T4 | T2 |
| | T25 | — | T15 | — | MC | — | — | T8 | — | I | T13 | — | — | — | — | MC | — | T17 | — | T33 | — | T2 | T16 | T33 | 6 |
| | T35 | T48 | — | T65 | T19 | — | 3 | 71 | — | MC | T58 | — | — | T2* | — | T6 | — | T4 | — | T8 | T5 | — | T27 | I | T7 |
| | — | T9 | MC | T32 | — | T68 | T7 | T63 | — | MC | — | 6 | T23 | I* | — | T44 | — | — | — | MC | 2* | T19 | T4 | T16 | T2 |
| | T54 | — | MC | — | MC | 2 | — | T50 | — | MC | T18 | — | — | T61 | — | T15 | — | T2 | — | T19 | — | T33 | T16 | T16 | T12 |
| | 3 | T30 | — | — | T19 | T27 | — | T41 | — | 2 | — | T21 | — | — | — | T22 | — | T53 | — | T8 | — | T25 | T13 | T4 | T14 |
| | — | T9 | I | — | MC | — | — | T41 | T10 | T4 | — | T61 | T30 | — | — | MC | T68 | T44 | — | MC | — | MC | T70 | T18 | T7 |
| | T20 | T24 | — | MC | MC | — | — | T4 | — | MC | — | I | T9 | — | — | MC | — | T7 | — | T25 | T20 | T25 | MC | T28 | T24 |
| | T25 | T42 | — | — | MC | — | T31 | T21 | — | MC | — | T44 | — | — | — | MC | T9 | T9 | — | 2 | — | T6 | T27 | 3 | T14 |
| | T20 | T35 | T42 | — | T62 | T33 | T46 | — | — | T4 | MC | — | — | — | — | T26 | — | T4 | — | I | — | T37 | T9 | T54 | T9 |
| | MC | T3 | — | T6 | T2 | — | MC | MC | — | MC | MC | — | — | T44 | — | T79 | — | T59 | — | T12 | — | T19 | T41 | T33 | T24 |
| | MC | 91 | — | T73 | T19 | — | T26 | T16 | — | T4 | T24 | MC | — | — | — | T9 | WD | — | — | T57 | — | T25 | T13 | T4 | T20 |
| | T13 | — | — | WD | — | — | — | MC | T10 | 55 | — | — | — | — | — | T32 | T2 | T33 | — | T8 | — | MC | T27 | T62 | 5 |
| | MC | 2 | — | T32 | T15 | — | — | MC | — | T32 | T5 | — | T41 | — | — | T64 | — | T14 | — | T25 | T11 | T15 | T53 | T24 | 4 |

# Tour Results 2013 (in chronological order)

*Players are of US nationality unless stated*

## Hyundai Tournament of Champions *Plantation Course, Kapalua, HI*   Jan 4–7   [7411–73]
| | | | |
|---|---|---|---|
| 1 | Dustin Johnson | 69-66-68—203 | $1,140,000 |
| 2 | Steve Stricker | 71-67-69—207 | 665,000 |
| 3 | Brandt Snedeker | 70-70-69—209 | 432,000 |

*Reduced to three rounds due to bad weather*

## Sony Open in Hawaii *Waialae CC, Honolulu, HI*   Jan 10–13   [7068–70]
| | | | |
|---|---|---|---|
| 1 | Russell Henley | 63-63-67-63—256 | $1,008,000 |
| 2 | Tim Clark (RSA) | 64-66-66-63—259 | 604,800 |
| 3 | Charles Howell III | 66-64-67-66—263 | 324,800 |
| | Scott Langley | 62-66-65-70—263 | 324,800 |

## Humana Challenge *PGA West (Palmer course), La Quinta, CA*   Jan 17–20   [6950–72]
| | | | |
|---|---|---|---|
| 1 | Brian Gay* | 67-66-67-63—263 | $1,008,000 |
| 2 | David Lingmerth | 68-64-69-62—263 | 492,800 |
| | Charles Howell III | 67-65-67-64—263 | 492,800 |

*\*Gay won at the second extra hole*

## Farmers Insurance Open *Torrey Pines (South course), La Jolla, CA*   Jan 24–27   [7569–72]
| | | | |
|---|---|---|---|
| 1 | Tiger Woods | 68-65-69-72—274 | $1,098,000 |
| 2 | Brandt Snedeker | 65-75-69-69—278 | 536,800 |
| | Josh Teater | 66-70-73-69—278 | 536,800 |

## Waste Management Phoenix Open *TPC Scottsdale, AZ*   Jan 31–Feb 3   [7216–71]
| | | | |
|---|---|---|---|
| 1 | Phil Mickelson | 60-65-64-67—256 | $1,116,000 |
| 2 | Brandt Snedeker | 64-66-65-65—260 | 669,600 |
| 3 | Scott Piercy | 70-66-64-61—261 | 421,600 |

## AT&T Pebble Beach National Pro-Am *Pebble Beach, CA*   Feb 7–10   [6816–72]
| | | | |
|---|---|---|---|
| 1 | Brandt Snedeker | 66-68-68-65—267 | $1,170,000 |
| 2 | Chris Kirk | 71-68-64-66—269 | 702,000 |
| 3 | James Hahn | 71-65-66-70—272 | 338,000 |
| | Kevin Stadler | 69-69-69-65—272 | 338,000 |
| | Jimmy Walker | 68-71-67-66—272 | 338,000 |

## Northern Trust Open *Riviera CC, Pacific Palisades, CA*   Feb 14–17   [7298–71]
| | | | |
|---|---|---|---|
| 1 | John Merrick* | 68-66-70-69—273 | $1,188,000 |

*\*Merrick won at the second extra hole*

| | | | |
|---|---|---|---|
| 2 | Charlie Beljan | 67-71-68-67—273 | 712,800 |
| 3 | Fredrik Jacobson (SWE) | 68-65-72-69—274 | 343,200 |
| | Bill Haas | 70-67-64-73—274 | 343,200 |
| | Charl Schwartzel (RSA) | 69-67-68-70—274 | 343,200 |

## WGC – Accenture Match Play Championship *Ritz-Carlton, Dove Mountain, AZ*
Feb 20–23   [7791–72]
| | | |
|---|---|---|
| Winner: | Matt Kuchar | $1,500,000 |
| Runner-up: | Hunter Mahan | 875,000 |
| Third place: | Jason Day (AUS) | 615,000 |

Full details of this event can be found on page 206

## Honda Classic *Palm Beach Gardens, FL*   Feb 28–Mar 3   [7158–70]

| | | | |
|---|---|---|---|
| 1 | Michael Thompson | 67-65-70-69—271 | $1,080,000 |
| 2 | Geoff Ogilvy (AUS) | 68-66-70-69—273 | 648,000 |
| 3 | Luke Guthrie | 68-63-71-73—275 | 408,000 |

## Puerto Rico Open *Rio Grande, Puerto Rico*   Mar 7–10   [7569–72]

| | | | |
|---|---|---|---|
| 1 | Scott Brown | 68-63-67-70—268 | $630,000 |
| 2 | Jordan Spieth | 69-66-67-67—269 | 308,000 |
| | Fabian Gomez (ARG) | 69-64-65-71—269 | 308,000 |

## WGC – Cadillac Championship *Doral, Orlando, FL*   Mar 7–10   [7334–72]

| | | | |
|---|---|---|---|
| 1 | Tiger Woods | 66-65-67-71—269 | $1,500,000 |
| 2 | Steve Stricker | 67-67-69-68—271 | 880,000 |
| 3 | Adam Scott (AUS) | 72-70-68-64—274 | 417,500 |
| | Sergio García (ESP) | 66-72-67-69—274 | 417,500 |
| | Phil Mickelson | 67-67-69-71—274 | 417,500 |
| | Graeme McDowell (NIR) | 66-67-69-72—274 | 417,500 |

Full details of this event can be found on page 207

## Tampa Bay Championship *Innisbrook, Copperhead, Palm Harbor, FL*   Mar 14–17   [7340-71]

| | | | |
|---|---|---|---|
| 1 | Kevin Streelman | 73-69-65-67—274 | $990,000 |
| 2 | Boo Weekley | 72-70-71-63—276 | 594,000 |
| 3 | Cameron Tringale | 71-70-70-66—277 | 374,000 |

## Arnold Palmer Invitational *Bay Hill, Orlando, FL*   Mar 21–24   [7381–72]

| | | | |
|---|---|---|---|
| 1 | Tiger Woods | 69-70-66-70—275 | $1,116,000 |
| 2 | Justin Rose (ENG) | 65-70-72-70—277 | 669,600 |
| 3 | Mark Wilson | 71-68-70-71—280 | 297,600 |
| | Keegan Bradley | 74-69-66-71—280 | 297,600 |
| | Gonzalo Fernandez-Castano (ESP) | 69-71-68-72—280 | 297,600 |
| | Rickie Fowler | 73-67-67-73—280 | 297,600 |

## Tavistock Cup *Isleworth G&CC, Windermere, FL*   Mar 25–26   [7442–72]

| | | | |
|---|---|---|---|
| 1 | Albany – Tim Clark (RSA), Ian Poulter (ENG), | | |
| | Justin Rose (ENG), Tiger Woods* | +7 | |
| 2 | Lake Nona – Ross Fisher (ENG), Peter Hanson (SWE), | | |
| | Graeme McDowell (NIR), Henrik Stenson (SWE) | +7 | |

*Poulter and Woods beat McDowell and Stenson in the best-ball playoff*

| | | | |
|---|---|---|---|
| 3 | Primland – Fred Couples, Bill Haas, Jay Haas, Webb Simpson | +8 | |

## Shell Houston Open *Redstone, Humble, TX*   Mar 28–31   [7457–72]

| | | | |
|---|---|---|---|
| 1 | DA Points | 64-71-71-66—272 | $1,116,000 |
| 2 | Henrik Stenson (SWE) | 69-70-68-66—273 | 545,600 |
| | Billy Horschel | 68-72-67-66—273 | 545,600 |

## Valero Texas Open *San Antonio, TX*   April 4–7   [7522–72]

| | | | |
|---|---|---|---|
| 1 | Martin Laird (SCO) | 70-71-70-63—274 | $1,116,000 |
| 2 | Rory McIlroy (NIR) | 72-67-71-66—276 | 669,600 |
| 3 | Billy Horschel | 68-68-70-71—277 | 322,400 |
| | Jim Furyk | 69-70-69-69—277 | 322,400 |
| | Charley Hoffman | 71-67-70-69—277 | 322,400 |

## THE MASTERS Augusta National, GA    April 11–13      [7435–72]

| | | | |
|---|---|---|---|
| 1 | Adam Scott (AUS)* | 69-72-69-69—279 | $1,440,000 |
| 2 | Angel Cabrera (ARG) | 71-69-69-70—279 | 864,000 |

*Scott won at the second extra hole

| | | | |
|---|---|---|---|
| 3 | Jason Day (AUS) | 70-68-73-70—281 | 544,000 |

Full details of this event can be found on page 82

## RBC Heritage Harbour Town Golf Links, Hilton Head Island, SC    April 18–21      [7101–71]

| | | | |
|---|---|---|---|
| 1 | Graeme McDowell (NIR) | 71-67-68-69—275 | $1,044,000 |
| 2 | Webb Simpson | 68-71-65-71—275 | 626,400 |
| 3 | Luke Donald (ENG) | 69-68-71-69—277 | 336,400 |
| | Kevin Streelman | 66-70-69-72—277 | 336,400 |

## Zurich Classic of New Orleans TPC Louisiana, Avondale, LA    April 25–28      [7341–72]

| | | | |
|---|---|---|---|
| 1 | Billy Horschel | 67-71-66-64—268 | $1,188,000 |
| 2 | DA Points | 66-68-70-65—269 | 712,800 |
| | Kyle Stanley | 72-67-65-67—271 | 448,800 |

## Wells Fargo Championship Quail Hollow, Charlotte, NC    May 2–5      [7442–72]

| | | | |
|---|---|---|---|
| 1 | Derek Ernst* | 67-71-72-70—280 | $1,206,000 |
| 2 | David Lynn (ENG) | 71-68-71-70—280 | 723,600 |

*Ernst won at the first extra hole

| | | | |
|---|---|---|---|
| 3 | Phil Mickelson | 68-67-73-73—281 | 455,600 |

## The Players Championship TPC, Sawgrass, Ponte Vedra Beach, FL    May 9–12      [7215-72]

| | | | |
|---|---|---|---|
| 1 | Tiger Woods | 67-67-71-70—275 | $1,710,000 |
| 2 | Kevin Streelman | 69-70-71-67—277 | 709,333 |
| | Jeff Maggert | 70-71-66-70—277 | 709,333 |
| | David Lingmerth (SWE) | 68-68-69-72—277 | 709,333 |
| 5 | Martin Laird (SCO) | 71-67-73-67—278 | 346,750 |
| | Henrik Stenson (SWE) | 68-67-71-72—278 | 346,750 |
| | Ryan Palmer | 67-69-70-72—278 | 346,750 |
| 8 | Ben Crane | 69-71-72-69—281 | 237,500 |
| | Rory McIlroy (NIR) | 66-72-73-70—281 | 237,500 |
| | Brandt Snedeker | 71-69-71-70—281 | 237,500 |
| | Marc Leishman (AUS) | 72-66-71-72—281 | 237,500 |
| | Lee Westwood (ENG) | 69-66-74-72—281 | 237,500 |
| | Casey Wittenberg | 67-69-70-75—281 | 237,500 |
| | Sergio García (ESP) | 68-65-72-76—281 | 237,500 |
| 15 | Jimmy Walker | 72-71-72-67—282 | 156,750 |
| | Tim Herron | 71-69-74-68—282 | 156,750 |
| | Webb Simpson | 67-71-74-70—282 | 156,750 |
| | Brendon de Jonge (RSA) | 72-69-70-71—282 | 156,750 |
| 19 | Jason Day (AUS) | 69-75-71-68—283 | 107,214 |
| | Luke Donald (ENG) | 72-69-73-69—283 | 107,214 |
| | Zach Johnson | 66-71-76-70—283 | 107,214 |
| | Adam Scott (AUS) | 69-68-75-71—283 | 107,214 |
| | Roberto Castro | 63-78-71-71—283 | 107,214 |
| | Louis Oosthuizen (RSA) | 69-75-67-72—283 | 107,214 |
| | Hunter Mahan | 67-70-71-75—283 | 107,214 |
| 26 | Graham DeLaet (CAN) | 71-70-74-69—284 | 67,450 |
| | David Hearn (CAN) | 72-71-71-70—284 | 67,450 |
| | James Driscoll | 75-68-70-71—284 | 67,450 |
| | Matt Every | 70-71-71-72—284 | 67,450 |
| | Daniel Summerhays | 69-74-69-72—284 | 67,450 |
| | Jeff Overton | 71-70-69-74—284 | 67,450 |
| | David Lynn (ENG) | 72-68-68-76—284 | 67,450 |
| 33 | Sang-Moon Bae (KOR) | 68-71-75-71—285 | 52,487 |

| 33T | Harris English | 70-71-73-71—285 | 52,487 |
| | Chris Stroud | 73-69-69-74—285 | 52,487 |
| | Kyle Stanley | 75-68-68-74—285 | 52,487 |
| 37 | Charley Hoffman | 70-74-71-71—286 | 41,800 |
| | Bubba Watson | 73-70-70-73—286 | 41,800 |
| | Jerry Kelly | 71-68-73-74—286 | 41,800 |
| | Andres Romero (ARG) | 69-72-71-74—286 | 41,800 |
| | Steve Stricker | 67-71-72-76—286 | 41,800 |
| | Greg Chalmers (AUS) | 68-73-68-77—286 | 41,800 |
| 43 | Martin Kaymer (GER) | 73-69-76-69—287 | 31,350 |
| | Chad Campbell | 71-72-74-70—287 | 31,350 |
| | John Senden (AUS) | 73-70-71-73—287 | 31,350 |
| | William McGirt | 70-74-70-73—287 | 31,350 |
| | Sean O'Hair | 70-71-69-77—287 | 31,350 |
| 48 | DA Points | 72-70-77-69—288 | 23,614 |
| | KJ Choi (KOR) | 69-73-74-72—288 | 23,614 |
| | Boo Weekley | 71-71-73-73—288 | 23,614 |
| | Freddie Jacobson (SWE) | 72-71-71-74—288 | 23,614 |
| | Matt Kuchar | 71-66-75-76—288 | 23,614 |
| | Davis Love III | 70-72-70-76—288 | 23,614 |
| | Branden Grace (RSA) | 73-71-67-77—288 | 23,614 |
| 55 | Charlie Wi (KOR) | 74-70-75-70—289 | 21,280 |
| | Charl Schwartzel (RSA) | 72-71-75-71—289 | 21,280 |
| | Justin Leonard | 70-74-74-71—289 | 21,280 |
| | Jason Bohn | 68-74-75-72—289 | 21,280 |
| | Michael Thompson | 69-75-72-73—289 | 21,280 |
| | Chris Kirk | 70-69-75-75—289 | 21,280 |
| | Angel Cabrera (ARG) | 74-70-69-76—289 | 21,280 |
| 62 | Bo Van Pelt | 69-74-79-68—290 | 20,235 |
| | Josh Teater | 72-72-76-70—290 | 20,235 |
| | James Hahn | 70-74-73-73—290 | 20,235 |
| | Jason Dufner | 71-67-72-80—290 | 20,235 |
| 66 | Seung-Yul Noh (KOR) | 70-74-73-74—291 | 19,665 |
| | Charles Howell III | 71-67-77-76—291 | 19,665 |
| 68 | Carl Pettersson (SWE) | 70-72-75-75—292 | 19,190 |
| | John Huh | 70-72-73-77—292 | 19,190 |
| | Kevin Chappell | 69-66-78-79—292 | 19,190 |
| 71 | Rory Sabbatini (RSA) | 75-68-76-74—293 | 18,810 |
| 72 | Brian Davis (ENG) | 78-66-75-75—294 | 18,430 |
| | Ricky Barnes | 71-71-74-78—294 | 18,430 |
| | Peter Hanson (SWE) | 70-70-72-82—294 | 18,430 |
| 75 | Ben Curtis | 69-72-80-74—295 | 17,955 |
| | Padraig Harrington (IRL) | 68-76-75-76—295 | 17,955 |
| 77 | Jonas Blixt (SWE) | 69-75-77-76—297 | 17,670 |

68 players missed the cut

## HP Byron Nelson Championship TPC Four Seasons, Irving, TX  May 16–19 [7166–70]

| 1 | Sang-Moon Bae (KOR) | 66-66-66-69—267 | $1,206,000 |
| 2 | Keegan Bradley | 60-69-68-72—269 | 723,600 |
| 3 | Charl Schwartzel (RSA) | 63-70-69-68—270 | 455,600 |

## Crowne Plaza Invitational Colonial, Forth Worth, TX  May 23–26 [7204–72]

| 1 | Boo Weekley | 67-67-66-66—266 | $1,152,000 |
| 2 | Matt Kuchar | 65-65-69-68—267 | 691,200 |
| 3 | Zach Johnson | 69-65-68-66—268 | 435,200 |

## Memorial Tournament *Muirfield Village, Dublin, OH*   May 30–June 2                    [7265–72]

| 1 | Matt Kuchar | 68-70-70-68—276 | $1,116,000 |
|---|---|---|---|
| 2 | Kevin Chappell | 71-71-68-68—278 | 669,600 |
| 3 | Kyle Stanley | 67-70-73-71—281 | 421,600 |

## Fedex St Jude Classic *TPC Southwind, Memphis, TN*   June 6–9                    [7244–70]

| 1 | Harris English | 66-64-69-69—268 | $1,026,000 |
|---|---|---|---|
| 2 | Scott Stallings | 67-68-67-68—270 | 501,600 |
|   | Phil Mickelson | 71-67-65-67—270 | 501,600 |

## 112th US OPEN CHAMPIONSHIP *Merion GC, Ardmore, PA*   June 13–16                    [6996–70]

| 1 | Justin Rose (ENG) | 71-69-71-70—281 | $1,440,000 |
|---|---|---|---|
| 2 | Jason Day (AUS) | 70-74-68-71—283 | 696,104 |
|   | Phil Mickelson | 67-72-70-74—283 | 696,104 |

Full details of this event can be found on page 71

## Travelers Championship *River Highlands, Cromwell, CT*   June 20–23                    [6844–70]

| 1 | Ken Duke* | 69-68-65-66—268 | $1,098,000 |
|---|---|---|---|
| 2 | Chris Stroud | 66-69-66-67—268 | 658,800 |
| *Duke won at the second extra hole | | | |
| 3 | Graham DeLaet (CAN) | 65-70-65-69—269 | 414,800 |

## AT&T National *Congressional Country Club, Bethesda, MD*   June 27–30                    [7569–71]

| 1 | Bill Haas | 70-68-68-66—272 | $1,170,000 |
|---|---|---|---|
| 2 | Roberto Castro | 66-69-71-69—275 | 702,000 |
| 3 | D H Lee (KOR) | 71-66-75-64—276 | 377,000 |
|   | Jason Kokrak | 71-66-70-69—276 | 377,000 |

## The Greenbrier Classic *White Sulphur Springs, WV*   July 4–7                    [7287–70]

| 1 | Jonas Blixt (SWE) | 66-67-67-67—267 | $1,134,000 |
|---|---|---|---|
| 2 | Steven Bowditch (AUS) | 65-67-69-68—269 | 415,800 |
|   | Matt Jones (AUS) | 69-66-66-68—269 | 415,800 |
|   | Johnson Wagner | 62-70-64-73—269 | 415,800 |
|   | Jimmy Walker | 69-65-64-71—269 | 415,800 |

## John Deere Classic *TPC Deere Run, Silvis, IL*   July 11–14                    [7257–71]

| 1 | Jordan Spieth* | 70-65-65-65—265 | $828,000 |
|---|---|---|---|
| 2 | Zach Johnson | 64-66-67-68—265 | 404,800 |
|   | David Hearn (CAN) | 66-66-64-69—265 | 404,800 |
| *Spieth won at the fifth extra hole | | | |

## Sanderson Farms Championship *Annandale GC, Madison, MS*   July 18–21                    [7199–72]

| 1 | Woody Austin* | 69-65-67-67—268 | $540,000 |
|---|---|---|---|
| 2 | Cameron Beckman | 72-64-65-67—268 | 264,000 |
|   | Daniel Summerhays | 63-67-69-69—268 | 264,000 |
| *Austin won at the first extra hole | | | |

## 142nd OPEN CHAMPIONSHIP *Muirfield, East Lothian, Scotland*   July 18–21                    [7192–71]

| 1 | Phil Mickelson | 69-74-72-66—281 | $1,400,000 |
|---|---|---|---|
| 2 | Henrik Stenson (SWE) | 70-70-74-70—284 | 826,874 |
| 3 | Ian Poulter (ENG) | 72-71-75-67—285 | 426,080 |
|   | Adam Scott (AUS) | 71-72-70-72—285 | 426,080 |
|   | Lee Westwood (ENG) | 72-68-70-75—285 | 426,080 |

Full details of this event can be found on page 54

## RBC Canadian Open Glen Abbey GC, Oakville, Ontario, Canada   July 25–28 [7253–72]

| | | | |
|---|---|---|---|
| 1 | Brandt Snedeker | 70-69-63-70—272 | $1,008,000 |
| 2 | William McGirt | 71-69-67-68—275 | 369,600 |
| | Dustin Johnson | 75-67-63-70—275 | 369,600 |
| | Matt Kuchar | 66-74-64-71—275 | 369,600 |
| | Jason Bohn | 70-68-66-71—275 | 369,600 |

## Reno-Tahoe Open Montreux G&CC, Reno, NV   Aug 1–4 [7472–72]
Modified Stableford

| | | | |
|---|---|---|---|
| 1 | Gary Woodland | 14-7-16-7—44 | $54,000 |
| 2 | Jonathan Byrd | 2-4-11-18—35 | 264,000 |
| | Andres Romero (ARG) | 8-14-5-8—35 | 264,000 |

## WGC – Bridgestone Invitational Firestone CC, Akron, OH   Aug 1–4 [7400–70]

| | | | |
|---|---|---|---|
| 1 | Tiger Woods | 66-61-68-70—265 | $1,500,000 |
| 2 | Keegan Bradley | 66-68-71-67—272 | 692,500 |
| | Henrik Stenson (SWE) | 65-70-67-70—272 | 692,500 |

Full details of this event can be found on page 208

## US PGA CHAMPIONSHIP Oak Hill CC, Rochester, NY   Aug 8–11 [7163–70]

| | | | |
|---|---|---|---|
| 1 | Jason Dufner | 68-63-71-68—270 | $1,445,000 |
| 2 | Jim Furyk | 65-68-68-71—272 | 865,000 |
| 3 | Henrik Stenson (SWE) | 68-66-69-70—273 | 545,000 |

Full details of this event can be found on page 91

## Wyndham Championship Sedgefield, Greensboro, NC   Aug 15–18 [7130–70]

| | | | |
|---|---|---|---|
| 1 | Patrick Reed* | 65-64-71-66—266 | $954,000 |
| 2 | Jordan Spieth | 65-66-70-65—266 | 572,400 |
| *Reed won at the second extra hole | | | |
| 3 | Brian Harman | 67-66-69-66—268 | 307,400 |
| | John Huh | 68-62-70-68—268 | 307,400 |

## The Barclays Liberty National GC, Jersey City, NJ   Aug 22–25 [7400–71]

| | | | |
|---|---|---|---|
| 1 | Adam Scott (AUS) | 69-66-72-66—273 | $1,440,000 |
| 2 | Graham DeLaet (CAN) | 67-73-69-65—274 | 528,000 |
| | Justin Rose (ENG) | 68-68-70-68—274 | 528,000 |
| | Tiger Woods | 67-69-69-69—274 | 528,000 |
| | Gary Woodland | 69-64-68-73—274 | 528,000 |

## Deutsche Bank Championship TPC Boston, Norton, MA   Aug 30–Sep 2 [7214–71]

| | | | |
|---|---|---|---|
| 1 | Henrik Stenson (SWE) | 67-63-66-66—262 | $1,440,000 |
| 2 | Steve Stricker | 66-68-63-67—264 | 864,000 |
| 3 | Graham DeLaet (CAN) | 67-68-62-69—266 | 544,000 |

## BMW Championship Conway Farms GC, Lake Forest, IL   Sep 12–15 [7149–71]

| | | | |
|---|---|---|---|
| 1 | Zach Johnson | 64-70-69-65—268 | $1,440,000 |
| 2 | Nick Watney | 67-69-70-64—270 | 864,000 |
| 3 | Jim Furyk | 72-59-69-71—271 | 544,000 |

## Tour Championship East Lake GC, Atlanta, GA   Sep 19–22 [7307–70]

| | | | |
|---|---|---|---|
| 1 | Henrik Stenson (SWE) | 64-66-69-68—267 | $1,440,000 |
| 2 | Jordan Spieth | 68-67-71-64—270 | 708,000 |
| | Steve Stricker | 66-71-68-65—270 | 708,000 |

## Presidents Cup Muirfield Village GC, Dublin, OH   Oct 3–6   [7265–72]
USA 18½, International 15½
Full details of this event can be found on page 230

## Frys.com Open CordeValle GC, San Martin, CA   Oct 7–13   [7379–71]
| 1 | Jimmy Walker | 70-69-62-66—267 | $900,000 |
| 2 | Vijay Singh (FIJ) | 69-67-65-68—269 | 540,000 |
| 3 | Kevin Na | 75-67-64-64—270 | 240,000 |
| | Scott Brown | 68-67-71-64—270 | 240,000 |
| | Hideki Matsuyama (JPN) | 70-66-68-66—270 | 240,000 |
| | Brooks Koepka | 67-64-67-72—270 | 240,000 |

## PGA Grand Slam of Golf Port Royal Golf Course, Bermuda   Oct 14–16   [6845–71]
| 1 | Adam Scott (AUS) | 70-64—134 | $600,000 |
| 2 | Justin Rose (ENG) | 67-69—136 | 300,000 |
| 3 | Jason Dufner | 69-70—139 | 250,000 |

## Shriners Hospitals for Children Open TPC Summerlin. Las Vegas, NV   Oct 14–20
[7223–71]
| 1 | Webb Simpson | 64-63-67-66—260 | $1,080,000 |
| 2 | Jason Bohn | 67-64-69-66—266 | 528,000 |
| | Ryo Ishikawa (JPN) | 67-66-68-65—266 | 528,000 |

## CIMB Classic Kuala Lumpur, Malaysia   Oct 24–27   [6951–72]
| 1 | Ryan Moore | 63-72-69-70—274 | $1,260,000 |
| 2 | Gary Woodland | 68-70-67-69—274 | 756,000 |
*Moore won at the first extra hole
| 3 | Kiradech Aphibarnrat (THA) | 67-69-69-70—275 | 406,000 |
| | Chris Stroud | 67-69-68-71—275 | 406,000 |

## WGC – HSBC Champions Sheshan International GC, Shanghai, China   Oct 31–Nov 3
[7266–72]
| 1 | Dustin Johnson | 69-63-66-66—264 | $1,400,000 |
| 2 | Ian Poulter (ENG) | 71-67-63-66—267 | 850,000 |
| 3 | Graeme McDowell (NIR) | 69-69-64-66—268 | 480,000 |
Full details of this event can be found on page 210

## The McGladrey Classic Sea Island, GA   Nov 7–10   [7055–70]
| 1 | Chris Kirk | 66-66-68-66—266 | $990,000 |
| 2 | Briny Baird | 63-70-67-67—267 | 484,000 |
| | Tim Clark (RSA) | 67-67-71-62—267 | 484,000 |

## Wendy's 3-Tour Challenge Nov 11–12   Rio Secco GC, NV
See page 252

## OHL Classic at Mayakoba El Camaleon GC at Mayakoba Resort, Playa del Carmen, Mexico
Nov 14–17   [6987–71]
| 1 | Harris English | 68-62-68-65—263 | $1,080,000 |
| 2 | Brian Stuard | 65-70-65-67—267 | 648,000 |
| 3 | Jason Bohn | 67-68-65-68—268 | 312,000 |
| | Chris Stroud | 66-68-66-68—268 | 312,000 |
| | Rory Sabbatini (RSA) | 68-65-65-70—268 | 312,000 |

## ISPS Handa World Cup of Golf *Royal Melbourne GC, Victoria, Australia* Nov 21–24 [6985–72]

| 1 | Australia | 143-138-134-136—551 |
|---|-----------|---------------------|
| 2 | USA | 137-137-142-145—561 |
| 3 | Denmark | 137-140-147-139—563 |
| | Japan | 143-138-141-141—563 |

Full details can be found on page 231

## Northwestern Mutual World Challenge *Sherwood CC, Thousand Oaks, CA* Dec 5–8

[7027–72]

| 1 | Zach Johnson* | 67-68-72-68—275 |
|---|---------------|-----------------|
| 2 | Tiger Woods | 71-62-72-70—275 |

*Johnson won at the first extra hole

| 3 | Bubba Watson | 70-70-69-70—279 |
|---|--------------|-----------------|
| | Matt Kuchar | 68-68-76-67—279 |

## Franklin Templeton Shootout *Tiburon GC, Naples, FL*   Dec 13–15   [7288–72]

| 1 | Harris English & Matt Kuchar | 64-60-58—182 | $385,000 each |
|---|------------------------------|--------------|---------------|
| 2 | Retief Goosen & Freddie Jacobson | 67-61-61—189 | $242,500 each |
| 3 | Ian Poulter & Lee Westwood | 70-61-59—190 | $145,000 each |

## Tiger is PGA Tour Golfer of the Year again

Thirty-seven-year old Tiger Woods was voted PGA Tour Player of the Year in 2013 for a record 11th time.

In 16 Tour starts Woods won five times – the tenth time he has compiled five or more victories in a season.

"It's been an incredible feeling to have won five times. It's an incredible feeling to be voted Player of the Year by your peers and have that respect. It is very humbling."

Woods also earned his 11th PGA of America Player of the Year award, his ninth Vardon Trophy for the adjusted scoring average (68.98) and his 10th Arnold Palmer award as the Tour's top money earner in 2013 ($8,553,439).

With 79 career victories, Woods starts 2014 three wins short of Sam Snead's all-time PGA Tour record of 82 victories

Tiger was selected for the Player of the Year award on the PGA Tour ahead of Matt Kuchar, Phil Mickelson, Adam Scott and Henrik Stenson.

## Putnam web.com Tour Player of the Year

Michael Putnam was near the bottom of the leaderboard when he finished his third round at The McGladrey Classic but still had plenty to smile about that Saturday.

That was the day he was named the web.com Tour Player of the Year after finishing the leading money winner with $450,184 and two wins.

The 30-year-old from Tacoma narrowly missed his PGA Tour card at the qualifying-school last December and entered the 2013 web.com Tour with one goal: To get it back – and it did not take long for him to do so.

Putnam won in back-to-back weeks in late May and early June at the Mexico Championship and the Mid-Atlantic Championship, locking up his status for the new 2013–14 wrap-around season on the PGA Tour. He wasn't done yet though.

From that point on his goal was to finish No 1 on the web.com Tour money list.

In addition to his two wins, Putnam tied for second at the South Georgia Classic and third at the Albertsons Boise Open.

He ended the season with nine top 10s and missed just four cuts.

# US Champions Tour 2013

www.pgatour.com

## Final Ranking  *Players are of American nationality unless stated*

| | | | | | | |
|---|---|---|---|---|---|---|
| 1 | Bernhard Langer (GER) | $2,448,428 | 26 | Chien Soon Lu (TPE) | 667,461 |
| 2 | Kenny Perry | 2,241,188 | 27 | Craig Stadler | 573,597 |
| 3 | David Frost (RSA) | 1,817,234 | 28 | John Riegger | 567,857 |
| 4 | Fred Couples | 1,706,812 | 29 | Dan Forsman | 539,854 |
| 5 | Russ Cochran | 1,458,583 | 30 | Steve Elkington (AUS) | 530,332 |
| 6 | Michael Allen | 1,454,841 | 31 | Rod Spittle | 484,431 |
| 7 | Tom Pernice Jr | 1,444,527 | 32 | Kohki Idoki (JPN) | 472,871 |
| 8 | Kirk Triplett | 1,390,059 | 33 | Bill Glasson | 459,277 |
| 9 | Duffy Waldorf | 1,353,947 | 34 | Tom Kite | 440,813 |
| 10 | Rocco Mediate | 1,341,098 | 35 | Loren Roberts | 425,039 |
| 11 | John Cook | 1,327,144 | 36 | Scott Hoch | 416,479 |
| 12 | Esteban Toledo (MEX) | 1,271,758 | 37 | Brad Faxon | 406,166 |
| 13 | Peter Senior (AUS) | 1,150,411 | 38 | Steve Pate | 393,653 |
| 14 | Corey Pavin | 1,088,648 | 39 | Olin Browne | 385,113 |
| 15 | Fred Funk | 1,079,919 | 40 | Jeff Hart | 380,128 |
| 16 | Jeff Sluman | 1,016,621 | 41 | John Huston | 377,416 |
| 17 | Mark O'Meara | 1,015,871 | 42 | Willie Wood | 341,671 |
| 18 | Bart Bryant | 953,893 | 43 | Gary Hallberg | 341,220 |
| 19 | Gene Sauers | 893,272 | 44 | Anders Forsbrand (SWE) | 339,649 |
| 20 | Tom Lehman | 871,912 | 45 | Tom Byrum | 336,342 |
| 21 | Jay Haas | 846,699 | 46 | Larry Mize | 326,762 |
| 22 | Mark Wiebe | 803,025 | 47 | Colin Montgomerie (SCO) | 322,945 |
| 23 | Jay Don Blake | 735,614 | 48 | Mark McNulty (IRL) | 317,366 |
| 24 | Mark Calcavecchia | 733,181 | 49 | Joe Daley | 310,774 |
| 25 | Mike Goodes | 677,843 | 50 | Roger Chapman (ENG) | 309,949 |

## Career Money List

| | | | | | | |
|---|---|---|---|---|---|---|
| 1 | Hale Irwin | $26,751,036 | 26 | Jim Dent | 9,022,981 |
| 2 | Gil Morgan | 20,375,204 | 27 | Vicente Fernandez (ARG) | 8,906,871 |
| 3 | Tom Kite | 15,836,651 | 28 | John Jacobs | 8,740,947 |
| 4 | Dana Quigley | 14,847,286 | 29 | Craig Stadler | 8,670,240 |
| 5 | Bruce Fleisher | 14,836,386 | 30 | Brad Bryant | 8,612,455 |
| 6 | Larry Nelson | 14,432,946 | 31 | Mark McNulty (IRL) | 8,462,391 |
| 7 | Jay Haas | 14,198,692 | 32 | Mike Hill | 8,383,104 |
| 8 | Jim Thorpe | 13,871,894 | 33 | Morris Hatalsky | 8,307,431 |
| 9 | Tom Watson | 13,818,322 | 34 | D A Weibring | 8,201,142 |
| 10 | Tom Jenkins | 13,684,849 | 35 | Tom Wargo | 8,003,930 |
| 11 | Allen Doyle | 13,401,250 | 36 | Tom Purtzer | 7,891,710 |
| 12 | Bernhard Langer (GER) | 12,490,555 | 37 | Doug Tewell | 7,739,606 |
| 13 | Loren Roberts | 12,235,442 | 38 | Jeff Sluman | 7,568,779 |
| 14 | Jim Colbert | 11,736,209 | 39 | Mike McCullough | 7,563,081 |
| 15 | Dave Stockton | 11,211,471 | 40 | John Bland | 7,511,059 |
| 16 | Bob Gilder | 11,093,619 | 41 | David Eger | 7,421,889 |
| 17 | John Cook | 9,949,618 | 42 | Bruce Lietzke | 7,416,223 |
| 18 | Lee Trevino | 9,869,613 | 43 | J C Snead | 7,406,161 |
| 19 | Jay Sigel | 9,497,195 | 44 | Bob Murphy | 7,221,956 |
| 20 | Raymond Floyd | 9,474,009 | 45 | Jose Maria Canizares (ESP) | 7,184,131 |
| 21 | Isao Aoki (JPN) | 9,368,335 | 46 | Dale Douglass | 7,019,089 |
| 22 | Graham Marsh (AUS) | 9,225,720 | 47 | Walter Hall | 7,007,368 |
| 23 | Fred Funk | 9,154,201 | 48 | Bobby Wadkins | 6,976,539 |
| 24 | Bruce Summerhays | 9,048,883 | 49 | Tom Lehman | 6,764,358 |
| 25 | Bob Charles (NZL) | 9,044,003 | 50 | Andy Bean | 6,711,480 |

# Tour Results

| | | | | |
|---|---|---|---|---|
| Jan 18–20 | Mitsubishi Electric C/ship | Hualalai, Ka'upulehu-Kona, HI | John Cook* | 199 (–17) |
| | *Beat David Frost (RSA) at the first extra hole | | | |
| Feb 8–10 | Allianz Championship | Broken Sound, Boca Raton, FL | Rocco Mediate | 199 (–17) |
| Feb 17–19 | The ACE Group Classic | TwinEagles, Naples, FL | Bernhard Langer (GER) | 204 (–12) |
| Mar 15–17 | Toshiba Classic | Newport Beach, CA | David Frost (RSA) | 194 (–6) |
| Mar 22–24 | Mississippi GR Classic | Fallen Oak, Biloxi, MI | Michael Allen | 205 (–11) |
| April 19–21 | Greater Gwinnett C/ship | TPC Sugarloaf, Duluth, GA | Bernhard Langer (GER) | 206 (–10) |
| April 26–28 | Liberty Mutual Legends of Golf | Savannah Harbor, GA | Brad Faxon and Jeff Sluman | 193 (–24) |
| May 3–5 | Insperity Championship | The Woodlands, TX | Esteban Toledo (MEX)* | 210 (–6) |
| | *Beat Gene Sauers and Mike Goodes at the third extra hole | | | |
| May 23–26 | **US Senior PGA Championship** | St Louis, MO | | |
| | 1 Kohki Idoki (JPN) | 71-69-68-65—273 | | |
| | 2 Kenny Perry | 69-66-68-72—275 | | |
| | Jay Haas | 66-72-67-70—275 | | |
| May 31– June 2 | Principal Charity Classic | Des Moines, IA | Russ Cochran | 205 (–11) |
| June 6–9 | Regions Tradition | Shoal Creek, AL | David Frost (RSA) | 272 (–16) |
| June 21–23 | Encompass Championship | Glen View, IL | Craig Stadler | 203 (–13) |
| June 27–30 | Constellation Senior Players Championship | Pittsburgh, PA | Kenny Perry | 261 (–19) |
| July 11–14 | **US Senior Open** | Omaha, NE | | |
| | 1 Kenny Perry | 67-73-64-63—267 | | |
| | 2 Fred Funk | 67-70-67-68—272 | | |
| | 3 Rocco Mediate | 68-67-72-66—273 | | |
| | Corey Pavin | 69-73-64-67—273 | | |
| July 25–28 | **The Senior Open** | Royal Birkdale, Southport, England | | |
| | 1 Mark Wiebe* | 70-65-70-66—271 | | |
| | 2 Bernhard Langer (GER) | 68-67-66-70—271 | | |
| | *Wiebe won at the fifth extra hole | | | |
| | 3 Corey Pavin | 69-71-69-65—274 | | |
| | Peter Senior (AUS) | 68-71-69-66—274 | | |
| | David Frost (RSA) | 68-68-68-70—274 | | |
| Aug 2–4 | 3M Championship | Blaine, MN | Tom Pernice Jr | 199 (–17) |
| Aug 16–18 | Dick's Sporting Goods Open | En-Joie GC, Endicott, NY | Bart Bryant | 200 (–16) |
| Aug 23–25 | Boeing Classic | Snoqualmie, WA | John Riegger | 201 (–15) |
| Aug 30– Sep 1 | Shaw Charity Classic | Calgary, Alberta, Canada | Rocco Mediate | 191 (–22) |
| Sep 6–8 | Montreal Championship | Sainte-Julie, Quebec, Canada | Esteban Toledo (MEX)* | 211 (–5) |
| | *Beat Kenny Perry at the third extra hole | | | |
| Sep 20–22 | Pacific Links Hawai'i Championship | Kapolei, HI | Mark Weibe* | 205 (–11) |
| | *Beat Corey Pavin at the second extra hole | | | |
| Sep 27–29 | Nature Valley First Tee Open | Pebble Beach, CA | Kirk Triplett | 205 (–11) |
| Oct 11–13 | SAS Championship | Prestonwood CC, Cary, NC | Russ Cochran | 199 (–17) |
| Oct 18–20 | Greater Hickory Classic | Rock Barn, Conover, NC | Michael Allen* | 197 (–13) |
| | *Beat Olin Browne at the first extra hole | | | |
| Oct 25–27 | AT&T Championship | San Antonio, TX | Kenny Perry* | 203 (–13) |
| | *Beat Bernhard Langer (GER) at the first extra hole | | | |
| Oct 31– Nov 3 | Charles Schwab Cup Championship | San Francisco, CA | Fred Couples | 267 (–17) |
| Nov 12 | Wendy's 3-Tour Challenge | Rio Secco GC, NV | See page 252 | |
| Dec 14–15 | PNC Father-Son Challenge | Ritz-Carlton GC, Orlando, FL | Stewart and Conner Cink | 122 (–23) |

# Tour Statistics

## Driving accuracy

| Pos | Name | Rounds | % |
|---|---|---|---|
| 1 | Jeff Hart | 56 | 81.14 |
| 2 | Fred Funk | 76 | 79.96 |
| 3 | Corey Pavin | 62 | 79.45 |
| 4 | Bart Bryant | 64 | 77.64 |
| 5 | Wayne Levi | 50 | 77.52 |
| 6 | Hale Irwin | 61 | 76.95 |
| 7 | Kohki Idoki (JPN) | 40 | 75.90 |
| 8 | Peter Jacobsen | 43 | 75.79 |
| 9 | Mark McNulty (IRL) | 74 | 75.74 |
| 10 | Tom Lehman | 56 | 75.26 |

## Driving distance

(Average yards per drive)

| Pos | Name | Rounds | Yds |
|---|---|---|---|
| 1 | Fred Couples | 50 | 296.7 |
| 2 | John Huston | 35 | 295.7 |
| 3 | John Riegger | 41 | 287.8 |
| 4 | Kenny Perry | 65 | 287.5 |
| 5 | Tom Lehman | 56 | 283.8 |
| 6 | Duffy Waldorf | 78 | 283.3 |
| 7 | Steve Elkington (AUS) | 77 | 282.3 |
| 8 | Jim Gallagher Jr | 60 | 282.1 |
| 9 | Russ Cochran | 70 | 280.6 |
| 10 | Sandy Lyle (SCO) | 61 | 280.5 |

## Greens in regulation

| Pos | Name | Rounds | % |
|---|---|---|---|
| 1 | Fred Couples | 50 | 77.26 |
| 2 | Tom Lehman | 56 | 75.96 |
| 3 | Bernhard Langer (GER) | 78 | 74.30 |
| 4 | Gene Sauers | 72 | 73.77 |
| 5 | Bart Bryant | 64 | 73.66 |
| 6 | John Cook | 74 | 73.47 |
| 7 | Kenny Perry | 65 | 72.99 |
| 8 | Mark O'Meara | 72 | 72.50 |
| 9 | Duffy Waldorf | 78 | 72.30 |
| 10 | Russ Cochran | 70 | 72.13 |

## Sand saves

| Pos | Name | Rounds | % |
|---|---|---|---|
| 1 | Corey Pavin | 62 | 65.08 |
| 2 | Tom Pernice Jr | 81 | 60.00 |
| 3 | Gary Hallberg | 75 | 59.84 |
| 4 | Fred Couples | 50 | 58.46 |
| 5 | Jeff Hart | 56 | 57.63 |
| 6 | Esteban Toledo (MEX) | 79 | 56.32 |
| 7 | Scott Hoch | 60 | 55.41 |
| 8 | Kirk Triplett | 71 | 55.29 |
| 9 | David Frost (RSA) | 80 | 55.21 |
| 10 | Steve Jones | 46 | 54.39 |

## Scrambling

(Made par after missing greens in regulation)

| Pos | Name | Rounds | % |
|---|---|---|---|
| 1 | Corey Pavin | 62 | 69.55 |
| 2 | Bernhard Langer (GER) | 78 | 67.42 |
| 3 | Scott Hoch | 60 | 66.67 |
| 4 | Fred Couples | 50 | 66.48 |
| 5 | Tom Byrum | 35 | 66.30 |
| 6 | David Frost (RSA) | 80 | 66.05 |
| 7 | Tom Pernice Jr | 81 | 65.53 |
| 8 | Jeff Hart | 56 | 65.36 |
| 9 | Russ Cochran | 70 | 65.27 |
| 10 | Kirk Triplett | 71 | 65.00 |

## Putts per round

| Pos | Name | Rounds | Avg. |
|---|---|---|---|
| 1 | Corey Pavin | 62 | 28.49 |
| 2 | Brian Henninger | 50 | 28.54 |
| 3 | David Frost (RSA) | 80 | 28.63 |
| 4 | Gary Hallberg | 75 | 28.64 |
| 5 | Olin Browne | 39 | 28.74 |
| 6 | Jeff Hart | 56 | 28.75 |
| 7 | Esteban Toledo (MEX) | 79 | 28.79 |
| 8 | Mark Mouland (WAL) | 61 | 28.80 |
| 9 | Bernhard Langer (GER) | 78 | 28.82 |
| 10 | Tom Pernice Jr | 81 | 28.86 |

## US Champions Tour Records 2013

### Multiple winners

| | |
|---|---|
| Michael Allen | Mississippi GR Classic; Greater Hickory Classic |
| Russ Cochran | Prinicipal Charity Classic; SAS Championship |
| David Frost (RSA) | Toshiba Classic; Regions Tradition |
| Bernhard Langer (GER) | ACE Group Classic; Greater Gwinnett Championship |
| Rocco Mediate | Allianz Championship; Shaw Charity Classic |
| Kenny Perry | Constellation Senior Players Championship; US Senior Open; AT&T Championship |
| Esteban Toledo (MEX) | Insperity Championship; Montreal Championship |
| Mark Weibe | The Senior Open; Pacific Links Hawai'i Championship |

# web.com Tour 2013
formerly the Nationwide Tour

www.pgatour.com

*Players are of American nationality unless stated*

## Final Ranking (Top 25 earned US Tour Card)

| | | | | | | |
|---|---|---|---|---|---|---|
| 1 | Chesson Hadley | $535,432 | | 51 | Joe Durant | 114,479 |
| 2 | Michael Putnam | 515,184 | | 52 | Kelly Kraft | 114,233 |
| 3 | Ben Martin | 508,332 | | 53 | Bhavik Patel | 113,102 |
| 4 | Edward Loar | 423,193 | | 54 | Ryan Spears | 111,136 |
| 5 | John Peterson | 364,569 | | 55 | Scott Dunlap | 110,506 |
| 6 | Andrew Svoboda | 332,607 | | 56 | Steve Wheatcroft | 109,319 |
| 7 | Bronson La'Cassie (AUS) | 288,300 | | 57 | Franklin Corpening | 108,369 |
| 8 | Kevin Tway | 266,766 | | 58 | Jason Gore | 108,354 |
| 9 | Alex Aragon | 255,867 | | 59 | Matt Davidson | 105,503 |
| 10 | Will Wilcox | 248,372 | | 60 | Troy Merritt | 104,249 |
| 11 | Brendon Todd | 247,948 | | 61 | Fernando Mechereffe (BRA) | 103,995 |
| 12 | Tim Wilkinson (NZL) | 246,540 | | 62 | Tom Hoge | 103,927 |
| 13 | Patrick Cantlay | 243,105 | | 63 | Andrew Loupe | 103,764 |
| 14 | Kevin Kisner | 238,491 | | 64 | Roland Thatcher | 101,268 |
| 15 | Will MacKenzie | 236,211 | | 65 | Brett Stegmaier | 98,490 |
| 16 | Mark Anderson | 232,341 | | 66 | Dawie van der Walt (RSA) | 94,497 |
| 17 | Alex Prugh | 223,583 | | 67 | Adam Crawford (AUS) | 94,356 |
| 18 | Brice Garnett | 217,785 | | 68 | Philip Pettitt Jr | 93,218 |
| 19 | Seung-Yul Noh (KOR) | 210,125 | | 69 | Len Mattiace | 91,375 |
| 20 | Danny Lee (NZL) | 209,153 | | 70 | Ryo Ishikawa (JPN) | 90,405 |
| 21 | Jamie Lovemark | 207,355 | | 71 | Richard Johnson (SWE) | 85,912 |
| 22 | Peter Malnati | 192,963 | | 72 | Aron Price (AUS) | 85,671 |
| 23 | Trevor Immelman (RSA) | 180,000 | | 73 | Alex Cejka (GER) | 84,772 |
| 24 | Chad Collins | 173,894 | | 74 | Adam Hadwin (CAN) | 81,182 |
| 25 | Russell Knox (SCO) | 168,710 | | 75 | Guy Boros | 80,615 |
| 26 | Wes Roach | 167,429 | | 76 | Nick Flanagan (AUS) | 76,579 |
| 27 | Jim Renner | 166,360 | | 77 | Ariel Canete (ARG) | 74,895 |
| 28 | Matt Bettencourt | 165,527 | | 78 | Nick O'Hern (AUS) | 73,909 |
| 29 | Daniel Chopra (SWE) | 164,826 | | 79 | Heath Slocum | 72,132 |
| 30 | Benjamin Alvarado (CHI) | 157,304 | | 80 | Scott Harrington | 72,104 |
| 31 | Miguel Angel Carballo (ARG) | 155,451 | | 81 | Oscar Fraustro (MEX) | 71,790 |
| 32 | Mathew Goggin (AUS) | 152,302 | | 82 | Brad Fritsch (CAN) | 66,000 |
| 33 | Alexandre Rocha (BRA) | 150,560 | | 83 | James Nitties (AUS) | 64,771 |
| 34 | Kevin Foley | 148,652 | | 84 | Kevin Kim | 64,531 |
| 35 | Billy Hurley III | 146,979 | | 85 | Michael Connell | 64,184 |
| 36 | Scott Parel | 143,044 | | 86 | Zack Sucher | 64,058 |
| 37 | Ashley Hall (AUS) | 142,838 | | 87 | Morgan Hoffmann | 63,120 |
| 38 | Steven Alker (NZL) | 142,588 | | 88 | Paul Claxton | 62,340 |
| 39 | Tyrone Van Aswegen (RSA) | 140,561 | | 89 | Scott Brown | 61,888 |
| 40 | Whee Kim (KOR) | 139,068 | | 90 | Bobby Gates | 61,484 |
| 41 | Hudson Swafford | 138,760 | | 91 | Randall Hutchison | 61,079 |
| 42 | D J Brigman | 135,016 | | 92 | Joe Affrunti | 59,367 |
| 43 | Spencer Levin | 129,352 | | 93 | Sean O'Hair | 59,333 |
| 44 | Scott Gardiner (AUS) | 127,533 | | 94 | Peter Tomasulo | 57,972 |
| 45 | Byron Smith | 127,129 | | 95 | Troy Matteson | 57,250 |
| 46 | Shane Bertsch | 119,904 | | 96 | Blayne Barber | 56,586 |
| 47 | Nick Rousey | 117,486 | | 97 | Sung Kang (KOR) | 56,075 |
| 48 | Camilo Benedetti (COL) | 117,329 | | 98 | Bud Cauley | 55,900 |
| 49 | Andrew Putnam | 115,608 | | 99 | Roger Sloan (CAN) | 54,613 |
| 50 | Hunter Haas | 114,604 | | 100 | I J Jang (KOR) | 54,048 |

# Tour Results

| Feb 21–24 | Panama Claro C/ship | Panama City | Kevin Foley | 272 (–8) |
|---|---|---|---|---|
| Feb 28–Mar 3 | Colombia Championship | Bogota | Patrick Cantlay | 266 (–22) |
| Mar 7–10 | Chile Classic | Santiago | Kevin Kisner | 267 (–21) |
| Mar 21–24 | Chitimacha Louisiana Open | Le Triomphe, Broussard, LA | Edward Loar | 267 (–17) |
| April 4–7 | Brasil Classic | Sao Paulo | Benjamin Alvarado (CHI) | 265 (–19) |
| April 11–14 | WNB Golf Classic | Midland, TX | Alex Aragon | 272 (–16) |
| April 25–28 | South Georgia Classic | Kinderlou Forest, Valdosta, GA | Will Wilcox | 273 (–15) |
| May 2–5 | Stadion Classic | Univ. of GA | Brendon Todd | 205 (–8) |
|  | *Reduced to three rounds due to bad weather* |  |  |  |
| May 16–18 | BMW Charity Pro-Am | Greer, SC | Mark Anderson | 259 (–27) |
| May 23–26 | Mexico Championship | El Bosque GC, Leon, Guanajuato, Mexico | Michael Putnam | 275 (–13) |
| May 30–June 2 | Mid-Atlantic Championship | Potomac, MD | Michael Putnam | 273 (–7) |
| June 13–16 | Air Capital Classic | Wichita, KS | Scott Parel | 266 (–18) |
| June 20–23 | Rex Hospital Open | Raleigh, NC | Chesson Hadley | 265 (–19) |
| June 27–30 | United Leasing C/ship | Newburgh, IN | Ben Martin* | 277 (–11) |
|  | *Beat Ashley Hall (AUS), Joe Affrunti and Bill Hurley III at the first extra hole* |  |  |  |
| July 11–14 | Utah Championship | Willow Creek CC, Sandy, UT | Steven Alker (NZL) | 262 (–22) |
|  | *Beat Ashley Hall (AUS) at the first extra hole* |  |  |  |
| July 18–21 | Midwest Classic | Overland Park, KS | Jamie Lovemark | 266 (–18) |
| July 25–28 | Albertsons Boise Open | Boise, ID | Kevin Tway* | 261 (–23) |
|  | *Beat Spencer Levin at the first extra hole* |  |  |  |
| Aug 1–4 | Mylan Classic | Canonsburg, PA | Ben Martin | 267 (–17) |
| Aug 8–11 | Price Cutter Charity C/ship | Springfield, MO | Andrew Svoboda | 266 (–22) |
| Aug 15–18 | News Sentinel Open | Knoxville, TN | Peter Mainati | 268 (–16) |
| Aug 22–25 | Cox Classic | Omaha, NE | Bronson La'Cassie (AUS)* | 263 (–21) |
|  | *Beat Matt Bettencourt at the third extra hole* |  |  |  |
| Aug 29–Sep 1 | Hotel Fitness Championship | Fort Wayne, IN | Trevor Immelman (RSA) | 268 (–16) |
| Sep 5–8 | Chiquita Classic | Davidson, NC | Andrew Svoboda* | 276 (–12) |
|  | *Beat Will MacKenzie at the first extra hole* |  |  |  |
| Sep 12–15 | Nationwide Children's Hospital Championship | Columbus, OH | Seung-Yul Noh (KOR) | 272 (–12) |
| Sep 26–29 | Web.com Tour C/ship | Ponte Vedra Beach, FL | Chesson Hadley | 270 (–10) |

## web.com Tour records 2013

### Multiple winners

Michael Putnam – Mexico Championship; Mid-Atlantic Championship
Ben Martin – United Leasing Championship; Mylan Classic

Andrew Svoboda – Price Cutter Charity Championship; Chiquita Classic
Chesson Hadley – Rex Hospital Open; Web.com Tour Championship

### Top 10 finishes (number of events in brackets)

| | | | | | | | | |
|---|---|---|---|---|---|---|---|---|
| 1 | Michael Putnam | (23) | 9 | | 4 | Edward Loar | (18) | 7 |
| 2 | Chesson Hadley | (22) | 8 | | 5 | John Peterson | (18) | 6 |
|   | Ben Martin | (22) | 8 | | | Tim Wilkinson | (19) | 6 |

### Scoring averages (number of rounds in brackets)

| | | | | | | | | |
|---|---|---|---|---|---|---|---|---|
| 1 | John Peterson | (68) | 68.94 | | 6 | Tim Wilkinson | (64) | 69.33 |
| 2 | Ben Martin | (81) | 69.00 | | 7 | Russell Knox | (53) | 69.58 |
| 3 | Edward Loar | (65) | 69.22 | | 8 | Will MacKenzie | (70) | 69.59 |
|   | Michael Putnam | (83) | 69.22 | | 9 | Chesson Hadley | (75) | 69.61 |
| 5 | Will Wilcox | (63) | 69.27 | | 10 | Peter Malnati | (42) | 69.62 |

# Asian Tour 2013
www.asiantour.com

| Feb 20–23 | WGC – Accenture Match | Ritz Carlton GC, AZ | Final: Matt Kuchar (USA) beat |
| | Play Championship | | Hunter Mahan (USA) 2 and 1 |
| Feb 2–5 | Zaykabar Myanmar Open | R Mingalardon G&CC, Yangon | Chawalit Plaphol (THA) 270 (–18) |
| Mar 6–9 | SAIL-SBI Open | Delhi GC, New Delhi | Anirban Lahiri (IND)* 273 (–15) |
| | *Beat Rashid Khan at the first extra hole | | |
| Mar 7–10 | WGC – Cadillac C/ship | TPC Blue Monster at Doral, FL | Tiger Woods (USA) 269 (–12) |
| Mar 14–17 | Avantha Masters | Delhi, India | Thomas Aiken (RSA) 265 (–23) |
| Mar 21–23 | Maybank Malaysian Open | Kuala Lumpur G&CC | Kiradech Aphibarnrat 203 (–13) |
| | | | (THA) |
| Mar 28–31 | Chiangmai Golf Classic | Chiangmai, Thailand | Scott Hend (AUS) 268 (–20) |
| April 4–7 | Panasonic Open India | Delhi GC, New Delhi | Wade Ormsby (AUS) 279 (–9) |
| April 11–14 | Solaire Open | Wack Wack G&CC, Manila | Lin Weng-tang (TPE) 285 (–3) |
| April 11–14 | Masters Tournament | Augusta National GC, GA | Adam Scott (AUS) 279 (–9) |
| April 25–28 | Ballantines Championship | Seoul, South Korea | Brett Rumford (AUS)* 277 (–11) |
| | *Beat Marcus Fraser (AUS) and Peter Whiteford (SCO) in the play-off | | |
| May 2–5 | Indonesian Masters | Royale Jakarta GC | Bernd Wiesberger (AUT) 273 (–15) |
| June 13–16 | US Open | Ardmore, PA, USA | Justin Rose (ENG) 281 (+1) |
| June 20–23 | Worldwide Holdings | Seri Selangor GC, | Pariya Junhasavasdikul 275 (–9) |
| | Selangor Masters | Petaling Jay, Malaysia | (THA) |
| July 18–21 | The Open Championship | Muirfield, Scotland | Phil Mickelson (USA) 281 (–5) |
| Aug 1–4 | WGC – Bridgestone Inv. | Akron, Ohio, USA | Tiger Woods (USA) 265 (–15) |
| Aug 8–11 | US PGA Championship | Rochester, NY, USA | Jason Dufner (USA) 270 (–10) |
| Sep 5–8 | Omega European Masters | Crans-sur-Sierre, | Thomas Björn (DEN) 264 (–20) |
| | | Switzerland | |
| Sep 12–15 | Yeangder Tournament | Linkou International | Thaworn Wiratchant 275 (–13) |
| | Players' Championship | G&CC, Taipei, Taiwan | (THA) |
| Sep 19–22 | Volvik-Sky Lake Vietnam | Sky Lake Golf Club, Hanoi | Postponed |
| | Masters | | |
| Sep 26–29 | Asia-Pacific Panasonic Open | Ibaraki CC, Osaka, Japan | Masahiro Kawamura (JPN) 275 (–9) |
| Oct 3–6 | Mercuries Taiwan Masters | Taiwan G&CC, Taipei | Scott Hend (AUS) 285 (–3) |
| Oct 10–13 | CJ Invitational | Nine Bridges GC, Korea | Sung-hoon Kang (KOR) 276 (–12) |
| Oct 17–20 | Venetian Macau Open | Macau G&CC | Scott Hend (AUS) 268 (–16) |
| Oct 24–27 | CIMB Classic | Kuala Lumpur, Malaysia | Ryan Moore (USA) 274 (–14) |
| Oct 31– | WGC – HSBC Champions | Shanghai, China | Dustin Johnson (USA) 264 (–24) |
| Nov 3 | | | |
| Nov 7–10 | Hero Indian Open | Delbhi GC | Mohd. Siddikur (BAN) 274 (–14) |
| Nov 14–17 | Resorts World Manila | Manila Southwoods G&CC, | Liang Wen-chong (CHN)* 272 (–16) |
| | Masters | Philippines | |
| | *Beat Prom Meesawat (THA) in the play-off | | |
| Nov 21–24 | World Cup of Golf | Melbourne, Australia | Jason Day (AUS) 274 (–10) |
| | | | Australia won the team event |
| Nov 28– | Indonesia Open | Jakarta | Gaganjeet Bhullar (IND) 268 (–16) |
| Dec 1 | | | |
| Dec 5–8 | Hong Kong Open | Hong Kong GC, Fanling | Miguel Angel Jiménez (ESP) 268 (–12) |
| Dec 12–15 | Thailand Golf Championship | Amata Spring CC, Bangkok | Sergio García (ESP) 266 (–22) |

## Final money list (Figures in brackets denote number of events played)

| | | | | | | | |
|---|---|---|---|---|---|---|---|
| 1 | Kiradech Aphibarnrat (THA) | (12) | US$1,127,855 | 6 Liang Wen-Chong (CHN) | (9) | 398,798 |
| 2 | Scott Hend (AUS) | (16) | 571,400 | 7 Baek Seuk-Hyun (KOR) | (19) | 336,993 |
| 3 | Siddikur Rahman (BAN) | (20) | 486,667 | 8 Prom Meesawat (THA) | (15) | 295,407 |
| 4 | Gaganjeet Bhullar (IND) | (16) | 479,978 | 9 Shiv Kapur (IND) | (15) | 289,871 |
| 5 | Anirban Lahiri (IND) | (20) | 465,696 | 10 Thongchai Jaidee (THA) | (11) | 280,297 |

# PGA Tour of Australasia 2013

*Players are of Australian nationality unless stated*                                    www.pgatour.com.au

| | | | | |
|---|---|---|---|---|
| Jan 17–20 | Turner Plumbing Victorian PGA Championship | Forest Resort, Creswick, Vic. | David McKenzie | 275 (–13) |
| Jan 24–27 | Lexus of Blackburn Heritage Classic | Heritage G&CC, Vic. | David Bransdon* | 274 (–14) |
| | *Beat Max McCardle and Lucas Hebert (am) in the play-off | | | |
| Feb 14–17 | Coca-Cola Queensland PGA | City GC, Toowoomba, Qld | Brad Kennedy | 254 (–18) |
| Feb 21–24 | Victorian Open | 13th Beach Golf Links, Vic. | Matthew Giles | 275 (–13) |
| Feb 28– Mar 3 | NZ PGA Championship | The Hills GC, Queenstown | Michael Hendry (NZL)* | 269 (–19) |
| | *Beat Scott Strange at the first extra hole | | | |
| Aug 22–25 | Isuzu Queensland Open | Brookwater G&CC, Qld | Nick Cullen | 279 (–9) |
| Sep 18–21 | South Pacific Golf Open Championship | Tina GC, New Caledonia | Andre Stolz* | 268 (–16) |
| | *Beat Michael Wright at the fifth extra hole | | | |
| Oct 3–6 | WA Goldfields PGA Championship | Kalgoorlie GC, Kalgoorlie, WA | Jack Wilson* | 278 (–10) |
| | *Beat Nick Gillespie (NZL) at the first extra hole | | | |
| Oct 10–13 | WA Open Championship | Mt Lawley Golf Crse, Perth, WA | Josh Geary (NZL) | 273 (–15) |
| Oct 17–20 | Perth International | Lake Karinyup CC, Perth, WA | Jin Jeong (KOR) | 278 (–10) |
| Nov 7–10 | Australian PGA Championship | RACV Royal Pines, Gold Coast, Qld | Adam Scott | 270 (–14) |
| Nov 14–17 | Talisker Masters | Royal Melbourne GC, Qld | Adam Scott | 270 (–14) |
| Nov 21–24 | NSW Open | Castle Hill CC, NSW | Aron Price | 269 (–19) |
| Nov 28– Dec 1 | **Emirates Australian Open** | Royal Sydney GC, NSW | Rory McIlroy (NIR) | 270 (–18) |

| | | | | | | | |
|---|---|---|---|---|---|---|---|
| 1904 | Hon Michael Scott (am) | 1934 | Bill Bolger | 1966 | Arnold Palmer (USA) | 1992 | Steve Elkington |
| 1905 | Dan Soutar | 1935 | F McMahon | 1967 | Peter Thomson | 1993 | Brad Faxon (USA) |
| 1906 | Carnegie Clark (am) | 1936 | Gene Sarazen (USA) | 1968 | Jack Nicklaus (USA) | 1994 | Robert Allenby |
| 1907 | Hon Michael Scott (am) | 1937 | George Naismith | 1969 | Gary Player (RSA) | 1995 | Greg Norman |
| | | 1938 | Jim Ferrier (am) | 1970 | Gary Player (RSA) | 1996 | Greg Norman |
| 1908 | Clyde Pearce (am) | 1939 | Jim Ferrier (am) | 1971 | Jack Nicklaus (USA) | 1997 | Lee Westwood (ENG) |
| 1909 | C Felstead (am) | 1940–1945 not played | | 1972 | Peter Thomson | 1998 | Greg Chalmers |
| 1910 | Carnegie Clark (am) | 1946 | Ossie Pickworth | 1973 | J C Snead (USA) | 1999 | Aaron Baddeley (am) |
| 1911 | Carnegie Clark (am) | 1947 | Ossie Pickworth | 1974 | Gary Player (RSA) | | |
| 1912 | Ivo Whitton (am) | 1948 | Ossie Pickworth | 1975 | Jack Nicklaus (USA) | 2000 | Aaron Baddeley |
| 1913 | Ivo Whitton (am) | 1949 | Eric Cremin | 1976 | Jack Nicklaus (USA) | 2001 | Stuart Appleby |
| 1914–1919 not played | | 1950 | Norman Von Nida | 1977 | David Graham | 2002 | Steve Allan |
| 1920 | Joe Kirkwood | 1951 | Peter Thomson | 1978 | Jack Nicklaus (USA) | 2003 | Peter Lonard |
| 1921 | A Le Fevre | 1952 | Norman Von Nida | 1979 | Jack Newton | 2004 | Peter Lonard |
| 1922 | C Campbell | 1953 | Norman Von Nida | 1980 | Greg Norman | 2005 | Robert Allenby |
| 1923 | T Howard | 1954 | Ossie Pickworth | 1981 | Bill Rogers (USA) | 2006 | John Senden |
| 1924 | A Russell (am) | 1955 | Bobby Locke (RSA) | 1982 | Bob Shearer | 2007 | Peter Lonard |
| 1925 | Fred Popplewell | 1956 | Bruce Crampton | 1983 | Peter Fowler | 2008 | Tim Clark* |
| 1926 | Ivo Whitton (am) | 1957 | Frank Phillips | 1984 | Tom Watson (USA) | *Beat Matthew Coggin at 1st extra hole | |
| 1927 | R Stewart | 1958 | Gary Player (RSA) | 1985 | Greg Norman | | |
| 1928 | Fred Popplewell | 1959 | Kel Nagle | 1986 | Rodger Davis | 2009 | Adam Scott |
| 1929 | Ivo Whitton (am) | 1960 | Bruce Devlin (am) | 1987 | Greg Norman | 2010 | Geoff Ogilvy |
| 1930 | F Eyre | 1961 | Frank Phillips | 1988 | Mark Calcavecchia (USA) | 2011 | Greg Chalmers |
| 1931 | Ivo Whitton (am) | 1962 | Gary Player (RSA) | | | 2012 | Peter Senior |
| 1932 | Mick Ryan (am) | 1963 | Gary Player (RSA) | 1989 | Peter Senior | | |
| 1933 | M Kelly | 1964 | Jack Nicklaus (USA) | 1990 | John Morse (USA) | | |
| | | 1965 | Gary Player (RSA) | 1991 | Wayne Riley | | |

## Final money list   (Figures in brackets denote number of events played)

| | | | | | | | | |
|---|---|---|---|---|---|---|---|---|
| 1 | Adam Scott | (3) | AU$538,620 | 6 | Gareth Paddison (NZL) | (10) | 108,644.97 |
| 2 | Jin Jeong (KOR) | (9) | 342,663 | 7 | Dimitrios Papadatos | (9) | 103,240.25 |
| 3 | Michael Hendry (NZL) | (5) | 118,782 | 8 | Nick Cullen | (10) | 100,958.59 |
| 4 | Brody Ninyette | (13) | 115,877.60 | 9 | David McKenzie | (9) | 95,654.22 |
| 5 | Jack Wilson | (7) | 108,758.33 | 10 | Matthew Griffin | (11) | 84,831.15 |

# PGA Tour Canada 2013

*Players are of Canadian nationality unless stated*                                www.cantour.com

| | | | | |
|---|---|---|---|---|
| June 7–10 | Times Colonist Island Savings Open | Uplands GC, BC | Stephen Gangluff (USA) | 269 (–11) |
| June 17–23 | ATB Financial Classic | Calgary, AB | *Cancelled due to flooding* | |
| July 1–7 | Dakota Dunes Open | Dakota Dunes, Saskatoon, SK | Will Collins (USA) | 267 (–21) |
| July 8–14 | Syncrude Boreal Open | Fort McMurray GC, AB | Riley Wheeldon | 275 (–13) |
| July 15–21 | The Players Cup | Pine Ridge GC, Winnipeg, MA | Carlos Sainz Jr (USA) | 271 (–17) |
| Aug 6–9 | ATB Financial Classic | Calgary, AB | Joe Panzeri (USA) | 271 (–17) |
| Aug 19–25 | Great Waterway Classic | Morrisburg, ON | Hugo Leon (CHI) | 266 (–22) |
| Aug 26–Sep 1 | The Wildfire Invitational | Peterborough, ON | Mark Hubbard (USA) | 264 (–20) |
| Sep 2–8 | Cape Breton Celtic Classic | Ben Eoin, NS | Mackenzie Hughes | 274 (–14) |
| Sep 9–15 | Canadian Tour C/ship | London, ON | Max Gilbert | 268 (–20) |

## Final Ranking (Figure in brackets indicates number of tournaments played)

| | | | | | | | | |
|---|---|---|---|---|---|---|---|---|
| 1 | Mackenzie Hughes | (9) | $52,114 | 6 | Joe Panzeri (USA) | (9) | 39,312 |
| 2 | Riley Wheeldon | (9) | 45,322 | 7 | Nick Taylor | (9) | 36,715 |
| 3 | Mark Hubbard (USA) | (9) | 40,696 | 8 | Chris Epperson (USA) | (9) | 36,295 |
| 4 | Hugo Leon (CHI) | (9) | 39,897 | 9 | Carlos Sainz Jr (USA) | (9) | 33,105 |
| 5 | Wil Collins (USA) | (9) | 39,708 | 10 | Kyle Stough (USA) | (9) | 32,920 |

## Henrik Stenson wins 2013 Golf Writers Trophy

Henrik Stenson is the winner of the 2013 Golf Writers Trophy following a magnificent season in which he became the first player to complete the lucrative double of the FedEx Cup and the Race to Dubai.

The 37 year old Swede topped the annual poll despite fierce competition from the likes of Justin Rose, who became the first Englishman in 43 years to win the United States Open, and Europe's Solheim Cup team, who made history by winning on American soil for the first time.

Stenson was clearly flattered to have come out on top and by a convincing margin as well with almost two-thirds of members of the Association of Golf Writers making him their first choice.

"I think when you look at what others achieved like Justin and the Solheim Cup team it does make it mean that little bit more," said Stenson. "It's a huge honour and a great reflection on the year I had. I'm looking forward to getting a few of these trophies I've won into the summer house in Sweden. It has been such a great year that I can have a few in Europe and a few in my house in America!

"What a great thrill it is going to be over Christmas to sit by the fire with my family and take stock of the season, look at trophies such as this one and reflect on the year of my life.

"I have always had a very good relationship with the media. I have tried to be accommodating and taken my time to give decent and honest responses. I think I have been treated very fairly by the media guys too. It is a give and take relationship and I've always understood that.

"I appreciate their support for what I've managed to accomplish."

Rose was a clear runner-up for his memorable first success in a major championship at Merion. Making up a glittering top-three were Europe's leading women, who survived the febrile atmosphere in Denver, Colorado to achieve their record-breaking success against all odds.

Given the nature of these feats, perhaps it wasn't surprising they dominated the leading positions, but members were also keen to recognise the achievement of Englishman Matthew Fitzpatrick in becoming the world's leading amateur golfer.

Voted on by members of the AGW and dating back to 1951, the award recognizes outstanding achievements during the year from golfers born or resident in Europe, and European teams.

Stenson is the first male Swedish golfer to win. Annika Sörenstam was victorious on two occasions, in 2003 and 2005.

Also featured in the voting this year were: Charley Hull, Graeme McDowell, Thomas Björn, Suzann Pettersen, Caroline Hedwall, Ian Poulter, Andrea Pavan, and Victor Dubuisson.

# Japan PGA Tour 2013

*Players are of Japanese nationality unless stated*                    www.jgto.org/jgto/WG01000000Init.do

| | | | | |
|---|---|---|---|---|
| Mar 14–17 | Thailand Open | Thana City Golf & Sports Club | Prayad Marksaeng (THA) | 264 (–24) |
| Mar 28–31 | Indonesia PGA C/ship | Emeralda GC | Ho-Sung Choi (KOR) | 269 (–19) |
| April 1114 | Masters Tournament | Augusta National GC, USA | Adam Scott (AUS)* | 279 (–9) |
| | *Beat Angel Cabrera (ARG) at the first extra hole | | | |
| April 18–21 | Token Homemate Cup | Token Tado CC, Nagoya | Yoshinobu Tsukada | 275 (–18) |
| April 25–28 | Tsuruya Open | Yamanohara GC, Hyogo | Hideki Matsuyama | 266 (–15) |
| May 2–5 | The Crowns | Nagoya GC (Wago course), Aichi | Michio Matsumura | 278 (–2) |
| May 16–19 | PGA Championship Nissin Cupnoodles Cup | Sobu CC, Chiba | Hyung-Sung Kim (KOR) | 279 (–5) |
| May 30– June 2 | Diamond Cup Golf | Oarai GC, Ibaraki | Hideki Matsuyama | 279 (–9) |
| June 16–13 | US Open | Ardmore, PA, USA | Justin Rose (ENG) | 281 (+1) |
| June 20–23 | Japan Tour Golf C/ship | Shishido Hills | Satoshi Kodaira | 274 (–14) |
| June 27–30 | Gateway to the Open Mizuno Open | JFE Setonakai GC, Okayama | Brendon Jones (AUS) | 269 (–19) |
| July 4–7 | Nagashime Shigeo Inv. (Sega Sammy Cup) | The North Country GC, Hokkaido | Shunsuke Sonoda | 268 (–20) |
| July 18–21 | The Open Championship | Muirfield, Scotland | Phil Mickelson (USA) | 281 (–5) |
| Aug 8–11 | US PGA Championship | Rochester, NY, USA | Jason Dufner (USA) | 270 (–10) |
| Aug 22–25 | Kansai Open | Olympic GC, Hyogo | Brad Kennedy (AUS) | 206 (–10) |
| Aug 29– Sep 1 | Vana H Cup KBC Augusta | Keya GC, Fukuoka | Sung-Joon Park (KOR) | 204 (–12) |
| Sep 5–8 | Fujisankei Classic | Fujizakura CC, Yamanashi | Hideki Matsuyama | 275 (–9) |
| Sep19–22 | ANA Open | Sapporo GC, Hokkaido | Koumei Oda | 273 (–15) |
| Sep 26–29 | Asia-Pacific Panasonic Open | Ibaraki CC, Osaka | Masahiro Kawamura | 275 (–9) |
| Oct 3–6 | Coca-Cola Tokai Classic | Miyoshi CC, Aichi | Shingo Katayama* | 281 (–7) |
| | *Beat Hidemasa Hoshino and Satoshi Tomiyama in the play-off | | | |
| Oct 10–13 | Toshin Golf Tournament | Toshin GC, Gifu | Yoshinori Fujimoto | 264 (–24) |
| Oct 17–20 | Japan Open | Ibaraki GC, Ibaraki | Masanori Kobayashi | 274 (–10) |
| Oct 24–27 | Bridgestone Open | Sodegaura CC, Chiba | Daisuke Maruyama | 203 (–10) |
| Oct 31– Nov 3 | Mynavi ABC Championship | ABC GC, Hyogo | Yuta Ikeda* | 269 (–15) |
| | *Beat S K Ho (KOR) in the play-off | | | |
| Nov 7–10 | Heiwa PGM Championship | Miho GC, Ibaraki | Ashun Wu (CHN) | 273 (–11) |
| Nov 14–17 | Mitsui Sumitomo VISA Taiheiyo Masters | Taiheiyo Club, Shizuoka | Hideto Tanihara | 275 (–13) |
| Nov 21–24 | Dunlop Phoenix | Phoenix CC, Miyazaki | Luke Donald (ENG) | 270 (–14) |
| Nov 28– Dec 1 | Casio World Open | Kochi Kuroshio CC, Kochi | Hideki Matsuyama | 276 (–12) |
| Dec 5–8 | Golf Nippon Series JT Cup | Tokyo Yomiuri CC, Tokyo | Yusaku Miyazato | 267 (–13) |

## Final money list (Japanese Tour events only)

| | | | | | |
|---|---|---|---|---|---|
| 1 | Hideki Matsuyama | ¥155,860,333 | 6 | Hideto Tanihara | 91,134,436 |
| 2 | Hyung-Sung Kim (KOR) | 125,824,405 | 7 | Yusaku Miyazato | 78,688,291 |
| 3 | Koumei Oda | 112,506,906 | 8 | Ashun Wu (CHN) | 78,347,975 |
| 4 | Shingo Katayama | 110,341,442 | 9 | Yuta Ikeda | 78,056,124 |
| 5 | Sung-Joon Park (KOR) | 93,402,445 | 10 | Yoshinori Fujimoto | 69,598,515 |

# Korean PGA Tour 2013

*Players are of Korean nationality unless stated*

http://eng.kgt.co.kr/main/english.aspx

| Date | Tournament | Venue | Winner | Score |
|---|---|---|---|---|
| April 25–28 | Ballantine's Championship | Blackstone Resort, Seoul | Brett Rumford (AUS) | 277 (–11) |
| May 9–12 | GS Caltex Maekyung Open | NamSeoul G&CC | Hyun Woo Ryu | 274 (–14) |
| May 16–19 | SK telecom Open | Pinx Golf Course | Matthew Griffin (AUS) | 203 (–13) |
| May 23–26 | Happiness Kwangju Bank Open | Happiness CC | Kyung Nam Kang | 268 (–20) |
| May 30– June 2 | Gunsan CC Open | GunSan CC | Soo Min Lee | 272 (–16) |
| Aug 1–4 | Bosung CC Classic | Bosung CC | Tae Hoon Kim | 267 (–21) |
| Aug 8–11 | SoLaSeaDo-Pine Beach Open | Pine Beach GL | Soon Sang Hong | 269 (–19) |
| Aug 15–18 | 56th KPGA Championship | Dongchon GC | Hyung Tae Kim | 271 (–17) |
| Sep 12–15 | Dongbu Promi Open | Wellihilli CC | Chang Woo Lee | 275 (–13) |
| Sep 26–29 | 29th Shinhan Donghae Open | Jack Nicklaus GC | Sang Moon Bae | 279 (–9) |
| Oct 4–6 | Munsingwear Match Play Championship | Maestro CC | Do-hoon Kim | |
| Oct 10–13 | CJ Invitational | Haesley Nine Bridges CC | Sung-hoon Kang | 276 (–12) |
| Oct 17–20 | 56th Kolon Korea Open | Woo Jung Hills GC | Sung-hoon Kang | 280 (–4) |
| Oct 24–27 | Tour Championship | Lotte Sky Hill Jeju CC | In Hoi Hur | 276 (–12) |

## Final Ranking

| | | | | | | |
|---|---|---|---|---|---|---|
| 1 | Sung Hoon Kang | ₩478,910,000 | 6 | Hyung Tae Kim | 242,787,936 |
| 2 | Hyun Woo Ryu | 445,974,458 | 7 | Hyung Sung Kim | 224,083,648 |
| 3 | Do Hoon Kim | 369,574,333 | 8 | Sang Hee Lee | 222,346,207 |
| 4 | Tae Hoon Kim | 259,419,333 | 9 | Matthew Griffin (AUS) | 210,720,000 |
| 5 | Kyung Nam Kang | 258,405,797 | 10 | Sang Moon Bae | 203,000,000 |

## Other Tours

Adams Tour – www.adamsgolfprotourseries.com
Alps Tour – www.alpstourgolf.com
Asean Tour – www.aseanpgatour.com
Asian Development Tour – www.asiantour.com
Charles Tour – www.golf.co.nz
Dakotas Tour – www.dakotastour.com
Ecco Tour – http://eccotour.org/
e-golf Tour – www.egolf.org.uk
EPD Tour – www.epdtour.de
Europro Tour – www.europrotour.com
Evolve Pro Tour – www.evolveprotour.com
France Tour – www.franceprogolftour.com

Golden State Tour – www.gstour.com
Hi5 Futures Tour – www.hi5futurestour.com
Iberian Tour – www.igtour.net
Italian Tour – www.italianprotour.com
Jamega Tour – www.jamegatour.co.uk
Japan Challenge Tour – www.jgto.org
NGA Tour – www.ngatour.com
PGTI Feeder Tour – www.pgtofindia.com
PGA New Zealand – www.pga.org.nz
Singha Tour – www.pgtofindia.com
Suncoast Tour – www.suncoastseries.com
TPGA Argentina – www.pgargentina.org.ar

Challenge Tour (Korean) –
http://eng.kgt.co.kr/tournaments/schedule.aspx?tour=bearriver&tour_code=12
Champions Tour (Korean Seniors) –
http://eng.kgt.co.kr/tournaments/schedule.aspx?tour=champions&tour_code=13
KPGA Academy Tour –
http://eng.kgt.co.kr/tournaments/schedule.aspx?tour=academy&tour_code=16

# PGA Tour Latinoamérica 2013

www.pgatourla.com

| | | | | |
|---|---|---|---|---|
| Mar 11–17 | Abierto Mexicano de Golf | Club de Golf Mexico | Ted Purdy (USA) | 281 (–7) |
| Mar 18–24 | TransAmerican Power Products Open | Atlas CC, Guadalajara, Mexico | Manuel Villegas (COL) | 276 (–8) |
| April 20–21 | Abierto OSDE del Centro | Córdoba, Argentina | Angel Cabrera (ARG)* | 284 (E) |
| | *Beat Rafael Gomez (ARG) at the first extra hole | | | |
| April 22–28 | Roberto De Vicenzo Inv. | Montevideo, Uruguay | José de Jesús Rodríguez (MEX)* | 271 (–17) |
| | *Beat Timothy O'Neal (USA) and Sebastian Saavedra (ARG) at the second extra hole | | | |
| April 29– May 5 | Arturo Calle Colombian Open | Pereiram Colombia | Timothy O'Neal (USA) | 268 (–16) |
| May 13–19 | Mundo Maya Open | Yucatan CC, Mérida, Mexico | Jorge Fernandez-Valdez (ARG) | 277 (–11) |
| May 27– June 1 | Dominican Republic Open | Cana Bay GC, Punta Cana | Ryan Blaum (USA) | 279 (–9) |
| Oct 7–13 | Puerto Rico Classic | San Juan, Puerto Rico | Ryan Sullivan (USA) | 205 (–11) |
| Oct 14–20 | Aberto do Brasil | Rio de Janeiro, Brazil | Ryan Blaum (USA)* | 265 (–11) |
| | *Beat Alan Wagner (ARG) at the first extra hole | | | |
| Nov 28– Nov 3 | Colombian Coffee Classic | Bogotá, Colombia | José de Jesús Rodríguez (MEX) | 270 (–14) |
| Nov 4–10 | Lexus Perú Open | Los Inkas GC, Lima | Julian Etulain (ARG) | 275 (–13) |
| Nov 18–24 | Abierto de Chile | Santiago, Chile | Timothy O'Neal (USA)* | 275 (–13) |
| | *Beat Sebastian Saavedra (ARG) and Ryan Blaum (USA) at the third extra hole | | | |
| Nov 25– Dec 1 | Personal Classic | Buenos Aires, Argentina | Fabián Gomez (ARG) | 269 (–19) |
| Dec 2–8 | 108th Argentine Open | Buenos Aries | Marcelo Rozo (COL) | 278 (–10) |

## Final Order of Merit   (Figures in brackets indicate number of events played)

| | | | | | | | | |
|---|---|---|---|---|---|---|---|---|
| 1 | Ryan Blaum (Usa) | (13) | US$99,135 | | 6 | Julian Etulain (ARG) | (14) | 52,566 |
| 2 | Jose De Jesus Rodriguez (MEX) | (13) | 98,383 | | 7 | Bronson Burgoon (USA) | (14) | 51,398 |
| 3 | Timothy O'Neal (USA) | (11) | 90,015 | | 8 | Sebastian Saavedra (ARG) | (14) | 45,924 |
| 4 | Jorge Fernandez-Valdes (ARG) | (14) | 65,178 | | 9 | Oscar Serna (MEX) | (11) | 45,619 |
| 5 | Manuel Villegas (COL) | (14) | 60,671 | | 10 | Marcelo Rozo (COL) | (14) | 42,154 |

## Month by month in 2013

Adam Scott hits back from his Open collapse to become Masters champion, beating Angel Cabrera in a play-off. Fourteen-year-old Guan Tianlang makes the cut despite a one-shot slow play penalty. Martin Laird and Graeme McDowell win the events before and after Augusta and Kraft Nabisco winner Inbee Park is the new women's world number one.

# PGTI Tour 2013

www.pgtofindia.com

*Players are of Indian nationality unless stated*

| Date | Tournament | Venue | Winner | Score |
|---|---|---|---|---|
| Jan 31–Feb 3 | Gujarat Kensville Challenge | Kensville G&CC, Ahmedabad | Shiv Kapur | 274 (–14) |
| Feb 13–15 | Louis Philippe Cup | Jaypee Greens, Greater Noida | Silverglades Delhi (Shamim Khan, Rashid Khan and Himmat Rai) | |
| Feb 19–22 | PGTI Players C/ship | Chandigarh GC | Mukesh Kumar | 275 (–13) |
| Feb 26–Mar 1 | PGTI Players C/ship *Beat Mukesh Kumar in the play-off | Classic Golf Resort, Haryana | Shamim Khan* | 276 (–12) |
| Mar 6–9 | SAIL-SBI Open *Beat Rashid Khan at the first extra hole | Delhi GC, New Delhi | Anirban Lahiri* | 273 (–15) |
| Mar 14–17 | Avantha Masters | Delhi, India | Thomas Aiken (RSA) | 265 (–23) |
| April 4–7 | Panasonic Open India | Delhi GC, New Delhi | Wade Ormsby (AUS) | 279 (–9) |
| April 9–12 | PGTI Players C/ship | Mewat, Haryana | Rashid Khan | 273 (–15) |
| April 16–19 | Sri Lanka Ports Auth. Open | R. Colombo GC, Sri Lanka | Chiragh Kumar | 273 (–11) |
| April 23–26 | Jaypee Greens Open | Jaypee Greens, Greater Noida | Manav Jaini | 275 (–13) |
| May 8–11 | Surya Nepal Masters | Gokarna GR, Kathmandu | Shiva Ram Shrestha | 270 (–18) |
| June 25–28 | PGTI Players C/ship *Beat Shamim Khan at the first extra hole | Oxford G&CC, Pune | Anirban Lahiri* | 278 (–10) |
| July 2–5 | PGTI Eaglesburg Open | The Golf Resort, Bengaluru | Anirban Lahiri | 268 (–20) |
| Sep 17–20 | PGTI Players C/ship | Chandigarh Golf Club | Rahil Gangjee | 275 (–13) |
| Oct 23–26 | Bilt Open *Beat Angad Cheema at the second extra hole | Jaypee Greens, Greater Noida | Rashid Khan* | 272 (–16) |
| Nov 7–10 | Hero Indian Open | Delhi GC | Mohd. Siddikur (BAN) | 274 (–14) |
| Nov 13–16 | IndianOil XtraPremium Masters | Digboi Golf Links, Assam | Kunal Bhasin (AUS) | 277 (–11) |
| Nov 27–30 | CG Open *Beat Rashid Khan at the first extra hole | Bombay Presidency GC, Mumbai | Seenappa Chikkarangappa* | 264 (–16) |
| Dec 5–8 | Dialog Enterprise Int. | Royal Colombo GC | Anghad Cheema | 66 pts |
| Dec 11–14 | PGTI Players C/ship *Beat N Thangaraja (SRI) in play-off | Noida GC | Vijay Kumar* | 284 (–4) |
| Dec 19–22 | 12th Tata Open | Golmuri GC, Jamshedpur | M Dharmar | 272 (–13) |
| Dec 26–29 | McLeod Russel Tour Championship | Royal Calcutta GC | Anirban Lahiri | 271 (–17) |

## Final Order of Merit

| | | | | | |
|---|---|---|---|---|---|
| 1 | Rashid Khan | ₹4,638,284 | 6 | Chiragh Kumar | 2,130,135 |
| 2 | Seenappa Chikkarangappa | 3,265,313 | 7 | Md Zamal Hossain Mollah | 1,906,180 |
| 3 | Angad Cheema | 2,650,448 | 8 | M Dharma | 1,821,539 |
| 4 | Shamim Khan | 2,608,508 | 9 | Shankar Das | 1,641,278 |
| 5 | Mukesh Kumar | 2,259,917 | 10 | Abhijit Singh Chadha | 1,511,702 |

## Typhoon claims eight relatives of Jason Day

Eight of Australian golfer Jason Day's relatives including his grandmother died last year in Typhoon Haiyan which hit the Philippines.

The player's uncle and six cousins were also victims of the typhoon, which killed nearly 4,000 people and left more than a thousand missing.

Day, who was scheduled to team with Adam Scott to represent Australia in the World Cup of Golf, did not withdraw and the Australian pair went on to win the event.

Day's mother, who migrated from the Philippines to Australia 30 years ago, said many of her family members lived in the area around Tacloban, the capital of hardest-hit Leyte province.

# OneAsia Tour 2013

www.oneasia.asia

| | | | | |
|---|---|---|---|---|
| Mar 14–17 | Thailand Open | Thana City Golf & Sports Club | Prayad Marksaeng (THA) | 264 (–24) |
| Mar 28–31 | Enjoy Jakarta Indonesian Open | Emeralda GC | Ho-sung Choi (KOR) | 269 (–19) |
| May 2–5 | Volvo China Open | Binhai Lake GC | Brett Rumford (AUS) | 272 (–16) |
| May 9–12 | GS Caltex Maekyung Open | Namseoul G&CC | Hyun-woo Ryo (KOR) | 274 (–14) |
| May 16–18 | SK Telecom Open | Pinx G&CC | Matthew Griffin (AUS) | 203 (–13) |
| Oct 10–13 | Nanshan China Masters | Nanshan Int. GC | Charl Schwartzel (RSA) | 279 (–9) |
| Oct 17–20 | Kolon Korea Open | Woo Jeong Hills CC | Sung-hoon Kang (KOR) | 280 (–4) |
| Nov 7–10 | Australian PGA Championship | RACV Royal Pines, Gold Coast, Qld. | Adam Scott (AUS) | 270 (–14) |
| Nov 28– Dec 1 | Emirates Australian Open | Royal Sydney GC | Rory McIlroy (NIR) | 270 (–18) |
| Dec 12–15 | Dongfeng Nissan Cup | CTS Tycoon GC, Shenzhen, China | China 12½, Asia–Pacific 11½ | |

*Full details can be found on page 231*

## Final money list (Figures in brackets denote number of events played)

| | | | | | | | | |
|---|---|---|---|---|---|---|---|---|
| 1 | Matthew Griffin (AUS) | (7) | US$257,480 | 6 | Nick Cullen (AUS) | (8) | | 124,902 |
| 2 | Ryu Hyun-Woo (KOR) | (5) | 207,990 | 7 | Kim Do-Hoon (KOR) | (5) | | 116,418 |
| 3 | Choi Ho-Sung (KOR) | (4) | 198,615 | 8 | Song Young-Han (KOR) | (5) | | 106,466 |
| 4 | Scott Strange (AUS) | (6) | 189,232 | 9 | David McKenzie (AUS) | (7) | | 103,117 |
| 5 | Liang Wen-Chong (CHN) | (3) | 130,609 | 10 | Rhein Gibson (AUS) | (5) | | 97,870 |

## Griffin wins OneAsia Order of Merit

Two-time OneAsia winner Matthew Griffin has set his sights on new horizons after clinching the tour's 2013 Order of Merit Title at the season-ending Emirates Australian Open.

The 30-year-old from Melbourne has led the money list since winning the weather-shortened SK Telecom Open on Korea's Jeju Island in May and has been such a consistent performer that he hasn't missed a cut on OneAsia all year.

Griffin earned US$257,480.20 in 2013, beating Ryu Hyun-woo ($207,990) and Choi Ho-sung ($198,615) into second and third respectively.

The title gives Griffin a three-year exemption to OneAsia's lucrative million-dollar-minimum events including those co-sanctioned with the European and Japan Tours such as the Volvo China Open and Thailand Open.

"I always try to set myself goals and this year was to win the OneAsia Order of Merit," Griffin said at the Emirates Australian Open where he finished joint 24th after closing with a two-under-par 70.

"My main goal for next year is to try to do well in the co-sanctioned events and try to get some status in Japan and Europe as well."

He would be following a trail blazed by Korean OneAsia regular Choi, who won the Japan–OneAsia co-sanctioned event Enjoy Jakarta Indonesian PGA Championship to gain full Japanese Tour status.

# South African Sunshine Tour
*Players are of South African nationality unless stated*                    www.sunshinetour.com

| Date | Tournament | Venue | Winner | Score |
|---|---|---|---|---|
| Jan 23–25 | Telkom PGA Pro-Am | Centurion CC, Tshwane | Oliver Bekker | 196 (–20) |
| Feb 7–10 | Joburg Open | Royal Johannesburg and Kensington GC | Richard Sterne | 260 (–27) |
| Feb 14–17 | Africa Open | East London GC | Darren Fitchardt | 272 (–16) |
| Feb 21–24 | Dimension Data Pro-am | Fancourt, George | Jaco Van Zyl | 272 (–17) |
| Feb 28– Mar 3 | Tshwane Open | The Els Club, Copperleaf, Tshwane | Dawie Van der Walt | 267 (–21) |
| Mar 14–17 | Telkom PGA C/ship | Country Club, Johannesburg | Jaco Van Zyl | 268 (–20) |
| Mar 21–24 | Investec Cup | Millvale, Rustenburg & Lost City | Jaco Van Zyl | 267 (–21) |
| Apr 18–21 | Golden Pilsner Zimbabwe Open | Royal Harare GC | Jake Roos | 274 (–14) |
| May 1–4 | Investec Royal Swazi Open | Royal Swazi Sun CC | James Kingston | 45 pts |
| May 16–19 | Zambia Sugar Open | Lusaka GC, Zambia | Adilson Da Silva (BRA) | 281 (–11) |
| May 31– June 2 | Lombard Insurance Classic | Royal Swazi Sun CC | Merrick Bremner | 199 (–17) |
| June 5–7 | Vodacom Origins of Golf | Simola | Jacques Blaauw | 204 (–12) |
| June 13–15 | Polokwane Classic | Polokwane GC, Limpopo | Dean Burmester | 204 (–12) |
| June 26–28 | Vodacom Origins of Golf | Selborne Park GC, Kwazulu-Natal | Jacques Blaauw | 198 (–18) |
| July 3–5 | Sun City Challenge | Lost City GC | Adilson Da Silva (BRA) | 207 (–9) |
| Aug 7–9 | Vodacom Origins of Golf | Euphoria Golf Est., Limpopo | Heinrich Bruiners | 208 (–8) |
| Aug 21–23 | Vodacom Origins of Golf | Langebaan Country Estate | Jean Hugo | 202 (–14) |
| Aug 27–29 | Wild Waves Golf Chall. | Wild Coast Sun CC | Andrew Curlewis | 194 (–16) |
| Sep 19–21 | Platinum Classic | Mooinooi GC | Neil Schietekat | 201 (–15) |
| Oct 9–11 | Vodacom Origins of Golf Final | St Francis Links | J J Senekal | 212 (–4) |
| Oct 18–20 | BMG Classic | Glendower GC | Ulrich van den Berg | 201 (–15) |
| Oct 31– Nov 3 | Lion of Africa Cape Town Open | Royal Cape GC | Tjaart van der Walt | 274 (–14) |
| Nov 5–7 | Nedbank Affinity Cup | Lost City GC, Sun City | Jacques Blaauw | 201 (–15) |
| Nov 21–24 | **South African Open Championship** | Glendower GC | Morten Ørum Madsen (DEN) | 269 (–19) |

| | | | |
|---|---|---|---|
| 1903 Laurie Waters | 1933 Sid Brews | 1963 Allan Henning | 1987 Mark McNulty (IRL) |
| 1904 Laurie Waters | 1934 Sid Brews | 1964 No tournament (two played in 1963) | 1988 Wayne Westner |
| 1905 AG Gray | 1935 Bobby Locke | | 1989 Fred Wadsworth |
| 1906 AG Gray | 1936 Clarence Olander | 1965 Gary Player | 1990 Trevor Dodds |
| 1907 Laurie Waters | 1937 Bobby Locke | 1966 Gary Player | 1990–91 Wayne Westner |
| 1908 George Fotheringham | 1938 Bobby Locke | 1967 Gary Player | 1991–92 Ernie Els |
| 1909 John Fotheringham | 1939 Bobby Locke | 1968 Gary Player | 1992–93 Clinton Whitelaw |
| 1910 George Fotheringham | 1940 Bobby Locke | 1969 Gary Player | 1993–94 Tony Johnstone |
| 1911 George Fotheringham | 1941–1945 Not played | 1970 Tommy Horton | 1994–95 Retief Goosen |
| 1912 George Fotheringham | 1946 Bobby Locke | 1971 Simon Hobday | 1995–96 Ernie Els |
| 1913 James Prentice | 1947 Ronnie Glennie (am) | 1972 Gary Player | 1996–97 Vijay Singh (FIJ) |
| 1914 George Fotheringham | 1948 Mickey Janks | 1973 Bob Charles (NZL) | 1997–98 Ernie Els |
| 1915–1918 Not played | 1949 Sid Brews | 1974 Bobby Cole | 1998–99 David Frost |
| 1919 WH Horne | 1950 Bobby Locke | 1975 Gary Player | 1999–2000 Matthias Grönberg (SWE) |
| 1920 Laurie Waters | 1951 Bobby Locke | 1976 Dale Hayes | |
| 1921 Jock Brews | 1952 Sid Brews | 1976 Gary Player | 2000–01 Mark McNulty (IRL) |
| 1922 F Jangle | 1953 Jimmy Boyd | 1977 Gary Player | 2001–02 Tim Clark |
| 1923 Jock Brews | 1954 Reg Taylor (am) | 1978 Hugh Baiocchi | 2002–03 Trevor Immelman |
| 1924 Bertie Elkin | 1955 Bobby Locke | 1979 Gary Player | 2003–04 Trevor Immelman |
| 1925 Sid Brews | 1956 Gary Player | 1980 Bobby Cole | 2004–05 Tim Clark |
| 1926 Jock Brews | 1957 Harold Henning | 1981 Gary Player | 2005–06 Retief Goosen |
| 1927 Sid Brews | 1958 Arthur Stewart (am) | 1982 No tournament (two played in 1976) | 2006–07 Ernie Els |
| 1928 Jock Brews | 1959 Denis Hutchinson (am) | | 2007 James Kingston |
| 1929 Archie Tosh | 1960 Gary Player | 1983 Charlie Bolling | 2008 Richard Sterne* |
| 1930 Sid Brews | 1961 Retief Waltman | 1984 Tony Johnstone | *Beat Gareth Maybin (NIR) at |
| 1931 Sid Brews | 1962 Harold Henning | 1985 Gavin Levenson | 1st extra hole |
| 1932 Charles McIlveny | 1963 Retief Waltman | 1986 David Frost | |

South African Sunshine Tour   *continued*

| | | |
|---|---|---|
| 2009 Richie Ramsay (SCO)* | 2010 Ernie Els | 2012 Henrik Stenson (SWE) |
| *Beat Shiv Kapur (IND) at 1st extra hole* | 2011 Hennie Otto | |

| | | | | |
|---|---|---|---|---|
| Nov 28–Dec 1 | Alfred Dunhill Championship | Leopard Creek GC | Charl Schwartzel | 271 (–17) |
| Dec 5–8 | Nedbank Golf Challenge | Gary Player CC, Sun City | Thomas Björn (DEN) | 268 (–20) |
| Dec 11–14 | Nelson Mandela Championship | Mount Edgecombe CC | Dawie Van der Walt | 195 (–15) |

## Final Order of Merit (Figures in brackets indicate number of events played)

| | | | | | | | | |
|---|---|---|---|---|---|---|---|---|
| 1 | Charl Schwartzel | (3) | SAR5,699,739 | 6 | Richard Finch (ENG) | (5) | 2,554,209 |
| 2 | Dawie Van der Walt | (10) | 5,082,292 | 7 | Richard Sterne | (3) | 2,517,955 |
| 3 | Darren Fichardt | (10) | 4,502,605 | 8 | Hennie Otto | (9) | 2,475,830 |
| 4 | Morten Ørum Madsen (DEN) | (6) | 3,197,582 | 9 | Romain Wattel (FRA) | (5) | 2,063,510 |
| 5 | Jaco Van Zyl | (8) | 3,027,749 | 10 | Jbe' Kruger | (10) | 2,045,404 |

---

# Distinguished Service Award for Trevino

Lee Trevino, the 73-year-old former double Open champion, has received the PGA of America's highest honour – the Distinguished Service Award. He was presented with it at the 95th PGA Championship at Oak Hill where he won one of his six major titles in 1968.

Inaugurated in 1988, the award honours outstanding individuals who display leadership and humanitarian qualities including integrity, sportsmanship and enthusiasm for the game.

"Lee is the classic rags to riches story in golf and throughout his life has never lost sight of his roots and his humble beginnings," said PGA of American President Ted Bishop, presenting the award.

"He was a self-made player who persevered and won championships because he owned his golf swing. He has also spent countless hours tirelessly helping others."

Born Lee Buck Trevino in Dallas, he was raised by his mother and his grandfather. Lee began picking cotton when he was just five years old and later became a caddie.

He left school at 14 to help raise money for his mother, grandfather, uncle and two sisters who lived in a small house across from the seventh hole at the Glen Lakes Country Club in Dallas. The house had no running water and no electricity.

After spending four years in the US Marine Corps he turned professional in 1960. At that time his talent talent was spotted by PGA of America life member Bill Eschenbrenner.

"When I saw what a great talent he was I told him that I would help him get a PGA card," said Eshenbrenner, who had noticed Lee working in the golf shop and managing the range at the Horizon Hills Country Club.

Joining the PGA Tour at the age of 27, Lee won the first of his two US Open Championships in 1968 at Oak Hill – the first of four times that he was to beat Jack Nicklaus into second place.

Trevino went on to win 29 times including his six majors – The Open in 1971 and 1972; the US Open in 1968 and 1971 and the US PGA Championship in 1974 and 1984. He played in six Ryder Cup sides and captained the Americans in 1985.

At the height of his career he was one of three players struck by lightning at the 1975 Western Open. He fought back from the injury and after a series of operations went on to win 29 titles on the Champions Tour including two Senior PGA Championships in 1992 and 1994.

For more than 25 years Trevino has supported countless charities for underpriviledged children, for shelters for abused women, for disease prevention and for research.

He has done much for the St Jude Children's Research Hospital including giving a $500,000 donation after he holed in one in a par3 shoot-out.

Trevino and his wife Claudia live in Dallas and have a daughter, Olivia, a University of Southern California graduate. He also has three further sons, a daughter, eight grandchildren and one great grandchild.

# Two players shoot 59 but both scores are unofficial

In the span of 10 minutes at the Nelson Mandela Championship in Durban, South Africa, two players registered an elusive 59 ... sort of.

Spain's Jorge Campillo and South Africa's Colin Nel each fired an 11-under-par 59 at Mount Edgecombe Country Club early in the second round but the scores were unofficial because a lift, clean and place provision was in place.

Lift, clean and place or not, a 59 is incredible. Two of them in one day is mind-blowing.

Campillo's 59 featured seven birdies and two eagles, while Nel's came as the result of nine birdies and an eagle.

Six players have shot 59 on the PGA Tour while the European Tour is still waiting for its first official 59. The last player to do so was Jim Furyk in the second round of the 2013 BMW Championship. Furyk made 11 birdies and holed out for an eagle in that round at Conway Farms Golf Club near Chicago and made a 3-footer at the par-4 ninth hole – his final hole – for a 12-under 59.

# Rookie Matsuyama tops Japanese Money List

Hideki Matsuyama, twice winner of what is now the Asia–Pacific Amateur Championship, has become the first rookie to claim the Japanese Tour's money title with a win at the Casio World Open.

Matsuyama, who turned pro in April, won four tournaments in Japan this season: The Tsuruya Open, the Diamond Cup Golf, the Fujisankei Classic and the Casio World Open. In seven tournaments he played in America, Matsuyama had six top-25 finishes. He plans to compete on the PGA Tour in 2014.

Matsuyama shot a 70 in the final round of the Casio event to finish at 12-under-par 276, one stroke ahead of Yuta Ikeda. The 21-year-old college student received $390,000 for his latest success, bringing his earnings this season to slightly more than $2 million.

In 2011 while still an amateur, Matsuyama gave an indication of his talent when he beat the professionals to win the Mitsui Sumitoma Visa Taiheiyo Masters on the Japanese circuit.

He clinched the No 1 spot with one tournament still to be played.

# Bizarre events in Hong Kong

One of the more bizarre events in professional tournament golf happened during the first round of the Hong Kong Open and the excellent Australian PGA website told the complicated story.

Fourth alternate Chih-Bing Lam got a last minute start in the field and, carrying his own bag, shot an opening 66 to be in third place after 18 holes. The sequence of events leading up to his start were unusual to say the least.

First alternate Anthony Kang assumed he would not get a call up to play the event so decided to caddie for his friend, Australia's Unho Park, instead.

When Finland's Joonas Granberg was disqualified for not making his tee time (his caddie had gone to the wrong tee with his clubs) his place in the field was given to second alternate Jeppe Huldahl who was mid swing when he was stopped and told he could not take the spot because he was not an Asian Tour member.

According to the tournament rules, because Granberg is an Asian Tour member he had to be replaced by an Asian Tour member after his disqualification.

That left Lam unexpectedly at the top of the alternate list. "I ran up to the tee," he said afterwards. "I had an extra club which I took out before I teed off, I had a bunch of old golf balls, no yardage book, no caddie but it worked out well for me."

In a further twist, Lam played in the same group as Unho Park whose caddie for the day, Anthony Kang, had inadvertently sparked the bizarre chain of events with his withdrawal.

Unfortunately, Lam could not sustain his first round brilliance and finished the tournament tied 65th.

# World Championship Events

## WGC – Accenture Match Play Championship

*Ritz-Carlton, Dove Mountain, AZ, USA*                                    [7791–72]

**First Round:**
Shane Lowry (IRL) beat Rory McIlroy (NIR)  I up
Carl Pettersson (SWE) beat Rickie Fowler (USA)  at 19th
Alexander Noren (SWE) beat Dustin Johnson (USA)  6 and 4
Graeme McDowell (NIR) beat Padraig Harrington (IRL)  2 up
Bubba Watson (USA) beat Chris Wood (ENG)  2 and I
Jim Furyk (USA) beat Ryan Moore (USA)  4 and 2
Russell Henley (USA) beat Charl Schwartzel (RSA)  I up
Jason Day (AUS) beat Zach Johnson (USA)  6 and 5

Charles Howell III (USA) beat Tiger Woods (USA)  2 and I
Gonzalo Fernandez-Castano (ESP) beat Francesco Molinari (ITA)  2 up
Webb Simpson (USA) beat David Lynn (ENG)  5 and 4
Peter Hanson (SWE) beat Thomas Björn (DEN)  3 and 2
Rafael Cabrera-Bello (ESP) beat Lee Westwood (ENG)  at 19th
Martin Kaymer (GER) beat George Coetze (RSA)  2 and I
Richard Sterne (RSA) beat Jason Dufner (USA)  I up
Hunter Mahan (USA) beat Matteo Manassero (ITA)  5 and 4

Louis Oosthuizen (RSA) beat Richie Ramsay (SCO)  2 and I
Robert Garrigus (USA) beat Branden Grace (RSA)  4 and 3
Marcus Fraser (AUS) beat Keegan Bradley (USA)  I up
Fredrik Jacobson (SWE) beat Ernie Els (RSA)  I up
Justin Rose (ENG) beat KJ Choi (KOR)  2 and I
Nicolas Colsaerts (BEL) beat Bill Haas (USA)  5 and 4
Sergio García (ESP) beat Thongchai Jaidee (THA)  at 20th
Matt Kuchar (USA) beat Hiroyuki Fujita (JPN)  3 and 2

Luke Donald (ENG) beat Marcel Siem (GER)  I up
Scott Piercy (USA) beat Paul Lawrie (SCO)  4 and 3
Steve Stricker (USA) beat Henrik Stenson (SWE)  5 and 4
Nick Watney (USA) beat David Toms (USA)  5 and 4
Tim Clark (RSA) beat Adam Scott (AUS)  2 and I
Thorbjørn Olesen (DEN) beat Jamie Donaldson (WAL)  3 and 2
Ian Poulter (ENG) beat Stephen Gallacher (SCO)  2 and I
Bo Van Pelt (USA) beat John Senden (AUS)  6 and 5

**Second Round:**

| | |
|---|---|
| Lowry beat Pettersson  6 and 5 | Garrigus beat Oosthuizen  3 and 2 |
| McDowell beat Noren  at 20th | Jacobson beat Fraser  4 and 3 |
| Watson beat Furyk at 22nd | Colsaerts beat Rose  4 and 2 |
| Day beat Henley  at 19th | Kuchar beat García  2 and I |
| Fernandez-Castano beat Howell  6 and 5 | Piercy beat Donald  7 and 8 |
| Simpson beat Hanson  I up | Stricker beat Watney  at 21st |
| Kaymer beat Cabrera-Bello  2 and I | Clark beat Olesen  3 and 2 |
| Mahan beat Sterne  4 and 3 | Poulter beat Van Pelt  3 and I |

**Third Round:**

| | |
|---|---|
| McDowell beat Lowry  3 and 2 | Garrigus beat Jacobson  3 and I |
| Day beat Watson  4 and 3 | Kuchar beat Colsaerts  4 and 3 |
| Simpson beat Fernandez-Castano  2 up | Stricket beat Piercy  I up |
| Mahan beat Kaymer  5 and 4 | Poulter beat Clark  5 and 3 |

**Quarter-finals:**

| | |
|---|---|
| Day beat McDowell  I up | Kuchar beat Garrigus  3 and 2 |
| Mahan beat Simpson  I up | Poulter beat Stricker  3 and 2 |

**Semi-finals:**
Kuchar beat Day  4 and 3
Mahan beat Poulter  4 and 3

**Final:**
Matt Kuchar beat Hunter Mahan  2 and 1

| Winner: | $1,500,000 | €1,148,809 |
|---|---|---|
| Runner-up: | $875,000 | €670,138 |
| 3rd Place: | $615,000 | €471,011 |

**Third Place Match:**
Day beat Poulter  1 up

2000  Darren Clarke (NIR) beat Tiger Woods (USA) 4 and 3 at La Costa, Carlsbad, CA, USA
2001  Steve Stricker (USA) beat Pierre Fulke (SWE) 4 and 3 at Metropolitan GC, Melbourne, Australia
2002  Kevin Sutherland (USA) beat Scott McCarron (USA) 1 hole at La Costa, Carlsbad, CA, USA
2003  Tiger Woods (USA) beat David Toms (USA) 2 and 1 at La Costa, Carlsbad, CA, USA
2004  Tiger Woods (USA) beat Davis Love III (USA) 3 and 2 at  La Costa, Carlsbad, CA, USA
2005  David Toms (USA) beat Chris DiMarco (USA) 6 and 5 at La Costa, Carlsbad, CA, USA
2006  Geoff Ogilvy (AUS) beat Davis Love III (USA) 3 and 2 at  La Costa, Carlsbad, CA, USA
2007  Henrik Stenson (SWE) beat Geoff Ogilvy (AUS) 2 and 1 at Gallery, Tucson, AZ, USA
2008  Tiger Woods (USA) beat Stewart Cink (USA) 8 and 7 at Gallery, Tucson, AZ, USA
2009  Geoff Ogilvy (AUS) beat Paul Casey (ENG) 4 and 3 at Dove Mountain, AZ, USA
2010  Ian Poulter (ENG) beat Paul Casey (ENG) 4 and 3 at Dove Mountain, AZ, USA
2011  Luke Donald (ENG) beat Martin Kaymer (GER) 3 and 2 at Dove Mountain, AZ, USA
2012  Hunter Mahan (USA) beat Rory McIlroy (NIR) 2 and 1 at Dove Mountain, AZ, USA

# WGC – Cadillac Championship  (formerly WGC – CA Championship)
*Doral, Orlando, FL, USA*                                                                [7334–72]

| 1 | Tiger Woods (USA) | 66-65-67-71—269 | $1,500,000 |
|---|---|---|---|
| 2 | Steve Stricker (USA) | 67-67-69-68—271 | 880,000 |
| 3 | Adam Scott (AUS) | 72-70-68-64—274 | 417,500 |
| | Sergio García (ESP) | 66-72-67-69—274 | 417,500 |
| | Phil Mickelson (USA) | 67-67-69-71—274 | 417,500 |
| | Graeme McDowell (NIR) | 66-67-69-72—274 | 417,500 |
| 7 | Keegan Bradley (USA) | 68-68-69-71—276 | 240,000 |
| 8 | Rory McIlroy (NIR) | 73-69-71-65—278 | 163,750 |
| | Justin Rose (ENG) | 68-72-70-68—278 | 163,750 |
| | Peter Hanson (SWE) | 67-71-70-70—278 | 163,750 |
| | Michael Thompson (USA) | 69-69-67-73—278 | 163,750 |
| 12 | Richard Sterne (RSA) | 70-71-71-67—279 | 113,750 |
| | Charles Howell III (USA) | 68-71-69-71—279 | 113,750 |
| | Jason Dufner (USA) | 69-69-69-72—279 | 113,750 |
| | Dustin Johnson (USA) | 68-69-70-72—279 | 113,750 |
| 16 | Freddie Jacobson (SWE) | 66-69-71-74—280 | 98,000 |
| | Charl Schwartzel (RSA) | 71-65-69-75—280 | 98,000 |
| 18 | Nicolas Colsaerts (BEL) | 71-71-67-72—281 | 93,000 |
| | Bubba Watson (USA) | 66-69-71-75—281 | 93,000 |
| 20 | Alexander Noren (SWE) | 69-70-72-71—282 | 88,000 |
| | Webb Simpson (USA) | 72-67-71-72—282 | 88,000 |
| | John Senden (AUS) | 69-69-70-74—282 | 88,000 |
| 23 | Matteo Manassero (ITA) | 71-71-75-66—283 | 83,000 |
| | Scott Jamieson (SCO) | 70-69-72-72—283 | 83,000 |
| 25 | Lee Westwood (ENG) | 73-69-71-71—284 | 79,000 |
| | Scott Piercy (USA) | 70-73-69-72—284 | 79,000 |
| | Hunter Mahan (USA) | 67-72-71-74—284 | 79,000 |
| 28 | Francesco Molinari (ITA) | 78-66-72-69—285 | 75,000 |
| | Ernie Els (RSA) | 73-69-72-71—285 | 75,000 |
| | Russell Henley (USA) | 70-72-70-73—285 | 75,000 |
| | Ian Poulter (ENG) | 68-70-72-75—285 | 75,000 |
| | John Huh (USA) | 71-67-71-76—285 | 75,000 |
| 33 | Jason Day (AUS) | 74-66-75-71—286 | 71,500 |
| | Louis Oosthuizen (RSA) | 70-75-69-72—286 | 71,500 |
| 35 | Matt Kuchar (USA) | 72-72-72-71—287 | 68,500 |
| | Jim Furyk (USA) | 72-70-72-73—287 | 68,500 |
| | Brian Gay (USA) | 70-76-69-72—287 | 68,500 |

## WGC – Cadillac Championship *continued*

| | | | |
|---|---|---|---|
| 35T | Rickie Fowler (USA) | 69-69-71-78—287 | 68,500 |
| 39 | Marcel Siem (GER) | 75-73-70-70—288 | 64,500 |
| | David Lynn (ENG) | 71-70-76-71—288 | 64,500 |
| | Padraig Harrington (IRL) | 76-72-68-72—288 | 64,500 |
| | Bo Van Pelt (USA) | 68-75-71-74—288 | 64,500 |
| 43 | Bill Haas (USA) | 72-73-72-72—289 | 60,500 |
| | Luke Donald (ENG) | 70-76-71-72—289 | 60,500 |
| | Chris Wood (ENG) | 71-74-71-73—289 | 60,500 |
| | Gonzalo Fernandez-Castano (ESP) | 72-70-73-74—289 | 60,500 |
| 47 | Geoff Ogilvy (AUS) | 69-74-73-74—290 | 57,500 |
| | Zach Johnson (USA) | 71-67-77-75—290 | 57,500 |
| 49 | Branden Grace (RSA) | 73-74-72-72—291 | 54,500 |
| | Nick Watney (USA) | 69-71-77-74—291 | 54,500 |
| | Martin Kaymer (GER) | 76-68-73-74—291 | 54,500 |
| | Carl Pettersson (SWE) | 71-75-71-74—291 | 54,500 |
| 53 | Thorbjørn Olesen (DEN) | 75-75-70-72—292 | 50,600 |
| | Stephen Gallacher (SCO) | 74-75-69-74—292 | 50,600 |
| | Ryan Moore (USA) | 73-71-72-76—292 | 50,600 |
| | Thaworn Wiratchant (THA) | 69-69-77-77—292 | 50,600 |
| | George Coetzee (RSA) | 70-69-73-80—292 | 50,600 |
| 58 | Paul Lawrie (SCO) | 78-73-72-70—293 | 48,750 |
| | Mike Hendry (NZL) | 72-66-78-77—293 | 48,750 |
| 60 | Marcus Fraser (AUS) | 73-72-77-73—295 | 47,500 |
| | John Merrick (USA) | 75-72-72-76—295 | 47,500 |
| | Tim Clark (RSA) | 72-73-71-79—295 | 47,500 |
| 63 | Jamie Donaldson (WAL) | 72-77-76-74—299 | 46,250 |
| | Rafael Cabrera-Bello (ESP) | 71-74-76-78—299 | 46,250 |
| 65 | Robert Garrigus (USA) | 75-75-74-76—300 | 45,500 |
| | Brandt Snedeker (USA) | DNS | |

| | | | |
|---|---|---|---|
| 1999 | Tiger Woods* (USA) | 71-69-70-68—278 | at Valderrama GC, Cadiz, Spain |

*Woods beat Miguel Angel Jiménez (ESP) at the first extra hole

| | | | |
|---|---|---|---|
| 2000 | Mike Weir (CAN) | 68-75-65-69—277 | at Valderrama GC, Cadiz, Spain |
| 2001 | Cancelled | | |
| 2002 | Tiger Woods (USA) | 65-65-67-66—263 | at Mount Juliet, Kilkenny, Ireland |
| 2003 | Tiger Woods (USA) | 67-66-69-72—274 | at Capital City, Atlanta, GA |
| 2004 | Ernie Els (RSA) | 69-64-68-69—270 | at Mount Juliet, Kilkenny, Ireland |
| 2005 | Tiger Woods* (USA) | 67-68-68-67—270 | at Harding Park, San Francisco, CA |

*Woods beat John Daly at the second extra hole

| | | | |
|---|---|---|---|
| 2006 | Tiger Woods (USA) | 63-64-67-67—261 | at The Grove, Chandlers Cross, Herts |
| 2007 | Tiger Woods (USA) | 71-66-68-73—278 | at Doral, Orlando, FL, USA |
| 2008 | Geoff Ogilvy (AUS) | 65-67-68-71—271 | at Doral, Orlando, FL, USA |
| 2009 | Phil Mickelson (AUS) | 65-66-69-69—269 | at Doral, Orlando, FL, USA |
| 2010 | Ernie Els (RSA) | 68-66-70-66—270 | at Doral, Orlando, FL, USA |
| 2011 | Nick Watney (USA) | 67-70-68-67—272 | at Doral, Orlando, FL, USA |
| 2012 | Justin Rose (ENG) | 69-64-69-70—272 | at Doral, Orlando, FL, USA |

## WGC – Bridgestone Invitational   *Firestone CC, Akron, OH, USA*   [7400–70]

| | | | |
|---|---|---|---|
| 1 | Tiger Woods (USA) | 66-61-68-70—265 | $1,500,000 |
| 2 | Keegan Bradley (USA) | 66-68-71-67—272 | 692,500 |
| | Henrik Stenson (SWE) | 65-70-67-70—272 | 692,500 |
| 4 | Zach Johnson (USA) | 69-70-68-67—274 | 321,666 |
| | Miguel Angel Jiménez (ESP) | 71-69-65-69—274 | 321,666 |
| | Jason Dufner (USA) | 67-69-67-71—274 | 321,666 |
| 7 | Bill Haas (USA) | 67-68-69-71—275 | 205,000 |
| | Chris Wood (ENG) | 66-68-70-71—275 | 205,000 |
| 9 | Martin Kaymer (GER) | 74-67-69-66—276 | 145,750 |
| | Jim Furyk (USA) | 67-69-72-68—276 | 145,750 |
| | Richard Sterne (RSA) | 70-68-70-68—276 | 145,750 |
| | Luke Donald (ENG) | 67-69-68-72—276 | 145,750 |
| 13 | Steve Stricker (USA) | 71-67-70-69—277 | 114,000 |
| 14 | Webb Simpson (USA) | 64-75-73-66—278 | 102,666 |

| 14T | Harris English (USA) | 70-68-72-68—278 | 102,666 |
| | Adam Scott (AUS) | 73-68-66-71—278 | 102,666 |
| 17 | Jamie Donaldson (WAL) | 70-69-71-69—279 | 93,000 |
| | Justin Rose (ENG) | 69-72-69-69—279 | 93,000 |
| 19 | Ian Poulter (ENG) | 69-72-69-70—280 | 89,000 |
| | John Merrick (USA) | 72-66-70-72—280 | 89,000 |
| 21 | Michael Thompson (USA) | 72-71-70-68—281 | 81,166 |
| | Charl Schwartzel (RSA) | 74-74-64-69—281 | 81,166 |
| | Bo Van Pelt (USA) | 71-73-68-69—281 | 81,166 |
| | Hideki Matsuyama (JPN) | 72-68-70-71—281 | 81,166 |
| | Phil Mickelson (USA) | 72-71-67-71—281 | 81,166 |
| | Rickie Fowler (USA) | 67-71-70-73—281 | 81,166 |
| 27 | Russell Henley (USA) | 72-69-75-66—282 | 73,500 |
| | Paul Casey (ENG) | 70-70-73-69—282 | 73,500 |
| | Paul Lawrie (SCO) | 69-72-71-70—282 | 73,500 |
| | Matt Kuchar (USA) | 72-71-69-70—282 | 73,500 |
| | Rory McIlroy (NIR) | 70-71-69-72—282 | 73,500 |
| | Bubba Watson (USA) | 67-69-72-74—282 | 73,500 |
| 33 | Dustin Johnson (USA) | 72-69-75-67—283 | 68,000 |
| | Boo Weekley (USA) | 73-70-70-70—283 | 68,000 |
| | Brandt Snedeker (USA) | 72-70-71-70—283 | 68,000 |
| | Peter Hanson (SWE) | 70-72-70-71—283 | 68,000 |
| | Ryan Moore (USA) | 66-74-70-73—283 | 68,000 |
| 38 | Gonzalo Fernandez-Castano (ESP) | 70-74-68-72—284 | 64,500 |
| | Angel Cabrera (ARG) | 72-68-70-74—284 | 64,500 |
| 40 | Sergio García (ESP) | 71-76-70-68—285 | 61,500 |
| | Graeme McDowell (NIR) | 71-71-71-72—285 | 61,500 |
| | Lee Westwood (ENG) | 71-71-71-72—285 | 61,500 |
| | Kiradech Aphibarnrat (THA) | 69-68-73-75—285 | 61,500 |
| 44 | Billy Horschel (USA) | 74-74-72-66—286 | 57,500 |
| | Stephen Gallacher (SCO) | 74-74-67-71—286 | 57,500 |
| | Nick Watney (USA) | 71-72-70-73—286 | 57,500 |
| | Francesco Molinari (ITA) | 70-70-72-74—286 | 57,500 |
| 48 | Martin Laird (SCO) | 77-70-71-69—287 | 53,000 |
| | Shane Lowry (IRL) | 72-76-70-69—287 | 53,000 |
| | Richie Ramsay (SCO) | 73-69-73-72—287 | 53,000 |
| | Thorbjørn Olesen (DEN) | 73-69-72-73—287 | 53,000 |
| | Ernie Els (RSA) | 71-72-70-74—287 | 53,000 |
| 53 | Jason Day (AUS) | 74-72-72-70—288 | 48,875 |
| | David Lynn (ENG) | 71-73-73-71—288 | 48,875 |
| | Sang-Moon Bae (KOR) | 73-73-70-72—288 | 48,875 |
| | Matteo Manassero (ITA) | 71-70-74-73—288 | 48,875 |
| 57 | Derek Ernst (USA) | 73-76-71-69—289 | 47,250 |
| | Nicolas Colsaerts (BEL) | 72-70-74-73—289 | 47,250 |
| 59 | Kevin Streelman (USA) | 76-73-71-70—290 | 45,750 |
| | Scott Piercy (USA) | 68-77-75-70—290 | 45,750 |
| | Jonas Blixt (SWE) | 70-75-73-72—290 | 45,750 |
| | D A Points (USA) | 73-69-75-73—290 | 45,750 |
| 63 | Brett Rumford (AUS) | 76-74-72-70—292 | 44,250 |
| | Brian Gay (USA) | 72-70-75-75—292 | 44,250 |
| 65 | Tommy Gainey (USA) | 74-71-76-72—293 | 42,800 |
| | Mikko Ilonen (FIN) | 73-73-73-74—293 | 42,800 |
| | Satoshi Kodaira (JPN) | 70-74-76-73—293 | 42,800 |
| | Ken Duke (USA) | 70-75-73-75—293 | 42,800 |
| | Branden Grace (RSA) | 70-75-70-78—293 | 42,800 |
| 70 | Carl Pettersson (SWE) | 72-73-73-77—295 | 42.000 |
| 71 | Toru Taniguchi (JPN) | 75-73-79-73—300 | 41,750 |
| 72 | Jaco Van Zyl (RSA) | 73-82-78-72—305 | 41,500 |
| 73 | Daniel Popovic (AUS) | 79-77-76-82—314 | 41,250 |
| | Louis Oosthuizen (RSA) | DNS | |

## WGC – Bridgestone Invitational   *continued*

| | | | |
|---|---|---|---|
| 1999 | T Woods (USA) | 66-71-62-71—270 | at Firestone CC, Akron, OH |
| 2000 | T Woods (USA) | 64-61-67-67—259 | at Firestone CC, Akron, OH |
| 2001 | T Woods (USA) | 66-67-66-69—268 | at Firestone CC, Akron, OH |
| 2002 | C Parry (AUS) | 72-65-66-65—268 | at Sahalee, Redmond, WA |
| 2003 | D Clarke (NIR) | 65-70-66-67—268 | at Firestone CC, Akron, OH |
| 2004 | S Cink (USA) | 63-68-68-70—269 | at Firestone CC, Akron, OH |
| 2005 | T Woods (USA) | 66-70-67-71—274 | at Firestone CC, Akron, OH |
| 2006 | T Woods (USA) | 67-64-71-68—270 | at Firestone CC, Akron, OH |
| 2007 | V Singh (FIJ) | 67-66-69-68—270 | at Firestone CC, Akron, OH |
| 2008 | V Singh (FIJ) | 67-66-69-68—270 | at Firestone CC, Akron, OH |
| 2009 | T Woods (USA) | 68-70-65-65—268 | at Firestone CC, Akron, OH |
| 2010 | H Mahan (USA) | 71-67-66-64—268 | at Firestone CC, Akron, OH |
| 2011 | A Scott (AUS) | 62-70-66-65—263 | at Firestone CC, Akron, OH |
| 2012 | K Bradley (USA) | 67-69-67-64—267 | at Firestone CC, Akron, OH |

## WGC – HSBC Champions Tournament   *Mission Hills GC, Shenzhen, China*   [725|-72]

| | | | | |
|---|---|---|---|---|
| 1 | Dustin Johnson (USA) | 69-63-66-66—264 | €1,012,146 |
| 2 | Ian Poulter (ENG) | 71-67-63-66—267 | 614,517 |
| 3 | Graeme McDowell (NIR) | 69-69-64-66—268 | 347,021 |
| 4 | Sergio García (ESP) | 70-68-69-63—270 | 263,881 |
| 5 | Justin Rose (ENG) | 68-71-65-68—272 | 216,888 |
| 6 | Graham DeLaet (CAN) | 71-68-65-69—273 | 167,366 |
| | Rory McIlroy (NIR) | 65-72-67-69—273 | 167,366 |
| 8 | Jamie Donaldson (WAL) | 67-74-66-67—274 | 116,879 |
| | Martin Kaymer (GER) | 70-74-62-68—274 | 116,879 |
| | Bubba Watson (USA) | 68-69-69-68—274 | 116,879 |
| 11 | Keegan Bradley (USA) | 71-68-68-68—275 | 84,345 |
| | Ernie Els (RSA) | 69-69-71-66—275 | 84,345 |
| | Boo Weekley (USA) | 70-67-69-69—275 | 84,345 |
| 14 | Phil Mickelson (USA) | 71-68-72-65—276 | 72,296 |
| 15 | Liang Wen-chong (CHN) | 72-67-72-66—277 | 67,597 |
| | Louis Oosthuizen (RSA) | 70-70-70-67—277 | 67,597 |
| 17 | Jordan Spieth (USA) | 68-71-70-69—278 | 65,067 |
| 18 | Tommy Fleetwood (ENG) | 68-70-69-72—279 | 62,898 |
| | Jin Jeong (KOR) | 70-69-71-69—279 | 62,898 |
| 20 | Paul Casey (ENG) | 69-73-69-69—280 | 60,729 |
| 21 | Grégory Bourdy (FRA) | 75-68-67-71—281 | 54,294 |
| | Bill Haas (USA) | 72-72-69-68—281 | 54,294 |
| | Peter Hanson (SWE) | 70-73-70-68—281 | 54,294 |
| | Scott Hend (AUS) | 69-74-66-72—281 | 54,294 |
| | Mikko Ilonen (FIN) | 72-69-72-68—281 | 54,294 |
| | Matteo Manassero (ITA) | 72-70-70-69—281 | 54,294 |
| | Francesco Molinari (ITA) | 72-69-70-70—281 | 54,294 |
| | Scott Piercy (USA) | 72-73-68-68—281 | 54,294 |
| | Bo Van Pelt (USA) | 77-67-66-71—281 | 54,294 |
| | Jaco van Zyl (RSA) | 72-73-68-68—281 | 54,294 |
| 31 | Luke Donald (ENG) | 70-71-70-71—282 | 49,161 |
| | Henrik Stenson (SWE) | 74-76-67-65—282 | 49,161 |
| | Nick Watney (USA) | 75-74-67-66—282 | 49,161 |
| 34 | Mark Brown (NZL) | 72-68-72-71—283 | 46,270 |
| | Jason Dufner (USA) | 73-67-71-72—283 | 46,270 |
| | Billy Horschel (USA) | 71-69-72-71—283 | 46,270 |
| | Huang Wen-yi (CHN) | 70-74-69-70—283 | 46,270 |
| | Kevin Streelman (USA) | 70-73-72-68—283 | 46,270 |
| 39 | Thomas Björn (DEN) | 74-72-70-68—284 | 41,932 |
| | Gonzalo Fernandez-Castaño (ESP) | 67-71-70-76—284 | 41,932 |
| | Branden Grace (RSA) | 77-71-67-69—284 | 41,932 |
| | Li Hao-tong (CHN) | 72-71-74-67—284 | 41,932 |
| | David Lynn (ENG) | 74-70-69-71—284 | 41,932 |
| | Richard Sterne (RSA) | 74-73-74-63—284 | 41,932 |
| | Chris Wood (ENG) | 71-71-73-69—284 | 41,932 |

| 46 | Ken Duke (USA) | 70-72-73-70—285 | 37,955 |
| | Brian Gay (USA) | 71-72-72-70—285 | 37,955 |
| | Thongchai Jaidee (THA) | 76-68-68-73—285 | 37,955 |
| | Jimmy Walker (USA) | 73-73-69-70—285 | 37,955 |
| 50 | Hiroyuki Fujita (JPN) | 75-70-68-73—286 | 35,425 |
| | Michael Hendry (NZL) | 72-73-73-68—286 | 35,425 |
| | Masahiro Kawamura (JPN) | 73-72-70-71—286 | 35,425 |
| | Ryan Moore (USA) | 70-74-69-73—286 | 35,425 |
| | Michael Thompson (USA) | 74-72-68-72—286 | 35,425 |
| 55 | Kiradech Aphibarnrat (THA) | 69-78-68-72—287 | 33,437 |
| | Rickie Fowler (USA) | 74-70-70-73—287 | 33,437 |
| | John Merrick (USA) | 72-75-69-71—287 | 33,437 |
| | Brandt Snedeker (USA) | 73-74-70-70—287 | 33,437 |
| | Peter Uihlein (USA) | 71-73-73-70—287 | 33,437 |
| | Lee Westwood (ENG) | 71-73-68-75—287 | 33,437 |
| 61 | Derek Ernst (USA) | 71-72-73-72—288 | 31,991 |
| | Darren Fichardt (RSA) | 70-74-75-69—288 | 31,991 |
| 63 | Gaganjeet Bhullar (IND) | 69-71-75-74—289 | 31,449 |
| | Jonas Blixt (SWE) | 70-75-74-70—289 | 31,449 |
| | Stephen Gallacher (SCO) | 73-73-72-71—289 | 31,449 |
| 66 | Ryo Ishikawa (JPN) | 81-72-68-69—290 | 30,997 |
| | Daniel Popovic (AUS) | 77-71-69-73—290 | 30,997 |
| 68 | D A Points (USA) | 72-74-70-75—291 | 30,635 |
| | Wu Ashun (CHN) | 74-75-70-72—291 | 30,635 |
| 70 | David Howell (ENG) | 72-75-73-72—292 | 30,364 |
| 71 | Seuk-hyun Baek (KOR) | 81-68-69-75—293 | 30,184 |
| 72 | Miguel Angel Jiménez (ESP) | 75-76-70-74—295 | 30,003 |
| 73 | Raphaël Jacquelin (FRA) | 81-70-71-74—296 | 29,822 |
| 74 | George Coetzee (RSA) | 75-77-74-71—297 | 29,641 |
| 75 | Hu Mu (CHN) | 76-75-73-75—299 | 29,461 |
| 76 | Brett Rumford (AUS) | 75-77-79-72—303 | 29,280 |
| 77 | Huang Ming-jie (CHN) | 83-77-80-83—323 | 29,099 |
| 78 | Hideki Matsuyama (JPN) | 71 WD | |

| | | |
|---|---|---|
| 2006 David Howell (ENG) | 2008 (2009 season) | 2011 M Kaymer (GER) |
| 2007 Yang-Eun Yang (KOR) | Sergio García (ESP)* | 2012 I Poulter (ENG) |
| 2008 Phil Mickelson (USA)* | *Beat O Wilson (ENG) at 2nd extra hole | |
| *Beat Ross Fisher (ENG) at 2nd extra hole | 2009 Phil Mickelson (USA) | |
| | 2010 F Molinari (ITA) | |

## DP World Tour Championship, Dubai  *Jumeirah Golf Estates, Dubai, UAE*

Full results can be found on page 166

## Month by month in 2013

A ban on anchoring putters, effective from 2016, is announced. Tiger Woods has his fourth victory of the year at the Players Championship and Graeme McDowell his second at the Volvo World Match Play, while 20-year-old Matteo Manassero becomes the youngest-ever BMW PGA champion at Wentworth – his fourth European Tour title.

# International Team Events 2013

## Ryder Cup – inaugurated 1927

2012 *Medinah, Chicago, IL* Sept 28–30
**Result: Europe 14½, USA 13½**
*Captains: Davis Love III (USA), José Maria Olazábal (Eur)*

**First Day – Foursomes**
Furyk & Snedeker lost to McIlroy & McDowell  1 up
Mickelson & Bradley beat Donald & García  4 and 3
Dufner & Johnson beat Westwood & Molinari  3 and 2
Woods & Stricker lost to Poulter & Rose  2 and 1

*Fourballs*
Watson & Simpson beat Lawrie and Hanson  5 and 4
Mickelson & Bradley beat McIlroy & McDowell  2 and 1
Woods & Stricker lost to Westwood & Colsaerts  1 up
Johnson & Kuchar beat Rose & Kaymer  3 and

**Second Day – Foursomes**
Watson & Simpson lost to Rose & Poulter  1 up
Bradley & Mickelson beat Westwood & Donald  7 and 6
Dufner & Johnson beat Colsaerts & García  2 and 1
Furyk & Snedeker beat McIlroy & McDowell  1 up

**Fourballs**
Johnson & Kuchar beat Colsaerts & Lawrie  1 up
Watson & Simpson beat Rose & Molinari  5 and 4
Woods & Stricker lost to García & Donald  1 up
Dufner & Johnson lost to McIlroy & Poulter  1 up

*Third Day – Singles*
Bubba Watson lost to Luke Donald (ENG)  2 and 1
Webb Simpson lost to Ian Poulter (ENG)  2 up
Keegan Bradley lost to Rory McIlroy (NIR)  2 and 1
Phil Mickelson lost to Justin Rose (ENG)  1 up
Brandt Snedeker lost to Paul Lawrie (SCO)  5 and 3
Dustin Johnson beat Nicolas Colsaerts (BEL)  3 and 2
Zach Johnson beat Graeme McDowell (NIR)  2 and 1
Jim Furyk lost to Sergio García (ESP)  1 up
Jason Dufner beat Peter Hanson (SWE)  2 up
Matt Kuchar lost to Lee Westwood (ENG)  3 and 2
Steve Stricker lost to Martin Kaymer (GER)  1 up
Tiger Woods halved with Francesco Molinari (ITA)

2010 *Celtic Manor, Wales* Oct 1–4
**Result: Europe 14½, USA 13½**
*Captains: Colin Montgomerie (Eur), Corey Pavin (USA)*

*Heavy rain delayed play from the first day forcing a departure from the customary format, requiring an extra day to complete all the matches*

**First Session – Fourballs**
Westwood & Kaymer beat Mickelson & Johnson  3 and 2
McIlroy & McDowell halved with Cink & Kuchar
Poulter & Fisher lost to Stricker & Woods  2 holes
Donald & Harrington lost to Watson & Overton  3 and 2

**Second Session – Foursomes**
E Molinari & F Molinari lost to Johnson & Mahan  2 holes
Westwood & Kaymer halved with Furyk & Fowler
Harrington & Fisher beat Mickelson & Johnson  3 and 2
Jiménez & Hanson lost to Stricker & Woods  4 and 3
Poulter & Donald Bubba Watson & Overton  2 and 1
McIlroy & McDowell lost to Cink & Kuchar  1 hole

*Third Session – Foursomes*
Donald & Westwood beat Stricker & Woods  6 and 5
McIlroy & McDowell beat Johnson & Mahan  3 and 1
**Fourballs**
Harrington & Fisher beat Furyk & Johnson  2 and 1
Jiménez & Hanson beat Watson & Overton  2 holes
E Molinari & F Molinari halved with Cink & Kuchar
Poulter & Kaymer beat Mickelson & Fowler  2 and 1

*Fourth Session – Singles*
Lee Westwood (ENG) lost to Steve Stricker  2 and 1
Rory McIlroy (NIR) halved with Stewart Cink
Luke Donald (ENG) beat Jim Furyk  1 hole
Martin Kaymer (GER) lost to Dustin Johnson  6 and 4
Ian Poulter (ENG) beat Matt Kuchar  5 and 4
Ross Fisher (ENG) lost to Jeff Overton  3 and 2
Miguel Angel Jiménez (ESP) beat Bubba Watson  4 and 3
Francesco Molinari (ITA) lost to Tiger Woods  4 and 3
Edoardo Molinari (ITA) halved with Rikki Fowler
Peter Hanson (SWE) lost to Phil Mickelson  4 and 2
Padraig Harrington (IRL) lost to Zach Johnson  3 and 2
Graeme McDowell (NIR) beat Hunter Mahan  2 and 1

2008 *Valhalla, Louisville, KY* Sept 18–20
**Result: USA 16½, Europe 11½**
*Captains: Paul Azinger (USA), Nick Faldo (Eur)*
**First Day, Morning – Foursomes**
Mickelson & Kim halved with Harrington & Karlsson
Leonard & Mahan beat Stenson & Casey  3 and 2
Cink & Campbell beat Poulter & Rose  1 hole
Perry & Furyk halved with Westwood & García

*Afternoon – Fourballs*
Mickelson & Kim beat Harrington & McDowell  2 holes
Stricker & Curtis lost to Poulter & Rose  4 and 2
Leonard & Mahan beat García & Jiménez  4 and 3
Holmes & Weekley halved with Westwood & Hansen

**Second Day, Morning – Foursomes**
Cink & Campbell lost to Poulter & Rose  4 and 3
Leonard & Mahan halved with Jiménez & McDowell
Mickelson & Kim lost to Stenson & Wilson  2 and 1
Perry & Furyk beat Harrington & Karlsson  3 and 1

*Afternoon – Fourballs*
Holmes & Weekley beat Westwood & Hansen  2 and 1
Stricker & Curtis halved with García & Casey
Perry & Furyk lost to Poulter & McDowell  1 hole
Mickelson & Mahan halved with Stenson & Karlsson

*Third Day – Singles*
Anthony Kim beat Sergio García (ESP)  5 and 4
Hunter Mahan halved with Paul Casey (ENG)
Justin Leonard lost to Robert Karlsson (SWE)  5 and 3
Phil Mickelson lost to Justin Rose (ENG)  3 and 2
Kenny Perry beat Henrik Stenson (SWE)  3 and 2
Boo Weekley beat Oliver Wilson (ENG)  4 and 2
J B Holmes beat Søren Hansen (DEN)  2 and 1
Jim Furyk beat Miguel Angel Jiménez (ESP)  2 and 1
Stewart Cink lost to Graeme McDowell (NIR)
  2 and 1
Steve Stricker lost to Ian Poulter (ENG)  3 and 2
Ben Curtis beat Lee Westwood (ENG)  2 and 1
Chad Campbell beat Padraig Harrington (IRL)
  2 and 1

## 2006 K Club, Straffan, Ireland  Sept 22–24
**Result: Europe 18½, USA 9½**
*Captains: Ian Woosnam (Eur), Tom Lehman (USA)*
**First Day, Morning – Fourballs**
Harrington & Montgomerie lost to Woods & Furyk  1 hole
Casey & Karlsson halved with Cink & Henry
García & Olazábal beat Toms & Wetterich  3 and 2
Clarke & Westwood beat Mickelson & DiMarco  1 hole
**Afternoon – Foursomes**
Harrington & McGinley halved with Campbell & Johnson
Howell & Stenson halved with Cink & Toms
Westwood & Montgomerie halved with Mickelson & DiMarco
Donald & García beat Woods & Furyk  2 holes
**Second Day, Morning – Fourballs**
Casey & Karlsson halved with Cink & Henry
García & Olazábal beat Mickelson & DiMarco  3 and 2
Clarke & Westwood beat Woods & Furyk  3 and 2
Stenson & Harrington lost to Verplank & Johnson  2 and 1
**Afternoon – Foursomes**
García & Donald beat Mickelson & Toms  2 and 1
Montgomerie & Westwood halved with Campbell & Taylor
Casey & Howell beat Cink & Johnson  5 and 4
Harrington & McGinley lost to Woods & Furyk  3 and 2
**Third Day – Singles**
Colin Montgomerie (sco) beat David Toms  1 hole
Sergio García (ESP) lost to Stewart Cink  4 and 3
Paul Casey (ENG) beat Jim Furyk  2 and 1
Robert Karlsson (SWE) lost to Tiger Woods  3 and 2
Luke Donald (ENG) beat Chad Campbell  2 and 1
Paul McGinley (IRL) halved with JJ Henry
Darren Clarke (NIR) beat Zach Johnson  3 and 2
Henrik Stenson (SWE) beat Vaughn Taylor  4 and 3
David Howell (ENG) beat Brett Wetterich  5 and 4
José María Olazábal (ESP) beat Phil Mickelson  2 and 1
Lee Westwood (ENG) beat Chris DiMarco  2 holes
Padraig Harrington (IRL) lost to Scott Verplank  4 and 3

## 2004 Oakland Hills Country Club, Bloomfield, Detroit, MI, USA  Sept 17–19
**Result: USA 9½, Europe 18½**
*Captains: Hal Sutton (USA), Bernhard Langer (Eur)*
**First Day, Morning – Fourball**
Woods & Mickelson lost to Montgomerie & Harrington  2 and 1
Love & Campbell lost to Clarke & Jiménez  5 and 4
Riley & Cink halved with McGinley & Donald
Toms & Furyk lost to García & Westwood  5 and 3
**Afternoon – Foursomes**
DiMarco & Haas beat Jiménez & Levet  3 and 2
Love & Funk lost to Montgomerie & Harrington  4 and 2
Mickelson & Woods lost to Clarke & Westwood  1 hole
Perry & Cink lost to García & Donald  2 and 1
**Second Day, Morning – Fourball**
Haas & DiMarco halved with García & Westwood
Woods & Riley beat Clarke & Poulter  4 and 3
Furyk & Campbell lost to Casey & Howell  1 hole
Cink & Love beat Montgomerie & Harrington  3 and 2
**Afternoon – Foursomes**
DiMarco & Haas lost to Clarke & Westwood  5 and 4
Mickelson & Toms beat Jiménez & Levet  4 and 3
Funk & Furyk lost to Donald & García  1 hole
Love & Woods lost to Harrington & McGinley  4 and 3
**Third Day – Singles**
Tiger Woods beat Paul Casey (ENG)  3 and 2
Phil Mickelson lost to Sergio García (ESP)  3 and 2

Davis Love III halved with Darren Clarke (NIR)
Jim Furyk beat David Howell (ENG)  6 and 4
Kenny Perry lost to Lee Westwood (ENG)  1 hole
David Toms lost to Colin Montgomerie (SCO)  1 hole
Chad Campbell beat Luke Donald (ENG)  5 and 3
Chris DiMarco beat Miguel Angel Jiménez (ESP)  1 hole
Fred Funk lost to Thomas Levet (FRA)  1 hole
Chris Riley lost to Ian Poulter (ENG)  3 and 2
Jay Haas lost to Padraig Harrington (IRL)  1 hole
Stewart Cink lost to Paul McGinley (IRL)  3 and 2

## 2002 The Brabazon Course, The De Vere Belfry, Sutton Coldfield, West Midlands, England  Sept
**Result: Europe 13½, USA 12½**
*Captains: Sam Torrance (Eur), Curtis Strange (USA)*
**First Day, Morning – Fourball**
Björn & Clarke beat Azinger & Woods  1 hole
García & Westwood beat Duval & Love  4 and 3
Langer & Montgomerie beat Furyk & Hoch  4 and 3
Fasth & Harrington lost to Mickelson & Toms  1 hole
**Afternoon – Foursomes**
Björn & Clarke lost to Sutton & Verplank  2 and 1
García & Westwood beat Calcavecchia & Woods  2 and 1
Langer & Montgomerie halved with Mickelson & Toms
Harrington & McGinley lost to Cink & Furyk  3 and 2
**Second Day, Morning – Foursomes**
Fulke & Price lost to Mickelson & Toms  2 and 1
García & Westwood beat Cink & Furyk  2 and 1
Langer & Montgomerie beat Hoch & Verplank  1 hole
Björn & Clarke lost to Love & Woods  4 and 3
**Afternoon – Fourball**
Fasth & Parnevik lost to Calcavecchia & Duval  1 hole
García & Westwood lost to Love & Woods  1 hole
Harrington & Montgomerie beat Mickelson & Toms  2 and 1
Clarke & McGinley halved with Furyk & Hoch
**Third Day – Singles**
Colin Montgomerie (SCO) beat Scott Hoch  5 and 4
Sergio García (ESP) lost to David Toms  1 hole
Darren Clarke (NIR) halved with David Duval
Bernhard Langer (GER) beat Hal Sutton  4 and 3
Padraig Harrington (IRL) beat Mark Calcavecchia  5 and 4
Thomas Björn (DEN) beat Stewart Cink  2 and 1
Lee Westwood (ENG) lost to Scott Verplank  2 and 1
Niclas Fasth (Swe) halved with Paul Azinger
Paul McGinley (IRL) halved with Jim Furyk
Pierre Fulke (SWE) halved with Davis Love III
Phillip Price (WAL) beat Phil Mickelson  3 and 2
Jesper Parnevik (SWE) halved with Tiger Woods

## 1999 The Country Club, Brookline, MA., USA  Sept 24–26
**Result: USA 14½, Europe 13½**
*Captains: Ben Crenshaw (USA), Mark James (Eur)*
**First Day: Morning – Foursomes**
Duval & Mickelson lost to Montgomerie & Lawrie  3 and 2
Lehman & Woods lost to Parnevik & García  2 and 1
Love & Stewart halved with Jiménez & Harrington
Sutton & Maggert beat Clarke & Westwood  3 and 2
**Afternoon – Fourball**
Love & Leonard halved with Montgomerie & Lawrie
Mickelson & Furyk lost to Parnevik & García  1 hole
Sutton & Maggert lost to Jiménez & Olazábal  2 and 1
Duval & Woods lost to Clarke & Westwood  1 hole

## 1999 *continued*

**Second Day: Morning – Foursomes**
Sutton & Maggert beat Montgomerie & Lawrie   1 hole
Furyk & O'Meara lost to Clarke & Westwood   3 and 2
Pate & Woods beat Jiménez & Harrington   1 hole
Stewart & Leonard lost to Parnevik & García
   3 and 2

**Afternoon – Fourball**
Mickelson & Lehman beat Clarke & Westwood
   2 and 1
Love & Duval halved with Parnevik & García
Leonard & Sutton halved with Jiménez & Olazábal
Pate & Woods lost to Montgomerie & Lawrie
   2 and 1

**Third Day – Singles**
Tom Lehman beat Lee Westwood   3 and 2
Hal Sutton beat Darren Clarke   4 and 2
Phil Mickelson beat Jarmo Sandelin   4 and 3
Davis Love III beat Jean Van de Velde   6 and 5
Tiger Woods beat Andrew Coltart   3 and 2
David Duval beat Jesper Parnevik   5 and 4
Mark O'Meara lost to Padraig Harrington   1 hole
Steve Pate beat Miguel Angel Jiménez   2 and 1
Justin Leonard halved with José Maria Olazábal
Payne Stewart lost to Colin Montgomerie   1 hole
Jim Furyk beat Sergio García   4 and 3
Jeff Maggert lost to Paul Lawrie   4 and 3

## 1997 *Valderrama Golf Club, Sotogrande, Cadiz, Spain* Sept 26–28

**Result: Europe 14½, USA 13½**
*Captains: Seve Ballesteros (Eur), Tom Kite (USA)*

**First Day: Morning – Fourball**
Olazábal & Rocca beat Love & Mickelson   1 hole
Faldo & Westwood lost to Couples & Faxon   1 hole
Parnevik & Johansson beat Lehman & Furyk   1 hole
Montgomerie & Langer lost to Woods & O'Meara
   3 and 2

**Afternoon – Foursomes**
Rocca & Olazábal lost to Hoch & Janzen   1 hole
Langer & Montgomerie beat O'Meara & Woods
   5 and 3
Faldo & Westwood beat Leonard & Maggert   3 and 2
Parnevik & Garrido halved with Lehman & Mickelson

**Second Day: Morning – Fourball**
Montgomerie & Clarke beat Couples & Love   1 hole
Woosnam & Björn beat Leonard & Faxon   2 and 1
Faldo & Westwood beat Woods & O'Meara   2 and 1
Olazábal & Garrido halved with Mickelson & Lehman

**Afternoon – Foursomes**
Montgomerie & Langer beat Janzen & Furyk   1 hole
Faldo & Westwood lost to Hoch & Maggert   2 and 1
Parnevik & Garrido halved with Leonard & Woods
Olazábal & Rocca beat Love & Couples   5 and 4

**Third Day – Singles**
Ian Woosnam lost to Fred Couples   8 and 7
Per-Ulrik Johansson lost to Davis Love III   3 and 2
Costantino Rocca beat Tiger Woods   4 and 2
Thomas Björn halved with Justin Leonard
Darren Clarke lost to Phil Mickelson   2 and 1
Jesper Parnevik lost to Mark O'Meara   5 and 4
José Maria Olazábal lost to Lee Janzen   1 hole
Bernhard Langer beat Brad Faxon   2 and 1
Lee Westwood lost to Jeff Maggert   3 and 2
Colin Montgomerie halved with Scott Hoch
Nick Faldo lost to Jim Furyk   3 and 2
Ignacio Garrido lost to Tom Lehman   7 and 6

## 1995 *Oak Hill Country Club, Rochester, NY, USA* Sept 22–24

**Result: USA 13½, Europe 14½**
*Captains: Lanny Wadkins (USA),
   Bernard Gallacher (Eur)*

**First Day: Morning – Foursomes**
Pavin & Lehman beat Faldo & Montgomerie   1 hole
Haas & Couples lost to Torrance & Rocca   3 and 2
Love & Maggert beat Clark & James   4 and 3
Crenshaw & Strange lost to Langer & Johansson   1 hole

**Afternoon – Fourball**
Faxon & Jacobsen lost to Gilford & Ballesteros   4 and 3
Maggert & Roberts beat Torrance & Rocca   6 and 5
Couples & Love beat Faldo & Montgomerie   3 and 2
Pavin & Mickelson beat Langer & Johansson   6 and 4

**Second Day: Morning – Foursomes**
Haas & Strange lost to Faldo & Montgomerie   4 and 2
Love & Maggert lost to Torrance & Rocca   6 and 5
Roberts & Jacobsen beat Woosnam & Walton   1 hole
Pavin & Lehman lost to Langer & Gilford   4 and 3

**Afternoon – Fourball**
Faxon & Couples beat Torrance & Montgomerie   4 and 2
Love & Crenshaw lost to Woosnam & Rocca   3 and 2
Haas & Mickelson beat Ballesteros & Gilford   3 and 2
Pavin & Roberts beat Faldo & Langer   1 hole

**Third Day – Singles**
Tom Lehman beat Seve Ballesteros   4 and 3
Peter Jacobsen lost to Howard Clark   1 hole
Jeff Maggert lost to Mark James   4 and 3
Fred Couples halved with Ian Woosnam
Davis Love III beat Costantino Rocca   3 and 2
Brad Faxon lost to David Gilford   1 hole
Ben Crenshaw lost to Colin Montgomerie   3 and 1
Nick Faldo beat Curtis Strange   1 hole
Loren Roberts lost to Sam Torrance   2 and 1
Corey Pavin beat Bernhard Langer   3 and 2
Jay Haas lost to Philip Walton   1 hole
Phil Mickelson beat Per-Ulrik Johansson   2 and 1

## 1993 *The Brabazon Course, The De Vere Belfry, Sutton Coldfield, West Midlands, England* Sept 24–26

**Result: Europe 13, USA 15**
*Captains: Bernard Gallacher (Eur), Tom Watson (USA)*

**First Day: Morning – Foursomes**
Torrance & James lost to Wadkins & Pavin   4 and 3
Woosnam & Langer beat Azinger & Stewart 7 and 5
Ballesteros & Olazábal lost to Kite & Love   2 and 1
Faldo & Montgomerie beat Floyd & Couples
   4 and 3

**Afternoon – Fourball**
Woosnam & Baker beat Gallagher & Janzen   1 hole
Lane & Langer lost to Wadkins & Pavin   4 and 2
Faldo & Montgomerie halved with Azinger & Couples
Ballesteros & Olazábal beat Kite & Love   4 and 3

**Second Day: Morning – Foursomes**
Faldo & Montgomerie beat Wadkins & Pavin   3 and 2
Langer & Woosnam beat Couples & Azinger   2 and 1
Baker & Lane lost to Floyd & Stewart   3 and 2
Ballesteros & Olazábal beat Kite & Love   2 and 1

**Afternoon – Fourball**
Faldo & Montgomerie lost to Beck & Cook   2 holes
James & Rocca lost to Pavin & Gallagher   5 and 4
Woosnam & Baker beat Couples & Azinger   6 and 5
Olazábal & Haeggman lost to Floyd & Stewart   2 and 1

**Third Day – Singles**
Ian Woosnam halved with Fred Couples
Barry Lane lost to Chip Beck 1 hole
Colin Montgomerie beat Lee Janzen 1 hole
Peter Baker beat Corey Pavin 2 holes
Joakim Haeggman beat J Cook 1 hole
Sam Torrance (withdrawn at start of day) halved with
 Lanny Wadkins (withdrawn at start of day)
Mark James lost to Payne Stewart 3 and 2
Constantino Rocca lost to Davis Love III 1 hole
Seve Ballesteros lost to Jim Gallagher Jr 3 and 2
José Maria Olazábal lost to Ray Floyd 2 holes
Bernhard Langer lost to Tom Kite 5 and 3
Nick Faldo halved with Paul Azinger

**1991** *The Ocean Course, Kiawah Island, SC, USA*
  Sept 26–29
**Result: USA 14½, Europe 13½**
*Captains: Dave Stockton (USA),*
 *Bernard Gallacher (Eur)*

**First Day: Morning – Foursomes**
Azinger & Beck lost to Ballesteros & Olazábal 2 and 1
Floyd & Couples beat Langer & James 2 and 1

**First Day: Morning – Foursomes (continued)**
Wadkins & Irwin beat Gilford & Montgomerie 4 and 2
Stewart & Calcavecchia beat Faldo & Woosnam 1 hole

**Afternoon – Fourball**
Wadkins & O'Meara halved with Torrance & Feherty
Azinger & Beck lost to Ballesteros & Olazábal 2 and 1
Pavin & Calcavecchia lost to Richardson & James 5 and 4
Floyd & Couples beat Faldo & Woosnam 5 and 3

**Second Day: Morning – Foursomes**
Irwin & Wadkins beat Torrance & Feherty 4 and 2
Calcavecchia & Stewart beat James & Richardson 1 hole
Azinger & O'Meara beat Faldo & Gilford 7 and 6
Couples & Floyd lost to Ballesteros & Olazábal 3 and 2

**Afternoon – Fourball**
Azinger & Irwin lost to Woosnam & Broadhurst 2 and 1
Pate & Pavin lost to Langer & Montgomerie 2 and 1
Wadkins & Levi lost to James & Richardson 3 and 1
Couples & Stewart halved with Ballesteros & Olazábal

**Third Day – Singles**
Ray Floyd lost to Nick Faldo 2 holes
Payne Stewart lost to David Feherty 2 and 1
Mark Calcavecchia halved with Colin Montgomerie
Paul Azinger beat José Maria Olazábal 2 holes
Corey Pavin beat Steven Richardson 2 and 1
Wayne Levi lost to Seve Ballesteros 3 and 2
Chip Beck beat Ian Woosnam 3 and 1
Mark O'Meara lost to Paul Broadhurst 3 and 1
Fred Couples beat Sam Torrance 3 and 2
Lanny Wadkins beat Mark James 3 and 2
Hale Irwin halved with Bernhard Langer
Steve Pate (withdrawn – injured) halved with David Gilford
 (withdrawn)

**1989** *The Brabazon Course, The De Vere Belfry,*
 *Sutton Coldfield, West Midlands, England*
  Sept 22–24
**Result: Europe 14, USA 14**
*Captains: Tony Jacklin (Eur), Ray Floyd (USA)*

**First Day: Foursomes – Morning**
Faldo & Woosnam halved with Kite & Strange
Clark & James lost to Stewart & Wadkins 1 hole
Ballesteros & Olazábal halved with Beck & Watson
Langer & Rafferty lost to Calcavecchia & Green 2 and 1

**Fourball – Afternoon**
Brand & Torrance beat Azinger & Strange 1 hole
Clark & James beat Couples & Wadkins 3 and 2
Faldo & Woosnam beat Calcavecchia & McCumber 1 hole
Ballesteros & Olazábal beat O'Meara & Watson 6 and 5

**Second Day: Foursomes – Morning**
Faldo & Woosnam beat Stewart & Wadkins 3 and 2
Brand & Torrance lost to Azinger & Beck 4 and 3
O'Connor & Rafferty lost to Calcavecchia & Green 3 and 2
Ballesteros & Olazábal beat Kite & Strange 1 hole

**Fourball – Afternoon**
Faldo & Woosnam lost to Azinger & Beck 2 and 1
Canizares & Langer lost to Kite & McCumber 2 and 1
Clark & James beat Stewart & Strange 1 hole
Ballesteros & Olazábal beat Calcavecchia & Green 4 and 2

**Third Day: Singles**
Seve Ballesteros lost to Paul Azinger 1 hole
Bernhard Langer lost to Chip Beck 3 and 1
José Maria Olazábal beat Payne Stewart 1 hole
Ronan Rafferty beat Mark Calvecchia 1 hole
Howard Clark lost to Tom Kite 8 and 7
Mark James beat Mark O'Meara 3 and 2
Christy O'Connor Jr beat Fred Couples 1 hole
José Maria Canizares beat Ken Green 1 hole
Gordon Brand Jr lost to Mark McCumber 1 hole
Sam Torrance lost to Tom Watson 3 and 1
Nick Faldo lost to Lanny Wadkins 1 hole
Ian Woosnam lost to Curtis Strange 1 hole

**1987** *Muirfield Village Golf Club, Dublin, OH, USA*
  Sept 25–27
**Result: Europe 15, USA 13**
*Captains: Jack Nicklaus (USA), Tony Jacklin (Eur)*

**First Day: Foursomes – Morning**
Kite & Strange beat Clark & Torrance 4 and 2
Pohl & Sutton beat Brown & Langer 2 and 1
Mize & Wadkins lost to Faldo & Woosnam 2 holes
Nelson & Stewart lost to Ballesteros & Olazábal 1 hole

**Fourball – Afternoon**
Crenshaw & Simpson lost to Brand & Rivero 3 and 2
Bean & Calcavecchia lost to Langer & Lyle 1 hole
Pohl & Sutton lost to Faldo & Woosnam 2 and 1
Kite & Strange lost to Ballesteros & Olazábal 2 and 1

**Second Day: Foursomes – Morning**
Kite & Strange beat Brand & Rivero 3 and 1
Mize & Sutton halved with Faldo & Woosnam
Nelson & Wadkins lost to Langer & Lyle 2 and 1
Crenshaw & Stewart lost to Ballesteros & Olazábal
 1 hole

**Fourball – Afternoon**
Kite & Strange lost to Faldo & Woosnam 5 and 4
Bean & Stewart beat Brand & Darcy 3 and 2
Mize & Sutton beat Ballesteros & Olazábal 2 and 1
Nelson & Wadkins lost to Langer & Lyle 1 hole

**Third Day: Singles**
Andy Bean beat Ian Woosnam 1 hole
Dan Pohl lost to Howard Clark 1 hole
Larry Mize halved with Sam Torrance
Mark Calcavecchia beat Nick Faldo 1 hole
Payne Stewart beat José Maria Olazábal 2 holes
Scott Simpson beat José Rivero 2 and 1
Tom Kite beat Sandy Lyle 3 and 2
Ben Crenshaw lost to Eamonn Darcy 1 hole
Larry Nelson halved with Bernhard Langer
Curtis Strange lost to Seve Ballesteros 2 and 1
Lanny Wadkins beat Ken Brown 3 and 2
Hal Sutton halved with Gordon Brand Jr

## 1985 The Brabazon Course, The De Vere Belfry, Sutton Coldfield, West Midlands, England Sept 13–15

### Result: Europe 16½, USA 11½
*Captains: Tony Jacklin (Eur), Lee Trevino (USA)*

**First Day: Foursomes – Morning**
Ballesteros & Pinero beat Strange & O'Meara  2 and 1
Faldo & Langer lost to Kite & Peete  3 and 2
Brown & Lyle lost to Floyd & Wadkins  4 and 3
Clark & Torrance lost to Stadler & Sutton  3 and 2

**Fourball – Afternoon**
Way & Woosnam beat Green & Zoeller  1 hole
Ballesteros & Pinero beat Jacobsen & North  2 and 1
Canizares & Langer halved with Stadler & Sutton
Clark & Torrance lost to Floyd & Wadkins  1 hole

**Second Day: Fourball – Morning**
Clark & Torrance beat Kite & North  2 and 1
Way & Woosnam beat Green & Zoeller  4 and 3
Ballesteros & Pinero lost to O'Meara & Wadkins  3 and 2
Langer & Lyle halved with Stadler & Strange

**Foursomes – Afternoon**
Canizares & Rivero beat Kite & Peete  7 and 5
Ballesteros & Pinero beat Stadler & Sutton  5 and 4
Way & Woosnam lost to Jacobsen & Strange  4 and 3
Brown & Langer beat Floyd & Wadkins  3 and 2

**Third Day: Singles**
Manuel Pinero beat Lanny Wadkins  3 and 1
Ian Woosnam lost to Craig Stadler  2 and 1
Paul Way beat Ray Floyd  2 holes
Seve Ballesteros halved with Tom Kite
Sandy Lyle beat Peter Jacobsen  3 and 2
Bernhard Langer beat Hal Sutton  5 and 4
Sam Torrance beat Andy North  1 hole
Howard Clark beat Mark O'Meara  1 hole
Nick Faldo lost to Hubert Green  3 and 1
José Rivero lost to Calvin Peete  1 hole
José Maria Canizares beat Fuzzy Zoeller  2 holes
Ken Brown lost to Curtis Strange  4 and 2

## 1983 PGA National Golf Club, Palm Beach Gardens, FL, USA  Oct 14–16

### Result: USA 14½, Europe 13½
*Captains: Jack Nicklaus (USA), Tony Jacklin (Eur)*

**First Day: Foursomes – Morning**
Watson & Crenshaw  beat Gallacher & Lyle  5 and 4
Wadkins & Stadler lost to Faldo & Langer  4 and 2
Floyd & Gilder lost to Canizares & Torrance  4 and 3
Kite & Peete beat Ballesteros & Way  2 and 1

**Fourball – Afternoon**
Morgan & Zoeller lost to Waites & Brown  2 and 1
Watson & Haas beat Faldo & Langer  2 and 1
Floyd & Strange lost to Ballesteros & Way  1 hole
Crenshaw & Peete halved with Torrance & Woosnam

**Second Day: Foursomes – Morning**
Floyd & Kite lost to Faldo & Langer  3 and 2
Wadkins & Morgan beat Canizares & Torrance  7 and 5
Gilder & Watson lost to Ballesteros & Way  2 and 1
Haas & Strange beat Waites & Brown  3 and 2

**Fourball – Afternoon**
Wadkins & Stadler beat Waites & Brown  1 hole
Crenshaw & Peete lost to Faldo & Langer  2 and 1
Haas & Morgan halved with Ballesteros & Way
Gilder & Watson beat Torrance & Woosnam  5 and 4

**Third Day: Singles**
Fuzzy Zoeller halved with Seve Ballesteros
Jay Haas lost to Nick Faldo  2 and 1
Gil Morgan lost to Bernhard Langer  2 holes
Bob Gilder beat Gordon J Brand  2 holes
Ben Crenshaw beat Sandy Lyle  3 and 1
Calvin Peete beat Brian Waites  1 hole
Curtis Strange lost to Paul Way  2 and 1
Tom Kite halved with Sam Torrance
Craig Stadler beat Ian Woosnam  3 and 2
Lanny Wadkins halved with José Maria Canizares
Ray Floyd lost to Ken Brown  4 and 3
Tom Watson beat Bernard Gallacher  2 and 1

## 1981 Walton Heath GC, Tadworth, Surrey, England Sept 18–20

### Result: USA 18½, Europe 9½
*Captains: John Jacobs (Eur), Dave Marr (USA)*

**First Day: Foursomes – Morning**
Langer & Pinero lost to Trevino & Nelson  1 hole
Lyle & James beat Rogers & Lietzke  2 and 1
Gallacher & Smyth beat Irwin & Floyd  3 and 2
Oosterhuis & Faldo lost to Watson & Nicklaus  4 and 3

**Fourball – Afternoon**
Torrance & Clark halved with Kite & Miller
Lyle & James beat Crenshaw & Pate  3 and 2
Smyth & Canizares beat Rogers & Lietzke  6 and 5
Gallacher & Darcy lost to Irwin & Floyd  2 and 1

**Second Day: Fourball – Morning**
Faldo & Torrance lost to Trevino & Pate  7 and 5
Lyle & James lost to Nelson & Kite  1 hole
Langer & Pinero beat Irwin & Floyd  2 and 1
Smyth & Canizares lost to Watson & Nicklaus  3 and 2

**Foursomes – Afternoon**
Oosterhuis & Torrance lost to Trevino & Pate  2 and 1
Langer & Pinero lost to Watson & Nicklaus  3 and 2
Lyle & James lost to Rogers & Floyd  3 and 2
Gallacher & Smyth lost to Nelson & Kite  3 and 2

**Third Day: Singles**
Sam Torrance lost to Lee Trevino  5 and 3
Sandy Lyle lost to Tom Kite  3 and 2
Bernard Gallacher halved with Bill Rogers
Mark James lost to Larry Nelson  2 holes
Des Smyth lost to Ben Crenshaw  6 and 4
Bernhard Langer halved with Bruce Lietzke
Manuel Pinero beat Jerry Pate  4 and 2
José Maria Canizares lost to Hale Irwin  1 hole
Nick Faldo beat Johnny Miller  2 and 1
Howard Clark beat Tom Watson  4 and 3
Peter Oosterhuis lost to Ray Floyd  2 holes
Eamonn Darcy lost to Jack Nicklaus  5 and 3
*From 1979 GB&I became a European team*

## 1979 The Greenbrier, White Sulphur Springs, WV, USA  Sept 14–16

### Result: USA 17, Europe 11
*Captains: Billy Casper (USA), John Jacobs (Eur)*

**First Day: Fourball – Morning**
Wadkins & Nelson beat Garrido & Ballesteros  2 and 1
Trevino & Zoeller beat Brown & James  3 and 2
Bean & Elder beat Oosterhuis & Faldo  2 and 1
Irwin & Mahaffey lost to Gallacher & Barnes  2 and 1

**Foursomes – Afternoon**
Irwin & Kite beat Brown & Smyth  7 and 6
Zoeller & Green lost to Garrido & Ballesteros  3 and 2
Trevino & Morgan halved with Lyle & Jacklin
Wadkins & Nelson beat Gallacher & Barnes  4 and 3

*Second Day:* Foursomes – Morning
Elder & Mahaffey lost to Lyle & Jacklin 5 and 4
Bean & Kite lost to Oosterhuis & Faldo 6 and 5
Zoeller & Hayes halved with Gallacher & Barnes
Wadkins & Nelson beat Garrido & Ballesteros 3 and 2
Fourball – Afternoon
Wadkins & Nelson beat Garrido & Ballesteros 5 and 4
Irwin & Kite beat Lyle & Jacklin 1 hole
Trevino & Zoeller lost to Gallacher & Barnes 3 and 2
Elder & Hayes lost to Oosterhuis & Faldo 1 hole
*Third Day:* Singles
Lanny Wadkins lost to Bernard Gallacher 3 and 2
Larry Nelson beat Seve Ballesteros 3 and 2
Tom Kite beat Tony Jacklin 1 hole
Mark Hayes beat Antonio Garrido 1 hole
Andy Bean beat Michael King 4 and 3
John Mahaffey beat Brian Barnes 1 hole
Lee Elder lost to Nick Faldo 3 and 2
Hale Irwin beat Des Smyth 5 and 3
Hubert Green beat Peter Oosterhuis 2 holes
Fuzzy Zoeller lost to Ken Brown 1 hole
Lee Trevino beat Sandy Lyle 2 and 1
Gil Morgan, Mark James: injury; match a half

1977 *Royal Lytham & St Annes GC, St Annes,*
*Lancs, England* Sept 15–17
**Result: USA 12½, GB&I 7½**
*Captains: Brian Huggett (GB&I),*
*Dow Finsterwald* (USA)
*First Day:* Foursomes
Gallacher & Barnes lost to Wadkins & Irwin 3 and 1
Coles & Dawson lost to Stockton & McGee 1 hole
Faldo & Oosterhuis beat Floyd & Graham 2 and 1
Darcy & Jacklin halved with Sneed & January
Horton & James lost to Nicklaus & Watson 5 and 4
*Second Day:* Fourball
Barnes & Horton lost to Watson & Green 5 and 4
Coles & Dawson lost to Sneed & Wadkins 5 and 3
Faldo & Oosterhuis beat Nicklaus & Floyd 3 and 1
Darcy & Jacklin lost to Hill & Stockton 5 and 3
James & Brown lost to Irwin & Graham 1 hole
*Third Day:* Singles
Howard Clark lost to Lanny Wadkins 4 and 3
Neil Coles lost to Lou Graham 5 and 3
Peter Dawson beat Don January 5 and 4
Brian Barnes beat Hale Irwin 1 hole
Tommy Horton lost to Dave Hill 5 and 4
Bernard Gallacher beat Jack Nicklaus 1 hole
Eamonn Darcy lost to Hubert Green 1 hole
Mark James lost to Ray Floyd 2 and 1
Nick Faldo beat Tom Watson 1 hole
Peter Oosterhuis beat Jerry McGee 2 holes

1975 *Laurel Valley Golf Club, Ligonier, PA, USA*
Sept 19–21
**Result: USA 21, GB&I 11**
*Captains: Arnold Palmer (USA),*
*Bernard Hunt (GB&I)*
*First Day:* Foursomes – Morning
Nicklaus & Weiskopf beat Barnes & Gallacher 5 and 4
Littler & Irwin beat Wood & Bembridge 4 and 3
Geiberger & Miller beat Jacklin & Oosterhuis 3 and 1
Trevino & Snead beat Horton & O'Leary 2 and 1
Fourball – Afternoon
Casper & Floyd lost to Jacklin & Oosterhuis 2 and 1
Weiskopf & Graham beat Darcy & Christy O'Connor Jr
3 and 2
Nicklaus & Murphy halved with Barnes & Gallacher
Trevino & Irwin beat Horton & O'Leary 2 and 1

*Second Day:* Fourball – Morning
Casper & Miller halved with Jacklin & Oosterhuis
Nicklaus & Snead beat Horton & Wood 4 and 2
Littler & Graham beat Barnes & Gallacher 5 and 3
Geiberger & Floyd halved with Darcy & Hunt
Foursomes – Afternoon
Trevino & Murphy lost to Jacklin & Barnes 3 and 2
Weiskopf & Miller beat O'Connor & O'Leary 5 and 3
Irwin & Casper beat Oosterhuis & Bembridge 3 and 2
Geiberger & Graham beat Darcy & Hunt 3 and 2
*Third Day:* Singles – Morning
Bob Murphy beat Tony Jacklin 2 and 1
Johnny Miller lost to Peter Oosterhuis 2 holes
Lee Trevino halved with Bernard Gallacher
Hale Irwin halved with Tommy Horton
Gene Littler beat Brian Huggett 4 and 2
Billy Casper beat Eamonn Darcy 3 and 2
Tom Weiskopf beat Guy Hunt 5 and 3
Jack Nicklaus lost to Brian Barnes 4 and 2

Singles – Afternoon
Ray Floyd beat Jacklin 1 hole
JC Snead lost to Oosterhuis 3 and 2
Al Geiberger halved with Gallacher
Lou Graham lost to Horton 2 and 1
Irwin beat John O'Leary 2 and 1
Murphy beat Maurice Bembridge 2 and 1
Trevino lost to Norman Wood 2 and 1
Nicklaus lost to Barnes 2 and 1

1973 *Honourable Company of Edinburgh Golfers,*
*Muirfield, Gullane, East Lothian, Scotland*
Sept 20–22
**Result: USA 19, GB&I 13**
*Captains: Bernard Hunt (GB&I), Jack Burke*
*(USA)*
*First Day:* Foursomes – Morning
Barnes & Gallacher beat Trevino & Casper 1 hole
O'Connor & Coles beat Weiskopf & Snead 3 and 2
Jacklin & Oosterhuis halved with Rodriguez & Graham
Bembridge & Polland lost to Nicklaus & Palmer 6 and 5

Fourball – Afternoon
Barnes & Gallacher beat Aaron & Brewer 5 and 4
Bembridge & Huggett beat Nicklaus & Palmer 3 and 1
Jacklin & Oosterhuis beat Weiskopf & Casper 3 and 1
O'Connor & Coles lost to Trevino & Blancas 2 and 1

*Second Day:* Foursomes – Morning
Barnes & Butler lost to Nicklaus & Weiskopf 1 hole
Jacklin & Oosterhuis beat Palmer & Hill 2 holes
Bembridge & Huggett beat Rodriguez & Graham
5 and 4
O'Connor & Coles lost to Trevino & Casper 2 and 1

Fourball – Afternoon
Barnes & Butler lost to Snead & Palmer 2 holes
Jacklin & Oosterhuis lost to Brewer & Casper
3 and 2
Clark & Polland lost to Nicklaus & Weiskopf 3 and 2
Bembridge & Huggett halved with Trevino & Blancas

*Third Day:* Singles – Morning
Brian Barnes lost to Billy Casper 2 and 1
Bernard Gallacher lost to Tom Weiskopf 3 and 1
Peter Butler lost to Homero Blancas 5 and 4
Tony Jacklin beat Tommy Aaron 3 and 1
Neil Coles halved with Gay Brewer
Christy O'Connor lost to JC Snead 1 hole
Maurice Bembridge halved with Jack Nicklaus
Peter Oosterhuis halved with Lee Trevino

1973 *continued*

**Singles – Afternoon**
Brian Huggett beat Blancas 4 and 2
Barnes lost to Snead 3 and 1
Gallacher lost to Brewer 6 and 5
Jacklin lost to Casper 2 and 1
Coles lost to Trevino 6 and 5
O'Connor halved with Weiskopf
Bembridge lost to Nicklaus 2 holes
Oosterhuis beat Arnold Palmer 4 and 2

1971 *Old Warson Country Club, St Louis, MO, USA*
Sept 16–18
**Result: USA 18½, GB&I 13½**
*Captains: Jay Hebert (USA), Eric Brown (GB&I)*
**First Day: Foursomes – Morning**
Casper & Barber lost to Coles & O'Connor 2 and 1
Palmer & Dickinson beat Townsend & Oosterhuis
2 holes
Nicklaus & Stockton lost to Huggett & Jacklin 3 and 2
Coody & Beard lost to Bembridge & Butler 1 hole
**Foursomes – Afternoon**
Casper & Barber lost to Bannerman & Gallacher 2 and 1
Palmer & Dickinson beat Townsend & Oosterhuis
1 hole
Trevino & Rudolph halved with Huggett and Jacklin
Nicklaus & Snead beat Bembridge & Butler 5 and 3
**Second Day: Fourball – Morning**
Trevino & Rudolph beat O'Connor & Barnes 2 and 1
Beard & Snead beat Coles & John Garner 2 and 1
Palmer & Dickinson beat Oosterhuis & Gallacher
5 and 4
Nicklaus & Littler beat Townsend & Bannerman 2 and 1
**Fourball – Afternoon**
Trevino & Casper lost to Oosterhuis & Gallacher 1 hole
Littler & Snead beat Huggett & Jacklin 2 and 1
Palmer & Nicklaus beat Townsend & Bannerman 1 hole
Coody & Beard halved with Coles & O'Connor
**Third Day: Singles – Morning**
Lee Trevino beat Tony Jacklin 1 hole
Dave Stockton halved with Bernard Gallacher
Mason Rudolph lost to Brian Barnes 1 hole
Gene Littler lost to Peter Oosterhuis 4 and 3
Jack Nicklaus beat Peter Townsend 3 and 2
Gardner Dickinson beat Christy O'Connor 5 and 4
Arnold Palmer halved with Harry Bannerman
Frank Beard halved with Neil Coles
**Singles – Afternoon**
Trevino beat Brian Huggett 7 and 6
JC Snead beat Jacklin 1 hole
Miller Barber lost to Barnes 2 and 1
Stockton beat Townsend 1 hole
Charles Coody lost to Gallacher 2 and 1
Nicklaus beat Coles 5 and 3
Palmer lost to Oosterhuis 3 and 2
Dickinson lost to Bannerman 2 and 1

1969 *Royal Birkdale Golf Club, Southport, Lancs,*
*England* Sept 18–20
**Result: USA 16, GB&I 16**
*Captains: Eric Brown (GB&I), Sam Snead (USA)*
**First Day: Foursomes – Morning**
Coles & Huggett beat Barber & Floyd 3 and 2
Gallacher & Bembridge beat Trevino & Still 2 and 1
Jacklin & Townsend beat Hill & Aaron 3 and 1
O'Connor & Alliss halved with Casper & Beard

**Foursomes – Afternoon**
Coles & Huggett lost to Hill & Aaron 1 hole
Gallacher & Bembridge lost to Trevino & Littler 2 holes
Jacklin & Townsend beat Casper & Beard 1 hole
Hunt & Butler lost to Nicklaus & Sikes
**Second Day: Fourball – Morning**
O'Connor & Townsend beat Hill & Douglass 1 hole
Huggett & Alex Caygill halved with Floyd & Barber
Barnes & Alliss lost to Trevino & Littler 1 hole
Jacklin & Coles beat Nicklaus & Sikes 1 hole
**Fourball – Afternoon**
Townsend & Butler lost to Casper & Beard 2 holes
Huggett & Gallacher lost to Hill & Still 2 and 1
Bembridge & Hunt halved with Aaron & Floyd
Jacklin & Coles halved with Trevino & Barber
**Third Day: Singles – Morning**
Peter Alliss lost to Lee Trevino 2 and 1
Peter Townsend lost to Dave Hill 5 and 4
Neil Coles beat Tommy Aaron 1 hole
Brian Barnes lost to Billy Casper 1 hole
Christy O'Connor beat Frank Beard 5 and 4
Maurice Bembridge beat Ken Still 1 hole
Peter Butler beat Ray Floyd 1 hole
Tony Jacklin beat Jack Nicklaus 4 and 3
**Singles – Afternoon**
Barnes lost to Hill 4 and 2
Bernard Gallacher beat Trevino 4 and 3
Bembridge lost to Miller Barber 7 and 6
Butler beat Dale Douglass 3 and 2
O'Connor lost to Gene Littler 2 and 1
Brian Huggett halved with Casper
Coles lost to Dan Sikes 4 and 3
Jacklin halved with Nicklaus

1967 *Champions Golf Club, Houston, TX, USA*
Oct 20–22
**Result: USA 23½, GB&I 8½**
*Captains: Ben Hogan (USA), Dai Rees (GB&I)*
**First Day: Foursomes – Morning**
Casper & Boros halved with Huggett & Will
Palmer & Dickinson beat Alliss & O'Connor 2 and 1
Sanders & Brewer lost to Jacklin & Thomas 4 and 3
Nichols & Pott beat Hunt & Coles 6 and 5
**Foursomes – Afternoon**
Boros & Casper beat Huggett & Will 1 hole
Dickinson & Palmer beat Gregson & Boyle 5 and 4
Littler & Geiberger lost to Jacklin & Thomas 3 and 2
Nichols & Pott beat Alliss & O'Connor 2 and 1
**Second Day: Fourball – Morning**
Casper & Brewer beat Alliss & O'Connor 3 and 2
Nichols & Pott beat Hunt & Coles 1 hole
Littler & Geiberger beat Jacklin & Thomas 1 hole
Dickinson & Sanders beat Huggett & Will 3 and 2
**Fourball – Afternoon**
Casper & Brewer beat Hunt & Coles 5 and 3
Dickinson & Sanders beat Alliss & Gregson 4 and 3
Palmer & Boros beat Will & Boyle 1 hole
Littler & Geiberger halved with Jacklin & Thomas
**Third Day: Singles – Morning**
Gay Brewer beat Hugh Boyle 4 and 3
Billy Casper beat Peter Alliss 2 and 1
Arnold Palmer beat Tony Jacklin 3 and 2
Julius Boros lost to Brian Huggett 1 hole
Doug Sanders lost to Neil Coles 2 and 1
Al Geiberger beat Malcolm Gregson 4 and 2
Gene Littler halved with Dave Thomas
Bobby Nichols halved with Bernard Hunt

## Singles – Afternoon

Palmer beat Huggett 5 and 3
Brewer lost to Alliss  2 and 1
Gardner Dickinson beat Jacklin  3 and 2
Nichols beat Christy O'Connor  3 and 2
Johnny Pott beat George Will 3 and 1
Geiberger beat Gregson  2 and 1
Boros halved with Hunt
Sanders lost to Coles  2 and 1

## 1965 *Royal Birkdale Golf Club, Southport, Lancs, England*  Oct 7–9

### Result: GB&I 12½, USA 19½

*Captains: Harry Weetman (GB&I), Byron Nelson (USA)*

### First Day: Foursomes – Morning

Thomas & Will beat Marr & Palmer  6 and 5
O'Connor & Alliss beat Venturi & January  5 and 4
Platts & Butler lost to Boros & Lema  1 hole
Hunt & Coles lost to Casper & Littler  2 and 1

### Foursomes – Afternoon

Thomas & Will lost to Marr & Palmer  6 and 5
Martin & Hitchcock lost to Boros & Lema  5 and 4
O'Connor & Alliss beat Casper & Littler  2 and 1
Hunt & Coles beat Venturi & January  3 and 2

### Second Day: Fourball – Morning

Thomas & Will lost to January & Jacobs  1 hole
Platts & Butler halved with  Casper & Littler
Alliss & O'Connor lost to Marr & Palmer  5 and 4
Coles & Hunt beat Boros & Lema  1 hole

### Fourball – Afternoon

Alliss & O'Connor beat Marr & Palmer  1 hole
Thomas & Will lost to January & Jacobs  1 hole
Platts & Butler halved with Casper & Littler
Coles &  Hunt lost to Lema & Venturi  1 hole

### Third Day: Singles – Morning

Jimmy Hitchcock lost to Arnold Palmer  3 and 2
Lionel Platts lost to Julius Boros  4 and 2
Peter Butler lost to Tony Lema  1 hole
Neil Coles lost to Dave Marr  2 holes
Bernard Hunt beat Gene Littler  2 holes
Peter Alliss beat Billy Casper  1 hole
Dave Thomas lost to Tommy Jacobs  2 and 1
George Will halved with Don January

### Singles – Afternoon

Butler lost to Palmer  2 holes
Hitchcock lost to Boros  2 and 1
Christy O'Connor lost to Lema  6 and 4
Alliss beat Ken Venturi  3 and 1
Hunt lost to Marr  1 hole
Coles beat Casper  3 and 2
Will lost to Littler  2 and 1
Platts beat Jacobs  1 hole

## 1963 *East Lake CC, Atlanta, GA, USA*    Oct 11–13

### Result: USA 23, GB&I 9

*Captains: Arnold Palmer (USA), John Fallon (GB&I)*

### First Day: Foursomes – Morning

Palmer &  Pott lost to Huggett & Will  3 and 2
Casper & Ragan beat Alliss & O'Connor  1 hole
Boros & Lema halved with Coles & B Hunt
Littler & Finsterwald halved with Thomas &  Weetman

### Foursomes – Afternoon

Maxwell & Goalby beat Thomas & Weetman  4 and 3
Palmer & Casper beat Huggett & Will  5 and 4
Littler & Finsterwald beat Coles & G Hunt  2 and 1
Boros & Lema beat Haliburton & B Hunt  1 hole

### Second Day: Fourball – Morning

Palmer & Finsterwald beat Huggett & Thomas  5 and 4
Littler & Boros halved with Alliss & B Hunt
Casper & Maxwell beat Weetman & Will  3 and 2
Goalby & Ragan lost to Coles & O'Connor  1 hole

### Fourball – Afternoon

Palmer & Finsterwald beat Coles & O'Connor
  3 and 2
Lema & Pott beat Alliss & B Hunt  1 hole
Casper & Maxwell beat Haliburton & G Hunt
  2 and 1
Goalby & Ragan halved with Huggett & Thomas

### Third Day: Singles – Morning

Tony Lema beat Geoffrey Hunt  5 and 3
Johnny Pott lost to Brian Huggett  3 and 1
Arnold Palmer lost to Peter Alliss  1 hole
Billy Casper halved with Neil Coles
Bob Goalby beat Dave Thomas  3 and 2
Gene Littler lost to Tom Haliburton  6 and 5
Julius Boros lost to Harry Weetman  1 hole
Dow Finsterwald lost to Bernard Hunt  2 holes

### Singles – Afternoon

Arnold Palmer beat George Will  3 and 2
Dave Ragan beat Neil Coles  2 and 1
Tony Lema halved with Peter Alliss
Gene Littler beat Tom Haliburton  6 and 5
Julius Boros beat Harry Weetman  2 and 1
Billy Maxwell beat Christy O'Connor  2 and 1
Dow Finsterwald beat Dave Thomas  4 and 3
Bob Goalby beat Bernard Hunt  2 and 1

## 1961 *Royal Lytham & St Annes GC, St Annes, Lancs, England*  Oct 13–14

### Result: USA 14½, GB&I 9½

*Captains: Jerry Barber (USA), Dai Rees (GB&I)*

### First Day: Foursomes – Morning

O'Connor & Alliss beat Littler & Ford  4 and 3
Panton & Hunt lost to Wall & Hebert  4 and 3
Rees & Bousfield lost to Casper & Palmer  2 and 1
Haliburton & Coles lost to Souchak & Collins
  1 hole

### Foursomes – Afternoon

O'Connor & Alliss lost to Wall & Hebert  1 hole
Panton & Hunt lost to Casper & Palmer  5 and 4
Rees & Bousfield beat Souchak & Collins  4 and 2
Haliburton & Coles lost to Barber & Finsterwald
  1 hole

### Second Day: Singles – Morning

Harry Weetman lost to Doug Ford  1 hole
Ralph Moffitt lost to Mike Souchak  5 and 4
Peter Alliss halved with Arnold Palmer
Ken Bousfield lost to Billy Casper  5 and 3
Dai Rees beat Jay Hebert  2 and 1
Neil Coles halved with Gene Littler
Bernard Hunt beat Jerry Barber  5 and 4
Christy O'Connor lost to Dow Finsterwald
  2 and 1

### Singles – Afternoon

Weetman lost to Wall  1 hole
Alliss beat Bill Collins  3 and 2
Hunt lost to Souchak  2 and 1
Tom Haliburton lost to Palmer  2 and 1
Rees beat Ford  4 and 3
Bousfield beat Barber  1 hole
Coles beat Finsterwald  1 hole
O'Connor halved with Littler

## 1959 *Eldorado Country Club, Palm Desert, CA, USA*
### Nov 6–7
## Result: USA 8½, GB&I 3½
*Captains: Sam Snead (USA), Dai Rees (GB&I)*

**Foursomes**
Rosburg & Souchak beat Hunt & Brown  5 and 4
Ford & Wall lost to O'Connor & Alliss  3 and 2
Boros & Finsterwald beat Rees & Bousfield  2 holes
Snead & Middlecoff halved with Weetman & Thomas

**Singles**
Doug Ford halved with Norman Drew
Mike Souchak beat Ken Bousfield  3 and 2
Bob Rosburg beat Harry Weetman  6 and 5
Sam Snead beat Dave Thomas  6 and 5
Dow Finsterwald beat Dai Rees  1 hole
Jay Hebert halved with Peter Alliss
Art Wall Jr beat Christy O'Connor  7 and 6
Cary Middlecoff lost to Eric Brown  4 and 3

## 1957 *Lindrick Golf Club, Sheffield, Yorks, England*
### Oct 4–5
## Result: GB&I 7½, USA 4½
*Captains: Dai Rees (GB&I), Jack Burke (USA)*
**Foursomes**
Alliss & Hunt lost to Ford & Finsterwald  2 and 1
Bousfield & Rees beat Art Wall Jr & Hawkins  3 and 2
Faulkner & Weetman lost to Kroll & Burke  4 and 3
O'Connor & Brown lost to Mayer & Bolt  7 and 5

**Singles**
Eric Brown beat Tommy Bolt  4 and 3
Peter Mills beat Jack Burke  5 and 3
Peter Alliss lost to Fred Hawkins  2 and 1
Ken Bousfield beat Lionel Hebert  4 and 3
Dai Rees beat Ed Furgol  7 and 6
Bernard Hunt beat Doug Ford  6 and 5
Christy O'Connor beat Dow Finsterwald  7 and 6
Harry Bradshaw halved with Dick Mayer

## 1955 *Thunderbird G and C Club, Palm Springs, CA, USA*  Nov 5–6
## Result: USA 8, GB&I 4
*Captains: Chick Harbert (USA), Dai Rees (GB&I)*

**Foursomes**
Harper & Barber lost to Fallon & Jacobs  1 hole
Ford & Kroll beat Brown & Scott  5 and 4
Burke & Bolt beat Lees & Weetman  1 hole
Snead & Middlecoff beat Rees & Bradshaw  3 and 2

**Singles**
Tommy Bolt beat Christy O'Connor  4 and 2
Chick Harbert beat Syd Scott  3 and 2
Cary Middlecoff lost to John Jacobs  1 hole
Sam Snead beat Dai Rees  3 and 1
Marty Furgol lost to Arthur Lees  3 and 1
Jerry Barber lost to Eric Brown  3 and 2
Jack Burke beat Harry Bradshaw  3 and 2
Doug Ford beat Harry Weetman  3 and 2

## 1953 *West Course, Wentworth GC, Surrey, England*  Oct 2–3
## Result: USA 6½, GB 5½
*Captains: Henry Cotton (GB), Lloyd Mangrum (USA)*
**Foursomes**
Weetman & Alliss lost to Douglas & Oliver  2 and 1
Brown & Panton lost to Mangrum & Snead  8 and 7

Adams & Hunt lost to Kroll & Burke  7 and 5
Daly & Bradshaw beat Burkemo & Middlecoff  1 hole
**Singles**
Dai Rees lost to Jack Burke  2 and 1
Fred Daly beat Ted Kroll  9 and 7
Eric Brown beat Lloyd Mangrum  2 holes
Harry Weetman beat Sam Snead  1 hole
Max Faulkner lost to Cary Middlecoff  3 and 1
Peter Alliss lost to Jim Turnesa  1 hole
Bernard Hunt halved with Dave Douglas
Harry Bradshaw beat Fred Haas Jr  3 and 2

## 1951 *Pinehurst No.2, Pinehurst, NC, USA*
### Nov 2–4
## Result: USA 9½, GB 2½
*Captains: Sam Snead (USA), Arthur Lacey (GB)*
**Foursomes**
Heafner & Burke beat Faulkner & Rees  5 and 3
Oliver & Henry Ransom lost to Ward & Lees  2 and 1
Mangrum & Snead beat Adams & Panton  5 and 4
Hogan & Demaret beat Daly & Bousfield  5 and 4

**Singles**
Jack Burke beat Jimmy Adams  4 and 3
Jimmy Demaret beat Dai Rees  2 holes
Clayton Heafner halved with Fred Daly
Lloyd Mangrum beat Harry Weetman  6 and 5
Ed Oliver lost to Arthur Lees  2 and 1
Ben Hogan beat Charlie Ward  3 and 2
Skip Alexander beat John Panton  8 and 7
Sam Snead beat Max Faulkner  4 and 3

## 1949 *Ganton Golf Club, Scarborough, Yorks, England*
### Sept 16–17
## Result: USA 7, GB 5
*Captains: Charles Whitcombe (GB), Ben Hogan (USA)*
**Foursomes**
Faulkner & Adams beat Harrison & Palmer  2 and 1
Daly & Ken Bousfield beat Hamilton & Alexander  4 and 2
Ward & King lost to Demaret & Heafner  4 and 3
Burton & Lees beat Snead & Mangrum  1 hole

**Singles**
Max Faulkner lost to Dutch Harrison  8 and 7
Jimmy Adams beat Johnny Palmer  2 and 1
Charlie Ward lost to Sam Snead  6 and 5
Dai Rees beat Bob Hamilton  6 and 4
Dick Burton lost to Clayton Heafner  3 and 2
Sam King lost to Chick Harbert  4 and 3
Arthur Lees lost to Jimmy Demaret  7 and 6
Fred Daly lost to Lloyd Mangrum  1 hole

## 1947 *Portland Golf Club, Portland, OR, USA*  Nov 1–2
## Result: USA 11, GB 1
*Captains: Ben Hogan (USA), Henry Cotton (GB)*
**Foursomes**
Oliver & Worsham beat Cotton & Lees  10 and 9
Snead & Mangrum beat Daly & Ward  6 and 5
Hogan & Demaret beat Adams & Faulkner  2 holes
Nelson & Herman Barron beat Rees & King  2 and 1

**Singles**
Dutch Harrison beat Fred Daly  5 and 4
Lew Worsham beat Jimmy Adams  3 and 2
Lloyd Mangrum beat Max Faulkner  6 and 5
Ed Oliver beat Charlie Ward  4 and 3
Byron Nelson beat Arthur Lees  2 and 1
Sam Snead beat Henry Cotton  5 and 4
Jimmy Demaret beat Dai Rees  3 and 2
Herman Keiser lost to Sam King  4 and 3

1937 *Southport & Ainsdale GC, Southport, Lancs,*
*England* June 29–30

**Result: USA 8, GB 4**
*Captains: Charles Whitcombe (GB),*
*Walter Hagen (USA)*

**Foursomes**
Padgham & Cotton lost to Dudley & Nelson   4 and 2
Lacey & Bill Cox lost to Guldahl & Manero   2 and 1
Whitcombe & Rees halved with Sarazen & Shute
Alliss & Burton beat Picard & Johnny Revolta   2 and 1

**Singles**
Alf Padgham lost to Ralph Guldahl   8 and 7
Sam King halved with Densmore Shute
Dai Rees beat Byron Nelson   3 and 1
Henry Cotton beat Tony Manero   5 and 3
Percy Alliss lost to Gene Sarazen   1 hole
Dick Burton lost to Sam Snead   5 and 4
Alf Perry lost to Ed Dudley   2 and 1
Arthur Lacey lost to Henry Picard   2 and 1

1935 *Ridgewood Country Club, Paramus, NJ, USA*
Sept 28–29

**Result: USA 9, GB 3**
*Captains: Walter Hagen (USA),*
*Charles Whitcombe (GB)*

**Foursomes**
Sarazen & Hagen beat Perry & Busson   7 and 6
Picard & Revolta beat Padgham & Alliss   6 and 5
Runyan & Smith beat Cox & Jarman   9 and 8
Dutra & Laffoon lost to C Whitcombe & E Whitcombe
1 hole

1935 *continued*

**Singles**
Gene Sarazen beat Jack Busson   3 and 2
Paul Runyon beat Dick Burton   5 and 3
Johnny Revolta beat Charles Whitcombe   2 and 1
Olin Dutra beat Alf Padgham   4 and 2
Craig Wood lost to Percy Alliss   1 hole
Horton Smith halved with Bill Cox
Henry Picard beat Ernest Whitcombe   3 and 2
Sam Parks halved with Alf Perry

1933 *Southport & Ainsdale GC, Southport, Lancs,*
*England* June 26–27

**Result: GB 6½, USA 5½**
*Captains: JH Taylor (GB), Walter Hagen (USA)*

**Foursomes**
Alliss & Whitcombe halved with Sarazen & Hagen
Mitchell & Havers beat Dutra & Shute   3 and 2
Davies & Easterbrook beat Wood & Runyan   1 hole
Padgham & Perry lost to Dudley & Burke   1 hole

**Singles**
Alf Padgham lost to Gene Sarazen   6 and 4
Abe Mitchell beat Olin Dutra   9 and 8
Arthur Lacey lost to Walter Hagen   2 and 1
William H Davies lost to Craig Wood   4 and 3
Percy Alliss beat Paul Runyan   2 and 1
Arthur Havers beat Leo Diegel   4 and 3
Syd Easterbrook beat Densmore Shute   1 hole
Charles Whitcombe lost to Horton Smith   2 and 1

1931 *Scioto Country Club, Columbus, OH, USA*
June 26–27

**Result: USA 9, GB 3**
*Captains: Walter Hagen (USA),*
*Charles Whitcombe (GB)*

**Foursomes**
Sarazen & Farrell beat Compston & Davies   8 and 7
Hagen & Shute beat Duncan & Havers   10 and 9
Diegel & Espinosa lost to Mitchell & Robson   3 and 1
Burke & Cox beat Easterbrook & E Whitcombe   3 and 2

**Singles**
Billy Burke beat Archie Compston   7 and 6
Gene Sarazen beat Fred Robson   7 and 6
Johnny Farrell lost to William H Davies   4 and 3
Wilfred Cox beat Abe Mitchell   3 and 1
Walter Hagen beat Charles Whitcombe   4 and 3
Densmore Shute beat Bert Hodson   8 and 6
Al Espinosa beat Ernest Whitcombe   2 and 1
Craig Wood lost to Arthur Havers   4 and 3

1929 *Moortown Golf Club, Leeds, Yorkshire,*
*England* May 26–27

**Result: GB 7, USA 5**
*Captains: George Duncan (GB),*
*Walter Hagen (USA)*

**Foursomes**
C Whitcombe & Compston halved with Farrell &
Turnesa
Boomer & Duncan lost to Diegel & Espinosa   7 and 5
Mitchell & Robson beat Sarazen & Dudley   2 and 1
E Whitcombe & Cotton lost to Golden & Hagen   2 holes

**Singles**
Charles Whitcombe beat Johnny Farrell   8 and 6
George Duncan beat Walter Hagen   10 and 8
Abe Mitchell lost to Leo Diegel   9 and 8
Archie Compston beat Gene Sarazen   6 and 4
Aubrey Boomer beat Joe Turnesa   4 and 3
Fred Robson lost to Horton Smith   4 and 2
Henry Cotton beat Al Watrous   4 and 3
Ernest Whitcombe halved with Al Espinosa

1927 *Worcester Country Club, Worcester, MA, USA*
June 3–4

**Result: USA 9½, GB 2½**
*Captains: W Hagen (USA), E Ray (GB)*

**Foursomes**
Hagen & Golden beat Ray & Robson   2 and 1
Farrell & Turnesa beat Duncan & Compston   8 and 6
Sarazen & Watrous beat Havers & Jolly   3 and 2
Diegel & Mehlhorn lost to Boomer & Whitcombe
7 and 5

**Singles**
Bill Mehlhorn beat Archie Compston   1 hole
Johnny Farrell beat Aubrey Boomer   5 and 4
Johnny Golden beat Herbert Jolly   8 and 7
Leo Diegel beat Ted Ray   7 and 5
Gene Sarazen halved with Charles Whitcombe
Walter Hagen beat Arthur Havers   2 and 1
Al Watrous beat Fred Robson   3 and 2
Joe Turnesa lost to George Duncan   1 hole

## Unofficial Ryder Cups
*Great Britain v USA*

**1926** *West Course,Wentworth GC, Surrey,
England*  June 4–5

**Result: GB 13½, USA 1½**

**Singles**
Abe Mitchell beat Jim Barnes  8 and 7
George Duncan beat Walter Hagen  6 and 5
Aubrey Boomer beat Tommy Armour  2 and 1
Archie Compston lost to Bill Mehlhorn  1 hole
George Gadd beat Joe Kirkwood  8 and 7
Ted Ray beat Al Watrous  6 and 5
Fred Robson beat Cyril Walker  5 and 4
Arthur Havers beat Fred McLeod  10 and 9
Ernest Whitcombe halved with Emmett French
Herbert Jolly beat Joe Stein  3 and 2

**Foursomes**
Mitchell & Duncan beat Barnes & Hagen  9 and 8
Boomer & Compston beat Armour & Kirkwood
3 and 2
Gadd & Havers beat Mehlhorn & Watrous  3 and 2
Ray & Robson beat Walker & McLeod  3 and 2
Whitcombe & Jolly beat French & Stein  3 and 2

**1921** *King's Course, Gleneagles Hotel, Perthshire,
Scotland*  June 6

**Result: GB 9 USA 3**
(no half points were awarded)

**Singles**
George Duncan beat Jock Hutchison  2 and 1
Abe Mitchell halved with Walter Hagen
Ted Ray lost to Emmet French  2 and 1
JH Taylor lost to Fred McLeod  1 hole
Harry Vardon beat Tom Kerrigan  3 and 1
James Braid beat Charles Hoffner  5 and 4
AG Havers lost to WE Reid  2 and 1
J Ockenden beat G McLean  5 and 4
J Sherlock beat Clarence Hackney  3 and 2
Joshua Taylor beat Bill Melhorn  3&2

**Foursomes**
George Duncan & Abe Mitchell halved with  Jock
Hutchison & Walter Hagen
Ted Ray & Harry Vardon beat Emmet French &
Tom Kerrigan  5 and 4
James Braid & JH Taylor halved with Charles Hoffner &
Fred McLeod
AG Havers & J Ockenden beat WE Reid & G McLean
6 and 5
J Sherlock & Joshua Taylor beat Clarence Hackney &
W Melhorn  1 hole

Three matches were halved

---

Although no matches were played between 1939 and 1945, Great Britain selected a side in 1939 and the Americans chose sides in 1939 to 1943. No alternative fixture was played in 1939 but the Americans played matches amongst themselves in the other four years. They resulted in:

|      |                                              |
|------|----------------------------------------------|
| 1940 | Cup Team 7, Gene Sarazen's Challengers 5     |
| 1941 | Cup Team 6½, Bobby Jones' Challengers 8½     |
| 1942 | Cup Team 10, Walter Hagen's Challengers 5    |
| 1943 | Cup Team 8½, Walter Hagen's Challengers 3½   |

---

## INDIVIDUAL RECORDS

Matches were contested as Great Britain v USA from 1927 to 1953; as Great Britain & Ireland v USA from 1955 to 1977 and as Europe v USA from 1979. Non-playing captains are shown in brackets.

### GB/GB&I/Europe

| Name | Year | Played | Won | Lost | Halved |
|------|------|--------|-----|------|--------|
| Jimmy Adams | *1939-47-49-51-53 | 7 | 2 | 5 | 0 |
| Percy Alliss | 1929-33-35-37 | 6 | 3 | 2 | 1 |
| Peter Alliss | 1953-57-59-61-63-65-67-69 | 30 | 10 | 15 | 5 |
| Laurie Ayton | 1949 | 0 | 0 | 0 | 0 |
| Peter Baker | 1993 | 4 | 3 | 1 | 0 |
| Severiano Ballesteros (ESP) | 1979-83-85-87-89-91-93-95-(97) | 37 | 20 | 12 | 5 |
| Harry Bannerman | 1971 | 5 | 2 | 2 | 1 |
| Brian Barnes | 1969-71-73-75-77-79 | 25 | 10 | 14 | 1 |
| Maurice Bembridge | 1969-71-73-75 | 16 | 5 | 8 | 3 |
| Thomas Björn (DEN) | 1997-2002 | 6 | 3 | 2 | 1 |
| Aubrey Boomer | 1927-29 | 4 | 2 | 2 | 0 |
| Ken Bousfield | 1949-51-55-57-59-61 | 10 | 5 | 5 | 0 |
| Hugh Boyle | 1967 | 3 | 0 | 3 | 0 |
| Harry Bradshaw | 1953-55-57 | 5 | 2 | 2 | 0 |
| Gordon J Brand | 1983 | 1 | 0 | 1 | 0 |
| Gordon Brand Jr | 1987-89 | 7 | 2 | 4 | 1 |
| Paul Broadhurst | 1991 | 2 | 2 | 0 | 0 |
| Eric Brown | 1953-55-57-59-(69)-(71) | 8 | 4 | 4 | 0 |
| Ken Brown | 1977-79-83-85-87 | 13 | 4 | 9 | 0 |

* In 1939 a GB team was named but the match was not played because of the Second World War

| Name | Year | Played | Won | Lost | Halved |
|---|---|---|---|---|---|
| Stewart Burns | 1929 | 0 | 0 | 0 | 0 |
| Dick Burton | 1935-37-*39-49 | 5 | 2 | 3 | 0 |
| Jack Busson | 1935 | 2 | 0 | 2 | 0 |
| Peter Butler | 1965-69-71-73 | 14 | 3 | 9 | 2 |
| José Maria Canizares (ESP) | 1981-83-85-89 | 11 | 5 | 4 | 2 |
| Paul Casey | 2004-06-08 | 9 | 3 | 2 | 4 |
| Alex Caygill | 1969 | 1 | 0 | 0 | 1 |
| Clive Clark | 1973 | 1 | 0 | 1 | 0 |
| Howard Clark | 1977-81-85-87-89-95 | 15 | 10 | 7 | 3 |
| Darren Clarke | 1997-99-2002-04-06 | 20 | 7 | 7 | 3 |
| Neil Coles | 1961-63-65-67-69-71-73-77 | 40 | 12 | 21 | 7 |
| Andrew Coltart | 1999 | 1 | 0 | 1 | 0 |
| Archie Compston | 1927-29-31 | 6 | 1 | 4 | 1 |
| Henry Cotton | 1929-37-*39-47-(53) | 6 | 2 | 4 | 0 |
| Bill Cox | 1935-37 | 3 | 0 | 2 | 1 |
| Allan Dailey | 1933 | 0 | 0 | 0 | 0 |
| Fred Daly | 1947-49-51-53 | 8 | 3 | 4 | 1 |
| Eamonn Darcy | 1975-77-81-87 | 11 | 1 | 8 | 2 |
| William Davies | 1931-33 | 4 | 2 | 2 | 0 |
| Peter Dawson | 1977 | 3 | 1 | 2 | 0 |
| Luke Donald | 2004-06-10 | 11 | 8 | 2 | 1 |
| Norman Drew | 1959 | 1 | 0 | 0 | 1 |
| George Duncan | 1927-29-31 | 5 | 2 | 3 | 0 |
| Syd Easterbrook | 1931-33 | 3 | 2 | 1 | 0 |
| Nick Faldo | 1977-79-81-83-85-87-89-91-93-95-97-(08) | 46 | 23 | 19 | 4 |
| John Fallon | 1955-(63) | 1 | 1 | 0 | 0 |
| Niclas Fasth (SWE) | 2002 | 3 | 0 | 2 | 1 |
| Max Faulkner | 1947-49-51-53-57 | 8 | 1 | 7 | 0 |
| David Feherty | 1991 | 3 | 1 | 1 | 1 |
| Ross Fisher | 2010 | 4 | 2 | 2 | 0 |
| Pierre Fulke (SWE) | 2002 | 2 | 0 | 1 | 1 |
| George Gadd | 1927 | 0 | 0 | 0 | 0 |
| Bernard Gallacher | 1969-71-73-75-77-79-81-83-(91)-(93)-(95) | 31 | 13 | 13 | 5 |
| Sergio García (ESP) | 1999-2002-04-06-08 | 24 | 14 | 6 | 4 |
| John Garner | 1971-73 | 1 | 0 | 1 | 0 |
| Antonio Garrido (ESP) | 1979 | 5 | 1 | 4 | 0 |
| Ignacio Garrido (ESP) | 1997 | 4 | 0 | 1 | 3 |
| David Gilford | 1991-95 | 6 | 3 | 3 | 0 |
| Eric Green | 1947 | 0 | 0 | 0 | 0 |
| Malcolm Gregson | 1967 | 4 | 0 | 4 | 0 |
| Joakim Haeggman (SWE) | 1993 | 2 | 1 | 1 | 0 |
| Tom Haliburton | 1961-63 | 6 | 0 | 6 | 0 |
| Søren Hansen (DEN) | 2008 | 3 | 0 | 2 | 1 |
| Peter Hanson (SWE) | 2010 | 3 | 1 | 2 | 0 |
| Jack Hargreaves | 1951 | 0 | 0 | 0 | 0 |
| Padraig Harrington | 1999-2002-04-06-08-10 | 25 | 9 | 13 | 3 |
| Arthur Havers | 1927-31-33 | 6 | 3 | 3 | 0 |
| Jimmy Hitchcock | 1965 | 3 | 0 | 3 | 0 |
| Bert Hodson | 1931 | 1 | 0 | 1 | 0 |
| Reg Horne | 1947 | 0 | 0 | 0 | 0 |
| Tommy Horton | 1975-77 | 8 | 1 | 6 | 1 |
| David Howell | 2004-06 | 5 | 3 | 1 | 1 |
| Brian Huggett | 1963-67-69-71-73-75-(77) | 25 | 9 | 10 | 6 |
| Bernard Hunt | 1953-57-59-61-63-65-67-69-(73)-(75) | 28 | 6 | 16 | 6 |
| Geoffrey Hunt | 1963 | 3 | 0 | 3 | 0 |
| Guy Hunt | 1975 | 3 | 0 | 2 | 1 |
| Tony Jacklin | 1967-69-71-73-75-77-79-(83)-(85)-(87)-(89) | 35 | 13 | 14 | 8 |
| John Jacobs | 1955-(79)-(81) | 2 | 2 | 0 | 0 |
| Mark James | 1977-79-81-89-91-93-95-(99) | 24 | 8 | 15 | 1 |
| Edward Jarman | 1935 | 1 | 0 | 1 | 0 |
| Miguel Angel Jiménez (ESP) | 1999-2004-08-10 | 15 | 4 | 8 | 3 |
| Per-Ulrik Johansson (SWE) | 1995-97 | 5 | 3 | 2 | 0 |
| Herbert Jolly | 1927 | 2 | 0 | 2 | 0 |
| Robert Karlsson (SWE) | 2006-08 | 7 | 1 | 2 | 4 |
| Martin Kaymer (GER) | 2010 | 4 | 2 | 1 | 0 |
| Michael King | 1979 | 1 | 0 | 1 | 0 |
| Sam King | 1937-*39-47-49 | 5 | 1 | 3 | 1 |
| Arthur Lacey | 1933-37-(51) | 3 | 0 | 3 | 0 |
| Barry Lane | 1993 | 3 | 0 | 3 | 0 |
| Bernhard Langer (GER) | 1981-83-85-87-89-91-93-95-97-2002-(04) | 42 | 21 | 15 | 6 |
| Paul Lawrie | 1999 | 5 | 3 | 1 | 1 |
| Arthur Lees | 1947-49-51-55 | 8 | 4 | 4 | 0 |
| Thomas Levet (FRA) | 2004 | 3 | 1 | 2 | 0 |

* In 1939 a GB team was named but the match was not played because of the Second World War

| Name | Year | Played | Won | Lost | Halved |
|------|------|--------|-----|------|--------|
| Sandy Lyle | 1979-81-83-85-87 | 18 | 7 | 9 | 2 |
| Graeme McDowell | 2008-10 | 8 | 4 | 2 | 2 |
| Paul McGinley | 2002-04-06 | 9 | 2 | 2 | 5 |
| Rory McIlroy (NIR) | 2010 | 4 | 1 | 1 | 2 |
| Jimmy Martin | 1965 | 1 | 0 | 1 | 0 |
| Peter Mills | 1957-59 | 1 | 1 | 0 | 0 |
| Abe Mitchell | 1929-31-33 | 6 | 4 | 2 | 0 |
| Ralph Moffitt | 1961 | 1 | 0 | 1 | 0 |
| Edoardo Molinari (ITA) | 2010 | 3 | 0 | 1 | 2 |
| Francesco Molinari (ITA) | 2010 | 3 | 0 | 2 | 1 |
| Colin Montgomerie | 1991-93-95-97-99-2002-04-06-(10) | 36 | 20 | 9 | 7 |
| Christy O'Connor Jr | 1975-89 | 4 | 1 | 3 | 0 |
| Christy O'Connor Sr | 1955-57-59-61-63-65-67-69-71-73 | 36 | 11 | 21 | 4 |
| José María Olazábal (ESP) | 1987-89-91-93-97-99-2006 | 31 | 18 | 8 | 5 |
| John O'Leary | 1975 | 4 | 0 | 4 | 0 |
| Peter Oosterhuis | 1971-73-75-77-79-81 | 28 | 14 | 11 | 3 |
| Alf Padgham | 1933-35-37-*39 | 6 | 0 | 6 | 0 |
| John Panton | 1951-53-61 | 5 | 0 | 5 | 0 |
| Jesper Parnevik (SWE) | 1997-99-2002 | 11 | 4 | 3 | 4 |
| Alf Perry | 1933-35-37 | 4 | 0 | 3 | 1 |
| Manuel Pinero (ESP) | 1981-85 | 9 | 6 | 3 | 0 |
| Lionel Platts | 1965 | 5 | 1 | 2 | 2 |
| Eddie Polland | 1973 | 2 | 0 | 2 | 0 |
| Ian Poulter | 2004-08-10 | 11 | 8 | 3 | 0 |
| Phillip Price | 2002 | 2 | 1 | 1 | 0 |
| Ronan Rafferty | 1989 | 3 | 1 | 2 | 0 |
| Ted Ray | 1927 | 2 | 0 | 2 | 0 |
| Dai Rees | 1937-*39-47-49-51-53-55-57-59-61-(67) | 18 | 7 | 10 | 1 |
| Steven Richardson | 1991 | 4 | 2 | 2 | 0 |
| José Rivero (ESP) | 1985-87 | 5 | 2 | 3 | 0 |
| Fred Robson | 1927-29-31 | 6 | 2 | 4 | 0 |
| Costantino Rocca (ITA) | 1993-95-97 | 11 | 6 | 5 | 0 |
| Justin Rose | 2008 | 4 | 3 | 1 | 0 |
| Jarmo Sandelin (SWE) | 1999 | 1 | 0 | 1 | 0 |
| Syd Scott | 1955 | 2 | 0 | 2 | 0 |
| Des Smyth | 1979-81 | 7 | 2 | 5 | 0 |
| Henrik Stenson (SWE) | 2006-08 | 7 | 2 | 3 | 2 |
| Dave Thomas | 1959-63-65-67 | 18 | 3 | 10 | 5 |
| Sam Torrance | 1981-83-85-87-89-91-93-95-(2002) | 27 | 7 | 15 | 5 |
| Peter Townsend | 1969-71 | 11 | 3 | 8 | 0 |
| Jean Van de Velde (FRA) | 1999 | 1 | 0 | 1 | 0 |
| Brian Waites | 1983 | 4 | 1 | 3 | 0 |
| Philip Walton | 1995 | 2 | 1 | 1 | 0 |
| Charlie Ward | 1947-49-51 | 6 | 1 | 5 | 0 |
| Paul Way | 1983-85 | 9 | 6 | 2 | 1 |
| Harry Weetman | 1951-53-55-57-59-61-63-(65) | 15 | 2 | 11 | 2 |
| Norman Wood | 1975 | 3 | 1 | 2 | 0 |
| Ian Woosnam | 1983-85-87-89-91-93-95-97-(2006) | 31 | 14 | 12 | 5 |
| Lee Westwood | 1997-99-2002-04-06-08-10 | 28 | 14 | 8 | 6 |
| Charles Whitcombe | 1927-29-31-33-35-37-*39-(49) | 9 | 3 | 2 | 4 |
| Ernest Whitcombe | 1929-31-35 | 6 | 1 | 4 | 1 |
| Reg Whitcombe | 1935-*39 | 1 | 0 | 1 | 0 |
| George Will | 1963-65-67 | 15 | 2 | 11 | 2 |
| Oliver Wilson | 2008 | 2 | 1 | 1 | 0 |

## United States of America

| Name | Year | Played | Won | Lost | Halved |
|------|------|--------|-----|------|--------|
| Tommy Aaron | 1969-73 | 6 | 1 | 4 | 1 |
| Skip Alexander | 1949-51 | 2 | 1 | 1 | 0 |
| Paul Azinger | 1989-91-93-2002-(08) | 16 | 5 | 8 | 3 |
| Jerry Barber | 1955-61 | 5 | 1 | 4 | 0 |
| Miller Barber | 1969-71 | 7 | 1 | 4 | 2 |
| Herman Barron | 1947 | 1 | 1 | 0 | 0 |
| Andy Bean | 1979-87 | 6 | 4 | 2 | 0 |
| Frank Beard | 1969-71 | 8 | 2 | 3 | 3 |
| Chip Beck | 1989-91-93 | 9 | 6 | 2 | 1 |
| Homero Blancas | 1973 | 4 | 2 | 1 | 1 |
| Tommy Bolt | 1955-57 | 4 | 3 | 1 | 0 |
| Julius Boros | 1959-63-65-67 | 16 | 9 | 3 | 4 |
| Gay Brewer | 1967-73 | 9 | 5 | 3 | 1 |
| Billy Burke | 1931-33 | 3 | 3 | 0 | 0 |

*In 1939 a GB team was named but the match was not played because of the Second World War*

| Name | Year | Played | Won | Lost | Halved |
|---|---|---|---|---|---|
| Jack Burke | 1951-53-55-57-59-(73) | 8 | 7 | 1 | 0 |
| Walter Burkemo | 1953 | 1 | 0 | 1 | 0 |
| Mark Calcavecchia | 1987-89-91-2002 | 14 | 6 | 7 | 1 |
| Chad Campbell | 2004-06-08 | 9 | 3 | 4 | 2 |
| Billy Casper | 1961-63-65-67-69-71-73-75-(79) | 37 | 20 | 10 | 7 |
| Stewart Cink | 2002-04-06-08-10 | 19 | 5 | 7 | 7 |
| Bill Collins | 1961 | 3 | 1 | 2 | 0 |
| Charles Coody | 1971 | 3 | 0 | 2 | 1 |
| John Cook | 1993 | 2 | 1 | 1 | 0 |
| Fred Couples | 1989-91-93-95-97 | 20 | 7 | 9 | 4 |
| Wilfred Cox | 1931 | 2 | 2 | 0 | 0 |
| Ben Crenshaw | 1981-83-87-95-(99) | 12 | 3 | 8 | 1 |
| Ben Curtis | 2008 | 3 | 1 | 1 | 1 |
| Jimmy Demaret | *1941-47-49-51 | 6 | 6 | 0 | 0 |
| Gardner Dickinson | 1967-71 | 10 | 9 | 1 | 0 |
| Leo Diegel | 1927-29-31-33 | 6 | 3 | 3 | 0 |
| Chris DiMarco | 2004-06 | 8 | 2 | 4 | 2 |
| Dale Douglass | 1969 | 2 | 0 | 2 | 0 |
| Dave Douglas | 1953 | 2 | 1 | 0 | 1 |
| Ed Dudley | 1929-33-37 | 4 | 3 | 1 | 0 |
| Olin Dutra | 1933-35 | 4 | 1 | 3 | 0 |
| David Duval | 1999-2002 | 7 | 2 | 3 | 2 |
| Lee Elder | 1979 | 4 | 1 | 3 | 0 |
| Al Espinosa | 1927-29-31 | 4 | 2 | 1 | 1 |
| Johnny Farrell | 1927-29-31 | 6 | 3 | 2 | 1 |
| Brad Faxon | 1995-97 | 6 | 2 | 4 | 0 |
| Dow Finsterwald | 1957-59-61-63-(77) | 13 | 9 | 3 | 1 |
| Ray Floyd | 1969-75-77-81-83-85-(89)-91-93 | 31 | 12 | 16 | 3 |
| Doug Ford | 1955-57-59-61 | 9 | 4 | 4 | 1 |
| Rikki Fowler | 2010 | 3 | 0 | 1 | 2 |
| Fred Funk | 2004 | 3 | 0 | 3 | 0 |
| Ed Furgol | 1957 | 1 | 0 | 1 | 0 |
| Marty Furgol | 1955 | 1 | 0 | 1 | 0 |
| Jim Furyk | 1997-99-2002-04-06-08-10 | 27 | 8 | 15 | 4 |
| Jim Gallagher Jr | 1993 | 3 | 2 | 1 | 0 |
| Al Geiberger | 1967-75 | 9 | 5 | 1 | 3 |
| Vic Ghezzi | *1939-*41 | 0 | 0 | 0 | 0 |
| Bob Gilder | 1983 | 4 | 2 | 2 | 0 |
| Bob Goalby | 1963 | 5 | 3 | 1 | 1 |
| Johnny Golden | 1927-29 | 3 | 3 | 0 | 0 |
| Lou Graham | 1973-75-77 | 9 | 5 | 3 | 1 |
| Hubert Green | 1977-79-85 | 7 | 4 | 3 | 0 |
| Ken Green | 1989 | 4 | 2 | 2 | 0 |
| Ralph Guldahl | 1937-*39 | 2 | 2 | 0 | 0 |
| Fred Haas Jr | 1953 | 1 | 0 | 1 | 0 |
| Jay Haas | 1983-95-2004 | 12 | 4 | 6 | 2 |
| Walter Hagen | 1927-29-31-33-35-(37) | 9 | 7 | 1 | 1 |
| Bob Hamilton | 1949 | 2 | 0 | 2 | 0 |
| Chick Harbert | 1949-55 | 2 | 2 | 0 | 0 |
| Chandler Harper | 1955 | 1 | 0 | 1 | 0 |
| EJ (Dutch) Harrison | 1947-49-51 | 3 | 2 | 1 | 0 |
| Fred Hawkins | 1957 | 2 | 1 | 1 | 0 |
| Mark Hayes | 1979 | 3 | 1 | 2 | 0 |
| Clayton Heafner | 1949-51 | 4 | 3 | 0 | 1 |
| Jay Hebert | 1959-61-(71) | 4 | 2 | 1 | 1 |
| Lionel Hebert | 1957 | 1 | 0 | 1 | 0 |
| J J Henry | 2006 | 3 | 0 | 0 | 3 |
| Dave Hill | 1969-73-77 | 9 | 6 | 3 | 0 |
| Jimmy Hines | *1939 | 0 | 0 | 0 | 0 |
| Scott Hoch | 1997-2002 | 7 | 2 | 3 | 2 |
| Ben Hogan | *1941-47-(49)-51-(67) | 3 | 3 | 0 | 0 |
| J B Holmes | 2008 | 3 | 2 | 0 | 1 |
| Hale Irwin | 1975-77-79-81-91 | 20 | 13 | 5 | 2 |
| Tommy Jacobs | 1965 | 4 | 3 | 1 | 0 |
| Peter Jacobsen | 1985-95 | 6 | 2 | 4 | 0 |
| Don January | 1965-77 | 7 | 2 | 3 | 2 |
| Lee Janzen | 1993-97 | 5 | 2 | 3 | 0 |
| Dustin Johnson | 2010 | 4 | 1 | 3 | 0 |
| Zach Johnson | 2006-10 | 7 | 3 | 3 | 1 |
| Herman Keiser | 1947 | 1 | 0 | 1 | 0 |
| Anthony Kim | 2008 | 4 | 2 | 1 | 1 |
| Tom Kite | 1979-81-83-85-87-89-93-(97) | 28 | 15 | 9 | 4 |
| Ted Kroll | 1953-55-57 | 4 | 3 | 1 | 0 |

* In 1939 a GB team was named but the match was not played because of the Second World War

| Name | Year | Played | Won | Lost | Halved |
|------|------|--------|-----|------|--------|
| Matt Kuchar | 2010 | 4 | 1 | 3 | 0 |
| Ky Laffoon | 1935 | 1 | 0 | 1 | 0 |
| Tom Lehman | 1995-97-99-(2006) | 10 | 5 | 3 | 2 |
| Tony Lema | 1963-65 | 11 | 8 | 1 | 2 |
| Justin Leonard | 1997-99-08 | 12 | 2 | 4 | 6 |
| Wayne Levi | 1991 | 2 | 0 | 2 | 0 |
| Bruce Lietzke | 1981 | 3 | 0 | 2 | 1 |
| Gene Littler | 1961-63-65-67-69-71-75 | 27 | 14 | 5 | 8 |
| Davis Love III | 1993-95-97-99-2002-04 | 26 | 9 | 12 | 5 |
| Jeff Maggert | 1995-97-99 | 11 | 6 | 5 | 0 |
| John Mahaffey | 1979 | 3 | 1 | 2 | 0 |
| Hunter Mahan | 2008-10 | 8 | 3 | 2 | 3 |
| Mark McCumber | 1989 | 3 | 2 | 1 | 0 |
| Jerry McGee | 1977 | 2 | 1 | 1 | 0 |
| Harold McSpaden | *1939-*41 | 0 | 0 | 0 | 0 |
| Tony Manero | 1937 | 2 | 1 | 1 | 0 |
| Lloyd Mangrum | *1941-47-49-51-53 | 8 | 6 | 2 | 0 |
| Dave Marr | 1965-(81) | 6 | 4 | 2 | 0 |
| Billy Maxwell | 1963 | 4 | 4 | 0 | 0 |
| Dick Mayer | 1957 | 2 | 1 | 0 | 1 |
| Bill Mehlhorn | 1927 | 2 | 1 | 1 | 0 |
| Dick Metz | *1939 | 0 | 0 | 0 | 0 |
| Phil Mickelson | 1995-97-99-2002-04-06-08–10 | 34 | 11 | 17 | 6 |
| Cary Middlecoff | 1953-55-59 | 6 | 2 | 3 | 1 |
| Johnny Miller | 1975-81 | 6 | 2 | 2 | 2 |
| Larry Mize | 1987 | 4 | 1 | 1 | 2 |
| Gil Morgan | 1979-83 | 6 | 1 | 2 | 3 |
| Bob Murphy | 1975 | 4 | 2 | 1 | 1 |
| Byron Nelson | 1937-*39-*41-47-(65) | 4 | 3 | 1 | 0 |
| Larry Nelson | 1979-81-87 | 13 | 9 | 3 | 1 |
| Bobby Nichols | 1967 | 5 | 4 | 0 | 1 |
| Jack Nicklaus | 1969-71-73-75-77-81-(83)-(87) | 28 | 17 | 8 | 3 |
| Andy North | 1985 | 3 | 0 | 3 | 0 |
| Ed Oliver | 1947-51-53 | 5 | 3 | 2 | 0 |
| Mark O'Meara | 1985-89-91-97-99 | 14 | 4 | 9 | 1 |
| Jeff Overton | 2010 | 4 | 2 | 2 | 0 |
| Arnold Palmer | 1961-63-65-67-71-73-(75) | 32 | 22 | 8 | 2 |
| Johnny Palmer | 1949 | 2 | 0 | 2 | 0 |
| Sam Parks | 1935 | 1 | 0 | 0 | 1 |
| Jerry Pate | 1981 | 4 | 2 | 2 | 0 |
| Steve Pate | 1991-99 | 4 | 2 | 2 | 0 |
| Corey Pavin | 1991-93-95–(2010) | 8 | 5 | 3 | 0 |
| Calvin Peete | 1983-85 | 7 | 4 | 2 | 1 |
| Kenny Perry | 2004-08 | 6 | 2 | 3 | 1 |
| Henry Picard | 1935-37-*39 | 4 | 3 | 1 | 0 |
| Dan Pohl | 1987 | 3 | 1 | 2 | 0 |
| Johnny Pott | 1963-65-67 | 7 | 5 | 2 | 0 |
| Dave Ragan | 1963 | 4 | 2 | 1 | 1 |
| Henry Ransom | 1951 | 1 | 0 | 1 | 0 |
| Johnny Revolta | 1935-37 | 3 | 2 | 1 | 0 |
| Chris Riley | 2004 | 3 | 1 | 1 | 1 |
| Loren Roberts | 1995 | 4 | 3 | 1 | 0 |
| Chi Chi Rodriguez | 1973 | 2 | 0 | 1 | 1 |
| Bill Rogers | 1981 | 4 | 1 | 2 | 1 |
| Bob Rosburg | 1959 | 2 | 2 | 0 | 0 |
| Mason Rudolph | 1971 | 3 | 1 | 1 | 1 |
| Paul Runyan | 1933-35-*39 | 4 | 2 | 2 | 0 |
| Doug Sanders | 1967 | 5 | 2 | 3 | 0 |
| Gene Sarazen | 1927-29-31-33-35-37-*41 | 12 | 7 | 2 | 3 |
| Densmore Shute | 1931-33-37 | 6 | 2 | 2 | 2 |
| Dan Sikes | 1969 | 3 | 2 | 1 | 0 |
| Scott Simpson | 1987 | 2 | 1 | 1 | 0 |
| Horton Smith | 1929-31-33-35-37-*39-*41 | 4 | 3 | 0 | 1 |
| C Snead | 1971-73-75 | 11 | 9 | 2 | 0 |
| Sam Snead | 1937-*39-*41-47-49-51-53-55-59-(69) | 13 | 10 | 2 | 1 |
| Ed Sneed | 1977 | 2 | 1 | 0 | 1 |
| Mike Souchak | 1959-61 | 6 | 5 | 1 | 0 |
| Craig Stadler | 1983-85 | 8 | 4 | 2 | 2 |
| Payne Stewart | 1987-89-91-93-99 | 19 | 7 | 10 | 2 |
| Ken Still | 1969 | 3 | 1 | 2 | 0 |
| Dave Stockton | 1971-77-(91) | 5 | 3 | 1 | 1 |
| Curtis Strange | 1983-85-87-89-95-2002 | 20 | 6 | 12 | 2 |
| Steve Stricker | 2008-10 | 7 | 3 | 3 | 1 |

* US teams were selected in 1939 and 1941, but did not play because of the Second World War

| Name | Year | Played | Won | Lost | Halved |
|---|---|---|---|---|---|
| Hal Sutton | 1985-87-99-2002-(04) | 16 | 7 | 5 | 4 |
| Vaughn Taylor | 2006 | 2 | 0 | 1 | 1 |
| David Toms | 2002-04-06 | 12 | 4 | 6 | 2 |
| Lee Trevino | 1969-71-73-75-79-81-(85) | 30 | 17 | 7 | 6 |
| Jim Turnesa | 1953 | 1 | 1 | 0 | 0 |
| Joe Turnesa | 1927-29 | 4 | 1 | 2 | 1 |
| Ken Venturi | 1965 | 4 | 1 | 3 | 0 |
| Scott Verplank | 2002-06 | 5 | 4 | 1 | 0 |
| Lanny Wadkins | 1977-79-83-85-87-89-91-93-(95) | 33 | 20 | 11 | 2 |
| Art Wall Jr | 1957-59-61 | 6 | 4 | 2 | 0 |
| Al Watrous | 1927-29 | 3 | 2 | 1 | 0 |
| Bubba Watson | 2010 | 4 | 1 | 3 | 0 |
| Tom Watson | 1977-81-83-89-(93) | 15 | 10 | 4 | 1 |
| Boo Weekley | 2008 | 3 | 2 | 0 | 1 |
| Tom Weiskopf | 1973-75 | 10 | 7 | 2 | 1 |
| Brett Wetterich | 2006 | 2 | 0 | 2 | 0 |
| Craig Wood | 1931-33-35-*41 | 4 | 1 | 3 | 0 |
| Tiger Woods | 1997-99-2002-04-06-10 | 29 | 13 | 14 | 2 |
| Lew Worsham | 1947 | 2 | 2 | 0 | 0 |
| Fuzzy Zoeller | 1979-83-85 | 10 | 1 | 8 | 1 |

## Seve Trophy by Golf+ (inaugurated 2000) St Nom La Bretche, France

**Captains:** Continental Europe – José Maria Olazábal (ESP); GB&I – Sam Torrance (SCO)

**First Day – Fourballs**
Thomas Björn & Miguel Angel Jiménez lost to Paul Lawrie & Stephen Gallacher  3 and 2
Mikko Ilonen & Thorbjørn Olesen beat Tommy Fleetwood & Chris Wood  1 hole
Francesco Molinari & Matteo Manassero halved with Paul Casey & Simon Khan
Joost Luiten & Grégory Bourdy beat Jamie Donaldson & David Lynn 2 and 1
Nicolas Colsaerts & Gonzalo Fernandez-Castaño beat Marc Warren & Scott Jamieson  5 and 3
**Match position:** Continental Europe 3½, GB&I 1½

**Second Day – Fourballs**
Mikko Ilonen & Thorbjørn Olesen lost to Paul Casey & Simon Khan  3 and 2
Francesco Molinari & Matteo Manassero lost to David Lynn & Scott Jamieson  1 hole
Thomas Björn & Miguel Angel Jiménez lost to Jamie Donaldson & Marc Warren  4 and 2
Joost Luiten & Grégory Bourdy beat Tommy Fleetwood & Chris Wood  1 hole
Nicolas Colsaerts & Gonzalo Fernandez-Castaño beat Paul Lawrie & Stephen Gallacher  6 and 5
**Match position:** Continental Europe 5½, GB&I 4½

**Third Day – Morning: Foursomes**
Nicolas Colsaerts & Gonzalo Fernandez-Castaño halved with Stephen Gallacher & Paul Lawrie
Joost Luiten & Grégory Bourdy beat Jamie Donaldson & Marc Warren  2 and 1
Thorbjørn Olesen & Francesco Molinari lost to Chris Wood & Scott Jamieson  2 and 1
Miguel Angel Jiménez & Matteo Manassero beat Paul Casey & Tommy Fleetwood  1 hole

**Afternoon: Foursomes**
Nicolas Colsaerts & Gonzalo Fernandez-Castaño lost to Paul Lawrie & Stephen Gallacher  2 and 1
Thomas Björn & Mikko Ilonen lost to Jamie Donaldson & Marc Warren  2 and 1
Joost Luiten & Grégory Bourdy beat Chris Wood & Scott Jamieson  2 holes
Miguel Angel Jiménez & Matteo Manassero beat Paul Casey & David Lynn  1 hole
**Match position:** Continental Europe 9, GB&I 9

**Fourth Day – Singles**
Gonzalo Fernandez-Castaño (ESP) halved with Jamie Donaldson (WAL)
Nicolas Colsaerts (BEL) beat Paul Casey (ENG)  1 hole
Joost Luiten (NED) lost to Tommy Fleetwood (ENG)  3 and 2
Thomas Björn (DEN) halved with Simon Khan (ENG)
Grégory Bourdy (FRA) beat Scott Jamieson (SCO)  4 and 3
Thorbjørn Olesen (DEN) lost to Marc Warren (SCO)  4 and 3
Matteo Manassero (ITA) beat Stephen Gallacher (SCO)  3 and 2
Mikko Ilonen (FIN) lost to Paul Lawrie (SCO)  2 and 1
Miguel Angel Jiménez (ESP) beat David Lynn (ENG)  6 and 4
Francesco Molinari (ITA) beat Chris Wood (ENG)  3 and 2
**Result:** Continental Europe 15, GB&I 13

---

*\* US teams were selected in 1939 and 1941, but did not play because of the Second World War*

## Seve Trophy *continued*

| | | | | | |
|---|---|---|---|---|---|
| 2000 | Sunningdale, England | GB&I 12½, Europe 13½ | 2009 | Golf de Saint-Nom-la- | GB&I 16½, Europe 11½ |
| 2002 | Druid's Glen, Ireland | Europe 12½, GB&I 14½ | | Bretèche, France | |
| 2003 | El Saler, Spain | Europe 13, GB&I 15 | 2011 | Golf de Saint-Nom-la- | GB&I 15½, Europe 12½ |
| 2005 | The Wynyard, England | GB&I 16½, Europe, 11½ | | Bretèche, France | |
| 2007 | The Heritage, Ireland | GB&I 16½, Europe 11½ | | | |

## 26th PGA Cup (Llandudno Trophy) (Instituted 1973)   *De Vere Slaley Hall, Hexham, England*
Great Britain and Ireland Club Professionals v United States Club Professionals

**Captains:** GB&I – Russell Weir; USA – Allen Wronowski

*GB&I names first*

### First Day – Morning: Foursomes
Gareth Wright (West Linton) and Richard Wallis (Walmer and Kingsdown) beat Mark Sheftic (Merion) and Chip Sullivan (Hanging Rock)  3 and 2
Benn Barham (Kings Hill) and David Callaway (Milford) lost to JC Anderson (Missouri Bluffs) and Kelly Mitchum (Pinehurst)  4 and 3
Graham Fox (Clydeway) and Jon Barnes (Ampfield Par 3) beat Rod Perry (Crane Lakes) and Jeff Sorenson (Columbia)  2 up
Greig Hutcheon (Banchory) and Scott Henderson (Kings Links) lost to Bob Sowards (Albany) and Mike Small (University of Illinois)  5 and 4

### First Day – Afternoon: Fourballs
Wright and Wallis lost to Matt Dobyns (Fresh Meadow) and Ryan Polzin (Royal Oaks)  3 and 2
Barham and Callaway lost to Sheftic and Sullivan  3 and 2
Nick Brennan (Borwood) and Dan Greenwood (Forest Pines) lost to Anderson and Mitchum  6 and 5
Hutcheon and Fox lost to Sowards and Small  2 up

**Match position:** GB&I 2, USA 6

### Second Day – Morning: Foursomes
Fox and Barnes lost to Anderson and Mitchum  5 and 4
Hutcheon and Henderson beat Dobyns and Polzin  1 up
Greenwood and Barham halved with Perry and Sorenson
Wallis and Wright halved with Sowards and Small

### Second Day – Afternoon: Fourball
Henderson and Hutcheon beat Anderson and Mitchum  6 and 5
Fox and Callaway lost to Sullivan and Sheftic  3 and 2
Brennan and Wright lost to Perry and Sorenson  3 and 2
Greenwood and Barham halved with Dobyns and Polzin

**Match position:** GB&I 5½, USA 10½

### Third Day: Singles
Barham beat Small  4 and 3
Wallis beat Sowards  3 and 2
Hutcheon lost to Mitchum  2 and 1
Henderson halved with Anderson
Wright beat Sorenson  2 and 1

Fox beat Perry  3 and 2
Greenwood Matt Dobyns  1 up
Callaway lost Ryan Polzin  3 and 2
Brennan beat Sullivan  2 and 1
Barnes beat Sheftic  3 and 2

**Result:** GB&I 13, USA 13 (USA retain the cup)

| | | | | | | | | |
|---|---|---|---|---|---|---|---|---|
| 1973 | USA | Pinehurst, NC | 13–3 | 1990 | USA | Turtle Point, Kiawah Island, SC | 19–7 | |
| 1974 | USA | Pinehurst, NC | 11½–4½ | 1992 | USA | K Club, Ireland | 15–11 | |
| 1975 | USA | Hillside, Southport, England | 9½–6½ | 1994 | USA | Palm Beach, Florida | 15–11 | |
| 1976 | USA | Moortown, Leeds, England | 9½–6½ | 1996 | Halved | Gleneagles, Scotland | 13–13 | |
| 1977 | Halved | Mission Hills, Palm Springs | 8½–8½ | 1998 | USA | The Broadmoor, Colorado | 11½–4½ | |
| 1978 | GB&I | St Mellion, Cornwall | 10½–6½ | | | Springs, CO | | |
| 1979 | GB&I | Castletown, Isle of Man | 12½–4½ | 2000 | USA | Celtic Manor, Newport, Wales | 13½–12½ | |
| 1980 | USA | Oak Tree, Edmond, OK | 15–6 | 2002 | *Cancelled* | | | |
| 1981 | Halved | Turnberry Isle, Miami, FL | 10½–10½ | 2003 | USA | Port St Lucie, FL | 19–7 | |
| 1982 | USA | Holston Hills, Knoxville, TN | 13–7 | 2005 | GB&I | K Club, Dublin, R.o.I. | 15–11 | |
| 1983 | GB&I | Muirfield, Scotland | 14½–6½ | 2007 | USA | Reynolds Plantation, GA | 13½–12½ | |
| 1984 | GB&I | Turnberry, Scotland | 12½–8½ | 2009 | USA | The Carrick, Loch Lomond, | 17½–8½ | |
| *Played alternate years from 1984* | | | | | | Scotland | | |
| 1986 | USA | Knollwood, Lake Fore, IL | 16–9 | 2011 | USA | CordeValle, San Martin, CA | 17½–8½ | |
| 1988 | USA | The Belfry, England | 15½–10½ | | | | | |

## PGAs of Europe International Team Championship
*Onyria Palmares Beach & Golf Resort, Portugal*

| | | |
|---|---|---|
| 1 | Netherlands (Robin Swane, Ralph Miller and Nicolas Nube) | 149-152-135-143—579 |
| 2 | Scotland (David Orr, Graham Fox and Greg McBain) | 150-150-138-143—581 |
| 3 | Denmark (Jacob Nordestgaard, Morten Hedegaard and Martin Hansen) | 149-149-142-142—582 |
| | Wales (Lee Rooke, Jon Bevan and Stuart Runcie) | 156-146-141-139—582 |
| | Ireland (John Kelly, Cian McNamara and Brendan McGovern) | 153-147-139-143—582 |

6 Italy 585; 7 Sweden 587; 8 Spain, France 588; 10 England 590; 11 Portugal 598; 12 Slovenia 602; 13 Germany 603; 14 South Africa 607; 15 Austria 610; 16 Switzerland 612; 17 Belgium 614; 18 Finland 616; 19 Greece 617; 20 Poland 619; 21 Czech Republic 625; 22 Iceland 630; 23 Croatia, Norway 631; 25 Slovakia 643; 26 Russia 660

**Individual:**

| | | |
|---|---|---|
| 1 | Graham Fox (SCO) | 72-76-67-71—286 |
| | Ralph Miller (NED) | 73-80-64-69—286 |
| 3 | Magnus Atlevi (SWE) | 74-71-73-69—287 |

| | | | | | | | | |
|---|---|---|---|---|---|---|---|---|
| 1990 | Scotland | 1995 | Spain | 2000 | Wales | 2005 | France | 2008 | Ireland |
| 1991 | Netherlands | 1996 | Scotland | 2001 | Spain | 2006 | Scotland | 2009 | Wales |
| 1992 | Scotland | 1997 | Scotland | 2002 | Spain | 2007 | Austria* | 2010 | England |
| 1993 | Scotland | 1998 | Ireland | 2003 | Spain | *Beat Wales at 2nd | 2011 | France |
| 1994 | Not played | 1999 | England | 2004 | England | extra hole | 2012 | Scotland |

---

## The Royal Trophy (Asia v Europe)  *Dragon Lake GC, Guangzhou, China*

*Asian names first*

**First Day – Foursomes**

Thongchai Jaidee (THA) and Kiradech Aphirbarnrat (THA) beat Paul Lawrie (SCO) and Stephen Gallacher (SCO) 5 and 3

Ryo Ishikawa (JPN) and Hiroyuki Fujita (JPN) beat Nicolas Colsaerts (BEL) and Bernd Wiesberger (AUT) 3 and 2

K T Kim (KOR) and H S Kim (KOR) beat Alvaro Quiros (ESP) and Thorbjørn Olesen (DEN) 4 and 2

Liang Wen-chong (CHN) and Wu Ashun (CHN) lost to David Howell (ENG) and Marc Warren (SCO) 2 and 1

**Second Day – Fourball**

Thongchai Jaidee and Kiradech Aphibarnrat beat Paul Lawrie and Stephen Gallacher 2 and 1

Liang Wen-chong and Wu Ashun halved with David Howell and Marc Warren

Ryo Ishikawa and Hiroyuki Fujita lost to Thorbjorn Olesen and Bernd Wiesberger 2 and 1

K T Kim and H S Kim halved with Nicolas Colsaerts and Alvaro Quiros

**Third Day – Singles**

Kiradech Aphirbarnrat beat Paul Lawrie 3 and 2

Thongchai Jaidee beat Stephen Gallacher 4 and 2

Ryo Ishikawa lost to Marc Warren 1 hole

H S Kim lost to David Howell 1 hole

**Result:** Asia 7½, Europe 8½

K T Kim halved with Alvaro Quiros

Wu Ashun lost to Thorbjørn Olesen 3 and 2

Hiroyuki Fujita lost to Bernd Wiesberger 3 and 2

Liang Wen-chong lost to Nicolas Colsaerts 2 holes

| | | | | | |
|---|---|---|---|---|---|
| 2006 | Europe 9, Asia 7 | Amata Spring CC, Chonburi, Thailand | 2010 | Europe 8½, Asia 7½ | Amata Spring CC, Chonburi, Thailand |
| 2007 | Europe 12½, Asia 3½ | Amata Spring CC, Chonburi, Thailand | 2011 | Europe 9, Asia 7 | Black Mountain CC, Hua Hin, Thailand |
| 2008 | Cancelled | | 2012 | Europe 8, Asia 8 | Empire CC, Brunei |
| 2009 | Asia 10, Europe 6 | Amata Spring CC, Chonburi, Thailand | | | |

---

## Captains roles for Jaidee and Jiménez

Thongchai Jaidee is captain of Team Asia and Miguel Angel Jiménez of Team Europe in the first EurAsia Cup presented by DRB-HICOM.

The Ryder Cup-styled match, played over three days, was scheduled for the Glenmarie Golf and Country Club in Kuala Lumpur at the end of March.

## 10th Presidents Cup (Instituted 1994)   *Muirfield Village GC, Dublin, Columbus, Ohio, USA*

**Captains:** Fred Couples (USA), Nick Price (International)   *USA names first*

### First Day – Fourballs
Hunter Mahan and Brandt Snedeker lost to Jason Day (AUS) and Graham DeLaet (CAN)   1 up
Bill Haas and Webb Simpson halved with Adam Scott (AUS) and Hideki Masuyama (JPN)
Phil Mickelson and Keegan Bradley lost to Louis Oosthuizen (RSA) and Charl Schwartzel (RSA)   2 and 1
Steve Stricker and Jordan Spieth beat Ernie Els (RSA) and Brendon de Jong (ZIM)   1 up
Matt Kuchar and Tiger woods beat Angel Cabrera (ARG) and Marc Leishman (AUS)   5 and 4
Zach Johnson and Jason Dufner beat Branden Grace (RSA) and Richard Sterne (RSA)   5 and 3

**Match position:** USA 3½, International 2½

### Second Day – Foursomes
Mickelson and Bradley beat Day and DeLaet
4 and 3
Haas and Maahan lost to Els and de Jong
4 and 3
Stricker and Spieth beat Grace and Sterne
2 and 1

Simpson and Snedeker lost to Cabrera and
Leishman   2 and 1
Woods and Kuchar beat Oosthuizen and
Schwartzel   4 and 2
Dufner and Johnson lost to Matsuyama and Scott
2 and 1

**Match position:** USA 6½, International 5½

### Third Day – Fourballs
Bradley and Mickelson beat Els and de Jong
2 and 1
Stricker and Spieth lost to Day and DeLaet
2 up
Haas and Simpson beat Cabrera and Grace
4 and 3
Snedeker and Mahan beat Oosthuizen and
Schwartzel   2 up
Woods and Kuchar beat Scott and Matsuyama
1 up

### Third Day – Foursomes
Mickelson and Bradley halved with Day and
DeLaet
Dufner and Johnson beat Sterne and Leishman
4 and 3
Haas and Stricker beat Scott and Matsuyama
4 and 3
Woods and Kuchar lost to Els and De Jonge
1 up
Simpson and Snedeker beat Oosthuizen and
Schwartzel   1 up

**Match position:** USA 14, International 8

### Fourth Day – Singles
Steve Stricker lost to Ernie Els   1 up
Hunter Mahan beat Hideki Matsuyama   3 and 2
Jason Dufner beat Brendon de Jong   4 and 3
Brandt Snedeker lost to Jason Day   6 and 4
Jordan Spieth lost to Graham DeLaet   1 up
Bill Haas lost to Adam Scott   2 and 1

Zach Johnson beat Branden Grace   4 and 2
Matt Kuchar lost to Marc Leishman   1 up
Tiger Woods beat Richard Sterne   1 up
Keegan Bradley lost to Charl Schwartzel   2 and 1
Webb Simpson halved with Louis Oosthuizen
Phil Mickelson lost to Angel Cabrara   1 up

**Result:** USA 18½, International 15½

1994 United States 20 International Team 12
  Captains: USA Hale Irwin; International David Graham
  Robert Trent Jones GC, Prince William County, Virginia
1996 United States 18½, International 15½
  Captains: USA Arnold Palmer; International Peter Thomson
  Robert Trent Jones GC, Prince William County, Virginia
1998 Interntational 20½, USA 12½
  Captains: USA Jack Nicklaus; Internationals Peter Thomson
  Royal Melbourne GC, Victoria , Australia
2000 United States 21½, Interntational 10½
  Captains: USA Ken Venturi; International Peter Thomson
  Robert Trent Jones GC, Prince William County, Virginia
2003 United States 17, International Team 17
  Captains: USA Jack Nicklaus; International Gary Player
  The Links at Fancourt Hotel and CC Estate, South Africa

2005 United States 18½, International 15½
  Captains: USA Jack Nicklaus; International Gary Player
  Robert Trent Jones GC, Prince William County, Virginia
2007 United States 19½, International 14½
  Captains: USA Jack Nicklaus; International Gary Player
  The Royal Montreal GC, Quebec, Canada
2009 United States 19½, International 14½
  Captains: USA Fred Couples; International Greg Norman
  Harding Park Golf Course, San Francisco, California
2011 United States 19, International 15
  Captains: USA Fred Couples; International Greg Norman
  Royal Melbourne GC, Victoria, Australia

This event will next be held in 2015 at the Jack Nicklaus GC, Incheon, Korea

# Dongfeng Nissan Cup (China v Asia–Pacific)  *CTS Tycoon Club, Shenzhen, China*

**Captains:** China: Wang Jun; Asia–Pacific: Peter Thomson (AUS)
*Chinese names first*

**Friday – Fourballs**
Wu Ashun & Wu Kangchun lost to Scott Laycock & Michael Long  7 and 6
Zhang Lianwei & Huang Wenyi beat Eric Mina and Choo Tze-huang  2 and 1
Yang Guangming & Yan Bin lost to Rory Hie & Thaworn Wiratchant  1 hole
Li Chao & Huang Mingjie lost to Kim Dae-sub & Choi Ho-sung  4 and 2
Wang Minghao & Li Xinyang lost to Masamichi Uehira & Kazuhiro Yamashita  4 and 3
Su Dong & Dou Zecheng halved with Matthew Griffin & Gareth Paddison
**Match position:** China 1½, Asia–Pacific 4½

**Saturday – Foursomes**
Zhang Lianwei & Huang Wenyi beat Scott Laycock & Michael Long  5 and 4
Yang Guangming & Yan Bin beat Choi Ho-sung & Kim Dae-sub  3 and 1
Huang Mingjie & Wu Kangchun lost to Rory Hie & Thaworn Wiratchant  3 and 2
Su Dong & Dou Zecheng beat Choi Ho-sung & Kim Dae-sub  3 and 1
Wu Ashun & Wang Minghao beat Kazuhiro Yamashita & Masamichi Uehira  1 hole
Li Chao & Li Xinyang lost to Matthew Griffin & Gareth Paddison  3 and 2
**Match position:** China 5½, Asia–Pacific 6½

**Sunday – Singles**
Wang Minghao lost to Masimichi Uehira (JPN)  3 and 1
Wu Ashun beat Michael Long (NZL)  4 and 3
Huang Wenyi halved with Choi Ho-sung (KOR)
Yang Guanming beat Kim Dae-sub (KOR)  1 hole
Yan Bin beat Eric Mina (PHI)  4 and 3
Dou Zecheng beat Thaworn Wiratchant (THA)  4 and 3
Li Xinyang lost to Kazuhiro Yamashita (JPN)  2 and 1
Wu Kangchun halved with Choo Tze-huang (SIN)
Huang Mingjie halved with Rory Hie (INA)
Zhang Lianwei halved with Matthew Griffin (AUS)
Su Dong beat Scott Laycock (AUS)  1 hole
Li Chao lost to Gareth Paddison (NZL)  2 and 1
**Result:** China 12½, Asia–Pacific 11½

2011 Asia–Pacific 12½, China 11½      2012 Asia–Pacific 14, China 10

# ISPS Handa World Cup of Golf  *Royal Melbourne GC, Victoria, Australia*  [6985–72]
*(formerly known as the Canada Cup but now run separately by the various world golf tours. In 2010, it was announced that the event would change from annual to biennial, held in odd-numbered years, to accommodate the 2016 inclusion of golf in the Olympics)*

| | | | | $ per team |
|---|---|---|---|---|
| 1 | Australia | Jason Day and Adam Scott | 143-138-134-136—551 | |
| 2 | USA | Matt Kuchar and Kevin Streelman | 137-137-142-145—561 | |
| 3 | Denmark | Thomas Björn and Thorbjørn Olesen | 137-140-147-139—563 | |
| | Japan | Ryo Ishikawa and Hideto Tanihara | 143-138-141-141—563 | |
| 5 | Canada | David Hearn and Brad Fritsch | 141-144-141-144—570 | |
| 6 | South Africa | George Coetzee and Branden Grace | 147-141-145-139—572 | |
| 7 | France | Grégory Bourdy and Victor Dubuisson | 145-140-145-143—573 | |
| | Germany | Maximilian Kieffer and Marcel Siem | 144-145-139-145—573 | |
| 9 | Thailand | Kiradech Aphibarnrat and Prayad Marksaeng | 143-142-143-147—575 | |
| 10 | Scotland | Martin Laird and Stephen Gallacher | 141-143-146-146—576 | |
| 11 | Ireland | Graeme McDowell and Shane Lowry | 147-143-138-149—577 | |
| | Sweden | Peter Hanson and Jonas Blixt | 148-143-147-139—577 | |
| 13 | England | Chris Wood and Danny Willett | 144-143-143-148—578 | |
| | Finland | Roope Kakko and Mikko Korhonen | 142-147-144-145—578 | |
| 15 | South Korea | K J Choi and Sang-Moon Bae | 141-148-144-147—580 | |

World Cup of Golf *continued*

| 16 | Netherlands | Robert-Jan Derksen and Tim Sluiter | 150-147-139-145—581 |
|----|-------------|-------------------------------------|---------------------|
| 17 | Argentina | Fabian Gomez and Emiliano Grillo | 149-146-146-141—582 |
|    | Portugal | Ricardo Santos and Jose-Filipe Lima | 140-142-146-154—582 |
|    | Spain | Miguel Angel Jiménez and Rafael Cabrera Bello | 148-144-141-149—582 |
| 20 | Brazil | Adilson da Silva and Alexandre Rocha | 144-143-141-155—583 |
|    | Italy | Francesco Molinari and Matteo Manassero | 151-141-142-149—583 |
|    | New Zealand | Mike Hendry and Tim Wilkinson | 154-144-141-144—583 |
| 23 | Philippines | Angelo Que and Tony Lascuna | 144-143-147-153—587 |
| 24 | Chile | Mark Tullo and Felipe Aguilar | 149-144-145-150—588 |
|    | China | A-shun Wu and Wen-Chong Liang | 152-145-148-143—588 |
| 26 | India | Anirban Lahiri and Gaganjeet Bhullar | 154-147-149-143—593 |

**Individual:**

| 1 | Jason Day (AUS) | 68-70-66-70—274 |
|----|-----------------|-----------------|
| 2 | Thomas Björn (DEN) | 66-68-71-71—276 |
| 3 | Adam Scott (AUS) | 75-68-68-66—277 |
| 4 | Matt Kuchar (USA) | 71-68-68-71—278 |
| 5 | Ryo Ishikawa (JPN) | 71-71-70-69—281 |
|   | Kiradech Aphibarnrat (THA) | 71-70-70-70—281 |
| 7 | Hideto Tanihara (JPN) | 72-67-71-72—282 |
| 8 | David Hearn (CAN) | 70-71-71-71—283 |
|   | Stuart Manley (WAL) | 67-72-72-72—283 |
|   | Kevin Streelman (USA) | 66-69-74-74—283 |
|   | Francesco Molinari (ITA) | 75-67-66-75—283 |
| 12 | Brendon de Jonge (ZIM) | 74-72-70-68—284 |
|   | Maximilian Kieffer (GER) | 73-71-70-70—284 |
|   | Bernd Wiesberger (AUT) | 71-72-69-72—284 |
| 15 | Roope Kakko (FIN) | 72-72-70-71—285 |
|   | Grégory Bourdy (FRA) | 72-69-72-72—285 |
|   | K J Choi (KOR) | 67-74-71-73—285 |
|   | Ricardo Santos (POR) | 69-69-73-74—285 |
|   | Graeme McDowell (IRL) | 72-71-67-75—285 |
| 20 | George Coetzee (RSA) | 74-71-73-68—286 |
|   | Branden Grace (RSA) | 73-70-72-71—286 |
|   | Martin Laird (SCO) | 67-72-74-73—286 |
|   | Miguel Angel Jiménez (ESP) | 73-69-71-73—286 |
|   | Oscar Fraustro (MEX) | 74-67-71-74—286 |
| 25 | Thorbjørn Olesen (DEN) | 71-72-76-68—287 |
|   | Vijay Singh (FIJ) | 73-69-75-70—287 |
|   | Nicolas Colsaerts (BEL) | 70-76-70-71—287 |
|   | Anirban Lahiri (IND) | 72-70-73-72—287 |
|   | Brad Fritsch (CAN) | 71-73-70-73—287 |
| 30 | Jonas Blixt (SWE) | 76-72-74-66—288 |
|   | Victor Dubuisson (FRA) | 73-71-73-71—288 |
| 32 | Fabian Gomez (ARG) | 72-75-72-70—289 |
|   | Chris Wood (ENG) | 75-70-72-72—289 |
|   | Mark Tullo (CHI) | 74-72-71-72—289 |
|   | Peter Hanson (SWE) | 72-71-73-73—289 |
|   | Marcel Siem (GER) | 71-74-69-75—289 |
|   | Danny Willett (ENG) | 69-73-71-76—289 |
| 38 | A-shun Wu (CHN) | 77-69-75-69—290 |
|   | Mike Hendry (NZL) | 75-73-71-71—290 |
|   | Robert-Jan Derksen (NED) | 74-75-70-71—290 |
|   | Stephen Gallacher (SCO) | 74-71-72-73—290 |
| 42 | Tim Sluiter (NED) | 76-72-69-74—291 |
|   | Adilson da Silva (BRA) | 72-71-71-77—291 |
| 44 | Shane Lowry (IRL) | 75-72-71-74—292 |
|   | Alexandre Rocha (BRA) | 72-72-70-78—292 |

| 46 | Emiliano Grillo (ARG) | 77-71-74-71—293 |
|---|---|---|
|  | Tim Wilkinson (NZL) | 79-71-70-73—293 |
|  | Mikko Korhonen (FIN) | 70-75-74-74—293 |
|  | Angelo Que (PHI) | 74-72-70-77—293 |
| 50 | Tony Lascuna (PHI) | 70-71-77-76—294 |
|  | Prayad Marksaeng (THA) | 72-72-73-77—294 |
| 52 | Sang-Moon Bae (KOR) | 74-74-73-74—295 |
|  | Rafael Cabrera Bello (ESP) | 75-75-70-76—296 |
| 54 | Jose-Filipe Lima (POR) | 71-73-73-80—297 |
| 55 | Wen-Chong Liang (CHN) | 75-76-73-74—298 |
|  | Siddikur Rahman (BAN) | 73-75-77-73—298 |
| 57 | Felipe Aguilar (CHI) | 75-72-74-78—299 |
| 58 | Matteo Manassero (ITA) | 76-74-76-74—300 |
| 59 | Espen Kofstad (NOR) | 72-75-74-82—303 |
| 60 | Gaganjeet Bhullar (IND) | 82-77-76-71—306 |

1953   I Argentina (A Cerda and R de Vicenzo); 2 Canada (S Leonard and B Kerr)                287   Montreal
   (Individual: A Cerda, Argentina, 140)
1954   I Australia (P Thomson and K Nagle); 2 Argentina (A Cerda and R de Vicenzo)              556   Laval-Sur-Lac
   (Individual: S Leonard, Canada, 275)
1955   I United States (C Harbert and E Furgol); 2 Australia (P Thomson and K Nagle)            560   Washington
   (Individual: E Furgol*, USA (*after a play-off with P Thomson and F van Donck, 279))
1956   I United States (B Hogan and S Snead); 2 South Africa (A Locke and G Player)             567   Wentworth
   (Individual: B Hogan, USA, 277)
1957   I Japan (T Nakamura and K Ono); 2 United States (S Snead and J Demaret)                  557   Tokyo
   (Individual: T Nakamura, Japan, 274)
1958   I Ireland (H Bradshaw and C O'Connor); 2 Spain (A Miguel and S Miguel)                   579   Mexico City
   (Individual: A Miguel*, Spain (*after a play-off with H Bradshaw, 286))
1959   I Australia (P Thomson and K Nagle); 2 United States (S Snead and C Middlecoff)          563   Melbourne
   (Individual: S Leonard*, Canada, 275 (*after a tie with P Thomson, Australia))
1960   I United States (S Snead and A Palmer); 2 England (H Weetman and B Hunt)                 565   Portmarnock
   (Individual: F van Donck, Belgium, 279)
1961   I United States (S Snead and J Demaret); 2 Australia (P Thomson and K Nagle)             560   Puerto Rico
   (Individual: S Snead, USA, 272)
1962   I United States (S Snead and A Palmer); 2 Argentina (F de Luca and R De Vicenzo)         557   Buenos Aires
   (Individual: R De Vicenzo, Argentina, 276)
1963   I United States (A Palmer and J Nicklaus); 2 Spain (S Miguel and R Sota)                 482   St Nom-La-
   (Individual: J Nicklaus, USA, 237 – tournament reduced to 36 holes because of fog)               Breteche
1964   I United States (A Palmer and J Nicklaus); 2 Argentina (R De Vicenzo and L Ruiz)         554   Maui, Hawaii
   (Individual: J Nicklaus, USA, 276)
1965   I South Africa (G Player and H Henning); 2 Spain (A Miguel and R Sota)                   571   Madrid
   (Individual: G Player, South Africa, 281)
1966   I United States (J Nicklaus and A Palmer); 2 South Africa (G Player and H Henning)       548   Tokyo
   (Individual: G Knudson* Canada, 272 (*after a play-off with H Sugimoto, Japan))
1967   I United States (J Nicklaus and A Palmer); 2 New Zealand (R Charles and W Godfrey)       557   Mexico City
   (Individual: A Palmer, USA, 276)
1968   I Canada (A Balding and G Knudson); 2 United States (J Boros and L Trevino)              569   Olgiata, Rome
   (Individual: A Balding, Canada, 274)
1969   I United States (O Moody and L Trevino); 2 Japan (T Kono and H Yasuda)                   552   Singapore
   (Individual: L Trevino, USA, 275)
1970   I Australia (B Devlin and D Graham); 2 Argentina (R De Vicenzo and V Fernandez)          545   Buenos Aires
   (Individual: R De Vicenzo, Argentina, 269)
1971   I United States (J Nicklaus and L Trevino); 2 South Africa (H Henning and G Player)      555   Palm Beach, Florida
   (Individual: J Nicklaus, USA, 271)
1972   I Taiwan (H Min-Nan and LL Huan); 2 Japan (T Kono and T Murakami)                        438   Melbourne
   (Three rounds only – Individual: H Min-Nan, Taiwan, 217)
1973   I United States (J Nicklaus and J Miller); 2 South Africa (G Player and H Baiocchi)      558   Marbella, Spain
   (Individual: J Miller, USA, 277)
1974   I South Africa (R Cole and D Hayes); 2 Japan (I Aoki and M Ozaki)                        554   Caracas
   (Individual: R Cole, South Africa, 271)
1975   I United States (J Miller and L Graham); 2 Taiwan (H Min-Nan and KC Hsiung)              554   Bangkok
   (Individual: J Miller, USA, 275)
1976   I Spain (S Ballesteros and M Pinero); 2 United States (J Pate and D Stockton)            574   Palm Springs
   (Individual: EP Acosta, Mexico, 282)
1977   I Spain (S Ballesteros and A Garrido); 2 Philippines (R Lavares and B Arda)              591   Manilla, Philippines
   (Individual: G Player, South Africa, 289)
1978   I United States (J Mahaffey and A North); 2 Australia (G Norman and W Grady)             564   Hawaii
   (Individual: J Mahaffey, USA, 281)

## World Cup of Golf continued

| | | |
|---|---|---|
| 1979 | 1 United States (J Mahaffey and H Irwin); 2 Scotland (A Lyle and K Brown) (Individual: H Irwin, USA, 285) | 575 Glyfada, Greece |
| 1980 | 1 Canada (D Halldorson and J Nelford); 2 Scotland (A Lyle and S Martin) (Individual: A Lyle, Scotland, 282) | 572 Bogota |
| 1981 | Not played | |
| 1982 | 1 Spain (M Pinero and JM Canizares); 2 United States (B Gilder and B Clampett) (Individual: M Pinero, Spain, 281) | 563 Acapulco |
| 1983 | 1 United States (R Caldwell and J Cook); 2 Canada (D Barr and J Anderson) (Individual: D Barr, Canada, 276) | 565 Pondok Inah, Jakarta |
| 1984 | 1 Spain (JM Canizares and J Rivero); 2 Scotland (S Torrance and G Brand Jr) (Played over 54 holes because of storms – Individual: JM Canizares, Spain, 205) | 414 Olgiata, Rome |
| 1985 | 1 Canada (D Halidorson and D Barr); 2 England (H Clark and P Way) (Individual: H Clark, England, 272) | 559 La Quinta, Calif. |
| 1986 | Not played | |
| 1987 | 1 Wales* (I Woosnam and D Llewelyn); 2 Scotland (S Torrance and A Lyle) (*Wales won play-off – Individual: I Woosnam, Wales, 274) | 574 Kapalua, Hawaii |
| 1988 | 1 United States (B Crenshaw and M McCumber); 2 Japan (T Ozaki and M Ozaki) (Individual: B Crenshaw, USA, 275) | 560 Royal Melbourne, Australia |
| 1989 | 1 Australia (P Fowler and W Grady); 2 Spain (JM Olazábal and JM Canizares) (Played over 36 holes because of storms – Individual: P Fowler) | 278 Las Brisas, Spain |
| 1990 | 1 Germany (B Langer and T Giedeon); 2 England (M James and R Boxall)   tied   Ireland (R Rafferty and D Feherty) (Individual: P Stewart, USA, 271) | 556 Grand Cypress Resort, Orlando, Florida |
| 1991 | 1 Sweden (A Forsbrand and P-U Johansson); 2 Wales (I Woosnam and P Price) (Individual: I Woosnam, Wales, 273) | 563 La Querce, Rome |
| 1992 | 1 USA (F Couples and D Love III); 2 Sweden (A Forsbrand and P-U Johansson) (Individual: B Ogle*, Australia, 270 (*after a tie with Ian Woosnam, Wales)) | 548 La Moraleja II, Madrid, Spain |
| 1993 | 1 USA (F Couples and D Love III); 2 Zimbabwe (N Price and M McNulty) (Individual: B Langer, Germany, 272) | 556 Lake Nona, Orlando, Forida |
| 1994 | 1 USA(F Couples and D Love III); 2 Zimbabwe (M McNulty and T Johnstone) (Individual: F Couples, USA, 265) | 536 Dorado Beach, Puerto Rico |
| 1995 | 1 USA (F Couples and D Love III); 2 Australia (B Ogle and R Allenby) (Individual: D Love III, USA, 267) | 543 Mission Hills, Shenzhen, China |
| 1996 | 1 South Africa (E Els and W Westner); 2 USA (T Lehman and S Jones) (Individual: E Els, S. Africa, 272) | 547 Erinvale, Cape Town South Africa |
| 1997 | 1 Ireland (P Harrington and P McGinley); 2 Scotland (C Montgomerie and R Russell) (Individual: C Montgomerie, Scotland, 266) | 545 Kiawah Island, SC |
| 1998 | 1 England (N Faldo and D Carter); 2 Italy (C Rocca and M Florioli) (Individual: Scott Verplank, USA, 279) | 568 Auckland, New Zealand |
| 1999 | 1 USA (T Woods and M O'Meara); 2 Spain (S Luna and MA Martin) (Individual: Tiger Woods, USA, 263) | 545 The Mines Resort, K Lumpur, Malaysia |
| 2000 | 1 USA (T Woods and D Duval); 2 Argentina (A Cabrera & E Romero) | 254 Buenos Aires GC Argentina |
| 2001 | 1 South Africa* (E Els and R Goosen); 2 New Zealand (M Campbell and D Smail) USA (D Duval and T Woods)   tied   Denmark (T Björn and S Hansen) *South Africa won at the second extra hole | 254 The Taiheiyo Club, Japan |
| 2002 | 1 Japan (S Maruyama and T Izawa); 2 USA (P Mickelson and D Toms) | 252 Puerto Vallarta, Mexico |
| 2003 | 1 South Africa (T Immelman and R Sabbatini); 2 England (J Rose and P Casey) | 275 Kiawah Island, SC |
| 2004 | 1 England (L Donald and P Casey); 2 Spain (MA Jiménez and S García) Reduced to 54 holes because of rain | 257 Real Club de Sevilla, Spain |
| 2005 | 1 Wales (B Dredge and S Dodd); 2 Sweden (N Fasth and H Stenson) Reduced to 54 holes because of bad weather | 189 Vilamoura, Portugal |
| 2006 | 1 Germany* (B Langer and M Siem); 2 Scotland (C Montgomerie and M Warren) *Germany beat Scotland at the first extra hole | 268 Sandy Lane Resort, Barbados |
| 2007 | 1 Scotland* (C Montgomerie and M Warren); 2 Germany (B Weekley and H Slocum) *Scotland beat USA at the third extra hole | 263 Shenzhen, China |
| 2008 | 1 Sweden (R Karlsson and H Stenson); 2 Spain (MA Jiménez and P Larrazabal) | 261 Shenzhen, China |
| 2009 | 1 Italy (E Molinari and F Molinari); 2T Ireland (G McDowell and R McIlroy)/ Sweden (R Karlsson and H Stenson) | 259 Shenzhen, China |
| 2010 | Not played – this event will now be held bienially in odd-numbered years | |
| 2011 | 1 USA (M Kuchar and G Woodland); 2T England (I Poulter and J Rose)/Germany (A Cejka and M Kaymer) | 264 Shenzhen, China |

# National Championships 2013

## Glenmuir PGA Professional Championship  *De Vere Slaley Hall*

| | | |
|---|---|---|
| 1 | Daniel Greenway (Forest Pines) | 71-69-72-68—280 |
| 2 | David Callaway (Milford) | 73-71-73-72—289 |
| 3 | Benn Barham (King's Hill) | 72-72-74-72—290 |

## ISPS Handa PGA Seniors Championship  *De Vere Mottram Hotel*

| | | |
|---|---|---|
| 1 | Paul Wesselingh (Keddleston Park) | 68-70-70-64—272 |
| 2 | Angel Franco (PAR) | 70-70-70-73—276 |
| 3 | Ian Woosnam (RAW Course Design) | 72-69-71-65—277 |

## PGA Senior Professional Championship  *Northampton GC*

| | | |
|---|---|---|
| 1 | Wraith Grant (Woodcote Park) | 72-68-72—212 |
| 2 | Robert Elliss (Newark) | 72-69-72—213 |
| 3 | Richard Masters (Baildon) | 70-71-73—214 |

## Powerade PGA Assistants' Championship  *Coventry GC*

| | | |
|---|---|---|
| 1 | Matthew Cort (Rothley Park) | 68-68-67—203 |
| 2 | Jack Harrison (Wildwood) | 69-67-68—204 |
| 3 | Robert Gower (South Winchester) | 70-69-69—208 |
| | Ben O'Dell (Best4balls Ltd) | 70-67-71—208 |

## Southern PGA Championship  *The Drift GC*

| | | |
|---|---|---|
| 1 | Matthew Ford (CK Group)* | 69-69-69—207 |
| 2 | Richard Wallis (Walmer and Kingsdown) | 71-67-69—207 |
| | Adam Wootton (Oxford Golf Centre) | 68-68-72—208 |

* Ford won at the first extra hole

## Cassidy Golf 103rd Irish PGA Championship  *Roganstown G&CC*

| | | |
|---|---|---|
| 1 | Michael McGeady | 66-72-70-67—275 |
| 2 | Damian Mooney (Monkstown) | 70-70-68-68—276 |
| | Cian McNamara (Ballyliffin) | 73-69-66-68—276 |

## Irish PGA Club Professional Championship  *Dundalk GC*

| | | |
|---|---|---|
| 1 | Brian McElhinney (Foyle Golf Centre) | 68-72—140 |
| 2 | Patrick Devine (Royal Dublin) | 71-70—141 |
| 3 | Robert Giles (Greenore ) | 73-69—142 |
| | John Kelly (St Margaret's) | 72-70—142 |
| | Damian Mooney (Ballyliffin) | 71-71—142 |

## Irish PGA Assistants' Championship  *Nuremore CC*

| | | |
|---|---|---|
| 1 | Brian McElhinney (Foyle Golf Centre)* | 72-71-73-73—289 |
| 2 | Dara Lernihan (Elm Park) | 76-73-71-69—289 |

*McElhinney won at the second extra hole

| | | |
|---|---|---|
| 3 | Enda Maguire (Dundalk) | 77-74-69-74—294 |

## Gleneagles Scottish PGA Championship  *Gleneagles Golf Resort, (King's course)*
| | | |
|---|---|---|
| I | Greig Hutcheon (Banchory) | 73-64-64-66—267 |
| 2 | Gareth Wright (West Linton) | 65-67-65-71—268 |
| 3 | Jason McCreadie (Buchanan Castle) | 64-66-73-70—273 |

## Scottish Young Professionals Championship  *West Lothian GC*
| | | |
|---|---|---|
| I | Paul O'Hara (Clydeway Golf) | 65-67-68-72—272 |
| 2 | Neil Fenwick (Dunbar) | 70-68-74-66—278 |
| | Daniel Flannery (Caldwell) | 70-66-70-72—278 |

## Paul Lawrie Invitational  *Desside GC (Haughton course)*
| | | |
|---|---|---|
| I | David Law (Paul Lawrie Golf Centre) | 66-64-69—199 |
| 2 | Paul Lawrie (Carnegie Club) | 69-69-64—202 |
| 3 | Graeme Brown (Montrose Golf Links Ltd) | 69-68-67—204 |

## Northern Open  *Meldrum House GC*
| | | |
|---|---|---|
| I | James Byrne (Banchory) | 67-66-63-65—261 |
| 2 | David Law | 63-65-68-66—262 |
| 3 | Graham Fox (Clydeway Golf) | 64-70-63-68—265 |

## Welsh National PGA Championship  *Royal St David's GC*
| | | |
|---|---|---|
| I | Lee Rooke (Royal St David's)* | 64-71—135 |
| 2 | Jon Bevan (Rhos on Sea) | 68-67—135 |

*Rooke won at the second extra hole
| | | |
|---|---|---|
| 3 | Garry Houston | 68-69—137 |

## Farmfoods British Par-3 Championship  *Nailcote Hall Hotel*
| | | |
|---|---|---|
| I | Tommy Fleetwood | 51-53—104 |
| 2 | Paul Broadhurst | 48-57—105 |
| 3 | Ian Woosnam | 56-50—106 |
| | Tony Johnstone | 53-53—106 |
| | Raymond Russell | 52-54—106 |
| | Carl Mason | 54-52—106 |

## PGAs of Europe Fourball Championship  *Lumine Golf and Beach Club, Spain*
| | | |
|---|---|---|
| I | Uli Weinhandl and Jurgen Maurer (AUT) | 68-64-61—193 |
| 2 | Mark Ridley and David Clark (ENG) | 65-63-66—194 |
| 3 | Nelson Cavalheiro and Hugo Santos (POR) | 66-64-67—197 |
| | Pablo Herreria and Ismael Del Castillo (ESP) | 65-65-67—197 |

## Unicredit PGAs of Europe Championship  *Pravets GR and Spa, Bulgaria*
| | | |
|---|---|---|
| I | Federico Elli (ITA) | 72-65-70-67—274 |
| 2 | Alec Roberts (SUI) | 70-67-73-70—280 |
| | Corsin Caviezel (POR) | 71-70-69-70—280 |

## Nedbank Golf Challenge  *Gary Player CC, Sun City, South Africa*
| | | |
|---|---|---|
| I | Thomas Björn (DEN) | 67-70-66-65—268 |
| 2 | Jamie Donaldson (WAL) | 67-66-67-70—270 |
| | Sergio García (ESP) | 66-73-66-65—270 |

## PGA National Pro-Am Final (Lombard Cup)  *Gleneagles Centenary course*
| | | |
|---|---|---|
| I | Keddleston Park GC (Ian Walley and Ian Neal) | 68-65—133 |
| 2 | Shirland GC (Tim Stevens and Keith Cornish) | 69-66—135 |
| 3 | Fynn Valley GC (Chris Smith and Kane Mayes) | 69-67—136 |
| | West Berkshire GC (Paul Simpson and Richard Muldoon) | 68-68—136 |

## PGA Southern Professional Championship   *Foxhills GC*

| | | |
|---|---|---|
| 1 | Robert Gowers (South Winchester) | 70-68-69—207 |
| 2 | James Ablett (Lee-on –the-Solent) | 71-70-69—210 |
| 3 | Paul Newman (East Berkshire) | 73-71-70—214 |
|   | James Harris (Nevill) | 69-70-75—214 |

## Paul Lawrie receives OBE for his work with children

Paul Lawrie, the 1999 Open champion and Ryder Cup player, has had his voluntary work off the golf course recognised with the award of an OBE.

Aberdeen-born and based Lawrie, a PGA-trained professional, received the award for 'voluntary services to golf' from Prince Charles in a ceremony at Buckingham Palace.

He was named in this year's Queen's Birthday Honours list for his work with the Paul Lawrie Foundation which he set up in 2001 and is now supported by The R&A.

Thousands of youngsters have already benefited from the Paul Lawrie Foundation which was set up to support junior golf in the north-east of Scotland but now includes a variety of sports such as football and hockey.

Paul was made an MBE in the New Year list in 2000 after winning the 1999 Open at Carnoustie in a dramatic play-off against Frenchman Jean Van de Velde and American Justin Leonard.

Lawrie said he and his wife Marian, who have two boys, Craig, who recently turned pro, and Michael, had spent of lot of time, effort and money on the Foundation.

"We started it in 2001 to help youngsters get started in golf and now we also have football, rugby, hockey and tennis included in our programme," he said of the Foundation.

The main focus is still the golf and the basic idea remains the same – to take the cost away from the parents so it's very cheap or free for their children, boys and girls, to learn how to play.

Stephen Gallacher, another Scottish pro, has used the Lawrie Foundation model as a basis for his own recently formed Foundation.

## Europe fights back to win Royal Trophy

When Paul McGinley leads his Ryder Cup side into action at Gleneagles later this year he will be hoping that he will be as successful as his predecessor José Maria Olazábal.

After leading his men to a spectacular come-from-behind triumph in the Ryder Cup at Medinah in 2012, Olazábal was equally successful as captain of the European side competing against Asia for the Royal Trophy.

Just as at Chicago, his team staged a dramatic comeback on the final day to win for the fifth time in seven matches.

The Europeans trailed 5–3 after the first two series and it got worse for the visitors at the Dragon Lake Golf Club in Guangzhou when Paul Lawrie and Stephen Gallacher lost their singles.

At 7–3, the Asian captain Y E Yang must have thought that victory was "in the bag" for his team but he was in for a shock. European won five and half of the remaining six points to win 8½–7½

Scotsman Mark Warren stood strong to start the fight back with a one hole win over Japan's Ryo Ishikawa then Dunhill Links champion David Howell came from three down with four to play for a vital victory over Korea's H S Kim.

Spain's Alvaro Quiros halved with K T Kim, Dane Thorbjørn Oleson was a 3 and 2 winner against Ashan Wu and Austrian Bernd Wiesberger won by a similar margin over Hiroyuki Fujita before Belgium's Nicolas Colsaerts clinched victory with his winning point against China's Liang Wen-chong.

"We came back from the dead," said Colsaerts, who will be hoping to retain his place in this year's Ryder Cup side for Gleneagles.

Olazábal said: "The European players did something extraordinary today. I am proud of the way they played."

Yang's response was predictable: "I never expected this to happen because we were so far in front. I congratulate Europe on an outstanding comeback."

# County, District and other Regional Championships

Berks, Bucks & Oxon: Matt Woods

Carnegie Invitational: Neil Fenwick

Channel Islands Challenge: Michael Durcan

Cheshire & North Wales: Andrew Barnett

Cornish Festival: Christopher Hudson

Cumbria Masters: Will Bowe

Devon Championship: Christian Vine

Dorset Open: Martyn Thompson

East Anglian Open: Crue Elliott

East Region Championship: Barrie Trainor

East Hertfordshire Classic: Glen Portelli

Essex Open: Jason Levermore

Essex PGA: Jason Levermore

Hampshire, Isle of Wight and
Channel Islands Open: Jon Barnes

Kent Open: Matthew Ford

Kent PGA: Charlie Wilson

Lancashire Open: Kris Andrews

Leeds Cup: Nicholas Ludwell

Manchester Open: David Shacklady

Midland Open: Matthew Cort

Midland PGA: Matthew Cort

Midland Masters: Matthew Cort

Middlesex PGA: Nick Pateman

Middlesex Open: Nick Pateman

Muir Deer Park Masters: Greig Hutcheon

Norfolk PGA: Ian Ellis

Norfolk Open: Luke Johnson (am)

Northamptonshire PGA: Simon Lilley

North East/North West: Craig Goodfellow

North Region PGA: Michael Jones

Northern Open: James Byrne

Paul Lawrie Invitational: David Law

Royal Cromer 125th Anniversary:
Nick Pateman

Shropshire & Hereford Open: Will Jones

Southern Open: Richard Wallis

Southern PGA: Robert Gowers

South Wales Festival: Cennydd Mills

Spey Valley Challenge: Stephen Gray

Suffolk PGA: Neil Mitchell (MP),
Lawrence Dodd (SP)

Surrey Open: Richard Wallis

Surrey Masters: Wraith Grant

Sussex Open: Wayne Hawes (am)

Ulster PGA: Niall Kearney

Welsh National PGA: Lee Rooke

West Region PGA: James Ruth

West Region Championship: James Ruth

Yorkshire Masters: David Shacklady

PART III

# Women's Professional Tournaments

# Rolex Women's World Golf
# Rankings at the end of the European, American and Japanese Tour seasons

| Rank | Name | Country | Events | Average points | Total points |
|------|------|---------|--------|----------------|--------------|
| 1 | Inbee Park | KOR | 63 | 11.47 | 722.59 |
| 2 | Suzann Pettersen | NOR | 50 | 10.83 | 541.45 |
| 3 | Stacy Lewis | USA | 54 | 9.61 | 518.91 |
| 4 | Lydia Ko | NZL | 25 | 7.78 | 272.20 |
| 5 | So Yeon Ryu | KOR | 56 | 7.01 | 392.63 |
| 6 | Shanshan Feng | CHN | 60 | 6.77 | 406.04 |
| 7 | Na Yeon Choi | KOR | 55 | 6.10 | 335.35 |
| 8 | Karrie Webb | AUS | 43 | 5.43 | 233.63 |
| 9 | Lexi Thompson | USA | 50 | 5.05 | 252.28 |
| 10 | I K Kim | KOR | 48 | 4.87 | 233.82 |
| 11 | Catriona Matthew | SCO | 45 | 4.76 | 214.06 |
| 12 | Cristie Kerr | USA | 46 | 4.63 | 212.86 |
| 13 | Paula Creamer | USA | 49 | 4.61 | 225.85 |
| 14 | Jiyai Shin | KOR | 55 | 4.31 | 237.14 |
| 15 | Amy Yang | KOR | 45 | 4.26 | 191.48 |
| 16 | Angela Stanford | USA | 49 | 4.11 | 201.51 |
| 17 | Hee Young Park | KOR | 55 | 3.97 | 218.57 |
| 18 | Ai Miyazato | JPN | 48 | 3.95 | 189.53 |
| 19 | Beatriz Recari | ESP | 55 | 3.94 | 216.91 |
| 20 | Lizette Salas | USA | 42 | 3.92 | 164.73 |
| 21 | Mika Miyazato | JPN | 50 | 3.85 | 192.28 |
| 22 | Ha Na Jang | KOR | 34 | 3.77 | 131.81 |
| 23 | Caroline Hedwall | SWE | 50 | 3.44 | 171.83 |
| 24 | Hyo-Joo Kim | KOR | 36 | 3.30 | 118.90 |
| 25 | Karine Icher | FRA | 51 | 3.26 | 166.25 |
| 26 | Anna Nordqvist | SWE | 57 | 3.19 | 181.95 |
| 27 | Sun Ju Ahn | KOR | 51 | 3.19 | 162.72 |
| 28 | Chella Choi | KOR | 58 | 3.11 | 180.21 |
| 29 | Yani Tseng | TPE | 49 | 2.97 | 145.72 |
| 30 | Azahara Muñoz | ESP | 55 | 2.96 | 162.98 |
| 31 | Se-Ri Pak | KOR | 34 | 2.96 | 103.53 |
| 32 | Ariya Jutanugarn | THA | 13 | 2.95 | 103.25 |
| 33 | Ilhee Lee | KOR | 51 | 2.83 | 144.38 |
| 34 | Sakura Yokomine | JPN | 67 | 2.76 | 184.71 |
| 35 | Sei Young Kim | KOR | 38 | 2.72 | 103.22 |
| 36 | Gerina Piller | USA | 50 | 2.70 | 135.02 |
| 37 | Rikako Morita | JPN | 70 | 2.69 | 188.51 |
| 38 | Pornanong Phatlum | THA | 56 | 2.68 | 149.93 |
| 39 | Jessica Korda | USA | 47 | 2.63 | 123.71 |
| 40 | Bo-Mee Lee | KOR | 60 | 2.61 | 156.84 |
| 41 | Carlota Ciganda | ESP | 49 | 2.61 | 127.69 |
| 42 | Hee Kyung Seo | KOR | 52 | 2.57 | 133.44 |
| 43 | Miki Saiki | JPN | 64 | 2.49 | 159.35 |
| 44 | Brittany Lincicome | USA | 49 | 2.46 | 120.71 |
| 45 | Ha Neul Kim | KOR | 46 | 2.46 | 113.16 |
| 46 | Sandra Gal | GER | 57 | 2.40 | 136.81 |
| 47 | Morgan Pressel | USA | 50 | 2.38 | 118.96 |
| 48 | Mi Jeong Jeon | KOR | 61 | 2.34 | 142.92 |
| 49 | Sun Young Yoo | KOR | 50 | 2.33 | 116.25 |
| 50 | Mamiko Higa | JPN | 51 | 2.25 | 114.83 |

# Ladies European Tour

www.ladieseuropeantour.com

## ISPS Handa Order of Merit

(figures in brackets show number of tournaments played)

| | | | | | | | | |
|---|---|---|---|---|---|---|---|---|
| 1 | Suzann Pettersen (NOR) | (3) | €518,448 | 51 | Stacy Lee Bregman (RSA) | (17) | 41,925 |
| 2 | Lee-Anne Pace (RSA) | (20) | 250,927 | 52 | Christina Kim (USA) | (7) | 41,380 |
| 3 | Lexi Thompson (USA) | (3) | 228,794 | 53 | Christel Boeljon (NED) | (7) | 38,731 |
| 4 | Gwladys Nocera (FRA) | (22) | 221,287 | 54 | Ai Miyazato (JPN) | (3) | 38,640 |
| 5 | Carlota Ciganda (ESP) | (13) | 173,328 | 55 | Whitney Hillier (AUS) | (15) | 38,252 |
| 6 | Charley Hull (ENG) | (15) | 135,994 | 56 | Caroline Afonso (FRA) | (17) | 36,123 |
| 7 | Holly Clyburn (ENG) | (17) | 116,100 | 57 | Dewi Claire Schreefel (NED) | (6) | 36,086 |
| 8 | Beatriz Recari (ESP) | (4) | 114,936 | 58 | Celine Herbin (FRA) | (12) | 36,078 |
| 9 | Shanshan Feng (CHN) | (4) | 106,166 | 59 | Vikki Laing (SCO) | (13) | 34,405 |
| 10 | Valentine Derrey (FRA) | (18) | 97,685 | 60 | Pamela Pretswell (SCO) | (16) | 34,094 |
| 11 | Catriona Matthew (SCO) | (4) | 96,903 | 61 | Karine Icher (FRA) | (4) | 34,080 |
| 12 | Mikaela Parmlid (SWE) | (17) | 96,709 | 62 | Louise Larsson (SWE) | (13) | 33,681 |
| 13 | Joanna Klatten (FRA) | (18) | 92,879 | 63 | Yu Yang Zhang (CHN) | (7) | 32,915 |
| 14 | Pornanong Phatlum (THA) | (5) | 89,411 | 64 | Kristie Smith (AUS) | (11) | 30,426 |
| 15 | Ashleigh Simon (RSA) | (10) | 88,592 | 65 | Titiya Plucksataporn (THA) | (18) | 29,427 |
| 16 | Rebecca Artis (AUS) | (18) | 87,960 | 66 | Sophie Giquel-Bettan (FRA) | (20) | 28,704 |
| 17 | Beth Allen (USA) | (20) | 84,436 | 67 | Melissa Reid (ENG) | (13) | 28,317 |
| 18 | Pernilla Lindberg (SWE) | (9) | 77,213 | 68 | Maria Hernandez (ESP) | (15) | 27,574 |
| 19 | Ariya Jutanugarn (THA) | (4) | 74,520 | 69 | Emily Taylor (ENG) | (18) | 27,413 |
| 20 | Anna Nordqvist (SWE) | (5) | 70,885 | 70 | Alexandra Vilatte (FRA) | (14) | 26,822 |
| 21 | Diana Luna (ITA) | (12) | 68,450 | 71 | Felicity Johnson (ENG) | (14) | 26,186 |
| 22 | Linda Wessberg (SWE) | (19) | 65,940 | 72 | Belen Mozo (ESP) | (5) | 25,672 |
| 23 | Liz Young (ENG) | (19) | 65,812 | 73 | Stefania Croce (ITA) | (14) | 25,375 |
| 24 | Ann-Kathrin Lindner (GER) | (16) | 65,083 | 74 | Kylie Walker (SCO) | (19) | 25,144 |
| 25 | Stacey Keating (AUS) | (16) | 65,024 | 75 | Carin Koch (SWE) | (9) | 24,889 |
| 26 | Marianne Skarpnord (NOR) | (21) | 64,888 | 76 | Jade Schaeffer (FRA) | (19) | 24,831 |
| 27 | Hannah Burke (ENG) | (20) | 64,379 | 77 | Julie Greciet (FRA) | (15) | 24,002 |
| 28 | Azahara Muñoz (ESP) | (4) | 64,277 | 78 | Cheyenne Woods (USA) | (11) | 24,000 |
| 29 | Sandra Gal (GER) | (3) | 62,767 | 79 | Sophie Walker (ENG) | (19) | 23,822 |
| 30 | Nontaya Srisawang (THA) | (19) | 62,447 | 80 | Margherita Rigon (Ita) | (17) | 23,795 |
| 31 | Nikki Campbell (AUS) | (20) | 60,956 | 81 | Connie Chen (RSA) | (19) | 23,587 |
| 32 | Sarah Kemp (AUS) | (16) | 60,336 | 82 | Noora Tamminen (FIN) | (11) | 23,349 |
| 33 | Laura Davies (ENG) | (16) | 59,141 | 83 | Stephanie Na (AUS) | (17) | 23,130 |
| 34 | Caroline Hedwall (SWE) | (5) | 57,440 | 84 | Jia Yun Li (CHN) | (9) | 23,087 |
| 35 | Florentyna Parker (ENG) | (19) | 56,989 | 85 | Giulia Sergas (ITA) | (5) | 22,487 |
| 36 | Cindy Lacrosse (USA) | (6) | 56,738 | 86 | Lindsey Wright (AUS) | (5) | 21,956 |
| 37 | Line Vedel (DEN) | (16) | 55,849 | 87 | Maria Balikoeva (RUS) | (6) | 21,466 |
| 38 | Veronica Zorzi (ITA) | (16) | 55,708 | 88 | Nikki Garrett (AUS) | (18) | 20,930 |
| 39 | Klara Spilkova (CZE) | (14) | 53,239 | 89 | Eleanor Givens (ENG) | (8) | 20,269 |
| 40 | Caroline Masson (GER) | (8) | 52,311 | 90 | Holly Aitchison (ENG) | (19) | 19,684 |
| 41 | Malene Jorgensen (DEN) | (12) | 51,682 | 91 | Mallory Fraiche (USA) | (15) | 19,054 |
| 42 | Xi Yu Lin (CHN) | (12) | 50,831 | 92 | Tania Elosegui (ESP) | (21) | 19,041 |
| 43 | Jessica Korda (USA) | (4) | 50,714 | 93 | Marion Ricordeau (FRA) | (16) | 18,945 |
| 44 | Trish Johnson (ENG) | (15) | 50,054 | 94 | Becky Morgan (WAL) | (9) | 18,163 |
| 45 | Camilla Lennarth (SWE) | (17) | 49,567 | 95 | Sahra Hassan (WAL) | (19) | 17,208 |
| 46 | Minea Blomqvist (FIN) | (15) | 48,287 | 96 | Alison Whitaker (AUS) | (16) | 16,016 |
| 47 | Katie Burnett (USA) | (9) | 43,797 | 97 | Marta Silva Zamora (ESP) | (8) | 15,958 |
| 48 | Bree Arthur (AUS) | (21) | 43,577 | 98 | Hannah Jun (USA) | (9) | 15,810 |
| 49 | Amelia Lewis (USA) | (7) | 42,476 | 99 | Rebecca Hudson (ENG) | (16) | 15,237 |
| 50 | Anne-Lise Caudal (FRA) | (18) | 42,062 | 100 | Cassandra Kirkland (FRA) | (15) | 14,632 |

# 2013 Tour Statistics

## Scoring average

| | | Points | | | | Points |
|---|---|---|---|---|---|---|
| 1 | Suzann Pettersen (NOR) | 68.20 | 6 | Karine Icher (FRA) | | 71.08 |
| 2 | Ariya Jutanugarn (THA) | 69.43 | 7 | Lee-Anne Pace (RSA) | | 71.15 |
| 3 | Azahara Muñoz (ESP) | 70.36 | 8 | Jessica Korda (USA) | | 71.17 |
| 4 | Shanshan Feng (CHN) | 70.90 | 9 | Charley Hull (ENG) | | 71.20 |
| 5 | Catriona Matthew (SCO) | 71.00 | 10 | Beatriz Recari (ESP) | | 71.27 |

## Driving distance

| | | Yards | | | | Yards |
|---|---|---|---|---|---|---|
| 1 | Morgana Robbertze (RSA) | 273.5 | 6 | Daniela Holmqvist (SWE) | | 263.3 |
| 2 | Jade Schaeffer (FRA) | 269.9 | 7 | Steffi Kirchmayr (GER) | | 262.3 |
| 3 | Bonita Bredenhann (NAM) | 268.3 | 8 | Joanna Klatten (FRA) | | 262.1 |
| 4 | Laura Davies (ENG) | 267.9 | 9 | Celine Herbin (FRA) | | 261.6 |
| 5 | Virginia Espejo (ESP) | 265.6 | 10 | Tania Elosegui (ESP) | | 260.8 |

## Greens in regulation

| | | % | | | | % |
|---|---|---|---|---|---|---|
| 1 | Maria Hernandez (ESP) | 80.08 | 6 | Gwladys Nocera (FRA) | | 76.94 |
| 2 | Dewi Claire Schreefel (NED) | 79.50 | 7 | Marianne Skarpnord (NOR) | | 75.70 |
| 3 | Celine Herbin (FRA) | 78.34 | 8 | Linda Wessberg (SWE) | | 75.64 |
| 4 | Charley Hull (ENG) | 78.04 | 9 | Ariya Jutanugarn (THA) | | 75.36 |
| 5 | Felicity Johnson (ENG) | 77.79 | 10 | Veronica Zorzi (ITA) | | 75.29 |

## Putts per round

| | | Av. | | | | Av. |
|---|---|---|---|---|---|---|
| 1 | Dawn Shockley (USA) | 28.8 | 6 | Carin Koch (SWE) | | 29.6 |
| 2 | Ashleigh Simon (RSA) | 29.1 | 7 | Line Vedel (DEN) | | 29.6 |
| 3 | Katie Burnett (USA) | 29.3 | 8 | Malene Jorgensen (DEN) | | 29.7 |
| 4 | Pernilla Lindberg (SWE) | 29.4 | 9 | Minea Blomqvist (FIN) | | 29.8 |
| 5 | Benedikte Grotvedt (NOR) | 29.4 | 10 | Stacey Keating (AUS) | | 29.9 |

## Total eagles

| | | Total | | | | Total |
|---|---|---|---|---|---|---|
| 1 | Stacey Keating (AUS) | 6 | 5T | Connie Chen (RSA) | | 4 |
| 2 | Hannah Burke (ENG) | 5 | | Veronica Zorzi (ITA) | | 4 |
| | Kylie Walker (SCO) | 5 | | Line Vedel (DEN) | | 4 |
| | Laura Davies (ENG) | 5 | | Camilla Lennarth (SWE) | | 4 |
| 5 | Rebecca Artis (AUS) | 4 | | Alison Whitaker (AUS) | | 4 |
| | Anne-Lise Caudal (FRA) | 4 | | Felicity Johnson (ENG) | | 4 |

## Total birdies

| | | Total | | | | Total |
|---|---|---|---|---|---|---|
| 1 | Lee-Anne Pace (RSA) | 170 | 6 | Line Vedel (DEN) | | 143 |
| 2 | Valentine Derrey (FRA) | 164 | 7 | Linda Wessberg (SWE) | | 142 |
| 3 | Gwladys Nocera (FRA) | 163 | 8 | Bree Arthur (AUS) | | 138 |
| 4 | Joanna Klatten (FRA) | 157 | 9 | Marianne Skarpnord (NOR) | | 135 |
| 5 | Nikki Campbell (AUS) | 144 | 10 | Beth Allen (USA) | | 134 |

# 2013 Tour Results (in chronological order)

For past results see earlier editions of *The R&A Golfer's Handbook*

## Volvik RACV Ladies' Masters *Royal Pines, Gold Coast, Queensland, Australia* Feb 1–3

[5182m–72]

| | | | |
|---|---|---|---|
| 1 | Karrie Webb (AUS) | 70-66-67—203 | €30,000 |
| 2 | Su-Hyun Oh (AUS) (am) | 70-64-71—205 | |
| | Chella Choi (KOR) | 69-67-69—205 | 17,150 |
| | Ariya Jutanugarn (THA) | 69-65-71—205 | 17,150 |

## ISPS Handa New Zealand Women's Open *Clearwater, Christchurch, New Zealand*

Feb 8–10    [5644m–72]

| | | | |
|---|---|---|---|
| 1 | Lydia Ko (NZL) (am) | 70-68-68—206 | |
| 2 | Amelia Lewis (USA) | 73-68-66—207 | €30,804 |
| 3 | Stacey Keating (AUS) | 73-68-67—208 | 20,844 |

## ISPS Handa Women's Australian Open *Royal Canberra, ACT, Australia* Feb 14–17 [6108–73]

| | | | |
|---|---|---|---|
| 1 | Jiyai Shin (KOR) | 65-67-70-72—274 | €135,090 |
| 2 | Yani Tseng (TPE) | 68-71-71-66—276 | 82,197 |
| 3 | Lydia Ko (NZL) (am) | 63-69-70-76—278 | |

## World Ladies Championships *Mission Hills, Hainan, China* Mar 7–10

[7363–72]

**Individual**

| | | | |
|---|---|---|---|
| 1 | Suzann Pettersen (NOR) | 70-67-67-66—270 | €57,560 |
| 2 | Inbee Park (KOR) | 68-65-69-69—271 | 38,949 |
| 3 | Shanshan Feng (CHN) | 70-69-72-66—277 | 26,861 |

**Team**

| | | | | |
|---|---|---|---|---|
| 1 | Korea | | 137-137-140-146—560 | €15,000 |
| | Inbee Park | 68-65-69-69—271 | | |
| | Ha-Neul Kim | 69-72-71-77—289 | | |
| 2 | Norway | | 142-139-142-141—565 | 13,000 |
| | Suzann Pettersen | 70-67-67-66—270 | | |
| | Marianne Skarpnord | 72-72-76-75—295 | | |
| 3 | Thailand | | 143-140-142-145—570 | 11,000 |
| | Ariya Jutanugarn | 69-71-69-73—282 | | |
| | Nontaya Srisawang | 74-69-73-72—288 | | |

4 England; 5 France; 6 Australia, China II; 8 China; 9 USA; 10 Spain; 11 Netherlands; 12 Scotland, RSA; 14 Italy; 15 Wales; 16 Finland; 17 Sweden; 18 Germany; 19 Japan

## Lalla Meryem Cup *Golf de l'Ocean, Agadir, Morocco* Mar 28–31

[5747m–71]

| | | | |
|---|---|---|---|
| 1 | Ariya Jutanugarn (THA) | 69-67-67-67—270 | €48,750 |
| 2 | Beth Allen (USA) | 70-68-67-68—273 | 27,868 |
| | Charley Hull (ENG) | 68-70-64-71—273 | 27,868 |

---

## Morita and Yokomine the big winners in Japan

Rikako Morita won the Japanese LPGA money list after a battle with last year's winner Sakura Yokomine that came to the wire but Sakura still was on the end of season awards lists with the Most Valuable Player award.

Morita and Yokomine both had four tournament successes during the 2013 season but Morita topped the money list with ¥126,675,049 – 1.3 million Yen ahead of Yokomine.

## South African Women's Open   Southbroom, Hibiscus Coast, RSA   April 19–21   [5564m–72]

| | | | |
|---|---|---|---|
| 1 | Marianne Skarpnord (NOR) | 69 | €14,500 |
| 2 | Stacy Lee Bregman (RSA) | 70 | 4,921 |
| | Charley Hull (ENG) | 70 | 4,921 |
| | Minea Blomqvist (FIN) | 70 | 4,921 |
| | Ashleigh Simon (RSA) | 70 | 4,921 |
| | Nina Holleder (GER) | 70 | 4,921 |
| | Camilla Lennarth (SWE) | 70 | 4,921 |
| | Katie Burnett (USA) | 70 | 4,921 |

Reduced to one round due to bad weather

## Turkish Airlines Ladies Open   National GC, Antalya, Turkey   May 9–12   [6279m–72]

| | | | |
|---|---|---|---|
| 1 | Lee-Anne Pace (RSA) | 70-77-70-72—289 | €37,500 |
| 2 | Minea Blomqvist (FIN) | 75-75-70-70—290 | 18,791 |
| | Carlota Ciganda (ESP) | 69-74-72-75—290 | 18,791 |
| | Charley Hull (ENG) | 75-71-69-75—290 | 18,791 |

## Deloitte Ladies Open   The International, Amsterdam, Netherlands   May 24–26   [5940m–73]

| | | | |
|---|---|---|---|
| 1 | Holly Clyburn (ENG) | 71-69-71—211 | €37,500 |
| 2 | Charley Hull (ENG) | 72-73-69—214 | 25,375 |
| 3 | Carin Koch (SWE) | 73-71-71—215 | 17,500 |

## UniCredit Ladies German Open   Gut Häusern, Munich   May 30–June 2   [5832m–72]

| | | | |
|---|---|---|---|
| 1 | Carlota Ciganda (ESP)* | 68-33—101 | €52,500 |
| 2 | Charley Hull (ENG) | 67-34—101 | 35,525 |

*Ciganda won at the first extra hole

| | | | |
|---|---|---|---|
| 3 | Rebecca Hudson (ENG) | 68-34—102 | 24,500 |

Reduced to two rounds due to bad weather

## Allianz Ladies Slovak Open   Tále, Slovakia   June 20-23

| | | | |
|---|---|---|---|
| 1 | Gwladys Nocera (FRA) | 70-68-71-70—279 | €37,500 |
| 2 | Lee-Anne Pace (RSA) | 71-70-70-72—283 | 25,375 |
| 3 | Whitney Hillier (AUS) | 75-70-69-70—284 | 17,500 |

## Open de España   Club de Campo Villa de Madrid, Madrid, Spain   July 18–21

| | | | |
|---|---|---|---|
| 1 | Lee-Anne Pace (RSA) | 67-69-68-71—275 | €52,500 |
| 2 | Mikaela Parmlid (SWE) | 69-71-66-70—276 | 35,535 |
| 3 | Joanna Klatten (FRA) | 69-71-67-72—279 | 24,500 |

## ISPS Handa Ladies European Masters   Denham, Buckinghamshire, England   July 26–28   [6401–72]

| | | | |
|---|---|---|---|
| 1 | Karrie Webb (AUS) | 68-67-65—200 | €60,000 |
| 2 | Ashleigh Simon (RSA) | 63-69-69—201 | 40,600 |
| 3 | Caroline Masson (GER) | 63-69-70—202 | 28,000 |

## RICOH WOMEN'S BRITISH OPEN   St Andrews (Old Course), Scotland   Aug 1–4   [6672–72]

| | | | |
|---|---|---|---|
| 1 | Stacy Lewis (USA) | 67-72-69-72—280 | €302,982 |
| 2 | Hee Young Park (KOR) | 70-69-70-73—282 | 161,437 |
| | Na Yeon Choi (KOR) | 67-67-75-73—282 | 161,437 |

Full details of this event can be found on page 105

## Honma Pilsen Golf Masters
Dýšina, Prague, Czech Republic  Aug 9–11  [5321m–71]

| 1 | Ann-Kathrin Lindner (GER) | 66-67-68—201 | €37,500 |
| 2 | Alexandra Vilatte (FRA) | 70-69-63—202 | 21,437 |
|   | Diana Luna (ITA) | 66-69-67—202 | 21,437 |

## The Solheim Cup
Colorado GC, Parker, Colorado, USA  Aug 16–18  [7604–72]

**Result:** Europe 18, USA 10
Full details of this event can be found on page 259

## Aberdeen Asset Management Ladies Scottish Open
Archerfield Links, East Lothian, Scotland  Aug 30–Sep 1  [6999–72]

| 1 | Catriona Matthew (SCO) | 71-67-70—208 | €31,536 |
| 2 | Hannah Burke (ENG) | 71-71-68—210 | 21,339 |
| 3 | Holly Clyburn (ENG) | 74-73-71—218 | 14,717 |

## The Helsingborg Open
Vasatorp GC, Helsingborg, Sweden  Sep 5–8

| 1 | Rebecca Artis (AUS) | 69-71-71-69—280 | €37,500 |
| 2 | Caroline Hedwall (SWE) | 69-70-67-75—281 | 25,375 |
| 3 | Valentine Derrey | 68-68-74-73—283 | 17,500 |

## The Evian Championship
Evian GC, Evian-Les-Bains, France  Sep 12–15  [6428–71]

| 1 | Suzann Pettersen (NOR) | 66-69-68—203 | €366,393 |
| 2 | Lydia Ko (NZL) (am) | 68-67-70—205 |  |
| 3 | Lexi Thompson (USA) | 72-67-68—207 | 223,963 |

Full details of this event can be found on page 144

## Lacoste Ladies Open de France
Chantaco GC, Aquitaine, France  Sep 26–29  [6104–70]

| 1 | Stacey Keating (AUS) | 62-71-69-64—266 | €37,500 |
| 1 | Azahara Muñoz (ESP) | 68-65-68-65—266 | €37,500 |
| 2 | Valentine Derrey (FRA) | 68-65-67-67—267 | 21,437 |
|   | Gwladys Nocera (FRA) | 67-63-70-67—267 | 21,437 |

## Sanya Ladies Open
Yalong Bay GC, Sanya, China  Oct 25–27  [7189–72]

| 1 | Lee-Anne Pace (RSA)* | 67-66-70—203 | €45,000 |
| 2 | Yu Yang Zhang (CHN) | 69-69-65—203 | 30,450 |

*Pace won at the first extra hole

| 3 | Ye Na Chung (KOR) | 64-68-72—204 | 21,000 |

## China Suzhou Taihu Open
Suzhou Taihu International Golf Club, Suzhou, China  Nov 1–3

| 1 | Gwladys Nocera (FRA) | 69-67-65—201 | €60,000 |
| 2 | Carlota Ciganda (ESP) | 67-68-68—203 | 40,600 |
| 3 | Jing Yan (CHN) (am) | 67-70-67—204 |  |

## Hero Women's Indian Open
Delhi GC, New Delhi, India  Nov 28–30  [6202–72]

| 1 | Thidapa Suwannapura (THA) | 66-74-68—208 | €33,113 |
| 2 | Valentine Derrey (FRA) | 66-75-70—211 | 22,406 |
| 3 | Hannah Burke (ENG) | 73-71-68—212 | 13,686 |
|   | Saraporn Chamchoi (THA) | 73-70-69—212 | 13,686 |

## Omega Dubai Ladies Masters  *Dubai, UAE*  Dec 4–7  [7301–72]

| | | | |
|---|---|---|---|
| 1 | Pornanong Phatlum (THA) | 68-70-69-66—273 | €75,000 |
| 2 | Stacy Lewis (USA) | 70-65-70-69—274 | 50,000 |
| 3 | Carlota Ciganda (ESP) | 67-70-73-71—281 | 35,000 |

## Women's World Cup
*Not played*
For list of past winners, see page 267

# LET Access Series  www.letaccess.com

| Mar 21–23 | Terre Blanche Ladies Open | Terre Blanche, Nice, France | Sophie Giquel-Bettan (FRA) | 211 (–8) |
|---|---|---|---|---|
| April 5–7 | Dinard Ladies Open | Dinard Golf, Saint Briac Sur Mer, France | Monica Christiansen (DEN) | 137 (–1) |
| | *Reduced to two rounds due to bad weather* | | | |
| May 1–3 | Ocho Golf Ladies Open | Augas Santas Balneario, Panton, Spain | Mireia Prat (ESP) | 202 (–8) |
| May 16–18 | Kristianstad Åhus Ladies Open | Kristianstad GC Åhus, Sweden | Linn Andersson (SWE) (am) | 220 (+4) |
| May 22–24 | Sölvesborg Ladies Open | Sölvesborg, Sweden | Heather MacRae (SCO)* | 214 (–2) |
| | *Beat Kym Larratt (ENG) and Chloe Leurquin (BEL) at the first extra hole* | | | |
| June 6–8 | Fourqueux Ladies Open | Golf de Fourqueux, Paris, France | Cassandra Kirkland (FRA) | 209 (–7) |
| July 25–27 | Ingarö Ladies Open | Stockholm, Sweden | Pamela Feggans (SCO) | 203 (–7) |
| Aug 9–11 | HLR Golf Academy Open | Hillside GC, Vihti, Finland | Nicole Broch Larsen (DEN) | 210 (–3) |
| Aug 30– Sep 1 | Norrporten Ladies Open | Kvissleby, Sweden | Lauren Taylor (ENG) (am) | 217 (–1) |
| Sep 18–20 | Ladies Norwegian Challenge | Oslo, Norway | Nicole Broch Larsen (NOR) | 212 (–4) |
| Sep 26–28 | WPGA International Chall. | Levenheath, England | Hannah Ralph (ENG) | 209 (–7) |
| Oct 4–6 | Azores Ladies Open | Terceira Island, Portugal | Fabienne In-Albon (SUI) | 212 (–4) |
| Oct 24–26 | Grecotel Amirandes Ladies Open | Hersonissos, Greece | Patricia Sanz Barrio (ESP)* | 213 (=) |
| | *Beat Julia Davidsson (SWE) at the first extra hole* | | | |
| Nov 18–20 | Costa Blanca Ladies Open | Alicante, Spain | Mireia Prat (ESP) | 226 (+10) |
| Nov 28–30 | The Mineks Ladies Classic | Antalya, Turkey | Chloe Leurquin (BEL) | 219 (=) |
| | *Beat Mireia Prat (ESP) at the first extra hole* | | | |

## Order of Merit

| | | | | | | |
|---|---|---|---|---|---|---|
| 1 | Mireia Prat (ESP) | 34,313 Pts | 6 | Heather MacRae (SCO) | 14,064 |
| 2 | Patricia Sanz Barrio (ESP) | 23,786 | 7 | Steffi Kirchmayr (GER) | 13,638 |
| 3 | Nicole Broch Larsen (DEN) | 17,724 | 8 | Caroline Martens (NOR) | 13,432 |
| 4 | Chloe Leurquin (BEL) | 17,494 | 9 | Chrisje De Vries (NED) | 13,378 |
| 5 | Fabienne In-Albon (SUI) | 14,106 | 10 | Pamela Feggans (SCO) | 11,930 |

# Six first time winners on the Ladies European Tour

The international nature of the LET (Ladies European Tour) was evident in the players who won their first events in 2013 and where they won their titles.

Two Thailanders, a New Zealander and an English golfer, along with an Australian and a German were the first time winner in New Zealand, Morocco, the Netherlands, the Czech Republic, Sweden and India.

Lydia Ko, who won the ISPS Handa New Zealand Women's Open as a 15-year-old amateur, was the youngest winner.

The winners were:

| | | |
|---|---|---|
| Lydia Ko (NZL) | ISPS Handa New Zealand Women's Open | 206 (–12) |
| Ariya Jutanugarn (THA) | Lalla Meryem Cup, Morocco | 270 (–14) |
| Holly Clyburn (ENG) | Deloitte Ladies Open, The Netherlands | 211 (–8) |
| Ann-Kathrin Lindner (GER) | Honma Pilsen Golf Masters, Czech Rep | 201 (–12) |
| Rebecca Artis (AUS) | The Helsingborg Open, Sweden | 280 (–8) |
| Thidapa Sunawannapura (THA) | Hero Women's Indian Open | 208 (–8) |

# Teenager Jaye Marie Green qualifies in style

She led from start to finish after opening with a 62 at LPGA International in Daytona Beach, Florida to finish the 90 hole third and final stage of the LPGA Qualifying School at 29-under-par 331.

Her 10-shot victory set the record for the lowest score at final qualifying beating the previous record set in 2008 by Stacy Lewis by 11 shots. Second placed was South Korean Mi Rim Lee.

Twenty players gained their full cards for the 2014 season – eight Americans, two South Koreans (Mi Rim Lee and Seon Hwa Lee), two South Africans (Paula Reto and Ashleigh Simon) Canadian Jennifer Kirby, China's Xiyu Lin, Spain's Maria Hernandez, Denmark's Line Vedel, Chile's Paz Echeverria, Italy's Silvia Cavalleri, Japan's Haru Nomura and the Malaysian amateur Kelly Tan.

Nomura and Simon earned their cards after a play-off for the last two spots with Americans Megan McChrystal and Jenny Suh.

| | | | |
|---|---|---|---|
| 1 | Jaye Marie Green (USA) | 62-68-66-67 - 68 - 331 (–29) | $5,000 |
| 2 | Mi Rim Lee (KOR) | 69-73-61-69 - 69 - 341 (–19) | 4,500 |
| 3 | Tiffany Joh (USA) | 66-70-70-68 - 71 - 345 (–15) | 4,000 |
| 4 | Amy Anderson (USA) | 68-69-70-70 - 69 - 346 (–14) | 3,500 |
| 5 | Jennifer Kirby (CAN) | 71-69-69-71 - 68 - 348 (–12) | 3,125 |
| 6 | Seon Hwa Lee (KOR) | 66-70-72-70 - 71 - 349 (–11) | 2,875 |
| 7 | Megan Grehan (USA) | 67-68-74-70 - 71 - 350 (–10) | 2,650 |
| | Kathleen Ekey (USA) | 67-72-69-70 - 72 - 350 (–10) | 2,650 |
| 9 | Xiyu Lin (CHN) | 69-71-73-69 - 70 - 352 (–8) | 2,181 |
| | Maria Hernandez (ESP) | 71-71-72-67 - 71 - 352 (–8) | 2,181 |
| | Line Vedel (DEN) | 67-75-69-70 - 71 - 352 (–8) | 2,181 |
| | Erica Popson (USA) | 71-70-71-67 - 73 - 352 (–8) | 2,181 |
| 13 | Victoria Elizabeth (USA) | 70-72-71-73 - 67 - 353 (–7) | 1,700 |
| | Kelly Tan (MAS) (am) | 72-72-71-70 - 68 - 353 (–7) | |
| | Lisa Ferrero (USA) | 73-71-69-71 - 69 - 353 (–7) | 1,700 |
| | Paula Reto (RSA) | 73-71-72-67 - 70 - 353 (–7) | 1,700 |
| | Paz Echeverria (CHI) | 71-68-73-71 - 70 - 353 (–7) | 1,700 |
| | Silvia Cavalleri (ITA) | 71-72-68-72 - 70 - 353 (–7) | 1,700 |
| 19 | Haru Nomura (JPN) | 67-75-69-74 - 69 - 354 (–6) | 694 |
| | Ashleigh Simon (RSA) | 72-67-73-68 - 74 - 354 (–6) | 694 |

# LPGA Tour

www.lpga.com

*Players are American unless stated*

## Money List

| | | | | | | | | |
|---|---|---|---|---|---|---|---|---|
| 1 | Inbee Park (KOR) | $2,456,619 | 34 | Se Ri Pak (KOR) | 440,162 | 67 | Christel Boeljon | 163,260 |
| 2 | Suzann Pettersen (NOR) | 2,296,106 | 35 | Sandra Gal (GER) | 420,137 | 68 | Jennifer Rosales (PHI) | 154,166 |
| | | | 36 | Mika Miyazato (JPN) | 417,658 | 69 | Juli Inkster | 150,628 |
| 3 | Stacy Lewis | 1,938,868 | 37 | Haeji Kang (KOR) | 408,641 | 70 | Jacqui Concolino | 150,573 |
| 4 | Shanshan Feng (CHN) | 1,716,657 | 38 | Yani Tseng (TPE) | 405,068 | 71 | Hee-Won Han (KOR) | 143,904 |
| 5 | So Yeon Ryu (KOR) | 1,278,864 | 39 | Sun Young Yoo (KOR) | 383,748 | 72 | Austin Ernst | 142,002 |
| 6 | Lexi Thompson | 1,206,109 | 40 | Carlota Ciganda (ESP) | 355,949 | 73 | Thidapa | 137,554 |
| 7 | I K Kim (KOR) | 1,125,389 | 41 | Michelle Wie | 355,853 | | Suwannapura (THA) | |
| 8 | Beatriz Recari (ESP) | 1,030,614 | 42 | Brittany Lang | 355,809 | 74 | Vicky Hurst | 135,119 |
| 9 | Na Yeon Choi (KOR) | 929,964 | 43 | Jenny Shin (KOR) | 332,461 | 75 | Mi Jung Hur (KOR) | 132,504 |
| 10 | Hee Young Park (KOR) | 848,676 | 44 | Eun-Hee Ji (KOR) | 332,012 | 76 | Christina Kim | 126,535 |
| 11 | Paula Creamer | 831,918 | 45 | Meena Lee (KOR) | 324,362 | 77 | Lindsey Wright (AUS) | 125,964 |
| 12 | Angela Stanford | 778,234 | 46 | Mo Martin, Mo | 319,244 | 78 | Lisa McCloskey | 123,886 |
| 13 | Karrie Webb (AUS) | 765,880 | 47 | Moriya Jutanugarn (THA) | 293,158 | 79 | Cindy LaCrosse | 121,693 |
| 14 | Caroline Hedwall (SWE) | 763,104 | 48 | Caroline Masson (GER) | 287,770 | 80 | Rebecca Lee-Bentham (CAN) | 118,441 |
| 15 | Lizette Salas | 759,323 | 49 | Mina Harigae | 285,195 | 81 | Belen Mozo (ESP) | 114,325 |
| 16 | Karine Icher (FRA) | 746,572 | 50 | Giulia Sergas (ITA) | 274,231 | 82 | Paola Moreno (COL) | 113,151 |
| 17 | Chella Choi (KOR) | 739,441 | 51 | Jane Park | 267,757 | 83 | Kristy McPherson | 108,615 |
| 18 | Amy Yang (KOR) | 719,481 | 52 | Irene Cho | 257,202 | 84 | Sydnee Michaels | 107,365 |
| 19 | Cristie Kerr | 710,946 | 53 | Alison Walshe | 245,515 | 85 | Ryann O'Toole | 100,554 |
| 20 | Anna Nordqvist (SWE) | 678,751 | 54 | Candie Kung (TPE) | 228,929 | 86 | Sarah Jane Smith | 92,883 |
| 21 | Catriona Matthew (SCO) | 643,896 | 55 | Julieta Granada (PAR) | 224,662 | 87 | Ji Young Oh (KOR) | 84,879 |
| 22 | Jiyai Shin (KOR) | 602,875 | 56 | Katherine Hull-Kirk (AUS) | 223,138 | 88 | Momoko Ueda (JPN) | 83,283 |
| 23 | Pornanong Phatlum (THA) | 600,210 | 57 | Danielle Kang | 221,649 | 89 | Heather Bowie Young | 81,924 |
| 24 | Ilhee Lee (KOR) | 595,800 | 58 | Ayako Uehara (JPN) | 212,788 | 90 | Moira Dunn | 73,873 |
| 25 | Jessica Korda | 593,389 | 59 | Nicole Castrale | 209,915 | 91 | Jeong Jang (KOR) | 73,123 |
| 26 | Gerina Piller | 572,690 | 60 | Pernilla Lindberg (SWE) | 206,926 | 92 | Mi Hyang Lee (KOR) | 69,181 |
| 27 | Ai Miyazato (JPN) | 526,968 | 61 | Chie Arimura (JPN) | 202,283 | 93 | Katie Futcher | 67,658 |
| 28 | Morgan Pressel | 504,188 | 62 | Mariajo Uribe (COL) | 197,839 | 94 | Mindy Kim | 67,370 |
| 29 | Jodi Ewart Shadoff (ENG) | 493,091 | 63 | Natalie Gulbis | 187,237 | 95 | Danah Bordner | 65,426 |
| 30 | Jennifer Johnson | 472,778 | 64 | Stacy Prammanasudh | 181,246 | 96 | Becky Morgan (WAL) | 64,593 |
| 31 | Azahara Muñoz (ESP) | 457,996 | 65 | Jee Young Lee (KOR) | 172,692 | 97 | Paige Mackenzie | 63,685 |
| 32 | Brittany Lincicome | 449,113 | 66 | Dewi Claire Schreefel (NED) | 164,767 | 98 | Brooke Pancake | 63,647 |
| 33 | Hee Kyung Seo (KOR) | 446,373 | | | | 99 | Katie Burnett | 53,377 |
| | | | | | | 100 | Sandra Changkija | 52,701 |

---

### Asian players lead the field again

Asian golfers have once more dominated the list of LPGA Tour event winners. Of the 28 events, 21 were won by non-American players with Asian golfers capturing 12 of these. Top of the list of multiple winners was Korea's Inbee Park with six victories followed by Norwegian Suzann Pettersen with four and Stacy Lewis from the USA with three. The USA's Lexi Thompson, Spain's Beatriz Recari and Shanshan Feng from China took two apiece.

# 2013 Tour Results (in chronological order)

## ISPS Handa Women's Australian Open  Royal Canberra, ACT, Australia  Feb 14–17   [6108–73]

| | | | |
|---|---|---|---|
| 1 | Jiyai Shin (KOR) | 65-67-70-72—274 | $180,000 |
| 2 | Yani Tseng (TPE) | 68-71-71-66—276 | 109,523 |
| 3 | Lydia Ko (NZL) (am) | 63-69-70-76—278 | |

## Honda LPGA Thailand  Chonburi, Thailand   Feb 20–24   [6469–72]

| | | | |
|---|---|---|---|
| 1 | Inbee Park (KOR) | 67-71-71-67—276 | $225,000 |
| 2 | Ariya Jutanugarn (THA) | 69-66-70-72—277 | 140,305 |
| 3 | Stacy Lewis | 63-69-76-70—278 | 73,935 |
| | Beatriz Recari (ESP) | 68-68-72-70—278 | 73,935 |
| | So Yeon Ryu (KOR) | 68-68-74-68—278 | 73,935 |
| | Yani Tseng (TPE) | 75-68-72-63—278 | 73,935 |

## HSBC Women's Champions  Sentosa GC, Singapore   Feb 27–Mar 3   [6600–72]

| | | | |
|---|---|---|---|
| 1 | Stacy Lewis | 67-66-69-71—273 | 210,000 |
| 2 | Na Yeon Choi (KOR) | 69-66-67-72—274 | 134,116 |
| 3 | Paula Creamer | 68-67-69-71—275 | 97,292 |

## RR Donnelley LPGA Founders Cup  Phoenix, AZ   Mar 14–17   [6583–72]

| | | | |
|---|---|---|---|
| 1 | Stacy Lewis | 68-65-68-64—265 | $225,000 |
| 2 | Ai Miyazato (JPN) | 63-67-67-71—268 | 138,527 |
| 3 | Angela Stanford | 68-70-65-68—271 | 100,492 |

## KIA Classic  Carlsbad, CA   Mar 21–24   [6493–72]

| | | | |
|---|---|---|---|
| 1 | Beatriz Recari (ESP) | 69-67-69-74—279 | $255,000 |
| 2 | IK Kim (KOR) | 71-67-70-71—279 | 156,616 |
| 3 | Cristie Kerr | 70-68-71-71—280 | 90,748 |
| | Mo Martin | 69-71-71-69—280 | 90,748 |
| | Pornanong Phatlum (THA) | 75-68-69-68—280 | 90,748 |

## KRAFT NABISCO CHAMPIONSHIP  Rancho Mirage, CA   April 4–7   [6738–72]

| | | | |
|---|---|---|---|
| 1 | Inbee Park (KOR) | 70-67-67-69—273 | $300,000 |
| 2 | So Yeon Ryu (KOR) | 73-71-68-65—277 | 187,073 |
| 3 | Suzann Pettersen (NOR) | 68-75-67-69—279 | 120,345 |
| | Caroline Hedwall (SWE) | 71-68-72-68—279 | 120,345 |

Full details of this event can be found on page 135

## LPGA LOTTE Championship  Kapolei, Oahu, HI   April 17–20   [6383–72]

| | | | |
|---|---|---|---|
| 1 | Suzann Pettersen (NOR) | 65-69-68-67—269 | $255,000 |
| 2 | Lizette Salas | 69-71-67-62—269 | 155,874 |
| 3 | Ariya Jutanugarn (THA) | 64-75-68-66—273 | 113,075 |

## North Texas LPGA Shootout  Irving, TX   April 25–28   [6410–71]

| | | | |
|---|---|---|---|
| 1 | Inbee Park (KOR) | 67-70-67-67—271 | $195,000 |
| 2 | Carlota Ciganda (ESP) | 66-70-66-70—272 | 118,649 |
| 3 | Suzann Pettersen (NOR) | 70-70-68-66—274 | 86,072 |

## Kingsmill Championship Williamsburg, VA   May 2–5                    [6379–71]

| | | | |
|---|---|---|---|
| 1 | Cristie Kerr | 66-71-66-69—272 | $195,000 |
| 2 | Suzann Pettersen (NOR) | 68-69-68-67—272 | 118,649 |
| 3 | Ilhee Lee (KOR) | 69-69-69-67—274 | 76,327 |
| | Ariya Jutanugarn (THA) | 64-71-73-66—274 | 76,327 |

## Mobile Bay LPGA Classic Mobile, AL   May 16–19                    [6521–72]

| | | | |
|---|---|---|---|
| 1 | Jennifer Johnson | 67-70-65-65—267 | $180,000 |
| 2 | Pornanong Phatlum (THA) | 69-65-71-63—268 | 94,065 |
| | Jessica Korda | 66-65-69-68—268 | 94,065 |

## Pure Silk-Bahamas LPGA Classic Paradise Island, Bahamas   May 24–26                    [6644–73]

| | | | |
|---|---|---|---|
| 1 | Ilhee Lee (KOR) | 41-43-42—126 | $195,000 |
| 2 | Irene Cho | 45-43-40—128 | 120,353 |
| 3 | Anna Nordqvist (SWE) | 40-44-45—129 | 87,308 |

## ShopRite LPGA Classic Dolce Seaview Resort, Galloway, NJ   May 31–June 2                    [6155–71]

| | | | |
|---|---|---|---|
| 1 | Karrie Webb (AUS) | 72-69-68—209 | $225,000 |
| 2 | Shanshan Feng (CHN) | 69-67-75—211 | 138,191 |
| 3 | Hee Young Park (KOR) | 69-72-71—212 | 100,248 |

## Wegmans LPGA Championship Locust Hill, Pittsford, NY   June 6–9                    [6534–72]

| | | | |
|---|---|---|---|
| 1 | Inbee Park (KOR)* | 72-68-68-75—283 | $337,500 |
| 2 | Catriona Matthew (SCO) | 71-71-73-68—283 | 206,304 |
| *Park won at the third extra hole | | | |
| 3 | Suzann Pettersen (NOR) | 72-73-74-65—284 | 132,716 |
| | Morgan Pressel | 68-70-71-75—284 | 132,716 |

Full details of this event can be found on page 125

## Walmart NW Arkansas Championship Rogers, AR   June 21–23                    [6389–71]

| | | | |
|---|---|---|---|
| 1 | Inbee Park (KOR)* | 69-65-67—201 | $300,000 |
| 2 | So Yeon Ryu (KOR) | 66-66-69—201 | 184,703 |
| *Park won at the first extra hole | | | |
| 3 | Mika Miyazato (JPN) | 65-70-67—202 | 133,989 |

## 68th US WOMEN'S OPEN CHAMPIONSHIP Southampton, NY   June 27–30
[6827–72]

| | | | |
|---|---|---|---|
| 1 | Inbee Park (KOR) | 67-68-71-74—280 | $585,000 |
| 2 | I K Kim (KOR) | 68-69-73-74—284 | 350,000 |
| 3 | So Yeon Ryu (KOR) | 73-69-73-72—287 | 217,958 |

Full details of this event can be found on page 115

## Manulife Financial LPGA Classic Waterloo, Ontario, Canada   July 11–14                    [6330–71]

| | | | |
|---|---|---|---|
| 1 | Hee Young Park (KOR)* | 65-67-61-65—258 | $195,000 |
| 2 | Angela Stanford | 63-67-64-64—258 | 120,353 |
| *Park won at the third extra hole | | | |
| 3 | Catriona Matthew (SCO) | 63-64-68-66—261 | 87,308 |

## Marathon Classic Sylvania, OH   July 18–21                    [6428–71]

| | | | |
|---|---|---|---|
| 1 | Beatriz Recari (ESP) | 69-65-67-66—267 | $195,000 |
| 2 | Paula Creamer | 66-68-67-67—268 | 120,655 |
| 3 | Jodi Ewart Shadoff (ENG) | 69-68-68-66—271 | 77,618 |
| | Lexi Thompson | 66-71-67-67—271 | 77,618 |

# RICOH WOMEN'S BRITISH OPEN St Andrews (Old Course), Scotland Aug 1–4 [6672–72]

| | | | |
|---|---|---|---|
| 1 | Stacy Lewis | 67-72-69-72—280 | $402,584 |
| 2 | Hee Young Park (KOR) | 70-69-70-73—282 | 198,296 |
| | Na Yeon Choi (KOR) | 67-67-75-73—282 | 198,296 |

Full details of this event can be found on page 105

# The Solheim Cup Parker, CO  Aug 16–18 [7604–72]
**Result:** Europe 18, USA 10
Full details of this event can be found on page 259

# CN Canadian Women's Open Edmonton, Alberta, Canada  Aug 22–25 [6403–70]

| | | | |
|---|---|---|---|
| 1 | Lydia Ko (NZL) (am) | 65-69-67-64—265 | |
| 2 | Karine Icher (FRA) | 67-66-70-67—270 | $300,000 |
| | Brittany Lincicome | 68-68-66-69—271 | 159,346 |
| | Caroline Hedwall (SWE) | 68-68-64-71—271 | 159,346 |

# Safeway Classic Portland, OR  Aug 29–Sep 1 [6465–72]

| | | | |
|---|---|---|---|
| 1 | Suzann Pettersen (NOR) | 68-63-70-67—268 | $195,000 |
| 2 | Stacy Lewis | 67-70-65-68—270 | 117,114 |
| 3 | Lizette Salas | 66-68-68-69—271 | 84,958 |

# The Evian Championship Evian GC, Evian-Les-Bains, France  Sep 12–15 [6428–71]

| | | | |
|---|---|---|---|
| 1 | Suzann Pettersen (NOR) | 66-69-68—203 | $487,500 |
| 2 | Lydia Ko (NZL) (am) | 68-67-70—205 | |
| 3 | Lexi Thompson | 72-67-68—207 | 297,994 |

Full details of this event can be found on page 144

# Reignwood LPGA Classic Beijing, China  Oct 3–6 [6596–73]

| | | | |
|---|---|---|---|
| 1 | Shanshan Feng (CHN) | 70-64-64-68—266 | $270,000 |
| 2 | Stacy Lewis | 68-66-65-68—267 | 165,043 |
| 3 | Inbee Park (KOR) | 69-68-66-68—271 | 119,727 |

# Sime Darby LPGA Malaysia Kuala Lumpur, Malaysia  Oct 10–13 [6246–71]

| | | | |
|---|---|---|---|
| 1 | Lexi Thompson | 67-63-66-69—265 | $300,000 |
| 2 | Shanshan Feng (CHN) | 67-65-70-67—269 | 186,577 |
| 3 | Suzann Pettersen (NOR) | 67-68-67-70—272 | 120,026 |
| | Ilhee Lee (KOR) | 64-65-70-73—272 | 120,026 |

# LPGA KEB HanaBank Championship Incheon, South Korea  Oct 18–20 [6364–72]

| | | | |
|---|---|---|---|
| 1 | Amy Yang (KOR)* | 67-71-69—207 | $285,000 |
| 2 | Hee Kyung Seo (KOR) | 71-68-68—207 | 173,411 |

*Yang beat Seo at the first extra hole

| | | | |
|---|---|---|---|
| 3 | Sei Young Kim (KOR) | 71-68-69—208 | 100,479 |
| | Suzann Pettersen (NOR) | 69-69-70—208 | 100,479 |
| | Michelle Wie | 69-73-66—208 | 100,479 |

# Sunrise LPGA Taiwan Championship Yang Mei, Taoyuan, Taiwan  Oct 24–27 [6390–72]

| | | | |
|---|---|---|---|
| 1 | Suzann Pettersen (NOR) | 68-69-73-69—279 | $300,000 |
| 2 | Azahara Muñoz (ESP) | 73-72-69-70—284 | 186,096 |
| 3 | Caroline Hedwall (SWE) | 71-73-72-70—286 | 135,000 |

## Mizuno Classic  Shima-Shi Mie, Japan   Nov 8–10                              [6506–72]

| 1 | Teresa Lu (TPE) | 70-68-64—202 | $180,000 |
| 2 | Chella Choi (KOR) | 69-69-66—204 | 109,773 |
| 3 | Mamiko Higa (JPN) | 70-66-70—206 | 70,617 |
|   | Yuki Ichinose (JPN) | 70-66-70—206 | 70,617 |

## Lorena Ochoa Invitational  Guadalajara CC, Jalisco, Mexico   Nov 14–17      [6626–72]

| 1 | Lexi Thompson | 72-64-67-69—272 | $200,000 |
| 2 | Stacy Lewis | 72-66-67-68—273 | 103,449 |
| 3 | So Yeon Ryu (KOR) | 68-67-71-69—275 | 75,045 |

## CME Group Titleholders  Naples, FL   Nov 21–24

| 1 | Shanshan Feng (CHN) | 66-74-67-66—273 | $700,000 |
| 2 | Gerina Piller | 71-67-67-69—274 | 139,713 |
| 3 | Pornanong Phatlum (THA) | 70-68-67-70—275 | 101,352 |

## Wendy's 3-Tour Challenge  Rio Secco GC, Henderson, NV   Nov 8–12

| 1 | LPGA Tour (Cristie Kerr, Natalie Gulbis, Stacey Lewis) | $500,000 |
| 2 | Champions Tour (Kenny Perry, Bernhard Langer, Fred Funk) | 270,000 |
| 3 | PGA Tour (Billy Horschel, Boo Weekley, Jason Day) | 230,000 |

To date, the PGA Tour have won on nine occasions, the Champions Tour seven times and the LPGA on six occasions

# Symetra Tour 2013 (formerly Futures Tour)

*Players are of American nationality unless stated*

www.symetratour.com

| Feb 22–24 | VisitMesa.com Gateway Classic | Mesa, AZ | Jaclyn Sweeney | 209 (–7) |
| Mar 22–24 | Florida's Natural Charity Classic | Winter Haven, FL | Melissa Eaton (RSA) | 206 (–10) |
| April 26–28 | Guardian Retirement C/ship | Sarasota, FL | Christine Song* | 211 (–5) |
|  | *Beat Isabelle Boineau (FRA) at the second extra hole |  |  |  |
| May 9–11 | Symetra Classic | Charlotte, NC | Laura Kueny | 210 (–6) |
| May 17–19 | Friends of Mission Charity Classic | Asheville, NC | Giulia Molinaro (ITA) | 203 (–13) |
| June 14–16 | Decatur-Forsyth Classic | Decatur, IL | Sue Kim (CAN) | 206 (–10) |
| June 21–23 | Four Winds Invitational | South Bend, IN | Cydney Clanton* | 208 (–8) |
|  | *Beat Marina Alex and Marissa Steen at the seventh extra hole |  |  |  |
| June 28–30 | Island Resort Championship | Harris, MI | Kim Kaufman | 213 (–3) |
| July 12–14 | Credit Union Challenge | Albany, NY | Wei-Ling Hsu (TPE) | 202 (–11) |
| July 19–21 | Northeast Delta Dental Int. | Concord, NH | P K Kongkraphan (THA) | 207 (–9) |
| July 26–28 | Credit Union Classic | Syracuse, NY | Olivia Jordan-Higgins (ENG) | 207 (–6) |
| Aug 9–11 | IOA Golf Classic | Palm Harbor, FL | Katy Harris | 209 (–7) |
| Aug 16–18 | Eagle Classic | Richmond, VA | Christine Song | 208 (–8) |
| Sep 20–22 | Volvik Championship | Kissimmee, FL | Hannah Yun | 202 (–14) |
| Sep 26–29 | Symetra Tour Championship | Daytona Beach, FL | Megan McChrystal | 275 (–13) |

## Final Ranking

| 1 P K Kongkraphan (THA) | $47,283 | 6 Sue Kim (CAN) | 37,850 |
| 2 Giulia Molinaro (ITA) | 39,848 | 7 Hannah Jun | 36,810 |
| 3 Marina Alex | 39,804 | 8 Perrine Delacour (FRA) | 34,577 |
| 4 Christine Song | 39,309 | 9 Alena Sharp (CAN) | 34,120 |
| 5 Cydney Clanton | 38,861 | 10 Jaclyn Sweeney | 33,609 |

# LPGA Tour statistics

## Scoring average

| | | Total Rounds | Average |
|---|---|---|---|
| 1 | Stacy Lewis | 93 | 69.48 |
| 2 | Suzann Pettersen (NOR) | 79 | 69.69 |
| 3 | Inbee Park (KOR) | 84 | 69.86 |
| 4 | So Yeon Ryu (KOR) | 85 | 70.29 |
| 5 | Na Yeon Choi (KOR) | 88 | 70.30 |
| 6 | Shanshan Feng (CHN) | 70 | 70.37 |
| 7 | I K Kim (KOR) | 84 | 70.48 |
| 8 | Karrie Webb (AUS) | 77 | 70.63 |
| 9 | Jiyai Shin (KOR) | 73 | 70.65 |
| 10 | Chella Choi (KOR) | 699 | 70.68 |

## Driving distance average

| | | Average |
|---|---|---|
| 1 | Nicole Smith | 274.875 |
| 2 | Lexi Thompson | 271.190 |
| 3 | Daniela Iacobelli | 268.281 |
| 4 | Tani Tseng (TPE) | 268.280 |
| 5 | Alena Sharp (CAN) | 266.840 |
| 6 | Brittany Lincicome | 266.808 |
| 7 | Gerina Piller | 266.506 |
| 8 | Maude-Aimee Leblanc (CAN) | 266.281 |
| 9 | Marina Stuetz (AUT) | 264.056 |
| 10 | Jessica Korda | 263.231 |

## Driving accuracy

| | | Fairways | Possible Fairways | % |
|---|---|---|---|---|
| 1 | Mo Martin | 1,003 | 1,170 | 85.7 |
| 2 | Jiyai Shin (KOR) | 853 | 1,020 | 83.6 |
| 3 | Jenny Shin (KOR) | 1,074 | 1,288 | 83.4 |
| 4 | I K Kim (KOR) | 968 | 1,174 | 82.5 |
| 5 | Ayako Uehara (JPN) | 633 | 772 | 82.0 |
| 6 | Eun-Hee Ji (KOR) | 1,053 | 1,287 | 81.8 |
| 7 | Paola Moreno (CHI) | 680 | 837 | 81.2 |
| 8 | Chie Arimura (JPN) | 683 | 841 | 81.2 |
| 9 | Jane Rah | 368 | 458 | 80.3 |
| 10 | Pornanong Phatlum (THA) | 963 | 1200 | 80.3 |

## Greens in Regulation

| | | % |
|---|---|---|
| 1 | Suzann Pettersen (NOR) | 75.9 |
| 2 | So Yeon Ryu (KOR) | 75.3 |
| 3 | Stacy Lewis, | 75.0 |
| 4 | Jodi Ewart-Shadoff (ENG) | 74.8 |
| 5 | Shanshan Feng (CHN) | 74.6 |
| 6 | Chella Choi (KOR) | 74.3 |
| 7 | Jessica Korda | 73.9 |
| 8 | Lexi Thompson, | 73.9 |
| 9 | Azahara Muñoz (ESP) | 73.6 |
| 10 | Anna Nordqvist (SWE) | 73.6 |

## Top ten finishes

| | | No. of Top 10 Finishes | Events Played | % |
|---|---|---|---|---|
| 1 | Stacy Lewis | 19 | 26 | 73 |
| 2 | Suzann Pettersen (NOR) | 15 | 23 | 65 |
| 3 | Shanshan Feng (CHN) | 10 | 19 | 53 |
| 4 | Inbee Park (KOR) | 11 | 23 | 48 |
| 5 | So Yeon Ryu (KOR) | 10 | 24 | 42 |
| 6 | I K Kim (KOR) | 9 | 23 | 39 |
| 7 | Beatriz Recari (ESP) | 9 | 25 | 36 |
| 8 | Na Yeon Choi (KOR) | 8 | 24 | 33 |
| 9 | Gerina Piller | 8 | 26 | 31 |
| 10 | Lizette Salas | 7 | 24 | 29 |
| | Lexi Thompson | 7 | 24 | 29 |
| | Karrie Webb (AUS) | 6 | 21 | 29 |
| | Jessica Korda | 6 | 21 | 29 |

## Top money earners on the LPGA Tour 1950–2013

| 1950 | Babe Zaharias | $14,800 |
|---|---|---|
| 1960 | Louise Suggs | $16,892 |
| 1970 | Kathy Whitworth | $30,235 |
| 1980 | Beth Daniel | $231,000 |
| 1990 | Beth Daniel | $863,578 |
| 2000 | Karrie Webb (AUS) | $1,876,853 |
| 2005 | Annika Sörenstam (SWE) | $2,588,240 |
| 2006 | Lorena Ochoa (MEX) | $2,592,872 |
| 2007 | Lorena Ochoa (MEX) | $4,364,994 |
| 2008 | Lorena Ochoa (MEX) | $2,763,193 |
| 2009 | Ji Yai Shin (KOR) | $1,807,334 |
| 2010 | Na Yeon Choi (KOR) | $1,871,166 |
| 2011 | Yani Tseng (TPE) | $2,921,713 |
| 2012 | Inbee Park (KOR) | $2,266,638 |
| 2012 | Inbee Park (KOR) | $2,456,629 |

# LPGA Legends Tour 2013

*Players are of American nationality unless stated*          www.thelegendstour.com

| | | | | |
|---|---|---|---|---|
| Feb 23–24 | Walgreens Charity Classic | Sun City West, AZ | Michele Redman | 139 (–5) |
| Mar 9 | Fry's Desert Golf Classic | Tucson, AZ | Jane Crafter and | 64 (–8) |
| | | | Betsy King | |
| April 26–28 | Walgreens Charity C/ship | The Villages, FL | Nancy Scranton | 136 (–8) |
| July 12–15 | Judson Collegiate & Legends | Roswell, GA | Alicia Dibos* | |
| | *Beat Nancy Scranton at the second extra hole* | | | |
| July 28–29 | Legends Swing for the Cure | Kenmore, WA | Sherri Turner | 70 (–3) |
| Aug 11–12 | Wendy's Charity Challenge | Jackson, MI | Sherri Steinhauer* | 68 (–4) |
| | *Beat Christa Johnson in play-off* | | | |
| Sep 12–15 | Harris Golf Charity Classic | Falmouth, ME | Rosie Jones* | 136 (–8) |
| | *Beat Lorie Kane (CAN) at the fifth extra hole* | | | |
| Sep 23–29 | Legends Tour C/ship | French Lick, IN | Lori Kane (CAN) | 213 (–3) |
| Oct 11–13 | ISPS Handa Cup | Nashville, TN | World 27, USA 21 | |
| | *Full details can be found on page 266* | | | |
| Nov 8–10 | ISPS Handa Legends Tour Open | Innisbrook, FL | Lauri Rinker | 141 (–5) |

## Final Money List

| | | | | | |
|---|---|---|---|---|---|
| 1 | Lorie Kane (CAN) | $103,333 | 6 | Val Skinner | 45,985 |
| 2 | Laurie Rinker | 84,650 | 7 | Michele Redman | 40,580 |
| 3 | Nancy Scranton | 52,827 | 8 | Jane Crafter (AUS) | 39,662 |
| 4 | Rosie Jones | 47,995 | 9 | Cindy Figg-Currier | 30,034 |
| 5 | Barb Mucha | 47,133 | 10 | Christa Johnson | 28,326 |

# Ladies Asian Golf Tour 2013

www.lagt.org

| | | | | |
|---|---|---|---|---|
| Jan 11–13 | Royal Open | Hsinchu, Taiwan | Titiya Plucksataporn (THA) | 210 (–6) |
| Jan 18–20 | Hitachi Classic | Linkou, Taiwan | Pornanong Phatlum (THA) | 210 (–6) |
| Jan 24–26 | Yeangder Open | Linkou, Taiwan | Phoebe Yao (TPE)* | 209 (–7) |
| | *Beat Ai-Chen Kuo (TPE) in play-off* | | | |
| Apr 11–13 | Yumeya Dream Cup | Hirao, Nagoya, Japan | Yumika Adachi (JPN) | 210 (=) |
| May 31–June 2 | Technology Cup | Hsinchu G&CC, Taiwan | Huei-Ju Shih (TPE) | 221 (+5) |
| July 19–21 | Chung Cheng Open | Linkou, Taiwan | Ssu-Chia Cheng (TPE) | 209 (–7) |
| July 24–26 | Kenda Tires Open | Linkou, Taiwan | Ainil Johani Abu Bakar (MAS) | 212 (–4) |
| Sep 19–21 | TLPGA CTBC Open | Taoyuan, Taiwan | Do-Yeon Kim (KOR) | 225 (+9) |
| Sep 27–29 | TLPGA Fubon Open | Taoyuan, Taiwan | Ssu-Chia Cheng (TPE) | 212 (–4) |
| Oct 25–27 | Sanya Ladies Open | Sanya City, China | Lee-Anne Pace (RSA)* | 203 (–13) |
| | *Beat Yu Yang Zhang (CHN) at the first extra hole* | | | |
| Nov 1–3 | Suzhou Taihu Ladies Open | Suzhou Taihu Int. GC, China | Gwladys Nocera (FRA) | 201 (–15) |
| Nov 7–9 | PTT Global Chemical Thailand Ladies Open | Siam CC, Pattaya, Thailand | Sherman Santiwiwatthanaphong (am) | 213 (–3) |
| Nov 13–15 | TLPGA South Taiwan Open | Takangshan, Taiwan | Ya-Huei Lu (TPE) | 206 (–10) |
| Nov 28–30 | Hero Women's Indian Open | Delhi GC | Thidapa Suwannapura (THA) | 211 (–8) |

## Order of Merit (Figures in brackets denote number of events played)

| | | | | | | | |
|---|---|---|---|---|---|---|---|
| 1 Pornanong Phatlum (THA) | (3) | US$116,295 | 6 Nontaya Srisawang (THA) | (9) | 56,153 | | |
| 2 Ye Na Chung, (KOR) | (8) | 103,156 | 7 Rungthiwa Pangjan (THA) | (13) | 39,538 | | |
| 3 Patcharachuta Kongkapan (THA) | (8) | 85,977 | 8 Orie Fujino (JPN) | (5) | 33,486 | | |
| 4 Titiya Plucksataporn (THA) | (7) | 63,113 | 9 Bo-Mi Suh (KOR) | (6) | 31,189 | | |
| 5 Thidapa Suwannapura (THA) | (4) | 59,603 | 10 Yumika Adachi (JPN) | (1) | 30,600 | | |

# Australian LPG Tour 2013

*Players are of Australian nationality unless stated*

www.alpg.com.au

| | | | | |
|---|---|---|---|---|
| Jan 14–15 | The Vintage Golf Club Pro Am | Rothbury, NSW | Stacey Keating | 139 (–3) |
| Jan 17 | Ingham Antill Park Ladies Pro Am | Picton, NSW | Emma de Groot* | 69 (–5) |
| | *Beat Esther Choe (USA) in play-off | | | |
| Jan 19–20 | Mount Broughton Classic | Sutton Forest, NSW | Caroline Hedwall (SWE) | 132 (–12) |
| Jan 25–27 | Bing Lee Samsung New South Wales Open | Oatlands GC | Caroline Hedwall (SWE) | 203 (–13) |
| Feb 1–3 | Volvik RACV Ladies Masters | RACV Royal Pines Resort | Karrie Webb | 203 (–13) |
| Feb 8–10 | ISPS Handa New Zealand Women's Open | Christchurch, NZ | Lydia Ko (NZL) (am) | 206 (–10) |
| Feb 14–17 | ISPS Handa Women's Australian Open | Royal Canberra Golf Club | Ji Yai Shin (KOR) | 274 (–18) |
| Feb 21–24 | Women's Victoria Open | Bellarine Peninsula, Vic | Stacey Keating | 278 (–18) |

## Order of Merit (tournaments played in brackets)

| | | | | | | |
|---|---|---|---|---|---|---|
| 1 Stacey Keating (VIC) | (8) | A$74,625 | 6 Whitney Hillier (WA) | (8) | 26,225 | |
| 2 Karrie Webb (QLD) | (2) | 41,520 | 7 Bree Arthur (QLD) | (8) | 21,855 | |
| 3 Sarah Jane Smith (QLD) | (7) | 34,428 | 8 Rebecca Artis (NSW) | (7) | 21,703 | |
| 4 Kristie Smith (WA) | (8) | 30,684 | 9 Nikki Campbell (ACT) | (4) | 21,444 | |
| 5 Katherine Hull-Kirk (QLD) | (2) | 29,953 | 10 Hannah Burke (ENG) | (8) | 21,219 | |

## Teenager Charley Hull is LET Rookie of the Year

It was close run affair with Holly Clyburn but a tie for eighth at the end-of-season Omega Dubai Ladies Masters was enough to clinch the rookie honours for 17-year old Charley Hull.

Hull finished sixth on the ISPS Handa Order of Merit, one place ahead of Clyburn who finished tied 39th in the last event of the season. Hull had year-long earnings of €135,994 while Clyburn's total was €116,100.

"It is an honour to win this," said Hull. "I have had tough competition from Holly who is a great player. You can see me and Holly battling it out in the future. This year has been good fun and the Solheim Cup was great for me."

Hull, the Tour's youngest member, only turned pro in January 2013 and started her competitive career by finishing second five times in a row. In all, she had ten top 10 finishes in 15 Tour starts.

Selected to play in the Solheim Cup, she was the youngest ever player in the match and on the final day beat Paula Creamer 5 and 4. She was pleased to be a member of the side that beat the Americans on home soil for the first time.

After Christmas she will be heading for Australia with an eye on her future goals including winning a major which is, as she puts it, "any golfer's dream."

At the moment she is concentrating on her golf and the global Ladies European Tour which visits so many countries. "It's just fantastic," she says, "you see all those different cultures. It's amazing."

# China LPGA Tour 2013

*Players are of Chinese nationality unless stated*                    www.clpga.org

| | | | | |
|---|---|---|---|---|
| Mar 7–10 | World Ladies Championship | Sandbelt Trails course, Mission Hills, Haikou | Suzann Pettersen (NOR) | 270 (–18) |
| Mar 28–30 | Shanghai Classic | Orient (Shanghai) Sports & CC | Ajira Nualraksa (THA) | 212 (–4) |
| Apr 4–6 | Ningbo Challenge *Beat Yang Taoli at the second extra hole* | Ningbo Orient GC | Lin Tzu-chi (TPE)* | 210 (–6) |
| May 10–12 | Srixon XXIO Ladies Open | Wuxi Jinyuan GC | Liu Yu (am) | 209 (–10) |
| May 23–25 | Beijing Challenge | Orient (Beijing) Pearl Golf CC | Wichanee Meechai | 206 (–10) |
| May 30–June 1 | Bank of Qingdao Golden Mountain Challenge | Qingdao Golden Mountain GC, Shandong Province | Lin Tzu-chi (TPE) | 223 (–3) |
| July 5–7 | Kumho Tires Ladies Open | Weihai Point Hotel and Golf Resort, Shandong Province | Dana Kim (KOR) | 208 (–8) |
| July 25–27 | Wuhan Challenge | Orient Golf (WuHan) CC | Kusuma Meechai (THA) | 215 (–1) |
| Sep 30–Oct 6 | Reignwood LPGA Classic | Beijing | Shanshan Feng | 266 (–26) |
| Oct 25–27 | Sanya Ladies Open *Beat Yu Yang Zhang (CHN) at the first extra hole* | Sanya City | Lee-Anne Pace (RSA)* | 203 (–13) |
| Nov 1–3 | Suzhou Taihu Ladies Open | Suzhou Taihu Int. GC | Gwladys Nocera (FRA) | 201 (–15) |
| Dec 13–15 | Hyundai China Ladies Open | Lion Lake CC, Qingyuan | Ha-Na Jang (KOR) | 216 (–3) |

## Final Order of Merit

| | | | | | |
|---|---|---|---|---|---|
| 1 | Ye-NaChung (KOR) | 378,484 pts | 6 | Lin Tzu-Chi (TPE) | 230,684 |
| 2 | Xiyu Lin | 297,662 | 7 | Na Zhang | 222,180 |
| 3 | Linyan Shang | 289,603 | 8 | Kongkraphan Patcharajutar (THA) | 214,506 |
| 4 | Yuyang Zhang | 284,497 | 9 | Jiayun Li | 211,676 |
| 5 | Shanshan Feng | 238,603 | 10 | Hong Tian | 190,122 |

---

## Lewis tops scoring averages but it was tight

No American since 1994 had won the Vare Trophy which goes to the player with the lowest scoring average on the on the LPGA Tour until Stacy Lewis, holder of the Ricoh Women's British Open title, won it in 2013.

Her average score was 69.484 the eighth lowest scoring average in the history of the Tour but it was not easy for her. She was pushed all the way by Norway's Suzann Pettersen and by Inbee Park, the South Korean golfer who won three majors last year.

With one tournament to go, Pettersen had a chance to finish No.1 if she could beat Lewis by nine in the CME Group Titleholders but it was Lewis who won by nine.

This was the first time that three players finished with scoring averages under 70. Pettersen was 69.696 and Park finished with an average of 69.869.

Since Beth Daniel won the Trophy for America 18 years earlier, the winners comprised Sweden's Annika Sörenstam six times, Mexico's Lorena Ochoa four times, Australian Karrie Webb three times and once by Se Ri Pak, Grace Park, Inbee Park and Choi Na Yeon of South Korea and by Yani Tseng of Taiwan.

Winning the trophy capped a great year for Lewis who won three times and had no fewer than 15 top-10 finishes.

# Japan LPGA Tour 2013

*Players are of Japanese nationality unless stated*   http://en.wikipedia.org/wiki/LPGA_of_Japan_Tour

| Mar 8–10 | Daikin Orchid Ladies | Okinawa | Rikako Morita* | 203 (–13) |
|---|---|---|---|---|
| | *Beat Sakura Yokomine at the first extra hole* | | | |
| Mar 15–17 | Yokohama Tire PRGR Ladies Cup | Kochi | Mi-jeong Jeon (KOR)* | 207 (–9) |
| | *Beat Young Kim (KOR) in play-off* | | | |
| Mar 22–24 | T Point Ladies | Kagoshima | Yuki Ichinose | 202 (–14) |
| Mar 29–31 | AXA Ladies Golf Tournament | Miyazaki | Natsuka Hori | 202 (–14) |
| April 4–7 | Yamaha Ladies Open | Shizuoka | Mamiko Higa* | 284 (–4) |
| | *Beat Kaori Ohe and Teresa Lou (TPE) in play-off* | | | |
| April 12–14 | Studio Alice Open | Hyago | Na-ri Kim (KOR) | 212 (–4) |
| April 19–21 | KKT Cup Banterin Ladies Open | Kumamoto | Miki Saiki | 212 (–4) |
| April 26–28 | Fuji Sankei Ladies Classic | Shizuoka | Miki Saiki | 202 (–14) |
| May 3–5 | CyberAgent Ladies Tournament | Chiba | Sakura Yokomine | 206 (–10) |
| May 9–12 | World Ladies Championship (Salonpas Cup) | Ibaraki | Hiromi Mogi | 279 (–9) |
| May 17–19 | Hokken No Madoguchi Ladies | Fukuoka | Onnarin Sattayabanphot (THA) | 210 (–6) |
| May 24–26 | Chukyo TV Bridgestone Ladies | Aichi | Rikako Morita | 208 (–8) |
| May 31–June 2 | Resort Trust Ladies | Hyogo | Mamiko Higa | 207 (–9) |
| June 7–9 | Yonex Ladies Golf Tournament | Niigata | Junko Omote | 206 (–10) |
| June 13–16 | Suntory Ladies Open | Hyogo | Rikako Morita | 278 (–10) |
| June 21–23 | Nicherei Ladies Championship | Chiba | Yumiko Yoshida | 205 (–11) |
| June 27–30 | Earth Mondahamin Cup | Chiba | Natsuka Hori | 267 (–21) |
| July 5–7 | Nichi-Iko Women's Open | Toyama | Kim Young (KOR) | 203 (–13) |
| July 19–21 | Samantha Thavasa Girls Collection Ladies Tournament | Ibaraki | Yumiko Yoshida* | 200 (–16) |
| | *Beat Junko Omote in play-off* | | | |
| Aug 9–11 | Meijii Cup | Hokkaido | Da-ye Na (KOR) | 204 (–12) |
| Aug 16–18 | NEC Karuizawa 72 | Nagano | Misuzu Narita* | 202 (–14) |
| | *Beat Esther Lee Riesudo (KOR) in play-off* | | | |
| Aug 23–25 | CAT Ladies | Kanagawa | Sun-ju Ahn (KOR) | 201 (–15) |
| Aug 30–Sep 1 | Nitori Ladies | Hokkaido | Sun-ju Ahn (KOR) | 205 (–11) |
| Sep 6–8 | Golf 5 Ladies | Hokkaido | Yumiko Yoshida* | 204 (–12) |
| | *Beat Miki Saiki at the fourth extra hole* | | | |
| Sep 12–15 | Japan LPGA Championship (Konica Minolta Cup) | Hokkaido | Bo-Mee Lee (KOR)* | 201 (–11) |
| | *Beat Mamiko Higa at the sixth extra hole – final round cancelled due to bad weather* | | | |
| Sep 20–22 | Munsingwear Ladies Tokai Classic | Aichi | Sakura Yokomine | 201 (–15) |
| Sep 27–29 | Miyagi TV Cup Dunlop Women's Open | Miyagi | Na-ri Lee (KOR) | 207 (–9) |
| Oct 3–6 | Japan Women's Open C/ship | Kanagawa | Mika Miyazato | 288 (=) |
| Oct 11–13 | Stanley Ladies Golf Tournament | Shizuoka | Soo-yun Kang (KOR) | |
| Oct 18–20 | Fujitsu Ladies | Chiba | Na-ri Lee (KOR) | 138 (–6) |
| | *Third round cancelled due to flooding* | | | |
| Oct 24–27 | Nobuta Group Masters GC Ladies | Hyogo | Sakura Yokomine | 134 (–12) |
| Nov 1–3 | Hisako Higuchi – Morinaga Wieder Ladies | Chiba | Bo-Mee Lee (KOR) | 201 (–15) |
| Nov 8–10 | Mizuno Classic | Mie | Teresa Lu (TPE) | 202 (–14) |
| Nov 15–17 | Ito-en Ladies | Chiba | Sakura Yokomine | 206 (–10) |
| Nov 21–24 | Daio Paper Elleair Ladies Open | Ehime | Rikako Morita | 206 (–10) |
| Nov 28–Dec 1 | Japan LPGA Tour Championship (Ricoh Cup) | Miyazaki | Shiho Oyama | 279 (–9) |

## Final Money List

| | | | | | |
|---|---|---|---|---|---|
| 1 | Rikako Morita | ¥126,675,049 | 6 | Miki Saiki | 83,949,162 |
| 2 | Sakura Yokomine | 125,371.638 | 7 | Bo-Mee Lee (KOR) | 80,837,099 |
| 3 | Teresa Lu (TPE) | 94,793,600 | 8 | Mamiko Higa | 78,655,413 |
| 4 | Sun-Ju Ahn (KOR) | 91.109.680 | 9 | Shiho Oyama | 71,859,084 |
| 5 | Yumiko Yoshida | 89,508,900 | 10 | Natsuka Hori | 65,165,644 |

# Korean LPGA Tour 2013

*Players are of Korean nationality unless stated*

http://en.m.wikipedia.org/wiki/LPGA_of_Korea_Tour

| Dec 14–16 2012 | Hyundai China Ladies Open | Orient Xiamin GC, Fujian | Hyo Joo Kim | 205 (–11) |
|---|---|---|---|---|
| April 12–14 | Lotte Mart Ladies Open | Jeju | Sei Young Kim | 287 (–1) |
| April 19–21 | Nexen Saint Nine Masters | Gimhae | Soo Jin Yang | |
| May 3–5 | KG-Edaily Ladies Open | Anseong | Mi Rim Lee | 209 (–7) |
| May 17–19 | Woori Ladies Championship | Yongin | Yoon Kyung Heo* | 207 (–9) |
| | *Beat Ha Na Jang, Jung Eun Lee and Hyun Min Pyun at the first extra hole | | | |
| May 26 | Doosan Match Play C/ship | Chooncheon | Final: Ha Na Jang beat Ji Jeon In  2 holes | |
| June 2 | E1 Charity Open | Phoenix Springs | Bo Kyung Kim | 206 (–10) |
| June 8–10 | Lotte Cantata Ladies Open | Lotte Sky Hill CC, Jeju | Bo Kyung Kim | 205 (–11) |
| June 15–17 | S-Oil Champions Invitational | Jeju City | Hyun Min Byun | 199 (–17) |
| July 20–23 | Kia Motors Korean Women's Open | Incheon | In Gee Chun | 275 (–13) |
| July 5–7 | Kumho Tires Ladies Open | Shandong Province, China | Dana Kim | 208 (–8) |
| July 19–21 | BS Financial Group Busan Bank Women's Open | Busan | *Cancelled* | |
| Aug 9–11 | Thani Women's Open | | *Cancelled* | |
| Aug 16–18 | Nefs Masterpiece | | Ji Hyun Kim | 278 (–10) |
| Aug 23–25 | MBN-KYJ Golf Ladies Open | Yangpyung TPC GC | Ha Neul Kim | 265 (–23) |
| Aug 30–Sep 1 | LIG Insurance Classic | | *Cancelled* | |
| Sep 6–8 | Hanwa Finance Classic | Golden Bay | Sei Young Kim* | 283 (–5) |
| | *Beat So Yeon Ryu at the first extra hole | | | |
| Sep 12–15 | MetLife Hankyung KLPGA Championship | Ansan | Sei Young Kim | 279 (–9) |
| Sep 21–23 | KDB Daewoo Securities Classic | Pyeongchang | Hee Kyung Bae | 205 (–11) |
| Oct 6–8 | Rush n Cash Classic | | Ha Na Jang | 206 (–10) |
| Oct 10–13 | Hite Jinro Championship | | Ha Na Jang | 276 (–16) |
| Oct 18–20 | LPGA KEB HanaBank Championship | Incheon | Amy Yang | 207 (–9) |
| Oct 24–27 | KB Financial Group STAR Championship | Incheon | Seung Hyun Lee | 281 (–7) |
| Nov 3 | Seoul Economy Women's Open | | *Cancelled* | |
| Nov 8–10 | ADT CAPS Championship | Sky Hill, Jeju | Yoo Rim Choi* | 211 (–5) |
| | *Beat Ha Na Jang at the second extra hole | | | |
| Nov 15–17 | Chosun Ilbo-Posco Championship | Suncheon | Min Young Lee | 210 (–6) |
| Dec 13–15 | Swinging Skirts World Ladies Masters | Taiwan | Lydia Ko (NZL) | 205 (–5) |
| Dec 22 | Korea v Japan Match Play Tournament | | *Cancelled* | |

## Final Money List

| | | | | | |
|---|---|---|---|---|---|
| 1 | Ha Na Jang | W689,542,549 | 6 | Bo Kyung Kim | 354,188,200 |
| 2 | Sei Young Kim | 670,197,815 | 7 | Sung Hyun Lee | 348,916,375 |
| 3 | In Gee Chun | 471,137,666 | 8 | Soo Jin Yang | 329,044,206 |
| 4 | Hyo Joo Kim | 464,686,379 | 9 | Min Young Lee | 296,707,368 |
| 5 | Yoo Rim Choi | 356,397,500 | 10 | Yoon Kyung Heo | 293,626,026 |

# International Team Events

## Hedwall's five out of five a Solheim record

Caroline Hedwall rewrote the history books at Colorado Golf Club when she sank a four foot birdie putt at the final hole to beat Michelle Wie and retain the Solheim Cup for Europe.

The 24-year-old Swede became the first player to win five out five matches – and by winning the 14th point for Europe she ensured that Europe retained the Cup.

The final result was 18–10: the biggest-ever margin of victory.

"I am still shaking but it is an unbelievable feeling," said the elated Hedwall, who was also a star of the win when a rookie at Killeen Castle in Ireland two years earlier. "I was so pumped and ready to go."

Minutes later and a half point from Catriona Matthew against Gerina Piller took the European tally to 14½ points and the Cup had been won outright for the first time on American soil.

After a stunning 4–0 whitewash in Saturday afternoon's fourballs, Liselotte Neumann's team needed just 3½ points from the 12 singles to retain the Cup and England's 17-year-old Charley Hull led the way with victory over Paula Creamer.

But the outcome remained in the balance as matches swung one way and then another and there was more drama when play was halted for thunder and lightning with Europe leading 13–7 – a tantalising one point from glory.

Before the one hour delay 17-year-old Hull, the youngest ever Solheim Cup player, had packed five birdies into 14 holes and beaten Creamer, the world No 11, by 5 and 4.

"I wasn't too nervous," said the super-talented English teenager who won two out of three points. "It's always the way I look at golf. I'm not going to die if I hit a bad shot."

Creamer, who lost 6 and 5 to Matthew in the top singles at Killeen Castle, was generous in defeat. "She played great but I just wish I could have given her more of a battle. The Solheim Cup seems to bring the best or the worst out in me and I just couldn't hit a fairway on the front nine."

Anna Nordqvist had added a half point for Europe in the top match against the Ricoh Women's British Open Champion, Stacy Lewis and then Spanish rookie Carlota Ciganda brought the historic win even closer with a 4 and 2 triumph over Morgan Pressel.

Brittany Lang finally got a full point on the board for the USA with a 2 and 1 victory over Azahara Muñoz.

Following the weather delay, Hedwall and Matthew did their stuff and after that everyone was playing for pride.

For Matthew, it was another great Solheim memory. The 43-year-old Scot, who has played in seven matches gained the winning point at Barsebäck in 2003.

"I was told coming up the 18th that if I got a half we would win outright so I was kind of shaking," said the mum of two who had parred the short 17th to draw level with Piller.

"I made a great par to win the 17th and then the five footer for the half at the last. Being able to celebrate with 11 team mates, the caddies and other helpers makes it far more exciting and more fun than an individual win.

"Lotte has done a great job. She inspired us and instilled confidence. We don't need much motivation to go out and play but she got the pairings absolutely right. The key was the rookies, and the 4–0 success yesterday afternoon in the fourballs."

With the match over as a contest, Suzann Pettersen, Giulia Sergas and Karine Icher all had halved matches and Jodi Ewart-Shadoff beat Brittany Lincicome before Beatriz Recari took her point against Angela Stanford.

Caroline Masson lost, but it didn't really matter. Europe. 5–3 up after the first day foursomes and fourballs, and five ahead after the second days series won the singles 7½–4½.

## The Solheim Cup   *Colorado Golf Club, Parker, Colorado, USA*   August 16–18          [7604–72]

**Captains:** USA: Meg Mallon; Europe: Liselotte Neumann

*First Day,* **Foursomes:**
Stacy Lewis and Lizette Salas lost to Anna Nordqvist (SWE) and Caroline Hedwall (SWE)  4 and 2
Brittany Lang and Angela Stanford lost to Suzann Pettersen (NOR) and Beatriz Recari (ESP)  2 and 1
Morgan Pressel and Jessica Korda beat Catriona Matthew (SCO) and Jodi Ewart-Shadoff (ENG)  3 and 2
Cristie Kerr and Paula Creamer lost to Azahara Muñoz (ESP) and Karen Icher (FRA)  2 and 1

*First Day,* **Fourballs:**
Stacy Lewis and Lexi Thompson lost to Suzann Pettersen and Carlota Ciganda (ESP)  1 up
Angela Stanford and Gerina Piller lost to Caroline Hedwall and Caroline Masson (GER)  2 and 1
Britanny Lincicombe and Brittany Lang beat Anna Nordqvist (SWE) and Giulia Sergas (ITA)  4 and 3
Cristie Kerr and Michelle Wie beat Catriona Matthew and Charley Hull (ENG)  2 and 1
**Match position:** USA 3, Europe 5

*Second Day,* **Foursomes:**
Morgan Pressel and Jessica Korda lost to Anna Nordqvist and Caroline Hedwall  2 and 1
Stacy Lewis and Paula Creamer beat Azahara Muñoz and Karine Icher  1 up
Brittany Lincicome and Lizette Salas halved with Catriona Matthew and Caroline Masson
Michelle Wie and Brittany Lang beat Suzann Pettersen and Beatriz Recari  2 and 1

*Second Day,* **Fourballs:**
Paula Creamer and Lexi Thompson lost to Jodi Ewart-Shadoff and Charley Hull  2 up
Gerina Piller and Angela Stanford lost to Azahara Muñoz and Carlota Ciganda  1 up
Michelle Wie and Jessica Korda lost to Caroline Hedwall and Caroline Masson  2 and 1
Cristie Kerr and Morgan Pressel lost to Beatriz Recari and Karine Icher  1 up
**Match position:** USA 5½, Europe 10½

*Third Day –* **Singles:**
Stacy Lewis halved with Anna Nordqvist
Paula Creamer lost to Charley Hull  5 and 4
Brittany Lang beat Azahara Muñoz  2 and 1
Morgan Pressel lost to Carlota Ciganda  4 and 2
Michelle Wie lost to Caroline Hedwall  1 up
Gerina Piller halved with Catriona Matthew
Lizette Salas halved with Suzann Pettersen
Jessica Korda halved with Giulia Sergas
Lexi Thompson beat Caroline Masson  4 and 3
Brittany Lincicome lost to Jodi Ewart-Shadoff  3 and 2
Angela Stanford lost to Beatriz Recari  2 and 1
Cristie Kerr halved with Karine Icher

**Final result:** Europe 18, USA 10

### Previous results

| | | | |
|------|-------------|-------------|-----------------------------|
| 1990 | USA 11½ | Europe 4½ | Lake Nona, Florida |
| 1992 | Europe 11½ | USA 6½ | Dalmahoy, Scotland |
| 1994 | USA 13 | Europe 7 | The Greenbrier, West Virginia |
| 1996 | USA 17 | Europe 11 | St Pierre, Wales |
| 1998 | USA 16 | Europe 12 | Muirfield Village, Ohio |
| 2000 | Europe 14½ | USA 11½ | Loch Lomond, Scotland |
| 2002 | USA 15½ | Europe 12½ | Interachen, Minnesota |
| 2003 | Europe 17½ | USA 10½ | Barseback, Sweden |
| 2005 | USA 15½ | Europe 12½ | Crooked Stick Indiana |
| 2007 | USA 16 | Europe 12 | Halmstad, Sweden |
| 2009 | USA 16 | Europe 12 | Rich Harvest Farms, Illinois |
| 2011 | Europe 15 | USA 13 | Killeen Castle, Ireland |

**2011** *Killeen Castle, Ireland* Sept 23–25
## Result: Europe 15, USA 13
*Captains: Alison Nicholas (Europe), Rosie Jones (USA)*
**First Day, Foursomes**
Maria Hjörth (SWE) and Anna Nordqvist (SWE) lost to
  Michell Wie and Cristie Kerr  2 and 1
Karen Stupples (ENG) and Melissa Reid (ENG) lost to
  Paula Creamer and Brittany Lincicome  1 hole
Catriona Matthew (SCO) and Azahara Muñoz (ESP) beat
  Stacey Lewis and Angela Stanford  3 and 2
Suzann Pettersen (NOR) and Sophie Gustafson (SWE) beat
  Brittany Lang and Julie Inkster  1 up

**First Day, Fourballs**
Laura Davies (ENG) and Reid lost to Morgan Pressell and
  Creamer  1 hole
Matthew and Sandra Gal (GER) halved with Christina Kim
  and Ryanne O'Toole
Gustafson and Caroline Hedwall (SWE) beat Vicky Hurst
  and Lincicome  5 and 4
Pettersen and Nordqvist beat Kerr and Wie  2 holes

**Second Day, Foursomes**
Hedwall and Gustafson beat Stanford and Lewis  6 and 5
Stupples and Christel Boeljon (NED) lost to Pressel and
  O'Toole  3 and 2
Hjörth and Nordqvist beat Lang and Inkster  3 and 2
Matthew and Muñoz halved with Kerr and Creamer

**Second Day, Fourballs**
Davies and Reid beat Lang and Wie  4 and 3
Pettersen and Hedwall lost to Pressel and Kerr  1 hole
Gal and Boeljon lost to Lewis and O'Toole  2 and 1
Hjörth and Muñoz lost to Creamer and Lincicome
  3 and 2

**Third Day – Singles**
Matthew beat Creamer  6 and 5
Gustafson beat Lewis  2 holes
Norqvist lost to Pressel  2 and 1
Davies halved with Inkster
Reid lost to Hurst  2 holes
Boeljon beat Lincicome  2 holes
Gal lost to Lang  6 and 5
Hjörth lost to Kim  4 and 2
Pettersen beat Wie  1 hole
Hedwall  halved with O'Toole
Muñoz beat Stanford  1 hole
Stupples beat Kerr (withdrew, wrist injury)

**2009** *Rich Harvest Farms, IL, USA* Aug 17–23
## Result: USA 16, Europe 12
*Captains: Beth Daniel (USA), Alison Nicholas
(Europe)*
**First Day – Fourballs**
Creamer and Kerr beat Pettersen and Gustafson  1 hole
Stanford and Inkster lost to Alfredsson and Elosegui
  1 hole
Lang and Lincicome beat Davies and Brewerton  5 and 4
Pressel and Wie halved with Matthew and Hjörth

**Foursomes**
Kim and Gulbis beat Pettersen and Gustafson  4 and 2
Stanford and Castrale lost to Brewerton and Nocera
  3 and 1
McPherson and Lincicome lost to Hjörth and Nordqvist
  3 and 2
Creamer and Inkster beat Matthew and Moodie  2 and 1

**Second Day – Fourballs**
Kim and Wie beat Alfredsson and Elosegui  5 and 4
Lang and Stanford halved with Luna and Matthew

Castrale and Kerr lost to Nordqvist and Pettersen
  1 hole
Lincicome and McPherson lost to Hjörth and Nocera
  1 hole
**Foursomes**
Creamer and Inkster lost to Gustafson and Moodie
  4 and 3
McPherson and Pressel beat Alfredsson and Pettersen
  2 holes
Gulbis and Kim lost to Brewerton and Nocera  5 and 4
Kerr and Wie beat Hjörth and Nordqvist  1 hole
**Third Day – Singles**
Paula Creamer beat Suzann Pettersen (NOR)  3 and 2
Angela Stanford beat Becky Brewerton (WAL)  5 and 4
Michelle Wie beat Helen Alfredsson (SWE)  1 hole
Brittany Lang halved with Laura Davies (ENG)
Juli Inkster halved with Gwladys Nocera (FRA)
Kristy McPherson lost to Catriona Matthew (SCO)
  3 and 2
Brittany Lincicome beat Sophie Gustafson (SWE)  3 and 2
Nicole Castrale lost to Diana Luna (ITA)  3 and 2
Christina Kim beat Tania Elosegui (ESP)  2 holes
Cristie Kerr halved with Maria Hjörth (SWE)
Morgan Pressel beat Anna Nordqvist (SWE)  3 and 2
Natalie Gulbis halved with Janice Moodie (SCO)

**2007** *Halmstad, Tylosand, Sweden* Sept 14–16
## Result: USA 16, Europe 12
*Captains: Helen Alfredsson (Europe),
  Betsy King (USA)*
**First Day – Foursomes**
Pettersen & Gustafson halved with Hurst & Kerr
Sörenstam & Matthew lost to Steinhauer & Diaz
  4 and 2
Davies & Brewerton lost to Inkster & Creamer  2 and 1
Nocera & Hjörth beat Gulbis & Pressel  3 and 2
**Fourballs**
Matthew & Iben Tinning beat Hurst & Lincicome  4 and 2
Sörenstam & Hjörth halved with Stanford &
  Prammanasudh
Gustafson & Nocera lost to Castrale & Kerr  3 and 2
Johnson & Davies halved with Creamer & Pressel
**Second Day – Foursomes**
Hjörth & Nocera halved with Steinhauer & Diaz
Gustafson & Pettersen halved with Inkster & Creamer
Tinning & Hauert lost to Hurst & Stanford  4 and 2
Sörenstam & Matthew beat Castrale & Kerr  1 hole
**Fourballs**
Wessberg & Hjörth halved with Creamer & Lincicome
Johnson & Tinning halved with Inkster & Prammanasudh
Brewerton & Davies beat Gulbis & Castrale  1 hole
Sörenstam & Pettersen beat Kerr & Pressel  3 and 2
**Third Day – Singles**
Catriona Matthew (SCO) beat Laura Diaz  3 and 2
Sophie Gustafson (SWE) lost to Pat Hurst  2 and 1
Suzann Pettersen (NOR) lost to Stacy Prammanasudh
  2 holes
Iben Tinning (DEN) lost to Juli Inkster  4 and 3
Becky Brewerton (WAL) halved with Sherri Steinhauer
Trish Johnson (ENG) lost to Angela Stanford  3 and 2
Annika Sörenstam (SWE) lost to Morgan Pressel  2 and 1
Laura Davies (ENG) beat Brittany Lincicome  4 and 3
Bettina Hauert (GER) lost to Nicole Castrale  3 and 2
Maria Hjörth (SWE) lost to Paula Creamer  2 and 1
Linda Wessberg (SWE) beat Cristie Kerr  1 hole
Gwladys Nocera (FRA) lost to Natalie Gulbis  4 and 3

**2005** *Crooked Stick GC, Carmel, IN, USA*  Sept 9–11
**Result: USA 15½, Europe 12½**
*Captains: Nancy Lopez (USA),*
*Catrin Nilsmark (Europe)*
**First Day – Foursomes**
Daniel & Creamer halved with Koch & Matthew
Kerr & Gulbis lost to Davies & Hjörth  2 and 1
Kim & Hurst halved with Gustafson & Johnson
Redman & Diaz lost to Sörenstam & Pettersen  1 hole
**Fourballs**
Jones & Mallon beat Hjörth & Tinning  3 and 2
Hurst & Ward beat Sörenstam & Matthew  2 and 1
Kerr & Gulbis lost to Gustafson & Stupples  2 and 1
Creamer & Inkster lost to Davies & Pettersen  4 and 3
**Second Day – Foursomes**
Kim & Gulbis beat Nocera & Kreutz  4 and 2
Creamer & Inkster beat Davies & Hjörth  3 and 2
Diaz & Ward lost to Gustafson & Koch  5 and 3
Redman & Hurst beat Sörenstam & Matthew  2 holes
**Fourballs**
Hurst & Kim lost to Davies & Sörenstam  4 and 2
Daniel & Inkster halved with Tinning & Johnson
Kerr & Creamer beat Koch & Matthew  1 hole
Jones & Mallon halved with Gustafson & Pettersen
**Third Day – Singles**
Juli Inkster beat Sophie Gustafson (SWE)  2 and 1
Paula Creamer beat Laura Davies (ENG)  7 and 5
Pat Hurst beat Trish Johnson (ENG)  2 and 1
Laura Diaz beat Iben Tinning (DEN)  6 and 5
Christina Kim beat Ludivine Kreutz (FRA)  5 and 4
Beth Daniel lost to Annika Sörenstam (SWE)  4 and 3
Natalie Gulbis beat Maria Hjörth (SWE)  2 and 1
Wendy Ward lost to Catriona Matthew (SCO)  3 and 2
Michele Redman lost to Carin Koch (SWE)  2 and 1
Cristie Kerr lost to Gwladys Nocera (FRA)  2 and 1
Meg Mallon beat Karen Stupples (ENG)  1 hole
Rosie Jones halved with Suzann Pettersen (NOR)

**2003** *Barsebäck, Sweden*  Sept 12–14
**Result: Europe 17½, USA 10½**
*Captains: Catrin Nilsmark (Europe),*
*Patty Sheehan (USA)*
**First Day – Foursomes**
Koch & Davies halved with Daniel & Robbins
Moodie & Matthew beat Inkster & Ward  5 and 3
Sörenstam & Pettersen beat Diaz & Bowie  4 and 3
Gustafson & Esterl beat Mallon & Jones  3 and 2
**Fourball**
Davies & Matthew lost to Kuehne & Kerr  2 and 1
Sörenstam & Koch lost to Inkster & Daniel  1 hole
Pettersen & Meunier-Labouc beat Stanford & Mallon  3 and 2
Tinning & Gustafson lost to Redman & Jones  2 holes
**Second Day – Foursomes**
Gustafson & Pettersen beat Kuehne & Kerr  3 and 1
Esterl & Tinning halved with Stanford & Redman
Sörenstam & Koch beat Ward and Bowie  3 and 4
Moodie & Matthew halved with Mallon & Robbins
**Fourball**
Sanchez & McKay lost to Daniel & Inkster  5 and 4
Gustafson & Davies lost to Kerr & Kuehne  2 and 1
Matthew & Moodie beat Ward & Jones  4 and 3
Sörenstam & Pettersen beat Robbins & Diaz  1 hole
**Third Day – Singles**
Janice Moodie (SCO) beat Kelli Kuehne  3 and 2
Carin Koch (SWE) lost to Juli Inkster  5 and 4
Sophie Gustafson (SWE) beat Heather Bowie  5 and 4

Iben Tinning (DEN) beat Wendy Ward  2 and 1
Ana Belen Sanchez (ESP) lost to Michele Redman  3 and 1
Catriona Matthew (SCO) beat Rosie Jones  2 and 1
Annika Sörenstam (SWE) beat Angela Stanford  3 and 2
Suzann Pettersen (NOR) lost to Cristie Kerr  conceded
Laura Davies (ENG) beat Meg Mallon  conceded
Elisabeth Esterl (GER) lost to Laura Diaz  5 and 4
Mhairi McKay (SCO) beat Beth Daniel  conceded
Patricia Meunier-Labouc (FRA) beat Kelly Robbins  conceded

**2002** *Interlachen CC, Madina, MN*  Sept 20–22
**Result: USA 15½, Europe 12½**
*Captains: Patty Sheehan (USA),*
*Dale Reid (Europe)*
**First Day – Foursomes**
Inkster & Diaz lost to Davies & Marti  2 holes
Daniel & Ward beat Carriedo & Tinning  1 hole
Hurst & Robbins lost to Alfredsson & Pettersen  4 and 2
Kuehne & Mallon lost to Koch & Sörenstam  3 and 2
**Fourball**
Jones & Kerr beat Davies & Marti  1 hole
Diaz & Klein beat Gustafson & Icher  4 and 3
Mallon & Redman beat Hjörth & Sörenstam  3 and 1
Inkster & Kuehne lost to Koch & McKay  3 and 2
**Second Day – Foursomes**
Kerr & Redman lost to Koch & Sörenstam  4 and 3
Klein & Ward beat McKay & Tinning  3 and 2
Inkster & Mallon beat Davies & Marti  2 and 1
Diaz & Robbins beat Alfredsson & Pettersen  3 and 1
**Fourball**
Daniel & Ward lost to Koch & Sörenstam  4 and 3
Hurst & Kuehne lost to Hjörth & Tinning  1 hole
Jones & Kerr lost to Carriedo & Icher  1 hole
Klein & Robbins lost to Davies & Gustafson  1 hole
**Third Day – Singles**
Juli Inkster beat Raquel Carriedo (ESP)  4 and 3
Laura Diaz beat Paula Marti (ESP)  5 and 3
Emilee Klein beat Helen Alfredsson (SWE)  2 and 1
Kelli Kuehne lost to Iben Tinning (DEN)  3 and 2
Michele Redman halved with Suzann Pettersen (NOR)
Wendy Ward halved with Annika Sörenstam (SWE)
Kelly Robbins beat Maria Hjörth (SWE)  5 and 3
Cristie Kerr lost to Sophie Gustafson (SWE)  3 and 2
Meg Mallon beat Laura Davies (ENG)  3 and 2
Pat Hurst beat Mhairi McKay (SCO)  4 and 2
Beth Daniel halved with Carin Koch (SWE)
Rosie Jones beat Karine Icher (FRA)  3 and 2

**2000** *Loch Lomond*  Oct 6–8
**Result: Europe 14½, USA 11½**
*Captains: Dale Reid (Europe), Pat Bradley (USA)*
**First Day – Foursomes**
Davies & Nicholas beat Pepper & Inkster  4 and 3
Johnson & Gustafson beat Robbins & Hurst  3 and 2
Nilsmark & Koch beat Burton & Iverson  2 and 1
Sörenstam & Moodie beat Mallon & Daniel  1 hole
**First Day – Foursomes**
Davies & Nicholas lost to Iverson & Jones  6 and 5
Johnson & Gustafson halved with Inkster & Steinhauer
Neumann & Alfredsson lost to Robbins & Hurst  2 holes
Moodie & Sörenstam beat Mallon & Daniel  1 hole
**Second Day – Fourball**
Nilsmark & Koch beat Scranton & Redman  2 and 1
Neumann & Meunier Labouc halved with Pepper & Burton
Davies & Carriedo halved with Mallon & Daniel

Sörenstam & Moodie lost to Hurst & Robbins  2 and 1
Johnson & Gustafson beat Jones & Iverson  3 and 2
Nicholas & Alfredsson beat Inkster & Steinhauer  3 and 2

**Third Day – Singles**
Annika Sörenstam lost to Juli Inkster  5 and 4
Sophie Gustafson lost to Brandie Burton  4 and 3
Helen Alfredsson beat  Beth Daniel  4 and 3
Trish Johnson lost to Dottie Pepper  2 and 1
Laura Davies lost to Kelly Robbins  3 and 2
Liselotte Neumann halved with Pat Hurst
Alison Nicholas halved with Sherri Steinhauer
Patricia Meunier Labouc lost to Meg Mallon  1 hole
Catrin Nilsmark beat Rosie Jones  1 hole
Raquel Carriedo lost to Becky Iverson  3 and 2
Carin Koch beat Michele Redman  2 and 1
Janice Moodie beat Nancy Scranton  1 hole

**1998** *Muirfield Village, Dublin, OH*  Sept 18–20
**Result: USA 16, Europe 12**
*Captains: Judy Rankin (USA), Pia Nilsson (Europe)*

**First Day – Foursomes**
Pepper & Inkster beat Davies & Johnson  3 and 1
Mallon & Burton beat Alfredsson & Nicholas  3 and 1
Robbins & Hurst beat Hackney & Neumann  1 hole
Andrews & Green beat  A Sörenstam & Matthew
  3 and 2

**Fourball**
King & Johnson halved with Davies & C Sörenstam
Hurst & Jones beat Hackney & Gustafson  7 and 5
Robbins & Steinhauer lost to Alfredsson & de Lorenzi
  2 and 1
Pepper & Burton beat A Sörenstam & Nilsmark  2 holes

**Second Day – Foursomes**
Andrews & Steinhauer beat A Sörenstam & Matthew
  3 and 2
Mallon & Burton lost to Davies & C Sörenstam  3 and 2
Pepper & Inkster beat Alfredsson & de Lorenzi  1 hole
Robbins & Hurst beat Neumann & Nilsmark  1 hole

**Fourball**
King & Jones lost to A Sörenstam & Nilsmark  5 and 3
Johnson & Green lost to Davies & Hackney  2 holes
Andrews & Steinhauer beat Alfredsson & de Lorenzi
  4 and 3
Mallon & Inkster beat Neumann & C Sörenstam  2 and 1

**Third Day – Singles**
Pat Hurst lost to Laura Davies  1 hole
Juli Inkster lost to Helen Alfredsson  2 and 1
Donna Andrews lost to Annika Sörenstam  2 and 1
Brandie Burton lost to Liselotte Neumann  1 hole
Dottie Pepper beat Trish Johnson  3 and 2
Kelly Robbins beat Charlotta Sörenstam  2 and 1
Chris Johnson lost to Marie Laure de Lorenzi  1 hole
Rosie Jones beat Catrin Nilsmark  6 and 4
Tammie Green beat Alison Nicholas  1 hole
Sherri Steinhauer beat Catriona Matthew 3 and 2
Betsy King lost to Lisa Hackney  6 and 5
Meg Mallon halved with Sophie Gustafson

**1996** *St Pierre, Chepstow*  Sept 20–22
**Result: USA 17, Europe 11**
*Captains: Judy Rankin (USA), Mickey Walker (Europe)*

**First Day – Foursomes**
Sörenstam & Nilsmark halved with Robbins & McGann
Davies & Nicholas lost to Sheehan & Jones  1 hole
de Lorenzi & Reid lost to Daniel & Skinner  1 hole
Alfredsson & Neumann lost to Pepper & Burton
  2 and 1

**Fourball**
Davies & Johnson beat Robbins & Bradley  6 and 5
Sörenstam & Marshall beat Skinner & Geddes  1 hole
Neumann & Nilsmark lost to Pepper & King  1 hole
Alfredsson & Nicholas halved with Mallon & Daniel

**Second Day – Foursomes**
Davies & Johnson beat Daniel & Skinner  4 and 3
Sörenstam & Nilsmark beat Pepper & Burton  1 hole
Neumann & Marshall halved with Mallon & Geddes
de Lorenzi & Alfredsson beat Robbins & McGann  4 and 3

**Fourball**
Davies & Hackney beat Daniel & Skinner  6 and 5
Sörenstam & Johnson halved with McGann & Mallon
de Lorenzi & Morley lost to Robbins & King  2 and 1
Nilsmark & Neumann beat Sheehan & Geddes  2 and 1

**Third Day – Singles**
Annika Sörenstam beat  Pat Bradley  2 and 1
Kathryn Marshall lost to Val Skinner  2 and 1
Laura Davies lost to Michelle McGann 3 and 2
Liselotte Neumann halved with Beth Daniel
Lisa Hackney lost to Brandie Burton  1 hole
Trish Johnson lost to Dottie Pepper  3 and 2
Alison Nicholas halved with Kelly Robbins
Marie Laure de Lorenzi lost to Betsy King  6 and 4
Joanne Morley lost to Rosie Jones  5 and 4
Dale Reid lost to Jane Geddes  2 holes
Catrin Nilsmark lost to Patty Sheehan  2 and 1
Helen Alfredsson lost to Meg Mallon  4 and 2

**1994** *The Greenbrier, WA*  Oct 21–23
**Result: USA 13, Europe 7**
*Captains: JoAnne Carner (USA),
  Mickey Walker (Europe)*

**First Day – Foursomes**
Burton & Mochrie beat Alfredsson & Neuman  3 and 2
Daniel & Mallon lost to Nilsmark & Sörenstam  1 hole
Green & Robbins lost to Fairclough & Reid  2 and 1
Andrews & King lost to Davies & Nicholas  2 and 1
Sheehan & Steinhauer beat Johnson & Wright  2 holes

**Second Day – Fourball**
Burton & Mochrie beat Davies & Nicholas  2 and 1
Daniel & Mallon beat Nilsmark & Sörenstam  6 and 5
Green & Robbins lost to Fairclough & Reid  4 and 3
Andrews & King beat Johnson & Wright 3 and 2
Sheehan & Steinhauer lost to Alfredsson & Neumann
  1 hole

**Third Day – Singles**
Betsy King lost to Helen Alfredsson  2 and 1
Dottie Pepper Mochrie beat Catrin Nilsmark  6 and 5
Beth Daniel beat Trish Johnson  1 hole
Kelly Robbins beat Lora Fairclough  4 and 2
Meg Mallon beat Pam Wright  1 hole
Patty Sheehan lost to Alison Nicholas  3 and 2
Brandie Burton beat Laura Davies  1 hole
Tammie Green beat Annika Sörenstam  3 and 2
Sherri Steinhauer beat Dale Reid  2 holes
Donna Andrews beat Liselotte Neumann  3 and 2

**1992** *Dalmahoy, Edinburgh*  Oct 2–4
**Result: Europe 11½, USA 6½**
*Captains: Mickey Walker (Europe),
  Kathy Whitworth (USA)*

**First Day – Foursomes**
Davies & Nicholas beat King & Daniel  1 hole
Neumann & Alfredsson beat Bradley & Mochrie  2 and 1
Descampe & Johnson lost to Ammaccapane & Mallon
  1 hole
Reid & Wright halved with Sheehan & Inkster

**1992 continued**

**Second Day – Fourball**
Davies & Nicholas beat Sheehan & Inkster 1 hole
Johnson & Descampe halved with Burton & Richard
Wright & Reid lost to Mallon & King 1 hole
Alfredsson & Neumann halved with Bradley & Mochrie

**Third Day – Singles**
Laura Davies beat Brandie Burton 4 and 2
Helen Alfredsson beat Danielle Ammaccapane 4 and 3
Trish Johnson beat Patty Sheehan 2 and 1
Alison Nicholas lost to Juli Inkster 3 and 2
Florence Descampe lost to Beth Daniel 2 and 1
Pam Wright beat Pat Bradley 4 and 3
Catrin Nilsmark beat Meg Mallon 3 and 2
Kitrina Douglas lost to Deb Richard 7 and 6
Liselotte Neumann beat Betsy King 2 and 1
Dale Reid beat Dottie Pepper Mochrie 3 and 2

**1990** *Lake Nona, FL* Nov 16–18
**Result: USA 11½, Europe 4½**
*Captains: Kathy Whitworth (USA),*
*Mickey Walker (Europe)*

**First Day – Foursomes**
Bradley & Lopez lost to Davies & Nicholas 2 and 1
Gerring & Mochrie beat Wright & Neumann 6 and 5
Sheehan & Jones beat Reid & Alfredsson 6 and 5
Daniel & King beat Johnson & de Lorenzi 5 and 4

**Second Day – Fourball**
Sheehan & Jones beat Johnson & de Lorenzi 2 and 1
Bradley & Lopez beat Reid & Alfredsson 2 and 1
King & Daniel beat Davies & Nicholas 4 and 3
Gerring & Mochrie lost to Neumann & Wright
4 and 2

**Third Day – Singles**
Cathy Gerring beat Helen Alfredsson 4 and 3
Rosie Jones lost to Laura Davies 3 and 2
Nancy Lopez beat Alison Nicholas 6 and 4
Betsy King halved with Pam Wright
Beth Daniel beat Liselotte Neumann 7 and 6
Patty Sheehan lost to Dale Reid 2 and 1
Dottie Mochrie beat Marie Laure de Lorenzi 4 and 2
Pat Bradley beat Trish Johnson 8 and 7

## Solheim Cup – Individual Records   Brackets indicate non-playing captain
### Europe

| Name | | Year | Played | Won | Lost | Halved |
|---|---|---|---|---|---|---|
| Helen Alfredsson | SWE | 1990-92-94-96-98-2000-02-(07)-09 | 28 | 11 | 15 | 2 |
| Becky Brewerton | WAL | 2007-09 | 7 | 3 | 3 | 1 |
| Christel Boeljon | NED | 2011 | 3 | 1 | 2 | 0 |
| Raquel Carriedo | ESP | 2000-02 | 5 | 1 | 3 | 1 |
| Carlota Ciganda | ESP | 2013 | 3 | 3 | 0 | 0 |
| Laura Davies | ENG | 1990-92-94-96-98-2000-02-03-05-07-09-11 | 46 | 22 | 18 | 6 |
| Florence Descampe | BEL | 1992 | 3 | 0 | 2 | 1 |
| Kitrina Douglas | ENG | 1992 | 1 | 0 | 1 | 0 |
| Tania Elosegui | ESP | 2009 | 3 | 1 | 2 | 0 |
| Elisabeth Esterl | GER | 2003 | 3 | 1 | 1 | 1 |
| Jodi Ewart-Shadoff | ENG | 2013 | 3 | 2 | 1 | 0 |
| Lora Fairclough | ENG | 1994 | 3 | 2 | 1 | 0 |
| Sandra Gal | GER | 2011 | 3 | 0 | 2 | 1 |
| Sophie Gustafson | SWE | 1998-2000-02-03-05-07-09-11 | 31 | 14 | 11 | 6 |
| Lisa Hackney | ENG | 1996-98 | 6 | 3 | 3 | 0 |
| Caroline Hedwall | SWE | 2011-13 | 9 | 7 | 1 | 1 |
| Bettina Hauert | GER | 2007 | 2 | 0 | 2 | 0 |
| Maria Hjörth | SWE | 2000-04-05-07-09-11 | 21 | 6 | 7 | 8 |
| Charley Hull | ENG | 2013 | 3 | 2 | 1 | 0 |
| Karine Icher | FRA | 2002-13 | 7 | 3 | 3 | 1 |
| Trish Johnson | ENG | 1990-92-94-96-98-2000-05-07 | 25 | 5 | 13 | 7 |
| Carin Koch | SWE | 2000-02-03-05 | 16 | 10 | 3 | 3 |
| Ludivine Kreutz | FRA | 2005 | 2 | 0 | 2 | 0 |
| Laure de Lorenzi | FRA | 1990-96-98 | 11 | 3 | 8 | 0 |
| Diana Luna | ITA | 2009 | 2 | 1 | 0 | 1 |
| Mhairi McKay | SCO | 2002-03 | 5 | 2 | 3 | 0 |
| Kathryn Marshall | SCO | 1996 | 3 | 1 | 1 | 1 |
| Paula Marti | ESP | 2002 | 4 | 1 | 3 | 0 |
| Caroline Masson | GER | 2013 | 4 | 2 | 1 | 1 |
| Catriona Matthew | SCO | 1998-03-05-07-09-11-13 | 29 | 11 | 10 | 8 |
| Patricia Meunier Labouc | FRA | 2000-03 | 4 | 2 | 1 | 1 |
| Janice Moodie | SCO | 2000-03-09 | 11 | 7 | 2 | 2 |
| Joanne Morley | ENG | 1996 | 2 | 0 | 2 | 0 |
| Azara Muñoz | ESP | 2011-13 | 8 | 4 | 3 | 1 |
| Liselotte Neumann | SWE | 1990-92-94-96-98-2000-(13) | 21 | 6 | 10 | 5 |
| Alison Nicholas | ENG | 1990-92-94-96-98-2000-(09)-(11) | 18 | 7 | 8 | 3 |
| Catrin Nilsmark | SWE | 1992-94-96-98-2000-(03)-(05) | 16 | 8 | 7 | 1 |

| Name | | Year | Played | Won | Lost | Halved |
|---|---|---|---|---|---|---|
| Pia Nilsson | SWE | (1998) | 0 | 0 | 0 | 0 |
| Gwladys Nocera | FRA | 2005-07-09 | 10 | 5 | 3 | 2 |
| Anna Nordqvist | SWE | 2009-11-13 | 12 | 6 | 5 | 1 |
| Suzann Pettersen | NOR | 2002-03-05-07-09-11-13 | 29 | 13 | 9 | 7 |
| Beatriz Recari | ESP | 2013 | 4 | 3 | 1 | 0 |
| Dale Reid | SCO | 1990-92-94-96-(2000-02) | 11 | 4 | 6 | 1 |
| Melissa Reid | ENG | 2011 | 4 | 1 | 3 | 0 |
| Ana Belen Sanchez | ESP | 2003 | 2 | 0 | 2 | 0 |
| Giula Sergas | ITA | 2013 | 2 | 0 | 1 | 1 |
| Annika Sörenstam | SWE | 1994-96-98-2000-02-03-05-07 | 37 | 21 | 12 | 4 |
| Charlotta Sörenstam | SWE | 1998 | 4 | 1 | 2 | 1 |
| Karen Stupples | ENG | 2005-11 | 5 | 2 | 3 | 0 |
| Iben Tinning | DEN | 2002-03-05-07 | 14 | 4 | 7 | 3 |
| Mickey Walker | ENG | (1990)-(92)-(94)-(96) | 0 | 0 | 0 | 0 |
| Linda Wessberg | SWE | 2007 | 2 | 1 | 0 | 1 |
| Pam Wright | SCO | 1990-92-94 | 6 | 1 | 4 | 1 |

## United States

| Name | Year | Played | Won | Lost | Halved |
|---|---|---|---|---|---|
| Danielle Ammaccapane | 1992 | 2 | 1 | 1 | 0 |
| Donna Andrews | 1994-98 | 7 | 4 | 3 | 0 |
| Heather Bowie | 2003 | 3 | 0 | 3 | 0 |
| Pat Bradley | 1990-92-96-(2000) | 8 | 2 | 5 | 1 |
| Brandie Burton | 1992-94-96-98-2000 | 14 | 8 | 4 | 2 |
| Jo Anne Carner | (1994) | 0 | 0 | 0 | 0 |
| Nicole Castrale | 2007-09 | 7 | 2 | 5 | 0 |
| Paula Creamer | 2005-07-09-11-13 | 23 | 12 | 9 | 2 |
| Beth Daniel | 1990-92-94-96-2000-02-03-05-(09) | 29 | 10 | 9 | 7 |
| Laura Diaz | 2002-03-05-07 | 13 | 6 | 6 | 1 |
| Jane Geddes | 1996 | 4 | 1 | 2 | 1 |
| Cathy Gerring | 1990 | 3 | 2 | 1 | 0 |
| Tammie Green | 1994-98 | 6 | 2 | 4 | 0 |
| Natalie Gulbis | 2005-07-09 | 10 | 4 | 5 | 1 |
| Pat Hurst | 1998-2000-02-05-07 | 20 | 11 | 6 | 3 |
| Vicky Hurst | 2011 | 2 | 1 | 1 | 0 |
| Juli Inkster | 1992-98-2000-02-03-05-07-09-11 | 34 | 15 | 14 | 5 |
| Becky Iverson | 2000 | 4 | 2 | 2 | 0 |
| Chris Johnson | 1998 | 3 | 0 | 3 | 0 |
| Rosie Jones | 1990-96-98-2000-02-03-05-(11) | 22 | 11 | 9 | 2 |
| Cristie Kerr | 2002-03-05-07-09-11-13 | 30 | 11 | 15 | 4 |
| Christina Kim | 2005-09-11 | 10 | 6 | 2 | 2 |
| Betsy King | 1990-92-94-96-98-(07) | 15 | 7 | 6 | 2 |
| Emilee Klein | 2002 | 4 | 3 | 1 | 0 |
| Jessica Korda | 2013 | 4 | 1 | 2 | 1 |
| Kelli Kuehne | 2002-03 | 8 | 2 | 6 | 0 |
| Brittany Lang | 2009-11-13 | 11 | 4 | 5 | 2 |
| Stacy Lewis | 2011-13 | 8 | 2 | 5 | 1 |
| Brittany Lincicome | 2007-09-11-13 | 14 | 6 | 7 | 1 |
| Nancy Lopez | 1990-(2005) | 3 | 2 | 1 | 0 |
| Michelle McGann | 1996 | 4 | 1 | 1 | 2 |
| Kristy McPherson | 2009 | 4 | 1 | 3 | 0 |
| Meg Mallon | 1992-94-96-98-2000-02-03-05-(13) | 29 | 13 | 9 | 7 |
| Alice Miller | (1992)* | 0 | 0 | 0 | 0 |
| Ryanne O'Toole | 2011 | 4 | 2 | 0 | 2 |
| Dottie Pepper | 1990-92-94-96-98-2000 | 20 | 13 | 5 | 2 |
| Gerina Piller | 2013 | 3 | 0 | 2 | 1 |
| Stacy Prammanasudh | 2007 | 3 | 1 | 1 | 1 |
| Morgan Pressel | 2007-09-11-13 | 15 | 8 | 5 | 2 |
| Judy Rankin | (1996)-(98) | 0 | 0 | 0 | 0 |
| Michele Redman | 2000-02-03-05 | 11 | 4 | 5 | 2 |
| Deb Richard | 1992 | 2 | 1 | 0 | 1 |
| Kelly Robbins | 1994-96-98-2000-02-03 | 24 | 10 | 10 | 4 |
| Lizette Salas | 2013 | 3 | 0 | 1 | 2 |
| Nancy Scranton | 2000 | 2 | 0 | 2 | 0 |
| Patty Sheehan | 1990-92-94-96-(2002)-(03) | 13 | 5 | 7 | 1 |
| Val Skinner | 1996 | 4 | 2 | 2 | 0 |
| Angela Stanford | 2003-07-09-11-13 | 14 | 4 | 8 | 2 |
| Sherri Steinhauer | 1994-98-2000-07 | 13 | 6 | 5 | 2 |
| Lexi Thompson | 2013 | 3 | 1 | 2 | 0 |

| Name | Year | Played | Won | Lost | Halved |
|------|------|--------|-----|------|--------|
| Wendy Ward | 2002-03-05 | 11 | 3 | 7 | 1 |
| Kathy Whitworth | (1990)-(92)* | 0 | 0 | 0 | 0 |
| Michelle Wie | 2009-11-13 | 12 | 6 | 5 | 1 |

*In 1992, Kathy Whitworth was named captain of the USA team but she had to leave the competition prior to the start of the matches, and Alice Miller was appointed in her place.

# Solheim Cup statistics

**Largest margin of victory (individual matches):**
In the 1990 Singles, Pat Bradley (USA) beat Trish Johnson by 8 and 7. Also in 1990, Cathy Gerring and Dottie Mochrie (USA) beat Pam Wright and Liselotte Neumann by 6 and 5 and Patty Sheehan and Rosie Jones (USA) beat Dale Reid and Helen Alfredsson by the same margin, both in Foursomes matches.

This margin was repeated in the 2000 Foursomes when Becky Iverson and Rosie Jones (USA) beat Laura Davies and Alison Nicholas.

In the 1998 Fourballs, Pat Hurst and Rosie Jones (USA) beat Lisa Hackney and Sophie Gustafson by 7 and 5.

**Largest margin of victory (overall competition):**
In 2013, Europe defeated the USA with a score of 18 to 10, a margin of eight points. The previous highest margin (seven points) occurred in 1990 when the USA defeated Europe by a score of 11½ to 4½, a margin repeated in 2003 when Europe were the victors with a score of 17½ to 10½.

**Most events played (from 13 contests):**
12 Laura Davies (EUR); 9 Juli Inkster (USA); 8 Beth Daniel (USA), Trish Johnson (EUR), Meg Mallon (USA); Annika Sörenstam (EUR), Helen Alfredsson (EUR), Sophie Gustafson (EUR); 7 Rosie Jones (USA), Catriona Matthew (EUR); 6 Liselotte Neumann (EUR), Alison Nicholas (EUR), Dottie Pepper (USA), Kelly Robbins (USA).

**Most matches won:**
22 Annika Sörenstam (EUR), Laura Davies (EUR); 15 Juli Inkster (USA).

**Most points earned:**
25 Laura Davies (EUR); 24 Annika Sörenstam (EUR); 18½ Juli Inkster (USA); 16½ Meg Mallon (USA).

**Teams' won and lost record (*denotes a home win):**
USA 8–5 (1990*; 1994*; 1996; 1998*; 2002*; 2005*; 2007; 2009*).
Europe 5–8 (1992*; 2000*; 2003*; 2011*; 2013).

**Most times as captain:**
4 Mickey Walker (EUR), 1990, 1992, 1994, 1996.

## LPGA Legends Handa Cup (USA v Rest of World) *Hermitage GC, Nashville, Tennessee, USA*
USA names first

**Saturday morning – Best ball:**
Pat Bradley and Betsy King 32 lost to Laura Davies and Trish Johnson 31
Nancy Lopez and Barb Mucha 35 lost to Lorie Kane and Alicia Dibos 33
Sherri Turner and Laurie Rinker 32 beat Liselotte Neumann and Jane Crafter 33
Cindy Figg-Currier and Christa Johnson 31 beat Gail Graham and Jenny Lidback 32
Nancy Scranton and Cindy Rarick 34 lost to Helen Alfredsson and Jan Stephenson 32
Beth Daniel and Rosie Jones 31 beat Alison Nicholas and Mieko Nomura 34

**Match position: USA 6, World 6**

**Saturday morning – Foursomes:**
Turner and Rinker 33 lost to Davies and Johnson 30
Bradley and King 35 lost to Neumann and Dibos 33
Figg-Currier and Christa Johnson 35 halved with Kane and Graham 35
Lopez and Mucha 36 lost to Alfredsson and Nicholas 31
Daniel and Jones 34 beat Crafter and Nomura 35
Scranton and Rarick 36 halved with Lidback and Stephenson 36

**Match position: USA 10, World 14**

**Sunday – Singles:**

Beth Daniel 66 beat Laura Davies (ENG) 67
Rosie Jones 69 lost to Trish Johnson (ENG) 66
Cindy Rarick 74 beat Jenny Lidback (PER) 78
Barb Mucha 69 lost to Helen Alfredsson (SWE) 66
Nancy Lopez 75 lost to Alison Nicholas (ENG) 72
Christa Johnson 73 lost to Lorie Kane (CAN) 69

Pat Bradley 76 lost to Mieko Nomura (JPN) 68
Laurie Rinker 67 beat Jane Crafter (AUS) 72
Nancy Scranton 72 beat Liselotte Neumann (SWE) 73
Cindy Figg-Currier 66 beat Alicia Dibos (PER) 73
Sherri Turner 72 lost to Jan Stephenson (AUS) 73
Betsy King 71 halved with Gail Graham (CAN) 71

**Result:** World 27, USA 21

| | |
|---|---|
| 2006 USA 27, World 11 | 2010 USA 27, World 21 |
| 2007 USA 26, World 22 | 2011 USA 34, World 14 |
| 2008 USA 31, World 17 | 2012 USA 24, World 24 – USA retained cup |
| 2009 USA 28, World 20 | |

---

## Lexus Cup (Team Asia v Team International)    (inaugurated 2005)

Inaugurated in 2005, this tournament was last contested in 2008 at which time victor's honours stood at two apiece

| | | | | | |
|---|---|---|---|---|---|
| 2005 | Asia 8, International 16 | Tanah Merah GC, Singapore | 2007 | Asia 15, International 9 | The Vines, Perth, Australia |
| 2006 | Asia 12½, International 11½ | Tanah Merah GC, Singapore | 2008 | Asia 11½, International 12½ | Singapore Island GC |

## Women's World Cup

Inaugurated in 2005, this tournament was last contested in 2008

| | | | | | |
|---|---|---|---|---|---|
| 2005 | Japan (A Miyazato and R Kitada) | 289 | 2007 | Paraguay (J Granada and C Troche) | 279 |
| 2006 | Sweden (A Sörenstam and L Neumann) | 281 | 2008 | Philippines (J Rosales and D Deelasin) | 198 |

---

# National Championships 2013

---

## Glenmuir Women's PGA Professional Championship    *De Vere Slaley Hall*

| | | |
|---|---|---|
| 1 | Lucy Williams (Mid Herts) | 74-74—148 |
| 2 | Sarah Walton (Kington) | 82-77—159 |
| 3 | Tracy Loveys (Bigbury) | 79-81—160 |

---

### Hazel Kavanagh makes history in Ireland

Hazel Kavanagh made history in 2013 by becoming the first woman to make the cut in the Irish PGA Championship.

In the tournament, the 103rd staging of the event, Hazel had good reason to doubt that she would qualify after posting a first round 78 but she improved to 74 for round two and just made the cut on 152.

At the tournament's end Hazel, of Carr Golf Services, finished in joint 38th position.

# Suzann Pettersen is Europe's No 1

Thirty-two-year-old Norwegian Suzann Pettersen has topped the Ladies European Tour's ISPS Handa Order of Merit for the first time in 13 years.

The award caps a brilliant year for her. She won five times around the world and had 11 additional top 10 finishes She sealed No 1 spot in September by winning the weather-shortened Evian Championship, the newest major in women's golf.

She played in three LET events and won two of them – the Evian and the Mission Hills World Ladies Championship and in the third finished fourth in the Ricoh Women's British Open at St Andrews behind Stacy Lewis.

In America she won four times and finished the year second in the Rolex World Rankings. She now has a ten year exemption to the Ladies European Tour.

# Eight countries, 32 players and one crown

Spain and Sweden are among the eight countries who have been named to play in the new biennial LPGA International Crown match play tournament being played at the Caves Valley Golf Club in Maryland from July 24–27.

The field was determined based on the Rolex World Golf rankings The top four ranked players from each country combined for a "country score" and the eight countries to be involved are: South Korea, America, Australia, Thailand, Japan, Chinese Taipei along with the two European countries.

Players from these countries will jockey for a team place through to the Kraft Nabisco Championship, the first major of the 2014 season when seeding will be decided.

# Quick professional success for Lydia

Teen sensation Lydia Ko did not take long to win her first event as a professional. The 16-year old triumphed in the Swinging Skirts World Ladies Masters in Taiwan beating a field that included five of the top 10 ranked women in the world.

Ko, who moved to fourth in the world rankings, started the final round one shot behind So Yeon Ryu but a 3-under-par 69 saw her win by three.

Ko turned Professional at the end of October and played her first event, the CME Titleholders Classic, on the LPGA in November. The Swinging Skirts event is a co-sanctioned tournament between the Korean LPGA and the Taiwan LPGA. The field included World No 1 Inbee Park who finished third, four shots behind Ko.

It is Ko's fifth professional title but her first since joining the pay-for-play ranks.

# Lee-Anne is the players' Player of the Year

South African Lee-Anne Pace, the only player during the 2013 Ladies European Tour to win three titles, has been voted the players' Player of the Year. It is the second time she has been so honoured having won it in 2010.

A model of consistency throughout the season, she won the Turkish Airlines Ladies Open in May at the National Golf Club, the Open de España at Club de Campo Villa de Madrid in July and the Sanya Ladies Open in a play-off against Yu Yang Zhang at Yalong Bay in China in October.

In addition, she had six more top 10 finishes and finished second in the ISPS Handa Order of Merit behind Suzann Pettersen.

"To be recognised by your peers for you achievements is a huge honour. I feel proud and humbled," said the 32-yer-old from Mossel Bay. As I did in 2010, I felt very focussed, relaxed and in control during the 2013 season."

She thanked her two coaches Val Holland and James Petts for the part they played in her success and also her caddie Mark Britton for a great and unforgettable year.

# PART IV

# Men's Amateur Tournaments

# World Amateur Golf Ranking

## Matthew Fitzpatrick is the first English winner of the McCormack Medal

Matthew Fitzpatrick powered his way to the top of the World Amateur rankings in the closing stages of the 52-week period that counts towards the Mark McCormack medal.

The medal, awarded annually since 2007 to the man who is top of the rankings following the US Amateur Championship or the European Amateur Championship which ever comes last in the season (this year it was the US event), saw Fitzpatrick move up from ninth spot before the Open.

© The R&A

*Matthew Fitzpatrick receives the McCormack Medal from Professor Wilson Sibbett, the Chairman of The R&A, and Glen Nager, the President of the USGA*

In a brilliant four week spell he was low amateur in The Open won by Phil Mickelson at Muirfield, runner-up to Callum Shinkwin in the English Amateur Championship at Frilford Heath then made his final medal-winning push by becoming the first Englishman to win the US Amateur since Harold Hilton 102 years ago.

You could say his timing was perfect as he overtook Cheng-tsung Pan from Taipei, Australian Brady Watt and the American trio of Michael Kim, Cory Whitsett and Patrick Rodgers.

By winning the US amateur title at the Country Club at Brookline, Boston, where amateur Francis Ouimet shook the golfing world with his play-off victory in the US Open in 1913 against profession-als Harry Vardon and Ted Ray, the 18-year-old From the Hallamshire Club in Sheffield earned a place in this year's Open at Hoylake, the US Open at Pinehurst and earned a coveted invitation to the Masters.

All this coming just a year after he was Britain's boy champion at Hollinwell. Fitzpatrick, who is attending Chicago's Northwestern University said: "I am absolutely delighted to win the McCormack Medal. For this to come at the same time as winning the US Amateur is really special. It has been an amazing few weeks for me and I am really happy to have achieved so much."

John Bodenhamer, Senior Managing Director, Rules, Competitions and Amateur Status, extended his congratulations on behalf of the USGA to Fitzpatrick for his outstanding performances in the last competitive year. "We are impressed by his and Women's World No 1 Lydia Ko's record of successes in spotlight events. He and Lydia have earned our respect for their talent as golfers."

Johnnie Cole-Hamilton, Executive Director – Championships at The R&A, also expressed his congratulations at the high level of achievement and consistency shown by Matthew and Lydia, who has been top woman amateur for the past three years.

"The World Rankings, initiated in 2007, are an important tool for measuring the performances of amateur players around the world and highlighting the quality of players we have at the elite level of the game."

In the Men's section the WAGR now encompasses 2,900 counting events involving over 6,500 players from 100 different countries.

Fitzpatrick finished joint 44th to win leading amateur spot at Muirfield from fellow Englishman Jimmy Mullen, the only other amateur to make the cut. He made the final of the English Amateur Championship but lost 4 and 3 to Callum Shinkwin and then took the US title with a 4 and 3 victory over Oliver Goss, ranked eighth in the world going into the Championship.

Only two other Englishman have held the No 1 spot – Jamie Moul for a short time in 2007 and Danny Willett who was No 1 in the spring of 2008. The McCormack Medal is presented in memory of golfing entrepreneur Mark H McCormack.

# R&A World Amateur Golf Ranking 2012–2013 – Top 100

Players from the USA occupy most places in the Top 100 with 46 entries, four in the top ten. England takes second place with 17 entries, two in the top ten. Australian players account for eight entries, two in the top ten, with Ireland on four and Canada, France, Mexico and Spain with three apiece. By region the totals are: Americas 54, Europe 33, Australasia 8; Asia 4 and Africa one.

| | | | Divisor | Points | | | | | Divisor | Points |
|---|---|---|---|---|---|---|---|---|---|---|
| 1 | Matthew Fitzpatrick | ENG | 42 | 1424.46 | | 51 | Kevin Phelan | IRL | 52 | 1031.13 |
| 2 | Michael Kim | USA | 68 | 1320.53 | | 52 | Brandon Hagy | USA | 82 | 1030.18 |
| 3 | Cory Whitsett | USA | 63 | 1308.33 | | 53 | Jon Rahm-Rodriguez | ESP | 54 | 1029.01 |
| 4 | Brady Watt | AUS | 93 | 1300.63 | | 54 | Dermot McElroy | IRL | 51 | 1028.10 |
| 5 | Patrick Rodgers | USA | 65 | 1290.00 | | 55 | Andrew Yun | USA | 48 | 1025.00 |
| 6 | Cheng-tsung Pan | TPE | 50 | 1283.25 | | 56 | Zac Blair | USA | 75 | 1024.33 |
| 7 | Max Orrin | ENG | 60 | 1250.67 | | 57 | Tomasz Anderson | ENG | 46 | 1018.21 |
| 8 | Oliver Goss | AUS | 65 | 1230.13 | | 58 | Ian Davis | USA | 51 | 1016.91 |
| 9 | Scottie Scheffler | USA | 43 | 1205.00 | | 59 | Benjamin Griffin | USA | 43 | 1016.40 |
| 10 | Sebastian Cappelen | DEN | 49 | 1203.16 | | 60 | Viraat Badhwar | AUS | 48 | 1012.50 |
| 11 | Callum Shinkwin | ENG | 59 | 1188.14 | | 61 | Carlos Ortiz | MEX | 65 | 1012.44 |
| 12 | Justin Thomas | USA | 62 | 1181.85 | | 62 | Jim Liu | USA | 58 | 1011.49 |
| 13 | Max Homa | USA | 68 | 1181.50 | | 63 | Brett Drewitt | AUS | 66 | 1010.45 |
| 14 | Julien Brun | FRA | 57 | 1174.78 | | 64 | Cory McElyea | USA | 62 | 1010.01 |
| 15 | Garrick Porteous | ENG | 63 | 1170.63 | | 65 | Jonathan Garrick | USA | 49 | 1009.18 |
| 16 | Jordan Smith | ENG | 50 | 1158.00 | | 66 | Rory McNamara | IRL | 42 | 1008.33 |
| 17 | Scott Fernandez | ESP | 51 | 1157.35 | | 67 | Tom Berry | ENG | 53 | 1007.55 |
| 18 | Neil Raymond | ENG | 66 | 1156.06 | | 68 | Reeve Whitson | IRL | 54 | 1007.41 |
| 19 | Sean Dale | USA | 62 | 1152.72 | | 69 | Jonathan Grey | ENG | 46 | 1004.89 |
| 20 | Nathan Kimsey | ENG | 58 | 1147.84 | | 70 | Mike Moyers | USA | 49 | 1003.94 |
| 21 | James Erkenbeck | USA | 52 | 1144.39 | | 71 | Matt Gilchrest | USA | 36 | 1002.78 |
| 22 | Michael Weaver | USA | 69 | 1139.13 | | 72 | Renato Paratore | ITA | 69 | 1000.72 |
| 23 | Jordan Niebrugge | USA | 71 | 1135.39 | | 73 | Michael Johnson | USA | 63 | 1000.40 |
| 24 | Gavin Kyle Green | MAS | 69 | 1104.53 | | 74 | M J Maguire | USA | 49 | 1000.26 |
| 25 | Corey Conners | CAN | 74 | 1104.22 | | 75 | Alejandro Tosti | ARG | 80 | 997.50 |
| 26 | Robby Shelton | USA | 36 | 1103.82 | | 76 | Benjamin Rusch | SUI | 37 | 997.30 |
| 27 | Bobby Wyatt | USA | 56 | 1097.54 | | 77 | Toby Tree | ENG | 52 | 996.15 |
| 28 | Ryan Evans | ENG | 55 | 1096.97 | | 78 | Kramer Hickok | USA | 51 | 994.12 |
| 29 | Daniel Hoeve | AUS | 41 | 1086.59 | | 79 | Nick Marsh | ENG | 54 | 993.98 |
| 30 | Gregory Eason | ENG | 49 | 1082.14 | | 80 | Jimmy Beck | USA | 50 | 991.00 |
| 31 | Thomas Elissalde | FRA | 56 | 1079.91 | | 81 | Zach Olsen | USA | 38 | 990.46 |
| 32 | Cameron Wilson | USA | 52 | 1073.24 | | 82 | Scott Strohmeyer | USA | 52 | 989.42 |
| 33 | Taylor Pendrith | CAN | 58 | 1072.63 | | 83 | Austin Cook | USA | 46 | 988.15 |
| 34 | Harry Casey | ENG | 38 | 1072.37 | | 84 | Scott Vincent | ZIM | 46 | 987.50 |
| 35 | Bryson Dechambeau | USA | 61 | 1068.24 | | 85 | Rick Lamb | USA | 60 | 984.79 |
| 36 | Guan Tianlang | CHN | 35 | 1065.71 | | 86 | Adam Schenk | USA | 52 | 982.94 |
| 37 | Soo-min Lee | KOR | 54 | 1059.64 | | 87 | Lucas Herbert | AUS | 58 | 981.03 |
| 38 | Thomas Detry | BEL | 61 | 1059.43 | | 88 | Carson Young | USA | 33 | 978.79 |
| 39 | Michael Miller | USA | 43 | 1057.85 | | 89 | Corey Pereira | USA | 32 | 978.12 |
| 40 | Nathan Holman | AUS | 87 | 1050.38 | | 90 | Adam Svensson | CAN | 47 | 977.66 |
| 41 | Adam Wood | USA | 43 | 1048.26 | | 91 | Mario Clemens | MEX | 47 | 977.13 |
| 42 | Ashley Chesters | ENG | 43 | 1045.74 | | 92 | Jack Perry | USA | 52 | 975.48 |
| 43 | Steven Ihm | USA | 55 | 1043.86 | | 93 | Bo Andrews | USA | 54 | 975.46 |
| 44 | Oliver Schniederjans | USA | 61 | 1041.80 | | 94 | Mario Galiano | ESP | 44 | 975.00 |
| 45 | Gavin Hall | USA | 34 | 1041.18 | | | Aguilar | | | |
| 46 | Rodolfo Cazaubon | MEX | 65 | 1036.41 | | 95 | Anders Albertson | USA | 58 | 974.14 |
| 47 | Joel Stalter | FRA | 56 | 1035.94 | | 96 | Talor Gooch | USA | 49 | 972.11 |
| 48 | Toni Hakula | FIN | 59 | 1032.84 | | 97 | James Ross | SCO | 37 | 971.62 |
| 49 | Taylor James | AUS | 73 | 1032.02 | | 98 | Brad Dalke | USA | 45 | 971.11 |
| | MacDonald | | | | | 99 | Denny McCarthy | USA | 59 | 970.34 |
| 50 | Jorge Garcia | VEN | 59 | 1031.57 | | 100 | Jamie Rutherford | ENG | 47 | 968.94 |

The European Amateur Ranking Top 100 can be found on page 287

# World Amateur Golf Ranking 2012–2013

The World Amateur Golf Ranking (WAGR), which comprises a women's ranking and a men's ranking for elite amateur players, is offered by The R&A and the United States Golf Association as a global service to golf.

Through incorporation and assessment worldwide of both amateur and professional events, WAGR encourages the international development of the competitive game. WAGR endeavours to be the most comprehensive and accurate ranking in golf by effectively comparing players from around the world who may never directly compete against one another. WAGR is available to national federations and organisers of amateur and professional events and tours as a criterion for tournament field selection and for purposes of exemptions, national team selection, and orders of merit.

WAGR currently processes information from over 4,500 Counting Events to rank over 10,000 players from more than 100 countries. Players are ranked on the basis of their average performance in those events over a rolling cycle of the previous 52 weeks. Counting Events are graded from A to G in accordance with the strength of the field, with the number of points awarded being proportionate to the event strength.

A Counting Event is an event, match play, stroke play or a combination, amateur or professional, selected and approved by the WAGR Committee to count for WAGR. Counting Events may be:
1.  Any elite stroke play event, decided by gross scores, played over a minimum of three rounds.
2.  Any elite match play event, decided by gross scores, played over a minimum of three match play rounds. Stroke play qualifying for a counting match play event will also be included in the results for that event if played over a minimum of 36 holes.
3.  Any elite team match play event that contains at least one round of singles matches.
4.  Any of the major championships or any official event from the professional tours that make up the International Federation of PGA Tours, or any official event from other professional tours, if the event meets 1 or 2 above.

In order to be included in WAGR, results of Counting Events must be submitted by event organisers in a timely manner. Reporting templates are available. To receive points in WAGR for the Counting Events in which they participate, and to receive event exemptions they may have earned with those points, players may wish to encourage event organisers to return event results to WAGR as soon as possible once Counting Events conclude.

Further information can be found in the Frequently Asked Questions (FAQ's) on the WAGA.com website

The rankings are displayed here by month and are subdivided into the following regions:

Africa
The Americas (North, South and Central America and the Caribbean)
Asia (incorporating the Middle East)
Australasia (incorporating the Pacific Islands)
Europe

Players are from the country hosting the event unless otherwise stated.
* Indicates a newly ranked player.
‡ Indicates that the player has since turned professional.
A list of country abbreviations can be found on page 51; WWAGR can be found on page 364.

# Elite and Category "A" Events

Elite

Week 25    **2013 Amateur Championship**    *Royal Cinque Ports and Prince's, England*

June 17–22    (RSS 78–74)

|              |                       |             | SP | MP  | Points |
|--------------|-----------------------|-------------|----|-----|--------|
| Winner       | Garrick Porteous (ENG) | 76-69—146  | 22 | 138 | 160    |
| Runner-up    | Tony Hakula (FIN)     | 77-70—147   | 21 | 105 | 126    |
| Semi-finalists | Max Orrin (ENG)     | 73-70—143   | 25 | 76  | 101    |
|              | James Liu (USA)       | 72-74—146   | 22 | 76  | 98     |

Full details can be found on page 291

Week 32　2013 International European Championship
*Real Club de Golf El Prat, Spain*　Aug 5–11　　　　　　　　　　(RSS 77-75-77-76)

| | | | SP | MP | Points |
|---|---|---|---|---|---|
| 1 | Ashley Chesters (ENG) | 73-65-70-76—284 | 53 | 48 | 101 |
| 2 | David Morago (ESP) | 75-68-69-73—285 | 52 | 36 | 88 |
| 3 | Wm Fernandez Scott (ESP) | 70-71-71-74—286 | 51 | 18 | 69 |

Full details can be found on page 297

---

Week 33　2013 US Amateur Championship　*Brookline, MA, USA*

(RSS 74-73)

| | | | SP | MP | Points |
|---|---|---|---|---|---|
| Winner | Matthew Fitzpatrick (ENG) | 67-70—137 | 26 | 138 | 170 |
| Runner-up | Oliver Goss (AUS) | 70-67—137 | 26 | 105 | 137 |
| Semi-finalists | Cory Conners (CAN) | 70-73—143 | 20 | 76 | 96 |
| | Brady Watt (AUS) | 68-66—134 | 29 | 76 | 126 |

Full details can be found on page 299

---

Week 43　2013 Asia–Pacific Amateur Championship　*Nanshan Int. GC, Longkou, China*

(RSS 78-77-73-74)

| | | | SP | Bonus | Pts | Div |
|---|---|---|---|---|---|---|
| 1 | Chang-woo Lee (KOR) | 70-72-69-70—281 | 53 | 48 | 101 | 4 |
| 2 | Shohei Hasegawa (JPN) | 72-70-71-71—284 | 50 | 36 | 86 | 4 |
| 3 | Kenta Konishi (JPN) | 76-71-68-70—285 | 49 | 18 | 67 | 4 |

Full details can be found on page 289

---

Category "A"

## 2012

Week 36　**Carpet Capital Collegiate**　*Rocky Face, Georgia, USA*　Sep 7–9　(RSS 74-73-75)

| | | | |
|---|---|---|---|
| 1 | Brandon Stone (RSA)‡ | 69-63-72—204 | 23 points |
| 2 | T J Mitchell | 65-68-73—206 | 17.083 |
| | Jordan Spieth‡ | 70-66-70—205 | 17.083 |

---

Week 39　**Ping Golf Week Preview**　*Alpharetta, Georgia, USA*　Sep 23–25　(RSS 73-72-73)

| | | | |
|---|---|---|---|
| 1 | Tom Berry (ENG) | 67-69-72—208 | 60 points |
| 2 | Gavin Kyle Green (MAS) | 71-67-72—210 | 34.75 |
| | Max Homa | 71-70-69—210 | 34.75 |
| | Cheng-tsung Pan (TPE) | 72-69-69—210 | 34.75 |
| | Kevin Penner‡ | 71-69-70—210 | 34.75 |
| | Nicholas Peach | 70-73-67—210 | 34.75 |
| | Seth Reeves | 73-71-66—210 | 34.75 |
| | Michael Weaver | 71-70-69—210 | 34.75 |
| | Chris Williams‡ | 69-72-69—210 | 34.75 |

---

Week 40　**Eisenhower Trophy**　*Antalya, Turkey*　Oct 4–7　(RSS 74-74-75-73)

| | | | |
|---|---|---|---|
| 1 | Sebastian Vazquez (MEX) | 64-67-66—197 | 71 points |
| 2 | Chris Williams (USA)‡ | 64-67-69—200 | 56.5 |
| 3 | Moritz Lampert (GER) | 70-66-65—201 | 51.00 |

*Third round cancelled due to bad weather*

---

Week 43　**Isleworth Collegiate Inv.**　*Windermere, Florida, USA*　Oct 21–23　(RSS 75-75-76)

| | | | |
|---|---|---|---|
| 1 | Michael Kim | 67-72-73—212 | 66 points |
| 2 | James Erkenbeck | 72-70-71—213 | 48.25 |
| | Justin Thomas | 73-70-70—213 | 48.25 |

Week 47 **Western Refining Col. All-Am.** *El Paso, Texas, USA* Nov 19–20

(RSS 70-68-69)

| | | | |
|---|---|---|---|
| 1 | Kevin Penner‡ | 65-66-68—192 | 59 points |
| 2 | Sebastian Cappelen (DEN) | 72-65-63—200 | 44.5 |
| 3 | Cory Whitsett | 66-65-70—201 | 39 |

# 2013

Week 2 **Australian Master of the Amateurs** *Royal Melbourne* Jan 8–11

(RSS 72-75-73-76)

| | | | |
|---|---|---|---|
| 1 | Viraat Badhwar | 67-74-68-70—279 | 85 points |
| 2 | Brady Watt | 67-68-68-78—281 | 65 |
| 3 | Geoffrey Drakewood | 67-70-70-75—282 | 46 |

Week 5 **Jones Cup Invitational** *Sea Island, Georgia, USA* Feb 1–3    (RSS 76-76-78)

| | | | |
|---|---|---|---|
| 1 | Sean Dale | 71-73-69—213 | 68 points |
| 2 | Alex Carpenter‡ | 72-72-71—215 | 50.25 |
| 3 | Cory Whitsett | 68-72-75—215 | 50.25 |

Week 6 **The Amer-Ari** *Kohala Coast, Hawaii, USA* Feb 6–8    (RSS 72-72-73)

| | | | |
|---|---|---|---|
| 1 | Domenic Bozzelli‡ | 70-68-67—205 | 63 points |
| 2 | David Fink | 68-70-69—207 | 45.25 |
| | Trevor Simsby | 72-66-69—207 | 45.25 |

Week 8 **Prestige at PGA West** *La Quinta, California, USA* Feb 18–24    (RSS 73-75-73)

| | | | |
|---|---|---|---|
| 1 | Pedro Figueiredo (POR)‡ | 71-67-67—205 | 67 points |
| 2 | Jordan Niebrugge | 68-73-69—210 | 44 |
| | Anthony Paolucci | 70-70-70—210 | 44 |
| | Chris Williams | 70-68-72—210 | 44 |

Week 9 **Spanish Amateur Championship** *La Managa GC, Cartagena* Feb 25–Mar 3

(RSS 78-77)

| | | | SP | MP | Points |
|---|---|---|---|---|---|
| Winner | Reeve Whitson (IRL) | 75-73—148 | 23 | 115 | 138 |
| Runner-up | Neil Raymond (ENG) | 76-72—148 | 23 | 84 | 107 |
| Semi-finalists | Adrien Saddier (FRA)‡ | 76-74—150 | 21 | 57 | 78 |
| | Edouard Amacher (SUI) | 74-78—152 | 19 | 57 | 76 |

Week 10 **SH Collegiate Masters** *Las Vegas, Nevada, USA* Mar 8–10    (RSS 75-75-76)

| | | | |
|---|---|---|---|
| 1 | Patrick Rodgers | 66-73-73—212 | 65 points |
| 2 | James Erkenbeck | 69-72-71—212 | 47 |
| | Michael Kim | 76-67-69—212 | 47 |
| | Cory Whitsett | 68-73-71—212 | 47 |

Week 11 **Schenkel Invitational** *Statesboro, Georgia, CA, USA* Mar 11–17    (RSS 74-74-74)

| | | | |
|---|---|---|---|
| 1 | Justin Thomas | 67-70-70—207 | 66 points |
| 2 | Brandon Stone (RSA)‡ | 68-73-69—210 | 49.5 |
| 3 | Sean Dale | 71-73-67—211 | 41.75 |
| | Bobby Wyatt | 70-70-71—211 | 41.75 |

Week 11 **European Nations Cup Individual** *Sotogrande, Spain* Mar 13–16

(RSS 76-74-75-73)

| | | | |
|---|---|---|---|
| 1 | Adrien Saddier (FRA)‡ | 72-70-67-74—283 | 83 points |
| 2 | Maximilian Roehig (GER) | 72-68-72-71—283 | 65 |
| 3 | Christian Hillersborg Gloet (AUT) | 72-74-71-69—286 | 53 |
| | Renato Paratore (ITA) | 74-72-71-69—286 | 53 |

## Week 14   Aggie Invitational   *Bryan, Texas, USA*   April 6–7   (RSS 75-74-74)

| | | | |
|---|---|---|---|
| 1 | Cory Whitsett | 69-69-70—208 | 66 points |
| 2 | Bobby Wyatt | 67-72-70—209 | 51.5 |
| 3 | Scott Strohmeyer | 67-71-72—210 | 46 |

## Week 16   SEC Championship   *Sea Island, Georgia, USA*   April 19–21   (RSS 73-73-75)

| | | | |
|---|---|---|---|
| 1 | Sebastian Capalan (DEN) | 69-67-66—202 | 70 points |
| 2 | Caleb Sturgeon | 65-67-73—205 | 53.5 |
| 3 | Tyler McCumber‡ | 72-68-69—209 | 42.75 |
| | Cory Whitsett | 69-67-73—209 | 42.75 |

## Week 18   Lytham Trophy   *Royal Lytham and St Annes, England*   May 3–5   (RSS 77-76-75-76)

| | | | |
|---|---|---|---|
| 1 | Albert Eckhardt (FIN) | 73-72-69-73—287 | 85 points |
| 2 | Jack Hume (IRL) | 72-77-70-68—287 | 67 |
| 3 | Kristian Johannessen (NOR) | 70-74-73-74—291 | 54 |
| | Julien Marot (FRA) | 75-74-70-72—291 | 54 |

## Week 18   PAC-12 Championship   *Los Angeles, California, USA*   April 29–May 1
(RSS 73-73-74-74)

| | | | |
|---|---|---|---|
| 1 | Max Homa | 61-70-71-69—271 | 91 points |
| 2 | Michael Weaver | 65-69-74-68—273 | 68 |
| 3 | Anton Arboleda (PHI) | 69-69-70-70—278 | 57 |
| | Chris Williams‡ | 68-68-72-70—278 | 57 |

## Week 20   NCAA Tallahassee Regional   *Tallahassee, Florida, USA*   May 16–18
(RSS 71-72-72)

| | | | |
|---|---|---|---|
| 1 | Cheng-tsung Pan (TPE) | 67-67-67—201 | 65 points |
| 2 | M J Maguire | 65-68-71—204 | 44 |
| | Chase Seiffert‡ | 66-68-70—204 | 44 |
| | Daniel Walker | 68-67-69—204 | 44 |

## Week 20   NCAA Columbus Regional   *Columbus, Ohio, USA*   May 16–18
(RSS 75-75-74)

| | | | |
|---|---|---|---|
| 1 | James Erkenbeck | 72-70-68—210 | 65 points |
| 2 | Domnic Bozzelli‡ | 71-74-69—214 | 43 |
| | Denny McCarthy | 74-74-66—214 | 43 |
| | Matthew NeSmith | 75-71-68—214 | 43 |

## Week 20   NCAA Pullman Regional   *Pullman, Washington, USA*   May 16–18
(RSS 70-73-73)

| | | | |
|---|---|---|---|
| 1 | Sam Smith | 62-64-76—202 | 58.25 points |
| | Michael Weaver | 65-67-70—202 | 58.25 |
| 3 | Joel Stalier (FRA) | 65-68-73—204 | 43 |

## Week 22   NCAA DI Medal and Team Match   *Atlanta, Georgia, USA*   May 28–June 2
(RSS 72-71-72)

| | | | SP | Bonus | MP | Points |
|---|---|---|---|---|---|---|
| 1 | Cory Whitsett | 69-68-70—207 | 32 | – | 51 | 83 |
| 2 | Max Homa | 70-65-66—201 | 32 | 27 | 11 | 76 |
| 3 | Brandon Hagy | 69-69-70—208 | 34 | – | 28 | 62 |

Week 23   **St Andrews Links Trophy**   *Jubilee and Old courses, St Andrews, Scotland*   June 7–9
(RSS 75-75-73-74)

| 1 | Neil Raymond (ENG) | 72-73-68-69—282 | 83 points |
| 2 | Ryan Evans (ENG) | 66-73-72-73—284 | 57 |
| | Nathan Kimsey (ENG) | 68-76-70-70—284 | 57 |
| | Max Orrin (ENG) | 73-70-70-71—284 | 57 |

Week 24   **Sunnehanna Amateur**   *Johnstown, Pennsylvania, USA*   June 13–16   (RSS 73-72-72-72)

| 1 | Steven Ihm | 66-71-68-67—272 | 85 points |
| 2 | Cory Whitsett | 69-70-68-67—274 | 65 |
| 3 | Rick Lamb | 73-67-69-68—277 | 53 |
| | Michael Miller | 72-67-70-68—277 | 53 |

Week 25   **Northeast Amateur**   *Wannamoisett CC, Rhode Island, USA*   June 19–22
(RSS 72-72-72-71)

| 1 | Cory Whitsett | 66-68-69-63—266 | 89 points |
| 2 | Bo Andrews | 66-69-71-62—268 | 69 |
| 3 | Patrick Rodgers | 71-65-67-68—271 | 60 |

Week 26   **Brabazon Trophy**   *Formby Golf Club, England*   June 26–29   (RSS 76-76-76-74)

| 1 | Jordan Smith | 71-69-76-70—286 | 85 points |
| 2 | Brian Casey (IRL) | 71-76-69-74—290 | 63 |
| 3 | Nathan Kimsey | 71-74-75-71—291 | 49.5 |
| | Jimmy Mullen | 75-73-72-71—291 | 49.5 |
| | Alfie Plant | 71-78-69-73—291 | 49.5 |
| | Ben Taylor | 74-76-73-68—291 | 49.5 |

Week 27   **Sahalee Players Championship**   *Sammamish, Washington, USA*   July 1–3
(RSS 74-74-75-76)

| 1 | Andrew Yun | 67-71-75-74—287 | 80 points |
| 2 | Zac Blair | 73-68-72-75—288 | 58 |
| 3 | Bryson de Chambeau | 75-71-71-71—288 | 58 |

Week 28   **The Players Amateur**   *Berkeley Hall, South Carolina, USA*   July 8–14
(RSS 73-73-72)

| 1 | Hunter Stewart | 64-68-70—202 | 67 points |
| 2 | Michael Weaver | 67-67-69—203 | 52.5 |
| 3 | Chase Kopeka | 67-70-71—208 | 43 |

Week 28   **European Amateur Team Championship**   *Silkeborg GC, Denmark*   July 9–13
(RSS 76-76)

| | | | SP | MP | Points |
|---|---|---|---|---|---|
| 1 | Graeme Robertson (SCO) | 72-74—146 | 22 | 51 | 73 |
| 2 | Bradley Neil (SCO) | 75-77—152 | 16 | 51 | 67 |
| 3 | Garrick Porteous (ENG) | 77-76—153 | 15 | 51 | 66 |

Week 29   **Southern Amateur Championship**   *The Club at Carlton Woods*   July 17–20
(RSS 72-72-72-73)

| 1 | Zach Olsen | 64-73-68-71—276 | 81 points |
| 2 | Joey Garber | 67-73-67-69—276 | 60 |
| | Sam Love | 70 -71-69 66—276 | 60 |

**For further information, visit www.RandA.org/wagr**

Week 30  **Porter Cup**  *Niagra Falls CC, New York USA*  July 24–27

(RSS 72-70-70-70)

| | | | |
|---|---|---|---|
| 1 | Taylor Pendrith (CAN) | 68-66-63-67—264 | 86 Points |
| 2 | Ty Dunlap | 65-65-70-69—269 | 63 |
| 3 | Justin Slim (CAN) | 64-67-67-72—270 | 53 |
| | Brady Watt (AUS) | 70-65-66-69—270 | 53 |

Week 31  **Western Amateur**  *The Alotian Club, Arkanzas, USA*  July 29–Aug 4

(RSS 72--73-72-73)

| | | | SP | Bonus | MP | Points |
|---|---|---|---|---|---|---|
| 1 | Jordan Niebrugge | 66-69-70-72—277 | 45 | 12 | 100 | 157 |
| 2 | Sean Dale | 69-68-76-70—283 | 39 | – | 69 | 108 |
| 3 | Kramer Hickok | 70-70-71-69—279 | 43 | 4.5 | 42 | 89.5 |

Week 31  **English Amateur Championship**  *Frilford Heath GC, England*  July 29–Aug 3

(RSS 71-72)

| | | | SP | Bonus | MP | Points |
|---|---|---|---|---|---|---|
| Winner | Callum Shinkwin | 71-68—139 | 20 | – | 126 | 146 |
| Runner-up | Matthew Fitzpatrick | 67-71—138 | 21 | 0.4 | 95 | 116.4 |
| Semi-finalists | Thomasz Anderson | 70-67—137 | 22 | 6 | 68 | 96 |
| | Max Orrin | 69-69—138 | 21 | 0.4 | 68 | 89.4 |

## September

### Americas

| | | | | | |
|---|---|---|---|---|---|
| A | Carpet Capital Collegiate | Rocky Face, GA | 7–9 | Brandon Stone (RSA) | USA |
| A | Ping-Golfweek Preview | Alpharetta, GA | 23–25 | Tom Berry (ENG) | USA |
| B | Junior Ryder Cup | Olympia Fields CC, IL | 24– 25 | Tom Berry (ENG) | USA |
| B | Kikkor Husky Invitational | Bremerton, WA | 17– 18 | Cheng-tsung Pan (TPE) | USA |
| B | The Gopher Invitational | Wayzata, MN | 9–10 | Corey Conners (CAN) | USA |
| B | Wolf Run Intercollegiate | Zionsville, IN | 15–16 | Brant Peaper | USA |
| C | California State Fair Am. | Sacramento, CA | 1–3 | Brandon Hagy | USA |
| C | D A Weibring Intercoll. | Normal, IL | 22–23 | Pep Angles Ros (ESP) | USA |
| C | Inverness Intercollegiate | Toledo, OH | 17–18 | Jack Perry/Kevin Miller | USA |
| C | Invitational at Kiawah | Kiawah Is., SC | 9–11 | Scott Wolfes | USA |
| C | Northern Intercollegiate | Sugar Grove, IL | 8–9 | Denny McCarthy | USA |
| C | Saint Mary's Invitational | Seaside, CA | 24–25 | Ben Geyer | USA |
| C | Tar Heel Intercollegiate | Chapel Hill, NC | 15–16 | Albin Choi (CAN) | USA |
| C | The Carmel Cup | Carmel, CA | 1–2 | Albin Choi (CAN) | USA |
| C | The Junior PLAYERS Championship | Ponte Vedra Beach, FL | A31–S2 | Robby Shelton | USA |
| C | US Mid-Amateur | Conway Farms GC | 8–13 | Nathan Smith | USA |
| C | USGA State Championship | Galloway, NJ | 19–21 | Michael Miller | USA |
| C | William H Tucker | Albuquerque, NM | 28–29 | Gavin Kyle Green (MAS) | USA |
| D | Adams Cup of Newport | Newport, RI | 17–18 | Sam Bernstein | USA |
| D | Crump Cup | Pine Valley GC, NJ | 27–30 | Michael P McDermott* | USA |
| D | Gene Miranda Falcon Invite | USAF Academy, CO | 9–10 | Jason Burstyn | USA |
| D | Golfweek Conference Challenge | Burlington, IA | 16–18 | Jace Long | USA |
| D | Graeme McDowell Shoal Creek Invitational | Birmingham, AL | 24–25 | Curtis Thompson/Rodolfo Cazaubon (MEX)/Stewart Jolly | USA |
| D | Mason Rudolph Championship | Franklin, TN | 21–23 | Jonathan Grey (ENG) | USA |
| D | North Carolina Mid-Amateur | Rocky Mount, NC | 14–16 | Scott Harvey | USA |
| D | The McLaughlin | Farmingdale, NY | 15–16 | Jake Mondy | USA |
| D | Windon Memorial | Glencoe, IL | 23–24 | John Callahan | USA |

## Asia

| | | | | | |
|---|---|---|---|---|---|
| C | Topy Cup – Japan Intercollegiate | Fukushima | 11–13 | Shinji Tomimura | JPN |
| D | September Grand Prix | Royal Colombo GC | 18–21 | Nadaraja Thangaraja | SRI |
| D | Southern India Amateur | KGA, Bengaluru | 18–21 | Khalin Joshi | IND |
| D | Tamilnadu Amateur Open | TNGF, Chennai | 11–14 | Senapaa Chikkarangappa | IND |

## Australasia

| | | | | | |
|---|---|---|---|---|---|
| C | City of Sydney Amateur | Moore Park GC | 29–30 | Jake Higginbottom | AUS |
| C | Mandurah Amateur Open | Mandurah CC, Perth | 15–17 | Nathan Holman | AUS |
| D | City of Perth Championship | Royal Perth GC | 2–9 | Brady Watt | AUS |

## Europe

| | | | | | |
|---|---|---|---|---|---|
| B | Jacques Leglise Trophy | Portmarnock GC | A31–S1 | James Johnson (BAR) | IRL |
| B | St Andrews Trophy | Portmarnock GC | A31–S1 | James Johnson (BAR) | IRL |
| C | Austrian International Amateur | GC Linz St Florian | 6–9 | Christopher Carstensen (GER) | AUT |
| C | Coupe de France – Coupe Lignel | Golf Club de Lyon | 14–16 | Christopher Carstensen (GER) | FRA |
| C | Duke of York Young Champions Trophy | Royal Troon | 11–13 | Ragnar Mar Gardarsson (ISL) | SCO |
| C | German National Amateur | Hardenberg | 6–9 | Sebastian Schwind | GER |

# October

## Americas

| | | | | | |
|---|---|---|---|---|---|
| A | Isleworth Collegiate Invitational | Windermere, FL | 21–23 | Michael Kim | USA |
| B | Alister MacKenzie Invitational | Fairfax, CA | 15–16 | Brandon Hagy | USA |
| B | Jack Nicklaus Invitational | Dublin, OH | 8–9/ | Gregory Eason (ENG) | USA |
| B | Jerry Pate National Intercollegiate | Birmingham, AL | 15–16 | Justin Thomas | USA |
| B | OFCC-Fighting Illini Invite | Oly Fields, IL | S30–O2 | Patrick Rodgers | USA |
| B | PAC-12 Preview | North Plains, OR | 8–9 | Trevor Simsby | USA |
| B | US Collegiate Championship | Alpharetta, GA | 19–21 | Patrick Rodgers | USA |
| C | AutoTrader.com Collegiate Classic | Duluth, GA | 15–16 | Dykes Harbin | USA |
| C | Bank of Tennessee @ Blackthorn | Jonesborough, TN | 12–14 | Grant Milner | USA |
| C | Brickyard Collegiate Championship | Macon, GA | 5–7 | Jonathan Grey (ENG)/Sam Straka (AUT) | USA |
| C | Bridgestone Collegiate | Greensboro, NC | 27–28 | Chris Robb (SCO) | USA |
| C | Herb Wimberly Intercollegiate | Las Cruces, NM | 22–23 | Blake Biddle/Chris Gilbert | USA |
| C | Rod Myers Invitational | Durham, NC | 13–14 | Clark Palmer/Julian Suri | USA |
| C | Royal Oaks Intercollegiate | Dallas, TX | 29–30 | Ian Davis/Ian Vandersee | USA |
| C | The Ping Invitational | Stillwater, OK | 6–8 | Gavin Hall | USA |
| D | Bill Cullum Invitational | Simi Valley, CA | 22–23 | Jon Rahm-Rodriguez (ESP) | USA |
| D | David Toms Intercollegiate | Baton Rouge, LA | 6–7 | Andrew Presley | USA |
| D | Fighting Irish Gridiron Classic | South Bend, IN | 7–9 | Thomas Bass | USA |
| D | Firestone Invitational by First Energy | Akron, OH | 8–9 | Sean Bosdosh | USA |
| D | McDonough Cup | Orlando, FL | 29–30 | Daniel Young (SCO) | USA |
| D | Price's Give Em Five Invite | El Paso, TX | 26–27 | Gordon Webb | USA |
| D | Rees Jones Invitational | Daufuskie Island, SC | 1–2 | Niklas Lindstrom (SWE) | USA |
| D | SCVB Pacific Invitational | Stockton, CA | 29–31 | Devon Purser | USA |
| D | UTSA – Lone Star Invitational | San Antonio, TX | 14–16 | Rodolfo Cazaubon (MEX) | USA |

## Big boost for Matthew

Less than a month after his victory in the British Boys' Amateur Championship in which he defeated Welshman Henry James 10 and 8 in the 36-hole final to record the fourth highest margin of victory since the championship began in 1921, English golfer Matthew Fitzpatrick finds himself ranked 12th on the World Amateur Golf Ranking after the success of the Great Britain & Ireland team in the Jacques Léglise Trophy.

| D | Wendy's Kiawah Classic | Kiawah, SC | 28–30 | Caleb Sturgeon | USA |
| D | Wolfpack Intercollegiate | Raleigh, NC | 19–20 | Brandon Dalinka | USA |

| | Asia | | | | |
|---|---|---|---|---|---|
| D | October Grand Prix | Royal Colombo GC | 9–12 | M Arumugam | SRI |
| D | Thailand Amateur Open | Panya Indra GC | 16–19 | Buranatanyarat Itthipat | THA |

| | Australasia | | | | |
|---|---|---|---|---|---|
| B | Keperra Bowl | Keperra GC | 16–19 | Brady Watt | AUS |
| D | Queensland Stroke Play & Amateur | Southport GC, Pacific Harbour G&CC | 21–27 | Dimitrios Papadatos/ Jake McLeod | AUS |

| | Europe | | | | |
|---|---|---|---|---|---|
| A | Eisenhower Trophy Rounds 1–2 | Antalya | 4–7 | Rodrigo Olivero (GUA) | TUR |
| C | European Club Trophy | Minthis Hills GC | 25–27 | Adrien Saddier (FRA) | CYP |
| D | Daily Telegraph Junior Championship | Close House, Colt Course | 23–25 | Matthew Fitzpatrick | ENG |

# November

| | Africa | | | | |
|---|---|---|---|---|---|
| C | International Teams Championship Individual | Maccauvei | 24–25 | Drikus Bruyns | RSA |
| D | Harry Oppenheimer Trophy | Maccauvie | 20–22 | Haydn Porteous | RSA |

| | Americas | | | | |
|---|---|---|---|---|---|
| A | Western Refining Col. All-Am. | El Paso, TX | 19–20 | Kevin Penner | USA |
| B | Gifford Collegiate–CordeValle | San Martin, CA | 5–7 | Rick Lamb | USA |
| C | Polo Junior Classic | Palm Beach Gardens, FL | 17–23 | Adam Wood | USA |
| C | Warrior Wave Invitational | Kauai, HI | 5–7 | Albin Choi (CAN) | USA |
| C | Campeonato Argentino de Aficionados | Estancias GC | 13–18 | Antoni Ferrer (ESP) | ARG |
| C | Copa Juan Carlos Tailhade | Los Lagartos CC | 8–11 | Geoffrey Drakeford (AUS) | ARG |
| D | Stetson – CFSC Invitational | DeLand, FL | 5–6 | Ricardo Gouveia (POR) | USA |
| D | Copa Los Andes | Lagunita CC | 21–25 | Geoffrey Drakeford (AUS) | VEN |

| | Asia | | | | |
|---|---|---|---|---|---|
| D | November Grand Prix | Royal Colombo GC | 20–23 | Nadaraja Thangaraja | SRI |

| | Australasia | | | | |
|---|---|---|---|---|---|
| C | Dunes Medal | The Dunes GC, Victoria | 27–30 | Brady Watt | AUS |
| C | Federal Amateur | Federal GC | 9–11 | Daniel Bringolf | AUS |

| | Europe | | | | |
|---|---|---|---|---|---|
| D | Grand Prix de la Ligue | Golfe de Barbaroux | 9–11 | Julien Marot | FRA |

# December

| | Americas | | | | |
|---|---|---|---|---|---|
| B | Patriot All-America | The Wigwam, AZ | 29–31 | Sebastian Cappelen (DEN) | USA |
| B | South Beach International Amateur | Miami Beach & Normandy Shores GCs | 18–21 | Juan Pablo Hernandez (MEX) | USA |
| C | Dixie Amateur | Heron Bay, Woodlands, Palm Aire | 18–21 | Daniel Berger | USA |
| C | Junior Orange Bowl International | Coral Gables, FL | 27–30 | Patrick Kelly (ENG) | USA |
| D | Jones Cup Junior Invitational | Sea Island GC, GA | 21–23 | K K Limbhasut | USA |

### Australasia

| C | Port Phillip Open Amateur & Victoria Amateur | Kingston Heath, Commonwealth, Yara Yarra" | 14–19 | Taylor MacDonald/Simon Viitakangas | AUS |
|---|---|---|---|---|---|

## January

### Africa

| D | Gauteng North Open | Wingate Park CC | 25–27 | Toby Tree (ENG) | RSA |
|---|---|---|---|---|---|
| D | Kwazulu Natal Stroke Play | Royal Durban GC | 18–20 | Lyle McNeil* | RSA |
| D | Prince's Grant Invitational | Prince's Grant, Kwa-Zulu Natal | 14–16 | Haydn Porteous | RSA |

### Americas

| B | Arizona Intercollegiate | Tucson, AZ | 28–29 | Joel Stalter (FRA)/Michael Kim | USA |
|---|---|---|---|---|---|
| C | Copa de las Americas | Doral Resort, FL | 3–6 | Carlos Ortiz (MEX) | USA |
| C | New Year's Invitational | St Petersburg CC, FL | 3–6 | Toni Hakula (FIN) | USA |
| C | South American Amateur | El Rincon, Bogota | 23–27 | Callum Shinkwin (ENG) | COL |

### Australasia

| A | Australian Master of the Amateurs | The Royal Melbourne GC | 8–11 | Viraat Badhwar | AUS |
|---|---|---|---|---|---|
| B | Australian Amateur | Commonwealth and Woodlands GCs | 15–20 | Cameron Smith | AUS |
| B | Lake Macquarie International | Belmont GC, NSW | 24–27 | Joshua Munn (NZL) | AUS |

### Europe

| D | Campeonato de Canarias | RCG Tenerife | 9–12 | Scott Fernandez | ESP |
|---|---|---|---|---|---|

## February

### Africa

| B | South African Stroke Play | Oubaai GC | 12–15 | Haydn Porteous | RSA |
|---|---|---|---|---|---|
| B | Ten Nations Cup | Kingswood Golf Estate | 6–9 | Brady Watt (AUS) | RSA |
| D | Free State Open | Bloemfontein | 1–3 | Jason Froneman | RSA |

### Americas

| A | Jones Cup Invitational | Sea Island, GA | 1–3 | Sean Dale | USA |
|---|---|---|---|---|---|
| A | Prestige at PGA West | La Quinta, CA | 18–20 | Pedro Figueiredo (POR) | USA |
| A | The Amer Ari Invitational | Kohala Coast, HI | 6–8 | Dominic Bozzelli | USA |
| B | Bayou City Collegiate | Humble, TX | 22–24 | Brandon Stone (RSA) | USA |
| B | John Burns Intercollegiate | Wahiawa, HI | 20–22 | Joel Stalter (FRA) | USA |
| B | John Hayt Collegiate Invitational | Ponte Vedra, FL | 24–25 | Kevin Phelan (IRL) | USA |
| B | Mobile Bay Intercollegiate | Mobile, AL | 18–19 | Niclas Carlsson (SWE) | USA |
| B | SunTrust Gator Invitational | Gainesville, FL | 9–10 | Daniel Berger | USA |
| B | Wyoming Desert Intercollegiate | Palm Desert, CA | 22–24 | Julien Brun (FRA) | USA |
| B | Puerto Rico Classic | Rio Grande | 17–19 | Ibin Choi (CAN) | PUR |
| C | Big Ten Match Play Championship | Bradenton, FL | 8–10 | Julien Brun (FRA) | USA |
| C | HP Boys at Carlton Woods | The Woodlands, TX | 16–18 | Brad Dalke | USA |
| C | North Ranch Intercollegiate | Westlake, CA | 25–26 | Yi Keun Chang (KOR) | USA |

## Big moves for Munn and Shinkwin

New Zealand's Joshua Munn and England's Callum Shinkwin earned big jumps in the World Amateur Golf Ranking in January. Munn climbed 95 places to 239th with his victory in the Lake Macquarie International in Australia, while Shinkwin jumped 163 places with his victory the South American Amateur Championship in Bogota, Colombia.

| C | SeaBest Invitational | Ponte Vedra, FL | 4–5 | Rick Lamb | USA |
| C | The Farms Collegiate Invite | Rancho Santa Fe | 11–12 | Emilio Cuartero (ESP) | USA |
| C | UTSA – Oak Hills Invitational | San Antonio, TX | 11–12 | Kyle Jones | USA |
| D | Wexford Plantation Intercollegiate | Hilton Head, SC | 18–19 | Trey Valentine | USA |
| D | WSU Snowman Getaway | Chandler, AZ | 25–26 | Jace Long/Michael Anderson | USA |

### Australasia

| C | Avondale Medal | Avondale GC | 8–9 | Callan O'Reilly | AUS |
| C | New South Wales Medal & Amateur | The Coast, Bonnie Doon, Royal Sydney | J1–F5 | Thomas Power Horan/ Ben Eccles | AUS |
| D | SBS Invitational-Individual | Invercargill GC | 23–24 | Brent McEwan | NZL |
| D | Tasmanian Open | CC Tasmania | 21–24 | Jordan Zunic | AUS |

### Europe

| B | Portuguese International Amateur | Montado Golf Resort | 13–16 | Goncalo Pinto | POR |

## March

### Africa

| C | Northern Amateur Championship | Randpark | 10–15 | Louis Taylor | RSA |
| C | South Africa v Scotland | Leopard Creek | 4–6 | Louis Taylor | RSA |
| C | South African Amateur | CC Johannesburg | F24–M1 | Thriston Lawrence | RSA |
| D | North West Open | Orkney GC | 22–24 | Callum Mowat | RSA |

### Americas

| A | Schenkel Invitational | Statesboro, GA | 15–17 | Justin Thomas | USA |
| A | SH Collegiate Masters | Las Vegas, NV | 8–10 | Patrick Rodgers | USA |
| B | Bandon Dunes Championship | Bandon, OR | 8–10 | Troix Tonkham | USA |
| B | Don Puckette NIT | Tucson, AZ | 16–17 | Julien Brun (FRA) | USA |
| B | Fresno State Lexus Classic | Fresno, CA | 4–5 | Michael Kim | USA |
| B | General Hackler Championship | Murrells Inlet, SC | 11–12 | Oliver Goss (AUS)/ Taylor Pendrith (CAN) | USA |
| B | Hootie @ Bulls Bay Intercollegiate | Awendaw, SC | 24–26 | Logan Harrell | USA |
| B | Lamkin Grips SD Classic | Chula Vista, CA | 11–12 | Jon Rahm-Rodriguez (ESP) | USA |
| B | Linger Longer Invitational | Greensboro, GA | 23–24 | Cory Whitsett | USA |
| B | Louisiana Classics | Lafayette, LA | 4–5 | Zachary Wright | USA |
| B | Stanford Intercollegiate | Stanford, CA | 28–30 | Paul Barjon (FRA) | USA |
| B | The Duck Invitational | Eugene, OR | 25–26 | Jonathan Ke-Jun Woo (SIN) | USA |
| B | Tiger Invitational | Opelika, AL | 11–12 | Chad Ramey | USA |
| B | USF Invitational | Dade City, FL | 3–5 | Albin Choi (CAN) | USA |
| C | Argent Financial Classic | Choudrant, LA | 11–12 | Rodolfo Cazaubon (MEX) | USA |
| C | Azelea Invitational | Country Club of Charleston, SC | 21–24 | Austin Langdale | USA |
| C | Border Olympics | Laredo, TX | 15–16 | James Newton (ENG) | USA |
| C | C&F Bank Intercollegiate | Williamsburg, VA | 26–26 | Casey Olsen | USA |
| C | Desert Shootout | Goodyear, AZ | 21–23 | Zac Blair | USA |
| C | Furman Intercollegiate | Greenville, SC | 22–24 | Drew Aimone/Scott Fernandez (ESP) | USA |
| C | Palmetto Invitational | Aiken, SC | 11–12 | Matt Atkins | USA |
| C | Seahawk Intercollegiate | Wilmington, NC | 24–25 | Payne McLeod | USA |
| C | Seminole Intercollegiate | Tallahassee, FL | 15–17 | Daniel Berger | USA |
| D | Anteater Invitational | Laguna Niguel, CA | 25–26 | Connor Campbell* | USA |
| D | Bobcat Invitational | Eatonton, GA | 18–19 | Gus Wagoner | USA |
| D | FAU Spring Break Championship | Lake Worth, FL | 29–31 | Tomasz Anderson (ENG) | USA |
| D | Memphis Intercollegiate | Memphis, TN | 25–26 | Dustin Korte | USA |
| D | Mission Inn Spring Spectacular | Howey In The Hills, FL | 16–17 | Jonathan Grey (ENG) | USA |
| D | Samford Intercollegiate | Hoover, AL | 4–5 | Hunter Stewart | USA |

## For further information, visit www.RandA.org/wagr

## Australasia

| | | | | | |
|---|---|---|---|---|---|
| B | Riversdale Cup | Melbourne, Victoria | 7–10 | Brady Watt | AUS |
| D | New Zealand Stroke Play | Paraparauna Beach GC | 21–24 | Cameron Jones | NZL |
| D | Western Australian Amateur | Royal Fremantle GC | 13–17 | Brady Watt | AUS |

## Europe

| | | | | | |
|---|---|---|---|---|---|
| A | European Nations Cup Individual | Sotogrande | 13–16 | Adrien Saddier (FRA) | ESP |
| A | Spanish Amateur | La Manga GC | F27–M3 | Reeve Whitson (IRL) | ESP |
| C | French International Juniors | Le Touquet | 27–31 | Dominic Foos (GER) | FRA |

# April

## Africa

| | | | | | |
|---|---|---|---|---|---|
| D | Sanlam Cape Province Open | George GC, Kingswood | 5–7 | Haydn Porteous | RSA |

## Americas

| | | | | | |
|---|---|---|---|---|---|
| A | Aggie Invitational | Bryan, TX | 6–7 | Cory Whitsett | USA |
| A | SEC Championship | Sea Island, GA | 19–21 | Sebastian Cappelen (DEN) | USA |
| B | ACC Championship | New London, NC | 26–28 | Anders Albertson | USA |
| B | ASU Thunderbird Invitational | Tempe, AZ | 5–7 | Nick Chianello | USA |
| B | Big 12 Championship | Hutchinson, KS | 22–24 | Brandon Stone (RSA) | USA |
| B | Gary Koch Invitational | Tampa, FL | 8–9 | Bo Andrews/Rowin Caron (NED) | USA |
| B | Insperity ASU Invitational | Augusta, GA | 6–7 | Sebastian Soderberg (SWE) | USA |
| B | Junior Invitational at Sage Valley GC | Graniteville, SC | 26–28 | Carson Young | USA |
| B | Morris Williams Intercollegiate | Austin, TX | 13–14 | Finley Ewing | USA |
| B | Terra Cotta Invitational | Naples, FL | 5–7 | Nathan Kimsey (ENG) | USA |
| B | Western Intercollegiate | Santa Cruz, CA | 13–14 | Pedro Figueiredo (POR) | USA |
| C | Atlantic Sun Championship | Braselton, GA | 21–23 | M J Maguire | USA |
| C | BancorpSouth Intercollegiate | Madison, MS | 1–2 | James Newton (ENG) | USA |
| C | Big Ten Championship | French Lick, IN | 26–28 | Thomas Pieters (BEL) | USA |
| C | Boilermaker Invitational | West Lafayette, IN | 20–21 | Robin Sciot-Siegrist (FRA) /Steven Ihm | USA |
| C | C-USA Championship | Texarkana, TX | 21–23 | Roman Robledo | USA |
| C | Irish Creek Collegiate | Kannapolis, NC | 6–7 | Jimmy Beck | USA |
| C | Old Waverly Collegiate Championship | West Point, MS | 8–9 | Emerson Newsome* | USA |
| C | West Coast Conference Championship | Bremerton, WA | 15–17 | Grant Forrest (SCO) | USA |
| C | Wyoming Cowboy Classic | Scottsdale, AZ | 8–9 | Glen Scher | USA |
| D | Big South Championship | Ninety-Six, SC | 21–23 | Mathieu Fenasse (FRA) | USA |
| D | COG Mizzou Intercollegiate | Columbia, MO | 8–9 | Dustin Korte | USA |
| D | Coleman Mid Amateur Invitational | Seminole GC | 25–27 | Michael McCoy | USA |
| D | Florida Blue SSC Championship | Dade City, FL | 14–16 | Ricardo Jose Celia (COL) | USA |
| D | Hawkeye-Great River Entertainment | Iowa City, IA | 13–14 | Chris Gilbert/Steven Ihm | USA |
| D | Ping Cougar Classic | Provo, UT | 26–27 | Zac Blair | USA |
| D | SoCon Championship | Charleston, SC | 21–23 | Josh Lorenzetti | USA |
| D | Sun Belt Conference Tournament | Muscle Shoals, AL | 22–24 | Lane Hulse | USA |
| D | Campeonato Internacional de Aficionados | Lima GC | 17–20 | Patricio Alzamora | PER |
| D | South American Junior Championship | Asuncion GC | 8–14 | Jorge Garcia (VEN) | PAR |

# Dunbar breaks into top 20

Amateur Champion Nothern Ireland's Alan Dunbar, 2012 Amateur Champion and 2013 Masters contestant, was been given a boost on March when he climbed to 20th place on the World Amateur Golf Ranking after climbing 13 places in the weekly re-rank.

## Australasia

| | | | | | |
|---|---|---|---|---|---|
| C | South Australia Amateur Classic | Glenelg GC | 4–7 | Daniel Hoeve | AUS |
| D | New Zealand Amateur Championship | Manawatu GC | 24–27 | Kadin Neho* | NZL |
| D | North Island Stroke Play | Poverty Bay GC | 4–7 | Oscar Cadenhead | NZL |

## Europe

| | | | | | |
|---|---|---|---|---|---|
| B | Hampshire Salver | Blackmoor & North Hants GCs | 19–21 | Callum Shinkwin | ENG |
| C | Coupe Mouchy | Golf de Fontainebleau | 25–28 | Thomas Elissalde | FRA |
| C | Spain v England Team Match | RCG El Prat, Barcelona | 27–28 | Thomas Elissalde (FRA) | ESP |
| C | West of Ireland Amateur Open | County Sligo GC | M29–A2 | Rory McNamara | IRL |
| D | Battle Trophy | Craighead Links, Crail | 20–21 | Graeme Robertson | SCO |
| D | Carey Cup | The European Club | 28–29 | Graeme Robertson (SCO) | IRL |
| D | Duncan Putter | Southerndown GC | 13–14 | Tim Harry | WAL |
| D | Italian Stroke Play – Franco Bevione Trophy | Torino GC | 25–28 | Edoardo Raffae Lipparelli | ITA |
| D | Scottish Champion of Champions | Leven Golfing Society | 5–7 | Scott Borrowman | SCO |

# May

## Africa

| | | | | | |
|---|---|---|---|---|---|
| D | Boland Amateur Open | Devonvale Golf & Wine Estate | A29–M1 | Haydn Porteous | RSA |
| D | Kwazulu-Natal Amateur Championship | Umhlali CC | 22–26 | Zander Lombard | RSA |

## Americas

| | | | | | |
|---|---|---|---|---|---|
| A | NCAA Columbus Regional | Columbus, OH | 16–18 | James Erkenbeck | USA |
| A | NCAA Pullman Regional | Pullman, WA | 16–18 | Michael Weaver/Sam Smith | USA |
| A | NCAA Tallahassee Regional | Tallahassee, FL | 16–18 | Cheng-tsung Pan (TPE) | USA |
| A | Pac-12 Championship | Los Angeles, CA | A29–M1 | Max Homa | USA |
| B | NCAA Baton Rouge Regional | Baton Rouge, LA | 16–18 | Scott Strohmeyer | USA |
| B | NCAA Fayetteville Regional | Fayetteville, AR | 16–18 | Mario Clemens (MEX) | USA |
| B | NCAA Tempe Regional | Tempe, AZ | 16–18 | Gregory Eason (ENG) | USA |
| C | Mountain West Championship | Tucson, AZ | 3–5 | Kevin Penner | USA |
| C | Thunderbird International Junior | Scottsdale, AZ | 25–27 | Jorge Garcia (VEN) | USA |
| D | Memorial Amateur | Ancil Hoffman Park GC | 25–27 | Joshua Stone | USA |
| D | Mid-American Conference Championship | Nashport, OH | 3–5 | Taylor Pendrith (CAN) | USA |
| D | NCAA D2 South – SE Region | Howie in the Hills, FL | 6–8 | Ben Taylor (ENG) | USA |
| D | NCAA Division II Championship | Hershey, PA | 19–24 | Tim Crouch | USA |
| D | WAC Championship | Henderson, NV | A29–M1 | Paul McConnell | USA |

## Asia

| | | | | | |
|---|---|---|---|---|---|
| C | Malaysian Amateur Open | Royal Pahang G&CC | 23–26 | Kevin Marques (AUS) | MAS |

## Australasia

| | | | | | |
|---|---|---|---|---|---|
| B | Australian Interstate Team Matches | Tasmania GC | A30–M3 | Doan Van Dinh (VIE)* | AUS |

---

# History-maker triumphs again

China's Tianlang Guan, who made history in April as the youngest ever competitor in the Masters, earned low amateur honours at Augusta National as the only one of six amateurs to make the cut. and as a result made it into the world top 100, improving 61 places to 100th.

## Europe

| | | | | | |
|---|---|---|---|---|---|
| A | The Lytham Trophy | Royal Lytham & St Annes | 3–5 | Albert Eckhardt (FIN) | ENG |
| B | International de France (Coupe Murat) | Chantilly | 24–26 | Adrien Saddier | FRA |
| B | Irish Amateur Open | The Royal Dublin GC | 10–12 | Robert Cannon | IRL |
| B | Welsh Amateur Open Stroke Play | Royal Porthcawl | 17–19 | Rhys Pugh | WAL |
| C | South East of England Links Championship | Royal Cinque Ports & Royal St George's GCs | 9–11 | Max Orrin | ENG |
| D | Italian International Amateur | Villa D'Este | 11–15 | Federico Zucchetti | ITA |
| D | Scottish Area Team Championship | Crail Golfing Society | 18–19 | Federico Zucchetti (ITA) | SCO |

# June

## Americas

| | | | | | |
|---|---|---|---|---|---|
| A | NCAA DI Medal & Team Match | Atlanta, GA | M28–J2 | Max Homa | USA |
| A | Northeast Amateur | Wannamoisett CC, RI | 19–22 | Cory Whitsett | USA |
| A | Sunnehanna Amateur | Johnstown, PA | 13–16 | Steven Ihm | USA |
| B | California Amateur Championship | Monterey Peninsula CC | 17–22 | Cory McElyea | USA |
| B | Dogwood Invitational | Druid Hills Golf Club | 24–29 | Michael Johnson | USA |
| B | Monroe Invitational | Pittsford, NY | 12–15 | Nicholas Palladino | USA |
| B | Palmer Cup | Wilmington CC | 7–9 | Nicholas Palladino | USA |
| B | Palmetto Amateur | Palmetto Golf Club | 5–8 | Nicholas Reach | USA |
| C | FJ Invitational | Sedgefield CC | 11–14 | Matt Gilchrist | USA |
| C | Greystone Invitational | Birmingham, AL | 20–23 | Tyler Hitchner* | USA |
| C | Mexican Amateur | Guadalajara CC | 6–9 | Mario Clemens | MEX |
| D | Alabama State Amateur | Hoover CC | 6–9 | Michael Johnson | USA |
| D | Birmingham National Invitational | Birmingham, AL | M31–J2 | John Engler | USA |
| D | Florida Amateur | Jupiter Hills Club, Jupiter, FL | 20–23 | Sam Horsfield | USA |
| D | Ike Championship | Wykagyl CC, NY | 24–25 | Cameron Wilson | USA |
| D | North Carolina Amateur | Forsyth CC, Winston Salem, NC | 13–16 | Steven Brame* | USA |
| D | Rice Planters Amateur | Snee Farm CC | 17–22 | Maverick Antcliff (AUS) | USA |
| D | Southeastern Amateur | CC of Colombus | 12–15 | Seth Reeves | USA |
| D | Southwestern Amateur | Desert Mountain Club, AZ | 18–21 | J T Poston | USA |
| D | Texas Amateur Championship | Lakeside CC, Houston, TX | 13–16 | Doug Manor* | USA |
| D | Virginia State Amateur | The Homestead (Cascades), VA | 25–29 | Brinson Paolini | USA |

## Asia

| | | | | | |
|---|---|---|---|---|---|
| C | Putra Cup | Sherwood Hills GC | 27–30 | Gavin Kyle Green (MAS) | PHI |
| C | Toyota Junior World Cup | Chukyo GC, Ishino Course | 18–21 | Jorge Garcia (VEN) | JPN |

## Europe

| | | | | | |
|---|---|---|---|---|---|
| A | Brabazon Trophy | Formby GC | 26–29 | Jordan Smith | ENG |
| A | St Andrews Links Trophy | St Andrews, Jubilee and Old | 7–9 | Neil Raymond (ENG) | SCO |
| A | The Amateur Championship | Royal Cinque Ports & Prince's | 17–22 | Garrick Porteous | ENG |
| B | Scottish Open Stroke Play | Southerness GC | M31–J2 | Garrick Porteous (ENG) | SCO |
| C | Danish International Championship | Silkeborg GC | M31–J2 | Thomas Elissalde (FRA) | DEN |
| C | Swiss International Championship | GC Lausanne | 28–30 | Mathieu Fenasse (FRA) | SUI |
| C | The Berkshire Trophy | The Berkshire GC | 22–23 | Ryan Evans | ENG |
| D | East of Scotland Championship | Lundin GC | 29–30 | Jamie Savage | SCO |
| D | Tennant Cup | Glasgow Gailes & Killermont | 22–23 | Jack McDonald | SCO |

## Finnish triumph at Lytham

While Finland's Albert Eckhardt may have been a relative unknown when he arrived to compete for the Lytham Trophy at the Open Champiuonship venue in May, he left as Finland's highest ranked amateur having jumped 286 places to 144th position.

# July

## Americas

| | | | | | |
|---|---|---|---|---|---|
| A | Porter Cup | Niagara Falls CC, NY | 24–27 | Taylor Pendrith (CAN) | USA |
| A | Sahalee Players Championship | Sammamish, WA | 1–3 | Andrew Yun | USA |
| A | Southern Amateur Championship | The Club at Carlton Woods | 17–20 | Zach Olsen | USA |
| A | The Players Amateur | Berkeley Hall GC, SC | 8–14 | Hunter Stewart | USA |
| B | North & South Amateur | Pinehurst, NC | 1–6 | Andrew Dorn | USA |
| B | Trans-Mississippi Championship | Fairfax, CA | 9–11 | Bryson Dechambeau | USA |
| B | US Amateur Public Links C/ship | Laurel Hill GC, VA | 15–20 | Jordan Niebrugge | USA |
| B | US Junior Amateur Championship | Truckee, CA | 22–27 | Scottie Scheffler | USA |
| C | Cardinal Amateur | Cardinal G&CC | 19–21 | Taylor Coalson | USA |
| C | Pacific Coast Amateur | Capilano G&CC, W. Vancouver, BC | 23–26 | Tyler Raber (USA) | CAN |
| C | Rolex Tournament of Champions | Lancaster CC, PA | 9–12 | Benjamin Griffin | USA |
| C | Wyndham Cup | The Bridges at Rancho Santa Fe, CA | 16–18 | Benjamin Griffin | USA |
| D | Callaway Junior World Championship | Torrey Pines | 16–19 | Jose Mendez (CRC) | USA |
| D | Carolinas Amateur | Kiawah Island, SC | 11–14 | Carter Jenkins | USA |
| D | Oglethorpe Invitational | Savannah, GA | 26–28 | Jack Hall | USA |
| D | Ontario Amateur | Oslerbrook G&CC | 9–12 | Stephane Dubois | CAN |
| D | Pacific Northwest Amateur | Bandon Dunes GC & Bandon Trails GC | 6–11 | Cameron Peck | USA |
| D | SCGA Amateur Championship | San Diego CC | 12–14 | Beau Hossler | USA |

## Asia

| | | | | | |
|---|---|---|---|---|---|
| D | Bear Creek Cup | Pocheon | 16–19 | Sang-yeop Lee | KOR |
| D | Neighbors Trophy | Nagano | 24–26 | Nam-hun Kim (KOR) | JPN |

## Europe

| | | | | | |
|---|---|---|---|---|---|
| A | European Amateur Team C\ship | Silkeborg Ry GC | 9–13 | Alvaro Ortiz (CRC) | DEN |
| B | South of England Open Amateur Championship | Walton Heath GC | 23–25 | Riccardo Michelini (ITA) | ENG |
| C | Biarritz Cup | Golf de Biarritz | 11–14 | Ryan Evans (ENG) | FRA |
| C | European Boys Team Championship | Murcar Links GC | 9–13 | Ryan Evans (ENG) | SCO |
| C | German International Amateur | Club – Golf Neuhof e.V. | 25–28 | Maximilian Rottluff | GER |
| D | Cameron Corbett Vase | Haggs Castle GC | 6–7 | Daniel Young | SCO |
| D | Campeonato de Espana | CG Lomas – Bosque | 25–28 | Emilio Cuartero | ESP |
| D | Dutch Junior Open | Toxandria GC | 17–20 | Michael Kraaij | NED |
| D | European Challenge Trophy Ind. | Kuneticka Hora | 11–13 | Thomas Detry (BEL) | CZE |
| D | Grand Prix de Chiberta | Golf de Chiberta Anglet | 4–7 | Victor Perez | FRA |
| D | North of Ireland Amateur | Royal Portrush GC | 8–12 | Chris Selfridge | IRL |
| D | Sutherland Chalice | Dumfries & Galloway GC | 13–14 | Matthew Clark | SCO |
| D | Tillman Trophy | Burnham & Berrow GC | 8–10 | Paul Kinnear/Ryan Cornfield | ENG |

# August

## Americas

| | | | | | |
|---|---|---|---|---|---|
| A | Western Amateur | The Alotian Club, AR | J29–A4 | Jordan Niebrugge | USA |
| B | Canadian Amateur Championship | Royal Colwood GC, Gorge Vale GC | 6–9 | Eli Cole (USA) | CAN |
| D | Junior PGA Championship | Trump National GC, Washington DC | J30–A2 | Tyler McDaniel | USA |
| D | N. California Amateur Match Play | Spyglass Hill GC, CA | 12–16 | Ben Geyer | USA |
| D | S. Carolina Amateur Championship | The Members Club At Woodcreek | 1–4 | Carson Young | USA |

For further information, visit www.RandA.org/wagr

| | | | | | |
|---|---|---|---|---|---|
| | | **Asia** | | | |
| D | Iksung Cup Maekyung Amateur | Lakeside CC, Seoul | 27–30 | Nam-hun Kim | KOR |
| D | Song Am Cup | DaeGu CC | 20–23 | Chang-woo Lee | KOR |
| D | Sri Lanka Amateur | Royal Colombo GC | 20–25 | Syed Saqib Ahmed (IND) | SRI |
| | | **Europe** | | | |
| A | English Amateur | Frilford Heath GC | J29–A3 | Callum Shinkwin | ENG |
| B | Home Internationals | Ganton GC | 14–16 | Callum Shinkwin | ENG |
| C | Boys Amateur Championship | Royal Liverpool/Wallasey GCs | 13–18 | Ewen Ferguson (SCO) | ENG |
| C | Jacques Léglise Trophy | Royal St David's | 30–31 | Ewen Ferguson (SCO) | WAL |
| C | Scottish Amateur Championship | Blairgowrie GC | J29–A3 | Alexander Culverwell | SCO |
| D | Finnish Amateur | Helsingin GC | 15–17 | Joel Girrbach (SUI) | FIN |
| D | Lee Westwood Trophy | Rotherham GC | 13–15 | Joe Dean | ENG |
| D | Midland Open Amateur | Gay Hill & Fulford Heath GCs | 23–24 | Jamie Bower | ENG |
| D | North of England Open Youths | Middlesborough GC | 6–8 | Andrew Wilson* | ENG |

## Season 2013–2014

The R&A Men's World Amateur Golf Ranking season runs from September until the following August when the Mark McCormack Medal is presented following the US Men's Amateur Championship. Results for the remainder of the calendar year will be included in the following year's edition of *The R&A Golfer's Handbook*.

## Previous McCormack Medal winners

| 2007 | Colt Knost (USA) | 5 weeks as No 1 |
|---|---|---|
| 2008 | Danny Lee (NZL) | 34 weeks as No 1 |
| 2009 | Nick Taylor (CAN) | 20 weeks as No 1 |
| 2010 | Peter Uihlein (USA) | 49 weeks as No 1 |
| 2011 | Patrick Cantlay (USA) | 55 weeks as No 1 |
| 2012 | Chris Williams (USA) | 46 weeks as No 1 |

## Month by month in 2013

Justin Rose becomes England's first US Open winner since Tony Jacklin in 1970 when he pushes Phil Mickelson into a sixth runner-up finish in the event at Merion. Inbee Park makes it three out of three in the women's majors, adding the LPGA Championship and US Open to the Kraft Nabisco, and the new Amateur champion is England's Garrick Porteous.

# European Amateur Ranking 2012–2013

English players dominated the European Amateur Ranking in 2012–2013 with 22 entries in the top 100. Ireland was second with 11 places and Scotland third with 10. France had eight players in the top 100 with France and Spain finishing the season with eight apiece. The European Rankings are extracted from WAGR and are finalised at the same time.

| | | | Divisor | Points | | | | | Divisor | Points |
|---|---|---|---|---|---|---|---|---|---|---|
| 1 | Matthew Fitzpatrick | ENG | 50 | 1,313.05 | | 52 | Martin Keskari | GER | 44 | 912.22 |
| 2 | Sebastian Cappelen | DEN | 53 | 1,195.28 | | 53 | Thomas Sorensen | DEN | 46 | 911.14 |
| 3 | Garrick Porteous | ENG | 68 | 1,131.62 | | 54 | Jimmy Mullen | ENG | 47 | 910.28 |
| 4 | Nathan Kimsey | ENG | 70 | 1,131.07 | | 55 | Paul Howard | ENG | 39 | 910.26 |
| 5 | Thomas Detry | BEL | 61 | 1,105.74 | | 56 | Riccardo Michelini | ITA | 54 | 906.94 |
| 6 | Jordan Smith | ENG | 54 | 1,103.70 | | 57 | Lauri Ruuska | FIN | 36 | 906.25 |
| 7 | Ryan Evans | ENG | 55 | 1,086.06 | | 58 | Cormac Sharvin | IRL | 60 | 904.17 |
| 8 | Julien Brun | FRA | 56 | 1,077.68 | | 59 | Graeme Robertson | SCO | 72 | 901.16 |
| 9 | Scott Fernandez | ESP | 53 | 1,075.94 | | 60 | Joe Dean | POL | 54 | 900.00 |
| 10 | Joel Stalter | FRA | 59 | 1,061.23 | | 61 | Adrian Meronk | ENG | 35 | 900.00 |
| 11 | Gregory Eason | ENG | 50 | 1,045.00 | | 62 | Ben Taylor | ENG | 42 | 898.21 |
| 12 | Harry Casey | ENG | 42 | 1,044.05 | | 63 | Kristoffer Ventura | NOR | 48 | 892.01 |
| 13 | Toni Hakula | FIN | 62 | 1,036.09 | | 64 | Kristian Johannessen | NOR | 64 | 891.02 |
| 14 | Renato Paratore | ITA | 60 | 1,031.67 | | 65 | Michael Kraaij | NED | 33 | 887.88 |
| 15 | Jon Rahm-Rodriguez | ESP | 54 | 1,026.93 | | 66 | Erik Myllymaki | FIN | 38 | 886.84 |
| 16 | Tomasz Anderson | ENG | 43 | 1,023.26 | | 67 | -Rhys Pugh | WAL | 55 | 886.36 |
| 17 | Benjamin Rusch | SUI | 38 | 1,022.37 | | 68 | Ryan Fricker | ENG | 46 | 884.51 |
| 18 | Ashley Chesters | ENG | 48 | 1,015.97 | | 69 | Pep Angles Ros | ESP | 46 | 883.42 |
| 19 | Dermot McElroy | IRL | 63 | 1,013.23 | | 70 | Ben Stow | ENG | 58 | 883.41 |
| 20 | Matthias Schwab | AUT | 35 | 1,009.64 | | 71 | Ivan Cantero | ESP | 46 | 880.98 |
| 21 | Jack Hume | IRL | 33 | 998.99 | | 72 | Chris Selfridge | IRL | 68 | 878.68 |
| 22 | Mario Galiano Aguilar | ESP | 49 | 997.96 | | 73 | Daniel Young | SCO | 45 | 878.61 |
| 23 | Rory McNamara | IRL | 47 | 996.81 | | 74 | Haraldur Franklin | ISL | 35 | 878.57 |
| 24 | Grant Forrest | SCO | 58 | 983.62 | | | Magnus | | | |
| 25 | Ricardo Gouveia | POR | 46 | 978.08 | | 75 | Erik Oja | SWE | 52 | 877.84 |
| 26 | Emilio Cuartero | ESP | 53 | 978.07 | | 76 | Edouard Amacher | SUI | 49 | 876.53 |
| 27 | Maximilian Roehrig | GER | 46 | 973.91 | | 77 | Andreas Halvorsen | NOR | 59 | 871.61 |
| 28 | James Newton | ENG | 31 | 973.79 | | 78 | Lars van Meijel | NED | 51 | 870.10 |
| 29 | Nick Marsh | ENG | 55 | 973.64 | | 79 | Richard O'Donovan | IRL | 39 | 869.66 |
| 30 | Mads Soegaard | DEN | 48 | 973.49 | | 80 | Ewan Scott | SCO | 71 | 869.48 |
| 31 | Maximilian Rottluff | GER | 45 | 972.22 | | 81 | Michael Saunders | ENG | 62 | 869.35 |
| 32 | Toby Tree | ENG | 55 | 965.45 | | 82 | Mathias Eggenberger | SUI | 53 | 866.04 |
| 33 | Rowin Caron | NED | 58 | 960.13 | | 83 | Clement Sordet | FRA | 53 | 865.09 |
| 34 | James Ross | SCO | 46 | 959.78 | | 84 | Ashton Turner | ENG | 45 | 864.44 |
| 35 | Reeve Whitson | IRL | 56 | 957.14 | | 85 | Mathieu Decottignies- | FRA | 59 | 863.35 |
| 36 | Dominic Foos | GER | 66 | 955.18 | | | Lafon | | | |
| 37 | Paul Barjon | FRA | 48 | 953.44 | | 86 | Marcus Kinhult | SCO | 56 | 862.50 |
| 38 | Robbie van West | NED | 47 | 952.13 | | 87 | Scott Borrowman | SWE | 26 | 862.50 |
| 39 | Tim Gornik | SLO | 29 | 944.83 | | 88 | Jamie Bower | ENG | 40 | 860.00 |
| 40 | Victor Perez | FRA | 60 | 941.88 | | 89 | Stefano Pitoni | ITA | 49 | 859.01 |
| 41 | Albert Eckhardt | FIN | 49 | 938.44 | | 90 | Kevin Hesbois | BEL | 55 | 857.27 |
| 42 | Jack McDonald | SCO | 70 | 936.19 | | 91 | Eamon Bradley | IRL | 45 | 857.00 |
| 43 | Bradley Neil | SCO | 53 | 935.85 | | 92 | Antoni Ferrer | ESP | 45 | 855.56 |
| 44 | Daniel Jennevret | SWE | 41 | 932.93 | | 93 | Charlie Bull | ENG | 53 | 854.72 |
| 45 | Paul Dunne | IRL | 50 | 932.80 | | 94 | Gary Hurley | IRL | 34 | 854.04 |
| 46 | Pontus Gad | SWE | 42 | 930.95 | | 95 | Jamie Savage | SCO | 55 | 850.91 |
| 47 | Mathieu Fenasse | FRA | 49 | 930.61 | | 96 | David Morago | ESP | 51 | 849.02 |
| 48 | Juuso Kahlos | FIN | 33 | 928.79 | | 97 | Ugo Coussaud | FRA | 37 | 848.65 |
| 49 | Niclas Carlsson | SWE | 47 | 924.47 | | 98 | Richard James | WAL | 60 | 848.38 |
| 50 | Nicolai Kristensen | DEN | 42 | 916.67 | | 99 | Robin Dawson | IRL | 32 | 843.75 |
| 51 | Gavin Moynihan | IRL | 24 | 912.50 | | 100 | David Boote | WAL | 62 | 843.55 |

For the full European Amateur Rankings, visit www.ega-golf.ch

# English players dominated amateur majors in 2013

The 2013 season was a great year for English amateur golfers who took three of the four major amateur titles.

Matthew Fitzpatrick, the 2012 Boys Amateur Champion, qualified for The Open Championship at Muirfield and beat the other five amateurs in the field to take the Silver Medal awarded to the low amateur. He then went on to win the US Amateur Championship at The Country Club in Brookline, Massachusetts where he beat Australia's Oliver Goss in the final. With this achievement, Fitzpatrick became the first Englishman since Harold Hilton in 1911 to win the event.

The teenager from Sheffield ended the season as number one on the World Amateur Golf Ranking and was duly awarded the Mark H. McCormack Medal.

Continuing England's dominance of the amateur majors, Garrick Porteous from Bamburgh Castle claimed the honours in the Amateur Championship at Royal Cinque Ports and Prince's Golf Clubs when he defeated Toni Hakula from Finland 6 and 5 in the final.

To complete the trio of victories, Ashley Chesters from Shropshire took the European Amateur Championship title at Real Club de Golf El Prat in Catalunya, Spain, when he defeated Spaniard David Morago. With his victory, Ashley earned a place in the 2014 Open Championship at Royal Liverpool.

The fourth major amateur title – the Asia-Pacific Amateur Championship – was won by Korea's Chang-woo Lee who defeated Japan's Shohei Hasegawa by three shots at Nanshan International Golf Club in Shandong Province, China.

# Homa adds his name to a prestigious list

To any aspiring amateur golfer, a list of past tournament winners that included Jack Nicklaus, Tiger Woods, Phil Mickelson, Luke Donald, Charles Howell III, Justin Leonard, Curtis Strange, Ben Crenshaw and Hale Irwin would be one to join and University of California student Max Homa did just that when he became the individual winner of the NCAA Division I Men's Golf Championship, college golf's most important tournament.

# Manawatu-Wanganui win at last

Manawatu-Wanganui had never won the New Zealand Interprovincials until 2013 when they beat seven-times winner Bay of Plenty 4 ½–½ in the final at the North Shore Golf Club. It was a revenge win because Bay of Plenty had beaten Manawatu-Wanganui in a play-off in 2012.

# A bumper year for English amateur golfers

Of the 33 European victors in the Top 100 of the Men's World Amateur Golf Ranking at the conclusion of the 2012–2013 season, no less than 17 of those were down to English players. In the previous two seasons, the respective figures were eight from 31 (2011–2012) and nine from 29 (2010–2011).

The USA continues to dominate the Top 100 with 46 entries in 2012–2013 where they recovered slightly from their 42 victories in 2011–2012, down from 56 in 2010–2011.

Players from Australasia took third place having ousted Asian players from the position they held in the previous two seasons.

# Major Amateur Championships 2013

## 5th Asia–Pacific Amateur Championship (Inaugurated 2009)
*Nanshan International GC, Longkou City, China* [7006–71]

### Lee is second Korean to win Asia–Pacific title

Nineteen-year-old Lee Chang-Woo is the new Asia–Pacific champion after shooting a final round 70 at Nanshan International Golf Club in China for a three shot victory over Shoihei Hasegawa from Japan.

Lee was the only golfer to break par in the gusty windy conditions fininishing with a four round aggregate of 281. Kenta Konishi, also from Japan, finished third on his own on 285.

Lee, who is the second Korean to win the title – Han Chang-won was the winner at the inaugural championship at Mission Hills in 2009 – earns a place in the 2014 Masters tournament at Augusta and is guaranteed a spot in the International Final Qualifying for the Open Championship at Royal Liverpool in July along with runner-up Hasegawa.

Going into the final round, Lee held a one stroke lead over 16-year-old Chinese golfer Dou Zecheng who was attempting to emulate fellow countryman Guan Tianling who won in Bangkok in 2012.

Having difficulty on the fast Garden Course greens on the final day, Zecheng slipped to a 75 and finished joint fourth with Lucas Herbert from Australia and Korea's Lee Soo-min.

Lee, who impressed with a superb display of ball striking, admitted that playing in the Masters had always been a dream of his. He arrived at Nanshan as one of the favourites having won the Dongbu Promi Open on the Korean professional circuit earlier in the year and then finishing tied second with former World No 1 Rory McIlroy in the Korean Open a week before the Asia–Pacific event.

Lee admitted to being "a bit nervous" on the last two days. "I kept looking at the leader boards. I have never been so excited but I just tried to keep calm. It worked. I held my nerve and knew, after my tee shot at the 17th, that I was going to win."

Defending champion Guan shot a third round 68 but the 15-year-old, who became the youngest golfer ever to play in the Masters, was not at his best and finished joint eighth alongside the 2012 runner-up Pan Cheng-tsung, Japan's Kazuya Koura and Brady Watt of Australia.

Another Australian, Oliver Goss, who finished seventh on 288, will join Lee at the Masters having qualified previously as runner-up to England's Matthew Fitzpatrick in the 2013 US Amateur Championship.

| | | |
|---|---|---|
| 1 | Chang-woo Lee (KOR) | 70-72-69-70—281 |
| 2 | Shohei Hasegawa (JPN) | 72-70-71-71—284 |
| 3 | Kenta Konishi (JPN) | 76-71-68-70—285 |
| 4 | Lucas Herbert (AUS) | 73-75-71-68—287 |
| | Soo-Min Lee (KOR) | 73-70-74-70—287 |
| | Dou Zecheng (CHN) | 68-75-69-75—282 |
| 7 | Oliver Goss (AUS) | 72-73-71-72—288 |
| 8 | Brady Watt (AUS) | 71-74-73-71—289 |
| | Cheng-tsung Pan (TPE) | 72-73-73-71—289 |
| | Kazuya Koura (JPN) | 74-69-74-71—289 |
| | Guan Tianlang (CHN) | 74-74-68-73—289 |
| 12 | Taihei Sato (JPN) | 73-71-74-73—291 |
| | Zhang Jin (CHN) | 72-76-71-72—291 |
| | Poom Saksansin (THA) | 72-75-71-73—291 |
| 15 | Tae Woo Kim (KOR) | 75-75-67-75—292 |
| 16 | Anton Arboleda (PHI) | 74-74-72-73—293 |
| 17 | Jin Cheng (CHN) | 76-72-75-71—294 |
| | Daniel Hoeve (AUS) | 77-75-70-72—294 |

## Asian Amateur Championship *continued*

| 19 | Sam An (NZL) | 74-74-74-73—295 |
|---|---|---|
| 20 | Eric Sugimoto (JPN) | 73-74-77-72—296 |
| | Taylor James MacDonald (AUS) | 72-74-75-75—296 |
| 22 | Sarit Suwannarut (THA) | 78-75-70-74—297 |
| | Blair Riordan (NZL) | 74-73-74-76—297 |
| | Vaughan McCall (NZL) | 73-76-72-76—297 |
| 25 | Chieh-Po Lee (TPE) | 79-75-70-74—298 |
| | Danthai Boonma (THA) | 76-74-75-73—298 |
| | Nam-Hun Kim (KOR) | 76-72-76-74—298 |
| | Gyu-Bin Kim (KOR) | 77-76-73-72—298 |
| | Luke Toomey (NZL) | 74-75-74-75—298 |
| 30 | Khai Jei Low (MAS) | 79-75-69-76—299 |
| | Teng Kao (TPE) | 78-71-78-72—299 |
| | Jonathan Woo (SIN) | 77-74-71-77—299 |
| 33 | Nick Voke (NZL) | 75-72-74-79—300 |
| 34 | Shinichi Mizuno (HKG) | 74-76-75-76—301 |
| | Trishul Chinnappa (IND) | 77-75-73-76—301 |
| | Joshua Shou (SIN) | 77-75-75-74—301 |
| | Viraj Madappa (IND) | 80-72-69-80—301 |
| | Wang Xichen (CHN) | 74-77-78-72—301 |
| 39 | Jerome Ng (SIN) | 75-75-75-77—302 |
| | Karan Taunk (IND) | 80-78-68-76—302 |
| | Udayan Mane (IND) | 80-77-72-73—302 |
| 42 | Tawan Phongphun (THA) | 74-79-74-76—303 |
| | Yu-Jui Liu (TPE) | 78-77-73-75—303 |
| 44 | Chang-Heng Lin (TPE) | 73-73-78-80—304 |
| | Mikumu Horikawa (JPN) | 77-75-76-76—304 |
| | Kyo-Won Koo (KOR) | 81-74-78-71—304 |
| | Joshua Munn (NZL) | 80-79-75-70—304 |
| 48 | Rupert Zaragosa (PHI) | 77-77-74-77—305 |
| 49 | Chen Zihao (CHN) | 75-80-75-76—306 |
| | Ned Howard (COK) | 81-76-76-73—306 |
| 51 | Marc Ong (SIN) | 75-75-77-80—307 |
| 52 | Johnson Poh (SIN) | 75-76-76-81—308 |
| | Chan Tuck Soon (MAS) | 75-77-77-79—308 |
| | Mohd Afif Mohd Razif (MAS) | 80-75-76-77—308 |
| | Nattawat Suvajanakorn (THA) | 77-76-83-72—308 |
| 56 | Vijitha Bandara (SRI) | 79-76-73-82—310 |
| 57 | Wafiyuddin Abdul Manaf (MAS) | 80-77-75-79—311 |
| | Yang Yinong (CHN) | 80-78-76-77—311 |
| | Niko Vui (SAM) | 79-80-76-76—311 |
| 60 | Andres Saldana (PHI) | 78-77-76-84—315 |
| 61 | Justin Quiban (PHI) | 78-80-77-81—316 |

The following players missed the cut:

| 62 | Manu Gandas (IND) | 83-77—160 |
|---|---|---|
| | Jieyu Xiao (MAC) | 81-79—160 |
| | Thammasack Bouahom (LAO) | 80-80—160 |
| | Anuresh Chandra (FIJ) | 81-79—160 |
| | Ghazanfar Mehmood (PAK) | 80-80—160 |
| | Wang Ziting (CHN) | 83-77—160 |
| | Tiger Lee (HKG) | 83-77—160 |
| | Ye Htet Aung (MYA) | 85-75—160 |
| | Abdul Hadi (SIN) | 78-82—160 |
| 71 | Luo Xuewen (CHN) | 83-78—161 |
| | Olaf Allen (FIJ) | 80-81—161 |
| | Muhammad Waseem Rana (PAK) | 83-78—161 |
| 74 | Doan Van Dinh (VIE) | 83-79—162 |
| | Syed Saqib Ahmed (IND) | 80-82—162 |

| 74T | Kirk Tuaiti (COK) | 81-81—162 |
|---|---|---|
| 77 | Pulou Faaaliga (SAM) | 78-85—163 |
| | Md Nazim (BAN) | 80-83—163 |
| | Muhd. Thaznim Hamdan (MAS) | 85-78—163 |
| 80 | Dechen Ugyen (BHU) | 85-79—164 |
| | Solomon Emilio Rosidin (MAS) | 82-82—164 |
| | Nasser Yacoob (BRN) | 84-80—164 |
| | Muhammad Rehman (PAK) | 79-85—164 |
| 84 | Salman Jehangir (PAK) | 84-81—165 |
| | Maung Maung Oo (MYA) | 76-89—165 |
| 86 | George Rukabo (SOL) | 84-82—166 |
| | Redge Camacho (GUM) | 86-80—166 |
| | Geoffrey Drakeford (AUS) | 88-78—166 |
| 89 | Sung-I Yu (TPE) | 84-83—167 |

| 90 | Vanseiha Seng (CAM) | 87-81—168 |
|---|---|---|
| | Chak Hou Tang (MAC) | 89-79—168 |
| | B A Rohana (SRI) | 90-78—168 |
| 93 | Nguyen Gia Hong (VIE) | 89-80—169 |
| 94 | Bishnu Sharma (NEP) | 87-83—170 |
| | Brian Taikiri (PNG) | 89-81—170 |
| | Sisira Kumara (SRI) | 79-91—170 |
| | Akl Rachid (LBN) | 85-85—170 |
| | Qu Hongxin (CHN) | 85-85—170 |
| 99 | Elki Kow (INA) | 84-87—171 |
| | Navinda Ranga (SRI) | 85-86—171 |
| 101 | M Arumugam (SRI) | 84-90—174 |
| | Tshendra Dorji (BHU) | 90-84—174 |
| 103 | Ulziidelger Delgermaa (MON) | 90-85—175 |
| | Morgan Annato (PNG) | 94-81—175 |
| 105 | Lon Lindsey (GUM) | 88-89—177 |

| 106 | Dinesh Prajapati (NEP) | 89-90—179 | 112 | Mohamed Diab | 92-93—185 | 116 | Osmonkulov | 94-108—202 |
|-----|------------------------|-----------|-----|--------------|-----------|-----|------------|------------|
| 107 | Ben Felani (SOL) | 91-89—180 | | Alnoaimi (BRN) | | | Kuban (KGZ) | |
| | Thammalack | 89-91—180 | 113 | Mendsaikhan Gangaa | 95-98—193 | | Ramzi Bahsoun (LIB) | WD |
| | Bouahom (LAO) | | | (MON) | | | Md Sajib Ali (BAN) | DQ |
| | N Amarapadma (SRI) | 90-90—180 | 114 | Sokhamony Thong | 94-100—194 | | | |
| 110 | Sajad Karampour | 93-90—183 | | (CAM) | | | | |
| | Barjoei (IRI) | | 115 | Imanaliev Nurmat | 108-92—200 | | | |
| | Ebrahim Nouri (IRI) | 89-94—183 | | (KGZ) | | | | |

| 2009 | Chang-Won Han (KOR) | 2011 | Hideki Matsuyama (JPN) |
|------|---------------------|------|------------------------|
| 2010 | Hideki Matsuyama (JPN) | 2012 | Guan Tianlang (CHN) |

## 118th British Amateur Championship (Inaugurated 1885)    June 17–22

*Royal Cinque Ports and Prince's*

## Bamburgh Castle's Garrick Porteous is humbled at winning the Amateur title in the wind at Deal

England's Garrick Porteous admitted he was humbled to have his name engraved alongside so many great players on the trophy at the 118th Amateur Championship after beating 21-year-old Finn Toni Hakula 6 and 5 in the 36-hole final at Royal Cinque Ports.

The 23 year old from Bamburgh Castle who is studying studio art, is the first Englishman to win the prestigious title since Gary Wolstenholme in 2003 but only made the final with a 19th hole victory over former US Junior champion James Liu.

The 17-year-old American, who attends Stanford university, was ahead most of the way in the semi-final against Porteous who edged ahead by winning the 13th and the 14th. Liu took the 15th and 17th but was in the rough and lost the last which meant the match went into extra holes … only one in fact.

Liu, again in the rough, lost out despite the fact that Porteous had found the burn with his second. "When I hit it into the water I thought it was a done deal but when he could only hack out I thought well if I get it up and down I have a chance," said Porteous.

Hakula, making his fourth appearance in the Championship, beat fancied Max Orrin 4 and 2 in the semi-final to earn his place against Porteous in the final which was played in winds gusting to 40 mph.

Porteous lost the first hole but won four in a row from the sixth and turned four up on the Finn who comes from Espoo near Helsinki. Hakula fought back to only one down but Porteous won the 17th and 18th to lunch three up and by the 27th hole was four up again.

After losing the final 6 and 5 Hakula, who is studying economics at the University of Texas, said: "It hurt to lose. I did not play as well as I could. I missed a lot of short putts in the morning and it was hard to get back."

Porteous, who earned a place in the 2013 Open, also qualified for the 2014 US Open at Pinehurst and gained an invitation to the 2014 Masters at Augusta.

After stroke play qualifying at Royal Cinque Ports GC and Princes GC, 72 players from 20 different countries were involved in the match play section. Leading medallists were 20 year old Pole Adrian Meronk and England's Craig Hinton both on 140 but a notable failure by just one shot was Welsh Walker Cup star Rhys Pugh.

### Stroke Play Qualifying:

| | | | | |
|---|---|---|---|---|
| Craig Hinton (Oxfordshire) | 73-67—140 | | Zander Lombard (RSA) | 76-68—144 |
| Adrian Meronk (POL) | 72-68—140 | | Charlie Bull (Lake Nona) | 70-74—144 |
| Scott Gibson (Southerness) | 73-68—141 | | Callan O'Reilly (AUS) | 74-70—144 |
| Graeme Robertson (Glenbervie) | 71-70—141 | | Cameron Smith (AUS) | 74-70—144 |
| Mads Soegaard (DEN) | 70-72—142 | | Clement Sordet (FRA) | 74-70—144 |
| Paul Barjon (FRA) | 74-68—142 | | Aaaron Kearney (Castleroc) | 73-71—144 |
| Richrd James (Aberystwyth) | 73-69—142 | | Alexander Culverwell (Dunbar) | 74-70—144 |
| Paul Dunne (Greystones) | 77-65—142 | | Cormac Sharvin (Ardglass) | 72-73—145 |
| Brett Drewitt (AUS) | 72-70—142 | | Benjamin Rusch (SUI) | 74-71—145 |
| Neil Raymond (Corhampton) | 72-71—143 | | Jordan Zunic (AUS) | 75-70—145 |
| Jimmy Mullen (Royal North Devon) | 75-68—143 | | Thomas Elissalde (FRA) | 72-73—145 |
| Niclas Carlsson (SWE) | 72-71—143 | | Fraser McKenna (Balmore) | 73-72—145 |
| Max Orrin (North Foreland) | 73-70—143 | | Robbie Van West (NED) | 73-72—145 |
| Jack Hume (Rathsallagh) | 71-72—143 | | Pontus Gad (SWE) | 78-68—146 |
| Callum Shinkwin (Moor Park) | 75-68—143 | | Nicolai Kristensen (DEN) | 72-74—146 |
| Haraldur Franklin Magnus (ISL) | 72-71—143 | | Grant Forrest (Craigielaw) | 72-74—146 |

British Amateur Championship *continued*

| | | | |
|---|---|---|---|
| Max Williams (Cuddington) | 73-73—146 | Scott Borrowman (Dollar) | 78-71—149 |
| Thomas Sorensen (DEN) | 73-73—146 | Stefano Pitoni (ITA) | 75-74—149 |
| Adam Dunton (McDonald) | 74-72—146 | Sam Binning (Ranfurly Castle) | 77-72—149 |
| Nathan Kimsey (Woodhall Spa) | 72-74—146 | Mathieu Fenasse (FRA) | 74-75—149 |
| Garrick Porteous (Bamburgh Castle) | 77-69—146 | James Fox (Portmarnock) | 74-75—149 |
| Julian Taylor (York) | 76-70—146 | Harry Casey (Enfield) | 75-74—149 |
| Jim Liu (USA) | 72-74—146 | Jack Hiluta (Chelmsford) | 82-67—149 |
| Edward Richardson (Rye) | 75-71—146 | Bradley Neil (Blairgowrie) | 78-71—149 |
| Daniel Wasteney (Lindrick) | 74-72—146 | Patrick Spraggs (Stowmarket) | 74-75—149 |
| Henry James (Kidderminster) | 74-72—146 | Daniel Young (Craigie Hill) | 75-74—149 |
| Ashley Chesters (Hawkstone Park) | 76-70—146 | Maximilian Rottluff (GER) | 75-74—149 |
| Tom Berry (Wentworth) | 76-70—146 | Sean Towndrow (Southport & Ainsdale) | 76-74—150 |
| Kasper Estrup (DEN) | 74-72—146 | Nicolas Manifacier (FRA) | 78-72—150 |
| Tyler Hogarty (Rodway Hill) | 74-72—146 | Richard O'Donovan (Lucan) | 70-80—150 |
| Niklas Moeller (DEN) | 72-74—146 | Daniel Jennevret (SWE) | 79-71—150 |
| Richard Bridges (Stackstown) | 73-73—146 | Jack McDonald (Kilmarnock (Barassie)) | 79-71—150 |
| Tim Gornik (SLO) | 80-66—146 | Darren Timms (Mid Kent) | 78-72—150 |
| Michael Saunders (Dartford) | 76-70—146 | Ricardo Melo Gouveia (POR) | 75-75—150 |
| Victor Lange (RSA) | 73-73—146 | Gregoire Schoeb (FRA) | 76-74—150 |
| Rentao Paratore (ITA) | 71-75—146 | Andrew Hogan (Newlands) | 76-74—150 |
| Geoff Drakeford (AUS) | 75-72—147 | Tom Wilde (Castle Royle) | 78-72—150 |
| Riccardo Michelini (ITA) | 77-70—147 | Anthony Blaney (Liberton) | 77-73—150 |
| Paul Kinnear (Formby) | 75-72—147 | Luke Johnson (Kings Lynn) | 79-71—150 |
| Mario Galiano (ESP) | 76-71—147 | Erik Oja (SWE) | 73-77—150 |
| Nathan Holman (AUS) | 75-72—147 | Gary Hurley (West Waterford) | 79-71—150 |
| Nick Marsh (Huddersfield) | 77-70—147 | Victor Henum (DEN) | 77-73—150 |
| Toby Crisp (Newmarket Links) | 77-70—147 | Francesco Testa (ITA) | 74-76—150 |
| Tobias Nemecz (AUT) | 75-72—147 | Patrick Hanauer (BEL) | 75-75—150 |
| Eamon Bradley (Mount Ellen) | 74-73—147 | Nicolas Thommen (SUI) | 75-75—150 |
| Matthew McAlpin (Royal Portrush) | 78-69—147 | Louis Tomlinson (West Lancashire) | 77-73—150 |
| Daniel Brown (Bedale) | 81-66—147 | Jamie Savage (Cawder) | 76-74—150 |
| Pep Angles (ESP) | 73-74—147 | Romain Langasque (FRA) | 79-71—150 |
| Julien Brun (FRA) | 76-71—147 | Joe Dean (Lindrick) | 76-74—150 |
| A J McInerney (USA) | 77-70—147 | Toby Tree (Worthing) | 77-73—150 |
| Oliver Carr (Heswall) | 73-74—147 | Craig Howie (Peebles) | 74-76—150 |
| Toni Hakula (FIN) | 77-70—147 | Jaime Lopez Rivarola (ARG) | 77-73—150 |
| Ashton Turnern (Kenwick Park) | 75-72—147 | Lauri Ruuska (FIN) | 79-71—150 |
| Shane McGlynnn (Carton House) | 75-72—147 | Sebastian Soderberg (SWE) | 77-73—150 |
| Ben Stow (Rushmore) | 74-73—147 | Jamie Rutherford (Knebworth) | 76-75—151 |
| Mathias Eggenberger (SUI) | 75-72—147 | Ryan Fricker (Yelverton) | 80-71—151 |
| Reeve Whitson (Mourne) | 73-75—148 | Alejandro Tosti (ARG) | 79-72—151 |
| Rory McNamara (Headfort) | 77-71—148 | Javier Gallegos (ESP) | 79-72—151 |
| Sean Dale (USA) | 77-71—148 | Jack Singh Brar (Brokenhurst Manor) | 80-71—151 |
| Ruben Sondjaja (AUS) | 77-71—148 | Tom Brown (Harpenden Common) | 77-74—151 |
| Jon Rahm (ESP) | 78-70—148 | Henry Todd (USA) | 75-76—151 |
| Mark Geddes (Prenton) | 74-74—148 | Matthew Moseley (Carmarthen) | 80-71—151 |
| Conor O'Neil (Pollok) | 77-71—148 | Henry Tomlinson (R. Lytham & St Annes) | 77-74—151 |
| Borja Virto (ESP) | 78-70—148 | Pierre Mazier (FRA) | 76-75—151 |
| Sebastian Crookall-Nixon (Workington) | 74-74—148 | Chris Selfridge (Moyola Park) | 76-75—151 |
| Greig Marchbank (Dumfries & County) | 77-71—148 | Chris Robb (Meldrum House) | 77-74—151 |
| Jack Bush (Morlais Castle) | 76-72—148 | Lorenzo Scalise (ITA) | 80-71—151 |
| Rhys Pugh (Vale Resort) | 73-75—148 | Thjomas Detry (BEL) | 80-71—151 |
| Gordon Stevenson (Whitecraigs) | 77-71—148 | Juan Francisco Sarasti (ESP) | 82-69—151 |
| Hunter Kraus (USA) | 75-73—148 | Callum Tarren (Wynyard) | 75-76—151 |
| Robbie Busher (Salisbury & S. Wilts) | 77-71—148 | Gudmunder Kristjansson (ISL) | 80-71—151 |
| Robin Sciot-Siegrist (FRA) | 77-72—149 | Florian Kolberg (TUR) | 77-74—151 |
| James White (Lundin) | 74-75—149 | Dermot McElroy (Ballymena) | 78-73—151 |
| Kristian Johannessen (NOR) | 81-68—149 | Maximilian Walz (GER) | 76-75—151 |
| Erik Myllymaki (FIN) | 78-71—149 | Robin Goger (AUT) | 76-75—151 |
| Jacopo Guasconi (ITA) | 79-70—149 | Patrick Kelly (Boston West) | 79-72—151 |
| Albert Eckhardt (FIN) | 76-73—149 | David Morago (ESP) | 72-79—151 |

| | | | | |
|---|---|---|---|---|
| Jeppe Kristian Andersen (DEN) | 80-71—151 | Michael Daily (Erskine) | 77-77—154 |
| Nicholas Grant (Knock) | 76-75—151 | Brian Casey (Headfort) | 78-76—154 |
| Geoff Lenehan (Portmarnock) | 76-75—151 | A J Crouch (USA) | 78-76—154 |
| Ewan Scott (St Andrews) | 78-73—151 | Thomas Dunne (USA) | 81-73—154 |
| Ben Wheeler (Purley Downs) | 78-73—151 | Trevor Simsby (USA) | 77-77—154 |
| Scott Crichton (Aberdour) | 79-72—151 | Jose Maria Joia (POR) | 77-77—154 |
| Jordan McColl (Scotscraig) | 73-78—151 | Craig Melding (Neath) | 81-73—154 |
| Ben Taylor (Walton Heath) | 79-73—152 | Kristoffer Ventura (NOR) | 70-84—154 |
| Todd Sinnott (AUS) | 76-76—152 | Leonard Bem (FRA) | 79-75—154 |
| Robbie Cannon (Balbriggan) | 76-76—152 | Enrico Di Nitto (ITA) | 76-78—154 |
| Robert Sutton (Dunstable Downs) | 83-69—152 | Joris Etlin (FRA) | 76-78—154 |
| Marc Dobias (SUI) | 76-76—152 | Teemu Toivonen (FIN) | 79-76—155 |
| Mac McLaughlin (USA) | 77-75—152 | Julien De Poyen (FRA) | 80-75—155 |
| Joao Carlota (POR) | 77-75—152 | Ryan Evans (Wellingborough) | 79-76—155 |
| Valerio Pelliccia (ITA) | 79-73—152 | Josh Loughrey (Wrag Barn) | 75-80—155 |
| Jean-Michel Hall (Woburn) | 78-74—152 | Harry Ellis (Meon Valley) | 76-79—155 |
| Ross Bell (Downfield) | 80-72—152 | Giorgio De Filippi (ITA) | 79-76—155 |
| Scott Fernandez (ESP) | 81-71—152 | Ben Loughrey (Wrag Barn) | 77-78—155 |
| Jonathan Grey (Hever Castle) | 80-72—152 | Edouard Amacher (SUI) | 79-76—155 |
| Ryan Cornfield (Enville) | 84-68—152 | Philip Bootsma (NED) | 76-79—155 |
| James Ross (Royal Burgess) | 75-77—152 | Kyle Kochevar (USA) | 80-76—156 |
| Jonny McAllister (Tankersley Park) | 78-74—152 | Jonathan Bale (Royal Porthcawl) | 84-72—156 |
| Hampus Nilsson (SWE) | 77-75—152 | Kit Holmes (Hunstanton) | 79-77—156 |
| Henry Smart (Banstead Downs) | 79-73—152 | Mervin Rocchi (FRA) | 81-75—156 |
| Jack Bartlett (Worthing) | 77-75—152 | Joel Stalter (FRA) | 77-79—156 |
| Antoni Ferrer (ESP) | 81-71—152 | Paul Elissalde (FRA) | 79-77—156 |
| Martin Kim (ARG) | 78-74—152 | Philip Geerts (ITA) | 82-74—156 |
| Robert Burlison (Oxley Park) | 77-75—152 | Alasdair Dalgliesh (Haywards Heath) | 76-80—156 |
| Harry Diamond (Belvoir Park) | 76-76—152 | Victor Perez (FRA) | 79-77—156 |
| Philipp Westermann (GER) | 75-77—152 | Bjorn Hellgren (SWE) | 80-76—156 |
| Gregory Eason (Kirby Muxloe) | 79-73—152 | Steffen Harm (GER) | 83-73—156 |
| Jordan Smith (Bowood) | 77-75—152 | Joshua White (Chipstead) | 80-76—156 |
| Oskar Arvidsson (SWE) | 80-72—152 | Jules Bordonado (FRA) | 82-75—157 |
| Goncalo Pinto (POR) | 73-79—152 | Jeremy Freiburghaus (SUI) | 83-74—157 |
| David Boote (Walton Heath) | 77-75—152 | Corrado De Stefani (ITA) | 82-75—157 |
| Martin Keskari (GER) | 80-73—153 | Mateusz Gradecki (POL) | 82-75—157 |
| Alexandre Daydou (FRA) | 83-70—153 | Marco Iten (SUI) | 82-75—157 |
| Will Jones (Oswestry) | 78-75—153 | Simon Christensen (DEN) | 85-72—157 |
| Rowin Caron (NED) | 81-72—153 | Antoine Le Saux (FRA) | 84-73—157 |
| Alfie Plant (Rochester & Cobham Park) | 79-74—153 | Edoardo Rafe Lipparelli (ITA) | 81-76—157 |
| Neil Henderson (Renaissance Club) | 79-74—153 | Peter Valasek (SVK) | 82-76—158 |
| Martin Leth Simonsen (DEN) | 79-74—153 | Hampus Bergman (SWE) | 85-73—158 |
| Viraat Badhwar (AUS) | 79-74—153 | Gregory Wiggins (GER) | 79-79—158 |
| Adrien Saddier (FRA) | 80-73—153 | Joel Girrbach (SUI) | 81-77—158 |
| Giacomo Garbin (ITA) | 80-73—153 | Alasdair McDougall (Elderslie) | 82-76—158 |
| Adam Eineving (SWE) | 84-69—153 | Hamza Hakan Sayin (TUR) | 81-77—158 |
| Dale Brandt-Richards (AUS) | 81-72—153 | Julien Marot (FRA) | 83-75—158 |
| Alexander Matlari (GER) | 77-76—153 | Tom Harris (Castletown) | 80-78—158 |
| Niklas Lindstrom (SWE) | 81-72—153 | Thomas Perrot (FRA) | 86-73—159 |
| Kevin Hesbois (BEL) | 82-71—153 | Chtristian Gloet (DEN) | 81-78—159 |
| Feddie Edmunds (Aldeburgh) | 77-76—153 | Felix Mory (FRA) | 81-78—159 |
| Lawrence Allan (Alva) | 73-80—153 | Kyle McClung (Wigtownshire County) | 84-75—159 |
| Jeronimo Esteve (PUR) | 79-74—153 | Philippe Schweizer (SUI) | 85-74—159 |
| Paul Howard (Southport & Ainsdale) | 80-74—154 | Victor Veyret (FRA) | 84-75—159 |
| Paul Lockwood (Hessle) | 80-74—154 | Federico Zucchetti (ITA) | 79-80—159 |
| Jacopo Jori (ITA) | 79-75—154 | Sebastian Schwind (GER) | 85-75—160 |
| Tomasz Anderson (Brocket Hall) | 78-76—154 | Brady Watt (AUS) | 82-78—160 |
| Jamie Bower (Meltham) | 81-73—154 | Austin Quick (USA) | 80-80—160 |
| Jerome Titlow (Knole Park) | 78-76—154 | Lars Van Meijel (NED) | 82-78—160 |
| Vaughan McCall (NZL) | 82-72—154 | Joss Gosling (Harpenden) | 82-79—161 |
| Liam Johnston (Dumfries & County) | 77-77—154 | Jonathan K-J Woo (SIN) | 80-81—161 |
| Axel Boasson (ISL) | 81-73—154 | Luigi Botta (ITA) | 85-76—161 |
| Jason Shufflebotham (Prestatyn) | 79-75—154 | Filippo Zucchetti (ITA) | 86-75—161 |

British Amateur Championship *continued*

| | |
|---|---|
| Sam Forgan (Stowmarket) | 81-80—161 |
| Haydn Porteous (RSA) | 85-77—162 |
| Ugo Coussaud (FRA) | 82-80—162 |
| Thomas Le Berre (FRA) | 86-76—162 |
| Baptiste Courtachon (FRA) | 85-77—162 |
| Niclas Hellberg (FIN) | 84-78—162 |
| Kenny Subregis (FRA) | 85-79—164 |
| Max Albertus (NED) | 87-84—171 |

**Round One:**

Paul Kinnear (Formby) beat Daniel Brown (Bedale)  3 and 2

Ben Stow (Rushmore) beat Mathias Eggenberger (SUI)  5 and 4

Pep Angles (ESP) beat Mario Galiano (ESP)  4 and 2

Riccardo Michelini (ITA) beat Matthew McAlpin (Royal Portrush)  2 holes

A J McInerney (USA) beat Eamon Bradley (Mount Ellen)  1 hole

Shane McGlynn (Carton House) beat Geoff Drakeford (AUS)  at 19th

Nick Marsh (Huddersfield) beat Julien Brun (FRA)  4 and 2

Toby Crisp (Newmarket Links) beat Nathan Holman (AUS)  2 and 1

**Round Two:**

Adrian Meronk (POL) beat Thomas Sorensen (DEN)  4 and 3

Renato Paratore (ITA) beat Richard Bridges (Stackstown)  4 and 3

Haraldur Franklin Magnus (ISL) beat Michael Saunders (Dartford)  2 holes

Victor Lange (RSA) beat Alexander Culverwell (Dunbar) 4 and 3

Brett Drewitt (AUS) beat Niklas Moeller (DEN)  3 and 2

Kasper Estrup (DEN) beat Thomas Elissalde (FRA)  2 and 1

Mads Soegaard (DEN) beat Nathan Kimsey (Woodhall Spa)  at 19th

Jim Liu (USA) beat Benjamin Rusch (SUI)  4 and 2

Pontus Gad (SWE) beat Scott Gibson (Southerness)  1 hole

Tim Gornik (SLO) beat Robbie Van West (NED)  5 and 4

Neil Raymond (Corhampton) beat Max Williams (Cuddington)  at 20th

Adam Dunton (McDonald) beat Charlie Bull (Lake Nona)  2 and 1

Paul Dunne (Greystones) beat Ashton Turner (Kenwick Park)  2 and 1

Garrick Porteous (Bamburgh Castle) beat Cormac Sharvin (Ardglass)  3 and 2

Jimmy Mullen (Royal North Devon) beat Daniel Wasteney (Lindrick)  2 holes

Aaron Kearney (Castlerock) beat Henry James (Kidderminster)  4 and 2

Zander Lombard (RSA) beat Tóbias Nemecz (AUT)  1 hole

Ashley Chesters (Hawkstone Park) beat Jack Hume (Rathsallagh)  2 and 1

Edward Richardson (Rye) beat Fraser McKenna (Balmore)  2 and 1

Paul Barjon (FRA) beat Oliver Carr (Heswall)  3 and 1

Grant Forrest (Craigielaw) beat Callan O'Reilly (AUS)  2 and 1

Toni Hakula (FIN) beat Niclas Carlsson (SWE)  1 hole

Tyler Hogarty (Rodway Hill) beat Nicolai Kristensen (DEN)  4 and 3

Tom Berry (Wentworth) beat Graeme Robertson (Glenbervie)  4 and 2

Paul Kinnear (Formby) beat Cameron Smith (AUS)  4 and 2

Max Orrin (North Foreland) beat Ben Stow (Rushmore)  4 and 3

Jordan Zunic (AUS) beat Pep Angles (ESP)  2 holes

Richard James (Aberystwyth) beat Riccardo Michelini (ITA)  2 and 1

A J McInerney (USA) beat Clement Sordet (FRA)  at 19th

Callum Shinkwin (Moor Park) beat Shane McGlynn (Carton House)  4 and 2

Nick Marsh (Huddersfield) beat Julian Taylor (York)  7 and 6

Toby Crisp (Newmarket Links) beat Craig Hinton (Oxfordshire)  2 and 1

**Round Three:**

Paratore beat Meronk  3 and 2
Magnus beat Lange  4 and 2
Estrup beat Drewitt  at 20th
Liu beat Soegaard  2 and 1
Gornik beat Gad  5 and 4
Raymond beat Dunton  3 and 2
Porteous beat Dunne  3 and 3
Kearney beat Mullen  5 and 3
Chesters beat Lombard  3 and 2
Barjon beat Richardson  at 19th
Hakula beat Forrest  2 holes
Berry beat Hogarty  5 and 4
Orrin beat Kinnear  3 and 2
Zunic beat James  2 and 1
Shinkwin beat McInerney  2 and 1
Marsh beat Crisp  1 hole

**Round Four:**

Paratore beat Magnus  at 19th
Liu beat Estrup  2 holes
Raymond beat Gornik  7 and 6
Porteous beat Kearney  2 and 1
Barjon beat Chesters  2 holes
Hakula beat Berry  3 and 2
Orrin beat Zunic  3 and 1
Marsh beat Shinkwin  1 hole

**Quarter Finals:**
Liu beat Paratore  3 and 2
Porteous beat Raymond  2 and 1
Hakula beat Barjon  4 and 3
Orrin beat Marsh  4 and 3

**Semi-Finals:**
Porteous beat Liu  at 19th
Hakula beat Orrin  4 and 2

**Final (36 holes):** Garrick Porteous (Bamburgh Castle) beat Toni Hakula (FIN)  6 and 5

| Year | Result | Score | Venue | Entrants |
|---|---|---|---|---|
| 1885 | A MacFie beat H Hutchinson | 7 and 6 | Hoylake, Royal Liverpool | entrants 44 |
| 1886 | H Hutchinson beat H Lamb | 7 and 6 | St Andrews | 42 |
| 1887 | H Hutchinson beat J Ball | 1 hole | Hoylake, Royal Liverpool | 33 |
| 1888 | J Ball beat J Laidlay | 5 and 4 | Prestwick | 38 |
| 1889 | J Laidlay beat L Melville | 2 and 1 | St Andrews | 40 |
| 1890 | J Ball beat J Laidlay | 4 and 3 | Hoylake, Royal Liverpool | 44 |
| 1891 | J Laidlay beat H Hilton | at 20th | St Andrews | 50 |
| 1892 | J Ball beat H Hilton | 3 and 1 | Sandwich, Royal St George's | 45 |
| 1893 | P Anderson beat J Laidlay | 1 hole | Prestwick | 44 |
| 1894 | J Ball beat S Fergusson | 1 hole | Hoylake, Royal Liverpool | 64 |
| 1895 | L Melville beat J Ball | at 19th | St Andrews | 68 |
| From 1896 final played over 36 holes | | | | |
| 1896 | F Tait beat H Hilton | 8 and 7 | Sandwich, Royal St George's | 64 |
| 1897 | A Allan beat J Robb | 4 and 2 | Muirfield | 74 |
| 1898 | F Tait beat S Fergusson | 7 and 5 | Hoylake, Royal Liverpool | 77 |
| 1899 | J Ball beat F Tait | at 37th | Prestwick | 101 |
| 1900 | H Hilton beat J Robb | 8 and 7 | Sandwich, Royal St George's | 68 |
| 1901 | H Hilton beat J Low | 1 hole | St Andrews | 116 |
| 1902 | C Hutchings beat S Fry | 1 hole | Hoylake, Royal Liverpool | 114 |
| 1903 | R Maxwell beat H Hutchinson | 7 and 5 | Muirfield | 142 |
| 1904 | W Travis (USA) beat E Blackwell | 4 and 3 | Sandwich, Royal St George's | 104 |
| 1905 | A Barry beat Hon O Scott | 3 and 2 | Prestwick | 148 |
| 1906 | J Robb beat C Lingen | 4 and 3 | Hoylake, Royal Liverpool | 166 |
| 1907 | J Ball beat C Palmer | 6 and 4 | St Andrews | 200 |
| 1908 | E Lassen beat H Taylor | 7 and 6 | Sandwich, Royal St George's | 197 |
| 1909 | R Maxwell beat Capt C Hutchison | 1 hole | Muirfield | 170 |
| 1910 | J Ball beat C Aylmer | 10 and 9 | Hoylake, Royal Liverpool | 160 |
| 1911 | H Hilton beat E Lassen | 4 and 3 | Prestwick | 146 |
| 1912 | J Ball beat A Mitchell | at 38th | Westward Ho!, Royal North Devon | 134 |
| 1913 | H Hilton beat R Harris | 6 and 5 | St Andrews | 198 |
| 1914 | J Jenkins beat C Hezlet | 3 and 2 | Sandwich, Royal St George's | 232 |
| 1915–19 | Not played | | | |
| 1920 | C Tolley beat R Gardner (USA) | 37th hole | Muirfield | 165 |
| 1921 | W Hunter beat A Graham | 12 and 11 | Hoylake, Royal Liverpool | 223 |
| 1922 | E Holderness beat J Caven | 1 hole | Prestwick | 252 |
| 1923 | R Wethered beat R Harris | 7 and 6 | Deal, Royal Cinque Ports | 209 |
| 1924 | E Holderness beat E Storey | 3 and 2 | St Andrews | 201 |
| 1925 | R Harris beat K Fradgley | 13 and 12 | Westward Ho!, Royal North Devon | 151 |
| 1926 | J Sweetser (USA) beat A Simpson | 6 and 5 | Muirfield | 216 |
| 1927 | Dr W Tweddell beat D Landale | 7 and 6 | Hoylake, Royal Liverpool | 197 |
| 1928 | T Perkins beat R Wethered | 6 and 4 | Prestwick | 220 |
| 1929 | C Tolley beat J Smith | 4 and 3 | Sandwich, Royal St George's | 253 |
| 1930 | R Jones (USA) beat R Wethered | 7 and 6 | St Andrews | 271 |
| 1931 | E Smith beat J De Forest | 1 hole | Westward Ho!, Royal North Devon | 171 |
| 1932 | J De Forest beat E Fiddian | 3 and 1 | Muirfield | 235 |
| 1933 | Hon M Scott beat T Bourn | 4 and 3 | Hoylake, Royal Liverpool | 269 |
| 1934 | W Lawson Little (USA) beat J Wallace | 14 and 13 | Prestwick | 225 |
| 1935 | W Lawson Little (USA) beat Dr W Tweddell | 1 hole | Royal Lytham and St Annes | 232 |
| 1936 | H Thomson beat J Ferrier (AUS) | 2 holes | St Andrews | 283 |
| 1937 | R Sweeney Jr (USA) beat L Munn | 3 and 2 | Sandwich, Royal St George's | 223 |
| 1938 | C Yates (USA) beat R Ewing | 3 and 2 | Troon | 241 |
| 1939 | A Kyle beat A Duncan | 2 and 1 | Hoylake, Royal Liverpool | 167 |
| 1940–45 | Not played | | | |
| 1946 | J Bruen beat R Sweeny (USA) | 4 and 3 | Birkdale | 263 |
| 1947 | W Turnesa (USA) beat R Chapman (USA) | 3 and 2 | Carnoustie | 200 |
| 1948 | F Stranahan (USA) beat C Stowe | 5 and 4 | Sandwich, Royal St George's | 168 |
| 1949 | S McCready beat W Turnesa (USA) | 2 and 1 | Portmarnock | 204 |
| 1950 | F Stranahan (USA) beat R Chapman (USA) | 8 and 6 | St Andrews | 324 |
| 1951 | R Chapman (USA) beat C Coe (USA) | 5 and 4 | Royal Porthcawl | 192 |
| 1952 | E Ward (USA) beat F Stranahan (USA) | 6 and 5 | Prestwick | 286 |
| 1953 | J Carr beat E Harvie Ward (USA) | 2 holes | Hoylake, Royal Liverpool | 279 |
| 1954 | D Bachli (AUS) beat W Campbell (USA) | 2 and 1 | Muirfield | 286 |
| 1955 | J Conrad (USA) beat A Slater | 3 and 2 | Royal Lytham and St Annes | 240 |
| 1956 | J Beharrell beat L Taylor | 5 and 4 | Troon | 200 |

## British Amateur Championship *continued*

| | | | | |
|---|---|---|---|---|
| 1957 | R Reid Jack beat H Ridgley (USA) | 2 and 1 | Formby | 200 |
| *In 1956 and 1957 the Quarter Finals, Semi-Finals and Final were played over 36 holes* | | | | |
| 1958 | J Carr beat A Thirlwell | 3 and 2 | St Andrews | 488 |
| *In 1958, Semi-Finals and Final only were played over 36 holes* | | | | |
| 1959 | D Beman (USA) beat W Hyndman (USA) | 3 and 2 | Sandwich, Royal St George's | 362 |
| 1960 | J Carr beat R Cochran (USA) | 8 and 7 | Royal Portrush | 183 |
| 1961 | MF Bonallack beat J Walker | 6 and 4 | Turnberry | 250 |
| 1962 | R Davies (USA) beat J Povall | 1 hole | Hoylake, Royal Liverpool | 256 |
| 1963 | M Lunt beat J Blackwell | 2 and 1 | St Andrews | 256 |
| 1964 | G Clark beat M Lunt | at 39th | Ganton | 220 |
| 1965 | MF Bonallack beat C Clark | 2 and 1 | Royal Porthcawl | 176 |
| 1966 | R Cole (RSA) beat R Shade | 3 and 2 | Carnoustie (18 holes) | 206 |
| *Final played over 18 holes because of sea mist* | | | | |
| 1967 | R Dickson (USA) beat R Cerrudo (USA) | 2 and 1 | Formby | |
| 1968 | MF Bonallack beat J Carr | 7 and 6 | Royal Troon | 249 |
| 1969 | MF Bonallack beat W Hyndman (USA) | 3 and 2 | Hoylake, Royal Liverpool | 245 |
| 1970 | MF Bonallack beat W Hyndman (USA) | 8 and 7 | Newcastle, Royal Co Down | 256 |
| 1971 | S Melnyk (USA) beat J Simons (USA) | 3 and 2 | Carnoustie | 256 |
| 1972 | T Homer beat A Thirlwell | 4 and 3 | Sandwich, Royal St George's | 253 |
| 1973 | R Siderowf (USA) beat P Moody | 5 and 3 | Royal Porthcawl | 222 |
| 1974 | T Homer beat J Gabrielsen (USA) | 2 holes | Muirfield | 330 |
| 1975 | M Giles (USA) beat M James | 8 and 7 | Hoylake, Royal Liverpool | 206 |
| 1976 | R Siderowf (USA) beat J Davies | at 37th | St Andrews | 289 |
| 1977 | P McEvoy beat H Campbell | 5 and 4 | Ganton | 235 |
| 1978 | P McEvoy beat P McKellar | 4 and 3 | Royal Troon | 353 |
| 1979 | J Sigel (USA) beat S Hoch (USA) | 3 and 2 | Hillside | 285 |
| 1980 | D Evans beat D Suddards (RSA) | 4 and 3 | Royal Porthcawl | 265 |
| 1981 | P Ploujoux (FRA) beat J Hirsch (USA) | 4 and 2 | St Andrews | 256 |
| 1982 | M Thompson beat A Stubbs | 4 and 3 | Deal, Royal Cinque Ports | 245 |
| *Qualifying round introduced* | | | | |
| 1983 | P Parkin beat J Holtgrieve (USA) | 5 and 4 | Turnberry | 288 |
| 1984 | JM Olazábal (ESP) beat C Montgomerie | 5 and 4 | Formby | 291 |
| 1985 | G McGimpsey beat G Homewood | 8 and 7 | Royal Dornoch | 457 |
| 1986 | D Curry beat G Birtwell | 11 and 9 | Royal Lytham and St Annes | 427 |
| 1987 | P Mayo beat P McEvoy | 3 and 1 | Prestwick | 373 |
| 1988 | C Hardin (SWE) beat B Fouchee (RSA) | 1 hole | Royal Porthcawl | 391 |
| 1989 | S Dodd beat C Cassells | 5 and 3 | Royal Birkdale | 378 |
| 1990 | R Muntz (NED) beat A Macara | 7 and 6 | Muirfield | 510 |
| 1991 | G Wolstenholme beat B May (USA) | 8 and 6 | Ganton | 345 |
| 1992 | S Dundas beat B Dredge | 7 and 6 | Carnoustie | 364 |
| 1993 | I Pyman beat P Page | at 37th | Royal Portrush | 279 |
| 1994 | L James beat G Sherry | 2 and 1 | Nairn | 288 |
| 1995 | G Sherry beat M Reynard | 7 and 6 | Hoylake, Royal Liverpool | 288 |
| 1996 | W Bladon beat R Beames | 1 hole | Turnberry | 288 |
| 1997 | C Watson beat T Immelman (RSA) | 3 and 2 | Royal St Georges, Royal Cinque Ports | 369 |
| 1998 | S García (ESP) beat C Williams | 7 and 6 | Muirfield | 537 |
| 1999 | G Storm beat A Wainwright | 7 and 6 | Royal County Down, Kilkeel | 433 |
| 2000 | M Ilonen (FIN) beat C Reimbold | 2 and 1 | Royal Liverpool and Wallasey | 376 |
| 2001 | M Hoey beat I Campbell | 1 hole | Prestwick & Kilmarnock | 288 |
| 2002 | A Larrazábal (ESP) beat M Sell | 1 hole | Royal Porthcawl and Pyle & Kenfig | 286 |
| 2003 | G Wolstenholme beat R De Sousa (SUI) | 6 and 5 | Royal Troon and Irvine | 289 |
| 2004 | S Wilson beat L Corfield | 4 and 3 | St Andrews, Old and Jubilee Courses | 288 |
| 2005 | B McElhinney beat J Gallagher | 5 and 4 | Royal Birkdale and Southport & Ainsdale | 406 |
| 2006 | J Guerrier (FRA) beat A Gee | 4 and 3 | Royal St George's and Prince's | 284 |
| 2007 | D Weaver (USA) beat T Stewart (AUS) | 2 and 1 | Royal Lytham & St Annes and St Annes Old Links | 284 |
| 2008 | R Saxton (NED) beat T Fleetwood (ENG) | 3 and 2 | Turnberry | 288 |
| 2009 | M Manassero (ITA) beat S Hutsby (ENG) | 4 and 3 | Formby and West Lancashire | 284 |
| 2010 | Jin Jeong (KOR) beat J Byrne (Banchory) | 5 and 4 | Muirfield and North Berwick | 288 |
| 2011 | B Macpherson (AUS) beat M Stewart (Troon Welbeck) | 3 and 2 | Hillside and Hesketh | 288 |
| 2012 | A Dunbar (Rathmore) beat M Schwab (AUT) | 1 hole | Royal Troon and Glasgow – Gailes Links | 288 |

The 2014 Championship will be played at Royal Portrush GC and Portstewart GC from June 16 – 21

# 24th European Amateur Championship (inaugurated 1986)  *El Prat, Spain*  Aug 7–10

## Magical second round 65 sets Chesters on route
## to European title success at El Prat in Spain

Shropshire's Ashley Chesters may have been 285th in the world amateur rankings when he started but he beat a strong field to land the 26th European Amateur Championship at the tough Real Club de Golf El Prat near Barcelona.

The 23-year old from Sandy Lyle's old club Hawkstone Park beat Spain's David Morago by a shot with a four round total of four under par 284. Scott William Fernandez, another Spaniard. was third a further shot behind.

Chesters' success was built around a second round of 65, the low score of the tournament ... but he had to hole a closing hole birdie to win the title. Only two other Englishmen, Jim Payne in 1991 and Matthew Richardson in 2004. have previously been successful.

"This is my best result by a mile," said Chesters. "My 65 was the best I have ever played. I don't think I hit a bad shot in it."

Following up with a 70 on the third day he took a satisfying four shot lead into the last round and was still four ahead coming to the turn but he hit out of bounds at the 10th and ran up a 7 and the field began closing in. After a bogey at the 17th Chesters was only one ahead.

He did not know how his main rivals, playing ahead, were doing and when he nervously holed the three foot birdie at the last he was not even sure he had won.

Both Morago and Fernandez had birdied the par 5 last but so too did Chesters for the fourth day in a row and the title was his.

Englishman Jamie Rutherford was the only played to finish with three sub-par rounds and he took fourth place and there were no fewer than four Irishmen in the top 12 – Paul Dunne, Gavin Moynihan and Dermot McIlrow all on 292 and Kevin Phelan on 294.

Chesters, who follows some impressive winners including Rory McIlroy and Sergio Garcia, earns a spot in the Open Championship being played this year at Hoylake.

| | | | |
|---|---|---|---|
| 1 | Ashley Chesters (ENG) | 73-65-70-76—284 | |
| 2 | David Morago (ESP) | 75-68-69-73—285 | |
| 3 | Scott William Fernandez (ESP) | 70-71-71-74—286 | |
| 4 | Jamie Rutherford (ENG) | 71-73-71-74—289 | |
| | Thomas Detry (BEL) | 72-71-78-68—289 | |
| 6 | Benjamin Rusch (SUI) | 73-71-72-75—291 | |
| 7 | Paul Dunne (IRL) | 74-74-73-71—292 | |
| | Gavin Moynihan (IRL) | 72-74-68-78—292 | |
| | Dermot McElroy (IRL) | 75-70-74-73—292 | |
| 10 | Iván Cantero (ESP) | 73-77-71-72—293 | |
| 11 | Kevin Phelan (IRL) | 75-73-73-73—294 | |
| | João Carlota (POR) | 72-74-74-74—294 | |
| | James Ross (SCO) | 74-69-74-77—294 | |
| 14 | Antoni Ferrer (ESP) | 77-72-72-74—295 | |
| | Maximilian Rottluff (GER) | 74-74-78-69—295 | |
| | Jose Bondia Gil (ESP) | 74-74-76-71—295 | |
| | Borja Virto (ESP) | 72-72-76-75—295 | |
| 18 | Robbie Van West (NED) | 74-75-73-74—296 | |
| | David Boote (WAL) | 72-76-70-78—296 | |
| | Seb Crookall-Nixon (ENG) | 74-73-75-74—296 | |
| 21 | Pontus Gad (SWE) | 80-70-71-76—297 | |
| | Marcus Kinhult (SWE) | 77-70-75-75—297 | |
| | Grant Forrest (SCO) | 71-74-77-75—297 | |
| 24 | Graeme Robertson (SCO) | 75-75-72-76—298 | |
| | Manuel Elvira (ESP) | 77-72-74-75—298 | |
| | Renato Paratore (ITA) | 74-73-79-72—298 | |
| | José-Maria Jóia (POR) | 73-74-75-76—298 | |
| | Toby Tree (ENG) | 76-71-74-77—298 | |
| | Rowin Caron (NED) | 74-73-74-77—298 | |
| | Emilio Cuartero (ESP) | 76-67-76-79—298 | |
| 31 | Gudmundur Agust Kristjansson (ISL) | 77-76-72-74—299 | |
| | Tobias Edén (SWE) | 76-74-75-74—299 | |
| | Joel Girrbach (SUI) | 74-75-73-77—299 | |

## European Amateur Championship *continued*

| | | |
|---|---|---|
| 31T | Lauri Ruuska (FIN) | 75-74-71-79—299 |
| | Javier Gallegos (ESP) | 74-74-72-79—299 |
| | Tomasz Anderson (ENG) | 74-73-79-73—299 |
| | Daniel Jennevret (SWE) | 73-74-75-77—299 |
| | Simon Zach (CZE) | 74-73-70-82—299 |
| 39 | Stefano Pitoni (ITA) | 77-75-74-74—300 |
| | Niclas Carlsson (SWE) | 80-71-74-75—300 |
| | Martin Keskari (GER) | 74-75-75-76—300 |
| | Tom Berry (ENG) | 78-69-78-75—300 |
| | Luke Johnson (ENG) | 71-74-76-79—300 |
| | Mathieu Fenasse (FRA) | 70-74-77-79—300 |
| 45 | Adrian Meronk (POL) | 71-77-76-77—301 |
| | Reeve Whitson (IRL) | 70-77-75-79—301 |
| | Lars Van Meijel (NED) | 74-73-75-79—301 |
| | Mathias Eggenberger (SUI) | 75-70-75-81—301 |
| | Michael Saunders (ENG) | 72-72-78-79—301 |
| 50 | Christian Gløët (DEN | 76-75-75-76—302 |
| | Riccardo Michelini (ITA) | 76-75-72-79—302 |
| | Liam Johnston (SCO) | 76-74-74-78—302 |
| | Brian Casey (IRL) | 72-73-75-82—302 |
| 54 | Dominic Foos (GER) | 76-76-73-78—303 |
| 55 | Jon Rahm (ESP) | 75-77-74-78—304 |
| 56 | Max Williams (ENG) | 77-76-73-79—305 |
| | Grégoire Schoeb (FRA) | 76-72-76-81—305 |
| | Kenny Subregis (FRA) | 73-73-78-81—305 |
| 59 | Matthew Moseley (WAL) | 77-73-75-82—307 |
| 60 | Javier Sainz (ESP) | 75-73-77-83—308 |
| 61 | Maximilian Walz (GER) | 79-76-69-86—310 |

The following players missed the cut after three rounds:

**62 (227)**
Tapio Pulkkanen (FIN)    77-72-70
Scott Borrowman (SCO)    81-72-74
Philippe Schweizer (SUI)    78-73-76
Victor Henum (DEN)    78-72-77
Thomas Perrot (FRA)    76-75-76
Jules Bordonado (FRA)    73-74-80
**68 (228)**
Cormac Sharvin (IRL)    79-72-77
Sebastian Schwind (GER)    79-72-77
Antoine Rozner (FRA)    76-73-79
Haraldur Magnus (ISL)    75-78-75
**72 (229)**
Erik Oja (SWE)    84-75-70
Pep Angles (ESP)    81-70-78
Oskar Arvidsson (SWE)    78-74-77
Tim Gornik (SLO)    78-73-78
Alexander Matlari (GER)    75-78-76
Robin Goger (AUT)    75-76-78
Ben Stow (ENG)    72-77-80
**79 (230)**
Bradley Neil (SCO)    79-74-77
Tobias Nemecz (AUT)    78-77-75
Florian Kolberg (TUR)    78-76-76
Chris Selfridge (IRL)    78-74-78
Daniel Young (SCO)    77-79-74
Cedric Van Wassenhove (BEL)    76-78-76
Niclas Hellberg (FIN)    74-78-78
Kasper Estrup (DEN)    74-74-82
Federico Zucchetti (ITA)    74-73-83
**88 (231)**
Erik Myllymäki (FIN)    82-76-73
Juan Francisco Sarasti (ESP)    80-75-76
Jacopo Jori (ITA)    78-76-77
Max Mehles (GER)    77-78-76
Jack McDonald (SCO)    76-77-78
Gonçalo Pinto (POR)    76-74-81

**94 (232)**
Jack Hume (IRL)    80-74-78
Edouard Amacher (SUI)    76-79-77
Enrico Di Nitto (ITA)    76-78-78
Richard James (WAL)    76-76-80
Jerome Titlow (ENG)    75-77-80
Teemu Toivonen (FIN)    74-78-80
David Van Den Dungen (NED)    74-77-81
Chris Robb, (SCO)    73-77-82
**102 (233)**
Bjorn Hellgren (SWE)    81-76-76
Sixto Casabona (ESP)    79-80-74
Neil Henderson (SCO)    79-77-77
Nicholas Grant (IRL)    79-77-77
Rory McNamara (IRL)    78-77-78
Teemu Bakker (FIN)    77-74-82
Jeppe Kristian Andersen    83-76-75
(DEN)
**109 (234)**
Francesco Testa (ITA)    82-76-76
Paul Barjon (FRA)    77-74-83
Filippo Zucchetti (ITA)    73-84-77
**112 (235)**
Robin Sciot-Siegrist (IRL)    83-74-78
Mads Søgaard (DEN)    78-77-80
Victor Gebhard Østerby    77-80-78
(DEN)
**115 (236)**
Marco Iten (SUI)    81-76-79
Thomas Sørensen (DEN)    80-78-78
Nicolas Thommen (SUI)    73-81-82
**118 (237)**
Marcel Ohorn (GER)    82-75-80
Sam Binning (SCO)    79-75-83
**120 (238)**
Niklas Lindström (SWE)    87-78-73
Peter Valasek (SVK)    83-76-79

Stanislas Gautier (FRA)    82-77-79
Mathias Schjoelberg (NOR)    82-75-81
Simon Willer Hauskjold    80-74-84
Christensen (DEN)
Mario Galiano (ESP)    77-82-79
**126 (239)**
Mateusz Gradecki (POL)    85-77-77
Ewan Scott (SCO)    81-82-76
Sondre Erevik Ronold (NOR)    80-83-76
Mathieu Decottignies Lafon    80-80-79
(FRA)
**130 (240)**
Axel Boasson (ISL)    81-80-79
Emil Søgaard (DEN)    78-79-83
Teremoana Beaucousin (FRA)    76-85-79
**133 (241)**
Albert Eckhardt (FIN)    81-83-77
Kevin Hesbois (BEL)    78-82-81
**135 (242)**
Lee Jones (WAL)    82-81-79
Ben Loughrey (ENG)    81-80-81
Ugo Coussaud (FRA)    77-76-89
**138 (243)**
Richard O'Donovan (IRL)    79-84-80
**139 (244)**
Pavel Goryainov (RUS)    84-77-83
**140 (248)**
Jordi Panes, (ESP)    86-73-89
Martin Stanic (SLO)    79-85-84
**142 (249)**
Jacopo Vecchi Fossa (ITA)    84-80-85

Craig Hinton (ENG)    77-75 DQ
Clément Sordet (FRA)    76-83 RTD
Nicolai Kristensen (DEN)    75-72 NR
Joshua White (ENG)    74-79 NR

| 1986 | Anders Haglund (SWE) | Eindhoven GC, Netherlands | 2002 | Ralph Peliciolli (FRA) | Troia GC, Portugal |
|---|---|---|---|---|---|
| 1988 | David Ecob (AUS) | Falkenstein GC, Germany | 2003 | Brian McElhinney (IRL) | Nairn GC, Scotland |
| 1990 | Klas Erikson (SWE) | Aalborg GC, Denmark | 2004 | Matthew Richardson | Skovde GC, Sweden |
| 1991 | Jim Payne (ENG) | Hillside GC, England | | (ENG) | |
| 1992 | Massimo Scarpa (ITA) | La Querce GC, Italy | 2005 | Marius Thorp (NOR) | Antwerp International GC, |
| 1993 | Morten Backhausen | Dalmahoy GC, Scotland | | | Belgium |
| | (DEN)* | | 2006 | Rory McIlroy (NIR) | Biella GC, Italy |

*after play-off with Lee Westwood (ENG)

| 1994 | Stephen Gallacher (SCO) | Aura GC, Finland | 2007 | Benjamin Hebert (FRA)* | Sporting Club, Berlin, |
|---|---|---|---|---|---|
| 1995 | Sergio Garcia (ESP) | El Prat GC, Spain | | | Germany |

*after play-off with Joel Sjoholm (SWE)

| 1997 | Didier de Voogt (BEL) | Domaine Imperial, | 2008 | Stephan Gross (GER) | Esberg GC, Denmark |
|---|---|---|---|---|---|
| | | Switzerland | 2009 | Victor Dubuisson (FRA) | Golf de Chantilly, France |
| 1998 | Gregory Havret (FRA) | Celtic Manor Resort, Wales | 2010 | Lucas Bjerregaard (DEN) | Vanajanlinna, Finland |
| 1999 | Paddy Gribben (IRL) | Golf du Medoc, France | 2011 | Manuel Trappel (AUT)* | Halmstad, Sweden |
| 2000 | Carl Pettersen (SWE) | Syrian GC, Austria | | *after play-off with Steven Brown (ENG) | |
| 2001 | Stephen Browne (IRL) | Odense Eventyr GC, | 2012 | Rhys Pugh (WAL) | Carton House, Ireland |
| | | Denmark | | | |

## 113th United States Amateur Championship
The Country Club, Brookline, Massachusetts
(US unless stated)
Aug 17–18

### Teenager Fitzpatrick takes the US Amateur title
### and ends a 102-year wait for an English victory

Matthew Fitzpatrick won the US Amateur Championship at The Country Club, Brookline, and moved to the top of The R&A and USGA Amateur rankings in the process.

With the 18-year-old's 4 and 3 victory over 19-year-old Australian Oliver Goss he won both the Havemeyer Trophy as champion and, as a consequemce, the McCormack Medal as the world's top amateur.

The last Englishman to win the title was Harold Hilton in 1902 at the Apawamis Club at Rye, New York, and his victory meant that Englishmen hold both the American amateur and professional Opens, Justin Rose having earlier won the US Open on the East course at Merion.

Mackenzie, from the Hallamshire Club in Sheffield, is a former British Boys champion and was runner-up to Callum Shinkwin in the 2013 English Amateur Championship. His US success came just a few weeks after finishing leading amateur and winning the Silver Medal in The Open Championship at Muirfield.

Fitzpatrick's success came on the course that hosted the famous 1913 US Open when US amateur Francis Ouimet beat professionals Harry Vardon and Ted Ray. Ouimet on that occasion had young Eddie Lowry as his caddie and Fitzpatrick had his younger brother Alex on the bag this time.

"This is absolutely amazing. This is what everyone wants in golf and it's nice to go down in the history books", said the delighted Fitzpatrick who is studying at Northwestern University in Chicago where Luke Donald earned his degree.

Goss, who was attempting to become the third Australian to win the title after Water Travis and Nick Flanagan, was one down at lunch but squared at the first in the afternoon. Fitzpatrick, whose short game was impressive throughout, quickly moved two up, however, and from then on "felt in control".

Goss commented after his defeat: "I couldn't get any momentum going, I just didn't play solid enough. I seemed to be close but not close enough."

For the first time since the start of the Championship in 1895 no American reached the last four. In the quarter finals Australian Brady Watt beat US Junior champion Scottie Scheffler to set up a semi-final against fellow countryman Oliver Goss, who beat American Brandon Matthews,

Fitzpatrick beat Adam Ball 4 and 3 in the quarter finals and then met Canadian Corey Conners who had beaten England's Neil Raymond in the last eight. In the semi-final Fitzpatrick holed from 18 feet for a winning birdie at the 17th against Conners, runner-up in the 2013 Canadian Championship, while Goss was a last green winner over Watt.

Twenty-seven-year-old Raymond and Watt were winners of the stroke-play qualifying firing six under par totals of 134 to lead by three.

### Stroke Play Qualifying:

| | | | | |
|---|---|---|---|---|
| Neil Raymond (ENG) | 67-67—134 | | Michael Miller (Brewster, NY) | 69-69—138 |
| Brady Watt (AUS) | 68-66—134 | | Nick Hardy (Northbrook, IL) | 65-73—138 |
| Oliver Goss (AUS) | 70-67—137 | | Bryson Dechambeau (Clovis, CA) | 67-71—138 |
| Justin Shin (CAN) | 71-66—137 | | Sean Dale (Jacksonville, FL) | 70-69—139 |
| Matt Fitzpatrick (ENG) | 67-70—137 | | Stewart Jolly (Birmingham, AL) | 74-65—139 |

## US Amateur Championship *continued*

| | | | | |
|---|---|---|---|---|
| Wyndham Clark (Greenwood Village, CO) | 71-68—139 | Adam Schenk (Vincennes, IN) | 74-69—143 |
| Bo Andrews (Raleigh, NC) | 76-63—139 | Corey Conners (CAN) | 70-73—143 |
| Max Orrin (ENG) | 69-70—139 | Michael Weaver (Fresno, CA) | 74-69—143 |
| Scott Wolfes (St Simons Island, GA) | 72-67—139 | Brandon Hagy (Westlake Village, CA) | 72-71—143 |
| Charlie Hughes (CAN) | 71-68—139 | Matt Pinizzotto (Salinas, CA) | 73-70—143 |
| Richy Werenski (South Hadley, MA) | 66-73—139 | Bobby Wyatt (Mobile, AL) | 71-72—143 |
| Nathan Holman (AUS) | 72-68—140 | Joey Petronio (Orlando, FL) | 70-73—143 |
| Sebastian Cappelen (DEN) | 73-67—140 | Richard Hearden III (Green Bay, WI) | 68-75—143 |
| Xander Schauffele (San Diego, CA) | 69-71—140 | Steven Zychowski (Mendham, NJ) | 70-73—143 |
| Adam Ball (Richmond, VA) | 72-69—141 | Andrew Price (Lake Bluff, IL) | 71-72—143 |
| Rico Hoey (Rancho Cucamonga, CA) | 73-68—141 | Blair Hamilton (CAN) | 70-73—143 |
| Brandon Matthews (Dupont, PA) | 69-72—141 | Sean Yu (TPE) | 75-69—144 |
| Ricardo Gouveia (POR) | 68-73—141 | Chase Koepka (Lake Worth, FL) | 76-68—144 |
| Greg Eason (ENG) | 70-71—141 | Gerrit Chambers (Brush Prairie, WA) | 76-68—144 |
| Rodolfo Cazaubon (MEX) | 71-70—141 | Gavin Hall (Pittsford, NY) | 73-71—144 |
| Matthias Schwab (AUT) | 71-70—141 | Jason Anthony (Fairfield, CA) | 72-72—144 |
| Eli Cole (Beverly Hills, CA) | 76-66—142 | Rhys Pugh (WAL) | 70-74—144 |
| Blake Morris (Waterbury, CT) | 73-69—142 | Jordan Smith (ENG) | 72-72—144 |
| Jim Liu (Smithtown, NY) | 72-70—142 | Ian Davis (Edmond, OK) | 76-68—144 |
| Carr Vernon (Poplar Bluff, MO) | 75-67—142 | Scottie Scheffler (Dallas, TX) | 74-70—144 |
| Seth Reeves (Duluth, GA) | 75-67—142 | Patrick Rodgers (Avon, IN) | 73-71—144 |
| Julian Suri (St Augustine, FL) | 71-71—142 | Sean Walsh (Keller, TX) | 71-73—144 |
| Zachary Olsen (Cordova, TN) | 75-67—142 | Jade Scott (Daingerfield, TX) | 74-70—144 |
| Jordan Niebrugge (Mequon, WI) | 69-73—142 | Zac Blair (Ogden, UT) | 69-75—144 |
| Matt Emery (Franklin, TN) | 71-71—142 | Tyler Klava (Pace, FL) | 67-77—144 |
| Chelso Barrett (Surry, NH) | 72-70—142 | Toni Hakula (FIN) | 70-74—144 |
| Cory McElyea (Santa Cruz, CA) | 73-69—142 | Mario Clemens (MEX) | 70-74—144 |
| Charlie Danielson (Osceola, WI) | 72-71—143 | Gavin Green (MAS) | 73-71—144 |

**First Round:**
Neil Raymond (ENG) beat Jason Anthony 1 up
Zachary Olsen beat Julian Suri 2 and 1
Blair Hamilton (CAN) beat Richy Werenski 4 and 2
Nathan Holman (AUS) beat Andrew Price 3 and 2
Bryson Dechambeau beat Sean Yu (TPE) 2 and 1
Corey Conners (CAN) beat Rodolfo Cazaubon
(MEX) 5 and 4
Patrick Rodgers beat Sean Dale 3 and 2
Greg Eason (ENG) beat Michael Weaver 3 and 2
Justin Shin (CAN) beat Tyler Klava 3 and 2
Chelso Barrett beat Jim Liu 3 and 2
Max Orrin (ENG) beat Rhys Pugh (WAL) 1 up
Adam Ball beat Joey Petronio 6 and 4
Matt Fitzpatrick (ENG) beat Gerrit Chambers
4 and 3
Blake Morris beat Cory McElyea 4 and 3
Gavin Hall beat Bo Andrews 2 and 1
Bobby Wyatt beat Rico Hoey 4 and 3
Brady Watt (AUS) beat Sean Walsh 5 and 3
Seth Reeves beat Jordan Niebrugge 1 up
Charlie Hughes (CAN) beat Ian Davis 3 and 3
Sebastian Cappelen (DEN) beat Steven Zychowski
4 and 2
Zac Blair beat Nick Hardy 1 up
Matthias Schwab (AUT) beat Adam Schenk 2 and 1
Scottie Scheffler beat Stewart Jolly at 20th
Brandon Hagy beat Ricardo Gouveia (POR) at 19th
Oliver Goss (AUS) beat Toni Hakula (FIN) 1 up
Carr Vernon beat Matt Emery at 19th

Scott Wolfes beat Mario Clemens (MEX) 2 and 1
Richard Hearden beat Xander Schauffele 2 and 1
Chase Koepka beat Michael Miller 2 and 1
Charlie Danielson beat Eli Cole 3 and 2
Gavin Green (MAS) beat Wyndham Clark 1 up,
Brandon Matthews beat Matt Pinizzotto 1 up
**Second Round:**
Neil Raymond beat Zachary Olsen 2 and 1
Nathan Holman beat Blair Hamilton 4 and 3
Corey Conners beat Bryson Dechambeau 2 and 1
Patrick Rodgers beat Greg Eason 3 and 2
Chelso Barrett beat Justin Shin 4 and 3
Adam Ball beat Max Orrin 2 and 1
Matt Fitzpatrick beat Blake Morris 4 and 3
Gavin Hall beat Bobby Wyatt 4 and 2
Brady Watt beat Seth Reeves 3 and 2
Charlie Hughes beat Sebastian Cappelen 4 and 3
Matthias Schwab beat Zac Blair 2 and 1
Scottie Scheffler beat Brandon Hagy at 20th
Oliver Goss beat Carr Vernon 2 up
Xander Schauffele beat Scott Wolfes 2 and 1
Charlie Danielson beat Chase Koepka 3 and 1
Brandon Matthews beat Gavin Green 4 and 3
**Third Round:**
Neil Raymond beat Nathan Holman 1 up
Corey Conners beat Patrick Rodgers 5 and 3
Adam Ball beat Chelso Barrett 6 and 5
Matt Fitzpatrick beat Gavin Hall 4 and 3
Brady Watt beat Charlie Hughes 2 and 1
Scottie Scheffler beat Matthias Schwab 1 up

Oliver Goss beat Xander Schauffele 3 and 1
Brandon Matthews beat Charlie Danielson 3 and 2
**Quarter Finals:**
Corey Conners beat Neil Raymond 5 and 3
Matt Fitzpatrick beat Adam Ball 4 and 3

Brady Watt beat Scottie Scheffler 1 up
Oliver Goss beat Brandon Matthews 5 and 3
**Semi-Finals:**
Matt Fitzpatrick beat Corey Conners 2 and 1
Oliver Goss beat Brady Watt 2 up

**Final:** Matt Fitzpatrick (ENG) beat Oliver Goss (AUS) 4 and 3

| Year | Result | Score | Venue | Entrants |
|---|---|---|---|---|
| 1895 | CB Macdonald beat C Sands | 12 & 11 | Newport GC, RI | *Entrants* 32 |
| 1896 | HJ Whigham beat JG Thorp | 8 & 7 | Shinnecock Hills GC, NY | 58 |
| 1897 | HJ Whigham beat WR Betts | 8 & 6 | Chicago GC, IL | 58 |
| 1898 | FS Douglas beat WB Smith | 5 & 3 | Morris County GC, NJ | 120 |
| 1899 | HM Harriman beat FS Douglas | 3 & 2 | Onwentsia Club, IL | 112 |
| 1900 | WJ Travis beat FS Douglas | 2 up | Garden City, GC NY | 120 |
| 1901 | WJ Travis beat WE Egan | 5 & 4 | CC of Atlantic City, NJ | 142 |
| 1902 | LN James beat EM Byers | 4 & 2 | Glenview Club, IL | 157 |
| 1903 | WJ Travis beat EM Byers | 5 & 4 | Nassau CC, NY | 140 |
| 1904 | HC Egan beat F Herreshof | 8 & 6 | Baltusrol GC, NJ | 142 |
| 1905 | HC Egan beat DE Sawyer | 6 & 5 | Chicago GC, IL | 146 |
| 1906 | EM Byers beat GS Lyon | 2 up | Englewood GC, NJ | 141 |
| 1907 | JD Travers beat A Graham | 6 & 5 | Euclid Club, OH | 118 |
| 1908 | JD Travers beat MH Behr | 8 & 7 | Garden City GC, NY | 145 |
| 1909 | RA Gardner beat HC Egan | 4 & 3 | Chicago GC, IL | 120 |
| 1910 | WC Fownes Jr beat WK Wood | 4 & 3 | The Country Club, Brookline, MA | 217 |
| 1911 | HH Hilton (ENG) beat F Herreshof | 1 up | Apawamis Club, Rye, NY | 186 |
| 1912 | JD Travers beat C Evans Jr | 7 & 6 | Chicago GC, IL | 86 |
| 1913 | JD Travers beat JG Anderson | 5 & 4 | Garden City, NY | 149 |
| 1914 | F Ouimet beat JD Travers | 6 & 5 | Ekwanok CC, VT | 115 |
| 1915 | RA Gardner beat JG Anderson | 5 & 4 | CC of Detroit, MI | 152 |
| 1916 | C Evans Jr beat RA Gardner | 4 & 3 | Merion Cricket Club (East), PA | 163 |
| 1917–18 | *Not played* | | | |
| 1919 | SD Herron beat RT Jones Jr | 5 & 4 | Oakmont CC, PA | 150 |
| 1920 | C Evans Jr beat F Ouimet | 7 & 6 | Engineers CC, NY | 235 |
| 1921 | JP Guildford beat RA Gardner | 7 & 6 | St Louis CC, MO | 159 |
| 1922 | JW Sweetser beat C Evans Jr | 3 & 2 | The Country Club, Brookline, MA | 161 |
| 1923 | MR Marston beat JW Sweetser | 1 up | Flossmoor, IL | 143 |
| 1924 | RT Jones Jr beat G Von Elm | 9 & 8 | Merion Cricket Club (East), PA | 142 |
| 1925 | RT Jones Jr beat W Gunn | 8 & 7 | Oakmont CC, PA | 141 |
| 1926 | G Von Elm beat RT Jones Jr | 2 & 1 | Baltusrol CC (Lower), NJ | 157 |
| 1927 | RT Jones Jr beat C Evans Jr | 8 & 7 | Minikahda Club, MN | 174 |
| 1928 | RT Jones Jr beat TP Perkins | 10 & 9 | Brae Burn CC, MA | 158 |
| 1929 | HR Johnston beat OF Willing | 4 & 3 | Del Monte G&CC, CA | 162 |
| 1930 | RT Jones Jr beat EV Homans | 8 & 7 | Merion Cricket Club (East), PA | 175 |
| 1931 | F Ouimet beat J Westland | 6 & 5 | Beverly CC, IL | 583 |
| 1932 | CR Somerville beat J Goodman | 2 & 1 | Five Farms GC (East), MD | 600 |
| 1933 | GT Dunlap Jr beat MR Marston | 6 & 5 | Kenwood CC, OH | 601 |
| 1934 | W Lawson Little Jr beat D Goldman | 8 & 7 | The Country Club, Brookline, MA | 758 |
| 1935 | W Lawson Little Jr beat W Emery | 4 & 2 | The Country Club, Cleveland, OH | 945 |
| 1936 | JW Fischer beat J McLean | 37 holes | Garden City GC, NY | 1,118 |
| 1937 | J Goodman beat RE Billows | 2 up | Alderwood CC, OR | 619 |
| 1938 | WP Turnesa beat BP Abbott | 8 & 7 | Oakmont CC, PA | 871 |
| 1939 | MH Ward beat RE Billows | 7 & 5 | North Shore CC, IL | 826 |
| 1940 | RD Chapman beat WB McCullough | 11 & 9 | Winged Foot GC (West), NY | 755 |
| 1941 | MH Ward beat BP Abbott | 4 & 3 | Omaha Field Club, NE | 637 |
| 1942–45 | *Not played* | | | |
| 1946 | SE Bishop beat S Quick | 1 up | Baltusrol CC (Lower), NJ | 899 |
| 1947 | RH Riegel beat JW Dawson | 2 & 1 | Del Monte G&CC, CA | 1,048 |
| 1948 | WP Turnesa beat RE Billows | 2 & 1 | Memphis CC, TN | 1,220 |
| 1949 | CR Coe beat R King | 11 & 10 | Oak Hill CC (East), NY | 1,060 |
| 1950 | S Urzetta beat FR Stranahan | 1 up | Minneapolis GC, MN | 1,025 |
| 1951 | WJ Maxwell beat J Gagliardi | 4 & 3 | Saucon Valley GC (Old), PA | 1,416 |
| 1952 | J Westland beat A Mengert | 3 & 2 | Seattle GC, WA | 1,029 |
| 1953 | G Littler beat D Morey | 1 up | Oklahoma City GC, OK | 1,284 |
| 1954 | A Palmer beat R Sweeney | 1 up | CC Of Detroit, MI | 1,278 |
| 1955 | E Harvie Ward beat W Hyndman | 9 & 8 | CC of Virginia (James River Course), VA | 1,493 |
| 1956 | E Harvie Ward beat C Kocsis | 5 & 4 | Knollwood Club, IL | 1,600 |
| 1957 | H Robbins beat FM Taylor | 5 & 4 | The Country Club (Anniversary Course), Brookline, MA | 1,578 |
| 1958 | CR Coe beat TD Aaron | 5 & 4 | The Olympic Club (Lake Course), CA | 1,472 |
| 1959 | JW Nicklaus beat CR Coe | 1 up | Broadmoor GC (East), CO | 1,696 |

## US Amateur Championship *continued*

| 1960 | DR Beman beat RW Gardner | 6 & 4 | St Louis CC, MO | 1,737 |
|------|--------------------------|-------|-----------------|-------|
| 1961 | JW Nicklaus beat HD Wysong | 8 & 6 | Pebble Beach GC, CA | 1,995 |
| 1962 | LE Harris Jr beat D Gray | 1 up | Pinehurst CC (No.2 Course), NC | 2,044 |
| 1963 | DR Beman beat RH Sikes | 2 & 1 | Wakonda Club, IA | 1,768 |
| 1964 | WC Campbell beat EM Tutweiler | 1 up | Canterbury GC, OH | 1,562 |

*Changed to stroke play*

| 1965 | Robert J Murphy Jr | 291 | Southern Hill CC, OK | 1.476 |
|------|--------------------|-----|----------------------|-------|
| 1966 | Gary Cowan (CAN)* | 285 | Merion GC (East), PA | 1,902 |

*\*Cowan beat Deane Beman 75-76 in 18-hole play-off*

| 1967 | RB Dickson | 285 | Broadmoor GC (West), CO | 1,784 |
|------|-----------|-----|------------------------|-------|
| 1968 | B Fleisher | 284 | Scioto GC, OH | 2,057 |
| 1969 | S Melnyk | 286 | Oakmont CC, PA | 2,142 |
| 1970 | L Wadkins* | 279 | Waverley GC, OR | 1,853 |
| 1971 | G Cowan (CAN) | 280 | Wilmington CC (South), DE | 2,327 |
| 1972 | Marvin Giles III | 285 | Charlotte CC, NC | 2,295 |

*Reverted to match play*

| 1973 | C Stadler beat D Strawn | 6 & 5 | Inverness Club OH | 2,110 |
|------|-------------------------|-------|-------------------|-------|
| 1974 | J Pate beat J Grace | 2 & 1 | Ridgewood CC, NJ | 2,420 |
| 1975 | F Ridley beat K Fergus | 2 up | CC of Virginia (James River Course), VA | 2,528 |
| 1976 | B Sander beat CP Moore | 8 & 6 | Bel Air CC, CA | 2,681 |
| 1977 | J Fought beat D Fischesser | 9 & 8 | Aromink GC, PA | 2,950 |
| 1978 | J Cook beat S Hoch | 5 & 4 | Plainfield GC, NJ | 3,035 |
| 1979 | M O'Meara beat J Cook | 8 & 7 | Canterbury GC, OH | 3,916 |
| 1980 | H Sutton beat B Lewis | 9 & 8 | CC of North Carolina, NC | 4,008 |
| 1981 | N Crosby beat B Lindley | 1 up | The Olympic Club (Lake Course), CA | 3,525 |
| 1982 | J Sigel beat D Tolley | 8 & 7 | The Country Club, Brookline, MA | 3,685 |
| 1983 | J Sigel beat C Perry | 8 & 7 | North Shore CC, IL | 3,553 |
| 1984 | S Verplank beat S Randolph | 4 & 3 | Oak Tree GC, OK | 3,679 |
| 1985 | S Randolph beat P Persons | 1 up | Montclair GC, NJ | 3,816 |
| 1986 | S Alexander beat C Kite | 5 & 3 | Shoal Creek GC, AL | 4,069 |
| 1987 | W Mayfair beat E Rebmann | 4 & 3 | Jupiter Hills Club (Hills Course), FL | 4,085 |
| 1988 | E Meeks beat D Yates | 7 & 6 | Hot Springs CC (Cascades Course), VA | 4,320 |
| 1989 | C Patton beat D Green | 3 & 1 | Merion GC (East), PA | 4,603 |
| 1990 | P Mickelson beat M Zerman | 5 & 4 | Cherry Hills CC, CO | 4,763 |
| 1991 | M Voges beat M Zerman | 7 & 6 | The Honors Course, TN | 4,985 |
| 1992 | J Leonard beat T Scherrer | 8 & 7 | Muirfield Village GC, OH | 5,758 |
| 1993 | J Harris beat D Ellis | 5 & 3 | Champions GC (Cypress Creek Course), TX | 5,614 |
| 1994 | T Woods beat T Kuehne | 2 up | TPC at Sawgrass (Stadium Course), FL | 5,128 |
| 1995 | T Woods beat G Marucci | 2 up | Newport CC, RI | 5,248 |
| 1996 | T Woods beat S Scott | 38 holes | Pumpkin Ridge GC, OR | 5,538 |
| 1997 | M Kuchar beat J Kribel | 2 & 1 | Cog Hill G&CC (No.4 Course), IL | 6,666 |
| 1998 | H Kuehne beat T McKnight | 2 and 1 | Oak Hill CC (East), NY | 6,627 |
| 1999 | D Gossett beat Sung Yoon Kim | 9 and 8 | Pebble Beach GC, CA | 7,920 |
| 2000 | J Quinney beat J Driscoll | 1 up | Baltusrol GC, NJ | 7,124 |
| 2001 | B Dickerson beat R Hamilton | 2 and 1 | Eastlake GC, GA | 7,762 |
| 2002 | R Barnes beat H Mahon | 2 and 1 | Oakland Hills CC (South Course), MI | 7,597 |
| 2003 | N Flanagan (AUS) beat C Wittenberg | 37 holes | Oakmont CC, PA | 7,541 |
| 2004 | R Moore beat L List | 2 up | Winged Foot GC (West Course), NY | 7,356 |
| 2005 | E Molinari (ITA) beat D Dougherty | 4 and 3 | Merion GC (East Course), PA | 7,320 |
| 2006 | R Ramsay (SCO) beat J Kelly | 4 and 2 | Hazeltine National GC, MN | 7,182 |
| 2007 | C Knost beat M Thompson | 2 and 1 | The Olympic Club (Lake Course), CA | 7,398 |
| 2008 | D Lee (NZL) beat D Kittleson | 5 and 4 | Pinehurst Resort and CC, NC | 7,298 |
| 2009 | B An (KOR) beat B Martin | 7 and 5 | Southern Hills CC, Tulsa, OK | 9,086 |
| 2010 | P Uihlein beat D Chung | 4 and 3 | Chambers Bay, WA | 6,485 |
| 2011 | K Kraft beat P Cantlay | 2 holes | Erin Hills CC, WI | 6,265 |
| 2012 | S Fox beat M Weaver | at 37th | Cherry Hills CC, CO | 7,002 |

# NCAA Championships (Men) *Capital City Club, Atlanta, Georgia*

## Corey Whitsett tears last year forgotten as Alabama clinch victory over Illinois

Alabama's men's team scored their first national championship by beating Illinois 4–1 in the final over the Crabapple course at Capital City GC, Milton, Georgia, to emulate the success of the University's women golfers in Tennessee in 2012.

California had led the stroke play section of the Championship but lost to Illinois in their semi final to maintain the unenviable record of no side having completed the stroke play and match play double.

The victory was particularly sweet for Cory Whitsett who had been involved in the vital last game against Texas last year. With the score 2–2 and the result dependent on Whitsett's match with Dylan Fritelli, the Alabama golfer made bogey 5 and Fritelli holes a 25 foot bidie putt for victory.

It seemed only fair that after his 2012 disappointment it should be Whitsett who clinched victory this time with a 4 and 3 win over Alex Burge ... but he made sure of victory by only 10 seconds. Almost immediately Scott Strohmeyer beat Brian Campbell but it will be Whitsett who will be remembered as the match winner.

Alabama, needing to win three of the five points for victory, could not have had a better start. Bobby Wyatt won his first seven holes against Thomas Detry and lost only one hole in a 6 and 5 success.

Then Trey Mullinax held his nerve againt Illinois' Charlie Danielson. All square playing the last. both missed the green with their approach shots but it was the Alabama player who got up and down for a one hole success.

By now victory was all but assured with Whitsett four up on the 15th green and Strophmeyer two up on the 16th. They both went on to win and Justin Thomas, one down after seventeen to Thomas Pieters, conceded to give Alabama a 4–1 win. It was their 24th Championship win and their eight in all sports since 2009.

Max Homa from California with rounds of 70, 65 and 66 for 201 won the individual prize by three shots from Brandon Stone (Texas), Kevin Penner (UNLV), Jon Rahm (Arizona State)., Danel Berger (Florida State), Rick Lamb (Tennessee) and Dominic Boezelli (Auburn).

### Stroke Play Championship – Team event:

| | | |
|---|---|---|
| 1 | California | 277-272-275—824 |
| 2 | Georgia Tech | 274-274-282—830 |
| 3 | Alabama | 275-276-282—833 |
| | Texas | 279-271-283—833 |

5 Illinois 835; 6 New Mexico, UNLV, Arizona State 842, Texas A&M 842; 10 Arkansas 843; 11 Oklahoma, Florida State 845; 13 Auburn 846; 14 Texas Tech, Oklahoma State 847; 16 Washington, UCF 848; 18 North Florida 849; 19 TCU, Georgia, Tennessee 850; 22 Coastal Carolina 851; 23 LSU, Southern California 854; 25 Florida 857; 26 UCLA 858; 27 South Carolina, Kent State 868; 29 St. Mary's (CA) 869; 30 Ball State 872

**Winning team:** Michael Weaver, Joel Stalter, Brandon Hagy, Max Homa, Michael Kim

### Individual Championship:

| | | | | | | |
|---|---|---|---|---|---|---|
| 1 | Max Homa (California) | 70-65-66—201 | | Yi Keun Chang (S. California) | 71-66-70—207 | |
| 2 | Daniel Berger (Florida State) | 69-67-68—204 | | Mario Clemens (SMU) | 69-68-70—207 | |
| | Dominic Bozzelli (Auburn) | 71-67-66—204 | | Thomas Pieters (Illinois) | 68-68-71—207 | |
| | Rick Lamb (Tennessee) | 68-67-69—204 | | Justin Thomas (Alabama) | 67-68-72—207 | |
| | Kevin Penner (UNLV) | 69-67-68—204 | | Cory Whitsett (Alabama) | 69-68-70—207 | |
| | Jon Rahm (Arizona State) | 61-72-71—204 | 22 | Julien Brun (TCU) | 74-64-70—208 | |
| | Brandon Stone (Texas) | 68-68-68—204 | | Jose Joia (UCF) | 72-66-70—208 | |
| 8 | Ian Davis (Oklahoma State) | 67-70-68—205 | | Denny McCarthy (Virginia) | 72-67-69—208 | |
| | Tyler Dunlap (Texas A&M) | 69-68-68—205 | | Beau Titsworth (Oklahoma) | 72-66-70—208 | |
| | Greg Eason (UCF) | 68-66-71—205 | 26 | Anders Albertson (Georgia Tech) | 69-67-73—209 | |
| | Brandon Hagy (California) | 66-69-70—205 | | | | |
| | Ollie Schniederjans (Georgia Tech) | 67-68-70—205 | | Oliver Goss (Tennessee) | 71-66-72—209 | |
| | | | | Gavin Green (New Mexico) | 73-70-66—209 | |
| 13 | Charlie Danielson (Illinois) | 70-66-70—206 | | Henry Todd (Texas Tech) | 73-68-68—209 | |
| | Nicolas Echavarria (Arkansas) | 70-64-72—206 | | Ben Wheeler (Coastal Carolina) | 70-71-68—209 | |
| | Seth Reeves (Georgia Tech) | 69-69-68—206 | | | | |
| 16 | Sebastian Cappelen (Arkansas) | 70-67-70—207 | 32 | Rodolfo Cazaubon (N. Texas) | 68-72-70—210 | |

NCAA Championships *continued*

| 32T | Sean Dale (North Florida) | 70-69-71—210 |
| | Shun Yat Hak (Georgia Tech) | 69-70-71—210 |
| | Kurt Kitayama (UNLV) | 71-72-67—210 |
| | Julio Vegas (Texas) | 68-68-74—210 |
| | Chris Williams (Washington) | 72-70-68—210 |
| 38 | John Catlin (New Mexico) | 74-67-70—211 |
| | Thomas Detry (Illinois) | 70-73-68—211 |
| | Joey Garber (Georgia) | 70-71-70—211 |
| | Talor Gooch (Oklahoma State) | 67-76-68—211 |
| | Kramer Hickok (Texas) | 72-66-73—211 |
| | Michael Johnson (Auburn) | 72-70-69—211 |
| | Spencer Lawson (Arizona State) | 71-70-70—211 |
| | Matthew NeSmith (South Carolina) | 70-75-66—211 |
| | Michael Schoolcraft (Oklahoma) | 72-69-70—211 |
| | Chase Seiffert (Florida State) | 70-69-72—211 |
| | Clement Sordet (Texas Tech) | 71-75-65—211 |
| 49 | Drew Evans (Texas A&M) | 74-68-70—212 |
| | Toni Hakula (Texas) | 71-69-72—212 |
| | Michael Kim (California) | 72-70-70—212 |
| | Doug Letson (Florida State) | 71-71-70—212 |
| | Trey Mullinax (Alabama) | 72-70-70—212 |
| | Victor Perez (New Mexico) | 72-69-71—212 |
| | Austin Quick (Arizona State) | 70-70-72—212 |
| | Trevor Simsby (Washington) | 68-72-72—212 |
| | Sam Smith (S. California) | 71-72-69—212 |
| | Joel Stalter (California) | 69-68-75—212 |
| | Pontus Widegren (UCLA) | 72-70-70—212 |
| 60 | Daniel Jennevret (TCU) | 72-70-71—213 |
| | Stewart Jolly (LSU) | 72-70-71—213 |
| | Lee McCoy (Georgia) | 74-70-69—213 |
| | Keith Mitchell (Georgia) | 70-72-71—213 |
| | Taylor Moore (Arkansas) | 74-70-69—213 |
| | Jordan Niebrugge (Oklahoma State) | 71-74-68—213 |
| | Cameron Peck (Texas A&M) | 72-69-72—213 |
| | Nicholas Reach (Georgia) | 72-70-71—213 |
| | Johannes Veerman (Texas A&M) | 71-70-72—213 |
| 69 | Roberto Ballesteros (Coastal Carolina) | 75-66-73—214 |
| | Eric Banks (Florida) | 72-73-69—214 |
| | Niclas Carlsson (Auburn) | 76-69-69—214 |
| | James Erkenbeck (N. Mexico) | 75-68-71—214 |
| | Pedro Figueiredo (UCLA) | 72-67-75—214 |
| | Jonathan Garrick (UCLA) | 73-71-70—214 |
| | Charlie Hughes (Washington) | 73-69-72—214 |
| | Tyler Klava (South Alabama) | 73-70-71—214 |
| | Tyler McCumber (Florida) | 72-69-73—214 |
| | Taylor Pendrith (Kent State) | 72-71-71—214 |
| | Esteban Restrepo (Texas Tech) | 71-70-73—214 |
| | Charlie Saxon (Oklahoma) | 69-74-71—214 |
| | Scott Strohmeyer (Alabama) | 71-70-73—214 |
| | T J Vogel (Florida) | 72-72-70—214 |
| | Michael Weaver (California) | 74-71-69—214 |
| | Zach Wright (LSU) | 68-74-72—214 |
| 85 | Alex Burge (Illinois) | 72-74-69—215 |
| | Corey Conners (Kent State) | 71-72-72—215 |
| | Andrew Dorn (Coastal Carolina) | 74-71-70—215 |
| | Cody Gribble (Texas) | 75-70-70—215 |
| | Taylor Hancock (N. Florida) | 69-76-70—215 |
| | M J Maguire (North Florida) | 70-71-74—215 |
| | Dalan Refioglu (St Mary's (CA)) | 71-73-71—215 |
| | Max Rottluff (Arizona State) | 68-76-71—215 |
| 93 | Paul Barjon (TCU) | 74-72-70—216 |
| | Benjamin Bauch (N. Mexico) | 73-74-69—216 |
| | Carl Jonson (UNLV) | 73-74-69—216 |
| | Smylie Kaufman (LSU) | 77-68-71—216 |
| | Tony Lazzara (Ball State) | 70-69-77—216 |
| | Anthony Paolucci (Southern California) | 69-71-76—216 |
| | Jonathan Sanders (Washington) | 69-72-75—216 |
| | Sebastian Soderberg (Coastal Carolina) | 74-67-75—216 |
| | Jay Vandeventer (Tennessee) | 75-71-70—216 |
| | Daniel Walker (Richmond) | 74-71-71—216 |
| 103 | Abraham Ancer (Oklahoma) | 65-77-75—217 |
| | Eli Cole (TCU | 76-68-73—217 |
| | Pontus Gad (TCU) | 74-70-73—217 |
| | Ricardo Gouveia (UCF) | 70-73-74—217 |
| | Mac McClung (St Mary's (CA)) | 73-73-71—217 |
| | Kevin Phelan (N. Florida) | 75-71-71—217 |
| 109 | Brian Campbell (Illinois) | 68-75-75—218 |
| | Austin Cook (Arkansas) | 73-70-75—218 |
| | A J McInerney (UNLV) | 73-77-68—218 |
| | Jake Mondy (Auburn) | 73-73-72—218 |
| | Cheng-Tsung Pan (Washington) | 72-74-72—218 |
| | Nicholas Scott (Kent State) | 68-75-75—218 |
| | Peter Valasek (Coastal Carolina) | 75-71-72—218 |
| 116 | Jonathan De Los Reyes (St Mary's (CA)) | 71-75-73—219 |
| | Kevin Dougherty (Oklahoma State) | 74-74-71—219 |
| | Ben Geyer (St Mary's (CA)) | 72-74-73—219 |
| | Stewart Hagestad (Southern California) | 80-69-70—219 |
| 116T | Dykes Harbin (S. Carolina) | 74-71-74—219 |
| | Dustin Korte (Austin Peay State) | 75-72-72—219 |
| | Joey Petronio (N. Florida) | 72-71-76—219 |
| | Andrew Presley (LSU) | 72-74-73—219 |
| | Will Starke (S.Carolina) | 70-75-74—219 |
| | Alex Stinson (Ball State) | 72-74-73—219 |
| | Curtis Thompson (LSU) | 73-70-76—219 |
| | Greg Yates (Texas A&M) | 73-72-74—219 |
| 128 | Anton Arboleda (UCLA) | 72-73-75—220 |
| | Finley Ewing IV (Texas Tech) | 73-71-76—220 |
| | Joe Gasser (Ball State) | 76-72-72—220 |
| | Nicholas Maruri (UNLV) | 76-71-73—220 |

| | | | | | | |
|---|---|---|---|---|---|---|
| 128T | Manav Shah (UCLA) | 73-74-73—220 | | 144T | Sean Kelly (South Carolina) | 73-76-74—223 |
| | Caleb Sturgeon (South Carolina) | 73-75-72—220 | | | Hank Lebioda (Florida State) | 77-72-74—223 |
| 134 | Tyler Merkel (Ball State) | 72-77-72—221 | | | Kyle Wilshire (UCF) | 77-69-77—223 |
| | Tommy Mou (Florida) | 75-75-71—221 | | 149 | Alex Bungert (St Mary's (CA)) | 75-74-76—225 |
| 136 | Matias Dominguez (Texas Tech) | 78-74-70—222 | | | Brandon Rodgers (Tennessee) | 75-74-76—225 |
| | Michael Hebert (Auburn) | 77-74-71—222 | | | | |
| | Will Kropp (Oklahoma) | 75-75-72—222 | | 151 | McCormick Clouser (Ball State) | 77-74-76—227 |
| | Kevin Miller (Kent State) | 71-75-76—222 | | | | |
| | T J Mitchell (Georgia) | 77-73-72—222 | | 152 | Kyle Kmiecik (Kent State) | 78-75-75—228 |
| | Mike Nagy (Tennessee) | 72-73-77—222 | | | Michael Visacki (UCF) | 80-76-72—228 |
| | Thomas Sorensen (Arkansas) | 73-72-77—222 | | 154 | Trey Ka'ahanui (Arizona State) | 75-80-79—234 |
| | J D Tomlinson (Florida) | 80-69-73—222 | | 155 | Patrick Winther (Oklahoma State) | 78-75-82—235 |
| 144 | Bo Andrews (Georgia Tech) | 78-72-73—223 | | | | |
| | Rowin Caron (Florida State) | 82-70-71—223 | | 156 | Jeffrey Kang (S. California) | 83-75-84—242 |

**Match Play Championship:**

**Quarter-finals:**  California 3, Arizona State 2
Illinois 3, Texas 2
Georgia Tech 3, UNLV 2
Alabanma 4, New Mexico 1

**Semi-finals:**  Alabama 3, Georgia Tech 0
Illinois 3, California 2

**Final:** Alabama 4, Illinois 1

Bobby Wyatt beat Thomas Detry 6 and 5
Trey Mullinax beat Charlie Danielson 1 up
Justin Thomas lost to Thomas Pieters 1 up
Scott Stroymeyer beat Brian Campbell 3 and 2
Cory Whitsett beat Alexz Burge 4 and 3

# Referees' school always a big success

The annual R&A Tournament Administrators' and Referees' school at St Andrews each year usually attracts more than 70 representatives of Golf Federations from all over the world. Last year was no exception when it was attended by delegates from more than 30 different countries from South America, Asia, Africa, Australia, Canada and Europe. The event, which is hosted each year by The R&A, is designed to assist its affiliated bodies with the training of referees and tournament officials.

The three-day school included practical demonstration sessions on a specially constructed indoor facility, instructional sessions and presentations on subjects including pace of play, starting and recording, course marking, amateur status and guidance on officiating.

Andy McFee, the Chief Referee on the European Tour, gave a presentation about refereeing at the professional level and R&A instructors for a role play session in which delegates gave rulings in realistic on-course situations.

The school culminated in the delegates sitting the Level Three Rules Exam. The R&A's Rules Education programme takes a three-tiered approach to guide people from gaining a basic knowledge of the Rules to reaching the standard of tournament officials and referees.

David Rickman, Executive Director – Rules and Equipment Standards at The R&A, said, "It is great to see such a high level of interest from so many different countries. The school covers the many different aspects of refereeing and administering tournaments and takes people through the situations they might face out on the course.

"The diverse range of countries represented again this year shows that golf is growing in many parts of the world and we are working hard to support its development wherever we can."

# National Championships 2013

For past winners see earlier editions of The R&A Golfer's Handbook

*Players are from the host nation unless stated*

### Africa

## Egyptian Amateur Open Championship *Mirage City Golf Course, Cairo*

| | | |
|---|---|---|
| 1 | Soliman El Asser | 77-73-74—224 |
| 2 | Abdelmonen El Shafei | 78-71-78—227 |
| 3 | Amr Abou El Ela | 74-76-78—228 |

## Egyptian Closed Amateur Championship *Alexandria Sporting Club*

| | | |
|---|---|---|
| 1 | Amr Aboul Elq | 69-73—142 |
| 2 | Ayman Mahmoud | 71-72—143 |
| 3 | MaherAbdel Nabi | 72-74—146 |

## Kenya Amateur Stroke Play Championship *Sigona GC*

| | | |
|---|---|---|
| 1 | John Karichu | 80-73-72-69—294 |
| 2 | Jay Sandhu | 76-79-71-70—296 |
| | Nelson Sima | 75-74-71-76—296 |

## South African Amateur Championship (inaugurated 1892) *Country Club Johannesburg*

Feb 25–Mar 1

**Semi-finals:** Thriston Lawrence beat Louis Taylor 2 and 1
Andrew Light beat Ewan Scott 3 and 2

**Final:** Thirsten Lawrence beat Andrew Light 9 and 8

**Medallist:** Haydn Porteous 66-68—134

## South African Amateur Stroke Play Championship (inaugurated 1969)

*Oubaai GC* Feb 11–15

| | | |
|---|---|---|
| 1 | Haydn Porteous | 69-67-70-69—275 |
| 2 | Werner Ferreira | 66-69-73-69—277 |
| 3 | Alejandro Tosti | 73-67-68-70—278 |

## South African Mid-Amateur Stroke Play Championship *Stellenbosch GC*

| | | |
|---|---|---|
| 1 | Greg Sheard (De Zalze ) | 69-70-71-72—282 |
| 2 | Cameron Johnston (Milnerton) | 72-71-73-70—286 |
| 3 | Graeme Watson (Ebotse G&CE) | 71-69-71-76—287 |
| | Jaco Rall (Ebotse G&CE) | 75-71-72-69—287 |
| | Grant Wood (Modderfontein) | 72-67-76-72—287 |

## South African Senior Championship *Fancourt CC*

| | | |
|---|---|---|
| 1 | Gavin Van Aswegen (R. Johannesberg and Kensington GC) | 71-74—145 |
| 2 | Mellette Hendrikse (Akasia CC) | 73-73—146 |
| | Thys Matthys Johannes Marais (Greenside Colliery GC) | 72-72—146 |
| | Francois Leroux (De Zalze GC) | 71-75—146 |

*Final round cancelled because of thunder, lightning and flooding*

## Zimbabwe Amateur Games *Bulawayo GC*

| | | |
|---|---|---|
| 1 | Benjamin Follett-Smith | 68-74-72-71—285 |
| 2 | Hanish Nagrani (CAN) | 72-72-72-73—289 |
| 3 | Clive Nguru | 76-72-70-74—292 |

## Americas

## Argentine Amateur Championship *Martindale CC*

**Semi-finals:** Marcos Montenegro beat Niklas Nörgaard Möller (DEN) 3 and 2
Jacopo Vecchi Fossa (ITA) beat Joaquin Bonjour 1 up
**Final:** Marcos Montenegro beat Jacopo Vecchi Fossa 4 and 3
**Leading qualifier:** Filippo Campigliita (ITA) 65-70—135

## 12th United Insurance Barbados Open *Apes Hill CC, Barbados GC and Royal Westmorland*

| | | |
|---|---|---|
| 1 | James Johnson | 76-70-73—219 |
| 2 | Trevor Levine | 68-76-78—222 |
| 3 | Scott Stollmeyer | 73-74-77—224 |

Seniors: Robert Piggott 230. Super Seniors: Bill Weir

## 109th Canadian Amateur Championship (inaugurated 1895)
*Royal Colwood GC and Gorge Vale GC*

| | | |
|---|---|---|
| 1 | Eli Cole (USA) | 71-66-69-70—276 |
| 2 | Taylor Pendrith | 69-71-69-68—277 |
| | Corey Connors | 66-70-70-71—277 |

## Canadian Mid Amateur Championship *Blackhawk GC*

| | | |
|---|---|---|
| 1 | Kevin Carrigan (Victoria) | 63-68-67-67—264 |
| 2 | Michael Rutgers (Windsor) | 68-69-71-67—275 |
| | Garrett Rank (Elmira) | 72-64-65-74—275 |

## Canadian Men's Senior Championship *The Briars GC, Ontario*

| | | |
|---|---|---|
| 1 | David Schultz | 68-69-72-69—278 |
| 2 | Chip Lutz (USA) | 67-69-75-68—279 |
| 3 | Duke Delcher (USA) | 70-70-71-69—280 |

## 57th Caribbean Amateur Championship (Hoerman Cup) *St Thomas, US Virgin Islands*

| | | |
|---|---|---|
| 1 | Lino Guerriero (DOM) | 72-71-70-69—282 |
| 2 | Calvesbert Robert (PUR) | 73-71-70-71—285 |
| 3 | Estave Jeronimo (PUR) | 74-70-72-71—287 |

## Colombian Open *CC Pereira*

| | | |
|---|---|---|
| 1 | Federico Arango* | 68-72-70-77—287 |
| 2 | Ivan Camilo Ramirez | 67-78-72-70—287 |

*Arango won in play-off*

| | | |
|---|---|---|
| 3 | Santiago Tobon (pro) | 72-74-73-74—293 |

## Mexican Amateur Championship *Guadalajara CC* April 26–29

| | | |
|---|---|---|
| 1 | Mario Clemens | 69-65-65-79—269 |
| 2 | Carloz Ortiz | 68-68-70-65—271 |
| 3 | Guillermo Silva | 66-68-69-69—272 |

## 113th North and South Men's Amateur Championship *Pinehurst Resort*

**Semi-finals:**  Andrew Dorn beat Max Greyserman  5 and 4
              Zachary Bauchou beat Grayson Murray  1 hole
**Final:**  Andrew Dorn beat Zachary Bauchou  1 hole
**Medallist:**  Adam Schenk  203

## South American Amateur Championship  *Rincon CC Bogota, Colombia*  Jan 23–26

| | | |
|---|---|---|
| 1 | Callum Shinkwin (ENG) | 75-70-70-78—293 |
| 2 | Erik Myllymaki (FIN) | 75-73-73-73—294 |
| 3 | Joaquin Lolas (PER) | 77-72-76-71—296 |

## US Amateur Championship  *see page 299*

## 33rd US Mid-Amateur Championship  *Country Club of Birmingham, Birmingham, Alabama*

**Semi-finals:**  Michael McCoy (West Des Moines, IA) beat Kevin Marsh (Henderson, NV)  4 and 3
              Bill Williamson (Cincinnati, OH) beat Kenneth McCready (San Diego, CA)  2 and 1
**Final:**  Michael McCoy beat Bill Williamson  8 and 6
**Medallist:**  Matthew Mattare (Jersey City, NJ)  67-69—136

## US Amateur Seniors Championship  *Wade Hampton GC, Cashiers, North Carolina*

**Semi-finals:**  Douglas Hanzel (Savannah, GA) beat Chip Lutz (Reading, PA)  3 and 2
              Pat O'Donnell (Happy Valley, OR) beat Buzz Fly (Memphis, TN)  2 and 1
**Final:**  Douglas Hanzel beat Pat O'Donnell  3 and 2
**Medallist:**  Chip Lutz  69-69—138

## US Amateur Public Links Championship  *Laurel Hill GC, Lorton, Virginia*

**Semi-finals:**  Jordan Niebrugge (Mequon, WI) beat James Erkenbeck (San Diego, CA)  3 and 2
              Michael Kim (Del Mar, CA) beat Eric Sugimoto (San Diego, CA)  4 and 3
**Final:**  Jordan Niebrugge beat Michael Kim  1 up

## Uruguay Stroke Play Championship  *La Tahona GC*

| | | |
|---|---|---|
| 1 | Juan Alvarez | 72-73-73—218 |
| 2 | Nicolas Teuten | 75-77-71—223 |
| 3 | Facundo Alvarez | 79-73-74—226 |

## Venezuela Amateur Championship  *Guataparo CC*

| | | |
|---|---|---|
| 1 | Luis Lopez | 74-75-79—228 |
| 2 | Juan Guillermo Degwitz | 78-76-79—233 |
| 3 | Angelo De Pietro | 74-80-85—239 |

## Asia–Pacific Amateur Championship  *see page 289*

## Bangladesh Amateur Championship  *Kurmitola GC*

| | | |
|---|---|---|
| 1 | Karan Taunk (IND) | 70-69-70-72—281 |
| 2 | Md Sajib Ali | 72-67-75-74—288 |
| 3 | Md Sagor | 68-72-75-74—289 |

## China Amateur Championship CGU Nanshan ITC (Cuigu course)

| 1 | Jin Zhang | 71-69-71—211 |
| 2 | Youxin Wang | 68-72-74—214 |
| 3 | Rongjian Tang | 75-70-71—216 |
|   | Chenlin Liu (TPE) | 73 -69 74—216 |

## Emirates Championship (Presidents Cup) Saadyat Beach

| 1 | Khalid Yousuf | 74-76—150 |
| 2 | Abdulla Al Musharrek | 76-75—151 |
| 3 | Saif Thabot | 74-71—155 |
|   | Sohail Al Maizonqui | 82-73—155 |

## Hong Kong Close Amateur Championship Hong Kong GC (New course)

| 1 | Chen Kun Mex Wong | 67-70-71-68—276 |
| 2 | Shinichi Mizuno | 73-73-69-68—283 |
| 3 | H H Matthew Cheung | 69-70-75-71—285 |

## Hong Kong Open and Mid-Amateur Championship Hong Kong GC

| 1 | Yu-Jui Liu (TPE) | 73-67-71—211 |
| 2 | Marc Ong (SIN) | 70-69-73—212 |
| 3 | Jerome Ng (SIN) | 71-70-72—213 |

## Hong Kong Seniors Close Championship Hong Kong GC (Old)

| 1 | William Douglas | 75-72-70—217 |
| 2 | Tony Taylor | 75-76-75—226 |
|   | Joseph Pethes | 77-73-76—226 |

## 113th Amateur Golf Championship of India Bombay Presidency GC,Mumbai

**Semi-finals:** Karan Taunk beat Md. Sajib Ali 1 up
Pratap Atwal beat Gagan Verma 4 and 3
**Final:** Pratap Atwal beat Karan Tuank at 37th
**Medallist:** Karan Tuank 131

## Israeli Amateur Championship Caesarea GC

| 1 | Assaf Cohen | 76-77-72—225 |
| 2 | Yair Thaler | 75-76-75—226 |
| 3 | Dolev Gueta | 79-80-81—240 |

## 98th Japanese Amateur Championship Tokyo GC

**Semi-finals:** Yujiro Ohori beat Soo-Min Lee (KOR) at 20th
Tomoyasu Sugiyama beat Cameron Davis (AUS) 2 and 1
**Final:** Yujiro Ohori beat Tomoyasu Sugiyama 9 and 8

## Japan Mid-Amateur Golf Championship Dazaifu GC, Fukuoka

| 1 | Hironobu Kin | 76-71-72—219 |
| 2 | Sumio Shiotsuki | 71-73-76—220 |
| 3 | Takayoshi Iseki | 73-73-76—222 |

## Korean Amateur Championship (Hur Chung Koo Cup) Nameseoul GC

| 1 | Chang-woo Lee | 70-66-67-66—269 |
| 2 | Tae-hyun Kong | 73-68-73-69—283 |
| 3 | En-ho Yeoum | 76-69-71-69—285 |
|   | Joon-Hyeong Jeon | 68-73-75-69—285 |

## 111th Malaysian Open Amateur Championship   Royal Pahang GC
| | | |
|---|---|---|
| 1 | Kevin Marques (AUS) | 68-66-72-68—274 |
| 2 | Poom Saksansin (THA) | 69-70-71-65—275 |
| 3 | Taylor Macdonald (AUS) | 68-67-71-70—276 |

## Myanmar Amateur Championship   Yangon GC
| | | |
|---|---|---|
| 1 | Myo Win Aung | 71-70-69-75—285 |
| 2 | Danthai Boonma (THA) | 72-75-71-70—288 |
| 4 | Tawan Phongphun (THA) | 76-72-72-72—292 |

## Pakistan Amateur Championship   Lahore Gymkhana GC
| | | |
|---|---|---|
| 1 | Md Sagor (BAN) | 74-73-73-70—290 |
| 2 | Muhammad Ali Hai | 80-69-74-70—293 |
| 3 | Taimoor Khan | 75-71-73-76—295 |

## Philippine Open Amateur Championship   Wack Wack G&CC
| | | |
|---|---|---|
| 1 | Jerome Ng (SIN) | 78-73-74-75—300 |
| 2 | Mohd Afif Mohd Razif (MAS) | 76-76-78-72—302 |
| | Jung Sang In (TPE) | 73-75-81-73—302 |
| | Rupert Zaragosa | 73-74-80-75—302 |

## 14th Singapore National Amateur Championship   Jarong CC
**Semi-finals:**   Marc Ong  beat Johnson Poh  4 and 3
Yash Majmuder beat Wong Qi Wen  1 hole

**Final:**   Yash Majmuder beat Marc Ong  3 and 2

**Medallist:**   Marc Ong 68-72—140

## 66th Singapore Open Amateur Championship   Singapore Island GC
| | | |
|---|---|---|
| 1 | Yu-Jui Liu (TPE) | 72-71-70-65—278 |
| 2 | Kasidit Lepkrut (THA) | 69-77-66-68—280 |
| 3 | Marc Ong | 71-73-68-71—283 |
| | Itthipat Buranatanyarat (THA) | 72-69-70-72—283 |
| | Justin Quiban (PHI) | 73-70-68-72—283 |

## Singapore National Senior Amateur   Raffles GC (Palm)
| | | |
|---|---|---|
| 1 | Francis Chia Kok Hui | 76-82-79—237 |
| 2 | Wong Yess Seong | 81-80-81—242 |
| | Chin Soon Chye | 81-80-81—242 |

## 126th Sri Lanka Amateur Championship   Victoria G&CC
**Semi-finals:**   Sayed Saqib Ahmed (IND) beat Md Saqib Ali (BAN)
Trishul Chinnappa (IND) beat B A Rohana (SRI)

**Final:**   Syed Saqib Ahmed beat Trishul Chinnappa  5 and 3

## Taiwan Amateur Championship   Sunrise G&CC, Taoyuan, Taipei
| | | |
|---|---|---|
| 1 | Teng Kao | 67-75-70-66—278 |
| 2 | Chieh-Po | 71-76-67-65—279 |
| | Yu-Jui Liu | 70-70-69-70—279 |

## Thailand Amateur Open Championship  *Panya Indra GC*

| | | |
|---|---|---|
| 1 | Suradit Yongcharoenchai* | 71-72-73-65—281 |
| 2 | Poom Saksansin | 72-69-70-70—281 |
| 3 | Jerome Ng (SIN) | 71-68-71-71—281 |

*Yongcharoenchai won at the first extra hole*

## Vietnam National Amateur Championship  *Montgomerie Links*

| | | |
|---|---|---|
| 1 | Do Le Gia Dat | 78-80-73-73—304 |
| 2 | Doan Van Dinh | 77-77-78-78—310 |

### Australasia

## Australian Amateur Championship  (inaugurated 1894)  *Commonwealth GC and Woodlands GC*

Jan 15–20

**Semi-finals:** Geoff Drakeford (VIC) beat An Sam (NZL) 6 and 4
Cameron Smith (QLD) beat Blair Riordan (NZL) 3 and 2

**Final:** Cameron Smith beat Geoff Drakeford 3 and 2

**Medallist:** Brady Watt (WA) 66-70—136

## Australian Men's Mid-Amateur Championship  *Moonah Links (Open course), Victoria*

| | | |
|---|---|---|
| 1 | Damien Jordan (Queensland) | 73-70—143 |
| 2 | Richard Macafee (Victoria) | 77-73—150 |
| 3 | Jason Cocks (South Australia) | 74-77—151 |

*Reduced to 36 holes because of bad weather on first day*

## Australian Men's Senior Amateur Championship  *Royal Queensland GC, Brisbane*

| | | |
|---|---|---|
| 1 | Murray Martin (NZL) | 74-74-74—222 |
| 2 | Samuel Christie (Queensland) | 79-78-71—228 |
| | Frank Borren (NZL) | 76-76-76—228 |

## Fiji Open Amateur Championship  *Fiji GC, Suva*

| | | |
|---|---|---|
| 1 | Sam Lee | 68-73-69-68—278 |
| 2 | Anuresh Chandra | 75-72-72-75—294 |
| 3 | Olaf Allen | 71-75-73-79—298 |

## New Zealand Amateur Championship  (inaugurated 1893)  *Manawatu GC*  April 24–28

**Semi-finals:** Kadin Neho beat Steven Kuggeleijn 2 holes
Ryan Chisnall beat Tae Koh 2 and 1

**Final:** Kadin Neho beat Ryan Chisnall 3 and 2

**Medallist:** Luke Toomey 70-61—131

## New Zealand Stroke Play Championship  (inaugurated 1969)  *Paraparaumu Beach GC*

Mar 20–24

| | | |
|---|---|---|
| 1 | Cameron Jones | 68-69-72-67—276 |
| 2 | Nick Voke | 68-69-72-69—278 |
| 3 | Hayden Beard | 71-72-71-69—282 |

## New Zealand Senior Championship  *Waitikiri GC*  Feb 4–10

| | | |
|---|---|---|
| 1 | Brent Paterson | 70-72-71—213 |
| 2 | Mike Leitch | 72-74-76—222 |
| 3 | Frank Borren | 76-74-74—224 |

# New Zealand Mid-Amateur Championship  *Wairakei GC*

| | | |
|---|---|---|
| 1 | Mark Boulton (AUS) | 79-74-75—228 |
| 2 | Stuart Duff (Hastings) | 78-75-78—231 |
| 3 | Diego Hugues  (FRA) | 87-80-77—244 |
| | Michael Ursin (Manor Park) | 84-80-80—244 |

# Austrian Stroke Play Championship  *Schloss Schonborn*

| | | |
|---|---|---|
| 1 | Felix Schulz | 77-71-77-72—297 |
| 2 | Nikolaus Wimmer | 78-74-75-71—298 |
| 3 | Sebastian Wittmann | 77-79-78-67—301 |

# Austrian International Men's Championship  *GC Linz St Florian*

| | | |
|---|---|---|
| 1 | Kristian Kulokorpi (FIN)* | 70-69-67-70—276 |
| 2 | Robin Goger | 70-71-69-66—276 |

*Kulokorpi beat Goger in play-off*

| | | |
|---|---|---|
| 3 | Federico Paez Weinbaum (ESP) | 69-71-68-73—281 |

# Belgian International Amateur Championship  *Royal Antwerp GC*

| | | |
|---|---|---|
| 1 | Thomas Detry (Royal GC of Belgium) | 67-70-66-63—266 |
| 2 | Jamie Donaldson (Antwerp Inter.) | 64-69-70-70—273 |
| 3 | Alan de Bondt (Royal Antwerp) | 67 69-70-70—276 |

# Belgian National Stroke Play Championship  *Golf de Mean*

| | | |
|---|---|---|
| 1 | Gaetan Van Baarle | 71-75-71-71—288 |
| 2 | Pierre-Alexis Rolland | 75-73-70-71—289 |
| | Cedric Van Wassenhove | 70-73-73-73—289 |

# British Amateur Championship  *see page 291*

# British Seniors Open Amateur Championship  (inaugurated 1969)  *Royal Aberdeen GC*

| | | |
|---|---|---|
| 1 | George Zahringer (USA) | 69-75-74—218 |
| 2 | Tom Brandes (USA) | 77-73-69—219 |
| 3 | Garth McGimpsey (IRL) | 71-72-77—220 |

# Bulgarian Amateur Championship  *Pravets CC*

| | | |
|---|---|---|
| 1 | Dimitar Lulov | 75-76—151 |
| 2 | Vladislav Marinov | 78-76—154 |
| 3 | Alexander Evtimov | 83-75—158 |
| | Radoslav Rashev | 76-82—158 |

# Cyprus Amateur Men's Open  *Aphrodite Hills GC*

| | | |
|---|---|---|
| 1 | Oliver Gabor (SVK) | 76-71-74—221 |
| 2 | Robert Reynolds (ENG) | 72-83-71—226 |
| | Andre Draslar (CZE) | 70-79-77—226 |

## Czech Republic Amateur Championship  *Karlovy Vary GC*

| | | |
|---|---|---|
| 1 | Tim Gornik | 70-64-71-72—277 |
| 2 | Vitek Novak | 73-66-74-68—281 |
| | Michal Pospisal | 71-69-69-72—281 |

## Danish International Open Championship  *Silkeborg GC*  May 30–June 2

| | | |
|---|---|---|
| 1 | Thomas Elissalde (FRA) | 70-76-69-71—286 |
| 2 | Benjamin Henry Poke | 70-75-71-73—289 |
| 3 | Nicolai Tinning | 76-71-70-74—291 |

## Dutch National Stroke Play Championship  *Houtrak GC*

| | | |
|---|---|---|
| 1 | Lars Van Meijel | 70-71-73-74—288 |
| 2 | Berend van Holthuijsen | 71-79-70-70—290 |
| | Lars Keunen | 77-71-69-73—290 |

## Dutch National Match Play Championship  *Broekpolder GC*

**Semi-Finals:** Severiano Prins beat Axel Geers  5 and 4
Darius van Driel beat Maarten Bosch  4 and 3
**Final:** Darius van Driel beat Severiano Prins  4 and 3

## English Open Amateur Stroke Play Championship  (Brabazon Trophy)  *Formby GC*

(inaugurated 1947)

| | | |
|---|---|---|
| 1 | Jordan Smith | 71-69-76-70—286 |
| 2 | Brian Casey | 71-76-69-74—290 |
| 3 | Ben Taylor | 74-76-73-68—291 |
| | Jimmy Mullen | 75-73-72-71—291 |
| | Alfie Plant | 71-78-69-73—291 |

## English Amateur Championship  (inaugurated 1925)  *Frilford Heath GC*

**Semi-Finals:** Matthew Fitzpatrick (Hallamshire) beat Tomasz Anderson (Brocket Hall)  7 and 6
Callum Shinkwin (Moor Park) beat Max Orrin (North Foreland)  one hole
**Final:** Callum Shinkwin beat Matthew Fitzpatrick  4 and 3

## English Seniors' Amateur Championship  *Bristol and Clifton GC, Long Ashton GC*

| | | |
|---|---|---|
| 1 | Richard Latham | 72-70-79—221 |
| 2 | Alan Squires | 74-72-78—224 |
| 3 | Andrew Stracey | 73-75-77—225 |
| | Stewart King | 73-71-81—225 |

## English Open Mid-Amateur Championship  (Logan Trophy)  *The Worcestershire GC*

| | | |
|---|---|---|
| 1 | John Kemp (Woburn) | 69-70-72—211 |
| 2 | Paul Scarrett (Blackwell) | 70-72-70—212 |
| | Paul Williams (Hillside) | 71-69-72—212 |

## England Men's County Champion of Champions  *Woodhall Spa (Hotchkin course)*

| | | |
|---|---|---|
| 1 | Bobby Keeble (Essex) | 73-73—146 |
| 2 | Chris Halley (Yorkshire) | 68-79—147 |
| 3 | Andrew Minnikin (Northumberland) | 78-74—152 |
| | John Longcake  (Cumbria) | 72-80—152 |
| | Alfie Plant (Kent) | 69-83—152 |

## Europe (continued)

### England Senior County Champion of Champions  *Woodhall Spa (Hotchkin course)*

| 1 | Anthony McLure (Northumberland) | 75-70—145 |
|---|---|---|
| 2 | Richard Latham (Lincolnshire) | 72-74—146 |
| 3 | Charles Banks (Nottinghamshire) | 75-73—148 |

### Estonian Open Amateur Championship  *Niitvalja GC*

| 1 | Johannes Diederichs (GER) | 71-73-71—222 |
|---|---|---|
| 2 | David Michel (GER) | 77-75-71—223 |
| 3 | Gerard O'Neil | 75-75-76—226 |

### Estonian National Championship  *Estonian G&CC (Sea course)*

| 1 | Egert Poldma | 73-75-76—224 |
|---|---|---|
| 2 | Martin Jarve | 79-72-76—227 |
| 3 | Sander Aadusaar | 80-80-74—234 |

### European Amateur Championship  *see page 297*

### European International Seniors Championship  *Estonia G&CC*  June 13–15

| 1 | Lorenzo Sartori (ITA) | 72-74-71—217 |
|---|---|---|
| 2 | Markus Frank (SUI) | 73-77-69—219 |
| 3 | Hans Beckkstrom (SWE) | 74-76-70—220 |

**Super Seniors (over 65):** Hans Stenderup (DEN) 74-74-73—221

### European International Mid-Amateur Championship  *(inaugurated 1999)*
*Penati GR (Legend course), Slovakia*  June 6–8

| 1 | Bertrand Noel (FRA)* | 70-74-76—220 |
|---|---|---|
| 2 | Richard Heath (AUT) | 73-74-73—220 |
| 3 | Albert Turklitz (GER) | 74-73-73—220 |

* Noel won at the third extra hole

### Finnish Open Amateur Championship  *(Erkko Trophy)*  *Helsingin GK*

| 1 | Joel Girrbach (SUI) | 70-68-67—205 |
|---|---|---|
| 2 | Lauri Ruuska | 68-67-72—207 |
| 3 | Ville Lagerblom | 75-64-69—208 |

### Finnish National Championship  *St Laurence Golf*

| 1 | Arto Pehkonen | 72-70-71-71—284 |
|---|---|---|
| 2 | Juuso Kahlos | 71-71-71-72—285 |
|   | Timo Tuunanen | 68-72-72-73—285 |

### French Open Stroke Play Championship  *Chantilly GC*  May 26–29

| 1 | Adrien Saddier | 71-71-74-64—280 |
|---|---|---|
| 2 | Martin Keskari (GER) | 71-70-71-73—285 |
| 3 | Maximilian Rohrig (GER) | 73-75-69-70—287 |
|   | Albert Eckhardt (FIN) | 74-71-69-73—287 |
|   | Ryan Evans (ENG) | 72-73-69-73—287 |

## French Closed Amateur Championship (Trophée Jaques Leglise) *RCF La Boulie*

**Semi-Finals:** Ugo Coussaud (Angouleme Hiron) beat Jeremy Gandon (RCF La Boulie) 2 and 1
Francois Censier (Amiens) beat Thibault Vieilledent (Cannes Mougins) 3 and 2
**Final:** Francois Censier beat Ugo Coussaud 2 and 1

## French Mid-Amateur Championship *Golf Albi Lasbordes* Sep 23–29

| | | |
|---|---|---|
| 1 | Fredrik Axelsson (SWE) | 68-68-69—205 |
| 2 | Ulf Blixberg (SWE) | 71-74-68—213 |
| 3 | Bertrand Noel | 72-70-76—218 |

## German International Amateur Championship *GC Neuhof Dreieich*

| | | |
|---|---|---|
| 1 | Maximilian Rottluff | 72-68-68-70—278 |
| 2 | Mads Soegard (DEN) | 75-70-65-69—279 |
| | Marcel Ohorn | 69-66-75-69—279 |

## German National Championship *GR Hardenberg*

| | | |
|---|---|---|
| 1 | Sebastian Schwind | 72-66-73-72—283 |
| 2 | Julian Gesell | 71-71-73-71—286 |
| 3 | Maximilian Roehrig | 74-71-71-72—288 |

## Hungarian Amateur Open Championship *Royal Balaton G and YC*

| | | |
|---|---|---|
| 1 | Vince van Veen (NED) | 72-72-72—216 |
| 2 | Patrick Kopp (GER) | 74-72-74—220 |
| 3 | Alan de Bondt (BEL) | 76-74-73—223 |
| | Yohann Cauwenbergh (BEL) | 73-76-74—223 |
| | Kevin Hesbois (BEL) | 72-76-75—223 |

## Irish Open Amateur Championship *Royal Dublin GC* May 10–12
(inaugurated 1892 but not contested between 1960 and 1994)

| | | |
|---|---|---|
| 1 | Robbie Cannon (Balbriggan)* | 70-75-75-75—287 |
| 2 | Gavin Moynihan (The Island) | 76-73-73-73—287 |
| 3 | Graeme Robertson (SCO) | 68-81-72-73—287 |

* Cannon won at the fourth extra hole

## Irish Close Amateur Championship (inaugurated 1893) *Connemara GC*

**Semi-Finals:** Cormac Sharvin (Ardglass) beat David Byrne (Greystones) 4 and 3
Paul Dunne (Greystones) beat Jonathan Yates (Naas) at 19th
**Final:** Cormac Sharvin beat Paul Dunne 1 hole

## Irish Seniors' Amateur Open Championship *Malone GC*

| | | |
|---|---|---|
| 1 | M Quirke (Doneraile)* | 70-76-76—222 |
| 2 | B Hargreaves (USA) | 75-75-72—222 |

*Quirke won at the third extra hole

| | | |
|---|---|---|
| 3 | T Tyrell (The Heath) | 74-75-75—224 |

## Irish Seniors' Amateur Close Championship *Portumna GC*

| | | |
|---|---|---|
| 1 | G McGimpsey (Bangor) | 75-75-69—219 |
| 2 | M Quirke (Doneraile) | 75-73-77—225 |
| 3 | A Smith (The Island) | 75-76-75—226 |

# Italian International Amateur Championship *Villa d'Este GC* May 10–15

**Semi-Finals:** Jacopi Jori beat Lorenzo Scalise 2 holes
Federico Zucchetti beat Francesco Testa
**Final:** Federico Zucchetti beat Jacopi Jori 6 and 5
**Medallist:** Ediz Kemalogu 70-67—137

# Italian Stroke Play Championship *Torino GC*

| | | |
|---|---|---|
| 1 | Edoardo Raffae Lipparelli | 72-65-73-72—282 |
| 2 | Lorenzo Scalise | 74-70-72-70—286 |
| 3 | Renato Paratore | 71-74-75-69—289 |
| | Federico Zucchetti | 73-71-70-75—289 |

# Italian Mid-Amateur Championship *Castello Tolcinasco GC*

| | | |
|---|---|---|
| 1 | Gianluca Bolla | 71-73-70—214 |
| 2 | Franz Pfoestl | 73-70-72—215 |
| 3 | Matteo Natoli | 76-73-70—219 |

# Italian Senior Championship *Franciacorta GC*

| | | |
|---|---|---|
| 1 | Vincenzo Sita | 76-74-77—227 |
| 2 | Lorenzo Sartori | 76-76-77—229 |
| 3 | Cesare Castellini | 82-81-76—239 |

# Latvian National Amateur Championship *Ozo GC*

| | | |
|---|---|---|
| 1 | Karlis Broders | 70-72-75—217 |
| 2 | Roberts Eihmanis | 74-75-78—227 |
| 3 | Mikus Gavars | 72-77-84—233 |

# Latvian Open Amateur Championship *Ozo GC*

| | | |
|---|---|---|
| 1 | Markus Maukner (AUT) | 70-71-75—216 |
| 2 | Thaler Yair | 71-77-72—220 |
| 3 | Karlis Broders | 80-75-68—223 |
| | Martin Jarve | 77-73-73—223 |
| | Kornelijus Baliukonis | 75-71-77—223 |

# Latvian Match Play Championship *Ozo GC*

**Semi-Finals:** Roberts Biss beat Kristaps Kristropans 3 and 2
Roberts Eimanhis beat Karlis Broders 1 hole
**Final:** Roberts Eimanhis beat Roberts Biss 4 and 3

# Liechtenstein Open Amateur Championship *GC Gams-Werdenberg*

| | | |
|---|---|---|
| 1 | Sebastian Schredt (GER) | 88-77—157 |
| 2 | Christian Walch | 80-78—158 |
| 3 | Ferdi Sele | 83-79—162 |

# Lithuanian Open Championship *Capitols GC*

| | | |
|---|---|---|
| 1 | Claas-Eric Borges (GER) | 70-76-78—224 |
| 2 | Johnnes Diederichs (GER) | 73-75-78—226 |
| 3 | David Michel (GER) | 76-78-73—227 |

## Luxembourg International Amateur Championship  *Kikuoka CC*

| | | |
|---|---|---|
| 1 | Edoardo Torrieri (ITA) | 74-72-67—213 |
| 2 | ValerioPelliccia (ITA) | 73-67-73—213 |
| 3 | Bernard Geelkerken (NED) | 73-70-71—214 |

## Luxembourg Men's Amateur Championship  *Golf de Luxembourg Belenhaff*

| | | |
|---|---|---|
| 1 | Max Biwar (Grand Ducal) | 66-75—151 |
| 2 | Liam Petit (Belenhaff) | 75-77—152 |
| 3 | Henri Karas (Grand Ducal) | 77-78—155 |

## Polish Amateur Championship  *Postolowo GC*

| | | |
|---|---|---|
| 1 | Mateusz Gradecki (Toya) | 74-65-73—212 |
| 2 | Adrian Meronk (Toya) | 66-77-70—213 |
| 3 | Jan Szmidt (Toya) | 76-69-69—214 |

## Polish Mid-Amateur Championship  *Sierra GC*

| | | |
|---|---|---|
| 1 | Michael Kasprowicz | 75-70-74—219 |
| 2 | William Carey | 73-72-78—233 |
| 3 | Michael Poniz | 73-77-76—226 |

## Polish Senior Championship  *Sierra GC*

| | | |
|---|---|---|
| 1 | Henryk Konopa | 75-70-78—223 |
| 2 | Klaus Schneider | 78-76-77—231 |
| 3 | Craig Ballantyne | 79-77-79—235 |

## Portuguese International Amateur Championship  *Montado GC  Feb 13–16*

| | | |
|---|---|---|
| 1 | Goncalo Pinto | 70-69-67-71—277 |
| 2 | Jerome Titlow (ENG) | 68-67-75-69—278 |
| 3 | Harry Casey (ENG) | 74-71-69-67—281 |
| | Mike Miller (USA) | 70-73-68-70—281 |

## Russian Amateur Championship  *Tsleevo GC*

| | | |
|---|---|---|
| 1 | Johannes Schwab (AUT) | 72-70-70-74—286 |
| 2 | Pavel Goryainov | 70-69-73-76—288 |
| 3 | Vasiliy Belov | 69-72-72-78—291 |
| | Alexander Kleszcz (AUT) | 71-73-73-74—291 |

## Scottish Amateur Championship  (inaugurated 1922)  *Blairgowrie GC (Lansdowne course)*

**Semi-Finals:**   Alexander Culverwell (Dunbar) beat Grant Forrest (Craigielaw) 4 and 3
James White (Lundin) beat Craig Ross (Kirkhill) 2 and 1
**Final:**   Alexander Culverwell beat James White 2 and 1

## Scottish Open Amateur Championship  (inaugurated 1967)  *Southerness GC*
May 30–June 1

| | | |
|---|---|---|
| 1 | Garrick Porteous (ENG) | 68-69-72-68—277 |
| 2 | Dermot McElroy (NIR) | 69-70-75-67—281 |
| | Richard O'Donovan (IRL) | 68-70-72-71—281 |
| | Callum Shinkwin (ENG) | 71-68-70-72—281 |

## Scottish Seniors Open Amateur Stroke Play Championship *The Golf House, Elie*

| | | |
|---|---|---|
| 1 | Richard Latham (ENG) | 70-69-69—208 |
| 2 | Richard Partridge (ENG) | 72-70-68—210 |
| 3 | Alan O'Neill | 73-70-73—216 |
| | Anthony McLure (ENG) | 70-73-73—216 |
| | Lindsay Blair | 71-72-73—216 |

## Scottish Seniors Match Play Championship *Alyth GC*

**Semi-Finals:** Jim Watt (Edzell) beat Billy Erskine (Kilsyth Lennox) 1 hole
Lindsay Blair (Grangemouth) beat Alan O'Neill (West Lothian) at 20th
**Final:** Jim Watt beat Lindsay Blair 1 hole
**Medallist:** Tony Patterson (Sunningdale) 70-70—140

## Scottish Champion of Champions *Leven GS*

| | | |
|---|---|---|
| 1 | Scott Barrowman (Dollar) | 70-67-72-71—280 |
| 2 | Matthew Ckark (Kilmacolm) | 71-69-73-70—283 |
| 3 | Alexander Culverwell (Dunbar) | 73-74-70-70—287 |
| | Graeme Robertson (Glenbervie) | 72-70-75-70—287 |
| | Craig Howie (Peebles) | 75-71-70-71—287 |

## Slovak Stroke Play Championship *GR Black Stork*

| | | |
|---|---|---|
| 1 | Peter Valasek Jr | 68-75—143 |
| 2 | Martin Tavoda | 74-79—153 |
| 3 | Jan Friesz Jr | 75-79—154 |

## Slovak Open Amateur Championship *Welten GR*

| | | |
|---|---|---|
| 1 | Vitek Novak (CZE) | 69-69-68—206 |
| 2 | Markus Habeler (AUT) | 71-70-65—206 |
| 3 | Michael Ludwig (GER) | 72-71-67—210 |
| | Adam Studeny (CZE) | 70-71-69—210 |

## Slovak National Match Play Championhip *Black Stork GR*

**Semi-finals:** Peter Valasek Jr beat Oliver Gabor 2 holes
Jan Friesz Jr beat Martin Tavoda 6 and 4
**Final:** Jan Friesz Jr beat Peter Valasek 4 and 2
**Third place play-off:** Oliver Gabor beat Tavoda Martin 2 and 1
**Medallist:** Peter Valasek 68-75—143

## Slovenian International Amateur Championship *Bled GC*

| | | |
|---|---|---|
| 1 | Teemu Bakker (FIN) | 71-68-70—209 |
| 2 | Vitek Novak (CZE) | 69-74-69—212 |
| 3 | Ediz Kemaloglu (TUR) | 73-67-74—214 |
| | Matthias Schwab (AUT) | 68-73-73—214 |
| | Simon Zach (CZE) | 70-72-72—214 |
| | Michael Pospisil (CZE) | 72-71-71—214 |

## Spanish Amateur Championship *Las Lomas-Bosque GC*

| | | |
|---|---|---|
| 1 | Emilio Cuartero Blanco | 71-69-69-70—279 |
| 2 | Mario Galiano Aguilar | 71-75-65-70—281 |
| 3 | Pep Angles Ros | 73-74-69-69—285 |
| | Javier Gallegos Marsal | 75-66-71-73—285 |

## Spanish International Championship (Copa SM El Rey) *La Manga GC*
**Semi-finals:** Neil Raymond (ENG) beat Edouard Amacher (SUI) 2 and 1
Reeve Whitson (IRL) beat Adrien Saddier (FRA) 5 and 4
**Final:** Reeve Whitson beat Neil Raymond 4 and 3
**Medallists:** Harry Casey (ENG) 73-72—145; Richard O'Donovan (IRL) 71-74—145

## Swiss International Amateur Championship *Lausanne GC*
| | | |
|---|---|---|
| 1 | Matthieu Fenasse (FRA) | 71-72-70—213 |
| 2 | Michele Cea (ITA) | 67-75-73—215 |
| 3 | Benjamin Rusch | 75-69-72—216 |
| | Mathias Schwab (AUT) | 74-70-72—216 |
| | Marc Dobias | 67-72-77—216 |

## Turkish Amateur Open Championship *National GC* May 29–June 2
| | | |
|---|---|---|
| 1 | Hamza Sayin | 70-76-72-77—295 |
| 2 | Philippe Schweizer (SUI) | 75-75-78-73—301 |
| | Lombardo Janes (GER) | 73-77-73-78—301 |

## Welsh Amateur Championship (inaugurated 1895) *Ashburnham GC*
**Semi-finals:** Mike Hearne beat Richard James 4 and 3
Jack Bush beat Ben Westgate at 21st
**Final:** Jack Bush beat Mike Hearne 9 and 8

## Welsh Open Amateur Championship (inaugurated 1967) *Royal Porthcawl GC* May 15–19
| | | |
|---|---|---|
| 1 | Rhys Pugh | 68-73-66-70—277 |
| 2 | Garrick Porteous (ENG) | 67-72-74-68—281 |
| 3 | James Ross (SCO) | 72-70-68-72—282 |

## Welsh Seniors' Close Amateur Championship (inaugurated 1975) *always at Aberdovey*
| | | |
|---|---|---|
| 1 | Basil Griffiths | 75-71-81—227 |
| 2 | Glynn Rees | 75-70-83—228 |
| 3 | Edgar M Powell | 74-74-81—229 |
| | Andrew Williams | 73-72-84—229 |

## Welsh Seniors' Open Championship *Abergele GC*
| | | |
|---|---|---|
| 1 | Andrew Stracey | 76-68-75—219 |
| 2 | Robert Aston | 72-78-71—221 |
| | Anthony McLure | 70-77-74—221 |

## Welsh Tournament of Champions *always at Cradoc*
| | | |
|---|---|---|
| 1 | Luke Thomas (Pontypridd GC) | 72-70—142 |
| 2 | Jack Bush (Morlais Castle GC) | 73-70—143 |
| 3 | Richard Tayler (Llanwern GC) | 73-71—144 |

# Work begins on the Olympic course in Rio

Clearing work has started at the site of the golf course for the Rio 2016 Olympic Games golf after the necessary permit for the removal of the non-native vegetation was issued by the city. The process to clear the way for construction to begin as planned this year is being conducted by Tanedo, the private company responsible for the construction.

Carlos Arthur Nuzman, President of the Rio 2016 Organising Committee for the Olympic and Paralympic Games (Rio 2016), said: "We are delighted that work has begun on the golf venue and we remain on track to deliver the golf course for a test event in 2015 as scheduled. This venue will provide a key element of the Rio 2016 legacy as the first public course in Rio de Janeiro, and it will play a pivotal role in the development of the sport of golf in Brazil."

Course designer Gil Hanse, from US-based Hanse Golf Course Design, commented: "We are very excited and pleased to have begun the initial clearing of the site. It is the start of a long process to transform this property into a beautiful golf course, and we are happy to get started."

Hanse Golf Course Design's proposal for the course was selected by Rio 2016 in March 2012 after a thorough selection process.

The golf course will be built in Barra, the area that will host around more than half of the Olympic sports in 2016. It is a privately funded project that will be located approximately five kilometres from the Athletes' Village and seven kilometres from the Main Press Centre and the International Broadcast Centre.

# Callaway Handicapping

It frequently occurs in social competitions such as office or business association outings that many of the competitors do not have official handicaps. In such cases the best solution is to use the Callaway handicapping system, so called after the name of its inventor, as it is simple to use yet has proved equitable.

Competitors complete their round marking in their gross figures at every hole and their handicaps are awarded and deducted at the end of the 18 holes using the following table:

| Competitor's Gross Score | Handicap Deduction |
|---|---|
| par or less | none |
| one over par – 75 | ½ worst hole |
| 76–80 | worst hole |
| 81–85 | worst hole plus ½ next worse |
| 86–90 | two worst holes |
| 91–95 | two worst holes plus ½ next |
| 96–100 | three worst holes |
| 101–105 | three worst holes plus ½ next |
| 106–110 | four worst holes |
| 111–115 | four worst holes plus ½ next |
| 116–120 | five worst holes |
| 121–125 | five worst holes plus ½ next |
| 126–130 | six worst holes |

Note 1: Worst hole equals highest score at any hole regardless of the par of the hole except that the maximum score allowed for any one hole is twice the par of the hole.

Note 2: The 17th and 18th holes are not allowed to be deducted.

Example: Competitor scores 104. From the table he should deduct as his handicap the total of his three worst (i.e. highest) individual hole scores plus half of his fourth worst hole. If he scored one 9, one 8 and several 7's he would therefore deduct a total of 27½ from his gross score of 104 to give a net score of 76½.

# USA State Championships 2013

US nationality unless stated

| | | | | | |
|---|---|---|---|---|---|
| Alabama | Michael Johnson (SP) | Maine | Ricky Jones (SP) | Oklahoma | Hayden Wood (SP) |
| | Thomas Sutton (MP) | | Matt Greenleaf (MP) | | Nathan Hughes (MP) |
| Alaska | Adam Baxter | Maryland | Denny McCarthy | Oregon | Nick Chianello |
| Arizona | Christian | Massachusetts | Mike Calef | Pennsylvania | Christopher Ault |
| | Colegrove | Michigan | Andrew Chapman | Rhode Island | Brad Valois |
| Arkansas | Wes McNulty (SP) | Minnesota | Jon Dutoit | S. Carolina | Carson Young (SP) |
| | Stan Lee (MP) | Mississippi | Steve Wilson | | Adam Goins (MP) |
| California | Cory McElyea | Missouri | Richard Berkmeyer | S. Dakota | Dylan Baker (SP) |
| Colorado | John Ahern (SP) | | (SP) | | Grant Smith (MP) |
| | David Oraee (MP) | | Joey Johnson (MP) | Tennessee | Steven Fox (pro) |
| Connecticut | Cody Paladino | Montana | Brandon McIver | | (SP) |
| Delaware | Christopher | Nebraska | Andy Sajevic (SP/MP) | | Zach Olsen (MP) |
| | Hickman | Nevada | Gregory | Texas | Doug Manor |
| Florida | Sam Horsfield | | Horodesky (SP) | Utah | Cole Ogden |
| Georgia | Jimmy Beck | | Zane Thomas (MP) | Vermont | Evan Russell |
| Hawaii | John Oda | N. Hampshire | Chelso Barrett | Virginia | Brinson Paolini |
| Idaho | Ty Travis | New Jersey | Michael | | (pro) |
| Illinois | Tee-k Kelly | | Stamberger | Washington | Cameron Peck |
| Indiana | Adam Schenk | New Mexico | Jere Pelletier | West Virginia | Sam O'Dell |
| Iowa | Gene Elliott (SP) | New York | Matthew Stasiak | Wisconsin | Jordan Niebrugge |
| | Ian Vandersee (MP) | N. Carolina | Steven Brame (SP) | | (SP/MP) |
| Kansas | Chase Hanna | | Carter Jenkins (MP) | Wyoming | Edward Stewart |
| Kentucky | Tyler McDaniel | N. Dakota | Bill Carlson (SP/MP) | | |
| Louisiana | Eric Ricard | Ohio | Andrew Dorne | | |

| | | | | |
|---|---|---|---|---|
| Metropolitan | Kyle Weldon | 111th Western Amateur | | Jordan Niebrugge |
| Carolinas | Carter Jenkins | North & South | | Andrew Dorn |

Further details of these and other US amateur events can be found on page 443

# Canadian Provincial Championships 2013

Canadian nationality unless stated

| | | | |
|---|---|---|---|
| Alberta | Riley Fleming | Prince Edward Is. | Martin O'Brien |
| British Columbia | Charlie Hughes | Quebec | Hugo Bernard (SP) |
| Manitoba | Aaron Cockerill | | Corey Eccles (MP) |
| New Brunswick | Justin Richard | Saskatchewan | David Stewart |
| Nova Scotia | Stephane Boudreau | | |
| Ontario | Stephane Dubois (SP) | | |
| | Zack Kempa (MP) | | |

Further details of these and other Canadian amateur events can be found on page 442

# Australian State Championships 2013

*Australian nationality unless stated*

| New South Wales | Ben Eccles/Thomas Power Horan | Tasmania | Jordan Zunic |
| Queensland | Dimitrios Papadatos (pro)/Jake McLeod | Victoria | Simon Viitakangas/Taylor James MacDonald |
| South Australia | Daniel Hoeve | Western Australia | Brady Watt |

Further details of these and other Australian amateur events can be found on page 445

# South African Provincial Championships 2013

*South African nationality unless stated*

| Cape Province Open | Haydon Porteous (pro) | Limpopo Open | Christiaan Bezuidenhout |
| Eastern Province | Paul De Beer | Mpumalanga Open | Christiaan Bezuidenhout |
| Ekurhuleni Open | Aubrey Beckley | N. Cape Open | Stephan Erasmus |
| Free State Open | Jason Froneman | North West Open | Callum John Mowat |
| Gauteng North Open | Toby Tree (ENG) | S. Cape Open | Callum John Mowat |
| KwaZulu Natal | Zander Lombard | Western Province | Christiaan Bezuidenhout |

Further details of these and other South African amateur events can be found on page 440

# New Zealand Provincial Championships 2013

*New Zealand nationality unless stated*

| North Island Stroke Play Championship | Oscar Cadenhead |
| South Island Stroke Play Championship | Peter Lee |

Further details of these and other New Zealand amateur events can be found on page 447

## Month by month in 2013

Phil Mickelson hits back from his US Open disappointment with an inspired Open Championship triumph at Muirfield. A week after winning the Scottish Open he closes with a 66 to beat Henrik Stenson by three, his fifth major title. Graeme McDowell's third victory of the year comes at the French Open, while Jordan Spieth becomes the first teenage winner on the PGA Tour in 82 years.

# National Orders of Merit 2013

## Titleist England Golf Rankings

| | | | | | |
|---|---|---|---|---|---|
| 1 | Max Orrin (North Foreland) | 122,056 | 6 | Nathan Kimsey (Woodhall Spa) | 94,435 |
| 2 | Callum Shinkwin (Moor Park) | 107,231 | 7 | Ryan Evans (Wellingborough) | 84,016 |
| 3 | Garrick Porteous (Bamburgh Castle) | 105,215 | 8 | Ashley Chesters (Hawkstone Park) | 65,739 |
| 4 | Jordan Smith (Bowood Park) | 103,648 | 9 | Nick Marsh (Huddersfield) | 56,123 |
| 5 | Neil Raymond (Corhampton) | 97,848 | 10 | Paul Kinnear (Formby) | 54,750 |

## Irish Rankings (Willie Gill Award)

| | | | | | |
|---|---|---|---|---|---|
| 1 | Reeve Whitson (Mourne) | 624 | 6 | Brian Casey (Headfort) | 448 |
| 2 | Dermot McElroy (Ballymena) | 570 | 7 | Rory McNamara (Headfort) | 417 |
| 3 | Paul Dunne (Greystones) | 480 | 8 | Richard O'Donovan (Lucan) | 378 |
| 4 | Jack Hume (Naas) | 476 | 9 | Robbie Cannon (Balbriggan) | 364 |
| 5 | Cormac Sharvin (Ardglass) | 455 | 10 | Harry Diamond (Belvoir Park) | 305 |

## Scottish Golf Union Order of Merit

| | | | | | |
|---|---|---|---|---|---|
| 1 | Jack McDonald (Kilmarnock Barassie) | 697.83 | 6 | Alexander Culverwell (Dunbar) | 440.50 |
| 2 | James White (Lundin) | 631.00 | 7 | Scott Borrowman (Dollar) | 423.50 |
| 3 | Adam Dunton (McDonald) | 523.00 | 8 | Michael Dally (Erskine) | 361.00 |
| 4 | Matthew Clark (Kilmacolm) | 475.00 | 9 | Scott Crichton (Aberdour) | 357.00 |
| | Craig Ross (Kirkhill) | 475.00 | 10 | Kyle McClung (Wigtownshire County) | 346.75 |

## Welsh Rankings

| | | | | | |
|---|---|---|---|---|---|
| 1 | Rhys Pugh (Vale Resort) | 400.00 | 6 | Tim Harry (Vale Resort) | 225.00 |
| 2 | Richard James (Aberystwyth) | 340.00 | 7 | Zach Galliford (Borth & Ynylas) | 235.65 |
| 3 | Lee Jones (Conwy) | 311.49 | 8 | Mike Hearne (Southerndown) | 220.00 |
| 4 | Jack Bush (Morlais Castle) | 299.66 | 9 | Ben Westgate (Trevose) | 206.33 |
| 5 | Alastair Jones (Radyr) | 234.50 | 10 | Craig Melding (Neath) | 184.00 |

## New Zealand Order of Merit
### (events played in brackets)

| | | | | | | | |
|---|---|---|---|---|---|---|---|
| 1 | Kadin Neho | (11) | 102.15 | 6 | Peter Lee | (20) | 86.79 |
| 2 | Vaughan McCall | (9) | 98.93 | 7 | Nick Voke | (14) | 86.79 |
| 3 | Joshua Munn | (14) | 96.20 | 8 | Tae Koh | (16) | 84.87 |
| 4 | Luke Toomey | (14) | 95.33 | 9 | Tyler Hodge | (19) | 82.27 |
| 5 | Sam An | (14) | 89.70 | 10 | Blair Riordan | (10) | 80.31 |

## Australian Order of Merit
### (events played in brackets)

| | | | | | | | |
|---|---|---|---|---|---|---|---|
| 1 | Brady Watt (WA) | (13) | 108.21 | 6 | Kevin Marques (QLD) | (10) | 71.27 |
| 2 | Taylor MacDonald (QLD) | (13) | 88.95 | 7 | Brett Drewitt (NSW) (pro) | (9) | 70.81 |
| 3 | Geoff Drakeford (VIC) | (9) | 81.89 | 8 | Aaron Wilkin (QLD) | (17) | 70.36 |
| 4 | Tom Power Horan (VIC) | (13) | 74.83 | 9 | Cameron Smith (QLD) (pro) | (5) | 67.58 |
| 5 | Chris Brown (SA) | (13) | 74.68 | 10 | Cameron Davis (NSW) | (11) | 66.18 |

## Canadian Order of Merit

(events played in brackets)

| | | | | | | | | |
|---|---|---|---|---|---|---|---|---|
| 1 | Corey Conners | (12) | 5,935 | 6 | Chris Hemmerich | (10) | 2,054 |
| 2 | Taylor Pendrith | (12) | 4,912 | 7 | Riley Fleming | (8) | 1,902 |
| 3 | Garrett Rank | (12) | 2,930 | 8 | Kevin Carrigan | (4) | 1,850 |
| 4 | Adam Svensson | (7) | 2,295 | 9 | Stephane Dubois | (11) | 1,792 |
| 5 | Charlie Hughes | (12) | 2,173 | 10 | Kevin Kwon | (6) | 1,355 |

## French Order of Merit

| | | | | | |
|---|---|---|---|---|---|
| 1 | Adrien Saddier | 1,886.84 | 6 | Thomas Elissalde | 1,141.08 |
| 2 | Julien Brun | 1,400.00 | 7 | Ugo Coussaud | 1,125.50 |
| 3 | Joël Stalter | 1,199.55 | 8 | Mathieu Decottignies-Lafon | 1,123.42 |
| 4 | Paul Barjon | 1,179.67 | 9 | Paul Elissalde | 1,107.25 |
| 5 | Grégoire Schoeb | 1,177.67 | 10 | Mathieu Fenasse | 913.40 |

## South African Order of Merit

| | | | | | |
|---|---|---|---|---|---|
| 1 | Zander Lombard | 55.3936 | 6 | N J Arnoldi | 33.1346 |
| 2 | Christiaan Bezuidenhout | 54.3169 | 7 | Teaghan Gauche | 31.2685 |
| 3 | Gerlou Roux | 40.3224 | 8 | Thriston Lawrence | 30.2262 |
| 4 | Louis Taylor | 36.8483 | 9 | Andrew Light | 28.7123 |
| 5 | Callum Mowat | 35.6215 | 10 | Werner Van Niekerk | 27.4913 |

## Italian Order of Merit

| | | | | | |
|---|---|---|---|---|---|
| 1 | Renato Paratore | 2,914,60 | 6 | Enrico Di Nitto | 801,66 |
| 2 | Riccardo Michelini | 1,974,25 | 7 | Francesco Testa | 726,66 |
| 3 | Filippo Zucchetti | 1,068,42 | 8 | Guido Migliozzi | 667,17 |
| 4 | Federico Zucchetti | 885,65 | 9 | Lorenzo Scalise | 659,28 |
| 5 | Stefano Pitoni | 880,50 | 10 | Edoardo Raffae Lipparelli | 631,78 |

Dictionary of Golfing Terms

**Birdie** – probably deriving from the American slang word for excellent (bird), its first use in golf is widely accepted to originate from a game at the   Country Club in Atlantic City when golfer Ab Smith's second shot on the par 4 2nd hole came to rest mere inches from the cup and he stated "That was a bird of a shot" and suggested that holing out one shot under par should be termed a 'birdie'.

# Team Events

For past winners not listed here, please see earlier editions of *The R&A Golfer's Handbook*

## Walker Cup (Instituted 1922)
USA v Great Britain & Ireland (*home team names first*)

*National Golf Links of America, Southampton, NY*   Sep 7–8

**Captains:** USA: Jim Holtgrieve (St Louis, MO); GB&I: Nigel Edwards (Whitchurch)

### First Day – Foursomes
Cory Whitsett and Bobby Wyatt halved with Nathan Kimsey and Max Orrin
Jordan Niebrugge and Nathan Smith lost to Matthew Fitzpatrick and Neil Raymond  1 up
Michael Weaver and Todd White lost to Garrick Porteous and Rhys Pugh  3 and 1
Patrick Rodgers and Justin Thomas beat Gavin Moynihan and Kevin Phelan  2 and 1
**Match position:** USA 1½, GB&I 2½

### Singles
Bobby Wyatt beat Neil Raymond  2 up
Max Homa beat Max Orrin  5 and 3
Michael Kim beat Callum Shinkwin  2 and 1
Cory Whitsett beat Jordan Smith  1 up
Jordan Niebrugge beat Garrick Porteous  1 up
Michael Weaver beat Matthew Fitzpatrick  3 and 1
Justin Thomas halved with Nathan Kimsey
Patrick Rodgers lost to Gavin Moynihan  2 and 1
**Match position:** USA 8, GB&I 4

### Second Day – Foursomes
Wyatt and Whitsett beat Kimsey and Orrin  2 and 1
Weaver and White lost to Fitzpatrick and Raymond  3 and 2
Homa and Kim beat Porteous and Pugh  1 up
Rodgers and Niebrugge lost to Moynihan and Phelan  2 up
**Match position:** USA 10, GB&I 6

### Singles
Wyatt beat Raymond  4 and 3
Thomas beat Orrin  6 and 4
Weaver lost to Fitzpatrick  3 and 2
White beat Pugh  4 and 3
Smith beat Kimsey  4 and 3
Whitsett lost to Shinkwin  2 up
Kim beat Porteous  4 and 2
Homa lost to Phelan  2 and 1
Niebrugge beat Smith  6 and 5
Rodgers beat Moynihan  1 up

**Result:** USA 17, GB&I 9

2011 *Royal Aberdeen GC, Scotland* Sept 10–11

**Result: GBI 14, USA 12**

*Captains: Nigel Edwards (GBI), Jim Holtgrieve (USA)*

*First Day – Foursomes*
Tom Lewis & Michael Stewart beat Peter Uihlein & Harris English 2 and 1
Jack Senior & Andy Sullivan beat Russell Henley & Kelly Kraft 2 and 1
Paul Cutler & Alan Dunbar beat Nathan Smith & Blayne Barber 5 and 4
Steven Brown & Stiggy Hodgson lost to Patrick Cantlay & Chris Williams 5 and 4

*Singles*
Tom Lewis lost to Peter Uihlein 2 and 1
Jack Senior lost to Jordan Spieth 3 and 2
Andy Sullivan lost to Harris English 2 and 1
Rhys Pugh beat Patrick Rodgers 2 and 1
Steven Brown beat Russell Henley 1 hole
James Byrne beat Nathan Smith 2 and 1
Paul Cutler beat Kelly Kraft 2 and 1
Michael Stewart lost to Patrick Cantlay 2 and 1

*Second Day – Foursomes*
Tom Lewis & Michael Stewart halved with Jordan Spieth & Patrick Rodgers
Jack Senior & Andy Sullivan beat Peter Uihlein & Harris English 3 and 2
Paul Cutler & Alan Dunbar beat Kelly Kraft & Blayne Barber 2 and 1
James Byrne & Rhys Pugh beat Patrick Cantlay & Chris Williams 5 and 3

*Singles*
Tom Lewis (Welwyn Garden City) lost to  Russell Henley (Macon, GA)  4 and 2
Andy Sullivan  (Nuneaton) lost to Jordan Speith (Dallas, TX) 3 and 2
Jack Senior (Heysham) halved with Nathan Smith (Pittsburgh, PA)
Michael Stewart (Troon Welbeck) beat Patrick Rodgers (Avon, IN) 3 and 2
Stiggy Hodgson (Sunningdale) lost to Peter Uihlein (Orlando, FL)  2 and 1
Steven Brown (Wentworth) halved with Blayne Barber (Lake City, FL) 1 hole
Rhys Pugh (Vale of Glamorgan) beat Kelly Kraft (Dallas, TX) 2 and 1
Alan Dunbar (Rathmore) lost to Chris Williams (Moscow. ID) 1 hole
James Byrne (Banchory) lost to Harris English (Thomasville, GA) 2 and 1
Paul Cutler (Portstewart) halved with Patrick Cantlay (Los Alamitos, CA)

2009 *Merion GC, Ardmore, PA* Sept 12–13

**Result: USA 16½, GB&I 9½**

*Captains: George Marucci (USA), Colin Dalgleish (GB&I)*

*First Day – Foursomes*
B Harman & M Hoffmann beat W Booth & S Hutsby 2 and 1
P Uihlein & N Smith beat G Dear & M Haines 1 hole
R Fowler & B Cauley beat L Goddard & D Whitnell 6 and 5
C Tringale & A Mitchell lost to S Hodgson & N Kearney 3 and 1

*Singles*
B Harman halved with G Dear
R Fowler beat S Hutsby 7 and 6
C Tringale halved with W Booth
M Hoffmann halved with M Haines

P Uihlein beat T Fleetwood 2 and 1
D Weaver halved with C Paisley
B Cauley beat N Kearney 2 and 1
B Gielow lost to S Hodgson 2 and 1

*Second Day – Foursomes*
B Harman & A Mitchell beat G Dear & M Haines 3 and 2
R Fowler & B Caley beat S Hodgson & N Kearney 1 hole
D Weaver & B Gielow lost to W Booth & S Hutsby 3 and 2
N Smith & P Uihlein beat C Paisley & D Whitnell 5 and 4

*Singles*
Brian Harman lost to Gavin Dear (SCO) 3 and 2
Ricki Fowler beat Matt Haines (ENG) 2 and 1
Peter Uihlein beat Stiggy Hodgson (ENG) 3 and 1
Morgan Hoffmann beat Wallace Booth (SCO) 1 hole
Bud Cauley halved with Chris Paisley (ENG)
Adam Mitchell lost to Sam Hutsby (ENG) 1 hole
Drew Weaver lost to Tommy Fleetwood (ENG) 1 hole
Cameron Tringale beat Luke Goddard (ENG) 8 and 6
Nathan Smith lost to Niall Kearney (IRL) 3 and 2
Brendan Gielow beat Dale Whitnell (ENG) 4 and 3

2007 *Royal County Down GC, Co Down* Sept 8–9

**Result: USA 12½, GB&I 11½**

*Captains: Colin Dalgliesh (GB&I), Buddy Marucci (USA)*

*First Day – Foursomes*
L Saltman & R Davies lost to B Horschel & R Fowler 4 and 3
R McIlroy & J Caldwell halved with C Knost & D Johnson
J Parry & D Horsey beat T Kuehne & K Stanley 2 and 1
J Moul & D Willett halved with W Simpson & J Moore

*Singles*
R McIlroy lost to B Horschel 1 hole
L Saltman lost to  R Fowler  5 and 4
R Davies beat D Johnson 5 and 4
D Willett lost to C Knost 2 holes
L Matthews lost to J Lovemark 5 and 4
N Edwards beat K Stanley 1 hole
J Moul beat C Kirk 1 hole
D Horsey beat W Simpson 1 hole

*Second Day – Foursomes*
Caldwell & McIlroy lost to Horschel & Fowler 2 and 1
Davies & Edwards lost to Knost & Johnson 1 hole
Moul & Willett lost to Kuehne & Moore 4 and 2
Horsey & Parry lost to  Kirk & Lovemark 1 hole

*Singles*
McIlroy beat Horschel 4 and 2
Davies beat Fowler 3 and 2
Willett halved with Knost
Saltman beat Kuehne 2 and 1
Caldwell beat Stanley 2 holes
Edwards lost to Moore 1 hole
Moul lost to Lovemark 4 and 3
Horsey beat Simpson 1 hole

2005 *Chicago GC, Wheaton, IL* Aug 13–14

**Result: USA 12½, GB&I 11½**

*Captains: Bob Lewis (USA),*
*Garth McGimpsey (GB&I)*

*First Day – Foursomes*
A Kim & B Harman halved with NB Edwards & R Davies
L Williams & M Every beat G Lockerbie & R Dinwiddie 1 hole
J Overton & M Putnam beat O Fisher & M Richardson 2 and 1
K Reifers & B Hurley lost to R Ramsay & L Saltman 4 and 3

**Singles**
M Every lost to R Davies  4 and 3
A Kim beat G Lockerbie  6 and 5
L Overton beat NB Edwards  5 and 4
M Putnam lost to O Fisher  2 holes
N Thompson lost to M Richardson  5 and 4
B Hurley lost to L Saltman  1 hole
J Holmes beat G Wolstenholme  1 hole
L Williams beat B McElhinney  2 and 1

*Second Day – Foursomes*
Kim & Harman beat Ramsay & Saltman  4 and 2
Every & Williams lost to Davies & Edwards  2 and 1
Thompson & Holmes beat Fisher & Richardson  2 and 1
Putnam & Overton lost to Lockerbie & Dinwiddie  5 and 3

**Singles**
Kim lost to Wolstenholme  1 hole
Harman beat Davies  6 and 5
Putnam halved with Fisher
Every halved with Dinwiddie
Holmes lost to Richardson  5 and 4
Reifers lost to Saltman  1 hole
Overton beat Edwards  1 hole
Williams beat Lockerbie  4 and 3

## 2003 *Ganton GC, North Yorkshire* Sept 6–7
**Result: GB&I 12½, USA 11½**
*Captains: Garth McGimpsey (GB&I), Bob Lewis (USA)*

**First Day – Foursomes**
GP Wolstenholme & M Skelton lost to W Haas
  & T Kuehne  2 and 1
S Wilson & D Inglis beat L Williams & G Zahringer  2 holes
NB Edwards & S Manley beat C Nallen & R Moore  3 and 2
N Fox & C Moriarty beat A Rubinson & C Wittenberg
  4 and 2

**Singles**
GP Wolstenholme lost to W Haas  1 hole
O Wilson halved with T Kuehne
D Inglis lost to B Mackenzie  3 and 2
S Wilson halved with M Hendrix
NB Edwards beat G Zahringer  3 and 2
C Moriarty lost to C Nallen  1 hole
N Fox lost to A Rubinson  3 and 2
G Gordon lost to C Wittenberg  5 and 4

**Second Day – *Foursomes***
GP Wolstenholme & O Wilson beat W Haas & T Kuehne
  5 and 4
N Fox & C Moriarty lost to B Mackenzie & M Hendrix
  6 and 5
S Wilson & D Inglis halved with C Wittenberg &
  A Rubinson
NB Edwards & S Manley halved with L Williams &
  G Zahringer

**Singles**
O Wilson beat W Haas  1 hole
GP Wolstenholme beat C Wittenberg  3 and 2
M Skelton beat A Rubinson  3 and 2
C Moriarty lost to B Mackenzie  3 and 1
S Wilson lost to M Hendrix  5 and 4
D Inglis beat R Moore  4 and 3
NB Edwards halved with L Williams
S Manley beat T Kuehne  3 and 2

## 2001 *Ocean Forest, Sea Island, GA* Aug 11–12
**Result: GB&I 15, USA 9**
*Captains: D Yates Jr (USA), P McEvoy (GB&I)*
**First Day – Foursomes**
D Green & DJ Trahan lost to S O'Hara &
  GP Wolstenholme  5 and 3

N Cassini & L Glover beat L Donald & N Dougherty
  4 and 3
D Eger & B Molder halved with J Elson & R McEvoy
J Driscoll & J Quinney lost to G McDowell & M Hoey
  3 and 1

**Singles**
E Compton beat G Wolstenholme  3 and 2
DJ Trahan beat S O'Hara  2 and 1
J Driscoll lost to N Dougherty  2 and 1
N Cassini beat N Edwards  5 and 4
J Harris lost to M Warren  5 and 4
J Quinney lost to L Donald  3 and 2
B Molder beat G McDowell  2 and 1
L Glover beat M Hoey  1 hole

*Second Day – Foursomes*
E Compton & J Harris lost to L Donald & N Dougherty
  3 and 2
N Cassini & L Glover lost to G McDowell & M Hoey
  2 and 1
D Eger & B Molder beat S O'Hara & M Warren
  7 and 6
D Green & DJ Trahan lost to J Elson & R McEvoy
  1 hole

**Singles**
L Glover lost to L Donald  3 and 2
J Harris lost to S O'Hara  4 and 3
DJ Trahan lost to N Dougherty  1 hole
J Driscoll lost to M Warren  2 and 1
B Molder beat G McDowell  1 hole
D Green lost to M Hoey  1 hole
E Compton halved with J Elson
N Cassini lost to GP Wolstenholme  4 and 3

## 1999 *Nairn GC, Nairnshire, Scotland* Sept 11–12
**Result: GB&I 15, USA 9**
*Captains: P McEvoy (GB&I), D Yates Jr (USA)*

**First Day – Foursomes**
Rankin & Storm lost to Haas & Miller  1 hole
Casey & Donald beat Byrd & Scott  5 and 3
Gribben & Kelly lost to Gossett & Jackson
  3 and 1
Rowe & Wolstenholme beat Kuchar & Molder
  1 hole

**Singles**
G Rankin lost to E Loar  4 and 3
L Donald beat T McKnight  4 and 3
G Storm lost to H Haas  4 and 3
P Casey beat S Scott  4 and 3
D Patrick lost to J Byrd  6 and 5
S Dyson halved with D Gossett
P Gribben halved with B Molder
L Kelly lost to T Jackson  3 and 1

*Second Day – Foursomes*
Rankin & Storm beat Loar & McKnight  4 and 3
Dyson & Gribben lost to Haas & Miller  1 hole
Casey & Donald beat Gossett & Jackson  1 hole
Rowe & Wolstenholme beat Kuchar & Molder
  4 and 3

**Singles**
Rankin beat Scott  1 hole
Dyson lost to Loar  5 and 4
Casey beat Miller  3 and 2
Storm beat Byrd  1 hole
Donald beat Molder  3 and 2
Rowe beat Kuchar  1 hole
Gribben beat Haas  3 and 2
Wolstenholme beat Gossett  1 hole

## 1997 *Quaker Ridge GC, NY*  Aug 9–10
### Result: USA 18, GB&I 6
*Captains: AD Gray Jr (USA), C Brown (GB&I)*

**First Day – Foursomes**
Elder & Kribel beat Howard & Young  4 and 3
Courville & Marucci beat Rose & Brooks  5 and 4
Gore & Harris beat Wolstenholme & Nolan  6 and 4
Leen & Wollman beat Coughlan & Park  1 hole

**Singles**
D Delcher lost to S Young  5 and 4
S Scott lost to C Watson  1 hole
B Elder beat B Howard  5 and 4
J Kribel lost to J Rose  1 hole
R Leen beat K Nolan  3 and 2
J Gore beat G Rankin  3 and 2
C Wollman halved with R Coughlan
J Harris beat GP Wolstenholme  1 hole

**Second Day – Foursomes**
Harris & Elder beat Young & Watson  3 and 2
Courville & Marucci beat Howard & Rankin  5 and 4
Delcher & Scott beat Coughlan & Park  1 hole
Leen & Wollman lost to Wolstenholme & Rose
   2 and 1

**Singles**
Kribel lost to Young  2 and 1
Gore halved with Watson
J Courville beat Rose  3 and 2
Elder beat Nolan  2 and 1
Harris beat M Brooks  6 and 5
G Marucci beat D Park  4 and 3
D Delcher beat Wolstenholme  2 and 1
Scott beat Coughlan  2 and 1

## 1995 *Royal Porthcawl GC, Mid Glamorgan, Wales*
Sept 9–10
### Result: GB&I 14, USA 10
*Captains: C Brown (GB&I), AD Gray Jr (USA)*

**First Day – Foursomes**
Sherry & Gallacher lost to Harris & Woods  4 and 3
Foster & Howell halved with Bratton & Riley
Rankin & Howard lost to Begay & Jackson  4 and 3
Harrington & Fanagan beat Cox & Kuehne  5 and 3

**Singles**
G Sherry beat N Begay  3 and 2
L James lost to K Cox  1 hole
M Foster beat B Marucci  4 and 3
S Gallacher beat T Jackson  4 and 3
P Harrington beat J Courville Jr  2 holes
B Howard halved with A Bratton
G Rankin lost to J Harris  1 hole
GP Wolstenholme beat T Woods  1 hole

**Second Day – Foursomes**
Sherry & Gallacher lost to Bratton & Riley  4 and 2
Howell & Foster beat Cox & Kuehne  3 and 2
Wolstenholme & James lost to Marucci & Courville
   6 and 5
Harrington & Fanagan beat Harris & Woods  2 and 1

**Singles**
Sherry beat Riley  2 holes
Howell beat Begay  2 and 1
Gallacher beat Kuehne  3 and 2
Fanagan beat Courville  3 and 2
Howard halved with Jackson
Foster halved with Marucci
Harrington lost to Harris  3 and 2
Wolstenholme lost to Woods  4 and 3

## 1993 *Interlachen GC, Edina, MN*  Aug 18–19
### Result: USA 19, GB&I 5
*Captains: M Giles III (USA), G Macgregor (GB&I)*

**First Day – Foursomes**
Abandoned – rain & flooding

**Singles**
A Doyle beat I Pyman  1 hole
D Berganio lost to M Stanford  3 and 2
J Sigel lost to D Robertson  3 and 2
K Mitchum halved with S Cage
T Herron beat P Harrington  1 hole
D Yates beat P Page  2 and 1
T Demsey beat R Russell  2 and 1
J Leonard beat R Burns  4 and 3
B Gay lost to V Phillips  2 and 1
J Harris beat B Dredge  4 and 3

**Second Day – Foursomes**
Doyle & Leonard beat Pyman & Cage  4 and 3
Berganio & Demsey beat Stanford & Harrington
   3 and 2
Sigel & Mitchum beat Dredge & Phillips  3 and 2
Harris & Herron beat Russell & Robertson  1 hole

**Singles**
Doyle beat Robertson  4 and 3
Harris beat Pyman  3 and 2
Yates beat Cage  2 and 1
Gay halved with Harrington
Sigel beat Page  5 and 4
Herron beat Phillips  3 and 2
Mitchum beat Russell  4 and 2
Berganio beat Burns  1 hole
Demsey beat Dredge  3 and 2
Leonard beat Stanford  5 and 4

## 1991 *Portmarnock GC, Co Dublin, Ireland*  Sept 5–6
### Result: USA 14, GB&I 10
*Captains: G Macgregor (GB&I),
JR Gabrielsen (USA)*

**First Day – Foursomes**
Milligan & Hay lost to Mickelson & May  5 and 3
Payne & Evans lost to Duval & Sposa  1 hole
McGimpsey & Willison lost to Voges & Eger  1 hole
McGinley & Harrington lost to Sigel & Doyle  2 and 1

**Singles**
A Coltart lost to P Mickelson  4 and 3
J Payne beat F Langham  2 and 1
G Evans beat D Duval  2 and 1
R Willison lost to B May  2 and 1
G McGimpsey beat M Sposa  1 hole
P McGinley lost to A Doyle  6 and 4
G Hay beat T Scherrer  1 hole
L White lost to J Sigel  4 and 3

**Second Day – Foursomes**
Milligan & McGimpsey beat Voges & Eger  2 and 1
Payne & Willison lost to Duval & Sposa  1 hole
Evans & Coltart beat Langham & Scherrer  4 and 3
White & McGinley beat Mickelson & May  1 hole

**Singles**
Milligan lost to Mickelson  1 hole
Payne beat Doyle  3 and 1
Evans lost to Langham  4 and 2
Coltart beat Sigel  1 hole
Willison beat Scherrer  3 and 2
Harrington lost to Eger  3 and 2
McGimpsey lost to May  4 and 3
Hay lost to Voges  3 and 1

## 1989 Peachtree GC, GA  Aug 16–17
**Result: GB&I 12½, USA 11½**
*Captains: F Ridley (USA), GC Marks (GB&I)*

**First Day – Foursomes**
Gamez & Martin beat Claydon & Prosser  3 and 2
Yates & Mickelson halved with Dodd & McGimpsey
Lesher & Sigel lost to McEvoy & O'Connell  6 and 5
Eger & Johnson lost to Milligan & Hare  2 and 1

**Singles**
R Gamez beat JW Milligan  7 and 6
D Martin lost to R Claydon  5 and 4
E Meeks halved with SC Dodd
R Howe lost to E O'Connell  5 and 4
D Yates lost to P McEvoy  2 and 1
P Mickelson beat G McGimpsey  4 and 2
G Lesher lost to C Cassells  1 hole
J Sigel halved with RN Roderick

**Second Day – Foursomes**
Gamez & Martin halved with McEvoy & O'Connell
Sigel & Lesher lost to Claydon & Cassells  3 and 2
Eger & Johnson lost to Milligan & Hare  2 and 1
Mickelson & Yates lost to McGimpsey & Dodd  2 and 1

**Singles**
Gamez beat Dodd  1 hole
Martin halved with Hare
Lesher beat Claydon  3 and 2
Yates beat McEvoy  4 and 3
Mickelson halved with O'Connell
Eger beat Roderick  4 and 2
Johnson beat Cassells  4 and 2
Sigel halved with Milligan

## 1987 Sunningdale GC, Berkshire, England  May 27–28
**Result: USA 16½, GB&I 7½**
*Captains: GC Marks (GB&I), F Ridley (USA)*

**First Day – Foursomes**
Montgomerie & Shaw lost to Alexander & Mayfair  5 and 4
Currey & Mayo lost to Kite & Mattice  2 and 1
Macgregor & Robinson lost to Lewis & Loeffler  2 and 1
McHenry & Girvan lost to Sigel & Andrade  3 and 2

**Singles**
D Currey beat B Alexander  2 holes
J Robinson lost to B Andrade  7 and 5
CS Montgomerie beat J Sorenson  3 and 2
R Eggo lost to J Sigel  3 and 2
J McHenry lost to B Montgomery  1 hole
P Girvan lost to B Lewis  3 and 2
DG Carrick lost to B Mayfair  2 holes
G Shaw beat C Kite  1 hole

**Second Day – Foursomes**
Currey & Carrick lost to Lewis & Loeffler  4 and 3
Montgomerie & Shaw lost to Kite & Mattice  5 and 3
Mayo & Macgregor lost to Sorenson & Montgomery  4 and 3
McHenry & Robinson beat Sigel & Andrade  4 and 2

**Singles**
Currey lost to Alexander  5 and 4
Montgomerie beat Andrade  4 and 2
McHenry beat Loeffler  3 and 2
Shaw halved with Sorenson
Robinson beat Mattice  1 hole
Carrick lost to Lewis  3 and 2
Eggo lost to Mayfair  1 hole
Girvan lost to Sigel  6 and 5

## 1985 Pine Valley GC, NJ  Aug 21–22
**Result: USA 13, GB&I 11**
*Captains: J Sigel (USA), CW Green (GB&I)*

**First Day – Foursomes**
Verplank & Sigel beat Montgomerie & Macgregor  1 hole
Waldorf & Randolph lost to Hawksworth & McGimpsey  4 and 3
Sonnier & Haas lost to Baker & McEvoy  6 and 5
Podolak & Love halved with Bloice & Stephen

**Singles**
S Verplank beat G McGimpsey  2 and 1
S Randolph beat P Mayo  5 and 4
R Sonnier halved with J Hawksworth
J Sigel beat CS Montgomerie  5 and 4
B Lewis lost to P McEvoy  2 and 1
C Burroughs lost to G Macgregor  2 holes
D Waldorf beat G Gilford  4 and 2
J Haas lost to AR Stephen  2 and 1

**Second Day – Foursomes**
Verplank & Sigel halved with Mayo & Montgomerie
Randolph & Haas beat Hawksworth & McGimpsey  3 and 2
Lewis & Burroughs beat Baker & McEvoy  2 and 1
Podolak & Love beat Bloice & Stephen  3 and 2

**Singles**
Randolph halved with McGimpsey
Verplank beat Montgomerie  1 hole
Sigel lost to Hawksworth  4 and 3
Love beat McEvoy  5 and 3
Sonnier lost to Baker  5 and 4
Burroughs lost to Macgregor  3 and 2
Lewis beat Bloice  4 and 3
Waldorf lost to Stephen  2 and 1

## 1983 Royal Liverpool GC, Merseyside, England  May 25–26
**Result: USA 13½, GB&I 10½**
*Captains: CW Green (GB&I), J Sigel (USA)*

**First Day – Foursomes**
Macgregor & Walton beat Sigel & Fehr  3 and 2
Keppler & Pierse lost to Wood & Faxon  3 and 1
Lewis & Thompson lost to Lewis & Holtgrieve  7 and 6
Mann & Oldcorn beat Hoffer & Tentis  5 and 4

**Singles**
P Walton beat J Sigel  1 hole
SD Keppler lost to R Fehr  1 hole
G Macgregor halved with W Wood
DG Carrick lost to B Faxon  3 and 1
A Oldcorn beat B Tuten  4 and 3
P Parkin beat N Crosby  5 and 4
AD Pierse lost to B Lewis Jr  3 and 1
LS Mann lost to J Holtgrieve  6 and 5

**Second Day – Foursomes**
Macgregor & Walton lost to Crosby & Hoffer  2 holes
Parkin & Thompson beat Faxon & Wood  1 hole
Mann & Oldcorn beat Lewis & Holtgrieve  1 hole
Keppler & Pierse halved with Sigel & Fehr

**Singles**
Walton beat Wood  2 and 1
Parkin lost to Faxon  3 and 2
Macgregor lost to Fehr  2 and 1
Thompson lost to Tuten  3 and 2
Mann halved with Tentis
Keppler lost to Lewis  6 and 5
Oldcorn beat Holtgrieve  3 and 2
Carrick lost to Sigel  3 and 2

1981 *Cypress Point Club, CA* Aug 28–29
**Result: USA 15, GB&I 9**
*Captains: J Gabrielsen (USA), R Foster (GB&I)*

**First Day – Foursomes**
Sutton & Sigel lost to Walton & Rafferty  4 and 2
Holtgrieve & Fuhrer beat Chapman & McEvoy
 1 hole
Lewis & von Tacky beat Deeble & Hutcheon  2 and 1
Commans & Pavin beat Evans & Way  5 and 4

**Singles**
H Sutton beat R Rafferty  3 and 1
J Rassett beat CR Dalgleish  1 hole
R Commans lost to P Walton  1 hole
B Lewis lost to R Chapman  2 and 1
J Mudd beat G Godwin  1 hole
C Pavin beat IC Hutcheon  4 and 3
D von Tacky lost to P Way  3 and 1
J Sigel beat P McEvoy  4 and 2

**Second Day – Foursomes**
Sutton & Sigel lost to Chapman & Way  1 hole
Holtgrieve & Fuhrer lost to Walton & Rafferty
 6 and 4
Lewis & von Tacky lost to Evans & Dalgleish
 3 and 2
Rassett & Mudd beat Hutcheon & Godwin  5 and 4

**Singles**
Sutton lost to Chapman  1 hole
Holtgrieve beat Rafferty  2 and 1
Fuhrer beat Walton  4 and 3
Sigel beat Way  6 and 5
Mudd beat Dalgleish  7 and 5
Commans halved with Godwin
Rassett beat Deeble  4 and 3
Pavin halved with Evans

1979 *Muirfield, East Lothian, Scotland* May 30–31
**Result: USA 15½, GB&I 8½**
*Captains: R Foster (GB&I), RL Siderowf (USA)*

**First Day – Foursomes**
McEvoy & Marchbank lost to Hoch & Sigel  1 hole
Godwin & Hutcheon beat West & Sutton  2 holes
Brand Jr & Kelley lost to Fischesser & Holtgrieve
 1 hole
Brodie & Carslaw beat Moody & Gove  2 and 1

**Singles**
P McEvoy halved with J Sigel
JC Davies lost to D Clarke  8 and 7
J Buckley lost to S Hoch  9 and 7
IC Hutcheon lost to J Holtgrieve  6 and 4
B Marchbank beat M Peck  1 hole
G Godwin beat G Moody  3 and 2
MJ Kelley beat D Fischesser  3 and 2
A Brodie lost to M Gove  3 and 2

**Second Day – Foursomes**
Godwin & Brand lost to Hoch & Sigel  4 and 3
McEvoy & Marchbank beat Fischesser & Holtgrieve  2 and 1
Kelley & Hutcheon halved with West & Sutton
Carslaw & Brodie halved with Clarke & Peck

**Singles**
McEvoy lost to Hoch  3 and 1
Brand lost to Clarke  2 and 1
Godwin lost to Gove  3 and 2
Hutcheon lost to Peck  2 and 1
Brodie beat West  3 and 2
Kelley lost to Moody  3 and 2
Marchbank lost to Sutton  3 and 1
Carslaw lost to Sigel  2 and 1

1977 *Shinnecock Hills GC, NY* Aug 26–27
**Result: USA 16, GB&I 8**
*Captains: LW Oehmig(USA),
 AC Saddler (GB&I)*

**First Day – Foursomes**
Fought & Heafner beat Lyle & McEvoy  4 and 3
Simpson & Miller beat Davies & Kelley  5 and 4
Siderowf & Hallberg lost to Hutcheon & Deeble  1 hole
Sigel & Brannan beat Brodie & Martin  1 hole

**Singles**
L Miller beat P McEvoy  2 holes
J Fought beat IC Hutcheon  4 and 3
S Simpson beat GH Murray  7 and 6
V Heafner beat JC Davies  4 and 3
B Sander lost to A Brodie  4 and 3
G Hallberg lost to S Martin  3 and 2
F Ridley beat AWB Lyle  2 holes
J Sigel beat P McKellar  5 and 3

**Second Day – Foursomes**
Fought & Heafner beat Hutcheon & Deeble  4 and 3
Miller & Simpson beat McEvoy & Davies  2 holes
Siderowf & Sander lost to Brodie & Martin  6 and 4
Ridley & Brannan lost to Murray & Kelley  4 and 3

**Singles**
Miller beat Martin  1 hole
Fought beat Davies  2 and 1
Sander lost to Brodie  2 and 1
Hallberg beat McEvoy  4 and 3
Siderowf lost to Kelley  2 and 1
Brannan lost to Hutcheon  2 holes
Ridley beat Lyle  5 and 3
Sigel beat Deeble  1 hole

1975 *St Andrews, Fife, Scotland* May 28–29
**Result: USA 15½, GB&I 8½**
*Captains: DM Marsh (GB&I), ER Updegraff (USA)*

**First Day – Foursomes**
James & Eyles beat Pate & Siderowf  1 hole
Davies & Poxon lost to Burns & Stadler  5 and 4
Green & Stuart lost to Haas & Strange  2 and 1
Macgregor & Hutcheon lost to Giles & Koch
 5 and 4

**Singles**
M James beat J Pate  2 and 1
JC Davies halved with C Strange
P Mulcare beat RL Siderowf  1 hole
HB Stuart lost to G Koch  3 and 2
MA Poxon lost to J Grace  3 and 1
IC Hutcheon halved with WC Campbell
GRD Eyles lost to J Haas  2 and 1
G Macgregor lost to M Giles III  5 and 4

**Second Day – Foursomes**
Mulcare & Hutcheon beat Pate & Siderowf  1 hole
Green & Stuart lost to Burns & Stadler  1 hole
James & Eyles beat Campbell & Grace  5 and 3
Hedges & Davies lost to Haas & Strange  3 and 2

**Singles**
Hutcheon beat Pate  3 and 2
Mulcare lost to Strange  4 and 3
James lost to Koch  5 and 4
Davies beat Burns  2 and 1
Green lost to Grace  2 and 1
Macgregor lost to Stadler  3 and 2
Eyles lost to Campbell  2 and 1
Hedges halved with Giles

## 1973 *The Country Club, Brookline, MA*  Aug 24–25
**Result: USA 14, GB&I 10**
*Captains: JW Sweetser (USA), DM Marsh (GB&I)*

**First Day – Foursomes**
Giles & Koch halved with King & Hedges
Siderowf & Pfeil beat Stuart & Davies  5 and 4
Edwards & Ellis beat Green & Milne  2 and 1
West & Ballenger beat Foster & Homer  2 and 1

**Singles**
M Giles III beat HB Stuart  5 and 4
RL Siderowf beat MF Bonallack  4 and 2
G Koch lost to JC Davies  1 hole
M West lost to HK Clark  2 and 1
D Edwards beat R Foster  2 holes
M Killian lost to MG King  1 hole
W Rodgers lost to CW Green  1 hole
M Pfeil lost to WT Milne  4 and 3

**Second Day – Foursomes**
Giles & Koch & Homer & Foster  7 and 5
Siderowf & Pfeil halved with Clark & Davies
Edwards & Ellis beat Hedges & King  2 and 1
Rodgers & Killian beat Stuart & Milne  1 hole

**Singles**
Ellis lost to Stuart  5 and 4
Siderowf lost to Davies  3 and 2
Edwards beat Homer  2 and 1
Giles halved with Green
West beat King  1 hole
Killian lost to Milne  2 and 1
Koch halved with Hedges
Pfeil beat Clark  1 hole

## 1971 *St Andrews, Fife, Scotland*  May 26–27
**Result: GB&I 13, USA 11**
*Captains: MF Bonallack (GB&I), JM Winters Jr (USA)*

**First Day – Foursomes**
Bonallack & Humphreys beat Wadkins & Simons
  1 hole
Green & Carr beat Melnyk & Giles  1 hole
Marsh & Macgregor beat Miller & Farquhar  2 and 1
Macdonald & Foster beat Campbell & Kite  2 and 1

**Singles**
CW Green lost to L Wadkins  1 hole
MF Bonallack lost to M Giles III  1 hole
GC Marks lost to AL Miller III  1 hole
JS Macdonald lost to S Melnyk  3 and 2
RJ Carr halved with W Hyndman III
W Humphreys lost to JR Gabrielsen  1 hole
HB Stuart beat J Farquhar  3 and 2
R Foster lost to T Kite  3 and 2

**Second Day – Foursomes**
Marks & Green lost to Melnyk & Giles  1 hole
Stuart & Carr beat Wadkins & Gabrielsen  1 hole
Marsh & Bonallack lost to Miller & Farquhar  5 and 4
Macdonald & Foster halved with Campbell & Kite

**Singles**
Bonallack lost to Wadkins  3 and 1
Stuart beat Giles  2 and 1
Humphreys beat Melnyk  2 and 1
Green beat Miller  1 hole
Carr beat Simons  2 holes
Macgregor beat Gabrielsen  1 hole
Marsh beat Hyndman  1 hole
Marks lost to Kite  3 and 2

## 1969 *Milwaukee GC, WI*  Aug 22–23
**Result: USA 10, GB&I 8[†]**
*Captains: WJ Patton (USA), MF Bonallack (GB&I)*

**First Day – Foursomes**
Giles & Melnyk beat Bonallack & Craddock  3 and 2
Fleisher & Miller halved with Benka & Critchley
Wadkins & Siderowf lost to Green & A Brooks
W Hyndman III & Inman Jr beat Foster & Marks  2 and 1

**Singles**
B Fleisher halved with MF Bonallack
M Giles III beat CW Green  1 hole
AL Miller III beat B Critchley  1 hole
RL Siderowf beat LP Tupling  6 and 5
S Melnyk lost to PJ Benka  3 and 1
L Wadkins lost to GC Marks  1 hole
J Bohmann beat MG King  2 and 1
ER Updegraff beat R Foster  6 and 5

**Second Day – Foursomes**
Giles & Melnyk halved with Green & Brooks
Fleisher & Miller lost to Benka & Critchley  2 and 1
Siderowf & Wadkins beat Foster & King  6 and 5
Updegraff & Bohmann lost to Bonallack & Tupling  4 and 3

**Singles**
Fleisher lost to Bonallack  5 and 4
Siderowf halved with Critchley
Miller beat King  1 hole
Giles halved with Craddock
Inman beat Benka  2 and 1
Bohmann lost to Brooks  4 and 3
Hyndman halved with Green
Updegraff lost to Marks  3 and 2

## 1967 *R. St George's GC, Kent, England*  May 19–20
**Result: USA 13, GB&I 7[†]**
*Captains: JB Carr (GB&I), JW Sweetser (USA)*

**First Day – Foursomes**
Shade & Oosterhuis halved with Murphy & Cerrudo
Foster & Saddler lost to Campbell & Lewis  1 hole
Bonallack & Attenborough lost to Gray & Tutwiler
  4 and 2
Carr & Craddock lost to Dickson & Grant  3 and 1

**Singles**
RDBM Shade lost to WC Campbell  2 and 1
R Foster lost to RJ Murphy Jr  2 and 1
MF Bonallack halved with AD Gray Jr
MF Attenborough lost to RJ Cerrudo  4 and 3
P Oosterhuis lost to RB Dickson  6 and 4
T Craddock lost to JW Lewis Jr  2 and 1
AK Pirie halved with DC Allen
AC Saddler beat MA Fleckman  2 and 1

**Second Day – Foursomes**
Bonallack & Craddock beat Murphy & Cerrudo  2 holes
Saddler & Pirie lost to Campbell & Lewis  1 hole
Shade & Oosterhuis beat Gray & Tutwiler  3 and 1
Foster & Millensted beat Allen & Fleckman  2 and 1

**Singles**
Shade lost to Campbell  3 and 2
Bonallack beat Murphy  4 and 2
Saddler beat Gray  3 and 2
Foster halved with Cerrudo
Pirie lost to Dickson  4 and 3
Craddock beat Lewis  5 and 4
Oosterhuis lost to Grant  1 hole
Millensted lost to Tutwiler  3 and 1

---

† *No points were given for halved matches between 1922 and 1969. There was a total of 12 points 1922–61 and 24 points 1963–69.*

**1965** *Baltimore GC, MD*  Sept 3–4
**Result: USA 11, GB&I 11**[†]
*Captains: JW Fischer (USA), JB Carr (GB&I)*

**First Day – Foursomes**
Campbell & Gray lost to Lunt & Cosh  1 hole
Beman & Allen halved with Bonallack & Clark
Patton & Tutwiler beat Foster & Clark  5 and 4
Hopkins & Eichelberger lost to Townsend & Shade
  2 and 1

**Singles**
WC Campbell beat MF Bonallack  6 and 5
DR Beman beat R Foster  2 holes
AD Gray Jr lost to RDBM Shade  3 and 1
JM Hopkins lost to CA Clark  5 and 4
WJ Patton lost to P Townsend  3 and 2
D Morey lost to AC Saddler  2 and 1
DC Allen lost to GB Cosh  2 holes
ER Updegraff lost to MSR Lunt  2 and 1

**Second Day – Foursomes**
Campbell & Gray beat Saddler & Foster  4 and 3
Beman & Eichelberger lost to Townsend & Shade
  2 and 1
Tutwiler & Patton beat Cosh & Lunt  2 and 1
Allen & Morey lost to CA Clark & Bonallack  2 and 1

**Singles**
Campbell beat Foster  3 and 2
Beman beat Saddler  1 hole
Tutwiler beat Shade  5 and 3
Allen lost to Cosh  4 and 3
Gray beat Townsend  1 hole
Hopkins halved with CA Clark
Eichelberger beat Bonallack  5 and 3
Patton beat Lunt  4 and 2

**1963** *Turnberry, Ayrshire, Scotland*  May 24–25
**Result: USA 12, GB&I 8**[†]
*Captains: CD Lawrie (GB&I), RS Tufts (USA)*

**First Day – Foursomes**
Bonallack & Murray beat Patton & Sikes  4 and 3
Carr & Green lost to Gray & Harris  2 holes
Lunt & Sheahan lost to Beman & Coe  5 and 3
Madeley & Shade halved with Gardner & Updegraff

**Singles**
SWT Murray beat DR Beman  3 and 1
MJ Christmas lost to WJ Patton  3 and 2
JB Carr beat RH Sikes  7 and 5
DB Sheahan beat LE Harris  1 hole
MF Bonallack beat RD Davies  1 hole
AC Saddler halved with CR Coe
RDBM Shade beat AD Gray Jr  4 and 3
MSR Lunt halved with CB Smith

**Second Day – Foursomes**
Bonallack & Murray lost to Patton & Sikes  1 hole
Lunt & Sheahan lost to Gray & Harris  3 and 2
Green & Saddler lost to Gardner & Updegraff  3 and 1
Madeley & Shade lost to Beman & Coe  3 and 2

**Singles**
Murray lost to Patton  3 and 2
Sheahan beat Davies  1 hole
Carr lost to Updegraff  4 and 3
Bonallack lost to Harris  3 and 2
Lunt lost to Gardner  3 and 2
Saddler halved with Beman
Shade beat Gray  2 and 1
Green lost to Coe  4 and 3

**1961** *Seattle GC, WA*  Sept 1–2
**Result: USA 11, GB&I 1**
*Captains: J Westland (USA), CD Lawrie (GB&I)*

**Foursomes**
Beman & Nicklaus beat Walker & Chapman  6 and 5
Coe & Cherry beat Blair & Christmas  1 hole
Hyndman & Gardner beat Carr & G Huddy  4 and 3
Cochran & Andrews beat Bonallack & Shade  4 and 3

**Singles**
DR Beman beat MF Bonallack  3 and 2
CR Coe beat MSR Lunt  5 and 4
FM Taylor Jr beat J Walker  3 and 2
W Hyndman III beat DW Frame  7 and 6
JW Nicklaus beat JB Carr  6 and 4
CB Smith lost to MJ Christmas  3 and 2
RW Gardner beat RDBM Shade  1 hole
DR Cherry beat DA Blair  5 and 4

**1959** *Muirfield, East Lothian, Scotland*  May 15–16
**Result: USA 9, GB&I 3**
*Captains: GH Micklem (GB&I), CR Coe (USA)*

**Foursomes**
Jack & Sewell lost to Ward & Taylor  1 hole
Carr & Wolstenholme lost to Hyndman & Aaron
  1 hole
Bonallack & Perowne lost to Patton & Coe  9 and 8
Lunt & Shepperson lost to Wettlander & Nicklaus
  2 and 1

**Singles**
JB Carr beat CR Coe  3 and 1
GB Wolstenholme lost to EH Ward Jr  9 and 8
RR Jack beat WJ Patton  5 and 3
DN Sewell lost to W Hyndman III  4 and 3
AE Shepperson beat TD Aaron  2 and 1
MF Bonallack lost to DR Beman  2 holes
MSR Lunt lost to HW Wettlander  6 and 5
WD Smith lost to JW Nicklaus  5 and 4

**1957** *The Minikahda Club, MN*  Aug 30–31
**Result: USA 8, GB&I 3**[†]
*Captains: CR Coe (USA), GH Micklem (GB&I)*

**Foursomes**
Baxter & Patton beat Carr & Deighton  2 and 1
Campbell & Taylor beat Bussell & Scrutton  4 and 3
Blum & Kocsis lost to Jack & Sewell  1 hole
Robbins & Rudolph halved with Shepperson &
  Wolstenholme

**Singles**
WJ Patton beat RR Jack  1 hole
WC Campbell beat JB Carr  3 and 2
R Baxter Jr beat A Thirlwell  4 and 3
W Hyndman III beat FWG Deighton  7 and 6
JE Campbell lost to AF Bussell  2 and 1
FM Taylor Jr beat D Sewell  1 hole
EM Rudolph beat PF Scrutton  3 and 2
H Robbins Jr lost to GB Wolstenholme  2 and 1

**1955** *St Andrews, Fife, Scotland*  May 20–21
**Result: USA 10, GB&I 2**
*Captains: GA Hill (GB&I), WC Campbell (USA)*

**Foursomes**
Carr & White lost to Ward & Cherry  1 hole
Micklem & Morgan lost to Patton & Yost  2 and 1
Caldwell & Millward lost to Conrad & Morey  3 and 2
Blair & Cater lost to Cudd & Jackson  5 and 4

---

† *No points were given for halved matches between 1922 and 1969. There was a total of 12 points 1922–61 and 24 points 1963–69.*

**Singles**
RJ White lost to EH Ward Jr  6 and 5
PF Scrutton lost to WJ Patton  2 and 1
I Caldwell beat D Morey  1 hole
JB Carr lost to DR Cherry  5 and 4
DA Blair beat JW Conrad  1 hole
EB Millward lost to BH Cudd  2 holes
RC Ewing lost to JG Jackson  6 and 4
JL Morgan lost to RL Yost  8 and 7

## 1953 The Kittansett, MA  Sept 4–5
**Result: USA 9, GB&I 3**
*Captains: CR Yates (USA), AA Duncan (GB&I)*

**Foursomes**
Urzetta & Venturi beat Carr & White  6 and 4
Ward & Westland beat Langley & AH Perowne  9 and 8
Jackson & Littler beat Wilson & MacGregor  3 and 2
Campbell & Coe lost to Micklem & Morgan  4 and 3

**Singles**
EH Ward Jr beat JB Carr  4 and 3
RD Chapman lost to RJ White  1 hole
GA Littler beat GH Micklem  5 and 3
J Westland beat RC MacGregor  7 and 5
DR Cherry beat NV Drew  9 and 7
K Venturi beat JC Wilson  9 and 8
CR Coe lost to JL Morgan  3 and 2
S Urzetta beat JDA Langley  3 and 2

## 1951 Birkdale GC, Lancashire, England  May 11–12
**Result: USA 6, GB&I 3†**
*Captains: RH Oppenheimer (GB&I),*
*WP Turnesa (USA)*

**Foursomes**
White & Carr halved with Stranahan & Campbell
Ewing & Langley halved with Coe & McHale
Kyle & Caldwell lost to Chapman & Knowles Jr  1 hole
Bruen Jr & Morgan lost to Turnesa & Urzetta  5 and 4

**Singles**
SM McCready lost to S Urzetta  4 and 3
JB Carr beat FR Stranahan  2 and 1
RJ White beat CR Coe  2 and 1
JDA Langley lost to JB McHale Jr  2 holes
RC Ewing lost to WC Campbell  5 and 4
AT Kyle beat WP Turnesa  2 holes
I Caldwell halved with HD Paddock Jr
JL Morgan lost to RD Chapman  7 and 6

## 1949 Winged Foot GC. NY  Aug 19–20
**Result: USA 10, GB&I 2**
*Captains: FD Ouimet (USA), PB Lucas (GB&I)*

**Foursomes**
Billows & Turnesa lost to Carr & White  3 and 2
Kocsis & Stranahan beat Bruen & McCready  2 and 1
Bishop & Riegel beat Ewing & Micklem  9 and 7
Dawson & McCormick beat Thom & Perowne  8 and 7

**Singles**
WP Turnesa lost to RJ White  4 and 3
FR Stranahan beat SM McCready  6 and 5
RH Riegel beat J Bruen Jr  5 and 4
JW Dawson beat JB Carr  3 and 3
CR Coe beat RC Ewing  1 hole
RE Billows beat KG Thom  2 and 1
CR Kocsis beat AH Perowne  4 and 2
JB McHale Jr beat GH Micklem  5 and 4

## 1947 St Andrews, Fife, Scotland  May 16–17
**Result: USA 8, GB&I 4**
*Captains: JB Beck (GB&I), FD Ouimet (USA)*

**Foursomes**
Carr & Ewing lost to Bishop & Riegel  3 and 2
Crawley & Lucas beat Ward & Quick  5 and 4
Kyle & Wilson lost to Turnesa & Kammer  5 and 4
White & Stowe beat Stranahan & Chapman  4 and 3

**Singles**
LG Crawley lost to MH Ward  5 and 3
JB Carr beat SE Bishop  5 and 3
GH Micklem lost to RH Riegel  6 and 5
RC Ewing lost to WP Turnesa  6 and 5
C Stowe lost to FR Stranahan  2 and 1
RJ White beat AF Kammer Jr  4 and 3
JC Wilson lost to SL Quick  8 and 6
PB Lucas lost to RD Chapman  4 and 3

## 1938 St Andrews, Fife, Scotland  June 3–4
**Result: GB&I 7, USA 4†**
*Captains: JB Beck (GB&I), FD Ouimet (USA)*

**Foursomes**
Bentley & Bruen halved with Fischer & Kocsis
Peters & Thomson beat Goodman & Ward  4 and 2
Kyle & Stowe beat Yates & Billows  3 and 2
Pennink & Crawley beat Smith & Haas  3 and 1

**Singles**
J Bruen Jr lost to CR Yates  2 and 1
H Thomson beat JG Goodman  6 and 4
LG Crawley lost to JW Fischer  3 and 2
C Stowe beat CR Kocsis  2 and 1
JJF Pennink lost to MH Ward  12 and 11
RC Ewing beat RE Billows  1 hole
GB Peters beat R Smith  9 and 8
AT Kyle beat F Haas Jr  5 and 4

## 1936 Pine Valley GC, NJ  Sept 2–3
**Result: USA 9, GB&I 0†**
*Captains: FD Ouimet (USA), W Tweddell (GB&I)*

**Foursomes**
Goodman & Campbell beat Thomson & Bentley  7 and 5
Smith & White beat McLean & Langley  8 and 7
Yates & Emery halved with Peters & Dykes
Givan & Voigt halved with Hill & Ewing

**Singles**
JG Goodman beat H Thomson  3 and 2
AE Campbell beat J McLean  5 and 4
JW Fischer beat RC Ewing  8 and 7
R Smith beat GA Hill  11 and 9
W Emery beat GB Peters  1 hole
CR Yates beat JM Dykes  8 and 7
GT Dunlap Jr halved with HG Bentley
E White beat JDA Langley  6 and 5

## 1934 St Andrews, Fife, Scotland  May 11–12
**Result: USA 9, GB&I 2†**
*Captains: Hon M Scott (GB&I), FD Ouimet (USA)*

**Foursomes**
Wethered & Tolley lost to Goodman & Little  8 and 6
Bentley & Fiddian lost to Moreland & Westland  6 and 5
Scott & McKinlay lost to Egan & Marston  3 and 2
McRuvie & McLean beat Ouimet & Dunlap  4 and 2

† *No points were given for halved matches between 1922 and 1969. There was a total of 12 points 1922–61 and 24 points 1963–69*

## 1934 continued

**Singles**
Hon M Scott lost to JG Goodman  7 and 6
CJH Tolley lost to WL Little Jr  6 and 5
LG Crawley lost to FD Ouimet  5 and 4
J McLean lost to GT Dunlap Jr  4 and 3
EW Fiddian lost to JW Fischer  5 and 4
SL McKinlay lost to GT Moreland  3 and 1
EA McRuvie halved with J Westland
TA Torrance beat MR Marston  4 and 3

## 1932 The Country Club, Brookline, MA  Sept 1–2
### Result: USA 8, GB&I 1[†]
*Captains: FD Ouimet (USA), TA Torrance (GB&I)*

**Foursomes**
Sweetser & Voigt beat Hartley & Hartley  7 and 6
Seaver & Moreland beat Torrance & de Forest  6 and 5
Ouimet & Dunlap beat Stout & Burke  7 and 6
Moe & Howell beat Fiddian & McRuvie  5 and 4

**Singles**
FD Ouimet halved with TA Torrance
JW Sweetser halved with JA Stout
GT Moreland beat RW Hartley  2 and 1
J Westland halved with J Burke
GJ Voigt lost to LG Crawley  1 hole
MJ McCarthy Jr beat WL Hartley  3 and 2
CH Seaver beat EW Fiddian  7 and 6
GT Dunlap Jr beat EA McRuvie  10 and 9

## 1930 Royal St George's GC, Sandwich, Kent
May 15–16
### Result: USA 10, GB&I 2
*Captains: RH Wethered (GB&I), RT Jones Jr (USA)*

**Foursomes**
Tolley & Wethered beat Von Elm & Voigt  2 holes
Hartley & Torrance lost to Jones & Willing  8 and 7
Holderness & Stout lost to MacKenzie & Moe
  2 and 1
Campbell & Smith lost to Johnston & Ouimet  2 and 1

**Singles**
CJH Tolley lost to HR Johnston  5 and 4
RH Wethered lost to RT Jones Jr  9 and 8
RW Hartley lost to G Von Elm  3 and 2
EWE Holderness lost to GJ Voigt  10 and 8
JN Smith lost to OF Willing  2 and 1
TA Torrance beat FD Ouimet  7 and 6
JA Stout lost to DK Moe  1 hole
W Campbell lost to RR MacKenzie  6 and 5

## 1928 Chicago GC, IL  Aug 30–31
### Result: USA 11, GB&I 1
*Captains: RT Jones Jr (USA), W Tweddell (GB&I)*

**Foursomes**
Sweetser & Von Elm beat Perkins & Tweddell  7 and 6
Jones & Evans beat Hezlet & Hope  5 and 3
Ouimet & Johnston beat Tolley & Storey  4 and 2
Gunn & MacKenzie beat Beck & Martin  7 and 5

**Singles**
RT Jones Jr beat TP Perkins  13 and 12
G Von Elm beat W Tweddell  3 and 2
FD Ouimet beat CO Hezlet  8 and 7
JW Sweetser beat WL Hope  5 and 4
HR Johnston beat EF Storey  4 and 2
C Evans Jr lost to TA Torrance  1 hole
W Gunn beat RH Hardman  11 and 10
RR MacKenzie beat GNC Martin  2 and 1

## 1926 St Andrews, Fife, Scotland  June 2–3
### Result: USA 6, GB&I 5[†]
*Captains: R Harris (GB&I), RA Gardner (USA)*

**Foursomes**
Wethered & Holderness beat Ouimet & Guilford
  5 and 4
Tolley & Jamieson lost to Jones & Gunn  4 and 3
Harris & Hezlet lost to Von Elm & Sweetser  8 and 7
Storey & Brownlow lost to Gardner & MacKenzie
  1 hole

**Singles**
CJH Tolley lost to RT Jones Jr  12 and 11
EWE Holderness lost to JW Sweetser  4 and 3
RH Wethered beat FD Ouimet  5 and 4
CO Hezlet halved with G Von Elm
R Harris beat JP Guilford  2 and 1
Hon WGE Brownlow lost to W Gunn  9 and 8
EF Storey beat RR MacKenzie  2 and 1
A Jamieson Jr beat RA Gardner  5 and 4

## 1924 Garden City GC, NY  Sept 12–13
### Result: USA 9, GB&I 3
*Captains: RA Gardner (USA), CJH Tolley (GB&I)*

**Foursomes**
Marston & Gardner beat Storey & Murray  3 and 1
Guilford & Ouimet beat Tolley & Hezlet  2 and 1
Jones & Fownes Jr lost to Scott & Scott Jr  1 hole
Sweetser & Johnston beat Torrance & Bristowe
  4 and 3

**Singles**
MR Marston lost to CJH Tolley  1 hole
RT Jones Jr beat CO Hezlet  4 and 3
C Evans Jr beat WA Murray  2 and 1
FD Ouimet beat EF Storey  1 hole
JW Sweetser lost to Hon M Scott  7 and 6
RA Gardner beat WL Hope  3 and 2
JP Guilford beat TA Torrance  2 and 1
OF Willing beat DH Kyle  3 and 2

## 1923 St Andrews, Fife, Scotland  May 18–19
### Result: USA 6, GB&I 5[†]
*Captains: R Harris (GB&I), RA Gardner (USA)*

**Foursomes**
Tolley & Wethered beat Ouimet & Sweetser  6 and 5
Harris & Hooman lost to Gardner & Marston
  7 and 6
Holderness & Hope beat Rotan & Herron  1 hole
Wilson & Murray beat Johnston & Neville  4 and 3

**Singles**
RH Wethered halved with FD Ouimet
CJH Tolley beat JW Sweetser  4 and 3
R Harris lost to RA Gardner  1 hole
WW Mackenzie lost to GV Rotan  5 and 4
WL Hope lost to MR Marston  6 and 5
EWE Holderness lost to FJ Wright Jr  1 hole
J Wilson beat SD Herron  1 hole
WA Murray lost to OF Willing  2 and 1

## 1922 National Golf Links, NY  Aug 28–29
### Result: USA 8, GB&I 4
*Captains: WC Fownes (USA), R Harris (GB&I)*

**Foursomes**
Guilford & Ouimet beat Tolley & Darwin  8 and 7
Evans & Gardner lost to Wethered & Aylmer  5 and 4
Jones & Sweetser beat Torrance & Hooman  3 and 2
Marston & Fownes beat Caven & Mackenzie  2 and 1

---

† *No points were given for halved matches between 1922 and 1969. There was a total of 12 points 1922–61 and 24 points 1963–69*

**Singles**
JP Guilford beat CJH Tolley  2 and 1
RT Jones Jr beat RH Wethered  3 and 2
C Evans Jr beat J Caven  5 and 4
FD Ouimet beat CC Aylmer  8 and 7
RA Gardner beat WB Torrance  7 and 5
MR Marston lost to WW Mackenzie  6 and 5
WC Fownes Jr lost to B Darwin  3 and 1
JW Sweetser lost to CVL Hooman  at 37th

**Singles**
CJH Tolley beat C Evans Jr  4 and 3
JLC Jenkins lost to FD Ouimet  6 and 5
RH de Montmorency lost to RT Jones Jr  4 and 3
JG Simpson lost to JP Guilford  2 and 1
CC Aylmer beat P Hunter  2 and 1
TD Armour beat JW Platt  2 and 1
EWE Holderness lost to F Wright  2 holes
RH Wethered lost to WC Fownes Jr  3 and 1

## Unofficial match
1921 *Hoylake* 21 May
**Result: USA 9, GB&I 3**
**Foursomes**
Simpson & Jenkins lost to Evans & Jones  5 and 3
Tolley & Holderness lost to Ouimet & Guilford  3 and 2
de Montmorency & Wethered lost to Hunter & Platt
  1 hole
Aylmer & Armour lost to Wright & Fownes  4 and 2

## Walker Cup – INDIVIDUAL RECORDS

Notes:  Bold type indicates captain; in brackets, did not play
         † indicates players who have also played in the Ryder Cup

### Great Britain and Ireland

| Name | | Year | Played | Won | Lost | Halved |
|---|---|---|---|---|---|---|
| MF Attenborough | ENG | 1967 | 2 | 0 | 2 | 0 |
| CC Aylmer | ENG | 1922 | 2 | 1 | 1 | 0 |
| †P Baker | ENG | 1985 | 3 | 2 | 1 | 0 |
| JB Beck | ENG | 1928-**(38)**-**(47)** | 1 | 0 | 1 | 0 |
| PJ Benka | ENG | 1969 | 4 | 2 | 1 | 1 |
| HG Bentley | ENG | 1934-36-38 | 4 | 0 | 2 | 2 |
| DA Blair | SCO | 1955-61 | 4 | 1 | 3 | 0 |
| C Bloice | SCO | 1985 | 3 | 0 | 2 | 1 |
| MF Bonallack | ENG | 1957-59-61-63-65-67-**69-71**-73 | 25 | 8 | 14 | 3 |
| JT Bookless | SCO | (1932) | 0 | 0 | 0 | 0 |
| W Booth | SCO | 2009 | 4 | 1 | 2 | 1 |
| †G Brand Jr | SCO | 1979 | 3 | 0 | 3 | 0 |
| OC Bristowe | ENG | (1923)-24 | 1 | 0 | 1 | 0 |
| A Brodie | SCO | 1977-79 | 8 | 5 | 2 | 1 |
| A Brooks | SCO | 1969 | 3 | 2 | 0 | 1 |
| M Brooks | SCO | 1997 | 2 | 0 | 2 | 0 |
| C Brown | WAL | **(1995-97)** | 0 | 0 | 0 | 0 |
| S Brown | ENG | 2011 | 3 | 1 | 1 | 1 |
| Hon WGE Brownlow | IRL | 1926 | 2 | 0 | 2 | 0 |
| J Bruen | IRL | 1938-49-51 | 5 | 0 | 4 | 1 |
| JA Buckley | WAL | 1979 | 1 | 0 | 1 | 0 |
| J Burke | IRL | 1932 | 2 | 0 | 1 | 1 |
| R Burns | IRL | 1993 | 2 | 1 | 1 | 0 |
| AF Bussell | SCO | 1957 | 2 | 1 | 1 | 0 |
| J Byrne | SCO | 2011 | 3 | 2 | 1 | 0 |
| S Cage | ENG | 1993 | 3 | 0 | 2 | 1 |
| I Caldwell | ENG | 1951-55 | 4 | 1 | 2 | 1 |
| J Caldwell | IRL | 2007 | 3 | 1 | 1 | 1 |
| W Campbell | SCO | 1930 | 2 | 0 | 2 | 0 |
| JB Carr | IRL | 1947-49-51-53-55-57-59-61-63-**(65)-67** | 20 | 5 | 14 | 1 |
| RJ Carr | IRL | 1971 | 4 | 3 | 0 | 1 |
| DG Carrick | SCO | 1983-87 | 5 | 0 | 5 | 0 |
| IA Carslaw | SCO | 1979 | 3 | 1 | 1 | 1 |
| †P Casey | ENG | 1999 | 4 | 4 | 0 | 0 |
| C Cassells | ENG | 1989 | 3 | 2 | 1 | 0 |
| JR Cater | SCO | 1955 | 1 | 0 | 1 | 0 |
| J Caven | SCO | 1922-(23) | 2 | 0 | 2 | 0 |
| BHG Chapman | ENG | 1961 | 1 | 0 | 1 | 0 |
| R Chapman | ENG | 1981 | 4 | 3 | 1 | 0 |
| MJ Christmas | ENG | 1961-63 | 3 | 1 | 2 | 0 |

| Name | | Year | Played | Won | Lost | Halved |
|------|---|------|--------|-----|------|--------|
| †CA Clark | ENG | 1965 | 4 | 2 | 0 | 2 |
| GJ Clark | ENG | 1965 | 1 | 0 | 1 | 0 |
| †HK Clark | ENG | 1973 | 3 | 1 | 1 | 1 |
| R Claydon | ENG | 1989 | 4 | 2 | 2 | 0 |
| †A Coltart | SCO | 1991 | 3 | 2 | 1 | 0 |
| GB Cosh | SCO | 1965 | 4 | 3 | 1 | 0 |
| R Coughlan | IRL | 1997 | 4 | 0 | 3 | 1 |
| T Craddock | IRL | 1967-69 | 6 | 2 | 3 | 1 |
| LG Crawley | ENG | 1932-34-38-47 | 6 | 3 | 3 | 0 |
| B Critchley | ENG | 1969 | 4 | 1 | 1 | 2 |
| D Curry | ENG | 1987 | 4 | 1 | 3 | 0 |
| P Cutler | IRL | 2011 | 4 | 3 | 0 | 1 |
| CR Dalgleish | SCO | 1981-(07)-(09) | 3 | 1 | 2 | 0 |
| B Darwin | ENG | 1922 | 2 | 1 | 1 | 0 |
| JC Davies | ENG | 1973-75-77-79 | 13 | 3 | 8 | 2 |
| R Davies | WAL | 2005-07 | 8 | 4 | 3 | 1 |
| G Dear | SCO | 2009 | 4 | 1 | 2 | 1 |
| P Deeble | ENG | 1977-81 | 5 | 1 | 4 | 0 |
| FWG Deighton | SCO | (1951)-57 | 2 | 0 | 2 | 0 |
| R Dinwiddie | ENG | 2005 | 3 | 1 | 1 | 3 |
| SC Dodd | WAL | 1989 | 4 | 1 | 1 | 2 |
| †L Donald | ENG | 1999-01 | 8 | 7 | 1 | 0 |
| N Dougherty | ENG | 2001 | 4 | 3 | 1 | 0 |
| B Dredge | WAL | 1993 | 3 | 0 | 3 | 0 |
| †NV Drew | IRL | 1953 | 1 | 0 | 1 | 0 |
| A Dunbar | IRL | 2011 | 3 | 2 | 1 | 0 |
| AA Duncan | WAL | (1953) | 0 | 0 | 0 | 0 |
| JM Dykes | SCO | 1936 | 2 | 0 | 1 | 1 |
| S Dyson | ENG | 1999 | 3 | 0 | 2 | 1 |
| NB Edwards | WAL | 2001-03-05-07-(2011) | 12 | 4 | 5 | 3 |
| R Eggo | ENG | 1987 | 2 | 0 | 2 | 0 |
| J Elson | ENG | 2001 | 3 | 1 | 0 | 2 |
| D Evans | WAL | 1981 | 3 | 1 | 1 | 1 |
| G Evans | ENG | 1991 | 4 | 2 | 2 | 0 |
| RC Ewing | IRL | 1936-38-47-49-51-55 | 10 | 1 | 7 | 2 |
| GRD Eyles | ENG | 1975 | 4 | 2 | 2 | 0 |
| J Fanagan | IRL | 1995 | 3 | 3 | 0 | 0 |
| EW Fiddian | ENG | 1932-34 | 4 | 0 | 4 | 0 |
| O Fisher | ENG | 2005 | 4 | 1 | 2 | 1 |
| T Fleetwood | ENG | 2009 | 2 | 1 | 1 | 0 |
| J de Forest | ENG | 1932 | 1 | 0 | 1 | 0 |
| M Foster | ENG | 1995 | 4 | 2 | 0 | 2 |
| R Foster | ENG | 1965-67-69-71-73-(79)-(81) | 17 | 2 | 13 | 2 |
| N Fox | IRL | 2003 | 3 | 1 | 2 | 0 |
| DW Frame | ENG | 1961 | 1 | 0 | 1 | 0 |
| S Gallacher | SCO | 1995 | 4 | 2 | 2 | 0 |
| †D Gilford | ENG | 1985 | 1 | 0 | 1 | 0 |
| P Girvan | SCO | 1987 | 3 | 0 | 3 | 0 |
| L Goddard | ENG | 2009 | 2 | 0 | 2 | 0 |
| G Godwin | ENG | 1979-81 | 7 | 2 | 4 | 1 |
| G Gordon | SCO | 2003 | 1 | 0 | 1 | 0 |
| CW Green | SCO | 1963-69-71-73-75-(83)-(85) | 17 | 4 | 10 | 3 |
| P Gribben | IRL | 1999 | 4 | 1 | 2 | 1 |
| M Haines | ENG | 2009 | 4 | 1 | 3 | 0 |
| RH Hardman | ENG | 1928 | 1 | 0 | 1 | 0 |
| A Hare | ENG | 1989 | 3 | 2 | 0 | 1 |
| †P Harrington | IRL | 1991-93-95 | 9 | 3 | 5 | 1 |
| R Harris | SCO | (1922)-23-26 | 4 | 1 | 3 | 0 |
| RW Hartley | ENG | 1930-32 | 4 | 0 | 4 | 0 |
| WL Hartley | ENG | 1932 | 2 | 0 | 2 | 0 |
| J Hawksworth | ENG | 1985 | 4 | 2 | 1 | 1 |
| G Hay | SCO | 1991 | 3 | 1 | 2 | 0 |
| P Hedges | ENG | 1973-75 | 5 | 0 | 2 | 3 |
| CO Hezlet | IRL | 1924-26-28 | 6 | 0 | 5 | 1 |
| GA Hill | ENG | 1936-(55) | 2 | 0 | 1 | 1 |
| S Hodgson | ENG | 2009-11 | 6 | 2 | 4 | 0 |
| M Hoey | IRL | 2001 | 4 | 3 | 1 | 0 |
| Sir EWE Holderness | ENG | 1923-26-30 | 6 | 2 | 4 | 0 |
| TWB Homer | ENG | 1973 | 3 | 0 | 3 | 0 |
| ‡CVL Hooman | ENG | 1922-23 | 3 | †1 | 2 | †0 |

| Name | | Year | Played | Won | Lost | Halved |
|---|---|---|---|---|---|---|
| WL Hope | SCO | 1923-24-28 | 5 | 1 | 4 | 0 |
| D Horsey | ENG | 2007 | 4 | 3 | 1 | 0 |
| DB Howard | SCO | 1995-97 | 6 | 0 | 4 | 2 |
| †D Howell | ENG | 1995 | 3 | 2 | 0 | 1 |
| G Huddy | ENG | 1961 | 1 | 0 | 1 | 0 |
| W Humphreys | ENG | 1971 | 3 | 2 | 1 | 0 |
| IC Hutcheon | SCO | 1975-77-79-81 | 15 | 5 | 8 | 2 |
| S Hutsby | ENG | 2009 | 4 | 2 | 2 | 0 |
| D Inglis | SCO | 2003 | 4 | 2 | 1 | 1 |
| RR Jack | SCO | 1957-59 | 4 | 2 | 2 | 0 |
| L James | ENG | 1995 | 2 | 0 | 2 | 0 |
| †M James | ENG | 1975 | 4 | 3 | 1 | 0 |
| A Jamieson Jr | SCO | 1926 | 2 | 1 | 1 | 0 |
| N Kearney | IRL | 2009 | 4 | 2 | 2 | 0 |
| MJ Kelley | ENG | 1977-79 | 7 | 3 | 3 | 1 |
| L Kelly | SCO | 1999 | 2 | 0 | 2 | 0 |
| SD Keppler | ENG | 1983 | 4 | 0 | 3 | 1 |
| †MG King | ENG | 1969-73 | 7 | 1 | 5 | 1 |
| AT Kyle | SCO | 1938-47-51 | 5 | 2 | 3 | 0 |
| DH Kyle | SCO | 1924 | 1 | 0 | 1 | 0 |
| JA Lang | SCO | (1930) | 0 | 0 | 0 | 0 |
| JDA Langley | ENG | 1936-51-53 | 6 | 0 | 5 | 1 |
| CD Lawrie | SCO | (1961)-(63) | 0 | 0 | 0 | 0 |
| ME Lewis | ENG | 1983 | 1 | 0 | 1 | 0 |
| T Lewis | ENG | 2011 | 4 | 1 | 2 | 1 |
| G Lockerbie | ENG | 2005 | 4 | 1 | 3 | 0 |
| PB Lucas | ENG | (1936)-47-(49) | 2 | 1 | 1 | 0 |
| MSR Lunt | ENG | 1959-61-63-65 | 11 | 2 | 8 | 1 |
| †AWB Lyle | SCO | 1977 | 3 | 0 | 3 | 0 |
| AR McCallum | SCO | 1928 | 1 | 0 | 1 | 0 |
| SM McCready | IRL | 1949-51 | 3 | 0 | 3 | 0 |
| JS Macdonald | SCO | 1971 | 3 | 1 | 1 | 1 |
| †G McDowell | IRL | 2001 | 4 | 2 | 2 | 0 |
| B McElhinney | IRL | 2005 | 1 | 0 | 1 | 0 |
| P McEvoy | ENG | 1977-79-81-85-89-(99)-(01) | 18 | 5 | 11 | 2 |
| R McEvoy | ENG | 2001 | 2 | 1 | 0 | 1 |
| G McGimpsey | IRL | 1985-89-91-(03)-(05) | 11 | 4 | 5 | 2 |
| †P McGinley | IRL | 1991 | 3 | 1 | 2 | 0 |
| G Macgregor | SCO | 1971-75-83-85-87-(91)-(93) | 14 | 5 | 8 | 1 |
| RC MacGregor | SCO | 1953 | 2 | 0 | 2 | 0 |
| J McHenry | IRL | 1987 | 4 | 2 | 2 | 0 |
| †R McIlroy | IRL | 2007 | 4 | 1 | 2 | 1 |
| P McKellar | SCO | 1977 | 1 | 0 | 1 | 0 |
| WW Mackenzie | SCO | 1922-23 | 3 | 1 | 2 | 0 |
| SL McKinlay | SCO | 1934 | 2 | 0 | 2 | 0 |
| J McLean | SCO | 1934-36 | 4 | 1 | 3 | 0 |
| EA McRuvie | SCO | 1932-34 | 4 | 1 | 2 | 1 |
| JFD Madeley | IRL | 1963 | 2 | 0 | 1 | 1 |
| S Manley | WAL | 2003 | 3 | 2 | 0 | 1 |
| LS Mann | SCO | 1983 | 4 | 2 | 1 | 1 |
| B Marchbank | SCO | 1979 | 4 | 2 | 2 | 0 |
| GC Marks | ENG | 1969-71-(87)-(89) | 6 | 2 | 4 | 0 |
| DM Marsh | ENG | (1959)-71-(73)-(75) | 3 | 2 | 1 | 0 |
| GNC Martin | IRL | 1928 | 1 | 0 | 1 | 0 |
| S Martin | SCO | 1977 | 4 | 2 | 2 | 0 |
| L Matthews | WAL | 2007 | 1 | 0 | 1 | 0 |
| P Mayo | WAL | 1985-87 | 4 | 0 | 3 | 1 |
| GH Micklem | ENG | 1947-49-53-55-(57)-(59) | 6 | 1 | 5 | 0 |
| DJ Millensted | ENG | 1967 | 2 | 1 | 1 | 0 |
| JW Milligan | SCO | 1989-91 | 7 | 3 | 3 | 1 |
| EB Millward | ENG | (1949)-55 | 2 | 0 | 2 | 0 |
| WTG Milne | SCO | 1973 | 4 | 2 | 2 | 0 |
| †CS Montgomerie | SCO | 1985-87 | 8 | 2 | 5 | 1 |
| JL Morgan | WAL | 1951-53-55 | 6 | 2 | 4 | 0 |
| C Moriarty | IRL | 2003 | 4 | 1 | 3 | 0 |
| J Moul | ENG | 2007 | 4 | 2 | 1 | 1 |
| P Mulcare | IRL | 1975 | 3 | 2 | 1 | 0 |
| GH Murray | SCO | 1977 | 2 | 1 | 1 | 0 |
| SWT Murray | SCO | 1963 | 4 | 2 | 2 | 0 |
| WA Murray | SCO | 1923-24-(26) | 4 | 1 | 3 | 0 |

‡In 1922 Hooman beat Sweetser at the 37th – on all other occasions halved matches have counted as such.

| Name | | Year | Played | Won | Lost | Halved |
|------|---|------|--------|-----|------|--------|
| K Nolan | IRL | 1997 | 3 | 0 | 3 | 0 |
| E O'Connell | IRL | 1989 | 4 | 2 | 0 | 2 |
| S O'Hara | SCO | 2001 | 4 | 2 | 2 | 0 |
| A Oldcorn | ENG | 1983 | 4 | 4 | 0 | 0 |
| †PA Oosterhuis | ENG | 1967 | 4 | 1 | 2 | 1 |
| R Oppenheimer | ENG | (1951) | 0 | 0 | 0 | 0 |
| P Page | ENG | 1993 | 2 | 0 | 2 | 0 |
| C Paisley | ENG | 2009 | 3 | 0 | 1 | 2 |
| D Park | WAL | 1997 | 3 | 0 | 3 | 0 |
| P Parkin | WAL | 1983 | 3 | 2 | 1 | 0 |
| J Parry | ENG | 2007 | 2 | 1 | 1 | 0 |
| D Patrick | SCO | 1999 | 1 | 0 | 1 | 0 |
| J Payne | ENG | 1991 | 4 | 2 | 2 | 0 |
| JJF Pennink | ENG | 1938 | 2 | 1 | 1 | 0 |
| TP Perkins | ENG | 1928 | 2 | 0 | 2 | 0 |
| GB Peters | SCO | 1936-38 | 4 | 2 | 1 | 1 |
| V Phillips | ENG | 1993 | 3 | 1 | 2 | 0 |
| AD Pierse | IRL | 1983 | 3 | 0 | 2 | 1 |
| AH Perowne | ENG | 1949-53-59 | 4 | 0 | 4 | 0 |
| AK Pirie | SCO | 1967 | 3 | 0 | 2 | 1 |
| MA Poxon | ENG | 1975 | 2 | 0 | 2 | 0 |
| D Prosser | ENG | 1989 | 1 | 0 | 1 | 0 |
| R Pugh | WAL | 2011 | 3 | 3 | 0 | 0 |
| I Pyman | ENG | 1993 | 3 | 0 | 3 | 0 |
| †R Rafferty | IRL | 1981 | 4 | 2 | 2 | 0 |
| R Ramsay | SCO | 2005 | 2 | 1 | 1 | 0 |
| G Rankin | SCO | 1995-97-99 | 8 | 2 | 6 | 0 |
| M Richardson | ENG | 2005 | 4 | 2 | 2 | 0 |
| D Robertson | SCO | 1993 | 3 | 1 | 2 | 0 |
| J Robinson | ENG | 1987 | 4 | 2 | 2 | 0 |
| RN Roderick | WAL | 1989 | 2 | 0 | 1 | 1 |
| J Rose | ENG | 1997 | 4 | 2 | 2 | 0 |
| P Rowe | ENG | 1999 | 3 | 3 | 0 | 0 |
| R Russell | SCO | 1993 | 3 | 0 | 3 | 0 |
| AC Saddler | SCO | 1963-65-67-(77) | 10 | 3 | 5 | 2 |
| L Saltman | SCO | 2005-07 | 7 | 4 | 3 | 0 |
| Hon M Scott | ENG | 1924-34 | 4 | 2 | 2 | 0 |
| R Scott, Jr | SCO | 1924 | 1 | 1 | 0 | 0 |
| PF Scrutton | ENG | 1955-57 | 3 | 0 | 3 | 0 |
| J Senior | ENG | 2011 | 4 | 2 | 1 | 1 |
| DN Sewell | ENG | 1957-59 | 4 | 1 | 3 | 0 |
| RDBM Shade | SCO | 1961-63-65-67 | 14 | 6 | 6 | 2 |
| G Shaw | SCO | 1987 | 4 | 1 | 2 | 1 |
| DB Sheahan | IRL | 1963 | 4 | 2 | 2 | 0 |
| AE Shepperson | ENG | 1957-59 | 3 | 1 | 1 | 1 |
| G Sherry | SCO | 1995 | 4 | 2 | 2 | 0 |
| AF Simpson | SCO | (1926) | 0 | 0 | 0 | 0 |
| M Skelton | ENG | 2003 | 2 | 1 | 1 | 0 |
| JN Smith | SCO | 1930 | 2 | 0 | 2 | 0 |
| WD Smith | SCO | 1959 | 1 | 0 | 1 | 0 |
| M Stanford | ENG | 1993 | 3 | 1 | 2 | 0 |
| AR Stephen | SCO | 1985 | 4 | 2 | 1 | 1 |
| M Stewart | SCO | 2011 | 4 | 2 | 1 | 1 |
| EF Storey | ENG | 1924-26-28 | 6 | 1 | 5 | 0 |
| G Storm | ENG | 1999 | 4 | 2 | 2 | 0 |
| JA Stout | ENG | 1930-32 | 4 | 0 | 3 | 1 |
| C Stowe | ENG | 1938-47 | 4 | 2 | 2 | 0 |
| HB Stuart | SCO | 1971-73-75 | 10 | 4 | 6 | 0 |
| A Sullivan | ENG | 2011 | 4 | 2 | 2 | 0 |
| A Thirlwell | ENG | 1957 | 1 | 0 | 1 | 0 |
| KG Thom | ENG | 1949 | 2 | 0 | 2 | 0 |
| MS Thompson | ENG | 1983 | 3 | 1 | 2 | 0 |
| H Thomson | SCO | 1936-38 | 4 | 2 | 2 | 0 |
| CJH Tolley | ENG | 1922-23-24-26-30-34 | 12 | 4 | 8 | 0 |
| TA Torrance | SCO | 1924-28-30-32-34 | 9 | 3 | 5 | 1 |
| WB Torrance | SCO | 1922 | 2 | 0 | 2 | 0 |
| †PM Townsend | ENG | 1965 | 4 | 3 | 1 | 0 |
| LP Tupling | ENG | 1969 | 2 | 1 | 1 | 0 |
| W Tweddell | ENG | 1928-(36) | 2 | 0 | 2 | 0 |
| J Walker | SCO | 1961 | 2 | 0 | 2 | 0 |

| Name | | Year | Played | Won | Lost | Halved |
|---|---|---|---|---|---|---|
| †P Walton | IRL | 1981-83 | 8 | 6 | 2 | 0 |
| M Warren | SCO | 2001 | 3 | 2 | 1 | 0 |
| C Watson | SCO | 1997 | 3 | 1 | 1 | 1 |
| †P Way | ENG | 1981 | 4 | 2 | 2 | 0 |
| RH Wethered | ENG | 1922-23-26-**30**-34 | 9 | 5 | 3 | 1 |
| L White | ENG | 1991 | 2 | 1 | 1 | 0 |
| RJ White | ENG | 1947-49-51-53-55 | 10 | 6 | 3 | 1 |
| D Whitnell | ENG | 2009 | 3 | 0 | 3 | 0 |
| D Willett | ENG | 2007 | 4 | 0 | 2 | 2 |
| R Willison | ENG | 1991 | 4 | 1 | 3 | 0 |
| J Wilson | SCO | 1923 | 2 | 2 | 0 | 0 |
| JC Wilson | SCO | 1947-53 | 4 | 0 | 4 | 0 |
| O Wilson | ENG | 2003 | 3 | 2 | 0 | 1 |
| S Wilson | SCO | 2003 | 4 | 1 | 1 | 2 |
| GB Wolstenholme | ENG | 1957-59 | 4 | 1 | 2 | 1 |
| GP Wolstenholme | ENG | 1995-97-99-01-03-05 | 19 | 10 | 9 | 0 |
| S Young | SCO | 1997 | 4 | 2 | 2 | 0 |

## United States of America

| Name | Year | Played | Won | Lost | Halved |
|---|---|---|---|---|---|
| †TD Aaron | 1959 | 2 | 1 | 1 | 0 |
| B Alexander | 1987 | 3 | 2 | 1 | 0 |
| DC Allen | 1965-67 | 6 | 0 | 4 | 2 |
| B Andrade | 1987 | 4 | 2 | 2 | 0 |
| ES Andrews | 1961 | 1 | 1 | 0 | 0 |
| D Ballenger | 1973 | 1 | 1 | 0 | 0 |
| B Barber | 2011 | 3 | 0 | 2 | 1 |
| R Baxter, Jr | 1957 | 2 | 2 | 0 | 0 |
| N Begay III | 1995 | 3 | 1 | 2 | 0 |
| DR Beman | 1959-61-63-65 | 11 | 7 | 2 | 2 |
| D Berganio | 1993 | 3 | 1 | 2 | 0 |
| RE Billows | 1938-49 | 4 | 2 | 2 | 0 |
| SE Bishop | 1947-49 | 3 | 2 | 1 | 0 |
| AS Blum | 1957 | 1 | 0 | 1 | 0 |
| J Bohmann | 1969 | 3 | 1 | 2 | 0 |
| M Brannan | 1977 | 3 | 1 | 2 | 0 |
| A Bratton | 1995 | 3 | 1 | 0 | 2 |
| GF Burns III | 1975 | 3 | 2 | 1 | 0 |
| C Burroughs | 1985 | 3 | 1 | 2 | 0 |
| J Byrd | 1999 | 3 | 1 | 2 | 0 |
| AE Campbell | 1936 | 2 | 2 | 0 | 0 |
| JE Campbell | 1957 | 1 | 0 | 1 | 0 |
| WC Campbell | 1951-53-(**55**)-57-65-67-71-75 | 18 | 11 | 4 | 3 |
| P Cantlay | 2011 | 4 | 2 | 1 | 1 |
| N Cassini | 2001 | 4 | 2 | 2 | 0 |
| B Cauley | 2009 | 4 | 3 | 0 | 1 |
| RJ Cerrudo | 1967 | 4 | 1 | 1 | 2 |
| RD Chapman | 1947-51-53 | 5 | 3 | 2 | 0 |
| D Cherry | 1953-55-61 | 5 | 5 | 0 | 0 |
| D Clarke | 1979 | 3 | 2 | 0 | 1 |
| RE Cochran | 1961 | 1 | 1 | 0 | 0 |
| CR Coe | 1949-51-53-(**57**)-**59**-61-63 | 13 | 7 | 4 | 2 |
| R Commans | 1981 | 3 | 1 | 1 | 1 |
| E Compton | 2001 | 3 | 1 | 1 | 1 |
| JW Conrad | 1955 | 2 | 1 | 1 | 0 |
| J Courville Jr | 1995-97 | 6 | 4 | 2 | 0 |
| K Cox | 1995 | 3 | 1 | 2 | 0 |
| N Crosby | 1983 | 2 | 1 | 1 | 0 |
| BH Cudd | 1955 | 2 | 2 | 0 | 0 |
| RD Davies | 1963 | 2 | 0 | 2 | 0 |
| JW Dawson | 1949 | 2 | 2 | 0 | 0 |
| D Delcher | 1997 | 3 | 2 | 1 | 0 |
| T Demsey | 1993 | 3 | 3 | 0 | 0 |
| RB Dickson | 1967 | 3 | 3 | 0 | 0 |
| A Doyle | 1991-93 | 6 | 5 | 1 | 0 |
| J Driscoll | 2001 | 3 | 0 | 3 | 0 |
| GT Dunlap Jr | 1932-34-36 | 5 | 3 | 1 | 1 |
| †D Duval | 1991 | 3 | 2 | 1 | 0 |

| Name | Year | Played | Won | Lost | Halved |
|------|------|--------|-----|------|--------|
| D Edwards | 1973 | 4 | 4 | 0 | 0 |
| HC Egan | 1934 | 1 | 1 | 0 | 0 |
| D Eger | 1989-91-01 | 8 | 4 | 3 | 1 |
| D Eichelberger | 1965 | 3 | 1 | 2 | 0 |
| B Elder | 1997 | 4 | 4 | 0 | 0 |
| J Ellis | 1973 | 3 | 2 | 1 | 0 |
| W Emery | 1936 | 2 | 1 | 0 | 1 |
| H English | 2011 | 4 | 2 | 2 | 0 |
| C Evans Jr | 1922-24-28 | 5 | 3 | 2 | 0 |
| M Every | 2005 | 4 | 1 | 2 | 1 |
| J Farquhar | 1971 | 3 | 1 | 2 | 0 |
| †B Faxon | 1983 | 4 | 3 | 1 | 0 |
| R Fehr | 1983 | 4 | 2 | 1 | 1 |
| JW Fischer | 1934-36-38-(65) | 4 | 3 | 0 | 1 |
| D Fischesser | 1979 | 3 | 1 | 2 | 0 |
| MA Fleckman | 1967 | 2 | 0 | 2 | 0 |
| B Fleisher | 1969 | 4 | 0 | 2 | 2 |
| J Fought | 1977 | 4 | 4 | 0 | 0 |
| †R Fowler | 2007-09 | 8 | 7 | 1 | 0 |
| WC Fownes Jr | **1922-24** | 3 | 1 | 2 | 0 |
| F Fuhrer III | 1981 | 3 | 2 | 1 | 0 |
| JR Gabrielsen | 1977-(81)-(91) | 3 | 1 | 2 | 0 |
| R Gamez | 1989 | 4 | 3 | 0 | 1 |
| RA Gardner | 1922-**23-24-26** | 8 | 6 | 2 | 0 |
| RW Gardner | 1961-63 | 5 | 4 | 0 | 1 |
| B Gay | 1993 | 2 | 0 | 1 | 1 |
| B Gielow | 2009 | 3 | 1 | 2 | 0 |
| M Giles III | 1969-71-73-75-(93) | 15 | 8 | 2 | 5 |
| HL Givan | 1936 | 1 | 0 | 0 | 1 |
| L Glover | 2001 | 4 | 2 | 2 | 0 |
| JG Goodman | 1934-36-38 | 6 | 4 | 2 | 0 |
| J Gore | 1997 | 3 | 2 | 0 | 1 |
| D Gossett | 1999 | 4 | 1 | 2 | 1 |
| M Gove | 1979 | 3 | 2 | 1 | 0 |
| J Grace | 1975 | 3 | 2 | 1 | 0 |
| JA Grant | 1967 | 2 | 2 | 0 | 0 |
| AD Gray Jr | 1963-65-67-(95)-(97) | 12 | 5 | 6 | 1 |
| D Green | 2001 | 3 | 0 | 3 | 0 |
| JP Guilford | 1922-24-26 | 6 | 4 | 2 | 0 |
| W Gunn | 1926-28 | 4 | 4 | 0 | 0 |
| B Haas | 2003 | 4 | 2 | 2 | 0 |
| †F Haas Jr | 1938 | 2 | 0 | 2 | 0 |
| H Haas | 1999 | 4 | 3 | 1 | 0 |
| †JD Haas | 1975 | 3 | 3 | 0 | 0 |
| J Haas | 1985 | 3 | 1 | 2 | 0 |
| G Hallberg | 1977 | 3 | 1 | 2 | 0 |
| GS Hamer Jr | (1947) | 0 | 0 | 0 | 0 |
| B Harman | 2005-09 | 7 | 4 | 1 | 2 |
| J Harris | 1993-95-97-01 | 14 | 10 | 4 | 0 |
| LE Harris Jr | 1963 | 4 | 3 | 1 | 0 |
| V Heafner | 1977 | 3 | 3 | 0 | 0 |
| M Hendrix | 2003 | 3 | 2 | 0 | 1 |
| R Henley | 2011 | 3 | 1 | 2 | 0 |
| SD Herron | 1923 | 2 | 0 | 2 | 0 |
| T Herron | 1993 | 3 | 3 | 0 | 0 |
| †S Hoch | 1979 | 4 | 4 | 0 | 0 |
| W Hoffer | 1983 | 2 | 1 | 1 | 0 |
| M Hoffmann | 2009 | 3 | 2 | 0 | 1 |
| J Holmes | 2005 | 3 | 2 | 1 | 0 |
| J Holtgrieve | 1979-81-83-(2011) | 10 | 6 | 4 | 0 |
| JM Hopkins | 1965 | 3 | 0 | 2 | 1 |
| B Horschel | 2007 | 4 | 3 | 1 | 0 |
| R Howe | 1989 | 1 | 0 | 1 | 0 |
| W Howell | 1932 | 1 | 1 | 0 | 0 |
| B Hurley | 2005 | 2 | 0 | 2 | 0 |
| W Hyndman III | 1957-59-61-69-71 | 9 | 6 | 1 | 2 |
| J Inman Jr | 1969 | 2 | 2 | 0 | 0 |
| JG Jackson | 1953-55 | 3 | 3 | 0 | 0 |
| T Jackson | 1995-99 | 6 | 3 | 2 | 1 |
| †D Johnson | 2007 | 3 | 1 | 1 | 1 |

| Name | Year | Played | Won | Lost | Halved |
|---|---|---|---|---|---|
| GK Johnson | 1989 | 3 | 1 | 2 | 0 |
| HR Johnston | 1923-24-28-30 | 6 | 5 | 1 | 0 |
| RT Jones Jr | 1922-24-26-**28-30** | 10 | 9 | 1 | 0 |
| AF Kammer Jr | 1947 | 2 | 1 | 1 | 0 |
| M Killian | 1973 | 3 | 1 | 2 | 0 |
| A Kim | 2005 | 4 | 2 | 1 | 1 |
| C Kirk | 2007 | 2 | 1 | 1 | 0 |
| C Kite | 1987 | 3 | 2 | 1 | 0 |
| †TO Kite Jr | 1971 | 4 | 2 | 1 | 1 |
| RE Knepper | (1922) | 0 | 0 | 0 | 0 |
| C Knost | 2007 | 4 | 2 | 0 | 2 |
| RW Knowles Jr | 1951 | 1 | 1 | 0 | 0 |
| G Koch | 1973-75 | 7 | 4 | 1 | 2 |
| CR Kocsis | 1938-49-57 | 5 | 2 | 2 | 1 |
| K Kraft | 2011 | 4 | 0 | 4 | 0 |
| J Kribel | 1997 | 3 | 1 | 2 | 0 |
| †M Kuchar | 1999 | 3 | 0 | 3 | 0 |
| T Kuehne | 1995-03-07 | 10 | 2 | 7 | 1 |
| F Langham | 1991 | 3 | 1 | 2 | 0 |
| R Leen | 1997 | 3 | 2 | 1 | 0 |
| †J Leonard | 1993 | 3 | 3 | 0 | 0 |
| G Lesher | 1989 | 4 | 1 | 3 | 0 |
| B Lewis Jr | 1981-83-85-87-**(03)-(05)** | 14 | 10 | 4 | 0 |
| JW Lewis | 1967 | 4 | 3 | 1 | 0 |
| WL Little Jr | 1934 | 2 | 2 | 0 | 0 |
| †GA Littler | 1953 | 2 | 2 | 0 | 0 |
| E Loar | 1999 | 3 | 2 | 1 | 0 |
| B Loeffler | 1987 | 3 | 2 | 1 | 0 |
| †D Love III | 1985 | 3 | 2 | 0 | 1 |
| J Lovemark | 2007 | 3 | 2 | 1 | 0 |
| B Mackenzie | 2003 | 3 | 3 | 0 | 0 |
| RR Mackenzie | 1926-28-30 | 6 | 5 | 1 | 0 |
| MJ McCarthy Jr | (1928)-32 | 1 | 1 | 0 | 0 |
| BN McCormick | 1949 | 1 | 1 | 0 | 0 |
| T McKnight | 1999 | 2 | 0 | 2 | 0 |
| JB McHale | 1949-51 | 3 | 2 | 0 | 1 |
| MR Marston | 1922-23-24-34 | 8 | 5 | 3 | 0 |
| D Martin | 1989 | 4 | 1 | 1 | 2 |
| G Marucci | 1995-97-**(07)-(09)** | 6 | 4 | 1 | 1 |
| L Mattiace | 1987 | 3 | 2 | 1 | 0 |
| R May | 1991 | 4 | 3 | 1 | 0 |
| B Mayfair | 1987 | 3 | 3 | 0 | 0 |
| E Meeks | 1989 | 1 | 0 | 0 | 1 |
| SN Melnyk | 1969-71 | 7 | 3 | 3 | 1 |
| †P Mickelson | 1989-91 | 8 | 4 | 2 | 2 |
| AL Miller III | 1969-71 | 8 | 4 | 3 | 1 |
| J Miller | 1999 | 3 | 2 | 1 | 0 |
| L Miller | 1977 | 4 | 4 | 0 | 0 |
| A MItchell | 2009 | 3 | 1 | 2 | 0 |
| K Mitchum | 1993 | 3 | 2 | 0 | 1 |
| DK Moe | 1930-32 | 3 | 3 | 0 | 0 |
| B Molder | 1999-01 | 8 | 3 | 3 | 2 |
| B Montgomery | 1987 | 2 | 2 | 0 | 0 |
| G Moody III | 1979 | 3 | 1 | 2 | 0 |
| J Moore | 2007 | 3 | 2 | 0 | 1 |
| R Moore | 2003 | 2 | 0 | 2 | 0 |
| GT Moreland | 1932-34 | 4 | 4 | 0 | 0 |
| D Morey | 1955-65 | 4 | 1 | 3 | 0 |
| J Mudd | 1981 | 3 | 3 | 0 | 0 |
| †RJ Murphy Jr | 1967 | 4 | 1 | 2 | 0 |
| C Nallen | 2003 | 2 | 1 | 1 | 0 |
| JF Neville | 1923 | 1 | 0 | 1 | 0 |
| †JW Nicklaus | 1959-61 | 4 | 4 | 0 | 0 |
| LW Oehmig | **(1977)** | 0 | 0 | 0 | 0 |
| FD Ouimet | 1922-23-24-26-28-30-**32-34-(36)-(38)-(47)-(49)** | 16 | 9 | 5 | 2 |
| †J Overton | 2005 | 4 | 3 | 1 | 0 |
| HD Paddock Jr | 1951 | 1 | 0 | 0 | 1 |
| †J Pate | 1975 | 4 | 0 | 4 | 0 |
| WJ Patton | 1955-57-59-63-65-**(69)** | 14 | 11 | 3 | 0 |

| Name | Year | Played | Won | Lost | Halved |
|------|------|--------|-----|------|--------|
| †C Pavin | 1981 | 3 | 2 | 0 | 1 |
| M Pfeil | 1973 | 4 | 2 | 1 | 1 |
| M Podolak | 1985 | 2 | 1 | 0 | 1 |
| M Putnam | 2005 | 4 | 1 | 2 | 1 |
| M Peck | 1979 | 3 | 1 | 1 | 1 |
| SL Quick | 1947 | 2 | 1 | 1 | 0 |
| J Quinney | 2001 | 2 | 0 | 2 | 0 |
| S Randolph | 1985 | 4 | 2 | 1 | 1 |
| J Rassett | 1981 | 3 | 3 | 0 | 0 |
| K Reifers | 2005 | 2 | 0 | 2 | 0 |
| F Ridley | 1977-(**87**)-(**89**) | 3 | 2 | 1 | 0 |
| RH Riegel | 1947-49 | 4 | 4 | 0 | 0 |
| C Riley | 1995 | 3 | 1 | 1 | 1 |
| H Robbins Jr | 1957 | 2 | 0 | 1 | 1 |
| P Rodgers | 2011 | 3 | 0 | 2 | 1 |
| †W Rogers | 1973 | 2 | 1 | 1 | 0 |
| GV Rotan | 1923 | 2 | 1 | 1 | 0 |
| A Rubinson | 2003 | 4 | 1 | 2 | 1 |
| †EM Rudolph | 1957 | 2 | 1 | 0 | 1 |
| B Sander | 1977 | 3 | 0 | 3 | 0 |
| T Scherrer | 1991 | 3 | 0 | 3 | 0 |
| S Scott | 1997-99 | 6 | 2 | 4 | 0 |
| CH Seaver | 1932 | 2 | 2 | 0 | 0 |
| RL Siderowf | 1969-73-75-77-(**79**) | 14 | 4 | 8 | 2 |
| J Sigel | 1977-79-81-**83-85**-87-89-91-93 | 33 | 18 | 10 | 5 |
| RH Sikes | 1963 | 3 | 1 | 2 | 0 |
| JB Simons | 1971 | 2 | 0 | 2 | 0 |
| †S Simpson | 1977 | 3 | 3 | 0 | 0 |
| W Simpson | 2007 | 3 | 0 | 2 | 1 |
| CB Smith | 1961-63 | 2 | 0 | 1 | 1 |
| N Smith | 2009-11 | 6 | 2 | 3 | 1 |
| R Smith | 1936-38 | 4 | 2 | 2 | 0 |
| R Sonnier | 1985 | 3 | 0 | 2 | 1 |
| J Sorensen | 1987 | 3 | 1 | 1 | 1 |
| J Speith | 2011 | 3 | 2 | 0 | 1 |
| M Sposa | 1991 | 3 | 2 | 1 | 0 |
| †C Stadler | 1975 | 3 | 3 | 0 | 0 |
| K Stanley | 2007 | 3 | 0 | 3 | 0 |
| FR Stranahan | 1947-49-51 | 6 | 3 | 2 | 1 |
| †C Strange | 1975 | 4 | 3 | 0 | 1 |
| †H Sutton | 1979-81 | 7 | 2 | 4 | 1 |
| ‡JW Sweetser | 1922-23-24-26-28-32-(**67**)-(73) | 12 | 7 | ‡4 | 1 |
| FM Taylor | 1957-59-61 | 4 | 4 | 0 | 0 |
| D Tentis | 1983 | 2 | 0 | 1 | 1 |
| N Thompson | 2005 | 2 | 1 | 1 | 0 |
| DJ Trahan | 2001 | 4 | 1 | 3 | 0 |
| C Tringale | 2009 | 3 | 1 | 1 | 1 |
| RS Tufts | (**1963**) | 0 | 0 | 0 | 0 |
| WP Turnesa | 1947-49-**51** | 6 | 3 | 3 | 0 |
| B Tuten | 1983 | 2 | 1 | 1 | 0 |
| EM Tutweiler Jr | 1965-67 | 6 | 5 | 1 | 0 |
| ER Updegraff | 1963-65-69-(**75**) | 7 | 3 | 3 | 1 |
| S Urzetta | 1951-53 | 4 | 4 | 0 | 0 |
| P Uihlein | 2009 | 8 | 6 | 2 | 0 |
| †K Venturi | 1953 | 2 | 2 | 0 | 0 |
| †S Verplank | 1985 | 4 | 3 | 0 | 1 |
| M Voges | 1991 | 3 | 2 | 1 | 0 |
| GJ Voigt | 1930-32-36 | 5 | 2 | 2 | 1 |
| G Von Elm | 1926-28-30 | 6 | 4 | 1 | 1 |
| D von Tacky | 1981 | 3 | 1 | 2 | 0 |
| †JL Wadkins | 1969-71 | 7 | 3 | 4 | 0 |
| D Waldorf | 1985 | 3 | 1 | 2 | 0 |
| EH Ward Jr | 1953-55-59 | 6 | 6 | 0 | 0 |
| MH Ward | 1938-47 | 4 | 2 | 2 | 0 |
| D Weaver | 2009 | 3 | 0 | 2 | 1 |
| M West III | 1973-79 | 6 | 2 | 3 | 1 |
| J Westland | 1932-34-53-(**61**) | 5 | 3 | 0 | 2 |
| HW Wettlaufer | 1959 | 2 | 2 | 0 | 0 |
| E White | 1936 | 2 | 2 | 0 | 0 |
| C Williams | 2011 | 3 | 2 | 1 | 0 |

‡In 1922 Hooman beat Sweetser at the 37th – on all other occasions halved matches have counted as such.

| Name | Year | Played | Won | Lost | Halved |
|------|------|--------|-----|------|--------|
| L Williams | 2003-05 | 7 | 3 | 2 | 2 |
| OF Willing | 1923-24-30 | 4 | 4 | 0 | 0 |
| JM Winters Jr | (1971) | 0 | 0 | 0 | 0 |
| C Wittenberg | 2003 | 4 | 1 | 2 | 1 |
| C Wollman | 1997 | 3 | 1 | 1 | 1 |
| W Wood | 1983 | 4 | 1 | 2 | 1 |
| †T Woods | 1995 | 4 | 2 | 2 | 0 |
| FJ Wright Jr | 1923 | 1 | 1 | 0 | 0 |
| CR Yates | 1936-38-(53) | 4 | 3 | 0 | 1 |
| D Yates III | 1989-93-(99)-01 | 6 | 3 | 2 | 1 |
| RL Yost | 1955 | 2 | 2 | 0 | 0 |
| G Zahringer | 2003 | 3 | 0 | 2 | 1 |

# World Amateur Team Championship (Eisenhower Trophy) (inaugurated 1958)

| | | |
|---|---|---|
| 1958 | 1 Australia* 918; 2 United States 918 | Old Course, St Andrews, Fife, Scotland |
| | *Play-off: Australia 222; United States 224* | |
| 1960 | 1 United States 834; 2 Australia 836 | Merion GC East, Ardmore, PA, USA |
| 1962 | 1 United States 854; 2 Canada 862 | Fuji GC, Kawana, Japan |
| 1964 | 1 Great Britain & Ireland 895; 2 Canada 897 | Olgiata GC, Rome, Italy |
| 1966 | 1 Australia 877; 2 United States 879 | Club de Golf, Mexico City, Mexico |
| 1968 | 1 United States 868; 2 Great Britain & Ireland 869 | Royal Melbourne GC, Australia |
| 1970 | 1 United States 854; 2 New Zealand 869 | Real Club de Puerta Hierro, Madrid, Spain |
| 1972 | 1 United States 865; 2 Australia 870 | Olivos GC 1980, Buenos Aires, Argentina |
| 1974 | 1 United States 888; 2 Japan 898 | Campo de Golf Cajules, Dominican Republic |
| 1976 | 1 Great Britain & Ireland 892; 2 Japan 894 | Penina GC, Portimão, Algarve, Portugal |
| 1978 | 1 United States 873; 2 Canada 886 | Pacific Harbour GC, Fiji |
| 1980 | 1 United States 848; 2 South Africa 875 | Pinehurst No.2, NC, USA |
| 1982 | 1 United States 859; 2 Sweden 866 | Lausanne GC, Switzerland |
| 1984 | 1 Japan 870; 2 United States 877 | Royal Hong Kong GC, Fanling, Hong Kong |
| 1986 | 1 Canada 838; 2 United States 841 | Lagunita CC, Caracas, Venezuela |
| 1988 | 1 Great Britain & Ireland 882; 2 United States 887 | Ullna GC, Stockholm, Sweden |
| 1990 | 1 Sweden 879; 2 New Zealand 892 | Christchurch GC, New Zealand |
| 1992 | 1 New Zealand 823; 2 United States 830 | Capilano G&CC and Marine Drive GC, Vancouver, BC, Canada |
| 1994 | 1 United States 838; 2 Great Britain & Ireland 849 | La Boulie GC and Le Golf National, Versailles, France |
| 1996 | 1 Australia 838; 2 Sweden 849 | Manila Southwoods (Masters and Legends) GC, Philippines |
| 1998 | 1 Great Britain and Ireland 852; 2 Australia 856 | Club de Golf los Leones and Club de Golf La Dehesa, Santiago, Chile |
| 2000 | 1 United States 841; 2 Great Britain & Ireland 857 | Berlin Sporting Club and Club de Golf Bad Saaron, Germany |
| 2002 | 1 United States 568; 2 France 571 | Sanyana G&CC (Palm and Bunga Raya Courses), Malaysia |
| 2004 | 1 United States 407; 2 Spain 416 | Rio Mar GC (Ocean and River Courses), Puerto Rico |
| 2006 | 1 Netherlands 554; 2 Canada 556 | De Zalse GC and Stellenbosch GC, South Africa |
| 2008 | 1 Scotland 560; 2 USA 569 | The Grange GC (West Course) and Royal Adelaide GC, Australia |
| 2010 | 1 France 423; 2 Denmark 427 | Buenos Aires GC and Olivos GC, Argentina |
| 2012 | 1 United States 404; 2 Mexico 409 | Antalya GC (Sultan course) and Camelia GC (Faldo course), Turkey |

The 2014 Eisenhower Trophy competition will be played in Japan and Mexico will host the event in 2016

Europe v Asia–Pacific (Sir Michael Bonallack Trophy)    (inaugurated 1998)
This event will next be held in 2014

St Andrews Trophy (Great Britain & Ireland v Continent of Europe)
*Match inaugurated 1956, trophy presented 1964*
*History:* Since 1956, Great Britain & Ireland have won 24 times, Continent of Europe on five occasions.
This event will next be held in 2014

Asia–Pacific Amateur Team Championship (Nomura Cup) *Santiburi CC, Thailand*

| | | |
|---|---|---|
| 1 | Australia | 211-208-208-201—828 |
| 2 | Korea | 208-213-209-207—837 |
| 3 | Thailand | 207-208-212-215—842 |
| 4 | China | 205-210-222-206—843 |
| | Japan | 206-208-220-209—843 |
| 6 | Singapore | 216-214-207-213—850 |
| 7 | Chinese Taipei | 217-211-214-213—855 |
| 8 | Indonesia | 211-217-212-220—860 |
| 9 | New Zealand | 212-209-226-215—862 |
| 10 | India | 215-215-223-210—863 |

11 Hong Kong 868; 12 Malaysia 874; 13 Myanmar 879; 14 Philippines 883; 15 Pakistan 906; 16 Fiji 918;
17 Guam 926; 18 Bahrain 928; 19 Vietnam 943; 20 Iran 960; 21 Nepal 975; 22 UAE 983; 23 Qatar 996;
24 Mongolia 1,068; 25 Bhutan 1,076; 26 Kyrgyzstan 1,122

**Winning team:** Cameron Davis, Geoff Frakeford, Taylor MacDonald, Aaron Wilkin

**Individual:**

| | | |
|---|---|---|
| 1 | Geoff Drakeford (AUS) | 75-66-69-67—277 |
| | Taylor MacDonald (AUS) | 71-69-69-68—277 |
| | Nam-Hun Kim (KOR) | 68-73-67-69—277 |

*History:* Australia has won ten times, Japan eight times, Chinese Taipei five times, India, South Korea and
New Zealand once.
This event will next be held in 2015

Ten Nations Cup *Kingswood Golf Estate, George, South Africa*

| | | |
|---|---|---|
| 1 | Australia | 216-202-203-205—826 |
| 2 | New Zealand | 209-215-200-203—827 |
| 3 | England | 212-208-207-206—833 |

4 Argentina 839; 5 Scotland 842; 6 Colombia 847; 7 South Africa 851; 8 Ireland 861; 9 France 877

**Winning team:** Brady Watt, Lucas Herbert, Ryan Ruffles and Geoff Drakeford

**Individual:**

| | | |
|---|---|---|
| 1 | Brady Watt (AUS) | 69-62-69-70—270 |
| 2 | Tyler Hodge (NZL) | 70-68-67-68—273 |
| 3 | Carlos Ernesto Rodriguez (COL) | 70-68-67-69—274 |

Juan Carlos Tailhade Cup *Los Lagartos G&CC, Buenos Aires, Argentina*

| | | |
|---|---|---|
| 1 | Spain | 578 |
| 2 | Australia | 580 |
| 3 | Argentina | 587 |

4 Ireland 596; 5 South Africa 597; 6 New Zealand 599; 7 Portugal 603; 8 Brazil 6069 Canada 607

**Winning team:** Mario Galiano Aguilar and David Morago Ayra

**Individual:**

| | | |
|---|---|---|
| 1 | Nicolai B Kristensen (DEN) | 70-72-69-73—284 |
| 2 | Mario Galiano Aguilar (ESP) | 73-69-71-73—286 |
| 3 | Jarryd Felton (AUS) | 75-76-65-71—287 |

## Africa

## 7th African Amateur Team Championship  *Royal Swazi Spa CC*

| | | |
|---|---|---|
| 1 | South Africa | 208-204-202-216—830 |
| 2 | Zimbabwe | 204-215-208-229—856 |
| 3 | Swaziland | 215-223-219-220—877 |
| 4 | Kenya | 217-227-219-229—892 |
| 5 | Réunion | 219-226-216-236—895 |
| 6 | Mauritius | 215-222-225-235—897 |
| 7 | Zambia | 228-220-220-233—901 |
| 8 | Uganda | 226-213-232-234—905 |
| 9 | Namibia | 234-223-232-239—928 |
| 10 | Botswana | 239-242-232-245—958 |

**Winning team:** Callum Mowat, Zander Lombard, N J Arnoldi and Gerlou Roux
**Individual:** Callum Mowatt (RSA) 67-67-71-75—280
This event will next be played in 2015

## 53rd South African Men's Inter-Provincial Championship  *Rustenburg GC*

**Day 1:** Boland 3, Southern Cape 9; Western Province 4, KwaZulu Natal 8; Central Gauteng 5½, Gauteng North 6½

**Day 2:** KwaZulu Natal 5, Central Gauteng 7; Southern Cape 4½, Western Province 7½; Gauteng North 6½, Boland 5½

**Day 3:** Western Province 6½, Central Gauteng 5½; Southern Cape 3½, Gauteng North 8½; Boland 7, KwaZulu Natal 5

**Day 4:** Boland 7, Central Gauteng 5; KwaZulu Natal 5½, Southern Cape 6½; Western Province 5, Gauteng North 7

**Day 5:** Gauteng North 9½, KwaZulu Natal 2½; Central Gauteng 4½, Southern Cape 7½; Western Province 9, Boland 3

**Final table:**

| | | P | W | D | L | Pts | Games |
|---|---|---|---|---|---|---|---|
| 1 | Gauteng North | 5 | 5 | 0 | 0- | 10 | 38 |
| 2 | Western Province | 5 | 3 | 0 | 2 | 6 | 32 |
| 3 | Southern Cape | 5 | 3 | 0 | 2 | 6 | 31 |
| 4 | Boland | 5 | 2 | 0 | 3 | 4 | 25½ |
| 5 | Central Gauteng | 5 | 1 | 0 | 4 | 2 | 27½ |
| 6 | KwaZulu Natal | 5 | 1 | 0 | 4 | 2 | 26 |

**Winning teams:** Russell Franz. Hendrikus Stoop, Philip Kruse, Werner Ferreira, Teagan Gauche, Tertius Van Den Berg, Werner Van Niekerk and Zander Lombard

## South African Mid-Amateur Inter-Provincial Tournament  *Durban CC*

**Day 1:** Cent. Gauteng 8, North West 4; W. Province 7, Boland 5; Ekurhuleni 4, KwaZulu Natal 8

**Day 2:** Boland 4, Ekurhuleni 8; North West 4, W. Province 8; KwaZulu Natal 6½, Cent. Gauteng 3½

**Day 3:** W. Province 9, Ekurhuleni 3; North West 4, KwaZulu Natal 8; Cent.l Gauteng 8, Boland 4

**Day 4:** Cent. Gauteng 4, Ekurhuleni 8; Boland 4, North West 8; W. Province 7½, KwaZulu Natal 4½

**Day 5:** KwaZulu Natal 6½, Boland 5½; Ekurhuleni 10½, North West 1½; W. Province 5, Cent. Gauteng 7

South African Mid-Amateur Inter-Provincial Tournament *continued*

| Final table | | P | W | D | L | Pts | Games won |
|---|---|---|---|---|---|---|---|
| I | Western Province | 5 | 4 | 0 | I | 10 | 36½ |
| 2 | KwaZulu Natal | 5 | 4 | 0 | I | 10 | 35½ |
| 3 | Ekurhuleni | 5 | 3 | 0 | 2 | 8 | 33½ |
| 4 | Central Gauteng | 5 | 3 | 0 | 2 | 8 | 20½ |
| 5 | North West | 5 | I | 0 | 7 | 5 | 21½ |
| 6 | Boland | 5 | 0 | 0 | 5 | 0 | 22½ |

**Winning team:** Elvin Nel, Gareth Johnson, Giles Buchanan, Cameron Johnston, Francois le Roux, Dirk Van der Merwe, Greg Sheard and Gerloux Roux

## South African Senior Men's Inter-Provincial Championship *Euphoria Golf Estate*

| I | Central Gauteng | 14 pts |
|---|---|---|
| 2 | Western Province | 11 |
| 3 | Gauteng North | 8 |

4 KwaZula Natal 7; 5 Eastern Province, Erkuhuleni 6; 7 Mpumalanga, Border 2

**Super Seniors:**

| I | Western Province | 10 pts |
|---|---|---|
| 2 | Erkhuleni | 8 |
| 3 | Gauteng North | 4 |

4 Central Gauteng, KwaZulu Natal 3; 6 Boland 2

## 14th Zone VI African Team Championship *Windhoek G&C, Namibia*

I South Africa 23 pts; 2 Zimbabwe 19; 3 Namibia 15; 4 Kenya, Malawi 11; 6 Zambia 10½; 7 Swaziland 8; 8 Botswana 7½; 9 Mozambique 3

**Winning team:** Andrew Light (Southern Cape), Thriston Lawrence (Mpumalanga), Eddie Taylor (Central Gauteng), Zander Lombard (Gauteng North), Louis Taylor (Central Gauteng), Werner Ferreira (Gauteng North), Gerlou Roux (Western Province) and Tokkie van den Berg (Gauteng North)

## East Africa Challenge *The Great Rift Valley Lodge and Game Reserve, Naivasha, Kenya*

**Final table:**

| | | Singles | Foursomes | Fourballs | Singles | Points |
|---|---|---|---|---|---|---|
| I | Kenya | 5 | 2 | 4 | 8 | 19 |
| 2 | Uganda | 7 | 4 | 4 | 3½ | 18½ |
| 3 | Tanzania | 6½ | 2 | 2 | 5 | 15½ |
| 4 | Rwanda | 3 | 1½ | I | 3 | 8½ |
| 5 | Ethiopia | 2½ | I | 0 | 3½ | 7 |
| 6 | Burundi | 0 | 1½ | I | I | 3½ |

**Winning team:** J Karichu, D Nduva,, A Balala, W Odera, T Omuli, R Owiti, J Madoya, M Wahome and Tahir

## USGA Men's State Team Championship
This event will next be played in 2014

# 33rd Pan Arab Championship   *Dreamland GR, Egypt*

| 1 | Morocco | 221-214-214-223—872 |
| 2 | Bahrein | 223-218-224 221—886 |
| 3 | Egypt | 221-221-222-228—892 |

4 Qatar; 5 Saudi Arabia; 6 UAE; 7 Lebanon; 8 Tunisia; 9 Oman; 10 Libya; 11 Palestine; 12 Kuwait

**Winning team:** Mustapha El Maouassa, Ahmed Marjan, Mehdi Saissi and Amin El Maiki

**Individual:**

| 1 | Ahmed Marjan (MAR) | 73-69-73-74 – 289 |
| 2 | Mustapha El Maouassa (MAR) | 75-72-70-72 – 289 |
| 3 | Amr Aboul Ela (EGY) | 73-74-73-72 – 292 |

## Etiqa Asean Cup
*Postponed*

# Australian Men's Interstate Team Championships   *Tasmania Golf Club*

Round 1 – Victoria 5, S. Australia 2; Queensland 5, W. Australia 2;  New South Wales 4½, Tasmania 2½
Round 2 – Victoria 4, W. Australia 3; S. Australia 4½, Tasmania 2½; New South Wales 3½, Queensland 2½
Round 3 – W. Australia 5½, New South Wales 1½;  Queensland 6, S. Australia 1; Tasmania 6, Victoria 1
Round 4 – Tasmania 3½, Queensland 3½; New South Wales 6½, Victoria ½; S. Australia 3½, W. Australia 3½
Round 5 – New South Wales 5, S. Australia 2; Tasmania 4½, W. Australia 2½; Victoria 3½, Queensland 3½

**Final table:** 1 Queensland – contests won 3½, matches won 21½; 2 New South Wales 3½–21; 3 Tasmania 3½–19; 4 Victoria 2½,–14; 5 W. Australia 1½–16½; 6 S. Australia 1½–13

**Final:** Queensland 4½, New South Wales 3½; 3rd place play-off: Tasmania 4, Victoria 4; 5th place play-off: S. Australia 6, W. Australia 2

**Winning team:** Cameron Smith, Taylor MacDonald, Aaron Wilkin, Viraat Badhwar, Kevin Marques, James Gebellini, Jake McLeod and Simon Viitakangas

## Australian Senior Interstate Championship   *Royal Queensland GC, Brisbane*

| 1 | New South Wales | 238-229-229—696 |
| 2 | Queensland | 234-238-238—710 |
| 3 | Western Australia | 240-244-230—714 |
| 4 | Victoria | 256 -240-242—738 |

**Winning team:** Stefan Albinski, Ross Bockman, Denis Dale and Robert Payne

# 114th *Edinburgh Evening News Dispatch* Trophy   (inaugurated 1890)   *always at Braid Hills*

**Semi-finals:**   Carrickvale beat Edinburgh Thistle  4 and 3
                    Silverknowes beat Caermount  5 and 3
**Final:**   Carrickvale beat Silverknowes  1 hole

**Winning team:** Craig Deerness, Craig Eliot, Allyn Dick and Thomas Beattie

**Europe (continued)**

## European Men's Challenge Trophy (inaug. 2002) *Kuneticka Hora Resort, Czech Republic*

| | | |
|---|---|---|
| 1 | Belgium | 373-373-359—1,105, |
| 2 | Iceland | 382-374-366—1122 |
| 3 | Czech Republic | 377-387-374—1,138 |
| 4 | Turkey | 389-380-371—1,140 |
| 5 | Russia | 383-390-368—1,141 |
| 6 | Slovakia | 386-376-382—1,144 |
| 7 | Slovenia | 404-399-378—1,181 |
| 8 | Estonia | 402-399-384—1,185 |
| 9 | Serbia | 406-399-391—1,196 |
| 10 | Hungary | 442-434-419—1,295 |

**Winning team:** Cedric Van Wassenhove, Patrick Hanauer, Mathias Boesmans, Pierre-Alescis Rolland, Kevin Hesbois and Thomas Detry

**Individual:**

| | | |
|---|---|---|
| 1 | Thomas Detry (BEL) | 70-70-69—209 |
| 2 | Kelvin Hesbois (BEL) | 70-73-74—217 |
| 3 | Andri Bjornsson (ISL) | 75-68-76—219 |

## European Amateur Team Championship (inaugurated 1959) *Silkeborg Golfklub, Denmark*

**Stroke Play qualification:** 1 France 735; 2 Ireland 741; 3 England, Germany 743

**Individual:**

| | | |
|---|---|---|
| 1 | Rory McNamara (IRL) | 70-73—143 |
| 2 | James Ross (SCO) | 72-71—143 |
| 3 | Mads Sogaard (DEN) | 72-72—144 |

**Final placings:** 1 England; 2 Scotland; 3 France; 4 Netherlands; 5 Denmark; 6 Austria; 7 Ireland; 8 Germany; 9 Spain; 10 Sweden; 11 Italy; 12 Switzerland; 13 Portugal; 14 Norway; 15 Finland; 16 Wales

**Winning team:** Max Orrin, Nathan Kimsey, Neil Raymond, Callum Shinkwin, Toby Tree and Garrick Porteous

**Team results:**

**"A" Flight – Day 1:** France 5½, Austria 1½; Scotland 4, Germany 3; England 5, Denmark 2; Netherlands 4, Ireland 3.

**Day 2:** Scotland 4½, France 2½; England 6, Netherlands 1; Austria 4, Germany 1; Denmark 4½, Ireland ½

**Day 3 – Final:** England 4½. Scotland 2½; France 5, Netherlands 2; Denmark 3½, Austria 1½; Ireland 4, Germany 1

**"B" Flight – Day 1 :** Italy 5, Portugal 0; Sweden 5, Wales 0; Switzerland 4½, Norway ½; Spain 4. Finland 1

**Day 2:** Sweden 3, Italy 2; Spain 3½, Switzerland 1½; Portugal 3½, Wales 1½; Norway 3, Finland 2

**Day 3:** Spain 4, Sweden 3; Italy 4, Switzerland 1; Portugal 3½, Norway 1½; Finland 3. Wales 2

This event will next be held in 2015

## European Senior Men's Team Championship (inaugurated 2006) *Pannonia G&CC, Hungary*

**Flight "A"**

**Stroke play qualifying:**

| | | |
|---|---|---|
| 1 | Ireland | 358-363—721 |
| 2 | England | 366-364—730 |
| 3 | Sweden | 368-384—752 |
| | Scotland | 380-372—752 |

5 Spain; 6 France; 7 Norway; 8 Germany; 9 Switzerland; 10 Finland; 11 Italy; 12 Belgium,;13 Netherlands; 14 Austria; 15 Czech Republic; 16 Slovenia; 17 Denmark; 18 Poland; 19 Luxembourg; 20 Portugal; 21 Slovakia; 22 Hungary

**Individual:** Richard Latham (ENG) 70-68—138

**Match Play:**
**Quarter-finals:** Ireland 3½, Germany 1½; Scotland 3, Spain 2; Sweden 3, France 2; England 4, Norway 1
**Semi-finals:** Ireland 3, Scotland 2; Sweden 3½, England 5½
Third place play-off: England 3, Scotland 2. Fifth place play-off: Spain 4, Germany 1; Seventh place play-off: France 3½, Noway 1½
**Final:** Ireland 4, Sweden 1
**Winning team:** Tom Cleary, Michael Quirke, Arthur Pierse, Maurice Kelly, Garth McGimpsey and Adrian Morrow
Flight "B" Final: Italy 4, Switzerland 1
Flight "C" Final: Denmark 4, Luxembourg 1

# EGA European Men's Club Trophy    *Aroeira GC, Portugal*

| | | |
|---|---|---|
| 1 | GC Vilamour (POR) | 140-139—279 |
| 2 | Prise D'Eau Golf (NED) | 141-141—282 |
| | Saint Nom la Bretèche (FRA) | 142-140—282 |
| 4 | GC Hubbelrath (GER) | 148-140—288 |
| | Frederikssund GK (DEN) | 143-145—288 |
| 6 | Coventry GC (ENG) | 148-141—289 |
| 7 | Lausanne GC (SUI) | 148-144—292 |
| 8 | Royal Antwerp GC (BEL) | 150-145—295 |
| | County Sligo GC (IRL) | 147-148—295 |
| | Real Golf Pedreña (ESP) | 145-150—295 |
| | Keilir GC (ISL) | 149-146—295 |
| 12 | Wrexham GC (WAL) | 143-153—296 |
| 13 | Kymen GC (FIN) | 144-153—297 |
| | Colony Club Gutenhof (AUT) | 148-149—297 |
| 15 | CG Torino La Mandria (ITA) | 147-153—300 |
| 16 | Glenbervie GC (SCO) | 151-151—302 |
| 17 | GC Weiten (SVK) | 156-150—306 |
| | GC Erpet Praha (CZE) | 155-151—306 |
| 19 | Toya GC (POL) | 152-158—310 |
| 20 | GK Velenje (SLO) | 158-157—315 |
| 21 | Golf Luxembourg (LUX) | 161-160—321 |
| 22 | GC Quercus (CRO) | 163-162—325 |
| 23 | Estonian G&CC (EST) | 167-165—332 |
| 24 | Superior G&S (UKR) | 170-169—339 |

**Winning team:** Joao Carlote, Goncalo Pinto and Nathan Brader
**Individual competition:**

| | | |
|---|---|---|
| 1 | Robbie Van West (Prise D'Eau) | 69-67—136 |
| 2 | Joao Carlota (Villamoura) | 70-68—138 |
| 3 | Maximillian Herter (Hubbelrath) | 71-68—139 |

*The event was reduced to two rounds due to bad weather*

# Home Internationals (Raymond Trophy) (inaug. 1932)    *Ganton GC*

**Day 1:**    Scotland 9½, Wales 5½; England 8, Ireland 7
**Day 2:**    Ireland 8½, Scotland 6½; England 11, Wales 4
**Day 3:**    Ireland 8, Wales 7; England 9, Scotland 6

| Final table: | P | W | L | D | Pts |
|---|---|---|---|---|---|
| 1  England | 3 | 3 | 0 | 0 | 28 |
| 2  Ireland | 3 | 2 | 0 | 1 | 23½ |
| 3  Scotland | 3 | 1 | 0 | 2 | 22 |
| 4  Wales | 3 | 0 | 0 | 0 | 16½ |

**Winning team:** Ben Stow, Michael Saunders, James Rutherford, Callum Shankwin, Toby Tree, Ryan Evans, Paul Howard, Harry Casey, Nick Marsh and Jimmy Mullen

*History:* England 37 wins, Scotland 21, Ireland 8, Wales 1. England, Ireland and Scotland have tied on four occasions, Ireland and Scotland once, England and Ireland once and Scotland and England once.

## Senior Home Internationals (inaugurated 2002)    *Royal County Down GC*

**Day 1:**      England 4½, Scotland 4½; Ireland 7½, Wales 1½
**Day 2:**      Scotland 5½, Ireland 3½; England 6½, Wales 2½
**Day 3:**      Scotland 5. Wales 4; England 6, Ireland 3

| **Final Table:** | P | W | D | L | *Games Won* |
|---|---|---|---|---|---|
| 1  England | 3 | 2 | 1 | 0 | 17 |
| 2  Scotland | 3 | 2 | 1 | 0 | 15 |
| 3  Ireland | 3 | 1 | 0 | 2 | 14 |
| 4  Wales | 3 | 0 | 0 | 3 | 8 |

**Winning team:** Richard Latham, John Ambridge, Richard Partridge, Andrew Stracey, Tyrone Canter, Chris Reynolds and Charles Bantz

## English County Championship (inaugurated 1928)    *Minchinhampton GC*

**Day 1:**      Leicestershire and Rutland 3½; Lancashire 5½
                Devon 3; Hampshire, Isle of Wight and Channel Islands 6
**Day 2:**      Lancashire 3½, Devon 5½
                Hampshire, Isle of Wight and Channel Islands 3½, Leicestershire and Rutland 5½
**Day 3:**      Devon 5½, Leicestershire and Rutland 3½
                Hampshire, Isle of Wight and Channel Islands 2½, Lancashire 6½

| **Final table** | P | W | D | L | *Games won* |
|---|---|---|---|---|---|
| 1  Lancashire | 3 | 2 | 0 | 1 | 15½ |
| 2  Devon | 3 | 2 | 0 | 1 | 14 |
| 3  Leicestershire and Rutland | 3 | 1 | 0 | 2 | 12½ |
| 4  Hampshire, IoW and CI | 3 | 1 | 0 | 2 | 12 |

**Winning team:** Paul Howard, Paul Kinnear, Jophn Carroll. Haydn McCullen, Mark Young, Sean Towndrow and Ciaran Doherty

*History:* Since 1928, the following countries have won: Yorkshire 19 times, Lancashire 11, Surrey 10, Staffordshire 6, Warwickshire 5, Northumberland 4, Berkshire, Buckinghamshire, Oxfordshire, Middlesex, Worcestershire 3, Gloucestershire, Wiltshire 2, Cheshire, Devon, Dorset, Essex, Hampshire, Hertfordshire, Kent, Lincolnshire 1. In 1985, Hertfordshire and Devon tied.

## England Senior Men's County Finals    *RAC Club, Epsom*

**Day 1:**      Devon 7½, Lincolnshire 1½
                Kent 5, Lancashire 4
**Day 2:**      Devon 1, Lancashire 8
                Kent 8, Lincolnshire 1
**Day 3:**      Lancashire 7. Lincolnshire 1
                Kent 5½, Devon 3½

| **Final table** | P | W | D | L | *Games won* |
|---|---|---|---|---|---|
| 1  Kent | 3 | 0 | 0 | 0 | 18½ |
| 2  Lancashire | 3 | 2 | 0 | 1 | 19 |
| 3  Devon | 3 | 1 | 0 | 2 | 12 |
| 4  Lincolnshire | 3 | 0 | 0 | 3 | 4½ |

**Winning team:** Christopher Hurst, Chris Reynolds, Ian Brooker, Ross Galgut, Richard Partridge, Jon Wright, Richard Moore and David Weighton

# English Champion Club Tournament (inaugurated 1984) *Dudsbury GC*

| | | |
|---|---|---|
| 1 | Coventry | 214-206—420 |
| 2 | King;s Lynn | 220-205—425 |
| 3 | Walsall | 213-212—425 |

4 Darlington 427; 5 Spalding 428; 6 Weymouth 428; 7 Hexham 430; 9 Castle Royle 430; 10 Cumberwell Park 430; 11 Worksop 432; 12 Farrington Park 432; 13 Northamptonshire County 434; 14 Brockenhurst Manor 435; 15 Cosby 436; 16 West Middlesex 437; 17 St Enedoc 438; 18 Wath 439; 19 Brampton Park 440; 20 Royal Wimbledon 441; 21 Chipping Sodbury 441; 22 Harpenden Common 447; 23 Castletown 447; 24 Dartford 448; 25 Kedleston Park 450; 26 Wrekin 450; 27 Dunstable Downs 452; 28 Workington 453; 29 Exeter 453; 30 Redditch 453; 31 Hillside 458; 32 Royal Ashdown Forest 459; 33 West Essex 464; 34 Haverhill 464

**Winning Team:** Robert Browning 67-69—136; Andrew Carman 75-72—147; Sam Dodds 72-65—137

## Irish Inter-Provincial Championship *Lee Valley GC*

**Final Placings:** 1 Ulster, 2 Leinster, 3 Munster , 4 Connacht.

| | |
|---|---|
| **Day 1:** | Munster 7½, Connacht 3½ |
| | Ulster 5½, Leinster 5½ |
| **Day 2:** | Leinster 10, Connacht 1 |
| | Ulster 6½, Munster 4½ |
| **Day 3:** | Munster 5½, Leinster 5½ |
| | Ulster 7, Connacht 4 |

**Winning team:** Chris Selfridge, Reeve Whitson, Cormac Sharvin, Dermot McElroy, Harry Diamond, Aaron Kearney and Nicky Grant

## Golfkings Scottish Area Team Championship (inaugurated 1990) *Crail GS*

| | |
|---|---|
| **Semi-finals:** | Lothians 4, Stirlingshire 1 |
| | Fife 3, Glasgow 2 |
| **Final:** | Fife 3½, Lothians 1½ |

**Winning team:** Ally Hain, Jordan McColl, Ewan Scott, James White, Scott Crighton and Scott Stewart-Cation

**Stroke Play competition:**

| | | |
|---|---|---|
| 1 | Fife | 156-138—294 |
| 2 | Lothians | 152-144—296 |
| 3 | Stirlingshire | 155-144—299 |
| 4 | Glasgow | 156-150—306 |

5 Clackmannanshire 307; 6 North-East, Renfrewshire 309; 8 Lanarkshire, North, Ayrshire 310; 11 Perth and Kinross 313; 12 Angus 318; 13 Argyll and Bute 319; 14 Dunbartonshire 321; 15 Borders, South 327

## Belhaven Best Scottish Club Handicap Championship *Fairmont Hotel (Torrance course)*

| | | |
|---|---|---|
| 1 | Edzell (William Bremner and Gary Tough) | 64 |
| 2 | Earlsferry Thistle (Andy Hodge and Vince Walker) | 65 |
| 3 | Port Glasgow (Gerard McGachy and Campbell Gisbey) | 66 |
| 4 | Routenburn (Ian Muir and Alastair McPhail) | 67 |

## TSG Scottish Club Championship (inaugurated 1985) *Luffness New GC*

| | | |
|---|---|---|
| 1 | Glenbervie | 144-146—290 |
| 2 | Southerness | 148-143—291 |
| | Craigiehill | 145-146—291 |

4 Monifieth 297; 5 Cawder, Duff House Royal 301; 7 Fortrose and Rosemarkie, Cochrane Castle 302; 9 Lundin, Strathaven 303; 11 Turnberry 306; 12 Hawick 309; 13 Alloa 317; 14 Duddingston 320; 15 Windyhill 323

**Winning team:** Mark Hislop, Fraser Moore and Colin Mundie
**Individual winner:** Scott Gibson (Southerness) 73-68—141

## Scottish Seniors Team Championship    *Murcar GC*

| | | |
|---|---|---|
| 1 | Glasgow | 383 |
| 2 | Angus | 386 |
| 3 | Stirlingshire | 392 |

4 North-East 394; 5 Fife 396; 6 South of Scotland 403; 7 Dunbartonshire 403; 8 Perth and Kinross 404; 9 Lothians 410; 10 Ayrshire 410; 11 Argyll and Bute 411

**Winning team:** Angus Lamond, John McDonald, Ian Gillon, Stuart Black, George Crawford and Graeme Cox

## Welsh Inter-Counties Championship    *Borth & Ynyslas GC*

| | | |
|---|---|---|
| 1 | Caernarvonshire | 708 |
| 2 | Glamorgan | 711 |
| 3 | Gwent | 718 |
| 4 | Flintshire | 720 |
| 5 | Dyfed | 733 |
| 6 | Denbighshire | 737 |
| 7 | Brecon and Radner | 755 |
| 8 | Angelsey | 772 |

**Winning team:** Alwyn Thomas, Eilir Angel, Paul Roberts, Evan Griffiths, Steve Evans, Lee Jones

## Welsh Team Championship    *Milford Haven*

**Semi-Finals:**    Milford Haven beat St Pierre  3 and 2
                    Wrexham beat Tenby  4 and 1
**Final:**          Wrexham beat Milford Haven  3 and 2

## Turkish Amateur Open Nations Cup    *National GC, Belek*

| | | |
|---|---|---|
| 1 | Turkey | 148-153-148—449 (Fahrettin Kök, Güray Yazıkı, Hamza Sayın) |
| 2 | Germany | 144-149-156—449 |
| 3 | England | 154-153-154—461 |

4 Serbia 481; 5 Switzerland 486; 6 Tunisia 490; 7 Greece 491; 8 UAE 503

---

## John Miller to captain next US Walker Cup side

John "Spider" Miller will captain the US team which will defend the Walker Cup at Royal Lytham and St Annes Golf Club in 2015.

Miller is a two-time US Mid-Amateur champion and was a member of the Walker Cup side in 1999 at Nairn.

"This is one of the goals that amateurs aspire to and I am very fortunate to follow Jim Holtgrieve. I will be reaching out to him and other captains, all of whom are my friends, to help me prepare," he said.

Thomas J. O'Toole, Chairman of the Championship Committee, said: "Spider's patriotism, competitive spirit, camaraderie and passion for the game will help make the 2015 match exceptional and memorable."

The R&A will announce the captain of the Great Britain and Ireland side at a later date.

# The British Golf Museum

## Home to Golf's History

The British Golf Museum is a five star museum and holds a Recognised Collection of National Significance. It is situated just yards from the 1st tee of the famous Old Course at St Andrews. Containing the largest collection of golf memorabilia in Europe, the museum offers a wealth of sporting heritage spanning more than three centuries. High quality displays bring to life the people and events that have shaped the game's history and influenced its growing popularity, not just in the UK, but worldwide.

The museum is home to star attractions such as the oldest known set of golf clubs in the world, the first Open Championship medal, which was presented to Tom Morris Jr following his 1872 win, and the oldest known footage of a golf match, dating back to 1898. Imaginative exhibitions and stunning displays set the museum apart as the world's premier heritage centre for golf.

Our galleries are a great place for young people to learn about the history of golf, and we offer a variety of events for schools and families. Discover fascinating histories, incredible facts and take part in fun hands-on activities. Visiting a museum is a fun and engaging learning experience and can help children develop a range of skills. We aim to provide a collaborative experience by concentrating on museum items that can be handled, and encouraging children to ask questions.

At the end of your visit you have the chance to sink a putt to win The Open and have your picture taken with the Claret Jug in The R&A Gallery. This exciting interactive space explores the global work of The R&A, from running international championships to protecting wildlife on the course.

The museum is open 7 days a week throughout the year

Every museum visitor is given a complimentary guidebook as a memento

We look forward to welcoming you in 2014

www.britishgolfmuseum.co.uk

# Other Tournaments 2013

For past results see earlier editions of *The R&A Golfer's Handbook*

---

**Amateur Champion Gold Medal** (inaugurated 1870)  *always at Leven Links, Fife*
Brian Soutar (Leven GS)                67-69-79-72—287

---

**Aberconwy Trophy** (inaugurated 1976)  *always at Conwy and Llandudno (Maesdu), Gwynedd*
Alistair Jones (Radyr)                73-74-70-70—287

---

**The Antlers** (inaugurated 1933)  *always at Royal Mid-Surrey*
*Not played because of course reconstruction*

---

**The Battle Trophy** (inaugurated 2011)  *Crail, Craighead*
Graeme Robertson (Glenbervie)                81-69-72-69—291

---

**Berkhamsted Trophy** (inaugurated 1960)  *always at Berkhamsted*
Jack Singh Brar (Brokenhurst Manor)                69-71—140
*Beat Gary Oliver (Hainault Forest) and Luke Johnson (King's Lynn) at the fourth extra hole*

---

**Berkshire Trophy** (inaugurated 1946)  *always at The Berkshire*
Ryan Evans (Wellingborough)                68-72-70-69—279

---

**Burhill Family Foursomes** (inaugurated 1937)  *always at Burhill, Surrey*
**Final:** Federica and Peter Cole

---

**Cameron Corbett Vase** (inaugurated 1897)  *always at Haggs Castle, Glasgow*
Daniel Young (Craigie Hill)                71-66-68-71—276

---

**Clwyd Open** (inaugurated 1991)  *always at Prestatyn and Wrexham*
Ashley Griffiths (Wrexham)                70-73-74-75—292
*Beat Lee Jones (Conwy) and Craig Melding (Neath) at the third extra hole*

---

**Craigmillar Park Open** (inaugurated 1961)  *always at Craigmillar Park, Edinburgh*
Craig Howie (Peebles)                66-70-65—201
*Beat Kyle McClung (Wigtownshire County) at the third extra hole*
*Reduced to 54 holes due to bad weather*

---

**Duncan Putter** (inaugurated 1959)  *always at Southerndown, Bridgend, Glamorgan*
Tim Harry (Vale of Glamorgan)                68-57-69-72—266 [69 holes]
*Second round reduced to 15 holes due to bad weather*

---

**East of Ireland Open Amateur** (inaugurated 1989)  *Co. Louth*
Paul Dunne (Greystones)                69 68 72 73—282

---

## East of Scotland Open Amateur Stroke Play    (inaugurated 1989)    *Lundin*
Jamie Savage (Cawder)                          72-68-74-71—285
*Beat Scott Crichton (Aberdour) at the third extra hole*

## Eden Tournament    (inaugurated 1919)    *New and Eden courses, St Andrews*
**Final:** Craig Smith (Pike Hill) beat Jack Yule (King's Lynn)  3 and 2
**Medallist:** Craig Smith (Pike Hill) 67-69—136

## Edward Trophy (inaugurated 1892)  *always at Glasgow Gailes GC*
Matthew Clark (Kilmacolm)                      70-73—143

## Fathers and Sons Foursomes    *always at West Hill, Surrey*
**Final:** Kevin Penfold (Bohunt Manor) and Ben Penfold (Liphook) beat Iain and Thomas Webb-Wilson (Rye)  2 holes

## Frame Trophy (inaugurated 1986 for players aged 50+)  *always at Worplesdon, Surrey*
David Niven (Newbury and Crookham)             78-71-76—225

## *Golf Illustrated* Gold Vase (inaugurated 1909, discontinued 2003)
*For results see 2007 edition of The R&A Golfer's Handbook*

## Hampshire Hog (inaugurated 1957)  *always at North Hants*
Jordan Smith (Bowood)                          69-67—136

## Hampshire Salver (inaugurated 1979)  *always at North Hants/Blackmoor*
Callum Shinkwin (Moor Park)                    66-69-73-65—273

## Hertfordshire Bowl  *Porters Park and Moor Park*
Robert Sutton (Dunstable Downs)                72-71-66-74 – 283

## John Cross Bowl (inaugurated 1957)  *always at Worplesdon, Surrey*
Callum MacKay (Burhill)                        67-69—136

## King George V Coronation Cup  *always at Porters Park, Herts*
Will Davenport (USA)                           74-65—139

## Lagonda Trophy  *1975–1989 at Camberley and from 1990 at The Gog Magog*
Max Orrin (North Foreland)                     66-67-65-70—270

## Lytham Trophy (inaugurated 1965)  *always at Royal Lytham & St Annes and Fairhaven*
Albert Eckhardt (FIN)                          73-72-69-73—287
*Beat Jack Anthony Hume (Rathsallagh) at the third extra hole*

## Midland Open (inaugurated 1976)  *Gay Hill*
J S Bower (Meltham)                            66-65-71-66—268

## Mullingar Grant Thornton Scratch Trophy  *Mullingar*
Daniel Holland (Castle)                    68-71-73-68—280

## Newlands Trophy  *Lanark*
Matthew Clark (Kilmacolm)                  66-71-67-72—276

## North of Ireland Open Amateur  (inaugurated 1989)  *always at Royal Portrush*
**Final:** Chris Selfridge (Moyola Park) beat Gary Hinley (West Waterford)  2 and 1

## North of Scotland Open Amateur Stroke Play  (David Blair Trophy)  *Murcar*
Bryan Innes (Murcar)                       72-71-73-77—293

## North-East Scotland Open  *Nairn*
Jack McDonald (Kilmarnock Barassie)        69-66-73-66—274

## Prince of Wales Challenge Cup  (inaugurated 1928)  *always at Royal Cinque Ports*
Max Orrin (North Foreland) and Callum Shankwin (Moor Park)  146

## Rosebery Challenge Cup  (inaugurated 1933)  *always at Ashridge*
Robert Sutton (Dunstable Downs)            68-69—137

## St Andrews Links Trophy  (inaugurated 1989)  *always at St Andrews (Old and New)*
Neil Raymond (Corhampton)                  72-73-68-69—282

## St David's Gold Cross  (inaugurated 1930)  *always at Royal St David's, Gwynedd*
Richard James (Aberystwyth)                72-71-69-72—284

## Selborne Salver  (inaugurated 1976)  *always at Blackmoor*
Harry Casey (Enfield)                      66-66—132

## South of England Open Amateur  (inaugurated 2005)  *Walton Heath*
Ricardo Michelini (ITA)                    285

## South East England Links Championship  (inaugurated 2010)
*Royal Cinque Ports and Royal St George's*
Max Orrin (North Foreland)                 76-76-75-71—298

## South of Ireland Open Amateur  *Lahinch*
**Final:** Simon Ward (Co Louth) beat Paul O'Hara (Kilkenny)  at 19th

## South-East Scotland District Championship  *West Linton*
Jack McDonald (Kilmarnock Barassie)        71-68-70-71—280

## Sunningdale Foursomes  (inaugurated 1934)  *always at Sunningdale*
**Final:** P Archer (Birchwood) and S Walker (The Belfry) beat S Tiley (Royal Cinque Ports) and R Neil Jones (Rochester and Cobham)  at 19th

## Sutherland Chalice (inaugurated 2000)   *Dumfries & Galloway*
Matthew Clark (Kilmacolm)                66-69-66-73—274

## Tenby Golden Eagle   *always at Tenby*
Ian Flower (Mountain Ash)                71-75—146

## Tennant Cup (inaugurated 1880)   *always at Glasgow GC (Glasgow Gailes and Killermont)*
Jack McDonald (Kilmarnock Barassie)      71-72-69-72—284

## Tillman Trophy (inaugurated 1980)   *always at Moor Park*
Paul Kinnear (Formby)                    71-73-71-72—287
Ryan Cornfield (Enville)                 72-69-73-73—287   tie
*Level after five extra holes when the match was abandoned due to darkness*

## Trubshaw Cup (inaugurated 1989)   *always at Ashburnham and Tenby*
Lee Jones (Conwy)                        66-74-78-74—292

## Tucker Trophy (inaugurated 1991)   *Whitchurch*
Zach Galliford (Borth & Ynyslas)         70-68-67-67—272

## West of England Open Amateur Match Play (inaugurated 1912)
*always at Burnham & Berrow*
**Final:** Lewis Pearce (Walsall) beat Jeremy Larcombe (Burnham and Berrow)  8 and 7

## West of England Open Amateur Stroke Play (inaugurated 1968)   *Saunton*
Edward Richardson (Rye)                  71-74-75-73—293

## West of Ireland Open Amateur (inaugurated 1989)   *Co. Sligo (Rosses Point)*
**Final:** Rory McNamara (Headfort) beat Niall Gorey (Muskerry)  5 and 4

## Worplesdon Mixed Foursomes (inaugurated 1921)   *always at Worplesdon, Surrey*
*Cancelled*

## Month by month in 2013

The USPGA Championship at Oak Hill goes to Jason Dufner two years after he blew a five-shot lead. Tiger Woods remains four shy of Jack Nicklaus's 18 majors, but he does have 18 World Golf Championships after an eighth win at the Bridgestone Invitational. Stacy Lewis takes the Ricoh Women's British Open at St Andrews, but Europe thrash America 18–10 at the Solheim Cup – their first away victory.

# University and School Events 2013

For past results see earlier editions of *The R&A Golfer's Handbook*

**Palmer Cup** (USA university students v European university students) *Wilmington CC, Delaware, USA*
June 8–11

**Round One – Fourball** (USA names first):
Sean Dale and Bobby Wyatt beat Sebastian Cappelen (DEN) and Pontus Widegren (SWE) 5 and 4
Patrick Rodgers and JustinThomas beat Greg Eason (ENG) and Ben Taylor (ENG) 5 and 3
Alex Carpenter and Cory Whitsett beat Julien Brun (FRA) and Joel Stalter (FRA) 3 and 2
Daniel Berger and James Erkenbeck beat Scott Fernandez (ESP) and Pedro Figueredo (POR) 4 and 3
Michael Kim and Michael Weaver halved with Gary Hurley (IRL) and Kevin Phelan (IRL)

**Round Two – Singles:**

| | |
|---|---|
| Wyatt beat Cappelen 3 and 2 | Whitsett halved with Fernandez |
| Thomas beat Eason 5 and 3 | Carpenter halved with Hurley |
| Rodgers beat Brun 4 and 3 | Erkenbeck halved with Stalter |
| Dale beat Widegren 2 holes | Weaver lost to Phelan 3 and 1 |
| Berger beat Taylor 2 and 1 | Kim halved with Figueiredo |

**Round Three – Fosursomes:**
Whitsett and Wyatt beat Hurley and Phelan 5 and 3
Carpenter and Kim beat Brun and Stalter 1 hole
Berger and Dale lost to Cappelen and Eason 1 hole
Erkenbeck and Weaver lost to Fernandez and Taylor 4 and 3
Rodger and Thomas halved with Figueiredo and Widegren

**Round Four – Singles:**

| | |
|---|---|
| Wyatt halved with Phelan | Kim lost to Widegren 1 hole |
| Whitsett beat Fernandez 3 and 2 | Carpenter halved with Eason |
| Dale halved with Brun | Weaver beat Stalter 3 and 1 |
| Berger lost to Taylor 2 and 1 | Thomas beat Cappelen 2 and 1 |
| Erkenbeck beat Figueiredo 2 and 1 | Rodger beat Hurley 3 and 2 |

**Result:** Europe 13½, USA 10½

*History:* The United States of America have won the event nine times, Europe on seven occasions and Great Britain and Ireland once with one match drawn

| | | |
|---|---|---|
| 1997 | USA 19, Great Britain and Ireland 5 | Bay Hill GC |
| 1998 | USA 12, Great Britain and Ireland 12 | Old Course, St Andrews |
| 1999 | USA 17½, Great Britain and Ireland 6½ | Honors GC, Chattanooga |
| 2000 | Great Britain and Ireland 12½, USA 11½ | Royal Liverpool GC |
| 2001 | USA 18, Great Britain and Ireland 6 | Baltusrol (Lower) GC |
| 2002 | USA 15½, Great Britain and Ireland 8½ | Doonbeg GC |
| 2003 | Europe 14, USA 10 | Cassique GC Kiawah |
| 2004 | Europe 14½, USA 9½ | Ballybunion GC. |
| 2005 | USA 14, Europe 10 | Whistling Straits GC |
| 2006 | Europe 19½, USA 4½ | Prestwick GC |
| 2007 | USA 18, Europe 6 | Caves Valley GC |
| 2008 | Europe 14, USA 10 | Glasgow Gailes GC |
| 2008 | Europe 14, USA 10 | Glasgow Gailes GC |
| 2009 | Europe 13, USA 11 | Cherry Hills CC, CO |
| 2010 | USA 13, Europe 11 | Royal Portrush |
| 2011 | USA 13, Europe 11 | The Stanwich Club, Connecticut |
| 2012 | Europe 13½, USA 10½ | Royal Portrush GC, Northern Ireland |

The 2014 match is scheduled for Walton Heath, England

# Halford-Hewitt Cup (inaugurated 1924)

*always at Royal Cinque Ports, Deal, and Royal St George's*

**Semi finals:**   Tonbridge 3, Charterhouse 2
            Eton 4, Epsom 1
**Final:**        Eton 3, Tonbridge 2

**Winning team:** Henry Dixon, Ed Greenhalgh, Ben Holden, Fred Irwin, Billal Ismail, Rupert Krefting, Aex Leslie, Will McPhail, James Rowland Clark and Johnnie Seabrook

The Prince's Plate was won by Haileybury, beating The Leys 2½–½

---

# Senior Halford-Hewitt Competitions (inaugurated 2000) *always at Woking GC, West Hill GC*

Bernard Darwin Trophy: Tonbridge                                    *and Worplesdon: GC*

Senior Bernard Darwin: Repton

Veteran Bernard Darwin: Wellington

GL Mellin Salver: Cheltonian 2, Hurstpierpoint 1

Cyril Gray Trophy: Watsonians 3, Merchant Taylors 0

---

# Grafton Morrish Trophy (inaugurated 1963)   *Hunstanton GC*

**Semi finals:**   Wellington 2½, Uppingham ½
            Merchant Taylors 2, Woodbridge 1
**Final:**        Merchant Taylors 2½, Wellington ½

Solihull Salver: Millfield

Committee Bowl: Birkenhead

---

# 124th Oxford v Cambridge University Match (inaugurated 1878)   *Royal Cinque Ports*
## (Oxford names first)

**Foursomes:**
M Reynolds and P Sharkey lost to P Schoenberger and D Clark   5 and 4
R Van Wijk and M Seeley halved with L Birrell-Gray and J Wiese
B Wilson and J Riley lost to J Gregson and D Flynn   1 hole
D Crummey and G  Burnik lost to J Cumberlandand N Ramskill   2 and 1
A Gems and J Mercurio beat A Silver and G Ting   7 and 6

**Singles:**

| | |
|---|---|
| Gems beat Silver  2 and 1 | Crummey halved with Clark |
| Mercurio beat O'Flynn  5 and 4 | Sharkey halved with Cumberland |
| Seely lost to Ramskill  1 hol | Burnik beat Birrell-Gray  4 and 3 |
| Van Wijk beat Wiese  5 and | Riley beat Schoenberger  2 and 1 |
| Wilson lost to Ting  2 and 1 | M Reynolds beat Gregson  1 hole |

**Result:** Oxford University 8½, Cambridge University 6½

*History:* Cambridge have won the match on 64 occasions, Oxford on 53. Seven matches were halved

---

# Oxford and Cambridge Golfing Society for the President's Putter

(inaugurated 1920)   *Rye GC*

**Semi finals:**   Ben Wescoe (Pembroke C) beat W H P Jackson (St Peter's)  1 hole
            Adrian West (Downing) beat C A Consul (Worcester)  2 and 1
**Final:**        Ben Wescoe beat Adrian West  6 and 5

## 65th Boyd Quaich (always at St Andrews (Old and New))

| 1 | Charlie McNeal (Louisville) | 69-66-72-71—278 |
| 2 | Jordon McColl (Lander) | 70-69-77-69—285 |
| 3 | Angus Carrick (Stirling) | 70-71-73-71—285 |

## 61st Queen Elizabeth Coronation Schools Trophy (inaugurated 1953)

*always at Royal Burgess, Barnton*

**Semi-finals:** Glasgow High School FP beat Glasgow Academicals 2–1
Daniel Stewart's–Melville FP beat Breadalbane Academicals 2–1

**Final** (Glasgow HS FP names first):
K J McNair and A Farmer beat K Cattenach and A Ritchie 4 and 3.
R Harvey and N Crilley lost to D Miller and D Hamilton 6 and 5
C Gray and K Shanks beat G Pollock and S McLaren 1 hole

**Result:** Glasgow HS FP 2, Stewart's-Melville FP 1

*History:* Winning teams: 11 Watsonians, Glasgow HSFP; 6 Merchistonians; 4 Daniel Stewart's FP; 3 Old Lorettonians, George Heriot's FP; 2 Dollar Academicals, Hillhead HSFP, Levinside Academy, Old Carthusians, Perth Academy FP, Breadalbane Academicals; 1 Glasgow Academicals, Fettesians, Morrisonians, Hutcheson GSFP, Old Uppinghamians, Ayr Academy FP, Gordonians, Madras College FP, Lenzie Academicals, Stewarts Melville

## BUCS Student Tour Finals    Crail GC (Red course)

| 1 | Jack McDonald (Barassie) | 73-73-73-72—291 |
| 2 | Ryan McInstry (Cairdhu) | 83-74-69-70—296 |
| 3 | Cormac Sharvin (Ardglass) | 82-72-73-70—297 |
| | Oliver Roberts (Hong Kong) | 79-75-72-71—297 |

## Scottish Student Golf Championship    Moray New

| 1 | Mathias Eggenberger | 66-73-71-70—280 |
| 2 | Jack McDonald (Barassie) | 72-71-69-70—282 |
| 3 | Kit Holmes (Hunstanton) | 71-72-70-76—289 |

## Canadian University and Colleges Championship    Val des Lacs Golf Club

| 1 | University of British Columbia Thunderbirds | 291-287-287-283—1,148 |
| 2 | Universite Laval Rouge et Or | 286-293-299-291—1,169 |
| 3 | Universite de Montreal Carabins | 293-299-295-288—1,175 |

**Winning team:** Connor Kozak, Kieren Standen, Jerry Christiansen, Andrew Ledger and Scott Second

**Individual:**

| 1 | Ugo Coussaud (Laval Rouge at Or) | 66-69-73-72—280 |
| 2 | Chris Hemmerich (Kitchener) | 71-68-70-72—281 |
| 3 | Andrew Ledger (Toronto) | 71-72-72-67—282 |

## World Universities Men's Championship

Switzerland will host the next Championship in 2014

## 67th Japanese Men's Collegiate Championship    Kakogawa GC

| 1 | Shun Murayama | 70-70-73-65—278 |
| 2 | Daisuke Matsubara | 73-67-71-68—279 |
| | Kenta Konishi | 68-71-70-70—279 |
| | Tomohiro Umeyama | 70-70-68-71—279 |

# 3rd European Universities Golf Championship   *Saint Saens, France*

**Individual:**

| | | |
|---|---|---|
| 1 | Markus Enoksson (SWE) | 69-68-71-66—274 |
| 2 | Alexander Culverwell (SCO) | 69-70-69-69—277 |
| 3 | Philip Eriksson (SWE) | 71-69-74-69—283 |
| | Mattias Eggenberger (BEL) | 71-68-72-72—283 |
| | Cormac Sharvin (IRL) | 70-70-71-72—283 |

**Team:**

| | | |
|---|---|---|
| 1 | University of Stirling | 207-208-212-208—835 |
| 2 | Scandinavian School of Golf | 212-209-216-204—841 |
| 3 | National University of Ireland, Maynooth | 216-212-219-212—859 |

4 University of Exeter 872; 5 University of Lausanne 878; 6 Karlsruhe Institute of Technology 891; 7 TU Darmstadt 898; 8 Université de Pau et des Pays de l'Adour 902; 9 ASU Bordeaux 906; 10 University of St Gallen 926; 11 University of Ports, As Rouen US SSE 932; 13 University of St Gallen II 954

## European title for Stirling University students

Congratulations to coach Dean Robertson, the former European Tour player, and his two Stirling teams.

The men won the 3rd European Universities Team Championship at Saint Saens in France and the women came second in their competition to the Swedish University of Hamistad.

In the individual competition, Markus Enoksson from the University of Hamistad edged Alexander Culverwell of Stirling into second place and Stirling University's Eilidh Briggs was runner up to another Hamistad golfer, Emma Vestin.

# County and other Regional Championships 2013

## England

Bedfordshire: Robert Sutton
Berks, Bucks & Oxon:
  Tom Lawson
Cambridgeshire: James Reeson
Cheshire: James Newton
Cornwall: Joe Yorke
Cumbria: John Longcake
Derbyshire: Craig Young
Devon: Ryan Pope
Dorset: Aaron Crabb
Durham: John Kirkpatrick
Essex: Bobby Keeble
Gloucestershire: Andy Hale

Hampshire, Isle of Wight and
  Channel Islands: Ryan Henley
Hertfordshire: William Symons
Isle of Man: Kevin Moore
Kent: Alfie Plant
Lancashire: Haydn McCullen
Leicestershire and Rutland:
  David Gibson
Lincolnshire: Simon Richardson
Middlesex: Matthew Alden
Norfolk: Jack Yule
Northamptonshire: Jack Brown
Northumberland:
  Andrew Minnikin

Nottinghamshire:
  Martin Foulkes
Shropshire and Herefordshire:
  Alex Allen
Somerset: Ellis Cook
Suffolk: Patrick Spraggs
Surrey: Mark Booker
Sussex: Andrew Smith
Warwickshire: James Carney
Wiltshire: Jack Charman
Worcestershire: Josh Carpenter
Yorkshire: Christopher Halley
NAPGC: Gareth Hawkins
Artisans: Graham Adamson

## Ireland

East of Ireland Open:
  Paul Dunne
North of Ireland Amateur:
  Chris Selfridge

North of Ireland Stroke Play:
  Dermot McElroy
South of Ireland Open:
  Simon Ward (Pro)

West of Ireland Open:
  Rory McNamara

## Scotland

Angus: Graham Scott (M),
  Gary Tough (S)
Argyll and Bute:
  Bobby Willan (M),
  Steven Gilmour (S)
Ayrshire: Michael Smyth (M),
  Stuart Robin (S)
Borders: Allan Ballantyne (M),
  Simon Fairburn (S)
Clackmannanshire:
  Allan Watson (M), Ian Ross (S)
Dunbartonshire:
  Steven Stewart (M+S)

Fife: Tom Watson (M),
  Steven Meiklejohn (S)
Glasgow: Fraser Grant (M+S)
Lanarkshire: John Ralston (M),
  Stewart Henderson (S)
Lothians: Alan Anderson (M),
  James McIntosh (S)
North: Jeff Wright (M),
  Kyle Godsman (S)
North-East: David Morrison (M),
  Bryan Innes (S)

Perth and Kinross:
  Stephen Carruthers (M),
  Nicky Barr (S)
Renfrewshire: Jack Currie (M),
  Grant Beaton (S)
South: Neil Hamilton (M),
  David Brodie (S)
Stirlingshire:
  Gary Shepherd (M),
  Hugh Nelson (S)

## Wales

Anglesey: Adam Warriner
Brecon and Radnor:
  Tim Iveson

Caernarfon and District:
  Alwyn Thomas
Denbigh: Alyn Torrence

Dyfed: Richard Scott
Glamorgan: Keith Stimpson

# PART V

# Women's Amateur Tournaments

# World Amateur Golf Ranking

## Teenager Lydia Ko wins the McCormack Medal again

She is still the World No 1. The amazing Korean-born teenager who is now a New Zealander, has won the McCormack Medal as leading amateur golfer for a third year. She knows no sign of wilting.

She raced to the top of the world amateur rankings when the women's version was initiated by The R&A and the USGA in 2011 and has virtually reigned supreme ever since. In fact she has held top spot in that period except for nine weeks when Japan's Mitsuke Katahira took over at the top and the one week when fellow New Zealander Cecilia Cho was No 1. Ko has been No 1 for 123 weeks.

*Lydia Ko receives the McCormack Medal from R&A Working for Golf Ambassador Suzann Pettersen*

The teenager, who shortly after ending the qualifying period in No 1 spot retained the Canadian Women's Open title on the LPGA circuit, now plays most of her golf in professional events.

"Winning the Medal means a lot and winning it three times in a row makes it even more special. It's awesome. To have retained the No 1 spot for three years has been so meaningful. In 2012 I won the US Amateur title, a Championship I had always wanted to win. Had I not done so I might not have been able to maintain my position.

Lydia was only 14 when she became the youngest winner of a professional tournament with victory in the South Wales Open on the Australian Ladies Professional Tour. She also won the Australian Women's Amateur and was runner-up in the Australian Women's Stroke Play Championship that year.

She was also silver medallist as leading amateur in the US Open and now the phenomenal schoolgirl golfer is anxious to win a major either as an amateur or as a professional when (rather than if) she joins the paid ranks.

If she had been eligible to win prize-money when she first started playing in professional events she would have amassed not far short of a million dollars.

Already she has moved to 7th in the professional world rankings and that is the highest any pro from New Zealand, man or woman, has been ranked. Michael Campbell in his golden year when he won the US Open and the much-loved World Match Play Championship at Wentworth only ever reached No 12 in the men's pro rankings.

Lydia has played tournaments in the 52 weeks which is the qualifying period for the Medal in Canada, America, England, Scotland, Thailand, Japan, Australia, Chinese Taipei, Turkey and, of course, New Zealand … and she is still only 16.

"Golf is like 99.9 percent of my life and then there is school," says Lydia, "I don't get much time to go out with my friends."

And there are other disadvantages to being an extra special golfing teenager. "I can only go out to the movies once or twice a year and I'd love to own a dog but we don't have anyone to care for it," she says.

Johnnie Cole-Hamilton, The R&A's Executive Director of Championships, and John Bodenhamer, a Senior Executive at the United States Golf Association, congratulated her on her performances and consistency.

The women's ranking comprises over 1,700 events involving 3,400 players in 78 countries but, for the moment, nobody can catch the fantastic Lydia Ko. The McCormack Medal was inaugurated in the memory of top entrepreneur the late Mark H McCormack.

# R&A World Amateur Golf Ranking 2012–13 – Top 100

Players from the USA occupy most places in the Top 100 with 28 entries (two in the top ten) with Australia second with 10 (two in the top ten). New Zealand takes third place with seven entries. Players from England and Spain accounted for five places apiece. By region the totals are: Americas 37, Europe 29, Australasia 17, Asia 12 and Africa five.

| # | Name | | Divisor | Points | # | Name | | Divisor | Points |
|---|---|---|---|---|---|---|---|---|---|
| 1 | Lydia Ko | NZL | 63 | 2383.33 | 51 | Emily Tubert | USA | 45 | 1158.11 |
| 2 | Su-Hyun Oh | AUS | 67 | 1731.34 | 52 | Camilla Hedberg | ESP | 53 | 1150.00 |
| 3 | Nobuhle Dlamini | SWZ | 49 | 1673.47 | 53 | Jo Charlton | AUS | 27(28) | 1142.86 |
| 4 | Minjee Lee | AUS | 68 | 1607.35 | 54 | Angel Yin | USA | 33 | 1142.42 |
| 5 | Annie Park | USA | 46 | 1583.70 | 55 | Clara Baena | ESP | 35 | 1138.57 |
| 6 | Emily Kristine Pedersen | DEN | 53 | 1464.54 | 56 | Lara Weinstein | RSA | 54 | 1138.19 |
| 7 | Alison Lee | USA | 24(28) | 1455.00 | 57 | Julie Yang | KOR | 41 | 1135.77 |
| 8 | Kim Williams | RSA | 46 | 1441.03 | 58 | Krista Puisite | LAT | 57 | 1133.84 |
| 9 | Georgia Hall | ENG | 47 | 1439.89 | 59 | Luna Sobron | ESP | 48 | 1129.17 |
| 10 | Stephanie Meadow | IRL | 50 | 1434.50 | 60 | Mun Chin Keh | NZL | 64 | 1128.91 |
| 11 | Brooke Mackenzie Henderson | CAN | 51 | 1390.49 | 61 | Charlotte Thomas | ENG | 42 | 1127.23 |
| | | | | | 62 | Laura Gonzalez-Escallon | BEL | 53 | 1126.89 |
| 12 | Nicole Morales | USA | 30 | 1376.67 | | | | | |
| 13 | Ally McDonald | USA | 49 | 1365.82 | 63 | Gabriela Lopez | MEX | 50 | 1125.50 |
| 14 | Karolin Lampert | GER | 42 | 1337.50 | 64 | Lauren Diaz-Yi | USA | 33 | 1124.24 |
| 15 | Emma Talley | USA | 45 | 1326.11 | 65 | Yueer Feng | CHN | 95 | 1120.20 |
| 16 | Chirapat Jao-Javanil | THA | 38 | 1324.01 | 66 | Lita Guo | NZL | 39 | 1119.87 |
| 17 | Kelly Shon | USA | 35 | 1308.93 | 67 | Katja Pogacar | SLO | 33 | 1115.15 |
| 18 | Ashlan Ramsey | USA | 55 | 1295.94 | 68 | Quirine Eijkenboom | GER | 28 | 1114.29 |
| 19 | Ji Sun Kang | KOR | 51 | 1285.78 | 69 | Cassy Isagawa | USA | 42 | 1111.76 |
| 20 | Doris Chen | USA | 61 | 1284.84 | 70 | Madelene Sagstrom | SWE | 43 | 1110.23 |
| 21 | Natalia Escuriola | ESP | 47 | 1265.96 | | Chloe Williams | WAL | 33 | 1110.23 |
| 22 | Hayley Bettencourt | AUS | 57 | 1257.89 | 72 | Bronte Law | ENG | 25(28) | 1106.55 |
| 23 | Grace Lennon | AUS | 60 | 1256.25 | 73 | Chantelle Cassidy | NZL | 38 | 1101.32 |
| 24 | Erynne Lee | USA | 45 | 1248.06 | 74 | Gurbani Singh | IND | 60 | 1095.00 |
| | Kyung Kim | USA | 43 | 1248.06 | 75 | Lauren Taylor | ENG | 47 | 1094.68 |
| 26 | Casie Cathrea | USA | 27(28) | 1245.00 | 76 | Princess Mary Superal | PHI | 75 | 1091.50 |
| 27 | Noemi Jimenez | ESP | 51 | 1234.07 | 77 | Delfina Acosta | ARG | 60 | 1089.17 |
| 28 | Laura Funfstuck | GER | 28 | 1233.04 | 78 | Tonje Daffinrud | NOR | 41 | 1080.73 |
| 29 | Daniela Darquea | ECU | 41 | 1231.10 | 79 | Casey Grice | USA | 38 | 1077.63 |
| 30 | Mariah Stackhouse | USA | 37 | 1229.73 | 80 | Andrea Lee | USA | 29 | 1069.09 |
| 31 | Casey Danielson | USA | 32 | 1222.66 | 81 | Simin Feng | CHN | 46 | 1066.58 |
| 32 | Hayley Davis | ENG | 47 | 1222.13 | 82 | Linnea Johansson | SWE | 29 | 1063.79 |
| 33 | Nicole Garcia | RSA | 46 | 1211.96 | 83 | Malene Krolboll | DEN | 43 | 1059.30 |
| 34 | Grace Na | USA | 39 | 1210.90 | 84 | Wenyung Keh | NZL | 56 | 1055.80 |
| 35 | Soo-Bin Kim | CAN | 41 | 1204.88 | 85 | Maribel Lopez | COL | 48 | 1055.73 |
| 36 | Yan Jing | CHN | 49 | 1200.51 | 86 | Maria Torres | PUR | 32 | 1055.47 |
| 37 | Linnea Strom | SWE | 40 | 1200.31 | 87 | Brittney Dryland | NZL | 51 | 1055.39 |
| 38 | Lindsey Weaver | USA | 28 | 1197.32 | 88 | Laetitia Beck | ISR | 31 | 1054.84 |
| 39 | Anne-Catherine Tanguay | CAN | 46 | 1195.98 | 89 | Isabelle Lendl | USA | 44 | 1052.84 |
| 40 | Vicky Villanueva | ARG | 29 | 1194.83 | 90 | Ali Orchard | AUS | 27(28) | 1052.68 |
| 41 | Hannah Green | AUS | 57 | 1192.98 | 91 | Manon Gidali | FRA | 46 | 1051.09 |
| 42 | Sophia Popov | GER | 50 | 1180.70 | 92 | Megan Khang | USA | 32 | 1050.39 |
| 43 | Cathleen Santoso | AUS | 45 | 1177.78 | 93 | Ji-Hyun Oh | KOR | 32 | 1046.88 |
| 44 | Julianne Alvarez | NZL | 52 | 1173.08 | 94 | Amy Boulden | WAL | 56 | 1043.75 |
| 45 | Kelly Tan | MAS | 47 | 1172.87 | 95 | Meghan Stasi | USA | 31 | 1043.55 |
| 46 | Celine Boutier | FRA | 53 | 1171.70 | 96 | Hannah O'Sullivan | USA | 34 | 1037.50 |
| 47 | Carrie Park | RSA | 35 | 1166.79 | 97 | Tatiana Jaqueline Wijaya | USA | 51 | 1036.60 |
| 48 | Nanna Madsen | DEN | 40 | 1166.56 | 98 | Julienne Soo | AUS | 54 | 1034.26 |
| 49 | Bethany Wu | USA | 40 | 1163.75 | 99 | Raychelle Santos | USA | 39 | 1033.33 |
| 50 | Karen Chung | USA | 31 | 1162.10 | | Shi Yuting | CHN | 51 | 1033.33 |

# World Amateur Golf Ranking 2012–2013

The World Amateur Golf Ranking (WAGR), which comprises a women's ranking and a men's ranking for elite amateur players, is offered by The R&A and the United States Golf Association as a global service to golf.

Through incorporation and assessment worldwide of both amateur and professional events, WAGR encourages the international development of the competitive game. WAGR endeavours to be the most comprehensive and accurate ranking in golf by effectively comparing players from around the world who may never directly compete against one another. WAGR is available to national federations and organisers of amateur and professional events and tours as a criterion for tournament field selection and for purposes of exemptions, national team selection, and orders of merit.

WAGR currently processes information from over 4,500 Counting Events to rank over 10,000 players from more than 100 countries. Players are ranked on the basis of their average performance in those events over a rolling cycle of the previous 52 weeks. Counting Events are graded from A to G in accordance with the strength of the field, with the number of points awarded being proportionate to the event strength.

A Counting Event is an event, match play, stroke play or a combination, amateur or professional, selected and approved by the WAGR Committee to count for WAGR. Counting Events may be:
1. Any elite stroke play event, decided by gross scores, played over a minimum of three rounds.
2. Any elite match play event, decided by gross scores, played over a minimum of three match play rounds. Stroke play qualifying for a counting match play event will also be included in the results for that event if played over a minimum of 36 holes.
3. Any elite team match play event that contains at least one round of singles matches.
4. Any of the major championships or any official event from the professional tours that make up the International Federation of PGA Tours, or any official event from other professional tours, if the event meets 1 or 2 above.

In order to be included in WAGR, results of Counting Events must be submitted by event organisers in a timely manner. Reporting templates are available. To receive points in WAGR for the Counting Events in which they participate, and to receive event exemptions they may have earned with those points, players may wish to encourage event organisers to return event results to WAGR as soon as possible once Counting Events conclude.

Further information can be found in the Frequently Asked Questions (FAQ's) on the WAGA.com website

The rankings are displayed here by month and are subdivided into the following regions:
Africa
The Americas (North, South and Central America and the Caribbean)
Asia (incorporating the Middle East)
Australasia (incorporating the Pacific Islands)
Europe
Players are from the country hosting the event unless otherwise stated.
\* Indicates a newly ranked player.
‡ Indicates that the player has since turned professional.
A list of country abbreviations can be found on page 51; MWAGR can be found on page 270

# Elite and Category "A" Events

| Elite |
|---|

Week 21   **NCAA Championship**   *Athens, GA, USA*   May 20–26   (RSS 75-74-75-78)

| | | | SP | Bonus | Points |
|---|---|---|---|---|---|
| 1 | Annie Park | 70-67-70-71—278 | 56 | 48 | 104 |
| 2 | Lindy Duncan* | 72-71-71-70—284 | 50 | 36 | 86 |
| 3 | Paula Reto (RSA)* | 71-73-70-72—286 | 48 | 18 | 66 |

Full details can be found on page 389

## Week 24 Ladies British Open Amateur Championship — Machynys Peninsula G&CC
June 16–10 (RSS 77-77)

| | | | SP | Bonus | Points |
|---|---|---|---|---|---|
| Winner | Georgia Hall (ENG) | 74-75—149 | 21 | 138 | 159 |
| Runner-up | Luna Sobron (ESP) | 75-77—152 | 18 | 105 | 123 |
| Semi-finalists | Noemi Jimenez (ESP) | 76-74—150 | 20 | 76 | 96 |
| | Karolin Lampert (SWE) | 74-76—150 | 20 | 76 | 96 |

Full details can be found on page 381

## Week 30 International European Championship — Aura Golf, Turku, Finland    July 22–28
(RSS 78-74)

| | | | SP | Bonus | Points |
|---|---|---|---|---|---|
| 1 | Emily Kristine Pedersen (DEN) | 67-73-64-72—276 | 55 | 11 | 103 |
| 2 | Laura Gonzalez-Escallion (GER) | 69-74-68-68—279 | 52 | 36 | 86 |
| 3 | Kirsta Bakker (FIN) | 75-68-73-66—282 | 49 | 12 | 61 |
| | Celine Boutier (FRA) | 73-69-72-68—282 | 49 | 12 | 61 |
| | Noemi Jiminez (ESP) | 71-69-71-71—282 | 49 | 12 | 61 |

Full details can be found on page 384

## Week 32 US Women's Amateur Championship — Charleston, South Carolina, USA
Aug 5–11 (RSS 77-74)

| | | | SP | Bonus | MP | Points |
|---|---|---|---|---|---|---|
| Winner | Emma Talley | 71-69—140 | 27 | 11 | 138 | 176 |
| Runner-up | Yueer Feng (CHN) | 72-68—140 | 27 | 11 | 105 | 143 |
| Semi-finalists | Alison Lee | 72-69—141 | 26 | 0.9 | 76 | 102.9 |
| | Doris Chen | 74-72—146 | 21 | – | 76 | 97 |

Full details can be found on page 386

### Category "A"

## 2012

### Week 37 Cougar Classic — Charleston, South Carolina, USA    Sept 9–11 (RSS 74-74-75)
| 1 | Camilla Hedberg (ESP) | 69-66-68—203 | 71.50 points |
|---|---|---|---|
| 2 | Lindy Duncan‡ | 69-70-68—207 | 53.50 |
| 3 | Erica Popson‡ | 73-70-68—211 | 42.75 |
| | Lauren Stratton‡ | 70-71-70—211 | 42.75 |

### Week 39 Espirito Santo — Gloria CC, Antalya, Turkey    Sept 27–30 (RSS 77-77-74-78)
| | | | SP | Bonus | Pts |
|---|---|---|---|---|---|
| 1 | Lydia Ko (NZL) | 70-69-67-68—274 | 56 | 36 | 92 |
| 2 | Krista Bakker (FIN) | 72-70-69-69—280 | 50 | 15 | 65 |
| | Camilla Hedberg (SWE) | 70-72-70-68—280 | 50 | 15 | 65 |

### Week 40 Liz Murphey Fall Preview — Athens, Georgia, USA    Oct 5–7 (RSS 75-75-75)
| 1 | Mary Michael Maggio | 72-74-67—213 | 63 points |
|---|---|---|---|
| 2 | Casey Grice | 73-70-71—214 | 48.5 |
| 3 | Brittany Altomare‡ | 70-73-72—215 | 40.75 |
| | Marta Sanz (ESP) | 71-69-75—215 | 40.75 |

### Week 42 Stanford Intercollegiate — Stanford, California, USA    Oct 19–21 (RSS 75-74-74)
| 1 | Kyung Kim | 72-66-68—206 | 68 points |
|---|---|---|---|
| 2 | Soo-Bin Kim (CAN) | 72-68-69—209 | 51.5 |
| 3 | Doris Chen | 69-70-73—212 | 41.75 |
| | Lauren Sewell | 71-70-71—212 | 41.75 |

Week 43    **Landfall Tradition**    *Wilmington, North Carolina, USA*    Oct 26    (RSS 76)

| | | | |
|---|---|---|---|
| I | Kimberly Kaufman‡ | 67 | 17 points |
| 2 | Kelsey Vines‡ | 69 | 15 |
| 3 | Johanna Bjoerk (SWE) | 70 | 14 |
| | Lindsey Weaver | 70 | 14 |

Week 47    **Polo Junior Classic**    *Palm Beach Gardens, Florida, USA*    Nov 17–23    (RSS 77-77)

| | | | |
|---|---|---|---|
| I | Ariya Jutanugarn (THA)‡ | 73-69—142 | 181.5 points |
| 2 | Angel Yin | 75-74—149 | 125 |
| 3 | Nicole Morales | 73-72—145 | 98 |

## 2013

Week 3    **Australian Amateur Championship**    *Commonwealth and Woodlands, Melbourne*
Jan 15–20    (RSS 76-80-80-78)

| | | | SP | Bonus | MP | Points |
|---|---|---|---|---|---|---|
| Winner | Minjee Lee | 68-74—142 | 30 | 3.5 | 115 | 148,5 |
| Runner-up | Jenny Lee | 77-82—154 | 13 | – | 84 | 97 |
| Semi-finalists | Hannah Green | 71-73—144 | 30 | – | 57 | 87 |
| | Julienne Soo | 83-73—156 | 16 | – | 57 | 73 |

Week 4    **Annika Invitational**    *Reunion Resort, Florida, USA*    Jan 18–21    (RSS 75-74-74)

| | | | |
|---|---|---|---|
| I | Bethany Wu | 68-71-67—206 | 68 points |
| 2 | Karen Chung | 70-72-67—209 | 49.25 |
| | Emily Kristine Pedersen (DEN) | 70-71-68—209 | 49.25 |

Week 7    **Northrup Grumman Reg. Challenge**    *Palos Verde, California, USA*    Feb 11–13
(RSS 76-77-77)

| | | | |
|---|---|---|---|
| I | Erynne Lee | 72-72-69—213 | 67 points |
| 2 | Kelsey Vines | 71-72-71—214 | 52.5 |
| 3 | Kyung Kim | 74-69-73—216 | 46 |

Week 9    **Spanish Ladies Amateur**    *Pula Golf, Mallorca, Spain*    Feb 27–Mar 3    (RSS 79-80)

| | | | SP | Bonus | MP | Points |
|---|---|---|---|---|---|---|
| Winner | Emily Kristine Pedersen (DEN) | 74-77—151 | 24 | 1 | 115 | 140 |
| Runner-up | Linnea Strom (SWE) | 72-79—151 | 24 | 1 | 84 | 109 |
| Semi-finalists | Katerina Vlasinova (CRO) | 77-75—152 | 23 | – | 57 | 80 |
| | Anyssia Herbaut (FRA) | 77-78—155 | 20 | – | 57 | 77 |

Week 9    **All State Sugar Bowl Intercollegiate**    *New Orleans, Louisiana, USA*    Feb 25–26
(RSS 74-77)

| | | | |
|---|---|---|---|
| I | Hayley Davis (ENG) | 72-68—140 | 45 points |
| 2 | Lee Lopez‡ | 69-73—142 | 31 |
| | Sophia Popov (GER) | 70-72—142 | 31 |
| | Kelsey Vines‡ | 72-70—142 | 31 |

Week 10    **Darius Rucker Intercollegiate**    *Hilton Head, South Carolina, USA*    Mar 8–10
(RSS 77-76-76)

| | | | |
|---|---|---|---|
| I | Noemi Jimenez (ESP) | 72-69-68—209 | 71 points |
| 2 | Madeleine Sagstrom (SWE) | 71-67-75—213 | 53.5 |
| 3 | Stephanie Meadow (NIR) | 77-70-67—214 | 48 |

Week 11    **SunTrust Gator Invite**    *Gainesville, Florida, USA*    Mar 15–17    (RSS 75-76-75)

| | | | |
|---|---|---|---|
| I | Chirapat Jao-Javanil (THA) | 69-68-69—206 | 71 points |
| 2 | Portland Rosen | 68-72-71—211 | 52.5 |
| 3 | Brittany Altomare‡ | 73-69-71—213 | 46 |

## Week 13 Bryan National Collegiate  Brown Summit, North Carolina, USA  Mar 25–31
(RSS 75-75-75)

| | | | |
|---|---|---|---|
| 1 | Emilie Burger‡ | 72-70-69—211 | 65 points |
| 2 | Brittany Altomare‡ | 70-70-72—212 | 50.5 |
| 3 | Sarah Schmeizel | 71-73-71—215 | 43 |

## Week 14 Internationaux de France Juniors (Trophée Esmond)  St Cloud
April 1–7  (RSS 75-74)

| | | | SP | Bonus | MP | Points |
|---|---|---|---|---|---|---|
| Winner | Laura Funfstuck (GER) | 65-71—136 | 29 | 9 | 115 | 153 |
| Runner-up | Natalia Escuriola (ESP) | 67-68—135 | 30 | 18 | 84 | 132 |
| Semi-finalists | Eilidh Briggs (SCO) | 68-73—141 | 24 | – | 57 | 81 |
| | Lauralie Migneaux | 74-70—140 | 21 | – | 57 | 78 |

## Week 15 Ping-ASU Invitational  Tempe, Arizona, USA  April 12–14  (RSS 74-74-74)

| | | | |
|---|---|---|---|
| 1 | Emma Talley | 68-69-70—207 | 66 points |
| 2 | Erynne Lee | 69-74-66—209 | 48.25 |
| | Demi Runas‡ | 71-68-70—209 | 48.25 |

## Week 16 SEC Championship  Birmingham, Alabama, USA  April 29–21  (RSS 78-78-78)

| | | | |
|---|---|---|---|
| 1 | Stephanie Meadow (IRL) | 75-69-72—216 | 69 points |
| 2 | Sarah Harris | 73-76-76—225 | 46.5 |
| 3 | Justine Dreher (FRA) | 74-76-76—226 | 37.25 |

## Week 17 PAC-12 Championship  Valencia, California, USA  April 22–24  (RSS 75-75-76)

| | | | |
|---|---|---|---|
| 1 | Annie Park | 70-70-69—209 | 68 points |
| 2 | Sophia Popov (GER) | 66-75-70—211 | 52.5 |
| 3 | Jennifer Coleman | 74-67-72—213 | 43.75 |
| | Mariah Stackhouse | 73-67-73—213 | 43.75 |

## Week 19 NCAA D1 East Regional  Auburn, Alabama, USA  May 19–11  (RSS 75-75-75)

| | | | |
|---|---|---|---|
| 1 | Stephanie Meadow (IRL) | 68-66-69—203 | 73 points |
| 2 | Kelly Shon | 71-68-70—209 | 53.5 |
| 3 | Madison Opfer | 70-69-71—210 | 48 |

## Week 19 NCAA D1 Central Regional  Norman, Oklahoma, USA  May 9–11  (RSS 74-76-75)

| | | | |
|---|---|---|---|
| 1 | Ally McDonald | 69-69-68—206 | 70 points |
| 2 | Alejandro Cangrejo (COL) | 72-69-70—211 | 47 |
| | Emily Collins | 67-70-74—211 | 47 |
| | Anne-Catherine Tanguay (CAN) | 71-70-70—211 | 47 |

## Week 19 NCAA D1 West Regional  Stanford, Caliifornia, USA  May 9–11  (RSS 76-76-75)

| | | | |
|---|---|---|---|
| 1 | Annie Park | 67-71-68—206 | 65.25 points |
| | Paula Reto (RSA)‡ | 71-69-66—206 | 65.25 |
| | Kendall Martindale | 71-71-68—210 | 47.75 |

## Week 25 US Amateur Public Links  Jimmie Austin OU GC. Norman, Oklahoma, USA
June 17–22  (RSS 75-75-75)

| | | | SP | Bonus | MP | Points |
|---|---|---|---|---|---|---|
| Winner | Lauren Diaz-Yi | 72-76—148 | 18 | – | 126 | 144 |
| Runner-up | Doris Chen | 68-68—136 | 30 | 13.5 | 95 | 138.5 |
| Semi-finalists | Julie Yang (KOR) | 70-72—142 | 24 | 0.1666 | 68 | 92.1666 |
| | Raychelle Santos | 73-75—148 | 18 | – | 68 | 86 |

Week 29 **North and South Amateur** *Pinehurst, North Carolina, USA* July 15–20

|  |  |  | SP | Bonus | MP | (RSS 75-74-74) Points |
|---|---|---|---|---|---|---|
| Winner | Ally McDonald | 70-70-73—213 | 34 | 2.5 | 100 | 136.5 |
| Runner-up | Yueer Feng (CHN) | 72-72-72—216 | 31 | – | 69 | 100 |
| Semi-finalists | Michelle Piyapattra | 69-75-72—216 | 31 | – | 42 | 73 |
|  | Demi Runas | 72-73-73—218 | 29 | – | 42 | 71 |

Week 30 **Canadian Amateur Championship** *Beloeri GC* July 23–26

| | | | | (RSS 77-76-75-76) |
|---|---|---|---|---|
| 1 | Brooke Mackenzie Henderson | 69-70-70-66—275 | 97 points | |
| 2 | Anne-Catherine Tanguay | 71-68-69-73—281 | 73 | |
| 3 | Gabriela Lopez (MEX) | 69-75-71-68—283 | 65 | |

## September

### Africa

| | | | | | |
|---|---|---|---|---|---|
| C | Southern Cape Open | Mosselbay, Western Cape | 15–16 | Ji Sun Kang (KOR) | RSA |

### Americas

| | | | | | |
|---|---|---|---|---|---|
| A | Cougar Classic | Charleston, SC | 9–11 | Camilla Hedberg (ESP) | USA |
| B | Branch Law Firm– Dick McGuire Invitational | Albuquerque, NM | 17–18 | Jennifer Coleman | USA |
| B | Golfweek Conference Challenge | Vail, CO | 24–26 | Demi Runas | USA |
| B | Junior Ryder Cup | Olympia Fields CC, IL | 24–25 | Demi Runas | USA |
| B | Mason Rudolph Championship | Franklin, TN | 21–23 | Emilie Burger | USA |
| C | AJGA Championship | Greenville, SC | 1–3 | Simin Feng (CHN) | USA |
| C | Cardinal Cup | Simpsonville, KY | 17–18 | Emily Haas | USA |
| C | Colonel Wollenberg's Ram Classic | Fort Collins, CO | 10–11 | Manon De Roey (BEL) | USA |
| C | Dale McNamara Invitational | Broken Arrow, OK | 17–18 | Isabelle Lendl | USA |
| C | Mary Fossum Invitational | East Lansing, MI | 15–16 | Krista Puisite (LAT) | USA |
| C | Old Waverly Bulldog Invite | West Point, MS | 10–12 | Gemma Dryburgh (SCO) | USA |
| C | Oregon State Invitational | Corvallis, OR | 17–18 | Charlotte Thomas (ENG) | USA |
| D | Chip-N Club Invitational | Lincoln, NE | 10–11 | Alexandra Rossi | USA |
| D | Chris Banister Gamecock Classic | Glencoe, AL | 2–4 | Maya Parsons (CAN)/ Valdis Jonsdottir (ISL) | USA |
| D | Marilynn Smith Sunflower Invite | Lawrence, KS | 24–25 | Abi Laker (ENG) | USA |
| D | Nittany Lion Invitational | State College, PA | 28–29 | Ellen Ceresko | USA |
| D | Yale Fall Intercollegiate | New Haven, CT | 21–23 | Daniela Ortiz (MEX) | USA |

### Asia

| | | | | | |
|---|---|---|---|---|---|
| C | Taiwan Amateur | Sunrise G&CC, Taoyuan County | 11–14 | Dottie Ardina (PHI) | TPE |
| D | Hong Kong Open | Discovery Bay GC | 5–7 | Cyna Rodriguez (PHI) | HKG |
| D | Topy Cup – Japan Intercollegiate | Fukushima | 11–13 | Cassy Isagawa (USA) | JPN |

## Another triumph for Ko

While the Korean team of Hyo-Joo Kim, Kyu-Jung Baek and Min-Sun Kim retained the Espirito Santo Trophy to win the World Amateur Team Championship in Antalya, Turkey, in September the individual honours went to New Zealander Lydia Ko, number one player on the World Amateur Golf Ranking and holder of the Mark McCormack Medal.

| C | New Zealand Under 19 | Waipu GC, Northland | 5–7 | Te Rongapai Clay | NZL |
|---|---|---|---|---|---|
| D | Auckland Provincial | Royal Auckland GC | 21–23 | Sai Ma | NZL |
| D | Girls Championship of Victoria | Kingswood/Heidelbergh/Latrobe/ Riversdale GC's | 24–28 | Julienne Soo | AUS |

## Europe

| A | Espirito Santo | Gloria GC | 27–30 | Rebecca Tsai* (NZL) | TUR |
|---|---|---|---|---|---|
| B | Ladies Home International | Cork GC | 4–6 | Rebecca Tsai* (NZL) | IRL |
| C | Annika Invitational Europe | Linkopings GC | A31–S9 | Linnea Strom | SWE |
| C | DM Slagspil | Lubker GC | 7–9 | Nicole Broch Larsen | DEN |
| C | Duke of York Young Champions Trophy | Royal Troon | 11–13 | Katja Pogacar (SLO) | SCO |
| C | German National Amateur | Hardenberg | 6–9 | Karolin Lampert | GER |
| D | Austrian International Amateur | GC Linz St Florian | 7–9 | Anne van Dam (NED) | AUT |
| D | European Club Trophy | Corfu GC | 27–29 | Katerina Vlasinova (CZE) | GRE |

# October

## Africa

| B | Ackerman Championship | Clovelly CC | 13–14 | Nobuhle Dlamini (SWZ) | RSA |
|---|---|---|---|---|---|
| B | Boland Championships | Hermanus GC | 7–10 | Ji Sun Kang (KOR) | RSA |

## Americas

| A | Landfall Tradition | Wilmington, NC | 26 | Kimberly Kaufman | USA |
|---|---|---|---|---|---|
| A | Liz Murphey Fall Preview | Athens, GA | 5–7 | Mary Michael Maggio | USA |
| A | Stanford Intercollegiate | Stanford, CA | 19–21 | Kyung Kim | USA |
| B | Betsy Rawls Longhorn Invite | Austin, TX | 28–30 | Camilla Hedberg (ESP) | USA |
| B | Mercedes-Benz Intercollegiate | Knoxville, TN | 12–14 | Paula Reto (RSA) | USA |
| B | Ruth's Chris Tar Heel | Chapel Hill, NC | 12–14 | Isabelle Lendl | USA |
| B | Susie Maxwell Berning Classic | Norman, OK | 15–17 | Chirapat Jao-Javanil (THA) | USA |
| B | The Alamo Invitational | San Antonio, TX | 28–30 | Maribel Lopez (COL) | USA |
| B | The Ping Invitational | Stillwater, OK | 6–8 | Alison Lee | USA |
| B | Windy City Collegiate Championship | Golf, Illinois | 1–2 | April McCoy | USA |
| C | Edean Ihlanfeldt Invitational | Sammamish, WA | 8–10 | Soo-Bin Kim (CAN) | USA |
| C | Lady Pirate Intercollegiate | Greenville, NC | 8–9 | Juliet Vongphaumy | USA |
| C | Las Vegas Collegiate Showdown | Las Vegas, NV | 21–23 | Ally McDonald/ Elizabeth Tong (CAN) | USA |
| C | Palmetto Intercollegiate | Kiawah Island, SC | 28–29 | Maria Jose Benavides | USA |
| C | Rainbow Wahine Invitational | Schofield, HI | 30–31 | Shelby Coyle | USA |
| D | Fed Ex Memphis Womens Intercoll. | Germantown, TN | 22–23 | Natalie Mitchell | USA |
| D | Fighting Camel Fall Classic | Buies Creek, NC | 22–23 | Kaylin Yost | USA |
| D | FIU Pat Bradley Invitational | Bradenton, FL | 21–23 | Meghan MacLaren (ENG) | USA |
| D | Hoosier Fall Invitational | Florence, IN | 13–14 | Lindsay Danielson | USA |
| D | Jackrabbit Fall Invitational | Sioux Falls, SD | S30–O1 | Amy Anderson | USA |
| D | Johnie Imes Invitational | Columbia, MO | 1–2 | Melanie White | USA |
| D | Lady Paladin Invitational | Greenville, SC | 26–28 | Marion Duvernay (FRA) | USA |
| D | UNCG Starmount Fall Classic | Greensboro, NC | 1–2 | Frida Gustafsson-Spang (SWE) | USA |
| D | US Women's Mid-Amateur | San Antonio, TX | 6–11 | Meghan Stasi | USA |

## Asia

| D | Thailand Amateur Open | Panya Indra GC | 16–19 | Benyapa Niphatsophon | THA |
|---|---|---|---|---|---|

| | | | | | |
|---|---|---|---|---|---|
| | **Australasia** | | | | |
| B | Queensland Stroke Play & Amateur | Pacific Harbour G&CC | 21–27 | Hayley Bettencourt | AUS |
| C | Grange Classic | Grange GC | 27–28 | Mun Chin Keh | NZL |
| C | John Jones Steel Harewood Open | Harewood GC | 19–22 | Julianne Alvarez | NZL |
| C | Srixon Int. Junior Girls Classic | Maitland GC | 2–5 | Su-Hyun Oh | AUS |

| | | | | | |
|---|---|---|---|---|---|
| | **Europe** | | | | |
| C | Trophee Rothschild – Internationaux de France | Saint Germain | 12–14 | Franziska Friedrich (GER) | FRA |
| D | Daily Telegraph Junior Championship | Close House, Colt Course | 23–25 | Emily Taylor | ENG |

## November

| | | | | | |
|---|---|---|---|---|---|
| | **Americas** | | | | |
| A | Polo Junior Classic | Palm Beach Gardens, FL | 17–23 | Ariya Jutanugarn (THA) | USA |
| C | Copa Los Andes | Lagunita CC | 21–25 | Shanequa Valentine (USA) | VEN |

| | | | | | |
|---|---|---|---|---|---|
| | **Asia** | | | | |
| D | Albatross Int. Junior Girls C/ship | Jaypee Greens, New Delhi | 20–23 | Benyapa Niphatsophon (THA) | IND |
| D | Johor Amateur Open | Horizon Hills G&CC | 28–30 | Kelly Tan | MAS |
| D | MGA v SGA | Kelab Golf Seri Selangor | 22–24 | Kelly Tan | MAS |
| D | Penang Amateur | Bukit Jawi Golf Resort | 6–8 | Dottie Ardina (PHI) | MAS |

| | | | | | |
|---|---|---|---|---|---|
| | **Australasia** | | | | |
| B | Dunes Medal | The Dunes GC, VIC | 27–30 | Su-Hyun Oh | AUS |
| B | Tasmanian Stroke Play | Royal Hobart GC | 18–20 | Minjee Lee | AUS |
| D | Omanu Classic | Omanu GC, BOP | 17–18 | Mun Chin Keh | NZL |

## December

| | | | | | |
|---|---|---|---|---|---|
| | **Africa** | | | | |
| D | KwaZulu Natal Nomads Girls | Selborne CC | N30–D1 | Magda Kruger | RSA |

| | | | | | |
|---|---|---|---|---|---|
| | **Americas** | | | | |
| B | Junior Orange Bowl International | Coral Gables, FL | 27–39 | Maria Torres (PUR) | USA |
| C | Doral-Publix Junior Classic | Doral Resort, FL | 21–23 | Emily Pedersen (DEN) | USA |
| C | Joanne Winter Arizona Silver Belle | ASU Karsten Golf Course | 28–30 | Hannah Suh | USA |

| | | | | | |
|---|---|---|---|---|---|
| | **Asia** | | | | |
| C | SICC DBS Junior Invitational | Singapore Island CC | 11–13 | Dottie Ardina (PHI) | SIN |
| D | Aaron Baddeley International Junior | Lion Lake CC, Guangzhou | N29–D2 | Yan Jing | CHN |
| D | All India Junior | Kolkata | 3–7 | Aditi Ashok | IND |
| D | All India Ladies Amateur | Tollygunge GC, Kolkata | 10–16 | Gurbani Singh | IND |
| D | TSM Challenge | Glenmarie G&CC | 14–16 | Kelly Tan | MAS |

## Player of the Year Award for Jutanugarn

Thailand's Ariya Jutanugarn, the number two golfer on the World Amateur Golf Ranking, was presented with the American Junior Golf Association Player of the Year Award in November 2012 then went on win AJGA tournament at Palm Beach Gardens, Florida.

## Australasia

| | | | | | |
|---|---|---|---|---|---|
| B | Port Phillip Open Amateur & Victoria Amateur | Kingston Heath, Commonwealth, Yarra Yarra | 14–19 | Su-Hyun Oh | AUS |
| C | New Zealand Interprovincial | St Clair GC | 11–15 | Su-Hyun Oh (AUS) | NZL |
| D | Greg Norman Junior Masters | Palmer Colonial, Palmer Gold Coast GCs | 14–18 | Annie Choi (KOR) | AUS |
| D | Queensland Girls Amateur | Indooroopilly GC | 10–12 | Shelly Shin (KOR) | AUS |

## January

### Americas

| | | | | | |
|---|---|---|---|---|---|
| A | ANNIKA Invitational | Reunion Resort | 18–21 | Bethany Wu | USA |
| B | Copa de las Americas | Doral Resort, FL | 3–6 | Erynne Lee | USA |
| B | Dixie Amateur | Coral Springs, FL | D30–J1 | Isabelle Lendl | USA |
| B | Sally Championship | Ormond Beach, FL | 9–12 | Kelly Shon | USA |
| B | South American Amateur | El Rincon, Bogota | 23–27 | Brooke Mackenzie Henderson (CAN) | COL |
| C | Harder Hall Invitational | Sebring, FL | 3–6 | Erica Popson | USA |
| C | Mexican Amateur | Club de Golf Bellavista | 8–11 | Marijosse Navarro | MEX |
| D | Ione D Jones-Doherty Championship | Coral Ridge CC | 14–19 | Kelsey MacDonald (SCO) | USA |

### Asia

| | | | | | |
|---|---|---|---|---|---|
| C | Philippine Amateur Open | Wack G&CC | 8–10 | Dottie Ardina | PHI |

### Australasia

| | | | | | |
|---|---|---|---|---|---|
| A | Australian Amateur | Commonwealth and Woodlands GCs | 15–20 | Minjee Lee | AUS |
| B | Lake Macquarie Amateur | Belmont GC | 8–11 | Su-Hyun Oh | AUS |
| C | Australian Youth Olympic Festival | Twin Creeks G&CC | 17–20 | Georgia Hall (ENG) | AUS |
| D | Danny Lee Springfield Ladies Open | Springfield GC | 12–13 | Brittney Dryland/Chantelle Cassidy | NZL |

## February

### Africa

| | | | | | |
|---|---|---|---|---|---|
| B | Eastern Cape Amateur | Humewood GC | 11–13 | Nobuhle Dlamini (SWZ) | RSA |
| C | Border Championship | East London GC | 23–24 | Lara Weinstein | RSA |

### Americas

| | | | | | |
|---|---|---|---|---|---|
| A | Allstate Sugar Bowl Intercollegiate | New Orleans, LA | 25–26 | Hayley Davis (ENG) | USA |
| A | NorthropGrumman Regional Challenge | Palos Verdes, CA | 11–13 | Erynne Lee | USA |
| B | Central District Invitational | Parrish, FL | 18–19 | Caroline Powers/Natalie Wille (SWE) | USA |
| B | Hurricane Invitational | Miami, FL | 4–5 | Kelsey Vines | USA |
| B | Seminole Match Up | Tallahassee, FL | 15–17 | Erica Popson/Rocio Sanchez Lobato (ESP) | USA |
| B | Terrapin Challenge | Miami Lakes, FL | 25–26 | Lindsay McGetrick | USA |
| B | UCF Challenge | Sorrento, FL | 10–12 | Briana Mao | USA |
| B | Westbrook Invitational | Peoria, AZ | 24–25 | Gabriela Lopez (MEX) | USA |
| B | Lady Puerto Rico Classic | San Juan, PR | 10–12 | Emily Tubert (usa) | PUR |
| C | Jim West Challenge | Blanco, TX | 17–18 | Iman Ahmad Nordin (MAS) | USA |
| D | Gold Rush by Farmers | Yorba Linda, CA | 11–12 | Raychelle Santos | USA |
| D | Islander Classic | Crp Christi, TX | 25–26 | Danielle Lemek | USA |
| D | Lady Moc Classic | Lakeland, FL | 25–26 | Linnea Johansson (SWE) | USA |
| D | Le Triomphe Collegiate Invite | Broussard, LA | 18–19 | Bao Nghi Ngo (VIE) | USA |
| D | UC Irvine Invitational | Santa Ana, CA | 25–26 | Alice Kim | USA |

## Americas (continued)

| | | | | | |
|---|---|---|---|---|---|
| D | Internacional de Menores Juvenil, Pre-Juvenil | Lima GC | 5–8 | Anneke Strobach | PER |

## Australasia

| | | | | | |
|---|---|---|---|---|---|
| C | Dunedin Stroke Play | St Clair GC, Dunedin | 16–17 | Mun Chin Keh | NZL |
| C | LawnMaster Ladies Classic | Manawatu GC, Manawatu | J31–F3 | Lita Guo | NZL |
| C | Tasmanian Stroke Play | CC Tasmania | 21–24 | Tatiana Wijaya | AUS |
| D | Grant Clements Memorial | Mt Maunganui GC, BOP | 9–10 | Brittney Dryland | NZL |

## Europe

| | | | | | |
|---|---|---|---|---|---|
| B | Portuguese International Amateur | Montado Golf Resort | J30–F2 | Clara Baena (ESP) | POR |
| C | Campeonato Absoluto C. Valenciana | Villaitana | 8–10 | Patricia Sanz | ESP |

# March

## Africa

| | | | | | |
|---|---|---|---|---|---|
| C | KeNako South African World Juniors | Kingswood GC, George | 5–7 | Lara Weinstein | RSA |
| C | Kwazulu-Natal Championship | Royal Durban GC | 3–5 | Nobuhle Dlamini (SWZ) | RSA |
| C | North West Championships | Rustenburg CC, North West Province | 9–10 | Nobuhle Dlamini (SWZ) | RSA |
| C | Western Province Championship | Mowbray GC | 17–19 | Kim Williams | RSA |

## Americas

| | | | | | |
|---|---|---|---|---|---|
| A | Bryan National Collegiate | Brown Summit, NC | 29–31 | Emilie Burger | USA |
| A | Darius Rucker Intercollegiate | Hilton Head, SC | 8–10 | Noemi Jimenez (ESP) | USA |
| A | SunTrust Gator Invite | Gainesville, FL | 15–17 | Chirapat Jao-Javanil (THA) | USA |
| B | Anuenue Spring Break Classic | Kapalua, HI | 25–27 | Grace Na | USA |
| B | Briar's Creek Invitational | Johns Isle, SC | 25–26 | Ashley Armstrong | USA |
| B | Bruin Wave Invitational | Tarzana, CA | 4–5 | Annie Park | USA |
| B | Clover Cup | Mesa, AZ | 9–10 | Kristina Merkle | USA |
| B | Insperity Lady Jaguar Intercollegiate | Augusta, GA | 15–17 | Ashley Armstrong | USA |
| B | Juli Inkster Spartan Invite | San Jose, CA | 4–5 | Mariah Stackhouse | USA |
| B | LSU Classic | Baton Rouge, LA | 22–24 | Emily Tubert | USA |
| B | Mountain View Collegiate | Tucson, AZ | 15–16 | Krista Puisite (LAT) | USA |
| C | Dr Donnis Thompson Invitational | Honolulu, HI | 12–13 | Manon Gidali (FRA) | USA |
| C | Goodman Networks Junior at Traditions | Traditions Golf Club at Texas A&M | 28–31 | Karen Chung | USA |
| C | JMU Eagle Landing Invite | Orange Park, FL | 8–10 | Frida Gustafsson-Spang (SWE) | USA |
| C | Kiawah Island Intercollegiate | Kiawah, SC | 3–5 | Julia Neumann (GER) | USA |
| C | Purdue Mount Vintage Invite | North Augusta, SC | 9–10 | Casey Kennedy | USA |
| C | TaylorMade-Adidas Junior at Innisbrook | Innisbrook Resort & Golf Club | 28–31 | Brogan McKinnon (CAN) | USA |
| C | Winn Grips Heather Farr Classic | Longbow GC | 28–31 | Krystal Quihuis | USA |
| D | BYU at Entrada Classic | St George, UT | 18–19 | Kimberly Dinh | USA |
| D | John Kirk-Panther Intercollegiate | Stockbridge, GA | 25–26 | Kim Bradbury (ENG) | USA |

## Big boost for Bethany

Sixteen-year-old Bethany Wu from Diamond Bar, California madw a significant leap on the World Amateur Golf Ranking in February following a record victory in the ANNIKA Invitational held at the Reunion Resort's Watson Course in Orlando, Florida. In this, her third American Junior Golf Association victory, Bethany finished three shots ahead of Denmark's Emily Pedersen and Karen Chung of the United States and climbed 41 places to world number 46.

| D | Peggy Kirk Bell Invitational | Winter Springs, FL | 4–5 | Linnea Johansson (SWE) | USA |
|---|---|---|---|---|---|
| D | Rio Verde Invitational | Rio Verde, AZ | 9–10 | Savana Bezdicek | USA |
| D | UALR Classic | Hot Springs, AR | 25–26 | Georgina Mundy (ENG)* | USA |
| D | University of Cincinnati Spring Invite | Crystal River, FL | 22–24 | Megan Kiley | USA |
| D | Abierto del Centro | Cordoba GC | 27–30 | Delfina Acosta | ARG |
| D | Copa Donovan | San Andres GC | 7–10 | Carolina Heredia Lozano | COL |

### Asia

| C | Thailand Amateur Open | Bangsai CC | 20–22 | Sherman Santiwiwattanapong | THA |
|---|---|---|---|---|---|
| D | Faldo Series Asia Grand Final | Mission Hills GC | 13–15 | Ssu-Chia Cheng (TPE) | CHN |
| D | TrueVisions International Junior # 12 | Windsor Park GC | 26–29 | Dottie Ardina (PHI) | THA |
| D | WWWExpress-DHL Amateur | Canlubang G&CC | 13–15 | Dottie Ardina | PHI |

### Australasia

| B | New Zealand Stroke Play | Paraparaumu Beach GC | 21–24 | Chantelle Cassidy | NZL |
|---|---|---|---|---|---|
| B | Riversdale Cup | Melbourne, VIC | 7–10 | Grace Lennon | AUS |
| C | Western Australian Amateur | Freemantle GC | 13–17 | Minjee Lee | AUS |
| D | South Australian Amateur | Tea Tree Gully, Flagstaff Hill, The Grange, Adelaide | 18–24 | Cyna Rodriguez (PHI) | AUS |

### Europe

| A | Spanish Ladies Amateur | Pula Golf | F27–M3 | Emily Pedersen (DEN) | ESP |
|---|---|---|---|---|---|
| B | European Nations Cup Individual | Sotogrande | 13–16 | Patricia Sanz | ESP |
| C | Campeonato de Madrid | El Encin | 15–17 | Nuria Iturrios | ESP |
| C | France v England Under 21 | Saint Cloud GC | 27–27 | Nuria Iturrios (ESP) | FRA |
| C | Italian International Ladies Amateur Championship | Castelgandolfo CC | 7–10 | Chloe Leurquin (BEL) | ITA |

# April

### Africa

| B | South African Stroke Play | Pretoria CC | 14–16 | Nobuhle Dlamini (SWZ) | RSA |
|---|---|---|---|---|---|
| C | Free State & Northern Cape Amateur | Clarens, Free State | 27–28 | Nicole Garcia | RSA |
| C | SA Girls Rose Bowl Stroke Play Championship | Selborne GC, Kwazulu-Natal | 2–3 | Catherine Lau* | RSA |

### Americas

| A | PAC-12 Championship | Valencia, CA | 22–24 | Annie Park | USA |
|---|---|---|---|---|---|
| A | PING – ASU Invitational | Tempe, AZ | 12–14 | Emma Talley | USA |
| A | SEC Championship | Birmingham, AL | 19–21 | Stephanie Meadow (IRL) | USA |
| B | ACC Championship | Greensboro, NC | 19–21 | Brittany Altomare | USA |
| B | Big 12 Championship | Rhodes, IA | 19–21 | Lauren Taylor (ENG) | USA |
| B | Big Ten Championship | French Lick, IN | 26–28 | Paula Reto (RSA) | USA |
| B | Lady Buckeye Spring Invite | Columbus, OH | 20–21 | Laura Gonzalez-Escallon (BEL) | USA |
| B | Rebel Intercollegiate | Oxford, MS | 5–7 | Jessica Alexander | USA |
| B | SDSU Farms Invitational | Rancho Santa Fe, CA | M31–A2 | Sophia Popov (GER) | USA |
| B | SMU Dallas Athletic Club Invitational | Dallas, TX | 5–7 | Julie Yang (KOR) | USA |
| B | Web.com Intercollegiate | Ponte Vedra Beach, FL | 8–9 | Paula Reto (RSA) | USA |
| C | Big East Championship | Orlando, FL | 21–23 | Lindsey Weaver/Talia Campbell | USA |
| C | Challenge at Onion Creek | Austin, TX | 1–2 | Han Wu/Krista Puisite (LAT) | USA |
| C | C-USA Championship | Gulf Shores, AL | 22–24 | Nicoline Skaug (NOR) | USA |
| C | Fresno State Lexus Classic | Fresno, CA | 15–16 | Simone Hoey | USA |
| C | Pinehurst Challenge | Pinehurst, NC | 1–2 | Caroline Lovette | USA |
| C | UNCW Seahawk Classic | Wallace, NC | 6–7 | Fanny Cnops (BEL) | USA |
| C | WAC Championship | Mesa, AZ | 22–24 | Tonje Daffinrud (NOR) | USA |

## Americas (continued)

| | | | | | |
|---|---|---|---|---|---|
| C | South American Junior Championship | Asuncion GC | 8–14 | Sofia Garcia | PAR |
| D | Big South Championship | Ninety-Six, SC | 14–16 | Brittany Henderson (CAN) | USA |
| D | Big West Championships | San Luis Obispo, CA | 21–23 | Demi Runas | USA |
| D | Florida Blue SSC Championship | Bradenton, FL | 15–16 | Liliana Cammisa (ARG) | USA |
| D | HBU Husky Invitational | Surgarland, TX | 1–2 | Julia Roth (SWE) | USA |
| D | Hoya Invitational | Beallsville, MD | 8–9 | Harin Lee (KOR) | USA |
| D | Indiana Invitational | Bloomington, IN | 13–14 | Elizabeth Tong (CAN) | USA |
| D | Mountain West Conference Championship | Mirage, CA | 25–27 | Manon De Roey (BEL) | USA |
| D | SoCon Championship | Hilton Head, SC | 14–16 | Agathe Sauzon (FRA) | USA |
| D | Sun Belt Conference Tournament | Muscle Shoals, AL | 15–17 | Meghan MacLaren (ENG) | USA |
| D | West Coast Conference Championship | Bremerton, WA | 15–17 | Grace Na | USA |
| D | Wyoming Cowgirl Classic | Chandler, AZ | 8–10 | Hayley Young | USA |
| D | Arturo Calle Colombian Open | CC Pereira | 25–28 | Maria Alejandra Hoyos | COL |

## Asia

| | | | | | |
|---|---|---|---|---|---|
| B | Queen Sirikit Cup | Sunrise G&CC | 17–19 | Supamas Sangchan (THA) | TPE |
| D | Sarawak Amateur | Sibu Sarawak | 26–28 | Kelly Tan | MAS |

## Australasia

| | | | | | |
|---|---|---|---|---|---|
| C | Australian Girls' Amateur | Mount Lawley GC | 10–12 | Minjee Lee | AUS |
| C | New Zealand Amateur Championship | Manawatu GC | 24–27 | Julianne Alvarez | NZL |
| C | North Island Stroke Play | Poverty Bay GC | 4–7 | Mun Chin Keh | NZL |
| C | Rene Erichsen Salver | Glenelg GC | 4–7 | Minjee Lee | AUS |
| C | WA 72 Hole Stroke Play | Lake Karrinyup CC | 22–24 | Hannah Green | AUS |
| D | Australian Girls Interstate Matches | Western Australian GC, Perth | 14–16 | Hannah Green | AUS |
| F | New Plymouth Open | New Plymouth | 11–14 | Hanna Seifert | NZL |

## Europe

| | | | | | |
|---|---|---|---|---|---|
| A | Internationaux De France Juniors (Trophée Esmond) | St Cloud | M28–A1 | Laura Funfstuck (GER) | FRA |
| B | Helen Holm Scottish Open Stroke Play | Troon Portland/Old Course Troon | 26–28 | Olivia Winning (ENG) | SCO |
| C | Copa Andalucia | Real Club de Golf Guadalmina | 12–14 | Ana Pelaez Trivino | ESP |
| C | Coupe de France Dames | St Germain | 19–21 | Elodie Bridenne | FRA |
| C | German Match Play | Frankfurter GC | 25–28 | Karolin Lampert | GER |
| D | Interprovincial Matches | Castle Dargan GC | 3–5 | Karolin Lampert (GER) | IRL |
| D | Italian Stroke Play Championship – I Goldschmid Trophy | Verona GC | 22–25 | Roberta Liti | ITA |
| D | R&A Foundation Scholars Tournament | Eden & Old GCs, St Andrews | 8–9 | Paula Grant (IRL) | SCO |

## May

## Africa

| | | | | | |
|---|---|---|---|---|---|
| B | Gauteng Amateur Championship | Randpark GC | 5–8 | Nobuhle Dlamini (SWZ) | RSA |
| B | WGSA 72 Hole Team Championship – Individual | Maccauvlei GC | 27–29 | Nobuhle Dlamini (SWZ) | RSA |
| D | Regional All-Africa Challenge Trophy | Centurion CC, Pretoria | 14–16 | Magda Kruger | RSA |

# For further information, visit www.RandA.org/wagr

## Americas

| | | | | | |
|---|---|---|---|---|---|
| A | NCAA D1 Central Regional | Norman, OK | 9–11 | Ally McDonald | USA |
| A | NCAA D1 East Regional | Auburn, AL | 9–11 | Stephanie Meadow (IRL) | USA |
| A | NCAA D1 West Regional | Stanford, CA | 9–11 | Annie Park/Paula Reto (RSA) | USA |
| B | Thunderbird International Junior | Scottsdale, AZ | 25–27 | Nicole Morales | USA |
| C | Scott Robertson Memorial | Roanoke, VA | 19–19 | Gabriella Then | USA |
| D | NCAA D2 Super Region 2 | Lakeland, FL | 5–7 | Annie Dulman | USA |
| D | Torneo Final Del Ranking De Jugadores | Club Campos De Golf Las Praderas De Lujan | 24–26 | Delfina Acosta | ARG |

## Asia

| | | | | | |
|---|---|---|---|---|---|
| B | SLGA Amateur Open | Laguna National G&CC | 28–30 | Princess Mary Superal (PHI) | SIN |
| C | Malaysian Amateur Open | Kuala Lumpur G&CC | 21–23 | Kelly Tan | MAS |
| D | TGA-CAT Junior World Championship | Naraihill G&CC | 2–5 | Ornicha Konsunthea | THA |

## Australasia

| | | | | | |
|---|---|---|---|---|---|
| B | Australian Interstate Team Matches | Royal Hobart GC | A30–M3 | Akiho Sato (JPN) | AUS |
| C | Muriwai Open | Muriwai GC, Auckland | 9–12/ | Mun Chin Keh | NZL |
| D | NT Amateur | Alice Springs GC | 10–12 | Tatiana Wijaya | AUS |

## Europe

| | | | | | |
|---|---|---|---|---|---|
| B | German International Amateur | GC Ulem e.V | 23–26 | Emma Broze (FRA) | GER |
| C | DGU Elite Tour Damer 1 | Asserbo GC | 11–12 | Caroline Nistrup | DEN |
| C | Spanish International Stroke Play | Las Colinas | 10–12 | Luna Sobron | ESP |
| C | Welsh Open Stroke Play | The Vale Resort – National Course | 4–5 | Amy Boulden | WAL |
| D | Coupe Didier Illouz | Racing Club de France | 18–20 | Marion Veysseyre | FRA |
| D | English Ladies Close Amateur | Kings Norton GC | 14–16 | Sarah-Jane Boyd | ENG |
| D | Irish Open Amateur Stroke Play | Castle GC | 25–26 | Meghan MacLaren (ENG) | IRL |
| D | Welsh Close Championship | Nefyn GC | 19–21 | Becky Harries | WAL |

# June

## Africa

| | | | | | |
|---|---|---|---|---|---|
| C | South African Girls | Orkney GC | 23–25 | Ji Sun Kang (KOR) | RSA |

## Americas

| | | | | | |
|---|---|---|---|---|---|
| A | US Amateur Public Links | Jimmie Austin OU GC, Norman, OK | 17–22 | Lauren Diaz-Yi | USA |
| B | Rolex Junior Championship | Dalhousie GC | 11–14 | Alison Lee | USA |
| B | Western Amateur | Dayton CC | 17–22 | Ashlan Ramsey | USA |
| C | BC Amateur | Pitt Meadows Golf Club | 25–28 | Cassy Isagawa (USA) | CAN |
| C | Eastern Amateur Championship | Kingsmill Resort, VA | 11–13 | Ashlan Ramsey | USA |
| C | Porter Cup | Niagara Falls CC | 12–14 | Casie Cathrea | USA |
| D | Club Corp Mission Hills Desert Junior | Mission Hills, CA | 18–20 | Alison Lee | USA |

# Big moves for Boyd, Khang, Liu and Then

May was a big month for England's Sarah-Jane Boyd and the USA's Megan Khang, Mika Liu and Gabriella Then. Then moved 449 places to world number 642 on the WAGR table while Liu climbed 331 places to 536. Boyd improveed her rankings by 262 places this week to reach 426th position and Khang Khang jumped 242 places to world number 269.

## Americas (continued)

| | | | | | |
|---|---|---|---|---|---|
| D | Under Armour – Steve Marino Championship | Weston Hills CC – Tour 17–20 Course | | Dylan Kim | USA |
| D | Abierto de Golf Ciudad de Ibague | Club Campestre de Ibague | 13–16/ | Maria Alejandra Hoyos | COL |

## Asia

| | | | | | |
|---|---|---|---|---|---|
| C | Santi Cup | Sherwood Hills GC | 27–30 | Benyapa Niphatsophon (THA) | PHI |
| D | Japan Amateur | Okayama GC | 25–29 | Haruka Morita | JPN |
| D | Kartini Cup | Sherwood Hills GC | 27–30 | Parinda Phokan (THA) | PHI |
| D | Philippine Junior Amateur Closed | Sherwood Hills GC | 6–9 | Regina De Guzman | PHI |
| D | Southern India Ladies Amateur | KGA, Bangalore | 10–12 | Gauri Monga | IND |

## Europe

| | | | | | |
|---|---|---|---|---|---|
| B | Campeonato de Espana Amateur | La Coruna | M30–J2 | Ainhoa Olarra | ESP |
| B | German Girls Open | GC ST Leon-Rot | 7–9 | Emily Kristine Pedersen (DEN) | GER |
| B | Vagliano Trophy | Chantilly GC | 28–29 | Emily Kristine Pedersen (DEN) | FRA |
| C | Danish International Championship | Silkeborg GC | M31–J2 | Nicole Broch Larsen | DEN |
| C | Irish Close Championship | Ballybunion | 20–23 | Paula Grant | IRL |
| C | St Rule Trophy | New/Old GCs, St Andrews | 1–2 | Ailsa Summers | SCO |
| C | Swiss International Championship | GC Lausanne | 28–30 | Ursa Orehek (SLO) | SUI |
| D | Belgian National Stroke Play | Golf de Mean | 23–30 | Manon De Roey | BEL |
| D | DM Hulspil | Varde GC | 21–23 | Henriette Nielsen | DEN |
| D | JSM Slag Flickor | Vasatorps Golf Club | 28–30 | Linn Andersson | SWE |
| D | Team Rudersdal Open | Fureso GC | 29–30 | Olafia Kristinsdottir (ISL) | DEN |
| D | Umberto Agnelli Trophy | Royal Park G&CC | M31–J2 | Bianca Fabrizio | ITA |

# July

## Africa

| | | | | | |
|---|---|---|---|---|---|
| B | Gauteng North Championship | Centurion CC | Jn30–Jy3 | Lara Weinstein | RSA |
| B | South African Womens Amateur Championship | Milnerton GC | 7–10 | Kim Williams | RSA |

## Americas

| | | | | | |
|---|---|---|---|---|---|
| A | Canadian Amateur Championship | Beloeri GC | 23–26 | Brooke Mackenzie Henderson | CAN |
| A | North & South Amateur | Pinehurst CC | 15–20 | Ally McDonald | USA |
| B | Rolex Tournament of Champions | Lancaster CC, PA | 9–12 | Alison Lee | USA |
| B | TRANS National Amateur | Truckee, CA | 9–12 | Hannah Suh | USA |
| B | US Junior Championship | Sycamore Hills GC, IN | 22–27 | Gabriella Then | USA |
| B | Wyndham Cup | The Bridges at Rancho Santa Fe, CA | 16–18 | Gabriella Then | USA |
| C | Callaway Junior World Championship | Torrey Pines | 16–19 | Mariel Galdiano | USA |
| D | Judson Collegiate Invitational | Country Club of Roswell | 13–15 | Maribel Lopez (COL) | USA |
| D | Pacific Northwest Amateur | Wine Valley GC, Walla Walla, WA | 15–19 | Jennifer Ha (CAN) | USA |
| D | San Diego Junior Masters | Sycuan Resort, Oak Glen | 8–10 | Princess Mary Superal (PHI) | USA |

## Asia

| | | | | | |
|---|---|---|---|---|---|
| D | China Amateur | CGA Nanshan International Training Center | 25–283 | Michelle Koh (MAS) | CHN |
| D | KB Financial Group Cup | Century 21 CC | 9–11 | Han-Sol Ji | KOR |
| D | Neighbors Trophy | Nagano | 24–26 | Asuka Kashiwabara | JPN |

## Australasia

| | | | | | |
|---|---|---|---|---|---|
| C | Ruth Middleton Classic | Matamata, Waikato | 13–14 | Chantelle Cassidy | NZL |

# For further information, visit www.RandA.org/wagr

## Europe

| A | European Amateur Team C\ship | Fulford GC | 9–13 | Wendy O'Connell (AUS)* | ENG |
|---|---|---|---|---|---|
| B | European Girls Team Championship | Linkopings GK | 9–13 | Wendy O'Connell (AUS)* | SWE |
| C | Dutch Junior Open | Toxandria GC | 17–20 | Lauren Taylor (ENG) | NED |
| C | European Young Masters | Hamburger GC | 25–27 | Cavadonga Sanjuan (ESP) | GER |
| D | Biarritz Cup | Golf de Biarritz | 11–14 | Emilie Alonso | FRA |
| D | Grand Prix de Chiberta | Golf de Chiberta Anglet | 4–7 | Celia Barquin (ESP) | FRA |
| D | Grand Prix des Landes | Golf Club D'Hossegor | 18–21 | Silvia Banon (ESP) | FRA |
| D | Scottish Junior Open Stroke Play | Inverness GC | 24–26 | Jessica Meek | SCO |

## August

### Africa

| C | Ekurhuleni Stroke Play Championship | Ebotse G and CE | 11–12 | Bertine Strauss | RSA |
|---|---|---|---|---|---|

### Americas

| A | PING Junior Solheim Cup | The Inverness GC | 12–14 | Gioia Carpinelli (SUI) | USA |
|---|---|---|---|---|---|
| C | Junior PGA Championship | Trump National GC, Washington DC | J30–A2 | Amy Lee | USA |
| D | AJGA Junior Challenge | Oak Valley GC | J29–A1 | Daniela Uy (PHI) | USA |
| D | Georgia Amateur | Glen Arven CC | J30–A1 | Ashlan Ramsey | USA |
| D | Royale Cup Canadian Junior C/ship | Cherry Downs G&CC, ON | J30–A2 | Maddie Szeryk (USA) | CAN |
| D | Torneo Aficionado Segunda Semana | Los Arrayanes | 1–4 | Maribel Lopez | COL |

### Asia

| C | Asian Youth Games | Zhongshan International GC | 18–20 | Clare Legaspi (PHI) | CHN |
|---|---|---|---|---|---|
| D | Japan Junior Championship | Kasumigaseki CC | 21–23 | Kotone Hori | JPN |
| D | Ryo Ishikawa World Junior Inv. | Royal Meadow Stadium | 26–30 | Ji-young Park (KOR) | JPN |

### Australasia

| C | Bay of Plenty Open | Whakatane GC | 2–4 | Wenyung Keh | NZL |
|---|---|---|---|---|---|
| C | Cambridge Classic | Cambridge | 9–11 | Mun Chin Keh | NZL |

### Europe

| B | English Women's Open Stroke Play | Mannings Heath GC | 6–8 | Amy Boulden (WAL) | ENG |
|---|---|---|---|---|---|
| B | Girls' British Open Amateur C/ship | Fairhaven GC | 12–16 | Yan Jing (CHN) | ENG |
| B | Ladies' British Open Amateur Stroke Play | Prestwick GC | 21–23 | Yan Jing (CHN) | SCO |
| C | Annika Invitational Europe | Landskrona GK | 6–9 | Malene Krolboll (DEN) | SWE |
| C | Championnat de France Coupe Gaveau | Les Aisses | 21–25 | Marion Veysseyre | FRA |
| C | Finnish Amateur | Helsingin GC | 15–17 | Anna Backman* | FIN |
| C | Harder German Junior Girls | Golfclub Heddesheim | 6–8 | Csilla Lajtai Rozsa (HUN) | GER |
| D | Belgian International Amateur | Royal Antwerp GC | J31–A3 | Laura Gonzalez-Escallon | BEL |
| D | German National Girls | GC Hannover | 23–25 | Amina Wolf | GER |
| D | Girls' Home International Matches | St Annes Old Links | 7–9 | Amina Wolf (GER) | ENG |
| D | JSM Match Play | Hills GC | 1–3 | Emma Svensson | SWE |

## Season 2013–2014

The R&A Women's World Amateur Golf Ranking season runs from September until the following August when the Mark McCormack Medal is presented following the US Women's Amateur Championship. Results for the remainder of the calendar year will be included in the following year's edition of The R&A Golfer's Handbook.

# European Amateur Ranking 2012–2013

Spanish players dominated the European Amateur Ranking in 2012–2013 with 16 entries in the top 100. Sweden and France were second with 14 places each and England was third with 13. The European Rankings are extracted from WAGR and are finalised at the same time.

| # | Name | | Divisor | Points | # | Name | | Divisor | Points |
|---|------|---|---------|--------|---|------|---|---------|--------|
| 1 | Stephanie Meadfow | IRL | 49 | 1,545.66 | 51 | Alexandra Peters | ENG | 39 | 955.13 |
| 2 | Emily Kristine Pedersen | DEN | 55 | 1,426.29 | 52 | Emily Penttila | FIN | 32 | 952.86 |
| 3 | Georgia Hall | ENG | 37 | 1,388.51 | 53 | Amber Ratcliffe | ENG | 37 | 947.30 |
| 4 | Noemi Jimenez | ESP | 57 | 1,244.08 | 54 | Justine Dreher | FRA | 43 | 946.80 |
| 5 | Natalia Escuriola | ESP | 51 | 1,230.39 | 55 | Sanna Nuutinen | FIN | 56 | 945.54 |
| 6 | Sophia Popov | GER | 46 | 1,229.35 | 56 | Virginia Elena Carta | ITA | 36 | 944.10 |
| 7 | Laura Funfstuck | GER | 38 | 1,215.13 | 57 | Emma Henrikson | SWE | 39 | 942.95 |
| 8 | Karolin Lampert | GER | 34 | 1,206.62 | 58 | Katerina Ruzickova | CZE | 35 | 934.29 |
| 9 | Linnea Strom | SWE | 50 | 1,198.00 | 59 | Leticia Ras-Anderica | ESP | 37 | 933.78 |
| 10 | Nanna Madsen | DEN | 49 | 1,193.37 | 60 | Eilidh Briggs | SCO | 54 | 932.18 |
| 11 | Celine Boutier | FRA | 51 | 1,176.96 | 61 | Anyssia Herbaut | FRA | 51 | 929.41 |
| 12 | Bronte Law | ENG | 32 | 1,161.72 | 62 | Emma Broze | FRA | 45 | 926.67 |
| 13 | Madelene Sagstrom | SWE | 39 | 1,159.62 | 63 | Marta Sanz | ESP | 48 | 926.56 |
| 14 | Laura Gonzalez-Escallon | BEL | 51 | 1,159.31 | 64 | Nicoline Skaug | NOR | 49 | 925.00 |
| 15 | Luna Sobron | ESP | 46 | 1,141.30 | 65 | Julia Roth | SWE | 32 | 919.53 |
| 16 | Chloe Williams | WAL | 30 | 1,138.75 | 66 | Clara Baena | ESP | 35 | 918.57 |
| 17 | Laetitia Beck | ISR | 33 | 1,129.55 | 67 | Olivia Cowan | GER | 35 | 910.00 |
| 18 | Caroline Nistrup | DEN | 38 | 1,113.16 | 68 | Bethan Popel | ENG | 28 | 908.93 |
| 19 | Charlotte Thomas | ENG | 47 | 1,104.12 | 69 | Ha Rang Lee | ESP | 48 | 903.12 |
| 20 | Hayley Davis | ENG | 47 | 1,079.26 | 70 | Camilla Hedberg | ESP | 46 | 900.00 |
| 21 | Tonje Daffinrud | NOR | 39 | 1,067.31 | 71 | Becky Harries | WAL | 35 | 900.00 |
| 22 | Matilda Castren | FIN | 45 | 1,053.33 | 72 | Andrea Vilarasau | ESP | 50 | 898.00 |
| 23 | Roberta Liti | ITA | 50 | 1,047.00 | 73 | Alexandra Bonetti | FRA | 41 | 896.95 |
| 24 | Ainhoa Olarra | ESP | 35 | 1,035.00 | 74 | Linnea Johansson | SWE | 23 | 888.39 |
| 25 | Krista Puisite | LAT | 53 | 1,031.21 | 75 | Gabriella Wahl | GER | 38 | 878.95 |
| 26 | Gabriella Cowley | ENG | 47 | 1,031.12 | 76 | Nicola Rossler | GER | 33 | 876.89 |
| 27 | Jenny Haglund | SWE | 32 | 1,011.33 | 77 | Alison Knowles | ENG | 26 | 872.32 |
| 28 | Anne van Dam | NED | 39 | 1,007.69 | 78 | Louise Ridderstrom | SWE | 46 | 872.28 |
| 29 | Ines Lescudier | FRA | 41 | 1,006.71 | 79 | Emma Svensson | SWE | 40 | 870.62 |
| 30 | Leona Maguire | IRL | 26 | 1,004.46 | 80 | Sarah-Jane Boyd | ENG | 38 | 868.42 |
| 31 | Manon Gidali | FRA | 42 | 1,003.57 | 81 | Silvia Banon | ESP | 36 | 865.97 |
| 32 | Malene Krolboll | DEN | 42 | 1,001.19 | 82 | Manon Molle | FRA | 45 | 861.67 |
| 33 | Alejandra Pasarin | ESP | 40 | 1,000.00 | 83 | Manon De Roey | BEL | 48 | 859.90 |
| 34 | Eva Gilly | FRA | 50 | 999.33 | 84 | Celia Mansour | FRA | 46 | 859.78 |
| 35 | Frida Gustafsson-Spang | SWE | 38 | 997.37 | 85 | Johanna Bjork | SWE | 30 | 856.67 |
| 36 | Mathilda Cappeliez | FRA | 46 | 996.56 | 86 | Katerina Vlasinova | CZE | 49 | 856.63 |
| 37 | Paula Grant | IRL | 34 | 993.38 | 87 | Leslie Cloots | BEL | 64 | 856.25 |
| 38 | Katja Pogacar | SLO | 34 | 991.91 | 88 | Ariane Provot | FRA | 42 | 855.36 |
| 39 | Csilla Lajtai Rozsa | HUN | 36 | 987.50 | 89 | Elin Arvidsson | SWE | 45 | 851.11 |
| 40 | Sarah Schober | AUT | 31 | 983.06 | 90 | Elizabeth Mallett | ENG | 36 | 851.04 |
| 41 | Jessica Vasilic | SWE | 31 | 980.65 | 91 | Rachael Watton | SCO | 39 | 850.00 |
| 42 | Lisa Maguire | IRL | 28 | 980.36 | 92 | Marta Perez Sanmartin | ESP | 32 | 846.88 |
| 43 | Vicki Troeltsch | GER | 28 | 980.36 | 93 | Antonia Scherer | GER | 38 | 846.05 |
| 44 | Meghan MacLaren | ENG | 49 | 980.10 | 94 | Henriette Nielsen | DEN | 39 | 844.55 |
| 45 | Nuria Iturrios | ESP | 30 | 978.33 | 95 | Sian Evans | ENG | 40 | 844.38 |
| 46 | Celia Barquin | ESP | 32 | 974.61 | 96 | Laura Lonardi | ITA | 50 | 841.50 |
| 47 | Gemma Dryburgh | SCO | 41 | 974.09 | 97 | Rocio Sanchez Lobato | ESP | 40 | 840.62 |
| 48 | Krista Bakker | FIN | 42 | 958.93 | 98 | Martina Edberg | SWE | 27 | 839.29 |
| 49 | Fanny Cnops | BEL | 43 | 957.85 | 99 | Cajsa Persson | SWE | 38 | 837.50 |
| 50 | Shannon Aubert | FRA | 43 | 957.56 | 100 | Marion Veysseyre | FRA | 48 | 836.98 |

For the full European Amateur Rankings, visit www.ega-golf.ch

# Major Amateur Championships 2013

## Ladies British Open Amateur Championship (inaugurated 1893)

*Machynys Peninsula* June 11–12

### Georgia clinches title victory in the best possible way with her first hole in one

Georgia Hall the 17 year old from Remedy Oaks who won the British Girl's Championship last year at Tenby is the 2013 British Ladies Amateur Open champion. She became the first to hold both titles concurrently when, helped by a hole in one, she came from behind to beat 18-year-old Madrid student Luna Sobron.

"To get my first hole in one and win the British championship is a dream come true," said Hall. I was behind all the way in the but I never gave up."

After a final played at windswept Machynys Golf and Country Club near Llanelli she took the title by one hole to continue the run of British winners – Kelly Tidy took the title in 2010 at Ganton, Lauren Taylor triumphed at Royal Portrush in 2011 and Stephanie Meadow was successful in 2012.

With winds gusting between 30 and 35 miles per hour playing conditions were far from easy on the final day and Hall found herself two down after eleven holes. She battled back to square matters at the 16th then pulled out a 9-iron at the 154 yards 17th and holed it to go one up for the first time. After a half at the last Hall was champion.

In her semi-final Hall was four under par in a nine birdie thriller with Noemi Jimenez from Spain. Hall won 3 and 1 against the Spaniard who is no relation to Miguel Angel Jiménez, the European Ryder Cup player.

Sobron beat the 2012 German Girls and Spanish Open champion Karolin Lampert from Germany putting in a storming finish to come from two down to win by one hole. Sobron won the 14th, 15th with a birdie and 16th to earn her final spot against Hall.

World No 2 Su-Hyun Oh, the South Korean born Australian who has a handicap of plus 7 and Nanna Madsen from Denmark led the qualifiers on 141 but Oh edged her for top seed. Curiously none of the top eight seeds survived the third round, Oh falling victim to Lisa Maguire from the Slieve Russell Club in Ireland.

### Stroke Play Qualifying (64 go to First Round):

| | | | | |
|---|---|---|---|---|
| Sally Watson (Elie & Earlsferry Ladies) | 72-69—141 | | Emily Pedersen (DEN) | 70-78—148 |
| Su-Hyun Oh (AUS) | 71-70—141 | | Alessandra Braida (ITA) | 77-72—149 |
| Nanna Madsen (DEN) | 69-72—141 | | Rachael Watton (Mortonhall) | 77-72—149 |
| Hayley Davis (Ferndown) | 71-72—143 | | Ines Lescudier (FRA) | 77-72—149 |
| Manon Gidali (FRA) | 72-72—144 | | Nuria Iturrios (ESP) | 76-73—149 |
| Amber Ratcliffe (Royal Cromer) | 71-73—144 | | Stephanie Meadow (Royal Portrush) | 76-73—149 |
| Celine Boutier (FRA) | 72-73—145 | | Linnea Strom (SWE) | 75-74—149 |
| Meghan Maclaren (Wellingborough) | 70-75—145 | | Georgia Hall (Remedy Oak) | 74-75—149 |
| Linnea Johansson (SWE) | 70-75—145 | | Jenny Haglund (SWE) | 74-75—149 |
| Gabriella Cowley (Brockett Hall) | 74-72—146 | | Lisa Maguire (Slieve Russell) | 71-78—149 |
| Bethany Garton (R. Lytham & St Annes) | 74-72—146 | | Shannon Aubert (FRA) | 76-74—150 |
| Harang Lee (ESP) | 73-73—146 | | Noemi Jimenez (ESP) | 76-74—150 |
| Leslie Cloots (BEL) | 75-72—147 | | Ariane Provot (FRA) | 75-75—150 |
| Alexandra Peters (Notts Ladies) | 74-73—147 | | Karolin Lampert (GER) | 74-76—150 |
| Anne Van Dam (NED) | 73-74—147 | | Lauren Taylor (Woburn) | 74-76—150 |
| Leona Maguire (Slieve Russell) | 72-75—147 | | Csilla Lajtai Rózsa (HUN) | 74-76—150 |
| Caroline Nistrup (DEN) | 68-79—147 | | Abi Laker (Frilford Heath) | 73-77—150 |
| Rachael Goodall (Heswall) | 78-70—148 | | Natalia Escuriola (ESP) | 80-71—151 |
| Sophia Popov (GER) | 77-71—148 | | Silvia Bañon (ESP) | 77-74—151 |
| Laura Fünfstück (GER) | 76-72—148 | | Eilidh Briggs (Kilmacolm) | 77-74—151 |
| Emma Henrikson (SWE) | 76-72—148 | | Abbey Gittings (Walmley) | 76-75—151 |
| Sanna Nuutinen (FIN) | 76-72—148 | | Tonje Daffinrud (NOR) | 74-77—151 |
| Ileen Domela Nieuwenhuis (NED) | 75-73—148 | | Marta Sanz (ESP) | 80-72—152 |

Ladies British Amateur Championship *continued*

| | | | |
|---|---|---|---|
| Sarah-Jane Boyd (Truro) | 78-74—152 | Mathilda Cappeliez (FRA) | 80-77—157 |
| Laura Lonardi (ITA) | 77-75—152 | Manon De Roey (BEL) | 79-78—157 |
| Roberta Liti (ITA) | 77-75—152 | Margaux Vanmol (BEL) | 78-79—157 |
| Jessica Meek (Carnoustie Ladies') | 77-75—152 | Olafia Kristinsdottir (ISL) | 77-80—157 |
| Adriana Brent (AUS) | 76-76—152 | Marlies Krenn (AUT) | 72-85—157 |
| Anyssia Herbaut (FRA) | 76-76—152 | Gemma Bradbury (Cottrell Park) | 79-79—158 |
| Sophie Keech (Lyme Regis) | 76-76—152 | Isabella Deilert (SWE) | 77-81—158 |
| Emma Tayler (Saunton) | 76-76—152 | Sophie Powell (Stockport) | 77-81—158 |
| Emma Nilsson (SWE) | 75-77—152 | Frida Gustafsson-Spang (SWE) | 77-81—158 |
| Emma Carberry (Highwoods) | 75-77—152 | Jessica Bradley (Tiverton) | 76-82—158 |
| Camilla Vik (NOR) | 75-77—152 | Amy Boulden (Conwy) | 74-84—158 |
| Luna Sobron (ESP)n | 75-77—152 | Eva Saulnier (FRA) | 85-74—159 |
| Lauren Hillier (Newport) | 74-78—152 | Anja Purgauer (AUT) | 84-75—159 |
| Nicoline Engstroem Skaug (NOR) | 74-78—152 | Fanny Cnops (BEL) | 83-76—159 |
| Justine Dreher (FRA) | 72-80—152 | Quirine Eijkenboom (GER) | 80-79—159 |
| Grace Lennon (AUS) | 79-74—153 | Hannah Mccook (Grantown On Spey) | 80-79—159 |
| ohanna Tillstrom (SWE) | 79-74—153 | Samantha Giles (St Mellion) | 78-81—159 |
| Jamila Jaxaliyeva (KAZ) | 78-75—153 | Sunna Vidisdottir (ISL) | 76-83—159 |
| Paula Grant (Lisburn) | 77-76—153 | Sarah Schober (AUT) | 84-76—160 |
| Bethan Popel (Long Ashton) | 77-76—153 | Bianca Ling (AUS) | 82-78—160 |
| Julienne Soo (AUS) | 77-76—153 | Jane Turner (Craigielaw) | 82-78—160 |
| Alexandra Bonetti (FRA) | 75-78—153 | Lauren Whyte (St Regulus) | 81-79—160 |
| Josephine Janson (SWE) | 81-73—154 | Gabriella Wahl (GER) | 78-82—160 |
| Joanna Charlton (AUS) | 79-75—154 | Mariell Bruun (NOR) | 81-80—161 |
| Chloe Ryan (Castletroy) | 79-75—154 | Gabrielle Macdonald (Craigielaw) | 83-79—162 |
| Roberta Roeller (GER) | 78-76—154 | Agathe Sauzon (FRA) | 79-83—162 |
| Laure Castelain (FRA) | 77-77—154 | Grace Danielle (AUS) | 82-81—163 |
| Laura Gonzalez Escallon (BEL) | 76-78—154 | Joëlle Van Baarle (BEL) | 80-83—163 |
| Clara Baena (ESP) | 76-78—154 | Hollie Vizard (Pleasington) | 79-84—163 |
| Virginia Elena Carta (ITA) | 75-79—154 | Manon Mollé (FRA) | 74-89—163 |
| Eva Gilly (FRA) | 75-79—154 | Susana Vik (NOR) | 86-79—165 |
| Becky Harries (Haverfordwest) | 72-82—154 | Marion Duvernay (FRA) | 85-80—165 |
| Madelene Sagstrom (SWE) | 81-74—155 | Maria Palacios Siegenthale (ESP) | 84-81—165 |
| Rocio Sanchez Lobato (ESP) | 80-75—155 | Julie Finne-Ipsen (DEN) | 81-84—165 |
| Andrea Vilarasau (ESP) | 80-75—155 | Gudrun Bjorgvinsdottir (ISL) | 79-86—165 |
| Jing Yan (CHN) | 80-75—155 | Gemma Clews (Delamere Forest) | 87-79—166 |
| Natalie Wille (SWE) | 79-76—155 | Lesley Atkins (Gullane Ladies') | 85-81—166 |
| Kerry Smith (Waterlooville) | 78-77—155 | Charlotte Thompson (ENG) | 83-85—168 |
| Shelby Smart (Knowle) | 77-78—155 | Brogan Townend (Pleasington) | 86-83—169 |
| Lucy Goddard (Mid Herts) | 75-80—155 | Marthe Wold (NOR) | 86-83—169 |
| Rosie Davies (Indiana University) | 75-80—155 | Poppy Finlay (Vicars Cross) | 85-85—170 |
| Antonia Scherer (GER) | 73-82—155 | Elise Boehmer (NED) | 91-82—173 |
| Vicki Troeltsch (GER) | 81-75—156 | Bronwyn Davies (Trentham) | 86-89—175 |
| Teresa Caballer (ESP) | 80-76—156 | Nastja Banovec (SLO) | 80 RTD |
| Alyson McKechin (Elderslie) | 79-77—156 | Sophia Zeeb (GER) | 73 DSQ |
| Elizabeth Mallett (Sutton Coldfield Ladies) | 79-77—156 | Charlotte De Corte (BEL) | DSQ |
| Jess Wilcox (Blankney) | 79-77—156 | Aedin Murphy (Carlow) | DSQ |
| Annette lucia Lyche (NOR)y | 78-78—156 | Maria Dunne (Skerries) | DSQ |

**First Round:**
Su-Hyun Oh (AUS) beat Paula Grant (Lisburn) 5 and 4
Lisa Maguire (Slieve Russell) beat Shannon Aubert (FRA) 2 and 1
Roberta Liti (ITA) beat Rachael Goodall (Heswall) 1 up
Caroline Nistrup (DEN) beat Jessica Meek (Carnoustie Ladies') at 20th
Gabriella Cowley (Brockett Hall) beat Camilla Vik (NOR) 4 and 3
Alessandra Braida (ITA) beat Silvia Bañon (ESP) 2 and 1
Rachael Watton (Mortonhall) beat Natalia Escuriola (ENP) 1 up
Luna Sobron (ESSP) beat Linnea Johansson (SWE) 4 and 2
Justine Dreher (FRA) beat Amber Ratcliffe (Royal Cromer) 4 and 3
Stephanie Meadow (Royal Portrush) beat Lauren Taylor (Woburn) 5 and 4
Tonje Daffinrud (NOR) beat Sanna Nuutinen (FIN) 2 and 1
Leslie Cloots (BEL) beat Emma Tayler (Saunton) 3 and 2

Alexandra Peters (Notts Ladies) beat Sophie Keech (Lyme Regis)  at 20th
Emma Henrikson (SWE) beat Marta Sanz (ESP) 2 and 1
Karolin Lampert (GER) beat Linnea Strom (SWE) 2 up
Manon Gidali (FRA) beat Grace Lennon (AUS) 1 up
Hayley Davis (Ferndown) beat Johanna Tillstrom (SWE) 3 and 1
Georgia Hall (Remedy Oak) beat Ariane Provot (FRA) 2 up
Laura Fünfstück (GER) beat Sarah-Jane Boyd (Truro) 5 and 4
Anyssia Herbaut (FRA) beat Anne Van Dam (NED) 1 up
Harang Lee (ESP) beat Emma Nilsson (SWE) 3 and 2
Ileen Domela Nieuwenhuis (NED) beat Abbey Gittings (Walmley) 4 and 3
Csilla Lajtai Rózsa (HUN) beat Nuria Iturrios (ESP) at 19th
Celine Boutier (FRA) beat Nicoline Engstroem Skaug (NOR) 2 up
Lauren Hillier (Newport) beat Meghan Maclaren (Wellingborough) 2 and 1
Ines Lescudier (FRA) beat Abi Laker (Frilford Heath) 7 and 6
Eilidh Briggs (Kilmacolm) beat Emily Pedersen (DEN) 2 up
Emma Carberry (Highwoods) beat Bethany Garton (Royal Lytham & St Annes)  at 19th
Leona Maguire (Slieve Russell) beat Adriana Brent (AUS) 6 and 4
Laura Lonardi (ITA) beat Sophia Popov (GER) at 19th
Noemi Jimenez (ESP) beat Jenny Haglund (SWE) 6 and 4
Nanna Madsen (DEN) beat Jamila Jaxaliyeva (KAZ) 2 and 1

**Second Round:**
Lisa Maguire beat Su-Hyun Oh 6 and 4
Roberta Liti beat Caroline Nistrup 2 and 1
Gabriella Cowley beat Alessandra Braida 2 and 1
Luna Sobron beat Rachael Watton 2 and 1
Justine Dreher beat Stephanie Meadow 2 up
Tonje Daffinrud beat Leslie Cloots 4 and 2
Alexandra Peters beat Emma Henrikson 5 and 3
Karolin Lampert beat Manon Gidali 3 and 2
Georgia Hall beat Hayley Davis 1 up
Laura Fünfstück beat Anyssia Herbaut 3 and 1
Harang Lee beat Ileen Domela Nieuwenhuis 1 up
Csilla Lajtai Rózsa beat Celine Boutier 2 and 1
Ines Lescudier beat Lauren Hillier 2 and 1
Emma Carberry beat Eilidh Briggs 2 up
Leona Maguire beat Laura Lonardi 2 up
Noemi Jimenez beat Nanna Madsen at 19th

**Third Round:**
Lisa Maguire beat Roberta Liti 2 and 1
Luna Sobron beat Gabriella Cowley 1 up
Justine Dreher beat Tonje Daffinrud 4 and 2
Karolin Lampert beat Alexandra Peters 1 up
Georgia Hall beat Laura Fünfstück 6 and 5
Harang Lee beat Csilla Lajtai Rózsa 7 and 6
Ines Lescudier beat Emma Carberry 4 and 3
Noemi Jimenez beat Leona Maguire 3 and 1

**Quarter Finals:**
Luna Sobron beat Lisa Maguire 3 and 2
Karolin Lampert beat Justine Dreher 4 and 3
Georgia Hall beat Harang Lee 4 and 3
Noemi Jimenez beat Ines Lescudier 5 and 4

**Semi-Finals:**
Luna Sobron beat Karolin Lampert 1 up
Georgia Hall beat Noemi Jimenez 3 and 1

**Final:** Georgia Hall (Remedy Oak) beat Luna Sobron (ESP) 1 up

| | |
|---|---|
| 1893 | M Scott beat I Pearson 7 and 5 |
| 1894 | M Scott beat I Pearson 2 and 2 |
| 1895 | M Scott beat E Lythgoe 5 and 4 |
| 1896 | Miss Pascoe beat L Thomson 2 and 2 |
| 1897 | EC Orr beat Miss Orr 4 and 2 |
| 1898 | L Thomson beat EC Neville 7 and 5 |
| 1899 | M Hezlet beat Magill 2 and 1 |
| 1900 | Adair beat Neville 6 and 5 |
| 1901 | Graham beat Adair 2 and 1 |
| 1902 | M Hezlet beat E Neville at 19th |
| 1903 | Adair beat F Walker-Leigh 4 and 3 |
| 1904 | L Dod beat M Hezlet 1 hole |
| 1905 | B Thompson beat ME Stuart 2 and 2 |
| 1906 | Kennon beat B Thompson 4 and 3 |
| 1907 | M Hezlet beat F Hezlet 2 and 1 |
| 1908 | M Titterton beat D Campbell at 19th |
| 1909 | D Campbell beat F Hezlet 4 and 3 |
| 1910 | Miss Grant Suttie beat L Moore 6 and 4 |
| 1911 | D Campbell beat V Hezlet 2 and 2 |
| 1912 | G Ravenscroft beat S Temple 2 and 2 |
| 1913 | M Dodd beat Miss Chubb 8 and 6 |
| 1914 | C Leitch beat G Ravenscroft 2 and 1 |
| 1915–18 | Not played |
| 1919 | Abandoned because of railway strike |
| 1920 | C Leitch beat M Griffiths 7 and 6 |
| 1921 | C Leitch beat J Wethered 4 and 3 |
| 1922 | J Wethered beat C Leitch 9 and 7 |
| 1923 | D Chambers beat A Macbeth 2 holes |
| 1924 | J Wethered beat Mrs Cautley 7 and 6 |
| 1925 | J Wethered beat C Leitch at 37th |
| 1926 | C Leitch beat Mrs Garon 8 and 7 |
| 1927 | T de la Chaume (FRA) beat Miss Pearson 5 and 4 |
| 1928 | N Le Blan (FRA) beat S Marshall 2 and 2 |
| 1929 | J Wethered beat G Collett (USA) 2 and 1 |
| 1930 | D Fishwick beat G Collett (USA) 4 and 3 |
| 1931 | E Wilson beat W Morgan 7 and 6 |
| 1932 | E Wilson beat CPR Montgomery 7 and 6 |
| 1933 | E Wilson beat D Plumpton 5 and 4 |
| 1934 | AM Holm beat P Barton 6 and 5 |
| 1935 | W Morgan beat P Barton 2 and 2 |
| 1936 | P Barton beat R Newell 5 and 3 |
| 1937 | J Anderson beat D Park 6 and 4 |
| 1938 | AM Holm beat E Corlett 4 and 3 |
| 1939 | P Barton beat T Marks 2 and 1 |
| 1940–45 | Not played |
| 1946 | GW Hetherington beat P Garvey 1 hole |
| 1947 | B Zaharias (USA) beat J Gordon 5 and 4 |
| 1948 | L Suggs (USA) beat J Donald 1 hole |

## Ladies British Amateur Championship *continued*

| | | | | |
|---|---|---|---|---|
| 1949 | F Stephens beat V Reddan 5 and 4 | | 1981 | IC Robertson beat W Aitken at 20th |
| 1950 | Vicomtesse de St Sauveur (FRA) beat J Valentine 3 and 2 | | 1982 | K Douglas beat G Stewart 4 and 2 |
| 1951 | PJ MacCann beat F Stephens 4 and 3 | | 1983 | J Thornhill beat R Lautens (SUI) 4 and 2 |
| 1952 | M Paterson beat F Stephens at 39th | | 1984 | J Rosenthal (USA) beat J Brown 4 and 3 |
| 1953 | M Stewart (CAN) beat P Garvey 7 and 6 | | 1985 | L Beman (IRL) beat C Waite 1 hole |
| 1954 | F Stephens beat E Price 4 and 3 | | 1986 | M McGuire (NZL) beat L Briars (AUS) 2 and 1 |
| 1955 | J Valentine beat B Romack (USA) 7 and 6 | | 1987 | J Collingham beat S Shapcott at 19th |
| 1956 | M Smith (USA) beat M Janssen (USA) 8 and 7 | | 1988 | J Furby beat J Wade 4 and 3 |
| 1957 | P Garvey beat J Valentine 4 and 3 | | 1989 | H Dobson beat E Farquharson 6 and 5 |
| 1958 | J Valentine beat E Price 1 hole | | 1990 | J Hall beat H Wadsworth 2 and 2 |
| 1959 | E Price beat B McCorkindale at 37th | | 1991 | V Michaud (FRA) beat W Doolan (AUS) 2 and 2 |
| 1960 | B McIntyre (USA) beat P Garvey 4 and 2 | | 1992 | P Pedersen (DEN) beat J Morley 1 hole |
| 1961 | M Spearman beat DJ Robb 7 and 6 | | 1993 | C Lambert beat K Speak 2 and 2 |
| 1962 | M Spearman beat A Bonallack 1 hole | | 1994 | E Duggleby beat C Mourgue d'Algue 2 and 1 |
| 1963 | B Varangot (FRA) beat P Garvey 2 and 1 | | 1995 | J Hall beat K Mourgue d'Algue 2 and 2 |
| 1964 | C Sorenson (USA) beat BAB Jackson at 37th | | 1996 | K Kuehne (USA) beat B Morgan 5 and 3 |
| 1965 | B Varangot (FRA) beat IC Robertson 4 and 3 | | 1997 | A Rose beat M McKay 4 and 3 |
| 1966 | E Chadwick beat V Saunders 2 and 2 | | 1998 | K Rostron beat G Nocera (FRA) 2 and 2 |
| 1967 | E Chadwick beat M Everard 1 hole | | 1999 | M Monnet (FRA) beat R Hudson 1 hole |
| 1968 | B Varangot (FRA) beat C Rubin (FRA) at 20th | | 2000 | R Hudson beat E Duggleby 5 and 4 |
| 1969 | C Lacoste (FRA) beat A Irvin 1 hole | | 2001 | M Prieto (ESP) beat E Duggleby 4 and 3 |
| 1970 | D Oxley beat IC Robertson 1 hole | | 2002 | R Hudson beat L Wright 5 and 4 |
| 1971 | M Walker beat B Huke 2 and 1 | | 2003 | E Serramia (ESP) beat P Odefey (GER) 2 holes |
| 1972 | M Walker beat C Rubin (FRA) 2 holes | | 2004 | L Stahle (SWE) beat A Highgate 4 and 2 |
| 1973 | A Irvin beat M Walker 2 and 2 | | 2005 | L Stahle (SWE) beat C Coughlan 2 and 2 |
| 1974 | C Semple (USA) beat A Bonallack 2 and 1 | | 2006 | B Mozo (ESP) beat A Nordqvist (SWE) 2 and 1 |
| 1975 | N Syms (USA) beat S Cadden 2 and 2 | | 2007 | C Ciganda (ESP) beat A Nordqvist (SWE) 4 and 3 |
| 1976 | C Panton beat A Sheard 1 hole | | 2008 | A Nordqvist (SWE) beat C Hedwall (SWE) 3 and 2 |
| 1977 | A Uzielli beat V Marvin 6 and 5 | | 2009 | A Muñoz (ESP) beat C Ciganda (ESP) 2 and 1 |
| 1978 | E Kennedy (AUS) beat J Greenhalgh 1 hole | | 2010 | K Tidy beat K MacDonald 2 and 1 |
| 1979 | M Madill beat J Lock (AUS) 2 and 1 | | 2011 | L Taylor beat A Bonetti (ITA) 6 and 5 |
| 1980 | A Quast (USA) beat L Wollin (SWE) 2 and 1 | | 2012 | S Meadow beat R Sanchez Lobato (ESP) 4 and 3 |

# European Ladies Amateur Championship  (inaugurated 1986)

*Aura GC (Turku), Finland*   July 24–27   [6113–73]

## Denmark's Emily Kristine Pedersen helped by a third round 64
### wins the European title in Finland

Danish teenager Emily Kristine Pedersen, who lives near Copenhagen, needed only shoot a par 72 in the final round to win the 2013 European Women's Amateur title at the Aura Club, Turku, Finland.

She produced a 64, the round of the tournament, on the third day to open up a commanding seven shot lead on the field and her clinical par-matching performance on the final day gave her an eight under par winning total of 276 and a three shot lead over Belgium's Laura Gonzalez Escallion with Finn Krista Bakker, who shot a closing 66, third a further three shots back.

Pedersen, who has been playing golf since she was 10, felt great after her 64 but admitted "I suddenly felt I had everything to lose. I felt the pressure."

On the last day her goal was to make four birdies – so that she did not need to think about what the other players were doing or focus on how far she was or was not ahead ... although she knew Noemi Jimenez from Spain had closed to with two after ten holes.

Pedersen credited the Junior Ryder Cup for helping her win the title. "To play in a team with such good players was amazing, It gave me lots of motivation. I realised I wanted to play at the top of world golf."

Pedersen was the first Dane to win the title since the event began in 1986.

| | | |
|---|---|---|
| 1 | Emily Kristine Pedersen (DEN) | 67-73-64-72—276 |
| 2 | Laura Gonzalez Escallon (BEL) | 69-74-68-68—279 |
| 3 | Krista Bakker (FIN) | 75-68-73-66—282 |
| | Céline Boutier (FRA) | 73-69-72-68—282 |
| | Noemi Jimenez (ESP) | 71-69-71-71—282 |
| 6 | Lisa Maguire (IRL) | 69-72-71-72—284 |
| | Karolin Lampert (GER) | 70-71-70-73—284 |
| 8 | Natalia Escuriola (ESP) | 72-70-70-73—285 |

| 8T | Amy Boulden (WAL) | 71-70-70-74—285 |
|---|---|---|
| 10 | Marika Voss (FIN) | 77-70-69-71—287 |
| | Manon de Roey (BEL) | 74-72-69-72—287 |
| | Marthe Wold (NOR) | 70-70-73-74—287 |
| 13 | Nanna Koerstz Madsen (DEN) | 70-72-74-72—288 |
| 14 | Annika Nykänen (FIN) | 74-71-74-70—289 |
| | Sophia Popov (GER) | 71-72-72-74—289 |
| 16 | Leslie Cloots (BEL) | 77-71-71-71—290 |
| | Nicoline Skaug (NOR) | 77-70-74-69—290 |
| | Bronte Law, Bronte (ENG) | 71-76-70-73—290 |
| | Hayley Davis (ENG) | 70-75-74-71—290 |
| 20 | Eva Gilly (FRA) | 73-76-73-69—291 |
| | Caroline Nistrup (DEN) | 73-73-70-75—291 |
| 22 | Luna Sobrón (ESP) | 73-79-72-68—292 |
| | Clara Baena (ESP) | 74-76-73-69—292 |
| 24 | Laura Lonardi (ITA) | 74-75-73-71—293 |
| | Fanny Cnops (BEL) | 72-76-73-72—293 |
| | Nicole Broch Larsen (DEN) | 68-80-72-72—293 |
| | Anne Van Dam (NED) | 76-71-73-73—293 |
| | Andrea Vilarasau Amorós (ESP) | 74-73-73-73—,293 |
| | Emma Henrikson (SWE) | 75-72-72-74—293 |
| | Roberta Liti (ITA) | 74-71-74-74—293 |
| 31 | Mathilda Cappeliez (FRA) | 72-78-72-72—294 |
| | Virginia Elena Carta (ITA) | 78-69-73-74—294 |
| | Franziska Friedrich (GER) | 75-71-75-73—294 |
| | Sarah Schober (AUT) | 74-72-72-76—294 |
| | Marlies Krenn (AUT) | 73-72-78-71—294 |
| 36 | Alexandra Peters (ENG) | 75-78-71-71—295 |
| | Antonia von Wnuck (GER) | 78-74-71-72—295 |
| | Krista Puisite (LAT) | 74-77-73-71—295 |
| | Antonia Scherer (GER) | 74-74-76-71—295 |
| | Sarah Jane Boyd (ENG) | 74-71-76-74—291 |
| | Amina Wolf (GER) | 72-73-76-74—295 |
| | Georgia Hall (ENG) | 71-73-78-73—295 |
| | Elin Arvidsson (SWE) | 72-69-77-77—295 |
| 44 | Iman Ahmad Nordin (MAS) | 77-74-70-75—296 |
| | Dewi Weber (NED) | 78-72-73-73—296 |
| | Laura Fünfstück (GER) | 76-73-74-73—296 |
| | Matilda Castren (FIN) | 71-76-75-74—296 |
| | Célia Gimblett (SUI) | 72-70-76-78—296 |
| | Tonje Frydenberg Daffinrud (NOR) | 69-68-85-74—296 |
| 50 | Vicki Troeltsch (GER) | 77-74-73-73—297 |
| | Louise Ridderstrom (SWE) | 77-74-73-73—297 |
| | Alexandra Bonetti (FRA) | 75-74-75-73—297 |
| | Becky Harries (WAL) | 77-70-75-75—297 |
| | Laura Kowohl (GER) | 72-74-76-75—297 |
| 55 | Bianca Maria Fabrizio (ITA) | 78-71-74-75—298 |
| 56 | Ariane Provot (FRA) | 72-75-77-75—299 |
| 57 | Olivia Cowan (GER) | 72-78-74-76—300 |
| | Chloe Williams (WAL) | 74-74-76-76—300 |
| 59 | Meghan MacLaren (ENG) | 76-76-72-77—301 |
| | Marion Duvernay (FRA) | 75-72-74-80—301 |
| 61 | Roberta Roeller (GER) | 78-73-72-80—303 |
| 62 | Leena Makkonen (FIN) | 76-76-71-82—305 |

The remaining 76 players missed the cut

| 1986 | Martina Koch (GER) | Morfontaine GC, France |
|---|---|---|
| 1988 | Florence Descampe (BEL)* | Pedrena GC, Spain |

*after a play-off with Delphine Bourson (FRA)

| 1990 | Matina Koch (GER) | Zumikon GC, Switzerland |
|---|---|---|
| 1991 | Delphine Bourson (FRA) | Schonborn GC, Austria |

| 1992 | Joanne Morton (ENG) | Estoril GC, Portugal |
|---|---|---|
| 1993 | Vibeke Stensrud (NOR) | Torino GC, Italy |
| 1994 | Martina Fischer (GER) | Bastadt GC, Sweden |
| 1995 | Maria Hjorth (SWE) | Berlin GC, Germany |
| 1996 | Silvia Cavalerri (ITA) | Furesoe GC, Denmark |
| 1997 | Silvia Cavalerri (ITA) | Formby GC, England |

European Ladies Amateur Championship *continued*

| | | | |
|---|---|---|---|
| 1998 Guilia Sergas (ITA) | Noordwijke GC, Netherlands | | Germany |
| 1999 Sofia Sandolo (ITA) | Karlovy Vary GC, Czech Rep. | 2007 Caroline Hedwall (SWE)* | Golf National, France |
| | | *after play-off with Carlota Ciganda (ESP) | |
| 2000 Emma Duggelby (ENG) | Amber Baltic GC, Poland | 2008 Carlota Ciganda (ESP)* | GC Schloss Schonborn, Austria |
| 2001 Martina Eberl (GER) | Biella GC, Italy | *after play-off with Maria Hernandez (ESP) | |
| 2002 Becky Brewerton (WAL) | Kristianstad GC, Sweden | 2009 Caroline Hedwall (SWE) | Falsterbo GC, Sweden |
| 2003 Virginie Beauchet (FRA) | Shannon GC, Ireland | 2010 Sophia Popov (GER) | Kunetickà Hora, Czech Rep. |
| 2004 Carlota Ciganda (ESP) | Ulzama GC, Spain | | |
| 2005 Jade Schaeffer (FRA) | Santo da Serra GC, Madeira | 2011 Lisa Maquire (IRL) | Noordwijksee, Netherlands |
| | | 2012 Celine Boutier (FRA) | Ljubljana, Slovenia |
| 2006 Belen Mozo (ESP) | Falkenstein GC, | 2013 Emily Kristine Pedersen | Aura GC (Turku), Finland |

# 113th United States Women's Amateur Championship (inaugurated 1895)

Charleston, South Carolina    (Players are of US nationality unless stated)    [6473/6479–71]

## Kentucky's Emma Talley survives the tiring heat in Charleston to win the US title

Her 10th USGA Championship proved to be a winning one for Princeton, Kentucky, golfer Emma Talley at the Country Club of Charleston when she beat Yueer Cindy Feng 2 and 1.

Talley, who won the Robert Cox Trophy, said: "This is a dream come true". Her win gave her great satisfaction but just as happy was her father Dan who caddied for her. "We always have a lot of fun together," said Talley, "He is a jokester and he was great for me this week."

Defeated Feng said "When she did not play in the morning I played worse and when she did play well after lunch I was not able to hold on as tight".

Talley was one up after eighteen holes and improved to three up but the match was square again before the turn in the afternoon. Talley won the 28th and was never headed after this.

In the quarter finals 18-year-old Doris Chen from Chinese Taipei, who had lost to Lauren Diaz-Yi 10 and 9 in the final of the US Public Links Championship, got her revenge. Chen Lost the first but squared at the second and was never headed again *en route* to a 4 and 3 success

Feng beat the NCAA champion Annie Park 6 and 4, Alison Lee ended Katelyn Sepmoree's Championship hopes and Talley's scalp was that of World No 2 Su-Hyun Oh, the South Korean born Australian. All square at the last, Oh left her birdie attempt short and Talley holed from four feet for par to keep the game alive. At the first extra hole Oh's four-footer lipped out and Talley was through to a semi-final with Alison Lee who despite suffering from nose bleeds, took the match all the way before admitting defeat. Talley had been four up at one stage. In the other semi-final Feng beat US Girls' Champion Chen by 3 and 2.

Medallist honours went to 14-yearold Japanese golfer Yumi Matsubara whose second round 64 helped her to a a seven under par 135 equalling the qualifying record set in 2002 by Courtney Trimble. The 64 was one shot better than the previous low qualifying score returned by Rachel Rohanna in 2010.

Matsubara finished five head of next best, Allisen Corpuz from Honolulu, and from Talley and Feng who would go on to contest the final.

### Stroke Play Qualifying:

| | | | |
|---|---|---|---|
| Hyo-Joo Kim (KOR) | 68-68—136 | Casie Cathrea (Livermore, CA) | 77-67—144 |
| Yumi Matsubara (JPN) | 71-64—135 | Carolin Pinegger (AUT) | 71-73—144 |
| Allisen Corpuz (Honolulu, HI) | 69-71—140 | Grace Na (Oakland, CA) | 75-70—145 |
| Emma Talley (Princeton, KY) | 71-69—140 | Stephanie Meadow (NIR) | 72-73—145 |
| Yueer Cindy Feng, (Orlando, FL) | 72-68—140 | Minjee Lee (AUS) | 73-72—145 |
| Brittany Fan (Pearl City, HI) | 72-69—141 | Erynne Lee (Silverdale, WA) | 75-70—145 |
| Emily Tubert (Burbank, CA) | 71-70—141 | Mariel Galdiano (Pearl City, HI) | 72-73—145 |
| Alison Lee (Valencia, CA) | 72-69—141 | Cammie Gray (Northport, AL) | 75-70—145 |
| Brooke Mackenzie Henderson (CAN) | 71-70—141 | Annie Park (Levittown, NY) | 74-71—145 |
| Kotone Hori (JPN) | 73-68—141 | Ember Schuldt (Sterling, IL) | 73-72—145 |
| Princess Superal (PHI) | 76-66—142 | Christine Meier (Rochester Hills, MI) | 75-71—146 |
| Su-Hyun Oh (AUS) | 73-69—142 | Katelyn Sepmoree (Tyler, TX) | 74-72—146 |
| Kelly Shon (Port Washington, NY) | 74-68—142 | Lauren Diaz-Yi (Thousand Oaks, CA) | 75-71—146 |
| Nicole Morales (South Salem, NY) | 75-68—143 | Desiree Dubreuil (Santa Ana, CA) | 75-71—146 |
| Cyna Marie Rodriguez (PHI) | 76-67—143 | Kyung Kim (Chandler, AZ) | 75-71—146 |
| Caroline Inglis (Eugene, OR) | 74-69—143 | Tatiana Wijaya (INA) | 74-72—146 |
| Lori Beth Adams (Burlington, NC) | 73-71—144 | Emily Collins (Colleyville, TX) | 76-70—146 |
| Kendall Prince (Lake Oswego, OR) | 71-73—144 | Lauren Stephenson (Lexington, SC) | 75-71—146 |
| Aurora Kan (Boothwyn, PA) | 73-71—144 | Simin Feng (CHN) | 76-70—146 |
| Ally McDonald (Fulton, MS) | 72-72—144 | Katelyn Dambaugh (Goose Creek, SC) | 74-72—146 |

| | | | | | |
|---|---|---|---|---|---|
| Doris Chen (TPE) | 74-72—146 | | Gabriella Lopez (MEX) | 76-72—148 |
| Elizabeth Nagel (Dewitt, MI) | 75-71—146 | | Jessie Gerry (Madison, WI) | 75-74—149 |
| Leona Maguire (IRL) | 75-71—146 | | Alexandra Harkins (Crystal Lake, IL) | 75-74—149 |
| Megan Khang (Rockland, MA) | 72-74—146 | | Kelly Grassel (Chesterton, IN) | 74-75—149 |
| Meghan Stasi (Oakland Park, FL) | 71-76—147 | | Kacie Komoto (Honolulu, HI) | 77-72—149 |
| Sophia Popov (GER) | 74-73—147 | | Dawn Woodard (Greer, SC) | 72-77—149 |
| Allyssa Ferrell (Edgerton, WI) | 72-75—147 | | Ashlan Ramsey (Milledgeville, GA) | 76-73—149 |
| Gabriella Then (Rancho Cucamonga, CA) | 73-74—147 | | Monica Petchakan (Encino, CA) | 76-73—149 |
| Casey Danielson (Osceola, WI) | 76-71—147 | | Laura Wearn (Charlotte, NC) | 79-71—150 |
| Clariss Guce (PHI) | 72-75—147 | | Lydia Choi (Beverly Hills, CA) | 76-74—150 |
| Elizabeth Wang (San Marino, CA) | 79-68—147 | | Saki Iida (Gilbert, AZ) | 75-75—150 |
| Maria Fassi (MEX) | 77-71—148 | | Bianca Maria Fabrizio (ITA) | 80-70—150 |
| Liv Cheng (NZL) | 77-71—148 | | | |

**First Round:**
Yumi Matsubara (JPN) beat Bianca Maria Fabrizio (ITA) 2 and 1
Lauren Diaz-Yi beat Desiree Dubreuil 4 and 3
Lori Beth Adams beat Clariss Guce (PHI) 2 up
Kendall Prince beat Casey Danielson at 20th
Kacie Komoto beat Brooke Mackenzie Henderson (CAN) 4 and 3
Doris Chen (TPE) beat Erynne Lee 1 up
Kotone Hori (JPN) beat Kelly Grassel 3 and 2
Minjee Lee (AUS) beat Elizabeth Nagel 6 and 4
Yueer Cindy Feng beat Saki Iida 5 and 4
Emily Collins beat Ember Schuldt 2 and 1
Nicole Morales beat Liv Cheng (NZL) 2 and 1
Casie Cathrea beat Sophia Popov (GER) 3 and 2
Brittany Fan beat Monica Petchakan 3 and 2
Annie Park beat Lauren Stephenson 4 and 3
Kelly Shon beat Gabriela Lopez (MEX) 1 up
Meghan Stasi beat Carolin Pinegger (AUT) 2 and 1

**Second Round:**
Lauren Diaz-Yi beat Yumi Matsubara 2 and 1
Kendall Prince beat Lori Beth Adams 2 up
Doris Chen beat Kacie Komoto 3 and 2
Minjee Lee beat Kotone Hori 4 and 3
Yueer Cindy Feng beat Emily Collins 4 and 2
Casie Cathrea beat Nicole Morales 2 and 1
Annie Park beat Brittany Fan 2 and 1
Kelly Shon beat Meghan Stasi 3 and 1
Katelyn Sepmoree beat Laura Wearn 2 and 1
Aurora Kan beat Caroline Inglis 2 up
Alison Lee beat Katelyn Dambaugh at 19th
Alexandra Harkins beat Leona Maguire 1 up
Emma Talley beat Tatiana Wijaya 8 and 7
Maria Fassi beat Ally McDonald at 19th
Cammie Gray beat Emily Tubert at 19th
Su-Hyun Oh beat Grace Na 2 and 1

Laura Wearn beat Allisen Corpuz 3 and 2
Katelyn Sepmoree beat Kyung Kim 2 and 1
Caroline Inglis beat Elizabeth Wang 2 and 1
Aurora Kan beat Gabriella Then 7 and 5
Alison Lee beat Dawn Woodard 3 and 1
Katelyn Dambaugh beat Mariel Galdiano 2 up
Alexandra Harkins beat Princess Superal (PHI) 3 and 2
Leona Maguire (IRL) beat Stephanie Meadow (NIR) 3 and 2
Emma Talley beat Lydia Choi 3 and 1
Tatiana Wijaya (INA) beat Christine Meier 1 up, ,
Maria Fassi (MEX) beat Cyna Marie Rodriguez (PHI) 3 and 2
Ally McDonald beat Allyssa Ferrell 2 and 1
Emily Tubert beat Ashlan Ramsey 2 and 1
Cammie Gray beat Simin Feng (CHN) 4 and
Su-Hyun Oh (AUS) beat Jessie Gerry 5 and 3
Grace Nabeat Megan Khang at 19th

**Third Round:**
Lauren Diaz-Yi beat Kendall Prince 4 and 3
Doris Chen beat Minjee Lee 2 and 1
Yueer Cindy Feng beat Casie Cathrea 1 up
Annie Park beat Kelly Shon 1 up
Katelyn Sepmoree beat Aurora Kan 1 up
Alison Lee beat Alexandra Harkins 3 and 2
Emma Talley beat Maria Fassi 2 up
Su-Hyun Oh beat Cammie Gray 5 and 4

**Quarter Finals:**
Doris Chen beat Lauren Diaz-Yi 4 and 3
Yueer Cindy Feng beat Annie Park 6 and 4
Alison Lee beat Katelyn Sepmoree 4 and 3
Emma Talley beat Su-Hyun Oh at 19th

**Semi-Finals:**
Yueer Cindy Feng beat Doris Chen 3 and 2
Emma Talley beat Alison Lee 1 up

**Final:** Emma Talley (Princeton, KY) beat Yueer Cindy Feng (Orlando, FL) 2 and 1

| | | | | |
|---|---|---|---|---|
| 1895 | LB Brown (132) beat N Sargent 134 | | Meadowbrook GC, NY | |
| *Changed to match play* | | | | |
| 1896 | B Hoyt beat A Tunure 2 and 1 | | Morris County GC, NJ | *Entrants* 29 |
| 1897 | B Hoyt beat N Sargent 5 and 4 | | Essex CC, MA | 29 |
| 1898 | B Hoyt beat M Wetmore 5 and 3 | | Ardsley Club, NY | 61 |
| 1899 | R Underhill beat M Fox 2 and 1 | | Philadelphia CC (Bala Course) | 78 |
| 1900 | FC Griscom beat M Curtis 6 and 5 | | Shinnecock Hills GC, NY | 62 |
| 1901 | G Hecker beat L Herron 5 and 3 | | Baltusrol GC, NJ | 89 |

## US Women's Amateur Championship *continued*

| | | | |
|---|---|---|---:|
| 1902 | G Hecker beat LA Wells 4 and 3 | The Country Club, Brookline, MA | 96 |
| 1903 | B Anthony beat JA Carpenter 7 and 6 | Chicago GC, IL | 64 |
| 1904 | GM Bishop beat EF Sanford 5 and 3 | Merion Cricket Club, PA | 86 |
| 1905 | P Mackay beat M Curtis 1 hole | Morris City GC, NJ | 69 |
| 1906 | HS Curtis beat MB Adams 2 and 1 | Brae Burn CC, MA | 75 |
| 1907 | M Curtis beat HS Curtis 7 and 6 | Midlothian CC (Blue Island Course), IL | 87 |
| 1908 | KC Harley beat TH Polhemus 6 and 5 | Chevy Chase GC, MD | 41 |
| 1909 | D Campbell beat N Barlow 3 and 2 | Merion Cricket Club, PA | 86 |
| 1910 | D Campbell beat GM Martin 2 and 1 | Homewood CC, IL | 57 |
| 1911 | M Curtis beat LB Hyde 5 and 4 | Baltusrol GC, NJ | 67 |
| 1912 | M Curtis beat N Barlow 3 and 2 | Essex CC, MA | 62 |
| 1913 | G Ravenscroft beat M Hollins 2 holes | Wilmington CC, DE | 88 |
| 1914 | KC Harley beat EV Rosenthal 1 hole | Nassau CC, NY | 93 |
| 1915 | F Vanderbeck beat M Gavin (ENG) 3 and 2 | Onwentsia Club, IL | 119 |
| 1916 | A Stirling beat M Caverly 2 and 1 | Belmont Springs CC, MA | 63 |
| 1917–1918 | *Not played* | | |
| 1919 | A Stirling beat M Gavin (ENG) 6 and 5 | Shawnee CC, De | 114 |
| 1920 | A Stirling beat D Campbell Hurd 5 and 4 | Mayfield CC, OH | 114 |
| 1921 | M Hollins beat A Stirling 5 and 4 | Hollywood GC, NJ | 181 |
| 1922 | G Collett beat M Gavin (ENG) 5 and 4 | Glenbrier GC, WV | 196 |
| 1923 | E Cummings beat A Stirling 3 and 2 | Westchester CC, NY | 196 |
| 1924 | D Campbell Hurd beat MK Browne 7 and 6 | Rhode Island CC, RI | 98 |
| 1925 | G Collett beat A Stirling Fraser 9 and 8 | St Louis CC, MO | 85 |
| 1926 | H Stetson beat E Goss 2 and 1 | Merion Cricket Club (East), PA | 134 |
| 1927 | MB Horn beat M Orcutt 5 and 4 | Cherry Valley Club, NY | 150 |
| 1928 | G Collett beat V Van Wie 13 and 12 | Hot Springs CC (Cascades Course), VA | 123 |
| 1929 | G Collett beat L Pressler 4 and 3 | Oakland Hills CC (South Course), MI | 98 |
| 1930 | G Collett beat V Van Wie 6 and 5 | Los Angeles CC (North Course), CA | 102 |
| 1931 | H Hicks beat G Collett Vare 2 and 1 | CC of Buffalo, NY | 102 |
| 1932 | V Van Wie beat G Collett Vare 10 and 8 | Salem CC, MA | 90 |
| 1933 | V Van Wie beat H Hicks 4 and 3 | Exmoor CC, IL | 120 |
| 1934 | V Van Wie beat D Traung 2 and 1 | Whitemarsh Valley CCm PA | 157 |
| 1935 | G Collett Vare beat P Berg 3 and 2 | Interlachen CC, MN | 94 |
| 1936 | P Barton (ENG) beat M Orcutt 4 and 3 | Canoe Brook CC (South Course), NJ | 188 |
| 1937 | EL Page beat P Berg 7 and 6 | Memphis CC, TN | 136 |
| 1938 | P Berg beat EL Page 6 and 5 | Westmoreland CC, IL | 118 |
| 1939 | B Jameson beat D Kirby 3 and 2 | Wee Burn CC, CT | 201 |
| 1940 | B Jameson beat J Cochran 6 and 5 | Del Monte G&CC, CA | 163 |
| 1941 | E Hicks Newell beat H Sigel 5 and 3 | The Country Club, Brookline, MA | 124 |
| 1942–1945 | *Not played* | | |
| 1946 | B Zaharias beat C Sherman 11 and 9 | Southern Hills CC, OK | 69 |
| 1947 | L Suggs beat D Kirby 2 holes | Franklin Hills CC, MI | 83 |
| 1948 | G Lenczyk beat H Sigel 4 and 3 | Del Monte G&CC, CA | 116 |
| 1949 | D Porter beat D Kielty 3 and 2 | Merion Cricket Club (East), PA | 171 |
| 1950 | B Hanson beat M Murray 6 and 4 | Atlanta Athletic Club, GA | 110 |
| 1951 | D Kirby beat C Doran 2 and 1 | Town and CC, MN | 79 |
| 1952 | J Pung beat S McFedters 2 and 1 | Waverley CC, OR | 159 |
| 1953 | ML Faulk beat P Riley 3 and 2 | Rhode Island CC, RI | 158 |
| 1954 | B Romack beat M Wright 4 and 2 | Allegheny CC, PA | 151 |
| 1955 | P Lesser beat J Nelson 7 and 6 | Myers Park CC, NC | 112 |
| 1956 | M Stewart beat J Gunderson 2 and 1 | Meridian Hills CC, IN | 116 |
| 1957 | J Gunderson beat AC Johnstone 8 and 6 | Del Paso CC, CA | 100 |
| 1958 | A Quast beat B Romack 3 and 2 | Wee Burn CC, CT | 195 |
| 1959 | B McIntyre beat J Goodwin 4 and 3 | Congressional CC, Washington, DC | 128 |
| 1960 | J Gunderson beat J Ashley 6 and 5 | Tulsa CC, OK | 109 |
| 1961 | A Quast beat P Preuss 14 and 13 | Tacoma G&CC, WA | 107 |
| 1962 | J Gunderson beat A Baker 9 and 8 | CC of Rochester, NY | 128 |
| 1963 | A Quast beat P Conley 2 and 1 | Taconic CC, MA | 128 |
| 1964 | B McIntyre beat J Gunderson 3 and 2 | Prairie Dunes CC, KS | 93 |
| 1965 | J Ashley beat A Quast 5 and 4 | Lakewood CC, CO | 88 |
| 1966 | J Gunderson Carner beat JD Stewart Streit at 41st | Sewickley Heights GC, PA | 115 |
| 1967 | ML Dill beat J Ashley 5 and 4 | Annandale GC, CA | 119 |
| 1968 | J Gunderson Carner beat A Quast 5 and 4 | Birmingham CC, MA | 110 |
| 1969 | C Lacoste (FRA) beat S Hamlin 3 and 2 | Las Colinas CC, TX | 103 |
| 1970 | M Wilkinson beat C Hill 3 and 2 | Wee Burn CC, CT | 139 |
| 1971 | L Baugh beat B Barry 1 hole | Atlanta CC, GA | 102 |
| 1972 | M Budke beat C Hill 5 and 4 | St Louis CC, MO | 134 |
| 1973 | C Semple beat A Quast 1 hole | Montclair GC, NJ | 142 |
| 1974 | C Hill beat C Semple 5 and 4 | Broadmoor GC, WA | 121 |

| | | | |
|---|---|---|---|
| 1975 | B Daniel beat D Horton 3 and 2 | Brae Burn CC, MA | 154 |
| 1976 | D Horton beat M Bretton 2 and 1 | Del Paso CC, CA | 157 |
| 1977 | B Daniel beat C Sherk 3 and 1 | Cincinnati GC, OH | 162 |
| 1978 | C Sherk beat J Oliver 4 and 3 | Sunnybrook GC, PA | 207 |
| 1979 | C Hill beat P Sheehan 7 and 6 | Memphis CC, TN | 273 |
| 1980 | J Inkster beat P Rizzo 2 holes | Prairie Dunes CC, KS | 281 |
| 1981 | J Inkster beat L Goggin (AUS) 1 hole | Waverley CC, OR | 240 |
| 1982 | J Inkster beat C Hanlon 4 and 3 | Broadmoor GC (South Course), CO | 262 |
| 1983 | J Pacillo beat S Quinlan 2 and 1 | Canoe Brook CC (North Course), NJ | 259 |
| 1984 | D Richard beat K Williams at 37th | Broadmoor GC, WA | 290 |
| 1985 | M Hattori (JPN) beat C Stacy 5 and 4 | Fox Chapel CC, PA | 329 |
| 1986 | K Cockerill beat K McCarthy 9 and 7 | Pasatiempo GC, CA | 387 |
| 1987 | K Cockerill beat T Kerdyk 3 and 2 | Rhode Island CC, RI | 359 |
| 1988 | P Sinn beat K Noble 6 and 5 | Minikahda Club, MN | 384 |
| 1989 | V Goetze beat B Burton 4 and 3 | Pinehurst CC (No.2), NC | 376 |
| 1990 | P Hurst beat S Davis at 37th | Canoe Brook CC (North Course), NJ | 384 |
| 1991 | A Fruhwirth beat H Voorhees 5 and 4 | Prairie Dunes CC, KS | 391 |
| 1992 | V Goetze beat A Söre nstam (SWE) 1 hole | Kemper Lakes GC, IL | 441 |
| 1993 | J McGill beat S Ingram 1 hole | San Diego CC, CA | 442 |
| 1994 | W Ward beat J McGill 2 and 1 | The Homestead (Cascades Course), VA | 451 |
| 1995 | K Kuehne beat A-M Knight 4 and 2 | The Country Club, Brookline, MA | 452 |
| 1996 | K Kuehne beat M Baena 2 and 1 | Firethorn GC, NE | 495 |
| 1997 | S Cavalleri (ITA) beat R Burke 5 and 4 | Brae Burn CC, MA | 557 |
| 1998 | G Park (KOR) beat J Chuasiriporn 7 and 6 | Barton Hills CC, MI | 620 |
| 1999 | D Delasin beat J Kang 4 and 3 | Biltmore Forest CC, NC | 676 |
| 2000 | N Newton beat L Myerscough 8 and 7 | Waverley CC, OR | 682 |
| 2001 | M Duncan beat N Perrot at 37th | Flint Hills National GC, KS | 768 |
| 2002 | B Lucidi beat B Jackson 3 and 2 | Sleepy Hollow CC, NY | 793 |
| 2003 | V Nirapathpongporn beat J Park 2 and 1 | Philadelphia CC, PA | 814 |
| 2004 | J Park beat A McCurdy 2 holes | The Kahkwa Club, PA | 868 |
| 2005 | M Pressel beat M Martinez 9 and 8 | Ansley GC (Settingdown Creek Course) | 873 |
| 2006 | K Kim* beat K Schallenberg | Pumpkin Ridge GC (Witch Hollow Course) | 969 |
| *at 14, the youngest-ever winner | | | |
| 2007 | MJ Uribe beat A Blumenherst 1 hole | Crooked Stick GC, IN | 935 |
| 2008 | A Blumenhurst beat A Muñoz (ESP) 2 and 1 | Eugene CC, OR | 920 |
| 2009 | J Song beat J Johnson 3 and 1 | St Louis, MO | 1,278 |
| 2010 | Danielle Kang beat Jessica Korda 2 and 1 | Charlotte CC, NC | 1,296 |
| 2011 | Danielle Kang beat Moriya Jutanugarn (THA) | Rhode Island CC | 1,013 |
| 2012 | Lydia Ko (NZL) beat Jaye marie Green 3 and 1 | Cleveland, OH | 1,170 |
| 1896–1952 | 18-hole stroke play qualifying before match play | | |
| 1953–1963 | All match play | | |
| 1964–1972 | 36-hole stroke play qualifying before match play | | |
| 1973–1979 | 18-hole stroke play qualifying before match play | | |
| 1980– | 36-hole stroke play qualifying before match play | | |

# NCAA Championships (Women) *University of Georgia Golf Course, Athens, Georgia*

## Annie Park leads Southern Callifornia to a record 21 shots NCAA victory

Unflappable freshman Annie Park raced to a six shot victory in the individual section of the NCAA Championship at the University of Georgia Golf Club in Athens and in the process helped Southern California win the team event by a record margin.

Park, from Levittown, NY, and her team mates Rachel Morris, Sophia Popov, Doris Chen and Kyung Kim finished with a 19 under par total of 1,133 giving the University of Southern California a staggering 21-shot winning margin over runners-up Duke with third placed Purdue 40 shots behind the winners.

Park was the seventh freshman to win the Championship since 1991 when Annika Sörenstam won as an Arizona University freshman. She was the fourth freshman to win the title from USC following Jennifer Rosales in 1998, Mikada Parmlid in 2003 and Dewi Claire Schreefel in 2006.

Park had rounds of 70, 67, 70 and 71 for her winning total of ten under par 278, six ahead of Duke's Lindy Duncan. After shooting 67 in the second round she completed a bogey-free 70 on the third day but had a much more topsy-turvy 71 on the final day when coach Andrea Gaston sent her assistant Justin Silverstein to walk with her just to give her any encouragement needed.

Park dropped two shots on the front nine but lipped out for a hole in one at the tricky short 13th before stumbling to drop four shots in three holes from the 15th. She remained calm, however, and a 220yds 5-wood second shot to the last gave her a chance of an eagle. She settled for a birdie.

Afterwards assistant coach Silverstein said that he was impressed with her unflappable ability to bounce back from bad shots or bad holes

## NCAA Championships (Women) continued

Her victory was the culmination of a great few weeks for her because she was joint first in the NCAA West Regional Championship and medallist in the PAC 12 Championship.

For the team it was an historic success making up for having let a five shot lead slip the previous year when Alabama finally triumphed by one. Their 1,133 winning total beat the previous record set by UCLA in 2004 by a massive 15 strokes

After an NCAA record low round team score of 276 in the second round which gave USC a 12 shot lead, coach Gaston had warned the girls that no lead was safe and that they needed to stay "in the moment". She need not have worried!

### Team event

| | | |
|---|---|---|
| 1 | S. California | 284-276-285-288—1,133 |
| 2 | Duke | 286-289-287-292—1,154 |
| 3 | Purdue | 289-289-295-300—1,173i |

4 UCLA 1,174; 5 Arizona State 1,181; 6 Auburn 1,183; 7 Alabama 1,189; 8 Arizona 1,190; 9 Oklahoma, Michigan State, Tulane 1,191; 12 Oklahoma State 1,193; 13 Arkansas, Stanford 1,200; 15 Northwestern 1,201; 16 UC Davis 1, 203; 17 Florida 1,205; 18 Vanderbilt 1,206; 19 San Jose State 1,209; 20 South Carolina 1,211; 21 Texas 1,213; 22 Oregon 1,217; 23 Wisconsin 1, 218; 24 Miss. State 1,221

**Winning team:** Annie Park, Kyung Kim, Rachel Morris, Doris Chen, Sophia Popov

### Individual Championship

| | | | | | | |
|---|---|---|---|---|---|---|
| 1 | Annie Park (S. California) | 70-67-70-71—278 | | | (Northwestern) | |
| 2 | Lindy Duncan (Duke) | 72-71-71-70—284 | 29 | Erica Popson (Tennessee) | 72-75-73-75—295 |
| 3 | Paula Reto (Purdue) | 71-73-70-72—286 | | Mariah Stackhouse | 72-68-74-81—295 |
| 4 | Celine Boutier (Duke) | 69-73-71-74—287 | | (Stanford | |
| | Erynne Lee (UCLA) | 71-70-73-73—287 | | Victoria Trapani (Auburn) | 80-72-69-74—295 |
| 6 | Kyung Kim (S. California) | 74-69-69-77—289 | 32 | Laura Blanco (Arizona | 74-70-73-79—296 |
| | Stephanie Meadow | 69-67-73-80—289 | | State) | |
| | (Alabama) | | | Betty Chen (UC Davis) | 73-73-72-78—296 |
| | Christine Meier (Michigan | 72-75-69-73—289 | | Taylor Schmidt | 71-73-74-78—296 |
| | State) | | | (Oklahoma) | |
| | Sophia Popov (Southern | 71-70-74-74—289 | | Carlie Yadloczky (Auburn) | 74-77-70-75—296 |
| | California) | | 36 | Irina Gabasa (Vanderbilt) | 74-72-77-74—297 |
| 10 | Noemi Jimenez (Arizona | 73-68-72-77—290 | 37 | Manon Gidali (Arizona) | 73-77-73-75—298 |
| | State) | | | Mia Piccio (Florida) | 73-75-75-75—298 |
| | Ally McDonald (Miss. | 70-69-70-81—290 | | Demi Runas (UC Davis) | 74-74-71-79—298 |
| | State) | | | Kelly Shon (Princeton) | 76-72-76-74—298 |
| | Marta Sanz (Auburn) | 79-69-68-74—290 | | Victoria Vela (Arkansas) | 74-71-77-76—298 |
| | Andrea Vilarasau (Arizona) | 72-72-76-70—290 | 42 | Regan De Guzman (San | 67-75-73-84—299 |
| 14 | Maribel Lopez Porras | 76-67-72-76—291 | | Jose State) | |
| | (Tulane) | | | Josephine Janson | 78-74-76-71—299 |
| 15 | Doris Chen (S. California) | 72-78-72-70—292 | | (Oklahoma State) | |
| | Aurora Kan (Purdue) | 71-71-77-73—292 | | Lauren Kim (Stanford) | 71-75-73-80—299 |
| 17 | Laetitia Beck (Duke) | 71-75-71-76—293 | | Kendall Prince (Arizona) | 74-73-74-78—299 |
| | Gemma Dryburgh | 71-74-74-74—293 | | Louise Ridderstrom | 72-74-75-78—299 |
| | (Tulane) | | | (UCLA) | |
| | Jenny Hahn (Vanderbilt) | 71-67-79-76—293 | | Kris Yoo (Wisconsin) | 75-74-73-77—299 |
| | Chirapat Jao-Javanil | 75-70-73-75—293 | 48 | Justine Dreher (South | 77-77-73-73—300 |
| | (Oklahoma) | | | Carolina) | |
| | Rachel Morris (Southern | 71-70-79-73—293 | | Hanule Sky Seo (Oregon) | 79-72-73-76—300 |
| | California) | | 50 | Courtney Ellenbogen | 74-72-74-81—301 |
| | Julie Yang (Oklahoma | 74-72-73-74—293 | | (Duke) | |
| | State) | | | Allyssa Ferrell (Michigan | 74-72-74-81—301 |
| 23 | Laura Gonzalez (Purdue) | 72-73-72-77—294 | | State) | |
| | Cassy Isagawa (Oregon) | 75-71-70-78—294 | | Camilla Hedberg (Florida) | 73-75-77-76—301 |
| | Lee Lopez (UCLA) | 73-69-77-75—294 | | Justine Lee (Arizona State) | 72-76-80-73—301 |
| | Tiffany Lua (UCLA) | 73-74-72-75—294 | | Ying Luo (Washington) | 72-74-77-78—301 |
| | Emma Talley (Alabama) | 71-71-77-75—294 | | Jayde Panos (Oklahoma | 75-74-73-79—301 |
| | Suchaya Tangkamolprasert | 71-72-76-75—294 | | State) | |

| | | | | | | |
|---|---|---|---|---|---|---|
| 50T | Caroline Powers (Michigan State) | 76-74-79-72—301 | 93 | Emilie Alonso (Arizona State) | 81-75-74-78—308 |
| | Emily Tubert (Arkansas) | 75-73-74-79—301 | | Desiree Dubreuil (Texas) | 75-74-77-82—308 |
| 58 | Jennifer Brumbaugh (San Jose State) | 73-76-71-82—302 | | Liz Nagel (Michigan State) | 78-74-76-80—308 |
| | Emilie Burger (Georgia) | 75-77-75-75—302 | | Lauren Weaver (Northwestern) | 79-73-77-79—308 |
| | Alejandra Cangrejo (Duke) | 77-73-80-72—302 | 97 | Patricia Garcia (Arizona) | 79-75-74-81—309 |
| | Silvia Garces (Tulane) | 74-75-75-78—302 | | Olafia Kristinsdottir (Wake Forest) | 79-75-77-78—309 |
| | Gabriela Lopez (Arkansas) | 74-76-75-77—302 | | Meredith Swanson (South Carolina) | 79-74-74-82—309 |
| | Daniela Ordonez (Arizona State) | 74-74-77-77—302 | 100 | Lindsay Danielson (Wisconsin) | 79-75-76-80—310 |
| | Bertine Strauss (Texas) | 73-77-74-78—302 | | Kaitlin Park (Northwestern) | 75-74-78-83—310 |
| | A C Tanguay (Oklahoma) | 75-71-75-81—302 | 102 | Caroline Inglis (Oregon) | 74-77-77-83—311 |
| 66 | Ursa Orehek (Florida) | 76-73-75-79—303 | | Amy Simanton (UC Davis) | 75-74-82-80—311 |
| | Aaren Ziegler (Wisconsin) | 76-81-73-73—303 | 104 | Kendall Martindale (Vanderbilt) | 77-75-75-85—312 |
| 68 | Hana Lee (Northwestern) | 73-74-77-80—304 | | Madison Opfer (Tulane) | 74-76-80-82—312 |
| | Suzie Lee (S. Carolina) | 74-78-75-77—304 | | Kathleen Rojas (San Jose State) | 72-86-74-80—312 |
| | Madison Pressel (Texas) | 77-72-77-78—304 | | Elena Warren (Miss. State) | 76-82-72-82—312 |
| | Kishi Sinha (Purdue) | 75-73-77-79—304 | | Trisha Witherby (Michigan State) | 76-71-86-79—312 |
| | Lauren Stratton (Vanderbilt) | 77-75-76-76—304 | 109 | Hannah Collier (Alabama) | 77-71-81-84—313 |
| 73 | Diana Fernandez (Auburn) | 72-75-78-80—305 | | Mary L Gallagher (Miss. State) | 78-74-77-84—313 |
| | Jennifer Kirby (Alabama) | 73-75-75-82—305 | | Mary Fran Hillow (South Carolina) | 77-76-79-81—313 |
| | Daniela Lendl (Alabama) | 75-75-76-79—305 | | Andrea Wong (UC Davis) | 77-79-75-82—313 |
| | Sarah Schmelzel (South Carolina) | 76-80-70-79—305 | | Anna Young (Florida) | 80-78-78-77—313 |
| | Elcin Ulu (Florida) | 77-75-78-75—305 | 114 | Kimberly Dinh (Wisconsin) | 73-83-75-83—314 |
| | Bev Vatananugulkit (UC Davis) | 77-76-76-76—305 | | Ani Gulugian (UCLA) | 77-74-82-81—314 |
| | Sally Watson (Stanford) | 76-73-77-79—305 | | Janie Jackson (Arizona) | 80-75-82-77—314 |
| 80 | Jennifer Ha (Kent State) | 79-70-80-77—306 | | Emily Penttila (Tulane) | 78-73-76-87—314 |
| | Katelyn Sepmoree (Texas) | 77-72-78-79—306 | | Rica Tse (Miss. State) | 76-78-75-85—314 |
| | Elizabeth Szokol (Northwestern) | 82-78-70-76—306 | 119 | Alexis Nelson (Wisconsin) | 77-79-79-81—316 |
| | Margaux Vanmol (Purdue) | 80-72-76-78—306 | 120 | Danielle Frasier (Stanford) | 84-76-77-81—318 |
| | Kelsey Vines (Oklahoma State) | 76-80-75-75—306 | | Cali Hipp (Oregon) | 76-75-77-90—318 |
| 85 | Emily Collins (Oklahoma) | 71-79-79-78—307 | | Megan Osland (San Jose State) | 80-76-79-83—318 |
| | Lauren Falley (Oklahoma State) | 78-80-73-76—307 | | Gabi Oubre (Miss. State) | 82-81-75-80—318 |
| | Emma Lavy (Arkansas) | 73-78-76-80—307 | | Jamie Yun (Auburn) | 81-76-83-78—318 |
| | Regina Plasencia (Arkansas) | 77-73-80-77—307 | 125 | Avery Sills (Oregon) | 76-79-84-87—326 |
| | Rachelle Reali (San Jose State) | 72-76-77-82—307 | 126 | Rene Sobolewski (Vanderbilt) | 85-80-84-87—336 |
| | Kaitlyn Rohrback (Oklahoma) | 74-77-78-78—307 | | | |
| | Haley Stephens (Texas) | 74-77-76-80—307 | | | |
| | Mariko Tumangan (Stanford) | 71-72-77-87—307 | | | |

# National Championships 2013

For past winners see earlier editions of *The R&A Golfer's Handbook*

*Players are from the host nation unless stated*

## Africa

### Regional All Africa Championship   *Centurion CC, South Africa*

| | | |
|---|---|---|
| 1 | Magda Kruger (Centurion) | 65-64-71—200 |
| 2 | Nobuhle Dlamini (Centurion) | 73-72-65—210 |
| 3 | Lara Weinstein (R. Joburg & Kensington) | 71-71-69—211 |

### South African Amateur Stroke Play Championship   *Pretoria CC*

| | | |
|---|---|---|
| 1 | Nobuhle Dlamini (SWZ) | 76-73-70—219 |
| 2 | Lara Weinstein | 75-82-74—231 |
| 3 | Danielle du Toit | 80-79-73—232 |
| | Gina Switala | 77-74-81—232 |

### South African Women's Amateur Championship   *Milnerton GC*

**Semi-Finals:**   Ji Sun Kang (KOR) beat Nicole Garcia  4 and 3
Kim Williams beat Kelly Erasmus  1 up
**Final:**   Kim Williams beat Ji Sun Kang  2 and 1

### South African Mid-Amateur Championship   *Graceland CC*

| | | |
|---|---|---|
| 1 | Sonja Bland (Fancourt CC) | 77-82-77—236 |
| 2 | Sheryl Matthews (Randpark GC) | 83-76-78—237 |
| 3 | Millie Dondashe (East London GC) | 83-80-82—245 |
| | Carina Theron (Bloemfontein GC) | 81-80-84—245 |

### WGSA 72-hole Championship   *Maccauvlei CC, South Africa*

| | | |
|---|---|---|
| 1 | Nobuhle Dlamini (Centurion) | 69-74-72-74—289 |
| 2 | Kim Williams (Els Club, Copperleaf) | 76-72-70-70—290 |
| 3 | Carrie Oark (Irene) | 77-73-74-72—296 |

**Team event** (Swiss Trophy):

| | | |
|---|---|---|
| 1 | Gauteng North "A" | 145-146-142-146—579 |
| 2 | Gauteng North "B" | 150-154-145-147—596 |
| 3 | Western Province "A" | 153-155-149-150—607 |

4 Gauteng "A" 610; 5 Boland "A" 623; 6 Mpumalanga 623; 7 Western Province "B" 625; 8 Gauteng "B" 625; 9 Ekurhuleni "A" 629; 10 KwaZulu Natal "A" 649; 11 Northwest "A" 655; 12 Southern Cape 658.

**Winning team:** Nobuhle Dlamini, Kim Williams and Magda Kruger

**Challenge Trophy:** Gauteng North "C" 632

### Zimbabwe Ladies Open Championship   *Borrowdale Brook GC*

| | | |
|---|---|---|
| 1 | Angel Eaton (TAN) | 78-76-77—231 |
| 2 | Batsirai Tilowakuti | 76-75-84—235 |

## Americas

# Argentine Women's Amateur Championship    *Martindale CC*
**Semi-finals:**  Luz Besio beat Agustina Zeballos 1 up
                  Ruiz Sofia Goicoechea beat Aldana Maira Foigel at 19th
**Final:**        Luz Besio beat Ruiz Sofia Goicoechea 3 and 2
**Leading qualifier:** Aylen Irizar 74-70—144

---

# 12th United Insurance Barbados Women's Open    *Apes Hill CC, Barbados GC and Royal Westmoreland*

| | | |
|---|---|---|
| 1 | Rae "Muffin" Stollmeyer | 76-75-78—229 |
| 2 | Mavi Vergos | 78-78-81—237 |
| 3 | Julia Stephenson | 80-81-83—244 |

---

# Royale Cup Canadian Women's Amateur Championship    *Club de Golf Beloeil*

| | | |
|---|---|---|
| 1 | Brooke Henderson (Smith Falls) | 69-70-70-66—275 |
| 2 | Anne-Catherine Tanguay (Quebec) | 71-68-69-73—281 |
| 3 | Gabrida Lopez (MEX) | 69-75-71-68—283 |

---

# Royale Cup Canadian Women's Senior Championship    *Spallumcheen G&CC.*

| | | |
|---|---|---|
| 1 | Mary Ann Hayward (Aurora) | 75-67-71—213 |
| 2 | Alison Murdoch (Victoria) | 74-72-72—218 |
| 3 | Dian Dolan (Gatinau) | 73-75-72—220 |
|   | Marie-Therese Torti (Candiac) | 77-72-71—220 |

---

# Caribbean Amateur Championship (George Teale Trophy)    *St Thomas, US Virgin Islands*

| | | |
|---|---|---|
| 1 | Monifa Sealy (TRI) | 71-77-71-77—296 |
| 2 | Samantha Widmer (CAY) | 78-79-76-76—309 |
| 3 | Ali Prazak (ISV) | 75-80-77-80—312 |

---

# 111th North and South Women's Championship    *Pinehurst Resort*
**Stroke Play:**

| | | |
|---|---|---|
| 1 | Mariah Stackhouse (Riverdale) | 69-73-70—212 |
|   | Hayley Bettencourt (Halls Head) | 71-73-68—212 |
|   | Ashlan Ramsey (Milledgeville) | 71-71-70—212 |

**Match Play:**
**Semi-Finals:**  Ally McDonald (Fulton) beat Michelle Piyapattra (Corona) 2 and 1
                  Yueer Cindy Feng (Orlando) beat Demi Runas (Torrance) 4 and 3
**Final:**        Ally McDonald beat Yueer Cindy Feng 3 and 2

---

# US Women's Mid-Amateur Championship    *Biltmore Forest CC, Asheville, N. Carolina*
**Semi-Finals:**  Julia Potter (Granger, IN) beat Stefi Markovich (CAN) 3 and 2
                  Margaret Shirley (Roswell, GA) beat Meghan Stasi (Oakland Park, FL) at 19th
**Final:**        Julia Potter beat Margaret Shirley at 19th
**Medallist:**    Julia Potter (Granger, IN) 69-74—143

---

# 52nd US Amateur Women's Senior Championship    *CordeValle, San Martin, California*
**Semi-Finals:**  Ellen Port (St Louis, MO) beat Mary Jane Hiestand (Naples, FL) 4 and 3
                  Susan Cohn (Palm Beach Gardens, FL) beat Caryn Wilson (Rancho Mirage, CA) 4 and 3
**Final:**        Ellen Port beat Susan Cohn 3 and 2

## US Amateur Public Links Championship  Norman, Oklahoma
**Semi-Finals:**    Lauren Diaz-Yi (Thousand Oaks, CA) beat Raychelle Santos (La Quinta, CA)  2 and 1
Doris Chen (Bradenton, FL) beat Julie Yang (Stillwater, OK)  at 19th
**Final:**    Lauren Diaz-Yi beat Doris Chen  4 and 3

## US Women's Amateur Championship  see page 386

## China National Amateur Championship  CGA Nanshan ITC (Cuigu course)
| | | |
|---|---|---|
| 1 | Michelle Koh (MAS) | 71-70-70—211 |
| 2 | Kelly Tanguat Chen (MAS) | 70-72-72—214 |
| 3 | Danting Cai | 75-70-70—215 |

## Hong Kong Ladies Open Amateur Championship  Clearwater Bay G&CC
| | | |
|---|---|---|
| 1 | Chayanid Prapassarangkul (THA) | 68-37—105 |
| 2 | Ornnicha Konsunthea (THA) | 77-33—110 |
| | Sherman Sanjiniwatthanapong (THA) | 74-36—110 |

## Hong Kong Ladies Close Amateur Championship  Clearwater Bay G&CC
| | | |
|---|---|---|
| 1 | Michelle Cheung (HKGC) | 79-75-73—227 |
| 2 | Yik Ching Kitty Tam (HKGC) | 81-74-74—229 |
| 3 | Ching Suet Michelle Lee (DBGC) | 83-78-76—237 |

## Hong Kong Open Mid-Amateur Championship  Clearwater Bay G&CC
| | | |
|---|---|---|
| 1 | Alice Kerr | 83-42—125 |
| 2 | Felicia Louey | 85-42—127 |
| 3 | Jane Lo | 88-42—130 |

## Hong Kong Close Mid-Amateur Championship  Clearwater Bay G&CC
| | | |
|---|---|---|
| 1 | Si Nga Cindy Lee | 89-82-79—250 |
| 2 | Alice Karr | 88-85-85—258 |
| 3 | Emma Pike | 86-90-88—264 |

## All-India Women's Amateur Championship  Bombay Presidency GC, Chembur
**Semi-finals:**    Gurbani Singh beat Ridhima Dilawari
Aditi Ashok beat Astha Madan
**Final:**    Gurbani Singh beat Aditi Ashok  5 and 4

## Israel Amateur Women's Open  Caesarea GC
| | | |
|---|---|---|
| 1 | Hadas Libman | 73-74-71—218 |
| 2 | Katharina Schulz (GER) | 76-76-72—224 |
| 3 | Ludovica Farina (ITA) | 75-76-80—231 |

## 55th Japanese Amateur Championship  Tojigaoka Marine Hills GC
**Semi-finals:**    Yumi Matsubara beat Mao Nozawa  1 up
Haruka Morita beat Hibiki Kitamura  1 up
**Final:**    Haruka Morita beat Yumi Matsubara  at 37th
**Third place play-off:** Mao Nozawa beat Hibiki Kitamura  1 up

## 30th Malaysian Women's Open Amateur Championship  *Kuala Lumpur G&CC*

| | | |
|---|---|---|
| I | Kelly Tan | 67-70-71—208 |
| 2 | Cyna Rodriguez (PHI) | 69-72-68—209 |
| | Princess Mary Superal (PHI) | 70-68-71—209 |

## Philippines Women's Open Amateur Championship  *Wack G&CC*

| | | |
|---|---|---|
| I | Dottie Ardina (pro) | 70-72-73—215 |
| 2 | Clare Legaspi | 75-74-74—223 |
| 3 | Princess Mary Superal | 76-77-76—229 |

## 14th Singapore National Championship  *Jurong CC*

**Semi-finals:** Joey Poh beat Elizabeth Ang  4 and 3
Koh Sock Hwee beat Low Si Xuan  6 and 4
**Final:** Koh Sock Hwee beat Joey Poh  7 and 6

## 126th Sri Lanka Ladies Amateur Match Play Championship  *Victoria G&CC*

**Semi-finals:** Gauri Monga (IND) beat S Selvaratnam  5 and 4
Rasika Ekanayake beat Millie Saroha (IND)  2 holes
**Final:** Gauri Monga beat Rasika Ekanayake  14 and 13

## Sri Lanka Ladies Stroke Play Championship  *Victoria G&CC*

| | | |
|---|---|---|
| I | Gauri Monga (IND) | 72-72—144 |
| 2 | Millie Saroha (IND) | 72-73—145 |
| 3 | Rasika Ekanayake | 82-80—162 |

## Singha Thailand Women's Open Amateur  *Panya Indra CC*

| | | |
|---|---|---|
| I | Busabakorn Sukphan* | 75-72-69-69—285 |
| 2 | Princess Superal (PHI) | 72-70-73-70—285 |
| *Sukphan won at the second extra hole | | |
| 3 | Suvathee Chanachai | 72-75-72-69—288 |
| | Supamas Sangchan | 74-71-71-72—288 |
| | Eri Okayama (JPN) | 70-75-71-72—288 |

## Australian Women's Amateur Championship  (inaugurated 1894)

*Commonwealth GC and Woodlands GC  Jan 15–20*
**Semi-finals:** Minjee Lee (WA) beat Julienne Soo (VIC)  7 and 6
Jenny Lee (SA) beat Hannah Green (WA)  2 and 1
**Final:** Minjee Lee beat Jenny Lee  6 and 5
**Medallists:** Grace Lennon (VIC) 70-70—140; Lydia Ko (NZL) 69-71—140

## Australian Women's Mid-Amateur Championship  *Moonah Links (Open course), Victoria*

| | | |
|---|---|---|
| I | Sue Wooster (Victoria) | 80-85—165 |
| 2 | Katrina Jones (Queensland) | 83-83—166 |
| 3 | Kerry Henningsen (Victoria) | 84-85—169 |
| *Reduced to 36 holes because of bad weather on first day* | | |

## New Zealand Amateur Championship (inaugurated 1893)    *Manawatu GC*    April 24–27
**Semi-finals:**    Hannah Seifert beat Chantelle Cassidy  6 and 4
Julianne Alvarez beat Munchin Keh  1 hole
**Final:**    Julianne Alvarez beat Hannah Seifert  7 and 6
**Medallist:**    Wenyung Keh 72-71—143

## New Zealand Stroke Play Championship (Mellsop Cup)    (inaugurated 1911)
*Paraparaumu Beach GC*

| | | |
|---|---|---|
| 1 | Chantelle Cassidy | 73-73-79-74—299 |
| 2 | Lita Guo | 74-72-80-76—302 |
| 3 | Te Rongapai Clay | 75-74-77-80—306 |

## New Zealand Mid-Amateur Championship    *Wairakei GC*

| | | |
|---|---|---|
| 1 | Jacqui Morgan (AUS) | 81-77-78—236 |
| 2 | Trish McBride (Ngahinapouri) | 82-85-83—250 |
| 3 | Kathy Olsen (Maraenui) | 90-80-84—254 |

## Austrian International Women's Championship    *Thermen GC*

| | | |
|---|---|---|
| 1 | Virginia Elena Carta (ITA) | 77-68-69—214 |
| 2 | Morgane Metraux | 71-78-66—215 |
| 3 | Antonia-Leonie Eberhard (GER) | 75-71-71—217 |
| | Anja Purgauer | 73-74-70—217 |

## Belgian International Championship    *Royal Antwerp GC*

| | | |
|---|---|---|
| 1 | Laura Gonzales Escallon (R. Waterloo) | 71-68-72-68—279 |
| 2 | Leslie Cloots (Ternesse) | 67-70-71-73—281 |
| 3 | Kim Metraux (Club of Guests) | 71-73-68-73—285 |

## Belgian National Championship    *Golf de Mean*

| | | |
|---|---|---|
| 1 | Manon de Roey | 72-76-69-72—289 |
| 2 | Laura Gonzalez Escallion | 71-75-72-73—291 |
| 3 | Leslie Cloots | 80-74-70-75—299 |

## Ladies British Amateur Championship    see page 381

## Ladies' British Open Amateur Stroke Play Championship (inaugurated 1969)
*Prestwick GC*

| | | |
|---|---|---|
| 1 | Jing Yan (CHN) | 68-72-73-69—282 |
| 2 | Gemma Dryburgh | 72-72-69-71—284 |
| 3 | Roberta Liti (ITA) | 72-70-77-68—287 |

## British Ladies' Open Championship    *Machynys Peninsula G&CC*
**Semi-Finals:**    Luna Sobron (ESP) beat Karolin Lampert (GER)  1 hole
Georgia Hall (ENG) beat Noemi Jimenez (ESP)  3 and 1
**Final:**    Gorgia Hall beat Luna Sobron  1 hole

## Senior Ladies' British Open Amateur Championship  *Royal Portrush GC*

| | | |
|---|---|---|
| 1 | Ann Lewis (Royal St David's) | 78-82—160 |
| 2 | Sheena McElroy (Grange) | 76-85—161 |
| | Minna Kaarnalahti (FIN) | 75-86—161 |

## Bulgarian Amateur Championship  *Pravets CC*

| | | |
|---|---|---|
| 1 | Maya Kucherkova | 75-84—159 |
| 2 | Ivana Simeonova | 93-89—182 |
| 3 | Stefani Skokanska | 86-99—185 |

## Czech Republic Amateur Championship  *Karlovy Vary GC*

| | | |
|---|---|---|
| 1 | Ursa Orehek (SLO) | 74-70-70-74—288 |
| 2 | Katerina Viasinova | 75-71-72-73—291 |
| 3 | Nemka Christine Gemmershaus | 73-73-72-74—292 |

## Danish International Ladies Championship  *Silkeborg GC*

| | | |
|---|---|---|
| 1 | Nicole Broch Larsen (pro) | 68-77-75-76—296 |
| 2 | Nanna Madsen | 79-67-73-79—298 |
| 3 | Caroline Nistrup | 76-77-70-76—299 |

## Dutch National Open Championship  *Rosendaelshe GC, Arnhem*

| | | |
|---|---|---|
| 1 | Dewi Weber | 75-74-69-73—291 |
| 2 | Myrte Eikenaar | 74-76-70-75—295 |
| 3 | Brit Steeghs | 76-72-75-74—297 |

## Dutch Women's National Stroke Play Championship  *Houtrak GC*

| | | |
|---|---|---|
| 1 | Myrte Eikenaar | 69-75-76-74—295 |
| 2 | Dewi Weber | 75-71-82-74—302 |
| 3 | Ileen Domela Nieuwenhuis | 79-76-74-76—305 |

## Dutch National Match Play Championship  *Broekpolder GC*

**Semi-finals:** Myrte Eikenaar beat Noelle Beijer 6 and 5
Floor Sinke beat Michelle Naafs 1 hole

**Final:** Myrte Eikenaar beat Floor Sinke 4 and 2

## English Ladies Close Amateur Championship  *Kings Norton GC*

| | | |
|---|---|---|
| 1 | Sarah-Jane Boyd | 73-70-72-75—290 |
| 2 | Alexandra Peters | 71-77-73-71—292 |
| 3 | Gabriella Cowley | 71-73-76-75—295 |

## English Women's Open Amateur Championship  *Mannings Heath GC*

| | | |
|---|---|---|
| 1 | Amy Boulden (Conway)* | 72-69-72-72—285 |
| 2 | Charlotte Thomas (Singapore) | 71-70-71-73—285 |
| *Boulden won at the first extra hole* | | |
| 3 | Hayley Davis (Ferndown) | 71-74-72-70—287 |

## English Women's Amateur Championship (inaugurated 1984)   *Kings Norton GC*

| | | |
|---|---|---|
| 1 | Sarah Jane Boyd (Truro) | 73-70-72-75—290 |
| 2 | Alexandra Peters (Notts Ladies) | 71-77-73-71—292 |
| 3 | Gabriella Cowley (Brocket Hall) | 71-73-76-75—295 |

## English Women's Open Mid-Amateur Championship (inaugurated 1982)
*John O'Gaunt GC*

**Semi-Finals:**   Charlotte Thomas (SIN) beat Samantha Giles (St Mellion)  2 and 1
Chloe Rogers (Braintree) beat Emma Taylor (Saunton)  5 and 4
**Final:**   Charlotte Thomas beat Chloe Rogers  4 and 3

## Senior Women's Open Amateur Stroke Play Championship   *Shanklin & Sandown GC*

| | | |
|---|---|---|
| 1 | Sue Dye (Delamere Forest) | 71-71-74—216 |
| 2 | Christine Quinn (Hockley) | 74-79-70—223 |
| 3 | Caroline Berry (Bromborough) | 78-78-69—225 |
| | Amanda Mayne (Saltford) | 74-77-74—225 |

## Senior Women's English Close Match Play Championship   *Sherwood Forest GC*

**Semi-Finals:**   Christine Quinn (Hockley) beat Karen Lobb (Northamptonshire County)  3 and 2
Janette Melville (Sherwood Forest) beat Catherine Rawthore (Sale)  at 20th
**Final:**   Janet Melville beat Christine Quinn  2 and 1
**Medallist:** Lula Housman (Highgate) 77-78—157

## Estonian Open Championship   *Niitvalja GC*

| | | |
|---|---|---|
| 1 | Antonia-Leonie Eberhard (GER) | 73-66-76—215 |
| 2 | Roosa Narhi | 79-75-74—228 |
| 3 | Anna Diana Svanka (LAT) | 74-77-78—229 |

## Estonian National Stroke Play Championship   *Estonian G&CC (Sea course)*

| | | |
|---|---|---|
| 1 | Mari Hutsi | 76-80-78—234 |
| 2 | Liis Kuuli | 82-82-73—237 |
| 3 | Cliona Georgia Dalberg | 85-79-81—245 |

## Ladies European Open Amateur Championship see page 384

## European International Senior Ladies Championship Estonia G&CC  June 13–15

| | | |
|---|---|---|
| 1 | Helen Maxe (SWE) | 73-71-77—221 |
| 2 | Anna-Maria Lehtonen (FIN) | 74-74-76—224 |
| 3 | Maria de Orueta (ESP) | 79-71-75—225 |

**Super Seniors (over 60):** Viveca Hoff (SWE) 72-77-79—228

## International European Ladies Amateur Championship   *Aura GC (Turku), Finland*

| | | |
|---|---|---|
| 1 | Emily Kristine Pedersen (DEN) | 67-73-64-72—276 |
| 2 | Laura Gonzalez Escallon (BEL) | 69-74-68-68—279 |
| 3 | Krista Bakker (FIN) | 75-68-73-76—282 |
| | Céline Boutier (FRA) | 73-69-72-68—282 |
| | Noemi Jimenez (ESP) | 71-69-71-71—282 |

## Finnish Amateur Championship  *Helsingin GK*

| | | |
|---|---|---|
| I | Anna Backman | 74-66-70—210 |
| 2 | Sanna Nuutinen | 66-71-74—211 |
| 3 | Marika Voss | 73-70-73—216 |
| | Matilda Castren | 68-75-73—216 |

## Finnish Women's Stroke Play Championship  *St Laurence GC*

| | | |
|---|---|---|
| I | Sanna Nuutinen | 74-69-69-75—287 |
| 2 | Marika Voss | 71-72-74-71—288 |
| 3 | Miia Pulliainen | 75-75 70-74—294 |

## French Closed Championship  (Coupe Pierre Deschamps)  *RCF La Boulie*

**Semi-finals:** Chloe Salort (RCF La Boulie) beat Emma Ambroise (Evian Resort) 6 and 5
Marion Veysseyre (Toulouse Viel) beat Loiuse Gateau-Chovelon 3 and 2
**Final:** Marion Veysseyre beat Chloe Salort 4 and 3

## German Women's Championship  *GR Hardenberg*

| | | |
|---|---|---|
| I | Olivia Cowan | 71-72-73-70—286 |
| 2 | Karolin Lampert | 73-70-76-69—288 |
| 3 | Franziska Friedrich | 71-72-68-80—291 |

## German International Women's Amateur Championship  *Golf Club Ulm*

| | | |
|---|---|---|
| I | Emma Broze (FRA) | 76-73-70-73—292 |
| 2 | Arina Wolf | 76-70-74-73—293 |
| 3 | Nicoline Skang Engstroem (NOR) | 71-77-73-73—294 |

## Hungarian Women's Amateur Open  *Balaton G&YC*

| | | |
|---|---|---|
| I | Csilla Lajtai Rozsa | 78-72-76—226 |
| 2 | Anja Purgauer (AUT) | 72-84-72—228 |
| | Camille Richelle (BEL) | 77-77-74—228 |

## Hungarian Open Championship  *Royal Balaton G&YC*

| | | |
|---|---|---|
| I | Csilla Lajtai Rozsa | 78-72-76—226 |
| 2 | Anja Purgauer (AUT) | 72-84-72—228 |
| | Camille Richelle (BEL) | 77-77-74—228 |
| | Marie Lunackova (CZE) | 78-74-76—228 |

## Irish Women's Close Amateur Championship  (inaugurated 1894)  *Ballybunion*

**Semi-Finals:** Lisa Maguire (Slieve Russell) beat Olivia Mehaffey (RCD Ladies) 5 and 4
Paula Grant (Lisburn) beat Jessica Carty (Holywood) 3 and 1
**Final:** Paula Grant beat Lisa Maguire at 19th

## Irish Women's Open Amateur Stroke Play Championship  (inaugurated 1993)
*The Castle GC, Dublin*

| | | |
|---|---|---|
| I | Meghan MacLaren (ENG) | 71-73-74—218 |
| 2 | Paula Grant (NIR) | 76-73-70—219 |
| 3 | Eilidh Briggs (SCO) | 76-71-80—227 |
| | Emma O'Driscoll | 74-76-77—227 |

## Irish Senior Women's Close Amateur Championship *Woodenbridge GC*

**Semi-Finals:** Suzanne Corcoran (Portumna) beat Gertie McMullan (The Island) 3 and 2
Carol Wickham (Laytown and Bettystown) beat Pat Doran (Donabate) 1 hole
**Final:** Corcoran beat Wickham 3 and 2
**Medallist:** Suzanne Corcoran 76-71—147

## Irish Women's Senior Open Championship *Castlerock GC*

| | | |
|---|---|---|
| 1 | Gertie McMullen (The Island) | 80-79-79—238 |
| 2 | Diane Williams (CAN) | 79-84-79—242 |
| 3 | Diane Nolan (CAN) | 86-79-78—243 |

**Nations Cup:**

| | | |
|---|---|---|
| 1 | Canada 'B' | 160-163-157—480 |
| 2 | Ireland 'A' | 162-162-162—486 |
| 3 | England 'A' | 167-161-158—486 |

4 Ireland 'B' 489; 5 Canada 'A' 490;6 USA 'A' 501; 7 Scotland 'A' 510; 8 England 'B' 513; 9 Scotland 'B' 535
**Winning team:** Diane Dolan, Diane Williams and Ivy Steinberg

## Italian Ladies Stroke Play Championship *Verona GC*

| | | |
|---|---|---|
| 1 | Roberta Liti | 76-71-72-73—292 |
| 2 | Martina Flori | 76-75-73-74—298 |
| 3 | Virginia Elena Carta | 74-72-80-73—299 |

## Latvian Amateur Championship *Ozo GC*

| | | |
|---|---|---|
| 1 | Linda Dobele | 226 |
| 2 | Anna Diana Svonky | 240 |
| 3 | Ieva Caca | 243 |

## Liechtenstein Open Ladies' Amateur Championship *GC Gams-Werdenberg*

| | | |
|---|---|---|
| 1 | Christine Tinner-Rampone (GER) | 81-85—166 |
| 2 | Jaimee Bodmer | 84-84—168 |
| 3 | Cornelia Fassold (SUI) | 93-90—183 |

## Lithuanian Open Championship *Capitals GC*

| | | |
|---|---|---|
| 1 | Anna Diana Svanka (LAT) | 88-84-77—249 |
| 2 | Indra Enina (LAT) | 89-88-86—263 |
| 3 | Ieva Cace (LAT) | 94-88-83—265 |

## Luxembourg Women's Amateur Championship *Golf Club Grand-Ducal*

| | | |
|---|---|---|
| 1 | Jacqueline Klepper (Belenhaff) | 83-91—174 |
| 2 | Marielle Marque (Belenhaff) | 93-84—177 |
| 3 | Christian Wanderschedit (Belenhaff) | 95-83—178 |

## Ping Grand Final (Four Ball Better Ball)   *Gainsborough Karsten GC*

| | | |
|---|---|---|
| 1 | Denise Page (11) and Sarah Dawson (5) (Willow Valley) 43 | 22pts |
| 2 | Cheryl Shepperson (14) and Pat Holloway (11) (Ormonde Fields) | 41 pts |
| 3 | Val Swales (8) and Pauline Bramley (4) (Hallamshire) | 41 pts |

## Polish Amateur Championship  Gradi CC

| | | |
|---|---|---|
| 1 | Ludovica Farina (ITA) | 70-75-71—216 |
| 2 | Dominika Gradecka | 78-72-72—222 |
| 3 | Dorota Zalewska | 78-74-76—228 |

## 83rd Portuguese Women's Championship  Montado Golf Resort, Lisbon

| | | |
|---|---|---|
| 1 | Clara Baena Sanchez (ESP) | 71-68-70—209 |
| 2 | Karolin Lampert (GER) | 70-72-69—211 |
| | Matilda Castren (FIN) | 70-72-69—211 |

## Russian Women's Amateur Championship  GC Agalarov

| | | |
|---|---|---|
| 1 | Nina Pegova | 68-69-71-73—281 |
| 2 | Angelina Monakhova | 81-74-72-78—305 |
| 3 | Vera Markevich | 80-75-77-80—312 |
| | Sofia Morozova | 76-78-75-83—312 |

## Scottish Ladies' Close Amateur Championship  (inaugurated 1903)  Tain

**Semi-Finals:** Clara Young (North Berwick) beat Rachel Polson (Peterculter) 4 and 3
Alyson McKechin (Elderslie) beat Megan Briggs (Kilmacolm) 2 and 1
**Final:** Alyson McKechin beat Clara Young 3 and 2

## Scottish Ladies' Open Stroke Play Championship  (Helen Holm Trophy)
(inaugurated 1973)  Troon Portland GC and Old Course Troon

| | | |
|---|---|---|
| 1 | Olivia Winning (Rotherham) | 70-72-78—220 |
| 2 | Alyson McKechin (Elderslie) | 76-72-74—222 |
| 3 | Poppy Finlay (Vicars Cross) | 72-74-76—142 |

## Scottish Senior Ladies' (Close) Amateur Championship  West Linton GC

**Stroke Play**

| | | |
|---|---|---|
| 1 | Anna Telfer | 76-79—155 |
| 2 | Heather Anderson | 78-78—156 |
| 3 | Margaret Tough | 79-78—157 |
| | Fiona De Vries | 77-80—158 |

**Match Play**
**Semi-Finals:** Fiona Hunter (Southerness) beat Kathleen Webster (Ladybank) at 19th
Kathleen Sutherland (Royal Montrose) beat Laura Bennett (Ladybank) 1 hole
**Final:** Fiona Hunter beat Kathleen Sutherland 2 and 1

## Scottish Women's Stroke Play Foursomes  Kirriemuir GC

| | | |
|---|---|---|
| 1 | Anne Laing and Lindsay Mathie (Vale of Leven and Playsport) | 80 |
| 2 | Mary Lou Watkins and Hazel Saunders (Gullane Ladies) | 81* |
| 3 | Sal Shepherd and Rachel Livingston (Craigmillar Park) | 83 |

*Watkins and Saunders won trophy because under the rules contestants must come from the same club*

## SLGA Medal Grand Final  King James VI GC, Perth

| | | |
|---|---|---|
| 1 | Heather Anderson (Blairgowrie) | 71 (4) 67 |
| 2 | Morag Wardrop (Turnhouse) | 81 (8) 73 |
| 3 | Lauren Lee (Musselburgh) | 85 (11) 74 |

## Scottish Champion of Champions   *Glasgow Gailes*

| | | |
|---|---|---|
| I | Megan Briggs (Renfrewshire) | 72 |
| 2 | Ailsa Summers (Angus) | 75 |
| 3 | Sammy Leslie (Aberdeenshire) | 78 |

## Scottish Veteran Ladies Championship   *Blairgowrie GC*

**Semi-Finals:**   Alison Bartlett beat Linda Dyball I hole
Alex Glennie beat Susan Arbuckle 4 and 3
**Final:**   Alison Bartlett beat Alex Glennie 5 and 4

## Slovak Amateur Stroke Play Championship   *GR Black Stork*

| | | |
|---|---|---|
| I | Natalia Heckova | 76-76—152 |
| 2 | Katerina Chovancova | 79-74—153 |
| 3 | Karolina Cordieri | 79-82—171 |
| 4 | Zuzana Bielikova | 79-82—171 |

## Slovak Women's Open Amateur Championship   *Welten GR*

| | | |
|---|---|---|
| I | Katerina Vlasinova (CZE) | 68-71-74—213 |
| 2 | Natalia Heckova | 74-71-72—217 |
| 3 | Nina Alexandra von Siebenthal (SUI) | 73-72-75—220 |

## Slovakian National Match Play Championship   *Black Stork GR*

**Semi-Finals:**   Natalia Heckova beat Zuzana Bielikova 3 and I
Lina Sekerkova beat Alexandra Patakova 3 and 2
**Final:**   Natalie Heckova beat Lina Sekerkova 2 and I
**Third-place play-off:** Alexandra Patakova beat Zuzana Bielikova at 19th

## Slovenian Women's International Championship   *GC Bled*

| | | |
|---|---|---|
| I | Katja Pogacar | 71-73-70—214 |
| 2 | Bianca Maria Fabrizio (ITA) | 75-77-75—227 |
| 3 | Lea Zeitler (AUT) | 75-77-76—228 |

## Spanish Amateur Championship (Copa de SM La Reina)   *Pula Golf*

**Semi-Finals:**   Emily Kristine Pedersen (DEN) beat Anyssia Herbaut (FRA) 3 and 2
Linnea Strom (SWE) beat Katerina Vlasinova (CZE) at 19th
**Final:**   Emily Kristine Pedersen beat Linnea Strom 5 and 3

## Spanish International Stroke Play Championship   *Las Colinas*

| | | |
|---|---|---|
| I | Luna Sobron | 70-72-70—212 |
| 2 | Natalia Escuriola | 73-72-68—213 |
| 3 | Mathilda Cappielez (FRA) | 73-72-69—214 |

## Swiss International Women's Amateur Championship   *Lausanne GC*

| | | |
|---|---|---|
| I | Ursa Orehek (SLO) | 150 |
| 2 | Manon Molle (FRA) | 151 |
| 3 | Nina von Sibenthal | 152 |
| | Justine Dreher (FRA) | 152 |

## 12th Turkish Women's Open Amateur Championship   *National GC*

| | | |
|---|---|---|
| 1 | Karolina Vlckova (CZE) | 81-75-76-79—311 |
| 2 | Leslie Cloots (BEL) | 79-84-74-77—314 |
| 3 | Tugce Erden | 82-77-78-80—317 |
| | Sena Ersoy | 83-76-82-76—317 |

## Welsh Ladies' Close Amateur Championship   (inaugurated 1905)   *Nefyn and District GC*

| | | |
|---|---|---|
| 1 | Amy Boulden | 69-73—142 |
| 2 | Katherine O'Connor | 71-73—144 |
| 3 | Chloe Williams | 71-74—145 |

## Welsh Ladies' Open Amateur Stroke Play Championship   (inaugurated 1976)

*The Vale Resort*

| | | |
|---|---|---|
| 1 | Amy Boulden | 75-75-74—224 |
| 2 | Alexandra Peters (ENG) | 75-77-76—228 |
| 3 | Samantha Burke | 76-77-76—229 |

## Welsh Senior Ladies' Open Championship   Denbigh GC

| | | |
|---|---|---|
| 1 | Jane Rees (Hendon) | 71-79—150 |
| 2 | Anna Lewis (Royal St Davids) | 77-75—155 |
| 3 | Sue Pidgeon (Wrekin) | 78-79—157 |

## Month by month in 2013

Jim Furyk becomes the sixth player in PGA Tour history to score 59, but finishes "only" third at the BMW Championship. Henrik Stenson wins two of the other three FedEx Cup play-off events, his victory at the Tour Championship giving the Swede the $10 million bonus. The Evian Masters is staged as a major for the first time and the title goes to Suzann Pettersen, while America have an easy 17–9 triumph at the Walker Cup.

# USA State Championships 2013

*US nationality unless stated*

| Alabama | Cammie Gray (SP/MP) | Idaho | Gabrielle Barker | N. Hampshire | Tracy Martin |
|---|---|---|---|---|---|
| Alaska | Terri McAngus | Illinois | Bing Singhsumalee | New Jersey | Alice Chen |
| Arizona | Kim Eaton (SP) | Indiana | Emily Podzielinski | New York | Jenna Hoecker |
| | Kylee Duede (MP) | Iowa | Megan Furnish (SP) | N. Carolina | Courtney McKim |
| Arkansas | Grier Bennett (SP) | Kansas | Laura Cilek (MP) | N. Dakota | Sarah Storandt |
| | Julie Oxendine | Kentucky | Lauren Falley | Ohio | Natalie Goodson |
| | (MP) | Louisiana | April Emerson | Oklahoma | Jade Staggs |
| California | Kaitlin Park | Maine | Sarah Davison | Oregon | Kendall Prince |
| Colorado | Melissa Martin (SP) | Maryland | Emily Bouchard | Pennsylvania | Ellen Ceresko |
| | Christina Spinzig | Massachusetts | Kaitlyn Rohrback | S. Dakota | Morgan Fitts |
| | (MP) | Michigan | Mary Mulcahy | | (SP/MP) |
| Connecticut | Kelly Whaley (SP) | Minnesota | Christine Meier | Tennessee | Sarah Harris |
| | Nicole Yatsenik | | Celia Kuenster | Texas | Christine Lin |
| | (MP) | | (SP) | Utah | Kelsey Chugg |
| Delaware | Emily Ransone | Mississippi | Anna Laorr (MP) | Vermont | Madison Corley |
| Florida | Mallory Viera | | Kathleen | Virginia | Lauren Coughlin |
| Georgia | Ashlan Ramsey | Missouri | Gallagher | Washington | Mallory Kent |
| | (SP/MP) | Montana | Catherine Dolan | West Virginia | Sydney Snodgrass |
| Hawaii | Nicole Sakamoto | Nebraska | Amber Lundskog | Wisconsin | Jessica Gerry |
| | (SP) | | Kayla Knopik (SP) | | (SP/MP) |
| | Kacie Komoto | | Morgan Smejkal | Wyoming | Sarah Bowman |
| | (MP) | | (MP) | | |
| | | Nevada | Hunter Pate | | |

North & South  Ally McDonald        Carolinas        Katy Rose Higgins (SP/MP)

Further details of these and other USA amateur events can be found on page 443

# Canadian Provincial Championships 2013

*Canadian nationality unless stated*

| Alberta | Jocelyn Alford | Ontario | Robyn Doig (SP/MP) |
|---|---|---|---|
| Brititish Columbia | Cassy Isagawa | Pacific Northwest | Jennifer Ha |
| Manitoba | Bri-ann Tokariwski (SP/MP) | Quebec | Anne-Catherine Tanguay (SP) |
| New Brunswick | Leanne Richardson | | Elyse Archambault (MP) |
| Nova Scotia | Brynn Tomie | Saskatchewan | Anna Young |

Further details of these and other Canadian amateur events can be found on page 442

# Australian State Championships 2013
*Australian nationality unless stated*

| | | | |
|---|---|---|---|
| New South Wales | Cancelled | Tasmania | Tatiana Jaqueline Wijaya |
| Northern Territory | Tatiana Wijaya | Victoria | Su-Hyun Oh |
| Queensland | Ashley Ona (SP and MP) | Western Australia | Minjee Lee |
| South Australia | Cyna Rodriguez (PHI) | | |

Further details of these and other Australian amateur events can be found on page 445

# South African Provincial Championships 2013
*South African nationality unless stated*

| | | | |
|---|---|---|---|
| Boland | Ji Sun Kang (KOR) | KwaZulu Natal | Nobuhle Dlamini (SWZ) |
| Border | Lara Weinstein | Limpopo | Monja Richards |
| Eastern Cape | Nobuhle Dlamini (SWZ) | Mpumalanga | Kaleigh Telfer |
| Ekurhuleni | Bertine Strauss | North West | Nobuhle Dlamini (SWZ) |
| Free State & | Nicole Garcia | Southern Cape | Bianca Theron |
| Northern Cape | | Western | Kim Williams |
| Gauteng | Nobuhle Dlamini (SWZ) | Province | |
| Gauteng North | Lara Weinstein | | |

Further details of these and other South African amateur events can be found on page 440

# New Zealand Provincial Championships 2013
*New Zealand nationality unless stated*

| | |
|---|---|
| North Island Stroke Play Championship | Mun Chin Keh |
| South Island Stroke Play Championship | Mun Chin Keh |
| New Zealand Interprovincial Championship | Auckland |

Further details of these and other New Zealand amateur events can be found on page 447

## Auckland dominate Women's Interprovincials

Auckland defeated Bay of Plenty 5–0 in the final of the Toro Women's New Zealand Interprovincial Championship at Muriwai GC to finish the week with 36.5 pts from a possible 40.

Auckland's Wenyung Keh and Brittney Dryland had perfect winning records as Auckland won the title for the third time in a row and extended their record number of wins in the event to 22 since the team's match-play competition began back in 1950.

# National Orders of Merit 2013

## England Golf Ladies Order of Merit

| | | |
|---|---|---|
| 1 Alexandra Peters (Notts Ladies) | 645.625 | |
| 2 Sarah Jane Boyd (Truro) | 638.500 | |
| 3 Meghan McLaren (Wellingborough) | 587.000 | |
| 4 Georgia Hall (Remedy Oak) | 550.000 | |
| 5 Gabriella Cowley (Brocket Hall) | 545.875 | |
| 6 Rachel Goodall (Heswall) | 511.000 | |
| 7 Charlote Thomas (Singapore) | 450.000 | |
| 8 Emma Taylor (Saunton) | 449.000 | |
| 9 Samantha Fuller (Roehampton) | 394.000 | |
| 10 Charlotte Thomson (Channels) | 375.625 | |

## Irish Ladies Golf Union Order of Merit

| | | |
|---|---|---|
| 1 Lisa Maguire* | 925 | |
| 2 Leona Maguire | 925 | |
| 3 Chloe Ryan | 823 | |
| 4 Paula Grant | 785 | |
| 5 Maria Dunne | 767 | |
| 6 Olivia Mehaffey | 635 | |
| 7 Stephanie Meadow | 597 | |
| 8 Jessica Carty | 577 | |
| 9 Amy Farrell | 537 | |
| 10 Emma O'Driscoll | 536 | |

*No 1 because of higher points at Irish Close Championship

## Scottish Ladies Golf Association Order of Merit

| | | |
|---|---|---|
| 1 Eilidh Briggs (Kilmacolm) | 2,075 | |
| 2 Alyson McKechin (Elderslie) | 1,613 | |
| 3 Ailsa Summers (Carnoustie Ladies) | 1,520 | |
| 4 Megan Briggs (Kilmacolm) | 1,410 | |
| 5 Clara Young (North Berwick) | 1,335 | |
| 6 Jessic Meek (Carnoustie Ladies) | 1,100 | |
| 7 Jane Turner (Craigielaw) | 1,065 | |
| 8 Lauren Whyte (St Regulus) | 970 | |
| 9 Rachel Polson (Peterculter) | 880 | |
| 10 Hannah Scott (Broomieknowe) | 770 | |

## Golf Union of Wales Ping Ladies Order of Merit

| | | |
|---|---|---|
| 1 Amy Boulden (Conwy) | 1,141.5 | |
| 2 Becky Harries (Haverfordwest) | 630.5 | |
| 3 Chloe Williams (Wrexham) | 280.0 | |
| 4 Sam Birks (Woolstanton) | 260.0 | |
| 5 Katherine O'Connor (West Byfleet) | 163.5 | |
| 6 Jess Evans (Newport) | 132.0 | |
| 7 Bethan Morris (Tenby) | 100.5 | |
| 8 Gemma Bradbury (Cottrell Park) | 70.0 | |
| 9 Sara Rees-Evans (Penrhos) | 50.0 | |
| 10 Rachel Lewis (Southerndown) | 13.0 | |
| Georgia Lewis (Llanishen) | 13.0 | |

## Australian Order of Merit
### (events played in brackets)

| | | | | |
|---|---|---|---|---|
| 1 Minjee Lee (WA) | (10) | 130.81 | | |
| 2 Su Hyun Oh (VIC) | (10) | 125.40 | | |
| 3 Grace Lennon (VIC) | (12) | 103.33 | | |
| 4 Hannah Green (WA) | (8) | 96.78 | | |
| 5 Tatiana Wijaya (WA) (pro) | (11) | 87.61 | | |
| 6 Lauren Hibbert (NSW) | (12) | 84.99 | | |
| 7 Hayley Bettancourt (WA) | (14) | 81.06 | | |
| 8 Cathleen Santoso (NSW) | (8) | 80.66 | | |
| 9 Lydia Ko (NZL) | (4) | 78.33 | | |
| 10 Ellen Davies-Graham (QLD) | (12) | 78.07 | | |

## New Zealand Order of Merit
### (events played in brackets)

| | | | | | | |
|---|---|---|---|---|---|---|
| 1 | Lydia Ko (pro) | (4) | 173.00 | 6 Hana-Rae Seifert | (16) | 88.19 |
| 2 | Lita Guo | (8) | 145.34 | 7 Wenyung Keh | (13) | 86.89 |
| 3 | Julianne Alvarez | (13) | 145.12 | 8 Sai Ma | (16) | 73.84 |
| 4 | Chantelle Cassidy | (14) | 124.91 | 9 Sarah Bradley | (10) | 57.20 |
| 5 | Mun Chin Keh | (18) | 122.13 | 10 Grace Senior | (12) | 57.07 |

## Canadian Order of Merit
### (events played in brackets)

| | | | | | | |
|---|---|---|---|---|---|---|
| 1 | Brooke Henderson | (12) | 6,069 | 6 Jennifer Ha | (12) | 2,699 |
| 2 | Anne-Catherine Tanguay | (10) | 4,257 | 7 Vivian Tsui | (11) | 1,754 |
| 3 | SooBin Kim | (12) | 3,892 | 8 Taylor Kim | (9) | 1,619 |
| 4 | Augusta James | (12) | 3,290 | 9 Robyn Doig | (11) | 1,539 |
| 5 | Brittany Marchand | (12) | 3,196 | 10 Josée Doyon | (11) | 1,533 |

## French Order of Merit

| | | | | |
|---|---|---|---|---|
| 1 | Céline Boutier Céline | 1,893.50 | 6 Anyssia Herbaut | 1,197.77 |
| 2 | Eva Gilly Eva | 1,333.67 | 7 Manon Gidali | 1,149.50 |
| 3 | Shannon Aubert | 1,329.46 | 8 Marion Veysseyre | 1,147.84 |
| 4 | Mathilda Cappeliez | 1,322.33 | 9 Justine Dreher | 1,044.33 |
| 5 | Emma Broze | 1,235.00 | 10 Ines Lescudier | 1,025.17 |

## South African Order of Merit

| | | | | |
|---|---|---|---|---|
| 1 | Kim Williams | 138,000 | 6 Bianca Theron | 80,833 |
| 2 | Nobuhle Dlamini | 134,000 | 7 Carrie Park | 76,033 |
| 3 | Lara Weinstein | 106,000 | 8 Magda Kruger | 74,166 |
| 4 | Nicole Garcia | 95,000 | 9 Ji Sun Kang | 64,333 |
| 5 | Monja Richards | 84,500 | 10 Kaleigh Telfer | 46,500 |

## Italian Order of Merit

| | | | | |
|---|---|---|---|---|
| 1 | Roberta Liti Roberta | 3,315,00 | 6 Alessandra Braida | 778,40 |
| 2 | Laura Lonardi | 2,065,60 | 7 Stefania Avanzo | 774,83 |
| 3 | Virginia Elena Carta | 1,211,89 | 8 Carlotta Ricolfi | 691,15 |
| 4 | Bianca Maria Fabrizio | 1,193,26 | 9 Camilla Mazzola | 637,34 |
| 5 | Martina Flori | 893,57 | 10 Barbara Borin | 631,58 |

## Month by month in 2013

Continental Europe enjoy their first Seve Trophy victory since the inaugural match in 2000, Gregory Bourdy's five points out of five creating history. Another member of the team, Gonzalo Fernandez-Castaño, boosts his hopes of a Ryder Cup début with victory at the BMW Masters in Shanghai and David Lynn, also a possible rookie in Paul McGinley's side, captures the Portugal Masters.

# Team Events

For past winners not listed here see earlier editions of *The R&A Golfer's Handbook*

International

## The Curtis Cup

2012 *Nairn GC, Scotland* June 8–10
**Result: GB&I 10½, USA 9½**
*Captains: Tegwen Matthews (GB&I),*
*Pat Cornett (USA)*
**First Day – Foursomes:**
Kelly Tidy & Amy Boulden lost to Austin Ernst &
Brooke Pancake 1 hole
Holly Clyburn & Bronte Law lost to Amy Anderson &
Tiffany Lua 2 and 1
Leona Maguire & Stephanie Meadow lost to
Lindy Duncan & Lisa McCloskey 5 and 4
**First Day – Fourball:**
Pamela Pretswell & Charley Hull lost to Amy Anderson
& Emily Tubert 4 and 3
Kelly Tidy & Holly Clyburn beat Brooke Pancake &
Erica Popson 2 and 1
Bronte Law & Amy Boulden beat Lindy Duncan &
Lisa McCloskey 3 and 2
**Second Day – Foursomes:**
Pretswell & Hull lost to Anderson & Lua 3 and 2
Clyburn & Boulden lost to Ernst & Pancake 2 holes
Meadow & Maguire beat Duncan & McCloskey 3 and 1
**Second Day – Fourball:**
Clyburn & Tidy beat Tubert & Anderson 1 hole
Maguire & Law halved with Pancake & Ernst
Meadow & Pretswell beat Lua & Popson 2 holes
**Third Day – Singles:**
Kelly Tidy beat Austin Ernst 2 and 1
Amy Boulden beat Emily Tubert 3 and 1
Holly Clyburn beat Erica Popson 3 and 2
Pamela Pretswell lost to Lisa McCloskey 4 and 3
Bronte Law lost to Tiffany Lua 2 holes
Charley Hull beat Lindy Duncan 5 and 3
Stephanie Meadow beat Amy Anderson 4 and 2
Leona Maguire lost to Brooke Pancake 6 and 5

2010 *Essex CC, Manchester-by-the-Sea, MA*
June 11–13
**Result: USA 12½, GB&I 7½**
*Captains: Noreen Mohler (USA),*
*Mary McKenna (GB&I)*
**First Day – Foursomes:**
Jennifer Song & Jennifer Johnson halved with Sally Watson
& Rachel Jennings
Alexis Thompson & Jessica Korda halved with Hannah
Barwood & Holly Clyburn
Cydnet Clanton & Stephanie Kono halved with Danielle
McVeigh & Leona Maguire
**First Day – Fourball:**
Song & Kimberly Kim lost to McVeigh & Pamela Pretswell
4 and 3
Thompson & Johnson beat Jennings & Leona Maguire
3 and 2

Korda & Tiffany Lua lost to Watson & Lisa Maguire
1 hole
**Second Day – Fourball:**
Thompson & Korda beat McVeigh & Pretswell 2 and 1
Song & Clanton beat Maguire & Maguire 3 and 2
Kono & Kim beat Watson & Jennings 2 holes
**Second Day – Foursomes:**
Thompson & Korda beat McVeigh & Leona Maguire
3 and 1
Song & Kono beat Barwood & Clyburn 3 and 1
Lua & Johnson beat Watson & Jennings 3 and 2
**Third Day – Singles:**
Jennifer Song lost to Danielle McVeigh (IRL) 3 and 2
Alexis Thompson beat Sally Watson (SCO) 6 and 5
Jennifer Johnson beat Rachel Jennings (ENG) 5 and 4
Kimberly Kim lost to Lisa Maguire (IRL) 1 hole
Cydney Clanton beat Hannah Barwood (ENG) 4 and 3
Tiffany Lua lost to Leona Maguire (IRL) 2 and 1
Jessica Korda beat Pamela Pretswell (SCO) 4 and 3
Stephanie Kono lost to Holly Clyburn (ENG) 2 and 1

2008 *Old Course, St Andrews* May 30–June 1
**Result: GB&I 7, USA 13**
*Captains: Mary McKenna (GB&I),*
*Carol Semple Thompson (USA)*
**First Day – Foursomes**
E Bennett & J Ewart lost to S Lewis & A Walshe
3 and 1
S Watson & M Thomson beat M Harigae & J Lee 1 hole
B Loucks & F Parker lost to A Blumenherst & T Joh
1 hole
**First Day – Fourballs**
C Booth & M Thomson lost to K Kim & M Harigae
3 and 2
S Watson & K Caithness beat T Joh & M Bolger 3 and 2
F Parker & E Bennett lost to A Blumenherst & S Lewis
3 and 1
**Second Day – Foursomes**
C Booth & B Loucks beat K Kim & J Lee 3 and 2
S Watson & M Thomson lost to A Walshe & S Lewis
5 and 4
E Bennett & J Ewart halved with A Blumenherst & T Joh
**Second Day – Fourballs**
C Booth & B Loucks lost to K Kim & M Harigae
2 and 1
S Watson & K Caithness beat A Blumenherst & M Bolger
3 and 2
E Bennett & F Parker lost to A Walshe & S Lewis 1 hole
**Third Day – Singles**
Breanne Loucks (WAL) lost to Kimberly Kim 3 and 1
Jodi Ewart (ENG) lost to Amanda Blumenherst 2 and 1
Elizabeth Bennett (ENG) lost to Stacy Lewis 3 and 2
Carly Booth (SCO) lost to Tiffany Joh 6 and 5
Michele Thomson (SCO) halved with Jennie Lee

Florentyna Parker (ENG) beat Meghan Bolger  6 and 4
Krystle Caithness (SCO) beat Mina Harigae  2 and 1
Sally Watson (SCO) lost to Alison Walshe  1 hole

**2006** *Bandon Dunes, OR*  July 29–30
**Result: USA 11½, GB&I 6½**
*Captains: Carol Semple Thompson (USA),
Ada O'Sullivan (Monkstown) (GB&I)*

**First Day: Foursomes**
P Mackenzie & A Blumenherst beat T Mangan &
K Matharu  5 and 4
D Grimes & A McCurdy beat M Gillen & N Edwards
2 holes
J Park & T Leon beat C Coughlan & M Reid  1 hole

**Singles**
Jenny Suh lost to Kiran Matharu (Cookridge Park)  2 and 1
Jennie Lee beat Martina Gillen (Beaverstown)  4 and 3
Amanda Blumenherst lost to Breanne Loucks (Wrexham)
5 and 4
Paige Mackenzie beat Melissa Reid (Chevin)  5 and 4
Jane Park beat Tara Delaney (Carlow)  3 and 2
Taylor Leon beat Claire Coughlan (Cork)  5 and 4

**Second Day: Foursomes**
J Park & T Leon halved with T Mangan & T Delaney
J Lee & J Suh lost to M Reid & B Loucks  7 and 5
P Mackenzie & A Blumenherst lost to M Gillen &
N Edwards  1 hole

**Singles**
Virginia Grimes lost to M Gillen  3 and 2
Amanda McCurdy lost to B Loucks  3 and 2
P Mackenzie beat Tricia Mangan (Ennis)  1 hole
T Leon beat Naomi Edwards (Ganton)  5 and 4
J Lee beat M Reid  3 and 2
J Park beat T Delaney  3 and 2

**2004** *Formby*  June 12–13
**Result: GB&I 8, USA 10**
*Captains: Ada O'Sullivan (Monkstown) (GB&I),
Martha Kironac (USA)*

**First Day: Foursomes**
S McKevitt & E Duggleby beat P Creamer & J Park  3 and 2
N Timmins & D Masters beat S Huarte & A Thurman
1 hole
A Laing & C Coughlan beat B Lang & M Wie  1 hole

**Singles**
Emma Duggleby beat Elizabeth Janangelo  3 and 2
Danielle Masters lost to Erica Blasberg  1 hole
Fame More lost to Paula Creamer  5 and 3
Anna Highgate lost to Michelle Wie  5 and 4
Shelley McKevitt lost to Jane Park  4 and 3
Anne Laing lost to Anne Thurman  4 and 3

**Second Day: Foursomes**
E Duggleby & S McKevitt beat E Blasberg & Sarah Huarte
2 and 1
A Laing & C Coughlan beat E Janangelo & M Wie  3 and 2
N Timmins & D Masters lost to B Lang & A Thurman
5 and 4

**Singles**
E Duggleby lost to P Creamer  3 and 2
A Laing beat J Park  3 and 1
S McKevitt lost to E Janangelo  1 hole
Nicola Timmins lost to M Wie  6 and 5
Claire Coughlan beat Brittany Lang  2 holes
D Masters lost to A Thurman  1 hole

**2002** *Fox Chapel, PA*  Aug 3–4
**Result: USA 11, GB&I 7**
*Captains: Mary Budke (USA), Pam Benka (GB&I)*

**First Day: Foursomes**
Duncan & Jerman beat Duggleby & Hudson  4 and 3
Fankhauser & Semple Thompson beat Laing & Stirling
1 hole
Myerscough & Swaim beat Coffey & Smith  3 and 2

**Singles**
Emily Bastel lost to Rebecca Hudson  2 holes
Leigh Anne Hardin beat Emma Duggleby  2 and 1
Meredith Duncan beat Fame More  5 and 4
Angela Jerman beat Sarah Jones  6 and 5
Courtney Swaim beat Heather Stirling  4 and 2
Mollie Fankhauser lost to Vikki Laing  1 hole

**Second Day: Foursomes**
Hardin & Bastel lost to Laing & Stirling  3 and 1
Myerscough & Swaim beat Hudson & Smith  4 and 2
Duncan & Jerman lost to Coffey & Dugglesby  4 and 2

**Singles**
Mollie Fankhauser beat Rebecca Hudson  3 and 1
Carol Semple Thompson Beat Vikki Laing  1 hole
Leigh Anne Hardin lost to Emma Duggleby  4 and 3
Laura Myerscough beat Heather Stirling  2 holes
Meredith Duncan beat Akison Coffey  3 and 1
Courtney Swaim lost to Sarah Jones  5 and 3

**2000** *Ganton*  June 24–25
**Result: USA 10, GB&I 8**
*Captains: Claire Hourihane Dowling (GB&I),
Jane Bastanchury Booth (USA)*

**First Day: Foursomes**
Andrew & Morgan lost to Bauer & Carol Semple
Thompson  1 hole
Brewerton & Hudson lost to Keever & Stanford  1 hole
Duggleby & O'Brien halved with Derby Grimes &
Homeyer

**Singles**
Kim Rostron Andrew lost to Beth Bauer  3 and 2
Fiona Brown lost to Robin Weiss  1 hole
Rebecca Hudson lost to Stephanie Keever  4 and 2
Lesley Nicholson halved with Angela Stanford
Suzanne O'Brien beat Leland Beckel  3 and 1
Emma Duggleby lost to Hilary Homeyer  1 hole

**Second Day: Foursomes**
Brewerton & Hudson beat Bauer & Thompson
2 and 1
Duggleby & O'Brien beat Keever & Stanford  7 and 6
Andrew & Morgan lost to Derby Grimes & Homeyer
3 and 1

**Singles**
Hudson lost to Bauer  1 hole
O'Brien beat Weiss  3 and 2
Duggleby beat Keever  4 and 2
Becky Brewerton lost to Homeyer  3 and 2
Becky Morgan beat Stanford  4 and 4
Andrew beat Virginia Derby Grimes  6 and 5

**1998** *Minikahda, Minneapolis, MN*  Aug 1–2
**Result: USA 10, GB&I 8**
*Captains: Barbara McIntire (USA),
Ita Burke Butler (GB&I)*

**First Day: Foursomes**
Bauer & Chuasiriporn lost to Ratcliffe & Rostron  1 hole
Booth & Corrie Kuehn beat Brown & Stupples  2 and 1
Burke & Derby Grimes beat Morgan & Rose  3 and 2

**1998** *continued*

**Singles**
Kellee Booth beat Kim Rostron 2 and 1
Brenda Corrie Kuehn beat Alison Rose 3 and 2
Jenny Chuasiriporn halved with Rebecca Hudson
Beth Bauer beat Hilary Monaghan 5 and 3
Jo Jo Robertson lost to Becky Morgan 2 and 1
Carol Semple Thompson lost to Elaine Ratcliffe 3 and 2
**Second Day: Foursomes**
Booth & Corrie Kuehn beat Morgan & Rose 6 and 5
Bauer & Chuasiriporn lost to Brown & Hudson 2 holes
Burke & Derby Grimes beat Ratcliffe & Rostron 2 and 1
**Singles**
Booth beat Rostron 2 and 1
Corrie Kuehn beat Morgan 2 and 1
Thompson lost to Karen Stupples 1 hole
Robin Burke lost to Hudson 2 and 1
Robertson lost to Fiona Brown 1 hole
Virginia Derby Grimes halved with Ratcliffe

**1996** *Killarney* June 21–22
**Result: GB&I 11½, USA 6½**
*Captains: Ita Burke Butler (GB&I),*
  *Martha Lang (USA)*
**First Day: Foursomes**
Lisa Walton Educate & Wade lost to K Kuehne & Port
  2 and 1
Lisa Dermott & Rose beat B Corrie Kuehn & Jemsek
  3 and 1
McKay & Moodie halved with Kerr & Thompson
**Singles**
Julie Wade lost to Sarah LeBrun Ingram 4 and 2
Karen Stupples beat Kellee Booth 3 and 2
Alison Rose beat Brenda Corrie Kuehn 5 and 4
Elaine Ratcliffe halved with Marla Jemsek
Mhairi McKay beat Cristie Kerr 1 hole
Janice Moodie beat Carol Semple Thompson 3 and 1
**Second Day: Foursomes**
McKay & Moodie beat Booth & Ingram 3 and 2
Dermott & Rose beat B Corrie Kuehn & Jemsek
  2 and 1
Educate & Wade lost to K Kuehne & Port 1 hole
**Singles**
Wade lost to Kerr 1 hole
Ratcliffe beat Ingram 3 and 1
Stupples lost to Booth 3 and 2
Rose beat Ellen Port 6 and 5
McKay halved with Thompson
Moodie beat Kelli Kuehne 2 and 1

**1994** *Chattanooga, TN* July 30–31
**Result: GB&I 9, USA 9**
*Captains: Lancy Smith (USA),*
  *Elizabeth Boatman (GB&I)*
**First Day: Foursomes**
Sarah LeBrun Ingram & McGill halved with Matthew
  & Moodie
Klein & Thompson beat McKay & Kirsty Speak
  7 and 5
Kaupp & Port lost to Wade & Walton 6 and 5
**Singles**
Jill McGill halved with Julie Wade
Emilee Klein beat Janice Moodie 3 and 2
Wendy Ward lost to Lisa Walton 1 hole
Carol Semple Thompson beat Myra McKinlay 2 and 1
Ellen Port beat Mhairi McKay 2 and 1
Stephanie Sparks lost to Catriona Lambert Matthew
  1 hole

**Second Day: Foursomes**
Ingram & McGill lost to Wade & Walton 2 and 1
Klein & Thompson beat McKinlay & Eileen Rose Power
  4 and 2
Sparks & Ward lost to Matthew & Moodie 3 and 2
**Singles**
McGill beat Wade 4 and 3
Klein lost to Matthew 2 and 1
Port beat McKay 7 and 5
Wendy Kaupp lost to McKinlay 3 and 2
Ward beat Walton 4 and 3
Thompson lost to Moodie 2 holes

**1992** *Hoylake* June 5–6
**Result: GB&I 10, USA 8**
*Captains: Elizabeth Boatman (GB&I),*
  *Judy Oliver (USA)*
**First Day: Foursomes**
Hall & Wade halved with Fruhwirth & Goetze
Lambert & Thomas beat Ingram & Shannon 2 and 1
Hourihane & Morley beat Hanson & Thompson 2 and 1
**Singles**
Joanne Morley halved with Amy Fruhwirth
Julie Wade lost to Vicki Goetze 3 and 2
Elaine Farquharson beat Robin Weiss 2 and 1
Nicola Buxton lost to Martha Lang 2 holes
Catriona Lambert beat Carol Semple Thompson 3 and 2
Caroline Hall beat Leslie Shannon 6 and 5
**Second Day: Foursomes**
Hall & Wade halved with Fruhwirth & Goetze
Hourihane & Morley halved with Lang & Weiss
Lambert & Thomas lost to Hanson & Thompson 3 and 2
**Singles**
Morley beat Fruhwirth 2 and 1
Lambert beat Tracy Hanson 6 and 5
Farquharson lost to Sarah LeBrun Ingram 2 and 1
Vicki Thomas lost to Shannon 2 and 1
Claire Hourihane lost to Lang 2 and 1
Hall beat Goetze 1 hole

**1990** *Somerset Hills, NJ* July 28–29
**Result: USA 14, GB&I 4**
*Captains: Leslie Shannon (USA), Jill Thornhill (GB&I)*
**First Day: Foursomes**
Goetze & Anne Quast Sander beat Dobson & Lambert
  4 and 3
Noble & Margaret Platt lost to Wade & Imrie 2 and 1
Thompson & Weiss beat Farquharson & Helen
  Wadsworth 3 and 1
**Singles**
Vicki Goetze lost to Julie Wade 2 and 1
Katie Peterson beat Kathryn Imrie 3 and 2
Brandie Burton beat Linzi Fletcher 3 and 1
Robin Weiss beat Elaine Farquharson 4 and 3
Karen Noble beat Catriona Lambert 1 hole
Carol Semple Thompson lost to Vicki Thomas 1 hole
**Second Day: Foursomes**
Goetze & Sander beat Wade & Imrie 3 and 1
Noble & Platt lost to Dobson & Lambert 1 hole
Burton & Peterson beat Farquharson & Wadsworth
  5 and 4
**Singles**
Goetze beat Helen Dobson 4 and 3
Burton beat Lambert 4 and 3
Peterson beat Imrie 1 hole
Noble beat Wade 2 holes
Weiss beat Farquharson 2 and 1
Thompson beat Thomas 3 and 1

## 1988 Royal St George's  June 10–11
**Result: GB&I 11, USA 7**
*Captains: Diane Robb Bailey (GB&I), Judy Bell (USA)*
**First Day: Foursomes**
Bayman & Wade beat Kerdyk & Scrivner  2 and 1
Davies & Shapcott beat Scholefield & Thompson  5 and 4
Thomas & Thornhill halved with Keggi & Shannon
**Singles**
Linda Bayman halved with Tracy Kerdyk
Julie Wade beat Cindy Scholefield  2 holes
Susan Shapcott lost to Carol Semple Thompson  1 hole
Karen Davies lost to Pearl Sinn  4 and 3
Shirley Lawson beat Pat Cornett-Iker  1 hole
Jill Thornhill beat Leslie Shannon  3 and 2
**Second Day: Foursomes**
Bayman & Wade lost to Kerdyk & Scrivner  1 hole
Davies & Shapcott beat Keggi & Shannon  2 holes
Thomas & Thornhill beat Scholefield & Thompson  6 and 5
**Singles**
Wade lost to Kerdyk  2 and 1
Shapcott beat Caroline Keggi  3 and 2
Lawson lost to Kathleen McCarthy Scrivner  4 and 3
Vicki Thomas beat Cornett-Iker  5 and 3
Bayman beat Sinn  1 hole
Thornhill lost to Thompson  3 and 2

## 1986 Prairie Dunes, KS  Aug 1–2
**Result: GB&I 13, USA 5**
*Captains: Judy Bell (USA),*
*Diane Robb Bailey (GB&I)*
**First Day: Foursomes**
Kessler & Schreyer lost to Behan & Thornhill  7 and 6
Ammaccapane & Mochrie lost to Davies & Johnson
2 and 1
Gardner & Scrivner lost to McKenna & Robertson  1 hole
**Singles**
Leslie Shannon lost to Patricia (Trish) Johnson  1 hole
Kim Williams lost to Jill Thornhill  4 and 3
Danielle Ammaccapane lost to Lillian Behan  4 and 3
Kandi Kessler beat Vicki Thomas  3 and 2
Dottie Pepper Mochrie halved with Karen Davies
Cindy Schreyer beat Claire Hourihane  2 and 1
**Second Day: Foursomes**
Ammaccapane & Mochrie lost to Davies & Johnson  1 hole
Shannon & Williams lost to Behan & Thornhill  5 and 3
Gardner & Scrivner halved with McKenna & Belle
McCorkindale Robertson
**Singles**
Shannon halved with Thornhill
Kathleen McCarthy Scrivner lost to Trish Johnson  5 and 3
Kim Gardner beat Behan  1 hole
Williams lost to Thomas  4 and 3
Kessler halved with Davies
Schreyer lost to Hourihane  5 and 4

## 1984 Muirfield  June 8–9
**Result: USA 9½, GB&I 8½**
*Captains: Diane Robb Bailey (GB&I),*
*Phyllis Preuss (USA)*
**First Day: Foursomes**
New & Waite beat Pacillo & Sander  2 holes
Grice & Thornhill halved with Rosenthal & Smith
Davies & McKenna lost to Farr & Widman  1 hole
**Singles**
Jill Thornhill halved with Joanne Pacillo
Claire Waite lost to Penny Hammel  4 and 2
Claire Hourihane lost to Jody Rosenthal  3 and 1

Vicki Thomas beat Dana Howe  2 and 1
Penny Grice beat Anne Quast Sander  2 holes
Beverley New lost to Mary Anne Widman  4 and 3
**Second Day: Foursomes**
New & Waite lost to Rosenthal & Smith  3 and 1
Grice & Thornhill beat Farr & Widman  2 and 1
Hourihane & Thomas halved with Hammel & Howe
**Singles**
Thornhill lost to Pacillo  3 and 2
Laura Davies beat Sander  1 hole
Waite beat Lancy Smith  5 and 4
Grice lost to Howe  2 holes
New lost to Heather Farr  6 and 5
Hourihane beat Hammel  2 and 1

## 1982 Denver, CO  Aug 5–6
**Result: USA 14½, GB&I 3½**
*Captains: Betty Probasco (USA),*
*Maire O'Donnell (GB&I)*
**First Day: Foursomes**
Inkster & Semple beat McKenna & Robertson  5 and 4
Baker & Smith halved with Douglas & Soulsby
Benz & Hanlon beat Connachan & Stewart  2 and 1
**Singles**
Amy Benz beat Mary McKenna  2 and 1
Cathy Hanlon beat Jane Connachan  5 and 4
Mari McDougall beat Wilma Aitken  2 holes
Kathy Baker beat Belle McCorkindale Robertson  7 and 6
Judy Oliver lost to Janet Soulsby  2 holes
Juli Inkster beat Kitrina Douglas  7 and 6
**Second Day: Foursomes**
Inkster & Semple beat Aitken & Connachan  3 and 2
Baker & Smith beat Douglas & Soulsby  1 hole
Benz & Hanlon lost to McKenna & Robertson  1 hole
**Singles**
Inkster beat Douglas  7 and 6
Baker beat Gillian Stewart  4 and 3
Oliver beat Vicki Thomas  5 and 4
McDougall beat Soulsby  2 and 1
Carol Semple beat McKenna  1 hole
Lancy Smith lost to Robertson  5 and 4

## 1980 St Pierre, Chepstow  June 6–7
**Result: USA 13, GB&I 5**
*Captains: Carol Comboy (GB&I),*
*Nancy Roth Syms (USA)*
**First Day: Foursomes**
McKenna & Nesbitt halved with Terri Moody & Smith
Stewart & Thomas lost to Castillo & Sheehan  5 and 3
Caldwell & Madill halved with Oliver & Semple
**Singles**
Mary McKenna lost to Patty Sheehan  3 and 2
Claire Nesbitt halved with Lancy Smith
Jane Connachan lost to Brenda Goldsmith  2 holes
Maureen Madill lost to Carol Semple  4 and 3
Linda Moore halved with Mary Hafeman
Carole Caldwell lost to Judy Oliver  1 hole
**Second Day: Foursomes**
Caldwell & Madill lost to Castillo & Sheehan  3 and 2
McKenna & Nesbitt lost to Moody & Smith  6 and 5
Moore & Thomas lost to Oliver & Semple  1 hole
**Singles**
Madill lost to Sheehan  5 and 4
McKenna beat Lori Castillo  5 and 4
Connachan lost to Hafeman  6 and 5
Gillian Stewart beat Smith  5 and 4
Moore beat Goldsmith  1 hole
Tegwen Perkins Thomas lost to Semple  4 and 3

## 1978 Apawamis, NY  Aug 4–5
### Result: USA 12, GB&I 6
*Captains: Helen Wilson (USA), Carol Comboy (GB&I)*
**First Day: Foursomes**
Daniel & Brenda Goldsmith lost to Greenhalgh &
 Marvin  3 and 2
Cindy Hill & Smith lost to Everard & Thomson  2 and 1
Cornett & Carolyn Hill halved with McKenna & Perkins
**Singles**
Beth Daniel beat Vanessa Marvin  5 and 4
Noreen Uihlein lost to Mary Everard  7 and 6
Lancy Smith beat Angela Uzielli  4 and 3
Cindy Hill beat Julia Greenhalgh  2 and 1
Carolyn Hill halved with Carole Caldwell
Judy Oliver beat Tegwen Perkins  2 and 1
**Second Day: Foursomes**
Cindy Hill & Smith beat Everard & Thomson  1 hole
Daniel & Goldsmith beat McKenna & Perkins  1 hole
Oliver & Uihlein beat Greenhalgh & Marvin  4 and 3
**Singles**
Daniel beat Mary McKenna  2 and 1
Patricia Cornett beat Caldwell  3 and 2
Cindy Hill lost to Muriel Thomson  2 and 1
Lancy Smith beat Perkins  2 holes
Oliver halved with Greenhalgh
Uihlein halved with Everard

## 1976 Royal Lytham & St Annes  June 11–12
### Result: USA 11½, GB&I 6½
*Captains: Belle McCorkindale Robertson (GB&I),
 Barbara McIntyre (USA)*
**First Day: Foursomes**
Greenhalgh & McKenna lost to Daniel & Hill
 3 and 2
Cadden & Henson lost to Horton & Massey
 6 and 5
Irvin & Perkins beat Semple & Syms  3 and 2
**Singles**
Ann Irvin lost to Beth Daniel  4 and 3
Dinah Oxley Henson beat Cindy Hill  1 hole
Suzanne Cadden lost to Nancy Lopez  3 and 1
Mary McKenna lost to Nancy Roth Syms  1 hole
Tegwen Perkins lost to Debbie Massey  1 hole
Julia Greenhalgh halved with Barbara Barrow
**Second Day: Foursomes**
Cadden & Irvin lost to Daniel & Hill  4 and 3
Henson & Perkins beat Semple & Syms  2 and 1
McKenna & Anne Stant lost to Barrow & Lopez
 4 and 3
**Singles**
Henson lost to Daniel  3 and 2
Greenhalgh beat Syms  2 and 1
Cadden lost to Donna Horton  6 and 5
Jennie Lee-Smith lost to Massey  3 and 2
Perkins beat Hill  1 hole
McKenna beat Carol Semple  1 hole

## 1974 San Francisco, CA  Aug 2–3
### Result: USA 13, GB&I 5
*Captains: Sis Choate (USA),
 Belle McCorkindale Robertson (GB&I)*
**First Day: Foursomes**
Hill & Semple halved with Greenhalgh & McKenna
Booth & Sander beat Lee-Smith & LeFeuvre  6 and 5
Budke & Lauer lost to Everard & Walker  5 and 4

**Singles**
Carol Semple lost to Mickey Walker  2 and 1
Jane Bastanchury Booth beat Mary McKenna
 5 and 3
Debbie Massey beat Mary Everard  1 hole
Bonnie Lauer beat Jennie Lee-Smith  6 and 5
Beth Barry beat Julia Greenhalgh  1 hole
Cindy Hill halved with Tegwen Perkins
**Second Day: Foursomes**
Booth & Sander beat McKenna & Walker  5 and 4
Budke & Lauer beat Everard & LeFeuvre  5 and 3
Hill & Semple lost to Greenhalgh & Perkins  3 and 2
**Singles**
Anne Quast Sander beat Everard  4 and 3
Booth beat Greenhalgh  7 and 5
Massey beat Carol LeFeuvre  6 and 5
Semple beat Walker  2 and 1
Mary Budke beat Perkins  5 and 4
Lauer lost to McKenna  2 and 1

## 1972 Western Gailes  June 9–10
### Result: USA 10, GB&I 8
*Captains: Frances Stephens Smith (GB&I),
 Jean Ashley Crawford (USA)*
**First Day: Foursomes**
Everard & Beverly Huke lost to Baugh & Kirouac
 2 and 1
Frearson & Robertson beat Booth & McIntyre  2 and 1
McKenna & Walker beat Barry & Hollis Stacy  1 hole
**Singles**
Mickey Walker halved with Laura Baugh
Belle McCorkindale Robertson lost to Jane Bastanchury
 Booth  3 and 1
Mary Everard lost to Martha Wilkinson Kirouac  4 and 3
Dinah Oxley lost to Barbara McIntire  4 and 3
Kathryn Phillips beat Lancy Smith  2 holes
Mary McKenna lost to Beth Barry  2 and 1
**Second Day: Foursomes**
McKenna & Walker beat Baugh & Kirouac  3 and 2
Everard & Huke lost to Booth & McIntyre  5 and 4
Frearson & Robertson halved with Barry & Stacy
**Singles**
Robertson lost to Baugh  6 and 5
Everard beat McIntyre  6 and 5
Walker beat Booth  1 hole
McKenna beat Kirouac  3 and 1
Diane Frearson lost to Smith  3 and 1
Phillips lost to Barry  3 and 1

## 1970 Brae Burn, MA  Aug 7–8
### Result: USA 11½, GB&I 6½
*Captains: Carolyn Cudone (USA),
 Jeanne Bisgood (GB&I)*
**First Day: Foursomes**
Bastanchury & Hamlin lost to McKenna & Oxley  4 and 3
Preuss & Wilkinson beat Irvin & Robertson  4 and 3
Jane Fassinger & Hill lost to Everard & Greenhalgh
 5 and 3
**Singles**
Jane Bastanchury beat Dinah Oxley  5 and 3
Martha Wilkinson beat Ann Irvin  1 hole
Shelley Hamlin halved with Belle McCorkindale
 Robertson
Phyllis Preuss lost to Mary McKenna  4 and 2
Nancy Hager beat Margaret Pickard  5 and 4
Alice Dye beat Julia Greenhalgh  1 hole

**Second Day: Foursomes**
Preuss & Wilkinson beat McKenna & Oxley  6 and 4
Dye & Hill halved with Everard & Greenhalgh
Bastanchury & Hamlin beat Irvin & Robertson  1 hole
**Singles**
Bastanchury beat Irvin  4 and 3
Hamlin halved with Oxley
Preuss beat Robertson  1 hole
Wilkinson lost to Greenhalgh  6 and 4
Hager lost to Mary Everard  4 and 3
Cindy Hill beat McKenna  2 and 1

## 1968 Newcastle, Co Down  June 14–15
**Result: USA 10½, GB&I 7½**
*Captains: Zara Bolton (GB&I), Evelyn Monsted (USA)*
**First Day: Foursomes**
Irvin & Robertson beat Hamlin & Welts  6 and 5
Pickard & Saunders beat Conley & Dill 3 and 2
Howard & Pam Tredinnick lost to Ashley & Preuss  1 hole
**Singles**
Ann Irvin beat Anne Quast Welts  3 and 2
Vivien Saunders lost to Shelley Hamlin  1 hole
Belle McCorkindale Robertson lost to Roberta Albers
  1 hole
Bridget Jackson halved with Peggy Conley
Dinah Oxley halved with Phyllis Preuss
Margaret Pickard beat Jean Ashley  2 holes
**Second Day: Foursomes**
Oxley & Tredinnick lost to Ashley & Preuss  5 and 4
Irvin & Robertson halved with Conley & Dill
Pickard & Saunders lost to Hamlin & Welts  2 and 1
**Singles**
Irvin beat Hamlin 3 and 2
Robertson halved with Welts
Saunders halved with Albers
Ann Howard lost to Mary Lou Dill  4 and 2
Pickard lost to Conley  1 hole
Jackson lost to Preuss 2 and 1

## 1966 Hot Springs, VA  July 29–30
**Result: USA 13, GB&I 5**
*Captains: Dorothy Germain Porter (USA),*
*Zara Bolton (GB&I)*
**First Day: Foursomes**
Ashley & Preuss beat Armitage & Bonallack  1 hole
Barbara McIntire & Welts halved with Joan Hastings &
  Robertson
Boddie & Flenniken beat Chadwick & Tredinnick  1 hole
**Singles**
Jean Ashley beat Belle McCorkindale Robertson  1 hole
Anne Quast Welts halved with Susan Armitage
Barbara White Boddie beat Angela Ward Bonallack  3 and 2
Nancy Roth Syms beat Elizabeth Chadwick  2 holes
Helen Wilson lost to Ita Burke  4 and 2
Carol Sorenson Flenniken beat Marjory Fowler  3 and 1
**Second Day: Foursomes**
Ashley & Preuss beat Armitage & Bonallack  2 and 1
McIntire & Welts lost to Burke & Chadwick  1 hole
Boddie & Flenniken beat Hastings & Robertson  2 and 1
**Singles**
Ashley lost to Bonallack  2 and 1
Welts halved with Robertson
Boddie beat Armitage  3 and 2
Syms halved with Pam Tredinnick
Phyllis Preuss beat Chadwick  3 and 2
Flenniken beat Burke  2 and 1

## 1964 Porthcawl  Sept 11–12
**Result: USA 10½, GB&I 1½**
*Captains: Elsie Corlett (GB&I), Helen Hawes (USA)*
**First Day: Foursomes**
Spearman & Bonallack beat McIntyre & Preuss  2 and 1
Sheila Vaughan & Porter beat Gunderson & Roth  3 and 2
Jackson & Susan Armitage lost to Sorenson & White
  8 and 6
**Singles**
Angela Ward Bonallack lost to JoAnne Gunderson
  6 and 5
Marley Spearman halved with Barbara McIntyre
Julia Greenhalgh lost to Barbara White  3 and 2
Bridget Jackson beat Carol Sorenson  4 and 3
Joan Lawrence lost to Peggy Conley  1 hole
Ruth Porter beat Nancy Roth  1 hole
**Second Day: Foursomes**
Spearman & Bonallack beat McIntyre & Preuss  6 and 5
Armitage & Jackson lost to Gunderson & Roth  2 holes
Porter & Vaughan halved with Sorenson & White
**Singles**
Spearman halved with Gunderson
Lawrence lost to McIntyre  4 and 2
Greenhalgh beat Phyllis Preuss  5 and 3
Bonallack lost to White  3 and 2
Porter lost to Sorenson  3 and 2
Jackson lost to Conley  1 hole

## 1962 Broadmoor, CO  Aug 17–18
**Result: USA 8, GB&I 1**
*Captains: Polly Riley (USA),*
*Frances Stephens Smith (GB&I)*
**Foursomes**
Decker & McIntyre beat Spearman & Bonallack
  7 and 5
Jean Ashley & Anna Johnstone beat Ruth Porter &
  Frearson 8 and 7
Creed & Gunderson beat Vaughan & Ann Irvin  4 and 3
**Singles**
Judy Bell lost to Diane Frearson  8 and 7
JoAnne Gunderson beat Angela Ward Bonallack
  2 and 1
Clifford Ann Creed beat Sally Bonallack  6 and 5
Anne Quast Decker beat Marley Spearman  7 and 5
Phyllis Preuss beat Jean Roberts  1 hole
Barbara McIntyre beat Sheila Vaughan  5 and 4

## 1960 Lindrick  May 20–21
**Result: USA 6½, GB&I 2½**
*Captains: Maureen Garrett (GB&I),*
*Mildred Prunaret (USA)*
**Foursomes**
Price & Bonallack beat Gunderson & McIntyre  1 hole
Robertson & McCorkindale lost to Eller & Quast  4 and 2
Frances Smith & Porter lost to Goodwin & Anna
  Johnstone 3 and 2
**Singles**
Elizabeth Price halved with Barbara McIntyre
Angela Ward Bonallack lost to JoAnne Gunderson
  2 and 1
Janette Robertson lost to Anne Quast  2 holes
Philomena Garvey lost to Judy Eller  4 and 3
Belle McCorkindale lost to Judy Bell  8 and 7
Ruth Porter beat Joanne Goodwin  1 hole

## 1958 Brae Burn, MA  Aug 8–9
**Result: GB&I 4½, USA 4½**
*Captains:Virginia Dennehy (USA),*
  *Daisy Ferguson (GB&I)*
**Foursomes**
Riley & Romack lost to Bonallack & Price  2 and 1
Gunderson & Quast lost to Robertson & Smith  3 and 2
Johnstone & McIntire beat Jackson & Valentine  6 and 5
**Singles**
JoAnne Gunderson beat Jessie Anderson Valentine  2 holes
Barbara McIntire halved with Angela Ward Bonallack
Anne Quast beat Elizabeth Price  4 and 2
Anna Johnstone lost to Janette Robertson  3 and 2
Barbara Romack beat Bridget Jackson  3 and 2
Polly Riley lost to Frances Stephens Smith  2 holes

## 1956 Prince's, Sandwich  June 8–9
**Result: GB&I 5, USA 4**
*Captains: Zara Davis Bolton (GB&I), Edith Flippin*
  *(USA)*
**Foursomes**
Valentine & Garvey lost to Lesser & Smith  2 and 1
Smith & Price beat Riley & Romack  5 and 3
Robertson & Veronica Anstey lost to Downey &
  Carolyn Cudone  6 and 4
**Singles**
Jessie Anderson Valentine beat Patricia Lesser
  6 and 4
Philomena Garvey lost to Margaret Smith  9 and 8
Frances Stephens Smith beat Polly Riley  1 hole
Janette Robertson lost to Barbara Romack  6 and 4
Angela Ward beat Mary Ann Downey  6 and 4
Elizabeth Price beat Jane Nelson  7 and 6

## 1954 Merion, PA  Sept 2–3
**Result: USA 6, GB&I 3**
*Captains: Edith Flippin (USA), Mrs JB Beck (GB&I)*
**Foursomes**
Faulk & Riley beat Stephens & Price  6 and 4
Doran & Patricia Lesser beat Garvey & Valentine  6 and 5
Kirby & Barbara Romack beat Marjorie Peel &
  Robertson  6 and 5
**Singles**
Mary Lena Faulk lost to Frances Stephens  1 hole
Claire Doran beat Jeanne Bisgood  4 and 3
Polly Riley beat Elizabeth Price  9 and 8
Dorothy Kirby lost to Philomena Garvey  3 and 1
Grace DeMoss Smith beat Jessie Anderson Valentine
  4 and 3
Joyce Ziske lost to Janette Robertson  3 and 1

## 1952 Muirfield  June 6–7
**Result: GB&I 5, USA 4**
*Captains: Lady Katherine Cairns (GB&I),*
  *Aniela Goldthwaite (USA)*
**Foursomes**
Donald & Price beat Kirby & DeMoss  3 and 2
Stephens & JA Valentine lost to Doran & Lindsay  6 and 4
Paterson & Garvey beat Riley & Patricia O'Sullivan  2 and 1
**Singles**
Jean Donald lost to Dorothy Kirby  1 hole
Frances Stephens beat Marjorie Lindsay  2 and 1
Moira Paterson lost to Polly Riley  6 and 4
Jeanne Bisgood beat Mae Murray  6 and 5
Philomena Garvey lost to Claire Doran  3 and 2
Elizabeth Price beat Grace DeMoss  3 and 2

## 1950 Buffalo, NY  Sept 4–5
**Result: USA 7½, GB&I 1½**
*Captains: Glenna Collett Vare (USA),*
  *Diana Fishwick Critchley (GB&I)*
**Foursomes**
Hanson & Porter beat Valentine & Donald  3 and 2
Helen Sigel & Kirk lost to Stephens & Price  1 hole
Dorothy Kirby & Kielty beat Garvey & Bisgood
  6 and 5
**Singles**
Dorothy Porter halved with Frances Stephens
Polly Riley beat Jessie Anderson Valentine  7 and 6
Beverly Hanson beat Jean Donald  6 and 5
Dorothy Kielty beat Philomena Garvey  2 and 1
Peggy Kirk beat Jeanne Bisgood  1 hole
Grace Lenczyk beat Elizabeth Price  5 and 4

## 1948 Birkdale  May 21–22
**Result: USA 6½, GB&I 2½**
*Captains: Doris Chambers (GB&I),*
  *Glenna Collett Vare (USA)*
**Foursomes**
Donald & Gordon beat Suggs & Lenczyk  3 and 2
Garvey & Bolton lost to Kirby & Vare  4 and 3
Ruttle & Val Reddan lost to Page & Kielty  5 and 4
**Singles**
Philomena Garvey halved with Louise Suggs
Jean Donald beat Dorothy Kirby  2 holes
Jacqueline Gordon lost to Grace Lenczyk  5 and 3
Helen Holm lost to Estelle Lawson Page  3 and 2
Maureen Ruttle lost to Polly Riley  3 and 2
Zara Bolton lost to Dorothy Kielty  2 and 1

## 1938 Essex, MA  Sept 7–8
**Result: USA 5½, GB&I 3½**
*Captains: Frances Stebbins (USA),*
  *Mrs RH Wallace-Williamson (GB&I)*
**Foursomes**
Page & Orcutt lost to Holm & Tiernan  2 holes
Vare & Berg lost to Anderson & Corlett  1 hole
Miley & Kathryn Hemphill halved with Walker &
  Phyllis Wade
**Singles**
Estelle Lawson Page beat Helen Holm  6 and 5
Patty Berg beat Jessie Anderson  1 hole
Marion Miley beat Elsie Corlett  1 and 1
Glenna Collett Vare beat Charlotte Walker  2 and 1
Maureen Orcutt lost to Clarrie Tiernan  2 and 1
Charlotte Glutting beat Nan Baird  1 hole

## 1936 Gleneagles  May 6
**Result: USA 4½, GB&I 4½**
*Captains: Doris Chambers (GB&I),*
  *Glenna Collett Vare (USA)*
**Foursomes**
Morgan & Garon halved with Vare & Berg
Barton & Walker  lost to Orcutt & Cheney  2 and 1
Anderson & Holm beat Hill & Glutting  3 and 2
**Singles**
Wanda Morgan lost to Glenna Collett Vare  3 and 2
Helen Holm lost to Patty Berg  4 and 3
Pamela Barton lost to Charlotte Glutting  1 hole
Charlotte Walker lost to Maureen Orcutt  1 hole
Jessie Anderson beat Leona Pressley Cheney  1 hole
Marjorie Garon beat Opal Hill  7 and 5

## 1934 Chevy Chase, MD Sept 27–28
**Result: USA 6½, GB&I 2½**
*Captains: Glenna Collett Vare (USA),*
*Doris Chambers (GB&I)*

**Foursomes**
Van Wie & Glutting halved with Gourlay & Barton
Orcutt & Cheney beat Fishwick & Morgan  2 holes
Hill & Lucille Robinson lost to Plumpton & Walker
  2 and 1

**Singles**
Virginia Van Wie beat Diana Fishwick  2 and 1
Maureen Orcutt beat Molly Gourlay  4 and 2
Leona Pressley Cheney beat Pamela Barton  7 and 5
Charlotte Glutting beat Wanda Morgan
Opal Hill beat Diana Plumpton  3 and 2
Aniela Goldthwaite lost to Charlotte Walker  3 and 2

## 1932 Wentworth  May 21
**Result: USA 5½, GB&I 3½**
*Captains: J Wethered (GB&I), M Hollins (USA)*

**Foursomes**
Wethered & Morgan lost to Vare & Hill  1 hole
Wilson & JB Watson lost to Van Wie & Hicks  2 and 1
Gourlay & Doris Park lost to Orcutt & Cheney
  1 hole

**Singles**
Joyce Wethered beat Glenna Collett Vare  6 and 4
Enid Wilson beat Helen Hicks  2 and 1
Wanda Morgan lost to Virginia Van Wie  2 and 1
Diana Fishwick beat Maureen Orcutt  4 and 3
Molly Gourlay halved with Opal Hill
Elsie Corlett lost to Leona Pressley Cheney  4 and 3

## Curtis Cup INDIVIDUAL RECORDS

Bold print: captain; bold print in brackets: non-playing captain
Maiden name in parentheses, former surname in square brackets

### Great Britain and Ireland

| Name | | Year | Played | Won | Lost | Halved |
|---|---|---|---|---|---|---|
| Jean Anderson (Donald) | SCO | 1948 | 6 | 3 | 3 | 0 |
| Kim Andrew (Rostron) | ENG | 1998-2000 | 8 | 2 | 6 | 0 |
| Diane Bailey [Frearson] (Robb) | ENG | 1962-72-**(84)-(86)-(88)** | 5 | 2 | 2 | 1 |
| Sally Barber (Bonallack) | ENG | 1962 | 1 | 0 | 1 | 0 |
| Pam Barton | ENG | 1934-36 | 4 | 0 | 3 | 1 |
| Hannah Barwood | ENG | 2010 | 3 | 0 | 2 | 1 |
| Linda Bayman | ENG | 1988 | 4 | 2 | 1 | 1 |
| Baba Beck (Pym) | IRL | **(1954)** | 0 | 0 | 0 | 0 |
| Charlotte Beddows [Watson] (Stevenson) | SCO | 1932 | 1 | 0 | 1 | 0 |
| Lilian Behan | IRL | 1986 | 4 | 3 | 1 | 0 |
| Veronica Beharrell (Anstey) | ENG | 1956 | 1 | 0 | 1 | 0 |
| Pam Benka (Tredinnick) | ENG | 1966-68 **(2002)** | 4 | 0 | 3 | 1 |
| Elizabeth Bennett | ENG | 2008 | 5 | 0 | 4 | 1 |
| Jeanne Bisgood | ENG | 1950-52-54-**(70)** | 4 | 1 | 3 | 0 |
| Elizabeth Boatman (Collis) | ENG | **(1992)-(94)** | 0 | 0 | 0 | 0 |
| Zara Bolton (Davis) | ENG | 1948-**(56)-(66)-(68)** | 2 | 0 | 2 | 0 |
| Angela Bonallack (Ward) | ENG | 1956-58-60-62-64-66 | 15 | 6 | 8 | 1 |
| Carly Booth | SCO | 2008 | 4 | 1 | 3 | 0 |
| Amy Boulden | WAL | 2012 | 8 | 4 | 3 | 1 |
| Becky Brewerton | WAL | 2000 | 3 | 1 | 2 | 0 |
| Fiona Brown | ENG | 1998-2000 | 4 | 2 | 2 | 0 |
| Ita Butler (Burke) | IRL | 1966-**(96)** | 3 | 2 | 1 | 0 |
| Lady Katherine Cairns | ENG | **(1952)** | 0 | 0 | 0 | 0 |
| Krystle Caithness | SCO | 2008 | 3 | 3 | 0 | 0 |
| Carole Caldwell (Redford) | ENG | 1978-80 | 5 | 0 | 3 | 2 |
| Doris Chambers | ENG | **(1934)-(36)-(48)** | 0 | 0 | 0 | 0 |
| Holly Clyburn | ENG | 2010-12 | 5 | 1 | 1 | 1 |
| Alison Coffey | IRL | 2002 | 3 | 1 | 2 | 0 |
| Carol Comboy (Grott) | ENG | **(1978)-(80)** | 0 | 0 | 0 | 0 |
| Jane Connachan | SCO | 1980-82 | 5 | 0 | 5 | 0 |
| Elsie Corlett | ENG | 1932-38-**(64)** | 3 | 1 | 2 | 0 |
| Claire Coughlan | IRL | 2004-06 | 5 | 3 | 2 | 0 |
| Diana Critchley (Fishwick) | ENG | 1932-34-**(50)** | 3 | 1 | 2 | 0 |
| Alison Davidson (Rose) | SCO | 1996-98 | 7 | 4 | 3 | 0 |
| Karen Davies | WAL | 1986-88 | 7 | 4 | 1 | 2 |
| Laura Davies | ENG | 1984 | 2 | 1 | 1 | 0 |
| Tara Delanbey | ENG | 2006 | 3 | 0 | 2 | 1 |
| Lisa Dermott | WAL | 1996 | 2 | 2 | 0 | 0 |
| Helen Dobson | ENG | 1990 | 3 | 1 | 2 | 0 |
| Kitrina Douglas | ENG | 1982 | 4 | 0 | 3 | 1 |
| Claire Dowling (Hourihane) | IRL | 1984-86-88-90-92-**(2000)** | 8 | 3 | 3 | 2 |
| Marjorie Draper [Peel] (Thomas) | SCO | 1954 | 1 | 0 | 1 | 0 |
| Emma Duggleby | ENG | 2000-04 | 8 | 5 | 2 | 1 |

| Name | | Year | Played | Won | Lost | Halved |
|---|---|---|---|---|---|---|
| Lisa Educate (Walton) | ENG | 1994-96 | 6 | 3 | 3 | 0 |
| Naomi Edwards | ENG | 2006 | 3 | 1 | 2 | 0 |
| Mary Everard | ENG | 1970-72-74-78 | 15 | 6 | 7 | 2 |
| Jodi Ewart | ENG | 2008 | 3 | 0 | 2 | 1 |
| Elaine Farquharson | SCO | 1990-92 | 6 | 1 | 5 | 0 |
| Daisy Ferguson | IRL | (1958) | 0 | 0 | 0 | 0 |
| Marjory Ferguson (Fowler) | SCO | 1966 | 1 | 0 | 1 | 0 |
| Elizabeth Price Fisher (Price) | ENG | 1950-52-54-56-58-60 | 12 | 7 | 4 | 1 |
| Linzi Fletcher | ENG | 1990 | 1 | 0 | 1 | 0 |
| Maureen Garner (Madill) | IRL | 1980 | 4 | 0 | 3 | 1 |
| Marjorie Ross Garon | ENG | 1936 | 2 | 1 | 0 | 1 |
| Maureen Garrett (Ruttle) | ENG | 1948-(60) | 2 | 0 | 2 | 0 |
| Philomena Garvey | IRL | 1948-50-52-54-56-60 | 11 | 2 | 8 | 1 |
| Carol Gibbs (Le Feuvre) | ENG | 1974 | 3 | 0 | 3 | 0 |
| Martine Gillen | IRL | 2006 | 4 | 2 | 2 | 0 |
| Jacqueline Gordon | ENG | 1948 | 2 | 1 | 1 | 0 |
| Molly Gourlay | ENG | 1932-34 | 4 | 0 | 2 | 2 |
| Julia Greenhalgh | ENG | 1964-70-74-76-78 | 17 | 6 | 7 | 4 |
| Penny Grice-Whittaker (Grice) | ENG | 1984 | 4 | 2 | 1 | 1 |
| Caroline Hall | ENG | 1992 | 4 | 2 | 0 | 2 |
| Marley Harris [Spearman] (Baker) | ENG | 1962-64 | 6 | 2 | 2 | 2 |
| Dorothea Hastings (Sommerville) | SCO | 1958 | 0 | 0 | 0 | 0 |
| Lady Heathcoat-Amory (Joyce Wethered) | ENG | 1932 | 2 | 1 | 1 | 0 |
| Dinah Henson (Oxley) | ENG | 1968-70-72-76 | 11 | 3 | 6 | 2 |
| Anna Highgate | WAL | 2004 | 1 | 0 | 1 | 0 |
| Helen Holm (Gray) | SCO | 1936-38-48 | 5 | 3 | 2 | 0 |
| Ann Howard (Phillips) | ENG | 1956-68 | 2 | 0 | 2 | 0 |
| Rebecca Hudson | ENG | 1998-2000-02 | 11 | 5 | 5 | 1 |
| Shirley Huggan (Lawson) | SCO | 1988 | 2 | 1 | 1 | 0 |
| Beverley Huke | ENG | 1972 | 2 | 0 | 2 | 0 |
| Charley Hull | ENG | 2012 | 3 | 1 | 2 | 0 |
| Ann Irvin | ENG | 1962-68-70-76 | 12 | 4 | 7 | 1 |
| Bridget Jackson | ENG | 1958-64-68 | 8 | 1 | 6 | 1 |
| Rachel Jennings | ENG | 2010 | 5 | 0 | 4 | 1 |
| Patricia Johnson | ENG | 1986 | 4 | 4 | 0 | 0 |
| Sarah Jones | WAL | 2002 | 2 | 1 | 1 | 0 |
| Anne Laing | SCO | 2004 | 4 | 3 | 1 | 0 |
| Vikki Laing | SCO | 2002 | 4 | 2 | 2 | 0 |
| Susan Langridge (Armitage) | ENG | 1964-66 | 6 | 0 | 5 | 1 |
| Bronte Law | ENG | 2012 | 4 | 1 | 2 | 1 |
| Joan Lawrence | SCO | 1964 | 2 | 0 | 2 | 0 |
| Wilma Leburn (Aitken) | SCO | 1982 | 2 | 0 | 2 | 0 |
| Jenny Lee Smith | ENG | 1974-76 | 3 | 0 | 3 | 0 |
| Breanne Loucks | WAL | 2006-08 | 7 | 4 | 3 | 0 |
| Kathryn Lumb (Phillips) | ENG | 1970-72 | 2 | 1 | 1 | 0 |
| Leona Maquire | IRL | 2010-12 | 9 | 2 | 5 | 2 |
| Lisa Maquire | IRL | 2010 | 3 | 2 | 1 | 0 |
| Mhairi McKay | SCO | 1994-96 | 7 | 2 | 3 | 2 |
| Mary McKenna | IRL | 1970-72-74-76-78-80-82-84-86-(2008-10) | 30 | 10 | 16 | 4 |
| Shelley McKevitt | ENG | 2004 | 4 | 2 | 2 | 0 |
| Myra McKinlay | SCO | 1994 | 3 | 1 | 2 | 0 |
| Suzanne McMahon (Cadden) | SCO | 1976 | 4 | 0 | 4 | 0 |
| Danielle McVeigh | IRL | 2010 | 5 | 2 | 2 | 1 |
| Sheila Maher (Vaughan) | ENG | 1962-64 | 4 | 1 | 2 | 1 |
| Tricia Mangan | IRL | 2006 | 3 | 0 | 2 | 1 |
| Kathryn Marshall (Imrie) | SCO | 1990 | 4 | 1 | 3 | 0 |
| Vanessa Marvin | ENG | 1978 | 4 | 1 | 3 | 0 |
| Danielle Masters | ENG | 2004 | 3 | 1 | 2 | 0 |
| Kiran Matharu | ENG | 2006 | 2 | 1 | 1 | 0 |
| Catriona Matthew (Lambert) | SCO | 1990-92-94 | 12 | 7 | 4 | 1 |
| Tegwen Matthews [Thomas] (Perkins) | WAL | 1974-76-78-80-(2012) | 14 | 4 | 8 | 2 |
| Stephanie Meadow | NIR | 2012 | 4 | 3 | 1 | 0 |
| Moira Milton (Paterson) | SCO | 1952 | 2 | 1 | 1 | 0 |
| Hilary Monaghan | SCO | 1998 | 1 | 0 | 1 | 0 |
| Janice Moodie | SCO | 1994-96 | 8 | 5 | 1 | 2 |
| Fame More | ENG | 2002-04 | 2 | 0 | 2 | 0 |
| Becky Morgan | WAL | 1998-2000 | 7 | 2 | 5 | 0 |
| Wanda Morgan | ENG | 1932-34-36 | 6 | 0 | 5 | 1 |

| Name | | Year | Played | Won | Lost | Halved |
|---|---|---|---|---|---|---|
| Joanne Morley | ENG | 1992 | 4 | 2 | 0 | 2 |
| Nicola Murray (Buxton) | ENG | 1992 | 1 | 0 | 1 | 0 |
| Beverley New | ENG | 1984 | 4 | 1 | 3 | 0 |
| Lesley Nicholson | SCO | 2000 | 1 | 0 | 0 | 1 |
| Suzanne O'Brien | IRL | 2000 | 4 | 3 | 0 | 1 |
| Maire O'Donnell | IRL | (1982) | 0 | 0 | 0 | 0 |
| Ada O'Sullivan | IRL | (2004-06) | 0 | 0 | 0 | 0 |
| Florentyna Parker | ENG | 2008 | 4 | 1 | 3 | 0 |
| Margaret Pickard (Nichol) | ENG | 1968-70 | 5 | 2 | 3 | 0 |
| Diana Plumpton | ENG | 1934 | 2 | 1 | 1 | 0 |
| Elizabeth Pook (Chadwick) | ENG | 1966 | 4 | 1 | 3 | 0 |
| Doris Porter (Park) | SCO | 1932 | 1 | 0 | 1 | 0 |
| Pamela Pretswell | SCO | 2010-12 | 7 | 2 | 5 | 0 |
| Eileen Rose Power (McDaid) | IRL | 1994 | 1 | 0 | 1 | 0 |
| Elaine Ratcliffe | ENG | 1996-98 | 6 | 3 | 1 | 2 |
| Clarrie Reddan (Tiernan) | IRL | 1938-48 | 3 | 2 | 1 | 0 |
| Joan Rennie (Hastings) | SCO | 1966 | 2 | 0 | 1 | 1 |
| Melissa Reid | ENG | 2006 | 4 | 1 | 3 | 0 |
| Maureen Richmond (Walker) | SCO | 1974 | 4 | 2 | 2 | 0 |
| Jean Roberts | ENG | 1962 | 1 | 0 | 1 | 0 |
| Belle Robertson (McCorkindale) | SCO | 1960-66-68-70-72-(74)-(76)-82-86 | 24 | 5 | 12 | 7 |
| Claire Robinson (Nesbitt) | IRL | 1980 | 3 | 0 | 1 | 2 |
| Vivien Saunders | ENG | 1968 | 4 | 1 | 2 | 1 |
| Susan Shapcott | ENG | 1988 | 4 | 3 | 1 | 0 |
| Linda Simpson (Moore) | ENG | 1980 | 3 | 1 | 1 | 1 |
| Ruth Slark (Porter) | ENG | 1960-62-64 | 7 | 3 | 3 | 1 |
| Anne Smith [Stant] (Willard) | ENG | 1976 | 1 | 0 | 1 | 0 |
| Frances Smith (Stephens) | ENG | 1950-52-54-56-58-60-(62)-(72) | 11 | 7 | 3 | 1 |
| Kerry Smith | ENG | 2002 | 2 | 0 | 2 | 0 |
| Janet Soulsby | ENG | 1982 | 4 | 1 | 2 | 1 |
| Kirsty Speak | ENG | 1994 | 1 | 0 | 1 | 0 |
| Gillian Stewart | SCO | 1980-82 | 4 | 1 | 3 | 0 |
| Heather Stirling | SCO | 2002 | 4 | 1 | 3 | 0 |
| Karen Stupples | ENG | 1996-98 | 4 | 2 | 2 | 0 |
| Vicki Thomas (Rawlings) | WAL | 1982-84-86-88-90-92 | 13 | 6 | 5 | 2 |
| Michele Thomson | SCO | 2008 | 4 | 1 | 2 | 1 |
| Muriel Thomson | SCO | 1978 | 3 | 2 | 1 | 0 |
| Jill Thornhill | ENG | 1984-86-88 | 12 | 6 | 2 | 4 |
| Kelly Tidy | ENG | 2012 | 4 | 3 | 1 | 0 |
| Nicola Timmins | ENG | 2004 | 3 | 1 | 2 | 0 |
| Angela Uzielli (Carrick) | ENG | 1978 | 1 | 0 | 1 | 0 |
| Jessie Valentine (Anderson) | SCO | 1936-38-50-52-54-56-58 | 13 | 4 | 9 | 0 |
| Julie Wade | ENG | 1988-90-92-94-96 | 19 | 6 | 10 | 3 |
| Helen Wadsworth | WAL | 1990 | 2 | 0 | 2 | 0 |
| Claire Waite | ENG | 1984 | 4 | 2 | 2 | 0 |
| Mickey Walker | ENG | 1972-74 | 4 | 3 | 0 | 1 |
| Pat Walker | IRL | 1934-36-38 | 6 | 2 | 3 | 1 |
| Verona Wallace-Williamson | SCO | (1938) | 0 | 0 | 0 | 0 |
| Nan Wardlaw (Baird) | SCO | 1938 | 1 | 0 | 1 | 0 |
| Sally Watson | SCO | 2008-10 | 10 | 4 | 5 | 1 |
| Enid Wilson | ENG | 1932 | 2 | 1 | 1 | 0 |
| Janette Wright (Robertson) | SCO | 1954-56-58-60 | 8 | 3 | 5 | 0 |
| Phyllis Wylie (Wade) | ENG | 1938 | 1 | 0 | 0 | 1 |

## United States of America

| Name | Year | Played | Won | Lost | Halved |
|---|---|---|---|---|---|
| Roberta Albers | 1968 | 2 | 1 | 0 | 1 |
| Danielle Ammaccapane | 1986 | 3 | 0 | 3 | 0 |
| Amy Anderson | 2012 | 5 | 3 | 2 | 0 |
| Kathy Baker | 1982 | 4 | 3 | 0 | 1 |
| Barbara Barrow | 1976 | 2 | 1 | 0 | 1 |
| Beth Barry | 1972-74 | 5 | 3 | 1 | 1 |
| Emily Bastel | 2002 | 2 | 0 | 2 | 0 |
| Beth Bauer | 1998-2000 | 7 | 4 | 3 | 0 |
| Laura Baugh | 1972 | 4 | 2 | 1 | 1 |
| Leland Beckel | 2000 | 1 | 0 | 1 | 0 |
| Judy Bell | 1960-62-(86)-(88) | 2 | 1 | 1 | 0 |
| Peggy Kirk Bell (Kirk) | 1950 | 2 | 1 | 1 | 0 |
| Amy Benz | 1982 | 3 | 2 | 1 | 0 |

| Name | Year | Played | Won | Lost | Halved |
|------|------|--------|-----|------|--------|
| Patty Berg | 1936-38 | 4 | 1 | 2 | 1 |
| Erica Blasberg | 2004 | 2 | 1 | 2 | 1 |
| Amanda Blumenherst | 2006-08 | 8 | 4 | 3 | 1 |
| Barbara Fay Boddie (White) | 1964-66 | 8 | 7 | 0 | 1 |
| Meghan Bolger | 2008 | 3 | 0 | 3 | 0 |
| Jane Booth (Bastanchury) | 1970-72-74-(2000) | 12 | 9 | 3 | 0 |
| Kellee Booth | 1996-98 | 7 | 5 | 2 | 0 |
| Mary Budke | 1974-(2002) | 3 | 2 | 1 | 0 |
| Robin Burke | 1998 | 3 | 2 | 1 | 0 |
| Brandie Burton | 1990 | 3 | 3 | 0 | 0 |
| Jo Anne Carner (Gunderson) | 1958-60-62-64 | 10 | 6 | 3 | 1 |
| Lori Castillo | 1980 | 3 | 2 | 1 | 0 |
| Leona Cheney (Pressler) | 1932-34-36 | 6 | 5 | 1 | 0 |
| Sis Choate | (1974) | 0 | 0 | 0 | 0 |
| Jenny Chuasiriporn | 1998 | 3 | 0 | 2 | 1 |
| Cydney Clanton | 2010 | 3 | 2 | 0 | 1 |
| Peggy Conley | 1964-68 | 6 | 3 | 1 | 2 |
| Mary Ann Cook (Downey) | 1956 | 2 | 1 | 1 | 0 |
| Patricia Cornett | 1978-88-(2012) | 4 | 1 | 2 | 1 |
| Brenda Corrie Kuehn | 1996-98 | 7 | 4 | 3 | 0 |
| ean Crawford (Ashley) | 1962-66-68-(72) | 8 | 6 | 2 | 0 |
| Paula Creamer | 2004 | 3 | 2 | 1 | 0 |
| Clifford Ann Creed | 1962 | 2 | 2 | 0 | 0 |
| Grace Cronin (Lenczyk) | 1948-50 | 3 | 2 | 1 | 0 |
| Carolyn Cudone | 1956-(70) | 1 | 1 | 0 | 0 |
| Beth Daniel | 1976-78 | 8 | 7 | 1 | 0 |
| Virginia Dennehy | (1958) | 0 | 0 | 0 | 0 |
| Virginia Derby Grimes | 1998-2000 | 6 | 3 | 1 | 2 |
| Mary Lou Dill | 1968 | 3 | 1 | 1 | 1 |
| Lindy Duncan | 2012 | 4 | 1 | 3 | 0 |
| Meredith Duncan | 2002 | 4 | 3 | 1 | 0 |
| Alice Dye | 1970 | 2 | 1 | 0 | 1 |
| Austin Ernst | 2012 | 4 | 2 | 1 | 1 |
| Mollie Fankhauser | 2002 | 3 | 1 | 2 | 0 |
| Heather Farr | 1984 | 3 | 2 | 1 | 0 |
| Jane Fassinger | 1970 | 1 | 0 | 1 | 0 |
| Mary Lena Faulk | 1954 | 2 | 1 | 1 | 0 |
| Carol Sorensen Flenniken (Sorensen) | 1964-66 | 8 | 6 | 1 | 1 |
| Edith Flippin (Quier) | (1954)-(56) | 0 | 0 | 0 | 0 |
| Amy Fruhwirth | 1992 | 4 | 0 | 1 | 3 |
| Kim Gardner | 1986 | 3 | 1 | 1 | 1 |
| Charlotte Glutting | 1934-36-38 | 5 | 3 | 1 | 1 |
| Vicki Goetze | 1990-92 | 8 | 4 | 2 | 2 |
| Brenda Goldsmith | 1978-80 | 4 | 2 | 2 | 0 |
| Aniela Goldthwaite | 1934-(52) | 1 | 0 | 1 | 0 |
| Joanne Goodwin | 1960 | 2 | 1 | 1 | 0 |
| Virginia Grimes | 2006 | 2 | 1 | 1 | 0 |
| Mary Hafeman | 1980 | 2 | 1 | 0 | 1 |
| Shelley Hamkin | 1968-70 | 8 | 3 | 3 | 2 |
| Penny Hammel | 1984 | 3 | 1 | 1 | 1 |
| Nancy Hammer (Hager) | 1970 | 2 | 1 | 1 | 0 |
| Cathy Hanlon | 1982 | 3 | 2 | 1 | 0 |
| Beverley Hanson | 1950 | 2 | 2 | 0 | 0 |
| Tracy Hanson | 1992 | 3 | 1 | 2 | 0 |
| Patricia Harbottle (Lesser) | 1954-56 | 3 | 2 | 1 | 0 |
| Leigh Anne Hardin | 2002 | 3 | 1 | 2 | 0 |
| Mina Harigae | 2008 | 4 | 2 | 2 | 0 |
| Helen Hawes | (1964) | 0 | 0 | 0 | 0 |
| Kathryn Hemphill | 1938 | 1 | 0 | 0 | 1 |
| Helen Hicks | 1932 | 2 | 1 | 1 | 0 |
| Carolyn Hill | 1978 | 2 | 0 | 0 | 2 |
| Cindy Hill | 1970-74-76-78 | 14 | 5 | 6 | 3 |
| Opel Hill | 1932-34-36 | 6 | 2 | 3 | 1 |
| Marion Hollins | (1932) | 0 | 0 | 0 | 0 |
| Hilary Homeyer | 2000 | 4 | 3 | 0 | 1 |
| Dana Howe | 1984 | 3 | 1 | 1 | 1 |
| Sarah Huarte | 2004 | 2 | 0 | 2 | 0 |
| Juli Inkster | 1982 | 4 | 4 | 0 | 0 |
| Elizabeth Janangelo | 2004 | 3 | 1 | 2 | 0 |
| Maria Jemsek | 1996 | 3 | 0 | 2 | 1 |

| Name | Year | Played | Won | Lost | Halved |
|---|---|---|---|---|---|
| Angela Jerman | 2002 | 3 | 2 | 1 | 0 |
| Tiffany Joh | 2008 | 4 | 2 | 1 | 1 |
| Jennifer Johnson | 2010 | 4 | 3 | 0 | 1 |
| Ann Casey Johnstone | 1958-60-62 | 4 | 3 | 1 | 0 |
| Mae Murray Jones (Murray) | 1952 | 1 | 0 | 1 | 0 |
| Wendy Kaupp | 1994 | 2 | 0 | 2 | 0 |
| Stephanie Keever | 2000 | 4 | 2 | 2 | 0 |
| Caroline Keggi | 1988 | 3 | 0 | 2 | 1 |
| Tracy Kerdyk | 1988 | 4 | 2 | 1 | 1 |
| Cristie Kerr | 1996 | 3 | 1 | 1 | 1 |
| Kandi Kessler | 1986 | 3 | 1 | 1 | 1 |
| Dorothy Kielty | 1948-50 | 4 | 4 | 0 | 0 |
| Kimberly Kim | 2008-10 | 7 | 4 | 3 | 0 |
| Dorothy Kirby | 1948-50-52-54 | 7 | 4 | 3 | 0 |
| Martha Kirouac (Wilkinson) | 1970-72-(2004) | 8 | 5 | 3 | 0 |
| Emilee Klein | 1994 | 4 | 3 | 1 | 0 |
| Nancy Knight (Lopez) | 1976 | 2 | 2 | 0 | 0 |
| Stephanie Kono | 2010 | 4 | 2 | 1 | 1 |
| Jessica Korda | 2010 | 5 | 3 | 1 | 1 |
| Kelli Kuehne | 1996 | 3 | 2 | 1 | 0 |
| Brittany Lang | 2004 | 3 | 1 | 2 | 0 |
| Martha Lang | 1992-(96) | 3 | 2 | 0 | 1 |
| Bonnie Lauer | 1974 | 4 | 2 | 2 | 0 |
| Sarah Le Brun Ingram | 1992-94-96 | 7 | 2 | 4 | 1 |
| Taylor Leon | 2006 | 4 | 3 | 0 | 1 |
| Tiffany Lua | 2010 | 7 | 3 | 3 | 1 |
| Stacy Lewis | 2008 | 5 | 5 | 0 | 0 |
| Marjorie Lindsay | 1952 | 2 | 1 | 1 | 0 |
| Patricia Lucey (O'Sullivan) | 1952 | 1 | 0 | 1 | 0 |
| Paige Mackenzie | 2006 | 4 | 3 | 1 | 0 |
| Lisa McCloskey | 2012 | 4 | 2 | 2 | 0 |
| Amanda McCurdy | 2006 | 2 | 1 | 1 | 0 |
| Mari McDougall | 1982 | 2 | 2 | 0 | 0 |
| Jill McGill | 1994 | 4 | 1 | 1 | 2 |
| Barbara McIntire | 1958-60-62-64-66-72-(76) | 16 | 6 | 6 | 4 |
| Lucile Mann (Robinson) | 1934 | 1 | 0 | 1 | 0 |
| Debbie Massey | 1974-76 | 5 | 5 | 0 | 0 |
| Marion Miley | 1938 | 2 | 1 | 0 | 1 |
| Dottie Mochrie (Pepper) | 1986 | 3 | 0 | 2 | 1 |
| Noreen Mohler (Uihlein) | 1978-(2010) | 3 | 1 | 1 | 1 |
| Evelyn Monsted | (1968) | 0 | 0 | 0 | 0 |
| Terri Moody | 1980 | 2 | 1 | 0 | 1 |
| Laura Myerscough | 2002 | 3 | 3 | 0 | 0 |
| Karen Noble | 1990 | 4 | 2 | 2 | 0 |
| Judith Oliver | 1978-80-82-(92) | 8 | 5 | 1 | 2 |
| Maureen Orcutt | 1932-34-36-38 | 8 | 5 | 3 | 0 |
| Joanne Pacillo | 1984 | 3 | 1 | 1 | 1 |
| Estelle Page (Lawson) | 1938-48 | 4 | 3 | 1 | 0 |
| Brooke Pancake | 2012 | 5 | 3 | 1 | 1 |
| Jane Park | 2004-06 | 7 | 4 | 2 | 1 |
| Katie Peterson | 1990 | 3 | 3 | 0 | 0 |
| Margaret Platt | 1990 | 2 | 0 | 2 | 0 |
| Frances Pond (Stebbins) | (1938) | 0 | 0 | 0 | 0 |
| Erica Popson | 2012 | 3 | 0 | 3 | 0 |
| Ellen Port | 1994-96 | 6 | 4 | 2 | 0 |
| Dorothy Germain Porter | 1950-(66) | 2 | 1 | 0 | 1 |
| Phyllis Preuss | 1962-64-66-68-70-(84) | 15 | 10 | 4 | 1 |
| Betty Probasco | (1982) | 0 | 0 | 0 | 0 |
| Mildred Prunaret | (1960) | 0 | 0 | 0 | 0 |
| Polly Riley | 1948-50-52-54-56-58-(62) | 10 | 5 | 5 | 0 |
| Jo Jo Robertson | 1998 | 2 | 0 | 2 | 0 |
| Barbara Romack | 1954-56-58 | 5 | 3 | 2 | 0 |
| Jody Rosenthal | 1984 | 3 | 2 | 0 | 1 |
| Anne Sander [Welts] [Decker] (Quast) | 1958-60-62-66-68-74-84-90 | 22 | 11 | 7 | 4 |
| Cindy Scholefield | 1988 | 3 | 0 | 3 | 0 |
| Cindy Schreyer | 1986 | 3 | 1 | 2 | 0 |
| Kathleen McCarthy Scrivner (McCarthy) | 1986-88 | 6 | 2 | 3 | 1 |
| Carol Semple Thompson | 1974-76-80-82-90-92-94-96-(98)-2000-02-(06)-(08) | 33 | 16 | 13 | 4 |
| Leslie Shannon | 1986-88-90-92 | 9 | 1 | 6 | 2 |

| Name | Year | Played | Won | Lost | Halved |
|------|------|--------|-----|------|--------|
| Patty Sheehan | 1980 | 4 | 4 | 0 | 0 |
| Pearl Sinn | 1988 | 2 | I | I | 0 |
| Grace De Moss Smith (De Moss) | 1952-54 | 3 | I | 2 | 0 |
| Lancy Smith | 1972-78-80-82-84-(94) | 16 | 7 | 5 | 4 |
| Margaret Smith | 1956 | 2 | 2 | 0 | 0 |
| Jennifer Song | 2010 | 5 | 2 | 2 | I |
| Stephanie Sparks | 1994 | 2 | 0 | 2 | I |
| Hollis Stacy | 1972 | 2 | 0 | I | I |
| Claire Stancik (Doran) | 1952-54 | 4 | 4 | 0 | 0 |
| Angela Stanford | 2000 | 4 | I | 2 | I |
| Judy Street (Eller) | 1960 | 2 | 2 | 0 | 0 |
| Louise Suggs | 1948 | 2 | 0 | I | I |
| Jenny Suh | 2006 | 2 | 0 | 2 | 0 |
| Courtney Swaim | 2002 | 4 | 3 | I | 0 |
| Nancy Roth Syms (Roth) | 1964-66-76-(80) | 9 | 3 | 5 | I |
| Alexis Thompson | 2010 | 5 | 4 | 0 | I |
| Anne Thurman | 2004 | 4 | 3 | I | 0 |
| Emily Tubert | 2012 | 3 | I | 2 | 0 |
| Virginia Van Wie | 1932-34 | 4 | 3 | 0 | I |
| Glenna Collett Vare (Collett) | 1932-(34)-36-38-48-(50) | 7 | 4 | 2 | I |
| Alison Walshe | 2008 | 4 | 4 | 0 | 0 |
| Wendy Ward | 1994 | 3 | I | 2 | 0 |
| Jane Weiss (Nelson) | 1956 | I | 0 | I | 0 |
| Robin Weiss | 1990-92-2000 | 7 | 4 | 2 | I |
| Donna White (Horton) | 1976 | 2 | 2 | 0 | 0 |
| Mary Anne Widman | 1984 | 3 | 2 | I | 0 |
| Michelle Wie | 2004 | 4 | 2 | 2 | 0 |
| Kimberley Williams | 1986 | 3 | 0 | 3 | 0 |
| Helen Sigel Wilson (Sigel) | 1950-66-(78) | 2 | 0 | 2 | 0 |
| Joyce Ziske | 1954 | I | 0 | I | 0 |

# Women's World Amateur Team Championship for the Espirito Santo Trophy
(Inaugurated 1964)

*History* – The United States of America have won the event on 13 occasions, Korea, France, Australia and Sweden twice and South Africa once.

| | | |
|---|---|---|
| 1964 | I France 588; 2 USA 589 | St Germain GC, Paris, France |
| 1966 | I USA 580; 2 Canada 589 | Mexico City GC, Mexico |
| 1968 | I USA 626; 2 Australia 622 | Victoria GC, Melbourne, Australia |
| 1970 | I USA 598; 2 France 599 | RSHE Club de Campo, Madrid, Spain |
| 1972 | I USA 583; 2 France 587 | The Hindu GC, Argentina |
| 1974 | I USA 620; 2 GB and I, Spain 636 | Campo de Golf Cajuiles, Dominican Republic |
| 1976 | I USA 605; 2 France 622 | Vilamoura GC, Portugal |
| 1978 | I Australia 596; 2 Canada 597 | Pacific Harbour GC, Fiji |
| 1980 | I USA 588; 2 Australia 595 | Pinehurst No.2, NC, USA |
| 1982 | I USA 579; 2 New Zealand 596 | Geneva GC, Switzerland |
| 1984 | I USA 585; 2 France 597 | Royal Hong Kong GC |
| 1986 | I Spain 580; 2 France 583 | Lagunita CC, Colombia |
| 1988 | I USA 587; 2 Sweden 588 | Drottningholm GC, Sweden |
| 1990 | I USA 585; 2 New Zealand 597 | Russley GC, Christchurch, New Zealand |
| 1992 | I Spain 588; 2 GB&I 599 | Marine Drive GC Vancouver, Canada |
| 1994 | I USA 569; 2 South Korea 573 | Golf National, Versailles, France |
| 1996 | I South Korea 438; 2 Italy 440 | St Elena GC, Philippines |
| 1998 | I USA 558; 2 Italy, Germany 579 | Prince of Wales GC, Santiago, Chile |
| 2000 | I France 580; 2 South Korea 587 | Sporting Club, Berlin (Faldo Course) and Bad Sarrow, GC, Germany |
| 2002 | I Australia* 578; 2 Thailand 578 | Saujana G&CC (Palm and Bunga Raya Courses), Malaysia |
| *Australia won play-off* | | |
| 2004 | I Sweden 567; 2 USA, Canada 570 | Rio Mar GC (River and Ocean Courses), Puerto Rico |
| 2006 | I South Africa* 566; 2 Sweden 566 | De Zalze GC and Stellenbosch GC South Africa |
| *South Africa won play-off* | | |
| 2008 | I Sweden 561; 2 Spain 573 | The Grange GC (East and West Courses), Adelaide, Australia |
| 2010 | I Korea 546; 2 USA 563 | Olivos Golf Club and Buenos Aires GC, Argentina |
| 2012 | I Korea 563; 2 Germany 566 | Gloria CC (New and Old courses), Antalya, Turkey |

Astor Trophy (Formerly the Commonwealth Trophy) (Inaugurated 1959)
This event will next be held in 2015

# Vagliano Trophy – Great Britain & Ireland v Continent of Europe

(Inaugurated 1959)    *Golf de Chantilly, France*
**Captains:** GB&I: Tegwen Matthews; Europe: Anne Lanrezac
**First Day: Foursomes** *(GB&I names first)*
Georgia Hall (ENG) and Hayley Davis (ENG) bet Nicole Larsen (DEN) and Emily Pedersen (DEN)  5 and 3
Bronte Law (ENG) and Gabriella Cowley (ENG) halved with Celine Boutier (FRA) and Natalia Escuriola
(ESP)
Amy Boulden (WAL) and Alexandra Peters (ENG) beat Sophia Popov (GER) and Karolin Lampert (GER)
3and 2
Stephanie Meadow (IRL) and Amber Ratcliffe ENG) halved with Camilla Hedberg (ESP) and Noemi Jimenez
(ESP)

**Singles**
Hall lost to Boutier 2 and 1                Boulden halved with Jimenez
Becky Harries (WAL) lost to Larsen  1 hole       Law beat Popov  2 holes
Peters lost to Lampert  1 hole             Cowley lost to Escuriola  2 and 1
Davis beat Quirine Eijkenboom (GER)  4 and 3     Meadow lost to Hedberg  4 and 2

**Second Day: Foursomes**
Hall and Davis beat Boutier and Escuriola  2 and 1
Law and Cowley lost to Larsen and Pedersen 2 and 1
Boulden and Peters lost to Hedberg and Jimene  3 and 2
Meadow and Ratcliffe lost to Popov and Lampert  2 and 1

**Singles**
Hall lost to Jimenez  4 and 3              Boulden lost to Pedersen  2 and 1
Harries lost to Boutier  3 and 1           Ratcliffe lost Escuriola  4 and 3
Law lost to Popov  4and 3                  Davis lost to Hedberg  1 hole
Peters beat Lampert  1 hole                Meadow lost to Larsen  4 and 3

**Result:** GB&I 7½, Continent of Europe 16½

*History:* Great Britain & Ireland have won the event 15 times, the Continent of Europe 12 and in 1979
the match was drawn.

| | | |
|---|---|---|
| 1973 | Great Britain and Ireland 20, Continent of Europe 10 | Eindhoven GC, Netherlands |
| 1975 | Great Britain and Ireland 13½, Continent of Europe 10½ | Muirfield, Scotland |
| 1977 | Great Britain and Ireland 15½, Continent of Europe 8½ | Llunghusen GC, Sweden |
| 1979 | Great Britain and Ireland 12, Continent of Europe 12 | Royal Porthcawl GC, Wales |
| 1981 | Continent of Europe 14, Great Britain and Ireland 10 | RC de Puerto de Hierro, Madrid, Spain |
| 1983 | Great Britain and Ireland 14, Continent of Europe 10 | Woodhall Spa GC, England |
| 1985 | Great Britain and Ireland 14, Continent of Europe 10 | Hamburg GC, Germany |
| 1987 | Great Britain and Ireland 15, Continent of Europe 9 | The Berkshire GC, England |
| 1989 | Great Britain and Ireland 14½, Continent of Europe 9½ | Venezia GC, Italy |
| 1991 | Great Britain and Ireland 13½, Continent of Europe 10½ | Nairn GC, Scotland |
| 1993 | Great Britain and Ireland13 ½, Continent of Europe  10½ | Morfontaine GC, France |
| 1995 | Continent of Europe 14, Great Britain and Ireland 10 | Ganton GC, England |
| 1997 | Continent of Europe 14, Great Britain and Ireland 10 | Halmstad GC, Sweden |
| 1999 | Continent of Europe 13, Great Britain and Ireland 11 | North Berwick GC, Scotland |
| 2001 | Continent of  Europe 13 Great Britain and Ireland 11 | Circolo GC, Italy |
| 2003 | Great Britain and Ireland 12½, Continent of Europe 11½ | Co. Louth GC, Ireland |
| 2005 | Great Britain and Ireland 13, Continent of Europe 11 | Chantilly GC, France |
| 2007 | Continent of Europe 15, Great Britain and Ireland 9 | Fairmont Hotel, Scotland |
| 2009 | Continent of Europe 13, Great Britain and Ireland 11 | Hamburg GC, Germany |
| 2011 | Continent of Europe 15½, Great Britain and Ireland 8½ | Royal Porthcawl GC, Wales |

This event will next be held in 2015

## 35th Queen Sirikit Cup (inaugurated 1979) *Sunrise Golf and Country Club, Taiwan* April 17–19

**Team event** (best two scores to count):
1   Australia (Minjee Lee 74-72-74; Grace Lennon 75-78-77; Su-hyun Oh 74-69-74) 437
2   Japan (Asuka Kashiwabara 78-75-76; Mayu Hosaka 75-70-76; Haruka Morita 70-77-72) 438
3   Thailand (Supamas Sangchan 75-70-69; Benyapa Niphatsophon 73-75-80; Ornnicha Konsunthea 72-75-82) 439
4 Philippines, South Korea 445; 6 Malaysia, Chinese Taipei 447; 8 Hong Kong, India 462; 10 New Zealand 463; 11 Singapore 486

**Individual event:**
| | | |
|---|---|---|
| 1 | Supamas Sangchan (THA) | 75-70-69—214 |
| 2 | Su-Hyun Oh (AUS) | 74-69-74—217 |
| 3 | Gyeol Park (KOR) | 72-71-75—218 |
| 4 | Haruka Morita (JPN) | 70-77-72—219 |
| | Kelly Tan (MAS) | 76-71-72—219 |
| 6 | Minjee Lee (AUS) | 74-72-74—220 |

*History:* South Korea have won 13 times, Australia 9, Japan 6, New Zealand 3, Chinese Taipei 2

## All-Africa Challenge (Central and Eastern) (inaugurated 1992) *Lusaka GC, Zambia*
| | | |
|---|---|---|
| 1 | Zambia | 238-239-240—717 |
| 2 | Tanzania | 258-244-248—750 |

3 Uganda 767; 4 Kenya 835; 5 Reunion 857; 6 Malawi 887
**Winning team:** Devanshi Naik, Hilda Edwards and Melissa Nawa

## WGSA 72 Hole Teams Championship *Graceland, Mpumalanga*
### Swiss Team Trophy
| | | |
|---|---|---|
| 1 | Gauteng North A Daisies | 151-145-138-141—575 |
| 2 | Western Province Waves | 151-151-149-147—598 |
| 3 | North West | 148-155-150-153—606 |

4 Southern Cape A Flyers 609; 5 Free State & Northern Cape A 612; 6 Gauteng A Lions, Kwazulu Natal A 616; 8 Gauteng North B Blommies 620; 9 Kwazulu Natal B 621; 10 Gauteng B Tigers 628; 11 Boland A 638; 12 Eastern Cape 645

**Winning team:** Connie Chen, Henriëtta Frylinck and Kim Williams

**Individual:**
| | | |
|---|---|---|
| 1 | Connie Chen (GN) | 75-73-69-69—286 |
| 2 | Kim Williams (GN) | 76-72-72-73—293 |
| 3 | Henriëtta Frylinck (GN) | 77-77-69-72—295 |
| | Lumien Orton (FS&NC) | 70-76-74-75—295 |

### Challenge Trophy
| | | |
|---|---|---|
| 1 | Mpumalanga A | 152-148-146-145—591 |
| 2 | SA Invitational | 163-157-153-150—623 |
| 3 | Western Province B Breakers | 156-153-161-154—624 |
| | Boland B | 156-154-152-162—624 |

5 Border 629; 6 Gauteng C Leopards 632; 7 Kwazulu Natal C, Western Province C 634; 9 Mpumalanga B 642; 10 Southern Cape B Rollers 647; 11 Gauteng North C 649; 12 Free State & Northern Cape B 676; 13 Limpopo 679

**Winning team:** Izel Pieters, Alra van den Berg and Alana van Gruening

## South African Women's Interprovincial Championships  *Port Elizabeth GC*
**Day One:** Gauteng North 'A' 8, Gauteng North 'B' 1
Gauteng 'A' 4½, Western Province 4½
**Day Two:** Western Province 7, Gauteng North 'B' 2
Gauteng North 'A' 5, Gauteng 'A' 4
**Day Three:** Gauteng North 'A' 7; Western Province 'A' 2
Gauteng 'A' 6½, Gauteng North 'B' 2½

**Final table:**

| | P | W | D | L | Pts | Games won |
|---|---|---|---|---|---|---|
| 1 Gauteng North 'A' | 3 | 3 | 0 | 0 | 6 | 20 |
| 2 Gauteng 'A' | 3 | 1 | 1 | 1 | 3 | 15 |
| 3 Western Province | 3 | 1 | 1 | 1 | 3 | 13½ |
| 4 Gauteng North 'B' | 3 | 0 | 0 | 3 | 0 | 5½ |

**Winning team:** Kim Williams, Magda Kruger, Nobuhle Dlamini, Carrie Park, Eugenie Clack and Marie Clark
KwaZulu Natal won the 'B' Division

### Americas

## US Women's State Team Championship  NCR CC *(South Course), Kettering, Ohio*
1 New Jersey  151-146-149—446
2 Florida  146-151-152—449
3 Virginia  152-152-146—450
4 Arizona 451; 5 Maryland 454; 6 Colorado 457; 7 Georgia 460; 8 Minnesota, New Mexico 461; 10 Hawaii, Oklahoma 464; 12 Tennessee 466; 13 Wisconsin 467; 14 Texas 471; 15 Michigan, Kentucky, Oregon 472; 18 North Carolina, Ohio 473; 20 Illinois, Louisiana 474; 22 California 476; 23 Idaho, South Carolina 478; 25 Indiana 479; 26 Missouri 481; 27 Pennsylvania 483. The following teams failed to qualify: Alabama, Alaska, Arkansas, Connecticut, Delaware, District of Columbia, Iowa, Kansas, Maine, Massachusetts, Mississippi, Montana, Nebraska, Nevada, New Hampshire, New York, North Dakota, Puerto Rico, Rhode Island, South Dakota, Utah, Vermont, Washington, West Virginia, Wyoming

**Individual:**
1 Bryana Nguyen (Maryland)  71-72-70—213
Alice Chen (New Jersey)  72-67-74—213
3 Hannah O'Sullivan (Arizona)  71-73-74—218
**Winning team:** Tara Fleming 85-79-82—246; Alice Chen 72-67-74—213; Cindy Ha 79-81-75—235
This event will next be held in 2015

### Australasia

## Australian Women's Interstate Team Championship
for the Gladys Hay Memorial Cup  *Royal Hobart Golf Club, Tasmania*
**Round 1:** Victoria 4½, S. Australia ½; W. Australia 3½, Queensland 1½; New South Wales 5, Tasmania 0
**Round 2:** Victoria 4½, W. Australia ½; S. Australia 3½, Tasmania 1½; New South Wales 2½; Queensland 2½
**Round 3:** W. Australia 3, New South Wales 2; Queensland 5, S. Australia 0; Victoria 5, Tasmania 0
**Round 4:** Queensland 4, Tasmania 1; Victoria 5, New South Wales 0; W. Australia 4, S. Australia 1
**Round 5:** New South Wales 4, S. Australia 1; W. Australia 5, Tasmania 0; Victoria 2½, Queensland 2½
**Final table:** 1 Victoria – matches won 21½, contests won 4; ½ 2 W. Australia 16–4; 3 Queensland 15½–3; 4 New South Wales 13½–2½; 5 South Australia 6–1; 6 Tasmania 2½–0
**Final:** Victoria 5, Western Australia 1; 3rd place play-off: Queensland 4, New South Wales 2; 5th place play-off: Tasmania 4, South Australia 2
**Winning team:** Caitlin Roberts, Cassidy Evreniadis, Kristalle Blum, Elysia Yap, Ella Adams and Deb Christie

## Europe

## British Amateur Championship Team Competition  *Formby GC*

```
I   Denmark       137-150—287
2   England       141-147—288
3   France        144-145—289
```

5 Australia, Germany 294; 7 Netherlands 295; 8 Ireland 296; 9 Sweden 297; 9 Spain, Belgium 299; 11 Italy 302; 12 Norway, Scotland 303; 14 Austria, Wales 307; 16 Iceland 316

**Winning team:** Emily Pedersen, Nanna Madsen and Caroline Nistrup

## English Ladies County Championship  *Wilmslow GC*

**Day 1::** Kent 2, Yorkshire 7
Gloucestershire 6, Warwickshire 3
Lincolnshire 5, Hertfordshire 4

**Day 2:** Gloucestershire 4½, Lincolnshire 4½
Yorkshire 5, Warwickshire 4
Hertfordshire 5½, Kent 3½

**Day 3:** Warwickshire 4, Hertfordshire 5
Kent 2½, Lincolnshire 6½
Gloucestershire 2, Yorkshire 7

**Day 4:** Yorkshire 7, Hertfordshire 2
Lincolnshire 5, Warwickshire 4
Kent 4, Gloucestershire 5

**Day 5:** Lincolnshire 4, Yorkshire 5
Gloucestershire 2½, Hertfordshire 6½
Warwickshire 3½, Kent 5½

| Final table | P | W | D | L | Pts | Games Won |
|---|---|---|---|---|---|---|
| I Yorkshire | 5 | 5 | 0 | 0 | 5 | 31 |
| 2 Lincolnshire | 5 | 3 | I | I | 3½ | 25 |
| 3 Hertfordshire | 5 | 3 | 0 | 2 | 3 | 23 |
| 4 Gloucestershire | 5 | 2 | I | 2 | 2½ | 20 |
| 5 Kent | 5 | I | 0 | 4 | I | 17½ |
| 6 Warwickshire | 5 | 0 | 0 | 5 | 0 | 18½ |

**Winning team:** Emma Brown, Becky Wood, Charlotte Austwick, Holly Morgan. Megan Lockett, Ellie Goodall, Kirsty Beckwith and Rochelle Morris

## European Ladies Club Trophy  *St Sofia GC&S, Bulgaria*

```
I   Smorum GC (DEN)          133-133-135—401
2   Golf de St Cloud (FRA)   136-142-142—420
3   RNCGSS Basozabal (ESP)   140-140-145—425
```

4 GC de Lausanne (SUI) 429; 5 Club de Golf de Castiello (ESP) 436; 6 GC Welten (SVK) 439; 7 Royal Golf Club du Sart-Tilman (BEL) 440; 8 GKG GC (ISL) 441; 9 Eindhovenesche Golf (NED) 442; 10 Park GC Ostrava (CZE) 453; 11 Niitvalja GC (EST) 466; 12 GC Linz-St Florian (AUT) 470; 13 St Sofia GC&S (BUL) 487; 14 Grand Ducal (LUX) 520; 15 Golfstream Kiev GC (RUS) 532

**Winning team:** Emily Pedersen, Nanna Madsen and Charlotte Lorentzen

**Individual:**
```
I   Nanna Madsen (Smorum)      65-66-65—196
2   Emily Pedersen (Smorum)    68-67-70—205
3   Ainhoa Olarra Mugsika      66-69-72—207
    (RNCGSS Basozabal)
```

## Home Internationals (Miller Trophy)  *Scotscraig GC*

**Day 1:** Scotland 4½, Ireland 4½; Wales 6½, England 2½
**Day 2:** Scotland 4, England 5; Wales 5, Ireland 4
**Day 3:** Wales 7, Scotland 2; Ireland 5, England 4

| Final table | W | D | L | Pts |
|---|---|---|---|---|
| Wales | 15 | 7 | 5 | 18½ |
| Ireland | 10 | 7 | 10 | 13½ |
| England | 10 | 3 | 14 | 11½ |
| Scotland | 9 | 3 | 15 | 10½ |

**Winning Team:** Amy Boulden, Becky Harries, Chloe Williams, Katie Bradbury, Samantha Birks, Katherine O'Connor, Jess Evans and Megan Lockett
*History:* England have been champions 40 times, Scotland 15, Ireland 4 and Wales three times. There have been three ties, once between England and Scotland, once between England, Scotland and Ireland and once between Scotland and Ireland.
This event will next be held in 2015

## European Ladies Team Championship  (Inaugurated 1959)   *Fulford GC, England*

**Stroke Play qualification:** 1 Denmark 701; Spain 732; 3 Netherlands 739

| Individual: | 1 Oona Vartiainen (FIN) | 69-67—136 |
|---|---|---|
| | 2 Madelene Sagstrom (SWE) | 67-69—136 |
| | 3 Stephanie Meadow (IRL) | 70-68—138 |
| | Daisy Nielsen (DEN) | 68-70—138 |

**Final placings:** 1 Spain; 2 Austria; 3 Finland; 4 England; 5 Denmark; 6 France; 7 Netherlands; 8 Sweden; 9 Germany; 10 Belgium; 11 Ireland; 12 Scotland; 13 Wales; 14 Italy; 15 Slovenia; 16 Norway; 17 Iceland; 18 Switzerland; 19 Slovakia

**Winning team:** Marta Sanz, Noemi Jimenez, Camilla Hedberg, Luna Sobron, Natalia Escuriola and Patricia Sanz

**Team results:**
**"A" Flight – Day 1:** Austria 4, Denmark 3; Finland 4, Sweden 3; England 4, Netherlands 3; Spain 5½, France 1½

**Day 2:** Austria 5½, Finland 1½; Spain 4½, England 2½; Denmark 3, Sweden 2; France 4, Netherlands 1

**Day 3 – Final:** Spain 5, Austria 2; Finland 4, England 3; Denmark 4, France 1; Netherlands 3, Sweden 2

**"B" Flight – Day 1:** Ireland 4½, Slovenia ½; Germany 3, Wales 2; Belgium 3½, Italy 1½; Scotland 3, Norway 2

**Day 2:** Germany 4, Ireland 1; Belgium 3, Scotland 2; Wales 4½, Slovenia ½; Italy 3½, Norway 1½.

**Day 3:** Germany 3½, Belgium 1½; Ireland 3, Scotland 2; Wales 3, Italy 2; Slovenia 4, Norway 1

**"C" Flight:** Iceland P2 W2 7½–2 ½; Switzerland P2 W1 L1 4–6; Slovakia P2 L2 3 ½–6½
This event will next be held in 2015

## European Senior Women's Team Championship   *Bled GC, Slovenia*

**Flight "A"**

**Stroke play qualifying**
| 1 | Netherlands | 388-389—777 |
|---|---|---|
| 2 | France | 394 386—780 |
| 3 | England | 396 396—792 |

4 Ireland; 5 Sweden; 6 Germany; 7 Italy; 8 Spain; 9 Switzerland; 10 Scotland; 11 Austria; 12 Belgium; 13 Finland; 14 Iceland  15 Slovenia

**Individual:** Nan Croockewit (NED)  72-72—144

**Match Play**
**Quarter-finals:** Netherlands 3, Spain 2; Ireland 3, Sweden 2; England 3½, Germany 1½; Italy 3, France 2
**Semi-finals:** Ireland 4½, Netherlands 3½; Italy 3½, England 1½
Third place play-off: England 4, Netherlands 1. Fifth place play-off: France 4½, Spain ½. Seventh place play-off: Sweden 3, Germany 2
**Final:** Ireland 3½, Italy 1½
**Winning team:** Sheena McElroy, Pat Doran, Suzanne Corcoran, Carol Wickham, Gertie McMullen and Laura Webb

**Flight "B" Final:** Belgium 3, Scotland 2

## Jamboree (Ladies Veterans)   *North Hants GC, Fleet*

**Day 1:**  South 7½, Scotland 1½
       Midlands 3, North 6

**Day 2:**  South 4½, Midlands 4½
       North 8, Scotland 1

**Day 3:**  South 3½, North 5½
       Scotland 7½, Midlands 1½

**Final Placings:** 1 North 19½ pts; 2 South 15½; 3 Scotland 10; 4 Midlands 9

## 13th Ladies Veterans Match (Mary McKenna Trophy)   *West Kilbride GC*

Ireland 6½, Scotland 5½

**Winning team:** Suzanne Corcoran, Pat Doran, Mary Dowling, Kate Evans, Helen Jones, Sheena McElroy, Gertie McMullen and Carol Wickham

---

## Senior Home Internationals (Sue Johnson Cup)   *Llandudno GC, Maesdu*

**Day 1:**  Ireland 8; Scotland 0; England 6, Wales 2
**Day 2:**  England 6½, Scotland 2½; Ireland 6, Wales 2
**Day 3:**  Wales 6; Scotland 2; Ireland 4, England 4

| Final table: | P | W | D | L | Games won |
|---|---|---|---|---|---|
| 1 Ireland | 3 | 2 | 1 | 0 | 18½ |
| 2 England | 3 | 2 | 1 | 0 | 16½ |
| 3 Wales | 3 | 1 | 0 | 2 | 10 |
| 4 Scotland | 3 | 0 | 0 | 3 | 4½ |

**Winning team:** Sheena McElroy, Carol Wickham, Suzanne Corcoran, Laura Webb, Helen Jones, Pat Doran and Gertie McMullen

---

## Scottish Ladies County Championship (inaugurated 1992)   *Stirling GC*

**Day 1:**  Aberdeenshire 5, Midlothian 4
       Renfrewshire 7, Borders 2

**Day 2:**  Aberdeenshire 8, Borders 1
       Midlothian 5, Renfrewshire 4

**Day 3:**  Midlothian 8. Borders 1
       Renfrewshire 5. Aberdeenshire 4

| Final table: | P | W | D | L | Games won |
|---|---|---|---|---|---|
| 1 Midlothian* | 3 | 2 | 0 | 1 | 17 |
| 2 Aberdeenshire | 3 | 2 | 0 | 1 | 17 |
| 3 Renfrewshire | 3 | 2 | 0 | 1 | 16 |
| 4 Borders | 3 | 0 | 0 | 3 | 4 |

*Midlothian won on a countback having played fewer holes: 252–253

**Winning team:** Hannah Scott, Wendy Nicholson, Kate McIntosh, Karen Marshall, Gabrielle MacDonald, Rachel Livingstone, Louise Frase and Emily Dalgetty

*History:* East Lothian have won 5 times, Northern Counties and Midlothian 3, Fife 2, Dunbartonshire & Ayrshire, Stirlingshire & Clackmannanshire, Renfrewshire and Angus 1

---

## Welsh Ladies Inter-Counties Stroke Play Championship   *Builth Wells*

| | | |
|---|---|---|
| 1 | Glamorgan | 734 |
| 2 | Mid Wales | 769 |
| 2 | Monmouthshire | 770 |
| 4 | Carmarthenshire and Pembrokeshire | 786 |
| 5 | Caernarvonshire and Angelsey | 792 |
| 6 | Denbighshire and Flintshire | 813 |

## Welsh Ladies Team Championship    (inaugurated 1992)    *Cardigan*

**Semi-Finals:**    Southerndown 4, Aberdovey 1
Newport 4, Tenby 1
**Final:**    Southerndown 4, Newport 1

## Turkish Amateur Open Nations Cup    *National GC, Belek*

| | | |
|---|---|---|
| 1 | Turkey | 165-153-160—478 (Begüm Yılmaz, Sena Ersoy, Tuğçe Erden) |
| 2 | Russia | 167-161-160—488 |
| | Slovakia | 157-160-171—488 |
| 4 | Tunisia | 184-196-194—574 |

## Presidential role for Pam Benka

Former Curtis Cup player and captain Pam Benka became the new President of England Golf – the organisation formed by the merger of the English Golf Union and the English Women's Golf Association – in 2013 becoming the organisation's first sole President.

"I have been involved with women's golf all my life and through my late husband Peter I gained much knowledge of the men's side of the game," said Mrs Benka. Her late husband Peter was a Walker Cup player and chairman of selectors for both England and The R&A.

A former British and French girl's champion she played in the Vagliano Trophy and won the Portuguese Ladies Championship in 1968.

Later she became a national and international selector and captained the Curtis Cup team in 2002, the England team at the European Junior Championship and the England team at the Commonwealth Trophy event now known as the Astor Trophy.

Prior to Pam's appointment the office of President was held jointly by Paul Baxter of Lincolnshire and Sue Johnson of Yorkshire.

Ray Saunders, a past President of Kent and a former Chairman of the EGU Championship Committee, accepted the nomination to become President Elect of England Golf for the year 2013 with a view to becoming President in 2014.

The 72 year old has been a keen supporter of golf and football for most of his life and is surprised and delighted to be considered for the presidency.

"I was surprised to be asked," he said. "Surprised, because at times I haven't conformed to convention. For example, when I was Chairman of the Championship Committee we changed the format of the English Amateur Championship, which didn't go down well in certain quarters."

## Month by month in 2013

Comeback king Henrik Stenson adds the European Tour's "Race to Dubai" money list title to his PGA Tour FedEx Cup crown. As in America he wins the final event, beating runner-up Ian Poulter by six at the DP World Tour Championship. Adam Scott has back-to-back victories at the Australian PGA and Masters and then at Royal Melbourne combines with individual winner Jason Day to give Australia their first World Cup triumph since 1989.

# Other Tournaments 2013

For past winners see earlier editions of *The R&A Golfer's Handbook*

---

**Astor Salver** (inaugurated 1951)   *always at The Berkshire*
Lauren Taylor (Woburn)                  70-68—138

---

**Bridget Jackson Bowl** (inaugurated 1982)   *always at Handsworth*
Samantha Fuller (Roehampton)            72-73—145

---

**Burhill Family Foursomes** (inaugurated 1937)   *always at Burhill, Surrey*
**Final:** Kika and Peter Coles beat Stephanie and Jeremy Williams

---

**Commonwealth Spoons**   *Fortrose & Rosemarkie*
Ingrid Elgsaas & Georgene Parsons (East Lothian)

---

**Critchley Salver** (inaugurated 1982)   *always at Sunningdale*
Gabriella Cowley (Brocket Hall)         71
*Reduced to one round*

---

**Hampshire Rose** (inaugurated 1973)   *always at North Hants*
Georgia Hall (Remedy Oak)               70-68—138

---

**The Leveret** (inaugurated 1986)   *always at Formby*
Amy Boulden (Conwy)                     69-69—138

---

**Liphook Scratch Cup** (inaugurated 1992)   *always at Liphook*
Kerry Smith (Waterlooville)             77-70--147
beat Charlotte Thompson (Channel)       68-79—147 (better second round)

---

**London Ladies Foursomes**   *The Berkshire*
*Abandoned – snow*

---

**Mackie Bowl** (inaugurated 1974)   *always at Gullane No 1*
*Abandoned – flooding*

---

**Mothers and Daughters Foursomes**   27-hole event   *Royal Mid-Surrey*
Glenna and Harriet Beasley (Woburn)     78-36—114

---

**Munross Trophy** (inaugurated 1986)   *always at Montrose Links*
Jane Turner (Craigielaw)                74-72—146

---

**Peugeot 208 LGU Coronation Foursomes**   *St Andrews (Eden course)*
Mary Shawley and Kate Helm (Meltham)    40 pts

**Pleasington Putter** (inaugurated 1995)  *always at Pleasington*
Catherine Roberts (Pleasington)            74-68—142

**Riccarton Rose Bowl** (inaugurated 1970)  *always at Hamilton*
Cancelled – lack of entries

**Roehampton Gold Cup** (inaugurated 1926)  *always at Roehampton*
(This event has included women professionals since 1982 and has been an open event since 1987)
Charlotte Ellis (Minchinhampton)            75-75—150

**Royal Birkdale Scratch Trophy** (inaugurated 1984)  *always at Royal Birkdale*
Hollie Muse West (Lancashire GC)            75-73—148

**Royal County Down Scratch Salver**  *always at Royal County Down*
Cancelled – bad weather

**St Rule Trophy** (inaugurated 1984)  *always at St Andrews (Old and New)*
Ailsa Summers (Carnoustie)            67-72-72—211
The International Trophy was won by France (Alexandra Bonetti, Celine Boutier and Manon Gidali)

**Scottish Ladies Foursomes**  *Kirriemuir GC*
**Semi-finals:**  Kilmarnock Barassie beat Deeside Ladies  2 and 1
            Turnhouse beat Braehead  2 and 1
**Final:**      Kilmarnock Barassie beat Turnhouse  2 and 1
**Third place play-off:** Deeside Ladies beat Braehead  3 and 1
**Winning team:** Alex Glennie and Debbie Peberdy

**SLGA Grand Medal Finals**  *King George VI GC, Perth*
**Silver:**      Heather Anderson (Blairgowrie)    nett 67
**Bronze:**      Vivien Mitchell (Lochend)        nett 74

**Tenby Ladies Open** (inaugurated 1994)  *always at Tenby*
Cancelled

**Whittington Trophy**  *always at Whittington Heath*
Cancelled

**Worplesdon Mixed Foursomes** (inaugurated 1921)  *always at Worplesdon, Surrey*
Cancelled

# University and School Events 2013

## Canadian University and Colleges Championship *Val des Lacs Golf Club*

| | | |
|---|---|---|
| 1 | Universite de Montreal Carabins | 223-231-219-230—903 |
| 2 | University of Victoria Vikes | 226-222-229-234—911 |
| 3 | Univerity of British Columbia Thunderbirds | 228-240-226-225—919 |

**Winning team:** Sabrina Sapone, Caroline Clot, Laurence Mignault and Sarah-Andrea Landry

**Individual:**

| | | |
|---|---|---|
| 1 | Sabrina Sapone (Montreal) | 74-74-71-74—280 |
| 2 | Megan Woodland (Victoria Vikes) | 71-68-70-72—281 |
| 3 | Brynn Tomie (Bedford) | 74-72-77-79—302 |

## World Universities Women's Championship

Switzerland will host the next Championship in 2014

## BUCS Student Tour Finals *Crail GC (Red course)*

| | | |
|---|---|---|
| 1 | Rebecca Gibbs (Burnham and Berrow) | 79-70-74-77—300 |
| 2 | Gabrielle MacDonald (Craigielaw) | 77-78-73-74—302 |
| 3 | Katie Bradbury (Cottrell Park) | 77-75-75-78—305 |

## Scottish Student Golf Championship *Moray Old*

| | | |
|---|---|---|
| 1 | Georgina Gilling (Stirling) | 76-72-78-82—308 |
| 2 | Gabrielle MacDonald (St Andrews) | 80-79-74-78—311 |
| | Iona Stephen | 78-75-74-84—311 |

## 50th Japanese Women's Collegiate Championship *Kakogawa GC*

| | | |
|---|---|---|
| 1 | Rikako Sakashita | 71-71-72—214 |
| 2 | Riko Inoue | 73-72-73—218 |
| 3 | Seira Oki | 71-76-72—219 |

## 3rd European Universities Golf Championship *Saint Saens, France*

**Individual:**

| | | |
|---|---|---|
| 1 | Emma Vestin (SWE) | 75-72-65-69—281 |
| 2 | Eilidh Briggs (SCO) | 75-72-68-68—283 |
| 3 | Therese Larsson (SWE) | 71-71-67-75—284 |

**Team:**

| | | |
|---|---|---|
| 1 | Scandinavian School of Golf | 144-141-132-140—557 |
| 2 | University of Stirling | 151-144-141-151—587 |
| 3 | National Iniversity of Ireland, Maynooth | 153-150-152-147—602 |
| 4 | University of Lausanne | 161-161-157-154—633 |
| 5 | University of Exeter | 171-158-155-155—639 |

# County and other Regional Championships 2013

## England

Bedfordshire: Sally Shayler
Berkshire: Laura Webb
Buckinghamshire: Charlotte West
Cambridgeshire & Huntingdonshire: Sarah Attwood
Cheshire: Emma Goddard
Cornwall: Emily Toy
Cumbria: Hannah Smith
Derbyshire: Aimee Wilson
Devon: Chloe Howard
Dorset: Kyra Horlock
Durham: Pauline Dobson
Essex: Charlotte Thompson

Gloucestershire: Joanne Hodge
Hampshire: Aimee Ponte
Hertfordshire: Lucyt Goddard
Kent: Emily Royer
Lancashire: Catherine Roberts
Leicestershire & Rutland: Helen Lowe
Lincolnshire: Helen Hewlett
Middlesex: Jane Rees
Norfolk: Sharon Black
Northamptonshire: Karen Lobb
Northumberland: Nicola Haynes

Nottinghamshire: Alexandra Peters
Oxfordshire: Cara Gainer
Shropshire: Katrina Gillum
Somerset: Victoria Watts
Staffordshire: Holly Langford
Suffolk: Sharon Luckman
Surrey: Annabel Dimmock
Sussex: Karen Sykes
Warwickshire: Melissa Nicol
Wiltshire: Jo Terry
Worcestershire & Herefordshire: Sarah Nicklin
Yorkshire: Emma Brown

## Ireland

Connacht: Amy Farrell
East Leinster: Emma O'Driscoll

Mid Leinster: Karen Delaney
Munster: Olivia Mehaffey

Ulster: Jessica Carty

## Scotland

Aberdeenshire: Sammy Leslie
Angus: Ailsa Summers
Ayrshire: nnie Jaffray
Border Counties: Judith Anderson
Dumfriesshire: Rachel Walker
Dunbartonshire: Lindsay McCubbin

Dunbartonshire and Argyll: Anne Laing
East Lothian: Clara Young
Fife: Susan Jackson
Galloway: Fiona Hunter
Lanarkshire: Fiona Morris
Midlothian: Belinda Murphy

North of Scotland: Claire Prouse
Northern Counties: Cara Thompson
Perth and Kinross: Emily Ogilvie
Renfrewshire: Donna Jackson
Stirling and Clackmannan: Louise MacGregor

## Wales

Carmarthen and Pembroke: Becky Harries
Denbighshire & Flintshire: Emma Pritchard
Glamorgan County: Fauve Birch

Mid-Wales: Sharon Roberts
Monmouthshire: Patricia Fernon

ROLEX AND THE RULES OF GOLF.
UNITED BY UNCOMPROMISING STANDARDS.

R&A, ST ANDREWS

OYSTER PERPETUAL DAY-DATE

# ROLEX

# data for :

the professional

Data can do amazing things. Helping people make the right decisions at the right time is what we do.

NTT DATA is here to provide professionals, across industries, with IT solutions that help store, organise and share data. Because we think data should always be there, wherever and whenever you need it. NTT DATA is a proud Patron of The Open Championship. Get to know us at nttdata.com.

**data for : the people**

NTT DATA is a proud Patron of The Open Championship.

Global IT Innova

# The R&A Rules Academy
# Online Rules Qualification

**LEARN AT YOUR OWN PACE**
When you want, how you want,
from wherever you want

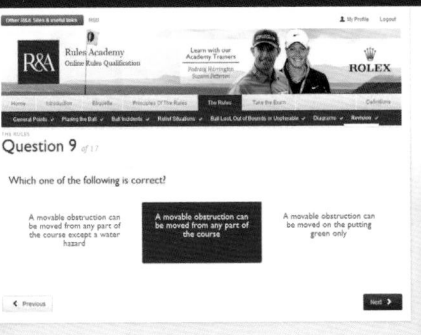

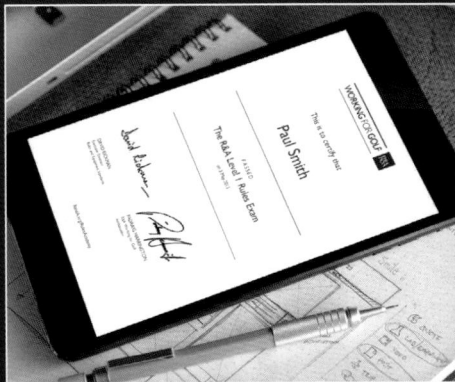

**INTERACTIVE EXPERIENCE**
Informative text, diagrams, photos, video
and revision questions

**OFFICIAL CERTIFICATE**
Receive an official R&A certificate when you
pass the Level 1 Exam

## Learn the basic Rules and etiquette, enjoy your game even more, get qualified.

**www.RandA.org/RulesAcademy**

WORKING FOR GOLF

# Doosan, your reliable partner in the infrastructure support business

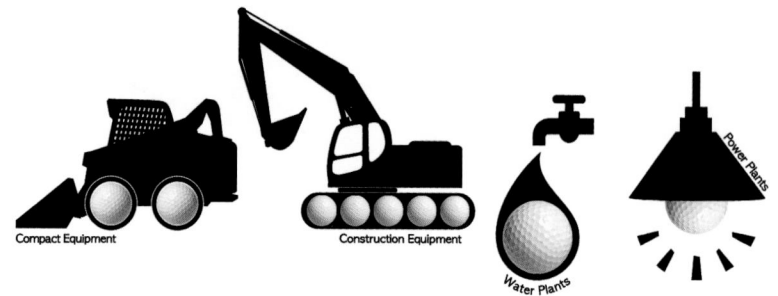

Compact Equipment

Construction Equipment

Water Plants

Power Plants

*Building your tomorrow today*

PATRON AND OFFICIAL OUTFITTER
OF THE OPEN CHAMPIONSHIP

POLO
RALPH LAUREN

THE OPEN
CHAMPIONSHIP

MEET THE GREATEST GOLFERS IN THE WORLD AND GET EXCLUSIVE VIDEO GOLF TIPS AT

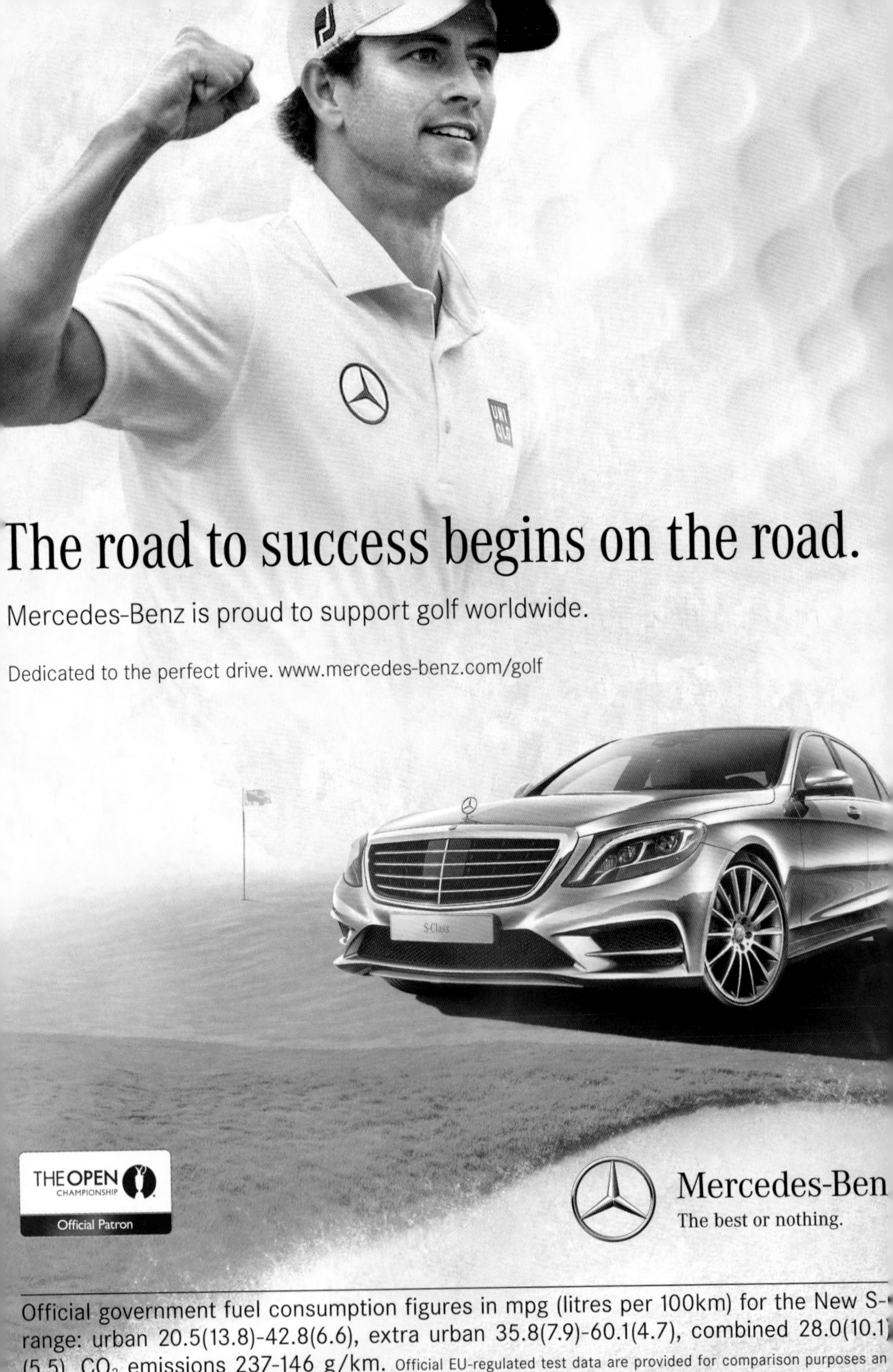

# The road to success begins on the road.

Mercedes-Benz is proud to support golf worldwide.

Dedicated to the perfect drive. www.mercedes-benz.com/golf

# coursetracker

IMPROVING YOUR GOLF COURSE

Developed by The R&A, CourseTracker is the free new digital business management tool for golf courses.

With the growing challenges facing our industry, CourseTracker will help your Club plan for a successful future.

Get started at www.coursetracker.org

# In the future, talent will emerge from anywhere.

Golf is one of the fastest growing sports in Asia and across emerging markets, where rising disposable income is helping to bring new talent into the game. HSBC is proud to be investing in golf in these territories.

From major tournaments to grassroots initiatives, we're opening up opportunities for both emerging talent and our customers.

There's more on emerging markets at
www.hsbc.com/inthefuture

Issued by HSBC Holdings plc.

# PART VI

# Mixed Men's and Women's Amateur Tournaments

For past results see earlier editions of *The R&A Golfer's Handbook*

## European Nations Cup   *Real Club de Golf Sotogrande, Spain*

**Men:**

| | | | | | | |
|---|---|---|---|---|---|---|
| 1 | England | 856 | | 4 | Portugal | 875 |
| 2 | France | 869 | | 5 | Denmark | 878 |
| 3 | Ireland | 874 | | 6 | Spain | 881 |

**Winning Team:** Max Orrin, Toby Tree, Garrick Porteous, Neil Kimsey

**Individual:**

| | | |
|---|---|---|
| 1 | Adrien Saddier (FRA) | 72-70-67-74—283 |
| 2 | Maximilian Rohrig (GER) | 72-68-72-71—283 |
| 3 | Christian Gloeet (DEN) | 72-74-71-69—286 |
| 4 | Renato Paratore (ITA) | 74-72-71-69—286 |

**Women:**

| | | | | | | |
|---|---|---|---|---|---|---|
| 1 | Spain | 565 | | 4 | England | 598 |
| 2 | Germany | 590 | | 5 | Italy | 605 |
| 3 | Wales | 596 | | 6 | Denmark | 601 |

**Individual:**

| | | |
|---|---|---|
| 1 | Patricia Sanz-Bario (ESP) | 74-71-69-73—287 |
| 2 | Chloe Williams (WAL) | 76-72-70-76—294 |
| 3 | Nicole Broche Larsen (DEN) | 76-74-71-76—297 |

**Winning Team:** Patricia Sanz Barrio, Clara Baena Sanchez, Silvia Banon Ibanez, Maria Orueta Pemartin

## Spirit International   *Whispering Pines, GC, Trinity, Texas, USA*

**Mixed competition:**

| | | |
|---|---|---|
| 1 | USA | 127-138-134—399 |
| 2 | France | 139-130-136—405 |
| 3 | Malaysia | 134-133-140—407 |

4 Finland 408; 5 South Africa 410; 6 Sweden 411; 7 Spain 413; 8 Canada 417; 9 Belgium; 418 10 Japan, Mexico 419; 12 Norway 420; 13 Australia 422; 14 Argentina, Scotland 424; 16 Denmark, Ireland 426; 18 Italy 429; 19 England 430; 20 India 439

**Winning team:** Scottie Sheffler, Jordan Niebrugge, Ally McDonald and Ashlan Ramsey

**Men's competition:**

| | | |
|---|---|---|
| 1 | USA | 61-69-64—194 |
| 2 | Finland | 71-66-63—200 |
| | Sweden | 64-68-58—200 |

4 France, Malaysia 201; 6 Spain 202; 7 Australia 203; 8 South Africa 204; 9 Norway, Argentina 205; 11 Denmark, Belgium, Mexico 209; 14 Canada 210; 15 England, Scotland 211; 17 Japan 212; 18 Ireland 216; 19 Italy 217; 20 India 224

| Men's Individual – Birdies: | | Eagles: | |
|---|---|---|---|
| Jordan Niebrugge (USA) | 14 | Daniel Jennevret (SWE) | 1 |
| Julien Brun (FRA) | 14 | Emilio Cuartero (ESP) | 1 |
| Scottie Scheffler (USA) | 14 | Richard O'Donovan (IRL) | 1 |
| Toni Hakula (FIN) | 14 | | |

**Women's competition:**

| | | |
|---|---|---|
| 1 | France | 71-64-69—204 |
| 2 | USA | 66-69-70—205 |
| 3 | Malaysia | 69-65-72—206 |
| | South Africa | 67-67-72—206 |

5 Japan, Canada 207; 7 Finland 208; 8 Belgium 209; 9 Mexico, Ireland 210; 11 Spain, Sweden 211; 13 Italy 212; 14 Scotland 213; 15 Norway, India 215; 17 Denmark 217; 18 Australia, England, Argentina 219

| Women's Individual – Birdies | | Eagles: | |
|---|---|---|---|
| Brooke Henderson (CAN) | 13 | Kelly Guat Chen Tan (MAS) | 1 |
| Mathilda Cappeliez (FRA) | 12 | Lara Weinstein (RSA) | 1 |
| Kim Williams (RSA) | 11 | | |
| Yumi Matsubara (JPN) | 11 | | |

*Event reduced to three rounds due to wet weather*

## Grand Prix de Chiberta  *Chiberta, Biarritz*
**Men:**
| | | |
|---|---|---|
| 1 | Victor Perez (FRA) | 66-68-66-71—271 |
| 2 | Michael Saunders (ENG) | 70-68-67-71—276 |
| | Thomas Grava (FRA) | 69-73-67-68—277 |

**Women:**
| | | |
|---|---|---|
| 1 | Célia Barquin Arozamena (ESP) | 66-70-69-69—274 |
| 2 | Laure Castelain (FRA) | 69-67-71-71—278 |
| 3 | Lauralie Migneaux (FRA) | 69-69-70-72—280 |

## Challenge International de la Ville d'Anglet  *Golf de Chiberta, Anglet*
**Men:**
| | | |
|---|---|---|
| 1 | England | 135 (Nick Marsh, Paul Howard, Michael Saunders) |
| 2 | Denmark | 139 |
| 3 | Chiberta I | 140 |

**Women:**
| | | |
|---|---|---|
| 1 | Spain I | 138 (Anna Sanjuan, Celia Barquin, Andrea Jonama) |
| 2 | Chiberta | 142 |
| 3 | France I | 143 |

## Copa Los Andes  *David Guiterez Field, Club Los Lagartos, Bogota, Columbia*
**Men's competition**
1 Argentina 13 pts*; 2 Colombia; 13 Chile, Brazil 11; 5 Peru 7; 6 Bolivia 6; 7 Venezuela 5; 8 Paraguay 4; 9 Uruguay 2
*won on countback with Argentina
**Winning team:** Alejandro Tosti, Santiago Bauni, Andrés Schonbaum, Jaime Lopéz, Granco Grillo

**Women's competition**
1 Colombia 13 pts*; 2 Argentina 13; 3 Peru, Paraguay 9; 5 Bolivia 7; 6 Brazil, Venezuela 6; 8 Ecuador 5; 9 Chile 4
*won on countback with Colombia
**Winning team:** María Alejandra Hoyos, Laura Sojo, laura Blanco, Maribel López, María Mercedes Rodríguez

## South-East Asia Amateur Team Championships  *Sherwood Hills CC, Philippines*
**53rd Putra Cup (men)**
| | | |
|---|---|---|
| 1 | Philippines | 213-210-208-209—840 |
| 2 | Singapore | 213-222-210-217—862 |
| 3 | Thailand | 216-221-216-211—864 |

4 Malaysia 873; 5 Hong Kong 877; 6 Indonesia 896; 7 Papua New Guinea 949; 7 Brunei 961
**Winning team:** Jonathan De Los Reyes, Jobin Antonio Carlos, Rico Hoey and Ruperto Zaragosa
| **Indvidual:** | 1 | Gavin Green (MAS) | 70-68-68-68 – 274 |
|---|---|---|---|
| | 2 | Jonathan de Los Reyes (PHI) | 66-69-71- 71 – 277 |
| | 3 | Rico Hoey (PHI) | 75-70-67-68 - 260 |

**5th Santi Cup (women)**
| | | |
|---|---|---|
| 1 | Malaysia | 149-147-141-139—576 |
| 2 | Thailand | 150-146-137-144—577 |
| 3 | Philippines | 150-148-144-151—593 |

4 Singapore 594; 5 Hong Kong 601; 6 Indonesia 618; 7 Brunei 709
**Winning team:** Kelly Tan, Michelle Koh and Ven Chin
| **Individual:** | 1 | Benyapa Niphatsophon (THA) | 74-73-67-72—286 |
|---|---|---|---|
| | 2 | Tiffany Chan (HKG) | 73-71-77-70—291 |
| | 3 | Kelly Tan (MAS) | 79-73-72-69—293 |
| | | Supamas Sangchan (THA) | 76-73-70-74—293 |

*For Boys' and Girls' events see page 470*

## Asian Games
*The next staging of this event (the 17th) will be held between September 18 to October 4, 2014 in Incheon, South Korea*

## Trans Tasman Cup
This event will next be held in 2014

## Copa de las Americas    *Doral Golf Resort and Spa, Florida, USA*
**Overall:**
| | | |
|---|---|---|
| 1 | Canada | 300-290-293-294—1,177 |
| 2 | Mexico | 298-296-294-290—1,178 |
| 3 | USA | 295-302-291-291—1,179 |

4 Argentina 1,203; 5 Colombia 1,203; 6 Trinidad and Tobago 1,250. Venezuela and Guatemala also played but did not complete four rounds

**Winning team:** Albin Choi, Corey Connors, Brooke Mackenzie Henderson and Augusta James.

**Men's competiton:**
| | | |
|---|---|---|
| 1 | Mexico | 145-144-143-143—575 |
| 2 | Canada | 153-137-142-147—579 |
| 3 | USA | 146-149-144-143—582 |

4 Venezuela 600; 5 Panama 604; 6 Puerto Rico 605; 7 Trinidad and Tobago 623. Guatemala played but did not complete four rounds

**Winning team:** Carlos Ortiz and Rodolfo Cazaubon

**Women's competition:**
| | | |
|---|---|---|
| 1 | USA | 149-153-147-148—597 |
| 2 | Canada | 147-153-151-147—598 |
| 3 | Mexico | 153-152-151-147—603 |

4 Colombia 614; 5 Argentina 619. Trinidad and Tobago, Venezuela and Guatemala played but did not complete four rounds

**Individual Competition – Men:**
| | | |
|---|---|---|
| 1 | Carlos Ortiz (MEX) | 68-74-72-73—287 |
| 2 | Rodolfo Cazaubon (MEX) | 77-70-71-70—288 |
| | Chris Williams (USA) | 71-75-70-72—288 |
| | Albin Choi (CAN) | 76-68-70-74—288 |

**Women:**
| | | |
|---|---|---|
| 1 | Erynne Lee (USA) | 73-75-71-72—291 |
| 2 | Gabriela Lopez (MEX) | 73-71-75-73—292 |
| 3 | Brooke Mackenzie Henderson (CAN) | 71-77-75-70—293 |

## 13th Neighbors Trophy    *Karuizawa 72 GC*
**Men:**
| | | |
|---|---|---|
| 1 | Korea | 197-199-195—591 |
| 2 | Japan | 213-208-207—628 |
| 3 | Chinese Taipei | 217-219-217—653 |

**Winning team:** Nam-Hin Kim, Sang-Yeop Lee, Soo-Min Lee and Chang-Woo Lee

**Women:**
| | | |
|---|---|---|
| 1 | Japan | 208-210-205—623 |
| 2 | Korea | 213-208-221—642 |
| 3 | Chinese Taipei | 215-222-219—656 |

**Winning team:** Kotoni Hori, Asuka Kashiwabara, Yumi Matsubara and Haruka Morita

## Irish Mixed Foursomes Championship    *Douglas GC*

**Semi-finals:** Newlands 3, Clonmel 2
Claremorris 4, Mannan Castle 1
**Final:** Claremorris 4, Newlands 1
**Winning team:** S Healy, H Grant, T Fanning, R Kean, D J Griffin, N McHugh, G Noone, C Rush, D Lambe and M Healy

## Scottish Mixed Foursomes    *Kirriemuir GC*

**Semi-finals:** Kilmarnock Barassie beat Deeside Ladies 1 hole
Turnhouse beat Braehead 2 and 1
**Final:** Kilmarnock Barassie beat Turnhouse 2 holes
**Winning team:** Alex Glennie and Debbie Peberdy

## Australian Mid-Amateur Team Championship    *Moonah Links (Open course), Victoria*

| 1 | Queensland | 232-236—468 |
|---|---|---|
| 2 | Victoria | 231-239—70 |
| 3 | ACT | 258-255—513 |
| 4 | Northern Territory | 269-257—526 |

**Winning team:** Damien Jordan, Michael Neaton and Katrina Jones
*Reduced to 36 holes because of inclement weather*

---

## What is the answer?

**Q:** Is it permitted to practice on the competition course before a match or a stroke play competition?

**A:** If the committee of the club where the match is being staged are agreeable and if there is nothing in the competition rules preventing you from doing so it is possible to practice on the competition course. No practice on the course or testing of the surface of the greens is permitted, however, in a stroke play competition unless permitted in the conditions of the competition.

# PART VII

# Amateur Golf
# Around the World

# Amateur Golf Around the World

Results from organisations affiliated to The R&A and the USGA

For results marked [1], [2], [3] or [4], further details can be found on pages 306–319, 392–403, 454–457 and 461–463

Players are from the host nation unless stated

## Africa

**Botswana**
Population: 2m          Golf Courses: 10
Men's Champion: Hamadzangu Kamunga

**Egypt**
Population: 83.6m          Golf Courses: 20
Egyptian Closed Championship: Amr Aboul Elq[1]
Egyptian Men's Open Championship: Soliman El Asser[1]

**Kenya**
Population: 44.3m          Golf Courses: 42
Men's Stroke Play Champion: John Karichu[1]
Men's Match Play Champion: Nelson Simwa
Junior Stroke Play Champion (Boys): Hennie du Plessis (RSA)
Junior Match Play Champion (Boys): Peter Muigai

**South Africa**
Population: 52.9m
Golfers: 500,000          Golf Courses: 451
South African Amateur Championship – CCJ-Rocklands GC: Thirston Lawrence beat Andrew Light 9 and 8[1]
South African Women's Amateur Championship – Milnerton GC: Kim Williams beat Ji Sun Kang (KOR) 2 and 1[2]
Stroke Play Championship (Men) – Oubaai: Haydn Porteous 275[1]
Stroke Play Championship (Women) – Pretoria CC: Nobuhle Dlamini (SWZ)[2]
Women's Team Championship – Maccauvlei GC: Nobuhle Dlamini (SWZ)
South African Men's Mid-Amateur Championship – Stellenbosch: Greg Sheard[1]
South African Women's Mid-Amateur Championship – Graceland CC: Sonja Bland[2]
Men's Senior Championship – Fancourt CC: Gavin Van Aswegen[1]
KeNako South African World Juniors – Jade Buitendag
Nomads Dr Bam NOOM Championship – Pollak Park GC: Thriston Lawrence
Nomads Inland NOOM Championship – Kempton Park CC: Keegan De Lange
Nomads WGWP Junior Championship – Metropolitan GC: Bianca Theron
Nomads Rose Bowl Girls Championship – Selborne GC: Catherine Lai
Nomads South African Boys Under 17 Stroke Play – Mt Edgecombe: Jovan Rebula 278

Nomads South African Boys Under 19 Stroke Play – Benoni GC: Zander Gous 205. Match Play – Benoni: Zander Gous beat Aneurin Gounden at 37th
Nomads South African Girls Championship – Orkney GC: Ji Sun Kang
The Players Invitational – Sun City: Peter Van Coller 144
Prince's Grant Invitational – Prince's Grant GC: Haydn Porteous 289
Retief Goosen High Schools Championship – Fish River Sun CC: Individual – Jovan Rebula 141; Team – King Edward VII (+15)
SA Boys Under-17 Championship: Jovan Rebula
SA Boys Under-19 Championship: Zander Gous
Nomads SA Girls Rose Bowl Championship – Selborne CC: Catherine Lau
WGSA 72-hole Championship – Maccauvlei CC: Nobuhle Dlamini (SWZ)[2]

Provincial Championships:
South African Men's Interprovincial Championship – Rustenberg GC: 1 Gauteng North; 2 Western Province; 3 Southern Cape. Winning team: Russell Franz, Hendrikus Stoop, Philip Kruse, Werner Ferreira, Teagan Gauche, Tertius Van Den Berg, Werner Van Niekerk and Zander Lombard[1]
South African Women's Interprovincial Championship – Port Elizabeth GC: 1 Gauteng North A; 2 Gauteng A; 3 Western Province; 4 Gauteng North B. Winning team: Kim Williams, Magda Kruger, Nobuhle Dlamini, Carrie Park, Eugenie Clack and Marie Clark[2]
South African Mid-Amateur Provincial Tournament – Durban GC: 1 Western Province; 2 KwaZulu Natal; 3 Ekurhuleni. Winning team: Elvin Nel, Gareth Johnson, Giles Buchanan, Cameron Johnston, Francois le Roux, Dirk Van der Merwe, Greg Sheard and Gerloux Roux[1]
Challenge Interprovincial – Maccauvlei GC: 1 SAGA Juniors 7pts; 2 Central Gauteng 7pts; 3 Gauteng North 6pts; 4 USSA 4pts; 5 Western Province 5pts; 6 President's Team 2pts. Winning team: SAGA Juniors – Jade Buitendag, Kyle McClatchie, Dylan Naidoo, Jovan Rebula, Rosswell Sinclair and Luke Trocado
Senior Inter-Provincial – Euphoria GE: 1 Central Gauteng; 2 Western Province; 3 Gauteng North1 Winning team: Richard Bruyns, Lawrence Franklin,

Colin Hayward, Schalke Naude, David Stratton, Stuart Till, Gavin Van Aswegen and Jock Wellington[1]
Super Senior Inter-Provincial – Euphoria GE: 1 Western Province; 2 Erkhuleni; 3 Gauteng North.[1]
Under 23 Interprovincial Championship – Nelspruit: 1 Gauteng North 9pts; 2 Ekurhuleni 7pts; Western Province 5pts; 4 Central Gauteng 4pts; 5 Limpopo 4pts; 6 Southern Cape 1pt. Winning team: Gauteng North – Matthew Bright, K De Lange, Teaghan Gauche, Warrick Moonieyan, Adriel Poonan, Jason Smith, Tristen Strydom and Werner Von Niekerk
South African Junior Inter-Provincial Championship – Bellville GC: Central Gautent (A Section); Southern Cape (B Section)
Boland Open – Devonvale: Haydn Porteous 202
Boland Women's Championship – Somerset West GC: Ji Sun Kang
Boland Mid-Amateur Championship – Stellenbosch GC: Francois Le Roux
Boland Senior Open – Paarl/Boschenmeer: Francois Le Roux 141
Boland Junior Girls Championship – Kuilsriver GC: Michaela Fletcher
Border Open – East London: Teaghan Gauche 212
Border Women's Championship – East London: Lara Weinstein
45th Border Stroke Play – East London GC: Teaghan Gauche
Border Senior Open – East London GC: Francois Le Roux
Cape Province Open – George and Kingswood: Haydn Porteous 273
Cape Winelands Senior Amateur Open – De Zalze: Francois Le Roux 144
Country Districts Championship – Uppington: 1 North West 8pts; 2 Mpumalanga 6pts; 3 Ekurhuleni 4pts; 4 Free State and North Cape 2pts; 5 KwaZulu Natal 0pts. Winning team: North West – Stephen Allen, Wade Jacobs, Johan Joubert, Patrick Maichotlo, Hugo Malan, Andre Pistorius, Henk Pretorius and Danie Van Niekerk
Eastern Cape Women's Championship – Humewood GC: Nobuhle Dlamini (swz)
Eastern Province – Humewood: Paul De Beer 214
Eastern Province and Border Open – Fish River Sun: Christiaan Bezuidenhout 207
Eastern Province Mid-Amateur – Humewood: Attie Burger 143
Ekurhuleni Mid Amateur – Benoni Lake GC: Graeme Watson
Ekurhuleni Mid-Amateur Open – Benoni Lake GC: Tyrol Auret
Ekurhuleni Open (Men) – Benoni CC: Aubrey Beckley
Ekurhuleni Seniors Open – Erpm GC: Gavin Van Aswegen
Ekurhuleni 54 Hole Stroke Play Championship– Ebotse GC: Bertine Strauss
Ekurhuleni Junior Championship (Girls) – Erpm GC: Cara Gorlei
Free State and Northern Cape Open – Bloemfontein: Jason Froneman 275
Free State and North Cape Women's Championship – Clarens GE: Nicole Garcia
Free State and Northern Cape Mid-Amateur – Vaal de Grace: Josef Fourie 136
Free State and Northern Cape Seniors – Harrismith: Ramon Rahme 144

Gauteng Women's Championship – Randpark GC: Nicole Garcia
Gauteng Stroke Play Championship – Country Club Johannesburg: Nobuhle Dlamini
Gauteng Girls' Junior Championship – Randpark GC: Carrie Park
Gauteng Seniors – Silver Lakes: Phillip Bierman 146
Gauteng Central Senior Open – Houghton: Lawrence Franklin 146
Gauteng North Open – Wingate Park: Toby Tree 281
Gauteng North Men's Championship – Wingate Park: Toby Tree 281
Gauteng North Mid Amateur – Wingate Park: Cameron Johnston 139
Gauteng North Senior Open – Silver Lakes CC: Phillipus Bierman
Highveld Mid Amateur – Middleburg: James Elton 68-137; Graeme Watson 137
KwaZulu Natal Open – Durban: Royal Durban: Lyle McNeil 280
KwaZulu Natal Women's Championship – Royal Durban GC: Nobuhle Dlamini
KwaZulu Natal Match Play – Umhiali: Zander Lombard beat Haydn Porteous 2 and 1
KwaZulu Natal Senior Open – Victoria: Francois Le Roux 140
KwaZulu Natal Junior Championship – Selborne CC: Kaleigh Telfer
Limpopo Open – Polokwane: Christiaan Bezuidenhout 205
Limpopo Women's Championship – Hans Merensky GC: Monja Richards
Mpumalanga Open – Middelburg CC: Christiaan Bezuidenhout
Mpumalanga Women's Championship – Middelburg GC: Kaleigh Telfer
North and South Juniors – Lake Club: Benoni Jovan Rebula 203
Northern Stroke Play – Randpark: Haydn Porteous 266
Northern Match Play – Randpark: Louis Taylor beat Tertius Van Den Berg 2 and 1
Northern Cape Open – Kimberley: Stephen Erasmus 212
North West Mid-Amateur Championship – Klerksdorp GC: David Muller
North West Open – Orkney: Callum Mowat 274
North West Women's Championship – Rustenburg CC: Nobuhle Dlamini
North West Senior Open – Rustenburg GC: Gavin Van Aswegen
Southern Cape Open – Plettenberg Bay CC: Callum Mowat
Southern Cape Mid Amateur – Fancourt: Graeme Watson 146
Southern Cape Women's Championship – Kingswood Golf Estate: Bianca Theron
Southern Cape Senior Amateur Championship – George GC: Ben Kleynhans
Southern Cape Senior Open – Fancourt CC: Francois Le Roux
Western Province Stroke Play – Strand: Christiaan Bezuidenhout 274
Western Province Match Play – Strand: Christiaan Bezhuidenhout beat N J Arnoldi 2 holes
Western Province Women's Championship – Mowbray GC: Monja Richards

## Africa (continued)

Western Province Senior Open – Mowbray: Francois Le Roux 147
WGSA Teams Championship (Swiss Team Trophy) – Graceland, Mpumalanga: 1 Gauteng North "A" 575; 2 Western Province 598; 3 North West 606. Winning team: Devanshi Naik, Hilda Edwards and Melissa Nawa[2]

WGSA Teams Championship (Challenge Trophy) – Graceland, Mpumalanga: 1 Mpumalanga A 591; 2 SA Invitational 623; 3 Western Province B, Boland B 624. Winning team: Izel Pieters, Alra van den Berg and Alana van Grueninga[2]

**Zimbabwe**                    Golf Courses: 40+
Population: 12.9m
Men's Champion: Benjamin Follett-Smith[1]
Women's Champion: Claire Angel Eaton (TAN)[2]

## Americas

**Argentina**
Population: 40.1m
Golfers: 100,000          Golf Courses: 310
Argentine Amateur Championship: Marcos Montenegro
  beat Jacopo Vecchi Fossa  4 and 3[1]
Women's Amateur Championship: Luz Besio beat Ruiz Sofia Goicoechea  3 and 2[2]
Men's Mid-Amateur Champion: Santiago Bauni
Junior Champion (Boys): Sebastian Bergagna
Junior Champion (Girls): Maria Belen Abrile

**Barbados**
Population: 274,200        Golf Courses: 5
Men's Champion: James Johnson[1]
Women's Champion: Muffin Stollmeyer[2]

**Bermuda**
Population: 64,237
Golfers: 2,960            Golf Courses: 7
Men's Match Play Champion: Jarryd Dillas
Men's Stroke Play Champion: William Haddrell
Women's Match Play Champion: Ann Symonds

**Brazil**
Population: 193.9m
Golfers: 25,000          Golf Courses: 107
Men's Champion: Andre Tourinho
Junior Champion (Boys): Pedro Junqueira
Regional championships:
  Brasilia (Men): Juan Ignacio Garmendia (ARG)
  Parana (Men): Luis Thiele
  Rio de Janeiro (Men): Tomaz Pimenta Pinheiro
  São Paulo (Men): Pedro Costa Lima

**Canada**
Population: 35.1m
Golfers: 5.95m           Golf Courses: 2,400
Men's Champion: Eli Cole (USA)[1]
Women's Champion – Club de Golf Beloeil: Brooke Henderson 275[2]
Mid-Amateur Champion (Men): Kevin Carrigan[1]
Senior Champion (Men): David Schultz[1]
Senior Champion (Women): Mary Ann Hayward[2]
Junior Champion (Boys) – Timberwood GC – Kevin Kwon 276[3]
Junior Champion (Girls) – Cherry Down G&CC: Maddie Szeryk (USA) 283

Canadian Universities/College Championship (Men): Ugo Coussaud (FRA)
Canadian Universities/College Championship (Women): Sabrina Sapone
Provincial Championships:
Alberta:
  Men's Champion – Sundre GC: Riley Fleming 281
  Women's Champion – Earl Grey GC, Calgary: Jocelyn Alford 141
  Mid-Amateur Champion (Men): Alan Stewart 215
  Senior Ladies Champion: Jackie Little 224
  Open Championship: R Fleming 138
  Junior Champion (Boys): Nicholas Scrimgeour 278
  Junior Champion (Girls): Jacklyn Lee 288
British Columbia:
  Men's Champion – Copperpoint CC: Charlie Hughes 272
  Women's Champion – Pitt Meadows GC: Cassy Isagawa 280
  Men's Mid-Amateur Champion: Kris Yardley 212
  Women's Mid-Amateur Champion: Christina Proteau 226
  Men's Senior Champion: Doug Roxburgh 210
  Women's Senior Champion: Lynda Palahniuk 146
  Junior Champion (Boys): Jared Dutoit 277 (after play-off with Jordan Lu and Kevin Vigna)
  Junior Champion (Girls): Janice Oleksiew 280
Manitoba:
  Men's Champion – Neepawaa G&CC: Derek East 275
  Women's Champion – Minniwasta GC: Bri-ann Tokariwski 239
  Men's Mid-Amateur Champion: Ben Bandura 214
  Men's Match Play Championship: Final – Aaron Cockerill beat Derek East  4 and 3
  Women's Match Play Championship: Final – Bri-ann Tokariwski beat Jenna Roadley  8 and 7
  Junior Champion (Boys): Travis Freeborg 289
  Junior Champion (Girls): Dana Todd 232
New Brunswick:
  Men's Champion – Fraser Edmundston GC: Justin Richard 285
  Women's Champion – The Riverside-Rothesay GC: Leanne Richardson 226
  Men's Mid-Amateur Champion: Mike Landry 139
  Men's Senior Champion: Mike Breen 213
  Junior Champion (Boys): Sam Young 219
Newfoundland and Labrador
  Junior Champion (Boys): Blair Bursay 224
  Junior Champion (Girls): Jillian Lawlor 285

Nova Scotia:
Men's Champion – Northumberland Links GC:
Stephane Boudreau
Women's Champion: Brynn Tomie 235
Men's Mid-Amateur Champion: Trevor Chow 220
Women's Senior Champion: Heather Grant 251
(after play-off with Debbi Karrel)
Junior Champion (Boys): Bruce Tomie 291
Ontario:
Men's Champion – OstlerBrook G&C: Stephane
Dubois 282
Women's Champion – Woodington Lake GC: Robyn
Doig 217
Men's Match Play Championship: Final – Zack
Kempa beat Lucas Kim 4 and 2
Women's Match Play Championship: Final – Robyn
Doig beat A Rogers 7 and 6
Men's Mid-Amateur Champion: Tyler McDannold
210
Men's Champion of Champions: Daley Byles
Men's Senior Champion of Champions: Rich Parsons
Women's Champion of Champions: Julia Hodgson
Men's Senior Champion: Michael Jackson 215) after
play-off With Larry Cooper and Christopher
Kertsos)
Somen's Senior Champion: Mary Ann Hayward
Junior Champion (Boys): Jake McNulty 278
Junior Boys Match Play Championship: Final – John
Boncoddo beat Maxwell Sear at 20th
Junior Champion (Girls): Kennedy Bodfield 309
Junior Girls Match Play Championship: Final –
Kennedy Bodfield beat Grace St Germain 2 holes
Prince Edward Island:
Men's Champion – Country View GC: Martin
O'Brien 144
Quebec:
Men's Champion – Royal Montreal GC: Hugo
Bernard 287
Women's Champion – Carleton G&YC: Anne-
Catherine Tanguay 218 (after play-off with Josee
Doyon)
Men's Match Play Championship: C Eccles beat M
Perron 3 and 2
Men's Mid-Amateur Champion: Luca Michielli 144
Women's Mid-Amateur Champion: Mary Ann
Hayward 153
Junior Champion (Boys): Etienne Papineau 281
Saskatchewan:
Men's Champion – Melfort CC: David Stewart 281
Women's Champion – Humboldt GC: Anna Young
219
Men's Mid-Amateur Champion: Ryan McNall 228
Senior Men's Champion: Colin Coben 217
Senior Women's Champion: Denise Wilson 248
Junior Champion (Boys): Tie – Mike Flegel and
Leighton Bearchell
Junior Champion (Girls): Brooke Hobson 237

## Chile
Population: 16.3m        Golf Courses: 12
Men's Match Play Champion: Guillermo Pereira
Women's Match Play Champion: Isidora San Martin
Junior Champion (Boys): Claudio Correa
Junior Champion (Girls): Aldana Foigel (ARG)

## Colombia
Population: 47.1m        Golf Courses: 49
Men's Champion: Federico Arango* (Beat Ivan Camilo
Ramirez on play-off)[1]
Women's Champion: Maria Alejandra Hoyos
Mid-Amateur Champion (Men): Juan Fernando Mejia
Mid-Amateur Champion (Women): Ana Maria Gonzalez
de Llano

## Costa Rica
Population: 4.6m
Golfers: 3,500          Golf Courses: 11
Men's Match Play Champion: Alvaro Ortiz
Men's Stroke Play Champion: Alvaro Ortiz
Women's Match Play Champion: Ximena Montealegre
Junior Champion (Boys): Jose Mendez

## Mexico
Population: 117.4m       Golf Courses: 150+
Men's Champion: Mario Clemens (pro)[1]
Women's Champion: Marijosse Navarro
Junior Champion (Boys): Aaron Terrazas
Junior Champion (Girls): Maria Fassi

## Puerto Rico
Population: 3.6m         Golf Courses: 28
Puerto Rico Classic: Albin Choi (CAN) (pro)
Lady Puerto Rico Classic: Emily Tubert (USA)
Men's Champion: Erick Morales
Junior Champion (Boys): Jorge Garcia (VEN)

## Trinidad and Tobago
Population: 1.3m         Golf Courses: 9
Men's Champion: Shane Costelloe

## Uruguay
Population: 3.2m         Golf Courses: 11
Men's Match Play Champion: Gregor Schmid
Men's Stroke Play Champion: Juan Alvarez[1]
Women's Champion: Manuela Barros

## USA
Population: 316.4m
Golfers: 26.2m          Golf Courses: 16,547
113th US Amateur Championship: Matt Fitzpatrick
(ENG) beat Oliver Goss (AUS) 4 and 3[1]
113th US Women's Amateur Championship: Emma
Talley (Princeton, NY) beat Yueer Cindy Feng
(Orlando, FL) 2 and 1[2]
North and South Championships (Men): Andrew Dorn
beat Zachary Bauchou 1 hole[1]
North and South Championships (Women):
Ally McDonald beat Yueer Cindy Feng 3 and 2[2]
Mid-Amateur Champion (Men): Michael McCoy beat
Bill Williamson 8 and 6[1]
Mid-Amateur Champion (Women): Julia Potter
(Granger,
IN) beat Margaret Shirley (Roswell, GA) at 19th[2]
Senior Champion (Men): Douglas Hanzel (Savannah,
GA) beat Pat O'Donnell (Happy Valley, OR) 3 and 2[1]
Senior Champion (Women): Ellen Port (St Louis, MO)
beat Susan Cohn (Palm Beach gardens, FL) 3 and 2[2]
North and South Senior Championship (Men): Andrew
Dorn
North and South Senior Championship (Women):
Ally McDonald

## Americas (continued

North and South Junior Championships (Boys):
Will Blalock
North and South Junior Championships (Girls):
Anna Redding
Junior Champion (Boys): Scottie Scheffler beat Davis
Riley  2 and 1[3]
Junior Champion (Girls): Gabriella Then beat Iakareber
Abe  2 and 1[4]
US Amateur Public Links Championship (Men):
Jordan Niebrugge (Mequon, WI) beat Michael Kim
(Del Mar, CA)  1 up[1]

US Amateur Public Links Championship (Women):
Laura Diaz-Yi (Thousand Oaks, CA) beat Doris
Chen (Bradenton, FL)  4 and 3[2]
For US State championships see pages 321 and 404

**Venezuela**
Population: 28.9m          Golf Courses: 22
Men's Amateur Champion: Jorge Garcia
Junior Champion (Boys): Alejandro Perazzo
Junior Champion (Girls): Valentina Gilly

## Asia and the Middle East

**Bangladesh**
Population: 152.5m
Men's Champion: Karan Taunk (IND)[1]

**China**
Population: 1,359.3m          Golf Courses: 200+
Men's Champion: Jin Zhang[1]
Women's Champion: Michelle Koh (MAS)[2]
Junior Champion (Boys): Khai Jei Low (USA)
Junior Champion (Girls): Jin Man

**Chinese Taipei (Taiwan)**
Population: 23.3m
Men's Champion: Teng Kao[1]
Women's Champion: Yi-Ching Wu
Junior Champion (Girls): Chih-Min Chen

**Hong Kong**
Population: 7.1m
Golfers: 200,000          Golf Courses: 6 (18), 4 (9)
Hong Kong Ladies Open Amateur Championship –
Clearwater Bay: Chayanid Prapassarangkul (THA)[2]
Mizuno Hong Kong Close Amateur Championship –
HKGC New: Chen Kun Max Wong
Mizuno Hong Kong Ladies Close Championship –
Clearwater Bay G&CC: Michelle Cheung[2]
Hong Kong Open Mid-Amateur (Women) –
Clearwater Bay: Alice Kerr[2]
Hong Kong Open and Mid-Amateur Championship –
Hong Kong GC: Yu-Jui Liu (TPE)[1]
Hong Kong Close Ladies Mid-Amateur
Championship – Clearwater Bay G&CC: Si Nga
Cindy Lee[2]
Men's Spring Tournament – Discovery Bay: Diamond/
Jade Kit Kan Byron Tan 31pts
Women's Spring Tournament – Discovery Bay:
Rungnapa Winchester 27 pts
Munsingwear Hong Kong Senior Close Championship:
William Douglas 217
Bushnell Mid-Summer Classic – HKGC New. Men:
Stroke Play – Stuart Murray 71; Stableford – Wai
Kwong JohnYiu 27 pts; Women: Stableford – Emily
Vickie Leung, Estee Vivian Leung 30 pts
Le Coq Sportif Hong Kong Junior Close
Championship – Clearwater Bay G&CC. Boys:
Chung Ho Justin Lok 152; Girls: Isabella Leung 150
Hong Kong Junior Open Championship (Boys) –
HKGC Deep Water Bay: Lucas Lam[3]

Hong Kong Junior Open Championship (Girls) –
HKGC Deepwater Bay: Chayanit Wangmahaporn
(THA)[4]
Hong Kong Junior Close Championship (Boys) –
Clearwater Bay G&CC: Chung Ho Justin Lok[3] (beat
Michael Regan Wong in play-off)
Hong Kong Junior Close Championship (Girls) –
Clearwater Bay G&CC: Isabella Leung[4]
EFG Bank 2012 Junior Tour Final HKGC: Deep Water
Bay. Boys: Yannick Nathan Artigolle 61; Girls: Cheryl
Man 69
Hong Kong Schools Team Championship – HKGC
New: 1 ICS 239; 2 KCVI 240; 3 HKIS 242
Hong Kong Inter-Club Championship – Clearwater
Bay G&CC: Day 1 – HKGC 2, Discovery Bay 4;
Clearwater 5, Shek O 1. Day 2 – HCGC 6.
Clearwater 0; Shek O 5. Discovery Bay 15

**India**
Population: 1,232.5m
All India Amateur (Men): Pratap Atwal[1]
All India Amateur (Women): Gurbani Singh
All India Mid-Amateur: Gagan Verma
All India Junior (Boys): Viraj Madappa
All India Junior (Girls): Aditi Ashok
All India Seniors: Vijay Kumar
NRC Cup: Vijitha Bandara (SRI)
Provincial Championships:
East India Amateur: Ashbeer Saini (pro)
Eastern India Junior: Viraj Madappa
Delhi Juniors: Manu Gandas
Haryana Amateur: Syed Saqib Ahmed
Haryana Junior: Feroz Singh Garewal
Northern India Amateur: Piyush Sangwan
Northern India Ladies & Junior Girls: Gaurika Bishnoi
Northern India Junior: Viraj Madappa
Karnataka Amateur (Ladies): Gurbani Singh
Rajasthan Junior: Viraj Madappa
Southern India Amateur: Trishul Chinnappa
Southern India Ladies: Gauri Monga
Southern India Junior: Manu Gandas
West Bengal Ladies & Junior Girls: Millie Saroha
Western India Amateur: Karan Taunk
Western India Junior: Pukhraj Singh Gill

**Israel**
Population: 8m
Golfers: 1,300          Golf Courses: 2
Men's Champion: Assaf Cohen[1]
Women's Champion: Hadas Libman[2]

**Japan**

Population: 127.3m   Golf Courses: 2,442
55th Japanese Amateur Championship – Tojigaoka
Marine Hills GC: Haruka Morita beat Yumi
Matsubara at 37th hole[1]
Women's Champion – Okayama GC: Lu Wanyao
(CHN)
Women's Senior Championship – Elleair GC.
Matsuyama:  Mayumi Tanaka
Men's Mid-Amateur – Naruo GC: Sumio Shiotsuki
Junior Golf Championship – Kasumigaseki GC: Boys –
Shoutarou Wada; Girls – Kotone Hori
Junior Players Championship (Boys) – Nasuogawa GC:
Kodai Igari
Junior Players Championship (Girls) – Nasuogawa GC:
Mana Shinozaki
67th Men's Collegiate Championship – Kakogawa GC,
Hyogo: Shun Murayama
50th Women's Collegiate Championship – Kakogawa
GC, Hyogo: Rikako Sakashita

**Korea**

Population: 50.2m
Men's Champion: Chang-woo Lee[1]
Mid-Amateur (Chammaroo Cup): Cheol-sik Yoon

**Malaysia**

Population: 29.7m
Golfers: 376,000   Golf Courses: 219
Malaysian Amateur Open (Men): Kevin Marques (AUS)[1]
Malaysian Amateur Open (Women): Kelly Tan[2]
Malaysian Junior Open (Boys): Amir Nazrin Jailani
Malaysian Junior Open (Girls): Budsabakorn Sukapan
(THA)
Malaysian School Sports (Boys): Solomon Emilio
Malaysian School Sports (Girls): Loy Hee Ying
Kuala Lumpur Amateur Open (Men) : Khai Jei Low
Kuala Lumpur Amateur Open (Women): Gavrilla
Christina Arya (INA)
Perlis Amateur Open: Ahmad Zahir Abd Ghani
29th Sabah Amateur Open – Sabah GC: Muhammad
Wafiyuddin Abdul Manas
Sabah Women's Amateur Open – Sabah GC: : Aretha
Herng Pan (pro)
North Malaysian Open – Royal Perak GC: Khai Jei
Low
Sabah International Junior Masters – Sabah G&CC:
Aretha Herng Pan (pro)
44th Sarawak Amateur Open – Sibu, Sarawak: Lee ka
Tung
30th Negeri Sembilan Amateur Open – Seremban
International GC: Abdul Hadi (SIN)
22nd Negeri Sembilan Amateur Open – Seremban
International GC: Nur Durriyah Damian
Sarawak Women's Amateur Championship – Sibu
Sarawak: Kelly Tan

Sarawak Chief Minister's Cup – Petra Jaya: Kelie Kan
Kah Yan

**Pakistan**

Population: 183.9m
Golfers: 5,528   Golf Courses: 8 (18), 11 (9)
Men's Champion: Md Sagor (BAN)[1]
Pakistan Open (Men): Ghazanfar Mehmood/Muhammad
Waseem Rana)

**Philippines**

Population: 98.2m
Philippine Amateur Open: Jerome Ng (SIN)[1]
Philippine Amateur Closed: Rupert Zaragosa
Women's Open Champion: Dottie Ardina (pro)[2]
Philippine Mid-Amateur & Seniors: Abraham Avena
Philippine Junior Amateur (Boys): Min Ung Park (TPE)
Philippine Junior Amateur (Girls): Princess Mary
Superal
Philippine Junior Amateur Closed (Boys): Rupert
Zaragosa

**Qatar**

Population: 1.9m
Qatar Open Amateur – Doha GC: Max Williams (ENG)

**Singapore**

Population: 5.3m
Open Amateur Champion: Yu-Jui Liu (TPE)[1]
National Amateur Champion (Men): Yash Majmuder
beat Marc Ong  3 and 2[1]
National Amateur Champion: (Women): Koh Sock
Hwee beat Joey Poh  7 and 6[1]
National Senior Champion: Francis Chia Kok Hui
Junior Champion (Boys): Edgar Oh
Junior Champion (Girls): Pornpawee Thammavichai
(THA)

**Sri Lanka**

Population: 20.2m
Sri Lanka Championship: Syed Saqib Ahmed beat Trishul
Chinnappa  5 and 3[1]
Women's Champion: Gauri Monga (IND)[2]

**Thailand**

Population: 65.9m
Thailand Amateur Open (Men): Suradit
Yongcharoenchai (won at 1st extra hole of play-off)
Thailand Amateur Open (Women): Sherman
Santiwiwattanapong (beat Pannarat Thanapolboonyaras
in play-off)

**Vietnam**

Population: 88.7m   Golf Courses: 1
National Amateur Championship: Do Le Gia Dat

## Australasia

### Australia

Population: 23.1m

Golfers: 450,000          Golf Courses: 1,511

Australian Amateur Championship – Commonwealth GC and Woodlands GC: Cameron Smith (pro) beat Geoff Drakeford 3 and 2. Medallist: Brady Watt

Australian Women's Amateur Championship – Commonwealth and Woodlands GCs: Minjee Lee beat Jenny Lee  6 and 5[2]

Australian Master of the Amateurs – R. Melbourne: GC:Viraat Badhwar (QLD)

Riversdale Cup (inst. 1896) – Riversdale GC, Melbourne. Men: Brady Wyatt (WA); Women: Grace Lennon (VIC)

Men's Mid-Amateur Championship – Moonah Links, Victoria: Damien Jordab (QLD)[1]

Women's Mid-Amateur Championship – Moonah Links, Victoria: Sue Wooster (VIC)[2]

Mid-Amateur Team Championship: Queensland

National Senior Masters – The National GC: Roy Vandersluis (NSW)

Senior Champion (Men) – Royal Queensland GC: Murray Martin (NZL)[1]

Senior Match Play Championship – 13th Beach Golf Links: Ian McPherson

Senior Champion (Women) – Tanunda Pines GC: Josie Ryan

Junior Boys Amateur – Pinjarra GC: Anthony Murdaca

Australian Girls' Amateur – Mount Lawley GC: Minjee Lee

Lake Macquarie Men's Amateur – Belmont GC: Josh Munn (NZL)

Lake Macquarie Women's Amateur – Belmont GC: Su-Hyun Oh (VIC)

Lake Karrinyup Men's Senior Classic: Graham Bowen (WA)

Rene Erichsen Salver – Glenelg GC: Minjee Lee (WA)

Ross Herbert National Tournament: 1 Victoria 571 (Geoff Drakeford, Todd Sinnott, Grace Lennon, Su Hyun Oh); 2 Western Australia 579) Michael Dennit, Brady Watt, Hayley Bettancourt, Minjee Lee); 3 Queensland 601 (Taylor MacDonald, Cameron Smith, Ali Orchard, Ellen Davies-Graham) 5 South Australie 403 (Chris Brown, Anthony Murdaca, Jenny Lee, Caitlin Roberts); 5 New South Wales 619 (Ricky kato, Brett Drewitt, Lauren Hibbert, Adriana Brent)

Ross Herbert International Tournament: 1 Australia 579 (Brett Drewitt, Cameron Smith, Minjee Lee, Su Hyun Oh); 2 New Zealand 589 (Vaughan McCall, Blair Riordan, Munchin Keh, Lydia, Ko); 3 Korea 605 (Nam-hun Kim, Soo-min Lee, Ji-soo park, Ji-hyun Oh) 4 Japan 609 (Kazuya Koura, Kazuki Higa, Kotone Hori, Yumi Matsubara)

Tamar Valley Cup – Greens Beach, GC Tasmania. Boys: Zach Murray (VIC); Girls: Hira Naveed (WA)

South Pacific Ladies Open Classic – Surfer's Paradise, Queensland: Ashley Ona (QLD)

South Pacific Ladies Senior Masters – Surfer's Paradise, Queensland: Wendy O'Connell (QLD)

Jack Newton International Classic – Maitland GC and Kurri Kurri GC, Newcastle: Boys: Harrison Endycott (NSW) (Boys); Shelly Shin (NSW) (Girls)

Greg Norman Junior Masters – Palmer Colonial GC Queensland: Jiwon Jeon & Jack Sullivan

Royal Melbourne Senior Classic: Rick Oliver (NSW)

State Championships:

NSW Men's Amateur Championship – Sydney: Ben Eccles (VIC)

NSW Medal: Thomas Horan (VIC)

NSW Women's Stroke Play Championship: *Cancelled*

NSW Men's Senior Amateur – Howlong CGC: Bill Banks (ACT)

NSW Men's Senior Classic – The Lakes GC and Australia GC: David Limbach (NSW)

NSW Women's Senior Amateur – Manly GC: Dierdre Brander (NSW)

NSW Men's Medal – Sydney: Thomas Horan (VIC)

NSW Junior Championship: Jack Sullivan (QLD) (Boys): Amy Walsh (QLD) (Girls)

N. Territories Men's Amateur– Darwin GC: David Micheluzzi (NT)

N. Territory Women's Amateur – Alice Springs GC: Tatiana Wijaya (WA)

N. Territories Men's Senior Amateur – Darwin GC: Tom Harold (NT)

N. Territory Women's Senior Amateur – Alice Springs GC: Glenys Ferguson (QLD)

N. Territory Boys Amateur – Darwin GC: David Micheluzzi (NT)

N. Territory Girls' Amateur – Alice Springs GC: Tatiana Wijaya (WA)

Queensland Men's Open – Brookwater G&CC: Nick Cullen (SA)

Queensland Amateur Championship (Women): Ashley Ona

Queensland Men's Stroke Play – Pacific Harbour G&CC: Callan O'Reilly (NSW)

Queensland Women's Stroke Play – Southport GC: Ashley Ona (QLD)

Men's Qld Senior Amateur – Oxley GC: Alan Bullas (VIC)

Women's Qld Senior Amateur – Horton Park GC: Wendy O'Connell (QLD)

Queensland Junior Amateur (Boys) – Indooroopilly GC: Matthew Samen-Curtis

Queensland Junior Amateur (Girls) – Indooroopilly GC: Samantha Foley

Queensland Junior Amateur (Boys 14 and Under) – Indooroopilly GC: Cameron John

Queensland Junior Amateur (Girls 14 and Under) – Indooroopilly GC: Rebecca Kay

SA Men's Amateur – Flagstaff Hill GC and Tea Tree Gully GC: Jordan Cooper (VIC)

SA Women's Amateur – Flagstaff Hill GC and Tea Tree Gully GC: Cyna Rodriguez (PHI)

SA Men's Classic – Glenelg GC: Daniel Hoeve (WA)

SA Junior Amateur Championship – Kooyonga GC and The Grange GC. Boys: Anthony Murdaca (SA); Girls: Rebecca Kay (QLD)

SA Senior Amateur – Gawler GC: Peter King

17th SA Junior Masters – Royal Adelaide: Anthony Murdaca (SA) (Boys); Amy Walsh (QLD) (Girls)

Tasmanian Men's Open – Prospect Vale GC: Jordan Zunic (TAS)

Tasmanian Women's Stroke Play Championship (Elvie Whiteside Trophy) – Prospect Vale GC: Tatiana Wijaya (WA)

Tasmanian Men's Senior Amateur – Mowbray GC: Stefan Albinski (NSW)

Tasmanian Women's Senior Amateur – Royal Hobart Golf Club: Tammy Hall (TAS)

Women's Tas 72-Hole Stroke Play (Elvie Whiteside) –
Country Club Tasmania: Tatiana Wijaya (WA)
Tasmanian Junior Masters – Tasmania GC.
Boys: Ben
Elliott (TAS); Girls: Georgia Macklin (VIC)
53rd Victorian Open (Men) – Thirteenth Beach GC:
Matthew Giles (NSW)
Victoria Open (Women) – Thirteenth Beach GC:
Stacey Keating (VIC)
Victorian Amateur Championship (Men) – Kingston
Heath GC: Simon Viitakangas and Taylor James
MacDonald
Victorian Amateur Championship (Women) –
Kingston Heath GC: Su-Hyun Oh
Victorian Men's Senior Amateur – Royal Perth GC:
Stefan Albinski (NSW)
Victorian Women's Senior Amateur – Horsham GC:
Jenny McRae
Victoria Junior Masters – Waverley GC: D J Loypur
(VIC (Boys)L Montanna Strauss (VIC) (Girls)
Victorian Boys' Championship – Northern GC: Frazer
Droop (VIC)
Victorian Girls' Championship – Yarra Yarra GC:
Celina Yuan (NSW)
WA Men's Amateur – Royal Fremantle GC: Brady
Wyatt (WA)
WA Women's Amateur – Royal Fremantle GC: Minjee
Lee (WA)
WA Women's Stroke Play – Lake Karrunyup GC:
Hannah Green (WA)
WA Men's Senior Amateur – Royal Perth GC: Stefan
Albinski (NSW)
WA Women's Senior Amateur – Royal Perth GC: Ros
Fisher (WA)
Men's Interstate Championship – Royal Hobart GC
and Tasmania GC: 1 Queensland (Cameron Smith,
Taylor MacDonald, Aaron Wilkin, Viraat Badhwar,
Kevin Marques, James Gibellini, Jake McLeod, Simon
Viitakangas); 2 New South Wales; 3 Victoria; 4
Victoria; 5 Western Australia; 8 South Australia[1]
Women's Interstate Championship – Royal Hobart
GC: 1 Victoria (Su-Hyun Oh, Hannah Green, Hayley
Bettancourt, Claudia Pisano, Alyssa Keir); 2 Western
Australia; 3 Queensland; 4 New South Wales; 5
South Australia; 6 Tasmania[2]
Boys Interstate Team Championship – Bunbury GC: 1
Queensland (Viraat Badhwar, Blake Proverbs, Jack
Sullivan, jack Hulyer, Shae Wools-Cobb); 2 Victoria; 3
New South Waless, South Australia; 5 Western
Australia; 6 Tasmania; 7 Australian Capital Territory; 8
Northern Territory
Girls' Interstate Championship (Burtta Cheney
Cup) – Western Australia GC: 1 Queensland (Amy
Walsh, Rebecca Kay, Dee Dee Russell, Samantha
Foley, Kate Law); 2 New South Wales, Victoria; 4
Western Australia; 5 South Australia

**Fiji**
Population: 858,038
Open Championship (Men): Sam Lee[1]
Stroke Play Champion (Men): Olaf Allen
Match Play Champion (Men): Anuresh Chandra

**New Zealand**
Population: 4.4m
Golfers: 482,000        Golf Courses: 400+
New Zealand Amateur Championship (Men) –
Manawata: Kadim Neho beat Ryan Chisnall 3 and 2.
Medallist: Luke Toomey 131[1]

New Zealand Amateur Championship (Women) –
Julianne Alvaraz beat Hannah Seifert[2]
New Zealand Stroke Play Championship (Men) –
Paraparaumu: Cameron Jones 276[1]
New Zealand Stroke Play Championship (Women) –
Paraparaumu Beach GC: Chantelle Cassidy[2]
New Zealand Mid-Amateur Championship (Men) –
Wairakei GC: Mark Boulton (AUS)[1]
New Zealand Mid-Amateur Championship (Women) –
Wairakei GC: Jacqui Morgan (AUS)[2]
New Zealand Seniors Championship (Men) – Waitikiri
GC: Brent Paterson
New Zealand Under-19 Championship (Men) –
Harewood: Peter Lee
New Zealand Under-19 Championship (Women) –
Templeton: Julianne Alvarez
Danny Lee Springfield Open – Men: Nick Voke 203;
Women: Brittney Dryland 221
Grant Clements Memorial – Men: Compton Pikari;
Women: Brittney Dryland 305
Lamb and Hayward Stroke Play – Clearwater. Men:
Ryan Chisnall 294; Women: Yee Yeon Kim 226
Ruth Middleton Classic – Matamata, Waikato: Chantelle
Cassidy
Tom Bonnington Cup – Mangawhai: Taylor Gill 143

Provincial Championships:
Millenium Auckland Anniversary Tournament –
Akarana: Nick Voke 210
Cambridge Classic (Men): Denzel Ieremia
Cambridge Classic (Women): Mun Chin Keh
Canterbury Match Play (Men) – Templeton GC:
Jordan Bakermans
Canterbury Match Play (Women) – Templeton GC:
Grace Senior
Canterbury Stroke Play (Men) – Clearwater: Ryan
Chisnall
Canterbury Stroke Play (Women) – Clearwater: Yee
Yeon Kim (KOR)
Dunedin Stroke Play (Men) – St Clair: Peter Lee
Dunedin Stroke Play (Women) – St Clair: Mun Chin
Keh
Hastings Open – Hastings. Men: Harry Bateman 282;
Women: Kate Chadwick 304
Kapi Tareha – Napier GC: Joshua Munn
North Island Men's Stroke Play – Poverty Bay: Oscar
Cadenhead 274
North Island Women's Stroke Play – Poverty Bay: Mun
Chin Keh 291
North Island Men's Under-19 – Hamilton: Trent Munn
211
North Island Women's Under-19 – Hamilton: Celeste
McLean 225
North Shore Women's Classic – North Shore: Sai Ma
224
Otago Men's Stroke Play: Brent McEwan
Rotorua Men's Open – Rotorua: Peter Lee 264
South Island Men's Stroke Play – St Clair: Peter Lee
267
South Island Women's Stroke Play – St Clair: Mun
Chin Keh 280
South Island Men's Under-19 – Timaru: Tyler King 219
South Island Women's Under-19 – Timaru: Laura
Hoskin 222
Waikato Winter Stroke Play – Lochiel GC: Lachie
McDonald
Waikato Classic (Men) – Ngaruawahia GC: Brad
Hayward

## Australasia (continued)

Waikato Classic (Women) – Ngaruawahia GC: Chantelle Cassidy
Wairapara Open – Masterton. Men: Marc Jennings 280; Women: Lucy Davis 322
Wellington Stroke Play (Men) – Waikanae GC: Fraser MacLachlan

Wellington Stroke Play (Women) – Waikanae GC: Te Rongapai Clay
Women's interprovincial final: Auckland 5, Bay of Plenty 0
Men's Interprovincial final: Manawatu-Wanganui 4½, Bay of Plenty ½

## Europe

### Austria
Population: 8.4m
Golfers: 104,736          Golf Courses: 156
Men's Stroke Play Champion: Felix Schulz[1]
Men's Match Play Champion: Lukas Lipold
Women's Stroke Play Champion: Nina Muehl
Women's Match Play Champion: Anja Purgauer
International Amateur Championship (Men): Kristian Kulokorpi (FIN) (beat Robin Goger in play-off)[1]
International Amateur Championship (Women): Virginia Elena Carta (ITA)[2]
Mid-Amateur Champion (Men): Helmut Konrad
Junior Champion (Boys): Florian Payr (U16); Tom Brennacher (U18); Markus Habeler (U21)
Junior Stroke Play Champion (Girls): Sophie Poll (U16); Marlene Krejcy (U18)
Austrian Junior Tour U16 Match Play (Girls): Sophie Poll

### Belgium
Population: 11.1m
Golfers: 57,074          Golf Courses: 80
International Men's Champion: Thomas Detry[1]
National Stroke Play (Men): Gaetan Van Baarle[1]
National Match Play (Men): Aurian Capart
International Ladies Champion: Laura Gonzalez-Escallon[2]
National Stroke Play (Women): Manon de Roey[2]
International Juniors (Girls): Agathe Laisne
Junior Champion (Boys): Jonathan Albert (U14); Giovanni Tadiotto (U16); Aurian Capart (U18)
Junior Champion (Girls): Valerie Serrien (U14); Diane Baillieux (U16); Clara Aveling (U18)

### Bulgaria
Population: 7.2m
Golfers: 639          Golf Courses: 7
Men's Champion: Dimitar Lulov[1]
Women's Champion: Maya Kucherkova[1]

### Cyprus
Population: 862,999
Golfers: 1,464          Golf Courses: 10
Cyprus Men's Open: Oliver Gabor (SVK)[1]
Cyprus Men's Senior Open: Bob Windsor (ENG)
Cyprus Women's Senior Open: Sofia Gerardi (GRE)
CGF Cup (Stableford): EGC (Martyn Anderton, David Pitts, Cliff Monks, Patrick O'Flynn, Dorothy Hudson, Bobby Johnson, Martin Pollard, Maureen Holland) 210 pts
Cyprus Youth Golf Open: Jessica Heap

### Czech Republic
Population: 10.5m
Golfers: 55,547          Golf Courses: 96
Czech Amateur Championship: Tim Gornik[1]
Czech National Match Play (Women): Lucie Hinnerova
Czech International Amateur (Women): Ursa Orehek (SLO)[2]
Czech International Mid-Amateur (Men): Marc Mazur (GER)
Czech International Mid-Amateur (Women): Marketa Subrtova
Czech International Senior Champion (Men): Gianluca Bolla (ITA)
Czech International Senior Champion (Women): Anna Dzurenda
Czech International Junior Champion (Boys): Vitek Novak
Faldo Series Czech Championship (Girls): Marie Lunackova
National Youth Championship (Boys): Erik Palkovsky
National Youth Championship (Girls): Johanka Steindlerova
Czech International Junior (Boys): Vitek Novak
Czech International Junior (Girls): Kristyna Frydlova
Czech Academic Championship (Men) – Martin Pospisil
Czech Academic Championship (Women): Lucie Hinnerova (pro)

### Denmark
Population: 5.6m
Golfers: 152,972          Golf Courses: 188
Danish International Open Championship (Men): Thomas Elissade (FRA)[1]
Danish International Open Championship (Women): Nicole Broch Larsen (pro)[2]
Danish International Youth Championship (Boys): Nicklas Munkebo
Danish International Youth Championship (Girls): Amber Lee Svendsen (ITA)

### England
Population: 53m
Golfers: 688,195 affiliated to the EGU; 115,456 affiliated to the EWGA
Golf Courses: 1,954 affiliated to the EGU; 1,774 affiliated to the EWGA
English Open Amateur Stroke Play Championship (Brabazon Trophy) – Formby: Jordan Smith[1]
English Amateur Championship – Frilford Heath GC: Callum Shinkwin beat Matthew Fitzpatrick 4 and 3[1]
English Ladies Close Amateur Championship – Kings Norton GC: Sarah-Jane Boyd[2]

English Women's Open Amater Stroke Play
Championship – Kings Norton: Sarah Jane Boyd[2]
English Open Mid-Amateur Championship (Logan
Trophy) – The Worcestersghire GC: John Kemp
(Woburn)[1]
English Women's Open Mid-Amateur Championship –
John O'Gaunt GC: Charlotte Thomas
English Seniors' Amateur Championship – Bristol and
Clifton/Long Ashton: Richard Latham[1]
Senior Women's English Close Match Play
Championship – Sherwood Forest: Janet Melville
(Sherwood Forest) beat Christine Quinn (Hockley)
2 and 1. Medallist: Lula Housman (Highgate) 157[2]
English Men's County Champion of Champions
Tournament – Woodhall Spa: Bobby Keeble (Essex)[1]
English Senior County Champion of Champions –
Woodhall Spa: Anthony McLure (Northumberland)[1]
English Boys' Under-16 Championship (McGregor
Trophy) – Seacroft GC: Marco Penge (Worthing)[3]
English Boys' Under-18 Championship (Carris
Trophy) –
West Lancs GC: Ben Amor (Marlborough)* (*beat*
*Adam Chapman (Windermere) at the 2nd extra hole*)[3]
English Junior County Champion of Champions –
Woodhall Spa GC: Jordan Winsdale (Boston)[3]

**Estonia**
Population: 1.2m
Golfers: 2,247          Golf Courses: 8
Estonian Amateur Open (Men): Johannes Diederichs
(GER)[1]
Estonian Amateur Open (Women): Antonia-Leonie
Eberhard (GER)[2]
Estonian National Stroke Play (Women): Mari Hutsi[2]

**Finland**
Population: 5.4m
Golfers: 144,221          Golf Courses: 129
Finnish Open Amateur Championship: Joel Girrbach
(SUI)[1]
Finnish National Championship: Arto Pehkonen[1]
Finnish Women's Champion: Anna Backman[2]
Finnish Women's StrokePlay Championship: Sanna
Nuutinen[2]
Finnish Mid-Amateur Match Play (Men): Marco
Willberg
Finnish International Junior (Boys): Sami Valimaki (U16);
Matias Sipponen (U18); Miki Kuronen (U21)
Finnish International Junior (Girls): Azelia Meichtry
(SUI) (U16); Karina Kukkonen (U18 & U21)
Finnish Junior Match Play (Boys): Oliver Lindell (U16);
Iiro Eskelinen (U18); Mikko Lehtovuori (U21)
Finnish Junior Match Play (Girls): Emmi Jalkanen (U16);
Ida Kaukinen (U18); Tiia Koivisto (U21)
Finnish Tour Kamppi Open: Lauri Ruuska
Finnish Tour Karsinta 2014: Juho Selesniemi
Finnish Tour Finaali: Kristian Kulokorpi

**France**
Population: 65.7m
Golfers: 422,761          Golf Courses: 583
French Open Stroke Play Championship – Chantilly:
Adrien Saddier[1]
French Closed Amateur Championship (Trophée
Jacques Leglise) – RCF La Boulie: Francois Censier
beat Ugo Coussaud 2 and 1[1]

French Closed Amateur Championship (Coupe Pierre
Deschamps) – RCF La Boulie: Marion Veysseyre beat
Chloe Salort 4 and 3[2]
French Mid-Amateur Championship – Golf Albi
Lasbordes: Fredrik Axelsson (SWE)[1]
Internationaux de France Seniors: Glyn Rees (WAL)
Regional Championships:
Grand Prix d'Aix en Provence (Men): Thomas Joly
Grand Prix d'Aix en Provence (Women): Lara
Plachetka
Grand Prix d'Amiens Metropole (Men): Louis Leysen
(BEL)
Grand Prix d'Amiens Metropole (Women): Carole
Danten-Azfi
Grand Prix d'Apremonte (Men): Dewi Merckx (BEL)
Grand Prix d'Apremonte (Women): Marie Beauvalet-
Boutouyrie
Grand Prix de La Baule (Men): Kevin Hesbois (BEL)
Grand Prix de La Baule (Women): Louise Gateau-
Chovelon
Grand Prix de Bordeaux-Lac (Men): Matthieu Pavon
Grand Prix de Bordeaux-Lac (Women): Florine
Gaillac
Grand Prix de Bondues (Men): Thibaut Courmont
Grand Prix de Bondues (Women): Diane Baillieux
(BEL)
Grand Prix de la Bresse (Men): Clement Hauchard
Grand Prix de la Bresse (Women): Alice Putoud
Grande Prix de Bretagne (Men): Baptiste Courtachon
Grande Prix de Bretagne (Women): Louise Gateau-
Chovelon
Grand Prix du Cap D'Agde (Men): Gregoire Schoeb
Grand Prix du Cap D'Agde (Women): Romane Juve
Grand Prix de Chiberta (Men): Victor Perez
Grand Prix de Chiberta (Women): Celia Barquin (ESP)
Grand Prix de la Cote d'Albatre (Men): Nicolas
Maheut
Grand Prix de la Cote d'Albatre (Women): Julie
Laisney
Grand Prix de la Cote D'Opale (Men): Anthony
Renard
Grand Prix de Haute Savoie (Men): Adrien Saddier
(pro)
Grand Prix de Haute Savoie (Women): Alexia Gleise
Grand Prix des Landes (Men): Juan Sarasti (ESP)
Grand Prix des Landes (Women): Silvia Banon (ESP)
Grand Prix de la Ligue Messieurs: Romain Langasque
Grand Prix de Limere (Men): Mathieu Decottignies-
Lafon
Grand Prix de Limere (Women): Charlotte Charrayre
Grand Prix de Lyon (Men): Charles Almeida
Grand Prix de Lyon (Women): Emilie Alonso
Grand Prix du Lys Chantilly (Men): Christophe De
Grancy
Grand Prix du Lys (Women): Geraldine Spencer
Grand Prix du Medoc (Men): Ugo Coussaud
Grand Prix du Medoc (Women): Laure Castelain
Grand Prix de Montpellier Massane (Men): Charles
Hebert
Grand Prix de Montpellier Massane (Women): Marion
Benzekri
Grand Prix de Nîmes Campagne (Men): Stephane
Soum
Grand Prix de Nîmes Campagne (Women): Emma
Lavigne
Grand Prix de la Nivelle (Men): Pierre-Auguste Mary
Grand Prix de la Nivelle (Women): Irene Rollan (ESP)

## Europe (continued)

Grand Prix de Palmola (Men): Nelson Da Silva Ramos
Grand Prix du Pau (Men): Maxime Radureau
Grand Prix du Pau (Women): Emma Grechi
Grand Prix de Savoie (Men): Gregoire Schoeb
Grand Prix de Savoie (Women): Julie Toletti
Grand Prix de Saint Germain (Men): Mathieu Decottignies-Lafon
Grand Prix de Saint Germain (Women): Anaelle Carnet
Grand Prix de Saint Malo (Men): Charly Venien
Grand Prix de Saint-Nom-La-Breteche (Men): Anthony Renard
Grand Prix de Saint-Nom-La-Breteche (Women): Pauline Loulier
Grand Prix de Troyes la Cordelieres (Men): Eric Pery
Grand Prix de Troyes la Cordelieres (Women): Orphee Bugnard
Grand Prix de Valgarde (Men): Anthony Tron
Grand Prix de Valgarde (Women): Emilie Alonso
Grand Prix du Vaudreuil (Men): Lambert Cochet
Grand Prix Vichy Val d'Allier (Men): Baptiste Courtachon
Grand Prix Vichy Val d'Allier (Women): Celia Mansour
Grand Prix of Volcanoes: Betrant Noel
Grand Prix Wallaert Devilder (Men): Felix Mory
Saint Donat Grand Prix (Men): Victor Veyret
Saint Donat Grand Prix (Women): Mathilda Cappeliez

### Germany
Population: 80.4m
Golfers: 635,079          Golf Courses: 719
Men's Stroke Play Champion: Sebastian Schwind[1]
Men's Match Play Champion: Nicolai von Dellingshausen
Women's Stroke Play Champion: Olivia Cowan[2]
Women's Match Play Champion: Karolin Lampert
International Men's Amateur Championship: Maximilian Rotluff[1]
International Women's Amateur Championship: Emma Broze (FRA)[2]
German National Girls: Amina Wolf
German Girls Open: Emily Kristine Pedersen (DEN)
Junior Champion (Boys): Max Schmitt

### Hungary
Population: 9.9m
Golfers: 1,419          Golf Courses: 15
Men's Champion: Vince van Veen (NED)[1]
Women's Champion: Csilla Lajtai Rozsa
Junior Champion (Boys): Yannick Schutz (GER)
Junior Champion (Girls): Csilla Lajtai Rozsa

### Iceland
Population: 323,810
Golfers: 16,641          Golf Courses: 65
Women's Champion: Olafia Kristinsdottir
Junior Stroke Play Champion (Boys): Isak Jasonarson
Junior Stroke Play Champion (Girls): Anna Solveig Snorradottir

### Ireland (N. Ireland and Rep. of Ireland)
Population: 6.3m
Golfers: 208,120          Golf Courses: 416
Irish Amateur Open Championship – Royal Dublin: Robbie Cannon (Balbriggan) (beat Gavin Moyniham and Graeme Robertson (SCO) at 4th extra hole)[1]
Irish Close Amateur Championship – Connemara: Cormac Sharvin (Ardglass) beat Paul Dunne (Greystones) 1 hole[1]
Irish Women's Close Amateur Championship – Ballybunion: Paula Grant (Lisburn) beat Lisa Maguire (Slieve Russell) at 19th[2]
Irish Women's Open Amateur Stroke Play Championship – The Castle, Dublin: Meghan MacLaren (ENG)[2]
Irish Seniors' Amateur Open Championship – Malone: M Quirke (Doneraile)[1]
Irish Seniors' Amateur Close Championship – Portumna: Garth McGimpsey (Bangor)[1]
Irish Senior Women's Close Amateur Championship – Woodenbridge: Suzanne Corcoran (Portumna) beat Carol Wickham (Laytown and Bettystown) 3 and 2. Medallist: Suzanne Corcoran 147[2]
Irish Women's Senior Championship – Castlerock GC: Gertie McMullen (The Island)[2]
Irish Boys' Open Championship – Lisburn: Robin Dawson[3]
Irish Youths Close Championship – Claremorris GC: Tiarnan McLarnon[3]
Irish Boys' Under-15 Open Championship – West Waterford CC: Kevin Le Blanc[3]
Irish Boys' Inter-Provincial Championship – Royal Co Down GC: Leinster
Irish U18 Open Stroke Play – Roganstown GC: Olivia Mehaffey
Irish Girls Amateur Close Championship – Ballyliffin,: Julie McCarthy
Irish Girls' Inter-Provincial Championship – Ballinrobe GC: Ulster

### Italy
Population: 59.7m
Golfers: 101,817          Golf Courses: 278
Italian International Amateur Championship (Men): Federico Zucchetti beat beat Jacopi Jori 6 and 5[1]
Italian International Amateur Championship (Women): Chloe Leurquin (BEL) (pro)
Men's Stroke Play Champion: Edoardo Raffae Lipparelli[1]
Women's Stroke Play Champion: Roberta Liti[2]
Women's Match Play Champion: Barbara Borin
Mid-Amateur Championship: (Men): Gianluca Bolla
Mid-Amateur Championship: (Women): Gianluca Bolla
Senior Champion (Men): Vincenzo Sita
Senior Champion (Women): Antonella Manuli
Junior Champion (Boys): Andrea Romano (U14); Kristoffer Reitan (NOR) (U16); Giacomo Garbin (U18)
Junior Champion (Girls): Amber Lee Svendsen (U14); Camilla Mazzola (U18)

**Latvia**
Population: 2m
Golfers: 900          Golf Courses: 3
Latvian National Amateur Championship (Men) – Ozo:
Karlis Broders[1]
Latvian National Amateur Championship (Women) –
Ozo: Linda Dobele[2]
Men's Match Play Champion: Roberts Eimanhis beat
Roberts Biss 4 and 3[1]
Women's Match Play Champion: Linda Dobele
Latvian Open Amateur Championship (Women): Mara
Puisite
Junior Champion (Boys): Roberts Biss

**Liechtenstein**
Population: 36,656
Golfers: 302          Golf Courses: 1
Liechtenstein Open Amateur Championship:
Sebastian Schredt (GER)[1]
Liechtenstein Open Ladies' Amateur Championship:
Christine Tinner-Rampone (GER)[2]

**Lithuania**
Population: 2.9m
Golfers: 500          Golf Courses: 6
Lithuanian Open Amateur (Men): Claas-Eric Borges
(GER)[1]
Lithuanian Open Amateur (Women): Anna Diana
Svanka (LAT)[2]

**Luxembourg**
Population: 537,000
Golfers: 3,890          Golf Courses: 6
Men's Champion: Mac Biwar[1]
International Men's Champion: Edoardo Torrieri (ITA)[1]
International Women's Champion: Leena Makkonen
(FIN)
Women's Champion: Jacqueline Klepper[2]

**The Netherlands**
Population: 16.7m
Golfers: 388,493          Golf Courses: 229
Men's Match Play Champion: Darius van Driel
Netherlands National Open Championship (Women):
Dewi Weber
U21 Match Play (Boys): Axel Geers
U21 Match Play (Girls): Dewi Weber
Dutch National Match Play Championship: Myrte
Eikenaar
Dutch Junior Open (Boys): Michael Kraaij
Dutch Junior Open (Girls): Lauren Taylor (ENG) (pro)

**Poland**
Population: 38.5m
Golfers: 3,008          Golf Courses: 27
Men's Champion: Mateusz Gradecki[1]
Polish Match Play Championship: Adrian Meronk
Women's Stroke Play Champion: Ludovica Farina (ITA)
Women's Match Play Champion: Katarzyna Selwent
Mid-Amateur Champion (Men): Michael Kasprowicz[1]
Senior Champion (Men): Henryk Konopa[1]
Polish Junior Championship (Boys): Jan Szmidt
Polish Junior Championship (Girls): Anna Diana Svanka
TOYA Polish Junior (Girls): Antonia von Wnuck (GER)
Polish 19-34 Championship: Adrian Kaczala

**Portugal**
Population: 10.5m
Golfers: 14,198          Golf Courses: 87
Portuguese International Amateur Championship:
Goncalo Pinto[1]
Portuguese International Ladies Amateur: Clara Baena
(ESP)
Portuguese Federation Cup (Men): Miguel Gaspar
Portuguese Federation Cup (Women): Susana Mendes
Ribeiro
Portuguese National Championship (Men): Pedro
Almeida
Portuguese National Championship (Women): Susana
Mendes Ribeiro
National Youths (Boys): Joao Magalhaes
National Youths (Girls): Leonor Bessa

**Russia**
Population: 143.4m
Golfers: 500          Golf Courses: 17
Men's Champion: Johannes Schwab (AUT)[1]
Women's Champion: Nina Pegova[2]

**Scotland**
Population: 5.2m
Golfers: 226,217          Golf Courses: 560
Scottish Amateur Championship – Blairgowrie GC
(Lansdowne course): Alexander Culverwell (Dunbar)
beat James White (Lundin) 2 and 1[1]
Scottish Open Amateur Stroke Play Championship –
Southerness: Garrick Porteous (ENG)[1]
Scottish Ladies' Close Amateur Championship –
Tain: Alyson McKechin (Elderslie) beat Clara Young
(North Berwick) 3 and 2[2]
Scottish Ladies' Open Stroke Play Championship
(Helen Holm Trophy) – Troon Portland & Old
Course Troon: Olivia Winning (Rotherham)[2]
Scottish Seniors Open Amateur Stroke Play
Championship – Elie: Richard Latham (ENG)[1]
Scottish Seniors Match Play Championship – Alyth: Jim
Watt (Edzell) beat Lindsay Blair (Grangemouth) 1
hole[1]
Scottish Senior Ladies' (Close) Amateur
Championship – West Linton: Stroke Play: Anna Telfer.
Match Play: Fiona Hunter (Southerness) beat
Kathleen Sutherland (Royal Montrose) 2 and 1[2]
Scottish Champion of Champions (Men) – Leven: Scott
Barrowman (Dollar)[1]
Scottish Champion of Champions (Women) – Glasgow
Gailes: Megan Briggs (Renfrewshire)[2]
Scottish Women's Stroke Play Foursomes: Anne Laing
and Lindsay Mathie[2]
Scottish Ladies County Championship – Stirling GC:
Aberdeenshire[2]
Scottish Veteran Ladies – Blairgowrie: Alison Bartlett
beat Alex Glennie 5 and 4[2]
Scottish Boys Championship – Monifieth: Bradley Neil
(Blairgowrie) beat Ewan Scott (St Andrews) 4 and 2[3]
Scottish Boys' Open Stroke Play Championship – The
Roxburghe Hotel & GC: Bob MacIntyre[3]
Scottish Boys Under-16 Open Stroke Play
Championship – Portlethen: Matthieu Caron (FRA)[3]
Scottish Youths Open Stroke Play Championship –
Lanark: Robert MacIntyre (Glencruitten)[3]
Scottish Junior Open Stroke Play – Inverness GC:
Jessica Meek

## Europe (continued)

Scottish Boys' Area Team Championship – Prestwick St Cuthbert: Glasgow[3]

Scottish Girls' (Close) Stroke Play – Ranfurly Castle GC: Connie Jaffrey

SLGA Under-16 Stroke Play Championship – Strathmore: Alice Hewson (Berkhamstead)[4]

### Slovakia
Population: 5.4m
Golfers: 7,200          Golf Courses: 14
Men's Champion: Peter Valasek Jr[1]
Open Amateur Champion (Men): Vitek Novak (CZE)[1]
Slovak National Match Play Championship: Jan Friesz Jr beat Peter Valasek  4 and 2[1]
Open Amateur Champion (Women): Katerina Vlasinova (CZE)[2]
Women's Stroke Play Champion: Natalie Heckova[2]
Women's Match Play Champion: Natalie Heckova beat Lina Sekerkova  2 and 1[2]
Mid-Amateur (Men): Tomas Vymazal
Junior Champion (Boys): Jan Friesz
Junior Champion (Girls): Natalia Heckova

### Slovenia
Population: 2m
Golfers: 8,762          Golf Courses: 13
Men's International Champion: Teemu Bakker (FIN)[1]
Women's International Champion: Katja Pogacar[2]
Mid-Amateur (Men): Marko Stirn

International Slovenian Boys: Vitek Novak
Slovenian Junior Masters: Lara Jecnik

### Spain
Population: 46.7m
Golfers: 313,787          Golf Courses: 345
Spanish Amateur Championship – Las Lomas-Bosque GC: Emilio Cuartero Blanco[1]
Spanish International Championship: Reeve Whitson (IRL) beat Neil Raymond (ENG)  4 and 3
Women's Amateur Champion: Emily Kristine Pedersen (DEN)
Spanish International Stroke Play (Women): Luna Sobron[2]
Spanish International Senior Amateur: Bart Nolte (NED)
Junior Champion (Boys): Jorge Simon
Spanish University Championship (Men): Angel Acha Sanchez
Spanish University Championship (Women): Luna Sobron

### Switzerland
Population: 8m
Golfers: 85,758          Golf Courses: 95
Men's Match Play Champion: Nicolas Thommen
Women's Match Play Champion: Albane Valenzuela
International Men's Champion: Matthie Fenasse (FRA)[1]

International Women's Champion: Ursa Orehek (SLO)[2]
Junior Champion (Boys): Jeremy Freiburghaus
Junior Champion (Girls): Azelia Meichtry

### Turkey
Population: 75.6m
Golfers: 5,649          Golf Courses: 20
Turkish Amateur Championship (Men): Hamza Sayin
Turkish Amateur Championship (Women): Elcin Ulu
Turkish Amateur Open (Men): Hamza Sayin[1]
Turkish Amateur Open (Women): Karolina Vlckova (CZE)[2]

### Ukraine
Population: 45.4m
Golfers: 547          Golf Courses: 4
Men's Champion: Zan Luka Stirn (SLO)

### Wales
Population: 3m
Golfers: 55,079          Golf Courses: 157
Welsh Amateur Championship – Ashburnham GC: Jack Bush beat Mike Hearne  9 and 8[1]
Welsh Open Amateur Stroke Play Championship – Royal Porthcawl: Rhys Pugh[1]
Welsh Ladies' Close Amateur Championship – Nefyn and District: Amy Boulden[2]
Welsh Ladies' Open Amateur Stroke Play Championship – The Vale: Amy Boulden[2]
Welsh Mid-Amateur – Machynys Peninsula G&CC: James Bunch (SCO)
Welsh Seniors' Close Amateur Championship – Aberdovey: Basil Griffiths[1]
Welsh Seniors' Open Championship – Abergele GC: Andrew Stracey[1]
Welsh Senior Ladies' Championship – Denbigh GC: Jane Rees (Hendon)[2]
Welsh Tournament of Champions: Luke Thomas (Pontypridd GC)[1]
Welsh Ladies County Championship: Mid Wales (Northern Division); Glamorgan (Southern Division)
Welsh Ladies Team Championship – Cardigan: Southerndown[2]
Welsh Boys' Championship – Glamorganshire GC: Kyle Harman (Cottrell Park) beat Joshua Davies (Celtic Manor)  one hole[3]
Welsh Boys' Under-13 Championship – Carmarthen GC: Sam Mayer (Whitchurch)[3]
Welsh Boys' Under-15 Championship – Carmarthen GC: Elis Lewis (Borth and Ynsylas)[3]
Welsh Open Youths' Championship – Monmouthshire: William Whiteoak[3]
Welsh Girls' Championship – Caernarfon GC: Nia Greville (Ashburnham) beat Megan Lockett (Huddersfield)  2 and 1[4]
Welsh Girls' Under-16 – Carnarfon GC: Nia Greville

# PART VIII

# Junior Tournaments and Events

# Boys' and Youths' Tournaments

For past results see earlier editions of *The R&A Golfer's Handbook*

## British Boys' Amateur Championship  *Royal Liverpool GC and Wallasey GC*

**Semi-Finals:**  Michael Hirmer (GER) beat Paul Elissalde (FRA)  1 hole
Ewen Ferguson (SCO) beat Bradley Moore (ENG)  4 and 3
**Final:**  Ewen Ferguson beat Michael Hirmer  10 and 9
**Medallist:** Jack Hermeston (ENG)  74-67—141

## British Youths Amateur Championship

This championship bridged the gap between the Boys and the Men's tournaments from 1954 until 1994, when it was discontinued because it was no longer needed. The date on the schedule was used to introduce the Mid Amateur Championship for players over 25 but this event was discontinued after 2007.

*For results see the R&A website – www.randa.org*

## Canadian International Junior Challenge  *OslerBrook G&CC*

| | | |
|---|---|---|
| 1 | Tony Gil | 70-72-72—214 |
| 2 | Patrick Murphy | 74-73-71—218 |
| | Billy Spooner (ENG) | 72-73-73—218 |

## Canadian Junior Boys' Championship  *Timberwolf GC*

| | | |
|---|---|---|
| 1 | Kevin Kwon | 64-74-69-69—276 |
| 2 | Matthew Scobie | 68-73-70-70—281 |
| 3 | Joseph Kremer | 72-70-75-65—282 |

## English Boys' Under-16 Championship  (McGregor Trophy)  *Seacroft GC*

| | | |
|---|---|---|
| 1 | Marco Penge (Worthing) | 70-73-67-73—283 |
| 2 | Billy Spooner (Boston) | 77-70-70-69—286 |
| | Bradley Moore (Kedlestone Park) | 70-72-70-74—286 |

## English Boys' Under-18 Championship  (Carris Trophy)  *West Lancs GC (Blue Tees)*

| | | |
|---|---|---|
| 1 | Ben Amor (Marlborough)* | 74-67-72-73—286 |
| 2 | Jamie Li (Bath) | 73-74-69-70—286 |
| | Renato Paratore (ITA) | 71-72-70-73—286 |

*Amor won at the second extra hole

## English Junior County Champion of Champions  *Woodhall Spa GC*

| | | |
|---|---|---|
| 1 | Jordan Winsdale (Boston) | 75-69—144 |
| 2 | Adam Chapman (Windermere) | 71-74—145 |
| 3 | Oliver Farrell (Evesham) | 74-74—148 |

## Highland Spring Junior Masters

This event will next be held in 2014

# Hong Kong Junior Close Championship  *Clearwater Bay G&CC*

| | | |
|---|---|---|
| 1 | Chung Ho Justin Lok* | 77-75—152 |
| 2 | Michael Regan Wong | 76-76—152 |

(*Lok won in play-off)

| | | |
|---|---|---|
| 3 | Ambrose Tam | 80-73—153 |
| | Shuai Ming Benjamin Wong | 79-74—153 |

# Hong Kong Junior Open Championship  *HKGC Deep Water Bay*

| | | |
|---|---|---|
| 1 | Lucas Lam | 72-69—141 |
| 2 | Ting Wei Hsieh (TPE) | 79-72—151 |
| | Leon Philip D'Souza | 77-74—151 |

# Irish Boys' Open Championship  (inaugurated 1983)  *Lisburn GC*

| | | |
|---|---|---|
| 1 | Robin Dawson (Fiathlegg)* | 67-69-72-74—282 |
| 2 | Marco Penge (ENG) | 69-72-72-69—282 |

*Dawson won at the third extra hole

| | | |
|---|---|---|
| 3 | Jack Singh Brar (ENG) | 70-68-72-73—283 |

Under 16 Trophy: M Penge; Under 17 Trophy: J Singh Brar

# Irish Boys' Under-15 Open Championship  *West Waterford GC*

| | | |
|---|---|---|
| 1 | Kevin Le Blanc (The Island) | 70-70—140 |
| 2 | John Gough (ENG) | 74-69—143 |
| 3 | Daniel List (AUS) | 79-68—147 |

# Irish Youths Amateur Close Championship  (inaugurated 1969)  *Claremorris GC*

| | | |
|---|---|---|
| 1 | Tiarnan McLarnon (Massareene) | 71-66-72-78—287 |
| 2 | Stuart Grehan (Tullamore) | 74-74-71-70—289 |
| | Alan Lowry (Esker Hills) | 75-72-71-71—289 |

# Scottish Boys' Championship  *Monifieth GC*

**Semi-Finals:**  Ewan Scott (St Andrews) beat Ben Kinsley (St Andrews) 2 and 1
Bradley Neil (Blairgowrie) beat Ben Craggs (Glenbervie) 4 and 3

**Final:**  Neil beat Scott 4 and 2

# Scottish Boys Under-16 Open Stroke Play Championship  (inaug. 1990)  *Portlethen*

| | | |
|---|---|---|
| 1 | Matthieu Caron (FRA) | 68-72-70-75—285 |
| 2 | Edgar Catherine (FRA) | 74-75-68-69—286 |
| | Guido Migliozzi (ITA) | 75-69-69-73—286 |

# Stephen Gallacher Foundation Scottish Boys Stroke Play Championship
*The Roxburghe GC*

| | | |
|---|---|---|
| 1 | Robert Macintyre (Glencruiten) | 66-66-66—198 |
| 2 | Ewen Ferguson (Bearsden) | 69-70-68—207 |
| | Connor Syme (Dumfries and County) | 67-70-70—207 |

# Golf Data Lab Scottish Youths Championship  (inaugurated 1979)  *Lanark GC*

| | | |
|---|---|---|
| 1 | Robert MacIntyre (Glencruitten) | 72-73-72-67—284 |
| 2 | Charlie Macneal (Prestwick) | 71-72-72-72—287 |
| 3 | Joey Lamb (Wilpshire) | 71-71-72-74—288 |

## Singapore Junior Championship *Keppel Club*

| | | |
|---|---|---|
| 1 | Yash Majmidar (IND) | 75-74-72—221 |
| 2 | Lucius Toh Zheng Xhan | 74-75-75—224 |
| 3 | Nicklaus Chiam Yew Chun | 76-74-76—226 |

## South African Under-19 Championship *Benoni CC*

| | | |
|---|---|---|
| 1 | Zander Gous (Piet Retief) | 69-63-73—205 |
| 2 | Kyle McClatchie (Serengeti) | 68-66-74—208 |
| 3 | Hennie du Plessis (Polokwane) | 71-68-73—212 |

## South African Boys Match Play Championship *Benoni CC*

**Semi-Finals:** Zander Gous beat P J Boshoff  2 holes
Aneurin Gounden beat Kyle McClatchie  5 and 3
**Final:** Zander Gous beat Aneurin Gounden  at 37th

## Welsh Boys' Championship (inaugurated 1954) *Glamorganshire GC*

**Leading qualifier:** Kyle Harman (Cotterell Park) 62-69—131
**Semi-Finals:** Kyle Harman (Cottrell Park) beat Thomas Davies (Penrhos) 3 and 2
Joshua Davies (Celtic Manor) beat Charlie Spencer-White (Llanrindod Wells) 5 and 4
**Final:** Kyle Harman beat Joshua Davies 1 hole

## Welsh Boys Under-13 Championship *Carmarthen GC*

| | | |
|---|---|---|
| 1 | Sam Mayer (Whitchurch) | 77 |
| 2 | Harry Watkins (The Grove) | 79 |
| | Archie Davies  (Spalding) | 79 |
| | Ian Price (Carmarthen) | 79 |

## Welsh Boys' Under-15 Championship (inaugurated 1985) *Carmarthen GC*

| | | |
|---|---|---|
| 1 | Elis Lewis (Borth and Ynsylas) | 74-70—144 |
| 2 | Tomos Jones (Aberdovey) | 73-75—148 |
| 3 | Laurence Vargas (St Pierre) | 74-76—150 |

## Welsh Open Youths' Championship (inaugurated 1993) *Monmouthshire GC*

| | | |
|---|---|---|
| 1 | William Whiteoak | 66-71-62-65—264 |
| 2 | Nick Marsh | 70-69-69-65—273 |
| 3 | Ben Amor | 76-67-66-65—274 |

## US Junior Amateur Championship *Martis Camp Club, Truckee, CA*

**Semi-finals:** Davis Riley beat John Augensteil 4 and 3
Scottie Scheffler beat Doug Ghim 6 and 4
**Finals:** Scheffler beat Riley 2 and 1

## Enjoy Jakarta World Junior Golf Championship *Damai Indah GC, Jakarta, Indonesia*

| | | |
|---|---|---|
| 1 | Sarit Suwannarut (THA) | 76-71-72-75—294 |
| 2 | Feroz Singh Garewal (IND) | 73-73-78-74—298 |
| 3 | Kevin C Akbar (INA) | 73-76-78-73—300 |

## Peter McEvoy Trophy (inaugurated 1988)   *always at Copt Heath*

| | | |
|---|---|---|
| 1 | Bradley Moore (Kedleston Park) | 69-74-71-73—287 |
| 2 | Ashton Turner (Kenwick Park) | 69-75-71-75—290 |
| 3 | Adam Chapman (Windermere) | 76-74-73-68—291 |
| | Harry Ellis (Windermere) | 74-74-73-70—291 |
| | Jack Singh Brar (Brockenhurst Manor) | 75-74-70-72—291 |

## Midland Boys' Amateur Championship   *Birstall GC*

| | | |
|---|---|---|
| 1 | Billy Spooner (Boston)* | 72-68—138 |
| 2 | Ben Robinson (Vale) | 70-68—138 |
| *(*Spooner won play-off)* | | |
| 3 | Richard Mansell (Beau Desert) | 72-67—139 |

## Midland Youths' Championship   *Stoke Rochford GC*

| | | |
|---|---|---|
| 1 | Josh Carpenter (Cleobury) | 71-67-69-69—276 |
| 2 | Sam Claypole (Horsley Lodge) | 69-71-69-68—277 |
| | Jordan Boulton (Notts) | 70-69-66-72—277 |

## Sir Henry Cooper Junior Masters   *Nizels G&CC. Kent*

| | | |
|---|---|---|
| 1 | Matty Lamb (Hexham) | 73-71-70-68—282 |
| 2 | Adam Chapman (Windermere) | 69-75-71-69—284 |
| 3 | Jordan Wrisdale (Boston) | 70-74-74-69—287 |
| | Jack Singh Brar (Brokenhurst Manor) | 71-74-70-72—287 |

## Paul Lawrie Golf Foundation Junior Open   *Deeside GC*

| | | |
|---|---|---|
| 1 | Sam Locke* (Banchory) | 69 |
| 2 | Michael Lawrie (Deeside) | 69 |
| *Locke won in play-off* | | |
| 3 | Craig Lawrie (Deeside) | 70 |

## Paul Lawrie Golf Foundation Match Play Championship   *Newmacher GC*

**Semi-Finals:**   Lewis McWilliam (Aboyne) beat Calvin Cheyne (Newmacher) 2 and 1
Craig Lawrie (Deeside) beat Lewys Anderson (Deeside) 6 and 5

**Final:**   Craig Lawrie beat Lewis McWilliam 4 and 3

**Mashie** – from the Scottish word *mash* or the French word *massé* meaning sledgehammer (originally mace), the term may have been borrowed from billiards where it is employed to describe a downward jabbing stroke. The mashie, a lofted iron club which is no longer in use, was introduced in c1880 and was employed for pitching with backspin.

# Team Events

## European Boys Team Championship   *Murcar GC, Scotland*

**Stroke Play qualification:** I Italy 715; 2 England 718; 3 Scotland 721; 4 France 726

| Individual: | | | |
|---|---|---|---|
| | I | Ashton Turner (ENG) | 70-64—134 |
| | 2 | Connor Syme (SCO) | 70-66—136 |
| | 3 | Robert McIntyre (SCO) | 74-67—137 |
| | | Teodoro Soldati (ITA) | 70-71—137 |

**Final team placings:** I France; 2 Norway; 3 Italy; 4 England; 5 Ireland; 6 Denmark; 7 Sweden; 8 Scotland; 9 Spain; 10 Austria; 11 Germany; 12 Netherlands; 13 Czech Republic; 14 Finland; 15 Belgium; 16 Switzerland

**Winning team:** Paul Elissalde, Joris Etliin, Romain Langasque, Nicolas Manifacier, Pierre Mazier and Victor Veyret

**Team Results:**

**"A" Flight – Day One:** Norway 4, Scotland 3; Italy 5, Sweden 2; France 5, Denmark 2; Ireland 1, England 6

**Day Two:** Italy 3; France 4; Norway 5, England 2; Sweden 1½, Denmark 3½; Scotland 1½, Ireland 3½

**Day Three – Final:** France 4, Norway 3; Italy 4½, England 2½; Ireland 3, Denmark 2; Sweden 4½, Scotland ½

**"B" Flight – Day One:** Belgium 2, Austria 3; Netherlands 5, Czech Republic 0; Spain 3½, Finland 1½; Switzerland 0, Germany 5

**Day Two:** Austria 3½, Netherlands 1½ ; Spain 3½, Germany 1½; Belgium 2, Czech Republic 3; Finland 3, Switzerland 2

**Day Three:** Austria ½, Spain 4½; Czech Republic 3, Finland 2; Netherland 1½, Germany 3½; Belgium 3, Switzerland 2

---

## Great Britain & Ireland v Continent of Europe   (Jacques Léglise Trophy)

*Royal St Davids GC, Wales*

**Captains:** GB&I: Ashton Turner (ENG), Europe: Miguel Franco de Sousa (POR)

GB&I names first:

*First Day* **– Foursomes**

Ewen Ferguson (SCO) and Bradley Neil (SCO) beat Dominic Foos (GER) and Renato Paratore (ITA)   5 and 4
Ashton Turner (ENG) and Marco Penge (ENG) lost to Mario Galiano (ESP) and Ivan Cantero (ESP)   4 and 3
Bradley Moore (ENG) and Robin Dawson (IRL) beat Kristoffer Ventura (NOR) and Michael Hirmer (GER)   1 hole
Robert MacIntyre (SCO) and Connor Syme (SCO) beat Romain Langasque (FRA) and Nicolas Manifacier (FRA)   3 and 2

**Singles**

| | |
|---|---|
| Ferguson lost to Foos 8 and 7 | Dawson beat Cantero 4 and 3 |
| Neil beat Paul Elissalde (FRA) 1 hole | Penge beat Ventura 4 and 2 |
| Turner halved with Galiano | MacIntyre lost Hirmer 1 hole |
| Ben Amor (ENG) lost to Paratore 6 and 4 | Syme beat Langasque 5 and 3 |

*Second Day* **– Foursomes**

Turner and Penge beat Paratore and Foos   5 and 4
Ferguson and Neil halved with Galiano and Cantera
Moore and Dawson halved with Elissalde and Langasque
MacIntyre and Syme beat Ventura and Manifacier   3 and 2

**Singles**

| | |
|---|---|
| Ferguson lost to Paratore 2 and 1 | Penge beat Langasque 3 and 2 |
| Turner halved with Hirmer | Dawson beat Manifacier 4 and 3 |
| Neil lost to Cantero 2 holes | Syme lost to Foos 3 and 2 |
| Moore beat Galiano 5 and 4 | MacIntyre beat Elissalde 4 and 2 |

**Match result:** Great Britain and Ireland 15, Continent of Europe 5

# European Boys Challenge Trophy  Skalica GC, Slovakia

| | | |
|---|---|---|
| 1 | Belgium | 368-360-369—1,097 |
| 2 | Wales | 369-361-368—1,098 |
| 3 | Iceland | 373-362-367—1,102 |

4 Finland 1,104; 5 Portugal 1,106; 6 Switzerland 1,112; 7 Slovenia 1,122; 8 Slovakia 1,149; 9 Poland 1,157; 10 Russia 1,160; 11 Hungary 1,233

**Individual competition:**

| | | |
|---|---|---|
| 1 | Gisli Sveinbergsson (ISL) | 72-69-70—211 |
| 2 | Ingi Fannar Steingrimsson (ISL) | 72-70-72—214 |
| 3 | Otto Vanhatalo (FIN) | 78-69-69—216 |
| | Jeremy Freiburghaus (SUI) | 76-70-70—216 |
| | Goncalo Costa (POR) | 75-70-71—216 |

**Winning team:** Gaetan van Baarle, Yohan Cauwembergh, Basile Devillet, Giovanni Tadiotto, Alan de Bondt, Aurian Capart

# Boys' Home Internationals (R&A Trophy)  (inaugurated 1985)  Forest Pines GC

| | |
|---|---|
| Day One: | England 10½, Wales 4½; Scotland 7½, Ireland 7½ |
| Day Two: | England 7, Ireland 8; Scotland 12½, Wales 2½ |
| Day Three: | Ireland 9½, Wales 5½; Scotland 6½, England 7½ |

| Final ranking | Games won | Points won |
|---|---|---|
| 1 Ireland | 25 | 2½ |
| 2 England | 26 | 2 |
| 3 Scotland | 26½ | 1½ |
| 4 Wales | 12½ | 0 |

**Winning Team:** Robin Dawson, James Sugrue, Paul McBride, Jack Walsh, Gareth Lappin, Justin Hood, Sean Flanagan, Ronan Mullarney, Alec Myles, Rowan Lester and David Carey

# English Boys County Championships  Keddleston Park GC

| | |
|---|---|
| **Day One:** | Yorkshire 5½, Staffordshire 3½ |
| | Devon 4, Hampshire, Isle of Wight and Channel Islands 5 |
| **Day Two:** | Yorkshire 3½, Devon 5½ |
| | Hampshire, Isle of Wight and Channel Islands 3½, Staffordshire 5½ |
| **Day Three:** | Yorkshire 6½, Hampshire, Isle of Wight and Channel Islands 2½ |
| | Devon 1, Staffordshire 8 |

| Final placings | P | W | D | L | Games won |
|---|---|---|---|---|---|
| 1 Staffordshire | 3 | 2 | 0 | 1 | 17 |
| 2 Yorkshire | 3 | 2 | 0 | 1 | 15½ |
| 3 Hampshire, Isle of Wight and Channel Islands | 3 | 1 | 0 | 2 | 11 |
| 4 Devon | 3 | 1 | 0 | 2 | 10½ |

**Winning Team:** Cameron Long, Peter Booker, Michael Dewsbury, Harrison Quirk, Robert Burlison, Daniel Sutton and Gian-Marco Petrozzi

# Irish Boys' Inter-Provincial Championship  Lee Valley GC

**Final Placings:** 1 Leinster, 2 Connacht, 3 Munster, 4 Ulster

**Day One:** Leinster 7, Connacht 3; Ulster 6, Munster 4
**Day Two:** Munster 7½, Leinster 2½; Connacht 6½, Ulster 3½
**Day Three:** Connacht 5½, Munster 4½; Leinster 6½, Ulster 3½

**Winning team:** Jack Walsh, Rowan Lester, Jake Whelan, Eoin Leonard, David Carey, Alex Myles and Paul McBride

## Dunfermline BS Scottish Boys Area Team Championship   *Prestwick St Cuthbert GC*

| | | Foursomes | Singles | |
|---|---|---|---|---|
| 1 | Glasgow | 147 | 206 | 353 |
| 2 | North-East | 150 | 210 | 360 |
| 3 | Angus | 142 | 218 | 360 |

4 Ayrshire 362; 5 Lothians, North 363; 7 Dunbartonshire 364; 8 Argyll and Bute 367; 9 Renfrewshire 371; 10 Perth and Kinross 372; 11 Fife 373; 12 South 374; 13 Lanarkshire 378; 14 Stirlingshire 380; 15 Clackmannanshire 396; 16 Borders 397

**Winning team:** George Burns. Alan Waugh, Callum Fyfe and Fraser Davren

---

## Toyota Junior World Cup   *Toyota City, Japan*

**Individual:**

| 1 | Jorge Garcia (VEN) | 69-67-67-69—272 |
|---|---|---|
| 2 | Lucas Herbert (AUS) | 71-66-68-70—275 |
| 3 | Thriston Lawrence (RSA) | 70-68-69-69—276 |

**Team event:**

| 1 | Venezuela | 207-210-208-211—836 |
|---|---|---|
| 2 | Australia | 209-205-212-211—837 |
| 3 | Mexico | 208-206-214-214—842 |

4 Japan 844; 5 South Africa 845; 6 USA 847; 7 Chinese Taipei 848; 8 Korea 850; 9 Sweden 853; 10 Chile 855; 11 Germany 862; 12 Costa Rica 879

**Winning team:** George Trujillo, Gustao Morantes, Gustavo Leon and Jorge Garcia

---

## All-Africa Junior Golf Challenge   *Le Touessrok, Mauritius*

| 1 | South Africa | 230-216-211-227—884 |
|---|---|---|
| 2 | Zimbabwe | 240-238-233-231—942 |
| 3 | Zambia | 244-244-242-241—971 |
| 4 | Uganda | 244-231-246-253—974 |
| 5 | Tunisia | 248-253-227-252—980 |
| 6 | Réunion | 248-244-244-250—986 |
| | Kenya | 252-246-237-251—986 |
| 8 | Namibia | 243-257-247-254—1,001 |
| 9 | Swaziland | 267-247-241-248—1,003 |
| 10 | Botswana | 261-250-266-255—1,032 |
| 11 | Mauritius | 269-263-247-280—1,059 |
| 12 | Madagascar | 293-294-291-289—1,167 |

**Winning team:** Thriston Lawrence, Jason Froneman, Tristen Strydom and James du Preez

---

## South African Under-19 Inter-Provincial Championship   *Bellville GC, Cape Town*

**A Section**

| | | Pld | W | L | D | Pts |
|---|---|---|---|---|---|---|
| 1 | Central Gauteng | 5 | 4 | 0 | 1 | 39 |
| 2 | Western Province | 5 | 3 | 1 | 1 | 36½ |
| 3 | Gauteng North | 5 | 3 | 2 | 0 | 30½ |
| 4 | Ekurhuleni | 5 | 2 | 1 | 2 | 31 |
| 5 | Eastern Province | 5 | 0 | 5 | 0 | 24 |
| 6 | Limpopo | 5 | 1 | 4 | 0 | 18½ |

**B Section**

| | | Pld | W | L | D | Pts |
|---|---|---|---|---|---|---|
| 1 | Southern Cape | 5 | 5 | 0 | 0 | 42 |
| 2 | North West | 6 | 3 | 1 | 2 | 40 |
| 3 | KwaZulu Natal | 5 | 3 | 1 | 1 | 36½ |
| 4 | Boland | 5 | 3 | 2 | 0 | 33 |
| 5 | Border | 5 | 1 | 3 | 1 | 24 |
| 6 | Mpumalanga | 6 | 0 | 6 | 0 | 22 |
| 7 | Free State & Northern Cape | 5 | 1 | 4 | 0 | 22½ |

# Girls' and Junior Ladies' Tournaments

For past results see earlier editions of *The R&A Golfer's Handbook*

## British Girls' Open Amateur Championship   *Fairhaven GC*

**Semi-Finals:**   Roberta Liti (ITA) beat Michaela Finn (SWE)   4 and 2
                   Jing Yan (CHN) beat Puk Lyng Thomsen (DEN)   1 hole
**Final:**         Jing Yan beat Roberta Liti   1 hole

## Royale Cup Canadian Junior Girls Championship   *Cherry Downs G&CC*

| | | |
|---|---|---|
| 1 | Maddie Szeryk (USA) | 71-69-73-70—283 |
| 2 | Brooke Henderson | 76-77-72-72—297 |
| 3 | Kim Taylor | 76-75-79-71—301 |

## PONcat Dutch Junior Open

| | | |
|---|---|---|
| 1 | Lauren Taylor (ENG) | 71-69-71-69—280 |
| 2 | Marit Harry Van | 73-75-66-68—282 |
|   | Anne van Dam | 67-70-75-70—282 |

## English Girls' Championship   *Oake Manor GC*

| | | |
|---|---|---|
| 1 | Sophie Keech (Parkstone) | 70-68-73-73—284 |
| 2 | Annabel Dimmock (Wentworth) | 68-73-74-74—289 |
| 3 | Emily Slater (Woodhall Spa) | 72-70-74-74—290 |

## English Girls Under 15/13 Championship   *Tiverton GC*

| | | |
|---|---|---|
| 1 | Harriet Allsebrook (Shifnal)* | 75-72-73-79—299 |
| 2 | Victoria Mallett (Sutton Coldfield) | 77-72-78-72—299 |

*Allsebrook won at the fifth extra hole*

| | | |
|---|---|---|
| 3 | Annabel Bailey (Notts Ladies) | 77-75-73-76—301 |

## Highland Spring Junior Masters

This event will next be held in 2014

## Hong Kong Junior Girls Close Championship   *Clearwater Bay G&CC*

| | | |
|---|---|---|
| 1 | Isabella Leung | 74-76—150 |
| 2 | Michelle Cheung | 73-79—152 |
| 3 | Mimi Ho | 78-76—154 |

## Hong Kong Junior Open Championship   *HKGC Deepwater Bay*

| | | |
|---|---|---|
| 1 | Chayanit Wangmahaporn (THA) | 76-73—149 |
| 2 | Kai Wing Li | 81-75—151 |
| 3 | Yu Lun Huang (TPE) | 78-86—164 |

## Irish Girls' Close Championship (Blake Cup) (inaugurated 1951)   *Ballyliffin GC*
**Semi-Finals:**    Olivia Mehaffey (RCD Ladies) beat Shannon Burke (Ballinrobe)  2 and 1
                    Julie McCarthy (Forrest Little) beat Mary Doyle (The Heath)  2 and 1
**Final:**          Julie McCarthy beat Olivia Mehaffey 3 and 2

## Irish Girls' Open Stroke Play Championship    *Roganstown G&CC*
| | | |
|---|---|---|
| 1 | Olivia Mehaffey (RCD Ladies) | 72-77-71—220 |
| 2 | Dulcie Sverdloff (ENG) | 75-73-74—222 |
|   | Marthe Wold (NOR) | 75-71-76—222 |
|   | Sophie Madden (ENG) | 74-74-74—222 |
|   | Marina Hedlund (SWE) | 72-76-74—222 |

## Scottish Junior Ladies Open Stroke Play Championship (inaugurated 1955)
(formerly Scottish Under-21 Girls Open Stroke Play Championship)    *Inverness GC*
| | | |
|---|---|---|
| 1 | Jessica Meek (Carnoustie Ladies) | 68-74-72—214 |
| 2 | Rachael Watton (Mortonhall) | 75-67-74—216 |
|   | Eilidh Briggs (Kilmacolm) | 67-74-75—216 |

## Scottish Girls, Close Amateur Championship    (inaugurated 1960)    *Ranfurly Castle GC*
| | | |
|---|---|---|
| 1 | Emily Dalgetty (Glencorse) | 74-78—152 |
| 2 | Tara MacTaggart (Minto) | 76-77—153 |
| 3 | Heather Munro (Monifieth) | 79-75—154 |
|   | Lauren Whyte (St Regulas) | 77-77—154 |
|   | Connie Jaffrey (Troon Ladies) | 76-78—154 |

## SLGA Under-16 Open Championship    *Strathmore Centre*
| | | |
|---|---|---|
| 1 | Alice Hewson (Berkhamsted) | 73-66—139 |
| 2 | Sophie Hadden (West Sussex) | 73-68—141 |
| 3 | Olivia Mehaffey (R. County Down Ladies) | 73-69—142 |

## St Andrews Junior Ladies
*Golf Monthly Trophy:*                                *St Andrews (Eden and Old Courses)*
**Semi-Finals:**    Rachel Walker (Dumfries and County) beat India Clyburn (Woburn) at 19th
                    Samantha Meese (South Staffordshire) beat Lianna Bailey (Notts Ladies)  1 hole
**Final:**          Samantha Meese beat Rachel Walker  5 and 4

*Girls' Open Quaich:*                                *St Andrews (Strathtyrumand Old Courses)*
**Semi-Finals:**    Courtney Boyes (Wrag Barr) beat Emily Brennan (Trentham)  3 and 2
                    Emma Kennedy (Dumfries and Galloway) beat Kirsty Burgess (Silverknowes)  3 and 2
**Final:**          Final: Emma Kennedy beat Courtney Boyes  3 and 2

## Welsh Girls' Championship (inaugurated 1957)   *Caernarfon GC*
**Leading Qualifier:** Nia Greville (Ashburnham) 73-76—149
**Semi-Finals:**    Nia Greville (Ashburnham) beat Rebecca Ogden (Rhuddian)  3 and 2
                    Megan Lockett (Huddersfield) beat Jordan Ryan (Newport)  8 and 6
**Final:**          Nia Greville beat Megan Lockett  2 and 1

## US Girls' Junior Amateur Championship    *Sycamore Hills GC*
**Semi-finals:**    Gabriella Then (Upland) beat Megan Khang (Rockland)  2 and 1
                    Lakareber Abe (Angleton) beat Bethany Wu (Daimond Bar)  1 hole
**Finals:**         Gabriella Then beat Lakareber Abe  2 and 1

## Enjoy Jakarta World Junior Golf Championship *Damai Indah GC, Jakarta, Indonesia*
| | | |
|---|---|---|
| 1 | Kanyalak Preedasuttijit (THA) | 72-74-69 – 215 |
| 2 | Gavrilla Christina Arya (INA) | 76-74-77 – 226 |
| 3 | Zhu Kai Lin (CHN) | 79-74-74 – 227 |

## Paul Lawrie Foundation Girls Grand Final *Newmacher GC*
**Semi-Finals:** Kimberley Beveridge (Aboyne) w.o. Lauren Watson (Deeside)
Shannon McWilliam (Aboyne) beat Emma Logie (Keith) 3 and 2
**Final:** Kimberley Beveridge beat Shannon McWilliam 4 and 3

## Tournament dedicated to Nelson Mandela

The South African Golf Association (SAGA) dedicated the South African Under-19 Inter-Provincial Championship (see page 460) to the memory of the country's founding president, Nelson Mandela.

SAGA president Andre Pieterse paid tribute to the former president, who passed away at his home on December 5, 2013, at the age of 95.

"We learned with great sadness of the passing of our country's former president," said Pieterse, adding: "Mandela believed that sport could do more to unite a nation that politics could, and everyone in the sporting industry respected him for his relentless efforts to unite the sporting codes in South Africa in order to create a united and proud nation."

## Record run for Sammy

Having won her age group in the Honda Junior Classic for the past three years, 14-year-old Samantha Fuller from Roehampton won for a record breaking fourth time when she beat Kanyanat Saithip from Thailand by a stroke to win the girls' 14–15-year age group in Florida, USA.

The England international who makes regular winter trips to Florida, also ran up her sixth consecutive win in the Pars Florida International Junior Championship during last year's trip.

Sammy's talent clearly runs in the family as her younger sister, Annabell, was the runner-up in the 10–11-year age group at the Honda Junior Classic.

During last winter's trip, Sammy teamed up with English boy champion Ben Amor from Marlborough to represent England Golf in the prestigious Junior Orange Bowl at Biltmore Golf Club, Florida. Sammy ended in 19th position while Ben tied for 28th place.

In another remarkable run of success, England international Lauren Taylor won the Dutch Junior Open girls' title at Golf Club Toxandria for the third consecutive year.

# Team Events

## European Lady Juniors Team Championship

*Discontinued – for past results see the 2008 edition of The R&A Golfer's Handbook*

## European Girls Team Championship   *Linkopings GC, Sweden*

**Stroke Play qualification:** I Spain 362; 2 France 363; England 368

| **Individual:** | I Alejandra Pasarin (ESP) | 69 |
|---|---|---|
| | 2 Amber Ratcliffe (ENG) | 70 |
| | Eva Gilly (FRA) | 70 |

Second round of qualifying cancelled due to inclement weather

**Final team placings:** I Sweden; 2 France; 3 Spain; 4 England; 5 Italy; 6 Scotland; 7 Norway; 8 Finland; 9 Netherlands; 10 Germany; II Ireland; 12 Denmark; 13 Switzerland; 14 Belgium; 15 Czech Republic; 16 Austria; 17 Turkey; 18 Russia; 19 Slovakia

**Winning team:** Linn Andersson. Linnea Strom, Martina Edberg, Emma Svensson Jessica Vasilic and Mia Landegrean

**Team Results:**

**"A" Flight – Day One:** France 5, Norway 2; England 4, Italy 3; Finland I ½, Sweden 5½; Scotland I, Spain 6

**Day Two:** England 3, France 4; Spain I ½, Sweden 5½; Italy 4½, Norway ½; Finland 2, Scotland 3.

**Day Three – Final:** Sweden 4½, France 2½; England I ½, Spain 5½; Italy 5, Scotland 0; Finland I ½ Norway 3½

**"B" Flight – Day One:** Czech Republic 2, Ireland 3; Germany 3½, Belgium I ½; Denmark 3, Switzerland 2; Austria 3, Netherlands 2

**Day Two:** Germany 4, Ireland 2; Denmark 2, Netherlands 3; Belgium 4½, Czech Republic ½; Austria I. Switzerland 4

**Day Three:** German I ½, Netherlands 3½; Denmark I ½, Ireland 3½; Belgium 0, Switzerland 5; Austria I ½, Czech Republic 3½

**"C" Flight – Day One:** Russia 3, Slovakia 2. **Day Two:** Slovakia I, Turkey 4. **Day Three:** Russia I, Turkey 4

---

## Girls Home Internationals *(Stroyan Cup)*   *St Anne's Old Links*

**Day I:**   England 7, Wales 2; Scotland 5, Ireland 4
**Day 2:**   Ireland 4½, Wales 4½ England 5½, Scotland 3½
**Day 3:**   Wales 5, Scotland 4; England 4, Ireland 5

| **Final ranking** | *Games won* | *Points won* |
|---|---|---|
| I England | 16½ | 2 |
| 2 Ireland | 13½ | I ½ |
| 3 Wales | 11½ | I ½ |
| 4 Scotland | 12 ½ | I |

**Winning team:** Gabriella Cowley, Sophie Lamb, Alice Dimmock, Sammy Fuller, Sophie Keech, Alice Hewson, Olivia Winning and Sophie Madden

---

## Junior Solheim Cup   *Englewood, Colorado, USA*

**Captains:** USA: kathy Whitworth; Europe: Janice Moody

**First day – Fourballs:**

Alison Lee and Casey Danielson lost to Shannon Aubert (FRA) and Karolin Lampert (GER) I up
Casie Cathrea and Samantha Wagner halved with Jessica Vasilic (SWE) and Linnea Strom (SWE)
Bethany Wu and Andrea Lee beat Anyssia Herbaut (FRA) and Anne van Dam (NED) 2 and I
Krystal Quihuis and Alexandra Kaui halved with Harang Lee (ESP) and Virginia Elena Carta (ITA)
Nicole Morales and Amy Lee beat Georgia Hall (ENG) and Amber Ratcliffe (ENG) 4 and 3
Ashlan Ramsey and Karen Chung halved with Bronte Law (ENG) and Emily Pedersen (DEN)

**First day – Foursomes:**
Alison Lee and Amy Lee lost to Jessica Vasilic and Anne van Dam  2 and 1
Andrea Lee and Bethany Wu beat Harang Lee and Amber Ratcliffe  3 and 2
Alexandra Kaui and Krystal Quihuis halved with Linnea Strom and Virginia Elena Carta
Casey Danielson and Karen Chung beat Anyssia Herbaut and Shannon Aubert  4 and 3
Nicole Morales and Ashlan Ramsey lost to Emily Pedersen and Karolin Lampert  1 up
Casie Cathrea and Samantha Wagner lost to Bronte Law and Georgia Hall  2 up

**Second day – Singles:**

Casey Danielson halved with Georgia Hall

Nicole Morales beat Amber Ratcliffe  3 and 2

Ashlan Ramsey lost to Karolin Lampert  1 up

Samantha Wagner halved with Emily Pedersen

DenmarkCasie Cathrea beat Shannon Aubert  1 up

Alexandra Kaui beat Anyssia Herbaut  2 and 1

Krystal Quihuis beat Virginia Elena Carta  1 up

Andrea Lee halved with Linnea Strom

Karen Chung beat Harang Lee  3 and 1

Bethany Wu beat Bronte Law  5 and 3

Amy Lee lost to Anne van Dam  3 and 1

Alison Lee beat Jessica Vasilic  3 and 1

**Result:** USA 14½, Europe 9½

| | | | | | | |
|---|---|---|---|---|---|---|
| 2002 | USA 17, Europe 7 | 2005 | USA 16, Europe 8 | 2009 | USA 15½, Europe 8½ |
| 2003 | Europe 12½, USA 11½ | 2007 | Europe 14, USA 10 | 2011 | USA 12, Europe 12 |

## Junior Vagliano Trophy   *Golf de Chantilly, France*

**Day One – Foursomes:**
Sophie Madden (ENG) and Samantha Fuller (ENG) lost to Covadonga Sanjuan (ESP) and Alejandra Pasarin (ESP)  2 holes
Sophie Lamb (ENG) and Fiona Liddell (SCO) beat Csilla Lajtai Rozsa (HUN) and Eva Gilly (GER)  4 and 2
Olivia Mehaffey (IRL) and Alice Hewson (ENG) lost Mathilda Cappeliez (FRA) and Albane Valenzuela (SUI)  1 hole

**Singles:**

Madden lost Sanjuan  6 and 5

Fuller lost to Pasarin  3 and 2

Hewson beat Rozsa  2 and 1

Liddell lost to Gilly  4 and 3

Lamb halved with Valenzuela

Mehaffey lost to Cappeliez  1 hole

**Day Two – Foursomes:**
Mehaffey and Hewson lost Sanjuan and Pasarin  2 holes
Lamb and Liddell lost to Rozsa and Valenzuela  3 and 2
Madden and Fuller lost to Cappeliez and Gilly  3and 2

**Singles:**

Mehaffey lost to Sanjuan  3 and 1

Lamb lost to Pasarin  3 and 2

Hewson lost to Rozsa  3 and 2

Liddell lost to Gilly  3 and 2

Fuller beat Valenzuela  6 and 5

Madden halved with Cappeliez

**Result:** Great Britain and Ireland 4, Continent of Europe 14

## Irish Girls' Inter-Provincial Championship   *Birr GC*

**Day One:**    Munster 6½, Connacht 1½
             Leinster 4, Ulster 4

**Day Two:**    Ulster 6, Connacht 2
             Leinster 4½, Munster 3½

**Day Three:**  Munster 2, Ulster 6
             Connacht 2½, Leinster 5½

| **Final table** | P | W | D | L | Pts |
|---|---|---|---|---|---|
| 1  Ulster | 24 | 18 | 0 | 4 | 2½ |
| 2  Leinster | 24 | 13 | 2 | 9 | 2½ |
| 3  Munster | 24 | 11 | 2 | 11 | 1 |
| 4  Connacht | 24 | 7 | 2 | 17 | 0 |

**Winning team:** Judithe Allen, Clare Calvert, Hannah Henderson, Laura McCaw, Niahm McShery, Niahm Ward, Chloe Weir and Annabel Wilson

# Mixed Boys' and Girls' Events

For past results see earlier editions of *The R&A Golfer's Handbook*

## R&A Junior Open Championship
This event will next be held in 2014

## European Young Masters   *Hamburger GC, Germany*
**Team competition:**

| | | |
|---|---|---|
| 1 | England | 209-210-208—627 |
| 2 | Spain | 211-208-214—633 |
| 3 | Finland | 221-210-203—634 |

4 Norway 640; 5 Denmark 647; 6 Belgium 648; 7 Portugal 652; 8 Sweden 655; 9 Germany 656;
10 Switzerland 657; 11 Italy 658; 12 Austria 659; Ireland 661; 14 France 662; 15 Czech Republic 665;
16 Scotland 670; 17 Netherlands 672; 18 Slovenia 677; 19 Iceland 681; 20 Wales 690; 21 Hungary 697;
22 Slovakia 698; 23 Poland 716; 24 Russia 722

**Winning team:** Bradley Moore, Alice Hewson, Marco Penge and Sophie Madden

**Boys Individual:**

| | | |
|---|---|---|
| 1 | Bradley Moore (ENG) | 67-66-71—204 |
| 2 | John Axelsen (DEN) | 71-67-68—206 |
| | Pedro Almeida (POR) | 66-71-69—206 |

**Girls Individual:**

| | | |
|---|---|---|
| 1 | Cavadonga Sanjuan (ESP) | 67-69-70—206 |
| 2 | Sandra Nordaas (NOR) | 71-71-69—211 |
| 3 | Morgane Metraux (SUI) | 76-72-66—214 |

## Faldo Series

| | | Boys: | Girls: |
|---|---|---|---|
| April | Moortown | Billy Spooner (ENG) | Ellie Goodall (ENG) |
| April | West Lancashire | Paul Kinnear (ENG) | Poppy Finlay (ENG) |
| April | Ireland | | Olivia Mehaffey (NIR) |
| April | Middle East | Eoin Cunniffe (IRL) | |
| April | R. Ashdown Forest | Thomas Robson (ENG) | Kyra Horlock (ENG) |
| May | Chile, CG La Dehesa | Gustavo Silva (CHI) | |
| May | Trentham | Oliver Farrell (ENG) | Natasha Fear (ENG) |
| June | Czech Rep., Telc GR | Vitek Novak (CZE) | |
| June | Panmure | Michael Brodie (SCO) | Heather Munro (SCO) |
| July | Old Fold Manor | Luke Groves (ENG) | Miranda Brain (ENG) |
| July | Austria, Waldhofen GR | | Michaela Gasplmayr (AUT) |
| July | Pyle and Kenfig | Nick Ward (ENG) | Samantha Fuller (ENG) |
| July | S. America, Damha GC | Luiz Jacintho (BRA) | |
| July | Italy, GC Toscanba | | Elena Pagni (ITA) |
| July | Netherlands, Bleijenbeek GC | Severiano Prins (NED) | |
| July | Germany, Sporting Club Berlin | Felix Bode (GER) | |
| August | Hollinwell | Nick Watson (ENG) | Annabel Dimmock (ENG) |
| August | Slovakia Black Stork GC | Simon Zach (CZE) | |
| September | Greece, Glyfada GC | Vasilis Koouympakis (GRE) | |

**Faldo Series Grand Final**   *The Greenbrier GC, Sulphur Springs, USA*
1   Megan Khang (USA)                    70-71-69—210
2   Paul Kinnear (ENG)                   71-69-72—212
3   Zachary Bauchou (USA)                72-74-68—214
    Simon Zach (CZE)                     71-70-73—214

Boys (Under-21)   Paul Kinnear          71-69-72—212
Boys (Under-18)   Zachary Bauchou       72-74-68—214
Boys (Under-16)   Brad Dalke (USA)      71-74-72—217
Girls (Under 21)  Michaela Gasplmayr    76-74-76—226
                  (AUT)
Girls (Under-16)  Megan Khang (USA)     70-71-69—210

**Faldo Series Asia:**

| | | |
|---|---|---|
| April | Philippines, Eagle Ridge | Marvi Monsalve (PHI) |
| May | Chinese Taipei, Sunrise G&CC | Wei Lun Wang (TPE) |
| June | Cambodia, Angkor Resort | Watcharasit Trachuentong (THA) |
| July | Shanghai, Taihu International | Rongjian Tang (CHN) |
| July | China, Mission Hills, Shenzhen | Chun Yu Shih (TPE) |
| July | Vietnam, Laguna Lang Co | Bao Nghi Ngo (VIE) |
| August | Hong Kong (Boys), Jockey Club | Michael Regan Wong (CHN) |
| August | Hong Kong (Girls), Jockey Club | Yik Ching Kitty Tam (CHN) |
| October | India (Girls), Chandigarh | Gurbani Singh (IND) |
| October | India (Boys), Chandigarh | Viraj Madappa (IND) |
| October | Malaysia, Samarahan | Solomon Emilio Rosidin (MAS) |
| October | Nepal, Gokarna Forest | Tanka Bahadur Karki (NEP) |
| November | Singapore, Selatar | Lucius Toh Zheng Xian (SIN) |
| November | Brunei, Empire Hotel | Marc Ong (SIN) |
| December | Japan, Shizu Hills | |
| January | Pakistan, venue to be announced | |
| January | Kunming, Lakeview | |
| February | Indonesia, Damai Indah Jakarta | |
| February | Thailand, venue to be announced | |
| March 8th | **Faldo Series Asian Grand Final** *Mission Hills GC (Faldo Course), Shenzhen, China* | |

## Fairhaven Trophies   *Fairhaven*

1   Marco Penge (Worthing)                   72-73-72-71—288
    Bradley Neil (Rosemount Blairgowrie)     69-72-70-77—288
3   Jonathan Thomson (Lindrick)              75-75-75-70—295

**Nations Cup**
1   Scotland 1        141-147—288
2   Ireland A         148-150—298
3   England 3         154-145—299

4 Scotland 2 299; 5 Germany 2 303;  6 England 1 304; 7 Finland 2 306; 8 Wales 1 306; 9 Finland 1 309;
10 England 4 309; 11 Scotland 3 310; 12 England 2 310; 13 Germany 1 310; 14 Sweden 310; 15 Ireland B
312; 16 Scotland 4 314; 17 Netherlands 317; 18 Switzerland 1 318; 19 Switzerland 3 318; 20 Switzerland
2 321; 21 Wales 3 321; 22 Wales 2 326; 23 Wales 4 340; 24 Brazil NR

**Winning team:** Bradley Neil, Ewen Ferguson, and Lauren Whyte

## The Junior Ryder Cup

| | | | | | | | |
|---|---|---|---|---|---|---|---|
| 1995 | Exhibition Match | 1999 | Europe | 2006 | Europe | 2012 | USA |
| | won by Europe | 2002 | Europe | 2008 | USA | | |
| 1997 | United States | 2004 | Europe | 2010 | USA | | |

## 13th Duke of York Young Champions Trophy   Royal St George's GC

55 players took part – 29 boys and 26 girls

| | | |
|---|---|---|
| 1 | Guido Migliozzi (ITA) | 73-70-72—215 |
| 2 | Jack Singh Brar (ENG) | 75-72-69—216 |
| 3 | Bradley Neil (SCO) | 75-74-71—220 |
| 4 | Nicole Morales (USA) | 75-75-71—221 |
| | Kristian Johannessen (NOR) | 74-76-71—221 |
| | Robin Dawson (IRL) | 75-75-71—221 |

## Junior Orange Bowl   Biltmore GC, Florida                    [Boys: 6742–71; Girls: 6089–71]

**Boys:**

| | | |
|---|---|---|
| 1 | Renato Paratore (ITA) | 67-67-71-70—275 |
| 2 | Dominic Foos (GER) | 71-68-68-69—276 |
| | Jorge Garcia (VEN) | 69-69-70-68—276 |

**Girls:**

| | | |
|---|---|---|
| 1 | Brooke Henderson (CAN) | 68-72-73-67—280 |
| 2 | Megan Khang (USA) | 71-70-76-68—285 |
| 3 | Linnea Strom (SWE) | 71-76-69-70—286 |

## Callaway Junior Golf Championship

**Boys:**

| | | | |
|---|---|---|---|
| 15–17 | Torrey Pines GC (South) | Jose Mendez (CRC) | 68-71-71-73—283 |
| 13–14 | Morgan Run Resort | Kristoffer Arevalo (PHI) | 70-68-68—204 |
| 11–12 | Sycun Resort | Mason Nome (USA) | 66-73-70—209 |
| 9–10 | Welk Resort | Alexander Yang (USA) | 60-57-64—181 |
| 7–8 | Oaks North GC | Kuranosuke Shimizu (JPN) | 62-59-60—181 |
| 6 and under | Colina Park GC | Ratchanon Chantananuwat (THA) | 58-53-53—164 |

**Girls:**

| | | | |
|---|---|---|---|
| 15–17 | Torrey Pines GC (North) | Mariel Galdiano (USA) | 70-69-69-71—279 |
| 13–14 | CC of Rancho Bernardo | Pauline Del Rosario (PHI) | 68-70-68—206 |
| 11–12 | Rancho Bernardo Inn | Miyabi Tezuka (JPN) | 72-72-71—215 |
| 9–10 | Lomas Santa Fe (South) | Miku Abe (JPN) | 57-54-60—171 |
| 7–8 | Sycun Resort | Alexa Pano (USA) | 58-57-59—174 |
| 6 and under | Colina Park GC | Maye Huang (USA) | 62-60-59—181 |

## 5th World Golf Schools Challenge   Hua Hin, Thailand

| | |
|---|---|
| Division I Boys | Chanachoke Dejpiratanamongkol (Bromsgrove International School, Bangkok, Thailand) |
| Division II Boys | Tyron Searle (Hilton College, KwaZulu Natal, South Africa) |
| Division III Boys | Carter Milne (John McGlashan College, Dunedin, New Zealand) |
| Division IV Boys | Huang Tzu Wei (American School of Bangkok, Thailand) |
| Division I Girls | Pannarat Thanapolboonyaran (American School of Bangkok, Thailand) |
| Division II Girls | Melanie Foster (Como Secondary School, Perth, Western Australia) |
| Mixed Teams | American School of Bangkok, Thailand (Panat Bodhidatta, Tisjaras Kovitprakornkul, Pannarat Thanapolboonyaran, Pajaree Anannarukarn) |
| Boys' Team | Whangarei Boys' High School, New Zealand (Julian Fowler, Braden Keown, Kadin Neho, Sam Purdie) |

The 6th World Schools Challenge will be hosted by Millfield School, Somerset, and staged at Burnham & Berrow GC, Mendip GC, Yeovil GC and Wells GC from April 13–18 2014

## KeNako South Africa World Juniors Championship    *Kingswood GC*

**Boys**

| | | |
|---|---|---|
| I | Jade Buitendag (RSA)* | 71-71-68—210 |
| 2 | Robert Burlison (ENG) | 72-70-68—210 |

*Buitendag won at the first exta hole*

| | | |
|---|---|---|
| 3 | Philip Kruse (RSA) | 74-71-67—212 |
| | Benjamin Follett-Smith (ZIM) | 72-69-71—212 |
| | HP Van der Merwe (RSA) | 68-73-71—212 |

**Girls**

| | | |
|---|---|---|
| I | Lara Weinstein (RSA) | 67-73-76—216 |
| 2 | Cara Gorlei (RSA) | 73-72-72—217 |
| 3 | Bianca Theron (RSA) | 76-75-71—222 |
| | Ji Sun Kang (RSA) | 75-73-74—222 |

## Trans Tasman Cup
This event will next be held in 2014

## USA v China Youths International    *Nanshan International GC, China*

**Day One – Foursomes:**
Patrick Martin (Alabama) and Wilson Furr (Jackson) beat Li Yuan and Jin Bo  2 holes
A J Beechler (Pinehurst) and Seiya Liu (Beverly Hills) lost to Bai Zhengkai and Wang Dongyu  5 and 4
Ciara Petronzio (Scottsdale) and Divye Manthena (Camarillo) lost to Goa Meiqi and Sui Xiang  6 and 5
Jean Tyrrell (Leawood) and Dree Fausnaugh (Maitland) lost to Shi Yutang and Wu Sha  6 and 5

**Fourballs:**
Martin and Beechler beat Wang Dongyu and Bai Zhengkat  3 and 1
Furr and Liu beat Li Yuan and Jin Bo  2 and 1
Petronzio and Tyrell lost to Shi Yutang and Sui Xiang  2 and 1
Fausnaugh and Manthena lost to Wu Sha and Goa Meiqi  5 and 4

**Match position:** China 5, USA 3

**Day Two – Singles:**
Furr beat Wang Dongyu  1 hole
Beechler lost to Jin Bo  4 and 2
Liu lost to Bai Zhengkai  one hole
Tyrell lost to Shi Yuting  6 and 5
Matches unfinished because of bad weather:
Martin two up on Li Yuan after 16
Fausnaugh three up on Wu Sha after 13
Petronzio three down to Sui  Xiang after 13
Manthena two down to Gao Meiqi after 12

**Final Result:** China 8, USA 4

## South-East Asia Amateur Team Championships    *Sherwood Hills CC, Philippines*

### 7th Lion City Cup (boys under 18)

| | | |
|---|---|---|
| I | Thailand | 143-142-145-150—580 |
| 2 | Indonesia | 149-150-147-142—590 |
| 3 | Malaysia | 152-143-153-151—599 |

4 Philippines 600; 5 Singapore 617; 6 Hong Kong 647; 7 Brunei 685

**Winning team:** Nattawat Suvajanakorn, Ethumrong Luanganuruk and Puwit Anupansuebsal

**Individual:**
|  | | | |
|---|---|---|---|
| I | Nattawat Suvajanakorn (THA) | 74-70-72-73—289 |
| 2 | Puwit Anupansuebsal (THA) | 69-72-73-77—291 |
| 3 | Jordan Surya Irawan (INA) | 77-71-72-72—292 |

South-East Asia Amateur Team Championship *continued*

## Katrina Cup (girls under 18)

| | | |
|---|---|---|
| 1 | Thailand | 143-146-142-146—577 |
| 2 | Philippines | 144-148-139-151—582 |
| 3 | Indonesia | 150-147-139-151—597 |

4 Hong Kong 615; 5 Malaysia 635; 6 Singapore 642

**Winning team:** Nattawat Suvajanakorn, Ethumrong Luanganuruk and Puwit Anupansuebsal

**Individual:**

| | | |
|---|---|---|
| 1 | Parinda Phokan (THA) | 71-73-74-74—292 |
| 2 | Budsabakorn Sukapan (THA) | 75-73-68-77—293 |
| 3 | Sherman Santiwiwatthanaphong (THA) | 72-76-74-72—294 |
| | Pauline del Rosario (PHI) | 74-75-70-75—294 |

*For Men's and Women's events see page 435*

*For Men's and Women's events see page 435*

---

## Loretto School Scottish Under-14 Championship  *Fortrose GC and  Rosemarkie GC*

**Boys:**  Charlie Strickland (Ham Manor)      70-72—142
**Girls:** Shannon McWilliam (Aboyne)      75-79—154

---

## Evian Junior Masters  *Evian Resort, France*

**Team competition:**

| | | |
|---|---|---|
| 1 | USA | 439 |
| 2 | France | 447 |
| 3 | Czech Republic | 450 |
| 4 | Germany | 458 |
| 5 | Japan | 460 |

**Winning team:** Elizabeth Wang, Mika Liu, Varun Chopra and J J Gresco.

**Individual:**

| | | |
|---|---|---|
| 1 | Elizabeth Wang (USA) | 73-66—139 |

## Month by month in 2013

Rory McIlroy grabs his first win for over a year at the Australian Open, a last-hole birdie ending Adam Scott's bid for a fourth successive victory. In the World Challenge, Zach Johnson comes from four behind to beat Tiger Woods in a play-off, while the European Tour fine Simon Dyson £30,000 and hand him a suspended two-month ban for flattening a spike mark in what the disciplinary panel decide was a "momentary aberration".

## PART IX

# Tournaments for the Disabled

# Tournaments for the Disabled

For past results see earlier editions of *The R&A Golfer's Handbook*

## British Blind Open *Forest Pines Resort, Scunthorpe, Lincolnshire*

**B1:** Billy McAllister     67-79—146
**B2:** Ian Moncrieff     74-77—151
**B3:** Chris Evans     73-70—143
**Stableford:**
Danny McElroy     37-27—64 points

## British Blind Masters *Belton Wood, Grantham*

| | | |
|---|---|---|
| 1 | Billy McAllister B1 | 75-63-65-68—271 |
| 2 | Chris Evans B3 | 68-70-70-67—275 |
| 3 | Allan Morgan B3 | 74-69-76-67—286 |

**Stableford:**
Nick Mills     19-20-17-17—73 points
Billy McAllister won the Terry Wallace Trophy for the best four day score by a B1 player

## English Match Play Championship (for blind golfers) *Gaudet Luce GC, Worcestershire*

Peter Hodgkinson beat Billy McAllister 5 and 4

## English Stroke Play Championship (for blind golfers) *Gaudet Luce GC, Worcestershire*

| | | |
|---|---|---|
| 1 | Billy McAllister B1 | 64-59—123 |
| 2 | Andy Gilford B2 | 62-73—135 |
| 3 | Ron Tomlinson B1 | 68-73—141 |

## Scottish Match Play Championship (for blind golfers) *Green Hotel, Kinross*

John Imrie beat Iain Prime 2 up

## Scottish Stroke Play Championship (for blind golfers) *Murrayshall Hotel, Scone*

| | | |
|---|---|---|
| 1 | Alistair Reid | 69-68—137 |
| 2 | John Miller | 81-66—147 |
| | John Imrie | 74-73—147 |

## The Auld Enemy Cup (for blind golfers) *Drumoig Golf Hotel*

England and Wales 16½, Scotland 7½

## The Celtic Cup (for blind golfers) *Westerwood GCC, Cumbernauld*

Scotland 7½, Ireland 1½

## World Blind Golf Championships

This event will next be held in 2014

---

**Blind Golf Categories:** B1 Totally blind; B2 From the ability to recognise the shape of a hand up to visual acuity of 20/600; B3 From visual acuity above 20/600 up to visual acuity of less than 20/200

## Auld Enemies Cup (for disabled golfers)    *Kinross GC*
England 14, Scotland 10

## Oldfield Trophy (for disabled golfers)    *Pontypridd GC, South Wales*
England 12, Wales 8

## 76th One-Armed Golf Society World Championships    (inaugurated 1932)
*Ballater GC, Aberdeenshire, Scotland*
**Match Play Final:** Alex Hjalmarsson (SWE) beat Reinhard Schuhknecht (RSA)
**Stroke Play Champion:** Reinhard Schuhknecht 146

## Disabled British Open    (inaugurated 2009)
This event will next be held in 2014

## International Cup    (formerly the College Park Cup)    *Wilderness Ridge CC, Lincoln, NE*
USA v International (USA names first)
**Morning – foursomes:**
Evan Mathias & Kim Moore beat Hideki Kobayashi and Yoshio Asano   4 and 3
Mike Carver & Kenny Bontz beat Josh Williams & Dallas Smith   2 and 1
Les Meade & John Benway halved with Chris Osborne and Johannes Grames
Dick Krapfl & Troy Callahan beat Jim McElhiney & Kellie Valentine   4 and 3
Lucian Newman & Toby Plasencio beat Jesse Florkowski & Masato Koyamada   3 and 2
Bill Halloway & Mandi Sedlak halved with Gwen Davies & Vic McClelland
Tracy Ramin & Adam Benza beat Yakashi Arisako & Woody Walker   1 up
Chad Pfeifer & Brent Bleyenberg lost to Ryan Brenden & Tim Hermann   2 up
**Match position:** USA 6, International 2

**Afternoon – singles:**

| | |
|---|---|
| Evan Mathias beat Tim Hermann 3 and 2 | Troy Callahan lost to Kellie Valentine 2 and 1 |
| Kenny Bontz beat Josh Williams 1 up | Mike Carver lost to Yoshio Asano 1 up |
| Brent Bleyenburg beat Dallas Smith 4 and 3 | Mandi Sedlak beat Gwen Davies 5 and 4 |
| Lucian Newman lost to Jesse Florkowski 2 and 1 | Toby Plasencio lost to Masato Koyamada 4 and 3 |
| Bill Holloway beat Viv McClelland 2 up | John Benway lost to Chris Osborne 1 up |
| Les Meade beat Jim McElhiney 5 and 4 | Adam Benza beat Hideki Kobayashi 4 and 3 |
| Dick Krapfl beat Ryan Brenden 1 up | Chad Pfeifer beat Yakashi Arisako 2 up |
| Tracy Ramin lost to Woody Walker 3 and 2 | Kim Moore lost to Johannes Grames 1 down |

*History:* The College Park Cup (formerly the Robinson Cup), a Ryder Cup-style competition for amputee golfers between US and International teams of 16 players apiece, was inaugurated in 1999 by College Park Industries of Fraser, Michigan, USA. Following the 2011 matches, College Park felt they were unable to continue as sole sponsors and the event was taken up by the US National Amputee Golf Association and renamed the International Cup. At the end of the 2013 season, the tally of victories was eight for the USA and six for the International team with one match rained off and declared a draw.

## Golf HandiCup    (Great Britain v France)    *St Omer, Calais*
Great Britain 6½, France 5½

## Fightmaster Cup
This event will next be held in 2014 in Scotland

## Swedish Invitational Golf Challenge  *Bokskogens GC*

**Men:**

| | | |
|---|---|---|
| 1 | Daniel Slabbert (RSA) | 72-74—146 |
| 2 | Johan Kammerstad (SWE) | 76-77—153 |
| 3 | Geoff Nicholas (AUS) | 77-79—156 |
| | Iglin Grobbelar (RSA) | 77-79—156 |

**Women:**

| | | |
|---|---|---|
| 1 | Caroline Larsson (SWE) | 75-77—152 |
| 2 | Mette Wegge Lynggaard (DEN) | 88-82—170 |
| 3 | Tineke Loogman (NED) | 98-90—188 |

This event will next be held in 2015

## BALASA National Championships  *Belton Woods*

**Gross Champion:** Kevin Harmison 159 (beat Duncan Hamilton-Martin on count-back)

| Category 1 Nett (hcps 0–12): | | Category 2 Nett (hcps 13–18): | | Category 3 Stableford: (hcps 19–28): | |
|---|---|---|---|---|---|
| 1 Chris Foster | 151* | 1 Mike Wraight | 146 | 1 Keith Wallace | 65 pts |
| 2 Maximilien Puget | 151 | 2 Richard Saunders | 149* | 2 Michael McGowen | 64 pts |
| 3 Duncan Hamilton-Martin | 149 | 3 Andy McDonald | 149 | 3 Andrew Spratt | 63 pts |
| *Won on count-back | | *Won on count-back | | | |

## Handigolf

UK National Championship – Tapton Park Chesterfield: Terry Kirby

UK Masters – Wavendon Golf Centre Milton Keynes: Tony Tofield

## SDGP Competitions

| | | |
|---|---|---|
| Alloa GC: 1 White | Kittocks GC: Bob Drysdale | Muckart GC: Trevor Crombie |
| Charleton GC: Derek Milne | Liberton GC: M Gerdes-Hansen | Swanston GC: Jim Gales |
| Cluny GC: Derek Milne | Melville GC: Steve Cunningham | |
| Dalmahoy GC: Garry McNulty | Morecambe GC: Peter Osborne | |
| The Dukes GC: Garry McNulty | (Rd 1); Jim Gales (Rd 2) | |

Scottish Championships – Elmwood GC, Fife and Carrick Knowe GC, Edinburgh: 1 C Corbett, 2 A McDonald, 3 Bob Drysdale

Scottish Order of Merit Championship final placings:

| | | | | | | |
|---|---|---|---|---|---|---|
| 1 | Trevor Crombie (Kirkcaldy) | 129 points | 6 | Jim McNab (Glenrothes) | 102 |
| 2 | Derek Milne (Upper Largo) | 124 | 7 | Steve Cunningham (Alloa) | 95 |
| | Peter Osborne (Carnforth) | 124 | 8 | Gary Gardner (Edinburgh) | 88 |
| 4 | Garry McNulty (Glasgow) | 107 | 9 | John Elliot (Edinburgh) | 84 |
| 5 | Scott Anderson (Aberdeen) | 104 | 10 | Jim Gales (Springfield) | 82 |

## The Malaga Tournament  *Paradore GC, Malaga Spain*

1 Jim Gales, 2 Garry McNulty, 3 Scott Anderson

## World Match Play Championship   *Rowega G&CC, Ohio USA*

Div. 1 Phil Blackwell, Div. 2 Bruce Hooper, Div. 3 Scott Aughtry

## The World Team Cup   *Westerwood Golf Hotel*

1 England (M McGoven, S Haxton, W West, R Saunders)
2 Battle Back Golf (G Meekins, A Carlton, P Swain, L Smit)
3 Austria (R Mayer, D Engel, F Monitzer, M Hirschbühl)
4 British Disabled Golf (T Williamson, B Parsons, J Holmes, J Riorden)
5 England #2 (M Jelley, M Helm, C Foster, J Jones)
6 Germany (J Audreas, M Clemens, P Haustein, R Wagner)
7 The 4 Stooges (G Gardner, K Harmison, J Davidson, A McDonald)
8 "3 off the T" (D Walker D Standing, B Savage, M Walters
9 "Social Golfer" (I Halliwell, R Hurcombe, A Gardner, D Grey)
10 Scotland (J Gales P Osborne, P Cunningham, H Hester)

## 18th Japan Open Golf Championship for the Disabled   *Three Lakes CC, Mie*

| | |
|---|---|
| Grand Prix Division: Masato Koyamada | 83-72—155 |
| Lower Limb Disability Division: Kojiro Ono | 93-92—185 |
| Upper Limb Disability Division: Masahide Kusakawa | 93-89—182 |
| Multiple Disability Division: Toshikazu Chiba | 110-111—198 |
| Mild Disability Division: Kyoji Takazawa | 98-100—198 |
| Wheelchair Division: Hiromu Fujita | 103-104—207 |
| Persons Recovered from Stroke: Sadao Kimura | 100-103—203 |
| Mental Disability Division: Dai Murakami | 128-140—268 |

## Deaf Golf Association Annual Tournament   *Berkshire Valley GC, Jefferson, NJ, USA*

| | |
|---|---|
| Flight A: Dennis Berrigan | 88-86—174 |
| Flight B: Dayleena Doan | 87-101—188 |

## Golf organisations for the disabled

| | |
|---|---|
| International Blind Golf Association | www.internationalblindgolf.org |
| English Blind Golf Association | www.blindgolf.co.uk |
| Scottish Blind Golf Association | www.scottishblindgolf.com |
| Blind Golf Australia | www.blindgolf.com.au |
| United States Blind Golf Association | www.usblindgolf.com |
| BALASA | 01773 715984 |
| British Amputee Golf Association | www.baga.org.uk |
| The Society of One Armed Golfers | www.onearmgolf.org |
| European Disabled Golf Association | www.edgagolf.com |
| Disabled Golf Association | www.disabledgolfsociety.com |
| Disabled British Open | www.disabledbritishopen.org |
| National Amputee Golf Association | www.nagagolf.org |
| Canadian Amputee Golf Association | www.caga.ca |
| Deaf Golf Association | www.deafgolf.com |

## Donations to special needs groups

The R&A supports several organisations which run golf events for players with special needs. In 2013, £50,000 was set aside for this purpose and a similar amount will be allocated this year. In addition, The R&A does, on occasion, send referees and other representatives to events run for disabled golfers.

## Other Events  (winners from host nation unless stated)

**Australian Blind Golf Open**
Overall Champion: Doug Burrows (B3)

**Australian Stableford Championship**
Champion: Graham Coulton (NSW); Runner-up:
Sean Witting (VIC)
B1: David Blyth (VIC)
B2: Gary Sargent (NSW)
B3: Rod Mills (NSW)

**BGC-Handisport, International Disabled Open**
Trofeo Princesa Letizia: Cohen Mordecai (ISR)

**Canadian Amputee National Open**
| | | |
|---|---|---|
| 1 | Josh Williams (BK) | 225 |
| 2 | Jesse Florkowski (AE) | 228 |
| 3 | Kelly Mason (BK) | 239 |

**Canadian Blind Golf Open**
Doug Stoutley

**Finnish Disabled Open**
Mads Lykke Nielsen (DEN) – Gross, category (A)
Miroslav Lidinsky (CZE) – Net, category (B)

**4th Italian Blind Golf Open**
B1: Andrea Calcaterra
B2: Malcolm Elrich (ENG)
B3: John Eakin (ENG)
Ladies Champion: Chiara Giacosa

**Japanese Blind Golf Open**
Sean Witting (AUS)    94-88—182

**Nedbank SA Disabled Golf Open**
Physically disabled: Chris Wood 87-86-78—251
Visually impaired: Leon Strydom 21-31-24—76

**New South Wales Blind Open**
Men: Rod Mills
Women: Elsie McCulloch

**NSW v Victoria Interstate Blind Golf Challenge**
Victoria

**Swedish Handigolf Open**
C Class: Fredrik Pettersson
D Class: Andre Toth (NOR)

**Swedish Invitational**
Men: Daniel Slabbert (RSA)  72-74—146
Women: Caroline Larsson  75-77—152

**65th USA National Amputee Championship**
National Champion – Men: Josh Williams (CAN);
Women: Kimberly Moore

**24th USA National Senior Amputee Championship**
National Champion – Men: Lucian Newman III

**USBGA National Championship**
B1: David Meador
B2: Jeremy Poincenot
B3: Ron Plath

**USBGA Open Championship**
B1: Andrea Calcaterra (ITA)
B2: Jeremy Poincenot
B3: Ron Plath
Ladies Champion: Chiara Giacosa (ITA)

**Victorian Blind Open**
Stephen Mitchell B3

**Western Australian Masters**
Ron Anderson Trophy: Takakazu Takahashi (JPN)
B1: Glenn Niciejewski
B2: Sean Witting
B3: Rod Mills

**Western Australian Blind Golf Open**
Overall winner: John White B2
B2 winner: Jenny McCallum
B3 winner: Doug Golding

---

**Blind Golf Categories:** B1 Totally blind; B2 From the ability to recognise the shape of a hand up to visual acuity of 20/600; B3 From visual acuity above 20/600 up to visual acuity of less than 20/200

---

## Sign language version of Rules

Working closely with Signworld, Britain's biggest British Sign Language (BSL) learning resource website, The R&A has recently launched a version of the Quick Guide to the Rules of Golf video with a BSL interpretation.

R&A Working for Golf Ambassador Padraig Harrington features in the short film, providing explanations and clear illustrations of the Rules. With the assistance of Signworld, the ten minute video has been made accessible to deaf people with the production of a signed version.

Linda Day, Signworld Director and keen golfer herself, commented: "I feel it's important to have the Rules of Golf translated into BSL. Information in written English isn't always clear to deaf people. I'd now expect to see deaf golfers understanding and interpreting the Rules more effectively."

The BSL interpretation can be viewed on The R&A's website and has already generated enthusiastic comments from around the Deaf community.

Craig Crowley, Chief Executive of Action Deafness and ex-President of the International Committee of Sports for the Deaf, said it was "Truly an excellent breakthrough. Hopefully this will lead on to further developments in future."

# PART X

# Record Scoring

# Record Scoring

In the Major Championships nobody has shot lower than 63. There have been eight 63s in the Open, four 63s in the US Open, two 63s in The Masters and 12 63s in the USPGA Championship. The lowest first 36 holes is 130 by Nick Faldo in the 1992 Open at Muirfield and Brandt Snedeker in the 2012 Open at Royal Lytham and the lowest 72 hole total is 265 by David Toms in the 2001 USPGA Championship at the Atlanta Athletic Club.

## The Open Championship

**Most times champions**
**6** Harry Vardon, 1896–98–99–1903–11–14
**5** James Braid, 1901–05–06–08–10; JH Taylor, 1894–95–1900–09–13; Peter Thomson, 1954–55–56–58–65; Tom Watson, 1975–77–80–82–83

**Most times runner-up**
**7** Jack Nicklaus, 1964–67–68–72–76–77–79
**6** JH Taylor, 1896–1904–05–06–07–14

**Oldest winner**
Old Tom Morris, 46 years 99 days, 1867
Roberto De Vicenzo, 44 years 93 days, 1967

**Youngest winner**
Young Tom Morris, 17 years 5 months 8 days, 1868
Willie Auchterlonie, 21 years 24 days, 1893
Severiano Ballesteros, 22 years 3 months 12 days, 1979

**Youngest and oldest competitor**
Young Tom Morris, 15 years, 4 months, 29 days, 1866
Gene Sarazen, 71 years 4 months 13 days, 1973

**Widest margin of victory**
**13 strokes** Old Tom Morris, 1862
**12 strokes** Young Tom Morris, 1870

**8 strokes** JH Taylor, 1900 and 1913; James Braid, 1908; Tiger Woods, 2000
**7 strokes** Louis Oosthuizen, 2010

**Lowest winning aggregates**
**267** Greg Norman, 66-68-69-64, Sandwich, 1993
**268** Tom Watson, 68-70-65-65, Turnberry, 1977; Nick Price, 69-66-67-66, Turnberry, 1994
**269** Tiger Woods, 67-66-67-69, St Andrews, 2000
**270** Nick Faldo, 67-65-67-71, St Andrews, 1990; Tiger Woods 67-65-71-67, Hoylake, 2006

**Lowest in relation to par**
**19 under** Tiger Woods, St Andrews, 2000
**18 under** Nick Faldo, St Andrews, 1990; Tiger Woods, Hoylake, 2006

**Lowest aggregate by runner-up**
**269** (68-70-65-66), Jack Nicklaus, Turnberry, 1977; (69-63-70-67), Nick Faldo, Sandwich, 1993; (68-66-68-67), Jesper Parnevik, Turnberry, 1994

**Lowest aggregate by an amateur**
**281** (68-72-70-71), Iain Pyman, Sandwich, 1993; (75-66-70-70), Tiger Woods, Royal Lytham, 1996

**Lowest round**
**63** Mark Hayes, second round, Turnberry, 1977; Isao Aoki, third round, Muirfield, 1980; Greg Norman,

## Prize Money

| Year | Total | First Prize £ | Year | Total | First Prize £ | Year | Total | First Prize £ |
|------|-------|---------------|------|-------|---------------|------|-------|---------------|
| 1860 | nil | nil | 1965 | 10,000 | 1,750 | 1993 | 1,000,000 | 100,000 |
| 1863 | 10 | nil | 1966 | 15,000 | 2,100 | 1994 | 1,100,000 | 110,000 |
| 1864 | 16 | 6 | 1968 | 20,000 | 3,000 | 1995 | 1,250,000 | 125,000 |
| 1876 | 20 | 20 | 1969 | 30,000 | 4,250 | 1996 | 1,400,000 | 200,000 |
| 1889 | 22 | 8 | 1970 | 40,000 | 5,250 | 1997 | 1,586,300 | 250,000 |
| 1891 | 28.50 | 10 | 1971 | 45,000 | 5,500 | 1998 | 1,774,150 | 300,000 |
| 1892 | 110 | (am) | 1972 | 50,000 | 5,500 | 1999 | 2,029,950 | 350,000 |
| 1893 | 100 | 30 | 1975 | 75,000 | 7,500 | 2000 | 2,722,150 | 500,000 |
| 1910 | 125 | 50 | 1977 | 100,000 | 10,000 | 2001 | 3,229,748 | 600,000 |
| 1920 | 225 | 75 | 1978 | 125,000 | 12,500 | 2002 | 3,880,998 | 700,000 |
| 1927 | 275 | 100 | 1979 | 155,000 | 15,500 | 2003 | 3,931,000 | 700,000 |
| 1930 | 400 | 100 | 1980 | 200,000 | 25,000 | 2004 | 4,006,950 | 720,000 |
| 1931 | 500 | 100 | 1982 | 250,000 | 32,000 | 2005 | 3,854,900 | 720,000 |
| 1946 | 1000 | 150 | 1983 | 300,000 | 40,000 | 2006 | 3,990,916 | 720,000 |
| 1949 | 1700 | 300 | 1984 | 451,000 | 55,000 | 2007 | 4,185,400 | 750,000 |
| 1953 | 2450 | 500 | 1985 | 530,000 | 65,000 | 2008 | 4,260,000 | 750,000 |
| 1954 | 3500 | 750 | 1986 | 600,000 | 70,000 | 2009 | 4,206,354 | 750,000 |
| 1955 | 3750 | 1,000 | 1987 | 650,000 | 75,000 | 2010 | 4,546,305 | 850,000 |
| 1958 | 4850 | 1,000 | 1988 | 700,000 | 80,000 | 2011 | 5,000,000 | 900,000 |
| 1959 | 5000 | 1,000 | 1989 | 750,000 | 80,000 | 2012 | 5,000,000 | 900,000 |
| 1960 | 7000 | 1,250 | 1990 | 815,000 | 85,000 | 2013 | 5,250,000 | 945,000 |
| 1961 | 8500 | 1,400 | 1991 | 900,000 | 90,000 | | | |
| 1963 | 8500 | 1,500 | 1992 | 950,000 | 95,000 | | | |

second round, Turnberry, 1986; Paul Broadhurst, third round, St Andrews, 1990; Jodie Mudd, fourth round, Royal Birkdale, 1991; Nick Faldo, second round, Payne Stewart, fourth round, Sandwich, 1993; Rory McIlroy, first round, St Andrews, 2010

**Lowest round by an amateur**
65 Tom Lewis, first round, Sandwich, 2011

**Lowest first round**
63 Rory McIlroy, St Andrews, 2010

**Lowest second round**
63 Mark Hayes, Turnberry, 1977; Greg Norman, Turnberry, 1986; Nick Faldo, Sandwich, 1993

**Lowest third round**
63 Isao Aoki, Muirfield, 1980; Paul Broadhurst, St Andrews, 1990

**Lowest fourth round**
63 Jodie Mudd, Royal Birkdale, 1991; Payne Stewart, Sandwich, 1993

**Lowest first 36 holes**
130 (66-64) Nick Faldo, Muirfield 1992; (66-64) Brandt Snedeker, Royal Lytham 2012
131 (64-67) Adam Scott, Royal Lytham 2012

**Lowest second 36 holes**
130 (65-65), Tom Watson, Turnberry, 1977; (64-66) Ian Baker-Finch, Royal Birkdale, 1991; (66-64) Anders Forsbrand, Turnberry, 1994

**Lowest first 54 holes**
198 (67-67-64), Tom Lehman, Royal Lytham, 1996
199 (67-65-67), Nick Faldo, St Andrews, 1990; (66-64-69), Nick Faldo, Muirfield, 1992; (64-67-68), Adam Scott, Royal Lytham 2012

**Lowest final 54 holes**
199 (66-67-66), Nick Price, Turnberry, 1994
200 (70-65-65), Tom Watson, Turnberry, 1977; (63-70-67), Nick Faldo, Sandwich, 1993; (66-64-70), Fuzzy Zoeller, Turnberry, 1994; (66-70-64), Nick Faldo, Turnberry 1994

**Lowest 9 holes**
28 Denis Durnian, first 9, Royal Birkdale, 1983

**Champions in three decades**
Harry Vardon, 1986, 1903, 1911; JH Taylor, 1894, 1900, 1913; Gary Player, 1959, 1968, 1974

**Biggest span between first and last victories**
19 years – JH Taylor, 1894–1913
18 years – Harry Vardon, 1896–1914
15 years – Willie Park, 1860–75
15 years – Gary Player, 1959–74
14 years – Henry Cotton, 1934–48

**Successive victories**
4 Young Tom Morris, 1868–72 (no championship 1871)
3 Jamie Anderson, 1877–79; Bob Ferguson, 1880–82, Peter Thomson, 1954–56
2 Old Tom Morris, 1861–62; JH Taylor, 1894–95; Harry Vardon, 1898–99; James Braid, 1905–06; Bobby Jones, 1926–27; Walter Hagen, 1928–29; Bobby Locke, 1949–50; Arnold Palmer, 1961–62; Lee Trevino, 1971–72; Tom Watson, 1982–83; Tiger Woods, 2005–06; Padraig Harrington, 2007–08

**Amateur champions**
John Ball, 1890, Prestwick; Harold Hilton, 1892, Muirfield and 1897, Royal Liverpool; Bobby Jones, 1926, Royal Lytham; 1927, St Andrews; 1930 Royal Liverpool

**Highest number of top five finishes**
16 JH Taylor and Jack Nicklaus
15 Harry Vardon and James Braid

**Players with four rounds under 70**
Ernie Els (68-69-69-68), Sandwich, 1993; Greg Norman (66-68-69-64), Sandwich, 1993; Jesper Parnevik (68-66-68-67), Turnberry, 1994; Nick Price (69-66-67-66), Turnberry, 1994; Tiger Woods (67-66-67-69), St Andrews, 2000; Ernie Els (69-69-68-68), Royal Troon, 2004

**Highest number of rounds under 70**
39 Ernie Els                29 Tom Watson
37 Nick Faldo               26 Greg Norman
33 Jack Nicklaus

**Outright leader after every round (since Championship became 72 holes in 1892)**
James Braid, 1908; Ted Ray, 1912; Bobby Jones, 1927; Gene Sarazen, 1932; Henry Cotton, 1934; Tom Weiskopf, 1973; Tiger Woods, 2005

**Record leads (since 1892)**
*After 18 holes:* 4 strokes – Bobby Jones, 1927; Henry Cotton, 1934; Christy O'Connor Jr, 1985
*After 36 holes:* 9 strokes – Henry Cotton, 1934
*After 54 holes:* 10 strokes – Henry Cotton, 1934.
7 strokes – Tony Lema, 1964. 6 strokes – James Braid, 1908; Tom Lehman, 1996; Tiger Woods, 2000

**Champions with each round lower than previous one**
Jack White, 1904, Sandwich, 80-75-72-69; James Braid, 1906, Muirfield, 77-76-74-73; Ben Hogan, 1953, Carnoustie, 73-71-70-68; Gary Player, 1959, Muirfield, 75-71-70-68

**Champion with four rounds the same**
Densmore Shute, 1933, St Andrews, 73-73-73-73 (excluding the play-off)

**Biggest variation between rounds of a champion**
14 strokes – Henry Cotton, 1934, second round 65, fourth round 79. 11 strokes – Jack White, 1904, first round 80, fourth round 69; Greg Norman, 1986, first round 74, second round 63, third round 74

**Biggest variation between two rounds**
20 strokes – RG French, 1938, second round 71, third round 91; Colin Montgomerie, 2002, second round 64, third round 84. 18 strokes – A Tingey Jr, 1923, first round 94, second 76. 17 strokes – Jack Nicklaus, 1981, first round 83, second round 66; Ian Baker-Finch, 1986, first round 86, second round 69; Rory McIlroy, 2010, first round 63, second round 80

**Best comeback by champions**
*After 18 holes:* Harry Vardon, 1896, 11 strokes behind the leader
*After 36 holes:* George Duncan, 1920, 13 strokes behind leader
*After 54 holes:* Paul Lawrie, 1999, 10 strokes behind the leader (won four-hole play-off)

## Open attendances

| Year | Attendance | Year | Attendance | Year | Attendance | Year | Attendance |
|------|-----------|------|-----------|------|-----------|------|-----------|
| 1962 | 37,098 | 1975 | 85,258 | 1988 | 191,334 | 2001 | 178,000 |
| 1963 | 24,585 | 1976 | 92,021 | 1989 | 160,639 | 2002 | 161,000 |
| 1964 | 35,954 | 1977 | 87,615 | 1990 | 207,000 | 2003 | 182,585 |
| 1965 | 32,927 | 1978 | 125,271 | 1991 | 192,154 | 2004 | 176,000 |
| 1966 | 40,182 | 1979 | 134,501 | 1992 | 150,100 | 2005 | 223,000 |
| 1967 | 29,880 | 1980 | 131,610 | 1993 | 140,100 | 2006 | 230,000 |
| 1968 | 51,819 | 1981 | 111,987 | 1994 | 128,000 | 2007 | 153,000 |
| 1969 | 46,001 | 1982 | 133,299 | 1995 | 180,000 | 2008 | 201,500 |
| 1970 | 82,593 | 1983 | 142,892 | 1996 | 170,000 | 2009 | 123,000 |
| 1971 | 70,076 | 1984 | 193,126 | 1997 | 176,797 | 2010 | 201,000 |
| 1972 | 84,746 | 1985 | 141,619 | 1998 | 180,000 | 2011 | 180,100 |
| 1973 | 78,810 | 1986 | 134,261 | 1999 | 158,000 | 2012 | 181,300 |
| 1974 | 92,796 | 1987 | 139,189 | 2000 | 230,000 | 2013 | 142,036 |

**Best comeback by non-champions**
Of non-champions, Greg Norman, 1989, seven strokes behind the leader and lost in a play-off

**Best finishing round by a champion**
**64** Greg Norman, Sandwich, 1993
**65** Tom Watson, Turnberry, 1977; Severiano Ballesteros, Royal Lytham, 1988; Justin Leonard, Royal Troon, 1997

**Worst finishing round by a champion since 1920**
**79** Henry Cotton, Sandwich, 1934
**78** Reg Whitcombe, Sandwich, 1938
**77** Walter Hagen, Hoylake, 1924

**Best opening round by a champion**
**65** Louis Oosthuizen, St Andrews, 2010

**Worst opening round by a champion since 1919**
**80** George Duncan, Deal, 1920 (he also had a second round of 80)
**77** Walter Hagen, Hoylake, 1924

**Biggest recovery in 18 holes by a champion**
George Duncan, Deal, 1920, was 13 strokes behind the leader, Abe Mitchell, after 36 holes and level after 54

**Most consecutive appearances**
**47** Gary Player, 1955–2001

**Championship since 1946 with the fewest rounds under 70**
St Andrews, 1946; Hoylake, 1947; Portrush, 1951; Hoylake, 1956; Carnoustie, 1968. All had only two rounds under 70

**Longest course**
Carnoustie, 2007, 7,421 yards (par 71)

**Largest entries**
2,499 in 2005, St Andrews

**Courses most often used**
St Andrews 28; Prestwick 24 (but not since 1925); Muirfield 16; Sandwich 13; Hoylake 11; Royal Lytham and St Annes 11; Royal Birkdale 8; Royal Troon 8; Carnoustie 7; Musselburgh 6; Turnberry 4; Deal 2; Royal Portrush and Prince's 1

**Albatrosses**
Both Jeff Maggert (6th hole, 2nd round) and Greg Owen (11th hole, 3rd round) made albatrosses during the 2001 Open Championship at Royal Lytham and St Annes. No complete record of albatrosses in the history of the event is available but since 1979 there have been only five others – by Johnny Miller (Muirfield 5th hole) in 1980, Bill Rogers (Royal Birkdale 17th) 1983, Manny Zerman (St Andrews 5th) 2000, Gary Evans (Royal Troon 4th) 2004 and Paul Lawrie (Turnberry 7th) 2009

## US Open

**Most times champion**
**4** Willie Anderson, 1901–03–04–05; Bobby Jones, 1923–26–29–30; Ben Hogan, 1948–50–51–53; Jack Nicklaus, 1962–67–72–80

**Most times runner-up**
**6** Phil Mickelson 1999–2002–04–06–09–13

**Oldest winner**
Hale Irwin, 45 years, 15 days, Medinah, 1990

**Youngest winner**
Johnny McDermott, 19 years, 10 months, 12 days, Chicago, 1911

**Amateur winners**
Francis Ouimet 1913, Jerome Travers 1915, Charles Evans 1916, Robert T Jones 1923–26–29–30, John Goodman 1933

**Youngest competitor**
Andy Zhang, 14 years 6 months, Olympic Club 2012

**Biggest winning margin**
**15 strokes** Tiger Woods, Pebble Beach, 2000

**Lowest winning aggregate**
**268** Rory McIlroy, Congressional, 2011

**Lowest in relation to par**
**16 under** Rory McIlroy, Congressional, 2011

**Lowest round**
**63** Johnny Miller, fourth round, Oakmont, 1973; Jack Nicklaus, first round, Baltusrol, 1980; Tom Weiskopf, first round, Baltusrol, 1980; Vijay Singh, second round, Olympia Fields, 2003

**Lowest 9 holes**
**29** Neal Lancaster, Shinnecock Hills, 1995, and Oakland Hills, 1996

**Lowest first 36 holes**
**131** Rory McIlroy, Congressional, 2011

**Lowest final 36 holes**
**132** Larry Nelson, Oakmont, 1983

**Lowest first 54 holes**
199 Rory McIlroy, Congressional, 2011

**Lowest final 54 holes**
203 Rory McIlroy, Congressional, 2011

**Most consecutive appearances**
44 Jack Nicklaus 1957 to 2000

**Successive victories**
3 Willie Anderson, 1903–04–05

**Players with four rounds under 70**
Lee Trevino, 69-68-69-69, Oak Hill, 1968; Lee Janzen, 67-67-69-69, Baltusrol, 1993; Rory McIlroy, 65-66-68-69, Congressional, 2011

**Oldest player to make cut**
Sam Snead 1973, 61 years

**Outright leader after every round**
Walter Hagen, Midlothian, 1914; Jim Barnes, Columbia, 1921; Ben Hogan, Oakmont, 1953; Tony Jacklin, Hazeltine, 1970; Tiger Woods, Pebble Beach, 2000; Tiger Woods, Bethpage, 2002; Rory McIlroy, Congressional, 2011

**Best opening round by a champion**
63 Jack Nicklaus, Baltusrol, 1980

**Worst opening round by a champion**
91 Horace Rawlins, Newport, RI, 1895
*Since World War II:* 76 Ben Hogan, Oakland Hills, 1951; Jack Fleck, Olympic, 1955

**Amateur champions**
Francis Ouimet, Brookline, 1913; Jerome Travers, Baltusrol, 1915; Chick Evans, Minikahda, 1916; Bobby Jones, Inwood, 1923, Scioto, 1926, Winged Foot, 1929, Interlachen, 1930; Johnny Goodman, North Shore, 1933

## The Masters

**Most times champion**
6 Jack Nicklaus, 1963–65–66–72–75–86
4 Arnold Palmer, 1958–60–62–64; Tiger Woods, 1997–2001–02–05

**Most times runner-up**
4 Ben Hogan, 1942–46–54–55; Jack Nicklaus, 1964–71–77–81

**Oldest winner**
Jack Nicklaus, 46 years, 2 months, 23 days, 1986

**Youngest winner**
Tiger Woods, 21 years, 3 months, 15 days, 1997

**Youngest competitor**
Tianlang Guan, 14 years 5 months 17 days, 2013 (made cut and finished tied 58th)

**Biggest winning margin**
12 strokes Tiger Woods, 1997

**Lowest winning aggregate**
270 Tiger Woods, 1997

**Lowest in relation to par**
18 under Tiger Woods, Augusta, 1997

**Lowest aggregate by an amateur**
281 Charles Coe, 1961 (joint second)

**Lowest round**
63 Nick Price, 1986; Greg Norman, 1996

**Lowest 9 holes**
29 Mark Calcavecchia, 1992; David Toms, 1998

**Lowest first 36 holes**
131 Raymond Floyd, 1976

**Lowest final 36 holes**
131 Johnny Miller, 1975

**Lowest first 54 holes**
201 Raymond Floyd, 1976; Tiger Woods, 1997

**Lowest final 54 holes**
200 Tiger Woods, 1997

**Most appearances**
52 Gary Player 1957–2009
50 Arnold Palmer 1955–2004

**Successive victories**
2 Jack Nicklaus, 1965–66; Nick Faldo, 1989–90; Tiger Woods, 2001–02

**Players with four rounds under 70**
None

**Outright leader after every round**
Craig Wood, 1941; Arnold Palmer, 1960; Jack Nicklaus, 1972; Raymond Floyd, 1976

**Best opening round by a champion**
65 Raymond Floyd, 1976

**Worst opening round by a champion**
75 Craig Stadler, 1982

**Worst closing round by a champion**
75 Trevor Immelman, 2008

**Albatrosses**
There have been four albatross twos in the Masters at Augusta National: by Gene Sarazen at the 15th, 1935; by Bruce Devlin at the eighth, 1967; by Jeff Maggert at the 13th, 1994 and Louis Oosthuizen at the 2nd in 2012.

## USPGA Championship

**Most times champion**
5 Walter Hagen, 1921–24–25–26–27; Jack Nicklaus 1963–71–73–75–80

**Most times runner-up**
4 Jack Nicklaus, 1964–65–74–83

**Oldest winner**
Julius Boros, 48 years 4 months 18 days, Pecan Valley, 1968

**Youngest winner**
Gene Sarazen, 20 years 5 months 22 days, Oakmont, 1922

**Biggest winning margin**
8 strokes Rory McIlroy, Kiawah Island, 2012

**Lowest winning aggregate**
265 –15: David Toms, Atlanta Athletic Club, 2001
267 –17: Steve Elkington and Colin Montgomerie, Riviera, 1995 (Elkington won in sudden death play-off)

**Lowest aggregate by runner-up**
266 –14: Phil Michelson, Atlanta Athletic Club, 2001
267 –17: Colin Montgomerie, Riviera, 1995 (lost sudden death play-off to Steve Elkington)

**Lowest in relation to par**
**18 under** Tiger Woods and Bob May, Valhalla, 2000 (May lost three-hole play-off); Tiger Woods, Medinah, 2006

**Lowest round**
**63** Bruce Crampton, Firestone, 1975; Raymond Floyd, Southern Hills, 1982; Gary Player, Shoal Creek, 1984; Vijay Singh, Inverness, 1993; Michael Bradley and Brad Faxon, Riviera, 1995; José Maria Olazábal, Valhalla, 2000; Mark O'Meara, Atlanta Athletic Club, 2001; Thomas Bjørn, Baltusrol, 2005; Tiger Woods, Southern Hills, 2007; Steve Stricker, Atlanta Athletic Club, 2011; Jason Dufner, Oak Hill, 2013

**Most successive victories**
**4** Walter Hagen, 1924–25–26–27

**Lowest 9 holes**
**28** Brad Faxon, Riviera, 1995

**Lowest first 36 holes**
**131** Hal Sutton, Riviera, 1983; Vijay Singh, Inverness, 1993; Ernie Els and Mark O'Meara, Riviera, 1995; Shingo Katayama and David Toms, Atlanta Athletic Club, 2001; Jason Dufner, Oak Hill, 2013

**Lowest final 36 holes**
**131** Mark Calcavecchia, Atlanta Athletic Club, 2001
**132** Miller Barber, Dayton, 1969; Steve Elkington and Colin Montgomerie, Riviera, 1995; Padraig Harrington, Oakland Hills, 2008

**Lowest first 54 holes**
**196** David Toms, Atlanta Athletic Club, 2001

**Lowest final 54 holes**
**199** Steve Elkington, Colin Montgomerie, Riviera, 1995; Mark Calcavecchia, David Toms, Atlanta Athletic Club, 2001; David Toms, Atlanta Athletic Club, 2011

**Most appearances**
**37** Arnold Palmer; Jack Nicklaus

**Outright leader after every round**
Bobby Nichols, Columbus, 1964; Jack Nicklaus, PGA National, 1971; Raymond Floyd, Southern Hills, 1982; Hal Sutton, Riviera, 1983

**Best opening round by a champion**
**63** Raymond Floyd, Southern Hills, 1982

**Worst opening round by a champion**
**75** John Mahaffey, Oakmont, 1978

**Worst closing round by a champion**
**76** Vijay Singh, Whistling Straits, 2004 (worst in any major since Reg Whitcombe's 78 in 1938 Open)

**Albatrosses**
Joey Sindelar had an albatross at the fifth hole at Medinah Country Club during the third round of the 2006 PGA Championship

## PGA European Tour

**Lowest 72-hole aggregate**
**258** –14: David Llewellyn, AGF Biarritz Open, 1988. –18: Ian Woosnam, Monte Carlo Open, 1990.
**259** –29: Ernie Els, Johnnie Walker Classic, Lake Karrinyup, 2003. –25: Mark McNulty, German Open, Frankfurt, 1987. –21: Tiger Woods, NEC Invitational, 2000 (Note: Sergio Garcia scored 257, 27 under par, at

the 2011 Castello Masters, but preferred lies were in operation)

**Lowest 9 holes**
**27** –9: José María Canizares, Swiss Open, Crans-sur-Sierre, 1978; Joakim Haeggman, Alfred Dunhill Cup, St Andrews, 1997; Simon Khan, Wales Open, Celtic Manor, 2004; –7: Andrew Coltart, KLM Open, Kennemer, 2007; Robert Lee, Johnnie Walker Monte Carlo Open, Mont Agel, 1985. –6: Robert Lee, Portuguese Open, Estoril, 1987. (Note: Rafa Echenique, BMW International Open, 2009, also scored 27 (–9), but preferred lies were in operation)

**Lowest 18 holes**
**60** –12: Jamie Spence, Canon European Masters, Crans-sur-Sierre, 1992; Bernhard Langer, Linde German Masters, Motzener See, 1997; Darren Clarke, Smurfit European Open, K Club, 1999; Fredrik Jacobson, Linde German Masters, Gut Larchenhof, 2003; Ernie Els, Heineken Classic, Royal Melbourne, 2004; Branden Grace, Dunhill Links Championship, Kingsbarns, 2012; Brandt Snedeker, WGC–HSBC Champions, Mission Hills, 2012; Peter Uihlein, Dunhill Links Championship, Kingsbarns, 2013. –11: Baldovino Dassu, Swiss Open, Crans-sur-Sierre, 1971; Rafael Cabrera-Bello, Austrian Open, Fontana GC, Vienna, 2009; Scott Jamieson, Portugal Masters, Oceanico Victoria, 2013. –10: Paul Curry, Bell's Scottish Open, Gleneagles, 1992; Tobias Dier, TNT Open, Hilversum, 2002; Kenneth Ferrie, Open de Andalucia, Parador del Golf Malaga, 2011. –9: Ian Woosnam, Torras Monte Carlo Open, Mont Agel, 1990; Darren Clarke and Johan Rystrom, Monte Carlo Open, Mont Agel, 1992; Phillip Archer, Celtic Manor Wales Open, Celtic Manor, 2006. –8: David Llewellyn, AGF Biarritz Open, Biarritz GC, 1988 (Note: Bradley Dredge, Madeira Island Open, 2003, Colin Montgomerie, Indonesia Open, 2005, Ross McGowan, Madrid Masters, 2009 and Ian Poulter, Hong Kong Open 2010, also scored 60, but preferred lies were in operation)

**Lowest 36 holes**
**124** –18: Colin Montgomerie, Canon European Masters, Crans-sur-Sierre, 1996 (3rd and 4th rounds). –14: Robert Karlsson, Celtic Manor Wales Open, Celtic Manor, 2006 (1st and 2nd rounds). (Note: Ian Poulter also scored 124 (–16, 60-64) in the 2nd and 3rd rounds of the 2010 UBS Hong Kong Open, but preferred lies were in operation)

**Lowest 54 holes**
**189** –18 Robert Karlsson, Celtic Manor Wales Open, 2006 (rounds 1-2-3). (Note: Sergio García scored 190, 23 under par, in rounds 2-3-4 at the 2011 Castello Masters, but preferred lies were in operation). Ernie Els shot a record 23 under par 193 in the 2003 Johnnie Walker Championship at Lake Karrinyup and David Howell equalled that in the 2006 TCL Classic at Yalong Bay.

**Lowest 54 holes under par**
**192** –24 Anders Forsbrand, Ebel European Masters Swiss Open, Crans-Sur-Sierre, 1987 (rounds 2-3-4). (Note: Ross McGowan, Madrid Masters 2009, rounds 1-2-3, and Mikko Ilonen, Madrid Masters 2009, rounds 2-3-4, also scored 192, 24 under par, but preferred lies were in operation)

**Lowest round by amateur**
**62** −10 Shane Lowry, 3 Irish Open, County Louth, 2009; −9 Sven Struver, German Open, Frankfurt GC, 1989; −8 David Palm, SAS Masters, Arlandastad 2008 (*Note:* Adam Scott's 63 at the 2000 Greg Norman Holden International at The Lakes was 10 under par)

**Lowest first 36 holes**
**124** −14 Robert Karlsson, Wales Open, Celtic Manor Roman Road, 2006
**125** −17: Frankie Minoza, Caltex Singapore Masters, Singapore Island, 2001. −15: Tiger Woods, NEC Invitational World Championship, Firestone, Akron, Ohio, 2000. The lowest under par was Ernie Els' 18 under 126 in the 2004 Heineken Classic at Royal Melbourne.

**Largest winning margin**
**15 strokes** Tiger Woods, United States Open, Pebble Beach, 2000. (*Note:* Bernhard Langer's 17-stroke victory in 1979 at Cacharel Under-25's Championship in Nîmes is not considered a full European Tour event)

**Highest winning score**
**306** Peter Butler, Schweppes PGA Close Championship, Royal Birkdale, 1963

**Youngest winner**
Matteo Manassero, 17 years 188 days, Castello Masters, 2010

**Youngest to make cut**
Tianlang Guan, 14 years 169 days, The Masters, 2013

**Oldest to make cut**
Bob Charles 71 years 261 days, 2007 Michael Hill New Zealand Open, The Hills Golf Club, Queenstown

**Oldest winner**
Miguel Angel Jiménez, 49 years 337 days, 2013 Hong Kong Open

**Most wins in one season**
**7** Norman von Nida, 1947

**Amateur winners**
Pablo Martin, Estoril Portuguese Open, 2007; Danny Lee, Johnnie Walker Classic, 2009; Shane Lowry, 3 Irish Open, 2009

**Youngest to play**
Ye Wo-cheng, 12 years 242 days, Volvo China Open, 2013

**Oldest to play**
Arnold Palmer, 74 years 211 days, The Masters, 2004

## US PGA Tour

**Lowest 72-hole aggregate**
**254** −26: Tommy Armour III, Valero Texas Open, 2003. (*Note:* Steve Stricker's 255 at the 2009 Bob Hope Classic was a record 33 under par)

**Lowest 54 holes**
**188** −25: Steve Stricker, John Deere Classic, 2010 (rounds 1-3). (*Note:* Tim Herron's 190 at the 2003 Bob Hope Chrysler Classic (rounds 2-4) was a record 26 under par)

**Lowest 36 holes**
**122** −18: Troy Matteson, 2009 Frys.com Open (2nd and 3rd rounds). (*Note:* record under par was 123

(−21) Steve Stricker, 2009 Bob Hope Classic (3rd and 4th rounds)

**Lowest first 36 holes**
**124** −20: Pat Perez, 2009 Bob Hope Classic; −16 David Toms, 2001 Crowne Plaza Invitational at Colonial

**Lowest 18 holes**
**59** −13: Al Geiberger, 2nd round, Memphis Classic Colonial CC, 1977 (preferred lies in operation); Chip Beck, 3rd round, Las Vegas Invitational, Sunrise, 1991; David Duval, final round, Bob Hope Chrysler Classic, PGA West Palmer Course, 1999 (won tournament with last hole eagle); −12: Paul Goydos, 1st round, John Deere Classic, TPC Deere Run, 2010 (preferred lies); −11: Stuart Appleby, final round, Greenbrier Classic, Old White course, The Greenbrier, 2010 (won by one with three closing birdies); Jim Furyk, 2nd round, BMW Championship, Conway Farms, 2013

**Lowest 9 holes**
**26** −8: Corey Pavin, US Bank Championship, 2006
**27** −9: Billy Mayfair, Buick Open, 2001; Robert Gamez, Bob Hope Chrysler Classic, 2004; Brandt Snedeker, Buick Invitational, 2007; Chris Riley, Reno-Tahoe Open, 2009. −8: Mike Souchak, Texas Open, 1955; Nick Watney, AT&T National, 2011. −7: Andy North, BC Open, 1975

**Lowest round by amateur**
**60** −10 Patrick Cantlay, Travelers Championship, TPC River Highlands, 2011

**Largest winning margin**
**16 strokes** J Douglas Edgar, Canadian Open Championship, 1919; Joe Kirkwood, Corpus Christi Open 1924; Sam Snead, West Virginia Championship, 1936; Bobby Locke, Chicago Victory National Championship, 1948

**Youngest winner**
Harry Cooper, 19 years 4 days, Galveston Open, 1923

**Youngest to make cut**
Bob Panasik, 15 years 8 months 20 days, Canadian Open, 1957

**Oldest winner**
Sam Snead, 52 years 10 months, Greater Greensboro Open, 1965

**Most wins in one season**
**18** Byron Nelson, 1945

**Most wins**
**82** Sam Snead 1936–65; **79** Tiger Woods 1996–2013; **73** Jack Nicklaus 1962–86

**Most consecutive years with a win**
**17** Arnold Palmer 1955–71, Jack Nicklaus 1962–78

**Most consecutive wins**
**11** Byron Nelson 1945

**Most consecutive birdies**
**9** Mark Calcavecchia, Canadian Open, 2009

**Most consecutive birdies to win**
**6** Mike Souchak, St Paul Open, 1956

**Most consecutive rounds par or better**
**52** Tiger Woods, 2000 Byron Nelson Classic to 2001 Phoenix Open

**Biggest last round comeback to win**
**10 strokes** Paul Lawrie, Open Championship, 1999

# National Opens – excluding Europe and USA

**Lowest 72-hole aggregate**
**255** Peter Tupling, Nigerian Open, Lagos, 1981

**Lowest 36-hole aggregate**
**124** −18: Sandy Lyle, Nigerian Open, Ikoyi GC, Lagos, 1978 (his first year as a professional)

**Lowest 18 holes**
**59** Gary Player, second round, Brazilian Open, Gavea GC (6,185 yards), Rio de Janeiro, 1974

# Professional events – excluding Europe and US PGA Tour

**Lowest 72-hole aggregate**
**260** Bob Charles, Spalding Masters at Tauranga, New Zealand, 1969; Jason Bohn, Bayer Classic, Huron Oaks, Canada, 2001; Brian Kontak, Alberta Open, Canada, 1998.

**Lowest 18-hole aggregate**
**58** −13: Jason Bohn, Bayer Classic, Huron Oaks, Canada, 2001; −12: Ryo Ishikawa, The Crowns, Japan, 2010
**59** Sam Snead, Greenbrier Open, The Greenbrier 1959; Miguel Angel Martin, South Argentine Open, 1987

**Lowest 9-hole aggregate**
**27** Bill Brask at Tauranga in the New Zealand PGA in 1976

**Amateur winners**
Charles Evans, 1910 Western Open, Beverly, Illinois; John Dawson, 1942 Bing Crosby, Rancho Santa Fe, California; Gene Littler, 1954 San Diego Open, Rancho Santa Fe, California; Doug Sanders, 1956 Canadian Open, Beaconsfield, Quebec; Scott Verplank 1985 Western Open, Butler National, Illinois; Phil Mickelson 1991 Northern Telecom Open, Tucson, Arizona; Brett Rumford, 1999 ANZ Players Championship, Royal Queensland; Aaron Baddeley, 1999 Australian Open, Royal Sydney

# Asian PGA Tour

**Lowest 72 holes**
**256** −32: Chapchai Nirat, 2009 SAIL Open, India
**259** −29: Ernie Els, 2003 Johnnie Walker Classic.
(Note: Thaworn Wiratchant achieved a 25 under par total of 255 in the 2005 Enjoy Jakarta Standard Chartered Indonesian Open, but preferred lies were in use as they were when Ian Poulter scored a 22 under par 258 in the 2010 UBS Hong Kong Open)

**Highest winning score**
**293** +5: Boonchu Ruangkit, 1996 Myanmar Open

**Lowest 54 holes**
**189** −27: Chapchai Nirat, 2009 SAIL Open, India
**193** −23: Ernie Els, 2003 Johnnie Walker Classic; David Howell, 2006 TCL Classic. (Note: Thaworn Wiratchant achieved an 18 under par total of 192 in the 2005 Enjoy Jakarta Standard Chartered Indonesia Open, but preferred lies were in use)

**Lowest 36 holes**
**124** −20 Chapchai Nirat, 2009 SAIL Open, India; Lee Westwood, 2011 Thailand Championship
**125** −17 Frankie Minoza, 2001 Caltex Singapore Masters (Note: Peter Karmis has an 18 under par 126 in the 2010 Handa Singapore Classic, but preferred lies were in operation)

**Lowest 18 holes**
**60** −12: Liang Wen-chong, 2008 Hero Honda Indian Open; Lee Westwood, 2011 Thailand Championship; Brandt Snedeker, 2012 WGC–HSBC Champions (Note: Kim Felton had an 11 under par 60 in the 2000 Omega Hong Kong Open, Colin Montgomerie a 10 under par 60 in the 2005 Enjoy Jakarta Standard Chartered Indonesian Open and Ian Poulter a 10 under par 60 in the 2010 UBS Hong Kong Open, but preferred lies were in operation)

**Lowest 9 holes**
**28** −8: Chung Chun-hsing, 2001 Maekyung LG Fashion Open; Liang Wen-chong, 2008 Hero Honda Indian Open; Chinnarat Phadungsil, 2013 Avantha Masters; Craig Lee, 2012 Omega European Masters. −7: Chinnarat Phadungsil, 2007 Midea China Classic; Henrik Bjornstad, 2001 Omega Hong Kong Open; Maarten Lafeber, 2005 UBS Hong Kong Open; Mardan Mamat, 2009 Singha Thailand Open; Brett Rumford, 2009 Omega European Masters; Masanori Kobayashi, 2012 Asia-Pacific Panasonic Open

**Biggest margin of victory**
**13 strokes** Ernie Els, 2005 BMW Asian Open
**12 strokes** Bradley Hughes, 1996 Players Championship

**Youngest winners**
Chinarat Phadungsil (am), 17 years 5 days, 2005 Double A International Open; Kim Dae-sub (am), 17 years 83 days, 1998 Korean Open; Noh Seung-yul, 17 years 143 days, 2008 Midea China Classic

**Youngest to play**
Ye Wo-cheng, 13 years 2 days, 2013 Omega European Masters
**Youngest to play in an Asian event**
Ye Jian-fe, 13 years and 20 days, 2004 Sanya Open

**Oldest winners**
Choi Sang-ho, 50 years and 145 days, 2005 Maekyung Open; Miguel Angel Jiménez, 48 years 318 days, 2012 USB Hong Kong Open

**Amateur winner**
Kim Dae-sub, 1998 Korean Open; Eddie Lee, 2002 Maekyung Open, South Korea; Chinnarat Phadungsil, 2005 Double A International, Thailand

**Most wins in a season**
**4** Thaworn Wiratchant, 2005

**Most wins on Tour**
**16** Thaworn Wiratchant

**Most consecutive birdies**
9 Colin Montgomerie, 2005 Indonesian Open

**First par 6 hole**
878-yard fourth, St Andrews Hill, Rayong, Thailand, 2005 Double A International Open

**Youngest player to make the cut**
Atiwit Janewattananond, 14 years 71 days, 2010 Asian Tour International

**Oldest player to make the cut**
Hsieh Min-nan, 70 years 53 days, 2010 Mercuries Taiwan Masters

**Holes in one at same hole**
Chen Chung-cheng, 2004 Thailand Open, fourth hole, days 1 and 3

**First woman to make halfway cut**
Michelle Wie, 2006 SK Telecom Open, Korea (finished tied 35th)

## Japan Golf Tour

**Lowest 72 holes**
260 −20: Masashi 'Jumbo' Ozaki, 1995 Chunichi Crowns, Nagoya Wago
262 −26: Masashi Ozaki, 1996 Japan Series, Tokyo Yomiuri
263 −17: Tetsuji Hiratsuka, 2009 The Crowns, Nagoya

**Lowest 54 holes**
192 −18 Shingo Katayama, The Crowns 2004 and 2006

**Lowest 36 holes**
126 −18: Masahiro Kuramoto, 1987 Maruman Open, Higashi Matsuyama

**Lowest 18 holes**
58 −12: Ryo Ishikawa, 2010 The Crowns (this is the lowest round on a major tour. He came from six behind to win by five, aged 18 at the time); 59 −12 Masahiro Kuramoto, 2003 Acom International

**Lowest 9 holes**
28 −8: Yoshinori Kaneko, 1994 Nikkei Cup, Mitsui-kanko Tomakomai; Masayuki Kawamura, 1995 Gene Sarazen Jun Classic; Tsuyoshi Yoneyama, 1998 Sapporo Tokyu, Sapporo Kokusai; Toshimitsu Izawa, 2000 TPC Iiyama Cup, Horai; Hideto Tanihara 2004; −7 Dinesh Chand 2005; Hideto Tanihara 2008; Ryo Ishikawa 2010; Masanori Kobayashi 2012

**Largest winning margin**
15 Masashi Ozaki, 1994 Daiwa International Hatoyama (pre-1973 tour formation: 19 Akira Muraki, 1930 Japan PGA Championship, Takarazuka)

**Youngest winner**
Ryo Ishikawa (amateur), 15 years 8 months, 2007 Munsingwear Open KBS Cup

**Oldest winner**
Masashi Ozaki, 55 years 8 months, 2002 ANA Open, Sapporo Wattsu

**Most wins in a season**
8 Tsuneyuki 'Tommy' Nakajima, 1983; Masashi 'Jumbo' Ozaki, 1996

**Amateur winners**
Masahiro Kuramoto, 1980 Chugoku-Shikoku Open; Ryo Ishikawa, 2007 Munsingwear Open KBS Cup; Hideki Matsuyama, 2011 Taiheiyo Masters

## South African Sunshine Tour

**Lowest 9-hole score**
28 Simon Hobday, 2nd round of the 1987 Royal Swazi Sun Pro Am at Royal Swazi Sun Country Club; Mark McNulty, 2nd round of 1996 Zimbabwe Open at Chapman Golf Club; David Frost, 2nd round of the 1997 Alfred Dunhill PGA Championship at Houghton Golf Club; Tertius Claassens, 1st round of the 1982 SAB Masters at Milnerton; Brenden Pappas, 2nd round of the 1996 Dimension Data Pro-Am at Gary Player Country Club; Murray Urquhart, 2nd round of the 2001 Royal Swazi Sun Open at Royal Swazi Sun CC

**Lowest 18-hole score**
60 Shane Pringle 30-30, 2002 Botswana Open, Gabarone Golf Club

**Lowest first 36 holes**
127 Barry Painting 62-65, 2004 FNB Botswana Open, Gabarone Golf Club

**Lowest last 36 holes**
126 Mark McNulty 64-62, 1987 Royal Swazi Sun Pro-Am, Royal Swazi Sun Country Club

**Lowest 54 holes**
195 Nick Price 61-69-65, 1994 ICL International; Barry Painting 62-65-68, 2004 FNB Botswana Open, Gaberone GC

**Lowest 72-hole score**
259 Mark McNulty 68-65-64-62, 1987 Royal Swazi Sun Pro-Am, Royal Swazi Sun Country Club; David Frost 64-67-65-63, 1994 Lexington PGA, Wanderers Golf Club

**Largest winning margin**
12 strokes Nick Price, 1993 Nedbank Million Dollar, Sun City (non-Order of Merit event)
11 strokes Nico van Rensburg, 2000 Vodacom Series Gauteng, Silver Lakes

**Most wins in a season**
Seven wins in 11 tournaments by Mark McNulty, 1986-87 season − Southern Suns SA Open, AECI Charity Classic, Royal Swazi Sun Pro-Am, Trust Bank Tournament of Champions, Germiston Centenary Golf Tournament, Safmarine Masters, Helix Wild Coast Sun Classic

**Most wins in succession**
Four Gary Player, 1979-80 − Lexington PGA, Krönenbrau SA Masters, B.A. / Yellow Pages SA Open, Sun City Classic; Mark McNulty, 1986-87 − Southern Suns SA Open, AECI Charity Classic, Royal Swazi Sun Pro-Am, Trust Bank Tournament of Champions

**Most birdies in one round**
11 Allan Henning, 1st round of the 1975 Rolux Toro Classic, Glendower Golf Club; John Bland, 1st round of the 1993 SA Open Championship, Durban Country Club; Mark McNulty, 2nd round of the 1996 Zimbabwe Open, Royal Harare Golf Club; Alan McLean, 3rd round of the 2005 Telkom PGA Championship at Woodhill

Country Club. (*Note:* Shane Pringle had 10 birdies and an eagle in the 2nd round of the 2002 FNB Botswana Open at Gaborone Golf Club; Marc Cayeux had nine birdies and an eagle in the final round of the 2004 Vodacom Players Championship at Country Club Johannesburg)

**Most birdies in a row**
9 Alan McLean, from the seventh to the 15th in the 3rd round of the 2005 Telkom PGA Championship at Woodhill Country Club
8 Bobby Lincoln, from the eighth to the 15th in the final round of the AECI Classic, Randpark Golf Club; Mark McNulty, from the ninth to the 16th in the 2nd round of the 1996 Zimbabwe Open, Royal Harare Golf Club

**Lowest finish by a winner**
62 Gavan Levenson, last round of the 1983 Vaal Reefs Open, Orkney Golf Club; Mark McNulty, 1987 Royal Swazi Sun Pro-Am, Royal Swazi Sun Country Club

**Most Order of Merit victories**
Eight Mark McNulty, 1981, 82, 85, 86, 87, 93, 98

**Youngest winners**
Anton Haig, 19 years 4 months, 2005 Seekers Travel Pro-Am, Dainfern; Dale Hayes, 19 years 5 months, Bert Hagerman Invitational, Zwartkops, Dec 1971; Charl Schwartzel, 20 years 3 months, 2004 dunhill championship at Leopard Creek. (*Note:* Dale Hayes was 18 years 6 months when he won the unofficial Newcastle Open at Newcastle Golf Club in 1971); Mark Murless, 20 years 5 months, 1996 Platinum Classic, Mooinooi Golf Club; Adam Scott, 20 years 6 months, 2001 Alfred Dunhill Championship, Houghton Golf Club; Marc Cayeux, 20 years 9 months, 1998 Zambia Open, Lusaka Golf Club; Trevor Immelman, 20 years 11 months, Vodacom Players Championship, Royal Cape Golf Club

**Oldest winner**
Mark McNulty, 49 years 44 days, 2003 Vodacom Players Championship, Royal Cape Golf Club

## Australasian Tour

**Most wins**
31 Greg Norman

**Youngest winner**
A Baddeley (19 years), 1999 Australian Open

**Oldest winner**
Kel Nagle (54 years), 1975 Clearwater Classic (now the New Zealand PGA Championship

**Lowest round**
60 −12: Paul Gow, 2001 Canon Challenge, Castle Hill; Ernie Els, 2004 Heineken Classic, Royal Melbourne

## Canadian Tour

**Lowest 72 holes**
256 −28: Brian Unk, 2009 Seaforth Country Classic

**Lowest 54 holes**
192 −21: Brian Unk, 2009 Seaforth Country Classic

**Lowest 36 holes**
126 −18: Matt Cole, 1988 Windsor Charity Classic.
−16: James Hahn, 2009 Seaforth Country Classic

**Lowest 18 holes**
58 −13: Jason Bohn, 2001 Bayer Championship

**Lowest 9 holes**
26 −9: Jason Bohn, 2001 Bayer Championship

**Most consecutive birdies**
8 Jason Bohn, 2002 Texas Challenge

**Most birdies in a round**
10 Jason Bohn, 2001 Bayer Championship

**Largest winning margin**
11 Arron Oberholser, 1999 Ontario Open Heritage Classic

**Most wins**
13 Moe Norman

**Most wins in a season**
4 Trevor Dodds (1996 Alberta Open, ED TEL Planet Open, Infiniti Championship, Canadian Masters); Moe Norman (1966 Manitoba Open, Canadian PGA Championship, Quebec Open, Alberta Open)

**Oldest winner**
Moe Norman, 46 years 11 months, 1976 Alberta Open

**Youngest winner**
James Lepp (amat.), 19 years 7 months, 2003 Greater Vancouver Charity Classic

**Youngest to play**
Michelle Wie, 13 years 10 months, 2003 Bay Mills Championship

**Oldest to make cut**
Jim Rutledge, 51 years 2 months, 2010 Players Cup

**Best last-day comeback to win**
8 strokes Brian Payne, 2001 Aliant Cup; Adrian Bland, 2007 San Jose International Classic; Spencer Levin, 2008 Spring International

## Tour de las Americas

**Lowest 72 holes**
265 −23: Jamie Donaldson, Telefonica de Guatemala Open, 2007; Felipe Aguilar, Chile Open, 2008

**Largest winning margin**
11 Felipe Aguilar, Chile Open, 2008

**Youngest winner**
Luciano Giometti, 18 years 9 months, Open del Sur Personal, Argentina, 2006

**Oldest winner**
Vicente Fernandez 54 years 7 months, Argentina Open, Jockey Club, Buenos Aires, 2002

**Highest winning aggregate**
289 +5: Rafael Gomez and Marco Ruiz, Costa Rica Open, 2002 (Gomez won play-off)

**Most wins in a season**
3 Jesus Amaya 2001-02; Rafael Gomez, 2008

**Most wins**
8 Rafael Gomez

**Lowest round**
59 –11: Cipriano Castro, Siemens Venezuela Open, Valle Arribe, Caracas, 2006

**Biggest comeback to win**
9 strokes Venezuela, Copa de Naciones, El Tigre, Nueva Vallarta, Mexico 2004; Rafael Ponce, Acapulco Fest, Fairmont Princess, Acapulco, Mexico, 2004 LPGA Tour

## LPGA Tour

**Lowest 72 holes**
258 –22: Karen Stupples, Welch's/Fry's Championship, Dell Urich, Arizona, 2004. (Note: Annika Sörenstam's 261 at 2001 Standard Register Ping, Moon Valley, Arizona, was a record 27 under par)

**Lowest 54 holes**
192 –24: Annika Sörenstam, Mizuno Classic, Shiga, Japan, 2003

**Lowest 36 holes**
124 –20: Annika Sörenstam, Standard Register Ping, Moon Valley, Arizona, 2001. –16: Meg Mallon, Welch's/Fry Championship, Dell Urich, Arizona, 2003

**Lowest 18 holes**
59 –13: Annika Sörenstam, Standard Register Ping, Moon Valley, Arizona, 2001

**Lowest 9 holes**
27 –8: Jimin Kang, ShopRite Classic, Seaview, New Jersey, 2005. –7: In-kyung Kim, Jamie Farr Owens Corning Classic, Highland Meadows, Ohio, 2007; Paula Creamer, Jamie Farr Corning Classic, Highland Meadows, Ohio, 2008 (Note: the 28s by Mary Beth Zimmerman, Rail Charity Classic, Springfield, Illinois, 1984, Annika Sörenstam, Standard Register Ping, Moon Valley, Arizona, 2001; Candie Kung, Wendy's Championship, Tartan Field, Ohio, 2006; Sarah Lee, Corona Championship, Tres Marias, Mexico, 2007; Sun Young Yoo, State Farm Classic, Panther Creek, Illinois, 2008 and Yani Tseng, Corning Classic, Corning CC, New York, 2009 were also 8 under par, as were the 29s by Nicky Le Roux, Rochester International, Locust Hill, New York, 1990, and Kris Tschetter, Weetabix Women's British Open, Royal Birkdale, England, 2005)

**Most birdies in a round**
13 Annika Sorenstam, Standard Register Ping, Moon Valley, Arizona, 2004

**Most consecutive birdies**
9 Beth Daniel, Philips Invitational, Onion Creek, Texas, 1999

**Largest winning margin**
14 strokes Cindy Mackey, MasterCard International Pro-am, Knollwood, New York, 1986

**Youngest winner**
Lydia Ko (amateur), 15 years 4 months 2 days, 2012 Canadian Women's Open

**Oldest winner**
Beth Daniel, 46 years 8 months 29 days, Canadian Open, 2003

**Most wins in a season**
13 Mickey Wright, 1963

**Most wins**
88 Kathy Whitworth

**Most majors**
15 Patty Berg

**Most majors won in a season**
3 Babe Zaharias (1950 US Women's Open, Titleholders, Western Open); Mickey Wright (1961 LPGA Championship, US Women's Open, Titleholders); Pat Bradley (1986 Nabisco Dinah Shore, LPGA Championship, Du Maurier Classic); Inbee Park (2013 Kraft Nabisco Championship, Wegmans LPGA Championship, US Women's Open)

**Most consecutive seasons with a victory**
17 Kathy Whitworth (1962–78)

**Biggest comeback to victory**
10 Mickey Wright (1964 Tall City Open); Annika Sörenstam (2001 Office Depot); Louise Friberg (2008 MasterCard Classic)

**Youngest major winner**
Morgan Pressel, 18 years 10 months 9 days, Kraft Nabisco Championship, 2007

**Oldest major winner**
Fay Crocker, 45 years 7 months 11 days, Titleholders Championship, 1960

**Youngest player**
Beverly Klass, 10 years 6 months 3 days, Dallas Civitan Open, 1967

**Oldest player**
JoAnne Carner, 65 years 11 months 21 days, Kraft Nabisco Championship, 2005

**Youngest to make cut**
Michelle Wie 13 years 5 months 17 days, Kraft Nabisco Championship, 2003

**Oldest to make cut**
JoAnne Carner, 64 years 26 days, Chick-fil-A Charity Championship, 2004

**Amateur winners**
Polly Riley, 1950 Tampa Open; Pat O'Sullivan, 1951 Titleholders Championship; Catherine LaCoste, 1967 US Women's Open; JoAnne Carner, 1969 Burdine's Invitational

**Lowest major round**
62 –10: Minea Blomqvist, 2004 Weetabix Women's British Open, Sunningdale; –10: Lorena Ochoa, 2006 Kraft Nabisco Championship, Rancho Mirage

**Most birdies in a round**
13 Annika Sörenstam, Moon Valley Country Club, Phoenix, 2001 Standard Register Ping

**Most consecutive birdies**
9 Beth Daniel, Onion Creek Club, Austin, 1999 Philips Invitational

## Ladies European Tour

**Lowest 72 holes**
249 –11: Dale Reid and Trish Johnson, 1991 Bloor Homes Eastleigh Classic, Fleming Park

**Lowest 72 holes in relation to par**
259 −29: Gwladys Nocera, 2008 Goteborg Masters, Lycke, Sweden

**Lowest 54 holes**
193 −23: Gwladys Nocera, 2008 Goteborg Masters, Lycke, Sweden

**Lowest 36 holes**
128 −16: Gwladys Nocera, 2008 Goteborg Masters, Lycke, Sweden. (Note: Sophie Gustafson's 129 at the 2003 Ladies Irish Open, Killarney, was a record 17 under)

**Lowest 18 holes**
58 −7: Dale Reid and Trish Johnson, 1991 Bloor Homes Eastleigh Classic, Fleming Park; Jane Connachan, 1991 Bloor Homes Eastleigh Classic, Fleming Park

**Lowest 18 holes in relation to par**
61 −11: Kirsty Taylor, 2005 Wales Ladies Championship, Machynys Peninsula; Nina Reis, 2008 Goteborg Masters, Lycke, Sweden; Karrie Webb, 2010 ANZ Ladies Masters, Royal Pines; So Yeon Ryu, 2012 Gold Coast RACV Australian Ladies Masters, Royal Pines
62 −11: Trish Johnson, 1996 Ladies French Open, Golf D'Arras; Lisa Holm Sorensen, 2009 SAS Masters, Larvik, Norway

**Lowest 9 holes**
28 −7: Tamie Durdin, 2010 ANZ Ladies Masters, Royal Pines

**Highest winning score**
292 +4: Raquel Carriedo, 2002 Tenerife Ladies Open, Golf del Sur; Sherri Steinhauer, 1998 Weetabix Women's British Open, Royal Lytham and St Annes

**Largest winning margin**
16 strokes  Laura Davies, 1995 Guardian Irish Holidays Open, St Margaret's

**Youngest winner**
Lydia Ko (amateur), 15 years 10 months, ISPS Handa New Zealand Women's Open, 2013

**Youngest to play**
Leona and Lisa Maguire, 12 years 6 months, 2007 BT Northern Ireland Ladies Open

**Youngest to make cut**
Ariya Jutanugarn, 12 years 9 months, 2008 Finnair Masters, Helsinki Golf Club

**Oldest winner**
Laura Davies, 47 years 1 month 8 days, 2010 Hero Honda Women's Indian Open

**Most wins**
45 Laura Davies

**Most wins in a year**
7  Marie-Laure de Lorenzi, 1988 (French Open, Volmac Open, Hennessy Cup, Gothenburg Open, Laing Charity Classic, Woolmark Matchplay, Qualitair Spanish Open)

**Most birdies in a round**
12  Kristie Smith, 2009 ANZ Masters, Royal Pines, Australia

## Miscellaneous British

**72-hole aggregate**
Andrew Brooks recorded a 72-hole aggregate of 259 in winning the Skol (Scotland) tournament at Williamwood in 1974.

**Lowest rounds**
Playing on the ladies' course (4,020 yards) at Sunningdale on 26th September, 1961, Arthur Lees, the professional there, went round in 52, 10 under par. He went out in 26 (2, 3, 3, 4, 3, 3, 3, 3, 2) and came back in 26 (2 3, 3, 3, 2, 3, 4, 3, 3).

On 1st January, 1936, AE Smith, Woolacombe Bay professional, recorded a score of 55 in a game there with a club member. The course measured 4,248 yards. Smith went out in 29 and came back in 26 finishing with a hole-in-one at the 18th.

Other low scores recorded in Britain are by CC Aylmer, an English International who went round Ranelagh in 56; George Duncan, Axenfels in 56; Harry Bannerman, Banchory in 56 in 1971; Ian Connelly Welwyn Garden City in 56 in 1972; James Braid Hedderwick near Dunbar in 57; H. Hardman, Wirral in 58; Norman Quigley, Windermere in 58 in 1937; Robert Webster, Eaglescliffe in 58, in 1970. Harry Weetman scored 58 in a round at the 6171 yards Croham Hurst on 30th January, 1956.

D Sewell had a round of 60 in an Alliance Meeting at Ferndown, Bournemouth, a full-size course. He scored 30 for each half and had a total of 26 putts. In September 1986, Jeffrey Burn, handicap 1, of Shrewsbury GC, scored 60 in a club competition, made up of 8 birdies, an eagle and 9 pars. He was 30 out and 30 home and no. 5 on his card. Andrew Sherborne, as a 20-year-old amateur, went round Cirencester in 60 strokes. Dennis Gray completed a round at Broome Manor, Swindon (6906 yards, SSS 73) in the summer of 1976 in 60 (28 out, 32 in).

Playing over Aberdour on 13th June, 1936, Hector Thomson, British Amateur champion, 1936, and Jack McLean, former Scottish Amateur champion, each did 61 in the second round of an exhibition. McLean in his first round had a 63, which gave him an aggregate 124 for 36 holes.

Steve Tredinnick in a friendly match against business tycoon Joe Hyman scored a 61 over West Sussex (6211 yards) in 1970. It included a hole-in-one at the 12th (198 yards) and a 2 at the 17th (445 yards).

Another round of 61 on a full-size course was achieved by 18-year-old Michael Jones on his home course, Worthing GC (6274 yards), in the first round of the President's Cup in May, 1974.

In the Second City Pro-Am tournament in 1970, at Handsworth, Simon Fogarty did the second 9 holes in 27 against the par of 36.

## Miscellaneous USA

**Lowest rounds**
The lowest known scores recorded for 18 holes in America are 55 by E F Staugaard in 1935 over the 6419 yards Montebello Park, California, and 55 by Homero Blancas in 1962 over the 5002 yards Premier course in Longview, Texas. Staugaard in his round had 2 eagles, 13 birdies and 3 pars.

In July 2010 Bobby Wyatt had a 14 under par 57 at the 6,628-yard Country Club of Mobile in the Alabama Boys State Junior Championship. He was 17 at the time. The round contained an eagle and 12 birdies and beat the course record by six.

Equally outstanding is a round of 58 (13 under par) achieved by a 13-year-old boy, Douglas Beecher, on 6th July, 1976, at Pitman CC, New Jersey. The course measured 6180 yards from the back tees, and the middle tees, off which Douglas played, were estimated by the club professional to reduce the yardage by under 180 yards.

In 1941 at a 6100 yards course in Portsmouth, Virginia, Chandler Harper scored 58.

Jack Nicklaus in an exhibition match at Breakers Club, Palm Beach, California, in 1973 scored 59 over the 6200-yard course.

The lowest 9-hole score in America is 25, held jointly by Bill Burke over the second half of the 6384 yards Normandie CC, St Louis in May, 1970 at the age of 29; by Daniel Cavin, who had seven 3s and two 2s on the par 36 Bill Brewer Course, Texas, in September, 1959; and by Douglas Beecher over the second half of Pitman CC, New Jersey, on 6th July, 1976, at the amazingly young age of 13. The back 9 holes of the Pitman course measured 3150 yards (par 35) from the back tees, but even though Douglas played off the middle tees, the yardage was still over 3000 yards for the 9 holes. He scored 8 birdies and 1 eagle.

Horton Smith scored 119 for two consecutive rounds in winning the Catalina Open in California in December, 1928. The course, however, measured only 4700 yards.

# Miscellaneous – excluding GB and USA

Tony Jacklin won the 1973 Los Lagartos Open with an aggregate of 261, 27 under par.

Henry Cotton in 1950 had a round of 56 at Monte Carlo (29 out, 27 in).

In a Pro-Am tournament prior to the 1973 Nigerian Open, British professional David Jagger went round in 59.

Max Banbury recorded a 9-hole score of 26 at Woodstock, Ontario, playing in a competition in 1952.

## Women

The lowest score recorded on a full-size course by a woman is 59 by Sweden's Annika Sörenstam on the 6459 yards, par 72 Moon Valley course in Phoenix, Arizona. It broke by two the previous record of 61 by South Korean Se Ri Pak. Sörenstam had begun the tournament with a 65 and by adding rounds of 69 and 68 she equalled the LPGA record of 261 set by Pak (71-61-63-66) at Highland Meadows in Ohio in 1998. Sörenstam's score represents 27 under par, Pak's 23 under.

The lowest 9-hole score on the US Ladies' PGA circuit is 28, first achieved by Mary Beth Zimmerman in the 1984 Rail Charity Classic and since equalled by Pat Bradley, Muffin Spencer-Devlin, Peggy Kirsch, Renee Heiken, Anika Sörenstam and Danielle Ammaccapane.

The Lowest 36-hole score is the 124 (20 under par) by Sörenstam at Moon Valley and the lowest 54-hole score 193 (23 under par) by Karrie Webb at Walnut Hills, Michigan, in the 2000 Oldsmobile Classic and equalled by Sörenstam at Moon Valley.

Patty Berg holds the record for the most number of women's majors with 15; Kathy Whitworth achieved a record number of tournament wins with 88; Mickey Wright's 13 wins in 1963 was the most in one season and the youngest and oldest winners of LPGA events were Marlene Hagge, 18 years and 14 days when she won the 1952 Sarasota Open and JoAnne Carner, 46 years 5 months 11 days when she won the 1985 Safeco Classic.

The lowest round on the European LPGA is 62 (11 under par) by Trish Johnson in the 1996 French Open. A 62 was also achieved by New Zealand's Janice Arnold at Coventry in 1990 during a Women's Professional Golfers' Association tournament.

The lowest 9-hole score on the European LPGA circuit is 29 by Kitrina Douglas, Regine Lautens, Laura Davies, Anne Jones and Trish Johnson.

In the Women's World Team Championship in Mexico in 1966, Mrs Belle Robertson, playing for the British team, was the only player to break 70. She scored 69 in the third round.

At Westgate-on-Sea GC (measuring 5002 yards), Wanda Morgan scored 60 in an open tournament in 1929.

Since scores cannot properly be taken in matchplay no stroke records can be made in matchplay events. Nevertheless we record here two outstanding examples of low scoring in the finals of national championships. Mrs Catherine Lacoste de Prado is credited with a score of 62 in the first round of the 36-hole final of the 1972 French Ladies' Open Championship at Morfontaine. She went out in 29 and came back in 33 on a course measuring 5933 yards. In the final of the English Ladies' Championship at Woodhall Spa in 1954, Frances Stephens (later Mrs Smith) did the first nine holes against Elizabeth Price (later Mrs Fisher) in 30. It included a hole-in-one at the 5th. The nine holes measured 3280 yards.

## Amateurs

### National championships

The following examples of low scoring cannot be regarded as genuine stroke play records since they took place in match play. Nevertheless they are recorded here as being worthy of note.

Michael Bonallack in beating David Kelley in the final of the English championship in 1968 at Ganton did the first 18 holes in 61 with only one putt under two feet conceded. He was out in 32 and home in 29. The par of the course was 71.

In 1948 Richard Chapman of America went out in 29 in the fourth round of the Amateur Championship at Sandwich eventually beating Hamilton McInally, Scottish Champion in 1937, 1939 and 1947, by 9 and 7.

Francis Ouimet in the first round of the American Amateur Championship in 1932 against George Voigt did the first nine holes in 30. Ouimet won by 6 and 5.

### Open competitions

The 1970 South African Dunlop Masters Tournament was won by an amateur, John Fourie, with a score of

266, 14 under par. He led from start to finish with rounds of 65, 68, 65, 68, finally winning by six shots from Gary Player.

Jim Ferrier from Manly won the New South Wales championship at Sydney in 1935 with 266. His rounds were: 67, 65, 70, 64, giving an aggregate 16 strokes better than that of the runner-up. At the time he did this amazing score Ferrier was 20 years old and an amateur.

Aaron Baddeley became the first amateur to win the Australian Open since Bruce Devlin in 1960 when he took the title at Royal Sydney in 1999. After turning pro he successfully defended the title the following year at Kingston Heath.

On the European Tour, Spaniard Pablo Martin won the Estoril Open de Portugal as an amateur in 2000 and both Danny Lee (AUS) and Shane Lowry (IRL) were amateur winners in 2009. Lee won the now defunct Johnnie Walker Classic at The Vines in Perth Australia and Lowry the 3 Irish Open at Baltray.

## Holes below par

**Most holes below par**

E.F. Staugaard in a round of 55 over the 6419 yards Montbello Park, California, in 1935, had two eagles, 13 birdies and three pars.

American Jim Clouette scored 14 birdies in a round at Longhills GC, Arkansas, in 1974. The course measured 6257 yards.

Jimmy Martin in his round of 63 in the Swallow-Penfold at Stoneham in 1961 had one eagle and 11 birdies.

In the Ricarton Rose Bowl at Hamilton, Scotland, in August, 1981, Wilma Aitken, a women's amateur internationalist, had 11 birdies in a round of 64, including nine consecutive birdies from the 3rd to the 11th.

Mrs Donna Young scored nine birdies and one eagle in one round in the 1975 Colgate European Women's Open.

Jason Bohn had two eagles and 10 birdies in his closing 58 at the 2001 Bayer Classic on the Canadian Tour at the par 71 Huron Oaks.

**Consecutive holes below par**

Lionel Platts had ten consecutive birdies from the 8th to 17th holes at Blairgowrie GC during a practice round for the 1973 Sumrie Better-Ball tournament.

Roberto de Vicenzo in the Argentine Centre of the Republic Championship in April, 1974 at the Cordoba GC, Villa Allende, broke par at each of the first nine holes. (By starting his round at the 10th hole they were in fact the second nine holes played by Vicenzo.) He had one eagle (at the 7th hole) and eight birdies. The par for the 3,602 yards half was 37, completed by Vicenzo in 27.

Nine consecutive holes under par have been recorded by Claude Harmon in a friendly match over Winged Foot GC, Mamaroneck, NY, in 1931; by Les Hardie at Eastern GC, Melbourne, in April, 1934; by Jimmy Smith at McCabe GC, Nashville, Tenn, in 1969; by 13-year-old Douglas Beecher, in 1976, at Pitman CC, New Jersey; by Rick Sigda at Greenfield CC, Mass, in 1979; and by Ian Jelley at Brookman Park in 1994.

TW Egan in winning the East of Ireland Championship in 1962 at Baltray had eight consecutive birdies (2nd to 9th) in the third round.

On the United States PGA tour, eight consecutive holes below par have been achieved by six players – Bob Goalby (1961 St Petersburg Open), Fuzzy Zoeller (1976 Quad Cities Open), Dewey Arnette (1987 Buick Open), Edward Fryatt (2000 Doral-Ryder Open), JP Hayes (2002 Bob Hope Chrysler Classic) and Jerry Kelly (2003 Las Vegas Invitational).

Fred Couples set a PGA European Tour record with 12 birdies in a round of 61 during the 1991 Scandinavian Masters on the 72-par Drottningholm course. This has since been equalled by Ernie Els (1994 Dubai Desert Classic), Russell Claydon (1995 German Masters) and Darren Clarke (1999 European Open). Ian Woosnam, Tony Johnstone, Severiano Ballesteros, John Bickerton, Mark O'Meara, Raymond Russell, Darren Clarke, Marcello Santi, Mårten Olander and Craig Spence share another record with eight successive birdies.

The United States Ladies' PGA record is seven consecutive holes below par achieved by Carol Mann in the Borden Classic at Columbus, Ohio in 1975.

Miss Wilma Aitken recorded nine successive birdies (from the 3rd to the 11th) in the 1981 Ricarton Rose Bowl.

**Low scoring rarities**

At Standerton GC, South Africa, in May 1937, F F Bennett, playing for Standerton against Witwatersrand University, did the 2nd hole, 110 yards, in three 2s and a 1 Standerton is a 9-hole course, and in the match Bennett had to play four rounds.

In 1957 a fourball comprising HJ Marr, E Stevenson, C Bennett and WS May completed the 2nd hole (160 yards) in the grand total of six strokes. Marr and Stevenson both holed in one while Bennett and May both made 2.

The old Meadow Brook Club of Long Island, USA, had five par 3 holes and George Low in a round there in the 1950s scored two at each of them.

In a friendly match on a course near Chicago in 1971, assistant professional Tom Doty (23 years) had a remarkable low run over four consecutive holes: 4th (500 yards) 2; 5th (360 yards, dogleg) 1; 6th (175 yards) 1; 7th (375 yards) 2.

R W Bishop, playing in the Oxley Park, July medal competition in 1966, scored three consecutive 2s. They occurred at the 12th, 13th and 14th holes which measured 151, 500 and 136 yards respectively.

In the 1959 PGA Close Championship at Ashburnham, Bob Boobyer scored five 2s in one of the rounds. American Art Wall scored three consecutive 2s in the first round of the US Masters in 1974. They were at the 4th, 5th and 6th holes, the par of which was 3, 4 and 3.

Nine consecutive 3s have been recorded by RH Corbett in 1916 in the semi-final of the Tangye Cup; by Dr James Stothers of Ralston GC over the 2056 yards 9-hole course at Carradale, Argyll, during the summer of 1971; by Irish internationalist Brian Kissock in the Homebright Open at Carnalea GC, Bangor, in June, 1975; and by American club professional Ben Toski.

The most consecutive 3s in a British PGA event is seven by Eric Brown in the Dunlop at Gleneagles (Queen's Course) in 1960.

Hubert Green scored eight consecutive 3s in a round in the 1980 US Open.

The greatest number of 3s in one round in a British PGA event is 11 by Brian Barnes in the 1977 Skol Lager tournament at Gleneagles.

**Fewest putts**
The lowest known number of putts in one round is 14, achieved by Colin Collen-Smith in a round at Betchworth Park, Dorking, in June, 1947. He single-putted 14 greens and chipped into the hole on four occasions.

Professional Richard Stanwood in a round at Riverside GC, Pocatello, Idaho on 17th May, 1976 took 15 putts, chipping into the hole on five occasions.

Several instances of 16 putts in one round have been recorded in friendly games.

For 9 holes, the fewest putts is five by Ron Stutesman for the first 9 holes at Orchard Hills G&CC, Washington, USA in 1978.

Walter Hagen in nine consecutive holes on one occasion took only seven putts. He holed long putts on seven greens and chips at the other two holes.

In competitive stroke rounds in Britain and Ireland, the lowest known number of putts in one round is 18, in a medal round at Portpatrick Dunskey GC, Wilmslow GC professional Fred Taggart is reported to have taken 20 putts in one round of the 1934 Open Championship. Padraigh Hogan (Elm Park), when competing in the Junior Scratch Cup at Carlow in 1976, took only 20 putts in a round of 67.

The fewest putts in a British PGA event is believed to be 22 by Bill Large in a qualifying round over Moor Park High Course for the 1972 Benson and Hedges Match Play.

Overseas, outside the United States of America, the fewest putts is 19 achieved by Robert Wynn in a round in the 1973 Nigerian Open and by Mary Bohen in the final round of the 1977 South Australian Open at Adelaide.

The USPGA record for fewest putts in one round is 18, achieved by Andy North (1990); Kenny Knox (1989); Mike McGee (1987) and Sam Trehan (1979). For 9 holes the record is eight putts by Kenny Knox (1989), Jim Colbert (1987) and Sam Trehan (1979).

The fewest putts recorded for a 72-hole US PGA Tour event is 93 by Kenny Knox in the 1989 Heritage Classic at Harbour Town Golf Links.

The fewest putts recorded by a woman is 17, by Joan Joyce in the Lady Michelob tournament, Georgia, in May, 1982.

# A short history of golf At St Andrews

When golf first started at St Andrews there were 11 holes on the outward half and 11 on the inward starting and finishing on a mound behind what is now the first tee.

Yet despite this unfamiliar description, today's golfers would recognise the 'Old' Course of the 1700s and note that the challenges it presented then have changed little in three centuries.

As legend has it, the game has been enjoyed en masse on the links since the 12th century, when shepherds would knock stones into rabbit holes with rudimentary clubs.

By 1457, the popularity of the game had reached such a level that King James II outlawed it for taking men away from their archery practice! But in 1552, on the proviso that Archbishop of St Andrews, John Hamilton, was able to retain possession of the rabbits on the course, the town's right to play golf on the links was officially established.

Fast-forward 200 years and the custodians of the course, by this time the Society of St Andrews Golfers – later to become The Royal and Ancient Golf Club of St Andrews – took the decision to reduce the number of holes from 22 to 18, so creating the format that we have come to recognize as the standard course layout.

There was still one hole on each green, which was played twice; the homeward groups taking priority over those on their way out. Teeing-off occurred by the hole-side and the course meandered around and through dunes and narrow corridors in the whins.

The next leap towards the modern game took place on the Old Course in 1832. Two holes were cut on the putting surfaces, creating the double-greens for which St Andrews has become so famous. Soon after, separate teeing-grounds were created, fairways were widened both naturally and unnaturally, and golf began to be played in a left-hand loop from – as today's golfer would understand it – the first tee to the 17th green and following the inland holes to the turn before returning on the seaward half.

It was quickly recognised that playing the 'right-hand loop', as it was known, had many virtues and for 30 or 40 years the layout was altered from day-to-day and from week-to-week. Indeed, on one day a year, golf is still played 'backwards' on the Old, bringing into play all those bunkers which, on first encounter, reveal no rhyme nor reason for their location.

The construction of the first green on the far side of the Swilcan Burn in 1870 represented a more permanent move towards the modern right-hand loop. Records of play on the left-hand-loop continue – including the Amateur Championship of 1886 when Tom Morris Senior, then the 65-year-old Keeper of the Green, forgot to set up the course correctly – but by 1873, the year of St Andrews' first Open Championship, the favoured loop was the one that would go on to welcome Arnold Palmer in 1960, Jack Nicklaus in 1970 and Tiger Woods in the year 2000.

The Old Course has now staged 28 Open Championships, most recently in 2010, and the event will be staged there again in 2015.

# PART XI

# Fixtures 2014

# European Tour Race to Dubai   www.europeantour.com

**2013**

| | |
|---|---|
| Nov 21–24 | South African Open Championship, Glendower GC, Gauteng, Johannesburg, South Africa |
| Nov 28–Dec 1 | Alfred Dunhill Championship, Leopard Creek CC, Malelane, South Africa |
| Dec 5–8 | Nedbank Golf Challenge, Gary Player CC, Sun City, South Africa |
| Dec 5–8 | Hong Kong Open, Hong Kong GC, Fanling, Hong Kong |
| Dec 12–15 | The Nelson Mandela Championship, Mount Edgecombe CC, Durban, Kwa-Zulu Natal, South Africa |

**2014**

| | |
|---|---|
| Jan 9–12 | Volvo Golf Champions, Durban CC, Durban, South Africa |
| Jan 16–19 | Abu Dhabi HSBC Golf Championship, Abu Dhabi GC, Abu Dhabi, UAE |
| Jan 22–25 | Commercialbank Qatar Masters, Doha GC, Doha, Qatar |
| Jan 30–Feb 2 | Omega Dubai Desert Classic, Emirates GC, Dubai, UAE |
| Feb 6–9 | Joburg Open, Royal Johannesburg & Kensington GC, Johannesburg, South Africa |
| Feb 13–16 | Africa Open, East London GC, East London, Eastern Cape, South Africa |
| Feb 19–23 | WGC–Accenture Match Play Championship, Ritz-Carlton GC, Dove Mountain, Marana, Arizona, USA |
| Feb 27–Mar 2 | Tshwane Open, Copperleaf Golf & Country Estate, Centurion, South Africa |
| Mar 6–9 | WGC–Cadillac Championship, Doral Golf Resort & Spa, Doral, Florida, USA |
| Mar 13–16 | Trophée Hassan II, Golf du Palais Royal, Agadir, Morocco |
| Mar 20–23 | Event and venue to be confirmed |
| Mar 28–30 | Eurasia Cup, Glenmarie G&CC, Kuala Lumpur, Malaysia |
| Apr 3–6 | Event and venue to be confirmed |
| Apr 10–13 | **Masters Tournament**, Augusta National, Georgia, USA |
| Apr 17–20 | Maybank Malaysian Open, Kuala Lumpur G&CC, Kuala Lumpur, Malaysia |
| Apr 24–27 | Volvo China Open, Genzon GC, Shenzhen, China |
| May 1–4 | The Championship, Blackstone GC, Icheon, Seoul, South Korea |
| May 8–11 | Madeira Islands Open, Clube de Golf Santo da Serra, Santo Antonio da Serra, Madeira |
| May 15–18 | Open de España, venue to be confirmed |
| May 22–25 | BMW PGA Championship, Wentworth Club, Surrey, England |
| May 29–June 1 | Nordea Masters, PGA Sweden National, Lake Course, Malmo, Sweden |
| June 5–8 | Lyoness Open, Diamond CC, Atzenbrugg, near Vienna, Austria |
| June 12–15 | **US Open Championship**, Pinehurst Resort, Pinehurst, North Carolina, USA |
| June 12–15 | Najeti Hotels et Golfs Open, Aa St Omer GC, Lumbres, France |
| June 19–22 | The Irish Open, venue to be confirmed |
| June 26–29 | BMW International Open, Golf Club Gut Lärchenhof, Cologne, Germany |
| July 3–6 | Alstom Open de France, Le Golf National, Paris, France |
| July 10–13 | Aberdeen Asset Management Scottish Open, Royal Aberdeen, Aberdeen, Scotland |
| July 17–20 | **143rd Open Championship**, Royal Liverpool GC, Hoylake, England |
| July 24–27 | M2M Russian Open, venue to be confirmed |
| July 31–Aug 3 | WGC – Bridgestone Invitational, Firestone GC, Akron, Ohio, USA |
| Aug 7–10 | **US PGA Championship**, Valhalla GC, Louisville, Kentucky, USA |
| Aug 14–17 | Made In Denmark, Himmerland Golf & Spa Resort, Denmark |
| Aug 21–24 | D+D Real Czech Masters, Albatross Golf Resort, Prague, Czech Republic |
| Aug 28–31 | Italian Open, Circolo Golf Torino – La Mandria, Fiano, Torino, Italy |
| Sept 4–7 | Omega European Masters, Crans-sur-Sierre GC, Crans Montana, Switzerland |
| Sept 11–14 | KLM Open, Kennemer G&CC, Zandvoort, The Netherlands |
| Sept 18–21 | ISPS Handa Wales Open, The Celtic Manor Resort, City of Newport, South Wales |
| Sept 26–28 | **The 2014 Ryder Cup**, Gleneagles, Scotland |
| Oct 2–5 | Alfred Dunhill Links Championship, Old Course St Andrews, Carnoustie and Kingsbarns, Scotland |
| Oct 9–12 | Portugal Masters, Oceânico Victoria GC, Vilamoura, Portugal |
| Oct 16–19 | Volvo World Match Play Championship, venue to be confirmed |
| Oct 23–26 | Perth International, venue to be confirmed |
| Oct 30–Nov 2 | BMW Masters, Lake Malaren GC, Shanghai, China |
| Nov 6–9 | WGC – HSBC Champion,s Sheshan International GC, Shanghai, China |
| Nov 13–16 | Turkish Airlines Open, The Montgomerie Maxx Royal, Antalya, Turkey |
| Nov 20–23 | **DP World Tour Championship**, Dubai Jumeirah Golf Estates, Dubai, UAE |

# US PGA Tour

www.pgatour.com

| | |
|---|---|
| Jan 3–6 | Hyundai Tournament of Champions, Plantation Course, Kapalua, Hawaii |
| Jan 9–12 | Sony Open in Hawaii, Waialae CC, Honolulu, Hawaii |
| Jan 16–19 | Humana Challenge, PGA West (Palmer), La Quinta, California |
| Jan 23–26 | Farmers Insurance Open, Torrey Pines (South), La Jolla, California |
| Jan 30–Feb 2 | Waste Management Phoenix Open, TPC Scottsdale, Scottsdale, Arizona |
| Feb 6–9 | AT&T Pebble Beach National Pro-Am, Pebble Beach Golf Links, California |
| Feb 13–16 | Northern Trust Open, Riviera CC, Pacific Palisades, California |
| Feb 19–23 | WGC–Accenture Match Play Championship, Dove Mountain, Marana, Arizona |
| Feb 27–Mar 2 | The Honda Classic, PGA National (Champion), Palm Beach Gardens, Florida |
| Mar 6–9 | Puerto Rico Open, Trump International GC–Puerto Rico, Rio Grande, Puerto Rico |
| Mar 6–9 | WGC–Cadillac Championship, TPC Blue Monster at Doral, Miami, Florida |
| Mar 13–16 | Valspar Championship, Innisbrook Resort–Copperhead, Palm Harbor, Florida |
| Mar 20–23 | Arnold Palmer Invitational, Bay Hill Club & Lodge, Orlando, Florida |
| Mar 27–30 | Valero Texas Open, JW Marriott, TPC San Antonio, San Antonio, Texas |
| Apr 3–6 | Shell Houston Open, Redstone GC (Tournament), Humble, Texas |
| Apr 10–13 | **Masters Tournament**, Augusta National GC, Augusta, Georgia |
| Apr 17–20 | RBC Heritage, Harbour Town Golf Links, Hilton Head, South Carolina |
| Apr 24–27 | Zurich Classic of New Orleans, TPC Louisiana, Avondale, Louisiana |
| May 1–4 | Wells Fargo Championship, Quail Hollow Club, Charlotte, North Carolina |
| May 8–11 | THE PLAYERS Championship, TPC Sawgrass, Ponte Vedra Beach, Florida |
| May 15–18 | HP Byron Nelson Championship, TPC Four Seasons Resort, Irving, Texas |
| May 22–25 | Crowne Plaza Invitational, Colonial CC, Fort Worth, Texas |
| May 29–Jun 1 | The Memorial Tournament, Muirfield Village GC, Dublin, Ohio |
| Jun 5–8 | FedEx St Jude Classic, TPC Southwind, Memphis, Tennessee |
| Jun 12–15 | **US Open**, Pinehurst No 2, Pinehurst, North Carolina |
| Jun 19–22 | Travelers Championship, TPC River Highlands, Cromwell, Connecticut |
| Jun 23–24 | CVS Caremark Charity Classic, Rhode Island CC, Barrington, Rhode Island |
| Jun 26–29 | AT&T National, Congressional CC, Bethesda, Maryland |
| Jul 3–6 | The Greenbrier Classic, The Old White TPC, White Sulphur Springs, West Virginia |
| Jul 10–13 | John Deere Classic, TPC Deere Run, Silvis, Illinois |
| Jul 17–20 | **The Open Championship**, Royal Liverpool GC, Hoylake, England |
| Jul 24–27 | RBC Canadian Open Royal Montreal GC (Blue Course), Ile Bizard, Quebec, Canada |
| Jul 31–Aug 3 | Reno-Tahoe Open, Montreux G&CC, Reno, Nevada |
| Jul 31–Aug 3 | WGC–Bridgestone Invitational, Firestone CC (South), Akron, Ohio |
| Aug 7–10 | **PGA Championship**, Valhalla GC, Louisville, Kentucky |
| Aug 14–17 | Wyndham Championship, Sedgefield CC, Greensboro, North Carolina |
| Aug 21–24 | The Barclays, Ridgewood CC, Paramus, New Jersey |
| Aug 29–Sep 1 | Deutsche Bank Championship, TPC Boston, Norton, Massachusetts |
| Sep 4–7 | BMW Championship, Cherry Hills CC, Englewood, Colorado |
| Sep 11–14 | TOUR Championship, East Lake GC, Atlanta, GA |

The PGA Tour Season officially ends with the TOUR Championship and the following season begins three weeks later with the first Fall Tournament

# European Golf Association Championships

www.ega-golf.ch

| | |
|---|---|
| Jan 29–Feb 1 | Portuguese International Ladies' Amateur Championship, Montado Golf Resort |
| Feb 12–15 | Portuguese International Amateur Championship, Montado Golf Resort |
| Feb 26–Mar 2 | Spanish International Ladies Amateur Championship, El Saler |
| Feb 26–Mar 2 | Spanish International Amateur Championship, La Reserva |
| Mar 20–23 | Italian International Ladies Stroke Play Championship, Castelgandolfo GC |
| Mar 20–23 | Italian International Amateur Stroke Play Championship, Is Molas GC |
| Apr 17–21 | French International Boys Championship (Michel Carlhian Trophy), Golf du Médoc |
| Apr 17–21 | French International Lady Juniors Championship (Esmond Trophy), Saint Cloud GC |
| Apr 25–27 | Scottish Ladies' Open Stroke Play C/ship (Helen Holm), Portland & Old Course, Troon |

EGA Championships *continued*

| | |
|---|---|
| May 2–4 | Lytham Trophy, Royal Lytham & St Annes |
| May 3–4 | Welsh Ladies' Open Stroke Play Championship, Prestatyn GC |
| May 9–11 | Spanish International Ladies' Stroke Play Championship, Panorámica |
| May 9–11 | Irish Amateur Open Championship, Royal Dublin |
| May 22–24 | Slovenian International Ladies Amateur Championship, Diners G&CC, Ljubljana |
| May 22–24 | Slovenian International Amateur Championship. Bled GC |
| May 22–25 | German International Ladies Amateur C/ship, Golf-Club Heilbronn-Hohenlohe e.V. |
| May 22–25 | Cyprus Amateur Men's Open, Elea Estate GC |
| May 23–25 | Lithuanian Ladies' Amateur Open Championship, The Capitals GC |
| May 23–25 | Lithuanian Amateur Open Championship (venue to be announced) |
| May 23–25 | Welsh Amateur Open Stroke Play Championship, Conwy GC |
| May 23–25 | French Men's Amateur Stroke Play Championship (Murat Cup), Golf de Chantilly |
| May 23–25 | Romanian Ladies' Amateur Open Championship, Sungarden GC, Cluj-Napoca |
| May 23–25 | Romanian Amateur Open Championship. Sungarden GC, Cluj-Napoca |
| May 24–25 | Irish Women's Open Stroke Play Championship, Douglas |
| May 29–June 1 | Turkish Open Amateur Championship (Ladies) (venue to be announced) |
| May 29–June 1 | Turkish Open Amateur Championship (Men) (venue to be announced) |
| May 30–Juen 1 | Scottish Open Stroke Play Championship, Panmure |
| May 31–June 1 | Welsh Open Youths Championship, Pennard GC |
| June 6–8 | German Girls Open, GC St. Leon-Rot e.V. |
| June 6–8 | German Boys Open, GC St. Leon-Rot e.V. |
| June 12–15 | Russian Ladies Amateur Open Championship, Agalarov GC |
| June 12–15 | Russian Amateur Open Championship, Agalarov GC |
| June 16–21 | **The Amateur Championship**, Royal Portrush & Portstewart |
| June 18–20 | Scottish Seniors (over 55's) Open Stroke Play Championship, Blairgowrie, Rosemount |
| June 24–28 | Ladies' British Open Amateur Championship, Royal St George's |
| June 25–28 | English Men's Open Amateur Stroke Play C/ship (Brabazon Trophy), Seaton Carew |
| June 26–28 | Estonian Open Ladies Amateur Championship, Saaremaa |
| June 26–28 | Estonian Open Amateur Championship, Saaremaa |
| June 27–29 | Macedonian Amateur Open Championship, St Sofia GC |
| June 27–29 | Swiss Ladies Amateur Championship, Genève GC |
| June 27–29 | Swiss Amateur Championship, Genève GC |
| July 2–5 | Danish International Ladies Amateur Championship, Silkeborg GC |
| July 2–5 | Danish International Amateur Championship, Silkeborg GC |
| July 3–5 | Balkan Challenge Trophy (venue to be announced) |
| July 3–6 | English Women's Open Mid Amateur Championship, Bath |
| July 4–6 | Ukrainian Open Amateur Championship, Superior GC, Kharkiv |
| July 4–6 | Ukrainian Ladies Open Amateur Championship (venue to be announced) |
| July 10–12 | Luxembourg Ladies Amateur Championship (venue to be announced) |
| July 10–12 | Luxembourg Men Amateur Championship (venue to be announced) |
| July 11–13 | French International Senior Men's Championship (venue to be announced) |
| July 14–16 | Scottish Youths Open Amateur Stroke Play Championship, St Andrews, Jubilee |
| July 15–17 | Danish International Lady Junior Championship, Smørum GC |
| July 15–17 | Danish International Youth Championship, Smørum GC |
| July 16–19 | Dutch Lady Junior International (PonCat), Toxandria GC |
| July 16–19 | Dutch Junior International (PonCat), Toxandria GC |
| July 22–24 | Scottish Boys (under 18's) Open Stroke Play Championship, Cruden Bay |
| July 22–25 | English Boys (under 18) Open Amateur Stroke Play C/ship (Carris Trophy), Moor Park |
| July 23–25 | Scottish Ladies' Junior Open Stroke Play Championship, Alloa |
| July 24–27 | German International Amateur Championship, GC Hamburg Wendlohe e.V. |
| July 25–27 | Polish Men's Amateur Open Championship, Postolowo GC |
| July 30–Aug 2 | Belgian International Ladies Amateur Championship. Royal Antwerp GC |
| July 30–Aug 2 | Belgian International Amateur Amateur Championship, Royal Antwerp GC |
| July 31–Aug 2 | Czech International Girls & Lady Juniors Championship (venue to be announced) |
| July 31–Aug 2 | Czech International Boys & Juniors Championship (venue to be announced) |
| Aug 5–7 | English Women's Open Amateur Stroke Play Championship, Tandridge |
| Aug 6–8 | British Senior Open Amateur Championship, Ganton |
| Aug 5–7 | ANNIKA Invitational (Girls), Forsgardens GC |
| Aug 8–10 | Hungarian Junior Amateur Open Championship, Royal Balaton G&YC, Balatonudvari |
| Aug 11–15 | Girls' British Open Amateur Championship, Massereene |

| Aug 12–14 | Slovak Ladies Amateur Open Championship (venue to be announced) |
| Aug 12–14 | Slovak Amateur Open Championship (venue to be announced) |
| Aug 12–17 | British Boys Championship, Prestwick & Dundonald Links, Scotland |
| Aug 13–16 | Czech International Ladies Amateur Championship, GC Mlada Boleslav |
| Aug 13–16 | Czech International Amateur Championship, GC Mlada Boleslav |
| Aug 15–17 | Latvian Ladies Amateur Open Championship, Ozo GC |
| Aug 15–17 | Latvian Amateur Open Championship, Ozo GC |
| Aug 15–17 | Dutch Brabants Open Ladies' Championship, Eindhovensche Golf |
| Aug 15–17 | Dutch Brabants Open Men's Championship, Eindhovensche Golf |
| Aug 21–23 | Finnish Ladies Amateur Championship, Helsinki GC |
| Aug 21–23 | Finnish Amateur Championship, Helsinki GC |
| Aug 20–22 | Ladies' British Open Amateur Stroke Play Championship, Ashburnham |
| Aug 21–23 | Hungarian Open Ladies' Amateur Championship, Royal Balaton G&YC, Balatonudvari |
| Aug 21–23 | Hungarian Open Amateur Championship, Royal Balaton G&YC, Balatonudvari |
| Aug 21–24 | Polish Junior Championship, Kalinowe Pola GC |
| Aug 27–30 | Belgian International Girls (U18) Championship, Royal Golf Club of Belgium |
| Aug 27–30 | Belgian International Boys (U18) Championship, Royal Golf Club of Belgium |
| Sep 2–4 | Italian International Individual (Under 16) Championship, Biella Le Betulle |
| Sep 2–4 | Bulgarian Open Ladies' Amateur Championship (venue to be announced) |
| Sep 4–7 | Austrian International Men's Amateur Championship (venue to be announced) |
| Sep 4–7 | Spanish International (U18) Stroke Play Championship, Hacienda del Álamo |
| Sep 10–12 | Irish Senior Women's Open Stroke Play Championship, Dundalk |
| Sep 12–13 | Serbian International Ladies' Amateur Championship (venue to be announced) |
| Sep 12–13 | Serbian International Amateur Championship (venue to be announced) |
| Sep 12–14 | Polish Ladies Amateur Open Championship, Gradi GC |
| Sep 12–14 | Skandia Lady Junior Open (Youth), Halmstad GC |
| Sep 12–14 | Skandia Junior Open (Youth), Halmstad GC |
| Sep 12–14 | Austrian International Ladies Amateur Championship (venue to be announced) |
| Sep 13–14 | Liechtenstein Open Ladies' Amateur Championship (venue to be announced) |

European Golf Association Championships continued

| Sep 13–14 | Liechtenstein Open Amateur Championship (venue to be announced) |
| Sep 16–18 | Senior Ladies' British Open Amateur Championship, Royal Dornoch |
| Sep 21–23 | Israel Juniors Boys and Girls Championship (venue to be announced) |
| Oct 6–9 | Israel Amateur Open Championship (venue to be announced) |
| Oct 7–9 | Israel Ladies Amateur Open Championship (venue to be announced) |
| Oct 10–12 | French International Ladies' Amateur Stroke Play Championship (Cécile de Rothschild Trophy) (venue to be announced) |

# European Team Championships

| July 8–12 | Ladies, G&CC Ljubljana, Slovenia |
| July 8–12 | Amateur, Linna Golf, Finland |
| July 8–12 | Girls, Golf Resort Skalica, Slovakia |
| July 8–12 | Boys, Oslo Golf Club, Norway |
| July 10–12 | Men's Challenge Trophy, Golf & Spa Resort Kunětická Hora, Czech Republic |
| Sep 2–6 | Senior Ladies', Gut Altentann GC, Austria |
| Sep 2–6 | Senior Men's, Sierra GC, Poland |
| Sep 18–20 | Boys' Challenge Trophy, Pannonia G&CC, Hungary |

# International European Championships

| June 5–7 | Mid-Amateur, Pravets GC, Bulgaria |
| June 12–14 | Seniors, RC Puerta De Hierro, Spain |
| July 23–26 | Ladies, Estonian G&CC, Estonia |
| July 24–26 | European Young Masters, Hamburger GC, Germany |
| Aug 6–9 | Men, The Duke's St Andrews, Scotland |
| Oct 2–4 | European Ladies' Club Trophy, Achental GC, Germany |
| Oct 23–25 | European Men's Club Trophy, Pravets GC, Bulgaria |

# International Matches

| Mar 26–28 | Sir Michael Bonallack Trophy, Karnataka Golf Ass., Bengaluru, India |
| Aug 29–30 | St Andrews Trophy, Barsebäck G&CC, Sweden |
| Aug 29–30 | Jacques Léglise Trophy, Barsebäck G&CC, Sweden |
| Sep 22–23 | Ryder Cup Junior Match, Blairgowrie GC, Scotland |

EGA Championships *continued*

## World Amateur Team Championships

Sep 3–6     Espirito Santo Trophy, Karuizawa, Japan
Sep 11–14   Eisenhower Trophy, Karuizawa, Japan

# United States Golf Association Championships

www.usga.org

| | |
|---|---|
| June 6–8 | **Curtis Cup**, St. Louis Country Club, St Louis, Missouri |
| June 12–15 | **US Open**, Pinehurst Resort & CC, Village of Pinehurst, North Carolina |
| June 19–22 | **US Women's Open**, Pinehurst Resort & CC, Village of Pinehurst, North Carolina |
| July 10–14 | US Senior Open, Oak Tree National, Edmond, Oklahoma |
| July 14–19 | US Women's Amateur Public Links, The Home Course, Dupont, Washington |
| July 14–19 | US Amateur Public Links, Sand Creek Station Golf Course, Newton, Kansas |
| July 21–26 | US Girls' Junior, Forest Highlands Golf Club, Flagstaff, Arizona |
| July 21–26 | US Junior Amateur, The Club at Carlton Woods, The Woodlands, Texas |
| Aug 4–10 | US Women's Amateur, Nassau Country Club, Glen Cove, New York |
| Aug 11–17 | US Amateur, Atlanta Athletic Club, Johns Creek, Georgia |
| Sep 3–6 | Women's World Amateur Team, Karuizawa 72 Golf Complex, Karuizawa, Japan |
| Sep 6–11 | US Mid-Amateur, Saucon Valley Country Club, Bethlethem, Pennsylvania |
| Sep 6–11 | US Women's Mid Amateur, Harbour Trees Golf Club, Noblesville, Indiana |
| Sep 11–14 | World Amateur Team, Karuizawa 72 Golf Complex, Karuizawa, Japan |
| Sep 13–18 | USGA Senior Women's Amateur, Hollywood Golf Club, Deal, New Jersey |
| Sep 13–18 | USGA Senior Amateur, Big Canyon Country Club, Newport Beach, California |
| Sep 30–Oct 2 | USGA Men's State Team, French Lick Resort (Pete Dye Course), French Lick, Indiana |

# LPGA Tour

www.lpga.com

| | |
|---|---|
| Jan 23–26 | Pure Silk Bahamas Classic, Paradise Island, Bahamas |
| Feb 13–16 | ISPS Handa Women's Australian Open, Victoria, Australia |
| Feb 20–23 | Honda LPGA Thailand Chonburi, Thailand |
| Feb 27–Mar 2 | HSBC Women's Champions, Singapore |
| Mar 20–23 | LPGA Founders Cup, Phoenix, AZ |
| Mar 27–30 | Kia Classi,c Carlsbad, CA |
| Apr 3–6 | **Kraft Nabisco Championship**, Rancho Mirage, CA |
| Apr 16–19 | LPGA LOTTE Championship, Oahu, HI |
| Apr 24–27 | Swinging Skirts LPGA Classic, San Francisco, CA |
| May 1–4 | North Texas LPGA Shootout Irving, TX |
| May 15–18 | Kingsmill Championship, Williamsburg, VA |
| May 22–25 | Mobile Bay LPGA Classic, Mobile, AL |
| May 30–Jun 1 | ShopRite LPGA Classic, Galloway, NJ |
| June 5–8 | Manulife Financial LPGA Classic, Waterloo, Ontario, Canada |
| June 19–22 | **US Women's Open**, Pinehurst, NC 3,250,000 |
| Juen 27–29 | Walmart NW Arkansas Championship, Rogers, AR |
| July 10–13 | **Ricoh Women's British Open**, Southport, Lancashire, England |
| July 17–20 | Marathon Classic, Sylvania, OH 1,400,000 |
| July 24–27 | International Crown  Owings Mills, MD |
| Aug 7–10 | Meijer LPGA Classic  Belmont, MI 1,500,000 |
| Aug 14–17 | **Wegmans LPGA Championship**, Pittsford, NY |
| Aug 21–24 | Canadian Pacific Women's Open  London, Ontario, Canada |
| Aug 28–31 | Portland Classic,Portland, OR – to be confirmed |
| Sept 11–14 | **The Evian Championship**, Evian-les-Bains, France |
| Sept 18–21 | Alabama LPGA Classic, Prattville, AL |
| Oct 2–5 | Reignwood LPGA Classic, Beijing, China |
| Oct 9–12 | Sime Darby LPGA Malaysia, Kuala Lumpur, Malaysia |
| Oct 17–19 | LPGA KEB – HanaBank Championship, Incheon, Korea |
| Oct 23–26 | LPGA Taiwan Championship, Taipei, Taiwan |

| | |
|---|---|
| Oct 30–<br>Nov 2 | Event and venue to be confirmed |
| Nov 7–9 | Mizuno Classic, Shima-Shi, Mie, Japan |
| Nov 13–16 | Lorena Ochoa Invitational, Mexico |
| Nov 20–23 | CME Group Titleholders, Naples, FL |

# Japan PGA Tour

www.jgto.org/jgto/WG01000000Initi.do

| | |
|---|---|
| Mar 13–16 | Thailand Open, Thana City Golf & Sports Club, Thailand |
| Mar 27–30 | Indonesia PGA Championship, Damai Indah Golf – Bumi Serpong Damai Course, Indonesia |
| Apr 10–13 | **Masters Tournament**, Augusta National GC, Atlanta, Georgia, USA |
| Apr 17–20 | Token Homemate Cup, Token Tado Country Club, Nagoya, Mie |
| Apr 24–27 | Tsuruya Open, Yamanohara Golf Club, Yamanohara Course, Hyogo |
| May 1–4 | The Crowns, Nagoya Golf Club, Wago Course, Aichi |
| May 22–25 | Kansai Open Golf Championship, Rokko Country Club, Hyogo |
| May 29–<br>June 1 | Gate Way to The Open Mizuno Open, JFE Setonaikai Golf Club, Okayama |
| June 5–8 | PGA Championship Nissin Cupnoodles Cup, Golden Valley Golf Club, Hyogo |
| June 12–16 | **US Open Championship**, Pinehurst Resort, North Carolina, USA |
| June 19–22 | Japan Golf Tour Championship, Shishido Hills, Shishido Hills CC, West Course, Ibaraki |
| July 3–6 | Nagashima Shigeo Invitational Sega Sammy Cup, The North Country GC, Hokkaido |
| July 17–20 | **British Open**, Royal Liverpool GC, Lancashire, England |
| Aug 7–10 | **US PGA Championship**, Valhalla GC, Louisville, Kentucky, USA |
| Aug 8–31 | KBC Augusta, Keya Golf Club, Fukuoka |
| Sep 4–7 | Fujisankei Classic, Fujizakura Country Club, Yamanashi |
| Sep 18–21 | ANA Open, Sapporo Golf Club, Wattsu Course, Hokkaido |
| Sep 25–28 | Asia-Pacific Diamond Cup Golf, Otone Country Club, West Course, Ibaraki |
| Oct 2–5 | Tokai Classic, Miyoshi Country Club, West Course, Aichi |
| Oct 9–12 | Toshin Golf Tournament, Toshin Golf Club, Central Course, Gifu |
| Oct 16–19 | Japan Open, Chiba Country Club, Umesato Course, Chiba |
| Oct 23–26 | Bridgestone Open, Sodegaura Country Club, Sodegaura Course, Chiba |
| Oct 30–<br>Nov 2 | Mynavi ABC Championship, ABC Golf Club, Hyogo |
| Nov 6–9 | Heiwa PGM Championship, Miho Golf Club, Ibaraki |
| Nov 13–16 | Mitsui Sumitomo VISA Taiheiyo Masters, Taiheiyo Club Gotemba Course, Shizuoka |
| Nov 20–23 | Dunlop Phoenix, Phoenix Country Club, Miyazaki |
| Nov 27–30 | Casio World Open, Kochi Kuroshio Country Club, Kochi |
| Dec 4–7 | Golf Nippon Series JT Cup, Tokyo Yomiuri Country Club, Tokyo |

# Ladies European Tour

www.ladieseuropeantour.com

| | |
|---|---|
| Jan 31–Feb 2 | ISPS Handa New Zealand Women's Open, Clearwater Golf Club, New Zealand |
| Feb 6–9 | Volvik RACV Australian Masters, Racv Royal Pines Resort, Gold Coast, Queensland, Australia |
| Feb 13–16 | ISPS Handa Women's Australian Open, Victoria Golf Club, Melbourne, Victoria, Australia |
| Mar 6–9 | World Ladies Championship, Mission Hills Hainan's Blackstone Course, Haikou, Hainan, China |
| Mar 6–9 | World Ladies Championship (Team), Mission Hills Hainan's Blackstone Course, Haikou, Hainan, China |
| Mar 13–16 | Lalla Meryem Cup, Golf De L'Ocean, Agadir, Morocco |
| May 8–11 | Turkish Ladies Open, National Golf Club, Belek, Antalya, Turkey |
| May 23–25 | Deloitte Ladies Open, The International Amsterdam, Netherlands |
| June 15–17 | Catalonia Ladies Masters, venue to be confirmed |
| June 20–22 | Ladies Slovak Open, Golf Resort Tale, Brezno, Tale, Slovakia |

## Ladies European Tour continued

| | |
|---|---|
| July 3–6 | ISPS Handa Ladies European Masters, Buckinghamshire Golf Club, Denham, Buckinghamshire, England |
| July 10–13 | **Ricoh Women's British Open**, Royal Birkdale Golf Club, Lancashire, England |
| July 17–20 | Ladies German Open, Wörthsee Golf Club, Wörthsee, Germany |
| Aug 7–10 | Pilsen Golf Masters, Golf Park Pizen – Dysina, Prague, Czech Republic |
| Aug 29–31 | Aberdeen Asset Management Ladies Scotland Open, Archerfield Links, East Lothian, Scotland |
| Sept 4–7 | The Helsingborg Open, Vasatorp Golf Club, Helsingborg, Sweden |
| Sept 11–14 | **The Evian Championship**, Evian Golf Club, Evian-les-Bains, France |
| Sept 18–21 | Open De España Femenino, venue to be confirmed |
| Oct 2–5 | Lacoste Ladies Open de France, Chantaco Golf Club, Saint-Jean-De-Luz, Aquitaine, France (date to be confirmed) |
| Oct 16–19 | The South African Women's Open, San Lameer Country Club, Hibiscus Coast, South Africa |
| Nov 7–9 | China Suzhou Taihu Open, Suzhou Taihu International Golf Club, Suzhou, China |
| Nov 14–16 | Sanya Ladies Open, Yalong Bay Golf Club, Sanya, Hainan Province, China |
| Nov 27–29 | Hero Honda Women's Indian Open, venue to be confirmed |
| TBC | Omega Dubai Ladies Masters, Emirates Golf Course (Majlis Course), Dubai, U.A.E. |

# PGA Tour Canada

www.cantour.com

| | |
|---|---|
| May 26–June 1 | PC Financial Open, Point Grey G&CC, Vancouver, British Columbia |
| June 2–8 | 32nd Bayview Place Island Savings Open, presented by Times Colonist, Uplands GC, Victoria, British Columbia |
| June 16–22 | Syncrude Boreal Open presented by AECON, Fort Murray GC, Alberta |
| June 30–July 6 | SIGA Dakota Dunes Open presented by SaskTel Dakota Dunes Links, Saskatoon, Saskatchewan |
| July 7–13 | The Players Cup, Pine Ridge GC Winnipeg, Manitoba |
| July 14–20 | Thunder Bay Golf Classic, Whitewater Bay GC, Ontario |
| July 28–Aug 3 | ATB Financial Classic, Sirocco GC, Calgary, Alberta |
| Aug 4–10 | Forces and Families Open, Hylands GC, Ottowa, Ontario |
| Aug 18–24 | The Great Waterway Classic, Loyalist G&CC, Kingston, Ontario |
| Aug 25–31 | The Wildfire Invitational presented by PC Financial, Peterborough, Ontario |
| Sep 1–7 | Cape Breton Celtic Classic presented by PC Financial, The Lakes GC, Sydney, Nova Scotia |
| Sep 8–14 | Tour Championship of Canada presented by Freedom 55 Financial, Sunningdale G&CC, London, Ontario |

# OneAsia Tour

www.oneasia.asia

| | |
|---|---|
| May 26– | PC Financial Open, Point Grey G&CC, Vancouver, British Columbia |
| Mar 13–16 | Thailand Open, Thana City Golf and Sports Club |
| Mar 27–30 | Indonesia PGA Championship, Damai Indah Golf (BSD) |
| Apr 24–27 | Volvo China Open, Genzon GC |
| May 8–11 | GS Caltex Maekyung Open, Namseoul CC |
| May 15–18 | SK Telecom Openm Pinx GC |
| TBA | Fiji International, Natadola Bay G&CC |
| Sep 25–28 | Nanshan China Mastersm Nanshan International GC |
| Oct 23–26 | Kolon Korea Open, Woo Jeong Hills CC |
| Dec 5–7 | Dongfeng Nissan Cup, CTS Tycoon Club |
| TBA | Emirates Australian Open, The Australian GC |
| TBA | Australian PGA Championship, RACV Royal Pines Resort |

# PART XII

# Annual Awards

# Annual Awards

## European

### European Tour Player of the Year

| | | |
|---|---|---|
| 1985 Bernhard Langer (GER) | 1995 Colin Montgomerie (SCO) | 2005 Michael Campbell (NZL) |
| 1986 Severiano Ballesteros (ESP) | 1996 Colin Montgomerie (SCO) | 2006 Paul Casey (ENG) |
| 1987 Ian Woosnam (WAL) | 1997 Colin Montgomerie (SCO) | 2007 Padraig Harrington (IRL) |
| 1988 Severiano Ballesteros (ESP) | 1998 Lee Westwood (ENG) | 2008 Padraig Harrington (IRL) |
| 1989 Nick Faldo (ENG) | 1999 Colin Montgomerie (SCO) | 2009 Lee Westwood (ENG) |
| 1990 Nick Faldo (ENG) | 2000 Lee Westwood (ENG) | 2010 Martin Kaymer (GER) and |
| 1991 Severiano Ballesteros (ESP) | 2001 Retief Goosen (RSA) | Graeme McDowell (NIR) |
| 1992 Nick Faldo (ENG) | 2002 Ernie Els (RSA) | 2011 Luke Donald (ENG) |
| 1993 Bernhard Langer (GER) | 2003 Ernie Els (RSA) | 2012 Rory McIlroy (NIR) |
| 1994 Ernie Els (RSA) | 2004 Vijay Singh (FIJ) | 2013 Henrik Stenson (SWE) |

### Association of Golf Writers' Trophy (Awarded to the man or woman who, in the opinion of golf writers, has done most for European golf during the year)

| | | |
|---|---|---|
| 1951 Max Faulkner (ENG) | 1973 Peter Oosterhuis (ENG) | 1993 Bernhard Langer (GER) |
| 1952 Miss Elizabeth Price (ENG) | 1974 Peter Oosterhuis (ENG) | 1994 Laura Davies (ENG) |
| 1953 Joe Carr (IRL) | 1975 Golf Foundation | 1995 European Ryder Cup Team |
| 1954 Mrs Roy Smith (Miss Frances | 1976 GB&I Eisenhower Trophy Team | (Bernard Gallacher capt.) |
| Stephens) (ENG) | (Sandy Saddler capt.) | 1996 Colin Montgomerie (SCO) |
| 1955 LGU's Touring Team | 1977 Christy O'Connor (IRL) | 1997 Alison Nicholas (ENG) |
| (Mrs BR Bostock capt.) | 1978 Peter McEvoy (ENG) | 1998 Lee Westwood (ENG) |
| 1956 John Beharrell (ENG) | 1979 Severiano Ballesteros (ESP) | 1999 Sergio García (ESP) |
| 1957 Dai Rees (WAL) | 1980 Sandy Lyle (SCO) | 2000 Lee Westwood (ENG) |
| 1958 Harry Bradshaw (IRL) | 1981 Bernhard Langer (GER) | 2001 GB&I Walker Cup Team |
| 1959 Eric Brown (SCO) | 1982 Gordon Brand Jr (SCO) | (Peter McEvoy capt.) |
| 1960 Sir Stuart Goodwin | 1983 Nick Faldo (ENG) | 2002 Ernie Els (RSA) |
| 1961 Commander Charles Roe | 1984 Severiano Ballesteros (ESP) | 2003 Annika Sörenstam (SWE) |
| 1962 Marley Spearman (ENG) | 1985 European Ryder Cup Team | 2004 European Ryder Cup team |
| 1963 Michael Lunt (ENG) | (Tony Jacklin capt.) | (Bernhard Langer capt.) |
| 1964 GB&I Eisenhower Trophy Team | 1986 GB&I Curtis Cup Team | 2005 Annika Sörenstam (SWE) |
| (Joe Carr capt.) | (Diane Bailey capt.) | 2006 European Ryder Cup team |
| 1965 Gerald Micklem (ENG) | 1987 European Ryder Cup Team | (Ian Woosnam capt.) |
| 1966 Ronnie Shade (SCO) | (Tony Jacklin capt.) | 2007 Padraig Harrington (IRL) |
| 1967 John Panton (SCO) | 1988 Sandy Lyle (SCO) | 2008 Padraig Harrington (IRL) |
| 1968 Michael Bonallack (ENG) | 1989 GB&I Walker Cup Team | 2009 Lee Westwood (ENG) |
| 1969 Tony Jacklin (ENG) | (Peter McEvoy capt.) | 2010 Graeme McDowell (NIR) |
| 1970 Tony Jacklin (ENG) | 1990 Nick Faldo (ENG) | 2011 Luke Donald (ENG) |
| 1971 GB&I Walker Cup Team | 1991 Severiano Ballesteros (ESP) | 2012 Rory McIlroy (NIR) |
| (Michael Bonallack capt.) | 1992 European Solheim Cup Team | 2013 Henrik Stenson (SWE) |
| 1972 Miss Michelle Walker (ENG) | (Mickey Walker capt.) | |

## McGinley honoured by PGA

Paul McGinley has followed in the footsteps of some illustrious past Ryder Cup captains by receiving the PGA Recognition Award for his outstanding contribution to golf.

Europe's skipper for the 2014 matches at Gleneagles has been a stalwart performer on the course since winning the Irish Amateur Championship in 1989, going on to become a four-time European Tour winner and member of three successive victorious Ryder Cup teams. He sank the decisive winning putt at The Belfry in 2002.

## European Tour Harry Vardon Trophy

(Awarded to the PGA member heading the Order of Merit at the end of the season)

| | | | | | | | |
|---|---|---|---|---|---|---|---|
| 1937 | Charles Whitcombe | 1960 | Bernard Hunt | 1978 | Severiano Ballesteros | 1996 | Colin Montgomerie |
| 1938 | Henry Cotton | 1961 | Christy O'Connor | 1979 | Sandy Lyle | 1997 | Colin Montgomerie |
| 1939 | Roger Whitcombe | 1962 | Christy O'Connor | 1980 | Sandy Lyle | 1998 | Colin Montgomerie |
| 1940–45 | In abeyance | 1963 | Neil Coles | 1981 | Bernhard Langer | 1999 | Colin Montgomerie |
| 1946 | Bobby Locke | 1964 | Peter Alliss | 1982 | Greg Norman | 2000 | Lee Westwood |
| 1947 | Norman Von Nida | 1965 | Bernard Hunt | 1983 | Nick Faldo | 2001 | Retief Goosen |
| 1948 | Charlie Ward | 1966 | Peter Alliss | 1984 | Bernhard Langer | 2002 | Retief Goosen |
| 1949 | Charlie Ward | 1967 | Malcolm Gregson | 1985 | Sandy Lyle | 2003 | Ernie Els |
| 1950 | Bobby Locke | 1968 | Brian Huggett | 1986 | Severiano Ballesteros | 2004 | Ernie Els |
| 1951 | John Panton | 1969 | Bernard Gallacher | 1987 | Ian Woosnam | 2005 | Colin Montgomerie |
| 1952 | Harry Weetman | 1970 | Neil Coles | 1988 | Severiano Ballesteros | 2006 | Padraig Harrington |
| 1953 | Flory van Donck | 1971 | Peter Oosterhuis | 1989 | Ronan Rafferty | 2007 | Justin Rose |
| 1954 | Bobby Locke | 1972 | Peter Oosterhuis | 1990 | Ian Woosnam | 2008 | Robert Karlsson |
| 1955 | Dai Rees | 1973 | Peter Oosterhuis | 1991 | Severiano Ballesteros | 2009 | Lee Westwood |
| 1956 | Harry Weetman | 1974 | Peter Oosterhuis | 1992 | Nick Faldo | 2010 | Martin Kaymer |
| 1957 | Eric Brown | 1975 | Dale Hayes | 1993 | Colin Montgomerie | 2011 | Luke Donald |
| 1958 | Bernard Hunt | 1976 | Severiano Ballesteros | 1994 | Colin Montgomerie | 2012 | Rory McIlroy |
| 1959 | Dai Rees | 1977 | Severiano Ballesteros | 1995 | Colin Montgomerie | 2013 | Henrik Stenson |

## Sir Henry Cotton European Rookie of the Year

| | | | | | | | |
|---|---|---|---|---|---|---|---|
| 1960 | Tommy Goodwin | 1976 | Mark James (ENG) | 1989 | Paul Broadhurst (ENG) | 2003 | Peter Lawrie (IRL) |
| 1961 | Alex Caygill (ENG) | 1977 | Nick Faldo (ENG) | 1990 | Russell Claydon (ENG) | 2004 | Scott Drummond |
| 1962 | No Award | 1978 | Sandy Lyle (SCO) | 1991 | Per-Ulrik Johansson | | (SCO) |
| 1963 | Tony Jacklin (ENG) | 1979 | Mike Miller (SCO) | | (SWE) | 2005 | Gonzolo Fernandez- |
| 1964 | No Award | 1980 | Paul Hoad (ENG) | 1992 | Jim Payne (ENG) | | Castano (ESP) |
| 1966 | Robin Liddle (SCO) | 1981 | Jeremy Bennett (ENG) | 1993 | Gary Orr (SCO) | 2006 | Marc Warren (SCO) |
| 1967 | No Award | 1982 | Gordon Brand Jr (SCO) | 1994 | Jonathan Lomas (ENG) | 2007 | Martin Kaymer (GER) |
| 1968 | Bernard Gallacher (SCO) | 1983 | Grant Turner (NZL) | 1995 | Jarmo Sandelin (SWE) | 2008 | Pablo Larrazabal (ESP) |
| 1969 | Peter Oosterhuis (ENG) | 1984 | Philip Parkin (WAL) | 1996 | Thomas Bjørn (DEN) | 2009 | Chris Wood (ENG) |
| 1970 | Stuart Brown (ENG) | 1985 | Paul Thomas (WAL) | 1997 | Scott Henderson (SCO) | 2010 | Matteo Manassero |
| 1971 | David Llewellyn (WAL) | 1986 | José Maria Olazàbal | 1998 | Olivier Edmond (FRA) | | (ITA) |
| 1972 | Sam Torrance (SCO) | | (ESP) | 1999 | Sergio García (ESP) | 2011 | Tom Lewis (ENG) |
| 1973 | Philip Elson (ENG) | 1987 | Peter Baker (ENG) | 2000 | Ian Poulter (ENG) | 2012 | Carlos Santos (POR) |
| 1974 | Carl Mason (ENG) | 1988 | Colin Montgomerie | 2001 | Paul Casey (ENG) | 2013 | Peter Uihlein (USA) |
| 1975 | No Award | | (SCO) | 2002 | Nick Dougherty (ENG) | | |

## PGAs of Europe Lifetime Achievement Award

2011  Severiano Ballesteros (ESP)
2012  Tony Jacklin CBE (ENG)
2013  Alison Nicholas MBE (ENG)

## PGAs of Europe Achievement Award for Alison Nicholas

Six time Solheim Cup player two time captain and former US Women's Open champion Alison Nicholas MBE has received the PGAs of Europe Life time Achievement award for her outstanding achievements and contribution to the game.

Nicholas, who is now coaching golf, receives the award which was presented posthumously to Severiano Ballesteros, her hero, in 2011 and to Tony Jacklin in 2012.

## Ladies European Tour ISPS Handa Order of Merit

| | | |
|---|---|---|
| 1979 Catherine Panton-Lewis (SCO) | 1991 Corinne Dibnah (AUS) | 2003 Sophie Gustafson (SWE) |
| 1980 Muriel Thomson (SCO) | 1992 Laura Davies (ENG) | 2004 Laura Davies (ENG) |
| 1981 Jenny Lee-Smith (ENG) | 1993 Karen Lunn (AUS) | 2005 Iben Tinning (DEN) |
| 1982 Jenny Lee-Smith (ENG) | 1994 Liselotte Neumann (SWE) | 2006 Laura Davies (ENG) |
| 1983 Muriel Thomson (SCO) | 1995 Annika Sörenstam (SWE) | 2007 Sophie Gustafson (SWE) |
| 1984 Dale Reid (SCO) | 1996 Laura Davies (ENG) | 2008 Gwladys Nocera (FRA) |
| 1985 Laura Davies (ENG) | 1997 Alison Nicholas (ENG) | 2009 Sophie Gustafson (SWE) |
| 1986 Laura Davies (ENG) | 1998 Helen Alfredsson (SWE) | 2010 Lee-Anne Pace (RSA) |
| 1987 Dale Reid (SCO) | 1999 Laura Davies (ENG) | 2011 Ai Miyazato (JPN) |
| 1988 Marie-Laure Taud (FRA) | 2000 Sophie Gustafson (SWE) | 2012 Carlota Ciganda (ESP) |
| 1989 Marie-Laure de Laurenzi (FRA) | 2001 Raquel Carriedo (ESP) | 2013 Suzann Pettersen (NOR) |
| 1990 Trish Johnson (ENG) | 2002 Paula Marti (ESP) | |

## Ladies European Tour Players' Player of the Year

| | | |
|---|---|---|
| 1995 Annika Sörenstam (SWE) | 2002 Annika Sörenstam (SWE) | 2009 Catriona Matthew (SCO) |
| 1996 Laura Davies (ENG) | 2003 Sophie Gustafson (SWE) | 2010 Lee-Anne Pace (RSA) |
| 1997 Alison Nicholas (ENG) | 2004 Stephanie Arricau (FRA) | 2011 Caroline Hedwall (SWE) |
| 1998 Sophie Gustafson (SWE) | 2005 Iben Tinning (DEN) | 2012 Carlota Ciganda (ESP) |
| 1999 Laura Davies (ENG) | 2006 Gwladys Nocera (FRA) | 2013 Lee-Anne Pace (RSA) |
| 2000 Sophie Gustafson (SWE) | 2007 Sophie Gustafson (SWE) | |
| 2001 Raquel Carriedo (ESP) | 2008 Gwladys Nocera (FRA) | |

## Ladies European Tour Rolex Rookie of the Year

| | | |
|---|---|---|
| 1984 Katrina Douglas (ENG) | 1994 Tracy Hansen (USA) | 2004 Minea Blomqvist (FIN) |
| 1985 Laura Davies (ENG) | 1995 Karrie Webb (AUS) | 2005 Elisa Serramia (ESP) |
| 1986 Patricia Gonzales (COL) | 1996 Anne-Marie Knight (AUS) | 2006 Nikki Garrett (AUS) |
| 1987 Trish Johnson (ENG) | 1997 Anna Berg (SWE) | 2007 Louise Stahle (SWE) |
| 1988 Laurette Maritz (USA) | 1998 Laura Philo (USA) | 2008 Melissa Reid (ENG) |
| 1989 Helen Alfredsson (SWE) | 1999 Elaine Ratcliffe (ENG) | 2009 Anna Norqvist (SWE) |
| 1990 Pearl Sinn (KOR) | 2000 Guila Sergas (ITA) | 2010 Kim In-Kyung (KOR) |
| 1991 Helen Wadsworth (WAL) | 2001 Suzann Pettersen (NOR) | 2011 Anna Nordqvist (SWE) |
| 1992 Sandrine Mendiburu (FRA) | 2002 Kirsty S Taylor (ENG) | 2012 Carlota Ciganda (ESP) |
| 1993 Annika Sörenstam (SWE) | 2003 Rebecca Stevenson (AUS) | 2013 Charley Hull (ENG) |

## *Daily Telegraph* Amateur Woman Golfer of the Year

| | | |
|---|---|---|
| 1982 Jane Connachan (SCO) | 1992 GBI Curtis Cup Team (Liz | 1999 Welsh International Team |
| 1983 Jill Thornhill (ENG) | Boatman capt.) | (Olwen Davies capt.) |
| 1984 Gillian Stewart and | 1993 Catriona Lambert and | 2000 Rebecca Hudson (ENG) |
| Claire Waite (ENG) | Julie Hall | 2001 Rebecca Hudson (ENG) |
| 1985 Belle Robertson (SCO) | 1994 GBI Curtis Cup Team (Liz | 2002 Becky Brewerton (WAL) |
| 1986 GBI Curtis Cup Team (Diane | Boatman capt.) | 2003 Becky Brewerton (WAL) |
| Bailey capt.) | 1995 Julie Hall (ENG) | 2004 Emma Duggleby (ENG) |
| 1987 Linda Bayman (ENG) | 1996 GBI Curtis Cup Team (Ita | 2005 Felicity Johnson (ENG) |
| 1988 GBI Curtis Cup Team | Butler capt.) | 2006 *Not awarded* |
| 1989 Helen Dobson (ENG) | 1997 Alison Rose (ENG) | 2007 Melissa Reid (ENG) |
| 1990 Angela Uzielli (ENG) | 1998 Kim Andrew | 2008 *Discontinued* |
| 1991 Joanne Morley (ENG) | | |

## Joyce Wethered Trophy (Awarded to the outstanding amateur under 25)

| | | | |
|---|---|---|---|
| 1994 Janice Moodie (SCO) | 1998 Liza Walters (ENG) | 2003 Sophie Walker (ENG) | 2007 Henrietta Brockway |
| 1995 Rebecca Hudson | 1999 Becky Brewerton | 2004 Melissa Reid (ENG) | (ENG) |
| (ENG) | (WAL) | 2005 Becky Harries (ENG) | 2008 *Discontinued* |
| 1996 Mhairi McKay (SCO) | 2000 Sophie Walker (ENG) | 2006 Sally Little (SCO) and | |
| 1997 Rebecca Hudson | 2001 Clare Queen (ENG) | Carly Booth (SCO) | |
| (ENG) | 2002 Sarah Jones (ENG) | | |

# American

*Winners American unless stated*

## Arnold Palmer Award (Awarded to the PGA Tour's leading money winner)

| | | | |
|---|---|---|---|
| 1981 Tom Kite | 1990 Greg Norman (AUS) | 1999 Tiger Woods | 2008 Vijay Singh (FIJ) |
| 1982 Craig Stadler | 1991 Corey Pavin | 2000 Tiger Woods | 2009 Tiger Woods |
| 1983 Hal Sutton | 1992 Fred Couples | 2001 Tiger Woods | 2010 Matt Kuchar |
| 1984 Tom Watson | 1993 Nick Price (ZIM) | 2002 Tiger Woods | 2011 Luke Donald (ENG) |
| 1985 Curtis Strange | 1994 Nick Price (ZIM) | 2003 Tiger Woods | 2012 Rory McIlroy (NIR) |
| 1986 Greg Norman (AUS) | 1995 Greg Norman (AUS) | 2004 Vijay Singh (FIJ) | 2013 Tiger Woods |
| 1987 Paul Azinger | 1996 Tom Lehman | 2005 Tiger Woods | |
| 1988 Curtis Strange | 1997 Tiger Woods | 2006 Tiger Woods | |
| 1989 Tom Kite | 1998 David Duval | 2007 Tiger Woods | |

## Jack Nicklaus Award (Player of the Year decided by player ballot)

| | | | |
|---|---|---|---|
| 1990 Wayne Levi | 1997 Tiger Woods | 2004 Vijay Singh (FIJ) | 2010 Jim Furyk |
| 1991 Fred Couples | 1998 Mark O'Meara | 2005 Tiger Woods | 2011 Luke Donald (ENG) |
| 1992 Fred Couples | 1999 Tiger Woods | 2006 Tiger Woods | 2012 Rory McIlroy (NIR) |
| 1993 Nick Price (ZIM) | 2000 Tiger Woods | 2007 Tiger Woods | 2013 Tiger Woods |
| 1994 Nick Price (ZIM) | 2001 Tiger Woods | 2008 Padraig Harrington | |
| 1995 Greg Norman (AUS) | 2002 Tiger Woods | (IRL) | |
| 1996 Tom Lehman | 2003 Tiger Woods | 2009 Tiger Woods | |

## PGA Tour Rookie of the Year (Decided by player ballot)

| | | | |
|---|---|---|---|
| 1990 Robert Gamez | 1997 Stewart Cink | 2004 Todd Hamilton | 2009 Marc Leishman (AUS) |
| 1991 John Daly | 1998 Steve Flesch | 2005 Sean O'Hair | 2010 Rickie Fowler |
| 1992 Mark Carnevale | 1999 Carlos Franco (PAR) | 2006 Trevor Immelman | 2011 Keegan Bradley |
| 1993 Vijay Singh (FIJ) | 2000 Michael Clark II | (RSA) | 2012 John Huh |
| 1994 Ernie Els (RSA) | 2001 Charles Howell III | 2007 Brandt Snedeker | 2013 Jordan Spieth |
| 1995 Woody Austin | 2002 Jonathan Byrd | 2008 Andres Romero | |
| 1996 Tiger Woods | 2003 Ben Curtis | (ARG) | |

## PGA of America Player of the Year (Decided on merit points)

| | | | |
|---|---|---|---|
| 1948 Ben Hogan | 1965 Dave Marr | 1982 Tom Watson | 1999 Tiger Woods |
| 1949 Sam Snead | 1966 Billy Casper | 1983 Hal Sutton | 2000 Tiger Woods |
| 1950 Ben Hogan | 1967 Jack Nicklaus | 1984 Tom Watson | 2001 Tiger Woods |
| 1951 Ben Hogan | 1968 not awarded | 1985 Lanny Wadkins | 2002 Tiger Woods |
| 1952 Julius Boros | 1969 Orville Moody | 1986 Bob Tway | 2003 Tiger Woods |
| 1953 Ben Hogan | 1970 Billy Casper | 1987 Paul Azinger | 2004 Vijay Singh (FIJ) |
| 1954 Ed Furgol | 1971 Lee Trevino | 1988 Curtis Strange | 2005 Tiger Woods |
| 1955 Doug Ford | 1972 Jack Nicklaus | 1989 Tom Kite | 2006 Tiger Woods |
| 1956 Jack Burke | 1973 Jack Nicklaus | 1990 Nick Faldo (ENG) | 2007 Tiger Woods |
| 1957 Dick Mayer | 1974 Johnny Miller | 1991 Corey Pavin | 2008 Padraig Harrington |
| 1958 Dow Finsterwald | 1975 Jack Nicklaus | 1992 Fred Couples | (IRL) |
| 1959 Art Wall | 1976 Jack Nicklaus | 1993 Nick Price (ZIM) | 2009 Tiger Woods |
| 1960 Arnold Palmer | 1977 Tom Watson | 1994 Nick Price (ZIM) | 2010 Jim Furyk |
| 1961 Jerry Barber | 1978 Tom Watson | 1995 Greg Norman (AUS) | 2011 Luke Donald (ENG) |
| 1962 Arnold Palmer | 1979 Tom Watson | 1996 Tom Lehman | 2012 Rory McIlroy (NIR) |
| 1963 Julius Boros | 1980 Tom Watson | 1997 Tiger Woods | 2013 Tiger Woods |
| 1964 Ken Venturi | 1981 Bill Rogers | 1998 Mark O'Meara | |

## PGA of America Vardon Trophy (For lowest scoring average over 60 PGA Tour rounds or more)

| Year | Name | Avg | Year | Name | Avg | Year | Name | Avg |
|---|---|---|---|---|---|---|---|---|
| 1937 | Harry Cooper | | 1966 | Billy Casper | 70.27 | 1991 | Fred Couples | 69.59 |
| 1938 | Sam Snead | | 1967 | Arnold Palmer | 70.18 | 1992 | Fred Couples | 69.38 |
| 1939 | Byron Nelson | | 1968 | Billy Casper | 69.82 | 1993 | Nick Price (ZIM) | 69.11 |
| 1940 | Ben Hogan | | 1969 | Dave Hill | 70.34 | 1994 | Greg Norman (AUS) | 69.81 |
| 1941 | Ben Hogan | | 1970 | Lee Trevino | 70.64 | 1995 | Steve Elkington (AUS) | 69.82 |
| 1942–46 | No Awards | | 1971 | Lee Trevino | 70.27 | 1996 | Tom Lehman | 69.32 |
| 1947 | Jimmy Demarel | 69.90 | 1972 | Lee Trevino | 70.89 | 1997 | Nick Price (ZIM) | 68.98 |
| 1948 | Ben Hogan | 69.30 | 1973 | Bruce Crampton (AUS) | 70.57 | 1998 | David Duval | 69.13 |
| 1949 | Sam Snead | 69.37 | 1974 | Lee Trevino | 70.53 | 1999 | Tiger Woods | 68.43 |
| 1950 | Sam Snead | 69.23 | 1975 | Bruce Crampton (AUS) | 70.51 | 2000 | Tiger Woods | 67.79 |
| 1951 | Lloyd Mangrum | 70.05 | 1976 | Don January | 70.56 | 2001 | Tiger Woods | 68.81 |
| 1952 | Jack Burke | 70.54 | 1977 | Tom Watson | 70.32 | 2002 | Tiger Woods | 68.56 |
| 1953 | Lloyd Mangrum | 70.22 | 1978 | Tom Watson | 70.16 | 2003 | Tiger Woods | 68.41 |
| 1954 | Ed Harrison | 70.41 | 1979 | Tom Watson | 70.27 | 2004 | Vijay Singh (FIJ) | 68.84 |
| 1955 | Sam Snead | 69.86 | 1980 | Lee Trevino | 69.73 | 2005 | Tiger Woods | 68.66 |
| 1956 | Cary Middlecoff | 70.35 | 1981 | Tom Kite | 69.80 | 2006 | Jim Furyk | 68.66 |
| 1957 | Dow Finsterwald | 70.30 | 1982 | Tom Kite | 70.21 | 2007 | Tiger Woods | 67.79 |
| 1958 | Bob Rosburg | 70.11 | 1983 | Ray Floyd | 70.61 | 2008 | Phil Mickelson | 69.17 |
| 1959 | Art Wall | 70.35 | 1984 | Calvin Peete | 70.56 | 2009 | Tiger Woods | 68.05 |
| 1960 | Billy Casper | 69.95 | 1985 | Don Pooley | 70.36 | 2010 | Matt Kuchar | 69.61 |
| 1961 | Arnold Palmer | 69.85 | 1986 | Scott Hoch | 70.08 | 2011 | Luke Donald (ENG) | 68.86 |
| 1962 | Arnold Palmer | 70.27 | 1987 | Dan Pohl | 70.25 | 2012 | Rory McIlroy (NIR) | 69.02 |
| 1963 | Billy Casper | 70.58 | 1988 | Chip Beck | 69.46 | 2013 | Tiger Woods | 68.98 |
| 1964 | Arnold Palmer | 70.01 | 1989 | Greg Norman (AUS) | 69.49 | | | |
| 1965 | Billy Casper | 70.85 | 1990 | Greg Norman (AUS) | 69.10 | | | |

## Payne Stewart Award (Presented for respecting and upholding the traditions of the game)

| Year | Name | Year | Name | Year | Name | Year | Name |
|---|---|---|---|---|---|---|---|
| 2000 | Byron Nelson, Jack Nicklaus, Arnold Palmer | 2002 | Nick Price | 2006 | Gary Player (RSA) | 2010 | Tom Lehman |
| 2001 | Ben Crenshaw | 2003 | Tom Watson | 2007 | Hal Sutton | 2011 | David Toms |
| | | 2004 | Jay Haas | 2008 | Davis Love III | 2012 | Steve Stricker |
| | | 2005 | Brad Faxon | 2009 | Kenny Perry | 2013 | Peter Jacobsen |

## Moriya Jutanugarn is first Thai Rookie of the Year

No player from Thailand had ever won the Louise Suggs Rolex Rookie of the Year award on the LPGA Tour until Moriya Jutanugarn was successful last year ... but she only beat Germany's Caroline Masson by a point.

The destination of the trophy was not decided until the last tournament on the LPGA circuit. Jutanugarn had led early in the season only to be overtaken by Masson who was 11 points clear coming into the season finale – the CME Group Titleholders event.

Jutanugarn fired 70-72-74-72 and holed a four foot putt on the last to finish in a tie for 33rd while Masson ended up in 61st spot to lose her lead and the Rookie of the Year prize.

"I wasn't nervous when I was playing but I was when it was all over," said Juanugarn who had six top 20 finishes in her first year.

"Winning this trophy has a lot of meaning for me. I feel like I did it for my family, my fans and for Thailand."

Jutganugarn's sister Ariya plays on the Ladies European Tour and was a first time winner at the Lalla Meryem Cup event in Morocco.

## PGA of America Distinguished Service Award

| | | | |
|---|---|---|---|
| 1988 Herb Graffis | 1995 Patty Berg | 2002 Tim Finchem | 2009 William J Powell |
| 1989 Bob Hope | 1996 Frank Chirkinian | 2003 Vince Gill | 2010 Billy Casper |
| 1990 No award | 1997 George Bush | 2004 Pete Dye | 2011 Larry Nelson |
| 1991 Gerald Ford | 1998 Paul Runyan | 2005 Wally Uihlein | 2012 Dave Stockton |
| 1992 Gene Sarazen | 1999 Bill Dickey | 2006 Fred Ridley | 2013 Lee Trevino |
| 1993 Byron Nelson | 2000 Jack Nicklaus | 2007 Jack Burke Jr | |
| 1994 Arnold Palmer | 2001 Mark McCormack | 2008 Dennis Walters | |

## Bob Jones Award (Awarded by USGA for distinguished sportsmanship in golf)

| | | | |
|---|---|---|---|
| 1955 Francis Ouimet | 1971 Arnold Palmer | 1986 Jess W Sweetser | 2002 Judy Rankin |
| 1956 Bill Campbell | 1972 Michael Bonallack | 1987 Tom Watson | 2003 Carol Semple |
| 1957 Babe Zaharias | (ENG) | 1988 Isaac B Grainger | Thompson |
| 1958 Margaret Curtis | 1973 Gene Littler | 1989 Chi-Chi Rodriquez | 2004 Jack Burke Jr |
| 1959 Findlay Douglas | 1974 Byron Nelson | (PUR) | 2005 Nick Price (ZIM) |
| 1960 Chick Evans | 1975 Jack Nicklaus | 1990 Peggy Kirk Bell | 2006 Jay Haas |
| 1961 Joe Carr (IRL) | 1976 Ben Hogan | 1991 Ben Crenshaw | 2007 Louise Suggs |
| 1962 Horton-Smith | 1977 Joseph C Dey | 1992 Gene Sarazen | 2008 George H W Bush |
| 1963 Patty Berg | 1978 Bob Hope and | 1993 P J Boatwright Jr | 2009 Gordon Brewer Jr |
| 1964 Charles Coe | Bing Crosby | 1994 Lewis Oehmig | 2010 Mickey Wright |
| 1965 Glenna Collett Vare | 1979 Tom Kite | 1995 Herbert Warren | 2011 Lorena Ochoa (MEX) |
| 1966 Gary Player (RSA) | 1980 Charles Yates | Wind | 2012 Annika Sörenstam |
| 1967 Richard Tufts | 1981 JoAnne Carner | 1996 Betsy Rawls | (SWE) |
| 1968 Robert Dickson | 1982 Billy Joe Patton | 1997 Fred Brand Jr | 2013 Davis Love III |
| 1969 Gerald Micklem | 1983 Maureen Garrett | 1998 Nancy Lopez | |
| (ENG) | (ENG) | 1999 Ed Updegraff | |
| 1970 Roberto De Vicenzo | 1984 Jay Sigel | 2000 Barbara McIntyre | |
| (ARG) | 1985 Fuzzy Zoeller | 2001 Thomas Cousins | |

## US LPGA Rolex Player of the Year

| | | | |
|---|---|---|---|
| 1966 Kathy Whitworth | 1978 Nancy Lopez | 1990 Beth Daniel | 2002 Annika Sörenstam (SWE) |
| 1967 Kathy Whitworth | 1979 Nancy Lopez | 1991 Pat Bradley | 2003 Annika Sörenstam (SWE) |
| 1968 Kathy Whitworth | 1980 Beth Daniel | 1992 Dottie Mochrie | 2004 Annika Sörenstam (SWE) |
| 1969 Kathy Whitworth | 1981 Jo Anne Carner | 1993 Betsy King | 2005 Annika Sörenstam (SWE) |
| 1970 Sandra Haynie | 1982 Jo Anne Carner | 1994 Beth Daniel | 2006 Lorena Ochoa (MEX) |
| 1971 Kathy Whitworth | 1983 Patty Sheehan | 1995 Annika Sörenstam (SWE) | 2007 Lorena Ochoa (MEX) |
| 1972 Kathy Whitworth | 1984 Betsy King | 1996 Laura Davies (ENG) | 2008 Lorena Ochoa (MEX) |
| 1973 Kathy Whitworth | 1985 Nancy Lopez | 1997 Annika Sörenstam (SWE) | 2009 Lorena Ochoa (MEX) |
| 1974 JoAnne Carner | 1986 Pat Bradley | 1998 Annika Sörenstam (SWE) | 2010 Yani Tseng (TPE) |
| 1975 Sandra Palmer | 1987 Ayako Okamoto (JPN) | 1999 Karrie Webb (AUS) | 2011 Yani Tseng (TPE) |
| 1976 Judy Rankin | 1988 Nancy Lopez | 2000 Karrie Webb (AUS) | 2012 Stacy Lewis |
| 1977 Judy Rankin | 1989 Betsy King | 2001 Annika Sörenstam (SWE) | 2013 Inbee Park (KOR) |

## Louise Suggs Rolex Rookie of the Year

| | | | |
|---|---|---|---|
| 1962 Mary Mills | 1978 Nancy Lopez | 1992 Helen Alfredsson | 2004 Shi Hyun Ahn (KOR) |
| 1963 Clifford Ann Creed | 1979 Beth Daniel | (SWE) | 2005 Paula Creamer |
| 1964 Susie Berning | 1980 Myra Van Hoose | 1993 Suzanne Strudwick | 2006 Seon-Hua Lee (KOR) |
| 1965 Margie Masters | 1981 Patty Sheehan | (ENG) | 2007 Angela Park (KOR) |
| 1966 Jan Ferraris | 1982 Patti Rizzo | 1994 Annika Sörenstam | 2008 Yani Tseng (KOR) |
| 1967 Sharron Moran | 1983 Stephanie Farwig | (SWE) | 2009 Ji-Yai Shin (KOR) |
| 1968 Sandra Post | 1984 Juli Inkster | 1995 Pat Hurst | 2010 Azahara Muños (ESP) |
| 1969 Jane Blalock | 1985 Penny Hammel | 1996 Karrie Webb (AUS) | 2011 Hee Kyung Seo (KOR) |
| 1970 JoAnne Carner | 1986 Jody Rosenthal | 1997 Lisa Hackney (ENG) | 2012 So Yeon Ryu (KOR) |
| 1971 Sally Little (RSA) | 1987 Tammi Green | 1998 Se Ri Pak (KOR) | 2013 Moriya Jutanugarn |
| 1972 Jocelyne Bourassa | 1988 Liselotte Neumann | 1999 Mi Hyun Kim (KOR) | (THA) |
| 1973 Laura Baugh | (SWE) | 2000 Dorothy Delasin | |
| 1974 Jan Stephenson | 1989 Pamela Wright (SCO) | (PHI) | |
| 1975 Amy Alcott | 1990 Hiromi Kobayashi | 2001 Hee Won Han (KOR) | |
| 1976 Bonnie Lauer | (JPN) | 2002 Beth Bauer | |
| 1977 Debbie Massey | 1991 Brandie Burton | 2003 Lorena Ochoa (MEX) | |

## LPGA Vare Trophy

| | Scoring av. | | | Scoring av. | | | Scoring av. |
|---|---|---|---|---|---|---|---|
| 1953 Patty Berg | 75.00 | 1976 Judy Rankin | 72.25 | 1997 Karrie Webb (AUS) | 70.01 |
| 1954 Babe Zaharias | 75.48 | 1977 Judy Rankin | 72.16 | 1998 Annika Sörenstam | 69.99 |
| 1955 Patty Berg | 74.47 | 1978 Nancy Lopez | 71.76 | (SWE) | |
| 1956 Patty Berg | 74.57 | 1979 Nancy Lopez | 71.20 | 1999 Karrie Webb (AUS) | 69.43 |
| 1957 Louise Suggs | 74.64 | 1980 Amy Alcott | 71.51 | 2000 Karrie Webb (AUS) | 70.05 |
| 1958 Beverly Hanson | 74.92 | 1981 Jo Anne Carner | 71.75 | 2001 Annika Sörenstam | 69.42 |
| 1959 Betsy Rawls | 74.03 | 1982 Jo Anne Carner | 71.49 | (SWE) | |
| 1960 Mickey Wright | 73.25 | 1983 Jo Anne Carner | 71.41 | 2002 Annika Sörenstam | 68.70 |
| 1961 Mickey Wright | 73.55 | 1984 Patty Sheehan | 71.40 | (SWE) | |
| 1962 Mickey Wright | 73.67 | 1985 Nancy Lopez | 70.73 | 2003 Se Ri Pak (KOR) | 70.03 |
| 1963 Mickey Wright | 72.81 | 1986 Pat Bradley | 71.10 | 2004 Grace Park (KOR) | 69.99 |
| 1964 Mickey Wright | 72.46 | 1987 Betsy King | 71.14 | 2005 Annika Sörenstam | 69.25 |
| 1965 Kathy Whitworth | 72.61 | 1988 Colleen Walker | 71.26 | (SWE) | |
| 1966 Kathy Whitworth | 72.60 | 1989 Beth Daniel | 70.38 | 2006 Lorena Ochoa (MEX) | 69.23 |
| 1967 Kathy Whitworth | 72.74 | 1990 Beth Daniel | 70.54 | 2007 Lorena Ochoa (MEX) | 69.68 |
| 1968 Carol Mann | 72.04 | 1991 Pat Bradley | 70.66 | 2008 Lorena Ochoa (MEX) | 69.58 |
| 1969 Kathy Whitworth | 72.38 | 1992 Dottie Mochrie | 70.80 | 2009 Lorena Ochoa (MEX) | 70.16 |
| 1970 Kathy Whitworth | 72.26 | 1993 Nancy Lopez | 70.83 | 2010 Choi Na Yeon (KOR) | 69.96 |
| 1971 Kathy Whitworth | 72.88 | 1994 Beth Daniel | 70.90 | 2011 Yani Tseng (TPE) | 69.66 |
| 1972 Kathy Whitworth | 72.38 | 1995 Annika Sörenstam | 71.00 | 2012 Inbee Park (KOR) | 70.21 |
| 1973 Judy Rankin | 73.08 | (SWE) | | 2013 Stacy Lewis (USA) | 69.48 |
| 1974 JoAnne Carner | 72.87 | 1996 Annika Sörenstam | 70.47 | | |
| 1975 JoAnne Carner | 72.40 | (SWE) | | | |

## First Lady of Golf Award

(PGA of America award for women who have made a significant contribution to the game)

From 2009 this award was presented every second year

| | | |
|---|---|---|
| 1998 Barbara Nicklaus (USA) | 2003 Renee Powell (USA) | 2008 Carol Mann (USA) |
| 1999 Judy Rankin (USA) | 2004 Alice Dye (USA) | 2009 Donna Caponi-Byrnes (USA) |
| 2000 No award given | 2005 Carole Semple-Thompson (USA) | 2011 Mary Bea Porter-King (USA) |
| 2001 Judy Bell (USA) | 2006 Kathy Whitworth (USA) | 2013 Annika Sörenstam (SWE) |
| 2002 Nancy Lopez (USA) | 2007 Peggy Kirk Bell (USA) | |

## Another award for Annika

Sweden's Annika Sörenstam, one of the most decorated golfers in women's golf, was awarded the 2013 PGA First Lady of Golf Award.

Inaugurated in 1998 and presented biennially since 2011, the award is made to a woman who has made significant contributions to the promotion of the game of golf.

The presentation will place at The PGA of America Awards in January 2014, at the Orange County Convention Center's Chapin Theater in Orlando, Florida.

Born in Bro in Sweden, Annika is the first internationally born golfer to receive the award and the third recipient with both PGA of America and LPGA membership, the others being Renee Powell (2003) and Carol Mann (2008).

Annika's tally of 89 wins in worldwide professional events on both the LPGA and Ladies European Tours includes 10 major championships. She was inducted into the World Golf Hall of Fame in 2013 retired from competitive golf in 2008. With earnings of $22 million, she remains the LPGA's all-time money leader.

# PART XIII

# Who's Who
# in Golf

# Who's Who in Golf – Men

Aaron, T.
Allenby, R.
Alliss, P.
An, B.H.
Aoki, I.
Atwal, A.
Azinger, P.
Baddeley, A.
Baker, P.
Baker-Finch, I.
Barnes, B.
Beem, R.
Bjørn, T.
Bonallack, M.
Bradley, K.
Brooks, M.
Brown, K.
Cabrera, A.
Cabrera Bello, R.
Calcavecchia, M.
Canizares, A.
Canizares, J.M.
Cantlay, P.
Casey, P.
Casper, B.
Chapman, R.
Charles, Sir Bob
Choi, K.-J.
Cink, S.
Clark, C.
Clark, H.
Clarke, D.
Coles, N.
Coltart, A.
Couples, F.
Crenshaw, B.
Curtis, B.
Daly, J.
Darcy, E.
Davis, R.
Day, J.
De Vincenzo, R.
Dickson, B.
Donald, L.
Drew, N.
Dufner, J.
Duval, D.
Dyson, S.

Edfors, J.
Edwards, N.
Elkington, S.
Els, E.
Faldo, Sir N.
Fasth, N.
Faxon, B.
Feherty, D.
Fernandez, V.
Fernandez-
   Castano, G.
Finsterwald, D.
Fisher, O.
Fisher, R.
Fitzpatrick, M.
Floyd, R.
Ford, D.
Frost, D.
Funk, F.
Furyk, J.
Gallacher, B.
García, S.
Garrido, A.
Garrido, I.
Goosen, R.
Grace, B.
Grady, W.
Graham, D.
Green, C,
Green, H.
Haas, B.
Haas, J.
Haeggman, J.
Hamilton, T.
Han, C.W.
Hansen, A.
Hansen, S.
Hanson, P.
Harrington, P.
Hayes, D.
Hoch, S.
Horton, T.
Howell, D.
Huggett, B.
Hunt, B.
Ilonen, M.
Immelman, T.
Irwin, H.

Ishikawa, R.
Jacklin, T.
Jacobs, J.
Jacquelin, R.
Jaidee, T.
James, M.
January, D.
Janzen, L.
Jiminéz, M.A.
Johansson, P.-U.
Johnson, D.
Johnson, Z.
Jones, S.
Karlsson, R.
Kaymer, M.
Kim, K.T.
Kuchar, M.
Kite, T.
Laird, M.
Lane, B.
Langer, B.
Lawrie, P.
Lee, D.
Lehman, T.
Leonard, J.
Levet, T.
Lewis, J.
Liang W.-C.
Littler, G.
Love III, D.
Lowry, S.
Lyle, S.
McDowell, G.
McEvoy, P.
McGimpsey, G.
McGinley, P.
Macgregor, G.
McIlroy, R.
McNulty, M.
Mahan, H.
Mamat, M.
Manassero, M.
Marsh, D.
Marsh, G.
Martin, P.
Mason, C.
Matsuyama, H.
Micheel, S.

Mickelson, P.
Miller, J.
Milligan, J.
Mize, L.
Molinari, E.
Molinari, F.
Montgomerie, C.
Nagle, K.
Nelson, L.
Newton, J.
Nicklaus, J.
Nirat, C.
Nobilo, F.
Noh, S.Y.
Norman, G.
North, A.
O'Connor, C., Sr
O'Connor, C., Jr
Ogilvy, G.
Olazábal, J.M.
O'Leary, J.
O'Meara, M.
Oosterhuis, P.
Oosthuizen, L.
Ozaki, M.
Pagunsan, J.
Palmer, A.
Parnevik, J.
Parry, C.
Pate, J.
Pavin, C.
Perry, K.
Phadungsil, C.
Player, G.
Poulter, I.
Price, N.
Price, P.
Quigley, D.
Quiros, A.
Rafferty, R.
Ramsay, R.
Randhawa, J.
Remesy, J.-F.
Rivero, J.
Roberts, L.
Rocca, C.
Rogers, B.
Romero, E.

Rose, J.
Sandelin, J.
Schwartzel, C.
Scott, A.
Senior, P.
Sigel, J.
Simpson, S.
Simpson, W.
Singh, J.M.
Singh, V.
Smyth, D.
Snedeker, B.
Stadler, C.
Stenson, H.
Strange, C.
Stricker, S.
Sutton, H.
Thomson, P.
Toms, D.
Torrance, S.
Townsend, P.
Trevino, L.
Van de Velde, J.
Verplank, S.
Wadkins, L.
Walton, P.
Warren, M.
Watney, N.
Watson, B.
Watson, T.
Weekley, B.
Weir, M.
Weiskopf, T.
Westwood, L.
Williams, C.
Wilson, O.
Wirachant, T.
Wolstenholme, G.
Wood, C.
Woods, E.
Woosnam, I.
Yang, Y-e
Yeh, W.-t.
Zhang, L.-W.
Zoeller, F.

## Aaron, Tommy (USA)
*Born Gainesville, Georgia, 22 February 1937*
*Turned professional 1961*
The 1973 Masters champion who, five years earlier inadvertently marked down a 4 on Roberto de Vicenzo's card for the 17th hole when the Argentinian had taken 3. De Vicenzo signed for the 4 and lost out by one shot on a play-off with Bob Goalby for the Green Jacket.

## Allenby, Robert (AUS)
*Born Melbourne, 12 July 1971*
*Turned professional 1992*
Pipped by a shot from winning the Australian Open as an amateur in 1991 by Wayne Riley's birdie, birdie, birdie finish at Royal Melbourne, he won the title three years later as a professional and won it again in 1955. After competing on the European Tour and winning four times, he now plays on the US Tour.

## Alliss, Peter (ENG)
*Born Berlin, 28 February 1931  Turned professional 1946*
Following a distinguished career as a tournament golfer in which he won 18 titles between 1954 and 1966 and played eight times in the Ryder Cup between 1953 and 1969, he turned to golf com- mentating. In Britain he works for the BBC and for the American network ABC at The Open. Twice captain of the PGA in 1962 and 1987 he won the Spanish, Italian and Portuguese Opens in 1958. Author or co- author of several golf books and a novel with a golfing background, he has also designed several courses including the Brabazon course at The Belfry in association with Dave Thomas. In 2003 he was awarded Life Membership of the PGA in honour of his lifelong contribution and commitment to the game. In 2005 he received an honorary degree from St Andrews University and in 2010 a PGA distinguished service award. He was selected through the international ballot to be inducted into the World Golf Hall of Fame in 2012.

## An, Byeong-Hun (Ben) (KOR)
*Born Korea, 17 September 1991*
When just 18 years old he became the youngest winner in the 109-year history of the US Amateur Championship when he beat Ben Martin 7 and 5 in the 2009 final at Southern Hills in Oklahoma. He was the 13th. Korean-born golfer to win a USGA title. An All-American at the University of California he was introduced to the game at the age of seven by his parents both of who were table tennis medallists in the 1988 Olympics in Seoul.

## Aoki, Isao (JPN)
*Born Abiko, Chiba, 31 August 1942*
*Turned professional 1964*
Successful international performer whose only victory on the PGA Tour came dramatically in Hawaii in 1983 when he holed a 128 yards pitch for an eagle 3 at the last at Waialae to beat Jack Renner. Only Japanese golfer to win on the European Tour taking the European Open in 1983. He also won the World Match

Play in 1978 beating Simon Owen and was runner up the following year. He holed in one at Wentworth in that event to win a condominium at Gleneagles. He was top earner five times in his own country and is the Japanese golfer who has come closest to winning a major title finishing runner-up two shots behind Jack Nicklaus in the 1980 US Open at Baltusrol. Inducted into the World Golf Hall of Fame in 2004.

## Atwal, Arjun (IND)
*Born Asansol, India, 20 March 1973*
*Turned professional 1995*
The first Indian golfer to win on the PGA Tour. In 2010 he triumphed at the Wyndham Championship and in the process became the first Monday qualifier for 24 years to win. When he won the 2002 Caltex Malaysian Open he became only the second Indian to earn a European To The first was Jeev Milkha Singh. He learned the game at Royal Calcutta.

## Azinger, Paul (USA)
*Born Holyoke, Massachusetts, 6 January 1960*
*Turned professional 1981*
Winner of the 1993 USPGA Championship at the Inverness CC by beating Greg Norman at the second leg of a play-off. He had finished joint runner-up with Rodger Davis to Nick Faldo in the 1987 Open at Muirfield. In 1994 he was diagnosed with lymphoma in his right shoulder blade but happily made a good recovery. He played in four Ryder Cup matches between 1989 and 2001 when he holed a bunker shot at the last to halve with Niclas Fasth. He successfully captained the US Ryder Cup side at Valhalla in 2008.

## Baddeley, Aaron (AUS)
*Born New Hampshire, USA, 17 March 1981*
*Turned professional 2000*
Became the first amateur to win the Australian Open since Bruce Devlin in 1969 and the youngest when he took the title at Royal Sydney in 2000. Then, having turned professional he successfully defended it at Kingston Heath. He had shown considerable promise when at age 15, he qualified for the Victorian Open. Represented Australia in the Eisenhower Trophy and holds both Australian and American passports. He led going into the last round at the US Open at Oakmont in 2007 but finished joint 13th. Now plays on the PGA Tour but returned to Australia to beat Swede Daniel Chopra in a play-off for the 2007 MasterCard Australian Masters at Huntingdale.

## Baker, Peter (ENG)
*Born Shifnal, Shropshire, 7 October 1967*
*Turned professional 1986*
Rookie of the year in 1987, Peter was hailed as the best young newcomer by Nick Faldo when he beat Faldo in a play-off for the Benson and Hedges International in 1988. Several times a winner since then he played in the 1993 Ryder Cup scoring three points out of four and in the singles beat former US Open champion Corey Pavin. He was a vice-captain to Ian Woosnam at the 2006 match.

## Baker-Finch, Ian (AUS)

*Born Namour, Queensland, 24 October 1960*
*Turned professional 1979*

Impressive winner of The Open Championship in 1991 at Royal Birkdale he lost his game completely when teeing up in Tour events and was forced, after an agonising spell, to retire prematurely. He commentated originally for Channel Seven in Australia then for ABC and now for CBS in America.

## Barnes, Brian (SCO)

*Born Addington, Surrey, 3 June 1945*
*Turned professional 1964*

Extrovert Scottish professional whose father-in-law was the late former Open champion Max Faulkner. He was a ten times winner on the European Tour between 1972 and 1981 and was twice British Seniors champion successfully defending the title in 1996. He played in six Ryder Cup matches most notably at Laurel Valley in 1975 when, having beaten Jack Nicklaus in the morning, he beat him again in the afternoon. Although he retired early because of ill-health caused by rheumatoid arthritis he has started to play and fish again after his rheumatic problem was re-diagnosed as caused by eating meat. He often commentates for Sky Television.

## Beem, Rich (USA)

*Born Phoenix Arizona, 24 August 1974*
*Turned professional 1994*

Playing in only his fourth major championship he hit the headlines in 2002 when he held off the spirited challenge of Tiger Woods to win the USPGA Championship at Hazeltine preventing Woods from winning three majors in one year for a second time. Rich, a winner of two previous Tour titles, admitted he was "flabbergasted to have won" having arrived with no expectations. On the final day at Hazeltine, Beem hit a fairway wood to to seven feet for an eagle at the at the 587 yards 11th and a holed a 40 foot putt for a birdie at the 16th to hold off Woods who finished with four birdies in a row. Just a year after turning professional Beem had given up the game to sell car stereos and mobile phones. After becoming an assistant club professional he returned once again to tournament play in 1999. In 2012 he took up the last year of an exemption on the European Tour where he competed regularly.

## Bjørn, Thomas (DEN)

*Born Silkeborg, 18 February 1971*
*Turned professional 1993*

A former Danish Amateur champion in 1990 and 1991, he became the first Dane to play in the Ryder Cup when he made the team in 1997. Four down after four holes against Justin Leonard in the last day singles at Valderrama he fought back to halve the match and gain a valuable half-point in the European victory. He missed out because of injury on the 1999 match but was back in the team in 2002 and 2004 and was a vice-captain at Celtic Manor in 2010. He has come close

four times to winning major titles. He was third to runaway winner Tiger Woods at Pebble Beach in the 2000 US Open and second to him at St Andrews in The Open a few weeks later. He looked set to win the 2003 Open at Royal St George's when three clear with four to play but dropped a shot at the 15th. and 17th and two shots after taking three to recover from a bunker at the short 16th. losing out eventually to Ben Curtis. In 2005 at Baltusrol he equalled the low round in a major with a 63 at the US PGA Championship but finished third to Phil Mickelson. In 2007 he became chairman of the European Tour Players' committee and in 2011 rediscovered his best form to win on the European Tour in Qatar, at Gleneagles and in Switzerland.

## Bonallack KT, OBE, Sir Michael (ENG)

*Born Chigwell, Essex, 31 December 1934*

One of only four golfing knights (the others are the late Sir Henry Cotton, Sir Bob Charles and Sir Nick Faldo) he won the Amateur Championship five times between 1961 and 1970 and was five times English champion between 1962 and 1968. He also won the English stroke play Championship (the Brabazon Trophy) four times and was twice leading amateur in The Open in 1968 and 1971. In his hugely impressive career he played in nine Walker Cup matches captaining the side on two occasions. He participated in five Eisenhower Trophy matches and five Commonwealth team competitions. He scored his first national title win in the 1952 British Boys' Championship and took his Essex County title 11 times between 1954 and 1972. After serving as secretary of The R&A from 1983 to 1999 he was elected captain for 1999/2000. Twice winner of the Association of Golf Writers' award in 1968 and 1999, he also received the Bobby Jones award for sportsmanship in 1972, the Donald Ross and Gerald Micklem awards in 1991 and the Ambassador of Golf award in 1995. In 2000 he was inducted into the World Hall Golf of Fame. A former chairman of The R&A selection committee, he served as chairman of the PGA from 1976 to 1981 and is now a non-executive director of the PGA European Tour. He served for a time as chairman of the Golf Foundation and was president of the English Golf Union in 1982. His wife is the former English champion Angela Ward.

## Bradley, Keegan (USA)

*Born Woodstock, Vermont, 1986*
*Turned professional 2008*

Winner of the US PGA Championship in 2011 after savouring a breakthrough success in the Byron Nelson, Bradley enjoyed a notable rookie season on the PGA Tour, earning $3.8 million in his first year among the elite. A graduate from the Nationwide Tour, he was the first golfer since Shaun Micheel in 2003 to win the PGA in his first appearance as well as the first player since Ben Curtis to win any major at the first attempt. In 2012 he won the Bridgestone Invitational, a World Golf Championship event, and made an impressive début for the USA in the Ryder

Cup, winning three matches in the company of Phil Mickelson. He hails from a golfing family and is the nephew of former LPGA player Pat Bradley.

## Brooks, Mark (USA)
Born Fort Worth, Texas, 25 March 1961
Turned professional 1983
Winner of the USPGA Championship title in 1996 after a play-off with Kenny Perry at Valhalla. On that occasion he birdied the 72nd hole and the first extra hole to win but lost b two shots to South African Retief Goosen in the 18-hole play-off for the 2000 US Open at Southern Hills in Tulsa.

## Brown, Ken (SCO)
Born Harpenden, Hertfordshire, 9 January 1957
Turned professional 1974
Renowned as a great short game exponent, especially with his hickory-shafted putter, he won four times in Europe between 1978 and 85, and took the Southern Open on the US tour in 1987. He played in five Ryder Cups and was on the winning side in 1985 and 1987. After retiring from professional tournament play he became an accomplished and highly respected television commentator working closely for the BBC (with Peter Alliss) and for The Golf Channel.

## Cabrera, Angel (ARG)
Born Córdoba, Argentina, September 12, 1969
Turned professional 1989
Big hitting Argentinian winner of two major titles who learned much from former Open champion Roberto de Vicenzo. He won his first major when he held off a strong challenge from Jim Furyk and Tiger Woods to win the 2007 US Open and two years later won The Masters in a play-off at Augusta with Chad Campbell and Kenny Perry.

## Cabrera Bello, Rafael (ESP)
Born Las Palmas, Gran Canaria, Spain, May 25, 1984
Turned professional 2005
Young Spanish golfer who won his first event on the European Tour in 2009 by firing a closing record 12-under-par 60 to win the Austrian Open at the Fontana Club in Vienna. Cabrera Bello, who started the final day eight off the lead, missed his eagle putt on the last for what would have been an historic 59. He was the 14th first-time winner of the season and the 13th person to shoot a 60 on the European Tour. His sister is a professional on the Ladies European Tour.

## Calcavecchia, Mark (USA)
Born Laurel, Nebraska, 12 June 1960
Turned professional 1981
Winner of the 1989 Open Championship at Royal Troon after the first four-hole play-off against Australians Greg Norman and Wayne Grady. He was runner-up in the 1987 Masters at Augusta to Sandy Lyle and came second to Jodie Mudd in the 1990 Players' Championship. He played in the 1987, 1989, 1991 and 2002 Ryder Cup sides.

## Canizares, Alejandro (ESP)
Born Manilva, Malaga, 9 January 1983
Turned professional 2006
A four-time All-American golfer when studying at Arizona State University, he is the son of José Maria Canizares. When he turned professional in July 2006 he won his third event – the Imperial Collection Russian Open in Moscow.

## Canizares, José Maria (ESP)
Born Madrid, 18 February 1947
Turned professional 1967
A popular seven-time winner on the European Tour between 1972 and 1992 the popular Spaniard retired after playing on the European Senior and US Champions Tours for a number of years. A former caddie, he played in four Ryder Cup matches in the 1980's winning five and halving two of his 11 games.

## Cantlay, Patrick (USA)
Born Long Beach, California, March 17, 1992
Turned professional 2012
Winner of the Mark H McCormack medal for the world's top ranked amateur male golfer at the end of 2011. His first appearance at the US Open in 2011 was auspicious since he finished 21st and during one round at Congressional covered the back nine in just 30 blows. He also signed for 60 in the Travelers Championship on the US PGA Tour, eventually finishing in 24th place. All told, he registered four top 25s in the four professional events he entered. He joined the paid ranks in the summer of 2012, missing out on an exempt amateur spot at The Open to play events on both the PGA and web.com Tours. His best finish was runner-up at the Chiquita Classic.

## Casey, Paul (ENG)
Born Cheltenham, 21 July 1977
Turned professional 2001
After successfully defending the English Amateur Championship in 2000, he attended Arizona State University where he was a three time All-American and broke records set by Phil Mickelson and Tiger Woods. In the 1999 Walker Cup match, which Great Britain and Ireland claimed at Nairn, he won all of his four games. After turning professional he earned his European Tour card after just five events and became a winner in only his 11th event when taking the Scottish PGA title at Gleneagles. He won the BMW PGA Championship in 2009, rising to No 3 in the world, but struggled with injury over the next three years and slipped outside the top 100.

## Casper, Billy (USA)
Born San Diego, California, 24 June 1931
Turned professional 1954
A three-time major title winner he took the US Open in 1959 and 1966 and the US Masters in 1970. In 1966 he came back from seven strokes behind Arnold Palmer with nine to play to force a play-off which he then won. Between 1956 and 1975 he picked up 51

# Sir Bob Charles (NZL)

*Born Auckland, 14 March 1936        Turned professional 1960*

The first left-handed golfer to win a major championship, Sir Bob became the only New Zealander so far to lift the Claret Jug in 1963 when, three years after turning professional, he defeated Phil Rodgers in a 36-hole play-off for the title at Royal Lytham. He carded 140 to the American's 148. Until the emergence of Mike Weir and Phil Mickelson, Charles was the game's pre-eminent left-hander – an ironic distinction since he does pretty much everything else right-handed apart from games which require the use of both hands.

While 40 years would elapse before another lefty won a major, Charles himself was a runner-up in The Open to Gary Player in 1968 at Carnoustie and to Tony Jacklin in 1969 at Lytham as well as to Julius Boros, the oldest major winner, at the PGA Championship in 1968 at Pecan Valley. He was also a contender at the US Open in 1964 and 1970 when he finished third both times. One of the reasons for his success was that he putted beautifully. When Charles won The Open, he averaged 30 putts per round over the course of 72 holes and just 26 putts during the first round of the play-off.

Blessed with a sure touch from long range on the greens, he was also nerveless from close range. He rarely missed from inside five feet and also holed the majority of ten footers. During the 1972 season, the former bank worker completed 11 successive rounds without a three-putt. That same season he received the OBE from Her Majesty the Queen before being awarded the CBE in 1992. He was knighted in 1999 for his services to golf.

The winner of more than 60 events around the world, Charles enjoyed a new lease of life after turning 50. He won 23 tournaments on the Champions Tour and posted the low scoring average three times in 1988, 1989 and 1993. He was the first left-hander to be inducted into the Hall of Fame and, at 71, he became the oldest player to make the cut on any of the world's Tours when he shot a second round 68 in the Michael Hill New Zealand Open in 2007.

first prize cheques on the US Tour. His European victories were the 1974 Trophée Lancôme and Lancia D'Oro and the 1975 Italian Open. As a senior golfer he won nine times between 1982 and 1989 including the US Senior Open in 1983. Played in eight Ryder Cups and captained the American side in 1979 at The Greenbrier. He and wife Shirley have 11 children several of them adopted. He was named Father of the Year in 1966. Started playing golf aged 5 and rates Ben Hogan, Byron Nelson and Sam Snead as his heroes. Five times Vardon Trophy winner (for low season stroke-average) and twice top money earner he was USPGA Player of the Year in 1966 and 1970. He was inducted into the World Golf Hall of Fame in 1978 and the USPGA Hall of Fame in 1982. Encouraged by his family to play in The Masters for one last time in 2005 he shot 106 but was disqualified for not handing in his card.

## Chapman, Roger (ENG)

*Born Nakuru, Kenya, 1 May 1959*
*Turned professional 1981*

He became the first English golfer to win the US Senior PGA Championship in August of 2012 at Harbor Shores in Michigan. Remarkably, on a visit to Michigan the month before, he also won the US Senior Open at Indianwood. He is only the fourth golfer after Gary Player, Jack Nicklaus and Hale Irwin to win both these senior majors in the same season. Chapman's astonishing success as a senior came after playing on the European Tour for 18 years without a victory. He lost his card and returned to the qualifying school in 1999. Regaining his playing privileges with a 12th place finish in the six round competition, he made his breakthrough win in his 472nd tournament

by beating Padraig Harrington at the second hole of a play-off in the Brazil Rio de Janeiro Five Hundred Years Open. A former English Amateur Champion in 1981 he played in the Walker Cup the same year beating Hal Sutton twice in a day at Cypress Point. In 2010 he earned his card to play the Champions Tour in America where his career would enjoy an Indian summer.

## Choi, K-J (KOR)

*Born Wando, South Korea, 19 May 1970*
*Turned professional 1994*

When his high school teacher suggested he take up golf, he studied all Jack Nicklaus' videos. Son of a rice farmer he was the first Korean to earn a PGA Tour card and in 2003 became the first Korean to win on the European Tour when he was successful in the Linde German Masters. Better known as KJ he finished fifth behind Tiger Woods on the 2007 American money list having earned over $4.5 million but failed to become the first Korean to win a major when YE Yang beat Woods in the 2009 US PGA Championship at Hazeltine.

## Cink, Stewart (USA)

*Born Huntsville, Alabama, 21 May 1973*
*Turned professional 1995*

In a dramatic play-off at Turnberry in 2009 he won his first major by beating Tom Watson by six shots in their four hole play-off after both had tied at the end of 72-holes. This win by the former PGA Tour Rookie of the Year made up for the two-foot putt he missed which would have earned him a play-off for the 2002 US Open won by Retief Goosen. He has played in every Ryder Cup since 2002. In the 2006 Cup match

## Darren Clarke OBE (NIR)

*Born Dungannon, Northern Ireland, 14 August 1968     Turned professional 1990*

Darren became the fourth golfer from Northern Ireland to win a major when he beat Dustin Johnson and Phil Mickelson in the 2011 Open at Royal St George's. The rough weather did not phase Clarke who learned his golf at Royal Portrush. His victory came weeks after another Ulsterman, Rory McIlroy, had been successful at the US Open and a year after Northern Ireland's Graeme McDowell had won the American title at Pebble Beach. The other Ulster winner of a major was Fred Daly who won The Open in 1947. Darren became the first European Tour player to shoot 60 twice when he returned a record equalling low score at the European Open at the K Club in 1999. Seven years earlier he had shot a nine under par 60 at Mont Angel in the Monte Carlo Open. His 60 in Dublin was 12 under. Tied second in the 1997 Open behind Justin Leonard at Royal Troon he was third behind David Duval at the 2001 Open at Royal Lytham and St Annes before winning the title at Sandwich in 2011. Cigar smoking Clarke became the first European to win a World Golf Championship event when he beat Tiger Woods 4 and 3 in the final of the 2000 Accenture Match Play Championship picking up a $1 million first prize.

He took a second World Championship event in 2003 when he was an impressive winner of the NEC Invitational at Firestone. He played in the 1997, 1999, 2002 and 2004 Ryder Cup matches and again in 2006, bravely competing just a few months after his wife Heather lost her battle with cancer. In that match he won twice with good friend Lee Westwood and gained a single point against Zach Johnson. In 2010 he was a vice captain at Celtic Manor but it was in 2011 that he scored his greatest success with victory at Royal St George's. He received the OBE in the 2011 Queen's New Year Honours list.

at the K Club, he beat Sergio García in the singles to prevent the Spaniard winning five points out of five.

## Clark, Clive (ENG)

*Born Winchester, 27 June 1945*
*Turned professional 1965*

In the 1965 Walker Cup at Five Farms East in Maryland, he holed a 35-foot putt to earn a half point against Mark Hopkins and ensure a first ever drawn match against the Americans on their home soil. After turning professional he played in the 1973 Ryder Cup. Following a career as commentator with the BBC he continued his golf course architecture work in America, and has received awards for his innovative designs.

## Clark, Howard (ENG)

*Born Leeds, 26 August 1954*
*Turned professional 1973*

A scratch player by the age of 16, he turned professional after playing in the 1973 Walker Cup. An eleven-time winner on the European tour he played in six Ryder Cups and was in the winning team three times – in 1985 at The Belfry, 1987 at Muirfield Village, when the Europeans won for the first time on American soil, and in 1995 when he gained a vital point helped by a hole in one in the last day singles against Peter Jacobsen. In the 1985 World Cup played at La Quinta in Palm Springs he was the individual champion. He played 494 tournaments before giving up full-time competition to concentrate on his job as a highly respected golf analyst for Sky television.

## Coles MBE, Neil (ENG)

*Born 26 September 1934     Turned professional 1950*

An Honorary Life Member of the European Tour he won golf tournaments in six decades. In 2003 he did not win but in the Travis Perkins event over Wentworth's Edinburgh Course (which he helped design) he shot a 64 – outstanding golf by a man who had been a pro at that

time for 54 years. He scored his first victory at the Gor-Ray tournament in 1956 when 22 and won the Lawrence Batley Seniors Open at Huddersfield in 2002 when 67 years and 276 days. From 1973 to 1979 he played in 56 events on the main European Tour without missing a half-way cut and became the then oldest winner when he won the Sanyo Open in Barcelona in 1982 at the age of 48 years and 14 days (Des Smyth has since become an even older winner). A member of eight Ryder Cup teams, he has represented his country 19 times since turning professional at the age of 16 with a handicap of 14. He has been chairman of the PGA European Tour's Board of Directors since its inception in 1971 and in 2000 was inducted into the World Golf Hall of Fame. Internationally respected he might well have won more in America but for an aversion to flying caused by a bad experience on an internal flight from Edinburgh to London.

## Coltart, Andrew (SCO)

*Born Dumfries, 12 May 1970     Turned professional 1991*

Twice Australian PGA champion in 1994 and 1997 he was the Australasian circuit's top money earner for the 1997/98 season. He made his Ryder Cup début in 1999 as a captain's pick and, having not been used in the foursomes and fourballs he lost in the singles on the final day to Tiger Woods. A former Walker Cup and Eisenhower Trophy player he was a member of the only Scottish team to win the Alfred Dunhill Cup at St Andrews in 1995. His sister Laurae is married to fellow professional Lee Westwood.

## Couples, Fred (USA)

*Born Seattle, Washington, 3 October 1959*
*Turned professional 1980*

Troubled continually with a back problem he has managed to win only one major – the 1992 US Masters but remains one of the most popular of all

American players. He has always been willing to travel and his overseas victories include two Johnnie Walker World Championships, the Johnnie Walker Classic, the Dubai Desert Classic and the Tournoi Perrier de Paris. On the US Tour he won 14 times between 1983 and 1998 and later won the Shell Houston Open. He played in five Ryder Cup matches and has teed up four times for the US in the Presidents Cup in which he acted as captain in 2009 and again in 2011. He will lead the side again in 2011. Couples kept up his winning ways on the Champions Tour in 2010 with a victory in only his second senior start at the Ace Group Classic. He also won the Toshiba Classic and the Cap Cana Championship to become the first 50-year-old to win three of the first four senior events in which he played. In 2011 he captained the US side in the President's Cup at Royal Melbourne.

## Crenshaw, Ben (USA)
*Born Austin, Texas, 11 January 1952*
*Turned professional 1973*

One of golf's great putters who followed up his victory in the 1984 Masters with an emotional repeat success in 1995 just a short time after the death of his long-time coach and mentor Harvey Pennick. He played in four Ryder Cup matches between 1981 and 1995 before captaining the side in 1999 when the Americans came from four points back to win with a scintillating last day singles performance. Winner of the Byron Nelson award in 1976 he was also named Bobby Jones award winner in 1991. Now combines playing with an equally successful career as a golf course designer and is an acknowledged authority on every aspect of the history of the game. In 2002 he won the Payne Stewart Award which recognises a player's respect for and upholding of the traditions of the game.

## Curtis, Ben (USA)
*Born Columbus, Ohio, 26 May 1977*
*Turned professional 2000*

Shock 750–1 outsider who played superbly at Royal St George's to get his name engraved with all the other golfing greats on the famous Claret Jug. His victory in the 2003 Open, while well deserved, was one of golf's biggest shocks in years. It was his first major appearance. He only qualified for the Championship with a 14th place finish in the Western Open in Chicago – a designated qualifying event. He had never played in Britain nor had he any experience of links golf but he outplayed Tiger Woods, Thomas Bjørn, David Love III and Vijay Singh to take the title with a score of 283. He learned the game in Ohio at the golf course his grandfather built at Ostrander. In 2008 he chased Padraig Harrington home to finish second behind the Irishman in the USPGA Championship at Oakland Hill. That year he made his début in captain Paul Azinger's Ryder Cup side which won the trophy back at Valhalla.

## Daly, John (USA)
*Born Sacramento, California, 28 April 1966*
*Turned professional 1987*

Winner of two majors – the 1991 USPGA Championship and the 1995 Open Championship at St Andrews after a play-off with Costantino Rocca, his career has not been without its ups and downs. He admits he has battled alcoholism and, on occasions has been his own worst enemy when having run-ins with officialdom but he remains popular because of his long hitting. His average drive is over 300 yards. When he won the USPGA Championship at Crooked Stick he got in as ninth alternate, drove through the night to tee it up without a practice round and shot 69, 67, 69, 71 to beat Bruce Lietzke by three. Given invaluable help by Fuzzy Zoeller he writes his own songs and is a mean performer on the guitar. Despite winning two majors he has never played in the Ryder Cup and now no longer holds a PGA Tour card. He had a stomach band inserted in 2009 in a successful bid to lose weight.

## Darcy, Eamonn (IRL)
*Born Dalgeny, 7 August 1952*
*Turned professional 1969*

One of Ireland's best known players who played more than 600 tournaments on the European Tour despite suffering for many years with back trouble. First played when he was 10 years old and is renowned for his very distinctive swing incorporating a flying right elbow. He played in four Ryder Cups including the memorable one at Muirfield Village in 1987 when Europe won for the first time in America. He scored a vital point in the last day singles holing a tricky left to right downhill seven footer for a valuable point against Ben Crenshaw. Now plays on the European Senior Tour.

## Davis, Rodger (AUS)
*Born Sydney, 18 May 1951   Turned professional 1974*

Experienced Australian who came joint second with Paul Azinger in the 1987 Open Championship behind Nick Faldo at Muirfield. A regular on the European Tour and for a time on the US Champions Tour he has won 27 titles – 19 of them on the Australasian circuit where, in 1988, he picked up an Aus $1 million first prize in the bicentennial event at Royal Melbourne. Usually played in trademark 'plus twos' but has now retired from all but Australian golf.

## Day, Jason (AUS)
*Born Beaudesert, Queensland, 1987*
*Turned professional 2006*

Already the winner of more than $9million in prize money after just four seasons on the PGA Tour, Day was runner-up in both the Masters and the US Open in 2011. These excellent performances in the majors followed on from a top ten finish at the US PGA in 2010. He also won the Byron Nelson in 2010. A successful amateur when he was growing up in Queensland, he won the 2006 Australian Amateur Stroke-Play

Championship as well as the Australian Junior Championship and the World Junior Cham-pionship.

## De Vicenzo, Roberto (ARG)

*Born Buenos Aires, 14 April 1923*
*Turned professional 1938*

Although he won The Open in 1967 at Royal Liverpool the impressive South American gentleman of the game is perhaps best known for the Major title he might have won. In 1968 he finished tied with Bob Goalby at Augusta or he thought he had. He had finished birdie, bogey to do so but sadly signed for the par 4 that had been inadvertently and carelessly put down for the 7th by Tommy Aaron who was marking his card. Although everyone watching on television and at the course saw the Argentinian make 3 the fact that he signed for 4 was indisputable and he had to accept that there would be no play-off. It remains one of the saddest incidents in golf with the emotion heightened by the fact that that Sunday was de Vicenzo's 45th birthday. The gracious manner in which he accepted the disappointment was remarkable. What a contrast to the scenes at Hoylake nine months earlier when, after years of trying, he finally won The Open beating Jack Nicklaus and Clive Clark in the process thanks to a pressure-packed brilliant last round 70. It was well deserved. He had been runner-up in 1950 and had finished third six times. The father of South American golf he was a magnificent driver and won over 200 titles in his extraordinary career including nine Argentinian Opens between 1944 and 1974 plus the 1957 Jamaican, 1950 Belgian, 1950 Dutch, 1950, 1960 and 1964 French, 1964 German Open and 1966 Spanish Open titles. He played 15 times for Argentina in the World Cup and four times for Mexico. Inducted into the World Golf Hall of Fame in 1989 he is an honorary member of the Royal and Ancient Golf Club of St Andrews. Although he was unable to return to Britain for the 2006 Open Championship at Hoylake were he won in 1967 he made it to the 150th. Anniversary celebrations of The Open at St Andrews in 2010. He was pleased when fellow Argentinian Angel Cabrera won the 2007 US Open but even more elated when Cabrera, inspired by him, became the first Argentinian winner of a Masters Green Jacket.

## Dickson, Bob (USA)

*Born McAlester, Oklahoma, 25 January 1944*
*Turned professional 1968*

Best remembered for being one of only four players to complete a Transatlantic amateur double. In 1967 he won the US Amateur Championship at Broadmoor with a total of 285 (the Championship was played over 72 holes from 1965 to 1972) and the British Amateur title with a 2 and 1 win over fellow American Ron Cerrudo at Formby.

## Donald, Luke (ENG)

*Born Hemel Hempstead, Herts., 7 December 1977*
*Turned professional 2001*

The game's outstanding golfer in 2011, Donald made history when he became the first ever player to top the money list on both the European and US PGA Tours. He was also named the PGA Tour's player of the year and enjoyed the same honour in Europe, where he was also celebrated by the Association of Golf Writers. Donald won four times in 2011, twice in America where he claimed the Accenture Match Play and the Childrens Miracle Network Hospital Classic; and twice in Europe at the BMW PGA and the Scottish Open. All told, he racked up 20 top ten finishes and missed only two cuts. His short game was second to none and he was the best putter on both sides of the Atlantic. A formidable amateur as well as a successful professional, he was a member of the winning Great Britain and Ireland team against the Americans in the 1999 Walker Cup at Nairnand again in 2001 before joining the paid ranks. In 1999 while attending the North-Western University in Chicago he won the NCAA Championship and was named NCAA Player of the Year. He was twice Big Ten Individual Championship winner and is a former Jack Nicklaus Trophy winner. Prior to 2011, he won three times on the European Tour in Sweden, Switzerland and Spain but went on to play more of his golf in America where he won the rain-shortened Southern Farms Bureau event in 2002 and the Honda tournament in 2006. He was one of five rookies in the winning 2004 European Ryder Cup team in Detroit having been a captain's pick and played again in 2006 and 2010 missing the chance of a place in the 2008 team because of a wrist injury that required surgery. He played an important part in the 2010 European Ryder Cup victory at Celtic Manor and in 2010 finished 15th in the Race to Dubai and 7th on the PGA Tour money list before moving from 28th to 9th in the world rankings. Made history with his consistency in 2011 when he finished the year as World No 1. In 2012 he lost the No 1 spot to Rory McIlroy but became only the third golfer to successfully defend the BMW PGA, was part of Europe's winning Ryder Cup team in Chicago and received the MBE for his services to golf.

## Drew, Norman (NIR)

*Born Belfast, 25 May 1932    Turned professional 1958*
Twice Irish Open Amateur champion in 1952 and 1953 he played in the 1953 Walker Cup and six years later represented Great Britain and Ireland in the Ryder Cup.

## Dufner, Jason (USA)

*Born Cleveland, Ohio, 24 March 1977*
*Turned professional 2000*

Winner of the US PGA Championship at Oak Hill, he didn't start playing golf until the age of 15 after his family moved to Florida. He went to college at Auburn in Alabama and was a finalist in the US Amateur Public Links at Torrey Pines in 1998 when he lost to Trevor Immelman. Between 2001 and 2006 he played mostly on the Nationwide Tour before establishing himself among the élite on the PGA Tour in 2009 when he produced six top ten finishes.

# Ernie Els (RSA)

*Born Johannesburg, 17 October 1969*     *Turned professional 1989*

Blessed with a powerful, smooth swing which laid the foundation for more than 65 tournament wins around the world, the big South African has lifted four major championships – two US Opens and The Open twice at Muirfield and Royal Lytham – while building a reputation as a formidable matchplay golfer, winning the World Matchplay on a record seven occasions. Although his nickname "the Big Easy" reflected an engaging personality as well as that rhythmic golf swing, it didn't tell the whole story. From his first victory at the Amatola Sun Classic in 1991 to The Open in 2012, Els was able to call upon the ruthless instincts of a serial winner.

As a youngster, he was a budding athlete and won a regional tennis tournament in South Africa at the age of 13. At 14, however, his career path was set after he won the world junior golf championship in California. After joining the professional ranks and following up wins on the Sunshine Tour with victories around the world, he first made his mark in the majors at the 1994 US Open. He came out on top at Oakmont after winning a play-off against Loren Roberts and Colin Montgomerie. The Scot was to regard Els as a nemesis in the majors since he also lost out to the South African in the 1997 US Open at Congressional. Long tipped by his compatriot, Gary Player, to lift the Claret Jug, Els realised his dream of glory in 2002 at The Open by defeating Thomas Levet in a sudden-death play-off. His triumph came at the first extra hole after a four hole play-off had eliminated the Australians Stuart Appleby and Steve Elkington. All four golfers had finished on the six-under-par total of 268. Els executed a brilliant recovery shot from an awkward lie in a greenside trap at the 18th to make the four foot putt for par which earned him his third major title.

His career was disrupted by an anterior cruciate ligament knee injury sustained during a sailing holiday with his family. It took time for Els to recover, though he was back in full cry at Doral and Bay Hill in 2010 when he won the World Golf Championship and the Arnold Palmer Invitational in the space of a couple of weeks. In 2012 he secured his first major since 2002 when he took advantage of Adam Scott's collapse over the closing four holes to win The Open for the second time. He's a Lytham specialist, having finished runner-up there in 1996 and third in 2001. His birdie on the 72nd hole marked only the second time in 20 years the champion had finished with a score below par.

In recent seasons, Els has also broadened his horizons beyond the golf course. He became involved in charity work through the Els for Autism Foundation which helps young people such as his son, Ben, who is autistic. He's active in course design and was involved in the re-design of Wentworth. He's also been in the wine business for ten years..

Leading by five strokes with four holes to play at the US PGA in 2011, he lost a play-off to Keegan Bradley. In 2012 he won twice and was a valued member of the US Ryder Cup team. A long time admirer of Ben Hogan, he broke his hero's course record at Oak Hill with a blistering 63 in 2013 and won his first major in Rochester thanks to a superb display of ball striking.

## Duval, David (USA)

*Born Jacksonville, Florida, 19 November 1971*
*Turned professional 1993*

A regular winner on the US Tour who wears dark glasses because of an eye stigmatism which is sensitive to light, he won his first major at Royal Lytham and St Annes in 2001 when he became only the second American professional to win The Open over that course. In 1998 and 2001 he was runner-up in The Masters and was third at Augusta in 2003. Although illness and injury affected his career he did finish second to Lucas Glover in the US Open at Bethpage Park black but failed to keep his US Tour card that year. He won the US Tour Championship in 1997 and the Players' Championship in 1999. As an amateur he played in the 1991 Walker Cup and was a member of the winning Ryder Cup side on his début in 1999 but on a losing side in 2002.

## Dyson, Simon (ENG)

*Born York, 21 December 1977*
*Turned professional 1999*

A three-time winner on the Asian Tour where he was top earner in 2000, he scored his first European Tour success in the joint Asian–European venture in Indonesia in 2006 and later in the season he beat Australian Richard Green in a play-off for the KLM Open at Zandvoort. He won that title again in 2009 and later in that season was successful in the Dunhill Links Championship played over the Old course, St Andrews, Carnoustie and Kingsbarns. In 2007 he shot 64 in the final round of the USPGA Championship to finish in joint sixth place – his best performance in a major. In 2011 he won the KLM Open for the second time and was also successful in the Irish Open. He was a member of the GB&I side in the Vivendi Seve Trophy.

## Edfors, Johan (SWE)

*Born Varberg, Sweden, 10 October 1975*
*Turned professional 1997*

The number one player on the 2003 Challenge Tour he had a brilliant year on the main Tour in 2006, winning three events – the TCL Classic in China, the Quinn Direct British Masters and the Barclays

Scottish Open at Loch Lomond. Since then he has won on the Asian Tour but has not had any more success on the European Tour.

## Edwards, Nigel (WAL)
*Born Caerphilly, 9 August 1968*

Top scoring member of the winning Walker Cup sides in 2001 and again in 2003 at Ganton, he captained the side that won the cup at Royal Aberdeen in 2011. In 2003 he had holed from off the green with the putter at the 17th to ensure a half point with Lee Williams and overall victory for the team. He was again involved in a dramatic finish to the 2005 Walker Cup but one down with one to play and needing to win the last against Jeff Overton his putt narrowly missed. Welshman Edwards also played in the match in 2007, inspired his side to a surprise victory over a talented US side in 2011 reminding his team that although on paper the Americans were the stronger side the game was not played on paper.

## Elkington, Steve (AUS)
*Born Inverell, 8 December 1962*
*Turned professional 1985*

A former Australian and New Zealand champion he was a regular winner on the PGA Tour despite an allergy to grass. Helped by a closing string of birdies at the Riviera CC in Los Angeles in 1995 he beat Colin Montgomerie in a play-off for the USPGA Championship. He has one of the finest swings in golf and is also an accomplished artist in his spare time. He played four times in the Presidents Cup. In 2002 after pre-qualifying for The Open at Dunbar he played off for the title at Muirfield with Thomas Levet, Stuart Appleby and eventual winner Ernie Els. He nearly won the USPGA Championship in 2005 finishing second with Thomas Bjørn behind Phil Mickelson at Baltusrol and was again in contention in the 2010 Championship at Whistling Straits.

## Fasth, Niclas (SWE)
*Born Gothenburg, Sweden, 29 April 1972*
*Turned professional 1989*

The studious-looking Swede made the headlines in 2001 when finishing second to David Duval in The Open. He played in the 2002 Ryder Cup and in 2007 he came a creditable fourth in the US Open at Oakmont. In 2008 he split with his long-time coach Graham Crisp who was working with him revamping his swing. The changes took time to settle and he missed out on a Ryder Cup place that year.

## Faxon, Brad (USA)
*Born Oceanport, New Jersey, 1 August 1961*
*Turned professional 1983*

A former Walker Cup player in 1983 match he has played in two Ryder Cup matches (1995 and 1997). A successful winner on the US Tour he also putted superbly to win the Australian Open at Metropolitan in 1993. In 2005 was named recipient of the Payne Stewart award for respecting and upholding the traditions of the game. He is a member of the PGA Tour Committee.

## Feherty, David (NIR)
*Born Bangor, Northern Ireland, 13 August 1958*
*Turned professional 1976*

Quick-witted Ulsterman who gave up his competitive golfing career to become a successful commentator for CBS in America where his one-liners are legendary. He had five European title wins and three victories on the South African circuit before switching his golf clubs for a much more lucrative career behind the microphone.

## Fernandez, Vicente (ARG)
*Born Corrientes, 5 May 1946*
*Turned professional 1964*

After playing on the European Tour where "Chino" won five times between 1975 and 1992 he joined the US Champions Tour competing with considerable success. Born with one leg shorter than the other he is remembered in Europe for the 87 foot putt he holed up three tiers on the final green at The Belfry in 1992 to win the Murphy's English Open.

## Fernandez-Castano, Gonzalo (ESP)
*Born Madrid, 13 October 1980*
*Turned professional 2004*

Twice Spanish amateur champion he began playing golf as a five-year-old and turned professional in 2004 when he was playing off plus 4. He represented Spain in the 2002 Eisenhower Trophy and played for the Continent of Europe against Great Britain and Ireland in 2004. He played twice in the Palmer Cup leading the European students to success against the Americans at Ballybunion in 2004. He won for the first time when he took the 2005 KLM Dutch Open title at Hilversum and was named Sir Henry Cotton Rookie of the Year. Since then he's won five more events in Europe, including the BMW Italian Open in 2012 for the second time when he shot a closing round of 64. His form last year was consistent enough to move inside the world's top 40.

## Finsterwald, Dow (USA)
*Born Athens, Ohio, 6 September 1929*
*Turned professional 1951*

Winner of the 1958 USPGA Championship he won 11 other competitions between 1955 and 1963. He played in four Ryder Cup matches in a row from 1957 and captained the side in 1977. He was USPGA Player of the Year in 1958.

## Fisher, Oliver (ENG)
*Born Chingford, Essex, 19 August 1988*
*Turned professional 2006*

Became the youngest ever Walker Cup player when he made the 2005 Great Britain and Ireland side at the age of 17. In 2006 he played in the Eisenhower and Bonallack Trophy matches and when he turned professional he was playing off plus 4 He won the Czech Open in 2011 but only came up with three top 20 finishes in 2012.

# Sir Nicholas A. Faldo (ENG)

*Born Welwyn Garden City, 18 July 1957     Turned professional 1976*

By a wide margin the most successful British golfer of the modern era – he spent 92 weeks in all as the world number one – his achievements were recognised in style when he became the first professional golfer since Sir Henry Cotton to receive a knighthood for his services to the game. Always single minded in his approach to winning tournaments, few would dispute Peter McEvoy's observation that Faldo sets the gold standard against which everyone else of recent vintage in English golf must be measured.

From the moment a careers officer at school warned him that only one in 10,000 made it as a professional – the Englishman insisted if that was the case then he would prove to be that solitary success – the golfer was as dedicated in his pursuit of glory as he was ambitious. At 14 he had never picked up a club, yet by 17 he was a top rank amateur. He won the British Youths and the English Amateur in 1975 before joining the paid ranks a year later. It was a measure of his rapid progress in the sport that by 20 he was playing in the Ryder Cup. He had only decided to take up the game after watching the Masters on his parents' new colour television when he followed the performance of Jack Nicklaus. "I was just absolutely mesmerised," he recalls.

He is Europe's most successful Major title winner having won three Open Championships in 1987 and 1992 at Muirfield and in 1990 at St Andrews along with three Masters titles in 1989, 1990 and 1996. Of contemporary players only Tiger Woods with 14 majors and Tom Watson with eight have won more majors. When he successfully defended the Masters in 1990 he became only the second golfer (after Nicklaus) to win in successive years. One of the most memorable moments of his career came when he staged a dramatic last day revival to win the 1996 Masters having started the last round six strokes behind Greg Norman.

Unkindly dubbed 'Nick Foldo' when he missed out on opportunities to win both The Open and The Masters in the early Eighties, Faldo nevertheless appreciated his swing was not good enough to win majors and completely revamped his action with the help of coach David Leadbetter. His revised swing and remarkable sense of poise under pressure duly helped him win more major titles than any other player between 1987 and 1996.

His 31 European Tour victories include a record three consecutive Irish Open victories. In 1992 he became the first player to win over £1 million in prize-money during a season. He also played with distinction in 11 Ryder Cup matches including the winning European teams in 1985, 1987, 1995 and 1997. He holds the record for most games played in the Cup, 46, and most points won, 25. In 1995 at Oak Hill he came from behind to score a vital last day point against Curtis Strange, the American who had beaten him in a play-off for the US Open title in 1988 at The Country Club in Boston. He also captained the Ryder Cup side at Valhalla in 2008 when Europe were disappointing and missed out on winning four in a row. His assistant, José Maria Olazábal, blamed Faldo's "poor communication" for the team's failure.

He became the first international player to be named USPGA Player of the Year in 1990 and led the official World Golf Rankings for 81 weeks in 1993–1994. After teaming up with Swedish caddie Fanny Sunesson for ten years, they split, only to be reunited as one of golf's most formidable partnerships in 2001 before parting company a second time.

His Faldo Junior Series, designed to encourage the best young players to improve, continues to expand. It organises more than 30 tournaments in 25 countries for boys and girls aged between 12 and 21. His company, Faldo Enterprises, runs a successful international golf course design business.

In 2006, he embarked on a TV commentating career with the Golf Channel and CBS. He signed an $8m eight-year contract with the American broadcaster and covers many PGA Tour events. He is an insightful analyst who sees his role as stimulating the interest of a broad audience. In 2009 he was knighted by Her Majesty the Queen for his services to golf.

## Fisher, Ross (ENG)

*Born Ascot, Berkshire, 22 November 1980*
*Turned professional 2004*

Attached to the Wentworh Club, he has been playing since he was three. In 2007 he won his first European Tour title at the KLM Open. Later in the season he won the European Open at the London Club leading from start to finish and ending up six clear of his nearest rival. He also won the Volvo Match Play Championship beating Anthony Kim at Finca Cortesin

in Spain. In 2010, helped by victory in the 3-Irish Open, he made his début in the Ryder Cup at Celtic Manor.In 2012 he missed out on a fifth victory when he was runner-up at both the Nordea Masters and the Portugal Masters.

## Fitzpatrick, Matthew (ENG)

*Born Sheffield, September 1 1994*

The first Englishman to win the US Amateur title since Harold Hilton overcame Fred Herreshoff in

1911, Fitzpatrick defeated Australia's Oliver Goss to secure victory at the 113th staging of the championship over the Country Club in Brookline. He was the first non-American, at the 16th time of asking, to win a title over the course where 100 years earlier Francis Ouimet had won the US Open. One of only two amateurs to play 72 holes at Muirfield in The Open, he won the Silver Medal in 2013 after posting 294, ten over par, good enough for a share of 44th. Fitzpatrick had played his way into The Open thanks to rounds of 68 and 72 in qualifying over Gullane No 1. He also won the Boys Amateur title at Notts Holinwell in 2012 by the huge margin of 10 and 8. After representing Great Britain and Ireland in the 44th Walker Cup match, he was presented with the Mark H McCormack Medal as the leading men's player in the World Amateur Golf Ranking for 2013.

## Floyd, Raymond (USA)

*Born Fort Bragg, North Carolina, 4 September 1942*
*Turned professional 1961*
A four time major winner whose failure to win an Open Championship title prevented his completing a Slam of Majors. He won the US Open in 1986, the Masters in 1976 when he matched the then 72-hole record set by Jack Nicklaus to win by eight strokes and took the USPGA title in 1969 and 1982. In addition to coming second and third in The Open he was also runner-up three times in the Masters and in the USPGA once. After scoring 22 victories on the main US Tour he has continued to win as a senior. Inducted into the World Golf Hall of Fame in 1989 he is an avid Chicago Cubs baseball fan. Played in eight Ryder Cup matches between 1969 and 1993 making history with his last appearance by being the oldest player to take part in the match. He was 49. He was non-playing captain in 1989 when the match was drawn at The Belfry and was an assistant to Paul Azinger at the 2008 match at Valhalla.

## Ford, Doug (USA)

*Born West Haven, Connecticut, 6 August 1922*
*Turned professional 1949*
His 25 wins on the PGA Tour between 1955 and 1963 included the 1975 Masters. USPGA Player of the Year in 1955, he competed in four Ryder Cup matches in succession from 1955.

## Frost, David (RSA)

*Born Cape Town, 11 September 1959*
*Turned professional 1981*
He has won as many titles overseas as on the US Tour and played regularly on the European Tour until 2009. The 1993 season was his best in America when he made over $1 million and finished fifth on the money list. He has established a vineyard in South Africa growing 100 acres of vines on the 300-acre estate and has very quickly earned a reputation for producing quality wines. He now plays on the Champions Tour in America and on Europe's Senior Tour.

## Funk, Fred (USA)

*Born Tacoma Park, Missouri, 14 June 1956*
*Turned professional 1981*
One of five rookies in the 2004 US Ryder Cup side, he scored his sixth US Tour success a few weeks later when he won the Southern Farm Bureau Classic. In 2005 he won the Tournament Players' Championship at Sawgrass and now plays on the Champions Tour. In 2009 he and Mark McNulty lost a play-off to Loren Roberts in the Senior Open at Sunningdale and then won the US Senior Open the following week at Crooked Stick.

## Furyk, Jim (USA)

*Born West Chester, Pennsylvania, 12 May 1970*
*Turned professional 1992*
One of only six golfers in US PGA Tour history to sign for 59, Furyk is a major champion who won the US Open at Olympia Fields, Chicago in 2003. He was one of four first-time major winners that year. He clearly enjoys playing in Las Vegas where he has won three Invitational events in 1995, 1999 and 1998. He has teed it up in five Presidents Cups and eight Ryder Cups, beating Nick Faldo in the singles at Valderrama in 1997. He has one of the most easily recognisable if idiosyncratic swings in golf. His father Mike has been his only coach. In 2006 he came second to Tiger Woods in the US Tour money list earning $7,213,316 but won the Harry Vardon Trophy for the best average of 68.66 for golfers who played 60 rounds or more. In 2010 he won three times on the PGA Tour, won the Fedex Cup $10 million bonus and was named Player of the Year. He won over $3 million in 2012 without adding to his 16 PGA Tour wins. Furyk was a wild card pick for the USA at the Ryder Cup in Medinah where he bogeyed the last two holes of a lost singles tie against Sergio García. In 2013 he shot 59 during the BMW Championship at Conway Farms in Illinois on a day when the scoring average was 71.

## Gallacher CBE, Bernard (SCO)

*Born Bathgate, Scotland, 9 February 1949*
*Turned professional 1967*
For many years he combined tournament golf with the club professional's post at Wentworth where he was honoured in 2000 by being appointed captain. He took up golf at the age of 11 and nine years later was European No 1. He has scored 30 victories world-wide. Gallacher was the youngest Ryder Cup player when he made his début in the 1969 match in which he beat Lee Trevino in the singles. He played in eight Cup matches and captained the side three times losing narrowly in 1991 at Kiawah Island and 1993 at The Belfry before leading the team to success at Oak Hill in 1995. A former member of the European Tour's Board of Directors, he was afforded honorary membership of the European Tour in 2003.

## García, Sergio (ESP)

*Born Castellon, 9 January 1980*
*Turned professional 1999*

The Spaniard, who was runner-up to Tiger Woods in the 1999 US PGA Championship, lost his best chance of winning a first major when he missed a putt on the final green at Carnoustie in 2007 and was beaten by Ireland's Padraig Harrington in the subsequent four-hole play-off. He had led for most of the four days. He was again pipped by Harrington in the 2008 USPGA Championship at Oakland Hills. Having won the British Boys' Championship in 1997, he took the Spanish and British Amateur titles in 1998 and in both years was the European Amateur Masters champion. Son of a greenkeeper/professional who now plays on the European Senior Tour, Sergio waited until after the 1999 Master before joining the paid ranks at the Spanish Open. Although only just starting to collect Ryder Cup points he easily made the 1999 team and formed an invaluable partnership with Jesper Parnevik at Brookline scoring three and a half points out of four on the first two days. The 1999 Sir Henry Cotton Rookie of the Year in Europe he again formed a useful partnership this time with Lee Westwood in the 2002 Cup match. Together they won three points out of four. They teamed up again in the winning 2004 side at Oakland Hills. He himself was unbeaten, winning 4½ out of five points including victory over Phil Mickelson in the singles. In the 2006 Ryder Cup at the K Club he again played well with José María Olazábal in the fourballs and Luke Donald in the foursomes. He scored four out of five points, losing only his single to Stewart Cink. His form dipped in the 2008 match at Valhalla but that year he did became the first European-born player since 1937 to win the Vardon Trophy on the PGA Tour with a low score average of 69.12. He ended the year as No. 2 in the World Rankings. Loss of confidence saw him take a break from the game and miss out on the 2010 Ryder Cup. By the end of 2010 he had slipped to 78th in the world rankings but improved to 18th in 2011 when he returned to winning ways with victories in successive weeks at his own event – the Castello Masters – and the Andalucia Masters. Last season he won the Wyndham Championship, his first success in America for four years, and returned to Ryder Cup action for Europe at Medinah.

## Garrido, Ignacio (ESP)

*Born Madrid 2 February 1944*
*Turned professional 1961*

Eldest son of Antonio Garrido who played in the 1979 Ryder Cup, Ignacio emulated his father when he made the team at the 1997 match at Valderrama having earlier that year won the Volvo German Open. A former English Amateur Stroke-play title-holder in 1992 his most impressive win on the European Tour was beating Trevor Immelman in a play-off for the 2003 Volvo PGA Championship at Wentworth. In the 80s used to caddie for his father who has since caddied for him on occasion.

## Goosen, Retief (RSA)

*Born Pietersburg, 3 February 1969*
*Turned professional 1990*

Introduced to golf at the age of 11 the former Sout| African amateur champion scored his first majo| professional success when leading from start to finis| at the 2001 US Open at Tulsa and then beating Mar| Brooks in the 18-hole play-off by two shots. Althoug| he suffered health problems after being hit by lightnin| as a teenager he has enjoyed a friendly rivalry wit| fellow South African Ernie Els whom he beat in the 2005 South African Airways Open at Fancourt. In 2004 he again won the US Open, this time a| Shinnecock Hills GC on Long Island producing, in the process, not only superb control through the gree| but inspirational form on the lightning fast putting surfaces to prevent Phil Mickelson winning wha| would have been his second major of the year| Goosen single-putted 11 of the first 17 holes of hi| final round of 71. In 2005 after finishing tied third a| The Masters, he was leading going into the last round of the US Open at Pinehurst No 2 but shot a closing 81 to miss out on a successful defence of his title. He finished 11th behind Michael Campbell but was fifth a| The Open and sixth at the USPGA that same year When he played again in the Presidents Cup later ir the year he beat Tiger Woods in the singles at Lake Mannassas. He continues to play well around the world.

## Grace, Branden (RSA)

*Born Pretoria, May 20, 1988*
*Turned professional 2007*

The latest in a long line of outstanding South African| golfers, Grace won four times on the European| Tour in 2012, kicking off the season with victories on home turf at the Joburg Open and the Volvo| Golf Champions before adding further triumphs at| the Volvo China Open and the Alfred Dunhill Links| in St Andrews. A graduate of the Ernie Els and Fancourt Foundation, he enjoyed a fine amateur career before making his mark in the paid ranks. During the Dunhill Links he matched the European| Tour's low score with a new course record, 60, at| Kingsbarns. He's the first ever player to win his first four events on the European Tour in the same| season.

## Grady, Wayne (AUS)

*Born Brisbane, 26 July 1957*
*Turned professional 1973 and again in 1978*

In 1990 he won the USPGA Championship at Shoal| Creek by three shots from Fred Couples. A year| earlier he had tied with Greg Norman and eventual| winner Mark Calcavecchia for The Open Champion-ship losing out in the first ever four-hole play-off for the title. He is a former chairman of the Australasian| Tour and with a reduced schedule on the Champions| Tour in America he manages to commentate| occasionally for the BBC.

## Graham, David (AUS)

*Born Windsor, Tasmania, 23 May 1946*
*Turned professional 1962*

Played superbly for a closing 67 round Merion to win the 1981 US Open Championship from George Burns and Bill Rogers. That day he hit every green in regulation. Two years earlier he had beaten Ben Crenshaw at the third extra hole at Oakland Hills to win the USPGA Championship. When he took up the game at age 14 he played with left-handed clubs before making the switch to a right-handed set. Awarded the Order of Australia for his services to golf he is a member of the Cup and Tee committee that sets up Augusta each year for the Masters. A regular winner around the world in the 70s and 80s he won eight times on the US Tour between 1972 and 1983 and has built up a considerable reputation as a course designer.

## Green OBE, Charlie (SCO)

*Born Dumbarton, 2 August 1932*

One of Scotland's most successful amateur golfers who was leading amateur in the 1962 Open Championship. A prolific winner he took the Scottish Amateur title three times in 1970, 1982 and 1983. He played in five and was non-playing captain in two more Walker Cups and was awarded the Frank Moran Trophy for his services to Scottish sport in 1974.

## Green, Hubert (USA)

*Born Birmingham, Alabama, 18 December 1946*
*Turned professional 1970*

In 1977 he beat Lou Graham at the 1977 US Open at Southern Hills despite being told with four holes to play that he had received a death threat. Three times a Ryder Cup player he also won the 1985 USPGA Championship. Best known for his unorthodox swing and distinctive crouching putting style. he has successfully beaten throat cancer – an illness that has prevented his competing on the US Champions Tour. He was inducted into the World Golf Hall of Fame in 2007.

## Haas, Bill (USA)

*Born Charlotte, North Carolina, 1982*
*Turned professional 2004*

Winner of three events on the PGA Tour, including the Tour Championship by Coca-Cola in 2011, Haas' victory in Atlanta was sufficient not only to collect the first prize of $1.44 million but also the FedEx Cup jackpot of $10m. The son of Jay Haas, who won nine times on the PGA Tour, Bill received a captain's pick from Fred Couples to play in the Presidents Cup at Royal Melbourne.

## Haas, Jay (USA)

*Born St Louis, Missouri, 2 December 1953*
*Turned professional 1976*

Winner of nine events on the USPGA Tour, he played in his third Ryder Cup as an invitee of the US captain Hal Sutton. He had played in 1983 and 1995.

He has played in three Presidents Cups and was a Walker Cup player in 1975. His uncle is former Masters champion Bob Goalby. In 2004 he was named recipient of the Payne Stewart award for respecting and upholding the traditions of the game and received the Bob Jones award for outstanding sportsmanship in 2005. In 2006 and 2007 he edged out Loren Roberts for the No 1 spot on the US Champions Tour winning five times in 2006 and a further four times in 2007.

## Haeggman, Joakim (SWE)

*Born Kalmar, 28 August 1969*
*Turned professional 1989*

Became the first Swedish player to play in the Ryder Cup when he made the side which lost to the Americans at The Belfry in 1993. He received one of team captain Bernard Gallacher's 'wild cards' and beat John Cook in his last day singles. Gave up ice hockey after dislocating his shoulder and breaking ribs in 1994. Realised then that ice hockey and golf do not mix but has become an enthusiastic angler when not on the links. Equalled the world record of 27 for the first nine holes in the Alfred Dunhill Cup over the Old course at St Andrews in 1997. Occasionally acts as commentator for Swedish TV and was a member of Sam Torrance's Ryder Cup backroom team at The Belfry in 2002 and Bernhard Langer's vice-captain at Oakland Hills in 2004. Returned to the winner's circle in 2004 at Qatar. It was only his second win on the European Tour and his first since 1993.

## Hamilton, Todd (USA)

*Born Galesburg, Illinois, 18 October 1965*
*Turned professional 1997*

Winner of the 2004 Open Championship at Royal Troon beating Ernie Els in a four-hole play-off after both had tied on ten-under-par 274. Having learned his craft on the Asian Tour and Japanese circuit where he won four times in 2003, he earned his US Tour card in 2004 and won the Honda Classic. His performance in The Open was flawless as he kept his nerve to win against Els, Phil Mickelson and World No 1 Tiger Woods among others. He was American Rookie of the Year in 2004 but has since lost his card to play there and has been a member of the European Tour.

## Han, Chang Won (KOR)

*Born Jeju Island*

The 17-year-old winner of the first Asian Amateur Championship played at Mission Hills in China, he shot a 12-under par score to earn a place in the 2010 Masters at Augusta joining two other foreign teenagers, US Amateur Champion Byeong-Hu An and British Champion Matteo Manassero there.

## Hansen, Anders (DEN)

*Born Sonderborg, 16 September 1970*
*Turned professional 1995*

Made up eight shots over the last 36 holes to win the BMW PGA Championship for a second time at

# Padraig Harrington (IRL)

*Born Dublin, Ireland, 31 August 1971        Turned professional 1995*

The winner of three major championships, Harrington is Ireland's most successful golfer thanks to his triumphs at The Open in 2007 and 2008 and the US PGA in 2007. He became only the second Irishman ever to hoist the Claret Jug when he overcame Sergio García in a four-hole play-off at Carnoustie, 60 years after Belfast's Fred Daly had won the title at Hoylake in 1947.

He savoured the season of his life in 2008 when he became the first European to win both The Open and US PGA titles in the same year and the first European to win the US PGA since Tommy Armour in 1930. At Royal Birkdale he defended the crown by holding off the challenge posed by Ian Poulter and Greg Norman with a closing 66. The highlight of the championship was the 5-wood he struck to two feet on the par 5 17th for a glorious eagle 3 which closed the door on his rivals. It was the first time since James Braid in 1906 that a European had retained the title. At Oakland Hills three weeks later his main challengers were García and Ben Curtis. Again a closing 66 did the trick for the talented Irishman. At the end of his extraordinary year, Harrington was named the European Tour, PGA Tour and PGA of America's Player of the Year. He was only the second European to be given this honour since it was first awarded in 1948.

A qualified accountant, Harrington played three times as an amateur in the Walker Cup before turning professional. He won the Spanish Open in 2006 and has gone on to lift 30 titles, including 14 on the European Tour. His career has been heavily influenced by input from both coach Bob Torrance and sports psychologist Bob Rotella. He won the European Order of Merit in 2006 and has featured on six Ryder Cup teams, four times as a winner. He has gone into the design business with his first course, The Marlbrook, in Co. Tipperary. In 2011, he was named as The R&A's first Working for Golf Ambassador, promoting the work of the game's governing body around the world.

---

Wentworth in 2007. He had also won the event in 2002. He ended top money winner on the South African Sunshine Tour in 2009. He won in 2011.

## Hansen, Søren (DEN)

*Born Copenhagen, 21 March 1974*
*Turned professional 1997*

Winner of the Murphy's Irish Open in 2002 and the Mercedes-Benz Championship in 2007, he made his début successfully in the 2008 Ryder Cup at Valhalla.

## Hanson, Peter (SWE)

*Born Svedala, 4 October 1977*
*Turned professional 1998*

In 1998 he won the English Amateur Stroke-play Championship (the Brabazon Trophy) and was also a member of the winning Swedish Eisenhower Trophy team. In 2005 he partnered Robert Karlsson for Sweden in the 2007 Mission Hills World Cup of Golf and in 2008 he ended a ten year wait for a home winner when he won the SAS Scandinavian Masters in poor weather at Arlandastat outside Stockholm. He won twice – at Majorca and the Czech Republic – in 2010 which helped him make his début in the Ryder Cup.

## Hayes, Dale (RSA)

*Born Pretoria, 1 July 1952*
*Turned professional 1970*

Former South African amateur stroke play champion who was a regular winner in South Africa and Europe after turning professional. He was Europe's top money earner in 1975 but retired from competitive golf to move into business. He is now a successful television commentator in South Africa with a weekly

programme of his own often working as a double act with veteran Denis Hutchinson.

## Hoch, Scott (USA)

*Born Raleigh, North Carolina, 24 November 1955*
*Turned professional 1979*

Ryder Cup, Presidents Cup, Walker Cup and Eisenhower Trophy player who was a regular winner on the US Tour soring 10 wins between 1980 and 2001 with six more victories worldwide. In 1989 he donated $100,000 of his Las Vegas Invitational winnings to the Arnold Palmer Children's Hospital in Orlando where his son Cameron had been successfully treated for a rare bone infection in his right knee. Also remembered for missing a short putt at the first extra hole of a play-off that would have won him a Masters Green Jacket and a first major.

## Horton MBE, Tommy (ENG)

*Born St Helens, Lancashire, 16 June 1941*
*Turned professional 1957*

A former Ryder Cup player who was No 1 earner on the European Seniors Tour in 1993 and for four successive seasons between 1996 and 1999. Awarded an MBE by Her Majesty the Queen for his services to golf, Tommy is a member of the European Tour Board and is chairman of the European Seniors Tour committee. A distinguished coach, broadcaster, author and golf course architect, Tommy retired as club professional at Royal Jersey in 1999 after 25 years in the post. He continues to play occasionally on the Senior Tour.

## Howell, David (ENG)

*Born Swindon, 23 June 1975 Turned professional 1995*
Winner of the 1999 Dubai Desert Classic, he made his Ryder Cup début in 2004 at Oakland Hills where he

teamed up with Paul Casey to gain a valuable foursomes point on the second day. He finished seventh in the 2005 European Tour money list making over £1.2 million and a year later despite his schedule being curtailed by injury, he made over £1.5 million and finished third. Although injury has severely restricted his play he remains an enthusiastic competitor and is often used as an expert analyst by Sky television.

## Huggett MBE, Brian (WAL)
*Born Porthcawl, Wales, 18 November 1936*
*Turned professional 1951*
Brian won the first of his 16 European Tour titles in Holland in 1962 and was still winning in 2000 when he landed the Beko Seniors Classic in Turkey after a play-off. A dogged competitor he played in six Ryder Cup matches before being given the honour of captaining the side in 1977 – the last year the Americans took on players from only Great Britain and Ireland. A respected golf course designer, Huggett was awarded the MBE for his services to golf and in particular Welsh golf.

## Hunt MBE, Bernard (ENG)
*Born Atherstone, Warwickshire, 2 February 1930*
*Turned professional 1946*
One of Britain's most accomplished professionals he won 22 times between 1953 and 1973. He was third in the 1960 Open at the Old Course behind Kel Nagle and fourth in 1964 when Tony Lema took the title at St Andrews. Among his other victories were successes in Egypt and Brazil. Having made eight appearances in the Ryder Cup he captained the side in 1973 and again in 1975. He was PGA captain in 1966 and won the Harry Vardon Trophy as leading player in the Order of Merit on three occasions.

## Ilonen, Mikko (FIN)
*Born Lahti, 18 December 1979*
*Turned professional 2001*
Became the first Finnish golfer to win the Amateur Championship when he beat Christian Reimbold from Germany 2 and 1 in the 2000 final at Royal Liverpool. He has won both the Finnish amateur match play and stroke play titles. He represented Finland in the 1998 and 2000 Eisenhower Trophy events. Now plays professionally on the European Tour and in 2007 won the Enjoy Jakarta Astro Indonesian Open, a joint venture with the Asian Tour and the Scandinavian Masters at Arlandastad. In 2008 he won the Indonesian Open title again.

## Immelman, Trevor (RSA)
*Born Cape Town, South Africa, 16 December 1979*
*Turned professional 1999*
The 2008 Masters champion is son of Johan Immelman, former executive director of the South African Sunshine Tour. A former South African Amateur Match Play and Stroke-play champion and twice South African Open champion Trevor played his early professional golf in Europe before moving to the United States where he scored a first major victory leading from start to finish in the 2008 Masters at Augusta. won his first PGA title when he held off a strong field at the Cialis Western Open at Cog Hill. He has played in two Presidents Cups but his career has been dogged by injury and illness causing him to miss three of the four 2009 majors.

## Irwin, Hale (USA)
*Born Joplin, Montana, 3 June 1945*
*Turned professional 1968*
A three time winner of the US Open (1974, 1979 and 1990) he has been a prolific winner on the main US Tour and, since turning 50, on the US Champions Tour. He had 20 wins on the main Tour including the 1990 US Open triumph where he holed a 45-foot putt on the final green at Medinah to force a play-off with Mike Donald then after both were still tied following a further 18 holes became the oldest winner of the Championship at 45 when he sank a 10-foot birdie putt at the first extra hole of sudden death. Joint runner-up to Tom Watson in the 1983 Open at Royal Birkdale where he stubbed the ground and missed a tap-in putt on the final day – a slip that cost him the chance of a play-off. Three times top earner on the Champions Tour where, prior to the start of the 2001 season, he had averaged $90,573 per start in 130 events coming in the top three in 63 of those events and finishing over par in only nine of them, he was inducted into the World Golf Hall of Fame in 2008.

## Ishikawa, Ryo (JPN)
*Born Saitama, 17 September 1991*
*Turned professional 2008*
Already established as one of the most exciting young players in world golf – he's nicknamed the "bashful prince" in Japan – the teenager captured headlines around the globe during 2010 when he carded 58 in the final round to win the Crowns tournament at Nagoya on the Japanese Tour. It was the lowest score ever recorded on a sanctioned Tour and included 12 birdies and six pars. The previous record of 59 was shared on the PGA Tour by the Americans Al Geiberger, Chip Beck, David Duval, Paul Goydos and Stuart Appleby. The Crowns tournament was Ishikawa's seventh victory of his career and followed on from an electrifying start to the final round when he birdied nine of the first 11 holes. He first won on the Japan Tour as an amateur at the 2007 Muningswear Open in Okayama. At just 15 years and 245 days he became the youngest man ever to win a professional event. He then went on to become the youngest player to compete in the US PGA Championship at Hazeltine in 2009 as well as the youngest ever to reach the top 50 of the World Golf Rankings.

## Jacobs OBE, John (ENG)
*Born Lindrick, Yorkshire, 14 March 1925*
The first Executive Director of the independently run PGA European Tour, John Jacobs was awarded the OBE in 2000 for his services to golf as a player, administrator and coach. Known as "Dr Golf" Jacobs

# Tony Jacklin CBE (ENG)

*Born Scunthorpe, 7 July 1944*     *Turned professional 1962*

A long and straight driver as well as a formidable ball striker at his peak, Jacklin was a significant force in the game between 1968 and 1974. It could even be argued that there were spells during his ascendancy when the Englishman was as good as anyone in the sport. In 1969 he won The Open Championship at Royal Lytham and St Annes, in the process becoming a national hero as the first British holder of the title since Max Faulkner in 1951. A year later he led from start to finish to win the US Open at Hazeltine by a seven shot margin – again underscoring his national standing as the first British player to win that event since Ted Ray had been successful in 1920. He was also the first Englishman since Harry Vardon to hold The Open and US Open titles simultaneously. He might well have won further Open championships but a thunderstorm thwarted his bid for the title at St Andrews in 1970, he came third in 1971 and in 1972 Lee Trevino chipped in at the 17th at Muirfield to win a title Jacklin had seemed destined to grasp.

The son of a Scunthorpe lorry driver who travelled by bus to play in assistants' events, he was rookie of the year on the European Tour in 1962 and went on to win 14 times on his home circuit. He was a driving force in the Ryder Cup as a player, taking part in seven consecutive matches from 1967. As a four-time captain of Europe, he twice led the Continent to victory including the first ever win on American soil in 1987. He also played an important and often under-rated role in the growth of the PGA European Tour after it became a self-supporting organisation in 1971. Although playing most of his golf in America he was encouraged by John Jacobs, the then executive director of the European Tour, to return to Europe to help build up the circuit.

He is an honorary member of the Royal and Ancient Golf Club of St Andrews having been elected in 2003 along with Lee Trevino. Played in his last Open in 2005. He has built in Florida with Jack Nicklaus a course known as The Concession, so named because of the putt Jack conceded him in the 1969 Ryder Cup to ensure the overall match was halved. He was awarded the OBE in 1970 and a CBE in 1990 in recognition of his influential Ryder Cup captaincy, which helped revive the standing of the match.

---

has built up an awesome reputation as a teacher around the world and is held in high esteem by the golfing fraternity. Top American coach Butch Harmon summed up John's contribution when he said: "There is not one teacher who does not owe something to John. He wrote the book on coaching." With 75 per cent of the votes he was inducted into the World Golf Teachers' Hall of Fame and was described at that ceremony as 'the English genius'. Last year he was also welcomed into the World Golf Hall of Fame in America. Having played in the 1955 Ryder Cup match he captained the side in 1979 when Continental players were included for the first time and again in 1981. Ken Schofield who succeeded him as European Tour supremo believes that John changed the face of golf sponsorship. In 2002 he received the Association of Golf Writers' award for outstanding services to golf.

## Jacquelin, Rafaël (FRA)

*Born Lyons, 8 May 1974*
*Turned professional 1995*

Ten years after turning professional and in his 238th event Rafaël Jacquelin a former French amateur champion, won his first event as a professional – the 2005 Madrid Open at Club de Campo. The Frenchman with a most graceful swing, who originlly wanted to be a soccer player but a knee injury thwarted his plans and he turned instead to tennis and later to golf. In 2007 he led wire-to-wire when winning the BMW Asian Open. He and Gregory Havret finished third

behind Scotland and the USA in the 2007 World Cup of Golf at Mission Hills in China. In 2011 he won the Sicilian Open and took over from the injured Alvaro Quiros in the Continental side captained by Jan Van de Velde against Great Britain and Ireland at St Nom la Breteche.

## Jaidee, Thongchai (THA)

*Born Lop Buri, Thailand, 8 November 1969*
*Turned professional 1999*

The first Thai golfer to win a title on the European Tour when he won the Carlsberg Malaysian Open in 2004. Learned his golf using a bamboo pole with an old 5-iron head and did not play his first nine holes until he was 16. An ex-paratrooper, Jaidee qualified and played all four rounds in the 2001 US Open. An impressive regular on the Asian Tour, he also competes on the European International schedule where in 2009 he won the Ballantines event in Korea and the Indonesian Open in Bali. Finished top money earner on the Asian Tour for the third time in 2009. He is still top career money earner on the Asian Tour with over $2 million.

## James, Mark (ENG)

*Born Manchester, 28 October 1953*
*Turned professional 1976*

Veteran of over 500 European tournaments he was for a time chairman of the European Tour's Tournament committee. A seven-time Ryder Cup player including the 1995 match at Oak Hill when he scored a vital early last day point against Jeff Maggert, he captained the side at Brookline in 1999. Four times a top five finisher in The Open Championship he has won 18 European Tour events and four elsewhere but caused some raised eyebrows with his comments in his book reviewing the 1999 Ryder Cup entitled *Into the Bear Pit*. Affectionately known as Jesse to his friends. he qualified for the US Champions Tour in 2004 and won one of that Tour's five majors – the Ford Senior Players Championship. Through 2008 continued to play on the US Champions Tour with only infrequent visits back to play in European Senior events or to join Ken Brown and Peter Alliss on the BBC golf commentating team. In his spare time he is an enthusiastic gardener.

## January, Don (USA)
*Born Plainview, Texas, 20 November 1929*
*Turned professional 1955*
Winner of the US Open in 1967 he followed up his successful main Tour career in which he had 11 wins between 1956 and 1976 with double that success as a Senior. Much admired for his easy rhythmical style.

## Janzen, Lee (USA)
*Born Austin, Minnesota, 28 August 1964*
*Turned professional 1986*
Twice a winner of the US Open in 1993 and in 1998 when he staged the best final round comeback since Johnny Miller rallied from six back to win the title 25 years earlier. Five strokes behind the late Payne Stewart after 54 holes at Baltusrol he closed with a 67 to beat Stewart with whom he had also battled for the title in 1993.

## Jiménez, Miguel Angel (ESP)
*Born Malaga, 4 January 1964*
*Turned professional 1982*
The oldest ever winner of a European Tour event, Jiménez was only five weeks shy of his 49th birthday when he claimed victory at the UBS Hong Kong Open in 2012. One of seven brothers, he did not take up golf until his mid-teens. Miguel loves cars, drives a Ferrari and has been nicknamed 'The Mechanic' by his friends. His best-remembered shot was the 3-wood he hit into the hole for an albatross 2 at the infamous 17th hole at Valderrama in the Volvo Masters. He was also credited with having played the Canon Shot of the Year when he chipped in at the last to win 1998 Trophée Lancôme. In 2000 lost in a play-off at Valderrama in a World Championship event to Tiger Woods. He played in the 2002, 2004, 2008 and 2010 European Ryder Cup sides gaining a vital point in the last day singles at Celtic Manor. He won four times during the 2004 European season, taking the Johnnie Walker Classic title in Bangkok, the Algarve Portuguese Open at Penina, the BMW Asian Open in Shanghai and the BMW German Open in Munich. and was a three time winner during the 2010 season succeeding in Dubai, Paris and at Crans. He was the 2008 BMW PGA champion beating Oliver Wilson in a play-off at Wentworth. He loves his rioja and is often seen smoking a cigar. At Medinah in 2012 he was one of Europe's four vice-captains at the Ryder Cup, a role he previously filled under Seve Ballesteros. His win in Hong Kong was the 19th of his career on the European Tour.

## Johansson, Per-Ulrik (SWE)
*Born Uppsala, 6 December 1966*
*Turned professional 1990*
A former amateur international at both junior and senior level he became the first Swede to play in two Ryder Cups when he made the 1995 and 1997 teams. In the 1995 match he lost to Phil Mickelson with whom he had studied at Arizona State University. In 1991 he was winner of the Sir Henry Cotton Rookie of the Year award in Europe. For a time, he played in America but returned to Europe, regaining his main Tour card with victory in the Russian Open in Moscow.

## Johnson, Dustin (USA)
*Born Columbia, South Carolina, 22 June 1984*
*Turned professional 2007*
Winner of the AT&T Pebble Beach Pro-am in both 2009 and 2010, he also led the US Open at Pebble Beach by three strokes after 54 holes but dropped back into a share of eighth place after carding 82 in the final round. Johnson also had a chance to win the US PGA in 2010 after making birdies in the final round at Whistling Straits on the 16th and 17th holes. Standing at 12 under par on the 72nd hole, he hit his tee shot right and landed in a sandy area. Unaware he was in a bunker he grounded his club in the dirt and thought he'd made a bogey to join Martin Kaymer and Bubba Watson in a play-off but he was penalised two strokes for grounding his club and finished in a share of fifth. His victory later in the season over Paul Casey in the BMW Championship, his fourth US PGA Tour win, proved his resilience. He was a member of the 2007 US Walker Cup side and made his début in the Ryder Cup at Celtic Manor in 2010. A year later he was runner-up to Darren Clarke in The Open losing his chance of possible victory by hitting his second shot out of bounds at the par 5 14th at Royal St George's.

## Johnson, Zach (USA)
*Born Iowa City, 24 February 1976*
*Turned professional 1998*
The winner of the 2004 BellSouth Classic, he made his début in the Ryder Cup at the K Club in 2006 and won The Masters at Augusta in 2007. Later, he won first prize in the AT&T Classic at TPC Sugarloaf and earned a Presidents Cup spot. Surprisingly missed out on Ryder Cup honours in 2008 but made the team in both 2010 and 2012. He made nearly $5 million and won twice on the PGA Tour last season – the John Deere Classic and the Crown Plaza – taking his victories there to nine.

## Jones, Steve (USA)
*Born Artesia, New Mexico, 27 December 1958*
*Turned professional 1981*
First player since Jerry Pate in 1976 to win the US Open after having had to qualify. His 1996 victory

was the result of inspiration he received from reading a Ben Hogan book given to him the week before the Championship at Oakland Hills. Uses a reverse over-lapping grip as a result of injury. Indeed his career was put on hold for three years after injury to his left index finger following a dirt-bike accident. He dominated the 1997 Phoenix Open shooting 62, 64, 65 and 67 for an 11 shot victory over Jesper Parnevik That week his 258 winning total was just one outside the low US Tour record set by Mike Souchak in 1955. Played in the 1999 Ryder Cup.

## Karlsson, Robert (SWE)

*Born St Malm, Sweden, 3 September 1969*
*Turned professional 1989*
The tall son of a greenkeeper is the most successful Swede on the European Tour having won 11 times by the end of 2010. He was a member of the winning 2006 Ryder Cup side and the losing 2008 team. He played with Peter Hanson in the 2007 Mission Hills World Cup of Golf in Shenzhen and in 2008 teamed up with Henrik Stenson to win the trophy for Sweden for a second time. It was a fitting finale to a year in which he made the cut in all four majors and towards the end of the season won the Mercedez-Benz German Masters and the Alfred Dunhill Links Championship to clinch the No 1 spot on the European Tour's Order of Merit. At one point during the summer of 2008 he was never out of the top four in five consecutive events finishing 3,3,3,2,4. An eye problem caused him to miss many tournaments in 2009. A year later, when back to full fitness he won the Dubai World Championship in 2010 and in 2011 played most of his golf in America.

## Kaymer, Martin (GER)

*Born Dusseldorf, Germany, 26 December 1984*
The 2010 US PGA champion produced an outstanding performance at Whistling Straits to secure his first Major title. Coached by Fanny Sunesson, who is better known as Nick Faldo's former caddie and bag carrier for Henrik Stenson, Kaymer was an out-standing amateur golfer who made an immediate impact as a professional. On a satellite circuit he made a name for himself by carding 59 before winning twice on the Challenge Tour in 2006. When he joined the European Tour the following year he ended up with five top ten finishes and won the Sir Henry Cotton Rookie of the Year award. He also won twice in 2008 at Abu Dhabi and Munich and just failed to make the Ryder Cup side, though he was invited to Valhalla as an observer by Faldo. In 2009 he won back to back titles at the French and Scottish Opens before an ankle injury sustained when go-karting in Arizona sidelined him for a spell. Victory in 2010 at the Abu Dhabi championship propelled Kaymer into the world's top ten. And when he defeated Bubba Watson in a play-off at Whistling Straits, Kaymer became only the second German after Bernhard Langer to become a major champion. He also won his next tournament,

the KLM Open, before making his Ryder Cup début at Celtic Manor then adding the Dunhill Links Championship to his list of successes. He went on to win the Race to Dubai and was jointly named European Golfer of the Year with Graeme McDowell. In 2011 he began with a third victory in four years at Abu Dhabi and moved to No 2 in the world but then his form deserted him.He was still out of sorts at the 2012 Ryder Cup but showed a true champion's mettle when he holed a vital putt on the 18th green at Medinah in a singles tie against Steve Stricker which retained the trophy for Europe.

## Kim Kyung-Tae (KOR)

*Born Seoul, South Korea, 2 September 1986*
*Turned professional: 2006*
It was no surprise that the 24-year-old South Korean topped the Japanese money list in 2010 with total earnings of over 181 million yen. He made it to the top with the help of three victories – the Diamond Cup, the Mynavi ABC Championship and the Japanese Open. His scoring average for the season was 69.41 and he hit more than three greens out of four in regulation during the season. As an amateur he had swept all before him earning a government exemption from National Service for his performance at the 2006 Asian Games where he won the individual honours and helped South Korea to victory in the team event. He won two events on the Korean professional Tour as an amateur and by the end of 2010 had moved from outdo the top 100 in the World Rankings to 30th.

## Kite, Tom (USA)

*Born Austin, Texas, 9 December 1949*
*Turned professional 1972*
He won the US Open at Pebble Beach in 1992 in difficult conditions when aged 42 to lose the 'best player around never to have won a Major' tag. With 19 wins on the main Tour he was the first to cash $6million, $7 million, $8 million and $9 million dollars in prize money. Has been playing since he was 11 and after a lifetime wearing glasses had laser surgery to correct acute near-sightedness. He played in seven Ryder Cups and was captain at Valderrama in 1997. He now plays the US Champions Tour and was inducted into the World Golf Hall of Fame in 2004.

## Kuchar, Matt (USA)

*Born Winter Park, Florida, 21 June 1978*
*Turned professional 2000*
A member of the US Walker Cup side which lost to GB&I at Nairn in 1999, Kuchar enjoyed a notable amateur career, winning the US Amateur in 1997. In 1998, he finished 14th at the US Open and 21st at the Masters while still at college. Since becoming a professional, the genial Kuchar has won four times on the PGA Tour as well as the Omega Mission Hills World Cup with Gary Woodland in 2011. His most significant victory to date came last year in the Players Championship at Sawgrass. He represented the USA at the Ryder Cup in both 2010 and 2012.

## Laird, Martin (SCO)
*Born Glasgow, Scotland, 1982*
*Turned professional 2004*

The Arizona based Scot enjoyed his best year so far on the PGA Tour in 2011, winning the Arnold Palmer Invitational at Bay Hill, the first European golfer ever to do so. He produced six top ten finishes and won $2.7 million. A graduate of the Nationwide Tour, his first PGA Tour win came at the Justin Timberlake Shriners Hospitals for Children Open. Laird's journey from junior captain and champion at Hilton Park in Glasgow to winner on the PGA Tour began in 2003. That was the summer he came from behind to clinch a three stroke victory in the Scottish Youths' Open Amateur Strokeplay Championship. He went to college at Colorado State and hasn't left America since, becoming first Scot in 20 years to play full-time on the PGA Tour.

## Lane, Barry (ENG)
*Born Hayes, Middlesex, 21 June 1960*
*Turned professional 1976*

After winning his way into the 1993 Ryder Cup he hit the headlines when he won the first prize of $1 million in the Andersen Consulting World Champion-ship beating David Frost in the final at Greyhawk in Arizona. He has played over 500 European events, winning five times between 1988 and 2008. In 2004, aged 44, he won the British Masters at Marriott Forest of Arden.

## Lawrie MBE, Paul (SCO)
*Born Aberdeen, 1 January 1969*
*Turned professional 1986*

Made golfing history when he came from 10 shots back on the final day to win the 1999 Open Cham- pionship at Carnoustie after a play-off against former winner Justin Leonard and Frenchman Jean Van de Velde. With his win he became the first home-based Scot since Willie Auchterlonie in 1893 to take the title. Still based in Aberdeen he hit the opening tee shot in the 1999 Ryder Cup and played well in partnership with Colin Montgomerie in foursomes and four balls and in the singles earned a point against Jeff Maggert. Originally an assistant at Banchory Golf Club on Royal Deeside Lawrie has had a hole named after him at the club. Lawrie was awarded an MBE for his achievements in golf and is a prominent supporter of junior golf in Scotland. In 2011 he won the Andalucian Masters in Malaga, his first victory in nine years. He was also runner-up in the season ending Dubai World Championship. Lawrie continued this run of good form into 2012 where he won twice on the European Tour – the Qatar Masters and the Johnnie Walker at Gleneagles – before moving into the world's top 30. He played in the Ryder Cup at Medinah for the first time since 1999 and demolished Brandt Snedeker by 5 and 3 in the singles.

## Lee, Danny (NZL)
*Born 24 July 1990*

Helped by his victory in the US Amateur Championship in 2008 he moved to the top of the Royal and Ancient Golf Club of St Andrews amateur rankings and the McCormack Trophy. Although Korean by birth he has been brought up in New Zealand and America. Late in 2008 he became a naturalised New Zealander and led his country in the Eisenhower Trophy competition won by Scotland in Adelaide. He is one of three amateurs to have won titles on the PGA European Tour. Pablo Martin won the Estoril Open de Portugal in 2007 as an amateur, Lee won the last Johnnie Walker Classic title at The Vines in Perth in 2009 and later that season Irish amateur Shane Lowry won the 3-Irish Open at Baltray.

## Lehman, Tom (USA)
*Born Austin, Minnesota, 7 March 1959*
*Turned professional 1982*

Winner of The Open Championship at Royal Lytham and St Annes in 1996 he was runner-up in the US Open that year and third in 1997. He was runner-up in the 1994 Masters having come third the previous year. He played in four Ryder Cup matches and led the US team in the 2006 Ryder Cup match at the K Club when the Americans lost 18½–9½ to the Europeans led by Ian Woosnam. In 2011 he was the Champions Tour player of the year, winning three times and earning over $2 milllion on the senior circuit.

## Leonard, Justin (USA)
*Born Dallas, Texas, 15 June 1972*
*Turned professional 1994*

Winner of the 1997 Open at Royal Troon when he beat Jesper Parnevik and Darren Clarke into second place with a closing 65 and nearly won the title again in 1999 when he lost to Paul Lawfrie in a four-hole play-off with the Scotsman and Jean Van de Velde at Carnoustie. In 1998 came from five back to beat Lee Janzen at the Players Championship and is remem- bered for his fight back against José Maria Olazábal on the final day of the 1999 Ryder Cup at Brookline. Four down after 11 holes he managed to share a half-point with the Spaniard to help America win the Cup. He was again a member of a winning Ryder Cup side when he played in the 2008 team captained by Paul Azinger at Valhalla but was in the losing side at Celtic Manor in 2010.

## Lewis, Tom (ENG)
*Born Welwyn Garden City, Hertfordshire, 5 January 1991  Turned professional 2011*

After a season in which he led The Open as an amateur and went on to surpass that feat in the paid ranks by winning in only his third start as a professional, it was fitting Lewis should be named the European Tour's rookie of the year in 2011. It was a 65 in the first round at Royal St George's – the lowest score ever recorded by an amateur at The Open – which first brought the

# Bernhard Langer (GER)

*Born Anhausen, 27 August 1957          Turned professional 1972*

While there have been many notable achievements during his enduring career, including collecting two Masters titles at Augusta, winning 40 titles on the European Tour and proving a mainstay of the European Ryder Cup side as both a player and a captain, the German's remarkable accomplishment in winning senior major titles in successive weeks during the summer of 2010 rivalled anything the veteran had accomplished in his prime. The first senior golfer to win back-to-back majors since Tom Watson in 2003, Langer's triumphs were all the more remarkable bearing in mind that his first success came in The Senior British Open at Carnoustie in Scotland and his second was in The US Senior Open in Seattle, Washington State, venues separated by thousands of miles as well as an eight hour time difference. Langer's success on the Champions' circuit, winning more than $2 million in each of his first three years on Tour, however, came as no surprise to those familiar with the track record of this determined champion.

His success at Carnoustie in The Senior British was particularly rewarding since he had come twice and finished third on three occasions in The Open without lifting the Claret Jug. A prolific winner throughout his career, Langer is the second most prolific champion, after Seve Ballesteros, in European Tour history. His most memorable victories, though, came in America where he won the Masters in 1985 and 1993. The latter triumph is best remembered for the eagle 3 he made at the 13th in the final round to set up a four stroke win over Chip Beck. Perhaps there was an element of irony attached to these triumphs at Augusta since Langer has frequently faced putting problems during his career and the Masters is widely regarded as the most demanding test of putting in championship golf. His most successful year as a pro came in 1985 when he won seven tournaments on five continents and was ranked No 1 in the world. Though far from the longest hitter, the consistency of Langer's game also made him a formidable match play golfer. He played in ten Ryder Cup matches and was an outstanding European captain at Oakland Hills in 2004. A member of the World Golf Hall of Fame, he was awarded an honorary OBE for his services to the game.

young Englishman, who won the Boys' Championship in 2009, to the attention of the wider golfing public. Just three months later in the final round of the Portugal Masters he uncorked another 65 to pull off the quickest victory by an affiliate member in Tour history. The son of Brian, a former Tour professional, Lewis' last act as an amateur was to help Great Britain and Ireland defeat the USA in the Walker Cup match at Royal Aberdeen

## Levet, Thomas (FRA)

*Born Paris, 9 September 1968*
*Turned professional 1988*

Although he was the first Frenchman to play full time on the US Tour and still has a home in Florida, he lost his card and only regained his European Tour card when he was invited, because of his French national ranking, to play in the 1998 Cannes Open – and won it. Sixth in the 1997 Open at Royal Troon he lost in a play-off to Ernie Els in the 2002 Open at Muirfield. Thomas made his Ryder Cup début at Oakland Hills in 2004, winning his singles game against Fred Funk. He is a gifted linguist speaking seven languages including Japanese. Has also turned his hand very successfully to commentating for French television. In 2011 he won the French Open but injured a food jumping into the lake at the 18th and had to withdraw from The Open at Royal St George's for which he had qualified earlier.

## Liang, Wen-Chong (CHN)

*Born Zhongshan, China, 2 August 1978*
*Turned professional 1999*

Became the second Chinese winner on the European Tour when he won the Clariden Leu Singapore Open in

2007. His friend and mentor has been Zhang Lian-wei Introduced to the game while still at school he plays with a most unorthodox swing but it works for him Finished second to Ian Poulter in the Barclays Singapore Open in 2009 he finished second to Thongchai Jaidee on the Asian Tour's Order of Merit and in 2010 was No 1 on the rival OneAsia Tour's final ranking.

## Littler, Gene (USA)

*Born San Diego, California, 21 July 1930*
*Turned professional 1954*

Winner of the 1953 US Amateur Championship he had a distinguished professional career scoring 26 victories on the US Tour between 1955 and 1977. He scored his only major triumph at Pebble Beach in 1971 when he beat Bob Goalby and Doug Sanders at Oakland Hills. He had been runner-up in the US Open in 1954 and was runner-up in the 1977 USPGA Championship and the 1970 US Masters. A seven-time Ryder Cup player between 1961 and 1977 he is a former winner of the Ben Hogan, Bobby Jones and Byron Nelson awards. He won the Hogan award after successfully beating cancer.

## Love III, Davis (USA)

*Born Charlotte, North Carolina, 13 April 1964*
*Turned professional 1985*

Son of one of America's most highly rated teachers who died in a plane crash in 1988, Love has won only one major – the 1997 USPGA Championship at Winged Foot where he beat Justin Leonard by five shots. He has been runner-up in the US Open (1996 and the US Masters (1999). In the World Cup of Golf he won the title in partnership with Fred Couples

## Sandy Lyle MBE (SCO)

*Born Shrewsbury, 9 February 1958        Turned professional 1977*

With his win in the 1985 Open Championship at Royal St George's he became the first British player to take the title since Tony Jacklin in 1969. He was also the first British player to win a Green Jacket in the Masters at Augusta in 1988 helped by a majestic 7-iron second shot out of sand at the last for a rare winning birdie 3. Although he represented England as an amateur at boys', youths' and senior level he became Scottish when he turned professional, something he was entitled to do at the time because his late father, the professional at Hawkstone Park, was a Scot. This is no longer allowed. He made his international début at age 14 and, two years later, qualified for and played 54 holes in the 1974 Open at Royal Lytham. A tremendously talented natural golfer who won 17 events on the European Tour, he fell a victim later in his career to becoming over-technical. Now lives in Perthshire and Florida. He was part of captain Ian Woosnam's backroom team for the 2006 Ryder Cup at the K Club in 2006. On the European Senior Tour, Sandy ended a 19 year wait for a tournament victory by winning the inaugural ISPS Handa Senior World Championship presented by Mission Hills China in 2011. He will be inducted into the World Golf Hall of Fame in 2012 after being selected through the international ballot.

our years in a row from 1992. He played in five Ryder Cups and was the losing captain of the US team at Medinah where he admitted to feeling "stunned" by urope's comeback on the final day.

## .owry, Shane (IRL)

*orn Clara, County Offaly, Ireland, 2 April 1987.*
*urned professional 2009*

The former Irish Amateur Close champion shot a 62 t County Louth GC in the Irish Open in 2009 and led om the second day. In the end in driving rain and a trong wind he held his nerve to beat Robert Rock in play-off for the title becoming only the third mateur to win on the European Tour. Pablo Martin on as an amateur in 2007 and earlier in 2009 Danny ee had won the Johnnie Walker Classic. Urged by ome to remain amateur until after the Walker Cup e chose to turn professional immediately.

## McDowell MBE, Graeme (NIR)

*orn Ballymoney, Northern Ireland, 30 July 1979*
*urned professional 2002*

The first European golfer to win the US Open since ony Jacklin 40 years earlier, he joined an elite group f golfers which includes Tiger Woods, Tom Watson nd Jack Nicklaus who have won America's oldest title t Pebble Beach. McDowell enjoyed the most uccessful season of his career to date in 2010. Two eeks before his triumph in the US Open he also won he Celtic Manor Wales Open thanks to a thrilling erformance over the weekend when he shot 63 and 4. The Ulsterman won the Andalucian Masters efore the end of the season and finished the year No. in the Race to Dubai. He was named Golfer of the ear by both the European and American Golf Vriters. Late in the year he beat Tiger Woods in a lay-off at Woods own tournament in California. A member of the winning Great Britain and Ireland Valker Cup team in 2001, he earned his European our card in just his fourth event as a professional. IcDowell, who had been signed up to represent the ungsangen Golf Club in Sweden just two weeks arlier, received a last minute sponsor's invitation to lay there in the Volvo Scandinavian Masters ... and

not only won the event but also broke the course record with an opening round of 64. He beat Trevor Immelman into second place with former USPGA champion Jeff Sluman third. McDowell's winning score of 270 – 14-under-par – earned him a first prize of over £200,000 and a place in the World Golf Championship NEC event at Sahalee in Washington. He was the European Tour's 12th first-time winner of the season and at 23 the youngest winner of the title. In 2008, helped by victories in the Ballantine's Championship in Korea and the Barclays Scottish Open at Loch Lomond, he qualified automatically for the Ryder Cup at Valhalla and was one of the team's most successful performers. He also represented Europe at Celtic Manor in 2010 when on a tense last day he scored the vital winning point with victory over Hunter Mahan. Crucially he holed tricky downhill putt for a winning birdie at the 16th. In his amateur days he attended the University of Alabama where he was rated No 1 Collegiate golfer winning six of 12 starts with a stroke average of 69.6. In 2004, scored his second European success when he won the Telecom Italia Open. At the end of the year he was voted Irish Sport Personality of the Year and was honoured with an MBE for his services to golf in the 2011 New Year's Honours List by Her Majesty the Queen.

## McEvoy OBE, Peter (ENG)

*Born London, 22 March 1953*

The most capped player for England who has had further success as a captain of Great Britain and Ireland's Eisenhower Trophy and Walker Cup sides. The Eisenhower win came in 1998 and the Walker Cup triumphs at Nairn in 1999 and at Ocean Forest, Sea Island, Georgia in 2001. On both occasions his team were 15–9. A regular winner of amateur events McEvoy was amateur champion in 1977 and 1978 and won the English stroke play title in 1980. He reached the final of the English Amateur the same year. In 1978 he played all four rounds of the Masters at Augusta and that year received the Association of Golf Writers' Trophy for his contribution to European golf. He was leading amateur in two Open Championships – 1978 and 1979. In 2003 he was awarded the OBE by Her

# Rory McIlroy MBE (NIR)

*Born Holywood, May 4 1989        Turned professional 2007*

Firmly established by the end of 2012 as the world's leading golfer, McIlroy enjoyed the best season of his fledgeling career last year when he won four times on the PGA Tour and earned over $8 million, thereby becoming the youngest golfer ever to reach $10 million in career earnings. The highlight of his season was a phenomenal eight shot victory in the US PGA Championship at Kiawah Island. It was the most emphatic triumph in the history of the tournament, surpassing even Jack Nicklaus' seven shot success in 1980.

The golfer from Holywood in County Down relished many other notable accomplishments in 2012 as he emulated Luke Donald's feat of winning the money lists in both America and Europe. He was named the PGA Tour's Player of the Year by his peers, won the Association of Golf Writers trophy and ranked as the second most marketable athlete in the world. In an unforgettable year for British sport, he was also shortlisted for the BBC's Sports Personality of the Year award.

The only active player under 40 with two major championship victories on his CV, the 23-year-old had also delivered the most exciting performance of 2011 when he led from the start to finish to win the US Open at Congressional, again by the breathtaking margin of eight strokes. It was the high point of another outstanding season in which he also won the Hong Kong Open by two shots and finished second behind Luke Donald in the Race to Dubai.

In 2010 he caught the attention of the golfing world thanks to a spectacular ten under par closing round of 62 to defeat Phil Mickelson by four shots in the Wells Fargo Championship. His eagle-birdie-par-birdie finish at Quail Hollow was electrifying.

Twice winner of the Irish and European Amateur titles – he was the youngest winner of the Irish event in 2005 – Rory won the silver medal as leading amateur in the 2007 Open at Carnoustie. After turning professional he won his European Tour card by finishing third in the Alfred Dunhill Links Championship, only his second event as a pro. In 2008 he missed a 15 inch putt to lose a play-off to Jean-François Lucquin at the Omega European Masters at Crans-sur-Sierre. In 2009 he won his first title – the Dubai Desert Classic – and finshed joint third in the USPGA Championship behind winner Yong-Eun Yang. He also finished third in the Race to Dubai after a season in which he had 12 top five finishes.

In 2010 he opened with 63 in The Open at St Andrews before carding an 80 on the second day which meant he had to settle for a share of third place. He was also third in the US PGA and made his début in the Ryder Cup at Celtic Manor. He returned to Ryder Cup action at Medinah in 2012, defeating Keegan Bradley in the singles, though only after speeding to the course on Sunday in a police car after a mix-up over his tee time.

Following Medinah, he turned his attention to winning the Race to Dubai, finishing second at the BMW Masters, third at the Barclays Singapore Open and ending the season with a notable victory in Dubai at the DP World Tour Championship thanks to a blistering closing run of five consecutive birdies.

Surprisingly overlooked for the Rookie of the Year award on the PGA Tour in 2010, he received the MBE in the 2011 Queen's New Year Honours List. Introduced to the game by his father, Gerry, Rory is coached by Michael Bannon, the professional at Holywood golf club.

---

Majesty the Queen for his services to golf. He received the Association of Golf Writers' Award in 2009 for his outstanding services to the game.

## McGimpsey, Garth (IRL)
*Born Bangor, 17 July 1955*

A long hitter who was Irish long-driving champion in 1977 and UK long-driving title holder two years later. He was amateur champion in 1985 and Irish champion the same year and again in 1988. He played in three Walker Cup matches and competed in the home internationals for Ireland in 1978 and from 1980 to 1998. He captained the winning Great Britain and Ireland Walker Cup side that beat American 12½–11½ at Ganton in 2003 and again two years later in Chicago when the Americans won by a point.

## McGinley, Paul (IRL)
*Born Dublin, 16 December 1966*
*Turned professional 1991*

Popular Irish golfer who turned to the game after breaking his left kneecap playing Gaelic football. With

Padraig Harrington won the 1977 World Cup at Kiawah and made his Ryder Cup début when the postponed 2001 match was played in 2002. In a tense finish to his match with Jim Furyk he holed from nine feet to get the half point the Europeans needed for victory. He made the side again in 2004 and was unbeaten as Europe beat the USA 18½–9½ and was one of three Irishmen who helped Europe win by the same margin in 2006. Europe might have won 19–9 had he not conceded a half to J.J. Henry at the last when a streaker ran over the line of the American's 20 foot downhill putt. In 2005 he finished third behind Coli Montgomerie and Michael Campbell in the European Tour Order of Merit making over £1.5 million. During the year he finished third behind Tiger Woods in the WGC–NEC Invitational at Firestone, lost the HSBC World Match-Play at Wentworth to Michael Campbell but ended the season on a high note with victory in the Volvo Masters of Andalucia. In 2007 he was appointed by Nick Faldo to be one of his vice-captains in the Ryder Cup but later declined in order to try and play himself into the side. He failed to do so. He was surprise omission from the Great Britain and Ireland side against the Continent of Europe for the Seve Trophy when it was played in Ireland in 2007 but led the Great Britain and Ireland side to victory at St Nom La Breteche in 2009. In 2010 he accepted a vice-captain's role from Colin Montgomerie at the Ryder Cup at Celtic Manor and reprised that position under Jose Maria Olazabal at Medinah.

## Macgregor, George (SCO)
*Born Edinburgh, 19 August 1944*
After playing in five Walker Cup matches he captained the side in 1991 and later served as chairman of The R&A Selection committee. He won the Scottish Stroke Play title in 1982 after having been runner up three times.

## McNulty, Mark (IRL)
*Born Zimbabwe, 25 October 1953*
*Turned professional 1977*
Recognised as one of the best putters in golf he was runner-up with the late Payne Stewart to Nick Faldo in the 1990 Open at St Andrews. Although hampered throughout his career by a series of injuries and illness he has scored 16 wins on the European Tour and 33 around the world including 23 on the South African Sunshine circuit. He won the South African Open in 1987 and again in 2001 holing an 18-foot putt on the last green at East London to beat Justin Rose. Qualified in 2004 to join the US Champions Tour and although originally from Zimbabwe he now plays out of Ireland. He lost a play-off at Sunningdale in the 2009 Senior Open to Loren Roberts. Injury prevented his playing much in 2010.

## Mahan, Hunter (USA)
*Born Orange, California, 17 May 1982*
*Turned professional 2003*
Although born in California, Mahan was raised in Texas where he went on to win the USGA Junior Championship. An outstanding amateur, he attended Oklahoma State and finished 28th on his début in the Masters before joining the professional ranks. In 2007 he finished sixth in the Open and played on the Presidents Cup. A year later he represented the US in the Ryder Cup and was their top scorer with 3½ points. In 2010 he enjoyed his most successful year to date, winning the Phoenix Open before shooting 64 in the final round to win the WGC–Bridgestone Invitational. He was second in the US Ryder Cup standings for Celtic Manor, earning one of the eight automatic qualifying spots but lost a crucial last day singles to Graeme McDowell. Although he won twice in 2012, including the WGC Match Play where he defeated Rory McIlroy in the final, Mahan missed out on the Ryder Cup at Medinah.

## Mamat, Mardan (SIN)
*Born Singapore, 31 October 1967*
*Turned professional 1994*
Became the first Singaporean to win an Asian/European joint venture in his home country when he took the Osim Singapore Masters in 2006.

## Manassero, Matteo (ITA)
*Born Verona, 19 April 1993*
Made history when he became not only the youngest but the first Italian to win the Amateur Championship with a 3 and 1 victory over Sam Hutsby in the final at Formby in 2009. He was only the third golfer in the 124-year history of the event to win after leading the qualifying. Later in the year earned the Silver Medal as leading amateur in The Open at Turnberry where he finished joint 13th. After playing all four rounds in The Masters he turned professional and made his début in the BMW Italian Open. He quickly secured his Tour card and when he won the Castello Masters he became the youngest title winner in European Tour history. In 2011 he won again in Malaysia and in 2012 was runner-up at the Andalucia Open and third at the Italian Open.

## Marsh MBE, Dr David (ENG)
*Born Southport, Lancashire, 29 April 1934*
Twice winner of the English Amateur Championship in 1964 and 1970, he was captain of The R&A in 1990/1991. He played in the 1971 Walker Cup match at St Andrews and helped the home side win by scoring a vital one hole victory in the singles against Bill Hyndman. He captained the team in 1973 and 1975 and had a distinguished career as a player and then captain for England between 1956 and 1972. He was chairman of The R&A selection committee from 1979 to 1983 and in 1987 was president of the English Golf Union. He was appointed an MBE in the 2011 New Year's Honours List for his voluntary services to amateur golf.

## Marsh, Graham (AUS)
*Born Kalgoorlie, Western Australia, 14 January 1944*
*Turned professional 1968*
A notable Australian who followed up his international playing career by gaining a reputation for designing fine courses. Although he played in Europe, America and Australasia he spent most of his time on the Japanese circuit where he had 17 wins between 1971 and 1982 . He won 11 times in Europe and scored victories also in the United States, India, Thailand and Malaysia.

## Martin, Pablo (ESP)
*Born Malaga, 20 April 1986*
*Turned professional 2007*
Became the first amateur to win on the PGA European Tour when he edged out Raphaël Jacquelin of France by a shot in the Estoril Open de Portugal in 2007. A former British Boys' champion in 2001, he played in two Eisenhower Trophy competitions and two Palmer Cups. Winner of the Jack Nicklaus award for top national amateur in 2006 when at Oklahoma State University he gave up his studies to join the professional rank. Curiously another Oklahoma "cowboy", Scott Verplank, has also won as an amateur in his case on the PGA Tour. Martin won the Alfred Dunhill Championship at the start of the 2010 and 2011 European seasons.

# Phil Mickelson (USA)

*Born San Diego, California, 16 June 1970*       *Turned professional 1992*

The winner of five major championships, Mickelson is the game's most successful left-handed golfer. He has won more than 50 events and has career earnings on the PGA Tour of $60 million. When he won The Open in 2013 by three strokes thanks to four birdies over the last six holes, he became one of only 15 golfers to win at least three of the four majors. He described his final round at Muirfield as the finest of his career. Mickelson has been particularly successful at Augusta where he won the Masters in 2004, 2006 and 2010. He also won the PGA Championship in 2005 at Baltusrol.

A hugely gifted amateur golfer, the left-hander won his first PGA Tour event when he was still a student at Arizona State University. When he was nine he watched on TV as Seve Ballesteros won the Masters and told his mother he would be a Masters' champion one day too. He was proved right 22 years later when he pulled off his first major success thanks to a run of five birdies over the closing seven holes, including an 18 foot putt on the last to thwart Ernie Els.

Right-handed in everything else, Mickelson played golf left-handed after watching his father swing a club and mirroring the action. The first left-hander to win the US Amateur, he was only the sixth amateur ever to win a PGA Tour event when he came out on top at the Northern Telecom Open in 1991. He turned professional a year later and broke into the world's top ten in 1996 where he has remained ever since.

His brilliant short game helped set up a second major triumph on the final hole at the PGA when he pitched from greenside rough to a couple of feet and finish a stroke in front of Thomas Bjørn. The following spring he won his second successive major and third in all thanks to another expert performance at Augusta. In 2010, he won the Masters for the third time by carding a final round of 67 to defeat Lee Westwood by three strokes. His total of 16 under par was the lowest score at Augusta since Tiger Woods in 2001. Perhaps the highlight of his fourth major victory came in Saturday's third round when he made back to back eagles on the 13th and 14th holes. Both his wife Amy and mother Mary have been recovering from breast cancer while Phil himself was diagnosed with arthritis. He won at Pebble Beach in 2012 and drew widespread admiration for both his play and sportsmanship in the Ryder Cup at Medinah. In 2013 he shot 60 *en route* to winning the Phoenix Open and bounced back from the disappointment of finishing runner-up at the US Open for the sixth time in his career with a fairytale fortnight in Scotland. He won the Scottish Open at Castle Stuart before coming from five shots behind to lift the Claret Jug at Muirfield, the first time any golfer had won both titles in the same season.

## Mason, Carl (ENG)

*Born Buxton, Derbyshire, 25 June 1953*
*Turned professional 1973*

Carl won twice on the main European Tour in 1994 but has played his best golf on the European Seniors Tour. He finished second on the money list in his first two years and first for the next three years. In 2004 and again in 2007 he won five events in a season.

## Matsuyama, Hideki (JPN)

*Born Japan, 25 February 1992*

Yet to join the paid ranks at the close of 2011, Matsuyama won his first professional event last year after beating an impressive field which included defending champion Ryo Ishikawa and the Masters champion Charl Schwartzel to win the Taiheiyo Masters in Japan. He was only the third amateur to win on the Japanese Tour and had to eagle the final hole to secure victory. The 19-year-old first caught the eye of the golfing world beyond Japan when he finished 27th on his début at the Masters and earned the accolade of low amateur at Augusta. Ranked fourth in the World Amateur Golf Ranking, he's won the Asian Amateur twice as well as the Japan Collegiate Championship and the World University Games.

## Micheel, Shaun (USA)

*Born Orlando, Florida, 5 January 1969*
*Turned professional 1962*

Surprise winner of the USPGA Championship at Oak Hill in 2003. He fired rounds of 69, 68, 69 and 70 for a winning total of 276. He completed his victory with one of the most brilliant approach irons from the rough to just one foot of the hole at the last. In 2006 at Medinah, he finished second to Tiger Woods again in the USPGA Championship. Later he beat Woods *en route* to the final of the HSBC World Match Play at Wentworth but lost in the final to Paul Casey.

## Milligan, Jim (SCO)

*Born Irvine, Ayrshire, 15 June 1963*

The 1988 Scottish Amateur champion had his moment of international glory in the 1989 Walker Cup which was won by the Great Britain and Ireland side for only the third time in the history of the event and for the first time on American soil. With GB&I leading by a point at Peachtree in Atlanta only Milligan and his experienced opponent Jay Sigel were left on the course. The American looked favourite to gain the final point and force a draw when two up with three to play but Milligan hit his approach from 100 yards to a few inches to win the 16th with a

# Johnny Miller (USA)

*Born San Francisco, California, 29 April 1947    Turned professional 1969*

Now perhaps best known as an often insightful and invariably acerbic TV commentator for NBC in America, Miller won two major titles, The Open and the US Open, during the early Seventies when he was one of the leading players in world golf. Like a comet, Miller's game burned brightly for a short period of time. During 1974, when he won five of the first 11 events on the PGA Tour, and 1975 he won 12 tournaments in total and was the most successful player in the game, earning a clothing sponsorship deal worth $1 million. He recalls that period of grace as a "sort of golfing Nirvana."

The high point of his career came at Royal Birkdale in 1976 when he followed in the footsteps of Tony Lema, a fellow member of the Olympic Club in San Francisco, and lifted the Claret Jug. He thwarted both Seve Ballesteros and Jack Nicklaus by the judicious use of a 1 iron off the tee which helped the American card a closing round of 66 and win the championship by six shots. He was also second behind Tom Weiskopf at Royal Troon in 1973. That was the season he secured victory in the US Open in spite of trailing the leader by six shots after 54 holes. He started the final round at Oakmont with four consecutive birdies and eventually posted 63 – the lowest closing score ever recorded in America's national championship. He found all 18 greens in regulation and racked up nine birdies after firing ten of his approach shots inside 15 feet.

After his success at Birkdale, however, Miller wouldn't win another tournament until 1980. He lost the burning desire to win which spurs on the greatest players and became a victim of the yips. Putting with his eyes closed for much of the time, Miller was a grandfather when he won his last PGA Tour event, the AT&T Pebble Beach Pro-Am in 1994. All told, he won 32 events as a professional around the world after first making a name for himself as an amateur in the Sixties by winning the US Junior Amateur title. A member of the World Golf Hall of Fame, he owns a golf design company.

---

birdie then chipped in after both had fluffed chips to square at the 17th. The last was halved leaving the Great Britain and Ireland side historic winners by a point.

## Mize, Larry (USA)

*Born Augusta, Georgia, 23 September 1958*
*Turned professional 1980*

Only local player ever to win the Masters and he did it in dramatic style holing a 140-foot pitch and run at the second extra hole to edge out Greg Norman and Seve Ballesteros. He had made the play-off by holing a 10-foot birdie on the final green. In 1993 he beat an international field to take the Johnnie Walker World Championship title at Tryall in Jamaica. His middle name is Hogan.

## Molinari, Edoardo (ITA)

*Born Turin, 11 February 1981*
*Turned professional 2006*

Became the first Italian to win the US Amateur Championship when he beat Dillon Dougherty 4 and 3 in the 2005 final at Merion, Pennsylvania. The 24-year-old, who has earned an engineering degree in his home country, joined his brother Francesco on the European Tour in 2006. He and his brother represented Italy in the 2007 and 2009 World Cup of Golf at Mission Hills in Shenzhen, China and were successful the second time. In 2009 he won three times and topped the Challenge Tour and then, a few weeks later, won the Dunlop Phoenix Tournament in Japan beating Robert Karlsson in a play-off. In 2010 he won twice in Scotland at Loch Lomond and Gleneagles where he finished with three birdies to

join his brother in the 2010 Ryder Cup team. He was troubled by a wrist injury last year and slipped from 15th in the rankings in 2010 to a spot outside the top 200 in 2012.

## Molinari, Francesco (ITA)

*Born Turin, 8 November 1982*
*Turned professional 2004*

Brother of Eduardo Molinari, winner of the US Amateur in 2005, he won his first European Tour title when he took the Italian Open at Castello di Tolcinasco in 2006. Partnering his brother Eduardo he gave Italy a first win in the World Cup of Golf in 2009. A year later he made his Ryder Cup début with his brother at Celtic Manor in 2010 and a few weeks later duelled with and beat the then World No 1 Lee Westwood in the WGC–HSBC Champions event in Shanghai. Played for the Continent in the Vivendi Seve Trophy in 2011 and enjoyed another consistent season last year, winning the Spanish Open as well as posting eight top ten finishes. He earned a half point against Tiger Woods in the final singles match at Medinah in 2012 to ensure Europe won the Ryder Cup.

## Montgomerie OBE, Colin (SCO)

*Born Glasgow, 23 June 1963*
*Turned professional 1987*

Europe's most consistent golfer who topped the Order of Merit an unprecedented seven years in a row between 1993 and 1999 and again in 2004. He never won a major but came close several times particularly in the US Open He lost a play-off for the US title to Ernie Els in 1994, was pipped by the South African again in 1997 and was joint second behind Geoff Ogilvy in 2006. In 1992 he was third to Tom Kite. He has come close in The Open and the US PGA Championship as well. He was Open runner-up to Tiger Woods in 2005 at St Andrews and in 1995 he was beaten in a play-off for the USPGA Championship at the Riviera CC in Los Angeles by Australian Steve Elkington who birdied the last three holes to force a play-off and the first extra hole to beat him.. He has had 31 victories around the world and has played with distinction in seven Ryder Cups matches. In 2010 he captained the side to victory at Celtic Manor. He has twice won the Association of Golf Writers' Golfer of the Year award and has been three times Golfer of the Year in Europe. He was honoured by Her Majesty the Queen for his record-breaking golfing exploits with an MBE which was later upgraded to OBE. In 2007 he teamed up with Marc Warren to win the World Cup of Golf at Mission Hills in China. It was Scotland's first win in the 54-year history of the event.  For one reason or another he has found it difficult to hit his best form in the past two years but, free of his Ryder Cup duties, he is determined to move back up the world rankings after dropping from inside the top 50 to outside the top 400. As an amateur he played in the 1985 and 1987 matches and is a former Scottish amateur champion.

## Nagle, Kel (AUS)

*Born North Sydney, 21 December 1920*
*Turned professional 1946*

In the dramatic Centenary Open at St Andrews in 1960 he edged out Arnold Palmer, winner already that year of the Masters and US Open, to become champion. It was the finest moment in the illustrious career of a golfer who has been a wonderful ambassador for his country. Along with Peter Thomson he competed nine times in the World Cup winning the event in 1954. He is an honorary member of the Royal and Ancient Golf Club of St Andrews and was inducted into the World Golf Hall of Fame in 2007.

## Nelson, Larry (USA)

*Born Fort Payne, Alabama, 10 September 1947*
*Turned professional 1971*

Often underrated he learned to play by reading Ben Hogan's The Five Fundamentals of Golf and broke 100 first time out and 70 after just nine months. Active as well these days on course design he has won the Jack Nicklaus award. He has been successful in the US Open (1983 at Oakmont) and two USPGA Championships (in 1981 at the Atlanta Athletic Club and in 1987 after a play-off with Lanny Wadkins at PGA National). Three times a Ryder Cup player he has competed equally successfully as a Senior having won 15 titles. He did not play as a youngster but visited a driving range after completing his military service and was hooked. He was named Senior PGA Tour Player of the Year for finishing top earner and winning six times in 2000. At the end of his third full season on the Senior Tour and after 87 events he had won just short of $10 million.

## Newton, Jack (AUS)

*Born Sydney, 30 January 1950*
*Turned professional 1969*

Runner-up to Tom Watson after a play-off in the 1975 Open at Carnoustie and runner-up to Seve Ballesteros in the 1980 Masters at Augusta, he was a popular personality on both sides of the Atlantic and in his native Australia only to have his playing career ended prematurely when he walked into the whirling propeller of a plane at Sydney airport. He lost an eye, an arm and had considerable internal injuries but the quick action of a surgeon who happened to be around saved his life. Learned to play one-handed and still competes in pro-ams successfully. Until his retirement in 2000 he was chairman of the Australasian Tour and for many years was Australia's most respected golf commentator in the days when Channel Seven organised the coverage.

## Nirat, Chapchai (THA)

*Born Pitsanulok. Thailand, 5 June 1983*
*Turned professional 1998*

Scored his first European Tour International circuit victory when he led from start to finish in the the TCL Classic. He was the 13th Asian to win and was the ninth first-time winner of the 2007 season. He covered the first 36 holes in 127 (61, 66).

## Nobilo, Frank (NZL)

*Born Auckland, 14 May 1960*
*Turned professional 1979*

Injury affected his playing career but he remains one of his country's most popular commentators with the Golf Channel. After winning regularly in Europe he moved to America where in 1997 he won the Greater Greensboro Classic. He has represented New Zealand in nine World Cup matches between 1982 and 1999, played in 11 Alfred Dunhill Cups and three Presidents Cup sides. In 2009 he was deputy captain to Greg Norman for the Rest of the World team.

## Noh Seung-Yul (KOR)

*Born Seoul 29 May 1991*
*Turned professional 2007*

Korean Junior Amateur and Amateur champion in 2005 Noh won his first professional event in 2008 at the Midea China Classic. He did even better in 2010 when he played a superb pitch at the last to beat KJ Choi in the Maybank Malaysian Masters which qualified him for a European Tour card. In his first season he finished 34th in the Race to Dubai and topped the Asian Tour's Order of Merit.

## North, Andy (USA)

*Born Thorp, Wisconsin, 9 March 1950*
*Turned professional 1972*

Although this tall American found it difficult to win Tour events he did pick up two US Open titles. His

# Jack Nicklaus (USA)

*Born Columbus, Ohio, 21 January 1940*
*Turned professional 1961*

In the course of a phenomenal playing career which spanned five decades and included 18 victories as a professional in the majors as well as 118 tournament wins around the world, the Golden Bear has been hailed as the outstanding golfer of the 20th century and perhaps the greatest player who ever lived. His career in golf was so illustrious that the magazine, *Sports Illustrated*, chose Nicklaus as the outstanding individual male athlete of the previous century in any sport.

As a fair haired bear of a boy with broad shoulders, a crew cut and the seeds of a revolutionary power game, Jack William Nicklaus from Ohio, in his autobiography, remembers his teenage self as junior version of "the ugly American". If that judgement from the elder statesman seems blunt, he developed the habits of an unrelenting serial winner as an amateur which served him well throughout his professional career. He won his first US national title at 17, made the cut in the US Open at 18 and, as a 19-year-old, won the US Amateur, played in a winning US Walker Cup side at Muirfield and reached the quarter-finals of The Amateur at Royal St George's.

Billed by the American media as "the kid who can beat the pros", in 1960 he was 13th at the Masters as well as runner-up to Arnold Palmer in the US Open at Cherry Hills, where he set a record score for an amateur. Before joining the paid ranks, he won the US Amateur again, was part of a winning US Walker Cup side on home turf and recorded another top four finish at the 1961 US Open.

If the success of his amateur career placed an onerous burden on Nicklaus when he joined the paid ranks in 1962, his first season as a pro made light of that load. From the moment he made his first start in the Los Angeles Open, Nicklaus set the bench mark for a rookie season in golf. He finished in the top ten 16 times and won three tournaments – notably the US Open at Oakmont, only his 17th event as a pro – where he defeated Arnold Palmer in a play-off. In a sign of what was to come in the championships which matter most, he also finished 15th at the Masters, 32nd at the Open and third at the US PGA.

By the time he crossed the Swilken Bridge for the last time in his final major appearance in The Open at St Andrews in 2005, he'd completed an astonishing record of achievment. He won The Open in 1966, 1970 and 1978, the last two at St Andrews. He was runner-up in the oldest major seven times and third on two further occasions. He followed up that US Open win in 1962 with more victories in 1967, 1972 and 1980 and came second four times. He won five US PGA titles in 1963, 1971, 1973, 1975 and 1980 and was runner-up four times and third on two further occasions. He won six Masters in 1963, 1965, 1966, 1972, 1975 and 1986 when, at the age of 46, he became the oldest champion to slip into a Green Jacket. In addition he was runner-up four times and twice third at Augusta. In 1966 he became the first player to successfully defend the Masters. When he retired from competition, Nicklaus had become the only golfer in history to win each of the majors at least three times.

Outisde the majors, he won the Players Championship three times, no fewer than six Australian Opens and played in six Ryder Cups, winning on five occasions, captaining two more in 1983 at Palm Beach Gardens when America won narrowly and in 1987 at Muirfield Village where his side were losers for the first time on home soil.

A shrewd thinker about the game, it was his idea Continental golfers should be included alongside British and Irish players in a European side from 1979. The change transformed the Ryder Cup. Ten years earlier, in a memorable act of sportsmanship, he conceded the 18-inch putt that Tony Jacklin needed to hole for a half at the last when the overall result of the match depended on the result of that game. "I don't think you would have missed," he told the Englishman, "but in the circumstances I would never give you the opportunity".

After winning 73 times on the PGA Tour, he won a further ten times on the US Champions Tour between 1990 and 1996. He has garnered every honour in golf including the Byron Nelson, Ben Hogan and Walter Hagen awards. He was the US top money earner in 1964, 1965, 1967, 1971, 1972, 1973, 1975 and 1976 and is an honorary member of the Royal and Ancient Golf Club of St Andrews. Bobby Jones once said of Nicklaus that 'he played a game with which I am not familiar'. With the constant support of his wife Barbara, Nicklaus has been the personification of all that is good about the game. He joined Arnold Palmer as an honorary starter at the Masters in 2010.

Nicklaus is also a renowned golf course architect who was instrumental in forging the signature design business. So far, he's designed 280 courses world-wide and his company, Nicklaus Design, has 350 courses open for play. He's captained the US Presidents Cup side against the Rest of the World on four occasions so far and when the match is held at his beloved Muirfield Village in 2013 it will mark " my last involvement in anything significant in the game of golf."

# Greg Norman (AUS)

*Born Mount Isa, Queensland, 10 February 1955*
*Turned professional 1976*

Three times the leading money winner on the PGA Tour, the Australian spent 331 weeks as world No 1 during a career in which he won 91 professional tournaments around the globe. The undoubted highlights of a successful career were his triumphs in 1986 and 1993 at The Open. The fact that he finished in the top ten at the four professional majors on no fewer than 29 occasions – more than 38 per cent of the championships he entered – stands as testimony to his consistency of performance.

If there's a debate that he lost majors he should have won, Norman's most noteworthy achievements came at Turnberry, where he carded a remarkable score of 63 as part of a five shot victory, and at Royal St George's, where his closing 64 set a low winning aggregate of 264 and overcame Nick Faldo by two strokes.

Fair and handsome as well as long off the tee, Norman was handed the moniker of "Great White Shark" during a staging of the Masters in 1981. The nickname was apt and today Norman's various business interests are named Great White Shark Enterprises. Perhaps an even more successful entrepreneur than he was a golfer, Norman didn't take up the sport until he was 15. He'd caddied for his mother and asked to borrow her clubs. Two years later he was a scratch player. He won for the first time as a pro in Australia at the West Lakes Classic in 1976, won the Martini in Europe a year later and first made his mark in the US at the Kemper in 1984. All told he won 20 times on the PGA Tour as well as 71 other events around the world.

For all his success, he also gained a reputation for coming up short in the biggest championships. He lost out in three different types of major play-offs – the 1987 Masters to Larry Mize and the 1993 US PGA to Paul Azinger in sudden death, The Open to Mark Calcavecchia at Royal Troon in a four-hole play-off in 1989 and the US Open over 18 holes to Fuzzy Zoeller at Winged Foot in 1984. In 1986 he led going into the final round of all four majors and won once. Perhaps his most painful loss was at the Masters in 1996 when he led by six strokes going into the final round and lost to Faldo by five shots.

Norman turned the clock back in 2008 at Birkdale to finish third behind Padraig Harrington in The Open after leading with nine holes to play. In 2011 and 2009 he captained the Rest of the World against America in the Presidents Cup. Due to business interests and back issues, he now only plays a handful of events each year.

first Championship success came at Cherry Hills in Denver in 1986 when he edged out Dave Stockton and J.C. Snead and the second at Oakland Hills in 1985 when he finished just a shot ahead of Dave Barr, T.C. Chen and Denis Watson who had been penalised a shot during the Championship for waiting longer than the regulation 10 seconds at one hole to see if his ball would drop into the cup. North is now a golf commentator.

## O'Connor Sr, Christy (IRL)

*Born Galway, 21 December 1924*
*Turned professional 1946*

Never managed to win The Open but came close on three occasions finishing runner-up to Peter Thomson in 1965 and being third on two other occasions. Played in ten Ryder Cup matches between 1955 and 1973 and scored 24 wins in tournament play between 1955 and 1972. Known affectionately as 'Himself' by Irish golfing fans who have long admired his talent with his clubs. He is a brilliant shot maker. He is an Honorary Member of the PGA European Tour. In 2006 a special dinner was staged in his honour in Dublin by the Irish Food Board on the eve of the Ryder Cup. In 2009 he was inducted into the World Golf Hall of Fame.

## O'Connor Jr, Christy (IRL)

*Born Galway, 19 August 1948*
*Turned professional 1965*

Nephew of Christy Sr, he finished third in the 1985 Open Championship. A winner on the European and Safari circuits he won the 1999 and 2000 Senior British Open – only the second man to successfully defend. Played in two Ryder Cup matches hitting a career best 2-iron to the last green at The Belfry in 1989 to beat Fred Couples and ensure a drawn match enabling Europe to keep the trophy. His US Champions Tour career was interrupted when he broke a leg in a motorcycle accident.

## Ogilvy, Geoff (AUS)

*Born Adelaide, South Australia*
*Turned professional 1998*

He became the first Australian to win a major since Steve Elkington's success in the USPGA Championship in 1992 when he won the US Open at Winged Foot beating Colin Montgomerie, Jim Furyk and Phil Mickelson into second place. In 2007 he was beaten by Henrik Stenson in the final of the Accenture Match Play Championship and finished 14th on the US money list. In 2009 he won the Accenture Match-play Championship beating Paul Casey in the final and in 2010 won the Australian Open for the first time.

## Olazábal, José María (ESP)

*Born Fuenterrabia, 5 February 1966*
*Turned professional 1985*

Twice a winner of the Masters, his second triumph was particularly emotional. He had won in 1994 but had to withdraw from the 1995 Ryder Cup with a foot problem eventually diagnosed as rheumatoid polyarthritis in three joints of the right foot and two of the left. He was out of golf for 18 months but treatment from Munich doctor Hans-Wilhelm Muller-Wohlfahrt helped him back to full fitness after a period when he was house bound and unable to walk. At that point it seemed as if his career was over, but he came back in 1999 to beat Davis Love III by two shots at Augusta. With over 20 victories in Europe and a further seven abroad, the son of a Real Sebastian greenkeeper who took up the game at the age of four has been one of the most popular players in the game. He competed in seven Ryder Cups between 1987 and 2006 frequently forming the most successful Cup partnership with Severiano Ballesteros winning 11 and losing only two of their 15 games together. He was Nick Faldo's backroom assistant at Valhalla in 2008 and will captain the side at some time in the future. Although he was sidelined again through rheumatic injury in 2008 he still believes he can make the side in 2010. He is a former British Boys', Youths' and Amateur champion. His best performances in The Open have been third behind Nick Faldo in the 1992 Championship at Muirfield and behind Tiger Woods in the 2005 event at St Andrews. Olazábal, who played on both sides of the Atlantic in 2005, finished 10th on the European Money list finishing strongly with a 2nd place finish in the Linde German Masters, victory in the Open de Mallorca and a third place behind Paul McGinley in the Volvo Masters of Andalucia. In 2006 he regained his place in the Ryder Cup team and played well with Sergio García in the fourballs, winning twice. He beat Phil Mickelson in the singles. He is now an irregular competitor on the European and PGA Tours as a result of his continuing rheumatic problems. In 2009 Olazabal, one of the most courageous of competitors, was inducted into the World Golf Hall of Fame. He asked close friend Severiano Ballesteros to do the oration. He was captain of the winning European Ryder Cup side at Medinah where he dedicated the victory to the memory of Ballesteros, who passed away in 2011. Olazabal described the experience as "torture".

## O'Leary, John (IRL)

*Born Dublin, 19 August 1949*
*Turned professional 1979*

After a successful career as a player including victory in the Carrolls Irish Open in 1982 he retired because of injury and now is director of golf at the Buckinghamshire Club. He is a member of the PGA European Tour Board of Directors.

## O'Meara, Mark (USA)

*Born Goldsboro, North Carolina, 13 January 1957*
*Turned professional 1980*

A former US Amateur Champion in 1979 Mark was 41 when he won his first Major – the US Masters at Augusta. That week in 1998 he did not three putt once on Augusta's glassy greens. Three months later he won The Open at Royal Birkdale battling with, among others, Tiger Woods with whom he has had a particular friendship. He is the oldest player to win two Majors in the same year and was chosen as PGA Player of the Year that season. When he closed birdie, birdie to win the Masters he joined Arnold Palmer and Art Wall as the only players to do that and became only the fifth player in Masters history to win without leading in the first three rounds. He won his Open championship title in a four hole play-off against Brian Watts. O'Meara played in five Ryder Cups between 1985 and 1999.

## Oosterhuis, Peter (ENG)

*Born London, 3 May 1948    Turned professional 1968*

Twice runner up in The Open Championship in 1974 and 1982, he was also the leading British player in 1975 and 1978. He finished third in the US Masters in 1973, had multiple wins on the European Tour and in Africa and won the Canadian Open on the US Tour in 1981. He played in six Ryder Cups partnering Nick Faldo at Royal Lytham and St Annes in 1977 when Faldo made his début. He was top earner in Europe four years in a row from 1971. Following his retirement from top-line golf he turned to commentary work for the Golf Channel CBS and SKY. His contribution to European professional golf is frequently underrated.

## Oosthuizen, Louis (RSA)

*Born Mossel Bay, 19 October 1982*
*Turned professional 2003*

One of the chosen few who have won The Open at St Andrews – he has Bobby Jones, Jack Nicklaus, Nick Faldo and Tiger Woods for company. His victory in the 150th anniversary staging of the game's oldest championship was as comprehensive as it was unexpected. Oosthuizen won by seven strokes from Lee Westwood in what was only his ninth appearance in a majors. He joined Bobby Locke, Gary Player and Ernie Els in the small band of South Africans who have their names on the Claret Jug. A graduate of the Ernie Els Foundation, Oosthuizen won the Irish Amateur and together with Charl Schwartzel won the World Junior Team Championship for South Africa before turning professional. He once shot 57 over his home course at Mossel Bay and had to persuade his family, who have strong connections with tennis, that he wanted to be a golfer. He enjoyed his breakthrough win on the European Tour in 2010 at the Open de Andalucia.

## Ozaki, 'Jumbo' Masashi (JPN)

*Born Kaiman Town, Tokushima, 24 January 1947*
*Turned professional 1980*

Along with Isao Aoki is Japan's best known player, but unlike Aoki has maintained his base in Japan where he has scored over 80 victories. His only overseas win was the New Zealand Open early in his career. He is a golfing icon in his native country. His two brothers Joe (Naomichi) and Jet also play professionally. In 2005 he was declared bankrupt. In 2011 he was elected into the World Golf Hall of Fame.

## Pagunsan, Juvic (PHI)

*Born Manila, 11 May 1978*
*Turned professional 2006*

Winner of the Asian Tour of Merit in 2011, he was the first golfer from the Phillipines to achieve that status. Although he didn't win in 2011, his second place finish after a play-off at the Barclays Singapore Open, where he won $666,660, propelled him to the top spot on the money list. Taught by his father, Juanito, Juvic took up the game at 13 and was a successful amateur, winning the Phillipine, Thailand and Malaysian championships in 2005. He joined the paid ranks a year later and his first win on the Asian Tour was the Pertamina Indonesia President Invitational in 2007.

## Parnevik, Jesper (SWE)

*Born Danderyd, Stockholm, 7 March 1965*
*Turned professional 1986*

Son of a well-known Swedish entertainer he is one of the most extrovert of golfers best known for his habit of wearing a baseball cap with the brim turned up and brightly coloured drain-pipe style trousers. Winner of events on both sides of the Atlantic he plays most of his golf these days in America. He made history in 1995 when he became the first Swede to win in Sweden when he took the Scandinavian Masters at Barsebäck in Malmo. Has twice finished runner-up in The Open. At Turnberry in 1994 he was two ahead but made a bogey at the last and was passed by Nick Price who finished with an eagle and a birdie in the last three holes. He led by two with a round to go in 1998 but shot 73 and finished tied second with Darren Clarke behind Justin Leonard at Royal Troon. Played in the 1997 and 1999 Ryder Cup teaming up successfully with Sergio García to win three and a half points in 1999. Was also in the 2002 team and halved with Tiger Woods in the singles. He has had two hip operations and at one stage began eating volcanic dust to cleanse his system.

## Parry Craig (AUS)

*Born Sunshine, Victoria, Australia, 12 January 1966*
*Turned professional 1985*

Australian Parry, winner of 18 titles internationally including the 2002 World Golf Championship NEC Invitational at Sahalee in Washington where he picked up his largest career cheque – $1 million. After 15 years of trying to win in America the chances of him being successful at Salahee seemed slim having missed the four previous cuts. However, the 300–1 long-shot played and putted beautifully covering the last 48 holes without making a bogey to win by four from another Australian Robert Allenby and American Fred Funk. Tiger Woods, trying to win the event for a record fourth-successive year was fourth. Only Gene Sarazen and Walter Hagen have ever won the same four titles in successive years. It was Parry's 236th tournament in the United States and moved him from 118th in the world to 45th. In 2004 he eagled the hardest hole on the US Tour in a play-off with Scott Verplank to win the Ford Championship in Florida.

## Pate, Jerry (USA)

*Born Macon, Georgia, 16 September 1953*
*Turned professional 1975*

Winner of the 1976 US Open when he hit a 5-iron across water to three feet at the 72nd hole at the Atlanta Athletic Club. He was a member of what is regarded as the strongest ever Ryder Cup side that beat the Europeans at Walton Heath in 1981. Has now retired from golf and commentates occasionally on American television.

## Pavin, Corey (USA)

*Born Oxnard, California, 26 May 1961*
*Turned professional 1983*

Although not one of golf's longer hitters he battled with powerful Greg Norman to take the 1995 US Open title at Shinnecock Hills. A runner-up in the 1994 USPGA Championship and third in the 1992 US Masters he won 14 times between 1984 and 2006. His only victory in Europe came when he took the German Open title in 1983 while on honeymoon. In 2006, he ended a ten-year winning drought by taking the US Bank Championship in Milwaukee and was one of Tom Lehman's vice-captains at the Ryder Cup at the K Club. He was selected to captain the US Ryder Cup side which lost by a point at Celtic Manor in 2010.

## Perry, Kenny (USA)

*Born Elizabethtown, Kentucky, 10 August 1960*
*Turned professional 1982*

After winning for times between 1991 and 2001, he had a marvellous 2003 winning the Bank of America Colonial, the Memorial Tournament and the Greater Milwaukee Open between May 25 and July 13. He made his Ryder Cup début at Detroit in 2004 having played in the 1996, 2003 and 2005 Presidents Cups. In 2008 he deliberately by-passed two major Championships in order to ensure he had a place in Paul Azinger's Ryder Cup side for the match against Europe at Valhalla in his home state of Kentucky. He achieved his goal and played with considerabie success. He tied with Angel Cabrera and Chad Campbell after 72 holes of the 2009 Masters Tournament but lost the play-off. Campbell went out at the first extra hole and Cabrera won The Green Jacket at the second extra hole.

# Arnold Palmer (USA)

*Born Latrobe, Pennsylvania, 10 September 1929     Turned professional 1954*

It is a measure of the charismatic appeal of Arnold Palmer that when *GQ* magazine listed the 25 "coolest" athletes of all time in 2011, the golfer from Latrobe should figure in the countdown some 38 years after his last PGA Tour win. For all the considerable success he enjoyed in the late Fifties and early Sixties, winning seven major titles between 1958 and 1964, it was the manner in which Palmer played the game rather than the championships he won which sealed his reputation. A handsome man with a thrillingly aggressive approach to the game, Palmer was hugely popular with the global audience for golf and when his competitive days were behind him he was able to build a lifelong career as a businessman and course designer because he connected so effectively with the public.

Palmer's high profile coincided with the expansion of televised golf. Unlike the more consistent power play produced by his rival and friend Jack Nicklaus, Palmer's risk-taking generated excitement for TV viewers. His flamboyant style duly helped to grow interest in the game as a spectator sport, both in America and around the world. At Augusta, "Arnie's Army" tracked his every move at The Masters while in Britain his decision to play in the oldest major is credited with helping Keith Mackenzie, then the secretary of the Royal and Ancient Golf Club of St Andrews, revive the fortunes of The Open. Palmer is now a distinguished honorary member of The R&A as well as Augusta National.

Born in Pennsylvania, he was taught by his father, Deacon, the professional and greenkeeper at Latrobe, before attending Wake Forest University on a golf scholarship. His amateur career between 1946 and 1954 delivered 26 victories, including the US Amateur title. After the death of his friend Bud Worsham, he spent three years with the US coastguard. Palmer then decided to try his luck as a professional. He recalls the season of 1954 as the turning point in his life, that victory in the US Amateur coinciding with the moment when the golf press first noticed his go-for-broke style, the habit of hitching up his pants as he walked the fairway and the open manner in which he shared his emotions and engaged with spectators. It was the summer when lightning struck.

In the early years of his career as a pro, Palmer was an irresistible force. His most dominant period was between 1960 and 1963 when he won 29 PGA Tour events in four seasons. In 1960 having already won The Masters and US Open he came to St Andrews for the Centenary Open, hoping to become the first golfer since Ben Hogan in 1953 to win three majors in a season. Although he lost out to Kel Nagle, Palmer would return to the British linksland and win consecutive stagings of The Open in 1961 and 1962. It was those victories which turned Palmer into an international sporting icon rather than just an American celebrity.

Along with Nicklaus and Gary Player he was a member of the Big Three – a concept developed by his manager, the late Mark McCormack – who signed Palmer as IMG's first client. It was the Big Three who effectively created the commercial environment which has made golf such a lucrative sport around the world. All told, Palmer won 61 tournaments in America and 92 around the world, including The Masters of 1958, 1960,1962 and 1964; the US Open of 1960 and the brace of Claret Jugs. He was second in the US PGA three times and narrowly missed out on the career Grand Slam. He played in six Ryder Cups and was US captain twice. He also captained the US in the 1996 Presidents Cup. He was the leading money winner on the PGA Tour four times. Palmer retired from competitive golf in October 2006.

At 81, he still features among the highest earners in the game. Palmer helped to launch the now hugely successful Golf Channel in the United States and presents the Palmer Cup for annual competition between the best young college golfers in America and Europe. He is an honorary starter at The Masters. The owner of Latrobe Country Club as well as Bay Hill in Orlando, he is arguably the most successfully marketed sportsman of all time.

## Phadungsil, Chinarat (THA)
*Born Bangkok, Thailand*
*Turned professional 2005*

He became the youngest winner on the Asian Tour when he beat Shiv Kapur at the second hole of their play-off for the Double A International title at the St Andrews Hill (2000) GC in Rayong, Thailand. The reigning World Junior champion, he was only 17 years and 5 days when he won that title and immediately turned professional.

## Poulter, Ian (ENG)
*Born Hitchen, England, 10 January 1976*
*Turned professional 1994*

One of golf's most extrovert personalities who insists he wants to be noticed for his golfing talent rather than his hairstyles and colourful clothing. Runner-up to Padraig Harrington in The Open at Royal Birkdale in 2008 he was a captain's pick on Nick Faldo's Ryder Cup side later that year at Valhalla. Europe lost but he was top scorer from either side. He also played in the

# Gary Player (RSA)

*Born Johannesburg, 1 November 1935    Turned professional 1953*

South Africa's pre-eminent sportsman of the 20th century, he celebrated his 50th anniversary as a professional in 2003 and continues to enjoy international admiration for a glorious career which saw the golfer win 176 titles around the world. The highlights of his playing days came in the majors where he won nine championships between 1959 and 1978 as well as nine senior major titles between 1986 and 1997. As the world's most travelled sportsman, clocking up over 14 million air miles, he won at least one tournament in 27 consecutive seasons.

Tipping 5ft 7ins and weighing 11 stone, he was often said to have done more with less than any other player. As well as introducing a revolutionary fitness programme to increase distance, Player's strength of mind was his most enduring asset. His craving for success was insatiable.

Although his swing was flat, Player was one of the most accomplished bunker players the game has ever seen. This prolific winner claimed the Claret Jug on three occasions, in 1959 at Muirfield, 1968 at Carnoustie and 1974 at Royal Lytham and St Annes. He's the only 20th century golfer who succeeded in winning The Open in three different decades.

He also won The Masters three times in 1961, 1974 and 1978, the US PGA championship in 1962 and 1972, and completed the Grand Slam of major titles when he succeeded at the US Open in 1965. His victory that summer at Bellrive at the age of 29, after a play-off against Kel Nagle, was the first by an international player since Ted Ray in 1920. Tiger Woods, Jack Nicklaus, Ben Hogan and Gene Sarazen are the only other players to win all four professional majors.

After taking up the sport at 14, Player spent much of his time during his teenage years on the golf course where all those diligent hours of practice made him a solid judge of distance and a perceptive reader of greens. Perhaps his greatest gift, though, was his indomitability. Player simply never gave up. When he won his first Open at Muirfield – this was in the era when the competitors played 36 holes on the last day – he started the third round eight strokes behind the leader. "Gary has that thing inside him, as much as anyone I ever saw, that champions have," observed Nicklaus.

Player's knack of winning tournaments from situations which many of his peers would have regarded as hopeless was perhaps best illustrated at The Masters in 1974 when, at 42, he went into the last round trailing Hubert Green by seven strokes. However, the South African came home in 30 and equalled the then record score of 64. He birdied seven of the last ten holes at Augusta to win by a stroke.

He was also once seven down to Tony Lema after 19 holes in the semi-final of the World Match Play in 1965 before securing safe passage into the final, where he defeated Peter Thomson, at the first extra hole. "My opponents knew I was like a bull terrier," he said. "I never gave up." One of the exceptional match-play golfers, Player won the World Match Play five times.

The son of a miner and a mother who died when he was eight, Player became a pro at 18 and won his first title, the Egyptian Match Play, in 1955. He liked to wear all black outfits and was one of the first golfers to rely on an exercise programme and a high fibre diet to improve his physique and hit the ball further. It was a regime which helped him to win the Australian Open seven times, the South African Open 13 times and sign for 59 in the 1974 Brazilian Open.

In 2006, he received the Payne Stewart award for his services to golf and charity work, especially in Africa. He has been a captain of the Rest of the World team in the Presidents Cup on three occasions. One of the game's 'Big Three' in the Sixties along with Nicklaus and Arnold Palmer, Player today has widespread global business interests through his company Black Knight International.

2004 and 2010 teams. In 2007 he was successful in Japan winning the Dunlop Phoenix event and in 2010 won for the first time on the PGA Tour in America when he beat Paul Casey in the final of the WGC-Accenture Match-play Championship in Arizona. Now based in Lake Nona, Florida he was in a play-off for the Dubai World Championship in 2010 and incurred a penalty when he inadvertently dropped his ball on his marker causing it to move. The highlight of his career to date came at Medinah in the 2012 Ryder Cup when he was the match's outstanding player, winning four points out of four and inspiring Europe to an improbable comeback victory. In 2013 he

finished second in the European Tour's Race to Dubai.

## Price, Nick (ZIM)

*Born Durban, South Africa, 28 January 1957*
*Turned professional 1977*

One of the game's most popular players his greatest season was 1994 when he took six titles including The Open at Turnberry when he beat Jesper Parnevik and the USPGA at Southern Hills when Corey Pavin was second. He had scored his first Major triumph two years earlier when he edged out John Cook, Nick

Faldo, Jim Gallagher Jr and Gene Sauers at the USPGA at Bellerive, St Louis. Along with Tiger Woods his record of 15 wins in the 90s was the most by any player. One of only eight players to win consecutive Majors, the others being Ben Hogan, Jack Nicklaus, Arnold Palmer, Lee Trevino, Tom Watson, Tiger Woods and Padraig Harrington. Four times a Presidents Cup player he jointly holds the Augusta National record of 63 with Greg Norman. One of only two players in the 90s to win two Majors in a year, the others being Nick Faldo in 1990 and Mark O'Meara in 1998. Born of English parents but brought up in Zimbabwe he played his early golf with Mark McNulty and Tony Johnstone. He was named recipient in 2002 of the Payne Stewart Award which goes to the player who respects the traditions of the game and works to uphold them. In 2003, ten years after being named PGA Tour Player of the Year, he was inducted into the World Golf Hall of Fame.He will captain the International team against the USA at the Presidents Cup in 2013 at Muirfield Village.

## Price, Phillip (WAL)

*Born Pontypridd, 21 October 1966*
*Turned professional 1989*

He made his Ryder Cup début in 2002 and produced a sterling last day performance when he beat the world No.2 Phil Mickelson 3 and 2 for a vital point. He played on the PGA Tour in 2005 with limited success and, back in Europe, has found it difficult to re-discover his old magic.

## Quigley, Dana (USA)

*Born Lynnfield Centre, Massachussetts, 14 April 1947*
*Turned professional 1971*

Iron man of the US Champions Tour who played in 278 consecutive events for which he was qualified before missing the 2005 Senior British Open at Royal Aberdeen. He had passed the million dollars mark in prize-money by early June that year and with official money of $2,170,258 he topped the Champions Tour money list at the end of the season.

## Quiros, Alvaro (ESP)

*Born Cadiz, Spain, 21 January 1983*
*Turned professional 2004*

The Spaniard became the first player in European Tour history to win on his first appearance when he won the 2007 dunhill championship at Leopard Creek in South Africa. He has won five times since then in Portugal, Qatar, Spain and Dubai twice. His victory at the Dubai World Championship in 2011 was the biggest of his career and earned him a cheque for more than €922,000. He has the reputation of being one of Europe's longest hitters averaging over 314 yards.

## Rafferty, Ronan (NIR)

*Born Newry, Northern Ireland, 13 January 1964*
*Turned professional 1981*

He won the Irish Amateur Championship as a 16 year old in 1980 when he also won the English Amateur

Open Stroke Play title, competed in the Eisenhower Trophy and played against Europe in the home internationals. Winner of the British Boys', Irish Youths' and Ulster Youths' titles in 1979, he also played in the senior Irish side against Wales that year. A regular winner on the European tour between 1988 and 1993 he was also victorious in tournaments played in South America, Australia and New Zealand. A wrist injury curtailed his career but he is active on the corporate golf front and has an impressive wine collection.

## Ramsay, Richie (SCO)

*Born Aberdeen, 15 June 1983*
*Turned professional 2007*

A student at Stirling University he became the first Scot since 1898 and the first British golfer since 1911 to win the US Amateur Championship when he beat John Kelly from St Louis 4 and 2 in the final A member of the 2005 Great Britain and Ireland Walker Cup team, he has played in the Palmer Cup and was the winner of the 2004 Scottish Open Amateur Stroke-play title and the 2005 Irish Open Amateur Stroke-play event. He has shot a 62 at Murcar in Aberdeenshire. Ramsay turned professional after the 2007 Open, missing the chance to play again in the Walker Cup. He failed to survive the first stage of the European Tour School and competed on the 2008 Challenge Tour winning twice and earning his card for the main Tour in 2009 winning the 2010 South African Open at Pearl Valley.

## Randhawa, Jyoti (IND)

*Born New Delhi, 4 May 1972*
*Turned professional 1994*

First Indian winner on the Japanese Tour when he triumphed in the 2003 Suntory Open. Son of an Indian general, he was top earner on the Asian PGA Tour in 2002 despite missing several events after breaking his collarbone in a motorcycle accident. Practices yoga and now plays on both the European and Asian Tours.

## Remesy, Jean-François (FRA)

*Born Nimes, 5 June 1964      Turned professional 1987*

In 2004 he became the first Frenchman since Jean Garaialde in 1969 to win the Open de France then successfully defended the title the following year at Golf National, Versailles beating Jean Van de Velde in a play-off. Now lives in the Seychelles.

## Rivero, José (ESP)

*Born Madrid, 20 September 1955*
*Turned professional 1973*

One of only eight Spaniards who have played in the Ryder Cup he was a member of the winning 1985 and 1987 sides. Worked as a caddie but received a grant from the Spanish Federation to pursue his golf career. With José Maria Canizares won the World Cup in 1984 at Olgiata in Italy.

## Roberts, Loren (USA)

*Born San Luis Obispo, California, 24 June 1955*
*Turned professional 1975*

An eight times winner on the PGA Tour, he earned the nickname "Boss of the Moss" because of his exceptional putting. He played in two Presidents Cup matches and the 1995 Ryder Cup before joining the Champions Tour. He had chalked up seven wins by the end of 2007 and for the second year running had the low average score on that Tour – an impressive 69.31. In a play-off for the 2009 Senior Open at Sunningdale he beat Mark McNulty and Fred Funk to win the title for a second time.

## Rocca, Costantino (ITA)

*Born Bergamo, 4 December 1956*
*Turned professional 1981*

The first and to date only Italian to play in the Ryder Cup. In the 1999 match at Valderrama he beat Tiger Woods 4 and 2 in a vital singles. Left his job in a polystyrene box making factory to become a club professional and graduated to the tournament scene through Europe's Challenge Tour. In 1995 he fluffed a chip at the final hole in The Open at St Andrews only to hole from 60 feet out of the Valley of Sin to force a play-off against John Daly which he then lost. Now plays on the European Senior Tour.

## Rogers, Bill (USA)

*Born Waco, Texas, 10 September 1951*
*Turned professional 1974*

USPGA Player of the Year in 1981 when he won The Open at Royal St George's and was runner-up in the US Open. That year he also won the Australian Open but retired from top line competitive golf not long after because he did not enjoy all the travelling. A former Walker Cup player in 1973 he only entered The Open in 1981 at the insistence of Ben Crenshaw. Now a successful club professional and sometime television commentator.

## Romero, Eduardo (ARG)

*Born Cordoba, Argentina, 12 July 1954*
*Turned professional 1982*

Son of the Cordoba club professional he learned much from former Open champion Roberto de Vicenzo and has inherited his grace and elegance as a competitor. A wonderful ambassador for Argentina he briefly held a US Tour card in 1994 but preferred to play his golf on the European Tour where he won seven times including the 1999 Canon European Masters. He improved his concentration after studying Indian yoga techniques. Used his own money to sponsor Angel Cabrera with whom he finished second in the 2000 World Cup in Buenos Aries behind Tiger Woods and David Duval. Joined the Senior ranks in July 2004 but still plays from time to time on the main European Tour. In 2008 he won the US Senior Open on the Champions Tour.

## Rose, Justin (ENG)

*Born Johannesburg, South Africa, 30 July 1980*
*Turned professional 1998*

Winner of the US Open at Merion in 2013, Rose was a Walker Cup player who shot to prominence during The Open Championship at Royal Birkdale in 1988. He finished as top amateur and third behind winner Mark O'Meara after holing his third shot at the last on the final day for a closing birdie. Immediately after that Open he turned professional and missed his first 21 half-way cuts before finding his feet. In 2002 was a multiple winner in Europe and also won in Japan and South Africa. Delighted his father who watched him win the Victor Chandler British Masters just a few weeks before he died of leukaemia. He has played most of his golf in America in recent years shooting 60 at the Funai Classic at Walt Disney World in 2006. Although he played only the minimum 12 events on the European Tour in 2007, he won the end of season Volvo Masters at Valderrama to finish No 1 on the money list and became the highest ranked British golfer, moving into seventh place. Later in the year he partnered Ian Poulter into fourth place in the Mission Hills World Cup of Golf in China. He made his début in the Ryder Cup in the 2008 match at Valhalla but failed to make the 2010 side despite winning two titles on the PGA Tour including the prestigious Memorial event at Muirfield Village. In 2011 he won the BMW Championship. And in 2012 he returned to Ryder Cup action at Medinah where he pulled off a remarkable comeback in the singles against Phil Mickelson thanks to birdies over the closing two holes. It was Rose's best season to date with a WGC victory in the Cadillac and earnings of over $4 million on the PGA Tour. In 2013, he again thwarted Mickelson at Merion when he won the US Open by two shots, the first Englishman to triumph at America's national championship since Tony Jacklin in 1970.

## Sandelin, Jarmo (SWE)

*Born Imatra, Finland, 10 May 1967*
*Turned professional 1987*

Extrovert Swede who made his début in the Ryder Cup at Brookline in 1999 although he did not play until the singles. Has always been a snazzy dresser on course where he is one of the game's longest hitters often using, in the early days, a 54-inch shafted driver. Five time winner on Tour he met his partner Linda when she asked to caddie for him at a Stockholm pro-am.

## Schwartzel, Charl (RSA)

*Born Johannesburg, 31 August 1984*
*Turned professional 2002*

The first Masters champion ever to birdie all four of the closing holes at Augusta, Schwartzel savoured one of the most thrilling finishes seen at the majors when he posted a closing round of 66 to earn a two stroke victory over Australians Jason Day and Adam

Scott. After claiming a Green Jacket, he was also ninth at the US Open, 16th at The Open and 12th at the US PGA in 2011. Since finishing 16th at the US Open in 2010 he's reeled off seven consecutive top 20 placings in the majors. Charl was playing off plus 4 when he turned professional after an amateur career that had seen him represent South Africa in the Eisenhower Trophy. In only his third event as a pro he finished joint third in the South African Airways Open and became a winner in his 56th event when he won the dunhill championship in a play-off at Leopard Creek. He was South African No 1 in season 2004–5 and was again No 1 in the 2005–6 season. In the 2007 European Tour season he won the Spanish Open but was winless in 2008 until he again played well in Spain to take the Madrid Masters title. He won the Joburg Open in 2010 and 2011 as well as the Africa Open in 2010. In 2012 he only posted two top finishes on the PGA Tour and the same number in Europe.

## Scott, Adam (AUS)

*Born Adelaide, 16 July 1980  Turned professional 2000*
Winner of The Masters in 2013, the first Australian in 77 years to triumph at Augusta, Scott was an outstanding amateur who reached World No 2 before turning professional in 2000. Coached in the early days by his father Phil, himself a golf professional, Scott also once worked with Butch Harmon whom he met while attending the University of Las Vegas. He made headlines as an amateur when he fired a 10-under-par 63 at the Lakes in the Greg Norman Holden International in 2000 before carding 62 in the US Junior Championship at Los Coyotes CC. Made his European Tour card in just eight starts and secured his first Tour win when beating Justin Rose in the 2001 Alfred Dunhill Championship at Houghton in Johannesburg. In 2002 he won at Qatar and at Gleneagles Hotel when he won the Diageo Scottish PGA Championship by ten shots with a 26 under total. He was 22 under par that week for the par 5 holes. In 2003 he was an impressive winner of the Scandinavian Masters at Barsebäck in Sweden and the Deutsche Bank Championship on the US Tour. In 2005 when he again played in the Presidents Cup, his victories included the Johnnie Walker Classic on the European and Asian Tours, the Singapore Open on the Asian Tour and the Nissan Open on the US Tour. In 2006, he won the Players Championship and Tour Championship in America, rising to third in the World rankings in mid November of that year. He also won the Singapore Open again. He continued to play well throughout 2008 but was less successful in 2009.He switched coaches and started working with Brad Malone, his brother-in-law. In 2010 he won the Valero Texas Open and in 2011, after switching to the broomhandle putter, won the Bridgestone and finished runner-up at the Masters. In 2012 he led The Open by four strokes going into the final round at Royal Lytham only to card four bogeys over the closing holes and lose out

to Ernie Els by a stroke. Undaunted, Scott bounced back at Augusta the following year, defeating Angel Cabrera in a play-off for the Green Jacket. He was also third in The Open at Muirfield and fifth in the US PGA.

## Senior, Peter (AUS)

*Born Singapore, 31 July 1959*
*Turned professional 1978*
One of Australia's most likeable and underrated performers who has been a regular winner over the years on the Australian, Japanese and European circuits. Converted to the broomstick putter by Sam Torrance – a move that saved his playing career. A former winner of the Australian Open, Australian PGA and Australian Masters titles he had considerable success off the course when he bought a share in a pawn-broking business. Senior now plays irregularly outside Australia where he has taken over as chairman of the Autralasian Tour from Wayne Grady. In 2010 he won the Handa Australian Seniors title and Australian PGA title for a third time.

## Sigel, Jay (USA)

*Born Narbeth, Pennsylvania, 13 November 1943*
*Turned professional 1993*
Winner of the Amateur Championship in 1979 when he beat Scott Hoch 3 and 2 at Hillside, he also won the US Amateur in 1982 and 1983. He was leading amateur in the US Open in 1984 and leading amateur in the US Masters in 1981, 1982 and 1988. He played in nine Walker Cup matches between 1977 and 1993 and has a record 18 points to his credit. Turned professional in order to join the US Senior Tour where he has had several successes.

## Simpson, Scott (USA)

*Born San Diego, California, 17 September 1955*
*Turned professional 1977*
Winner of the US Open in 1987 at San Francisco's Olympic Club, he was beaten in a play-off for the title four years later at Hazeltine when the late Payne Stewart won the 18-hole play-off.

## Simpson, Webb (USA)

*Born Raleigh, North Carolina, 1985*
*Turned professional 2008*
Thanks to a pair of 68s compiled on the week-end over an exceptionally tricky set-up at the Olympic golf club in San Francisco, Simpson won the US Open by a stroke from Graeme McDowell after setting the one over par mark of 281. His first major title was the highlight of a consistent year in which he finished in the top ten seven times. The previous year he earned nearly $5.8 million thanks to two wins in the space of just three weeks at the Wyndham and Deutche Bank championships. A talented amateur golfer, he was a member of the American Walker Cup team in 2007 which defeated

Great Britain and Ireland at Royal County Down. He made his Ryder Cup début for the USA in 2012, winning two points at Medinah in the defeat from Europe.

## Singh, Jeev Milkha (IND)

*Born Chandigarh, India, 15 December 1971*
*Turned professional 1993*

Stylish swinger, he won his first European event when he took the Volvo China Open in Beijing in 2006 but he scored an even greater triumph when he picked up the first prize at the Volvo Masters at Valderrama later in the year. He is the son of the former Olympian Milkha Singh who won a medal in the 1980 games. His victory in the 2007 Barclays Singapore Open enabled him to became the first player to make US $1 million in one season on the Asian Tour and helped him top the money list for the second time. His Singapore win also moved him into the top 50 in the world rankings for the second time. In 2012 he won the first prize of £470,000 at the Aberdeen Asset Scottish Open after defeating Francesco Molinari in a play-off.

## Singh, Vijay (FIJ)

*Born Lautoka, 22 February 1963*
*Turned professional 1982*

An international player who began his career in Australasia, he became the first Fijian to win a major when he won the 1998 USPGA Championship at Sahalee but may well be remembered more for his victory in the 2000 US Masters which effectively prevented Tiger Woods winning all four Majors in a year. Tiger went on to win the US Open, Open and USPGA Championship that year and won the Masters the following year to hold all four Major titles at the one time. Introduced to golf by his father, an aeroplane technician, Vijay modelled his swing on that of Tom Weiskopf. Before making the grade on the European Tour where he won the 1992 Volvo German Open by 11 shots he was a club professional in Borneo. He has won tournaments in South Africa, Malaysia, the Ivory Coast, Nigeria, France, Zimbabwe, Morocco, Spain, England, Germany, Sweden, Taiwan and the United States. He ended Ernie Els' run of victories in the World Match Play Championship when he beat him in the final by one hole in 1997 when the South African was going for a fourth successive title. One of the game's most dedicated practisers. In 2003 he won the Phoenix Open, the EDS Byron Nelson Championship, the John Deere Classic and the Funai Classic. On the PGA Tour in 2003 Singh ended Woods' run as top money earner when he finished with prize-money totalling $7,753,907 – the second largest total in Tour history – but he was not named Player of the Year. Woods was again the players' choice. In 2004 he had his best ever season and by mid-October was approaching $10 million in year-long winnings on the US Tour, having won eight times, matching Johnnie Miller's eight wins in 1974. Although finally edged out by Woods for the No 1 spot he earned his third

major and second USPGA Championship title with a play-off victory at Whistling Straits.

## Smyth, Des (IRL)

*Born Drogheda, Ireland, 12 February 1953*
*Turned professional 1973*

Became the oldest winner on the PGA European Tour when he won the Madeira Island Open in 2001. Smyth was 48 years and 34 days – 20 days older than Neil Coles had been when he won the Sanyo Open in Barcelona in 1982. One of the Tour's most consistent performers – he played 592 events before switching to the European Seniors Tour and qualifying for the US Champions Tour where he has been a winner. Five times Irish National champion he was a member of the winning Irish side in the 1988 Alfred Dunhill Cup. Won twice on US Champions Tour in 2005 and In Abu Dhabi on the European Senior Tour. He was a vice-captain for the European team in the 2006 Ryder Cup.

## Snedeker, Brandt (USA)

*Born Nashville, Tennessee, 12 August 1980*
*Turned professional 2004*

Winner of the FedEx Cup title in 2012 and a $10 million bonus for his efforts thanks to a three shot victory at PGA Tour Championship, Snedeker earned nearly $15m last year and described his success as " like winning the lottery." He also won the Farmers Insurance in 2012 and was third in The Open Championship. One of the best putters in golf, Snedeker won two points for the USA in the Ryder Cup match at Medinah before losing to Paul Lawrie in singles. Won the US Amateur Public Links in 2003 and finished 41st as an amateur on his Masters debut the following year.

## Stadler, Craig (USA)

*Born San Diego, California, 2 June 1953*
*Turned professional 1975*

Nicknamed "The Walrus" because of his moustache and stocky build, he won the 1982 Masters at Augusta. Winner of 12 titles on the US Tour between 1980 and 1996 he played in two Ryder Cups (1983 and 1985). As an amateur he played in the 1975 Walker Cup two years after winning the US Amateur. He won his first senior major title when he took the Ford Senior Players' Championship just a few weeks after turning 50 then went back to the main tour the following week and won the BC Open against many players half his age. In 2004 he was top earner on the US Champions Tour with over $2 million. His son Kevin, who is also a professional golfer, won the Johnnie Walker Classic at The Vines in 2006.

## Stenson, Henrik (SWE)

*Born Gothenburg, 5 April 1976*
*Turned professional 1998*

He enjoyed the best season of his career in 2013 thanks to an extraordinary run of performances between the Scottish Open in July and the DP World Tour Championship in Dubai in November. During this five month stretch there was a run of eight events where he finished as follows: 3, 2, 2, 3, 43, 1, 33, 1. His six top three finishes included a runner-up spot at The Open and third in the US PGA as well as winning the PGA Tour Championship and becoming the first European golfer to triumph in the Fed-Ex Cup. He earned more than $15 million for his trouble during this surge. He then went on to claim a historic double as he stormed to victory at the DP World Tour Championship, thereby becoming the first man to win The Race to Dubai and the FedEx Cup in the same season. Henrik first made his name on the European Tour in 2001 with a win at the Benson and Hedges over The Belfry. All told he's won seven events on the European Tour. He played for Sweden in the 1998 Eisenhower Trophy and made the 2006 Ryder Cup side helping Europe beat America 18½–9½ at the K Club. In the singles he beat Vaughn Taylor. He again played in the 2008 match at Valhalla. Stenson finished the 2006 season in seventh place with €1.7 million earned in prize-money. He played the first part of 2007 in America and was quickly a winner of the Accenture Match-Play Championship. Earlier, he had picked up first prize in the Dubai Desert Classic. Stenson rounded off 2008 in style by winning the World Cup at Mission Hils with Robert Karlsson. In 2009 he won the Players' Championship at Sawgrass to further underline his international reputation. Thereafter, his career was in the doldrums, a reaction to losing a fortune in the care of fraudster Allen Stanford. He was outside the world's top 200 at the beginning of 2012 and bounced back to the top five in 2013.

## Strange, Curtis (USA)

*Born Norfolk, Virginia, 20 January 1955*
*Turned professional 1976*

Winner of successive US Opens in 1988 and in 1989 when he beat Nick Faldo in an 18-hole play-off at The Country Club Brookline after getting up and down from a bunker at the last to tie on 278. Winner of 17 US Tour titles he won at least one event for seven successive years from 1983. Having played in five Ryder Cup matches he captained the US side when the 2001 match was played at The Belfry in 2002. In 2007 he was inducted into the World Golf Hall of Fame.

## Stricker, Steve (USA)

*Born Egerton, Wisconsin, 23 February 1967*
*Turned professional 1990*

Started 2001 by winning the $1 million first prize in the Accenture Match Play Championship, one of the World Golf Championship series. In the final he beat Pierre Fulke. Was a member of the winning American Alfred Dunhill Cup side in 1996. In 2007 he won the Barclays Championship … one of the four end of season Fedex Cup events. In 2008 he was a captain's pick in the US Ryder Cup side at Valhalla. He carded 63 in the first round of the PGA Championship in 2011 but is still without a major victory. He won his 12th title on the PGA Tour in 2012 at the Hyundai

Tournament of Champions. Was out of sorts at the 2012 Ryder Cup when he lost all four matches. When he started on Tour his wife Nikki caddied for him until having a daughter, Bobbi Maria, in 1998. Her father Dennis Tiziani was his coach.

## Sutton, Hal (USA)

*Born Shreveport, Louisiana, 28 April 1958*
*Turned professional 1981*

Winner of the 1983 USPGA Championship at the Riviera CC in Los Angeles beating Jack Nicklaus into second place. Played in the 1985, 1987 ,1999 and 2002 Ryder Cup matches. He captained the American team which lost to the Europeans at Oakland Hills in 2004 and in 2007 was given the Payne Stewart award for respecting and upholding the traditions of the game.

## Toms, David (USA)

*Born Monroe, LA, 4 January 1967*
*Turned professional 1989*

Highlight of his career was beating Phil Mickelson into second place at the 2001 USPGA Championship at the Atlanta Athletic Club with rounds of 66, 65, 65 and 69 for 265 a record winning Championship aggregate and the lowest aggregate in any Major. Made his Ryder Cup début in 2002, when he was the American side's top points scorer with 3½ points, and played again in 2004. In 2005 Toms won the WGC Accenture Match-play title beating Chris DiMarco 6 and 5 in the final He's won more than $38 million on the PGA Tour with 13 victories, most recently at Colonial in 2011. His best performance last season was fourth at the US Open.

## Torrance OBE, Sam (SCO)

*Born Largs, Ayrshire, 24 August 1953*
*Turned professional 1970*

Between 1976 and 1998 he won 21 times on the European Tour in which he has played over 700 events hitting that mark as the Barclays Scottish Open at Loch Lomond in 2010. Captain of the 2002 European Ryder Cup side having previously played in eight matches notably holing the winning putt in 1985 to end a 28-year run of American domination. He was an inspired captain when the 2001 match was played in September 2002. Tied 8 points each, Torrance's men won the singles for only the third time since 1979 to win 15½–12½. His father Bob, who has been his only coach, looks after the swings these days of several others on the European Tour including Paul McGinley who holed the nine foot putt that brought the Ryder Cup back to Europe in 2002. He was awarded the MBE in 1996. European Tour officials worked out that in his first 28 years Torrance walked an estimated 14,000 miles and played 15,000 shots earning at the rate of £22 per stroke. In 2003 he retired from full-time competition on the European Tour to play on the European Senior Tour and in 2005, 2006 and 2009 was top earner. He is often a member of the BBC commentary team working with Peter Alliss and Ken Brown.

## Peter Thomson CBE (AUS)

*Born Melbourne, 23 August 1929*          *Turned professional 1949*

The first golfer who was ever shown live on television winning The Open – the occasion was his triumph at St Andrews in 1955 – Peter Thomson enjoys a deserved reputation as one of the most astute links golfer to emerge since young Tom Morris won four consecutive Open titles. One of only four champions to capture five Opens – his other triumphs were at Birkdale twice, in 1954 and 1965, Hoylake in 1956 and Lytham in 1958 – Thomson was placed in the spotlight when the BBC used just three cameras for their first live broadcast from the Old Course.

The Australian found the incentive to win three consecutive Open titles lay in financial necessity. Prize money was relatively modest in the Fifties and sponsorship deals were scarce. Luckily, this largely self-taught golfer with a fluent swing and a knack of eliminating mistakes produced the kind of low ball flight which reaps dividends on the linksland. He made his début in the oldest major at Portrush in 1951 and between 1952 and 1958 never finished outside the first two. His run of extraordinary results during that seven year stretch was second, second, first, first, first, second and first. During that spell he also became the only golfer in the modern era to win three consecutive championships on three different links. (Jamie Anderson in the 1870s and Bob Ferguson in the 1880s are the other Open champions with this distinction.)

One of only four players to win five Opens – Harry Vardon, with six, has the most victories – he matched the feats of J.H. Taylor and James Braid while Tom Watson also won five in eight years from 1975. Thomson's fifth victory, arguably his most impressive, came at Royal Birkdale in 1965 when more Americans, including Jack Nicklaus, Arnold Palmer and Tony Lema, were in the field. He says that the reason for his success in The Open was simple – he built his career around the championship. In the American majors, he played only three times in the US Open, finishing fourth in 1956. He played at Augusta in five Masters with fifth his best finish in 1957. He also won three Australian Opens and in Europe savoured 24 victories between 1954 and 1972. His first victory in 1950 was at the New Zealand Open, a tournament he would win nine times. All told, he won over 100 tournaments around the world.

Raised in the Brunswick suburb of Melbourne, Thomson took up golf as a 12-year-old and was club champion at 15. He studied to become an industrial chemist and first worked for Spalding before becoming a professional in 1949. With one of the most fluent and reliable swings, gripping the club lightly, he made the links game look deceptively easy. Perhaps the greatest Australian player, he was instrumental in developing golf throughout Asia. Thomson placed a premium on accuracy rather than power and, like his rival Bobby Locke, often used a 3 wood from the tee.

When Thomson was ready to retire from competitive golf, he thought about pursuing a career in Australian politics but narrowly missed out on a seat in a state election. He turned instead to the US Senior Tour where he won 11 titles, including a remarkable nine victories in 1985, a record matched only by Hale Irwin. Thomson was also president of the Australian PGA between 1962 and 1994.

He was elected to the World Golf Hall of Fame in 1988, the year he won the Seniors British PGA, his last title, and is an honorary member of the Royal and Ancient Golf Club of St Andrews. His fondness for the Auld Toun persuaded the Australian to keep a house in St Andrews as well as a place in his heart for the Old Course. After his retirement from golf he concentrated on journalism and a successful golf course design business which built more than 100 courses. He's captained the Rest of the World side at the Presidents Cup, including a notable win over the US at Royal Melbourne in 1998. A member of Victoria golf club since 1949, the club celebrated his 80th birthday in 2009 by unveiling a bronze statue of him. He continues to regard the values of common sense, planning and clear thinking among the most useful golfing assets.

## Townsend, Peter (ENG)

*Born Cambridge, 16 September 1946*
*Turned professional 1966*

An outstanding amateur golfer regarded as one of the best prospects of the post war era who won the British Boys twice, the British Youths, the Lytham Trophy and the English Amateur titles. He was selected to play for GB&I in the 1965 Walker Cup match, partnering Ronnie Shade in foursomes, contributing three points, and emerging as one of the heroes of a drawn match against the USA. He turned professional the following season, initially struggled with swing changes, but went on to win 14 times, including the Swiss and Dutch Opens on the European Tour. He also won the Western Australian Open as well as recording numerous victories in South America and Africa. Keen to play around the globe, he qualified for the PGA Tour in America where he finished in the top ten three times. Once regarded as a rival to Tony Jacklin, he finished in the

## Lee Trevino, (USA)

*Born Dallas, Texas, I December 1939*     *Turned professional 1961*

The winner of six major championships and an enduring success over nearly half a century of competition, "Supermex" won as many tournaments on the senior circuit, 29, as he did on the PGA Tour. Using a distinctive swing with an open stance and a strong grip, Trevino was a golfer with a hook who faded the ball. His action was once described as five wrongs which make an immaculate right. If his style of play was unusual, it was his personality which struck a chord with the public. He was a charismatic figure with a sense of humour who played a huge role in the emergence of the Champions Tour. He once quipped that "you can talk to a fade but a hook won't listen."

Born in Texas to a family of Mexican ancestry, he left school at 14 and worked as a caddy. He spent four years with the US Marines before becoming an assistant pro in El Paso. Although he joined the paid ranks in 1960, it wasn't until 1967 that he joined the PGA Tour and was named rookie of the year. The following season he made his name with an outstanding performance in the US Open at Oak Hill. He won by four shots from Jack Nicklaus and his total of 275 – made up of scores of 69, 68, 69 and 69 – was the first in America's national championship to break 70 in each round.

The consistency of Trevino's game was never more evident than in the summer of 1971 when, between May 30 and July 10, he won four events, including The Open and the US Open. At Merion he defeated Nicklaus in a play-off while at Royal Birkdale he thwarted Mr Lu and Tony Jacklin. The following year at Muirfield, Trevino again crossed swords with Jacklin. This time the Englishman and the American were paired together over the closing 36 holes and Trevino's chip-in on the penultimate hole proved decisive. He would enjoy further major success in the PGA Championships of 1974 and 1984. His last major win came at the age of 44 over Shoal Creek in Alabama when once more he shot four rounds below 70.

Trevino never finished higher than tenth in the Masters where he felt a course with so many dog-legs did not suit his game. He was a low fader and believed Augusta required a high draw. He was an outstanding Ryder Cup player, playing six times as well as captaining the US in 1985. He won the Vardon Trophy for low scoring average five times in his career and recovered from being struck by lightning while playing in the Western Open in Chicago. He had to undergo back surgery before returning to competition. He was involved in one of the low scoring matches in the World Match Play Championship with Jacklin in 1972 when again he came out on top. In 2003 he was made an honorary member of the Royal and Ancient Golf Club of St Andrews. Trevino was a blue collar hero with a splash of showmanship who broadened the appeal of the game.

top 20 at The Open four times and played in the Ryder Cup matches of 1969 and 1971. A former captain of the PGA he now lives in Sweden.

## Van de Velde, Jean (FRA)

*Born Mont de Marsan, 29 May 1966*
*Turned professional 1987*

Who ever remembers who came second? Few do but almost everyone recalls Frenchman Jean Van de Velde finishing runner-up after a play-off with eventual winner Paul Lawrie and American Justin Leonard when The Open returned to a somewhat tricked-up Carnoustie in 1999. Playing the last hole he led by three but refused to play safe and paid a severe penalty. He ran up a triple bogey 7 after seeing his approach ricochet off a stand into the rough and hitting his next into the Barry Burn. He appeared to contemplate playing the half-submerged ball when taking off his shoes and socks and wading in but that was never a possibility. Sadly, he was an absentee at the 2007 Open at the same venue. Took up the game as a youngster when holidaying with his parents in Biarritz. Has scored only one win in Europe (the Roma Masters in 1993) and has returned to the European Tour after a spell in America. Made his Ryder Cup début at Brookline in 1999. Injury

prevented him competing regularly in 2003 and 2004 during which time he was part of the BBC Golf Commentary team with, among others, Peter Alliss, Sam Torrance, Mark James and Ken Brown. Came close to winning his national title but lost out in a play-off to fellow Frenchman Jean-François Remesy at Golf National in 2005. Created headlines later in the year when he said that if it was to be made easier for women to play in The Open he thought it only fair that he should be allowed to enter the British Women's Open but never followed through on his threat. Captained the Continental side which lost to Great Britain and Ireland in the 2011 Vivendi Seve Trophy.

## Verplank, Scott (USA)

*Born Dallas, Texas, 9 July 1964*
*Turned professional 1986*

When he won the Western Open as an amateur in 1985 he was the first to do so since Doug Sanders took the 1956 Canadian Open. Missed most of the 1991 and 1992 seasons because of an elbow injury and the injury also affected his 1996 season. He has diabetes and wears an insulin pump while playing to regulate his medication. Curtis Strange chose him as one of his two picks for the 2002 US Ryder Cup side.

# Tom Watson (USA)

*Born Kansas City, Missouri, 4 September 1949*
*Turned professional 1971*

For all the victories he's savoured during an enduringly brilliant career, it was Tom Watson's narrow loss in The Open at Turnberry in 2009, when he was nearing his 60th birthday, which will be discussed and remembered as long as the game of golf is played. A year after undergoing hip replacement surgery, he came within eight feet of relishing a record-equalling sixth championship success. Remarkably, a quarter of a century had elapsed since he'd won his fifth Open. While he missed the putt for glory on the 72nd hole and lost the subsequent play-off for the Claret Jug to Stewart Cink, Watson's performance on the Ailsa, nevertheless, struck a chord with the public and breathed new life into a career already notable for 39 PGA Tour wins, including no fewer than eight major titles. It also led, indirectly, to his appointment as captain of America's Ryder Cup side at Gleneagles.

Born in Missouri, Watson today remains true to his roots and still lives in the midwest of America on a farm near Kansas City. He was introduced to the game by his father, Ray, a scratch golfer, at the age of six. By the time he was 19, he was the state amateur champion, a feat he repeated on three more occasions. After studying psychology at Stanford University, where he graduated in 1971, Watson joined the PGA Tour and earned his first winner's cheque as a pro in 1974 at the Western Open.

When he came up short and twice failed to win the US Open in 1974 and 1975, he was branded as a choker in America. Whether that reputation was deserved or not is moot. But Watson produced the perfect response later in the summer of 1975 when he travelled to Scotland and won The Open on his début at Carnoustie after a play-off with Jack Newton. It was the beginning of the American's life-long affair with the home of golf in which he matched the success rate of J H Taylor, James Braid and Peter Thomson by winning the oldest major five times. He also missed out on an opportunity to collect a sixth Open title by a whisker at St Andrews in 1984 when he struck his second shot close to the wall through the green at the Road Hole and was thwarted by Seve Ballesteros.

Of all his Open triumphs, surely none was more memorable than the "Duel in the Sun" at Turnberry in 1977. At an event many regarded as the greatest championship of modern times, Watson edged out Jack Nicklaus by shooting closing rounds of 65,65 to Nicklaus' 65,66. His other successes on the linksland came in 1980 at Muirfield where he defeated Lee Trevino; in 1982 at Royal Troon where Peter Oosterhuis and Nick Price came second and in 1983 when Andy Bean and Hale Irwin were runners-up.

If his story at The Open provides the legendary narrative for Watson's career, he also produced a spectacular performance in the 1982 US Open at Pebble Beach. Watson's chip shot for birdie from the rough on the short 17th has been immortalised as the most memorable of his life. As at Turnberry, Nicklaus was the man he defeated. He also secured two green jackets at Augusta in 1977 and 1981 where Nicklaus finished second on both occasions. It was this talent for defeating arguably the game's greatest player in the tournaments which mattered most that separated Watson from his peers.

However, since he was never better than a runner-up at the US PGA Championship, Watson was unable to join Gene Sarazen, Ben Hogan, Gary Player, Nicklaus and Tiger Woods in the élite club of Grand Slam golfers who have won all four professional majors. Perhaps it's the only accolade missing from his career. He became the oldest winner on the PGA Tour when he won the Mastercard Colonial in 1998 almost 24 years after his first win. And he was the PGA Tour's player of the year six times and the leading moneywinner five times.

Watson played in four Ryder Cups in 1977, 1981, 1983 and 1989 before captaining the US side to victory in 1993 at The Belfry. Such is his standing in the game, he will become the oldest captain in the history of the match when he leads the USA at the age of 65 years and 22 days in the 2014 event at Gleneagles. He's also the first man to captain America twice since Jack Nicklaus in 1987.

He was inducted into the World Golf Hall of Fame in 1988 and is an honorary member of the Royal and Ancient Golf Club of St Andrews. He also succeeded Sam Snead as the golf professional emeritus at the Greenbrier.

After turning 50, he joined the Champions Tour. He's won 13 events since 1999 in the company of his senior peers, most recently in Hawaii in 2010. Perhaps his finest moment as a senior came at his beloved Turnberry in 2003 when he lifted the Senior British Open title 26 years after the Duel in the Sun.

As a direct consequence of his performance over the Ailsa in 2009, The R&A changed the entry rules and introduced a five year exemption for former champions who finish in the top ten. When the BBC conducted a poll to identify the greatest ever Open champion, it was entirely fitting that Watson was chosen by the British public as the recipient.

In the singles on the final day he beat Lee Westwood 2 and 1. He was again a captain's pick in Tom Lehman's side in 2006 and again won his singles, this time against Padraig Harrington. Surprisingly he failed to make the 2008 US side.

## Wadkins, Lanny (USA)

*Born Richmond, Virginia, 5 December 1949*
*Turned professional 1971*

His 21 victories on the US Tour between 1972 and 1992 include the 1977 USPGA Championship, his only Major. He won that after a play-off with Gene Littler at Pebble Beach but lost a play-off for the same title in 1987 to Larry Nelson at Palm Beach Gardens. He was second on two other occasions to Ray Floyd in 1982 and to Lee Trevino in 1984. In other Majors his best finish was third three times in the US Masters (1990, 1991 and 1993), tied second in the US Open (1986) and tied fourth in the 1984 Open at St Andrews. One of the fiercest of competitors he played eight Ryder Cups between 1977 and 1993 winning 20 of his 33 games, but was a losing captain at Oak Hill in 1995. In 2009 he was inducted into the World Golf Hall of Fame.

## Walton, Philip (IRL)

*Born Dublin, 28 March 1962*
*Turned professional 1983    Turned professional 1983*

Twice a Walker Cup player he is best remembered for two-putting the last to beat Jay Haas by one hole and clinch victory in the 1995 Ryder Cup at Oak Hill. He played in five Alfred Dunhill Cup competitions at St Andrews and was in the winning side in 1990.

## Warren, Marc (SCO)

*Born Rutherglen, near Glasgow, 1 April 1981*
*Turned professional 2002*

Holed the winning putt in Great Britain and Ireland's Walker Cup victory over America in 2001. Enjoyed two play-off victories on the European Challenge Tour in 2005 and finished top money Earner in the Ireland Ryder Cup Challenge and the Rolex Trophy. In 2006 Warren scored his first victory on the main Tour when he beat Robert Karlsson in a play-off for the Eurocard Masters at Barsebäck. At the start of the 2007 season he finished fifth behind winner Yang Yong-eun, Tiger Woods, Michael Campbell and Retief Goosen in the HSBC Champions event in Shanghai. He scored his second win in the Johnnie Walker Championship at Gleneagles Hotel by beating Simon Wakefield in a play-off. He was a wild card pick for the GB&I team in the Seve Trophy match and partnered Colin Montgomerie to a first-ever success for Scotland in the 2007 World Cup of Golf at Mission Hills in China. He lost his Tour card in 2010 but won it back in 2011. In 2012 he threw away a three shot lead and an opportunity to win the Aberdeen Asset Management Scottish Open at Castle Stuart when he ran up a double bogey at the 15th and bogeys at the 16th and 17th holes.

## Watney, Nick (USA)

*Born Sacramento, California, 1981*
*Turned professional 2003*

Enjoyed the best season of his five year career on the PGA Tour in 2011, winning nearly $5.3 million and relishing victories at the AT&T National and the Cadillac Championship. His record of ten top ten finishes was a model of consistency. Also won the Zurich Classic in 2007 and the Buick Invitational in 2009. Made his Presidents Cup début in 2011.

## Watson, Bubba (USA)

*Born Bagdad, Florida, 11 May 1978*
*Turned professional 2003*

Winner of four events on the PGA Tour, by far the most significant victory of Watson's career came at Augusta last year when he defeated Louis Oosthuizen in a play-off to clinch the Masters. His winning par on the second extra hole, the 18th, was notable for a miraculous recovery shot from the woods. Along with Mike Weir and Phil Mickelson, who won three titles, Watson's success was the fifth in ten Masters by a southpaw. As well as his short game skills, Watson is renowned for his power, once hitting a drive 422 yards in a Nationwide Tour event. His swing is self-taught and the left-hander has never had a lesson. Won two points for the USA at the 2012 Ryder Cup.

## Weekley, Boo (USA)

*Born Milton, Florida, 23 July 1973*
*Turned professional 1997*

One of six players who made their débuts in the 2008 Ryder Cup at Valhalla. He played well and enjoyed every minute of the American success. Nicknamed Boo after Yogi Bear's sidekick, he made $500,000 on the Nationwide Tour before joining the main Tour. Studied at the Abraham Baldwin Agricultural College and won the Verizon Open in 2007 and 2008.

## Weir, Mike (CAN)

*Born Sarnia, Ontario, 12 May 1970*
*Turned professional 1992*

A left-hander, he was the first Canadian to play in the Presidents Cup when he made the side in 2000 and the first from his country to win a World Golf Championship event when he took the American Express Championship at Valderrama in 2000. Wrote to Jack Nicklaus as a 13-year-old to enquire whether or not he should switch from playing golf left-handed to right-handed and was told not to switch. In 1997 he led the averages on the Canadian Tour with a score of 69.29 but his greatest triumph came when he became only the third left-hander to win a major when he played beautifully and putted outstandingly to beat Len Mattiace for a Masters Green Jacket in 2003. He had had to hole from 15 feet at the last to take the tournament into extra holes and won at the first when Mattiace failed to make par. He has now assumed hero status in Canada and has been inducted into the Canadian Golf Hall of Fame.

# Eldrick 'Tiger' Woods (USA)

*Born Cypress, California, 30 December 1975     Turned professional 1996*

By a wide margin the dominant golfer of the early 21st century, Woods has been the player to beat around the world ever since he became a professional in the late summer of 1996. His 95 tournament victories include no fewer than 14 major titles – the 1997, 2001, 2002 and 2005 Masters, 1999, 2000, 2006 and 2007 US PGA Championships, 2000, 2002, and 2008 US Open Championships, and The Open Championships of 2000, 2005 and 2006. When he won the Masters for the second time in 2001, Woods became the first golfer in the game's history to hold all four majors at the same time. If the "Tiger Slam" was the highlight to date of a spectacular career, Woods can reflect on many other significant accomplishments. His haul of 79 victories on the US PGA Tour is surpassed only by Sam Snead with 82. His career earnings from prize money in America are in excess of $109 million. According to *Forbes Magazine*, he became the first golfer to earn more than a billion dollars from a combination of prize money, sponsorship, appearance fees and golf course design.

From the moment he appeared as a two-year-old child prodigy on the Mike Douglas Show with Bob Hope, Woods carried a gilded reputation. He aced his first hole-in-one at the age of six and was a scratch golfer by 13. He won the US Junior Amateur three times between the ages of 15 and 17 and the US Amateur in three consecutive stagings between 1994 and 1996, the only golfer ever to record 18 consecutive match play wins at that event.

When he left university at Stanford and joined the professional ranks as a 20-year-old in 1996, Woods won twice at Las Vegas and Disney World as well as reeling off five consecutive top five finishes and rocketing up the World Golf Ranking. In 1997, his first full season as a pro, Woods won five of the first 16 events he entered, including his first appearance as a pro at Augusta. The youngest Masters champion at the age of 21 years, three months and 14 days, he won the tournament by 12 strokes and set a record 72 hole score of 270 thanks to rounds of 70,66,65 and 69.

It was a demolition of Augusta National which took the breath away and eventually led to the lengthening and toughening of the course as well as introducing the concept of "Tiger proofing" to the golfing lexicon. He became world No 1 in just 42 weeks as a pro. While this was a frightening pace to set, Woods had no qualms about continuing to floor the accelerator. In 1999 his scoring average of 68.43 was low enough to win eight times on the PGA Tour and 11 times around the globe. There was no let-up in 2000 when he won nine times, including three majors, thereby matching Ben Hogan's feat in 1953. His 15 stroke victory at Pebble Beach was the greatest margin of victory in US Open history. When Woods won The Open at St Andrews in 2000, he became the youngest to complete the career Grand Slam of professional majors and only the fifth golfer ever to do so.

Today, Woods holds or shares the record for the low score in relation to par in each of the four major championships. His records are 270 in the Masters, 272 in the US Open, 269 in The Open, and he shares the record of 270 with Bob May in the 2000 PGA Championship. The US Open and Masters victories came by record margins, 15 strokes and 12 strokes respectively, and the US Open triumph swept aside the 13-stroke major championship standard which had stood for 138 years, established by Old Tom Morris in the 1862 Open. The record margin for the US Open had been 11 strokes by Willie Smith in 1899. In the Masters, Woods broke the record margin of nine strokes set by Nicklaus in 1965. Tiger also won The Open by eight strokes, the largest margin since J.H. Taylor in 1913. Perhaps his most remarkable win of all came at the 2008 US Open at Torrey Pines when he defeated Rocco Mediate in a play-off in spite of suffering from a knee injury and a double stress fracture of his left tibia. When the championship was over, he underwent surgery on his anterior cruciate ligament and missed the rest of the season. All of those extraordinary accomplishments were the work of the son of the late Earl Woods, a retired lieutenant-colonel in the US Army, and Kultida, a native of Thailand. Woods was nicknamed Tiger after a Vietnamese soldier and friend of his father, Vuong Dang Phong, to whom he had also given that nickname.

When Tiger married Elin and the couple had two children, Sam and Charlie, Woods' life seemed blessed. However, controversy surrounding infidelity in his private life led to a divorce from Elin, as well as the loss of numerous sponsorship deals with Gatorade, AT&T, Accenture, Gillette and *Golf Digest*. For the first time in 15 years he failed to win during 2010 and was dethroned as world No 1 after a total of 623 weeks by Lee Westwood before falling out of the world's top 5 golfers after an injury-blighted season. In 2011 he split with long time caddie Steve Williams and fell as low as 58th in the world rankings. However, he ended a winless streak of 107 weeks when he captured the Chevron World Challenge and rose to 23rd in the world. In 2012, though another major title eluded him, he won three times on the PGA Tour and rose to second in the world rankings. By 2013, he was again World No 1, winning five times, including a record eighth triumph at Torrey Pines and a second Players Championship victory.

# Weiskopf, Tom (USA)

*Born Massillon, Ohio, 9 November 1942*
*Turned professional 1964*

Winner of only one Major – the 1973 Open Championship at Royal Troon, he lived in the shadow of Jack Nicklaus throughout his competitive career. He was runner-up in the 1976 US Open to Jerry Pate and was twice third in 1973 and 1977. His best finish in the USPGA Championship was third in 1975 – the year he had to be content for the fourth time with second place at the US Masters. He had been runner-up for a Green Jacket in 1969, 1972 and 1974 but played perhaps his best golf ever in 1975 only to be pipped at the post by Nicklaus. With 22 wins to his name he now plays the US Senior Tour with a curtailed schedule because of his course design work for which he and his original partner Jay Morrish have received much praise. One of their designs is Loch Lomond, venue for several years of the revived Scottish Open. Played in just two Ryder Cup matches giving up a place in the team one year in order to go Bighorn sheep hunting in Alaska.

## Westwood, Lee (ENG)

*Born Worksop, Nottinghamshire, 24 April 1973*
*Turned professional 1993*

The year 2010 was very special for Lee Westwood. The consistent Englishman was the man who finally prised Tiger Woods out of the No 1 spot in the World Rankings he had held for five years. He beat Phil Mickelson and Martin Kaymer to top spot following Tiger Woods dramatic loss of form following an off the course scandal. It was just reward for one of the most consistent of golfers who battled back and made it to the top after having very nearly quit the game a few years earlier. His own loss of form had seen him slump from No,. 4 in the world rankings to a position outside the top 250. He credits David Leadbetter for sorting out his game A former British Youths' champion who missed out on Walker Cup honours, he quickly made the grade in the professional ranks and, in 2000 ended the seven-year reign of Colin Montgomerie by taking the top spot in the Volvo Order of Merit. He was a six-time winner that year in Europe and beat Montgomerie at the second extra hole of the Cisco World Match Play final at Wentworth. He has won titles on every major circuit in the world including three victories at the Taiheiyo Masters in Japan, the Australian Open in 1997 when he beat Greg Norman in a play-off and the Freeport McDermott Classic and the New Orleans and St Jude Fedex titles on the US PGATour. He has been a member of the last eight European Ryder Cup teams including the 2012 match at Medinah where he won his singles tie against Matt Kuchar. His victory at the Nordea Masters last year was his 22nd success on the European Tour.

## Williams, Chris (USA)

*Born Moscow, Idaho, 21 June 1991*

The world's top ranked amateur golfer in 2012, Williams won the Mark H McCormack Award for his achievements. He helped the USA win the Eisenhower Trophy, the World Amateur team Championship, in Turkey last year, after winning the Western Amateur. He also represented the USA in the Walker Cup match against GB&I at Royal Aberdeen. Williams is exempt for this year's US Open at Merion and The Open Championship at Muirfield.

## Wilson, Oliver (ENG)

*Born Mansfield, 14 September 1980*
*Turned professional 2003*

He played his way into the 2008 Ryder Cup side at Valhalla and impressed as a rookie, Having attended Augusta College he now lives much of the time in America. He was a member of the winning Great Britain and Ireland Walker Cup side in 2003. Like Padraig Harrington who had so many runner-up finishes before becoming a regular winner, Wilson is still awaiting his first victory.

## Wirachant, Thawarn (THA)

*Born Bangkok, Thailand, 28 December 1966*
*Turned professional 1987*

He earned a full year's exemption on the European Tour when he won the Enjoy Jakarta Standard Chartered Indonesian Open – a joint venture between the Asian and European Tours. It was his sixth win on the Asian Tour which he joined 10 years earlier. Wirachant is best known for his unorthodox swing which works effectively for him. He is a former Thai Amateur champion.

## Wolstenholme, Gary (ENG)

*Born Egham, Surrey, 21 August 1960*
*Turned professional 2008*

Nobody has played more often for England. Between 1988 and 2008 when he turned professional to prepare for the European Senior Tour – he represented England an incredible 218 times. Although he can remember swinging a club at the age of 4½ when he started playing seriously at the age of 17. Within six years he was scratch and by the age of 23 he had started representing England. During his amateur career he played in seven St Andrews Trophy matches against the Continent of Europe between 1992 and 2004 during which time he amassed a P19 W10 L9 H0 points record. In six Walker Cups between 1995 and 2005 he had the most individual and team wins. Awarded the MBE for his services to golf in the 2007 New Year's honours list and the recipient of an honorary MA degree from Northampton University, he represented Leicestershire and Rutland from 1981 to 2007 and Cumbria in 2008. He was playing off plus 4 when he turned professional but at one point was a plus 5 golfer. He has honorary membership of 13 clubs and Associations. Amateur champion at Ganton in 1991 and Royal Troon in 2003 he has also won titles in China. the UAE, Finland, Luxembourg Australia and Spain. He has had 13 holes in one, five of them in competition. Highlights of his outstanding career were beating Tiger Woods at Porthcawl in the 1995

Walker Cup and, more importantly, helping Luke
Donald, Paddy Gribben and Lorn Kelly win the World
Amateur Team Championship in Chile in 1998. Since
becoming a professional, he's won three times on the
European Senior Tour, including victories in 2012 at
the Mallorca Senior Open and the Benahavis Senior
Masters.

## Wood, Chris (ENG)
*Born Bristol, 26 November 1987*
*Turned professional 2008*
First made the national newspaper headlines when he
finished fifth behind Padraig Harrington at the 2008
Open at Royal Birkdale. He turned professional
immediately and earned his Tour card at the 2009
European Qualifying School. In 2009 he went even
better in The Open when he finished joint third
behind Stewart Cink. A bogey at his final hole
prevented his being included in the play-off for the
title between Cink and Tom Watson. He ended the
season being named the Sir Henry Cotton Rookie of
the Year. The tallest player on the European Tour at
6ft 5ins, he was runner-up at the Sicilian Open in 2012
and is still seeking his first Tour victory.

## Woosnam MBE, Ian (WAL)
*Born Oswestry, Shropshire, 2 March 1958*
*Turned professional 1976*
Highlight of his career was winning the Green Jacket at
the Masters in 1991 after a last day battle with Spaniard
José Maria Olazábal who went on to win in 1994 and
again in 1999. Teamed up very successfully with Nick
Faldo in Ryder Cup golf and was in four winning teams
in 1985, 1987, 1995 and 1997 and was vice-captain in
2001 to Sam Torrance at The K Club before captaining
the side to victory in 2006 at the K Club. He scored 28
European Tour victories and twice won the World
Match Play Championship in 1987 when he beat Sandy
Lyle, with whom he used to play boys' golf in
Shropshire, in 1990 when his opponent was Mark
McNulty and in 2001 when he beat Retief Goosen,
then US Open Champion, Colin Montgomerie, Lee
Westwood and then Padraig Harrington in the final. In
1989 he lost a low-scoring final to Nick Faldo on the
last green. His lowest round was a 60 he returned in
the 1990 Monte Carlo Open at Mont Agel. Partnered
by David Llewellyn he won the World Cup of Golf in
1987 beating Scotland's Sam Torrance and Sandy Lyle
in a play-off. Honoured with an MBE from Her Majesty
the Queen he now lives with his family in Jersey.
Finished joint third in the 2001 Open at Lytham after
having been penalised two shots for discovering on the
second tee he had 15 clubs (one over the limit) in his
bag. He now plays on the European Senior Tour and
when he topped the money list in 2008 he became the

first player to make it to No 1 on the European Tour
and the European Seniors Tour.

## Yang, Yong-Eun (KOR)
*Born Seoul, Korea, 15 January 1972*
*Turned professional 1996*
Winner of events on his home circuit in Korea and
also in Japan, he shot to prominence first when
beating Tiger Woods into second place in the 2006
HSBC Champions event in Shanghai – a win that
earned him his European Tour card. These days he
plays mostly in the United States where he followed
up his victory in the 2009 Honda Classic with a first
major triumph at Hazeltine in the USPGA Championship. Playing with favourite Tiger Woods on the
final day he outscored him and outputted the World
No 1 to become the first Asian to win a major. It
earned him $1.35 million and he moved from 110th in
the world rankings to 34th.

## Yeh, Wei-tze (TPE)
*Born Taiwan, 20 February 1973*
*Turned professional 1994*
Fisherman's son who became the third Asia golfer
after "Mr Lu" and Isao Aoki to win on the European
Tour when he won the 2000 Benson and Hedges
Malaysian Open. In 2003 he won the ANA Open on
the Japanese Tour.

## Zhang, Lian-Wei (CHN)
*Born Shenzhen, 2 May 1965*
*Turned professional 1994*
Leading Chinese player whose victory in the 2003
Caltex Singapore Open when he edged out Ernie Els
was the first by a Chinese golfer on Tour. Initially he
trained as a javelin thrower before turning to golf.
Self-taught he was also the first Asian golfer to win on
the Canadian Tour but remains a stalwart on the
Asian circuit. In 2009 he was pipped by Ian Poulter for
the Barclays Singapore Open and finished the year in
second spot on the Asian Tour Order of Merit to
Thongchai Jaidee.

## Zoeller, Fuzzy (USA)
*Born New Albany, Indiana, 11 November 1951*
*Turned professional 1973*
Winner of the US Masters in 1979 after a play-off
with Ed Sneed (who had dropped shots at the last
three holes in regulation play) and Tom Watson and
was victorious US Open in 1984 at Winged Foot after
an 18-hole play-off with Greg Norman. A regular
winner on the US Tour between 1979 and 1980, he
played on three Ryder Cups in 1979, 1983 and 1985.
He announced that the 2008 Masters would be his
final appearance at the event.

# Who's Who in Golf – Women

| | | | | |
|---|---|---|---|---|
| Ahn, S-J. | Haynie, S. | Lewis, S. | Okamoto, A. | Steinhauer, S. |
| Alfredsson, H. | Higuchi, H. | Lincicome, B. | Otto, J. | Stephenson, J. |
| Andrew, K. | Hjörth, M. | Lopez, N. | Pace, L-A. | Streit, M.S. |
| Bailey, D. | Hudson, R. | De Lorenzi, M.-L. | Pak, S.R. | Stupples, K. |
| Bisgood, J. | Inkster, J. | Lunn, K. | Panton-Lewis, C. | Suggs, L. |
| Bonallack, A. | Irvin, A. | McIntire, B. | Park, G. | Thomas, V. |
| Bradley, P. | Jackson, B. | McKay, M. | Park, I. | Thompson, A. |
| Butler, I. | Jang, J. | McKenna, M. | Pepper, D. | Tseng, Y. |
| Caponi, D. | Ji, E.-H. | Mallon, M. | Pettersen, S. | Varangot, B. |
| Carner, J.A. | Johnson, T. | Mann, C. | Prado, C. | Walker, M. |
| Cavalleri, S. | Kerr, C. | Massey, D. | Rawls, B. | Webb, K. |
| Choi, N.Y. | Kim, B. | Matthew, C. | Reid, D. | Whitworth, K. |
| Creamer, P. | Kim, C. | Meunier-Lebouc, P. | Robertson, B. | Wie, M. |
| Daniel. B. | King, B. | Miyazato, A. | Sander, A. | Wright, J. |
| Davies, L. | Ko, L. | Moodie, J. | Saunders, V. | Wright, M. |
| Dibnah, C. | Klein, E. | Muñoz, A. | Segard, P. | Yang, A. |
| Dowling, C. | Koch, K. | Neumann, L. | Semple Thompson, | Yokomine, S. |
| Duggleby, E. | Kuehne, K. | Nicholas, A. | C. | Yoo, S.Y. |
| Feng, S. | Laing, A. | Nilsmark, C. | Sheehan, P. | |
| Fudoh, Y. | Lawrence, J. | Nordqvist, A. | Shin, J.-Y. | |
| Gustafson, S. | Lee-Smith, J. | Ochoa, L. | Sörenstam, A. | |

## Ahn, Sun-Ju (KOR)

*Born South Korea, 31 August 1987*
*Turned professional 2006*
The first Korean golfer to top the Japan LPGA Tour money list and be Japanese Rookie of the Year as well in 2010. Only other non-Japanese golfer to finish No.1 in Japan has been Chinese Taipei's Ai Yu Tu. In 2010, Ahn won four events and earned 145,07 million Yen. She topped the money list that season as well as in 2011. In 2012, she won three more events in Japan, taking her number of professional victories to 18.

## Alfredsson, Helen (SWE)

*Born Gothenburg, 9 April 1965*
*Turned professional 1989*
After earning Rookie of the Year on the 1989 European Tour she won the 1992 Ladies' British Open. Two years later she was Gatorade Rookie of the Year on the American LPGA Tour. She has competed in seven Solheim Cup matches and captained the 2007 Cup side before becoming the first player in the event's history to qualify as a past captain two years later.She has won titles in Europe, America, Japan and Australia and earned nearly $5.7 million during her career on the LPGA.

## Andrew, Kim (née Rostron) (ENG)

*Born 12 February 1974*
After taking the English and Scottish Ladies' stroke play titles in 1997 she won the Ladies' British Open Amateur a year later. She played in the 1998 and 2000 Curtis Cup matches.

## Bailey MBE, Mrs Diane (Frearson née Robb) (ENG)

*Born Wolverhampton, 31 August 1943*
After playing in the 1962 and 1972 Curtis Cup matches she captained the side in 1984, 1986 and 1988. In 1984 at Muirfield the Great Britain and Ireland side lost narrowly to the Americans but she led the side to a first ever victory on American soil at Prairie Dunes in Kansas two years later. The result was a convincing 13–5. She was in charge again when the GB&I side held on to the Cup two years later this time by 11–7 at Royal St George's.

## Bisgood CBE, Jeanne (ENG)

*Born Richmond, Surrey, 11 August 1923*
Three times English Ladies champion in 1951, 1953 and 1957. Having played in three Curtis Cups she captained the side in 1970. Between 1952 and 1955 she won the Swedish, Italian, German, Portuguese and Norwegian Ladies titles.

## Bonallack, Lady (née Angela Ward) (ENG)

*Born Birchington, Kent, 7 April 1937*
Wife of Sir Michael Bonallack OBE, she played in six Curtis Cup matches. She was leading amateur in the 1975 and 1976 Colgate European Opens, won two English Ladies' titles and had victories, too, in the Swedish, German, Scandinavian and Portuguese Championships.

## Bradley, Pat (USA)

*Born Westford, Massachusetts, 24 March 1951*
*Turned professional 1974*

Winner of four US LPGA majors – the Nabisco Championship, the US Women's Open, the LPGA Championship and the du Maurier Classic, she won 31 times on the American circuit. An outstanding skier and ski instructor as well, she started playing golf when she was 11. Every time she won her mother would ring a bell on the porch of the family home whatever the time of day. The bell is now in the World Golf Hall of Fame. She played in four Solheim Cup sides and captained the team in 2000 at Loch Lomond. Inducted into the LPGA Hall of Fame in 1991 she was Rolex Player of the Year in 1986 and 1991. In 2011 her nephew Keegan Bradley won the USPGA Championship.

## Butler, Ita (née Burke) (IRL)

*Born Nenagh, County Tipperary*

Having played in the Curtis Cup in 1966, she captained the side that beat the Americans by 5 points at Killarney thirty years later.

## Caponi, Donna (USA)

*Born Detroit, Michigan, 29 January 1945*
*Turned professional 1965*

Twice winner of the US Women's Open in 1969 and 1970 she collected 24 titles on the LPGA Tour between 1969 and 1981. Winner of the 1975 Colgate European Open at Sunningdale, she is now a respected commentator/analyst for The Golf Channel in Orlando.

## Carner, Jo Anne (née Gunderson) (USA)

*Born Kirkland, Washington, 4 April 1939*
*Turned professional 1970*

Had five victories in the US Ladies' Amateur Championship (1957, 1960, 1962, 1966 and 1968) before turning professional and winning the 1971 and 1976 US Women's Open. She remains the last amateur to win on the LPGA Tour after having taken the 1969 Burdine's Invitational. Between 1970 and 1985 scored 42 victories on the LPGA Tour and was Rolex Player of the Year in 1974, 1981 and 1982. She was inducted into the LPGA Hall of Fame in 1982 and the World Golf Hall of Fame in 1985. She won the Bobby Jones award in 1981 and the Mickey Wright award in 1974 and 1982.

## Cavalleri, Silvia (ITA)

*Born Milan, 10 October 1972*
*Turned professional 1997*

Became the first Italian to win the US Amateur when she beat Robin Burke 5 and 4 at Brae Burn in the 1997 final. She was five times Italian National Junior champion and won the British Girls' title in 1990 with a 5 and 4 success over E. Valera at Penrith.

## Choi, Na Yeon (KOR)

*Born Seoul, 28 October 1987*
*Turned professional 2004*

Winner of the US Women's Open in 2012, Choi was third in the Rolex world rankings thanks to a consistent season in which recorded seven top ten finishes. Started playing golf at 11 and as an amateur played for the Korean national team. She was pipped by Yani Tseng for rookie of the year on the LPGA in 2008 and won twice the following year. She won the money list and recorded the low stroke average on the LPGA in 2010. Her first major success arrived at Blackwolf Run courtesy of a four shot win over Amy Yang.

## Creamer, Paula (USA)

*Born Pleasanton, California, 5 August 1986*
*Turned professional 2005*

The youngest and first amateur to win the LPGA qualifying school in 2004. As an amateur she was top ranked American junior in 2003 and 2004 winning 19 national titles. After turning professional she became a winner on the LPGA Tour in her ninth start when she won the Sybase Classic. She began playing golf at the age of 10. Despite being sidelined with a hand injury and undergoing surgery on a thumb in 2010, she won her first major with a victory at the US Women's Open. She has played in four Solheim Cup matches. In 2012 she posted seven top ten finishes on the LPGA and has career earnings of more than $9.5million.

## Daniel, Beth (USA)

*Born Charleston, South Carolina, 14 October 1956*
*Turned professional 1978*

A member of the LPGA Hall of Fame, she won 32 times between 1979 and 1995 including the 1990 US LPGA Championship. She was Rolex Player of the Year in 1980, 1990 and 1994. Before turning professional she won the US Women's Amateur title in 1975 and 1977 and played in the 1976 and 1978 Curtis Cup teams. She has played in eight Solheim Cup competitions since 1990 and was named as vice-captain to Betsy King at the 2007 match in Sweden. She captained of the US side in 2009 at Rich Harvest Farm in Sugar Grove, Illinois. During her career she has won 33 LPGA events and has won $8.7m in prize money. She works as an analyst for the Golf Channel.

## Dibnah, Corinne (AUS)

*Born Brisbane, 29 July 1962*
*Turned professional 1984*

A former Australian and New Zealand amateur champion, she joined the European Tour after turning professional and won 13 times between 1986 and 1994. A pupil of Greg Norman's first coach Charlie Earp, she was Europe's top earner in 1991.

# Laura Davies CBE (ENG)

*Born 10 October 1963        Turned professional 1985*

Record-breaking performer who has won 77 events worldwide including the US and British Women's Opens. For six days in 1987 she held both titles having won the American event before joining the US Tour. She was a founder member of the Women's Tour in Europe.. She still holds the record for the number of birdies in a round – 11 which she scored in the 1987 Open de France Feminin. Her 16-shot victory, by a margin of five shots, in the 1995 Guardian Irish Holidays Open at St Margaret's remains the biggest in European Tour history. Her 267 totals in the 1988 Biarritz Ladies' Open and the 1995 Guardian Irish Holidays Open are the lowest on Tour and have been matched only by Julie Inkster in the 2002 Evian Masters. Other major victories include the LPGA Championship twice and the du Maurier Championship. In 1999 she became the first European Tour player to pass through the £1 million in prize-money earnings and finished European No. 1 that year for a record fifth time. She was No.1 again in 2004. The 1996 Rolex Player of the Year in America, she has won almost $5.5 million in US prize-money. Originally honoured with an MBE by Her Majesty the Queen in 1988, she became a CBE in 2000. Enjoys all sports including soccer (she supports Liverpool FC). Among other awards she has received during her career have been the Association of Golf Writers' Trophy for her contribution to European golf in 1994 and the American version in 1994 and 1996 for her performances on the US Tour.

In 1994 she became the first golfer to score victories on five different Tours – European, American, Australasian, Japanese and Asian in one calendar year. As an amateur she played for Surrey and was a Curtis Cup player in 1984. She has competed in all 11 Solheim Cup matches. In 2000 was recognised by the LPGA in their top 50 players' and teachers' honours list. Laura proved how strong a competitor she still is when she took the No.1 spot on the women's tour in Europe for a seventh time in 2006. Although she only won once she had six second-place finishes and ended the year with a total of €471,727 from the 11 events she played. By the end of 2006 she had stretched her winning record to 67 titles and in 2007 made it 68 with victory in the Austrian Open a week after missing the cut in the Scottish Open, the first time she had missed in 23 years competing in events organised solely by the Ladies European Tour. She has failed only once – in 2005 – to win an event. When she successfully defended the Uniqa Ladies' Golf Open in 2008 she took her victory tally to 69.

Her 2010 season was better than average because she won five titles in as many different lands – Australia, Germany, Austria, Spain and India –taking her tally of victories to 77. In amongst her haul of titles there are four majors, starting with the US Women's Open of 1987. Since then, she has bagged a couple of US LPGA championships and a du Maurier, while she also captured the British Women's Open in the days before the event was given major status. She is the oldest player on the Ladies European Tour but was still a force in 2012, finishing runner-up at the Ladies German Open and the UNIQA Ladies Open.

## Dowling, Clare (née Hourihane) (IRL)

*Born 18 February 1958*

Won three Irish Ladies' Championships in a row – 1983, 1984 and 1985 and won the title again in 1987 and 1991. She won the 1986 British Ladies' Stroke play amateur title. Two earlier she had made the first of five playing appearances in the Curtis Cup before acting as non-playing captain in 2000.

## Duggelby, Emma (ENG)

*Born Fulford, York, 5 October 1971*

Talented English golfer who won the British Ladies' Open Amateur Championship in 1994 and the English Ladies in 2000 when she made her Curtis Cup début. She also played in the 2004 match winning three points out of four.

## Feng, Shanshan (CHN)

*Born Guangzhou, 5 August 1989*
*Turned professional 2007*

The first Chinese golfer to become a member of the LPGA, Feng won her first major title in 2012 when she won the LPGA Championship. Ranked fourth in the Rolex world rankings last year after a consistent season in which she won over $1m and recorded seven top ten finishes. She won nine events as an amateur in China before turning pro in 2007 after finishing ninth in qualifying for the LPGA. Now coached by Gary Gilchrist, who also teaches world No 1 Yani Tseng.

## Fudoh, Yuri (JPN)

*Born Kumamoto, 14 October 1976*
*Turned professional 1996*

A multiple winner on the Japanese Tour who won her first Japanese event in 2003 when she took the Japan LPGA Championship title. She has won 20 events on the Japanese Tour and her winnings in 2000 of ¥120,443,924 was a record. By the end of 2010 she had become a yen billionaire in prize-money.

## Gustafson, Sophie (SWE)

*Born Saro, 27 December 1973*
*Turned professional 1992*

Winner of the 2000 Weetabix Women's British Open she had studied marketing, economics and law before turning to professional golf. Credits Seve

Ballesteros and Laura Davies as the two players most influencing her career. Her first European victory was the 1996 Swiss Open and her first on the LPGA Tour was the Chick-fil-A Charity Cup in 2000. She has played in every Solheim Cup match since 1998. Previously married to administrator Ty Votaw, the couple later divorced.

## Haynie, Sandra (USA)

*Born Fort Worth, Texas, 4 June 1943*
*Turned professional 1961*

Twice a winner of the US Women's Open (1965 and 1974) she won 42 times between 1962 and 1982 on the US LPGA Tour. She was elected to the LPGA Hall of Fame in 1977.

## Higuchi, Hisako "Chako" (JPN)

*Born Saitama Prefecture, Japan, 13 October 1945*
*Turned professional 1967*

A charter member and star of the Japan LPGA Tour, she won 72 victories worldwide during her career. In 2003 she was elected to the World Golf Hall of Fame.

## Hjörth, Maria (SWE)

*Born Falun, 10 October 1973*
*Turned professional 1996*

After an excellent amateur career when she won titles in Finland, Norway and Spain, she attended Stirling University in Scotland on a golf bursary and graduated with a BA honours degree in English before turning professional. She has played in the Solheim Cup, most notably in 2011. In 2008 she was beaten in a play-off for the McDonald's LPGA Championship by Yani Tseng.

## Hudson, Rebecca (ENG)

*Born Doncaster, Yorkshire, 13 June 1979*
*Turned professional 2002*

A member of the 1998, 2000 and 2002 Curtis Cup teams she won both the British Match Play and Stroke Play titles, the Scottish and English Stroke play Championships and the Spanish Women's Open in 2000. In addition she made the birdie that ensured Great Britain and Ireland won a medal in the World Team Championship for the Espirito Santo Trophy in Berlin in 2000.

## Inkster, Juli (USA)

*Born Santa Cruz, California, 24 June 1960*
*Turned professional 1983*

Winner of two majors in 1984 (the Nabisco Championship and the du Maurier) she also had a double Major year in 1999 when she won the US Women's Open and the LPGA Championship which she won for a second time in 2000. In 2002 she won the US Women's Open for a second time. In all she has won seven major titles. In her amateur career she became the first player since 1934 to win the US Women's amateur title three years in a row (1980, 81, 82). Only four other women and one man (Tiger Woods) have successfully defended their national titles twice in a row. Coached for a time by the late

London-based Leslie King at Harrods Store. She is a regular in the Solheim Cup competition having played nine times between between 1992 and 2011. By 2012her career earnings had surpassed $13.4m and she'd won 45 tournaments.

## Irvin, Ann (ENG)

*Born 11 April 1943*

Winner of the British Ladies' title in 1973, she played in four Curtis Cup matches between 1962 and 1976. She was Daks Woman Golfer of the Year in 1968 and 1969 and has been active in administration at junior and county level.

## Jackson, Bridget (ENG)

*Born Birmingham, 10 July 1936*

A former President of the Ladies' Golf Union she played in three Curtis Cup matches and captained the Vagliano Trophy side twice after having played four times. Although the best she managed in the British Championship was runner-up in 1964 she did win the English, German and Canadian titles.

## Jang, Jeong (KOR)

*Born Daejeon, Korea, 11 June 1980*
*Turned professional 1999*

She scored her breakthrough win on the LPGA Tour when winning the Weetabix Women's British Open at Royal Birkdale. She led from start to finish. As an amateur she won the Korean Women's Open in 1997 and the following year was Korean Women's Amateur champion. Just 5ft tall, she started playing golf at age 13 and has been influenced throughout her career by her father.

## Ji, Eun-Hee (KOR)

*Born Gapyeong, South Korea, 13 May 1986*
*Turned professional 2004*

A former Korean and Japanese Ladies Tour member she won her first major in 2009 when she was successful in the US Women's Open. She holed a 20-foot putt for a winning birdie at the last to collect a first prize of $580,000.

## Johnson, Trish (ENG)

*Born Bristol, 17 January 1966*
*Turned professional 1987*

Another stalwart of the Women's Tour in Europe who learned the game at windy Westward Ho. Regular winner on Tour both in Europe and America, she scored two and a half points out of four in Europe's dramatic Solheim Cup win over the Americans at Loch Lomond in 2000. She has played in eight Solheim Cup matches. She was European No.1 earner in 1990. A loyal supporter of Arsenal FC she regularly attends games at The Emirates Stadium.

## Kerr, Cristie (USA)

*Born Florida, 1977  Turned professional 1997*

She relished the second major success of her career in 2010 when she ran away with the LPGA Championship, defeating Song-Hee Kim by a record breaking margin of 12 shots. The first American to hold the No.1 spot in the world rankings, she finished in the top 20 at all four majors in 2010. Her previous major title victory came in the 2007 US Women's Open at Pine Needles, her favourite course. Kerr's official career earnings on the LPGA Tour amount to nearly $12m. In 2006 she had 19 top 10 finishes. In 1996 she played in the Curtis Cup and was low amateur in the US Women's Open. Since turning professional, she's won 14 events and played six times for the USA in the Solheim Cup. Unfortunately, she had to withdraw from the singles in 2011 because of injury, fofeiting a crucial point in the match won by Europe.

## Kim, Birdie (KOR)

*Born Ik-San, Korea, 26 August 1981*
*Turned professional 2000*
She became the 14th player in the history of the LPGA Tour to score her first win at the US Women's Open and she did it dramatically holing a bunker shot at the last to beat amateurs Brittany Lang and Morgan Pressel by two shots at Cherry Hills, Colorado. A silver medallist at the 1998 Asian Games she won 19 events as an amateur before joining the US Futures Tour in 2001.

## Kim, Christina (USA)

*Born California, 1984    Turned professional 2002*
One of the LPGA's most flamboyant and popular players, the American has won nearly $4m since becoming a regular Tour player in 2003. She's won twice and was a member of the US Solheim Cup teams on three occasions. In 2010 she recorded top ten finishes at both the US Women's Open and the Women's British Open.

## King, Betsy (USA)

*Born Reading, Pennsylvania, 13 August 1955*
*Turned professional 1977*
Another stalwart of the LPGA Tour in America she won 34 times between 1984 and 2001. Winner of the British Open in 1985 she has also won the US Women's Open in 1989 and 1990, the Nabisco Championship three times in 1987, 1990 and 1997 and the LPGA Championship in 1990. She never managed to win the du Maurier event although finishing in the top six on nine occasions. Three times Rolex Player of the Year in 1984, 1989 and 1993 she was elected to the LPGA Hall of Fame in 1995.

## Klein, Emilee (USA)

*Born Santa Monica, California, 11 June 1974*
*Turned professional 1994*
The former Curtis Cup player who played in the 1994 match scored her biggest triumph as a professional when winning the Weetabix British Women's Open at Woburn in 1996.

## Ko, Lydia (NZL)

*Born Korea, April 24 1997*
She became the youngest player in 2012 ever to win on the LPGA when she claimed victory at the CN Canadian Women's Open with a 13 under par total of 275. She was 15 years and four months old, 15 months younger than Lexi Thompson when she won in 2011. As the world's leading amateur, she was ineligible for the prize money of $300,000. She also won the NSW Women's Open on the ALPG Tour when she was still 14. The inaugural recipient in 2011 of the Mark H McCormack medal for the top ranked female amateur golfer, she collected the same honour again in 2012. Among her notable amateur successes, she won the US Women's Amateur at the Country Club in Cleveland. The Kiwi (she was born in Korea but is a New Zealand citizen) was the first golfer to win both the Australian and New Zealand women's strokeplay championships in the same year. She won four other amateur tournaments in New Zealand in 2011. She became the youngest player ever to make a cut in a Ladies European Tour event after finishing seventh as a 12-year-old at the NZ Women's Open in 2010. On her debut at the Womens British Open she finished 17th at Hoylake. In 2013 she successfully defended her CN Canadian Open title, the first amateur ever to win two LPGA events, and was runner-up to Suzann Pettersen in The Evian Championship. At the end of last season, her phenomenal amateur career ended and she joined the professional ranks.

## Koch, Carin (SWE)

*Born Kungalv, Sweden, 2 February 1971*
*Turned professional 1992*
She has been playing golf since she was nine and in the 2000 and 2002 Solheim Cup matches was unbeaten. In 2000 she won three points out of three and in 2002 she won 2½ points out of three. She also played in the 2003 and 2005 matches.

## Kuehne, Kelli (USA)

*Born Dallas, Texas, 11 May 1977*
*Turned professional 1998*
Having won the US Women's Amateur Championship in 1995 she successfully defended the title the following year when she also won the British Women's title – the first player to win both in the same year. She was also the first player to follow up her win in the US Junior Girls' Championship in 1994 with victory in the US Women's event the following year. Her brother Hank is also a professional.

## Laing, Anne (SCO)

*Born Alexandria, Dunbartonshire, 14 March 1975*
Winner of three Scottish Championships in 1996, 2003 and 2004. She made her début in the Curtis Cup in 2004 having played in the Vagliano Trophy in 2003.

## Lawrence, Joan (SCO)

*Born Kinghorn, Fife, 20 April 1930*
After a competitive career in which she three times won the Scottish championship and played in the

# Nancy Lopez, (née Knight) (USA)

*Born Torrance, California, 6 January 1957      Turned professional 1977*

One of the game's bubbliest personalities and impressive performers who took her first title – the New Mexico Women's Amateur title at age 12. Between 1978 and 1995 she won 48 times on the LPGA Tour and was Rolex Player of the Year on four occasions (1978, 79, 85 and 88). In 1978, her rookie year, she won nine titles including a record five in a row. That year she also lost two play-offs and remains the only player to have won the Rookie of the Year, Player of the Year and Vare Trophy (scoring average) in the same season. A year later she won eight tournaments. Three times a winner of the LPGA Championship in 1978, 1985 and 1989 she has never managed to win the US Women's Open although she was runner-up in 1975 as an amateur, in 1977, 1989 and most recently 1997 when she lost out to Britain's Alison Nicholas. She retired from competitive golf and in 2002 was awarded the PGA's First Lady in Golf award for the contribution she has made to the game. In 2005 she captained the winning American Solheim Cup side at Crooked Stick. She started playing competitively again on a limited basis in 2007.

1964 Curtis Cup, she has played her part in golf administration. She had two four-year spells as an LGU selector, is treasurer of the Scottish Ladies' Golf Association and has also served on the LGU executive.

## Lee-Smith, Jennifer (ENG)

*Born Newcastle-upon-Tyne, 2 December 1948*
*Turned professional 1977*

After winning the Ladies' British Open as an amateur in 1976 was named Daks Woman Golfer of the Year. She played twice in the Curtis Cup before turning professional and winning nine times in a six year run from 1979. For a time she ran her own driving range in southern England and is back living in Kent again after having spent time in Florida.

## Lewis, Stacy (USA)

*Born Toledo, Ohio, 1985    Turned professional 2008*

She enjoyed her first LPGA win in the majors by lifting the Kraft Nabisco Championship in 2011. After trailing Yani Tseng by two strokes going into the final round, she rallied behind to overtake the world No 1 and win by three shots. In 2012 she won four times on the LPGA and rose to second in the Rolex world rankings, also becoming the first American since Beth Daniels in 1994 to win the LPGA player of the year award. A formidable amateur golfer who became the first player in the history of the Curtis Cup to win all five of her matches over the Old Course in St Andrews, Lewis suffered from scoliosis and spent nearly eight years in a back brace before undergoing spinal surgery which left her unsure if she would be able to walk again.

## Lincicome, Britanny (USA)

*Born St Petersburg, Florida, 19 September 1985*
*Turned professional 2004*

She won the first 2009 major in spectacular fashion when eagling the final hole at Mission Hills to edge clear of Cristie Kerr and Kristie McPherson. Later in the year played in the Solheim Cup match. As an amateur she won the American Junior Golf Association Championship twice and first hit the headlines as a professional when she won the HSBC Women's World Match-play Championship beating Michelle Wie and Lorena Ochoa on the way to the final where she triumphed over Juli Inkster. She was a member of the 2007, 2009 and 2011 US Solheim Cup sides.

## De Lorenzi, Marie-Laure (FRA)

*Born Biarritz, 21 January 1961*
*Turned professional 1986*

The stylish French golfer won 20 titles in Europe between 1987 and 1997 setting a record in 1988 when she won eight times but for family reasons never spent time on the US Tour.

## Lunn, Karen (AUS)

*Born Sydney, 21 March 1966*
*Turned professional 1985*

A former top amateur she won the British Women's Open in 1993 at Woburn following the success in the European Ladies' Open earlier in the year by her younger sister Mardi.She is a former chairman of the LET.

## McIntire, Barbara (USA)

*Born Toledo, Ohio, 1935*

One of America's best amateurs who finished runner-up in the 1956 US Women's Open to Kathy Cornelius at Northland Duluth. Winner of the US Women's Amateur title in 1959 and 1964 she also won the British Amateur title in 1960. She played in six Curtis Cups between 1958 and 1962.

## McKay, Mhairi (SCO)

*Born Glasgow, 18 April 1975*
*Turned professional 1997*

Former British Girls' Champion (1992 and 1993) she has played in the Vagliano Trophy and Curtis Cup. She was an All-American when studying at Stanford University, where she was a contemporary of Tiger Woods, and made her first appearance in the Solheim Cup at Barsebäck, Sweden, in 2003.

## McKenna, Mary (IRL)

*Born Dublin, 29 April 1949*

Winner of the British Ladies' Amateur Stroke play title in 1979 and eight times Irish champion between 1969 and 1989. One of Ireland's most successful golfers she played in nine Curtis Cup matches and nine Vagliano Trophy matches between 1969 and 1987. She captained the Vagliano team in 1995 and 2009. Three times a member of the Great Britain and Ireland Espirito Santo Trophy side she went on to captain the team in 1986. She was Daks Woman Golfer of the Year in 1979. She captained the Cutis Cup team beaten by the Americans at St Andrews in 2008 and was re-appointed captain for that event in 2010.

## Mallon, Meg (USA)
*Born Natwick, Maryland, 14 April 1963*
*Turned professional 1986*
Winner of the 1991 US Women's Open, 1991 Mazda LPGA Championship, the 2000 du Maurier Classic and 11 other events between 1991 and 2002. In 2004 she won the US Women's Open for the second time. She holed the winning putt in the 2005 Solheim Cup.

## Mann, Carole (USA)
*Born Buffalo, New York, 3 February 1940*
*Turned professional 1960*
Winner of 38 events on the LPGA Tour in her 22 years on Tour. A former president of the LPGA she was a key figure in the founding of the Tour and received the prestigious Babe Zaharias award. In 1964 she won the Western Open, then a Major, and in 1965 the US Women's Open but in 1968 she had a then record 23 rounds in the 60s, won 11 times and won the scoring averages prize with a score of 72.04. Enjoys a hugely successful corporate career within golf. In 2008 she was awarded the prestigious First Lady of Golf award from the PGA of America.

## Massey, Debbie (USA)
*Born Grosse Pointe, Michigan, 5 November 1950*
*Turned professional 1977*
Best known for winning the British Women's Open in 1980 and 1981.

## Matthew, Catriona (SCO)
*Born Edinburgh, 25 August 1969*
*Turned professional 1995*
Former Scottish Girls Under-21 and Scottish Amateur champion, Catriona also won the British Amateur in 1993. She played in the 1990, 1992 and 1994 Curtis Cup matches and made her début in the Solheim Cup at Barsebäck in 2003 and had the honour of holing the winning putt. She performed impressively throughout, showing considerable coolness under pressure. She was also a member of the 2005, 2007, 2009 and 2011 European teams. Now plays on both sides of the Atlantic. With Janice Moodie came second to Sweden's Annika Sörenstam and Liselotte Neumann in the 2006 Women's World Cup of Golf. In 2007 made the cut in all four women's majors and finished tied second in the Kraft Nabisco Championship. Sixteen years after she had won the Amateur Championship at Royal Lytham and St

Annes she won her first major at that course when she won the Ricoh Women's British Open in 2009. Her victory came just two months after giving birth to her second daughter and a week after escaping with her husband who caddies for her, from a fire in the building they were staying in during the Evian Masters. In 2011 she returned to winning ways in the Aberdeen Scottish Open at Archerfield. The Scot also savoured an end of season victory in 2011 when she won the Lorena Ochoa Invitational in Mexico, her fourth career success on the LPGA Tour. And in 2012 she was pipped in a play-off by Suzann Pettersen for the LPGA Hana Bank Championship.

## Meunier-Lebouc, Patricia (FRA)
*Born Dijon, 16 November 1972*
*Turned professional 1993*
French amateur champion in 1992, she has been a regular winner in Europe. She played in the 2000 and 2002 Solheim Cup matches and won her first major when she took first prize in the Kraft-Nabisco Championship at Mission Hills in California

## Miyazato, Ai (JPN)
*Born Okinawa, Japan, 19 June, 1985*
*Turned professional 2004*
Miyazato became the first Japanese golfer ever to top the Order of Merit on the Ladies European Tour when she earned more than 363,000 euros from just two appearances in 2011. She earned all of her money from winning the Evian Masters for the second time. She donated a substantial portion of her earnings to the tsunami relief efforts in Japan. She topped the Rolex world rankings for 11 weeks in 2010 and has won nine times on the LPGA, including two victories in 2012.

## Moodie, Janice (SCO)
*Born Glasgow, 31 May 1973*
*Turned professional 1997*
The 1992 Scottish Women's Stroke play champion played in two winning Curtis Cup teams and earned All American honours at San José State University where she graduated with a degree in psychology. She has won twice on the LPGA, is married to an American and has a young son, Craig. Started playing at age 11 and was helped considerably by Cawder professional Ken Stevely. In the 2000 Solheim Cup she won three out of four points but was controversially left out of the 2002 team. She was reinstated by captain Catrin Nilsmark for the 2003 match at Barsebäck in Sweden where she teamed up with fellow Scot Catriona Matthew and won her singles. She was a wild card pick for the 2009 Solheim Cup but only had one top ten finish in 2010.

## Muñoz, Azahara (ESP)
*Born Malaga, 19 November 1987*
*Turned professional 2009*
After winning the British Girls Championship at Lanark in 2004, 21-year-old Muñoz won the British Women's Amateur title with a 2 and 1 victory in an

# Lorena Ochoa (MEX)

*Born Guadalajara, 15 November 1981      Turned professional 2003*

Announced her retirement from the LPGA as world No 1 in the spring of 2010 and finished sixth in her last event. She was thrillingly consistent throughout her career, finishing in the top ten at 109 of the 173 events she entered in America. Ochoa won her first major when she took the Ricoh British Women's Open when it was held for the first time over the Old Course at St Andrews. She was the fastest player to reach $3million in prize-money on the LPGA Tour in 2006, although she did not win a major that season, losing the Kraft Nabisco to Karrie Webb in a play-off at Palm Springs. However, she topped the money list and was Player of the Year. In 2006 she had six victories, five second place finishes, two thirds, two fourths and a fifth earning more than $2.5million. She fared even better in 2007 when she won eight times and pocketed $4.36 million in prize-money. In 2008 she won another major – the Kraft Nabisco. From the beginning of March to April 20 she won five times and enjoyed two more late season victories by the end of September. In 2009, she edged Ji Yai Shin for the Rolex Player of the Year Award by a single point. All told she won 27 times between 2004 and 2010 and earned nearly $15m. She chose to step down at the tender age of 29 because she had achieved her professional goals and wanted to start a family.

all-Spanish final against Carlota Ciganda. She immediately turned professional and in her rookie year won the Madrid Ladies Masters. Later she qualified to play on the LPGA Tour and ended the 2010 season winning the leading rookie award.

## Neumann, Liselotte (SWE)

*Born Finspång, 20 May 1966*
*Turned professional 1985*

Having won the US Women's Open in 1988 she won the Weetabix British Women's Open title in 1990 to become one of six players to complete the Transatlantic double. The others are Laura Davies, Alison Nicholas, Jane Geddes, Betsy King and Patty Sheehan. The 1988 Rookie of the Year on the LPGA Tour she played in the first six Solheim Cup matches but was a surprising omission from the team in 2005 when she had one of her best years on the US Tour. With Annika Sörenstam won the 2006 World Cup of Golf in South Africa.

## Nicholas MBE, Alison (ENG)

*Born Gibraltar, 6 February 1978*

In Solheim Cup golf had a successful partnership with Laura Davies. In addition they have both won the British and US Open Championships. Alison's first win on the European Tour came in the 1987 Weetabix British Open and she added the US Open ten years later after battling with Nancy Lopez who was trying to win her national title for the first time. Alison is a former winner of the Association of Golf Writers' Golfer of the Year award and has been honoured with an MBE. She announced her retirement from top-line competition in 2004. She captained the European Solheim Cup side in America in 2009. Europe lost but it was much closer than most people imagined it would be. Two year later, however, she led Europe to a famous victory at Killeen Castle.

## Nilsmark, Catrin (SWE)

*Born Gothenburg, Sweden, 28 Aug 1967*
*Turned professional 1987*

Holed the winning putt in Europe's Solheim Cup victory in 1992. Her early career was affected by

whiplash injury after a car crash. Used to hold a private pilot's licence but now rides Harley Davidson motorcycles. She captained the European team to victory in the 2003 Solheim Cup matches at Barsebäck in Sweden and captained the team again at Crooked Stick when America regained the trophy.

## Nordqvist, Anna (SWE)

*Born Esilstuna, Sweden, 10 June 1987*
*Turned professional 2008*

Swedish Junior Player of the Year in 2004 and 2005 and Swedish Player of the Year in 2005 she won the British Girls' Championship in 2005 and the British Women's title in 2008 the year she was a member of the winning Swedish side in the World Amateur Team Championship for the Espirito Santo Trophy at Adelaide. After a hugely successful amateur career while attending Arizona State University. she turned professional and in only her fifth event on the LPGA Tour she won her first major – the McDonald's LPGA Championship. She credited Annika Sörenstam for the advice that helped her win a major so quickly in her professional career. She was a member of the 2009 European Solheim Cup side.

## Okamoto, Ayako (JPN)

*Born Hiroshima, 12 April 1951*
*Turned professional 1976*

Although she won the British Women's Open in 1984 she managed only a runner-up spot in the US Women's Open and US LPGA Championship despite finishing in the top 20 28 times and missing the cut only four times. In the LPGA Championship she finished second or third five times in six years from 1986. She scored 17 victories in the USA between 1982 and 1992, won the 1990 German Open and was Japanese Women's champion in 1993 and 1997. The LPGA Tour's Player of the Year in 1987, she was inducted into the World Golf Hall of Fame in 2005.

## Otto, Julie (née Wade) (ENG)

*Born Ipswich, Suffolk, 10 March 1967*

Secretary of the Ladies' Golf Union from 1996 to 2000 she was one of the most successful competitors in both individual and team golf. Among the many titles she won were the English Stroke Play in 1987 and 1993, the British Ladies' Stroke Play in 1993 and the Scottish Stroke Play in 1991 and 1993. She shared Britain's Golfer of the Year award in 1993 and won it again in 1995 on her own. She played in five Curtis Cup matches including the victories at Royal Liverpool in 1992 and Killarney in 1996 and the drawn match in 1994 at Chattanooga.

## Pace, Lee-Anne (RSA)
*Born 15 February 1981, Mosel Bay, South Africa*
*Turned professional 2005*
Became the first South African to top the Ladies European Tour money list when she earned €339,517 from 25 events in 2010 and was named Players' Player of the Year. She won five times in 2010 in Switzerland, Wales, Finland, China and South Korea. She studied at the University of Tulsa and has a degree in Psychology.

## Pak, Se Ri (KOR)
*Born Daejeon, 28 September 1977*
*Turned professional 1996*
In 1998 she was awarded the Order of Merit by the South Korean government – the highest honour given to an athlete – for having won two Majors in her rookie year on the US Tour. She won the McDonald's LPGA Championship matching Liselotte Neumann in making a major her first tour success. When she won the US Women's Open later that year after an 18-hole play-off followed by two extra holes of sudden death against amateur Jenny Chuasiriporn, she became the youngest golfer to take that title. By the middle of 2001 she had won 12 events on the US tour including the Weetabix Women's British Open at Sunningdale – an event included on the US Tour as well as the European Circuit for the first time. In 2002 she was again a multiple winner on the US Tour adding to her majors by winning the McDonald's LPGA Championship. As an amateur in Korea she won 30 titles and became the first lady professional to make the cut in a men's professional event for 58 years when she played four rounds in a Korean Tour event. In 2006 she returned to the major winner's circle when she beat Karrie Webb in a play off for the McDonald's LPGA Championship. It was her fifth major victory but her first since 2002. In 2007 she was inducted into the World Golf Hall of Fame, the first player from South Korea to be honoured. She posted five top ten finished on the LPGA in 2012 where she's won 25 times.

## Panton-Lewis, Cathy (SCO)
*Born Bridge of Allan, Stirlingshire, 14 June 1955*
*Turned professional 1978*
A former Ladies' British Open Amateur Champion in 1976 when she was named Scottish Sportswoman of the year. She notched up 13 victories as a professional on the European tour between 1979 and 1988. Daughter of the late John Panton, MBE, former

honorary professional to the Royal and Ancient Golf Club of St Andrews.

## Park, Grace (KOR)
*Born Seoul, Korea, 6 March 1979*
*Turned professional 1999*
After having lost a sudden-death play-off to Annika Sörenstam at the McDonald's LPGA Championship in 2003 she did win her first major in 2004 when she was successful in the Nabisco Dinah Shore at Mission Hills in Palm Springs. She was a graduate of the Futures Tour where in 1999 she won five of the ten events. Before turning professional she attended Arizona State University and in 1998 became the first player since Patty Berg in 1931 to win the US Amateur, Western Amateur and Trans-Amateur titles in the same year. She won 55 national junior, college and amateur titles and tied eighth as an amateur in the 1999 US Women's Open. After years of back, neck and hip injuries, she announced her retirement from the game last year at the age of 33. All told, she won six events on the LPGA with career earnings of $5.4m.

## Park, Inbee (KOR)
*Born South Korea, 1988*
*Turned professional 2006*
In what was arguably the greatest season of golf ever completed by a woman, Park won three consecutive major titles during 2013. While she triumphed at six events in all and was firmly established as world number one, the highlights of the year for Park were undoubtedly the headline grabbing victories in the Kraft Nabisco, the LPGA Championship and the US Women's Open. Although she came up short in St Andrews at the Ricoh British Women's Open when she was striving to become the first golfer to win four consecutive professional majors in the same season, Park still earned her place in the record books. She started playing golf at the age of 10 and won nine events on the American Junior Golf Association circuit. She earned her LPGA card in 2006 and won her first major – the 2008 US Women's Open at Interlachen by four shots from Sweden's Helen Alfredsson. In 2012 she rose to fifth in the world rankings after winning the Evian Masters and the Sime Darby LPGA Malaysia. Her form in 2013 was even more spectacular as she won six times and reeled off a barrage of top ten finishes. She won the LPGA money list and was the Rolex player of the year.

## Pepper (Mochrie, Scarinzi), Dottie (USA)
*Born Saratoga Springs, Florida, 17 August 1965*
*Turned professional 1987*
Winner of 17 events on the LPGA Tour including two majors. She ranks 13th on the all-time money list with earnings of nearly $7 million. A fierce competitor she won the Nabisco Dinah Shore title in 1992 and again in 1999. She played in the Solheim Cup matches up to 2000. In 2004 she announced her retirement from the US LPGA Tour because of injury. The following year she started work as a TV commentator for NBC

and the Golf Channel, notoriously describing the US team at the 2007 Solheim Cup as "choking freaking dogs". While she apologised for her poor choice of words, a repu-tation for plain speaking has enhanced her broad-casting career.

## Pettersen, Suzann (NOR)

*Born Oslo, April 7 1981   Turned professional 2000*

Winner of two major championships, Pettersen is a five time Norwegian Amateur champion. She was also World Amateur champion in 2000. Suzann won the French Open in 2001 and made her Solheim Cup début in the 2002 match at Barsebäck. One of the best performers on the week , she was unbeaten going into the singles. She also played in the 2003, 2005, 2007, 2009, 2011 and 2013 matches. She earned her first major success when she won the McDonald's LPGA Championship in 2007, going on that year to finish second to Lorena Ochoa in the LPGA money list. She won three times in 2011, twice on the LPGA and once on the LET, to finish the season in second place on the Rolex rankings She won the Hanabank Championship in 2012, defeating Catriona Matthew in a play-off. The 14th victory of her career took her earnings past the $9m mark. In 2013 she won the Evian Championship after the tournament was elevated to major status. She has been a Working for Golf Ambassador on behalf of The R&A since 2011.

## Prado, Catherine (née Lacoste) (FRA)

*Born Paris 27 June 1945*

The only amateur golfer ever to win the US Women's Open she won the title at Hot Springs, Virginia in 1967. She was also the first non-American to take the title and the youngest. Two years later she won both the US and British Amateur titles. She was a four times winner of her own French Championship in 1967, 1969, 1970 and 1972 and won the Spanish title in 1969, 1972 and 1976. She comes from a well-known French sporting family.

## Rawls, Betsy (USA)

*Born Spartanburg, South Carolina, 4 May 1928*
*Turned professional 1951*

Winner of the 1951, 1953, 1957 and 1960 US Women's Open and the US LPGA Championship in 1959 and 1969 as well as two Western Opens when the Western Open was a Major. She scored 55 victories on the LPGA Tour between 1951 and 1972. One of the best shot makers in women's golf who was noted for her game around and on the greens.

## Reid MBE, Dale (SCO)

*Born Ladybank, Fife, 20 March 1959*
*Turned professional 1979*

Scored 21 wins in her professional career between 1980 and 1991 and was so successful in leading Europe's Solheim Cup side to victory against the Americans at Loch Lomond in 2000 that she wa again captain in 2002 when the Americans won. She had played in the 1990, 1992, 1994 and 1996 matche Following the team's success in the 2000 Solheim Cup she received an MBE.

## Robertson MBE, Belle (SCO)

*Born Southend, Argyll, 11 April 1936*

One of Scotland's most talented amateur golfers who was Scottish Sportswoman of the Year in 1968, 1971 1978 and 1981. She was Woman Golfer of the Yea in 1971, 1981 and 1985. A former Ladies' Britis Open Amateur Champion and six times Scottis Ladies' Champion, she competed in nine Curtis Cup acting as non-playing captain in 1974 and 1976.

## Sander, Anne (Welts, Decker, née Quast) (USA)

*Born Marysville, 1938*

A three times winner of the US Ladies' title in 1958 1961 and 1963, she also won the British Ladies' titl in 1980. She made eight appearances in the Curti Cup stretching from 1958 to 1990. Only Carol Semple Thompson has played more often, havin played ten times.

## Saunders, Vivien (ENG)

*Born Sutton, Surrey, 24 November 1946*
*Turned professional 1969*

Founder of the Women's Professional Golfers Association (European Tour) in 1978 and chairmar for the first two years. In 1969 she was the firs European golfer to qualify for the LPGA Tour ir America. She is keen to become a re-instatee amateur again.

## Segard, Mme Patrick (de St Saveur, née Lally Vagliano) (FRA)

Former chairperson of the Women's Committee o the World Amateur Golf Council holding the pos from 1964 to 1972. A four times French champior (1948, 50, 51 and 52) she also won the British (1950) Swiss (1949 and 1965), Luxembourg (1949), Italia (1949 and 1951) and Spanish (1951) amateur titles She represented France from 1937 to 1939, fron 1947 to 1965 and again in 1970.

## Semple Thompson, Carol (USA)

*Born 1950*

Winner of six titles including the US Ladies' in 197 and the British Ladies in 1974, he has played in 1 Curtis Cups between 1974 and 2002 and holed th 27-foot winning putt in the 2002 match. At 53 she i the oldest US Curtis Cup Player. She captained th side in 1998, 2006 and 2008 when the match wa played over the Old Course at St Andrews for th first time. In 2003 she was named winner of the Bol Jones award for sportsmanship and in 2005 receive the PGA of America Lady of the Year trophy.

# Annika Sörenstam (SWE)

*Born Stockholm, 9 October 1970*      *Turned professional 1992*

Winner of the US Women's Open in 1995 and 1996 she and Karrie Webb of Australia have battled for the headlines on the LPGA Tour over the past few years. A prolific winner of titles in America. She won four in a row in early summer 2000 as she and Webb battled again for the No. 1 spot in 2001. Sörenstam was the No. 1 earner in 1995, 1997 and 1998, Webb in 1996, 1999 and 2000. At the Standard Register Ping event she became the first golfer to shoot 59 on the LPGA Tour. Her second round score 59 included 13 birdies, 11 of them in her first 12 holes. Her 36-hole total of 124 beat the record set by Webb the previous season by three. Her 54-hole score of 193 matched the record set by Karrie Webb and her 72-hole total of 261 which gave her victory by three shots from Se Ri Pak matched the low total on Tour set by Se Ri Pak in 1998. Sörenstam's 27-under-par winning score was a new record for the Tour beating the 26-under-par score Webb returned in the Australian Ladies' Masters in 1999. Her sister Charlotta also plays on the LPGA and Evian Tours.

Before turning professional she finished runner-up in the 1992 US Women's Championship. Sörenstam continued on her winning way in 2002 when her victories included another major – the Kraft Nabisco Championship. By the end of August she had won six times in the US and once more in Europe. By the beginning of October she had won nine times on the 2002 LPGA Tour and collected her 40th LPGA title. Only four players have won more than 9 events in one LPGA season. By October she had won $2.5 million world wide. In 2003 she was awarded the Golf Writers award in Britain for the golfer who had done most for European golf. In 2004 she quickly passed through the 50 mark in titles won in America. Before the middle of October her tally was 54 she had passed the $2 million mark in American Tour earnings for the year. In 2004 she added another major to her list of achievements winning the McDonald's LPGA Championship. She remains the dominant force in women's professional golf. When Annika won the Mizuno Classic in Japan she became the first player for 34 years to win 10 titles in a season.

In 2003 she took up the challenge of playing on the US Men's Tour teeing up in a blaze of publicity in the Colonial event in Texas but missed the half-way cut. She won her fifth Major when she took the McDonald's LPGA Championship in June and when she won the Weetabix British Women's Open at Royal Lytham and St Annes she completed a Grand Slam of major titles. Her tally is now six Majors. Her win at Lytham was her sixth major success. By the end of August 2003 she had won 46 LPGA tournaments and was inducted into the World Golf Hall of Fame. When she won the Mizuno Classic for the third successive year she was winning her 46th LPGA title and had wrapped up the Player of the Year and top money earner award. In 2004 she quickly passed through the 50 mark in titles won and before the middle of October had passed the $2 million mark in US PGA Tour earnings for a fourth successive year. She added another major to her personal tally when she won the McDonald's LPGA Championship. 2005 was another stellar year for Annika who took her career wins on the LPGA Tour to 66 with 10 more victories from her 20 starts. She easily topped the money list with over $2 million and moved her career earnings on the US Tour to $18,332,764. During the year she also won her own event in Sweden.

Her majors total at the end of 2005 after further Grand Slam victories in the Kraft Nabisco Championship and McDonald's LPGA Championship moved to nine. Although she did not win Player of the Year honours in 2006 – that went to Mexico's Lorena Ochoa – Annika again had an excellent season, winning three times and coming second on a further five occasions. She has now won 69 times and her earnings in America have gone through $20 million. She added a further major win to her list of Grand Slam successes and with Liselotte Neumann won the World Cup of Golf in South Africa early in the year. She also hosted and then won her own event in Sweden and beat Helen Alfredsson and Karrie Webb to the first prize at the Dubai Ladies Masters in November. In 2007 her appearances were curtailed because of injury and she announced her retirement from full-time professional golf in 2008 despite having won the SBS Open in Hawaii, the Stanford International and the Michelob Ultra Open in the United States. In her last season she earned $1,617,411 taking her total on Tour since 1994 to $22,454,692. Now runs her own event in Sweden. Appointed an ambassador in the bid to have golf included in the Olympic Games, she gave birth to her first child in 2009. She announced in 2010 she was expecting her second child.

# Sheehan, Patty (USA)

*Born Middlebury, Vermont, 27 October 1956*
*Turned professional 1980*

Scored 35 victories between 1981 and 1996 including six Majors – the LPGA Championship in 1983, 1984 and 1994, the US Women's Open in 1993 and 1994 and the Nabisco Championship in 1996. She also won the British Women's Open at Woburn in 1992 before it was designated a major. As an amateur she won all her four games in the 1980 Curtis Cup. She is a member of the LPGA Hall of Fame. She played in four Solheim Cup games between 1990 and 1996 and captained the side in 2002 and 2003.

## Shin, Ji-Yai (KOR)

*Born Chonnam, Korea, 28 April 1988*
*Turned professional 2006*

She played 18 events on the Korean LPGA Tour in 2007 and won nine times, winning twice as much as her nearest rival with a then record total of $725,000. She was Korea's Player of the Year – a title she retained in 2008 when she became the first player to win all three events that comprise that circuit's Grand Slam. She had broken almost every record set on the Korean Tour by Se Ri Pak before the start of the 2008 season. In 2008 she won her first major – the Ricoh British Women's Open at Sunningdale – and went on to win two more times on the LPGA Tour taking the Mizuno Classic and the end-of-season ADT Championship in which she beat Karrie Webb by a shot to win US $1 million. She was the first non-member to win three times on that Tour. In addition she had three other top 10 finishes and earned US$1.77 million in prize-money. In 2008 she won 11 times – the three on the LPGA Tour, seven times in Korea and once in Japan. In 2009 she earned LPGA Rookie of the Year honours but was pipped at the post by Lorena Ochoa for the Rolex Player of the Year. By the end of 2010 she had played 60 events on the LPGA Tour and missed just one cut. Without a win in 2011, she relished two victories in the space of six days in 2012, following up her success over Paula Creamer at the ninth extra hole in the Kingsmill Championship with a nine stroke romp in the British Women's Open at Hoylake, the largest margin in the event's history.

## Steinhauer, Sherri (USA)

*Born Madison, Wisconsin, 27 December 1962*
*Turned professional 1985*

Winner of the Weetabix Women's British Open at Woburn in 1999 and at Royal Lytham and St Annes in 1998 and again there in 2006. Her third victory was her first major success because the British Women's Open had been awarded major status. She has also played in four Solheim Cup matches.

## Stephenson, Jan (AUS)

*Born Sydney, 22 December 1951*
*Turned professional 1973*

She won three majors on the LPGA Tour – the 1981 du Maurier Classic, the 1982 LPGA Championship and the 1983 US Women's Open. She was twice Australian Ladies champion in 1973 and 1977.

## Streit, Marlene Stewart (CAN)

*Born Cereal, Alberta, 9 March 1934*

One of Canada's most successful amateurs she won her national title ten times between 1951 and 1973. She won the 1953 British Amateur, the US Amateur in 1956 and the Australian Ladies in 1963. She was Canadian Woman Athlete of the Year in 1951, 1953, 1956, 1960 and 1963.

## Stupples, Karen (ENG)

*Born Dover, England, 24 June 1973*

English professional who lives in Orlando but hit the headlines at Sunningdale in the summer of 2004 when she won the Weetabix British Women's Open with a 19 under par total of 269. In the final round she began by making an eagle at the first and holing her second shot for an eagle 2 at the second. She finally clinched victory with the help of three birdies in a row on the back nine. Earlier in the year she had won on the LPGA Tour which she had joined in 1999. She has played golf since she was 11. She made her début in the Solheim Cup in 2005 and in 2011 gained a point for Europe without playing in the singles after Cristie Kerr pulled out through injury.

## Suggs, Louise (USA)

*Born Atlanta, Georgia, 7 September 1923*
*Turned professional 1948*

Winner of 58 titles on the LPGA Tour after a brilliant amateur career which included victories in the 1947 US Amateur and the 1948 British Amateur Championships. She won 11 Majors including the US Women's Open in 1949 and 1952 and the LPGA Championship in 1957. A founder member of the US Tour she was an inaugural honoree when the LPGA Hall of Fame was instituted in 1967. In 2006 she was awarded the Bob Jones award for outstanding sportsmanship and for being a perfect ambassador for the game. She comes from Atlanta and knew Bobby Jones when she was younger.

## Thomas, Vicki (née Rawlings) (WAL)

*Born Northampton, 27 October 1954*

One of Wales' most accomplished players who took part in six Curtis Cup matches between 1982 and 1992. She won the Welsh Championship eight times between 1979 and 1994 as well as the British Ladies' Stroke Play in 1990.

## Thompson, Alexis (USA)

*Born Florida, 10 February 1995*
*Turned professional 2010*

An outstanding amateur who won the US Junior girls in 2008, she was the youngest player at the age of 12 ever to qualify for the US Women's Open. After winning four and halving one of her matches in the Curtis Cup, she turned professional at 15 in the summer of 2010. She finished 10th at the US Women's Open and two weeks later at the Evian Masters was runner-up. After just three professional events she'd won $314,842. The LGU caused a stir when they declined to give the teenager an exemption into qualifying for the 2010 Women's British Open at Birkdale. In 2011 Alexis won the Navistar LPGA Classic in Alabama by five shots to become the youngest ever winner on the LPGA circuit. Better known as Lexi, she then became the second youngest ever winner on the LET as she won the Dubai Ladies Masters by four strokes. Aware of her exceptional talent, the LPGA changed their rules – which did not allow players to compete

# Yani Tseng (TPE)

*Born Taoyuan, near Teipei, Taiwan, 1989      Turned professional 2007*

With 11 victories around the world – including seven titles on the LPGA where she won nearly $3 million during 2011 –Tseng became the dominant player in women's golf. At just 22-years-old, she's won five major titles, the youngest golfer, male or female, ever to do so. A top-ranked Taiwanese amateur, she was the Asia-Pacific Junior Champion in 2003 and 2005. In 2004 she won the USGA Women's Amateur Public Links Championship, defeating Michelle Wie in the final. After turning professional, she competed initially on the Asian Golf Tour and in Canada. She joined the LPGA in 2008 and won her first major on the circuit that summer when she outlasted Sweden's Maria Hjörth at the fourth extra hole of a play-off for the McDonald's LPGA Championship. She enjoyed an even more successful season in 2010 when she won two more majors – the Kraft Nabisco and the Ricoh Women's British Open. Her victory at Birkdale meant she became the youngest woman ever to win three major titles.

Living in a house in Florida formerly owned by Annika Sörenstam, she has been mentored by the Swede, effectively succeeding both Sörenstam and Lorena Ochoa, who shared the No 1 spot for a decade, as the game's best player. By any standard, 2011 was an extraordinary season for the Taiwanese golfer. She won all of the first five tournaments she entered around the globe: the Taifong Ladies Open on the LPGA of Taiwan Tour; the ISPS Handa Women's Australian Open and ANZ RACV Ladies Open on the Australian Ladies Professional Golf Tour and the Ladies European Tour (LET) and the Honda LPGA Thailand, the season-opener on the LPGA. Thereafter, she was runner up at the Kraft Nabisco, the first major of the season, before adding to her impressive haul of victories in the most prized events with wins at the Wegmans LPGA and the Women's British Open. At Carnoustie, she was the first champion to mount a successful defence. And on the LPGA, where she posted 14 top tens in 22 events, she was only the 17th golfer since 1950 to win six tournaments or more in a single season.By those lofty standards, 2012 was more of a routine season, though she still won three times on the LPGA and earned more than $1.2m.

on Tour until they were 18 – in order that the teenager could play full time on the Tour in 2012.

## Varangot, Brigitte (FRA)
*Born Biarritz, 1 May 1940*

Winner of the French Amateur title five times in six years from 1961 and again in 1973. Her run in the French Championship was impressive from 1960 when her finishes were 2, 1, 1, 2, 1, 1, 2. She was also a triple winner of the British Championship in 1963, 1965 and 1968. One of France's most successful players she also won the Italian title in 1970.

## Walker OBE, Mickey (ENG)
*Born Alwoodley, Yorkshire, 17 December 1952*
*Turned professional 1973*

Always a popular and modest competitor she followed up an excellent amateur career by doing well as a professional. Twice a Curtis Cup player she won the Ladies' British Open Amateur in 1971 and 1972, the English Ladies' in 1973 and had victories, too, in Portugal, Spain and America where she won the 1972 Trans-Mississippi title. She won six times as a professional but is perhaps best known for her stirring captaincy of the first four European Solheim Cup sides leading them to a five point success at Dalmahoy. In 1992 she galvanised her side by playing them tapes of the men's Ryder Cup triumphs. Now a club professional she also works regularly as a television commentator for Sky

## Whitworth, Kathy (USA)
*Born Monahans, Texas, 27 September 1939*
*Turned professional 1958*

Won 88 titles on the LPGA Tour between 1959 and 1991 – more than any one else male or female. Her golden period was in the 1960s when she won eight events in 1965, nine in 1966, eight in 1967 and 10 in 1968. When she finished third in the 1981 US Women's Open she became the first player to top $1 million in prize money on the LPGA Tour. She was the seventh member of the LPGA Tour Hall of Fame when inducted in 1975. Began playing golf at the age of 15 and made golfing history when she teamed up with Mickey Wright to play in the previously all male Legends of Golf event. Winner of six Majors – including three LPGA Championship wins in 1967, 1971 and 1975. In addition she won two Titleholders' Championships (1966 and 1967) and the 1967 Western Open when they were Majors. Enjoyed a winning streak of 17 successive years on the LPGA Tour.

## Wie, Michelle (USA)
*Born Hawaii, 11 October 1989*
*Turned professional 2005*

As an amateur she finished third in the Weetabix British Women's Open in July 2005 and turned professional in October as a 16-year-old with multi-million contract guarantees. In her first event as a professional in the Samsung Championship she finished fourth behind Annika Sörenstam but then

# Karrie Webb (AUS)

*Born Ayr, Queensland, 21 December 1974      Turned professional 1994*

Blonde Australian who is rewriting the record books with her performances on the LPGA Tour. Peter Thomson, the five times Open champion considers she is the best golfer male or female there is and Greg Norman, who was her inspiration as a teenager, believes she can play at times better than Tiger Woods although Webb herself hates comparisons. She scored her first Major win in 1995 when she took the Weetabix Women's British Open – a title she won again in 1997. When she joined the LPGA Tour she won the 1999 du Maurier Classic, the 2000 Nabisco Championship and the 2000 and 2001 US Women's Open – five Majors out of eight (by the end of July 2001) – the most impressive run since Mickey Wright won five out of six in the early 1960s. In 2002 she became the first player to complete a career Grand Slam when she won her third Weetabix British Open which had become an official major on the US LPGA Tour. It was her sixth major title in four years. Her winning total at Turnberry was 15 under par 273. Enjoyed a close rivalry with Annika Sörenstam. In 2005 she was inducted into the World Golf Hall of Fame. She added to her majors tally in 2006 when she beat Lorena Ochoa in a play-off for the Kraft Nabisco Championship. Later she lost a play-off to Se Ri Pak for another major – the McDonald's LPGA Championship. She is the only player to have victories in the current four majors and the du Maurier event, now discarded as a major. She added more than $800,000 to her career earnings of $17.3m in 2012 thanks to six top ten finishes on the LPGA.

was disqualified for a dropped ball infringement incurred in the third round – and spotted by an American journalist who did not report it until the following day. In 2006 she continued to play in a few men's events including the Omega European Masters at Crans-sur-Sierre but failed to make the cut in any. She did make the cut in all four majors in 2006. She combines her professional career with her school work in Hawaii and it is reported she hopes to go eventually to Stanford University. In 2008 she earned a card on the LPGA Tour at the Qualifying School. She was chosen as a wild card and played with distinction in the 2009 Solheim Cup side won by the Americans and later in the year won her first event on the LPGA Tour when she took the Lorena Ochoa Mexico Classic.

## Wright, Janette (née Robertson) (SCO)
*Born Glasgow, 7 January 1935*

Another of Scotland's most accomplished amateur players she competed four times in the Curtis Cup and was four times Scottish champion between 1959 and 1973. Formerly married to the late Innes Wright. Her daughter Pamela was Collegiate Golfer of the Year 1988 and LPGA Rookie of the Year in 1989.

## Wright, Mickey (USA)
*Born San Diego, California, 14 February 1935*
*Turned professional 1954*

Her 82 victories on the LPGA Tour between 1956 and 1973 was bettered only by Kathy Whitworth who has 88 official victories. One of the greatest golfers in the history of the Tour she had a winning streak of 14 successive seasons. Winner of 13 Major titles she is the only player to date to have won three in one season. In 1961 she took the US Women's Open, the LPGA Championship and the Titleholders' Championship. That year she became only the second player to win both the US Women's Open and LPGA Championship in the same year having done so previously in 1958. Scored 79 of her victories between 1956 and 1969 when averaging almost eight wins a season. During this time she enjoyed a tremendous rivalry with Miss Whitworth.

## Yang, Amy (KOR)
*Born South Korea 28 July 1989*
*Turned professional 2006*

Only 16 when she won the ANZ Ladies Masters on the LET in 2006, Yang took up the game at the age of ten before emigrating to Australia when she was 15. Her family moved to Florida in 2007 when she took up membership of the LPGA. Runner-up at the US Women's Open and fourth at the Kraft Nabisco in 2012, she's won three times on the LET but is still seeking her first success on the LPGA.

## Yokomine, Sakura (JPN)
*Born Konoya Kagoshima, 13 December 1985*
*Turned professional 2005*

Winner of 17 events on the Japan LPGA Tour. She was top earner in Japan in 2009 but took second spot in 2010 to Korean golfer Ahn Sun-Ju.

## Yoo, Sun Young (KOR)
*Born Seoul, 13 December 1986*
*Turned professional 2004*

Winner of the Kraft Nabisco in 2012, her first major title, thanks to a sudden death play-off win over I.K. Kim, who had missed a short putt for victory on the 72nd hole. It was only her second victory on the LPGA after the Sybase Match Play in 2010. As an amateur, she reached the quarter-finals of the US Women's Amateur in 2004 before turning professional later that year.

# The earliest recorded Rules of Golf

In July 2013, The Open Championship returned to Muirfield, home of the Honourable Company of Edinburgh Golfers. If we owe the governance of the game of golf from the late 19th Century onwards to The Royal and Ancient Golf Club, then it is to the Gentlemen Golfers of Edinburgh (later the Honourable Company of Edinburgh Golfers) that we owe the earliest recorded Rules of Golf.

Written in 1744 and known as the Thirteen Articles, these rules were conceived for the first Challenge for the Silver Club, played over Leith Links. The rules were copied almost identically ten years later when a similar Challenge was instituted at St Andrews. The rules appear on the very first page of the St Andrews Golfers' first minute book and are entitled The Articles & Laws in Playing the Golf. The first competition, played on 14 May 1754, is taken as the start date of what eventu-ally became known as The Royal and Ancient Golf Club of St Andrews.

The first winner at Leith in 1744 was John Rattray, an Edinburgh surgeon. It was Rattray's signature that appeared at the end of the Thirteen Articles, which were enshrined in the minute book of the Edinburgh Golfers. By virtue of his victory he became 'Captain of the Golf'. Rattray won again the following year and for a third time in 1748. In addition to cementing his place in golfing history as the signatory of the first written Rules of Golf, in the years separating his second and third victories, Rattray found himself playing a part, albeit against his will, in the Jacobite Rebellion.

Rattray was persuaded to tend the Highlanders wounded at the Battle of Prestonpans in 1745. When Prince Charles Edward Stuart decided to make his way to England, Rattray was prevailed upon to accompany the Jacobite troops. He made it to Derby before returning with the retreating army to Culloden Moor, where he was forced to surrender himself. He was imprisoned in Inverness and only escaped slaughter due to the fact that his role was to tend the wounded and not bear arms. He was released thanks to the intervention of the Lord President of the Court of Session, Duncan Forbes, a friend and fellow golfer. Forbes had played his own part in the campaign. Following the 1745 Silver Club Challenge, he travelled north to try and persuade the Highland clans not to join the Jacobite cause. He later died, on 10 December 1747, at Culloden.

The annual Silver Club Challenges were the bedrock on which early golfing societies were founded and flourished. In the 18th and for most of the 19th century, each society was at liberty to follow its own rules and these were determined by factors specific to their own course. In 1754, the St Andrews Golfers made a slight alteration to Rule 5 of the Edinburgh Challenge to read: "If your Ball come among water, or any watery filth, you are at liberty to take out your Ball, and throw it behind the hazard, six yards at least". In the Edinburgh version, the wording was "bringing it behind the hazard and teeing it".

This amendment was presumably to reflect the course conditions at St Andrews, where teeing would be unnecessary as the ground was firmer. It could also have been that in the mid-18th century, teeing the ball simply meant placing it on a favourable piece of ground. According to Rule 2: "Your tee must be on the ground".

# Famous Personalities of the Past

In making the difficult choice of the names to be included, effort has been made to acknowledge the outstanding players and personalities of each successive era from the early pioneers to the stars of recent times.

| | | | | |
|---|---|---|---|---|
| Alliss, Percy | Compston, Archie | King, Sam | Park, Mungo | Tait, Freddie |
| Anderson, Jamie | Cotton, Sir Henry | Kirkaldy, Andrew | Park, Willie | Taylor, JH |
| Anderson, Willie | Crawley, Leonard | Laidlay, John | Park, Willie Jr | Thomas, D. |
| Archer, George | Curtis, The Sisters | Leitch, Cecil | Patton, Billy Joe | Tolley, Cyril |
| Armour, Tommy | Daly, Fred | Lema, Tony | Philp, Hugh | Travis, Walter |
| Auchterlonie, | Darwin, Bernard | Little, Lawson | Picard, Henry | Tumba, Sven |
| Willie | Demeret, Jimmy | Locke, Bobby | Price-Fisher, | Valentine, Jessie |
| Balding, Al | Dobereiner, Peter | Longhurst, Henry | Elizabeth | Van Donck, Flory |
| Ballesteros, | Duncan, George | Lunt, Michael | Ray, Ted | Vardon, Harry |
| Severiano | Faulkner, Max | McCormack, Mark | Rees, Dai | Vare, Glenna |
| Ball, John | Ferguson, Bob | McDonald, CB | Robertson, Allan | Venturi, Ken |
| Barnes, Jim | Fernie, Willie | Mackenzie, Alister | Rosburg, Bob | Von Nida, Norman |
| Barton, Pamela | Garrett, Maureen | Mackenzie, Keith | Ryder, Samuel | Walker, George |
| Berg, Patty | Garvey, Philomena | Massy, Arnaud | Sarazen, Gene | Ward, Charlie |
| Bolt, Tommy | Goldschmid, Isa | Micklem, Gerald | Sayers, Ben | Ward, Harvie |
| Boros, Julis | Hagen, Walter | Middlecoff, Cary | Sewgolum, | Wethered, Joyce |
| Bousfield, Ken | Harper, Chandler | Minoprio, Gloria | Sewunker | Wethered, Roger |
| Bradshaw, Harry | Henning, Harold | Mitchell, Abe | Shade, Ronnie | Whitcombes, The |
| Braid, James | Herd, Sandy | Moody, Orville | Smith, Frances | White, Ronnie |
| Brewer, Gay | Hilton, Harold | Morgan, Wanda | Smith, Horton | Will, George |
| Brown, Eric | Hogan, Ben | Morris, Old Tom | Smith, Macdonald | Wilson, Enid |
| Bruen, Jimmy | Howard, Barclay | Morris, Young Tom | Snead, Sam | Wind, Herbert |
| Camicia, Mario | Hunt, Bernard | Nelson, Byron | Solheim, Karsten | Warren |
| Campbell, Bill | Hutchinson, | Norman, Moe | Souchak, Mike | Wood, Craig |
| Campbell, Dorothy | Horace | Ortiz-Patino, Jaime | Spearman, Marley | Wooldridge, Ian |
| Carr, Joe | Jarman, Ted | Ouimet, Francis | Stewart, Payne | Yates, Charlie |
| Coe, Charlie | Jones, Bob | Panton, John | Stranrahan, Frank R. | Zaharias, "Babe" |

## Alliss, Percy  (1897–1975)

Father of Peter Alliss he finished in the top six in The Open Championship seven times, including joint third at Carnoustie in 1931, two strokes behind winner Tommy Armour. Twice winner of the Match Play Championship, five times German Open champion and twice winner of the Italian Open. He was a Ryder Cup player in 1933–35–37, an international honour also gained by his son. Spent six yesrs as professional at the Wansee Club in Berlin before moving back to Britain to work at Beaconsfield, Temple Newsam and for 30 years at Ferndown in Dorset.

## Anderson, Jamie  (1842–1912)

Winner of three consecutive Open Championships – 1877–78–79. A native St Andrean, he once claimed to have played 90 consecutive holes on the Old Course without a bad or unintended shot. He was noted for his straight hitting and accurate putting.

## Anderson, Willie  (1878–1910)

Took his typically Scottish flat swing to America where he won the US Open four times in a five year period from 1901. Only Bobby Jones, Ben Hogan and Jack Nicklaus have also won the US Open four times.

## Archer, George  (1940–2005)

The 6ft 5in tall former cowboy won The Masters in 1969 – one of four golfers who won their first major that year. A superb putter Archer was dogged throughout his career by injury but he won 12 times on the PGA Tour and a further 19 times on the US Senior Tour now the Champions Tour. Elizabeth, one of his two daughters, made headlines when she caddied for her father and became the first woman to do so at Augusta.

## Armour, Tommy  (1896–1968)

Born in Edinburgh, he played for Britain against America as an amateur and, after emigrating, for America against Britain as a professional in the forerunners of the Walker and Ryder Cup matches. Won the US Open in 1927, the USPGA in 1930 and the 1931 Open at Carnoustie. Became an outstanding coach and wrote several bestselling instruction books. Known as "The Silver Scot".

## Auchterlonie, Willie (1872–1963)
Won The Open at Prestwick in 1893 at the age of 21 with a set of seven clubs he had made himself. Founded the famous family club-making business in St Andrews. He believed that golfers should master half, three-quarter and full shots with each club. Appointed Honorary Professional to The R&A in 1935.

## Balding, Al (1924–2006)
A lovely swinger of the club, he was the first Canadian to win on the US Tour when he took the Mayfair Inn Open in Florida in 1955. In 1968, in partnership with Stan Leonard, he won the World Cup in Rome and was himself low individual scorer that year.

## Ball, John (1861–1940)
Finished fourth in The Open of 1878 at the age of 16 and became the first amateur to win the title in 1890 when The Open was played at Prestwick. He won the Amateur Championship eight times and shares with Bobby Jones the distinction of being the winner of The Open and Amateur in the same year – 1890. He grew up on the edge of the links area which became the Royal Liverpool Golf Club and the birthplace of the Amateur. He was a master at keeping the ball low in the wind, but with the same straight-faced club could cut the ball up for accurate approach shots. His run of success could have been greater but for military service in the South African campaign and the First World War.

## Barnes, Jim (1887–1966)
Raised in Cornwall before emigrating to California, where he took US citizenship, the 6ft 4ins golfer enjoyed outstanding success in the professional major championships of the early 20th century. He won The Open at Prestwick in 1925 and enjoyed a consistent record in the oldest major throughout the 1920s. He also made his mark with a string of top ten finishes in the US Open before winning America's national championship in 1921 in Maryland by nine strokes, a record which stood for nearly 80 years. And in the US PGA Championship, which was initially a match-play tournament, he won the first two stagings in 1916 and 1919.

## Barton, Pamela (1917–1943)
At the age of 19 she held both the British and American Ladies Championships in 1936. She was French champion at 17, runner-up in the British in both 1934 and '35 and won the title again in 1939. A Curtis Cup team member in 1934 and '36 she was a Flight Officer in the WAAF when she was killed in a plane crash at an RAF airfield in Kent.

## Berg, Patty (1915–2006)
The golf pioneer who won an LPGA Tour record 15 major titles and was one of the 13 founding members of the tour in 1950. She was the LPGA Tour's first president from 1950–52 and was the tour's money leader in 1954, '55 and '57 ending her career with 60 victories. She was a member of the LPGA Tour and World Golf Halls of Fame. She was described as a pioneer, an athlete, a mentor, a friend and an entertainer and had a great sense of humour.

## Bolt, Tommy (1916–2008)
The 1958 US Open champion and two-time Ryder Cup player who is remembered as much for his short temper as his short game. He had a penchant for throwing clubs insisting it was better to throw them ahead of you in order to avoid having to walk back for them! Known as "Terrible Tommy" he was a founding member of the US Champions Tour. In the 1957 Ryder Cup at Lindrick he lost a bad-tempered game to fiery Scot Eric Brown.

## Boros, Julius (1920–1994)
Became the oldest winner of a major championship when he won the USPGA in 1968 at the age of 48. He twice won the US Open, in 1952 and again 11 years later at Brookline when he was 43. In a play-off he beat Jackie Cupit by three shots and Arnold Palmer by six. He played in four Ryder Cup matches between 1959–67, winning nine of his 16 matches and losing only three.

## Bousfield, Ken (1919–2000)
Although a short hitter even by the standards of his era, he won five out of 10 matches in six Ryder Cup appearances from 1949–61. He captured the PGA Match Play Championship in 1955, one of eight tournament victories in Britain, and also won six European Opens. He represented England in the World Cup at Wentworth in 1956 and Tokyo in 1957.

## Bradshaw, Harry (1913–1950)
One of Ireland's most loved golfers whose swing Bernard Darwin described as "rustic and rugged". With Christy O'Connor he won the Canada Cup (World Cup) for Ireland in Mexico in 1958 but he is also remembered for losing the 1949 Open to Bobby Locke after having hit one shot out of a bottle at the fifth on the second day. That bit of bad luck, it was later considered, cost him £10,000.

## Braid, James (1870–1950)
Together with Harry Vardon and J.H. Taylor he formed the Great Triumvirate and dominated the game for 20 years before the 1914–18 war. In a 10-year period from 1901 he became the first player in the history of the event to win The Open five times – and also finished second on three occasions. In that same period he won the Match Play Championship four times and the French Open. He was a tall, powerful player who hit the ball hard but always retained an appearance of outward calm. He was one of the founder members of the Professional Golfers' Association and did much to elevate the status of the professional golfer. He was responsible for the design of many golf courses and served as professional at Walton Heath for 45 years. He was an honorary

# Severiano Ballesteros

## 1957–2011

Adventurous, exciting to watch and always unpredictable, the qualities which laid the foundation for the success of Severiano Ballesteros as a driven stroke-play champion were, if anything, even more formidable assets when the Spaniard conquered the arena of match-play. As well as his five major titles, the crowning achievement of a charismatic career cut short at the early age of 54, was an example he set for European golf in the Ryder Cup.

Of the many attributes Ballesteros shared with Arnold Palmer, the swashbuckling adventurer to whom he was most often compared, fearlessness was perhaps the most significant trait. His whole career was governed by passion and romanticism. And, just like Palmer in America, his blows of brilliance enlarged the audience for professional golf in Europe through TV exposure.

While the world of golf loved Seve's ebullience, he was held in particularly high esteem in the British Isles. The galleries in the UK were smitten from the moment at Royal Birkdale in 1976 when he executed a devious chip sending it running between the bunkers on the home hole rather than taking the aerial route. It was a shot of such sublime touch and imagination, no one who saw the teenager pull it off would have been surprised when the Spaniard went to have his name inscribed on the Claret Jug three times in 1979, 1984 and 1988. All told he won 52 titles between 1976 and 1999 including two stagings of The Masters at Augusta in 1980 and 1983.

When asked to choose the greatest player he'd ever seen, Lee Trevino selected the Spaniard. "Jack Nicklaus made a plan," he said. "Tiger Woods makes a plan. Seve never made a plan. He just made things happen. He had something we didn't have."

Born in a small village near Santander in the north of Spain, Seve was surrounded by family who played the game and caddied at Pedrena. As a boy, his brother Manuel gave him the gift of a 3 iron and the youngster used the club to perfect a variety of shots on a local beach. He became a professional before celebrating his 17th birthday and two years later made his mark in The Open at Birkdale when he led for three days and finished runner-up alongside Jack Nicklaus to Johnny Miller.

Apart from his triumphs on the British linksland, Ballesteros was more at home at Augusta National than anywhere else. It's worth recalling, before chronic back trouble sapped his power, how long Seve was off the tee. The combination of distance and touch was perfect for the Masters. His performances in Georgia in 1980 and 1983 were as dazzling as anything ever produced at Augusta. The bogeys which punished Seve's wayward tendencies were exceeded by electrifying surges of birdies and eagles. When Seve was around, the game was always human, never robotic. For example, in Friday's second round of the 1980 Masters, Seve struck a hook so far left on the 17th hole that his ball finished on the seventh green. However, after taking a free drop, he launched a blind iron shot onto the correct green and recovered by holing the improbable birdie putt.

When the 23-year-old slipped into a Green Jacket, church bells in his home town of Pedrena rang out in celebration. There was more music in 1983 when he started his final round at Augusta with a devastating flurry of birdie, eagle, par, birdie – four under par for the opening four holes – which the Spaniard regarded as "the best I ever played in my life." The greatest stroke, though, was surely that 15 foot birdie putt on the 18th green at St Andrews which sealed his second Open triumph. Ballesteros calls it "El Momento" and a silhouette of his ensuing celebration is surely the defining image of his career.

In the Ryder Cup, the arrival of Ballesteros and the example he set to others changed everything. There was an intensity about Ballesteros' play which galvanised the European cause. In many respects, the story of the modern Ryder Cup can be told in two distinct phases: before and after Seve. He played eight times in the match, finishing on the winning side four times, and was a winning captain in 1997.

Problems in his lower back caused a deterioration in his game in the Nineties and the last of his 50 European Tour wins came at the Spanish Open in 1995. He was diagnosed with a brain tumour after collapsing with an epileptic fit at Madrid Airport in 2008. Caught up in the most daunting challenge of his life, Ballesteros endured four operations, six subsequent courses of chemotherapy and radio-therapy treatment with the resilience of a champion before passing away in 2010. He may have died tragically early but the passion with which he played the game ensures his memory will live for ever.

member of that club for 25 years and became one of its directors. He was also an honorary member of The R&A.

## Brewer, Gay (1932–2007)

Winner of the 1967 Masters he was one of the most popular figures on the US Tour and later the Champions Tour. His love of the game, his joviality and his story-telling were all part of the legacy of the man from Lexington, Kentucky, whose loopy swing was one of the most unorthodox.

## Brown, Eric (1925–1986)

Twice captained the Ryder Cup side and for many years partnered John Panton for Scotland in the World Cup. A larger-than-life personality, he was one of two Cup captains who came from the Bathgate club. The other was Bernard Gallacher, who played in the 1969 match which Brown captained.

## Bruen, Jimmy (1920–1972)

Won the Irish Amateur at the age of 17 and defended the title successfully the following year. At 18 he became the youngest ever Walker Cup player at that time and in practice for the match at St Andrews in 1938 equalled the then amateur course record of 68 set by Bobby Jones.

## Camicia, Mario (1941–2011)

Often referred to as Italy's "Mr Golf" Mario was a passionate lover of the game who did much to make Italians more aware of and more interested in the game. For many years he ran the Italian Open, wrote in magazines and newspapers and became the country's first television golf commentator. He was the voice of golf in Italy who enjoyed the success Costantino Rocca, the Molinari brothers and Matteo Manassero had on the international scene. Commenting on his death Franco Chimenti, President of the Italian Federation, said: "The game has lost a good friend."

## Campbell, Bill (1923–2013)

One of America's most distinguished golfers and administrators, Campbell won the US Amateur Championship in 1964 at the age of 41, ten years after finishing runner-up in The Amateur Championship to Australian Doug Bachli at Muirfield. A career amateur, he teed up in 33 consecutive US Amateurs between 1941 and 1977. All told he played in the event 37 times after making his debut at 15 in 1938. He was the first man to serve as both President of the United States Golf Association (in 1983) and captain of the Royal and Ancient Golf Club of St Andrews (in 1987–88). He played in eight Walker Cup matches between 1951 and 1975 and was captain of the USA in 1955 at St Andrews. The native of West Virginia loved Scotland and was a member of the World Golf Hall of Fame. He was educated at Princeton, was a captain in the US Army, and made more appearances, 17, at the Masters than any other amateur. He also played in the US Open 14 times. When he became only the third American to captain the Royal and Ancient, his tee shot at the driving-in

ceremony was worthy of his illustrious predecessor, Francis Ouimet. In 1988, at the age of 65, he became the first serving Royal and Ancient Captain since Cyril Tolley in 1948 to play in The Amateur Championship during his year in office. He sat on the USGA executive committee from 1962–65 and again from 1977–84, serving as treasurer in 1978–79, vice-president in 1980–81 and president in 1982–83. He became a life member of The R&A in 2011 during his 60th year of membership.

## Campbell, Dorothy Iona (1883–1946)

One of only two golfers to win the British, American and Canadian Ladies titles. In total she won these three major championships seven times.

## Carr, Joe (1922–2004)

The first Irishman to captain the Royal and Ancient Golf Club of St Andrews, he was winner of three British Amateur Championship titles in 1953, 1958 and 1960. He played in or captained Walker Cup sides from 1947 to 1963 making a record 11 appearances. He was the first Irishman to play in The Masters at Augusta, made 23 consecutive appearances for Ireland in the Home Internationals and was a regular winner of the West of Ireland and East of Ireland Championships. At one point in an illustrious career he held 18 different course records. An ebullient, fast-talking personality with a somewhat eccentric swing, he was one of Ireland's best known and best loved golfers. In 2007 he was inducted posthumously into the World Golf Hall of Fame in St Augustine, Florida.

## Coe, Charlie (1923–2007)

Another fine American amateur golfer who finished runner-up with Arnold Palmer to Gary Player in the 1961 Masters at Augusta. Twice US Amateur champion in 1949 and 1958, he played in six Walker Cup matches and was non-playing captain in 1959. He won seven and halved two of the 13 games he played. Winner of the Bobby Jones award in 1964. Born in Oklahoma City, he never considered turning professional.

## Compston, Archie (1893–1962)

Beat Walter Hagen 18 and 17 in a 72-hole challenge match at Moor Park in 1928 and tied for second place in the 1925 Open. Played in the Ryder Cup in 1927–29–31.

## Cotton, Sir Henry (1907–1987)

The first player to be knighted for services to golf, he died a few days before the announcement of the award was made. He won The Open Championship three times, which included a round of 65 at Royal St George's in 1934 after which the famous Dunlop golf ball was named. His final 71 at Carnoustie to win the 1937 Championship in torrential rain gave him great satisfaction and he set another record with a 66 at Muirfield on the way to his third triumph in 1948 watched by King George VI. He won the Match Play Championship three times and was runner-up on three occasions. He also won 11 Open titles in

Europe, played three times in the Ryder Cup and was non-playing captain in 1953. Sir Henry worked hard to promote the status of professional golf and also championed the cause of young golfers, becoming a founder member of the Golf Foundation. He was a highly successful teacher, author and architect, spending much time at Penina, a course he created in southern Portugal. He was an honorary member of The R&A.

## Crawley, Leonard  (1903–1981)
Played four times in the Walker Cup in 1932–34–38–47 and won the English Amateur in 1931. He also played first-class cricket for Worcestershire and Essex and toured the West Indies with the MCC in 1936. After the Second World War he was golf correspondent for the *Daily Telegraph* for 30 years.

## The Curtis sisters, Harriet  (1878–1944)
## Margaret  (1880–1965)
Donors of the Curtis Cup still contested biennially between the USA and GB&I. Harriet won the US Women's Amateur in 1906 and lost in the following year's final to her sister Margaret, who went on to win the championship three times.

## Daly, Fred  (1911–1990)
Daly won The Open at Royal Liverpool in 1947 and in four of the next five years was never out of the top four in the Championship. At Portrush, where he was born, he finished fourth to Max Faulkner in 1951, the only time The Open has been played in Northern Ireland. He was Ulster champion 11 times and three times captured the prestigious PGA Match Play Championship. He was a member of the Ryder Cup team four times, finishing on a high note at Wentworth in 1953 when he won his foursomes match in partnership with Harry Bradshaw and then beat Ted Kroll 9 and 7 in the singles.

## Darwin, Bernard  (1876–1961)
One of the most gifted and authoritative writers on golf, he was also an accomplished England international player for more than 20 years. While in America to report the 1922 Walker Cup match for The Times, he was called in to play and captain the side when Robert Harris became ill. A grandson of Charles Darwin, he was Captain of the Royal and Ancient Golf Club of St Andrews in 1934–35. In 1937 he was awarded the CBE for services to literature. He was inducted posthumously into the World Golf Hall of Fame in 2005.

## Demaret, Jimmy  (1910–1983)
Three times Masters champion, coming from five strokes behind over the final six holes to beat Jim Ferrier by two in 1950, he also won six consecutive tournaments in 1940 while still performing as a night club singer. He won all six games he played in the 1947, 1949 and 1951 Ryder Cup matches.

## Dey, Joseph C (Joe)  (1907–1991)
A former sportswriter who covered the final leg of Bobby Jones' Grand Slam in 1930 he joined the USGA and srved as executive director from 1934 to 1968. Following his retirement he was appointed the first Commissioner of the PGA Tour – a post he held from 1969 to 1974. Dey also helped to synchronise the rules of golf around the world, instigated the PGA Tour's Players Championship and in 1975 was honorary captain of the Royal and Ancient Golf Club of St Andrews.

## Dobereiner, Peter  (1925–1996)
A multi-talented journalist in various fields who wrote eloquently, knowledgeably and amusingly on golf in many books, *Golf Digest*, and *Golf World* magazines and in *The Observer* and *Guardian* newspapers for whom he was correspondent for many years. Born of English-Scottish-Danish-Red Indian and German parentage he claimed he stubbornly refused all efforts by King's College, Taunton and Lincoln College, Oxford to impart a rudimentary education so chose journalism as a profession.

## Duncan, George  (1884–1964)
Won The Open in 1920 by making up 13 shots on the leader over the last two rounds and came close to catching Walter Hagen for the title two years later. Renowned as one of the fastest players, his book was entitled *Golf at the Gallop*.

## Faulkner, Max  (1916–2005)
One of the game's most extrovert and colourful personalities, who won the 1951 Open Championship at Royal Portrush, the only time the event was played in Northern Ireland. He played in five Ryder Cups and was deservedly if belatedly recognised for his contribution to the game with an honour in 2001 when he was awarded the OBE. His son-in-law is Brian Barnes, another golfing extrovert.

## Ferguson, Bob  (1848–1915)
The Open Championship winner three times in succession between 1880–82. He then lost a 36-hole play-off for the title by one stroke to Willie Fernie in 1883. He had shown his potential when, at the age of 18, he had won a tournament at Leith Links against the game's leading professionals.

## Fernie, Willie  (1851–1924)
In 1882 he was second to Bob Ferguson in The Open over his home course at St Andrews. The following year he beat the same player in a 36-hole play-off for the championship over Ferguson's home links at Musselburgh.

## Garrett, Maureen (née Ruttle)  (1922–2011)
President of the Ladies' Golf Union from 1982 to 1985, she captained the Curtis Cup (1960) and Vagliano Trophy (1961) teams. In 1983 won the Bobby Jones award presented annually by the United States Golf Association to a person who emulates Jones' spirit, personal qualities and attitude to the game and its players.

## Garvey, Philomena  (1927–2009)
Born in Drogheda she was one of Ireland's most successful competitors winning the Irish Ladies title 15

times between 1946 and 1970. She played six times in the Curtis Cup between 1948 and 1960 and won the British Ladies Amateur title in 1957. In 1964 she turned professional but was later re-instated an amateur.

## Goldschmid Isa (née Bevione)   (1925–2002)

One of Italy's greatest amateurs, she won her national title 21 times between 1947 and 1974 and was ten times Italian Open champion between 1952 and 1969. Among her other triumphs were victories in the 1952 Spanish Ladies and the 1973 French Ladies.

## Hagen, Walter   (1892–1969)

A flamboyant character who used a hired Rolls Royce as a changing room because professionals were not allowed in many clubhouses, he once gave his £50 cheque for winning The Open to his caddie. He won four consecutive USPGA Championships from 1924 when it was still decided by matchplay. He was four times a winner of The Open, in 1922–24–28–29 and captured the US Open title in 1914 and 1919. He captained and played in five Ryder Cup encounters between 1927–35, winning seven of his nine matches and losing only once. He was non-playing captain in 1937.

## Harper, Chandler   (1914–2004)

Born in Portsmouth, VA, he was winner of the 1950 US PGA Championship. He won over ten tournaments and was elected to the US PGA Hall of Fame in 1969. Once shot 58 (29-29) round a 6100 yards course in Portsmouth.

## Henning, Harold   (1934–2005)

One of three brothers from a well-known South African golf family he was a regular winner of golf events in his home country and Europe and had two wins on the US Tour. Played ten times for South Africa in the World Cup winning the event with Gary Player in Madrid in 1965.

## Herd, Alexander 'Sandy'   (1868–1944)

When he first played in The Open at the age of 17 he possessed only four clubs. His only Championship success came in the 1902 Open at Hoylake, the first player to capture the title using the new rubber-cored ball. He won the Match Play Championship at the age of 58 and took part in his last Open at St Andrews in 1939 at the age of 71.

## Hilton, Harold   (1869–1942)

Winner of the Amateur Championship four times between 1900 and 1913, he also became the first player and the only Briton to hold both the British and US Amateur titles in the same year 1911. He won The Open in 1892 at Muirfield, the first time the Championship was extended to 72 holes, and again in 1897 at Hoylake. A small but powerful player he was the first editor of Golf Monthly.

## Hogan, Ben   (1912–1997)

One of only five players to have won all four major championships, his record of capturing three in the same season has been matched by Tiger Woods. He dominated the golfing scene in America after the Second World War and in 1953 won the Masters, US Open and The Open Championship. A clash of dates between The Open and USPGA Championship prevented an attempt on the Grand Slam, but his poor state of health after a near fatal car crash four years earlier would have made the matchplay format of 10 rounds in six days in the USPGA an impossibility. After his car collided with a Greyhound bus in fog, it was feared that Hogan might never walk again. He had won three majors before the accident and he returned to capture six more. His only appearance in The Open was in his tremendous season of 1953 and he recorded rounds of 73-71-70-68 to win by four strokes at Carnoustie. His dramatic life story was made into a Hollywood film entitled Follow the Sun starring Glenn Ford as Hogan.

## Howard, Barclay   (1953–2008)

Leading amateur in the 1997 Open at Royal Troon he battled leukemia which had been diagnosed after he played in his second Walker Cup in 1997. When Dean Robertson won the 1999 Italian Open he dedicated his victory to Barclay as tribute to the courage and adversity he showed in attempting to beat the disease.

## Hunt, Bernard   (1930–2013)

A founder member of the European Tour and the European Senior Tour, he played in eight Ryder Cups including the winning side at Lindrick in 1957 and the side which drew with America in 1969 at Royal Birkdale. He and his brother Geoff played together in the 1963 side. He later captained the 1973 and 1975 teams. He won the European Order of Merit three times, won 30 titles and had four top 5 finishes in The Open Championship. He captained the PGA in 1966 and again from 1975–77. He was honoured with an MBE.

## Hutchinson, Horace   (1859–1932)

Runner-up in the first Amateur Championship in 1885, he won the title in the next two years and reached the final again in 1903. Represented England from 1902–07. He was a prolific writer on golf and country life and became the first English Captain of the Royal and Ancient Golf Club of St Andrews in 1908.

## Jarman, Ted   (1907–2003)

He competed in the 1935 Ryder Cup at Ridgewood, New Jersey, and until his death in 2003 he had been the oldest living Cup golfer. When he was 76 years old and before he had to stop playing because of arthritis he shot a 75.

## Jones, Bobby   (1902–1971)

Always remembered for his incredible and unrepeatable achievement in 1930 of winning The Open and Amateur Championships of Britain and America in one outstanding season – the original and unchallenged Grand Slam. At the end of that year he retired from competitive golf at the age of 28. His victories included four US Opens, five US Amateur titles, three Opens in Britain and one Amateur Championship. Although his swing was stylish and fluent, he suffered badly from nerves and was often sick and unable to eat during championships. He was also an accomplished scholar, gaining first-class honours degrees in law, English literature and mechanical engineering at three different universities. He subsequently opened a law practice in Atlanta and developed the idea of creating the Augusta National course and staging an annual invitation event which was to become known as The Masters. He was made an honorary member of the Royal and Ancient Golf Club in 1956 and two years later was given the freedom of the Burgh of St Andrews at an emotional ceremony. He died after many years of suffering from a crippling spinal disease. The tenth hole on the Old Course bears his name.

## King, Sam (1911–2003)

He played Ryder Cup golf immediately before and after World War II and came third in the 1939 Open behind Dick Burton at St Andrews. In the 1947 Ryder Cup he prevented an American whitewash in the singles by beating Herman Kaiser. He was British Senior Champion in 1961 and 1962 and was often described as "the old master" – a golfer noted for his long, straight drives and superb putting.

## Kirkaldy, Andrew (1860–1934)

First honorary professional appointed by The R&A, he lost a play-off for The Open Championship of 1889 to Willie Park at Musselburgh. He was second in the championship three times, a further three times finished third and twice fourth. A powerful player, he was renowned for speaking his mind.

## Laidlay, John Ernest (1860–1940)

The man who first employed the overlapping grip which was later credited to Harry Vardon and universally known as the Vardon grip, Laidlay was a finalist in the Amateur Championship six times in seven years from 1888, winning the title twice at a time when John Ball, Horace Hutchinson and Harold Hilton were at their peak. He was runner-up in The Open to Willie Auchterlonie at Prestwick in 1893. Among the 130 medals he won, were the Gold Medal and Silver Cross in R&A competitions.

## Leitch, Charlotte Cecilia "Cecil" (1891–1977)

Christened Charlotte Cecilia, but universally known as Cecil, her list of international victories would undoubtedly have been greater but for the blank golfing years of the first world war. She first won the British Ladies Championship in 1908 at the age of 17. In 1914 she took the English, French and British titles and successfully defended all three when competition was resumed after the war. In all she won the French Championship five times, the British four times, the English twice, the Canadian once. Her total of four victories in the British has never been beaten and has been equalled only by her great rival Joyce

Wethered. The victory in Canada was by a margin of 17 and 15 in the 36-hole final.

## Lema, Tony (1934–1966)

His first visit to Britain, leaving time for only 27 holes of practice around the Old Course at St Andrews, culminated in Open Championship victory in 1964 by five shots over Jack Nicklaus. He had won three tournaments in four starts in America before arriving in Scotland and gave great credit for his Open success to local caddie Tip Anderson and to the putter Arnold Palmer had loaned him for the week. He played in the Ryder Cup in 1963 and 1965 with an outstanding record. He lost only once in 11 matches, halved twice and won eight. Lema and his wife were killed when a private plane in which they were travelling to a tournament crashed in Illinois.

## Little, Lawson (1910–1968)

Won the Amateur Championships of Britain and America in 1934 and successfully defended both titles the following year. He then turned his amateur form into a successful professional career, starting in 1936 with victory in the Canadian Open. He won the US Open in 1940 after a play-off against Gene Sarazen.

## Locke, Bobby (1917–1987)

The son of Northern Irish emigrants to South Africa, Arthur D'Arcy Locke was playing off plus four by the age of 18 and won the South African Boys, Amateur and Open Championships. On his first visit to Britain in 1936 he was leading amateur in The Open Championship. Realising that his normal fade was leaving him well short of the leading players, he deliberately developed the hook shot to get more run on the ball. It was to become his trade-mark throughout a long career. He was encouraged to try the American tour in 1947 and won five tournaments, one by the record margin of 16 shots. More successes followed and the USPGA framed a rule which banned him from playing in their events, an action described by Gene Sarazen as "the most disgraceful action by any golf organisation". Disillusioned by the American attitude, Locke then played most of his golf in Europe, winning The Open four times. He shared a period of domination with Peter Thomson between 1949–1958 when they won the championship four times each, only Max Faulker in 1951 and Ben Hogan in 1953 breaking the sequence. In his final Open victory at St Andrews in 1957 he failed to replace his ball in the correct spot on the 18th green after moving it from fellow competitor Bruce Crampton's line. The mistake, which could have led to disqualification, was only spotted on television replays. The R&A Championship Committee rightly decided that Locke, who had won by three strokes, had gained no advantage, and allowed the result to stand. Following a career in which he won over 80 events around the world he was made an honorary member of The R&A in 1976.

## Longhurst, Henry (1909–1978)

Golf captain of Cambridge University he was winner of the German Amateur title and runner-up in the French and Swiss Championships in 1936. He became the most perceptive and readable golf correspondent of his time and a television commentator who never wasted a single word. His relaxed, chatty style was based on the premise that he was explaining the scene to a friend in his favourite golf club bar. For 25 years his *Sunday Times* column ran without a break and became compulsory reading for golfers and non-golfers alike. He had a brief spell as a member of parliament and was awarded the CBE for services to golf.

## Lunt, Michael (1935–2007)
The former Amateur and English Amateur champion who played most of his golf at Walton Heath died during his captaincy of the Royal and Ancient Golf Club of St Andrews – an honour which was well-deserved for a golfer who was liked and admired as much for his work as an administrator as his prowess on the links. Son of Stanley Lunt, the 1934 English amateur champion, Michael played on four Walker Cup teams including the one that shocked the Americans by drawing at Five Farms in 1965. He was also a member of the winning Great Britain and Ireland side captained by Joe Carr in the World Amateur Team Championship for the Eisenhower Trophy a year earlier at Olgiata in Rome. After working in the family business he moved to the Slazenger company and later was secretary manager at the Royal Mid-Surrey club before he retired. He is survived by his wife Vicki and son and daughter.

## McCormack, Mark (1931–2003)
The Cleveland lawyer who created a golf management empire after approaching Arnold Palmer to look after his affairs. A keen golfer himself, he became one of the most influential and powerful men in sport, managing many golfing legends including Tiger Woods. He was responsible for the development of the modern game commercially and started the World Match Play Championship at Wentworth in 1964.

## McDonald, C.B. (1855–1939)
Credited with building the first 18-hole golf course in the United States and instrumental in forming the United States Golf Association. He won the first US Amateur Championship in 1895. He was elected posthumously into the World Golf Hall of Fame in 2007.

## Mackenzie, Alister (1870–1934)
A family doctor and surgeon, he became involved with Harry S. Colt in the design of the Alwoodley course in Leeds, where he was a founder member and honorary secretary. He eventually abandoned his medical career and worked full time at golf course architecture. There are many outstanding examples of his work in Britain, Australia, New Zealand and America. His most famous creation, in partnership with Bobby Jones, is the Augusta National course in Georgia, home of The Masters.

## Mackenzie, Keith (1921–1990)
The commanding secretary of the Royal and Ancient Golf Club of St Andrews from 1967 to 1983 who,

along with Arnold Palmer, Jack Nicklaus and Gary Player ensured The Open, the oldest of the four majors, remained a truly international event. In addition to his normal club duties, he travelled extensively as an ambassador for The Open making friends with the professionals and encouraging foreign participation in the Championship.

## Massy, Arnaud (1877–1958)
The first non-British player to win The Open Championship. Born in Biarritz, France, he defeated J.H. Taylor by two strokes at Hoylake in 1907. Four years later he tied for the title with Harry Vardon at Royal St George's, but in the play-off conceded at the 35th hole when he was five strokes behind. He won the French Open four times, the Spanish on three occasions and the Belgian title once.

## Micklem, Gerald (1911–1988)
A pre-war Oxford Blue, he won the English Amateur Championship in 1947 and 1953 and played in the Walker Cup team four times between 1947 and 1955. He was non-playing captain in 1957 and 1959. In 1976 he set a record of 36 consecutive appearances in the President's Putter, an event that he won in 1953. In addition to his playing success he was a tireless administrator, serving as chairman of The R&A Rules, Selection and Championship Committees. He was president of the English Golf Union and the European Golf Association and Captain of the Royal and Ancient Golf Club of St Andrews. In 1969 he received the Bobby Jones award for distinguished sportsmanship and services to the game. He was elected posthumously into the World Golf Hall of Fame in 2007.

## Middlecoff, Cary (1921–1998)
Dentist turned golf professional, he became one of the most prolific winners on the US tour, with 37 victories that included two US Opens and a Masters victory. In the US Open of 1949 he beat Sam Snead and Clayton Heafner at Medinah, and seven years later recaptured the title by one shot ahead of Ben Hogan and Julius Boros at Oak Hill. His Masters success came in 1955 when he established a record seven-shot winning margin over Hogan.

## Minoprio, Gloria (1907–1958)
Striking a telling blow for women's liberty on the links, Minopro was the first female golfer to wear trousers when competing in the 1933 English Ladies Close Championship. Her stylish navy outfit, white makeup and scarlet lipstick sparked controversy among the Ladies Golf Union which duly condemned the departure at Westward Ho! from billowing skirts. In a further break with convention, she played with only one club, a cleek, similar to a 3 iron. Her striking ensemble is on display today at the British Golf Museum in St Andrews. Outwith golf, she was a magician who performed for the maharajahs.

## Mitchell, Abe (1897–1947)
Said by J.H. Taylor to be the finest player never to win an Open, he finished in the top six five times. He was

more successful in the Match Play Championship, with victories in 1919, 1920 and 1929. He taught the game to St Albans seed merchant Samuel Ryder and is the figure depicted on top of the famous golf trophy.

## Moody, Orville (1933–2008)

His only victory on the PGA Tour came in the 1969 US Open for which he had had to qualify. A descendent of the native American Choctaw tribe, he is best remembered, however, for popularising the long-shafted (broom handle) putter which he had first seen used by Charlie Owens, another "yips" sufferer. If Owens invented the 50in shafted putter Moody brought it to everyone's attention when he won the 1989 US Senior Open using one. Sam Torrance, Peter Senior and Bernhard Langer all started using it after golf's ruling bodies declared the putter legal.

## Morgan, Wanda (1910–1995)

Three-time English Amateur champion, in 1931–36–37, she also captured the British title in 1935 and played three times in the Curtis Cup from 1932–36.

## Morris, Old Tom (1821–1908)

Apprenticed as a feathery ball maker to Allan Robertson in St Andrews at the age of 18 he was one of the finest golfers of his day when he took up the position of Keeper of the Green at Prestwick, where he laid out the original 12-hole course. He was 39 when he finished second in the first Open in 1860, but subsequently won the title four times. His success rate might have been much greater if he had been a better putter. His son once said: "He would be a much better player if the hole was a yard closer." A man of fierce conviction, he returned to St Andrews to take up the duties of looking after the Old Course at a salary of £50 per year, paid by The R&A. He came to regard the course as his own property and was once publicly reprimanded for closing it without authority because he considered it needed a rest. A testimonial in 1896 raised £1,240 pounds towards his old age from golfers around the world and when he retired in 1903 The R&A continued to pay his salary. He died after a fall on the stairs of the New Club in 1908, having outlived his wife, his daughter and his three sons.

## Morris, Young Tom (1851–1875)

Born in St Andrews, but brought up in Prestwick, where his father had moved to become Keeper of the Green, he won a tournament against leading professionals at the age of 13. He was only 17 when he succeeded his father as Open champion in 1868 and then defended the title successfully in the following two years to claim the winner's belt outright. There was no championship in 1871, but when the present silver trophy – the Claret Jug – became the prize in 1872, Young Tom's was the first name engraved thereon. His prodigious talent was best demonstrated in his third successive Open victory in 1870 when he played 36 holes at Prestwick in 149 strokes, 12 shots ahead of his nearest rival, superb scoring given the equipment and the condition of the course at that

time. He married in November 1874 and was playing with his father in a money match at North Berwick the following year when a telegram from St Andrews sent them hurrying back across the Firth of Forth in a private yacht. Young Tom's wife and baby had both died in childbirth. He played golf only twice after that, in matches that had been arranged long in advance, and fell into moods of deep depression. He died on Christmas morning of that same year from a burst artery in the lung. He was 24 years old. A public subscription paid for a memorial which still stands above his grave in the cathedral cemetery.

## Nelson, Byron (1912–2006)

John Byron Nelson left a legacy which many will aspire to emulate but which few will achieve. He joined the professional circuit in 1935 after a caddie shack apprenticeship which he shared with Ben Hogan and quickly established himself, winning the New Jersey Open in 1935 and going on to take The Masters title two years after. Between 1935 and 1946 he had 54 wins but although he won The Masters in 1937 and 1942, the US Open in 1939 and the US PGA Championship in 1940 and 1945 he didn't manage to pull off a Grand Slam having never won The Open Championship. The 1939 US Open is probably best remembered as the tournament Sam Snead threw away, history tending to overlook the achievement of Byron Nelson, the man who eventually took the title. After a three-way play-off with Craig Wood and Densmore Shute, Nelson went on to win the decisive 18 holes by three shots from Wood. America's entry into the second world war called a temporary halt to competitive golf for many. Nelson, denied the opportunity to serve his country due to a blood disorder, continued to play throughout 1943 and 1944, re-establishing his prominent position when full competition resumed in 1945, winning 18 times including 11 events in a row between March and August – a record unlikely ever to be broken. He was twice a member of US Ryder Cup teams – in 1937 and 1947 and had been picked for the postponed matches in 1939 and 1941. He returned to that competition in 1965 when he captained the victorious US team. His only win in Europe was the 1955 French Open. He was a father figure in US golf and until he retired in 2001 was one of The Masters honorary starters along with the late Gene Sarazen and Sam Snead. In company with Snead and his old sparring partner Ben Hogan, Byron Nelson was one of the sport's most revered figures and had a particularly close friendship with five times Open champion Tom Watson.

## Norman, Moe (1929–2004)

Eccentric Canadian golf star who was renowned for the accuracy of his unusual swing. Twice Canadian Amateur Champion and winner of 13 Canadian Tour titles, he was inducted into the Canadian Golf Hall of Fame in 1995. He played very quickly, seldom slowing to line up a putt. He never had a lesson. He was such a character that Wally Uihlein, president of Titleist and Footjoy, paid him $5,000 a month for the last 10 years of his life for just "being himself".

**Ortiz-Patino, Jaime (1930–2013)**
Will always be remembered for bringing the Ryder Cup to Europe for the first time when he hosted the 1997 match at Valderrama, his course in Southern Spain which he and architect Robert Trent Jones turned into one of the best in Europe. Respected for his drive and dedication to perfection, Ortiz-Patino was awarded with an Honorary Lifetime Membership of the European Tour for his unfailing support over a long number of years.

**Ouimet, Francis (1893–1967)**
Regarded as the player who started the American golf boom after beating Harry Vardon and Ted Ray in a play-off for the 1913 US Open as a young amateur. Twice a winner of the US Amateur, he was a member of every Walker Cup team from 1922 to 1934 and non-playing captain from then until 1949. In 1951 he became the first non-British national to be elected Captain of the Royal and Ancient Golf Club of St Andrews and was a committee member of the USPGA for many years.

**Panton, John (1926–2009)**
Former honorary Professional to the Royal and Ancient Golf Club of St Andrews he was one of Scotland's best known, admired and loved profesionals who spent most of his working life at the Glenbervie Club near Stirling. A renowned iron-player he was leading British player in the 1956 Open and beat Sam Snead for the World Seniors' title in 1967 at Southport. He played in three Ryder Cup matches and was 12 times a contestant in the World Cup with the late Eric Brown as his regular partner. It was a partnership that earned considerable admiration although the two were so different in character – Panton quiet and unassuming, Brown extrovert and noisy! He won the Association of Golf Writers Trophy in 1967 for his contribution to the game and was honoured by The Queen with an MBE for his services to the game. In later years he lived with his daughter, herself a professional player of note, at Sunningdale. The ginger beer and lime drink now available in golf clubhouses was John's normal tipple and now bears his name! Over the years he took his film camera with him and left a unique library of some of the golfing greats in action.

**Park, Mungo (1839–1904)**
Younger brother to Willie Park, he spent much of his early life at sea, but won The Open Championship in 1874 at the age of 35, beating Young Tom Morris into second place by two shots on his home course at Musselburgh.

**Park, Willie (1834–1903)**
Winner of the first Open Championship in 1860. He won the title three more times, in 1863, 1866 and 1875, and was runner-up on four occasions. For 20 years he issued a standing challenge to play any man in the world for £100 a side. His reputation was built largely around a successful putting stroke and he always stressed the importance of never leaving putts short.

**Park Jr, Willie (1864–1925)**
Son of the man who won the first Open Championship, Willie Park Jr captured the title twice – in 1887 and 1889 – and finished second to Harry Vardon in 1898. He was also an accomplished clubmaker who did much to popularise the bulger driver with its convex face. He patented the wry-neck putter in 1891. One of the first and most successful professionals to design golf courses, he was responsible for many layouts in Britain, Europe and America and also wrote two highly successful books on the game.

**Patton, Billy Joe (1922–2011)**
Educated at Wake Forest, he is best remembered for holing out in one at the sixth hole en route to a closing 71 in the 1954 Masters at Augusta and failing by just one shot to play off for the Green Jacket with eventual winner Sam Snead and Ben Hogan. He played in five Walker Cups and captained the US side in 1969. In 1962 he won the USGA Bob Jones award for outstanding sportsmanship.

**Philp, Hugh (1782–1856)**
One of the master craftsmen in St Andrews in the early days of the 19th century, he was renowned for his skill in creating long-nosed putters. After his death his business was continued by Robert Forgan. Philp's clubs are much prized collector's items.

**Picard, Henry (1907–1997)**
Winner of The US Masters in 1938 and the 1939 USPGA Championship, where he birdied the final hole to tie with Byron Nelson and birdied the first extra hole for the title. Ill health cut short a career in which he won 27 tournaments.

**Price-Fisher, Elizabeth (1923–2008)**
Born in London she played in six Curtis Cup matches and, in addition to winning the 1959 British Women's Championship took titles in Denmark and Portugal, She turned professional in 1968 but was later reinstated as an amateur in 1971. For many years she worked as the ladies golf correspondent for the Daily Telegraph in London.

**Ray, Ted (1877–1943)**
Born in Jersey, his early years in golf were in competition with Channel Islands compatriot Harry Vardon and his fellow members of the Great Triumvirate, J.H. Taylor and James Braid. His only victory in The Open came in 1912, but he was runner-up to Taylor the following year and second again, to Jim Barnes of America, in 1925 when he was 48 years of age. He claimed the US Open title in 1920 and remains one of only three British players to win The Open and the US Open on both sides of the Atlantic. The others are Harry Vardon and Tony Jacklin.

**Rees, Dai (1913–1983)**
One of Britain's outstanding golfers for three decades, he played in nine Ryder Cup matches between 1937 and 1961 and was playing captain of the 1957 team which won the trophy for the first

time since 1933. He was non-playing captain in 1967. He was runner-up in The Open three times and won the PGA Match Play title four times. He was made an honorary member of the Royal and Ancient Golf Club in 1976.

### Robertson, Allan    (1815–1859)

So fearsome was Robertson's reputation as a player that when The R&A staged an annual competition for local professionals, he was not allowed to take part in order to give the others a chance. A famous maker of feather golf balls, he strongly resisted the advance of the more robust gutta percha. Tom Morris senior was his apprentice and they were reputed never to have lost a foursomes match in which they were partners.

### Rosburg, Bob    (1926–2009)

Winner of the 1959 US PGA Championship, he also made a name for himself as a golf commentator. After his playing days were over he was employed by Roone Arledge, the head of sport for ABC television, as golf's first on-course reporter – a job he did for 30 years. His characteristic "say-it-as-it-is" style means he will always be remembered by his response to the question regularly posed by one of his fellow commentators in the box … when asked how the ball was lying Rossie's regular reply was "He's got no chance!"

### Ryder, Samuel    (1858–1936)

The prosperous seed merchant was so impressed with the friendly rivalry between British and American professionals at an unofficial match at Wentworth in 1926 that he donated the famous gold trophy for the first Ryder Cup match the following year. The trophy is still presented today for the contest between America and Europe.

### Sarazen, Gene    (1902–1999)

Advised to find an outdoor job to improve his health, Sarazen became a caddie and then an assistant professional. At the age of 20 he became the first player to win the US Open and PGA titles in the same year. In claiming seven major titles he added The Open at Prince's in 1932 and when he won the second Masters tournament in 1935 he became the first of only five players to date who have won all four Grand Slam trophies during their careers. He played "the shot heard around the world" on his way to his 1935 Masters victory, holing a four-wood across the lake at the 15th for an albatross (double eagle) two. At the age of 71 he played in The Open at Troon and holed-in-one at the Postage Stamp eighth. The next day be holed from a bunker for a two at the same hole. He acted as an honorary starter at the Masters, hitting his final shot only a month before his death at 97.

### Sayers, Ben    (1857–1924)

A twinkling, elphin figure, the diminutive Sayers played a leading part in the game for more than four decades. He represented Scotland against England from 1903 to 1913 and played in every Open from 1880 to 1923.

### Sewgolum, Sewsunker "Pappa"    (1930–1978)

A former caddie he played every shot unconventionally with his left hand on the club beneath his right. He first made headlines when he beat a field of white golfers in the Natal Open at the prestigious Durban Country Club. He won the Dutch Open title three times in 1959, 1960 and 1964. The municipal course in Durban bears his name and in 2003 he received a posthumous achievement award.

### Shade, Ronnie D.B.M.    (1938–1984)

One of Scotland's greatest golfers whom many considered the world's top amateur in the mid 60s. After losing the 1962 Scottish Amateur Golf Championship final to Stuart Murray, he won that title five years in a row winning 43 consecutive ties before losing in the fourth round to Willie Smeaton at Muirfield in 1968. Taught by his father John, professional at the Duddingston club in Edinburgh, he was often referred to as "Right Down the Bloody Middle" because of his initials and consistent play. Shade won the Scottish and Irish Open Championships as a professional but was re-instated as an amateur before his death from cancer at the age of 47.

### Smith, Frances – née Bunty Stephens    (1925–1978)

Dominated post-war women's golf, winning the British Ladies Championship in 1949 and 1954, was three times a winner of the English and once the victor in the French Championship. She represented Great Britain & Ireland in six consecutive encounters from 1950, losing only three of her 11 matches, and was non-playing captain of the team in 1962 and 1972. She was awarded the OBE for her services to golf.

### Smith, Horton    (1908–1963)

In his first winter on the US professional circuit as a 20-year-old in 1928–29 he won eight out of nine tournaments. He was promoted to that year's Ryder Cup team and played again in 1933 and 1935 and remained unbeaten He won the first Masters in 1934 and repeated that success two year's later. He received the Ben Hogan Award for overcoming illness or injury and the Bobby Jones Award for distinguished sportsmanship in golf.

### Smith, Macdonald    (1890–1949)

Born into a talented Carnoustie golfing family, he was destined to become one of the finest golfers never to win The Open. He was second in 1930 and 1932, was twice third and twice fourth. His best chance came at Prestwick in 1925 when he led the field by five strokes with one round to play, but the enthusiastic hordes of Scottish supporters destroyed his concentration and he finished with an 82 for fourth place.

### Snead, Sam    (1912–2002)

Few would argue that "Slammin' Sam Snead" possessed the sweetest swing in the history of the game. 'He just walked up to the ball and poured honey all over it', it was said. Raised during the Depression in

Hot Springs, Virginia, he also died there on May 23 2002, four days short of his 90th birthday. His seven major titles comprised three Masters, three USPGA Championships and the 1946 Open at St Andrews, while he was runner-up four times but never won the US Open. But for the Second World War he would surely have added several more. He achieved a record 82 PGA Tour victories in America, the last of them at age 52, and was just as prolific round the world across six decades. He played in seven Ryder Cup matches, captained the 1969 United States team which tied at Royal Birkdale and after his retirement acted as honorary starter at The Masters until his death. Perhaps his greatest achievement came in the 1979 Quad Cities Open when he scored 67 and 66. He was 67 years of age at the time.

## Solheim, Karsten (1912–2000)
A golfing revolutionary who discovered the game at the age of 42 and, working in his garage, invented the Ping putter with its unique heel-toe weighting design, later adopted in his irons. A keen supporter of women's golf, he presented the Solheim Cup for a biennial competition between the American and European Ladies' Tours.

## Souchak, Mike (1927–2008)
He won 15 times on the PGA Tour in the 1950's and 1960's, competed in the 1959 and 1961 Ryder Cups and played for 11 years on the Champions Tour before retiring. Although he never won a major title he finished 11 times in the top 10 in majors coming third twice in the US Open.

## Spearman, Marley (1938–2011)
Superb ambassador for golf in the 1950s and 1960s whose exuberance and joie de vivre is legendary. Three times a Curtis Cup player she won the British Ladies in 1961 and again in 1962. She was English champion in 1964. In 1962 was awarded the Association of Golf Writers' Trophy for her services to golf.

## Stewart, Payne (1957–1999)
Four months after winning his second US Open title Payne Stewart was killed in a plane crash. Only a month earlier he had been on the winning United States Ryder Cup team. His first major victory was in the 1989 USPGA Championship and he claimed his first US Open title two years later after a play-off against Scott Simpson. In 1999 he holed an 18-foot winning putt to beat Phil Mickelson for the US title he was never able to defend. In 1985 he finished a stroke behind Sandy Lyle in The Open at Royal St George's and five years later he shared second place when Nick Faldo won the Championship at St Andrews.

## Stranahan, Frank R. (1922–2013)
One of golf's most successful amateurs, Stranahan won the Amateur championship at Royal St George's in 1948 and at St Andrews in 1950. He won the Mexican Amateur in 1946, 1948 and 1951 and the Canadian title in 1947 and 1948. The son of a wealthy industrialist family in Ohio, he was also leading amateur in The Open in 1947, 1949, 1950, 1951 and 1953 as well as the low amateur at The Masters four times. He played in three Walker Cups in 1947, 1949 and 1951. All told, he won more than 50 amateur titles and six US PGA Tour events. He turned professional at 32 in 1954 after again missing out on the US Amateur. A strict vegetarian, he ran in more than 100 marathons. Taught by Byron Nelson, he was twice runner-up at The Open in 1947 and 1953. The American was a dedicated supporter of The Open in the years after the Second World War when it was not fashionable for golfers on the other side of the Atlantic to enter the oldest major. One of the first golfers to put a premium on physical fitness, he was a body builder who traveled with weights and was known as the Toledo strongman. The American endured tragedy in his personal life when his wife, Ann, also a fine amateur golfer, died at 45 of cancer. His son, Frank, died of the same disease at 11 and his second son, Jimmy, died of a drug overdose at 19. He is survived by a third son, Lance.

## Tait, Freddie (1870–1900)
In 1890 Tait set a new record of 77 for the Old Course, lowering that to 72 only four years later. He was three times the leading amateur in The Open Championship and twice won the Amateur Championship, in 1896 and 1898. The following year he lost at the 37th hole of an historic final to John Ball at Prestwick. He was killed while leading a charge of the Black Watch at Koodoosberg Drift in the Boer War.

## Taylor, J.H. (1871–1963)
Winner of The Open Championship five times between 1894 and 1913, Taylor was part of the Great Triumvirate with James Braid and Harry Vardon. He tied for the title with Vardon in 1896, but lost in the play-off and was runner-up another five times. He also won the French and German Opens and finished second in the US Open. A self-educated man, he was a thoughtful and compelling speaker and became the founding father of the Professional Golfers' Association. He was made an honorary member of The R&A in 1949.

## Thomas, Dave (1934–2013)
Better known in later life as a course designer – he was the architect of more than 100 around the globe – Dave Thomas was a household name as player in the Fifties and Sixties thanks to his ability to drive the ball long and straight. Twice runner-up in The Open Championship, Welshman Thomas lost a 36 hole play-off to Peter Thomson in 1958 and was runner-up to Jack Nicklaus in 1966. He played 11 times in the World Cup for Wales and four times in the Ryder Cup. He partnered Tony Jacklin in Houston in 1967, winning two and a half points. In all he won 10 tournaments between 1961 and 1969 before retiring to concentrate on golf course design. Along with Peter Alliss he designed the Ryder Cup course at The Belfry. Some of his other best known courses are San Roque, Slaley Hall, La Manga, the Roxburgh and St Leon Rot, which will host the Solheim Cup in 2015.

He was captain of the Professional Golfers' Association for their Centenary year in 2001.

## Tolley, Cyril (1896–1978)

Won the first of his two Amateur Championships in 1920 while still a student at Oxford and played in the unofficial match which preceded the Walker Cup a year later. He played in six Walker Cup encounters and was team captain in 1924. Tolley is the only amateur to have won the French Open, a title he captured in 1924 and 1928. After winning the Amateur for the second time in 1929 he was favourite to retain the title at St Andrews the following summer but was beaten by a stymie at the 19th hole in the fourth round by Bobby Jones in the American's Grand Slam year.

## Travis, Walter (1862–1925)

Born in Australia, he won the US Amateur Championship in 1900 at the age of 38, having taken up the game only four years earlier. He won again the following year and in 1903. He became the first overseas player to win the Amateur title in Britain in 1904, using a centre-shafted Schenectady putter he had just acquired. The club was banned a short time later. He was 52 years old when he last reached the semi-finals of the US Amateur in 1914.

## Tumba, Sven (1931–2011)

A legendary ice-hockey player who played 245 times for his country and a top class soccer player he turned to golf in 1970 and was responsible for popularising the game in Sweden. Having played in the Eisenhower Trophy and won the Swedish Match Play Championship he founded his own club at Ullna and later opened the first golf course in Moscow. Helped by some of the biggest world stars including Jack Nicklaus he introduced top class professional golf with his Scandinavian Enterprise Open. Later in life he organised the World Golfers' Championship, played in 40 different countries. Always enthusiastic and well-loved, Sven was truly a Swedish sporting legend to whom golf owes much.

## Valentine, Jessie (1915–2006)

A winner of titles before and after World War II, she was an impressive competitor and was one of the first ladies to make a career out of professional golf. She won the British Ladies as an amateur in 1937 and again in 1955 and 1958 and was Scottish champion in 1938 and 1939 and four times between 1951 and 1956. But for the war years it is certain she would have had more titles and victories. She played in seven Curtis Cups between 1936 and 1958 and represented Scotland in the Home Internationals on 17 occasions between 1934 and 1958.

## Van Donck, Flory (1912–1992)

Although his style was unorthodox he will always be remembered as a great putter. He remains Belgium's most successful player. He won the Belgian title 16 times between 1939 and 1956 and was successful, too, often more than once in the Dutch, Italian, French, German, Swiss and Portuguese Cham-pionships. In 1963 he won seven titles in Europe. Twice runner-up in The Open in 1956 to Peter Thomson at Hoylake and in 1959 to Gary Player at Muirfield he represented 19 times in the World Cup including the 1967 competition at the age of 67.

## Vardon, Harry (1870–1937)

Still the only player to have won The Open Championship six times, Vardon, who was born in Jersey, won his first title in 1896, in a 36-hole play-off against J.H. Taylor and his last in 1914, this time beating Taylor by three shots. He won the US Open in 1900 and was beaten in a play-off by Francis Ouimet in 1913. He was one of the most popular of the players at the turn of the century and did much to popularise the game in America with his whistle-stop exhibition tours. He popularised the overlapping grip which still bears his name, although it was first used by Johnny Laidlay. He was also the originator of the modern upright swing, moving away from the flat sweeping action of previous eras. After his Open victory of 1903, during which he was so ill he thought he would not be able to finish, he was diagnosed with tuberculosis. His legendary accuracy and low scoring are commemorated with the award of two Vardon Trophies – in America for the player each year with the lowest scoring average and in Europe for the golfer who tops the money list.

## Vare, Glenna – née Collett (1903–1989)

Won the first of her six US Ladies Amateur titles at the age of 19 in 1922 and the last in 1935. A natural athlete, she attacked the ball with more power than was normal in the women's game. The British title eluded her, although at St Andrews in 1929 she was three-under par and five up on Joyce Wethered after 11 holes, but lost to a blistering counter-attack. She played in the first Curtis Cup match in 1932 and was a member of the team in 1936, 1938 and 1948 and was captain in 1934 and 1950.

## Venturi, Ken (1931–2013)

A member of the World Golf Hall of Fame, Venturi was a US Open champion who became a respected broadcaster in America after injury cut short his playing career. The winner of 14 events on the US PGA Tour, the highlight of his career came in 1964 at Congressional when he defied medical advice in sweltering temperatures to win his only major by four strokes from Tommy Jacobs. Told by doctors to withdraw or risk heat stroke, Venturi chose to carry on and came from two behind in the final round to win by four shots. A Ryder Cup golfer and captain of the USA at the Presidents Cup, Venturi was a runner-up at The Masters as an amateur. Taught by Byron Nelson, he was forced to retire from the game because of carpal tunnel syndrome in 1967. He then joined the American TV network, CBS, and went on to enjoy a 35 year career as a broadcaster.

## Von Nida, Norman (1914–2007)

Generally considered the father of Australian golf, he won over 80 titles worldwide. The Australian development Tour is named after him. Played extensively in Britain in the 1940s and 1960s. In later life he was registered bind. Generally regarded as the first golfer to make his income on Tour rather than being based at a club. In 1947 he won seven times in Europe.

## Walker, George (1874–1953)
The President of the United States Golf Association who donated the trophy for the first match in 1922, at Long Island, New York, and which is still presented to the winning team in the biennial matches between the USA and Great Britain & Ireland. His grandson and great grandson, George Walker Bush and George Bush Jr have both become Presidents of the United States.

## Ward, Charles Harold (1911–2001)
Charlie Ward played in three Ryder Cup matches from 1947–1951 and was twice third in The Open, behind Henry Cotton at Muirfield in 1948 and Max Faulkner at Royal Portrush in 1951.

## Ward, Harvie (1926–2004)
Born in Tarboro, North Carolina, he was winner of the Amateur Championship in 1952 when he beat Frank Stranahan 6 and 5 at Prestwick, he went on to win the US title in 1955 and 1956 and the Canadian Amateur in 1964. He played in the 1953, 1955 and 1959 Walker Cup matches and won all of his six games.

## Wethered, Joyce – Lady Heathcoat-Amory (1901–1997)
Entered her first English Ladies Championship in 1920 at the age of 18 and beat holder Cecil Leitch in the final. She remained unbeaten for four years, winning 33 successive matches. After they had played together at St Andrews, Bobby Jones remarked: "I have never played golf with anyone, man or woman, amateur or professional, who made me feel so utterly outclassed."

## Wethered, Roger (1899–1983)
Amateur champion in 1923 and runner-up in 1928 and 1930, he played five times in the Walker Cup, acting as playing captain at Royal St George's in 1930, and represented England against Scotland every year from 1922 to 1930. In The Open Championship at St Andrews in 1921 he tied with Jock Hutchison despite incurring a penalty for treading on his own ball. Due to play in a cricket match in England the following day, he was persuaded to stay in St Andrews for the play-off, but lost by 150–159 over 36 holes.

## Whitcombe, Ernest (1890–1971)
## Charles (1895–1978)
## Reginald (1898–1957)
The remarkable golfing brothers from Burnham, Somerset, were all selected for the Ryder Cup team of 1935. Charlie and Eddie were paired together and won the only point in the foursomes in a heavy 9–3 defeat by the American team. Reg won the gale-lashed Open at Royal St George's in 1938, with a final round of 78 on a day when the exhibition tent was blown

into the sea. Ernest finished second to Walter Hagen in 1924 and Charlie was third at Muirfield in 1935.

## White, Ronnie (1921–2005)
A five times Walker Cup team member between 1947 and 1953 he was one of the most impressive players in post-war amateur golf. He won six and halved one of the 10 games he played in the Walker Cup. He won the English Amateur Championship in 1949, the English Amateur Stroke-play title the following two years and was silver medallist as leading amateur in The Open Championship in 1961 played at his home club of Royal Birkdale.

## Will, George (1937–2010)
George Will from Ladybank in Fife was a three-time Ryder Cup player in 1963–65 and 67. He was for many years the club professional at Sundridge Park where he was longtime coach to former Walker Cup and European Tour player Roger Chapman but was also long-time coach to the Belgian National team. An always stylish player he was a former Scottish Boys, British Youths and Army champion.

## Wilson, Enid (1910–1996)
Completed a hat-trick of victories in the Ladies British Amateur Championship from 1931–33. She was twice a semi-finalist in the American Championship, won the British Girls' and English Ladies' titles and played in the inaugural Curtis Cup match, beating Helen Hicks 2 and 1 in the singles. Retiring early from competitive golf, she was never afraid to express strongly held views on the game in her role as women's golf correspondent of the Daily Telegraph.

## Wind, Herbert Warren (1917–2005)
One of if not the most distinguished writers on golf in America, he authored 14 books on the game he loved with a passion. A long-time contributor to the New Yorker magazine, he is still the only writer to have received the United States Golf Association's Bobby Jones award for distinguished sportsmanship – an honour bestowed on him in 1995, the year the Association celebrated its centenary. The award was appropriate because he was a life-long admirer of Jones and was a regular at The Masters each year where he has been given the credit for naming, in 1958, the difficult stretch of holes from the 11th to the 13th as Amen Corner, arguing you said "Amen" if you negotiated them without dropping a shot.

## Wood, Craig (1901–1968)
Both Masters and US Open champion in 1941, Wood finally made up for a career of near misses, having lost play-offs for all four major championships between 1933 and 1939. He was three times a member of the American Ryder Cup team.

## Wooldridge, Ian (1932–2007)
One of the most respected sports writers who enjoyed nothing more than covering golf. His Daily Mail column was required reading for 40 years.

## Yates, Charlie   (1913–2005)
Great friend of the late Bobby Jones he was top amateur in the US Masters in 1934, 1939 and 1940. In 1938 came to Royal Troon and won the British Amateur title beating R. Ewing 3 and 2. For many years acted as chairman of the press committee at The Masters and staged annual parties for visiting golf writers in the Augusta Clubhouse. He was a longtime Vice President of the Association of Golf Writers.

## Zaharias, Mildred "Babe" – née Didrickson  (1915–1956)
As a 17-year-old, Babe, as she was universally known, broke three records in the 1932 Los Angeles Olympics – the javelin, 80 metres hurdles and high jump, but her high jump medal was denied her when judges decided her technique was illegal. Turning her attention to golf, she rapidly established herself as the most powerful woman golfer of the time and in 1945 played and made the cut in the LA Open on the men's PGA Tour. She won the final of the US Amateur by 11 and 9 in 1946, became the first American to win the British title the following year, then helped launch the women's professional tour. She won the US Women's Open in 1948, 1950 and 1954 and in 1950 won six of the nine events on the tour. In 1952 she had a major operation for cancer, but when she won her third and final Open two years later it was by the margin of 12 shots. She was voted Woman Athlete of the Year five times between 1932 and 1950 and Greatest Female Athlete of the Half-Century in 1949.

# The R&A and the USGA announce final approval for Rule 14-1b

The R&A and the United States Golf Association (USGA), golf's governing bodies, have announced the adoption of Rule 14-1b of the Rules of Golf that prohibits anchoring the club in making a stroke. The new Rule will take effect on 1 January 2016 in accordance with the regular four-year cycle for changes to the Rules of Golf.

Rule 14-1b, which was proposed on 28 November 2012, has now been given final approval by The R&A and the USGA following an extensive review by both organisations. The decision to adopt the new Rule came after a comprehensive process in which comments and suggestions from across the golf community were collected and thoroughly considered.

The R&A and the USGA have prepared a detailed report to explain the reasons for the decision to adopt Rule 14-1b. The report explains the principles on which the Rules of Golf are founded, why freely swinging the entire club is the essence of the traditional method of stroke, and why anchoring is a substantially different form of stroke that may alter and diminish the fundamental challenges of the game. It points out that the Rule will still allow the use of belly-length and long putters and that a wide variety of types of strokes remain for players to use. The report concludes that the new Rule should not adversely affect participation in the game, that it is not too late or unfair to require players to comply with it and that it will remove concerns about any potential advantage that anchoring provides. It also makes clear that one set of Rules is essential to the future health of the game. The report, entitled Explanation of Decision to Adopt Rule 14-1b of the Rules of Golf, can be found at www.RandA.org/anchoring or at www.usga.org/anchoring.

Peter Dawson, Chief Executive of The R&A said: "We took a great deal of time to consider this issue and received a variety of contributions from individuals and organisations at all levels of the game."

USGA President Glen D. Nager commented. "The new Rule upholds the essential nature of the traditional method of stroke and eliminates the possible advantage that anchoring provides, ensuring that players of all skill levels face the same challenge inherent in the game of golf."

The current Rule 14-1 of the Rules of Golf will be re-numbered as Rule 14-1a, and new Rule 14-1b will be established as follows:

**14-1b Anchoring the Club**
In making a stroke, the player must not anchor the club, either "directly" or by use of an "anchor point."
Note 1: The club is anchored "directly" when the player intentionally holds the club or a gripping hand in contact with any part of his body, except that the player may hold the club or a gripping hand against a hand or forearm.
Note 2: An "anchor point" exists when the player intentionally holds a forearm in contact with any part of his body to establish a gripping hand as a stable point around which the other hand may swing the club.

Rule 14-1b will not alter current equipment rules and allows for the continued use of all conforming golf clubs, including belly-length and long putters, provided such clubs are not anchored during a stroke. The new Rule, which comes into effect on January 1 2016, narrowly targets only a few types of strokes, while preserving a golfer's ability to play a wide variety of strokes in his or her individual style.

# PART XIV

# Governance of the Game

## R&A Rules Limited

With effect from 1st January 2004, the responsibilities and authority of The Royal and Ancient Golf Club of St Andrews in making, interpreting and giving decisions on the Rules of Golf and on the Rules of Amateur Status were transferred to R&A Rules Limited.

## Gender

In the Rules of Golf, the gender used in relation to any person is understood to include both genders.

## Golfers with Disabilities

The R&A publication entitled "A Modification of the Rules of Golf for Golfers with Disabilities", that contains permissible modifications of the Rules of Golf to accommodate disabled golfers, is available through The R&A.

## Handicaps

The Rules of Golf do not legislate for the allocation and adjustment of handicaps. Such matters are within the jurisdiction of the National Union concerned and queries should be directed accordingly.

# RULES
# OF GOLF

### As Approved by
### R&A Rules Limited
### and the
### United States Golf Association

32nd Edition
Effective 1 January 2012

# Principle changes introduced in the 2012 Code

## Definitions

### Addressing the Ball
The Definition is amended so that a player has addressed the ball simply by grounding his club immediately in front of or behind the ball, regardless of whether or not he has taken his stance. Therefore, the Rules generally no longer provide for a player addressing the ball in a hazard. (See also related change to Rule 18-2b)

## Rules

### Rule 1-2. Exerting Influence on Movement of Ball or Altering Physical Conditions
The Rule is amended to establish more clearly that, if a player intentionally takes an action to influence the movement of a ball or to alter physical conditions affecting the playing of a hole in a way that is not permitted by the Rules, Rule 1-2 applies only when the action is not already covered in another Rule. For example, a player improving the lie of his ball is in breach of Rule 13-2 and therefore that Rule would apply, whereas a player intentionally improving the lie of a fellow-competitor's ball is not a situation covered by Rule 13-2 and, therefore, is governed by Rule 1-2.

### Rule 6-3a. Time of Starting
Rule 6-3a is amended to provide that the penalty for starting late, but within five minutes of the starting time, is reduced from disqualification to loss of the first hole in match play or two strokes at the first hole in stroke play. Previously this penalty reduction could be introduced as a condition of competition.

### Rule 12-1. Seeing Ball; Searching for Ball
Rule 12-1 is reformatted for clarity. In addition, it is amended to (i) permit a player to search for his ball anywhere on the course when it may be covered by sand and to clarify that there is no penalty if the ball is moved in these circumstances, and (ii) apply a penalty of one stroke under Rule 18-2a if a player moves his ball in a hazard when searching for it when it is believed to be covered by loose impediments.

### Rule 13-4. Ball in Hazard; Prohibited Actions
Exception 2 to Rule 13-4 is amended to permit a player to smooth sand or soil in a hazard at any time, including before playing from that hazard, provided it is for the sole purpose of caring for the course and Rule 13-2 is not breached.

### Rule 18-2b. Ball Moving After Address
A new Exception is added that exonerates the player from penalty if his ball moves after it has been addressed when it is known or virtually certain that he did not cause the ball to move. For example, if it is a gust of wind that moves the ball after it has been addressed, there is no penalty and the ball is played from its new position.

### Rule 19-1. Ball in Motion Deflected or Stopped; By Outside Agency
The note is expanded to prescribe the various outcomes when a ball in motion has been deliberately deflected or stopped by an outside agency.

### Rule 20-7c. Playing from Wrong Place; Stroke Play
Note 3 is amended so that if a player is to be penalised for playing from a wrong place, in most cases the penalty will be limited to two strokes, even if another Rule has been breached prior to his making the stroke.

## Appendix IV
A new Appendix is added to prescribe general regulations for the design of devices and other equipment, such as tees, gloves and distance measuring devices.

## Rules of Amateur Status
### Definitions

#### Amateur Golfer
The Definition is amended to establish more clearly that an "amateur golfer", regardless of whether he plays competitively or recreationally, is one who plays golf for the challenge it presents, not as a profession and not for financial gain.

#### Golf Skill or Reputation
A time limit of five years is introduced for the retention of "golf reputation" after the player's golf skill has diminished.

#### Prize Vouchers
The Definition is expanded to allow prize vouchers to be used for the purchase of goods or services from a golf club.

### Rules

#### Rule 1-3 Amateurism; Purpose of the Rules
Rule 1-3 is amended to re-state why there is a distinction between amateur and professional golf and why certain limits and restrictions are needed in the amateur game.

#### Rule 2-1 Professionalism; General
The existing Rules on professionalism are consolidated and re-formatted into new Rule 2-1.

#### Rule 2-2 Professionalism; Contracts and Agreements
National Golf Unions or Associations – New Rule 2-2(a) is added to allow an amateur golfer to enter into a contract and/or agreement with his national golf union or association, provided he does not obtain any financial gain, directly or indirectly, while still an amateur golfer.

Professional Agents, Sponsors and Other Third Parties – New Rule 2-2(b) is added to allow an amateur golfer, who is at least 18 years of age, to enter into a contract and/or agreement with a third party solely in relation to the golfer's future as a professional golfer, provided he does not obtain any financial gain, directly or indirectly, while still an amateur golfer.

#### Rule 3-2b Hole-in-One Prizes
New Rule 3-2b excludes from the general prize limit prizes (including cash prizes) awarded for achieving a hole-in-one while playing a round of golf. This exception is specific to prizes for holes-in-one (not longest drive or nearest the hole) and neither separate events nor multiple-entry events qualify.

#### Rule 4-3 Subsistence Expenses
New Rule added to allow an amateur golfer to receive subsistence expenses to assist with general living costs, provided the expenses are approved by and paid through the player's national golf union or association.

# How to use the rule book

It is understood that not everyone who has a copy of the Rules of Golf will read it from cover to cover. Most golfers only consult the Rule book when they have a Rules issue on the course that needs to be resolved. However, to ensure that you have a basic understanding of the Rules and that you play golf in a reasonable manner, it is recommended that you at least read the Quick Guide to the Rules of Golf and the Etiquette Section contained within this publication.

In terms of ascertaining the correct answer to Rules issues that arise on the course, use of the Rule book's Index should help you to identify the relevant Rule. For example, if a player accidentally moves his ball-marker in the process of lifting his ball on the putting green, identify the key words in the question, such as "ball-marker", "lifting ball" and "putting green" and look in the Index for these headings. The relevant Rule (Rule 20-1) is found under the headings "ball-marker" and "lifted ball" and a reading of this Rule will confirm the correct answer.

In addition to identifying key words and using the Index in the Rules of Golf, the following points will assist you in using the Rule book efficiently and accurately:

## Understand the Words
The Rule book is written in a very precise and deliberate fashion. You should be aware of and understand the following differences in word use:

- may     =   optional
- should   =   recommendation
- must     =   instruction (and penalty if not carried out)
- a ball    =   you may substitute another ball (e.g. Rules 26, 27 and 28)
- the ball   =   you must not substitute another ball (e.g. Rules 24-2 and 25-1)

## Know the Definitions
There are over fifty defined terms (e.g. abnormal ground condition, through the green, etc) and these form the foundation around which the Rules of Play are written. A good knowledge of the defined terms (which are italicised throughout the book) is very important to the correct application of the Rules.

## The Facts of the Case
To answer any question on the Rules you must consider the facts of the case in some detail. You should identify:

- The form of play (e.g. match play or stroke play, single, foursome or four-ball)
- Who is involved (e.g. the player, his partner or caddie, an outside agency)
- Where the incident occurred (e.g. on the teeing ground, in a bunker or water hazard, on the putting green)
- What actually happened
- The player's intentions (e.g. what was he doing and what does he want to do)
- The timing of the incident (e.g. has the player now returned his score card, has the competition closed)

## Refer to the Book
As stated above, reference to the Rule book Index and the relevant Rule should provide the answer to the majority of questions that can arise on the course. If in doubt, play the course as you find it and play the ball as it lies. On returning to the Clubhouse, refer the matter to the Committee and it may be that reference to the "Decisions on the Rules of Golf" will assist in resolving any queries that are not entirely clear from the Rule book itself.

# Contents

# Section I —
# Etiquette; Behaviour on the Course

## Introduction

This section provides guidelines on the manner in which the game of golf should be played. If they are followed, all players will gain maximum enjoyment from the game. The overriding principle is that consideration should be shown to others on the course at all times.

## The Spirit of the Game

Golf is played, for the most part, without the supervision of a referee or umpire. The game relies on the integrity of the individual to show consideration for other players and to abide by the Rules. All players should conduct themselves in a disciplined manner, demonstrating courtesy and sportsmanship at all times, irrespective of how competitive they may be. This is the spirit of the game of golf.

## Safety

Players should ensure that no one is standing close by or in a position to be hit by the club, the ball or any stones, pebbles, twigs or the like when they make a stroke or practice swing.

Players should not play until the players in front are out of range.

Players should always alert greenstaff nearby or ahead when they are about to make a stroke that might endanger them.

If a player plays a ball in a direction where there is a danger of hitting someone, he should immediately shout a warning. The traditional word of warning in such situations is "fore".

## Consideration for Other Players

### No Disturbance or Distraction

Players should always show consideration for other players on the course and should not disturb their play by moving, talking or making unnecessary noise.

Players should ensure that any electronic device taken onto the course does not distract other players.

On the teeing ground, a player should not tee his ball until it is his turn to play.

Players should not stand close to or directly behind the ball, or directly behind the hole, when a player is about to play.

### On the Putting Green

On the putting green, players should not stand on another player's line of putt or, when he is making a stroke, cast a shadow over his line of putt.

Players should remain on or close to the putting green until all other players in the group have holed out.

### Scoring

In stroke play, a player who is acting as a marker should, if necessary, on the way to the next tee, check the score with the player concerned and record it.

## Pace of Play

### Play at Good Pace and Keep Up

Players should play at a good pace. The Committee may establish pace of play guidelines that all players should follow.

It is a group's responsibility to keep up with the group in front. If it loses a clear hole and it is delaying the group behind, it should invite the group behind to play through, irrespective of the number of players in that group. Where a group has not lost a clear hole, but it is apparent that the group behind can play faster, it should invite the faster moving group to play through.

### Be Ready to Play

Players should be ready to play as soon as it is their turn to play. When playing on or near the putting green, they should leave their bags or carts in such a position as will enable quick movement off the green and towards the next tee. When the play of a hole has been completed, players should immediately leave the putting green.

### Lost Ball

If a player believes his ball may be lost outside a water hazard or is out of bounds, to save time, he should play a provisional ball.

Players searching for a ball should signal the players in the group behind them to play through as soon as it becomes apparent that the ball will not easily be found. They should not search for five minutes before doing so. Having allowed the group behind to play through, they should not continue play until that group has passed and is out of range.

### Priority on the Course

Unless otherwise determined by the Committee, priority on the course is determined by a group's pace of play. Any group playing a whole round is entitled to pass a group playing a shorter round. The term "group" includes a single player.

## Care of the Course

### Bunkers

Before leaving a bunker, players should carefully fill up and smooth over all holes and footprints made by them and any nearby made by others. If a rake is within reasonable proximity of the bunker, the rake should be used for this purpose.

### Repair of Divots, Ball-Marks and Damage by Shoes

Players should carefully repair any divot holes made by them and any damage to the putting green made by the impact of a ball (whether or not made by the player himself). On completion of the hole by all players in the group, damage to the putting green caused by golf shoes should be repaired.

### Preventing Unnecessary Damage

Players should avoid causing damage to the course by removing divots when taking practice swings or by hitting the head of a club into the ground, whether in anger or for any other reason.

Players should ensure that no damage is done to the putting green when putting down bags or the flagstick.

In order to avoid damaging the hole, players and caddies should not stand too close to the hole and should take care during the handling of the flagstick and the removal of a ball from the hole. The head of a club should not be used to remove a ball from the hole.

Players should not lean on their clubs when on the putting green, particularly when removing the ball from the hole.

The flagstick should be properly replaced in the hole before the players leave the putting green.

Local notices regulating the movement of golf carts should be strictly observed.

**Conclusion; Penalties for Breach**

If players follow the guidelines in this section, it will make the game more enjoyable for everyone.

If a player consistently disregards these guidelines during a round or over a period of time to the detriment of others, it is recommended that the Committee considers taking appropriate disciplinary action against the offending player. Such action may, for example, include prohibiting play for a limited time on the course or in a certain number of competitions. This is considered to be justifiable in terms of protecting the interests of the majority of golfers who wish to play in accordance with these guidelines.

In the case of a serious breach of etiquette, the Committee may disqualify a player under Rule 33-7.

---

# Section II — Definitions

The Definitions are listed alphabetically and, in the Rules themselves, defined terms are in *italics*.

**Abnormal Ground Conditions**

An *"abnormal ground condition"* is any *casual water, ground under repair* or hole, cast or runway on the *course* made by a *burrowing animal,* a reptile or a bird.

**Addressing the Ball**

A player has *"addressed the ball"* when he has grounded his club immediately in front of or immediately behind the ball, whether or not he has taken his *stance.*

**Advice**

*"Advice"* is any counsel or suggestion that could influence a player in determining his play, the choice of a club or the method of making a *stroke.*

Information on the *Rules,* distance or matters of public information, such as the position of *hazards* or the *flagstick* on the *putting green,* is not *advice.*

**Ball Deemed to Move**

See *"Move or Moved".*

**Ball Holed**

See *"Holed".*

**Ball Lost**

See *"Lost Ball".*

**Ball in Play**

A ball is *"in play"* as soon as the player has made a *stroke* on the *teeing ground.* It remains *in play* until it is *holed,* except when it is *lost, out of bounds* or lifted, or another ball has been *substituted,* whether or not the substitution is permitted; a ball so *substituted* becomes the *ball in play.*

If a ball is played from outside the *teeing ground* when the player is starting play of a hole, or when attempting to correct this mistake, the ball is not *in play* and Rule 11-4 or 11-5 applies. Otherwise, *ball in play* includes a ball played from outside the *teeing ground* when the player elects or is required to play his next *stroke* from the *teeing ground.*

*Exception in match play: Ball in play* includes a ball played by the player from outside the *teeing ground* when starting play of a hole if the *opponent* does not require the *stroke* to be cancelled in accordance with Rule 11-4a.

**Best-Ball**

See *"Forms of Match Play".*

**Bunker**

A *"bunker"* is a *hazard* consisting of a prepared area of ground, often a hollow, from which turf or soil has been removed and replaced with sand or the like.

Grass-covered ground bordering or within a *bunker,* including a stacked turf face (whether grass-covered or earthen), is not part of the *bunker.* A wall or lip of the *bunker* not covered with grass is part of the *bunker.* The margin of a *bunker* extends vertically downwards, but not upwards.

A ball is in a *bunker* when it lies in or any part of it touches the *bunker.*

**Burrowing Animal**

A *"burrowing animal"* is an animal (other than a worm, insect or the like) that makes a hole for habitation or shelter, such as a rabbit, mole, groundhog, gopher or salamander.

*Note:* A hole made by a non-burrowing animal, such as a dog, is not an *abnormal ground condition* unless marked or declared as *ground under repair.*

**Caddie**

A *"caddie"* is one who assists the player in accordance with the *Rules,* which may include carrying or handling the player's clubs during play.

When one *caddie* is employed by more than one player, he is always deemed to be the *caddie* of the player sharing the *caddie* whose ball (or whose *partner's* ball) is involved, and *equipment* carried by him is deemed to be that player's *equipment,* except when the *caddie* acts upon specific directions of another player (or the *partner* of another player) sharing the *caddie,* in which case he is considered to be that other player's *caddie.*

**Casual Water**

*"Casual water"* is any temporary accumulation of water on the *course* that is not in a *water hazard* and is visible before or after the player takes his *stance.* Snow and natural ice, other than frost, are either *casual water* or *loose impediments,* at the option of the player. Manufactured ice is an *obstruction.* Dew and frost are not *casual water.*

A ball is in *casual water* when it lies in or any part of it touches the *casual water.*

**Committee**

The *"Committee"* is the committee in charge of the competition or, if the matter does not arise in a competition, the committee in charge of the *course.*

**Competitor**

A *"competitor"* is a player in a stroke play competition. A *"fellow-competitor"* is any person with whom the *competitor* plays. Neither is *partner* of the other.

In stroke play *foursome* and *four-ball* competitions, where the context so admits, the word *"competitor"* or *"fellow-competitor"* includes his *partner.*

## Course

The "course" is the whole area within any boundaries established by the Committee (see Rule 33-2).

## Equipment

"Equipment" is anything used, worn or carried by the player or anything carried for the player by his partner or either of their caddies, except any ball he has played at the hole being played and any small object, such as a coin or a tee, when used to mark the position of a ball or the extent of an area in which a ball is to be dropped. Equipment includes a golf cart, whether or not motorised.

> Note 1: A ball played at the hole being played is equipment when it has been lifted and not put back into play.

> Note 2: When a golf cart is shared by two or more players, the cart and everything in it are deemed to be the equipment of one of the players sharing the cart.
> If the cart is being moved by one of the players (or the partner of one of the players) sharing it, the cart and everything in it are deemed to be that player's equipment. Otherwise, the cart and everything in it are deemed to be the equipment of the player sharing the cart whose ball (or whose partner's ball) is involved.

## Fellow-Competitor

See "Competitor".

## Flagstick

The "flagstick" is a movable straight indicator, with or without bunting or other material attached, centred in the hole to show its position. It must be circular in cross-section. Padding or shock absorbent material that might unduly influence the movement of the ball is prohibited.

## Forecaddie

A "forecaddie" is one who is employed by the Committee to indicate to players the position of balls during play. He is an outside agency.

## Forms of Match Play

Single: A match in which one player plays against another player.

Threesome: A match in which one player plays against two other players, and each side plays one ball.

Foursome: A match in which two players play against two other players, and each side plays one ball.

Three-Ball: Three players play a match against one another, each playing his own ball. Each player is playing two distinct matches.

Best-Ball: A match in which one player plays against the better ball of two other players or the best ball of three other players.

Four-Ball: A match in which two players play their better ball against the better ball of two other players.

## Forms of Stroke Play

Individual: A competition in which each competitor plays as an individual.

Foursome: A competition in which two competitors play as partners and play one ball.

Four-Ball: A competition in which two competitors play as partners, each playing his own ball. The lower score of the partners is the score for the hole. If one partner fails to complete the play of a hole, there is no penalty.

> Note: For bogey, par and Stableford competitions, see Rule 32-1.

## Four-Ball

See "Forms of Match Play" and "Forms of Stroke Play".

## Foursome

See "Forms of Match Play" and "Forms of Stroke Play".

## Ground Under Repair

"Ground under repair" is any part of the course so marked by order of the Committee or so declared by its authorised representative. All ground and any grass, bush, tree or other growing thing within the ground under repair are part of the ground under repair. Ground under repair includes material piled for removal and a hole made by a greenkeeper, even if not so marked. Grass cuttings and other material left on the course that have been abandoned and are not intended to be removed are not ground under repair unless so marked.

When the margin of ground under repair is defined by stakes, the stakes are inside the ground under repair, and the margin of the ground under repair is defined by the nearest outside points of the stakes at ground level. When both stakes and lines are used to indicate ground under repair, the stakes identify the ground under repair and the lines define the margin of ground under repair. When the margin of ground under repair is defined by a line on the ground, the line itself is in the ground under repair. The margin of ground under repair extends vertically downwards but not upwards.

A ball is in ground under repair when it lies in or any part of it touches the ground under repair.

Stakes used to define the margin of or identify ground under repair are obstructions.

> Note: The Committee may make a Local Rule prohibiting play from ground under repair or an environmentally-sensitive area defined as ground under repair.

## Hazards

A "hazard" is any bunker or water hazard.

## Hole

The "hole" must be 4¼ inches (108 mm) in diameter and at least 4 inches (101.6 mm) deep. If a lining is used, it must be sunk at least 1 inch (25.4 mm) below the putting green surface, unless the nature of the soil makes it impracticable to do so; its outer diameter must not exceed 4 1/4 inches (108 mm).

## Holed

A ball is "holed" when it is at rest within the circumference of the hole and all of it is below the level of the lip of the hole.

## Honour

The player who is to play first from the teeing ground is said to have the "honour".

## Lateral Water Hazard

A "lateral water hazard" is a water hazard or that part of a water hazard so situated that it is not possible, or is deemed by the Committee to be impracticable, to drop a ball behind the water hazard in accordance with Rule 26-1b. All ground and water within the margin of a lateral water hazard are part of the lateral water hazard.

When the margin of a lateral water hazard is defined by stakes, the stakes are inside the lateral water hazard, and the margin of the hazard is defined by the nearest outside points of the stakes at ground level. When both stakes and lines are used to indicate a lateral water hazard, the stakes identify the hazard and the lines define the hazard margin. When the margin of a lateral water hazard is defined by a line on the ground, the line itself is in the lateral water hazard. The margin of a lateral water hazard extends vertically upwards and downwards.

A ball is in a lateral water hazard when it lies in or any part of it touches the lateral water hazard.

Stakes used to define the margin of or identify a lateral water hazard are obstructions.

> Note 1: That part of a water hazard to be played as a lateral water hazard must be distinctly marked. Stakes or

lines used to define the margin of or identify a *lateral water hazard* must be red.

*Note 2:* The *Committee* may make a Local Rule prohibiting play from an environmentally-sensitive area defined as a *lateral water hazard*.

*Note 3:* The *Committee* may define a *lateral water hazard* as a *water hazard*.

## Line of Play

The *"line of play"* is the direction that the player wishes his ball to take after a *stroke*, plus a reasonable distance on either side of the intended direction. The *line of play* extends vertically upwards from the ground, but does not extend beyond the *hole*.

## Line of Putt

The *"line of putt"* is the line that the player wishes his ball to take after a *stroke* on the *putting green*. Except with respect to Rule 16-1e, the *line of putt* includes a reasonable distance on either side of the intended line. The *line of putt* does not extend beyond the *hole*.

## Loose Impediments

*"Loose impediments"* are natural objects, including:
- stones, leaves, twigs, branches and the like,
- dung, and •
- worms, insects and the like, and the casts and heaps made by them,

provided they are not:
- fixed or growing,
- solidly embedded, or
- adhering to the ball.

Sand and loose soil are *loose impediments* on the *putting green*, but not elsewhere.

Snow and natural ice, other than frost, are either *casual water* or *loose impediments*, at the option of the player.

Dew and frost are not *loose impediments*.

## Lost Ball

A ball is deemed *"lost"* if:
a.  It is not found or identified as his by the player within five minutes after the player's *side* or his or their *cad dies* have begun to search for it; or
b.  The player has made a *stroke* at a *provisional ball* from the place where the original ball is likely to be or from a point nearer the *hole* than that place (see Rule 27-2b); or
c.  The player has put another *ball into play* under penalty of stroke and distance under Rule 26-1a, 27-1 or 28a; or
d.  The player has put another *ball into play* because it is known or virtually certain that the ball, which has not been found, has been *moved* by an *outside agency* (see Rule 18-1), is in an *obstruction* (see Rule 24-3), is in an *abnormal ground condition* (see Rule 25-1c) or is in a *water hazard* (see Rule 26-1b or c); or
e.  The player has made a *stroke* at a *substituted ball*.

Time spent in playing a *wrong ball* is not counted in the five-minute period allowed for search.

## Marker

A *"marker"* is one who is appointed by the *Committee* to record a *competitor's* score in stroke play. He may be a *fellow-competitor*. He is not a *referee*.

## Move or Moved

A ball is deemed to have *"moved"* if it leaves its position and comes to rest in any other place.

## Nearest Point of Relief

The *"nearest point of relief"* is the reference point for taking relief without penalty from interference by an immovable *obstruction* (Rule 24-2), an *abnormal ground condition* (Rule 25-1) or a *wrong putting green* (Rule 25-3).

It is the point on the *course* nearest to where the ball lies:
(i)   that is not nearer the *hole*, and
(ii)  where, if the ball were so positioned, no interference by the condition from which relief is sought would exist for the *stroke* the player would have made from the original position if the condition were not there.

*Note:* In order to determine the *nearest point of relief* accurately, the player should use the club with which he would have made his next *stroke* if the condition were not there to simulate the *address* position, direction of play and swing for such a *stroke*.

## Observer

An *"observer"* is one who is appointed by the *Committee* to assist a *referee* to decide questions of fact and to report to him any breach of a *Rule*. An *observer* should not attend the *flagstick*, stand at or mark the position of the *hole*, or lift the ball or mark its position.

## Obstructions

An *"obstruction"* is anything artificial, including the artificial surfaces and sides of roads and paths and manufactured ice, except:
a.  Objects defining *out of bounds*, such as walls, fences, stakes and railings;
b.  Any part of an immovable artificial object that is *out of bounds*; and
c.  Any construction declared by the *Committee* to be an integral part of the *course*.

An *obstruction* is a movable *obstruction* if it may be moved without unreasonable effort, without unduly delaying play and without causing damage. Otherwise, it is an immovable *obstruction*.

*Note:* The *Committee* may make a Local Rule declaring a movable *obstruction* to be an immovable *obstruction*.

## Opponent

An *"opponent"* is a member of a *side* against whom the player's *side* is competing in match play.

## Out of Bounds

*"Out of bounds"* is beyond the boundaries of the *course* or any part of the *course* so marked by the *Committee*.

When *out of bounds* is defined by reference to stakes or a fence or as being beyond stakes or a fence, the *out of bounds* line is determined by the nearest inside points at ground level of the stakes or fence posts (excluding angled supports). When both stakes and lines are used to indicate *out of bounds*, the stakes identify *out of bounds* and the lines define *out of bounds*. When *out of bounds* is defined by a line on the ground, the line itself is *out of bounds*. The *out of bounds* line extends vertically upwards and downwards.

A ball is *out of bounds* when all of it lies *out of bounds*. A player may stand *out of bounds* to play a ball lying within bounds.

Objects defining *out of bounds* such as walls, fences, stakes and railings are not *obstructions* and are deemed to be fixed. Stakes identifying *out of bounds* are not *obstructions* and are deemed to be fixed.

*Note 1:* Stakes or lines used to define *out of bounds* should be white.

*Note 2:* A *Committee* may make a Local Rule declaring stakes identifying but not defining *out of bounds* to be *obstructions*.

## Outside Agency

In match play, an *"outside agency"* is any agency other than either the player's or *opponent's side*, any *caddie* of either *side*, any ball played by either *side* at the hole being played or any *equipment* of either *side*.

In stroke play, an *outside agency* is any agency other than the *competitor's side*, any *caddie* of the *side*, any ball played by the side at the hole being played or any equipment of the side.

An outside agency includes a referee, a marker, an observer and a forecaddie. Neither wind nor water is an outside agency.

**Partner**

A "partner" is a player associated with another player on the same side. In threesome, foursome, best-ball or four-ball play, where the context so admits, the word "player" includes his partner or partners.

**Penalty Stroke**

A "penalty stroke" is one added to the score of a player or side under certain Rules. In a threesome or foursome, penalty strokes do not affect the order of play.

**Provisional Ball**

A "provisional ball" is a ball played under Rule 27-2 for a ball that may be lost outside a water hazard or may be out of bounds.

**Putting Green**

The "putting green" is all ground of the hole being played that is specially prepared for putting or otherwise defined as such by the Committee. A ball is on the putting green when any part of it touches the putting green.

**R&A**

The "R&A" means R&A Rules Limited.

**Referee**

A "referee" is one who is appointed by the Committee to decide questions of fact and apply the Rules. He must act on any breach of a Rule that he observes or is reported to him.

A referee should not attend the flagstick, stand at or mark the position of the hole, or lift the ball or mark its position.

Exception in match play: Unless a referee is assigned to accompany the players throughout a match, he has no authority to intervene in a match other than in relation to Rule 1-3, 6-7 or 33-7.

**Rub of the Green**

A "rub of the green" occurs when a ball in motion is accidentally deflected or stopped by any outside agency (see Rule 19-1).

**Rule or Rules**

The term "Rule" includes:

a. The Rules of Golf and their interpretations as contained in "Decisions on the Rules of Golf";

b. Any Conditions of Competition established by the Committee under Rule 33-1 and Appendix I;

c. Any Local Rules established by the Committee under Rule 33-8a and Appendix I; and

d. The specifications on:

(i) clubs and the ball in Appendices II and III and their interpretations as contained in "A Guide to the Rules on Clubs and Balls"; and

(ii) devices and other equipment in Appendix IV.

**Side**

A "side" is a player, or two or more players who are partners. In match play, each member of the opposing side is an opponent. In stroke play, members of all sides are competitors and members of different sides playing together are fellow-competitors.

**Single**

See "Forms of Match Play" and "Forms of Stroke Play".

**Stance**

Taking the "stance" consists in a player placing his feet in position for and preparatory to making a stroke.

**Stipulated Round**

The "stipulated round" consists of playing the holes of the course in their correct sequence, unless otherwise authorised by the Committee. The number of holes in a stipulated round is 18 unless a smaller number is authorised by the Committee. As to extension of stipulated round in match play, see Rule 2-3.

**Stroke**

A "stroke" is the forward movement of the club made with the intention of striking at and moving the ball, but if a player checks his downswing voluntarily before the clubhead reaches the ball he has not made a stroke.

**Substituted Ball**

A "substituted ball" is a ball put into play for the original ball that was either in play, lost, out of bounds or lifted.

**Teeing Ground**

The "teeing ground" is the starting place for the hole to be played. It is a rectangular area two club-lengths in depth, the front and the sides of which are defined by the outside limits of two tee-markers. A ball is outside the teeing ground when all of it lies outside the teeing ground.

**Three-Ball**

See "Forms of Match Play".

**Threesome**

See "Forms of Match Play".

**Through the Green**

"Through the green" is the whole area of the course except:

a. The teeing ground and putting green of the hole being played; and

b. All hazards on the course.

**Water Hazard**

A "water hazard" is any sea, lake, pond, river, ditch, surface drainage ditch or other open water course (whether or not containing water) and anything of a similar nature on the course. All ground and water within the margin of a water hazard are part of the water hazard.

When the margin of a water hazard is defined by stakes, the stakes are inside the water hazard, and the margin of the hazard is defined by the nearest outside points of the stakes at ground level. When both stakes and lines are used to indicate a water hazard, the stakes identify the hazard and the lines define the hazard margin. When the margin of a water hazard is defined by a line on the ground, the line itself is in the water hazard. The margin of a water hazard extends vertically upwards and downwards.

A ball is in a water hazard when it lies in or any part of it touches the water hazard.

Stakes used to define the margin of or identify a water hazard are obstructions.

Note 1: Stakes or lines used to define the margin of or identify a water hazard must be yellow.

Note 2: The Committee may make a Local Rule prohibiting play from an environmentally-sensitive area defined as a water hazard.

**Wrong Ball**

A "wrong ball" is any ball other than the player's:

• ball in play;
• provisional ball; or
• second ball played under Rule 3-3 or Rule 20-7c in stroke play;

and includes:

• another player's ball;
• an abandoned ball; and
• the player's original ball when it is no longer in play.

Note: Ball in play includes a ball substituted for the ball in play, whether or not the substitution is permitted.

**Wrong Putting Green**

A "wrong putting green" is any putting green other than that of the hole being played. Unless otherwise prescribed by the Committee, this term includes a practice putting green or pitching green on the course.

# Section III — The Rules of Play

## The Game

### Rule 1 – The Game

**Definitions**
All defined terms are in *italics* and are listed alphabetically in the Definitions section – see pages 592–595.

**1-1. General**
The Game of Golf consists of playing a ball with a club from the *teeing ground* into the *hole* by a *stroke* or successive *strokes* in accordance with the *Rules*.

**1-2. Exerting Influence on Movement of Ball or Altering Physical Conditions**
A player must not (i) take an action with the intent to influence the movement of a *ball in play* or (ii) alter physical conditions with the intent of affecting the playing of a hole.

*Exceptions:* An action expressly permitted or expressly prohibited by another *Rule* is subject to that other *Rule*, not Rule 1-2.

An action taken for the sole purpose of caring for the *course* is not a breach of Rule 1-2.

**\*PENALTY FOR BREACH OF RULE 1-2:**
Match play – Loss of hole; Stroke play – Two strokes.

*\*In the case of a serious breach of Rule 1-2, the Committee may impose a penalty of disqualification.*

*Note 1:* A player is deemed to have committed a serious breach of Rule 1-2 if the *Committee* considers that the action taken in breach of this Rule has allowed him or another player to gain a significant advantage or has placed another player, other than his *partner*, at a significant disadvantage.

*Note 2:* In stroke play, except where a serious breach resulting in disqualification is involved, a player in breach of Rule 1-2 in relation to the movement of his own ball must play the ball from where it was stopped, or, if the ball was deflected, from where it came to rest. If the movement of a player's ball has been intentionally influenced by a *fellow-competitor* or other *outside agency*, Rule 1-4 applies to the player (see Note to Rule 19-1).

**1-3. Agreement to Waive Rules**
Players must not agree to exclude the operation of any *Rule* or to waive any penalty incurred.

PENALTY FOR BREACH OF RULE 1-3:
Match play – Disqualification of both *sides*;
Stroke play – Disqualification of *competitors* concerned.

(Agreeing to play out of turn in stroke play – see Rule 10-2c)

**1-4. Points Not Covered by Rules**
If any point in dispute is not covered by the *Rules*, the decision should be made in accordance with equity.

### Rule 2 – Match Play

**Definitions**
All defined terms are in *italics* and are listed alphabetically in the Definitions section – see pages 592–595.

**2-1. General**
A match consists of one *side* playing against another over a *stipulated round* unless otherwise decreed by the *Committee*.

In match play the game is played by holes.

Except as otherwise provided in the *Rules*, a hole is won by the *side* that *holes* its ball in the fewer *strokes*. In a handicap match, the lower net score wins the hole.

The state of the match is expressed by the terms: so many "holes up" or "all square", and so many "to play".

A *side* is "dormie" when it is as many holes up as there are holes remaining to be played.

**2-2. Halved Hole**
A hole is halved if each *side holes* out in the same number of *strokes*.

When a player has *holed* out and his *opponent* has been left with a *stroke* for the half, if the player subsequently incurs a penalty, the hole is halved.

**2-3. Winner of Match**
A match is won when one *side* leads by a number of holes greater than the number remaining to be played.

If there is a tie, the *Committee* may extend the *stipulated round* by as many holes as are required for a match to be won.

**2-4. Concession of Match, Hole or Next Stroke**
A player may concede a match at any time prior to the start or conclusion of that match.

A player may concede a hole at any time prior to the start or conclusion of that hole.

A player may concede his *opponent's* next *stroke* at any time, provided the *opponent's* ball is at rest. The *opponent* is considered to have *holed* out with his next *stroke*, and the ball may be removed by either *side*.

A concession may not be declined or withdrawn.

(Ball overhanging hole – see Rule 16-2)

**2-5. Doubt as to Procedure; Disputes and Claims**
In match play, if a doubt or dispute arises between the players, a player may make a claim. If no duly authorised representative of the *Committee* is available within a reasonable time, the players must continue the match without delay. The *Committee* may consider a claim only if it has been made in a timely manner and if the player making the claim has notified his *opponent* at the time (i) that he is making a claim or wants a ruling and (ii) of the facts upon which the claim or ruling is to be based. A claim is considered to have been made in a timely manner if, upon discovery of circumstances giving rise to a claim, the player makes his claim (i) before any player in the match plays from the next *teeing ground*, or (ii) in the case of the last hole of the match, before all players in the match leave the *putting green*, or (iii) when the circumstances giving rise to the claim are discovered after all the players in the match have left the *putting green* of the final hole, before the result of the match has been officially announced.

A claim relating to a prior hole in the match may only be considered by the *Committee* if it is based on facts previously unknown to the player making the claim and he had been given wrong information (Rules 6-2a or 9) by an *opponent*. Such a claim must be made in a timely manner.

Once the result of the match has been officially announced, a claim may not be considered by the *Committee*, unless it is satisfied that (i) the claim is based on facts which were previously unknown to the player making the claim at the time the result was officially announced, (ii) the player making the claim had been given wrong information by an *opponent* and (iii) the *opponent* knew he was giving wrong information. There is no time limit on considering such a claim.

*Note 1:* A player may disregard a breach of the *Rules* by his *opponent* provided there is no agreement by the *sides* to waive a *Rule* (Rule 1-3).

*Note 2:* In match play, if a player is doubtful of his rights or the correct procedure, he may not complete the play of the hole with two balls.

## 2-6. General Penalty

The penalty for a breach of a *Rule* in match play is loss of hole except when otherwise provided.

## Rule 3 – Stroke Play

### Definitions

All defined terms are in *italics* and are listed alphabetically in the Definitions section – see pages 592–595.

### 3-1. General; Winner

A stroke play competition consists of *competitors* completing each hole of a *stipulated round* or rounds and, for each round, returning a score card on which there is a gross score for each hole. Each *competitor* is playing against every other *competitor* in the competition.

The *competitor* who plays the *stipulated round* or rounds in the fewest *strokes* is the winner.

In a handicap competition, the *competitor* with the lowest net score for the *stipulated round* or rounds is the winner.

### 3-2. Failure to Hole Out

If a *competitor* fails to hole out at any hole and does not correct his mistake before he makes a *stroke* on the next *teeing ground* or, in the case of the last hole of the round, before he leaves the *putting green*, he is disqualified.

### 3-3. Doubt as to Procedure

#### a. Procedure

In stroke play, if a *competitor* is doubtful of his rights or the correct procedure during the play of a hole, he may, without penalty, complete the hole with two balls.

After the doubtful situation has arisen and before taking further action, the *competitor* must announce to his *marker* or *fellow-competitor* that he intends to play two balls and which ball he wishes to count if the *Rules* permit.

The *competitor* must report the facts of the situation to the *Committee* before returning his score card. If he fails to do so, he is disqualified.

*Note:* If the *competitor* takes further action before dealing with the doubtful situation, Rule 3-3 is not applicable. The score with the original ball counts or, if the original ball is not one of the balls being played, the score with the first ball put into play counts, even if the *Rules* do not allow the procedure adopted for that ball. However, the *competitor* incurs no penalty for having played a second ball, and any penalty strokes incurred solely by playing that ball do not count in his score.

#### b. Determination of Score for Hole

(i) If the ball that the *competitor* selected in advance to count has been played in accordance with the *Rules*, the score with that ball is the *competitor's* score for the hole. Otherwise, the score with the other ball counts if the *Rules* allow the procedure adopted for that ball.

(ii) If the *competitor* fails to announce in advance his decision to complete the hole with two balls, or which ball he wishes to count, the score with the original ball counts, provided it has been played in accordance with the *Rules*. If the original ball is not one of the balls being played, the first ball put into play counts, provided it has been played in accordance with the *Rules*. Otherwise, the score with the other ball counts if the *Rules* allow the procedure adopted for that ball.

*Note 1:* If a *competitor* plays a second ball under Rule 3-3, the *strokes* made after this Rule has been invoked with the ball ruled not to count and *penalty strokes* incurred solely by playing that ball are disregarded.

*Note 2:* A second ball played under Rule 3-3 is not a *provisional ball* under Rule 27-2.

### 3-4. Refusal to Comply with a Rule

If a *competitor* refuses to comply with a *Rule* affecting the rights of another *competitor*, he is disqualified.

### 3-5. General Penalty

The penalty for a breach of a *Rule* in stroke play is two strokes except when otherwise provided.

## Clubs and the Ball

The *R&A* reserves the right, at any time, to change the *Rules* relating to clubs and balls (see Appendices II and III) and make or change the interpretations relating to these *Rules*.

## Rule 4 – Clubs

A player in doubt as to the conformity of a club should consult the *R&A*.

A manufacturer should submit to the *R&A* a sample of a club to be manufactured for a ruling as to whether the club conforms with the *Rules*. The sample becomes the property of the *R&A* for reference purposes. If a manufacturer fails to submit a sample or, having submitted a sample, fails to await a ruling before manufacturing and/or marketing the club, the manufacturer assumes the risk of a ruling that the club does not conform with the *Rules*.

### Definitions

All defined terms are in *italics* and are listed alphabetically in the Definitions section – see pages 592–595.

### 4-1. Form and Make of Clubs

#### a. General

The player's clubs must conform with this Rule and the provisions, specifications and interpretations set forth in Appendix II.

*Note:* The *Committee* may require, in the conditions of a competition (Rule 33-1), that any driver the player carries must have a clubhead, identified by model and loft, that is named on the current List of Conforming Driver Heads issued by the *R&A*.

#### b. Wear and Alteration

A club that conforms with the *Rules* when new is deemed to conform after wear through normal use. Any part of a club that has been purposely altered is regarded as new and must, in its altered state, conform with the *Rules*.

### 4-2. Playing Characteristics Changed and Foreign Material

#### a. Playing Characteristics Changed

During a *stipulated round*, the playing characteristics of a club must not be purposely changed by adjustment or by any other means.

#### b. Foreign Material

Foreign material must not be applied to the club face for the purpose of influencing the movement of the ball.

*PENALTY FOR CARRYING, BUT NOT MAKING STROKE WITH, CLUB OR CLUBS IN BREACH OF RULE 4-1 or 4-2:*

Match play – At the conclusion of the hole at which the breach is discovered, the state of the match is adjusted by deducting one hole for each hole at which a breach occurred; maximum deduction per round – Two holes.

Stroke play – Two strokes for each hole at which any breach occurred; maximum penalty per round – Four strokes (two strokes at each of the first two holes at which any breach occurred).

Match play or stroke play – If a breach is discovered between the play of two holes, it is deemed to have been discovered during play of the next hole, and the penalty must be applied accordingly.

Bogey and par competitions – See Note 1 to Rule 32-1a.

Stableford competitions – See Note 1 to Rule 32-1b.

*Any club or clubs carried in breach of Rule 4-1 or 4-2 must be declared out of play by the player to his *opponent* in match play or his *marker* or a *fellow-competitor* in stroke play immediately upon discovery that a breach has occurred. If the player fails to do so, he is disqualified.

PENALTY FOR MAKING STROKE WITH CLUB IN
BREACH OF RULE 4-1 or 4-2:
Disqualification.

### 4-3. Damaged Clubs: Repair and Replacement
**a. Damage in Normal Course of Play**

If, during a *stipulated round*, a player's club is damaged in the normal course of play, he may:

(i) use the club in its damaged state for the remainder of the *stipulated round*; or

(ii) without unduly delaying play, repair it or have it repaired; or

(iii) as an additional option available only if the club is unfit for play, replace the damaged club with any club. The replacement of a club must not unduly delay play (Rule 6-7) and must not be made by borrowing any club selected for play by any other person playing on the *course* or by assembling components carried by or for the player during the *stipulated round*.

PENALTY FOR BREACH OF RULE 4-3a:
See Penalty Statements for Rule 4-4a or b, and Rule 4-4c.

*Note:* A club is unfit for play if it is substantially damaged, e.g. the shaft is dented, significantly bent or breaks into pieces; the clubhead becomes loose, detached or significantly deformed; or the grip becomes loose. A club is not unfit for play solely because the club's lie or loft has been altered, or the clubhead is scratched.

**b. Damage Other Than in Normal Course of Play**

If, during a *stipulated round*, a player's club is damaged other than in the normal course of play rendering it non-conforming or changing its playing characteristics, the club must not subsequently be used or replaced during the round.

PENALTY FOR BREACH OF RULE 4-3b: Disqualification.

**c. Damage Prior to Round**

A player may use a club damaged prior to a round, provided the club, in its damaged state, conforms with the *Rules*.

Damage to a club that occurred prior to a round may be repaired during the round, provided the playing characteristics are not changed and play is not unduly delayed.

PENALTY FOR BREACH OF RULE 4-3c:
See Penalty Statement for Rule 4-1 or 4-2.

(Undue delay – see Rule 6-7)

### 4-4. Maximum of Fourteen Clubs
**a. Selection and Addition of Clubs**

The player must not start a *stipulated round* with more than fourteen clubs. He is limited to the clubs thus selected for that round, except that if he started with fewer than fourteen clubs, he may add any number, provided his total number does not exceed fourteen.

The addition of a club or clubs must not unduly delay play (Rule 6-7) and the player must not add or borrow any club selected for play by any other person playing on the *course* or by assembling components carried by or for the player during the *stipulated round*.

**b. Partners May Share Clubs**

*Partners* may share clubs, provided that the total number of clubs carried by the *partners* so sharing does not exceed fourteen.

PENALTY FOR BREACH OF RULE 4-4a or b,
REGARDLESS OF NUMBER OF EXCESS CLUBS
CARRIED:

Match play – At the conclusion of the hole at which the breach is discovered, the state of the match is adjusted by deducting one hole for each hole at which a breach occurred; maximum deduction per round – Two holes.

Stroke play – Two strokes for each hole at which any breach occurred; maximum penalty per round – Four strokes (two strokes at each of the first two holes at which any breach occurred).

Match play or stroke play – If a breach is discovered between the play of two holes, it is deemed to have been discovered during play of the hole just completed, and the penalty for a breach of Rule 4-4a or b does not apply to the next hole.

Bogey and par competitions – See Note 1 to Rule 32-1a.

Stableford competitions – See Note 1 to Rule 32-1b.

**c. Excess Club Declared Out of Play**

Any club or clubs carried or used in breach of Rule 4-3a(iii) or Rule 4-4 must be declared out of play by the player to his *opponent* in match play or his *marker* or a *fellow-competitor* in stroke play immediately upon discovery that a breach has occurred. The player must not use the club or clubs for the remainder of the *stipulated round*.

PENALTY FOR BREACH OF RULE 4-4c:
Disqualification.

## Rule 5 – The Ball

A player in doubt as to the conformity of a ball should consult the *R&A*.

A manufacturer should submit to the *R&A* samples of a ball to be manufactured for a ruling as to whether the ball conforms with the *Rules*. The samples become the property of the *R&A* for reference purposes. If a manufacturer fails to submit samples or, having submitted samples, fails to await a ruling before manufacturing and/or marketing the ball, the manufacturer assumes the risk of a ruling that the ball does not conform with the *Rules*.

**Definitions**

All defined terms are in *italics* and are listed alphabetically in the Definitions section – see pages 592–595.

**5-1. General**

The ball the player plays must conform to the requirements specified in Appendix III.

*Note:* The *Committee* may require, in the conditions of a competition (Rule 33-1), that the ball the player plays must be named on the current List of Conforming Golf Balls issued by the *R&A*.

**5-2. Foreign Material**

The ball the player plays must not have foreign material applied to it for the purpose of changing its playing characteristics.

PENALTY FOR BREACH OF RULE 5-1 or 5-2:
Disqualification.

**5-3. Ball Unfit for Play**

A ball is unfit for play if it is visibly cut, cracked or out of shape. A ball is not unfit for play solely because mud or other materials adhere to it, its surface is scratched or scraped or its paint is damaged or discoloured.

If a player has reason to believe his ball has become unfit for play during play of the hole being played, he may lift the ball, without penalty, to determine whether it is unfit.

Before lifting the ball, the player must announce his intention to his *opponent* in match play or his *marker* or a *fellow-competitor* in stroke play and mark the position of the ball. He may then lift and examine it, provided that he gives his *opponent*, *marker* or *fellow-competitor* an opportunity to examine the ball and observe the lifting and replacement. The ball must not be cleaned when lifted under Rule 5-3.

If the player fails to comply with all or any part of this procedure, or if he lifts the ball without having reason to believe that it has become unfit for play during play of the hole being played, he incurs a penalty of one stroke.

If it is determined that the ball has become unfit for play during play of the hole being played, the player may *substitute* another ball, placing it on the spot where the original ball lay. Otherwise, the original ball must be replaced. If a player *substitutes* a ball when not permitted and makes a *stroke* at the wrongly *substituted ball*, he incurs the general penalty for a breach of Rule 5-3, but there is no additional penalty under this Rule or Rule 15-2.

If a ball breaks into pieces as a result of a *stroke*, the *stroke* is cancelled and the player must play a ball, without penalty, as nearly as possible at the spot from which the original ball was played (see Rule 20-5).

**\*PENALTY FOR BREACH OF RULE 5-3:**
Match play – Loss of hole; Stroke play – Two strokes.

*\*If a player incurs the general penalty for a breach of Rule 5-3, there is no additional penalty under this Rule.*

*Note 1:* If the *opponent, marker* or *fellow-competitor* wishes to dispute a claim of unfitness, he must do so before the player plays another ball.

*Note 2:* If the original lie of a ball to be placed or replaced has been altered, see Rule 20-3b.

(Cleaning ball lifted from putting green or under any other Rule – see Rule 21)

## Player's Responsibilities

### Rule 6 – The Player

**Definitions**
All defined terms are in *italics* and are listed alphabetically in the Definitions section – see pages 592–595.

**6-1. Rules**
The player and his *caddie* are responsible for knowing the *Rules*. During a *stipulated round*, for any breach of a *Rule* by his *caddie*, the player incurs the applicable penalty.

**a. Match Play**
Before starting a match in a handicap competition, the players should determine from one another their respective handicaps. If a player begins a match having declared a handicap higher than that to which he is entitled and this affects the number of strokes given or received, he is disqualified; otherwise, the player must play off the declared handicap.

**b. Stroke Play**
In any round of a handicap competition, the *competitor* must ensure that his handicap is recorded on his score card before it is returned to the *Committee*. If no handicap is recorded on his score card before it is returned (Rule 6-6b), or if the recorded handicap is higher than that to which he is entitled and this affects the number of strokes received, he is disqualified from the handicap competition; otherwise, the score stands.

*Note:* It is the player's responsibility to know the holes at which handicap strokes are to be given or received.

**6-3. Time of Starting and Groups**
**a. Time of Starting**
The player must start at the time established by the *Committee*.

**PENALTY FOR BREACH OF RULE 6-3a:**
If the player arrives at his starting point, ready to play, within five minutes after his starting time, the penalty for failure to start on time is loss of the first hole in match play or two strokes at the first hole in stroke play. Otherwise, the penalty for breach of this Rule is disqualification.

Bogey and par competitions – See Note 2 to Rule 32-1a.
Stableford competitions – See Note 2 to Rule 32-1b.

*Exception:* Where the *Committee* determines that exceptional circumstances have prevented a player from starting on time, there is no penalty.

**b. Groups**
In stroke play, the *competitor* must remain throughout the round in the group arranged by the *Committee*, unless the *Committee* authorises or ratifies a change.

**PENALTY FOR BREACH OF RULE 6-3b:**
Disqualification.

(Best-ball and four-ball play – see Rules 30-3a and 31-2)

**6-4. Caddie**
The player may be assisted by a *caddie*, but he is limited to only one *caddie* at any one time.

**\*PENALTY FOR BREACH OF RULE 6-4:**
Match play – At the conclusion of the hole at which the breach is discovered, the state of the match is adjusted by deducting one hole for each hole at which a breach occurred; maximum deduction per round – Two holes.
Stroke play – Two strokes for each hole at which any breach occurred; maximum penalty per round – Four strokes (two strokes at each of the first two holes at which any breach occurred).
Match play or stroke play – If a breach is discovered between the play of two holes, it is deemed to have been discovered during play of the next hole, and the penalty must be applied accordingly.

Bogey and par competitions – See Note 1 to Rule 32-1a.
Stableford competitions – See Note 1 to Rule 32-1b.

*\*A player having more than one caddie in breach of this Rule must immediately upon discovery that a breach has occurred ensure that he has no more than one caddie at any one time during the remainder of the stipulated round. Otherwise, the player is disqualified.*

*Note:* The *Committee* may, in the conditions of a competition (Rule 33-1), prohibit the use of *caddies* or restrict a player in his choice of *caddie*.

**6-5. Ball**
The responsibility for playing the proper ball rests with the player. Each player should put an identification mark on his ball.

**a. Recording Scores**
After each hole the *marker* should check the score with the *competitor* and record it. On completion of the round the *marker* must sign the score card and hand it to the *competitor*. If more than one *marker* records the scores, each must sign for the part for which he is responsible.

**b. Signing and Returning Score Card**
After completion of the round, the *competitor* should check his score for each hole and settle any doubtful points with the *Committee*. He must ensure that the *marker* or *markers* have signed the score card, sign the score card himself and return it to the *Committee* as soon as possible.

**PENALTY FOR BREACH OF RULE 6-6b:**
Disqualification.

## c. Alteration of Score Card

No alteration may be made on a score card after the *competitor* has returned it to the *Committee*.

## d. Wrong Score for Hole

The *competitor* is responsible for the correctness of the score recorded for each hole on his score card. If he returns a score for any hole lower than actually taken, he is disqualified. If he returns a score for any hole higher than actually taken, the score as returned stands.

*Note 1:* The *Committee* is responsible for the addition of scores and application of the handicap recorded on the score card – see Rule 33-5.

*Note 2:* In *four-ball* stroke play, see also Rules 31-3 and 31-7a.

## 6-7. Undue Delay; Slow Play

The player must play without undue delay and in accordance with any pace of play guidelines that the *Committee* may establish. Between completion of a hole and playing from the next *teeing ground*, the player must not unduly delay play.

PENALTY FOR BREACH OF RULE 6-7:

Match play – Loss of hole; Stroke play – Two strokes.
Bogey and par competitions – See Note 2 to Rule 32-1a.
Stableford competitions – See Note 2 to Rule 32-1b.
For subsequent offence – Disqualification.

*Note 1:* If the player unduly delays play between holes, he is delaying the play of the next hole and, except for bogey, par and Stableford competitions (see Rule 32), the penalty applies to that hole.

*Note 2:* For the purpose of preventing slow play, the *Committee* may, in the conditions of a competition (Rule 33-1), establish pace of play guidelines including maximum periods of time allowed to complete a *stipulated round*, a hole or a *stroke*.

In match play, the *Committee* may, in such a condition, modify the penalty for a breach of this Rule as follows:

First offence – Loss of hole;
Second offence – Loss of hole;
For subsequent offence – Disqualification.

In stroke play, the *Committee* may, in such a condition, modify the penalty for a breach of this Rule as follows:

First offence – One stroke;
Second offence – Two strokes;
For subsequent offence – Disqualification.

## 6-8. Discontinuance of Play; Resumption of Play

## a. When Permitted

The player must not discontinue play unless:

(i)   the *Committee* has suspended play;
(ii)  he believes there is danger from lightning;
(iii) he is seeking a decision from the *Committee* on a doubtful or disputed point (see Rules 2-5 and 34-3); or
(iv)  there is some other good reason such as sudden illness. Bad weather is not of itself a good reason for discontinuing play.

If the player discontinues play without specific permission from the *Committee*, he must report to the *Committee* as soon as practicable. If he does so and the *Committee* considers his reason satisfactory, there is no penalty. Otherwise, he is disqualified.

*Exception in match play:* Players discontinuing match play by agreement are not subject to disqualification, unless by so doing the competition is delayed.

*Note:* Leaving the *course* does not of itself constitute discontinuance of play.

## b. Procedure When Play Suspended by Committee

When play is suspended by the *Committee*, if the players in a match or group are between the play of two holes, they must not resume play until the *Committee* has ordered a resumption of play. If they have started play of the hole, they may discontinue play immediately or continue play of the hole, provided they do so without delay. If the players choose to continue play of the hole, they are permitted to discontinue play before completing it. In any case, play must be discontinued after the hole is completed.

The players must resume play when the *Committee* has ordered a resumption of play.

PENALTY FOR BREACH OF RULE 6-8b:
Disqualification.

*Note:* The *Committee* may provide, in the conditions of a competition (Rule 33-1), that in potentially dangerous situations play must be discontinued immediately following a suspension of play by the *Committee*. If a player fails to discontinue play immediately, he is disqualified, unless circumstances warrant waiving the penalty as provided in Rule 33-7.

## c. Lifting Ball When Play Discontinued

When a player discontinues play of a hole under Rule 6-8a, he may lift his ball, without penalty, only if the *Committee* has suspended play or there is a good reason to lift it. Before lifting the ball the player must mark its position. If the player discontinues play and lifts his ball without specific permission from the *Committee*, he must, when reporting to the *Committee* (Rule 6-8a), report the lifting of the ball.

If the player lifts the ball without a good reason to do so, fails to mark the position of the ball before lifting it or fails to report the lifting of the ball, he incurs a penalty of one stroke.

## d. Procedure When Play Resumed

Play must be resumed from where it was discontinued, even if resumption occurs on a subsequent day. The player must, either before or when play is resumed, proceed as follows:

(i)   if the player has lifted the ball, he must, provided he was entitled to lift it under Rule 6-8c, place the original ball or a *substituted ball* on the spot from which the original ball was lifted. Otherwise, the original ball must be replaced;

(ii)  if the player has not lifted his ball, he may, provided he was entitled to lift it under Rule 6-8c, lift, clean and replace the ball, or substitute a ball, on the spot from which the original ball was lifted. Before lifting the ball he must mark its position; or

(iii) if the player's ball or ball-marker is moved (including by wind or water) while play is discontinued, a ball or ball-marker must be placed on the spot from which the original ball or ball-marker was moved.

*Note:* If the spot where the ball is to be placed is impossible to determine, it must be estimated and the ball placed on the estimated spot. The provisions of Rule 20-3c do not apply.

*PENALTY FOR BREACH OF RULE 6-8d:
Match play – Loss of hole; Stroke play – Two strokes.

*If a player incurs the general penalty for a breach of Rule 6-8d, there is no additional penalty under Rule 6-8c.

# Rule 7 – Practice

## Definitions

All defined terms are in *italics* and are listed alphabetically in the Definitions section – see pages 592–595.

## 7-1. Before or Between Rounds
### a. Match Play
On any day of a match play competition, a player may practise on the competition *course* before a round.

### b. Stroke Play
Before a round or play-off on any day of a stroke play competition, a *competitor* must not practise on the competition *course* or test the surface of any *putting green* on the *course* by rolling a ball or roughening or scraping the surface.

When two or more rounds of a stroke play competition are to be played over consecutive days, a *competitor* must not practise between those rounds on any competition *course* remaining to be played, or test the surface of any *putting green* on such *course* by rolling a ball or roughening or scraping the surface.

*Exception:* Practice putting or chipping on or near the first *teeing ground* or any practice area before starting a round or play-off is permitted.

PENALTY FOR BREACH OF RULE 7-1b:
Disqualification.

*Note:* The *Committee* may, in the conditions of a competition (Rule 33-1), prohibit practice on the competition *course* on any day of a match play competition or permit practice on the competition *course* or part of the *course* (Rule 33-2c) on any day of or between rounds of a stroke play competition.

## 7-2. During Round
A player must not make a practice *stroke* during play of a hole.

Between the play of two holes a player must not make a practice *stroke*, except that he may practise putting or chipping on or near:
a. the *putting green* of the hole last played,
b. any practice *putting green*, or
c. the *teeing ground* of the next hole to be played in the round, provided a practice *stroke* is not made from a *hazard* and does not unduly delay play (Rule 6-7).

*Strokes* made in continuing the play of a hole, the result of which has been decided, are not practice *strokes*.

*Exception:* When play has been suspended by the *Committee*, a player may, prior to resumption of play, practise
(a) as provided in this Rule,
(b) anywhere other than on the competition *course* and
(c) as otherwise permitted by the *Committee*.

PENALTY FOR BREACH OF RULE 7-2:
Match play – Loss of hole; Stroke play – Two strokes.
In the event of a breach between the play of two holes, the penalty applies to the next hole.

*Note 1:* A practice swing is not a practice *stroke* and may be taken at any place, provided the player does not breach the *Rules*.

*Note 2:* The *Committee* may, in the conditions of a competition (Rule 33-1), prohibit:
(a) practice on or near the *putting green* of the hole last played, and
(b) rolling a ball on the *putting green* of the hole last played.

## Rule 8 – Advice; Indicating Line of Play
### Definitions
All defined terms are in *italics* and are listed alphabetically in the Definitions section – see pages 592–595.

### 8-1. Advice
During a *stipulated round*, a player must not:
a. give *advice* to anyone in the competition playing on the *course* other than his *partner*, or
b. ask for *advice* from anyone other than his *partner* or either of their *caddies*.

## 8-2. Indicating Line of Play
### a. Other Than on Putting Green
Except on the *putting green*, a player may have the *line of play* indicated to him by anyone, but no one may be positioned by the player on or close to the line or an extension of the line beyond the *hole* while the *stroke* is being made. Any mark placed by the player or with his knowledge to indicate the line must be removed before the *stroke* is made.

*Exception: Flagstick* attended or held up – see Rule 17-1.

### b. On the Putting Green
When the player's ball is on the *putting green*, the player, his *partner* or either of their *caddies* may, before but not during the *stroke*, point out a line for putting, but in so doing the *putting green* must not be touched. A mark must not be placed anywhere to indicate a line for putting.

PENALTY FOR BREACH OF RULE:
Match play – Loss of hole; Stroke play – Two strokes.

*Note:* The *Committee* may, in the conditions of a team competition (Rule 33-1), permit each team to appoint one person who may give *advice* (including pointing out a line for putting) to members of that team. The *Committee* may establish conditions relating to the appointment and permitted conduct of that person, who must be identified to the *Committee* before giving *advice*.

## Rule 9 – Information as to Strokes Taken
### Definitions
All defined terms are in *italics* and are listed alphabetically in the Definitions section – see pages 592–595.

### 9-1. General
The number of *strokes* a player has taken includes any *penalty strokes* incurred.

### 9-2. Match Play
#### a. Information as to Strokes Taken
An *opponent* is entitled to ascertain from the player, during the play of a hole, the number of *strokes* he has taken and, after play of a hole, the number of *strokes* taken on the hole just completed.

#### b. Wrong Information
A player must not give wrong information to his *opponent*. If a player gives wrong information, he loses the hole.

A player is deemed to have given wrong information if he:
(i) fails to inform his *opponent* as soon as practicable that he has incurred a penalty, unless (a) he was obviously proceeding under a *Rule* involving a penalty and this was observed by his *opponent*, or (b) he corrects the mistake before his *opponent* makes his next *stroke*; or
(ii) gives incorrect information during play of a hole regarding the number of *strokes* taken and does not correct the mistake before his *opponent* makes his next *stroke*; or
(iii) gives incorrect information regarding the number of *strokes* taken to complete a hole and this affects the *opponent's* understanding of the result of the hole, unless he corrects the mistake before any player makes a *stroke* from the next *teeing ground* or, in the case of the last hole of the match, before all players leave the *putting green*.

A player has given wrong information even if it is due to the failure to include a penalty that he did not know he had incurred. It is the player's responsibility to know the *Rules*.

### 9-3. Stroke Play
A *competitor* who has incurred a penalty should inform his *marker* as soon as practicable.

## Order of Play

### Rule 10 – Order of Play
**Definitions**
All defined terms are in *italics* and are listed alphabetically in the Definitions section – see pages 592–595.
**10-1. Match Play**
**a. When Starting Play of Hole**
The *side* that has the *honour* at the first *teeing ground* is determined by the order of the draw. In the absence of a draw, the *honour* should be decided by lot.

The *side* that wins a hole takes the *honour* at the next *teeing ground*. If a hole has been halved, the *side* that had the *honour* at the previous *teeing ground* retains it.
**b. During Play of Hole**
After both players have started play of the hole, the ball farther from the *hole* is played first. If the balls are equidistant from the *hole* or their positions relative to the *hole* are not determinable, the ball to be played first should be decided by lot.

*Exception:* Rule 30-3b (*best-ball* and *four-ball* match play).

*Note:* When it becomes known that the original ball is not to be played as it lies and the player is required to play a ball as nearly as possible at the spot from which the original ball was last played (see Rule 20-5), the order of play is determined by the spot from which the previous *stroke* was made. When a ball may be played from a spot other than where the previous *stroke* was made, the order of play is determined by the position where the original ball came to rest.
**c. Playing Out of Turn**
If a player plays when his *opponent* should have played, there is no penalty, but the *opponent* may immediately require the player to cancel the *stroke* so made and, in correct order, play a ball as nearly as possible at the spot from which the original ball was last played (see Rule 20-5).
**10-2. Stroke Play**
**a. When Starting Play of Hole**
The *competitor* who has the *honour* at the first *teeing ground* is determined by the order of the draw. In the absence of a draw, the *honour* should be decided by lot.

The *competitor* with the lowest score at a hole takes the *honour* at the next *teeing ground*. The *competitor* with the second lowest score plays next and so on. If two or more *competitors* have the same score at a hole, they play from the next *teeing ground* in the same order as at the previous *teeing ground*.

*Exception:* Rule 32-1 (handicap bogey, par and Stableford competitions).
**b. During Play of Hole**
After the *competitors* have started play of the hole, the ball farthest from the *hole* is played first. If two or more balls are equidistant from the *hole* or their positions relative to the *hole* are not determinable, the ball to be played first should be decided by lot.

*Exceptions:* Rules 22 (ball assisting or interfering with play) and 31-4 (*four-ball* stroke play).

*Note:* When it becomes known that the original ball is not to be played as it lies and the *competitor* is required to play a ball as nearly as possible at the spot from which the original ball was last played (see Rule 20-5), the order of play is determined by the spot from which the previous *stroke* was made. When a ball may be played from a spot other than where the previous *stroke* was made, the order of play is determined by the position where the original ball came to rest.

**c. Playing Out of Turn**
If a *competitor* plays out of turn, there is no penalty and the ball is played as it lies. If, however, the *Committee* determines that *competitors* have agreed to play out of turn to give one of them an advantage, they are disqualified.

(Making stroke while another ball in motion after stroke from putting green – see Rule 16-1f)

(Incorrect order of play in foursome stroke play – see Rule 29-3)
**10-3. Provisional Ball or Another Ball from Teeing Ground**
If a player plays a *provisional ball* or another ball from the *teeing ground*, he must do so after his *opponent* or *fellow-competitor* has made his first *stroke*. If more than one player elects to play a *provisional ball* or is required to play another ball from the *teeing ground*, the original order of play must be retained. If a player plays a *provisional ball* or another ball out of turn, Rule 10-1c or 10-2c applies.

## Teeing Ground

### Rule 11 – Teeing Ground
**Definitions**
All defined terms are in *italics* and are listed alphabetically in the Definitions section – see pages 592–595.
**11-1. Teeing**
When a player is putting a ball into play from the *teeing ground*, it must be played from within the *teeing ground* and from the surface of the ground or from a conforming tee (see Appendix IV) in or on the surface of the ground.

For the purposes of this Rule, the surface of the ground includes an irregularity of surface (whether or not created by the player) and sand or other natural substance (whether or not placed by the player).

If a player makes a *stroke* at a ball on a non-conforming tee, or at a ball teed in a manner not permitted by this Rule, he is disqualified.

A player may stand outside the *teeing ground* to play a ball within it.
**11-2. Tee-Markers**
Before a player makes his first *stroke* with any ball on the *teeing ground* of the hole being played, the tee-markers are deemed to be fixed. In these circumstances, if the player moves or allows to be moved a tee-marker for the purpose of avoiding interference with his *stance*, the area of his intended swing or his *line of play*, he incurs the penalty for a breach of Rule 13-2.
**11-3. Ball Falling off Tee**
If a ball, when not *in play*, falls off a tee or is knocked off a tee by the player in *addressing* it, it may be re-teed, without penalty. However, if a *stroke* is made at the ball in these circumstances, whether the ball is moving or not, the *stroke* counts, but there is no penalty.
**11-4. Playing from Outside Teeing Ground**
**a. Match Play**
If a player, when starting a hole, plays a ball from outside the *teeing ground*, there is no penalty, but the *opponent* may immediately require the player to cancel the *stroke* and play a ball from within the *teeing ground*.
**b. Stroke Play**
If a *competitor*, when starting a hole, plays a ball from outside the *teeing ground*, he incurs a penalty of two strokes and must then play a ball from within the *teeing ground*.

If the *competitor* makes a *stroke* from the next *teeing ground* without first correcting his mistake or, in the case of the last hole of the round, leaves the *putting green* without first declaring his intention to correct his mistake, he is disqualified.

The *stroke* from outside the *teeing ground* and any subsequent *strokes* by the *competitor* on the hole prior to his correction of the mistake do not count in his score.

**11-5. Playing from Wrong Teeing Ground**
The provisions of Rule 11-4 apply.

## Playing the Ball

### Rule 12 – Searching for and Identifying Ball
**Definitions**
All defined terms are in *italics* and are listed alphabetically in the Definitions section – see pages 592–595.

**12-1. Seeing Ball; Searching for Ball**
A player is not necessarily entitled to see his ball when making a *stroke*.

In searching for his ball anywhere on the *course*, the player may touch or bend long grass, rushes, bushes, whins, heather or the like, but only to the extent necessary to find or identify the ball, provided that this does not improve the lie of the ball, the area of his intended *stance* or swing or his *line of play*; if the ball is *moved*, Rule 18-2a applies except as provided in clauses a–d of this Rule.

In addition to the methods of searching for and identifying a ball that are otherwise permitted by the *Rules*, the player may also search for and identify a ball under Rule 12-1 as follows:

**a. Searching for or Identifying Ball Covered by Sand**
If the player's ball lying anywhere on the *course* is believed to be covered by sand, to the extent that he cannot find or identify it, he may, without penalty, touch or move the sand in order to find or identify the ball. If the ball is found, and identified as his, the player must re-create the lie as nearly as possible by replacing the sand. If the ball is *moved* during the touching or moving of sand while searching for or identifying the ball, there is no penalty; the ball must be replaced and the lie re-created.

In re-creating a lie under this Rule, the player is permitted to leave a small part of the ball visible.

**b. Searching for or Identifying Ball Covered by Loose Impediments in Hazard**
In a *hazard*, if the player's ball is believed to be covered by *loose impediments* to the extent that he cannot find or identify it, he may, without penalty, touch or move *loose impediments* in order to find or identify the ball. If the ball is found or identified as his, the player must replace the *loose impediments*. If the ball is *moved* during the touching or moving of *loose impediments* while searching for or identifying the ball, Rule 18-2a applies; if the ball is *moved* during the replacement of the *loose impediments*, there is no penalty and the ball must be replaced.

If the ball was entirely covered by *loose impediments*, the player must re-cover the ball but is permitted to leave a small part of the ball visible.

**c. Searching for Ball in Water in Water Hazard**
If a ball is believed to be lying in water in a *water hazard*, the player may, without penalty, probe for it with a club or otherwise. If the ball in water is accidentally *moved* while probing, there is no penalty; the ball must be replaced, unless the player elects to proceed under Rule 26-1. If the *moved* ball was not lying in water or the ball was accidentally *moved* by the player other than while probing, Rule 18-2a applies.

**d. Searching for Ball Within Obstruction or Abnormal Ground Condition**
If a ball lying in or on an *obstruction* or in an *abnormal ground condition* is accidentally *moved* during search, there is no penalty; the ball must be replaced unless the player elects to proceed under Rule 24-1b, 24-2b or 25-1b as applicable. If the player replaces the ball, he may still proceed under one of those Rules, if applicable.

PENALTY FOR BREACH OF RULE 12-1:
Match Play – Loss of Hole; Stroke Play – Two Strokes.

(Improving lie, area of intended stance or swing, or line of play – see Rule 13-2)

**Rule 12-2. Lifting Ball for Identification**
The responsibility for playing the proper ball rests with the player. Each player should put an identification mark on his ball.

If a player believes that a ball at rest might be his, but he cannot identify it, the player may lift the ball for identification, without penalty. The right to lift a ball for identification is in addition to the actions permitted under Rule 12-1.

Before lifting the ball, the player must announce his intention to his *opponent* in match play or his *marker* or a *fellow-competitor* in stroke play and mark the position of the ball. He may then lift the ball and identify it, provided that he gives his *opponent*, *marker* or *fellow-competitor* an opportunity to observe the lifting and replacement. The ball must not be cleaned beyond the extent necessary for identification when lifted under Rule 12-2.

If the ball is the player's ball and he fails to comply with all or any part of this procedure, or he lifts his ball in order to identify it without having good reason to do so, he incurs a penalty of one stroke. If the lifted ball is the player's ball, he must replace it. If he fails to do so, he incurs the general penalty for a breach of Rule 12-2, but there is no additional penalty under this Rule.

*Note:* If the original lie of a ball to be replaced has been altered, see Rule 20-3b.

*PENALTY FOR BREACH OF RULE 12-2:
Match Play – Loss of hole; Stroke Play – Two strokes.

*If a player incurs the general penalty for a breach of Rule 12-2, there is no additional penalty under this Rule.

### Rule 13 – Ball Played as It Lies
**Definitions**
All defined terms are in *italics* and are listed alphabetically in the Definitions section – see pages 592–595.

**13-1. General**
The ball must be played as it lies, except as otherwise provided in the *Rules*. (Ball at rest moved – see Rule 18)

**13-2. Improving Lie, Area of Intended Stance or Swing, or Line of Play**
A player must not improve or allow to be improved:
• the position or lie of his ball,
• the area of his intended *stance* or swing,
• his *line of play* or a reasonable extension of that line beyond the *hole*, or
• the area in which he is to drop or place a ball, by any of the following actions:
• pressing a club on the ground,
• moving, bending or breaking anything growing or fixed (including immovable *obstructions* and objects defining *out of bounds*),
• creating or eliminating irregularities of surface,
• removing or pressing down sand, loose soil, replaced divots or other cut turf placed in position, or
• removing dew, frost or water.
However, the player incurs no penalty if the action occurs:

- in grounding the club lightly when *addressing the ball*,
- in fairly taking his *stance*,
- in making a *stroke* or the backward movement of his club for a *stroke* and the *stroke* is made,
- in creating or eliminating irregularities of surface within the *teeing ground* or in removing dew, frost or water from the *teeing ground*, or
- on the *putting green* in removing sand and loose soil or in repairing damage (Rule 16-1).

*Exception:* Ball in *hazard* – see Rule 13-4.

### 13-3. Building Stance
A player is entitled to place his feet firmly in taking his *stance*, but he must not build a *stance*.

### 13-4. Ball in Hazard; Prohibited Actions
Except as provided in the *Rules*, before making a *stroke* at a ball that is in a *hazard* (whether a *bunker* or a *water hazard*) or that, having been lifted from a *hazard*, may be dropped or placed in the *hazard*, the player must not:
a. Test the condition of the *hazard* or any similar *hazard*;
b. Touch the ground in the *hazard* or water in the *water hazard* with his hand or a club; or
c. Touch or move a *loose impediment* lying in or touching the *hazard*.

*Exceptions:*
1. Provided nothing is done that constitutes testing the condition of the *hazard* or improves the lie of the ball, there is no penalty if the player (a) touches the ground or *loose impediments* in any *hazard* or water in a *water hazard* as a result of or to prevent falling, in removing an *obstruction*, in measuring or in marking the position of, retrieving, lifting, placing or replacing a ball under any *Rule* or (b) places his clubs in a *hazard*.
2. At any time, the player may smooth sand or soil in a *hazard* provided this is for the sole purpose of caring for the *course* and nothing is done to breach Rule 13-2 with respect to his next *stroke*. If a ball played from a *hazard* is outside the *hazard* after the *stroke*, the player may smooth sand or soil in the *hazard* without restriction.
3. If the player makes a *stroke* from a *hazard* and the ball comes to rest in another *hazard*, Rule 13-4a does not apply to any subsequent actions taken in the *hazard* from which the *stroke* was made.

*Note:* At any time, including at *address* or in the backward movement for the *stroke*, the player may touch, with a club or otherwise, any *obstruction*, any construction declared by the *Committee* to be an integral part of the *course* or any grass, bush, tree or other growing thing.

PENALTY FOR BREACH OF RULE:
Match play – Loss of hole; Stroke play – Two strokes.
(Searching for ball – see Rule 12-1)
(Relief for ball in water hazard – see Rule 26)

## Rule 14 – Striking the Ball

### Definitions
All defined terms are in *italics* and are listed alphabetically in the Definitions section – see pages 592–595.

### 14-1. Ball to be Fairly Struck At
The ball must be fairly struck at with the head of the club and must not be pushed, scraped or spooned.

### 14-2. Assistance
#### a. Physical Assistance and Protection from Elements
A player must not make a *stroke* while accepting physical assistance or protection from the elements.

#### b. Positioning of Caddie or Partner Behind Ball
A player must not make a *stroke* with his *caddie*, his *partner* or his *partner's caddie* positioned on or close to an extension of the *line of play* or *line of putt* behind the ball.

Exception: There is no penalty if the player's *caddie*, his *partner* or his *partner's caddie* is inadvertently located on or close to an extension of the *line of play* or *line of putt* behind the ball.

PENALTY FOR BREACH OF RULE 14-1 or 14-2:
Match play – Loss of hole; Stroke play – Two strokes.

### 14-3. Artificial Devices, Unusual Equipment and Unusual Use of Equipment
The *R&A* reserves the right, at any time, to change the *Rules* relating to artificial devices, unusual *equipment* and the unusual use of *equipment*, and to make or change the interpretations relating to these *Rules*.

A player in doubt as to whether use of an item would constitute a breach of Rule 14-3 should consult the *R&A*.

A manufacturer should submit to The *R&A* a sample of an item to be manufactured for a ruling as to whether its use during a *stipulated round* would cause a player to be in breach of Rule 14-3. The sample becomes the property of The *R&A* for reference purposes. If a manufacturer fails to submit a sample or, having submitted a sample, fails to await a ruling before manufacturing and/or marketing the item, the manufacturer assumes the risk of a ruling that use of the item would be contrary to the *Rules*.

Except as provided in the *Rules*, during a *stipulated round* the player must not use any artificial device or unusual *equipment* (see Appendix IV for detailed specifications and interpretations), or use any *equipment* in an unusual manner:
a. That might assist him in making a *stroke* or in his play; or
b. For the purpose of gauging or measuring distance or conditions that might affect his play; or
c. That might assist him in gripping the club, except that:
   (i)   gloves may be worn provided that they are plain gloves;
   (ii)  resin, powder and drying or moisturising agents may be used; and
   (iii) a towel or handkerchief may be wrapped around the grip.

*Exceptions:*
1. A player is not in breach of this Rule if (a) the *equipment* or device is designed for or has the effect of alleviating a medical condition, (b) the player has a legitimate medical reason to use the *equipment* or device, and (c) the *Committee* is satisfied that its use does not give the player any undue advantage over other players.
2. A player is not in breach of this Rule if he uses *equipment* in a traditionally accepted manner.

PENALTY FOR BREACH OF RULE 14-3:
Disqualification.

*Note:* The *Committee* may make a Local Rule allowing players to use devices that measure or gauge distance only.

### 14-4. Striking the Ball More Than Once
If a player's club strikes the ball more than once in the course of a *stroke*, the player must count the *stroke* and add a *penalty stroke*, making two strokes in all.

### 14-5. Playing Moving Ball
A player must not make a *stroke* at his ball while it is moving.

*Exceptions:*
- Ball falling off tee – Rule 11-3
- Striking the ball more than once – Rule 14-4
- Ball moving in water – Rule 14-6

When the ball begins to *move* only after the player has begun the *stroke* or the backward movement of his club for the *stroke*, he incurs no penalty under this Rule for playing a moving ball, but he is not exempt from any penalty under the following Rules:

- Ball at rest *moved* by player – Rule 18-2a
- Ball at rest moving after *address* – Rule 18-2b
(Ball purposely deflected or stopped by player, partner or caddie – see Rule 1-2)

**14-6. Ball Moving in Water**
When a ball is moving in water in a *water hazard*, the player may, without penalty, make a *stroke*, but he must not delay making his *stroke* in order to allow the wind or current to improve the position of the ball. A ball moving in water in a *water hazard* may be lifted if the player elects to invoke Rule 26.

PENALTY FOR BREACH OF RULE 14-5 or 14-6:
Match play – Loss of hole; Stroke play – Two strokes.

## Rule 15 – Substituted Ball; Wrong Ball

**Definitions**
All defined terms are in *italics* and are listed alphabetically in the Definitions section – see pages 592–595.

**15-1. General**
A player must hole out with the ball played from the *teeing ground*, unless the ball is *lost* or *out of bounds* or the player *substitutes* another ball, whether or not substitution is permitted (see Rule 15-2). If a player plays a *wrong ball*, see Rule 15-3.

**15-2. Substituted Ball**
A player may *substitute* a ball when proceeding under a *Rule* that permits the player to play, drop or place another ball in completing the play of a hole. The *substituted ball* becomes the *ball in play*.
If a player *substitutes* a ball when not permitted to do so under the *Rules*, that *substituted ball* is not a *wrong ball*; it becomes the *ball in play*. If the mistake is not corrected as provided in Rule 20-6 and the player makes a *stroke* at a wrongly *substituted ball*, he loses the hole in match play or incurs a penalty of two strokes in stroke play under the applicable *Rule* and, in stroke play, must play out the hole with the *substituted ball*.
*Exception:* If a player incurs a penalty for making a *stroke* from a wrong place, there is no additional penalty for substituting a ball when not permitted.
(Playing from wrong place – see Rule 20-7)

**15-3. Wrong Ball**
**a. Match Play**
If a player makes a *stroke* at a *wrong ball*, he loses the hole.
If the *wrong ball* belongs to another player, its owner must place a ball on the spot from which the *wrong ball* was first played.
If the player and *opponent* exchange balls during the play of a hole, the first to make a *stroke* at a *wrong ball* loses the hole; when this cannot be determined, the hole must be played out with the balls exchanged.
*Exception:* There is no penalty if a player makes a *stroke* at a *wrong ball* that is moving in water in a *water hazard*. Any *strokes* made at a *wrong ball* moving in water in a *water hazard* do not count in the player's score. The player must correct his mistake by playing the correct ball or by proceeding under the *Rules*.
(Placing and Replacing – see Rule 20-3)

**b. Stroke Play**
If a *competitor* makes a *stroke* or *strokes* at a *wrong ball*, he incurs a penalty of two strokes.
The *competitor* must correct his mistake by playing the correct ball or by proceeding under the *Rules*. If he fails to correct his mistake before making a *stroke* on the next *teeing ground* or, in the case of the last hole of the round, fails to declare his intention to correct his mistake before leaving the *putting green*, he is disqualified.

*Strokes* made by a *competitor* with a *wrong ball* do not count in his score. If the *wrong ball* belongs to another *competitor*, its owner must place a ball on the spot from which the *wrong ball* was first played.
*Exception:* There is no penalty if a *competitor* makes a *stroke* at a *wrong ball* that is moving in water in a *water hazard*. Any *strokes* made at a *wrong ball* moving in water in a *water hazard* do not count in the *competitor's* score.
(Placing and Replacing – see Rule 20-3)

# The Putting Green

## Rule 16 – The Putting Green

**Definitions**
All defined terms are in *italics* and are listed alphabetically in the Definitions section – see pages 592–595.

**16-1. General**
**a. Touching Line of Putt**
The *line of putt* must not be touched except:
(i) the player may remove *loose impediments*, provided he does not press anything down;
(ii) the player may place the club in front of the ball when *addressing* it, provided he does not press anything down;
(iii) in measuring – Rule 18-6;
(iv) in lifting or replacing the ball – Rule 16-1b;
(v) in pressing down a ball-marker;
(vi) in repairing old *hole* plugs or ball marks on the *putting green* – Rule 16-1c; and
(vii) in removing movable *obstructions* – Rule 24-1.
(Indicating line for putting on putting green – see Rule 8-2b)

**b. Lifting and Cleaning Ball**
A ball on the *putting green* may be lifted and, if desired, cleaned. The position of the ball must be marked before it is lifted and the ball must be replaced (see Rule 20-1). When another ball is in motion, a ball that might influence the movement of the ball in motion must not be lifted.

**c. Repair of Hole Plugs, Ball Marks and Other Damage**
The player may repair an old *hole* plug or damage to the *putting green* caused by the impact of a ball, whether or not the player's ball lies on the *putting green*. If a ball or ball-marker is accidentally *moved* in the process of the repair, the ball or ball-marker must be replaced. There is no penalty, provided the movement of the ball or ball-marker is directly attributable to the specific act of repairing an old *hole* plug or damage to the *putting green* caused by the impact of a ball. Otherwise, Rule 18 applies.
Any other damage to the *putting green* must not be repaired if it might assist the player in his subsequent play of the hole.

**d. Testing Surface**
During the *stipulated round*, a player must not test the surface of any *putting green* by rolling a ball or roughening or scraping the surface.
*Exception:* Between the play of two holes, a player may test the surface of any practice *putting green* and the *putting green* of the hole just played, unless the Committee has prohibited such action (see Note 2 to Rule 7-2).

**e. Standing Astride or on Line of Putt**
The player must not make a *stroke* on the *putting green* from a *stance* astride, or with either foot touching, the *line of putt* or an extension of that line behind the ball.
*Exception:* There is no penalty if the *stance* is inadvertently taken on or astride the *line of putt* (or an extension of that line behind the ball) or is taken to avoid standing on another player's *line of putt* or prospective *line of putt*.

### f. Making Stroke While Another Ball in Motion

The player must not make a *stroke* while another ball is in motion after a *stroke* from the *putting green*, except that if a player does so, there is no penalty if it was his turn to play.

(Lifting ball assisting or interfering with play while another ball in motion – see Rule 22)

PENALTY FOR BREACH OF RULE 16-1:

Match play – Loss of hole; Stroke play – Two strokes.

(Position of caddie or partner – see Rule 14-2)
(Wrong putting green – see Rule 25-3)

### 16-2. Ball Overhanging Hole

When any part of the ball overhangs the lip of the *hole*, the player is allowed enough time to reach the *hole* without unreasonable delay and an additional ten seconds to determine whether the ball is at rest. If by then the ball has not fallen into the *hole*, it is deemed to be at rest. If the ball subsequently falls into the *hole*, the player is deemed to have *holed* out with his last *stroke*, and must add a *penalty stroke* to his score for the hole; otherwise, there is no penalty under this Rule.

(Undue delay – see Rule 6-7)

## Rule 17 – The Flagstick

**Definitions**

All defined terms are in *italics* and are listed alphabetically in the Definitions section – see pages 592–595.

### 17-1. Flagstick Attended, Removed or Held Up

Before making a *stroke* from anywhere on the *course*, the player may have the *flagstick* attended, removed or held up to indicate the position of the *hole*.

If the *flagstick* is not attended, removed or held up before the player makes a *stroke*, it must not be attended, removed or held up during the *stroke* or while the player's ball is in motion if doing so might influence the movement of the ball.

*Note 1:* If the *flagstick* is in the *hole* and anyone stands near it while a *stroke* is being made, he is deemed to be attending the *flagstick*.

*Note 2:* If, prior to the *stroke*, the *flagstick* is attended, removed or held up by anyone with the player's knowledge and he makes no objection, the player is deemed to have authorised it.

*Note 3:* If anyone attends or holds up the *flagstick* while a *stroke* is being made, he is deemed to be attending the *flagstick* until the ball comes to rest.

(Moving attended, removed or held-up flagstick while ball in motion – see Rule 24-1)

### 17-2. Unauthorised Attendance

If an *opponent* or his *caddie* in match play or a *fellow-competitor* or his *caddie* in stroke play, without the player's authority or prior knowledge, attends, removes or holds up the *flagstick* during the *stroke* or while the ball is in motion, and the act might influence the movement of the ball, the *opponent* or *fellow-competitor* incurs the applicable penalty.

\*PENALTY FOR BREACH OF RULE 17-1 or 17-2:

Match play – Loss of hole; Stroke play – Two strokes.

*\*In stroke play, if a breach of Rule 17-2 occurs and the competitor's ball subsequently strikes the flagstick, the person attending or holding it or anything carried by him, the competitor incurs no penalty. The ball is played as it lies, except that if the stroke was made on the putting green, the stroke is cancelled and the ball must be replaced and replayed.*

### 17-3. Ball Striking Flagstick or Attendant

The player's ball must not strike:

a. The *flagstick* when it is attended, removed or held up;

b. The person attending or holding up the *flagstick* or anything carried by him; or

c. The *flagstick* in the *hole*, unattended, when the *stroke* has been made on the *putting green*.

*Exception:* When the *flagstick* is attended, removed or held up without the player's authority – see Rule 17-2.

PENALTY FOR BREACH OF RULE 17-3:

Match play – Loss of hole; Stroke play – Two strokes and the ball must be played as it lies.

### 17-4. Ball Resting Against Flagstick

When a player's ball rests against the *flagstick* in the *hole* and the ball is not *holed*, the player or another person authorised by him may move or remove the *flagstick*, and if the ball falls into the *hole*, the player is deemed to have *holed* out with his last *stroke*; otherwise, the ball, if *moved*, must be placed on the lip of the *hole*, without penalty.

## Ball Moved, Deflected or Stopped

## Rule 18 – Ball at Rest Moved

**Definitions**

All defined terms are in *italics* and are listed alphabetically in the Definitions section – see pages 592–595.

### 18-1. By Outside Agency

If a ball at rest is *moved* by an *outside agency*, there is no penalty and the ball must be replaced. Note: It is a question of fact whether a ball has been *moved* by an *outside agency*. In order to apply this Rule, it must be known or virtually certain that an *outside agency* has *moved* the ball. In the absence of such knowledge or certainty, the player must play the ball as it lies or, if the ball is not found, proceed under Rule 27-1.

(Player's ball at rest moved by another ball – see Rule 18-5)

### 18-2. By Player, Partner, Caddie or Equipment
**a. General**

Except as permitted by the *Rules*, when a player's ball is in play, if

(i)  the player, his *partner* or either of their *caddies*:
- lifts or *moves* the ball,
- touches it purposely (except with a club in the act of *addressing* the ball), or
- causes the ball to *move*, or

(ii)  the *equipment* of the player or his *partner* causes the ball to *move*,

the player incurs a penalty of one stroke.

If the ball is *moved*, it must be replaced, unless the movement of the ball occurs after the player has begun the *stroke* or the backward movement of the club for the *stroke* and the *stroke* is made.

Under the *Rules* there is no penalty if a player accidentally causes his ball to *move* in the following circumstances:

- In searching for a ball covered by sand, in the replacement of *loose impediments* moved in a *hazard* while finding or identifying a ball, in probing for a ball lying in water in a *water hazard* or in searching for a ball in an *obstruction* or an *abnormal ground condition* – Rule 12-1
- In repairing a *hole* plug or ball mark – Rule 16-1c
- In measuring – Rule 18-6
- In lifting a ball under a *Rule* – Rule 20-1
- In placing or replacing a ball under a *Rule* – Rule 20-3a
- In removing a *loose impediment* on the *putting green* – Rule 23-1
- In removing movable *obstructions* – Rule 24-1

**b. Ball Moving After Address**

If a player's *ball in play moves* after he has *addressed* it (other than as a result of a *stroke*), the player is deemed to have *moved* the ball and incurs a penalty of one stroke.

The ball must be replaced, unless the movement of the ball occurs after the player has begun the *stroke* or the backward movement of the club for the *stroke* and the *stroke* is made.

*Exception:* If it is known or virtually certain that the player did not cause his ball to *move*, Rule 18-2b does not apply.

### 18-3. By Opponent, Caddie or Equipment in Match Play

**a. During Search**

If, during search for a player's ball, an *opponent*, his *caddie* or his *equipment moves* the ball, touches it or causes it to *move*, there is no penalty. If the ball is *moved*, it must be replaced.

**b. Other Than During Search**

If, other than during search for a player's ball, an *opponent*, his *caddie* or his *equipment moves* the ball, touches it purposely or causes it to *move*, except as otherwise provided in the *Rules*, the opponent incurs a penalty of one stroke. If the ball is *moved*, it must be replaced.

(Playing a wrong ball – see Rule 15-3)
(Ball moved in measuring – see Rule 18-6)

### 18-4. By Fellow-Competitor, Caddie or Equipment in Stroke Play

If a *fellow-competitor*, his *caddie* or his *equipment moves* the player's ball, touches it or causes it to *move*, there is no penalty. If the ball is *moved*, it must be replaced.

(Playing a wrong ball – see Rule 15-3)

### 18-5. By Another Ball

If a *ball in play* and at rest is *moved* by another ball in motion after a *stroke*, the *moved* ball must be replaced.

### 18-6. Ball Moved in Measuring

If a ball or ball-marker is *moved* in measuring while proceeding under or in determining the application of a *Rule*, the ball or ball-marker must be replaced. There is no penalty, provided the movement of the ball or ball-marker is directly attributable to the specific act of measuring. Otherwise, the provisions of Rule 18-2a, 18-3b or 18-4 apply.

***PENALTY FOR BREACH OF RULE:***
Match play – Loss of hole; Stroke play – Two strokes.

*If a player who is required to replace a ball fails to do so, or if he makes a *stroke* at a ball *substituted* under Rule 18 when such substitution is not permitted, he incurs the general penalty for breach of Rule 18, but there is no additional penalty under this Rule.

*Note 1:* If a ball to be replaced under this Rule is not immediately recoverable, another ball may be *substituted*.

*Note 2:* If the original lie of a ball to be placed or replaced has been altered, see Rule 20-3b.

*Note 3:* If it is impossible to determine the spot on which a ball is to be placed or replaced, see Rule 20-3c.

## Rule 19 – Ball in Motion Deflected or Stopped

**Definitions**

All defined terms are in *italics* and are listed alphabetically in the Definitions section – see pages 592–595.

### 19-1. By Outside Agency

If a player's ball in motion is accidentally deflected or stopped by any *outside agency*, it is a *rub of the green*, there is no penalty and the ball must be played as it lies, except:

a. If a player's ball in motion after a *stroke* other than on the *putting green* comes to rest in or on any moving or animate *outside agency*, the ball must *through the green* or in a *hazard* be dropped, or on the *putting green* be placed, as near as possible to the spot directly under the place where the ball came to rest in or on the *outside agency*, but not nearer the *hole*, and

b. If a player's ball in motion after a *stroke* on the *putting green* is deflected or stopped by, or comes to rest in or on, any moving or animate *outside agency*, except a worm, insect or the like, the *stroke* is cancelled. The ball must be replaced and replayed.

If the ball is not immediately recoverable, another ball may be *substituted*.

*Exception:* Ball striking person attending or holding up *flagstick* or anything carried by him – see Rule 17-3b.

*Note:* If a player's ball in motion has been deliberately deflected or stopped by an *outside agency*:

(a) after a *stroke* from anywhere other than on the *putting green*, the spot where the ball would have come to rest must be estimated. If that spot is:

   (i) *through the green* or in a *hazard*, the ball must be dropped as near as possible to that spot;

   (ii) *out of bounds*, the player must proceed under Rule 27-1; or

   (iii) on the *putting green*, the ball must be placed on that spot.

(b) after a *stroke* on the *putting green*, the *stroke* is cancelled. The ball must be replaced and replayed.

If the *outside agency* is a *fellow-competitor* or his *caddie*, Rule 1-2 applies to the *fellow-competitor*.

(Player's ball deflected or stopped by another ball – see Rule 19-5)

### 19-2. By Player, Partner, Caddie or Equipment

If a player's ball is accidentally deflected or stopped by himself, his *partner* or either of their *caddies* or *equipment*, the player incurs a penalty of one stroke. The ball must be played as it lies, except when it comes to rest in or on the player's, his *partner's* or either of their *caddies'* clothes or *equipment*, in which case the ball must *through the green* or in a *hazard* be dropped, or on the *putting green* be placed, as near as possible to the spot directly under the place where the ball came to rest in or on the article, but not nearer the *hole*.

*Exceptions:*

1. Ball striking person attending or holding up *flagstick* or anything carried by him – see Rule 17-3b.

2. Dropped ball – see Rule 20-2a.

(Ball purposely deflected or stopped by player, partner or caddie – see Rule 1-2)

### 19-3. By Opponent, Caddie or Equipment in Match Play

If a player's ball is accidentally deflected or stopped by an *opponent*, his *caddie* or his *equipment*, there is no penalty. The player may, before another *stroke* is made by either side, cancel the *stroke* and play a ball, without penalty, as nearly as possible to the spot from which the original ball was last played (Rule 20-5) or he may play the ball as it lies. However, if the player elects not to cancel the *stroke* and the ball has come to rest in or on the *opponent's* or his *caddie's* clothes or *equipment*, the ball must *through the green* or in a *hazard* be dropped, or on the *putting green* be placed, as near as possible to the spot directly under the place where the ball came to rest in or on the article, but not nearer the *hole*.

*Exception:* Ball striking person attending or holding up *flagstick* or anything carried by him – see Rule 17-3b.

(Ball purposely deflected or stopped by opponent or caddie – see Rule 1-2)

### 19-4. By Fellow-Competitor, Caddie or Equipment in Stroke Play

See Rule 19-1 regarding ball deflected by *outside agency*.

*Exception:* Ball striking person attending or holding up *flagstick* or anything carried by him – see Rule 17-3b.

## 19-5. By Another Ball
### a. At Rest
If a player's ball in motion after a *stroke* is deflected or stopped by a *ball in play* and at rest, the player must play his ball as it lies. In match play, there is no penalty. In stroke play, there is no penalty, unless both balls lay on the *putting green* prior to the *stroke*, in which case the player incurs a penalty of two strokes.

### b. In Motion
If a player's ball in motion after a *stroke* other than on the *putting green* is deflected or stopped by another ball in motion after a *stroke*, the player must play his ball as it lies, without penalty.

If a player's ball in motion after a *stroke* on the *putting green* is deflected or stopped by another ball in motion after a *stroke*, the player's *stroke* is cancelled. The ball must be replaced and replayed, without penalty.

*Note:* Nothing in this Rule overrides the provisions of Rule 10-1 (Order of Play in Match Play) or Rule 16-1f (Making Stroke While Another Ball in Motion).

PENALTY FOR BREACH OF RULE:
Match play – Loss of hole; Stroke play – Two strokes.

## Relief Situations and Procedure

### Rule 20 – Lifting, Dropping and Placing; Playing from Wrong Place

**Definitions**
All defined terms are in *italics* and are listed alphabetically in the Definitions section – see pages 592–595.

### 20-1. Lifting and Marking
A ball to be lifted under the *Rules* may be lifted by the player, his *partner* or another person authorised by the player. In any such case, the player is responsible for any breach of the Rules.

The position of the ball must be marked before it is lifted under a *Rule* that requires it to be replaced. If it is not marked, the player incurs a penalty of one stroke and the ball must be replaced. If it is not replaced, the player incurs the general penalty for breach of this Rule but there is no additional penalty under Rule 20-1.

If a ball or ball-marker is accidentally *moved* in the process of lifting the ball under a *Rule* or marking its position, the ball or ball-marker must be replaced. There is no penalty, provided the movement of the ball or ballmarker is directly attributable to the specific act of marking the position of or lifting the ball. Otherwise, the player incurs a penalty of one stroke under this Rule or Rule 18-2a.

*Exception:* If a player incurs a penalty for failing to act in accordance with Rule 5-3 or 12-2, there is no additional penalty under Rule 20-1.

*Note:* The position of a ball to be lifted should be marked by placing a ball-marker, a small coin or other similar object immediately behind the ball.

If the ball-marker interferes with the play, *stance* or *stroke* of another player, it should be placed one or more clubhead-lengths to one side.

### 20-2. Dropping and Re-Dropping
### a. By Whom and How
A ball to be dropped under the Rules must be dropped by the player himself. He must stand erect, hold the ball at shoulder height and arm's length and drop it. If a ball is dropped by any other person or in any other manner and the error is not corrected as provided in Rule 20-6, the player incurs a penalty of one stroke.

If the ball, when dropped, touches any person or the *equipment* of any player before or after it strikes a part of

the *course* and before it comes to rest, the ball must be re-dropped, without penalty. There is no limit to the number of times a ball must be re-dropped in these circumstances.

(Taking action to influence position or movement of ball – see Rule 1-2)

### b. Where to Drop
When a ball is to be dropped as near as possible to a specific spot, it must be dropped not nearer the *hole* than the specific spot which, if it is not precisely known to the player, must be estimated.

A ball when dropped must first strike a part of the *course* where the applicable *Rule* requires it to be dropped. If it is not so dropped, Rules 20-6 and 20-7 apply.

### c. When to Re-Drop
A dropped ball must be re-dropped, without penalty, if it:
(i) rolls into and comes to rest in a *hazard;*
(ii) rolls out of and comes to rest outside a *hazard;*
(iii) rolls onto and comes to rest on a *putting green;*
(iv) rolls and comes to rest *out of bounds;*
(v) rolls to and comes to rest in a position where there is interference by the condition from which relief was taken under Rule 24-2b (immovable obstruction), Rule 25-1 (abnormal ground conditions), Rule 25-3 (wrong putting green) or a Local Rule (Rule 33-8a), or rolls back into the pitch-mark from which it was lifted under Rule 25-2 (embedded ball);
(vi) rolls and comes to rest more than two club-lengths from where it first struck a part of the *course;* or
(vii) rolls and comes to rest nearer the *hole* than:
(a) its original position or estimated position (see Rule 20-2b) unless otherwise permitted by the *Rules;* or
(b) the *nearest point of relief* or maximum available relief (Rule 24-2, 25-1 or 25-3); or
(c) the point where the original ball last crossed the margin of the *water hazard* or *lateral water hazard* (Rule 26-1).

If the ball when re-dropped rolls into any position listed above, it must be placed as near as possible to the spot where it first struck a part of the *course* when re-dropped.

*Note 1:* If a ball when dropped or re-dropped comes to rest and subsequently *moves*, the ball must be played as it lies, unless the provisions of any other *Rule* apply.

*Note 2:* If a ball to be re-dropped or placed under this Rule is not immediately recoverable, another ball may be *substituted.*

(Use of dropping zone – see Appendix1; Part B; Section 8)

### 20-3. Placing and Replacing
### a. By Whom and Where
A ball to be placed under the *Rules* must be placed by the player or his *partner*.

A ball to be replaced under the *Rules* must be replaced by any one of the following: (i) the person who lifted or *moved* the ball, (ii) the player, or (iii) the player's *partner*. The ball must be placed on the spot from which it was lifted or *moved*. If the ball is placed or replaced by any other person and the error is not corrected as provided in Rule 20-6, the player incurs a penalty of one stroke. In any such case, the player is responsible for any other breach of the *Rules* that occurs as a result of the placing or replacing of the ball.

If a ball or ball-marker is accidentally *moved* in the process of placing or replacing the ball, the ball or ball-marker must be replaced. There is no penalty, provided the movement of the ball or ball-marker is directly attributable to the specific act of placing or replacing the ball or removing the ball-marker. Otherwise, the player incurs a penalty of one stroke under Rule 18-2a or 20-1.

If a ball to be replaced is placed other than on the spot from which it was lifted or *moved* and the error is not corrected as provided in Rule 20-6, the player incurs the general penalty, loss of hole in match play or two strokes in stroke play, for a breach of the applicable *Rule*.

### b. Lie of Ball to be Placed or Replaced Altered

If the original lie of a ball to be placed or replaced has been altered:

(i) except in a *hazard*, the ball must be placed in the nearest lie most similar to the original lie that is not more than one club-length from the original lie, not nearer the *hole* and not in a *hazard*;

(ii) in a *water hazard*, the ball must be placed in accordance with Clause (i) above, except that the ball must be placed in the *water hazard*;

(iii) in a *bunker*, the original lie must be re-created as nearly as possible and the ball must be placed in that lie.

*Note:* If the original lie of a ball to be placed or replaced has been altered and it is impossible to determine the spot where the ball is to be placed or replaced, Rule 20-3b applies if the original lie is known, and Rule 20-3c applies if the original lie is not known.

*Exception:* If the player is searching for or identifying a ball covered by sand – see Rule 12-1a.

### c. Spot Not Determinable

If it is impossible to determine the spot where the ball is to be placed or replaced:

(i) *through the green*, the ball must be dropped as near as possible to the place where it lay but not in a *hazard* or on a *putting green*;

(ii) in a *hazard*, the ball must be dropped in the *hazard* as near as possible to the place where it lay;

(iii) on the *putting green*, the ball must be placed as near as possible to the place where it lay but not in a *hazard*.

*Exception:* When resuming play (Rule 6-8d), if the spot where the ball is to be placed is impossible to determine, it must be estimated and the ball placed on the estimated spot.

### d. Ball Fails to Come to Rest on Spot

If a ball when placed fails to come to rest on the spot on which it was placed, there is no penalty and the ball must be replaced. If it still fails to come to rest on that spot:

(i) except in a *hazard*, it must be placed at the nearest spot where it can be placed at rest that is not nearer the *hole* and not in a *hazard*;

(ii) in a *hazard*, it must be placed in the *hazard* at the nearest spot where it can be placed at rest that is not nearer the *hole*. If a ball when placed comes to rest on the spot on which it is placed, and it subsequently *moves*, there is no penalty and the ball must be played as it lies, unless the provisions of any other *Rule* apply.

\*PENALTY FOR BREACH OF RULE 20-1, 20-2 or 20-3:
Match play – Loss of hole; Stroke play – Two strokes.

*\*If a player makes a stroke at a ball substituted under one of these Rules when such substitution is not permitted, he incurs the general penalty for breach of that Rule, but there is no additional penalty under that Rule. If a player drops a ball in an improper manner and plays from a wrong place or if the ball has been put into play by a person not permitted by the Rules and then played from a wrong place, see Note 3 to Rule 20-7c.*

### 20-4. When Ball Dropped or Placed is in Play

If the player's *ball in play* has been lifted, it is again in play when dropped or placed.

A *substituted* ball becomes the *ball in play* when it has been dropped or placed.

(Ball incorrectly substituted – see Rule 15-2)

(Lifting ball incorrectly substituted, dropped or placed – see Rule 20-6)

### 20-5. Making Next Stroke from Where Previous Stroke Made

When a player elects or is required to make his next *stroke* from where a previous *stroke* was made, he must proceed as follows:

(a) On the Teeing Ground: The ball to be played must be played from within the *teeing ground*. It may be played from anywhere within the *teeing ground* and may be teed.

(b) Through the Green: The ball to be played must be dropped and when dropped must first strike a part of the *course through the green*.

(c) In a Hazard: The ball to be played must be dropped and when dropped must first strike a part of the *course* in the *hazard*.

(d) On the Putting Green: The ball to be played must be placed on the *putting green*.

PENALTY FOR BREACH OF RULE 20-5:
Match play – Loss of hole; Stroke play – Two strokes.

### 20-6. Lifting Ball Incorrectly Substituted, Dropped or Placed

A ball incorrectly *substituted*, dropped or placed in a wrong place or otherwise not in accordance with the *Rules* but not played may be lifted, without penalty, and the player must then proceed correctly.

### 20-7. Playing from Wrong Place

#### a. General

A player has played from a wrong place if he makes a *stroke* at his *ball in play*:

(i) on a part of the *course* where the *Rules* do not permit a *stroke* to be made or a ball to be dropped or placed; or

(ii) when the *Rules* require a dropped ball to be re-dropped or a *moved* ball to be replaced.

*Note:* For a ball played from outside the *teeing ground* or from a wrong *teeing ground* – see Rule 11-4.

#### b. Match Play

If a player makes a *stroke* from a wrong place, he loses the hole.

#### c. Stroke Play

If a *competitor* makes a *stroke* from a wrong place, he incurs a penalty of two strokes under the applicable *Rule*. He must play out the hole with the ball played from the wrong place, without correcting his error, provided he has not committed a serious breach (see Note 1).

If a *competitor* becomes aware that he has played from a wrong place and believes that he may have committed a serious breach, he must, before making a *stroke* on the next *teeing ground*, play out the hole with a second ball played in accordance with the *Rules*. If the hole being played is the last hole of the round, he must declare, before leaving the *putting green*, that he will play out the hole with a second ball played in accordance with the *Rules*.

If the *competitor* has played a second ball, he must report the facts to the *Committee* before returning his score card; if he fails to do so, he is disqualified. The *Committee* must determine whether the *competitor* has committed a serious breach of the applicable *Rule*. If he has, the score with the second ball counts and the competitor must add two penalty strokes to his score with that ball. If the *competitor* has committed a serious breach and has failed to correct it as outlined above, he is disqualified.

*Note 1:* A *competitor* is deemed to have committed a serious breach of the applicable *Rule* if the *Committee* considers he has gained a significant advantage as a result of playing from a wrong place.

*Note 2:* If a *competitor* plays a second ball under Rule 20-7c and it is ruled not to count, *strokes* made with that ball and *penalty strokes* incurred solely by playing that ball are disregarded. If the second ball is ruled to count, the *stroke* made from the wrong place and any *strokes* subsequently taken with the original ball including *penalty strokes* incurred solely by playing that ball are disregarded.

*Note 3:* If a player incurs a penalty for making a *stroke* from a wrong place, there is no additional penalty for:
(a)  *substituting* a ball when not permitted;
(b)  dropping a ball when the *Rules* require it to be placed, or placing a ball when the *Rules* require it to be dropped;
(c)  dropping a ball in an improper manner; or
(d)  a ball being put into play by a person not permitted to do so under the *Rules.*

## Rule 21 – Cleaning Ball
**Definitions**
All defined terms are in *italics* and are listed alphabetically in the Definitions section – see pages 592–595.

A ball on the *putting green* may be cleaned when lifted under Rule 16-1b. Elsewhere, a ball may be cleaned when lifted, except when it has been lifted:
a.  To determine if it is unfit for play (Rule 5-3);
b.  For identification (Rule 12-2), in which case it may be cleaned only to the extent necessary for identification; or
c.  Because it is assisting or interfering with play (Rule 22).

If a player cleans his ball during play of a hole except as provided in this Rule, he incurs a penalty of one stroke and the ball, if lifted, must be replaced. If a player who is required to replace a ball fails to do so, he incurs the general penalty under the applicable *Rule*, but there is no additional penalty under Rule 21.

*Exception:* If a player incurs a penalty for failing to act in accordance with Rule 5-3, 12-2 or 22, there is no additional penalty under Rule 21.

## Rule 22 – Ball Assisting or Interfering with Play
**Definitions**
All defined terms are in *italics* and are listed alphabetically in the Definitions section – see pages 592–595.

### 22-1. Ball Assisting Play
Except when a ball is in motion, if a player considers that a ball might assist any other player, he may:
a.  Lift the ball if it is his ball; or
b.  Have any other ball lifted.

A ball lifted under this Rule must be replaced (see Rule 20-3). The ball must not be cleaned, unless it lies on the *putting green* (see Rule 21).

In stroke play, a player required to lift his ball may play first rather than lift the ball.

In stroke play, if the *Committee* determines that *competitors* have agreed not to lift a ball that might assist any *competitor*, they are disqualified.

*Note:* When another ball is in motion, a ball that might influence the movement of the ball in motion must not be lifted.

### 22-2. Ball Interfering with Play
Except when a ball is in motion, if a player considers that another ball might interfere with his play, he may have it lifted.

A ball lifted under this Rule must be replaced (see Rule 20-3). The ball must not be cleaned, unless it lies on the *putting green* (see Rule 21).

In stroke play, a player required to lift his ball may play first rather than lift the ball.

*Note 1:* Except on the *putting green*, a player may not lift his ball solely because he considers that it might interfere with the play of another player. If a player lifts his ball without being asked to do so, he incurs a penalty of one stroke for a breach of Rule 18-2a, but there is no additional penalty for a breach of Rule 22.

*Note 2:* When another ball is in motion, a ball that might influence the movement of the ball in motion must not be lifted.

PENALTY FOR BREACH OF RULE:
Match play – Loss of hole; Stroke play – Two strokes.

## Rule 23 – Loose Impediments
**Definitions**
All defined terms are in *italics* and are listed alphabetically in the Definitions section – see pages 592–595.

### 23-1. Relief
Except when both the *loose impediment* and the ball lie in or touch the same *hazard*, any *loose impediment* may be removed without penalty.

If the ball lies anywhere other than on the *putting green* and the removal of a *loose impediment* by the player causes the ball to *move*, Rule 18-2a applies.

On the *putting green*, if the ball or ball-marker is accidentally *moved* in the process of the player removing a *loose impediment*, the ball or ball-marker must be replaced. There is no penalty, provided the movement of the ball or ball-marker is directly attributable to the removal of the *loose impediment*. Otherwise, if the player causes the ball to *move*, he incurs a penalty of one stroke under Rule 18-2a.

When a ball is in motion, a *loose impediment* that might influence the movement of the ball must not be removed.

*Note:* If the ball lies in a *hazard*, the player must not touch or move any *loose impediment* lying in or touching the same *hazard* – see Rule 13-4c.

PENALTY FOR BREACH OF RULE:
Match play – Loss of hole; Stroke play – Two strokes.

(Searching for ball in hazard – see Rule 12-1)
(Touching line of putt – see Rule 16-1a)

## Rule 24 – Obstructions
**Definitions**
All defined terms are in *italics* and are listed alphabetically in the Definitions section – see pages 592–595.

### 24-1. Movable Obstruction
A player may take relief, without penalty, from a movable *obstruction* as follows:
a.  If the ball does not lie in or on the *obstruction*, the *obstruction* may be removed. If the ball *moves*, it must be replaced, and there is no penalty, provided that the movement of the ball is directly attributable to the removal of the *obstruction*. Otherwise, Rule 18-2a applies.
b.  If the ball lies in or on the *obstruction*, the ball may be lifted and the *obstruction* removed. The ball must through the green or in a *hazard* be dropped, or on the *putting green* be placed, as near as possible to the spot directly under the place where the ball lay in or on the *obstruction*, but not nearer the *hole*.

The ball may be cleaned when lifted under this Rule.

When a ball is in motion, an *obstruction* that might influence the movement of the ball, other than *equipment* of any player or the *flagstick* when attended, removed or held up, must not be moved.

(Exerting influence on ball – see Rule 1-2)

*Note:* If a ball to be dropped or placed under this Rule is not immediately recoverable, another ball may be *substituted*.

## 24-2. Immovable Obstruction
### a. Interference
Interference by an immovable *obstruction* occurs when a ball lies in or on the *obstruction*, or when the *obstruction* interferes with the player's *stance* or the area of his intended swing. If the player's ball lies on the *putting green*, interference also occurs if an immovable *obstruction* on the *putting green* intervenes on his *line of putt*. Otherwise, intervention on the *line of play* is not, of itself, interference under this Rule.

### b. Relief
Except when the ball is in a *water hazard* or a *lateral water hazard*, a player may take relief from interference by an immovable *obstruction* as follows:
(i)  Through the Green: If the ball lies *through the green*, the player must lift the ball and drop it, without penalty, within one club-length of and not nearer the *hole* than the *nearest point of relief*. The *nearest point of relief* must not be in a *hazard* or on a *putting green*. When the ball is dropped within one club-length of the nearest *point of relief*, the ball must first strike a part of the *course* at a spot that avoids interference by the immovable *obstruction* and is not in a *hazard* and not on a *putting green*.
(ii)  In a Bunker: If the ball is in a *bunker*, the player must lift the ball and drop it either:
  (a)  Without penalty, in accordance with Clause (i) above, except that the *nearest point of relief* must be in the *bunker* and the ball must be dropped in the *bunker*; or
  (b)  Under penalty of one stroke, outside the *bunker* keeping the point where the ball lay directly between the *hole* and the spot on which the ball is dropped, with no limit to how far behind the *bunker* the ball may be dropped.
(iii)  On the Putting Green: If the ball lies on the *putting green*, the player must lift the ball and place it, without penalty, at the *nearest point of relief* that is not in a *hazard*. The *nearest point of relief* may be off the *putting green*.
(iv)  On the Teeing Ground: If the ball lies on the *teeing ground*, the player must lift the ball and drop it, without penalty, in accordance with Clause (i) above.
The ball may be cleaned when lifted under this Rule.
(Ball rolling to a position where there is interference by the condition from which relief was taken – see Rule 20-2c(v))
*Exception:* A player may not take relief under this Rule if (a) interference by anything other than an immovable *obstruction* makes the *stroke* clearly impracticable or (b) interference by an immovable *obstruction* would occur only through use of a clearly unreasonable *stroke* or an unnecessarily abnormal *stance*, swing or direction of play.
*Note 1:* If a ball is in a *water hazard* (including a *lateral water hazard*), the player may not take relief from interference by an immovable *obstruction*. The player must play the ball as it lies or proceed under Rule 26-1.
*Note 2:* If a ball to be dropped or placed under this Rule is not immediately recoverable, another ball may be *substituted*.
*Note 3:* The *Committee* may make a Local Rule stating that the player must determine the *nearest point of relief* without crossing over, through or under the *obstruction*.

## 24-3. Ball in Obstruction Not Found
It is a question of fact whether a ball that has not been found after having been struck toward an *obstruction* is in the *obstruction*. In order to apply this Rule, it must be known or virtually certain that the ball is in the *obstruction*.

In the absence of such knowledge or certainty, the player must proceed under Rule 27-1.

### a. Ball in Movable Obstruction Not Found
If it is known or virtually certain that a ball that has not been found is in a movable *obstruction*, the player may *substitute* another ball and take relief, without penalty, under this Rule. If he elects to do so, he must remove the *obstruction* and through the green or in a *hazard* drop a ball, or on the *putting green* place a ball, as near as possible to the spot directly under the place where the ball last crossed the outermost limits of the movable *obstruction*, but not nearer the *hole*.

### b. Ball in Immovable Obstruction Not Found
If it is known or virtually certain that a ball that has not been found is in an immovable *obstruction*, the player may take relief under this Rule. If he elects to do so, the spot where the ball last crossed the outermost limits of the *obstruction* must be determined and, for the purpose of applying this Rule, the ball is deemed to lie at this spot and the player must proceed as follows:
(i)  Through the Green: If the ball last crossed the outermost limits of the immovable *obstruction* at a spot *through the green*, the player may *substitute* another ball, without penalty, and take relief as prescribed in Rule 24-2b(i).
(ii)  In a Bunker: If the ball last crossed the outermost limits of the immovable *obstruction* at a spot in a *bunker*, the player may *substitute* another ball, without penalty, and take relief as prescribed in Rule 24-2b(ii).
(iii)  In a Water Hazard (including a Lateral Water Hazard): If the ball last crossed the outermost limits of the immovable *obstruction* at a spot in a *water hazard*, the player is not entitled to relief without penalty. The player must proceed under Rule 26-1.
(iv)  On the Putting Green: If the ball last crossed the outermost limits of the immovable *obstruction* at a spot on the *putting green*, the player may *substitute* another ball, without penalty, and take relief as prescribed in Rule 24-2b(iii).

PENALTY FOR BREACH OF RULE:
Match play – Loss of hole; Stroke play – Two strokes.

## Rule 25 – Abnormal Ground Conditions, Embedded Ball and Wrong Putting Green
### Definitions
All defined terms are in *italics* and are listed alphabetically in the Definitions section – see pages 592–595.

### 25-1. Abnormal Ground Conditions
#### a. Interference
Interference by an *abnormal ground condition* occurs when a ball lies in or touches the condition or when the condition interferes with the player's *stance* or the area of his intended swing. If the player's ball lies on the *putting green*, interference also occurs if an *abnormal ground condition* on the *putting green* intervenes on his *line of putt*. Otherwise, intervention on the *line of play* is not, of itself, interference under this Rule.
*Note:* The *Committee* may make a Local Rule stating that interference by an *abnormal ground condition* with a player's *stance* is deemed not to be, of itself, interference under this Rule.

#### b. Relief
Except when the ball is in a *water hazard* or a *lateral water hazard*, a player may take relief from interference by an *abnormal ground condition* as follows:
(i)  Through the Green: If the ball lies *through the green*, the player may lift the ball and drop it, without penalty, within one club-length of and not nearer the *hole*

than the *nearest point of relief*. The *nearest point of relief* must not be in a *hazard* or on a *putting green*. When the ball is dropped within one club-length of the *nearest point of relief*, the ball must first strike a part of the *course* at a spot that avoids interference by the condition and is not in a *hazard* and not on a *putting green*.

(ii) In a Bunker: If the ball is in a *bunker*, the player must lift the ball and drop it either:

(a) Without penalty, in accordance with Clause (i) above, except that the *nearest point of relief* must be in the *bunker* and the ball must be dropped in the *bunker* or, if complete relief is impossible, as near as possible to the spot where the ball lay, but not nearer the *hole*, on a part of the *course* in the *bunker* that affords maximum available relief from the condition; or

(b) Under penalty of one stroke, outside the *bunker* keeping the point where the ball lay directly between the *hole* and the spot on which the ball is dropped, with no limit to how far behind the *bunker* the ball may be dropped.

(iii) On the Putting Green: If the ball lies on the *putting green*, the player must lift the ball and place it, without penalty, at the *nearest point of relief* that is not in a *hazard* or, if complete relief is impossible, at the nearest position to where it lay that affords maximum available relief from the condition, but not nearer the *hole* and not in a *hazard*. The *nearest point of relief* or maximum available relief may be off the *putting green*.

(iv) On the Teeing Ground: If the ball lies on the *teeing ground*, the player must lift the ball and drop it, without penalty, in accordance with Clause (i) above.

The ball may be cleaned when lifted under Rule 25-1b.

(Ball rolling to a position where there is interference by the condition from which relief was taken – see Rule 20-2c(v))

*Exception:* A player may not take relief under this Rule if (a) interference by anything other than an *abnormal ground condition* makes the *stroke* clearly impracticable or (b) interference by an *abnormal ground condition* would occur only through use of a clearly unreasonable *stroke* or an unnecessarily abnormal *stance*, swing or direction of play.

*Note 1:* If a ball is in a *water hazard* (including a *lateral water hazard*), the player is not entitled to relief, without penalty, from interference by an *abnormal ground condition*. The player may play the ball as it lies (unless prohibited by Local Rule) or proceed under Rule 26-1.

*Note 2:* If a ball to be dropped or placed under this Rule is not immediately recoverable, another ball may be *substituted*.

**c. Ball in Abnormal Ground Condition Not Found**

It is a question of fact whether a ball that has not been found after having been struck toward an *abnormal ground condition* is in such a condition. In order to apply this Rule, it must be known or virtually certain that the ball is in the *abnormal ground condition*. In the absence of such knowledge or certainty, the player must proceed under Rule 27-1.

If it is known or virtually certain that a ball that has not been found is in an *abnormal ground condition*, the player may take relief under this Rule. If he elects to do so, the spot where the ball last crossed the outermost limits of the *abnormal ground condition* must be determined and, for the purpose of applying this Rule, the ball is deemed to lie at this spot and the player must proceed as follows:

(i) Through the Green: If the ball last crossed the outermost limits of the *abnormal ground condition* at a spot *through the green*, the player may *substitute* another

ball, without penalty, and take relief as prescribed in Rule 25-1b(i).

(ii) In a Bunker: If the ball last crossed the outermost limits of the *abnormal ground condition* at a spot in a *bunker*, the player may *substitute* another ball, without penalty, and take relief as prescribed in Rule 25-1b(ii).

(iii) In a Water Hazard (including a Lateral Water Hazard): If the ball last crossed the outermost limits of the *abnormal ground condition* at a spot in a *water hazard*, the player is not entitled to relief without penalty. The player must proceed under Rule 26-1.

(iv) On the Putting Green: If the ball last crossed the outermost limits of the *abnormal ground condition* at a spot on the *putting green*, the player may *substitute* another ball, without penalty, and take relief as prescribed in Rule 25-1b(iii).

**25-2. Embedded Ball**

A ball embedded in its own pitch-mark in the ground in any closely-mown area *through the green* may be lifted, cleaned and dropped, without penalty, as near as possible to the spot where it lay but not nearer the *hole*. The ball when dropped must first strike a part of the *course through the green*. "Closely-mown area" means any area of the *course*, including paths through the rough, cut to fairway height or less.

**25-3. Wrong Putting Green**
**a. Interference**

Interference by a *wrong putting green* occurs when a ball is on the *wrong putting green*. Interference to a player's *stance* or the area of his intended swing is not, of itself, interference under this Rule.

**b. Relief**

If a player's ball lies on a *wrong putting green*, he must not play the ball as it lies. He must take relief, without penalty, as follows: The player must lift the ball and drop it within one club-length of and not nearer the *hole* than the *nearest point of relief*. The *nearest point of relief* must not be in a *hazard* or on a *putting green*. When dropping the ball within one club-length of the *nearest point of relief*, the ball must first strike a part of the *course* at a spot that avoids interference by the *wrong putting green* and is not in a *hazard* and not on a *putting green*. The ball may be cleaned when lifted under this Rule.

PENALTY FOR BREACH OF RULE:
Match play – Loss of hole; Stroke play – Two strokes.

# Rule 26 – Water Hazards (Including Lateral Water Hazards)

**Definitions**
All defined terms are in italics and are listed alphabetically in the Definitions section – see pages 592–595.

**26-1. Relief for Ball in Water Hazard**

It is a question of fact whether a ball that has not been found after having been struck toward a *water hazard* is in the *hazard*. In the absence of knowledge or virtual certainty that a ball struck toward a *water hazard*, but not found, is in the *hazard*, the player must proceed under Rule 27-1.

If a ball is found in a *water hazard* or if it is known or virtually certain that a ball that has not been found is in the *water hazard* (whether the ball lies in water or not), the player may under penalty of one stroke:

a. Proceed under the stroke and distance provision of Rule 27-1 by playing a ball as nearly as possible at the spot from which the original ball was last played (see Rule 20-5); or

b. Drop a ball behind the *water hazard*, keeping the point at which the original ball last crossed the margin of the *water hazard* directly between the *hole* and the spot on which the ball is dropped, with no limit to how far behind the *water hazard* the ball may be dropped; or

c.  As additional options available only if the ball last crossed the margin of a *lateral water hazard*, drop a ball outside the *water hazard* within two club-lengths of and not nearer the *hole* than (i) the point where the original ball last crossed the margin of the *water hazard* or (ii) a point on the opposite margin of the *water hazard* equidistant from the *hole*.

When proceeding under this Rule, the player may lift and clean his ball or *substitute* a ball.

(Prohibited actions when ball is in a hazard – see Rule 13-4)

(Ball moving in water in a water hazard – see Rule 14-6)

**26-2. Ball Played Within Water Hazard**

**a. Ball Comes to Rest in Same or Another Water Hazard**

If a ball played from within a *water hazard* comes to rest in the same or another *water hazard* after the *stroke*, the player may:

(i)  proceed under Rule 26-1a. If, after dropping in the hazard, the player elects not to play the dropped ball, he may:

(a) proceed under Rule 26-1b, or if applicable Rule 26-1c, adding the additional penalty of one stroke prescribed by the Rule and using as the reference point the point where the original ball last crossed the margin of this *hazard* before it came to rest in this *hazard*; or

(b) add an additional penalty of one stroke and play a ball as nearly as possible at the spot from which the last *stroke* from outside a *water hazard* was made (see Rule 20-5); or

(ii)  proceed under Rule 26-1b, or if applicable Rule 26-1c; or

(iii)  under penalty of one stroke, play a ball as nearly as possible at the spot from which the last *stroke* from outside a *water hazard* was made (see Rule 20-5).

**b. Ball Lost or Unplayable Outside Hazard or Out of Bounds**

If a ball played from within a *water hazard* is *lost* or deemed unplayable outside the *hazard* or is *out of bounds*, the player may, after taking a penalty of one stroke under Rule 27-1 or 28a:

(i)  play a ball as nearly as possible at the spot in the *hazard* from which the original ball was last played (see Rule 20-5); or

(ii)  proceed under Rule 26-1b, or if applicable Rule 26-1c, adding the additional penalty of one stroke prescribed by the Rule and using as the reference point the point where the original ball last crossed the margin of the *hazard* before it came to rest in the *hazard*; or

(iii)  add an additional penalty of one stroke and play a ball as nearly as possible at the spot from which the last *stroke* from outside a *water hazard* was made (see Rule 20-5).

Note 1: When proceeding under Rule 26-2b, the player is not required to drop a ball under Rule 27-1 or 28a. If he does drop a ball, he is not required to play it. He may alternatively proceed under Rule 26-2b(ii) or (iii).

Note 2: If a ball played from within a *water hazard* is deemed unplayable outside the *hazard*, nothing in Rule 26-2b precludes the player from proceeding under Rule 28b or c.

PENALTY FOR BREACH OF RULE:
Match play – Loss of hole; Stroke play – Two strokes.

**Rule 27 – Ball Lost or Out of Bounds; Provisional Ball**

**Definitions**
All defined terms are in *italics* and are listed alphabetically in the Definitions section – see pages 592–595.

**27-1. Stroke and Distance; Ball Out of Bounds; Ball Not Found Within Five Minutes**

**a. Proceeding Under Stroke and Distance**
At any time, a player may, under penalty of one stroke, play a ball as nearly as possible at the spot from which the original ball was last played (see Rule 20-5), i.e. proceed under penalty of stroke and distance.

Except as otherwise provided in the *Rules*, if a player makes a *stroke* at a ball from the spot at which the original ball was last played, he is deemed to have proceeded under penalty of stroke and distance.

**b. Ball Out of Bounds**
If a ball is *out of bounds*, the player must play a ball, under penalty of one stroke, as nearly as possible at the spot from which the original ball was last played (see Rule 20-5).

**c. Ball Not Found Within Five Minutes**
If a ball is *lost* as a result of not being found or identified as his by the player within five minutes after the player's *side* or his or their *caddies* have begun to search for it, the player must play a ball, under penalty of one stroke, as nearly as possible at the spot from which the original ball was last played (see Rule 20-5).

*Exception:* If it is known or virtually certain that the original ball, that has not been found, has been moved by an *outside agency* (Rule 18-1), is in an *obstruction* (Rule 24-3), is in an *abnormal ground condition* (Rule 25-1) or is in a *water hazard* (Rule 26-1), the player may proceed under the applicable Rule.

PENALTY FOR BREACH OF RULE 27-1:
Match play – Loss of hole; Stroke play – Two strokes.

**27-2. Provisional Ball**
**a. Procedure**
If a ball may be *lost* outside a *water hazard* or may be *out of bounds*, to save time the player may play another ball provisionally in accordance with Rule 27-1. The player must inform his *opponent* in match play or his *marker* or a *fellow-competitor* in stroke play that he intends to play a *provisional ball*, and he must play it before he or his *partner* goes forward to search for the original ball.

If he fails to do so and plays another ball, that ball is not a *provisional ball* and becomes the *ball in play* under penalty of stroke and distance (Rule 27-1); the original ball is *lost*.

(Order of play from teeing ground – see Rule 10-3)
Note: If a *provisional ball* played under Rule 27-2a might be *lost* outside a *water hazard* or *out of bounds*, the player may play another *provisional ball*. If another *provisional ball* is played, it bears the same relationship to the previous *provisional ball* as the first *provisional ball* bears to the original ball.

**b. When Provisional Ball Becomes Ball in Play**
The player may play a *provisional ball* until he reaches the place where the original ball is likely to be. If he makes a *stroke* with the *provisional ball* from the place where the original ball is likely to be or from a point nearer the *hole* than that place, the original ball is *lost* and the *provisional ball* becomes the *ball in play* under penalty of stroke and distance (Rule 27-1).

If the original ball is *lost* outside a *water hazard* or is *out of bounds*, the *provisional ball* becomes the *ball in play*, under penalty of stroke and distance (Rule 27-1).

*Exception:* If it is known or virtually certain that the original ball, that has not been found, has been moved by an *outside agency* (Rule 18-1), or is in an *obstruction* (Rule 24-3) or an *abnormal ground condition* (Rule 25-1c), the player may proceed under the applicable *Rule*.

**c. When Provisional Ball to be Abandoned**
If the original ball is neither *lost* nor *out of bounds*, the player must abandon the *provisional ball* and continue playing the original ball. If it is known or virtually certain that the original ball is in a *water hazard*, the player may proceed in accordance with Rule 26-1. In either situation, if the player makes any further *strokes* at the *provisional ball,* he is playing a *wrong ball* and the provisions of Rule 15-3 apply.

*Note:* If a player plays a *provisional ball* under Rule 27-2a, the *strokes* made after this Rule has been invoked with a *provisional ball* subsequently abandoned under Rule 27-2c and penalties incurred solely by playing that ball are disregarded.

### Rule 28 – Ball Unplayable
**Definitions**
All defined terms are in *italics* and are listed alphabetically in the Definitions section – see pages 592–595.

The player may deem his ball unplayable at any place on the *course,* except where the ball is in a *water hazard.* The player is the sole judge as to whether his ball is unplayable.

If the player deems his ball to be unplayable, he must, under penalty of one stroke:
a.   Proceed under the stroke and distance provision of Rule 27-1 by playing a ball as nearly as possible at the spot from which the original ball was last played (see Rule 20-5); or
b.   Drop a ball behind the point where the ball lay, keeping that point directly between the *hole* and the spot on which the ball is dropped, with no limit to how far behind that point the ball may be dropped; or c. Drop a ball within two club-lengths of the spot where the ball lay, but not nearer the *hole.*

If the unplayable ball is in a *bunker,* the player may proceed under Clause a, b or c. If he elects to proceed under Clause b or c, a ball must be dropped in the *bunker.*

When proceeding under this Rule, the player may lift and clean his ball or *substitute* a ball.

PENALTY FOR BREACH OF RULE:
Match play – Loss of hole; Stroke play – Two strokes.

## Other Forms of Play

### Rule 29 – Threesomes and Foursomes
**Definitions**
All defined terms are in *italics* and are listed alphabetically in the Definitions section – see pages 592–595.

**29-1. General**
In a *threesome* or a *foursome,* during any *stipulated round* the *partners* must play alternately from the *teeing grounds* and alternately during the play of each hole. *Penalty strokes* do not affect the order of play.

**29-2. Match Play**
If a player plays when his *partner* should have played, his *side* loses the hole.

**29-3. Stroke Play**
If the *partners* make a *stroke* or *strokes* in incorrect order, such *stroke* or *strokes* are cancelled and the *side* incurs a penalty of two strokes. The *side* must correct the error by playing a ball in correct order as nearly as possible at the spot from which it first played in incorrect order (see Rule 20-5). If the *side* makes a *stroke* on the next *teeing ground* without first correcting the error or, in the case of the last hole of the round, leaves the *putting green* without declaring its intention to correct the error, the *side* is disqualified.

### Rule 30 – Three-Ball, Best-Ball and Four-Ball Match Play
**Definitions**
All defined terms are in *italics* and are listed alphabetically in the Definitions section – see pages 592–595.

**30-1. General**
The Rules of Golf, so far as they are not at variance with the following specific Rules, apply to *three-ball, best-ball* and *four-ball* matches.

**30-2. Three-Ball Match Play**
**a. Ball at Rest Moved or Purposely Touched by an Opponent**
If an *opponent* incurs a penalty stroke under Rule 18-3b, that penalty is incurred only in the match with the player whose ball was touched or *moved.* No penalty is incurred in his match with the other player.

**b. Ball Deflected or Stopped by an Opponent Accidentally**
If a player's ball is accidentally deflected or stopped by an *opponent,* his *caddie* or *equipment,* there is no penalty. In his match with that *opponent* the player may, before another *stroke* is made by either *side,* cancel the *stroke* and play a ball, without penalty, as nearly as possible at the spot from which the original ball was last played (see Rule 20-5) or he may play the ball as it lies. In his match with the other *opponent,* the ball must be played as it lies.

*Exception:* Ball striking person attending or holding up *flagstick* or anything carried by him – see Rule 17-3b.

(Ball purposely deflected or stopped by *opponent* – see Rule 1-2)

**30-3. Best-Ball and Four-Ball Match Play**
**a. Representation of Side**
A *side* may be represented by one *partner* for all or any part of a match; all *partners* need not be present. An absent *partner* may join a match between holes, but not during play of a hole.

**b. Order of Play**
Balls belonging to the same *side* may be played in the order the *side* considers best.

**c. Wrong Ball**
If a player incurs the loss of hole penalty under Rule 15-3a for making a *stroke* at a *wrong ball,* he is disqualified for that hole, but his *partner* incurs no penalty even if the *wrong ball* belongs to him. If the *wrong ball* belongs to another player, its owner must place a ball on the spot from which the *wrong ball* was first played.

(Placing and Replacing – see Rule 20-3)

**d. Penalty to Side**
A *side* is penalised for a breach of any of the following by any *partner:*
• Rule 4        Clubs
• Rule 6-4      Caddie
• Any Local Rule or Condition of Competition for which the penalty is an adjustment to the state of the match.

**e. Disqualification of Side**
(i)   A *side* is disqualified if any *partner* incurs a penalty of disqualification under any of the following:
• Rule 1-3      Agreement to Waive Rules
• Rule 4        Clubs
• Rule 5-1 or 5-2   The Ball
• Rule 6-2a     Handicap
• Rule 6-4      Caddie
• Rule 6-7      Undue Delay; Slow Play
• Rule 11-1     Teeing
• Rule 14-3     Artificial Devices, Unusual Equipment and Unusual Use of Equipment

- Rule 33-7      Disqualification Penalty Imposed by
                Committee
(ii) A *side* is disqualified if all *partners* incur a penalty of dis-
     qualification under any of the following:
  - Rule 6-3      Time of Starting and Groups
  - Rule 6-8      Discontinuance of Play
(iii) In all other cases where a breach of a *Rule* would
      result in disqualification, the player is disqualified for
      that hole only.

### f. Effect of Other Penalties
If a player's breach of a *Rule* assists his *partner's* play or
adversely affects an *opponent's* play, the *partner* incurs the
applicable penalty in addition to any penalty incurred by the
player.

In all other cases where a player incurs a penalty for
breach of a *Rule*, the penalty does not apply to his *partner*.
Where the penalty is stated to be loss of hole, the effect is
to disqualify the player for that hole.

## Rule 31 – Four-Ball Stroke Play
### Definitions
All defined terms are in *italics* and are listed alphabetically
in the Definitions section – see pages 592–595.

### 31-1. General
The Rules of Golf, so far as they are not at variance with
the following specific Rules, apply to *four-ball* stroke play.

### 31-2. Representation of Side
A *side* may be represented by either *partner* for all or any
part of a *stipulated round*; both *partners* need not be present. An absent *competitor* may join his *partner* between
holes, but not during play of a hole.

### 31-3. Scoring
The *marker* is required to record for each hole only the
gross score of whichever *partner's* score is to count. The
gross scores to count must be individually identifiable; otherwise, the *side* is disqualified. Only one of the *partners*
need be responsible for complying with Rule 6-6b.
(Wrong score – see Rule 31-7a)

### 31-4. Order of Play
Balls belonging to the same *side* may be played in the order
the *side* considers best.

### 31-5. Wrong Ball
If a *competitor* is in breach of Rule 15-3b for making a *stroke*
at a *wrong ball*, he incurs a penalty of two strokes and must
correct his mistake by playing the correct ball or by proceeding under the *Rules*. His *partner* incurs no penalty, even
if the *wrong ball* belongs to him.

If the *wrong ball* belongs to another *competitor*, its owner
must place a ball on the spot from which the *wrong ball* was
first played.
(Placing and Replacing – see Rule 20-3)

### 31-6 Penalty to Side
A *side* is penalised for a breach of any of the following by
any *partner*:
- Rule 4          Clubs
- Rule 6-4        Caddie
- Any Local Rule or Condition of Competition for
  which there is a maximum penalty per round.

### 31-7. Disqualification Penalties
#### a. Breach by One Partner
A *side* is disqualified from the competition if either *partner*
incurs a penalty of disqualification under any of the follow-
ing:
- Rule 1-1        Agreement to Waive Rules
- Rule 3-4        Refusal to Comply with a Rule
- Rule 4          Clubs
- Rule 5-1 or 5-2 The Ball

- Rule 6-2b       Handicap
- Rule 6-4        Caddie
- Rule 6-6b       Signing and Returning Score Card
- Rule 6-6d       Wrong Score for Hole
- Rule 6-7        Undue Delay; Slow Play
- Rule 7-1        Practice Before or Between Rounds
- Rule 10-2c      Sides Agree to Play Out of Turn
- Rule 11-1       Teeing
- Rule 14-3       Artificial Devices, Unusual Equip-
                  ment and Unusual Use of Equipment
- Rule 22-1       Ball Assisting Play
- Rule 31-3       Gross Scores to Count Not Individu-
                  ally Identifiable
- Rule 33-7       Disqualification Penalty Imposed by
                  Committee

#### b. Breach by Both Partners
A *side* is disqualified from the competition:
(i) if each *partner* incurs a penalty of disqualification for a
    breach of Rule 6-3 (Time of Starting and Groups) or
    Rule 6-8 (Discontinuance of Play), or
(ii) if, at the same hole, each *partner* is in breach of a *Rule*
     the penalty for which is disqualification from the com-
     petition or for a hole.

#### c. For the Hole Only
In all other cases where a breach of a *Rule* would result in
disqualification, the *competitor* is disqualified only for the
hole at which the breach occurred.

### 31-8. Effect of Other Penalties
If a *competitor's* breach of a *Rule* assists his *partner's* play, the
*partner* incurs the applicable penalty in addition to any
penalty incurred by the *competitor*.

In all other cases where a *competitor* incurs a penalty for
breach of a *Rule*, the penalty does not apply to his *partner*.

## Rule 32 – Bogey, Par and
## Stableford Competitions
### Definitions
All defined terms are in *italics* and are listed alphabetically
in the Definitions section – see pages 592–595.

### 32-1. Conditions
Bogey, par and Stableford competitions are forms of
stroke play in which play is against a fixed score at each
hole. The *Rules* for stroke play, so far as they are not at
variance with the following specific Rules, apply.

In handicap bogey, par and Stableford competitions, the
*competitor* with the lowest net score at a hole takes the
*honour* at the next *teeing ground*.

#### a. Bogey and Par Competitions
The scoring for bogey and par competitions is made as in
match play.

Any hole for which a *competitor* makes no return is
regarded as a loss. The winner is the *competitor* who is
most successful in the aggregate of holes.

The *marker* is responsible for marking only the gross
number of *strokes* for each hole where the *competitor*
makes a net score equal to or less than the fixed score.

Note 1: The *competitor's* score is adjusted by deducting a
hole or holes under the applicable *Rule* when a penalty
other than disqualification is incurred under any of the following:
- Rule 4          Clubs
- Rule 6-4        Caddie
- Any Local Rule or Condition of Competition for
  which there is a maximum penalty per round.

The *competitor* is responsible for reporting the facts
regarding such a breach to the *Committee* before he

returns his score card so that the *Committee* may apply the penalty.

If the *competitor* fails to report his breach to the *Committee*, he is disqualified.

*Note 2:* If the *competitor* is in breach of Rule 6-3a (Time of Starting) but arrives at his starting point, ready to play, within five minutes after his starting time, or is in breach of Rule 6-7 (Undue Delay; Slow Play), the *Committee* will deduct one hole from the aggregate of holes. For a repeated offence under Rule 6-7, see Rule 32-2a.

### b. Stableford Competitions
The scoring in Stableford competitions is made by points awarded in relation to a fixed score at each hole as follows:

| Hole Played In | Points |
|---|---|
| More than one over fixed score or no score returned | 0 |
| One over fixed score | 1 |
| Fixed score | 2 |
| One under fixed score | 3 |
| Two under fixed score | 4 |
| Three under fixed score | 5 |
| Four under fixed score | 6 |

The winner is the *competitor* who scores the highest number of points.

The *marker* is responsible for marking only the gross number of *strokes* at each hole where the *competitor's* net score earns one or more points.

*Note 1:* If a *competitor* is in breach of a *Rule* for which there is a maximum penalty per round, he must report the facts to the *Committee* before returning his score card; if he fails to do so, he is disqualified. The *Committee* will, from the total points scored for the round, deduct two points for each hole at which any breach occurred, with a maximum deduction per round of four points for each *Rule* breached.

*Note 2:* If the *competitor* is in breach of Rule 6-3a (Time of Starting) but arrives at his starting point, ready to play, within five minutes after his starting time, or is in breach of Rule 6-7 (Undue Delay; Slow Play), the *Committee* will deduct two points from the total points scored for the round. For a repeated offence under Rule 6-7, see Rule 32-2a.

*Note 3:* For the purpose of preventing slow play, the *Committee* may, in the conditions of a competition (Rule 33-1), establish pace of play guidelines, including maximum periods of time allowed to complete a *stipulated round*, a hole or a *stroke*.

The *Committee* may, in such a condition, modify the penalty for a breach of this Rule as follows: First offence − Deduction of one point from the total points scored for the round; Second offence − Deduction of a further two points from the total points scored for the round; For subsequent offence − Disqualificatio

### 32-2. Disqualification Penalties
#### a. From the Competition
A *competitor* is disqualified from the competition if he incurs a penalty of disqualification under any of the following:

| | |
|---|---|
| • Rule 1-3 | Agreement to Waive Rules |
| • Rule 3-4 | Refusal to Comply with a Rule |
| • Rule 4 | Clubs |
| • Rule 5-1 or 5-2 | The Ball |
| • Rule 6-2b | Handicap |
| • Rule 6-3 | Time of Starting and Groups |
| • Rule 6-4 | Caddie |
| • Rule 6-6b | Signing and Returning Score Card |
| • Rule 6-6d | Wrong Score for Hole, i.e. when the recorded score is lower than actually taken, except that no penalty is incurred when a breach of this Rule does not affect the result of the hole |

| | |
|---|---|
| • Rule 6-7 | Undue Delay; Slow Play |
| • Rule 6-8 | Discontinuance of Play |
| • Rule 7-1 | Practice Before or Between Rounds |
| • Rule 11-1 | Teeing |
| • Rule 14-3 | Artificial Devices, Unusual Equipment and Unusual Use of Equipment |
| • Rule 22-1 | Ball Assisting Play |
| • Rule 33-7 | Disqualification Penalty Imposed by Committee |

#### b. For a Hole
In all other cases where a breach of a *Rule* would result in disqualification, the *competitor* is disqualified only for the hole at which the breach occurred.

## Administration

### Rule 33 − The Committee
**Definitions**
All defined terms are in *italics* and are listed alphabetically in the Definitions section − see pages 592–595.

#### 33-1. Conditions; Waiving Rule
The *Committee* must establish the conditions under which a competition is to be played.

The *Committee* has no power to waive a Rule of Golf.

Certain specific *Rules* governing stroke play are so substantially different from those governing match play that combining the two forms of play is not practicable and is not permitted. The result of a match played in these circumstances is null and void and, in the stroke play competition, the *competitors* are disqualified.

In stroke play, the *Committee* may limit a *referee's* duties.

#### 33-2. The Course
##### a. Defining Bounds and Margins
The *Committee* must define accurately:
(i)    the *course* and *out of bounds*,
(ii)   the margins of *water hazards* and *lateral water hazards*,
(iii)  *ground under repair*, and
(iv)   *obstructions* and integral parts of the *course*.

##### b. New Holes
New *holes* should be made on the day on which a stroke play competition begins and at such other times as the *Committee* considers necessary, provided all *competitors* in a single round play with each *hole* cut in the same position.

*Exception:* When it is impossible for a damaged *hole* to be repaired so that it conforms with the Definition, the *Committee* may make a new *hole* in a nearby similar position.

*Note:* Where a single round is to be played on more than one day, the *Committee* may provide, in the conditions of a competition (Rule 33-1), that the *holes* and *teeing grounds* may be differently situated on each day of the competition, provided that, on any one day, all *competitors* play with each *hole* and each *teeing ground* in the same position.

##### c. Practice Ground
Where there is no practice ground available outside the area of a competition *course*, the *Committee* should establish the area on which players may practise on any day of a competition, if it is practicable to do so. On any day of a stroke play competition, the *Committee* should not normally permit practice on or to a *putting green* or from a *hazard* of the competition *course*.

##### d. Course Unplayable
If the *Committee* or its authorised representative considers that for any reason the *course* is not in a playable condition or that there are circumstances that render the proper playing of the game impossible, it may, in match play or stroke play, order a temporary suspension of play or, in stroke play, declare play null and void and cancel all scores

for the round in question. When a round is cancelled, all penalties incurred in that round are cancelled.
(Procedure in discontinuing and resuming play – see Rule 6-8)

## 33-3. Times of Starting and Groups
The *Committee* must establish the times of starting and, in *stroke play*, arrange the groups in which *competitors* must play.

When a match play competition is played over an extended period, the *Committee* establishes the limit of time within which each round must be completed. When players are allowed to arrange the date of their match within these limits, the *Committee* should announce that the match must be played at a stated time on the last day of the period, unless the players agree to a prior date.

## 33-4. Handicap Stroke Table
The *Committee* must publish a table indicating the order of holes at which handicap strokes are to be given or received.

## 33-5. Score Card
In *stroke play*, the *Committee* must provide each *competitor* with a score card containing the date and the *competitor's* name or, in *foursome* or *four-ball* stroke play, the *competitors'* names.

In *stroke play*, the *Committee* is responsible for the addition of scores and application of the handicap recorded on the score card.

In *four-ball* stroke play, the *Committee* is responsible for recording the better-ball score for each hole and in the process applying the handicaps recorded on the score card, and adding the better-ball scores.

In bogey, par and Stableford competitions, the *Committee* is responsible for applying the handicap recorded on the score card and determining the result of each hole and the overall result or points total.

*Note:* The *Committee* may request that each *competitor* records the date and his name on his score card.

## 33-6. Decision of Ties
The *Committee* must announce the manner, day and time for the decision of a halved match or of a tie, whether played on level terms or under handicap.

A halved match must not be decided by stroke play. A tie in stroke play must not be decided by a match.

## 33-7. Disqualification Penalty; Committee Discretion
A penalty of disqualification may in exceptional individual cases be waived, modified or imposed if the *Committee* considers such action warranted.

Any penalty less than disqualification must not be waived or modified.

If a *Committee* considers that a player is guilty of a serious breach of etiquette, it may impose a penalty of disqualification under this Rule.

## 33-8. Local Rules
### a. Policy
The *Committee* may establish Local Rules for local abnormal conditions if they are consistent with the policy set forth in Appendix I.

### b. Waiving or Modifying a Rule
A Rule of Golf must not be waived by a Local Rule. However, if a *Committee* considers that local abnormal condi-

tions interfere with the proper playing of the game to the extent that it is necessary to make a Local Rule that modifies the Rules of Golf, the Local Rule must be authorised by The R&A.

# Rule 34 – Disputes and Decisions
## Definitions
All defined terms are in *italics* and are listed alphabetically in the Definitions section – see pages 592–595.

## 34-1. Claims and Penalties
### a. Match Play
If a claim is lodged with the *Committee* under Rule 2-5, a decision should be given as soon as possible so that the state of the match may, if necessary, be adjusted. If a claim is not made in accordance with Rule 2-5, it must not be considered by the *Committee*.

There is no time limit on applying the disqualification penalty for a breach of Rule 1-3.

### b. Stroke Play
In stroke play, a penalty must not be rescinded, modified or imposed after the competition has closed. A competition is closed when the result has been officially announced or, in stroke play qualifying followed by match play, when the player has teed off in his first match.

*Exceptions:* A penalty of disqualification must be imposed after the competition has closed if a *competitor*:

(i) was in breach of Rule 1-3 (Agreement to Waive Rules); or
(ii) returned a score card on which he had recorded a handicap that, before the competition closed, he knew was higher than that to which he was entitled, and this affected the number of strokes received (Rule 6-2b); or
(iii) returned a score for any hole lower than actually taken (Rule 6-6d) for any reason other than failure to include a penalty that, before the competition closed, he did not know he had incurred; or
(iv) knew, before the competition closed, that he had been in breach of any other *Rule* for which the penalty is disqualification.

## 34-2. Referee's Decision
If a *referee* has been appointed by the *Committee*, his decision is final.

## 34-3. Committee's Decision
In the absence of a *referee*, any dispute or doubtful point on the *Rules* must be referred to the *Committee*, whose decision is final.

If the *Committee* cannot come to a decision, it may refer the dispute or doubtful point to the Rules of Golf Committee of the R&A, whose decision is final.

If the dispute or doubtful point has not been referred to the Rules of Golf Committee, the player or players may request that an agreed statement be referred through a duly authorised representative of the *Committee* to the Rules of Golf Committee for an opinion as to the correctness of the decision given. The reply will be sent to this authorised representative.

If play is conducted other than in accordance with the Rules of Golf, the Rules of Golf Committee will not give a decision on any question.

## Appendix I – Contents

## Appendix I – Local Rules; Conditions of the Competition

**Definitions**

All defined terms are in *italics* and are listed alphabetically in the Definitions section – see pages 592–595.

## Part A – Local Rules

As provided in Rule 33-8a, the Committee may make and publish Local Rules for local abnormal conditions if they are consistent with the policy established in this Appendix. In addition, detailed information regarding acceptable and prohibited Local Rules is provided in "Decisions on the Rules of Golf" under Rule 33-8 and in "Guidance on Running a Competition".

If local abnormal conditions interfere with the proper playing of the game and the Committee considers it necessary to modify a Rule of Golf, authorisation from the *R&A* must be obtained.

### 1. Defining Bounds and Margins

Specifying means used to define out *of bounds, water hazards, lateral water hazards, ground under repair, obstructions* and integral parts of the course (Rule 33-2a).

### 2. Water Hazards
### a. Lateral Water Hazards

Clarifying the status of water hazards that may be *lateral water hazards* (Rule 26).

### b. Ball Played Provisionally Under Rule 26-1

Permitting play of a ball provisionally under Rule 26-1 for a ball that may be in a *water hazard* (including a *lateral water hazard*) of such character that, if the original ball is not found, it is known or virtually certain that it is in the *water hazard* and it would be impracticable to determine whether the ball is in the *hazard* or to do so would unduly delay play.

### 3. Areas of the Course Requiring Preservation; Environmentally-Sensitive Areas

Assisting preservation of the *course* by defining areas, including turf nurseries, young plantations and other parts of the *course* under cultivation, as *ground under repair* from which play is prohibited.

When the *Committee* is required to prohibit play from environmentally-sensitive areas that are on or adjoin the *course*, it should make a Local Rule clarifying the relief procedure.

### 4. Course Conditions – Mud, Extreme Wetness, Poor Conditions and Protection of Course
### a. Lifting an Embedded Ball, Cleaning

Temporary conditions that might interfere with proper playing of the game, including mud and extreme wetness, warranting relief for an embedded ball anywhere *through the green* or permitting lifting, cleaning and replacing a ball anywhere *through the green* or on a closely-mown area *through the green*.

### b. "Preferred Lies" and "Winter Rules"

Adverse conditions, including the poor condition of the *course* or the existence of mud, are sometimes so general, particularly during winter months, that the *Committee* may decide to grant relief by temporary Local Rule either to protect the *course* or to promote fair and pleasant play. The Local Rule should be withdrawn as soon as the conditions warrant.

### 5. Obstructions
### a. General

Clarifying status of objects that may be *obstructions* (Rule 24).

Declaring any construction to be an integral part of the *course* and, accordingly, not an *obstruction*, e.g. built-up sides of *teeing grounds, putting greens* and *bunkers* (Rules 24 and 33-2a).

### b. Stones in Bunkers

Allowing the removal of stones in *bunkers* by declaring them to be movable *obstructions* (Rule 24-1).

**c. Roads and Paths**
(i)   Declaring artificial surfaces and sides of roads and paths to be integral parts of the course, or
(ii)  Providing relief of the type afforded under Rule 24-2b from roads and paths not having artificial surfaces and sides if they could unfairly affect play.

**d. Immovable Obstructions Close to Putting Green**
Providing relief from intervention by immovable *obstructions* on or within two club-lengths of the putting green when the ball lies within two clublengths of the immovable *obstruction*.

**e. Protection of Young Trees**
Providing relief for the protection of young trees.

**f. Temporary Obstructions**
Providing relief from interference by temporary obstructions (e.g. grandstands, television cables and equipment, etc).

**6. Dropping Zones**
Establishing special areas on which balls may or must be dropped when it is not feasible or practicable to proceed exactly in conformity with Rule 24-2b or 24-3 (Immovable Obstruction), Rule 25-1b or 25-1c (Abnormal Ground Conditions), Rule 25-3 (Wrong Putting Green) or Rule 26-1 (Water Hazards and Lateral Water Hazards) or Rule 28 (Ball Unplayable).

## Part B Specimen Local Rules

Within the policy established in Part A of this Appendix, the Committee may adopt a Specimen Local Rule by referring, on a score card or notice board, to the examples given below. However, Specimen Local Rules of a temporary nature should not be printed on a score card.

**1. Water Hazards; Ball Played Provisionally Under Rule 26-1**
If a *water hazard* (including a *lateral water hazard*) is of such size and shape and/or located in such a position that:
(i)   it would be impracticable to determine whether the ball is in the *hazard* or to do so would unduly delay play, and
(ii)  if the original ball is not found, it is known or virtually certain that it is in the *water hazard*, the *Committee* may introduce a Local Rule permitting the play of a ball provisionally under Rule 26-1. The ball is played provisionally under any of the applicable options under Rule 26-1 or any applicable Local Rule. In such a case, if a ball is played provisionally and the original ball is in a *water hazard*, the player may play the original ball as it lies or continue with the ball played provisionally, but he may not proceed under Rule 26-1 with regard to the original ball.

In these circumstances, the following Local Rule is recommended:
"If there is doubt whether a ball is in or is lost in the water hazard (specify location), the player may play another ball provisionally under any of the applicable options in Rule 26-1.

If the original ball is found outside the water hazard, the player must continue play with it.

I f the original ball is found in the water hazard, the player may either play the original ball as it lies or continue with the ball played provisionally under Rule 26-1.

If the original ball is not found or identified within the five-minute search period, the player must continue with the ball played provisionally.

PENALTY FOR BREACH OF LOCAL RULE:
Match play – Loss of hole; Stroke play – Two strokes."

**2. Areas of the Course Requiring Preservation; Environmentally- Sensitive Areas**
**a. Ground Under Repair; Play Prohibited**
If the *Committee* wishes to protect any area of the *course*, it should declare it to be *ground under repair* and prohibit play from within that area. The following Local Rule is recommended:
"The _____(defined by ___) is ground under repair from which play is prohibited. If a player's ball lies in the area, or if it interferes with the player's stance or the area of his intended swing, the player must take relief under Rule 25-1.

PENALTY FOR BREACH OF LOCAL RULE:
Match play – Loss of hole; Stroke play – Two strokes."

**b. Environmentally-Sensitive Areas**
If an appropriate authority (i.e. a Government Agency or the like) prohibits entry into and/or play from an area on or adjoining the *course* for environmental reasons, the *Committee* should make a Local Rule clarifying the relief procedure.

The *Committee* has some discretion in terms of whether the area is defined as *ground under repair*, a *water hazard* or *out of bounds*. However, it may not simply define the area to be a *water hazard* if it does not meet the Definition of a "*Water Hazard*" and it should attempt to preserve the character of the hole.

The following Local Rule is recommended:
**"I. Definition**
An environmentally-sensitive area (ESA) is an area so declared by an appropriate authority, entry into and/or play from which is prohibited for environmental reasons. These areas may be defined as ground under repair, a water hazard, a lateral water hazard or out of bounds at the discretion of the Committee, provided that in the case of an ESA that has been defined as a water hazard or a lateral water hazard, the area is, by definition, a water hazard.
Note: The Committee may not declare an area to be environmentally-sensitive.

**II. Ball in Environmentally-Sensitive Area**
**a. Ground Under Repair**
If a ball is in an ESA defined as ground under repair, a ball must be dropped in accordance with Rule 25-1b.

If it is known or virtually certain that a ball that has not been found is in an ESA defined as ground under repair, the player may take relief, without penalty, as prescribed in Rule 25-1c.

**b. Water Hazards and Lateral Water Hazards**
If the ball is found in or if it is known or virtually certain that a ball that has not been found is in an ESA defined as a water hazard or lateral water hazard, the player must, under penalty of one stroke, proceed under Rule 26-1.
Note: If a ball, dropped in accordance with Rule 26 rolls into a position where the ESA interferes with the player's stance or the area of his intended swing, the player must take relief as provided in Clause III of this Local Rule.

**c. Out of Bounds**
If a ball is in an ESA defined as out of bounds, the player must play a ball, under penalty of one stroke, as nearly as possible at the spot from which the original ball was last played (see Rule 20-5).

**III. Interference with Stance or Area of Intended Swing**
Interference by an ESA occurs when the ESA interferes with the player's stance or the area of his intended swing. If interference exists, the player must take relief as follows:
(a)  Through the Green: If the ball lies through the green, the point on the course nearest to where the ball lies must be determined that (a) is not nearer the hole, (b)

avoids interference by the ESA and (c) is not in a hazard or on a putting green. The player must lift the ball and drop it, without penalty, within one club-length of the point so determined on a part of the course that fulfils (a), (b) and (c) above.

(b) In a Hazard: If the ball is in a hazard, the player must lift the ball and drop it either:

(i)  Without penalty, in the hazard, as near as possible to the spot where the ball lay, but not nearer the hole, on a part of the course that provides complete relief from the ESA; or

(ii) Under penalty of one stroke, outside the hazard, keeping the point where the ball lay directly between the hole and the spot on which the ball is dropped, with no limit to how far behind the hazard the ball may be dropped. Additionally, the player may proceed under Rule 26 or 28 if applicable.

(c) On the Putting Green: If the ball lies on the putting green, the player must lift the ball and place it, without penalty, in the nearest position to where it lay that affords complete relief from the ESA, but not nearer the hole or in a hazard.

The ball may be cleaned when lifted under Clause III of this Local Rule.

*Exception:* A player may not take relief under Clause III of this Local Rule if (a) interference by anything other than an ESA makes the stroke clearly impracticable or (b) interference by an ESA would occur only through use of a clearly unreasonable stroke or an unnecessarily abnormal stance, swing or direction of play.

PENALTY FOR BREACH OF LOCAL RULE:
Match play – Loss of hole; Stroke play – Two strokes.

*Note:* In the case of a serious breach of this Local Rule, the Committee may impose a penalty of disqualification."

### 3. Protection of Young Trees
When it is desired to prevent damage to young trees, the following Local Rule is recommended:

"Protection of young trees identified by _____. If such a tree interferes with a player's stance or the area of his intended swing, the ball must be lifted, without penalty, and dropped in accordance with the procedure prescribed in Rule 24-2b (Immovable Obstruction). If the ball lies in a water hazard, the player must lift and drop the ball in accordance with Rule 24-2b(i), except that the nearest point of relief must be in the water hazard and the ball must be dropped in the water hazard or the player may proceed under Rule 26. The ball may be cleaned when lifted under this Local Rule.

*Exception:* A player may not obtain relief under this Local Rule if (a) interference by anything other than such a tree makes the stroke clearly impracticable or (b) interference by such a tree would occur only through use of a clearly unreasonable stroke or an unnecessarily abnormal stance, swing or direction of play.

PENALTY FOR BREACH OF LOCAL RULE:
Match play – Loss of hole; Stroke play – Two strokes."

### 4. Course Conditions – Mud, Extreme Wetness, Poor Conditions and Protection of the Course
#### a. Relief for Embedded Ball
Rule 25-2 provides relief, without penalty, for a ball embedded in its own pitch-mark in any closely-mown area *through the green*. On the *putting green*, a ball may be lifted and damage caused by the impact of a ball may be repaired (Rules 16-1b and c). When permission to take relief for an embedded ball anywhere *through the green* would be warranted, the following Local Rule is recommended:

"Through the green, a ball that is embedded in its own pitch-mark in the ground may be lifted, without penalty, cleaned and dropped as near as possible to where it lay but not nearer the hole. The ball when dropped must first strike a part of the course through the green.

*Exceptions:*
A player may not take relief under this Local Rule if the ball is embedded in sand in an area that is not closely mown.

A player may not take relief under this Local Rule if interference by anything other than the condition covered by this Local Rule makes the stroke clearly impracticable.

PENALTY FOR BREACH OF LOCAL RULE:
Match play – Loss of hole; Stroke play – Two strokes."

#### b. Cleaning Ball
Conditions, such as extreme wetness causing significant amounts of mud to adhere to the ball, may be such that permission to lift, clean and replace the ball would be appropriate. In these circumstances, the following Local Rule is recommended:

"(Specify area) a ball may be lifted, cleaned and replaced without penalty.

*Note:* The position of the ball must be marked before it is lifted under this Local Rule – see Rule 20-1.

PENALTY FOR BREACH OF LOCAL RULE:
Match play – Loss of hole; Stroke play – Two strokes."

#### c. "Preferred Lies" and "Winter Rules"
Ground under repair is provided for in Rule 25 and occasional local abnormal conditions that might interfere with fair play and are not widespread should be defined as *ground under repair.*

However, adverse conditions, such as heavy snows, spring thaws, prolonged rains or extreme heat can make fairways unsatisfactory and sometimes prevent use of heavy mowing equipment. When such conditions are so general throughout a *course* that the *Committee* believes "preferred lies" or "winter rules" would promote fair play or help protect the *course*, the following Local Rule is recommended:

"A ball lying on a closely-mown area through the green (or specify a more restricted area, e.g. at the 6th hole) may be lifted, without penalty, and cleaned. Before lifting the ball, the player must mark its position. Having lifted the ball, he must place it on a spot within (specify area, e.g. six inches, one club-length, etc.) of and not nearer the hole than where it originally lay, that is not in a hazard and not on a putting green.

A player may place his ball only once, and it is in play when it has been placed (Rule 20-4). If the ball fails to come to rest on the spot on which it is placed, Rule 20-3d applies. If the ball when placed comes to rest on the spot on which it is placed and it subsequently moves, there is no penalty and the ball must be played as it lies, unless the provisions of any other Rule apply.

If the player fails to mark the position of the ball before lifting it or moves the ball in any other manner, such as rolling it with a club, he incurs a penalty of one stroke.

*Note:* "Closely-mown area" means any area of the course, including paths through the rough, cut to fairway height or less.

*PENALTY FOR BREACH OF LOCAL RULE:
Match play – Loss of hole; Stroke play – Two strokes.
*If a player incurs the general penalty for a breach of this Local Rule, no additional penalty under the Local Rule is applied."

#### d. Aeration Holes
When a *course* has been aerated, a Local Rule permitting relief, without penalty, from an aeration hole may be warranted. The following Local Rule is recommended:

"Through the green, a ball that comes to rest in or on an aeration hole may be lifted, without penalty, cleaned and dropped, as near as possible to the spot where it lay but not nearer the hole. The ball when dropped must first strike a part of the course through the green.

On the putting green, a ball that comes to rest in or on an aeration hole may be placed at the nearest spot not nearer the hole that avoids the situation.

PENALTY FOR BREACH OF LOCAL RULE: Match play – Loss of hole; Stroke play – Two strokes."

### e. Seams of Cut Turf

If a Committee wishes to allow relief from seams of cut turf, but not from the cut turf itself, the following Local Rule is recommended:

"Through the green, seams of cut turf (not the turf itself) are deemed to be ground under repair. However, interference by a seam with the player's stance is deemed not to be, of itself, interference under Rule 25-1. If the ball lies in or touches the seam or the seam interferes with the area of intended swing, relief is available under Rule 25-1. All seams within the cut turf area are considered the same seam.

PENALTY FOR BREACH OF LOCAL RULE: Match play – Loss of hole; Stroke play – Two strokes."

### 5. Stones in Bunkers

Stones are, by definition, loose impediments and, when a player's ball is in a hazard, a stone lying in or touching the hazard may not be touched or moved (Rule 13-4). However, stones in bunkers may represent a danger to players (a player could be injured by a stone struck by the player's club in an attempt to play the ball) and they may interfere with the proper playing of the game.

When permission to lift a stone in a bunker is warranted, the following Local Rule is recommended:

"Stones in bunkers are movable obstructions (Rule 24-1 applies)."

### 6. Immovable Obstructions Close to Putting Green

Rule 24-2 provides relief, without penalty, from interference by an immovable obstruction, but it also provides that, except on the putting green, intervention on the line of play is not, of itself, interference under this Rule.

However, on some courses, the aprons of the putting greens are so closely mown that players may wish to putt from just off the green. In such conditions, immovable obstructions on the apron may interfere with the proper playing of the game and the introduction of the following Local Rule providing additional relief, without penalty, from intervention by an immovable obstruction would be warranted:

"Relief from interference by an immovable obstruction may be taken under Rule 24-2.

In addition, if a ball lies through the green and an immovable obstruction on or within two club-lengths of the putting green and within two club-lengths of the ball intervenes on the line of play between the ball and the hole, the player may take relief as follows:

The ball must be lifted and dropped at the nearest point to where the ball lay that (a) is not nearer the hole, (b) avoids intervention and (c) is not in a hazard or on a putting green.

If the player's ball lies on the putting green and an immovable obstruction within two club-lengths of the putting green intervenes on his line of putt, the player may take relief as follows:

The ball must be lifted and placed at the nearest point to where the ball lay that (a) is not nearer the hole, (b) avoids intervention and (c) is not in a hazard.

The ball may be cleaned when lifted.

Exception: A player may not take relief under this Local Rule if interference by anything other than the immovable obstruction makes the stroke clearly impracticable.

PENALTY FOR BREACH OF LOCAL RULE: Match play – Loss of hole; Stroke play – Two strokes."

Note: The Committee may restrict this Local Rule to specific holes, to balls lying only in closely-mown areas, to specific obstructions, or, in the case of obstructions that are not on the putting green, to obstructions in closely-mown areas if so desired. "Closely-mown area" means any area of the course, including paths through the rough, cut to fairway height or less.

### 7. Temporary Obstructions

When temporary obstructions are installed on or adjoining the course, the Committee should define the status of such obstructions as movable, immovable or temporary immovable obstructions.

### a. Temporary Immovable Obstructions

If the Committee defines such obstructions as temporary immovable obstructions, the following Local Rule is recommended:

"I. Definition

A temporary immovable obstruction (TIO) is a non-permanent artificial object that is often erected in conjunction with a competition and is fixed or not readily movable.

Examples of TIOs include, but are not limited to, tents, scoreboards, grandstands, television towers and lavatories. Supporting guy wires are part of the TIO, unless the Committee declares that they are to be treated as elevated power lines or cables.

II. Interference

Interference by a TIO occurs when (a) the ball lies in front of and so close to the TIO that the TIO interferes with the player's stance or the area of his intended swing, or (b) the ball lies in, on, under or behind the TIO so that any part of the TIO intervenes directly between the player's ball and the hole and is on his line of play; interference also exists if the ball lies within one club-length of a spot equidistant from the hole where such intervention would exist.

Note: A ball is under a TIO when it is below the outermost edges of the TIO, even if these edges do not extend downwards to the ground.

III. Relief

A player may obtain relief from interference by a TIO, including a TIO that is out of bounds, as follows:

(a) Through the Green: If the ball lies through the green, the point on the course nearest to where the ball lies must be determined that (a) is not nearer the hole, (b) avoids interference as defined in Clause II and (c) is not in a hazard or on a putting green. The player must lift the ball and drop it, without penalty, within one club-length of the point so determined on a part of the course that fulfils (a), (b) and (c) above.

(b) In a Hazard: If the ball is in a hazard, the player must lift and drop the ball either:

(i) Without penalty, in accordance with Clause III(a) above, except that the nearest part of the course affording complete relief must be in the hazard and the ball must be dropped in the hazard or, if complete relief is impossible, on a part of the course within the hazard that affords maximum available relief; or

(ii) Under penalty of one stroke, outside the hazard as follows: the point on the course nearest to where the ball lies must be determined that (a) is not nearer the hole, (b) avoids interference as defined in Clause II and (c) is not in a hazard. The player must drop the ball within one club-length of the point so determined on a part of the course that fulfils (a), (b) and (c) above.

The ball may be cleaned when lifted under Clause III.

*Note 1:* If the ball lies in a hazard, nothing in this Local Rule precludes the player from proceeding under Rule 26 or Rule 28, if applicable.

*Note 2:* If a ball to be dropped under this Local Rule is not immediately recoverable, another ball may be substituted.

*Note 3:* A Committee may make a Local Rule (a) permitting or requiring a player to use a dropping zone when taking relief from a TIO or (b) permitting a player, as an additional relief option, to drop the ball on the opposite side of the TIO from the point established under Clause III, but otherwise in accordance with Clause III.

*Exceptions:* If a player's ball lies in front of or behind the TIO (not in, on or under the TIO), he may not obtain relief under Clause III if:

Interference by anything other than the TIO makes it clearly impracticable for him to make a stroke or, in the case of intervention, to make a stroke such that the ball could finish on a direct line to the hole;

Interference by the TIO would occur only through use of a clearly unreasonable *stroke* or an unnecessarily abnormal stance, swing or direction of play; or

In the case of intervention, it would be clearly impracticable to expect the player to be able to strike the ball far enough towards the hole to reach the TIO.

A player who is not entitled to relief due to these exceptions may, if the ball lies through the green or in a bunker, obtain relief as provided in Rule 24-2b, if applicable. If the ball lies in a water hazard, the player may lift and drop the ball in accordance with Rule 24-2b(i), except that the nearest point of relief must be in the water hazard and the ball must be dropped under Rule 26-1.

**IV. Ball in TIO Not Found**

If it is known or virtually certain that a ball that has not been found is in, on or under a TIO, a ball may be dropped under the provisions of Clause III or Clause V, if applicable. For the purpose of applying Clauses III and V, the ball is deemed to lie at the spot where it last crossed the outermost limits of the TIO (Rule 24-3).

**V. Dropping Zones**

If the player has interference from a TIO, the Committee may permit or require the use of a dropping zone. If the player uses a dropping zone in taking relief, he must drop the ball in the dropping zone nearest to where his ball originally lay or is deemed to lie under Clause IV (even though the nearest dropping zone may be nearer the hole).

*Note:* A Committee may make a Local Rule prohibiting the use of a dropping zone that is nearer the hole.

PENALTY FOR BREACH OF LOCAL RULE:
Match play – Loss of hole; Stroke play – Two strokes."

**b. Temporary Power Lines and Cables**

When temporary power lines, cables, or telephone lines are installed on the *course*, the following Local Rule is recommended:

"Temporary power lines, cables, telephone lines and mats covering or stanchions supporting them are obstructions:

1. If they are readily movable, Rule 24-1 applies.
2. If they are fixed or not readily movable, the player may, if the ball lies through the green or in a bunker, obtain relief as provided in Rule 24-2b. If the ball lies in a water hazard, the player may lift and drop the ball in accordance with Rule 24-2b(i), except that the nearest point of relief

must be in the water hazard and the ball must be dropped in the water hazard or the player may proceed under Rule 26.

3. If a ball strikes an elevated power line or cable, the stroke is cancelled and the player must play a ball as nearly as possible at the spot from which the original ball was played in accordance with Rule 20-5 (Making Next Stroke from Where Previous Stroke Made).

*Note:* Guy wires supporting a temporary immovable obstruction are part of the temporary immovable obstruction, unless the Committee, by Local Rule, declares that they are to be treated as elevated power lines or cables.

*Exception:* A stroke that results in a ball striking an elevated junction section of cable rising from the ground must not be replayed.

4. Grass-covered cable trenches are ground under repair, even if not marked, and Rule 25-1b applies.

PENALTY FOR BREACH OF LOCAL RULE:
Match play – Loss of hole; Stroke play – Two strokes."

**8. Dropping Zones**

If the *Committee* considers that it is not feasible or practicable to proceed in accordance with a Rule providing relief, it may establish dropping zones in which balls may or must be dropped when taking relief. Generally, such dropping zones should be provided as an additional relief option to those available under the Rule itself, rather than being mandatory.

Using the example of a dropping zone for a *water hazard*, when such a dropping zone is established, the following Local Rule is recommended:

"If a ball is in or it is known or virtually certain that a ball that has not been found is in the water hazard (specify location), the player may:

(i) proceed under Rule 26; or
(ii) as an additional option, drop a ball, under penalty of one stroke, in the dropping zone.

PENALTY FOR BREACH OF LOCAL RULE:
Match play – Loss of hole; Stroke play – Two strokes."

*Note:* When using a dropping zone the following provisions apply regarding the dropping and re-dropping of the ball:

(a) The player does not have to stand within the dropping zone when dropping the ball.
(b) The dropped ball must first strike a part of the *course* within the dropping zone.
(c) If the dropping zone is defined by a line, the line is within the dropping zone.
(d) The dropped ball does not have to come to rest within the dropping zone.
(e) The dropped ball must be re-dropped if it rolls and comes to rest in a position covered by Rule 20-2c(i-vi).
(f) The dropped ball may roll nearer the *hole* than the spot where it first struck a part of the *course*, provided it comes to rest within two club-lengths of that spot and not into any of the positions covered by (e).
(g) Subject to the provisions of (e) and (f), the dropped ball may roll and come to rest nearer the *hole* than:
• its original position or estimated position (see Rule 20-2b);
• the *nearest point of relief* or maximum available relief (Rule 24-2, 25-1 or 25-3); or
• the point where the original ball last crossed the margin of the *water hazard* or *lateral water hazard* (Rule 26-1).

**9. Distance-Measuring Devices**

If the *Committee* wishes to act in accordance with the Note under Rule 14-3, the following wording is recommended:

"(Specify as appropriate, e.g. In this competition, or For all play at this course, etc.), a player may obtain distance information by using a device that measures distance only. If, during a stipulated round, a player uses a distance-measuring device that is designed to gauge or measure other conditions that might affect his play (e.g. gradient, windspeed, temperature, etc.), the player is in breach of Rule 14-3, for which the penalty is disqualification, regardless of whether any such additional function is actually used."

## Part C – Conditions of the Competition

Rule 33-1 provides, "The Committee must establish the conditions under which a competition is to be played." The conditions should include many matters such as method of entry, eligibility, number of rounds to be played, etc. which it is not appropriate to deal with in the Rules of Golf or this Appendix. Detailed information regarding these conditions is provided in "Decisions on the Rules of Golf" under Rule 33-1 and in "Guidance on Running a Competition".

However, there are a number of matters that might be covered in the Conditions of the Competition to which the Committee's attention is specifically drawn. These are:

### 1. Specification of Clubs and the Ball
The following conditions are recommended only for competitions involving expert players:

#### a. List of Conforming Driver Heads
On its website (www.randa.org) the R&A periodically issues a List of Conforming Driver Heads that lists driving clubheads that have been evaluated and found to conform with the Rules of Golf. If the Committee wishes to limit players to drivers that have a clubhead, identified by model and loft, that is on the List, the List should be made available and the following condition of competition used:

"Any driver the player carries must have a clubhead, identified by model and loft, that is named on the current List of Conforming Driver Heads issued the R&A.

*Exception:* A driver with a clubhead that was manufactured prior to 1999 is exempt from this condition.

*PENALTY FOR CARRYING, BUT NOT MAKING STROKE WITH, CLUB OR CLUBS IN BREACH OF CONDITION:*

Match play – At the conclusion of the hole at which the breach is discovered, the state of the match is adjusted by deducting one hole for  each hole at which a breach occurred; maximum deduction per round – Two holes.
Stroke play – Two strokes for each hole at which any breach occurred; maximum penalty per round – Four strokes (two strokes at each of the first two holes at which any breach occurred).
Match play or stroke play – If a breach is discovered between the play of two holes, it is deemed to have been discovered during play of the next hole, and the penalty must be applied accordingly.
Bogey and par competitions – See Note 1 to Rule 32-1a.
Stableford competitions – See Note 1 to Rule 32-1b.

*Any club or clubs carried in breach of this condition must be declared out of play by the player to his opponent in match play or his marker or a fellow-competitor in stroke play immediately upon discovery that a breach has occurred. If the player fails to do so, he is disqualified.

PENALTY FOR MAKING STROKE WITH CLUB IN BREACH OF CONDITION:
Disqualification."

#### b. List of Conforming Golf Balls
On its website (www.randa.org) the *R&A* periodically issues a List of Conforming Golf Balls that lists balls that have been tested and found to conform with the Rules of Golf. If the Committee wishes to require players to play a model of golf ball on the List, the List should be made available and the following condition of competition used:

"The ball the player plays must be named on the current List of Conforming Golf Balls issued by the R&A.
PENALTY FOR BREACH OF CONDITION:
Disqualification."

#### c. One Ball Condition
If it is desired to prohibit changing brands and models of golf balls during a *stipulated round*, the following condition is recommended:
"Limitation on Balls Used During Round: (Note to Rule 5-1)

##### (i) "One Ball" Condition
During a stipulated round, the balls a player plays must be of the same brand and model as detailed by a single entry on the current List of Conforming Golf Balls.
*Note:* If a ball of a different brand and/or model is dropped or placed it may be lifted, without penalty, and the player must then proceed by dropping or placing a proper ball (Rule 20-6).
PENALTY FOR BREACH OF CONDITION:
Match play – At the conclusion of the hole at which the breach is discovered, the state of the match is adjusted by deducting one hole for each hole at which a breach occurred; maximum deduction per round – Two holes.
Stroke play – Two strokes for each hole at which any breach occurred; maximum penalty per round – Four strokes (two strokes at each of the first two holes at which any breach occurred).
Bogey and Par competitions – See Note 1 to Rule 32-1a.
Stableford competitions – See Note 1 to Rule 32-1b.

##### (ii) Procedure When Breach Discovered
When a player discovers that he has played a ball in breach of this condition, he must abandon that ball before playing from the next teeing ground and complete the round with a proper ball; otherwise, the player is disqualified. If discovery is made during play of a hole and the player elects to substitute a proper ball before completing that hole, the player must place a proper ball on the spot where the ball played in breach of the condition lay."

### 2. Caddie (Note to Rule 6-4)
Rule 6-4 permits a player to use a *caddie*, provided he has only one *caddie* at any one time. However, there may be circumstances where a *Committee* may wish to prohibit *caddies* or restrict a player in his choice of *caddie*, e.g. professional golfer, sibling, parent, another player in the competition, etc. In such cases, the following wording is recommended:

#### Use of Caddie Prohibited
"A player is prohibited from using a caddie during the stipulated round.

#### Restriction on Who May Serve as Caddie
"A player is prohibited from having _____ serve as his caddie during the stipulated round.

*PENALTY FOR BREACH OF CONDITION:
Match play – At the conclusion of the hole at which the breach is discovered, the state of the match is adjusted by deducting one hole for each hole at which a breach occurred; maximum deduction per round – Two holes.
Stroke play – Two strokes for each hole at which any breach occurred; maximum penalty per round – Four strokes (two strokes at each of the first two holes at which any breach occurred).
Match play or stroke play – If a breach is discovered between the play of two holes, it is deemed to have been discovered during play of the next hole, and the penalty must be applied accordingly.
Bogey and par competitions – See Note 1 to Rule 32-1a.
Stableford competitions – See Note 1 to Rule 32-1b.

*A player having a caddie in breach of this condition must immediately upon discovery that a breach has occurred ensure that he conforms with this condition for the remainder of the stipulated round. Otherwise, the player is disqualified."

### 3. Pace of Play (Note 2 to Rule 6-7)

The *Committee* may establish pace of play guidelines to help prevent slow play, in accordance with Note 2 to Rule 6-7.

### 4. Suspension of Play Due to a Dangerous Situation (Note to Rule 6-8b)

As there have been many deaths and injuries from lightning on golf courses, all clubs and sponsors of golf competitions are urged to take precautions for the protection of persons against lightning. Attention is called to Rules 6-8 and 33-2d. If the *Committee* desires to adopt the condition in the Note under Rule 6-8b, the following wording is recommended:

"When play is suspended by the Committee for a dangerous situation, if the players in a match or group are between the play of two holes, they must not resume play until the Committee has ordered a resumption of play. If they are in the process of playing a hole, they must discontinue play immediately and not resume play until the Committee has ordered a resumption of play. If a player fails to discontinue play immediately, he is disqualified, unless circumstances warrant waiving the penalty as provided in Rule 33-7.

The signal for suspending play due to a dangerous situation will be a prolonged note of the siren."

The following signals are generally used and it is recommended that all *Committees* do similarly:

Discontinue Play Immediately: One prolonged note of siren.

Discontinue Play: Three consecutive notes of siren, repeated.

Resume Play: Two short notes of siren, repeated.

### 5. Practice
#### a. General

The *Committee* may make regulations governing practice in accordance with the Note to Rule 7-1, Exception (c) to Rule 7-2, Note 2 to Rule 7 and Rule 33-2c.

#### b. Practice Between Holes (Note 2 to Rule 7)

If the *Committee* wishes to act in accordance with Note 2 to Rule 7-2, the following wording is recommended:

"Between the play of two holes, a player must not make any practice stroke on or near the putting green of the hole last played and must not test the surface of the putting green of the hole last played by rolling a ball.

PENALTY FOR BREACH OF CONDITION:
Match play – Loss of next hole.
Stroke play – Two strokes at the next hole.
Match play or stroke play – In the case of a breach at the last hole of the stipulated round, the player incurs the penalty at that hole."

### 6. Advice in Team Competitions (Note to Rule 8)

If the *Committee* wishes to act in accordance with the Note under Rule 8, the following wording is recommended:

"In accordance with the Note to Rule 8 of the Rules of Golf, each team may appoint one person (in addition to the persons from whom advice may be asked under that Rule) who may give advice to members of that team. Such person (if it is desired to insert any restriction on who may be nominated insert such restriction here) must be identified to the Committee before giving advice."

### 7. New Holes (Note to Rule 33-2b)

The *Committee* may provide, in accordance with the Note to Rule 33-2b, that the *holes* and *teeing grounds* for a single round of a competition being held on more than one day may be differently situated on each day.

### 8. Transportation

If it is desired to require players to walk in a competition, the following condition is recommended:

"Players must not ride on any form of transportation during a stipulated round unless authorised by the Committee.

*PENALTY FOR BREACH OF CONDITION:
Match play – At the conclusion of the hole at which the breach is discovered, the state of the match is adjusted by deducting one hole for each hole at which a breach occurred; maximum deduction per round – Two holes.
Stroke play – Two strokes for each hole at which any breach occurred; maximum penalty per round – Four strokes (two strokes at each of the first two holes at which any breach occurred).
Match play or stroke play – If a breach is discovered between the play of two holes, it is deemed to have been discovered during play of the next hole, and the penalty must be applied accordingly.
Bogey and par competitions – See Note 1 to Rule 32-1a.
Stableford competitions – See Note 1 to Rule 32-1b.

*Use of any unauthorised form of transportation must be discontinued immediately upon discovery that a breach has occurred. Otherwise, the player is disqualified."

### 9. Anti-Doping

The *Committee* may require, in the conditions of competition, that players comply with an anti-doping policy.

### 10. How to Decide Ties

In both match play and stroke play, a tie can be an acceptable result. However, when it is desired to have a sole winner, the *Committee* has the authority, under Rule 33-6, to determine how and when a tie is decided. The decision should be published in advance.

The *R&A* recommends:

**Match Play**

A match that ends all square should be played off hole by hole until one side wins a hole. The play-off should start on the hole where the match began. In a handicap match, handicap strokes should be allowed as in the stipulated round.

**Stroke Play**

(a) In the event of a tie in a scratch stroke play competition, a play-off is recommended. The play-off may be over 18 holes or a smaller number of holes as specified by the Committee. If that is not feasible or there is still a tie, a hole-by-hole play-off is recommended.

(b) In the event of a tie in a handicap stroke play competition, a play-off with handicaps is recommended. The play-off may be over 18 holes or a smaller number of holes as specified by the Committee. It is recommended that any such play-off consist of at least three holes.

In competitions where the handicap stroke allocation table is not relevant, if the play-off is less than 18 holes, the percentage of 18 holes played should be applied to the players' handicaps to determine their play-off handicaps. Handicap stroke fractions of one half stroke or more should count as a full stroke and any lesser fraction should be disregarded.

In competitions where the handicap stroke table is relevant, such as four-ball stroke play and bogey, par and Stableford competitions, handicap strokes should be taken as they were assigned for the competition using the players' respective stroke allocation table(s).

(c) If a play-off of any type is not feasible, matching score cards is recommended. The method of matching score cards should be announced in advance and should also provide what will happen if this procedure does not produce a winner. An acceptable method of matching cards is to determine the winner on the basis of the best score for the last nine holes. If the tying players have the same score for the last nine, determine the winner on the basis of the last six holes, last three holes and finally the 18th hole. If this method is used in a competition with a multiple tee start, it is recommended that the "last nine holes, last six holes, etc." is considered to be holes 10-18, 13-18, etc.

For competitions where the handicap stroke table is not relevant, such as individual stroke play, if the last nine, last six, last three holes scenario is used, one-half, one-third, one-sixth, etc. of the handicaps should be deducted from the score for those holes. In terms of the use of fractions in such deductions, the Committee should act in accordance with the recommendations of the relevant handicapping authority.

In competitions where the handicap stroke table is relevant, such as four-ball stroke play and bogey, par and Stableford competitions, handicap strokes should be taken as they were assigned for the competition, using the players' respective stroke allocation table(s).

## 1. Draw for Match Play

Although the draw for match play may be completely blind or certain players may be distributed through different quarters or eighths, the General Numerical Draw is recommended if matches are determined by a qualifying round.

### General Numerical Draw

For purposes of determining places in the draw, ties in qualifying rounds other than those for the last qualifying place are decided by the order in which scores are returned, with the first score to be returned receiving the lowest available number, etc. If it is impossible to determine the order in which scores are returned, ties are determined by a blind draw.

| UPPER HALF | LOWER HALF |
|---|---|
| **64 QUALIFIERS** | |
| 1 vs. 64 | 2 vs. 63 |
| 32 vs. 33 | 31 vs. 34 |
| 16 vs. 49 | 15 vs. 50 |
| 17 vs. 48 | 18 vs. 47 |
| 8 vs. 57 | 7 vs. 58 |
| 25 vs. 40 | 26 vs. 39 |
| 9 vs. 56 | 10 vs. 55 |
| 24 vs. 41 | 23 vs. 42 |
| 4 vs. 61 | 3 vs. 62 |
| 29 vs. 36 | 30 vs. 35 |
| 13 vs. 52 | 14 vs. 51 |
| 20 vs. 45 | 19 vs. 46 |
| 5 vs. 60 | 6 vs. 59 |
| 28 vs. 37 | 27 vs. 38 |
| 12 vs. 53 | 11 vs. 54 |
| 21 vs. 44 | 22 vs. 43 |
| **32 QUALIFIERS** | |
| 1 vs. 32 | 2 vs. 31 |
| 16 vs. 17 | 15 vs. 18 |
| 8 vs. 25 | 7 vs. 26 |
| 9 vs. 24 | 10 vs. 23 |
| 4 vs. 29 | 3 vs. 30 |
| 13 vs. 20 | 14 vs. 19 |
| 5 vs. 28 | 6 vs. 27 |
| 12 vs. 21 | 11 vs. 22 |
| **16 QUALIFIERS** | |
| 1 vs. 16 | 2 vs. 15 |
| 8 vs. 9 | 7 vs. 10 |
| 4 vs. 13 | 3 vs. 14 |
| **8 QUALIFIERS** | |
| 1 vs. 8 | 2 vs. 7 |
| 4 vs. 5 | 3 vs. 6 |

## Appendices II, III and IV

### Definitions

All defined terms are in italics and are listed alphabetically in the Definitions section – see pages 592–595.

The R&A reserves the right, at any time, to change the Rules relating to clubs, balls, devices and other equipment and make or change the interpretations relating to these Rules. For up to date information, please contact the R&A or refer to www.randa.org/equipmentrules.

Any design in a club, ball, device or other equipment that is not covered by the Rules, which is contrary to the purpose and intent of the Rules or that might significantly change the nature of the game, will be ruled on by the R&A.

The dimensions and limits contained in Appendices II, III and IV are given in the units by which conformance is determined. An equivalent imperial/metric conversion is also referenced for information, calculated using a conversion rate of 1 inch = 25.4 mm.

## Appendix II – Design of Clubs

A player in doubt as to the conformity of a club should consult the R&A.

A manufacturer should submit to the R&A a sample of a club to be manufactured for a ruling as to whether the club conforms with the Rules. The sample becomes the property of the R&A for reference purposes. If a manufacturer fails to submit a sample or, having submitted a sample, fails to await a ruling before manufacturing and/or marketing the club, the manufacturer assumes the risk of a ruling that the club does not conform with the Rules.

The following paragraphs prescribe general regulations for the design of clubs, together with specifications and interpretations. Further information relating to these regulations and their proper interpretation is provided in "A Guide to the Rules on Clubs and Balls".

Where a club, or part of a club, is required to meet a specification within the Rules, it must be designed and manufactured with the intention of meeting that specification.

### 1. Clubs

#### a. General

A club is an implement designed to be used for striking the ball and generally comes in three forms: woods, irons and putters distinguished by shape and intended use. A putter is a club with a loft not exceeding ten degrees designed primarily for use on the *putting green*.

The club must not be substantially different from the traditional and customary form and make. The club must be composed of a shaft and a head and it may also have material added to the shaft to enable the player to obtain a firm hold (see 3 below). All parts of the club must be fixed so that the club is one unit, and it must have no external attachments. Exceptions may be made for attachments that do not affect the performance of the club.

#### b. Adjustability

All clubs may incorporate features for weight adjustment. Other forms of adjustability may also be permitted upon evaluation by the R&A. The following requirements apply to all permissible methods of adjustment:

(i)   the adjustment cannot be readily made;
(ii)  all adjustable parts are firmly fixed and there is no reasonable likelihood of them working loose during a round; and

(iii)  all configurations of adjustment conform with the *Rules*.
   During a *stipulated round*, the playing characteristics of a club must not be purposely changed by adjustment or by any other means (see Rule 4-2a).

**c. Length**
The overall length of the club must be at least 18 inches (0.457 m) and, except for putters, must not exceed 48 inches (1.219 m).

For woods and irons, the measurement of length is taken when the club is lying on a horizontal plane and the sole is set against a 60 degree plane as shown in Fig. I. The length is defined as the distance from the point of the intersection between the two planes to the top of the grip. For putters, the measurement of length is taken from the top of the grip along the axis of the shaft or a straight line extension of it to the sole of the club.

**d. Alignment**
When the club is in its normal address position the shaft must be so aligned so that:
(i)   the projection of the straight part of the shaft on to the vertical plane through the toe and heel must diverge from the vertical by at least 10 degrees (see Fig. II). If the overall design of the club is such that the player can effectively use the club in a vertical or close-to-vertical position, the shaft may be required to diverge from the vertical in this plane by as much as 25 degrees;
(ii)  the projection of the straight part of the shaft on to the vertical plane along the intended *line of play* must not diverge from the vertical by more than 20 degrees forwards or 10 degrees backwards (see Fig. III).

Except for putters, all of the heel portion of the club must lie within 0.625 inches (15.88 mm) of the plane containing the axis of the straight part of the shaft and the intended (horizontal) *line of play* (see Fig. IV).

**2. Shaft**
**a. Straightness**
The shaft must be straight from the top of the grip to a point not more than 5 inches (127 mm) above the sole, measured from the point where the shaft ceases to be straight along the axis of the bent part of the shaft and the neck and/or socket (see Fig. V).

**b. Bending and Twisting Properties**
At any point along its length, the shaft must:
(i)   bend in such a way that the deflection is the same regardless of how the shaft is rotated about its longitudinal axis; and

(ii)  twist the same amount in both directions.

**c. Attachment to Clubhead**
The shaft must be attached to the clubhead at the heel either directly or through a single plain neck and/or socket. The length from the top of the neck and/or socket to the sole of the club must not exceed 5 inches (127 mm), measured along the axis of, and following any bend in, the neck and/or socket (see Fig. VI).

*Exception for Putters:* The shaft or neck or socket of a putter may be fixed at any point in the head.

**3. Grip (see Fig. VII)**
The grip consists of material added to the shaft to enable the player to obtain a firm hold. The grip must be fixed to the shaft, must be plain in form, must not be moulded for any part of the hands. If no material is added, that portion of the shaft designed to be held by the player must be considered the grip.
(i)   For clubs other than putters the grip must be circular in cross-section, except that a continuous, straight, slightly raised rib may be incorporated along the cross-section (putters only) full length of the grip, and a slightly indented spiral is permitted on a wrapped grip or a replica of one.
(ii)  A putter grip may have a non-circular cross-section, provided the cross-section has no concavity, is symmetrical and remains generally similar throughout the length of (not permitted) the grip. (See Clause (v) overleaf). Bulge (not permitted)
(iii) The grip may be tapered but must not have any bulge or waist. Its cross-sectional dimensions measured in any direction must not exceed 1.75 inches (44.45 mm).
(iv)  For clubs other than putters the axis of the grip must coincide with the axis of the shaft.
(v)   A putter may have two grips provided each is circular in cross-section, the axis of each coincides with the axis of the shaft, and they are separated by at least 1.5 inches (38.1 mm).

**4. Clubhead**
**a. Plain in Shape**
The clubhead must be generally plain in shape. All parts must be rigid, structural in nature and functional. The clubhead or its parts must not be designed to resemble any other object. It is not practicable to define plain in shape precisely and comprehensively. However, features that are deemed to be in breach of this requirement and are therefore not permitted include, but are not limited to:

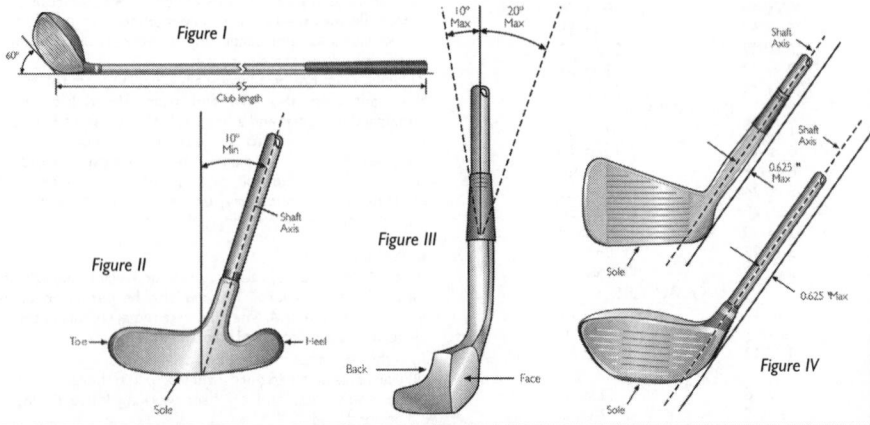

Figure I

Figure II

Figure III

Figure IV

**(i) All Clubs**
- holes through the ace;
- holes through the head (some exceptions may be made for putters and cavity back irons);
- features that are for the purpose of meeting dimensional specifications;
- features that extend into or ahead of the face;
- features that extend significantly above the top line of the head;
- furrows in or runners on the head that extend into the face (some exceptions may be made for putters); and
- optical or electronic devices.

**(ii) Woods and Irons**
- all features listed in (i) above;
- cavities in the outline of the heel and/or the toe of the head that can be viewed from above;
- severe or multiple cavities in the outline of the back of the head that can be viewed from above;
- transparent material added to the head with the intention of rendering conforming a feature that is not otherwise permitted; and
- features that extend beyond the outline of the head when viewed from above.

**b. Dimensions, Volume and Moment of Inertia**
**(i) Woods**
When the club is in a 60 degree lie angle, the dimensions of the clubhead must be such that:
- the distance from the heel to the toe of the clubhead is greater than the distance from the face to the back;
- the distance from the heel to the toe of the clubhead is not greater than 5 inches (127 mm); and
- the distance from the sole to the crown of the clubhead, including any permitted features, is not greater than 2.8 inches (71.12 mm).

These dimensions are measured on horizontal lines between vertical projections of the outermost points of:
- the heel and the toe; and
- the face and the back (see Fig. VIII, dimension A);
and on vertical lines between the horizontal projections of the outermost points of the sole and the crown (see Fig. VIII, dimension B). If the outermost point of the heel is not clearly defined, it is deemed to be 0.875 inches (22.23 mm) above the horizontal plane on which the club is lying (see Fig. VIII, dimension C).

The volume of the clubhead must not exceed 460 cubic centimetres (28.06 cubic inches), plus a tolerance of 10 cubic centimetres (0.61 cubic inches).

When the club is in a 60 degree lie angle, the moment of inertia component around the vertical axis through the clubhead's centre of gravity must not exceed 5900 g cm$^2$ (32.259 oz in$^2$), plus a test tolerance of 100 g cm$^2$ (0.547 oz in$^2$).

**(ii) Irons**
When the clubhead is in its normal address position, the dimensions of the head must be such that the distance from the heel to the toe is greater than the distance from the face to the back.

**(iii) Putters (see Fig. IX)**
When the clubhead is in its normal address position, the dimensions of the head must be such that:
- the distance from the heel to the toe is greater than the distance from the face to the back;
- the distance from the heel to the toe of the head is less than or equal to 7 inches (177.8 mm);
- the distance from the heel to the toe of the face is greater than or equal to two thirds of the distance from the face to the back of the head;
- the distance from the heel to the toe of the face is greater than or equal to half of the distance from the heel to the toe of the head; and
- the distance from the sole to the top of the head, including any permitted features, is less than or equal to 2.5 inches (63.5 mm).

For traditionally shaped heads, these dimensions will be measured on horizontal lines between vertical projections of the outermost points of:
- the heel and the toe of the head;
- the heel and the toe of the face; and
- the face and the back;
and on vertical lines between the horizontal projections of the outermost points of the sole and the top of the head.

For unusually shaped heads, the toe to heel dimension may be made at the face.

**c. Spring Effect and Dynamic Properties**
The design, material and/or construction of, or any treatment to, the clubhead (which includes the club face) must not:
(i) have the effect of a spring which exceeds the limit set forth in the Pendulum Test Protocol on file with the *R&A*; or
(ii) incorporate features or technology including, but not limited to, separate springs or spring features, that have the intent of, or the effect of, unduly influencing the clubhead's spring effect; or
(iii) unduly influence the movement of the ball.
    *Note:* (i) above does not apply to putters.

**d. Striking Faces**
The clubhead must have only one striking face, except that a putter may have two such faces if their characteristics are the same, and they are opposite each other.

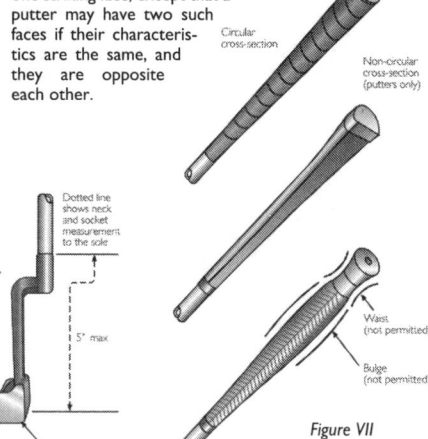

Figure VII

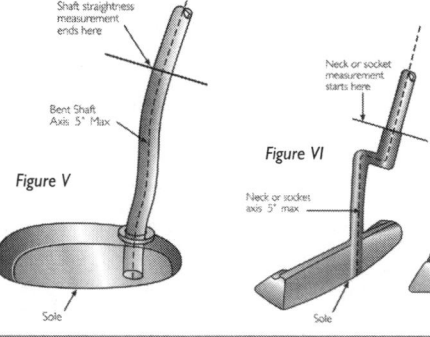

Figure V

Figure VI

## 5. Club Face
### a. General
The face of the club must be hard and rigid and must not impart significantly more or less spin to the ball than a standard steel face (some exceptions may be made for putters). Except for such markings listed below, the club face must be smooth and must not have any degree of concavity.

### b. Impact Area Roughness and Material
Except for markings specified in the following paragraphs, the surface roughness within the area where impact is intended (the "impact area") must not exceed that of decorative sandblasting, Illustrative or of fine milling (see Fig. X).

The whole of the impact area must be of the same material (exceptions may be made for clubheads made of wood).

### c. Impact Area Markings
If a club has grooves and/or punch marks in the impact area they must meet the following specifications:

#### (i) Grooves
- Grooves must be straight and parallel.
- Grooves must have a symmetrical cross-section and have sides which do not converge (see Fig. XI).
- *For clubs that have a loft angle greater than or equal to 25 degrees, grooves must have a plain cross-section.
- The width, spacing and cross-section of the grooves must be consistent throughout the impact area (some exceptions may be made for woods).
- The width (W) of each groove must not exceed 0.035 inches (0.9 mm), using the 30 degree method of measurement on file with the R&A.
- The depth of any punch mark must not exceed 0.040 inches (1.02 mm).
- Punch marks must not have sharp edges or raised lips.
- *For clubs that have a loft angle greater than or equal to 25 degrees, punch mark edges must be substantially in the form of a round having an effective radius which is not less than 0.010 inches (0.254 mm) when measured as shown in Figure XIII, and not greater than 0.020 inches (0.508 mm). Deviations in effective radius within 0.001 inches (0.0254 mm) are permissible.

*Note 1:* The groove and punch mark specifications above indicated by an asterisk (*) apply only to new models of clubs manufactured on or after 1 January 2010 and any club where the face markings have been purposely altered, for example, by re-grooving. For further information on the status of clubs available before 1 January 2010, refer to the "Equipment Search" section of www.randa.org.

*Note 2:* The Committee may require, in the conditions of competition, that the clubs the player carries must con-

form to the groove and punch mark specification above indicated by an asterisk (*). This condition is recommended only for competitions involving expert players. For further information, refer to Decision 4-1/1 in "Decisions on the Rules of Golf".

### d. Decorative Markings
The centre of the impact area may be indicated by a design within the boundary of a square whose sides are 0.375 inches (9.53 mm) in length. Such a design must not unduly influence the movement of the ball. Decorative markings are permitted outside the impact area.

### e. Non-Metallic Club Face Markings
The above specifications do not apply to clubheads made of wood on which the impact area of the face is of a material of hardness less than the hardness of metal and whose loft angle is 24 degrees or less, but markings which could unduly influence the movement of the ball are prohibited.

### f. Putter Face Markings
Any markings on the face of a putter must not have sharp edges or raised lips. The specifications with regard to roughness, material and markings in the impact area do not apply.

## Appendix III – The Ball

### 1. General
The ball must not be substantially different from the traditional and customary form and make. The material and construction of the ball must not be contrary to the purpose and intent of the *Rules*.

### 2. Weight
The weight of the ball must not be greater than 1.620 ounces avoirdupois (45.93 g).

### 3. Size
The diameter of the ball must not be less than 1.680 inches (42.67mm).

### 4. Spherical Symmetry
The ball must not be designed, manufactured or intentionally modified to have properties which differ from those of a spherically symmetrical ball.

### 5. Initial Velocity
The initial velocity of the ball must not exceed the limit specified under the conditions set forth in the Initial Velocity Standard for golf balls on file with the R&A.

### 6. Overall Distance Standard
The combined carry and roll of the ball, when tested on apparatus approved by the R&A, must not exceed the distance specified under the conditions set forth in the Overall Distance Standard for golf balls on file with the R&A.

## Appendix IV – Devices and Other Equipment

A player in doubt as to whether use of a device or other equipment would constitute a breach of the *Rules* should consult the R&A.

A manufacturer should submit to the R&A a sample of a device or other equipment to be manufactured for a ruling as to whether its use during a *stipulated round* would cause a player to be in breach of Rule 14-3. The sample becomes the property of the R&A for ref-

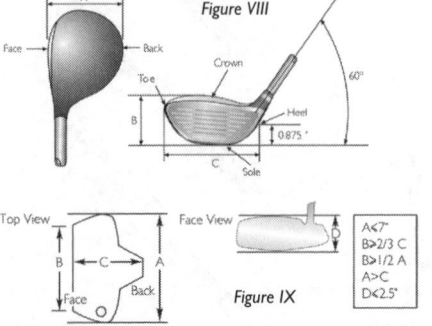

Figure VIII

Figure IX

A<7"
B>2/3 C
B>1/2 A
A>C
D<2.5"

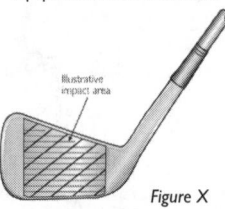

Figure X

erence purposes. If a manufacturer fails to submit a sample or, having submitted a sample, fails to await a ruling before manufacturing and/or marketing the device or other equipment, the manufacturer assumes the risk of a ruling that use of the device or other equipment would be contrary to the *Rules*.

The following paragraphs prescribe general regulations for the design of devices and other equipment, together with specifications and interpretations. They should be read in conjunction with Rule 11-1 (Teeing) and Rule 14-3 (Artificial Devices, Unusual Equipment and Unusual Use of Equipment).

## 1. Tees (Rule 11)

A tee is a device designed to raise the ball off the ground. A tee must not:

- be longer than 4 inches (101.6 mm);
- be designed or manufactured in such a way that it could indicate *line of play*;
- unduly influence the movement of the ball; or
- otherwise assist the player in making a *stroke* or in his play.

## 2. Gloves (Rule 14-3)

Gloves may be worn to assist the player in gripping the club, provided they are plain.

A "plain" glove must:

- consist of a fitted covering of the hand with a separate sheath or opening for each digit (fingers and thumb); and
- be made of smooth materials on the full palm and gripping surface of the digits.

A "plain" glove must not incorporate:

- material on the gripping surface or inside of the glove, the primary purpose of which is to provide padding or which has the effect of providing padding. Padding is defined as an area of glove material which is more than 0.025 inches (0.635 mm) thicker than the adjacent areas of the glove without the added material;

Note: Material may be added for wear resistance, moisture absorption or other functional purposes, provided it does not exceed the definition of padding (see above).

- straps to assist in preventing the club from slipping or to attach the hand to the club;
- any means of binding digits together;
- material on the glove that adheres to material on the grip;
- features, other than visual aids, designed to assist the player in placing his hands in a consistent and/or specific position on the grip;
- weight to assist the player in making a *stroke*;
- any feature that might restrict the movement of a joint; or

- any other feature that might assist the player in making a *stroke* or in his play.

## 3. Shoes (Rule 14-3)

Shoes that assist the player in obtaining a firm *stance* may be worn. Subject to the conditions of competition, features such as spikes on the sole are permitted, but shoes must not incorporate features:

- designed to assist the player in taking his *stance* and/or building a *stance*;
- designed to assist the player with his alignment; or
- that might otherwise assist the player in making a *stroke* or in his play.

## 4. Clothing (Rule 14-3)

Articles of clothing must not incorporate features:

- designed to assist the player with his alignment; or
- that might otherwise assist the player in making a *stroke* or in his play.

## 5. Distance-Measuring Devices (Rule 14-3)

During a *stipulated round*, the use of any distance measuring device is not permitted unless the Committee has introduced a Local Rule to that effect (see Note to Rule 14-3 and Appendix I; Part B; Section 9).

Even when the Local Rule is in effect, the device must be limited to measuring distance only. Features that would render use of the device contrary to the Local Rule include, but are not limited to:

- the gauging or measuring of slope;
- the gauging or measuring of other conditions that might affect play (e.g. wind speed or direction, or other climate-based information such as temperature, humidity, etc.);
- recommendations that might assist the player in making a *stroke* or in his play (e.g. club selection, type of shot to be played, green reading or any other advice related matter); or
- calculating the effective distance between two points based on slope or other conditions affecting shot distance.

Such non-conforming features render use of the device contrary to the *Rules*, irrespective of whether or not:

- the features can be switched off or disengaged; and
- the features are switched off or disengaged.

A multi-functional device, such as a smartphone or PDA, may be used as a distance measuring device provided it contains a distance measuring application that meets all of the above limitations (i.e. it must measure distance only). In addition, when the distance measuring application is being used, there must be no other features or applications installed on the device that, if used, would be in breach of the *Rules*, whether or not they are actually used.

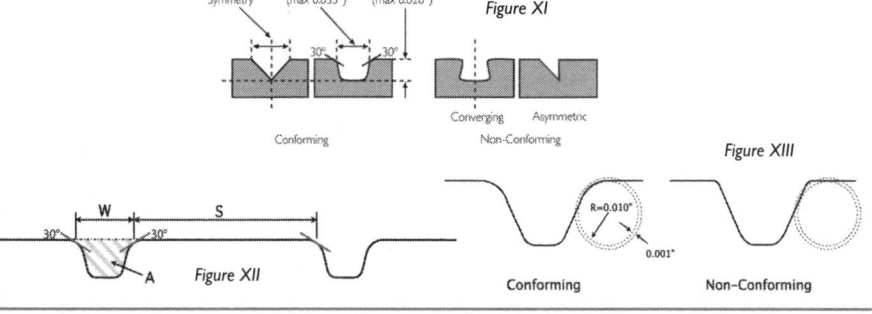

Axis of Symmetry    Groove width (max 0.035")    Groove depth (max 0.020")

Conforming

*Figure XI*

Converging    Asymmetric
Non-Conforming

*Figure XII*

*Figure XIII*

Conforming      Non-Conforming

# RULES OF AMATEUR STATUS
## As approved by R&A Rules Limited
### Effective from 1st January 2012

**Preamble**

The *R&A* reserves the right to change the Rules of Amateur Status and to make and change the interpretations of the Rules of Amateur Status at any time. For up to date information, please contact the *R&A* or refer to www.randa.org. In the Rules of Amateur Status, the gender used in relation to any person is understood to include both genders.

**Definitions**

The Definitions are listed alphabetically and, in the *Rules* themselves, defined terms are in *italics*.

**Amateur Golfer**

An "*amateur golfer*", whether he plays competitively or recreationally, is one who plays golf for the challenge it presents, not as a profession and not for financial gain.

**Committee**

The "*Committee*" is the appropriate *Committee* of the *Governing Body*.

**Golf Skill or Reputation**

It is a matter for the *Governing Body* to decide whether a particular *amateur golfer* has *golf skill or reputation*.

Generally, an *amateur golfer* is only considered to have *golf skill* if he:
(a) has had competitive success at regional or national level or has been selected to represent his national, regional, state or county golf union or association; or
(b) competes at an elite level.

*Golf reputation* can only be gained through *golf skill* and such *reputation* is deemed to continue for five years after that player's *golf skill* has fallen below the standard set by the *Governing Body*.

**Governing Body**

The "*Governing Body*" for the administration of the Rules of Amateur Status in any country is the national golf union or association of that country.

*Note:* In Great Britain and Ireland, the *R&A* is the *Governing Body*.

**Instruction**

"*Instruction*" covers teaching the physical aspects of playing golf, i.e. the actual mechanics of swinging a golf club and hitting a golf ball.

*Note: Instruction* does not cover teaching the psychological aspects of the game or the etiquette or Rules of Golf.

**Junior Golfer**

A "*junior golfer*" is an *amateur golfer* who has not reached a specified age as determined by the *Governing Body*.

**Prize Voucher**

A "*prize voucher*" is a voucher, gift certificate, gift card, or the like approved by the Committee in charge of a competition for the purchase of goods or services from a professional's shop, a golf club or other retail source.

**R&A**

The "*R&A*" means R&A Rules Limited.

**Retail Value**

The "*retail value*" of a prize is the price at which the prize is generally available from a retail source at the time of the award.

**Rule or Rules**

The term "*Rule*" or "*Rules*" refers to the Rules of Amateur Status and their interpretations as contained in "Decisions on the Rules of Amateur Status".

**Symbolic Prize**

A "*symbolic prize*" is a trophy made of gold, silver, ceramic, glass or the like that is permanently and distinctively engraved.

**Testimonial Award**

A "*testimonial award*" is an award for notable performances or contributions to golf as distinguished from competition prizes. A *testimonial award* may not be a monetary award.

**USGA**

The "*USGA*" means the United States Golf Association.

## Rule 1 – Amateurism

**1-1. General**

An amateur golfer must play the game and conduct himself in accordance with the Rules.

**1-2. Amateur Status**

Amateur Status is a universal condition of eligibility for playing in golf competitions as an *amateur golfer*. A person who acts contrary to the *Rules* may forfeit his amateur status and as a result will be ineligible to play in amateur competitions.

**1-3. Purpose of the Rules**

The purpose of the *Rules* is to maintain the distinction between amateur and professional golf and to ensure that amateur golf, which is largely self-regulating with regard to the Rules of Golf and handicapping, is free from the pressures that may follow from uncontrolled sponsorship and financial incentive.

Through appropriate limits and restrictions, the *Rules* are also intended to encourage amateur golfers to focus on the game's challenges and inherent rewards, rather than any financial gain.

**1-4. Doubt as to Rules**

A person who is in doubt as to whether taking a proposed course of action is permitted under the *Rules* should consult the *Governing Body*.

An organiser or sponsor of an amateur golf competition or a competition involving *amateur golfers* who is in doubt as to whether a proposal is in accordance with the *Rules* should consult the *Governing Body*.

## Rule 2 – Professionalism

**2-1. General**

An amateur golfer must not conduct or identify himself as a professional golfer.

For the purpose of applying these *Rules*, a professional golfer is one who:
• plays the game as his profession; or
• works as a professional golfer; or
• enters a golf competition as a professional; or
• holds or retains membership of any Professional Golfers' Association (PGA); or
• holds or retains membership of a Professional Tour limited exclusively to professional golfers.

*Exception:* An *amateur golfer* may hold or retain a category of PGA membership, provided this category does not confer any playing rights and it is purely for administrative purposes.

*Note 1:* An *amateur golfer* may enquire as to his likely prospects as a professional golfer, including applying unsuccessfully for the position of a professional golfer, and he may work in a professional's shop and receive payment or compensation, provided he does not infringe the *Rules* in any other way.

*Note 2:* If an *amateur golfer* must compete in one or more qualifying competitions in order to be eligible for membership of a Professional Tour, he may enter and play in such qualifying competitions without forfeiting his Amateur Status, provided, in advance of play and in writing, he waives his right to any prize money in the competition.

### 2-2. Contracts and Agreements
#### (a) National Golf Unions or Associations
An *amateur golfer* may enter into a contract and/or an agreement with his national golf union or association, provided that he does not obtain payment, compensation or any financial gain, directly or indirectly, whilst still an *amateur golfer*, except as otherwise provided in the *Rules*.

#### (b) Professional Agents, Sponsors and Other Third Parties
An *amateur golfer* may enter into a contract and/or an agreement with a third party (including but not limited to a professional agent or a sponsor), provided:
(i) the golfer is at least 18 years of age,
(ii) the contract or agreement is solely in relation to the golfer's future as a professional golfer and does not stipulate playing in certain amateur or professional events as an *amateur golfer*, and
(iii) except as otherwise provided in the *Rules*, the *amateur golfer* does not obtain payment, compensation or any financial gain, directly or indirectly, whilst still an *amateur golfer*.

*Exception:* In special individual circumstances, an *amateur golfer* under the age of 18 may apply to the *Governing Body* to be allowed to enter into such a contract, provided it is of no more than 12 months duration and it is non-renewable.

*Note 1:* An *amateur golfer* is advised to consult the *Governing Body* prior to signing any such third party contract and/or agreement to ensure that it complies with the *Rules*.

*Note 2:* If an *amateur golfer* is in receipt of an educational golf scholarship (see Rule 6-5), or may apply for such a scholarship in the future, he is advised to contact the national body regulating such scholarships and/or the relevant educational institution to ensure that any third party contracts and/ or agreements are allowable under the applicable scholarship regulations.

## Rule 3 – Prizes
### 3-1. Playing for Prize Money
An *amateur golfer* must not play golf for prize money or its equivalent in a match, competition or exhibition.

However, an *amateur golfer* may participate in a golf match, competition or exhibition where prize money or its equivalent is offered, provided that prior to participation he waives his right to accept prize money in that event.

*Exception:* Where prize money is offered for a hole-in-one made while playing a round of golf, an *amateur golfer* is not required to waive his right to accept that prize money prior to participation (see Rule 3-2b).

(Conduct contrary to the purpose of the Rules – see Rule 7-2)

(Policy on gambling – see Appendix)

### 3-2. Prize Limits
#### a. General
An *amateur golfer* must not accept a prize (other than a *symbolic prize*) or *prize voucher* of *retail value* in excess of £500 or the equivalent, or such a lesser figure as may be decided by the *Governing Body*. This limit applies to the total

prizes or *prize vouchers* received by an *amateur golfer* in any one competition or series of competitions.

*Exception:* Hole-in-one prizes – see Rule 3-2b.

*Note 1:* The prize limits apply to any form of golf competition, whether on a golf course, driving range or golf simulator, including nearest the hole and longest drive competitions.

*Note 2:* The responsibility to prove the *retail value* of a particular prize rests with the Committee in charge of the competition.

*Note 3:* It is recommended that the total value of prizes in a gross competition, or each division of a handicap competition, should not exceed twice the prescribed limit in an 18-hole competition, three times in a 36-hole competition, five times in a 54-hole competition and six times in a 72-hole competition.

#### b. Hole-in-One Prizes
An *amateur golfer* may accept a prize in excess of the limit in Rule 3-2a, including a cash prize, for a hole-in-one made while playing a round of golf.

*Note:* The hole-in-one must be made during a round of golf and be incidental to that round. Separate multiple-entry contests, contests conducted other than on a golf course (e.g. on a driving range or golf simulator) and putting contests do not qualify under this provision and are subject to the restrictions and limits in Rules 3-1 and 3-2a.

### 3-3. Testimonial Awards
#### a. General
An *amateur golfer* must not accept a *testimonial award* of *retail value* in excess of the limits prescribed in Rule 3-2.

#### b. Multiple Awards
An *amateur golfer* may accept more than one testimonial award from different donors, even though their total retail value exceeds the prescribed limit, provided they are not presented so as to evade the limit for a single award.

## Rule 4 – Expenses
### 4-1. General
Except as provided in the Rules, an *amateur golfer* must not accept expenses, in money or otherwise, from any source to play in a golf competition or exhibition.

### 4-2. Receipt of Competition Expenses
An *amateur golfer* may receive reasonable competition expenses, not exceeding the actual expenses incurred, to play in a golf competition or exhibition as prescribed in clauses a-g of this Rule.

If an *amateur golfer* is in receipt of an educational golf scholarship (see Rule 6-5), or may apply for such a scholarship in the future, he is advised to contact the national body regulating such scholarships and/or the relevant educational institution to ensure that any competition expenses are allowable under the applicable scholarship regulations.

#### a. Family Support
An *amateur golfer* may receive expenses from a member of his family or a legal guardian.

#### b. Junior Golfers
A *junior golfer* may receive expenses when competing in a competition limited exclusively to *junior golfers*.

*Note:* If a competition is not limited exclusively to *junior golfers*, a *junior golfer* may receive expenses when competing in that competition, as prescribed in Rule 4-2c.

#### c. Individual Events
An *amateur golfer* may receive expenses when competing in individual events provided he complies with the following provisions:
(i) Where the competition is to take place in the player's own country the expenses must be approved by and

paid through the player's national, regional, state or county golf union or association, or with the approval of such body, may be paid by the player's golf club.

(ii) Where the competition is to take place in another country the expenses must be approved by and paid through the player's national, regional, state or county golf union or association or, subject to the approval of the player's national union or association, paid by the body controlling golf in the territory in which he is competing.

The *Governing Body* may limit the receipt of expenses to a specific number of competitive days in any one calendar year and an *amateur golfer* must not exceed any such limit. In such a case, the expenses are deemed to include reasonable travel time and practice days in connection with the competitive days.

*Exception:* An *amateur golfer* must not receive expenses, directly or indirectly, from a professional agent (see Rule 2-2) or any other similar source as may be determined by the *Governing Body*.

*Note:* Except as provided in the *Rules*, an *amateur golfer* of *golf skill or reputation* must not promote or advertise the source of any expenses received (see Rule 6-2).

### d. Team Events

An *amateur golfer*, may receive expenses when he is representing:

* his country,
* his regional, state or county golf union or association,
* his golf club,
* his business or industry, or
* a similar body

in a team competition, practice session or training camp.

*Note 1:* A "similar body" includes a recognised educational institution or military service.

*Note 2:* Unless otherwise stated, the expenses must be paid by the body that the *amateur golfer* is representing or the body controlling golf in the country in which he is competing.

### e. Invitation Unrelated to Golf Skill

An *amateur golfer* who is invited for reasons unrelated to *golf skill* (e.g. a celebrity, a business associate or customer) to take part in a golf event may receive expenses.

### f. Exhibitions

An *amateur golfer* who is participating in an exhibition in aid of a recognised charity may receive expenses, provided that the exhibition is not run in connection with another golfing event in which the player is competing.

### g. Sponsored Handicap Competitions

An *amateur golfer* may receive expenses when competing in a sponsored handicap competition, provided the competition has been approved as follows:

(i) Where the competition is to take place in the player's own country, the annual approval of the *Governing Body* must first be obtained in advance by the sponsor; and

(ii) Where the competition is to take place in more than one country or involves golfers from another country, the annual approval of each *Governing Body* must first be obtained in advance by the sponsor. The application for this approval should be sent to the *Governing Body* in the country where the competition commences.

### 4-3. Subsistence Expenses

An *amateur golfer* may receive reasonable subsistence expenses, not exceeding actual expenses incurred, to assist with general living costs, provided the expenses are approved by and paid through the player's national golf union or association.

In determining whether such subsistence expenses are necessary and/ or appropriate, the national golf union or asso-ciation, which has the sole discretion in the approval of such expenses, should consider, among other factors, applicable socio-economic conditions.

*Exception:* An *amateur golfer* must not receive subsistence expenses, directly or indirectly, from a professional agent (see Rule 2-2) or any other similar source as may be determined by the *Governing Body*.

## Rule 5 – Instruction

### 5-1. General

Except as provided in the Rules, an *amateur golfer* must not receive payment or compensation, directly or indirectly, for giving golf *instruction*.

### 5-2. Where Payment Permitted
### a. Schools, Colleges, Camps, etc.

An *amateur golfer* who is (i) an employee of an educational institution or system or (ii) a counsellor at a camp or other similar organised programme, may receive payment or compensation for golf instruction to students in the institu-tion, system or camp, provided that the total time devoted to such instruction comprises less than 50 percent of the time spent in the performance of all duties as such an employee or counsellor.

### b. Approved Programmes

An *amateur golfer* may receive expenses, payment or com-pensation for giving golf *instruction* as part of a programme that has been approved in advance by the *Governing Body*.

### 5-3. Instruction in Writing

An *amateur golfer* may receive payment or compensation for golf *instruction* in writing, provided his ability or reputa-tion as a golfer was not a major factor in his employment or in the commission or sale of his work.

## Rule 6 – Use of Golf Skill or Reputation

The following regulations under Rule 6 only apply to *ama-teur golfers* of *golf skill* or *reputation*.

### 6-1. General

Except as provided in the *Rules*, an *amateur golfer* of *golf skill* or *reputation* must not use that skill or reputation for any financial gain.

### 6-2. Promotion, Advertising and Sales

An *amateur golfer* of *golf skill* or *reputation* must not use that skill or reputation to obtain payment, compensation, per-sonal benefit or any financial gain, directly or indirectly, for (i) promoting, advertising or selling anything, or (ii) allowing his name or likeness to be used by a third party for the promotion, advertisement or sale of anything.

*Exception:* An *amateur golfer* of *golf skill* or *reputation* may allow his name or likeness to be used to promote:

(a) his national, regional, state or county golf union or association; or

(b) a recognised charity (or similar good cause); or

(c) subject to the permission of his national golf union or association, any golf competition or other event that is considered to be in the best interests of, or would contribute to the development of, the game.

The *amateur golfer* must not obtain any payment, com-pensation or financial gain, directly or indirectly, for allow-ing his name or likeness to be used in these ways.

*Note 1:* An *amateur golfer* of *golf skill* or *reputation* may accept golf equipment from anyone dealing in such equip-ment provided no advertising is involved.

*Note 2:* Limited name and logo recognition is allowed on golf equipment and clothing. Further information relating to this Note and its proper interpretation is provided in "Decisions on the Rules of Amateur Status".

### 6-3. Personal Appearance

An *amateur golfer* of *golf skill or reputation* must not use that skill or reputation to obtain payment, compensation, personal benefit or any financial gain, directly or indirectly, for a personal appearance.

*Exception:* An *amateur golfer* of *golf skill or reputation* may receive actual expenses in connection with a personal appearance provided no golf competition or exhibition is involved.

### 6-4. Broadcasting and Writing

An *amateur golfer* of *golf skill or reputation* may receive payment, compensation, personal benefit or financial gain from broadcasting or writing provided:

(a) the broadcasting or writing is part of his primary occupation or career and golf *instruction* is not included (Rule 5); or

(b) if the broadcasting or writing is on a part-time basis, the player is actually the author of the commentary, articles or books and golf *instruction* is not included.

*Note:* An *amateur golfer* of *golf skill or reputation* must not promote or advertise anything within the commentary, article or books (see Rule 6-2).

### 6-5. Educational Grants, Scholarships and Bursaries

An *amateur golfer* of *golf skill or reputation* may accept the benefits of an educational grant, scholarship or bursary, the terms and conditions of which have been approved by the *Governing Body.*

A *Governing Body* may pre-approve the terms and conditions of educational grants, scholarships and bursaries, such as those that comply with the regulations of the National Collegiate Athletic Association (NCAA) in the United States of America, or other similar organisations governing athletes at educational institutions.

If an *amateur golfer* is in receipt of an educational golf scholarship, or may apply for such a scholarship in the future, he is advised to contact the national body regulating such scholarships and/or the relevant educational institution to ensure that any third party contracts and/or agreements (Rule 2-2b) or competition expenses (Rule 4-2) are allowable under the applicable scholarship regulations.

### 6-6. Membership

An *amateur golfer* of *golf skill or reputation* may accept an offer of membership of a Golf Club or privileges at a golf course, without full payment for the class of membership or privilege, unless such an offer is made as an inducement to play for that Club or course.

## Rule 7 – Other Conduct Incompatible with Amateurism

### 7-1. Conduct Detrimental to Amateurism

An *amateur golfer* must not act in a manner that is detrimental to the best interests of the amateur game.

### 7-2. Conduct Contrary to the Purpose of the Rules

An *amateur golfer* must not take any action, including actions relating to golf gambling, that is contrary to the purpose of the *Rules.*

(Policy on gambling – see Appendix)

## Rule 8 – Procedure for Enforcement of the Rules

### 8-1. Decision on a Breach

If a possible breach of the *Rules* by a person claiming to be an *amateur golfer* comes to the attention of the *Committee*, it is a matter for the *Committee* to decide whether a breach has occurred. Each case will be investigated to the extent deemed appropriate by the *Committee* and considered on its merits. The decision of the *Committee* is final, subject to an appeal as provided in these *Rules.*

### 8-2. Enforcement

Upon a decision that a person has breached the *Rules*, the *Committee* may declare the Amateur Status of the person forfeited or require the person to refrain or desist from specified actions as a condition of retaining his Amateur Status.

The *Committee* should notify the person and may notify any interested golf union or association of any action taken under Rule 8-2.

### 8-3. Appeals Procedure

Each *Governing Body* should establish a process or procedure through which any decision concerning enforcement of these *Rules* may be appealed by the person affected.

## Rule 9 – Reinstatement of Amateur Status

### 9-1. General

The *Committee* has the sole authority to:

- reinstate to Amateur Status a professional golfer and/or other persons who have infringed the *Rules*,
- prescribe a waiting period necessary for reinstatement, or
- deny reinstatement, subject to an appeal as provided in the *Rules.*

### 9-2. Applications for Reinstatement

Each application for reinstatement will be considered on its merits, with consideration normally being given to the following principles:

#### a. Awaiting Reinstatement

Amateur and professional golf are two distinct forms of the game which provide different opportunities and neither benefits if the process of changing status from professional to amateur is too easy. Furthermore, there needs to be a deterrent against all breaches of the *Rules.* Therefore, an applicant for reinstatement to Amateur Status must undergo a period awaiting reinstatement as prescribed by the *Committee.*

The period awaiting reinstatement generally starts from the date of the person's last breach of the *Rules* unless the *Committee* decides that it starts from either (a) the date when the person's last breach became known to the *Committee*, or (b) such other date determined by the *Committee.*

#### b. Period Awaiting Reinstatement
#### (i) Professionalism

Generally, the period awaiting reinstatement is related to the period the person was in breach of the *Rules.* However, no applicant is normally eligible for reinstatement until he has conducted himself in accordance with the *Rules* for a period of at least one year.

It is recommended that the following guidelines on periods awaiting reinstatement be applied by the *Committee*:

| Period of Breach | Period Awaiting Reinstatement: |
|---|---|
| under 5 years | 1 year |
| 5 years or more | 2 years |

However, the period may be extended if the applicant has played extensively for prize money, regardless of performance. In all cases, the *Committee* reserves the right to extend or to shorten the period awaiting reinstatement.

#### (ii) Other Breaches of the Rules

A period awaiting reinstatement of one year will normally be required. However, the period may be extended if the breach is considered serious.

### c. Number of Reinstatements

A person is not normally eligible to be reinstated more than twice.

### d. Players of National Prominence

A player of national prominence who has been in breach of the *Rules* for more than five years is not normally eligible for reinstatement.

### e. Status While Awaiting Reinstatement

An applicant for reinstatement must comply with these *Rules*, as they apply to an *amateur golfer*, during his period awaiting reinstatement.

An applicant for reinstatement is not eligible to enter competitions as an *amateur golfer*. However, he may enter competitions and win a prize solely among members of a Club where he is a member, subject to the approval of the Club. He must not represent such a Club against other Clubs unless with the approval of the Clubs in the competition and/or the organising Committee.

An applicant for reinstatement may enter competitions that are not limited to *amateur golfers*, subject to the conditions of competition, without prejudicing his application, provided he does so as an applicant for reinstatement. He must waive his right to any prize money offered in the competition and must not accept any prize reserved for an *amateur golfer* (Rule 3-1).

### 9-3. Procedure for Applications

Each application for reinstatement must be submitted to the *Committee*, in accordance with such procedures as may be laid down and including such information as the *Committee* may require.

### 9-4. Appeals Procedure

Each *Governing Body* should establish a process or procedure through which any decision concerning reinstatement of Amateur Status may be appealed by the person affected.

## Rule 10 – Committee Decision

### 10-1. Committee's Decision

The *Committee's* decision is final, subject to an appeal as provided in Rules 8-3 and 9-4.

### 10-2. Doubt as to Rules

If the *Committee* of a *Governing Body* considers the case to be doubtful or not covered by the *Rules*, it may, prior to making its decision, consult with the Amateur Status Committee of the R&A.

## Appendix – Policy of Gambling

### General

An "amateur golfer", whether he plays competitively or recreationally, is one who plays golf for the challenge it presents, not as a profession and not for financial gain.

Excessive financial incentive in amateur golf, which can result from some forms of gambling or wagering, could give rise to abuse of the *Rules* both in play and in manipulation

of handicaps to the detriment of the integrity of the game.

There is a distinction between playing for prize money (Rule 3-1), gambling or wagering that is contrary to the purpose of the *Rules* (Rule 7-2), and forms of gambling or wagering that do not, of themselves, breach the *Rules*. An *amateur golfer* or a Committee in charge of a competition where *amateur golfers* are competing should consult with the *Governing Body* if in any doubt as to the application of the *Rules*. In the absence of such guidance, it is recommended that no cash prizes be awarded so as to ensure that the *Rules* are upheld.

### Acceptable Forms of Gambling

There is no objection to informal gambling or wagering among individual golfers or teams of golfers when it is incidental to the game. It is not practicable to define informal gambling or wagering precisely, but features that would be consistent with such gambling or wagering include:

• the players in general know each other;
• participation in the gambling or wagering is optional and is limited to the players;
• the sole source of all money won by the players is advanced by the players; and
• the amount of money involved is not generally considered to be excessive.

Therefore, informal gambling or wagering is acceptable provided the primary purpose is the playing of the game for enjoyment, not for financial gain.

### Unacceptable Forms of Gambling

Other forms of gambling or wagering where there is a requirement for players to participate (e.g. compulsory sweepstakes) or that have the potential to involve considerable sums of money (e.g. calcuttas and auction sweepstakes – where players or teams are sold by auction) are not approved.

Otherwise, it is difficult to define unacceptable forms of gambling or wagering precisely, but features that would be consistent with such gambling or wagering include:

• participation in the gambling or wagering is open to non-players; and
• the amount of money involved is generally considered to be excessive.

An *amateur golfer's* participation in gambling or wagering that is not approved may be considered contrary to the purpose of the *Rules* (Rule 7-2) and may endanger his Amateur Status.

Furthermore, organised events designed or promoted to create cash prizes are not permitted. Golfers participating in such events without first irrevocably waiving their right to prize money are deemed to be playing for prize money, in breach of Rule 3-1.

*Note:* The Rules of Amateur Status do not apply to betting or gambling by *amateur golfers* on the results of a competition limited to or specifically organised for professional golfers.

# INDEX

The Rules of Golf are here indexed according to the
pertinant rule number, definition or appendix that has gone before.
Items marked with as asterisk refer to Rules of Amateur Status

# The role of The R&A today

## What is The R&A?

The R&A takes its name from The Royal and Ancient Golf Club of St Andrews, which traces its origins back over 250 years. Although the golf club still exists to meet the needs of more than 2,000 international members, The R&A has grown apart to focus on its role as golf's world governance and development body and organiser of The Open Championship.

The R&A operates with the consent of 149 national and international amateur and professional organisations from almost 135 countries and on behalf of an estimated 30 million golfers in Europe, Africa, Asia Pacific and the Americas.

The R&A and the United States Golf Association have jointly issued the Rules of Golf since 1952. The USGA is the governing body for the Rules of Golf in the United States and Mexico.

By making The Open Championship one of the world's great sporting events and an outstanding commercial success, The R&A is able to invest a substantial annual surplus for the development of the game through The R&A Foundation. The Foundation is the charitable body that channels money from The Open directly into grassroots development projects around the world.

Particular emphasis is placed on the encouragement of junior golf, on the development of the game in emerging golfing nations, on coaching and the provision of more accessible courses and improved practice facilities.

The R&A also provides best practice guidance on all aspects of golf course management, to help golf grow throughout the world in a commercially and environmentally sustainable way.

## Useful links

RandA.org
RandA.org/Rules
RandA.org/Equipment
RandA.org/WorkingForGolf
RandA.org/GolfCourseManagement
RandA.org/Heritage
Championships.RandA.org
WAGR.com
TheOpen.com
TheRoyalandAncientGolfClub.org

## The future of the game

The R&A is committed to promoting and developing golf both nationally and internationally. Two factors make this possible. One is the annual surplus from The Open Championship and the other is The R&A's position of global influence. Combined, these give scope for the worldwide advancement of golf.

A major priority for The R&A is providing funding for training and the development of the game around the world. In recent years, a determined effort has been directed towards financing development in countries where golf is a relatively new sport. Major contributions are made to women's golf and the Golf Foundation receives substantial help to assist with its work of introducing young people to the game.

The R&A is highly conscious of the need and its obligation to serve the game worldwide. Since 1997 The R&A has provided financial support towards the African VI Tournament. The South American Men's and Women's Amateur Team Championship are also supported as are the equivalent events in the Asia-Pacific region.

The R&A Foundation supports university golf throughout Great Britain and Ireland with the aim of encouraging students to remain competitive while completing their formal education.

The R&A takes a lead in and offers advice on all aspects of golf course management worldwide, with sustainability and environmental issues foremost among its concerns.

## Funding the future

Most of The R&A's funding comes from staging The Open Championship. Television rights sales and corporate sponsorship arrangements are negotiated worldwide and a loyal spectator following translates into strong gate receipts and other on course spending. The Open on global television has a broadcast reach of over half a billion households and is screened by 41 separate rights holders across 107 channels. It is the world's largest annual televised sports event alongside Wimbledon. The benefit of staging The Open is shared widely and independent research shows that it confers an economic benefit of up to £100m on each local host economy.

In recent years The R&A has been at the forefront of modern technology, extending its range of activities to Digital Media rights, whereby income is generated through the internet, and mobile communication devices. These, combined with merchandising, licensing and publishing, increase the ways in which The R&A is able to provide financial assistance for the development of golf throughout the world.

In 2004, Rolex began to sponsor the publication and distribution of the Rules of Golf book, ensuring that golfers worldwide can have a copy of the current Rules of Golf free of charge. Over three million copies are distributed and the book is available in over 30 different languages.

Ralph Lauren, Doosan, HSBC, Mercedes-Benz, Nikon, Rolex, MasterCard and NTT Data are Patrons of The Open Championship. Through their association with The Open, the Patrons provide additional income for the funding of golf development projects worldwide.

## The Rules of the game

In almost every country where the game is played, the Rules followed are those set by The R&A. The exceptions are the USA and Mexico, where the code is set by the United States Golf Association, and Canada, which is self-governing but affiliated to The R&A. There are 149 associations and unions affiliated to The R&A.

The R&A is responsible for the Rules of Golf, the Rules affecting equipment standards and the Rules of Amateur Status. The Rules of Golf Committee reviews the Rules of Golf and interprets and makes decisions on the playing Rules. The Equipment Standards Committee interprets and gives decisions on those Rules that deal with the form and make of golf clubs and the specifications of the ball. The Amateur Status Committee reviews, interprets and amends the Rules of Amateur Status. All work closely with the equivalent committees of the USGA.

To meet the needs of golfers worldwide the Rules of Golf are published in over 30 languages and in audio CD format. Supplementing these are the biennial decisions on the Rules of Golf. Each volume contains over 1,100 decisions. Together, these help to ensure a consistent interpretation of the Rules throughout the world. The R&A also publish modifications of the Rules for golfers with disabilities.

The Rules Department answers thousands of queries from golf clubs, associations and professional tours on the playing Rules, the equipment Rules and on the Amateur Code.

Rules education is a priority for The R&A. Each year a Referees School is held in St Andrews, and overseas Rules Schools are held on a regular basis. Since the beginning of 2001, countries visited include Argentina, Brazil, the Dominican Republic, Ecuador, Germany, Guatemala, Japan, Luxembourg, New Zealand, Poland, Russia, Singapore, South Africa, South Korea, Thailand and the United Arab Emirates. In 2013, schools were also held in India, Hong Kong and Laos.

## R&A Championships

The R&A promotes, organises and controls a number of championships and matches at both national and international level. Of these events, the biggest and most prestigious is The Open Championship.

In 1920, The Royal and Ancient Golf Club took over the running of the Amateur and Open Championships. The Boys Amateur Championship followed in 1948 and the British Youths Open Championship in 1963. The British Mid-Amateur Championship replaced the Youths event in 1995 but was discontinued in 2007.

In 1969, the Club introduced the Seniors Open Amateur Championship for players aged 55 and over. In 1991, it became involved with and now organises The Senior Open Championship, in conjunction with the PGA European Senior Tour. The Junior Open Championship, first played in 1994, came under The R&A umbrella in 2000.

The Walker Cup, which is the most famous of the international amateur matches, is played between teams from Great Britain & Ireland and the United States and is run jointly with the United States Golf Association.

The R&A also administers the St Andrews Trophy, inaugurated in 1956, and the Jacques Leglise Trophy, an event for boys. Both are played between teams from Great Britain & Ireland and the Continent of Europe. When these matches are played in Europe, they are organised by the European Golf Association.

The Great Britain and Ireland team selection for the Walker Cup and the St Andrews Trophy is undertaken by The R&A.

In 2004, The Royal and Ancient Golf Club transferred to The R&A the responsibilities and authority of the Club for all aspects of running championships and matches at national and international level.

# Governing Organisations – Professional Golf

## The Professional Golfers' Association (PGA)

The PGA was founded in 1901 and is the oldest PGA in the world. It has continued to develop steadily over the years; in the mid seventies major re-structuring of the Association took place with the development of two separate divisions. The administrative operation moved to The Belfry in 1977 to advance and develop the services available to club professionals, and shortly afterwards the Tournament Division established a new base at the Wentworth Club.

In 1984 it was decided that the interests of the members of each division would be best served by forming two separate organisations and on 1st January 1985 The Professional Golfers' Association and the European Tour became independent of each other.

The PGA's activities include training and further education of assistants and members and the organisation of tournaments at national level. National Headquarters is also the administrative base to accounts, marketing, media and the commercial activities of the Association.

There are seven regional headquarters located throughout Great Britain and Ireland and each region organises its own tournaments.

## Classes of Membership

### Class AA

Only Professionals who have a PGA Qualification; have been qualified for at least three years, and who have engaged in (at least) the minimum amount of proessional development are recognised as class 'AA'.

### Class A

A class 'A' status designation is carried by PGA Professionals who have a PGA Qualification and who have either been qualified for less than three years, and/or who have not engaged in sufficient recognised professional devlopment at the time of the annual re-grading of PGA membership status.

### Class TP1

Must be a current full member of either the European Tour, Ladies' European Tour, European Seniors' Tour or any tour belonging to the International Federation of PGA Tours subject to the relevant categories as defined by the Association at the time.

### Class TP2

Must be a current full member of either the European Tour, Ladies' European Tour or European Seniors' Tour subject to the relevant categories as defined by the Association at the time.

### Class TP3

Must be a member of the PGA Europro Tour finishing 1–80 in the immediately preceding year's Order of Merit.

### Class TP4

Must be qualified as an active playing Member within PGA Tournaments where Tournament entry criteria so permit and be in the top 100 players in the preceding year home region Order of Merit.

### Life Member

Must be a member of the Association who has been recommended by the Board of Directors to Special General Meeting of the Association for appointment as a Life Member and whose recommendation has been approved.

### Honorary Member

Must be a member who in the opinion of the Executive Committee through their past or continuing membership and contribution to the Association justifies retaining full privileges of membership as an Honorary Member.

### Inactive Member

Shall have been a member for a continuous period of 10 years and no longer engaged in a direct or commercial capacity in the golf industry.

### Retired Member

Shall have been a member for a periods of at least 35 years and not be engaged in a direct or commercial capacity in the golf industry.

As well as the class 'A/AA' status, PGA Members are also differentiated through formal recognition of their previous exerience, further education, achievements, accreditation, etc. Once qualified, and with a minimum length of time served in the golf industry, a Member can submit an application to be awarded any one of four additional titles. They rank hierarchically from PGA Advanced Professional up to PGA Master Professional – as below:

### Advanced Professional

Qualified members for a minimum of three years. Over a long period of time have demonstrated a strong desire to improve understanding and knowlededge. Through attendance at courses, seminars and by taking qualifications related to golf, have shown commitment and willingness to develop self. Written articles and/or delivered seminars. Recognised by peers as having a high level of skill and knowledge, or qualified through the PGA Advanced Diploma programme.

**Fellow Professional**
Qualified members for a minimum of eight years. Consistently demonstrated an ability to work at a very high level with contribution to: development of players at different levels and/or a very strong reputation as an ethical business person who has established an extensive business that has benefited the golfing community and/or a strong reputation in equipment technology and/or repairs, which has enhanced the reputations of golf professionals and/or has written articles/books and presented at conferences.

**Advanced Fellow Professional**
Qualified members for a minimum of ten years. Very strong national – possibly international reputation in one or more areas – coaching, course design, business, retail, equipment technology. Someone who has demonstrated strong leadership and has enhanced the world of golf and may have coached at the highest level or developed a programme method that has enabled ordinary players to play the game and/or designed a number of recognised golf courses and/or developed a strong golf business that has brought benefits to golf and golfers and/or innovative in the retail world with a strong sense of business ethics and/or designed/developed/improved some aspect of equipment (to include training aids or computer software) that has benefited a wide range of people in golf and/or a golf writer whose work has contributed strongly to the understanding and development of golf performance and/or a charity worker whose contribution has helped improve the lot of the disadvantaged through golf or in golf and/or written a number of books, articles and presented at prestigious conferences and seminars.

**Master Professional**
Qualified member for a minimum of fifteen years. Held in high national or international esteem. Made a significant contribution to the development of golf as a player, coach, administrator or course designer. Someone who has left their mark at conferences and/or through books, articles or videos.

*Tel* 01675 470333     *Fax* 01675 477888

# The Professional Golfers' Associations of Europe

The PGAs of Europe is an Association of 39 National PGAs (32 European and 7 international) with a col-

lective membership in excess of 21,000 golf professionals.

Our core mission is to represent, promote and provide advice to develop professional golf and ensure that the administration of the professional game throughout the continent delivers excellence in the services provided to ensure highly qualified, highly skilled PGA Professionals who lead the advancement of the game around the world.

The PGAs of Europe is also a partner in the Ryder Cup with specific responsibility for the management of the Ryder Cup European Development Trust and is widely acknowledged as a lead body in the delivery of golf development expertise on a global basis through its collaboration with The R&A in implementing its Working for Golf development programme.

*Website*   www.pgae.com
*Email*     info@pgae.com
*Tel*       +44(0)1675 477899
*Fax*       +44(0)1675 477890
*Twitter*   @PGAsofEurope

# European Tour
The European Tour offers Membership rights and playing opportunities for those players who have earned an Exempt Category on the Tour. To be eligible to become a Full Member of The European Tour for the first time a player must have either graduated from the European Challenge Tour by virtue of his performance in the previous season, gained one of the exemptions available at the annually competed European Tour Qualifying School or won a European Tour/Challenge Tour sanctioned event.

Full details are available from The Wentworth Headquarters:

*Tel* +44 1344 840400     *Fax* +44 1344 840500

*Website* www.europeantour.com

# Ladies' European Tour
The Ladies European Tour was founded in 1978 to further the development of women's professional golf with a focus in Europe and its membership is open to all nationalities. A qualifying school is held annually and an amateur wishing to participate must have a handicap of 3 or less. Full details can be obtained from the Tour Headquarters at Buckinghamshire Golf Club.

*Tel* 01895 831028     *Fax* 01895 832301

*Website* www.ladieseuropeantour.com

# Governing Organisations – Amateur Golf

## Home Unions

### The English Golf Union

The English Golf Union was founded in 1924 and embraces 35 County Unions with 1,949 affiliated clubs. Its objects are:

(1) To further the interests of Amateur Golf in England.

(2) To assist in maintaining a uniform system of handicapping.

(3) To arrange an English Championship; an English Strokeplay Championship; an English County Championship, International and other Matches and Competitions.

(4) To cooperate with The Royal and Ancient Golf Club of St Andrews and the Council of National Golf Unions.

(5) To cooperate with other National Golf Unions and Associations in such manner as may be decided.

*Tel* 01526 354500      *Fax* 01526 354020

The previously separate English Golf Union and English Women's Golf Association have merged and from January 2012 became one governing body entitled England Golf which will represent all amateur golfers in England. For further information, see pages 702 and 706.

### The Scottish Golf Union

The Scottish Golf Union, the governing body for men's golf in Scotland, is dedicated to inspiring people to play golf and to developing and sustaining the game throughout the country. Its over-arching intention is to make golf available to everyone, in an environment that will actively encourage players to fulfil their potential.

Its aims are to:

• **Grow the game** – work with others to develop and grow golf in Scotland by increasing the number of people playing and enjoying golf.

• **Develop talent** – ensure that the pathways to develop young talent are in place to produce excellent golfers at all levels.

• **Support Clubs** – provide core services including handicapping, course rating, membership, marketing and advice on Governance and Legislation to support affiliated clubs.

The organisation is governed by a non executive board of directors who oversee the management of the organisation and an executive council, comprising

representatives from 16 area associations, which pr[o]vides the board with advice on policy matters.

*Tel* 01334 466477      *Fax* 01334 461361

### Golfing Union of Ireland

The Golfing Union of Ireland, founded in 189[ ] embraces 430 Clubs. Its objects are:

(1) Securing the federation of the various Clubs.

(2) Arranging Amateur Championships, Inter-Provi[n]cial and Inter-Club Competitions, and Interr[na]tional Matches.

(3) Securing a uniform standard of handicapping.

(4) Providing for advice and assistance, other th[an] financial, to affiliated Clubs in all matters appe[r]taining to Golf, and generally to promote t[he] game in every way, in which this can be bett[er] done by the Union than by individual Clubs.

Its functions include the holding of the Open a[nd] Close Championships for Amateur Golfers a[nd] Tournaments for Team Matches.

Its organisation consists of Provincial Councils each of the four Provinces elected by the Clubs in t[he] Province – each province electing a limited numb[er] of delegates to the Central Council which mee[ts] annually.

*Tel* 00 353 1 505 4000      *Fax* 00 353 1 505 4001

### The Golf Union of Wales

The Golf Union of Wales was founded in 2007 follow[ing] the merger of the Welsh Golfing Union (1895) a[nd] the Welsh Ladies Golf Union (1904). The GUW, t[he] first of the Home Unions to merge, has 158 affiliat[ed] clubs and its mission statement is:-

To encourage participation and excellence for golfers at all levels whilst maintaining and preservi[ng] the traditions of honesty, integrity and fair play.

The GUW's key goals are:

(1) To develop a network of thriving clubs to "secu[re] the future of Welsh Golf.

(2) To provide competition opportunities for golfe[rs] of all ages and standards.

(3) To achieve international success for Wales and [its] players and produce world class golfers.

The Golf Union of Wales is a limited company wi[th] a board of non-executive directors and a Council of [club] members elected by the clubs.

*Tel* 01633 435040    *Fax* 01633 693568

*E-mail* office@golfunionwales.org

## The Council of National Golf Unions

The British Golf Unions Joint Advisory Committee, later The Council of National Golf Unions (CONGU), came into existence at a conference held in York on 14th February 1924. The conference was convened by the Royal and Ancient Golf Club of St Andrews as a means of enabling the representatives of the Golf Unions of Great Britain and Ireland to formulate a definitive system of calculating Scratch Scores and to arrive at a uniform system of handicapping based on Scratch Scores.

The Consultative Committee was appointed to receive and consider schemes for calculating and allocating the Scratch Scores and adjustments to handicaps throughout Great Britain and Ireland. The Standard Scratch Score and Handicapping Scheme was prepared by the Council in 1925 and has been in operation throughout Great Britain and Ireland since 1st March 1926.

In 2000/2001 discussions began between CONGU and the Ladies Golf Union (LGU), who were reviewing their own system. From these discussions the Unified Handicap System (UHS) emerged. It was passed by CONGU in September 2003 and by the LGU in January 2004. The joint system for men and ladies became effective from 1st February 2004.

The Constitution of CONGU was amended in 2004 to reflect the joint system. This has been further amended in 2007/2008 to recognise the amalgamation of the Welsh Unions and will again be changed to recognise the formation of England Golf following the merger of the English Unions. The CONGU Council now consists of an independent chairperson and sixteen representatives nominated by the six Unions/Associations in Great Britain and Ireland. The six are: England Golf, Golf Union of Wales, Golfing Union of Ireland, Irish Ladies' Golf Union, Scottish Golf Union and Scottish Ladies' Golfing Association. The Royal and Ancient Golf Club of St. Andrews and The Ladies' Golf Union have one representative each on The Council.

March 2012 will see the introduction of the latest updates to the UHS, which is part of the continual process of review and improvement. CONGU have a number of sub-committees, the two most active being the Statistics and Technical Committees. These two Committees continually listen to comments and suggestions, analyse results and data, project the effect any changes would make, and make recommendations for changes to the Board, who must then give approval before they are accepted into the system. This continual process ensures that we have an effective and relevant handicap system. Contact with other handicapping authorities, particularly the EGA, is maintained so that research and technical developments are shared.

*Tel* 0151 336 3936

## Government of the Amateur and Open Golf Championships

In December 1919, on the invitation of the clubs who had hitherto controlled the Amateur and Open Golf Championships, The Royal and Ancient Golf Club took over the government of those events. These two championships are now controlled by a committee appointed by The R&A.

*Tel* 01334 460000    *Fax* 01334 460001

## European Golf Association
## Association Européenne de Golf

Formed at a meeting held 20 November 1937 in Luxembourg, membership is restricted to European national amateur golf associations or unions. The Association concerns itself solely with matters of an international character. The association is presently composed of 30 member countries and is governed by the following committees:

- Executive Committee
- Championship Committee
- Professional Technical Committee
- EGA Handicapping & Course Rating Committee

Prime objectives are:

(a) To encourage international development of golf, to strengthen bonds of friendship existing between it members.

(b) To encourage the formation of new golf organisations representing the golf activities of European countries.

(c) To co-ordinate the dates of the Open and Amateur championships of its members and to arrange, in conjuction with host Federations, European championships and specific matches of international character.

(d) To ratify and publish the calendar dates of the major Amateur and Professional championships and international matches in Europe.

(e) To create and maintain international relationships in the field of golf and undertake any action useful to the cause of golf on an international level.

The headquarters are situated in Epalinges, Switzerland.

# Ladies' Golf Union (LGU)

Founded in 1893, the Ladies' Golf Union (LGU) is the encompassing body for ladies' amateur golf in Great Britain & Ireland. The LGU's administrative base is in St. Andrews, Fife, Scotland, while activities, championships, matches and events take place in Great Britain & Ireland and internationally.

The organisation's strategic objectives have been defined as follows:

To provide ladies and girls with opportunities to participate in the highest standard elite golf competitions;

To achieve international success for Great Britain & Ireland lady and girl golfers and teams;

To increase awareness and raise the profile of ladies' and girls' golf through the Ricoh Women's British Open and other golf events;

To provide a collective strong voice for, and represent the interests of, ladies' and girls' golf in proactive collaboration with the National Organisation and other organisations, both in and outwith the sport;

To actively demonstrate and grow the LGU's key advocacy role as the encompassing body for ladies' golf; and

To build on the present platform of operational and financial sustainability and progress strategically towards financial independence, with reduced reliance on subscription income.

The members of the LGU are the national governing bodies for ladies' golf in the Home Countries – England Golf, the Irish Ladies Golf Union Limited, the Scottish Ladies Golfing Association Limited and the Golf Union of Wales Limited. Clubs affiliated to these bodies pay a small annual subscription for each playing lady member, which is remitted to the LGU as a contribution to its activities.

A number of overseas unions, associations and clubs are also affiliated to the LGU.

The LGU's Executive Council is led by a Chairman whose term of office is three years, and comprises a representative from each of the national governing bodies, two members appointed for reasons of specific skills and contributions, and a non-voting President.

Operational activities are undertaken by a wholly owned subsidiary, LGU Championships Limited (LGUCL), while the LGU holds the assets of the organisation, including property and memorabilia. The members of the Executive Council also serve as members of the Board of LGUCL. Collectively, the LGU and LGUCL are referred to as the LGU Group. The strategic direction and policies of the LGU Group are determined by the Executive Council/Board members, while responsibility for implementing these policies and strategies is vested in a team of staff, headed by the CEO.

The Annual General Meeting of the LGU is held in February, with the National Organisations being the voting members.

The LGU Group owns and runs the Ricoh Women's British Open, founded by the LGU in 1976 and one of the five Major Tournaments for professional lady golfers. LGUCL also has responsibility for running, on an annual basis:

- the Ladies' British Open Amateur Championship
- the Ladies' British Open Amateur Stroke Play Championship
- the Girls' British Open Amateur Championship
- the Senior Ladies' British Open Amateur Championship
- the three sets of Home International Matches

In addition, international events involving Great Britain & Ireland teams, such as the Curtis Cup (against the USA) and Vagliano and Junior Vagliano Trophies (against the Continent of Europe) are organised and controlled by LGUCL on home soil. Both at home and abroad, the LGU Group selects and prepares the teams, provides uniforms and meets the costs of participation in these matches.

The LGU acts as the co-coordinating body for the Astor Trophy (former Commonwealth Trophy) matches in whichever one of the five participating countries (GB&I, Australia, Canada, South Africa, New Zealand) it is held, four yearly, by rotation.

The LGU also maintains and regulates a number of competitions played under handicap and aimed at supporting participation in the game by club golfers. The Peugeot 208 LGU Coronation Foursomes attracts over 35,000 participants each year, while the

Brigid McCaw, President of the Ladies' Golf Union

Breakthrough Brooch attracts over 1200 clubs and raises significant funds for the LGU's partner charity. Other handicap competitions – the Australian (Commonwealth) spoons and the Challenge Bowls are delivered with the support of the National Organisations.

A Yearbook is published annually, detailing regulations and venues for forthcoming championships and matches, results of past events and other relevant useful information.

In endeavouring to advance and safeguard ladies' golf, the LGU actively maintains contact with other golfing organisations – The R&A, CONGU, the United States Golf Association, the Professional Golfers Association, the European Golf Association, the Ladies' European Tour, the European Tour and the Ladies' Professional Golf Association. The organisation is also represented on the Rolex Rankings Committee which maintains and publishes the ladies' professional rankings.

Maintaining contact with these organisations keeps the LGU at the forefront of developments and emerging issues and provides an active opportunity to influence and protect the future of the ladies' game.

*Tel* 01334 475811    *Fax* 01334 472818

# United States Golf Association

The USGA is dedicated to promoting and conserving the best interests and true spirit of the game of golf. Founded on December 22, 1894 by representatives of five American golf clubs, the USGA was originally charged with conducting national championships, implementing a uniform code of rules and maintaining a national system of handicapping.

Today, the USGA comprises more than 9,000 member clubs and courses and its principal functions remain largely unchanged. The USGA annually conducts the U.S. Open, U.S. Women's Open, U.S. Senior Open and 10 national amateur championships. On a biennial basis, it also conducts two state team championships and helps conduct the Walker Cup Match, Curtis Cup Match and World Amateur Team Championships. More than 35,000 players representing more than 80 countries submit entries to play in USGA championships each year.

The USGA and The R&A together govern the game worldwide, including joint administration of the Rules of Golf, Rules of Amateur status and equipment standards. The organizations also work in partnership to administer the World Amateur Golf Rankings, the world's pre-eminent amateur golf ranking system for men and women.

The USGA maintains Handicap and Course Rating and Systems used on six continents in more than 50 countries and also provides handicap computation services to more than 70 national, regional and state golf associations through the Golf Handicap and Information Network.

Additional responsibilities assumed by the association encompass turfgrass and environmental research conducted by the USGA Green Section, a global leader in the development and support of sustainable golf course management practices since 1920; and preservation and promotion of the game's rich history in the USGA Museum and Arnold Palmer Center for Golf History, which houses the world's largest and most complete golf library. Since 1965, the USGA has supported philanthropic activities dedicated to maintaining and improving the opportunities for all individuals to partake fully in the game.

*Tel* 001 908 234 2300    *Fax* 001 908 234 9687

Thomas J O'Toole of St Louis, Missouri, is to be the new President of the United States Golf Association.

As President, 56-year-old O'Toole will lead the Association's staff of more than 300 along with nearly 1,200 volunteers who serve on more than 30 committees.

"I am truly honoured and deeply humbled to have been nominated as the next President," said O'Toole "It has been my priviledge to serve the organisation for 25 years as a Rules official at the US Open and other USGA Championships.

"During that time I have come to have a deep admiration for the Association and its important work. I look forward to working closely with my colleagues on the executive committee, staff and with executive director Mike Davis. Together we will continue to work with our valued partners in the golf industry to foster long-term sustainability of this great game."

Mr O'Toole is a partner in the law firm of Mickes Goldman O'Toole LLC. He chairs the firm's Business and Corporate Group while his practice specialises on real estate zoning. He is a graduate of St Louis University. He will hold the post for a year.

# Major Championship and International Conditions

## UK CHAMPIONSHIPS

### Men

#### Amateur Championship
The Championship, until 1982, was decided entirely by match play over 18 holes except for the final which was over 36 holes. Since 1983 the Championship has comprised two stroke play rounds of 18 holes each from which the leading 64 players and ties over the 36 holes qualify for the match play stages. Matches are over 18 holes except for the final which is over 36 holes. Full particulars can be obtained from the Entries Department, R&A, St Andrews, Fife KY16 9JD. Tel: 01334 460000; Fax 01334 460005; e-mail entries@randa.org

#### Seniors Open Amateur Championship
The Championship consists of 18 holes on each of two days, the leading 60 players and ties over the 36 holes then playing a further 18 holes the following day. Entrants must have attained the age of 55 years prior to the first day of the Championship. Full particulars can be obtained from the Entries Department, R&A, St Andrews, Fife KY16 9JD. Tel 01344 460000; fax 01334 460005; e-mail entries@randa.org

#### National Championships
The English, Irish, Scottish and Welsh Amateur Championships are played by holes, each match consisting of one round of 18 holes except the final which is contested over 36 holes. Only the English Golf Union hold a 36-hole qualifier for their event. Full particulars of conditions of entry and method of play can be obtained from the secretaries of the respective national Unions.

#### English Open Amateur Stroke Play Championship (The Brabazon)
The Championship consists of one round of 18 holes on each of two days after which the leading 60 and those tying for 60th place play a further two rounds. The remainder are eliminated.

Conditions for entry include: entrants must have a handicap not exceeding one; the maximum number of entries eligible for qualifying shall be 264 (132 to play at each of the Regional Qualifying courses. Certain players are exempt from qualifying.

Full particulars of conditions of entry and method of play can be obtained from the Secretary, English Golf Union, National Golf Centre, The Broadway, Woodhall Spa, Lincs LN10 6PU. Tel: 01526 354500; Fax: 01526 354020.

#### Scottish Open Amateur Stroke Play Championship
The Championship consists of one round of 18 holes on each of two days after which the leading 40 and those tying for 40th place play a further two rounds. The remainder are eliminated. Full particulars of conditions of entry and method of play can be obtained from the Events Department of the Scottish Golf Union, The Duke's, St Andrews, Fife KY16 8NX. Tel: 01334 466477; Fax: 01334 461361.

### Boys

#### Boys Amateur Championship
The Championship, until 2009, was decided entirely by match play over 18 holes except for the final which was over 36 holes. Since 2010 the Championship has comprised two stroke play rounds of 18 holes each from which the leading 64 players and ties over the 36 holes qualify for the match play stages. Matches are over 18 holes except for the final which is over 36 holes. Full particulars can be obtained from the Entries Department, R&A, St Andrews, Fife KY16 9JD. Tel: 01334 460000; Fax 01334 460005; e-mail entries@randa.org

### Ladies

#### Ladies' British Open Amateur Championship
The Championship consists of one 18-hole qualifying round on each of two days. The players returning the 64 lowest scores over 36 holes shall qualify for match play. Ties for the last place(s) shall be decided by card countback using the 18 hole second round score.

#### Ladies' British Open Amateur Stroke Play Championship
The Championship consists of 72 holes stroke play; 18 holes are played on each of two days after which

the first 40 and all ties for 40th place qualify for a further 36 holes on the third day. Handicap limit is 6.4. Full details can be obtained from LGU Championships Ltd, The Scores, St Andrews, Fife KY16 9AT.

## Ricoh Women's British Open Championship

The Ricoh Women's British Open is a designated major in ladies' professional golf and is the only such major played outside the USA. Owned by LGU Championships Ltd, the championship consists of 72 holes stroke play. 18 holes are played on each of four days, the field being reduced after the first 36 holes. Certain categories of players gain automatic entry to the championship because of past performance in the Ricoh Women's British Open or from current performance in the Rolex Rankings and the LET, LPGA and JLPGA money lists. Those not automatically exempt can gain entry through pre-qualifying and final qualifying competitions.

Full particulars of the above three championships can be obtained from the LTU Championships Ltd, The Scores, St Andrews, Fife KY16 9AT.

Tel: 01334 475811; Fax: 01334 472818.

## National Championships

Conditions of entry and method of play for the English, Scottish, Welsh and Irish Ladies' Close Championships can be obtained from the Registered Offices of the respective associations.

Other championships organised by the respective national associations, from whom full particulars can be obtained, include English Ladies', Intermediate, English Ladies' Stroke Play, Scottish Girls' Open Amateur Stroke Play (under 21) and Welsh Ladies' Open Amateur Stroke Play.

## Girls

### Girls' British Open Amateur Championship

The Championship consists of two 18-hole qualifying rounds, followed by match play. The players returning the 64 lowest scores over 36 holes qualify for the match play. Ties for the last place(s) shall be decided by card countback using the 18 hole second round score.

Entrants must be under 18 years of age on the 1st January in the year of the Championship.

The Championship is open to players of the female gender who are members of a recognised golf club, who have amateur status in accordance with the current rules and who hold a CONGU exact handicap of not more than 8.4 or overseas equivalent at the date of entry.

Full particulars can be obtained from the Administrator, LGU, The Scores, St Andrews, Fife KY16 9AT. Tel: 01334 475811; Fax: 01334 472818.

## National Championships

The English, Scottish, Irish and Welsh Girls' Close Championships are open to all girls of relevant nationality and appropriate age which may vary from country to country. A handicap limit may be set by some countries. Full particulars can be obtained via the secretaries of the respective associations.

# EUROPEAN CHAMPIONSHIPS

Founded in 1986 by the European Golf Association, the International Amateur and Ladies Amateur Championships are held on an annual basis since 1990. These Championships consist of one round of 18 holes on each of three days after which the leading 70 and those tying for 70th place play one further round.

Full particulars of conditions of entry and method of play can be obtained from the European Golf Association.

Since 1991, the European Golf Association also holds an International Mid-Amateur Championship on an annual basis. The Championship consist of one round of 18 holes on each of two days after which the leading 90 and those tying for 90th place play one further round.

Full particulars of conditions of entry and method of play can be obtained from the European Golf Association.

Since 1996, the European Golf Association holds an International Seniors Championship for ladies and men on an annual basis.

The Championship consists of one round of 18 holes on each of two days after which there is a cut in both ladies and men categories. The competitors who pass the cut play one further round.

Additionally, a nation's cup is played within the tournament on the first two days. Teams are composed of three players. The two best gross scores out of three will count each day. The total aggregate of the four scores over two days will constitute the team's score.

Full particulars of conditions of entry and method of play can be obtained from the European Golf Association, Place de la Croix-Blanche 19, PO Box CH-1066 Epilanges, Switzerland. Tel: +41 21 784 32 32; Fax: +412 1 784 35 91.

# TEAM CHAMPIONSHIPS

## Men's Amateur

### Walker Cup – Great Britain and Ireland v United States of America

Mr George Herbert Walker of the United States presented a Cup for international competition to be known as *The United States Golf Association International Challenge Trophy*, popularly described as *The Walker Cup*.

The Cup shall be played for by teams of amateur golfers selected from Clubs under the jurisdiction of the United States Golf Association on the one side and from England, Ireland, Scotland and Wales on the other.

The Walker Cup shall be held every two years in the United States of America and Great Britain and Ireland alternately.

The teams shall consist of not more than ten players and a captain.

The contest consists of four foursomes and eight singles matches over 18 holes on the first day and four foursomes and 10 singles on the final day.

### St Andrews Trophy – Great Britain and Ireland v Continent of Europe

First staged in 1956, the St Andrews Trophy is a biennial international match played between two selected teams of amateur golfers representing Great Britain and Ireland and the Continent of Europe. Each team consists of nine players and the match is played over two consecutive days with four morning foursomes followed each afternoon by eight singles. Selection of the Great Britain and Ireland team is carried out by the R&A Selection Committee. The European Golf Association select the Continent of Europe team.

### Eisenhower Trophy – Men's World Team Championship

Founded in recognition of the need for an official world amateur team championship, the first event was played at St Andrews in 1958 and the Trophy has been played for every second year in different countries around the world.

Each country enters a team of four players who play strokeplay over 72 holes, the total of the three best individual scores to be counted for each round.

### European Team Championship

Founded in 1959 by the European Golf Association for competition among member countries of the Association. The Championship has recently been changed to be played on an annual basis and played in rotation round the countries, which are grouped in four geographical zones.

Each team consists of six players who play two qualifying rounds of 18 holes, the five best scores of

each round constituting the team aggregate. Flights for match play are then arranged according to qualifying rankings. The match play consists of two foursomes and five singles on each of three days.

A similar championship is held in alternate years for Youths teams, under 21 years of age and every year for Boys teams, under 18 years of age.

### Raymond Trophy – Home Internationals

The first official International Match recorded was in 1902 at Hoylake between England and Scotland who won 32 to 25 on a holes up basis.

In 1932 International Week was inaugurated under the auspices of the British Golf Unions' Joint Advisory Council with the full approval of the four National Golf Unions who are now responsible for running the matches. Teams of 11 players from England, Ireland, Scotland and Wales engage in matches consisting of five foursomes and ten singles over 18 holes, the foursomes being in the morning and the singles in the afternoon. Each team plays every other team.

The eligibility of players to play for their country shall be their eligibility to play in the Amateur Championship of their country.

### Sir Michael Bonallack Trophy – Europe v Asia/Pacific

First staged in 1998, the Sir Michael Bonallack Trophy is a biennial international match played between two selected teams of amateur golfers representing Europe and Asia/Pacific. Each team consists of 12 players and the match is played over three days with five four balls in the morning and five foursomes in the afternoon of the first two days, followed by 12 singles on the last day. Selection of the European team is carried out by the European Golf Association. The Asia/Pacific Golf Confederation selects the Asia/Pacific team.

## Men's Professional

### The Ryder Cup

This is a biennial match now played between 12-man professional teams from Europe and the United States. The competition started in 1927 between teams from Great Britain and the United States. In 1926 an unofficial match took place at Wentworth Club, Surrey, England, following which Samuel Ryder, a prosperous businessman who owned the Heath and Heather Seed Company, famous for their penny packets of seeds which garden lovers adored, in St Albans, England, famously remarked: "We must do this again." Samuel Ryder donated a trophy – a golden chalice – at a cost of £250. The first official match took place in 1927 at the Worcester Country Club in Worcester, Massachusetts. The United States led 18-3 with one match tied before in 1979 players from the Continent of Europe became eligible. Between 1979 and 2010 Europe has eight victories and the United States seven with one tie. The United States will be seeking their 26th win overall and Europe their 12th when The 2012 Ryder Cup takes place at Medinah Country Club, Illinois, with the format of eight fourballs, eight foursomes and 12 singles which was introduced in 1981

## The World Cup of Golf

This is an annual competition founded in 1953 as the Canada Cup – it became The World Cup of Golf in 1967 – by John Jay Hopkins, the noted Canadian industrialist. It has since the start brought together countries each represented by two man teams with the winning team having the lowest aggregate score over 72-holes. Italy became the 16th different country to win The World Cup and in 2011 they defended the 56th edition at the 25th destination to be visited – the Mission Hills Resort, Hainan Island, China – when the format comprised fourballs on the first and third days and foursomes on the second and final day with 28 teams, each one of different nationality, competing at the final stage following a series of World Qualifying Competitions.

## Vivendi Seve Trophy

This is a biennial match between ten-man teams from Continental Europe and Great Britain and Ireland. Instigated by the late Seve Ballesteros in 2000 as a team competition to be contested in non-Ryder Cup years, Great Britain and Ireland gained their sixth win in seven editions when they won at Saint-Nom-la-Bretèche, Paris, France, in 2011. The match comprises of two series of five fourball matches; four greensomes; four foursomes; and ten singles on the final day.

## Llandudno Trophy (PGA Cup) – Great Britain and Ireland v United States of America

The Llandudno International Trophy was first awarded to England in 1939 after winning the first Home Tournament Series against Ireland, Scotland and Wales. With the outbreak of war the series was abolished and the Trophy formed part of Percy Alliss's personal collection. After Percy's death his son Peter donated the Llandudno Trophy to be awarded to the winner of the then annual PGA Cup Match. Now it is a biennial match played since 1973 in Ryder Cup format between Great Britain and Ireland and the United States of America involving top club professionals. No prize money is awarded to the competitors who compete solely for their country. Selection of the Great Britain and Ireland team is determined following completion of the Glenmuir PGA Club Professionals Championship.

# Ladies Amateur

## Curtis Cup – Great Britain and Ireland v United States

For a trophy presented by the late Misses Margaret and Harriot Curtis of Boston, USA, for biennial competition between amateur teams from the United States of America and Great Britain and Ireland. The match is sponsored jointly by the United States Golf Association and the Ladies' Golf Union who may select teams of not more than eight players.

The match, held over three days, consists of three foursomes and three four-ball matches on each of the first two days and eight singles of 18 holes on the final day.

## Vagliano Trophy – Great Britain and Ireland v Continent of Europe

For a trophy presented to the Comité des Dames de la Fédération Française de Golf and the Ladies' Golf Union by Monsieur AA Vagliano, originally for annual competition between teams of women amateur golfers from France and Great Britain and Ireland but, since 1959, by mutual agreement, for competition between teams from the Continent of Europe and Great Britain and Ireland.

The match is played biennially, alternately in Great Britain and Ireland and on the Continent of Europe, with teams of not more than nine players plus a non-playing captain. The match consists of four foursomes and eight singles of 18 holes on each of two days. The foursomes are played each morning.

## Espirito Santo Trophy – Women's World Team Championship

Presented by Mrs Ricardo Santo of Portugal for biennial competition between teams of not more than three women amateur golfers who represent a national association affiliated to the World Amateur Golf Council. First competed for in 1964. The Championship consists of 72 holes strokeplay, 18 holes on each of four days, the two best scores in each round constituting the team aggregate.

## Lady Astor Trophy – Five Nations Tournament (formerly Commonwealth Tournament)

For a trophy presented by Nancy, Viscountess Astor CH, and the Ladies' Golf Union for competition once in every four years between teams of women amateur golfers from Commonwealth countries.

The inaugural Commonwealth Tournament was played at St Andrews in 1959 between teams from Australia, Canada, New Zealand, South Africa and Great Britain and was won by the British team. The tournament is played in rotation in the competing countries, Great Britain, Australia, Canada, New Zealand and South Africa, each country being entitled to nominate six players including a playing or non-playing captain. In 2011, a Great Britain and Ireland team will compete for the first time.

Each team plays every other team and each team match consists of two foursomes and four singles over 18 holes. The foursomes are played in the morning.

## European Team Championships

Founded in 1959 by the European Golf Association for competition among member countries of the Association. The Championship is held annually and played in rotation round the countries, which are grouped in four geographical zones.

Each team consists of six players who play two qualifying rounds of 18 holes, the five best scores of each round constituting the team aggregate. Flights for matchplay are then arranged according to qualifying rankings. The matchplay consists of two foursomes and five singles on each of three days.

A similar championship is held in alternate years for Lady Juniors teams, under 21 years of age and every year for Girls teams, under 18 years of age.

## Home Internationals

Teams from England, Scotland, Ireland and Wales compete annually for a trophy presented to the LGU by the late Mr TH Miller. The qualifications for a player being eligible to play for her country are the same as those laid down by each country for its Close Championship.

Each team, consisting of not more than eight players, plays each other team, a draw taking place to decide the order of play between the teams. The matches consist of three foursomes and six singles, each of 18 holes.

# Ladies Professional

## Solheim Cup – Europe v United States

The Solheim Cup, named after Karsten Solheim who founded the sponsoring Ping company, is the women's equivalent of the Ryder Cup. In 1990 the inaugural competition between the top women professional golfers from Europe and America took place in Florida.

The matches are played biennially in alternate continents. The format is foursomes and fourball matches on the first two days, followed by singles on the third in accordance with the conditions as agreed between the Ladies European Tour and the United States LPGA Tour.

# Juniors

## R&A Trophy – Boys' Home Internationals

Teams comprising 11 players from England, Scotland, Ireland and Wales compete against one another over three days in a single round robin for-

mat. Each fixture comprises five morning foursomes followed by ten afternoon singles.

To be eligible for selection, players must be under the age of 18 at 00.00 hours on 1st January in the year of the matches and have eligibility to play in their national championships.

## Jacques Léglise Trophy – Great Britain and Ireland v Continent of Europe

The Jacques Léglise Trophy is an annual international match played between two selected teams of amateur boy golfers representing Great Britain and Ireland and the Continent of Europe. Each team consists of nine players and the match is played over two consecutive days with four morning foursomes followed each afternoon by eight singles. Selection of the Great Britain and Ireland team is carried out by the R&A Selection Committee. The European Golf Association selects the Continent of Europe team

To be eligible for selection, players must be under the age of 18 at 00.00 hours on 1st January in the year of the matches.

## Junior Ryder Cup

First staged in 1995, the Junior Ryder Cup is a biennial international match played between two selected teams of amateur golfers representing Europe and the USA, prior to the Ryder Cup. Each team consists of four girls and four boys under 16 as well as two girls and two boys under 18. The match is played over two consecutive days with six four balls on the first day and six mixed four balls on the second day.

Selection of the European team is carried out by the European Golf Association. Players and captains are then invited to watch the Ryder Cup.

## Girls' Home Internationals

Teams from England, Ireland, Scotland and Wales compete annually for the Stroyan Cup. The qualifications for a player for the Girls' International Matches shall be the same as those laid down by each country for its Girls' Close Championship except that a player shall be under 18 years on the 1st January in the year of the Tournament.

Each team, consisting of not more than eight players, plays each other team, a draw taking place to decide the order of play between the teams. The matches consist of three foursomes and six singles, each of 18 holes.

## The Junior Open

Run by The R&A every two years for junior golfers nominated by their various Federations. It is always held during The Open week at a venue close to the course where the Championship is being played.

# PART XV

# Golf History

# R&A Championships and Team Events

In 2004, The Royal and Ancient Golf Club of St Andrews devolved responsibility for the running of The Open Championship and other key golfing events to The R&A. The history of championships and team events organised by The R&A and by The R&A and other golfing bodies are outlined below. Current championship and match conditions are defined elsewhere in the volume.

**Championships solely under the administration of The R&A:**
The Open Championship
The Amateur Championship
The Seniors Open Amateur Championship
The Boys Amateur Championship
The Junior Open Championship

**Team events organised by The R&A:**
The Boys Home Internationals

**Team events organised by The R&A and other golfing bodies:**
The Walker Cup (R&A/USGA)
The World Amateur Team Championships (R&A as part of the International Golf Federation)
The St Andrews Trophy (R&A/EGA)
The Jacques Léglise Trophy (R&A/EGA)
The Senior Open Championship

## The Open Championship

The Open Championship began in 1860 at the Prestwick Golf Club and the original trophy was an ornate Challenge Belt, which was subscribed for and presented by the members of Prestwick Golf Club. What is now recognised as the first Open Championship was played on October 17, 1860 at the end of the club's autumn meeting. A total of eight players competed in three rounds of the 12 hole course. No prize money for The Open was awarded until 1863, the winner simply received the Belt for a year. In 1863 it was decided to give money prizes to those finishing second, third and fourth but the winner still only received the Belt. It was not until 1864 that the winner received £6. The average field in the 1860s was only 12 players.

The original rules of the competition stated that the Belt "becomes the property of the winner by being won three years in succession". In 1870 Tom Morris Junior won for the third year in a row and took possession of the Belt. He won £6 for his efforts out of a total prize fund of £12. No Championship was held in 1871 whilst the Prestwick Club entered into discussions with The Royal and Ancient Golf Club and the Honourable Company of Edinburgh Golfers over the future of the event.

One of the key turning points in the history of The Open took place at the Spring Meeting of the Prestwick Club in April 1871. At that meeting it was proposed that "in contemplation of St Andrews, Musselburgh and other clubs joining in the purchase of a Belt to be played for over four or more greens, it is not expedient for the Club to provide a Belt to be played solely for at Prestwick". From that date onwards, The Open ceased to be under the sole control of the Prestwick Golf Club.

The Championship was played again under this new agreement in 1872. A new trophy, the now famous Claret Jug, was purchased for presentation to the winner. Until 1891, the host club remained responsible for all arrangements regarding the Championship, which continued to be played over 36 holes in one day.

In 1892, the Honourable Company of Edinburgh Golfers took four radical steps to transform The Open Championship. It extended play to 72 holes over two days, imposed an entrance charge for all competitors, changed the venue to a new course at Muirfield and increased the total prize fund from £28 10s to £100. These actions were all taken unilaterally by the club. The increased purse to counter a rival tournament held at Musselburgh.

A meeting was held between the three host clubs on June 9, 1893, for the purpose of "placing the competition for The Open Championship on a basis more commensurate with its importance than had hitherto existed". Three resolutions were agreed. Two English clubs, St George's, Sandwich and Royal Liverpool, would be invited to stage the Championship and join the rota, now of five clubs. Four rounds of 18 holes would be played over five days. Each of the five clubs would contribute £15 to the cost and the balance would come from an entry fee for all competitors. The prize money would total £100, with £30 for the winner. The date of each year's championship would be set by the host club, which would also bear any additional necessary expenses. The representatives of the five clubs became known as the Delegates of the Associated Clubs.

The increasing number of entrants caused a cut to be introduced after two rounds in 1898 and between 1904 and 1906 the Championship was played over three days. It then reverted to two days in 1907 with the introduction of qualifying rounds. The entire field had to qualify and there were no exemptions.

On January 24, 1920, the Delegates of the Associated Clubs asked The Royal and Ancient Golf Club to take over "the management of the Championship and the custody of the Challenge Cup". The new Championship Committee was responsible for running both The Open and Amateur Championships and in 1922 it was decided that The Open should only be played over links courses. The venues included in today's circuit are: Carnoustie, Muirfield, Royal Birkdale, Royal Liverpool, Royal Lytham & St Annes, Royal St George's, Royal Troon, the Old Course, St Andrews and Turnberry.

Prestwick, birth place of The Open, played host to the Championship 24 times, the last in 1925. Other courses that have been used in the past are: Musselburgh (1874, 1877, 1880, 1883, 1886, 1889); Royal Cinque Ports, Deal (1909, 1920); Princes, Sandwich (1932) and Royal Portrush (1951).

The Open was played regularly over three days starting in 1926, with a round on each of the first two days and two rounds on the final day, which from 1927 onwards was a Friday. The total prize money had reached £500 by 1939. The prize money was increased to £1000 in 1946 and reached £5000 in 1959.

As The Open went into its second century in the 1960s, it grew tremendously both as a Championship and a spectator event. In 1963, exemptions from pre-qualifying were introduced for the leading players. Play was extended to four days in 1966, with the Championship finishing with a single round on the Saturday. In 1968, a second cut after 54 holes was introduced to further reduce the field on the final day and this remained in effect until 1985. To cope with the increasing spectator numbers, facilities were much improved. Grandstands were first introduced at The Open in 1960 and they became a standard feature from 1963 onwards.

Regional qualifying had been tried as an experiment for one year in 1926, but did not become a regular feature until 1977. Some players were exempt but had to take part in final qualifying, while others were exempt from both regional and final qualifying. In 2004, International Final Qualifying was introduced, enabling players around the world to qualify on five different Continents.

Since 1980, the Championship has been scheduled to end on a Sunday instead of a Saturday. In the event of a tie for first place, play-offs took place over 36 holes up until 1963, when they were reduced to 18 holes. In 1985 a four-hole play-off, followed by sudden death, was introduced.

The Open Championship was first televised live in 1955 and was shown on the BBC. In 2013, the total coverage was 4,468 hours worldwide. Forty-one broadcasters showed coverage of The Open Championship to a potential 501 million households.

Admission charges to watch The Open were introduced in 1926. Paid admissions went over 50,000 for the first time in 1968 at Carnoustie and over 100,000 for the first time at St Andrews in

1978. The 200,000 attendance figure was reached for the first time at St Andrews in 1990. A new record was set at the Home of Golf in 2000 when 238,787 watched the Millennium Open.

### Growth of prize money

| Year | Total Prize Money | First Prize |
|---|---|---|
| 1861 | £0 | £0 |
| 1860 | £0 | £0 |
| 1863 | £10 | £10 |
| 1873 | Not known | £11 |
| 1883 | £20 | £8 |
| 1893 | £100 | £30 |
| 1903 | £125 | £50 |
| 1913 | £135 | £50 |
| 1923 | £225 | £75 |
| 1933 | £500 | £100 |
| 1943 | No Championship | |
| 1953 | £2,500 | £500 |
| 1963 | £8,500 | £1,500 |
| 1973 | £50,000 | £5,500 |
| 1983 | £310,000 | £40,000 |
| 1993 | £1,000,000 | £100,000 |
| 2003 | £3,900,000 | £700,000 |
| 2013 | £5,250,000 | £945,000 |

Harry Vardon has scored most victories in The Open Championship. He won it six times between 1896 and 1914. JH Taylor, James Braid, Peter Thomson and Tom Watson have each won The Open five times. Between 1860 and 1889, all of The Open winners were Scottish. John Ball Jr became the first Englishman and the first amateur to claim the title in 1890. Arnaud Massy from France was the first Continental winner in 1907.

Four players have completed a hat trick of Open wins: Tom Morris Jr 1868–1870; Jamie Anderson 1877–1879; Bob Ferguson 1880–1882; Peter Thomson 1954–1956.

The Open Championship has been won by an amateur player six times – John Ball in 1890, Harold Hilton in 1892 and 1897 and Bobby Jones in 1926, 1927 and 1930. Walter Hagen was the first native born American to win The Open when he triumphed in 1922. Jock Hutchison, who had won the previous year, was resident in America at the time of his victory although he was born in St Andrews.

### The Amateur Championship

What became recognised as the first Amateur Championship was held at Hoylake in 1885, although earlier national amateur competitions had been played at St Andrews in 1857, 1858 and 1859. The Royal and Ancient Golf Club had considered holding a national amateur tournament in 1876 but decided not to proceed with the idea.

In December 1884, Thomas Owen Potter, the Secretary of Royal Liverpool Golf Club, proposed holding a championship for amateur players. The event was to be open to members of recognised clubs and it was hoped that it would make the game more popular and lead to improved standards of play.

A total of 44 players from 12 clubs entered the first championship. The format was matchplay, with the ruling that if two players tied they would both advance to the following round and play one another again. There were three semi-finalists: John Ball, Horace Hutchinson and Allan Macfie. After a bye to the final, Macfie beat Hutchinson 7 and 6.

Following the success of the first tournament, it was agreed that a championship open to all amateurs should be played at St Andrews, Hoylake and Prestwick in rotation.

Twenty-four golf clubs subscribed for the trophy, which was acquired in 1886. They were:

| | |
|---|---|
| Alnmouth | Royal Aberdeen |
| Bruntsfield | Royal Albert (Montrose) |
| Dalhousie | Royal and Ancient |
| Formby | Royal Blackheath |
| Gullane | Royal Burgess |
| Honourable Company | Royal Liverpool |
| Innerleven | Royal North Devon |
| Kilspindie | Royal St George's |
| King James VI | Royal Wimbledon |
| North Berwick New | Tantallon |
| Panmure | Troon |
| Prestwick | West Lancashire |

Representatives, known as Delegates of the Associated Clubs, were elected from these clubs to run the Championship and in 1919 they approached The Royal and Ancient Golf Club to accept future management. The Club agreed and in 1920 the Championship Committee was formed. This committee became responsible for organising the Amateur and Open and for making decisions on the conditions of play. It was not until 1922, however, that the 1885 tournament was officially recognised as the first Amateur Championship and Allan Macfie the first winner.

The venue circuit gradually increased. Sandwich was added in 1892, Muirfield in 1897 and Westward Ho! in 1912. The Championship was first played in Ireland in 1949 (Portmarnock) and Wales in 1951 (Porthcawl).

Prior to 1930, only two non-British players won the Amateur Championship title, Walter Travis, in 1904, and Jesse Sweetser, in 1926. Both hailed from the United States, the former via Australia.

The Americans began to make their presence felt more strongly in the 1930s, with four Americans winning five Amateur Championships. Bobby Jones took the title at St Andrews 1930, the year in which he achieved the Grand Slam. Lawson Little won in 1934 and 1935, Robert Sweeney in 1937 and Charles Yates in 1938.

Following a break during World War II, the Amateur Championship resumed in 1946 at Birkdale when the handicap limit was raised from one to two as an encouragement to those amateurs who had been on war service.

Attempts were made during the 1950s and 1960s to control large numbers of entries. In 1956 the field was limited to 200 so that the quarter-finals, semi-

finals and the final could be played over 36 holes. This experiment lasted two years, when it was decided that only the semi-finals and final should be played over two rounds.

Regional qualifying over 36 holes was introduced in 1958 when 14 courses throughout the UK were selected. Using this method, the original entry of 500 was reduced to 200. Any player with a handicap of 3 or better could enter.

In 1961 regional qualifying was scrapped and the quarter-finals and semi-finals were played over 18 holes. Then in 1983 at Turnberry, 36 holes of strokeplay qualifying were introduced during the first two days. This format continues, with the leading 64 players and ties qualifying for the matchplay stages.

## The Senior Open Championship

The Senior Open Championship has been part of the European Seniors Tour since 1987, and in 2003 was added to the Champions Tour as one of the five major world events in senior golf. The European Seniors Tour jointly administers the event alongside The R&A. Previous winners include former Open champions Gary Player, Bob Charles and Tom Watson.

## The Seniors Open Amateur Championship

The Seniors Open Amateur Championship was the first tournament to be initiated by The Royal and Ancient Golf Club. Prestwick Golf Club had been responsible for starting the Open Championship while Royal Liverpool Golf Club had introduced the Amateur Championship. Other events, such as the Boys Amateur Championship and Boys Home Internationals were introduced by private individuals and then handed over, by agreement, to The R&A.

The Seniors Open Amateur Championship made its début at Formby in 1969. It started as a means to help choose a Great Britain and Ireland team for the World Senior Amateur Team Championship which had begun in 1967 at Pinehurst, North Carolina, under the auspices of the World Amateur Golf Council.

Initially, the World Senior team event was to be played every two years, alternating with the competition for the Eisenhower Trophy, but it did not survive beyond 1969. The success of the Seniors Open Amateur Championship, however, was evident from the start and it became a popular event in its own right.

It began as a 36-hole strokeplay event, held over two days for players over the age of 55. The handicap limit was 5 and the field was restricted to 100. The winner was Reg Pattinson, who duly played his way onto the World Amateur Senior team in which he was partnered by Alan Cave, AL Bentley and AT Kyle. The short-lived World Senior event was played in 1969 over the Old Course at St Andrews and was won for the second time by the United States. Great Britain and Ireland finished third out of an entry of only 13 teams.

Before the present format was introduced, various alternatives were tried, in order to satisfy increasing entry demands. Two courses were used in 1971, allowing an entry of 250 with the handicap limit being increased to 9. In 1974, a limit of 130 was imposed. Subsidiary competitions were introduced according to age group: 55–59, 60–64 and 65 and over. A fourth age group was added in 1975 for the over 70s and the entry limit was increased to 140. The special categories changed in 1999, to one only for the 65 and over age group.

Today, the Seniors Open Amateur Championship attracts a wide international field, with 144 competitors playing two rounds and the leading 60 players and ties completing a further 18 holes.

## The Boys Amateur Championship
The Boys Amateur Championship was introduced in 1921 for the under-16 age group. For the first two years it was played at Royal Ascot under the guidance of DM Mathieson and Colonel Thomas South. In 1948, Colonel South announced his intention to retire from his duties in connection with the event, declaring that "nothing would give him greater pleasure than that The Royal and Ancient Golf Club should take over the conduct of the Championship".

The venue for the first Boys Amateur Championship to be played under the administration of The Royal and Ancient Golf Club was the Old Course, St Andrews. A sub-committee ran the event until 1952 when it was finally handed over to the Championship Committee.

Since that year a prize has been presented to the best performing 16-year-old. This, the Peter Garner Bowl, commemorates the death of a competitor who was killed in a road accident while returning from the 1951 Championship.

Sir Michael Bonallack enjoyed early success in the Boys Amateur Championship. He won in 1952, and went on to win the Amateur Championship in 1961, 1965, 1968, 1969 and 1970.

Professionals who won the title earlier in their careers include Ronan Rafferty (1979), José Maria Olazábal (1983) and more recently Sergio García (1997).

## The Junior Open Championship
Inaugurated in 1994, the Junior Open Championship came under The R&A's administrative control in 2000. All national golf unions and federations are invited to send their leading boy and girl under the age of 16 to compete in the three-day event. In previous years, only one player from each union or federation could enter. The biennial event is run on a course close to The Open Championship and in the same week so that all participants can spend time watching the world's finest players in action.

To encourage entries worldwide, there are three categories of competition defined by varying handicap limits. Gold is for those with a handicap of 3 and under, silver 4–9 and bronze 10–18.

## TEAM EVENTS

### The Walker Cup
The United States Golf Association International Challenge Trophy was originally intended to be presented to the winners of a contest to which all golf playing nations would be invited to compete. However, as The R&A tactfully pointed out to their counterparts in the USGA in 1921, the only two countries capable of entering a team were Great Britain and America.

By this simple process of elimination the trophy presented by USGA President George Herbert Walker became the focal point of a biennial series between the finest amateur players of the two countries. The first unofficial match was played in 1921 on the eve of the Amateur Championship at Hoylake when 19-year-old Bobby Jones helped the American team to a 9–3 victory. For the next three years the event was played annually, but settled into its biennial pattern after 1924.

It was not until 1938 at St Andrews that Great Britain and Ireland recorded a first victory. In 1965 the score was 11–11. There were 2 halved matches.

Only after the first success in America, with a 12½–11½ victory at Peachtree in Georgia in 1989, did the GB&I team finally end American domination of the matches. In the years that followed there were home wins at Porthcawl in 1995 and Nairn in 1999. The GB&I run of victories continued at Ocean Forest in 2001 and Ganton in 2003, before winning most recently at Royal Aberdeen in 2011.

The man after whom the trophy and the matches are named has another claim to a place in world history. His grandson, George Herbert Walker Bush and his great-grandson have both held office as President of the United States of America.

### The Eisenhower Trophy
The United States Golf Association approached The Royal and Ancient Golf Club in 1958 with the proposal that the two bodies should sponsor a worldwide amateur golf event. The new competition would take place biennially in non-Walker Cup years, with the first being played at St Andrews in 1958. All golfing bodies that observed the Rules of Golf and Amateur Status as approved by The R&A and the USGA were invited to send one representative to a meeting in Washington at which President Dwight D Eisenhower presented a trophy to be awarded to the winning country. The committee of the event was to be known as the World Amateur Golf Council, which is now the International Golf Federation.

The key objective of the new council was "to foster friendship and sportsmanship among the peoples of the world through the conduct of an Amateur Team Championship for The Eisenhower Trophy". In a meeting with the President in the Rose Garden of the White House, Eisenhower offered his advice to the delegates: "I suggest, aside from the four hotshot golfers you bring, that you take along some high-handicap fellows and let them play at their full handicaps ...

This way golf doesn't become so important". This observation led to the creation of a "Delegates and Duffers Cup" for officials and non-playing captains.

The format decided for the Eisenhower Trophy was strokeplay. Each team consisted of four players who would play four rounds. The team score for each round was the three best individual scores. The first competition was held in St Andrews and attracted teams from 29 countries. After 72 holes of golf, the American and Australian teams were both tied on an aggregate score of 918. A play-off was held and the Australian team won by two strokes. So far this has been the only play-off in the history of the event.

Australia went on to win the trophy twice more, in 1966 and 1996. However, the USA have dominated the event, winning it 13 times in total. The Great Britain and Ireland team have won four times, in 1964, 1976, 1988 and 1998. In 2002 teams were reduced from four to three players with the best two scores counting in each round and for the first time England, Ireland, Scotland and Wales entered separate teams. In 2008, Scotland claimed its first victory in the Eisenhower Trophy at the Royal Adelaide Golf Club, Australia. Fifty years after the Australians won the first Championship at the Old Course in St Andrews, the Scots took the Trophy home from Australia. A parallel event for women, playing for the Espirito Santo Trophy, is held at the same venue prior to the Eisenhower.

## The St Andrews Trophy

In November 1955 the Championship Committee of The Royal and Ancient Golf Club put forward a recommendation that "the European Golf Association should be approached with a view to arranging an international match between a Great Britain and Ireland and European side".

The GB&I team, captained by Gerald Micklem, duly triumphed by a score of 12½ to 2½ in the first match played over the West Course at Wentworth in 1956. A resounding success, it was immediately established as a biennial event in non-Walker Cup years and in 1964 the Club donated the St Andrews Trophy to be presented to the winning team.

Although Great Britain and Ireland have dominated the match, winning 24 of the 28 encounters, the Continent of Europe had a convincing victory at Villa d'Este in Italy in 1998 and suffered only a narrow 13–11 defeat at Turnberry in 2000. The Continent of Europe are the current holders of the trophy, winning in 2012 by a score of 12½ to 11½ at Portmarnock, County Dublin, Ireland.

## The Jacques Léglise Trophy

The annual boys international match involving GB&I against a team from the Continent of Europe was introduced in 1958. This event was dominated originally by the British and Irish side, which won every match through 1966 prompting the match to be discontinued because it was a one-sided affair.

The match was revived in 1977 when the Continental team won by 7 points to 6. A new trophy donated by Jean-Louis Dupont on behalf of Golf de Chantilly in memory of Jacques Léglise, a leading French golf administrator, was presented for the first time in 1978 when the Continental team again won. Since then the Continental side has triumphed a further nine times, most recently in 2012. The 2012 match at Portmarnock resulted in a 13½–10½ victory for the Continent of Europe. The 2013 match at Royal St David's resulted in a 15–9 victory for GB&I. The 2010 match at Castelconturbia resulted in a 15½–8½ victory for the Continent of Europe. The 2008 match at Kingsbarns resulted in a 14–10 victory for GB&I. Great Britain and Ireland won the 2011 match with an impressive 14½–9½ victory over the Continent of Europe. The match was played in conjunction with the Boys Amateur Championship and Home International events until 1995. Since 1996 it has been played concurrently with the St Andrews Trophy, although the Jacques Léglise Trophy remains an annual competition.

## The Boys Home Internationals

Introduced at Dunbar in 1923, the Boys Home Internationals started off as a match played between England and Scotland. It was traditionally associated with the Boys Amateur Championship, being played the day before and acting as a prelude to the main event.

The Royal and Ancient Golf Club accepted responsibility for the Boys Amateur Championship in 1949 and with it the running of the England v Scotland match. The Championship Committee originally carried out team selection. Today, representatives from the four Home Unions select the teams.

In 1972, a team match between Ireland and Wales was added to the fixture and the current format was established in 1996. The four home countries compete against one another over three consecutive days in a round robin series. Each fixture comprises five morning foursomes, followed by ten afternoon singles.

In 1997, there was a significant break with the past when, for the first time, the venue chosen for the Boys Home Internationals differed to that for the Boys Amateur Championship. This practice has remained, helping to shape the individual identity of the international matches. Since 1985, the R&A Trophy has been awarded to the winning team.

# Important dates in the history of St Andrews, The Open Championship and The R&A

1457    Golf is banned by King James II of Scotland; instead, archery is encouraged.

1552    Archbishop John Hamilton grants citizens rights to play games, including golf, on the links.

1744    First set of 13 rules laid out by golfers at Leith.

1754    Twenty-two noblemen and gentlemen of Fife form Society of St Andrews Golfers.

1764    A round at St Andrews changes from 22 to 18 holes and becomes the standard.

1834    King William IV confers his patronage and the Society of St Andrews Golfers becomes The Royal and Ancient Golf Club.

1854    The Royal and Ancient Clubhouse is built.

1860    First Open Championship is held at Prestwick and won by Willie Park Sr.

1870    Tom Morris Jr wins Open Belt for third time and gets to keep it.

1872    The Royal and Ancient Golf Club, Prestwick and Honourable Company of Edinburgh Golfers take over the running of The Open.

1873    First time The Open is played at St Andrews and first time the Claret Jug is presented.

1894    United States Golf Association is formed.

1897    The R&A becomes accepted authority for golf and forms the Rules of Golf Committee.

1904    Lost ball search time reduced from 10 to five minute.

1919    The R&A takes over the running of the Amateur Championship.

1920    The R&A takes responsibility for The Open Championship

1920    First R&A–USGA rules conference

1926    The Open is first played over three days.

1929    USGA legitimises larger ball (1.68in). Smaller ball (1.62in) still used elsewhere.

1929    Steel shafts are legalised.

1951    The R&A and USGA meet to unify rules.

1952    The R&A and USGA standardise rules except for ball size. Stymie is abolished.

1955    First live television coverage of The Open Championship by the BBC.

1956    First four-yearly rules revision.

1960    First grandstands erected at The Open Championship.

1963    Last 36-hole play-off for The Open Championship.

1966    First live coverage of The Open Championship in America.

1966    Open played over four days for first time at Muirfield.

1974    1.68in ball becomes compulsory in The Open Championship for first time.

1980    The Open ends on a Sunday for the first time at Muirfield.

1984    New dropping procedure at arms length from the shoulder.

1985    The R&A change play-off arrangements for The Open to four holes.

1990    The American size 1.68in ball becomes the only legal ball.

2004    The Royal and Ancient Golf Club celebrates its 250th anniversary. Responsibility for external activities, such as running The Open and administering the Rules, is devolved to a newly formed group of companies known as The R&A.

2007    Old Course first used for the Ricoh Women's British Open Championship.

2008    Curtis Cup played over the Old Course for the first time.

2010    The Open celebrates 150 years and is played at the Home of Golf for the 28th time

# Interesting Facts and Unusual Incidents

## Royal golf clubs

● The right to the designation *Royal* is bestowed by the favour of the Sovereign or a member of the Royal House. In most cases the title is granted along with the bestowal of royal patronage on the club. The Perth Golfing Society was the first to receive the designation *Royal*. That was accorded in June 1833. King William IV bestowed the honour on The Royal and Ancient Club in 1834. The most recent Club to be so designated is Royal Mayfair Golf & Country Club in Edmonton, Canada. The club was granted Royal status in October 2005. The next most recent was Royal Mariánské Lázně in the Czech Republic. In 2003, the club was given the Royal title as a result of its association in the early part of the 20th century with King Edward VII. A full list of Royal clubs can be found on pages 696–697.

## Royal and Presidential golfers

● In the long history of the Royal and Ancient game no reigning British monarch has played in an open competition. In 1922 the Duke of Windsor, when Prince of Wales, competed in The Royal and Ancient Autumn Medal at St Andrews. He also took part in competitions at Mid-Surrey, Sunningdale, Royal St George's and in the Parliamentary Handicap. He occasionally competed in American events, sometimes partnered by a professional. On a private visit to London in 1952, he competed in the Autumn competition of Royal St George's at Sandwich, scoring 97. As Prince of Wales he played on courses all over the world and, after his abdication, as Duke of Windsor he continued to enjoy the game for many years.

● King George VI, when still Duke of York, in 1930, and the Duke of Kent, in 1937, also competed in the Autumn Meeting of The Royal and Ancient, when they had formally played themselves into the Captaincy of the Club and each returned his card in the medal round. So too did Prince Andrew, the Duke of York, when he became captain in 2003. He also played in the medal and won the mixed foursomes the following day playing with former British ladies champion Julie Otto.

● King Leopold of Belgium played in the Belgian Amateur Championship at Le Zoute, the only reigning monarch ever to have played in a national championship. The Belgian King played in many competitions subsequent to his abdication. In 1949 he reached the quarter-finals of the French Amateur Championship at St Cloud, playing as Count de Rethy.

● King Baudouin of Belgium in 1958 played in the triangular match Belgium–France–Holland and won his match against a Dutch player. He also took part in the Gleneagles Hotel tournament (playing as Mr B. de Rethy), partnered by Dai Rees in 1959.

● United States President George Bush accepted an invitation in 1990 to become an Honorary Member of The Royal and Ancient Golf Club of St Andrews. The honour recognised his long connection and that of his family with golf and The R&A. Both President Bush's father, Prescott Bush Sr, and his grandfather, George Herbert Walker – who donated the Walker Cup – were presidents of the United States Golf Association. Other Honorary Members of The R&A include Kel Nagle, Jack Nicklaus, Arnold Palmer, Gene Sarazen, Peter Thomson, Roberto de Vicenzo, Gary Player and five-times Open Championship winner Tom Watson, who was made an honorary member in 1999 on his 50th birthday.

● In September 1992, The Royal and Ancient Golf Club of St Andrews announced that His Royal Highness The Duke of York had accepted the Club's invitation of Honorary Membership. The Duke of York is the sixth member of the Royal Family to accept membership along with Their Royal Highnesses The Duke of Edinburgh and The Duke of Kent. He has since become a single handicapper, and has appeared in a number of pro-ams, partnering The Open and Masters champion Mark O'Meara to victory in the Alfred Dunhill Cup pro-am at St Andrews in 1998. His Royal Highness was Captain for 2003–2004, the year in which the Club celebrated its 250th anniversary.

## First lady golfer

● Mary Queen of Scots, who was beheaded on 8th February, 1587, was probably the first lady golfer so mentioned by name. As evidence of her indifference to the fate of Darnley, her husband who was murdered at Kirk o' Field, Edinburgh, she was charged at her trial with having played at golf in the fields beside Seton a few days after his death.

## Record championship victories

● In the Amateur Championship at Muirfield, 1920, Captain Carter, an Irish golfer, defeated an American entrant by 10 and 8. This is the only known instance where a player has won every hole in an Amateur Championship tie.

● In the final of the Canadian Ladies' Championship at Rivermead, Ottawa, in 1921, Cecil Leitch defeated Mollie McBride by 17 and 15. Miss Leitch lost only 1 hole in the match, the ninth. She was 14 up at the end of the first round, making only 3 holes necessary in the second. She won 18 holes out of 21 played, lost 1, and halved 2.

● In the final of the French Ladies' Open Championship at Le Touquet in 1927, Mlle de la Chaume (St Cloud) defeated Mrs Alex Johnston (Moor Park) by 15 and 14, the largest victory in a European golf championship.

● At Prestwick in 1934, W. Lawson Little of Presidio, San Francisco, defeated James Wallace, Troon Portland, by 14 and 13 in the final of the Amateur Championship, the record victory in the Championship. Wallace failed to win a single hole.

## Players who have won two or more majors in the same year
*(The first Masters Tournament was played in 1934)*

1922  Gene Sarazen – USPGA, US Open
1924  Walter Hagen – USPGA, The Open
1926  Bobby Jones – US Open, The Open
1930  Bobby Jones – US Open, The Open (Bobby Jones also won the US Amateur and British Amateur in this year)
1932  Gene Sarazen – US Open, The Open
1941  Craig Wood – Masters, US Open
1948  Ben Hogan – USPGA, US Open
1949  Sam Snead – USPGA, Masters
1951  Ben Hogan – Masters, US Open
1953  Ben Hogan – Masters, US Open, The Open
1956  Jack Burke – USPGA, Masters
1960  Arnold Palmer – Masters, US Open
1962  Arnold Palmer – Masters, The Open
1963  Jack Nicklaus – USPGA, Masters
1966  Jack Nicklaus – Masters, The Open
1971  Lee Trevino – US Open, The Open
1972  Jack Nicklaus – Masters, The Open
1974  Gary Player – Masters, The Open
1975  Jack Nicklaus – USPGA, Masters
1977  Tom Watson – Masters, The Open
1980  Jack Nicklaus – USPGA, US Open
1982  Tom Watson – US Open, The Open
1990  Nick Faldo – Masters, The Open
1994  Nick Price – The Open, US PGA
1998  Mark O'Meara – Masters, The Open
2000  Tiger Woods* – US Open, The Open, USPGA
2008  Padraig Harrington – The Open, US PGA
2010  Yani Tseng – Women's British Open, Kraft Nabisco
2011  Yani Tseng – Women's British Open, LPGA
2013  Inbee Park – US Women's Open, LPGA, Kraft Nabisco

*Woods also won the 2001 Masters to become the first player to hold all four Majors at the same time. He was 65-under-par for the four events.

## Outstanding records in championships, international matches and on the professional circuit
● The record number of victories in The Open Championship is six, held by Harry Vardon who won in 1896-98-99-1903-11-14.

● Five-time winners of the Championship are J.H. Taylor in 1894-95-1900-09-13; James Braid in 1901-05-06-08-10; Peter Thomson in 1954-55-56-58-65 and Tom Watson in 1975-77-80-82-83. Thomson's 1965 win was achieved when the Championship had become a truly international event. In 1957 he finished second behind Bobby Locke. By winning again in 1958 Thomson was prevented only by Bobby Locke from winning five consecutive Open Championships.

● Four successive victories in The Open by *Young* Tom Morris is a record so far never equalled. He won in 1868-69-70-72. (The Championship was not played in 1871.) Other four-time winners are Bobby Locke in 1949-50-52-57, Walter Hagen in 1922-24-28-29, Willie Park 1860-63-66-75, and *Old* Tom Morris 1861-62-64-67.

● Since the Championship began in 1860, players who have won three times in succession are Jamie Anderson, Bob Ferguson, and Peter Thomson.

● Robert Tyre Jones won The Open three times in 1926-27-30; the Amateur in 1930; the American Open in 1923-26-29-30; and the American Amateur in 1924-25-27-28-30. In winning the four major golf titles of the world in one year (1930) he achieved a feat unlikely ever to be equalled. Jones retired from competitive golf after winning the 1930 American Open, the last of these Championships, at the age of 28.

● Jack Nicklaus has had the most wins (six) in the US Masters Tournament, followed by Arnold Palmer with four.

● In modern times there are four championships generally regarded as standing above all others – The Open, US Open, US Masters, and USPGA. Five players have held all these titles, Gene Sarazen, Ben Hogan, Gary Player, Jack Nicklaus and Tiger Woods in that order. In 1978 Nicklaus became the first player to have held each of them at least three times. His record in these events is: The Open 1966-70-78; US Open 1962-67-72-80; US Masters 1963-65-66-72-75-86; USPGA 1963-71-73-75-80. His total of major championships is now 18. In 1998 at the age of 58, Nicklaus finished joint sixth in the Masters. By not playing in The Open Championship that year, he ended a run of 154 successive major championships for which he was eligible (stretching back to 1957).

In 1953 Ben Hogan won the Masters, US Open and The Open, but did not compete in the USPGA because of a dates clash with The Open.

In 2000 Tiger Woods won the US Open by 15 strokes (a major championship record), The Open by eight strokes, and the USPGA in the play-off. In 2001 he then added the Masters winning by two shots to become the first player to hold all four major titles at the same time. He was 65-under-par for the four events.

● In the 1996 English Amateur Championship at Hollinwell, Ian Richardson (50) and his son, Carl, of Burghley Park, Lincolnshire, both reached the semi-finals. Both lost.

● The record number of victories in the US Open is four, held by Willie Anderson, Bobby Jones, Ben Hogan and Jack Nicklaus.

● Bobby Jones (amateur), Gene Sarazen, Ben Hogan, Lee Trevino, Tom Watson and Tiger Woods are the only players to have won The Open and US Open Championships in the same year. Tony Jacklin won The Open in 1969 and the US Open in 1970 and for a few weeks was the holder of both.

● In winning the Amateur Championship in 1970 Michael Bonallack became the first player to win in three consecutive years.

● The English Amateur record number of victories is held by Michael Bonallack, who won the title five times.

● John Ball holds the record number of victories in the Amateur Championship, which he won eight times. Next comes Michael Bonallack (who was internationally known as *The Duke*) with five wins.

● Cecil Leitch and Joyce Wethered each won the British Ladies' title four times.

● The Scottish Amateur record was held by Ronnie Shade, who won five titles in successive years, 1963 to 1967. His long reign as Champion ended when he was beaten in the fourth round of the 1968 Championship after winning 44 consecutive matches.

● Joyce Wethered established an unbeaten record by winning the English Ladies' in five successive years from 1920 to 1924 inclusive.

● In winning the Amateur Championships of Britain and America in 1934 and 1935 Lawson Little won 31 consecutive matches. Other dual winners of these championships in the same year are R.T. Jones (1930) and Bob Dickson (1967).

● Peter Thomson's victory in the 1971 New Zealand Open Championship was his ninth in that event.

● In a four-week spell in 1971, Lee Trevino won in succession the US Open, the Canadian Open and The Open Championship.

● Michael Bonallack and Bill Hyndman were the Amateur Championship finalists in both 1969 and 1970. This was the first time the same two players reached the final in successive years.

● On the US professional circuit the greatest number of consecutive victories is 11, achieved by Byron Nelson in 1945. Nelson also holds the record for most victories in one calendar year, again in 1945 when he won a total of 18 tournaments.

● Raymond Floyd, by winning the Doral Classic in March 1992, joined Sam Snead as the only winners of US Tour events in four different decades.

● Sam Snead won tournaments in six decades. His first win was the 1936 West Virginia PGA. In 1980 he won the *Golf Digest* Commemorative and in 1982 the Legends of Golf with Don January.

● Neil Coles has won official Tour events in six decades. His first victory was in 1958 and he was a winner on the European Senior Tour in June 2000 when he took the Microlease Jersey Senior Open. Coles still plays well enough to beat his age. Now 67, he shot a closing 64 in the final round of the 2003

Travis Perkins Senior Open over the Edinburgh course he helped design.

● Jack Nicklaus and the late Walter Hagen have had five wins each in the USPGA Championship. All Hagen's wins were at match play; all Nicklaus's at stroke play.

● In 1953 Flory van Donck of Belgium had seven major victories in Europe, including The Open Championships of Switzerland, Italy, Holland, Germany and Belgium.

● Mrs Anne Sander won four major amateur titles each under a different name. She won the US Ladies' in 1958 as Miss Quast, in 1961 as Mrs Decker, in 1963 as Mrs Welts and the British Ladies' in 1980 as Mrs Sander.

● The highest number of appearances in the Ryder Cup matches is held by Nick Faldo who made his eleventh appearance in 1997.

● The greatest number of appearances in the Walker Cup matches is held by Irishman Joe Carr who made his tenth appearance in 1967.

● In the Curtis Cup Mary McKenna made her ninth consecutive appearance in 1986.

● Players who have represented their country in both Walker and Ryder Cup matches are: for the United States, Fred Haas, Ken Venturi, Gene Littler, Jack Nicklaus, Tommy Aaron, Mason Rudolph, Bob Murphy, Lanny Wadkins, Scott Simpson, Tom Kite, Jerry Pate, Craig Stadler, Jay Haas, Bill Rodgers, Hal Sutton, Curtis Strange, Davis Love III, Brad Faxon, Scott Hoch, Phil Mickelson, Corey Pavin, Justin Leonard, Tiger Woods, David Duval, Anthony Kim, Dustin Johnson and Rickie Fowler; and for Great Britain & Ireland, Norman Drew, Peter Townsend, Clive Clark, Peter Oosterhuis, Howard Clark, Mark James, Michael King, Gordon Brand Jr, Paul Way, Ronan Rafferty, Sandy Lyle, Philip Walton, David Gilford, Colin Montgomerie, Peter Baker, Padraig Harrington, Andrew Coltart, Oliver Wilson, Justin Rose, Luke Donald, Paul Casey, Graeme McDowell and Rory McIlroy.

## Remarkable recoveries in matchplay

● There have been two remarkable recoveries in the Walker Cup Matches. In 1930 at Sandwich, J.A. Stout, Great Britain, round in 68, was 4 up at the end of the first round against Donald Moe. Stout started in the second round, 3, 3, 3, and was 7 up. He was still 7 up with 13 to play. Moe, who went round in 67, won back the 7 holes to draw level at the 17th green. At the 18th or 36th of the match, Moe, after a long drive placed his iron shot within three feet of the hole and won the match by 1 hole.

● In 1936 at Pine Valley, George Voigt and Harry Girvan for America were 7 up with 11 to play against Alec Hill and Cecil Ewing. The British pair drew level at the 17th hole, or the 35th of the match, and the last hole was halved.

● In the 1965 Piccadilly Match Play Championship Gary Player beat Tony Lema after being 7 down with 17 to play.

● Bobby Cruickshank, the old Edinburgh player, had an extraordinary recovery in a 36-hole match in a USPGA Championship for he defeated Al Watrous after being 11 down with 12 to play.

● In a match at the Army GC, Aldershot, on 5th July, 1974, for the Gradoville Bowl, M.C. Smart was 8 down with 8 to play against Mike Cook. Smart succeeded in winning all the remaining holes and the 19th for victory.

● In the 1982 Suntory World Match Play Championship Sandy Lyle beat Nick Faldo after being 6 down with 18 to play.

● In the 1991 Ryder Cup at Kiawah, Colin Montgomerie, on his début, was five down to Mark Calcavecchia at the turn. The American was still four up with four to play. Although the Scot finished double bogey, par, double bogey, par, he won all the closing holes and squared the match when the American missed the hole from two feet on the last.

## Oldest champions

*The Open Championship: Belt* Tom Morris in 1867 – 46 years 99 days. *Cup* Roberto de Vicenzo, 44 years 93 days, in 1967; Harry Vardon, 44 years 42 days, in 1914; J.H. Taylor, 42 years 97 days, in 1913; Darren Clarke, 42 years 11 months, in 2011.

*Amateur Championship* Hon. Michael Scot, 54, at Hoylake in 1933.

*British Ladies Amateur* Mrs Jessie Valentine, 43, at Hunstanton in 1958.

*Scottish Amateur* J.M. Cannon, 53, at Troon in 1969.

*English Amateur* Terry Shingler, 41 years 11 months at Walton Heath 1977; Gerald Micklem, 41 years 8 months, at Royal Birkdale 1947.

*Welsh Amateur* John Jermine, 56, at St David's, in 2000

*US Open* Hale Irwin, 45, at Medinah, Illinois, in 1990.

*US Amateur* Jack Westland, 47, at Seattle in 1952 (He had been defeated in the 1931 final, 21 years previously, by Francis Ouimet).

*US Masters* Jack Nicklaus, 46, in 1986.

*European Tour* Des Smyth, 48 years, 14 days, Madeira Open 1982; Neil Coles, 48 years 14 days, Sanyo Open 1982

*European Senior Tour* Neil Coles, 65, in 2000

*USPGA* Julius Boros, 48, in 1968. Lee Trevino, 44, in 1984.

*USPGA Tour* Sam Snead, 52, at Greensborough Open in 1965. Sam Snead, 61, equal second in Glen Campbell Open 1974.

## Youngest champions

*The Open Championship: Belt* Tom Morris, Jr, 17 years 5 months, in 1868. *Cup* Willie Auchterlonie, 21 years 24 days, in 1893; Tom Morris, Jr, 21 years 5 months, in 1872; Severiano Ballesteros, 22 years 103 days, in 1979.

*US Open Championship:* In 2011 Rory McIlroy, at the age of 22, became the youngest player to win the event since Bobby Jones' victory in 1923 at the age of 21.

*Amateur Championship* J.C. Beharrell, 18 years 1 month, at Troon in 1956; R. Cole (RSA) 18 years 1 month, at Carnoustie in 1966.

*British Ladies Amateur* May Hezlett, 17, at Newcastle, Co. Down, in 1899; Michelle Walker, 18, at Alwoodley in 1971.

*English Amateur* Nick Faldo, 18, at Lytham St Annes in 1975; Paul Downes, 18, at Birkdale in 1978; David Gilford, 18, at Woodhall Spa in 1984; Ian Garbutt, 18, at Woodhall Spa in 1990; Mark Foster, 18, at Moortown in 1994.

*English Amateur Strokeplay* Ronan Rafferty, 16, at Hunstanton in 1980.

*British Ladies Open Strokeplay* Helen Dobson, 18, at Southerness in 1989.

*British Boys Championship* Mark Mouland (WAL) 15 years 120 days at Sunningdale in 1976; Pablo Martin (ESP) 15 years 120 days at Ganton 2001.

**More records can be found on pages 478–491**

## Disqualifications

*Disqualifications are now numerous, usually for some irregularity over signing a scorecard or for late arrival at the first tee. We therefore show here only incidents in major events involving famous players or players who were in a winning position or incidents which were in themselves unusual.*

● J.J. McDermott, the American Open Champion 1911–12, arrived for The Open Championship at Prestwick in 1914 to discover that he had made a mistake of a week in the date the championship began. The American could not play, as the qualifying rounds were completed on the day he arrived.

● In the Amateur Championship at Sandwich in 1937, Brigadier-General Critchley, arriving at Southampton from New York on the *Queen Mary*, which had been delayed by fog, flew by specially chartered aeroplane to Sandwich. He circled over the clubhouse, so the officials knew he was nearly there, but he arrived six minutes late, and his name had been struck out. At the same championship a player, entered from Burma, who had travelled across the Pacific and the American Continent, and was also on the *Queen Mary*, travelled from Southampton by motor car and arrived four hours after his starting time to find after journeying more than halfway round the world he was struck out.

● An unprecedented disqualification was that of A. Murray in the New Zealand Open Championship, 1937. Murray, who was New Zealand Champion in 1935, was playing with J.P. Hornabrook, New Zealand Amateur Champion, and at the 8th hole in the last round, while waiting for his partner to putt, Murray dropped a ball on the edge of the green and made a practice putt along the edge. Murray returned the lowest score in the championship, but he was disqualified for taking the practice putt.

● At The Open Championship at St Andrews in 1946, John Panton, Glenbervie, in the evening practised putting on a green on the New Course, which was one of the qualifying courses. He himself reported his inadvertence to The Royal and Ancient and he was disqualified.

● At The Open Championship, Sandwich, 1949, C. Rotar, an American, qualified by four strokes to compete in the championship but he was disqualified because he had used a putter which did not conform to the accepted form and make of a golf club, the socket being bent over the centre of the club head. This is the only case where a player has been disqualified in The Open Championship for using an illegal club.

● In the 1957 American Women's Open Championship, Mrs Jackie Pung had the lowest score, 298 over four rounds, but lost the championship. The card she signed for the final round read *five* at the 4th hole instead of the correct *six*. Her total of 72 was correct but the error, under rigid rules, resulted in her disqualification. Betty Jameson, who partnered Mrs Pung and also returned a wrong score, was also disqualified.

● Mark Roe and Jesper Parnevik were disqualified in bizarre circumstances in the 2003 Open at Royal St George's, Sandwich. Roe had shot 67 to move into contention but it was discovered after they left the recorder's hut that they had not exchanged cards. Roe's figures were returned on a card with Parnevik's name on it and vice versa. The R&A have since changed the rules to allow the official scorer to erase the wrong name and put the correct one on the card ensuring a Roe–Parnevik incident can never happen again.

● Teenager Michelle Wie will not be allowed to forget her début on the LPGA Tour as a professional in the Samsung World Championship. Although she completed four rounds and finished fourth behind Annika Sörenstam, she was disqualified for taking a drop nearer to the hole in the third round. A reporter, Michael Bamberger from *Sports Illustrated*, saw the incident but did not report it to officials until the next day after he had spoken with his editor. Officials only decided to disqualify the youngster after measuring out distances at the spot where she took the drop with a yard of string.

● Kevin Stadler, son of Ryder Cup and former Masters champion Craig Stadler, was disqualified in the 2005 Funai Classic in Orlando for disclosing he had a bent shaft in his wedge. Lying 163rd in the money list and needing a good finish to keep his card, he was lying joint fifth going into the final round. He discovered the shaft of his wedge was bent on the second hole on the final day and was disqualified for playing with an illegal club – ironically, one that could never have helped him play a decent shot.

## Longest match

● W.R. Chamberlain, a retired farmer, and George New, a postmaster at Chilton Foliat, on 1st August, 1922, met at Littlecote, the 9-hole course of Sir Ernest Wills, and agreed to play every Thursday afternoon over the course. This continued until New's sudden death on 13th January, 1938. An accurate record of the match was kept, giving details of each round including wind direction and playing conditions. In the elaborate system nearly two million facts were recorded. They played 814 rounds, and aggregated 86,397 strokes, of which Chamberlain took 44,008 and New 42,371. New, therefore, was 1,637 strokes up. The last round of all was halved, a suitable end to such an unusual contest.

## Longest ties

● The longest known ties in 18-hole match play rounds in major events were in an early round of the News of the World Match Play Championship at Turnberry in 1960, when W.S. Collins beat W.J. Branch at the 31st hole, and in the third round of the same tournament at Walton Heath in 1961 when Harold Henning beat Peter Alliss also at the 31st hole.

● In the 1970 Scottish Amateur Championship at Balgownie, Aberdeen, E. Hammond beat J. McIvor at the 29th hole in their second round tie.

● C.A. Palmer beat Lionel Munn at the 28th hole at Sandwich in 1908. This is the record tie of the British Amateur Championship. Munn has also been engaged in two other extended ties in the Amateur Championship. At Muirfield, in 1932, in the semi-final, he was defeated by John de Forest, the ultimate winner, at the 26th hole, and at St Andrews, in 1936, in the second round he was defeated by J.L. Mitchell, again at the 26th hole.

*The following examples of long ties are in a different category for they occurred in competitions, either stroke play or match play, where the conditions stipulated that in the event of a tie, a further stated number of holes had to be played – in some cases 36 holes, but mostly 18. With this method a vast number of extra holes was sometimes necessary to settle ties.*

● The longest known was between two American women in a tournament at Peterson (New Jersey) when 88 extra holes were required before Mrs Edwin Labaugh emerged as winner.

● In a match on the Queensland course, Australia, in October, 1933, H.B. Bonney and Col H.C.H. Robertson versus B.J. Canniffe and Dr Wallis Hoare required to play a further four 18-hole matches after being level at the end of the original 18 holes. In the fourth replay Hoare and Caniffe won by 3 and 2 which meant that 70 extra holes had been necessary to decide the tie.

● After finishing all square in the final of the Dudley GC's foursomes competition in 1950, F.W. Mannell and A.G. Walker played a further three 18-hole replays against T. Poole and E. Jones, each time finishing all square. A further 9 holes were arranged and Mannell and Walker won by 3 and 2 making a total of 61 extra holes to decide the tie.

● R.A. Whitcombe and Mark Seymour tied for first prize in the Penfold £750 Tournament at St Annes-on-Sea, in 1934. They had to play off over 36 holes and tied again. They were then required to play another 9 holes when Whitcombe won with 34 against 36. The tournament was over 72 holes. The first tie added 36 holes and the extra 9 holes made an aggregate of 117 holes to decide the winner. This is a record in first-class British golf but in no way compares with other long ties as it involved only two replays – one of 36 holes and one of 9.

● In the American Open Championship at Toledo, Ohio, in 1931, G. Von Elm and Billy Burke tied for the title. Each returned aggregates of 292. On the first replay both finished in 149 for 36 holes but on the second replay Burke won with a score of 148 against 149. This is a record tie in a national open championship.

● Cary Middlecoff and Lloyd Mangrum were declared co-winners of the 1949 Motor City Open on the USPGA Tour after halving 11 sudden death holes.

● Australian David Graham beat American Dave Stockton at the tenth extra hole in the 1998 Royal Caribbean Classic, a record on the US Senior Tour.

● Paul Downes was beaten by Robin Davenport at the 9th extra hole in the 4th round of the 1981 English Amateur Championship, a record marathon match for the Championship.

● Severiano Ballesteros was beaten by Johnny Miller at the 9th extra hole of a sudden-death play-off at the 1982 Million Dollar Sun City Challenge.

● José Maria Olazábal beat Ronan Rafferty at the 9th extra hole to win the 1989 Dutch Open on the Kennemer Golf and Country Club course. Roger Chapman had been eliminated at the first extra hole.

## Long drives

It is impossible to state with any certainty what is the longest ever drive. Many long drives have never been measured and many others have most likely never been brought to our attention. Then there are several outside factors which can produce freakishly long drives, such as a strong following wind, downhill terrain or bonehard ground. Where all three of these favourable conditions prevail outstandingly long drives can be achieved. Another consideration is that a long drive made during a tournament is a different proposition from one made for length alone, either on the practice ground, a long driving competition or in a game of no consequence. All this should be borne in mind when considering the long drives shown here.

● When professional Carl Hooper hit a wayward drive on the 3rd hole (456 yards) at the Oak Hills Country Club, San Antonio, during the 1992 Texas Open, he wrote himself into the record books but out of the tournament. The ball kept bouncing and rolling on a tarmac cart path until it was stopped by a fence – 787 yards away. It took Hooper two recovery shots with a 4-iron and then an 8-iron to return to the fairway. He eventually holed out for a double bogey six and failed to survive the half-way qualifying cut.

● Tommie Campbell of Portmarnock hit a drive of 392 yards at Dun Laoghaire GC in July 1964.

● Playing in Australia, American George Bayer is reported to have driven to within chipping distance of a 589 yards hole. "It was certainly a drive of over 500 yards", said Bayer acknowledging the strong fol-

lowing wind, sharp downslope where his ball landed and the bone-hard ground.

● In September, 1934, over the East Devon course, T.H.V. Haydon, Wimbledon, drove to the edge of the 9th green which was a hole of 465 yards, giving a drive of not less than 450 yards.

● E.C. Bliss drove 445 yards at Herne Bay in August, 1913. The drive was measured by a government surveyor who also measured the drop in height from tee to resting place of the ball at 57 feet.

## Long carries

● At Sitwell Park, Rotherham, in 1935 the home professional, W. Smithson, drove a ball which carried a dyke at 380 yards from the 2nd tee.

● George Bell, of Penrith GC, New South Wales, Australia, using a number 2 wood drove across the Nepean River, a certified carry of 309 yards in a driving contest in 1964.

● After the 1986 Irish Professional Championship at Waterville, Co. Kerry, four long-hitting professionals tried for the longest-carry record over water, across a lake in the Waterville Hotel grounds. Liam Higgins, the local professional, carried 310 yards and Paul Leonard 311, beating the previous record by 2 yards.

● In the 1972 Algarve Open at Penina, Henry Cotton vouched for a carry of 305 yards over a ditch at the 18th hole by long-hitting Spanish professional Francisco Abreu. There was virtually no wind assistance.

● At the Home International matches at Portmarnock in 1949 a driving competition was held in which all the players in all four teams competed. The actual carry was measured and the longest was 280 yards by Jimmy Bruen.

● On 6th April, 1976, Tony Jacklin hit a number of balls into Vancouver harbour, Canada, from the 495-foot high roof of a new building complex. The longest carry was measured at 389 yards.

## Long hitting

There have been numerous long hits, not on golf courses, where an outside agency has assisted the length of the shot. Such an example was a "drive" by Liam Higgins in 1986, on the Airport runway at Baldonal, near Dublin, of 632 yards.

● How's this for a long shot? Odd Marthinussen was holidaying in Haparanda in Sweden when he holed in one at the 14th. So what! The curious thing about this ace is that while he teed up in Sweden the green is in Finland which is in a different time zone. Registered as an ace in both countries, the time it took for the ball to go from tee to cup  was estimated at 1 hour and 4 seconds ... surely the longest hole ever reported by Simon Pia in his column in The Scotsman newspaper.

## Longest albatrosses

● The longest-known albatrosses (three under par) recorded at par 5 holes are:
● 647 yards-2nd hole at Guam Navy Club by Chief Petty Officer Kevin Murray of Chicago on 3rd January, 1982.

● 609 yards-15th hole at Mahaka Inn West Course, Hawaii, by John Eakin of California on 12th November, 1972.

● 602 yards-16th hole at Whiting Field Golf Course, Milton, Florida, by 27-year-old Bill Graham with a drive and a 3-wood, aided by a 25 mph tail wind.

● The longest-known albatrosses in open championships are: 580 yards 14th hole at Crans-sur-Sierre, by American Billy Casper in the 1971 Swiss Open; 558 yards 5th hole at Muirfield by American Johnny Miller in the 1972 Open Championship.

● In the 1994 German Amateur Championship at Wittelsbacher GC, Rohrenfield, Graham Rankin, a member of the visiting Scottish national team, had a two at the 592 yard 18th.

### Eagles (multiple and consecutive)

● Wilf Jones scored three consecutive eagles at the first three holes at Moor Hall GC when playing in a competition there on August Bank Holiday Monday 1968. He scored 3, 1, 2 at holes measuring 529 yards, 176 yards and 302 yards.

● In a round of the 1980 Jubilee Cup, a mixed foursomes match play event of Colchester GC, Mrs Nora Booth and her son Brendan scored three consecutive gross eagles of 1, 3, 2 at the eighth, ninth and tenth holes.

● Three players in a four-ball match at Kington GC, Herefordshire, on 22nd July, 1948, all had eagle 2s at the 18th hole (272 yards). They were R.N. Bird, R. Morgan and V. Timson.

● Four Americans from Wisconsin on holiday at Gleneagles in 1977 scored three eagles and a birdie at the 300-yard par-4 14th hole on the King's course. The birdie was by Dr Kim Lulloff and the eagles by Dr Gordon Meiklejohn, Richard Johnson and Jack Kubitz.

● In an open competition at Glen Innes GC, Australia on 13th November, 1977, three players in a four-ball scored eagle 3s at the 9th hole (442 metres). They were Terry Marshall, Roy McHarg and Jack Rohleder.

● David McCarthy, a member of Moortown Golf Club, Leeds, had three consecutive eagles (3, 3, 2) on the 4th, 5th and 6th holes during a Pro-Am competition at Lucerne, Switzerland, on 7th August, 1992.

### Speed of golf ball and club head and effect of wind and temperature

● In *The Search for the Perfect Swing*, a scientific study of the golf swing, a first class golfer is said to have the club head travelling at 100 mph at impact. This will cause the ball to leave the club at 135 mph. An outstandingly long hitter might manage to have the club head travelling at 130 mph which would produce a ball send-off speed of 175 mph. The resultant shot would carry 280 yards.

● According to Thomas Hardman, Wilson's director of research and development, wind will reduce or increase the flight of a golf ball by approximately 1½ yards for every mile per hour of wind. Every two degrees of temperature will make a yard difference in a ball's flight.

### Most northerly course

● Although the most northerly course used to be in Iceland, Björkliden Arctic Golf Club, Sweden, 250 km north of the Arctic Circle, has taken over that role. This may soon change, however, when a course opens in Narvic, Norway, which could be a few metres further north than Björkliden.

### Most southerly course

● Golf's most southerly course is Scott Base Country Club, 13° north of the South Pole. The course is run by the New Zealand Antarctic Programme and players must be kitted in full survival gear. The most difficult aspect is finding the orange golf balls which tend to get buried in the snow. Other obstacles include penguins, seals and skuas. If the ball is stolen by a skua then a penalty of one shot is incurred; but if the ball hits a skua it counts as a birdie.

"I'm sure they shouldn't have been allowed on. I don't think they're members"

### Highest golf courses

● The highest golf course in the world is thought to be the Tuctu GC in Peru which is 14,335 feet above sea-level. High courses are also found in Bolivia with the La Paz GC being about 13,500 feet. In the Himalayas, near the border with Tibet, a 9-hole course at 12,800 feet has been laid out by keen golfers in the Indian Army.

● The highest course in Europe is at Sestriere in the Italian Alps, 6,500 feet above sea-level.

● The highest courses in Great Britain are West Monmouthshire in Wales at 1,513 feet, Leadhills in Scotland at 1,500 feet and Kington in England at 1,284 feet.

### Longest courses

● The longest course in the world is Dub's Dread GC, Piper, Kansas, USA measuring 8,101 yards (par 78).

● The longest course for The Open Championship was 7,361 yards at Carnoustie in 1999.

## Longest holes

● The longest hole in the world, as far as is known, is the 6th hole measuring 782 metres (860 yards) at Koolan Island GC, Western Australia. The par of the hole is 7. There are several holes over 700 yards throughout the world.

● The longest hole for The Open Championship is the 577 yards 6th hole at Royal Troon.

## Longest tournaments

● The longest tournament held was over 144 holes in the World Open at Pinehurst, N Carolina, USA, first held in 1973. Play was over two weeks with a cut imposed at the halfway mark.

● An annual tournament, played in Germany on the longest day of the year, comprises 100 holes' medal play. Best return, in 1995, was 399 strokes.

## Largest entries

● The Open – 2,500, St Andrews, 2010.

● The Amateur – 537, Muirfield, 1998.

● US Open – 9,086, Bethpage Park GC, NY, 2009.

● The largest entry for a PGA European Tour event was 398 for the 1978 Colgate PGA Championship. Since 1985, when the all-exempt ruling was introduced, all PGA tournaments have had 144 competitors, slightly more or less.

● In 1952, Bobby Locke, The Open Champion, played a round at Wentworth against any golfer in Britain. Cards costing 2s. 6d. each (12½p), were taken out by 24,000 golfers. The challenge was to beat the local par by more than Locke could beat the par at Wentworth. 1,641 competitors, including women, succeeded in *beating* the Champion and each received a certificate signed by him. As a result of this challenge the British Golf Foundation benefited to the extent of £3,026, the proceeds from the sale of cards. A similar tournament was held in the US and Canada when 87,094 golfers participated; 14,667 players bettered Ben Hogan's score under handicap. The fund benefited by $80,024.

## Largest prize money

● The Machrie Tournament of 1901 was the first tournament with a first prize of £100. It was won by J.H. Taylor, then The Open Champion, who beat James Braid in the final.

● The richest events (at time of writing) are the – US Open and US PGA Championships which carry a prize-fund of $7.5 million. The bonus for victory in the Fedex Cup is $10 million. The biggest first prize is the $1,710,000 which goes to the winner of The Players' Championship on the PGA Tour in America.

## Holing-in-one – odds against

● At the Wanderers Club, Johannesburg in January, 1951, forty-nine amateurs and professionals each played three balls at a hole 146 yards long. Of the 147 balls hit, the nearest was by Koos de Beer, professional at Reading Country Club, which finished 10½ inches from the hole. Harry Bradshaw, the Irish professional who was touring with the British team in South Africa, touched the pin with his second shot, but the ball rolled on and stopped 3 feet 2 inches from the cup.

● A competition on similar lines was held in 1951 in New York when 1,409 players who had done a hole-in-one held a competition over several days at short holes on three New York courses. Each player was allowed a total of five shots, giving an aggregate of 7,045 shots. No player holed-in-one, and the nearest ball finished 3½ inches from the hole.

● A further illustration of the element of luck in holing-in-one is derived from an effort by Harry Gonder, an American professional, who in 1940 stood for 16 hours 25 minutes and hit 1,817 balls trying to do a 160 yard hole-in-one. He had two official witnesses and caddies to tee and retrieve the balls and count the strokes. His 1,756th shot struck the hole but stopped an inch from the hole. This was his nearest effort.

● From this and other similar information an estimate of the odds against holing-in-one at any particular hole within the range of one shot was made at somewhere between 1,500 and 2,000 to 1 by a proficient player. Subsequently, however, statistical analysis in America has come up with the following odds: a male professional or top amateur 3,708 to 1; a female professional or top amateur 4,648 to 1; an average golfer 42,952 to 1.

## Hole-in-one first recorded

● The earliest recorded hole-in-one was in 1869 at The Open Championship when Tom Morris Jr completed the 145-yard 8th hole at Prestwick in one. This was the first ace in competition for The Open Championship Challenge Belt.

● The first hole-in-one recorded with the 1.66 inch ball was in 1972 by John G. Salvesen, a member of The R&A Championship Committee. At the time this size of ball was only experimental. Salvesen used a 7-iron for his historical feat at the 11th hole on the Old Course, St Andrews.

## Holing-in-one in important events

*Since the day of the first known hole-in-one by Tom Morris Jr, at the 8th hole (145 yards) at Prestwick in the 1869 Open Championship, holes-in-one, even in championships, have become too numerous for each to be recorded. Only where other unusual or interesting circumstances prevailed are the instances shown here.*

● All hole-in-one achievements are remarkable. Many are extraordinary. Among the more amazing was that of 2-handicap Leicestershire golfer Bob Taylor, a member of the Scraptoft Club. During the final practice day for the 1974 Eastern Counties Foursomes Championship on the Hunstanton Links, he holed his tee shot with a one-iron at the 188-yard 16th. The next day, in the first round of the competition, he repeated the feat, the only difference being that because of a change of wind he used a six-iron. When he stepped on to the 16th tee the following day his partner jokingly offered him odds of 1,000,000 to one against holing-in-one for a third successive time. Taylor again used his six-iron – and holed in one!

● 1878 – Jamie Anderson, competing in The Open Championship at Prestwick, holed in one at the 11th. In these days The Open was played over three rounds of 12 holes so his ace, the first hole-in-one in competition for the Claret Jug – came at his penultimate hole in his third round. Although it seemed then that he was winning easily, it turned out afterwards that if he had not taken this hole in one stroke he would very likely have lost. Anderson was just about to make his tee shot when Andy Stuart (winner of the first Irish Open Championship in 1892), who was acting as marker to Anderson, remarked he was standing outside the teeing ground, and that if he played the stroke from there he would be disqualified. Anderson picked up his ball and teed it in a proper place. Then he holed-in-one. He won the Championship by one stroke.

● On a Friday the 13th in 1990, Richard Allen holed-in-one at the 13th at the Barwon Heads Golf Club, Victoria, Australia, and then lost the hole. He was giving a handicap stroke to his opponent, brother-in-law Jason Ennels, who also holed-in-one.

● 1906 – R. Johnston, North Berwick, competing in The Open Championship, did the 14th hole at Muirfield in one. Johnston played with only one club throughout – an adjustable head club.

● 1959 – The first hole-in-one in the US Women's Open Championship was recorded. It was by Patty Berg on the 7th hole (170 yards) at Churchill Valley CC, Pittsburgh.

● 1962 – On 6th April, playing in the second round of the Schweppes Close Championship at Little Aston, H. Middleton of Shandon Park, Belfast, holed his tee shot at the 159-yard 5th hole, winning a prize of £1,000. Ten minutes later, playing two matches ahead of Middleton, R.A. Jowle, son of the professional, Frank Jowle, holed his tee shot at the 179-yard 9th hole. As an amateur he was rewarded by the sponsors with a £30 voucher.

● 1963 – By holing out in one stroke at the 18th hole (156 yards) at Moor Park on the first day of the Esso Golden round-robin tournament, H.R. Henning, South Africa, won the £10,000 prize offered for this feat.

● 1967 – Tony Jacklin in winning the Masters tournament at St George's, Sandwich, did the 16th hole in one. His ace has an exceptional place in the records for it was seen by millions on TV, the ball was in view in its flight till it went into the hole in his final round of 64.

● 1971 – John Hudson, 25-year-old professional at Hendon, achieved a near miracle when he holed two consecutive holes-in-one in the Martini Tournament at Norwich. They were at the 11th and 12th holes (195 yards and 311 yards respectively) in the second round.

● 1971 – In The Open Championship at Birkdale, Lionel Platts holed-in-one at the 212-yard 4th hole in the second round. This was the first instance of an Open Championship hole-in-one being recorded by television. It was incidentally Platts' seventh ace of his career.

● In the 2006 Ryder Cup at the K Club, Ireland, Paul Casey holed his 4-iron shot at the 14th to score the fifth ace in the history of the competition. The following day, at the same hole, Scott Verplank became the first American to score a Ryder Cup hole-in-one. Others who have enjoyed aces in the match include Peter Butler in 1973, Nick Faldo in 1993 and Costantino Rocca and Howard Clark in 1995 at Oak Hill.

● 1973 – In the 1973 Open Championship at Troon, two holes-in-one were recorded, both at the 8th hole, known as the Postage Stamp, in the first round. They were achieved by Gene Sarazen and amateur David Russell, who were by coincidence respectively the oldest and youngest competitors.

● Mrs Argea Tissies, whose husband Hermann took 15 at Royal Troon's Postage Stamp 8th hole in the 1950 Open, scored a hole-in-one at the 2nd hole at Punta Ala in the second round of the Italian Ladies' Senior Open of 1978. Exactly five years later on the same date, at the same time of day, in the same round of the same tournament at the same hole, she did it again with the same club.

● In less than two hours play in the second round of the 1989 US Open at Oak Hill Country Club, Rochester, New York, four competitors – Doug Weaver, Mark Wiebe, Jerry Pate and Nick Price – each holed the 167-yard 6th hole in one. The odds against four professionals achieving such a record in a field of 156 are reckoned at 332,000 to 1.

● On 20th May, 1998, British golf journalist Derek Lawrenson, an eight-handicapper, won a Lamborghini Diablo car, valued at over £180,000, by holing his three-iron tee shot to the 175-yard 15th hole at Mill Ride, Berkshire. He was taking part in a charity day and was partnering England football stars Paul Ince and Steve McManaman.

● David Toms took the lead in the 2001 USPGA Championship at Atlanta Athletic Club with a hole-in-one at the 15th hole in the third round and went on to win. Nick Faldo (4th hole) and Scott Hoch (17th hole) also had holes-in-one during the event.

● In the 2006 Ryder Cup at the K Club, Ireland, Paul Casey holed his 4-iron shot at the 14th to score the fifth ace in the history of the competition. The following day, at the same hole, Scott Verplank became the first American to score a Ryder Cup hole-in-one.

## Holing-in-one – longest holes

● Bob Mitera, as a 21-year-old American student, standing 5 feet 6 inches and weighing under 12 stones, claimed the world record for the longest hole-in-one. Playing over the appropriately named Miracle Hill course at Omaha, on 7th October, 1965, Bob holed his drive at the 10th hole, 447 yards long. The ground sloped sharply downhill.

● Two longer holes-in-one have been achieved, but because they were at dog-leg holes they are not generally accepted as being the longest holes-in-one. They were 496 yards (17th hole, Teign Valley) by Shaun Lynch in July 1995 and 480 yards (5th hole, Hope CC, Arkansas) by L. Bruce on 15th November, 1962.

● In March, 1961, Lou Kretlow holed his tee shot at the 427-yard 16th hole at Lake Hefner course, Oklahoma City, USA.

● The longest known hole-in-one in Great Britain was the 393-yard 7th hole at West Lancashire GC, where in 1972 the assistant professional Peter Parkinson holed his tee shot.

● Paul Neilson, a 34-year-old golfer at South Winchester, holed in one at the club's par 4 fifth hole – 391 yards.

● Other long holes-in-one recorded in Great Britain have been 380 yards (5th hole at Tankersley Park) by David Hulley in 1961; 380 yards (12th hole at White Webbs) by Danny Dunne on 30th July, 1976; 370 yards (17th hole at Chilwell Manor, distance from the forward tee) by Ray Newton in 1977; 365 yards (10th hole at Harewood Downs) by K. Saunders in 1965; 365 yards (7th hole at Catterick Garrison GC) by Leslie Bruckner on 18th July, 1980.

● The longest-recorded hole-in-one by a woman was that accomplished in September, 1949 by Marie Robie – the 393-yard hole at Furnace Brook course, Wollaston, Mass, USA.

## Holing-in-one – greatest number by one person

59–Amateur Norman Manley of Long Beach, California.

50–Mancil Davis, professional at the Trophy Club, Fort Worth, Texas.

31–British professional C.T. le Chevalier who died in 1973.

22–British amateur, Jim Hay of Kirkintilloch GC.

*At One Hole*

13–Joe Lucius at 15th hole of Mohawk, Ohio.

5–Left-hander, the late Fred Francis at 7th (now 16th) hole of Cardigan GC.

## Holing-in-one – greatest frequency

● The record for the greatest number of holes-in-one in a calendar year is 14, claimed in 2007 by Californian Jacqueline Gagne who hit her fourteenth ace at Mission Hills in front of a television crew who had been sent to check if her claims for the previous 13 were true.

● J.O. Boydstone of California made 11 aces in 1962.

● John Putt of Frilford Heath GC had six holes-in-one in 1970, followed by three in 1971.

● Douglas Porteous, of Ruchill GC, Glasgow, achieved seven holes-in-one in the space of eight months. Four of them were scored in a five-day period from 26th to 30th September, 1974, in three consecutive rounds of golf. The first two were achieved at Ruchill GC in one round, the third there two days later, and the fourth at Clydebank and District GC after another two days.

The following May, Porteous had three holes-in-one, the first at Linn Park GC incredibly followed by two more in the one round at Clober GC.

● Mrs Kathleen Hetherington of West Essex has holed-in-one five times, four being at the 15th hole at West Essex. Four of her five aces were within seven months in 1966.

● Mrs Dorothy Hill of Dumfries and Galloway GC holed-in-one three times in 11 days in 1977.

● James C. Reid of Brodick, aged 59 and 8 handicap in 1987, achieved 14 holes-in-one, all but one on Isle of Arran courses. His success was in spite of severe physical handicaps of a stiff left knee, a damaged right ankle, two discs removed from his back and a hip replacement.

● Jean Nield, a member at Chorlton-cum-Hardy and Bramall Park, has had eleven holes-in-one and her husband Brian, who plays at Bramall Park, has had five – a husband and wife total of 16.

● Peter Gibbins holed his tee shot at the 359 yards par 4 13th hole at Hazlemere on November 2 1984 using a 3-wood that was in his bag for the first time. That spectacular ace was his third but he has had nine more since then.

## Holing successive holes-in-one

● Successive holes-in-one are rare; successive par 4 holes-in-one may be classed as near miracles. N.L. Manley performed the most incredible feat in September, 1964, at Del Valle Country Club, Saugus, California, USA. The par 4 7th (330 yards) and 8th (290 yards) are both slightly downhill, dog-leg holes. Manley had aces at both, en route to a course record of 61 (par 71).

● The first recorded example in Britain of a player holing-in-one stroke at each of two successive holes was achieved on 6th February, 1964, at the Walmer and Kingsdown course, Kent. The young assistant professional at that club, Roger Game (aged 17) holed out with a 4-wood at the 244-yard 7th hole, and repeated the feat at the 256-yard 8th hole, using a 5-iron.

● The first occasion of holing-in-one at consecutive holes in a major professional event occurred when John Hudson, 25-year-old professional at Hendon, holed-in-one at the 11th and 12th holes at Norwich during the second round of the 1971 Martini tournament. Hudson used a 4-iron at the 195-yard 11th and a driver at the 311-yard downhill 12th hole.

● Assistant professional Tom Doty (23 years), playing in a friendly match on a course near Chicago in October, 1971, had a remarkable four-hole score which included two consecutive holes-in-one, sandwiched either side by an albatross and an eagle: 4th hole (500 yards)-2; 5th hole (360 yards dog-leg)-1; 6th hole (175 yards)-1; 7th hole (375 yards)-2. Thus he was 10 under par for four consecutive holes.

● At the Standard Life Loch Lomond tournament on the European Tour in July 2000 Jarmo Sandelin holed-in-one at the 17th with the final shot there in the third round and fellow Swede Mathias Gronberg holed-in-one with the first shot there in the last round. A prize of $100,000 was only on offer in the last round.

## Holing-in-one twice (or more) in the same round by the same person

*What might be thought to be a very rare feat indeed – that of holing-in-one twice in the same round – has in fact happened on many occasions as the following instances show. It is, nevertheless, compared to the number of golfers in the world, still something of an outstanding achievement. The first known occasion was in 1907 when J. Ireland playing in a three-ball match at Worlington holed the 5th and 18th holes in one stroke and two years later in 1909 H.C. Josecelyne holed the 3rd (175 yards) and the 14th (115 yards) at Acton on 24th November.*

● The first mention of two holes-in-one in a round by a woman was followed later by a similar feat by another lady at the same club. On 19th May, 1942, Mrs W. Driver, of Balgowlah Golf Club, New South Wales, holed out in one at the 3rd and 8th holes in the same round, while on 29th July, 1948, Mrs F. Burke at the same club holed out in one at the second and eighth holes.

● The Rev Harold Snider, aged 75, scored his first hole-in-one on 9th June, 1976 at the 8th hole of the Ironwood course, near Phoenix. By the end of his round he had scored three holes-in-one, the other two being at the 13th (110 yards) and 14th (135 yards). Ironwood is a par-3 course, giving more opportunity for scoring holes-in-one, but, nevertheless, three holes-in-one in one round on any type of course is an outstanding achievement.

● When the Hawarden course in North Wales comprised only nine holes, Frank Mills in 1994 had two holes-in-one at the same hole in the same round. Each time, he hit a seven iron to the 134-yard 3rd and 12th.

● The youngest player to achieve two holes-in-one in the same round is thought to be Christopher Anthony Jones on 14 September, 1994. At the age of 14 years and 11 months he holed-in-one at the Sand Moor, Leeds, 137-yard 10th and then at the 156-yard 17th.

● The youngest woman to have performed the feat was a 17-year-old, Marjorie Merchant, playing at the Lomas Athletic GC, Argentina, at the 4th (170 yards) and 8th (130 yards) holes.

● Tony Hannam, left-handed, handicap 16 and age 71, followed a hole-in-one at the 142 yards 4th of the Bude and North Cornwall Golf Club course with another at the 143-yard 10th on Friday, 18th September, 1992.

● Brothers Eric and John Wilkinson were playing together at the Ravensworth Golf Club on Tyneside in 2001 and both holed-in-one at the 148 yards eighth. Eric (46) played first and then John to the hidden green but there is no doubting this unusual double ace. The club's vice-captain Dave Johnstone saw both balls go in! Postman Eric plays off 9. John, a county planner, has a handicap of 20. Next time they played the hole both missed the green.

● Chris Valerro, a 22-handicapper from the Liberty Lake Golf Club, Spokane, Washington, aced the 143 yards 3rd hole at his home club with a 7-iron and then the 140 yards 11th hole with his 8-iron.

● Edinburgh golfer, 25-year-old Chris Tugwell, was representing the Lothianburn club when he aced the 157-yard seventh with a nine iron and then went on to hole-in-one again at the 168-yard 12th with a five iron.

● Eugene O'Brien scored a hole-in-one double on one of Britain's most difficult courses when he aced the 13th and 16th holes at Carnoustie.

● Yusuka Miyazato, a multiple winner on the Japanese circuit, had two holes in one in the same round on the second day at the Montreux Golf Club in 2006.

● Milwaukee resident Sanjay Kuttemperoor scored two aces in 2006 at the Treetops Resort, Michigan, the first on the 150-yard fifth and the second on the 135-yard ninth.

● Some golfers go through their life without ever having a coveted hole-in-one but Alan Domingo had two within an hour in the same round at the Hawick Club in 2011. He aced the 144 yards eighth and then did the same at the 198 yards 13th.

● 75-year-old Peter Wafford, who plays off 13 at Bush Hill Park Golf Club, had a red letter day when playing in a match against Chigwell at Chigwell in 2011. Although only having recently taken up golf he had two holes in one in the same round beating estimated odds of 67 million to one against that happening.

## Holes-in-one on the same day

● In July 1987, at the Skerries Club, Co Dublin, Rank Xerox sponsored two tournaments, a men's 18-hole four-ball with 134 pairs competing and a 9-hole mixed foursomes with 33 pairs. During the day each of the four par-3 holes on the course were holed-in-one: the 2nd by Noel Bollard, the 5th by Bart Reynolds, the 12th by Jackie Carr and the 15th by Gerry Ellis.

● Wendy Russell holed-in-one at the consecutive par threes in the first round of the British Senior Ladies' at Wrexham in 1989.

● Clifford Briggs, aged 65, holed-in-one at the 14th at Parkstone GC on the same day as his wife Gwen, 60, aced the 16th.

● In the final round of the 2000 Victor Chandler British Masters at Woburn Alastair Forsyth holed-in-one at the second. Playing partner Roger Chapman then holed-in-one at the eighth.

## Two holes-in-one at the same hole in the same game

● *First in World:* George Stewart and Fred Spellmeyer at the 18th hole, Forest Hills, New Jersey, USA in October 1919.

● *First in Great Britain:* Miss G. Clutterbuck and Mrs H.M. Robinson at the 15th hole (120 yards), St Augustine GC, Ramsgate, on 8th May, 1925.

● *First in Denmark:* In a Club match in August 1987 at Himmerland, Steffan Jacobsen of Aalborg and Peter Forsberg of Himmerland halved the 15th hole in one shot, the first known occasion in Denmark.
● *First in Australia:* Dr & Mrs B. Rankine, playing in a mixed "Canadian foursome" event at the Osmond Club near Adelaide, South Australia in April 1987, holed-in-one in consecutive shots at the 2nd hole (162 metres), he from the men's tee with a 3-iron and his wife from the ladies' tee with a 1½ wood.
● Jack Ashton, aged 76, holed-in-one at the 8th hole of the West Kent Golf Club at Downe but only got a half. Opponent Ted Eagle, in receipt of shot, made a 2, net 1.
● Dr Martin Pucci and Trevor Ironside will never forget one round at the Macdonald Club in Ellon last year. Playing in an open competition the two golfers with Jamie Cowthorne making up the three-ball reached the tee at the 169yards short 11th. Dr Pucci, with the honour, hit a 5-iron, Mr Ironside a 6-iron at the hole where only the top of the flag is visible. Both hit good shots but when they reached the green they could spot only one ball  and that was Mr Cowthorne's. Then they realised that something amazing might have happened. When they reached the putting surface they discovered that both Dr Pucci's and Mr Ironside's balls were wedged into the hole. Both had made aces. It was Dr Pucci's sixth and Mr Ironside's second.
● Eric and John Wilkinson went out for their usual weekly game at the Ravensworth Golf Club in Wrekenton on Tyneside in 2001 and both holed in one at the 148 yards eighth. Neither Eric, a 46-year-old 9-handicapper who has been playing golf since he was 14, nor John, who has been playing golf for ten years and has a handicap of 20, saw the balls go in because the green is over a hill but club vice-captain Dave Johnston did and described the incident as "amazing". Next time the brothers played the hole both missed the green!
● Richard Evans and Mark Evans may not be related but they have one thing in common – they both holed in one at the same hole when playing in a club competition. The double ace occurred in 2003 at Glynhir Golf Club's third hole which measures 189 yards. Thirty-seven-year-old surveyor Richard, who plays off 7, hit first and made his first hole-in-one in the 15 years he has played the game. His opponent, car worker Mark whose handicap is 12, then followed him in.
● Richard Hall, who plays off 12, and high handicapper Peter McEvoy had never had a hole-in-one until one Saturday night in 2003 at Shandon Park Golf Club in Belfast. Friends since their schooldays they play a lot of golf together so there was much excitement when Hall holed his 5-iron shot for an ace at the 180 yards eighth. Then he challenged McEvoy to match it. And he did!
● Brothers Hanks and Davis Massey were playing a late afternoon practice round at TPC Sawgrass in Florida in 2008 when they came to the par 3 third. Eleven-year-old Hanks was up first and hit a 9-iron

108 yards into the hole. He and his father Scott ran up to the green in wild celebration forgetting that nine-year-old Davis had still to play. When he did he pulled out an 8-iron and also aced.
● Ross Roger and John Downie, two 13-year-olds playing in a foursomes match at the Clober Club in Milngavie near Glasgow, Scotland, made their own little bit of golfing history when they stepped on to the 15th tee and both holed out in one. Ross, teeing up first, watched his ball drop into the hole for his first ace then stepped back and saw John do the same thing.

Three holes-in-one at the same hole in the same game

● During the October monthly medal at Southport & Ainsdale Golf Club on Saturday October 18, 2003, three holes-in-one were achieved at the 153-yard 8th by Stuart Fawcett (5 handicap), Brian Verinder (17 handicap) and junior member Andrew Kent (12 handicap). The players were not playing in the same group.

Holing-in-one – youngest and oldest players

● Elsie McLean, 102, from Chico, California, holed-in-one in April 2007.
● In January 1985 Otto Bucher of Switzerland holed-in-one at the age of 99 on La Manga's 130-yard 12th hole.
● In 2005, Bim Smith, a member of Rochester & Cobham Park Golf Club, Kent, hit a hole-in-one – his fourth – three days before his 91st birthday.
● Bob Hope had a hole-in-one at Palm Springs, California, at the age of 90.
● 76-year-old lady golfer Mrs Felicity Sieghart achieved two holes-in-one when playing in a club Stableford competition at the Aldeburgh club in 2003. Mrs Sieghart aced the 134 yards eighth and the 130 yards 17th – but sadly did not win the competition.
● The youngest player ever to achieve a hole in one is now believed to be Matthew Draper, who was only five when he aced the 122-yard fourth hole at Cherwell Edge, Oxfordshire, in June 1997. He used a wood.
● Six-year-old Tommy Moore aced the 145-yard fourth hole at Woodbrier, West Virginia, in 1968. He had another at the same hole before his seventh birthday.

● Keith Long was just five when he aced on a Mississippi golf course in 1998.

● Five-year-old Eleanor Gamble became one of the youngest to have a hole in one when she made an ace at the Cambridge Lakes club in 2011.

● Alex Evans, aged eight, holed-in-one with a 4-wood at the 136-yard 4th hole at Bromborough, Merseyside, in 1994.

● Nine-year-old Kate Langley from Scotter in Lincolnshire, is believed to have became the youngest girl to score an ace. It is reported that she holed in one at the 134 yards first hole at Forest Pines Beeches in Scunthorpe after having had a lesson from local professional David Edwards. Kate was nine years and 166 days when she hit the ace – 199 days younger than Australian Kathryn Webb who had held the record previously.

● In 2007, 13-year-old Lauren Taylor from Rugby scored two aces and made history at her club. Her first ace was scored on the 145 yard 12th, where she used a seven iron for her shot over the brook whilst playing in a junior medal competition. Her second came during the second round of the 36-hole Junior Championship This time it was achieved on the 100 yard 8th (which plays much harder due to it being all up-hill), using a pitching wedge. From the tee you cannot see what is happening on the green.

## Holing-in-one – miscellaneous incidents

● Chemistry student Jason Bohn, aged 19, of State College, Pennsylvania, supported a charity golf event at Tuscaloosa, Alabama, in 1992 when twelve competitors were invited to try to hole-in-one at the 135-yard second hole for a special prize covered by insurance. One attempt only was allowed. Bohn succeeded and was offered US$1m (paid at the rate of $5,000 a month for the next 20 years) at the cost of losing his amateur status. He took the money.

● The late Harry Vardon, who scored the greatest number of victories in The Open Championship, only once did a hole-in-one. That was in 1903 at Mundesley, Norfolk, where Vardon was convalescing from a long illness.

● In a guest day at Rochford Hundred, Essex, in 1994, there were holes-in-one at all the par threes. First Paul Cairns, of Langdon Hills, holed a 4-iron at the 205-yard 15th, next Paul Francis, a member of the home club, sank a 7-iron at the 156-yard seventh and finally Jim Crabb, of Three Rivers, holed a 9-iron at the 136-yard 11th.

● In April 1988, Mary Anderson, a bio-chemistry student at Trinity College, Dublin, holed-in-one at the 290-yard 6th hole at Island GC, Co Dublin.

● In April 1984 Joseph McCaffrey and his son, Gordon, each holed-in-one in the Spring Medal at the 164-yard 12th hole at Vale of Leven Club, Dunbartonshire.

● In 1977, 14-year-old Gillian Field after a series of lessons holed-in-one at the 10th hole at Moor Place GC in her first round of golf.

● When he holed-in-one at the second hole in a match against D. Graham in the 1979 Suntory World Match Play at Wentworth, Japanese professional Isao

Aoki won himself a Bovis home at Gleneagles worth, inclusive of furnishings, £55,000. Brian Barnes has aced the short 10th and Thomas Bjørn won a car when he aced the short 14th in 2003.

● On the morning after being elected captain for 1973 of the Norwich GC, J.S. Murray hit his first shot as captain straight into the hole at the 169-yard 1st hole.

● At Nuneaton GC in 1999 the men's captain and the ladies' captain both holed-in-one during their captaincies.

● Using the same club and ball, 11-handicap left-hander Christopher Smyth holed-in-one at the 2nd hole (170 yards) in two consecutive medal competitions at Headfort GC, Co. Meath, in January, 1976.

● Playing over Rickmansworth course at Easter, 1960, Mrs A.E. (Paddy) Martin achieved a remarkable sequence of aces. On Good Friday she sank her tee shot at the 3rd hole (125 yards). The next day, using the same ball and the same 8-iron, at the same hole, she scored another one. And on the Monday (same ball, same club, same hole) she again holed out from the tee.

● At Barton-on-Sea in February 1989 Mrs Dorothy Huntley-Flindt, aged 91, holed-in-one at the par-3 13th. The following day Mr John Chape, a fellow member in his 80s, holed the par- 3 5th in one.

● In 1995 Roy Marsland of Ratho Park, Edinburgh, had three holes-in-one in nine days: at Prestonfield's 5th, at Ratho Park's 3rd and at Sandilands' 2nd.

● Michael Monk, age 82, a member of Tandridge Golf Club, Surrey, waited until 1992 to record his first hole-in-one. It continued a run of rare successes for his family. In the previous 12 months, Mr Monk's daughter, Elizabeth, 52, daughter-in-law, Celia, 48, and grandson, Jeremy, 16, had all holed-in-one on the same course.

● Lou Holloway, a left-hander, recorded his second hole-in-one at the Mount Derby course in New Zealand 13 years after acing the same hole while playing right-handed.

● Ryan Procop, an American schoolboy, holed-in-one at a 168-yard par 3 at Glen Eagles GC, Ohio, with a putter. He confessed that he was so disgusted with himself after a 12 on the previous hole that he just grabbed his putter and hit from the tee.

● Ernie and Shirley Marsden, of Warwick Golf Club, are believed in 1993 to have equalled the record for holes-in-one by a married couple. Each has had three, as have another English couple, Mr and Mrs B.E. Simmonds.

● Russell Pughe, a 12-handicapper from Nottinghamshire, holed-in-one twice in three days at the 274-yard par-4 18th hole at Sidmouth in Devon in 1998. The hole has a blind tee shot.

● Robert Looney aced the 170 yards 13th at the Thorny Lea Golf Club in Brockton, Massachussetts, 30 years after his father made a hole-in-one at the same hole.

● The odds on the chances of two players having a hole in one when playing together are long but it happened to former club captain Robert Smallwood, a 58-year-old retired IBM manager, and current captain Mike Wheeler, a 57-year-old retired financial consultant, when they went out for a round at Irvine Golf Club in Ayrshire in 2005. Playing in the rain, Mr Smallwood, using a driver, had his ace at the 289 yards fourth before Mr Wheeler holed in one at the 279 yards fifth.

● Texan blind golfer Charles Adams, sank his tee shot on the 102-yard 14th hole at Stone Creek Golf Club, Oregon City, Oregon, on October 4, 2006, during the US Blind Golf Association National Championship, the first hole-in-one in the 61-year history of the tournament.

● Blind golfer Sheila Drummond, a member of the US Blind Golf Association, is believed to be the only blind woman golfer to have holed-in-one. Sheila's feat was accomplished in August 2007 at the 144-yard par-3 at Mahoning Valley CC in Lehighton, PA.

● Jim Gales, who was awarded the MBE for his services to blind golf, scored a hole in one in 2010 at Wellsgreen, Fife, while practising in the Scottish Pan-Disability Open. Other blind golfers who have scored aces include Jan Dinsdale (NIR), Joel Ludvicek (USA) and Zohar Sharon (ISR).

● Bob Taylor, a Leicestershire County player, achieved what many would consider the impossible when he holed in one at the same hole on three successive days at the Hunstanton Club. Playing in the Eastern Counties Foursomes in 1974 he aced the 188 yards 16th using first a 1-iron and then a 6-iron on the next two occasions.

## Challenge matches

One of the first recorded professional challenge matches was in 1843 when Allan Robertson beat Willie Dunn in a 20-round match at St Andrews over 360 holes by 2 rounds and 1 to play. Thereafter until about 1905 many matches are recorded, some for up to £200 a side – a considerable sum for the time. The Morrises, the Dunns and the Parks were the main protagonists until Vardon, Braid and Taylor took over in the 1890s. Often matches were on a home-and-away basis over 72 holes or more, with many spectators; Vardon and Willie Park Jr attracted over 10,000 at North Berwick in 1899.

Between the wars Walter Hagen, Archie Compston, Henry Cotton and Bobby Locke all played several such matches. Compston surprisingly beat Hagen by 18 up and 17 to play at Moor Park in 1928; yet typically Hagen went on to win The Open the following week at Sandwich. Cotton played classic golf at Walton Heath in 1937 when he beat Densmore Shute for £500-a-side at Walton Heath by 6 and 5 over 72 holes.

## Curious and large wagers

*(See also bets recorded under Cross-Country Matches and in Challenge Matches)*

● In The Royal and Ancient Golf Club minutes an entry on 3rd November, 1820 was made in the following terms:

*Sir David Moncrieffe, Bart, of Moncrieffe, backs his life against the life of John Whyte-Melville, Esq, of Strathkinnes, for a new silver club as a present to the St Andrews Golf Club, the price of the club to be paid by the survivor and the arms of the parties to be engraved on the club, and the present bet inscribed on it. No balls to be attached to it. In testimony of which this bet is subscribed by the parties thereto.*

Thirteen years later, Mr Whyte-Melville, in a feeling and appropriate speech, expressed his deep regret at the lamented death of Sir David Moncrieffe, one of the most distinguished and zealous supporters of the club. Whyte-Melville, while lamenting the cause that led to it, had pleasure in fulfilling the duty imposed upon him by the bet, and accordingly delivered to the captain the silver putter. Whyte-Melville in 1883 was elected captain of the club a second time; he died in his eighty-sixth year in July, 1883, before he could take office and the captaincy remained vacant for a year. His portrait hangs in The Royal and Ancient clubhouse is one of the finest and most distinguished pictures in the smoking room.

● In 1914 Francis Ouimet, who in the previous autumn had won the American Open Championship after a triangular tie with Harry Vardon and Ted Ray, came to Great Britain with Jerome D. Travers, the holder of the American amateur title, to compete in the British Amateur Championship at Sandwich. An American syndicate took a bet of £30,000 to £10,000 that one or other of the two United States champions would be the winner. It only took two rounds to decide the bet against the Americans. Ouimet was beaten by a then quite unknown player, H.S. Tubbs, while Travers was defeated by Charles Palmer, who was 56 years of age at the time.

● In 1907 John Ball for a wager undertook to go round Hoylake during a dense fog in under 90, in not more than two and a quarter hours and without losing a ball. Ball played with a black ball, went round in 81, and also beat the time.

● The late Ben Sayers, for a wager, played the 18 holes of the Burgess Society course scoring a four at every hole. Sayers was about to start against an American, when his opponent asked him what he could do the course in. *Fours* replied Sayers, meaning 72, or an average of 4s for the round. A bet was made, then the American added, *Remember a three or a five is not a four.* There were eight bogey 5s and two 3s on the Burgess course at the time Old Ben achieved his feat.

## Feats of endurance

*Although golf is not a game where endurance, in the ordinary sense in which the term is employed in sport, is required, there are several instances of feats on the links which demanded great physical exertion.*

● Four British golfers, Simon Gard, Nick Harley, Patrick Maxwell and his brother Alistair Maxwell, completed 14 rounds in one day at Iceland's Akureyri Golf Club, the most northern 18-hole course in the world, during June 1991 when there was 24-hour daylight. It was claimed a record and £10,000 was raised for charity.

● In 1971 during a 24-hour period from 6 pm on 27th November until 5.15 pm on 28th November, Ian Colston completed 401 holes over the 6,061 yards Bendigo course, Victoria, Australia. Colston was a top marathon athlete but was not a golfer. However prior to his golfing marathon he took some lessons and became adept with a 6-iron, the only club he used throughout the 401 holes. The only assistance Colston had was a team of harriers to carry his 6-iron and look for his ball, and a band of motorcyclists who provided light during the night. This is, as far as is known, the greatest number of holes played in 24 hours on foot on a full-size course.

● In 1934 Col Bill Farnham played 376 holes in 24 hours 10 minutes at the Guildford Lake Course, Guildford, Connecticut, using only a mashie and a putter.

● To raise funds for extending the Skipton GC course from 12 to 18 holes, the club professional, 24-year-old Graham Webster, played 277 holes in the hours of daylight on Monday 20th June, 1977. Playing with nothing longer than a 5-iron he averaged 81 per 18-hole round. Included in his marathon was a hole-in-one.

● Michael Moore, a 7 handicap 26-year-old member of Okehampton GC, completed on foot 15 rounds 6 holes (276 holes) there on Sunday, 25th June, 1972, in the hours of daylight. He started at 4.15 am and stopped at 9.15 pm. The distance covered was estimated at 56 miles.

● On 21st June, 1976, 5-handicapper Sandy Small played 15 rounds (270 holes) over his home course Cosby GC, length 6,128 yards, to raise money for the Society of Physically Handicapped Children. Using only a 5-iron, 9-iron and putter, Small started at 4.10 am and completed his 270th hole at 10.39 pm with the aid of car headlamps. His fastest round was his first (40 minutes) and slowest his last (82 minutes). His best round of 76 was achieved in the second round.

● During the weekend of 20th–21st June, 1970, Peter Chambers of Yorkshire completed over 14 rounds of golf over the Scarborough South Cliff course. In a non-stop marathon lasting just under 24 hours, Chambers played 257 holes in 1,168 strokes, an average of 84.4 strokes per round.

● Bruce Sutherland, on the Craiglockhart Links, Edinburgh, started at 8.15 pm on 21st June, 1927, and played almost continuously until 7.30 pm on 22nd June, 1927. During the night four caddies with acetylene lamps lit the way, and lost balls were reduced to a minimum. He completed fourteen rounds. Mr Sutherland, who was a physical culture teacher, never recovered from the physical strain and died a few years later.

● Sidney Gleave, motorcycle racer, and Ernest Smith, golf professional at Davyhulme Club, Manchester, on 12th June, 1939, played five rounds of golf in five different countries – Scotland, Ireland, Isle of Man, England and Wales. Smith had to play the five rounds under 80 in one day to win the £100 wager. They travelled by plane, and the following was their programme:

Start 3.40a.m. at Prestwick St Nicholas (Scotland), finished 1 hour 35 minutes later on 70.
2nd Course – Bangor, Ireland. Started at 7.15 a.m. and took 1 hour 30 minutes to finish on 76.
3rd Course – Castletown, Isle of Man. Started 10.15 am, scored 76 in 1 hour 40 minutes.
4th Course – Blackpool, Stanley Park, England. Started at 1.30 pm and scored 72 in 1 hour 55 minutes.
5th Course – Hawarden, Wales, started at 6 pm and finished 2 hours 15 minutes later with a score of 72.

● On 19th June, 1995, Ian Botham, the former England cricketer, played four rounds of golf in Ireland, Wales, Scotland and England. His playing companions were Gary Price, the professional at Branston, and Tony Wright, owner of Craythorne, Burton-on-Trent, where the last 18 holes were completed. The other courses were St Margaret's, Anglesey and Dumfries & Galloway. The first round began at 4.30 am and the last was completed at 8.30 pm.

● On Wednesday, 3rd July, 1974, E.S. Wilson, Whitehead, Co. Antrim and Dr G.W. Donaldson, Newry, Co. Down, played a nine-hole match in each of seven countries in the one day. The first 9 holes was at La Moye (Channel Islands) followed by Hawarden (Wales), Chester (England), Turnberry (Scotland), Castletown (Isle of Man), Dundalk (Eire) and Warrenpoint (N Ireland). They started their first round at 4.25 am and their last round at 9.25 pm. Wilson piloted his own plane throughout.

● In June 1986 to raise money for the upkeep of his medieval church, the Rector of Mark with Allerton, Somerset, the Rev Michael Pavey, played a sponsored 18 holes on 18 different courses in the Bath & Wells Diocese. With his partner, the well-known broadcaster on music, Antony Hopkins, they played the 1st at Minehead at 5.55 am and finished playing the 18th at Burnham and Berrow at 6.05 pm. They covered 240 miles in the "round" including the distances to reach the correct tee for the "next" hole on each course. Par for the "round" was 70. Together the pair raised £10,500 for the church.

● To raise funds for the Marlborough Club's centenary year (1988), Laurence Ross, the Club professional, in June 1987, played eight rounds in 12 hours. Against a par of 72, he completed the 576 holes in 3 under par, playing from back tees and walking all the way.

● As part of the 1992 Centenary Celebrations of the Royal Cinque Ports Golf Club at Deal, Kent, and to support charity, a six-handicap member, John Brazell, played all 37 royal courses in Britain and Ireland in 17 days. He won 22 matches, halved three, lost 12; hit 2,834 shots for an average score of 76.6; lost 11 balls and made 62 birdies. The aim was to raise £30,000 for Leukaemia Research and the Spastics Society.

● To raise more than £500 for the Guide Dogs for the Blind charity in the summer of 1992, Mrs Cheryle Power, a member of the Langley Park Golf Club,

Beckenham, Kent, played 100 holes in a day – starting at 5 am and finishing at 8.45 pm.

● David Steele, a former European Tour player, completed 17½ rounds, 315 holes, between 6 am and 9.45 pm in 1993 at the San Roque club near Gibraltar in a total of 1,291 shots. Steele was assisted by a caddie cart and raised £15,000 for charity.

● In 2005 Bernard Wood, a member of Rossendale Golf Club, played all the 18-hole courses in Scotland – 377 in all – to raise money for the Kirsty Appeal which supports the Frances House Children's Hospice in Manchester.

## Fastest rounds

● Dick Kimbrough, 41, completed a round on foot on 8th August, 1972, at North Platte CC, Nebraska (6,068 yards) in 30 minutes 10 seconds. He carried only a 3-iron.

● At Mowbray Course, Cape Town, November 1931, Len Richardson, who had represented South Africa in the Olympic Games, played a round which measured 6,248 yards in 31 minutes 22 seconds.

● The women's all-time record for the fastest round played on a course of at least 5,600 yards is held by Sue Ledger, 20, who completed the East Berks course in 38 minutes 8 seconds, beating the previous record by 17 minutes.

● In April, 1934, after attending a wedding in Bournemouth, Hants, Captain Gerald Moxom hurried to his club, West Hill in Surrey, to play in the captain's prize competition. With daylight fading and still dressed in his morning suit, he went round in 65 minutes and won the competition with a net 71 into the bargain.

● On 14th June, 1922, Jock Hutchison and Joe Kirkwood (AUS) played round the Old Course at St Andrews in 1 hour 20 minutes. Hutchison, out in 37, led by three holes at the ninth and won by 4 and 3.

● Fastest rounds can also take another form – the time taken for a ball to be propelled round 18 holes. The fastest known round of this type is 8 minutes 53.8 seconds on 25th August, 1979 by 42 members at Ridgemount CC Rochester, New York, a course measuring 6,161 yards. The Rules of Golf were observed but a ball was available on each tee; to be driven off the instant the ball had been holed at the preceding hole.

● The fastest round with the same ball took place in January 1992 at the Paradise Golf Club, Arizona. It took only 11 minutes 24 seconds; 91 golfers being positioned around the course ready to hit the ball as soon as it came to rest and then throwing the ball from green to tee.

● In 1992 John Daly and Mark Calcavecchia were both fined by the USPGA Tour for playing the final round of the Players' Championship in Florida in 123 minutes. Daly scored 80, Calcavecchia 81.

## Curious scoring

● C.W. Allen of Leek Golf Club chipped-in four times in a round in which he was partnered by K. Brint against G. Davies and R. Hollins. The shortest chip was a yard, the longest 20 yards.

● Tony Blackwell, playing off a handicap of four, broke the course record at Bull Bay, Anglesey, by four strokes when he had a gross 60 (net 56) in winning the club's town trophy in 1996. The course measured 6,217 yards.

● In the third round of the 1994 Volvo PGA Championship at Wentworth, Des Smyth, of Ireland, made birdie twos at each of the four short holes, the 2nd, 5th, 10th and 14th. He also had a two at the second hole in the fourth round.

● Also at Wentworth, in the 1994 World Match Play Championship, Seve Ballesteros had seven successive twos at the short holes – and still lost his quarter-final against Ernie Els.

● R.H. Corbett, playing in the semi-final of the Tangye Cup at Mullion in 1916, did a score of 27. The remarkable part of Corbett's score was that it was made up of nine successive 3s, bogey being 5, 3, 4, 4, 5, 3, 4, 4, 3.

● At Little Chalfont in June 1985 Adrian Donkersley played six successive holes in 6, 5, 4, 3, 2, 1 from the 9th to the 14th holes against a par of 4, 4, 3, 4, 4, 3.

● On 2nd September, 1920, playing over Torphin, near Edinburgh, William Ingle did the first five holes in 1, 2, 3, 4, 5.

● In the summer of 1970, Keith McMillan, on holiday at Cullen, had a remarkable series of 1, 2, 3, 4, 5 at the 11th to the 15th holes.

● Marc Osborne was only 14 years of age when he equalled the Betchworth Park amateur course record with a 66 in July, 1993. He was playing in the Mortimer Cup, a 36-hole medal competition, and had at the time a handicap of 6.8.

● Playing at Addington Palace, July, 1934, Ronald Jones, a member of Hendon Club, holed five consecutive holes in 5, 4, 3, 2, 1.

● Harry Dunderdale of Lincoln GC scored 5, 4, 3, 2, 1 in five consecutive holes during the first round of his club championship in 1978. The hole-in-one was the 7th, measuring 294 yards.

● At the Open Amateur Tournament of the Royal Ashdown Forest in 1936 Bobby Locke in his morning round had a score of 72, accomplishing every hole in 4.

● George Stewart of Cupar had a four at every hole over the Queen's course at Gleneagles despite forgetting to change into his golf shoes and therefore still wearing his street shoes.

● Nick Faldo scored par figures at all 18 holes in the final round of the 1987 Open Championship at Muirfield to win the title.

● During the Colts Championship at Knowle Golf Club, Bristol, Chris Newman (Cotswold Hills) scored eight consecutive 3s with birdies at four of the holes.

● At the Toft Hotel Golf Club captain's day event L. Heffernan had an ace, D. Patrick a 2, R. Barnett a 3 and D. Heffernan a 4 at the 240 yard par-4 ninth.

● In the European Club Championship played at the Parco de Medici Club in Rome in 1998, Belgian Dimitri van Hauwaert from Royal Antwerp had an albatross 2, Norwegian Marius Bjornstad from Oslo an eagle 3 and Scotsman Andrew Hogg from Turriff a birdie 4 at the 486 metre par-5 eighth hole.

● Henry Cotton told of one of the most extra-ordinary scoring feats ever. With some other professionals he was at Sestrieres in the 30s for the Italian Open Championship and Joe Ezar, a colourful character in those days on both sides of the Atlantic, accepted a wager from a club official – 1,000 lira for a 66 to break the course record; 2,000 for a 65; and 4,000 for a 64. *I'll do 64*, said Ezar, and proceeded to jot down the hole-by-hole score figures he would do next day for that total. With the exception of the ninth and tenth holes where his predicted score was 3, 4 and the actual score was 4, 3, he accomplished this amazing feat exactly as nominated.

● Earle F. Wilson from Brewerton, Alabama, has had an ace, an albatross and has fired eight birdies in a row.

## High scores

● In the qualifying competition at Formby for the 1976 Open Championship, Maurice Flitcroft, a 46-year-old crane driver from Barrow-in-Furness, took 121 strokes for the first round and then withdrew saying, *I have no chance of qualifying*. Flitcroft entered as a professional but had never before played 18 holes. He had taken the game up 18 months previously but, as he was not a member of a club, had been limited to practising on a local beach. His round was made up thus: 7, 5, 6, 6, 6, 6, 12, 6, 7-61; 11, 5, 6, 8, 4, 9, 5, 7, 5-60, total 121. After his round Flitcroft said, "I've made a lot of progress in the last few months and I'm sorry I did not do better. I was trying too hard at the beginning but began to put things together at the end of the round". R&A officials, who were not amused by the bogus professional's efforts, refunded the £30 entry money to Flitcroft's two fellow-competitors. Flitcroft has since tried to qualify for The Open under assumed names: Gerard Hoppy from Switzerland and Beau Jolley (as in the wine)!

● Playing in the qualifying rounds of the 1965 Open Championship at Southport, an American self-styled professional entrant from Milwaukee, Walter Danecki, achieved the inglorious feat of scoring a total of 221 strokes for 36 holes, 81 over par. His first round over the Hillside course was 108, followed by a second round of 113. Walter, who afterwards admitted he felt *a little discouraged and sad*, declared that he entered because he was *after the money*.

● The highest individual scoring ever known in the rounds connected with The Open Championship occurred at Muirfield, 1935, when a Scottish professional started 7, 10, 5, 10, and took 65 to reach the 9th hole. Another 10 came at the 11th and the player decided to retire at the 12th hole. There he was in a bunker, and after playing four shots he had not regained the fairway.

● In 1883 in The Open Championship at Musselburgh, Willie Fernie, the winner, had a 10, the only time double figures appeared on the card of The Open Champion of the year. Fernie won after a tie with Bob Ferguson, and his score for the last hole in the tie was 2. He holed from just off the green to win by one stroke.

● In the French Open at St Cloud, in 1968, Brian Barnes took 15 for the short 8th hole in the second round. After missing putts at which he hurriedly snatched while the ball was moving he penalised himself further by standing astride the line of a putt. The amazing result was that he actually took 12 strokes from about three feet from the hole. The highest scores on the European Tour were also recorded in the French Open. Philippe Porquier had a 20 at La Baule in 1978 and Ian Woosnam a 16 at La Boulie in 1986.

● US professional Dave Hill 6-putted the fifth green at Oakmont in the 1962 US Open Championship.

● Many high scores have been made at the Road Hole at St Andrews. Davie Ayton, on one occasion, was coming in a certain winner of The Open Championship when he got on the road and took 11. In 1921, at The Open Championship, one professional took 13. In 1923, competing for the Autumn Medal of The Royal and Ancient, J.B. Anderson required a five and a four to win the second award, but he took 13 at the Road Hole. Anderson was close to the green in two, was twice in the bunkers in the face of the green, and once on the road. In 1935, R.H. Oppenheimer tied for the Royal Medal (the first award) in the Autumn Meeting of The Royal and Ancient. On the play-off he was one stroke behind Captain Aitken when they stood on the 17th tee. Oppenheimer drove three balls out of bounds and eventually took 11 to the Road Hole.

● In the first Open Championship at Prestwick in 1860 a competitor took 21, the highest score for one hole ever recorded in this event. The record is preserved in the archives of the Prestwick Golf Club, where the championship was founded.

"I wish he'd hurry up and sink this ... I'd like to be home in time for Christmas"

● In the first round of the 1980 US Masters, Tom Weiskopf hit his ball into the water hazard in front of the par-3 12th hole five times and scored 13 for the hole.

● British professional Mark James scored 111 in the second round of the 1978 Italian Open. He played the closing holes with only his right hand due to an injury to his left hand.

● In the 1927 Shawnee Open, Tommy Armour took 23 strokes to the 17th hole. Armour had won the American Open Championship a week earlier. In an effort to play the hole in a particular way, Armour hooked ball after ball out of bounds and finished with a 21 on the card. There was some doubt about the accuracy of this figure and on reaching the clubhouse Armour stated that it should be 23. This is the highest score by a professional in a tournament.

## Freak matches

● In 1912, the late Harry Dearth, an eminent vocalist, attired in a complete suit of heavy armour, played a match at Bushey Hall. He was beaten 2 and 1.

● Captain Pennington took part in a match *from the air* against A.J. Young, the professional at Sonning. Captain Pennington, with 80 golf balls in the locker of his machine, had to find the Sonning greens by dropping the balls as he circled over the course. The balls were covered in white cloth to ensure that they did not bounce once they struck the ground. The airman completed the course in 40 minutes, taking 29 *strokes*, while Young occupied two hours for his round of 68. Captain Pennington was eventually killed in an air crash in 1933.

● In 1914, at the start of the First World War, J.N. Farrar, a native of Hoylake, was stationed at Royston, Herts. A bet was made of 10-1 that he would not go round Royston under 100 strokes, equipped in full infantry marching order, water bottle, full field kit and haversack. Farrar went round in 94. At the camp were several golfers, including professionals, who tried the same feat but failed.

"I don't think the greenkeepers will be overjoyed at his choice of buggy"

● In April 1924, at Littlehampton, Harry Rowntree, an amateur golfer, played the better ball of Edward Ray and George Duncan, receiving an allowance of 150 yards to use as he required during the round. Rowntree won by 6 and 5 and had used only 50 yards 2 feet of his handicap. At one hole Duncan had a two – Rowntree, who was 25 yards from the hole, took this distance from his handicap and won the hole in

one. Ray (died 1945) afterwards declared that, conceding a handicap of one yard per round, he could win every championship in the world. And he might, when reckoning is taken of the number of times a putt just stops an inch or two or how much difference to a shot three inches will make for the lie of the ball, either in a bunker or on the fairway. Many single matches on the same system have been played. An 18 handicap player opposed to a scratch player should make a close match with an allowance of 50 yards.

● The first known instance of a golf match by telephone occurred in 1957, when the Cotswold Hills Golf Club, Cheltenham, England, won a golf tournament against the Cheltenham Golf Club, Melbourne, Australia, by six strokes. A large crowd assembled at the English club to wait for the 12,000 miles telephone call from Australia. The match had been played at the suggestion of a former member of the Cotswold Hills Club, Harry Davies, and was open to every member of the two clubs. The result of the match was decided on the aggregate of the eight best scores on each side and the English club won by 564 strokes to 570.

## Golf matches against other sports

● H.H. Hilton and Percy Ashworth, many times racket champion, contested a driving match, the former driving a golf ball with a driver, and the latter a racket ball with a racket. Best distances: Against breeze – Golfer 182 yards; Racket player 125 yards. Down wind – Golfer 230 yards; Racket player 140 yards. Afterwards Ashworth hit a golf ball with the racket and got a greater distance than with the racket ball, but was still a long way behind the ball driven by Hilton.

● In December, 1913, F.M.A. Webster, of the London Athletic Club, and Dora Roberts, with javelins, played a match with the late Harry Vardon and Mrs Gordon Robertson, who used the regulation clubs and golf balls. The golfers conceded two-thirds in the matter of distance, and they won by 5 up and 4 to play in a contest of 18 holes. The javelin throwers had a mark of two feet square in which to *hole out* while the golfers had to get their ball into the ordinary golf hole. Mr Webster's best throw was one of 160 feet.

● In 1913, at Wellington, Shropshire, a match between a golfer and a fisherman casting a 2½ oz weight was played. The golfer, Rupert May, took 87; the fisherman J.J.D. Mackinlay, in difficulty because of his short casts, 102. His longest cast, 105 yards, was within 12 yards of the world record at the time, held by French angler, Decautelle. When within a rod's length of a hole he ran the weight to the rod end and dropped into the hole. Five times he broke his line, and was allowed another shot without penalty.

● In 1954, at the Southbroom Club, South Africa, a match over 9 holes was played between an archer and a fisherman against two golfers. The participants were all champions of their own sphere and consisted of Vernon Adams (archer), Dennis Burd (fisherman), Jeanette Wahl (champion of Southbroom and Port Shepstone), and Ron Burd (professional at

Southbroom). The conditions were that the archer had holed out when his arrows struck a small leather bag placed on the green beside the hole and in the event of his placing his approach shot within a bow's length of the pin he was deemed to have 1-putted. The fisherman, to achieve a 1-putt, had to land his sinker within a rod's length of the pin. The two golfers were ahead for brief spells, but it was the opposition who led at the deciding 9th hole where *Robin Hood* played a perfect approach for a birdie.

● An *Across England* combined match was begun on 11th October, 1965, by four golfers and two archers from Crowborough Beacon Golf Club, Sussex, accompanied by *Penny*, a white Alsatian dog, whose duty it was to find lost balls. They teed off from Carlisle Castle via Hadrian's Wall, the Pennine Way, finally holing out in the 18th hole at Newcastle United GC in 612 teed shots. Casualties included 110 lost golf balls and 19 lost or broken arrows. The match took 5½ days, and the distance travelled was about 60 miles. The golfers were Miss P. Ward, K. Meaney, K. Ashdown and C.A. Macey; the archers were W.H. Hulme and T. Scott. The first arrow was fired from the battlements of Carlisle Castle, a distance of nearly 300 yards, by Cumberland Champion R. Willis, who also fired the second arrow right across the River Eden. R. Clough, president of Newcastle United GC, holed the last two putts. The match was in aid of *Guide Dogs for the Blind* and *Friends of Crowborough Hospital.*

● Several matches have taken place between a golfer on the one side and an archer on the other. The wielder of the bow and arrow has nearly always proved the victor. In 1953 at Kirkhill Golf Course, Lanarkshire, five archers beat six golfers by two games to one. There were two special rules for the match; when an archer's arrow landed six feet from the hole or the golfer's ball three feet from the hole, they were counted as holed. When the arrows landed in bunkers or in the rough, archers lifted their arrow and added a stroke. The sixth archer in this match called off and one archer shot two arrows from each of the 18 tees.

"This doesn't appear to be covered by the Rules"

## Cross-country matches

● Taking 1 year, 114 days, Floyd Rood golfed his way from coast to coast across the United States. He took 114,737 shots including 3,511 penalty shots for the 3,397 mile course.

● Two Californian teenagers, Bob Aube (17) and Phil Marrone (18) went on a golfing safari in 1974 from San Francisco to Los Angeles, a trip of over 500 miles lasting 16 days. The first six days they played alongside motorways. Over 1,000 balls were used.

● In 1830, the Gold Medal winner of The Royal and Ancient backed himself for 10 sovereigns to drive from the 1st hole at St Andrews to the toll bar at Cupar, distance nine miles, in 200 teed shots. He won easily.

● In 1848, two Edinburgh golfers played a match from Bruntsfield Links to the top of Arthur's Seat – an eminence overlooking the Scottish capital, 822 feet above sea level.

● On a winter's day in 1898, Freddie Tait backed himself to play a gutta ball in 40 teed shots from Royal St George's Clubhouse, Sandwich, to the Cinque Ports Club, Deal. He was to hole out by hitting any part of the Deal Clubhouse. The distance as the crow flies was three miles. The redoubtable Tait holed out with his 32nd shot, so effectively that the ball went through a window.

● In 1900 three members of the Hackensack (NJ) Club played a game of four-and-a-half hours over an extemporised course six miles long, which stretched from Hackensack to Paterson. Despite rain, cornfields, and wide streams, the three golfers – J.W. Hauleebeek, Dr E.R. Pfaare, and Eugene Crassons – completed the round, the first and the last named taking 305 strokes each, and Dr Pfaare 327 strokes. The players used only two clubs, the mashie and the cleek.

● On 3rd December, 1920, P. Rupert Phillips and W. Raymond Thomas teed up on the first tee of the Radyr Golf Club and played to the last hole at Southerndown. The distance as the crow flies was 15½ miles, but circumventing swamps, woods, and plough, they covered, approximately, 20 miles. The wager was that they would not do the hole in 1,000 strokes, but they holed out at their 608th stroke two days later. They carried large ordnance maps.

● On 12th March, 1921, A. Stanley Turner, Macclesfield, played from his house to the Cat and Fiddle Inn, five miles distance, in 64 strokes. The route was broken and hilly with a rise of nearly 1,000 feet. Turner was allowed to tee up within two club lengths after each shot and the wagering was 6-4 against his doing the distance in 170 strokes.

● In 1919, a golfer drove a ball from Piccadilly Circus and, proceeding via the Strand, Fleet Street and Ludgate Hill, *holed out* at the Royal Exchange, London. The player drove off at 8 am on a Sunday, a time when the usually thronged thoroughfares were deserted.

● On 23rd April, 1939, Richard Sutton, a London stockbroker, played from Tower Bridge, London, to

White's Club, St James's Street, in 142 strokes. The bet was he would not do *the course* in under 200 shots. Sutton used a putter, crossed the Thames at Southwark Bridge, and hit the ball short distances to keep out of trouble.

● Golfers produced the most original event in Ireland's three-week national festival of An Tostal, in 1953 – a cross-country competition with an advertised £1,000,000 for the man who could hole out in one. The 150 golfers drove off from the first tee at Kildare Club to hole out eventually on the 18th green, five miles away, on the nearby Curragh course, a distance of 8,800 yards. The unusual hazards to be negotiated included the main Dublin-Cork railway line and highway, the Curragh Racecourse, hoofprints left by Irish thoroughbred racehorses out exercising on the plains from nearby stables, army tank tracks and about 150 telephone lines. The Golden Ball Trophy, which is played for annually – a standard size golf ball in gold, mounted on a black marble pillar beside the silver figure of a golfer on a green marble base, designed by Captain Maurice Cogan, Army GHQ, Dublin – was for the best gross. And it went to one of the longest hitters in international golf – Amateur Champion, Irish internationalist and British Walker Cup player Joe Carr, with the remarkable score of 52.

● In 1961, as a University Charities Week stunt, four Aberdeen University students set out to golf their way up Ben Nevis (4,406 feet). About half-way up, after losing 63 balls and expending 659 strokes, the quartet conceded victory to Britain's highest mountain.

● Among several cross-country golfing exploits, one of the most arduous was faced by Iain Williamson and Tony Kent, who teed off from Cained Point on the summit of Fairfield in the Lake District. With the hole cut in the lawn of the Bishop of Carlisle's home at Rydal Park, it measured 7,200 yards and passed through the summits of Great Rigg Mann, Heron Pike and Nab Scar, descending altogether 1,900 feet. Eight balls were lost and the two golfers holed out in a combined total of 303 strokes.

● In 2011, Trevor Sandford from Bearsted in Kent played golf on each of  the 31 days of August on 31 different courses close to the 31 junctions of the M25 motorway. During Trevor's feat, in which he raised over £8,000 for Cancer Research UK, he walked 210 miles and took 2,789 strokes.

## Long-lived golfers

● James Priddy, aged 80, played in the Seniors' Open at his home club, Weston-super-Mare, Avon, on 27th June, 1990, and scored a gross 70 to beat his age by ten shots.

● The oldest golfer who ever lived is believed to have been Arthur Thompson of British Columbia, Canada. He equalled his age when 103 at Uplands GC, a course of over 6,000 yards. He died two years later.

● Nathaniel Vickers celebrated his 103rd birthday on Sunday, 9th October, 1949, and died the following day. He was the oldest member of the United States Senior Golf Association and until 1942 he competed regularly in their events and won many trophies in the various age divisions. When 100 years old, he apologised for being able to play only nine holes a day. Vickers predicted he would live until 103 and he died a few hours after he had celebrated his birthday.

● American George Miller, who died in 1979 aged 102, played regularly when 100 years old.

● In 1999 94-year-old Mr W. Seneviratne, a retired schoolmaster who lived and worked in Malaysia, was still practising every day and regularly competing in medal competitions at the Royal Colombo Golf Club which was founded in 1879.

● Bim Smith, a member of Rochester & Cobham Park Golf Club, Kent, achieved a hole-in-one three days before his 91st birthday.

● Phyllis Tidmarsh, aged 90, won a Stableford competition at Saltford Golf Club, near Bath, when she returned 42 points. Her handicap was cut from 28 to 27.

● George Swanwick, a member of Wallasey, celebrated his 90th birthday with a lunch at the club on 1st April, 1971. He played golf several times a week, carrying his own clubs, and had holed-in-one at the ages of 75 and 85. His ambition was to complete the sequence aged 95 ... but he died in 1973 aged 92.

● The 10th Earl of Wemyss played a round on his 92nd birthday, in 1910, at Craigielaw. At the age of 87 the Earl was partnered by Harry Vardon in a match at Kilspindie, the golf course on his East Lothian estate at Gosford. After playing his ball the venerable earl mounted a pony and rode to the next shot. He died on 30th June, 1914.

● F.L. Callender, aged 78, in September 1932, played nine consecutive rounds in the Jubilee Vase, St Andrews. He was defeated in the ninth, the final round, by 4 and 2. Callender's handicap was 12. This is the best known achievement of a septuagenarian in golf.

● George Evans shot a remarkable one over par 71 at Brockenhurst Manor – remarkable because Mr Evans was 87 at the time. Playing with him that day was Hampshire, Isle of Wight and Channel Islands President John Nettell and former Ferndown pro Doug Sewell. "It's good to shoot a score under your age, but when its 16 shots better than must be a record", said Mr Nettell. Mr Evans qualified for four opens while professional at West Hill, Surrey.

● Bernard Matthews, aged 82, of Banstead Downs Club, handicap 6, holed the course in 72 gross in August 1988. A week later he holed it in 70, twelve shots below his age. He came back in 31, finishing 4, 3, 3, 2, 3, against a par of 5, 4, 3, 3, 4. Mr Matthews's eclectic score at his Club is 37, or one over 2's.

## Playing in the dark

*On numerous occasions it has been necessary to hold lamps, lighted candles, or torches at holes in order that players might finish a competition. Large entries, slow play, early darkness and an eclipse of the sun have all been causes of playing in darkness.*

● Since 1972, the Whitburn Golf Club at South Shields, Tyne and Wear, has held an annual Summer Solstice Competition. All competitors, who draw lots for starting tees, must begin before 4.24 and 13 seconds am, the time the sun rises over the first hole on the longest day of the year.

● At The Open Championship in Musselburgh in November 1889 many players finished when the light had so far gone that the adjacent street lamps were lit. The cards were checked by candlelight. Several players who had no chance of the championship were paid small sums to withdraw in order to permit others who had a chance to finish in daylight. This was the last championship at Musselburgh.

● At the Southern Section of the PGA tournament on 25th September, 1907, at Burnham Beeches, several players concluded the round by the aid of torch lights placed near the holes.

● In the Irish Open Championship at Portmarnock in September, 1907, a tie in the third round between W.C. Pickeman and A. Jeffcott was postponed owing to darkness, at the 22nd hole. The next morning Pickeman won at the 24th.

● The qualifying round of the American Amateur Championship in 1910 could not be finished in one day, and several competitors had to stop their round on account of darkness, and complete it early in the morning of the following day.

● On 10th January, 1926, in the final of the President's Putter, at Rye, E.F. Storey and R.H. Wethered were all square at the 24th hole. It was 5 pm and so dark that, although a fair crowd was present, the balls could not be followed. The tie was abandoned and the Putter held jointly for the year. Each winner of the Putter affixes the ball he played; for 1926 there are two balls, respectively engraved with the names of the finalists.

● In the 1932 Walker Cup contest at Brooklyn, a total eclipse of the sun occurred.

● At Perth, on 14th September, 1932, a competition was in progress under good clear evening light, and a full bright moon. The moon rose at 7.10 and an hour later came under eclipse to the earth's surface. The light then became so bad that on the last three greens competitors holed out by the aid of the light from matches.

● At Carnoustie, 1932, in the competition for the Craw's Nest Tassie the large entry necessitated competitors being sent off in 3-ball matches. The late players had to be assisted by electric torches flashed on the greens.

● In February, 1950, Max Faulkner and his partner, R. Dolman, in a Guildford Alliance event finished their round in complete darkness. A photographer's flash bulbs were used at the last hole to direct Faulkner's approach. Several of the other competitors also finished in darkness. At the last hole they had only the light from the clubhouse to aim at and one played his approach so boldly that he put his ball through the hall doorway and almost into the dressing room.

● On the second day of the 1969 Ryder Cup contest, the last 4-ball match ended in near total darkness on the 18th green at Royal Birkdale. With the help of the clubhouse lights the two American players, Lee Trevino and Miller Barber, along with Tony Jacklin for Britain each faced putts of around five feet to win their match. All missed and their game was halved.

*The occasions mentioned above all occurred in competitions where it was not intended to play in the dark. There are, however, numerous instances where players set out to play in the dark either for bets or for novelty.*

● On 29th November, 1878, R.W. Brown backed himself to go round the Hoylake links in 150 strokes, starting at 11 pm. The conditions of the match were that Mr Brown was only to be penalised *loss of distance* for a lost ball, and that no one was to help him to find it. He went round in 147 strokes, and won his bet by the narrow margin of three strokes.

● In 1876 David Strath backed himself to go round St Andrews under 100, in moonlight. He took 95, and did not lose a ball.

● In September 1928, at St Andrews, the first and last holes were illuminated by lanterns, and at 11 pm four members of The Royal and Ancient set out to play a foursome over the 2 holes. Electric lights, lanterns, and rockets were used to brighten the fairway, and the headlights of motor cars parked on Links Place formed a helpful battery. The 1st hole was won in four, and each side got a five at the 18th. About 1,000 spectators followed the freak match, which was played to celebrate the appointment of Angus Hambro to the captaincy of the club.

● In 1931, Rufus Stewart, professional, Kooyonga Club, South Australia, and former Australian Open Champion, played 18 holes of exhibition golf at night without losing a single ball over the Kooyonga course, and completed the round in 77.

● At Ashley Wood Golf Club, Blandford, Dorset, a night-time golf tournament was arranged annually with up to 180 golfers taking part over four nights. Over £6000 has been raised in four years for the Muscular Dystrophy Charity.

● At Pannal, 3rd July, 1937, R.H. Locke, playing in bright moonlight, holed his tee shot at the 15th hole, distance 220 yards, the only known case of holing-in-one under such conditions.

## Fatal and other accidents on the links

*The history of golf is, unfortunately, marred by a great number of fatal accidents on or near the course. In the vast majority of such cases they have been caused either by careless swinging of the club or by an uncontrolled shot when the ball has struck a spectator or bystander. In addition to the fatal accidents there is an even larger number on record which have resulted in serious injury or blindness. We do not propose to list these accidents except where they have some unusual feature. We would remind all golfers of the tragic consequences which have so often been caused by momentary carelessness. The fatal accidents which follow have an unusual cause and other accidents given may have their humorous aspect.*

● English tournament professional Richard Boxall was three shots off the lead in the third round of the 1991 Open Championship when he fractured his left leg driving from the 9th tee at Royal Birkdale. He was taken from the course to hospital by ambulance and was listed in the official results as "retired" which entitled him to a consolation prize of £3000.

A month later, Russell Weir of Scotland, was competing in the European Teaching Professionals' Championship near Rotterdam when he also fractured his left leg driving from the 7th tee in the first round.

● In July, 1971, Rudolph Roy, aged 43, was killed at a Montreal course; in playing out of woods, the shaft of his club snapped, rebounded off a tree and the jagged edge plunged into his body.

● Harold Wallace, aged 75, playing at Lundin Links with two friends in 1950, was crossing the railway line which separates the fifth green and sixth tee, when a light engine knocked him down and he was killed instantly.

● In the summer of 1963, Harold Kalles, of Toronto, Canada, died six days after his throat had been cut by a golf club shaft, which broke against a tree as he was trying to play out of a bunker.

● At Jacksonville, Florida, on 18th March, 1952, two women golfers were instantly killed when hit simultaneously by the whirling propeller of a navy fighter plane. They were playing together when the plane with a dead engine coming in out of control, hit them from behind.

● In May, 1993, at Ponoka Community GC, Alberta, Canada, Richard McCulough hit a poor tee shot on the 13th hole and promptly smashed his driver angrily against a golf cart. The head of the driver and six inches of shaft flew through the air, piercing McCulough's throat and severing his carotid artery. He died in hospital.

● Britain's first national open event for competitors aged over 80, at Moortown, Leeds in September, 1992, was marred when 81-year-old Frank Hart collapsed on the fourth tee and died. Play continued and Charles Mitchell, aged 80, won the Stableford competition with a gross score of 81 for 39 points.

● Playing in the 1993 Carlesburg-Tetley Cornish Festival at Tehidy Park, Ian Cornwell was struck on the leg by a wayward shot from a player two groups behind. Later, as he was leaving the 16th green, he was hit again, this time below the ear, by the same player, knocking him unconscious. This may be the first time that a player has been hit twice in the same round by the same player.

## Lightning on the links

*There have been a considerable number of fatal and serious accidents through players and caddies having been struck by lightning on the course. The Royal and Ancient and the USGA have, since 1952, provided for discontinuance of play during lightning storms under the Rules of Golf (Rule 37, 6) and the United States Golf Association has given the following guide for personal safety during thunderstorms:*

(a) Do not go out of doors or remain out during thunderstorms unless it is necessary. Stay inside of a building where it is dry, preferably away from fireplaces, stoves, and other metal objects.

(b) If there is any choice of shelter, choose in the following order:
1. Large metal or metal-frame buildings.
2. Dwellings or other buildings which are protected against lightning.
3. Large unprotected buildings.
4. Small unprotected buildings.

(c) If remaining out of doors is unavoidable, keep away from:
1. Small sheds and shelters if in an exposed location.
2. Isolated trees.
3. Wire fences.
4. Hilltops and wide open spaces.

(d) Seek shelter in:
1. A cave.
2. A depression in the ground.
3. A deep valley or canyon.
4. The foot of a steep or overhanging cliff.
5. Dense woods.
6. A grove of trees.

**Note** – Raising golf clubs or umbrellas above the head is dangerous.

● A serious incident with lightning involving well-known golfers was at the 1975 Western Open in Chicago when Lee Trevino, Jerry Heard and Bobby Nichols were all struck and had to be taken to hospital. At the same time Tony Jacklin had a club thrown 15 feet out of his hands.

● Two well-known competitors were struck by lightning in European events in 1977. They were Mark James of Britain in the Swiss Open and Severiano Ballesteros of Spain in the Scandinavian Open. Fortunately neither appeared to be badly injured.

● Two spectators were killed by lightning in 1991: one at the US Open and the other at US PGA Championship.

## Spectators interfering with balls

● Deliberate interference by spectators with balls in play during important money matches was not unknown in the old days when there was intense rivalry between the *schools* of Musselburgh, St Andrews, and North Berwick, and disputes arose in stake matches caused by the action of spectators in kicking the ball into either a favourable or an unfavourable position.

● Tom Morris, in his last match with Willie Park at Musselburgh, refused to go on because of interference by the spectators, and in the match on the same course about 40 years later, in 1895, between Willie Park Jr and J.H. Taylor, the barracking of the crowd and interference with play was so bad that when the Park-Vardon match came to be arranged in 1899, Vardon refused to accept Musselburgh as a venue.

● Even in modern times spectators have been known to interfere deliberately with players' balls, though it is usually by children. In the 1972 Penfold Tournament at Queen's Park, Bournemouth, Christy O'Connor Jr had his ball stolen by a young boy, but not being told of this at the time had to take the penalty for a lost ball. O'Connor finished in a tie for first place, but lost the play-off.

● In 1912 in the last round of the final of the Amateur Championship at Westward Ho! between Abe Mitchell and John Ball, the drive of the former to the short 14th hit an open umbrella held by a lady protecting herself from the heavy rain, and instead of landing on the green the ball was diverted into a bunker. Mitchell, who was leading at the time by 2 holes, lost the hole and Ball won the Championship at the 38th hole.

● In the match between the professionals of Great Britain and America at Southport in 1937 a dense crowd collected round the 15th green waiting for the Sarazen-Alliss match. The American's ball landed in the lap of a woman, who picked it up and threw it so close to the hole that Sarazen got a two against Alliss' three.

● In a memorable tie between Bobby Jones and Cyril Tolley in the 1930 Amateur Championship at St Andrews, Jones' approach to the 17th green struck spectators massed at the left end of the green and led to controversy as to whether it would otherwise have gone on to the famous road. Jones himself had deliberately played for that part of the green and had requested stewards to get the crowd back. Had the ball gone on to the road, the historic Jones Quadrilateral of the year – The Open and Amateur Championships of Britain and the United States – might not have gone into the records.

● In the 1983 Suntory World Match Play Championship at Wentworth Nick Faldo hit his second shot over the green at the 16th hole into a group of spectators. To everyone's astonishment and discomfiture the ball reappeared on the green about 30ft from the hole, propelled there by a thoroughly misguided and anonymous spectator. The referee ruled that Faldo should play the ball where it lay on the green. Faldo's opponent, Graham Marsh, understandably upset by the incident, took three putts against Faldo's two, thus losing a hole he might well otherwise have won. Faldo won the match 2 and 1, but lost in the final to Marsh's fellow Australian Greg Norman by 3 and 2.

## Golf balls killing animals and fish, and incidents with animals

● An astounding fatality to an animal through being hit by a golf ball occurred at St Margaret's-at-Cliffe Golf Club, Kent on 13th June, 1934, when W.J. Robinson, the professional, killed a cow with his tee shot to the 18th hole. The cow was standing in the fairway about 100 yards from the tee, and the ball struck her on the back of the head. She fell like a log, but staggered to her feet and walked about 50 yards before dropping again. When the players reached her she was dead.

● J.W. Perret, of Ystrad Mynach, playing with Chas R. Halliday, of Ralston, in the qualifying rounds of the Society of One Armed Golfers' Championship over the Darley course, Troon, on 27th August, 1935, killed two gulls at successive holes with his second shots. The *deadly* shots were at the 1st and 2nd holes.

● On the first day of grouse shooting of the 1975 season (12th August), 11-year-old schoolboy Willie Fraser, of Kingussie, beat all the guns when he killed a grouse with his tee shot on the local course.

● On 10th June, 1904, while playing in the Edinburgh High Constables' Competition at Kilspindie, Captain Ferguson sent a long ball into the rough at the Target hole, and on searching for it found that it had struck and killed a young hare.

● Playing in a mixed open tournament at the Waimairi Beach Golf Club in Christchurch, New Zealand, in the summer of 1961, Mrs R.T. Challis found her ball in fairly long spongy grass where a placing rule applied. She picked up, placed the ball and played her stroke. A young hare leaped into the air and fell dead at her feet. She had placed the ball on the leveret without seeing it and without disturbing it.

● In 1906 in the Border Championship at Hawick, a gull and a weasel were killed by balls during the afternoon's play.

● A golfer at Newark, in May, 1907, drove his ball into the river. The ball struck a trout 2lb in weight and killed it.

● On 24th April, 1975, at Scunthorpe GC, Jim Tollan's drive at the 14th hole, called *The Mallard*, struck and killed a female mallard duck in flight. The duck was stuffed and is displayed in the Scunthorpe Clubhouse.

● A. Samuel, Melbourne Club, at Sandringham, was driving with an iron club from the 17th tee, when a kitten, which had been playing in the long grass, sprang suddenly at the ball. Kitten and club arrived at the objective simultaneously, with the result that the kitten took an unexpected flight through the air, landing some 20 yards away.

● As Susan Rowlands was lining up a vital putt in the closing stages of the final of the 1978 Welsh Girls' Championship at Abergele, a tiny mouse scampered up her trouser leg. After holing the putt, the mouse ran down again. Susan, who won the final, admitted that she fortunately had not known it was there.

## Interference by birds and animals

● Crows, ravens, hawks and seagulls frequently carry off golf balls, sometimes dropping the ball actually on the green, and it is a common incident for a cow to swallow a golf ball. A plague of crows on the Liverpool course at Hoylake are addicted to golf balls – they stole 26 in one day – selecting only new balls. It was suggested that members should carry shotguns as a 15th club!

● A match was approaching a hole in a rather low-lying course, when one of the players made a crisp chip from about 30 yards from the hole. The ball trickled slowly across the green and eventually disappeared into the hole. After a momentary pause, the ball was suddenly ejected on to the green, and out jumped a large frog.

● A large black crow named Jasper which frequented the Lithgow GC in New South Wales, Australia, stole 30 golf balls in the club's 1972 Easter Tournament.

● As Mrs Molly Whitaker was playing from a bunker at Beachwood course, Natal, South Africa, a large monkey leaped from a bush and clutched her round the neck. A caddie drove it off by clipping it with an iron club.

● In Massachusetts a goose, having been hit rather hard by a golf ball which then came to rest by the side of a water hazard, took revenge by waddling over to the ball and kicking it into the water.

● In the summer of 1963, S.C. King had a good drive to the 10th hole at the Guernsey Club. His partner, R.W. Clark, was in the rough, and King helped him to search. Returning to his ball, he found a cow eating it. Next day, at the same hole, the positions were reversed, and King was in the rough. Clark placed his woollen hat over his ball, remarking, *I'll make sure the cow doesn't eat mine*. On his return he found the cow thoroughly enjoying his hat; nothing was left but the pom-pom.

● On 5 August 2000 in the first round of the Royal Westmoreland Club Championship in Barbados, Kevin Edwards, a five-handicapper, hit a tee shot at the short 15th to a few feet of the hole. A monkey then ran onto the green, picked up the ball, threw it into the air a few times, then placed it in the hole before running off. Mr Edwards had to replace his ball, but was obliged afterwards to buy everyone a drink at the bar by virtue of a newly written rule.

## Armless, one-armed, legless and ambidextrous players

● In September, 1933, at Burgess Golfing Society of Edinburgh, the first championship for one-armed golfers was held. There were 43 entries and 37 of the competitors had lost an arm in the 1914–18 war. Play was over two rounds and the championship was won by W.E. Thomson, Eastwood, Glasgow, with a score of 169 (82 and 87) for two rounds. The Burgess course was 6,300 yards long. Thomson drove the last green, 260 yards. The championship and an international match are played annually.

● In the Boys' Amateur Championship 1923, at Dunbar and 1949 at St Andrews, there were competitors each with one arm. The competitor in 1949, R.P. Reid, Cupar, Fife, who lost his arm working a machine in a butcher's shop, got through to the third round.

● There have been cases of persons with no arms playing golf. One, Thomas McAuliffe, who held the club between his right shoulder and cheek, once went round Buffalo CC, USA, in 108.

● Group Captain Bader, who lost both legs in a flying accident prior to the World War 1939–45, took part in golf competitions and reached a single-figure handicap in spite of his disability.

● In 1909, Scott of Silloth, and John Haskins of Hoylake, both one-armed golfers, played a home and

away match for £20-a-side. Scott finished five up at Silloth. He was seven up and 14 to play at Hoylake but Haskins played so well that Scott eventually only won by 3 and 1. This was the first match between one-armed golfers. Haskins in 1919 was challenged by Mr Mycock, of Buxton, another one-armed player. The match was 36 holes, home and away. The first half was played over the Buxton and High Peak Links, and the latter half over the Liverpool Links, and resulted in a win for Haskins by 11 and 10. Later in the same year Haskins received another challenge to play against Alexander Smart of Aberdeen. The match was 18 holes over the Balgownie Course, and ended in favour of Haskins.

● In a match, November, 1926, between the Geduld and Sub Nigel Clubs – two golf clubs connected with the South African gold mines of the same names – each club had two players minus an arm. The natural consequence was that the quartet were matched. The players were – A.W.P. Charteris and E. Mitchell, Sub Nigel; and E.P. Coles and J. Kirby, Geduld. This is the first record of four one-armed players in a foursome.

● At Joliet Country Club, USA, a one-armed golfer named D.R. Anderson drove a ball 300 yards.

● Left-handedness, but playing golf right-handed, is prevalent and for a man to throw with his left hand and play golf right-handed is considered an advantage, for Bobby Jones, Jesse Sweetser, Walter Hagen, Jim Barnes, Joe Kirkwood and more recently Johnny Miller were eminent golfers who were left-handed and ambidextrous.

● In a practice round for The Open Championship in July, 1927, at St Andrews, Len Nettlefold and Joe Kirkwood changed sets of clubs at the 9th hole. Nettlefold was a left-handed golfer and Kirkwood right-handed. They played the last nine, Kirkwood with the left-handed clubs and Nettlefold with the right-handed clubs.

● The late Harry Vardon, when he was at Ganton, got tired of giving impossible odds to his members and beating them, so he collected a set of left-handed clubs, and rating himself at scratch, conceded the handicap odds to them. He won with the same monotonous regularity.

● Ernest Jones, who was professional at the Chislehurst Club, was badly wounded in the war in France in 1916 and his right leg had to be amputated below the knee. He persevered with the game, and before the end of the year he went round the Clacton course balanced on his one leg in 72. Jones later settled in the United States where he built fame and fortune as a golf teacher.

● Major Alexander McDonald Fraser of Edinburgh had the distinction of holding two handicaps simultaneously in the same club – one when he played left-handed and the other for his right-handed play. In medal competitions he had to state before teeing up which method he would use.

● Former England test cricketer Brian Close once held a handicap of 2 playing right-handed, but after retiring from cricket in 1977 decided to apply himself as a left-handed player. His left-handed handicap at the time of his retirement was 7. Close had the distinction of once beating Ted Dexter, another distinguished test cricketer and noted golfer twice in the one day, playing right-handed in the morning and left-handed in the afternoon.

## Blind and blindfolded golf

● Major Towse, VC, whose eyes were shot out during the South African War, 1899, was probably the first blind man to play golf. His only stipulations when playing the game were that he should be allowed to touch the ball with his hands to ascertain its position, and that his caddie could ring a small bell to indicate the position of the hole. Major Towse, who played with considerable skill, was also an expert oarsman and bridge player. He died in 1945, aged 81.

● The United States Blind Golfers' Association in 1946 promoted an Invitational Golf Tournament for the blind at Inglewood, California, to be held annually. In 1953 there were 24 competitors, of which 11 completed the two rounds of 36 holes. The winner was Charley Boswell who lost his eyesight leading a tank unit in Germany in 1944.

● In July, 1954, at Lambton Golf and Country Club, Toronto, the first international championship for the blind was held. It resulted in a win for Joe Lazaro, of Waltham, Mass., with a score of 220 for the two rounds. He drove the 215-yard 16th hole and just missed an ace, his ball stopping 18 inches from the hole. Charley Boswell, who won the United States Blind Golfers' Association Tournament in 1953, was second. The same Charles Boswell, of Birmingham, Alabama, holed the 141-yard 14th hole at the Vestavia CC in one in October, 1970.

● Another blind person to have holed-in-one was American Ben Thomas while on holiday in South Carolina in 1978.

● Rick Sorenson undertook a bet in which, playing 18 holes blindfolded at Meadowbrook Course, Minneapolis, on 25th May, 1973, he was to pay $10 for every hole over par and receive $100 for every hole in par or better. He went round in 86 losing $70 on the deal.

● Alfred Toogood played blindfolded in a match against Tindal Atkinson at Sunningdale in 1912. Toogood was beaten 8 and 7. Previously, in 1908, I. Millar, Newcastle-upon-Tyne, played a match blindfolded against A.T. Broughton, Birkdale, at Newcastle, County Down.

● Wing-Commander *Laddie* Lucas, DSO, DFC, MP, played over Sandy Lodge golf course in Hertfordshire on 7th August, 1954, completely blindfolded and had a score of 87.

## Trick shots

● Joe Kirkwood, Australia, specialised in public exhibitions of trick and fancy shots. He played all kinds of strokes after nominating them, and among his ordinary strokes nothing was more impressive than those hit for low flight. He played a full drive from the face of a wrist watch, and the toe of a spectator's shoe, full strokes at a suspended ball, and played for slice and pull at will, and exhibited his ambidexterity by playing left-handed strokes with right-handed clubs. Holing six balls, stymieing, a full shot at a ball catching it as it descended, and hitting 12 full shots in rapid succession, with his face turned away from the ball, were shots among his repertoire. In playing the last named Kirkwood placed the balls in a row, about six inches apart, and moved quickly along the line. Kirkwood, who was born in Australia lived for many years in America. He died in November, 1970 aged 73.

● On 2nd April, 1894, a 3-ball match was played over Musselburgh course between Messrs Grant, Bowden, and Waggot, the clubmaker, the latter teeing on the face of a watch at each tee. He finished the round in 41 the watch being undamaged in any way.

● In a match at Esher on 23rd November, 1931, George Ashdown, the professional, played his tee shot for each of the 18 holes from a rubber tee strapped to the forehead of Miss Ena Shaw.

● E.A. Forrest, a South African professional in a music hall turn of trick golf shots, played blindfolded shots, one being from the ball teed on the chin of his recumbent partner.

● The late Paul Hahn, an American trick specialist could hit four balls with two clubs. Holding a club in each hand he hit two balls, hooking one and slicing the other with the same swing. Hahn had a repertoire of 30 trick shots. In 1955 he flew round the world, exhibiting in 14 countries and on all five continents.

## Balls colliding and touching

● Competing in the 1980 Corfu International Championship, Sharon Peachey drove from one tee and her ball collided in mid-air with one from a competitor playing another hole. Her ball ended in a pond.

● Playing in the Cornish team championship in 1973 at West Cornwall GC Tom Scott-Brown, of West Cornwall GC, and Paddy Bradley, of Tehidy GC, saw their drives from the fourth and eighth tees collide in mid-air.

● During a fourball match at Guernsey Club in June, 1966, near the 13th green from the tee, two of the players, D.G. Hare and S. Machin, chipped up simultaneously; the balls collided in mid-air and Machin's ball hit the green, then the flagstick, and dropped into the hole for a birdie 2.

● In May, 1926, during the meeting of the Army Golfing Society at St Andrews, Colonel Howard and Lieutenant-Colonel Buchanan Dunlop, while playing in the foursomes against J. Rodger and J. Mackie, hit full iron shots for the seconds to the 16th green. Each thought he had to play his ball first, and hidden by a bunker the players struck their balls simultaneously. The balls, going towards the hole about 20 yards from the pin and five feet in the air, met with great force and dropped either side of the hole five yards apart.

● In 1972, before a luncheon celebrating the centenary year of the Ladies' Section of Royal Wimbledon GC, a 12-hole competition was held during which two competitors, Mrs L. Champion and Mrs A. McKendrick, driving from the eighth and ninth tees respectively, saw their balls collide in mid-air.

● In 1928, at Wentworth Falls, Australia, Dr Alcorn and E.A. Avery, of Leura Club, were playing with professional E. Barnes. The tee shots of Avery and Barnes at the 9th hole finished on opposite sides of the fairway. Both players unknowingly hit their seconds (chip shots) at the same time. Dr Alcorn, standing at the pin, suddenly saw two balls approaching the hole from different angles. They met in the air and dropped into the hole.

● At Rugby, 1931, playing in a 4-ball match, H. Fraser pulled his drive from the 10th tee in the direction of the ninth tee. Simultaneously a club member, driving from the ninth tee, pulled his drive. The tees were about 350 yards apart. The two balls collided in mid-air.

● Two golf balls, being played in opposite directions, collided in flight over Longniddry Golf Course on 27th June, 1953. Immediately after Stewart Elder, of Longniddry, had driven from the third tee, another ball, which had been pulled off line from the second fairway, which runs alongside the third, struck his ball about 20 feet above the ground. S.J. Fleming, of Tranent, who was playing with Elder, heard a loud crack and thought Elder's ball had exploded. The balls were found undamaged about 70 yards apart.

### Three and two balls dislodged by one shot

● In 1934 on the short 3rd hole (now the 13th) of Olton Course, Warwickshire, J.R. Horden, a scratch golfer of the club, sent his tee shot into long wet grass a few feet over the back of the green. When he played an *explosion* shot three balls dropped on to the putting green, his own and two others.

● A.M. Chevalier, playing at Hale, Cheshire, March, 1935, drove his ball into a grass bunker, and when he reached it there was only part of it showing. He played the shot with a niblick and to his amazement not one but three balls shot into the air. They all dropped back into the bunker and came to rest within a foot of each other. Then came another surprise. One of the *finds* was of the same manufacture and bore the same number as the ball he was playing with.

● Playing to the 9th hole, at Osborne House Club, Isle of Wight, George A. Sherman lost his ball which had sunk out of sight on the sodden fairway. A few weeks later, playing from the same tee, his ball again was plugged, only the top showing. Under a local rule he lifted his ball to place it, and exactly under it lay the ball he had lost previously.

### Balls in strange places

● Playing at the John O' Gaunt Club, Sutton, near Biggleswade (Beds), a member drove a ball which did not touch the ground until it reached London – over 40 miles away. The ball landed in a vegetable lorry which was passing the golf course and later fell out of a package of cabbages when they were unloaded at Covent Garden, London.

● In the English Open Amateur Stroke Play at Moortown in 1974, Nigel Denham, a Yorkshire County player, in the first round saw his overhit second shot to the 18th green bounce up some steps into the clubhouse. His ball went through an open door, ricocheted off a wall and came to rest in the men's bar, 20 feet from the windows. As the clubhouse was not out of bounds Denham decided to play the shot back to the green and opened a window 4 feet by 2 feet through which he pitched his ball to 12 feet from the flag. (Several weeks later The R&A declared that Denham should have been penalised two shots for opening the window. The clubhouse was an immovable obstruction and no part of it should have been moved.)

● In The Open Championship at Sandwich, 1949, Harry Bradshaw, Kilcroney, Dublin, at the 5th hole in his second round, drove into the rough and found his ball inside a beer bottle with the neck and shoulder broken off and four sharp points sticking up. Bradshaw, if he had treated the ball as in an unplayable lie might have been involved in a disqualification, so he decided to play it where it lay. With his blaster he smashed the bottle and sent the ball about 30 yards. The hole, a par 4, cost him 6.

● Kevin Sharman of Woodbridge GC hit a low, very straight drive at the club's 8th hole in 1979. After some minutes' searching, his ball was found embedded in a plastic sphere on top of the direction post.

● On the Dublin Course, 16th July, 1936, in the Irish Open Championship, A.D. Locke, the South African, played his tee shot at the 100-yard 12th hole, but the ball could not be found on arrival on the green. The marker removed the pin and it was discovered that the ball had been entangled in the flag. It dropped near the edge of the hole and Locke holed the short putt for a birdie two.

● While playing a round on the Geelong Golf Club Course, Australia, Easter, 1923, Captain Charteris topped his tee shot to the short 2nd hole, which lies over a creek with deep and steep clay banks. His ball came to rest on the near slope of the creek bank. He elected to play the ball as it lay, and took his niblick. After the shot, the ball was nowhere to be seen. It was found later embedded in a mass of gluey clay stuck fast to the face of the niblick. It could not be shaken off. Charteris did what was afterwards approved by The R&A, cleaned the ball and dropped it behind without penalty.

● In October, 1929, at Blackmoor Golf Club, Bordon, Hants, a player driving from the first tee holed out his ball in the chimney of a house some 120 yards distant and some 40 yards out of bounds on the right. The owner and his wife were sitting in front of the fire when they heard a rattle in the chimney and were astonished to see a golf ball drop into the fire.

● A similar incident occurred in an inter-club match between Musselburgh and Lothianburn at Prestongrange in 1938 when a member of the former team hooked his ball at the 2nd hole and gave it up for lost. To his amazement a woman emerged from one of the houses adjacent to this part of the course and handed back the ball which she said had come down the chimney and landed on a pot which was on the fire.

● In July, 1955, J. Lowrie, starter at the Eden Course, St Andrews, witnessed a freak shot. A visitor drove from the first tee just as a north-bound train was passing. He sliced the shot and the ball disappeared through an open window of a passenger compartment. Almost immediately the ball emerged again, having been thrown back on to the fairway by a man in the compartment, who waved a greeting which presumably indicated that no one was hurt.

● At Coombe Wood Golf Club, a player hit a ball towards the 16th green where it landed in the vertical exhaust of a tractor which was mowing the fairway. The greenkeeper was somewhat surprised to find a temporary loss of power in the tractor. When sufficient compression had built up in the exhaust system, the ball was forced out with tremendous velocity, hit the roof of a house nearby, bounced off and landed some three feet from the pin on the green.

● There have been many occasions when misdirected shots have finished in strange places after an unusual line of flight and bounce. At Ashford, Middlesex, John Miller, aged 69, hit his tee shot out of bounds at the 12th hole (237 yards). It struck a parked car, passed through a copse, hit more cars, jumped a canopy, flew through the clubhouse kitchen window, finishing in a cooking stock-pot, without once touching the ground. Mr Miller had previously done the hole in one on four occasions.

"Waiter. There's a golf ball in my soup"

● When carrying out an inspection of the air conditioning system at St John's Hospital, Chelmsford, in 1993, a golf ball was found in the ventilator immediately above the operating theatre. It was probably the result of a hooked drive from the first tee at Chelmsford Golf Club, which is close by, but the ball can only have entered the duct on a rebound through a three-inch gap under a ventilator hood and then descended through a series of sharp bends to its final resting place.

## Balls Hit To and From Great Heights

● In 1798 two Edinburgh golfers undertook to drive a ball over the spire of St Giles' Cathedral, Edinburgh, for a wager. Mr Sceales, of Leith, and Mr Smellie, a printer, were each allowed six shots and succeeded in sending the balls well over the weather-cock, a height of more than 160 feet from the ground.

● Some years later Donald McLean, an Edinburgh lawyer, won a substantial bet by driving a ball over the Melville Monument in St Andrew Square, Edinburgh – height, 154 feet.

● Tom Morris in 1860, at the famous bridge of Ballochmyle, stood in the quarry beneath and, from a stick elevated horizontally, attempted to send golf balls over the bridge. He could raise them only to the pathway, 400 feet high, which was in itself a great feat with the gutta ball.

● Captain Ernest Carter, on 28th September, 1922, drove a ball from the roadway at the 1st tee on Harlech Links against the wall of Harlech Castle. The embattlements are 200 feet over the level of the roadway, and the point where the ball struck the embattlements was 180 yards from the point where the ball was teed. Captain Carter, who was laid odds of £100 to £1, used a baffy.

● In 1896 Freddie Tait, then a subaltern in the Black Watch, drove a ball from the Rookery, the highest building on Edinburgh Castle, in a match against a brother officer to hole out in the fountain in Princes Street Gardens 350 feet below and about 300 yards distant.

● Prior to the 1977 Lancôme Tournament in Paris, Arnold Palmer hit three balls from the second stage of the Eiffel Tower, over 300 feet above ground. The longest was measured at 403 yards. One ball was hooked and hit a bus but no serious damage was done as all traffic had been stopped for safety reasons.

● Long drives have been made from mountain peaks, across the gorge at Victoria Falls, from the Pyramids, high buildings in New York, and from many other similar places. As an illustration of such freakish *drives* a member of the New York Rangers' Hockey Team from the top of Mount Edith Cavell, 11,033 feet high, drove a ball which struck the Ghost Glacier 5000 feet below and bounced off the rocky ledge another 1000 feet – a total drop of 2000 yards. Later, in June, 1968, from Pikes Peak, Colorado (14,110 feet), Arthur Lynskey hit a ball which travelled 200 yards horizontally but 2 miles vertically.

## Remarkable Shots

● Remarkable shots are as numerous as the grains of sand; around every 19th hole, legends are recalled of astounding shots. One shot is commemorated by a memorial tablet at the 17th hole at the Lytham and St Annes Club. It was made by Bobby Jones in the final round of The Open Championship in 1926. He was partnered by Al Watrous, another American player. They had been running neck and neck and at the end of the third round, Watrous was just leading Jones with 215 against 217. At the 16th Jones drew level then on the 17th he drove into a sandy lie in broken ground. Watrous reached the green with his second. Jones took a mashie-iron (the equivalent to a 4-iron today) and hit a magnificent shot to the green to get his 4. This remarkable recovery unnerved Watrous, who 3-putted, and Jones, getting another 4 at the last hole against 5, won his first Open Championship with 291 against Watrous' 293. The tablet is near the spot where Jones played his second shot.

● Arnold Palmer (USA), playing in the second round of the Australian Wills Masters tournament at Melbourne, in October, 1964, hooked his second shot at the 9th hole high into the fork of a gum tree. Climbing 20 feet up the tree, Palmer, with the head of his 1-iron reversed, played a hammer stroke and knocked the ball some 30 yards forward, followed by a brilliant chip to the green and a putt.

● In the foursome during the Ryder Cup at Moortown in 1929, Joe Turnesa hooked the American side's second shot at the last hole behind the marquee adjoining the clubhouse, Johnny Farrel then pitched the ball over the marquee on to the green only feet away from the pin and Turnesa holed out for a 4.

## Miscellaneous Incidents and Strange Golfing Facts

● Gary Player of South Africa was honoured by his country by having his portrait on new postage stamps which were issued on 12th December, 1976. It was the first time a specific golfer had ever been depicted on any country's postage stamps. In 1981 the US Postal Service introduced stamps featuring Bobby Jones and Babe Zaharias. They are the first golfers to be thus honoured by the United States.

● Gary Harris, aged 18, became the first player to make five consecutive appearances for England in the European Boys Team Championship at Vilamoura, Portugal, in 1994.

● In February, 1971, the first ever golf shots on the moon's surface were played by Captain Alan Shepard, commander of the Apollo 14 spacecraft. Captain Shepard hit two balls with an iron head attached to a makeshift shaft. With a one-handed swing he claimed he hit the first ball 200 yards aided by the reduced force of gravity on the moon. Subsequent findings put this distance in doubt. The second was a shank. Acknowledging the occasion The R&A sent Captain Shepard the following telegram: *Warmest congratulations to all of you on your great achievement and safe return. Please refer to Rules of Golf section on etiquette, paragraph 6, quote – before leaving a bunker a player should carefully fill up all holes made by him therein, unquote.* Shepard presented the club to the USGA Museum in 1974.

● Charles (Chick) Evans competed in every US Amateur Championship held between 1907 and 1962 by which time he was 72 years old. This amounted to 50 consecutive occasions discounting the six years of the two World Wars when the championship was not held.

● In winning the 1977 US Open at Southern Hills CC, Tulsa, Oklahoma, Hubert Green had to contend with a death threat. Coming off the 14th green in the final round, he was advised by USGA officials that a phone call had been received saying that he would be killed. Green decided that play should continue and happily he went on to win, unharmed.

● It was discovered at the 1977 USPGA Championship that the clubs with which Tom Watson had won The Open Championship and the US Masters earlier in the year were illegal, having grooves which exceeded the permitted specifications. The set he used in winning the 1975 Open Championship were then flown out to him and they too were found to be illegal. No retrospective action was taken.

● Mrs Fred Daly, wife of the former Open champion, saved the clubhouse of Balmoral GC, Belfast, from destruction when three men entered the professional's shop on 5th August, 1976, and left a bag containing a bomb outside the shop beside the clubhouse when refused money. Mrs Daly carried the bag over to a hedge some distance away where the bomb exploded 15 minutes later. The only damage was broken windows. On the same day several hours afterwards, Dungannon GC in Co. Tyrone suffered extensive damage to the clubhouse from terrorist bombs. Co. Down GC, proposed venue of the 1979 home international matches suffered bomb damage in May that year and through fear for the safety of team members the 1979 matches were cancelled.

● The Army Golfing Society and St Andrews on 21st April, 1934, played a match 200-a-side, the largest golf match ever played. Play was by foursomes. The Army won 58, St Andrews 31 and 11 were halved.

● Jamie Ortiz-Patino, owner of the Valderrama Golf Club at Sotogrande, Spain, paid a record £84,000 (increased to £92,400 with ten per cent buyers premium) for a late seventeenth- or early eighteenth-century rake iron offered at auction in Musselburgh in July, 1992. The iron, which had been kept in a garden shed, was bought to be exhibited in a museum being created at Valderrama.

● In 1986 Alistair Risk and three colleagues on the 17th green at Brora, Sutherland, watched a cow giving birth to twin calves between the markers on the 18th tee, causing them to play their next tee shots from in front of the tee. Their application for a ruling from The R&A brought a Rules Committee reply that while technically a rule had been broken, their action was considered within the spirit of the game and there should be no penalty. The Secretary added that the Rules Committee hoped that mother and twins were doing well.

● In view of the increasing number of people crossing the road (known as Granny Clark's Wynd) which runs across the first and 18th fairways of the Old Course, St Andrews, as a right of way, the St Andrews Links committee decided in 1969 to control the flow by erecting traffic lights, with appropriate green for go, yellow for caution and red for stop. The lights are controlled from the starter's box on the first tee. Golfers on the first tee must wait until the lights turn to green before driving off and a notice has been erected at the Wynd warning pedestrians not to cross at yellow or stop.

● A traffic light for golfers was also installed in 1971 on one of Japan's most congested courses. After putting on the uphill 9th hole of the Fukuoka course in Southern Japan, players have to switch on a go-ahead signal for following golfers waiting to play their shots to the green.

● A 22-year-old professional at Brett Essex GC, Brentwood, David Moore, who was playing in the Mufulira Open in Zambia in 1976, was shot dead it is alleged by the man with whom he was staying for the duration of the tournament. It appeared his host then shot himself.

● Peggy Carrick and her daughter, Angela Uzielli, won the Mothers and Daughters Tournament at Royal Mid-Surrey in 1994 for the 21st time.

● Patricia Shepherd has won the ladies' club championship at Turriff GC Aberdeenshire 30 consecutive times from 1959 to 1988.

● Mrs Jackie Mercer won the South African Ladies' Championship in 1979, 31 years after her first victory in the event as Miss Jacqueline Smith.

● During The Royal and Ancient Golf Club of St Andrews' medal meeting on 25th September, 1907, a member of The Royal and Ancient drove a ball which struck the sharp point of a hatpin in the hat of a lady who was crossing the course. The ball was so firmly impaled that it remained in position. The lady was not hurt.

● John Cook, former English Amateur Champion, narrowly escaped death during an attempted coup against King Hassan of Morocco in July 1971. Cook had been playing in a tournament arranged by King Hassan, a keen golfer, and was at the King's birthday party in Rabat when rebels broke into the party demanding that the King give up his throne. Cook and many others present were taken hostage.

● When playing from the 9th tee at Lossiemouth golf course in June, 1971, Martin Robertson struck a Royal Navy jet aircraft which was coming in to land at the nearby airfield. The plane was not damaged.

● At a court in Inglewood, California, in 1978, Jim Brown was convicted of beating and choking an opponent during a dispute over where a ball should have been placed on the green.

● During the Northern Ireland troubles a home-made hand grenade was found in a bunker at Dungannon GC, Co. Tyrone, on Sunday, 12th September, 1976.

● Tiger Woods, 18, became both the youngest and the first black golfer to win the United States Amateur Championship at Sawgrass in 1994. He went on to win the title three years in a row and then won the first major championship he played as a professional, the 1997 Masters, by a record 12 strokes and with a record low aggregate of 270, 18 under par.

● To mark the centenary of the Jersey Golf Club in 1978, the Jersey Post Office issued a set of four special stamps featuring Jersey's most famous golfer, Harry Vardon. The background of the 13p stamp was a brief biography of Vardon's career reproduced from the Golfer's Handbook.

● Forty-one-year-old John Mosley went for a round of golf at Delaware Park GC, Buffalo, New York, in July, 1972. He stepped on to the first tee and was challenged over a green fee by an official guard. A scuffle developed, a shot was fired and Mosley, a bullet in his chest, died on the way to hospital. His wife was awarded $131,250 in an action against the City of Buffalo and the guard. The guard was sentenced to 7¹/₂ years for second-degree manslaughter.

● When three competitors in a 1968 Pennsylvania pro-am event were about to drive from the 16th tee, two bandits (one with pistol) suddenly emerged from the bushes, struck one of the players and robbed them of wristwatches and $300.

● In the 1932 Walker Cup match at Brooklyn, Leonard Crawley succeeded in denting the cup. An errant iron shot to the 18th green hit the cup, which was on display outside the clubhouse.

● In Johannesburg, South Africa, three golf officials appeared in court accused of violating a 75-year-old Sunday Observance Law by staging the final round of the South African PGA championship on Sunday, 28th February, 1971. The Championship should have been completed on the Saturday but heavy rain prevented any play.

● In The Open Championship of 1876, at St Andrews, Bob Martin and David Strath tied at 176. A protest was lodged against Strath alleging he played his approach to the 17th green and struck a spectator. The Royal and Ancient ordered the replay, but Strath refused to play off the tie until a decision had been given on the protest. No decision was given and Bob Martin was declared the Champion.

● At Rose Bay, New South Wales, on 11th July, 1931, D.J. Bayly MacArthur, on stepping into a bunker, began to sink. MacArthur, who weighed 14 stone, shouted for help. He was rescued when up to the armpits. He had stepped on a patch of quicksand, aggravated by excess of moisture.

● The late Bobby Cruickshank was the victim of his own jubilation in the 1934 US Open at Merion. In the 4th round while in with a chance of winning he half-topped his second shot at the 11th hole. The ball was heading for a pond in front of the green but instead of ending up in the water it hit a rock and bounced on to the green. In his delight Cruickshank threw his club into the air only to receive a resounding blow on the head as it returned to earth.

● A dog with an infallible nose for finding lost golf balls was, in 1971, given honorary membership of the Waihi GC, Hamilton, New Zealand. The dog, called Chico, was trained to search for lost balls, to be sold back to the members, the money being put into the club funds.

● By 1980 Waddy, an 11-year-old beagle belonging to Bob Inglis, the secretary of Brokenhurst Manor GC, had found over 35,000 golf balls.

● Herbert M. Hepworth, Headingley, Leeds, Lord Mayor of Leeds in 1906, scored one thousand holes in 2, a feat which took him 30 years to accomplish. It was celebrated by a dinner in 1931 at the Leeds club. The first 2 of all was scored on 12th June, 1901, at Cobble Hall Course, Leeds, and the 1,000th in 1931 at Alwoodley, Leeds. Hepworth died in November, 1942.

● Fiona MacDonald was the first female to play in the Oxford and Cambridge University match at Ganton in 1986.

● Mrs Sara Gibbon won the Farnham (Surrey) Club's Grandmother's competition 48 hours after her first grand-child was born.

● At Carnoustie in the first qualifying round for the 1952 Scottish Amateur Championship a competitor drove three balls in succession out of bounds at the 1st hole and thereupon withdrew.

● In 1993, the Clark family from Hagley GC, Worcs, set a record for the county's three major professional events. The Worcestershire Stroke Play Championship was won by Finlay Clark, the eldest son, who beat his father Iain and younger brother Cameron, who tied second. In the Match Play Iain beat his son Finlay by 2 and 1 in the final; Cameron won the play-off for third place. Then in the Worcestershire Annual Pro-Am it was Cameron's turn to win, with his brother Finlay coming second and father Iain third. To add to the achievements of the family, Cameron also won the Midland Professional Match Play Championship.

● During a Captain–Pro foursomes challenge match at Chelmsford in 1993, Club Professional Dennis Bailey, put the ball into a hole only once in all 18 holes – when he holed-in-one at the fourth.

● In 1891, a new kind of matchplay – bogey – was introduced at Great Yarmouth Golf Club where the scratch score of the course was taken and each hole given a value known as the ground score. One of the club's members was described as a "regular bogey-man", a name suggested by a music hall song that was currently popular ... and the name stuck.

● Mrs C.C. Gray was Todmorden Golf Club's Ladies Champion 38 out of 42 times between 1951 and 1992, a fact recorded in the Guinness Book of Records.

● Llanymynech is a golf club situated in two countries with 15 holes in Wales and three in England. On the fourth tee, players drive from England and putt out in Wales.

● Gary Sutherland, with only his golf bag as his suitcase and using public transport, competed an unusual tribute to his late father by playing 18 rounds on 18 courses on 18 different islands in Scotland. His travels began on the 13-hole course at Port Bannatyne on Bute, took him among other islands to Orkney, Shetland, Harris, South Uist, Arran and ended at Machrie on Islay. Accompanied by his friend golf architect Brian Noble, Sutherland found the trip rekindled his own love of a game his father had enjoyed so much. ... and he has recorded his adventures in a new book The Fairway Isles.

● In 1913, the last playing of the Irish Amateur Championship prior to the outbreak of World War I was held at Dollymount where it was won by C.A. Palmer from Handsworth GC in Warwickshire. The Championship was not held again until 1919 when not only was the winning player's club once again Handsworth GC but the victor was C.A. Palmer's ward, C.A Bretherton.

## Strange local rules

● The Duke of Windsor, who played on an extraordinary variety of the world's courses, once took advantage of a local rule at Jinja in Uganda and lifted his ball from a hippo's footprint without penalty.

● At the Glen Canyon course in Arizona a local rule provides that *If your ball lands within a club length of a rattlesnake you are allowed to move the ball.*

● Another local rule in Uganda reads: *If a ball comes to rest in dangerous proximity to a crocodile, another ball may be dropped.*

"I reckon that qualifies as dangerous proximity"

● The 6th hole at Koolan Island GC, Western Australia, also serves as a local air strip and a local rule reads: *Aircraft and vehicular traffic have right of way at all times.*

● A local rule at the RAF Waddington GC reads: *When teeing off from the 2nd, right of way must be given to taxiing aircraft.*

# Open Championship Timeline

**1860** The first Open Championship is played at Prestwick. There are eight competitors and the trophy, an ornate red leather belt, is won by Willie Park Sr.

**1863** Prize money is first awarded, but only to second, third and fourth place finishers. The winner first receives a cash prize of £6 in 1864.

**1870** Tommy Morris Jr takes possession of the Challenge Belt after winning The Open for the third consecutive year.

**1873** The Claret Jug is first awarded. Played at St Andrews, it is the first time the Championship is held outside Prestwick.

**1890** John Ball becomes the first amateur and the first Englishman to win The Open.

**1892** Play is extended to two days over 72 holes at Muirfield. Competitors are charged an entrance fee.

**1898** The "cut" is introduced after 36 holes.

**1907** Arnaud Massy from France is the first continental player to win The Open. Qualifying rounds are first played.

**1909** The Golf Exhibition tent makes its first appearance, as a display venue for leading manufacturers.

**1922** It is decided that The Open should only be played over links courses.

**1925** Prestwick hosts its 24th and final Open Championship.

**1926** Admission charges are introduced. Play is extended to three days.

**1955** The Open is broadcast live on television by the BBC.

**1960** Grandstands are introduced at the Centenary Open played in St Andrews.

**1963** Exemptions from pre-qualifying are introduced for the leading players.

**1966** America receives its first live Open broadcast. The Championship is played over three days.

**1968** The double cut is introduced after 54 holes and remains in effect until 1985.

**1970** Jack Nicklaus and Doug Sanders became the first duo to compete in an 18-hole play-off.

**1973** The 1.62 inch ball is last used at The Open.

**1976** Japan receives its first live Open transmission.

**1977** Regional qualifying is introduced as a preliminary to Final Qualifying for most players.

**1980** The Championship ends on a Sunday for the first time.

**1985** The four-hole play-off, followed by sudden death, is introduced.

**2000** A new record is set at the Home of Golf when 238,787 watch the Millennium Open.

**2002** History is made when The Open ends for the first time in a four-way tie. In another first, the four-hole play-off results in a tie.

**2004** International Final Qualifying is introduced, allowing players to qualify at five international locations.

**2006** The 135th Open Championship is broadcast globally for 2,051 hours. Fifty-seven broadcasters across 162 territories show coverage of The Open to a potential household reach of 410 million.

**2007** Ireland's Padraig Harrington becomes the first European to win The Open since Paul Lawrie in 1999 and only the second Irishman. Fred Daly preceded him in 1947.

**2009** Tom Watson, aged 59 years, 10 months, 15 days, becomes the oldest ever runner-up. Matteo Manassero, aged 16 years and 3 months, becomes the youngest winner of the Silver Medal for the leading amateur.

**2010** Golf's oldest Major celebrates its 150th anniversary as The Open is played at the Home of Golf for the 28th time.

# Timeline for the Rules of Golf

The earliest known Rules of Golf were drawn up in 1744 by what was to become the Honourable Company of Edinburgh Golfers. For the next 100 years, each club could issue and revise its own code of Rules, and these were mainly based on the codes issued by The Royal and Ancient Golf Club, the Edinburgh Burgess Golfing Society or the Honourable Company. Some of the rules followed by individual clubs were identical to one of these codes, while others were worded with reference to the features of a particular course.

Starting in the second half of the 19th century, more and more clubs based their codes on those issued by The Royal and Ancient Golf Club. In 1897 its governance role was formalised with the creation of the Rules of Golf Committee.

**1744** The Honourable company of Edinburgh Golfers produce a written code of rules. Known as the Thirteen Articles, Rule 1 states: "You must tee your ball within a club-length of the hole".

**1754** Largely copying from the 1744 Rules, the Society of St Andrews Golfers (later to become The Royal and Ancient Golf Club) record their own Rules in the minutes.

**1775** Methods of settling disputes first appear in the Honourable Company's Rules. "Any dispute arising between parties on the green shall be determined by the Captain for the time, if present, or by the latest Captain who may be on the ground".

**1812** The R&A's 1754 code is revised and for the first time the Rules of Golf refer to bunkers and the putting green.

**1842** The revised R&A code stipulates that "one round of the links, or 18 holes, is reckoned a match" for the first time.

**1851** A revised R&A code is issued. In response to the advent of the gutta percha ball, a new rule allows that: "If a ball shall split into two or more pieces, a fresh ball shall be put down in playing for a medal".

**1875** Attending the flagstick and dealing with balls resting against the flagstick appear in the Rules for the first time.

**1882** The revised R&A code contains an index and a glossary of terms for the first time.

**1882** The glossary of terms in the R&A code defines the size of the hole as being four inches in diameter and lined with iron.

**1886** The Royal Isle of Wight Golf Club issues a version of the Rules of Golf, which defines the size of the hole as being four inches in diameter and six inches deep.

**1888** Local Rules for Playing the Links at St Andrews are separated out from the main Rules of Golf for the first time by The R&A.

**1891** The revised R&A code defines the hole as being four and a quarter inches in diameter and at least four inches deep. This remains the definition.

**1897** The Royal and Ancient Golf Club is officially recognised as the game's governing body for the Rules of Golf.

**1909** Limits on the form and make of clubs are applied for the first time.

**1920** The R&A and the USGA agreed that from May 1st, 1921, "the weight of the ball should be no greater than 1.62 ounces and the size not less than 1.62 inches in diameter".

**1929** Steel shafts are legalised.

**1939** The maximum number of clubs that can be carried is 14.

**1952** The R&A and the USGA establish a unified code of Rules.

**1960** Distance measuring devices are banned.

**1984** The ball is no longer dropped over the player's shoulder, but at arm's length and at shoulder height.

**1988** First Joint Decisions on the Rules of Golf book published by The R&A and the USGA.

**1990** The 1.68-inch ball becomes the only legal ball, marking the demise of the 1.62-inch British ball.

**2002** The R&A announces its decision to limit driver 'spring-like' effect from 2008, with an elite level Condition of Competition effective 1 January 2003.

**2004** Entire Rule book redrafted for clarity, adopting a more modern style. Etiquette section amended and expanded. Limits introduced on size and dimensions of wood heads and club length (excluding putters).

**2010** New groove specifications introduced, effective immediately at elite level by Condition of Competition. Club level golfers exempt until at least 2024.

# Royal Clubs

There are currently 64 clubs with royal titles granted by the British Royal family. In 2013, Homburger Golf Club in Germany was granted Royal status by Her Majesty Queen Elizabeth II who also bestowed this honour on Auckland Golf Club, New Zealand (2009) and the Mayfair Golf Club in Edmonton, Canada (2005). In 2004, Wellington Golf Club received the title from HRH The Duke of York. Mariánské Lázně Golf Club was honoured in 2003. The club had strong connections with British Royalty in the past; King Edward VII holidayed there, in what is now the Czech Republic. Apart from Mariánské Lázně and Royal Homburger, the Royal Clubs are in the United Kingdom or the Commonwealth. The oldest club with Royal connections is The Royal and Ancient Golf Club of St Andrews, founded in 1754 and given Royal patronage by King William IV in 1834. Royal Perth Golf Club, which was founded in 1824, received the patronage of King William IV a year earlier, in 1833.

| Club | Year Founded | Year of Royal Patronage | Royal Patron |
|---|---|---|---|
| Royal Ancient Golf Club, St Andrews | 1754 | 1834 | William IV |
| Royal Aberdeen | 1780 | 1903 | Edward VII (Leopold patron in 1872) |
| Royal Adelaide | 1892 | 1923 | George V |
| Royal Ascot | 1887 | 1887 | Victoria 1887; Elizabeth II 1977 |
| Royal Ashdown Forest | 1888 | 1893 | Victoria |
| Royal Auckland | 1894 | 2010 | Elizabeth II |
| Royal Belfast | 1881 | 1885 | Edward, Prince of Wales (later Edward VII) |
| Royal Birkdale | 1889 | 1951 | George VI |
| Royal Blackheath | 1766 | 1857 | Not known |
| Royal Burgess | 1773 | 1929 | George V |
| Royal Calcutta | 1829 | 1912 | George V |
| Royal Canberra | 1926 | 1933 | George V |
| Royal Cape | 1885 | 1910 | George V |
| Royal Cinque Ports | 1892 | 1910 | George V |
| Royal Colombo | 1879 | 1928 | George V |
| Royal Colwood | 1913 | 1931 | George V |
| Royal County Down | 1889 | 1908 | Edward VII |
| Royal Cromer | 1888 | 1887 | Edward, Prince of Wales (later Edward VII) |
| Royal Dornoch | 1877 | 1906 | Edward VII |
| Royal Dublin | 1885 | 1891 | Victoria |
| Duff House Royal | 1909 | 1925 | Princess Louise, Dowager Duchess of Fife |
| Royal Durban | 1892 | 1932 | George V |
| Royal Eastbourne | 1887 | 1887 | Victoria |
| Royal Epping Forest | 1888 | 1888 | Victoria |
| Royal Fremantle | 1905 | 1930 | George V |
| Royal Guernsey | 1890 | 1891 | Victoria |

| Club | Year Founded | Year of Royal Patronage | Royal Patron |
|---|---|---|---|
| Royal Harare | 1898 | 1929 | George V |
| Royal Hobart | 1900 | 1925 | George V |
| Royal Homburger | 1899 | 2013 | Elizabeth II |
| The Royal Household | 1901 | 1901 | Edward VII |
| Royal Jersey | 1878 | 1879 | Victoria |
| Royal Johannesburg | 1890 | 1931 | George V |
| Royal Liverpool | 1869 | 1871 | Prince Arthur, Duke of Connaught |
| Royal Lytham | 1886 | 1926 | George V |
| Royal Malta | 1888 | 1888 | Prince Alfred, Duke of Edinburgh |
| Royal Mariánské Lázně | 1905 | 2003 | Elizabeth II |
| Royal Mayfair | 1922 | 2005 | Elizabeth II |
| Royal Melbourne | 1891 | 1895 | Victoria |
| Royal Mid Surrey | 1892 | 1926 | George V |
| Royal Montreal | 1873 | 1884 | Victoria |
| Royal Montrose | 1810 | 1845 | Prince Albert |
| Royal Musselburgh | 1774 | 1876 | Prince Arthur, Duke of Connaught |
| Royal Nairobi | 1906 | 1935 | George V |
| Royal North Devon | 1864 | 1866 | Edward, Prince of Wales (later Edward VII) |
| Royal Norwich | 1893 | 1893 | George, Duke of York (later George V) |
| Royal Ottawa | 1891 | 1912 | George V |
| Royal Perth | 1824 | 1833 | William IV |
| Royal Perth (Australia) | 1895 | 1937 | George VI |
| Royal Port Alfred | 1907 | 1924 | George V |
| Royal Porthcawl | 1891 | 1909 | Edward VII |
| Royal Portrush | 1888 | 1892 | George, Duke of York (later George V) |
| Royal Quebec | 1874 | 1934 | George V |
| Royal Queensland | 1920 | 1921 | George V |
| Royal Regina | 1899 | 1999 | Elizabeth II |
| Royal St Davids | 1894 | 1908 | Edward, Prince of Wales (later Edward VII) |
| Royal St George's | 1887 | 1902 | Edward VII |
| Royal Sydney | 1893 | 1897 | Victoria |
| Royal Tarlair | 1926 | 1926 | Princess Louise, Dowager Duchess of Fife |
| Royal Troon | 1878 | 1978 | Elizabeth II |
| Royal Wellington | 1895 | 2004 | Prince Andrew, Duke of York |
| Royal West Norfolk | 1892 | 1892 | Edward, Prince of Wales (later Edward VII) |
| Royal Wimbledon | 1865 | 1882 | Victoria |
| Royal Winchester | 1888 | 1913 | George V |
| Royal Worlington and Newmarket | 1893 | 1895 | Victoria |

# Websites

| | |
|---|---|
| **The R&A** | www.randa.org |
| **United States Golf Association** | www.usga.org |
| **English Golf Union** | www.englishgolfunion.org |
| **Golf Union of Ireland** | www.gui.ie |
| **Scottish Golf Union** | www.scottishgolfunion.org |
| **Welsh Golf Union** | www.welshgolf.org |
| **European Golf Association** | www.ega-golf.ch |
| **Ladies Golf Union (LGU)** | www.lgu.org |
| **English Ladies (ELGA)** | www.englishladiesgolf.org |
| **Irish Ladies (ILGU)** | www.ilgu.ie |
| | |
| **European Tour** | www.europeantour.com |
| **US PGA Tour** | www.pgatour.com |
| **Australasian Tour** | www.pgatour.com.au |
| **Asian Tour** | www.asiantour.com |
| **Japanese Tour** | www.jgto.org |
| **South African Sunshine Tour** | www.sunshinetour.com |
| **LPGA Tour** | www.lpga.com |
| **Ladies European Tour (LET)** | www.ladieseuropeantour.com |
| **Japanese Ladies Tour** | www.lpga.or.jp (Japanese only) |
| **Asian Ladies Tour** | www.lagt.org |
| **Australian Ladies Tour** | www.alpgtour.com |
| **South African Ladies Tour** | www.wpga.co.za |
| **Futures Tour** | www.duramedfuturestour.com |
| | |
| **The Open** | www.opengolf.com |
| **US Open** | www.usopen.com |
| **The Masters** | www.masters.org |
| **US PGA Championship** | www.pga.com/pgachampionship/2010 |
| | |
| **PGA (The Belfry)** | www.pga.info |
| **PGAs of Europe** | www.pgae.com |
| **PGA of America** | www.pga.com |

| | |
|---|---|
| Severiano Ballesteros | www.seveballesteros.com |
| Angel Cabrera | www.angelcabrera.com |
| Michael Campbell | www.cambogolf.com |
| Paul Casey | www.paul-casey.com |
| Darren Clarke | www.darrenclarke.com |
| Ernie Els | www.ernieels.com |
| Nick Faldo | www.nickfaldo.com |
| Niclas Fasth | www.niclasfasth.com |
| Sergio García | www.sergiogarcia.com |
| Retief Goosen | www.retiefgoosen.com |
| Padraig Harrington | www.padraigharrington.com |
| David Howell | www.davidhowellgolf.com |
| Miguel Angel Jiménez | www.mmiworldwide.com |
| Bernhard Langer | www.bernhardlanger.de |
| Thomas Levet | www.thomas-levet.com |
| Paul McGinley | www.paulmcginley.net |
| Rory McIlroy | www.rorymcilroy,com |
| Phil Mickelson | www.phil-mickelson.com |
| Colin Montgomerie | www.colinmontgomerie.com |
| Jack Nicklaus | www.nicklaus.com |
| Greg Norman | www.shark.com |
| Lorena Ochoa | www.lorenaochoa.com |
| Geoff Ogilvy | www.prosportmanagement.com |
| José Maria Olazábal | www.gmi.com |
| Arnold Palmer | www.arnoldpalmer.com |
| Ian Poulter | www.ianpoulter.co.uk |
| Eduardo Romero | www.eduardoromero.com |
| Justin Rose | www.justinrose.com |
| Adam Scott | www.adamscott.com.au |
| Jeev Milkha Singh | www.jeevmilkhasingh.net |
| Annika Sörenstam | www.annikasorenstam.com |
| Henrik Stenson | www.henrikstenson.com |
| Lee Westwood | www.westyuk.com |
| Tiger Woods | www.tigerwoods.com |
| Ian Woosnam | www.woosie.com |

PART XVI

# Directory of Golfing Organisations Worldwide

# Directory of Golfing Organisations Worldwide

## National Associations

**The R&A**
Ch Exec, Peter Dawson, Beach House, Golf Place, St Andrews, Fife KY16 9JD
Tel (01334) 460000     Fax (01334) 460001
E-mail thechiefexecutive@randa.org
Website www.randa.org

**CONGU – Council of National Golf Unions**
Sec, Melvyn Goddard, 1 Peerswood Court, Little Neston, Neston CH64 0US
Tel (0151) 336 3936 – office
E-mail secretary@congu.com
Website www.congu.com

**IGF – International Golf Federation**
Exec Dir, Antony Scanlon, Maison Du Sport International, Av De Rhodanie 54, 1007 Lausanne, Switzerland
Tel +41 21 623 1212     Fax +41 21 601 6477
E-mail info@igfmail.org
Website www.internationalgolffederation.org

**LET – Ladies European Tour**
Exec Dir, Ivan Khodabakhsh, Buckinghamshire GC, Denham Court Drive, Denham UB9 5PG
Tel (01895) 831028     Fax (01895) 832301
E-mail mail@ladieseuropeantour.com
Website www.ladieseuropeantour.com

**LGU – Ladies' Golf Union**
Ch Exec, S Malcolm, The Scores, St Andrews, Fife KY16 9AT
Tel (01334) 475811     Fax (01334) 472818
E-mail info@lgu.org     Website www.lgu.org

**PGA – The Professional Golfers' Association**
Ch Exec, Sandy Jones, Centenary House, The Belfry, Sutton Coldfield B76 9PT
Tel (01675) 470333     Fax (01675) 477888
Email sandy.jones@pga.org.uk
Website www.pga.info

**PGA European Tour**
Exec Dir, G O'Grady, PGA European Tour, Wentworth Drive, Virginia Water, Surrey GU25 4LX
Tel (01344) 840400     Fax (01344) 840500
E-mail info@europeantour.com
Website www.europeantour.com

**PGAs of Europe**
Ch Exec, I Randell, Centenary House, The Belfry, Sutton Coldfield, B76 9PT
Tel (01675) 477899     Fax (01675) 477890
E-mail info@pgae.com
Website www.pgae.com

**Artisan Golfers' Association**
Hon Sec, W Johns. 6 Rennets Close, Eltham Heights, Eltham, London SE9 2NQ
Tel (020) 8850 1234
E-mail sec@agagolf.co.uk
Website www.agagolf.co.uk

**Association of Golf Writers**
A group of 30 newspapermen attending the Walker Cup match at St Andrews in 1938 founded the Association to protect the interests of golf writers. The principal objective is to maintain a close liaison with all the governing bodies and promoters to ensure good working conditions.

Hon Sec, Peter Dixon, 36 Gravett Close, Henley-on-Thames, Oxfordshire RG9 1XW
Tel (07770) 536094
E-mail enquiries@agwgolf.org
Website www.agwgolf.org

**BAGCC – British Association of Golf Course Constructors**
The BAGCC has a small but highly prestigious membership of constructors who have performed work to the highest standard from initial consultation to survey work and design through to the construction of a course and then its regular maintenance. Membership is granted only if the candidates satisfy the demanding criteria of experience, professionalism and workmanship set down by the Association.

Sec, Brian Pierson, 32 New Rd, Ringwood BH24 3AU
Tel (01425) 475584
E-mail brian.pierson@btopenworld,com
Website www.bagcc.org.uk

**BALASA – British Amputee & Les Autres Sports Association**
Golf Coordinator, Richard Saunders, 25 Kiln Lane, Manningtree, Essex CO11 1HQ
Tel (07967) 169951
E-mail richardsaundersfingers32@btinternet.com

**British Golf Collectors' Society**
Sec, A Thorpe, 22 Cherry Tree Close, Brinsley, Nottingham NG16 5BA
Tel/Fax (01773) 780420
E-mail anthonythorpe@ntlworld.com
Website www.britgolfcollectors.wyenet.co.uk

**BGIA – British Golf Industry Association**
Federation House, Stoneleigh Park, Warks CV8 2RF
Tel (024) 7641 4999 (x207)    Fax (024) 7641 4990
E-mail info@bgia.org.uk
Website www.bgia.org.uk

**British Golf Museum**
Dir, Angela Howe, Bruce Embankment, St Andrews,
Fife KY16 9AB
Tel (01334) 460046    Fax (01334) 460064
Website www.britishgolfmuseum.co.uk

**BIGGA – British & International Golf
Greenkeepers Association**
The British & International Golf Greenkeepers Associa-
tion has over 6,000 members and is dedicated to the
continuing professional development of its members
and strives, by education and training, for standards of
excellence in golf course management. BIGGA organise
an annual education conference and Europe's largest
indoor turf show.
Ch Exec, J Croxton, BIGGA House, Aldwark, Alne,
York YO61 1UF
Tel (01347) 833800    Fax (01347) 833801
E-mail info@bigga.co.uk
Website www.bigga.org.uk

**BRTMA – British Rootzone & Topdressing
Manufacturers Association**
Federation House, Stoneleigh Park, Warks CV8 2RF
Tel (024) 7641 4999    Fax (024) 7641 4990
E-mail brtma@sportsandplay.com
Website www.brtma.com

**BTLIA – British Turf & Landscape
Irrigation Association**
Sec, M Jones, Hinton House, Hinton Rd,
Bournemouth, Dorset BH1 2EN
Tel/Fax (01995) 670675
E-mail btlisecretary@btconnect.com
Website www.btlia.org.uk

**Club Managers Association of Europe**
CEO, Jerry Kilby, Federation House, Stoneleigh Park,
Warks CV8 2RF
Tel (024) 7669 2359    Fax (024) 7641 4990
E-mail jerry.kilby@cmaeurope.eu
Website www.cmaeurope.org

**EDGA – European Disabled Golf
Association**
Vice Pres, Pieter van Duijn, Wederikhof 8, NL-2215 GJ
Voorhout, The Netherlands
Tel +31 252 224161    E-mail mail@edgagolf.com
Website www.edgagolf.com

**EGIA – European Golf Industry Association**
Federation House, Stoneleigh Park, Warks CV8 2RF
Tel (024) 7641 4999    Fax (024) 7641 4990
E-mail egia@sportsandplay.com

**EIGCA – European Institute of Golf Course
Architects**
The EIGCA represents the vast majority of qualified
and experienced golf course architects throughout
Europe. Its goals are to enhance its professional status
and to provide educational courses to train future
architects.

Exec Off, Mrs Julia Green, Meadow View House,
Tannery Lane, Bramley, Surrey GU5 0AJ
Tel/Fax (01483) 891831    Fax (01483) 891846
E-mail enquiries@eigca.org    Website www.eigca.org

**Golf Club Managers' Association**
Membership of the Association is approximately
2,300, consisting of managers/secretaries and owners
of clubs and golfing associations situated mainly in the
UK and Europe. The Association offers advice on all
aspects of managing a golf club and has an extensive
information library available to its members through
its website.
Ch Exec, Bob Williams, 7a Beaconsfield Rd,
Weston-super-Mare BS23 1YE
Tel (01934) 641166    Fax (01934) 644254
E-mail hq@gcma.org.uk
Website www.gcma.org.uk

**Golf Club Stewards' Association**
The Golf Club Stewards' Association was founded in
1912 to promote the interests of members and to
serve as an employment agency for golf club stewards
and caterers.
Sec, KG Brothwell, 11 King Charles Court,
Sunderland, Tyne & Wear SR5 4PD
Tel (01915) 190137
E-mail k.brothwell@sky.com
Website www.club-noticeboard.co.uk

**Golf Consultants Association**
Federation House, Stoneleigh Park, Warks CV8 2RF
Tel (024) 7641 4999    Fax (024) 7641 4990
E-mail gca@sportsandplay.com
Website www.golfconsultants.org.uk

**Golf Foundation**
Ch. Exec, Michael Round, The Spinning Wheel, High St,
Hoddesdon, Herts EN11 8BP
Tel (01992) 449830
Fax (01992) 449840
E-mail info@golf-foundation.org
Website www.golf-foundation.org

**Golf Society of Great Britain**
Founded in 1955 by the late Sir Aynsley Bridgland of
Prince's Golf Club with the object of promoting good-
will and providing funds to further the interest of the
game in all its aspects, the Society now has about 850
members and continues its founder's aims of promot-
ing amateur golf through the sponsorship of junior golf
tournaments and through donations to the Junior Sec-
tion of the Society's participating clubs. Five to six
meetings are held each year in the UK plus Spring and
Autumn Tours abroad.
Sec, Brian Ward, Parkhouse Lodge, Mill Lane, Holmes
Chapel, Cheshire CW4 8AU
Tel (07760) 777736
E-mail secretary@golfsocietygb.com
Website www.golfsocietygb.com

**Handigolf Foundation**
Sec, Terry Kirby
Tel (07817) 515006
E-mail terry1.kirby@virgin.net
Website www.handigolf.org

**National Association of Public Golf Courses**
Affiliated to the English Golf Union, the Association was founded in 1927 by golf course architect FG Hawtree and five times Open champion JH Taylor to provide a relationship between public and proprietory golf clubs, and local councils and course owners.
*Hon Sec,* E Mitchell, 12 Newton Close, Redditch B98 7YR
*Tel* (01527) 542106
*E-mail* secretary@napgc.org.uk
*Website* www.napgc.org.uk

**National Golf Clubs' Advisory Association**
Founded in 1922, the Association's aims are to protect the interests of golf clubs in general; to give legal advice and direction, under the opinion of Counsel, on the administrative and legal responsibilities of golf clubs;.and to provide a mediation service to members' clubs within the UK.
*Ch Exec,* Michael Shaw LLM
*Nat Sec,* J Howe, The Threshing Barn, Homme Castle Barns, Shelsley Walsh, Worcs WR6 6RR
*Tel* (01886) 812943      *Fax* (01886) 812935
*E-mail* jackie.ngaa@idealnet.co.uk
*Website* www.ngcaa.org.uk

**One-Armed Golfers, Society of**
*Hon Sec,* Jerry Woodley, 56 Hillfield Rd, Little Sutton, Ellesmere Port, Cheshire CH66 1JD
*Tel* (01513) 399 630
*E-mail* jedro1@sky.com
*Website* www.onearmgolf.org

**Public Schools Old Boys Golf Association**
*Hon Sec,* P de Pinna, Bruins, Wythwood, Haywards Heath, West Sussex RH16 4RD
*Tel* (01444) 454883
*Email* fred-.die_@tiscali.co.uk
*Website* www.grafton.morrish.org.uk

**Public Schools' Golfing Society**
*Hon Sec,* N D Owen,1 Bruce Grove, Orpington, Kent BR6 0HF
*Tel* (01689) 810225
*E-mail* nick.owen@ndowen.com

**STRI – Sports Turf Research Institute**
STRI is an independent consultancy and research organisation specialising in golf courses. Recognised throughout the world for its expertise in both agronomic and environmental issues relating to golf, STRI is the official adviser to The R&A's Championship Committee for all 'Open' venues. STRI undertakes research into turfgrass and sports surface science, promoting innovative solutions. For golf courses, it provides advisory and architectural services and gives ecological advice. In addition, STRI organises training and produces publications.
*Ch Exec,* Dr I G McKillop; *Marketing,* Carolyn Beadsmoore, St Ives Estate, Bingley, West Yorks BD16 1AU
*Tel* (01274) 565131
*Fax* (01274) 561891
*E-mail* info@stri.co.uk
*Website* www.stri.co.uk

# Country and Regional Unions and Associations
Every effort has been made to ensure the accuracy of the information

## England

**England Golf**
*CEO,* David Joy, National Golf Centre, The Broadway, Woodhall Spa, Lincs LN10 6PU
*Tel* (01526) 354500
*Fax* (01526) 354020
*E-mail* info@englandgolf.org
*Website* www.englandgolf.org

**Midland Golf Union**
*Sec,* N Harris, 24 Ayston Rd, Uppingham, Rutland LE15 9RL
*Tel* (01572) 823036      *Mobile* (07906) 156701
*E-mail* secretary@midlandgolfunion.co.uk
*Website* www.midlandgolfunion.co.uk

**North Golf Union**
*Sec,* J D Trickett, 8 Derriman Grove, Sheffield S11 9LE
*Tel/Fax* (0114) 219 1625      *Mobile* (07756) 764240
*E-mail* dennistrickett@yahoo.co.uk
*Website* www.ncgu.co.uk

**South East Golf Union**
*Sec,* A Sigee, 7 Bosmore Rd, Luton LU3 2TR
*Tel* (01582) 651948
*E-mail* secretary@southeastgolfunion.co.uk
*Website* www.southeastgolfunion.co.uk

**South West Golf Union**
*Sec,* T C Reynolds, The Haven, Velator, Nr Braunton, N Devon EX33 2DX
*Tel/Fax* (01271) 812228
*E-mail* swcga@talktalk.net
*Website* www.swcga.co.uk

### English Men's County Unions

**Bedfordshire CGU**
*Sec,* S K Goode, 54 Swasedale Rd, Luton LU3 2UD
*Tel* (01582) 521716
*E-mail* secretary@bedsgolfunion.org.uk
*Website* www.bedsgolfunion.org

**Berks, Bucks & Oxon UGC**
*Sec,* P M J York, Bridge House, Station Approach, Great Missenden HP16 9AZ
*Tel* (01494) 867341
*E-mail* secretary@bbogolf.com
*Website* www.bbogolf.com

**Cambridgeshire Area GU**
*Sec,* H S Fleming, The Old Chapel, New Path, Fordham CB7 5JX
*Tel* (01638) 723028      *Mobile* (07760) 557622
*E-mail* hamishfleming@fordhamchapel.plus.com
*Website* www.cagu.co.uk

**Cheshire UGC**
Sec, S J Foster, County Office Chester GC, Curzon
Park North, Chester CH4 8AR
Tel (01244) 678004
E-mail secretary@cheshiregolf.org.uk
Website www.cheshiregolf.org.uk

**Cornwall GU**
Sec, C Pountney, South Court, South Hill Rd,
Callington PL17 7LG
Tel (01579) 384233
Mobile (07767) 418500
E-mail secretary@cornwallgolfunion.org.uk
Website www.cornwallgolfunion.org.uk

**Cumbria UGC**
Hon Sec, T F Stout, Kingston House, Moresby,
Whitehaven CA28 8UW
Tel (01946) 693036
E-mail cumbriaugcsec@yahoo.co.uk
Website www.cumbria-golf-union.org.uk

**Derbyshire UGC**
Hon Sec, P McGrath, 36 Ilkeston Rd, Stapleford,
Notts NG9 8JL
Tel (01159) 223606
E-mail pmcgd20147@aol.com
Website www.dugc.co.uk

**Devon CGU**
Sec, R J Hirst, Unit 1,Tavy Business Centre, Pitts
Cleave,Tavistock PL19 0NU
Tel (01822) 610640
Fax (01822) 610540
E-mail info@devongolfunion.org.uk
Website www.devongolfunion.org.uk

**Dorset CGU**
Sec, I L Hulse, 5 St James Rd, Ferndown, Dorset
BH22 9NY
Tel (01202) 861185
Mobile (07815) 144582
E-mail secretary@dcgu.org.uk
Website www.dcgu.org.uk

**Durham CGU**
Sec, G P Hope, 7 Merrion Close, Moorside,
Sunderland SR3 2QP
Tel/Fax (0191) 522 8605
E-mail secretary@durhamcountygolfunion.co.uk
Website www.durhamcountygolfunion.co.uk

**Essex GU**
Sec, A T Lockwood, 2d Maldon Rd, Witham, Essex
CM8 2AB
Tel (01376) 500998
Fax (01376) 500842
E-mail info@essexgolfunion.org
Website www.essexgolfunion.org

**Gloucestershire GU**
Sec, I Watkins, The Vyse, Olde Lane,
Toddington, Glos GL54 5DQ
Tel/Fax (01242) 621476
E-mail secretary@gloucestershiregolfunion.co.uk
Website www.gloucestershiregolfunion.co.uk

**Hampshire GU**
Sec, David Wheeler County Office, Hockley GC,
Winchester Rd, Twyford Winchester SO21 1PL
Tel/Fax (01962) 711532
Mobile (07568) 372893

**Hampshire, Isle of Wight &
Channel Islands GU**
Sec, Barry Morgan, c/o Liphook GC, Wheatsheaf
Enclosure, Liphook, Hampshire GU30 7EH
Tel (01428) 725580
E-mail hgu@hampshiregolf.co.uk
Website www.hampshiregolf.org.uk

**Hertfordshire GU**
Sec, L Matamala, Chesfield Downs GC, Jacks Hill,
Graveley, Herts SG4 7EQ
Tel (08081) 682333
E-mail secretary@hertsgolfunion.com
Website www.hertsgolfunion.com

**Isle of Man GU**
Sec, C Taylor Ballabrune, Dog Mills, Ramsey, Isle of
Man IM7 4AD
Tel (01624) 814028    Mobile (076244) 34778
E-mail joyboyd@manx.net
Website www.isleofmangolf.im

**Kent GU**
Sec, J G Young, Littlestone GC, St Andrew's Rd,
Littlestone, New Romney, Kent TN28 8RB
Tel (01797) 367725    Fax (01797) 367726
E-mail kcgu@kentgolf.co.uk
Website www.kentgolf.org

**Lancashire UGC**
Hon Sec, A V Moss, Ashton & Lea GC, Tudor Ave,
Lea, Preston PR4 0XA
Tel (01772) 731330    Fax (01772) 727776
E-mail secretary@lancashiregolf.org
Website www.lancashiregolf.org

**Leicestershire & Rutland GU**
Hon Sec, B Tuttle, 63 Gwendoline Dr., Countesthor-
pe, Leicester LE8 5SJ
Tel (01162) 771900    Mobile (07967) 873500
E-mail lrgusecretary@gmail.com
Website www.lrgu.net

**Lincolnshire UGC**
Hon Sec, H Harrison, 27 Orchard Close, Morton,
Gainsborough DN21 3BP
Tel (01427) 616904    Mobile (07885) 787622
E-mail secretary@lugc.co.uk
Website www.lugc.co.uk

**Middlesex GU**
Sec, R Blower, Northwick Park Golf Centre, Wat-
ford Rd, Harrow HA1 3TZ
Tel (0208) 864 4744    Mobile (07840) 531974
Fax (0208) 864 4554
E-mail secretary@mcgu.co.uk
Website www.mcgu.co.uk

**Norfolk CGU**
Hon Sec, M Devlin, Acacia House, The Street,
Tibenham, Norwich NR16 1QA
Tel (013789) 674516    Mobile (07922) 202848
E-mail niblick@btinternet.com
Website www.norfolkcountygolfunion.co.uk

**Northamptonshire GU**
Hon Sec, J Pearson, 150 Church Green Rd, Bletchley,
Milton Keynes MK3 6DD
Tel (01908) 648657    Mobile (07951) 123099
E-mail secretary@northantsgolfunion.co.uk
Website www.northantsgolfunion.co.uk

## Northumberland UGC
*Hon Sec,* W E Procter, Eastfield House, Moor Rd
South, Gosforth, Newcastle upon Tyne NE3 1NP
*Tel* (0191) 285 4981
*Mobile* (07946) 417416
*E-mail* secretary@nugc.org.uk
*Website* www.nugc.org.uk

## Nottinghamshire UGC
*Hon Sec,* C Bee, 270 Wollaton Road, Wollaton
Nottinghamshire NG8 1GN
*Tel* (01159) 284891      *Mobile* (07814) 433095
*E-mail* secretary@nottsgolfunion.co.uk
*Website* www.nottsgolf.com

## Shropshire & Herefordshire UGC
*Sec,* P D Simmonds, Grove Farm House, Dorrington,
Nr Shrewsbury SY5 7JD
*Tel* (01743) 718388
*E-mail* secretary@shugc.com
*Website* www.shugc.com

## Somerset GU
*Sec,* D Longden, 2 The Rectory, 71 Upper Church Rd,
Weston-super-Mare BS23 2HX
*Tel/fax* (01934) 632687      *Mobile* (07741) 283741
*E-mail* secretary@somersetgolfunion.co.uk
*Website* www.somersetgolfunion.co.uk

## Staffordshire UGC
*Sec,* M A Payne, 20 Kingsbrook Drive, Hillfield, Solihull
B91 3UU
*Tel* (0121) 704 4779   *Mobile* (07730) 891172
*E-mail* martin.payne11@btinternet.com
*Website* www.golfinstaffs.co.uk

## Suffolk GU
*Hon Sec,* C A Wilderspin, 10a Chestnut Avenue,
Oulton Broad, Lowestoft, Suffolk, NR32 3JA
*Tel* (01502) 588028
*E-mail* charles.wilderspin632@btinternet.com
*Website* www.suffolkgolfunion.co.uk

## Surrey CGU
*Sec,* J A Davies, Sutton Green GC, New Lane,
Sutton Green GU4 7QF
*Tel* (01483) 755788      *Fax* (01483) 751771
*E-mail* secretary@surreygolf.org
*Website* www.surreygolf.org

## Sussex CGU
*Sec,* A Vasant, J.P., Eastbourne Down GC, East Dean
Rd, Eastbourne, East Sussex BN20 8ES
*Tel* (01323) 746677      *Fax* (01323) 746777
*E-mail* countyoffice@sussexgolf.org
*Website* www.sussexgolf.org

## Warwickshire UGC
*Sec,* M Nixon, PO Box 6184, Stratford upon Avon,
Warks CV37 1NG
*Tel* (01789) 297198      *Mobile* (07813) 932318
*E-mail* matt@warwickshiregolf.com
*Website* www.warksgolf.co.uk

## Wiltshire CGU
*Sec,* D J Lewis, 39 Ashley Piece, Ramsbury, SN8 2QE
*Tel* (01672) 520008
*E-mail* secretary@wcgu.org.uk
*Website* www.wcgu.org.uk

## Worcestershire UGC
*Hon Sec,* A Boyd, The Bear's Den, Upper St,
Defford, Worcester WR8 9BG
*Tel* (01386) 750657      *Fax* (01386) 750472
*Mobile* (07953) 26922
*E-mail* menssecretary
                    @worcestershireamateurgolf.co.uk
*Website* www.worcestershireamateurgolf.co.uk

## Yorkshire UGC
*Hon Sec,* K H Dowswell, 33 George St, Wakefield
WF1 1LX
*Tel* (01924) 383869      *Fax* (01924) 383634
*Mobile* (07860) 391380
*E-mail* yorkshiregolf@lineone.net
*Website* www.yorkshireunionofgolf.co.uk

### English Women's County Associations
## Bedfordshire LCGA
*Hon Sec,* Mrs Gwen Walpole, 2 Thornbridge Close,
Rushden, Northants NN10 9NJ
*Tel* (01933) 318736
*E-mail* gwenwalpole@gmail.com
*Website* blcga.co.uk

## Berkshire CLGA
*Hon Sec,* Mrs Nicky Luff, 7 Bass Mead, Cookham,
Maidenhead, Berkshire SL6 9DJ
*Tel* (07885) 028440
*E-mail* nicky.luff@btinternet.com
*Website* www.bclga.co.uk

## Buckinghamshire CLGA
*Hon Sec,* Mrs Helen Mines, Sobalym, Manor Rd,
Princes Risborough, HP27 9DJ
*Tel* (07538) 306496
*E-mail* helen_mines@btinternet.com
*Website* bclga.org.uk

## Cambs & Hunts LCGA
*Hon Sec,* Mrs Jacquie Richardson, Peel House,
11 Doddington Rd, Benwick, March, Cambridge
PE15 0UT
*Tel* (01354) 677856
*E-mail* j.s.richardson@btinternet.com
*Website* chlgca.co.uk

## Cheshire CLGA
*Hon Sec,* Mrs A McCormick, 1 Grange Close, Weston,
Disley, Crewe CW2 5FL
*Tel* (07918) 672497
*E-mail* ann.mccormick4@ntlworld.com
*Website* www.cheshireladiesgolf.org

## Cornwall LCGA
*Hon Sec,* Mrs Pat Crowson, 41 Old Coach Road,
Playing Place, Truro TR3 6ET
*Tel* (01872) 864412
*E-mail* pat_pmc41@yahoo.co.uk      *Website* clga.co.uk

## Cumbria LCGA
*Hon Sec,* Mrs Sandra Stoker, Yew Tree Cottage, Main
Rd, Endmoor, Kendal LA8 0EU
*Tel* (01539) 567826
*E-mail* stokers1985@btinternet.com
*Website* www.cumbria-lcga.co.uk

## Derbyshire LCGA
*Hon Sec,* Mrs Tracy Pierrepont, 22 Arnos Grove,
Nuthall, Notts NG16 1QA

*Tel* (01159) 750107
*E-mail* ladysecretary@dugc.co.uk
*Website* www.derbyshiregolf.org

**Devon CLGA**
*Hon Sec,* Mrs Rickie Pawsey, 33 Prince of Wales Rd,
Crediton EX17 2AG
*Tel* (01363) 772141
*E-mail* devonladiessecretary@hotmail.com
*Website* www.devonladiesgolf.org

**Dorset LCGA**
*Hon Sec,* Mrs Zoe Ashley, Honeypot Cottage, 12
Glenwood Rd, West Moor, Ferndown BH22 0EP
*Tel* (01202) 872277
*E-mail* zoe.odlcga@yahoo.co.uk
*Website* www.dorsetladiesgolf.org

**Durham LGA**
*Hon Sec,* Mrs Ann Corbett, 1 Corby Mews,
Ashbrooke Rd, Sunderland SR2 7HQ
*Tel* (0191) 522 9448
*E-mail* secretary@durhamladiesgolf.org.uk
*Website* www.durhamladiesgolf.org.uk

**Essex LGA**
*Hon Sec,* Mrs Nicola Thomas, 6 Heathgate, Wickham
Bishops, Witham CM8 3NZ
Tel (01621) 891592
*E-mail* ath1343349@aol.com
*Website* essexladiesgolf.org

**Gloucestershire LCGA**
*Hon Sec,* Mrs Debbie Casling, 27 Tallis Rd,
Churchdown GL3 1LX
*Tel* (01452) 857500
*E-mail* secretary@glcga.co.uk
*Website* www.glcga.co.uk

**Hampshire LCGA**
*Hon Sec,* Mrs Gill Staley, Garth House, 55 Elvetham
Rd, Fleet GU51 4QP
*Tel* (01252) 616442
*E-mail* gill@staley.org.uk
*Website* www.hampshireladiesgolf.co.uk

**Hertfordshire CLGA**
*Hon Sec,* Mrs Linda Battye 12 Manor Links, Bishop's
Stortford, Herts CM23 5RA
*Tel* (01279) 505393
*E-mail* lindabattye@gmail.com
*Website* www.hclga.co.uk

**Kent CLGA**
*Hon Sec,* Mrs Sarah Brooks, 10 Hayle Mill, Hayle Mill
Rd, Maidstone ME15 6JW
*Tel* (01622) 761841
*E-mail* pumplodge@aol.com
*Website* kentladiesgolf.org.uk

**Lancashire LCGA**
*Hon Sec,* Mrs Margaret Milne, The Rough, 39
Longmeadow Rd, Knowsley Village, Prescot L34 0HN
*Tel* (0151) 546 0479
*E-mail* margaretmilne52@yahoo.co.uk
*Website* www.llcga.org.uk

**Leicestershire & Rutland LCGA**
*Hon Sec,* Mrs Anita Higginson, The Old Rectory, Main
St, Peatling Parva, Leics LE17 5QA
*Tel* (01162) 478240

*E-mail* higginsons@talk21.com
*Website* www.lrlcga.co.uk

**Lincolnshire LCGA**
*Hon Sec,* Mrs Beverley Dolman, Long Barn, Wakerley
Rd, Harringworth NN17 3AH
*Tel* (01572) 747385
*E-mail* secretary@lincolnshireladiesgolf.co.uk
*Website* www.lincolnshireladiesgolf.co.uk

**Middlesex LCGA**
*Hon Sec,* Mrs Sue Katz, 18 Pyke's End, Pinner
HA5 2EX
*Tel* (0208) 866 2295
*E-mail* suekatz@ideasint.demon.co.uk
*Website* www.mlcga.co.uk

**Norfolk LCGA**
*Hon Sec,* Mrs Margaret Watson, Dunham House,
Litcham Rd, Great Dunham PE32 2LJ
*Tel* (01328) 701982
*E-mail* quesol@btinternet.com
*Website* www.norfolkladiesgolf.co.uk

**Northamptonshire LCGA**
*Hon Sec,* Miss April Owens, Oakham Cottage, Croft
Lane, Staverton NN1 6JE
*Tel* (01327) 872324
*E-mail* nlcga.countysec@rocketmail.com
*Website* www.nlcga.org.uk

**Northumberland LCGA**
*Hon Sec,* Mrs Janette Fellows, 19 Holystone Av.,
Newcastle upon Tyne NE3 3HN
*Tel* (0191) 385 5185
*E-mail* nlcga.sec@gmail.com
*Website* www.nlcga.co.uk

**Nottinghamshire CLGA**
*Hon Sec/Treas,* Mrs Bridgett Patrick
*Tel* (01159) 373237
*E-mail* contactus@nclga.org
*Website* www.nclga.org.uk

**Oxfordshire LCGA**
*Hon Sec,* Mrs Iona Smith
*Tel* (01235) 526718
*E-mail* nsirsmith@btopenworld.com
*Website* olcga.org.uk

**Shropshire LCGA**
*E-mail* shropslcga@gmail.com

**Somerset LCGA**
*Hon Sec,* Mrs Margaret Allen, 21 Walnut Grove,
Shepton Mallet BA4 4HX
*Tel* (01749) 347886
*E-mail* secretary@somersetladiesgolf.org.uk
*Website* www. somersetladiesgolf.org.uk

**Staffordshire LCGA**
*Hon Sec,* Penny Small, 6 Rowley Close, Edingale
B79 9LN
*Tel* (07899) 916852
*E-mail* honsec@staffsladiesgolf.org
*Website* www.staffsladiesgolf.org

**Suffolk LCGA**
*Hon Sec,* Mrs Jeanette Longman, The Old School
House, Chillesford, IP12 3PS
*Tel* (01394) 450939
*E-mail* jeanette.longman@gmail.com
*Website* suffolkladiesgolf.org.uk

**Surrey LCGA**
*Sec,* Mrs Penelope Hall, SLCGA, c/o Sutton Green
GC, Sutton Green, Guildford GU4 7QF
*Tel* (01483) 751622
*Fax* (01483) 751771
*E-mail* secretary@slcga.org
*Website* www.slcga.org

**Sussex CLGA**
*Hon Sec,* Mrs Ann Carnegie, 7 The Wad, West
Wittering, West Sussex PO20 8AH
*Tel* (01243) 511307
*E-mail* ann@thecarnegies.net
*Website* www.sclga.com

**Warwickshire LCGA**
*Hon Sec,* Mrs Elizabeth Murdoch, Plestowes House,
Hareway Lane, Barford, Warwick CV35 8DD
*Tel* (01926) 624503
*E-mail* liz@murdochonline.co.uk
*Website* www.warwickshiregolf.com

**Wiltshire LCGA**
*Hon Sec,* Irene Tomkinson, Chirton Lodge, 63 The
Street, Chirton, Devizes SN10 3QS
*Tel* (01380) 848477
*E-mail* tomkinsons2@btinternet.com
*Website* www.wlcga.com

**Worcestershire and Herefordshire LCGA**
*Hon Sec,* Mrs Sue Birch, 159 Hither Green Lane,
Abbey Park, Redditch B98 9AZ
*Tel* (01527) 61958
*Mobile* (07801) 437942
*E-mail* suebirch@btinternet.com
*Website* www.ladies.worcestershireamateurgolf.co.uk

**Yorkshire LCGA**
*Hon Sec,* Mrs Dawn Clegg, 10 Usher Park Rd, Haxby,
York YO32 3RY
*Tel* (01904) 761987
*E-mail* dawnhclegg@hotmail.com
*Website* www.ylcga.org

**English Regional and County PGAs**

**The PGA in England (East)**
*Sec,* J Smith, Bishop's Stortford GC, Dunmow Road,
Bishop's Stortford, Herts CM23 5HP
*Tel* (01279) 652070
*Fax* (01279) 652732
*E-mail* john.smith@pga.org.uk

**The PGA in England (Midland)**
*Sec,* J Brown, Forward House, 17 High Street, Henley
In Arden, Warwickshire B95 5AA
*Tel* (01564) 330635    *Fax* (01564) 797410
*E-mail* james.brown@pga.org.uk

**The PGA in England &Wales (North)**
*Sec,* G Maly, No 2 Cottage, Bolton GC, Lostock Park,
Chorley New Rd, Bolton, Lancs BL6 4AJ
*Tel* (01204) 496137    *Fax* (01204) 847959
*E-mail* graham.maly@pga.org.uk

**The PGA in England (South)**
*Sec,* S Smith, Clandon Regis GC, Epsom Rd, West
Clandon, Guildford, Surrey GU4 7TT
*Tel* (01483) 224200
*E-mail* sam.smith@pga.org.uk

**The PGA in England &Wales (South West)**
*Sec,* G Ross, The Lodge House, Woodbury Park
H&GC, Woodbury Castle, Woodbury, Exeter, EX5 1JJ
*Tel* (01395) 232288    *Fax* (01395) 232383
*E-mail* glenn.ross@ pga.org.uk

**Bedfordshire & Cambridgeshire PGA**
*Sec,* Simon Fitton  Thorpe Wood Golf Course and
Driving Range, Thorpe Wood, Peterborough
PE3 6SE
*Tel* (01733) 267701
*E-mail* simon@neneparkgolf.com

**Berks, Bucks & Oxon PGA**
*Hon Sec,* Martin Morbey, Valderrama, Haywards Road,
Drayton, Oxon OX14 4LB
*Tel* (07803) 499567
*E-mail* admin@bbopga.co.uk
*Website* www.bbopga.co.uk

**Cheshire and North Wales PGA**
*Sec,* G Maly, No 2 Cottage, Bolton GC, Lostock Park,
Chorley New Road, Bolton BL6 4AJ
*Tel* (01204) 496137
*Fax* (01204) 847959
*E-mail* graham.maly@pga.org.uk

**Cornwall PGA**
*Sec,* Dave Higman
*Tel* (07717) 792687
*E-mail* davehigman@hotmail.co.uk

**Derbyshire PGA**
*Sec,* Andrew Smith, Ashbourne GC, Wyaston Rd,
Ashbourne DE6 1NB
*Tel* (01335) 342078
*E-mail* ashbournegc@tiscali.co.uk
*Website* www.ashbournegc.co.uk

**Devon PGA**
*Sec,* Dan Hendriksen, Churston GC, Churston, Brixham
TQ5 0LA
*Tel* (07971) 821550
*E-mail* dcpga@hotmail.com
*Website* www.devonpga.co.uk

**Dorset PGA**
*Sec,* D Parsons, Bridport & West Dorset GC, Burton
Rd, Bridport, Dorset DT6 4PS
*Tel* (01308) 421491
*E-mail* bridproshop@tesco.net

**Essex PGA**
*Sec,* Suzy Garland-Collins, 27 Willowdene Court,
Brentwood, Essex CM14 5ET
*Tel/Fax* (01277) 223510
*E-mail* essexpga@googlemail.com
*Website* www.essexpga.com

**Gloucestershire & Somerset PGA**
*Secretaries,* Pat Baker
*Tel* (01934) 852322
*Mobile* (07775) 503698
*E-mail* info@mendipspringgolfclub.com
Mike Laband
*Tel* (07809) 243839
*E-mail* lairdlaband@googlemail.com
Daryl Kelley
*Tel* (01179) 696968

## Hampshire PGA
Sec, Paul Brown, HPGA Office, South Winchester GC,
Pitt, Winchester SO22 5QX
Tel (01962) 860928
E-mail secretary@hampshirepga.co.uk
Website www.hampshire-pga.co.uk

## Hertfordshire PGA
Sec, M E Plumbley, Stavonga Dell, 21 Pasture Rd,
Letchworth SG6 3LP
Tel/Fax (01462) 670774
E-mail meplumbley@hertspga.org
Website www.hertspga.org

## Kent PGA
Contact South Region PGA

## Lancashire PGA
Sec, Jeff Matthews 14 Long Meadow, Mellor Brook,
Blackburn, Lancashire BB2 7NX
Tel (07931) 587304
E-mail graham.maly@pga.org.uk

## Leicestershire & Rutland PGA
Sec, Mark Hatton, Golfing Days Ltd, 1 Royal Mews,
Station Rd, Ashby de la Zouch LE65 2GJ
Tel (07784) 783299      Mobile 07920 113 463
E-mail mark@golfingdays.co.uk
Website www.golfingdays.co.uk

## Lincolnshire PGA
Sec, D Drake, 23 Manor Rd, Saxilby, Lincoln  LN1 2HX
Tel (01522) 703331

## Middlesex PGA
Sec, S Rist, 64 Dorchester Avenue, Palmers Green
London N13 5DX
Tel (0208) 803 9702
E-mail steve@mdxpga.co.uk
Website www.mdxpga.co.uk

## Norfolk PGA
Sec, John Paling, Squirrels Reach, Folgate Lane,
Old Costessey, Norwich NR8 5EF
Tel (01603) 741301      Mobile (07778) 577590
E-mail jandjpaling@uwclub.net
Website www.club-noticeboard.co.uk

## North East & North West PGA
Hon Sec, T Flowers, 10 Rosedale Rd, Belmont,
Durham DH1 2AS
Tel (0191) 383 9385
Mobile (07958) 043403
E-mail tom.flowers@nenwpga.co.uk

## Northamptonshire PGA
Sec, R Lobb, 15 Manor Rd, Pitsford, Northampton
NN6 9AR
Tel (01604) 881367      Mobile (07968) 164151
E-mail richard.lobb@northamptonshiregolf.org.uk
Website www.northamptonshirepga.co.uk

## Nottinghamshire PGA
Hon Sec, Tel (07806) 592419
E-mail secretary@nottspga.co.uk
Website www.nottspga.co.uk

## Shropshire & Hereford PGA
Sec, P Hinton, 29 Stourbridge Rd, Bridgnorth,
WV15 5AZ
Tel (01746) 762045

E-mail paulhinton@enta.net
Website www.a1golf.biz

## Staffordshire PGA
Sec, R Hill, 80 Old Town Mews, Stratford upon Avon
CV37 6GR
Tel (07791) 289 941

## Suffolk PGA
Sec, Terry Broome, 2 The Crescents, Reydon,
Southwold IP18 6RT
Tel (01502) 722506      Mobile (07814) 676770
E-mail tmb.suffolkpga@gmail.com

## Surrey PGA
Contact South Region PGA

## Sussex PGU
Sec, C Pluck, 96 Cranston Ave, Bexhill,
East Sussex TN39 3NL
Tel (01424) 221298      Mobile (07841) 929866
E-mail sussexpgu@g.mail.com
Website www.spgu.co.uk

## Warwickshire PGA
Sec, N Selwyn-Smith, 18 Cornfield Ave, Stoke Heath,
Bromsgrove B60 3QU
Tel (01527) 875750      Mobile (07973) 863578
E-mail neilss@execgolf.co.uk

## Wiltshire PGA
Sec, M Walters, Erlestoke Sands GC, Erlestoke,
Devizes SN10 5UB
Tel (01380) 831027

## Worcestershire PGA
Sec, K Ball, 136 Alvechurch Rd, West Heath,
Birmingham B31 3PW
Tel (0121) 475 7400      E-mail kenball@talktalk.net

## Yorkshire PGA
Sec, J Pape, 22 The Locks, Pottery Lane, Woodlesford,
Leeds LS26 8PU
Tel (01132) 828984      Mobile (07891) 104633

## England and Wales Blind Golf
Sec, Barry Ritchie
Tel (02476) 414166
Website www.blindgolf.co.uk

# Ireland

## Golfing Union of Ireland
Gen Sec, Pat Finn, National Headquarters, Carton
Demesne, Maynooth, Co. Kildare
Tel +353 1 505 4000  Fax +353 1 505 4001
E-mail information@gui.ie
Website www.gui.ie

### Irish Men's Branches
**Connacht Branch:** Gen Sec, E Lonergan, Breaffy
Business Centre, Breaffy, Castlebar, Mayo
Tel +353 (0) 94 90 28141
E-mail guibc@eircom.net
Website gui@ie/connacht

**Leinster Branch:** Exec Off T Thompson, Carton
Demesne, Maynooth, Co.Kildare
Tel +353 1 601 6842  Fax +353 1 6016858
E-mail info@leinster.gui.ie

**Munster Branch:** *Exec Off,* K Walsh, 6 Townview,
Mallow, Co Cork
*Tel* +353 22 21026    *Fax* +353 22 42373
*E-mail* info@munster.gui.ie

**Ulster Branch:** *Gen Sec,* K Stevens, Unit 5,
Forestgrove Business Park, Newtownbreda Rd, Belfast
BT8 6AW
*Tel* (028) 9049 1891
*Fax* (028) 9049 1615
*E-mail* info@gui-ulster.co.uk

**Irish Ladies' Golf Union**
*Ch Exec,* Sinead Heraty, 103-105 Q House, 76 Furze
Rd, Sandyford Ind. Est., Dublin 18
*Tel* +353 1 293 4833
*E-mail* info@ilgu.ie    *Website* www.ilgu.ie

*Irish Ladies' Districts*
**Connacht District:** *Hon Sec,* Kate O'Meara,
Lenarevagh, Bearna, Co.Galway
*Tel* +353 (0) 83 404 7131
*E-mail* ilguwest@eircom.net

**East Leinster District:** *Hon Sec,* Mrs Lucia Farrell,
Bannonstown, Hayes, Navan, Co Meath
*Tel* +353 (0) 46 902 4707
*Mobile* +353 (0) 86 806 3667
*E-mail* easterndistrict@eircom.net

**Mid Leinster District:** *Hon Sec,* Mrs Yvonne Mac-
Sweeney, Old Town Lane, Castlebridge, County
Wexford
*Tel* +353 (0) 83 404 7246
*E-mail* midlanddistrict@gmail.com

**Munster District:** *Hon Sec,* Mrs Marion
Pattenden, Abbeystrewery, Skibbereen. Co Cork
*Tel* +353 (0) 83 404 3481
*Mobile* +353 (0)282 2955
*E-mail* ilgusoutherndistrict@gmail.com

**Ulster District:** *Hon Sec* Mrs Joyce Hughes,
1 Beech Hill Park, Lisburn, Co Antrim BT28 3HP
*Tel* (02892) 92675605
*Mobile* (07881) 955738
*E-mail* joycehughes16@yahoo.co.uk

**PGA Irish Region**
*Sec,* M McCumiskey, Dundalk GC, Blackrock,
Dundalk, Co Louth, Eire
*Tel* +353 42 932 1193    *Fax* +353 42 932 1899
*E-mail* michael.mccumiskey@pga.org.uk

## Scotland

**Scottish Golf Union**
*Ch Exec,* H Grey, The Duke's, St Andrews KY16 8NX
*Tel* (01334) 466477    *Fax* (01334) 461361
*E-mail* sgu@scottishgolf.org
*Website* www.scottishgolf.org

*Scottish Men's Associations/Unions*
**Angus CGA**
*Sec,* W Miller, 48 Buddon Drive, Monifieth DD5 4TJ
*Tel* (01382) 533728
*E-mail* billhmill@blueyonder.co.uk

**Argyll & Bute GU**
*Sec,* L. Pirie, 54 Banchory Ave, Inchinnan,
Renfrewshire PA4 9PZ
*Tel* (0141) 561 0535    *Mobile* (07815) 564001
*E-mail* lrpirie@aol.com
*Website* www.argyllandbutegolfunion.com

**Ayrshire GA**
*Sec,* A J Malcolm, 17 Auchincruive Ave, Prestwick
KA9 2DT
*Tel* (01292) 477657
*E-mail* ayrshiregolf@fsmail.net
*Website* www.ayrshiregolf.blogspot.com

**Borders GA**
*Sec,* D Little, Greenyard, Drove Rd, Langholm
DG13 0JW
*Tel* (01387) 381308
*E-mail* dennis.little@btinternet.com
*Website* www.bordergolf.co.uk

**Clackmannanshire CGU**
*Sec,* T Johnson, 75 Dewar Ave, Kincardine on Forth
FK10 4RR
*Tel* 01259) 731168    *Fax* (01259) 769445
*E-mail* thjohn01@aol.com

**Dunbartonshire GU**
*Sec,* A Harris, 11 Millersneuk Dr, Lenzie, Kirkintilloch,
Glasgow G66 5JF
*Tel* (0141) 776 3535
*E-mail* secretary@dgu.org.uk
*Website* www.dgu.org.uk

**Fife GA**
*Sec,* J Scott, Lauriston, East Links, Leven KY8 4JL
*Tel* (01333) 423798    *Fax* (01333) 439910
*E-mail* jscottfga@blueyonder.co.uk
*Website* www.fifegolf.org

**Glasgow GU**
*Sec,* R J G Jamieson, 32 Eglinton St, Beith KA15 1AQ
*Tel/Fax* (01505) 503000
*E-mail* r.jamieson-accountants@fsmail.net
*Website* www.glasgowgolfunion.org

**Lanarkshire GA**
*Sec,* Position vacant, 3 Westerhouse Court, Carluke,
South Lanarkshire ML8 5UP
*E-mail* business@lanarkshiregolf.com

**Lothians GA**
*Sec,* Neil F Park  43 Hopetoun Terrace, Gullane
EH31 2DD
*Tel* (01620) 844795
*Mobile* (07787) 156685
*E-mail* lga@edgewood.org.uk
*Website* www.lothiansgolfassociation.org.uk

**North District GU**
*Sec,* P L Abbott, 21 Manse Rd, Nairn IV12 4RW
*Tel* (01667) 453625
*E-mail* secretary@sgunorthgolf.com
*Website* www.sgunorth.com

**North-East District GA**
*Sec,* G M Young, 24 Shore St, Cairnbulg, Fraserburgh
AB43 8YL
*Tel* (01346) 582324
*E-mail* georgemyoung24@btinternet.com
*Website* www.sgunortheast.com

**Perth & Kinross CGU**
Sec, J J E Simpson, 11 Dunbarney Av, Bridge of Earn,
Perth PH2 9BP
Tel (01738) 812588      Mobile (07850) 724740
E-mail auntyeedie@hotmail.com
Website www.perthandkinrosscountygolf.net

**Renfrewshire GU**
Sec, I Storie, 35 Balmoral Rd, Elderslie PA5 9RA
Tel (01505) 343872
E-mail ian.storie@ntlworld.com
Website www.renfrewshiregolfunion.co.uk

**South of Scotland GA**
Sec, I Robin, 62 Albert Rd, Dumfries DG2 9DL
Tel (01387) 252004
E-mail iainrobin@tiscali.co.uk

**Stirlingshire GU**
Sec, J Elliott, 65 Rosebank Ave, Falkirk FK1 5JR
Tel (01324) 634118      Mobile (07979) 798160
E-mail johnelliott65@btinternet.com
Website www.stirlingshiregolfunion.co.uk

**PGA Scottish Region**
Sec, Brian Mair, King's Lodge, Gleneagles,
Auchterarder PH3 1NE
Tel (01764) 661840      Fax (01764) 661841
E-mail pgainscotland@oga.org.uk

**Scottish Ladies' Golfing Association**
Sec, Dr S Hartley, Caledonia House 1 Redheughs Rigg,
South Gyle, Edinburgh EH12 9DQ
Tel (0131) 339 3987
E-mail secretary@slga.co.uk
Website www.slga.co.uk

*Scottish Ladies' County Associations*

**Aberdeen LCGA**
Hon Sec, Miss K Stalker, 2 Braemar Court,
Fraserburgh AB43 9XE
Tel (01346) 513308
E-mail karen@fairways.eclipse.co.uk
Website www.alcga.co.uk

**Angus LCGA**
Hon Sec, Edna Jane Wallwork, The Shilling, 12d Rossie
Island Road, Montrose DD10 9NN
Tel (01674) 673478

**Ayrshire LCGA**
Hon Sec, Fiona Collier, Monkton Hall Lodge,
Southwoods, Monkton, Prestwick KA9 1UR
Tel (01292) 315982
E-mail secretary@alcga.com

**Border Ladies' CGA**
Hon Sec, Julie Birdsall, Highridgehall, Kelso
TD5 7QD
Tel (01890) 830605      Mobile (07973) 441381
E-mail highridgehall@btinternet.com
Website www.borderladiesgolf.com

**Dumfriesshire LCGA**
Hon Sec, Mrs E C Scott, Treweryn, 24 Carlisle Rd,
Lockerbie DG11 2DN
Tel (01576) 203507
E-mail malcolmscott228@btinternet.com

**Dunbartonshire & Argyll LCGA**
Hon Sec, Mrs J Shankland, 25 Thorn Dr., Bearsden,
Glasgow G61 4ND
Tel (0141) 942 4696
E-mail je.shankland@btinternet.com
Website www.dalcga.ik.com

**East Lothian LCGA**
Hon Sec, Liz McLelland, Elmsford, Main Street, Gullane
EH31 2DR
Tel (01620) 843131
Mobile (07968) 007269
E-mail lizbeak@hotmail.com

**Fife CLGA**
Hon Sec, Ms Liz Childs, 10 Woodlands Road, Lundin
Links KY8 6HG
Tel (01333) 320503
E-mail secretaryfclga@gmail.com

**Galloway CLGA**
Hon Sec, Sally Huntly, Tramerry, Wigtown DG8 9JP
Tel (01988) 402309

**Lanarkshire LCGA**
Capt, Anne Lloyd, 9 Jardine Ter., Gartcosh, Glasgow
G69 8AR
Tel (0781) 887 8187
E-mail anne.Lloyd@hotmail.co.uk
Website www.llcga.co.uk

**Midlothian CLGA**
Hon Sec, Mrs H Anderson, 10 Woodhall Bank,
Colinton, Edinburgh EH13 0HJ
Tel (0131) 477 1131
E-mail mclga66@hotmail.co.uk
Website www.mclga.co.uk

**Northern Counties' LGA**
Hon Sec, Mrs Alison Bartlett
Tel (01408) 633180
E-mail secretary@northerncounties.com

**Perth & Kinross LCGA**
Hon Sec, Mrs Pat Hebner, 5 West Mains Avenue, Perth
PH1 1QZ
Tel (01738) 626582
E-mail jilliancmilne@hotmail.com

**Renfrewshire LCGA**
Hon Sec, Mrs J Irvine, Wrayburn, Woodside Lane,
Brookfield PA5 8UW
Tel (01505) 328411
E-mail jean.Irvine@sky.com
Website rlgca.co.uk

**Stirling & Clackmannan CLGA**
Hon Sec, Mrs A Hunter, 22 Muirhead Rd,
Stenhousemuir, FK5 4JA
Tel (01324) 554515
E-mail annathunter@btinternet.com

**Scottish Veteran Ladies' Golfing
Association**
Hon Sec, Mrs J C Lambert, Balcary, Barcloy Rd,
Rockcliffe, Dalbeattie DG5 4QJ
Tel (01556) 630419
E-mail jeanc.lambert@btinternet.com
Website www.svlga.co.uk

**Scottish Blind Golf Society**
Sec, R Clayden, 5 The Round, Dunfermline, Fife
KY12 7YH
Tel (01383) 737717
Website www.scottishblindgolf.com

**Scottish Midland Golfing Alliance**
Sec, E Sherry, Lundin Tower, Pilmuir Rd, Lundin Links
KY8 6BD

## Wales

**Golf Union of Wales**
Ch Exec, Richard Dixon, Catsash, Newport, Gwent
NP18 1JQ
Tel (01633) 436040    Fax (01633) 430843
E-mail office@golfunionwales.org
Website www.golfunionwales.org

*Welsh Men's Unions*
**Anglesey GU**
Hon Sec, GP Jones, 20 Gwelfor Estate, Cemaes Bay,
Anglesey LL67 0NL
Tel (01407) 710755
E-mail garethgwelfor@aol.com
Website www.anglestgolfunion.co.uk

**Brecon & Radnor GU**
Hon Sec, Martyn Hughes, 1 Wool Row, Brecon Rd,
Builth Wells LD2 3ED
Tel (01982) 552852
E-mail martynhughes49@googlemail.com

**Caernarfonshire & District GU**
Hon Sec, EG Angel, 13 Glanrafon Est., Bontnewydd,
Caernarfon, Gwynedd LL55 2UW
Tel (01286) 675798
E-mail einionecdgu@talktalk.net

**Denbighshire GU**
Sec, D Ethelston, Gwylfa, Garth Rd, Garth, Llangollen
LL20 7UR
Tel (01978) 820722    E-mail eric.mai@talktalk.net
Website www.dgugolf.co.uk

**Dyfed GU**
Sec, J Harries, Ffynnon Werdd, Station Hill, St Clears,
Carmarthen SA 33 4DL
Tel (01994) 230634
Website www.dyfedgolf.co.uk

**Union of Flintshire Golf Clubs**
Hon Sec, Mrs G Snead, 1 Cornist Cottages, Flint
CH6 5RH
Tel (01352) 733461
E-mail gsnead@hotmail.co.uk

**Glamorgan County GU**
Hon Sec, P Austerberry, 10 Chestnut Tree Close,
Radyr, Cardiff CF15 8RY
Tel (02920) 419823
E-mail p.austerberry@ntlworld.com

**Gwent GU**
Sec, WG Harris, 4 Rolls Walk, Mount Pleasant,
Rogerstone, Gwent NP10 0AE
Tel (01633) 663750
E-mail w.graham.harris@ntlworld.com
Website www.gwentgolfunion.eu

**North Wales PGA**
See Cheshire & North Wales PGA, page 708

**South Wales PGA**
See The PGA in England &Wales (South West), page
708

*Welsh Ladies' County Associations*
**Caernarvonshire & Anglesey LCGA**
Hon Sec, Mrs J Harvey, 10 Craig y Don, Pensarn,
Abergele LL22 7RL
Tel (01745) 827239
E-mail alecharvey32@btinternet.com

**Carmarthenshire & Pembrokeshire LCGA**
Sec, Paula James
Website carmspembscountylga.co.uk

**Denbighshire & Flintshire LCGA**
Hon Sec, Mrs K Harcombe, 6 Birch Drive, Gresford,
Wrexham LL12 8YZ
Tel (01978) 855933
E-mail kim.harcombe@btinternet.com

**Glamorgan LCGA**
Hon Sec, Mrs Sybil Thomas
Website www.glamorganladiesgolf.co.uk

**Mid Wales LCGA**
Hon Sec, Mrs L Price, Coygen, Lower Chapel, Brecon,
Powys LD3 9RE
Tel (01874) 690258
E-mail coygen@btclick.com

**Monmouthshire LCGA**
Hon Sec, Mrs Libby Hutchings
E-mail libby.hutchings@talktalk.net

## Europe

**European Golf Association**
Gen Sec, Richard Heath, Place de la Croix Blanche 19,
Case Postale CH-1066 Epalinges, Switzerland
Tel +41 21 785 7060    Fax +41 21 785 7069
E-mail info@ega-golf.ch
Website www.ega-golf.ch

**Albanian Golf Federation**
Gen Sec, Marin Harxhi, Rr.Sulevman Delvina-Haxhi
Kika, P.142/3 Ap.12, AL-Tiranë
Tel +355 68 603 3626
E-mail info@fshgolf.org    Website www.fshgolf.org

**National Golf Federation of Armenia**
Pres, Vahag Hovnanian, 50 G Chaush Str, Yerevan
0088, Armenia
Tel +374 10 394085/+374 55 050913
E-mail golfarmenia@gmail.com

**Austrian Golf Association (Österreichischer
  Golf Verband)**
Gen Sec, Robert Fiegl, Marxergasse 25, AT-1030 Wien
Tel +43 1 505 324515
E-mail oegv@golf.at    Website www.golf.at

**Azerbaijan Golf Federation**
657 Sarabski Street, Baku, Azerbaijan AZ1022
Tel +994 12 499 8686
E-mail info@agf.az

**Royal Belgian Golf Federation**
Gen Sec, Christian Moyson, Boulevard Louis Schmidt
37/6, BE-1040 Brussels
Tel +32 2 672 2389
Fax +32 2 675 4619
E-mail info@golfbelgium.be
Website www.golfbelgium.be

**Bulgarian Golf Association**
Gen Sec, Seth Underwood, 19 Oborishte Street,
1 504 Sofia
Tel +359 2943 0610
Fax +359 2946 3740
E-mail office@golfbg.com
Website www.golfbg.com

**Croatian Golf Federation**
Chair, Dino Klisovic, Esplanade Hotel, Mihanoviceva 1,
HR-10000 Zagreb
Tel +385 1 456 6050
E-mail hgs@golf.hr
Website www.golf.hr

**Cyprus Golf Federation**
Gen Sec, Nick Rossides, Olympic House, Amfipoleos
21, Office B208, CY-2025 Nicosia
Tel +357 22 449874    Fax +357 22 449876
E-mail cgf@cgf.org.cy    Website www.cgf.org.cy

**Czech Golf Federation**
Gen Sec, Lubos Klikar, Erpet Golf Centre,
Strakonickà 2860, CZ-150 00 Pragha
Tel  +420 603 890 961
E-mail secretary@cgf.cz
Website www.cgf.cz

**Danish Golf Union (Dansk Golf Union)**
Dir, Morten Backhausen, Idrættens Hus, Brøndby
Stadion 20, DK-2605 Brøndby
Tel +45 43 262 700    Fax +45 43 262 701
E-mail info@dgu.org    Website www.dgu.org

**Estonian Golf Association**
Livalaia 9 , 101 18 Talinn
Tel +372 566 86206
E-mail info@golf.ee    Website www.golf.ee

**Finnish Golf Union**
Gen Sec, Petri Peltoniemi, Radiokatu 20, Fin-00093
SLU, Helsinki
Tel +358 9 3481 2520    Fax +358 9 147 145
E-mail office@golf.fi
Website www.golf.fi

**French Golf Federation (Federation Française
de Golf)**
Exec Dir, Christophe Muniesa, 68 rue Anatole France,
FR-92309 Levallois-Perret Cedex
Tel +33 1 41 49 77 00    Fax +33 1 49 77 01/33
E-mail ffgolf@ffgolf.org
Website www.ffgolf.org

**German Golf Association (Deutscher Golf
Verband e.V.)**
Sec Gen, Alexander Klose and Klaus Dallmeyer
Kreuzberger Ring 64, 65202 Weisbaden
Tel +49 611 99020 130-0
Fax +49 611 99020 163-170
E-mail info@dgv.golf.de    Website www.golf.de

**Hellenic Golf Federation**
Gen Sec, Tommy Tokas, PO Box 70003,
GR-166 10 Glyfada, Athens
Tel +30 210 894 1933    Fax +30 210 894 5162
E-mail info@hgf.gr    Website www.hgf.gr

**Hungarian Golf Federation**
Gen Sec, Istvanmezei út 1-3, HU-1146 Budapest
Tel/Fax +36 1 460 6859
E-mail hungolf@hungolf.hu
Website: www.hungolf.hu

**Golf Union of Iceland**
Gen Sec, Hordur Thorsteinsson, Sport Center,
Laugardal, IS-104 Reykjavik
Tel +354 514 4050    Fax +354 514 4051
E-mail gsi@isisport.is    Website www.golf.is

**Italian Golf Federation (Federazione Italiana
Golf)**
Sec Gen, Stefano Manca, Viale Tiziano 74, IT-00196
Roma
Tel +39 06 323 1825    Fax +39 06 322 0250
E-mail fig@federgolf.it    Website www.federgolf.it

**Latvia Golf Federation**
Gen Sec, Milgrãvja lela 16, LV-1034 Riga
Tel +371 6739 4399
Fax +371 6739 4034
E-mail info@golfaskola.lv    Website www.lgf.lv

**Liechtenstein Golf Association (Golfverband
Liechtenstein)**
Pres, Carlo Rampone, Postfach 264, LI-9490 Vaduz
Tel +42 3 232 1991    Fax +42 3 232 1992
E-mail info@golf-verband.li
Website www.golf.li

**Lithuanian Golf Federation**
Veiveriu Str 142 B, 46353 Kaunas
E-mail info@golfofederacija.lt
Website www.golfofederacija.lt

**Luxembourg Golf Federation (Federation
Luxemburgeoise de Golf)**
Sec, Roger Weber, Domaine de Belenhaff, LU-6141
Junglinster
Tel +352 26 78 2383    Fax +352 26 78 2393
E-mail flgsecretariat@flgolf.lu
Website www.flgolf.lu

**Macedonian Golf Federation**
Gen Sec, Marijan Pop-Angelov, Tone Tomsic 3A,
MK-1000 Skopje
Tel 389 2 2774 071    Fax +389 2 2774 072
E-mail mkgolffederation@gmail.com

**Malta Golf Association**
Pres, William Beck, Aldo Moro Str, Marsa MRS 9064,
Malta
Tel +356 2122 3704    Fax +356 2122 7020
E-mail association@maltagolf.org
Website www.maltagolf.org

**Netherlands Golf Federation (Nederlandse
Golf Federation)**
Gen Sec, Jeroen Stevens, PO Box 8585, NL-3503 RN
Utrecht
Tel +31 30 242 6370    Fax +31 30 242 6380
E-mail golf@ngf.nl    Website www.ngf.nl

**Norwegian Golf Federation**
*Gen Sec,* Tor-Anders Hanssen, NO-0840 Oslo
*Tel* +47 22 029 150
*E-mail* post@golfforbundet.no
*Website* www.golfforbundet.no

**Polish Golf Union**
*Gen Sec,* Bartlomiej Chelmecki, Lim Centre, Al.Jero-
zolimskie 65/79, PL-00-697 Warszawa
*Tel* +48 22 630 5560    *Fax* +48 22 630 5561
*E-mail* secretarz@pzgolf.pl
*Website* www.pzgolf.pl

**Portuguese Golf Federation (Federacao
Portuguesa de Golfe)**
*Gen Sec,* Miguel Franco De Sousa, Av das Túlipas No
6, Edifico Miraflores17°, Miraflores, 1495-061 Algés
*Tel* +351 21 412 3780
*Fax* +351 21 410 7972
*E-mail* fpg@fpg.pt    *Website* www.fpg.pt

**Romanian Golf Federation**
*Gen Sec,* Corin Comsulea, 44 Carierei Str., Breaza,
RO-105 400 Prahova
*Tel* +40 727 700 987
*E-mail* office@frgolf.ro
*Website* www.romaniangolffederation.com

**Russian Golf Association**
*Int. Rel. Man.,* Mrs Ekaterina Popova, Office 378, 8
Luzhnetskaya nab, RU – 119991 Moskva
*Tel* +7 495 363 2385    *Fax* +7 495 725 4719
*E-mail* info@mail.ru    *Website* www.rusgolf.ru

**San Marino Golf Federation**
*Sec Gen,* Dr Guilio Caramaschi, Via Rancagalia 30,
SM-47899 Serravalle, San Marino
*Tel* +378 0549 885 600
*Fax* +378 0549 885 651
*E-mail* federgolfsm@gmail.com
*Website* www.cons.sm

**Golf Association of Serbia**
*Gen Sec,* Mrs Irena Suturovic Bogdanovic, Ada Ciganlija
2, RS-11000 Belgrad
*Tel* +381 11 333 2851    *Fax* +381 11 305 6837
*E-mail* office@golfas.rs
*Website* www.golfasocijacijasrbije.rs

**Slovak Golf Association**
*Gen Sec,* Juraj Špánik, Kukucínova, Kukucínova 26,
SK-831 02 Bratislava, Slovakia
*Tel/Fax* +421 2 4445 0727
*E-mail* skga@skga.sk    *Website* www.skga.sk

**Slovenian Golf Association**
Golf Zvoza Slovenije, Smartinska Cesta 152 PP4002,
1000 Ljubljana
*Tel* +386 1 430 3200    *Fax* +386 1 430 3201
*E-mail* golfzveza@golfzveza-slovenije.si

**Royal Spanish Golf Federation (Real
Federacion Espanola de Golf)**
*Man Dir,* Jorge Sagardoy Fidalgo, Arroyo del Fresno
Dos 5, ES-28035 Madrid
*Tel* +34 91 555 2682    *Fax* +34 91 556 3290
*E-mail* rfeg@golfspain.com
*Website* www.golfspainfederacion.com

**Swedish Golf Federation (Svenska
Golfforbundet)**
*Gen Sec,* Gunnar Håkansson, PO Box 84, SE-182 11
Danderyd
*Tel* +46 8 622 1500    *Fax* +46 8 755 8439
*E-mail* info@sgf.golf.se
*Website* www.sgf.golf.se

**Swiss Golf Association (Association Suisse de
Golf)**
*Gen Sec,* Christian Bohn, Place de la Croix Blanche 19,
Case Postale, CH-1066 Epalinges
*Tel* +41 21 785 7000    *Fax* +41 21 785 7009
*E-mail* info@asg.ch    *Website* www.asg.ch

**Turkish Golf Federation**
*Pres,* Ahmet Agaoglu, GSGM Ulus Is Hani A Blok 2.,
Kat 205 Ulus 06050, TR-Ankara
*Tel* +90 312 309 3945    *Fax* +90 312 309 1840
*E-mail* info@tgf.org.tr
*Website* www.tgf.org.tr

**Ukrainian Golf Federation**
*Gen Sec,* Sergey Kozyrenko, 39 Pushkinskya str. Suite
38, 01004 Kyiv
*Tel* +380 67 231 8949
*E-mail* skozyrenko@gmail.com
*Website* www.ukrgolf.com

*Professional Associations*

**Austria PGA**
*Contact:* Monika Goss, Grabentrasse 26/1a, AT-8010
Graz
*Tel* +43 316 890 503    *Fax* +43 316 890 50315
*E-mail* office@apga.info
*Website* www.apga.info

**Belgian PGA**
*Contact:* Bernard de Bruyckere, PO Box 1062, BE-8300
Knokke-Heist
*Tel* +32 476 645 414
*E-mail* info@pga.be    *Website* www.pga.be

**Bulgarian PGA**
*Contact:* Robin McGarr, Oborishte Street 19. BG-1504
Sofia
*Tel /Fax* +359 2 943 0610
*E-mail* info@pga-bulgaria.com
*Website* www.pga-bulgaria.com

**Croatia PGA**
*Contact:* Nikola Smoljenovic, Fancevljec Prilaz 16,
HR-100 00 Zagreb
*Tel* +385 1 667 3308    *Fax* +385 1 660 6798
*E-mail* pga@pga.hr
*Website* www.pga.hr

**Czech Republic PGA**
*Gen Sec,* Michael Jon, Villa Golfista, Amerika 782/1C,
CZ-353 01 Marianske Lazne
*Tel* +420 354 623071
*E-mail* pga@pga.cz    *Website* www.pga.cz

**Denmark PGA**
*Contact:* Joan Ejlertsen, Kong Chr. Alle 37, Bygaden
20A, DK-9000, Aalborg
*Tel* +45 20 73 00 41    *Fax* +45 98 662 236
*E-mail* info@pga.dk    *Website* www.pga.dk

**Estonia PGA**
*Gen Sec,* Paul Pohi, Kauge Tee 3, Harjumaa, EE-11215
Tallinn
*Tel* +372 53 48 12 36
*E-mail* info@pga.ee    *Website* www.pga.ee

**Finland PGA**
*Contact;,* Teemu Laakso, Radiokatu 20, FI-00093 SLU
*Tel* +358 9 3481 2377    *Fax* +358 9 3481 2378
*E-mail* pgafinland@pga.fi    *Website* www.pga.fi

**France PGA**
*Contact:* Adelaide Vannier, National Golf Club, 2
Avenue du Golf, FR-78 280 Guyancourt
*Tel* +33 1 3452 0846
*Fax* +33 1 3057 4704
*E-mail* contact@pgafrance.org
*Website* www.pgafrance.org

**PGA of Germany**
*Ch Exec,* Rainier Goldrain, Professional Golf AG,
Landsbergerstr. 290, DE-80687 München
*Tel* +49 8917 95880    *Fax* +49 8917 958829
*E-mail* info@pga.de    *Website* www.pga.de

**Greece PGA**
*Gen Sec,* Adonis Sotiropoulos, 9 Harilaou Trikoupi str,
2nd Fl, GR-166 75 Glyfada Athens
*Tel* +30 22410 52798
*E-mail* info@greekpga.com
*Website* www.greekpga.com

**Hungary PGA**
*Gen Sec,* Áron Makszin, 1016 Krisztina Krt 71 4/1
Budapest
*Tel* +36 23 545 440    *Fax* +36 70 454 5663
*E-mail* makszin@yahoo.com
*Website* www.pgah.hu

**Iceland PGA**
*Gen Sec,* Agnar Már Jonsson, Engjavegur 6, IS-104
Reykjavik
*Tel* +354 514 4050    *Fax* +354 514 4051
*E-mail* agnarj@pga.is    *Website* www.pga.is

**Italy PGA**
*Contact:* Laura Rendina, Via Marangoni 3, IT-20124
Milano
*Tel* +39 02 670 5670    *Fax* +39 02 669 3600
*E-mail* pgaitaly@tin.it    *Website* www.pga.it

**Luxembourg PGA**
*Contact:* Leon Marks, Luxembourg GC Belenhaff,
LU-26141 Junglinster
*Tel/Fax* +352 348394
*E-mail* leon@golfpro.lu    *Website* www.pga.lu

**Malta PGA**
*Contact:* Kenneth Cachia, The Royal Malta GC, Aldo
Moro St, Marsa LQA 06
*Tel* +356 212 39302
*Fax* +356 212 27020
*E-mail* info@pgamalta.com
*Website* www.pgamalta.com

**Netherlands PGA (Holland PGA)**
Po Box 642, 6200 AP Maastricht
*Tel* +31 30 228 7018    *Fax* +31 30 225 0261
*E-mail* info@pgaholland.nl
*Website* www.pgaholland.nl

**Norway PGA**
*Contact:* Trond Baardseng, PO Box 135, NO-2401
Elverum
*Tel* +47 993 44000
*E-mail* trond.bardseng@pganorway.no
*Website* www.pganorway.no

**Poland PGA**
*Contact:* Anna Maliszewska, ul.Kwiatowa 16,
PL-81638 Gdynia
*Tel* +48 664 941994
*E-mail* biuro@pgapolska.pl
*Website* www.pgapolska.com

**Portugal PGA**
*Gen Sec,* Nelson Cavalheiro, Av Das Túlipas 6-Edif.,
Miraflores 17°, Miraflores, PT-1495-161 Algés
*Tel* +351 21 962 6640    *Fax* +351 21 962 6641
*E-mail* nelsoncavalheiro@gmail.com
*Website* www.pgaportugal.pt

**Russia PGA**
*Contact:* Maria Milovidova, Office 242a, Build 8,
Luzhnetskaya nab, RU-119992 Moscow
*Tel* +7 495 363 2385    *Fax* +7 495 725 4719
*E-mail* maria.milovidova@mail.ru
*Website* www.rusga.ru

**Serbian PGA**
Ada Ciganlija 2, 11030 Belgrade
*Tel* +381 11 33 32 851
*E-mail* office@spgu.rs

**Slovakia PGA**
Lopuchova 9, 83101 Bratislava, Slovak Republic
*Tel* +421 905 305 246
*E-mail* info@pga.sk    *Website* www.pga.sk

**Slovenia PGA**
Smartinska 152, PP4002, SL 1122 Ljubljana
*Tel* +386 4 148 7280    *Fax* +386 1430 3201
*E-mail* info@pgaslo.si    *Website* www.pgaslo.si

**Spain PGA**
*Contact:* Mercedes Santamaria, c/ Capitán Haya 22-5C,
ES-28020 Madrid
*Tel* +34 91 555 1393    *Fax* +34 91 597 0170
*E-mail* pga@pgaspain.com
*Website* www.pgaspain.com

**Swedish PGA**
*Contact:* Anna Svantesson, Malmovagen 647-36,
SE-230 40 Bara
*Tel* +46 35 320 30    *Fax* +46 4044 7656
*E-mail* pga@pgasweden.com
*Website* www.pgasweden.com

**Swiss PGA**
*Gen Sec,* Peter Schwager, Zürcherstrasse 204,
CH-9014 St Gallen
*Tel* +41 71 277 1717    *Fax* +41 71 277 7317
*E-mail* info@swisspga.ch
*Website* www.swisspga.ch

**Turkey PGA**
*Gen Sec,* Andrew McNabola, Doktorlar Sitesi A7 Blok
Daire 6, Nato Yolu, Bosna Bulvari, Cengelkoy, Istanbul
*Tel* +90 533 773 3019
*E-mail* andrewmmcnabola@gmail.com

## North America: Canada and USA

**Royal Canadian Golf Association**
*Exec Dir*, Scott Simmons, Suite 1 1333 Dorval Drive,
Oakville, Ontario L6M 4X7
*Tel* +1 905 849 9700    *Fax* +1 905 845 7040
*E-mail* info@golfcanada.ca
*Website* www.rcga.org

**Canadian Ladies' Golf Association**
See Royal Canadian Golf Association

**National Golf Foundation**
*Ch Exec*, Joseph Beditz, 1150 South US Highway One,
Suite 401, Jupiter, Florida 33477
*Tel* +1 561 744 6006    *Fax* +1 561 744 6107
*E-mail* general@ngf.org
*Website* www.ngf.org

**United States Golf Association**
*Pres*, Thomas J O'Toole, Golf House, PO Box 708, Far
Hills, NJ 07931-0708
*Tel* +1 908 234 2300    *Fax* +1 908 234 9687
*E-mail* usga@usga.org
*Website* www.usga.org

### Professional Associations

**Canadian PGA**
*Ch Exec*, Gary Bernard, 13450 Dublin Line RR#1,
Acton, Ontario L7J 2W7
*Tel* +1 519 853 5450 (Ext 221)
*Fax* +1 519 853 5449
*E-mail* gary@pgaofcanada.com
*Website* www.cpga.com

**Ladies' Professional Golf Association**
*Comm*, Mike Whan, 100 International Golf Drive,
Daytona Beach, Florida 32124-1092
*Tel* +1 386 274 6260
*Website* www.lpga.com

**PGA of America**
Mike Abramowitz, Julius Mason, 100 Avenue of the
Champions, Palm Beach Gardens, Florida 33410-9601
*Tel* +1 561 624 8400    *Fax* +1 561 624 8448
*E-mail* jmason@pgahq.com
*Website* www.pgaonline.com

**PGA Tour**
*Comm*, Tim Finchem, PGA Tour, 112 PGA Tour
Boulevard, Ponte Vedra Beach, Florida 32082
*Tel* +1 904 285 3700
*E-mail* tyvotaw@pgatourhq.com
*Website* www.pgatour.com

**PGA Tour Canada**
See PGA Tour

**PGA Tour Latinoamérica**
See PGA Tour

## The Caribbean and Central America

**Belize Amateur Golf Association**
*Sec*, Andrew Hunt, PO Box 107, Belmopan, Belize
*Tel* +501 651 9929
*E-mail* bagabze@gmail.com
*Website* www.belizegolf.blogspot.com

**Caribbean Golf Association**
*Sec*, Karen Calvesbert, 262 Matadero Street, Puerto
Nuevo PR 00920
*Tel* +787 293 7302
*E-mail* kcalvesbert@hotmail.com
*Website* www.cgagolfnet.com

**Bahamas Golf Federation**
*Sec*, Dudley Martinborough, PO Box SS-19092,
Nassau, Grand Bahama
*Tel* +1 242 394 3134
*E-mail* admin@bgfnet.com
*Website* www.bgfnet.com

**Barbados Golf Association**
*Sec*, Trenton Weekes, PO Box 149W, Worthing,
Christ Church, Barbados BB-15000
*Tel* +1 246 826 3626
*E-mail* secretary@barbadosgolfassociation.com
*Website* www.barbadosgolfassociation.com

**Bermuda Golf Association**
*Sec*, Susie Kendell Marshall, Victoria Place Building, 31
Victoria Street, Hamilton, HM 10, Bermuda
*Tel* +1 441 295 9972    *Fax* +1 441 295 0304
*E-mail* info@bermudagolf.org
*Website* www.bermudagolfasociation.net

**Cayman Islands Golf Association**
*Sec*, David G Bird, PO Box 31329, Grand Cayman,
KY1-1206
*Tel* +1 345 947 1903    *Fax* +1 345 947 3439
*E-mail* info@clga.ky
*Website* www.ciga.ky

**Costa Rica Golf Federation**
*Pres*, Arnoldo Madrigal, PO Box 10969, San José 1000
*Tel* +506 296 5772    *Fax* +506 231 1914
*E-mail* info@anagolf.com
*Website* www.anagolf.com

**Fedogolf (Dominican Republic)**
*Exec Dir*, Carlos Lizarazo, Calle Macao No.7,
Urbanizacion Tenis Club, Arroyo Hondo, Santo
Domingo, Dominican Republic
*Tel* +1 809 338 1005
*Fax* +1 809 338 1008
*E-mail* administracion@fedogolf.org.do
*Website* www.golfdominicano.com

**El Salvador Golf Federation**
Resedencial Escalon Sobre, 89 Av Norte Entre 1y3,
Calle Pte 2, San Salvador
*Tel* +503 2264 1584    *Fax* +503 2264 1582
*E-mail* fesagolf@yahoo.com

**National Golf Association of Guatemala**
*Exec Asst*, Nancy Fuentes, Avenida delas Americas
18-81 Zona 14, Guatemala Cuidad 01010
*Tel* +502 2363 1734    *Fax* +502 2363 1754
*E-mail* asogolf@asogolfguatemala.org
*Website* www.asogolfguatemala.org

**Hondureña Golf Association**
*Pres*, Henry Kattan, Residential Piñares, Km 6.5
Paseo al Hatillo, PO Box 3555, Tegucigalpa, Honduras
*Tel* +504 211 9260    *Fax* +504 227 3105
*E-mail* Hondurasgolf@gmail.com
*Website* www.hondurasgolf.org

## Jamaica Golf Association
Hon Sec, William Brown, 7 Courtney Walsh Drive, Kingston 10
Tel +1 876 755 3593 +1 876 969 6233
Fax +1 876 924 7635
E-mail jamgolf2@cwjamaica.com
Website www.jagolfassociation.com

## Mexican Golf Federation
Sec Gen, Federico Valdez, Av.Insurgentes Sur 1605
10° Piso Torre Mural, Col. San Jose Insurgentes, C.P. 03900 México, D.F.
Tel +1 525 55 1084 2170    Fax +1 525 55 1084 2179
E-mail ivaldez@fmg.org.mx
Website www.fmg.org.mx

## Nicaraguan Golf Federation
Sec Gen, Jorge Palisso, Nicabox 2464. POBox 02-5640. Miami, Florida 33102
Tel +505 8882 5522    Fax +505 2266 1973
E-mail jorge-palliso@fenigolf.org

## OECS Golf Association
Sec, Cedric Jeffers, c/o PO Box 895, Basseterre, St Kitts
Tel +1 869 662 3036
E-mail golftoddler2009@gmail.com

## Panama Golf Association
Exec Dir, Luiz Heley Bárcenas, Panama 0823-02719
Tel +507 264 6655    Fax +507 264 5204
E-mail jmc@cableonda.net

## Puerto Rico Golf Association
Exec Dir, Julio Soto, 264 Matadero – Suite 11, San Juan, Puerto Rico 00920
Tel +1 787 793 3444    Fax +1 787 723 3138
E-mail swolf00@gmail.com
Website www.prga.org

## St Maarten Golf Association
Pres, Keith Graham, PO Box 720, Philipsburg, St Maarten, Netherlands Antilles
Tel +44 599 551 2105    Fax +44 599 542 1261
E-mail stmaartengolf@gmail.com

## Trinidad & Tobago Golf Association
Sec, Clyde Abder, c/o St Andrews GC, PO Box 3403, Moka, Maraval, T&T, W.I.
Tel +1 868 629 7127
Fax +1 868 629 0411
E-mail ttga@live.com
Website www.trinidadandtobagogolfassociation.com

## Turks & Caicos Golf Association
PO box 319, Suite C12 Providenciales
Tel +649 946 4109    Fax +649 946 4939
E-mail thomas@tciway.tc

## Virgin Islands Golf Federation
Pres, Nevin Phillips, PMB 1126002, Diamond Ruby Suite 3, Christiansted 00820
Tel +305 281 2670
E-mail vipterf@aol.com

### Professional Association

## Jamaica PGA
Chairman, O Marshall, 9 Park Ave., Kingston 5
Tel +1 876 881 4444    E-mail pgajamaica@gmail.com

## Mexico PGA
Off, D Ross, Nadadores 30, Col.Country Club, Mexico DF, CP 04210
Tel +52 55 5544 6644    Fax +52 55 5689 4254
E-mail info@pgamexico.org
Website www.pgamexico.org

# South America

## South American Golf Federation
Carrera 12, No 79-43 Oficina 704,Bogota
Tel +571 691 8985    Fax +571 691 8640
E-mail enetero@cable.net.co

## Argentine Golf Association
Exec Dir, Mark Lawrie, Av Corrientes 538-Pisos 11y12, 1043 CF, Buenos Aires C1043AAS
Tel +54 11 4325 1113
E-mail golf@aag.org.ar    Website www.aag.org.ar

## Bolivian Golf Federation
Sec Gen, Gabriele Cruz Cabral, Calle 1 Norte Nro 297, Zona Equipetrol, Faremafu, Casilla de Coreos 359, Santa Cruz
Tel/Fax +591 333 9403
E-mail fbgolf@entelnet.bo
Website www.boliviagolf.com

## Brasilian Golf Confederation
Exec Sec, M A Aguiar Giusti, Rua Paez de Araújo 29 conj 42/43, CEP 04531-090, São Paulo
Tel/Fax +55 11 3168 4366
E-mail golfe@cbg.com.br    Website www.cbg.com.br

## Chilean Golf Federation
Sec Gen, Andres Delano, Málaga 665, Las Condes, Santiago
Tel +56 2 690 8700    Fax +56 2 690 8720
E-mail secretaria@chilegolf.cl
Website www.chilegolf.cll

## Colombian Golf Federation
Sec Gen, Felipe Harker S, cra. 7#72-64 Int 26, Bogotá DC
Tel +57 1 310 7664    Fax +57 1 235 5091
E-mail fedegolf@federacioncolombianadegolf.com
Website www.federacioncolombianadegolf.com

## Ecuador Golf Federation
Sec, Juan Fernando Moscoso, Av Amazonas N.28-17 y Alemania, Edif. Scorpios Piso 8 Of.812, Quito
Tel +593 2 2922 128    Fax +593 2 2442 989
E-mail fedecuat@feg.org.ec
Website www.feg.org.ec

## Falkland Islands Golf Association
Sec, Troyd Bowles, Stanley F100 1ZZ
Tel +2731 00500 22976
E-mail bowles@horizon.co.fk

## Guyana Golf Union
Sec, c/o Demerara Bauxite Co Ltd, Mackenzie, Guyana

## Paraguay Golf Association
Eduardo Victor Haedo, N407 c/o Alberdi Ediificio, Libra Planta, Baja
Tel +595 21 491 217
E-mail secretaria@apg.org.py
Website www.apg.org.py

**Peru Golf Federation**
*Exec Dir*, Martin Alarco, Calle Conde de la Monclova
315 Of 308, San Isidro, Lima
*Tel* +51 1 441 1500   *Fax* +51 1 441 1992
*E-mail* fepegolf@terra.com.pe
*Website* www.fpg.org.pe

**Uruguay Golf Association**
Jose Ellauri 357 apto 303, Montevideo CP11300
*Tel/Fax* +598 2 711 5385
*E-mail* augolf@adinet.com.uy
*Website* www.aug.com.uy

**Venezuela Golf Federation**
*Exec Dir*, Carlos Waithe, Av. Eugenio Mendoza, Edif.
IASA, Mezzanina Of 2, La Castellana,  Municipio
Chacoa, Caracas 1061
*Tel* +58 212 263 5043   *Fax* +58 212 265 2839
*E-mail* fvg@fvg.org
*Website* www.fvg.org

*Professional Association*

**Brazil PGA**
*Contact,* Claci Schneider, Rua Francisco de Paula Brito,
317-Planalto Paulista, cep 04071 050 São Paulo-SP
*Tel* +55 11 2276 0745   *Fax* +55 11 2276 0789
*E-mail* pgabrasil@uol.com.br
*Website* www.pgadobrasil.com.br

## Africa

**African Golf Confederation**
*Sec Gen,* Hugh Mortimer, PO Box 2122, Windhoek,
Namibia
*Tel* +264 61 205 5223   *Fax* +264 61 205 5220
*E-mail* gm@wccgolf.com.na

**Algerian Golf Federation**
*Sec Gen,* Youcef Yakhief  Centre de Federations
Sportif, Cite Olympique, Mohamed Boudiaf, Dely-
Ibrahim, Alger 16320
*Tel* 213 21 926916   *Fax* 213 31 91892
*E-mail* djoudimn@hotmail.com

**Arab Golf Federation**
*Sec Gen,* Adel Zarouni, PO Box 31410, Dubai, UAE
*Tel* +9714 295 2277   *Fax* +9714 95 2288
*E-mail* info@ugagolf.com
*Website* www.arabgolf.org

**Botswana Golf Union**
*Sec Gen,* Mpho Kelosiwang, PO Box 1033, Gaborone
*Tel/Fax* +267 316 1116
*E-mail* bgu@bgu.org.bw

**Cameroon Golf Federation**
*Pres,* Dr Yves Martin Ahanda Assiga, 295 Rue 1810,
Montée Mini prix Bastos-BP 3, 35091 Yaoundé
*Tel* +237 22 20 4968
*E-mail* camergreen.golf@yahoo.fr
*Website* www.federationcamerounaisedegolf.com

**D R of Congo Golf Federation**
*Pres,* Alain Nitu, c/o Rainbow Connections, Carrefour
des Jeunes, 5151 Avenue Kasa-Vuba, Q/Matonge,
Commune Kalamu, Kinshasa
*Tel* +243 081 540 1140
*E-mail* alainnitu@hotmail.com
*Website* www.rainbowconnections.biz

**Egyptian Golf Federation**
*Golf Man,* Gerard Bent, 6 Rd 301,Fifth Sector, New
Maadi, Cairo
*Tel* +201 222 141961
*E-mail* s.omar@egyptiangolffederation.com
*Website* www.egyptiangolffederation.com

**Gabonese Golf Federation**
*Sec,* 11492,Mindouve, Libreville
*Tel* +241 760 378
*E-mail* golfclublibreville@gmail.com
*Website* fggolf.org

**Ghana Golf Association**
*Hon Sec,* George Lee Mensah, c/o National Sport
Council, PO Box 8 Achimota, Accra
*Tel* +233 244 318 500   *Fax* +233 302 220 953
*E-mail* ghanagolfass@yahoo.co.uk
*Website* www.ghanagolfassociation.com

**Ghana Ladies Golf Union**
*Hon Sec,* Mrs E Amedzro, PO Box 8, Achimota, Accra
*E-mail* estheramedzro@yahoo.com

**Ivory Coast (Côte d'Ivoire) Golf Federation**
*Pres,* Diaby Laye, 01 BP1554, Abidjan 01
*Tel* +225 2243 1076   *Fax* +225 2243 3772
*E-mail* f.golfci@aviso.ci   *Website* www.fgolfci.com

**Kenya Golf Union**
*Man.* Jessee M Mungai, PO Box 49609 Nairobi 00100
*Tel* +254 715 457906
*E-mail* info@kgu.or.ke   *Website* www.kgu.org.ke

**Kenya Ladies' Golf Union**
*Hon Secs,* A Sangar, S Hoare, PO Box  16751 Nairobi
*Tel* +254 2 733 794
*E-mail* klgukenya@gmail.com

**KwaZulu-Natal Golf Union**
77 Bulwen Road, Glenwood, Durban 4001
*Tel* +27 (0)31 202 7636   *Fax* +27 (0)31 202 1022
*E-mail* kzngu@kzngolf.co.za

**Liberia Golf Association**
*Pres,* Dr C Nelson Oniyama, c/o Monrovia Breweries
Inc., Monrovia
*Tel* +231 6 510788
*E-mail* cnonlyama@yahoo.com

**Libyan Golf Federation**
*Pres,* Dr Salem Mohamed Musq, PO Box  13304,
Alfeteh University Post Office, Tripoli
*Tel* +218 21 478 0485
*E-mail* sm_musa@yahoo.com

**Golf Union of Malawi**
*Pres* Hudson Kantwanje, PO Box 1198, Blantyre 8
*Tel* +265 1 830201
*E-mail* gkambala@msn.com

**Mauritius Golf Federation**
3rd Floor, Discovery House, St Jean Road, Quatre
Bornes
*Tel* +230 454 1676
*E-mail* mgolffed@internet.mw

**The Royal Moroccan Golf Federation**
*Sec Gen,* Abdelal Latif Benali, Route des Zaers, Rabat,
Dar El Salam
*Tel* +212 3775 5636   *Fax* +212 3775 1026
*E-mail* abdellatif.benali@manara.ma

**Mozambique Golfe**
*Exec*, Fernando Manhica
*Tel* +258 847 236988    *Fax* +258 214 17966
*E-mail* clubegolfe@gmail.com

**Namibia Golf Federation**
*Treas*, Hugh Mortimer, PO Box 2122, Windhoek,
Namibia
*Tel* +264 61 205 5223    *Fax* +264 61 205 5220
*E-mail* gm@wccgolf.com.na
*Website* www.wccgolf.com.na

**Nigeria Golf Federation**
*Sec*, Patrick Uwagbale, National Stadium Surulere,
PO Box 145, Lagos
*Tel* +234 1 897 9436
*E-mail* nigeriagolffederation@yahoo.com

**Nigerian Ladies Golf Union**
*Sec*, Mrs K Odukola, c/o Benin GC, Golf Course
Road, Benin City

**Réunion Golfe**
*VicePres*, Hoarau J Maric
*E-mail* as@bassinbleu.fr

**Senegalese Golf Federation**
*Dep Gen Sec*, Mr Moustaph Baïdy Bâ, BP 24105
Ouakam Dakar, Senegal
*E-mail* moustaph@senelec.sn

**Sierra Leone Golf Federation**
Freetown GC, PO Box 237, Lumley Beach Rd,
Freetown
*E-mail* eric@djibo.com

**South African Golf Association**
*Exec Dir*, BA Younge, PO Box 65303, Benmore 2010
RSA
*Tel* +27 11 476 1713    *Fax* +27 11 476 1714
*E-mail* bruce@saga.co.za    *Website* www.saga.co.za

**Women's Golf South Africa**
*Pres*, Mrs Cynthia Rayner, PO Box 2921 Somerset
West 7129
*Tel* +27 82 416 6356
*E-mail* president@wgsa.co.za

**Swaziland Golf Union**
*Pres*, Sibusiso Motsa, PO Box 1739, Mbabane, H100
Swaziland
*Tel* +268 602 4488    *Fax* +268 404 6400
*E-mail* sbmotsa@realnet.co.sz

**Tanzania Golf Union**
*Golf Dir*, Farayi Chitengwa, c/o Gymkhana Club,
PO Box 286, Dar Es Salaam
*Tel* +255 789 186203
*E-mail* info@tgu.or.tz    *Website* www.tgu.com

**Tunisian Golf Federation**
*Sec Gen*, Mohamed Moncef Gaida, Maison de Fédéra-
cions Sportives, 1004 Cité Olympique, Tunis
*Tel* +216 71 238 113    *Fax* +216 71 237087
*E-mail* ftg@ftg.org.tn    *Website* www.ftg.org.tn

**Uganda Golf Union**
*Hon Sec*, Johnson Omolo, Kitante Road, PO Box 2574,
Kampala
*Tel* +256 711 761526
*E-mail* jomolo@ntvuganda.co.ug

**Uganda Ladies Golf Union**
*Hon Sec*, Ms Sheila Keslime, PO Box 624, Kampala
*E-mail* ugandaladiesgolfunion@ymail.com

**Zaire Golf Federation**
*Pres*, Tshilombo Mwin Tshitol, BP 1648, Lubumbashi

**Zambia Golf Union**
*Sec Gen*, Charles Mwanza
*Tel* +260 2 097 778 7037
*Fax* +260 2 095 529 6852
*E-mail* mwanzac@indini.com.zm

**Zambia Ladies Golf Union**
*Pres*, Ms Moono Mwila, PO Box 31185, Lusaka
*E-mail* mmoonoeuphrazia@yahoo.com

**Zimbabwe Golf Association**
PO Box 404, Harare
*Tel* +263 746141
*E-mail* fuelink@africaonline.co.zw

*Professional Associations*

**South African PGA**
*Sec*, Anne Du Toit, PO Box 949 Bedfordview 2008, RSA
*Tel* +27 11 485 1370    *Fax* +27 11 640 1612
*E-mail* admin@pga.co.za
*Website* www.pga.co.za

**South African Women's PGA**
*Sec*, Barbara Pestana, PO Box 781547, Sandton 2146
*Tel/Fax* +27 82 781 4653

**South Africa Sunshine Tour**
*Exec Dir*, Selwyn Nathan, 15 Postnet Suite #185,
Private Bag X15, Somerset West 7129
*Tel* +27 21 850 6500    *Fax* +27 21 852 8271

## Middle East

**Bahrain Golf Association**
*Sec Gen*, Abdulla Al Kaabi, PO Box 38938, Riffa,
Kingdom of Bahrain
*Tel* +973 1777 7179    *Fax* +973 1776 9484
*E-mail* bgassoc@batelco.com.bh

**Emirates Golf Association**
*Sec*, Khalid Mubarak Al Shamsi, PO Box 31410, Dubai,
UAE
*Tel* +971 4 295 2277    *Fax* +971 4 295 2288
*E-mail* info@ugagolf.com    *Website* www.ugagolf.com

**Islamic Republic of Iran Golf Federation**
*Sec Gen*, Mohammad Reza Naddafpour, Enghelab Club,
Vali-e-asr Avenue, PO Box 15815-1881, Tehran
*Tel/Fax* +98 21 2201 15617
*E-mail* info@golfir.com    *Website* www.golfir.com

**Israel Golf Federation**
*Vice Chair*, Avi Dagan, PO Box 141, IL-38900 Caesarea
*Tel* +972 4 610 9600
*E-mail* info@israelgolffed.org
*Website* www.israelgolffed.org

**Jordan Golf Federation**
*Sec*, Ali A Shahin, PO Box 141331, Amman 11814
*Tel* +962 795 525187    *Fax* +962 658 56913
*E-mail* ashahin70@yahoo.com

**Kuwait Golf Federation**
*Pres*, Saud Al Hajeri, PO Box 1192, Fintas Z-code
51013
*Tel* +965 390 5287

**Lebanese Golf Federation**
*Sec*, c/o Golf Club of Lebanon, PO Box 11-3099,
Beirut, Lebanon
*Tel* +961 11 861862
*E-mail* info@lebanesegolffederation.org

**Oman Golf Committee**
*Contact*, Maria Nordberg, PO Box 2618, Post code 11
CPO, Muscat, Sultanate of Oman
*Tel* +968 993 30217
*E-mail* argam@oman-golf.org
*Website* www.ogchandicap.com

**Qatar Golf Association**
*Sec*,Mike Shoueiry, PO Box 6177, Doha
*Tel* +974 4483 7815 or +974 4483 7809 or +974 4483
2667
*E-mail* info@qga,com,qa
*Website* www.qga.com.qa

**Saudi Arabian Golf Federation**
PO Box 325422, Riyadh 11371
*Tel* +996 1409 0004
*E-mail* saudigolf@yahoo.com
*Website* www.ksagolf.com

*Professional Associations*

**Israel PGA**
*Contact*, Basil Katz, Sintat Hahoma 3 / 4, Raanana
43331
*Tel* +972 4 6636 1172
*Fax* +972 4 6636 1173
*E-mail* basad@013.net
*Website* www.pgaisrael.com

**United Arab Emirates PGA**
*Off*, J Danby, Nad Al Sheba Golf, PO Box 52872,
Dubai
*Tel* +971 4 336 3666    *Fax* +971 4 336 1624
*E-mail* jdanby@dubaigolf.com

## Asia

**Asia-Pacific Golf Confederation**
*Hon Gen*, Kyungjae Lee
*E-mail* KFL.APGC@leema.co.kr
*Website* www.asiapacificgolf.org

**Afghanistan Golf Federation**
*Gen Sec*, Azizulah Attaei, Shahr-E-Naw, Charahi
Ansari, Shah Bobo Jan St, Kabul
*Tel* +93 752 12 86 45
*E-mail* afgolffederation@yahoo.com
*Website* www.afghangolf.af

**Azerbaijan Golf Federation**
*Gen Man*, Dominik Naughton, 657 Sarabski Str, Baku
AZ 1022
*Tel* +994 12 4998686
*E-mail* info@agf.az

**Bangladesh Golf Federation**
c/o Kurmitola GC, Dhaka Cantonment, Dhaka-1206,
Bangladesh
*Tel* +800 2 8752520/8752523
*E-mail* kgcdhaka@hotmail.com
*Website* www.kgc-bd.com

**Bhutan Golf Confederation**
*Sec Gen*, Tshenchok Thinlay, PO Box 423, Thimphu,
Bhutan
*Tel* +975 77 222 222    *Fax* +975 2 323 666
*E-mail* tsenchok@gmail.com

**Cambodian Golf Federation**
*Sec Gen*, Ek Sonnchan, 295 Eo Kampuchea Krom,
Kahn 7 Makuni, Phnom Penh, Cambodia
*Tel* +855 977 711 111
*E-mail* eksonnchan@ppwsa.com.kh
*Website* www.cambodiangolf-federation.com

**China Golf Federation**
5 Tiyuguan Rd, Beijing, 100763 China
*Tel* +86 10 87 183910
*Fax* +86 87 183989
*E-mail* chinagolf@263.net
*Website* www.golf.org.cn

**Chinese Taipei Golf Association**
*Sec Gen*, Wen-Kuei Chung, 12 F-1 125 Nanking East
Rd, Section 2, Taipei, Taiwan 104, Chinese Taipei
*Tel* +886 22 516 5611    *Fax* +886 22 516 5904
*E-mail* garoc.tw@msa.hinet.net
*Website* www.taiwangolf.org

**Hong Kong Golf Association**
*Ch Exec*, Tom Phillips, Suite 2003, Olympic House,
1 Stadium Path, So Kon Po, Causeway Bay,
Hong Kong
*Tel* +852 2504 8196    *Fax* +852 2845 1553
*E-mail* hkgolf@hkga.com
*Website* www.hkga.com

**Indian Golf Union**
*Sec Gen*, Maj Gen A Parmar, First Floor,24 Adchini,
New Delhi 110017
*E-mail* abhi.parmar@indiangolfunion.org
*Website* indiangolfunion.org

**Indonesian Golf Association**
*Capt*, Rizal Aya, Gedung Medico, JL Ampera No 18-20
Cilandak, Senayan, Jakarta 12560
*Tel* +021 2937 5521    *Mobile* 0812 9056 182
*E-mail* info@pbpgi.org
*Website* www.pgionline.org

**Japan Golf Association**
*Chief Sec*, Aijiro Uchida, Kyobashi YS Building 2nd
Floor, 1-12-5 Kyobashi Chuo-Ku, Tokyo 104-0031,
Japan
*Tel* +81 3 3566 0003    *Fax* +81 3 3566 0003
*E-mail* info@jga.or.jp
*Website* www.jga.or.jp

**Kazakhstan Golf Federation**
*Gen Sec*, Konstantin Lifanov, c/o Nurtau GC, Alatau
Sanatorium, Karasayskiy Region, Kamenka Village,
KZ-040918 Almat obl. Kazakhstan
*Tel* +7 727 295 8823
*E-mail* golfpro1@yandex.ru

**Korea Golf Association**
*Exec Dir,* Wonn Ko, 513-12 Munbal Road,
Gyoha-eup, Korea
*Tel* +82 31 955 2255
*E-mail* kga@kgagolf.or.kr   *Website* www.kgagolf.or.kr

**Kyrgyzstan Golf**
*Sec,* Andrej Mymrin, Maldybaeva 1/2 Str, 1st.
Floor, Bishkek City, Kyrgyz Republic
*Tel* +996 555 733786
*E-mail* golf_kg@mail.ru

**Lao National Golf Federation**
PO Box 4300, 33 Wat Xiengnhum St, Sethathirat Rd,
Vientiane, Lao PDR
*Tel/Fax* +85 621 217294
*E-mail* sangkhom52@hotmail.com

**Golf Association of Macau**
*Sec,* Johnny Senna Fernandes, Room 15 Estrada Vitoria
S/N, Centro Desportivo Vitoria, Macau
*Tel* +853 288 31555    *Fax* +853 288 32555
*Email* macaugolfassociation@yahoo.com

**Malaysian Golf Association**
*Hon Sec,* Ms.Sara Ismail, No 14, Jalan 4/76C Desa
Pandan, 55100 Kuala Lumpur, Malaysia
*Tel* +603 9283 7300    *Fax* +603 9282 9300
*E-mail* mga@tm.net.my
*Website* www.mgaonline.com.my

**Mongolian Golf Association**
*Sec Gen,* Enkh-Amgalan, MCS Plaza, 3 Seoul Street,
Ulaanbatar 210644, Mongolia
*Tel* +976 991 18982
*E-mail* zoljargal@mongolbank.mn

**Golf Federation of the Union of Myanmar**
*Gen Sec,* Aung Hia Han, Room-002, Building 17-B
Shwegabar Housing, Lane 1 3 Ward Mayangone Tsp
Yangon
*Tel* +95 9 43095678    *Fax* +95 1 9669526
*E-mail* admin@myanmargolffederation.org

**Nepal Golf Association**
Royal Singi Hotel, GPO Box 1665, Naya Baneshwar,
Kathmandu, Nepal
*E-mail* hotel@rsingi.wlink.com.np

**Pakistan Golf Federation**
*Pres,* Nayyar Afzal, Jhelum Road, PO Box 1295,
Rawalpindi, Pakistan
*Tel* +92 51 556 8177
*E-mail* info@pakistangolffederation.com

**National Golf Association of the
Philippines**
*Board Sec,* Susana S Facundo, Room 307, Building B,
Philsports Complex , Meralco Building, Pasig City,
Manila 1603
*Tel* +63 2 517 9778    *Fax* +63 2 706 5926
*E-mail* ngapgolf@rocketmail.com

**Singapore Golf Association**
*Gen Man,* Peter Teo, Tanglin Post Office, PO Box 457,
Singapore 9124162
*Tel* +65 6755 5976
*E-mail* peter@sga.org.sg
*Website* www.sga.org.sg

**Sri Lanka Golf Union**
*Hon Sec,* Ana Punchihewa, PO Box 309, 223 Model
Farm Road, Colombo 8, Sri Lanka
*Tel* +94 11 266 7771
*E-mail* info@golfsrilanka.org
*Website* www.golfsrilanka.org

**Thailand Golf Association**
286 Rajmangala National Stadium, Room211-213,
Ramkamhaeng Road, Huamark, Bangkok
*Tel* +66 2 369 3777/8/9
*E-mail* thailandgolfassociation@hotmail.com
*Website* www.tga.or.th

**Vietnam Golf Association**
*Sec Gen,* Nguyen Ngoc Chu, Suite 114, National
Convention Centre, Me Tri, Tu Liem, Hanoi
*Tel* +84 4 783 3194
*E-mail* info@vga.com.vn
*Website* www.vga.com.vn

*Professional Associations*

**ASEAN PGA Ltd**
20 Maxwell Road, 07-18K Maxwell House, Singapore
069113
*Tel* +65 6226 1318    *Fax* +65 6226 1120
*E-mail* annieloo@aseanpga.com

**Asian PGA**
*Sec,* Ramlan Dato Harun, 415-417 Block A Kelana
Business Centre, 97 Jalan SS 7/2 Kelana Jaya,
Selangor, Malaysia
*Tel* +603 7492 0099    *Fax* +603 7492 0098
*Website* www.asianpgatour.com

**Asian Tour**
*Chief Exec,* Mike Kerr, 108 Pasir Panjang Road 03-06,
Singapore 118535
*Tel* +65 67 20 8990    *Fax* +65 67 20 8997
Also at Level 1.01A Wisma Prosper, Block B, Kelana
Centre Point, No 3 Jalan SS7/19,   47301, Kelana Jaya,
Petaling Jaya, Selangor Malaysia
*Tel* +603 7880 4714/5    *Fax* +603 7880 1141
*E-mail* apgtour@asiaonline.net
*Website* www.asiantour.com

**PGA Republic of China**
2nd Floor 196 Cheng-Teh Road, Taipei, Taiwan
*Tel* +886 2 8220318    *Fax* +886 2 8229684
*E-mail* garoc.tw@msa.hinet.net
*Website* www.twgolf.org

**Hong Kong PGA**
*Contact,* Viola Wong, 70 Ting Kok Rd, Tai Po, N.T.
Hong Kong
*Tel* +852 2761 7455    *Fax* +852 2761 1489
*E-mail* info@hkpga.com.hk
*Website* www.hkpga.com.hk

**Indian PGA**
33 Poorvi Marg, Vasant Vihar, New Delhi 110-057
*Tel* +91 11 3250 5456    *Fax* +91 11 2461 6331
*E-mail* pgaofindia@gmail.com

**Japan PGA**
Top Hamamatsucho Bldg, 1-5-12 Shiba.Minato-Ku,
8FL, Tokyo 105-0014
*Tel* +81 3 5419 2614    *Fax* +81 3 5419 2622
*E-mail* bp@pga.or.jp

## Japan Ladies PGA
*Pres*, Hiromi Kobayashi, 7-16-3 Ginza, Nitetsu Kobiki Bldg 8F, Chuo-ku, Tokyo 104-0061
*Tel* +81 3 3546 7801    *Fax* +81 3 3546 7805

## OneAsia Tour
Unit 14-15, 20/F Hutchison House, 10 Harcourt Road Central, Hong Kong
*Tel* +852 2523 3660    *Fax* +852 2523 3622
*E-mail* info@oneasia.asia
*Website* www.oneasia.asia

## PGA of Malaysia
*Sec*, Brig-Gen Mahendran, 1B Jalan Mamanda 7, Ampang Point, 6800 Selangor Darul Ehsan, Malaysia

## Australasia and the Pacific

## Golf Australia
*Ch Exec*, Stephen Pitt, Level 3,95 Coventry St, South Melbourne, Victoria-3205
*Tel* +613 9626 5050    *Fax* +613 9626 5095
*E-mail* info@golfaustralia.org.au
*Website* www.golfaustralia.org.au

## Cook Islands Golf Association
*Sec*, Mrs Tereapii Urlich, c/o Rarotonga Golf Club, PO Box 151, Avarua, Rarotonga, Cook Islands
*Tel* +682 20621
*E-mail* golf@rarogolf.co.ck

## National Golf Association of Fiji
*Gen Sec*, GPO Box 5363, Raiwaqa, Suva, Fiji
*Tel/Fax* +679 338 5089
*E-mail* ngaf@connect.com.fi

## Guam National Golf Federation
*Contact*, Joe Couch, PO Box 6572, Tamuning, Guam 96931
*Tel* +1 671 472 6621    *Fax* +1 671 734 3702
*E-mail* couchjoe@hotmail.com

## New Zealand Golf Incorporated
*Ch Exec*, Dean Murphy, Level 1, Quadrant House, 1 Papuke Takapuna, North Shore City, 0704 New Zealand
*Tel* +644 471 0990
*E-mail* nzgolf@nzgolf.org.nz
*Website* www.nzgolf.org.nz

## Oceana Golf Union
*Sec*, Mosese Waqavonovono, GPO Box 18505, Suva, Fiji
*Tel* +679 331 0738
*E-mail* shamozen@connect.com.fj

## Papua New Guinea Golf Association
PO Box 4632, Boroko National Capital District. Papua New Guinea
*Tel* +675 323 110    *Fax* +675325 8418
*E-mail* jbrazier@remington.com.pg

## Papua New Guinea Ladies Golf Association
*Hon Sec*, Mrs L Illidge, PO Box 348, Lae MP 411

## Samoa Golf Incorporated
*Sec*, Sam Sesega, PO Box 3770, Apia, Samoa
*Tel* +685 24839    *Fax* 685 22457
*E-mail* samsesega@conservation.ws

## Solomon Islands
PO Box 3770 Apia, Samoa
*Tel* +685 31490
*E-mail* samesega@conservation.ws

## Tonga Golf Union
*Sec*, Piveni Piukala
*E-mail* piveni@hotmail.com

## Vanuatu Golf Association
*Chairman*, Bernie Cain, PO Box 358, Port Vila, Vanuatu, Pacific Ocean
*Tel* +678 22178
*E-mail* bernie@vanuatu.com.vu

### *Professional Associations*

## Australian PGA
*Ch Exec*, Brian Thorburn, 600 Thompson Rd, Sandhurst, Victoria 3977
Tel +61 3 8320 1911
*E-mail* info@pga.org.au
*Website* www.pga.org.au

## Australian Ladies Professional Golf
*Ch Exec*, Karen Lunn, PO Box 447, Mudgeeraba, Queensland 4213
*Tel* +61 7 5669 9706
*E-mail* Karen@algp.com.au
*Website* www.alpg.com.au

## PGA Tour Australasia
See Australian PGA

## New Zealand PGA
*Ch Exec*, Duncan Simpson, 1 Papuke Rd, PO Box 33-678, North Shore City 0740
*Tel* +64 9 488 6616    *Mobile* +64 21 756 801
*E-mail* duncan.simpson@pga.org.nz
*Website* www.pga.org.nz

## PART XVI

# Clubs and Courses

*Compiled by Paula Taylor*

# Club Centenaries

## 1913

The Addington
Ashton & Lea
Ashton-under-Lyne
Baxenden & District
Bidston
Blackmoor
Bowring
Bramley
Bull Bay
Castle
Clones
Coxmoor
Davenport
Dore & Totley
Dukinfield
Ellesmere
Ferndown
Garforth
Gathurst
Gay Hill
Hazel Grove
Highcliffe Castle
Letterkenny
Linlithgow
Lytham Green Drive
Milford Haven
Okehampton
Oxley Park
Portumna
Redditch
Royal Automobile Club
St Regulus Ladies'
Sale
Seahouses
Sitwell Park
Stocksfield
Tynemouth

## 1914

Anglesey
Apsley Guise and Woburn
  Sands
Balmoral
Blackwood
Buckingham
Burnside
Crosland Heath
Eaglescliffe
Eden Course (St Andrews)
Green Hawarth
Hockley
Nevill
Newtownstewart
Oakdale
Routenburn
Shirley Park
Sonning
Sutton Bridge
Thirsk & Northallerton
Wheatley
Whitchurch (Cardiff)

## 1915

Brokenhurst Manor
Llandudno (Maesdu)
Lowes Park
Spanish Point

## 1916

Crews Hill
Howth
Rossmore
West Kent

# Golf Clubs and Courses

## How to use this section

Clubs in England, Ireland and Wales are listed in alphabetical order by country and county. Note that some clubs and courses are affiliated to a county different to that in which they are physically located. Clubs in Scotland are grouped under recognised administrative regions. The Great Britain and Ireland county index can be found on page 682.

European clubs and clubs from the rest of the world are listed alphabetically by country and grouped under regional headings. The index for Europe can be found on page 805 and the index for the rest of the world is on page 855. In most European countries, only 18 hole courses are included.

All clubs and courses are listed in the the general index at the back of the book.

With the publication of the 2010 edition, we began introducing a new international look to the R&A Golfer's Handbook and to accommodate our global expansion of results and club information, we have modified entries to the Club's Directory as detailed below.

It is apparent that information previously displayed of green fees, membership, personnel, additional features, etc., can be best imparted as current data via the websites that the majority of clubs now operate. Currently, nearly 80 per cent of golf clubs operate websites, a number that is growing by around four per cent per annum.

### Club details (see Key to Symbols below)
The date after the name of the club indicates the year it was founded. Courses are private unless otherwise stated. Many public courses play host to members' clubs. Information on these can be obtained from the course concerned.

*We are indebted to club secretaries in the British Isles and continental Europe for the information supplied.*

### Key to Symbols

| | | | |
|---|---|---|---|
| ☎ | Telephone | ✍ | Secretary |
| 📠 | Fax | ⊕ | Additional information in the absence of a website |
| ✉ | E-mail | | |
| 🖥 | Website | | |

### European Dialling Codes

| | | |
|---|---|---|
| Austria +43 | Iceland +354 | Poland +48 |
| Belgium +32 | Repubic of | Portugal +351 |
| Cyprus +357 | Ireland +353 | Slovenia +386 |
| Czech Republic +420 | Italy +39 | Spain +34 |
| Denmark +45 | Latvia +371 | Sweden +46 |
| Finland +358 | Luxembourg +352 | Switzerland +41 |
| France +33 | Malta +356 | Turkey +90 |
| Germany +49 | Netherlands +31 | |
| Greece +30 | Norway +47 | |
| Hungary +36 | | |

# Great Britain and Ireland County Index

# England

## Bedfordshire

### Aspley Guise & Woburn Sands (1914)

West Hill, Aspley Guise, Milton Keynes
MK17 8DX
☎ (01908) 583596
📠 (01908) 288140
✉ info@aspleyguisegolfclub.co.uk
✍ Karen Evans (01908) 583596
🖳 www.aspleyguisegolfclub.co.uk

### Aylesbury Vale (1991)

Proprietary
Wing, Leighton Buzzard LU7 0UJ
☎ (01525) 240196
📠 (01525) 240848
✉ info@avgc.co.uk
✍ C Wright (Sec/Mgr)
🖳 www.avgc.co.uk

### Beadlow Manor Hotel G&CC (1973)

Proprietary
Beadlow, Shefford SG17 5PH
☎ (01525) 860800
📠 (01525) 861345
✉ office@beadlowmanor.co.uk
✍ Graham Wilson (Gen Mgr)
🖳 www.beadlowmanor.co.uk

### The Bedford (1999)

Proprietary
Carnoustie Drive, Great Denham Golf
Village, Biddenham MK40 4FF
☎ (01234) 320022
📠 (01234) 320023
✉ geoff@thebedfordgc.com
✍ Geoff Swain
🖳 www.thebedfordgc.com

### Bedford & County (1912)

Green Lane, Clapham, Bedford MK41 6ET
☎ (01234) 352617
📠 (01234) 357195
✉ office@bandcgc.co.uk
✍ John Olds (Gen Mgr)
🖳 www.bandcgc.co.uk

### Bedfordshire (1891)

Spring Lane, Stagsden, Bedford MK43 8SR
☎ (01234) 822555
📠 (01234) 825052
✉ office@bedfordshiregolf.com
✍ Geraint Dixon (Gen Mgr)
🖳 www.bedfordshiregolf.com

### Caddington (1985)

Proprietary
Chaul End Road, Caddington LU1 4AX
☎ (01582) 415573
📠 (01582) 415314
✉ info@caddingtongolfclub.co.uk
✍ D Isger
🖳 www.caddingtongolfclub.co.uk

### Chalgrave Manor (1994)

Proprietary
Dunstable Road, Chalgrave, Toddington
LU5 6JN
☎ (01525) 876556
📠 (01525) 876556
✉ steve@chalgravegolf.co.uk
✍ S Rumball
🖳 www.chalgravegolf.co.uk

### Colmworth (1992)

Proprietary
New Road, Colmworth MK44 2NN
☎ (01234) 378181
📠 (01234) 376678
✉ info@colmworthgolfclub.co.uk
✍ C Porch (01933) 412398
🖳 www.colmworthgolfclub.co.uk

### Colworth (1985)

Colworth House, Sharnbrook, Bedford
MK44 1LQ
☎ (01234) 782442
✉ secretary@colworthgolf.co.uk
✍ Dennis Scott (Sec)
⊕ Visitors can only play as Members
   guests.
🖳 www.colworthgolf.co.uk

### Dunstable Downs (1906)

Whipsnade Road, Dunstable LU6 2NB
☎ (01582) 604472
📠 (01582) 478700
✉ dunstabledownsgc@btconnect.com
✍ Alan Sigee
🖳 www.dunstabledownsgolf.co.uk

### Henlow (1985)

RAF Henlow, Henlow SG16 6DN
☎ (01462) 851515 Ext 7083
📠 (01462) 816780
✍ S Bowen (01462) 851515
🖳 www.henlowgolfclub.co.uk

### John O'Gaunt (1948)

Sutton Park, Sandy, Biggleswade SG19 2LY
☎ (01767) 260360
📠 (01767) 262834
✉ simon@johnogauntgolf.co.uk
✍ Simon Davis (Gen Mgr)
🖳 www.johnogauntgolf.co.uk

### Leighton Buzzard (1925)

Plantation Road, Leighton Buzzard
LU7 3JF
☎ (01525) 244800
📠 (01525) 244801
✉ secretary@leightonbuzzardgolf.net
✍ D Mutton (01525) 244800
🖳 www.leightonbuzzardgolf.net

### Mentmore G&CC (1992)

Mentmore, Leighton Buzzard LU7 0UA
☎ (01296) 662020
📠 (01296) 662592
✉ enquiries@mentmorecountryclub
   .co.uk

✍ Clint Moore
🖳 www.mentmorecountryclub.co.uk

### The Millbrook (1980)

Ampthill MK45 2JB
☎ (01525) 840252
📠 (01525) 406249
✉ info@themillbrook.com
✍ DC Cooke (01525) 840252
🖳 www.themillbrook.com

### Mount Pleasant (1992)

Proprietary
Station Road, Lower Stondon, Henlow
SG16 6JL
☎ (01462) 850999
📠 (01462) 850257
✉ tarasimkins
   @mountpleasantgolfclub.co.uk
✍ Tara Simkins (Gen Mgr)
🖳 www.mountpleasantgolfclub
   .co.uk

### Mowsbury (1975)

Public
Kimbolton Road, Bedford MK41 8BJ
☎ (01234) 772700
✍ TW Gardner (01234) 771041

### Pavenham Park (1994)

Proprietary
Pavenham, Bedford MK43 7PE
☎ (01234) 822202
📠 (01234) 826602
✉ office@pavenhampark.com
✍ S Pepper
🖳 www.pavenhampark.com

### South Beds (1892)

Warden Hill Road, Luton LU2 7AE
☎ (01582) 591500
📠 (01582) 495381
✉ office@southbedsgolfclub.co.uk
✍ MT Seaton (01582) 591500
🖳 www.southbedsgolfclub.co.uk

### Stockwood Park (1973)

Public
Stockwood Park, London Rd, Luton
LU1 4LX
☎ (01582) 413704
📠 (01582) 481001
✉ spgc@hotmail.co.uk
✍ Brian E Clark (Club Admin
   Officer)
🖳 www.activeluton.co.uk

### Tilsworth (1972)

Pay and play
Dunstable Rd, Tilsworth, Dunstable
LU7 9PU
☎ (01525) 210721/210722
📠 (01525) 210465
✉ info@tilsworthgolf.co.uk
✍ N Webb
🖳 www.tilsworthgolf.co.uk

## Wyboston Lakes   (1978)
Public
Wyboston Lakes, Wyboston MK44 3AL
☎ (01480) 223004
🖳 (01480) 407330
✍ DJ Little (Mgr)
🖥 www.wybostonlakes.co.uk

## Berkshire

### Bearwood Golf Club   (1986)
Mole Road, Sindlesham, Berkshire
RG11 5DB
☎ (0118) 976 0060
🖳 (0118) 977 2687
✉ barrytustin@btconnect.com
✍ BFC Tustin (Mgr)
🖥 www.bearwoodgolfclub.com

### Bearwood Lakes   (1996)
Proprietary
Bearwood Road, Sindlesham RG41 4SJ
☎ (0118) 979 7900
🖳 (0118) 979 2911
✉ info@bearwoodlakes.co.uk
✍ Carl Rutherford (MD)
🖥 www.bearwoodlakes.co.uk

### The Berkshire   (1928)
Swinley Road, Ascot SL5 8AY
☎ (01344) 621495
🖳 (01344) 623328
✉ admin@theberkshire.co.uk
✍ Lt Col JCF Hunt (01344) 621496
🖥 www.theberkshire.co.uk

### Billingbear Park   (1985)
Pay and play
The Straight Mile, Wokingham RG40 5SJ
☎ (01344) 869259
🖳 (01344) 869259
✉ info@billingbearpark.com
✍ Mrs JR Blainey
🖥 www.billingbearpark.co.uk

### Bird Hills Golf Centre   (1985)
Public
Drift Road, Hawthorn Hill, Maidenhead
SL6 3ST
☎ (01628) 771030
🖳 (01628) 631023
✉ info@birdhills.co.uk
✍ Hannah Edwards
🖥 www.birdhills.co.uk

### Blue Mountain Golf Centre
(1993)
Pay and play
Wood Lane, Binfield RG42 4EX
☎ (01344) 300200
🖳 (01344) 360960
✉ bluemountain@crown-golf.co.uk
✍ Grant Convey (Gen Mgr)
🖥 www.crown-golf.co.uk

### Calcot Park   (1930)
Bath Road, Calcot, Reading RG31 7RN
☎ (0118) 942 7124
🖳 (0118) 945 3373
✉ info@calcotpark.com
✍ Kim Brake
🖥 www.calcotpark.com

### Castle Royle   (1994)
Knowl Hill, Reading RG10 9XA
☎ (01628) 825442
✍ Pam Sutcliffe

### Caversham Heath   (2000)
Proprietary
Chazey Heath, Mapledurham, Reading
RG4 7UT
☎ (0118) 947 8600
🖳 (0118) 947 8700
✉ info@cavershamgolf.co.uk
✍ Michael Palk
🖥 www.cavershamgolf.co.uk

### Datchet   (1890)
Buccleuch Road, Datchet SL3 9BP
☎ (01753) 543887 (Clubhouse)
🖳 (01753) 541872
✉ secretary@datchetgolfclub.co.uk
✍ J R Staniford (01753) 543887
🖥 www.datchetgolfclub.co.uk

### Deanwood Park   (1995)
Pay and play
Stockcross, Newbury RG20 8JP
☎ (01635) 48772
🖳 (01635) 48772
✉ golf@deanwoodpark.co.uk
✍ John Bowness
🖥 www.deanwoodpark.co.uk

### Donnington Grove Country Club
Donnington Grove, Grove Road, Donnington
RG14 2LA
☎ (01635) 581000
🖳 (01635) 552259
✉ enquiries@donnington-grove.com

✍ S Greenacre (Mgr)
🖥 www.donnington-grove.com

### Donnington Valley   (1985)
Proprietary
Snelsmore House, Snelsmore Common,
Newbury RG14 3BG
☎ (01635) 568142
🖳 (01635) 41889
✉ golf@donningtonvalley.co.uk
✍ Peter Smith (01635) 568144
🖥 www.donningtonvalleygolfclub.co.uk

### Downshire Golf Complex
(1973)
Public
Easthampstead Park, Wokingham
RG40 3DH
☎ (01344) 302030
🖳 (01344) 301020
✉ downshiregc@bracknell-forest.gov.uk
✍ P Stanwick (Golf Mgr)
🖥 www.bracknell-forest.gov.uk/downshiregolf

### East Berkshire   (1903)
Ravenswood Ave, Crowthorne RG45 6BD
☎ (01344) 772041
🖳 (01344) 777378
✉ thesecretary@eastberkshiregolfclub.com
✍ C Day
🖥 www.eastberkshiregolfclub.com

### Goring & Streatley   (1895)
Rectory Road, Streatley-on-Thames
RG8 9QA
☎ (01491) 873229
🖳 (01491) 875224
✉ secretary@goringgolf.co.uk
✍ M Evans
🖥 www.goringgolf.co.uk

### Hennerton   (1992)
Proprietary
Crazies Hill Road, Wargrave RG10 8LT
☎ (0118) 940 1000
🖳 (0118) 940 1042
✉ info@hennertongolfclub.co.uk
✍ G Johnson (0118) 940 1000
🖥 www.hennertongolfclub.co.uk

### Hurst Ladies   (1979)
Public
c/o Dinton Pastures Country Park, Davis
Street, Hurst, Wokingham RG10 0SU
☎ (01189) 751693

---

## The Berkshire Trophy

The Berkshire Trophy, an important 72-hole Tournament in The R&A Calendar for Amateurs with a handicap of +1 or better. Hosted by the Berkshire Golf Club (founded in 1928), the Trophy was first contested in 1946. Its distinquished list of past winners includes Sir Michael Bonallack, Peter Oosterhuis, Nick Faldo, Sandy Lyle and Ross Fisher.

The Club also hosts The Lady Astor Salver for for Amateur Ladies, first contested in 1951.

△ Mrs A Haynes
⊕ Mens Club have disbanded – Ladies continues. Course still operating under countryside services

## Lavender Park
Swinley Road, Ascot SL5 8BD
☎ (01344) 893344
🖳 www.lavenderparkgolf.co.uk

## Maidenhead (1896)
Shoppenhangers Road, Maidenhead SL6 2PZ
☎ (01628) 624693
🖳 (01628) 780758
✉ manager@maidenheadgolf.co.uk
△ J Pugh
🖳 www.maidenheadgolf.co.uk

## Mapledurham (1992)
Mapledurham, Reading RG4 7UD
☎ (0118) 946 3353
🖳 (0118) 946 3363
✉ mapledurham.info
@theclubcompany.com
△ R Davies
🖳 www.theclubatmapledurham.com

## Mill Ride (1990)
Mill Ride, Ascot SL5 8LT
☎ (01344) 886777
🖳 (01344) 886820
✉ r.greenwood@mill-ride.com
△ Robin Greenwood (Gen Mgr)
🖳 www.mill-ride.com

## Newbury & Crookham (1873)
Bury's Bank Road, Greenham Common, Newbury RG19 8BZ
☎ (01635) 40035
✉ ed.richardson@newburygolf.co.uk
△ E Richardson (01635) 40035
🖳 www.newburygolf.co.uk

## Newbury Racecourse (1994)
The Racecourse, Newbury RG14 7NZ
☎ (01635) 551464
△ N Mitchell
🖳 www.nrgc.co.uk

## Reading (1910)
17 Kidmore End Road, Emmer Green, Reading RG4 8SG
☎ (0118) 947 2909
🖳 (0118) 946 4468
✉ secretary@readinggolfclub.com
🖳 www.readinggolfclub.com

## Royal Ascot (1887)
Winkfield Road, Ascot SL5 7LJ
☎ (01344) 625175
🖳 (01344) 872330
✉ admin@royalascotgolfclub.co.uk
△ Mrs S Thompson (01344) 625175
🖳 www.royalascotgolfclub.co.uk

## The Royal Household (1901)
Buckingham Palace, London SW1 1AA
☎ (0207) 930 4832
✉ rhgc@royal.gsx.gov.uk
△ Peter Walter (Secretary)
⊕ Members and guests only

## Sand Martins (1993)
Proprietary
Finchampstead Road, Wokingham RG40 3RQ
☎ (0118) 979 2711
🖳 (0118) 977 0282
✉ info@sandmartins.com
△ Andrew Hall (Man Dir) (01189) 029964
🖳 www.sandmartins.com

## Sonning (1914)
Proprietary
Duffield Road, Sonning, Reading RG4 6GJ
☎ (0118) 969 3332
✉ secretary@sonning-golf-club.co.uk
△ Guy Stacey
🖳 www.sonning-golf-club.co.uk

## Swinley Forest (1909)
Coronation Road, Ascot SL5 9LE
☎ (01344) 620197
🖳 (01344) 874733
✉ office@swinleyfgc.co.uk
△ Stewart Zuill (01344) 295283
⊕ 18h L6062 Par 69 SSS 70

## Temple (1909)
Henley Road, Hurley, Maidenhead SL6 5LH
☎ (01628) 824795
✉ secretary@templegolfclub.co.uk
△ KGM Adderley (01628) 824795
🖳 www.templegolfclub.co.uk

## Theale Golf Club (1996)
Proprietary
North Street, Theale, Reading RG7 5EX
☎ (01189) 305331
✉ info@thealegolf.com
△ M Lowe
🖳 www.thealegolf.com

## West Berkshire (1975)
Proprietary
Chaddleworth, Newbury RG20 7DU
☎ (01488) 638574
🖳 (01488) 638781
✉ info@thewbgc.co.uk
△ Mrs CM Clayton
🖳 www.thewbgc.co.uk

## Winter Hill (1976)
Proprietary
Grange Lane, Cookham SL6 9RP
☎ (01628) 527613
🖳 (01628) 527479
✉ derek_bond@johnlewis.co.uk
△ Clare Leech (01628) 536071
🖳 www.winterhillgolfclub.net

## Wokefield Park (1998)
Proprietary
Goodboys Lane, Mortimer, Reading RG7 3AH
☎ (0118) 933 4072
🖳 (0118) 933 4031
✉ wokgolfteam@deverevenues.co.uk
△ Tim Gilpin (Mgr)
🖳 www.deveregolf.co.uk

## Buckinghamshire

## Aylesbury Golf Centre (1992)
Public
Hulcott Lane, Bierton HP22 5GA
☎ (01296) 393644
✉ kevinpartington@hotmail.co.uk
△ K Partington (Mgr)
🖳 www.aylesburygolfclub.co.uk

## Aylesbury Park (1996)
Proprietary
Andrews Way, Oxford Road, Aylesbury HP17 8QQ
☎ (01296) 399196
✉ info@aylesburyparkgolf.com
△ Carole Barnes
🖳 www.aylesburyparkgolf.com

## Beaconsfield (1902)
Seer Green, Beaconsfield HP9 2UR
☎ (01494) 676545
🖳 (01494) 681148
✉ secretary@beaconsfieldgolfclub.co.uk
△ D Cliffe
🖳 www.beaconsfieldgolfclub.co.uk

## Buckingham (1914)
Tingewick Road, Buckingham MK18 4AE
☎ (01280) 815566
✉ admin@buckinghamgolfclub.co.uk
△ Peter Frost
🖳 www.buckinghamgolfclub.co.uk

## Buckinghamshire (1992)
Proprietary
Denham Court Mansion, Denham Court Drive, Denham UB9 5PG
☎ (01895) 835777
🖳 (01895) 835210
✉ info@buckinghamshiregc.co.uk
△ D Griffiths (01895) 836803
🖳 www.buckinghamshiregc.com

## Burnham Beeches (1891)
Green Lane, Burnham, Slough SL1 8EG
☎ (01628) 661448
🖳 (01628) 668968
✉ enquiries@bbgc.co.uk
△ P C Dawson (Mgr)
🖳 www.bbgc.co.uk

## Chartridge Park (1989)
Chartridge, Chesham HP5 2TF
☎ (01494) 791772
🖳 (01494) 786462
✉ info@cpgc.co.uk
△ E Roca
🖳 www.cpgc.co.uk

## Chesham & Ley Hill (1900)
Ley Hill, Chesham HP5 1UZ
☎ (01494) 784541
🖳 (01494) 785506
✉ secretary@cheshamgolf.co.uk
△ James Short
🖳 www.cheshamgolf.co.uk

## Chiltern Forest (1979)
Aston Hill, Halton, Aylesbury HP22 5NQ
☎ (01296) 631267

☎ (01296) 632709
✉ generalmanager@chilternforest
.co.uk
✍ Neil Clayton (Gen Mgr)
🖳 www.chilternforest.co.uk

## Denham    (1910)
*Tilehouse Lane, Denham UB9 5DE*
☎ **(01895) 832022**
☐ (01895) 835340
✍ JW Tucker
🖳 www.denhamgolfclub.co.uk

## Ellesborough    (1906)
*Butlers Cross, Aylesbury HP17 0TZ*
☎ **(01296) 622114**
☐ (01296) 622114
✉ office@ellesboroughgolf.co.uk
✍ Mr Andy Hayes
🖳 www.ellesboroughgolf.co.uk

## Farnham Park    (1974)
**Public**
*Park Road, Stoke Poges, Slough SL2 4PJ*
☎ **(01753) 643332**
☐ (01753) 646617
✉ farnhamparkgolf@southbucks.gov.uk
✍ Nigel Whitton Golf Mgr
🖳 www.farnhamparkgolfcourse.co.uk

## Flackwell Heath    (1904)
*Treadaway Road, Flackwell Heath, High Wycombe HP10 9PE*
☎ **(01628) 520929**
☐ (01628) 530040
✉ secretary@fhgc.co.uk
✍ P Clarke
🖳 www.fhgc.co.uk

## Gerrards Cross    (1921)
*Chalfont Park, Gerrards Cross SL9 0QA*
☎ **(01753) 883263**
☐ (01753) 883593
✉ secretary@gxgolf.co.uk
✍ Simon Maynard
🖳 www.gxgolf.co.uk

## Harewood Downs    (1907)
*Cokes Lane, Chalfont St Giles HP8 4TA*
☎ **(01494) 762184**
✉ office@hdgc.co.uk
✍ Nigel Daniel
🖳 www.hdgc.co.uk

## Harleyford    (1996)
*Harleyford Estate, Henley Road, Marlow SL7 2SP*
☎ **(01628) 816161**
☐ (01628) 816160
✉ info@harleyfordgolf.co.uk
✍ Trevor Collingwood 01628 816164
🖳 www.harleyfordgolf.co.uk

## Hazlemere    (1982)
*Penn Road, Hazlemere, High Wycombe HP15 7LR*
☎ **(01494) 719300**
☐ (01494) 713914
✉ enquiries@hazlemeregolfclub.co.uk
✍ Chris Mahoney
🖳 www.hazlemeregolfclub.co.uk

## Hedsor    (2000)
**Pay and play**
*Broad Lane, Wooburn Common, Bucks HP10 0JW*
☎ **(01628) 851285**
✉ info@hedsorgolfcourse.co.uk
✍ Stuart Cannon
🖳 www.hedsorgolfcourse.co.uk

## Huntswood    (1996)
**Pay and play**
*Taplow Common Road, Burnham SL1 8LS*
☎ **(01628) 667144**
☐ (01628) 663145
✉ huntswoodgc@btconnect.com
✍ Sue Morris (Mgr)
🖳 www.huntswoodgolf.com

## Iver    (1983)
*Hollow Hill Lane, Iver SL0 0JJ*
☎ **(01753) 655615**
☐ (01753) 654225
✉ ivergolf@fsmail.net
✍ J Lynch (Golf Dir) - Fellow PGA
🖳 www.ivergolfcourse.co.uk

## Ivinghoe    (1967)
**Proprietary**
*Wellcroft, Ivinghoe, Leighton Buzzard LU7 9EF*
☎ **(01296) 668696**
☐ (01296) 662755
✉ info@ivinghoegolfclub.co.uk
✍ Mrs E Culley (01296) 668696
🖳 www.ivinghoegolfclub.co.uk

## Kingfisher CC    (1995)
**Proprietary**
*Buckingham Road, Deanshanger, Milton Keynes MK19 6JY*
☎ **(01908) 560354**
☐ (01908) 260857
✉ sales.kingfisher@btopenworld.com
✍ Matthew Brand (01908) 562332
🖳 www.kingfisher-uk.com

## The Lambourne Club    (1992)
**Proprietary**
*Dropmore Road, Burnham SL1 8NF*
☎ **(01628) 666755**
☐ (01628) 663301
✉ info@lambourneclub.co.uk
✍ D Hart (Gen Mgr)
🖳 www.lambourneclub.co.uk

## Little Chalfont    (1981)
*Lodge Lane, Chalfont St Giles HP8 4AJ*
☎ **(01494) 764877**
✍ JM Dunne (01494) 762942

## Magnolia Park
*Arncott Road, Boarstall HP18 9XX*
☎ **(01844) 239700**
☐ (01844) 238991
✉ info@magnoliapark.co.uk
✍ Debbie Ludlow
🖳 www.magnoliapark.co.uk

## Oakland Park    (1994)
**Proprietary**
*Three Households, Chalfont St Giles HP8 4LW*
☎ **(01494) 871277**

☐ (01494) 874692
✉ info@oaklandparkgolf.co.uk
✍ I Donnelly (Gen Mgr)
🖳 www.oaklandparkgolf.co.uk

## Princes Risborough    (1990)
*Lee Road, Saunderton Lee, Princes Risborough HP27 9NX*
☎ **(01844) 346989 (Clubhouse)**
☐ (01844) 274938
✉ info@prgc.co.uk
✍ J Murray (Man Dir)
🖳 www.prgc.co.uk

## Richings Park    (1994)
**Proprietary**
*North Park, Iver SL0 9DL*
☎ **(01753) 655352**
☐ (01753) 655409
✉ info@richingspark.co.uk
✍ Carl Lindsay (01753) 655370
🖳 www.richingspark.co.uk

## Silverstone    (1992)
**Proprietary**
*Silverstone Road, Stowe, Buckingham MK18 5LH*
☎ **(01280) 850005**
☐ (01280) 850156
✉ proshop@silverstonegolfclub.co.uk
✍ S Barnes
🖳 www.silverstonegolfclub.co.uk

## Stoke Park Club    (1908)
*Park Road, Stoke Poges SL2 4PG*
☎ **(01753) 717171**
☐ (01753) 717181
✉ info@stokepark.com
✍ Mrs Kelly Gorry (01753) 717116
🖳 www.stokepark.com

## Stowe    (1974)
*Stowe, Buckingham MK18 5EH*
✍ D Procter (01280) 818024

## Thorney Park    (1992)
**Proprietary**
*Thorney Mill Road, Iver SL0 9AL*
☎ **(01895) 422095**
☐ (01895) 431307
✉ sales@thorneypark.com
✍ P Gray
🖳 www.thorneypark.com

## Three Locks    (1992)
*Great Brickhill, Milton Keynes MK17 9BH*
☎ **(01525) 270050**
☐ (01525) 270470
✉ info@threelocksgolfclub.co.uk
✍ P Critchley
🖳 www.threelocksgolfclub.co.uk

## Wavendon Golf Centre    (1990)
**Pay and play**
*Lower End Road, Wavendon, Milton Keynes MK17 8DA*
☎ **(01908) 281811**
☐ (01908) 281257
✉ wavendon@hotmail.co.uk
✍ G Iron
🖳 www.jackbarker.com

*For key to symbols see page 725*

## Weston Turville   (1973)
**Proprietary**
*New Road, Weston Turville, Aylesbury HP22 5QT*
☎ **(01296) 424084**
📠 (01296) 395376
📧 enquiries@westonturvillegolfclub .co.uk
✍ D Allen
🖥 www.westonturvillegolfclub.co.uk

## Wexham Park   (1977)
**Pay and play**
*Wexham Street, Wexham, Slough SL3 6ND*
☎ **(01753) 663271**
📠 (01753) 663318
📧 info@wexhamparkgolfcourse.co.uk
✍ J Kennedy
🖥 www.wexhamparkgolfcourse.co.uk

## Whiteleaf   (1907)
*Whiteleaf, Princes Risborough HP27 0LY*
☎ **(01844) 343097/274058**
📧 info@whiteleafgolfclub.co.uk
✍ M Piercy (01844) 345472
🖥 www.whiteleafgolfclub.co.uk

## Windmill Hill   (1972)
**Pay and play**
*Tattenhoe Lane, Bletchley MK3 7RB*
☎ **(01908) 631113 (Bookings)**
📧 whgolf@milton-keynes.gov.uk
✍ Diana Allen (01908) 647615
🖥 www.milton-keynes.gov.uk

## Woburn   (1976)
*Little Brickhill, Milton Keynes MK17 9LJ*
☎ **(01908) 370756**
📠 (01908) 378436
📧 enquiries@woburngolf.com
✍ Jason O'Malley (Gen Mgr)
🖥 www.discoverwoburn.co.uk

## Wycombe Heights   (1991)
**Pay and play**
*Rayners Avenue, Loudwater, High Wycombe HP10 9SZ*
☎ **(01494) 816686**
📠 (01494) 816728
📧 info@wycombeheightsgc.co.uk
✍ Steve West
🖥 www.wycombeheightsgc.co.uk

# Cambridgeshire

## Abbotsley   (1986)
**Proprietary**
*Potton Road, St Neots PE19 6XN*
☎ **(01480) 474000**
📠 (01480) 471018
📧 sales@abbotsley.com
✍ Helen Lavis (01480) 474000
🖥 www.abbotsley.com

## Bourn   (1991)
**Proprietary**
*Toft Road, Bourn, Cambridge CB23 2TT*
☎ **(01954) 718057**
📠 (01954) 718908
📧 info@bourngolfandleisure.co.uk
🖥 www.bourngolf and leisure.co.uk

## Brampton Park   (1991)
*Buckden Road, Brampton, Huntingdon PE28 4NF*
☎ **(01480) 434700**
📧 admin@bramptonparkgc.co.uk
✍ Lisa Charlton (Gen Mgr)
🖥 www.bramptonparkgc.co.uk

## Cambridge   (1995)
*Station Road, Longstanton, Cambridge CB4 5DS*
☎ **(01954) 789388**
📧 klgcambridgegolf@tiscali.co.uk
✍ K Green

## Cambridge Meridian   (1944)
**Proprietary**
*Comberton Road, Toft, Cambridge CB23 2RY*
☎ **(01223) 264700**
📠 (01223) 264701
📧 meridian@golfsocieties.com
✍ Steve Creighton
🖥 www.golfsocieties.com

## Cromwell   (1986)
**Pay and play**
*Potton Road, St Neots PE19 6XN*
☎ **(01480) 408900**
📠 (01480) 471018
📧 sales@abbotsley.com
✍ Helen Lavis (01480) 474000
🖥 www.abbotsley.com

## Elton Furze   (1993)
**Proprietary**
*Bullock Road, Haddon, Peterborough PE7 3TT*
☎ **(01832) 280189**
📠 (01832) 280299
✍ Fiona Martin (Sec)
🖥 www.eltonfurzegolfclub.co.uk

## Ely City   (1961)
*107 Cambridge Road, Ely CB7 4HX*
☎ **(01353) 662751**
📠 (01353) 668636
📧 info@elygolf.co.uk
✍ Tom Munt (Mgr) (01353) 662751
🖥 www.elygolf.co.uk

## Girton   (1936)
*Dodford Lane, Girton CB3 0QE*
☎ **(01223) 276169**
📠 (01223) 277150
📧 info@girtongolf.co.uk
✍ Miss VM Webb
🖥 www.girtongolf.co.uk

## The Gog Magog   (1901)
*Shelford Bottom, Cambridge CB22 3AB*
☎ **(01223) 247626**
📠 (01223) 414990
📧 secretary@gogmagog.co.uk
✍ Mr K Mader
🖥 www.gogmagog.co.uk

## Hemingford Abbots Golf Club   (1991)
**Proprietary**
*New Farm Lodge, Cambridge Road, Hemingford Abbots, Cambs PE18 9HQ*
☎ **(01480) 495000**

📠 (01480) 496000
✍ RD Paton
🖥 www.astroman.co.uk

## Heydon Grange G&CC   (1994)
*Heydon, Royston SG8 7NS*
☎ **(01763) 208988**
📠 (01763) 208926
📧 enquiries@heydongrange.co.uk
✍ S Akhtar
🖥 www.heydongrange.co.uk

## Lakeside Lodge   (1992)
**Public & Proprietary**
*Fen Road, Pidley, Huntingdon PE28 3DF*
☎ **(01487) 740540**
📠 (01487) 740852
📧 info@lakeside-lodge.co.uk
✍ Mrs J Hopkins
🖥 www.lakeside-lodge.co.uk

## March   (1922)
*Frogs Abbey, Grange Rd, March PE15 0YH*
☎ **(01354) 652364**
📧 secretary@marchgolfclub.co.uk
✍ M Simpson
🖥 www.marchgolfclub.co.uk

## Menzies Cambridgeshire   (1974)
**Proprietary**
*Bar Hill, Cambridge CB23 8EU*
☎ **(01954) 780098**
📠 (01954) 780010
📧 cambridge.golfpro@menzieshotels .co.uk
✍ Tom Turner (Golf Ops Mgr)
🖥 www.menzieshotels.co.uk

## New Malton   (1993)
**Proprietary/Members**
*Malton Lane, Meldreth, Royston SG8 6PE*
☎ **(01763) 262200**
📠 (01763) 262209
📧 brian@newmaltongolfcambridge .co.uk
✍ Brian Mudge (Professional)
🖥 www.newmaltongolfcambridge.co.uk

## Old Nene G&CC   (1992)
*Muchwood Lane, Bodsey, Ramsey PE26 2XQ*
☎ **(01487) 815622**
📠 (01487) 813519
📧 george.stoneman@virgin.net
✍ GHD Stoneman

## Orton Meadows   (1987)
**Public**
*Ham Lane, Peterborough PE2 5UU*
☎ **(01733) 237478**
📧 omgc@btinternet.com
✍ WL Stocks (01733) 237478
🖥 www.omgc.co.uk

## Peterborough Milton   (1937)
*Milton Ferry, Peterborough PE6 7AG*
☎ **(01733) 380489**
📠 (01733) 380489
📧 admin@pmgc.org.uk
✍ Andy Izod (01733) 380489
🖥 www.pmgc.org.uk

## Ramsey    (1964)
*4 Abbey Terrace, Ramsey, Huntingdon PE26 1DD*
- ☎ **(01487) 812600**
- 🖥 (01487) 815746
- ✉ admin@ramseyclub.co.uk
- 🖊 John Bufton
- 🖥 www.ramseyclub.co.uk

## St Ives    (1923)
*Needingworth Road, St Ives PE27 6NB*
- ☎ **(01480) 499920 Ext 4**
- 🖥 (01480) 301489
- ✉ manager@stivesgolfclub.co.uk
- 🖊 Mike Kjenstad (01480) 499920 Ext 4
- 🖥 www.stivesgolfclub.co.uk

## St Neots    (1890)
*Crosshall Road, St Neots PE19 7GE*
- ☎ **(01480) 472363**
- 🖥 (01480) 472363
- ✉ office@stneots-golfclub.co.uk
- 🖊 M.V.Truswell
- 🖥 www.stneots-golfclub.co.uk

## Stilton Oaks    (1997)
**Proprietary**
*High Street, Stilton, Cambridgeshire PE7 3RB*
- ☎ **(01733) 245233**
- 🖊 Mr D Darke (Mgr)

## Thorney Golf Centre    (1991)
**Public**
*English Drove, Thorney, Peterborough PE6 0TJ*
- ☎ **(01733) 270570**
- 🖥 (01733) 270842
- ✉ info@thorneygolfcentre.com
- 🖊 Jane Hind
- 🖥 www.thorneygolfcentre.com

## Thorpe Wood    (1975)
**Pay and play**
*Nene Parkway, Peterborough PE3 6SE*
- ☎ **(01733) 267701**
- 🖥 (01733) 332774
- 🖥 www.thorpewoodgolfcourse.co.uk

## Tydd St Giles Golf & Leisure Estate    (1993)
**Proprietary**
*Kirkgate, Tydd St Giles, Cambridgeshire PE13 5NZ*
- ☎ **(01945) 871007**
- ✉ enquiries@tyddgolf.com
- 🖊 Daniel Newell
- 🖥 www.pureleisuregroup.com

## Waterbeach    (1968)
**Public**
*Waterbeach Barracks, Waterbeach, Cambridge CB5 9PA*
- ☎ **(01223) 441199 (Sec)**
- 🖥 (01223) 204636
- ✉ waterbeach.golfclub@btconnect.com
- 🖊 Maj (Retd) DA Hornby (Hon)
- 🖥 www.waterbeachgolfclub.co.uk

# Channel Islands

## Alderney
*Route des Carrieres, Alderney GY9 3YD*
- ☎ **(01481) 822835**
- 🖥 (01481) 823609
- 🖊 Ken Bithell (01481) 822835

## La Grande Mare    (1994)
**Proprietary**
*Vazon Bay, Castel, Guernsey GY5 7LL*
- ☎ **(01481) 253544**
- 🖥 (01481) 255194
- ✉ golf@lagrandemare.com
- 🖊 N Graham
- 🖥 www.lagrandemare.com

## Les Mielles G&CC    (1994)
**Public**
*St Ouens Bay, Jersey JE3 7FQ*
- ☎ **(01534) 482787**
- 🖥 (01534) 485414
- ✉ golf@lesmielles.co.je
- 🖊 J Le Brun (Golf Dir)
- 🖥 www.lesmielles.com

## La Moye    (1902)
*La Moye, St Brelade, Jersey JE3 8GQ*
- ☎ **(01534) 743401**
- 🖥 (01534) 747289
- ✉ secretary@lamoyegolfclub.co.uk
- 🖊 Sue Biard
- 🖥 www.lamoyegolfclub.co.uk

## Les Ormes    (1996)
*Mont à la Brune, St Brelade, Jersey JE3 8FL*
- ☎ **(01534) 497000**
- 🖥 (01534) 499122
- ✉ reception@lesormesjersey.co.uk
- 🖊 M Harris (01534) 497015
- 🖥 www.lesormes.je

## Royal Guernsey    (1890)
*L'Ancresse, Guernsey GY3 5BY*
- ☎ **(01481) 246523**
- 🖥 (01481) 243960
- ✉ clubmanager @royalguernseygolfclub.com
- 🖊 Roy Bushby (01481) 246523
- 🖥 www.royalguernseygolfclub.com

## Royal Jersey    (1878)
*Grouville, Jersey JE3 9BD*
- ☎ **(01534) 854416**
- ✉ thesecretary@royaljersey.com
- 🖊 DJ Attwood
- 🖥 www.royaljersey.com

## St Clements    (1925)
**Public**
*St Clements, Jersey JE2 6QN*
- ☎ **(01534) 721938**
- 🖥 (01534) 721938
- ✉ manager@stclementsgolfandsports centre.co.uk

## St Pierre Park    (1986)
*Rohais, St Peter Port, Guernsey GY1 1FD*
- ☎ **(01481) 727039**
- 🖥 (01481) 712041
- ✉ golf@stpierrepark.co.uk
- 🖊 James Child
- 🖥 www.stpierreparkgolf.co.uk

## Wheatlands Golf Club    (2004)
*Off Old Beaumont Hill, St Peter, Jersey JE3 7ED*
- ☎ **(01534) 888877**
- 🖥 (01534) 769880
- ✉ info@wheatlandsjersey.com
- 🖥 www.wheatlandsgolf.com

# Cheshire

## Alder Root    (1993)
**Proprietary**
*Alder Root Lane, Winwick, Warrington WA2 8RZ*
- ☎ **(01925) 291919**
- 🖥 (01925) 291961
- ✉ office@alderrootgolfclub.com
- 🖊 E Lander
- 🖥 www.alderroot.com

## Alderley Edge    (1907)
*Brook Lane, Alderley Edge SK9 7RU*
- ☎ **(01625) 586200**
- ✉ office@aegc.co.uk
- 🖊 Club Administrator (01625) 586200 Option 1
- 🖥 www.aegc.co.uk

## Aldersey Green    (1993)
**Proprietary**
*Aldersey, Chester CH3 9EH*
- ☎ **(01829) 782157**
- ✉ bradburygolf@aol.com
- 🖊 S Bradbury
- 🖥 alderseygreengolfclub.co.uk

## Altrincham Municipal    (1893)
**Public**
*Stockport Road, Timperley, Altrincham WA15 7LP*
- ☎ **(0161) 928 0761**
- 🖊 C J Schofield 0161 861 0201
- 🖥 www.altrinchamgolfclub.org

## Alvaston Hall    (1992)
**Proprietary**
*Middlewich Road, Nantwich CW5 6PD*
- ☎ **(01270) 628473**
- 🖥 (01270) 623395
- 🖊 N Walkington (01270) 628473

## Antrobus    (1993)
**Proprietary**
*Foggs Lane, Antrobus, Northwich CW9 6JQ*
- ☎ **(01925) 730890**
- 🖊 Vacant
- 🖥 www.antrobusgolfclub.co.uk

## Ashton-on-Mersey    (1897)
*Church Lane, Sale M33 5QQ*
- ☎ **(0161) 976 4390 (Clubhouse)**
- 🖥 (0161) 976 4390
- ✉ golf.aomgc@btconnect.com
- 🖊 R Coppock (0161) 976 4390
- 🖥 www.aomgc.co.uk

## Astbury    (1922)
*Peel Lane, Astbury, Congleton CW12 4RE*
- ☎ **(01260) 272772**
- 🖥 (01260) 276420

admin@astburygolfclub.com
P Bentley (01260) 272772
www.astburygolfclub.com

## Birchwood   (1979)
Kelvin Close, Birchwood, Warrington
WA3 7PB
☎ **(01925) 818819,
Pro Shop (01925) 225216**
(01925) 822403
enquiries@birchwoodgolfclub.co.uk
A Harper (Facilities Mgr)
www.birchwoodgolfclub.co.uk

## Bramall Park   (1894)
20 Manor Road, Bramhall, Stockport
SK7 3LY
☎ **(0161) 485 3119 (Clubhouse)**
(0161) 485 7101
secretary@bramallparkgolfclub
.co.uk
J R Cambbell
www.bramallparkgolfclub.co.uk

## Bramhall   (1905)
Ladythorn Road, Bramhall, Stockport
SK7 2EY
☎ **(0161) 439 6092**
(0161) 439 6092
office@bramhallgolfclub.com
D O'Brien (Hon) (0161) 439 6092
www.bramhallgolfclub.com

## Carden Park Hotel Golf Resort & Spa
Chester CH3 9DQ
☎ **(01829) 731534**
(01829) 731599
reservations.carden@devere-hotels.com
K Proctor (01829) 731000
www.cardenpark.co.uk

## Cheadle   (1885)
Shiers Drive, Cheadle Road, Cheadle
SK8 1HW
☎ **(0161) 491 4452**
cheadlegolfclub@msn.com
Mrs Vera Moore
www.cheadlegolfclub.com

## Chester   (1901)
Curzon Park, Chester CH4 8AR
☎ **(01244) 677760**
secretary@chestergolfclub.co.uk
Mark J Williams (01244) 677760
www.chestergc.co.uk

## Congleton   (1898)
Biddulph Road, Congleton CW12 3LZ
☎ **(01260) 273540**
(01260) 290902
congletongolfclub@btconnect.com
D Lancake
www.congletongolf.co.uk

## Crewe   (1911)
Fields Road, Haslington, Crewe CW1 5TB
☎ **(01270) 584227 (Steward)**
(01270) 256482
secretary@crewegolfclub.co.uk
H Taylor (01270) 584099
www.crewegolfclub.co.uk

## Davenport   (1913)
Worth Hall, Middlewood Road, Poynton
SK12 1TS
☎ **(01625) 876951**
(01625) 877489
admin@davenportgolf.co.uk
J E Roome (01625) 876951
www.davenportgolf.co.uk

## Delamere Forest   (1910)
Station Road, Delamere, Northwich
CW8 2JE
☎ **(01606) 883800**
sec@delameregolf.co.uk
M Towers (01606) 883800
www.delameregolf.co.uk

## Disley   (1889)
Stanley Hall Lane, Disley, Stockport
SK12 2JX
☎ **(01663) 764001**
secretary@disleygolfclub.co.uk
Howard Orton
www.disleygolfclub.co.uk

## Dukinfield   (1913)
Yew Tree Lane, Dukinfield SK16 5GF
☎ **(0161) 338 2340**
(0161) 303 0205
secretary@dukinfieldgolfclub.co.uk
K Marsh (0161) 338 2340
www.dukinfieldgolfclub.co.uk

## Dunham Forest G&CC   (1961)
Oldfield Lane, Altrincham WA14 4TY
☎ **(0161) 928 2605**
(0161) 929 8975
enquiries@dunhamforest.com
Mrs A Woolf
www.dunhamforest.com

## Eaton   (1965)
Guy Lane, Waverton, Chester CH3 7PH
☎ **(01244) 335885**
(01244) 335782
office@eatongolfclub.co.uk
K Brown
www.eatongolfclub.co.uk

## Ellesmere Port   (1971)
**Public**
Chester Road, Childer Thornton, South
Wirral CH66 1QF
☎ **(0151) 339 7689**
C Craggs

## Frodsham   (1990)
Simons Lane, Frodsham WA6 6HE
☎ **(01928) 732159**
(01928) 734070
paulw@frodshamgolf.co.uk
El Roylance
www.frodshamgolf.co.uk

## Gatley   (1912)
Waterfall Farm, Styal Road, Heald Green,
Cheadle SK8 3TW
☎ **(0161) 437 2091**
secretary@gatleygolfclub.com
Michael J Coffey
www.gatleygolfclub.com

## Hale   (1903)
Rappax Road, Hale, Altrincham
WA15 0NU
☎ **(0161) 980 4225**
secretary@halegolfclub.com
C E J Wright (Hon Sec)
www.halegolfclub.com

## Hartford Golf Club   (2000)
Burrow Hill, Hartford, Cheshire CW8 3AP
☎ **(01606) 871162**
(01606) 872182
info@hartfordgolf.co.uk
www.hartfordgolf.co.uk

## Hazel Grove   (1913)
Buxton Road, Hazel Grove, Stockport
SK7 6LU
☎ **(0161) 483 3978 (Office)**
(0161) 483 3978
secretary@hazelgrovegolfclub.com
Jane Hill (0161) 483 3978 Opt 4
www.hazelgrovegolfclub.com

## Heaton Moor   (1892)
Mauldeth Road, Heaton Mersey, Stockport
SK4 3NX
☎ **(0161) 432 2134**
(0161) 432 2134
heatonmoorgolfclub@yahoo.co.uk
A C Brook (Hon Sec)
www.heatonmoorgolfclub.co.uk

## Helsby   (1901)
Tower's Lane, Helsby WA6 0JB
☎ **(01928) 722021**
(01928) 726816
secretary@helsbygolfclub.org
C A Stubbs
www.helsbygolfclub.org

## Heyrose   (1989)
**Proprietary**
Budworth Road, Tabley, Knutsford
WA16 0HZ
☎ **(01565) 733664**
(01565) 734578
info@heyrosegolfclub.com
Mrs H Marsh
www.heyrosegolfclub.com

## High Legh Park Golf Club
**Pay and play**
Warrington Road, High Legh, Knutsford,
Cheshire WA16 0WA
☎ **(01565) 830888**
(01565) 830999
info@highleghpark.com
Martin Cooper (Course Director)
www.highleghpark.com

## Houldsworth   (1910)
Houldsworth Park, Houldsworth Street,
Reddish, Stockport SK5 6BN
☎ **(0161) 442 1712**
(0161) 947 9678
houldsworthsecretary@hotmail
.co.uk
K Smith (Sec) (0161) 442 1712
www.houldsworthgolfclub.co.uk

## Knights Grange (1983)
**Public**
Grange Lane, Winsford CW7 2PT
☎ (01606) 552780
✉ golf@brioleisure.org
🖎 Mrs P Littler (Mgr)

## Knutsford (1891)
Mereheath Lane, Knutsford WA16 6HS
☎ (01565) 633355
✉ secretary@knutsfordgolf.com
🖎 Stuart Blake
🖳 www.knutsfordgolf.com

## Leigh (1906)
Kenyon Hall, Broseley Lane, Culcheth, Warrington WA3 4BG
☎ (01925) 763130
🖥 (01925) 765097
✉ golf@leighgolf.fsnet.co.uk
🖎 Antony O'Neill (01925) 762943
🖳 www.leighgolf.co.uk

## Lymm (1907)
Whitbarrow Road, Lymm WA13 9AN
☎ (01925) 755020
🖥 (01925) 755020
✉ lymmgolfclub@btconnect.com
🖎 A Scully
🖳 www.lymm-golf-club.co.uk

## Macclesfield (1889)
The Hollins, Macclesfield SK11 7EA
☎ (01625) 423227
🖥 (01625) 260061
✉ secretary@maccgolfclub.co.uk
🖎 B Littlewood
🖳 www.maccgolfclub.co.uk

## Malkins Bank Golf Course (1980)
**Public**
Betchton Road, Malkins Bank, Sandbach CW11 4XN
☎ (01270) 765931/767878 (Pro shop/Clubhouse)
🖥 (01270) 764730
✉ proshop@malkinsbankgolfclub.co.uk
🖎 Tony Minshall (Director of Golf)
🖳 www.malkinsbankgolfclub.co.uk

## Marple (1892)
Barnsfold Road, Hawk Green, Marple, Stockport SK6 7EL
☎ (0161) 427 2311 Ext 1
🖥 (0161) 427 2311
✉ secretary@marple-golf-club.co.uk
🖎 W Hibbert (0161) 427 2311/ 427 9525
🖳 www.marplegolfclub.co.uk

## Mellor & Townscliffe (1894)
Tarden, Gibb Lane, Mellor, Stockport SK6 5NA
☎ (0161) 427 9700 (Clubhouse)
🖥 (0161) 427 9700
🖎 J V Dixon (0161) 427 2208
🖳 www.mellorgolf.co.uk

## Mere G&CC (1934)
Chester Road, Mere, Knutsford WA16 6LJ
☎ (01565) 830155

🖥 (01565) 830713
✉ sales@meregolf.co.uk
🖎 P Whitehead
🖳 www.meregolf.co.uk

## Mersey Valley (1995)
**Proprietary**
Warrington Road, Bold Heath, Widnes WA8 3XL
☎ (0151) 424 6060
🖥 (0151) 257 9097
✉ chrismgerrard@yahoo.co.uk
🖎 RM Bush (Man Dir)
🖳 www.merseyvalleygolfclub.co.uk

## Mobberley (1996)
Burleyhurst Lane, Mobberley, Knutsford WA16 7JZ
☎ (01565) 880188
🖥 (01565) 880178
✉ info@mobgolfclub.co.uk
🖎 Gary Donnison (Golf Director)
🖳 www.mobgolfclub.co.uk

## Mollington Grange (1999)
Townfield Lane, Mollington, Chester CH1 6NJ
☎ (01244) 851185
🖥 (01244) 851349
✉ info@mollingtongolfclub.co.uk
🖎 Ray Stringer
🖳 www.mollingtongolfclub.co.uk

## Mottram Hall Hotel (1991)
**Proprietary**
Wilmslow Road, Mottram St Andrew, Prestbury SK10 4QT
☎ (01625) 820064
🖥 (01625) 829284
✉ mhgolf@devere-hotels.com
🖎 Tim Hudspith (Head Golf & Leisure)
🖳 www.deveregolf.co.uk

## Peover (1996)
**Proprietary**
Plumley Moor Road, Lower Peover WA16 9SE
☎ (01565) 723337
🖥 (01565) 723311
✉ mail@peovergolfclub.co.uk
🖎 B Pearson (Gen Mgr)
🖳 www.peovergolfclub.co.uk

## Portal G&CC (1992)
Cobblers Cross Lane, Tarporley CW6 0DJ
☎ (0844) 879 9082
🖥 (01829) 733928
✉ enquiries@portalgolf.co.uk
🖎 D Wills (Golf Dir)
🖳 www.macdonaldhotels.co.uk

## Poulton Park (1978)
Dig Lane, Cinnamon Brow, Warrington WA2 0SH
☎ (01925) 812034/822802
🖥 (01925) 822802
✉ secretary@poultonparkgolfclub.co.uk
🖎 Jeff Perkin (01925) 822802
🖳 www.poultonparkgolfclub.co.uk

## Prestbury (1920)
Macclesfield Road, Prestbury, Macclesfield SK10 4BJ
☎ (01625) 828241
🖥 (01625) 828241
✉ office@prestburygolfclub.com
🖎 N Young (Gen Mgr)
🖳 www.prestburygolfclub.com

## Pryors Hayes (1993)
**Proprietary**
Willington Road, Oscroft, Tarvin CH3 8NL
☎ (01829) 741250
🖥 (01829) 749077
✉ info@pryors-hayes.co.uk
🖎 JM Quinn
🖳 www.pryorshayes.com

## Queens Park (1985)
**Public**
Queens Park Drive, Crewe CW2 7SB
☎ (01270) 662378
🖎 T J Weston (01270) 662887

## Reaseheath (1987)
1 Ash Grove, Nantwich, Cheshire CW5 7DQ
☎ (01270) 625131
🖥 (01270) 625665
✉ j.soddy@sky.com
🖎 John Soddy (01270) 629869
🖳 www.reaseheath.ac.uk

## Reddish Vale (1912)
Southcliffe Road, Reddish, Stockport SK5 7EE
☎ (0161) 480 2359
🖥 (0161) 480 2359
✉ admin@rvgc.co.uk
🖎 D J Sanders
🖳 www.rvgc.co.uk

## Ringway (1909)
Hale Mount, Hale Road, Hale Barns, Altrincham WA15 8SW
☎ (0161) 980 2630
🖥 (0161) 980 4414
✉ fiona@ringwaygolfclub.co.uk
🖎 Ms F Cornelius
🖳 www.ringwaygolfclub.co.uk

## Romiley (1897)
Goosehouse Green, Romiley, Stockport SK6 4LJ
☎ (0161) 430 2392
✉ office@romileygolfclub.org
🖎 C D Haworth
🖳 www.romileygolfclub.org

## Runcorn (1909)
Clifton Road, Runcorn WA7 4SU
☎ (01928) 572093 (Members)
🖥 (01928) 574214
✉ secretary@runcorngolfclub.co.uk
🖎 B R Griffiths (01928) 574214
🖳 www.runcorngolfclub.co.uk

## Sale (1913)
Sale Lodge, Golf Road, Sale M33 2XU
☎ (0161) 973 1638
🖥 (0161) 962 4217
✉ mail@salegolfclub.com

🖉 CJ Boyes (Hon Sec)
🖥 www.salegolfclub.com

## Sandbach    (1895)
*Middlewich Road, Sandbach, Cheshire
CW11 9EA*
☎ **(01270) 762117**
✉ sec@sandbachgolfclub.co.uk
🖉 D Ludley
🖥 www.sandbachgolfclub.co.uk

## Sandiway    (1920)
*Chester Road, Sandiway CW8 2DJ*
☎ **(01606) 883247**
✉ information@sandiwaygolf.co.uk
🖉 Yvonne Bould (01606) 880811
🖥 www.sandiwaygolf.co.uk

## Stamford    (1901)
*Oakfield House, Huddersfield Road,
Stalybridge SK15 3PY*
☎ **(01457) 832126**
✉ admin@stamfordgolfclub.co.uk
🖉 J Kitchen
🖥 www.stamfordgolfclub.co.uk

## Stockport    (1905)
*Offerton Road, Offerton, Stockport
SK2 5HL*
☎ **(0161) 427 8369**
🖥 (0161) 427 8369
✉ info@stockportgolf.co.uk
🖉 J O Bolt
🖥 www.stockportgolf.co.uk

## Styal    (1994)
**Proprietary**
*Station Road, Styal SK9 4JN*
☎ **(01625) 531359 (Bookings)**
🖥 (01625) 416373
✉ gtraynor@styalgolf.co.uk
🖉 G Traynor
🖥 www.styalgolf.co.uk

## Sutton Hall    (1995)
**Proprietary**
*Aston Lane, Sutton Weaver, Runcorn
WA7 3ED*
☎ **(01928) 790747**
🖥 (01928) 759174
✉ info@suttonhallgolf.co.uk
🖉 M Faulkner
🖥 www.suttonhallgolf.co.uk

## The Tytherington Club    (1986)
*Macclesfield SK10 2JP*
☎ **(01625) 506000**
🖥 (01625) 506040
✉ tytherington.events
@theclubcompany.com
🖉 James Gathercole
🖥 www.theclubcompany.com

## Upton-by-Chester    (1934)
*Upton Lane, Chester CH2 1EE*
☎ **(01244) 381183**
🖥 (01244) 376955
✉ annejennings@uptongolf.co.uk
🖉 Anne Jennings (Mgr)
🖥 www.uptonbychestergolfclub
.co.uk

## Vale Royal Abbey    (1998)
**Proprietary**
*Whitegate, Northwich CW8 2BA*
☎ **(01606) 301291**
🖥 (01606) 301784
✉ secretary@vra.co.uk
🖉 Ian Embury
🖥 www.vra.co.uk

## Vicars Cross    (1939)
*Tarvin Road, Great Barrow, Chester
CH3 7HN*
☎ **(01244) 335174**
🖥 (01244) 335686
✉ manager@vicarscrossgolf.co.uk
🖉 Mrs K Hunt
🖥 www.vicarscrossgolf.co.uk

## Walton Hall    (1972)
**Public**
*Warrington Road, Higher Walton,
Warrington WA4 5LU*
☎ **(01925) 266775**
✉ theclub@waltonhallgolfclub.co.uk
🖉 John Diprose
🖥 www.waltonhallgolfclub.co.uk

## Warrington    (1903)
*Hill Warren, London Road, Appleton
WA4 5HR*
☎ **(01925) 261775**
🖥 (01925) 265933
✉ secretary@warringtongolfclub.co.uk
🖉 D S Macphee (01925) 261775
🖥 www.warringtongolfclub.co.uk

## Werneth Low    (1912)
*Werneth Low Road, Gee Cross, Hyde
SK14 3AF*
☎ **(0161) 368 2503**
🖥 (0161) 320 0053
🖉 M Gregg (0161) 336 9496

## Widnes    (1924)
*Highfield Road, Widnes WA8 7DT*
☎ **(0151) 424 2995**
🖥 (0151) 495 2849
✉ office@widnesgolfclub.co.uk
🖉 Mrs Nicola Ogburn
🖥 www.widnesgolfclub.co.uk

## Wilmslow    (1889)
*Great Warford, Mobberley, Knutsford
WA16 7AY*
☎ **(01565) 872148**
🖥 (01565) 872172
✉ admin@wilmslowgolfclub.co.uk
🖉 Keith Melia (Gen Mgr)
🖥 www.wilmslowgolfclub.co.uk

## Woodside    (1999)
**Proprietary**
*Knutsford Road, Cranage, Holmes Chapel,
Cheshire CW4 8HJ*
☎ **(01477) 532388**
🖥 (01477) 549207
✉ info@woodsidegolf.co.uk
🖉 Marie-Therese Whelan
🖥 www.woodsidegolf.co.uk

## Cornwall

## Bowood Park    (1992)
*Valley Truckle, Lanteglos, Camelford
PL32 9RF*
☎ **(01840) 213017**
🖥 (01840) 212622
✉ info@bowood-park.co.uk
🖉 Gerald Simmons
🖥 www.bowood-park.co.uk

## Bude & North Cornwall
(1891)
*Burn View, Bude EX23 8DA*
☎ **(01288) 352006**
🖥 (01288) 356855
✉ secretary@budegolf.co.uk
🖉 Mr I V Roddy (Mgr/Sec)
🖥 www.budegolf.co.uk

## Budock Vean Hotel Golf &
Country Club    (1932)
*Mawnan Smith, Falmouth TR11 5LG*
☎ **(01326) 252102**
🖥 (01326) 250892
✉ relax@budockvean.co.uk
🖉 Keith Rashleigh (01326) 377091

## Cape Cornwall G&CC    (1990)
*St Just, Penzance TR19 7NL*
☎ **(01736) 788611**
🖥 (01736) 788611
✉ golf@capecornwall.com
🖉 Ben Ludwell (Mgr)
🖥 www.capecornwall.com

## Carlyon Bay    (1926)
**Proprietary**
*Carlyon Bay, St Austell PL25 3RD*
☎ **(01726) 814250**
🖥 (01726) 814250
✉ golf@carlyonbay.com
🖉 P Martin
🖥 www.carlyongolf.com

## China Fleet CC    (1991)
*Saltash PL12 6LJ*
☎ **(01752) 848668**
🖥 (01752) 848456
✉ golf@china-fleet.co.uk
🖉 Mrs L Goddard
🖥 www.china-fleet.co.uk

## Falmouth    (1894)
**Proprietary**
*Swanpool Road, Falmouth TR11 5BQ*
☎ **(01326) 311262/314296**
🖥 (01326) 211447
✉ clubsec@falmouthgolfclub.com
🖉 Steve Burrows (Director)
🖥 www.falmouthgolfclub.com

## Isles of Scilly    (1904)
*Carn Morval, St Mary's, Isles of Scilly
TR21 0NF*
☎ **(01720) 422692**
✉ iosgcsec@googlemail.com
🖉 Peter Leahy (Hon Sec)
🖥 www.islesofscillygolfclub.co.uk

## Killiow    (1987)
**Proprietary**
Killiow, Kea, Truro TR3 6AG
☎ **(01872) 270246**
🖷 (01872) 240915
📧 killiowsec@yahoo.co.uk
🏌 J Crowson (01872) 266876

## Lanhydrock Hotel & Golf Club
(1991)
**Proprietary**
Lostwithiel Road, Bodmin PL30 5AQ
☎ **(01208) 262570**
🖷 (01208) 262579
📧 info@lanhydrockhotel.com
🏌 G Bond (Dir)
🖥 www.lanhydrockhotel.com

## Launceston    (1927)
St Stephens, Launceston PL15 8HF
☎ **(01566) 773442**
🖷 (01566) 777506
📧 secretary@launcestongolfclub
.co.uk
🏌 Alan Creber
🖥 www.launcestongolfclub.co.uk

## Looe    (1933)
Bin Down, Looe PL13 1PX
☎ **(01503) 240239**
🖷 (01503) 240864
📧 enquiries@looegolfclub.co.uk
🏌 M D Joy (Hon)
🖥 www.looegolfclub.co.uk

## Lostwithiel G&CC    (1990)
Lower Polscoe, Lostwithiel PL22 0HQ
☎ **(01208) 873550**
🖷 (01208) 873479
📧 reception@golf-hotel.co.uk
🏌 D Higman
🖥 www.golf-hotel.co.uk

## Merlin    (1991)
**Proprietary**
Mawgan Porth, Newquay TR8 4DN
☎ **(01841) 540222**
🖷 (01841) 541031
📧 play@merlingolfcourse.co.uk
🏌 Mr Richard Burrough
🖥 www.merlingolfcourse.co.uk

## Mullion    (1895)
Cury, Helston TR12 7BP
☎ **(01326) 240276**
🖷 (01326) 241527
📧 secretary@mulliongolfclub.plus.com
🏌 R Griffiths (01326) 240685
🖥 www.mulliongolfclub.co.uk

## Newquay    (1890)
Tower Road, Newquay TR7 1LT
☎ **(01637) 872091/874354
(clubhouse/office)**
📧 info@newquaygolfclub.co.uk
🏌 P F Batty (Sec/Mgr)/Mrs K
    Chapman (Assist. Sec/Mgr)
🖥 www.newquaygolfclub.co.uk

## Perranporth    (1927)
Budnic Hill, Perranporth TR6 0AB
☎ **(01872) 572454**

📧 secretary@perranporthgolfclub
.co.uk
🏌 DC Mugford
🖥 www.perranporthgolfclub.co.uk

## Porthpean    (1992)
**Proprietary**
Porthpean, St Austell PL26 6AY
☎ **(01726) 64613**
🖷 (01726) 64613
📧 porthpeangolfclub@hotmail.co.uk
🏌 Michelle Baily (Mgr)
🖥 www.porthpeangolfclub.co.uk

## Praa Sands Golf and Country
Club    (1971)
**Public**
Praa Sands, Penzance TR20 9TQ
☎ **(01736) 763445**
🖷 (01736) 763741
📧 praasands2@haulfryn.co.uk
🏌 Simon Spencer 01736 762201
🖥 www.praa-sands.com

## Radnor    (1988)
**Proprietary**
Radnor Road, Treleigh, Redruth, Cornwall
TR16 5EL
☎ **(01209) 211059**
📧 jonradnor@btconnect.com
🏌 Jon Barber
🖥 www.radnorgolfandleisure.co.uk

## St Austell    (1911)
Tregongeeves Lane, St Austell PL26 7DS
☎ **(01726) 74756**
🖷 (01726) 71978
📧 office@staustellgolf.co.uk
🏌 P Clemo
🖥 www.staustellgolf.co.uk

## St Enodoc    (1890)
Rock, Wadebridge PL27 6LD
☎ **(01208) 863216**
🖷 (01208) 862976
📧 enquiries@st-enodoc.co.uk
🏌 TD Clagett
🖥 www.st-enodoc.co.uk

## St Kew    (1993)
**Proprietary**
St Kew Highway, Wadebridge, Bodmin
PL30 3EF
☎ **(01208) 841500**
🖷 (01208) 841500
📧 stkewgolf@btconnect.com
🏌 J Brown (Prop)

## Tehidy Park    (1922)
Camborne TR14 0HH
☎ **(01209) 842208**
🖷 (01209) 842208
📧 secretary-
    manager@tehidyparkgolfclub.co.uk
🏌 I J Veale (Sec/Mgr)
🖥 www.tehidyparkgolfclub.co.uk

## The Point at Polzeath    (1996)
**Proprietary**
The Point at Polzeath, St. Minver, Polzeath
PL27 6QT
☎ **(01208) 863000**

📧 info@thepointatpolzeath.co.uk
🖥 www.thepointatpolzeath.co.uk

## Tregenna Castle Hotel    (1982)
St Ives TR26 2DE
☎ **(01736) 795254**
🖷 (01736) 796066
📧 hotel@tregenna-castle.co.uk
🏌 S Davey
🖥 www.tregenna-castle.co.uk

## Treloy    (1991)
Treloy, Newquay TR8 4JN
☎ **(01637) 878554**
🏌 J Paull
🖥 www.treloygolfclub.co.uk

## Trethorne    (1991)
Kennards House, Launceston PL15 8QE
☎ **(01566) 86903**
🖷 (01566) 86929
📧 gen@trethornegolfclub.com
🏌 M Boundy
🖥 www.trethornegolfclub.com

## Trevose    (1924)
Constantine Bay, Padstow PL28 8JB
☎ **(01841) 520208**
🖷 (01841) 521057
📧 info@trevose-gc.co.uk
🏌 P Gammon (Prop),
🖥 www.trevose-gc.co.uk

## Truro    (1937)
Treliske, Truro TR1 3LG
☎ **(01872) 278684**
🖷 (01872) 225972
📧 trurogolfclub@tiscali.co.uk
🏌 L Booker (Sec/Mgr)
🖥 www.trurogolf.co.uk

## West Cornwall    (1889)
Lelant, St Ives TR26 3DZ
☎ **(01736) 753401**
📧 secretary@westcornwallgolfclub
.co.uk
🏌 GM Evans
🖥 www.westcornwallgolfclub.co.uk

## Whitsand Bay Hotel    (1906)
Portwrinkle, Torpoint PL11 3BU
☎ **(01503) 230276 (Clubhouse)**
🖷 (01503) 230329
🏌 Paul Phillips
🖥 www.whitsandbayhotel.co.uk

## Cumbria

## Alston Moor    (1906)
The Hermitage, Alston CA9 3DB
☎ **(01434) 381675**
📧 secretary@alstonmoorgolfclub
.org.uk
🏌 Paul Parkin (01434) 381704
🖥 www.alstonmoorgolfclub.org.uk

## Appleby    (1903)
Brackenber Moor, Appleby CA16 6LP
☎ **(017683) 51432**
🖷 (017683) 52773

📧 enquiries@applebygolfclub.co.uk
✏ JMF Doig (Hon)
🖥 www.applebygolfclub.co.uk

## Barrow (1922)
*Rakesmoor Lane, Hawcoat, Barrow-in-Furness LA14 4QB*
☎ (01229) 825444
📧 barrowgolf@supanet.com
✏ S G Warbrick (Hon)
🖥 www.barrowgolfclub.co.uk

## Brampton (Talkin Tarn) (1909)
*Tarn Road, Brampton CA8 1HN*
☎ (0169) 772255
📠 (0169) 7741487
📧 sec@bramptongolfclub.com
✏ Diana Banks
🖥 www.bramptongolfclub.com

## Brayton Park (1986)
**Pay and play**
*The Garth, Home Farm, Brayton, Aspatria CA7 3SX*
☎ (01697) 323539
✏ J Gibson (01697) 322517

## Carlisle (1908)
*Aglionby, Carlisle CA4 8AG*
☎ (01228) 513029
📠 (01228) 513303
📧 secretary@carlislegolfclub.org
✏ Roger Johnson
🖥 www.carlislegolfclub.org

## Carus Green (1996)
**Proprietary**
*Burneside Road, Kendal LA9 6EB*
☎ (01539) 721097
📠 (01539) 721097
📧 info@carusgreen.co.uk
✏ G Curtin or W Dand
🖥 www.carusgreen.co.uk

## Casterton (1955)
**Proprietary**
*Sedbergh Road, Casterton, Nr Kirkby Lonsdale LA6 2LA*
☎ (015242) 71592
📧 castertongc@hotmail.com
✏ J & E Makinson (Props)
🖥 www.castertongolf.co.uk

## Cockermouth (1896)
*Embleton, Cockermouth CA13 9SG*
☎ (017687) 76223/76941
📠 (017687) 76941
📧 secretary@cockermouthgolf.co.uk
✏ RS Wimpress (01900) 825431
🖥 www.cockermouthgolf.co.uk

## Dalston Hall (1990)
**Pay and play**
*Dalston Hall, Dalston, Carlisle CA5 7JX*
☎ (01228) 710165
📠 (01228) 710165
📧 info@dalstonholidaypark.com
✏ PS Holder
🖥 www.dalstonhallholidaypark.co.uk

## The Dunnerholme Golf Club (1905)
*Duddon Road, Askam-in-Furness LA16 7AW*
☎ (01229) 462675
📠 (01229) 462675
📧 dunnerholmegolfclub@btinternet.com
✏ Lynda Preston (Sec)
🖥 www.thedunnerholmegolfclub.co.uk

## Eden (1992)
**Proprietary**
*Crosby-on-Eden, Carlisle CA6 4RA*
☎ (01228) 573003
📠 (01228) 818435
🖥 www.edengolf.co.uk

## Furness (1872)
*Central Drive, Walney Island, Barrow-in-Furness LA14 3LN*
☎ (01229) 471232
📠 (01229) 475100
📧 furnessgolfclub@chessbroadband.co.uk
✏ Mr R S Turner (Secretary)
🖥 www.furnessgolfclub.co.uk

## Grange Fell (1952)
*Fell Road, Grange-over-Sands LA11 6HB*
☎ (015395) 32536
📧 gfgc@etherway.net
✏ JG Park (015395) 58513

## Grange-over-Sands (1919)
*Meathop Road, Grange-over-Sands LA11 6QX*
☎ (015395) 33180
📠 (015395) 33754
📧 office@grangegolfclub.co.uk
✏ G Whitfield (015395) 33180
🖥 www.grangegolfclub.co.uk

## Haltwhistle (1967)
*Wallend Farm, Greenhead, Carlisle CA8 7HN*
☎ (01697) 747367
✏ Patrick Peace (Hon Sec)
🖥 www.haltwhistlegolf.co.uk

## Kendal (1891)
*The Heights, Kendal LA9 4PQ*
☎ (01539) 723499 (Bookings)
📧 secretary@kendalgolfclub.co.uk
✏ I Clancy (01539) 733708
🖥 www.kendalgolfclub.co.uk

## Keswick (1978)
*Threlkeld Hall, Threlkeld, Keswick CA12 4SX*
☎ (017687) 79324
📠 (017687) 79861
📧 secretary@keswickgolfclub.com
✏ May Lloyd (017687) 79324 ext 1
🖥 www.keswickgolfclub.com

## Kirkby Lonsdale (1906)
*Scaleber Lane, Barbon, Kirkby Lonsdale LA6 2LJ*
☎ (015242) 76366
📠 (015242) 76503
📧 info@kirkbylonsdalegolfclub.com

✏ D Towers (015242) 76365
🖥 www.kirkbylonsdalegolfclub.com

## Maryport (1905)
*Bankend, Maryport CA15 6PA*
☎ (01900) 812605
📠 (01900) 815626
✏ Mrs L Hayton (01900) 815626
🖥 www.maryportgolfclub.co.uk

## Penrith (1890)
*Salkeld Road, Penrith CA11 8SG*
☎ (01768) 891919
📠 (01768) 891919
📧 secretary@penrithgolfclub.co.uk
✏ S D Wright (01768) 891919
🖥 www.penrithgolfclub.com

## Seascale (1893)
*Seascale CA20 1QL*
☎ (019467) 28202/28800
📠 (019467) 28042
📧 seascalegolfclub@googlemail.com
✏ JDH Stobart (019467) 28202
🖥 www.seascalegolfclub.co.uk

## Sedbergh (1896)
**Proprietary**
*Dent Road, Sedbergh LA10 5SS*
☎ (015396) 21551
📠 (015396) 21827
📧 info@sedberghgolfclub.com
✏ Craig or Steve Gardner
🖥 www.sedberghgolfclub.com

## Silecroft (1903)
*Silecroft, Millom LA18 4NX*
☎ (01229) 774250
📧 sgcsecretary@hotmail.co.uk
✏ K Newton (01229) 770467
🖥 www.silecroftgolfclub.co.uk

## Silloth-on-Solway (1892)
*Silloth, Wigton CA7 4BL*
☎ (016973) 31304
📠 (016973) 31782
📧 office@sillothgolfclub.co.uk
✏ Alan Oliver
🖥 www.sillothgolfclub.co.uk

## Silverdale (1906)
*Red Bridge Lane, Silverdale, Carnforth LA5 0SP*
☎ (01524) 701300
📠 (01524) 701986
📧 info@silverdalegolfclub.co.uk
✏ Mr R A Whitaker (Sec) (01524) 702074
🖥 www.silverdalegolfclub.co.uk

## St Bees (1929)
*Peckmill, Beach Road, St Bees CA27 0EJ*
☎ (01946) 820319
📧 lhinde21@btinternet.com
✏ L Hinde
🖥 www.stbeesgolfclub.org.uk

## Stony Holme (1974)
**Public**
*St Aidan's Road, Carlisle CA1 1LS*
☎ (01228) 625511
✏ A McConnell (01228) 625511

## Ulverston    (1895)
*Bardsea Park, Ulverston LA12 9QJ*
☎ **(01229) 582824**
🖷 (01229) 588910
📧 enquiries@ulverstongolf.co.uk
✍ Mr Charles Dent
🖳 www.ulverstongolf.co.uk

## Windermere    (1891)
*Cleabarrow, Windermere LA23 3NB*
☎ **(015394) 43123**
🖷 (015394) 46370
📧 office@windermeregc.co.uk
✍ Carol Slater (Sec/Mgr)
🖳 www.windermeregolfclub.co.uk

## Workington    (1893)
*Branthwaite Road, Workington CA14 4SS*
☎ **(01900) 603460**
📧 secretary@workingtongolfclub.com
✍ P Hoskin (Sec)
🖳 www.workingtongolfclub.com

## Derbyshire

## Alfreton    (1892)
*Oakerthorpe, Alfreton DE55 7LH*
☎ **(01773) 832070**
✍ S Bradley (07712) 136647
🖳 www.alfretongolfclub.co.uk

## Allestree Park    (1949)
**Public**
*Allestree Hall, Allestree, Derby DE22 2EU*
☎ **(01332) 550616**
📧 mail@allestreeparkgolfclub.co.uk
✍ M Wightman (Hon Sec)
⊕ For tee bookings, green fees,
   societies, please use the following
   e-mail address: golf@derby.gov.uk
🖳 www.allestreeparkgolfclub.co.uk

## Ashbourne    (1886)
*Wyaston Road, Ashbourne DE6 1NB*
☎ **(01335) 342078**
🖷 (01335) 347937
📧 ashbournegc@tiscali.co.uk
✍ Andrew Smith
🖳 www.ashbournegolfclub.co.uk

## Bakewell    (1899)
*Station Road, Bakewell DE4 1GB*
☎ **(01629) 812307**
📧 administrator@bakewellgolfclub
   .co.uk
✍ Mr G Holmes
🖳 www.bakewellgolfclub.co.uk

## Birch Hall
*Sheffield Road, Unstone S18 5DH*
☎ **(01246) 291979**
✍ E Gallagher (Hon Gen)

## Bondhay    (1991)
*Bondhay Lane, Whitwell, Worksop S80 3EH*
☎ **(01909) 723608**
🖷 (01909) 720226
📧 enquiries@bondhaygolfclub.com
✍ M Hardisty (Mgr)
🖳 www.bondhaygolfclub.com

## Brailsford    (1994)
**Proprietary**
*Pools Head Lane, Brailsford, Ashbourne DE6 3BU*
☎ **(01335) 360096**
🖷 (01335) 360077
📧 vivian.craig@clowes-
   developments.com
✍ T Payne (tpayne@talktalk.net)
🖳 www.brailsfordgolfcourse.co.uk

## Breadsall Priory Hotel G&CC
   (1976)
*Moor Road, Morley, Derby DE7 6DL*
☎ **(01332) 836016**
🖷 (01332) 836089
📧 mhrs.emags.golf@marriotthotels
   .com
✍ I Knox (Dir of Golf)
🖳 www.marriottgolf.com

## Broughton Heath    (1988)
**Proprietary**
*Bent Lane, Church Broughton DE65 5BA*
☎ **(01283) 521235**
📧 info@broughtonheathgc.co.uk
✍ J Bentley (Mgr)
🖳 www.broughtonheathgc.co.uk

## Burton-on-Trent    (1894)
*43 Ashby Road East, Burton-on-Trent DE15 0PS*
☎ **(01283) 544551**
📧 clubmanager
   @burtonontrentgolfclub.co.uk
✍ S A Dixon (01283) 544551
🖳 www.burtonontrentgolfclub.co.uk

## Buxton & High Peak    (1887)
*Townend, Buxton SK17 7EN*
☎ **(01298) 26263**
🖷 (01298) 26333
📧 sec@bhpgc.co.uk
✍ Garry Bagguley (Sec)
🖳 www.bhpgc.co.uk

## Cavendish    (1925)
*Watford Road, Buxton SK17 6XF*
☎ **(01298) 79708**
🖷 (01298) 79708
📧 admin@cavendishgolfclub.com
✍ S A Davis
🖳 www.cavendishgolfclub.com

## Chapel-en-le-Frith    (1905)
*The Cockyard, Manchester Road, Chapel-en-le-Frith SK23 9UH*
☎ **(01298) 812118**
🖷 (01298) 814990
📧 info@chapelgolf.co.uk
✍ Denise Goldfinch (01298) 813943
🖳 www.chapelgolf.co.uk

## Chesterfield    (1897)
*Walton, Chesterfield S42 7LA*
☎ **(01246) 279256**
🖷 (01246) 276622
📧 secretary@chesterfieldgolfclub
   .co.uk
✍ T H Glover
🖳 www.chesterfieldgolfclub.co.uk

## Chevin    (1894)
*Duffield DE56 4EE*
☎ **(01332) 841864**
🖷 (01332) 844028
📧 manager@chevingolf.co.uk
✍ John A Jenkins (Gen Mgr)
🖳 www.chevingolf.co.uk

## Derby    (1923)
**Public**
*Wilmore Road, Sinfin, Derby DE24 9HD*
☎ **(01332) 766323**
📧 secretary@derbygolfclub.co.uk
✍ DP Anderson
🖳 www.derbygolfclub.co.uk

## Erewash Valley    (1905)
*Stanton-by-Dale DE7 4QR*
☎ **(0115) 932 3258**
📧 manager@erewashvalley.co.uk
✍ Andrew Burrows (Gen Mgr)
🖳 www.erewashvalley.co.uk

## Glossop & District    (1894)
*Sheffield Road, Glossop SK13 7PU*
☎ **(01457) 865247 (Clubhouse)**
🖷 (01457) 864003
📧 glossopgolfclub@talktalk.net
✍ Steve Mycio
🖳 www.glossopgolfclub.co.uk

## Grassmoor Golf Centre    (1990)
**Proprietary**
*North Wingfield Road, Grassmoor, Chesterfield S42 5EA*
☎ **(01246) 856044**
🖷 (01246) 853486
📧 enquiries@grassmoorgolf.co.uk
✍ H Hagues (Club Manager)
🖳 www.grassmoorgolf.co.uk

## Horsley Lodge    (1990)
**Proprietary**
*Smalley Mill Road, Horsley DE21 5BL*
☎ **(01332) 780838**
🖷 (01332) 781118
📧 richard@horsleylodge.co.uk
✍ Dennis Wake (07771) 874 882
🖳 www.horsleylodge.co.uk

## Kedleston Park    (1946)
*Kedleston, Quarndon, Derby DE22 5JD*
☎ **(01332) 840035**
🖷 (01332) 840035
📧 secretary@kedlestonparkgolfclub
   .co.uk
✍ R Simpson (Gen Mgr)
🖳 www.kedlestonparkgolfclub.co.uk

## Lafarge Golf Club    (1985)
*Lafarge Cement, Hope Works, Hope Valley, Derbyshire S33 6RP*
☎ **(01433) 622315**
✍ DS Smith

## Matlock    (1906)
*Chesterfield Road, Matlock Moor, Matlock DE4 5LZ*
☎ **(01629) 582191**
🖷 (01629) 582135
📧 secretary@matlockgolfclub.co.uk
✍ Mick Wain (01629) 582191 opt 4
🖳 www.matlockgolfclub.co.uk

**Maywood** (1990)
*Proprietary*
*Rushy Lane, Risley, Derby DE72 3SW*
☎ **(0115) 939 2306**
📧 maywoodgolfclub@btinternet.com
✍ WJ Cockeram (0115) 932 6772
🖥 www.maywoodgolfclub.com

**Mickleover** (1923)
*Uttoxeter Road, Mickleover DE3 9AD*
☎ **(01332) 516011 (Clubhouse)**
☐ (01332) 516011
📧 secretary@mickleovergolfclub.com
✍ GW Finney (01332) 516011
🖥 www.mickleovergolfclub.com

**New Mills** (1907)
*Shaw Marsh, New Mills, High Peak
SK22 4QE*
☎ **(01663) 743485**
✍ Margaret Palmer (01663) 744330 (Sec)
🖥 www.newmillsgolfclub.co.uk

**Ormonde Fields** (1926)
*Nottingham Road, Codnor, Ripley DE5 9RG*
☎ **(01773) 742987**
☐ (01773) 744848
📧 info@ormondefieldsgolfclub.co.uk
✍ K Constable
🖥 www.ormondefieldsgolfclub.co.uk

**Shirland** (1977)
*Proprietary*
*Lower Delves, Shirland DE55 6AU*
☎ **(01773) 834935**
📧 geofftowle@hotmail.com
✍ G Towle (01773) 874224

**Sickleholme** (1898)
*Bamford, Sheffield S33 0BH*
☎ **(01433) 651306**
☐ (01433) 659498
📧 sickleholme.gc@btconnect.com
✍ PH Taylor (Mgr)
🖥 www.sickleholme.co.uk

**Stanedge** (1934)
*Walton Hay Farm, Chesterfield S45 0LW*
☎ **(01246) 566156**
📧 chrisshaw56@tiscali.co.uk
✍ Mr Chris Shaw 0776 742 6584
🖥 www.stanedgegolfclub.co.uk

## Devon

**Ashbury** (1991)
*Higher Maddaford, Okehampton
EX20 4NL*
☎ **(01837) 55453**
☐ (01837) 55468
✍ I Gill
🖥 www.ashburyhotel.co.uk

**Axe Cliff** (1894)
*Proprietary*
*Squires Lane, Axmouth, Seaton EX12 4AB*
☎ **(01297) 21754**
☐ (01297) 24371
📧 D.Quinn@axecliff.co.uk

✍ David Quinn
🖥 www.axecliff.co.uk

**Bigbury** (1923)
*Bigbury-on-Sea, South Devon TQ7 4BB*
☎ **(01548) 810557**
📧 enquiries@bigburygolfclub.co.uk
✍ Nigel Blenkarne (Director of Golf)
🖥 www.bigburygolfclub.com

**Bovey Castle** (1929)
*Proprietary*
*North Bovey, Devon TQ13 8RE*
☎ **(01647) 445009**
☐ (01647) 440961
📧 richard.lewis@boveycastle.com
✍ R Lewis
🖥 www.boveycastle.com

**Bovey Tracey Golf Club** (2006)
*Pay and play*
*Monks Way, Bovey Tracey, Newton Abbot,
Devon TQ13 9NG*
☎ **(01626) 836464**
📧 tonyv.btgc@gmail.com
✍ A Vincent (Sec)
🖥 www.boveytraceygolfclub.co.uk

**Chulmleigh** (1976)
*Pay and play*
*Leigh Road, Chulmleigh EX18 7BL*
☎ **(01769) 580519**
☐ (01769) 580519
📧 chulmleighgolf@aol.com
✍ RW Dow
🖥 www.chulmleighgolf.co.uk

**Churston** (1890)
*Churston, Dartmouth Road, Brixham
TQ5 0LA*
☎ **(01803) 842751**
☐ (01803) 845738
📧 manager@churstongolf.com
✍ SR Bawden (01803) 842751
🖥 www.churstongolf.com

**Dainton Park** (1993)
*Proprietary*
*Totnes Road, Ipplepen, Newton Abbot
TQ12 5TN*
☎ **(01803) 815000**
☐ (01803) 815001
📧 info@daintonparkgolf.co.uk
✍ Mr Daniel Wood
🖥 www.daintonparkgolf.co.uk

**Dartmouth G&CC** (1992)
*Blackawton, Nr Dartmouth, Devon
TQ9 7DE*
☎ **(01803) 712686**
☐ (01803) 712628
📧 info@dgcc.co.uk
✍ J Waugh (Sec), A Chappell (Assist. Sec)
🖥 www.dgcc.co.uk

**Dinnaton – McCaulays Health
Club, Ivybridge Fitness &
Golf** (1989)
*Ivybridge PL21 9HU*
☎ **(01752) 892512**
☐ (01752) 698334

📧 info@mccaulays.com
✍ P Hendriksen
🖥 www.mccaulays.com

**Downes Crediton** (1976)
*Hookway, Crediton EX17 3PT*
☎ **(01363) 773025**
☐ (01363) 775060
📧 golf@downescreditongc.co.uk
✍ Robin Goodey (01363) 773025
🖥 www.downescreditongc.co.uk

**East Devon** (1902)
*Links Road, Budleigh Salterton EX9 6DG*
☎ **(01395) 443370**
☐ (01395) 445547
📧 secretary@edgc.co.uk
✍ J Reynolds (01395) 443370
🖥 www.edgc.co.uk

**Elfordleigh Hotel G&CC**
(1932)
*Proprietary*
*Colebrook, Plympton, Plymouth PL7 5EB*
☎ **(01752) 348425**
☐ (01752) 344581
📧 reception@elfordleigh.co.uk
✍ Derek Mills (01752) 556205
🖥 www.elfordleigh.co.uk

**Exeter G&CC** (1895)
*Countess Wear, Exeter EX2 7AE*
☎ **(01392) 874139**
📧 golf@exetergcc.co.uk
✍ Russell Mayne (Golf Manager)
🖥 www.exetergcc.co.uk

**Fingle Glen** (1989)
*Proprietary*
*Tedburn St Mary, Exeter EX6 6AF*
☎ **(01647) 61817**
☐ (01647) 61135
📧 mail@fingleglengolfhotel.co.uk
✍ P Miliffe
🖥 www.fingleglengolfhotel.co.uk

**Great Torrington** (1895)
*The Club House, Weare Trees, Torrington
EX38 7EZ*
☎ **(01805) 622229**
☐ (01805) 623878
📧 torringtongolfclub@btconnect .com
✍ Mr G S C Green
🖥 www.torringtongolfclub.co.uk

**Hartland Forest** (1980)
*Hartland Forest Golf & Leisure Parc,
Woolsery, Bideford EX39 5RA*
☎ **(01237) 431777**
📧 hfgadmin@gmail.com
🖥 www.hartlandforestgolf.co.uk

**Hele Park Golf Centre** (1993)
*Proprietary*
*Ashburton Road, Newton Abbot TQ12 6JN*
☎ **(01626) 336060**
☐ (01626) 332661
📧 info@heleparkgolf.co.uk
✍ Wendy Stanbury
🖥 www.heleparkgolf.co.uk

## Highbullen Hotel G&CC
(1961)
**Proprietary**
*Chittlehamholt, Umberleigh EX37 9HD*
☎ **(01769) 540561**
📠 (01769) 540492
📧 info@highbullen.co.uk
🏌 John Aryes (01769) 540664
🖥 www.highbullen.co.uk

## Holsworthy    (1937)
*Killatree, Holsworthy EX22 6LP*
☎ **(01409) 253177**
📠 (01409) 255393
📧 info@holsworthygolfclub.co.uk
🏌 Mrs J Carter
🖥 www.holsworthygolfclub.co.uk

## Honiton    (1896)
*Middlehills, Honiton EX14 9TR*
☎ **(01404) 44422**
📧 secretary@honitongolfclub.fsnet
.co.uk
🏌 Graham Burch (Administrator)
🖥 www.honitongolf club.co.uk

## Hurdwick    (1990)
*Tavistock Hamlets, Tavistock PL19 0LL*
☎ **(01822) 612746**
📧 info@hurdwickgolf.com
🏌 Mr M J Wood (Mgr)
🖥 www.hurdwickgolf.com

## Ilfracombe    (1892)
*Hele Bay, Ilfracombe EX34 9RT*
☎ **(01271) 862176**
📧 ilfracombegolfclub@btinternet.com
🏌 Mr D Cook
🖥 www.ilfracombegolfclub.com

## Libbaton    (1988)
*High Bickington, Umberleigh EX37 9BS*
☎ **(01769) 560269**
📠 (01769) 560342
📧 enquiries.libbatongolfclub.co.uk
🏌 Gerald Herniman
🖥 www.libbatongolfclub.co.uk

## Mortehoe & Woolacombe
(1992)
*Easewell, Mortehoe, Ilfracombe EX34 7EH*
☎ **(01271) 870566**
🏌 M Wilkinson (01271) 870745

## Okehampton    (1913)
*Okehampton EX20 1EF*
☎ **(01837) 52113**
📧 secretary@okehamptongolfclub
.co.uk
🏌 Beverley Lawson
🖥 www.okehamptongolfclub.co.uk

## Padbrook Park    (1992)
**Proprietary**
*Cullompton EX15 1RU*
☎ **(01884) 836100**
📠 (01884) 836101
📧 info@padbrookpark.co.uk
🏌 Cary Rawlings (Mgr)
⊕ 40 Bed Hotel, 10 bay Driving Range
🖥 www.padbrookpark.co.uk

## Portmore Golf Park    (1993)
**Proprietary**
*Landkey Road, Barnstaple EX32 9LB*
☎ **(01271) 378378**
📧 contact@portmoregolf.co.uk
🏌 C Webber
🖥 www.portmoregolf.co.uk

## Royal North Devon    (1864)
*Golf Links Road, Westward Ho! EX39 1HD*
☎ **(01237) 473817 (Clubhouse)**
📠 (01237) 423456
📧 mark@rndgc.co.uk
🏌 M Evans (01237) 473817
🖥 www.royalnorthdevongolfclub
.co.uk

## Saunton    (1897)
*Saunton, Braunton EX33 1LG*
☎ **(01271) 812436**
📠 (01271) 814241
📧 gm4@sauntongolf.co.uk
🏌 P McMullen (Mgr)
🖥 www.sauntongolf.co.uk

## Sidmouth    (1889)
*Cotmaton Road, Sidmouth EX10 8SX*
☎ **(01395) 513451**
📠 (01395) 514661
📧 secretary@sidmouthgolfclub.co.uk
🏌 JP Lee (Mgr) (01395) 513451
🖥 www.sidmouthgolfclub.co.uk

## Sparkwell    (1993)
**Pay and play**
*Sparkwell, Plymouth PL7 5DF*
☎ **(01752) 837219**
📠 (01752) 837219
🏌 G Adamson

## Staddon Heights    (1904)
*Plymstock, Plymouth PL9 9SP*
☎ **(01752) 402475**
📠 (01752) 401998
📧 golf@shgc.uk.net
🏌 TJH Aggett (01752) 402475
🖥 www.staddonheightsgolf.co.uk

## Stover    (1930)
*Bovey Road, Newton Abbot TQ12 6QQ*
☎ **(01626) 352460**
📠 (01626) 330210
📧 info@stovergolfclub.co.uk
🏌 W Hendry
🖥 www.stovergolfclub.co.uk

## Tavistock    (1890)
*Down Road, Tavistock PL19 9AQ*
☎ **(01822) 612344**
📠 (01822) 612344
📧 info@tavistockgolfclub.org.uk
🏌 J Coe
🖥 www.tavistockgolfclub.org.uk

## Teign Valley    (1995)
*Christow, Exeter EX6 7PA*
☎ **(01647) 253026**
📠 (01647) 253026
📧 andy@teignvalleygolf.co.uk
🏌 Andy Stubbs
🖥 www.teignvalleygolf.co.uk

## Teignmouth    (1924)
*Haldon Moor, Exeter Road, Teignmouth
TQ14 9NY*
☎ **(01626) 777070**
📧 info@teignmouthgolfclub.co.uk
🏌 Mark Haskell
🖥 www.teignmouthgolfclub.co.uk

## Thurlestone    (1897)
*Thurlestone, Kingsbridge TQ7 3NZ*
☎ **(01548) 560405**
📧 info@thurlestonegolfclub.co.uk
🏌 Steve Gledhill (Gen Mgr)
🖥 www.thurlestonegolfclub.co.uk

## Tiverton    (1932)
*Post Hill, Tiverton EX16 4NE*
☎ **(01884) 252114 (Clubhouse)**
📧 tivertongolfclub@lineone.net
🏌 R Jessop (Gen Mgr)
🖥 www.tivertongolfclub.co.uk

## Torquay    (1909)
*Petitor Road, St Marychurch, Torquay
TQ1 4QF*
☎ **(01803) 314591**
📠 (01803) 316116
📧 secretary@torquaygolfclub.co.uk
🏌 Daniel C Hendriksen (Sec/Mgr)
🖥 www.torquaygolfclub.co.uk

## Warren    (1892)
*Dawlish Warren EX7 0NF*
☎ **(01626) 862255**
📧 assistant@dwgc.co.uk
🏌 Cathie Stokes
🖥 www.dwgc.co.uk

## Waterbridge    (1992)
**Pay and play**
*Down St Mary, Crediton EX17 5LG*
☎ **(01363) 85111**
🏌 G & A Wren (Props)
🖥 www.waterbridgegc.co.uk

## Willingcott Valley    (1996)
*Willingcott, Woolacombe EX34 7HN*
☎ **(01271) 870173**
📠 (01271) 870800
📧 holidays@willingcott.co.uk
🏌 Andy Hodge
🖥 www.willingcott.co.uk

## Woodbury Park    (1992)
*Woodbury Castle, Woodbury EX5 1JJ*
☎ **(01395) 233500**
📠 (01395) 233384
🏌 A Richards (Mgr)

## Wrangaton    (1895)
*Golf Links Road, Wrangaton, South Brent
TQ10 9HJ*
☎ **(01364) 73229**
📠 (01364) 73341
📧 wrangatongolf@btconnect.com
🏌 R Clark
🖥 www.wrangatongolfclub.co.uk

## Yelverton    (1904)
*Golf Links Road, Yelverton PL20 6BN*
☎ **(01822) 852824**
📠 (01822) 854869

secretary@yelvertongolf.co.uk
Steve West (01822) 852824
www.yelvertongolf.co.uk

# Dorset

## The Ashley Wood (1896)
Wimborne Road, Blandford Forum
DT11 9HN
☎ (01258) 452253
(01258) 450590
generalmanager
@ashleywoodgolfclub.com
M Batty
www.ashleywoodgolfclub.com

## Bridport & West Dorset (1891)
The Clubhouse, Burton Road, Bridport
DT6 4PS
☎ (01308) 421095/422597
(Clubhouse)
secretary@bridportgolfclub.org.uk
R Wilson (01308) 421095
www.bridportgolfclub.org.uk

## Broadstone (Dorset) (1898)
Wentworth Drive, Broadstone BH18 8DQ
☎ (01202) 692595
office@broadstonegolfclub.com
David Morgan (Gen
Mgr) (01202) 642521
www.broadstonegolfclub.com

## Bulbury Woods (1989)
Bulbury Lane, Lytchett Minster, Poole
BH16 6EP
☎ (01929) 459574
(01929) 459000
bulbury-woods@hoburne.com
www.bulbury-woods.co.uk

## Came Down (1896)
Higher Came, Dorchester DT2 8NR
☎ (01305) 813494
(01305) 815122
manager@camedowngolfclub.co.uk
Matthew Staveley (Gen Mgr)
www.camedowngolfclub.co.uk

## Canford Magna (1994)
Proprietary
Knighton Lane, Wimborne BH21 3AS
☎ (01202) 592552
(01202) 592550
admin@canfordmagnagc.co.uk
S Hudson (Dir) (01202) 592505
www.canfordmagnagc.co.uk

## Canford School (1987)
Canford School, Wimborne BH21 3AD
☎ (01202) 841254
(01202) 881009
steve.ronaldson@talk21.com
Steve Ronaldson
(Mgr) (01202) 881232
www.canford.com

## Charminster (1998)
Proprietary
Wolfedale Golf Course, Charminster,
Dorchester DT2 7SG
☎ (01305) 260186

(01305) 257074
D Cox (Prop/Mgr)

## Crane Valley (1992)
Proprietary
The Clubhouse, Verwood BH31 7LH
☎ (01202) 814088
(01202) 813407
andrew.blackwell@hoburne.com
A Blackwell (Gen Mgr)
www.crane-valley.co.uk

## The Dorset G&CC (1978)
Hyde, Bere Regis, Nr. Poole, Wareham
BH20 7NT
☎ (01929) 472244
(01929) 471294
admin@dorsetgolfresort.com
G Packer (Mgr)
www.dorsetgolfresort.com

## Dudmoor Golf Course (1985)
Pay and play
Dudmoor Farm Road, (off Fairmile Road),
Christchurch, Dorset BH23 6AQ
☎ (01202) 473826
(01202) 480207
peter@dudmoorgolfcourse.co.uk
Peter Hornsby
www.dudmoorfarm.co.uk

## Dudsbury (1992)
Proprietary
64 Christchurch Road, Ferndown BH22 8ST
☎ (01202) 593499
(01202) 594555
info@dudsburygolfclub.co.uk
Steve Pockneall
www.dudsburygolfclub.co.uk

## Ferndown (1913)
119 Golf Links Road, Ferndown BH22 8BU
☎ (01202) 653950
(01202) 653960
golf@ferndowngolfclub.co.uk
Ian Walton (Gen Mgr)
www.ferndowngolfclub.co.uk

## Ferndown Forest (1993)
Forest Links Road, Ferndown BH22 9PH
☎ (01202) 876096
(01202) 894095
golf@ferndownforestgolf.co.uk
Chris Lawford
www.ferndownforestgolf.co.uk

## Folke Golf Centre (1995)
Proprietary
c/o Folke Golf Centre, Alweston, Sherborne,
Dorset DT9 5HR
☎ (01963) 23330
(01963) 23330
info@folkegolfcentre.co.uk
Steve Harris
www.folkegolfcentre.co.uk

## Highcliffe Castle (1913)
107 Lymington Road, Highcliffe-on-Sea,
Christchurch BH23 4LA
☎ (01425) 272210/272953
(01425) 272953
secretary@highcliffecastlegolfclub
.co.uk

G Fisher (01425) 272210
www.highcliffecastlegolfclub.co.uk

## Isle of Purbeck (1892)
Proprietary
Studland BH19 3AB
☎ (01929) 450361
(01929) 450501
iop@purbeckgolf.co.uk
Mrs C Robinson
www.purbeckgolf.co.uk

## Knighton Heath (1976)
Francis Avenue, Bournemouth BH11 8NX
☎ (01202) 572633
(01202) 590774
manager@khgc.co.uk
Reunert Bauser
www.knightonheathgolfclub.co.uk

## Lyme Regis (1893)
Timber Hill, Lyme Regis DT7 3HQ
☎ (01297) 442963
(01297) 444368
secretary@lymeregisgolfclub.co.uk
Mr Mark Betteridge
(01297) 442963
www.lymeregisgolfclub.co.uk

## Meyrick Park (1890)
Pay and play
Central Drive, Meyrick Park, Bournemouth
BH2 6LH
☎ (01202) 786000
meyrickpark.info
@theclubcompany.com
www.theclubatmeyrickpark.com

## Moors Valley Golf Course
(1988)
Proprietary
Horton Road, Ashley Heath, Ringwood
BH24 2ET
☎ (01425) 479776
golf@moorsvalleygolf.co.uk
Desmond Meharg (Mgr)
www.moors-valley.co.uk/golf

## Parkstone (1909)
49a Links Road, Parkstone, Poole
BH14 9QS
☎ (01202) 707138
(01202) 706027
admin@parkstonegolfclub.co.uk
Gary Peddie (Gen Mgr)
www.parkstonegolfclub.co.uk

## Parley Court (1992)
Proprietary
Parley Green Lane, Hurn, Christchurch
BH23 6BB
☎ (01202) 591600
(01202) 579043
info@parleygolf.co.uk
Mr Adrian Perry
www.parleygolf.co.uk

## Playgolf Bournemouth (1977)
Pay and play
Riverside Avenue, Bournemouth BH7 7ES
☎ (01202) 436436 (Bookings)
(01202) 436400

✉ bournemouth@playgolfworld.com
✍ Ben Chant
🖥 www.playgolfbournemouth.com

## Queens Park (Bournemouth)
(1905)
**Public**
Queens Park West Drive, Queens Park,
Bournemouth BH8 9BY
☎ **(01202) 302611 Secretary**
🖳 (01202) 302611
✉ secretary@queensparkgolfclub
  .co.uk
✍ P Greenwood (01202) 302611
🖥 www.queensparkgolfclub.co.uk

## Remedy Oak   (2006)
**Proprietary**
Horton Road, Woodlands, Dorset
BH21 8ND
☎ **(01202) 812070**
🖳 (01202) 812071
✉ info@remedyoak.com
✍ Nigel Tokely
🖥 www.remedyoak.com

## Sherborne   (1894)
Higher Clatcombe, Sherborne DT9 4RN
☎ **(01935) 814431**
🖳 (01935) 814218
✉ office@sherbornegolfclub.co.uk
✍ Office Manager
🖥 www.sherbornegolfclub.co.uk

## Solent Meads Golf Centre
(1965)
**Public**
Rolls Drive, Southbourne, Bournemouth
BH6 4NA
☎ **(01202) 420795**
✉ solentmeads@yahoo.co.uk
✍ Matt Steward (01202) 420795
🖥 www.solentmeads.com

## Sturminster Marshall   (1992)
**Pay and play**
Moor Lane, Sturminster Marshall
BH21 4AH
☎ **(01258) 858444**
✉ mike@smgc.eu
✍ Mike Dodd
🖥 www.smgc.eu

## Wareham   (1908)
Sandford Road, Wareham BH20 4DH
☎ **(01929) 554147**
🖳 (01929) 557993
✉ secretary@warehamgolfclub.com
✍ Richard Murgatroyd
🖥 www.warehamgolfclub.com

## Weymouth   (1909)
Links Road, Weymouth DT4 0PF
☎ **(01305) 750831**
🖳 (01305) 788029
✉ weymouthgolfclub@googlemail
  .com
✍ John Northover (Sec/Treasurer)
🖥 www.weymouthgolfclub.co.uk

# Durham

## Barnard Castle   (1898)
Harmire Road, Barnard Castle DL12 8QN
☎ **(01833) 638355**
🖳 (01833) 695551
✍ J A Saunders
🖥 www.barnardcastlegolfclub.org

## Beamish Park   (1906)
Beamish, Stanley DH9 0RH
☎ **(0191) 370 1382**
🖳 (0191) 370 2937
✉ beamishgolf@btconnect.com
✍ John Bosanko (Hon
  Sec) (0191) 370 1382
🖥 www.beamishgolfclub.co.uk

## Billingham   (1967)
Sandy Lane, Billingham TS22 5NA
☎ **(01642) 533816/554494**
🖳 (01642) 533816
✉ billinghamgc@btconnect.com
✍ Julie Lapping
  (Sec/Mgr) (01642) 533816
🖥 www.billinghamgolfclub.com

## Bishop Auckland   (1894)
High Plains, Durham Road, Bishop Auckland
DL14 8DL
☎ **(01388) 661618**
🖳 (01388) 607005
✉ enquiries@bagc.co.uk
✍ D J Perriss
🖥 www.bagc.co.uk

## Blackwell Grange   (1930)
Briar Close, Blackwell, Darlington DL3 8QX
☎ **(01325) 464458**
✉ secretary@blackwellgrangegolf.com
✍ D C Christie (Hon)
🖥 www.blackwellgrangegolf.com

## Brancepeth Castle   (1924)
The Clubhouse, Brancepeth Village, Durham
DH7 8EA
☎ **(0191) 378 0075**
🖳 (0191) 378 3835
✉ enquiries@brancepeth-castle-golf
  .co.uk
✍ Arthur Chadwick
🖥 www.brancepeth-castle-golf.co.uk

## Castle Eden   (1927)
Castle Eden, Hartlepool TS27 4SS
☎ **(01429) 836510**
✉ castleedengolfclub@hotmail.com
✍ S J Watkin (0794) 114 1057
🖥 www.castleedengolfclub.co.uk

## Chester-Le-Street   (1908)
Lumley Park, Chester-Le-Street DH3 4NS
☎ **(0191) 388 3218**
🖳 none
✉ clsgcoffice@tiscali.co.uk
✍ Bill Routledge
🖥 www.clsgolfclub.co.uk

## Consett & District   (1911)
Elmfield Road, Consett DH8 5NN
☎ **(01207) 502186 (Clubhouse)**
🖳 (01207) 505060

✉ consettgolfclub@btconnect.com
✍ Vincent Kelly (Sec/Treasurer)
🖥 www.consettgolfclub.com

## Crook   (1919)
Low Job's Hill, Crook, Co Durham
DL15 9AA
☎ **(01388) 762429**
✉ secretary@crookgolfclub.co.uk
✍ Mr D Hanlon (Sec)
🖥 www.crookgolfclub.co.uk

## Darlington   (1908)
Haughton Grange, Darlington DL1 3JD
☎ **(01325) 355324**
✉ office@darlington-gc.co.uk
✍ M Etherington
🖥 www.darlington-gc.co.uk

## Dinsdale Spa   (1910)
Neasham Road, Middleton, St George,
Darlington DL2 1DW
☎ **(01325) 332297**
🖳 (01325) 332297
✉ martynstubbings@hotmail.co.uk
✍ A Patterson
🖥 www.dinsdalespagolfclub.co.uk

## Durham City   (1887)
Littleburn, Langley Moor, Durham
DH7 8HL
☎ **(0191) 378 0069**
🖳 (0191) 378 4265
✉ enquiries@durhamcitygolf.co.uk
✍ David Stainsby (0191) 378 0069
🖥 www.durhamcitygolf.co.uk

## Eaglescliffe   (1914)
Yarm Road, Eaglescliffe, Stockton-on-Tees
TS16 0DQ
☎ **(01642) 780238 (Clubhouse)**
🖳 (01642) 781128
✉ secretary@eaglescliffegolfclub
  .co.uk
✍ Alan McNinch (01642) 780238
🖥 www.eaglescliffegolfclub.co.uk

## Hartlepool   (1906)
Hart Warren, Hartlepool TS24 9QF
☎ **(01429) 274398**
🖳 (01429) 274129
✉ hartlepoolgolf@btconnect.com
✍ G Laidlaw (Mgr) (01429) 274398
🖥 www.hartlepoolgolfclub.com

## High Throston   (1997)
**Proprietary**
Hart Lane, Hartlepool TS26 0UG
☎ **(01429) 275325**
✍ Mrs J Sturrock

## Knotty Hill Golf Centre
(1992)
**Pay and play**
Sedgefield, Stockton-on-Tees TS21 2BB
☎ **(01740) 620320**
🖳 (01740) 622227
✉ knottyhill@btconnect.com
✍ D Craggs (Mgr)
🖥 www.knottyhill.com

## Mount Oswald (1934)
**Pay and play**
South Road, Durham City DH1 3TQ
☎ **(0191) 386 7527**
🖥 (0191) 386 0975
✉ info@mountoswald.co.uk
✍ N Galvin
🖳 www.mountoswald.co.uk

## Norton (1989)
**Pay and play**
Junction Road, Norton, Stockton-on-Tees
TS20 1SU
☎ **(01642) 676385**
🖥 (01642) 608467

## Oakleaf Golf Complex (1993)
**Pay and play**
School Aycliffe Lane, Newton Aycliffe
DL5 6QZ
☎ **(01325) 310820**
🖥 (01325) 300873
✉ info@great-aycliffe.gov.uk
✍ A Bailey (Mgr)
🖳 www.great-aycliffe.gov.uk

## Ramside (1995)
**Proprietary**
Ramside Hall Hotel, Carrville, Durham
DH1 1TD
☎ **(0191) 386 9514**
🖥 (0191) 386 9519
✉ kevin.jackson@ramsidehallhotel
.co.uk
✍ Kevin Jackson
🖳 www.ramsidehallhotel.co.uk

## Roseberry Grange (1987)
**Public**
Grange Villa, Chester-Le-Street DH2 3NF
☎ **(0191) 370 0660**
🖥 (0191) 370 2047
✉ chrisjones@chester-le-
street.gov.uk
✍ R McDermott (Hon)

## Royal Hobson (1978)
Hobson, Burnopfield, Newcastle-upon-Tyne
NE16 6BZ
☎ **(01207) 271605**
✉ secretary@hobsongolfclub.co.uk
✍ A J Giles (01207) 270941
🖳 www.hobsongolfclub.co.uk

## Seaham (1908)
Shrewsbury Street, Dawdon, Seaham
SR7 7RD
☎ **(0191) 581 2354**
✉ seahamgolfclub@btconnect.com
✍ T Johnson (0191) 581 1268
🖳 www.seahamgolfclub.com

## Seaton Carew (1874)
Tees Road, Hartlepool TS25 1DE
☎ **(01429) 266249**
✉ secretary@seatoncarewgolfclub
.co.uk
✍ Secretary (01429) 266249 Ext 2
🖳 www.seatoncarewgolfclub.co.uk

## South Moor (1923)
The Middles, Craghead, Stanley DH9 6AG
☎ **(01207) 232848/283525**

🖥 (01207) 284616
✉ secretary@southmoorgc.co.uk
✍ Peter Johnson
🖳 www.southmoorgc.co.uk

## Stressholme (1976)
**Public**
Snipe Lane, Darlington DL2 2SA
☎ **(01325) 461002**
🖥 (01325) 461002
✉ stressholme@btconnect.com
✍ R Givens
🖳 www.darlington.gov.uk/golf

## Woodham G&CC (1983)
**Proprietary**
Burnhill Way, Newton Aycliffe DL5 4PN
☎ **(01325) 320574**
🖥 (01325) 315254
✉ woodhamproshop@googlemail.com
✍ Ernie Wilson (Mgr)
🖳 www.woodhamgolfandcountryclub
.co.uk

## The Wynyard Club (1996)
**Proprietary**
Wellington Drive, Wynyard Park, Billingham
TS22 5QJ
☎ **(01740) 644399**
🖥 (01740) 644599
✉ chris@wynyardgolfclub.co.uk
✍ C Mounter (Golf Dir)
🖳 www.wynyardgolfclub.co.uk

## Essex

## Abridge G&CC (1964)
Epping Lane, Stapleford Tawney RM4 1ST
☎ **(01708) 688396**
✉ info@abridgegolf.com
🖳 www.abridgegolf.com

## Ballards Gore G&CC (1980)
**Proprietary**
Gore Road, Canewdon, Rochford SS4 2DA
☎ **(01702) 258917**
🖥 (01702) 258571
✉ secretary@ballardsgore.com
✍ Susan May (Sec)
🖳 www.ballardsgore.com

## Basildon (1967)
**Pay and play**
Clay Hill Lane, Sparrow's Hearne, Basildon,
Essex SS16 5HL
☎ **(01268) 533297**
✉ basildongc@uk6.net
✍ G Eaton
🖳 www.basgolfclub.uk7.net

## Belfairs (1926)
**Public**
Eastwood Road North, Leigh-on-Sea
SS9 4LR
☎ **(01702) 525345 (Starter)**

## Belhus Park G&CC (1972)
**Pay and play**
Belhus Park, South Ockendon RM15 4QR
☎ **(01708) 854260**
✍ D Clifford

## Bentley (1972)
Ongar Road, Brentwood CM15 9SS
☎ **(01277) 373179**
🖥 (01277) 375097
✉ info@bentleygolfclub.com
✍ Andy Hall
🖳 www.bentleygolfclub.com

## Benton Hall Golf & Country Club (1993)
**Proprietary**
Wickham Hill, Witham CM8 3LH
☎ **(01376) 502454**
🖥 (01376) 521050
✉ bentonhall.retail@theclubcompany
.com
✍ Scott Clark
🖳 www.theclubcompany.com

## Birch Grove (1970)
Layer Road, Colchester CO2 0HS
☎ **(01206) 734276**
✉ maureen@birchgrove.fsbusiness
.co.uk
✍ Mrs M Marston
🖳 www.birchgrovegolfclub.co.uk

## Boyce Hill (1922)
Vicarage Hill, Benfleet SS7 1PD
☎ **(01268) 793625**
🖥 (01268) 750497
✉ secretary@boycehillgolfclub.co.uk
✍ D Kelly
🖳 www.boycehillgolfclub.co.uk

## Braintree (1891)
Kings Lane, Stisted, Braintree
CM77 8DD
☎ **(01376) 346079**
🖥 (01376) 348677
✉ info@braintreegolfclub.co.uk
✍ Mr N Hawkins
🖳 www.braintreegolfclub.co.uk

## Braxted Park (1953)
Braxted Park, Witham CM8 3EN
☎ **(01376) 572372**
🖥 (01376) 572372
✉ golf@braxtedpark.com
✍ Mr P Keeble
🖳 www.braxtedpark.com

## Bunsay Downs Golf Club (1982)
**Proprietary**
Little Baddow Road, Woodham Walter,
Maldon CM9 6RU
☎ **(01245) 222648/222369**
✉ info@bunsaydownsgc.co.uk
✍ J Durham (01245) 223258
🖳 www.bunsaydownsgc.co.uk

## Burnham-on-Crouch (1923)
Ferry Road, Creeksea, Burnham-on-Crouch
CM0 8PQ
☎ **(01621) 782282**
🖥 (01621) 784489
✉ enquiries@burnhamgolfclub.co.uk
✍ S K Golf Ltd
🖳 www.burnhamgolfclub.co.uk

## The Burstead   (1993)
**Proprietary**
Tye Common Road, Little Burstead,
Billericay CM12 9SS
☎ **(01277) 631171**
🖷 (01277) 632766
✉ info@thebursteadgolfclub.com
✍ Stuart Mence (Managing Director)
🖥 www.thebursteadgolfclub.com

## Canons Brook   (1962)
Elizabeth Way, Harlow CM19 5BE
☎ **(01279) 421482**
🖷 (01279) 626393
✉ manager@canonsbrook.com
✍ Mrs SJ Langton
🖥 www.canonsbrook.com

## Castle Point   (1988)
**Public**
Waterside Farm, Somnes Avenue, Canvey
Island SS8 9FG
☎ **(01268) 510830**
✍ Mrs B de Koster

## Channels   (1974)
Belsteads Farm Lane, Little Waltham,
Chelmsford CM3 3PT
☎ **(01245) 440005**
🖷 (01245) 442032
✉ info@channelsgolf.co.uk
✍ Mrs SJ Larner
🖥 www.channelsgolf.co.uk

## Chelmsford   (1893)
Widford Road, Chelmsford CM2 9AP
☎ **(01245) 256483**
🖷 (01245) 256483
✉ office@chelmsfordgc.co.uk
✍ G Winckless (01245) 256483
🖥 www.chelmsfordgc.co.uk

## Chigwell   (1925)
High Road, Chigwell IG7 5BH
☎ **(020) 8500 2059**
🖷 (020) 8501 3410
✉ info@chigwellgolfclub.co.uk
✍ James Fuller (Gen Mgr)
🖥 www.chigwellgolfclub.com

## Chingford   (1923)
158 Station Road, Chingford, London
E4 6AN
☎ **(0208) 529 2107**
✍ B W Woods

## Clacton-on-Sea   (1892)
West Road, Clacton-on-Sea CO15 1AJ
☎ **(01255) 421919**
🖷 (01255) 424602
✉ secretary@clactongolfclub.com
✍ Brian Telford
🖥 www.clactongolf.com

## Colchester GC   (1907)
21 Braiswick, Colchester CO4 5AU
☎ **(01206) 853396**
🖷 (01206) 852698
✉ secretary@colchestergolfclub.com
✍ Julie Ruscoe
🖥 www.colchestergolfclub.com

## Colne Valley   (1991)
Station Road, Earls Colne CO6 2LT
☎ **(01787) 224343**
🖷 (01787) 224126
✉ info@colnevalleygolfclub.co.uk
✍ T Smith (01787) 224343
🖥 www.colnevalleygolfclub.co.uk

## Crondon Park   (1994)
**Proprietary**
Stock Road, Stock CM4 9DP
☎ **(01277) 841115**
🖷 (01277) 841356
✉ info@crondon.com
✍ P Cranwell
🖥 www.crondon.com

## Crowlands Heath Golf Club
(2000)
**Pay and play**
Wood Lane, Dagenham, Essex RM8 1JX
☎ **(020) 8984 7373**
🖷 (020) 8984 0505
✉ chris@chrisjenkinsgolf.com
✍ Marcus Radmore (Mgr)
🖥 www.chrisjenkinsgolf.com

## Elsenham Golf and Leisure
(1997)
**Proprietary**
Hall Road, Elsenham, Bishop's Stortford
CM22 6DH
☎ **(01279) 812865**
✉ info@elsenhamgolfandleisure.co.uk
✍ Martin McKenna (Gen Mgr)
🖥 www.egcltd.co.uk

## Epping Golf Club   (1996)
**Proprietary**
Flux Lane, Epping, Essex CM16 7NJ
☎ **(01992) 572282**
🖷 (01992) 575512
✉ info@eppinggolfcourse.org.uk
✍ Mr Neil Sjöberg
⊕ Half mile walk from Epping Central
Line Underground Station.
🖥 www.eppinggolfcourse.org.uk

## Essex G&CC   (1990)
Earls Colne, Colchester CO6 2NS
☎ **(01787) 224466**
🖷 (01787) 224410
✉ essex.golfops@theclubcompany
.com
✍ J Gathercole (Mgr)
🖥 www.theclubcompany.com

## Five Lakes Resort   (1995)
Colchester Road, Tolleshunt Knights,
Maldon CM9 8HX
☎ **(01621) 868888 (Hotel)**
🖷 (01621) 869696
✉ office@fivelakes.co.uk
✍ AD Bermingham (Dir)
🖥 www.fivelakes.co.uk

## Forrester Park   (1975)
Beckingham Road, Great Totham, Maldon
CM9 8EA
☎ **(01621) 891406**
🖷 (01621) 891903
✉ housemanager@forresterparkltd
.com
✍ T Forrester-Muir
🖥 www.forresterparkltd.com

## Frinton   (1895)
1 The Esplanade, Frinton-on-Sea CO13 9EP
☎ **(01255) 674618**
🖷 (01255) 682450
✉ enquiries@frintongolfclub.com
✍ Deborah Rablin
🖥 www.frintongolfclub.com

## Garon Park Golf Complex
(1993)
**Pay and play**
Eastern Avenue, Southend-on-Sea, Essex
SS2 4FA
☎ **(01702) 601701**
🖷 (01702) 601033
✉ debbie@garonparkgolf.co.uk
✍ Mrs Debbie Wright
🖥 www.garonparkgolf.co.uk

## Gosfield Lake   (1986)
Hall Drive, Gosfield, Halstead CO9 1SE
☎ **(01787) 474747**
🖷 (01787) 476044
✉ gosfieldlakegc@btconnect.com
✍ JA O'Shea (Sec/Mgr)
🖥 www.gosfield-lake-golf-club.co.uk

## Hainault Golf Club   (1912)
**Public**
Romford Road, Chigwell Row IG7 4QW
☎ **(020) 8500 2131
(Proshop/Reception)**
✍ Gary Ivory (Mgr)
🖥 www.hainaultgolfclub.co.uk

## Hartswood   (1967)
**Pay and play**
King George's Playing Fields, Brentwood
CM14 5AE
☎ **(01277) 214830 (Bookings)**
🖷 (01277) 218850
✍ D Bonner (01227) 218850

## Harwich & Dovercourt
(1906)
Station Road, Parkeston, Harwich
CO12 4NZ
☎ **(01255) 503616**
🖷 (01255) 503323
✉ secretary@harwichanddovercourt
golfclub.com
✍ K Feaviour (Hon Sec)
🖥 www.harwichanddovercourt
golfclub.com

## Ilford   (1907)
291 Wanstead Park Road, Ilford IG1 3TR
☎ **(020) 8554 2930**
🖷 (020) 8554 0822
✉ secretary@ilfordgolfclub.com
✍ Janice Pinner (Mgr)
🖥 www.ilfordgolfclub.com

## Langdon Hills   (1991)
**Proprietary**
Lower Dunton Road, Bulphan RM14 3TY
☎ **(01268) 548444/544300**

☎ (01268) 490084
✉ secretary@golflangdon.co.uk
✍ K Thompson (01268) 400064
🖥 www.langdonhillsgolfclub.co.uk

**Loughton** (1981)
**Pay and play**
Clays Lane, Debden Green, Loughton
IG10 2RZ
☎ (020) 8502 2923
✍ A Day

**Maldon** (1891)
Beeleigh Langford, Maldon CM9 4SS
☎ (01621) 853212
🖥 (01621) 855232
✉ maldon.golf@virgin.net
✍ Viv Locke
🖥 www.maldon-golf.co.uk

**Maylands** (1936)
**Proprietary**
Colchester Road, Harold Park, Romford
RM3 0AZ
☎ (01708) 341777
🖥 (01708) 343777
✉ maylands@maylandsgolf.com
✍ (01708) 341777
🖥 www.maylandsgolf.com

**North Weald** (1996)
**Proprietary**
Rayley Lane, North Weald, Epping
CM16 6AR
☎ (01992) 522118
✉ info@northwealdgolfclub.co.uk
✍ T Lloyd-Skinner
🖥 www.northwealdgolfclub.co.uk

**Orsett** (1899)
Brentwood Road, Orsett RM16 3DS
☎ (01375) 891352
🖥 (01375) 892471
✉ suecoleman@orsettgolfclub.co.uk
✍ GH Smith (01375) 893409
🖥 www.orsettgolfclub.co.uk

**Playgolf Colchester** (1993)
**Proprietary**
Bakers Lane, Colchester CO3 4AU
☎ (01206) 843333
🖥 (01206) 854775
✉ colchester@playgolfworld.com
✍ K Hanvey
🖥 www.playgolfcolchester.com

**Regiment Way** (1995)
**Pay and play**
Pratts Farm Lane West, Little Waltham,
Chelmsford CM3 3PR
☎ (01245) 361100 (Golf)
   362210 (General)
🖥 (01245) 442032
✉ info@littlechannelsce.co.uk
✍ D A Wallbank
🖥 www.cliffordsestate.co.uk

**Risebridge Golf Centre** (1972)
**Pay and play**
Risebridge Chase, Lower Bedfords Road,
Romford RM1 4DG
☎ (01708) 741429
✉ risebridge@btconnect.com

✍ P Jennings
🖥 www.risebridgegolf.com

**Rivenhall Oaks Golf Centre**
(1994)
**Pay and play**
Forest Road, Witham, Essex CM8 2PS
☎ (01376) 510222
🖥 (01376) 500316
✉ info@rivenhalloaksgolf.com
✍ B Chapman
🖥 www.rivenhalloaksgolf.com

**Rochford Hundred Golf Club**
(1893)
Rochford Hall, Hall Road, Rochford
SS4 1NW
☎ (01702) 544302
🖥 (01702) 541343
✉ admin@rochfordhundredgolfclub
   .co.uk
✍ N T Wells
🖥 www.rochfordhundredgolfclub.co.uk

**Romford** (1894)
Heath Drive, Gidea Park, Romford
RM2 5QB
☎ (01708) 740007 (Members)
🖥 (01708) 752157
✉ info@romfordgolfclub.co.uk
✍ M R J Hall (01708) 740986
🖥 www.romfordgolfclub.com

**Royal Epping Forest** (1888)
Forest Approach, Station Road, Chingford,
London E4 7AZ
☎ (020) 8529 2195
✉ office@refgc.co.uk
✍ Mrs D Woodland (0208) 529 2195
🖥 www.refgc.co.uk

**Saffron Walden** (1919)
Windmill Hill, Saffron Walden CB10 1BX
☎ (01799) 522786
🖥 (01799) 520313
✉ office@swgc.com
✍ Mrs Stephanie Standen
🖥 www.swgc.com

**South Essex G&CC**
Herongate, Brentwood CM13 3LW
☎ (01277) 811289
🖥 (01277) 811304
✉ enquiry@crown-golf.co.uk
✍ P Lecras (Gen Mgr)
🖥 www.crown-golf.co.uk

**St Cleres** (1994)
**Proprietary**
St Cleres Hall, Stanford-le-Hope
SS17 0LX
☎ (01375) 361565
🖥 (01375) 361565
✉ david.wood@foremostgolf.com
✍ D Wood (01375) 361565

**Stapleford Abbotts** (1989)
**Proprietary**
Horseman's Side, Tysea Hill, Stapleford
Abbotts RM4 1JU
☎ (01708) 381108
🖥 (01708) 386345

✉ staplefordabbotts@crown-
   golf.co.uk
✍ C Whittaker (Gen Mgr)
🖥 www.staplefordabbotts.golf.co.uk

**Stock Brook Manor** (1992)
**Proprietary**
Queen's Park Avenue, Stock, Billericay
CM12 0SP
☎ (01277) 658181
🖥 (01277) 633063
✉ events@stockbrook.com
✍ C Laurence (Golf Dir)
🖥 www.stockbrook.com

**The Rayleigh Club** (1995)
Hullbridge Road, Rayleigh SS6 9QS
☎ (01702) 232377
🖥 (01702) 233725
✉ info@therayleighclub.com
🖥 www.therayleighclub.com

**The Warren** (1932)
**Proprietary**
Woodham Walter, Maldon CM9 6RW
☎ (01245) 223258/223198
🖥 (01245) 223989
✉ enquiries@warrengolfclub.co.uk
✍ J Durham (01245) 223258
🖥 www.warrengolfclub.co.uk

**Theydon Bois** (1897)
Theydon Road, Theydon Bois, Epping
CM16 4EH
☎ (01992) 813054
🖥 (01992) 815602
✉ theydonboisgolf@btconnect.com
✍ D Bowles (01992) 813054
🖥 www.theydongolf.co.uk

**Thorndon Park** (1920)
Ingrave, Brentwood CM13 3RH
☎ (01277) 810345
🖥 (01277) 810645
✉ office@thorndonpark.com
✍ Mr G Thomas (mgr)
🖥 www.thorndonparkgolfclub.com

**Thorpe Hall** (1907)
Thorpe Hall Avenue, Thorpe Bay SS1 3AT
☎ (01702) 582205/
   (01702) 588195 Pro Shop
🖥 (01702) 584498
✉ sec@thorpehallgc.co.uk
✍ Ms F Gale
🖥 www.thorpehallgc.co.uk

**Three Rivers G&CC** (1973)
Stow Road, Purleigh, Chelmsford CM3 6RR
☎ (01621) 828631
🖥 (01621) 828060
✍ F Teixeira (Gen Mgr)
🖥 www.threeriversclub.com

**Toot Hill** (1991)
**Proprietary**
School Road, Toot Hill, Ongar CM5 9PU
☎ (01277) 365747
🖥 (01277) 364509
✉ office@toothillgolfclub.co.uk
✍ Mrs Cameron
🖥 www.toothillgolfclub.co.uk

## Top Meadow    (1986)
*Fen Lane, North Ockendon RM14 3PR*
- ☎ **(01708) 852239 (Clubhouse)**
- ✉ info@topmeadow.co.uk
- ✍ D Stock
- 🖥 www.topmeadow.co.uk

## Upminster    (1928)
*114 Hall Lane, Upminster RM14 1AU*
- ☎ **(01708) 222788**
- 🖥 (01708) 222484
- ✉ secretary@upminstergolfclub.co.uk
- ✍ RP Winmill
- 🖥 www.upminstergolfclub.co.uk

## Wanstead    (1893)
*Overton Drive, Wanstead, London E11 2LW*
- ☎ **(0208) 989 3938**
- ✉ info@wansteadgolfclub.com
- ✍ J P Nolan
- 🖥 www.wansteadgolf.org.uk

## Warley Park    (1975)
*Magpie Lane, Little Warley, Brentwood CM13 3DX*
- ☎ **(01277) 224891**
- 🖥 (01277) 200679
- ✉ enquiries@warleyparkgc.co.uk
- ✍ N Hawkins
- 🖥 www.warleyparkgc.co.uk

## Weald Park    (1994)
*Coxtie Green Road, South Weald, Brentwood CM14 5RJ*
- ☎ **(01277) 375101**
- 🖥 (01277) 374888
- ✍ M Orwin (Gen Mgr)
- 🖥 www.wealdparkhotel.co.uk

## West Essex    (1900)
*Bury Road, Sewardstonebury, Chingford, London E4 7QL*
- ☎ **(020) 8529 7558**
- 🖥 (020) 8524 7870
- ✉ sec@westessexgolfclub.co.uk
- ✍ Mrs Emma Clifford
- 🖥 www.westessexgolfclub.co.uk

## Woodford    (1890)
*2, Sunset Avenue, Woodford Green IG8 0ST*
- ☎ **(020) 8504 0553 (Clubhouse)**
- 🖥 (020) 8559 0504
- ✉ office@woodfordgolf.co.uk
- ✍ PS Willett (020) 8504 3330
- 🖥 www.woodfordgolf.com

## Woolston Manor    (1994)
*Woolston Manor, Abridge Road, Chigwell, Essex IP7 6BX*
- ☎ **(020) 8500 2549**
- 🖥 (020) 8501 5452
- ✉ bradley@woolstonmanor.co.uk
- ✍ P Spargo
- 🖥 www.woolstonmanor.co.uk

## Gloucesteershire

## Brickhampton Court Golf Complex    (1995)
**Proprietary**
*Cheltenham Road East, Churchdown, Gloucestershire GL2 9QF*
- ☎ **(01452) 859444**
- 🖥 (01452) 859333
- ✉ info@brickhampton.co.uk
- ✍ Natalie Dyke
- 🖥 www.brickhampton.co.uk

## Bristol & Clifton    (1891)
*Beggar Bush Lane, Failand, Clifton, Bristol BS8 3TH*
- ☎ **(01275) 393474/393117**
- 🖥 (01275) 394611
- ✉ office@bristolgolf.co.uk
- ✍ (01275) 393474
- 🖥 www.bristolgolf.co.uk

## Broadway    (1895)
*Willersey Hill, Broadway, Worcs WR12 7LG*
- ☎ **(01386) 853683**
- 🖥 (01386) 858643
- ✉ secretary@broadwaygolfclub.co.uk
- ✍ Mr V Tofts
- 🖥 www.broadwaygolfclub.co.uk

## Canons Court    (1982)
**Pay and play**
*Bradley Green, Wotton-under-Edge GL12 7PN*
- ☎ **(01453) 843128**
- ✍ A Bennett
- 🖥 www.canonscourtgolf.co.uk

## Chipping Sodbury    (1905)
*Trinity Lane, Chipping Sodbury, Bristol BS37 6PU*
- ☎ **(01454) 319042 (Members)**
- ✉ info@chippingsodburygolfclub.co.uk
- ✍ Robin Goodey
- 🖥 www.chippingsodburygolfclub.co.uk

## Cirencester    (1893)
*Cheltenham Road, Bagendon, Cirencester GL7 7BH*
- ☎ **(01285) 652465**
- ✉ info@cirencestergolfclub.co.uk
- ✍ R Collishaw (01285) 652465
- 🖥 www.cirencestergolfclub.co.uk

## Cleeve Hill    (1892)
**Pay and play**
*Cleeve Hill, Cheltenham GL52 3PW*
- ☎ **(01242) 678666**
- ✉ hugh.fitzsimons@btconnect.com
- ✍ Hugh Fitzsimons (Dir of Golf)
- 🖥 www.cleevehillgolfclub.co.uk

## Cotswold Edge    (1980)
*Upper Rushmire, Wotton-under-Edge GL12 7PT*
- ☎ **(01453) 844167**
- 🖥 (01453) 845120
- ✉ cotswoldedge@freenetname.co.uk
- ✍ NJ Newman
- 🖥 www.cotswoldedgegolfclub.org.uk

## Cotswold Hills    (1902)
*Ullenwood, Cheltenham GL53 9QT*
- ☎ **(01242) 515264**
- 🖥 (01242) 515317
- ✉ tania@cotswoldhills-golfclub.com
- ✍ Mrs A Hale (Club Mgr)
- 🖥 www.cotswoldhills-golfclub.com

## Dymock Grange    (1995)
*The Old Grange, Leominster Road, Dymock GL18 2AN*
- ☎ **(01531) 890840**
- 🖥 (01531) 890860
- ✍ B Crossman

## Filton    (1909)
*Golf Course Lane, Bristol BS34 7QS*
- ☎ **(0117) 969 4169**
- 🖥 (0117) 931 4359
- ✉ secretary@filtongolfclub.co.uk
- ✍ T Atkinson (0117) 969 4169
- 🖥 www.filtongolfclub.co.uk

## Forest Hills    (1992)
**Proprietary**
*Mile End Road, Coleford GL16 7BY*
- ☎ **(01594) 810620**
- 🖥 (01594) 810823
- ✍ D Bowen (01594) 837134
- 🖥 www.fweb.org.uk/forestgolf

## Forest of Dean    (1973)
*Lords Hill, Coleford GL16 8BE*
- ☎ **(01594) 832583**
- 🖥 (01594) 832584
- ✉ enquiries@bells-hotel.co.uk
- ✍ H Wheeler (Hon Sec)
- 🖥 www.bells-hotel.co.uk

## Gloucester Golf & Country Club    (1976)
*Matson Lane, Gloucester, Gloucestershire GL4 6EA*
- ☎ **(01452) 525653**
- ✍ K Wood (01452) 411311 (Mgr)

## Henbury    (1891)
*Henbury Road, Westbury-on-Trym, Bristol BS10 7QB*
- ☎ **(0117) 950 0044**
- 🖥 (0117) 959 1928
- ✉ thesecretary@henburygolfclub.co.uk
- ✍ Derek Howell (0117) 950 0044
- 🖥 www.henburygolfclub.co.uk

## Hilton Puckrup Hall Hotel    (1992)
*Puckrup, Tewkesbury GL20 6EL*
- ☎ **(01684) 296200/271591**
- 🖥 (01684) 850788
- ✍ R Lazenby
- 🖥 www.puckrupgolf.co.uk

## The Kendleshire    (1997)
**Proprietary**
*Henfield Road, Coalpit Heath, Bristol BS36 2TG*
- ☎ **(0117) 956 7007**
- 🖥 (0117) 957 3433
- ✉ info@kendleshire.com

P Murphy
www.kendleshire.com

## Knowle (1905)
Fairway, West Town Lane, Brislington, Bristol BS4 5DF
☎ (0117) 977 0660
✉ admin@knowlegolfclub.co.uk
🖳 (0117) 977 0660
🖥 www.knowlegolfclub.co.uk

## Lilley Brook (1922)
Cirencester Road, Charlton Kings, Cheltenham GL53 8EG
☎ (01242) 526785
✉ caroline@lilleybrook.co.uk
🖊 Mrs C Martin (Sec)
🖥 www.lilleybrook.co.uk

## Long Ashton (1893)
Clarken Coombe, Long Ashton, Bristol BS41 9DW
☎ (01275) 392229
🖳 (01275) 394395
✉ secretary@longashtongolfclub .co.uk
🖊 Victoria Rose
🖥 www.longashtongolfclub.co.uk

## Lydney (1909)
Naas Course, Naas Lane, Lydney GL15 5ES
☎ (01594) 842775
🖊 J Mills (01594) 841186
🖥 www.lydneygolfclub.co.uk

## Minchinhampton (1889)
Minchinhampton, Stroud GL6 9BE
☎ (01453) 832642 (Old) 833866 (New)
🖳 (01453) 837360
✉ rob@mgcnew.co.uk
🖊 R East (01453) 833866
🖥 www.minchinhamptongolfclub .co.uk

## Naunton Downs (1993)
Proprietary
Naunton, Cheltenham GL54 3AE
☎ (01451) 850090
✉ admin@nauntondowns.co.uk
🖊 Nick Ellis
🖥 www.nauntondowns.co.uk

## Newent Golf Club and Lodges (1994)
Pay and play
Coldharbour Lane, Newent GL18 1DJ
☎ (01531) 820478
✉ newentgolf@btconnect.com
🖊 T Brown
🖥 www.newentgolf.co.uk

## Painswick (1891)
Golf Course Road, Painswick, Stroud GL6 6TL
☎ (01452) 812180
✉ secretary.painswick@virginmedia .com
🖊 Mrs Ann Smith
🖥 www.painswickgolf.com

## Rodway Hill (1991)
Pay and play
Newent Road, Highnam GL2 8DN
☎ (01452) 384222
🖳 (01452) 313814
✉ info@rodway-hill-golf-course.co.uk
🖊 A Price
🖥 www.rodway-hill-golf-course.co.uk

## Sherdons Golf Centre (1993)
Pay and play
Tredington, Tewkesbury GL20 7BP
☎ (01684) 274782
🖳 (01684) 275358
✉ info@sherdons.co.uk
🖊 R Chatham
🖥 www.sherdons.co.uk

## Shirehampton Park (1904)
Park Hill, Shirehampton, Bristol BS11 0UL
☎ (0117) 982 2083
🖳 (0117) 982 5280
✉ info@shirehamptonparkgolfclub .co.uk
🖊 Karen Rix (0117) 982 2083
🖥 www.shirehamptonparkgolfclub .co.uk

## Stinchcombe Hill (1889)
Stinchcombe Hill, Dursley GL11 6AQ
☎ (01453) 542015
🖳 (01453) 549545
✉ secretary@stinchcombehill.plus.com
🖊 Leigh Topping
🖥 www.stinchcombehillgolfclub.com

## Tewkesbury Park Hotel (1976)
Lincoln Green Lane, Tewkesbury GL20 7DN
☎ (01684) 295405 (Hotel)
🖳 (01684) 292386
✉ reservations@tewkesburypark.co.uk
🖊 Club Golf Sec (01684) 272322
🖥 www.tewkesburypark.co.uk

## Thornbury Golf Centre (1992)
Bristol Road, Thornbury BS35 3XL
☎ (01454) 281144
🖳 (01454) 281177
✉ info@thornburygc.co.uk
🖊 Mr Richard Dakin (Gen Mgr)
🖥 www.thornburygc.co.uk

## Woodlands G&CC (1989)
Pay and play
Trench Lane, Almondsbury, Bristol BS32 4JZ
☎ (01454) 619319
🖳 (01454) 619397
✉ info@woodlands-golf.com
🖊 D Knipe
🖥 www.woodlands-golf.com

## Woodspring G&CC (1994)
Proprietary
Yanley Lane, Long Ashton, Bristol BS41 9LR
☎ (01275) 394378
🖳 (01275) 394473
✉ info@woodspring-golf.com
🖊 D Knipe
🖥 www.woodspring-golf.com

## Alresford (1890)
Cheriton Road, Tichborne Down, Alresford SO24 0PN
☎ (01962) 733746
🖳 (01962) 736040
✉ secretary@alresfordgolf.co.uk
🖊 D Maskery
🖥 www.alresfordgolf.co.uk

## Alton (1908)
Old Odiham Road, Alton GU34 4BU
☎ (01420) 82042
🖊 R Keeling

## Ampfield Par Three (1962)
Proprietary
Winchester Road, Ampfield, Romsey SO51 9BQ
☎ (01794) 368480
🖊 Mark Hazell (MD) 01794 368 480
🖥 www.ampfieldgolf.com

## Andover (1907)
51 Winchester Road, Andover SP10 2EF
☎ (01264) 323980
🖳 (01264) 358040
✉ secretary@andovergolfclub.co.uk
🖊 Jon Lecisie (01264) 358040
🖥 www.andovergolfclub.co.uk

## Army (1883)
Laffan's Road, Aldershot GU11 2HF
☎ (01252) 337272
🖳 (01252) 337562
✉ secretary@armygolfclub.com
🖊 Jim Galley
🖥 www.armygolfclub.com

## Barton-on-Sea (1897)
Milford Road, New Milton BH25 5PP
☎ (01425) 615308
🖳 (01425) 621457
✉ info@barton-on-sea-golf.co.uk
🖊 I Prentice
🖥 www.barton-on-sea-golf.co.uk

## Basingstoke (1907)
Kempshott Park, Basingstoke RG23 7LL
☎ (01256) 465990
🖳 (01256) 331793
✉ office@basingstokegolfclub.co.uk
🖊 John Hiscock
🖥 www.basingstokegolfclub.co.uk

## Bishopswood (1978)
Proprietary
Bishopswood Lane, Tadley, Basingstoke RG26 4AT
☎ (01189) 408600
✉ kpickett@bishopswoodgc.co.uk
🖊 Mrs J Jackson-Smith (0118) 982 0312 (Sec)
🖥 www.bishopswoodgc.co.uk

## Blackmoor (1913)
Whitehill, Bordon GU35 9EH
☎ (01420) 472775
🖳 (01420) 487666
✉ admin@blackmoorgolf.co.uk
🖊 Mrs J Dean (Admin Mgr)
🖥 www.blackmoorgolf.co.uk

## Blacknest    (1993)
Blacknest GU34 4QL
- ☎ **(01420) 22888**
- 🖳 (01420) 22001
- 📧 reception@blacknestgolf.co.uk
- ⛳ Tim Russell

## Botley Park Hotel G&CC
(1989)
Winchester Road, Boorley Green, Botley SO3 2UA
- ☎ **(01489) 780888 Ext 451**
- 🖳 (01489) 789242
- 📧 golf.botley@macdonald-hotels.co.uk
- ⛳ Dean Rossilli (Gen Mgr)
- 🖳 www.macdonald-hotels.co.uk

## Bramshaw    (1880)
Brook, Lyndhurst SO43 7HE
- ☎ **(023) 8081 3433**
- 🖳 (023) 8081 3460
- 📧 golf@bramshaw.co.uk
- ⛳ Stuart James
- 🖳 www.bramshaw.co.uk

## Brokenhurst Manor    (1915)
Sway Road, Brockenhurst SO42 7SG
- ☎ **(01590) 623332**
- 🖳 (01590) 624691
- 📧 secretary@brokenhurst-manor.org.uk
- ⛳ Neil Hallam Jones
- 🖳 www.brokenhurst-manor.org.uk

## Burley    (1905)
Cott Lane, Burley, Ringwood BH24 4BB
- ☎ **(01425) 402431**
- 🖳 (01425) 404168
- 📧 secretary@burleygolfclub.co.uk
- ⛳ Mrs L J Harfield (01425) 402431
- 🖳 www.burleygolfclub.co.uk

## Cams Hall Estate    (1993)
Proprietary
Cams Hall Estate, Fareham PO16 8UP
- ☎ **(01329) 827222**
- 🖳 (01329) 827111
- 📧 camshall@crown-golf.co.uk
- ⛳ R Climas (Sec/Mgr)
- 🖳 www.camshallgolf.co.uk

## Chilworth    (1989)
Main Road, Chilworth, Southampton SO16 7JP
- ☎ **(023) 8074 0544**
- 🖳 (023) 8073 3166
- ⛳ F Bendall

## Corhampton    (1891)
Corhampton, Southampton SO32 3GZ
- ☎ **(01489) 877279**
- 🖳 (01489) 877680
- 📧 secretary@corhamptongc.co.uk
- ⛳ Bob Ashton
- 🖳 www.corhamptongc.co.uk

## Dibden Golf Centre    (1974)
Public
Main Road, Dibden, Southampton SO45 5TN
- ☎ **(023) 8020 7508 (Bookings)**
- 🖳 www.nfdc.gov.uk/golf

## Dummer    (1992)
Proprietary
Dummer, Basingstoke RG25 2AD
- ☎ **(01256) 397950 (Pro Shop)**
- 📧 enquiries@dummergolfclub.com
- ⛳ Steve Wright (Mgr) (01256) 397888
- 🖳 www.dummergolfclub.com

## Dunwood Manor    (1969)
Danes Road, Awbridge, Romsey SO51 0GF
- ☎ **(01794) 340549**
- 🖳 (01794) 341215
- 📧 admin@dunwood-golf.co.uk
- ⛳ Hazel Johnson/Kenny Bygate
- 🖳 www.dunwood-golf.co.uk

## Fleetlands    (1961)
Fareham Road, Gosport PO13 0AW
- ☎ **(023) 9254 4492**
- ⛳ J Watmore (07762) 230 4344

## Four Marks    (1994)
Headmore Lane, Four Marks, Alton GU34 3ES
- ☎ **(01420) 587214**
- 🖳 (01420) 587324
- ⛳ General Manager
- 🖳 www.fourmarksgolf.co.uk

## Furzeley    (1993)
Pay and play
Furzeley Road, Denmead PO7 6TX
- ☎ **(023) 9223 1180**
- 🖳 (023) 9223 0921
- 📧 furzeleygc@btinternet.com
- ⛳ R Brown

## Gosport & Stokes Bay    (1885)
Fort Road, Haslar, Gosport PO12 2AT
- ☎ **(023) 925 27941**
- 🖳 (023) 925 27941
- 📧 secretary@gosportandstokesbay golfclub.co.uk
- ⛳ Clun Manager (023) 925 27941
- 🖳 www.gosportandstokesbaygolfclub.co.uk

## The Hampshire    (1993)
Pay and play
Winchester Road, Goodworth Clatford, Andover SP11 7TB
- ☎ **(01264) 357555**
- 🖳 (01264) 356606
- 📧 enquiries@thehampshiregolfclub.co.uk
- ⛳ J Miles
- 🖳 www.thehampshiregolfclub.co.uk

## Hartley Wintney    (1891)
London Road, Hartley Wintney, Hook RG27 8PT
- ☎ **(01252) 844211**
- 🖳 (01252) 844211
- 📧 office@hartleywintneygolfclub.com
- ⛳ P J Gaylor
- 🖳 www.hartleywintneygolfclub.com

## Hayling    (1883)
Links Lane, Hayling Island PO11 0BX
- ☎ **(023) 9246 4446**
- 📧 members@haylinggolf.co.uk

- ⛳ Ian Walton (023) 9246 4446
- 🖳 www.haylinggolf.co.uk

## Hockley    (1914)
Twyford, Winchester SO21 1PL
- ☎ **(01962) 713165**
- 📧 admin@hockleygolfclub.com
- ⛳ Mrs A Pfam
- 🖳 www.hockleygolfclub.com

## Lee-on-the-Solent    (1905)
Brune Lane, Lee-on-the-Solent PO13 9PB
- ☎ **(023) 9255 1170**
- 🖳 (023) 9255 4233
- 📧 enquiries@leegolf.co.uk
- ⛳ Rob Henderson (Mgr) (023) 9255 1170
- 🖳 www.leegolf.co.uk

## Liphook    (1922)
Liphook GU30 7EH
- ☎ **(01428) 723271/723785**
- 🖳 (01428) 724853
- 📧 secretary@liphookgolfclub.com
- ⛳ John Douglass
- 🖳 www.liphookgolfclub.com

## Meon Valley Marriott Hotel & Country Club    (1979)
Proprietary
Sandy Lane, Shedfield, Southampton SO32 2HQ
- ☎ **(01329) 833455**
- 🖳 (01329) 834411
- 📧 george.mcmenemy@marriotthotels.com
- ⛳ GF McMenemy (Golf Dir)
- 🖳 www.marriottgolf.co.uk

## New Forest    (1888)
Southampton Road, Lyndhurst SO43 7BU
- ☎ **(023) 8028 2752**
- 🖳 (023) 8028 4030
- 📧 secretarynfgc@aol.com
- ⛳ Derek Hurlstone/Graham Lloyd
- 🖳 www.newforestgolf.co.uk

## North Hants    (1904)
Minley Road, Fleet GU51 1RF
- ☎ **(01252) 616443**
- 🖳 (01252) 811627
- 📧 secretary@northhantsgolf.co.uk
- ⛳ C J Gotla
- 🖳 www.northhantsgolf.co.uk

## Old Thorns    (1982)
Longmoor Road, Griggs Green, Liphook GU30 7PE
- ☎ **(01428) 724555**
- 🖳 (01428) 725036
- 📧 proshop@oldthorns.com
- ⛳ Greg Knights
- 🖳 www.oldthorns.com

## Otterbourne Golf Centre    (1995)
Pay and play
Poles Lane, Otterbourne, Winchester SO21 2EL
- ☎ **(01962) 775225**
- 📧 info@chilworthgolfclub.com
- ⛳ C Garner
- 🖳 www.chilworthgolfclub.com

**Park** (1995)
Pay and play
Avington, Winchester SO21 1BZ
☎ (01962) 779945 (Clubhouse)
🖥 (01962) 779530
📧 office@avingtongolf.co.uk
✍ R Stent (Prop)
🖳 www.avingtongolf.co.uk

**Paultons Golf Centre** (1922)
Pay and play
Old Salisbury Road, Ower, Romsey
SO51 6AN
☎ (023) 8081 3992
🖥 (023) 8081 3993
✍ M Rollinson
🖳 www.crown-golf.co.uk

**Petersfield** (1892)
Tankerdale Lane, Liss GU33 7QY
☎ (01730) 895165
📧 manager@petersfieldgolfclub.co.uk
✍ PD Badger
🖳 www.petersfieldgolfclub.co.uk

**Petersfield Pay and Play**
Pay and play
139 Sussex Road, Petersfield GU31 4LE
☎ (01730) 267732
✍ PD Badger

**Portsmouth** (1926)
Pay and play
Crookhorn Lane, Widley, Waterlooville
PO7 5QL
☎ (023) 9237 2210
📧 portsmouthgc@btconnect.com
✍ Mr Iden Adams (Sec)
 (023) 9220 1827
🖳 www.portsmouthgc.com

**Quindell** (1997)
Skylark Meadows, Whiteley, Fareham
PO15 6RS
☎ (01329) 844441
🖥 (01329) 836736
📧 sales@quindell.com
✍ Rob Terry
🖳 www.quindell.com

**Romsey** (1900)
Nursling, Southampton SO16 0XW
☎ (023) 8073 4637
🖥 (023) 8074 1036
📧 secretary@romseygolfclub.co.uk
✍ Mike Batty
🖳 www.romseygolfclub.com

**Rowlands Castle** (1902)
Links Lane, Rowlands Castle PO9 6AE
☎ (023) 9241 2784
🖥 (023) 9241 3649
📧 manager@rowlandscastlegc.co.uk
✍ KD Fisher (023) 9241 2784
🖳 www.rowlandscastlegolfclub.co.uk

**Royal Winchester** (1888)
Sarum Road, Winchester SO22 5QE
☎ (01962) 852462
🖥 (01962) 865048
📧 manager@royalwinchestergolfclub
 .com

✍ A Buck
🖳 www.royalwinchestergolfclub.com

**Sandford Springs** (1988)
Wolverton, Tadley RG26 5RT
☎ (01635) 296800
🖥 (01635) 296801
📧 info@sandfordsprings.co.uk
✍ Andrew Wild (01635) 296800
🖳 www.sandfordsprings.co.uk

**Somerley Park** (1995)
Somerley, Ringwood BH24 3PL
☎ (01425) 461496
📧 gordon@somerleyparkgolfclub.co.uk
✍ Gordon Scott
🖳 www.somerleyparkgolfclub.co.uk

**South Winchester**
Pitt, Winchester, Hampshire SO22 5QX
☎ (01962) 877800
🖥 (01962) 877900
📧 winchester-sales@crown-golf.co.uk
✍ L Ross (Gen Mgr) (01962) 877800
🖳 www.crown-golf.co.uk

**Southampton Municipal**
(1935)
Public
1 Golf Course Road, Bassett, Southampton
SO16 7AY
☎ (023) 807 60546
📧 mick.carter7@ntlworld.com
✍ E Hemsley
🖳 www.southamptongolfclub.co.uk

**Southsea** (1972)
Public
The Clubhouse, Burrfields Road, Portsmouth
PO3 5JJ
☎ (023) 9266 8667
🖥 (023) 9266 8667
📧 southseagolfclub@tiscali.co.uk
✍ R Collinson (02392) 699110
🖳 www.southsea-golf.co.uk

**Southwick Park** (1977)
Pinsley Drive, Southwick PO17 6EL
☎ (023) 9238 0131 Option 1
🖥 (0871) 855 6809
📧 jameslever@southwickparkgolfclub
 .co.uk
✍ J R Lever
🖳 www.southwickparkgolfclub.co.uk

**Southwood** (1977)
Public
Ively Road, Farnborough GU14 0LJ
☎ (01252) 548700
🖥 (01252) 549091
✍ Chris Hudson (01252) 665452
🖳 www.southwoodgolfclub.co.uk

**Stoneham** (1908)
Monks Wood Close, Bassett, Southampton
SO16 3TT
☎ (023) 8076 9272
🖥 (023) 8076 6320
📧 richard@stonehamgolfclub.org.uk
✍ R Penley-Martin (Mgr)
🖳 www.stonehamgolfclub.org.uk

**Test Valley** (1992)
Micheldever Road, Overton, Basingstoke
RG25 3DS
☎ (01256) 771737
🖥 (01256) 771285
📧 info@testvalleygolf.com
✍ A Briggs (Mgr)
🖳 www.testvalleygolf.com

**Tylney Park** (1973)
Proprietary
Rotherwick, Hook RG27 9AY
☎ (01256) 762079
🖥 (01256) 763079
📧 contact@tylneypark.co.uk
✍ Alasdair Hay (Mgr)
🖳 www.tylneypark.co.uk

**Waterlooville** (1907)
Cherry Tree Ave, Cowplain, Waterlooville
PO8 8AP
☎ (023) 9226 3388
🖥 (023) 9224 2980
📧 secretary@waterloovillegolfclub
 .co.uk
✍ J Hay
🖳 www.waterloovillegolfclub.co.uk

**Wellow** (1991)
Proprietary
Ryedown Lane, East Wellow, Romsey
SO51 6BD
☎ (01794) 322872
🖥 (01794) 323832
✍ Mrs C Gurd
🖳 www.wellowgolfclub.co.uk

**Weybrook Park** (1971)
Rooksdown Lane, Basingstoke RG24 9NT
☎ (01256) 320347
🖥 (01256) 812973
📧 info@weybrookpark.co.uk
✍ Mrs S Bowen (Sec)/Mr A Dillon
 (Mgr)
🖳 www.weybrookpark.co.uk

**Wickham Park** (1991)
Proprietary
Titchfield Lane, Wickham, Fareham
PO17 5PJ
☎ (01329) 833342
🖥 (01329) 834798
📧 wickhampark@crown-golf.co.uk
✍ Jonathan Tubb
🖳 www.crown-golf.co.uk

**Worldham** (1993)
Proprietary
Cakers Lane, Worldham, Alton GU34 3BF
☎ (01420) 543151/544606
📧 office@worldhamgolfclub.co.uk
✍ Ian Yates (01420) 544606
🖳 www.worldhamgolfclub.co.uk

## Herefordshire

**Belmont Lodge** (1983)
Ruckhall Lane, Belmont, Hereford HR2 9SA
☎ (01432) 352666
🖥 (01432) 358090

✉ info@belmont-hereford.co.uk
✍ Christopher T Smith (Gen Mgr)
🖥 www.belmont-hereford.co.uk

## Burghill Valley    (1991)
**Proprietary**
Tillington Road, Burghill, Hereford
HR4 7RW
☎ **(01432) 760456**
✉ admin@bvgc.co.uk
✍ Mrs D Harrison (Office Mgr)
🖥 www.bvgc.co.uk

## Cadmore Lodge    (1990)
**Pay and play**
Berrington Green, Tenbury Wells, Worcester
WR15 8TQ
☎ **(01584) 810044**
📠 (01584) 810044
✉ reception.cadmore
    @cadmorelodge.com
✍ Mike Miles
🖥 www.cadmorelodge.co.uk

## Hereford Golf Club    (1983)
**Public**
Hereford Halo Leisure & Golf Club, Holmer
Road, Hereford HR4 9UD
☎ **(01432) 344376**
📠 (01432) 266281
✍ G Morgan (Mgr)

## Herefordshire    (1896)
Raven's Causeway, Wormsley, Hereford
HR4 8LY
☎ **(01432) 830219/830465**
✉ herefordshire.golf@breathe.com
✍ Miss Sarah Lawrence (Sec)
⊕ Twitter; @HerefordshireGC
Like us on Facebook at
    HerefordshireGC
🖥 www.herefordshiregolfclub.co.uk

## Kington    (1925)
Bradnor Hill, Kington HR5 3RE
☎ **(01544) 230340**
✉ info@kingtongolf.co.uk
✍ N P Venables (01544) 388259
🖥 www.kingtongolf.co.uk

## Leominster    (1967)
Ford Bridge, Leominster HR6 0LE
☎ **(01568) 610055**
📠 (01568) 610055
✉ contact@leominstergolfclub.co.uk
✍ Mr Dilwyn James
🖥 leominstergolfclub.co.uk

## Ross-on-Wye    (1803)
Two Park, Gorsley, Ross-on-Wye HR9 7UT
☎ **(01989) 720267**
📠 (01989) 720212
✉ admin@therossonwyegolfclub
    .co.uk
✍ Ian Griffiths
🖥 www.therossonwyegolfclub.co.uk

## Sapey    (1991)
**Proprietary**
Upper Sapey, Worcester WR6 6XT
☎ **(01886) 853288**
📠 (01886) 853485
✉ anybody@sapeygolf.co.uk

✍ Miss L Stevenson
    (01886) 853506
🖥 www.sapeygolf.co.uk

## South Herefordshire    (1992)
Twin Lakes, Upton Bishop, Ross-on-Wye
HR9 7UA
☎ **(01989) 780535**
📠 (01989) 740611
✉ info@herefordshiregolf.co.uk
✍ James Leaver
🖥 www.herefordshiregolf.co.uk

## Summerhill    (1994)
**Proprietary**
Clifford, Nr. Hay-on-Wye, Hereford
HR3 5EW
☎ **(01497) 820451**
✉ competitions
    @summerhillgolfcourse.co.uk
✍ Michael Tom
🖥 www.summerhillgolfcourse.co.uk

# Hertfordshire

## Aldenham G&CC    (1975)
**Proprietary**
Church Lane, Aldenham, Watford
WD25 8NN
☎ **(01923) 853929**
📠 (01923) 858472
✉ info@aldenhamgolfclub.co.uk
✍ Mrs J Phillips
🖥 www.aldenhamgolfclub.co.uk

## Aldwickbury Park    (1995)
**Proprietary**
Piggottshill Lane, Wheathampstead Road,
Harpenden AL5 1AB
☎ **(01582) 760112**
📠 (01582) 760113
✉ info@aldwickburyparkgc.co.uk
✍ A Shewbridge
🖥 www.aldwickburyparkgolfclub
    .co.uk

## Arkley    (1909)
Rowley Green Road, Barnet EN5 3HL
☎ **(020) 8449 0394**
✉ office@arkleygc.co.uk
✍ A N Welsh
🖥 www.arkleygolfclub.co.uk

## Ashridge    (1932)
Little Gaddesden, Berkhamsted HP4 1LY
☎ **(01442) 842244**
📠 (01442) 843770
✉ info@ashridgegolfclub.ltd.uk
✍ Secretary
🖥 www.ashridgegolfclub.ltd.uk

## Barkway Park    (1992)
**Proprietary**
Nuthampstead Road, Barkway, Royston
SG8 8EN
☎ **(01763) 849070**
✉ gc@barkwaypark.fsnet.co.uk
✍ GS Cannon
🖥 www.barkwaypark.co.uk

## Batchwood Hall    (1935)
**Pay and play**
Batchwood Drive, St Albans AL3 5XA
☎ **(01727) 844250**
✉ batchwood@leisureconnection
    .co.uk
✍ Luke Askew
🖥 www.leisureconnection.co.uk

## Batchworth Park    (1996)
London Road, Rickmansworth WD3 1JS
☎ **(01923) 711400**
📠 (01923) 710200
✉ batchworthpark-sales@crown-
    golf.co.uk
✍ Rob Davies
🖥 www.batchworthparkgolf.co.uk

## Berkhamsted    (1890)
The Common, Berkhamsted HP4 2QB
☎ **(01442) 865832**
📠 (01442) 863730
✉ Steve@berkhamstedgc.co.uk
✍ S H Derbyshire
🖥 www.berkhamstedgolfclub.co.uk

## Bishop's Stortford    (1910)
Dunmow Road, Bishop's Stortford
CM23 5HP
☎ **(01279) 654715**
📠 (01279) 655215
✉ office@bsgc.co.uk
✍ Judy Barker
🖥 www.bsgc.co.uk

## Boxmoor    (1890)
18 Box Lane, Hemel Hempstead HP3 0DJ
☎ **(01442) 242434 (Clubhouse)**
✍ B Swann
🖥 www.boxmoorgolfclub.co.uk

## Brickendon Grange    (1964)
Pembridge Lane, Brickendon, Hertford
SG13 8PD
☎ **(01992) 511258**
📠 (01992) 511411
✉ play@bggc.org.uk
✍ Martin Bennet (Gen Mgr) Jane
    Coulcher (Sec)
🖥 www.bggc.org.uk

## Briggens Park    (1988)
**Proprietary**
Briggens Park, Stanstead Road, Stanstead
Abbotts SG12 8LD
☎ **(01279) 793867**
📠 (01279) 793867
✉ briggensparkgolf@aol.co.uk
✍ Trevor Mitchell
🖥 www.briggensparkgolfclub.co.uk

## Brocket Hall    (1992)
**Proprietary**
Welwyn AL8 7XG
☎ **(01707) 368808**
📠 (01707) 390052
✉ louis.matamala@brocket-hall
    .co.uk
✍ Louis Matamala (01707) 368740
🖥 www.brocket-hall.co.uk

## Brookmans Park (1930)
Brookmans Park, Hatfield AL9 7AT
- ☎ (01707) 652487
- 📠 (01707) 661851
- ✉ info@bpgc.co.uk
- Una Handley
- 🖥 www.bpgc.co.uk

## Bushey G&CC (1980)
High Street, Bushey WD23 1TT
- ☎ (020) 8950 2283
- Pro Shop (020) 8950 2215
- 📠 (020) 8386 1181
- ✉ info@busheycountryclub.com
- Mark Young
- 🖥 www.busheycountryclub.com

## Bushey Hall (1890)
Proprietary
Bushey Hall Drive, Bushey WD23 2EP
- ☎ (01923) 222253
- 📠 (01923) 229759
- ✉ info@golfclubuk.co.uk
- Gordon Dawson
- 🖥 www.busheyhallgolfclub.co.uk

## Chadwell Springs GC (1974)
Pay and play
Hertford Road, Ware SG12 9LE
- ☎ (01920) 462075/61447
- ✉ chadwell.golfshop@virgin.net
- David Smith PGA Pro/Manager
- 🖥 www.chadwellspringsgolfshop.co.uk

## Chesfield Downs (1991)
Pay and play
Jack's Hill, Graveley, Stevenage SG4 7EQ
- ☎ (08707) 460020
- 📠 (08707) 460021
- P Barnfather

## Cheshunt (1976)
Public
Park Lane, Cheshunt EN7 6QD
- ☎ (01992) 629777
- ✉ accounts.cpgc@btconnect.com
- B Furne

## Chorleywood (1890)
Common Road, Chorleywood WD3 5LN
- ☎ (01923) 282009
- 📠 (01923) 286739
- ✉ secretary@chorleywoodgolfclub.co.uk
- RA Botham
- 🖥 www.chorleywoodgolfclub.co.uk

## Dyrham Park CC (1963)
Galley Lane, Barnet EN5 4RA
- ☎ (020) 8440 3361
- 📠 (020) 8441 9836
- ✉ enquiries@dyrhampark.com
- David Adams
- 🖥 www.dyrhampark.com

## East Herts (1899)
Hamels Park, Buntingford SG9 9NA
- ☎ (01920) 821978
- 📠 (01920) 823700
- ✉ gm@easthertsgolfclub.co.uk
- Ms A McDonald
- 🖥 www.easthertsgolfclub.co.uk

## Great Hadham (1993)
Proprietary
Great Hadham Road, Bishop's Stortford SG10 6JE
- ☎ (01279) 843558
- 📠 (01279) 842122
- ✉ ian@ghgcc.co.uk
- I Bailey
- 🖥 www.ghgcc.co.uk

## The Grove (2003)
Pay and play
Chandler's Cross, Rickmansworth WD3 4TG
- ☎ (01923) 294266
- 📠 (01923) 294268
- ✉ golf@thegrove.co.uk
- Anna Darnell (Dir of Golf)
- 🖥 www.thegrove.co.uk

## Hadley Wood (1922)
Beech Hill, Hadley Wood, Barnet EN4 0JJ
- ☎ (020) 8449 4328
- 📠 (020) 8364 8633
- ✉ gm@hadleywoodgc.com
- WM Beckett (Gen Mgr)
- 🖥 www.hadleywoodgc.com

## Hanbury Manor G&CC (1990)
Ware SG12 0SD
- ☎ (01920) 487722
- 📠 (01920) 487692
- ✉ mhrs.stngs.golfevents @marriotthotels.com
- Mike Harrison (Director of Clubs)
- 🖥 www.hanbury-manor.co.uk

## Harpenden (1894)
Hammonds End, Redbourn Lane, Harpenden AL5 2AX
- ☎ (01582) 712580
- 📠 (01582) 712725
- ✉ office@harpendengolfclub.co.uk
- Frank Clapp (Gen Mgr)
- 🖥 www.harpendengolfclub.co.uk

## Harpenden Common (1931)
East Common, Harpenden AL5 1BL
- ☎ (01582) 711320
- 📠 (01582) 711321
- ✉ admin@hcgc.co.uk
- Terry Crump (01582) 711325
- 🖥 www.harpendencommongolfclub .co.uk

## Hartsbourne G&CC (1946)
Hartsbourne Avenue, Bushey Heath WD23 1JW
- ☎ (020) 8421 7272
- 📠 (020) 8950 5357
- ✉ ian@hartsbournecountryclub.co.uk
- I Thomas
- 🖥 www.hartsbournecountryclub.co.uk

## Hatfield London CC (1976)
Bedwell Park, Essendon, Hatfield AL9 6HN
- ☎ (01707) 260360
- 📠 (01707) 278475
- ✉ info@hatfieldlondon.co.uk
- H Takeda
- 🖥 www.hatfieldlondon.co.uk

## The Hertfordshire (1995)
Proprietary
Broxbournebury Mansion, White Stubbs Lane, Broxbourne EN10 7PY
- ☎ (01992) 466666
- 📠 (01992) 470326
- ✉ hertfordshire-manager@crown-golf.co.uk
- Nikki Blacker
- 🖥 www.thehertfordshire-golf.co.uk

## Kingsway Golf Centre (1991)
Proprietary
Cambridge Road, Melbourn, Royston SG8 6EY
- ☎ (01763) 262943
- 📠 (01763) 263038
- ✉ kingswaygolf@btconnect.com
- Chris Page
- 🖥 www.kingswaygolfcentre.co.uk

## Knebworth (1908)
Deards End Lane, Knebworth SG3 6NL
- ☎ (01438) 812752 (Clubhouse)
- 📠 (01438) 815216
- ✉ admin@knebworthgolfclub.com
- Steve Barrett
- 🖥 www.knebworthgolfclub.com

## Lamerwood (1996)
Codicote Road, Wheathampstead AL4 8RH
- ☎ (01582) 833013
- 📠 (01582) 832604
- ✉ lamerwood.cc@virgin.net
- R Darling (Gen Mgr)
- 🖥 www.lamerwood.humaxuk.com

## Letchworth (1905)
Letchworth Lane, Letchworth Garden City SG6 3NQ
- ☎ (01462) 683203
- 📠 (01462) 484567
- ✉ secretary@letchworthgolfclub.com
- Mrs Niki Hunter
- 🖥 www.letchworthgolfclub.com

## Little Hay Golf Complex (1977)
Pay and play
Box Lane, Bovingdon, Hemel Hempstead HP3 0XT
- ☎ (01442) 833798
- 📠 (01442) 831399
- ✉ membership@sportspace.co.uk
- George Reid (Mgr)
- 🖥 www.sportspace.co.uk

## Manor of Groves G&CC (1992)
Proprietary
High Wych, Sawbridgeworth CM21 0JU
- ☎ (01279) 603559
- 📠 (01279) 603543
- ✉ golfsecretary@manorofgroves .co.uk
- Bob Walker (01279) 603559
- 🖥 www.manorgolf.net

## Mid Herts (1892)
Gustard Wood, Wheathampstead AL4 8RS
- ☎ (01582) 832242

(01582) 834834
secretary@mid-hertsgolfclub.co.uk
Martin Bennet
www.mid-hertsgolfclub.co.uk

## Mill Green   (1994)
Proprietary
Gypsy Lane, Mill Green, Welwyn Garden
City AL7 4TY
☎ **(01707) 276900**
(01707) 276898
millgreen@crown-golf.co.uk
Tim Hudson
www.millgreengolf.co.uk

## Moor Park   (1923)
Rickmansworth WD3 1QN
☎ **(01923) 773146**
(01923) 777109
jon.moore@moorparkgc.co.uk
JM Moore (01923) 773146
www.moorparkgc.co.uk

## Old Fold Manor   (1910)
Old Fold Lane, Hadley Green, Barnet
EN5 4QN
☎ **(020) 8440 9185**
(020) 8441 4863
manager@oldfoldmanor.co.uk
B Cullen (Mgr)
www.oldfoldmanor.co.uk

## Oxhey Park   (1991)
Pay and play
Prestwick Road, South Oxhey, Watford
WD19 7EX
☎ **(01923) 248213/210118**
oxheyparkgolfclub@live.com
James Wright (Prop)
www.oxheyparkgolfclub.co.uk

## Panshanger Golf Complex
   (1976)
Public
Old Herns Lane, Welwyn Garden City
AL7 2ED
☎ **(01707) 333312/333350
(Bookings)**
(01707) 390010
trish.skinner@talk21.com
Trish Skinner (07982) 259475
www.finesseleisure.com

## Porters Park   (1899)
Shenley Hill, Radlett WD7 7AZ
☎ **(01923) 854127**
enquiries@porterspark.com
P Marshall
www.porterspark.com

## Potters Bar   (1923)
Darkes Lane, Potters Bar, Hertfordshire
EN6 1DF
☎ **(01707) 652020**
(01707) 655051
louise@pottersbargolfclub.com
Louise Alabaster
www.pottersbargolfclub.com

## Radlett Park Golf Club   (1984)
Proprietary
Watling Street, Nr. Radlett WD6 3AA
☎ **(0208) 953 6115**

(0208) 207 6390
info@radlettparkgolfclub.com
Marc Warwick
(Mgr/Pro) (0208) 238694
www.radlettparkgolfclub.com

## Redbourn   (1970)
Proprietary
Kinsbourne Green Lane, Redbourn, St
Albans AL3 7QA
☎ **(01582) 793493**
(01582) 794362
info@redbourngc.co.uk
T Hall (01582) 793493
www.redbourngolfclub.com

## Rickmansworth   (1937)
Public
Moor Lane, Rickmansworth WD3 1QL
☎ **(01923) 775278**
(01923) 775278

## Royston   (1892)
Baldock Road, Royston SG8 5BG
☎ **(01763) 243476**
(01763) 246910
roystongolf@btconnect.com
S Clark (Mgr)
www.roystongolfclub.co.uk

## Sandy Lodge   (1910)
Sandy Lodge Lane, Northwood, Middx
HA6 2JD
☎ **(01923) 825429**
(01923) 824319
clivebailey@sandylodge.co.uk
C H Bailey
www.sandylodge.co.uk

## Shendish Manor Hotel & Golf
## Course   (1988)
Pay and play
Shendish Manor, London Road, Apsley
HP3 0AA
☎ **(01442) 251806**
(01442) 230683
golfmanager@shendish-manor.com
Bronwen Pateman (Membership
Co-ordinator)
www.shendish-manor.com

## South Herts   (1899)
Links Drive, Totteridge, London N20 8QU
☎ **(020) 8445 2035**
(020) 8445 7569
secretary@southhertsgolfclub
.co.uk
John Charlton (020) 8445 2035
www.southhertsgolfclub.co.uk

## Stevenage   (1980)
Public
Aston Lane, Stevenage SG2 7EL
☎ **(01438) 880424**
P Winston

## Verulam   (1905)
226 London Road, St Albans AL1 1JG
☎ **(01727) 853327**
(01727) 812201
gm@verulamgolf.co.uk
R Farrer
www.verulamgolf.co.uk

## Welwyn Garden City   (1923)
Mannicotts, High Oaks Road, Welwyn
Garden City AL8 7BP
☎ **(01707) 325243**
(01707) 393213
secretary@welwyngardencitygolfcl
ub.co.uk
D Spring (Gen Mgr)
www.welwyngardencitygolfclub.co.
uk

## West Herts   (1890)
Cassiobury Park, Watford WD3 3GG
☎ **(01923) 236484**
(01923) 222300
gm@westhertsgolf.demon.co.uk
R M McCue
www.westhertsgolfclub.co.uk

## Wheathampstead   (2001)
Pay and play
Harpenden Road, Wheathampstead, St
Albans AL4 8EZ
☎ **(01582) 833941**
(01582) 833941
nlawrencegolfacademy@hotmail.
co.uk
N Lawrence
www.wheathampstead.net
/golf-course

## Whipsnade Park   (1974)
Studham Lane, Dagnall HP4 1RH
☎ **(01442) 842330**
(01442) 842090
secretary@whipsnadeparkgolf.co.uk
R Whalley
www.whipsnadeparkgolf.co.uk

## Whitehill   (1990)
Proprietary
Dane End, Ware SG12 0JS
☎ **(01920) 438495**
(01920) 438891
andrew@whitehillgolf.co.uk
Mr A Smith (Prop)
www.whitehillgolf.co.uk

## Isle of Man

## Castletown Golf Links   (1892)
Proprietary
Fort Island, Derbyhaven IM9 1UA
☎ **(01624) 822211**
(01624) 829661
probbo@manx.net
Peter Robertson
www.castletowngolflinks.com

## Douglas   (1891)
Public
Pulrose Road, Douglas IM2 1AE
☎ **(01624) 675952 (Clubhouse)**
(01624) 616865
douglasgolfclub@manx.net
Mrs J Murley (01624) 616865
www.douglasgolfclub.com

## King Edward Bay (1893)
Groudle Road, Onchan IM3 2JR
- ☎ **(01624) 620430/673821**
- 🖳 (01624) 676794
- ✍ C Kelly (01624) 836556

## Mount Murray G&CC (1994)
Proprietary
Santon IM4 2HT
- ☎ **(01624) 695308**
- 🖳 (01624) 611116
- ✉ manager@mountmurraygolfclub
.com
- ✍ Andrew Seddon (golf club mgr)
- 🖥 www.mountmurray.com

## Peel (1895)
Rheast Lane, Peel IM5 1BG
- ☎ **(01624) 843456**
- ✉ peelgc@manx.net
- ✍ Guy Smith
- 🖥 www.peelgolfclub.com

## Port St Mary (1903)
Public
Kallow Road, Port St Mary IM9 5EJ
- ☎ **(01624) 834932**
- 🖳 (01624) 837231
- ✍ N Swimmin (07624) 498848

## Ramsey (1891)
Brookfield Avenue, Ramsey IM8 2AH
- ☎ **(01624) 813365/812244**
- 🖳 (01624) 815833
- ✉ ramseygolfclub@manx.net
- ✍ Mr J M Ferrier (01624) 812244
- 🖥 www.ramseygolfclub.im

## Rowany (1895)
Rowany Drive, Port Erin IM9 6LN
- ☎ **(01624) 834108**
- 🖳 (01624) 834072
- ✉ rowany@iommail.net
- ✍ CA Corrin (Mgr)
- 🖥 www.rowanygolfclub.com

# Isle of Wight

## Cowes (1909)
Crossfield Avenue, Cowes PO31 8HN
- ☎ **(01983) 280135 (Steward)**
- 🖳 (01983) 292303
- ✉ secretary@cowesgolfclub.co.uk
- ✍ C lacey (01983) 292303
- 🖥 www.cowesgolfclub.co.uk

## Freshwater Bay (1894)
Afton Down, Freshwater, Isle of Wight
PO40 9TZ
- ☎ **(01983) 752955**
- 🖳 (01983) 756704
- ✉ secretary@freshwaterbaygolfclub
.co.uk
- ✍ Kevin Garrett (01983) 752955
- 🖥 www.freshwaterbaygolfclub.co.uk

## Newport (1896)
St George's Lane, Shide, Newport
PO30 3BA
- ☎ **(01983) 525076**

- 🖳 (01983) 526711
- ✉ newportgc@btconnect.com
- ✍ Dean Faulkner (01983) 525076
- 🖥 www.newportgolfclub.co.uk

## Osborne (1904)
Osborne House Estate, East Cowes
PO32 6JX
- ☎ **(01983) 295421**
- 🖳 (01983) 292781
- ✉ manager@osbornegolfclub.co.uk
- ✍ AC Waite
- 🖥 www.osbornegolfclub.co.uk

## Ryde (1895)
Binstead Road, Ryde PO33 3NF
- ☎ **(01983) 614809**
- 🖳 (01983) 567418
- ✉ ryde.golfclub@btconnect.com
- ✍ RA Dean
- 🖥 www.rydegolf.co.uk

## Shanklin & Sandown (1900)
The Fairway, Lake, Sandown PO36 9PR
- ☎ **(01983) 403217**
- 🖳 (01983) 403007
- ✉ club@ssgolfclub.com
- ✍ AC Creed
- 🖥 www.ssgolfclub.com

## Ventnor (1892)
Steephill Down Road, Ventnor PO38 1BP
- ☎ **(01983) 853326/853388**
- 🖳 (01983) 853326
- ✉ secretary@ventnorgolfclub.co.uk
- ✍ S Blackmore
- 🖥 www.ventnorgolfclub.co.uk

## Westridge (1990)
Pay and play
Brading Road, Ryde PO33 1QS
- ☎ **(01983) 613131**
- 🖳 (01983) 567017
- ✉ westgc@aol.com
- ✍ Simon Hayward
- 🖥 www.westridgegolfcentre.co.uk

# Kent

## Aquarius (1912)
Marmora Rd, Honor Oak, London
SE22 0RY
- ☎ **(020) 8693 1626**
- ✉ secretary@aquariusgolfclub.co.uk
- ✍ J Halliday
- 🖥 www.aquariusgolfclub.co.uk

## Ashford (Kent) (1903)
Sandyhurst Lane, Ashford TN25 4NT
- ☎ **(01233) 622655**
- 🖳 (01233) 627494
- ✉ secretary@ashfordgolfclub.co.uk
- ✍ K Osbourne (01233) 622655
- 🖥 www.ashfordgolfclub.co.uk

## Austin Lodge (1991)
Upper Auston Lodge Road, Eynsford,
Swanley DA4 0HU
- ☎ **(01322) 863000**
- 🖳 (01322) 862406
- ✍ G Haenen (Mgr)

## Barnehurst (1903)
Public
Mayplace Road East, Bexley Heath
DA7 6JU
- ☎ **(01322) 523746**
- 🖳 (01322) 523860
- ✍ Freda Sunley

## Bearsted (1895)
Ware Street, Bearsted, Maidstone
ME14 4PQ
- ☎ **(01622) 738198**
- 🖳 (01622) 735608
- ✉ bearstedgolfclub@tiscali.co.uk
- ✍ Stuart Turner (01622) 738198
- 🖥 www.bearstedgolfclub.co.uk

## Beckenham Place Park (1907)
Public
Beckenham Hill Road, Beckenham BR3 2BP
- ☎ **(020) 8650 2292**
- 🖳 (020) 8663 1201
- ✉ beckenhamgolf@glendale-
services.co.uk
- 🖥 www.glendale-services.co.uk

## Bexleyheath (1909)
Mount Road, Bexleyheath DA6 8JS
- ☎ **(020) 8303 6951**
- ✉ bexleyheathgolf@btconnect.com
- ✍ Mrs J Smith

## Birchwood Park (1990)
Birchwood Road, Wilmington, Dartford
DA2 7HJ
- ☎ **(01322) 662038**
- 🖳 (01322) 667283
- ✍ Mr SA Morley (Mgr)
- 🖥 www.birchwoodparkgc.co.uk

## Boughton (1993)
Pay and play
Brickfield Lane, Boughton, Faversham
ME13 9AJ
- ☎ **(01227) 752277**
- 🖳 (01227) 752361
- ✉ greg@pentlandgolf.co.uk
- ✍ Sue Coleman
- 🖥 www.pentlandgolf.co.uk

## Broke Hill (1993)
Sevenoaks Road, Halstead TN14 7HR
- ☎ **(01959) 533225**
- 🖳 (01959) 532680
- ✉ broke-sales@crows-golf.co.uk
- ✍ Mark Clarke
- 🖥 www.brokehillgolf.com

## Bromley (1948)
Pay and play
Magpie Hall Lane, Bromley BR2 8JF
- ☎ **(020) 8462 7014**
- 🖳 (020) 8462 6916
- ✉ bromley@mytimegolf.co.uk
- ✍ Dave Langford (01959) 573376
- 🖥 www.mytimegolf.co.uk

## Broome Park (1981)
Broome Park Estate, Barham, Canterbury
CT4 6QX
- ☎ **(01227) 830728**
- 🖳 (01227) 832591

✉ golf@broomepark.co.uk
✍ Mrs D Burtenshaw
🖳 www.broomepark.co.uk

## Canterbury   (1927)
Scotland Hills, Littlebourne Road,
Canterbury CT1 1TW
☎ **(01227) 453532**
✉ secretary@canterburygolfclub
.co.uk
✍ Jonathan Webb (Secretary)
🖳 www.canterburygolfclub.co.uk

## Chart Hills   (1993)
**Proprietary**
Weeks Lane, Biddenden, Ashford TN27 8JX
☎ **(01580) 292222**
🖳 (01580) 292233
✉ info@charthills.co.uk
✍ David Colyer
🖳 www.charthills.co.uk

## Chelsfield Lakes Golf Centre
(1992)
**Pay and play**
Court Road, Orpington BR6 9BX
☎ **(01689) 896266**
✉ manager@chelsfieldlakesgolf.co.uk
✍ Colin White (Group Dir. of Golf)
🖳 www.chelsfieldlakesgolf.co.uk

## Cherry Lodge   (1969)
Jail Lane, Biggin Hill, Westerham TN16 3AX
☎ **(01959) 572250**
✉ info@cherrylodgegc.co.uk
✍ Craig Sutherland
🖳 www.cherrylodgegc.co.uk

## Chestfield   (1925)
103 Chestfield Road, Whitstable CT5 3LU
☎ **(01227) 794411**
🖳 (01227) 794454
✉ generalmanager@chestfield-
golfclub.co.uk
✍ Alan Briggs
🖳 www.chestfield-golfclub.co.uk

## Chislehurst   (1894)
Camden Place, Camden Park Road,
Chislehurst BR7 5HJ
☎ **(020) 8467 6798**
🖳 (020) 8295 0874
✉ thesecretary@chislehurstgolfclub
.co.uk
✍ Mark Hickson (020) 8467 2782
🖳 www.chislehurstgolfclub.co.uk

## Cobtree Manor Park   (1984)
**Public**
Chatham Road, Boxley, Maidstone
ME14 3AZ
☎ **(01622) 753276**
✉ cobtree@mytimegolf.co.uk
✍ Steve Miller
🖳 www.cobtreemanorparkgolfcourse
.co.uk

## Darenth Valley   (1973)
**Pay and play**
Station Road, Shoreham, Sevenoaks
TN14 7SA
☎ **(01959) 522944 (Clubhouse)**

🖳 (01959) 525089
✉ enquiries@dvgc.co.uk
✍ Deborah Terry
🖳 www.dvgc.co.uk

## Dartford   (1897)
The Clubhouse, Heath Lane (Upper),
Dartford DA1 2TN
☎ **(01322) 223616**
🖳 (01322) 278690
✉ dartfordgolf@hotmail.com
✍ Mrs Amanda Malas (01322) 226455
🖳 www.dartfordgolfclub.co.uk

## Deangate Ridge Golf & Sports Complex   (1972)
**Public**
Duxcourt Road, Hoo, Rochester ME3 8RZ
☎ **(01634) 254481 (Gen Mgr)**
✉ leisure@medway.gov.uk
✍ Lee Mills (Gen
Mgr) (01634) 254481
🖳 www.deangateridge.co.uk

## Eastwell Manor   (2008)
Boughton Lees, Ashford, Kent TN25 4HR
☎ **(01233) 213100**
🖳 (01233) 213105
✉ enquiries@eastwellmanor.co.uk
✍ Phil Redman (Mgr)
🖳 www.eastwellmanor.co.uk

## Eltham Warren   (1890)
Bexley Road, Eltham, London SE9 2PE
☎ **(0208) 850 4477**
🖳 (0208) 850 0522
✉ secretary@elthamwarrengolfclub
.co.uk
✍ D J Mabbott
🖳 www.elthamwarrengolfclub.co.uk

## Etchinghill   (1995)
**Pay and play**
Canterbury Road, Etchinghill, Folkestone
CT18 8FA
☎ **(01303) 863863**
🖳 (01303) 863210
✉ deb@pentlandgolf.co.uk
✍ D Francis (01303) 864576
🖳 www.pentlandgolf.co.uk

## Faversham   (1902)
Belmont Park, Faversham ME13 0HB
☎ **(01795) 890561**
✉ themanager@favershamgolf.co.uk
✍ Paul Smith
🖳 www.favershamgolf.co.uk

## Fawkham Valley   (1987)
Gay Dawn Farm, Fawkham, Dartford
DA3 8LZ
☎ **(01474) 707144**
✉ fvgolfcourse@googlemail.com
✍ J Marchant
🖳 www.fawkhamvalleygolf.co.uk

## Gillingham   (1905)
Woodlands Road, Gillingham ME7 2AP
☎ **(01634) 853017/855862**
✉ golf@gillinghamgolf.idps.co.uk
✍ Miss K Snow (01634) 853017
🖳 www.gillinghamgolfclub.co.uk

## Hawkhurst   (1968)
High Street, Hawkhurst TN18 4JS
☎ **(01580) 752396**
🖳 (01580) 754074
✉ hawkhurstgolfclub@tiscali.co.uk
🖳 HawkhurstGolfClub.org.uk

## Hemsted Forest   (1969)
**Proprietary**
Golford Road, Cranbrook TN17 4AL
☎ **(01580) 712833**
🖳 (01580) 714274
✉ golf@hemstedforest.co.uk
✍ K Stevenson
🖳 www.hemstedforest.co.uk

## Hever Castle   (1992)
**Proprietary**
Hever Road, Hever, Edenbridge TN8 7NP
☎ **(01732) 700771**
🖳 (01732) 700775
✉ mail@hever.co.uk
✍ Jon Wittenberg
🖳 www.hever.co.uk

## High Elms   (1969)
**Public**
High Elms Road, Downe, Orpington
BR6 7SZ
☎ **(01689) 858175**
🖳 (01689) 856326
✍ Mrs P O'Keeffe (Hon)
🖳 www.highelmsgolfclub.com

## Hilden Golf Centre
**Pay and play**
Rings Hill, Hildenborough, Tonbridge
TN11 8LX
☎ **(01732) 833607**
🖳 (01732) 834484
✉ info@hildenpark.co.uk
✍ Jan Parfett
🖳 www.hildenpark.co.uk

## Hythe Imperial   (1950)
Prince's Parade, Hythe CT21 6AE
☎ **(01303) 233745**
🖳 (01303) 267554 (Professional)
✉ h6862-th@accor.com
✍ Clare Gibson (01303) 233724
🖳 www.mercure-uk.com

## The Kent & Surrey G&CC
(1972)
**Proprietary**
Crouch House Road, Edenbridge TN8 5LQ
☎ **(01732) 867381**
🖳 (01732) 867167
✉ info@thekentandsurrey.com
✍ David Taylor/Richard Thorpe
🖳 www.thekentandsurrey.com

## Kings Hill   (1996)
**Proprietary**
Fortune Way, Kings Hill, West Malling, Kent
ME19 4GF
☎ **(01732) 875040/842121**
    **(Bookings)**
🖳 (01732) 875019
✉ office@kingshillgolf.co.uk
✍ Margaret Gilbert (Mgr)
🖳 www.kingshillgolf.co.uk

## Knole Park (1924)
Seal Hollow Road, Sevenoaks TN15 0HJ
- ☎ (01732) 452150
- 🖬 (01732) 463159
- ✉ secretary@knoleparkgolfclub.co.uk
- ✍ N Statham (01732) 452150
- 🖥 www.knoleparkgolfclub.co.uk

## Lamberhurst (1890)
Church Road, Lamberhurst TN3 8DT
- ☎ (01892) 890591
- 🖬 (01892) 891140
- ✉ secretary@lamberhurstgolfclub.com
- ✍ Mrs S Deadman (01892) 890591
- 🖥 www.lamberhurstgolfclub.com

## Langley Park (1910)
Barnfield Wood Road, Beckenham BR3 6SZ
- ☎ (020) 8658 6849
- 🖬 (020) 8658 6310
- ✉ manager@langleyparkgolf.co.uk
- ✍ S Naylor (Gen Mgr)
- 🖥 www.langleyparkgolf.co.uk

## Leeds Castle (1928)
Pay and play
Leeds Castle, Hollingbourne, Maidstone
ME17 1PL
- ☎ (01622) 880467/767828
- 🖬 (01622) 735616
- ✉ stevepurves@leeds-castle.co.uk
- 🖥 www.leeds-castle.com

## Littlestone (1888)
St Andrews Road, Littlestone, New Romney
TN28 8RB
- ☎ (01797) 362310
- 🖬 (01797) 362740
- ✉ secretary@littlestonegolfclub
  .org.uk
- ✍ S Fullager (01797) 363355
- 🖥 www.littlestonegolfclub.org.uk

## Littlestone Warren (1993)
Pay and play
St Andrews Road, Littlestone, New Romney
TN28 8RB
- ☎ (01797) 362231
- 🖬 (01797) 362740
- ✉ secretary@littlestonegolf.org.uk
- ✍ S Fullager 01797 363355
- 🖥 www.romneywarrengolfclub.org.uk

## London Beach Golf Club (1998)
Pay and play
Ashford Road, St Michaels, Tenterden
TN30 6HX
- ☎ (01580) 767616
- 🖬 (01580) 763884
- ✉ enquiries@londonbeach.com
- ✍ P Edmonds
- 🖥 www.londonbeach.com

## London Golf Club (1993)
Stansted Lane, Ash, Nr Brands Hatch, Kent
TN15 7EH
- ☎ (01474) 879899
- 🖬 (01474) 879912
- ✉ golf@londongolf.co.uk
- ✍ Austen Gravestock
- 🖥 www.londongolf.co.uk

## Lullingstone Park (1967)
Public
Parkgate Road, Chelsfield, Orpington
BR6 7PX
- ☎ (01959) 533793
- ✍ CJ Pocock (0208) 303 9535
- 🖥 www.lullingstoneparkgolfclub.com

## Lydd (1994)
Proprietary
Romney Road, Lydd, Romney Marsh
TN29 9LS
- ☎ (01797) 320808
- ✉ golf@lyddgolfclub.co.uk
- ✍ Carole Harradine
- 🖥 www.lyddgolfclub.co.uk

## Mid Kent (1908)
Singlewell Road, Gravesend DA11 7RB
- ☎ (01474) 568035
- 🖬 (01474) 564218
- ✉ pamholden@mkgc.co.uk
- ✍ Mrs P Holden (01474) 568035
- 🖥 www.mkgc.co.uk

## Nizels (1992)
Nizels Lane, Hildenborough, Tonbridge
TN11 8NU
- ☎ (01732) 833833
- 🖬 (01732) 835492
- ✉ nizels@theclubcompany.com
- ✍ Vanessa Machen (Gen Mgr)
- 🖥 www.theclubcompany.com

## North Foreland (1903)
Convent Road, Broadstairs, Kent CT10 3PU
- ☎ (01843) 862140
- 🖬 (01843) 862663
- ✉ office@northforeland.co.uk
- ✍ AJ Adams (01843) 862140
- 🖥 www.northforeland.co.uk

## Oastpark (1992)
Pay and play
Malling Road, Snodland ME6 5LG
- ☎ (01634) 242661
- 🖬 (01634) 240744
- ✉ oastparkgolfclub@btconnect.com
- ✍ Lesley Murrock (01634) 242818

## Park Wood (1994)
Proprietary
Chestnut Avenue, Tatsfield, Westerham
TN16 2EG
- ☎ (01959) 577744
- 🖬 (01959) 577765
- ✉ mail@parkwoodgolf.co.uk
- ✍ John Hemphrey (Gen Mgr)
- 🖥 www.parkwoodgolf.co.uk

## Pedham Place Golf Centre (1996)
Proprietary
London Road, Swanley BR8 8PP
- ☎ (01322) 867000
- 🖬 (01322) 861646
- ✉ info@pppc.co.uk
- ✍ Tim Milford (Head Pro)
- 🖥 www.pppc.co.uk

## Poult Wood (1974)
Public
Higham Lane, Tonbridge TN11 9QR
- ☎ (01732) 364039 (Bookings)
- ✍ S Taylor

## Prince's (1906)
Proprietary
Sandwich Bay, Sandwich CT13 9QB
- ☎ (01304) 611118
- 🖬 (01304) 612000
- ✉ office@princesgolf.co.uk
- ✍ J T George (Dir) (01304) 626909
- 🖥 www.princesgolf.co.uk

## Redlibbets (1996)
Proprietary
West Yoke, Ash, Nr Sevenoaks TN15 7HT
- ☎ (01474) 879190
- 🖬 (01474) 879290
- ✉ info@redlibbets.com
- ✍ K Morris
- 🖥 www.redlibbets.co.uk

## The Ridge (1993)
Proprietary
Chartway Street, Sutton Valence, Maidstone
ME17 3JB
- ☎ (01622) 844382
- ✉ mike@theridgegolfclub.co.uk
- ✍ Jemma Stoner (Gen Mngr)
- 🖥 www.theridgegolfclub.co.uk

## Rochester & Cobham Park (1891)
Park Pale, by Rochester ME2 3UL
- ☎ (01474) 823411
- 🖬 (01474) 824446
- ✉ rcpgc@talk21.com
- ✍ J S Aughterlony
- 🖥 www.rochesterandcobhamgc.co.uk

## Royal Blackheath (1608)
Court Road, Eltham, London SE9 5AF
- ☎ (020) 8850 1795
- 🖬 (020) 8859 0150
- ✉ gm@rbgc.com
- ✍ M Evans (01237) 473817
- 🖥 www.royalblackheath.com

## Royal Cinque Ports (1892)
Golf Road, Deal CT14 6RF
- ☎ (01304) 374007 (Office)
- 🖬 (01304) 379530
- ✉ Martin.bond@royalcinqueports
  .com
- ✍ Martin Bond
- 🖥 www.royalcinqueports.com

## Royal St George's (1887)
Sandwich CT13 9PB
- ☎ (01304) 613090
- 🖬 (01304) 611245
- ✉ office@royalstgeorges.com
- ✍ Colonel T J Checketts OBE
- 🖥 www.royalstgeorges.com

## Sene Valley (1888)
Sene, Folkestone CT18 8BL
- ☎ (01303) 268513
- 🖬 (01303) 237513

senevalleygolf@btconnect.com
Gordon Syers (Mgr)
www.senevalleygolfclub.co.uk

## Sheerness    (1909)
Power Station Road, Sheerness ME12 3AE
☎ (01795) 662585
✉ secretary@sheernessgolfclub.co.uk
🖉 A Tindall
🖥 www.sheernessgolfclub.co.uk

## Shooter's Hill    (1903)
Lowood, Eaglesfield Road, London
SE18 3DA
☎ (020) 8854 6368
📠 (020) 8854 0469
✉ john@shgc.uk.com
🖉 J Clement (020) 8854 6368
🖥 www.shgc.uk.com

## Shortlands    (1894)
Meadow Road, Shortlands, Bromley
BR2 0DX
☎ (020) 8460 2471
📠 (020) 8460 8828
✉ enquiries@shortlandsgolfclub.co.uk
🖉 PS May (020) 8460 8828
🖥 www.shortlandsgolfclub.co.uk

## Sidcup    (1891)
Hurst Road, Sidcup DA15 9AW
☎ (020) 8300 2150
📠 (020) 8300 2150
✉ sidcupgolfclub@googlemail.com
🖉 Steve Armstrong (020) 8300 2150
🖥 www.sidcupgolfclub.co.uk

## Sittingbourne & Milton Regis
(1929)
Wormdale, Newington, Sittingbourne
ME9 7PX
☎ (01795) 842261
✉ sittingbournegc@btconnect.com
🖉 Charles Maxted
🖥 www.sittingbournegolfclub.com

## Southern Valley    (1999)
Pay and play
Thong Lane, Gravesend, Kent DA12  4LT
☎ (01474) 568568
📠 (01474) 360366
✉ info@southernvalley.co.uk
🖉 Paul Thornberry (Managing
    Director)
🖥 www.southernvalley.co.uk

## St Augustines    (1907)
Cottington Road, Cliffsend, Ramsgate
CT12 5JN
☎ (01843) 590333
📠 (01843) 590444
✉ sagc@ic24.net
🖉 R M Cooper
🖥 www.staugustinesgolfclub.co.uk

## Staplehurst Golf Centre
Cradducks Lane, Staplehurst TN12 0DR
☎ (01580) 893362
📠 (01580) 893372
🖉 C Jenkins
🖥 www.staplehurstgolfcentre.co.uk

## Sundridge Park    (1901)
Garden Road, Bromley BR1 3NE
☎ (020) 8460 0278
📠 (020) 8289 3050
✉ luke@spgc.co.uk
🖉 Luke Edgcumbe (020) 8460 0278
🖥 www.spgc.co.uk

## Sweetwoods Park    (1994)
Proprietary
Cowden, Edenbridge TN8 7JN
☎ (01342) 850729
📠 (01342) 850866
✉ golf@sweetwoodspark.com
🖥 www.sweetwoodspark.com

## Tenterden    (1905)
Woodchurch Road, Tenterden TN30 7DR
☎ (01580) 763987
📠 (01580) 763430
✉ enquiries@tenterdengolfclub.co.uk
🖉 Mrs Teresa Cuff
🖥 www.tenterdengolfclub.co.uk

## Thamesview Golf Centre
(1991)
Pay and play
Fairway Drive, Summerton Way,
Thamesmead, London SE28 8PP
☎ (020) 8310 7975
📠 (020) 8312 0546
✉ golf@tvgc.co.uk
🖉 Stephen Lee
🖥 www.tvgc.co.uk

## Tudor Park    (1988)
Proprietary
Ashford Road, Bearsted, Maidstone
ME14 4NQ
☎ (01622) 739412
📠 (01622) 735360

brad.mclean1@marriotthotels.com
Brad McLean
www.marriottgolf.com

## Tunbridge Wells    (1889)
Langton Road, Tunbridge Wells TN4 8XH
☎ (01892) 523034
✉ tunbridgewelgolf@btconnect.com
🖉 Peter Annington (01892) 536918
🖥 www.tunbridgewellsgolf.com

## Upchurch River Valley
(1991)
Pay and play
Oak Lane, Upchurch, Sittingbourne
ME9 7AY
☎ (01634) 360626
📠 (01634) 387784
✉ secretary@urvgc.co.uk
🖉 Graham Driscoll (01634) 260594
🖥 www.urvgc.co.uk

## Walmer & Kingsdown    (1909)
The Leas, Kingsdown, Deal CT14 8EP
☎ (01304) 373256
📠 (01304) 382336
✉ info@kingsdowngolf.co.uk
🖉 David Nehra
🖥 www.kingsdowngolf.co.uk

## Weald of Kent    (1992)
Proprietary
Maidstone Road, Headcorn TN27 9PT
☎ (01622) 890866
📠 (01622) 890070
✉ proshop@weald-of-kent.co.uk
🖉 Matt Pickard (Golf Operations
    Mgr)
🖥 www.weald-of-kent.co.uk

## West Kent    (1916)
Milking Lane, Downe, Orpington
BR6 7LD
☎ (01689) 851323
📠 (01689) 858693
✉ golf@wkgc.co.uk
🖉 Sean Trussell
🖥 www.wkgc.co.uk

## West Malling    (1974)
Addington, Maidstone ME19 5AR
☎ (01732) 844785
📠 (01732) 844795
✉ greg@westmallinggolf.com
🖉 MR Ellis
🖥 www.westmallinggolf.com

---

# The Halford-Hewitt Cup

The Halford Hewitt Cup was founded in 1924 as a competition for old boys of 64 English and Scottish public schools.

Described as "the greatest of all truly amateur tournaments", the cup is hosted by the Royal Cinque Ports Golf Club. In 1950, the competition became too large for a single club to host so Royal St George's Golf Club was asked to help. Since then, half the field has played its initial two rounds at Royal St George's.

## Westerham (1997)

**Proprietary**
Valence Park, Brasted Road, Westerham
TN16 1LJ
☎ (01959) 567100
🖷 (01959) 567101
🖂 info@westerhamgc.co.uk
🖳 R Sturgeon (Gen Mgr)
🖳 www.westerhamgc.co.uk

## Westgate & Birchington
(1893)
176 Canterbury Road, Westgate-on-Sea
CT8 8LT
☎ (01843) 831115/833905
🖂 wandbgc@tiscali.co.uk
🖳 TJ Sharp
🖳 www.westgate-and-birchington-golfclub.co.uk

## Whitstable & Seasalter
(1911)
Collingwood Road, Whitstable CT5 1EB
☎ (01227) 272020
🖷 (01227) 280822
🖂 wandsgolfclub@talktalk.net
🖳 MD Moore
🖳 www.whitstableandseasaltergolfclub
.co.uk

## Wildernesse (1890)
Park Lane, Seal, Kent TN15 0JE
☎ (01732) 761199
🖷 (01732) 763809
🖂 golf@wildernesse.co.uk
🖳 Mr A D Lawrence
🖳 www.wildernesse.co.uk

## Woodlands Manor (1928)
Woodlands, Tinkerpot Lane, Sevenoaks
TN15 6AB
☎ (01959) 523806
🖂 pro@woodlandsmanorgolf.co.uk
🖳 CG Robins (01959) 523806
🖳 www.woodlandsmanorgolf.co.uk

## Wrotham Heath (1906)
Seven Mile Lane, Comp, Sevenoaks
TN15 8QZ
☎ (01732) 884800
🖂 wrothamheathgolf@btconnect.com
🖳 J Hodgson
🖳 www.wrothamheathgolfclub.co.uk

# Lancashire

## Accrington & District (1893)
West End, Oswaldtwistle, Accrington
BB5 4LS
☎ (01254) 381614
🖷 (01254) 350111
🖂 info@accringtongolfclub.com
🖳 Paul A Wright (01254) 350112
⊕ Twitter: @accringtongolf &
@Eliotaccygolf
🖳 www.accringtongolfclub.com

## Ashton & Lea (1913)
Tudor Ave, Off Blackpool Rd, Lea, Preston
PR4 0XA
☎ (01772) 735282
🖷 (01772) 735762
🖂 info@ashtonleagolfclub.co.uk
🖳 S Plumb (01772) 735282
🖳 www.ashtonleagolfclub.co.uk

## Ashton-in-Makerfield (1902)
Garswood Park, Liverpool Road, Ashton-in-Makerfield, Wigan WN4 0YT
☎ (01942) 719330
🖷 (01942) 719330
🖂 secretary@ashton-in-makerfieldgolfclub.co.uk
🖳 G S Lacy
🖳 www.ashton-in-makerfieldgolfclub
.co.uk

## Ashton-under-Lyne (1913)
Gorsey Way, Hurst, Ashton-under-Lyne
OL6 9HT
☎ (0161) 330 1537
🖂 secretary@ashtongolfclub.co.uk
🖳 www.ashtongolfclub.co.uk

## Bacup (1910)
Maden Road, Bankside Lane, Bacup
OL13 8HN
☎ (01706) 873170
🖂 secretary_bgc@btconnect.com
🖳 Sue Styles (07792) 810877
🖳 www.bacupgolfclub.com

## Baxenden & District (1913)
Top o' th' Meadow, Baxenden, Accrington
BB5 2EA
☎ (01254) 234555
🖂 baxgolf@hotmail.com
🖳 N Turner (01706) 225423
🖳 www.baxendengolf.co.uk

## Beacon Park G&CC (1982)
**Public**
Beacon Lane, Dalton, Up Holland
WN8 7RU
☎ (01695) 625551
🖂 info@beaconparkgolf.com
🖳 Mark Prosser
🖳 www.westlancsleisure.com

## Blackburn (1894)
Beardwood Brow, Blackburn BB2 7AX
☎ (01254) 51122
🖷 (01254) 665578
🖂 sec@blackburngolfclub.com
🖳 I A McGowan (Hon Sec)
🖳 www.blackburngolfclub.com

## Blackpool North Shore
(1904)
Devonshire Road, Blackpool FY2 0RD
☎ (01253) 352054
🖷 (01253) 591240
🖂 office@bnsgc.com
🖳 Mrs C L Woosnam
(01253) 352054 ext 1
🖳 www.bnsgc.com

## Blackpool Park (1925)
**Public**
North Park Drive, Blackpool FY3 8LS
☎ (01253) 397916
🖷 (01253) 397916
🖂 secretary@blackpoolparkgc.co.uk
🖳 Don McLeod
🖳 www.blackpoolparkgc.co.uk

## Bolton (1891)
Lostock Park, Bolton BL6 4AJ
☎ (01204) 843067
🖂 secretary@boltongolfclub.co.uk
🖳 S Kay (01204) 843067
🖳 www.boltongolfclub.co.uk

## Bolton Old Links (1891)
Chorley Old Road, Montserrat, Bolton
BL1 5SU
☎ (01204) 842307
🖷 (01204) 497549
🖂 mail@boltonoldlinksgolfclub.com
🖳 Mrs J Boardman (01204) 842307
🖳 www.boltonoldlinksgolfclub.co.uk

## Bolton Open Golf Course
**Pay and play**
Longsight Park, Longsight Lane, Harwood
BL2 4JX
☎ (01204) 597659/309778
🖳 H Swindells (Sec/Mgr)

---

# The St George's Grand Challenge Cup

Inaugurated in 1888, the St George's Grand Challenge Cup is open to amateur golfers from recognised golf clubs and is presented by Royal St George's Golf Club, host to many top amateur and professional tournaments including The Open Championship, the Walker Cup, the Curtis Cup and the PGA Championship.

Sir Michael Bonallack (successful on three occasions), Jack Nicklaus and Lee Westwood are among the competition's prestigious winners.

---

## Brackley Municipal    (1977)
**Public**
*Bullows Road, Little Hulton, Worsley M38 9TR*
☎ **(0161) 790 6076**

## Breightmet    (1911)
*Red Bridge, Ainsworth, Bolton BL2 5PA*
☎ **(01204) 527381**
✍ R K Green
🖥 www.breightmetgolfclub.co.uk

## Brookdale    (1896)
*Medlock Road, Woodhouses, Failsworth M35 9WQ*
☎ **(0161) 681 4534**
🖳 (0161) 688 6872
✉ brookdalegolf@btconnect.com
✍ P Brownlow
🖥 www.brookdalegolf.co.uk

## Burnley    (1905)
*Glen View, Burnley BB11 3RW*
☎ **(01282) 455266**
✉ secretary@burnleygolfclub.co.uk
✍ Mr A Green
🖥 www.burnleygolfclub.com

## Bury    (1890)
*Unsworth Hall, Blackford Bridge, Bury BL9 9TJ*
☎ **(0161) 766 4897**
🖳 (0161) 796 3480
✉ secretary@burygolfclub.com
✍ David Parkinson
🖥 www.burygolfclub.com

## Castle Hawk    (1975)
*Chadwick Lane, Castleton, Rochdale OL11 3BY*
☎ **(01706) 640841**
🖳 (01706) 860587
✉ teeoff@castlehawk.co.uk
✍ L Entwistle

## Chorley    (1897)
*Hall o' th' Hill, Heath Charnock, Chorley PR6 9HX*
☎ **(01257) 480263**
🖳 (01257) 480722
✉ secretary@chorleygolfclub .freeserve.co.uk
✍ Mrs A Green (01257) 480263
🖥 www.chorleygolfclub.co.uk

## Clitheroe    (1891)
*Whalley Road, Clitheroe BB7 1PP*
☎ **(01200) 422292**
🖳 (01200) 422292
✉ secretary@clitheroegolfclub.com
✍ Michael Walls
🖥 www.clitheroegolfclub.com

## Colne    (1901)
*Law Farm, Skipton Old Road, Colne BB8 7EB*
☎ **(01282) 863391**
🖳 (01282) 870547
✉ colnegolfclub@hotmail.com
✍ A Turpin (Hon)
🖥 www.colnegolfclub.com

## Crompton & Royton    (1908)
*High Barn, Royton, Oldham OL2 6RW*
☎ **(0161) 624 0986**
🖳 (0161) 652 4711
✉ secretary@cromptonandroyton golfclub.co.uk
✍ J A Osbaldeston (0161) 624 0986
⊕ New driving range opened August 2012
🖥 www.cromptonandroytongolfclub .co.uk

## Darwen    (1893)
*Winter Hill, Duddon Avenue, Darwen BB3 0LB*
☎ **(01254) 701287**
🖳 (01254) 773833
✉ admin@darwengolfclub.com
✍ J Howarth (01254) 704367
🖥 www.darwengolfclub.com

## Dean Wood    (1922)
*Lafford Lane, Up Holland, Skelmersdale WN8 0QZ*
☎ **(01695) 622219**
🖳 (01695) 622245
✉ ray.benton@deanwoodgolfclub .co.uk
✍ WR Benton
🖥 www.deanwoodgolfclub.co.uk

## Deane    (1906)
*Broadford Road, Deane, Bolton BL3 4NS*
☎ **(01204) 61944**
🖳 (01204) 652047
✉ secretary@deanegolfclub.com
✍ Frank Hodgkiss (01204) 651808
🖥 www.deanegolfclub.co.uk

## Dunscar    (1908)
*Longworth Lane, Bromley Cross, Bolton BL7 9QY*
☎ **(01204) 303321**
🖳 (01204) 303321
✉ dunscargolfclub@uk2.net
✍ Mrs A E Jennings (01204) 303321
🖥 www.dunscargolfclub.co.uk

## Duxbury Park    (1975)
**Public**
*Duxbury Hall Road, Duxbury Park, Chorley PR7 4AS*
☎ **(01257) 235095**
🖳 (01257) 241378
✉ fholding2008@hotmail.co.uk
✍ F Holding (01257) 262209

## Fairhaven    (1895)
*Oakwood Avenue, Ansdell, Lytham St Annes FY8 4JU*
☎ **(01253) 736741**
🖳 (01253) 736741
✉ secretary@fairhavengolfclub.co.uk
✍ R Thompson
🖥 www.fairhavengolfclub.co.uk

## Fishwick Hall    (1912)
*Glenluce Drive, Farringdon Park, Preston PR1 5TD*
☎ **(01772) 798300**
🖳 (01772) 704600
✉ fishwickhallgolfclub@supanet.com

✍ Secretary
🖥 www.fishwickhallgolfclub.co.uk

## Fleetwood    (1932)
*Golf House, Princes Way, Fleetwood FY7 8AF*
☎ **(01253) 773573**
✉ secretary@fleetwoodgolf.co.uk
✍ Ernie Langford
🖥 www.fleetwoodgolf.co.uk

## Gathurst Golf Club Ltd    (1913)
*62 Miles Lane, Shevington, Wigan WN6 8EW*
☎ **(01257) 255882 (Pro Shop)**
🖳 (01257) 255953
✉ secretary@gathurstgolfclub.co.uk
✍ Barbara Wood (01257) 255235
🖥 www.gathurstgolfclub.co.uk

## Ghyll    (1907)
*Ghyll Brow, Skipton Row, Barnoldswick BB18 6JH*
☎ **(01282) 842466**
✉ secretary@ghyllgolfclub.co.uk
✍ R Presland (01282) 844359
🖥 www.ghyllgolfclub.co.uk

## Great Harwood    (1896)
*Harwood Bar, Whalley Road, Great Harwood BB6 7TE*
☎ **(01254) 884391**
✍ J Spibey
🖥 www.greatharwoodgolfclub.co.uk

## Green Haworth    (1914)
*Green Haworth, Accrington BB5 3SL*
☎ **(01254) 237580**
🖳 (01254) 396176
✉ green-haworth-gc1@talktalk.net
✍ W Halstead
🖥 www.green-haworth-gc.talktalk.net

## Greenmount    (1920)
*Greenmount, Bury BL8 4LH*
☎ **(01204) 883712**
✉ secretary@greenmountgolfclub .co.uk
✍ D Beesley
🖥 www.greenmountgolfclub.co.uk

## Haigh Hall    (1972)
**Public**
*Haigh Hall Country Park, Haigh, Wigan WN2 1PE*
☎ **(01942) 833337 (Clubhouse)**
✉ secretary@haighhall-golfclub.co.uk
✍ SG Eyres
🖥 www.haighhall-golfclub.co.uk

## Hart Common    (1995)
**Proprietary**
*Westhoughton Golf Centre, Wigan Road, Westhoughton BL5 2BX*
☎ **(01942) 813195**
✍ B Hill (01942) 813195

## Harwood    (1926)
*Roading Brook Road, Bolton BL2 4JD*
☎ **(01204) 522878**
✉ secretary@harwoodgolfclub.com /info@harwoodgolfclub.com

### D A Johnston
www.harwoodgolfclub.com

## De Vere Herons Reach (1993)
**Proprietary**
East Park Drive, Blackpool FY3 8LL
☎ (01253) 766156
📠 (01253) 798800
✉ richard.bowman@devere-hotels
.com
🖎 P Heaton
🖥 www.deveregolf.co.uk

## Heysham (1910)
Trumacar Park, Middleton Road, Heysham,
Morecambe LA3 3JH
☎ (01524) 851011
📠 (01524) 853030
✉ secretary@heyshamgolfclub.co.uk
🖎 Mrs G E Gardner
🖥 www.heyshamgolfclub.co.uk

## Hindley Hall (1905)
Hall Lane, Hindley, Wigan WN2 2SQ
☎ (01942) 255131
✉ secretary@hindleyhallgolfclub.co.uk
🖎 Ian Rimmer (01942) 255131
🖥 www.hindleyhallgolfclub.co.uk

## Horwich (1895)
Victoria Road, Horwich BL6 5PH
☎ (01204) 696980
📠 (01942) 205316
🖎 R Swift

## Hurlston Hall Golf & Country Club (1994)
**Proprietary**
Hurlston Lane, Southport, Scarisbrick
L40 8HB
☎ (01704) 840400
📠 (01704) 841404
✉ info@hurlstonhall.co.uk
🖎 Aoife O'Brien (MD)
🖥 www.hurlstonhall.co.uk

## Ingol (1981)
**Proprietary**
Tanterton Hall Road, Ingol, Preston
PR2 7BY
☎ (01772) 734556
📠 (01772) 729815
✉ ingol@golfers.net
🖎 M Ross
🖥 www.ingolgolfclub.co.uk

## Knott End (1910)
Wyreside, Knott End-on-Sea, Poulton-le-
Fylde FY6 0AA
☎ (01253) 810576
📠 (01253) 813446
✉ louise@knottendgolfclub.com
🖎 Louise Freeman (01253) 810576
🖥 www.knottendgolfclub.com

## Lancaster (1889)
Ashton Hall, Ashton-with-Stodday, Lancaster
LA2 0AJ
☎ (01524) 751247 (Secretary)
✉ secretary@lancastergc.co.uk
🖎 G Yates (01524) 751247
🖥 www.lancastergc.co.uk

## Lansil (1947)
Caton Road, Lancaster LA4 3PE
☎ (01524) 39269
🖎 M Lynch (01524) 62785
🖥 www.lansilgolfclub.org.uk

## Leyland (1924)
Wigan Road, Leyland PR25 5UD
☎ (01772) 436457
📠 (01772) 435605
✉ manager@leylandgolfclub.co.uk
🖎 S Drinkall
🖥 www.leylandgolfclub.co.uk

## Lobden (1888)
Whitworth, Rochdale OL12 8XJ
☎ (01706) 343228
📠 (01706) 343228
✉ golf@lobdengolfclub.co.uk
🖎 B Harrison (01706) 852752

## Longridge (1877)
Fell Barn, Jeffrey Hill, Longridge, Preston
PR3 2TU
☎ (01772) 783291
📠 (01772) 783022
✉ secretary@longridgegolfclub.co.uk
🖎 D Carling
🖥 www.longridgegolfclub.co.uk

## Lowes Park (1915)
Hilltop, Lowes Road, Bury BL9 6SU
☎ (0161) 764 1231
✉ lowesparkgc@btconnect.com
🖎 Alan Taylor
🖥 www.lowesparkgc.co.uk

## Lytham Green Drive (1913)
Ballam Road, Lytham St Annes FY8 4LE
☎ (01253) 737390
📠 (01253) 731350
✉ secretary@lythamgreendrive.co.uk
🖎 I Stewart (01253) 737390 Opt 4
🖥 www.lythamgreendrive.co.uk

## Marland (1928)
**Public**
Springfield Park, Bolton Road, Rochdale
OL11 4RE
☎ (01706) 649801
📠 (01706) 523082
🖎 J Wallis

## Marsden Park (1969)
**Public**
Townhouse Road, Nelson BB9 8DG
☎ (01282) 661912
📠 (01282) 661384
✉ martin.robinson
@pendleleisuretrust.com
🖎 D Walton (01282) 835833
🖥 www.pendleleisuretrust.co.uk

## Morecambe (1905)
Bare, Morecambe LA4 6AJ
☎ (01524) 412841
📠 (01524) 400088
✉ secretary@morecambegolfclub.com
🖎 Mr Steven Alcock (01524) 412841
🖥 www.morecambegolfclub.com

## Mossock Hall (1996)
**Proprietary**
Liverpool Road, Bickerstaffe L39 0EE
☎ (01695) 421717
📠 (01695) 424961
✉ info@mossockhallgolfclub.co.uk
🖎 Mel Brooke
🖥 www.mossockhallgolfclub.co.uk

## Mytton Fold Hotel & Golf Complex (1994)
**Proprietary**
Whalley Road, Langho BB6 8AB
☎ (01254) 245392
📠 (01254) 248119
✉ golfshop@myttonfold.co.uk
🖎 Nigel Alcock
🖥 www.myttonfold.co.uk

## Nelson (1902)
Kings Causeway, Brierfield, Nelson BB9 0EU
☎ (01282) 611834
📠 (01282) 611834
✉ secretary@nelsongolfclub.com
🖎 Richard M Lees
🖥 www.nelsongolfclub.com

## Oak Royal Golf & Country Club (2008)
**Proprietary**
Bury Lane, Withnell, Nr Chorley PR6 8SW
☎ 01254 830616
✉ enquiries@oakroyalgolf-
countryclub.co.uk
🖎 Kath Downes
🖥 www.oakroyalgolf-
countryclub.co.uk

## Oldham (1892)
Lees New Road, Oldham OL4 5PN
☎ (0161) 624 4986
📠 (0161) 624 4986
✉ info@oldhamgolfclub.com
🖎 J Brooks

## Ormskirk (1899)
Cranes Lane, Lathom, Ormskirk L40 5UJ
☎ (01695) 572112
📠 (01695) 572227
✉ mail@ormskirkgolfclub.com
🖎 R K Oakes (01695) 572227
🖥 www.ormskirkgolfclub.com

## Pennington (1977)
**Public/Municipal**
Pennington Country Park, St Helens Road,
Leigh WN7 3PA
☎ (01942) 741873/
(01942) 682852 Shop
✉ penningtongolfclub@blueyonder
.co.uk
🖎 Mr B W Lythgoe
🖥 www.penningtongolfclub.co.uk

## Penwortham (1908)
Blundell Lane, Penwortham, Preston
PR1 0AX
☎ (01772) 744630
📠 (01772) 740172
✉ admin@penworthamgc.co.uk
🖎 N Annandale
🖥 www.penworthamgc.co.uk

## Pleasington   (1891)
Pleasington, Blackburn BB2 5JF
☎ **(01254) 202177**
✉ secretary-manager@pleasington-golf.co.uk
✍ C J Williams
🖥 www.pleasington-golf.co.uk

## Poulton-le-Fylde   (1982)
**Public**
Myrtle Farm, Breck Road, Poulton-le-Fylde
FY6 7HJ
☎ **(01253) 892444**
✉ greenwood-golf@hotmail.co.uk
✍ S Wilkinson
🖥 www.poultonlefyldegolfclub.co.uk

## Preston   (1892)
Fulwood Hall Lane, Fulwood, Preston
PR2 8DD
☎ **(01772) 700011**
🖳 (01772) 794234
✉ secretary@prestongolfclub.com
✍ Ed Burrow
🖥 www.prestongolfclub.com

## Regent Park (Bolton)   (1931)
**Pay and play**
Links Road, Chorley New Road, Bolton
BL6 4AF
☎ **(01204) 495421**
✍ N Brazell
(Professional) (01204) 495421
⊕ 18 hole Pay and Play. Food
Available. Club comps on
Saturdays.

## Rishton   (1927)
Eachill Links, Hawthorn Drive, Rishton
BB1 4HG
☎ **(01254) 884442**
🖳 (01254) 887701
✉ info@rishtongolfclub.co.uk
✍ Mr J Hargreaves MBE (Gen Mgr)
🖥 www.rishton-golf-club.co.uk

## Rochdale   (1888)
Edenfield Road, Bagslate, Rochdale
OL11 5YR
☎ **(01706) 643818 (Clubhouse)**
🖳 (01706) 861113
✉ admin@rochdalegolfclub.co.uk
✍ P Kershaw (01706) 643818 (opt 2)
🖥 www.rochdalegolfclub.co.uk

## Rossendale   (1903)
Ewood Lane Head, Haslingden, Rossendale
BB4 6LH
☎ **(01706) 831339**

🖳 (01706) 228669
✉ admin@rossendalegolfclub.net
✍ Mr J Pink
🖥 www.rossendalegolfclub.net

## Royal Lytham & St Annes
(1886)
Links Gate, Lytham St Annes FY8 3LQ
☎ **(01253) 724206**
🖳 (01253) 780946
✉ bookings@royallytham.org
✍ RJG Cochrane
🖥 www.royallytham.org

## Saddleworth   (1904)
Mountain Ash, Uppermill, Oldham OL3 6LT
☎ **(01457) 873653**
🖳 (01457) 820647
✉ generalmanager@saddleworthgolfcl ub.org.uk
✍ Alastair Griffiths
🖥 www.saddleworthgolfclub.co.uk

## Shaw Hill Hotel G&CC
(1925)
**Proprietary**
Preston Road, Whittle-le-Woods, Chorley
PR6 7PP
☎ **(01257) 269221**
🖳 (01257) 261223
✉ info@shaw-hill.co.uk
✍ Lawrence Bateson (Secretary)
🖥 www.shaw-hill.co.uk

## St Annes Old Links   (1901)
Highbury Road East, Lytham St Annes
FY8 2LD
☎ **(01253) 723597**
🖳 (01253) 781506
✉ secretary@stannesoldlinks.com
✍ Mrs Jane Donohoe
🖥 www.stannesoldlinks.com

## Standish Court   (1995)
**Pay and play**
Rectory Lane, Standish, Wigan WN6 0XD
☎ **(01257) 425777**
🖳 (01257) 425777
✉ info@standishgolf.co.uk
✍ S McGrath
🖥 www.standishgolf.co.uk

## Stonyhurst Park   (1979)
Stonyhurst, Hurst Green, Clitheroe BB7 9QB
☎ **(01254) 826072 (not manned)**
✉ gmonkspgc@gmail.com
✍ Mr Graham Monk (01200) 423191
🖥 www.stonyhurstpark.co.uk

## Towneley   (1932)
**Public**
Towneley Park, Todmorden Road, Burnley
BB11 3ED
☎ **(01282) 451636**
✉ secretary@towneleygolfclub.co.uk
✍ Peter Witt
🖥 www.towneleygolfclub.co.uk

## Tunshill   (1901)
Kiln Lane, Milnrow, Rochdale OL16 3TS
☎ **(01706) 342095**
✉ secretary@tunshillgolfclub.co.uk
✍ S Reade (01706) 342095
🖥 www.tunshillgolfclub.co.uk

## Turton   (1908)
Wood End Farm, Hospital Road, Bromley
Cross, Bolton BL7 9QD
☎ **(01204) 852235**
🖳 (01204) 856921
✉ info@turtongolfclub.com
✍ John Drabble
🖥 www.turtongolfclub.com

## Walmersley   (1906)
Garrett's Close, Walmersley, Bury BL9 6TE
☎ **(0161) 764 1429**
🖳 (0161) 764 7770
✉ walmersleygc@btconnect.com
✍ V Slater (0161) 764 7770
🖥 www.walmersleygolfclub.co.uk

## Werneth   (1909)
Green Lane, Garden Suburb, Oldham
OL8 3AZ
☎ **(0161) 624 1190**
✉ secretary@wernethgolfclub.co.uk
✍ JH Barlow
🖥 www.wernethgolfclub.co.uk

## Westhoughton   (1929)
Long Island, Westhoughton, Bolton BL5 2BR
☎ **(01942) 811085**
✉ honsec.wgc@btconnect.com
✍ Neil Robinson (07760) 754933
🖥 www.westhoughtongolfclub.co.uk

## Whalley   (1912)
Long Leese Barn, Clerkhill Road, Whalley
BB7 9DR
☎ **(01254) 822236**
🖳 (01254) 824766
✍ P R Benson (01282) 773354
🖥 www.whalleygolfclub.co.uk

## Whittaker   (1906)
Littleborough OL15 0LH
☎ **(01706) 378310**

---

# The Lytham Trophy

Founded by the Royal Lytham & St Annes Golf Club in 1965, the Lytham Trophy is a 72 hole scratch stroke play competition for amateur golfers and is classified as a Category A event by The R&A's World Amateur Golf Rankings.

Notable past winners include Sir Michael Bonallack, Peter McEvoy, Paul Broadhurst and Lloyd Saltman.

---

Paul Jones (07930) 569260
www.secretarywgc.com

## Wigan (1898)
Arley Hall, Haigh, Wigan WN1 2UH
☎ (01257) 421360
📠 (01257) 426500
✉ info@wigangolfclub.co.uk
✍ A Lawless (Ass Sec)
🖥 www.wigangolfclub.co.uk

## Wilpshire (1890)
72 Whalley Road, Wilpshire, Blackburn BB1 9LF
☎ (01254) 248260
📠 (01254) 246745
✉ admin@wilpshiregolfclub.co.uk
✍ D Hawksworth
🖥 www.wilpshiregolfclub.co.uk

# Leicestershire

## Beedles Lake (1993)
170 Broome Lane, East Goscote LE7 3WQ
☎ (0116) 260 6759/7086
📠 (0116) 269 4127
✉ joncoleman@jelson.co.uk
✍ Jon Coleman (Mgr)
🖥 www.beedleslake.co.uk

## Birstall (1900)
Station Road, Birstall, Leicester LE4 3BB
☎ (0116) 267 4450
✉ sue@birstallgolfclub.co.uk
✍ Mrs SE Chilton (0116) 267 4322
🖥 www.birstallgolfclub.co.uk

## Breedon Priory Golf Centre
(1990)
Green Lane, Wilson, Derby DE73 8LG
☎ (01332) 863081
✉ lee@breedonpriory.co.uk
✍ Lee Sheldon (Mgr)

## Charnwood Forest (1890)
Breakback Road, Woodhouse Eaves, Loughborough LE12 8TA
☎ (01509) 890259
✉ secretary@charnwoodforestgolfclub
   .com
✍ PK Field
🖥 www.charnwoodforestgolfclub.com

## Cosby (1895)
Chapel Lane, Broughton Road, Cosby, Leicester LE9 1RG
☎ (0116) 286 4759
📠 (0116) 286 4484
✉ secretary@cosbygolfclub.co.uk
✍ Frazer Baxter (0116) 286 4759 Opt 1
🖥 www.cosbygolfclub.co.uk

## Enderby (1986)
Public
Mill Lane, Enderby, Leicester LE19 4LX
☎ (0116) 284 9388
📠 (0116) 284 9388
🖥 www.enderbygolfshopandcourse
   .co.uk

## Forest Hill (1991)
Proprietary
Markfield Lane, Botcheston LE9 9FH
☎ (01455) 824800
📠 (01455) 828522
✉ admin@foresthillgolfclub.co.uk
✍ Rachel Crowden
🖥 www.foresthillgolfclub.co.uk

## Glen Gorse (1933)
Glen Road, Oadby, Leicester LE2 4RF
☎ (0116) 271 4159
📠 (0116) 271 4159
✉ secretary@gggc.org
✍ Mrs J James (0116) 271 4159
🖥 www.gggc.org

## Hinckley (1894)
Leicester Road, Hinckley LE10 3DR
☎ (01455) 615124
📠 (01455) 890841
✉ proshop@hinckleygolfclub.com
✍ R Mather (Sec) Catherine Merrie
   (Finance & Admin)
🖥 www.hinckleygolfclub.com

## Humberstone Heights (1978)
Public
Gipsy Lane, Leicester LE5 0TB
☎ (0116) 299 5570/1
✉ hhgc@talktalk.net
✍ Mrs M Weston
🖥 www.humberstoneheightsgc.co.uk

## Kibworth (1904)
Weir Road, Kibworth Beauchamp, Leicestershire LE8 0LP
☎ (0116) 279 2301
📠 (0116) 279 6434
✉ secretary@kibworthgolfclub
   .freeserve.co.uk
🖥 www.kibworthgolfclub.co.uk

## Kilworth Springs (1993)
Proprietary
South Kilworth Road, North Kilworth, Lutterworth LE17 6HJ
☎ (01858) 575082
📠 (01858) 575078
✉ admin@kilworthsprings.co.uk
✍ Jeremy Wilkinson (Manager)
🖥 www.kilworthsprings.co.uk

## Kirby Muxloe (1893)
Station Road, Kirby Muxloe, Leicester LE9 2EP
☎ (0116) 239 3457
📠 (0116) 238 8891
✉ kirbymuxloegolf@btconnect.com
✍ B N Whipham
   (Mgr/Professional) (0116) 239 3457
🖥 www.kirbymuxloe-golf.co.uk

## Lingdale (1967)
Joe Moore's Lane, Woodhouse Eaves, Loughborough LE12 8TF
☎ (01509) 890703
📠 (01509) 890703
✉ secretary@lingdalegolfclub.co.uk
✍ T Walker
🖥 www.lingdalegolfclub.co.uk

## Longcliffe (1906)
Snells Nook Lane, Nanpantan, Loughborough LE11 3YA
☎ (01509) 239129
📠 (01509) 231286
✉ secretary@longcliffegolf.co.uk
✍ Mr B Jones
🖥 www.longcliffegolf.co.uk

## Lutterworth (1904)
Rugby Road, Lutterworth, Leicestershire LE17 4HN
☎ (01455) 552532
📠 (01455) 553586
✉ sec@lutterworthgc.co.uk
✍ J Faulks (01455) 552532
🖥 www.lutterworthgc.co.uk

## Market Harborough (1898)
Great Oxendon Road, Market Harborough NE16 9NB
☎ (01858) 463684
📠 (01858) 432906
✉ proshop@mhgolf.co.uk
✍ F J Baxter
🖥 www.mhgolf.co.uk

## Melton Mowbray (1925)
Waltham Rd, Thorpe Arnold, Melton Mowbray LE14 4SD
☎ (01664) 562118
📠 (01664) 562118
✉ meltonmowbraygc@btconnect
   .com
✍ Sue Millward/Marilyn Connelly
🖥 www.mmgc.org

## Oadby (1974)
Public
Leicester Road, Oadby, Leicester LE2 4AJ
☎ (0116) 270 9052/270 0215
✉ secretaryogc@talktalk.net
✍ RA Primrose (0116) 270 3828
🖥 www.oadbygolfclub.co.uk

## Park Hill Golf Club (1994)
Proprietary
Park Hill, Seagrave LE12 7NG
☎ (01509) 815454
📠 (01509) 816062
✉ mail@parkhillgolf.co.uk
✍ JP Hutson
🖥 www.parkhillgolf.co.uk

## Rothley Park (1911)
Westfield Lane, Rothley, Leicester LE7 7LH
☎ (0116) 230 2809
📠 (0116) 237 4847
✉ clubmanager@rothleypark.co.uk
✍ Danny Spillane (Mgr) (0116) 230 2809
🖥 www.rothleypark.com

## Scraptoft (1928)
Beeby Road, Scraptoft, Leicester LE7 9SJ
☎ (0116) 241 9000
📠 (0116) 241 9000
✉ secretary@scraptoft-golf.co.uk
✍ Andy Mee (0116) 241 9000
🖥 www.scraptoft-golf.co.uk

## Six Hills   (1986)
**Pay and play**
*Six Hills, Melton Mowbray LE14 3PR*
☎ (01509) 881225
🖳 (01509) 881846
✍ Mrs J Showler

## Stapleford Park   (2000)
*Stapleford park, Melton Mowbray LE14 2EF*
☎ (01572) 787044
🖳 (01572) 787001
📧 clubs@stapleford.co.uk
✍ Richard Alderson
🖥 www.staplefordpark.com

## The Leicestershire   (1890)
*Evington Lane, Leicester LE5 6DJ*
☎ (0116) 273 8825
📧 secretary@theleicestershiregolfclub
.co.uk
✍ AJ Baxter (0116) 273 8825
🖥 www.theleicestershiregolfclub.co.uk

## Ullesthorpe Court Hotel
(1976)
**Proprietary**
*Frolesworth Road, Ullesthorpe, Lutterworth
LE17 5BZ*
☎ (01455) 209023
🖳 (01455) 202537
📧 bookings@ullesthorpecourt.co.uk
✍ AP Parr (ext 2446)
🖥 www.bw-ullesthorpecourt.co.uk

## Western Park   (1910)
**Public**
*Scudamore Road, Leicester LE3 1UQ*
☎ (0116) 287 5211
✍ Paul Williams
🖥 www.westerpkgc.co.uk

## Whetstone   (1965)
**Proprietary**
*Cambridge Road, Cosby, Leicester LE9 1SJ*
☎ (0116) 286 1424
🖳 (0116) 286 1424
✍ N Morris
🖥 www.whetstonegolfclub.co.uk

## Willesley Park   (1921)
*Measham Road, Ashby-de-la-Zouch
LE65 2PF*
☎ (01530) 414596
🖳 (01530) 564169
📧 info@willesleypark.com
✍ Tina Harlow (01530) 414596
🖥 www.willesleypark.com

## Lincolnshire

## Ashby Decoy   (1936)
*Ashby Decoy, Burringham Road, Scunthorpe
DN17 2AB*
☎ (01724) 866561
🖳 (01724) 271708
📧 secretary@ashbydecoy.co.uk
✍ Mrs J Harrison (01724) 866561
🖥 www.ashbydecoy.co.uk

## Belton Park   (1890)
*Belton Lane, Londonthorpe Road, Grantham
NG31 9SH*
☎ (01476) 567399
🖳 (01476) 592078
📧 greatgolf@beltonpark.co.uk
✍ S Rowley (01476) 542900
🖥 www.beltonpark.co.uk

## De Vere Belton Woods Hotel
(1991)
*Belton, Grantham NG32 2LN*
☎ (01476) 593200
🖳 (01476) 574547
📧 golf@devere.co.uk
✍ A Cameron (01476) 514364
🖥 www.devere.co.uk

## Blankney   (1904)
**Proprietary**
*Blankney, Lincoln LN4 3AZ*
☎ (01526) 320263
🖳 (01526) 322521
📧 manager@blankneygolfclub.co.uk
✍ G Bradley (01526) 320202
🖥 www.blankneygolfclub.co.uk

## Boston   (1900)
*Cowbridge, Horncastle Road, Boston
PE22 7EL*
☎ (01205) 350589
🖳 (01205) 367526
📧 secretary@bostongc.co.uk
✍ Nick Hiom (Dir of
   Golf) (01205) 362306
🖥 www.bostongc.co.uk

## Boston West   (1995)
**Proprietary**
*Hubbert's Bridge, Boston PE20 3QX*
☎ (01205) 290670
🖳 (01205) 290725
📧 info@bostonwestgolfclub.co.uk
✍ MJ Couture (01205) 290670
🖥 www.bostonwestgolfclub.co.uk

## Burghley Park   (1890)
*St Martin's, Stamford PE9 3JX*
☎ (01780) 753789
📧 secretary@burghleyparkgolfclub
.co.uk
✍ S Last (Sec/Mgr)
🖥 www.burghleyparkgolfclub.co.uk

## Canwick Park   (1893)
*Canwick Park, Washingborough Road,
Lincoln LN4 1EF*
☎ (01522) 542912/522166
📧 manager@canwickpark.org
✍ N Porteus (01522) 542912
🖥 www.canwickpark.org

## Carholme   (1906)
*Carholme Road, Lincoln LN1 1SE*
☎ (01522) 523725
🖳 (01522) 533733
📧 secretary@carholmegolfclub
.co.uk
✍ J Lammin
🖥 www.carholmegolfclub.co.uk

## Cleethorpes   (1894)
*Kings Road, Cleethorpes DN35 0PN*
☎ (01472) 816110 option 1
📧 secretary@cleethorpesgolfclub
.co.uk
✍ A J Thompson (01472) 816110
   option 3
🖥 www.cleethorpesgolfclub.co.uk

## Elsham   (1900)
*Barton Road, Elsham, Brigg DN20 0LS*
☎ (01652) 680291
🖳 (0872) 1113238
📧 office@elshamgolfclub.co.uk
✍ T Hartley (Mgr)
🖥 www.elshamgolfclub.co.uk

## Forest Pines Hotel & Golf
   Resort   (1996)
**Proprietary**
*Ermine Street, Brigg DN20 0AQ*
☎ (01652) 650756 Golf Shop
🖳 (01652) 650495
📧 forestpines@qhotels.co.uk
✍ Andrew Cook (Director of Golf)
🖥 www.qhotels.co.uk

## Gainsborough   (1894)
**Proprietary**
*Thonock, Gainsborough DN21 1PZ*
☎ (01427) 613088
📧 info@gainsboroughgc.co.uk
✍ S Keane (Operations Manager)
🖥 www.gainsboroughgc.co.uk

## Gedney Hill   (1991)
**Public**
*West Drove, Gedney End Hill PE12 0NT*
☎ (01406) 330922
🖳 (01945) 581903
✍ R Newns (01945) 581903

## Grange Park   (1992)
**Proprietary**
*Butterwick Road, Messingham, Scunthorpe
DN17 3PP*
☎ (01724) 762945
📧 info@grangepark.com
✍ I Cannon (Mgr)
🖥 www.grangepark.com

## Grimsby   (1922)
*Littlecoates Road, Grimsby DN34 4LU*
☎ (01472) 342630 (Clubhouse)
   356981 (Pro-S
🖳 (01472) 342630
📧 manager@grimsbygolfclub.co.uk
✍ Jon Tyson (01472) 342630
🖥 www.grimsbygolfclub.com

## Holme Hall   (1908)
*Holme Lane, Bottesford, Scunthorpe
DN16 3RF*
☎ (01724) 862078
🖳 (01724) 862081
📧 secretary@holmehallgolf.co.uk
✍ Gerald Pearce
🖥 www.holmehallgolf.co.uk

## Horncastle   (1990)
*West Ashby, Horncastle LN9 5PP*
☎ (01507) 526800

- (01507) 517069
- info@horncastlegolfclub.co.uk
- C Redfearn
- www.horncastlegolfclub.co.uk

## Humberston Park
Humberston Avenue, Humberston
DN36 4SJ
- **(01472) 210404**
- RTrish Neal (01472) 825822

## Immingham    (1975)
St Andrews Lane, Off Church Lane,
Immingham DN40 2EU
- **(01469) 575298**
- (01469) 577636
- C Todd (Mgr)
- www.immgc.com

## Kenwick Park    (1992)
Kenwick, Louth LN11 8NY
- **(01507) 605134**
- (01507) 606556
- secretary@kenwickparkgolf.co.uk
- C James (Gen Mgr)
- www.kenwickparkgolf.co.uk

## Kirton Holme    (1992)
**Proprietary**
Holme Road, Kirton Holme, Boston
PE20 1SY
- **(01205) 290669**
- Mrs T Welberry
- www.kirtonholmegolfcourse.com

## Lincoln    (1891)
Torksey, Lincoln LN1 2EG
- **(01427) 718721**
- (01427) 718721
- manager@lincolngc.co.uk
- Craig Innes
- ⊕ Twitter;- @lincolngc
- www.lincolngc.co.uk

## Louth    (1965)
Crowtree Lane, Louth LN11 9LJ
- **(01507) 603681**
- (01507) 608501
- louthgolfclub@btconnect.com
- Simon Moody (Gen Mgr)
- www.louthgolfclub.com

## Market Rasen & District
(1912)
Legsby Road, Market Rasen LN8 3DZ
- **(01673) 842319**
- (01673) 849245
- marketrasengolf@onetel.net
- JP Smith
- www.marketrasengolfclub.co.uk

## Market Rasen Racecourse
(1990)
**Pay and play**
Legsby Road, Market Rasen LN8 3EA
- **(01673) 843434**
- (01673) 844532
- marketrasen
  @jockeyclubracecourses.com
- www.marketrasenraces.co.uk

## Martin Moor    (1993)
**Proprietary**
Martin Road, Blankney LN4 3BE
- **(01526) 378243**
- enquiries@martinmoorgolfclub
  .co.uk
- Alan Roberts/Carole Roberts
- ⊕ 9 hole course with 18 seperate
  tees. Visitors/Societies/Corporate
  events welcome

## Millfield    (1984)
**Proprietary**
Laughterton, Lincoln LN1 2LB
- **(01427) 718473**
- millfieldgolfclub@gmail.com
- John Thomson (Sec)
- www.millfieldgolfclub.co.uk

## North Shore    (1910)
**Proprietary**
North Shore Road, Skegness PE25 1DN
- **(01754) 763298**
- (01754) 761902
- info@northshorehotel.co.uk
- B Howard (07765 223848)
- www.northshorehotel.co.uk

## Pottergate    (1992)
Moor Lane, Branston, Lincoln
- **(01522) 794867**
- (01522) 794867
- pottergategc@hotmail.co.uk
- Lee Tasker
- www.pottergategolfclub.co.uk

## RAF Coningsby    (1972)
RAF Coningsby, Lincoln LN4 4SY
- **(01526) 342581 Ext 6828**
- N Parsons (01526) 347946

## Sandilands    (1901)
**Proprietary**
Sandilands, Sutton-on-Sea LN12 2RJ
- **(01507) 441432**
- (01507) 441617
- sandilandsgolf@googlemail.com
- Simon Sherratt (Pro/Mgr)
- www.sandilandsgolfclub.co.uk

## Seacroft    (1895)
Drummond Road, Seacroft, Skegness
PE25 3AU
- **(01754) 763020**
- (01754) 763020
- enquiries@seacroft-golfclub.co.uk
- R England (Mgr)
- www.seacroft-golfclub.co.uk

## Sleaford    (1905)
Willoughby Road, Greylees, Sleaford, Lincs
NG34 8PL
- **(01529) 488273**
- manager@sleafordgolfclub.co.uk
- Mr N Porteus
- www.sleafordgolfclub.co.uk

## South Kyme    (1990)
Skinners Lane, South Kyme, Lincoln
LN4 4AT
- **(01526) 861113**
- (01526) 861080

- southkymegc@hotmail.com
- P Chamberlain
- www.skgc.co.uk

## Spalding    (1907)
Surfleet, Spalding PE11 4EA
- **(01775) 680386**
- (01775) 680988
- secretary@spaldinggolfclub.co.uk
- Mr Chris Huggins (01775) 680386
- www.spaldinggolfclub.co.uk

## Stoke Rochford    (1924)
Great North Rd, Grantham NG33 5EW
- **(01476) 530275**
- (01476) 530237
- secretary@stokerochfordgolfclub
  .co.uk
- A J Wheeler
- www.stokerochfordgolfclub.co.uk

## Sudbrook Moor    (1991)
**Public**
Charity Street, Carlton Scroop, Grantham
NG32 3AT
- **(01400) 250796 all enquiries**
- Judith Hutton
- www.sudbrookmoor.co.uk

## Sutton Bridge    (1914)
New Road, Sutton Bridge, Spalding
PE12 9RQ
- **(01406) 350323 (Clubhouse)**
- secretary@sbgolfclub.plus.com
- Colin Fawcett (01945) 583656
- www.club-noticeboard.co.uk
  /suttonbridge

## Tetney    (1993)
Station Road, Tetney, Grimsby DN36 5HY
- **(01472) 211644**
- (01472) 211644
- J Abrams

## The Manor Golf Club Laceby
(1992)
**Proprietary**
Laceby Manor, Laceby, Grimsby DN37 7LD
- **(01472) 873468**
- gemma@lacebymanorgolfclub
  .co.uk
- Mrs Gemma Gibney (Club Sec)
- www.lacebymanorgolfclub.co.uk

## Toft Hotel    (1988)
**Proprietary**
Toft, Bourne PE10 0JT
- **(01778) 590616**
- (01778) 590264
- R Morris (01778) 590654
- www.thetofthotelgolfclub.com

## Waltham Windmill    (1997)
**Proprietary**
Cheapside, Waltham, Grimsby
DN37 0HT
- **(01472) 824109**
- (01472) 828391
- S Bennett (01472) 821883
- www.walthamgolf.co.uk

## Welton Manor    (1995)
**Proprietary**
*Hackthorn Road, Welton LN2 3PA*
- ☎ **(01673) 862827**
- 📠 (01673) 861888
- 📧 info@weltonmanorgolfcentre.co.uk
- ✍ David Ottenell/Hayley Olliver
- 🖥 www.weltonmanorgolfcentre.co.uk

## Woodhall Spa    (1891)
**Proprietary**
*Woodhall Spa LN10 6PU*
- ☎ **(01526) 352511**
- 📠 (01526) 351817
- 📧 booking@woodhallspagolf.com
- ✍ Richard A Latham
- 🖥 www.woodhallspagolf.com

## Woodthorpe Hall    (1986)
*Woodthorpe, Alford LN13 0DD*
- ☎ **(01507) 450000**
- 📠 (01507) 450000
- 📧 woodthorpehallgolfclub@live.co.uk
- ✍ Joan Smith (01507) 450000
- 🖥 www.woodthorpehall.co.uk

### London Clubs

**Aquarius** *Kent*
**Bush Hill Park** *Middlesex*
**Central London Golf Centre** *Surrey*
**Chingford** *Essex*
**Dulwich & Sydenham Hill** *Surrey*
**Eltham Warren** *Kent*
**Finchley** *Middlesex*
**Hampstead** *Middlesex*
**Hendon** *Middlesex*
**Highgate** *Middlesex*
**Leaside** *Middlesex*
**London Scottish** *Surrey*
**Mill Hill** *Middlesex*
**Muswell Hill** *Middlesex*
**North Middlesex** *Middlesex*
**Richmond Park** *Surrey*
**Roehampton Club** *Surrey*
**Royal Blackheath** *Kent*
**Royal Epping Forest** *Essex*
**Royal Mid-Surrey** *Surrey*
**Royal Wimbledon** *Surrey*
**Shooter's Hill** *Kent*
**South Herts** *Hertfordshire*
**Thameside Golf Centre** *Kent*
**Trent Park** *Middlesex*
**Wanstead** *Essex*
**West Essex** *Essex*
**Wimbledon Common** *Surrey*
**Wimbledon Park** *Surrey*

### Manchester

## Blackley    (1907)
*Victoria Avenue East, Manchester M9 7HW*
- ☎ **(0161) 643 2980**
- 📠 (0161) 653 8300
- 📧 office@blackleygolfclub.com
- ✍ B Beddoes (0161) 654 7770
- 🖥 www.blackleygolfclub.com

## Boysnope Park    (1998)
**Proprietary**
*Liverpool Road, Barton Moss, Eccles M30 7RF*
- ☎ **(0161) 707 6125**
- 📠 (0161) 707 1888
- 📧 karensmith63@btconnect.com
- ✍ Jean Stringer (0161) 707 6125
- 🖥 www.boysnopegolfclub.co.uk

## Chorlton-cum-Hardy    (1902)
*Barlow Hall, Barlow Hall Road, Manchester M21 7JJ*
- ☎ **(0161) 881 3139**
- 📠 (0161) 881 4532
- 📧 chorltongolf@hotmail.com
- ✍ IR Booth (0161) 881 5830
- 🖥 www.chorltoncumhardygolfclub.co.uk

## Davyhulme Park    (1911)
*Gleneagles Road, Davyhulme, Manchester M41 8SA*
- ☎ **(0161) 748 2260**
- 📠 (0161) 747 4067
- 📧 davyhulmeparkgolfclub@email.com
- ✍ GR Swarbrick
- 🖥 www.davyhulmeparkgc.info

## Denton    (1909)
*Manchester Road, Denton, Manchester M34 2GG*
- ☎ **(0161) 336 3218**
- 📠 (0161) 336 4751
- 📧 info@dentongolfclub.com
- ✍ ID McIlvanney
- 🖥 www.dentongolfclub.com

## Didsbury    (1891)
*Ford Lane, Northenden, Manchester M22 4NQ*
- ☎ **(0161) 998 9278**
- 📠 (0161) 902 3060
- 📧 golf@didsburygolfclub.com
- ✍ John K Mort (Mgr)
- 🖥 www.didsburygolfclub.com

## Ellesmere    (1913)
*Old Clough Lane, Worsley, Manchester M28 7HZ*
- ☎ **(0161) 790 2122**
- 📠 (0161) 790 2122
- 📧 honsec@ellesmeregolfclub.co.uk
- ✍ Mrs J A Westley (Hon Sec)
- 🖥 www.ellesmeregolfclub.co.uk

## Fairfield Golf & Sailing Club    (1892)
*Booth Road, Audenshaw, Manchester M34 5QA*
- ☎ **(0161) 301 4528**
- 📧 manager@fairfieldgolfclub.co.uk
- ✍ John Paton (Mgr)
- 🖥 www.fairfieldgolfclub.co.uk

## Flixton    (1893)
*Church Road, Flixton, Urmston, Manchester M41 6EP*
- ☎ **(0161) 748 2116**
- 📠 (0161) 748 2116
- 📧 flixtongolfclub@mail.com
- ✍ A Braithwaite
- 🖥 www.flixtongolfclub.co.uk

## Great Lever & Farnworth    (1901)
*Plodder Lane, Farnworth, Bolton BL4 0LQ*
- ☎ **(01204) 656493**
- 📠 (01204) 656137
- 📧 greatlever@btconnect.com
- ✍ MJ Ivill (01204) 656137

## Heaton Park Golf Centre    (1912)
**Pay and play**
*Heaton Park, Middleton Road, Prestwich M25 2SW*
- ☎ **(0161) 654 9899**
- 📠 (0161) 653 2003
- 📧 hpbookings@macktrading.net
- ✍ Brian Dique (Gen Mgr)
- 🖥 www.mackgolf.co.uk

## New North Manchester    (1923)
*Rhodes House, Manchester Old Road, Middleton M24 4PE*
- ☎ **(0161) 643 9033**
- 📠 (0161) 643 7775
- 📧 tee@nmgc.co.uk
- ✍ G Heaslip
- 🖥 www.northmanchestergolfclub.co.uk

## Northenden    (1913)
*Palatine Road, Manchester M22 4FR*
- ☎ **(0161) 998 4738**
- 📠 (0161) 945 5592
- 📧 secretary@northendengolfclub.com
- ✍ Paul Bayley (Gen Mgr)
- 🖥 www.northendengolfclub.com

## Old Manchester    (1818)
**Club**
- ☎ **(0161) 766 4157**
- ✍ PT Goodall

## Pike Fold    (1909)
*Hills Lane, Pole Lane, Unsworth, Bury BL9 8QP*
- ☎ **(0161) 766 3561**
- 📠 (0161) 351 2189
- 📧 secretary@pikefold.co.uk
- ✍ Martin Jeffs (Secretary)
- 🖥 www.pikefold.co.uk

## Prestwich    (1908)
*Hilton Lane, Prestwich M25 9XB*
- ☎ **(0161) 772 0700**
- 📠 (0161) 772 0700
- 📧 prestwichgolf@btconnect.com
- ✍ R Mason
- 🖥 www.prestwichgolf.co.uk

## Stand    (1904)
*The Dales, Ashbourne Grove, Whitefield, Manchester M45 7NL*
- ☎ **(0161) 766 2388**
- 📠 (0161) 796 3234
- 📧 secretary@standgolfclub.co.uk
- ✍ M A Cowsill (0161) 766 3197
- 🖥 www.standgolfclub.co.uk

## Swinton Park (1906)
*East Lancashire Road, Swinton, Manchester M27 5LX*
- ☎ (0161) 794 0861
- 🖴 (0161) 281 0698
- ✉ info@spgolf.co.uk
- ✎ Barbara Wood
- 🖥 www.spgolf.co.uk

## The Manchester (1882)
*Hopwood Cottage, Rochdale Road, Middleton, Manchester M24 6QP*
- ☎ (0161) 643 3202
- 🖴 (0161) 643 3202
- ✉ secretary@mangc.co.uk
- ✎ Stephen Armstead
- 🖥 www.mangc.co.uk

## Whitefield (1932)
*Higher Lane, Whitefield, Manchester M45 7EZ*
- ☎ (0161) 351 2700
- 🖴 (0161) 351 2712
- ✉ enquiries@whitefieldgolfclub.com
- ✎ Mrs M Rothwell
- 🖥 www.whitefieldgolfclub.co.uk

## Withington (1892)
*243 Palatine Road, West Didsbury, Manchester M20 2UE*
- ☎ (0161) 445 9544
- 🖴 (0161) 445 5210
- ✉ secretary@withingtongolfclub.co.uk
- ✎ PJ Keane
- 🖥 www.withingtongolfclub.co.uk

## Worsley (1894)
*Stableford Avenue, Monton Green, Eccles, Manchester M30 8AP*
- ☎ (0161) 789 4202
- 🖴 (0161) 789 3200
- ✉ office@worsleygolfclub.co.uk
- ✎ J D Clarke
- 🖥 www.worsleygolfclub.co.uk

# Merseyside

## Allerton Municipal (1934)
**Public**
*Allerton Road, Liverpool L18 3JT*
- ☎ (0151) 428 1046

## Arrowe Park (1931)
**Public**
*Arrowe Park, Woodchurch, Birkenhead CH49 5LW*
- ☎ (0151) 677 1527,
  (0151) 678 5285
- ✉ contact@arroweparkgolfclub.co.uk
- ✎ P Hickey
- 🖥 www.arroweparkgolfclub.co.uk

## Bidston (1913)
*Bidston Link Road, Wallasey, Wirral CH44 2HR*
- ☎ (0151) 638 3412
- ✉ info@bidstongolf.co.uk
- 🖥 www.bidstongolf.co.uk

## Bootle (1934)
**Pay and play**
*Dunnings Bridge Road, Litherland L30 2PP*
- ☎ (0151) 928 1371
- 🖴 (0151) 949 1815
- ✉ bootlegolfcourse@btconnect.com
- ✎ G Howarth

## Bowring (1913)
**Public**
*Bowring Park, Roby Road, Huyton L36 4HD*
- ☎ (0151) 489 1901
- ✉ dgwalker36@tiscali.co.uk
- ✎ W Earps (0151) 480 6859

## Brackenwood (1933)
**Public**
*Bracken Lane, Bebington, Wirral L63 2LY*
- ☎ (0151) 608 3093
- ✉ secretary@brackenwoodgolf.co.uk
- ✎ GW Brogan (0151) 339 9817
- 🖥 www.brackenwoodgolf.co.uk

## Bromborough (1903)
*Raby Hall Road, Bromborough CH63 0NW*
- ☎ (0151) 334 2155
- 🖴 (0151) 334 7300
- ✉ enquiries@bromboroughgolfclub.org.uk
- ✎ Alisdair Mackay (0151) 334 2155
- 🖥 www.bromboroughgolfclub.org.uk

## Caldy (1907)
*Links Hey Road, Caldy, Wirral CH48 1NB*
- ☎ (0151) 625 5660
- 🖴 (0151) 625 7394
- ✉ secretarycaldygc@btconnect.com
- ✎ Gail M Copple
- 🖥 www.caldygolfclub.co.uk

## Childwall (1912)
*Naylors Road, Gateacre, Liverpool L27 2YB*
- ☎ (0151) 487 0654
- 🖴 (0151) 487 0654
- ✉ office@childwallgolfclub.co.uk
- ✎ Peter Bowen
- 🖥 www.childwallgolfclub.co.uk

## Eastham Lodge (1973)
*117 Ferry Road, Eastham, Wirral CH62 0AP*
- ☎ (0151) 327 3003 (Clubhouse)
- 🖴 (0151) 327 7574
- ✉ easthamlodge.g.c@btinternet.com
- ✎ Mr Nick Sargent (Director of Golf)
- 🖥 www.easthamlodgegolfclub.co.uk

## Formby (1884)
*Golf Road, Formby, Liverpool L37 1LQ*
- ☎ (01704) 872164
- 🖴 (01704) 833028
- ✉ info@formbygolfclub.co.uk
- ✎ M Betteridge (01704) 872164
- 🖥 www.formbygolfclub.co.uk

## Formby Hall Golf Resort & Spa (1996)
**Proprietary**
*Southport Old Road, Formby L37 1NN*
- ☎ (01704) 875699
- 🖴 (01704) 832134
- ✉ golf@formbyhallgolfresort.co.uk
- 🖥 www.formbyhallgolfresort.co.uk

## Formby Ladies' (1896)
*Golf Road, Formby, Liverpool L37 1YH*
- ☎ (01704) 873493
- 🖴 (01704) 874127
- ✉ secretary@formbyladiesgolfclub.co.uk
- ✎ Mrs CA Bromley (01704) 873493
- 🖥 www.formbyladiesgolfclub.co.uk

## Grange Park (1891)
*Prescot Road, St Helens WA10 3AD*
- ☎ (01744) 22980 (Members)
- 🖴 (01744) 26318
- ✉ secretary@grangeparkgolfclub.co.uk
- ✎ G Brown (01744) 26318
- 🖥 www.grangeparkgolfclub.co.uk

## Haydock Park (1877)
*Golborne Park, Newton Lane, Newton-le-Willows WA12 0HX*
- ☎ (01925) 228525
- 🖴 (01925) 224984
- ✉ secretary@haydockparkgc.co.uk
- ✎ David Hughes
- 🖥 www.haydockparkgc.co.uk

## Hesketh (1885)
*Cockle Dick's Lane, Cambridge Road, Southport PR9 9QQ*
- ☎ (01704) 536897
- 🖴 (01704) 539250
- ✉ secretary@heskethgolfclub.co.uk
- ✎ N P Annandale
  (Sec) (01704) 536897 ext 1
- 🖥 www.heskethgolfclub.co.uk

## Heswall (1902)
*Cottage Lane, Gayton, Heswall CH60 8PB*
- ☎ (0151) 342 1237
- 🖴 (0151) 342 6140
- ✉ dawn@heswallgolfclub.com
- ✎ Graham Capewell (Manager)
- 🖥 www.heswallgolfclub.com

## Hillside (1911)
*Hastings Road, Hillside, Southport PR8 2LU*
- ☎ (01704) 567169
- 🖴 (01704) 563192
- ✉ secretary@hillside-golfclub.co.uk
- ✎ SH Newland (01704) 567169
- 🖥 www.hillside-golfclub.co.uk

## Houghwood (1996)
**Proprietary**
*Billinge Hill, Crank Road, Crank, St Helens WA11 8RL*
- ☎ (01744) 894754
- ✉ office@houghwoodgolf.co.uk
- ✎ P Turner (Man Dir)
- 🖥 www.houghwoodgolfclub.co.uk

## Hoylake Municipal (1933)
**Public**
*Carr Lane, Hoylake, Wirral CH47 4BG*
- ☎ (0151) 632 2956/4883 (Bookings)
- ✎ P Davies (0151) 632 0523
- 🖥 www.hoylakegolfclub.com

## Huyton & Prescot    (1905)
*Hurst Park, Huyton Lane, Huyton L36 1UA*
- ☎ **(0151) 489 3948**
- 🖥 (0151) 489 0797
- ✉ secretary@huytonandprescotgolf
  .co.uk
- ⛳ L Griffin(0151) 489 3948
- 🖥 www.huytonandprescot
  .myprogolfer.co.uk

## Leasowe    (1891)
*Leasowe Road, Moreton, Wirral CH46 3RD*
- ☎ **(0151) 677 5852**
- 🖥 (0151) 641 8519
- ✉ secretary@leasowegolfclub.co.uk
- ⛳ David Knight (0151) 677 5852
- 🖥 www.leasowegolfclub.co.uk

## Lee Park    (1954)
*Childwall Valley Road, Gateacre, Liverpool L27 3YA*
- ☎ **(0151) 487 3882 (Clubhouse)**
- 🖥 (0151) 498 4666
- ✉ lee.park@virgin.net
- ⛳ Steve Settle
- 🖥 www.leepark.co.uk

## Prenton    (1905)
*Golf Links Road, Prenton, Birkenhead CH42 8LW*
- ☎ **(0151) 609 3426**
- ✉ nigel.brown@prentongolfclub
  .co.uk
- ⛳ N Brown
- 🖥 www.prentongolfclub.co.uk

## RLGC Village Play    (1895)
**Club**
*c/o 18 Waverley Road, Hoylake, Wirral CH47 3DD*
- ☎ **(07885) 507263**
- 🖥 (0151) 632 5156
- ✉ pdwbritesparks@sky.com
- ⛳ PD Williams (0151) 632 5156

## Royal Birkdale    (1889)
*Waterloo Road, Birkdale, Southport PR8 2LX*
- ☎ **(01704) 552020**
- 🖥 (01704) 552021
- ✉ secretary@royalbirkdale.com
- ⛳ Mike Gilyeat (Sec)
- 🖥 www.royalbirkdale.com

## Royal Liverpool    (1869)
*Meols Drive, Hoylake CH47 4AL*
- ☎ **(0151) 632 3101/3102**
- 🖥 (0151) 632 6737
- ✉ secretary@royal-liverpool-golf.com
- ⛳ D R Cromie
- 🖥 www.royal-liverpool-golf.com

## Sherdley Park Municipal    (1974)
**Public**
*Eltonhead Road, Sutton, St Helens, Merseyside WA9 5DE*
- ☎ **(01744) 813149**
- 🖥 (01744) 817967
- ✉ sherdleyparkgolfcourse@sthelens
  .gov.uk
- ⛳ Ian Corice (Mgr)
- 🖥 www.sthelens.gov.uk/goactive

## Southport & Ainsdale    (1906)
*Bradshaws Lane, Ainsdale, Southport PR8 3LG*
- ☎ **(01704) 578000**
- 🖥 (01704) 570896
- ✉ secretary@sandagolfclub.co.uk
- ⛳ Ryan O'Connor
- 🖥 www.sandagolfclub.co.uk

## Southport Golf Links    (1912)
**Public**
*Park Road West, Southport PR9 0JS*
- ☎ **(01704) 535286**

## Southport Old Links    (1926)
*Moss Lane, Southport PR9 7QS*
- ☎ **(01704) 228207**
- ✉ secretary
  @southportoldlinksgolfclub.co.uk
- ⛳ BE Kenyon
- 🖥 www.southportoldlinksgolfclub
  .co.uk

## Wallasey    (1891)
*Bayswater Road, Wallasey CH45 8LA*
- ☎ **(0151) 691 1024**
- 🖥 (0151) 638 8988
- ✉ office@wallaseygolfclub.com
- ⛳ John K Mort (Mgr)
- 🖥 www.wallaseygolfclub.com

## Warren    (1911)
**Public**
*Grove Road, Wallasey, Wirral CH45 0JA*
- ☎ **(0151) 639 8323 (Clubhouse)**
- ⛳ KE McCormack (0151) 678 0330
- 🖥 www.warrengc.freeserve.co.uk

## West Derby    (1896)
*Yew Tree Lane, Liverpool L12 9HQ*
- ☎ **(0151) 254 1034**
- 🖥 (0151) 259 0505
- ✉ secretary@westderbygc.co.uk
- ⛳ Karen Buck
- 🖥 www.westderbygc.co.uk

## West Lancashire    (1873)
*Hall Road West, Blundellsands, Liverpool L23 8SZ*
- ☎ **(0151) 924 1076**
- 🖥 (0151) 931 4448
- ✉ sec@westlancashiregolf.co.uk
- ⛳ S King (0151) 924 1076
- 🖥 www.westlancashiregolf.co.uk

## Wirral Ladies    (1894)
*93 Bidston Road, Birkenhead, Wirral CH43 6TS*
- ☎ **(0151) 652 1255**
- 🖥 (0151) 651 3775
- ✉ wirral.ladies@btconnect.com
- ⛳ Mr P Greville
- 🖥 www.wirral-ladies-golf-club.co.uk

## Woolton    (1900)
*Doe Park, Speke Road, Woolton, Liverpool L25 7TZ*
- ☎ **(0151) 486 2298**
- 🖥 (0151) 486 1664
- ✉ golf@wooltongolf.co.uk
- ⛳ Miss T Rawlinson (0151) 486 2298 opt 4
- 🖥 www.wooltongolf.com

# Middlesex

## Airlinks    (1984)
**Public**
*Southall Lane, Hounslow TW5 9PE*
- ☎ **(020) 8561 1418**
- 🖥 (020) 8813 6284
- ⛳ S Brewster

## Ashford Manor    (1898)
*Fordbridge Road, Ashford TW15 3RT*
- ☎ **(01784) 424644**
- 🖥 (01784) 424649
- ✉ secretary@amgc.co.uk
- ⛳ Peter Dawson (Business Manager)
- 🖥 www.amgc.co.uk

## Brent Valley    (1909)
**Public**
*Church Road, Hanwell, London W7 3BE*
- ☎ **(020) 8567 4230 (Clubhouse)**
- ⛳ Ms M Griffin

## Bush Hill Park    (1895)
*Bush Hill, Winchmore Hill, London N21 2BU*
- ☎ **(020) 8360 5738**
- 🖥 (020) 8360 5583
- ✉ chris@bhpgc.com
- ⛳ Lee Fickling (Director of Golf)
- 🖥 www.bhpgc.com

## Crews Hill    (1916)
*Cattlegate Road, Crews Hill, Enfield EN2 8AZ*
- ☎ **(020) 8363 6674**
- ✉ manager@crewshillgolfclub.com
- ⛳ Brian Cullen
- 🖥 www.crewshillgolfclub.com

## David Lloyd Hampton Golf Club    (1977)
**Pay and play**
*Staines Road, Twickenham TW2 5JD*
- ☎ **(0208) 783 1698**
- 🖥 (0208) 783 9475
- ✉ golf.hampton@davidlloyd.co.uk
- ⛳ Jamie Skinner
- 🖥 www.davidlloyd.co.uk

## Ealing    (1898)
*Perivale Lane, Greenford UB6 8TS*
- ☎ **(020) 8997 0937**
- 🖥 (020) 8998 0756
- ✉ info@ealinggolfclub.co.uk
- ⛳ David Jones
- 🖥 www.ealinggolfclub.co.uk

## Enfield    (1893)
*Old Park Road South, Enfield EN2 7DA*
- ☎ **(020) 8363 3970**
- 🖥 (020) 8342 0381
- ✉ secretary@enfieldgolfclub.co.uk
- 🖥 www.enfieldgolfclub.co.uk

## Finchley    (1929)
*Nether Court, Frith Lane, London NW7 1PU*
- ☎ **(020) 8346 2436**
- 🖥 (020) 8343 4205
- ✉ secretary@finchleygolfclub.co.uk
- 🖥 www.finchleygolfclub.co.uk

## Fulwell (1904)
Wellington Road, Hampton Hill TW12 1JY
- ☎ (020) 8977 2733
- 🖶 (020) 8977 7732
- ✉ secretary@fulwellgolfclub.co.uk
- 🖎 Sean Whelan
- 🖥 www.fulwellgolfclub.co.uk

## Grim's Dyke (1909)
Oxhey Lane, Hatch End, Pinner HA5 4AL
- ☎ (020) 8428 4539
- 🖶 (020) 8421 5494
- ✉ secretary@grimsdyke.co.uk
- 🖎 R Jones (020) 8428 4539
- 🖥 www.club-noticeboard.co.uk /grimsdyke

## Hampstead (1893)
82 Winnington Road, London N2 0TU
- ☎ (020) 8455 0203
- 🖶 (020) 8731 6194
- ✉ secretary@hampsteadgolfclub.co.uk
- 🖎 Mark Smith
- 🖥 www.hampsteadgolfclub.co.uk

## Harrow Hill Golf Course (1982)
Public
Kenton Road, Harrow, Middx HA1 2BW
- ☎ (0208) 8643754
- ✉ info@harrowgolf.co.uk
- 🖎 S Bishop
- 🖥 www.harrowgolf.co.uk

## Harrow School (1978)
High Street, Harrow-on-the-Hill HA1 3HP
- ☎ (0208) 872 8000
- ✉ hsgcsecretary@harrowschool.org.uk
- 🖎 W K Driver (0208) 423 0604
- 🖥 www.harrowschoolgolfclub.co.uk

## Haste Hill (1930)
Public
The Drive, Northwood HA6 1HN
- ☎ (01923) 825224
- 🖶 (01923) 826485
- ✉ hastehillgc@yahoo.co.uk
- 🖎 S Cella

## Heath Park (1975)
Stockley Road, West Drayton UB7 9NA
- ☎ (01895) 444232
- ✉ heathparkgolf@yahoo.co.uk
- 🖎 B Sharma (Prop)
- 🖥 www.heathparkgolf.com

## Hendon (1903)
Ashley Walk, Devonshire Road, London NW7 1DG
- ☎ (020) 8346 6023
- 🖶 (020) 8343 1974
- ✉ admin@hendongolf.com
- 🖎 Gabriela Segal (Asst. Sec)
- 🖥 www.hendongolf.com

## Highgate (1904)
Denewood Road, Highgate, London N6 4AH
- ☎ (020) 8340 1906
- 🖶 (020) 8348 9152
- ✉ admin@highgategc.co.uk
- 🖎 N Sinclair (020) 8340 1906
- 🖥 www.highgategc.co.uk

## Horsenden Hill (1935)
Public
Woodland Rise, Greenford UB6 0RD
- ☎ (020) 8902 4555
- ✉ hhgchonsec@aol.com
- 🖎 John Leach (0208) 922 3472
- 🖥 www.horsendenhillgolfclub.co.uk

## Hounslow Heath (1979)
Public
Staines Road, Hounslow TW4 5DS
- ☎ (020) 8570 5271
- 🖶 (020) 8570 5205
- ✉ golf@hhgc.uk.com
- 🖎 J Swanson
- 🖥 www.hhgc.uk.com

## Leaside GC (1974)
Pay and play
Lee Valley Leisure, Picketts Lock Lane, Edmonton, London N9 0AS
- ☎ (020) 8803 3611

## Mill Hill (1925)
100 Barnet Way, Mill Hill, London NW7 3AL
- ☎ (020) 8959 2339
- 🖶 (020) 8906 0731
- ✉ cluboffice@millhillgc.co.uk
- 🖎 David Beal
- 🖥 www.millhillgc.co.uk

## Muswell Hill (1893)
Rhodes Avenue, London N22 7UT
- ☎ (020) 8888 1764
- 🖶 (020) 8889 9380
- ✉ manager@muswellhillgolfclub.co.uk
- 🖎 A Hobbs (020) 8888 1764
- 🖥 www.muswellhillgolfclub.co.uk

## North Middlesex (1905)
The Manor House, Friern Barnet Lane, Whetstone, London N20 0NL
- ☎ (020) 8445 1604
- 🖶 (020) 8445 5023
- ✉ manager@northmiddlesexgc.co.uk
- 🖎 Mr Howard Till
- 🖥 www.northmiddlesexgc.co.uk

## Northwood (1891)
Rickmansworth Road, Northwood HA6 2QW
- ☎ (01923) 821384
- 🖶 (01923) 840150
- ✉ secretary@northwoodgolf.co.uk
- 🖎 S Proudfoot
- 🖥 www.northwoodgolf.co.uk

## Perivale Park (1932)
Public
Stockdove Way, Argyle Road, Greenford UB6 8JT
- ☎ (020) 8575 7116
- 🖎 J Mealyer

## Pinner Hill (1927)
Southview Road, Pinner Hill HA5 3YA
- ☎ (020) 8866 0963
- 🖶 (020) 8868 4817
- ✉ phgc@pinnerhillgc.com
- 🖎 Alan Findlater (Gen Mgr)
- 🖥 www.pinnerhillgc.com

## Playgolf London
Watford Road, Harrow HA1 3TZ
- ☎ (0208) 864 2020
- ✉ london@playgolfworld.com
- 🖥 www.playgolf-london.com

## Ruislip (1936)
Public
Ickenham Road, Ruislip HA4 7DQ
- ☎ (01895) 277777
- 🖶 (01895) 635780
- ✉ ruislipgc@hillingdon.gov.uk
- 🖎 N Jennings
- 🖥 www.hillingdon.gov.uk

## Stanmore (1893)
29 Gordon Avenue, Stanmore HA7 2RL
- ☎ (020) 8954 2599
- 🖶 (020) 8954 2599
- ✉ secretary@stanmoregolfclub.co.uk
- 🖎 Allan Knott (020) 8954 2599
- 🖥 www.stanmoregolfclub.co.uk

## Stockley Park (1993)
Pay and play
The Clubhouse, Stockley Park, Uxbridge UB11 1AQ
- ☎ (020) 8813 5700/561 6339 (Bookings)
- 🖶 (020) 8813 5655
- ✉ proshop@stockleypines.com
- 🖎 K Soper
- 🖥 www.stockleyparkgolf.com

## Strawberry Hill (1900)
Wellesley Road, Strawberry Hill, Twickenham TW2 5SD
- ☎ (020) 8894 0165
- ✉ secretary@shgc.net
- 🖎 Secretary (020) 8894 0165
- 🖥 www.shgc.net

## Sudbury (1920)
Bridgewater Road, Wembley HA0 1AL
- ☎ (020) 8902 3713 (office)
- 🖶 (020) 8902 3713
- ✉ enquiries@sudburygolfclubltd.co.uk
- 🖎 N Cropley (Gen Mgr)
- 🖥 www.sudburygolfclubltd.co.uk

## Sunbury (1993)
Proprietary
Charlton Lane, Shepperton TW17 8QA
- ☎ (01932) 771414
- 🖶 (01932) 789300
- ✉ sunbury@crown-golf.co.uk
- 🖎 P Dawson (Gen Mgr)
- 🖥 www.crown-golf.co.uk

## Trent Park (1973)
Pay and play
Bramley Road, Southgate, London N14 4UW
- ☎ (020) 8367 4653
- 🖶 (020) 8366 4581
- ✉ info@trentparkgolf.co.uk
- 🖥 www.trentparkgolf.co.uk

## Uxbridge (1947)
Public
The Drive, Harefield Place, Uxbridge UB10 8AQ
- ☎ (01895) 556750 (Pro Shop)

☎ (01895) 810262
✉ uxbridgegolfclub@btconnect.com
✍ Mrs A James (01895) 272457
🖥 www.uxbridgegolf.co.uk

## West Middlesex (1891)
*Greenford Road, Southall UB1 3EE*
☎ (020) 8574 3450
🖫 (020) 8574 2383
✉ westmid.gc@virgin.net
✍ Miss R Khanna
🖥 www.westmiddxgolfclub.co.uk

## Wyke Green (1928)
*Syon Lane, Isleworth, Osterley TW7 5PT*
☎ (020) 8560 8777
🖫 (020) 8569 8392
✉ office@wykegreengolfclub.co.uk
✍ D Pearson
🖥 www.wykegreengolfclub.co.uk

# Norfolk

## Barnham Broom Hotel (1977)
*Honingham Road, Barnham Broom,
Norwich NR9 4DD*
☎ (01603) 759393 (Hotel)
🖫 (01603) 758224
✉ golf@barnham-broom.co.uk
✍ M Breen (01603) 757504
🖥 www.barnham-broom.co.uk

## Bawburgh (1978)
*Glen Lodge, Marlingford Road, Bawburgh,
Norwich NR9 3LU*
☎ (01603) 740404
🖫 (01603) 740403
✉ info@bawburgh.com
✍ I Ladbrooke (Gen Mgr)
🖥 www.bawburgh.com

## Caldecott Hall (1993)
**Pay and play**
*Caldecott Hall, Beccles Road, Fritton, Great
Yarmouth NR31 9EY*
☎ (01493) 488488
🖫 (01493) 488561
✉ info@caldecotthall.co.uk
✍ Jill Braybrooke
🖥 www.caldecotthall.co.uk

## Costessey Park (1983)
*Costessey Park, Costessey, Norwich
NR8 5AL*
☎ (01603) 746333
🖫 (01603) 746185
✉ enquiry@costesseypark.com
✍ GC Stangoe
🖥 www.costesseypark.com

## Dereham (1934)
*Quebec Road, Dereham NR19 2DS*
☎ (01362) 695900
✉ office@derehamgolfclub.com
✍ Mr Tim Evans
🖥 www.derehamgolfclub.com

## Dunham (1979)
**Proprietary**
*Little Dunham, Swaffham PE32 2DF*
☎ (01328) 701906

✉ garympotter@hotmail.com
✍ G & S Potter (Props)
🖥 www.dunhamgolfclub.com

## De Vere Dunston Hall (1994)
**Pay and play**
*Ipswich Road, Dunston, Norwich NR14 8PQ*
☎ (01508) 470178
🖫 (01508) 471499
✍ P Briggs

## Eagles (1990)
**Pay and play**
*39 School Road, Tilney All Saints, Kings
Lynn PE34 4RS*
☎ (01553) 827147
🖫 (01553) 829777
✉ shop@eagles-golf-tennis.co.uk
✍ D W Horn
🖥 www.eagles-golf-tennis.co.uk

## Eaton (1910)
*Newmarket Road, Norwich NR4 6SF*
☎ (01603) 451686
🖫 (01603) 457539
✉ admin@eatongc.co.uk
✍ P Johns
🖥 www.eatongc.co.uk

## Fakenham (1973)
*The Race Course, Hempton Road,
Fakenham NR21 7NY*
☎ (01328) 855678
🖫 (01328) 855678
✉ fakenhamgolf@tiscali.co.uk
✍ G Cocker (01328) 855678
🖥 www.fakenhamgolfclub.co.uk

## Feltwell (1976)
*Thor Ave, Wilton Road, Feltwell, Thetford
IP26 4AY*
☎ (01842) 827644
🖫 (01842) 829065
✉ sec.feltwellgc@virgin.net
✍ Jonathan Moore
🖥 www.club-noticeboard.co.uk

## Gorleston (1906)
*Warren Road, Gorleston, Gt Yarmouth
NR31 6JT*
☎ (01493) 661911
🖫 (01493) 661911
✉ manager@gorlestongolfclub.co.uk
✍ David James (01493) 661911
🖥 www.gorlestongolfclub.co.uk

## Great Yarmouth & Caister (1882)
*Beach House, Caister-on-Sea, Gt Yarmouth
NR30 5TD*
☎ (01493) 728699
🖫 (01493) 728831
✉ office@caistergolf.co.uk
✍ Brian Lever
🖥 www.caistergolf.co.uk

## Hunstanton (1891)
*Golf Course Road, Old Hunstanton
PE36 6JQ*
☎ (01485) 532811
🖫 (01485) 532319
✉ secretary@hunstantongolfclub.com

✍ BRB Carrick
🖥 www.hunstantongolfclub.com

## King's Lynn (1923)
*Castle Rising, King's Lynn PE31 6BD*
☎ (01553) 631654
🖫 (01553) 631036
✉ secretary@kingslynngc.co.uk
✍ M Bowman
🖥 www.kingslynngc.co.uk

## Links Country Park Hotel & Golf Club (1903)
*West Runton, Cromer NR27 9QH*
☎ (01263) 838383
🖫 (01263) 838264
✉ links@mackenziehotels.com
✍ Marc Mackenzie
🖥 www.links-hotel.co.uk

## Marriott Sprowston Manor Hotel (1980)
*Wroxham Road, Sprowston, Norwich
NR7 8RP*
☎ (0870) 400 7229
🖫 (0870) 400 7329
✉ keith.grant@marriotthotels.com
✍ Keith Grant
🖥 www.marriott.co.uk/nwigs

## Mattishall (1990)
**Proprietary**
*South Green, Mattishall, Dereham*
☎ (01362) 850464
✍ B Hall
🖥 www.mattishallgolfclub.co.uk

## Middleton Hall (1989)
**Proprietary**
*Middleton, King's Lynn PE32 1RY*
☎ (01553) 841800
✉ enquiries@middletonhallgolfclub
    .com
✍ M Johnson
🖥 www.middletonhallgolfclub.co.uk

## Mundesley (1901)
*Links Road, Mundesley NR11 8ES*
☎ (01263) 720095
🖫 (01263) 722849
✉ manager@mundesleygolfclub.com
✍ R Pudney
🖥 www.mundesleygolfclub.com

## RAF Marham (1974)
*RAF Marham, Kings Lynn PE33 9NP*
☎ (01760) 337261 ext 7262
✍ PG Williams (ext 7387)
🖥 www.marhamgolf.co.uk

## Richmond Park (1990)
*Saham Road, Watton IP25 6EA*
☎ (01953) 881803
🖫 (01953) 881817
✉ info@richmondpark.co.uk
✍ Simon Jessop
🖥 www.richmondpark.co.uk

## Royal Cromer (1888)
*Overstrand Road, Cromer NR27 0JH*
☎ (01263) 512884
🖫 (01263) 512430

general.manager@royal-cromer.com
Gary Richardson
www.royalcromergolfclub.com

## Royal Norwich    (1893)
Drayton High Road, Hellesdon, Norwich NR6 5AH
☎ (01603) 429928
📠 (01603) 417945
info mail@royalnorwichgolf.co.uk
Phil Grice (Gen Mgr)
www.royalnorwichgolf.co.uk

## Royal West Norfolk    (1892)
Brancaster, King's Lynn PE31 8AX
☎ (01485) 210087
📠 (01485) 210087
secretary@rwngc.org
Ian Symington
www.rwngc.org

## Ryston Park    (1932)
Ely Road, Denver, Downham Market PE38 0HH
☎ (01366) 382133
📠 (01366) 383834
rystonparkgc@talktalkbusiness.net
WJ Flogdell
www.club-noticeboard.co.uk

## Sheringham    (1891)
Sheringham NR26 8HG
☎ (01263) 823488
📠 (01263) 826129
info@sheringhamgolfclub.co.uk
N R Milton
www.sheringhamgolfclub.co.uk

## Swaffham    (1922)
Cley Road, Swaffham PE37 8AE
☎ (01760) 721621
📠 (01760) 336998
manager@swaffhamgc.co.uk
www.club-noticeboard.co.uk

## Thetford    (1912)
Brandon Road, Thetford IP24 3NE
☎ (01842) 752258 (Clubhouse)
📠 (01842) 766212
thetfordgolfclub@btconnect.com
Mrs Diane Hopkins (01842) 752169
www.thetfordgolfclub.co.uk

## Wensum Valley    (1990)
Proprietary
Beech Avenue, Taverham, Norwich NR8 6HP
☎ (01603) 261012
📠 (01603) 261664
enqs@wensumvalleyhotel.co.uk
Mrs B Hall
www.wensumvalleyhotel.co.uk

## Weston Park    (1993)
Proprietary
Weston Longville, Norwich NR9 5JW
☎ (01603) 872998
📠 (01603) 873040
pro@weston-park.co.uk
Michael R Few (PGA Pro)
www.weston-park.co.uk

# Northamptonshire

## Brampton Heath    (1995)
Pay and play
Sandy Lane, Church Brampton NN6 8AX
☎ (01604) 843939
📠 (01604) 843885
info@bhgc.co.uk
Carl Sainsbury (Head Pro)
www.bhgc.co.uk

## Cold Ashby    (1974)
Proprietary
Stanford Road, Cold Ashby, Northampton NN6 6EP
☎ (01604) 740548
📠 (01604) 743025
info@coldashbygolfclub.com
DA Croxton (Prop)
www.coldashbygolfclub.com

## Collingtree Park Golf Course    (1990)
Proprietary
Windingbrook Lane, Northampton NN4 0XN
☎ (01604) 700000
📠 (01604) 702600
enquiries@collingtreeparkgolf.com
Kevin Whitehouse (Dir of Golf)
www.collingtreeparkgolf.com

## Daventry & District    (1907)
Norton Road, Daventry NN11 2LS
☎ (01327) 702829
ddgc@hotmail.co.uk
Colin Long
www.daventrygolfclub.co.uk

## Delapre    (1976)
Pay and play
Eagle Drive, Nene Valley Way, Northampton NN4 7DU
☎ (01604) 764036
📠 (01604) 706378
delapre@jbgolf.co.uk
Greg Iron (Centre Mgr) John Cuddiny (PGA Pro)
www.delapregolfcentre.co.uk

## Farthingstone Hotel    (1974)
Farthingstone, Towcester NN12 8HA
☎ (01327) 361291
📠 (01327) 361645
interest@farthingstone.co.uk
C Donaldson
www.farthingstone.co.uk

## Hellidon Lakes Hotel G&CC    (1991)
Hellidon, Nr. Daventry, Northamptonshire NN11 6LN
☎ (01327) 262550
📠 (01327) 262559
MA Thomas
www.hellidon.co.uk

## Kettering    (1891)
Headlands, Kettering NN15 6XA
☎ (01536) 511104
📠 (01536) 523788

secretary@kettering-golf.co.uk
JM Gilding (01536) 511104
www.kettering-golf.co.uk

## Kingfisher Hotel    (1995)
Proprietary
Buckingham Road, Deanshanger, Milton Keynes MK19 6JY
☎ (01908) 560354/562332
📠 (01908) 260857
sales.kingfisher@btopenworld.com
Roland Carlish
www.kingfisher-hotelandgolf.co.uk

## Kingsthorpe    (1908)
Kingsley Road, Northampton NN2 7BU
☎ (01604) 711173
📠 (01604) 710610
secretary@kingsthorpe-golf.co.uk
DS Wade (01604) 710610
www.kingsthorpe-golf.co.uk

## Northampton    (1893)
Harlestone, Northampton NN7 4EF
☎ (01604) 845155
📠 (01604) 820262
golf@northamptongolfclub.co.uk
B Randall (Director of Golf)
www.northamptongolfclub.co.uk

## Northamptonshire County    (1909)
Church Brampton, Northampton NN6 8AZ
☎ (01604) 843025
📠 (01604) 843463
secretary@countygolfclub.org.uk
Peter Walsh (01604) 843025
www.countygolfclub.org.uk

## Oundle    (1893)
Benefield Road, Oundle PE8 4EZ
☎ (01832) 273267
📠 (01832) 273008
office@oundlegolfclub.com
L Quantrill (01832) 272267
www.oundlegolfclub.com

## Overstone Park    (1994)
Proprietary
Overstone Park Ltd, Billing Lane, Northampton NN6 0AS
☎ (01604) 647666
📠 (01604) 642635
enquiries@overstonepark.com
Nigel Wardle (Gen Mgr)
www.overstonepark.com

## Priors Hall    (1965)
Public
Stamford Road, Weldon, Corby NN17 3JH
☎ (01536) 260756
📠 (01536) 260756
p.ackroyd1@btinternet.com
P Ackroyd (01536) 263722

## Rushden    (1919)
Kimbolton Road, Chelveston, Wellingborough, Northamptonshire NN9 6AN
☎ (01933) 418511
📠 (01933) 418511
secretary@rushdengolfclub.org

✍ EJ Williams
🖳 www.rushdengolfclub.org

## Staverton Park    (1977)
*Staverton Park, Staverton, Daventry NN11 6JT*
☎ **(01327) 302000/302118**
🖳 (01327) 311428
✍ I Conder (Gen Mgr),

## Stoke Albany    (1995)
**Proprietary**
*Ashley Road, Stoke Albany, Market Harborough LE16 8PL*
☎ **(01858) 535208**
✉ info@stokealbanygolfclub.co.uk
✍ R Want
🖳 www.stokealbanygolfclub.com

## Wellingborough    (1893)
*Harrowden Hall, Great Harrowden, Wellingborough NN9 5AD*
☎ **(01933) 677234**
🖳 (01933) 679379
✉ info@wellingboroughgolfclub.com
✍ David Waite (01933) 677234
🖳 www.wellingboroughgolfclub.com

## Whittlebury Park G&CC
(1992)
**Proprietary, Public,**
*Whittlebury, Towcester NN12 8WP*
☎ **(01327) 850000**
🖳 (01327) 850001
✉ sales@whittlebury.com
✍ Alison Trubshaw
🖳 www.whittlebury.com

# Northumberland

## Allendale    (1906)
*High Studdon, Allenheads Road, Allendale, Hexham NE47 9DH*
☎ **(0700) 580 8246**
✉ secretary@allendale-golf.co.uk
✍ Mrs A Woodcock (Hon Sec)
🖳 www.allendale-golf.co.uk

## Alnmouth    (1869)
*Foxton Hall, Alnmouth NE66 3BE*
☎ **(01665) 830231**
🖳 (01665) 830922
✉ secretary@alnmouthgolfclub.com
✍ P Simpson
🖳 www.alnmouthgolfclub.com

## Alnmouth Village    (1869)
*Marine Road, Alnmouth NE66 2RZ*
☎ **(01665) 830370**
✉ bobhill53@live.co.uk
✍ R A Hill (01665) 833189
🖳 www.alnmouthvillagegolfclub.co.uk

## Alnwick Castle    (1907)
**Proprietary**
*Swansfield Park, Alnwick NE66 2AB*
☎ **(01665) 602632**
✉ secretary@alnwickgolfclub.co.uk
✍ Club Manager (01665) 602632
🖳 www.alnwickcastlegolfclub.co.uk

## Arcot Hall    (1909)
*Dudley, Cramlington NE23 7QP*
☎ **(0191) 236 2794**
🖳 (0191) 217 0370
✉ arcothall@tiscali.co.uk
✍ Brian Rumney (0191) 236 2794
🖳 www.arcothall.co.uk

## Bamburgh Castle    (1904)
*The Club House, 40 The Wynding, Bamburgh NE69 7DE*
☎ **(01668) 214378**
🖳 (01668) 214607
✉ sec@bamburghcastlegolfclub.co.uk
✍ MND Robinson (01668) 214321
🖳 www.bamburghcastlegolfclub.co.uk

## Bedlingtonshire    (1972)
*Acorn Bank, Hartford Road, Bedlington NE22 6AA*
☎ **(01670) 822457**
🖳 (01670) 823048
✉ secretary@bedlingtongolfclub.com
✍ J Laverick (01670) 822457
🖳 www.bedlingtongolfclub.com

## The Belford    (1993)
*South Road, Belford NE70 7DP*
☎ **(01668) 213323**
🖳 (01668) 213282
✍ HS Adair
🖳 www.thebelford.com

## Bellingham    (1893)
*Boggle Hole, Bellingham NE48 2DT*
☎ **(01434) 220530/220152**
✉ admin@bellinghamgolfclub.com
✍ Jamie Rickleton (Club Steward)
🖳 www.bellinghamgolfclub.com

## Berwick-upon-Tweed
(Goswick)    (1890)
*Goswick, Berwick-upon-Tweed TD15 2RW*
☎ **(01289) 387256**
🖳 (01289) 387392
✉ goswickgc@btconnect.com
✍ IAM Alsop
🖳 www.goswicklinksgc.co.uk

## Blyth    (1905)
*New Delaval, Blyth NE24 4DB*
☎ **(01670) 540110**
🖳 (01670) 540134
✉ clubmanager@blythgolf.co.uk
✍ J C Hall
🖳 www.blythgolf.co.uk

## Burgham Park Golf & Leisure
Club    (1994)
**Proprietary**
*Felton, Morpeth NE65 9QP*
☎ **(01670) 787898**
🖳 (01670) 787164
✉ info@burghampark.co.uk
✍ William Kiely
🖳 www.burghampark.co.uk

## Close House Hotel & Golf
(1968)
**Proprietary**
*Close House, Heddon-on-the-Wall, Newcastle-upon-Tyne NE15 0HT*
☎ **(01661) 852255**
🖳 (01661) 853322
✉ events@closehouse.co.uk
✍ John Glendinning
🖳 www.closehouse.co.uk

## Dunstanburgh Castle    (1900)
*Embleton NE66 3XQ*
☎ **(01665) 576562**
🖳 (01665) 576562
✉ enquiries@dunstanburgh.com
✍ Irene Williams (Mgr)
🖳 www.dunstanburgh.com

## Hexham    (1892)
*Spital Park, Hexham NE46 3RZ*
☎ **(01434) 603072**
🖳 (01434) 601865
✉ info@hexhamgolf.co.uk
✍ Dawn Wylie (01434) 603072
🖳 www.hexhamgolf.co.uk

## Linden Hall    (1997)
**Proprietary**
*Longhorsley, Morpeth NE65 8XF*
☎ **(0844) 879 9084**
🖳 www.macdonaldhotels.co.uk/lindenhall

## Longhirst Hall Golf Course
(1997)
*Longhirst Hall, Longhirst NE61 3LL*
☎ **(01670) 791562 (Clubhouse)**
🖳 (01670) 791768
✉ enquiries@longhirstgolf.co.uk
✍ Graham Chambers (01670) 791562
🖳 www.longhirstgolf.co.uk

## Magdalene Fields    (1903)
**Pay and play**
*Magdalene Fields, Berwick-upon-Tweed TD15 1NE*
☎ **(01289) 306130**
✉ secretary.magdalenefields@hotmail.co.uk
✍ S Eddington (Sec)
🖳 www.magdalene-fields.co.uk

## Matfen Hall Hotel    (1994)
**Proprietary**
*Matfen, Hexham NE20 0RH*
☎ **(01661) 886400 (golf)**
🖳 (01661) 886055
✉ golf@matfenhall.com
✍ Peter Smith
🖳 www.matfenhall.com

## Morpeth    (1906)
*The Clubhouse, Morpeth NE61 2BT*
☎ **(01670) 504942**
🖳 (01670) 504918
✉ admin@morpethgolf.co.uk
✍ Terry Minett
🖳 www.morpethgolf.co.uk

**Newbiggin**   (1884)
*Newbiggin-by-the-Sea NE64 6DW*
☎ **(01670) 817344 (Clubhouse)**
📧 info@newbiggingolfclub.co.uk
✍ J Oliphant (Sec)/J Young (Mgr)
🖥 www.newbiggingolfclub.co.uk

**Percy Wood Golf & Country Retreat**   (1993)
*Coast View, Swarland, Morpeth NE65 9JG*
☎ **(01670) 787940 (Clubhouse)**
📧 enquiries@percywood.com
✍ (01670) 787010
🖥 www.percywood.co.uk

**Ponteland**   (1927)
*53 Bell Villas, Ponteland, Newcastle-upon-Tyne NE20 9BD*
☎ **(01661) 822689**
📠 (01661) 860077
📧 secretary@thepontelandgolfclub.co.uk
✍ G Waugh
🖥 www.thepontelandgolfclub.co.uk

**Prudhoe**   (1930)
*Eastwood Park, Prudhoe-on-Tyne NE42 5DX*
☎ **(01661) 832466 ext 20**
📠 (01661) 830710
📧 secretary@prudhoegolfclub.co.uk
✍ ID Pauw
🖥 www.prudhoegolfclub.co.uk

**Rothbury**   (1891)
*Whitton Bank Road, Rothbury, Morpeth NE65 7RX*
☎ **(01669) 621271 Ext 2**
📧 secretary@rothburygolfclub.com
✍ M Arkle (01669) 620487
🖥 www.rothburygolfclub.com

**Seahouses**   (1913)
*Beadnall Road, Seahouses NE68 7XT*
☎ **(01665) 720794**
📧 secretary@seahousesgolf.co.uk
✍ Ian Wort
🖥 www.seahousesgolf.co.uk

**De Vere Slaley Hall**   (1988)
*Slaley, Hexham NE47 0BX*
☎ **(01434) 673154**
📠 (01434) 673350
📧 slaley.hall@devere-hotels.com
✍ M Stancer (Golf Mgr)
🖥 www.devere.co.uk

**Stocksfield**   (1913)
*New Ridley, Stocksfield NE43 7RE*
☎ **(01661) 843041**
📠 (01661) 843046
📧 info@sgcgolf.co.uk
✍ B Garrow (Acting Sec)
🖥 www.sgcgolf.co.uk

**Warkworth**   (1891)
*The Links, Warkworth, Morpeth, Northumberland NE65 0SW*
☎ **(01665) 711596**
✍ David Arkley
🖥 www.warkworthgolfclub
   @btconnect.com

**Wooler**   (1975)
*Dod Law, Doddington, Wooler NE71 6AL*
☎ **(01668) 282135**
✍ S Lowrey (01668) 281631
🖥 www.woolergolf.co.uk

## Nottinghamshire

**Beeston Fields**   (1923)
*Old Drive, Wollaton Road, Beeston, Nottingham NG9 3DD*
☎ **(0115) 925 7062**
📠 (0115) 925 4280
📧 info@beestonfields.co.uk
✍ G Conrad
⊕ Sat Nav. Post Code NG9 3DA
🖥 www.beestonfields.co.uk

**Brierley Forest**   (1993)
*Main Street, Huthwaite, Sutton-in-Ashfield NG17 2LG*
☎ **(01623) 550761**
📠 (01623) 550761
✍ D Crafts (01623) 514234

**Bulwell Forest**   (1902)
*Hucknall Road, Bulwell, Nottingham NG6 9LQ*
☎ **(0115) 976 3172 (secretary)**
📧 secretary@bulwellforestgolfclub
   .co.uk
✍ R D Savage
🖥 www.bulwellforestgolfclub.co.uk

**Chilwell Manor**   (1906)
*Meadow Lane, Chilwell, Nottingham NG9 5AE*
☎ **(0115) 925 8958**
📠 (0115) 922 0575
📧 info@chilwellmanorgolfclub.co.uk
✍ D B Reynolds
🖥 www.chilwellmanorgolfclub.co.uk

**College Pines**   (1994)
**Proprietary**
*Worksop College Drive, Sparken Hill, Worksop S80 3AL*
☎ **(01909) 501431**
📧 snelljunior@btinternet.com
✍ C Snell (Golf Dir)
🖥 www.collegepinesgolfclub.co.uk

**Coxmoor**   (1913)
*Coxmoor Road, Sutton-in-Ashfield NG17 5LF*
☎ **(01623) 557359**
📠 (01623) 557435
📧 secretary@coxmoorgolfclub.co.uk
✍ Mrs J Chambers
🖥 www.coxmoorgolfclub.co.uk

**Edwalton**   (1982)
**Pay and play**
*Wellin Lane, Edwalton, Nottingham NG12 4AS*
☎ **(0115) 923 4775**
📠 (0115) 923 1647
📧 edwalton@glendale-services.co.uk
✍ Ms D J Kerrison
🖥 www.glendale-golf.com

**Kilton Forest**   (1978)
**Public**
*Blyth Road, Worksop S81 0TL*
☎ **(01909) 486563**
✍ JA Eyre (Hon)

**Leen Valley Golf Club**   (1994)
**Pay and play**
*Wigwam Lane, Hucknall NG15 7TA*
☎ **(0115) 964 2037**
📠 (0115) 964 2724
📧 leenvalley@live.co.uk
✍ Robert Kerr
🖥 www.leenvalleygolfclub.co.uk

**Mapperley**   (1907)
*Central Avenue, Plains Road, Mapperley, Nottingham NG3 6RH*
☎ **(0115) 955 6672**
📠 (0115) 955 6670
📧 secretary@mapperleygolfclub.org
✍ Michael Mulhern
🖥 www.mapperleygolfclub.org

**Newark**   (1901)
*Coddington, Newark NG24 2QX*
☎ **(01636) 626282**
📠 (01636) 626497
📧 manager@newarkgolfclub.co.uk
✍ S D Collingwood (01636) 626282
🖥 www.newarkgolfclub.co.uk

**Norwood Park Golf Centre**   (1999)
**Proprietary**
*Norwood Park, Southwell NG25 0PF*
☎ **(01636) 816626**
📧 golf@norwoodpark.co.uk
✍ Paul Thornton
🖥 www.norwoodgolf.co.uk

**Nottingham City**   (1910)
**Public**
*Norwich Gardens, Bulwell, Nottingham NG6 8LF*
☎ **(0115) 927 2767 (Pro Shop)**
📧 garyandkate1@talktalk.net
✍ GJ Chappell (07740) 288694
🖥 www.nottinghamcitygolfclub.co.uk

**Notts**   (1887)
*Hollinwell, Kirkby-in-Ashfield NG17 7QR*
☎ **(01623) 753225**
📠 (01623) 753655
📧 office@nottsgolfclub.co.uk
✍ S E Lawrence
🖥 www.nottsgolfclub.co.uk

**Oakmere Park**   (1974)
*Oaks Lane, Oxton NG25 0RH*
☎ **(0115) 965 3545**
📠 (0115) 965 5628
📧 enquiries@oakmerepark.co.uk
✍ D St-John Jones
🖥 www.oakmerepark.co.uk

**Radcliffe-on-Trent**   (1909)
*Dewberry Lane, Cropwell Road, Radcliffe-on-Trent NG12 2JH*
☎ **(0115) 933 3000**
📠 (0115) 911 6991
📧 bill.dunn@radcliffeontrentgc.co.uk

✍ B Dunn
🖥 www.radcliffeontrentgc.co.uk

## Ramsdale Park Golf Centre
(1992)
**Pay and play**
Oxton Road, Calverton NG14 6NU
☎ **(0115) 965 5600**
🖳 (0115) 965 4105
📧 info@ramsdaleparkgc.co.uk
✍ N Birch (Mgr)
🖥 www.ramsdaleparkgc.co.uk

## Retford   (1920)
Brecks Road, Ordsall, Retford DN22 7UA
☎ **(01777) 703733/711188**
🖳 (01777) 710412
📧 office@retfordgolfclub.co.uk
✍ Lesley Redfearn & Diane Moore
🖥 www.retfordgolfclub.co.uk

## Ruddington Grange   (1988)
Wilford Road, Ruddington, Nottingham
NG11 6NB
☎ **(0115) 984 6141**
🖳 (0115) 940 5165
📧 info@ruddingtongrange.co.uk
✍ P Deacon
🖥 www.ruddingtongrange.co.uk

## Rufford Park G&CC   (1990)
**Proprietary**
Rufford Lane, Rufford, Newark NG22 9DG
☎ **(01623) 825253**
🖳 (01623) 825254
📧 enquiries@ruffordpark.co.uk
✍ Club Manager (01623) 825253
🖥 www.ruffordpark.co.uk

## Rushcliffe   (1909)
Stocking Lane, East Leake, Loughborough
LE12 5RL
☎ **(01509) 852959**
🖳 (01509) 852688
📧 secretary@rushcliffegolfclub.com
✍ C Bee
🖥 www.rushcliffegolfclub.com

## Serlby Park   (1906)
Serlby, Doncaster DN10 6BA
☎ **(01777) 818268**
📧 serlbysec@talktalkbusiness.net
✍ KJ Crook (01302) 742280

## Sherwood Forest   (1895)
Eakring Road, Mansfield NG18 3EW
☎ **(01623) 626689/627403**
📧 info@sherwoodforestgolfclub
.co.uk
✍ Mrs Ellen Matthews (Sec)
🖥 www.sherwoodforestgolfclub.co.uk

## Southwell   (1993)
**Proprietary**
Southwell Racecourse, Rolleston, Newark
NG25 0TS
☎ **(01636) 813706**
🖳 (01636) 812271
📧 golf@southwell-racecourse.co.uk
✍ Mrs S Pawson (Sec) (01636) 659905
thepawsons1@gmail.com
🖥 www.southwellgolfclub.com

## Springwater   (1991)
**Proprietary**
Moor Lane, Calverton, Nottingham
NG14 6FZ
☎ **(0115) 965 4946**
🖳 (0115) 965 2344
📧 dave.pullan@springwatergolfclub
.com
✍ E Brady (0115) 952 3956
🖥 www.springwatergolfclub.com

## Stanton-on-the-Wolds   (1906)
Golf Course Road, Stanton-on-the-Wolds,
Nottingham NG12 5BH
☎ **(0115) 937 4885**
🖳 (0115) 937 1652
📧 info@stantongolfclub.co.uk
✍ Michael Gurney (0115) 937 1650
🖥 www.stantongolfclub.co.uk

## The Nottinghamshire G&CC
(1991)
Stragglethorpe, Nr Cotgrave Village,
Cotgrave NG12 3HB
☎ **(0115) 933 3344**
🖳 (0115) 933 4567
📧 general@thenottinghamshire.com
✍ Nick Lenty
🖥 www.thenottinghamshire.com

## Trent Lock Golf Centre   (1991)
**Proprietary**
Lock Lane, Sawley, Long Eaton NG10 2FY
☎ **(0115) 946 4398**
🖳 (0115) 946 1183
📧 enquiries@trentlockgolf.com
✍ R Prior (F & B Mgr)
🖥 www.trentlock.co.uk

## Wollaton Park   (1927)
Wollaton Park, Nottingham NG8 1BT
☎ **(0115) 978 7574**
📧 secretary@wollatonparkgolfclub
.com
✍ Avril J Jamieson
🖥 www.wollatonparkgolfclub.com

## Worksop   (1914)
Windmill Lane, Worksop S80 2SQ
☎ **(01909) 477731**
🖳 (01909) 530917
📧 thesecretary@worksopgolfclub
.com
✍ Mr A D Mansbridge
(01909) 477731
🖥 www.worksopgolfclub.com

## Oxfordshire

## Aspect Park   (1988)
Remenham Hill, Henley-on-Thames
RG9 3EH
☎ **(01491) 578306**
🖳 (01491) 578306
✍ T Notley (Mgr) (01491) 578306

## Badgemore Park   (1972)
**Proprietary**
Henley-on-Thames RG9 4NR
☎ **(01491) 637300**
🖳 (01491) 576899
📧 info@badgemorepark.com
✍ A Smith (Club Sec)
(01491) 637300
🖥 www.badgemorepark.com

## Banbury Golf Club   (1993)
**Pay and play**
Aynho Road, Adderbury, Banbury
OX17 3NT
☎ **(01295) 810419**
🖳 (01295) 810056
✍ Mr M Reed
🖥 www.banburygolfclub.co.uk

## Bicester Hotel Golf and Spa
(1973)
Chesterton, Bicester OX26 1TE
☎ **(01869) 241204**
📧 jamie.herbert
@bicesterhotelgolfandspa.com
✍ M Odom (01869) 241204
🖥 www.bicestergolf.co.uk

## Burford   (1936)
Burford OX18 4JG
☎ **(01993) 822583**
🖳 (01993) 822801
📧 secretary@burfordgolfclub
.co.uk
✍ RP Thompson
🖥 www.burfordgolfclub.co.uk

## Carswell CC   (1993)
Carswell, Faringdon SN7 8PU
☎ **(01367) 870422**
🖳 (01367) 870592
📧 info@carswellgolfandcountryclub
.co.uk
✍ G Lisi (Prop)
🖥 www.carswellgolfandcountryclub
.co.uk

## Cherwell Edge   (1980)
Chacombe, Banbury OX17 2EN
☎ **(01295) 711591**
🖳 (01295) 713674
📧 enquiries@cherwelledgegolfclub
.co.uk
✍ Dave Bridger (Sec)
🖥 www.cherwelledgegolfclub.co.uk

## Chipping Norton   (1890)
Southcombe, Chipping Norton OX7 5QH
☎ **(01608) 642383**
🖳 (01608) 645422
📧 golfadmin@chippingnortongolfclub
.com
✍ Lindsey Dray (Operations Mgr)
🖥 www.chippingnortongolfclub.com

## Drayton Park   (1992)
**Pay and play**
Steventon Road, Drayton, Abingdon,
OX14 4IA
☎ **(01235) 550607/528989**
🖳 (01235) 525731
📧 draytonpark@btclick.com
✍ Rob Bolton (01235) 528989
🖥 www.draytonparkgolfclubabingdon
.co.uk

## Feldon Valley   (1992)
**Proprietary**
*Sutton Lane, Lower Brailes, Banbury
OX15 5BB*
- ☎ **(01608) 685633**
- ✉ info@feldonvalley.co.uk
- ✍ Neil Simpson (Dir) (01608) 685633
- 🖥 www.feldonvalley.co.uk

## Frilford Heath   (1908)
*Frilford Heath, Abingdon OX13 5NW*
- ☎ **(01865) 390864**
- 🖳 (01865) 390823
- ✉ generalmanager@frilfordheath.co.uk
- ✍ A B W James
- 🖥 www.frilfordheath.co.uk

## Hadden Hill   (1990)
**Proprietary**
*Wallingford Road, Didcot OX11 9BJ*
- ☎ **(01235) 510410**
- 🖳 (01235) 511260
- ✉ info@haddenhillgolf.co.uk
- ✍ M V Morley
- 🖥 www.haddenhillgolf.co.uk

## Henley   (1907)
*Harpsden, Henley-on-Thames RG9 4HG*
- ☎ **(01491) 575742**
- 🖳 (01491) 412179
- ✉ info@henleygc.com
- ✍ Gary Oatham (01491) 635305
- 🖥 www.henleygc.com

## Hinksey Heights   (1995)
**Public**
*South Hinksey, Oxford OX1 5AB*
- ☎ **(01865) 327775**
- ✉ admin@oxford-golf.co.uk
- ✍ Jane Binning
- 🖥 www.oxford-golf.co.uk

## Huntercombe   (1901)
*Nuffield, Henley-on-Thames RG9 5SL*
- ☎ **(01491) 641207**
- 🖳 (01491) 642060
- ✉ office@huntercombegolfclub.co.uk
- ✍ GNV Jenkins
- 🖥 www.huntercombegolfclub.co.uk

## Kirtlington   (1995)
**Proprietary**
*Kirtlington, Oxon OX5 3JY*
- ☎ **(01869) 351133**
- 🖳 (01869) 331143
- ✉ info@kirtlingtongolfclub.com
- ✍ Miss P Smith (Sec/Mgr)
- 🖥 www.kirtlingtongolfclub.com

## North Oxford   (1907)
*Banbury Road, Oxford OX2 8EZ*
- ☎ **(01865) 554415**
- 🖳 (01865) 554924
- ✍ R J Harris (Mgr) (01865) 554924
  opt 2
- 🖥 www.nogc.co.uk

## Oxford Golf Club   (1875)
*Hill Top Road, Oxford OX4 1PF*
- ☎ **(01865) 242158**
- 🖳 (01865) 250023
- ✉ sgcltd@btopenworld.com

---

- ✍ C G Whittle (01865) 242158
- 🖥 www.oxfordgolfclub.net

## The Oxfordshire   (1993)
**Proprietary**
*Rycote Lane, Milton Common, Thame
OX9 2PU*
- ☎ **(01844) 278300**
- 🖳 (01844) 278003
- ✉ info@theoxfordshire.com
- ✍ Mr C Hanks
- 🖥 www.theoxfordshiregolfclub.com

## RAF Benson   (1975)
*Royal Air Force, Benson, Wallingford
OX10 6AA*
- ☎ **(01491) 837766 Ext 7322**
- ✍ A Molloy (01491) 827017

## Rye Hill   (1992)
**Proprietary**
*Milcombe, Banbury OX15 4RU*
- ☎ **(01295) 721818**
- 🖳 (01295) 720089
- ✉ info@ryehill.co.uk
- ✍ Tony Pennock
- 🖥 www.ryehill.co.uk

## The Springs Hotel & Golf Club   (1998)
**Proprietary**
*Wallingford Road, North Stoke, Wallingford
OX10 6BE*
- ☎ **(01491) 827310**
- 🖳 (01491) 827312
- ✉ proshop@thespringshotel.com
- ✍ M Ackerman (01491) 827315
- 🖥 www.thespringshotel.com

## Studley Wood   (1996)
**Proprietary**
*The Straight Mile, Horton-cum-Studley,
Oxford OX33 1BF*
- ☎ **(01865) 351144**
- 🖳 (01865) 351166
- ✉ admin@studleywoodgolfclub.co.uk
- ✍ Ken Heathcote (01865) 351144
- 🖥 www.studleywoodgolfclub.co.uk

## Tadmarton Heath   (1922)
*Wigginton, Banbury OX15 5HL*
- ☎ **(01608) 737278**
- 🖳 (01608) 730548
- ✉ secretary@tadmartongolf.com
- ✍ JR Cox (01608) 737278
- 🖥 www.tadmartongolf.com

## Waterstock   (1994)
**Proprietary**
*Thame Road, Waterstock, Oxford
OX33 1HT*
- ☎ **(01844) 338093**
- 🖳 (01844) 338036
- ✉ wgc_oxford@btinternet.com
- ✍ AJ Wyatt
- 🖥 www.waterstockgolf.com

## Witney Lakes   (1994)
*Downs Road, Witney OX29 0SY*
- ☎ **(01993) 893011**
- 🖳 (01993) 778866
- ✉ golf@witney-lakes.co.uk

---

- ✍ G Brown
- 🖥 www.witney-lakes.co.uk

## The Wychwood   (1992)
**Proprietary**
*Lyneham, Chipping Norton OX7 6QQ*
- ☎ **(01993) 831841**
- 🖳 (01993) 831775
- ✉ info@thewychwood.com
- ✍ Mrs S J Lakin (administrator)
- 🖥 www.thewychwood.com

## Greetham Valley   (1992)
**Proprietary**
*Greetham, Oakham LE15 7SN*
- ☎ **(01780) 460444**
- 🖳 (01780) 460623
- ✉ info@greethamvalley.co.uk
- ✍ RE Hinch
- 🖥 www.greethamvalley.co.uk

## Luffenham Heath   (1911)
*South Luffenham, Stamford PE9 3UU*
- ☎ **(01780) 720205**
- 🖳 (01780) 722146
- ✉ tstephens@theluffenhamheathgc
  .co.uk
- ✍ Tim Stephens (Mgr)
- 🖥 www.luffenhamheath.org

## Rutland County Golf Club   (1991)
**Proprietary**
*Pickworth, Stamford PE9 4AQ*
- ☎ **(01780) 460239/460330**
- 🖳 (01780) 460437
- ✉ info@rutlandcountygolf.co.uk
- ✍ G Lowe (Golf Dir)
- 🖥 www.rutlandcountygolf.co.uk

## Aqualate   (1995)
**Pay and play**
*Stafford Road, Newport TF10 9DB*
- ☎ **(01952) 811699**
- 🖳 (01952) 825343
- ✍ HB Dawes (Mgr) (01952) 811699
- 🖥 www.aqualategolf..co.uk

## Arscott   (1992)
**Proprietary**
*Arscott, Pontesbury, Shrewsbury SY5 0XP*
- ☎ **(01743) 860114**
- 🖳 (01743) 860114
- ✉ golf@arscott.dydirect.net
- ✍ Sian Hinkins
- 🖥 www.arscottgolfclub.co.uk

## Bridgnorth   (1889)
*Stanley Lane, Bridgnorth WV16 4SF*
- ☎ **(01746) 763315**
- 🖳 (01746) 763315
- ✉ secretary@bridgnorthgolfclub
  .co.uk
- ✍ A M Jones
- 🖥 www.bridgnorthgolfclub.co.uk

---

## Brow
Proprietary
*Welsh Frankton, Ellesmere SY12 9HW*
☎ **(01691) 622628**
📧 browgolf@btinternet.com
✍ David Davies
🖥 www.thebrowgolfclub.com

## Chesterton Valley   (1993)
Proprietary
*Chesterton, Worfield, Bridgnorth WV15 5NX*
☎ **(01746) 783682**
📧 cvgc@hotmail.co.uk
✍ P Hinton
🖥 www.a1golf.biz

## Church Stretton   (1898)
*Trevor Hill, Church Stretton SY6 6JH*
☎ **(01694) 722281**
📧 secretary@churchstrettongolfclub
.co.uk
✍ J Townsend (Mgr) (07973) 762510
🖥 www.churchstrettongolfclub.co.uk

## Cleobury Mortimer   (1993)
Proprietary
*Wyre Common, Cleobury Mortimer DY14 8HQ*
☎ **(01299) 271112 (Clubhouse)**
🖥 (01299) 271468
📧 pro@cleoburygolfclub.com
✍ G Pain (Gen Mgr)
🖥 www.cleoburygolfclub.com

## Hawkstone Park Golf Club
(1920)
Proprietary
*Weston-under-Redcastle, Shrewsbury SY4 5UY*
☎ **(01939) 200365**
🖥 (01939) 200365
📧 secretary@hpgcgolf.com
✍ Jane Lloyd
🖥 www.hpgcgolf.com

## Hill Valley G&CC   (1975)
Proprietary
*Tarporley Road, Whitchurch SY13 4HA*
☎ **(0844) 879 9049**
🖥 (01948) 665927
📧 general.hillvalley@mcdonald-hotels.co.uk
✍ A De Barro (01948) 664039
🖥 www.hillvalleygolfclub.co.uk

## Horsehay Village Golf Centre
(1999)
Pay and play
*Wellington Road, Horsehay, Telford TF4 3BT*
☎ **(01952) 632070**
🖥 (01952) 632074
📧 horsehayvillagegolfcentre@telford
.gov.uk
✍ M Maddison (Mgr)
🖥 www.telford.gov.uk/golf

## Lilleshall Hall   (1937)
*Abbey Road, Lilleshall, Newport TF10 9AS*
☎ **(01952) 604776**

🖥 (01952) 604272
📧 honsec@lilleshallhallgolfclub.co.uk
✍ A Marklew (01952) 604776
🖥 www.lilleshallhallgolfclub.co.uk

## Llanymynech   (1933)
*Pant, Oswestry SY10 8LB*
☎ **(01691) 830983**
🖥 (01691) 183 9184
📧 secretary@llanymynechgolfclub
.co.uk
✍ Howard Jones
🖥 www.llanymynechgolfclub.co.uk

## Ludlow   (1889)
*Bromfield, Ludlow SY8 2BT*
☎ **(01584) 856285**
🖥 (01584) 856366
📧 secretary@ludlowgolfclub.com
✍ R Price (01584) 856285
🖥 www.ludlowgolfclub.com

## Market Drayton   (1906)
*Sutton, Market Drayton TF9 2HX*
☎ **(01630) 652266**
📧 market.draytongc@btconnect.com
✍ CK Stubbs
🖥 www.marketdraytongolfclub.co.uk

## Mile End   (1992)
Proprietary
*Mile End, Oswestry SY11 4JF*
☎ **(01691) 671246**
🖥 (01691) 670580
📧 info@mileendgolfclub.co.uk
✍ R Thompson
🖥 www.mileendgolfclub.co.uk

## Oswestry   (1903)
*Aston Park, Queens Head, Oswestry SY11 4JJ*
☎ **(01691) 610535**
🖥 (01691) 610535
📧 secretary@oswestrygolfclub.co.uk
✍ John Evans (01691) 610535
🖥 www.oswestrygolfclub.co.uk

## Patshull Park Hotel G&CC
(1980)
*Pattingham WV6 7HR*
☎ **(01902) 700100**
🖥 (01902) 700874
✍ John Poole
🖥 www.patshull-park.co.uk

## Shifnal   (1929)
*Decker Hill, Shifnal TF11 8QL*
☎ **(01952) 460330**
🖥 (01952) 460330
📧 secretary@shifnalgolf.com
✍ Miss L Law/Mr C Hayes
🖥 www.shifnalgolf.com

## Shrewsbury   (1891)
*Condover, Shrewsbury SY5 7BL*
☎ **(01743) 872977**
🖥 (01743) 872977
📧 info@shrewsburygolfclub.co.uk
✍ Anthony Rowe (01743) 872977
🖥 www.shrewsburygolfclub.co.uk

## The Shropshire   (1992)
*Muxton, Telford TF2 8PQ*
☎ **(01952) 677800**
🖥 (01952) 677622
📧 info@theshropshire.co.uk
✍ Stuart Perry (Gen Mgr)
🖥 www.theshropshire.co.uk

## Telford   (1976)
Proprietary
*Great Hay Drive, Sutton Heights, Telford TF7 4DT*
☎ **(01952) 429977**
🖥 (01952) 586602
📧 ibarklem@aol.com
✍ I Lucas
🖥 www.telford-golfclub.co.uk

## Worfield   (1991)
Proprietary
*Worfield, Bridgnorth WV15 5HE*
☎ **(01746) 716541**
🖥 (01746) 716302
📧 enquiries@worfieldgolf.co.uk
✍ W Weaver (Gen Mgr)
🖥 www.worfieldgolf.co.uk

## Wrekin   (1905)
*Wellington, Telford TF6 5BX*
☎ **(01952) 244032**
🖥 (01952) 252906
📧 secretary@wrekingolfclub.co.uk
✍ B P Everitt
🖥 www.wrekingolfclub.co.uk

# Somerset

## Bath   (1880)
*Sham Castle, North Road, Bath BA2 6JG*
☎ **(01225) 463834**
🖥 (01225) 331027
📧 enquiries@bathgolfclub.org.uk
✍ (01225) 463834
🖥 www.bathgolfclub.org.uk

## Brean   (1973)
*Coast Road, Brean, Burnham-on-Sea TA8 2QY*
☎ **(01278) 752111**
🖥 (01278) 752111
📧 proshop@brean.com
✍ D Haines (Director of Golf)
🖥 www.breangolfclub.co.uk

## Burnham & Berrow   (1890)
*St Christopher's Way, Burnham-on-Sea TA8 2PE*
☎ **(01278) 785760**
🖥 (01278) 795440
📧 secretary.bbgc@btconnect.com
✍ MA Blight (01278) 785760
🖥 www.burnhamandberrowgolfclub
.co.uk

## Cannington   (1993)
Pay and play
*Cannington Centre for Land Based Studies, Bridgwater TA5 2LS*
☎ **(01278) 655050**
🖥 (01278) 655055

macrowr@bridgwater.ac.uk
R Macrow (Mgr)
www.canningtongolfcentre
.co.uk

## Clevedon (1891)
Castle Road, Clevedon BS21 7AA
- **(01275) 874057**
- (01275) 341228
- secretary@clevedongolfclub
.co.uk
- J Cunning (01275) 874057
- www.clevedongolfclub.co.uk

## Enmore Park (1906)
Enmore, Bridgwater TA5 2AN
- **(01278) 672100**
- (01278) 672101
- manager@enmorepark.co.uk
- S.Varcoe (01278) 672100
- www.enmorepark.co.uk

## Farrington (1992)
Proprietary
Marsh Lane, Farrington Gurney, Bristol
BS39 6TS
- **(01761) 451596**
- (01761) 451021
- info@farringtongolfclub.net
- J Cowgill
- www.farringtongolfclub.net

## Fosseway CC (1970)
Charlton Lane, Midsomer Norton, Radstock
BA3 4BD
- **(01761) 412214**
- (01761) 418357
- club@centurionhotel.co.uk
- Mark Manley
- www.centurionhotel.co.uk

## Frome (1994)
Proprietary
Critchill Manor, Frome BA11 4LJ
- **(01373) 453410**
- secretary@fromegolfclub.co.uk
- Mrs S Austin/Mrs J Vowell
- www.fromegolfclub.co.uk

## Isle of Wedmore (1992)
Proprietary
Lineage, Lascots Hill, Wedmore
BS28 4QT
- **(01934) 712452**
- office@wedmoregolfclub.com
- AC Edwards (01934) 712222
- www.wedmoregolfclub.com

## Kingweston (1983)
(Sec) 12 Lowerside Road, Glastonbury,
Somerset BA6 9BH
- **(01458) 834086**
- I Price

## Lansdown (1894)
Lansdown, Bath BA1 9BT
- **(01225) 422138**
- (01225) 339252
- admin@lansdowngolfclub.co.uk
- Mrs E Bacon
- www.lansdowngolfclub.co.uk

## Long Sutton (1991)
Pay and play
Long Load, Langport TA10 9JU
- **(01458) 241017**
- (01458) 241022
- info@longsuttongolf.com
- Graham Holloway
- www.longsuttongolf.com

## The Mendip (1908)
Gurney Slade, Radstock BA3 4UT
- **(01749) 840570**
- secretary@mendipgolfclub.com
- J Scott (Managing Secretary)
- www.mendipgolfclub.com

## Mendip Spring (1992)
Proprietary
Honeyhall Lane, Congresbury BS49 5JT
- **(01934) 852322**
- (01934) 853021
- info@mendipspringgolfclub.com
- A Melhuish
- www.mendipspringgolfclub.com

## Minehead & West Somerset (1882)
The Warren, Minehead TA24 5SJ
- **(01643) 702057**
- (01643) 705095
- secretary@mineheadgolf.co.uk
- www.minehead-golf-club.co.uk

## Oake Manor (1993)
Oake, Taunton TA4 1BA
- **(01823) 461993**
- (01823) 461996
- golf@oakemanor.com
- R Gardner (Golf Mgr)
- www.oakemanor.com

## Orchardleigh Golf Club (1996)
Proprietary
Frome BA11 2PH
- **(01373) 454200**
- (01373) 454202
- info@orchardleighgolf.co.uk
- Peter Holloway (Director of Golf)
- www.orchardleighgolf.co.uk

## Saltford (1904)
Golf Club Lane, Saltford, Bristol BS31 3AA
- **(01225) 873513**
- (01225) 873525
- secretary@saltfordgolfclub.co.uk
- M Penn (01225) 873513
- www.saltfordgolfclub.co.uk

## Stockwood Vale (1991)
Public
Stockwood Lane, Keynsham, Bristol
BS31 2ER
- **(0117) 986 6505**
- (0117) 986 8974
- stockwoodvale@aol.com
- M Edenborough
- www.stockwoodvale.com

## Tall Pines (1990)
Proprietary
Cooks Bridle Path, Downside, Backwell,
Bristol BS48 3DJ
- **(01275) 472076**

- (01275) 474869
- T Murray
- www.tallpinesgolf.co.uk

## Taunton & Pickeridge (1892)
Corfe, Taunton TA3 7BY
- **(01823) 421537**
- (01823) 421742
- mail@tauntongolf.co.uk
- S Stevenson (Golf Professional)
- www.tauntongolf.co.uk

## Taunton Vale (1991)
Proprietary
Creech Heathfield, Taunton TA3 5EY
- **(01823) 412220**
- (01823) 413583
- admin@tauntonvalegolf.co.uk
- Reuben Evans
- www.tauntonvalegolf.co.uk

## Tickenham (1994)
Proprietary
Clevedon Road, Tickenham, Bristol
BS21 6RY
- **(01275) 856626**
- play@tickenhamgolf.co.uk
- Joint Head Pro's Andrew Sutcliffe
and Sarah Sutcliffe
- www.tickenhamgolf.co.uk

## Vivary Park (1928)
Public
Fons George, Taunton TA1 3JW
- **(01823) 333875**
- r.coffin@toneleisure.com
- Bob Stout
- www.toneleisure.co.uk

## Wells (1893)
East Horrington Road, Wells BA5 3DS
- **(01749) 675005**
- (01749) 683170
- secretary@wellsgolfclub.co.uk
- Eira Powell (01749) 675005
- www.wellsgolfclub.co.uk

## Weston-super-Mare (1892)
Uphill Road North, Weston-super-Mare
BS23 4NQ
- **(01934) 626968**
- (01934) 621360
- wsmgolfclub@eurotelbroadband
.com
- Mrs K Drake (01934) 626968
- www.westonsupermaregolfclub
.com

## Wheathill (1993)
Proprietary
Wheathill, Somerton TA11 7HG
- **(01963) 240667**
- (01963) 240230
- wheathill@wheathill.fsnet.co.uk
- A England
- www.wheathillgc.co.uk

## Wincanton Golf Course (1994)
Proprietary
The Racecourse, Wincanton BA9 8BJ
- **(01963) 435850**

📞 (01963) 34668
✉ wincanton@thejockeyclub.co.uk
✍ Andrew England
🖥 wincantonracecourse.co.uk

## Windwhistle    (1932)
Cricket St Thomas, Chard TA20 4DG
📞 **(01460) 30231**
📠 (01460) 30055
✉ info@windwhistlegolfclub.co.uk
✍ Miss Sarah Wills
🖥 www.windwhistlegolfclub.co.uk

## Worlebury    (1908)
Monks Hill, Worlebury, Weston-super-Mare
BS22 9SX
📞 **(01934) 625789**
📠 (01934) 621935
✉ secretary@worleburygc.co.uk
✍ A S Horsburgh
🖥 www.worleburygc.co.uk

## Yeovil    (1907)
Sherborne Road, Yeovil BA21 5BW
📞 **(01935) 422965**
📠 (01935) 411283
✉ office@yeovilgolfclub.com
✍ S Greatorex (01935) 422965
🖥 www.yeovilgolfclub.com

## Staffordshire

## 3 Hammers Golf Complex
(1964)
**Pay and play**
Old Stafford Road, Coven, Wolverhampton
WV10 7PP
📞 **(01902) 790428**
📠 (01902) 791777
✉ Info@3hammers.co.uk
✍ Mr Nick Forbes
🖥 www.3hammers.co.uk

## Alsager G&CC    (1992)
Audley Road, Alsager, Stoke-on-Trent
ST7 2UR
📞 **(01270) 875700**
📠 (01270) 875008
✉ admin@alsagergolfclub.com
✍ Margaret Davenport
🖥 www.alsagergolfclub.com

## Aston Wood    (1994)
Blake Street, Sutton Coldfield B74 4EU
📞 **(0121) 580 7803**
📠 (0121) 353 0354
✉ events@astonwoodgolfclub
.co.uk
✍ Simon Smith
🖥 www.astonwoodgolfclub.co.uk

## Barlaston    (1987)
Meaford Road, Stone ST15 8UX
📞 **(01782) 372867 (Admin)**
    **372795 (Pro-Shop)**
📠 (01782) 373648
✉ info@barlastongolfclub.co.uk
✍ C P Holloway (01782 372867)
🖥 www.barlastongolfclub.co.uk

## Beau Desert    (1911)
Hazel Slade, Cannock WS12 0PJ
📞 **(01543) 422626/422773**
📠 (01543) 451137
✉ enquiries@bdgc.co.uk
✍ Stephen Mainwaring
    01543) 422626
🖥 www.bdgc.co.uk

## Bloxwich    (1924)
136 Stafford Road, Bloxwich WS3 3PQ
📞 **(01922) 476593**
📠 (01922) 493449
✉ secretary@bloxwichgolfclub.com
✍ RJ Wormstone
🖥 www.bloxwichgolfclub.com

## Branston G&CC    (1975)
Burton Road, Branston, Burton-on-Trent
DE14 3DP
📞 **(01283) 528320**
📠 (01283) 566984
✉ golflodge@branstonclub.co.uk
✍ Richard Odell (Director of Golf)
🖥 www.branstonclub.co.uk

## Brocton Hall    (1894)
Brocton, Stafford ST17 0TH
📞 **(01785) 661901**
📠 (01785) 661591
✉ secretary@broctonhall.com
✍ JDS Duffy (01785) 661901
🖥 www.broctonhall.com

## Burslem    (1907)
Wood Farm, High Lane, Stoke-on-Trent
ST6 7JT
📞 **(01782) 837006**
✉ alanbgc@talktalkbusiness.net
✍ A Porter

## Calderfields    (1983)
**Proprietary**
Aldridge Road, Walsall WS4 2JS
📞 **(01922) 632243**
📠 (01922) 640540
✉ GM@calderfieldsgolfclub.com
✍ MR Andrews
🖥 www.calderfieldsgolfclub.co.uk

## Cannock Park    (1993)
**Public**
Stafford Road, Cannock WS11 2AL
📞 **(01543) 578850**
📠 (01543) 578850
✉ seccpgc@yahoo.co.uk
✍ CB Milne (01543) 571091
🖥 www.cpgc.freeserve.co.uk

## The Chase    (1991)
**Proprietary**
Pottal Pool Road, Penkridge ST19 5RN
📞 **(01785) 712888**
📠 (01785) 712692
✉ manager@thechasegolf.co.uk
✍ Bryan Davies
🖥 www.thechasegolf.co.uk

## The Craythorne    (1974)
Craythorne Road, Rolleston on Dove, Burton
upon Trent DE13 0AZ
📞 **(01283) 564329**

📠 (01283) 511908
✉ admin@craythorne.co.uk
✍ AA Wright (Man Dir/Owner)
🖥 www.craythorne.co.uk

## Dartmouth    (1910)
Vale Street, West Bromwich B71 4DW
📞 **(0121) 588 2131**
📠 (0121) 588 5746
✍ CF Wade (0121) 532 4070
🖥 www.dartmouthgolfclub.co.uk

## Denstone College    (1991)
Denstone, Uttoxeter ST14 5HN
📞 **(01889) 590484**
📠 (01889) 590744
✉ andy.oakes@uwclub.net
✍ Andy Oakes
🖥 www.denstonecollege.org

## Drayton Park    (1897)
Drayton Park, Tamworth B78 3TN
📞 **(01827) 251139**
📠 (01827) 284035
✉ admin@draytonparkgc.com
✍ Jon Northover
🖥 www.draytonparkgc.com

## Druids Heath    (1974)
Stonnall Road, Aldridge WS9 8JZ
📞 **(01922) 455595**
✉ admin@druidsheathgc.co.uk
✍ KI Taylor
🖥 www.druidsheathgc.co.uk

## Enville    (1935)
Highgate Common, Enville, Stourbridge
DY7 5BN
📞 **(01384) 872074**
✉ manager@envillegolfclub.com
✍ H L Mulley (Mgr)
🖥 www.envillegolfclub.com

## Great Barr    (1961)
Chapel Lane, Birmingham B43 7BA
📞 **(0121) 358 4376**
📠 (0121) 358 4376
✉ info@greatbarrgolfclub.co.uk
✍ Miss L Pollard (0121) 358 4376
🖥 www.greatbarrgolfclub.co.uk

## Greenway Hall    (1909)
**Proprietary**
Stockton Brook, Stoke-on-Trent ST9 9LJ
📞 **(01782) 503158**
✉ contact@greenwayhallgolfclub.co.uk
✍ Simon Arnold (Golf Pro)
🖥 www.greenwayhallgolfclub.co.uk

## Hawkesyard    (1995)
Hawkesyard Hall and Golf Club, Armitage
Park, Nr. Lichfield WS15 1PU
📞 **(01543) 491911**
📠 (01543) 492096
✉ info@hawkesyardestate.com
✍ RMR O'Hanlon
🖥 www.hawkesyardestate.com

## Himley Hall    (1980)
**Pay and play**
Himley Hall Park, Dudley DY3 4DF
📞 **(01902) 895207**

(01902) 895207
himleygolf@hotmail.co.uk
B Sparrow (01902) 894973 mobile
07515 284196
www.himleyhallgolfclub.com

## Ingestre Park (1977)
*Ingestre, Stafford ST18 0RE*
☎ **(01889) 270845**
📠 (01889) 271434
📧 manager@ingestregolf.co.uk
D Warrilow (Mgr)
www.ingestregolf.com

## Izaak Walton (1993)
*Cold Norton, Stone ST15 0NS*
☎ **(01785) 760900**
📠 (01785) 760900 (opt 4)
📧 secretary@izaakwaltongolfclub
.co.uk
Charlie Lightbown
www.izaakwaltongolfclub.co.uk

## Keele Golf Centre (1973)
**Pay and play**
*Keele Road, Newcastle-under-Lyme
ST5 5AB*
☎ **(01782) 627596**
📠 (01782) 714555
L Harris (01782) 751173

## Lakeside (1969)
*Rugeley Power Station, Rugeley WS15 1PR*
☎ **(01889) 575667**
📧 lakeside.golfclub@unicombox.co.uk
TA Yates
www.lakesidegolf.co.uk

## Leek (1892)
*Birchall, Leek ST13 5RE*
☎ **(01538) 384779**
📠 (01538) 384779
📧 enquiries@leekgolfclub.co.uk
DT Brookhouse
www.leekgolfclub.co.uk

## Lichfield Golf and Country Club (1991)
**Proprietary**
*Elmhurst, Lichfield WS13 8HE*
☎ **(01543) 417333**
📠 (01543) 418098
📧 r.gee@theclubcompany.com
Richard Gee
www.theclubcompany.com

## Little Aston (1908)
*Roman Road, Streetly, Sutton Coldfield
B74 3AN*
☎ **(0121) 353 2942**
📠 (0121) 580 8387
📧 manager@littleastongolf.co.uk
Glyn Ridley (Mgr) (0121) 353 2942
www.littleastongolf.co.uk

## Manor (Kingstone) (1991)
**Proprietary**
*Leese Hill, Kingstone, Uttoxeter ST14 8QT*
☎ **(01889) 563234**
📠 (01889) 563234
📧 manorgc@btinternet.com
S Foulds
www.manorgolfclub.net

## Newcastle-under-Lyme (1908)
*Whitmore Road, Newcastle-under-Lyme
ST5 2QB*
☎ **(01782) 617006**
📠 (01782) 617531
📧 info@newcastlegolfclub.co.uk
Joe Hyde (Manager)
www.newcastlegolfclub.co.uk

## Onneley (1968)
*Onneley, Crewe, Cheshire CW3 9QF*
☎ **(01782) 750577**
📧 admin@onneleygolfclub.co.uk
Iain Colville (Mgr)
www.onneleygolf.co.uk

## Oxley Park (1913)
*Stafford Road, Bushbury, Wolverhampton
WV10 6DE*
☎ **(01902) 773989**
📠 (01902) 773981
📧 office@oxleyparkgolfclub.co.uk
www.oxleyparkgolfclub.co.uk

## Parkhall (1989)
**Public**
*Hulme Road, Weston Coyney, Stoke-on-
Trent ST3 5BH*
☎ **(01782) 599584**
📠 (01782) 599584
M Robson

## Penn (1908)
*Penn Common, Wolverhampton WV4 5JN*
☎ **(01902) 341142**
📠 (01902) 620504
📧 secretary@penngolfclub.co.uk
Rob Hickman
www.penngolfclub.co.uk

## Perton Park (1990)
**Proprietary**
*Wrottesley Park Road, Perton,
Wolverhampton WV6 7HL*
☎ **(01902) 380073**
📠 (01902) 326219
📧 admin@pertongolfclub.co.uk
Mark Allen (Gen Mgr)
www.pertongolfclub.co.uk

## Sandwell Park (1895)
*Birmingham Road, West Bromwich B71 4JJ*
☎ **(0121) 553 4637**
📠 (0121) 525 1651
📧 secretary@sandwellparkgolfclub
.co.uk
www.sandwellparkgolfclub.co.uk

## Sedgley (1992)
**Pay and play**
*Sandyfields Road, Sedgley, Dudley DY3 3DL*
☎ **(01902) 880503**
📧 admin@sedgleygolfcentre.co.uk
David Cox

## South Staffordshire (1892)
*Danescourt Road, Tettenhall,
Wolverhampton WV6 9BQ*
☎ **(01902) 751065**
📠 (01902) 751159
📧 suelebeau@southstaffsgc.co.uk

P Baker (Professional)
www.southstaffsgc.co.uk

## Stafford Castle (1906)
**Proprietary**
*Newport Road, Stafford ST16 1BP*
☎ **(01785) 223821**
📠 (01785) 223821
📧 sharonscgc@btconnect.com
Mrs S Calvert
www.staffordcastlegolf.com

## Stone (1896)
*The Fillybrooks, Stone ST15 0NB*
☎ **(01785) 813103**
D M Cole (01785) 817746
www.stonegolfclub.co.uk

## Swindon (1976)
**Proprietary**
*Bridgnorth Road, Swindon, Dudley DY3 4PU*
☎ **(01902) 897031**
📠 (01902) 326219
📧 admin@swindongolfclub.co.uk
Mark Allen (Mgr)
www.swindongolfclub.co.uk

## Tamworth (1976)
**Public**
*Eagle Drive, Amington, Tamworth B77 4EG*
☎ **(01827) 709303**
📠 (01827) 709304
Elaine Pugh

## Trentham (1894)
*14 Barlaston Old Road, Trentham, Stoke-
on-Trent ST4 8HB*
☎ **(01782) 658109**
📠 (01782) 644024
📧 secretary@trenthamgolf.org
Richard Minton (Gen Mgr)
www.trenthamgolf.org

## Trentham Park (1936)
*Trentham Park, Stoke-on-Trent ST4 8AE*
☎ **(01782) 642245**
📠 (01782) 658800
📧 manager@trenthamparkgolfclub
.com
Gordon Martin (01782) 658800
www.trenthamparkgolfclub.com

## Uttoxeter (1970)
*Wood Lane, Uttoxeter ST14 8JR*
☎ **(01889) 566552**
📠 (01889) 566552
📧 admin@uttoxetergolfclub.com
Mr A McCanaless
www.uttoxetergolfclub.com

## Walsall (1907)
*Broadway, Walsall WS1 3EY*
☎ **(01922) 613512**
📠 (01922) 616460
📧 secretary@walsallgolfclub.co.uk
P Thompson (01922) 613512
www.walsallgolfclub.co.uk

## Wergs (1990)
**Pay and play**
*Keepers Lane, Tettenhall WV6 8UA*
☎ **(01902) 742225**

(01902) 844553
wergs.golfclub@btinternet.com
Tina Bennett (Mgr)
www.wergs.com

## Westwood   (1923)
Newcastle Road, Wallbridge, Leek
ST13 7AA
☎ (01538) 398385
(01538) 382485
westwoodgolfclubleek@btconnect
.com
Mr W Walker (Hon Sec)
www.westwoodgolfclubleek.co.uk

## Whiston Hall   (1971)
Whiston, Cheadle ST10 2HZ
☎ (01538) 266260
(01538) 266820
info@whistonhall.co.uk
LC & RM Cliff (Mgr)
www.whistonhall.com

## Whittington Heath   (1886)
Tamworth Road, Lichfield WS14 9PW
☎ (01543) 432317 (Admin)
    432212 (Steward)
(01543) 433962
info@whittingtonheathgc.co.uk
Mrs JA Burton
www.whittingtonheathgc.co.uk

## Wolstanton   (1904)
Dimsdale Old Hall, Hassam Parade,
Wolstanton, Newcastle ST5 9DR
☎ (01782) 622413
(01782) 622413
Mrs VJ Keenan (01782) 622413
www.wolstantongolfclub.com

## Suffolk

## Aldeburgh   (1884)
Saxmunden Road, Aldeburgh IP15 5PE
☎ (01728) 452890
(01728) 452937
info@aldeburghgolfclub.co.uk
Bill Beckett (Sec)
www.aldeburghgolfclub.co.uk

## Beccles   (1899)
The Common, Beccles NR34 9BX
☎ (01502) 712244
alan@ereira.wanadoo.co.uk
A Ereira (07896) 087297
www.becclesgolfclub.co.uk

## Brett Vale   (1992)
Proprietary
Noakes Road, Raydon, Ipswich IP7 5LR
☎ (01473) 310718
info@brettvalegolf.co.uk
L Williams
www.brettvale.co.uk

## Bungay & Waveney Valley
(1889)
Outney Common, Bungay NR35 1DS
☎ (01986) 892337
(01986) 892222

golf@bungaygc.co.uk
A Collison (Director of golf)
www.club-noticeboard.co.uk
/bungay

## Bury St Edmunds   (1924)
Tut Hill, Fornham All Saints, Bury St
Edmunds IP28 6LG
☎ (01284) 755979
(01284) 763288
secretary@burygolf.co.uk
M Verhelst
www.burystedmundsgolfclub.co.uk

## Cretingham   (1984)
Grove Farm, Cretingham, Woodbridge
IP13 7BA
☎ (01728) 685275
(01728) 685488
cretinghamgolf@tiscali.co.uk
Mrs K Jackson
www.cretinghamgolfclub.co.uk

## Diss   (1903)
Stuston Common, Diss IP21 4AA
☎ (01379) 641025
(01379) 644586
sec.dissgolf@virgin.net
Graham Weeks
www.club-noticeboard.co.uk

## Felixstowe Ferry   (1880)
Ferry Road, Felixstowe IP11 9RY
☎ (01394) 286834
(01394) 273679
secretary@felixstowegolf.co.uk
R Baines (01394) 286834
www.felixstowegolf.co.uk

## Flempton   (1895)
Flempton, Bury St Edmunds IP28 6EQ
☎ (01284) 728291
secretary@flemptongolfclub.co.uk
MS Clark
www.flemptongolfclub.co.uk

## Fynn Valley   (1991)
Proprietary
Witnesham, Ipswich IP6 9JA
☎ (01473) 785267
(01473) 785632
enquiries@fynn-valley.co.uk
AR Tyrrell (01473) 785267
www.fynn-valley.co.uk

## Halesworth   (1990)
Proprietary
Bramfield Road, Halesworth IP19 9XA
☎ (01986) 875567
(01986) 874565
info@halesworthgc.co.uk
Chris Aldred (Mgr)
www.halesworthgc.co.uk

## Haverhill   (1974)
Coupals Road, Haverhill CB9 7UW
☎ (01440) 761951
(01440) 761951
admin@haverhillgc.co.uk
Mrs K Wilby (Mgr)
www.club-noticeboard.co.uk

## Hintlesham   (1991)
Proprietary
Hintlesham, Ipswich IP8 3JG
☎ (01473) 652761
(01473) 652750
sales@hintleshamgolfclub.com
Henry Roblin (Owner/Director)
www.hintleshamgolfclub.com

## Ipswich Golf Club (Purdis
Heath)   (1895)
Purdis Heath, Bucklesham Road, Ipswich
IP3 8UQ
☎ (01473) 728941
(01473) 715236
neill@ipswichgolfclub.com
Neill Ellice (01473) 728941
www.ipswichgolfclub.com

## Links (Newmarket)   (1902)
Cambridge Road, Newmarket CB8 0TG
☎ (01638) 663000
(01638) 661476
secretary@linksgolfclub.co.uk
ML Hartley
www.linksgolfclub.co.uk

## Newton Green   (1907)
Newton Green, Sudbury CO10 0QN
☎ (01787) 377217
info@newtongreengolfclub.co.uk
Mrs C List
www.newtongreengolfclub.co.uk

## Rookery Park   (1891)
Beccles Road, Carlton Colville, Lowestoft
NR33 8HJ
☎ (01502) 509190
office@rookeryparkgolfclub.co.uk
R Pettett
www.rookeryparkgolfclub.co.uk

## Royal Worlington &
Newmarket   (1893)
Golf Links Road, Worlington, Bury St
Edmunds IP28 8SD
☎ (01638) 717787 Sec/
    (01638) 712216 Clubhouse
secretary@royalworlington.co.uk
S Ballentine (01638) 717787
www.royalworlington.co.uk

## Rushmere   (1927)
Rushmere Heath, Ipswich IP4 5QQ
☎ (01473) 725648
(01473) 273852
rushmeregolfclub@btconnect
.com
RWG Tawell (01473) 725648
www.club-
noticeboard.co.uk/rushmere

## Seckford   (1991)
Seckford Hall Road, Great Bealings,
Woodbridge IP13 6NT
☎ (01394) 388000
(01394) 382818
secretary@seckfordgolf.co.uk
G Cook
www.seckfordgolf.co.uk

**Southwold**  (1884)
*The Common, Southwold IP18 6TB*
☎ **(01502) 723234**
✉ mail@southwoldgolfclub.co.uk
✍ R Wilshaw (01502) 723248
🖳 www.southwoldgolfclub.co.uk

**Stoke-by-Nayland**  (1972)
*Keepers Lane, Leavenheath, Colchester CO6 4PZ*
☎ **(01206) 262836**
🖳 (01206) 265840
✉ golfsecretary@stokebynayland.com
✍ A Bullock (01206) 265815
🖳 www.stokebynayland.com

**Stowmarket**  (1902)
*Lower Road, Onehouse, Stowmarket IP14 3DA*
☎ **(01449) 736473**
🖳 (01449) 736826
✉ mail@stowmarketgolfclub.co.uk
✍ Geoff Scott (01449) 736473
🖳 www.club-noticeboard.co.uk /stowmarket

**Thorpeness Hotel & Golf Course**  (1923)
**Proprietary**
*Thorpeness, Leiston IP16 4NH*
☎ **(01728) 452176**
🖳 (01728) 453868
✉ christopher@thorpeness.co.uk
✍ Christopher Oldrey (01728) 454926
🖳 www.thorpeness.co.uk

**Ufford Park Hotel Golf & Spa**
(1992)
**Pay and play**
*Yarmouth Road, Melton, Woodbridge, Suffolk IP12 1QW*
☎ **(01394) 382836**
🖳 (01394) 383582
✉ enquiries@uffordpark.co.uk
✍ Michael Halliday
🖳 www.uffordpark.co.uk

**Waldringfield**  (1983)
*Newbourne Road, Waldringfield, Woodbridge IP12 4PT*
☎ **(01473) 736768**
✉ enquiries@waldringfieldgc.co.uk
✍ Pat Whitham
🖳 www.waldringfieldgc.co.uk

**Woodbridge**  (1893)
*Bromeswell Heath, Woodbridge IP12 2PF*
☎ **(01394) 382038**
🖳 (01394) 382392
✉ info@woodbridgegolfclub.co.uk
✍ AJ Bull
🖳 www.woodbridgegolfclub.co.uk

## Surrey

**Abbey Moor**  (1991)
**Pay and play**
*Green Lane, Addlestone KT15 2XU*
☎ **(01932) 570741/570765**

🖳 (01932) 561313
✍ Richard Payne (01932) 570741

**The Addington**  (1913)
**Proprietary**
*205 Shirley Church Road, Croydon CR0 5AB*
☎ **(020) 8777 1055**
🖳 (020) 8777 6661
✉ info@addingtongolf.com
✍ Oliver Peel
🖳 www.addingtongolf.com

**Addington Court**  (1932)
**Pay and play**
*Featherbed Lane, Addington, Croydon CR0 9AA*
☎ **(020) 8657 0281 (Bookings)**
🖳 (020) 8651 0282
✉ addington@crown-golf.co.uk
✍ B Chard (020) 657 0281
🖳 www.addingtoncourt-golfclub.co.uk

**Addington Palace**  (1930)
*Addington Park, Gravel Hill, Addington CR0 5BB*
☎ **(020) 8654 3061**
🖳 (020) 8655 3632
✉ info@addingtonpalacegolf.co.uk
✍ Roger Williams
🖳 www.addingtonpalacegolf.co.uk

**Banstead Downs**  (1890)
*Burdon Lane, Belmont, Sutton SM2 7DD*
☎ **(020) 8642 2284**
🖳 (020) 8642 5252
✉ secretary@bansteaddowns.com
✍ R D Bauser
🖳 www.bansteaddowns.com

**Barrow Hills**  (1970)
*Longcross, Chertsey KT16 0DS*
☎ **(01344) 635770**
✍ R Hammond (01483) 234807

**Betchworth Park**  (1911)
*Reigate Road, Dorking RH4 1NZ*
☎ **(01306) 882052**
✉ manager@betchworthparkgc.co.uk
✍ Timothy Lowe (Sec/Mgr)
🖳 www.betchworthparkgc.co.uk

**Bletchingley**  (1993)
**Proprietary**
*Church Lane, Bletchingley RH1 4LP*
☎ **(01883) 744666 Functions 744848 Golf**
🖳 (01883) 744284
✉ stevec1412@yahoo.co.uk
✍ Steven Cookson (Golf Operations Mgr)
🖳 www.bletchingleygolf.co.uk

**Bowenhurst Golf Centre**
(1994)
*Mill Lane, Crondall, Farnham GU10 5RP*
☎ **(01252) 851695**
🖳 (01252) 852225
✍ GL Corbey (01252) 851695

**Bramley**  (1913)
*Bramley, Guildford GU5 0AL*
☎ **(01483) 892696**
🖳 (01483) 894673
✉ secretary@bramleygolfclub.co.uk
✍ Jeremy Lucas (Club Mgr) (01483) 892696
🖳 www.bramleygolfclub.co.uk

**Broadwater Park**  (1989)
**Pay and play**
*Guildford Road, Farncombe, Godalming GU7 3BU*
☎ **(01483) 429955**
✉ info@broadwaterparkgolf.co.uk
✍ Kevin Milton
🖳 www.broadwaterparkgolfclub.co.uk

**Burhill**  (1907)
*Burwood Road, Walton-on-Thames KT12 4BL*
☎ **(01932) 227345**
🖳 (01932) 267159
✉ info@burhillgolf-club.co.uk
✍ D Cook (Gen Mgr)
🖳 www.burhillgolf-club.co.uk

**Camberley Heath**  (1912)
*Golf Drive, Camberley GU15 1JG*
☎ **(01276) 23258**
🖳 (01276) 692505
✉ info@camberleyheathgolfclub.co.uk
✍ Stuart Dubber
🖳 www.camberleyheathgolfclub.co.uk

**Central London Golf Centre**
(1992)
**Public**
*Burntwood Lane, Wandsworth, London SW17 0AT*
☎ **(020) 8871 2468**
🖳 (020) 8874 7447
✉ info@clgc.co.uk
✍ Michael Anscomb (Mgr)
🖳 www.clgc.co.uk

**Chessington Golf Centre**
(1983)
**Pay and play**
*Garrison Lane, Chessington KT9 2LW*
☎ **(020) 8391 0948**
🖳 (020) 8397 2068
✉ info@chessingtongolf.co.uk
✍ M Bedford
🖳 www.chessingtongolf.co.uk

**Chiddingfold**  (1994)
*Petworth Road, Chiddingfold GU8 4SL*
☎ **(01428) 685888**
🖳 (01428) 685939
✉ enquiries@chiddingfoldgolf.co.uk

**Chipstead**  (1906)
*How Lane, Chipstead, Coulsdon CR5 3LN*
☎ **(01737) 555781**
🖳 (01737) 555404
✉ office@chipsteadgolf.co.uk
✍ Gary Torbett (Director)
🖳 www.chipsteadgolf.co.uk

### Chobham (1994)
*Chobham Road, Knaphill, Woking GU21 2TZ*
☎ **(01276) 855584**
📠 (01276) 855663
📧 info@chobhamgolfclub.co.uk
🔏 Adrian Wratting
🖥 www.chobhamgolfclub.co.uk

### Clandon Regis (1994)
*Epsom Road, West Clandon GU4 7TT*
☎ **(01483) 224888**
📠 (01483) 211781
📧 office@clandonregis-golfclub.co.uk
🔏 Paul Napier (Gen Mgr)
🖥 www.clandonregis-golfclub.co.uk

### Coombe Hill (1911)
*Golf Club Drive, Coombe Lane West, Kingston KT2 7DF*
☎ **(0208) 336 7600**
📠 (0208) 336 7601
📧 office@chgc.net
🔏 Colin Chapman (CEO)
🖥 www.coombehillgolfclub.com

### Coombe Wood (1904)
*George Road, Kingston Hill, Kingston-upon-Thames KT2 7NS*
☎ **(0208) 942 0388 (Clubhouse)**
📠 (0208) 942 5665
📧 geoff.seed@coombewoodgolf.com
🔏 G Seed (0208) 942 0388
🖥 www.coombewoodgolf.com

### Coulsdon Manor (1937)
**Pay and play**
*Coulsdon Court Road, Old Coulsdon, Croydon CR5 2LL*
☎ **(0843) 178 7149**
📠 (0843) 178 7150
📧 reservations.coulsdon @bespokehotels.com
🔏 A Oxby (020) 8668 0414
🖥 www.bespokehotels.com /coulsdonmanorandgolf

### The Cranleigh (1985)
*Barhatch Lane, Cranleigh GU6 7NG*
☎ **(01483) 268855**
📠 (01483) 267251
📧 clubshop@cranleighgolfandleisure .co.uk
🔏 MG Kateley
🖥 www.cranleighgolfandleisure.co.uk

### Croham Hurst (1911)
*Croham Road, South Croydon CR2 7HJ*
☎ **(020) 8657 5581**
📠 (020) 8657 3229
📧 secretary@chgc.co.uk
🔏 S Mackinson
🖥 www.chgc.co.uk

### Cuddington (1929)
*Banstead Road, Banstead SM7 1RD*
☎ **(020) 8393 0952**
📠 (020) 8786 7025
📧 secretary@cuddingtongc.co.uk
🔏 John Robinson
🖥 www.cuddingtongc.co.uk

### Dorking (1897)
*Deepdene Avenue, Chart Park, Dorking RH5 4BX*
☎ **(01306) 886917**
📠 (01306) 886917
📧 info@dorkinggolfclub.co.uk
🔏 A Smeal (Mgr)
🖥 www.dorkinggolfclub.co.uk

### Drift (1975)
**Proprietary**
*The Drift, East Horsley KT24 5HD*
☎ **(01483) 284641**
📠 (01483) 284642
📧 info@driftgolfclub.com
🔏 Ben Beagley (GM)
🖥 www.driftgolfclub.com

### Dulwich & Sydenham Hill (1894)
*Grange Lane, College Road, London SE21 7LH*
☎ **(020) 8693 3961**
📠 (020) 8693 2481
📧 info@dulwichgolf.co.uk
🔏 MP Hickson
🖥 www.dulwichgolf.co.uk

### Effingham (1927)
*Guildford Road, Effingham KT24 5PZ*
☎ **(01372) 452203**
📠 (01372) 459959
📧 secretary@effinghamgolfclub .com
🔏 Robin Easton (Business Mgr)
🖥 www.effinghamgolfclub.com

### Epsom (1889)
*Longdown Lane South, Epsom Downs, Surrey KT17 4JR*
☎ **(01372) 721666**
📠 (01372) 817183
📧 stuart@epsomgolfclub.co.uk
🔏 Stuart Walker (Pro)
🖥 www.epsomgolfclub.co.uk

### Farnham (1896)
*The Sands, Farnham GU10 1PX*
☎ **(01252) 782109**
📠 (01252) 781185
📧 farnhamgolfclub@tiscali.co.uk
🔏 G Cowlishaw (01252) 782109
🖥 www.farnhamgolfclub.co.uk

### Farnham Park (1966)
**Pay and play**
*Folly Hill, Farnham GU9 0AU*
☎ **(01252) 715216**
📧 farnhamparkgolf@googlemail .com
🔏 J Van Der Merwe
🖥 www.fpgc.co.uk

### Foxhills (1975)
*Stonehill Road, Ottershaw KT16 0EL*
☎ **(01932) 872050**
📠 (01932) 874762
📧 golfservices@foxhills.co.uk
🔏 R Hyder
🖥 www.foxhills.co.uk

### Gatton Manor Hotel & Golf Club (1969)
**Proprietary**
*Standon Lane, Ockley, Dorking, Surrey RH5 5PQ*
☎ **(01306) 627555**
📠 (01306) 627713
📧 info@gattonmanor.co.uk
🔏 Patrick Kiely (owner)
🖥 www.gattonmanor.co.uk

### Goal Farm Par Three (1978)
**Proprietary**
*Gole Road, Pirbright GU24 0PZ*
☎ **(01483) 473183**
📠 (01483) 473205
📧 secretary@goalfarmgolfclub.co.uk
🔏 R Little
🖥 www.goalfarmgolfclub.co.uk

### Guildford (1886)
*High Path Road, Merrow, Guildford GU1 2HL*
☎ **(01483) 563941**
📧 secretary@guildfordgolfclub.co.uk
🔏 Adam Bodimeade (Gen Mgr)
🖥 www.guildfordgolfclub.co.uk

### Hampton Court Palace (1895)
*Hampton Wick, Kingston-upon-Thames KT1 4AD*
☎ **(020) 8977 2423**
📠 (020) 8614 4747
📧 hamptoncourtpalace@crown-golf .co.uk
🔏 Matthew Hazelden

### Hankley Common (1896)
*Tilford, Farnham GU10 2DD*
☎ **(01252) 792493**
📠 (01252) 795699
📧 lynne@hankley.co.uk
🔏 IM McColl (01252) 797711
🖥 www.hankley.co.uk

### Hazelwood Golf Centre (1992)
**Pay and play**
*Croysdale Avenue, Green Street, Sunbury-on-Thames TW16 6QU*
☎ **(01932) 770932**
📠 (01932) 770933
📧 hazelwoodgolf@btconnect.com
🔏 Roger Ward

### Hersham Golf Club (1997)
**Proprietary**
*Assher Road, Hersham, Surrey KT12 4RA*
☎ **(01932) 267666**
📠 (01932) 240975
📧 hvgolf@tiscali.co.uk
🔏 R Hutton (Golf Dir)
🖥 www.hershamgolfclub.co.uk

### The Hindhead (1904)
*Churt Road, Hindhead GU26 6HX*
☎ **(01428) 604614**
📠 (01428) 608508
📧 secretary@the-hindhead-golf-club.co.uk
🖥 www.the-hindhead-golf-club.co.uk

## Hoebridge Golf Centre
(1982)
**Public**
*Old Woking Road, Old Woking GU22 8JH*
- ☎ **(01483) 722611**
- 📠 (01483) 740369
- ✉ info@hoebridgegc.co.uk
- ✍ M O'Connell (Senior Gen Mgr)
- 🖥 www.hoebridgegc.co.uk

## Horne Park (1994)
**Proprietary**
*Croydon Barn Lane, Horne, South Godstone RH9 8JP*
- ☎ **(01342) 844443**
- 📠 (01342) 841828
- ✉ info@hornepark.co.uk
- ✍ Neil Burke
- 🖥 www.hornepark.co.uk

## Horton Park Golf Club
(1987)
**Pay and play**
*Hook Road, Epsom KT19 8QG*
- ☎ **(020) 8393 8400 (Enquiries)**
- 📠 (020) 8394 3854
- ✉ info@hortonparkgolf.com
- ✍ Wendy Wright
- 🖥 www.hortonparkgolf.com

## Hurtmore (1992)
**Pay and play**
*Hurtmore Road, Hurtmore, Surrey GU7 2RN*
- ☎ **(01483) 426492**
- 📠 (01483) 426121
- ✉ hurtmore@hoburne.com
- ✍ Maxine Burton (01483) 426492
- 🖥 www.hurtmore-golf.co.uk

## Kingswood (1928)
**Proprietary**
*Sandy Lane, Kingswood, Tadworth KT20 6NE*
- ☎ **(01737) 832188**
- 📠 (01737) 833920
- ✉ sales@kingswood-golf.co.uk
- ✍ Mark Stewart (Secretary)
- 🖥 www.kingswood-golf.co.uk

## Laleham (1903)
**Proprietary**
*Laleham Reach, Chertsey KT16 8RP*
- ☎ **(01932) 564211**
- ✉ info@laleham-golf.co.uk
- ✍ Managing Director
- 🖥 www.laleham-golf.co.uk

## Limpsfield Chart (1889)
*Westerham Road, Limpsfield RH8 0SL*
- ☎ **(01883) 723405/722106**
- ✉ secretary@limpsfieldchartgolf.co.uk
- ✍ K Johnson
- 🖥 www.limpsfieldchartgolf.co.uk

## Lingfield Park (1987)
*Racecourse Road, Lingfield RH7 6PQ*
- ☎ **(01342) 834602**
- 📠 (01342) 836077
- ✉ cmorley@lingfieldpark.co.uk
- ✍ C Morley

## London Scottish (1865)
*Windmill Enclosure, Wimbledon Common, London SW19 5NQ*
- ☎ **(020) 8788 0135**
- 📠 (020) 8789 7517
- ✉ secretary.lsgc@btconnect.com
- ✍ S Barr (020) 8789 1207
- ⊕ Red upper outer garment must be worn
- 🖥 www.londonscottishgolfclub.co.uk

## Malden (1893)
*Traps Lane, New Malden KT3 4RS*
- ☎ **(020) 8942 0654**
- 📠 (020) 8336 2219
- ✉ manager@maldengolfclub.com
- ✍ Mr Neil Coulson-Bence (Mgr)
- 🖥 www.maldengolfclub.com

## Merrist Wood (1997)
*Coombe Lane, Worplesdon, Guildford GU3 3PE*
- ☎ **(01483) 238890**
- 📠 (01483) 238896
- ✍ Martin Huckleby
- 🖥 www.merristwood-golfclub.co.uk

## Milford (1993)
**Proprietary**
*Station Lane, Milford GU8 5HS*
- ☎ **(01483) 419200**
- 📠 (01483) 419199
- ✉ milford-manager@crown-golf.co.uk
- ✍ Rebecca Prout
- 🖥 www.milfordgolf.co.uk

## Mitcham (1924)
*Carshalton Road, Mitcham Junction CR4 4HN*
- ☎ **(020) 8640 4197**
- 📠 (020) 8648 4197
- ✉ mitchamgc@hotmail.co.uk
- ✍ DJ Tilley (020) 8648 4197
- 🖥 www.mitchamgolfclub.co.uk

## Moore Place (1926)
**Public**
*Portsmouth Road, Esher KT10 9LN*
- ☎ **(01372) 463533**
- 📠 (01372) 463533
- ✍ R Egan (020) 8715 8851
- 🖥 www.moore-place.co.uk

## New Zealand (1895)
*Woodham Lane, Addlestone KT15 3QD*
- ☎ **(01932) 345049**
- ✉ roger.marrett@nzgc.org
- ✍ RA Marrett (01932) 342891

## North Downs (1899)
*Northdown Road, Woldingham, Caterham CR3 7AA*
- ☎ **(01883) 652057**
- 📠 (01883) 652832
- ✉ secretary@northdownsgolfclub.co.uk
- ✍ K R Robinson (Sec)
- 🖥 www.northdownsgolfclub.co.uk

## Oak Park (1984)
**Proprietary**
*Heath Lane, Crondall, Farnham GU10 5PB*
- ☎ **(01252) 850850**
- 📠 (01252) 850851
- ✉ oakpark@crown-golf.co.uk
- ✍ S Edwin
- 🖥 www.oakparkgolf.co.uk

## Oaks Sports Centre (1973)
**Public**
*Woodmansterne Road, Carshalton SM5 4AN*
- ☎ **(020) 8643 8363**
- 📠 (020) 8661 7880
- ✉ info@theoaksgolf.co.uk
- ✍ G Edginton
- 🖥 www.theoaksgolf.co.uk

## Pachesham Park Golf Centre
(1990)
**Pay and play**
*Oaklawn Road, Leatherhead KT22 0BP*
- ☎ **(01372) 843453**
- 📠 (01372) 841796
- ✉ enquiries@pacheshamgolf.co.uk
- ✍ P Taylor
- 🖥 www.pacheshamgolf.co.uk

## Pine Ridge (1992)
**Pay and play**
*Old Bisley Road, Frimley, Camberley GU16 9NX*
- ☎ **(01276) 675444**
- 📠 (01276) 678837
- ✉ pineridge@crown-golf.co.uk
- ✍ Elaine Jackson (Sec/Mgr)
- 🖥 www.pineridgegolf.co.uk

## Playgolf Leatherhead (1903)
**Proprietary**
*Kingston Road, Leatherhead KT22 0EE*
- ☎ **(01372) 849413**
- 📠 (01372) 842241
- ✉ leatherhead@playgolfworld.com
- ✍ Timothy Lowe
- 🖥 www.playgolfleatherhead.com

## Purley Downs (1894)
*106 Purley Downs Road, South Croydon CR2 0RB*
- ☎ **(020) 8657 8347**
- 📠 (020) 8651 5044
- ✉ info@purleydowns.co.uk
- ✍ Mr S Graham
- 🖥 www.purleydowns.co.uk

## Puttenham (1894)
*Puttenham, Guildford GU3 1AL*
- ☎ **(01483) 810498**
- 📠 (01483) 810988
- ✉ enquiries@puttenhamgolfclub.co.uk
- ✍ G Simmons
- 🖥 www.puttenhamgolfclub.co.uk

## Pyrford (1993)
*Warren Lane, Pyrford GU22 8XR*
- ☎ **(01483) 723555**
- 📠 (01483) 729777
- ✉ pyrford@crown-golf.co.uk
- ✍ Andrew Lawrence
- 🖥 www.pyrfordgolf.co.uk

## Redhill    (1993)
**Pay and play**
*Canada Avenue, Redhill RH1 5BF*
☎ **(01737) 770204**
✉ info@redhillgolfcentre.co.uk
🏌 S Furlonger
🖥 www.redhillgolfcentre.co.uk

## Redhill & Reigate    (1887)
**Members Club**
*Clarence Lodge, Pendleton Road, Redhill RH1 6LB*
☎ **(01737) 240777/244433**
🖬 (01737) 242117
✉ mail@rrgc.net
🏌 D Simpson (01737) 240777
🖥 www.rrgc.net

## Reigate Heath    (1895)
*The Club House, Reigate Heath RH2 8QR*
☎ **(01737) 242610**
✉ manager@reigateheathgolfclub .co.uk
🏌 Richard Arnold (01737) 242610
🖥 www.reigateheathgolfclub.co.uk

## Reigate Hill
**Proprietary**
*Gatton Bottom, Reigate RH2 0TU*
☎ **(01737) 645577**
🖬 (01737) 642650
✉ proshop@reigatehillgolfclub.co.uk
🏌 John Holmes
🖥 www.reigatehillgolfclub.co.uk

## The Richmond    (1891)
*Sudbrook Park, Richmond TW10 7AS*
☎ **(020) 8940 4351**
🖬 (020) 8332 7914
✉ gm@richmondgolfclub.co.uk
🏌 J Maguire (020) 8940 4351
🖥 www.therichmondgolfclub.com

## Richmond Park    (1923)
**Public**
*Roehampton Gate, Richmond Park, London SW15 5JR*
☎ **(020) 8876 3205/1795**
🖬 (020) 8878 1354
✉ richmondpark@glendale-services.co.uk
🏌 A J Gourvish
🖥 www.richmondparkgolf.co.uk

## Roehampton Club    (1901)
*Roehampton Lane, London SW15 5LR*
☎ **(020) 8480 4200**
🖬 (020) 8480 4265
✉ tristan.mcillroy@roehamptonclub .co.uk
🏌 Tristan McIllroy
🖥 www.roehamptonclub.co.uk

## Rokers Golf Course    (1993)
**Pay and play**
*Holly Lane, Aldershot Road, Guildford GU3 3PB*
☎ **(01483) 236677**
✉ golf@rokers.co.uk
🏌 C Tegg
🖥 www.rokersgolf.co.uk

## Royal Automobile Club    (1913)
*Woodcote Park, Wilmerhatch Lane, Epsom KT18 7EW*
☎ **(01372) 273091**
🖬 (01372) 276117
✉ golf@royalautomobileclub.co.uk
🏌 Jason Neve (Dir. of Golf)
🖥 www.royalautomobileclub.co.uk

## Royal Mid-Surrey    (1892)
*Old Deer Park, Twickenham Road, Richmond TW9 2SB*
☎ **(020) 8940 1894**
🖬 (020) 8939 0150
✉ secretary@rmsgc.co.uk
🏌 Luke Edgcumbe
🖥 www.rmsgc.co.uk

## Royal Wimbledon    (1865)
*29 Camp Road, Wimbledon, London SW19 4UW*
☎ **(020) 8946 2125**
🖬 (020) 8944 8652
✉ secretary@rwgc.co.uk
🏌 R J Brewer (Sec)
🖥 www.rwgc.co.uk

## Rusper    (1992)
**Proprietary**
*Rusper Road, Newdigate, Dorking RH5 5BX*
☎ **(01293) 871871/871456**
✉ nikki@ruspergolfclub.co.uk
🏌 Miss Nikki Sanders (Sec)/Mr Simon Adby (Man Dir.)
🖥 www.ruspergolfclub.co.uk

## Sandown Park Golf Centre    (1960)
**Public**
*More Lane, Esher KT10 8AN*
☎ **(01372) 469260**
🏌 Nick Jones & Craig Morley (Directors)
🖥 www.sandownparkgolf.com

## Selsdon Park Hotel    (1929)
**Proprietary**
*Addington Road, Sanderstead, South Croydon CR2 8YA*
☎ **(020) 768 3116**
🖬 (020) 8657 3401
✉ enquiries@principal-hayley.com
🏌 Mr C Baron
🖥 www.principal-hayley.com

## Shirley Park    (1914)
*194 Addiscombe Road, Croydon CR0 7LB*
☎ **(020) 8654 1143**
🖬 (020) 8654 6733
✉ secretary@shirleyparkgolfclub .co.uk
🏌 Steve Murphy
🖥 www.shirleyparkgolfclub.co.uk

## Silvermere    (1976)
**Pay and play**
*Redhill Road, Cobham KT11 1EF*
☎ **(01932) 584300**
🖬 (01932) 584301
✉ sales@silvermere-golf.co.uk
🏌 Mrs P Devereux (01932) 584306
🖥 www.silvermere-golf.co.uk

## St George's Hill    (1912)
*Golf Club Road, St George's Hill, Weybridge KT13 0NL*
☎ **(01932) 847758**
🖬 (01932) 821564
✉ admin@stgeorgeshillgolfclub.co.uk
🏌 B J Hill
🖥 www.stgeorgeshillgolfclub.co.uk

## Sunningdale    (1900)
*Ridgemount Road, Sunningdale, Berks SL5 9RR*
☎ **(01344) 621681**
🖬 (01344) 624154
✉ info@sunningdalegolfclub.co.uk
🏌 S Toon
🖥 www.sunningdale-golfclub.co.uk

## Sunningdale Ladies    (1902)
*Cross Road, Sunningdale SL5 9RX*
☎ **(01344) 620507**
✉ golf@sunningdaleladies.co.uk
🏌 Samantha Lamb
🖥 www.sunningdaleladies.co.uk

## Surbiton    (1895)
*Woodstock Lane, Chessington KT9 1UG*
☎ **(020) 8398 3101**
🖬 (020) 8339 0992
✉ enqs@surbitongolfclub.com
🏌 CJ Cornish
🖥 www.surbitongolfclub.com

## Surrey Downs    (2001)
**Proprietary**
*Outwood Lane, Kingswood KT20 6JS*
☎ **(01737) 839090**
🖬 (01737) 839080
✉ booking@surreydownsgc.co.uk
🏌 P Townson
🖥 www.surreydownsgc.co.uk

## Surrey National    (1999)
*Rook Lane, Chaldon, Caterham CR3 5AA*
☎ **(01883) 344555**
✉ caroline@surreynational.co.uk
🏌 R Sturgeon (Gen Mgr)
🖥 www.surreynational.co.uk

## Sutton Green    (1994)
*New Lane, Sutton Green, Guildford GU4 7QF*
☎ **(01483) 747898**
🖬 (01483) 750289
✉ admin@suttongreengc.co.uk
🏌 J Buchanan
🖥 www.suttongreengc.co.uk

## The Swallow Farleigh Court    (1997)
**Proprietary**
*Old Farleigh Road, Farleigh CR6 9PX*
☎ **(01883) 627711**
🖬 (01883) 627722
✉ enquiries@farleighfox.co.uk
🏌 Scott Graham (Mgr)
🖥 www.farleighfox.co.uk

## Tandridge    (1924)
*Oxted RH8 9NQ*
☎ **(01883) 712273 (Clubhouse)**
🖬 (01883) 730537

secretary@tandridgegolfclub.com
A J Tanner
www.tandridgegolfclub.com

**Thames Ditton & Esher** (1892)
Portsmouth Road, Esher KT10 9AL
☎ (020) 8398 1551
D Dodge

**Tyrrells Wood** (1924)
The Drive, Tyrrells Wood, Leatherhead
KT22 8QP
☎ (01372) 376025 (2 lines)
(01372) 360836
office@tyrrellswoodgolfclub.com
www.tyrrellswoodgolfclub.com

**Walton Heath** (1903)
Deans Lane, Walton-on-the-Hill, Tadworth
KT20 7TP
☎ (01737) 812060
(01737) 814225
secretary@waltonheath.com
Stuart Christie (01737) 812380
www.waltonheath.com

**Wentworth Club** (1924)
Wentworth Drive, Virginia Water GU25 4LS
☎ (01344) 842201
(01344) 842804
Stuart Christie (Admin)
www.wentworthclub.com

**West Byfleet** (1906)
Sheerwater Road, West Byfleet KT14 6AA
☎ (01932) 343433
admin@wbgc.co.uk
I R Attoe (Gen Mgr) (01932) 343433
www.wbgc.co.uk

**West Hill** (1909)
Bagshot Road, Brookwood GU24 0BH
☎ (01483) 474365
(01483) 474252
secretary@westhill-golfclub.co.uk
Gina Rivett
www.westhill-golfclub.co.uk

**West Surrey** (1910)
Enton Green, Godalming GU8 5AF
☎ (01483) 421275
(01483) 415419
office@wsgc.co.uk
Richard Hall (Sec/Mgr)
www.wsgc.co.uk

**Wildwood Golf & CC** (1992)
Proprietary
Horsham Road, Alfold GU6 8JE
☎ (01403) 753255
(01403) 752005
info@wildwoodgolf.co.uk
J Hansen
www.wildwoodgolf.co.uk

**Wimbledon Common** (1908)
19 Camp Road, Wimbledon Common,
London SW19 4UW
☎ (020) 8946 0294 (Pro Shop)
(020) 8947 8697
office@wcgc.co.uk

Jeff Jukes (Golf Mgr/Pro)
www.wcgc.co.uk

**Wimbledon Park** (1898)
Home Park Road, London SW19 7HR
☎ (020) 8946 1250
(020) 8944 8688
secretary@wpgc.co.uk
P Shanahan
www.wpgc.co.uk

**Windlemere** (1978)
Pay and play
Windlemere Road, West End, Woking
GU24 9QL
☎ (01276) 858727 or (01276) 858271
(01276) 858271
mikew@windlemeregolf.co.uk
C D Smith/M Walsh

**Windlesham** (1994)
Proprietary
Grove End, Bagshot GU19 5HY
☎ (01276) 452220
(01276) 452290
admin@windleshamgolf.com
Scott Patience
www.windleshamgolf.com

**The Wisley** (1991)
Ripley, Woking GU23 6QU
☎ (01483) 212110
(01483) 211662
reception@thewisley.com
Wayne Sheffield
www.thewisley.com

**Woking** (1893)
Pond Road, Hook Heath, Woking
GU22 0JZ
☎ (01483) 760053
(01483) 772441
info@wokinggolfclub.co.uk
G Ritchie
www.wokinggolfclub.co.uk

**Woldingham** (1996)
proprietary
Halliloo Valley Road, Woldingham CR3 7HA
☎ (01883) 653501
(01883) 653502
info@woldingham-golfclub.com
Michael Chubb
www.woldingham-golfclub.co.uk

**Woodcote Park** (1912)
Meadow Hill, Bridle Way, Coulsdon
CR5 2QQ
☎ (0208) 668 2788
(0208) 660 0918
info@woodcotepgc.com
AP Dawson
www.woodcotepgc.com

**Worplesdon** (1908)
Heath House Road, Woking GU22 0RA
☎ (01483) 472277
(01483) 473303
office@worplesdongc.co.uk
CK Symington
www.worplesdongc.co.uk

## Sussex (East)

**Beauport Park Golf Course** (1973)
Pay and play
Battle Road, St Leonards-on-Sea, East
Sussex TN37 7BP
☎ (01424) 854245
(01424) 854245
info@beauportparkgolf.co.uk
C Giddins
www.beauportparkgolf.co.uk

**Brighton & Hove** (1887)
Devils Dyke Road, Brighton BN1 8YJ
☎ (01273) 556482
(01273) 554247
phil@brightongolf.co.uk
P Bonsall (Golf Dir)
www.brightonandhovegolfclub.co.uk

**Cooden Beach** (1912)
Cooden Sea Road, Bexhill-on-Sea
TN39 4TR
☎ (01424) 842040
(01424) 842040
enquiries@coodenbeachgc.com
KP Wiley (01424) 842040
www.coodenbeachgc.com

**Crowborough Beacon** (1895)
Beacon Road, Crowborough TN6 1UJ
☎ (01892) 661511
office@cbgc.co.uk
John Holmes (Mgr)
www.cbgc.co.uk

**Dale Hill Hotel & GC** (1973)
Ticehurst, Wadhurst TN5 7DQ
☎ (01580) 201090
(01580) 201249
golf@dalehill.co.uk
John Tolliday (Dir of Golf)
www.dalehill.co.uk

**Dewlands Manor** (1992)
Cottage Hill, Rotherfield TN6 3JN
☎ (01892) 852266
(01892) 853015
T Robins
⊕ 15 minute Tee Times relaxed golf

**Dyke Golf Club** (1906)
Devil's Dyke, Devil's Dyke Road, Brighton
BN1 8YJ
☎ (01273) 857296
(01273) 857078
manager@dykegolfclub.co.uk
Megan Bibby (Gen Mgr)
www.dykegolf.com

**East Brighton** (1893)
Roedean Road, Brighton BN2 5RA
☎ (01273) 604838
(01273) 680277
office@ebgc.co.uk
James Malliff
www.ebgc.co.uk

## East Sussex National Golf Resort and Spa (1989)
**Proprietary**
*Little Horsted, Uckfield TN22 5ES*
☎ **(01825) 880088**
📠 (01825) 880066
📧 reception@eastsussexnational.co.uk
✍ DT Howe
🖥 www.eastsussexnational.co.uk

## Eastbourne Downs (1908)
*East Dean Road, Eastbourne BN20 8ES*
☎ **(01323) 720827**
📧 secretary@ebdownsgolf.co.uk
✍ Lorna Hardy & Sandra McKay
🖥 www.ebdownsgolf.co.uk

## Eastbourne Golfing Park Ltd (1992)
**Pay and play**
*Lottbridge Drove, Eastbourne BN23 6QJ*
☎ **(01323) 520400**
📠 (01323) 520400
📧 egpltd@hotmail.co.uk
✍ Maggie Garbutt
🖥 www.eastbournegolfingpark.co.uk

## Highwoods (1925)
*Ellerslie Lane, Bexhill-on-Sea TN39 4LJ*
☎ **(01424) 212625**
📠 (01424) 216866
📧 highwoods@btconnect.com
✍ AP Moran
🖥 www.highwoodsgolfclub.co.uk

## Hollingbury Park (1908)
**Public**
*Ditchling Road, Brighton BN1 7HS*
☎ **(01273) 552010**
📠 (01273) 552010
✍ Mrs M Bailey
🖥 www.hollingburygolfclub.co.uk

## Holtye (1893)
*Holtye Common, Cowden, Nr Edenbridge TN8 7ED*
☎ **(01342) 850635**
📧 secretary@holtye.com
✍ Mrs I Martin (01342) 850635 opt 2
🖥 www.holtye.com

## Horam Park (1985)
**Pay and play**
*Chiddingly Road, Horam TN21 0JJ*
☎ **(01435) 813477**
📠 (01435) 813677
📧 angie@horampark.com
✍ Mrs A Briggs
🖥 www.horamparkgolfclub.co.uk

## Lewes (1896)
*Chapel Hill, Lewes BN7 2BB*
☎ **(01273) 473245**
📠 (01273) 483474
📧 secretary@lewesgolfclub.co.uk
✍ Mr L C Dorn (01273) 483474
🖥 www.lewesgolfclub.co.uk

## Mid Sussex (1995)
**Proprietary**
*Spatham Lane, Ditchling BN6 8XJ*
☎ **(01273) 846567**
📠 (01273) 847815
📧 admin@midsussexgolfclub.co.uk
✍ Lee Andrews
🖥 www.midsussexgolfclub.co.uk

## Nevill (1914)
*Benhall Mill Road, Tunbridge Wells TN2 5JW*
☎ **(01892) 525818**
📠 (01892) 517861
📧 manager@nevillgolfclub.co.uk
✍ FW Prescott
🖥 www.nevillgolfclub.co.uk

## Peacehaven (1895)
**Proprietary**
*Brighton Road, Newhaven BN9 9UH*
☎ **(01273) 514049**
📧 henry@golfatpeacehaven.co.uk
✍ Henry Hilton (01273) 514049
🖥 www.golfatpeacehaven.co.uk

## Piltdown (1904)
*Piltdown, Uckfield TN22 3XB*
☎ **(01825) 722033**
📠 (01825) 724192
📧 secretary@piltdowngolfclub.co.uk
✍ Mike Miller
🖥 www.piltdowngolfclub.co.uk

## Royal Ashdown Forest (1888)
*Chapel Lane, Forest Row, East Sussex RH18 5LR*
☎ **(01342) 822018**
📠 (01342) 825211
📧 david@royalashdown.co.uk
✍ D S Holmes
🖥 www.royalashdown.co.uk

## Royal Eastbourne (1887)
*Paradise Drive, Eastbourne BN20 8BP*
☎ **(01323) 744045**
📧 sec@regc.co.uk
✍ David Lockyer (01323) 744045
🖥 www.regc.co.uk

## Rye (1894)
*New Lydd Road, Camber, Rye TN31 7QS*
☎ **(01797) 225241**
📠 (01797) 225460
📧 links@ryegolfclub.co.uk
✍ J H Laidler (Sec)
🖥 www.ryegolfclub.co.uk

## Seaford (1887)
*111 Firle Road, Seaford BN25 2JD*
☎ **(01323) 892442**
📠 (01323) 894113
📧 secretary@seafordgolfclub.co.uk
✍ LM Dennis-Smither (Gen Sec)
🖥 www.seafordgolfclub.co.uk

## Seaford Head (1887)
**Public**
*Southdown Road, Seaford BN25 4JS*
☎ **(01323) 890139**
📠 (01323) 890139

📧 seafordheadproshop@hotmail.co.uk
✍ RW Andrews (01323) 894843
🖥 www.seafordheadgolfcourse.co.uk

## Sedlescombe (1990)
*Kent Street, Sedlescombe TN33 0SD*
☎ **(01424) 871700**
📠 (01424) 871712
📧 golf@golfschool.co.uk
✍ Dan Gale

## Wellshurst G&CC (1992)
**Proprietary**
*North Street, Hellingly BN27 4EE*
☎ **(01435) 813636**
📠 (01435) 812444
📧 info@wellshurst.com
✍ M Adams (Man Dir)
🖥 www.wellshurst.com

## West Hove (1910)
*Badgers Way, Hangleton, Hove BN3 8EX*
☎ **(01273) 413411 (Clubhouse)**
📠 (01273) 439988
📧 info@westhovegolfclub.co.uk
✍ Gary Salt (Mgr) (01273) 419738
🖥 www.westhovegolfclub.info

## Willingdon (1898)
*Southdown Road, Eastbourne BN20 9AA*
☎ **(01323) 410981**
📠 (01323) 411510
📧 secretary@willingdongolfclub.co.uk
✍ Mrs J Packham (01323) 410981
🖥 www.willingdongolfclub.co.uk

# Sussex (West)

## Avisford Park (1990)
**Pay and play**
*Yapton Lane, Walberton, Arundel BN18 0LS*
☎ **(01243) 554611**
📠 (01243) 554958
📧 avisfordparkgolf@aol.com
✍ Sarah Chitty
🖥 www.avisfordparkgolfclub.com

## Bognor Regis (1892)
*Downview Road, Felpham, Bognor Regis PO22 8JD*
☎ **(01243) 821929**
📠 (01243) 860719
📧 sec@bognorgolfclub.co.uk
🖥 www.bognorgolfclub.co.uk

## Burgess Hill Golf Centre (1995)
**Pay and play**
*Cuckfield Road, Burgess Hill*
☎ **(01444) 258585 (shop)**
📠 (01444) 247318
📧 enquiries@burgesshillgolfcentre.co.uk
✍ CJ Collins (Mgr)
🖥 www.burgesshillgolfcentre.co.uk

## Chartham Park   (1993)
**Proprietary**
*Felcourt, East Grinstead RH19 2JT*
☎ **(01342) 870340**
🖳 (01342) 870719
✉ d.hobbs@theclubcompany.com
⛳ David Hobbs (PGA Pro)
🖥 www.theclubcompany.com

## Chichester   (1990)
**Proprietary**
*Hunston Village, Chichester PO20 1AX*
☎ **(01243) 533833**
🖳 (01243) 538989
✉ info@chichestergolf.com
⛳ Helen Howard (01243) 536666
🖥 www.chichestergolf.com

## Copthorne   (1892)
*Borers Arms Road, Copthorne RH10 3LL*
☎ **(01342) 712508**
🖳 (01342) 717682
✉ info@copthornegolfclub.co.uk
⛳ R Moan (01342) 712033
🖥 www.copthornegolfclub.co.uk

## Cottesmore   (1975)
**Proprietary**
*Buchan Hill, Pease Pottage, Crawley RH11 9AT*
☎ **(01293) 528256**
🖳 (0844) 8717221
✉ info@cottesmoregolf.co.uk
⛳ N Miller
🖥 www.cottesmoregolf.co.uk

## Cowdray Park   (1904)
**Proprietary**
*Petworth Road, Midhurst GU29 0BB*
☎ **(01730) 813599**
🖳 (01730) 815900
✉ enquiries@cowdraygolf.co.uk
⛳ M Purves
🖥 www.cowdraygolf.co.uk

## Effingham Park   (1980)
**Proprietary**
*West Park Road, Copthorne RH10 3EU*
☎ **(01342) 716528**
🖳 (0870) 890 0215
✉ mark.root@mill-cop.com
⛳ IWB McRobbie (Hon)
🖥 www.effinghamparkgc.co.uk

## Foxbridge   (1993)
*Foxbridge Lane, Plaistow RH14 0LB*
☎ **(01403) 753303 (Bookings)**
🖳 (01403) 753303
⛳ PA Clark

## Golf At Goodwood   (1892)
*Kennel Hill, Goodwood, Chichester PO18 0PN*
☎ **(01243) 755130**
🖳 (01243) 755135
✉ golf@goodwood.com
🖥 www.goodwood.com

## Ham Manor   (1936)
*West Drive, Angmering, Littlehampton BN16 4JE*
☎ **(01903) 783288**

🖳 (01903) 850886
✉ secretary@hammanor.co.uk
⛳ Paul Bodle
🖥 www.hammanor.co.uk

## Hassocks   (1995)
**Pay and play**
*London Road, Hassocks BN6 9NA*
☎ **(01273) 846990**
🖳 (01273) 846070
✉ admin@hassocksgolfclub.co.uk
⛳ Mr Michael Ovett (Gen Mgr)
🖥 www.hassocksgolfclub.co.uk

## Haywards Heath   (1922)
*High Beech Lane, Haywards Heath RH16 1SL*
☎ **(01444) 414457**
🖳 (01444) 458319
✉ info@haywardsheathgolfclub.co.uk
⛳ Graham White
🖥 www.haywardsheathgolfclub.co.uk

## Hill Barn   (1935)
**Public**
*Hill Barn Lane, Worthing BN14 9QE*
☎ **(01903) 237301**
🖳 (01903) 217613
✉ info@hillbarn.com
⛳ R Haygarth (01903) 237301
🖥 www.hillbarngolf.com

## Horsham   (1993)
**Pay and play**
*Worthing Road, Horsham RH13 0AX*
☎ **(01403) 271525**
🖳 (01403) 274528
✉ secretary@horshamgolfandfitness.co.uk
⛳ Warren Pritchard
🖥 www.horshamgolfandfitness.co.uk

## Ifield   (1927)
*Rusper Road, Ifield, Crawley RH11 0LN*
☎ **(01293) 520222**
🖳 (01293) 612973
⛳ J Earl

## Lindfield   (1990)
**Proprietary**
*East Mascalls Lane, Lindfield RH16 2QN*
☎ **(01444) 484467**
🖳 (01444) 482709
✉ info@thegolfcollege.com
⛳ Paul Lyons
🖥 www.thegolfcollege.com

## Littlehampton   (1889)
*170 Rope Walk, Littlehampton BN17 5DL*
☎ **(01903) 717170**
🖳 (01903) 726629
✉ lgc@talk21.com
⛳ S Graham
🖥 www.littlehamptongolf.co.uk

## Mannings Heath   (1905)
**Proprietary**
*Fullers, Hammerpond Road, Mannings Heath, Horsham RH13 6PG*
☎ **(01403) 210228**
🖳 (01403) 270974
✉ enquiries@manningsheath.com

⛳ Steve Slinger (01403) 220340
🖥 www.exclusivehotels.co.uk

## Pease Pottage Golf Centre   (1986)
*Horsham Road, Pease Pottage, Crawley RH11 9AP*
☎ **(01293) 521706**
🖳 (01293) 521706
⛳ A Venn (01293) 521766

## Petworth Downs Golf Club   (1989)
**Pay and play**
*London Road, Petworth GU28 9LX*
☎ **(01798) 344097**
✉ petworthdowns@hotmail.co.uk
⛳ Annabel Hall (0771) 156 7466
🖥 www.petworthgolf.com

## Pyecombe   (1894)
*Clayton Hill, Pyecombe, Brighton BN45 7FF*
☎ **(01273) 845372**
🖳 (01273) 843338
✉ info@pyecombegolfclub.com
⛳ Alan Davey
🖥 www.pyecombegolfclub.com

## Rustington   (1992)
**Public**
*Golfers Lane, Angmering BN16 4NB*
☎ **(01903) 850790**
🖳 (01903) 850982
✉ info@rgcgolf.com
⛳ Mr S Langmead
🖥 www.rgcgolf.com

## Selsey   (1908)
*Golf Links Lane, Selsey PO20 9DR*
☎ **(01243) 605176 (Members)**
🖳 (01243) 607101
✉ secretary@selseygolfclub.co.uk
⛳ BE Rogers (01243) 608935
🖥 www.selseygolfclub.co.uk

## Shillinglee Park   (1980)
**Pay and play**
*Chiddingfold, Godalming GU8 4TA*
☎ **(01428) 653237**
🖳 (01428) 644391
⛳ G Baxter (Prop)

## Singing Hills   (1992)
**Proprietary**
*Muddleswood Road, Albourne, Brighton BN6 9EB*
☎ **(01273) 835353**
🖳 (01273) 835444
✉ golfsecretary@singinghills.co.uk
⛳ Jane Covey
🖥 www.singinghills.co.uk

## Slinfold Golf & Country Club   (1993)
**Proprietary**
*Stane Street, Slinfold, Horsham RH13 0RE*
☎ **(01403) 791154 (Clubhouse)**
🖳 (01403) 791465
✉ info.slinfold@ccgclubs.com
⛳ S Blake (Gen Mgr)
🖥 www.ccgslinford.com

## Tilgate Forest   (1982)
**Public**
*Titmus Drive, Tilgate, Crawley RH10 5EU*
- ☎ **(01293) 530103**
- 📠 (01293) 523478
- ✍ I Bourton

## West Chiltington   (1988)
**Proprietary**
*Broadford Bridge Road, West Chiltington RH20 2YA*
- ☎ **(01798) 813574**
- 📠 (01798) 812631
- ✉ debbie@westchiltgolf.co.uk
- ✍ D Haines
- 🖳 www.westchiltgolf.co.uk

## West Sussex   (1931)
*Golf Club Lane, Wiggonholt, Pulborough RH20 2EN*
- ☎ **(01798) 872563**
- 📠 (01798) 872033
- ✉ secretary@westsussexgolf.co.uk
- ✍ A D Stubbs
- 🖳 www.westsussexgolf.co.uk

## Worthing   (1905)
*Links Road, Worthing BN14 9QZ*
- ☎ **(01903) 260801**
- 📠 (01903) 694664
- ✉ enquiries@worthinggolf.com
- ✍ John Holton
- 🖳 www.worthinggolf.co.uk

# Tyne & Wear

## Backworth   (1937)
*The Hall, Backworth, Shiremoor, Newcastle-upon-Tyne NE27 0AH*
- ☎ **(0191) 268 1048**
- ✉ backworth.miners@virgin.net
- ✍ J A Wilkinson
- 🖳 www.backworthgolf.co.uk

## Birtley   (1922)
*Birtley Lane, Birtley DH3 2LR*
- ☎ **(0191) 410 2207**
- 📠 (0191) 410 2207
- ✉ birtleygolfclub@aol.com
- ✍ K Self
- 🖳 www.birtleyportobellogolfclub.co.uk

## Boldon   (1912)
*Dipe Lane, East Boldon, Tyne & Wear NE36 0PQ*
- ☎ **(0191) 536 5360 (Clubhouse)**
- 📠 (0191) 537 2270
- ✉ info@boldongolfclub.co.uk
- ✍ Chris Brown (0191) 536 5360
- 🖳 www.boldongolfclub.co.uk

## City of Newcastle   (1891)
*Three Mile Bridge, Gosforth, Newcastle-upon-Tyne NE3 2DR*
- ☎ **(0191) 285 1775**
- 📠 (0191) 284 0700
- ✉ info@cityofnewcastlegolfclub.co.uk
- ✍ AJ Matthew (Mgr)
- 🖳 www.cityofnewcastlegolfclub.co.uk

## Garesfield   (1922)
*Chopwell NE17 7AP*
- ☎ **(01207) 561309**
- 📠 (01207) 561073
- ✉ garesfieldgc@btconnect.com
- ✍ Mr Alan Hill (Hon Sec)
- 🖳 www.garesfieldgolfclub.co.uk

## Gosforth   (1906)
*Broadway East, Gosforth, Newcastle upon Tyne NE3 5ER*
- ☎ **(0191) 285 0553**
- ✉ gosforth.golf@virgin.net
- ✍ Grahame Garland
- 🖳 www.gosforthgolfclub.co.uk

## Hetton-le-Hill Community Golf Club
*Easington Lane, Co. Durham DH5 0QB*
- ☎ **(0191) 517 3057**
- 📠 (0191) 517 3054
- ✉ elemortgolfclub@talktalkbusiness.net
- ✍ William Allen
- 🖳 www.elemort.co.uk

## Heworth   (1912)
*Gingling Gate, Heworth, Gateshead NE10 8XY*
- ☎ **(0191) 469 9832**
- 📠 (0191) 469 9898
- ✉ heworthgc@tiscali.co.uk
- ✍ G Peters
- 🖳 www.theheworthgolfclub.co.uk

## Houghton-le-Spring   (1908)
*Copt Hill, Houghton-le-Spring, Tyne & Wear DH5 8LU*
- ☎ **(0191) 584 7421 (Pro Shop)**
- 📠 (0191) 584 0048
- ✉ houghton.golf@virgin.net
- ✍ Graeme Robinson
- 🖳 www.houghtongolfclub.co.uk

## Newcastle United   (1892)
*Ponteland Road, Cowgate, Newcastle-upon-Tyne NE5 3JW*
- ☎ **(0191) 286 9998 (Clubhouse)**
- 📠 (0191) 286 4323
- ✉ info@newcastleunitedgolfclub.co.uk
- ✍ P Jobe (Sec/Treasurer)
- 🖳 www.newcastleunitedgolfclub.co.uk

## Northumberland   (1898)
*High Gosforth Park, Newcastle-upon-Tyne NE3 5HT*
- ☎ **(0191) 236 2498/2009**
- 📠 (0191) 236 2036
- ✉ gm@thengc.co.uk
- ✍ Richard Breakey
- 🖳 www.thengc.co.uk

## Parklands   (1971)
**Proprietary**
*High Gosforth Park, Newcastle-upon-Tyne NE3 5HQ*
- ☎ **(0191) 236 3322**
- ✉ parklands@newcastle-racecourse.co.uk
- ✍ G Brown (Hon Sec)
- 🖳 www.parklandsgolf.co.uk

## Ravensworth   (1906)
*Angel View, Long Bank, Gateshead NE9 7NE*
- ☎ **(0191) 487 6014**
- ✉ secretary@ravensworthgolfclub.co.uk
- ✍ Marcus Humphrey
- 🖳 www.ravensworthgolfclub.co.uk

## Ryton   (1891)
*Doctor Stanners, Clara Vale, Ryton NE40 3TD*
- ☎ **(0191) 413 3253**
- 📠 (0191) 413 1642
- ✉ secretary@rytongolfclub.co.uk
- ✍ Mr K McLeod
- 🖳 www.rytongolfclub.co.uk

## South Shields   (1893)
*Cleadon Hills, South Shields NE34 8EG*
- ☎ **(0191) 456 0475**
- ✉ thesecretary@south-shields-golf.freeserve.co.uk
- ✍ R Stanness (0191) 456 8942

## Tynemouth   (1913)
*Spital Dene, Tynemouth, North Shields NE30 2ER*
- ☎ **(0191) 257 4578**
- 📠 (0191) 259 5193
- ✉ secretary@tynemouthgolfclub.com
- ✍ TJ Scott (0191) 257 3381
- 🖳 www.tynemouthgolfclub.com

## Tyneside   (1879)
*Westfield Lane, Ryton NE40 3QE*
- ☎ **(0191) 413 2742**
- 📠 (0191) 413 0199
- ✉ secretary@tynesidegolfclub.co.uk
- ✍ Alastair Greenfield (Club Manager)
- 🖳 www.tynesidegolfclub.co.uk

## Wallsend   (1973)
*Rheydt Avenue, Bigges Main, Wallsend NE28 8SU*
- ☎ **(0191) 262 1973**
- ✍ D Souter

## Washington   (1979)
*Stone Cellar Road, High Usworth, Washington NE37 1PH*
- ☎ **(0191) 417 8346**
- 📠 (0191) 415 1166
- ✉ graeme.amanda@btopenworld.com
- 🖳 www.georgewashington.co.uk

## Westerhope   (1941)
*Whorlton Grange, Westerhope, Newcastle-upon-Tyne NE5 1PP*
- ☎ **(0191) 286 7636**
- 📠 (0191) 214 6287
- ✉ wgc@btconnect.com
- ✍ D Souter (Sec)
- 🖳 www.westerhopegolfclub.com

## Whickham   (1911)
*Hollinside Park, Fellside Road, Whickham, Newcastle-upon-Tyne NE16 5BA*
- ☎ **(0191) 488 1576 (Clubhouse)**
- 📠 (0191) 488 1577
- ✉ enquiries@whickhamgolfclub.co.uk

✍ Mr M E Pearse
🖥 www.whickhamgolfclub.co.uk

## Whitburn (1931)
Lizard Lane, South Shields NE34 7AF
☎ (0191) 529 2177
📧 wgcsec@hotmail.com
✍ Mr R Button (Sec) (0191) 529 2177
option 1
🖥 www.whitburngolfclub.co.uk

## Whitley Bay (1890)
Claremont Road, Whitley Bay NE26 3UF
☎ (0191) 252 0180
🖵 (0191) 297 0030
📧 whtglfclb@aol.com
✍ F Elliott
🖥 www.whitleybaygolfclub.co.uk

# Warwickshire

## Ansty (1990)
Pay and play
Brinklow Road, Ansty, Coventry CV7 9JL
☎ (024) 7662 1341/7660 2568
🖵 (024) 7660 2568
✍ K Smith
🖥 www.anstygolfandconference.co.uk

## Atherstone (1894)
The Outwoods, Coleshill Road, Atherstone
CV9 2RL
☎ (01827) 713110
🖵 (01827) 715686
✍ VA Walton (01827) 892568

## The Belfry (1977)
Pay and play
Wishaw, Sutton Coldfield B76 9PR
☎ (01675) 470301
🖵 (01675) 470178
📧 enquiries@thebelfry.com
✍ Gary Silcock (Dir. of Golf)
🖥 www.thebelfry.com

## Boldmere (1936)
Public
Monmouth Drive, Sutton Coldfield,
Birmingham BJ3 6JR
☎ (0121) 354 3379
🖵 (0121) 353 5576
📧 boldmeregolfclub@hotmail.com
✍ R Leeson
🖥 www.boldmeregolfclub.co.uk

## Bramcote Waters (1995)
Pay and play
Bazzard Road, Bramcote, Nuneaton
CV11 6QJ
☎ (01455) 220807
📧 bwgc@hotmail.co.uk
✍ Sara Britain (01455) 220807
🖥 www.bramcotewatersgolfclub
.co.uk

## City of Coventry (Brandon Wood) (1977)
Public
Brandon Lane, Coventry CV8 3GQ
☎ (024) 7654 3141

🖵 (024) 7654 5108
📧 info@brandonwood.co.uk
✍ N Orton (Mgr)
🖥 www.brandonwood.co.uk

## Copsewood Grange (1924)
Allard Way, Copsewood, Coventry CV3 1JP
☎ (024) 76448355
✍ REC Jones (024) 7645 2973
🖥 www.copsewoodgrange.co.uk

## Copt Heath (1907)
1220 Warwick Road, Knowle, Solihull
B93 9LN
☎ (01564) 731620
🖵 (01564) 731621
📧 golf@copt-heath.co.uk
✍ J A Moon
🖥 www.coptheathgolf.co.uk

## Coventry (1887)
St Martins Road, Finham, Coventry CV3 6RJ
☎ (024) 7641 4152
📧 secretary@coventrygolf.co.uk
✍ Kay Forrester (024) 7641 4152
🖥 www.coventrygolf.co.uk

## Coventry Hearsall (1894)
Beechwood Avenue, Coventry CV5 6DF
☎ (024) 7671 3470
🖵 (024) 7669 1534
📧 secretary@hearsallgolfclub.co.uk
✍ R Meade
🖥 www.hearsallgolfclub.co.uk

## Edgbaston (1896)
Church Road, Edgbaston, Birmingham
B15 3TB
☎ (0121) 454 1736
🖵 (0121) 454 2395
📧 secretary@edgbastongc.co.uk
✍ AD Grint
🖥 www.edgbastongc.co.uk

## Harborne (1893)
40 Tennal Road, Harborne, Birmingham
B32 2JE
☎ (0121) 427 3058
🖵 (0121) 427 4039
📧 adrian@harbornegolfclub
.org.uk
✍ Adrian Cooper (0121) 427 3058
🖥 www.harbornegolfclub.com

## Harborne Church Farm (1926)
Public
Vicarage Road, Harborne, Birmingham
B17 0SN
☎ (0121) 427 1204
🖵 (0121) 428 3126
🖥 www.golfbirmingham.co.uk

## Hatchford Brook (1969)
Public
Coventry Road, Sheldon, Birmingham
B26 3PY
☎ (0121) 743 9821
📧 idthbgc@hotmail.com
✍ I D Thomson (07457 37320)

## Henley G&CC (1994)
Proprietary
Birmingham Road, Henley-in-Arden
B95 5QA
☎ (01564) 793715
🖵 (01564) 795754
📧 enquiries@henleygcc.co.uk
✍ G Waller (Director)
🖥 www.henleygcc.co.uk

## Hilltop (1979)
Public
Park Lane, Handsworth, Birmingham
B21 8LJ
☎ (0121) 554 4463
✍ K Highfield (Mgr & Professional)

## Ingon Manor (1993)
Ingon Lane, Snitterfield, Stratford-on-Avon
CV37 0QE
☎ (01789) 731857
📧 golf@ingonmanor.co.uk
✍ Richard James Hampton
🖥 www.ingonmanor.co.uk

## Kenilworth (1889)
Crewe Lane, Kenilworth CV8 2EA
☎ (01926) 854296
🖵 (01926) 864453
📧 secretary@kenilworthgolfclub
.co.uk
✍ Rob Griffiths (01926) 858517
🖥 www.kenilworthgolfclub.co.uk

## Ladbrook Park (1908)
Poolhead Lane, Tanworth-in-Arden, Solihull
B94 5ED
☎ (01564) 742264
📧 secretary@ladbrookparkgolf.co.uk
✍ Caroline Hopkins/Sally Dawson
🖥 www.ladbrookparkgolf.co.uk

## Lea Marston Hotel & Leisure Complex (2002)
Proprietary
Haunch Lane, Lea Marston, Warwicks
B76 0BY
☎ (01675) 470707
🖵 (01675) 470871
📧 golf.shop@leamarstonhotel.co.uk
✍ Darren Lewis (Mgr)
🖥 www.leamarstonhotel.co.uk

## Leamington & County (1907)
Golf Lane, Whitnash, Leamington Spa
CV31 2QA
☎ (01926) 425961
📧 secretary@leamingtongolf.co.uk
✍ David M Beck
🖥 www.leamingtongolf.co.uk

## Marriott Forest of Arden Hotel (1970)
Maxstoke Lane, Meriden, Coventry
CV7 7HR
☎ (01676) 526113
🖵 (01676) 523711
📧 mhrs.cvtgs.golf@marriotthotels
.com
✍ I Burns (Golf Dir)
🖥 www.marriott.com/cvtgs

## Maxstoke Park    (1898)
*Castle Lane, Coleshill, Birmingham B46 2RD*
☎ **(01675) 466743**
🖥 (01675) 466185
📧 info@maxstokeparkgolfclub.com
🖳 www.maxstokeparkgolfclub.com

## Menzies Welcombe Hotel, Spa & Golf Club
*Warwick Road, Stratford-on-Avon CV37 0NR*
☎ **(01789) 413800**
🖥 (01789) 262028
✍ Dan Hacker (Director)
🖳 www.welcombehotelstratford.co.uk

## Moor Hall    (1932)
*Moor Hall Drive, Four Oaks, Sutton Coldfield B75 6LN*
☎ **(0121) 308 6130**
🖥 (0121) 308 9560
📧 secretary@moorhallgolfclub.co.uk
✍ DJ Etheridge
🖳 www.moorhallgolfclub.co.uk

## Newbold Comyn    (1973)
**Public**
*Newbold Terrace East, Leamington Spa CV32 4EW*
☎ **(01926) 421157**
📧 ian@viscount5.freeserve.co.uk
✍ I Shepherd (07799) 248759

## North Warwickshire    (1894)
*Hampton Lane, Meriden, Coventry CV7 7LL*
☎ **(01676) 522464 (Clubhouse)**
🖥 (01676) 523004
📧 nwgcltd@btconnect.com
✍ Bob May (Hon) (01676) 522915
🖳 www.northwarwickshiregolfclubltd.co.uk

## Nuneaton    (1905)
*Golf Drive, Whitestone, Nuneaton CV11 6QF*
☎ **(024) 7634 7810**
🖥 (024) 7632 7563
📧 nuneatongolfclub@btconnect.com
✍ Tracey Carpenter
🖳 www.nuneatongolfclub.co.uk

## Oakridge    (1993)
**Proprietary**
*Arley Lane, Ansley Village, Nuneaton CV10 9PH*
☎ **(01676) 541389**
🖥 (01676) 542709
📧 oakridgegolfclub@hotmail.com
✍ Kym Allen (Admin Mgr)
🖳 www.oakridgegolfclub.co.uk

## Olton    (1893)
*Mirfield Road, Solihull B91 1JH*
☎ **(0121) 704 1936**
🖥 (0121) 711 2010
📧 secretary@oltongolfclub.co.uk
✍ R Gay (0121) 704 1936
🖳 www.oltongolfclub.co.uk

## Purley Chase    (1980)
*Pipers Lane, Ridge Lane, Nuneaton CV10 0RB*
☎ **(024) 7639 3118**
🖥 (024) 7639 8015
📧 events@purleychase.com
✍ Linda Jackson

## Pype Hayes    (1932)
**Public**
*Eachelhurst Road, Walmley, Sutton Coldfield, West Midlands B76 1EP*
☎ **(0121) 351 1014**
🖥 (0121) 313 0206
✍ C Marson

## Robin Hood    (1893)
*St Bernards Road, Solihull B92 7DJ*
☎ **(0121) 706 0061**
🖥 (0121) 700 7502
📧 manager@robinhoodgolfclub.co.uk
✍ M J Ward
🖳 www.robinhoodgolfclub.co.uk

## Rugby    (1891)
*Clifton Road, Rugby CV21 3RD*
☎ **(01788) 544637 (Clubhouse)**
🖥 (01788) 542306
📧 rugbygolfclub@tiscali.co.uk
✍ John Drake (01788) 542306
🖳 www.rugbygc.co.uk

## Shirley    (1955)
*Stratford Road, Monkspath, Solihull B90 4EW*
☎ **(0121) 744 6001 opt 5**
🖥 (0121) 746 5645
📧 enquiries@shirleygolfclub.co.uk
✍ Patricia Harris (Mgr)
🖳 www.shirleygolfclub.co.uk

## Stonebridge    (1996)
**Proprietary**
*Somers Road, Meriden CV7 7PL*
☎ **(01676) 522442**
🖥 (01676) 522447
📧 sales@stonebridgegolf.co.uk
✍ Darren Murphy
🖳 www.stonebridgegolf.co.uk

## Stoneleigh Deer Park Golf Club    (1991)
**Proprietary**
*The Clubhouse, Coventry Road, Stoneleigh CV8 3DR*
☎ **(024) 7663 9991**
🖥 (024) 7651 1533
📧 info@stoneleighdeerparkgolfclub.com
✍ C Reay
🖳 www.stoneleighdeerparkgolfclub.com

## Stratford Oaks    (1991)
**Proprietary**
*Bearley Road, Snitterfield, Stratford-on-Avon CV37 0EZ*
☎ **(01789) 731980**
🖥 (01789) 731981
📧 admin@stratfordoaks.co.uk
✍ ND Powell (Golf Dir)
🖳 www.stratfordoaks.co.uk

## Stratford-on-Avon    (1894)
*Tiddington Road, Stratford-on-Avon CV37 7BA*
☎ **(01789) 205749**
🖥 (01789) 414909
📧 sec@stratfordgolf.com
✍ C J Hughes (01789) 205749
🖳 www.stratfordgolf.co.uk

## Sutton Coldfield    (1889)
*110 Thornhill Road, Sutton Coldfield B74 3ER*
☎ **(0121) 353 9633**
🖥 (0121) 353 5503
📧 admin@suttoncoldfieldgc.com
✍ I H Phillips, KM Tempest
🖳 www.suttoncoldfieldgc.com

## Walmley    (1902)
*Brooks Road, Wylde Green, Sutton Coldfield B72 1HR*
☎ **(0121) 373 0029**
🖥 (0121) 377 7272
📧 secretary@walmleygolfclub.co.uk
✍ J C Shakespeare
🖳 www.walmleygolfclub.co.uk

## Warwick    (1971)
**Public & Proprietary**
*Warwick Racecourse, Warwick CV34 6HW*
☎ **(01926) 494316**
📧 info@warwickgolfcentre.co.uk
✍ Mrs R Dunkley
🖳 www.warwickgolfcentre.co.uk

## The Warwickshire    (1993)
**Proprietary**
*Leek Wootton, Warwick CV35 7QT*
☎ **(01926) 409409**
🖥 (01926) 408409
✍ B Fotheringham (Golf Mgr)

## West Midlands    (2003)
*Marsh House Farm Lane, Barston, Solihull B92 0LB*
☎ **(01675) 444890**
🖥 (01675) 444891
📧 mark@wmgc.co.uk
✍ Mark Harrhy (01675) 444890
🖳 www.wmgc.co.uk

## Whitefields Golf Club & Draycote Hotel    (1992)
**Proprietary**
*London Road, Thurlaston, Rugby CV23 9LF*
☎ **(01788) 815555**
🖥 (01788) 521695
📧 mail@draycotehotel.co.uk
✍ B Coleman (01788) 815555
🖳 www.draycote-hotel.co.uk

## Widney Manor    (1993)
**Pay and play**
*Saintbury Drive, Widney Manor, Solihull B91 3SZ*
☎ **(0121) 704 0704**
🖥 (0121) 704 7999
✍ Tim Atkinson

## Windmill Village   (1990)
Proprietary
Birmingham Road, Allesley, Coventry
CV5 9AL
☎ (024) 7640 4041
🖷 (024) 7640 4042
📧 leisure@windmillvillagehotel.co.uk
✍ Oliver Thomas (Mgr)
🖳 www.windmillvillagehotel.co.uk

## Wishaw   (1992)
Proprietary
Bulls Lane, Wishaw, Sutton Coldfield
B76 9QW
☎ (0121) 313 2110
📧 golf@wishawgc.co.uk
✍ PH Burwell
🖳 www.wishawgc.co.uk

## Wiltshire

## Bowood Hotel, Spa and Golf
## Resort   (1992)
Proprietary
Derry Hill, Calne SN11 9PQ
☎ (01249) 822228
🖷 (01249) 822218
📧 p.mclean@bowood.org
✍ Paul McLean
🖳 www.bowood.org

## Broome Manor   (1976)
Public
Pipers Way, Swindon SN3 1RG
☎ (01793) 532403
📧 secretary@bmgc.co.uk
✍ C Beresford 01793 526544
🖳 www.bmgc.co.uk

## Chippenham   (1896)
Malmesbury Road, Chippenham SN15 5LT
☎ (01249) 652040
🖷 (01249) 446681
📧 chippenhamgolf@btconnect.com
✍ Mr W Williams (General Manager)
🖳 www.chippenhamgolfclub.com

## Cricklade House   (1992)
Pay and play
Common Hill, Cricklade SN6 6HA
☎ (01793) 750751
🖷 (01793) 751767
📧 reception@crickladehotel.co.uk
✍ C Withers/P Butler
🖳 www.crickladehotel.co.uk

## Cumberwell Park   (1994)
Proprietary
Bradford-on-Avon BA15 2PQ
☎ (01225) 863322
🖷 (01225) 868160
📧 enquiries@cumberwellpark.com
✍ Alistair James
🖳 www.cumberwellpark.com

## Defence Academy   (1953)
Shrivenham, Swindon SN6 8LA
☎ (01793) 785725
📧 golfclub.hq@da.mod.uk
✍ A Willmett (Mgr)
🖳 www.dagc.org.uk

## Erlestoke   (1992)
Proprietary
Erlestoke, Devizes SN10 5UB
☎ (01380) 831069
📧 info@erlestokegolfclub.co.uk
✍ R Goboroonsingh
🖳 www.erlestokegolfclub.co.uk

## Hamptworth G&CC   (1994)
Elmtree Farmhouse, Hamptworth Road,
Landford SP5 2DU
☎ (01794) 390155
🖷 (01794) 390022
📧 info@hamptworthgolf.co.uk
✍ Janet Facer
🖳 www.hamptworthgolf.co.uk

## High Post   (1922)
Great Durnford, Salisbury SP4 6AT
☎ (01722) 782356
🖷 (01722) 782674
📧 manager@highpostgolfclub.co.uk
✍ P Hickling (01722) 782356
🖳 www.highpostgolfclub.co.uk

## Highworth   (1990)
Public
Swindon Road, Highworth SN6 7SJ
☎ (01793) 766014
✍ Geoff Marsh

## Kingsdown   (1880)
Kingsdown, Corsham SN13 8BS
☎ (01225) 743472
🖷 (01225) 743472
📧 secretary@kingsdowngolfclub
.co.uk
✍ N Newman
🖳 www.kingsdowngolfclub.co.uk

## Manor House   (1992)
Proprietary
Castle Combe SN14 7JW
☎ (01249) 782982
🖷 (01249) 782992
📧 enquiries@manorhousegolf.co.uk
✍ Stephen Browning
🖳 www.manorhousegolf.co.uk

## Marlborough   (1888)
The Common, Marlborough SN8 1DU
☎ (01672) 512147
🖷 (01672) 513164
📧 gm@marlboroughgolfclub.co.uk
✍ L J Trute
🖳 www.marlboroughgolfclub.co.uk

## Monkton Park Par Three
(1965)
Pay and play
Chippenham SN15 3PP
☎ (01249) 653928
✍ MR & BJ Dawson (Props)
🖳 www.pitchandputtgolf.com

## North Wilts   (1890)
Bishops' Cannings, Devizes SN10 2LP
☎ (01380) 860257
📧 secretary@northwiltsgolf.com
✍ Mrs P Stephenson
🖳 www.northwiltsgolf.com

## Oaksey Park   (1991)
Pay and play
Oaksey, Malmesbury SN16 9SB
☎ (01666) 577995
🖷 (01666) 577174
📧 info@oakseypark.co.uk
✍ John Cooper
🖳 www.oakseyparkgolf.co.uk

## Ogbourne Downs   (1907)
Ogbourne St George, Marlborough
SN8 1TB
☎ (01672) 841327
📧 office@ogbournedowns.co.uk
✍ John Edwards (01672) 841327
🖳 www.ogbournedowns.co.uk

## Rushmore   (1997)
Proprietary
Tollard Royal, Salisbury SP5 5QB
☎ (01725) 516326
🖷 (01725) 516437
📧 golfmanager@rushmoreuk.com
✍ Declan Healy (Gen
Mgr) (01725) 516391
🖳 www.rushmoregolfclub.co.uk

## Salisbury & South Wilts
(1888)
Netherhampton, Salisbury SP2 8PR
☎ (01722) 742645 ext.1
🖷 (01722) 742676
📧 mail@salisburygolf.co.uk
✍ Alex Taylor (Secretary)
🖳 www.salisburygolf.co.uk

## Shrivenham Park   (1967)
Pay and play
Pennyhooks Lane, Shrivenham, Swindon
SN6 8EX
☎ (01793) 783853
📧 gplatt@aol.com
✍ G Platt (01793) 783853
🖳 www.shrivenhampark.com

## Tidworth Garrison   (1908)
Bulford Road, Tidworth SP9 7AF
☎ (01980) 842301 (Clubhouse)
🖷 (01980) 842301
📧 secretary@tidworthgolfclub.co.uk
✍ Gwen Phillips
🖳 www.tidworthgolfclub.co.uk

## Upavon   (1912)
Douglas Avenue, Upavon SN9 6BQ
☎ (01980) 630281
📧 richard@richardblake.co.uk
✍ Richard Blake
🖳 www.upavongolfclub.co.uk

## West Wilts   (1891)
Elm Hill, Warminster BA12 0AU
☎ (01985) 213133
📧 sec@westwiltsgolfclub.co.uk
✍ GN Morgan
🖳 www.westwiltsgolfclub.co.uk

## Whitley   (1993)
Pay and play
Corsham Road, Whitley, Melksham
SN12 8EQ
☎ (01225) 790099

info@whitleygolfclub.com
Jack Nicholas
www.whitleygolfclub.com

## The Wiltshire   (1991)
**Proprietary**
*Vastern, Wootton Bassett, Swindon
SN4 7PB*
- ☎ **(01793) 849999**
- 🖷 (01793) 849988
- ✉ reception@the-wiltshire.co.uk
- ✍ Jennifer Shah (Gen Mgr)
- 🖥 www.the-wiltshire.co.uk

## Wrag Barn G&CC   (1990)
*Shrivenham Road, Highworth, Swindon
SN6 7QQ*
- ☎ **(01793) 861327**
- 🖷 (01793) 861325
- ✉ manager@wragbarn.com
- ✍ T Lee
- 🖥 www.wragbarn.com

## Worcestershire

## Royal Worlington & Newmarket   (1985)
*Dagnell End Road, Redditch B98 9BE*
- ☎ **(01638) 712216 (Clubhouse)**
- ✉ secretary@royalworlington.co.uk
- ✍ S Ballentine (01638) 717787
- 🖥 www.royalworlington.co.uk

## Blackwell   (1893)
*Blackwell, Bromsgrove, Worcestershire
B60 1PY*
- ☎ **(0121) 445 1994**
- 🖷 (0121) 445 4911
- ✉ secretary@blackwellgolfclub.com
- ✍ Finlay Clark
- 🖥 www.blackwellgolfclub.com

## Brandhall   (1906)
**Public**
*Heron Road, Oldbury, Warley B68 8AQ*
- ☎ **(0121) 552 2195**
- 🖷 (0121) 552 1758
- ✉ john_robinson@sandwell.gov.uk
- ✍ J Robinson
- 🖥 www.slt@sandwell.gov.uk

## Bransford   (1992)
*Bank House Hotel, Bransford, Worcester
WR6 5JD*
- ☎ **(01886) 833545**
- 🖷 (01886) 833545
- ✉ sales@bankhouseworcester.com
- ✍ Matt Nixon
- 🖥 www.bransfordgolfclub.com

## Bromsgrove Golf Centre (1992)
**Proprietary**
*Stratford Road, Bromsgrove B60 1LD*
- ☎ **(01527) 575886**
- 🖷 (01527) 570964
- ✉ enquiries@bromsgrovegolfcentre.com
- ✍ P Morris (Director) P Brothwood (Sec)
- 🖥 www.bromsgrovegolfcentre.com

## Churchill & Blakedown   (1926)
*Churchill Lane, Blakedown, Kidderminster
DY10 3NB*
- ☎ **(01562) 700018**
- ✉ admin@churchillblakedowngolfclub.co.uk
- ✍ Trevor Hare
- 🖥 www.churchillblakedowngolfclub.co.uk

## Cocks Moor Woods   (1926)
**Public**
*Alcester Road South, King's Heath,
Birmingham, West Midlands B14 6ER*
- ☎ **(0121) 464 3584**
- ✍ P J Ellison
- 🖥 www.golfbirmingham.co.uk

## Droitwich G&CC   (1897)
*Ford Lane, Droitwich WR9 0BQ*
- ☎ **(01905) 774344**
- 🖷 (01905) 796503
- ✍ CS Thompson
- 🖥 www.droitwichgolfclub.co.uk

## Dudley   (1893)
*Turners Hill, Rowley Regis B65 9DP*
- ☎ **(01384) 233877**
- 🖷 (01384) 233877
- ✉ secretary@dudleygolfclub.com
- ✍ W B Whitcombe
- 🖥 www.dudleygolfclub.com

## Evesham   (1894)
*Craycombe Links, Fladbury, Pershore
WR10 2QS*
- ☎ **(01386) 860395**
- ✉ eveshamgolf@btopenworld.com
- ✍ Mr Jerry Cain
- 🖥 www.eveshamgolfclub.co.uk

## Fulford Heath   (1933)
*Tanners Green Lane, Wythall, Birmingham
B47 6BH*
- ☎ **(01564) 822806 (Clubhouse)**
- 🖷 (01564) 822629
- ✉ secretary@fulfordheathgolfclub.co.uk
- ✍ Mrs J Morris (01564) 824758
- 🖥 www.fulfordheathgolfclub.co.uk

## Gay Hill   (1913)
*Hollywood Lane, Birmingham B47 5PP*
- ☎ **(0121) 430 8544**
- 🖷 (0121) 436 7796
- ✉ secretary@ghgc.org.uk
- ✍ Mrs D L O'Reilly (0121) 430 8544
- 🖥 www.ghgc.org.uk

## Habberley   (1924)
*Low Habberley, Kidderminster DY11 5RF*
- ☎ **(01562) 745756**
- ✉ info@habberleygolfclub.co.uk
- ✍ DS McDermott
- 🖥 www.habberleygolfclub.co.uk

## Hagley   (1980)
**Proprietary**
*Wassell Grove, Hagley, Stourbridge
DY9 9JW*
- ☎ **(01562) 883701**

- 🖷 (01562) 887518
- ✉ enquiries@HagleyGCC.co.uk
- ✍ GF Yardley (01562) 883701
- 🖥 www.hagleygolfandcountryclub.co.uk

## Halesowen   (1906)
*The Leasowes, Halesowen B62 8QF*
- ☎ **(0121) 501 3606**
- ✉ office@halesowengc.co.uk
- ✍ Mrs N Heath
- 🖥 www.halesowengc.co.uk

## Handsworth   (1895)
*11 Sunningdale Close, Handsworth Wood,
Birmingham B20 1NP*
- ☎ **(0121) 554 3387**
- 🖷 (0121) 554 6144
- ✉ info@handsworthgolfclub.net
- ✍ PS Hodnett (Hon)
- 🖥 www.handsworthgolfclub.com

## Kidderminster   (1909)
*Russell Road, Kidderminster DY10 3HT*
- ☎ **(01562) 822303**
- 🖷 (01562) 827866
- ✉ info@thekidderminstergolfclub.com
- ✍ Nina Cruyer
- 🖥 www.thekidderminstergolfclub.com

## Kings Norton   (1892)
*Brockhill Lane, Weatheroak, Alvechurch,
Birmingham B48 7ED*
- ☎ **(01564) 826789**
- 🖷 (01564) 826955
- ✉ info@kingsnortongolfclub.co.uk
- ✍ T Webb (Mgr)
- 🖥 www.kingsnortongolfclub.co.uk

## Little Lakes   (1975)
*Lye Head, Bewdley, Worcester DY12 2UZ*
- ☎ **(01299) 266385**
- 🖷 (01299) 266398
- ✉ info@littlelakes.co.uk
- ✍ J Dean (01562) 741704
- 🖥 www.littlelakes.co.uk

## Moseley   (1892)
*Springfield Road, Kings Heath, Birmingham
B14 7DX*
- ☎ **(0121) 444 4957**
- 🖷 (0121) 441 4662
- ✉ secretary@moseleygolfclub.co.uk
- ✍ Mr M W Wake
- 🖥 www.moseleygolf.co.uk

## North Worcestershire   (1907)
*Frankley Beeches Road, Northfield,
Birmingham B31 5LP*
- ☎ **(0121) 475 1047**
- 🖷 (0121) 476 8681
- ✉ secretary@nwgolfclub.com
- ✍ Alex Brophy
- 🖥 www.nwgolfclub.com

## Ombersley Golf Club   (1991)
**Pay and play**
*Bishopswood Road, Ombersley, Droitwich
WR9 0LE*
- ☎ **(01905) 620747**
- 🖷 (01905) 620047
- ✉ enquiries@ombersleygolfclub.co.uk

✍ G Glenister (Gen Mgr)
🖥 www.ombersleygolfclub.co.uk

## Perdiswell Park (1978)
**Pay and play**
Bilford Road, Worcester WR3 8DX
☎ **(01905) 754668**
📠 (01905) 756608
✉ perdiswell@leisureconnection
.co.uk
✍ B F Hodgetts (01905) 640456
🖥 www.harpersfitness.co.uk

## Pitcheroak (1973)
**Public**
Plymouth Road, Redditch B97 4PB
☎ **(01527) 541054**
✍ R Barnett

## Ravenmeadow (1995)
Hindlip Lane, Claines, Worcester
WR3 8SA
☎ **(01905) 757525**
📠 (01905) 458876
✍ James Leaver
(Mgr) (01905) 458876
🖥 info@ravenmeadowgolf.co.uk

## Redditch (1913)
Lower Grinsty, Green Lane, Callow Hill,
Redditch B97 5PJ
☎ **(01527) 543079**
📠 (01527) 547413
✉ info@redditchgolfclub.com
✍ S Mee
🖥 www.redditchgolfclub.com

## Rose Hill (1921)
**Public**
Lickey Hills, Rednal, Birmingham
B45 8RR
☎ **(0121) 453 3159**
📠 (0121) 457 8779
✉ rosehillgolfclub@hotmail.com
✍ D C Walker
🖥 www.rosehill-golfclub.co.uk

## Stourbridge (1892)
Worcester Lane, Pedmore, Stourbridge
DY8 2RB
☎ **(01384) 395566**
📠 (01384) 444660
✉ secretary@stourbridgegolfclub
.co.uk
✍ Mr M Hughes
🖥 www.stourbridgegolfclub.co.uk

## Tolladine (1898)
The Fairway, Tolladine Road, Worcester
WR4 9BA
☎ **(01905) 21074 (Clubhouse)**
✍ P Lynas

## The Vale (1991)
**Proprietary**
Hill Furze Road, Bishampton, Pershore
WR10 2LZ
☎ **(01386) 462781 ext 309**
📠 (01386) 462597
✉ admin@thevalegolf.co.uk
✍ Simon Williams
🖥 www.thevalegolf.co.uk

## Warley Woods (1921)
**Pay and play**
The Pavilion, 101 Lightwoods Hill,
Smethwick, West Midlands B67 5ED
☎ **(0121) 429 2440**
✉ golfshop@warleywoods.org.uk
🖥 www.warleywoods.org.uk

## Wharton Park (1992)
**Proprietary**
Longbank, Bewdley DY12 2QW
☎ **(01299) 405222 (restaurant)**
📠 (01299) 405121
✉ enquiries@whartonpark.co.uk
✍ Kevin Fincher
🖥 www.whartonpark.co.uk

## Worcester G&CC (1898)
Boughton Park, Worcester WR2 4EZ
☎ **(01905) 422555**
📠 (01905) 749090
✉ worcestergcc@btconnect.com
✍ PA Tredwell (01905) 422555
🖥 www.worcestergcc.co.uk

## Worcestershire (1879)
Wood Farm, Malvern Wells WR14 4PP
☎ **(01684) 575992**
📠 (01684) 893334
✉ secretary@worcsgolfclub.co.uk
✍ Terry Smith (Sec/Mgr)
🖥 www.worcsgolfclub.co.uk

## Wyre Forest Golf Centre
**Pay and play**
Zortech Avenue, Kidderminster DY11 7EX
☎ **(01299) 822682**
📠 (01299) 879433
✉ wyreforestgc@hotmail.co.uk
✍ C Botterill

# Yorkshire (East)

## Allerthorpe Park (1994)
**Proprietary**
Allerthorpe, York YO42 4RL
☎ **(01759) 306686**
📠 (01759) 305106
✉ enquiries@allerthorpeparkgolfclub
.com
✍ Alex Drinkall/Jan Drinkall
🖥 www.allerthorpeparkgolfclub.com

## Beverley & East Riding
(1889)
The Westwood, Beverley HU17 8RG
☎ **(01482) 868757**
📠 (01482) 868757
✉ golf@beverleygolfclub.karoo.co.uk
✍ A Ashby (01482) 869519
🖥 www.beverleygolfclub.co.uk

## Boothferry (1982)
**Proprietary**
Spaldington Lane, Spaldington, Nr Howden
DN14 7NG
☎ **(01430) 430364**
✉ info@boothferrygolfclub.co.uk
✍ Ben McAllister
🖥 www.boothferrygolfclub.co.uk

## Bridlington (1905)
Belvedere Road, Bridlington YO15 3NA
☎ **(01262) 672092/606367**
✉ enquiries@bridlingtongolfclub
.co.uk
✍ ARA Howarth (01262) 606367
🖥 www.bridlingtongolfclub.co.uk

## Bridlington Links (1993)
**Pay and play**
Flamborough Road, Marton, Bridlington
YO15 1DW
☎ **(01262) 401584**
📠 (01262) 401702
✉ bridlington@pureleisuregroup.com
✍ Wayne Stephens (Sec)
🖥 www.bridlington-links.co.uk

## Brough (1893)
Cave Road, Brough HU15 1HB
☎ **(01482) 667291**
📠 (01482) 669873
✉ gt@brough-golfclub.co.uk
✍ G W Townhill (Professional)
🖥 www.brough-golfclub.co.uk

## Cave Castle (1989)
South Cave, Nr Brough HU15 2EU
☎ **(01430) 421286**
📠 (01430) 421118
✉ admin@cavecastlegolf.co.uk
✍ J Simpson (Admin)
🖥 www.cavecastlegolf.co.uk

## Cherry Burton (1993)
**Proprietary**
Leconfield Road, Cherry Burton, Beverley
HU17 7RB
☎ **(01964) 550924**
✉ jonnygrayroll@europe.com
✍ John Gray 01964 550924
🖥 cherryburtongolf.co.uk

## Cottingham (1994)
**Proprietary**
Woodhill Way, Cottingham, Hull
HU16 5SW
☎ **(01482) 846030**
📠 (01482) 845932
✉ info@cottinghamparks.co.uk
✍ RJ Wiles (01482) 846030
🖥 www.cottinghamparks.co.uk

## Driffield (1923)
Sunderlandwick, Driffield YO25 9AD
☎ **(01377) 253116**
📠 (01377) 240599
✉ info@driffieldgolfclub.co.uk
✍ Maxine Moorhouse (Assist. Sec)
🖥 www.driffieldgolfclub.co.uk

## Flamborough Head (1931)
Lighthouse Road, Flamborough, Bridlington
YO15 1AR
☎ **(01262) 850333**
✉ enquiries
@flamboroughheadgolfclub.co.uk
✍ GS Thornton (Sec)
🖥 www.flamboroughheadgolfclub
.co.uk

## Ganstead Park    (1976)
**Proprietary**
*Longdales Lane, Coniston, Hull HU11 4LB*
- ☎ **(01482) 811280 (Steward)**
- 🖵 (01482) 817754
- 🖂 secretary@gansteadpark.co.uk
- ✍ M Milner (01482) 817754
- 🖹 www.gansteadpark.co.uk

## Hainsworth Park    (1983)
*Brandesburton, Driffield YO25 8RT*
- ☎ **(01964) 542362**
- 🖵 (01964) 544666
- 🖂 sec@hainsworthparkgolfclub.co.uk
- ✍ A Higgins, BW Atkin (Prop)
- 🖹 www.hainsworthparkgolfclub.co.uk

## Hessle    (1898)
*Westfield Road, Raywell, Cottingham HU16 5ZA*
- ☎ **(01482) 306840**
- 🖵 (01482) 652679
- 🖂 secretary@hesslegolfclub.co.uk
- ✍ Paul Haddon
- 🖹 www.hesslegolfclub.co.uk

## Hornsea    (1898)
*Rolston Road, Hornsea HU18 1XG*
- ☎ **(01964) 532020**
- 🖵 (01964) 532080
- 🖂 office@hornseagolfclub.co.uk
- ✍ Stretton Wright (Dir of Golf)/Yvonne Wright (Admin)
- 🖹 www.hornseagolfclub.co.uk

## Hull    (1904)
*The Hall, 27 Packman Lane, Kirk Ella, Hull HU10 7TJ*
- ☎ **(01482) 660970**
- 🖵 (01482) 660978
- 🖂 secretary@hullgolfclub1921.karoo.co.uk
- ✍ DJ Crossley
- 🖹 www.hullgolfclub.com

## KP Club    (1995)
**Proprietary**
*Pocklington, York, East Yorkshire YO42 1UF*
- ☎ **(01759) 303090**
- 🖂 info@kpclub.co.uk
- ✍ Aaron Pheasant
- 🖹 www.kpclub.co.uk

## Springhead Park    (1930)
**Public**
*Willerby Road, Hull HU5 5JE*
- ☎ **(01482) 656309**
- ✍ P Smith

## Sutton Park    (1935)
**Public**
*Salthouse Road, Hull HU8 9HF*
- ☎ **(01482) 374242**
- 🖵 (01482) 701428
- ✍ S J Collins

## Withernsea    (1909)
*Egroms Lane, Withernsea HU19 2NA*
- ☎ **(01964) 612258 (Clubhouse)**
- 🖵 (01964) 612078
- 🖂 info@withernseagolfclub.co.uk
- ✍ S Dale (Admin)
- 🖹 www.withernseagolfclub.co.uk

# Yorkshire (North)

## Aldwark Manor    (1978)
*Aldwark, Alne, York YO61 1UF*
- ☎ **(01347) 838353**
- 🖵 (01347) 833991
- ✍ A Grindlay (01347) 838353
- 🖹 www.Qhotels.co.uk

## Ampleforth College    (1972)
*Castle Drive, Gilling East, York YO62 4HP*
- ☎ **(01439) 788274**
- 🖂 sec@ampleforthgolf.co.uk
- ✍ Ian Henley
- 🖹 www.ampleforthgolf.co.uk

## Bedale    (1894)
*Leyburn Road, Bedale DL8 1EZ*
- ☎ **(01677) 422451**
- 🖵 (01677) 427143
- 🖂 office@bedalegolfclub.com
- ✍ Mike Mayman (01677) 422451
- 🖹 www.bedalegolfclub.com

## Bentham    (1922)
**Proprietary**
*Robin Lane, Bentham, Lancaster LA2 7AG*
- ☎ **(015242) 62455**
- 🖂 golf@benthamgolf.co.uk
- ✍ C Cousins (Pro)
- 🖹 www.benthamgolfclub.co.uk

## Catterick    (1930)
*Leyburn Road, Catterick Garrison DL9 3QE*
- ☎ **(01748) 833268**
- 🖂 secretary@catterickgolfclub.co.uk
- ✍ M Young
- 🖹 www.catterickgolfclub.co.uk

## Cleveland    (1887)
*Majuba Road, Redcar TS10 5BJ*
- ☎ **(01642) 471798**
- 🖵 (01642) 487619
- 🖂 majuba@btconnect.com
- 🖹 www.clevelandgolfclub.co.uk

## Crimple Valley    (1976)
**Pay and play**
*Hookstone Wood Road, Harrogate HG2 8PN*
- ☎ **(01423) 883485**
- 🖵 (01423) 881018
- ✍ Paul Johnson

## Drax    (1989)
*Drax, Selby YO8 8PJ*
- ☎ **(01757) 617228**
- 🖵 (01757) 617228
- 🖂 draxgolfclub@btinternet.com
- ✍ Denise Smith
- 🖹 www.draxgolfclub.com

## Easingwold    (1930)
*Stillington Road, Easingwold, York YO61 3ET*
- ☎ **(01347) 822474**
- 🖵 (01347) 823948
- 🖂 enquiries@easingwoldgolfclub.co.uk
- ✍ Mrs C Readman
- 🖹 www.easingwoldgolfclub.co.uk

## Filey    (1897)
*West Ave, Filey YO14 9BQ*
- ☎ **(01723) 513293**
- 🖂 secretary@fileygolfclub.com
- ✍ Mrs V Gilbank
- 🖹 www.fileygolfclub.com

## Forest of Galtres    (1993)
**Proprietary**
*Moorlands Road, Skelton, York YO32 2RF*
- ☎ **(01904) 766198**
- 🖵 (01904) 769400
- 🖂 secretary@forestofgaltres.co.uk
- ✍ Mrs SJ Procter
- 🖹 www.forestofgaltres.co.uk

## Forest Park    (1991)
**Proprietary**
*Stockton-on Forest, York YO32 9UW*
- ☎ **(01904) 400425**
- 🖂 admin@forestparkgolfclub.co.uk
- ✍ S Crossley (01904) 400688
- 🖹 www.forestparkgolfclub.co.uk

## Fulford (York) Golf Club    (1906)
*Heslington Lane, York YO10 5DY*
- ☎ **(01904) 413579**
- 🖵 (01904) 416918
- 🖂 info@fulfordgolfclub.co.uk
- ✍ GS Pearce
- 🖹 www.fulfordgolfclub.co.uk

## Ganton    (1891)
*Station Road, Ganton, Scarborough YO12 4PA*
- ☎ **(01944) 710329**
- 🖵 (01944) 710922
- 🖂 secretary@gantongolfclub.com
- ✍ R Penley-Martin
- 🖹 www.gantongolfclub.com

## Harrogate    (1892)
*Forest Lane Head, Harrogate HG2 7TF*
- ☎ **(01423) 863158 (Clubhouse)**
- 🖵 (01423) 798310
- 🖂 secretary@harrogate-gc.co.uk
- ✍ Ruth Skaife-Clarke
- 🖹 www.harrogate-gc.co.uk

## Heworth    (1911)
*Muncaster House, Muncastergate, York YO31 9JY*
- ☎ **(01904) 424618**
- 🖵 (01904) 426156
- 🖂 golf@heworth-gc.fsnet.co.uk
- ✍ RJ Hunt (01904) 426156
- 🖹 www.heworthgolfclub.co.uk

## Hunley Hall    (1993)
*Brotton, Saltburn TS12 2FT*
- ☎ **(01287) 676216**
- 🖵 (01287) 678250
- 🖂 enquiries@hhgc.co.uk
- ✍ G Briffa (01287) 676216
- 🖹 www.hhgc.co.uk

## Kirkbymoorside    (1951)
*Manor Vale, Kirkbymoorside, York YO62 6EG*
- ☎ **(01751) 431525**
- 🖵 (01751) 433190

enqs@kirkbymoorsidegolf.co.uk
Mrs R Rivis
www.kirkbymoorsidegolf.co.uk

## Knaresborough   (1920)
*Boroughbridge Road, Knaresborough HG5 0QQ*
☎ **(01423) 862690**
📠 (01423) 869345
✉ secretary@kgc.uk.com
✍ M Taylor
🖥 www.knaresboroughgolfclub.co.uk

## Malton & Norton   (1910)
*Welham Park, Welham Road, Norton, Malton YO17 9QE*
☎ **(01653) 697912**
📠 (01653) 697844
✉ maltonandnorton@btconnect.com
✍ Mr N J Redman
🖥 www.maltonandnortongolfclub.co.uk

## Masham   (1895)
*Burnholme, Swinton Road, Masham, Ripon HG4 4NS*
☎ **(01765) 688054**
✉ info@mashamgolfclub.co.uk
✍ S Blades
🖥 www.mashamgolfclub.co.uk

## Middlesbrough   (1908)
*Brass Castle Lane, Marton, Middlesbrough TS8 9EE*
☎ **(01642) 311515**
📠 (01642) 319607
✉ enquiries@middlesbroughgolfclub.co.uk
🖥 www.middlesbroughgolfclub.co.uk

## Middlesbrough Municipal   (1977)
**Public**
*Ladgate Lane, Middlesbrough TS5 7YZ*
☎ **(01642) 315533**
📠 (01642) 300726
✉ enquiriesgolfcentre@middlesbrough.gov.uk
✍ M Gormley (Mgr)
🖥 www.middlesbrough.gov.uk

## Oakdale   (1914)
*Oakdale, Oakdale Glen, Harrogate HG1 2LN*
☎ **(01423) 567162**
📠 (01423) 536030
✉ manager@oakdalegolfclub.co.uk
✍ MJ Cross
🖥 www.oakdalegolfclub.co.uk

## The Oaks   (1996)
**Proprietary**
*Aughton Common, Aughton, York YO42 4PW*
☎ **(01757) 288577 (Office)**
📠 (01757) 288232
✉ sheila@theoaksgolfclub.co.uk
✍ Mrs S Nutt (01757) 288577
🖥 www.theoaksgolfclub.co.uk

## Pannal   (1906)
*Follifoot Road, Pannal, Harrogate HG3 1ES*
☎ **(01423) 872628**

📠 (01423) 870043
✉ secretary@pannalgolfclub.co.uk
✍ NG Douglas
🖥 www.pannalgolfclub.co.uk

## Pike Hills   (1904)
*Tadcaster Road, Askham Bryan, York YO23 3UW*
☎ **(01904) 700797**
📠 (01904) 700797
✉ secretary@pikehillsgolfclub.co.uk
✍ David Winterburn (Secretary)
🖥 www.pikehillsgolfclub.co.uk

## Richmond   (1892)
*Bend Hagg, Richmond DL10 5EX*
☎ **(01748) 825319**
📠 (01748) 821709
✉ secretary@richmondyorksgolfclub.co.uk
✍ Amy Lancaster (01748) 823231
🖥 www.richmondyorksgolfclub.co.uk

## Ripon City Golf Club   (1907)
*Palace Road, Ripon HG4 3HH*
☎ **(01765) 603640**
📠 (01765) 692880
✉ secretary@riponcitygolfclub.com
✍ MJ Doig MBE
🖥 www.riponcitygolfclub.co.uk

## Romanby Golf and Country Club   (1993)
**Pay and play**
*Yafforth Road, Northallerton DL7 0PE*
☎ **(01609) 778855**
📠 (01609) 779084
✉ info@romanby.com
✍ R Boucher (Gen Mgr)
🖥 www.romanby.com

## Rudding Park   (1995)
**Pay and play**
*Rudding Park, Harrogate HG3 1JH*
☎ **(01423) 872100**
📠 (01423) 873011
✉ sales@ruddingpark.com
✍ J King
🖥 www.ruddingpark.com

## Saltburn-By-The-Sea   (1894)
*Hob Hill, Saltburn-by-the-Sea TS12 1NJ*
☎ **(01287) 622812**
✉ secretary@saltburngolf.co.uk
✍ Mrs Julie Annis (Secretary)
🖥 www.saltburngolf.co.uk

## Sandburn Hall   (2005)
**Proprietary**
*Scotchman Lane, Flaxton, York YO60 7RB*
☎ **(01904) 469929**
📠 (01904) 469923
✉ info@sandburnhall.co.uk
✍ Emma Brown (Clubhouse Manager)
🖥 www.sandburnhall.co.uk

## Scarborough North Cliff   (1909)
*North Cliff Avenue, Burniston Road, Scarborough YO12 6PP*
☎ **(01723) 355397**
✉ info@northcliffgolfclub.co.uk

✍ Miss J Duck
🖥 www.northcliffgolfclub.co.uk

## Scarborough South Cliff   (1902)
*Deepdale Avenue, Scarborough YO11 2UE*
☎ **(01723) 360522**
📠 (01723) 360523
✉ clubsecretary@southcliffgolfclub.com
✍ S F Smith
🖥 www.southcliffgolfclub.com

## Scarthingwell   (1993)
*Scarthingwell, Tadcaster LS24 9DG*
☎ **(01937) 557878**
📠 (01937) 557909
✉ ben.burlingham@scarthingwellgolfcourse.co.uk
✍ Ben Burlingham
🖥 www.scarthingwellgolfcourse.co.uk

## Selby   (1907)
*Mill Lane, Brayton, Selby YO8 9LD*
☎ **(01757) 228622**
📠 (01757) 229286
✉ secretary@selbygolfclub.co.uk
✍ Sally McHale
🖥 www.selbygolfclub.co.uk

## Settle   (1895)
*Giggleswick, Settle BD24 0DH*
☎ **(01729) 825288**
✉ drabwright@hotmail.com
✍ Alan Wright (07801) 550 358
🖥 www.settlegolfclub.co.uk

## Skipton   (1893)
*Short Lee Lane, Skipton BD23 3LF*
☎ **(01756) 793257 Pro**
**(01756) 795657 Office**
✉ enquiries@skiptongolfclub.co.uk
✍ Beverley Keyworth
🖥 www.skiptongolfclub.co.uk

## Teesside   (1900)
*Acklam Road, Thornaby TS17 7JS*
☎ **(01642) 676249**
📠 (01642) 676252
✉ teessidegolfclub@btconnect.com
✍ M Fleming (01642) 616516
🖥 www.teessidegolfclub.co.uk

## Thirsk & Northallerton   (1914)
*Thornton-le-Street, Thirsk YO7 4AB*
☎ **(01845) 525115**
📠 (01845) 525119
✉ secretary@tngc.co.uk
✍ Secretary (01845) 525115 ext 1
🖥 www.tngc.co.uk

## Whitby   (1892)
*Sandsend Road, Low Straggleton, Whitby YO21 3SR*
☎ **(01947) 602719**
📠 (01947) 600660
✉ office@whitbygolfclub.co.uk
✍ T Mason
🖥 www.whitbygolfclub.co.uk

## Wilton   (1952)
*Wilton, Redcar, Cleveland TS10 4QY*
☎ **(01642) 465265**
✉ secretary@wiltongolfclub.co.uk
✍ C Harvey (01642) 465265
🖥 www.wiltongolfclub.co.uk

## York   (1890)
*Lords Moor Lane, Strensall, York YO32 5XF*
☎ **(01904) 491840**
📠 (01904) 491852
✉ secretary@yorkgolfclub.co.uk
✍ MJ Wells
🖥 www.yorkgolfclub.co.uk

## Yorkshire (South)

## Abbeydale   (1895)
*Twentywell Rise, Twentywell Lane, Dore, Sheffield S17 4QA*
☎ **(0114) 236 0763**
📠 (0114) 236 0762
✉ abbeygolf@btconnect.com
✍ Mrs JL Wing (Office Mgr)
🖥 www.abbeydalegolfclub.co.uk

## Barnsley   (1925)
**Public**
*Wakefield Road, Staincross, Barnsley S75 6JZ*
☎ **(01226) 382856**
✉ barnsleygolfclub@btconnect.com
✍ Trevor Jones
🖥 www.barnsleygolfclub.co.uk

## Bawtry   (1974)
*Cross Lane, Austerfield, Doncaster DN10 6RF*
☎ **(01302) 711409**
📠 (01302) 711445
✉ enquiries@bawtrygolfclub.co.uk
🖥 www.bawtrygolfclub.co.uk

## Beauchief   (1925)
**Public**
*Abbey Lane, Beauchief, Sheffield S8 0DB*
☎ **(0114) 236 7274**
✉ e-mail@beauchiefgolfclub.co.uk
✍ Mrs B Fryer
🖥 www.beauchiefgolfclub.co.uk

## Birley Wood   (1974)
**Public**
*Birley Lane, Sheffield S12 3BP*
☎ **(0114) 264 7262**
✉ birleysec@hotmail.com
✍ P Renshaw (0114) 265 3784
🖥 www.birleywood.free-online.co.uk

## Concord Park   (1952)
**Pay and play**
*Shiregreen Lane, Sheffield S5 6AE*
☎ **(0114) 257 7378**
📠 (0114) 234 7792
✉ concordparkgc@tiscali.co.uk
✍ PJ Wilson (0114) 234 7792
🖥 www.concordparkgolfclub.co.uk

## Crookhill Park   (1974)
**Public**
*Carr Lane, Conisborough, Doncaster DN12 2AH*
☎ **(01709) 862979**
✉ secretary@crookhillpark.co.uk
✍ A Goddard (Sec)
🖥 www.crookhillpark.co.uk

## Doncaster   (1894)
*Bawtry Road, Bessacarr, Doncaster DN4 7PD*
☎ **(01302) 865632**
📠 (01302) 865994
✉ doncastergolf@aol.com
✍ Malcolm Macphee
🖥 www.doncastergolfclub.co.uk

## Doncaster Town Moor   (1895)
*Bawtry Road, Belle Vue, Doncaster DN4 5HU*
☎ **(01302) 533167**
📠 (01302) 533448
✉ dtmgc@btconnect.com
✍ Mike Pears
🖥 www.doncastertownmoorgolfclub.co.uk

## Dore & Totley   (1913)
*Bradway Road, Bradway, Sheffield S17 4QR*
☎ **(0114) 236 0492**
📠 (0114) 235 3436
✉ dore.totley@btconnect.com
✍ Mrs SD Haslehurst (0114) 236 9872
🖥 www.doreandtotleygolfclub.co.uk

## Grange Park   (1972)
**Pay and play**
*Upper Wortley Road, Kimberworth, Rotherham S61 2SJ*
☎ **(01709) 558884**
✍ RP Townley (01709) 558884

## Hallamshire   (1897)
*Sandygate, Sheffield S10 4LA*
☎ **(0114) 230 2153**
📠 (0114) 230 5413
✉ secretary@hallamshiregolfclub.com
✍ Bob Hill (0114) 230 2153
🖥 www.hallamshiregolfclub.co.uk

## Hallowes   (1892)
*Dronfield, Sheffield S18 1UR*
☎ **(01246) 413734**
📠 (01246) 413753
✉ secretary@hallowesgolfclub.org
✍ N Ogden
🖥 www.hallowesgolfclub.org

## Hickleton   (1909)
*Lidget Lane, Hickleton, Doncaster DN4 6UT*
☎ **(01709) 896081**
✉ info@hickletongolfclub.co.uk
✍ Susan Leach (Sec)
🖥 www.hickletongolfclub.co.uk

## Hillsborough   (1920)
*Worrall Road, Sheffield S6 4BE*
☎ **(0114) 234 9151 (Secretary)**
📠 (0114) 229 4105

✉ admin@hillsboroughgolfclub.co.uk
✍ Lewis Horsman (0114) 234 9151
🖥 www.hillsboroughgolfclub.co.uk

## Lees Hall   (1907)
*Hemsworth Road, Norton, Sheffield S8 8LL*
☎ **(0114) 255 4402**
✉ secretary@leeshallgolfclub.co.uk
✍ J Clegg (0114) 255 4402
🖥 www.leeshallgolfclub.co.uk

## Lindrick   (1891)
*Lindrick Common, Worksop, Notts S81 8BH*
☎ **(01909) 475282**
📠 (01909) 488685
✉ briannoble@lindrickgolfclub.co.uk
✍ Mr Brian Noble (01909) 475282
🖥 www.lindrickgolfclub.co.uk

## Owston Hall (the Robin Hood golf course)   (1996)
**Proprietary**
*Owston Hall, Owston, Doncaster DN6 9JF*
☎ **(01302) 722800**
📠 (01302) 728885
✉ proshop@owstonhall.com
✍ Gerry Briggs
🖥 www.owstonhall.com

## Owston Park   (1988)
**Public**
*Owston Lane, Owston, Carcroft DN6 8EF*
☎ **(01302) 330821**
✉ michael.parker@foremostgolf.com
✍ MT Parker
🖥 www.owstonparkgolfcourse.co.uk

## Phoenix   (1932)
*Pavilion Lane, Brinsworth, Rotherham S60 5PA*
☎ **(01709) 363788**
📠 (01709) 363788
✉ secretary@phoenixgolfclub.co.uk
✍ I Gregory (01709) 363788
🖥 www.phoenixgolfclub.co.uk

## Renishaw Park   (1911)
*Golf House, Mill Lane, Renishaw, Sheffield S21 3UZ*
☎ **(01246) 432044**
📠 (01246) 432116
✉ secretary@renishawparkgolf.co.uk
✍ Mark Nelson
🖥 www.renishawparkgolf.co.uk

## Rother Valley Golf Centre   (1997)
**Proprietary**
*Mansfield Road, Wales Bar, Sheffield S26 5PQ*
☎ **(0114) 247 3000**
📠 (0114) 247 6000
✉ info@rothervalleygolfcentre.co.uk
✍ Mr R Hanson
🖥 www.rothervalleygolfcentre.co.uk

## Rotherham   (1902)
*Thrybergh Park, Rotherham S65 4NU*
☎ **(01709) 850466**
✉ manager@rotherhamgolfclub.com

✍ Mr Chris Allen
   (Secretary/Chairman)
🖳 www.rotherhamgolfclub.com

## Roundwood    (1976)
*Green Lane, Rawmarsh, Rotherham
S62 6LA*
☎ **(01709) 826061**
📠 (01709) 523478
📧 golf.secretary@roundwoodgolfclub
   .co.uk
✍ G Billups (01709) 525208
🖳 www.roundwoodgolfclub.co.uk

## Sandhill    (1993)
**Proprietary**
*Little Houghton, Barnsley S72 0HW*
☎ **(01226) 753444**
📠 (01226) 753444
📧 steven.gavin409@googlemail.com
✍ S Gavin (01226) 780025
🖳 www.sandhillgolfclub.co.uk

## Sheffield Transport    (1923)
*Meadow Head, Sheffield S8 7RE*
☎ **(0114) 237 3216**
✍ AE Mason

## Silkstone    (1893)
*Field Head, Elmhirst Lane, Silkstone,
Barnsley S75 4LD*
☎ **(01226) 790328**
📠 (01226) 794902
📧 silkstonegolf@hotmail.co.uk
✍ Alan Cook
🖳 www.silkstone-golf-club.co.uk

## Sitwell Park    (1913)
*Shrogs Wood Road, Rotherham S60 4BY*
☎ **(01709) 541046**
📠 (01709) 703637
📧 secretary@sitwellgolf.co.uk
✍ S G Bell
🖳 www.sitwellgolf.co.uk

## Stocksbridge & District
(1924)
*Royd Lane, Deepcar, Sheffield S36 2RZ*
☎ **(0114) 288 7479/288 2003**
📠 (0114) 283 1460
📧 stocksbridgegolf@live.co.uk
✍ Mrs A Methley (0114) 288 2003
🖳 www.stocksbridgeanddistrictgolfclub
   .com

## Styrrup Hall    (2000)
**Proprietary**
*Main Street, Styrrup, Doncaster DN11 8NB*
☎ **(01302) 751112 (Golf)**
   **759933 (Clubhouse)**
📠 (01302) 750622
📧 office@styrrupgolf.co.uk
✍ Dianne Stokoe (Sec/Mgr)
🖳 www.styrrupgolf.co.uk

## Tankersley Park    (1907)
*Park Lane, High Green, Sheffield S35 4LG*
☎ **(0114) 246 8247**
📠 (0114) 245 7818
📧 secretary@tpgc.freeserve.co.uk
✍ A Brownhill (0114) 246 8247
🖳 www.tankersleyparkgolfclub.org.uk

## Thorne    (1980)
**Pay and play**
*Kirton Lane, Thorne, Doncaster DN8 5RJ*
☎ **(01405) 815173**
   **(bookings 01405 812084)**
📠 (01405) 741899
📧 carolinehighfield@live.co.uk
✍ E Highfield (Golf Shop)
🖳 www.thornegolf.co.uk

## Tinsley Park    (1920)
**Public**
*High Hazels Park, Darnall, Sheffield S9 4PE*
☎ **(0114) 244 8974**
✍ Wayne Yellott (Professional)
🖳 www.tinsleyparkgolfcourse.co.uk

## Wath    (1904)
*Abdy Rawmarsh, Rotherham S62 7SJ*
☎ **(01709) 878609**
📠 (01709) 877097
📧 golf@wathgolfclub.co.uk
✍ I Gregory (01709) 878609 ext 1
🖳 www.wathgolfclub.co.uk

## Wheatley    (1914)
*Armthorpe Road, Doncaster DN2 5QB*
☎ **(01302) 831655**
📠 (01302) 812736
📧 secretary@wheatleygolfclub.co.uk
✍ Ken Gosden
🖳 www.wheatleygolfclub.co.uk

## Wortley    (1894)
*Hermit Hill Lane, Wortley, Sheffield
S35 7DF*
☎ **(0114) 288 8469**
📠 (0114) 288 8488
📧 wortley.golfclub@btconnect.com
✍ Roy Cooke
🖳 www.wortleygolfclub.co.uk

# Yorkshire (West)

## The Alwoodley    (1907)
*Wigton Lane, Alwoodley, Leeds LS17 8SA*
☎ **(0113) 268 1680**
📧 alwoodley@btconnect.com
✍ Mrs J Slater
🖳 www.alwoodley.co.uk

## Bagden Hall Hotel    (1993)
*Wakefield Road, Scissett HD8 9LE*
☎ **(01484) 865330**
📠 (01484) 861001
✍ J Rinder

## Baildon    (1896)
*Moorgate, Baildon, Shipley BD17 5PP*
☎ **(01274) 584266**
📧 secretary@baildongolfclub.com
✍ Paul Weatherill
🖳 www.baildongolfclub.com

## Ben Rhydding    (1947)
*High Wood, Ben Rhydding, Ilkley LS9 8SB*
☎ **(01943) 608759**
📧 secretary@benrhyddinggc
   .freeserve.co.uk
✍ J D B Watts
🖳 www.benrhyddinggolfclub.com

## Bingley St Ives    (1931)
*St Ives Estate, Bingley BD16 1AT*
☎ **(01274) 562436**
📠 (01274) 511788
📧 secretary@bingleystivesgc.co.uk
✍ A M Weaver
🖳 www.bingleystivesgc.co.uk

## Bracken Ghyll    (1993)
*Skipton Road, Addingham, Ilkley LS29 0SL*
☎ **(01943) 831207**
📠 (01943) 839453
📧 office@brackenghyll.co.uk
✍ Peter Knowles
🖳 www.brackenghyll.co.uk

## The Bradford Golf Club
(1891)
*Hawksworth Lane, Guiseley, Leeds
LS20 8NP*
☎ **(01943) 875570**
📧 secretary@bradfordgolfclub.co.uk
✍ James Washington
🖳 www.bradfordgolfclub.co.uk

## Bradford Moor    (1906)
*Scarr Hall, Pollard Lane, Bradford
BD2 4RW*
☎ **(01274) 771716**
📧 bfdmoorgc@hotmail.co.uk
✍ C P Bedford (01274) 771693
🖳 www.bradfordmoorgolfclub.co.uk

## Bradley Park    (1978)
**Public**
*Bradley Road, Huddersfield HD2 1PZ*
☎ **(01484) 223772**
📠 (01484) 451613
📧 parnellreilly@btconnect.com
✍ Derek M Broadbent
🖳 www.bradleyparkgolf.co.uk

## Branshaw    (1912)
*Sykes Head, Oakworth, Keighley BD22 7ES*
☎ **(01535) 643235**
📠 (01535) 643235
📧 enquiries@branshawgolfclub.co.uk
✍ Simon Jowitt
🖳 www.branshawgolfclub.co.uk

## Calverley    (1980)
*Woodhall Lane, Pudsey LS28 5QY*
☎ **(0113) 256 9244**
📠 (0113) 256 4362
📧 calverleygolf@btconnect.com
✍ N Wendel-Jones (Mgr)

## Castlefields    (1903)
*Rastrick Common, Brighouse HD6 3HL*
📧 secretary@castlefieldsgolfclub
   .co.uk
✍ David Bartliff
🖳 www.castlefieldsgolfclub.co.uk

## City Golf Course    (1997)
**Pay and play**
*Red Cote Lane, Kirkstall Road, Leeds
LS4 2AW*
☎ **(0113) 263 3030**
📠 (0113) 263 3044
✍ P Cole (Mgr)

## City of Wakefield    (1936)
**Public**
*Lupset Park, Horbury Road, Wakefield
WF2 8QS*
☎ **(01924) 367442**

## Clayton    (1906)
*Thornton View Road, Clayton, Bradford
BD14 6JX*
☎ **(01274) 880047**
✉ secretary@claytongc.plus.com
✍ DA Stevens (01274) 572311
🖥 www.claytongolfclub.co.uk

## Cleckheaton & District    (1900)
*483 Bradford Road, Cleckheaton
BD19 6BU*
☎ **(01274) 851266 (Secretary)**
📠 (01274) 871382
✉ info@cleckheatongolfclub.co.uk
✍ Dick Guiver
🖥 www.cleckheatongolfclub.com

## Cookridge Hall    (1997)
**Proprietary**
*Cookridge Lane, Cookridge, Leeds
LS16 7NL*
☎ **(0113) 230 0641**
📠 (0113) 203 0198
✉ info@cookridgehall.co.uk
✍ Gary Day
🖥 www.cookridgehall.co.uk

## Crosland Heath    (1914)
*Felks Stile Road, Crosland Heath,
Huddersfield HD4 7AF*
☎ **(01484) 653216**
📠 (01484) 461079
✉ golf@croslandheath.co.uk
✍ Mrs L Salvini
🖥 www.croslandheath.co.uk

## Crow Nest Park    (1995)
*Coach Road, Hove Edge, Brighouse
HD6 2LN*
☎ **(01484) 401121**
✉ info@crownestgolf.co.uk
✍ L Holmes
🖥 www.crownestgolf.co.uk

## De Vere Oulton Park Golf Club    (1990)
**Public**
*Rothwell Lane, Oulton, Leeds, West
Yorkshire LS26 8HN*
☎ **(0113) 282 3152**
📠 (0113) 282 6290
✍ A Cooper (Mgr)

## Dewsbury District    (1891)
*The Pinnacle, Sands Lane, Mirfield
WF14 8HJ*
☎ **(01924) 492399**
📠 (01924) 491928
✉ info@dewsburygolf.co.uk
✍ A M Thorpe
🖥 www.dewsburygolf.co.uk

## East Bierley    (1928)
*South View Road, Bierley, Bradford
BD4 6PP*
☎ **(01274) 681023**

✉ rjwelch@talktalk.net
✍ RJ Welch (01274) 683666

## Elland    (1910)
*Hammerstone Leach Lane, Hullen Edge,
Elland HX5 0TA*
☎ **(01422) 372505**
✉ secretary@ellandgolfclub.plus.com
✍ PA Green (01422) 251431
🖥 www.ellandgolfclub.plus.com

## Fardew    (1993)
**Pay and play**
*Nursery Farm, Carr Lane, East Morton,
Keighley BD20 5RY*
☎ **(01274) 561229**
✉ davidheaton@btconnect.com
✍ A Stevens
🖥 www.fardewgolfclub.co.uk

## Ferrybridge    (2002)
*PO Box 39, Stranglands Lane, Knottingley
WF11 8SQ*
☎ **(01977) 884165**
📠 (01977) 884001
✉ Trevor.Ellis@Scottish-southern
✍ TD Ellis

## Fulneck    (1892)
*Fulneck, Pudsey LS28 8NT*
☎ **(0113) 256 5191**
✉ fulneckgolf@aol.com
✍ Mr J McLean (Hon Sec)
🖥 www.fulneckgolfclub.co.uk

## Garforth    (1913)
*Long Lane, Garforth, Leeds LS25 2DS*
☎ **(0113) 286 3308**
📠 (0113) 286 3308
✉ garforthgcltd@lineone.net
✍ D R Carlisle
🖥 www.garforthgolfclub.co.uk

## Gotts Park    (1933)
**Public**
*Armley Ridge Road, Armley, Leeds
LS12 2QX*
☎ **(0113) 234 2019**
✍ M Gill (0113) 256 2994

## Halifax    (1895)
*Union Lane, Ogden, Halifax HX2 8XR*
☎ **(01422) 244171**
📠 (01422) 241459
✉ halifax.golfclub@virgin.net
🖥 www.halifaxgolfclub.co.uk

## Halifax Bradley Hall    (1907)
*Holywell Green, Halifax HX4 9AN*
☎ **(01422) 374108**
✉ bhgc@gotadsl.co.uk
✍ Mrs J Teale
🖥 www.bradleyhallgolfclub.co.uk

## Halifax West End    (1906)
*Paddock Lane, Highroad Well, Halifax
HX2 0NT*
☎ **(01422) 341878**
📠 (01422) 410540
✉ manager@westendgc.co.uk
✍ S J Boustead (01422) 341878
🖥 www.westendgc.co.uk

## Hanging Heaton    (1922)
*Whitecross Road, Bennett Lane, Dewsbury
WF12 7DT*
☎ **(01924) 461606**
📠 (01924) 430100
✉ derek.atkinson@hhgc.org
✍ Derek Atkinson (01924) 430100
🖥 www.hangingheatongolfclub.co.uk

## Headingley    (1892)
*Back Church Lane, Adel, Leeds LS16 8DW*
☎ **(0113) 267 9573 (Clubhouse)**
📠 (0113) 281 7334
✉ manager@headingleygolfclub.co.uk
✍ Mr J L Hall
🖥 www.headingleygolfclub.co.uk

## Headley    (1907)
*Headley Lane, Thornton, Bradford
BD13 3LX*
☎ **(01274) 833481**
📠 (01274) 833481
✉ admin@headleygolfclub.co.uk
✍ D Britton
🖥 www.headleygolfclub.co.uk

## Hebden Bridge    (1930)
*Great Mount, Wadsworth, Hebden Bridge
HX7 8PH*
☎ **(01422) 842896**
✉ hbgc@btconnect.com
✍ Stepney Calvert (01422) 842896
🖥 www.hebdenbridgegolfclub.co.uk

## Horsforth    (1906)
*Layton Rise, Layton Road, Horsforth, Leeds
LS18 5EX*
☎ **(0113) 258 6819**
📠 (0113) 258 9336
✉ secretary@horsforthgolfclub.co.uk
✍ Mrs LA Harrison-Elrick
🖥 www.horsforthgolfclub.co.uk

## Howley Hall    (1900)
*Scotchman Lane, Morley, Leeds LS27 0NX*
☎ **(01924) 350100**
📠 (01924) 350104
✉ office@howleyhall.co.uk
✍ D Jones (01924) 350100
🖥 www.howleyhall.co.uk

## Huddersfield    (1891)
*Fixby Hall, Lightridge Road, Huddersfield
HD2 2EP*
☎ **(01484) 426203**
📠 (01484) 424623
✉ secretary@huddersfield-golf.co.uk
✍ S.A.Jones
🖥 www.huddersfield-golf.co.uk

## Ilkley    (1890)
*Myddleton, Ilkley LS29 0BE*
☎ **(01943) 607277**
📠 (01943) 816130
✉ honsec@ilkleygolfclub.co.uk
✍ Robert G Lambert (Hon
   Sec) (01943) 600214
🖥 www.ilkleygolfclub.co.uk

## Keighley    (1904)
*Howden Park, Utley, Keighley BD20 6DH*
☎ **(01535) 604778**

(01535) 604778
manager@keighleygolfclub.com
G Cameron Dawson
www.keighleygolfclub.com

## Leeds (1896)
*Elmete Lane, Roundhay, Leeds LS8 2LJ*
☎ (0113) 265 9203
admin@leedsgolfclub.co.uk
P Mawman (0113) 265 9203
www.leedsgolfclub.co.uk

## Leeds Golf Centre (1994)
**Proprietary**
*Wike Ridge Lane, Shadwell, Leeds LS17 9JW*
☎ (0113) 288 6000
(0113) 288 6185
info@leedsgolfcentre.com
A Herridge (Director of Golf)
www.leedsgolfcentre.com

## Lightcliffe (1907)
*Knowle Top Road, Lightcliffe HX3 8SW*
☎ (01422) 202459
RP Crampton (01484) 384672

## Lofthouse Hill
*Leeds Road, Lofthouse Hill, Wakefield WF3 3LR*
☎ (01924) 823703
(01924) 823703
P Moon
www.lofthousehillgolfclub.co.uk

## Longley Park (1910)
*Maple Street, Huddersfield HD5 9AX*
☎ (01484) 426932
(01484) 515280
longleyparkgolfclub@12freeukisp.co.uk
J Ambler (01484) 431885

## Low Laithes (1925)
*Park Mill Lane, Flushdyke, Ossett WF5 9AP*
☎ (01924) 266067
(01924) 266266
info@lowlaithesgolfclub.co.uk
P Browning (Sec/Mgr)
www.lowlaithesgolfclub.co.uk

## The Manor
**Proprietary**
*Bradford Road, Drighlington, Bradford BD11 1AB*
☎ (01132) 852644
(01332) 879961
themanorgolfclub@hotmail.co.uk
G Thompson (Sec/Mgr)
www.themanorgolfclub.co.uk

## Marriott Hollins Hall Hotel (1999)
*Hollins Hill, Baildon, Shipley BD17 7QW*
☎ (01274) 534212
(01274) 534220
mhrs.lbags.golf@marriotthotels.com
Stuart Carnie (01274) 534250
www.hollinshallgolf.com

## Marsden (1921)
*Hemplow, Marsden, Huddersfield HD7 6NN*
☎ (01484) 844253
secretary@marsdengolf.co.uk
R O'Brien
www.marsdengolf.co.uk

## Meltham (1908)
*Thick Hollins Hall, Meltham, Huddersfield HD9 4DQ*
☎ (01484) 850227
admin@meltham-golf.co.uk
J R Dixon (Hon)
www.meltham-golf.co.uk

## Mid Yorkshire (1993)
**Proprietary**
*Havercroft Lane, Darrington, Pontefract WF8 3BP*
☎ (01977) 704522
(01977) 600823
admin@midyorkshiregolfclub.com
Robert Pointon
www.midyorkshiregolfclub.com

## Middleton Park (1933)
**Public**
*Ring Road, Beeston Park, Middleton LS10 3TN*
☎ (0113) 270 0449
secretary@middletonparkgolfclub.co.uk
www.middletonparkgolfclub.co.uk

## Moor Allerton (1923)
*Coal Road, Wike, Leeds LS17 9NH*
☎ (0113) 266 1154
(0113) 268 0589
info@magc.co.uk
G Pretty (Mgr)
www.magc.co.uk

## Moortown (1909)
*Harrogate Road, Leeds LS17 7DB*
☎ (0113) 268 6521
(0113) 268 0986
secretary@moortown-gc.co.uk
Mr Peter Rishworth
www.moortown-gc.co.uk

## Normanton (1903)
*Hatfield Hall, Aberford Road, Stanley, Wakefield WF3 4JP*
☎ (01924) 377943
(01924) 200777
office@normantongolf.co.uk
Lynne Pickles
www.normantongolf.co.uk

## Northcliffe (1921)
*High Bank Lane, Shipley, Bradford BD18 4LJ*
☎ (01274) 584085
(01274) 584148
sec@northcliffegc.org.uk
C Malloy (01274) 596731
www.northcliffegolfclub.co.uk

## Otley (1906)
*West Busk Lane, Otley LS21 3NG*
☎ (01943) 465329

(01943) 850387
office@otleygolfclub.co.uk
PJ Clarke Ext 1
www.otleygolfclub.co.uk

## Outlane (1906)
*Slack Lane, off New Hey Road, Outlane, Huddersfield HD3 3FQ*
☎ (01422) 374762
(01422) 311789
secretary@outlanegolfclub.ltd.uk
P Turner
www.outlanegolfclub.ltd.uk

## Pontefract & District (1904)
*Park Lane, Pontefract WF8 4QS*
☎ (01977) 781940
(01977) 792241
manager@pdgc.co.uk
Malcolm Huddlestone (Mgr)
www.pdgc.co.uk

## Queensbury (1923)
*Brighouse Road, Queensbury, Bradford BD13 1QF*
☎ (01274) 882155
(01274) 882155
queensburygolf@talktalk.net
MH Heptinstall
www.queensburygc.co.uk

## Rawdon (1896)
*Buckstone Drive, Micklefield Lane, Rawdon LS19 6BD*
☎ (0113) 250 6040
info@rgltc.co.uk
Phil Denison
www.rgltc.co.uk

## Riddlesden (1927)
*Howden Rough, Riddlesden, Keighley BD20 5QN*
☎ (01535) 602148
S Morton (01535) 602148

## Roundhay (1923)
**Public**
*Park Lane, Leeds LS8 2EJ*
☎ (0113) 266 2695
geoff.hodgson@sky.com
G M Hodgson (Hon Sec)
www.roundhaygc.com

## Ryburn (1910)
*Norland, Sowerby Bridge, Halifax HX6 3QP*
☎ (01422) 831355
secretary@ryburngolfclub.co.uk
Raymond Attiwell (07904) 834320
www.ryburngolfclub.co.uk

## Sand Moor (1926)
*Alwoodley Lane, Leeds LS17 7DJ*
☎ (0113) 268 5180
(0113) 266 1105
info@sandmoorgolf.co.uk
Jackie Hogan (0113) 268 5180
www.sandmoorgolf.co.uk

## Scarcroft (1937)
*Syke Lane, Scarcroft, Leeds LS14 3BQ*
☎ (0113) 289 2311
(0113) 289 3835

✉ secretary@scarcroftgolfclub.co.uk
✍ R A Simpson (Sec/Mgr)
🖥 www.scarcroftgolfclub.co.uk

## Shipley    (1896)
Beckfoot Lane, Cottingley Bridge, Bingley
BD16 1LX
☎ **(01274) 568652**
📠 (01274) 567739
✉ office@shipleygc.co.uk
✍ Mrs MJ Simpson (01274) 568652
🖥 www.shipleygolfclub.com

## Silsden    (1911)
Brunthwaite Lane, Brunthwaite, Silsden
BD20 0ND
☎ **(01535) 652998**
✉ info@silsdengolfclub.co.uk
✍ M Twigg
🖥 www.silsdengolfclub.co.uk

## South Bradford    (1906)
Pearson Road, Odsal, Bradford BD6 1BH
☎ **(01274) 679195**
✉ secsouthbradford@btconnect.com
✍ B Broadbent (01274) 679195
🖥 www.southbradfordgolfclub.co.uk

## South Leeds    (1906)
Gipsy Lane, Ring Road, Beeston, Leeds
LS11 5TU
☎ **(0113) 277 1676**
📠 (0113) 277 1676
✉ south-leeds@btconnect.com
✍ B Clayton (0113) 277 1676
🖥 www.southleedsgolfclub.co.uk

## Temple Newsam    (1923)
**Public**
Temple Newsam Road, Halton, Leeds
LS15 0LN
☎ **(0113) 264 5624**
✉ secretary@tngc.co.uk

✍ Mrs Christine P Wood
🖥 www.tngolfclub.co.uk

## Todmorden    (1894)
Rive Rocks, Cross Stone, Todmorden
OL14 8RD
☎ **(01706) 812986**
✉ secretarytodgolfclub@msn.com
✍ Peter H Eastwood
🖥 www.todmordengolfclub.co.uk

## Wakefield    (1891)
28 Woodthorpe Lane, Sandal, Wakefield
WF2 6JH
☎ **(01924) 258778**
📠 (01924) 242752
✉ wakefieldgolfclub
  @woodthorpelane.freeserve
  .co.uk
✍ Elizabeth Newton (01924) 258778
🖥 www.wakefieldgolfclub.co.uk

## Waterton Park    (1995)
The Balk, Walton, Wakefield WF2 6QL
☎ **(01924) 259525**
📠 (01924) 256969
✉ wparkgolfclub@btconnect.com
✍ M Pearson (01924) 255557

## West Bradford    (1900)
Chellow Grange Road, Haworth Road,
Bradford BD9 6NP
☎ **(01274) 542767**
✉ secretary@westbradfordgolfclub
  .co.uk
✍ Tad Janzio (Hon Sec)
🖥 www.westbradfordgolfclub.co.uk

## Wetherby    (1910)
Linton Lane, Linton, Wetherby LS22 4JF
☎ **(01937) 580089**
📠 (01937) 581915
✉ manager@wetherbygolfclub.co.uk

✍ Darren Tear
🖥 www.wetherbygolfclub.co.uk

## Whitwood    (1987)
**Public**
Altofts Lane, Whitwood, Castleford
WF10 5PZ
☎ **(01977) 512835**
✍ J Deakin

## Willow Valley Golf    (1993)
**Pay and play**
Clifton, Brighouse HD6 4JB
☎ **(01274) 878624**
✉ sales@wvgc.co.uk
✍ H Newton
🖥 www.wvgc.co.uk

## Woodhall Hills    (1905)
Woodhall Road, Calverley, Pudsey
LS28 5UN
☎ **(0113) 256 4771 (Clubhouse)**
📠 (0113) 255 4594
✉ woodhallgolf@btconnect.com
✍ J Hayes (0113) 255 4594
🖥 www.woodhallhillsgolfclub.com

## Woodsome Hall    (1922)
Woodsome Hall, Fenay Bridge,
Huddersfield HD8 0LQ
☎ **(01484) 602971**
📠 (01484) 608260
✍ TJ Mee (01484) 602739 (Gen Mgr)
🖥 www.woodsomehall.co.uk

## Woolley Park    (1995)
**Proprietary**
New Road, Woolley, Wakefield WF4 2JS
☎ **(01226) 380144 (Bookings)**
📠 (01226) 390295
✉ woolleyparkgolf@yahoo.co.uk
✍ RP Stoffel (01226) 382209
🖥 www.woolleyparkgolfclub.co.uk

# Ireland

## Antrim (1997)
**Public**
Allen Park Golf Centre, 45 Castle Road,
Antrim BT41 4NA
☎ (028) 9442 9001
✉ allenpark@antrim.gov.uk
✍ Marie Agnew (Mgr)
🖳 www.antrim.gov.uk

## Ballycastle (1890)
Cushendall Road, Ballycastle BT64 6QP
☎ (028) 2076 2536
🖳 (028) 2076 9909
✉ info@ballycastlegolfclub.com
✍ Mr Mark Steen
🖳 www.ballycastlegolfclub.com

## Ballyclare (1923)
25 Springvale Road, Ballyclare BT39 9JW
☎ (028) 9332 2696 (Clubhouse)
🖳 (028) 9332 2696
✉ info@ballyclaregolfclub.com
✍ Michael Stone
🖳 www.ballyclaregolfclub.com

## Ballymena (1903)
128 Raceview Road, Ballymena BT42 4HY
☎ (028) 2586 1207/1487
🖳 (028) 2586 1487
✉ admin@ballymenagolfclub.com
✍ Ken Herbison (Hon Sec)

## Bentra
**Public**
Slaughterford Road, Whitehead BT38 9TG
☎ (028) 9335 8000
🖳 (028) 9336 6676
✉ greenspace@carrickfergus.org
✍ S Daye (028) 9335 8039
🖳 www.bentragolf.co.uk

## Burnfield House
10 Cullyburn Road, Newtownabbey
BT36 5BN
☎ (028) 9083 8737
✉ burnfieldhouse@gmail.com
🖳 www.burnfieldhouse.co.uk

## Bushfoot (1890)
50 Bushfoot Road, Portballintrae BT57 8RR
☎ (028) 2073 1317
🖳 (028) 2073 1852
✉ bushfootgolfclub@btconnect.com
✍ T McFaull (Hon Sec)
🖳 www.bushfootgolfclub.co.uk

## Cairndhu (1928)
192 Coast Road, Ballygally, Larne
BT40 2QG
☎ (028) 2858 3324
🖳 (028) 2858 3324
✉ cairndhugc@btconnect.com
✍ N McKinstry (Sec/Mgr)
(028) 2858 3324
🖳 www.cairndhugolfclub.co.uk

## Carrickfergus (1926)
35 North Road, Carrickfergus BT38 8LP
☎ (028) 9336 3713
🖳 (028) 9336 3023
✉ carrickfergusgc@btconnect.com
✍ I McLean (Hon Sec)
🖳 www.carrickfergusgolfclub.com

## Cushendall (1937)
21 Shore Road, Cushendall BT44 0NG
☎ (028) 2177 1318
🖳 (028) 2177 1318
✉ cushendallgc@btconnect.com
✍ S McLaughlin (028) 2175 8366

## Down Royal (1990)
**Proprietary**
6 Dungarton Road, Maze, Lisburn
BT27 5RT
☎ (028) 9262 1339
🖳 (028) 9262 1339
✉ info@downroyalgolf.com
✍ Bill McCappin (Mgr)
🖳 www.downroyalgolf.com

## Galgorm Castle (1997)
**Proprietary**
200 Galgorm Road, Ballymena BT42 1HL
☎ (028) 256 46161
🖳 (028) 256 51151
✉ golf@galgormcastle.com
✍ G Henry (Gen Mgr)
🖳 www.galgormcastle.com

## Gracehill (1995)
**Proprietary**
141 Ballinlea Road, Stranocum, Ballymoney
BT53 8PX
☎ (028) 2075 1209
🖳 (028) 2075 1074
✉ info@gracehillgolfclub.co.uk
✍ M McClure (Mgr)
🖳 www.gracehillgolfclub.co.uk

## Greenacres (1996)
153 Ballyrobert Road, Ballyclare BT39 9RT
☎ (028) 933 54111
🖳 (028) 933 44509
✍ Colin Crawford
🖳 www.greenacresgolfclub.co.uk

## Greenisland (1894)
156 Upper Road, Greenisland,
Carrickfergus BT38 8RW
☎ (028) 9086 2236
✉ greenisland.golf@btconnect.com
✍ FF Trotter (Hon)
🖳 www.greenislandgolfclub.co.uk

## Hilton Templepatrick (1999)
**Proprietary**
Castle Upton Estate, Paradise Walk,
Templepatrick BT39 0DD
☎ (028) 9443 5542
🖳 (028) 9443 5511
✉ eamonn.logue@hilton.com
✍ Eamonn Logue (Golf Ops Mgr)
🖳 www.hiltontemplepatrickgolf.com

## Larne (1894)
54 Ferris Bay Road, Islandmagee, Larne
BT40 3RJ
☎ (028) 9338 2228
🖳 (028) 9338 2088
✉ info@larnegolfclub.co.uk
✍ RI Johnston

## Lisburn (1891)
68 Eglantine Road, Lisburn BT27 5RQ
☎ (028) 9267 7216
🖳 (028) 9260 3608
✉ info@lisburngolfclub.com
✍ John McKeown (Gen Mgr)
🖳 www.lisburngolfclub.com

## Mallusk (1992)
Antrim Road, Glengormley, Newtownabbey
BT36 4RF
☎ (028) 9084 3799
✍ J Patterson

## Massereene (1895)
51 Lough Road, Antrim BT41 4DQ
☎ (028) 9442 8096 (office)
🖳 (028) 9448 7661
✉ info@massereene.com
✍ G Henry (028) 9442 8096
🖳 www.massereene.com

## Rathmore (1947)
Bushmills Road, Portrush BT56 8JG
☎ (028) 7082 2996
✉ info@rathmoregolfclub.co.uk
✍ Stan Short (Club Admin)
⊕ For queries regarding the Valley
  Links Course, please contact Royal
  Portrush Golf Club (02870)
  822311
🖳 www.rathmoregolfclub.com

## Royal Portrush (1888)
Dunluce Road, Portrush BT56 8JQ
☎ (028) 7082 2311
🖳 (028) 7082 3139
✉ wilma.erskine
  @royalportrushgolfclub.com
✍ Miss W Erskine
🖳 www.royalportrushgolfclub.com

## Whitehead (1904)
McCrae's Brae, Whitehead, Carrickfergus
BT38 9NZ
☎ (028) 9337 0820
🖳 (028) 9337 0825
✉ robin@whiteheadgc.fsnet.co.uk
✍ RA Patrick (Hon)
🖳 www.whiteheadgolfclub.com

## Ashfield (1990)
Freeduff, Cullyhanna, Newry BT35 0JJ
☎ (028) 3086 8180
✍ J Quinn (Sec/Mgr)

## Cloverhill    (1999)
Proprietary
*Lough Road, Mullaghbawn BT35 9XP*
- ☎ **(028) 3088 9374**
- ✉ info@cloverhillgolfclub.co.uk
- ✍ Colin Pilkington
- 🖥 www.cloverhillgolfclub.co.uk

## County Armagh    (1893)
*7 Newry Road, Armagh BT60 1EN*
- ☎ **(028) 37 525861/(028) 37 525864 (Pro Sh**
- 📠 (028) 3752 8768
- ✉ lynne@golfarmagh.co.uk
- ✍ Mrs Lynne Fleming (028) 3752 5861
- 🖥 www.golfarmagh.co.uk

## Edenmore G&CC    (1992)
*Edenmore House, 70 Drumnabreeze Road, Magheralin, Craigavon BT67 0RH*
- ☎ **(028) 9261 9241**
- 📠 (028) 9261 3310
- ✉ info@edenmore.com
- ✍ K Logan (Sec/Mgr)
- 🖥 www.edenmore.com

## Loughgall Country Park & Golf Course
*11-14 Main Street, Loughgall*
- ☎ **(028) 3889 2900**
- 📠 (028) 3889 2902
- ✉ g.ferson@btinternet.com
- ✍ G Ferson (Mgr)
- 🖥 www.armagh.gov.uk

## Lurgan    (1893)
*The Demesne, Windsor Avenue, Lurgan BT67 9BN*
- ☎ **(028) 3832 2087 (Clubhouse)**
- 📠 (028) 3831 6166
- ✉ lurgangolfclub@btconnect.com
- ✍ Muriel Gamble
- 🖥 www.lurgangolfclub.com

## Portadown    (1902)
*192 Gilford Road, Portadown BT63 5LF*
- ☎ **(028) 383 55356**
- 📠 (028) 383 91394
- ✉ info@portadowngolfclub.co.uk
- ✍ Barbara Currie (Sec/Mgr)
- 🖥 www.portadowngolfclub.co.uk

## Silverwood    (1983)
*Turmoyra Lane, Silverwood, Lurgan BT66 6NG*
- ☎ **(028) 3832 5380**
- 📠 (028) 3834 7272
- ✉ silverwoodgolfclub@myrainbow.com
- ✍ S Ashe
- 🖥 www.silverwoodgolfclub.com

## Tandragee    (1922)
*Markethill Road, Tandragee BT62 2ER*
- ☎ **(028) 3884 1272 (Clubhouse)**
- 📠 (028) 3884 0664
- ✉ office@tandragee.co.uk
- ✍ A Hewitt (028) 3884 1272
- 🖥 www.tandragee.co.uk

# Belfast

## Ballyearl Golf Centre
Public
*585 Doagh Road, Newtownabbey BT36 5RZ*
- ☎ **(028) 9084 8287**
- 📠 (028) 9084 4896
- ✉ sbartley@newtownabbey.gov.uk
- 🖥 wwwnewtownabbey.gov.uk

## Balmoral    (1914)
*518 Lisburn Road, Belfast BT9 6GX*
- ☎ **(028) 9038 1514**
- 📠 (028) 9066 6759
- ✉ admin@balmoralgolf.com
- ✍ JT Graham (Ch Exec)
- 🖥 www.balmoralgolf.com

## Belvoir Park    (1927)
*73 Church Road, Newtownbreda, Belfast BT8 7AN*
- ☎ **(028) 9049 1693**
- 📠 (028) 9064 6113
- ✉ info@belvoirparkgolfclub.com
- ✍ Ann Vaughan (028) 9049 1693
- 🖥 www.belvoirparkgolfclub.com

## Castlereagh Hills Golf Course    (2005)
Pay and play
*73 Upper Braniel Road, Belfast BT5 7TX*
- ☎ **(028) 9044 8477**
- ✉ golfclub@castlereagh.gov.uk
- ✍ Lea Booth
- 🖥 www.castlereaghhills.com

## Dunmurry    (1905)
*91 Dunmurry Lane, Dunmurry, Belfast BT17 9JS*
- ☎ **(028) 9061 0834**
- 📠 (028) 9060 2540
- ✉ dunmurrygc@hotmail.com
- ✍ T Cassidy (Golf Mgr)
- 🖥 www.dunmurrygolfclub.co.uk

## Fortwilliam    (1891)
*8A Downview Avenue, Belfast B15 4EZ*
- ☎ **(028) 9037 0770**
- 📠 (028) 9078 1891
- ✉ office@fortwilliamgc.co.uk
- ✍ Pat Toal CB (Hon Sec)
- 🖥 www.fortwilliamgc.co.uk

## The Knock Club    (1895)
*Summerfield, Dundonald, Belfast BT16 2QX*
- ☎ **(028) 9048 3251**
- 📠 (028) 9048 7277
- ✉ knockgolfclub@btconnect.com
- ✍ Anne Armstrong
- 🖥 www.knockgolfclub.co.uk

## Malone    (1895)
*240 Upper Malone Road, Dunmurry, Belfast BT17 9LB*
- ☎ **(028) 9061 2758**
- 📠 (028) 9043 1394
- ✉ manager@malonegolfclub.co.uk
- ✍ Peter Kelly (028) 9061 2758
- 🖥 www.malonegolfclub.co.uk

## Ormeau    (1893)
*50 Park Road, Belfast BT7 2FX*
- ☎ **(028) 9064 1069 (Members)**
- 📠 (028) 9064 6250
- ✍ J Duggan (028) 9064 0700

## Shandon Park    (1926)
*73 Shandon Park, Belfast BT5 6NY*
- ☎ **(028) 9080 5030**
- ✉ shandonpark@btconnect.com
- ✍ GA Bailie ( Gen Mgr)
- 🖥 www.shandonpark.net

# Co Carlow

## Borris    (1907)
*Deerpark, Borris*
- ☎ **(059) 977 3310 (office)**
- 📠 (059) 977 3750
- ✉ borrisgolfclub@eircom.net
- ✍ Shena Walsh (059) 977 3310

## Carlow    (1899)
*Deer Park, Dublin Road, Carlow*
- ☎ **(059) 913 1695**
- 📠 (059) 914 0065
- ✉ carlowgolfclub@eircom.net
- ✍ D MacSweeney (Gen Mgr)
- 🖥 www.carlowgolfclub.com

# Co Cavan

## Belturbet    (1950)
*Erne Hill, Belturbet*
- ☎ **(049) 952 2287**
- ✍ PF Coffey (049) 22498

## Blacklion    (1962)
*Toam, Blacklion, via Sligo*
- ☎ **(071) 985 3024**
- 📠 (071) 985 3024
- ✍ P Gallery (Hon)
- 🖥 www.blackliongolf.eu

## Cabra Castle    (1978)
*Kingscourt*
- ☎ **(042) 966 7030**
- 📠 (042) 966 7039
- ✉ kevcarry@gmail.com
- ✍ Kevin Carry (087) 655 7538

## County Cavan    (1894)
*Arnmore House, Drumelis, Cavan*
- ☎ **(049) 433 1541**
- 📠 (049) 433 1541
- ✉ info@cavangolf.ie
- ✍ James Fraker
- 🖥 www.cavangolf.ie

## Slieve Russell G&CC    (1994)
*Ballyconnell*
- ☎ **(049) 952 5090**
- 📠 (049) 952 6046
- ✉ golf@slieverussell.ie
- ✍ (049) 952 5091
- 🖥 www.slieverussellgolf.ie

## Virginia (1945)
Park Hotel, Virginia
☎ (049) 854 8066
✍ P Gill (087) 681 3387

---

# Co Clare

## Clonlara (1993)
Clonlara
☎ (061) 354141
✉ clonlaragolfclub@eircom.net
✍ Tom Carroll

## Doonbeg (2002)
Doonbeg, Co Clare
☎ (065) 905 5600
🖳 (065) 905 5247
✉ reservations@doonbeggolfclub.com
✍ Joe Russell (Gen Mgr)
🖥 www.doonbeggolfclub.com

## Dromoland Castle (1964)
Newmarket-on-Fergus
☎ 353 (61) 368444
🖳 353 (61) 368498
✉ golf@dromoland.ie
✍ J O'Halloran
🖥 www.dromoland.ie

## East Clare (1992)
Bodyke
☎ (061) 921322
✍ Michael O'Hanlon

## Ennis (1907)
Drumbiggle, Ennis
☎ (065) 682 4074
🖳 (065) 684 1848
✉ info@ennisgolfclub.com
✍ Pat McCarthy
🖥 www.ennisgolfclub.com

## Kilkee (1896)
East End, Kilkee
☎ (065) 905 6048
🖳 (065) 905 6977
✉ kilkeegolfclub@eircom.net
✍ Jim Leyden (Sec/Mgr)
🖥 www.kilkeegolfclub.ie

## Kilrush (1934)
Parknamoney, Kilrush
☎ (065) 905 1138
🖳 (065) 905 2633
✉ info@kilrushgolfclub.com
🖥 www.kilrushgolfclub.com

## Lahinch (1892)
Liscannor Road, Lahinch
☎ (065) 708 1003
🖳 (065) 708 1592
✉ info@lahinchgolf.com
✍ Paddy Keane (Gen Mgr)
🖥 www.lahinchgolf.com

## Shannon (1966)
Shannon
☎ (061) 471849
🖳 (061) 471507
✉ info@shannongolfclub.ie
✍ M Corry (061) 471849
🖥 www.shannongolfclub.ie

## Spanish Point (1915)
Spanish Point, Miltown Malbay
☎ (065) 708 4219
✍ D Fitzgerald
🖥 www.spanish-point.com

## Woodstock (1993)
Shanaway Road, Ennis
☎ (065) 682 9463
🖳 (065) 682 0304
✉ proshopwoodstock@eircom.net
✍ Avril Guerin (Sec/Mgr)
🖥 www.woodstockgolfclub.com

---

# Co Cork

## Bandon (1909)
Castlebernard, Bandon
☎ (023) 88 41111
🖳 (023) 88 20819
✉ enquiries@bandongolfclub.com
✍ Kay Walsh
🖥 www.bandongolfclub.com

## Bantry Bay (1975)
Donemark, Bantry, West Cork
☎ (027) 50579
🖳 (027) 53790
✉ info@bantrygolf.com
✍ Steve Ellis (Mgr) (027) 50579
🖥 www.bantrygolf.com

## Berehaven (1902)
Millcove, Castletownbere
☎ (027) 70700
🖳 (027) 71957
✉ info@berehavengolf.com
✍ Damien O'Sullivan (Hon Sec)
🖥 www.berehavengolf.com

## Charleville (1909)
Ardmore, Charleville
☎ 353 63 81257
🖳 353 63 81274
✉ info@charlevillegolf.com
✍ Patrick Nagle (Sec/Mgr)
🖥 www.charlevillegolf.com

## Cobh (1987)
Ballywilliam, Cobh
☎ (021) 812399
🖳 (021) 812615
✍ H Cunningham

## Coosheen (1989)
Coosheen, Schull
☎ (028) 28182
✍ L Morgan

## Cork (1888)
Little Island, Cork
☎ (021) 435 3451/3037
🖳 (021) 435 3410
✉ info@corkgolfclub.ie
✍ M Sands (021) 435 3451
🖥 www.corkgolfclub.ie

## Doneraile (1927)
Doneraile
☎ (022) 24137
✉ info@donerailegolfclub.com
✍ J O'Leary (022) 24379
🖥 www.donerailegolfclub.com

## Douglas (1909)
Douglas, Cork
☎ (021) 489 1086
🖳 (021) 436 7200
✉ admin@douglasgolfclub.ie
✍ Ronan Burke (Mgr)
🖥 www.douglasgolfclub.ie

## Dunmore Golf Club (1967)
Muckross, Clonakilty
☎ 023 8834644
✉ dunmoregolfclub@gmail.com
✍ Liam Santry
🖥 www.dunmoregolfclub.ie

## East Cork (1971)
Gortacrue, Midleton
☎ (021) 463 1687
🖳 (021) 461 3695
✉ eastcorkgolfclub@eircom.net
✍ M Moloney (Sec/Mgr)
🖥 www.eastcorkgolfclub.com

## Fermoy (1892)
Corrin, Fermoy
☎ (025) 32694
🖳 (025) 33072
✉ fermoygolfclub@eircom.net
✍ K Murphy
🖥 www.fermoygolfclub.ie

## Fernhill (1994)
Carrigaline
☎ (021) 437 2226
🖳 (021) 437 1011
✉ info@fernhillgolfhotel.com
✍ A Bowes (Mgr)
🖥 www.fernhillgolfhotel.com

## Fota Island Resort (1993)
Proprietary
Fota Island, Cork
☎ (021) 488 3700
🖳 (021) 488 3713
✉ reservations@fotaisland.ie
✍ Jonathon Woods
🖥 www.fotaisland.ie

## Frankfield (1984)
Frankfield, Douglas
☎ (0214) 363124/3611299
🖳 (01214) 366205
✉ frankfieldhouse@gmail.com
✍ James St Leger
🖥 www.frankfieldhouse.com

## Glengarriff (1935)
Droumgarriff
☎ (027) 63150
🖳 (027) 63575
✉ info@glengarriffgolfclub.com
✍ N Deasy (Hon)
🖥 www.glengarriffgolfclub.com

## Harbour Point   (1991)
**Proprietary**
*Clash Road, Little Island*
☎ (021) 435 3094
📠 (021) 435 4408
📧 hpoint@iol.ie
✍ Aylmer Barrett
🖥 www.harbourpointgolfclub.com

## Kanturk   (1971)
*Fairyhill, Kanturk*
☎ (029) 50534
✍ T McAuliffe

## Kinsale Farrangalway   (1993)
*Farrangalway, Kinsale*
☎ (021) 477 4722
📠 (021) 477 3114
📧 office@kinsalegolf.com
✍ Michael Power
🖥 www.kinsalegolf.com

## Kinsale Ringenane   (1912)
*Ringenane, Belgooly, Kinsale*
☎ (021) 477 2197
✍ Michael Power

## Lee Valley G&CC   (1993)
*Clashanure, Ovens, Cork*
☎ (021) 733 1721
📠 (021) 733 1695
📧 reservations@leevalleygcc.ie
✍ D Keohane
🖥 www.leevalleygcc.ie

## Macroom   (1924)
*Lackaduve, Macroom*
☎ (026) 41072
📠 (026) 41391
📧 mcroomgc@lol.ie
✍ C O'Sullivan (Mgr)
🖥 www.macroomgolfclub.com

## Mahon   (1980)
*Clover Hill, Blackrock, Cork*
☎ (021) 429 2543
📠 (021) 429 2604
📧 mahon@golfnet.ie
✍ Martin Groeger (086) 813 5769
🖥 www.mahongolfclub.com

## Mallow   (1948)
*Ballyellis, Mallow*
☎ (022) 21145
📠 (022) 42501
📧 mallowgolfclubmanager@eircom
.net
✍ D Curtin (Sec/Mgr)
🖥 www.mallowgolfclub.net

## Mitchelstown   (1910)
*Gurrane, Mitchelstown*
☎ (025) 24072
📠 (025) 86631
📧 info@mitchelstown-golf.com
✍ Dan Kelleher
🖥 www.mitchelstown-golf.com

## Monkstown   (1908)
*Parkgarriffe, Monkstown*
☎ (021) 484 1376
📠 (021) 484 1722
📧 office@monkstowngolfclub.com
✍ H Madden (Sec/Mgr)
🖥 www.monkstowngolfclub.com

## Muskerry   (1907)
*Carrigrohane, Co. Cork*
☎ (021) 438 5297
📠 (021) 451 6860
📧 muskgc@eircom.net
✍ H Gallagher
🖥 www.muskerrygolfclub.ie

## Old Head Golf Links   (1997)
*Kinsale*
☎ (021) 477 8444
📠 (021) 477 8022
📧 info@oldhead.com
✍ Danny Brassil (Dir of Golf)
🖥 www.oldhead.com

## Raffeen Creek   (1989)
*Ringaskiddy*
☎ (021) 437 8430
✍ J Kiely

## Skibbereen   (1904)
*Licknavar, Skibbereen*
☎ (028) 21227
📠 (028) 22994
📧 info@skibbgolf.com
✍ Club Aministrator
🖥 www.skibbgolf.com

## Youghal   (1898)
*Knockaverry, Youghal*
☎ (024) 92787/92861
📠 (024) 92641
📧 youghalgolfclub@eircom.net
✍ Margaret O'Sullivan
🖥 www.youghalgolfclub.ie

# Co Donegal

## Ballybofey & Stranorlar   (1957)
*The Glebe, Stranorlar*
☎ (074) 913 1093
📠 (074) 913 0158
📧 info@ballybofeyandstranorlar
golfclub.com
✍ Cathal Patton (074) 913 1093
🖥 www.ballybofeyandstranorlar
golfclub.com

## Ballyliffin   (1947)
*Ballyliffin, Inishowen*
☎ (07493) 76119
📠 (07493) 76672
📧 info@ballyliffingolfclub.com
✍ John Farren (Gen Mgr)
🖥 www.ballyliffingolfclub.com

## Buncrana   (1951)
**Public**
*Ballymacarry*
☎ (07493) 62279
📧 buncranagc@eircom.net
✍ F McGrory (Hon) (07493) 62279
🖥 www.buncranagolf.com

## Bundoran   (1894)
*Bundoran*
☎ (07198) 41302
📠 (07198) 42014
📧 bundorangolfclub@eircom.net
✍ Noreen Allen (Sec/Mgr)
🖥 www.bundorangolfclub.com

## Cruit Island   (1985)
*Kincasslagh, Dunglow*
☎ (074) 954 3296
📠 (074) 954 8029
✍ D Devenney
🖥 www.homepage.eircom.net
/~cruitisland

## Donegal   (1959)
*Murvagh, Laghey*
☎ (074) 973 4054
📠 (074) 973 4377
📧 info@donegalgolfclub.ie
✍ Grainne Dorrian
🖥 www.donegalgolfclub.ie

## Dunfanaghy   (1906)
*Kill, Dunfanaghy, Letterkenny*
☎ (074) 913 6335
📠 (074) 913 6684
📧 dunfanaghygolf@eircom.net
✍ Mary Lafferty
🖥 www.dunfanaghygolfclub.com

## Greencastle   (1892)
*Greencastle*
☎ (074) 93 81013
📠 (074) 93 81015
📧 b_mc_caul@yahoo.com
✍ Billy McCaul
🖥 www.greencastlegc.com

## Gweedore   (1926)
**Pay and play**
*Magheragallon, Derrybeg, Letterkenny*
☎ (07495) 31140
📧 eugenemccafferty@hotmail.com
✍ Eugene McCafferty
🖥 www.gweedoregolfclub.com

## Letterkenny   (1913)
*Barnhill, Letterkenny*
☎ (+353) 7491 21150
📠 (+353) 7491 21175
📧 info@letterkennygolfclub.com
✍ Cynthia Fuery (Hon
Sec) (+353) 7491 21150
🖥 www.letterkennygolfclub.com

## Narin & Portnoo   (1930)
*Narin, Portnoo*
☎ (074) 954 5107
📠 (074) 945 5994
📧 narinportnoo@eircom.net
✍ Daragh Lyons (PGA Professional)
🖥 www.narinportnoogolfclub.ie

## North West   (1891)
*Lisfannon, Buncrana*
☎ (074) 936 0127
📠 (074) 936 3284
📧 secretary@northwestgolfclub.com
✍ Eddie Curran (086) 604 7299
🖥 www.northwestgolfclub.com

**Otway** (1893)
Saltpans, Rathmullan, Letterkenny
☎ **(074) 915 1665**
✉ tolandkevin@eircom.net
✍ Kevin Toland

**Portsalon** (1891)
Portsalon, Fanad
☎ **(074) 915 9459**
📠 (074) 915 9919
✉ portsalongolfclub@eircom.net
✍ P Doherty
🖥 www.portsalongolfclub.com

**Redcastle** (1983)
Redcastle, Moville
☎ **(074) 938 5555**
📠 (074) 938 2214
✍ M Wilson

**Rosapenna** (1894)
Downings, Rosapenna
☎ **(074) 55301**
📠 (074) 55128
✉ rosapenna@eircom.net
✍ Frank Casey
🖥 www.rosapenna.ie

**St Patricks Courses** (1994)
Carrigart
☎ **(074) 55114**
📠 (074) 55250
✍ D Walsh (Mgr)

## Co Down

**Ardglass** (1896)
Castle Place, Ardglass BT30 7PP
☎ **(028) 4484 1219**
📠 (028) 4484 1841
✉ info@ardglassgolfclub.com
✍ Mrs D Turley
🖥 www.ardglassgolfclub.com

**Ardminnan** (1995)
Pay and play
15 Ardminnan Road, Portaferry BT22 1QJ
☎ **(028) 4277 1321**
📠 (028) 4277 1321
✉ lesliejardine104@yahoo.co.uk
✍ L Jardine

**Banbridge** (1912)
116 Huntly Road, Banbridge BT32 3UR
☎ **(028) 4066 2211 (office)**
📠 (028) 4066 9400
✉ info@banbridgegolfclub.com
✍ Mrs Sandra Duprey (Club Mgr)
🖥 www.banbridgegolfclub.com

**Bangor** (1903)
Broadway, Bangor BT20 4RH
☎ **(028) 9127 0922**
✉ office@bangorgolfclubni.co.uk
✍ Mr Stephen Bell
🖥 www.bangorgolfclubni.co.uk

**Blackwood** (1995)
150 Crawfordsburn Road, Bangor
BT19 1GB
☎ **(028) 9185 2706**

📠 (028) 9185 3785
✉ info@blackwoodgolfcentre.com
✍ Chris Widdowson
🖥 www.blackwoodgolfcentre.com

**Bright Castle** (1970)
14 Coniamstown Road, Bright, Downpatrick
BT30 8LU
☎ **(028) 4484 1319**
✍ J McCawl (Hon)

**Carnalea** (1927)
Station Road, Bangor BT19 1EZ
☎ **(028) 9127 0368**
📠 (028) 9127 3989
✉ nicola@carnaleagolfclub.com
✍ Nicola Greene (028) 9127 0368
🖥 www.carnaleagolfclub.com

**Clandeboye** (1933)
Conlig, Newtownards BT23 7PN
☎ **(028) 9127 1767 (office)**
📠 (028) 9147 3711
✉ info@cgc.ni.com
✍ Gary Steele (Gen Mgr)
🖥 www.cgc-ni.com

**Crossgar** (1993)
231 Derryboye Road, Crossgar BT30 9DL
☎ **(028) 4483 1523**
✍ J McKinley (Hon)

**Donaghadee** (1899)
84 Warren Road, Donaghadee BT21 0PQ
☎ **(028) 9188 3624**
📠 (028) 9188 8891
✉ office@donaghadeegolfclub.com
✍ Jim Cullen
🖥 www.donaghadeegolfclub.com

**Downpatrick** (1930)
Saul Road, Downpatrick BT30 6PA
☎ **(028) 4461 5947**
✉ office@downpatrickgolf.org.uk
✍ Elaine Carson (028) 4461 5947
🖥 www.downpatrickgolfclub.org.uk

**Helen's Bay** (1896)
Golf Road, Helen's Bay, Bangor BT19 1TL
☎ **(028) 9185 2815 (office)**
📠 (028) 9185 2660
✉ mail@helensbaygc.com
✍ John McCullough (Sec)
🖥 www.helensbaygc.com

**Holywood** (1904)
Nuns Walk, Demesne Road, Holywood
BT18 9LE
☎ **(028) 9042 2138**
📠 (028) 9042 5040
✉ mail@holywoodgolfclub.co.uk
✍ Paul Gray (Gen Mgr)
🖥 www.holywoodgolfclub.co.uk

**Kilkeel** (1948)
Mourne Park, Kilkeel BT34 4LB
☎ **(028) 4176 2296/5095**
📠 (028) 4176 5579
✉ info@kilkeelgolfclub.org
✍ SC McBride (Hon)
🖥 www.kilkeelgolfclub.org

**Kirkistown Castle** (1902)
142 Main Road, Cloughey, Newtownards
BT22 1JA
☎ **(028) 4277 1233**
📠 (028) 4277 1699
✉ kirkistown@supanet.com
✍ R Coulter (028) 4277 1233
🖥 www.linksgolfkirkistown.com

**Mahee Island** (1929)
Comber, 14 Mahee Island, Newtownlands
BT23 6EP
☎ **(028) 9754 1234**
📠 (028) 9754 1234
✉ info@maheegolf.com
✍ M Marshall (Hon)
🖥 www.maheegolf.com

**Mount Ober G&CC** (1985)
Ballymaconaghy Road, Knockbracken,
Belfast BT8 6SB
☎ **(028) 9079 2108 (Bookings)**
📠 (028) 9070 5862
✉ info@mountober.com
✍ E Williams (Sec/Mgr)
🖥 www.mountober.com

**Mourne** (1946)
Club
36 Golf Links Road, Newcastle BT33 0AN
☎ **(028) 4372 3218/3889**
📠 (028) 4372 2575
✉ info@mournegolfclub.co.uk
✍ P Keown (Hon)
🖥 www.mournegolfclub.co.uk

**Rockmount** (1995)
Proprietary
28 Drumalig Road, Carryduff, Belfast
BT8 8EQ
☎ **(028) 9081 2279**
📠 (028) 9081 5851
✉ info@rockmountgolfclub.com
✍ D Patterson (Mgr)
🖥 www.rockmountgolfclub.com

**Royal Belfast** (1881)
Holywood, Craigavad BT18 0BP
☎ **(028) 9042 8165**
📠 (028) 9042 1404
✉ admin@royalbelfast.com
✍ Mrs SH Morrison
🖥 www.royalbelfast.com

**Royal County Down** (1889)
Newcastle BT33 0AN
☎ **(028) 4372 3314**
📠 (028) 4372 6281
✉ wilson@royalcountydown.org
✍ David Wilson
🖥 www.royalcountydown.org

**Scrabo** (1907)
233 Scrabo Road, Newtownards BT23 4SL
☎ **(028) 9181 2355**
📠 (028) 9182 2919
✉ admin.scrabogc@btconnect.com
🖥 www.scrabo-golf-club.org

**The Spa** (1907)
Grove Road, Ballynahinch BT24 8PN
☎ **(028) 9756 2365**

☎ (028) 9756 4158
✉ spagolfclub@btconnect.com
✍ TG Magee
▤ www.spagolfclub.net

## Temple   (1994)
60 Church Road, Boardmills, Lisburn
BT27 6UP
☎ **(028) 9263 9213**
☐ (028) 9263 8637
✉ info@templegolf.com
✍ B McConnell (Mgr)
▤ www.templegolf.com

## Warrenpoint   (1893)
Lower Dromore Rd, Warrenpoint
BT34 3LN
☎ **(028) 4175 3695**
☐ (028) 4175 2918
✉ office@warrenpointgolf.com
✍ D Moan
▤ www.warrenpointgolf.com

## Co Dublin

## Balbriggan   (1945)
Blackhall, Balbriggan
☎ **(01) 841 2229**
☐ (01) 841 3927
✉ balbriggangolfclub@eircom.net
✍ Brian Finn (Hon Sec)
▤ www.balbriggangolfclub.com

## Balcarrick   (1972)
Corballis, Donabate
☎ **(01) 843 6957**
☐ (01) 843 6228
✉ balcarr@iol.ie
✍ Ms. Patricia Fennelly (Office Admin)
▤ www.balcarrickgolfclub.com

## Beaverstown   (1985)
Beaverstown, Donabate
☎ **(01) 843 6439/6721**
☐ (01) 843 5059
✉ office@beaverstown.com
✍ Gillian Harris (Administrator)
▤ www.beaverstown.com

## Beech Park   (1983)
Johnstown, Rathcoole
☎ **(01) 458 0522**
☐ (01) 458 8365
✉ info@beechpark.ie
✍ Mr K M Young (Gen Mgr)
▤ www.beechpark.ie

## Coldwinters   (1994)
Newtown House, St Margaret's
☎ **(01) 864 0324**
☐ (01) 834 1400
✍ Mrs K Yates

## Corrstown Golf Club   (1993)
Corrstown, Killsallaghan
☎ **(01) 864 0533**
☐ (01) 864 0537
✉ info@corrstowngolfclub.com
✍ M Jeanes
▤ www.corrstowngolfclub.com

## Donabate   (1925)
Balcarrick, Donabate
☎ **(01) 843 6346**
☐ (01) 843 4488
✉ info@donabategolfclub.com
✍ Betty O'Connor (01) 843 6346
▤ www.donabategolfclub.com

## Dublin Mountain   (1993)
Gortlum, Brittas
☎ **(01) 458 2622**
☐ (01) 458 2048
✉ info@dublinmountaingolf.com
✍ F Carolan
▤ www.dublinmountaingolf.com

## Dun Laoghaire   (1910)
Eglinton Park, Tivoli Road, Dun Laoghaire
☎ **(01) 280 3916**
☐ (01) 280 4868
✍ D Murphy (Gen Mgr)
▤ www.dunlaoghairegolfclub.ie

## Forrest Little   (1940)
Forrest Little, Cloghran, Swords
☎ **(01) 840 1763**
☐ (01) 840 1000
✉ margaret@forrestlittle.ie
✍ Kevin McIntyre
▤ www.forrestlittle.com

## Glencullen
Glencullen, Co Dublin
☎ **(01) 295 2895**
✍ G Davy
▤ www.glencullengc.ie

## Hermitage   (1905)
Lucan
☎ **(01) 626 5396**
☐ (01) 623 8881
✉ hermitagegolf@eircom.net
✍ Eddie Farrell
▤ www.hermitagegolf.ie

## Citywest   (1998)
City West Hotel, Saggert
☎ **(01) 401 0878**
☐ (01) 458 8756
✍ Tony Shine
▤ www.citywesthotel.com

## Hollywood Lakes   (1992)
Ballyboughal, Co Dublin
☎ **(01) 843 3406/7**
☐ (01) 843 3002
✉ hollywoodlakesgc@eircom.net
✍ Seamus Kelly (Gen Mgr)
▤ www.hollywoodlakesgolfclub.com

## The Island Golf Club   (1890)
Corballis, Donabate
☎ **+353 1843 6205**
☐ +353 1843 6860
✉ info@theislandgolfclub.com
✍ Ronan Smyth
▤ www.theislandgolfclub.com

## Killiney   (1903)
Ballinclea Road, Killiney
☎ **(01) 285 2823**
☐ (01) 285 2861
✉ killineygolfclub@eircom.net

✍ MF Walsh CCM
▤ www.killineygolfclub.ie

## Kilternan   (1987)
Enniskerry Road, Kilternan
☎ **(01) 295 5559**
☐ (01) 295 5670
✉ kgc@kilternan-hotel.ie
▤ www.kilternangolfclub.ie

## Lisheen Springs   (2002)
Lisheen Road, Brittas, Co Dublin
☎ **(01) 458 2965**
✉ info@lisheenspringsgolfclub.ie
✍ Michael Diskin (Gen Mgr)
▤ www.lisheenspringsgolfclub.ie

## Lucan   (1897)
Celbridge Road, Lucan
☎ **(01) 628 0246**
☐ (01) 628 2929
✉ admin@lucangolf.ie
✍ Francis Duffy (Sec/Mgr)
▤ www.lucangolfclub.ie

## Luttrellstown Castle G&CC   (1993)
Porterstown Road, Castleknock, Dublin 15
☎ **(353) 1 860 9600**
☐ (353) 1 860 9601
✉ info@luttrellstown.ie
✍ Colm Haunon
▤ www.luttrellstowncastleresort.com

## Malahide   (1892)
Beechwood, The Grange, Malahide
☎ **(01) 846 1611**
☐ (01) 846 1270
✉ manager@malahidegolfclub.ie
✍ Mark Gannon (Gen Mgr)
▤ www.malahidegolfclub.ie

## Milltown   (1907)
Lower Churchtown Road, Milltown,
Dublin 14
☎ **(01) 497 6090**
☐ (01) 497 6008
✉ info@milltowngolfclub.ie
✍ J Burns (Gen Mgr)
▤ www.milltowngolfclub.ie

## Portmarnock   (1894)
Portmarnock
☎ **(01) 846 2968 (Clubhouse)**
☐ (01) 846 2601
✍ JJ Quigley (01) 846 2968 (Gen Mgr)
▤ www.portmarnockgolfclub.ie

## Portmarnock Hotel & Golf Links   (1995)
Proprietary
Strand Road, Portmarnock
☎ **(01) 846 1800**
☐ (01) 846 2442
✉ golfres@portmarnock.com
✍ Moira Cassidy (Golf Dir)
▤ www.portmarnock.com

## Rush   (1943)
Rush
☎ **(01) 843 8177**
☐ (01) 843 8177
✉ info@rushgolfclub.com

✍ Noeline Quirke (Sec/Mgr)
🖥 www.rushgolfclub.com

## Silloge Park Golf Club (2010)
*Old Ballymun Road, Swords*
☎ **(01) 842 9956**
📧 info@sillogeparkgolfclub.com
✍ Damien Connolly
🖥 www.sillogeparkgolfclub.com

## Skerries (1905)
*Hacketstown, Skerries*
☎ **(01) 849 1567 (Clubhouse)**
📠 (01) 849 1591
📧 admin@skerriesgolfclub.ie
✍ I Fraher (01) 849 1567
🖥 www.skerriesgolfclub.ie

## Slade Valley (1970)
*Lynch Park, Brittas*
☎ **(01) 458 2183**
📠 (01) 458 2784
📧 info@sladevalleygolfclub.ie
✍ D Clancy
🖥 www.sladevalleygolfclub.ie

## St Margaret's G&CC (1992)
*St Margaret's, Dublin*
☎ **(01) 864 0400**
📠 (01) 864 0408
📧 reservations@stmargaretsgolf.com
✍ Gary Kearney (Gen Mgr)
🖥 www.stmargaretsgolf.com

## Swords (1996)
*Balheary Avenue, Swords*
☎ **(01) 840 9819/890 1030**
📠 (01) 840 9819
📧 info@swordsopengolfcourse.com
✍ O McGuinness (Mgr)
🖥 www.swordsopengolfcourse.com

## Turvey (1994)
*Turvey Avenue, Donabate*
☎ **(01) 843 5169**
📠 (01) 843 5179
📧 turveygc@eircom.net
✍ Aoife Griffin
🖥 www.turveygolfclub.com

## Westmanstown (1988)
*Clonsilla, Dublin 15*
☎ **(01) 820 5817**
📠 (01) 820 5858
📧 info@westmanstowngolfclub.ie
✍ Edward Doyle (Director of Golf)
🖥 www.westmanstowngolfclub.ie

## Woodbrook (1926)
*Dublin Road, Bray*
☎ **(01) 282 4799**
📠 (01) 282 1950
📧 golf@woodbrook.ie
✍ Jim Melody (Gen Mgr)
🖥 www.woodbrook.ie

## Dublin City

## Carrickmines (1900)
*Golf Lane, Carrickmines, Dublin 18*
☎ **(01) 295 5972**

📠 (01) 214 9674
📧 carrickminesgolf@eircom.net
✍ B Levis 00353 871682150 (Mobile)

## Castle (1913)
*Woodside Drive, Rathfarnham, Dublin 14*
☎ **(01) 490 4207**
📠 (01) 492 0264
📧 info@castlegc.ie
✍ John McCormack (Gen Mgr)
🖥 www.castlegc.ie

## Clontarf (1912)
*Donnycarney House, Malahide Road, Dublin 3*
☎ **(01) 833 1892**
📠 (01) 833 1933
📧 info@clontarfgolfclub.ie
✍ A Cahill (Mgr)
🖥 www.clontarfgolfclub.ie

## Deer Park (1974)
*Deer Park Hotel, Howth*
☎ **(01) 832 6039**
✍ BM Dunne (Hon)

## Edmondstown (1944)
*Rathfarnham, Dublin 16*
☎ **(01) 493 2461**
📠 (01) 493 3152
📧 info@edmondstowngolfclub.ie
✍ Mark Lynch (01) 493 1082
🖥 www.edmondstowngolfclub.ie

## Elm Park (1925)
*Nutley House, Donnybrook, Dublin 4*
☎ **(01) 269 3438/269 3014**
📠 (01) 269 4505
📧 office@elmparkgolfclub.ie
✍ A McCormack (01) 269 3438
🖥 www.elmparkgolfclub.ie

## Grange (1910)
*Whitechurch Road, Rathfarnham, Dublin 14*
☎ **(01) 493 2889**
📠 (01) 493 9490
📧 administration@grangegolfclub.ie
✍ Billy Meehan (Gen Mgr)
🖥 www.grangegolfclub.ie

## Hazel Grove (1988)
*Mount Seskin Road, Jobstown, Dublin 24*
☎ **(01) 452 0911**
✍ Paddy Massey (+353 86 235 9624)

## Howth (1916)
*Carrickbrack Road, Sutton, Dublin 13*
☎ **(01) 832 3055**
📠 (01) 832 1793
📧 gm@howthgolfclub.ie
✍ Darragh Tighe MPGA
(01) 832 3055
🖥 www.howthgolfclub.ie

## Kilmashogue (1994)
*St Columba's College, Whitechurch, Dublin 16*
☎ **(087) 274 9844**
✍ H Farrell

## Newlands (1910)
*Newlands Cross, Dublin 22*
☎ **(01) 459 3157**

📠 (01) 459 3498
📧 info@newlandsgolfclub.com
✍ Gay Nolan (Gen Mgr)
🖥 www.newlandsgolf.com

## Rathfarnham (1899)
*Newtown, Dublin 16*
☎ **(01) 493 1201/493 1561**
📠 (01) 493 1561
📧 info@rathfarnhamgolfclub.com
✍ John Lawler (01) 493 1201
🖥 www.rathfarnhamgolfclub.ie

## Royal Dublin (1885)
*North Bull Island Nature Reserve, Dollymount, Dublin 3*
☎ **(01) 833 6346**
📠 (01) 833 6504
📧 info@theroyaldublingolfclub.com
✍ Sam O'Beirne (Hon Sec)/Eoin O'Sullivan (Gen Mgr)
🖥 www.theroyaldublingolfclub.com

## St Anne's (1921)
*North Bull Nature Reserve, Dollymount, Dublin 5*
☎ **(01) 833 6471**
📠 (01) 833 4618
📧 info@stanneslinksgolf.com
✍ Ted Power
🖥 www.stanneslinksgolf.com

## Stackstown (1975)
*Kellystown Road, Rathfarnham, Dublin 16*
☎ **(01) 494 1993**
📠 (01) 493 3934
📧 info@stackstowngolfclub.ie
✍ Raymond Murphy (Gen Mgr)
🖥 www.stackstowngolfclub.com

## Sutton (1890)
*Cush Point, Sutton, Dublin 13*
☎ **(01) 832 3013**
📠 (01) 832 1603
📧 info@suttongolfclub.org
✍ Frank Kennedy (Hon Sec)
🖥 www.suttongolfclub.org

## Co Fermanagh

## Castle Hume (1991)
*Belleek Road, Enniskillen BT93 7ED*
☎ **(028) 6632 7077**
📠 (028) 6632 7076
📧 info@castlehumegolf.com
✍ Patrick Duffy (Admin)
🖥 www.castlehumegolf.com

## Enniskillen (1896)
*Castlecoole, Enniskillen BT74 6HZ*
☎ **(028) 6632 5250**
📠 (028) 6632 5250
📧 enniskillengolfclub@mail.com
✍ Darryl Robinson (Club Steward)
🖥 www.enniskillengolfclub.com

## Co Galway

## Ardacong
*Milltown Road, Tuam, Co Galway*
☎ **(093) 25525**
✍ Catherine Hahessy

## Athenry (1902)
Palmerstown, Oranmore
☎ **(091) 794466**
🖷 (091) 794971
📧 athenrygc@eircom.net
🖥 www.athenrygolfclub.net

## Ballinasloe (1894)
Rosgloss, Ballinasloe
☎ **(0905) 42126**
🖷 (0905) 42538
✍ M Kelly

## Bearna (1996)
Corboley, Bearna
☎ **(091) 592677**
🖷 (091) 592674
📧 info@bearnagolfclub.com
✍ Pat Donnellan
🖥 www.bearnagolfclub.com

## Connemara (1973)
**Public**
Ballyconneely, Clifden
☎ **(095) 23502/23602**
🖷 (095) 23662
📧 info@connemaragolflinks.net
✍ Kathleen Burke (Sec/Mgr)
🖥 www.connemaragolflinks.com

## Connemara Isles
Annaghvane, Lettermore, Connemara
☎ **(091) 572498**
🖷 (091) 572498
✍ J Lynch

## Curra West (1996)
Curra, Kylebrack, Loughrea
☎ **(091) 45121**

## Galway (1895)
Blackrock, Salthill, Galway
☎ **(091) 522033**
🖷 (091) 529783
📧 info@galwaygolf.com
✍ P Fahy
🖥 www.galwaygolf.com

## Galway Bay Golf Resort
(1993)
Renville, Oranmore
☎ **+353 (91) 790711/2**
🖷 +353 (91) 792510
✍ Ann Hanley (Golf Dir)
🖥 www.galwaybaygolfresort.com

## Glenlo Abbey
Glenlo Abbey Hotel, Bushy Park, Galway
☎ **(091) 519698**
🖷 (091) 519699
✍ P Murphy (Sec/Mgr)
🖥 www.glenlo.com

## Gort (1924)
Castlequarter, Gort
☎ **(091) 632244**
🖷 (091) 632387
📧 info@gortgolf.com
✍ J Skehill (Hon)
🖥 www.gortgolf.com

## Loughrea (1924)
Graigue, Loughrea
☎ **(091) 841049**
🖷 (091) 847472
📧 loughreagolfclub@eircom.net

## Mountbellew (1929)
Shankill, Mountbellew, Ballinasloe
☎ **(090) 967 9259**
📧 mountbellewgc@eircom.net
✍ Padraic Costello
🖥 www.mountbellewgolfclub.com

## Oughterard (1973)
Gortreevagh, Oughterard
☎ **(091) 552131**
🖷 (091) 552733
📧 oughterardgc@eircom.net
✍ Richard McNamarg
🖥 www.oughterardgolfclub.com

## Portumna (1913)
Ennis Road, Portumna
☎ **(090) 97 41059**
🖷 (090) 97 41798
📧 portumnagc@eircom.net
✍ Michael Ryan (Secretary)
🖥 www.portumnagolfclub.ie

## Tuam (1904)
Barnacurragh, Tuam
☎ **(093) 28993**
🖷 (093) 26003
📧 tuamgolfclub@eircom.net
✍ Mary Burns (Sec/Mgr)
🖥 www.tuamgolfclub.com

# Co Kerry

## Ardfert (1993)
Sackville, Ardfert, Tralee
☎ **(066) 713 4744**
🖷 (066) 713 4744
✍ T Lawlor

## Ballybeggan Park
Ballybeggan, Tralee, Co Kerry
☎ **(066) 712 6188**
✍ P Colleran

## Ballybunion Golf Club (1893)
Sandhill Road, Ballybunion, Ireland
☎ **+353 (68) 27146**
🖷 +353 (68) 27387
📧 info@ballybuniongolfclub.ie
✍ Vari McGreevy
🖥 www.ballybuniongolfclub.ie

## Ballyheigue Castle (1995)
Ballyheigue, Tralee
☎ **(066) 713 3555**
🖷 (066) 713 3934
✍ J Casey (Sec/Mgr)
🖥 www.ballyheiguecastlegolfclub.com

## Beaufort (1994)
Churchtown, Beaufort, Killarney
☎ **(064) 44440**
🖷 (064) 44752
📧 beaufortgc@eircom.net

✍ C Kelly
🖥 www.beaufortgolfclub.com

## Castlegregory (1989)
Stradbally, Castlegregory
☎ **(066) 713 9444**
🖷 (066) 713 9958
📧 info@castlegregorygolflinks.com
✍ M Keane (Hon Sec)
🖥 www.castlegregorygolfclub.com

## Ceann Sibeal (1924)
Ballyferriter
☎ **(066) 915 6255/6408**
🖷 (066) 915 6409
📧 dinglegc@iol.ie
✍ S Fahy (Mgr)
🖥 www.dinglelinks.com

## Dooks (1889)
Glenbeigh
☎ **(066) 976 8205**
🖷 (066) 976 8476
📧 office@dooks.com
✍ Brian Hurley
🖥 www.dooks.com

## Kenmare (1903)
Kenmare
☎ **(064) 6641291**
🖷 (064) 6642061
📧 info@kenmaregolfclub.com
✍ John Sullivan
🖥 www.kenmaregolfclub.com

## Kerries (1995)
Tralee
☎ **(066) 712 2112**
✍ H Barrett

## Killarney (1893)
Mahoney's Point, Killarney
☎ **(064) 31034**
🖷 (064) 33065
📧 reservations@killarney-golf.com
✍ Maurice O'Meara (Gen Mgr)
🖥 www.killarney-golf.com

## Killorglin (1992)
Stealroe, Killorglin
☎ **00353 (66) 9761 979**
🖷 00353 (66) 9761 437
📧 kilgolf@iol.ie
✍ Mike Ashe
🖥 www.killorglingolf.ie

## Parknasilla (1974)
Parknasilla, Sneem
☎ **(064) 66 45145**
🖷 (064) 66 45323
📧 parknasillagolfclub@eircom.net
✍ Mr Sean McCarthy (Secretary)
🖥 www.parknasillahotel.ie

## Ring of Kerry G&CC (1998)
**Proprietary**
Templenoe, Killarney
☎ **(064) 66 42000**
🖷 (064) 66 42533
📧 james@ringofkerrygolf.com
✍ James Mitchell (Gen Mgr)
🖥 www.ringofkerrygolf.com

**Tralee** (1896)
*West Barrow, Ardfert, Tralee*
☎ **(066) 713 6379**
📠 (066) 713 6008
📧 info@traleegolfclub.com
✍ A Byrne (Gen Mgr)
🖥 www.traleegolfclub.com

**Waterville Golf Links** (1889)
*Waterville Golf Links, Ring of Kerry, Waterville*
☎ **+353-66-947 4102**
📠 +353-66-947 4482
📧 wvgolf@iol.ie
✍ Noel Cronin (Sec/Mgr)
🖥 www.watervillegolflinks.ie

## Co Kildare

**Athy** (1906)
*Geraldine, Athy*
☎ **(059) 863 1729**
📠 (059) 863 4710
📧 info@athygolfclub.com
✍ Kathleen Gray (Sec/Administrator)
🖥 www.athygolfclub.com

**Bodenstown** (1972)
*Bodenstown, Sallins*
☎ **(045) 897096**
📠 (045) 898126
📧 bodenstown@eircom.net
✍ Tom Keightley (0872 264133
🖥 www.bodenstown.com

**Carton House** (2002)
*Carton House, Maynooth*
☎ **+353 (0)1 505 2000**
📠 +353 (0)1 651 7703
📧 reservations@cartonhouse.com
✍ Francis Howley (Director of Golf)
🖥 www.cartonhouse.com

**Castlewarden** (1989)
*Straffan*
☎ **(01) 458 9254**
📠 (01) 458 8972
📧 info@castlewardengolfclub.ie
✍ Andy Callanan
🖥 www.castlewardengolfclub.ie

**Celbridge Elm Hall**
*Elmhall, Celbridge, Co Kildare*
☎ **(01) 628 8208**
✍ S Lawless

**Cill Dara** (1920)
*Little Curragh, Kildare Town*
☎ **(045) 521295**
✍ R Hill (Hon)

**Craddockstown** (1991)
*Blessington Road, Naas*
☎ **(045) 897610**
📠 (045) 896968
📧 enquiries@craddockstown.com
✍ Pat Meagher
🖥 www.craddockstown.com

**The Curragh** (1883)
*Curragh*
☎ **(045) 441238/441714**

📠 (045) 442476
📧 curraghgolf@eircom.net
✍ Ann Culliton (045) 441714
🖥 www.curraghgolf-club.com

**Highfield Golf & Country Club** (1992)
**Proprietary**
*Carbury, Co. Kildare*
☎ **(046) 973 1021**
📠 (046) 973 1021
📧 highfieldgolf@eircom.net
✍ Philomena Duggan (Sec/Mgr)
🖥 www.highfield-golf.ie

**The K Club** (1991)
*Straffan*
☎ **(01) 601 7300**
📠 (01) 601 7399
📧 golf@kclub.ie
✍ B Donald (Golf Dir) (01) 601 7302
🖥 www.kclub.ie

**Kilkea Castle** (1995)
*Castledermot*
☎ **(059) 914 5555**
📠 (059) 914 5505
📧 kilkeagolfclub@eircom.net
✍ J Kissane (Gen Mgr)
🖥 www.kilkeacastlehotelgolf.com

**Killeen** (1986)
*Killeenbeg, Kill*
☎ **(045) 866003**
📠 (045) 875881
📧 admin@killeengc.ie
✍ M Kelly
🖥 www.killeengolf.com

**Knockanally** (1985)
*Donadea, Naas, North Kildare*
☎ **(045) 869322**
📧 golf@knockanally.com
✍ Seamus Fennessy
🖥 www.knockanally.com

**Naas** (1896)
*Kerdiffstown, Naas*
☎ **(045) 874644**
📠 (045) 896109
📧 info@naasgolfclub.com
✍ Denis Mahon (Mgr)
🖥 www.naasgolfclub.com

**Newbridge** (1997)
*Tankardsgarden, Newbridge*
☎ **(045) 486110**
📠 (045) 446840
✍ Jamie Stafford (Mgr)

## Co Kilkenny

**Callan** (1929)
*Geraldine, Callan*
☎ **(056) 7725136**
📠 (056) 7755155
📧 info@callangolfclub.com
✍ Deirdre Power (Sec/Mgr) (056) 77 25136
🖥 www.callangolfclub.com

**Castlecomer** (1935)
*Dromgoole, Castlecomer*
☎ **(056) 4441139**
📠 (056) 4441139
📧 castlecomergolf@eircom.net
✍ Marnie Brennan (Hon Sec)
🖥 www.castlecomergolfclub.com

**Kilkenny** (1896)
*Glendine, Kilkenny*
☎ **(087) 125 0853**
📠 (056) 772 3593
📧 enquiries@kilkennygolfclub.com
✍ Sean Boland (056) 776 5400
🖥 www.kilkennygolfclub.com

**Mount Juliet** (1991)
*Thomastown*
☎ **(056) 777 3071**
📠 (056) 777 3078
📧 info@mountjuliet.com
✍ William Kirby
🖥 www.mountjuliet.com

## Co Laois

**Abbeyleix** (1895)
*Rathmoyle, Abbeyleix*
☎ **(057) 8731450**
📧 abbeyleixgolfclub_shirley@hotmail.com
✍ Gery O'Hara (Hon Sec)
🖥 www.abbeyleixgolfclub.ie

**The Heath** (1930)
*The Heath, Portlaoise*
☎ **(057) 864 6533**
📠 (057) 864 6735
📧 info@theheathgc.ie
✍ Christy Crawford (Hon)
🖥 www.theheathgc.ie

**The Heritage Golf & Spa Resort** (2004)
**Proprietary**
*The Heritage Golf & Spa Resort, Killenard*
☎ **(057) 864 2321**
📠 (057) 864 2392
📧 info@theheritage.com
✍ Niall Carroll (Golf Ops Mgr)
🖥 www.theheritage.com

**Mountrath** (1929)
*Knockanina, Mountrath*
☎ **(0502) 32558/32643**
📠 (0502) 56735
📧 mountrathgc@eircom.net
✍ Lar Sculls (057) 862 0375
🖥 www.mountrathgolfclub.ie

**Portarlington** (1908)
*Garryhinch, Portarlington*
☎ **(057) 862 23115**
📠 (057) 862 23044
📧 portarlingtongc@eircom.net
✍ Jerry Savage
🖥 www.portarlingtongolf.com

**Rathdowney** (1930)
*Coulnaboul West, Rathdowney*
☎ **(0505) 46170**

rathdowneygolf@eircom.net
Sean Bolger 087 9356509
www.rathdowneygolfclub.com

## Co Leitrim

### Ballinamore    (1941)
Creevy, Ballinamore
☎ (078) 964 4346
G Mahon (078) 964 4031,

## Co Limerick

### Abbeyfeale    (1993)
Dromtrasna, Collins Abbeyfeale
☎ (068) 32033
(068) 51871
abbeyfealegolf@eircom.net
Conleth Dillon (Hon Sec)
www.abbeyfealegolfclub.com

### Adare Manor    (1900)
Adare
☎ (061) 396204
(061) 396800
info@adaremanorgolfclub.com
Michael O'Donnell (Hon Sec)
www.adaremanorgolfclub.com

### Castletroy    (1937)
Golf Links Road, Castleroy, Co. Limerick
☎ (061) 335753 (club)
(061) 335373
golf@castletroygolfclub.ie
Louis Keegan (Gen Mgr)
www.castletroygolfclub.ie

### Limerick    (1891)
Ballyclough, Limerick
☎ (061) 414083
(061) 319219
information@limerickgolfclub.ie
P Murray (Gen Mgr) (061) 415146
www.limerickgolfclub.ie

### Limerick County G&CC
(1994)
Ballyneety, Co. Limerick
☎ (061) 351881
(061) 351384
info@limerickcounty.com
www.limerickcounty.com

### Newcastle West    (1938)
Rathgonan, Ardagh, Co. Limerick
☎ (069) 76500
(069) 76511
info@newcastlewestgolf.com
John Whelan (Sec/Mgr)
www.newcastlewestgolf.com

### Rathbane    (1998)
Public
Rathbane, Crossagalla, Limerick
☎ (061) 313655
(061) 313655
John O'Sullivan

## Co Londonderry

### Benone Par Three
53 Benone Avenue, Benone, Limavady
BT49 0LQ
☎ (028) 7775 0555
Ml Clark

### Brown Trout    (1984)
209 Agivey Road, Aghadowey, Coleraine
BT51 4AD
☎ (028) 7086 8209
(028) 7086 8878
bill@browntroutinn.com
B O'Hara (Sec/Mgr)
www.browntroutinn.com

### Castlerock    (1901)
65 Circular Road, Castlerock BT51 4TJ
☎ (028) 7084 8314
(028) 7084 9440
info@castlerockgc.co.uk
M Steen (Sec/Mgr)
www.castlerockgc.co.uk

### City of Derry    (1912)
49 Victoria Road, Londonderry BT47 2PU
☎ (028) 7134 6369
(028) 7131 0008
info@cityofderrygolfclub.com
Andrew A Meenagh
www.cityofderrygolfclub.com

### Foyle    (1994)
Proprietary
12 Alder Road, Londonderry BT48 8DB
☎ (028) 7135 2222
(028) 7135 3967
giftshop@foylegolfcentre.co.uk
Rob Gallagher (028) 71 352222
www.foylegolfcentre.co.uk

### Kilrea    (1919)
47a Lisnagrot Road, Kilrea BT51 5SF
☎ (028) 295 40044
kilreagc@hotmail.co.uk
M R Dean (028) 295 40044
www.kilreagolfclub.co.uk

### Moyola Park    (1976)
15 Curran Road, Castledawson,
Magherafelt BT45 8DG
☎ (028) 7946 8468
(028) 7946 8626
moyolapark@btconnect.com
S McKenna (Hon)
www.moyolapark.com

### Portstewart    (1894)
117 Strand Road, Portstewart BT55 7PG
☎ (028) 7083 2015
(028) 7083 4097
info@portstewartgc.co.uk
M Moss BA (028) 7083 3839
www.portstewartgc.co.uk

### Roe Park    (1993)
Public/Hotel
Roe Park Resort, Linmavady BT49 9LB
☎ (028) 777 2222
Reservations@RoeParkResort.com
Terry Kelly (028) 777 60105
www.roeparkresort.com

### Traad Ponds
Shore Road, Magherafelt BT45 6LR
☎ (028) 7941 8865
R Gribben

## Co Longford

### County Longford    (1894)
Glack, Dublin Road, Longford
☎ (043) 334 6310
(043) 334 7082
colonggolf@eircom.net
Ms Pauline Corry
www.countylongfordgolfclub.com

## Co Louth

### Ardee    (1911)
Townparks, Ardee
☎ (041) 685 3227
(041) 685 6137
ardeegolfclub@eircom.net
Noel Malone (Sec)
www.ardeegolfclub.com

### Carnbeg    (1996)
Carnbeg, Dundalk, Co Louth
☎ (042) 933 2518
(042) 939 5731
carnbeggolfcourse@eircom.net
P Kirk
www.dundalk.parkinn.ie

### County Louth    (1892)
Baltray, Drogheda
☎ (041) 988 1530
(041) 988 1531
reservations@countylouthgolfclub
.com
Liam Murphy
www.countylouthgolfclub.com

### Dundalk    (1904)
Blackrock, Dundalk
☎ (042) 932 1731
(042) 932 2022
manager@dundalkgolfclub.ie
R Woods (Sec/Mgr)
www.dundalkgolfclub.ie

### Greenore    (1896)
Greenore
☎ (042) 937 3212/3678
(042) 937 3678
greenoregolfclub@eircom.net
Linda Clarke
www.greenoregolfclub.com

### Killinbeg    (1991)
Killin Park, Dundalk
☎ (042) 933 9303
(042) 932 0848
Pat Reynolds (Sec/Mgr)

### Seapoint    (1993)
Termonfeckin, Drogheda
☎ (041) 982 2333
(041) 982 2331
golflinks@seapoint.ie
www.seapointgolflinks.ie

**Townley Hall** (1994)
*Tullyallen, Drogheda*
☎ **(041) 984 2229**
🖳 (041) 984 2229
📧 townleyhall@oceanfree.net
✍ M Foley (Hon)

## Co Mayo

**Achill** (1951)
*Keel, Achill*
☎ **(098) 43456**
🖳 (098) 43456
📧 achillislandgolfclub@gmail.com
✍ Hugo Boyle (087) 798 1225
🖥 www.achillgolf.com

**Ashford Castle**
*Cong*
☎ **(092) 46003**

**Ballina** (1910)
*Mossgrove, Shanaghy, Ballina*
☎ **(096) 21050**
🖳 (096) 21718
📧 ballinagc@eircom.net
✍ Dick Melrose
🖥 www.ballina-golf.com

**Ballinrobe** (1895)
*Cloonacastle, Ballinrobe, Co Mayo*
☎ **(094) 954 1118**
🖳 (094) 954 1889
📧 info@ballinrobegolfclub.com
✍ John G Burke
🖥 www.ballinrobegolfclub.com

**Ballyhaunis** (1929)
*Coolnaha, Ballyhaunis*
☎ **(0907) 30014**
✍ J Mooney (Hon)

**Belmullet** (1925)
*Carne, Belmullet*
☎ **(00353) 97 82292**
📧 pmcintyrecarne@gmail.com
✍ Patrick Mc Intyre (Hon Sec)
🖥 www.belmulletgolfclub.ie

**Castlebar** (1910)
*Hawthorn Avenue, Rocklands, Castlebar*
☎ **(094) 21649**
🖳 (094) 26088
📧 info@castlebargolfclub.ie
✍ Bernie Murray/Stephanie Ryan
🖥 www.castlebargolfclub.ie

**Claremorris** (1917)
Pay and play
*Castlemacgarrett, Claremorris*
☎ **(094) 937 1527**
🖳 (094) 937 2919
📧 info@claremorrisgolfclub.com
✍ N McCarthy (Hon)
🖥 www.claremorrisgolfclub.com

**Mulranny** (1968)
*Mulranny, Westport*
☎ **(098) 36262**
✍ C Moran (Hon)

**Swinford** (1922)
*Brabazon Park, Swinford*
☎ **(+353) 94 925 1378**
🖳 (+353) 94 925 1378
✍ T Regan (087) 291 3067

**Westport** (1908)
*Carrowholly, Westport*
☎ **(098) 28262**
🖳 (098) 24648
📧 info@westportgolfclub.com
✍ Sean Durkan
🖥 www.westportgolfclub.com

## Co Meath

**Ashbourne** (1991)
*Archerstown, Ashbourne, Co.Meath*
☎ **(01) 835 2005**
🖳 (01) 835 9261
📧 info@ashbournegolfclub.ie
✍ Paul Wisniewski
🖥 www.ashbournegolfclub.ie

**Black Bush** (1987)
*Thomastown, Dunshaughlin*
☎ **(01) 825 0021**
🖳 (01) 825 0400
📧 info@blackbushgolfclub.ie
✍ Kate O'Rourke (Admin)
(01) 825 0021
🖥 www.blackbushgolfclub.ie

**County Meath** (1898)
*Newtownmoynagh, Trim*
☎ **(046) 9431463**
🖳 (046) 9437554
✍ J Higgins
🖥 www.trimgolf.net

**Glebe**
*Kildalkey Road, Trim, Meath*
☎ **(00353) 4694 31926**
🖳 (00353) 4694 31926
📧 glebegc@eircom.net
✍ Chris Bligh
🖥 www.glebegolfclub.com

**Gormanston College** (1961)
*Franciscan College, Gormanston*
☎ **(01) 841 2203**
🖳 (01) 841 2685
✍ Br Laurence Brady
🖥 www.gormanstoncollege.ie

**Headfort** (1928)
*Kells*
☎ **(046) 924 0146**
🖳 (046) 924 9282
📧 hgcadmin@eircom.net
✍ Nora Murphy (Admin)
🖥 www.headfortgolfclub.ie

**Kilcock** (1985)
*Gallow, Kilcock*
☎ **(01) 628 7592**
🖳 (01) 628 7283
📧 info@kilcockgolfclub.ie
✍ Martha Dalton (Sec)
🖥 www.kilcockgolfclub.ie

**Laytown & Bettystown**
(1909)
*Golf Links Road, Bettystown*
☎ **(041) 982 7170**
🖳 (041) 982 8506
📧 links@landb.ie
✍ Helen Finnegan
🖥 www.landb.ie

**Moor Park** (1993)
*Moortown, Navan*
☎ **(046) 27661**
✍ M Fagan (Mgr)

**Navan** (1996)
Public
*Proudstown, Navan, Co Meath*
☎ **(046) 907 2888**
🖳 (046) 907 6722
📧 info@navangolfclub.ie
✍ Sheila Slattery
🖥 www.navangolfclub.ie

**Royal Tara** (1906)
*Bellinter, Navan*
☎ **(046) 902 5508/902 5584**
🖳 (046) 902 6684
📧 info@royaltaragolfclub.com
✍ John McGarth (Hon)
🖥 www.royaltaragolfclub.com

**Summerhill**
*Agher, Rathmoylan, Co Meath*
☎ **(046) 955 7857**
✍ M Nangle

## Co Monaghan

**Castleblayney Golf Club, Concrawood** (1985)
*Onomy, Castleblayney*
☎ **(042) 974 9485**
🖳 (042) 975 4576
📧 info@concrawood.ie
✍ Adrian Kelly
🖥 www.concrawood.ie

**Clones** (1913)
*Hilton Demesne, Clones*
☎ **(047) 56017**
🖳 (047) 56017
📧 clonesgolfclub@eircom.net
✍ Paul Fitzpatrick (087) 766 1778
🖥 www.clonesgolfclub.com

**Nuremore Hotel & CC** (1964)
*Nuremore Hotel, Carrickmacross*
☎ **(042) 966 1438**
🖳 (042) 966 1853
📧 info@nuremore.com
✍ Maurice Cassidy (Director)
🖥 www.nuremore.com

**Rossmore** (1916)
*Rossmore Park, Cootehill Road, Monaghan*
☎ **(047) 81316**
🖳 (047) 71227
📧 rossmoregolfclub@eircom.net
✍ J McKenna (Hon)
🖥 www.rossmoregolfclub.com

## Co Offaly

**Birr**   (1893)
*The Glenns, Birr*
☎ (057) 91 20082
📠 (057) 91 22155
✉ birrgolfclub@eircom.net
✍ Tony Hogan (Hon)
🖥 www.birrgolfclub.ie

**Castle Barna**   (1992)
*Castlebarnagh, Daingean, Offaly*
☎ (057) 935 3384
📠 (057) 935 3077
✉ info@castlebarna.ie
✍ E Mangan
🖥 www.castlebarna.ie

**Edenderry**   (1910)
*Kishawanny, Edenderry*
☎ (046) 973 1072
📠 (046) 973 3911
✉ info@edenderrygolfclub.ie
✍ Noel Usher
🖥 www.edenderrygolfclub.ie

**Esker Hills G&CC**   (1996)
Proprietary
*Tullamore, Co Offaly*
☎ (057) 93 55999
📠 (057) 93 55021
✉ info@eskerhillsgolf.com
✍ C Guinan
🖥 www.eskerhillsgolf.com

**Tullamore**   (1896)
*Brookfield, Tullamore*
☎ (057) 93 21439
📠 (057) 83 41806
✉ tullamoregolfclub@eircom.net
✍ Ann Marie Cunniffe (057) 93 21439
🖥 www.tullamoregolfclub.ie

## Co Roscommon

**Athlone**   (1892)
*Hodson Bay, Athlone*
☎ (090) 649 2073
📠 (090) 649 4080
✉ athlonegolfclub@eircom.net
✍ Admin Office or Hon. Sec.
🖥 www.athlonegolfclub.ie

**Boyle**   (1911)
*Knockadoo, Brusna, Boyle*
☎ (071) 966 2594
✍ J Mooney (Hon) (087) 776 0161

**Castlerea**   (1905)
*Clonallis, Castlerea*
☎ (0871) 278066
✉ castlereagolfclub@gmail.com
✍ Cathering O'Loughlin
🖥 www.castlereagolfclub.ie

**Roscommon**   (1904)
*Mote Park, Roscommon*
☎ (09066) 26382
📠 (09066) 26043
✉ info@roscommongolfclub.ie
✍ M Dolan (087) 225 4695
🖥 www.roscommongolfclub.ie

**Strokestown**   (1995)
*Strokestown, Co Roscommon*
☎ (07196) 33660
✉ strokestowngolfclub@gmail.com
✍ L Glover (Hon)
🖥 www.strokestowngolfclub.com

## Co Sligo

**Ballymote**   (1943)
*Ballinascarrow, Ballymote*
☎ (087) 218 7054/(087) 277 9974
📠 (071) 918 3504
✉ ballymotegolfclub@gmail.com
✍ Trevor Mattimoe
🖥 www.ballymotegolfclub.ie

**County Sligo**   (1894)
*Rosses Point*
☎ (071) 9177134/9177186
📠 (071) 9177460
✉ teresa@countysligogolfclub.ie
✍ David O'Donovan
🖥 www.countysligogolfclub.ie

**Enniscrone**   (1918)
*Ballina Road, Enniscrone*
☎ (096) 36297
✉ enniscronegolf@eircom.net
✍ Albie O'Connor (Hon Sec)
🖥 www.enniscronegolf.com

**Strandhill**   (1932)
*Strandhill*
☎ (00353) 71 91 68188
📠 (00353) 71 91 68811
✉ strandhillgc@eircom.net
✍ Sandra Corcoran
🖥 www.strandhillgc.com

**Tubbercurry**   (1990)
*Ballymote Road, Tubbercurry*
☎ (071) 918 5849 (Societies)
(086) 8306174
✉ info@tubbercurrygolfclub.ie
✍ Billy Kilgannon (071) 918 6124
🖥 www.tubbercurrygolfclub.com

## Co Tipperary

**Ballykisteen Hotel & Golf Resort**   (1994)
Proprietary
*Ballykisteen, Limerick Junction*
☎ (+353) 062 33333 (hotel)
📠 (+353) 062 31555
✉ golf.ballykisteen@ballykisteenhotel.com
✍ Mike Keegan (+353 087 667 9495)
🖥 www.ballykisteenhotel.com

**Cahir Park**   (1967)
*Kilcommon, Cahir, Co Tipperary*
☎ (052) 7441474
📠 (052) 7442717
✉ cahirgolfclub@hotmail.com
✍ Paul Adamson (Club Sec)
🖥 www.cahirgolfclub.com

**Carrick-on-Suir**   (1939)
*Garravoone, Carrick-on-Suir, County Tipperary*
☎ (051) 640047
📠 (051) 640558
✉ info@carrickgolfclub.com
✍ Michael Kelly (Hon Sec)
🖥 www.carrickgolfclub.com

**Clonmel**   (1911)
*Lyreanearla, Mountain Road, Clonmel*
☎ (052) 61 24050
📠 (052) 61 83349
✉ cgc@indigo.ie
✍ A Myles-Keating (052) 6124050 (Ext 20)
🖥 www.clonmelgolfclub.com

**Dundrum Golf & Leisure Resort**   (1993)
*Dundrum, Cashel*
☎ (062) 71717
✉ golfshop@dundrumhouse.ie
✍ William Crowe (Mgr) (062) 71717
🖥 www.dundrumhousehotel.com

**Nenagh**   (1929)
*Beechwood, Nenagh*
☎ (067) 31476
📠 (067) 34808
✉ nenaghgolfclub@eircom.net
✍ Maeve De Loughry
🖥 www.nenaghgolfclub.com

**Roscrea**   (1892)
*Derryvale, Roscrea*
☎ 00353 (0) 505 21130
📠 00353 (0) 505 23410
✉ info@roscreagolfclub.ie
✍ Steve Crofton
🖥 www.roscreagolfclub.ie

**Slievenamon**   (1999)
Proprietary
*Clonacody, Lisronagh, Co Tipperary*
☎ (052) 61 32213
📠 (052) 61 30875
✉ info@slievenamongolfclub.com
✍ B Kenny (052) 61 32213
🖥 www.slievenamongolfclub.com

**Templemore**   (1970)
*Manna South, Templemore*
☎ (0504) 32923/31400
✉ johnkm@tinet.ie
✍ John Hackett

**Thurles**   (1909)
*Turtulla, Thurles*
☎ (0504) 21983
📠 (0504) 90806
✉ office@thurlesgolfclub.com
✍ Tom Ryan (Hon Sec)
🖥 www.thurlesgolfclub.com

**Tipperary**   (1896)
*Rathanny, Tipperary*
☎ (062) 51119
✉ tipperarygolfclub@eircom.net
✍ Michael Tobin (Sec/Mgr)
🖥 www.tipperarygolfclub.com

# Co Tyrone

## Auchnacloy (1995)
**Pay and play**
99A Tullyvar Road, Auchnacloy BT69 6BL
☎ (028) 8255 7050
🖥 (028) 8555 7050
🖂 Sidney.houston@yahoo.co.uk
🖎 Sidney Houston
🖥 www.irishgolfcourses.co.uk
/auchnacloy

## Benburb Valley
Maydown Road, Benburb BT71 7LJ
☎ (028) 3754 9868
🖎 T McKillion

## Dungannon (1890)
34 Springfield Lane, Mullaghmore,
Dungannon BT70 1QX
☎ (028) 8772 2098
🖥 (028) 8772 7338
🖂 dungannongolfclub2009@hotmail
.co.uk
🖎 ST Hughes
🖥 www.dungannongolfclub.com

## Fintona (1904)
Eccleville Desmesne, 1 Kiln Street, Fintona
BT78 2BJ
☎ (028) 8284 1480
🖥 (028) 8284 1480
🖂 fintonagolfclub@btconnect.com
🖎 Raymond D Scott

## Killymoon (1889)
200 Killymoon Road, Cookstown BT80 8TW
☎ (028) 8676 3762
🖥 (028) 8676 3762
🖂 killymoongolf@btconnect.com
🖎 N Weir
🖥 www.killymoongolfclub.com

## Newtownstewart (1914)
38 Golf Course Road, Newtownstewart
BT78 4HU
☎ (028) 8166 1466
🖥 (028) 8166 2506
🖂 info@newtownstewartgolfclub.com
🖎 Lorraine Donnell (Administrator)
🖥 www.newtownstewartgolfclub.com

## Omagh (1910)
83A Dublin Road, Omagh BT78 1HQ
☎ (028) 8224 3160/1442
🖥 (028) 8224 3160
🖎 Mrs F Caldwell

## Strabane (1908)
Ballycolman, Strabane BT82 9PH
☎ (028) 7138 2271/2007
🖥 (028) 7188 6514
🖂 strabanegc@btconnect.com
🖎 Claire Keys
🖥 www.strabanegolfclub.co.uk

# Co Waterford

## Dungarvan (1924)
Knocknagranagh, Dungarvan
☎ (058) 43310/41605

🖥 (058) 44113
🖂 dungarvangc@eircom.net
🖎 Irene Lynch (Mgr)
🖥 www.dungarvangolfclub.com

## Dunmore East (1993)
**Proprietary**
Dunmore East
☎ (051) 383151
🖥 (051) 383151
🖂 info@dunmoreeastgolfclub.ie
🖎 Alan Skehan
🖥 www.dunmoreeastgolfclub.ie

## Faithlegg (1993)
Faithlegg House, Faithlegg
☎ (051) 380587/380592
🖥 (051) 382010
🖂 reservations@fhh.ie
🖎 Ryan Hunt (051) 380588
🖥 www.faithlegg.com

## Gold Coast (1993)
Ballinacourty, Dungarvan
☎ (058) 44055
🖥 (058) 43378
🖂 info@goldcoastgolfclub.com
🖎 Mark Lenihan/Brendan O'Brien
🖥 www.goldcoastgolfclub.com

## Lismore (1965)
Ballyin, Lismore
☎ (058) 54026
🖥 (058) 53338
🖂 lismoregolfclub@eircom.net
🖎 W Henry
🖥 www.lismoregolf.org

## Tramore (1894)
Newtown, Tramore
☎ (051) 386170/381247
🖥 (051) 390961
🖂 info@tramoregolfclub.com
🖎 Richard Walsh (Hon Sec)
🖥 www.tramoregolfclub.com

## Waterford (1912)
Newrath, Waterford
☎ +353 (0) 51 876748
🖂 info@waterfordgolfclub.com
🖎 Damien Maquire (Gen Mgr)
🖥 www.waterfordgolfclub.com

## Waterford Castle (1991)
**Proprietary**
The Island, Ballinakill, Waterford
☎ (051) 871633
🖥 (051) 871634
🖂 golf@waterfordcastle.com
🖎 M Garland (Dir. of Golf)
🖥 www.waterfordcastle.com

## West Waterford G&CC
(1993)
Dungarvan
☎ (058) 43216/41475
🖥 (058) 44343
🖂 info@westwaterfordgolf.com
🖎 A Spratt (Director)
🖥 www.westwaterfordgolf.com

# Co Westmeath

## Ballinlough Castle
Clonmellon, Co Westmeath
☎ (044) 64544
🖎 T Brady

## Delvin Castle (1992)
Clonyn, Delvin
☎ (044) 96 64315
🖂 info@delvincastlegolf.com
🖎 F Dillon
🖥 www.delvincastlegolf.com

## Glasson Country House Hotel and Golf Club (1993)
Glasson, Athlone
☎ 00353 (0) 90 6485120
🖥 00353 (0) 90 6485444
🖂 info@glassongolf.ie
🖎 Gareth Jones
🖥 www.glassoncountryhouse.ie

## Moate (1900)
Aghanargit, Moate
☎ (090) 648 1271
🖥 (090) 648 2645
🖂 moategolfclub@eircom.net
🖎 A O'Brien
🖥 www.moategolfclub.ie

## Mount Temple G&CC (1991)
**Proprietary**
Mount Temple, Moate
☎ (090) 648 1841
🖂 mounttemple@eircom.net
🖎 M Dolan
🖥 www.mounttemplegolfclub.com

## Mullingar (1894)
Belvedere, Mullingar
☎ (0 353 44) 934 8366
🖥 (0 353 44) 934 1499
🖂 mullingargolfclub@hotmail.com
🖎 Sean Finnegan (Gen Mgr)
🖥 www.mullingargolfclub.com

# Co Wexford

## Courtown (1936)
Kiltennel, Gorey
☎ (053) 942 5166
🖥 (053) 942 5553
🖂 info@courtowngolfclub.com
🖎 S O'Hara
🖥 www.courtowngolfclub.com

## Enniscorthy (1906)
Knockmarshall, Enniscorthy
☎ (053) 92 33191
🖥 (053) 92 37637
🖂 honsec@enniscorthygc.ie
🖎 John Cullen
🖥 www.enniscorthygc.ie

## New Ross (1905)
Tinneranny, New Ross
☎ (051) 421433
🖥 (051) 420098
🖂 newrossgolf@eircom.net
🖎 Kathleen Daly (Sec/Mgr)
🖥 www.newrossgolfclub.net

### Rosslare (1905)
*Rosslare Strand, Rosslare*
- ☎ **(053) 913 2203 (office)**
- 📠 (053) 913 2263
- ✉ office@rosslaregolf.com
- ✍ Frank Codd (Hon Sec)
- 🖥 www.rosslaregolf.com

### St Helen's Bay (1993)
**Proprietary**
*St Helen's, Kilrane, Rosslare Harbour*
- ☎ **(053) 91 33234**
- 📠 (053) 91 33803
- ✉ info@sthelensbay.com
- ✍ A Howard
- 🖥 www.sthelensbay.com

### Tara Glen (1984)
*Ballymoney, Gorey, Co Wexford*
- ☎ **(053) 942 5413**
- 📠 (053) 942 5612
- ✉ taraglenplc@eircom.net
- ✍ Marion Siggins
- 🖥 www.tataglen.ie

### Wexford (1960)
*Mulgannon, Wexford*
- ☎ **(05391) 42238**
- 📠 (05391) 42243
- ✉ info@wexfordgolfclub.ie
- ✍ Roy Doyle (Hon Sec)
- 🖥 www.wexfordgolfclub.ie

## Co Wicklow

### Arklow (1927)
*Abbeylands, Arklow*
- ☎ **(0402) 32492**
- 📠 (0402) 91604
- ✉ arklowgolflinks@eircom.net
- ✍ D Canavan (Hon Sec)
- 🖥 www.arklowgolfclublinks.com

### Baltinglass (1928)
*Baltinglass*
- ☎ **(059) 648 1350**
- 📠 (059) 648 2842
- ✉ baltinglassgolfclub@eircom.net
- 🖥 www.baltinglassgolfclub.ie

### Blainroe (1978)
*Blainroe*
- ☎ **(0404) 68168**
- 📠 (0404) 69369
- ✉ info@blainroe.com
- ✍ Patrick Bradshaw
- 🖥 www.blainroe.com

### Boystown
*Baltyboys, Blessington, Co Wicklow*
- ☎ **(045) 867146**
- ✍ D McEvoy

### Bray (1897)
*Greystones Road, Bray*
- ☎ **(01) 276 3200**
- 📠 (01) 276 3262
- ✉ info@braygolfclub.com
- ✍ Alan Threadgold (Gen Mgr)
- 🖥 www.braygolfclub.com

### Charlesland (1992)
*Greystones*
- ☎ **(01) 287 4350**
- 📠 (01) 287 0078
- ✉ teetimes@charlesland.com
- ✍ Gerry O'Brien (Mgr)
- 🖥 www.charlesland.com

### Delgany (1908)
*Delgany*
- ☎ **(01) 287 4536**
- 📠 (01) 287 3977
- ✉ delganygolf@eircom.net
- ✍ Denzil Jones (Hon Sec)
- 🖥 www.delganygolfclub.com

### Djouce (1995)
*Roundwood*
- ☎ **(01) 281 8585**
- ✉ djoucegolfclub@gmail.com
- ✍ D McGillycuddy (Mgr)
- 🖥 www.djoucegolfclub.com

### Druid's Glen (1995)
*Newtownmountkennedy*
- ☎ **(01) 287 3600**
- 📠 (01) 287 3699
- ✉ info@druidsglen.ie
- ✍ D Flinn (Gen Mgr)
- 🖥 www.druidsglen.ie

### Druid's Heath (2003)
*Newtownmountkennedy*
- ☎ **(01) 287 3600**
- 📠 (01) 287 3699
- ✉ info@druidsglen.ie
- ✍ D Flinn (Gen Mgr)
- 🖥 www.druidsglen.ie

### The European Club (1987)
*Brittas Bay, Wicklow*
- ☎ **(0404) 47415**
- 📠 (0404) 47449
- ✉ info@theeuropeanclub.com
- ✍ P Ruddy
- 🖥 www.theeuropeanclub.com

### Glen of the Downs (1998)
*Coolnaskeagh, Delgany, Co Wicklow*
- ☎ **(01) 287 6240**
- 📠 (01) 287 0063
- ✉ info@glenofthedowns.com
- ✍ Derek Murphy
- 🖥 www.glenofthedowns.com

### Glenmalure (1991)
*Greenane, Rathdrum*
- ☎ **(0404) 46679**
- ✉ info@glenmalure.com
- ✍ Tina O'Shaughnessy (Hon Sec)
- 🖥 www.glenmalure.com

### Greystones (1895)
*Whitshed Road, Greystones*
- ☎ **(01) 287 4136**
- 📠 (01) 287 3749
- ✉ administration@greystonegc.com
- ✍ Angus Murray (Mgr)
- 🖥 www.greystonesgc.com

### Kilcoole (1992)
*Kilcoole*
- ☎ **(01) 287 2066**

---

- 📠 (01) 201 0497
- ✉ adminkg@eircom.net
- ✍ E Lonergan
- 🖥 www.kilkoolegolfclub.com

### Old Conna (1987)
*Ferndale Road, Bray*
- ☎ **(01) 282 6055**
- 📠 (01) 282 5611
- ✉ info@oldconna.com
- ✍ Tom Sheridan (Gen Mgr)
- 🖥 www.oldconna.com

### Powerscourt (East) (1996)
*Powerscourt Estate, Enniskerry*
- ☎ **(01) 204 6033**
- 📠 (01) 276 1303
- ✍ B Gibbons (Mgr)
- 🖥 www.powerscourt.ie

### Powerscourt (West) (2003)
*Powerscourt Estate, Enniskerry*
- ☎ **(01) 204 6033**
- 📠 (01) 276 1303
- ✍ B Gibbons (Mgr)
- 🖥 www.powerscourt.ie

### Rathsallagh (1993)
**Proprietary**
*Dunlavin*
- ☎ **(045) 403316**
- 📠 (045) 403295
- ✉ golf@rathsallagh.com
- ✍ J O'Flynn (045) 403316
- 🖥 www.rathsallagh.com

### Roundwood (1995)
*Ballinahinch, Newtownmountkennedy*
- ☎ **(01) 281 8488**
- 📠 (01) 284 3642
- ✉ rwood@indigo.ie
- ✍ M McGuirk
- 🖥 www.roundwoodgolf.com

### Tulfarris (1987)
*Blessington Lakes, Blessington*
- ☎ **(045) 867644**
- 📠 (045) 867601
- ✉ golf@tulfarris.com
- ✍ A Williams (Mgr)

### Vartry Lakes (1997)
**Proprietary**
*Roundwood*
- ☎ **(01) 281 7006**
- 📠 (01) 281 7006
- ✍ J & A McDonald
- 🖥 www.wicklow.ie

### Wicklow (1904)
*Dunbur Road, Wicklow*
- ☎ **(0404) 67379**
- 📠 (0404) 64756
- ✉ info@wicklowgolfclub.ie
- ✍ J Kelly
- 🖥 www.wicklowgolfclub.ie

### Woodenbridge (1884)
*Vale of Avoca, Arklow*
- ☎ **(0402) 35202**
- 📠 (0402) 35754
- ✉ reception@woodenbridge.ie
- ✍ Gerry Coleman
- 🖥 www.woodenbridgegolfclub.com

---

# Scotland

## Aberdeenshire

### Aboyne (1883)
Formaston Park, Aboyne AB34 5HP
☎ (013398) 86328
🖥 (013398) 87078
📧 aboynegolfclub@btconnect.com
✍ Mr Allan Taylor (013398) 87078
🌐 www.aboynegolfclub.co.uk

### Aboyne Loch Golf Centre
(2000)
**Pay and play**
Aboyne Loch, Aboyne AB34 5BR
☎ (013398) 86444
🖥 (013398) 86488
📧 info@thelodgeontheloch.com
✍ Derek McCulloch
🌐 www.thelodgeontheloch.com

### Alford (1982)
Montgarrie Road, Alford AB33 8AE
☎ (019755) 62178
📧 info@alford-golf-club.co.uk
✍ Mrs Julie Alexander
🌐 www.alford-golf-club.co.uk

### Auchenblae Golf Course
(1894)
**Pay and play**
Auchenblae, Laurencekirk AB30 1TX
☎ (01561) 320002
**(Group Bookings)**
✍ J Thomson (01561) 320245
🌐 www.auchenblaegolfcourse.co.uk

### Ballater (1892)
Victoria Road, Ballater AB35 5LX
☎ (013397) 55567
📧 sec@ballatergolfclub.co.uk
✍ Colin Smith
🌐 www.ballatergolfclub.co.uk

### Ballindalloch Castle (2003)
**Pay and play**
Lagmore, Ballindalloch, Banffshire AB37 9AA
☎ (01807) 500305
📧 golf@ballindallochcastle.co.uk
🌐 www.ballindallochcastle.co.uk

### Banchory (1904)
Kinneskie Road, Banchory AB31 5TA
☎ (01330) 822365
🖥 (01330) 822491
📧 bgc.secretary@btconnect.com
✍ Mrs A Smart
🌐 www.banchorygolfclub.co.uk

### Braemar (1902)
Cluniebank Road, Braemar AB35 5XX
☎ (013397) 41618
📧 info@braemargolfclub.co.uk
✍ E Myers (013397) 41618
🌐 www.braemargolfclub.co.uk

### Craibstone (1999)
**Public**
Craibstone Estate, Bucksburn, Aberdeen AB29 9YA
☎ (01224) 716777
📧 golf@marshall-leisure.co.uk
✍ Iain Buchan

### Cruden Bay (1899)
Aulton Road, Cruden Bay, Peterhead AB42 0NN
☎ (01779) 812285
🖥 (01779) 812945
📧 les@crudenbaygolfclub.co.uk
✍ Mr Les Durno (Gen Mgr)
🌐 www.crudenbaygolfclub.co.uk

### Cullen (1879)
The Links, Cullen, Buckie AB56 4WB
☎ (01542) 840685
📧 info@cullengolfclub.co.uk
✍ Mrs H Bavidge
🌐 www.cullengolfclub.co.uk

### Duff House Royal Golf Club
(1910)
The Barnyards, Banff AB45 3SX
☎ (01261) 812062
🖥 (01261) 812224
📧 manager@duffhouseroyal.com
✍ Gerry Fitzpatrick
🌐 www.duffhouseroyal.com

### Fraserburgh (1777)
Philorth Links, Fraserburgh AB43 8TL
☎ (01346) 516616
📧 secretary@fraserburghgolfclub.org
✍ Lindsay Schuitema
🌐 www.fraserburghgolfclub.org

### Huntly (1892)
Cooper Park, Huntly AB54 4SH
☎ (01466) 792643
🖥 (01466) 792643
📧 huntlygc@btconnect.com
✍ A Donald/Kathleen Raeburn
🌐 www.huntlygc.com

### Inchmarlo (1995)
**Proprietary**
Glassel Road, Banchory AB31 4BQ
☎ (01330) 826424
🖥 (01330) 826425
📧 reception@inchmarlo-golf.com
✍ Andrew Shinie (01330) 826427
🌐 www.inchmarlo-golf.com

### Insch (1906)
Golf Terrace, Insch AB52 6JY
☎ (01464) 820363
📧 administrator@inschgolfclub.co.uk
✍ Sarah Ellis (Administrator)
🌐 www.inschgolfclub.co.uk

### Inverallochy
**Public**
Whitelink, Inverallochy, Fraserburgh AB43 8XY
☎ (01346) 582000

### (continued)
☎ (01346) 582000
📧 inverallochygolf@btconnect.com
✍ GM Young
🌐 www.inverallochygolfclub.com

### Inverurie (1923)
Davah Wood, Inverurie AB51 5JB
☎ (01467) 624080
🖥 (01467) 672869
📧 administrator@inveruriegc.co.uk
✍ Alan Donald (01467) 624080
🌐 www.inveruriegolfclub.co.uk

### Keith (1963)
Mar Court, Fife Keith, Keith AB55 5GF
☎ (01542) 882469
📧 secretary@keithgolfclub.co.uk
✍ Diane Morrison
🌐 www.keithgolfclub.co.uk

### Kemnay (1908)
Monymusk Road, Kemnay AB51 5RA
☎ (01467) 642225
🖥 (01467) 643561
📧 administrator@kemnaygolfclub.co.uk
✍ F Webster (Secretary)
🌐 www.kemnaygolfclub.co.uk

### Kintore (1911)
Balbithan Road, Kintore AB51 0UR
☎ (01467) 632631
🖥 (01467) 632995
📧 kintoregolfclub@lineone.net
✍ C Lindsay
🌐 www.kintoregolfclub.net

### Longside (1973)
West End, Longside, Peterhead AB42 4XJ
☎ (01779) 821558
📧 info@longsidegolf.wanadoo.co.uk
✍ J Taylor
🌐 www.longsidegolfclub.co.uk

### Lumphanan (1924)
**Owned privately**
Main Road, Lumphanan, Banchory AB31 4PW
☎ (01339) 883480
📧 info@lumphanangolfclub.co.uk
✍ Y Taite/J Wilson (Hon Sec) (01224) 312226
🌐 www.lumphanangolfclub.co.uk

### McDonald (1927)
Hospital Road, Ellon AB41 9AW
☎ (01358) 720576
📧 mcdonald.golf@virgin.net
✍ G Ironside
🌐 www.ellongolfclub.co.uk

### Meldrum House (1998)
Meldrum House Estate, Oldmeldrum AB51 0AE
☎ (01651) 873553
🖥 (01651) 873635
📧 info@meldrumhousegolfclub.co.uk
✍ B Smith (Operations Mgr)
🌐 www.meldrumhousegolfclub.co.uk

### Newburgh-on-Ythan    (1888)
*Beach Road, Newburgh, Aberdeenshire AB41 6BY*
- ☎ **(01358) 789058**
- 🖳 (01358) 788104
- ✉ secretary@newburghgolfclub.co.uk
- ✍ Administrator: (01358) 789084
- 🖥 www.newburghgolfclub.co.uk

### Newmachar    (1989)
*Swailend, Newmachar, Aberdeen AB21 7UU*
- ☎ **(01651) 863002**
- 🖳 (01651) 863055
- ✉ info@newmachargolfclub.co.uk
- ✍ Alasdair MacGregor
- 🖥 www.newmachargolfclub.co.uk

### Oldmeldrum    (1885)
*Kirk Brae, Oldmeldrum AB51 0DJ*
- ☎ **(01651) 872648**
- ✉ admin@oldmeldrumgolf.co.uk
- ✍ Hamish Dingwall (Club Co-ordinator)
- 🖥 www.oldmeldrumgolf.co.uk

### Peterhead    (1841)
*Craigewan Links, Peterhead AB42 1LT*
- ☎ **(01779) 472149/480725**
- 🖳 (01779) 480725
- ✉ enquiries@peterheadgolfclub.co.uk
- ✍ D.G.Wood
- 🖥 www.peterheadgolfclub.co.uk

### Rosehearty    (1874)
*c/o Mason's Arms Hotel, Rosehearty, Fraserburgh AB43 7JJ*
- ☎ **(01346) 571250 (Capt)**
- 🖳 (01346) 571306
- ✉ scotthornal@cbtinternet.com
- ✍ S Hornal

### Rothes    (1990)
**Proprietary**
*Blackhall, Rothes, Aberlour AB38 7AN*
- ☎ **(01340) 831443**
- 🖳 (01340) 831443
- ✉ rothesgolfclub@tiscali.co.uk
- ✍ Kenneth MacPhee (01340) 831676
- 🖥 www.rothesgolfclub.co.uk

### Royal Tarlair    (1926)
*Buchan Street, Macduff AB44 1TA*
- ☎ **(01261) 832897**
- 🖳 (01261) 833455
- ✉ info@royaltarlair.co.uk
- ✍ Mrs Muriel McMurray
- 🖥 www.royaltarlair.co.uk

### Stonehaven    (1888)
*Cowie, Stonehaven AB39 3RH*
- ☎ **(01569) 762124**
- 🖳 (01569) 765973
- ✉ info@stonehavengolfclub.com
- ✍ Mrs M H Duncan
- 🖥 www.stonehavengolfclub.com

### Strathlene    (1877)
*Portessie, Buckie AB56 4DJ*
- ☎ **(01542) 831798**
- ✉ strathlenegc@gmail.com
- ✍ David Lyon
- 🖥 www.strathlenegolfclub.co.uk

### Tarland    (1908)
*Aberdeen Road, Tarland AB34 4TB*
- ☎ **(013398) 81000**
- 🖳 (013398) 81000
- ✉ secretary@tarlandgolfclub.co.uk
- ✍ Mrs C Foreman (admin) (019756) 51484
- 🖥 www.tarlandgolfclub.co.uk

### Torphins    (1896)
*Bog Road, Torphins AB31 4JU*
- ☎ **(013398) 82115**
- ✉ stuartmacgregor5@btinternet.com
- ✍ S MacGregor (013398) 82402
- 🖥 www.torphinsgolfclub.com

### Turriff    (1896)
*Rosehall, Turriff AB53 4HD*
- ☎ **(01888) 562982 Pro Shop**
  **(01888) 563025**
- 🖳 (01888) 568050
- ✉ secretary@turriffgolf.sol.co.uk
- ✍ D Purdie
- 🖥 www.turriffgolfclub.com

## Aberdeen Clubs

### Bon Accord    (1872)
**Club**
*19 Golf Road, Aberdeen AB24 5QB*
- ☎ **(01224) 633464**
- ✍ JA Morrison

### Caledonian    (1899)
**Club**
*20 Golf Road, Aberdeen AB2 1QB*
- ☎ **(01224) 632443**
- ✍ JA Bridgeford

### Northern    (1897)
**Public**
*22 Golf Road, Aberdeen AB24 5QB*
- ☎ **(01224) 636440**
- 🖳 (01224) 622679
- ✉ ngcgolf@hotmail.com
- ✍ D Johnstone
- 🖥 www.northerngolfclub.co.uk

## Aberdeen Courses

### Auchmill    (1975)
*Bonnyview Road, West Heatheryfold, Aberdeen AB16 7FQ*
- ☎ **(01224) 715214**
- 🖳 (01224) 715226
- ✉ auchmill.golf@btconnect.com
- ✍ Yvonne Sangster (01224) 715214
- 🖥 www.auchmill.co.uk

### Balnagask    (1955)
**Public**
*St Fitticks Road, Aberdeen*
- ☎ **(01224) 871286**
- 🖳 (01224) 873418
- ✉ information@sportaberdeen.co.uk
- ✍ W Gordon
- 🖥 www.aberdeencity.gov.uk

### Deeside    (1903)
*Golf Road, Bieldside, Aberdeen AB15 9DL*
- ☎ **(01224) 869457**
- 🖳 (01224) 861800
- ✉ admin@deesidegolfclub.com
- ✍ Ms D Pern (01224) 869457
- 🖥 www.deesidegolfclub.com

### Fyvie    (2003)
**Pay and play**
*Fyvie, Turriff, Aberdeenshire AB53 8QR*
- ☎ **(01651) 891166**
- 🖳 (01651) 891166
- ✉ info@fyviegolfcourse.co.uk
- ✍ Alexander Rankin
- 🖥 www.fyviegolfcourse.co.uk

### Murcar Links    (1909)
*Bridge of Don, Aberdeen AB23 8BD*
- ☎ **(01224) 704354**
- 🖳 (01224) 704354
- ✉ golf@murcarlinks.com
- ✍ Carol O'Neill
- 🖥 www.murcarlinks.com

### Peterculter    (1989)
**Proprietary**
*Oldtown, Burnside Road, Peterculter AB14 0LN*
- ☎ **(01224) 735245**
- 🖳 (01224) 735580
- ✉ info@petercultergolfclub.co.uk
- ✍ D Vannet
- 🖥 www.petercultergolfclub.co.uk

### Portlethen    (1983)
*Badentoy Road, Portlethen, Aberdeen AB12 4YA*
- ☎ **(01224) 781090**
- 🖳 (01224) 783383
- ✉ admin@portlethengolfclub.com
- 🖥 www.portlethengolfclub.com

### Royal Aberdeen    (1780)
*Links Road, Bridge of Don, Aberdeen AB23 8AT*
- ☎ **(01224) 702571**
- 🖳 (01224) 826591
- ✉ ronnie@royalaberdeengolf.com
- ✍ Ronnie Macaskill (Director of Golf)
- 🖥 www.royalaberdeengolf.com

### Westhill    (1977)
*Westhill Heights, Westhill AB32 6RY*
- ☎ **(01224) 742567**
- 🖳 (01224) 749124
- ✉ westhillgolf@btconnect.com
- ✍ George Bruce (Admin)
- 🖥 www.westhillgolfclub.co.uk

## Angus

### Arbroath    (1903)
**Public**
*Elliot by Arbroath DI1 2PT*
- ☎ **(01241) 872069**
- 🖳 (01241) 875837
- ✉ lindsay.ewart@btconnect.com
- ✍ J.Lindsay Ewart (PGA Qual. Pro)
- 🖥 www.arbroathgolfcourse.co.uk

### Ballumbie Castle    (2000)
*3 Old Quarry Road, Dundee DD4 0SY*
- ☎ **(01382) 770028**
- 🖳 (01382) 730008
- ✉ ballumbie2000@yahoo.com

&#9856; Stephen Harrod
&#9906; www.ballumbiecastlegolfclub.com

## Brechin (1893)
*Trinity, Brechin DD9 7PD*
&#9742; **(01356) 625270 (bookings/pro)**
&#9000; (01356) 625270
&#9993; brechingolfclub@tiscali.co.uk
&#9856; S Rennie (Manager)
&#9906; www.brechingolfclub.co.uk

## Caird Park (1926)
**Public**
*Mains Loan, Caird Park, Dundee DD4 9BX*
&#9742; **(01382) 453606/461460**
&#9000; (01382) 461460
&#9993; cp.golf.club@btconnect.com
&#9856; G Martin (07961) 159636

## Camperdown (1960)
**Public**
*Camperdown Park, Dundee DD2 4TF*
&#9742; **(01382) 623398**
&#9856; T Finegan (01382) 459524

## Downfield (1932)
*Turnberry Ave, Dundee DD2 3QP*
&#9742; **(01382) 825595**
&#9000; (01382) 813111
&#9993; downfieldgc@aol.com
&#9856; Mrs M Campbell
&#9906; www.downfieldgolf.co.uk

## Edzell (1895)
*High St, Edzell DD9 7TF*
&#9742; **(01356) 647283**
&#9000; (01356) 648094
&#9993; secretary@edzellgolfclub.com
&#9856; AA Turnbull
&#9906; www.edzellgolfclub.com

## Forfar (1871)
*Cunninghill, Arbroath Road, Forfar DD8 2RL*
&#9742; **(01307) 463773/462120**
&#9000; (01307) 468495
&#9993; info@forfargolfclub.co.uk
&#9856; S Wilson
&#9906; www.forfargolfclub.com

## Kirriemuir (1884)
*Shielhill Road, Northmuir, Kirriemuir DD8 4LN*
&#9742; **(01575) 573317**
&#9000; (01575) 575247
&#9993; enquiries@kirriemuirgolfclub.co.uk
&#9856; Charlie Gowrie
&#9906; www.kirriemuirgolfclub.co.uk

## Monifieth Golf Links
*Medal Starter's Box, Princes Street, Monifieth DD5 4AW*
&#9742; **(01382) 532767 (Bookings)**
&#9000; (01382) 535816
&#9993; secretary@monifiethlinks.com
&#9856; J Brodie (Managing Sec),
&#9906; www.monifiethgolf.co.uk

## Montrose Golf Links (1562)
**Public**
*Traill Drive, Montrose DD10 8SW*
&#9742; **(01674) 672932**
&#9000; (01674) 671800

&#9993; secretary@montroselinks.co.uk
&#9856; Miss Claire Penman
&#9906; www.montroselinks.co.uk

## Montrose Caledonia (1896)
**Club**
*Dorward Road, Montrose DD10 8SW*
&#9742; **(01674) 672313**
&#9856; Mrs S Burness (01674 672416)

## Panmure (1845)
*Burnside Road, Barry, Carnoustie DD7 7RT*
&#9742; **(01241) 855120**
&#9000; (01241) 859737
&#9993; secretary@panmuregolfclub.co.uk
&#9856; Ian W Gordon
&#9906; www.panmuregolfclub.co.uk

## Royal Montrose (1810)
**Club**
*Traill Drive, Montrose DD10 8SW*
&#9742; **(01674) 672376**
&#9993; secretary@royalmontrosegolf.com
&#9856; Michael Cummings
&#9906; www.royalmontrosegolf.com

### Carnoustie Clubs

## Carnoustie Caledonia (1887)
**Club**
*Links Parade, Carnoustie DD7 7JF*
&#9742; **(01241) 852115**
&#9856; R Reyner
&#9906; www.carnoustiecaledonia.co.uk

## Carnoustie Ladies (1873)
**Club**
*12 Links Parade, Carnoustie DD7 7JF*
&#9742; **(01241) 855252**
&#9856; Mrs JM Mitchell (01241) 855035

## Carnoustie Mercantile (1896)
**Club**
*Links Parade, Carnoustie DD7 7JE*
&#9856; GJA Murray (01241) 854420

## The Carnoustie Golf Club (1842)
**Club**
*3 Links Parade, Carnoustie DD7 7JF*
&#9742; **(01241) 852480**
&#9993; admin@carnoustiegolfclub.co.uk
&#9856; AJR MacKenzie
&#9906; www.carnoustiegolfclub.co.uk

### Carnoustie Courses

## Buddon Links (1981)
**Public**
*20 Links Parade, Carnoustie DD7 7JF*
&#9742; **(01241) 802270**
&#9000; (01241) 802271
&#9993; golf@carnoustiegolflinks.co.uk
&#9856; G Duncan
&#9906; www.carnoustiegolflinks.co.uk

## Burnside (1914)
**Public**
*20 Links Parade, Carnoustie DD7 7JF*
&#9742; **(01241) 802270**
&#9000; (01241) 802271

&#9993; golf@carnoustiegolflinks.co.uk
&#9856; G Duncan
&#9906; www.carnoustiegolflinks.co.uk

## Carnoustie Championship (1842)
**Public**
*20 Links Parade, Carnoustie DD7 7JF*
&#9742; **(01241) 802270**
&#9000; (01241) 802271
&#9993; golf@carnoustiegolflinks.co.uk
&#9856; G Duncan
&#9906; www.carnoustiegolflinks.co.uk

## Argyll & Bute

## Blairmore & Strone (1896)
*High Road, Strone, Dunoon PA23 8TH*
&#9742; **(01369) 840676**
&#9993; thompsongg@talk21.com
&#9856; Graham Thompson
(01369) 840208
&#9906; www.blairmoregc.co.uk

## Bute (1888)
*32 Marine Place, Ardbeg, Rothesay, Isle of Bute PA20 0LF*
&#9742; **(01700) 503091**
&#9993; administrator@butegolfclub.com
&#9856; F Robinson (01700) 503091
&#9906; www.butegolfclub.com

## Carradale (1906)
*Airds, Carradale, Campbeltown PA28 6RY*
&#9742; **(01583) 431788**
&#9993; margaretrichardson1977
@live.co.uk
info@carradalegolf.com
&#9856; Margaret Richardson (Sec)
&#9906; www.carradalegolf.

## Colonsay
**Owned privately**
*Isle of Colonsay PA61 7YR*
&#9742; **(01951) 200200**
&#9000; (01951) 200290
&#9856; Eleanor McNeill (01951) 200210

## Cowal (1891)
*Ardenslate Road, Dunoon PA23 8LT*
&#9742; **(01369) 705673**
&#9000; (01369) 705673
&#9993; secretary@cowalgolfclub.com
&#9856; A Douglas (01369) 705673
&#9906; www.cowalgolfclub.com

## Craignure (1895)
*Scallastle, Craignure, Isle of Mull PA65 6BA*
&#9742; **(01688) 302517**
&#9993; info@craignuregolfclub.co.uk
&#9856; PA Vanniekerk
&#9906; www.craignuregolfclub.co.uk

## Dalmally (1986)
*Old Saw Mill, Dalmally PA33 1AE*
&#9742; **(01838) 200619**
&#9993; dalmallygolfclub@btinternet.com
&#9856; S Tollan (01631) 710401
&#9906; www.dalmallygolfclub.co.uk

## Dunaverty    (1889)
*Southend, Campbeltown PA28 6RW*
☎ **(01586) 830677**
🖷 (01586) 830677
✉ dunavertygc@aol.com
✍ Bill Brannigan
🖥 www.dunavertygolfclub.com

## Gigha    (1992)
**Pay and play**
*Isle of Gigha, Kintyre PA41 7AA*
☎ **(01583) 505242**
✉ johngigha@hotmail.co.uk
✍ J Bannatyne
🖥 www.gigha.org

## Glencruitten    (1908)
*Glencruitten Road, Oban PA34 4PU*
☎ **(01631) 562868**
✉ enquiries@obangolf.com
✍ David Finlayson (01631) 566186
🖥 www.obangolf.com

## Helensburgh    (1893)
*25 East Abercromby Street, Helensburgh G84 9HZ*
☎ **(01436) 674173**
🖷 (01436) 671170
✉ secretary@helensburghgolfclub
   .co.uk
✍ Martyn Lawrie (Gen
   Mgr) (01436) 674173
🖥 www.helensburghgolfclub.co.uk

## Innellan    (1891)
*Knockamillie Road, Innellan, Dunoon*
☎ **(01369) 830242**
✉ innellangolfclub@btconnect.com
✍ R Milliken (01369) 830415

## Inveraray    (1893)
*North Cromalt, Inveraray, Argyll*
☎ **(01499) 600286**
✍ D MacNeill

## Islay    (1891)
*25 Charlotte St, Port Ellen, Isle of Islay PA42 7DF*
☎ **(01496) 300094**
✍ T Dunn
🖥 www.islay.golf.btinternet.co.uk

## Kyles of Bute    (1906)
*The Moss, Kames, Tighnabruaich PA21 2AB*
✍ Dr J Thomson 01700 811 603
🖥 www.kylesofbutegolfclub.co.uk

## Lochgilphead    (1963)
*Blarbuie Road, Lochgilphead PA31 8LE*
☎ **(01546) 602340**
✍ Bill Dick
🖥 www.lochgilphead-golf.com

## Lochgoilhead    (1994)
**Public**
*Drimsynie Estate, Lochgoilhead PA24 8AD*
☎ **(01301) 703247**
🖷 (01301) 703538
✉ info@argyllholidays.com
✍ Colin Park
🖥 www.argyllholidays.com

## Machrihanish    (1876)
*Machrihanish, Campbeltown PA28 6PT*
☎ **(01586) 810213**
🖷 (01586) 810221
✉ secretary@machgolf.com
✍ Mrs A Anderson
🖥 www.machgolf.com

## Millport    (1888)
*Millport, Isle of Cumbrae KA28 0HB*
☎ **(01475) 530311**
✉ secretary@millportgolfclub.co.uk
✍ William Reid (01475) 530306
🖥 www.millportgolfclub.co.uk

## Port Bannatyne    (1912)
*Bannatyne Mains Road, Port Bannatyne, Isle of Bute PA20 0PH*
☎ **(01700) 504544**
✍ R Jardine (01700) 500195
🖥 www.portbannatynegolf.co.uk

## Rothesay    (1892)
*Canada Hill, Rothesay, Isle of Bute PA20 9HN*
☎ **(01700) 503554**
✉ rothesaygolfclub@btconnect.com
✍ Joan Torrence
🖥 www.rothesaygolfclub.com

## Tarbert    (1910)
*Kilberry Road, Tarbert PA29 6XX*
☎ **(01880) 820565**
✍ P Cupples (01546) 606896

## Taynuilt    (1987)
*Golf Club House, Taynuilt, Argyll PA35 1JH*
☎ **(01866) 822429**
🖷 (01866) 822255 (phone first)
✉ secretary@taynuiltgolfclub.com
✍ J J Church (01631) 770 633
🖥 www.taynuiltgolfclub.co.uk

## Tobermory    (1896)
*Erray Road, Tobermory, Isle of Mull PA75 6PS*
☎ **(01688) 302387**
🖷 (01688) 302140
✉ secretary@tobermorygolfclub.com
✍ M Campbell (01688) 302743
🖥 www.tobermorygolfclub.com

---

# Ayrshire

## Annanhill    (1957)
**Public**
*Irvine Road, Kilmarnock KA1 2RT*
☎ **(01563) 521512 (Starter)**
✉ annanhillgolfclub@btconnect.com
✍ T Denham (01563) 521644/525557
🖥 www.annanhillgc.co.uk

## Ardeer    (1880)
*Greenhead Avenue, Stevenston KA20 4LB*
☎ **(01294) 464542**
🖷 (01294) 464542
✉ info@ardeergolfclub.co.uk
✍ John Boyle (01294) 464542
🖥 www.ardeergolfclub.co.uk

## Ayr Seafield    (1930)
**Public**
*Belleisle Park, Doonfoot Road, Ayr KA7 4DU*
☎ **(01292) 441258**
🖷 (01292) 442632
✉ secretary@ayrseafieldgolfclub.com
✍ Brian Milligan (01292) 445144
🖥 www.ayrseafieldgolfclub.com

## Ballochmyle    (1937)
*Ballochmyle, Mauchline KA5 6LE*
☎ **(01290) 550469**
✉ ballochmylegolf@btconnect.com
✍ J Davidson
🖥 www.ballochmylegolfclub.co.uk

## Beith    (1896)
*Threepwood Road, Beith KA15 2JR*
☎ **(01505) 503166 (Clubhouse)**
✍ Joe McSorley (Captain)
🖥 www.beithgolfclub.co.uk

## Brodick    (1897)
*Brodick, Isle of Arran KA27 8DL*
☎ **(01770) 302349**
🖷 (01770) 302349
✉ enquiries@brodickgolf.com
✍ Ann Hart (Sec)
🖥 www.brodickgolfclub.com

## Brunston Castle    (1992)
*Golf Course Road, Dailly, Girvan KA26 9GD*
☎ **(01465) 811471**
🖷 (01465) 811545
✉ golf@brunstoncastle.co.uk
✍ M Edens
🖥 www.brunstoncastle.co.uk

## Caprington    (1958)
**Public**
*Ayr Road, Kilmarnock KA1 4UW*
☎ **(01563) 53702 (Club)**
✉ caprington.golf@btconnect.com
✍ Michael McDonnell
   Mob 0791 564 8834

## Corrie    (1892)
*Corrie, Sannox, Isle of Arran KA27 8JD*
☎ **(01770) 810223/810606**
✍ George E Welford (01770) 600403
🖥 www.corriegolf.com

## Dalmilling    (1961)
**Public**
*Westwood Avenue, Ayr KA8 0QY*
☎ **(01292) 263893**
🖷 (01292) 610543
✍ G Campbell (01292) 521351

## Doon Valley    (1927)
*1 Hillside, Patna, Ayr KA6 7JT*
☎ **(01292) 531607**
🖷 (01292) 532489
✍ H Johnstone

## Dundonald Links    (2003)
**Pay and play**
*Ayr Road, Gailes, Ayrshire KA11 5BF*
☎ **(01294) 314000**
🖷 (01294) 314001
✉ reservations@dundonaldlinks.com
✍ Guy Redford
🖥 www.dundonaldlinks.com

## Girvan (1860)
Public
Golf Course Road, Girvan KA26 9HW
☎ (01465) 714272/714346
(Starter)
🖳 (01465) 714346
✍ WB Tait

## Glasgow GC Gailes Links
(1892)
Gailes, Irvine KA11 5AE
☎ (01294) 311258
🖳 (01294) 279366
✉ secretary@glasgowgolfclub.com
✍ AG McMillan (0141) 942 2011
🖥 www.gaileslinks.com

## Irvine (1887)
Bogside, Irvine KA8 8SN
☎ (01294) 275979
🖳 (01294) 278209
✉ secretary@theirvinegolfclub.co.uk
✍ W McMahon
🖥 www.theirvinegolfclub.co.uk

## Irvine Ravenspark (1907)
Public
Kidsneuk Lane, Irvine KA12 8SR
☎ (01294) 271293
✉ secretary@irgc.co.uk
✍ T McFarlane (01294) 213537
🖥 www.irgc.co.uk

## Kilbirnie Place (1925)
Largs Road, Kilbirnie KA25 7AT
☎ (01505) 683398
🖳 01505 684444
✉ kilbirnie.golfclub@tiscali.co.uk
✍ Mr J Melvin
🖥 www.kilbirnieplacegolfclub.webs
.com

## Kilmarnock (Barassie) (1887)
29 Hillhouse Road, Barassie, Troon
KA10 6SY
☎ (01292) 313920/311077
🖳 (01292) 318300
✉ golf@kbgc.co.uk
✍ D Wilson (01292) 313920
🖥 www.kbgc.co.uk

## Lamlash (1889)
Lamlash, Isle of Arran KA27 8JU
☎ (01770) 600296 (Clubhouse)

✉ lamlashgolfclub@btconnect.com
✍ D Bilsland
🖥 www.lamlashgolfclub.co.uk

## Largs (1891)
Irvine Road, Largs KA30 8EU
☎ (01475) 673594
(Secretary's office)
🖳 (01475) 673594
✉ secretary@largsgolfclub.co.uk
✍ Barry Streets
🖥 www.largsgolfclub.co.uk

## Lochranza Golf Course (1899)
Pay and play
Lochranza, Isle of Arran KA27 8HL
☎ (0177083) 0273
✉ office@lochgolf.demon.co.uk
✍ N Wells
🖥 www.lochranzagolf.com

## Loudoun Gowf (1909)
Galston KA4 8PA
☎ (01563) 821993
🖳 (01563) 820011
✉ secy@loudoungowfclub.co.uk
✍ WB Buchanan
🖥 www.loudoungowfclub.co.uk

## Machrie Bay (1900)
Pay and play
Machrie Bay, Brodick, Isle of Arran
KA27 8DZ
☎ (01770) 840310
✉ machriebayclubsec@googlemail
.com
✍ E Ross
🖥 www.machriebay.com

## Muirkirk (1991)
Pay and play
c/o 65 Main Street, Muirkirk KA18 3QR
☎ (01290) 660184 (night)
✍ R Bradford

## New Cumnock (1902)
Lochill, Cumnock Road, New Cumnock
KA18 4BQ
☎ (01290) 332761
✍ J McGinn

## Prestwick (1851)
2 Links Road, Prestwick KA9 1QG
☎ (01292) 477404
🖳 (01292) 477255

✉ bookings@prestwickgc.co.uk
✍ K W Goodwin
🖥 www.prestwickgc.co.uk

## Prestwick St Cuthbert
(1899)
East Road, Prestwick KA9 2SX
☎ (01292) 477101
🖳 (01292) 671730
✉ secretary@stcuthbert.co.uk
✍ Jim Jess
🖥 www.stcuthbert.co.uk

## Prestwick St Nicholas
(1851)
Grangemuir Road, Prestwick KA9 1SN
☎ (01292) 477608
🖳 (01292) 473900
✉ secretary@prestwickstnicholas
.com
✍ Eddie Prentice
🖥 www.prestwickstnicholas.com

## Routenburn (1914)
Routenburn Road, Largs KA30 8QS
☎ (01475) 686475
Steward/Clubhouse
✍ RB Connal (01475) 672757

## Royal Troon (1878)
Craigend Road, Troon KA10 6EP
☎ (01292) 311555
🖳 (01292) 318204
✉ secretary@royaltroon.com
✍ D L K Brown (Sec) (01292) 310060
🖥 www.royaltroon.com

## Shiskine (1896)
Shiskine, Blackwaterfoot, Isle of Arran
KA27 8HA
☎ (01770) 860226
🖳 (01770) 860205
✉ info@shiskinegolf.com
✍ Pietre Johnston
🖥 www.shiskinegolf.com

## Skelmorlie (1891)
Skelmorlie PA17 5ES
☎ (01475) 520152
✉ sec@skelmorliegolf.co.uk
✍ Mrs Shelagh Travers (Hon)
🖥 www.skelmorliegolf.co.uk

---

# The Edward Trophy

The Edward family, well-known Glasgow jewellers, presented the trophy in 1892 for all amateurs whose handicaps did not exceed three and who were members of any club in membership with the Scottish Golf Union in the counties of Lanark, Ayrshire, Dunbarton. Stirling, Renfrew, Argyll, Bute and Glasgow. The event was, therefore, originally created as a competition for West of Scotland golfers.

Until 1927 it was played over 36 holes at various venues but the Edward family asked Glasgow Golf Club if they would consider playing it annually on the club's course at Gailes in Ayrshire. The club agreed and so the event has been played at Gailes every year since.

William Tulloch's feat of winning the trophy five times in the 1920s and 30s has not been equalled. In 2008, it became an SGU Order of Merit event over 72 holes.

## Troon Municipal
**Public**
*Harling Drive, Troon KA10 6NF*
- ☎ **(01292) 312464**
- 📠 (01292) 312578

## Troon Portland   (1894)
**Club**
*1 Crosbie Road, Troon  KA10*
- ☎ **(01292) 313488**
- ✍ R McEwan (01292) 313602

## Troon St Meddans   (1909)
**Club**
*Harling Drive, Troon KA10 6NF*
- ✉ secretary@troonstmeddansgolfclub .com
- ✍ Jim Pennington (01563) 851339

## Turnberry Hotel   (1906)
*Turnberry KA26 9LT*
- ☎ **(01655) 331000**
- 📠 (01655) 331069
- ✉ turnberry@luxurycollection.com
- ✍ Richard Hall (Head golf Proff)
- 🖥 www.westin.com/turnberry

## West Kilbride   (1893)
*33-35 Fullerton Drive, Seamill, West Kilbride KA23 9HT*
- ☎ **(01294) 823911**
- 📠 (01294) 829573
- ✉ golf@westkilbridegolfclub.com
- ✍ Gordon Clark
- 🖥 www.westkilbridegolfclub.com

## Western Gailes   (1897)
*Gailes, Irvine KA11 5AE*
- ☎ **(01294) 311649**
- 📠 (01294) 312312
- ✉ enquiries@westerngailes.com
- ✍ Jerry Kessell
- 🖥 www.westerngailes.com

## Whiting Bay   (1895)
*Golf Course Road, Whiting Bay, Isle of Arran KA27 8QT*
- ☎ **(01770) 700487**
- ✉ info@whitingbaygolf.com
- ✍ Mr Richard Fletcher (Hon Sec)
- 🖥 www.whitingbaygolf.com

## Borders

## Duns   (1894)
*Hardens Road, Duns TD11 3NR*
- ☎ **(01361) 882194**
- ✉ secretary@dunsgolfclub.com
- ✍ G Clark (01361) 883599
- 🖥 www.dunsgolfclub.com

## Eyemouth   (1894)
*Gunsgreen House, Eyemouth TD14 5DX*
- ☎ **(018907) 50551 (Clubhouse)**
- ✍ M Gibson (018907) 50004

## Galashiels   (1884)
*Ladhope Recreation Ground, Galashiels TD1 2NJ*
- ☎ **(01896) 753724**
- ✉ secretary@galashiels-golfclub.co.uk

- ✍ R Gass (01896) 755307
- 🖥 www.galashiels-golfclub.co.uk

## Hawick   (1877)
*Vertish Hill, Hawick TD9 0NY*
- ☎ **(01450) 372293**
- 📠 (01450) 372293
- ✉ reillyjh@aol.com
- ✍ J Reilly
- 🖥 www.hawickgolfclub.com

## The Hirsel   (1948)
*Kelso Road, Coldstream TD12 4NJ*
- ☎ **(01890) 882678**
- 📠 (01890) 882233
- ✉ info@hirselgc.co.uk
- ✍ Mr Allan Rodger
- 🖥 www.hirselgc.co.uk

## Jedburgh   (1892)
*Dunion Road, Jedburgh TD8 6TA*
- ☎ **(01835) 863587**
- ✉ info@jedburghgolfclub.co.uk
- ✍ R Nagle (01835) 866271
- 🖥 www.jedburghgolfclub.co.uk

## Kelso   (1887)
*Golf Course Road, Kelso TD5 7SL*
- ☎ **(01573) 223009**
- 📠 (01573) 228490
- ✉ secretary@kelsogolfclub.com
- ✍ DR Jack
- 🖥 www.kelsogolfclub.com

## Langholm   (1892)
*Langholm DG13 0JR*
- ☎ **(07724) 875151**
- ✉ golf@langholmgolfclub.co.uk
- ✍ Pauline Irving
- 🖥 www.langholmgolfclub.co.uk

## Lauder   (1896)
**Pay and play**
*Galashiels Road, Lauder TD2 6RS*
- ☎ **(01578) 722526**
- 📠 (01578) 722526
- ✉ secretary@laudergolfclub.co.uk
- ✍ R Towers (01578) 722240
- 🖥 www.laudergolfclub.co.uk

## Melrose   (1880)
*Dingleton Road, Melrose TD6 9HS*
- ☎ **(01896) 822855**
- 📠 (01896) 822855
- ✉ info@melrosegolfcourse.co.uk
- ✍ LM Wallace (01835) 823553
- 🖥 www.melrosegolfcourse.co.uk

## Minto   (1928)
*Denholm, Hawick TD9 8SH*
- ☎ **(01450) 870220**
- 📠 (01450) 870126
- ✉ mintogolfclub@btconnect.com
- ✍ J Simpson
- 🖥 www.mintogolf.co.uk

## Newcastleton   (1894)
**Pay and play**
*Holm Hill, Newcastleton TD9 0QD*
- ☎ **(013873) 75608**
- ✍ GA Wilson

## Peebles   (1892)
*Kirkland Street, Peebles EH45 8EU*
- ☎ **(01721) 720197**
- ✉ secretary@peeblesgolfclub.com
- ✍ William Baird (Administrator)
- 🖥 www.peeblesgolfclub.com

## The Roxburghe Hotel & Golf Course   (1997)
**Proprietary**
*Heiton, Kelso TD5 8JZ*
- ☎ **(01573) 450333**
- 📠 (01573) 450611
- ✉ golf@roxburghe.net
- ✍ Craig Montgomerie (Director of Golf)
- 🖥 www.roxburghegolfclub.co.uk

## Selkirk   (1883)
*The Hill, Selkirk TD7 4NW*
- ☎ **(01750) 20621**
- ✉ secretary@selkirkgolfclub.co.uk
- ✍ A Robertson (01750) 20519 (pm)
- 🖥 www.selkirkgolfclub.co.uk

## St Boswells   (1899)
*Braeheads, St Boswells, Melrose TD6 0DE*
- ☎ **(01835) 823527**
- ✉ secretary@stboswellsgolfclub.co.uk
- ✍ Sue Brooks (Secretary)
- 🖥 www.stboswellsgolfclub.co.uk

## Torwoodlee   (1895)
*Edinburgh Road, Galashiels, Torwoodlee TD1 2NE*
- ☎ **(01896) 752260**
- ✉ torwoodleegolfclub @torwoodleegolfclub.com
- ✍ Stan Irvine (Sec)
- 🖥 www.torwoodleegolfclub.co.uk

## West Linton   (1890)
*Medwyn Road, West Linton EH46 7HN*
- ☎ **(01968) 660970**
- 📠 (01968) 660622
- ✉ secretarywlgc@btinternet.com
- ✍ John Johnson (01968) 661121
- 🖥 www.wlgc.co.uk

## Woll Golf Course   (1993)
**Proprietary**
*New Woll Estate, Ashkirk, Selkirkshire TD7 4PE*
- ☎ **(01750) 32711**
- ✉ wollgolf@tiscali.co.uk
- ✍ Nicholas Brown (01750) 32711
- 🖥 www.wollgolf.co.uk

## Clackmannanshire

## Alloa   (1891)
*Schawpark, Sauchie, Alloa FK10 3AX*
- ☎ **(01259) 722745**
- 📠 (01259) 218796
- ✉ secretary@alloagolfclub.co.uk
- ✍ Secretary
- 🖥 www.alloagolfclub.co.uk

## Alva
*Beauclerc Street, Alva FK12 5LH*
- ☎ **(01259) 760431**

## Braehead (1891)
Cambus, Alloa FK10 2NT
- ☎ (01259) 725766
- ⬛ (01259) 214070
- ✉ enquiries@braeheadgolfclub.co.uk
- ✍ Gus Ferguson
- 🖥 www.braeheadgolfclub.com

## Dollar (1890)
Brewlands House, Dollar FK14 7EA
- ☎ (01259) 742400
- ⬛ (01259) 743497
- ✉ info@dollargolfclub.com
- ✍ W D Carln
- 🖥 www.dollargolfclub.com

## Tillicoultry (1899)
Alva Road, Tillicoultry FK13 6BL
- ☎ (01259) 750124
- ⬛ (01259) 750124
- ✉ tillygolf@btconnect.com
- ✍ M Todd
- 🖥 www.tillygc.co.uk

## Tulliallan (1902)
Kincardine, Alloa FK10 4BB
- ☎ (01259) 730396
- ⬛ (01259) 731395
- ✉ tulliallangolf@btconnect.com
- ✍ Amanda Maley
- 🖥 www.tulliallangolf.co.uk

# Dumfries & Galloway

## Brighouse Bay (1999)
Pay and play
Borgue, Kirkcudbright DG6 4TS
- ☎ (01557) 870509
- ⬛ (01557) 870409
- ✉ enquiries@brighousebay-golfclub.co.uk
- ✍ E Diamond (01557) 870509
- 🖥 www.brighousebay-golfclub.co.uk

## Castle Douglas (1905)
Abercromby Road, Castle Douglas DG7 1BA
- ☎ (01556) 502801
- ✉ cdgolfclub@aol.com
- ✍ J Duguid (01556) 503527
- 🖥 www.cdgolf.co.uk

## Colvend (1905)
Sandyhills, Dalbeattie DG5 4PY
- ☎ (01556) 630398
- ✉ secretary@colvendgolfclub.co.uk
- ✍ R N Bailey
- ⊕ For Tee times and catering email
  steward@colvendgolfclub.co.uk
- 🖥 www.colvendgolfclub.co.uk

## Crichton Golf Club (1884)
Public/Private
Bankend Road, Dumfries DG1 4TH
- ☎ (01387) 254946 or
  (07770) 553320
- ✉ crichtongolf@hotmail.co.uk
- ✍ Lee Sterritt (Match Sec)
- 🖥 www.crichtongolfclub.limewebs.com

## Dalbeattie (1894)
Maxwell Park, Dalbeattie DG5 4JR
- ☎ (01556) 611421
- ✉ steveandpen@btinternet.com
- ✍ Mrs P Smith
- 🖥 www.dalbeattiegc.co.uk

## Dumfries & County (1912)
Nunfield, Edinburgh Road, Dumfries
DG1 1JX
- ☎ (01387) 253585
- ⬛ (01387) 253585
- ✉ admin@thecounty.co.uk
- ✍ Vivien Tipping (Asst Sec)
- 🖥 www.thecounty.org.uk

## Dumfries & Galloway (1880)
2 Laurieston Avenue, Maxwelltown,
Dumfries DG2 7NY
- ☎ (01387) 253582
- ⬛ (01387) 263848
- ✉ info@dandggolfclub.co.uk
- ✍ Joe Fergusson
  (Professional) (01387) 256902
- 🖥 www.dandggolfclub.com

## Gatehouse (1921)
Lauriston Road, Gatehouse of Fleet, Castle
Douglas DG7 2BE
- ☎ (01557) 814766
  (Clubhouse – unmanned)
- ✉ info@gatehousegolfclub.com
- ✍ M Ashmore (01559) 814884
- 🖥 www.gatehousegolfclub.com

## Hoddom Castle (1973)
Pay and play
Hoddom Bridge, Ecclefechan DG11 1AS
- ☎ (01576) 300251
- ⬛ (01576) 300757
- ✉ hoddomcastle@aol.com
- ✍ G Condron
- 🖥 www.hoddomcastle.co.uk

## Kirkcudbright (1893)
Stirling Crescent, Kirkcudbright DG6 4EZ
- ☎ (01557) 330314
- ⬛ (01557) 330314
- ✉ info@kirkcudbrightgolf.co.uk
- ✍ Bill Roff (Captain)
- 🖥 www.kirkcudbrightgolf.com

## Lochmaben (1926)
Castlehill Gate, Lochmaben DG11 1NT
- ☎ (01387) 810552
- ✉ enquiries@lochmabengolf.co.uk
- ✍ JM Dickie (Sec)
- 🖥 www.lochmabengolf.co.uk

## Lockerbie (1889)
Corrie Road, Lockerbie DG11 2ND
- ☎ (01576) 203363
- ⬛ (01576) 203363
- ✉ enquiries@lockerbiegolf.co.uk
- ✍ Gillian Shanks
- 🖥 www.lockerbiegolf.co.uk

## Moffat (1884)
Coatshill, Moffat DG10 9SB
- ☎ (01683) 220020
- ✉ bookings@moffatgolfclub.co.uk
- ✍ Club Manager (01683) 220020
- 🖥 www.moffatgolfclub.co.uk

## New Galloway (1902)
New Galloway, Dumfries DG7 3RN
- ☎ (01644) 420737
- ✉ brown@nggc.co.uk
- ✍ Ian Brown
- 🖥 www.nggc.co.uk

## Newton Stewart (1981)
Kirroughtree Avenue, Minnigaff, Newton
Stewart DG8 6PF
- ☎ (01671) 402172
- ✉ newtonstewartgc@btconnect.com
- ✍ Russell McClymont (Hon Sec)
- 🖥 www.newtonstewartgolfclub.com

## Dumfriesshire Golf Academy – Pines Golf Centre (1998)
Pay and play
Lockerbie Road, Dumfries DG1 3PF
- ☎ (01387) 247444
- ⬛ (01387) 249600
- ✉ info@dumfriesshiregolfcentre.com
- ✍ B Macleod
- 🖥 www.dumfriesgolf.com

## Portpatrick (1903)
Golf Course Road, Portpatrick DG9 8TB
- ☎ (01776) 810273
- ⬛ (01776) 810811
- ✉ enquiries@portpatrickgolfclub.com
- ✍ James Gaffney (Mgr)
- 🖥 www.portpatrickgolfclub.com

## Powfoot (1903)
Cummertrees, Annan DG12 5QE
- ☎ (01461) 204100
- ⬛ (01461) 204111
- ✉ info@powfootgolfclub.com
- ✍ SR Gardner (Mgr)
- 🖥 www.powfootgolfclub.com

## Sanquhar (1894)
Blackaddie Road, Sanquhar, Dumfries
DG4 6JZ
- ☎ (01659) 50577
- ✉ tich@rossirene.fsnet.co.uk
- ✍ Ian Macfarlane
- 🖥 www.scottishgolf.com

## Southerness (1947)
Southerness, Dumfries DG2 8AZ
- ☎ (01387) 880677
- ⬛ (01387) 880471
- ✉ southerness@btconnect.com
- ✍ R G Blar (Hon Sec)
- 🖥 www.southernessgolfclub.com

## St Medan (1904)
Monreith, Newton Stewart DG8 8NJ
- ☎ (01988) 700358
- ✉ mail@stmedangolfclub.com
- ✍ William G McKeand
  (01988) 700804
- 🖥 www.stmedangolfclub.com

## Stranraer (1905)
Creachmore, Leswalt, Stranraer DG9 0LF
- ☎ (01776) 870245
- ⬛ (01776) 870445
- ✉ stranraergolf@btclick.com
- ✍ J Burns
- 🖥 www.stranraergolfclub.net

## Thornhill   (1893)
*Blacknest, Thornhill DG3 5DW*
☎ **(01848) 330546 (clubhouse)/**
     **331779 (office)**
✉ info@thornhillgolfclub.co.uk
✍ A Hillier (Administrator)
🖥 www.thornhillgolfclub.co.uk

## Wigtown & Bladnoch   (1960)
*Lightlands Terrace, Wigtown DG8 9DY*
☎ **(01988) 403354**
✍ IM Thin

## Wigtownshire County   (1894)
*Mains of Park, Glenluce, Newton Stewart
DG8 0NN*
☎ **(01581) 300420**
🖳 (01581) 300420
✉ enquiries
     @wigtownshirecountygolfclub.com
✍ Mr Jimmy Caldwell (Steward)
🖥 www.wigtownshirecountygolfclub
     .com

## Dunbartonshire

## Balmore   (1894)
*Balmore, Torrance G64 4AW*
☎ **(01360) 620284**
🖳 (01360) 622742
✉ balmoregolf@btconnect.com
✍ Karen Dyer (01360) 620284
🖥 www.balmoregolfclub.co.uk

## Bearsden   (1891)
*Thorn Road, Bearsden, Glasgow G61 4BP*
☎ **(0141) 586 5300**
🖳 (0141) 586 5300
✉ secretary@bearsdengolfclub.com
✍ Alan Harris
🖥 www.bearsdengolfclub.com

## Cardross   (1895)
*Main Road, Cardross, Dumbarton G82 5LB*
☎ **(01389) 841213 (Clubhouse)**
🖳 (01389) 842162
✉ golf@cardross.com
✍ G A Mill (01389) 841754
🖥 www.cardross.com

## Clober   (1951)
*Craigton Road, Milngavie, Glasgow G62 7HP*
☎ **(0141) 956 1685**
✉ clobergolfclub@gmail.com
✍ Gary McFarlane
🖥 www.clobergolfclub.co.uk

## Clydebank & District   (1905)
*Glasgow Road, Hardgate, Clydebank
G81 5QY*
☎ **(01389) 383831**
🖳 (01389) 383831
✉ admin@clydebankanddistrictgolfclub
     .co.uk
✍ Miss M Higgins
🖥 www.clydebankanddistrictgolfclub
     .co.uk

## Clydebank Overtoun   (1927)
**Public**
*Overtoun Road, Dalmuir, Clydebank G81 3RE*
☎ **(0141) 952 2070 (Clubhouse)**
✍ Jim Woolfries (01389) 876869

## Dougalston   (1977)
*Strathblane Road, Milngavie, Glasgow
G62 8HJ*
☎ **(0141) 955 2400**
🖳 (0141) 955 2406
✉ secretary.esportadougalstongc
     @hotmail.co.uk
✍ Mr S Gilbey
🖥 www.esporta.com

## Douglas Park   (1897)
*Hillfoot, Bearsden, Glasgow G61 2TJ*
☎ **(0141) 942 2220 (Clubhouse)**
🖳 (0141) 942 0985
✉ secretary@douglasparkgolfclub
     .co.uk
✍ Christine Scott (0141) 942 0985
🖥 www.douglasparkgolfclub.co.uk

## Dullatur   (1896)
*1a Glendouglas Drive, Craigmarloch,
Cumbernauld G68 0DW*
☎ **(01236) 723230**
🖳 (01236) 727271
✉ generalmanager@dullaturgolf.com
✍ John Bryceland B.E.M
     (01236) 723230
🖥 www.dullaturgolf.com

## Dumbarton   (1888)
*Broadmeadow, Dumbarton G82 2BQ*
☎ **(01389) 765995**
✉ secretary@dumbartongolfclub.co.uk
✍ M Buchanan
🖥 www.dumbartongolfclub.co.uk

## Hayston   (1926)
*Campsie Road, Kirkintilloch, Glasgow
G66 1RN*
☎ **(0141) 775 0723**
🖳 (0141) 776 9030
✉ secretary@haystongolf.com
✍ Jim Smart
🖥 www.haystongolf.com

## Hilton Park   (1927)
*Auldmarroch Estate, Stockiemuir Road,
Milngavie G62 7HB*
☎ **(0141) 956 4657**
🖳 (0141) 956 1215
✉ office@hiltonpark.co.uk
✍ Mr Craig Bell
🖥 www.hiltonpark.co.uk

## Kirkintilloch   (1895)
*Todhill, Campsie Road, Kirkintilloch
G66 1RN*
☎ **(0141) 776 1256**
🖳 (0141) 775 2424
✉ secretary@kirkintillochgolfclub
     .co.uk
✍ T Cummings (0141) 775 2387
🖥 www.kirkintillochgolfclub.co.uk

## Lenzie   (1889)
*19 Crosshill Road, Lenzie G66 5DA*
☎ **(0141) 776 1535**
🖳 (0141) 777 7748
✉ club-secretary@ntlbusiness.com
✍ Roy McKee (0141) 776 1535
🖥 www.lenziegolfclub.co.uk

## Loch Lomond   (1994)
*Rossdhu House, Luss G83 8NT*
☎ **(01436) 655555**
🖳 (01436) 655500
✉ info@lochlomond.com
✍ Bill Donald (Gen Mgr)
🖥 www.lochlomond.com

## Milngavie   (1895)
*Laighpark, Milngavie, Glasgow G62 8EP*
☎ **(0141) 956 1619**
🖳 (0141) 956 4252
✉ secretary@milngaviegolfclub.co.uk
✍ S Woods
🖥 www.milngaviegolfclub.com

## Palacerigg   (1975)
**Public**
*Palacerigg Country Park, Cumbernauld
G67 3HU*
☎ **(01236) 734969**
🖳 (01236) 721461
✉ palacerigg.golfclub@lineone.net
✍ P O'Hara
🖥 www.palacerigg.co.uk

## Ross Priory   (1978)
**Proprietary**
*Ross Loan, Gartocharn, Alexandria
G83 8NL*
☎ **(01389) 830398**
🖳 (01389) 830357
✉ ross.priory@strath.ac.uk
✍ R Cook 0141 548 2960
🖥 www.strath.ac.uk/rosspriory/golf

## Vale of Leven   (1907)
*Northfield Road, Bonhill, Alexandria
G83 9ET*
☎ **(01389) 752351**
🖳 (01389) 758866
✉ rbarclay@volgc.org
✍ R Barclay
🖥 www.volgc.org

## Westerwood Hotel G&CC
(1989)
**Pay and play**
*St Andrews Drive, Cumbernauld G68 0EW*
☎ **(01236) 725281**
🖳 (01236) 738478
✉ westerwoodgolf@qhotels.co.uk
✍ Iain Baird
🖥 www.qhotels.co.uk

## Windyhill   (1908)
*Baljaffray Road, Bearsden G61 4QQ*
☎ **(0141) 942 2349**
🖳 (0141) 942 5874
✉ secretary@windyhill.co.uk
✍ Chris Duffy (PGA Pro)
🖥 www.windyhillgolfclub.co.uk

## Fife

## Aberdour   (1896)
*Seaside Place, Aberdour KY3 0TX*
☎ **(01383) 860256**
🖳 (01383) 860050
✉ manager@aberdourgolfclub.co.uk

✍ Jane Cuthill
🖥 www.aberdourgolfclub.co.uk

## Anstruther (1890)
*Marsfield Shore Road, Anstruther KY10 3DZ*
☎ (01333) 310956
🖥 (01333) 310956
✉ secretary@anstruthergolf.co.uk
✍ D Malden
🖥 www.anstruthergolf.co.uk

## Auchterderran (1904)
**Public**
*Woodend Road, Cardenden KY5 0NH*
☎ (01592) 721579
✍ C Taylor (01592) 720080

## Balbirnie Park (1983)
*Balbirnie Park, Markinch, Fife KY7 6NR*
☎ (01592) 612095
🖥 (01592) 612383
✉ administrator@balbirniegolf.com
✍ J Donnelly (Club Sec)
🖥 www.balbirniegolf.com

## Ballingry (1981)
**Pay and play**
*Lochore Meadows Country Park, Crosshill, Lochgelly KY5 8BA*
☎ (01592) 860086
✉ terryir@hotmail.co.uk
✍ Terry Ironside

## Burntisland (1797)
**Club**
*51 Craigkennochie Terrace, Burntisland KY3 9EN*
☎ (01592) 872728
✉ bgc1797@gmail.com
✍ AD McPherson
🖥 www.burntislandgolfclub.co.uk

## Burntisland Golf House Club
(1898)
*Dodhead, Kircaldy Road, Burntisland KY3 9LQ*
☎ (01592) 874093
✉ info@burntislandgolfhouseclub .co.uk
✍ Administration (01592) 874093 Ext 4
🖥 www.burntislandgolfhouseclub .co.uk

## Canmore (1897)
*Venturefair Avenue, Dunfermline KY12 0PE*
☎ (01383) 724969
✉ canmoregolfclub@btconnect.com
✍ D Maccallum (Sec)
🖥 www.canmoregolfclub.co.uk

## Charleton (1994)
**Proprietary**
*Charleton, Colinsburgh KY9 1HG*
☎ (01333) 340505
🖥 (01333) 340583
✉ clubhouse@charleton.co.uk
✍ John Priestley
🖥 www.charleton.co.uk

## Cowdenbeath (1991)
**Public**
*Seco Place, Cowdenbeath KY4 8PD*
☎ (01383) 511918/ (01383) 513079 (Starter)
✉ mail@cowdenbeath-golfclub.com
✍ Secretary
🖥 www.cowdenbeath-golfclub.com

## Crail Golfing Society (1786)
*Balcomie Clubhouse, Fifeness, Crail KY10 3XN*
☎ (01333) 450686
🖥 (01333) 450416
✉ info@crailgolfingsociety.co.uk
✍ D Roy
🖥 www.crailgolfingsociety.co.uk

## Cupar (1855)
*Hilltarvit, Cupar KY15 5JT*
☎ (01334) 653549
🖥 (01334) 653549
✉ cupargc@fsmail.net
✍ James Elder
🖥 www.cupargolfclub.co.uk

## Drumoig (1996)
*Drumoig Hotel, Drumoig, Leuchars, St Andrews, Fife KY16 0BE*
☎ (01382) 541898
🖥 (01382) 541898
✉ drumoiggolf@btconnect.com
✍ Gordon Taylor
🖥 www.drumoigleisure.com

## Dunfermline (1887)
*Pitfirrane, Crossford, Dunfermline KY12 8QW*
☎ (01383) 723534
✉ secretary@dunfermlinegolfclub.com
✍ R De Rose
🖥 www.dunfermlinegolfclub.com

## Dunnikier Park (1963)
**Public**
*Dunnikier Way, Kirkcaldy KY1 3LP*
☎ (01592) 261599
✉ dunnikierparkgolfclub@btinternet .com
✍ G Macdonald
🖥 www.dunnikierparkgolfclub.com

## Earlsferry Thistle (1875)
**Club**
*Melon Park, Elie KY9 1AS*
✍ J Peters (01333) 424315

## Elmwood Golf Course (1997)
**Pay and play**
*Stratheden, Nr Cupar KY15 5RS*
☎ (01334) 658780
🖥 (01334) 658781
✉ Elmwoodclubhouse@sruc.ac.uk
✍ Sharif Sulaiman (Golf Admin) (01334) 658780
🖥 www.elmwoodgc.co.uk

## Falkland (1976)
*The Myre, Falkland KY15 7AA*
☎ (01337) 857404
✉ falklandgolfclub@gmail.com
✍ Mrs H Brough
🖥 www.falklandgolfclub.com

## Glenrothes (1958)
**Public**
*Golf Course Road, Glenrothes KY6 2LA*
☎ (01592) 754561/758686
🖥 (01592) 754561
✉ secretary@glenrothesgolf.org.uk
✍ Miss C Dawson
🖥 www.glenrothesgolf.org.uk

## Golf House Club (1875)
*Elie, Leven KY9 1AS*
☎ (01333) 330301
🖥 (01333) 330895
✉ secretary@golfhouseclub.org
✍ Gordon Fleming
🖥 www.golfhouseclub.org

## Kinghorn (1887)
**Public**
*Burntisland Road, Kinghorn KY3 9RS*
☎ (01592) 890345
✉ kgclub123@btconnect.co.uk
✍ Mrs Joan Tulloch
🖥 www.kinghorngolfclub.co.uk

## Kinghorn Ladies (1894)
**Club**
*Golf Clubhouse, Burntisland Road, Kinghorn KY3 9RS*
☎ (01592) 890345
✉ kgclub@tiscali.co.uk
🖥 www.kinghorngolfclub.co.uk

## Kingsbarns Golf Links (2000)
**Pay and play**
*Kingsbarns, Fife KY16 8QD*
☎ (01334) 460860
🖥 (01334) 460877
✉ info@kingsbarns.com
✍ Alan Hogg (Chief Executive)
🖥 www.kingsbarns.com

## Kirkcaldy (1904)
*Balwearie Road, Kirkcaldy KY2 5LT*
☎ (01592) 205240
✉ enquiries@kirkcaldygolfclub.co.uk
✍ M Langstaff
🖥 www.kirkcaldygolfclub.co.uk

## Ladybank (1879)
*Annsmuir, Ladybank, Fife KY15 7RA*
☎ (01337) 830814
🖥 (01337) 831505
✉ info@ladybankgolf.co.uk
✍ FH McCluskey
🖥 www.ladybankgolf.co.uk

## Leslie (1898)
*Balsillie Laws, Leslie, Glenrothes KY6 3EZ*
☎ (01592) 620040
✉ secretarylgc@hotmail.com
✍ G Lewis
🖥 www.lesliegolfclub.com

## Leven Golfing Society (1820)
**Club**
*Links Road, Leven KY8 4HS*
☎ (01333) 426096/424229
🖥 (01333) 424229
✉ secretary@levengolfingsociety.co.uk
✍ Verne Greger
🖥 www.levengolfingsociety.co.uk

## Leven Links   (1846)
*The Promenade, Leven KY8 4HS*
☎ **(01333) 421390 (Starter)**
🖥 (01333) 428859
📧 secretary@leven-links.com
✍ Jen Low (01333) 428859
🖳 www.leven-links.com

## Leven Thistle   (1867)
Club
*Balfour Street, Leven KY8 4JF*
☎ **(01333) 426333**
🖥 (01333) 439910
📧 secretary@leventhistlegolf.org.uk
✍ Ian Winn (01333) 426333
🖳 www.leventhistlegolf.org.uk

## Lundin   (1868)
*Golf Road, Lundin Links KY8 6BA*
☎ **(01333) 320202**
🖥 (01333) 329743
📧 secretary@lundingolfclub.co.uk
✍ AJ McDonald
🖳 www.lundingolfclub.co.uk

## Lundin Ladies   (1891)
*Woodielea Road, Lundin Links KY8 6AR*
☎ **(01333) 320832 (Office)/**
   **(01333) 320022 (Starter)**
📧 llgolfclub@gmail.co.uk
✍ Lilian Spence (Secretary)
🖳 www.lundinladiesgolfclub.co.uk

## Methil   (1892)
Club
*Links House, Links Road, Leven KY8 4HS*
☎ **(01333) 425535**
🖥 (01333) 425187

📧 andrew.traill@btconnect.com
✍ ATJ Traill

## Pitreavie   (1922)
*Queensferry Road, Dunfermline KY11 8PR*
☎ **(01383) 722591**
🖥 (01383) 722592
📧 secretary@pitreaviegolfclub.co.uk
✍ Malcom A Brown
🖳 www.pitreaviegolfclub.co.uk

## Saline   (1912)
*Kinneddar Hill, Saline KY12 9LT*
☎ **(01383) 852591**
🖥 (01383) 852591
📧 salinegolfclub@btconnect.com
✍ D Hatton
🖳 www.saline-golf-club.co.uk

## Scoonie   (1951)
Public
*North Links, Leven KY8 4SP*
☎ **(01333) 307007**
🖥 (01333) 307008
📧 manager@scooniegolfclub.com
✍ Mr J Divers
🖳 www.scooniegolfclub.com

## Scotscraig   (1817)
*Golf Road, Tayport DD6 9DZ*
☎ **(01382) 552515**
🖥 (01382) 553130
📧 scotscraig@scotscraiggolfclub.com
✍ BD Liddle
🖳 www.scotscraiggolfclub.com

## St Michaels   (1903)
*Gallow Hill, Leuchars KY16 0DX*
☎ **(01334) 839365 (Clubhouse)**

📧 (01334) 838789
📧 stmichaelsgc@btclick.com
✍ D S Landsburgh (01334) 838666
🖳 www.stmichaelsgolfclub.co.uk

## Thornton   (1921)
*Station Road, Thornton KY1 4DW*
☎ **(01592) 771173 (Starter)**
🖥 (01592) 774955
📧 thorntongolf@btconnect.com
✍ WD Rae (01592) 771111
🖳 www.thorntongolfclub.co.uk

### St Andrews Clubs

## The Royal and Ancient Golf Club of St Andrews   (1754)
Club
*St Andrews KY16 9JD*
☎ **(01334) 460000**
🖥 (01334) 460001
📧 thesecretary@randagc.org
✍ P Dawson
🖳 www.RandA.org

## St Andrews Thistle Golf Club   (1817)
Club
*c/o Links House, 13 The Links, S Andrews, Fife KY16 9JB*
☎ **(01334) 478789**
📧 thistle.secretary@gmail.com
✍ Iain Ross (Secretary)

## St Regulus Ladies'   (1913)
Club
*9 Pilmour Links, St Andrews KY16 9JG*
☎ **(01334) 477797**

---

# The Standard Life Amateur Champion Gold Medal

It was on July 11th 1870 that the Captain and Council of Innerleven Golf Club, the forerunner to Leven Golfing Society, were notified by their Secretary that the Standard Assurance Company (now Standard Life plc) had presented a Gold Medal for annual competition and Thursday 4th August had been fixed for the event.

The inaugural competition was won by James Elder of Leven Golf Club with a single round score of 85. The competition was, "open to members of Innerleven, Leven and Lundin Golf Clubs and the members of such other clubs as the Captain and Council of Innerleven shall approve, but makers of clubs or balls, or professionals, may not compete".

The competition, hosted annually by Leven Golfing Society and Standard Life plc, continued over 18 holes until 1966 when a 36 holes event was introduced and three years later it moved to the current 72 hole format over two days.

From that historic date, Standard Life has each year presented a gold medallion to the winner and, in more recent times, silver and bronze medallions to the second and third.

Over the decades the tournament, which is played in early August over the classic Leven Links, has grown in stature and is now considered one of the most prestigious competitions in Scottish Golf.

One of the great winners from the past was former Walker Cup player Eric McCruvie who won the medal on no fewer than seven occasions between 1927 and 1950, whilst previous winners who have subsequently gone on to successful professional careers include Pierre Ulrich Johansson, Andrew Coltart and Lee Westwood.

While winning the medal remains a much sought-after prize, each year, every entrant who takes the tee can proudly claim to have played in the world's oldest open amateur stroke-play competition at the eleventh oldest club.

(01334) 477797
admin@st-regulus-lgc.co.uk
Honorary Secretary
www.st-regulus-lgc.co.uk

### The St Rule Club (1898)
**Club**
12 The Links, St Andrews KY16 9JB
☎ (01334) 472988
(01334) 472988
admin@thestruleclub.co.uk
Mr Neil Doctor

### The New Golf Club (1902)
3-5 Gibson Place, St Andrews KY16 9JE
☎ (01334) 473426
(01334) 472988
admin@newgolfclubstandrews.co.uk
The Secretary
www.newgolfclubstandrews.co.uk

### The St Andrews (1843)
Links House, 13 The Links, St Andrews KY16 9JB
☎ (01334) 479799
(01334) 479577
sec@thestandrewsgolfclub.co.uk
T Gallacher
www.thestandrewsgolfclub.co.uk

*St Andrews Courses*

### Balgove Course (1993)
**Public**
St Andrews Links, Pilmour House, St Andrews KY16 9SF
☎ (01334) 466666
(01334) 479555
reservations@standrews.org.uk
Euan Loudon (Chief Executive)
Twitter: @thehomeofgolf
www.standrews.org.uk

### The Castle Course (2008)
**Public**
St Andrews Links, Pilmour House, St Andrews KY16 9SF
☎ (01334) 466666
(01334) 479555
reservations@standrews.org.uk
Euan Loudon (Chief Executive)
Twitter: @thehomeofgolf
www.standrews.org.uk

### Duke's (1995)
Craigtoun, St Andrews KY16 8NX
☎ (01334) 470214
(01334) 479456
reservations@oldcoursehotel.co.uk
David Scott (Mgr) (01334) 470214
www.playthedukes.com

### Eden Course (1914)
**Public**
St Andrews Links, Pilmour House, St Andrews KY16 9SF
☎ (01334) 466666
(01334) 479555
reservations@standrews.org.uk
Euan Loudon (Chief Executive)
Twitter: @thehomeofgolf
www.standrews.org.uk

### Jubilee Course (1897)
**Public**
St Andrews Links, Pilmour House, St Andrews KY16 9SF
☎ (01334) 466666
(01334) 479555
reservations@standrews.org.uk
Euan Loudon (Chief Executive)
Twitter: @thehomeofgolf
www.standrews.org.uk

### New Course (1895)
**Public**
St Andrews Links, Pilmour House, St Andrews KY16 9SF
☎ (01334) 466666
(01334) 479555
reservations@standrews.org.uk
Euan Loudon (Chief Executive)
Twitter: @thehomeofgolf
www.standrews.org.uk

### Old Course (c1400)
**Public**
St Andrews Links, Pilmour House, St Andrews KY16 9SF
☎ (01334) 466666
(01334) 479555
reservations@standrews.org.uk
Euan Loudon (Chief Executive)
Twitter: @thehomeofgolf
www.standrews.org.uk

### Strathtyrum Course (1993)
**Public**
St Andrews Links, Pilmour House, St Andrews KY16 9SF
☎ (01334) 466666
(01334) 479555
reservations@standrews.org.uk
Euan Loudon (Chief Executive)
Twitter: @thehomeofgolf
www.standrews.org.uk

## Glasgow

### Alexandra Park (1880)
**Public**
Alexandra Park, Dennistoun, Glasgow G31 8SE
☎ (0141) 276 0600
F Derwin

### Bishopbriggs (1906)
Brackenbrae Road, Bishopbriggs, Glasgow G64 2DX
☎ (0141) 772 1810
(0141) 762 2532
thesecretarybgc@yahoo.co.uk
A Smith (0141) 772 8938
www.thebishopbriggsgolfclub.com

### Cathcart Castle (1895)
Mearns Road, Clarkston G76 7YL
☎ (0141) 638 9449
(0141) 638 1201
secretary@cathcartcastle.com
IG Sutherland (0141) 638 9449
www.cathcartcastle.com

### Cawder (1933)
Cadder Road, Bishopbriggs, Glasgow G64 3QD
☎ (0141) 761 1281
(0141) 761 1285
secretary@cawdergolfclub.com
Fraser Gemmell (0141) 761 1281
www.cawdergolfclub.com

### Cowglen (1906)
301 Barrhead Road, Glasgow G43 1EU
☎ (0141) 632 7463
(0141) 632 7463

## The Tennant Cup

The Tennant Cup, presented by Glasgow Golf Club Captain Sir Charles Tennant in 1880, is the oldest golfing trophy in the world for open competition among amateur golfers under medal conditions.

Originally played over two 10-hole rounds at Alexandra Park, it became an 18-hole competition when the course was extended in 1885.

In 1893, the event was transferred to the club's Gailes course and was played there before moving to Killermont in 1906.

In 1927, the competition was extended to two rounds over Killermont and that event was won by William Tulloch of Cathkin Braes, who had been the last player to win in over 18 holes.

In 1976, it was extended to 72 holes with two rounds at Gailes on the Saturday and two at Killermont the following day. That has been the format ever since.

*For key to symbols see page 725*

✉ secretary@cowglengolfclub.co.uk
✍ Mrs Anne Burnside
🌐 www.cowglengolfclub.co.uk

## Glasgow   (1787)
*Killermont, Bearsden, Glasgow G61 2TW*
☎ (0141) 942 1713
📠 (0141) 942 0770
✉ secretary@glasgowgolfclub.com
✍ A G McMillan (0141) 942 2011
🌐 www.glasgowgolfclub.com

## Haggs Castle   (1910)
*70 Dumbreck Road, Dumbreck, Glasgow G41 4SN*
☎ (01141) 427 1157
✉ secretary@haggscastlegolfclub .com
✍ A Williams (0141) 427 1157
🌐 www.haggscastlegolfclub.com

## Knightswood   (1929)
**Public**
*Knightswood Park, Lincoln Avenue, Glasgow G13 3DN*
☎ (0141) 959 6358
✍ D Gardner (0141) 959 8158

## Lethamhill   (1933)
**Public**
*Cumbernauld Road, Glasgow G33 1AH*
☎ (0141) 770 6220
📠 (0141) 770 0520

## Linn Park   (1924)
**Public**
*Simshill Road, Glasgow G44 5TA*
☎ (0141) 633 0377

## Pollok   (1892)
*90 Barrhead Road, Glasgow G43 1BG*
☎ (0141) 632 1080
📠 (0141) 649 1398
✉ secretary@pollokgolf.com
✍ D McKellar (0141) 632 4351
🌐 www.pollokgolf.com

## Ralston   (1904)
*Strathmore Avenue, Ralston, Paisley PA1 3DT*
☎ (0141) 882 1349
📠 (0141) 883 9837
✉ thesecretary@ralstongolf.co.uk
✍ B W Hanson
🌐 www.ralstongolfclub.com

## Rouken Glen   (1922)
**Pay and play**
*Stewarton Road, Thornliebank, Glasgow G46 7UZ*
☎ (0141) 638 7044
📠 (0141) 638 6115
✉ deaconsbank@ngclubs.co.uk
✍ S Armstrong

## Sandyhills   (1905)
*223 Sandyhills Road, Glasgow G32 9NA*
☎ (0141) 778 1179
✉ admin@sandyhillsgolfclub.co.uk
✍ J Thomson
🌐 www.sandyhillsgolfclub.co.uk

## Williamwood   (1906)
*Clarkston Road, Netherlee, Glasgow G44 3YR*
☎ (0141) 637 1783
📠 (0141) 571 0166
✉ secretary@williamwoodgc.co.uk
✍ LW Conn (0141) 629 1981
🌐 www.williamwoodgc.co.uk

# Highland

## Caithness & Sutherland

## Bonar Bridge/Ardgay   (1904)
*Migdale Road, Bonar-Bridge, Sutherland IV24 3EJ*
☎ (01863) 766199 (Clubhouse)
✉ nielsenhunter@btinternet.com
✍ Jeani Hunter (01863) 766 199
⊕ 9 hole scenic course. Catering available May - Sept.
🌐 www.bbagc.co.uk

## Brora   (1891)
*Golf Road, Brora KW9 6QS*
☎ (01408) 621417
📠 (01408) 622157
✉ secretary@broragolf.co.uk
✍ AJA Gill
🌐 www.broragolf.co.uk

## The Carnegie Club   (1995)
*Skibo Castle, Dornoch, Sutherland IV25 3RQ*
☎ (01862) 881 260
📠 (01862) 881 260
✉ katy.renwick@carnegieclub.co.uk
✍ Sharon Stewart
🌐 www.carnegieclubs.com

## Durness   (1988)
**Pay and play**
*Balnakeil, Durness IV27 4PN*
☎ (01971) 511364
📠 (01971) 511321
✉ lucy@durnessgolfclub.org
✍ Mrs L Mackay (01971) 511364
🌐 www.durnessgolfclub.org

## Golspie   (1889)
**Visitors welcome**
*Ferry Road, Golspie KW10 6ST*
☎ (01408) 633266
✉ info@golspie-golf-club.co.uk
✍ RI Beaton (Hon) (01408 633927)
🌐 www.golspie-golf-club.co.uk

## Helmsdale   (1895)
*Strath Road, Helmsdale KW8 6JL*
☎ (01431) 821063
✍ R Sutherland
🌐 www.helmsdale.org

## Lybster   (1926)
*Main Street, Lybster KW1 6BL*
☎ (01593) 721316
✍ AG Calder (01593) 721316
🌐 www.lybstergolfclub.co.uk

## Reay   (1893)
*Reay, Thurso, Caithness KW14 7RE*
☎ (01847) 811288
✉ info@reaygolfclub.co.uk
✍ J Disbury (Sec)
🌐 www.reaygolfclub.co.uk

## Royal Dornoch   (1877)
*Golf Road, Dornoch IV25 3LW*
☎ (01862) 810219
📠 (01862) 810792
✉ neil@royaldornoch.com
✍ Neil Hampton (Gen Mgr)
🌐 www.royaldornoch.com

## Thurso   (1893)
**Pay and play**
*Newlands of Geise, Thurso KW14 7XD*
☎ (01847) 893807
📠 (01847) 892575
✉ thursogolfclub@gmail.com
✍ RM Black
🌐 www.thursogolfclub.co.uk

## Ullapool   (1998)
**Pay and play**
*North Road, Ullapool IV26 2TH*
☎ (01854) 613323
✉ mail@ullapoolgolfclub.co.uk
✍ A Paterson
🌐 www.ullapoolgolfclub.co.uk

## Wick   (1870)
*Reiss, Wick KW1 4RW*
☎ (01955) 602726
✉ wickgolfclub@hotmail.com
✍ Rognvald Taylor (Secretary)
🌐 www.wickgolfclub.org.uk

## Inverness

## Abernethy   (1893)
*Nethy Bridge PH25 3EB*
☎ (01479) 821305/ (07938) 968102
✉ info@abernethygolfclub.com
✍ Hamish Fraser (Secretary)
🌐 www.abernethygolfclub.com

## Aigas   (1993)
**Proprietary**
*mains of Aigas, Beauly, Inverness IV4 7AD*
☎ (01463) 782942
✉ info@aigas-holidays.co.uk
🌐 www.aigas-holidays.co.uk

## Alness   (1904)
*Ardross Rd, Alness, Ross-shire IV17 0QA*
☎ (01349) 883877
✉ info@alnessgolfclub.co.uk
✍ Mr Richard Green
🌐 www.alnessgolfclub.co.uk

## Boat of Garten   (1898)
*Boat of Garten, Inverness-shire PH24 3BQ*
☎ (01479) 831282
📠 (01479) 831523
✉ office@boatgolf.com
✍ W.N McConachie (clubsec@boatgolf.com)
🌐 www.boatgolf.com

## Carrbridge (1980)

Inverness Road, Carrbridge PH23 3AU

☎ **(01479) 841623 (Clubhouse)**
✉ secretary@carrbridgegolf.co.uk
✍ The Secretary
🖥 www.carrbridgegolf.co.uk

## Fort Augustus (1904)

**Pay and play**
Markethill, Fort Augustus PH32 4DS

☎ **(01320) 366660**
✉ fortaugustusgc@aol.com
✍ K Callow
🖥 www.fortaugustusgc.webeden
   .co.uk

## Fort William (1974)

North Road, Fort William PH33 6SN

☎ **(01397) 704464**
✉ fortwilliam01@btconnect.com
✍ Ian Robertson
🖥 www.fortwilliamgolf.co.uk

## Fortrose & Rosemarkie (1888)

Ness Road East, Fortrose IV10 8SE

☎ **(01381) 620529/620733**
🖳 (01381) 621328
✉ secretary@fortrosegolfclub.co.uk
✍ M MacDonald
🖥 www.fortrosegolfclub.co.uk

## Grantown-on-Spey (1890)

Golf Course Road, Grantown-on-Spey
PH26 3HY

☎ **(01479) 872079**
🖳 (01479) 873725
✉ secretary
   @grantownonspeygolfclub.co.uk
✍ PR Mackay
🖥 www.grantownonspeygolfclub
   .co.uk

## Invergordon (1893)

King George Street, Invergordon IV18 0BD

☎ **(01349) 852715**
✉ invergordongolf@tiscali.co.uk
✍ David Jamieson
🖥 www.invergordongolf.co.uk

## Inverness (1883)

Culcabock Road, Inverness IV2 3XQ

☎ **(01463) 239882**
🖳 (01463) 240616
✉ manager@invernessgolfclub.co.uk
✍ E Forbes
🖥 www.invernessgolfclub.co.uk

## Kingussie (1891)

**Pay and play**
Gynack Road, Kingussie PH21 1LR

☎ **(01540) 661600 (Office)**
🖳 (01540) 662066
✉ sec@kingussie-golf.co.uk
✍ Ian Chadburn
🖥 www.kingussie-golf.co.uk

## Loch Ness (1996)

**Proprietary**
Fairways, Castle Heather, Inverness
IV2 6AA

☎ **(01463) 713335**
🖳 (01463) 712695

✉ info@golflochness.com
✍ Secretary (01463) 713335
🖥 www.golflochness.com

## Muir of Ord (1875)

Great North Road, Muir of Ord IV6 7SX

☎ **(01463) 870825**
✉ muir.golf@btconnect.com
✍ Mr N Strachan
🖥 www.muirofordgolfclub.co.uk

## Nairn (1887)

Seabank Road, Nairn IV12 4HB

☎ **(01667) 453208**
🖳 (01667) 456328
✉ bookings@nairngolfclub.co.uk
✍ Yvonne Forgan (Mgr)
🖥 www.nairngolfclub.co.uk

## Nairn Dunbar (1899)

Lochloy Road, Nairn IV12 5AE

☎ **(01667) 452741**
🖳 (01667) 456897
✉ secretary@nairndunbar.com
✍ J Gibson
🖥 www.nairndunbar.com

## Newtonmore (1893)

**Owned privately**
Golf Course Road, Newtonmore PH20 1AT

☎ **(01540) 673878**
✉ secretary@newtonmoregolf.com
✍ Heather Bruce (Office Mgr)
🖥 www.newtonmoregolf.com

## Strathpeffer Spa (1888)

Golf Course Road, Strathpeffer IV14 9AS

☎ **(01997) 421219**
🖳 (01997) 421011
✉ mail@strathpeffergolf.co.uk
✍ Mrs Margaret Spark
🖥 www.strathpeffergolf.co.uk

## Tain (1890)

Chapel Road, Tain IV19 1JE

☎ **(01862) 892314**
🖳 (01862) 892099
✉ info@tain-golf.co.uk
✍ Mrs Magi Vass (Sec)
🖥 www.tain-golf.co.uk

## Tarbat (1909)

**Pay and play**
Portmahomack, Tain IV20 1YB

☎ **(01862) 871278**
🖳 (01862) 871598

## Torvean (1962)

**Public**
Glenurquhart Road, Inverness IV3 8JN

☎ **(01463) 225651**
🖳 (01463) 711417
✉ admin@torveangolfclub.co.uk
✍ John Robertson (Administrator)
🖥 www.torveangolfclub.co.uk

## Orkney and Shetland

## Orkney (1889)

Grainbank, Kirkwall, Orkney KW15 1RD

☎ **(01856) 872457**

🖳 (01856) 872457
✍ Gary Farqumar
🖥 www.orkneygolfclub.co.uk

## Sanday (1977)

**Pay and play**
Sanday, Orkney KW17 2BW

☎ **(01857) 600341**
🖳 (01857) 600341
✉ nearhouse@triscom.co.uk
✍ R Thorne
⊕ Day Fee £5, Associate Membership
   (no further fees) £20

## Shetland (1891)

Dale, Gott, Shetland ZE2 9SB

☎ **(01595) 840369**
✉ info@shetlandgolfclub.co.uk
✍ S Lamb
🖥 www.shetlandgolfclub.co.uk

## Stromness (1890)

Stromness, Orkney KW16 3DU

☎ **(01856) 850772**
✍ Colin McLeod
🖥 www.stromnessgc.co.uk

## Whalsay (1976)

**Public**
Skaw Taing, Whalsay, Shetland ZE2 9AL

☎ **(01806) 566450/566481**
✉ alan.solvei@lineone.net
✍ HA Sandison, C Hutchison
🖥 www.whalsaygolfclub.com

## West Coast

## Askernish (1891)

**Pay and play**
Lochboisdale, Askernish, South Uist
HS81 5ST

☎ **(01878) 710312**
✉ rthomp4521@btinternet.com
✍ A MacIntyre
🖥 www.askernishgolfclub.com

## Gairloch (1898)

Gairloch, Ross-Shire IV21 2BE

☎ **(01445) 712407**
✉ gairlochgolfclub@hotmail.co.uk
✍ J Powell
🖥 www.gairlochgolfclub.co.uk

## Isle of Harris (1975)

**Pay and play**
Scarista, Isle of Harris HS3 3HX

☎ **(01859) 550226**
🖳 (01859) 550226
✉ harrisgolf@ic24.net
✍ R A MacDonald
🖥 www.harrisgolf.com

## Isle of Skye (1964)

Sconser, Isle of Skye IV48 8TD

☎ **(01478) 650414**
✍ I Macmillan

## Lochcarron (1908)

Lochcarron, Strathcarron, Ross Shire
IV54 8YS

☎ **(01520) 722744**
✉ info@lochcarrongolfclub.co.uk
🖥 www.lochcarrongolfclub.co.uk

**Skeabost**    (1982)
*Skeabost Bridge, Isle of Skye IV51 9NP*
☎ (01470) 532202
🖳 (01470) 532454
🖉 DJ Matheson (01470) 532202

**Stornoway**    (1890)
*Lady Lever Park, Stornoway, Isle of Lewis HS2 0XP*
☎ (01851) 702240
✉ admin@stornowaygolfclub.co.uk
🖉 KW Galloway (01851) 702533
🖳 www.stornowaygolfclub.co.uk

**Traigh**    (1947)
*Arisaig, Inverness-shire PH39 4NT*
☎ (01687) 450337
🖉 R Burt (01687) 462 512
🖳 www.traighgolf.co.uk

## Lanarkshire

**Airdrie**    (1877)
*Glenmavis Road, Rochsoles, Airdrie ML6 0PQ*
☎ (01236) 762195
🖳 (01236) 760584
✉ airdriegolfclub@gmail.com
🖉 W Campbell

**Bellshill**    (1905)
*Community Road, Orbiston, Bellshill ML4 2RZ*
☎ (01698) 745124
🖳 (01698) 292576
✉ info@bellshillgolfclub.com
🖉 Tony Deerin (Secretary)
🖳 www.bellshillgolfclub.com

**Biggar**    (1895)
Public
*Park House, Broughton Road, Biggar ML12 6HA*
☎ (01899) 220618 (Clubhouse)
✉ secretary@biggargolfclub.org.uk
🖉 Frazer Andrews
🖳 www.biggargolfclub.com

**Blairbeth**    (1910)
*Burnside, Rutherglen, Glasgow G73 4SF*
☎ (0141) 634 3355 (Clubhouse)
🖳 (0141) 634 3355
✉ secretary@blairbethgolfclub.co.uk
🖉 (0141) 634 3325
🖳 www.blairbethgolfclub.co.uk

**Bothwell Castle**    (1922)
*Uddington Road, Bothwell, Glasgow G71 8TD*
☎ (01698) 801971
🖳 (01698) 801971
✉ secretary@bcgolf.co.uk
🖉 Jim Callaghan CCM
   (01698) 801971
🖳 www.bcgolf.co.uk

**Calderbraes**    (1891)
*57 Roundknowe Road, Uddingston G71 7TS*
☎ (01698) 813425
✉ calderbraesgolfclub@tiscali.co.uk

🖉 S McGuigan (0141) 573 2497
🖳 www.calderbraesgolfclub.com

**Cambuslang**    (1892)
*30 Westburn Drive, Cambuslang G72 7NA*
☎ (0141) 641 3130
🖳 (0141) 641 3130
✉ cambuslanggolfclub@tiscali.co.uk
🖉 RM Dunlop
🖳 www.cambuslandgolf.org

**Carluke**    (1894)
*Hallcraig, Mauldslie Road, Carluke ML8 5HG*
☎ (01555) 770574/771070
🖳 (01555) 770574
✉ carlukegolfsecy@tiscali.co.uk
🖉 G White (01555) 770574
🖳 www.carlukegolfclub.com

**Carnwath**    (1907)
*1 Main Street, Carnwath ML11 8JX*
☎ (01555) 840251
🖳 (01555) 841070
✉ carnwathgc@hotmail.co.uk
🖉 Mrs L Jardine
🖳 www.carnwathgc.co.uk

**Cathkin Braes**    (1888)
*Cathkin Road, Rutherglen, Glasgow G73 4SE*
☎ (0141) 634 6605
✉ secretary@cathkinbraesgolfclub.co.uk
🖉 DE Moir
🖳 www.cathkinbraesgolfclub.co.uk

**Coatbridge Municipal**    (1971)
Public
*Townhead Road, Coatbridge ML52 2HX*
☎ (01236) 28975

**Colville Park**    (1923)
*Jerviston Estate, Motherwell ML1 4UG*
☎ (01698) 263017
🖳 (01698) 230418
🖉 L Innes (01698) 262808
🖳 www.colvillepark.co.uk

**Crow Wood**    (1925)
*Cumbernauld Road, Muirhead, Glasgow G69 9JF*
☎ (0141) 799 1943
🖳 (0141) 779 4873
✉ secretary@crowwoodgolfclub.co.uk
🖉 Margaret Laughrey
   (0141) 779 4954
🖳 www.crowwoodgolfclub.co.uk

**Dalziel Park**    (1997)
*100 Hagen Drive, Motherwell ML1 5RZ*
☎ (01698) 862862
🖳 (01698) 862863
🖉 I Donnachie

**Douglas Water**    (1922)
*Rigside, Lanark ML11 9NB*
☎ (01555) 880361
🖳 (01555) 880361
🖉 S Hogg
🖳 www.douglaswatergolf.co.uk

**Drumpellier**    (1894)
*Drumpellier Ave, Coatbridge ML5 1RX*
☎ (01236) 424139
🖳 (01236) 428723
✉ administrator@drumpelliergolfclub.com
🖉 JM Craig
⊕ Visitors: Weekdays only
   Round £35.00 / Day £50.00

**East Kilbride**    (1900)
*Chapelside Road, Nerston, East Kilbride G74 4PH*
☎ (01355) 581805 (Pro Shop)
🖳 (01355) 581807
✉ secretary@ekgolfclub.co.uk
🖉 Fraser Gow (01355) 581800
🖳 www.ekgolfclub.co.uk

**Easter Moffat**    (1922)
*Mansion House, Plains, Airdrie ML6 8NP*
☎ (01236) 842878
🖳 (01236) 842904
✉ secretary@emgc.org.uk
🖉 John Dunlop
🖳 www.emgc.org.uk

**Hamilton Golf Club**    (1892)
*Riccarton, Ferniegair, Hamilton ML3 7UE*
☎ (01698) 282872
🖳 (01698) 204650
✉ secretary@hamiltongolfclub.co.uk
🖉 G B Mackenzie (Mgr)
🖳 www.hamiltongolfclub.co.uk

**Hollandbush**    (1954)
Public
*Acretophead, Lesmahagow, Coalburn ML11 0JS*
☎ (01555) 893484
✉ mail@hollandbushgolfclub.co.uk
🖉 J Hamilton (Secretary)
🖳 www.hollandbushgolfclub.co.uk

**Kirkhill**    (1910)
*Greenlees Road, Cambuslang, Glasgow G72 8YN*
☎ (0141) 641 3083 (Clubhouse)
🖳 (0141) 641 8499
✉ secretary@kirkhillgolfclub.org.uk
🖉 C Downes (0141) 641 8499
🖳 www.kirkhillgolfclub.org.uk

**Lanark**    (1851)
*The Moor, Lanark ML11 7RX*
☎ (01555) 663219
🖳 (01555) 663219
✉ lanarkgolfclub@supanet.com
🖉 George H Cuthill
🖳 www.lanarkgolfclub.co.uk

**Langlands**    (1985)
Public
*Langlands Road, East Kilbride G75 0QQ*
☎ (01355) 248173
🖳 (01355) 248121
🖉 A Craik (01355) 248401

**Larkhall**    (1909)
Public
*Burnhead Road, Larkhall, Glasgow*
☎ (01698) 881113
🖉 M Mallinson

## Leadhills (1895)

1 New Row, Wanlockhead, Leadhills, Nr
Biggar ML12 6UJ
☎ (01659) 74272
✉ jack@gsx-r750cc.fsnet.co.uk
✍ Jack Arrigoni
🖥 See Golf Central

## Mount Ellen (1904)

Lochend Road, Gartcosh, Glasgow G69 9EY
☎ (01236) 872277
🖷 (01236) 872249
✉ secretary@mountellengolfclub
.co.uk
✍ Robert Watt
🖥 www.mountellengolfclub.co.uk

## Mouse Valley (1993)

East End, Cleghorn, Lanark ML11 8NR
☎ (01555) 870015
🖷 (01555) 870022
✉ info@kames-golf-club.com
✍ Helen Howitt
🖥 www.kames-golf-club.com

## Shotts (1895)

Blairhead, Benhar Road, Shotts
ML7 5BJ
☎ (01501) 820431
🖷 (01501) 825868
✉ info@shottsgolfclub.co.uk
✍ GT Stoddart (01501) 825868
🖥 www.shottsgolfclub.co.uk

## Strathaven (1908)

Glasgow Road, Strathaven ML10 6NL
☎ (01357) 520421
🖷 (01357) 520539
✉ info@strathavengc.com
✍ IF Neil
🖥 www.strathavengc.com

## Strathclyde Park (1936)

Public
Mote Hill, Hamilton ML3 6BY
☎ (01698) 429350
✍ K Will
⊕ 24-bay driving range. Large practice
area. Large putting green

## Torrance House (1969)

Public
Strathaven Road, East Kilbride, Glasgow
G75 0QZ
☎ (01355) 248638
✉ secretary@torrancehousegc
.co.uk
✍ Margaret D McKerlie
(01355) 249720

## Wishaw (1897)

55 Cleland Road, Wishaw ML2 7PH
☎ (01698) 372869 (Clubhouse)
🖷 (01698) 356930
✉ jwdouglas@btconnect.com
✍ JW Douglas (01698) 357480
⊕ WD-U until 4.00pm NA-Sat
U-Sun

## Lothians

### East Lothian

## Aberlady (1912)

Club
Aberlady EH32 0RB
✉ ithomps3@aol.com
✍ I Thompson (01875) 870029

## Archerfield Links (2004)

Dirleton, East Lothian EH39 5HU
☎ (01620) 897050
🖷 (08700) 515487
✉ mail@archerfieldgolfclub.com
✍ Stuart Bayne (Dir of Golf)
🖥 www.archerfieldgolfclub.com

## Bass Rock (1873)

Club
43a High Street, North Berwick EH39 4HH
☎ (01620) 895182
✉ bassrockgolfclub@hotmail.com
✍ Tom McGinley

## Castle Park (1994)

Pay and play
Gifford, Haddington EH41 4PL
☎ (01620) 810733
✉ castleparkgolf@hotmail.com
✍ JT Wilson (01620) 810733
🖥 www.castleparkgolfclub.co.uk

## Dirleton Castle (1854)

Club
15 The Pines, Gullane EH31 2DT
☎ (01620) 843591
✍ J Taylor
🖥 www.dirletoncastlegolfclub.org.uk

## Dunbar (1856)

East Links, Dunbar EH42 1LL
☎ (01368) 862317
🖷 (01368) 865202
✉ secretary@dunbargolfclub.com
✍ John Barber (Sec to Council)
🖥 www.dunbargolfclub.com

## Gifford (1904)

Edinburgh Road, Gifford EH41 4JE
☎ (01620) 810591 (Starter)
✉ secretary@giffordgolfclub.com
✍ Robert Stewart (01620) 810267
🖥 www.giffordgolfclub.com

## Glen (North Berwick) (1906)

East Links, Tantallon Terrace, North
Berwick EH39 4LE
☎ (01620) 892726
🖷 (01620) 895447
✉ secretary@glengolfclub.co.uk
✍ Rita Wilson (Office Mgr)
🖥 www.glengolfclub.co.uk

## Gullane (1882)

West Links Road, Gullane, East Lothian
EH31 2BB
☎ (01620) 842255
🖷 (01620) 842327
✉ secretary@gullanegolfclub.com
✍ S Anthony
🖥 www.gullanegolfclub.com

## Haddington (1865)

Amisfield Park, Haddington EH41 4PT
☎ (01620) 823627
🖷 (01620) 826580
✉ info@haddingtongolf.co.uk
✍ Jane Helmn (Accounts
Administrator)
🖥 www.haddingtongolf.co.uk

## The Honourable Company of Edinburgh Golfers (1744)

Duncur Road, Muirfield, Gullane EH31 2EG
☎ (01620) 842123
🖷 (01620) 842977
✉ hceg@muirfield.org.uk
✍ ANG Brown
🖥 www.muirfield.org.uk

## Kilspindie (1867)

Aberlady EH32 0QD
☎ (01875) 870358
✉ kilspindie@btconnect.com
✍ J R Leslie
🖥 www.kilspindlegolfclub.com

## Longniddry (1921)

Links Road, Longniddry EH32 0NL
☎ (01875) 852141
🖷 (01875) 853371
✉ secretary@longniddrygolfclub
.co.uk
✍ RMS Gunning
🖥 www.longniddrygolfclub.co.uk

## Luffness New (1894)

Aberlady EH32 0QA
☎ (01620) 843114
🖷 (01620) 842933
✉ secretary@luffnessnew.com
✍ Gp Capt AG Yeates
(01620) 843336
🖥 www.luffnessgolf.com

## Musselburgh (1938)

Monktonhall, Musselburgh EH21 6SA
☎ (0131) 665 2005
🖷 (0131) 665 4435
✉ secretary@themusselburghgolfclub
.com
✍ B Knowles
🖥 www.themusselburghgolfclub.com

## Musselburgh Old Course (1982)

Public
10 Balcarres Road, Musselburgh EH21 7SD
☎ (0131) 665 6981
🖷 (0131) 653 1770
✉ oldcourseclub@unicombox.com
✍ K Bentley (Sec) (0131) 665 6981
🖥 www.mocgc.com

## North Berwick (1832)

West Links, Beach Road, North Berwick
EH39 4BB
☎ (01620) 895040
🖷 (01620) 893274
✉ secretary@northberwickgolfclub
.com
✍ Christopher Spencer
(01620) 895040
🖥 www.northberwickgolfclub.com

## Royal Musselburgh    (1774)
*Prestongrange House, Prestonpans*
*EH32 9RP*
☎ **(01875) 810276**
   **(advance bookings) opt 3**
🖳 (01875) 810276
📧 johnhenderson@royalmusselburgh
   .co.uk
✍ Colin Ramsey
🖥 www.royalmusselburgh.co.uk

## Tantallon    (1853)
**Club**
*32 Westgate, North Berwick EH39 4AH*
☎ **(01620) 892114**
🖳 (01620) 894399
📧 secretary@tantallongolfclub.co.uk
✍ I F Doig
🖥 www.north-berwick.co.uk
   /tantallon

## Thorntree Golf Club
   (1856)
**Club**
*Prestongrange House, Prestonpans*
*EH32 9RP*
☎ **(0131) 552 3559**
✍ Arthur Reid

## Whitekirk    (1995)
**Pay and play**
*Whitekirk, North Berwick EH39 5PR*
☎ **(01620) 870300**
🖳 (01620) 870330
📧 countryclub@whitekirk.com
✍ D Brodie
🖥 www.whitekirk.com

## Winterfield    (1935)
**Public**
*St Margarets, Back Road, Dunbar*
*EH42 IXE*
☎ **(01368) 863562**
📧 kevinphillips@tiscali.co.uk
✍ Kevin Phillips
🖥 www.winterfieldgolfclub.info

*Midlothian*

## Baberton    (1893)
*55 Baberton Avenue, Juniper Green,*
*Edinburgh EH14 5DU*
☎ **(0131) 453 4911**
📧 manager@baberton.co.uk
✍ K A Nicholson
🖥 www.baberton.co.uk

## Braid Hills    (1893)
**Public**
*Braid Hills Road, Edinburgh EH10 6JY*
☎ **(0131) 447 6666 (Starter)**

## Braids United    (1897)
**Club**
*22 Braid Hills Approach, Edinburgh*
*EH10 6JY*
☎ **(07541) 136133**
📧 mail@braids-united.co.uk
✍ WJ Mitchell (0131) 476 2238
🖥 www.braids-united.co.uk

## Broomieknowe    (1905)
*36 Golf Course Road, Bonnyrigg*
*EH19 2HZ*
☎ **(0131) 663 9317**
🖳 (0131) 663 2152
📧 administrator@broomieknowe
   .com
✍ R H Beattie
🖥 www.broomieknowe.com

## Bruntsfield Links Golfing Society    (1761)
*The Clubhouse, 32 Barnton Avenue,*
*Edinburgh EH4 6JH*
☎ **(0131) 336 1479**
🖳 (0131) 336 5538
📧 secretary@bruntsfield.sol.co.uk
✍ Alan Feltham
🖥 www.bruntsfieldlinks.co.uk

## Carrick Knowe    (1930)
**Public**
*Glendevon Park, Edinburgh EH12 5VZ*
☎ **(0131) 337 1096 (Starter)**

## Craigmillar Park    (1895)
*I Observatory Road, Edinburgh EH9 3HG*
☎ **(0131) 667 2837**
🖳 (0131) 662 8091
📧 secretary@craigmillarpark.co.uk
✍ Mrs D Nichol (0131) 667 0047
🖥 www.craigmillarpark.co.uk

## Duddingston    (1895)
*Duddingston Road West, Edinburgh*
*EH15 3QD*
☎ **(0131) 661 7688**
🖳 (0131) 652 6057
📧 secretary@duddingstongolf.co.uk
✍ Duncan Ireland
🖥 www.duddingstongolfclub.co.uk

## Glencorse    (1890)
*Milton Bridge, Penicuik EH26 0RD*
☎ **(01968) 677177**
🖳 (01968) 674399
📧 secretary@glencorsegolfclub.com
✍ W Oliver (01968) 677189
🖥 www.glencorsegolfclub.com

## Gogarburn    (1975)
**Members and Visitors**
*Hanley Lodge, Newbridge, Midlothian*
*EH28 8NN*
☎ **(0131) 333 4718**
🖳 (0131) 333 2496
📧 secretary@gogarburngc.com
✍ Gregg Murie
🖥 www.gogarburngc.com

## Kings Acre    (1997)
**Proprietary**
*Lasswade EH18 IAU*
☎ **(0131) 663 3456**
🖳 (0131) 663 7076
📧 info@kings-acregolf.com
✍ Alan Murdoch (Dir of Golf)
🖥 www.kings-acregolf.com

## Kingsknowe    (1907)
*326 Lanark Road, Edinburgh EH14 2JD*
☎ **(0131) 441 1145**

🖳 (0131) 441 2079
📧 clubmanager@kingsknowe.com
✍ Colin Pearson
🖥 www.kingsknowe.com

## Liberton    (1920)
*Kingston Grange, 297 Gilmerton Road,*
*Edinburgh EH16 5UJ*
☎ **(0131) 664 3009**
📧 info@libertongc.co.uk
✍ John Masterton
🖥 www.libertongc.co.uk

## Lothianburn    (1893)
*106a Biggar Road, Edinburgh EH10 7DU*
☎ **(0131) 445 5067**
📧 info@lothianburngc.co.uk
✍ (0131) 445 5067
🖥 www.lothianburngc.co.uk

## Marriott Dalmahoy Hotel & CC
*Dalmahoy, Kirknewton EH27 8EB*
☎ **(0131) 335 8010**
🖳 (0131) 335 3577
✍ Neal Graham (Golf Dir),

## Melville Golf Centre    (1995)
**Pay and play**
*Lasswade, Edinburgh EH18 IAN*
☎ **(0131) 663 8038**
   **(range, shop, tuition)**
🖳 (0131) 654 0814
📧 golf@melvillegolf.co.uk
✍ Mr & Mrs MacFarlane (Props)
🖥 www.melvillegolf.co.uk

## Merchants of Edinburgh
   (1907)
*10 Craighill Gardens, Morningside,*
*Edinburgh EH10 5PY*
☎ **(0131) 447 1219**
🖳 (0131) 446 9833
📧 admin@merchantsgolf.com
✍ J W B Harwood
🖥 www.merchantsgolf.com

## Mortonhall    (1892)
*231 Braid Road, Edinburgh EH10 6PB*
☎ **(0131) 447 6974**
🖳 (0131) 447 8712
📧 clubhouse@mortonhallgc.co.uk
✍ Ms BM Giefer
🖥 www.mortonhallgc.co.uk

## Murrayfield    (1896)
*43 Murrayfield Road, Edinburgh EH12 6EU*
☎ **(0131) 337 3478**
🖳 (0131) 313 0721
📧 john@murrayfieldgolfclub.co.uk
✍ Mr J A Fraser (0131) 337 3478
🖥 www.murrayfieldgolfclub.co.uk

## Newbattle    (1896)
*Abbey Road, Eskbank, Dalkeith EH22 3AD*
☎ **(0131) 663 2123**
🖳 (0131) 654 1810
📧 mail@newbattlegolfclub.com
✍ HG Stanners (0131) 663 1819
🖥 www.newbattlegolfclub.com

## Prestonfield (1920)

6 Priestfield Road North, Edinburgh
EH16 5HS
- ☎ (0131) 667 9665
- 🖷 (0131) 777 2727
- ✉ generalmanager@prestonfieldgolf.com
- ✍ Carol King (Sec)
- 🖳 www.prestonfieldgolf.com

## Ratho Park (1928)

Ratho, Edinburgh EH28 8NX
- ☎ (0131) 335 0068
- ✉ secretary@rathoparkgolfclub.co.uk
- ✍ D A Scott
- 🖳 www.rathoparkgolfclub.co.uk

## Ravelston (1912)

24 Ravelston Dykes Road, Edinburgh
EH4 3NZ
- ☎ (0131) 315 2486
- 🖷 (0131) 315 2486
- ✉ ravelstongc@hotmail.com
- ✍ Jim Lowrie
- 🖳 www.ravelstongolfclub.com

## Royal Burgess Golfing Society of Edinburgh (1735)

181 Whitehouse Road, Barnton, Edinburgh
EH4 6BU
- ☎ (0131) 339 2075
- ✉ graham@royalburgess.co.uk
- ✍ G Callander
- 🖳 www.royalburgess.co.uk

## Silverknowes (1947)

Public
Silverknowes Parkway, Edinburgh EH4 5ET
- ☎ (0131) 336 3843 (Starter)

## Swanston New Golf Course (1927)

111 Swanston Road, Fairmilehead,
Edinburgh EH10 7DS
- ☎ (0131) 445 2239
- 🖷 (0131) 445 5720
- ✉ golf@swanston.co.uk
- ✍ Colin McClung
- 🖳 www.swanstongolf.co.uk

## Torphin Hill (1895)

37-39 Torphin Road, Edinburgh EH13 0PG
- ☎ (0131) 441 1100
- 🖷 (0131) 441 7166
- ✉ torphinhillgc@aol.co.uk
- ✍ Secretary
- 🖳 www.torphinhillgc.com

## Turnhouse (1897)

154 Turnhouse Road, Corstorphine,
Edinburgh EH12 0AD
- ☎ (0131) 339 1014
- ✉ secretary@turnhousegc.com
- ✍ Lindsay Gordon (Secretary)
- 🖳 www.turnhousegc.com

### West Lothian

## Bathgate (1892)

Edinburgh Road, Bathgate EH48 1BA
- ☎ (01506) 630505
- 🖷 (01506) 636775
- ✉ bathgate.golfclub@lineone.net
- ✍ G Flannigan (01506) 630505
- 🖳 www.bathgategolfclub.com

## Bridgend & District (1994)

Willowdean, Bridgend, Linlithgow
EH49 6NW
- ☎ (01506) 834140
- 🖷 (01506) 834706
- ✍ George Green
- 🖳 www.bridgendgolfclub.com

## Deer Park G&CC (1978)

Golf Course Road, Knightsridge, Livingston
EH54 8AB
- ☎ (01506) 446699
- 🖷 (01506) 435608
- ✉ jdouglas@muir-group.co.uk
- ✍ John Douglas (Gen Mgr)
- 🖳 www.deer-park.co.uk

## Dundas Parks (1957)

South Queensferry EH30 9SS
- ☎ (0131)331 4252
- ✉ cmkwood@btinternet.com
- ✍ Mrs C Wood (07747) 854802
- 🖳 www.dundasparks.co.uk

## Greenburn (1953)

6 Greenburn Road, Fauldhouse EH47 9HJ
- ☎ (01501) 770292
- 🖷 (01501) 772615
- ✉ administrator@greenburngolfclub.co.uk
- ✍ Adrian McGowan
- 🖳 www.greenburngolfclub.com

## Harburn (1932)

West Calder EH55 8RS
- ☎ (01506) 871131
- 🖷 (01506) 870286
- ✉ info@harburngolf.co.uk
- ✍ H Warnock (01506) 871131
- 🖳 www.harburngolfclub.co.uk

## Linlithgow (1913)

Braehead, Linlithgow EH49 6QF
- ☎ (01506) 842585
- 🖷 (01506) 842764
- ✉ linlithgowgolfclub@talk21.com
- ✍ TI Adams
- 🖳 www.linlithgowgolf.co.uk

## Niddry Castle (1983)

Castle Road, Winchburgh EH52 2RQ
- ☎ (01506) 891097
- ✉ secretary@niddrycastlegc.co.uk
- ✍ B Brooks
- 🖳 www.niddrycastlegc.co.uk

## Oatridge (2000)

Pay and play
Ecclesmachen, Broxburn, West Lothian
EH52 6NH
- ☎ (01506) 859636
- ✉ info@oatridge.ac.uk
- ✍ Jim Thomson
- 🖳 www.oatridge.ac.uk

## Polkemmet (1981)

Public
Whitburn, Bathgate EH47 0AD
- ☎ (01501) 743905
- 🖷 (01501) 744780
- ✉ polkemmet@westlothian.gov.uk
- ✍ Stuart Mungall (01501) 743905
- 🖳 www.beecraigs.com

## Pumpherston (1895)

Drumshoreland Road, Pumpherston
EH53 0LH
- ☎ (01506) 432869/433336
- 🖷 (01506) 438250
- ✉ sheena.corner@tiscali.co.uk
- ✍ James Taylor (01506) 433336
- 🖳 www.pumpherstongolfclub.co.uk

## Rutherford Castle (1998)

Proprietary
West Linton EH46 7AS
- ☎ (01968) 661233
- 🖷 (01968) 661233
- ✉ clubhouse@rutherfordcastle.org.uk
- ✍ Derek Mitchell (Mgr)
- 🖳 www.rutherfordcastlegc.org.uk

## Uphall (1895)

Houston Mains, Uphall EH52 6JT
- ☎ (01506) 856404
- 🖷 (01506) 855358
- ✉ uphallgolfclub@btconnect.com
- ✍ Gordon Law (Club Administrator Mgr)
- 🖳 www.uphallgolfclub.com

## West Lothian (1892)

Airngath Hill, Bo'ness EH49 7RH
- ☎ (01506) 826030
- 🖷 (01506) 826030
- ✉ manager@westlothiangc.com
- ✍ Alan E Gibson (01506) 826030
- 🖳 www.westlothiangc.com

## Moray

## Buckpool (1933)

Barhill Road, Buckie AB56 1DU
- ☎ (01542) 832236
- ✉ golf@buckpoolgolf.com
- ✍ Mrs I Coull
- 🖳 www.buckpoolgolf.com

## Dufftown (1896)

Tomintoul Road, Dufftown AB55 4BS
- ☎ (01340) 820325
- 🖷 (01340) 820325
- ✉ admin@dufftowngolfclub.com
- ✍ Richard Dix
- 🖳 www.dufftowngolfclub.com

## Elgin (1906)

Hardhillock, Birnie Road, Elgin IV30 8SX
- ☎ (01343) 542338
- 🖷 (01343) 542341
- ✉ secretary@elgingolfclub.com
- ✍ Gary J Abel
- 🖳 www.elgingolfclub.com

## Forres (1889)

Muiryshade, Forres IV36 2RD
- ☎ (01309) 672949
- 🖷 (01309) 672261
- ✉ secretary@forresgolfclub.co.uk
- ✍ David Mackintosh
- 🖳 www.forresgolfclub.co.uk

## Garmouth & Kingston    (1932)
*Spey Street, Garmouth, Fochabers IV32 7NJ*
- ☎ **(01343) 870388**
- 📠 (01343) 870388
- ✉ garmouthgolfclub@aol.com
- 🖊 Mrs I Fraser
- 🖥 www.garmouthkingstongolfclub
  .com

## Hopeman    (1909)
*Hopeman, Moray IV30 5YA*
- ☎ **(01343) 830578**
- 📠 (01343) 830152
- ✉ hopemangc@aol.com
- 🖊 J Fraser (01343) 835068
- 🖥 www.hopemangc.co.uk

## Moray    (1889)
*Stotfield Road, Lossiemouth IV31 6QS*
- ☎ **(01343) 812018**
- 📠 (01343) 815102
- ✉ secretary@moraygolf.co.uk
- 🖊 Stevie Grant
- 🖥 www.moraygolf.co.uk

## Spey Bay    (1904)
**Proprietary**
*The Links, Spey Bay, Fochabers IV32 7PJ*
- ☎ **(01343) 820424**
- ✉ info@speybay.co
- 🖊 Mr Iain Ednie
- 🖥 www.speybay.co

## Perth & Kinross

## Aberfeldy    (1895)
*Taybridge Road, Aberfeldy PH15 2BH*
- ☎ **(01887) 820535**
- 📠 (01887) 820535
- ✉ aberfeldygolfclub@btconnect.com
- 🖊 Jim Adams
- 🖥 www.aberfeldy-golf-club.co.uk

## Alyth    (1894)
*Pitcrocknie, Alyth PH11 8HF*
- ☎ **(01828) 632268**
- 📠 (01828) 633491
- ✉ enquiries@alythgolfclub.co.uk
- 🖊 J Docherty
- 🖥 www.alythgolfclub.co.uk

## Auchterarder    (1892)
*Orchil Road, Auchterarder PH3 1LS*
- ☎ **(01764) 662804**
- 📠 (01764) 664423
- ✉ secretary@auchterardergolf.co.uk
- 🖊 D.D.Smith
- 🖥 www.auchterardergolf.co.uk

## Bishopshire    (1903)
**Pay and play**
*Kinnesswood, Woodmarch, Kinross KY13 9HX*
- ✉ ian-davidson@tiscali.co.uk
- 🖊 Ian Davidson (01592) 773224
- 🖥 www.bishopshiregolfclub.com

## Blair Atholl    (1896)
*Invertilt Road, Blair Atholl PH18 5TG*
- ☎ **(01796) 481407**
- 🖊 T Boon 01796 481611

## Blairgowrie    (1889)
*Golf Course Road, Rosemount, Blairgowrie PH10 6LG*
- ☎ **(01250) 872622**
- 📠 (01250) 875451
- ✉ office@theblairgowriegolfclub.co.uk
- 🖊 Douglas Cleeton (Managing Secretary)
- 🖥 www.theblairgowriegolfclub.co.uk

## Callander    (1890)
*Aveland Road, Callander FK17 8EN*
- ☎ **(01877) 330090**
- 📠 (01877) 330062
- ✉ callandergolf@btconnect.com
- 🖊 Miss E Macdonald
- 🖥 www.callandergolfclub.co.uk

## Comrie    (1891)
*Laggan Braes, Comrie PH6 2LR*
- ☎ **(01764) 670055**
- ✉ enquiries@comriegolf.co.uk
- 🖊 Manager
- 🖥 www.comriegolf.co.uk

## Craigie Hill    (1909)
*Cherrybank, Perth PH2 0NE*
- ☎ **(01738) 622644**
- 📠 (01738) 620829
- ✉ admin@craigiehill.co.uk
- 🖊 Administration (01738) 620829
- 🖥 www.craigiehill.co.uk

## Crieff    (1891)
*Perth Road, Crieff PH7 3LR*
- ☎ **(01764) 652909 (Bookings)**
- 📠 (01764) 653803
- ✉ secretary@crieffgolf.co.uk
- 🖊 Lesley Mackenzie (01764) 652397
- 🖥 www.crieffgolf.co.uk

## Dalmunzie    (1948)
*Glenshee, Blairgowrie PH10 7QE*
- ☎ **(01250) 885226**
- ✉ info@dalmunzieestate.com
- 🖊 Simon Winton
- 🖥 www.dalmunzieestate.com

## Dunkeld & Birnam    (1892)
*Fungarth, Dunkeld PH8 0ES*
- ☎ **(01350) 727524**
- 📠 (01350) 728660
- ✉ secretary-dunkeld@tiscali.co.uk
- 🖊 Jane Burnett
- 🖥 www.dunkeldandbirnamgolfclub
  }.co.uk

## Dunning    (1907)
*Rollo Park, Dunning PH2 0QX*
- ☎ **(01764) 684747**
- ✉ secretary@dunninggolfclub.co.uk
- 🖊 Neil C Morton (01738) 626701
- 🖥 www.dunninggolfclub.co.uk

## Foulford Inn    (1995)
**Pay and play**
*Crieff PH7 3LN*
- ☎ **(01764) 652407**
- 📠 (01764) 652407
- ✉ foulford@btconnect.com
- 🖊 M Beaumont
- 🖥 www.foulfordinn.co.uk

## The Gleneagles Hotel    (1924)
*Auchterarder PH3 1NF*
- ☎ **(01764) 662231**
- 📠 (01764) 662134
- ✉ resort.sales@gleneagles.com
- 🖊 Bernard Murphy (Hotel)
- 🖥 www.gleneagles.com

## Glenisla    (1998)
**Proprietary**
*Pitcrocknie Farm, Alyth PH11 8JJ*
- ☎ **(01828) 632445**
- 📠 (01828) 633749
- 🖊 Alison Stubbington (Mgr)
- 🖥 www.golf-glenisla.co.uk

## Killin    (1911)
*Killin FK21 8TX*
- ☎ **(01567) 820312**
- 📠 (01567) 820312
- ✉ info@killingolfclub.co.uk
- 🖥 www.killingolfclub.co.uk

## King James VI    (1858)
*Moncreiffe Island, Perth PH2 8NR*
- ☎ **(01738) 632460**
- ✉ mansec@kingjamesvi.com
- 🖊 Mike Brown (Managing Secretary)
- 🖥 www.kingjamesvi.com

## Kinross Golf Courses    (1900)
*c/o The Green Hotel, 2 The Muirs, Kinross KY13 8AS*
- ☎ **(01577) 863407**
- 📠 (01577) 863180
- ✉ reception@green-hotel.com
- 🖊 Eileen Gray
- 🖥 www.golfkinross.com

## Mains of Taymouth Golf Course    (1992)
**Pay and play**
*Mains of Taymouth, Kenmore, Aberfeldy PH15 2HN*
- ☎ **(01887) 830226**
- 📠 (01887) 830775
- ✉ info@taymouth.co.uk
- 🖊 R Menzies (Mgr)
- 🖥 www.taymouth.co.uk

## Milnathort    (1910)
*South Street, Milnathort, Kinross KY13 9XA*
- ☎ **(01577) 864069**
- ✉ milnathort.gc@btconnect.com
- 🖊 K Dziennik (Admin. Mgr)
- 🖥 www.milnathortgolfclub.co.uk

## Muckhart    (1908)
*Drumburn Road, Muckhart, Dollar FK14 7JH*
- ☎ **(01259) 781423**
- ✉ enquiries@muckhartgolf.com
- 🖊 A Houston
- 🖥 www.muckhartgolf.com

## Murrayshall    (1981)
*Murrayshall, New Scone, Perth PH2 7PH*
- ☎ **(01738) 554804**
- 📠 (01738) 552595
- ✉ info@murrayshall.co.uk
- 🖊 M Lloyd (Mgr)
- 🖥 www.murrayshall.co.uk

## Muthill (1911)

Peat Road, Muthill PH5 2DA
- ☎ (01764) 681523
- 🖵 (01764) 681557
- ✉ muthillgolfclub@btconnect.com
- ✍ Nan Shaw
- 🖥 www.muthillgolfclub.co.uk

## North Inch (1892)

**Public**

c/o Perth & Kinross Council, The Environment Services, Pullar House, 35 Kinnoull St, Perth PH1 5GD
- ☎ (01738) 636481 (Starter)
- 🖵 (01738) 476410
- ✉ northinchgolf@pkc.gov.uk
- ✍ Alison White
- 🖥 www.pkc.gov.uk/northinchgolf

## Pitlochry (1909)

**Proprietary**

Golf Course Road, Pitlochry PH16 5QY
- ☎ (01796) 472792 (Bookings)
- 🖵 (01796) 473947 (bookings)
- ✉ pro@pitlochrygolf.co.uk
- ✍ Mark Pirie (01796) 472792
- 🖥 www.pitlochrygolf.co.uk

## Royal Perth Golfing Society (1824)

**Club**

1/2 Atholl Crescent, Perth PH1 5NG
- ☎ (01738) 622265
- ✉ secretary@rpgs.org.uk
- ✍ DP McDonald (Gen Sec) (01738) 622265,
- 🖥 www.rpgs.org.uk

## St Fillans (1903)

South Loch Earn Rd, St Fillans PH6 2NJ
- ☎ (01764) 685312
- 🖵 01764 685312
- ✉ stfillansgc@aol.com
- ✍ G Hibbert (01764) 685312
- 🖥 www.st-fillans-golf.com

## Strathmore Golf Centre (1995)

**Proprietary**

Leroch, Alyth, Blairgowrie PH11 8NZ
- ☎ (01828) 633322
- 🖵 (01828) 633533
- ✉ enquiries@strathmoregolf.com
- ✍ David Norman
- 🖥 www.strathmoregolf.com

## Strathtay (1909)

Donfield, Strathtay, Pitlochry PH9 0PG
- ☎ (01887) 840493
- ✍ James Wilson
- 🖥 www.strathtaygolfclub.com

## Taymouth Castle (1923)

Kenmore, Aberfeldy PH15 2NT
- ☎ (01887) 830234
- 🖵 (01887) 830234
- ✉ secretary@taymouthcastlegolfclub.com
- ✍ W R McGregor (Sec)
- 🖥 www.taymouthcastlegolfclub.com

## Whitemoss (1994)

Whitemoss Road, Dunning, Perth PH2 0QX
- ☎ (01738) 730300
- 🖵 (01738) 730490
- ✉ info@whitemossgolf.com
- ✍ A Nicolson
- 🖥 www.whitemossgolf.com

# Renfrewshire

## Barshaw (1927)

**Public**

Barshaw Park, Glasgow Road, Paisley, PA2
- ☎ (0141) 889 2908
- 🖵 (0141) 840 2148
- ✍ W Collins (0141) 884 2533

## Bonnyton (1957)

Eaglesham, Glasgow G76 0QA
- ☎ (01355) 303030
- 🖵 (01355) 303151
- ✉ secretarybgc@btconnect.com
- ✍ Mags Crichton
- 🖥 www.bonnytongolfclub.com

## Caldwell (1903)

Caldwell, Uplawmoor G78 4AU
- ☎ (01505) 850329
- 🖵 (01505) 850604
- ✉ Secretary@caldwellgolfclub.co.uk
- ✍ Alan Ferguson (01505) 850366
- 🖥 www.caldwellgolfclub.co.uk

## Cochrane Castle (1895)

Scott Avenue, Craigston, Johnstone PA5 0HF
- ☎ (01505) 320146
- 🖵 (01505) 325338
- ✉ secretary@cochranecastle.com
- ✍ Mrs PlJ Quin
- 🖥 www.cochranecastle.com

## East Renfrewshire (1922)

Pilmuir, Newton Mearns G77 6RT
- ☎ (01355) 500256
- 🖵 (01355) 500323
- ✉ secretary@eastrengolfclub.co.uk
- ✍ G J Tennant (01355) 500256
- 🖥 www.eastrengolfclub.co.uk

## Eastwood (1893)

Muirshield, Loganswell, Newton Mearns, Glasgow G77 6RX
- ☎ (01355) 500285
- 🖵 (01355) 500333
- ✉ eastwoodgolfclub@btconnect.com
- ✍ I Brown (01355) 500280
- 🖥 www.eastwoodgolfclub.co.uk

## Elderslie (1908)

63 Main Road, Elderslie PA5 9AZ
- ☎ (01505) 323956
- 🖵 (01505) 340346
- ✉ eldersliegolfclub@btconnect.com
- ✍ Mrs A Anderson
- 🖥 www.eldersliegolfclub.com

## Erskine (1904)

Golf Road, Bishopton PA7 5PH
- ☎ (01505) 862302
- 🖵 (01505) 862898
- ✉ secretary_erskinegolfclub@btconnect.com
- ✍ Christine Campbell
- 🖥 www.erskinegolfclublimited.co.uk

## Fereneze (1904)

Fereneze Avenue, Barrhead G78 1HJ
- ☎ (0141) 881 1519
- 🖵 (0141) 881 7149
- ✉ ferenezegc@lineone.net
- ✍ G McCreadie (0141) 881 7149
- 🖥 www.ferenezegolfclub.co.uk

## Gleddoch (1974)

Langbank PA14 6YE
- ☎ (01475) 540711
- ✍ DW Tierney

## Gourock (1896)

Cowal View, Gourock PA19 1HD
- ☎ (01475) 631001
- ✉ secretary@gourockgolfclub.com
- ✍ Margaret Paterson
- 🖥 www.gourockgolfclub.com

## Greenock (1890)

Forsyth Street, Greenock PA16 8RE
- ☎ (01475) 720793
- ✉ secretary@greenockgolfclub.co.uk
- ✍ Mrs Heather Sinclair (01475) 791912
- 🖥 www.greenockgolfclub.co.uk

## Kilmacolm (1891)

Porterfield Road, Kilmacolm PA13 4PD
- ☎ (01505) 872139
- 🖵 (01505) 874007
- ✉ secretary@kilmacolmgolfclub.com
- ✍ VR Weldin
- 🖥 www.kilmacolmgolfclub.com

## Lochwinnoch (1897)

Burnfoot Road, Lochwinnoch PA12 4AN
- ☎ (01505) 842153
- 🖵 (01505) 843668
- ✉ admin@lochwinnochgolf.co.uk
- ✍ Elaine Boyle
- 🖥 www.lochwinnochgolf.co.uk

## Old Course Ranfurly Golf Club (1905)

Ranfurly Place, Bridge of Weir PA11 3DE
- ☎ (01505) 613612 (Clubhouse)
- 🖵 (01505) 613214
- ✉ secretary@oldranfurly.com
- ✍ J M R Doyle (01505) 613214
- 🖥 www.oldranfurly.com

## Paisley (1895)

Braehead Road, Paisley PA2 8TZ
- ☎ (0141) 884 2292 (Clubhouse)
- 🖵 (0141) 884 3903
- ✉ paisleygolfclub@btconnect.com
- ✍ John Devenny (Sec/Mgr)
- 🖥 www.paisleygolfclub.com

## Port Glasgow (1895)

Devol Road, Port Glasgow PA14 5XE
- ☎ (01475) 704181
- 🖵 01475 700334
- ✉ contact@portglasgowgolfclub.co.uk
- ✍ James Downie
- 🖥 www.portglasgowgolfclub.com

## Ranfurly Castle    (1889)
Golf Road, Bridge of Weir PA11 3HN
☎ **(01505) 612609**
✉ secranfur@btconnect.com
♘ Ronnie Carswell (Sec)
🖥 www.ranfurlycastlegolfclub.co.uk

## Renfrew    (1894)
Blythswood Estate, Inchinnan Road, Renfrew PA4 9EG
☎ **(0141) 886 6692**
📠 (0141) 886 1808
✉ secretary@renfrewgolfclub.net
♘ Kenny Morrison
🖥 www.renfrewgolfclub.net

## Whitecraigs    (1905)
72 Ayr Road, Giffnock, Glasgow G46 6SW
☎ **(0141) 639 4530**
📠 (0141) 616 3648
✉ admin@whitecraigsgolfclub.com
♘ Ian Brown
🖥 www.whitecraigsgolfclub.com

## Stirlingshire

## Aberfoyle    (1890)
Braeval, Aberfoyle FK8 3UY
☎ **(01877) 382493**
✉ secretary@aberfoylegolf.co.uk
♘ EJ Barnard (Sec) (01360) 550847
🖥 www.aberfoylegolf.com

## Balfron    (1992)
Kepculloch Road, Balfron G63 0QP
☎ **(0781) 482 7620**
✉ brian.a.davidson23@btinternet.com
♘ Brian Davidson (01360) 550613
🖥 www.balfrongolfsociety.org.uk

## Bonnybridge    (1925)
Larbert Road, Bonnybridge, Falkirk FK4 1NY
☎ **(01324) 812822/812323**
📠 (01324) 812323

✉ bgc1925@hotmail.co.uk
♘ Alexander Nolton (01324) 812323
🖥 www.bonnybridgegc.co.uk

## Bridge of Allan    (1895)
Sunnylaw, Bridge of Allan, Stirling FK9 4LY
☎ **(01786) 832332**
✉ secretary@bofagc.com
♘ Scott Benson
🖥 www.bofagc.com

## Buchanan Castle    (1936)
Proprietary
Drymen G63 0HY
☎ **(01360) 660307**
✉ info@buchanancastlegolfclub.co.uk
♘ Ms JA Dawson
🖥 www.buchanancastlegolfclub.com

## Campsie    (1897)
Crow Road, Lennoxtown, Glasgow G66 7HX
☎ **(01360) 310244**
✉ campsiegolfclub@aol.com
♘ K Stoddart (Administrator)
🖥 www.campsiegolfclub.org.uk

## Dunblane New    (1923)
Perth Road, Dunblane FK15 0LJ
☎ **(01786) 821527**
📠 (01786) 825066
✉ secretary@dngc.co.uk
♘ RD Morrison
🖥 www.dngc.co.uk

## Falkirk    (1922)
Stirling Road, Camelon, Falkirk FK2 7YP
☎ **(01324) 611061/612219**
📠 (01324) 639573
✉ secretary@falkirkgolfclub.co.uk
♘ Aileen Jenkins
🖥 www.falkirkgolfclub.co.uk

## Falkirk Tryst    (1885)
86 Burnhead Road, Larbert FK5 4BD
☎ **(01324) 562415**
📠 (01324) 562054
✉ secretary@falkirktrystgolfclub.com

♘ Mhairi Kemp (01324) 562054
🖥 www.falkirktrystgolfclub.com

## Glenbervie    (1932)
Stirling Road, Larbert FK5 4SJ
☎ **(01324) 562605**
📠 (01324) 551054
✉ secretary@glenberviegolfclub.com
♘ IR Webster CA
🖥 www.glenberviegolfclub.com

## Grangemouth    (1973)
Public
Polmonthill, Polmont FK2 0YA
☎ **(01324) 711500**
✉ info@grangemouthgolfclub.co.uk
♘ Anne Cunningham
🖥 www.grangemouthgolfclub.co.uk

## Kilsyth Lennox    (1905)
Tak-Ma-Doon Road, Kilsyth G65 0RS
☎ **(01236) 824115 (Bookings)**
📠 (01236) 823089
✉ admin@kilsythlennox.com
♘ L Reeds (01236) 824115
🖥 www.kilsythlennox.com

## Polmont    (1901)
Manuel Rigg, Maddiston, Falkirk FK2 0LS
☎ **(01324) 711277 (Clubhouse)**
📠 (01324) 712504
✉ polmontgolfclub@btconnect.com
♘ Mrs M Fellows

## Stirling    (1869)
Queen's Road, Stirling FK8 3AA
☎ **(01786) 464098**
📠 (01786) 460090
✉ enquiries@stirlinggolfclub.tv
♘ AMS Rankin (01786) 464098 Option 2
🖥 www.stirlinggolfclub.com

## Strathendrick    (1901)
Glasgow Road, Drymen G63 0AA
☎ **(01360) 660695**
♘ M Quyn (01360) 660733
🖥 www.strathendrickgolfclub.co.uk

# Wales

## Cardiganshire

### Aberystwyth (1911)
*Brynymor Road, Aberystwyth SY23 2HY*
- ☎ **(01970) 615104**
- ✉ secretary@aberystwythgolfclub .com
- Emlyn Thomas
- 🖳 www.aberystwythgolfclub.com

### Borth & Ynyslas (1885)
*Borth, Ceredigion SY24 5JS*
- ☎ **(01970) 871202**
- 🖵 (01970) 871202
- ✉ secretary@borthgolf.co.uk
- Owen Lawrence
- 🖳 www.borthgolf.co.uk

### Cardigan (1895)
*Gwbert-on-Sea, Cardigan SA43 1PR*
- ☎ **(01239) 621775**
- 🖵 (01239) 621775
- ✉ cgc@btconnect.com
- Clive Day (Sec) (01239) 621775
- 🖳 www.cardigangolf.co.uk

### Cilgwyn (1905)
*Llangybi, Lampeter SA48 8NN*
- ☎ **(01570) 493286**
- J M Jones
- 🖳 www.cilgwyngolf.co.uk

### Penrhos G&CC (1991)
*Llanrhystud, Ceredigion SY23 5AY*
- ☎ **(01974) 202999**
- 🖵 (01974) 202100
- ✉ info@penrhosgolf.co.uk
- R Rees-Evans
- 🖳 www.penrhosgolf.co.uk

## Carmarthenshire

### Ashburnham (1894)
*Cliffe Terrace, Burry Port SA16 0HN*
- ☎ **(01554) 832269**
- 🖵 (01554) 836974
- ✉ golf@ashburnhamgolfclub.co.uk
- Mr Huw Morgan
- 🖳 www.ashburnhamgolfclub.co.uk

### Carmarthen (1907)
*Blaenycoed Road, Carmarthen SA33 6EH*
- ☎ **(01267) 281588**
- 🖵 (01267) 281493
- ✉ carmarthengolfclub@btinternet .com
- Shan Lewis
- 🖳 www.carmarthengolf.com

### Derllys Court (1993)
**Proprietary**
*Derllys Court, Llysonnen Road, Carmarthen SA33 5DT*
- ☎ **(01267) 211575**
- 🖵 (01267) 211575
- ✉ derllys@hotmail.com

- R Walters
- 🖳 www.derllyscourtgolfclub.com

### Garnant Park (1997)
*Garnant, Ammanford SA18 1NP*
- ☎ **(01269) 823365**
- 🖵 (01269) 823365
- ✉ garnantgolf@carmarthenshire .gov.uk
- Vince Mosson
- 🖳 www.parcgarnantgolf.co.uk

### Glyn Abbey (1992)
**Proprietary**
*Trimsaran SA17 4LB*
- ☎ **(01554) 810278**
- 🖵 (01554) 810889
- ✉ info@glynabbey.co.uk
- Dafydd Latham (Manager)
- 🖳 www.glynabbey.co.uk

### Glynhir (1909)
*Glynhir Road, Llandybie, Ammanford SA18 2TF*
- ☎ **(01269) 851365**
- 🖵 (01269) 851365
- ✉ glynhirgolfclub@tiscali.co.uk
- Mr Roburt Edwards
- 🖳 www.glynhirgolfclub.co.uk

### Saron Golf Course (1990)
**Pay and play**
*Penwern, Saron, Llandysul SA44 4EL*
- ☎ **(01559) 370705**
- 🖵 (01559) 370705
- ⊕ Answer telephone 24hrs

## Conwy

### Abergele (1910)
*Tan-y-Gopa Road, Abergele LL22 8DS*
- ☎ **(01745) 824034**
- 🖵 (01745) 824772
- ✉ secretary@abergelegolfclub.co.uk
- CP Langdon
- 🖳 www.abergelegolfclub.co.uk

### Betws-y-Coed (1977)
*Clubhouse, Betws-y-Coed LL24 0AL*
- ☎ **(01690) 710556**
- ✉ info@golf-betws-y-coed.co.uk/betwsycoedgclub @btinternet.com
- Adam Brown
- 🖳 www.golf-betws-y-coed.co.uk

### Conwy (Caernarvonshire) (1890)
*Beacons Way, Morfa, Conwy LL32 8ER*
- ☎ **(01492) 592423**
- 🖵 (01492) 593363
- ✉ secretary@conwygolfclub.com
- Chris Chance (01492) 592423
- 🖳 www.conwygolfclub.com

### Llandudno (Maesdu) (1915)
*Hospital Road, Llandudno LL30 1HU*
- ☎ **(01492) 876450**
- 🖵 (01492) 876450
- ✉ secretary@maesdugolfclub.co.uk
- Miss S Thomas
- 🖳 www.maesdugolfclub.co.uk

### Llanfairfechan (1971)
*Llannerch Road, Llanfairfechan LL33 0EB*
- ☎ **(01248) 680144**
- K V Williams

### North Wales (Llandudno) (1894)
*72 Bryniau Road, West Shore, Llandudno LL30 2DZ*
- ☎ **(01492) 875325**
- 🖵 (01492) 872420
- ✉ enquiries@northwalesgolfclub .co.uk
- Nick Kitchen
- 🖳 www.northwalesgolfclub.co.uk

### Old Colwyn (1907)
*Woodland Avenue, Old Colwyn LL29 9NL*
- ☎ **(01492) 515581**
- ✉ colwyngolf@tiscali.co.uk
- Mike Eccles (07760) 119445
- 🖳 www.oldcolwyngolfclub.co.uk

### Penmaenmawr (1910)
*Conway Old Road, Penmaenmawr LL34 6RD*
- ☎ **(01492) 623330**
- 🖵 (01492) 622105
- ✉ clubhouse@pengolf.co.uk
- Mrs A H Greenwood
- 🖳 www.pengolf.co.uk

### Rhos-on-Sea (1899)
*Penrhyn Bay, Llandudno LL30 3PU*
- ☎ **(01492) 549641**
- 🖵 (01492) 549100
- ✉ rhosonseagolfclub@btinternet.com
- G Simmonds & I Taylor
- 🖳 www.rhosgolf.co.uk

## Denbighshire

### Bryn Morfydd Hotel (1982)
*Llanrhaeadr, Denbigh LL16 4NP*
- ☎ **(01745) 589090**
- 🖵 (01745) 890488
- ✉ Reception@Brynmorfyddhotelgolf .co.uk
- BW Astle (07752) 527257
- 🖳 www.brynmorfyddhotelgolf.co.uk

### Denbigh (1908)
*Henllan Road, Denbigh LL16 5AA*
- ☎ **(01745) 816669**
- 🖵 (01745) 814888
- ✉ denbighgolfclub@aol.com
- JR Williams (01745) 816669
- 🖳 www.denbighgolfclub.co.uk

## Kinmel Park    (1989)
**Pay and play**
Bodelwyddan LL18 5SR
☎ **(01745) 833548**
✉ info@kinmelgolf.co.uk
✍ Mrs Fetherstonhaugh
🖳 www.kinmelgolf.co.uk

## Prestatyn    (1905)
Marine Road East, Prestatyn LL19 7HS
☎ **(01745) 854320**
🖥 (01745) 834320
✉ enquiries@prestatyngolfclub.co.uk
✍ Chris Owens (Sec)
🖳 www.prestatyngolfclub.co.uk

## Rhuddlan    (1930)
Meliden Road, Rhuddlan LL18 6LB
☎ **(01745) 590217**
🖥 (01745) 590472
✉ secretary@rhuddlangolfclub.co.uk
✍ Mr J M Wood
🖳 www.rhuddlangolfclub.co.uk

## Rhyl    (1890)
Coast Road, Rhyl LL18 3RE
☎ **(01745) 353171**
🖥 (01745) 353171
✉ rhylgolfclub@btconnect.com
✍ Gill Davies
🖳 www.rhylgolfclub.co.uk

## Ruthin-Pwllglas    (1920)
Pwllglas, Ruthin LL15 2PE
☎ **(01824) 702296**
✉ secretary@ruthinpwliglasgc.co.uk
✍ Neil L Roberts 01824 704651
🖳 www.ruthinpwllglasgc.co.uk

## St Melyd    (1922)
The Paddock, Meliden Road, Prestatyn
LL19 8NB
☎ **(01745) 854405**
🖥 (01745) 856908
✉ office@stmelydgolf.co.uk
✍ Janette Williams
🖳 www.stmelydgolf.co.uk

## Vale of Llangollen    (1908)
Holyhead Road, Llangollen LL20 7PR
☎ **(01978) 860906**
🖥 (01978) 869165
✉ secretary@vlgc.co.uk
✍ Bob Hardy
🖳 www.vlgc.co.uk

## Flintshire

## Caerwys    (1989)
**Pay and play**
Caerwys, Mold CH7 5AQ
☎ **(01352) 721222**
✍ G Nicholls (01352) 720692

## Hawarden    (1911)
Groomsdale Lane, Hawarden, Deeside
CH5 3EH
☎ **(01244) 531447**
🖥 (01244) 536901
✉ secretary@hawardengolfclub.co.uk
✍ A Rowland
🖳 www.hawardengolfclub.co.uk

## Holywell    (1906)
Brynford, Holywell CH8 8LQ
☎ **(01352) 710040 opt 2**
✉ secretary@holywellgc.co.uk
✍ Matt Parsley (01352 710040)
🖳 www.holywellgc.co.uk

## Kinsale    (1996)
**Pay and play**
Llanerchymor, Holywell CH8 9DX
☎ **(01745) 561080**
✍ S Leverett
🖳 www.kinsalegolf.wordpress.com

## Mold    (1909)
Cilcain Road, Pantymwyn, Mold CH7 5EH
☎ **(01352) 740318/741513**
🖥 (01352) 741517
✉ info@moldgolfclub.co.uk
✍ C Mills (01352) 741513
🖳 www.moldgolfclub.co.uk

## Northop Country Park    (1994)
Northop, Chester CH7 6WA
☎ **(01352) 840440**
🖥 (01352) 840445
✉ john@northoppark.co.uk
✍ John Nolan (01352) 840440 press 1
🖳 www.northoppark.co.uk

## Old Padeswood    (1978)
**Proprietary**
Station Road, Padeswood, Mold CH7 4JL
☎ **(01244) 547401 Ext 2**
   **(Clubhouse)**
🖥 (01244) 545082
✉ sec@oldpadeswoodgolfclub.co.uk
✍ Robert Jones (01244) 550414
🖳 www.oldpadeswoodgolfclub.co.uk

## Padeswood & Buckley    (1933)
The Caia, Station Lane, Padeswood, Mold
CH7 4JD
☎ **(01244) 550537**
🖥 (01244) 541600
✉ admin@padeswoodgolf.plus.com
✍ Mrs S A Davies
🖳 www.padeswoodgolfclub.co.uk

## Pennant Park    (1998)
**Proprietary**
Whitford, Holywell CH8 9AE
☎ **(01745) 563000**
✍ M Foster
🖳 www.pennant-park.co.uk

## Gwynedd

## Aberdovey    (1892)
Aberdovey LL35 0RT
☎ **(01654) 767493**
🖥 (01654) 767027
✉ sec@aberdoveygolf.co.uk
✍ Gareth Pritchard (Mgr)
🖳 www.aberdoveygolf.co.uk

## Abersoch    (1907)
Golf Road, Abersoch LL53 7EY
☎ **(01758) 712636**
🖥 (01758) 712777
✉ manager@abersochgolf.co.uk

✍ Dai Davies
🖳 www.abersochgolf.co.uk

## Bala    (1973)
Penlan, Bala LL23 7YD
☎ **(01678) 520359**
🖥 (01678) 521361
✉ balagolf@btconnect.com
✍ G Rhys Jones
🖳 www.golffbala.co.uk

## Bangor St Deiniol    (1906)
Penybryn, Bangor LL57 1PX
☎ **(01248) 353098**
✉ secretary@bangorgolf.co.uk
✍ David T Davies (Hon Sec)
🖳 www.bangorgolf.co.uk

## Clwb Golff Pwllheli    (1900)
Golf Road, Pwllheli LL53 5PS
☎ **(01758) 701644**
🖥 (01758) 701644
✉ admin@pwllheligolfclub.co.uk
✍ Dennis Moore (Gen Mgr)
🖳 www.clwbgolffpwllheli.com

## Dolgellau    (1910)
**Proprietary**
Hengwrt Estate, Pencefn Road, Dolgellau
LL40 2ES
☎ **(01341) 422603**
✉ info@dolgellaugolfclub.com
✍ M White
🖳 www.dolgellaugolfclub.com

## Ffestiniog    (1893)
Y Cefn, Ffestiniog
☎ **(01766) 762637 (Clubhouse)**
✉ info@ffestinioggolf.org
✍ G Hughes (01766) 590617
🖳 www.ffestinioggolf.org

## Nefyn & District    (1907)
Lon Golff, Morfa Nefyn, Pwllheli LL53  6DA
☎ **(01758) 720966 (Clubhouse)**
🖥 (01758) 720476
✉ secretary@nefyn-golf-club.com
✍ S Dennis (Sec/Mgr) (01758) 720966
   ext 1
🖳 www.nefyn-golf-club.com

## Porthmadog    (1905)
Morfa Bychan, Porthmadog LL49 9UU
☎ **(01766) 514124**
🖥 (01766) 514124
✉ secretary@porthmadog-golf-
   club.co.uk
✍ GT Jones (Mgr)
🖳 www.porthmadog-golf-club.co.uk

## Royal St David's    (1894)
Harlech LL46 2UB
☎ **(01766) 780361**
🖥 (0844) 811 1484
✉ secretary@royalstdavids.co.uk
✍ T Davies (01766) 780361
🖳 www.royalstdavids.co.uk

## Royal Town of Caernarfon
   (1909)
Aberforeshore, LLanfaglan, Caernarfon
LL54 5RP
☎ **(01286) 673783**

▯ (01286) 673783
✉ secretary@caernarfongolfclub
.co.uk
✍ EG Angel
▤ www.caernarfongolfclub.co.uk

## Isle of Anglesey

**Anglesey** (1914)
*Station Road, Rhosneigr LL64 5QX*
☎ **(01407) 811127**
✉ info@theangleseygolfclub.com
✍ M Tommis (01407) 811127
▤ www.angleseygolfclub.co.uk

**Baron Hill** (1895)
*Beaumaris LL58 8YW*
☎ **(01248) 810231**
▯ (01248) 810231
✉ golf@baronhill.co.uk
✍ A Pleming
▤ www.baronhill.co.uk

**Bull Bay** (1913)
*Bull Bay Road, Amlwch LL68 9RY*
☎ **(01407) 830960**
▯ (01407) 832612
✉ info@bullbaygc.co.uk
✍ John Burns
▤ www.bullbaygc.co.uk

**Henllys Hall** (1996)
*Llanfaes, Beaumaris LL58 8HU*
☎ **(01248) 811717**
▯ (01248) 811511
✉ hg@hpb.co.uk
✍ Peter Maton
▤ www.henllysgolfclub.co.uk

**Holyhead** (1912)
*Trearddur Bay, Anglesey LL65 2YL*
☎ **(01407) 763279/762119**
▯ (01407) 763279
✉ holyheadgolfclub@tiscali.co.uk
✍ S Elliott (01407) 763279
▤ www.holyheadgolfclub.co.uk

**Llangefni** (1983)
**Public**
*Llangefni LL77 8YQ*
☎ **(01248) 722193**

**RAF Valley**
*Anglesey LL65 3NY*
☎ **(01407) 762241**
▯ (01407) 762241 ext 7705
✉ constables@constables.wanadoo
.com
✍ MJ Constable (Mgr) ext 7716
▤ www.rafvalleygolfclub.co.uk

**Storws Wen** (1996)
**Proprietary**
*Brynteg, Benllech LL78 8JY*
☎ **(01248) 852673**
✉ storws.wen.golf@hotmail.com
✍ E Rowlands (Gen Mgr)
▤ www.storwswen.org

## Mid Glamorgan

**Aberdare** (1921)
**Proprietary**
*Abernant, Aberdare CF44 0RY*
☎ **(01685) 871188 (Clubhouse)**
▯ (01685) 872797
✉ aberdaregolfclub@hotmail.co.uk
✍ Mark Male (Mgr)
▤ www.aberdaregolfclub.com

**Bargoed** (1910)
*Heolddu, Bargoed CF81 9GF*
☎ **(01443) 830143**
▯ (01443) 830608
✍ Mrs Denise Richards
(01443) 830608

**Bryn Meadows Golf Hotel**
(1973)
*Maes-y-Cwmmer, Ystrad Mynach, Nr
Caerphilly CF82 7SN*
☎ **(01495) 225590/224103**
▯ (01495) 228272
✉ reception@brynmeadows.co.uk
✍ S Mayo
▤ www.brynmeadows.co.uk

**Caerphilly** (1905)
*Pencapel, Mountain Road, Caerphilly
CF83 1HJ*
☎ **(029) 2086 3441**
✉ secretary@caerphillygolfclub.com
✍ Howard Mallett
▤ www.caerphillygolfclub.com

**Coed-y-Mwstwr** (1994)
*Coychurch, Bridgend CF35 6AF*
☎ **(01656) 864934**
▯ (01656) 864934
✉ secretary@coed-y-mwstwr.co.uk
✍ Gareth Summerton
▤ www.coed-y-mwstwr.co.uk

**Creigiau** (1921)
*Creigiau, Cardiff CF15 9NN*
☎ **(029) 2089 0263**
▯ (029) 2089 0706
✉ creigiaugolfclub@btconnect.com
✍ Gareth Morgan
▤ www.creigiaugolfclub.co.uk

**Grove** (1996)
**Proprietary**
*South Cornelly, Bridgend CF33 4RP*
☎ **(01656) 788771**
▯ (01656) 788414
✉ enquiries@grovegolf.com
✍ M Thomas
▤ www.grovegolf.com

**Llantrisant & Pontyclun**
(1927)
*Ely Valley Road, Talbot Green, Llantrisant
CF72 8AL*
☎ **(01443) 224601**
▯ (01443) 224601
✉ llantrisantgolf@btconnect.com
✍ Andrew Bowen (Professional)
▤ www.llantrisantgolfclub.co.uk

**Maesteg** (1912)
*Mount Pleasant, Neath Road, Maesteg
CF34 9PR*
☎ **(01656) 734106**
▯ (01656) 731822
✉ manager@maesteg-golf.co.uk
✍ Mr Mark Wilson (Gen Mgr)
▤ www.maesteg-golf.co.uk

**Merthyr Tydfil** (1909)
*Cloth Hall Lane, Cefn Coed, Merthyr Tydfil
CF48 2NU*
☎ **(01685) 373131**
✍ K Anderson
▤ www.merthyrtydfilgolfclub.co.uk

**Mountain Ash** (1907)
*Cefnpennar, Mountain Ash CF45 4DT*
☎ **(01443) 479459 (office)**
▯ (01443) 479628
✉ sec@mountainashgc.co.uk
✍ (01443) 479459 ext 1
▤ www.mountainashgc.co.uk

**Mountain Lakes** (1988)
*Heol Penbryn, Blaengwynlais, Caerphilly
CF83 1NG*
☎ **(029) 2086 1128**
▯ (029) 2086 3243
✍ GM Richards (Hon)

**Pontypridd** (1905)
*Ty Gwyn Road, Pontypridd CF37 4DJ*
☎ **(01443) 409904**
▯ (01443) 491622
✉ rebekah.craven
@pontypriddgolfclub.co.uk
✍ Rebekah Craven (01443) 409904
▤ www.pontypriddgolfclub.co.uk

**Pyle & Kenfig** (1922)
*Waun-y-Mer, Kenfig, Bridgend CF33 4PU*
☎ **(01656) 783093**
▯ (01656) 772822
✉ secretary@pandkgolfclub.co.uk
✍ Mr Simon Hopkin (01656) 771613
▤ www.pandkgolfclub.co.uk

**Rhondda** (1910)
*Penrhys, Ferndale, Rhondda CF43 3PW*
☎ **(01443) 441384**
▯ (01443) 441384
✉ manager@rhonddagolf.co.uk
✍ Ian Ellis (01443) 441384
▤ www.rhonddagolf.co.uk

**Ridgeway** (1997)
**Proprietary**
*Caerphilly Mountain, Caerphilly CF83 1LY*
☎ **(029) 2088 2255**
✉ petethepro@tiscali.co.uk
✍ Hilary Mears
▤ www.ridgeway-golf.co.uk

**Royal Porthcawl** (1891)
*Rest Bay, Porthcawl CF36 3UW*
☎ **(01656) 782251**
▯ (01656) 771687
✉ office@royalporthcawl.com
✍ Michael Newland
▤ www.royalporthcawl.com

*For key to symbols see page 725*

## Southerndown   (1905)
*Ogmore-by-Sea, Bridgend CF32 0QP*
- ☎ **(01656) 880476**
- 🖶 (01656) 880317
- ✉ admin@southerndowngolfclub.com
- ✍ AJ Hughes (01656) 881111
- 🖳 www.southerndowngolfclub.com

## Whitehall   (1922)
*The Pavilion, Nelson, Treharris CF46 6ST*
- ☎ **(01443) 740245**
- ✉ m.wilde001@tiscali.co.uk
- ✍ PM Wilde
- 🖳 www.whitehallgolfclub1922.co.uk

## Monmouthshire

## Alice Springs   (1989)
**Proprietary**
*Kemeys Commander, Usk NP15 1PP*
- ☎ **(01873) 880914**
- 🖶 (01873) 881381
- ✉ golf@alicespringsgolfclub.co.uk
- 🖳 www.alicespringsgolfclub.co.uk

## Blackwood   (1914)
*Cwmgelli, Blackwood NP12 1BR*
- ☎ **(01495) 223152**
- ✉ blackwoodgolfclub@btconnect
  .com
- ✍ Mr John Bills
- 🖳 www.blackwoodgolfclub.org.uk

## The Celtic Manor Resort
(1995)
**Proprietary**
*Coldra Woods, The Usk Valley, NP18 1HQ*
- ☎ **(01633) 413000**
- 🖶 (01633) 410309
- ✉ postbox@celtic-manor.com
- ✍ Matthew Lewis
  (Director of Golf)
- 🖳 www.celtic-manor.com

## Dewstow   (1988)
**Proprietary**
*Caerwent, Monmouthshire NP26 5AH*
- ☎ **(01291) 430444**
- 🖶 (01291) 425816
- ✉ info@dewstow.com
- ✍ D Bradbury
- 🖳 www.dewstow.com

## Greenmeadow G&CC
(1979)
*Treherbert Road, Croesyceiliog, Cwmbran NP44 2BZ*
- ☎ **(01633) 869321**
- 🖶 (01633) 868430
- ✉ info@greenmeadowgolf.com
- ✍ PJ Richardson (01633) 869321
- 🖳 www.greenmeadowgolf.com

## Llanwern   (1928)
*Tennyson Avenue, Llanwern, Newport NP18 2DY*
- ☎ **(01633) 412029**
- 🖶 (01633) 412260
- ✉ llanwerngolfclub@btconnect.com
- ✍ Mrs A Webber
- 🖳 www.llanwerngolfclub.co.uk

## Marriott St Pierre Hotel & CC   (1962)
*St Pierre Park, Chepstow NP16 6YA*
- ☎ **(01291) 625261**
- 🖶 (01291) 629975
- ✉ chepstow.golf@btconnect.com
- ✍ Mr Arnie Pidgeon (01291) 635218

## Monmouth   (1896)
*Leasbrook Lane, Monmouth NP25 3SN*
- ☎ **(01600) 712212**
- 🖶 (01600) 772399
- ✉ sec@monmouthgolfclub.co.uk
- ✍ Club Manager/Club Secretary
- 🖳 www.monmouthgolfclub.co.uk

## Monmouthshire   (1892)
*Llanfoist, Abergavenny NP7 9HE*
- ☎ **(01873) 852606**
- 🖶 (01873) 850470
- ✉ monmouthshiregc@btconnect.com
- ✍ C Sobik (Gen Mgr)
- 🖳 www.monmouthshiregolfclub
  .co.uk

## Newport   (1903)
*Great Oak, Rogerstone, Newport NP10 9FX*
- ☎ **(01633) 892643**
- 🖶 (01633) 896676
- ✉ newportgolfclub@btconnect.com
- ✍ R Thomas (01633) 892643
- 🖳 www.newportgolfclub.org.uk

## Oakdale   (1990)
**Pay and play**
*Llwynon Lane, Oakdale NP12 0NF*
- ☎ **(01495) 220044**
- ✍ M Lewis (Dir)
- ⊕ 18 bay floodlit golf practice range.
  Snooker, Pool, Darts, Licensed Bar.
  PGA Professional Mathew Griffiths.

## Pontnewydd   (1875)
*West Pontnewydd, Cwmbran, Gwent NP44 1AB*
- ☎ **(01633) 482170**
- 🖶 (01633) 838598
- ✉ secretary@pontnewyddgolf.co.uk
- ✍ CT Phillips (01633) 484447
- 🖳 www.pontnewyddgolf.co.uk

## Pontypool   (1903)
*Lasgarn Lane, Trevethin, Pontypool NP4 8TR*
- ☎ **(01495) 763655**
- 🖶 (01495) 755564
- ✉ pontypoolgolf@btconnect.com
- ✍ L Dodd
- 🖳 www.pontypoolgolf.co.uk

## Raglan Parc   (1994)
*Parc Lodge, Raglan NP5 2ER*
- ☎ **(01291) 690077**
- 🖶 (01291) 69075
- ✉ info@raglanparc.co.uk
- ✍ S Dobney
- 🖳 www.raglanparc.co.uk

## The Rolls of Monmouth
(1982)
*The Hendre, Monmouth NP25 5HG*
- ☎ **(01600) 715353**
- 🖶 (01600) 713115
- ✉ enquiries@therollsgolfclub.co.uk
- ✍ Mrs SJ Orton
- 🖳 www.therollsgolfclub.co.uk

## Shirenewton   (1995)
*Shirenewton, Chepstow NP16 6RL*
- ☎ **(01291) 641642**
- 🖶 (01291) 641472
- ✍ T Morgan (Mgr)

## Tredegar & Rhymney   (1921)
*Tredegar, Rhymney NP22 5HA*
- ☎ **(01685) 840743**
- ✉ tandrgc@googlemail.com

---

# The Duncan Putter

The Duncan Putter was started in 1959 by ex-Walker Cup Captain Tony Duncan in memory of his father, John Duncan – one of the founders of Southerndown Golf Club where the tournament is staged evey April.

A 72-hole scratch competiton, it was originally an invitation event designd to give young Welsh golfers the opportunity to compete against top English amateurs. It is now a Welsh Order of Merit open-entry event which attracts aspiring young golfers from all parts of the UK and occasionally from Europe.

Former winners include Peter McEvoy, Gary Wolstenholme and Nigel Edwards.

---

🖉 Will Price (07761) 005184
🖥 www.tandrgc.co.uk

## Tredegar Park (1923)
Parc-y-Brain Road, Rogerstone, Newport NP10 9TG
☎ (01633) 894433
📧 secretary@tredegarparkgolfclub.co.uk
🖉 S Salway
🖥 www.tredegarparkgolfclub.co.uk

## Wernddu Golf Centre (1992)
**Proprietary**
Old Ross Road, Abergavenny NP7 8NG
☎ (01873) 856223
📠 (01873) 852177
📧 info@wernddu-golf-club.co.uk
🖉 S Cole (Sec)
🖥 www.wernddu-golf-club.co.uk

## West Monmouthshire (1906)
Golf Road, Pond Road, Nantyglo, Ebbw Vale NP23 4QT
☎ (01495) 310233
📧 care@westmongolfclub.co.uk
🖉 L B Matthews (01495) 310233
🖥 www.westmongolfclub.co.uk

## Woodlake Park (1993)
**Proprietary**
Glascoed, Usk NP4 0TE
☎ (01291) 673933
📠 (01291) 673811
📧 golf@woodlake.co.uk
🖉 MJ Wood
🖥 www.woodlake.co.uk

# Pembrokeshire

## Haverfordwest (1904)
Arnolds Down, Haverfordwest SA61 2XQ
☎ (01437) 764523
📠 (01437) 764143
📧 secretary@haverfordwestgolfclub.com
🖉 M Davies (01437) 764523
🖥 www.haverfordwestgolfclub.co.uk

## Milford Haven (1913)
Clay Lane, Hubberston, Milford Haven SA72 3RX
☎ (01646) 697822
📧 fran@mhgc.co.uk
🖉 Frances Cooke (Admin)
🖥 www.mhgc.co.uk

## Newport Links (1925)
Newport SA42 0NR
☎ (01239) 820244
📠 (01239) 821338
📧 info@newportlinks.co.uk
🖉 Mrs A Payne (Mgr)
🖥 www.newportlinks.co.uk

## Priskilly Forest (1992)
Castle Morris, Haverfordwest SA62 5EH
☎ (01348) 840276
📠 (01348) 840276
📧 jevans@priskilly-forest.co.uk
🖉 P Evans
🖥 www.priskilly-forest.co.uk

## South Pembrokeshire (1970)
Military Road, Pembroke Dock SA72 6SE
☎ (01646) 621453
📧 spgc06@tiscali.co.uk
🖉 P Fisher (01646) 621453
🖥 www.southpembsgolf.co.uk

## St Davids City (1903)
Whitesands Bay, St Davids SA62 6PT
☎ (01437) 721751 (Clubhouse)
📧 sdcgc@mail.com
🖉 S Jarvis (01437) 720781
🖥 www.stdavidscitygolfclub.co.uk

## Tenby (1888)
The Burrows, Tenby SA70 7NP
☎ (01834) 842978
📠 (01834) 845603
📧 info@tenbygolf.co.uk
🖉 DJ Hancock (01834) 842978
🖥 www.tenbygolf.co.uk

## Trefloyne (1996)
**Proprietary**
Trefloyne Park, Penally, Tenby SA70 7RG
☎ (01834) 842165
📠 (01834) 844288
📧 sarah@trefloyne.com
🖉 Sarah Knight
🖥 www.trefloyne.com

# Powys

## Brecon (1902)
Newton Park, Llanfaes, Brecon LD3 8PA
☎ (01874) 622004
📧 info@brecongolfclub.co.uk
🖉 I Chambers (01874) 611545
🖥 www.brecongolfclub.co.uk

## Builth Wells (1923)
Golf Links Road, Builth Wells LD2 3NF
☎ (01982) 553296
📧 info@builthwellsgolf.co.uk
🖉 S Edwards (Professional) (01982) 551155
🖥 www.builthwellsgolf.co.uk

## Cradoc (1967)
Penoyre Park, Cradoc, Brecon LD3 9LP
☎ (01874) 623658
📠 (01874) 611711
📧 secretary@cradoc.co.uk
🖉 Robert Southcott (01874) 623658
🖥 www.cradoc.co.uk

## Knighton (1906)
Ffrydd Wood, Knighton LD7 1DL
☎ (01547) 528646
🖉 DB Williams (Hon)
🖥 www.knightongolfclub.co.uk

## Llandrindod Wells (1905)
The Clubhouse, Llandrindod Wells LD1 5NY
☎ (01597) 823873
📠 (01597) 828881
📧 secretary@lwgc.co.uk
🖉 Mrs Terry Evans (01597) 823873
🖥 www.lwgc.co.uk

## Machynlleth (1904)
Felingerrig, Machynlleth SY20 8UH
☎ (01654) 702000
📧 machgolf2@tiscali.co.uk
🖉 John Lewis (Secretary)
🖥 www.machynllethgolfclub.com

## Mid-Wales Golf Centre (1992)
Maesmawr Golf Club, Caersws, Nr Newtown SY17 5SB
☎ (01686) 688303
📠 (01686) 688303
🖉 Mrs Penny Dewinton Davies

## Rhosgoch (1984)
Rhosgoch, Builth Wells LD2 3JY
☎ (01497) 851251
📧 rhosgochgolf@yahoo.co.uk
🖉 C Dance (Sec) N Lloyd (Mgr)
🖥 www.rhosgoch-golf.co.uk

## St Giles Newtown (1895)
Pool Road, Newtown SY16 3AJ
☎ (01686) 625844
📧 stgilesgolf@gmail.com
🖉 John Evans (07739 884198)
🖥 www.stgilesgolf.co.uk

## St Idloes (1906)
Penrhallt, Llanidloes SY18 6LG
☎ (01686) 412559
📧 st.idloesgolfclub@btconnect.com
🖉 Mr E Parry (Sec)
🖥 www.stidloesgolfclub.co.uk

## Welsh Border Golf Complex (1991)
**Pay and play**
Bulthy Farm, Bulthy, Middletown SY21 8ER
☎ (01743) 884247
📧 info@welshbordergolf.com
🖉 K Farr (07966) 530042
🖥 www.welshbordergolf.com

## Welshpool (1894)
Y Golfa, Welshpool, Powys SY21 9AQ
☎ (01938) 850249
📧 secretary@welshpoolgolfclub.co.uk
🖉 Sally Marshall
🖥 www.welshpoolgolfclub.co.uk

# South Glamorgan

## Brynhill (1921)
Port Road, Barry CF62 8PN
☎ (01446) 720277
📠 (01446) 740422
📧 louise@brynhillgolfclub.co.uk
🖉 Louise Edwards
🖥 www.brynhillgolfclub.co.uk

## Cardiff (1922)
Sherborne Avenue, Cyncoed, Cardiff CF23 6SJ
☎ (02920) 753320
📧 russell@cardiffgolfclub.co.uk
🖉 Mr Russell Thomas (Chief Exec) (029) 2075 3320
🖥 www.cardiffgolfclub.co.uk

## Cottrell Park Golf Resort
(1996)
**Proprietary**
*St Nicholas, Cardiff CF5 6SJ*
☎ **(01446) 781781**
🖷 (01446) 781187
🖳 sales@cottrellpark.com
✍ Mr Derek Smith
🖦 www.cottrellpark.com

## Dinas Powis   (1914)
*Old Highwalls, Dinas Powis CF64 4AJ*
☎ **(029) 2051 2727**
🖷 (029) 2051 2727
🖳 dinaspowisgolfclub@yahoo.co.uk
✍ Sally Phelps/Roger Davies
🖦 www.dpgc.co.uk

## Glamorganshire   (1890)
*Lavernock Road, Penarth CF64 5UP*
☎ **(029) 2070 1185**
🖷 (029) 2071 3333
🖳 glamgolf@btconnect.com
✍ BM Williams (029) 2070 1185
🖦 www.glamorganshiregolfclub.co.uk

## Llanishen   (1905)
*Heol Hir, Cardiff CF14 9UD*
☎ **(029) 207 55078**
🖳 manager@llanishengolfclub.com
✍ Colin Duffield (029) 207 55078
🖦 www.llanishengc.co.uk

## Peterstone Lakes   (1990)
**Proprietary**
*Peterstone, Wentloog, Cardiff CF3 2TN*
☎ **(01633) 680009**
🖷 (01633) 680563
🖳 info@peterstonelakes.com
✍ P Millar
🖦 www.peterstonelakes.com

## Radyr   (1902)
*Drysgol Road, Radyr, Cardiff CF15 8BS*
☎ **(029) 2084 2408**
🖷 (029) 2084 3914
🖳 office@radyrgolf.co.uk
✍ Manager
🖦 www.radyrgolf.co.uk

## RAF St Athan   (1977)
*Golf Club Lane, St Athan CF62 4LJ*
☎ **(01446) 751043**
🖷 (01446) 751862
🖳 rafstathan@golfclub.fsbusiness
.co.uk
✍ A McKinstry (01446) 751043
🖦 www.rafstathangc.co.uk

## St Andrews Major   (1993)
**Proprietary**
*Coldbrook Road East, Cadoxton, Barry CF6 3BB*
☎ **(01446) 722227**
🖷 (01446) 748953
🖳 info@standrewsmajorgolfclub.com
✍ A Edmunds
🖦 www.standrewsmajorgolfclub.com

## St Mellons   (1937)
*St Mellons, Cardiff CF3 2XS*
☎ **(01633) 680408**

🖷 (01633) 681219
🖳 secretary@stmellonsgolfclub.co.uk
✍ R Haggerty (01633) 680408
🖦 www.stmellonsgolfclub.co.uk

## Vale Hotel Golf & Spa Resort
(1994)
*Hensol Park, Hensol CF7 8JY*
☎ **(01443) 665899**
🖷 (01443) 222120
🖳 golf@vale-hotel.com
✍ Clive Coombs
🖦 www.vale-hotel.com

## Wenvoe Castle   (1936)
*Wenvoe, Cardiff CF5 6BE*
☎ **(029) 205 94371**
🖷 (029) 205 94371
🖳 wenvoecastle@btconnect.com
✍ Nicola Sims
🖦 www.wenvoecastlegolfclub.co.uk

## Whitchurch (Cardiff)   (1914)
*Pantmawr Road, Whitchurch, Cardiff CF14 7TD*
☎ **(029) 2062 0985**
🖷 (029) 2052 9860
🖳 secretary
@whitchurchcardiffgolfclub.com
✍ G Perrott
🖦 www.whitchurchcardiffgolfclub.com

## West Glamorgan

## Allt-y-Graban   (1993)
*Allt-y-Graban Road, Pontlliw, Swansea SA4 1DT*
☎ **(01792) 885757**
✍ P Gillis (Prop)

## Clyne   (1920)
*120 Owls Lodge Lane, Mayals, Swansea SA3 5DP*
☎ **(01792) 401989**
🖷 (01792) 401078
🖳 manager@clynegolfclub.com
✍ N John Hollis (Gen Mgr)
🖦 www.clynegolfclub.com

## Fairwood Park   (1969)
**Proprietary**
*Blackhills Lane, Fairwood, Swansea SA2 7JN*
☎ **(01792) 297849**
🖷 (01792) 297849
🖳 info@fairwoodpark.com
✍ E Golbas (Mgr)
🖦 www.fairwoodpark.com

## Glynneath   (1931)
*Penygraig, Pontneathvaughan, Glynneath SA11 5UH*
☎ **(01639) 720452**
🖷 (01639) 720452
🖳 enquiries@glynneathgolfclub.co.uk
✍ Shane McMenamin
🖦 www.glynneathgolfclub.co.uk

## Gower
*Cefn Goleu, Three Crosses, Gowerton, Swansea SA4 3HS*
☎ **(01792) 872480**

🖷 (01792) 872480
🖳 info@gowergolf.com
✍ A Richards (01792) 872480
🖦 www.gowergolf.co.uk

## Lakeside   (1992)
*Water Street, Margam, Port Talbot SA13 2PA*
☎ **(01639) 899959**
✍ B Channell
🖦 www.lakesidegolf.co.uk

## Langland Bay   (1904)
*Langland Bay Road, Langland, Swansea SA3 4QR*
☎ **(01792) 361721**
🖳 info@langlandbaygolfclub.com
✍ Mr A Minty (Director of Golf)
🖦 www.langlandbaygolfclub.com

## Morriston   (1920)
*160 Clasemont Road, Morriston, Swansea SA6 6AJ*
☎ **(01792) 796528**
🖷 (01792) 796528
🖳 morristongolf@btconnect.com
✍ Robert Howells (01792) 796528
🖦 www.morristongolfclub.co.uk

## Neath   (1934)
*Cadoxton, Neath SA10 8AH*
☎ **(01639) 632759**
🖷 (01639) 639955
🖳 info@neathgolfclub.co.uk
✍ D M Gee
🖦 www.neathgolfclub.co.uk

## Palleg & Swansea Valley Golf Course   (1930)
**Proprietary**
*Palleg Road, Lower Cwmtwrch, Swansea Valley SA9 2QQ*
☎ **(01639) 842193**
🖷 (01639) 845661
🖳 gc.gcgs@btinternet.com
✍ Graham Coombe (PGA Pro/Director)
🖦 www.palleg-golf.com

## Pennard   (1896)
*2 Southgate Road, Southgate, Swansea SA3 2BT*
☎ **(01792) 233131**
🖷 (01792) 235125
🖳 sec@pennardgolfclub.com
✍ Mrs S Crowley (01792) 235120
🖦 www.pennardgolfclub.com

## Pontardawe   (1924)
*Cefn Llan, Pontardawe, Swansea SA8 4SH*
☎ **(01792) 863118**
🖷 (01792) 830041
🖳 enquiries@pontardawegolfclub
.co.uk
✍ R W Grove (Hon)
🖦 www.pontardawegolfclub.co.uk

## Swansea Bay   (1892)
**Proprietary**
*Jersey Marine, Neath SA10 6JP*
☎ **(01792) 812198**
🖳 swanseabaygolfclub@hotmail.co.uk
✍ Mrs J Richardson (01792) 812198

**Tawe Vale** (1965)
*Clydach, Swansea SA6 5QR*
☎ **(01792) 841257**
✉ secretarytawevalegolfclub
  @btconnect.com
✍ DE Jones (01792) 842929
▤ www.tawevalegolfclub.co.uk

## Wrexham

**Clays Golf Centre** (1992)
Proprietary
*Bryn Estyn Road, Wrexham LL13 9UB*
☎ **(01978) 661406**

▭ (01978) 661406
✉ sales@claysgolf.co.uk
✍ Steve Williams
▤ www.claysgolf.co.uk

**Moss Valley** (1990)
*Moss Road, Wrexham LL11 6HA*
☎ **(01978) 720518**
▭ (01978) 720518
✉ info@mossvalleygolf.co.uk
✍ John Nolan (07588) 104761
▤ www.mossvalleygolf.co.uk

**Plassey** (1992)
*Eyton, Wrexham LL13 0SP*
☎ **(01978) 780020**

▭ (01978) 781397
✉ enquiries@plasseygolfclub.com
✍ OJ Jones (01978) 780020
▤ www.plasseygolfclub.com

**Wrexham** (1906)
*Holt Road, Wrexham LL13 9SB*
☎ **(01978) 364268**
▭ (01978) 362168
✉ info@wrexhamgolfclub.co.uk
✍ R West (01978) 364268
▤ www.wrexhamgolfclub.co.uk

*For key to symbols see page 725*

---

## Gallacher campaigns for defibrillators in clubs

Last year Bernard Gallacher, former Ryder Cup player and former winning captain, suffered a sudden cardiac arrest while speaking at dinner in Aberdeen.

His life was saved by the instant treatment he received and by use of a defibrillator which was available at the hotel. Without this he may not have survived.

He was for a time in intensive care but has made a complete recovery. It is important to know that there is a difference between a heart attack – a blockage to the artery that supplies blood to the heart with the result that the heart muscle begins to die – and what Bernard experienced.

He had a sudden cardiac arrest when the heart suddenly and unexpectedly stops due to a malfunction of its electrical system. The malfunction is a life threatening arrhythmia, most commonly ventricular fibrillation.

There is only a five per cent chance of survival unless there is immediate CPR (cardiopulmonary resuscitation) and AED (the use of a defibrillator) when the chance of survival improves to 50 percent.

Aware how lucky he was, Bernard and his wife Lesley together with the PGA and the Arrhythmia Alliance – the Heart Rhythm Charity – have begun a campaign to get defibrillators into every golf club.

A recent survey indicated there were 3,000 golf courses and a further 84 driving ranges across Great Britain and Ireland but only three in ten had a public access defibrillator available.

A campaign entitled "Play Golf – help save lives" is being organized in conjunction with the PGA to run special events open to both members and non-members with the sole purpose of financing the scheme.

---

## First public golf course in Estonia

The Estonian Golf Association has launched an ambitious plan to build the country's first public golf facility. The new 9-hole golf course and driving range, to be built on an attractive inner city site in the country's capital city of Tallinn, is part of the Association's on-going campaign to bring golf to a wider cross section of the nation's 1.4 million population.

Golf was introduced to Estonia back in 1993 when the country's first facility was opened for play at Niitvälja. It now boasts seven courses including the impressive Sea Course at the Estonian G&CC. Estonia currently has around 2,000 regular golfers.

# Continent of Europe –
# Country and Region Index

# Austria

## Innsbruck & Tyrol

### Achensee    (1934)
Golf und Landclub Achensee,
6213 Pertisau/Tirol
☎ **(05243) 5377**
📠 (05243) 6202
📧 info@golfclub-achensee.at
🖥 www.golfclub-achensee.com

### Innsbruck-Igls    (1935)
Oberdorf 11, 6074 Rinn
☎ **43 (5223) 78177**
📠 43 (5223) 78177-77
📧 office@golfclub-innsbruck-igls.at
🔑 Martin Sterzinger (President Mgr) & Michael Raggl (Mgr)
🖥 www.golfclub-innsbruck-igls.at

### Kaiserwinkl GC Kössen    (1988)
6345 Kössen, Mühlau 1
☎ **(05375) 2122**
📠 (05375) 2122-13
📧 club@golf-koessen.at
🔑 Stefan Emberger
🖥 www.golf-koessen.at

### Golfclub Kitzbühel    (1955)
Ried Kaps 3, 6370 Kitzbühel
☎ **(05356) 63007 Members**
📠 (05356) 630077
📧 gckitzbuehel@golf.at
🔑 Werner Gandler
🖥 www.golfclub-kitzbuehel.at

### Kitzbühel-Schwarzsee
(1988)
6370 Kitzbühel, Golfweg Schwarzsee 35
☎ **(05356) 66660 70**
📠 (05356) 66660 71

### Seefeld-Wildmoos    (1969)
6100 Seefeld, Postfach 22
☎ **(0699) 1-606606-0**
📠 (0699) 4-606606-3
📧 info@seefeldgolf.com
🔑 Mr Werner Seelos
🖥 www.seefeldgolf.com

## Klagenfurt & South

### Bad Kleinkirchheim-
### Reichenau    (1977)
9564 Padergassen, Plass 19
☎ **(04275) 594**
📠 (04275) 594-4

### Golfpark Klopeinersee-
### Sudkarnten    (1988)
9122 St Kanzian, Grabelsdorf 94
☎ **(04239) 3800-0**
📠 (04239) 3800-18
📧 office@golfklopein.at
🖥 www.golfklopein.at

### Kärntner GC Dellach    (1927)
Golfstrasse 3, 9082 Maria Wörth, Golfstr 3
☎ **(04273) 2515**
📠 (04273) 2515-20
📧 office@kgcdellach.at
🔑 Ronald Krach (Mgr)
🖥 www.kgcdellach.at

### Golfclub Klagenfurt-
### Seltenheim    (1996)
Seltenheimerstr. 137, A-9061 Wolfnitz
☎ **0043 463 40223**
📠 0043 463 4022320
📧 office@gcseltenheim.at
🖥 www.gcseltenheim.at

### Golfclub Millstatter See
Am Golfplatz 1, 9872 Millstatt
☎ **+43 (0)4762 82542**
📠 +43 (0)4762 82548-10
📧 gcmillstatt@golf.at
🖥 www.golf-millstatt.at

### Moosburg-Pörtschach    (1986)
9062 Moosburg, Golfstr 2
☎ **(04272) 83486**
📠 (04272) 834 8620
📧 moosburg@golfktn.at
🔑 Tanja Starzacher
🖥 www.golfmoosburg.at

### Wörthersee-Velden    (1988)
9231 Köstenberg, Golfweg 41
☎ **(04274) 7045**
📠 (04274) 7087-15
📧 golf-velden@golfktn.at
🔑 Map. Roland Sint (Mgr)
🖥 www.golfvelden.at

## Linz & North

### Amstetten-Ferschnitz    (1972)
3325 Ferschnitz, Gut Edla 18
☎ **(07473) 8293**
📠 (07473) 82934
📧 office@golfclub-amstetten.at
🖥 www.golfclub-amstetten.at

### Böhmerwald GC Ulrichsberg
(1990)
4161 Ulrichsberg, Seitelschlag 50
☎ **(07288) 8200**
📠 (07288) 82004
📧 office@boehmerwaldgolf.at
🖥 www.boehmerwaldgolf.at

### Celtic Golf Course –
### Schärding    (1994)
Maad 2, 4775 Taufkirchen/Pram
☎ **(0043) 7719 8110**
📠 (0043) 7719 811015
📧 office@gcschaerding.at
🖥 www.gcschaerding.at

### Golfresort Haugschlag    (1987)
3874 Haugschlag 160
☎ **(02865) 8441**
📠 (02865) 8441-522
📧 info@golfresort.at
🖥 www.golfresort.at

### Herzog Tassilo    (1991)
Blankenbergerstr 30, 4540 Bad Hall
☎ **(07258) 5480**
📠 (07258) 29858
📧 gcherzogtassilo@golf.at
🖥 www.gcherzogtassilo.at/

### Golf Resort Kremstal    (1989)
Am Golfplatz 1, 4531 Kematen/Krems
☎ **0043 (0)7228 7644**
📠 0043 (0)7228 7644 7
📧 info@golfresort-kremstal.at
🔑 Günter Obermayr
🖥 www.golfresort-kremstal.at
   www.golfvillage.at

### Linz-St Florian    (1960)
4490 St Florian, Tillysburg 28
☎ **(07223) 828730**
📠 (07223) 828737
📧 gclinz@golf.at
🖥 www.gclinz.at

### Linzer Golf Club Luftenberg
(1990)
4222 Luftenberg, Am Luftenberg 1a
☎ **(07237) 3893**
📠 (07237) 3893-40
📧 gclinz-luftenberg@golf.at
🖥 www.gclinz-luftenberg.at

### Maria Theresia    (1989)
Letten 5, 4680 Haag am Hausruck
☎ **(07732) 3944**
📠 (07732) 3944-9
🖥 www.members.eunet.at
   /gcmariatheresia

### Ottenstein    (1988)
3532 Niedergrünbach 60
☎ **(02826) 7476**
📠 (02826) 7476-4
📧 info@golfclub-ottenstein.at
🖥 www.golfclub-ottenstein.at

### St Oswald-Freistadt
(1988)
Am Golfplatz 1, 4271 St Oswald
☎ **(07945) 7938**
📠 (07945) 79384

### St Pölten Schloss Goldegg
(1989)
3100 St Pölten Schloss Goldegg
☎ **(02741) 7360/7060**
📠 (02741) 73608

### Union Golfclub Schloss
### Ernegg    (1973)
3261 Steinakirchen, Ernegg 4
☎ **+43 (0) 7488) 76770**
📠 +43 (0) 7488) 71171
📧 gcernegg@golf.at
🔑 Kristel Josel (Mgr)
🖥 www.ernegg.at

### Traunsee Kircham
4656 Kircham, Kampesberg 38
☎ **(07619) 2576**
📠 (07619) 2576-11

**Weitra**    (1989)
*3970 Weitra, Hausschachen*
☎ **(02856) 2058**
🖷 (02856) 2058-4
📧 gcweitra@golf.at
🖥 www.gcweitra.at

**Wels**    (1981)
*4616 Weisskirchen, Golfplatzstrasse 2*
☎ **(07243) 56038**
🖷 (07243) 56685
📧 gcwels@golf.at
🖥 www.golfclub-wels.at

## Salzburg Region

**Bad Gastein**    (1960)
*5640 Bad Gastein, Golfstrasse 6*
☎ **0043 (6434) 2775**
🖷 0043 (6434) 2775-4
📧 info@golfclub-gastein.com
✍ Verena Kuhlank
🖥 www.golfclub-gastein.com

**GC Sonnberg**    (1993)
*5241 Höhnart, Strass 1*
☎ **0043 (7743) 20066**
🖷 0043 (7743) 20077
📧 golf@gcsonnberg.at
🖥 www.gcsonnberg.at

**Goldegg**
*5622 Goldegg, Maierhof 4*
☎ **(06415) 8585**
🖷 (06415) 8585-4
📧 info@golfclub-goldegg.com
🖥 www.golfclub-goldegg.com

**Gut Altentann**    (1989)
*Hof 54, 5302 Henndorf am Wallersee*
☎ **(06214) 6026-0**
🖷 (06214) 6105-81
📧 office@gutaltentann.com
✍ Catarina Hofmann
🖥 www.gutaltentann.com

**Gut Brandlhof G&CC**
   (1983)
*5760 Saalfelden am Steinernen Meer,
Hohlwegen 4*
☎ **(06582) 7800-555**
🖷 (06582) 7800-529

**Lungau**    (1991)
*5582 St Michael, Feldnergasse 165*
☎ **(06477) 7448**
🖷 (06477) 7448-4
📧 gclungau@golf.at
🖥 www.golfclub-lungau.at

**Am Mondsee**    (1986)
*St Lorenz 400, 5310 Mondsee*
☎ **(06232) 3835-0**
🖷 (06232) 3835-83
📧 gcmondsee@golf.at
✍ Frank Riedel (Senior Golf Mgr)
   (FH)
🖥 www.golfclubmondsee.at

**Radstadt Tauerngolf**    (1991)
*Römerstrasse 18, 5550 Radstadt*
☎ **(06452) 5111**
🖷 (06452) 5111/15
📧 info@radstadtgolf.at
🖥 www.radstadtgolf.at

**G&CC Salzburg-Klessheim**
   (1955)
*Klessheim 21, 5071 Wals*
☎ **(0662) 850851**
🖷 (0662) 857925
📧 office@gccsalzburg.at
🖥 www.golfclub-klessheim.com

**Salzburg Romantikourse
Schloss Fuschl**    (1865)
*5322 Hof/Salzburg*
☎ **(06229) 2390**
🖷 (06229) 2390
📧 fuschl@golfclub-salzburg.at
🖥 www.golfclub-salzburg.at

**Salzkammergut**    (1933)
*Wirling 36, 5360 St. Wolfgang*
☎ **(06132) 26340**
🖷 (06132) 26708
📧 office@salzkammergut-golf.at
✍ Cornelia Kogler
🖥 www.salzkammergut-golf.at

**Urslautal**    (1991)
*Schinking 81, 5760 Saalfelden*
☎ **(06584) 2000**
🖷 (06584) 7475-10
📧 info@golf-urslautal.at
🖥 www.golf-urslautal.at

**Zell am See-Kaprun**    (1983)
*Golfstrasse 25, A-5700 Zell am See*
☎ **+43 6542 56161**
🖷 +43 6542 56161-16
📧 golf@zellamsee-kaprun.at
✍ Roland Geringer (Manager)
🖥 www.golf-zellamsee.at

## Steiermark

**Bad Gleichenberg**    (1984)
*Am Hoffeld 3, 8344 Bad Gleichenberg*
☎ **(03159) 3717**
🖷 (03159) 3065
📧 gcgleichenberg@golf.at
🖥 www.golf-badgleichenberg.at

**Dachstein Tauern**    (1990)
*8967 Haus/Ennstal, Oberhaus 59*
☎ **(03686) 2630**
🖷 (03686) 2630-15
📧 gccschladming@golf.at
🖥 www.schladming-golf.at

**Ennstal-Weissenbach G&LC**
   (1977)
*Austria 8940 Liezen, Postfach 193*
☎ **(03612) 24821**
🖷 (03612) 24821-4
📧 glcennstal@golf.at
✍ Thomas Aigner
🖥 www.glcennstal.at

**Graz**    (1989)
*8051 Graz-Thal, Windhof 137*
☎ **(0316) 572867**
🖷 (0316) 572867-4

**Gut Murstätten**    (1989)
*8403 Lebring, Oedt 14*
☎ **(03182) 3555**
🖷 (03182) 3688
📧 gcmurstaetten@golf.at
🖥 www.gcmurstaetten.at

**Maria Lankowitz**    (1992)
*Puchbacher Str 109, 8591 Maria Lankowitz*
☎ **(03144) 6970**
🖷 (03144) 6970-4

**Murhof**    (1963)
*8130 Frohnleiten, Adriach 53*
☎ **(03126) 3010-40**
🖷 (03126) 3000-28
📧 gcmurhof@golf.at
🖥 www.murhof.at

**Murtal**    (1995)
*Frauenbachstr 51, 8724 Spielberg*
☎ **(03512) 75213**
🖷 (03512) 75213
📧 gcmurtal@golf.at
🖥 www.gcmurtal.at

**Reiting G&CC**    (1990)
*8772 Traboch, Schulweg 7*
☎ **(0663) 833308/(03847) 5008**
🖷 (03847) 5682

**St Lorenzen**    (1990)
*8642 St Lorenzen, Gassing 22*
☎ **(03864) 3961**
🖷 (03864) 3961-2
📧 gclorenzen@golf.at
🖥 www.gclorenzen.at

**Schloss Frauenthal**    (1988)
*8530 Deutschlandsberg, Ulrichsberg 7*
☎ **(03462) 5717**
🖷 (03462) 5717-5
📧 office@gcfrauenthal.at
🖥 www.gcfrauenthal.at

**Golf & Country Club Schloss
Pichlarn**    (1972)
*8952 Irdning/Ennstal, Zur Linde 1*
☎ **+43 3682-24440-540**
🖷 +43 3682-24440-580
📧 golf@pichlarn.at
🖥 www.pichlarn.at

**TGC Füerstenfeld-
Loipersdorp**    (1984)
*8282 Loipersdorf, Gillersdorf 50*
☎ **(03382) 8533**
🖷 (03382) 8533-33
📧 office@thermengolf.at
🖥 www.thermengolf.at

## Vienna & East

**Adamstal**    (1994)
*Gaupmannsgraben 21, 3172 Ramsal*
☎ **(02764) 3500**

☎ (02764) 3500-15
🖥 www.adamstal.at

## Bad Tatzmannsdorf Reiters G&CC (1991)
Am Golfplatz 2, 7431 Bad Tatzmannsdorf
☎ (0043) 3353 8282-0
🖥 (0043) 3353 8282-1735
✉ golfclub@burgenlandresort.at
🖥 www.reitersburgenlandresort.at

## Brunn G&CC (1988)
2345 Brunn/Gebirge, Rennweg 50
☎ (02236) 33711
🖥 (02236) 33863
✉ club@gccbrunn.at
🖥 www.gccbrunn.at

## Colony Club Gutenhof (1988)
2325 Himberg, Gutenhof
☎ (02235) 87055-0
🖥 (02235) 87055-14
✉ club@colonygolf.com
✍ Magira-Xenia Glatz
🖥 www.colonygolf.com

## Eldorado Bucklige Welt (1990)
Golfplatz 1, 2871 Zöbern
☎ (02642) 8451
🖥 (02642) 8451-52
🖥 www.golf1.at

## Enzesfeld (1970)
2551 Enzesfeld
☎ (02256) 81272
🖥 (02256) 81272-4
✉ office@gcenzesfeld.at
🖥 www.gcenzesfeld.at

## Föhrenwald (1968)
2700 Wiener Neustadt, Postfach 105
☎ (02622) 29171
🖥 (02622) 29171-4
✉ office@gcf.at
✍ Zelester Elgar (Mgr)
🖥 www.gcf.at

## Fontana (1996)
Fontana Allee 1, 2522 Oberwaltersdorf
☎ (02253) 6062202
🖥 (02253) 6062200
✉ gcfontana@fontana.at
✍ Mag. Matthias Wagner
🖥 www.fontana.at

## Hainburg/Donau (1977)
2410 Hainburg, Auf der Heide 762
☎ (02165) 62628
🖥 (02165) 626283
✉ gchainburg@golf.at
✍ Dietmar Haderer (Mgr)
🖥 www.golfclub-hainburg.at

## Lengenfeld (1995)
Am Golfplatz 1, 3552 Lengenfeld
☎ (02719) 8710
🖥 (02719) 8738

## Neusiedlersee-Donnerskirchen (1988)
7082 Donnerskirchen
☎ (02683) 8171
🖥 (02683) 817231

## Schloss Ebreichsdorf (1988)
2483 Ebreichsdorf, Schlossallee 1
☎ (02254)73888
🖥 (02254) 73888-13
✉ office@gcebreichsdorf.at
🖥 www.gcebreichsdorf.at

## Schloss Schönborn (1987)
2013 Schönborn 4
☎ (02267) 2863/2879
🖥 (02267) 2879-19
✉ golfclub@gcschoenborn.com
🖥 www.gcschoenborn.com

## Schönfeld (1989)
A-2291 Schönfeld, Am Golfplatz 1
☎ +43 (02213) 2063
🖥 +43 (02213) 20631
✉ gcschoenfeld@golf.at
🖥 www.golf.at
    /clubdetail.asp?clubnr=315

## Semmering (1926)
2680 Semmering
☎ (02664) 8154
🖥 (02664) 2114

## Golfclub Spillern (1993)
Wiesenerstrasse 100, A-2104 Spillern
☎ +43 (0)22 668 1211
🖥 +43 (0)22 668 121120
✉ gcspillern@golf.at
✍ J Culen
🖥 www.gcspillern.at

## Thayatal Drosendorf (1994)
Autendorf 18, 2095 Drosendorf
☎ (02915) 62625
🖥 (02915) 62625

## Wien (1901)
1020 Wien, Freudenau 65a
☎ (01) 728 9564 (Clubhouse)
🖥 (01) 728 9564-20
✉ gcwien@golf.at
🖥 www.gcwien.at

## Wien-Süssenbrunn (1995)
Weingartenallee 22, 1220 Wien
☎ +43 (01) 256 8282
🖥 +43 (01) 246 8282 -44
✉ golf@sportparkwien.at
✍ Andreas Artner
🖥 www.gcwien-sb.at

## Wienerwald (1981)
1130 Wien, Altgasse 27
☎ (0222) 877 3111 (Sec)

## Bludenz-Braz (1996)
Oberradin 60, 6751 Braz bei Bludenz
☎ (05552) 33503
🖥 (05552) 33503-3
✉ gcbraz@golf.at
🖥 www.gc-bludenz-braz.at

## Bregenzerwald (1997)
Unterlitten 3a, 6943 Riefensberg
☎ (05513) 8400
🖥 (05513) 8400-4

✉ office@golf-bregenzerwald.com
🖥 www.golf-bregenzerwald.com

## Montafon (1992)
6774 Tschagguns, Zelfenstrasse 110
☎ (05556) 77011
🖥 (05556) 77045
✉ info@golfclub-montafon.at
🖥 www.golfclub-montafon.at

# Belgium

## Antwerp Region

## Bossenstein (1989)
Moor 16, Bossenstein Kasteel, 2520 Broechem
☎ (03) 485 64 46
🖥 (03) 485 78 41
✉ bossenstein.shop@skynet.be

## Cleydael G&CC (1988)
Groenenhoek 7-9, 2630 Aartselaar
☎ (03) 870 56 80
🖥 (03) 887 14 75
✉ secretariaat@cleydael.be
✍ Maryse Bal (Gen Sec)
🖥 www.cleydael.be

## Kempense (1986)
Kiezelweg 78, 2400 Mol-Rauw
☎ 00 32 (0)14 81 46 41
   (Clubhouse)
🖥 00 32 (0)14 81 62 78
✉ kempense@pandora.be
🖥 www.golf.be/kempense

## Lilse Golf & Country (1987)
Haarlebeek 3, 2275 Lille
☎ (014) 55 19 30
🖥 (014) 55 19 31
✉ info@lilsegolfcountry.be
✍ Vink Nienue
🖥 www.lilsegolfcountry.be

## Golf Club Nuclea Mol (1984)
Goorstraat, 2400 Mol
☎ +32 14 37 0915
✉ info@golfclubnucleamol.be
✍ André Verbruggen
🖥 www.golfclubnucleamol.be

## Rinkven G&CC (1980)
Sint Jobsteenweg 120, 2970 Schilde
☎ (03) 380 12 80
🖥 (03) 384 29 33
✉ info@rinkven.be
🖥 www.rinkven.be

## Royal Antwerp (1888)
Georges Capiaulei 2, 2950 Kapellen
☎ (03) 666 84 56
🖥 (03) 666 44 37
✉ info@ragc.be
✍ Jean-Noel Raymakers (Mgr)
🖥 www.ragc.be

## Steenhoven (1985)
Steenhoven 89, 2400 Postel-Mol
- ☎ (014) 37 36 61
- 📠 (014) 37 36 62
- 📧 info@steenhoven.be
- 🖎 Luc Hannes (Mgr/Sec)
- 🖥 www.steenhoven.be

## Ternesse G&CC (1976)
Uilenbaan 15, 2160 Wommelgem
- ☎ (03) 355 14 30
- 📠 (03) 355 14 35
- 📧 info@ternessegolf.be
- 🖎 Piet Vandenbussche
- 🖥 www.ternessegolf.be

## Ardennes & South

## Andenne (1988)
Ferme du Moulin 52, Stud, 5300 Andenne
- ☎ (085) 84 34 04
- 📠 (085) 84 34 04
- 📧 jojadin@hotmail.com
- 🖎 Josiane Colson
- 🖥 www.golfclubandenne.be

## Château Royal d'Ardenne
Tour Léopold, Ardenne 6, 5560 Houyet
- ☎ (082) 66 62 28
- 📠 (082) 66 74 53

## Falnuée (1987)
Rue E Pirson 55, 5032 Mazy
- ☎ (081) 63 30 90
- 📠 (081) 63 21 41
- 📧 info@falnuee.be
- 🖎 Eric Jottrand/Anne Sophie Jottrand
- 🖥 www.falnuee.be

## Five Nations C C (1990)
Ferme du Grand Scley, 5372 Méan (Havelange)
- ☎ (086) 32 32 32
- 📠 (086) 32 30 11

## Mont Garni Golf Club (1990)
Rue du Mont Garni, 3 7331 Saint Ghislain
- ☎ +32 65.52.94.10
- 📠 +32 65 62 34 10
- 📧 secretariat@golfmontgarni.be
- 🖎 Marie van der Schueren/Jodi De Frenne
- 🖥 www.golfmontgarni.be

## Rougemont (1987)
Chemin du Beau Vallon 45, 5170 Profondeville
- ☎ +32 81 41 21 31
- 📠 +32 81 41 21 42
- 📧 rougemont@skynet.be
- 🖎 Jean-Louis Rousseau (Hon Sec)
- 🖥 www.golfderougemont.be

## Royal GC du Hainaut (1933)
Rue de la Verrerie 2, 7050 Erbisoeul
- ☎ (065) 22 96 10 (Clubhouse)
- 📠 (065) 22 02 09
- 📧 info@golfhainaut.be
- 🖥 www.golfhainaut.be

## Brussels & Brabant

## Bercuit (1965)
Les Gottes 3, 1390 Grez-Doiceau
- ☎ (010) 84 15 01
- 📠 (010) 84 55 95
- 📧 info@golfdubercuit.be
- 🖥 www.golfdubercuit.be

## Brabantse Golf (1982)
Steenwagenstraat 11, 1820 Melsbroek
- ☎ (02) 751 82 05
- 📠 (02) 751 84 25
- 📧 secretariaat@brabantsegolf.be
- 🖎 Rob Houben (Mgr/Sec)
- 🖥 www.brabantsegolf.be

## La Bruyère (1988)
Rue Jumerée 1, 1495 Sart-Dames-Avelines
- ☎ (071) 87 72 67
- 📠 (071) 87 43 38
- 📧 info@golflabruyere.be
- 🖥 www.golflabruyere.be

## Golf du Château de la Bawette (1988)
Chaussée du Chateau de la Bawette 5, 1300 Wavre
- ☎ (010) 22 33 32
- 📠 (010) 22 90 04
- 📧 info@labawette.com
- 🖥 www.golflabawette.com

## L'Empereur (1989)
Rue Emile François No.31, 1474 Ways (Genappe)
- ☎ (067) 77 15 71
- 📠 (067) 77 18 33
- 📧 info@golfempereur.com
- 🖎 Capart
- 🖥 www.golfempereur.com

## Golf Château de la Tournette (1988)
Chemin de Baudemont 21, B-1400 Nivelles
- ☎ +32-(067)-89 42 66
- 📠 +32-(067)-21 95 17
- 📧 info@tournette.com
- 🖥 www.tournette.com

## Hulencourt (1989)
Bruyère d'Hulencourt 15, 1472 Vieux Genappe
- ☎ (067) 79 40 40
- 📠 (067) 79 40 48
- 📧 info@golfhulencourt.be
- 🖥 www.golfhulencourt.be

## Kampenhout (1989)
Wildersedreef 56, 1910 Kampenhout
- ☎ (016) 65 12 16
- 📠 (016) 65 16 80
- 📧 info@golfclubkampenhout.be
- 🖥 www.golfclubkampenhout.be

## Keerbergen (1968)
Vlieghavenlaan 50, 3140 Keerbergen
- ☎ (015) 22 68 78
- 📠 (015) 23 57 37
- 📧 info@golfkeerbergen.be
- 🖥 www.golfkeerbergen.be

## Louvain-la-Neuve (1989)
Rue A Hardy 68, 1348 Louvain-la-Neuve
- ☎ (010) 45 05 15
- 📠 (010) 45 44 17
- 📧 info@golflln.com
- 🖥 www.golflln.com

## Overijse (1986)
Gemslaan 55, 3090 Overijse
- ☎ (02) 687 50 30
- 📧 ogc@golf-overijse.be
- 🖥 www.overijsegolfclub.be

## Pierpont (1992)
Chemin Grand Pierpont 1, B-6210 Frasnes-lez-Gosselies
- ☎ +32-(071)-880 830
- 📠 +32-(071)-851543
- 📧 info@pierpont.be
- 🖎 Gary Nisbet
- 🖥 www.pierpont.be

## Rigenée (1981)
Rue de Châtelet 62, 1495 Villers-la-Ville
- ☎ (071) 87 77 65
- 📠 (071) 87 77 83
- 📧 golf@rigenee.be
- 🖥 www.rigenee.be

## Royal Amicale Anderlecht (1987)
Rue Schollestraat 1, 1070 Brussels
- ☎ (02) 521 16 87
- 📠 (02) 521 51 56
- 📧 info@golf-anderlecht.com
- 🖥 www.golf-anderlecht.com

## Royal Golf Club de Belgique (1906)
Château de Ravenstein, 3080 Tervuren
- ☎ +32 (0) 2 767 58 01
- 📠 +32 (0) 2 767 28 41
- 📧 info@rgcb.be
- 🖎 Jos Vankriekelsienne (Dir)
- 🖥 www.rgcb.be

## Royal Waterloo Golf Club (1923)
Vieux Chemin de Wavre 50, 1380 Lasne
- ☎ (00) 322 633 1850
- 📠 (00) 322 633 2866
- 📧 infos@golfwaterloo.be
- 🖎 Henri Bailly
- 🖥 www.rwgc.be

## Sept Fontaines (1987)
1021, Chaussée d'Alsemberg, 1420 Braine L'Alleud
- ☎ (02) 353 02 46/353 03 46
- 📠 (02) 354 68 75
- 📧 info@golf7fontaines.be
- 🖎 Manuel Weymeersch
- 🖥 www.golf7fontaines.be

## Winge G&CC (1988)
Leuvensesteenweg 252, B-3390 Sint Joris Winge
- ☎ (016) 63 40 53
- 📠 (016) 63 21 40
- 📧 info@wingegolf.be
- 🖎 Chris Morton
- 🖥 www.wingegolf.be

## East

**Avernas** ( 199)
*Route de Grand Hallet 19A, 4280 Hannut*
☎ **(019) 51 30 66**
📠 (019) 51 53 43
📧 info@golfavernas.be
🖥 www.golfavernas.be

**Durbuy** (1991)
*Route d'Oppagne 34, 6940 Barvaux-su-Ourthe*
☎ **(086) 21 44 54**

**Flanders Nippon Hasselt**
(1988)
*Vissenbroekstraat 15, 3500 Hasselt*
☎ **(011) 26 34 82**
📠 (011) 26 34 83
📧 flanders.nippon.golf@pandora.be
🖥 www.flandersnippongolf.be

**Henri-Chapelle** (1988)
*Rue du Vivier 3, B-4841 Henri-Chapelle*
☎ **(087) 88 19 91**
📠 (087) 88 36 55
📧 info@golfhenrichapelle.be
🖥 www.golfhenrichapelle.be

**International Gomze Golf Club** (1986)
*Sur Counachamps 8, 4140 Gomze Andoumont*
☎ **(04) 360 92 07/**
 **(04) 278 75 00**
📠 (04) 360 92 06
📧 gomzegolf@skynet.be
✍ Michele Quertainmont
🖥 www.gomze.be

**Limburg G&CC** (1966)
*Golfstraat 1, 3530 Houthalen*
☎ **(089) 38 35 43**
📠 (089) 84 12 08
📧 limburggolf@telenet.be
✍ Jan Hendrikx
🖥 www.lgcc.be

**Royal GC du Sart Tilman**
(1939)
*Route du Condroz 541, 4031 Liège*
☎ **(041) 336 20 21**
📠 (041) 337 20 26
📧 secretariat@rgcst.be
🖥 www.rgcst.be

**Royal Golf des Fagnes** (1930)
*1 Ave de l'Hippodrome, 4900 Spa*
☎ **(087) 79 30 30**
📠 (087) 79 30 39
📧 info@golfdespa.be
🖥 www.golfdespa.be

**Spiegelven GC Genk** (1988)
*Wiemesmeerstraat 109, 3600 Genk*
☎ **(0032) 893 59616**
📠 (0032) 893 64184
📧 info@spiegelven.be
🖥 www.spiegelven.be

## West & Oost Vlanderen

**Damme G&CC** (1987)
*Doornstraat 16, 8340 Damme-Sijsele*
☎ **(050) 35 35 72**
📠 (050) 35 89 25
📧 info@dammegolf.be
✍ Chris Morton
🖥 www.dammegolf.be

**Oudenaarde G&CC** (1975)
*Kasteel Petegem, Kortrykstraat 52, 9790 Wortegem-Petegem*
☎ **(055) 33 41 61**
📠 (055) 31 98 49
📧 oudenaarde@golf.be
🖥 www.golfoudenaarde.be

**Palingbeek** (1991)
*Eekhofstraat 14, 8902 Hollebeke-Ieper*
☎ **(057) 20 04 36**
📠 (057) 21 89 58
📧 golfpalingbeek@skynet.be
✍ Ian Connerty
🖥 www.golfpalingbeek.be

**Royal Latem** (1909)
*9830 St Martens-Latem, Latemstraat 120*
☎ **+32 9 282 54 11**
📠 +32 9 282 90 19
📧 secretary@latemgolf.be
✍ Ph Buysse
🖥 www.latemgolf.be

**Royal Ostend** (1903)
*Koninklijke Baan 2, 8420 De Haan*
☎ **(059) 23 32 83**
📠 (059) 23 37 49
🖥 www.golfoostende.be

**Royal Zoute** (1899)
*Caddiespad 14, 8300 Knokke-le-Zoute*
☎ **(050) 60 16 17 (Clubhouse)**
📠 (050) 62 30 29
📧 golf@zoute.be
✍ (050) 60 12 27
🖥 www.zoute.be

**Waregem** (1988)
*Bergstraat 41, 8790 Waregem*
☎ **(056) 60 88 08**
📠 (056) 62 18 23
📧 onthaal.golf@waregemgolf.be
🖥 www.golf.be/waregem

# Cyprus

**Aphrodite Hills GC** (2002)
*3 Aphrodite Avenue, Aphrodite Hills, Kouklia, 8509 Paphos*
☎ **00357 2682 8200**
📠 00357 2695 6706
📧 golfreservations@aphroditehills.com
✍ Nuno T Bastos
🖥 www.aphroditehills.com

**Minthis Hills GC** (1994)
*P O Box 62085, 8060 Paphos*
☎ **00357 2664 2774/5**
📠 00357 2664 2776
📧 golfers2@cytanet.com.cy
✍ Mr Stelios Patsalides (Manager)
🖥 www.minthishills.com

**Vikla G&CC** (1992)
*Vikla Village, Kellaki, Limassol*
☎ **00 357 99 674 218**
📧 viklagolf@cytanet.com.cy
 /info@vikla4golf.com
✍ Robin Houry
🖥 www.vikla4golf.com

**Paphos Golfers Association**
(2006)
*D105 Antonescos Gardens, Pafiou Street, Chloraka, Paphos 8220*
☎ **00357 99394164/**
 **00357 26100684**
📧 mike_emmett@hotmail.co.uk
✍ Mr Michael Emmett (Secretary)
🖥 www.cgf.org.cy/Memb

# Czech Republic

**Karlovy Vary** (1904)
*Prazska 125, PO Box 67, 360 01 Karlovy Vary*
☎ **(017) 333 1001-2**
📠 (017) 333 1101

**Lísnice** (1928)
*252 10 Mnísek pod Brdy*
☎ **(0318) 599 151**
📠 (0318) 599 151
🖥 www.gkl.cz

**Royal Golf Club Mariánské Lázne** (1905)
*Mariánské Lázne c.p. 582, 353 01 Mariánské Lázne*
☎ **+420 354 604300**
📠 +420 354 625195
📧 office@golfml.cz
✍ Martin Fucik
🖥 www.golfml.cz

**Park Golf Club Mittal Ostrava**
(1968)
*Dolni 412, 747 15 Silherovice*
☎ **(+420) 595 054 144**
📠 (+420) 595 054 144
📧 golf@golf-ostrava.cz
✍ Ing. Paval Pniak
🖥 www.golf-ostrava.cz

**Podebrady** (1964)
*Na Zalesi 530, 29080 Podebrady*
☎ **(0324) 610928**
📠 (0324) 610981
🖥 www.golfpodebrady.cz

**Semily**   (1970)
*Bavlnarska 521, 513 01 Semily*
☎ **(0431) 622443/624428**
🖥 (0431) 623000
📧 www.semily.cz

# Denmark

## Bornholm Island

**Bornholm**   (1972)
*Plantagevej 3B, 3700 Rønne*
☎ **56 95 68 54**
🖥 56 95 68 53
📧 info@bornholmsgolfklub.dk
📧 www.bornholmsgolfklub.dk

**Nexø**
*Dueodde Golfbane, Strandmarksvejen 14, 3730 Nexø*
☎ **56 48 89 87**
🖥 56 48 89 69
📧 ngk@dueodde-golf.dk
📧 www.dueodde-golf.dk

**Nordbornholm-Rø**   (1987)
*Spellingevej 3, Rø, 3760 Gudhjem*
☎ **56 48 40 50**
🖥 56 48 40 52
📧 mail@roegolfbane.dk
📧 www.roegolfbane.dk

## Funen

**Faaborg**   (1989)
*Dalkildegards Allee 1, 5600 Faaborg*
☎ **62 61 77 43**
🖥 62 61 79 34

**Lillebaelt**   (1990)
*O.Hougvej 130, 5500 Middelfart*
☎ **64 41 80 11**
🖥 64 41 14 11
📧 gkl@post10.tele.dk
📧 www.gkl.dk

**Odense**   (1927)
*Hestehaven 200, 5220 Odense SØ*
☎ **65 95 90 00**
📧 sekretariatet@odensegolfklub.dk
✍ Hans Henrik Burkal
📧 www.odensegolfklub.dk

**Proark Golf Odense Eventyr**
(1993)
*Falen 227, 5250 Odense SV*
☎ **7021 1900**
🖥 6562 2021
📧 pgoe@proarkgolf.dk
✍ Ulla Vahl-Møller (Golf Mgr)
📧 www.proarkgolf.dk

**Sct. Knuds Golfklub**   (1954)
*Slipshavnsvej 16, 5800 Nyborg*
☎ **65 31 12 12**
🖥 65 30 28 04

📧 mail@sct-knuds.dk
✍ Margit Madsen
📧 www.sct-knuds.dk

**Svendborg**   (1970)
*Tordensgaardevej 5, Sørup, 5700 Svendborg*
☎ **62 22 40 77**
🖥 62 20 29 77
📧 info@svendborg-golf.dk
📧 www.svendborg-golf.dk

**Vestfyns**   (1974)
*Rønnemosegård, Krengerupvej 27, 5620 Glamsbjerg*
☎ **63 72 19 20**
🖥 63 72 19 26
📧 info@vestfynsgolfklub.dk
📧 www.vestfynsgolfklub.dk

## Jutland

**Circolo Golf Ugolino**   (1933)
*Jaegersprisvej 35, 50023 Impruneta (FI), 9000 Aalborg*
☎ **(055) 230 1009/1085**
🖥 (055) 230 1141
📧 info@golfugolino.it
✍ Fausto Siddu/Christiano Bevilacqua
📧 www.golfugolino.it

**Aarhus**   (1931)
*Ny Moesgaardvej 50, 8270 Hojbjerg*
☎ **86 27 63 22**
🖥 86 27 63 21
📧 aarhusgolf@mail.dk
📧 www.aarhusgolf.dk

**Blokhus Golfcentre**   (1993)
*Hunetorpvej 115, Box 37, 9492 Blokhus*
☎ **98 20 95 00**
🖥 98 20 95 01
📧 reception@blokhusgolfcenter.dk
📧 www.blokhusgolfcenter.dk

**Breinholtgård**   (1992)
*Koksspangvej 17-19, 6710 Esbjerg V*
☎ **75 11 57 00**
🖥 75 11 55 12
📧 bgk@tiscali.dk
📧 www.bggc.dk

**Brønderslev Golfklub**   (1971)
*Golfvejen 83, 9700 Brønderslev*
☎ **98 82 32 81**
📧 info@broenderslevgolfklub.dk
✍ Ulla Gade
📧 www.broenderslevgolfklub.dk

**Bruntland Golfcenter**   (2000)
*Bruntland Allé 1-3, 6520 Toftlund*
☎ **73 83 16 00**
🖥 73 83 16 19
📧 info@brundtlandgolfcenter.dk
📧 www.brundtlandgolfcenter.dk

**Dejbjerg**   (1966)
*Letagervej 1, Dejbjerg, 6900 Skjern*
☎ **97 35 00 09**
🖥 96 80 11 18
📧 kontor@dejbjerggk.dk
✍ Hanne Häggavist
📧 www.dejbjerggk.dk

**Ebeltoft**   (1966)
*Galgebakken 14, 8400 Ebeltoft*
☎ **87 59 6000**
📧 post@ebeltoft-golfclub.dk

**Esbjerg**   (1921)
*Sønderhedevej 11, Marbaek, 6710 Esbjerg*
☎ **75 26 92 19**
🖥 75 26 94 19
📧 kontor@egk.dk
📧 www.egk.dk

**Fanø Golf Links**   (1901)
*Golfvejen 5, 6720 Fanø*
☎ **76 66 00 77**
🖥 76 66 00 44
📧 golf@fanonet.dk
📧 www.fanoe-golf-links.dk

**Grenaa**   (1981)
*Vestermarken 1, DK-8500 Grenaa*
☎ **+45 863 27929**
🖥 +45 863 09654
📧 info@grenaagolfklub.dk
📧 www.grenaagolfklub.dk

**Gyttegård**   (1974)
*Billundvej 43, 7250 Hejnsvig*
☎ **+45 75 33 63 82**
🖥 +45 75 33 68 20
📧 info@gyttegaardgolfklub.dk
📧 www.gyttegaardgolfklub.dk

**Haderslev**   (1971)
*Viggo Carstensvej 7, 6100 Haderslev*
☎ **74 52 83 01**
🖥 74 53 36 01

**Han Herreds**
*Starkaervej 20, 9690 Fjerritslev*
☎ **98 21 26 66 / 98 21 26 78**
🖥 98 21 26 77

**Henne**   (1989)
*Hennebysvej 30, 6854 Henne*
☎ **75 25 56 10**
📧 post@hennegolfklub.dk
✍ Beverley Elston
📧 www.hennegolfklub.dk

**Herning**   (1964)
*Golfvej 2, 7400 Herning*
☎ **97 21 00 33**
🖥 97 21 00 34
📧 info@herninggolfklub.dk
📧 www.herninggolfklub.dk

**Himmerland G&CC**   (1979)
*Centervej 1, Gatten, 9640 Farsö*
☎ **96 49 61 00**
🖥 98 66 14 56
📧 hgcc@himmerlandgolf.dk
📧 www.himmerlandgolf.dk

**Hirtshals**   (1990)
*Kjulvej 10, PO Box 51, 9850 Hirtshals*
☎ **98 94 94 08**
🖥 98 94 19 35

**Hjarbaek Fjord**   (1992)
*Lynderup, 8832 Skals*
☎ **86 69 62 88**
🖥 86696268

pghf@proarkgolf.dk
www.proarkgolf.dk

## Hjorring (1985)
Vinstrupvej 30, 9800 Hjorring
☎ 98 91 18 28
📠 98 90 31 00
✉ info@hjoerringgolf.dk
🖥 www.hjoerringgolf.dk

## Holmsland Klit
Klevevej 19, Søndervig, 6950 Ringkøbing
☎ 97 33 88 00
📠 97 33 86 80
🖥 www.holmslandklitgolf.dk

## Holstebro Golf Klub (1970)
Brandsbjergvej 4, 7570 Vemb
☎ (+45) 97 48 51 55
✉ post@holstebro-golfklub.dk
✍ Kjeld Rasmussen
🖥 www.holstebro-golfklub.dk

## Horsens (1972)
Silkeborgvej 44, 8700 Horsens
☎ 75 61 51 51
📠 75 61 40 51
🖥 www.horsensgolf.dk

## Hvide Klit (1972)
Hvideklitvej 28, 9982 Aalbaek
☎ 98 48 90 21
📠 98 48 91 12
✉ info@hvideklit.dk
🖥 www.hvideklit.dk

## Juelsminde (1973)
Bobroholtvej 11a, 7130 Juelsminde
☎ 75 69 34 92
📠 75 69 46 11
✉ golf@juelsmindegolf.dk
🖥 www.juelsmindegolf.dk

## Kaj Lykke (1988)
Kirkebrovej 5, 6740 Bramming
☎ 00 45 - 75 10 22 46
📠 00 45 - 75 10 26 68
✉ post@kajlykkegolfklub.dk
✍ Mrs Susanne Noergaard (Sec)
🖥 www.kajlykkegolfklub.dk

## Kalo (1992)
Aarhusvej 32, 8410 Rønde
☎ 86 37 36 00
📠 86 37 36 46

## Kolding (1933)
Egtved Alle 10, 6000 Kolding
☎ 75 52 37 93
📠 75 52 42 42
✉ kgc@koldinggolfclub.dk
✍ Ronny Kert (Mgr)
🖥 www.koldinggolfclub.dk

## Lemvig (1986)
Søgårdevejen 6, 7620 Lemvig
☎ 97 81 09 20
📠 97 81 09 20
✉ lemviggolfklub
@lemviggolfklub.dk
🖥 www.lemviggolfklub.dk

## Løkken (1990)
Vrenstedvej 226, PO Box 43, 9480 Løkken
☎ 98 99 26 57
📠 98 99 26 58
✉ info@loekken-golfklub.dk
🖥 www.loekken-golfklub.dk

## Nordvestjysk (1971)
Nystrupvej 19, 7700 Thisted
☎ 97 97 41 41

## Odder (1990)
Akjaervej 200, Postbox 46, 8300 Odder
☎ 86 54 54 51
📠 86 54 54 58
✉ oddergolf@oddergolf.dk
✍ Karen Frederiksen
🖥 www.oddergolf.dk

## Ornehoj Golfklub
Lundegard 70, 9260 Gistrup-Aalborg
☎ 98 31 43 44
📠 98 32 39 45
✉ golfklubben@mail.dk
🖥 www.ornehojgolfklub.dk

## Randers (1958)
Himmelbovej 22, Fladbro, 8900 Randers
☎ 86 42 88 69
📠 86 40 88 69
✉ postmaster@randersgolf.dk
🖥 www.randersgolf.dk

## Ribe (1979)
Rønnehave, Snepsgårdevej 14, 6760 Ribe
☎ 30 73 65 18

## Rold Skov (1991)
Golfvej 1, 9520 Skørping
☎ 96 82 8300
📠 96 82 8309
✉ info@roldskovgolf.dk
🖥 www.roldskovgolf.dk

## Royal Oak (1992)
Golfvej, Jels, 6630 Rødding
☎ 74 55 32 94
📠 74 55 32 95
✉ golf@royaloak.dk
🖥 www.royaloak.dk

## Silkeborg (1966)
Sommervej 50, 8600 Silkeborg
☎ 86 85 33 99
✉ welcome@srgolf.dk
✍ Mads Rügholm (Mgr)
🖥 www.srgolf.dk

## Sønderjyllands (1968)
Uge Hedegård, 6360 Tinglev
☎ 74 68 75 25
📠 74 68 75 05
✉ sonderjylland@mail.dk
🖥 www.sdj-golfklub.dk

## Varde (1991)
Gellerupvej 111b, 6800 Varde
☎ +45 75 22 49 44
✉ kontor@vardegolfklub.dk
✍ Lene Godtfredsen
🖥 www.vardegolfklub.dk

## Vejle (1970)
Faellessletgard, Ibaekvej, 7100 Vejle
☎ 75 85 81 85
📠 75 85 83 01
✉ info@vgc.dk
🖥 www.vgc.dk

## Viborg (1973)
Spangsbjerg Alle 50, Overlund, 8800 Viborg
☎ 86 67 30 10
📠 86 67 34 15
✉ mail@viborggolfklub.dk
🖥 www.viborggolfklub.dk

# Zealand

## Asserbo Golf Club (1946)
Bødkergaardsvej 9, 3300 Frederiksvaerk
☎ 47 72 14 90
📠 47 72 14 26
✉ agc@agc.dk
✍ Arne Larsen
🖥 www.agc.dk

## Copenhagen (1898)
Dyrehaven 2, 2800 Kgs. Lyngby
☎ 39 63 04 83
✉ info@kgkgolf.dk
✍ S Pedersen (Mgr)
🖥 www.kgkgolf.dk

## Dragør Golfklub (1991)
Kalvebodvej 100, 2791 Dragør
☎ 32 53 89 75
✉ post@dragor-golf.dk
🖥 www.dragor-golf.dk

## Falster (1994)
Virketvej 44, 4863 Eskilstrup, Falster Island
☎ 54 43 81 43
📠 54 43 81 23
✉ info@falster-golfklub.dk
✍ Knud Erik Melgaard
🖥 www.falster-golfklub.dk

## Frederikssund (1974)
Egelundsgården, Skovnaesvej 9,
3630 Jaegerspris
☎ +45 47 31 08 77
✉ fgk@fgkgolf.dk
✍ Jorgen Bundgaard (Mgr)
🖥 www.frederikssundgolfklub.dk

## Furesø (1974)
Hestkøbgård, Hestkøb Vaenge 4,
3460 Birkerød
☎ +45 45 81 74 44
✉ info@fggolf.dk
✍ Lars Lindegren
🖥 www.fggolf.dk

## Gilleleje (1970)
Ferlevej 52, 3250 Gilleleje
☎ 49 71 80 56
📠 49 71 80 86
✉ info@gillelejegolfklub.dk
🖥 www.gillelejegolfklub.dk

## Hedeland (1980)
Staerkendevej 232A, 2640 Hedehusene
☎ 46 13 61 88

**46 13 62 78**
klub@hedeland-golf.dk
www.hedeland-golf.dk

**Helsingør**
GL Hellebaekvej, 3000 Helsingør
☎ 49 21 29 70
🖬 49 21 09 70

**Hillerød**    (1966)
Nysøgårdsvej 9, Ny Hammersholt,
3400 Hillerød
☎ 48 26 50 46/48 25 40 30 (Pro)
🖬 48 25 29 87
klubben@hillerodgolf.dk
www.hillerodgolf.dk

**Hjortespring Golfklub**    (1980)
Klausdalsbrovej 602, 2750 Ballerup
☎ 44 68 90 09
🖬 44 68 90 04
post@hjgk.dk
Jens Åge Dalby
www.hjgk.dk

**Holbaek**    (1964)
Dragerupvej 50, 4300 Holbaek
☎ 59 43 45 79
🖬 59 43 51 61
info@holbakgolfklub.dk
Jorgen Buur (Mgr)
www.holbakgolfklub.dk

**Køge Golf Klub**    (1970)
Gl.Hastrupvej12, 4600 Køge
☎ +45 56 65 10 00
🖬 +45 56 65 13 45
admin@kogegolf.dk
Helge Caspersen
www.kogegolf.dk

**Kokkedal**    (1971)
Kokkedal Alle 9, 2970 Horsholm
☎ 45 76 99 59
🖬 45 76 99 03
kg@kokkedalgolf.dk
Ken Lauritsen (Golf Mgr)
www.kokkedalgolf.dk

**Korsør Golf Club**    (1964)
Ornumuey 8, Postbox 53, 4220 Korsør
☎ 58 37 18 36
🖬 58 37 18 39
golf@korsoergolf.dk
Kevin O'Donoghue
www.korsoergolf.dk

**Mølleåens**    (1970)
Stenbaekgård, Rosenlundvej 3, 3540 Lynge
☎ 48 18 86 31/48 18 86 36 (Pro)
🖬 48 18 86 43

**Odsherred**    (1967)
Stårupvej 2, 4573 Hojby
☎ 59 30 20 76
sek@odsherredgolf.dk
www.odsherredgolf.dk

**Roskilde**    (1973)
Gedevad, Kongemarken 34, 4000 Roskilde
☎ 46 37 01 81
🖬 46 32 85 79

**Rungsted**    (1937)
Vestre Stationsvej 16, 2960 Rungsted Kyst
☎ +45 45 86 34 44
info@rungstedgolfklub.dk
Jens Holm Boye (Club Mgr)/Claus
Preetzmann (Club Sec)
www.rungstedgolfklub.dk

**Simon's**    (1993)
Nybovej 5, 3490 Kvistgaard
☎ +45 49 19 14 78
🖬 +45 49 19 14 70
info@simonsgolf.dk
Mrs Helle Kongsted
www.simonsgolf.dk

**Skjoldenaesholm**    (1992)
Skjoldenaesvej 101, 4174 Jystrup
☎ +45 57 53 88 10
pgs@proarkgolf.dk
www.proarkgolf.dk

**Søllerød**    (1972)
Brillerne 9, 2840 Holte
☎ 45 80 17 84
info@sollerodgolf.dk
Helle Hessellund
www.sollerodgolf.dk

**Sorø**    (1979)
Suserupvej 7a, 4180 Sorø
☎ 57 84 93 95
🖬 57 84 85 58
www.soroegolf.dk

**Sydsjaellands**    (1974)
Borupgården, Mogenstrup, 4700 Naestved
☎ (+45) 55 76 15 55
🖬 (+45) 55 76 15 88
sydsjaelland@golfonline.dk
www.sydsjaellandsgolfklub.dk

**Vaerloese Golfklub**    (1993)
Christianshoejvej 22, 3500 Vaerloese
☎ (+45) 4447 2124
🖬 (+45) 4447 2128
mail@vaerloese-golfklub.dk
Tine Lunding (Sec)
www.vaerloese-golfklub.dk

# Finland

## Central

**Etelä-Pohjanmaan**    (1986)
P O Box 136, 60101 Seinäjoki
☎ (06) 423 4545
🖬 (06) 423 4547
www.ruuhikoskigolf.fi

**Karelia Golf**    (1987)
Vaskiportintie, 80780 Kontioniemi
☎ (013) 732411
🖬 (013) 732472

**Kokkolan**    (1957)
P O Box 164, 67101 Kokkola
☎ (06) 823 8600
toimisto@kokkolangolf.fi
www.kokkolangolf.fi

**Laukaan Peurunkagolf**    (1989)
Valkolantie 68, 41530 Laukaa
☎ (014) 3377 300
🖬 (014) 3377 305
www.golfpiste.com/lpg

**Tarina Golf**    (1988)
Tarinagolfintie 19, 71800 Siilinjärvi
☎ 02 01 87 87 02
toimisto@tarinagolf.fi
www.tarinagolf.fi

**Vaasan Golf**    (1969)
Golfkenttätie 61, 65380 Vaasa
☎ (06) 356 9989
🖬 (06) 356 9091
toimisto@vaasangolf.fi
Mr Petri Jolkkonen (Mgr)
www.vaasangolf.fi

## Helsinki & South

**Aura Golf**    (1958)
Ruissalon Puistotie 536, 20100 Turku
☎ (02) 258 9201/9221
🖬 (02) 258 9121
office@auragolf.fi
www.auragolf.fi

**Espoo Ringside Golf**    (1990)
Nurmikartanontie 5, 02920 Espoo
☎ (09) 849 4940
🖬 (09) 853 7132
caddie@ringsidegolf.fi
Ari Vepsä
www.ringsidegolf.fi

**Espoon Golfseura**    (1982)
Mynttiläntie 1, 02780 Espoo
☎ (09) 8190 3444
🖬 (09) 8190 3434
www.espoongolfseura.fi

**Harjattula G&CC**    (1989)
Harjattulantie 84, 20960 Turku
☎ (02) 276 2180
🖬 (02) 258 7218
www.harjattula.fi

**Helsinki Golf Club**    (1932)
Talin Kartano, 00350 Helsinki
☎ +358 9 225 23710
🖬 +358 9 225 23737
toimisto@helsingingolfklubi.fi
Markku Ignatius
www.helsingingolfklubi.fi

**Hyvinkään**    (1989)
Golftie 63, 05880 Hyvinkää
☎ (019) 456 2400
🖬 (019) 456 2410
caddiemaster@hyvigolf.fi
www.hyvigolf.fi

**Keimola Golf**    (1988)
Kirkantie 32, 01750 Vantaa
☎ (09) 276 6650
🖬 (09) 896790

**Kurk Golf**    (1985)
02550 Evitskog
☎ (09) 819 0480

☎ (09) 819 04810
✉ kurk@kurkgolf.fi
🖳 www.kurkgolf.fi

**Master Golf** (1988)
*Bodomin kuja 7, 02940 Espoo*
☎ **(09) 849 2300**
🖳 (09) 849 23011
🖳 www.mastergolf.fi

**Meri-Teijo** (1990)
*Mathildedalin Kartano, 25660 Mathildedal*
☎ **(02) 736 3955**
🖳 (02) 736 3945

**Messilä** (1988)
*Messiläntie 240, 15980 Messilä*
☎ **(03) 884040**
🖳 (03) 884 0440

**Nevas Golf** (1988)
*01150 Söderkulla*
☎ **(010) 400 6400**
✉ ng@nevasgolf.fi
🖳 www.nevasgolf.fi

**Nordcenter G&CC** (1988)
*10410 Aminnefors*
☎ **(019) 2766850**
🖳 (019) 238871
🖳 www.nordcenter.com

**Nurmijärven** (1990)
*Ratasillantie 70, 05100 Röykkä*
☎ **(09) 276 6230**
🖳 (09) 276 62330
✉ caddiemaster@nurmijarvi-golf.fi
🖳 www.nurmijarvi-golf.fi

**Peuramaa Golf** (1991)
*Peuramaantie 152, 02400 Kirkkonummi*
☎ **(09) 295 588**
🖳 (09) 295 58210
✉ office@peuramaagolf.com
🖳 www.peuramaagolf.com

**Pickala Golf** (1986)
*Golfkuja 5, 02580 Siuntio*
☎ **(09) 221 9080**
🖳 (09) 221 90899
✉ toimisto@pickalagolf.fi
🖳 www.pickalagolf.fi

**Ruukkigolf** (1986)
*PL 9, 10420 Skuru*
☎ **(019) 245 4485**
🖳 (019) 245 4285
✉ toimisto@ruukkigolf.fi
🖳 www.ruukkigolf.fi

**Sarfvik** (1984)
*P O Box 27, 02321 Espoo*
☎ **(09) 221 9000**
🖳 (09) 297 7134
✉ sarfvik@golfsarfvik.fi

**Sea Golf Rönnäs** (1989)
*Kabbölentie 319, 07750 Isnäs*
☎ **+358 (0) 19 634 434**
🖳 +358 (0) 19 634 458
✉ toimisto@seagolf.fi
🖳 www.seagolf.fi

**St Laurence Golf** (1989)
*Kaivurinkatu 133, 08200 Lohja*
☎ **+358 (0)19 357 821**
🖳 +358 (0)19 386 666
✉ caddie.master@stlaurencegolf.fi
🖳 www.stlaurencegolf.fi

**Suur-Helsingin Golf** (1965)
*Rinnekodintie 29, 02980 Espoo*
☎ **+358 9 4399 7110**
🖳 +358 9 437121
✉ toimisto@shg.fi
🖳 www.shg.fi

**Golf Talma** (1989)
*Nygårdintie 115-6, 04240 Talma*
☎ **+358 9 274 6540**
🖳 +358 9 274 654 32
✉ golftalma@golftalma.fi
✍ Ismo Haaponiemi (Mgr)
🖳 www.golftalma.fi

**Tuusula** (1983)
*Kirkkotie 51, 04301 Tuusula*
☎ **(042) 410241**
🖳 (09) 274 60860
🖳 www.golfpiste.com/tgk

**Virvik Golf** (1981)
*Virvik, 06100 Porvoo*
☎ **(915) 579292**
🖳 (915) 579292

### North

**Green Zone Golf** (1987)
*Näräntie, 95400 Tornio*
☎ **(016) 431711**
🖳 (016) 431710

**Katinkulta** (1990)
*Pisterinniementie 2, 88610 Voukatti*
☎ **(030) 686 3488**
✉ toimisto@katinkultagolf.fi
🖳 www.katinkultagolf.fi

**Oulu** (1964)
*Sankivaaran Golfkeskus, 90650 Oulu*
☎ **(08) 531 5222**
🖳 (08) 531 5129
✉ caddiemaster@oulugolf.fi
🖳 www.oulugolf.fi

### South East

**Imatran Golf** (1986)
*Golftie 11, 55800 Imatra*
☎ **(05) 473 4954**
🖳 (05) 473 4953

**Kartano Golf** (1988)
*P O Box 60, 79601 Joroinen*
☎ **(017) 572257**
🖳 (017) 572263

**Kerigolf** (1990)
*Kerimaantie 65, 58200 Kerimäki*
☎ **(015) 252600**
🖳 (015) 252606
✉ clubhouse@kerigolf.fi
🖳 www.kerigolf.fi

**Koski Golf** (1987)
*Eerolanväylä 126, 45700 Kuusankoski*
☎ **+358 207 129 820**
🖳 +358 207 129 829
✉ toimisto@koskigolf.fi
🖳 www.koskigolf.fi

**Kymen Golf** (1964)
*Mussalo Golfcourse, 48310 Kotka*
☎ **(05) 210 3700**
🖳 (05) 210 3730
🖳 www.kymengolf.fi

**Lahden Golf** (1959)
*Takkulantie, 15230 Lahti*
☎ **(03) 784 1311**
🖳 (03) 784 1311

**Porrassalmi** (1989)
*Annila, 50100 Mikkeli*
☎ **(015) 335518/335446**
🖳 (015) 335682

**Vierumäki Golf** (1988)
*Kaskelantie 10, 19120 Vierumäki*
☎ **+358 (0) 40 837 6149**
🖳 +358 (0) 3 8424 7015
✉ jan.ruoho@vierumaki.fi
✍ Jan Ruoho (Dir)
🖳 www.vierumakigolf.fi

### South West

**Porin Golfkerho** (1939)
*P O Box 25, 28601 Pori*
☎ **(02) 630 3888**
🖳 (02) 630 38813
✉ toimisto@kalafornia.com
🖳 www.kalafornia.com

**River Golf** (1988)
*Taivalkunta, 37120 Nokia*
☎ **(03) 340 0234**
🖳 (03) 340 0235

**Salo Golf** (1988)
*Anistenkatu 1, 24100 Salo*
☎ **(02) 721 7300**
🖳 (02) 721 7310
✉ caddiemaster@salogolf.fi
✍ Mr Mika Havulinna
🖳 www.salogolf.fi

**Tammer Golf** (1965)
*Toimelankatu 4, 33560 Tampere*
☎ **(03) 261 3316**
🖳 (03) 261 3130

**Tawast Golf** (1987)
*Tawastintie 48, 13270 Hämeenlinna*
☎ **(03) 630 610**
🖳 (03) 630 6120
✉ tawast@tawastgolf.fi
🖳 www.tawastgolf.fi

**Vammala** (1991)
*38100 Karkku*
☎ **(03) 513 4070**
🖳 (03) 513 90711

**Wiurila G&CC** (1990)
*Viurilantie 126, 24910 Halikko*
☎ **+35 8272 78100**

+35 8272 78107
toimisto@wgcc.fi
www.wgcc.fi

**Yyteri Golf**   (1988)
*Karhuluodontie 85, 28840 Pori*
(02) 638 0380
(02) 638 0385
www.yyterilinks.com

# France

## Bordeaux & South West

**Albret**   (1986)
*Le Pusocq, 47230 Barbaste*
05 53 65 53 69
05 53 65 61 19

**Arcachon**   (1955)
*Golf International d'Arcachon, 35 Bd d'Arcachon, 33260 La Teste De Buch*
05 56 54 44 00
05 56 66 86 32
golfarcachon@free.fr

**Arcangues**   (1991)
*64200 Arcangues*
05 59 43 10 56
05 59 43 12 60
golf.arcangues@orange.fr
www.golfdarcangues.com

**Biarritz**   (1888)
*Ave Edith Cavell, 64200 Biarritz*
05 59 03 71 80
05 59 03 26 74
info@golfbiarritz.com
www.golf-biarritz.com

**Biscarrosse**   (1989)
*Avenue du Golf, F-40600 Biscarrosse*
05 58 09 84 93
05 58 09 84 50
golfdebiscarrosse@wanadoo.fr
www.biscarrossegolf.com

**Blue Green-Artiguelouve**   (1986)
*Domaine St Michel, Pau-Artiguelouve, 64230 Artiguelouve*
05 59 83 09 29
05 59 83 14 05

**Blue Green-Seignosse**   (1989)
*Avenue du Belvédère, 40510 Seignosse*
05 58 41 68 30
05 58 41 68 31
golfseignosse@wanadoo.fr
www.golfseignosse.com

**Bordeaux-Cameyrac**   (1972)
*33450 St Sulpice-et-Cameyrac*
(+33) (0)5 56 72 96 79
(+33) (0)5 56 72 86 56
contact@golf-bordeaux-cameyrac.com
www.golf-bordeaux-cameyrac.com

**Bordeaux-Lac**   (1976)
*Public*
*Avenue de Pernon, 33300 Bordeaux*
05 56 50 92 72
05 56 29 01 84
bordeaux.lac@bluegreen.com
www.bluegreen.com

**Bordelais**   (1900)
*Domaine de Kater, Allee F Arago, 33200 Bordeaux-Caudéran*
05 56 28 56 04
05 56 28 59 71
golfbordelais@wanadoo.fr
Franck Koenig
www.golf-bordelais.fr

**Casteljaloux**   (1989)
*Route de Mont de Marsan, 47700 Casteljaloux*
05 53 93 51 60
05 5320 90 98
golfdecasteljaloux@wanadoo.fr
www.golfdecasteljaloux.com

**Chantaco**   (1928)
*Route d'Ascain, 64500 St Jean-de-Luz*
05 59 26 14 22/05 59 26 19 22
05 59 26 48 37
contact@chantaco.com
www.golfdechantaco.com

**Château des Vigiers G&CC**   (1992)
*24240 Monestier*
05 53 61 50 33
05 53 61 50 31
golf@vigiers.com
Matthew Storm
www.vigiers.com

**Chiberta**   (1926)
*Boulevard des Plages, 64600 Anglet*
05 59 63 83 20
05 59 63 30 56

**Domaine de la Marterie**   (1987)
*St Felix de Reillac, 24260 Le Bugue*
05 53 05 61 00
05 53 05 61 01
www.marterie.fr

**Graves et Sauternais**   (1989)
*St Pardon de Conques, 33210 Langon*
05 56 62 25 43
05 56 76 83 72
Golf-des-graves@wanadoo.fr
www.golf-des-graves.com

**Gujan**   (1990)
*Route de Souguinet, 33470 Gujan Mestras*
05 57 52 73 73
05 56 66 10 93

**Hossegor**   (1930)
*333 Ave du Golf, 40150 Hossegor*
05 58 43 56 99
05 58 43 98 52
golf.hossegor@wanadoo.fr
Christophe Raillard
www.golfhossegor.com

**Lacanau Golf & Hotel**   (1980)
*Domaine de l'Ardilouse, 33680 Lacanau-Océan*
(+33) 556 039292
(+33) 556 263057
info@golf-hotel-lacanau.fr
www.golf-hotel-lacanau.fr

**Makila**
*Route de Cambo, 64200 Bassussarry*
05 59 58 42 42
05 59 58 42 48

**Médoc**
*Chemin de Courmateau, Louens, 33290 Le Pian Médoc*
05 56 70 11 90
05 56 70 11 99

**Moliets**   (1989)
*Public*
*Rue Mathieu Desbieys, 40660 Moliets*
05 58 48 54 65
05 58 48 54 88
resa@golfmoliets.com
Breton
www.golfmoliets.com

**Pau**   (1856)
*Rue du Golf, 64140 Billère*
+33 (05) 5913 1856
+33 (0) 5913 1857
pau.golf.club@wanadoo.fr
www.paugolfclub.com

**Pessac**   (1989)
*Rue de la Princesse, 33600 Pessac*
05 57 26 03 33
05 56 36 52 89

**Stade Montois**   (1993)
*Pessourdat, 40090 Saint Avit*
05 58 75 63 05
05 58 06 80 72

**Villeneuve sur Lot G&CC**   (1987)
*'La Menuisière', 47290 Castelnaud de Gratecambe*
05 53 01 60 19
05 53 01 78 99
info@vslgolf.com
Jenny Lyon
www.vslgolf.com

## Brittany

**Ajoncs d'Or**   (1976)
*Kergrain Lantic, 22410 Saint-Quay Portrieux*
02 96 71 90 74
02 96 71 40 83
golfdesajoncsdor@wanadoo.fr

**Baden**
*Kernic, 56870 Baden*
02 97 57 18 96
02 97 57 22 05

**Belle Ile en Mer**   (1987)
*Les Poulins, 56360 Belle-Ile-en-Mer*
02 97 31 64 65

**Brest Les Abers**   (1990)
*Kerhoaden, 29810 Plouarzel*
☎   02 98 89 68 33
🖳   golf@abersgolf.com
🖳   www.abersgolf.com

**Brest-Iroise**   (1976)
*Parc de Lann-Rohou, Saint-Urbain,
29800 Landerneau*
☎   02 98 85 16 17
🖳   02 98 85 19 39
🖂   golfhotel@brest-iroise.com
🖳   www.brest-iroise.com

**Dinard**   (1887)
*53 Boulevard de la Houle, 35800 St-Briac-
sur-Mer*
☎   02 99 88 32 07
🖳   02 99 88 04 53
🖂   dinardgolf@dinardgolf.com
✍   Jean-Guillaurne Legros
🖳   www.dinardgolf.com

**La Freslonnière**   (1989)
*Le Bois Briand, 35650 Le Rheu*
☎   02 99 14 84 09
🖳   02 99 14 94 98
🖂   lafreslo@wanadoo.fr
🖳   www.lafreslonniere.com

**L'Odet**   (1986)
*Clohars-Fouesnant, 29950 Benodet*
☎   02 98 54 87 88
🖳   02 98 54 61 40
🖂   odet@bluegreen.com
✍   Jean-Luc Leroux
🖳   www.bluegreen.com

**Les Ormes**   (1988)
*Château des Ormes, Epiniac, 35120 Dol-
de-Bretagne*
☎   02 99 73 54 44
🖳   02 99 73 53 65

**Pléneuf-Val André**
*Rue de la Plage des Vallées, 22370 Pléneuf-
Val André*
☎   02 96 63 01 12
🖳   02 96 63 01 06

**Ploemeur Océan Formule
  Golf**   (1990)
*Kerham Saint-Jude, 56270 Ploemeur*
☎   02 97 32 81 82
🖳   02 97 32 80 90
🖳   www.formule-golf.com

**Quimper-Cornouaille**   (1959)
*Manoir du Mesmeur, 29940 La Forêt-
Fouesnant*
☎   02 98 56 97 09
🖳   02 98 56 86 81
🖂   golf-de-cornouaille@wanadoo.fr
🖳   www.golfdecornouaille.com

**Rennes St Jacques**   (1957)
*Le Temple du Cerisier, 35136 St-Jacques-
de-la-Lande*
☎   02 99 30 18 18
🖳   02 99 30 10 25
🖂   asgolfrennes@wanadoo.fr
🖳   www.golfderennes.net

**Les Rochers**   (1989)
*Route d'Argentré du Plessis 3, 35500 Vitré*
☎   02 99 96 52 52
🖳   02 99 96 79 34

**Sables-d'Or-les-Pins**   (1925)
*22240 Fréhel*
☎   02 96 41 42 57
🖳   02 96 41 51 44

**St Laurent**   (1975)
*Ploemel, 56400 Auray*
☎   02 97 56 85 18
🖳   02 97 56 89 99
🖂   st.laurent@bluegreen.com
🖳   www.bluegreen.com

**St Malo Hotel G&CC**   (1986)
*Le Tronchet, 35540 Miniac-Morvan*
☎   02 99 58 96 69
🖳   02 99 58 10 39
🖂   saintmalogolf@st-malo.com
🖳   www.saintmalogolf.com

**St Samson**   (1965)
*Route de Kérénoc, 22560 Pleumeur-Bodou*
☎   02 96 23 87 34
🖳   02 96 23 84 59

**St Cast Pen Guen**   (1926)
*22380 Saint-Cast-le-Guildo*
☎   02 96 41 91 20
🖳   02 96 41 77 62
🖂   golf.stcast@wanadoo.fr
✍   Jean Marie Vilpasteur
🖳   www.golf-st-cast.com

**Val Queven**   (1990)
**Public**
*Kerruisseau, 56530 Queven*
☎   02 97 05 17 96
🖳   02 97 05 19 18
🖳   www.formule-golf.com

## Burgundy & Auvergne

**Aubazine**   (1977)
**Public**
*19190 Aubazine*
☎   03 55 27 25 66
🖳   03 55 27 29 33

**Beaune-Levernois**   (1990)
*21200 Levernois*
☎   03 80 24 10 29
🖳   03 80 24 03 78
🖂   golfdebeaune@wanadoo.fr
🖳   www.golfbeaune.free.fr

**Chalon-sur-Saône**   (1976)
*Parc de Saint Nicolas, 71380 Chatenoy-en-
Bresse*
☎   03 85 93 49 65
🖳   03 85 93 56 95
🖂   contact@golfchalon.com
🖳   www.golf_chalon_sur_saone.com

**Chambon-sur-Lignon**   (1986)
*Riondet, La Pierre de la Lune, 43400
Le Chambon-sur-Lignon*
☎   04 71 59 28 10

🖳   04 71 65 87 14
🖳   www.golf-chambon.com

**Château d'Avoise**   (1992)
*9 Rue de Mâcon, 71210 Montchanin*
☎   03 85 78 19 19
🖳   03 85 78 15 16

**Château de Chailly**   (1990)
*Chailly-sur-Armançon, 21320 Pouilly-en-
Auxois*
☎   03 80 90 30 40
🖳   03 80 90 30 05
🖂   reservation@chailly.com
🖳   www.chailly.com

**Domaine de Roncemay**   (1989)
*89110 Aillant-sur-Tholon*
☎   03 86 73 50 50
🖳   03 86 73 69 46
🖂   info@roncemay.com
✍   Franzoise Couilloud
🖳   www.roncemay.com

**Jacques Laffite Dijon-
  Bourgogne**   (1972)
*Bois des Norges, 21490 Norges-la-Ville*
☎   03 80 35 71 10
🖳   03 80 35 79 27
🖂   contacts@golfdijonbourgogne.com
🖳   www.golfdijonbourgogne.com

**Limoges-St Lazare**   (1976)
**Public**
*Avenue du Golf, 87000 Limoges*
☎   05 55 28 30 02

**Mâcon La Salle**   (1989)
*La Salle-Mâcon Nord, 71260 La Salle*
☎   03 85 36 09 71
🖳   03 85 36 06 70
🖂   golf.maconlasalle@wanadoo.fr
🖳   www.golfmacon.com

**Le Nivernais**
**Public**
*Le Bardonnay, 58470 Magny Cours*
☎   03 58 18 30
🖳   03 58 04 04

**La Porcelaine**
*Célicroux, 87350 Panazol*
☎   05 55 31 10 69
🖳   05 55 31 10 69
🖂   golf@golf.porcelaine.com
🖳   www.golf-porcelaine.com

**St Junien**   (1997)
*Les Jouberties, 87200 Saint Junien*
☎   05 55 02 96 96
🖳   05 55 02 32 52
🖂   info@golfdesaintjunien.com
🖳   www.golfdesaintjunien.com

**Sporting Club de Vichy**   (1907)
*Allée Baugnies, 03700 Bellerive/Allier*
☎   04 70 32 39 11
🖳   04 70 32 00 54

**Val de Cher**   (1975)
*03190 Nassigny*
☎   04 70 06 71 15
🖳   04 70 06 70 00

golfvaldecher@free.fr
http://golfclub.valdecher.free.fr

**Les Volcans**   (1984)
*La Bruyère des Moines, 63870 Orcines*
☎ 04 73 62 15 51
📠 04 73 62 26 52
✉ accueil@golfdesvolcans.com
✍ Gabriel Martin
🖥 www.golfdesvolcans.com

## Centre

**Les Aisses**   (1992)
*RN20 Sud, 45240 La Ferté St Aubin*
☎ 02 38 64 80 87
📠 02 38 64 80 85
✉ golfdesaisses@wanadoo.fr
🖥 www.aissesgolf.com

**Ardrée**   (1988)
*37360 St Antoine-du-Rocher*
☎ 02 47 56 77 38
📠 02 47 56 79 96
✉ tours.ardree@bluegreen.com
🖥 www.bluegreen.com/tours
www.golf-ardree.com

**Aymerich Golf 'Les Dryades'**
(1987)
*Domaine Les Dryades, 28 rue Golf
(36160), Pouligny-Notre Dame*
☎ 02 54 06 60 66
📠 02 54 30 10 24
✉ info@lesdryades.com
🖥 www.lesdryadesgolf.com

**Les Bordes**   (1987)
*41220 Saint Laurent-Nouan*
☎ 02 54 87 72 13
📠 02 54 87 78 61
✉ reception@lesbordes.com
✍ Mark Vickery (Managing Director)
🖥 www.lesbordes.com

**Château de Cheverny**   (1989)
*La Rousselière, 41700 Cheverny*
☎ 02 54 79 24 70
📠 02 54 79 25 52
✉ contact@golf-cheverny.com
✍ Aurélie Rigault
🖥 www.golf-cheverny.com

**Château de Maintenon**   (1989)
*Route de Gallardon, 28130 Maintenon*
☎ 02 37 27 18 09
📠 02 37 27 10 12

**Château des Sept Tours**   (1989)
*Le Vivier des Landes, 37330 Courcelles
de Touraine*
☎ 02 47 24 69 75
📠 02 47 24 23 74

**Cognac**   (1987)
*Saint-Brice, 16100 Cognac*
☎ 05 45 32 18 17
📠 05 45 35 10 76

**Le Connétable**   (1987)
*Parc Thermal, 86270 La Roche Posay*
☎ 05 49 86 25 10
📠 05 49 19 48 40

**Domaine de Vaugouard**   (1987)
*Chemin des Bois, Fontenay-sur-Loing,
45210 Ferrières*
☎ 02 38 89 79 00
📠 02 38 89 79 01

**Haut-Poitou**   (1987)
*86130 Saint-Cyr*
☎ 05 49 62 53 62
📠 05 49 88 77 14
✉ contact@golfduhautpoitou.com
🖥 www.golfduhautpoitou.com

**Loudun-Roiffe**   (1985)
*Domaine St Hilaire, 86120 Roiffe*
☎ 05 49 98 78 06
📠 05 49 98 72 57
🖥 www.golf-loudun.com

**Marcilly**   (1986)
*Domaine de la Plaine, 45240 Marcilly-en-
Villette*
☎ 02 38 76 11 73
📠 02 38 76 18 73
✉ golf@marcilly.com
✍ Emilie/Sophie
🖥 www.marcilly.com

**Niort**   (1984)
*Chemin du Grand Ormeau, 79000
Niort Romagne*
☎ 05 49 09 01 41
📠 05 49 73 41 53
✉ contact@golfclubniort.fr
✍ Eric Fleury
🖥 www.golfclubniort.fr

**Orléans Donnery**
*Château de la Touche, 45450 Donnery*
☎ 02 38 59 25 15
📠 02 38 57 01 98

**Golf du Perche**   (1987)
*La Vallée des Aulnes, 28400 Souancé
au Perche*
☎ 02 37 29 17 33
📠 02 37 29 12 88
✉ golfduperche@wanadoo.fr
🖥 www.golfduperche.fr

**Petit Chêne**   (1987)
*Le Petit Chêne, 79310 Mazières-en-Gâtine*
☎ 05 49 63 20 95
📠 05 49 63 33 75

**La Picardière**
*Chemin de la Picardière, 18100 Vierzon*
☎ 02 48 75 21 43
📠 02 48 71 87 61

**Poitiers**
*635 route de Beauvoir, 86550
Mignaloux Beauvoir*
☎ 05 49 55 10 50
📠 05 49 62 26 70
✉ asgcp@wanadoo.fr

**Poitou**   (1991)
*Domaine des Forges, 79340 Menigoute*
☎ 0549 69 91 77
📠 0549 69 96 84
✉ info@golfdesforges.com
🖥 www.golfdesforges.com

**La Prée-La Rochelle**   (1988)
*La Richardière, 17137 Marsilly*
☎ 05 46 01 24 42
📠 05 46 01 25 84
✉ golflarochelle@wanadoo.fr
🖥 www.golflarochelle.com

**Royan**   (1977)
*Maine-Gaudin, 17420 Saint-Palais*
☎ 05 46 23 16 24
📠 05 46 23 23 38
✉ golfderoyan@wanadoo.fr
🖥 www.golfderoyan.com

**Saintonge**   (1953)
*Fontcouverte, 17100 Saintes*
☎ 05 46 74 27 61
📠 05 46 92 17 92

**Sancerrois**   (1989)
*St Thibault, 18300 Sancerre*
☎ 02 48 54 11 22
📠 02 48 54 28 03
✉ golf.sancerre@wanadoo.fr
✍ D Gaucher
🖥 www.golf-sancerre.com

**Touraine**   (1971)
*Château de la Touche, 37510 Ballan-Miré*
☎ 02 47 53 20 28
📠 02 47 53 31 54

**Val de l'Indre**   (1989)
*Villedieu-sur-Indre, 36320 Tregonce*
☎ 02 54 26 59 44
📠 02 54 26 06 37

## Channel Coast & North

**Abbeville**   (1989)
*Route du Val, 80132 Grand-Laviers*
☎ 03 22 24 98 58
📠 03 22 24 98 58
✉ abbeville.golfclub@wanadoo.fr
🖥 www.golf.abbeville.com

**L'Ailette**   (1985)
*02860 Cerny en Laonnais*
☎ 03 23 24 83 99
📠 03 23 24 84 66
✉ golf@ailette.org
✍ Philippe Courtin (Dir)
🖥 www.golfailette.fr

**Amiens**   (1925)
*Route départementale 929
80115, Querrieu*
☎ 03 22 93 04 26
📠 03 22 93 04 61
✉ contact@golfamiens.fr
✍ Antoine Monfort (Mgr)/Audrey
Guinault (Sec)
🖥 www.golfamiens.fr

**Apremont Golf Country Club**
(1992)
*60300 Apremont*
☎ 03 44 25 61 11
📠 03 44 25 11 72
✉ apremont@club-albatros.com
✍ E Jacob
🖥 www.apremont-golf.com

## Arras (1989)
*Rue Briquet Taillandier, 62223 Anzin-St-Aubin*
- ☎ 03 21 50 24 24
- 📠 03 21 50 29 71
- ✉ golf@golf-arras.com
- 🖥 www.golf-arras.com

## Belle Dune
*Promenade de Marquenterre, 80790 Fort-Mahon-Plage*
- ☎ 03 22 23 45 50
- 📠 03 22 23 93 41

## Bois de Ruminghem (1992)
*1625 Rue St Antoine, 62370 Ruminghem*
- ☎ 03 21 35 31 37
- ✉ mail@golfdubois.com
- ✍ Boris & Els Janjic
- 🖥 www.golfdubois.com

## Bondues (1968)
*Château de la Vigne, 5910 Bondues*
- ☎ 03 20 23 20 62
- 📠 03 20 23 24 11
- ✉ contact@golfdebondues.com
- 🖥 www.golfdebondues.com

## Champagne (1986)
*02130 Villers-Agron*
- ☎ 03 23 71 62 08
- 📠 03 23 71 50 40
- ✉ golf.de.champagne@wanadoo.fr
- ✍ Camille Piquer (Mgr)
- 🖥 www.golf-de-champagne.com

## Chantilly (1909)
*Allée de la Ménagerie, 60500 Chantilly*
- ☎ +33 (0) 3 44 57 04 43
- 📠 +33 (0) 3 44 57 26 54
- ✉ contact@golfdechantilly.com
- ✍ Remy Dorbeau
- 🖥 www.golfdechantilly.com

## Chaumont-en-Vexin (1968)
*Château de Bertichère, 60240 Chaumont-en-Vexin*
- ☎ 03 44 49 00 81
- 📠 03 44 49 32 71
- ✉ golfdechaumont@golf-paris.net
- 🖥 www.golf-paris.net

## Club du Lys - Chantilly (1929)
*Rond-Point du Grand Cerf, 60260 Lamorlaye*
- ☎ 03 44 21 26 00
- 📠 03 44 21 35 52
- ✉ clubdulys@wanadoo.fr
- ✍ Christophe Rondelé
- 🖥 www.club-lys-chantilly.com

## Compiègne (1896)
*Avenue Royale, 60200 Compiègne*
- ☎ 03 44 38 48 00
- 📠 03 44 40 23 59
- ✉ directeur-golfcompiegne@orange.fr
- ✍ Stephane Banteilla (Director)
- 🖥 www.golf-compiegne.com

## Deauville l'Amiraute (1992)
*CD 278, Tourgéville, 14800 Deauville*
- ☎ 02 31 14 42 00

- 📠 02 31 88 32 00
- 🖥 www.amiraute-resort.com

## Domaine du Tilleul (1984)
*Landouzy-la-Ville, 02140 Vervins*
- ☎ 03 23 98 48 00
- 📠 03 23 98 46 46

## Dunkerque (1991)
**Public**
*Fort Vallières, Coudekerque-Village, 59380 Coudekerque*
- ☎ 03 28 61 07 43
- 📠 03 28 60 05 93
- ✉ golf@golf-dk.com
- 🖥 www.golf-dk.com

## Golf de Raray (1987)
*4 Rue Nicolas de Lancy, 60810 Raray*
- ☎ 03 44 54 70 61
- 📠 03 44 54 72 51
- ✉ contact@exclusivgolf-raray.fr
- 🖥 www.golfraray.com

## Golf Dolce Chantilly (1991)
*Route d'Apremont, 60500 Vineuil St-Firmin*
- ☎ 03 44 58 47 74
- 📠 03 44 58 50 28
- ✉ golf.chantilly@dolce.com
- ✍ Pierre Jacob (Mgr)
- 🖥 www.dolce.com

## Hardelot Dunes Course (1991)
*Ave du Golf, 62152 Hardelot*
- ☎ 03 21 83 73 10
- 📠 03 21 83 24 33
- ✉ hardelot@opengolfclub.com
- ✍ Ken Strachan (Mgr)
- 🖥 www.hardelot-golf.com

## Hardelot Pins Course (1931)
*Ave du Golf, 62152 Hardelot*
- ☎ 03 21 83 73 10
- 📠 03 21 83 24 33
- ✉ hardelot@opengolfclub.com
- ✍ Ken Strachan (Mgr)
- 🖥 www.hardelot-golf.com

## Morfontaine (1913)
*60128 Mortefontaine*
- ☎ 03 44 54 68 27
- 📠 03 44 54 60 57
- ✉ morfontaine@wanadoo.fr
- ✍ Jean-Maurice Dulout
- 🖥 www.golfdemorfontaine.fr

## Mormal (1991)
*Bois St Pierre, 59144 Preux-au-Sart*
- ☎ 03 27 63 07 00
- 📠 03 27 39 93 62
- ✉ info@golf-mormal.com
- 🖥 www.golf-mormal.com

## Nampont-St-Martin (1978)
*Maison Forte, 80120 Nampont-St-Martin*
- ☎ 03 22 29 92 90/03 22 29 89 87
- 📠 03 22 29 97 54
- ✉ golfdenampont@wanadoo.fr
- 🖥 www.golfdenampont.com

## Rebetz (1988)
*Route de Noailles, 60240 Chaumont-en-Vexin*
- ☎ 03 44 49 15 54

- 📠 03 44 49 14 26
- 🖥 www.rebetz.com

## Saint-Omer
*Chemin des Bois, Acquin-Westbécourt, 62380 Lumbres*
- ☎ 03 21 38 59 90
- 📠 03 21 93 02 47

## Le Sart (1910)
*5 Rue Jean-Jaurès, 59650 Villeneuve D'Ascq*
- ☎ 03 20 72 02 51
- 📠 03 20 98 73 28
- ✉ contact@golfdusart.com
- 🖥 www.golfdusart.com

## Thumeries (1935)
*Bois Lenglart, 59239 Thumeries*
- ☎ 03 20 86 58 98
- 📠 03 20 86 52 66
- ✉ golfdethumeries@free.fr
- ✍ Fransoise Dumoulin
- 🖥 www.golfdethumeries.com

## Le Touquet 'La Forêt' (1904)
*Ave du Golf, BP 41, 62520 Le Touquet*
- ☎ 03 21 06 28 00
- 📠 03 21 06 28 01
- ✉ letouquet@opengolfclub.com
- ✍ Gilles Grattepanche
- 🖥 www.opengolfclub.com

## Le Touquet 'La Mer' (1931)
*Ave du Golf, BP 41, 62520 Le Touquet*
- ☎ 03 21 06 28 00
- 📠 03 21 06 28 01
- ✉ letouquet@opengolfclub.com
- ✍ Gilles Grattepanche
- 🖥 www.opengolfclub.com

## Le Touquet 'Le Manoir' (1994)
*Ave du Golf, BP 41, 62520 Le Touquet*
- ☎ 03 21 06 28 00
- 📠 03 21 06 28 01
- ✉ letouquet@opengolfclub.com
- ✍ Gilles Grattepanche
- 🖥 www.opengolfclub.com

## Val Secret (1984)
*Brasles, 02400 Château Thierry*
- ☎ 03 23 83 07 25
- 📠 03 23 83 92 73
- ✉ contact@golfvalsecret.com
- 🖥 www.golfvalsecret.com

## Vert Parc (1991)
*3 Route d'Ecuelles, 59480 Illies*
- ☎ 03 20 29 37 87
- 📠 03 20 49 76 39
- ✉ golfduvertparc@sfr.fr
- 🖥 www.golflevertparc.com

## Wimereux (1901)
*Avenue F. Mitterrand, 62930 Wimereux*
- ☎ 03 21 32 43 20
- 📠 03 21 33 62 21
- ✉ accueil@golf-wimereux.com
- 🖥 www.golf-wimereux.com

## Corsica

**Sperone**    (1990)
*Domaine de Sperone, 20169 Bonifacio*
☎    04 95 73 17 13
🖥    04 95 73 17 85
📧    golf@sperone.com
🖳    www.sperone.com

## Ile de France

**Ableiges**    (1989)
*95450 Ableiges*
☎    01 30 27 97 00
🖥    01 30 27 97 10
📧    golf@ableigesgolf.com
🖳    www.ableiges-golf.com

**Bellefontaine**    (1987)
*Route du Pulseux, 95270 Bellefontaine*
☎    01 34 71 05 02
🖥    01 34 71 90 90
📧    contact@golf-bellefontaine.fr
🖳    www.bellefontainegolfclub.com

**Bussy-St-Georges**    (1988)
*Promenade des Golfeurs, 77600 Bussy-St-Georges*
☎    01 64 66 00 00
🖥    01 64 66 22 92

**Cély**    (1990)
*Le Château, Route de Saint-Germain, 77930 Cély-en-Bière*
☎    01 64 38 03 07
🖥    01 64 38 08 78
🖳    www.celygolf.com

**Cergy Pontoise**    (1988)
*2 Allee de l'Obstacle d'Eau, 95490 Vaureal*
☎    01 34 21 03 48
🖥    01 34 21 03 34

**Chevannes-Mennecy**    (1994)
*Chemin de l'Avenue, 91750 Chevannes*
☎    01 64 99 88 74
🖥    01 64 99 88 67
📧    legolfdechevannes@wanadoo.fr
🖳    www.golfdechevannes.fr

**Clement Ader**    (1990)
*Avenue Charles de Gaulle, Domaine du Château Péreire, 77220 Gretz-Armainvilliers*
☎    01 64 07 82 18
🖥    01 64 07 82 10
📧    contact@golfclementader.com
🖳    www.golfclementader.com

**Coudray**    (1960)
*Ave du Coudray, 91830 Le Coudray-Montceaux*
☎    01 64 93 81 76
🖥    01 64 93 99 95
📧    golf.du.coudray@wanadoo.fr
🖳    www.golfcoudray.org

**Courson Monteloup**    (1991)
*91680 Bruyères-le-Chatel*
☎    01 64 58 80 80
🖥    01 64 58 83 06
🖳    www.golf-stadefrancais.com

**Crécy-la-Chapelle**    (1987)
*Domaine de la Brie, Route de Guérard, F 77580 Crécy-la-Chapelle*
☎    01 64 75 34 44
🖥    01 64 75 34 45
📧    info@domainedelabrie.com
🖳    www.crecygolfclub.com

**Le Golf d'Etiolles**    (1990)
*Vieux Chemin de Paris, 91450 Étiolles*
☎    01 69 89 59 59
🖥    01 69 89 59 62
🖳    www.golf-etiolles.com

**Disneyland Golf**    (1992)
*1 Allee de la Mare Houleuse, 77700 Magny-le-Hongre*
☎    01 60 45 68 90
🖥    01 60 45 68 33
📧    dlp.golf.disneyland@disney.com
🖳    www.disneylandparis.co.uk

**Domaine de Belesbat**    (1989)
*Courdimanche-sur-Essonne, 91820 Boutigny-sur-Essonne*
☎    01 69 23 19 10
🖥    01 69 23 19 01
🖳    www.belesbat.com

**Domont-Montmorency**
*Route de Montmorency, 95330 Domont*
☎    01 39 91 07 50
🖥    01 39 91 25 70

**Fontainebleau**    (1909)
*Route d'Orleans, 77300 Fontainebleau*
☎    01 64 22 22 95
🖥    01 64 22 63 76
📧    golf.fontainebleau@orange.fr
✍    Christian Majcher
🖳    www.golfdefontainebleau.org

**Fontenailles**    (1991)
*Domaine de Bois Boudran, 77370 Fontenailles*
☎    01 64 60 51 00
🖥    01 60 67 52 12

**Forges-les-Bains**    (1989)
*Rue du Général Leclerc, 91470 Forges-les-Bains*
☎    01 64 91 48 18
🖥    01 64 91 40 52
📧    infos@golf-forgeslesbains.com
🖳    www.golf-forgeslesbains.com

**Greenparc**    (1993)
*Route de Villepech, 91280 St Pierre-du-Perray*
☎    01 60 75 40 60
🖥    01 60 75 40 04

**L'Isle Adam**    (1995)
*1 Chemin des Vanneaux, 95290 L'Isle Adam*
☎    01 34 08 11 11
🖥    01 34 08 11 19

**Marivaux**    (1992)
*Bois de Marivaux, 91640 Janvry*
☎    01 64 90 85 85
🖥    01 64 90 82 22
📧    contact@golfmarivaux.com
🖳    www.golfmarivaux.com

**Meaux-Boutigny**    (1985)
*Rue de Barrois, 77470 Boutigny*
☎    01 60 25 63 98
🖥    01 60 25 60 58

**Mont Griffon**    (1990)
*RD 909, 95270 Luzarches*
☎    01 34 68 10 10
🖥    01 34 68 04 10
📧    golf@golfmontgriffon.com
🖳    www.golfmontgriffon.com

**Montereau La Forteresse**    (1989)
*Domaine de la Forteresse, 77940 Thoury-Ferrottes*
☎    (+33) 01 60 96 95 10
🖥    (+33) 01 60 96 01 41
📧    contact@golf-forteresse.com
✍    Aurelie Maloubier
🖳    www.golf-forteresse.com

**Ormesson**    (1969)
*Chemin du Belvedère, 94490 Ormesson-sur-Marne*
☎    01 45 76 20 71
🖥    01 45 94 86 85

**Ozoir-la-Ferrière**    (1926)
*Château des Agneaux, 77330 Ozoir-la-Ferrière*
☎    01 60 02 60 79
🖥    01 64 40 28 20

**Paris International**    (1991)
*18 Route du Golf, 95560 Baillet-en-France*
☎    01 34 69 90 00
🖥    01 34 69 97 15

**St Germain-les-Corbeil**
*6 Ave du Golf, 91250 St Germain-les-Corbeil*
☎    01 60 75 81 54
🖥    01 60 75 52 89

**Seraincourt**    (1964)
*Gaillonnet-Seraincourt, 95450 Vigny*
☎    01 34 75 47 28
🖥    01 34 75 75 47

**Villarceaux**    (1971)
*Château du Couvent, 95710 Chaussy*
☎    01 34 67 73 83
🖥    01 34 67 72 66
📧    villarceaux@wanadoo.fr
🖳    www.villarceaux.com

**Villeray**    (1974)
Public
*Melun-Sénart, St Pierre du Perray, 91100 Corbeil*
☎    01 60 75 17 47
🖥    01 69 89 00 73

## Languedoc-Roussillon

**Cap d'Agde**    (1989)
Public
*4 Ave des Alizés, 34300 Cap d'Agde*
☎    04 67 26 54 40
🖥    04 67 26 97 00

✉ golf@ville-agde.fr
🖥 www.ville-agde.fr

## Carcassonne   (1988)
Route de Ste-Hilaire, 11000 Carcassonne
☎ 06 13 20 85 43
🖥 04 68 72 57 30

## Coulondres   (1984)
72 Rue des Erables, 34980 Saint-Gely-du-Fesc
☎ 04 67 84 13 75
🖥 04 67 84 06 33
🖥 www.coulondres.com

## Domaine de Falgos   (1992)
BP 9, 66260 St Laurent-de-Cerdans
☎ 04 68 39 51 42
🖥 04 68 39 52 30
✉ contact@falgos.com
🖥 www.falgos.com

## Fontcaude   (1991)
Route de Lodève, Domaine de Fontcaude, 34990 Juvignac
☎ 04 67 45 90 10
🖥 04 67 45 90 20
✉ golf@golfhotelmontpellier.com
🖥 www.golfhotelmontpellier.com

## La Grande-Motte   (1987)
Clubhouse du Golf, 34280 La Grande-Motte
☎ 04 67 56 05 00
🖥 04 67 29 18 84

## Montpellier Massane   (1988)
Domaine de Massane, 34670 Baillargues
☎ 04 67 87 87 87
🖥 04 67 87 87 90

## Nîmes Campagne   (1968)
1360 chemin du Mas de Campagne, 30900 Nîmes
☎ 04 66 70 17 37
🖥 04 66 70 03 14
✉ resa@golfnimescampagne.fr
✍ Ruven Estelle
🖥 www.golfnimescampagne.fr

## Nîmes-Vacquerolles   (1990)
1075 chemin du golf, 30900 Nîmes
☎ 04 66 23 33 33
🖥 04 66 23 94 94
✉ vacquerolles.opengolfclub @wanadoo.fr
🖥 www.golf-nimes.com

## Saint Cyprien Golf Resort   (1976)
Le Mas D'Huston, 66750 St Cyprien Plage
☎ 04 68 37 63 63
🖥 04 68 37 64 64
✉ golf@saintcyprien-golfresort.com
🖥 www.saintcyprien-golfresort.com

## St Thomas   (1992)
Route de Bessan, 34500 Béziers
☎ 04 67 39 03 09
🖥 04 67 39 10 65
✉ info@golfsaintthomas.com
🖥 www.golfsaintthomas.com

## Loire Valley

## Avrillé   (1988)
Château de la Perrière, 49240 Avrillé
☎ 02 41 69 22 50
🖥 02 41 34 44 60
✉ avrille@bluegreen.com
✍ J Goudard (Dir)
🖥 www.bluegreen.com

## Baugé-Pontigné   (1994)
Public
Route de Tours, 49150 Baugé
☎ 02 41 89 01 27
🖥 02 41 89 05 50
✉ golf.bauge@wanadoo.fr
🖥 www.golf-bauge.fr

## La Bretesche   (1967)
Domaine de la Bretesche, 44780 Missillac
☎ 02 51 76 86 86
🖥 02 40 88 36 28

## Carquefou   (1991)
Boulevard de l'Epinay, 44470 Carquefou
☎ 02 40 52 73 74
🖥 02 40 52 73 20

## Cholet   (1989)
Allée du Chêne Landry, 49300 Cholet
☎ 02 41 71 05 01
🖥 02 41 56 06 94

## La Domangère
La Roche-sur-Yon, Route de la Rochelle, 85310 Nesmy
☎ 02 51 07 65 90
🖥 02 51 07 65 95
🖥 www.golf-domangere.com

## Fontenelles
Public
Saint-Gilles-Croix-de-Vie, 85220 Aiguillon-sur-Vie
☎ 02 51 54 13 94
🖥 02 51 55 45 77

## Golf D'Anjou   (1990)
Route de Cheffes, 49330 Champigné
☎ 02 41 42 01 01
🖥 02 41 42 04 37
✉ accueil@anjougolf.com
✍ Sean Adamson
🖥 www.anjougolf.com

## Ile d'Or   (1988)
BP 90410, 49270 La Varenne
☎ 02 40 98 58 00
🖥 02 40 98 51 62
✉ nantesiledor@wanadoo.fr

## International Barriere-La Baule   (1976)
44117 Saint-André-des Eaux
☎ 02 40 60 46 18
🖥 02 40 60 41 41
✉ golfinterlabaule@lucienbarriere .com
✍ Nathalie Primas
🖥 www.lucienbarriere.com

## Laval-Changé   (1972)
La Chabossiere, 53000 Changé-les-Laval
☎ 02 43 53 16 03
🖥 02 43 49 35 15
✉ laval53.golf@sfr.fr
🖥 www.laval53-golf.com

## Le Mansgolfier   (1990)
Rue du Golf, 72190 Sargé les Le Mans
☎ 02 43 76 25 07
🖥 02 43 76 45 25
✉ lemansgolfier@wanadoo.fr

## Le Mans Mulsanne   (1961)
Route de Tours, 72230 Mulsanne
☎ 02 43 42 00 36
🖥 02 43 42 21 31

## Le Mansgolfier Golf Club   (1990)
Rue du Golf, 72190 Sarge les Le Mans
☎ 02 43 76 25 07
🖥 02 43 76 45 25
✉ lemansgolfier@wanadoo.fr
🖥 www.lemansgolfier.com

## Nantes   (1967)
44360 Vigneux de Bretagne
☎ 02 40 63 25 82
🖥 02 40 63 64 86
✉ golfclubdenantes@aol.com
🖥 www.golfclubnantes.com

## Nantes Erdre   (1990)
Chemin du Bout des Landes, 44300 Nantes
☎ 02 40 59 21 21
🖥 02 40 94 14 32
✉ golf.nanteserdre@nge-nantes.fr
🖥 www.nge.fr

## Les Olonnes
Gazé, 85340 Olonne-sur-Mer
☎ 02 51 33 16 16
🖥 02 51 33 10 45

## Pornic   (1912)
49 Boulevard de l'Océan, Sainte-Marie/Mer, 44210 Pornic
☎ 02 40 82 06 69
🖥 02 40 82 80 65

## Port Bourgenay   (1990)
Avenue de la Mine, Port Bourgenay, 85440 Talmont-St-Hilaire
☎ 02 51 23 35 45
🖥 02 51 23 35 48

## Sablé-Solesmes   (1991)
Domaine de l'Outinière, Route de Pincé, 72300 Sablé-sur-Sarthe
☎ 02 43 95 28 78
🖥 02 43 92 39 05
✉ golf-sable-solesmes@wanadoo.fr
✍ Yves Pironneau
🖥 www.golf-sable-solesmes.com

## St Jean-de-Monts   (1988)
Ave des Pays de la Loire, 85160 Saint Jean-de-Monts
☎ 02 51 58 82 73
🖥 02 51 59 18 32

**Savenay** (1990)
*44260 Savenay*
☎ 02 40 56 88 05
📠 02 40 56 89 04

## Normandy

**Bellême-St-Martin** (1988)
*Les Sablons, 61130 Bellême*
☎ 02 33 73 00 07
📠 02 33 73 00 17

**Cabourg-Le Home** (1907)
*38 Av Président Réné Coty, Le Home
Varaville, 14390 Cabourg*
☎ 02 31 91 25 56
📠 02 31 91 18 30
📧 golf-cabourg-le-
home@worldonline.fr
🌐 www.golfclubdecabourglehome
.com

**Caen** (1990)
*Le Vallon, 14112 Bieville-Beuville*
☎ 02 31 94 72 09
📠 02 31 47 45 30

**Champ de Bataille** (1988)
*Château du Champ de Bataille, 27110
Le Neubourg*
☎ 02 32 35 03 72
📠 02 32 35 83 10
📧 info@champdebataille.com
🌐 www.champdebataille.com

**Clécy** (1988)
*Manoir de Cantelou, 14570 Clécy*
☎ 02 31 69 72 72
📠 02 31 69 70 22
📧 golf-de-clecy@golf-de-clecy.com
🌐 www.golf-de-clecy.com

**Coutainville** (1925)
*Ave du Golf, 50230 Agon-Coutainville*
☎ 02 33 47 03 31
📠 02 33 47 38 42

**Deauville St Gatien** (1987)
*14130 St Gatien-des-Bois*
☎ 02 31 65 19 99
📠 02 31 65 11 24
📧 contact@golfdeauville.com
🌐 www.golfdeauville.com

**Dieppe-Pourville** (1897)
*51 Route de Pourville, 76200 Dieppe*
☎ 02 35 84 25 05
📠 02 35 84 97 11
📧 golf-de-dieppe@wanadoo.fr
🌐 www.golf-dieppe.com

**Étretat** (1908)
*BP No 7, Route du Havre, 76790
Étretat*
☎ 02 35 27 04 89

**Forêt Verte**
*Bosc Guerard, 76710 Montville*
☎ 02 35 33 62 94

**Golf barrière de Deauville**
(1929)
*14 Saint Arnoult, 14800 Deauville*
☎ 02 31 14 24 24
📠 02 31 14 24 25
📧 golfdeauville@lucienbarriere.com
🌐 www.lucienbarriere.com

**Golf de Jumièges** (1991)
*Jumièges, 76480 Duclair*
☎ 02 35 05 32 97
📠 02 35 37 99 97
📧 jumieges.golf@ucpa.asso.fr

**Granville** (1912)
*Bréville, 50290 Bréhal*
☎ 02 33 50 23 06
📠 02 33 61 91 87
📧 contact@golfdegranville.com
🌐 www.golfdegranville.com

**Le Havre** (1933)
*Hameau Saint-Supplix, 76930 Octeville-sur-
Mer*
☎ 02 35 46 36 50
📠 02 35 46 32 66
📧 contact@golfduhavre.com
✍ Christian Coty (President)
🌐 www.golfduhavre.com

**Houlgate** (1981)
*Route de Gonneville, 14510 Houlgate*
☎ 02 31 24 80 49
📠 02 31 28 04 48

**Omaha Beach** (1986)
*Ferme St Sauveur, 14520 Port-en-Bessin*
☎ 02 31 22 12 12
📠 02 31 22 12 13
📧 omaha.beach@wanadoo.fr
🌐 www.omahabeachgolfclub.com

**Rouen-Mont St Aignan** (1911)
*Rue Francis Poulenc, 76130 Mont St Aignan*
☎ 02 35 76 38 65
📠 02 35 75 13 86

**Golf-hotel St Saëns** (1987)
*Domaine du Vaudichon, 76680 St Saëns*
☎ 02 35 34 25 24
📠 02 35 34 43 33
📧 golf@golfdesaintsaens.com
🌐 www.golfdesaintsaens.com

**Golf barrière de St Julien**
(1987)
*St Julien-sur-Calonne, 14130 Pont-l'Évêque*
☎ 02 31 64 30 30
📠 02 31 64 12 43
📧 golfsaintjulien@lucienbarriere.com
🌐 www.lucienbarriere.com

**Le Vaudreuil** (1962)
*27100 Le Vaudreuil*
☎ 02 32 59 02 60
📠 02 32 59 43 88

## North East

**Ammerschwihr** (1990)
*Allée du golf, 68770 Ammerschwihr*
☎ +33 3 89 47 17 30

📱 +33 3 89 47 17 77
📧 golf-mail@golf-ammerschwihr.com
🌐 www.golf-ammerschwihr.com

**Bâle G&CC** (1926)
*Rue de Wentzwiller, 68220 Hagenthal-le-
Bas*
☎ +33 (0)3 89 68 50 91
📠 +33 (0)3 89 68 55 66
📧 info@gccbasel.ch
🌐 www.gccbasel.ch

**Besançon** (1968)
*La Chevillotte, 25620 Mamirolle*
☎ 03 81 55 73 54
📠 03 81 55 88 64
🌐 www.golfbesancon.com

**Bitche** (1988)
*Rue des Prés, 57230 Bitche*
☎ 03 87 96 15 30
📠 03 87 96 08 04

**Château de Bournel** (1990)
*25680 Cubry*
☎ 03 81 86 00 10
📠 03 81 86 01 06
📧 info@bournel.com
🌐 www.bournel.com

**Combles-en-Barrois**
(1948)
*14 Rue Basse, 55000 Combles-en-Barrois*
☎ 03 29 45 16 03
📠 03 29 45 16 06

**Épinal** (1985)
**Public**
*Rue du Merle-Blanc, 88001 Épinal*
☎ 03 29 34 65 97

**Golf de Faulquemont-
Pontpierre** (1993)
*Avenue Jean Monnett, 57380 Faulquemont*
☎ 03 87 81 30 52
📠 03 87 81 30 62
📧 golf.faulquemont@gmail.com
✍ Michel Goedert (Pres)
🌐 www.golf-faulquemont.com

**Golf Hotel Club de la Forêt
d'Orient** (1990)
*Route de Geraudot, 10220 Rouilly Sacey*
☎ 03 25 43 80 80
📠 03 25 41 57 58
📧 contact@hotel-foret-orient.com
🌐 www.hotel-foret-orient.com

**Gardengolf Metz**
*3 Rue Félix Savart, 57070 Metz
Technopole 2000*
☎ 03 87 78 71 04
📠 03 87 78 68 98
📧 contact@gardengolfmetz.com
🌐 www.gardengolfmetz.com

**Grande Romanie** (1988)
*La Grande Romanie, 51460 Courtisols*
☎ 03 26 66 65 97
📠 03 26 66 65 97
📧 contact@par72.net
🌐 wwwpar72.net

## La Grange aux Ormes   (1990)
*Golf de La Grange aux Ormes, Rue de la Grange aux Ormes, 57155 Marly*
☎ +33 (0)3 87 63 10 62
🖥 +33 (0)3 87 55 01 77
📧 info@grange-aux-ormes.com
✍ Pierre Bogenez
⊕ Facebook: www.facebook.com /GolfdelaGrangesauxOrmes
🖃 www.grange-aux-ormes.com

## Kempferhof   (1988)
*Golf-Hôtel-Restaurant, 67115 Plobsheim*
☎ 0033 (0) 3 88 98 72 72
🖥 0033 (0) 3 88 98 74 76
📧 info@golf-kempferhof.com
🖃 www.golf-kempferhof.com

## La Largue G&CC   (1988)
*25 Rue du Golf, 68580 Mooslargue*
☎ 03 89 07 67 67
🖥 03 89 25 62 83
📧 lalargue@golf-lalargue.com
🖃 www.golf-lalargue.com

## Les Rousses   (1986)
*1305 Route du Noirmont, 39220 Les Rousses*
☎ 03 84 60 06 25
🖥 03 84 60 01 73

## Metz-Cherisey   (1963)
*Château de Cherisey, 57420 Cherisey*
☎ 03 87 52 70 18
🖥 03 87 52 42 44

## Nancy-Aingeray   (1962)
*Aingeray, 54460 Liverdun*
☎ 03 83 24 53 87

## Nancy-Pulnoy   (1993)
*10 Rue du Golf, 54425 Pulnoy*
☎ 03 83 18 10 18
🖥 03 83 18 10 19

## Reims-Champagne   (1928)
*Château des Dames de France, 51390 Gueux*
☎ 03 26 05 46 10
🖥 03 26 05 46 19

## Golf du Rhin   (1969)
*Ile du Rhin, F-68490 Chalampé*
☎ +33 3 89 83 28 32
🖥 +33 3 89 83 28 42
📧 golfdurhin@wanadoo.fr
✍ Mr Michel Zimmerlin
🖃 www.golfdurhin.com

## Rougemont-le-Château   (1990)
*Route de Masevaux, 90110 Rougemont-le-Château*
☎ 03 84 23 74 74
🖥 03 84 23 03 15
📧 golf.rougemont@wanadoo.fr
✍ Lionel Burnet
🖃 www.golf.rougemont.com

## Strasbourg   (1934)
*Route du Rhin, 67400 Illkirch*
☎ 03 88 66 17 22
🖥 03 88 65 05 67

📧 golf.strasbourg@wanadoo.fr
🖃 www.golf-strasbourg.com

## Domaine du Val de Sorne   (1989)
*Domaine de Val de Sorne, 39570 Vernantois*
☎ 03 84 43 04 80
🖥 03 84 47 31 21
📧 info@valdesorne.com
🖃 www.valdesorne.com

## La Wantzenau   (1991)
*C D 302, 67610 La Wantzenau*
☎ 03 88 96 37 73
🖥 03 88 96 34 71

---

## Paris Region

## Béthemont-Chisan CC   (1989)
*12 Rue du Parc de Béthemont, 78300 Poissy*
☎ 01 39 75 51 13
🖥 01 39 75 49 90

## La Boulie
*La Boulie, 78000 Versailles*
☎ 01 39 50 59 41

## Feucherolles   (1992)
*78810 Feucherolles*
☎ 01 30 54 94 94
🖥 01 30 54 92 37
📧 contact @exclusivgolf-feucherolles.fr
🖃 www.ngf-golf.com /exclusivgolf-feucherolles

## Fourqueux   (1963)
*Rue Saint Nom 36, 78112 Fourqueux*
☎ 01 34 51 41 47
🖥 01 39 21 00 70

## Golf National   (1990)
*2 Avenue du Golf, 78280 Guyancourt*
☎ 00 33 1 30 43 36 00
🖥 0 33 1 30 43 85 58
📧 gn@golf-national.com
✍ Olivier Roche (Gen Mgr)
🖃 www.golf-national.com

## Isabella   (1969)
*RN12, Sainte-Appoline, 78370 Plaisir*
☎ 01 30 54 10 62
🖥 01 30 54 67 58
📧 info@golfisabella.com
🖃 www.golfisabella.com

## Joyenval   (1992)
*Chemin de la Tuilerie, 78240 Chambourcy*
☎ 01 39 22 27 50
🖥 01 39 79 12 90
📧 joyenval@golfdejoyenval.com
🖃 www.joyenval.fr

## Rochefort   (1964)
*78730 Rochefort-en-Yvelines*
☎ 01 30 41 31 81
🖥 01 30 41 94 01

## St Cloud   (1911)
*60 Rue du 19 Janvier, Garches 92380*
☎ 01 47 01 01 85
🖥 01 47 01 19 57

## St Germain   (1922)
*Route de Poissy, 78100 St Germain-en-Laye*
☎ 01 39 10 30 30
🖥 01 39 10 30 31
📧 info@golfsaintgermain.org
🖃 www.golfsaintgermain.org

## St Quentin-en-Yvelines
**Public**
*RD 912, 78190 Trappes*
☎ 01 30 50 86 40

## St Nom-La-Bretêche   (1959)
*Hameau Tuilerie-Bignon, 78860 St Nom-La-Bretèche*
☎ 01 30 80 04 40
🖥 01 34 62 60 44

## La Vaucouleurs   (1987)
*Rue de l'Eglise, 78910 Civry-la-Forêt*
☎ 01 34 87 62 29
🖥 01 34 87 70 09
📧 vaucouleurs@vaucouleurs.fr
✍ J Pelard
🖃 www.vaucouleurs.fr

## Les Yvelines   (1989)
*Château de la Couharde, 78940 La-Queue-les-Yvelines*
☎ 01 34 86 48 89
🖥 01 34 86 50 31
📧 lesyvelines@opengolfclub.com
🖃 www.opengolfclub.com

---

## Provence & Côte d'Azur

## Aix Marseille   (1935)
*13290 Les Milles, Domaine Riquetti, 13290 Les Milles*
☎ 04 42 24 40 41/04 42 24 23 01
🖥 04 42 39 97 48
📧 golfaixmarseille@aol.com
✍ Mme Roseline Maillet
🖃 www.golfaixmarseille.com

## Barbaroux   (1989)
*Route de Cabasse, 83170 Brignoles*
☎ 04 94 69 63 63
🖥 04 94 59 00 93
📧 contact@barbaroux.com
🖃 www.barbaroux.com

## Les Baux de Provence   (1989)
*Domaine de Manville, 13520 Les Baux-de-Provence*
☎ 04 90 54 40 20
🖥 04 90 54 40 93
📧 golfbauxdeprovence@wanadoo.fr
🖃 www.golfbauxdeprovence.com

## Beauvallon-Grimaud
*Boulevard des Collines, 83120 Sainte-Maxime*
☎ 04 94 96 16 98

**Biot**   (1930)
La Bastide du Roy, 06410 Biot
☎ 04 93 65 08 48
🖳 04 93 65 05 63

**Cannes Mandelieu**   (1891)
Route de Golf, 06210 Mandelieu
☎ 04 92 97 32 00
🖳 04 93 49 92 90

**Cannes Mandelieu Riviera**
(1990)
Avenue des Amazones, 06210 Mandelieu
☎ 04 92 97 49 49
🖳 04 92 97 49 42

**Cannes Mougins**   (1923)
175 Avenue du Golf, 06250 Mougins
☎ 04 93 75 79 13
🖳 04 93 75 27 60
✉ golf-cannes-mougins@wanadoo.fr
✍ Monsieur Bernard Biard
🖥 www.golf-cannes-mougins.com

**Châteaublanc**
Les Plans, 84310 Morières-les-Avignon
☎ 04 90 33 39 08
🖳 04 90 33 43 24
✉ info@golfchateaublanc.com
🖥 www.golfchateaublanc.com

**Digne-les-Bains**   (1990)
**Public**
57 Route du Chaffaut, 0400 Digne-les-Bains
☎ 04 92 30 58 00
🖳 04 92 30 58 13
✉ contact@golfdignelalavande.com
🖥 www.golfdignelalavande.com

**Estérel Latitudes**   (1989)
Ave du Golf, 83700 St Raphaël
☎ 04 94 52 68 30
🖳 04 94 52 68 31

**Frégate**   (1992)
Dolce Frégate Provence, RD 559, 83270
St Cyr-sur-Mer
☎ 04 94 29 38 00
🖳 04 94 29 96 94
✉ golf-fregate@dolce.com
🖥 www.golfdolcefregate.com

**Gap-Bayard**   (1988)
Centre d'Oxygénation, R.N. 85 Col Bayard,
05000 Gap
☎ 04 92 50 16 83
🖳 04 92 50 17 05
✉ gap-bayard@wanadoo.fr
✍ Rostaing
🖥 www.gap-bayard.com

**Golf Claux-Amic**   (1992)
1 Route des Trois Ponts, 06130 Grasse
☎ 04 93 60 55 44
🖳 04 93 60 55 19
✉ info@claux-amic.com
🖥 www.chateau-taulane.com

**Golf de Roquebrune**   (1989)
Golf de Roquebrune, CD7,
83520 Roquebrune-sur-Argens
☎ 04 94 19 60 35

✉ contact@golfderoquebrune.com
✍ Mathieu Sevestre (Mgr)
🖥 www.golfderoquebrune.com

**Grand Avignon**   (1989)
Les Chênes Verts, 84270 Vedene - Avignon
☎ 04 90 31 49 94
🖳 04 90 31 01 21
✉ info@golfgrandavignon.com
🖥 www.golfgrandavignon.com

**La Grande Bastide**   (1990)
Chemin des Picholines 761, 06740
Châteauneuf de Grasse
☎ 04 93 77 70 08
🖳 04 93 77 72 36
✉ grandebastide@opengolfclub.com
✍ Alexis Davet (Mgr)
🖥 www.opengolfclub.com

**Luberon**   (1986)
La Grande Gardette, 04860 Pierrevert
☎ 04 92 72 17 19
🖳 04 92 72 59 12
✉ info@golf-du-luberon.com
✍ Philippe Berrut
🖥 www.golf-du-luberon.com

**Marseille La Salette**   (1988)
65 Impasse des Vaudrans, 13011 La
Valentine Marseille
☎ 04 91 27 12 16
🖳 04 91 27 21 33
✉ lasalette@opengolfclub.com
🖥 www.opengolfclub.com

**Miramas**   (1993)
Mas de Combe, 13140 Miramas
☎ 04 90 58 56 55
🖳 04 90 17 38 73

**Monte Carlo**   (1910)
Route du Mont-Agel, 06320 La Turbie
☎ 04 92 41 50 70
🖳 04 93 41 09 55
✉ monte-carlo-golf-club
   @wanadoo.fr

**Opio-Valbonne**   (1966)
Route de Roquefort-les-Pins, 06650 Opio
☎ 04 93 12 00 08
🖳 04 93 12 26 00
🖥 www.opengolfclub.com

**Pont Royal**   (1992)
Pont Royal, 13370 Mallemort
☎ 04 90 57 40 79
🖳 04 90 57 50 19

**Royal Mougins**   (1993)
424 Avenue du Roi, 06250 Mougins
☎ 04 92 92 49 69 (reception)
🖳 04 92 92 49 70
✉ contact@royalmougins.fr
🖥 www.royalmougins.fr

**Saint Donat G&CC**   (1993)
270 Route de Cannes, 06130 Grasse
☎ +33 493 097660
🖳 +33 493 097663
✉ info@golfsaintdonat.com
✍ Gaelle Secretary
🖥 www.golfsaintdonat.com

**Les Domaines de Saint
Endréol Golf & Spa Resort**
(1992)
Route de Bagnols-en-Fôret, 83 920
La Motte-en-Provence
☎ 04 94 51 89 89
🖳 04 94 51 89 90
✉ accueil.golf@st-endreol.com
🖥 www.st-endreol.com

**Sainte Victoire**   (1985)
Domaine de Château L'Arc, 13710 Fuveau
☎ 0442 298343
🖳 0442 534268
✉ saintevictoiregolfclub@wanadoo.fr
🖥 www.saintevictoiregolfclub.com

**La Sainte-Baume**   (1988)
Golf Hotel, Domaine de Châteauneuf,
83860 Nans-les-Pins
☎ 04 94 78 60 12
🖳 04 94 78 63 52
✉ saintebaume@opengolfclub.com
✍ Marie-Pierre Picard
🖥 www.opengolfclub.com

**Sainte-Maxime**
Route de Débarquement, 83120 Sainte-Maxime
☎ 04 94 55 02 02
🖳 04 94 55 02 03

**Servanes**   (1989)
Domaine de Servanes, 13890 Mouriès
☎ 04 90 47 59 95
🖳 04 90 47 52 58
✉ servanes@opengolfclub.com
🖥 www.opengolfclub.com

**Taulane**
Domaine du Château de Taulane, RN 85,
83840 La Martre
☎ 04 93 60 31 30
🖳 04 93 60 33 23
✉ resagolf@chateau-taulane.com
🖥 www.chateau-de-taulane.com

**Valcros**   (1964)
Domaine de Valcros, 83250 La Londe-les-Maures
☎ 04 94 66 81 02
🖳 04 94 66 90 48
✉ golfdevalcros@wanadoo.fr

**Valescure**   (1895)
BP 451, 83704 St-Raphaël Cedex
☎ 04 94 82 40 46
🖳 04 94 82 41 42

## Rhone-Alps

**Aix-les-Bains**   (1904)
Avenue du Golf, 73100 Aix-les-Bains
☎ 04 79 61 23 35
🖳 04 79 34 06 01
✉ info@golf-aixlesbains.com
✍ Gerard Bourge
🖥 www.golf-aixlesbains.com

**Albon** (1989)
*Domaine de Senaud, Albon, 26140 St Rambert d'Albon*
☎ 04 75 03 03 90
📠 04 75 03 11 01
✉ golf.albon@wanadoo.fr
🖥 www.golf-albon.com

**Annecy** (1953)
*Echarvines, 74290 Talloires*
☎ (0033)4 50 60 12 89
📠 (0033)4 50 60 08 80
✉ accueil@golf-lacannecy.com
✍ Emmanuelle Kipper (Mgr)
🖥 www.golf-lacannecy.com

**Annonay-Gourdan** (1988)
*Domaine de Gourdan, 07430 Saint Clair*
☎ 04 75 67 03 84
📠 04 75 67 79 50

**Les Arcs**
*B P 18, 73706 Les Arcs Cedex*
☎ 04 79 07 43 95
📠 04 79 07 47 65

**Bossey G&CC** (1985)
*Château de Crevin, 74160 Bossey*
☎ 04 50 43 95 50
📠 04 50 95 32 57
✉ gccb@golfbossey.com
🖥 www.golfbossey.com

**La Bresse**
*Domaine de Mary, 01400 Condessiat*
☎ 04 74 51 42 09
📠 04 74 51 40 09

**Chamonix** (1934)
*35 Route du Golf, 74400 Chamonix*
☎ +33 4 50 53 06 28
📠 +33 4 50 53 38 69
✉ info@golfdechamonix.com
✍ David Richalot (Manager)
🖥 www.golfdechamonix.com

**Le Clou** (1985)
*01330 Villars-les-Dombes*
☎ 04 74 98 19 65
📠 04 74 98 15 15
✉ golfduclou.fr@freesbee.fr
🖥 www.golfduclou.fr

**Divonne** (1931)
*Ave des Thermes, 01220 Divonne-les-Bains*
☎ 04 50 40 34 11
📠 04 50 40 34 25
✉ golf@domaine-de-divonne.com
🖥 www.domaine-de-divonne.com

**Esery** (1990)
*Esery, 74930 Reignier*
☎ 00334 50 36 58 70
📠 00334 50 36 57 62
✉ info@golf-club-esery.com
✍ Emmanuel Ballongue
🖥 www.golf-club-esery.com

**Evian Resort** (1904)
*Route du golf, 74500 Évian-les-bains*
☎ 04 50 75 46 66
📠 04 50 75 65 54
✉ golf@evianresort.com

✍ Christine Lagarde (Exec Mgr)
🖥 www.evianresort.com

**Giez** (1991)
*Lac d'Annecy, 74210 Giez*
☎ 04 50 44 48 41
📠 04 50 32 55 93
✉ as.golfdegiez@wanadoo.fr
🖥 www.golfdegiez.fr

**Le Gouverneur**
*Château du Breuil, 01390 Monthieux*
☎ 04 72 26 42 20
📠 04 72 26 41 61
✉ golfgouverneur@worldonline.fr
🖥 www.golfgouverneur.fr

**Grenoble-Bresson** (1990)
*Route de Montavie, 38320 Eybens*
☎ 04 76 73 65 00
📠 04 76 73 65 51

**Grenoble-Charmeil** (1988)
*38210 St Quentin-sur-Isère*
☎ 04 76 93 67 28
📠 04 76 93 62 04
✉ info@golfhotelgrenoble.com
🖥 www.golfhotelgrenoble.com

**Grenoble-Uriage** (1921)
*Les Alberges, 38410 Vaulnaveys-le-haut*
☎ 04 76 89 03 47
📠 04 76 73 15 80
✉ golfuriage@wanadoo.fr
🖥 www.golfuriage.com

**Golf Club de Lyon** (1921)
*38280 Villette-d'Anthon*
☎ 04 78 31 11 33
📠 04 72 02 48 27
✉ info@golfclubdelyon.com
✍ F Barba
🖥 www.golfclubdelyon.com

**Lyon-Verger** (1977)
*69360 Saint-Symphorien D'Ozon*
☎ 04 78 02 84 20
📠 04 78 02 08 12

**Maison Blanche G&CC** (1991)
*01170 Echenevex*
☎ 04 50 42 44 42
📠 04 50 42 44 43

**Méribel** (1966)
*BP 54, 73550 Méribel*
☎ 04 79 00 52 67
📠 04 79 00 38 85
✉ info@golf-meribel.com
🖥 www.golf-meribel.com

**Mionnay La Dombes** (1986)
*Chemin de Beau-Logis, 01390 Mionnay*
☎ 04 78 91 84 84
📠 04 78 91 02 73

**Mont-d'Arbois** (1964)
*74120 Megève*
☎ 04 50 21 29 79
📠 04 50 93 02 63

**Pierre Carée** (1984)
*74300 Flaine*
☎ 04 50 90 85 44
📠 04 50 90 88 21

**St Etienne** (1989)
*62 Rue St Simon, 42000 St Etienne*
☎ 04 77 32 14 63
📠 04 77 33 61 23

**Salvagny** (1987)
*100 Rue des Granges, 69890 La Tour de Salvagny*
☎ 04 78 48 88 48
📠 04 78 48 00 16
✉ accueil@golf-salvagny.com
🖥 www.lyon-salvagny-golf-club.com

**La Sorelle** (1991)
*Domaine de Gravagnieux, 01320 Villette-sur-Ain*
☎ 04 74 35 47 27
📠 04 74 35 44 51

**Tignes** (1968)
*Val Claret, 73320 Tignes*
☎ 04 79 06 37 42 (Summer)
📠 04 79 00 53 17
✉ golf.tignes@compagniedesalpes.fr
✍ Fred Scuiller (Mgr)
🖥 www.tignes.net

**Valdaine** (1989)
*Domaine de la Valdaine, Montboucher/Jabron, 26740 Montelimar-Montboucher*
☎ 04 75 00 71 33
📠 04 75 01 24 49
🖥 www.domainedelavaldaine.com

**Valence St Didier** (1983)
*26300 St Didier de Charpey*
☎ 04 75 59 67 01
📠 04 75 59 68 19

## Toulouse & Pyrenees

**Albi Lasbordes** (1989)
*Château de Lasbordes, 81000 Albi*
☎ 05 63 54 98 07
📠 05 63 54 98 06
✉ contact@golfalbi.com
🖥 www.golfalbi.com

**Ariège** (1986)
*Unjat, 09240 La Bastide-de-Serou*
☎ 05 61 64 56 78
📠 05 61 64 57 99

**Auch Embats** (1970)
*Route de Montesquiou, 32000 Auch*
☎ 05 62 61 10 11/06 81 18 41 43
📠 05 62 611057
🖥 www.golf-auch-embats.com

**Golf County Club de Bigorre** (1992)
*65200 Pouzac, Bagnères de Bigorre*
☎ (33) (0) 5 62 91 06 20
📠 (33) (0) 5 62 91 38 00
✉ contact@golf-bigorre.fr
🖥 www.golf-bigorre.fr

**Étangs de Fiac**   (1987)
*Brazis, 81500 Fiac*
☎ 05 63 70 64 70
🖳 05 63 75 32 91
📧 golf.fiac-sw@wanadoo.fr
🖥 www.etangsdefiac.com

**Florentin-Gaillac**   (1990)
*Le Bosc, Florentin, 81150 Marssac-sur-Tarn*
☎ 05 63 55 20 50
🖳 05 63 53 26 41

**Golf de tarbes**   (1987)
*1 Rue du Bois, 65310 Laloubère*
☎ 05 62 45 14 50
🖳 05 62 45 11 78
📧 golf.des.tumulus@wanadoo.fr
🖥 www.perso.wanadoo.fr/tumulus

**Guinlet**   (1986)
*32800 Eauze*
☎ 05 62 09 80 84
🖳 05 62 09 84 50
🖥 www.guinlet.fr

**Lannemezan**   (1962)
*250 Rue uu Dr Vererschlag,
65300 Lannemezan*
☎ 0562 98 01 01
🖳 0562 98 52 32
📧 golflannemezan@wanadoo.fr
🖎 Valerie Lasserre (Assistant Mgr)
🖥 www.golflannemezan.com

**Lourdes**   (1988)
*Chemin du Lac, 65100 Lourdes*
☎ 05 62 42 02 06
🖳 05 62 42 02 06
📧 golf.lourdes@wanadoo.fr

**Mazamet-La Barouge**   (1956)
*81660 Pont de l'Arn*
☎ 05 63 61 08 00/05 63 67 06 72
🖳 05 63 61 13 03
📧 golf.labarouge@wanadoo.fr
🖥 www.golf-mazamet.net

**Toulouse**   (1951)
*31320 Vieille-Toulouse*
☎ 05 61 73 45 48
🖳 05 62 19 04 67

**Toulouse-Palmola**   (1974)
*Route d'Albi, 31660 Buzet-sur-Tarn*
☎ 05 61 84 20 50
🖳 05 61 84 48 92
📧 golf.palmola@wanadoo.fr

---

# Germany

## Berlin & East

**Balmer See**   (1995)
*Drewinscher Weg 1, 17429 Benz/Otbalm*
☎ (038379) 28199
🖳 (038379) 28200
📧 info@golfhotel-usedom.de
🖥 www.golfhotel-usedom.de

**Golf- und Land-Club Berlin-
Wannsee e.V.**   (1895)
*Golfweg 22, 14109 Berlin*
☎ +49 (030) 806 7060
🖳 +49 (030) 806 706-10
📧 info@wannsee.de
🖥 www.wannsee.de

**Berliner G&CC Motzener See**
(1991)
*Am Golfplatz 5, 15749 Mittenwalde
OT Motzen*
☎ (033769) 50130
🖳 (033769) 50134
📧 info@golfclubmotzen.de
🖥 www.golfclubmotzen.de

**GC Dresden Elbflorenz**   (1992)
*Ferdinand von Schillstr 4a,
01728 Possendorf*
☎ (035206) 2430
🖳 (035206) 24317
📧 info@golfclub-dresden.de
🖎 Alfred Hagh
🖥 www.golfclub-dresden.de

**Potsdamer GC**   (1990)
*Zachower Strasse, 14669 Ketzin
OT Tremmen*
☎ (033233) 7050
🖳 (033233) 70519
📧 clubsekretariat
    @potsdamergolfclub.de
🖥 www.pgc.de

**Schloss Meisdorf**   (1996)
*Petersberger Trift 33, 06463 Meisdorf*
☎ (034743) 98450
🖳 (034743) 98499

**Golfpark Schloss Wilkendorf**
(1991)
*Am Weiher 1, 15345 Altlandsberg-
Wilkendorf*
☎ (0049) 3341 330960
🖳 (0049) 3341 330961
📧 service@golfpark-schloss-
    wilkendorf.com
🖥 www.golfpark-schloss-
    wilkendorf.com

**Golf-und Country Club
Seddiner See**   (1994)
*Zum Weiher 44, 14552 Michendorf*
☎ (033205) 7320
🖳 (036) 308140
📧 info@gccseddinersee.de
🖎 Mr Horst Schubert (Mgr)
🖥 www.gccseddinersee.de

**Seddiner See**   (1993)
*Zum Weiher 44, 14552 Wildenbruch*
☎ (033205) 7320
🖳 (033205) 73229
📧 info@gccseddiner-see.de
🖥 www.gccseddiner-see.de

**Golfresort Semlin am See**
(1992)
*Ferchesarerstrasse 8b, 14712 Semlin*
☎ (03385) 554410

☎ (03385) 554400
📧 golf@golfresort-semlin.de
🖥 www.golfresort-semlin.de

**Sporting Club Berlin
Schwantzelsee e.V**   (1992)
*Parkallee 3, 15526 Bad Sarrow*
☎ (033631) 63300
🖳 (033631) 63310
📧 info@sporting-club-berlin.de
🖥 www.sporting-club-berlin.com

## Bremen & North West

**Bremer Schweiz e.v.**   (1991)
*Wölpscherstr 4, 28779 Bremen*
☎ (0421) 609 5331
🖳 (0421) 609 5333
📧 info@golfclub-bremerschweiz.de
🖥 www.golfclub-bremerschweiz.de

**Herzogstadt Celle**   (1985)
*Beukenbusch 1, D 29229 Celle*
☎ (05086) 395
🖳 (05086) 8288
📧 golfclub-celle@t-online.de
🖎 Godlind Reif/Michael Olville
⊕ English Speaking
🖥 www.golf-celle.de

**Küsten GC Hohe Klint**   (1978)
*Hohe Klint, 27478 Cuxhaven*
☎ (04723) 2737
🖳 (04723) 5022
🖥 www.golf-cuxhaven.de

**Münster-Wilkinghege**   (1963)
*Steinfurter Str 448, 48159 Münster*
☎ (0251) 214090
🖳 (0251) 214 0940
📧 kontakt@golfclub-wilkinghege.de
🖥 www.golfclub-wilkinghege.de

**Oldenburgischer**   (1964)
*Wemkenstr. 13, 26180 Rastede*
☎ (04402) 7240
🖳 (04402) 70417
📧 info@oldenburgischer-golfclub.de
🖥 www.oldenburgischer-golfclub.de

**Ostfriesland**   (1980)
*Fliederstrasse 5, 26639 Wiesmoor*
☎ (04944) 6440
🖳 (04944) 6441
📧 golf@golfclubostfriesland.de
🖎 Stephan Hueller
🖥 www.golfclub-ostfriesland.de

**Soltau**   (1982)
*Hof Loh, 29614 Soltau*
☎ (05191) 967 63 33
🖳 (05191) 967 63 34
📧 info@golf-soltau.de
🖎 Bernd Ingendahl
🖥 www.golf-soltau.de

**Syke**   (1989)
*Schultenweg 1, 28857 Syke-Okel*
☎ (04242) 8230
🖳 (04242) 8255

---

## Tietlingen (1979)
*29683 Fallingbostel*
- ☎ **(05162) 3889**
- 📠 (05162) 7564
- ✉ info@golfclub-tietlingen.de
- 🖥 www.golfclub-tietlingen.de

## Verden (1988)
*Holtumer Str 24, 27283 Verden*
- ☎ **(04230) 1470**
- 📠 (04230) 1550

## Worpswede (1974)
*Giehlermühlen, 27729 Vollersode*
- ☎ **(04763) 7313**
- 📠 (04763) 6193

## Club Zur Vahr (1905)
*Bgm-Spitta-Allee 34, 28329 Bremen*
- ☎ **Bremen (0421) 204480**
- 📠 (0421) 244 9248
- ✉ info@club-zur-vahr-bremen.de
- 🖥 www.club-zur-vahr-bremen.de

## Central North

### Dillenburg
*Auf dem Altscheid, 35687 Dillenburg*
- ☎ **(02771) 5001**
- 📠 (02771) 5002
- ✉ info@gc-dillenburg.de
- 🖥 www.gc-dillenburg.de

### Golfclub Lauterbach Schloss Sickendorf e.V. (1990)
*Schloss Sickendorf, 36341 Lauterbach*
- ☎ **(06641) 96130**
- 📠 (06641) 961335
- ✉ sickendorf@sommerfeld-golf.de
- 🖥 www.gc-lauterbach.de

### Hofgut Praforst (1992)
*Dr-Detlev-Rudelsdorff-Allee 3, 36088 Hünfeld*
- ☎ **(06652) 9970**
- 📠 (06652) 99755
- ✉ info@praforst.de
- 🖥 www.praforst.de

### Kassel-Wilhelmshöhe (1958)
*Ehlenerstr 21, 34131 Kassel*
- ☎ **(0561) 33509**
- 📠 (0561) 37729
- ✉ mail@golfclub-kassel.de
- 🖥 www.golfclub-kassel.de

### Kurhessischer GC Oberaula (1987)
*Am Golfplatz, 36278 Oberaula*
- ☎ **(06628) 91540**
- 📠 (06628) 915424
- ✉ info@golfclub-oberaula.de
- 🖥 www.golf-oberaula.de

### Licher Golf Club (1992)
*35423 Lich, Golfplatz Kolnhausen*
- ☎ **(06404) 91071**
- 📠 (06404) 91072
- ✉ info@licher-golf-club.de
- 🖥 www.licher-golf-club.de

## Fulda Rhoen (1971)
*Am Golfplatz, 36145 Hofbieber*
- ☎ **(06657) 1334**
- 📠 (06657) 914809
- ✉ info@golfclub-fulda.de
- ⚐ Nick Staples
- 🖥 www.golfclub-fulda.de

### Schloss Braunfels (1970)
*Homburger Hof, 35619 Braunfels*
- ☎ **(06442) 4530**
- 📠 (06442) 6683
- ✉ info@golfclub-braunfels.de
- ⚐ Gregor Sommer
- 🖥 www.golfclub-braunfels.de

### Winnerod (1999)
*Parkstr 22, 35447 Reiskirchen*
- ☎ **(06408) 9513-0**
- 📠 (06408) 9513-13
- ✉ info@golfpark.de
- ⚐ Michael Sonnenstatter (Mgr)
- 🖥 www.golfpark.de

### Zierenberg Gut Escheberg (1995)
*Gut Escheberg, 34289 Zierenberg*
- ☎ **(05606) 2608**
- 📠 (05606) 2609
- 🖥 www.golfclub-escheberg.de

## Central South

### Bad Kissingen (1910)
*Euerdorferstr 11, 97688 Bad Kissingen*
- ☎ **(0971) 3608**
- 📠 (0971) 60140

### Bad Vilbeler Golfclub Lindenhof e.V. (1994)
*61118 Bad Vilbel-Dortelweil*
- ☎ **+49 (0)6101 5245200**
- 📠 +49 (0)6101 5245202
- ✉ info@bvgc.de
- 🖥 www.bvgc.de

### Golfclub Eschenrod e.V. (1996)
*Postfach 1227, Lindenstr. 46, 63679 Schotten*
- ☎ **(06044) 8401**
- 📠 (06044) 951159
- ✉ br.golf@t-online.de
- 🖥 www.eschenrod.de

### Frankfurter Golf Club (1913)
*Golfstrasse 41, 60528 Frankfurt/Main*
- ☎ **(069) 666 2318 0**
- 📠 (069) 666 2318 20
- ✉ info@fgc.de
- ⚐ Mrs Sanja Bradley
- 🖥 www.fgc.de

### Hanau-Wilhelmsbad (1958)
*Franz-Ludwig-von-Cancrin-Weg 1a, 63454 Hanau*
- ☎ **(06181) 1 80 19 0**
- 📠 (06181) 1 80 19 10

## Hof Trages
*Hofgut Trages, 63579 Freigericht*
- ☎ **(06055) 91380**
- 📠 (06055) 913838
- 🖥 www.hoftrages.de

### Idstein (2001)
*Am Nassen Berg, 65510 Idstein*
- ☎ **(06126) 9322-13**
- 📠 (06126) 9322-33
- 🖥 www.golfpark-idstein.de

### Idstein-Wörsdorf (1989)
*Gut Henriettenthal, 65510 Idstein*
- ☎ **(06126) 9322-0**
- 📠 (06126) 9322-22
- 🖥 www.golfpark-idstein.de

### Kitzingen (1980)
*Zufahrt über Steigweg, 97318 Kitzingen*
- ☎ **(09321) 4956**
- 📠 (09321) 21936
- ✉ golfkitzingen@aol.com
- 🖥 www.golfclub-kitzingen.de

### Kronberg G&LC (1954)
*Schloss Friedrichshof, Hainstr 25, 61476 Kronberg/Taunus*
- ☎ **(06173) 1426**
- 📠 (06173) 5953
- 🖥 www.gc-kronberg.de

### Main-Spessart (1990)
*Postfach 1204, 97821 Marktheidenfeld-Eichenfürst*
- ☎ **(09391) 8435**
- 📠 (09391) 8816
- ✉ info@main-spessart-golf.de
- 🖥 www.main-spessart-golf.de

### Main-Taunus (1979)
*Lange Seegewann 2, 65205 Wiesbaden*
- ☎ **(06122) 588680 (Sec)**
- 📠 (06122) 936099
- ✉ clubinfo@golfclub-maintaunus.de
- ⚐ Markus Erdmann
- 🖥 www.golfclub-maintaunus.de

### Mannheim-Viernheim (1930)
*Alte Mannheimer Str 3, 68519 Viernheim*
- ☎ **(06204) 6070-0**
- 📠 (06204) 607044
- ✉ info@gcmv.de
- 🖥 www.gcmv.de

### Maria Bildhausen (1992)
*Rindhof 1, 97702 Münnerstadt*
- ☎ **(09766) 1601**
- 📠 (09766) 1602
- ✉ info@maria-bildhausen.de
- 🖥 www.maria-bildhausen.de

### Neuhof
*Hofgut Neuhof, 63303 Dreieich*
- ☎ **(06102) 327927/327010**
- 📠 (06102) 327012
- ✉ info@golfclubneuhof.de
- 🖥 www.golfclubneuhof.de

### Rhein Main (1977)
*Steubenstrasse 9, 65189 Wiesbaden*
- ☎ **(0611) 373014**

## Rheinblick
*Weisser Weg, 65201 Wiesbaden-Frauenstein*
☎ **(0611) 420675**
🖳 (0611) 941 0434

## Rheintal    (1971)
*An der Bundesstrr 291, 68723 Oftersheim*
☎ **(06202) 56390**

## Royal Homburger    (1899)
*Saalburgchaussee 2, 61350 Bad Homburg*
☎ **(06172) 306808**
🖳 (06172) 32648

## St. Leon-Rot
## Betriebsgesellschaft mbH & Co.KG    (1996)
*Opelstrasse 30, 68789 St. Leon-Rot*
☎ **+49 62 27 86 08- 0**
🖳 +49 62 27 86 08-88
📧 info@gc-slr.de
🖳 www.gc-slr.de

## Spessart    (1972)
*Golfplatz Alsberg, 63628 Bad Soden-Salmünster*
☎ **(06056) 91580**
🖳 (06056) 915820
🖳 www.gc-spessart.com

## Taunus Weilrod    (1979)
*Merzhäuser Strasse, 61276 Weilrod-Altweilnau*
☎ **(06083) 95050**
🖳 (06083) 950515
📧 kontakt@gc-weilrod.de
🖳 www.gc-weilrod.de

## Wiesbadener Golf Club e.v.    (1893)
*Chausseehaus 17, 65199 Wiesbaden*
☎ **(0611) 460238**
🖳 (0611) 463251
📧 info@wiesbadener-golfclub.de
🖳 www.wiesbadener-golfclub.de

## Golf- und Landclub Wiesloch    (1983)
*Hohenhardter Hof, 69168 Wiesloch-Baiertal*
☎ **(06222) 78811-0**
🖳 (06222) 78811-11
📧 info@golfclub-wiesloch.de
🖳 www.golfclub-wiesloch.de

# Hamburg & North

## Altenhof    (1971)
*Eckernförde, 24340 Altenhof*
☎ **(04351) 41227**
🖳 (04351) 751304

## An der Pinnau e.V.    (1982)
*Pinneberger strasse 81a, 25451 Quickborn-Renzel*
☎ **(04106) 81800**
🖳 (04106) 82003
📧 info@pinnau.de
✍ Christoph Lampe
🖳 www.pinnau.de

## Behinderten Golf Club Deutschland e.V.    (1994)
*Hauptstrausse 3 c, 37434 Bodensee*
☎ **+49 (0) 55079799108**
🖳 +49 (0) 5507 979144
📧 rollydrive@aol.com
🖳 www.bgc-golf.de

## Brodauer Mühle    (1986)
*Baumallee 14, 23730 Gut Beusloe*
☎ **(04561) 8140**
🖳 (04561) 407397
📧 gc-brodauermuehle@t-online.de
🖳 www.gc-brodauermuehle.de

## Buchholz-Nordheide    (1982)
*An der Rehm 25, 21244 Bucholz*
☎ **(04181) 36200**
🖳 (04181) 97294
📧 gc-buchholz@t-online.de
🖳 www.golfclub-buchholz.de

## Buxtehude    (1982)
*Zum Lehmfeld 1, 21614 Buxtehude*
☎ **(04161) 81333**
🖳 (04161) 87268
📧 post@golfclubbuxtehude.de
🖳 www.golfclubbuxtehude.de

## Deinster Mühle    (1994)
*Im Mühlenfeld 30, 21717 Deinste*
☎ **(04149) 925112**
🖳 (04149) 925111
📧 golfpark@allesistgdm.de
🖳 www.allesistgdm.de

## Föhr    (1925)
*25938 Nieblum*
☎ **(04681) 580455**
🖳 (04681) 580456
📧 info@golfclubfoehr.de
🖳 www.golfclubfoehr.de

## Golf Club Hoisdorf    (1977)
*Hof Bornbek/Hoisdorf, 22952 Lütjensee*
☎ **(04107) 7831**
🖳 (04107) 9934
📧 info@gc-hoisdorf.com
✍ Petra Bröcker (Secretary)
🖳 www.gc-hoisdorf.com

## Gut Apeldör    (1996)
*Apeldör 2, 25779 Hennstedt*
☎ **(04836) 9960-0**
🖳 (04836) 9960-33
📧 info@apeldoer.de
✍ Karsten Voss
🖳 www.apeldoer.de

## Gut Grambek    (1981)
*Schlosstr 21, 23883 Grambek*
☎ **(04542) 841474**
🖳 (04542) 841476
📧 info@gcgrambek.de
🖳 www.gcgrambek.de

## Gut Kaden    (1984)
*Kadenerstrasse 9, 25486 Alveslohe*
☎ **(04193) 9929-0**
🖳 (04193) 992919

## Gut Uhlenhorst    (1989)
*24229 Daenischenhagen, Mühlenstrasse 37*
☎ **(04349) 91700**
🖳 (04349) 919400
📧 golf@gut-uhlenhorst.de
🖳 www.gut-uhlenhorst.de

## Gut Waldhof    (1969)
*Am Waldhof, 24629 Kisdorferwohld*
☎ **(04194) 99740**
🖳 (04194) 997425
🖳 www.gut-waldhof.de

## Gut Waldshagen    (1996)
*24306 Gut Waldshagen*
☎ **(04522) 766766**
🖳 (04522) 766767
📧 info@gut-golf.de
🖳 www.gut-golf.de

## Hamburger Golf-Club Falkenstein    (1906)
*In de Bargen 59, 22587 Hamburg*
☎ **(040) 812177**
🖳 (040) 817315
📧 info@golfclub-falkenstein.de
✍ Berthold Apel
🖳 www.golfclub-falkenstein.de

## Hamburg Ahrensburg    (1964)
*Am Haidschlag 39-45, 22926 Ahrensburg*
☎ **(04102) 51309**
🖳 (04102) 81410

## Hamburg Hittfeld    (1957)
*Am Golfplatz 24, 21218 Seevetal*
☎ **(04105) 2331**
🖳 (04105) 52571

## Hamburg Holm    (1993)
*Haverkamp 1, 25488 Holm*
☎ **(04103) 91330**
🖳 (04103) 913313
📧 info@hchh.de
🖳 www.gchh.de

## Hamburg Walddörfer    (1960)
*Schevenbarg, 22949 Ammersbek*
☎ **(040) 605 1337**
🖳 (040) 605 4879
📧 info@gchw.de
🖳 www.gchw.de

## Golfclub Hohen Wieschendorf e.V.    (1992)
*Am Golfplatz 1, 23968 Hohen Wieschendorf*
☎ **(0049) 384 28660**
🖳 (0049) 384 286666
📧 info@howido-ostsee.de
🖳 www.howido-golfclub.de

## Jersbek    (1986)
*GolfClub Jersbek e.V., Oberteicher Weg, 22941 Jersbek*
☎ **(04532) 20950**
🖳 (04532) 24779
📧 mail@golfclub-jersbek.de
🖳 www.golfclub-jersbek.de

## Kieler GC Havighorst   (1988)
*Havighorster Weg 20, 24211 Havighorst*
- ☎ **(04302) 965980**
- 📞 (04302) 965981
- 📧 golfclub.havighorst@t-online.de

## Lübeck-Travemünder Golf Klub e.V   (1921)
*Kowitzberg 41, 23570 Lübeck-Travemünde*
- ☎ **(04502) 74018**
- 📞 (04502) 72184
- 📧 info@ltgk.de
- 🖥 www.ltgk.de

## Mittelholsteinischer Aukrug (1969)
*Zum Glasberg 9, 24613 Aukrug-Bargfeld*
- ☎ **(04873) 595**
- 📞 (04873) 1698

## Peiner Hof
*Peiner Hag, 25497 Prisdorf*
- ☎ **(04101) 73790**
- 📞 (04101) 76640
- 🖥 www.peinerhof.de

## Am Sachsenwald   (1985)
*Am Riesenbett, 21521 Dassendorf*
- ☎ **(04104) 6120**
- 📞 (04104) 6551
- 📧 gc-sachsenwald@t-online.de
- 🖥 www.gc-sachsenwald.de

## Golf Club Schloss Breitenburg e.v
*25524 Breitenburg*
- ☎ **(04828) 8188**
- 📞 (04828) 8100
- 📧 info@gcsb.de
- 🚹 Elke Gräfin zu Rantzau
- 🖥 www.golfclubschlossbreitenburg.de

## Schloss Lüdersburg   (1985)
*Lüdersburger Strasse 21, 21379 Lüdersburg*
- ☎ **(04139) 6970-0**
- 📞 (04139) 6970 70
- 📧 info@luedersburg.de
- 🖥 www.luedersburg.de

## St Dionys   (1972)
*Widukindweg, 21357 St Dionys*
- ☎ **(04133) 213311**
- 📞 (04133) 213313
- 📧 info@golfclub-st-dionys.de
- 🖥 www.golfclub-st-dionys.de

## GC Sylt e.V.   (1982)
*Norderrung 5, 25996 Wenningstedt*
- ☎ **(04651) 99598-0**
- 📞 (04651) 99598-19
- 📧 info@gcsylt.de
- 🖥 www.golfclubsylt.de

## Golfanlage Seeschlösschen Timmendorfer Strand   (1973)
*Am Golfplatz 3, 23669 Timmendorfer Strand*
- ☎ **(04503) 704400**
- 📞 (04503) 704400-14
- 📧 info@gc-timmendorf.de
- 🚹 Mrs Birgit Krause (Club Mgr)
- 🖥 www.gc-timmendorf.de

## G&CC Treudelberg   (1990)
*Lemsahler Landstr 45, 22397 Hamburg*
- ☎ **(040) 608 228877**
- 📞 (040) 608 228879
- 📧 golf@treudelberg.com
- 🖥 www.treudelberg.com

## Wentorf-Reinbeker Golf-Club e.V.   (1901)
*Golfstrasse 2, 21465 Wentorf*
- ☎ **(040) 72 97 80 68**
- 📞 (040) 72 97 80 67
- 📧 sekretariat@wrgc.de
- 🖥 www.wrgc.de

# Hanover & Weserbergland

## Bad Salzuflen G&LC   (1956)
*Schwaghof 4, 32108 Bad Salzuflen*
- ☎ **(05222) 10773**
- 📞 (05222) 13954

## British Army Golf Club (Sennelager)   (1963)
*Bad Lippspringe, BFPO 16*
- ☎ **(05252) 53794**
- 📞 (05252) 53811
- 📧 manager@sennelagergolfclub.de
- 🖥 www.sennelagergolfclub.de

## Burgdorf   (1969)
*Waldstr 27, 31303 Burgdorf-Ehlershausen*
- ☎ **(05085) 7628**
- 📞 (05085) 6617
- 📧 info@burgdorfergolfclub.de
- 🖥 www.burgdorfergolfclub.de

## Gifhorn   (1982)
*Wilscher Weg 69, 38518 Gifhorn*
- ☎ **(05371) 16737**
- 📞 (05371) 51092

## Gütersloh Garrison   (1963)
*Princess Royal Barracks, BFPO 47*
- ☎ **(05241) 236938**
- 📞 (01241) 236838
- 📧 timothyholt14@hotmail.com

## Hamelner Golfclub e.V.   (1985)
*Schwöbber 8, 31855 Aerzen*
- ☎ **(05154) 987 0**
- 📞 (05154) 987 111
- 📧 info@hamelner-golfclub.de
- 🖥 www.hamelner-golfclub.de

## Hannover   (1923)
*Am Blauen See 120, 30823 Garbsen*
- ☎ **(05137) 73068**
- 📞 (05137) 75851
- 📧 info@golfclub-hannover.de
- 🖥 www.golfclub-hannover.de

## Hardenberg   (1969)
*Gut Levershausen, 37154 Northeim*
- ☎ **(05551) 908380**
- 📞 (05551) 9083820
- 📧 info@gchardenberg.de
- 🚹 Norbert Hoffmann (Manager)
- 🖥 www.gchardenberg.de

## Isernhagen   (1983)
*Auf Gut Lohne 22, 30916 Isernhagen*
- ☎ **(05139) 893185**
- 📞 (05139) 27033
- 🖥 www.golfclub-isernhagen.de

## GC Langenhagen e.v.   (1989)
*Hainhaus 22, D-30855 Langenhagen*
- ☎ **(0511) 736832**
- 📞 (0511) 726 1990
- 📧 golfclub-langenhagen@t-online.de
- 🖥 www.golfclub-langenhagen.de

## Lippischer Golfclub e.V.   (1980)
*Huxoll 14, 32825 Blomberg-Cappel*
- ☎ **(05236) 459**
- 📞 (05236) 8102
- 📧 sekretariat@lippischergolfclub.de
- 🖥 www.lippischergolfclub.de

## Marienfeld   (1986)
*Remse 27, 33428 Marienfeld*
- ☎ **(05247) 8880**
- 📞 (05247) 80386
- 📧 info@gc-marienfeld.de
- 🚹 John Pollitt (Mgr)
- 🖥 www.gc-marienfeld.de

## Paderborner Land   (1983)
*Wilseder Weg 25, 33102 Paderborn*
- ☎ **(05251) 4377**

## Ravensberger Land
*Sudstrasse 96, 32130 Enger-Pödinghausen*
- ☎ **(09224) 79751**
- 📞 (09224) 699446
- 📧 golfclub-ravensberger-land@teleos-web.de
- 🖥 www.golfclub-ravensberger-land.de

## Senne-Golf gut Welschof (1992)
*Augustdorferstr 72, 33758 Schloss Holte-Stukenbrock*
- ☎ **(05207) 920936**
- 📞 (05207) 88788
- 📧 info@sennegolfclub.de
- 🖥 www.sennegolfclub.de

## Sieben-Berge Rheden   (1965)
*Schloss Str 1a, 31039 Rheden*
- ☎ **(05182) 52336**
- 📞 (05182) 923350
- 📧 info@gc7berge.de
- 🖥 www.gc7berge.de

## Weserbergland   (1982)
*Weissenfelder Mühle, 37647 Polle*
- ☎ **(05535) 8842**
- 📞 (05535) 1225

## Westfälischer Gütersloh
*Gütersloher Str 127, 33397 Rietberg*
- ☎ **(05244) 2340/10528**
- 📞 (05244) 1388
- 📧 golf-club@golf-gt.de
- 🖥 www.golf-gt.de

## Widukind-Land   (1985)
*Auf dem Stickdorn 63, 32584 Löhne*
- ☎ **(05228) 7050**
- 📞 (05228) 1039

## Munich & South Bavaria

### Allgäuer G&LC    (1984)
Hofgut Boschach, 87724 Ottobeuren
- ☎ (08332) 9251-0
- 📠 (08332) 5161
- ✉ info@aglc.de
- 🖥 www.aglc.de

### Altötting-Burghausen    (1986)
Piesing 4, 84533 Haiming
- ☎ (08678) 986903
- 📠 (08678) 986905
- ✉ office@gc-altoetting-burghausen.de
- ✍ Johann Brehm (President)
- 🖥 www.gc-altoetting-burghausen.de

### Augsburg    (1959)
Engelshofer Str 2, 86399 Bobingen-Burgwalden
- ☎ (08234) 5621
- 📠 (08234) 7855
- 🖥 www.golfclub-augsburg.de

### Bad Tölz    (1973)
83646 Wackersberg
- ☎ (08041) 9994
- 📠 (08041) 2116

### Beuerberg    (1982)
Gut Sterz, 82547 Beuerberg
- ☎ (08179) 671 or 782
- 📠 (08179) 5234
- ✉ info@gc-beuerberg.de
- 🖥 www.gc-beuerberg.de

### Chieming    (1982)
Kötzing 1, D-83339 Chieming
- ☎ (08669) 87330
- 📠 (08669) 873333
- ✉ info@golfchieming.de
- ✍ Inger Schmid
- 🖥 www.golfchieming.de

### Donauwörth    (1995)
Lederstatt 1, 86609 Donauwörth
- ☎ (0906) 4044
- 📠 (0906) 999 8164
- ✉ info@gc-donauwoerth.de
- ✍ Claudia Slimpfie-Taslican
- 🖥 www.gc-donauwoerth.de

### Ebersberg    (1988)
Postfach 1351, 85554 Ebersberg
- ☎ (08094) 8106
- 📠 (08094) 8386
- ✉ info@gc-ebersberg.de
- ✍ Stefan Schreyer (Mgr)
- 🖥 www.gc-ebersberg.de

### Erding-Grünbach    (1973)
Am Kellerberg, 85461 Grünbach
- ☎ (08122) 49650
- 📠 (08122) 49684

### Eschenried    (1983)
Kurfürstenweg 10, 85232 Eschenried
- ☎ (08131) 56740
- 📠 (08131) 567418
- ✉ info@golf-eschenried.de
- 🖥 www.gc-eschenried.de

### Feldafing    (1926)
Tutzinger Str 15, 82340 Feldafing
- ☎ (08157) 9334-0
- 📠 (08157) 9334-99
- ✉ info@golfclub-Feldafing.de
- 🖥 www.golfclub-Feldafing.de

### Garmisch-Partenkirchen    (1928)
Gut Buchwies, 82496 Oberau
- ☎ (08824) 8344
- 📠 (08824) 944198
- ✉ golfclubGAP@onlinehome.de
- 🖥 www.golfclub-garmisch-partenkirchen.de

### Golfclub Wörthsee e.V.    (1982)
Gut Schluifeld, 82237 Wörthsee
- ☎ (08153) 93477-0
- 📠 (08153) 93477-40
- ✉ info@golfclub-woerthsee.de
- ✍ Andrè Mosig (Manager)
- 🖥 www.golfclub-woerthsee.de

### Gut Ludwigsberg    (1989)
Augsburgerstr 51, 86842 Turkheim
- ☎ (08245) 3322
- 📠 (08245) 3789

### Gut Rieden
Gut Rieden, 82319 Starnberg
- ☎ (08151) 90770
- 📠 (08151) 907711

### Hohenpähl    (1988)
82396 Pähl
- ☎ (08808) 9202-0
- 📠 (08808) 9202-22
- ✉ info@gchp.de
- ✍ Claus Ammer
- 🖥 www.gchp.de

### Holledau
Weihern 3, 84104 Rudelzhausen
- ☎ (08756) 96010
- 📠 (08756) 815

### Höslwang im Chiemgau    (1975)
Kronberg 3, 83129 Höslwang
- ☎ (08075) 714
- 📠 (08075) 8134
- ✉ info@golfclub-hoeslwang.de
- 🖥 www.golfclub-hoeslwang.de

### Iffeldorf    (1989)
Gut Rettenberg, 82393 Iffeldorf
- ☎ 0049 (8856) 92550
- 📠 0049 (8856) 925559
- ✉ sekretariat@golf-iffeldorf.de
- ✍ Uwe Hinz
- 🖥 www.golf-iffeldorf.de

### Landshut    (1989)
Oberlippach 2, 84095 Furth-Landshut
- ☎ (08704) 8378
- 📠 (08704) 8379
- ✉ gc.landshut@t-online.de
- 🖥 www.golf-landshut.de

### Mangfalltal G&LC
Oed 1, 83620 Feldkirchen-Westerham
- ☎ (08063) 6300
- 📠 (08063) 6958
- 🖥 www.glcm.de

### Margarethenhof    (1982)
Gut Steinberg, 83666 Waakirchen/Marienstein
- ☎ (08022) 7506-0
- 📠 (08022) 74818
- ✉ info@margarethenhof.com
- 🖥 www.margarethenhof.com

### Memmingen Gut Westerhart    (1994)
Westerhart 1b, 87740 Buxheim
- ☎ (08331) 71016
- 📠 (08331) 71018
- ✉ gc-memmingen@t-online.de
- 🖥 www.golfclub-memmingen.de

### Golfclub München Eichenried    (1989)
Münchner Strasse 57, 85452 Eichenried
- ☎ (08123) 93080
- 📠 (08123) 930893
- ✉ info@gc-eichenried.de
- 🖥 www.gc-eichenried.de

### München West-Odelzhausen    (1988)
Gut Todtenried, 85235 Odelzhausen
- ☎ (08134) 1618
- 📠 (08134) 7623

### München-Riedhof e.V.    (1991)
82544 Egling-Riedhof, Riedhof 16
- ☎ (08171) 21950
- 📠 (08171) 219511
- ✉ info@riedhof.de
- 🖥 www.riedhof.de

### Münchener    (1910)
Tölzerstrasse 95, 82064 Strasslach
- ☎ (08170) 450
- 📠 (08170) 611

### Olching    (1980)
Feursstrasse 89, 82140 Olching
- ☎ (08142) 48290
- 📠 (08142) 482914
- ✉ sportbuero@golfclub-olching.de
- 🖥 www.golfclub-olching.de

### Pfaffing Wasserburger
Golfclub Pfaffing München-Ost e.V, wsw Golf AG, Köckmühle 132, 83539 Pfaffing
- ☎ (08076) 1718
- 📠 (08076) 8594
- ✉ club@gcpwl.de
- 🖥 www.gc-pfaffing-wasserburger-land.de

### Reit im Winkl-Kössen    (1986)
Postfach 1101, 83237 Reit im Winkl
- ☎ (08640) 798250
- 📠 (08640) 798252

### Rottaler G&CC    (1972)
Am Fischgartl 2, 84332 Hebertsfelden
- ☎ (08561) 5969
- 📠 (08561) 2646
- ✉ info@rottaler-gc.de
- 🖥 www.rottaler-gc.de

**Rottbach** (1997)
*Weiherhaus 5, 82216 Rottbach*
☎ **(08135) 93290**
📠 (08135) 932911
📧 info@rottbach.de
🖥 www.golfanlage-rottbach.de

**Schloss Maxlrain**
*Freiung 14, 83104 Maxlrain-Tuntenhausen*
☎ **(08061) 1403**
📠 (08061) 30146
📧 info@golfclub-maxlrain.de
🖥 www.golfclub-maxlrain.de

**Sonnenalp Oberallgäu** (1976)
*Hotel Sonnenalp, 87527 Ofterschwang*
☎ **(08321) 272181/**
  **(08326) 3859410**
📠 (08326) 3859412
📧 info@golfresort-sonnenalp.de
🖥 www.golfresort-sonnenalp.de

**Starnberg** (1986)
*Uneringerstr, 82319 Starnberg*
☎ **(08151) 12157**
📠 (08151) 29115
📧 club@gcstarnberg.de
🖥 www.gcstarnberg.de

**Tegernseer GC Bad Wiessee**
(1958)
*Rohbognerhof, 83707 Bad Wiessee*
☎ **(08022) 271130**
📠 (08022) 2711333
📧 info@tegernseer-golf-club.de
👤 Eva Meisinger
🖥 www.tegernseer-golf-club.de

**Tutzing** (1983)
*82327 Tutzing-Deixlfurt*
☎ **(08158) 3600**
📠 (08158) 7234

**Waldegg-Wiggensbach** (1988)
*Hof Waldegg, 87487 Wiggensbach*
☎ **(08370) 93073**
📠 (08370) 93074
📧 info@golf-wiggensbach.com
🖥 www.golf-wiggensbach.com

**Wittelsbacher GC
Rohrenfeld-Neuburg** (1988)
*Rohrenfeld, 86633 Neuburg/Donau*
☎ **(08431) 90859-0**
📠 (08431) 90859-99
📧 info@wbgc.de
👤 Frank Thonig (Gen Mgr)
🖥 www.wbgc.de

## Nuremberg & North Bavaria

**Abenberg** (1988)
*Am Golfplatz 19, 91183 Abenberg*
☎ **(09178) 98960**
📠 (09178) 989696

**Bad Windsheim** (1992)
*Otmar-Schaller-Alleen, 91438
Bad Windsheim*
☎ **(09841) 5027**

📠 (09841) 3448
📧 gc.badwindsheim@t-online.de
🖥 www.golf-bw.de

**Bamberg** (1973)
*Golfclub Bamberg e.V., Gut Leimershof 5,
96149 Breitengüssbach*
☎ **(09547) 8709939**
📠 (09547) 8709940
📧 gc-leimershof@t-online.de
🖥 www.golfclubbamberg.de

**Donau GC Passau-Rassbach**
(1986)
*Rassbach 8, 94136 Thyrnau-Passau*
☎ **(08501) 91313**
📠 (08501) 91314
📧 info@golf-passau.de
👤 Anetseder Leonhard
🖥 www.golf-passau.de

**Fränkische Schweiz** (1974)
*Kanndorf 8, 91316 Ebermannstadt*
☎ **(09194) 4827**
📠 (09194) 5410
📧 gc.fraenkischeschweix@t-online.de
👤 Astrid Quarte
🖥 www.gc-fs.de

**Golf Club Fürth e.V.** (1951)
*Am Golfplatz 10, 90768 Fürth*
☎ **(0911) 757522**
📠 (0911) 973 2989
📧 info@golfclub-fuerth.de
🖥 www.golfclub-fuerth.de

**Gäuboden** (1992)
*Gut Fruhstorf, 94330 Aiterhofen*
☎ **(09421) 72804**
📠 (09421) 72804

**Golf Resort Bad Griesbach**
(1989)
*Holzhäuser 8, 94086 Bad Griesbach*
☎ **(08532) 790-0**
📠 (08532) 790-45
📧 golfresort@hartl.de
🖥 www.hartl.de

**Hof** (1985)
*Postfach 1324, 95012 Hof*
☎ **(09281) 470155**
📠 (09821) 470157

**Lauterhofen** (1987)
*Ruppertslohe 18, 92283 Lauterhofen*
☎ **(09186) 1574**
📠 (09186) 1527

**Lichtenau-Weickershof**
(1980)
*Weickershof 1, 91586 Lichtenau*
☎ **(09827) 92040**
📠 (09827) 9204-44

**Oberfranken Thurnau**
(1965)
*Postfach 1349, 95304 Kulmbach*
☎ **(09228) 319**
📠 (09228) 7219

**Oberpfälzer Wald G&LC**
(1977)
*Ödengrub, 92431 Kemnath bei Fuhrn*
☎ **(09439) 466**
📠 (09439) 1247

**Oberzwieselau** (1990)
*94227 Lindberg*
☎ **(01049) 9922/2367**
📠 (01049) 9922/2924
🖥 www.golfpark-oberzwieselau.de

**Golf-und Land-club
Regensburg e.V.** (1966)
*93093 Jagdschloss Thiergarten*
☎ **(09403) 505**
📠 (09403) 4391
📧 sekretariat@golfclub-regensburg.de
👤 Christian Früh
🖥 www.golfclub-regensburg.de

**Am Reichswald** (1960)
*Schiestlstr 100, 90427 Nürnberg*
☎ **(0911) 305730**
📠 (0911) 301200
📧 info@golfclub-nuernberg.de
👤 Kornelia Knoblich/Petra Ketzmer
🖥 www.golfclub-nurnburg.de

**Sagmühle** (1984)
*Golfplatz Sagmühle 1, 94086
Bad Griesbach*
☎ **(08532) 2038**
📠 (08532) 3165

**Schloss Fahrenbach** (1993)
*95709 Tröstau*
☎ **(09232) 882-256**
📠 (09232) 882-345
🖥 www.golfhotel-fahrenbach.de

**Schloss Reichmannsdorf**
(1991)
*Schlosshof 4, 96132 Schlüsselfeld*
☎ **(09546) 9215-10**
📠 (09546) 9215-20
📧 info@golfanlage-reichmannsdorf
  .de
👤 Franz von Schrottenberg
🖥 www.golfanlage-reichmannsdorf
  .de

**Schlossberg** (1985)
*Grünbach 8, 94419 Reisbach*
☎ **(08734) 7035**
📠 (08734) 7795

**Schwanhof** (1994)
*Klaus Conrad Allee 1, 92706 Luhe-
Wildenau*
☎ **(09607) 92020**
📠 (09607) 920248

**Die Wutzschleife** (1997)
*Hillstett 40, 92444 Rötz*
☎ **(09976) 184460**
📠 (09976) 18180
📧 info@golfanlage-wutzschleife
  .de
🖥 www.golfanlage-wutzschleife
  .de

## Rhineland North

### Golf und Landclub Ahaus
(1987)
*Schmäinghook 36, 48683 Ahaus-Alstätte*
- ☎ (02567) 405
- 🖷 (02567) 3524
- ✉ info@glc-ahaus.de
- 🖳 www.glc-ahaus.de

### Alten Fliess (1995)
*Am Alten Fliess 66, 50129 Bergheim*
- ☎ (02238) 94410
- 🖷 (02238) 944119

### Artland (1988)
*Westerholte 23, 49577 Ankum*
- ☎ (05466) 301
- 🖷 (05466) 91081
- ✉ info@artlandgolf.de
- 🖳 www.artlandgolf.de

### Bergisch-Land (1928)
*Siebeneickerst 386, 42111 Wuppertal*
- ☎ (02053) 7177
- 🖷 (02053) 7303
- ✉ info@golfclub-bergischland.de
- ♟ Philipp Pfannkuche
- 🖳 www.golfclub-bergischland.de

### Bochum (1982)
*Im Mailand 127, 44797 Bochum*
- ☎ (0234) 799832
- 🖷 (0234) 795775

### Dortmund (1956)
*Reichmarkstr 12, 44265 Dortmund*
- ☎ (0231) 774133/774609
- 🖷 (0231) 774403

### Düsseldorfer GC (1961)
*Rommeljansweg 12, D-40882 Ratingen*
- ☎ 0049 (0) 2102 81092
- 🖷 0049 (0) 2102 81782
- ✉ info@duesseldorfer-golf-club.de
- ♟ Henrike Kleyoldt
- 🖳 www.duesseldorfer-golf-club.de

### Elfrather Mühle (1991)
*An der Elfrather Mühle 145, 47802 Krefeld*
- ☎ (02151) 4969-0
- 🖷 (02151) 477459
- ✉ info@gcem.de
- 🖳 www.gcem.de

### Erftaue (1991)
*Zur Mühlenerft 1, 41517 Grevenbroich*
- ☎ (02181) 280637
- 🖷 (02181) 280639
- ✉ gc.erftaue@t-online.de
- 🖳 www.golf-erftaue.de

### Essener Golfclub Haus Oefte
(1959)
*Laupendahler Landstr, 45219 Essen-Kettwig*
- ☎ (02054) 83911
- 🖷 (02054) 83850
- ✉ info@golfclub-oefte.de
- ♟ Heidrün Vodnik (Sec)
- 🖳 www.golfclub-oefte.de

### Euregio Bad Bentheim (1987)
*Postbox 1205, Am Hauptelick 8, 48443 Bad Bentheim*
- ☎ (05922) 7776-0
- 🖷 (05922) 7776-18
- 🖳 www.golfclub-euregio.de

### Grevenmühle Ratingen (1988)
*Grevenmühle, 40882 Ratingen-Homberg*
- ☎ (02102) 9595-0
- 🖷 (02102) 959515

### Haus Bey (1992)
*An Haus Bey 16, 41334 Nettetal*
- ☎ (02153) 9197-0
- 🖷 (02153) 919750
- ✉ golf@hausbey.de
- ♟ Elmar Claus
- 🖳 www.hausbey.de

### Haus Kambach (1989)
*Kambachstrasse 9-13, 52249 Eschweiler-Kinzweiler*
- ☎ (02403) 50890
- 🖷 (02403) 21270
- ✉ info@golf-kambach.de
- 🖳 www.golf-kambach.de

### Hubbelrath (1961)
*Bergische Landstr 700, 40629 Düsseldorf*
- ☎ (02104) 72178
- 🖷 (02104) 75685
- ✉ info@gc-hubbelrath.de
- ♟ Dr Gerd W Thörner
- 🖳 www.gc-hubbelrath.de

### Hummelbachaue Neuss (1987)
*Norfer Kirchstrasse, 41469 Neuss*
- ☎ (02137) 91910
- 🖷 (02137) 4016

### Issum-Niederrhein (1973)
*Pauenweg 68, 47661 Issum 1*
- ☎ (02835) 92310
- 🖷 (02835) 9231-20
- 🖳 www.gc-issum.de

### Golf- and Land-Club Köln e.V.
(1906)
*Golfplatz 2, 51429 Bergisch Gladbach*
- ☎ 0049 (0) 2204-9276-0
- 🖷 0049 (0) 2204-9276-15
- ✉ info@glckoeln.de
- ♟ Achim Lehmstardt (Gen Mgr)
- 🖳 www.glckoeln.de

### Kosaido International
(1989)
*Am Schmidtberg 11, 40629 Düsseldorf*
- ☎ (02104) 77060
- 🖷 (02104) 770611
- ✉ info@kosaido.de
- 🖳 www.kosaido.de

### Krefeld (1930)
*Eltweg 2, 47809 Krefeld*
- ☎ (02151) 156030
- 🖷 (02151) 15603 222
- ✉ kgc@krefelder-gc.de
- ♟ Ula Weinforth
- 🖳 www.krefelder-gc.de

### Mühlenhof G&CC (1990)
*Greilack 29, 47546 Kalkar*
- ☎ 0049 (2824) 924092
- 🖷 0049 (2824) 924093
- ✉ awilmsen@muehlenhof.net
- ♟ Annette Wilmsen
- 🖳 www.muehlenhof.net

### Nordkirchen (1974)
*Am Golfplatz 6, 59394 Nordkirchen*
- ☎ (02596) 9191
- 🖷 (02596) 9195
- 🖳 www.glc-nordkirchen.de

### Op de Niep (1995)
*Bergschenweg 71, 47506 Neukirchen-Vluyn*
- ☎ (02845) 28051
- 🖷 (02845) 28052

### Osnabrück (1955)
*Am Golfplatz 3, 49143 Bissendorf*
- ☎ (05402) 5636
- 🖷 (05402) 5257
- ✉ info@ogc.de
- ♟ Thomas Page
- 🖳 www.ogc.de

### Rheine/Mesum (1998)
*Wörstr 201, 48432 Rheine*
- ☎ (05975) 9490
- 🖷 (05975) 9491
- ✉ info@golfclub-rheine.de
- 🖳 www.golfclub-rheine.de

### Rittergut Birkhof (1996)
*Rittergut Birkhof, 41352 Korschenbroich*
- ☎ (02131) 510660
- 🖷 (02131) 510616

### St Barbara's Royal Dortmund
(1969)
*Hesslingweg, 44309 Dortmund*
- ☎ (0231) 202551
- 🖷 (0231) 259183

### Schloss Georghausen (1962)
*Georghausen 8, 51789 Lindlar-Hommerich*
- ☎ (02207) 4938
- 🖷 (02207) 81230
- ✉ info@gcsg.de
- 🖳 www.golfclub-schloss-georghausen.de

### Schloss Haag (1996)
*Bartelter Weg 8, 47608 Geldern*
- ☎ (02831) 94777
- 🖷 (02831) 94778

### Schloss Myllendonk (1965)
*Myllendonkerstr 113, 41352 Korschenbroich 1*
- ☎ (02161) 641049
- 🖷 (02161) 648806
- ✉ info@gcsm.de
- ♟ Peter Géronne
- 🖳 www.gcsm.de

### Golfclub Schloss Westerholt
e.V. (1993)
*Schloss Strasse 1, 45701 Herten-Westerholt*
- ☎ (0209) 165840

☎ (0209) 1658415
✉ info@gc-westerholt.de
🖳 www.gc-westerholt.de

## Golf- und Landclub Schmitzhof (1975)
Arsbeckerstr 160, 41844 Wegberg
☎ (02436) 39090
🖳 (02436) 390915
✉ info@golfclubschmitzhof.de
🖳 www.golfclubschmitzhof.de

## Siegen-Olpe (1966)
Am Golfplatz, 57482 Wenden
☎ (02762) 9762-0
🖳 (02762) 9762-12
✉ info@gcso.de
✍ Stefan Eisenschmitt
🖳 www.gcso.de

## Golfclub Siegerland e.V. (1993)
Berghäuser Weg, 57223 Kreuztal-Mittelhees
☎ (02732) 59470
🖳 (02732) 594724
✉ info@golfclub-siegerland.de
✍ Ursula Kaidel
🖳 www.golfclub-siegerland.de

## Teutoburger Wald (1990)
Eggeberger Strasse 13, D-33790 Halle/Westfalen
☎ +49 5201 6279
🖳 +49 5201 6222
✉ post@gctw.de
🖳 www.gctw.de

## Unna-Fröndenberg (1985)
Schwarzer Weg 1, 58730 Fröndenberg
☎ (02373) 70068
🖳 (02373) 70069
✉ info@gcuf.de
✍ Mariya Mikli
🖳 www.gcuf.de

## Vechta-Welpe (1989)
Welpe 2, 49377 Vechta
☎ (04441) 5539/82168
🖳 (04441) 852480
✉ info@golfclub-vechta.de
✍ Maria Kortenbusch
🖳 www.golfclub-vechta.de

## Velbert - Gut Kuhlendahl
Kuhlendahler Str 283, 42553 Velbert
☎ (02053) 923290
🖳 (02053) 923291
✉ golfclub-velbert@t-online.de
✍ Michael Ogger (Director)
🖳 www.golfclub-velbert.de

## Golf & Country Club Velderhof (1997)
Velderhof, 50259 Pulheim
☎ (02238) 923940
🖳 (02238) 9239440
✉ info@velderhof.de
✍ Eva Harzheim
🖳 www.velderhof.de

## Vestischer GC Recklinghausen (1974)
Bockholterstr 475, 45659 Recklinghausen
☎ (02361) 93420
🖳 (02361) 934240
✉ vest.golfclub@t-online.de
🖳 www.gc-recklinghausen.de

## Wasserburg Anholt (1972)
Schloss 3, 46419 Isselburg Anholt
☎ (02874) 915120
🖳 (02874) 915128
✉ sekretariat@golfclub-anholt.de
🖳 www.golfclub-anholt.de

## Golfclub Weselerwald (1988)
Steenbecksweg 12, 46514 Schermbeck
☎ (02856) 91370
🖳 (02856) 913715
✉ info@gcww.de
✍ John Emery
🖳 www.gcww.de

## West Rhine (1954)
Javelin Barracks, BFPO 35, British Army of Germany
☎ +49 2163 974463
🖳 +49 2163 80049
✉ secretary@westrhinegc.co.uk
✍ David W Hampson
🖳 www.westrhinegc.co.uk

## Westerwald (1979)
Steinebacherstr, 57629 Dreifelden
☎ (02666) 8220
🖳 (02666) 8493
✉ gcwesterwald@t-online.de
🖳 ww.gc-westerwald.de

## Rhineland South

## Bad Neuenahr G&LC (1979)
Remagener Weg, 53474 Bad Neuenahr-Ahrweiler
☎ (02641) 950950
🖳 (02641) 950 9595

## Golf-Resort Bitburger Land (1995)
Zur Weilersheck 1, 54636 Wissmannsdorf
☎ (06527) 9272-0
🖳 (06527) 9272-30
✉ info@bitgolf.de
🖳 www.bitgolf.de

## Bonn-Godesberg in Wachtberg (1960)
Landgrabenweg, 53343 Wachtberg-Niederbachen
☎ (0228) 344003
🖳 (0228) 340820

## Burg Overbach (1984)
Postfach 1213, 53799 Much
☎ (02245) 5550
🖳 (02245) 8247
✉ widl@golfclub-burg-overbach.de
✍ Günter Widl
🖳 www.golfclub-burg-overbach.de

## Burg Zievel (1994)
Burg Zievel, 53894 Mechernich
☎ (02256) 1651
🖳 (02256) 3479

## Eifel (1977)
Kölner Str, 54576 Hillesheim
☎ (06593) 1241
🖳 (06593) 9421

## Gut Heckenhof (1993)
53783 Eitorf
☎ (02243) 9232-0
🖳 (02243) 923299
✉ info@gut-heckenhof.de
🖳 www.gut-heckenhof.de

## Internationaler GC Bonn (1992)
Gut Grossenbusch, 53757 St Augustin
☎ (02241) 39880
🖳 (02241) 398888
✉ info@gcbonn.de
🖳 www.golf-course-bonn.de

## Jakobsberg (1990)
Im Tal der Loreley, 56154 Boppard
☎ (06742) 808491
🖳 (06742) 808493
✉ golf@jakobsberg.de
🖳 www.jakobsberg.de

## Kyllburger Waldeifel
Lietzenhof, 54597 Burbach
☎ (06553) 961039
🖳 (06553) 3282
🖳 www.golf-lietzenhof.de

## Mittelrheinischer Bad Ems (1938)
Denzerheide, 56130 Bad Ems
☎ (02603) 6541
🖳 (02603) 13995
✉ info@mgcbadems.de
🖳 ww3w.mgcbadems.de

## Nahetal (1971)
Drei Buchen, 55583 Bad Münster am Stein
☎ (06708) 2145
🖳 (06708) 1731
🖳 www.golfclub-nahetal.de

## Stromberg-Schindeldorf (1987)
Park Village Golfanlagen, Buchenring 6, 55442 Stromberg
☎ (06724) 93080
🖳 (06724) 930818

## Trier (1977)
54340 Ensch-Birkenheck
☎ (06507) 993255
🖳 (06507) 993257
✉ info@golf-club-trier.de
🖳 www.golf-club-trier.de

## Waldbrunnen (1983)
Brunnenstr 11, 53578 Windhagen
☎ (02645) 8041
🖳 (02645) 8042
✉ info@golfclub-waldbrunnen.de
✍ Mrs B Thomas
🖳 www.golfclub-waldbrunnen.de

**Wiesensee** (1992)
*Am Wiesensee, 56459 Westerburg-Stahlhofen*
☎ **(02663) 991192**
📠 (02663) 991193
📧 golfclub.wiesensee@lindner.de
🖥 www.golfclub-wiesensee.de

## Saar-Pfalz

**Pfalz Neustadt** (1971)
*Im Lochbusch, 67435 Neustadt-Geinsheim*
☎ **(06327) 97420**
📠 (06327) 974218
📧 info@gc-pfalz.de
🖥 www.gc-pfalz.de

**Saarbrücken** (1961)
*Oberlimbergerweg, 66798 Wallerfangen-Gisingen*
☎ **(06837) 91800/1584**
📠 (06837) 91801
🖥 www.golfclub-saarbruecken.de

**Websweiler Hof** (1991)
*Websweiler Hof, 66424 Homburg/Saar*
☎ **(06841) 7777-60**
📠 (06841) 7777-666
🖥 www.golf-saar.de

**Westpfalz Schwarzbachtal**
(1988)
*66509 Rieschweiler*
☎ **(06336) 6442**
📠 (06336) 6408
📧 egw@golf.de
🖥 www.gcwestpfalz.de

**Woodlawn Golf Course**
*6792 Ramstein Flugplatz*
☎ **(06371) 476240**
📠 (06371) 42158
✍ R Nichols (Gen Mgr)
🖥 www.ramsteingolf.com

## Stuttgart & South West

**Bad Liebenzell**
*Golfplatz 1-9, 75378 Bad Liebenzell*
☎ **(07052) 9325-0**
📠 (07052) 9325-25
📧 info@gcbl.de
🖥 www.gcbl.de

**Bad Rappenau** (1989)
*Ehrenbergstrasse 25a, 74906 Bad Rappenau*
☎ **(07264) 3666**
📠 (07264) 3838

**Bad Salgau** (1995)
*Koppelweg 103, 88348 Bad Salgau*
☎ **(07581) 527459**
📠 (07581) 527487
📧 info@gc-bs.de
🖥 www.gc-bs.de

**Baden Hills Golf & Curling Club e.v.** (1982)
*Cabot Trail G208, 77836 Rheinmünster*
☎ **(07229) 185100**
📠 (07229) 1851011
📧 info@baden-hills.de
🖥 www.baden-hills.de

**Baden-Baden** (1901)
*Fremersbergstr 127, 76530 Baden-Baden*
☎ **(07221) 23579**
📠 (07221) 3025659
📧 info@golfclub-baden-baden.de
✍ Gerhard Kaufmann (Mgr)
🖥 www.golfclub-baden-baden.de

**GC Bodensee Weissenberg eV** (1986)
*Lampertsweiler 51, D-88138 Weissensberg*
☎ +41 (8389) 89190
📠 +41 (8389) 923907
📧 info@gcbw.de
🖥 www.gcbw.de

**Freiburg** (1970)
*Krüttweg 1, 79199 Kirchzarten*
☎ **(07661) 9847-0**
📠 (07661) 984747
📧 fgc@freiburger-golfclub.de
✍ Andrea Bührer
🖥 www.freiburger-golfclub.de

**Fürstlicher Golfclub Waldsee**
(1998)
*Hopfenweiler, 88339 Bad Waldsee*
☎ **(07524) 4017 200**
📠 (07524) 4017 100
📧 club@waldsee-golf.de
🖥 www.waldsee-golf.de

**Hechingen Hohenzollern**
(1955)
*Postfach 1124, 72379 Hechingen*
☎ **(07471) 6478**
📠 (07471) 14776
📧 info@golfclub-hechingen.de
🖥 www.golfclub-hechingen.de

**Heidelberg-Lobenfeld**
(1968)
*Biddersbacherhof, 74931 Lobbach- Lobenfeld*
☎ **(06226) 952110**
📠 (06226) 952111
📧 golf@gchl.de
🖥 www.gchl.de

**Heilbronn-Hohenlohe** (1964)
*Hofgasse, 74639 Zweiflingen-Friedrichsruhe*
☎ **(07941) 920810**
📠 (07941) 920819
🖥 www.friedrichsruhe.de

**Hetzenhof**
*Hetzenhof 7, 73547 Lorch*
☎ **(07172) 9180-0**
📠 (07172) 9180-30
📧 info@golfclub-hetzenhof.de
🖥 www.golfclub-hetzenhof.de

**Hohenstaufen** (1959)
*Unter den Ramsberg, 73072 Donzdorf-Reichenbach*
☎ **(07162) 27171**
📠 (07162) 25744
📧 info@gc-hohenstaufen.de
🖥 www.gc-hohenstaufen.de

**Kaiserhöhe** (1995)
*Im Laber 4a, 74747 Ravenstein*
☎ **(06297) 399**
📠 (06297) 599
📧 info@golfclub-kaiserhoehe.de
✍ Martin Arzberger
🖥 www.gc-kaiserhoehe.de

**Golf-Club Konstanz e.V.**
(1965)
*Hofgut Kargegg 1, D-78476 Allensbach-Langenrain*
☎ +49 (0) 75 33 93 03 - 0
📠 +49 (o) 75 33 93 03 - 30
📧 info@golfclubkonstanz.de
🖥 www.golfclubkonstanz.de

**Lindau-Bad Schachen** (1954)
*Am Schönbühl 5, 88131 Lindau*
☎ **(08382) 96170**
📠 (08382) 961750
📧 info@golflindau.de
🖥 www.gc-lindau-bad-schachen.de

**Markgräflerland Kandern**
(1984)
*Feuerbacher Str 35, 79400 Kandern*
☎ **(07626) 97799-0**
📠 (07626) 97799-22
📧 info@gc-mk.com
✍ Graham Currie
🖥 www.gc-mk.com

**Neckartal** (1974)
*Aldinger Str. 975, 70806 Kornwestheim*
☎ **(07141) 871319**
📠 (07141) 81716
📧 info@gc-neckartal.de
🖥 www.gc-neckartal.de

**Nippenburg** (1993)
*Nippenburg 21, 71701 Schwieberdingen*
☎ **(07150) 39530**
📠 (07150) 353518

**Obere Alp** (1989)
*Am Golfplatz 1-3, 79780 Stühlingen*
☎ **(07703) 9203-0**
📠 (07703) 9203-18
📧 sekretariat@golf-oberealp.de
🖥 www.golf-oberealp.de

**Oberschwaben-Bad Waldsee**
(1968)
*Hopfenweiler 2d, 88339 Bad Waldsee*
☎ **(07524) 5900**
📠 (07524) 6106

**Oeschberghof L & GC**
(1976)
*Golfplatz 1, 78166 Donaueschingen*
☎ **(0771) 84525**
📠 (0771) 84540

## Land-und Golfclub Oschberghof (1976)
*Golfplatz 1, 78166 Donaueschingen*
☎ **(0771) 84525**
🖬 (0771) 84540
🖾 golf@oeschberghof.com
🖹 www.oeschberghof.com

## Owingen-Überlingen e.V – Hofgut Lugenhof (1989)
*Alte Owinger Str 93, 88696 Owingen*
☎ **(07551) 83040**
🖬 (07551) 830422
🖾 welcome@golfclub-owingen.de
🖹 www.golfclub-owingen.de

## Pforzheim Karlshäuser Hof (1987)
*Karlshäuser Weg, 75248 Ölbronn-Dürrn*
☎ **(07237) 9100**
🖬 (07237) 5161
🖾 info@gc-pf.de
✍ Andreas List (CM)
🖹 www.gc-pf.de

## Reischenhof (1987)
*Industriestrasse 12, 88489 Wain*
☎ **(07353) 1732**
🖬 (07373) 3824
🖹 www.golf.de/gc-reischenhof

## Reutlingen-Sonnenbühl (1987)
*Im Zerg, 72820 Sonnenbühl*
☎ **(07128) 92660**
🖬 (07128) 926692

## Rhein Badenweiler (1971)
*79401 Badenweiler*
☎ **(07632) 7970**
🖬 (07632) 797150

## Rickenbach (1979)
*Hennematt 20, 79736 Rickenbach*
☎ **(07765) 777**
🖬 (07765) 544
🖾 info@golfclub-rickenbach.de
🖹 www.golfclub-rickenbach.de

## Schloss Klingenburg e.v. (1978)
*Schloss Klingenburg, 89343 Jettingen-Scheppach*
☎ **(08225) 3030**
🖬 (08225) 30350
🖾 info@golf-klingenburg.de
🖹 www.golf-klingenburg.de

## Schloss Langenstein (1991)
*Schloss Langenstein, 78359 Orsingen-Nenzingen*
☎ **(07774) 50651**
🖬 (07774) 50699
🖾 golf-sekretariat@schloss-langenstein.com
🖹 www.schloss-langenstein.com

## Schloss Liebenstein (1982)
*Postfach 27, 74380 Neckarwestheim*
☎ **(07133) 9878-0**
🖬 (07133) 9878-18
🖾 info@gc-sl.de

✍ Rüdiger Schmid
🖹 www.golfclubliebenstein.de

## Schloss Weitenburg (1984)
*Sommerhalde 11, 72181 Starzach-Sulzau*
☎ **(07472) 15050**
🖬 (07472) 15051
🖾 info@gcsw.de
🖹 www.gcsw.de

## Sinsheim-Buchenauerhof (1993)
*Buchenauerhof 4, 74889 Sinsheim*
☎ **(07265) 7258**
🖬 (07265) 7379
🖾 mail@golfclubsinsheim.de
✍ Marion Bonn
🖹 www.golfclubsinsheim.de

## Steisslingen (1991)
*Brunnenstr 4b, 78256 Steisslingen-Wiechs*
☎ **(07738) 7196**
🖬 (07738) 923297
🖾 info@golfclub-steisslingen.de
✍ Peter Ridley
🖹 www.golfclub-steisslingen.de

## Stuttgarter Golf-Club Solitude e.V. (1927)
*Schlossfeld/Golfplatz 71297, Mönsheim*
☎ **(07044) 911 0410**
🖬 (07044) 911 0420
🖾 info@golfclub-stuttgart.com
✍ Birgit Geise
🖹 www.golfclub-stuttgart.com

## Ulm e.V. (1963)
*Wochenauer Hof 2, 89186 Illerrieden*
☎ **(07306) 929500**
🖬 (07306) 9295025
🖾 GolfClubUlm@t-online.de
🖹 www.GolfClubUlm.de

---

# Greece

## Afandou (1973)
*Afandou, Rhodes*
☎ **(0241) 51255**

## Corfu (1972)
*PO Box 71, Ropa Valley, 49100 Corfu*
☎ **(26610) 94220**
🖬 (26610) 94221
🖾 cfugolf@hol.gr
🖹 www.corfugolfclub.com

## Glyfada Golf Club of Athens (1966)
*PO Box 70116, 166-10 Glyfada, Athens*
☎ **+30 210 894 6459**
🖬 +30 210 894 6834
🖾 info@ggca.gr
✍ Nicole Cavadia
🖹 www.ggca.gr

# Hungary

## Birdland G&CC (1991)
*Thermal krt.10, 9740 Bükfürdö*
☎ **(+36) 94 358060**
🖬 (+36) 94 359000
🖾 golf@greenfieldhotel.net
🖹 www.birdlandresort.hu

## Budapest G&CC
*Golf u.1, 2024 Kisoroszi*
☎ **(1) 36 26 392 465**
🖬 (1) 36 26 392 465

## European Lakes G&CC (1994)
*Kossuth u.3, 7232 Hencse*
☎ **(82) 481245**
🖬 (82) 481248
🖾 info@europeanlakes.com
✍ Medea Zag
⊕ Soft spikes only - No metal spikes
🖹 www.europeanlakes.com

## Old Lake (1998)
*PO Box 127, 2890 Tata-Remeteségpuszta*
☎ **(34) 587620**
🖬 (34) 587623
🖾 club@oldlakegolf.com
✍ Dr Ba'bos Réka (Club Director)
🖹 www.oldlakegolf.com

## Pannonia Golf & Country Club (1996)
*Alcsútdoboz, 8087 Mariavölgy*
☎ **0036 (22) 594200**
🖬 0036 (22) 594205
🖾 info@golfclub.hu
✍ Damian MacPherson
🖹 www.golfclub.hu

## St Lorence G&CC
*Pellérdi ut 55, 7634 Pécs*
☎ **(72) 252844/252142**
🖬 (72) 252844/252173

---

# Iceland

## Akureyri (1935)
*PO Box 317, 602 Akureyri*
☎ **+354 4622974**
🖾 gagolf@gagolf.is
✍ Halla Sif Svavarsdóttir
🖹 www.gagolf.is

## Borgarness (1973)
*Hamar, 310 Borgarnes*
☎ **(345) 437 1663**
🖾 gbgolf@simnet.is
🖹 www.gbgolf.is

## Golfklubbur Sudurnesja (1964)
*PO Box 112, 232 Keflavik*
☎ **(421) 4100**
🖾 gs@gs.is
✍ Gunnar Johannsson
🖹 www.gs.is

**Húsavík**   (1967)
*PO Box 23, Kötlum, 640 Húsavík*
☎ **(464) 1000**
📠 (464) 1678
✉ palmi.palmason@tmd.is

**Isafjardar**   (1978)
*PO Box 367, 400 Isafjördur*
☎ **(456) 5081**
📠 (456) 4547
✉ gi@snerpa.is

**Jökull**   (1973)
*Postholf 67, 355 Olafsvík*
☎ **(436) 1666**

**Keilir**   (1967)
*Box 148, 222 Hafnarfjördur*
☎ **(565) 3360**
📠 (565) 2560
✉ keilir@keilir.is
🖥 www.keilir.is

**Kopavogs og Gardabaejar**
(1994)
*Postholf 214, 212 Gardabaer*
☎ **(+354) 565 7373**
📠 (+354) 565 9190
✉ gkg@gkg.is
✍ Agnar Mar Jonsson (Manager)
🖥 www.gkg.is

**Leynir**   (1965)
*PO Box 9, Akranes*
☎ **(00354) 431 2771**
📠 (00354) 431 3711
✉ leynir@simnet.is
🖥 www.golf.is/gl    www.leynir.is

**Ness-Nesklúbburinn**   (1964)
*PO Box 66, 172 Seltjarnarnes*
☎ **(561) 1930**
📠 (561) 1966
✉ nk@centrum.is
🖥 www.golf.is/nk

**Oddafellowa**   (1990)
*Urridavatnsdölum, 210 Gardabaer*
☎ **(565) 9094**
📠 (565) 9074
🖥 www.oddur.is

**Olafsfjardar**   (1968)
*Skeggjabrekku, 625 Olafsfjördur*
☎ **(466) 2611**
📠 (466) 2611

**Reykjavíkur**   (1934)
*Grafarholt, 112 Reykjavik*
☎ **+354 (585) 0200/0210**
📠 +354 (585) 0201
✉ gr@grgolf.is
🖥 www.grgolf.is

**Saudárkróks**   (1970)
*Hlidarendi, Postholf 56, 550 Saudárkrókur*
☎ **(453) 5075**

**Vestmannaeyja**   (1938)
*Postholf 168, 902 Vestmannaeyar*
☎ **(481) 2363**
📠 (481) 2362

# Italy

## Como/Milan/Bergamo

**Ambrosiano**   (1994)
*Cascina Bertacca, 20080 Bubbiano-Milan*
☎ **(0290) 840820**
📠 (0290) 849365
✉ info@golfclubambrosiano.com
🖥 www.golfclubambrosiano.com

**Barlassina CC**   (1956)
*Via Privata Golf 42, 20030 Birago di Camnago (MI)*
☎ **(0362) 560621/2**
📠 (0362) 560934
✉ bccgolf@libero.it

**Bergamo L'Albenza**   (1961)
*Via Longoni 12, 24030 Almenno S. Bartolomeo (BG)*
☎ **(035) 640028**
📠 (035) 643066
✉ segreteria@golfbergamo.it
✍ Achille Ridamouti (Sec)
🖥 www.golfbergamo.it

**Bogogno**   (1996)
*Via Sant'Isidoro 1, 28010 Bogogno*
☎ **(0322) 863794**
📠 (0322) 863798
✉ info@circologolfbogogno.com
✍ Tiziano Capello
🖥 www.circolo9golfbogogno.com

**Golf Brianza Country Club**
(1996)
*Cascina Cazzu, 4, 20040 Usmate Velate (Mi)*
☎ **(039) 682 9089/079**
📠 (039) 682 9059
✉ brianzagolf@tin.it
✍ Francesco Alajmo (Mgr)
🖥 www.brianzagolf.it

**Carimate**   (1962)
*Via Airoldi 2, 22060 Carimate (CO)*
☎ **(031) 790226**
📠 (031) 791927
✉ info@golfcarimate.it
✍ Giuseppe Nava
🖥 www.golfcarimate.it

**Castelconturbia**   (1984)
*Via Suno, 28010 Agrate Conturbia*
☎ **(0322) 832093**
📠 (0322) 832428
✉ castelconturbia@tin.it
🖥 www.golfclubcastelconturbia.it

**Castello di Tolcinasco**   (1993)
*20090 Pieve Emanuele (MI)*
☎ **(02) 9042 8035**
📠 (02) 9078 9051
✉ golf@golftolcinasco.it
🖥 www.golftolcinasco.it

**Franciacorta**   (1986)
*Via Provinciale 34b, 25040 Nigoline di Corte Franca, (Brescia)*
☎ **(030) 984167**

📠 (030) 984393
✉ franciacortagolfclub@libero.it

**Menaggio & Cadenabbia**   (1907)
*Via Golf 12, 22010 Grandola E Uniti*
☎ **(0344) 32103**
📠 (0344) 30780
✉ reception@golfclubmenaggio.it
🖥 www.menaggio.it

**Milano**   (1928)
*20.900 Parco di Monza (MI)*
☎ **(039) 303081/2/3**
📠 (039) 304427
✉ info@golfclubmilano.com
✍ Arnaldo Cocuzza (Mgr)
🖥 www.golfclubmilano.it

**Molinetto CC**   (1982)
*SS Padana Superiore 11, 20063 Cernusco S/N (MI)*
☎ **(02) 9210 5128/9210 5983**
📠 (02) 9210 6635

**Monticello**   (1975)
*Via Volta 63, 22070 Cassina Rizzardi (Como)*
☎ **(031) 928055**
📠 (031) 880207
✉ monticello@tin.it
🖥 www.golfmonticello.it

**La Pinetina Golf Club**
(1971)
*Via al Golf 4, 22070 Appiano Gentile (CO)*
☎ **(031) 933202**
📠 (031) 890342
✉ info@golfpinetina.it
✍ Simone Laureti (Club Mgr)
🖥 www.golfpinetina.it

**Le Robinie**   (1992)
*Via per Busto Arsizio 9, 21058 Solbiate Olona (VA)*
☎ **(039) 331 329260**
📠 (039) 331 329266
✉ info@lerobinie.com
🖥 www.lerobinie.com

**La Rossera**   (1970)
*Via Montebello 4, 24060 Chiuduno*
☎ **(035) 838600**
📠 (035) 442 7047
✉ segreteria@rossera.it
🖥 www.rossera.it

**Le Rovedine**   (1978)
*Via Karl Marx, 20090 Noverasco di Opera (Mi)*
☎ **(02) 5760 6420**
📠 (02) 5760 6405
✉ info@rovedine.com
🖥 www.rovedone.com

**Varese**   (1934)
*Via Vittorio Veneto 59, 21020 Luvinate (VA)*
☎ **(0332) 229302/821293**
📠 (0332) 811293
✉ info@golfclubvarese.it
✍ Carlo Giraldi
🖥 www.golfclubvarese.it

**Vigevano** (1974)
*Via Chitola 49, 27029 Vigevano (PV)*
☎ **(0381) 346628/346077**
🖶 (0381) 346091
📧 golfvigevano@yahoo.it

**Villa D'Este** (1926)
*Via Cantù 13, 22030 Montorfano (CO)*
☎ **(031) 200200**
🖶 (031) 200786
📧 info@golfvilladeste.com
✍ Andrea Contigiani
🖥 www.golfvilladeste.com

**Zoate**
*20067 Zoate di Tribiano (MI)*
☎ **(02) 9063 2183/9063 1861**
🖶 (02) 9063 1861

### Elba

**Acquabona** (1971)
*57037 Portoferraio, Isola di Elba (LI)*
☎ **(0565) 940066**
🖶 (0565) 933410

### Emilia Romagna

**Adriatic GC Cervia** (1985)
*Via Jelenia Gora No 6, 48016 Cervia-Milano Marittima*
☎ **(0544) 992786**
🖶 (0544) 993410

**Bologna** (1959)
*Via Sabattini 69, 40050 Monte San Pietro (BO)*
☎ **(051) 969100**
🖶 (051) 672 0017

**Croara Country Club** (1976)
*Loc. Croara Nuova 23010 Gazzola (PC)*
☎ **(0523) 977105**
🖶 (0523) 977100
📧 info@golfcroara.it
🖥 www.golfcroara.it

**Matilde di Canossa** (1987)
*Via Casinazzo 1, 42100 San Bartolomeo, Reggio Emilia*
☎ **(0522) 371295**
🖶 (0522) 371204
📧 golfcanossa@libero.it
🖥 www.tiscali.it/golfcanossa

**Modena G&CC** (1987)
*Via Castelnuovo Rangone 4, 41050 Colombaro di Formigine (MO)*
☎ **(059) 553482**
🖶 (059) 553696
📧 segretaria@modenagolf.it
✍ Davide Colombarini
🖥 www.modenagolf.it

**Riolo Golf La Torre** (1992)
*Via Limisano 10, Riolo Terme (RA)*
☎ **(0546) 74035**
🖶 (0546) 74076
📧 info@golflatorre.it
✍ Lamberto Di Giacinto
🖥 www.golflatorre.it

**La Rocca** (1985)
*Via Campi 8, 43038 Sala Baganza (PR)*
☎ **(0521) 834037**
🖶 (0521) 834575
🖥 www.officeitalia.it/golflarocca

### Gulf of Genoa

**Garlenda** (1965)
*Via Golf 7, 17033 Garlenda*
☎ **(0182) 580012**
🖶 (0182) 580561
📧 info@garlendagolf.it
✍ Claudio Rota
🖥 www.garlendagolf.it

**Marigola** (1975)
*Via Biaggini 5, 19032 Lerici (SP)*
☎ **(0187) 970193**
🖶 (0187) 970193
📧 info@golfmarigola.it
🖥 www.golfmarigola.it

**Pineta di Arenzano** (1959)
*Piazza del Golf 3, 16011 Arenzano (GE)*
☎ **(010) 911 1817**
🖶 (010) 911 1270

**Rapallo** (1930)
*Via Mameli 377, 16035 Rapallo (GE)*
☎ **(0185) 261777**
🖶 (0185) 261779

**Sanremo-Circolo Golf degli Ulivi** (1932)
*Via Campo Golf 59, 18038 Sanremo*
☎ **(0184) 557093**
🖶 (0184) 557388
📧 info@golfsanremo.com
✍ Vittorio Bersotti
🖥 www.golfsanremo.com

**Versilia** (1990)
*Via Sipe 100, 55045 Pietrasanta (LU)*
☎ **(0584) 88 15 74**
🖶 (0584) 75 22 72

### Lake Garda & Dolomites

**Asiago** (1967)
*Via Meltar 2, 36012 Asiago (VI)*
☎ **(0424) 462721**
🖶 (0424) 465133
🖥 www.golfasiago.it

**Bogliaco** (1912)
*Via Golf 21, 25088 Toscolano-Maderno*
☎ **(0365) 643006**
🖶 (0365) 643006
📧 golfbogliaco@tin.it
🖥 www.bogliaco.com

**Campo Carlo Magno** (1922)
*Golf Hotel, 38084 Madonna di Campiglio (TN)*
☎ **(0465) 440622**
🖶 (0465) 440298

**Folgaria** (1987)
*Loc Costa di Folgaria, 38064 Folgaria (TN)*
☎ **(0464) 720480**
🖶 (0464) 720480

**Gardagolf CC** (1985)
*Via Angelo Omodeo 2, 25080 Soiano Del Lago (BS)*
☎ **(0365) 674707 (Sec)**
🖶 (0365) 674788
📧 info@gardagolf.it
🖥 www.gardagolf.it

**Il Golf Ca' degli Ulivi** (1988)
*Via Ghiandare 2, 37010 Marciaga di Costermano (VR)*
☎ **(045) 627 9030**
🖶 (045) 627 9039
📧 info@golfcadegliulivi.it
🖥 www.golfcadegliulivi.it

**Karersee-Carezza**
*Loc Carezza 171, 39056 Welschofen-Nova Levante*
☎ **(0471) 612200**
🖶 (0471) 612200

**Petersberg** (1987)
*Unterwinkel 5, 39050 Petersberg (BZ)*
☎ **+39 0471 615122**
🖶 +39 0471 615229
📧 info@golfclubpetersberg.it
✍ Hans-Peter Thaler
🖥 www.golfclubpetersberg.it

**Ponte di Legno** (1980)
*Corso Milano 36, 25056 Ponte di Legno (BS)*
☎ **(0364) 900306**
🖶 (0364) 900555

**Verona** (1963)
*Ca' del Sale 15, 37066 Sommacampagna*
☎ **(045) 510060**
🖶 (045) 510242
📧 golfverona@libero.it
🖥 www.golfclubverona.com

### Naples & South

**Riva Dei Tessali** (1971)
*74011 Castellaneta*
☎ **(099) 843 9251**
🖶 (099) 843 9255

**San Michele**
*Loc Bosco 8/9, 87022 Cetraro (CS)*
☎ **(0982) 91012**
🖶 (0982) 91430
📧 sanmichele@sanmichele.it
🖥 www.sanmichele.it

### Rome & Centre

**Country Club Castelgandolfo** (1987)
*Via Santo Spirito 13, 00040 Castelgandolfo*
☎ **(06) 931 2301**
🖶 (06) 931 2244
📧 info@golfclubcastelgandolfo.it
🖥 www.countryclubcastelgandolfo.it

---

*For key to symbols and European dialling codes see page 725*

## Fioranello
*CP 96, 00134 Roma (RM)*
☎ **(06) 713 8080 - 213**
🖳 (06) 713 8212
📧 info@fioranellogolf.it
🖥 www.fioranellogolf.com

## Marco Simone    (1989)
*Via di Marco Simone, 00012
Guidonia (RM)*
☎ **(0774) 366469**
🖳 (0774) 366476

## Marediroma
*Via Enna 30, 00040 Ardea (RM)*
☎ **(06) 913 3250**
🖳 (06) 913 3592
📧 info@golfmarediroma.it
🖥 www.golfmarediroma.it

## Nazionale
*Via Cassia, Km 44,5, San Martino I-01015
Sutri (VT)*
☎ **(0761) 609 308**
🖳 (0761) 600142
📧 info@golfnazionale.it
🖥 www.golfnazionale.it

## Nettuno
*Via della Campana 18, 00048
Nettuno (RM)*
☎ **(06) 981 9419**
🖳 (06) 989 88142

## Oasi Golf Club    (1988)
*Via Cogna 5, 04011 Aprilia (Roma)*
☎ **0039-06-92746252/9268120**
🖳 0039-06-9268502
📧 info@oasigolf.it
✍ Marina Lanza (President)
🖥 www.oasigolf.it

## Olgiata    (1961)
*Largo Olgiata 15, 00123 Roma*
☎ **(06) 308 89141**
🖳 (06) 308 89968
📧 secretaria@olgiatagolfclub.it
🖥 www.olgiatagolfclub.it

## Parco de' Medici    (1989)
*Viale Salvatore Rebecchini, 00148 Roma*
☎ **(06) 655 3477**
🖳 (06) 655 3344
📧 info@sheratongolf.it
🖥 www.sheraton.com/golfrome
   www.golfclubparcodemedici.com

## Pescara    (1992)
*Contrado Cerreto 58, 66010
Miglianico (CH)*
☎ **(0871) 959566**
🖳 (0871) 950363

## Roma    (1903)
*Via Appia Nuova 716A, 00178 Roma*
☎ **(06) 780 3407**
🖳 (06) 783 46219

## Tarquinia
*Loc Pian di Spille, Via degli Alina 271,
01016 Marina Velca/Tarquinia (VT)*
☎ **(0766) 812109**

# Sardinia

## Is Molas    (1975)
*CP 49, 09010 Pula*
☎ **(070) 924 1013/4**
🖳 (070) 924 2121
📧 ismolasgolf@ismolas.it
🖥 www.ismolas.it

## Pevero GC Costa Smeralda
(1972)
*Cala di Volpe, 07021 Porto Cervo (SS)*
☎ **+39 0789 958000**
🖳 +39 0789 96572
📧 pevero@starwoodhotels.com
✍ Richard Cau (Sec)
🖥 www.golfclubpevero.com

# Sicily

## Il Pìcciolo    (1988)
*S.S. 120 Km 200, 95012 Castiglione di
Sicilia (CT)*
☎ **+39 (0942) 986252**
🖳 +39 (0942) 986138
📧 info@ilpicciologolf.com
✍ Alfredo Petralia
🖥 www.ilpicciologolf.com

# Turin & Piemonte

## Alpino Di Stresa    (1924)
*Viale Golf Panorama 48, 28839 Vezzo (VB)*
☎ **(0323) 20642**
🖳 (0323) 208900
📧 info@golfalpino.it
✍ Alessandro Aina
🖥 www.golfalpino.it

## Biella Le Betulle    (1958)
*Regione Valcarozza, 13887 Magnano (BI)*
☎ **(015) 679151**
🖳 (015) 679276
📧 info@golfclubbiella.it
✍ Riccardo Valzorio (Sec)
🖥 www.golfclubbiella.it

## Golf Club del Cervino
(1955)
*11021 Breuil- Cervinia (AO)*
☎ **+39 0166 949131**
🖳 +39 0166 940700
📧 info@golfcervino.com
🖥 www.golfcervino.com

## Cherasco CC    (1982)
*Via Fraschetta 8, 12062 Cherasco (CN)*
☎ **(0172) 489772/488489**
🖳 (0172) 488320
📧 info@golfcherasco.com
✍ Corrado Graglia (Dir)
🖥 www.golfcherasco.com

## Cuneo    (1990)
*Via degli Angeli 3, 12012 Mellana-
Bóves (CN)*
☎ **(0171) 387041**
🖳 (0171) 390763

## Le Fronde    (1973)
*Via Sant-Agostino 68, 10051 Avigliana (TO)*
☎ **(011) 932 8053/0540**
🖳 (011) 932 0928

## I Girasoli    (1991)
*Via Pralormo 315, 10022 Carmagnola (TO)*
☎ **(011) 979 5088**
🖳 (011) 979 5228
📧 info@girasoligolf.it
✍ Renzo Dutto
🖥 www.girasoligolf.it

## Iles Borromees    (1987)
*Loc Motta Rossa, 28833 Brovello
Carpugnino (VB)*
☎ **(0323) 929285**
🖳 (0323) 929190
📧 info@golfdesiles.it
✍ Marco Garbaccio
🖥 www.golfdesiles.it

## Golf dei Laghi    (1993)
*Via Trevisani 6, 21028 Travedona
Monate (VA)*
☎ **(0332) 978101**
🖳 (0332) 977532

## Margara    (1975)
*Via Tenuta Margara 7, 15043 Fubine (AL)*
☎ **(0131) 778555**
🖳 (0131) 778772
📧 margara@golfmargara.com
✍ Gian Marco Griffi
🖥 www.golfmargara.it

## La Margherita
*Strada Pralormo, 29 - 1 10022
Carmagnola (TO)*
☎ **(011) 979 5113**
🖳 (011) 979 5204
📧 info@golfclublamargherita.it
🖥 www.golfclublamargherita.it

## La Serra    (1970)
*Via Astigliano 42, 15048 Valenza (AL)*
☎ **(0131) 954778**
🖳 (0131) 928294
📧 golfclublaserra@tin.it

## Sestrieres    (1932)
*Piazza Agnelli 4, 10058 Sestriere (TO)*
☎ **(0122) 755170/76243**
🖳 (0122) 76294

## Stupinigi    (1972)
*Corso Unione Sovietica 506, 10135 Torino*
☎ **(011) 347 2640**
🖳 (011) 397 8038

## Torino    (1924)
*Via Agnelli 40, 10070 Fiano Torinese*
☎ **+39 (011) 923 5440/923 5670**
🖳 +39 (011) 923 5886
📧 info@circologolftorino.it
✍ Mr Mauro Stroppiana
🖥 www.circologolftorino.it

## Vinovo    (1986)
*Via Stupinigi 182, 10048 Vinovo (TO)*
☎ **(011) 965 3880**
🖳 (011) 962 3748

## Tuscany & Umbria

**Casentino**    (1985)
6 Via Fronzola, 52014 Poppi (Arezzo)
☎ **(0575) 529810**
🖳 (0575) 520167
📧 info@golfclubcasentino.it
🖉 Luca Alterini
🖥 www.golfclubcasentino.it

**Circolo Golf Ugolino**    (1933)
Strada Chiantigiana 3, 50015 Grassina
☎ **(055) 230 1009/1085**
🖳 (055) 230 1141
📧 info@golfugolino.it

**Conero GC Sirolo**    (1987)
Via Betellico 6, 60020 Sirolo (AN)
☎ **(071) 736 0613**
🖳 (071) 736 0380

**Cosmopolitan G&CC**    (1992)
Viale Pisorno 60, 56018 Tirrenia
☎ **(050) 33633**
🖳 (050) 384707
📧 info@cosmopolitangolf.it
🖥 www.cosmopolitangolf.it

**Lamborghini-Panicale**    (1992)
Loc Soderi 1, 06064 Panicale (PG)
☎ **(075) 8350029**
📧 info@lamborghinionline.it
🖉 Zeke Martinez
🖥 www.lamborghinionline.it

**Montecatini**    (1985)
Via Dei Brogi 1652, Loc Pievaccia, 51015
Monsummano Terme (Pistoia)
☎ **(0572) 62218**
🖳 (0572) 617435
📧 info@montecatinigolf.com
🖉 Giannini Maria Stella
🖥 www.montecatinigolf.com

**Le Pavoniere**    (1986)
Via Traversa Il Crocifisso, 59100 Prato
☎ **(0574) 620855**
🖳 (0574) 624558

**Golf Club Perugia**    (1959)
Loc S.Sabina, 06132 - Perugia (PG)
☎ **(075) 517 2204**
🖳 (075) 517 2370
📧 info@golfclubperugia.it
🖉 Matteo Bragone (Mgr)
🖥 www.golfclubperugia.it

**Poggio dei Medici**    (1995)
Via San Gavino, 27 - Loc. Cignano, I-50038
Scarperia, (Florence)
☎ **(+39) 055 84350**
🖳 (+39) 055 843439
📧 info@golfpoggiodeimedici.com
🖉 Cristiano Bevilacqua (Mgr)
🖥 www.golfpoggiodeimedici.com

**Punta Ala**    (1964)
Via del Golf 1, 58040 Punta Ala (GR)
☎ **(0564) 922121/922719**
🖳 (0564) 920182
🖥 www.puntaAla.net/golf

**Tirrenia**    (1968)
Viale San Guido, 56018 Tirrenia (PI)
☎ **(050) 37518**
🖳 (050) 33286

## Venice & North East

**Albarella Golf Club**
Isola di Albarella, 45010 Rosolina (RO)
☎ **(0426) 330124**
🖳 (0426) 330830
🖉 Gabriele Marangon

**Cansiglio**    (1956)
CP 152, 31029 Vittorio Veneto
☎ **(0438) 585398**
🖳 (0438) 585398
📧 golfcansiglio@tin.it
🖥 www.golfclubcansiglio.it

**Colli Berici**    (1986)
Strada Monti Comunali, 36040
Brendola (VI)
☎ **(0444) 601780**
🖳 (0444) 400777

**Frassanelle**    (1990)
Via Rialto, 5/A - 35030 Rovolon (PD)
☎ **(049) 991 0722**
🖳 (049) 991 0691
📧 info@golffrassanelle.it
🖥 www.golffrassanelle.it

**Lignano**
Via Bonifica 3, 33054 Lignano
Sabbiadoro (UD)
☎ **(0431) 428025**
🖳 (0431) 423230
🖥 www.golflignano.it

**La Montecchia**    (1989)
Via Montecchia 12, 35030
Selvazzano (PD)
☎ **(049) 805 5550**
🖳 (049) 805 5737
📧 info@golfmontecchia.it
🖥 www.golfmontecchia.it

**Padova**    (1964)
35050 Valsanzibio di Galzigano
Terme (PD)
☎ **(049) 913 0078**
🖳 (049) 913 1193
📧 info@golfpadova.it
🖥 www.golfpadova.it

**San Floriano-Gorizia**    (1987)
Castello di San Floriano, 34070 San
Floriano del Collio (GO)
☎ **(0481) 884252/884234**
🖳 (0481) 884252/884052

**Trieste**    (1954)
Via Padriciano 80, 34012 Trieste
☎ **(040) 226159/226270**
🖳 (040) 226159

**Udine**    (1971)
Via dei Faggi 1, Località Villaverde, 33034
Fagagna (UD)
☎ **(0432) 800418**
🖳 (0432) 801312

📧 info@golfudine.com
🖥 www.golfudine.com

**Venezia**    (1928)
Strada Vecchia 1, 30126 Alberoni (Venezia)
☎ **(041) 731333**
🖳 (041) 731339
📧 info@circologolfvenezia.it
🖥 www.circologolfvenezia.it

**Villa Condulmer**    (1960)
Via della Croce 3, 31020 Zerman di
Mogliano Veneto - Tv
☎ **(041) 457062**
🖳 (041) 457202
📧 info@golfvillacondulmer.com
🖥 www.golfvillacondulmer.com

# Latvia

**Ozo Golf Club**    (2002)
Milgravju iela 16, Riga, LV-1034
☎ **+371 6739 4399**
🖳 +371 6739 4034
📧 ozogolf@apollo.lv
🖥 www.ozogolf.lv

**Saliena**    (2006)
Egluciems, Babites pagasts, Rigas rajons LV-2107
☎ **+371 6716 0300**
🖳 +371 6714 6322
📧 golf@salienagolfcourse.com
🖥 www.saliena.com

**Viesturi Golf Club**    (1998)
Viesturi-1, Jaunmärupe, Märupes
pagasts, LV-2166
☎ **+371 2921 9699**
🖳 +371 6747 0030
📧 sandra@golfsviesturi.lv
🖥 www.golfsviesturi.lv

# Luxembourg

**Christnach**    (1993)
Am Lahr, 7641 Christnach
☎ **87 83 83**
🖳 87 95 64
📧 gcc@gms.lu
🖉 Claus Uwe Leske (Mgr)
🖥 www.golfclubchristnach.lu

**Clervaux**    (1992)
Mecherwee, 9748 Eselborn
☎ **92 93 95**
🖳 92 94 51
📧 gcclerv@pt.lu
🖥 www.golfclervaux.lu

**Gaichel**
Rue de Eischen, 8469 Gaichel
☎ **39 71 08**
🖳 39 00 75
📧 infogolf@golfgaichel.com
🖥 www.golfgaichel.com

874   Clubs and Courses

## Golf de Luxembourg   (1993)
*Domaine de Belenhaff, L-6141 Junglinster*
☎ **(00252) 78 00 68-1**
📠 (00352) 78 71 28
📧 info@golfdeluxembourg.lu
🖥 www.golfdeluxembourg.lu

## Grand-Ducal de Luxembourg
(1936)
*1 Route de Trèves, 2633 Senningerberg*
☎ **34 00 90-1**
📠 34 83 91
📧 gcgd@pt.lu
🖊 Mr Philippe Dewolf
🖥 www.gcgd.lu

## Kikuoka Country Club   (1991)
*Scheierhaff, L-5412 Canach*
☎ **+352 35 61 35**
📠 +352 35 74 50
📧 kikuoka@kikuoka.lu
🖊 Patrick Platz (Gen Mgr)
🖥 www.kikuoka.lu

# Malta

## Royal Malta   (1888)
*Aldo Moro Street, Marsa MRS 9064*
☎ **(356) 21 22 70 19**
📠 (356) 21 22 70 20
📧 sales@royalmaltagolfclub.com
🖥 www.royalmaltagolfclub.com

# Netherlands

## Amsterdam & Noord Holland

## Amsterdam Old Course (1990)
*Zwarte Laantje 4, 1099 CE Amsterdam*
☎ **(020) 663 1766**
📠 (020) 663 4621
📧 info@amsterdamoldcourse.nl
🖊 Mr B Flik
🖥 www.amsterdamoldcourse.nl

## Amsterdamse   (1934)
*Bauduinlaan 35, 1047 HK Amsterdam*
☎ **(020) 497 7866**
📠 (020) 497 5966
📧 agc1934@wxs.nl
🖥 www.amsterdamsegolfclub.nl

## BurgGolf Purmerend   (1989)
*Westerweg 60, 1445 AD Purmerend*
☎ **(029) 948 1666**
📠 (029) 948 1697
📧 purmerend@burggolf.nl
🖥 www.burggolf.nl

## Haarlemmermeersche Golf Club   (1986)
*Spieringweg 745, 2142 ED Cruquius*
☎ **(023) 558 9000**

📠 (023) 558 9009
📧 info@haarlemmermeerschegolfclub.nl
🖥 www.haarlemmermeerschegolfclub.nl

## Heemskerkse   (1998)
*Communicatieweg 18, 1967 PR Heemskerk*
☎ **(0251) 250088**
📠 (0251) 241627
📧 manager@heemskerksegolfclub.nl
🖊 Pien van Nass (Manager)
🖥 www.heemskerksegolfclub.nl

## Kennemer G&CC   (1910)
*Kennemerweg 78, 2042 XT Zandvoort*
☎ **+31 (0)23 571 2836/8456**
📠 +31 (0)23 571 9520
📧 info@kennemergolf.nl
🖊 Mr J Gelderman
🖥 www.kennemergolf.nl

## De Noordhollandse   (1982)
*Sluispolderweg 6, 1817 BM Alkmaar*
☎ **(072) 515 6807**
📠 (072) 520 9918
📧 secretariaat @denoordhollandsegolfclub.nl
🖊 Anita Von Schie (Club Mgr)
🖥 www.denoordhollandsegolfclub.nl

## Olympus   (1976)
*Abcouderstraatweg 46, 1105 AA Amsterdam Zuid-Oost*
☎ **(0294) 281241**
📠 (0294) 286347
🖥 www.olympusgolf.nl

## Spaarnwoude   (1977)
*Het Hoge Land 5, 1981 LT Velsen-Zuid*
☎ **(023) 538 2708 (club)**
📠 (023) 538 7274
🖥 www.gcspaarnwoude.nl

## Waterlandse   (1990)
*Buikslotermeerdijk 141, 1027 AC Amsterdam*
☎ **(020) 636 1040**
📠 (020) 634 3506
📧 info@golfbaanamsterdam.nl
🖥 www.golfbaanamsterdam.nl

## Zaanse   (1988)
*Zuiderweg 68, 1456 NH Wijdewormer*
☎ **(0299) 438199**
📠 (0299) 474416
📧 secretariaat@zaansegolfclub.nl
🖥 www.zaansegolfclub.com

## Breda & South West

## Brugse Vaart   (1993)
*Brugse Vaart 10, 4501 NE Oostburg*
☎ **(0117) 453410**
📠 (0117) 455511
📧 info@golfoostburg.com
🖥 www.golfoostburg.com

## Domburgsche   (1914)
*Schelpweg 26, 4357 BP Domburg*
☎ **(0118) 586106**
📠 (0118) 586109

📧 secretariaat @domburgschegolfclub.nl
🖥 www.domburgschegolfclub.nl

## Efteling Golf Park   (1995)
*Postbus 18, 5170 AA Kaatsheuvel, Holland*
☎ **+31 (0) 416 288 499**
📧 golfpark@efteling.com
🖥 www.efteling.nl

## Grevelingenhout   (1988)
*Oudendijk 3, 4311 NA Bruinisse*
☎ **(0111) 482650**
📠 (0111) 481566

## Oosterhoutse   (1985)
*Dukaatstraat 21, 4903 RN Oosterhout*
☎ **(0162) 458759**
📠 (0162) 433285
📧 info@ogcgolf.nl
🖥 www.ogcgolf.nl

## Princenbosch   (1991)
*Bavelseweg 153, 5126 PX Molenschot*
☎ **(0161) 431811**
📠 (0161) 434254
📧 golfclub@princenbosch.nl
🖊 Mr R C J Beenackers
🖥 www.princenbosch.nl

## Toxandria   (1928)
*Veenstraat 89, 5124 NC Molenschot*
☎ **(0161) 411200**
📠 (0161) 411715
📧 secretariaat@toxandria.nl
🖊 Mw E Nollen
🖥 www.toxandria.nl

## De Woeste Kop   (1986)
*Justaasweg 4, 4571 NB Axel*
☎ **(0115) 564467**
📧 dewoestekop@planet.nl
🖥 www.dewoestekop.nl

## Wouwse Plantage   (1981)
*Zoomvlietweg 66, 4624 RP Bergen op Zoom*
☎ **(0165) 377100**
📠 (0165) 377101
📧 secretariaat@golfwouwseplantage.nl
🖊 R W Van de Pol
🖥 www.golfwouwseplantage.nl

## East Central

## Breuninkhof
*Bussloselaan 6, 7383 RP Bussloo*
☎ **(0571) 261955**
📠 (0571) 262089
📧 secretariaat@debreuninkhof.nl
🖥 www.debreuninkhof.nl

## Edese   (1978)
*Papendallaan 22, 6816 VD Arnhem*
☎ **(026) 482 1985**
📧 info@edesegolf.nl
🖥 www.edesegolf.nl

## Hattemse G&CC   (1930)
*Veenwal 11, 8051 AS Hattem*
☎ **(038) 444 1909**

*For key to symbols and European dialling codes see page 725*

secretariaat@golfclub-hattem.nl
www.golfclub-hattem.nl

## Keppelse (1926)
Oude Zutphenseweg 15, 6997 CH Hoog-Keppel
☎ (0314) 301416
✉ dekeppelse@planet.nl
🖥 www.keppelse.com

## De Koepel (1983)
Postbox 88, 7640 AB Wierden
☎ (0546) 576150/574070
🖥 (0546) 578109
✉ info@golfclubdekoepel.nl
🖥 www.golfclubdekoepel.nl

## Lochemse Golf & Countryclub 'De Graafschap' (1987)
Sluitdijk 4, 7241 RR Lochem
☎ (0573) 254323
🖥 (0573) 258450
✉ info@lochemsegolfclub.nl
✍ P Grootoonk
🖥 www.lochemsegolfclub.nl

## Golfbaan Het Rijk van Nunspeet (1987)
Public
Plesmanlaan 30, 8072 PT Nunspeet
☎ (0341) 255255
🖥 (0341) 255285
✉ info@golfbaanhetrijkvannunspeet.nl
🖥 www.golfenophetrijk.nl

## Rosendaelsche (1895)
Apeldoornseweg 450, 6816 SN Arnhem
☎ +31 26 442 1438
✉ info@rosendaelsche.nl
✍ F J M König (Secretary)
🖥 www.rosendaelsche.nl

## Sallandsche De Hoek (1934)
Golfweg 2, 7431 PR Diepenveen
☎ (0570) 593269
🖥 (0570) 590102
✉ secretariaat@sallandsche.nl
✍ Mrs J Visschers
🖥 www.sallandsche.nl

## Golfbaan Het Rijk van Sybrook (1992)
Veendijk 100, 7525 PZ Enschede
☎ (0541) 530331
🖥 (0541) 531690
✉ info@golfbaanhetrijkvansybrook.nl
🖥 www.golfengohetrijk.nl

## Twentsche (1926)
Almelosestraat 17, 7495 TG Ambt Delden
☎ (074) 384 1167
🖥 (074) 384 1067
✉ info@twentschegolfclub.nl
✍ Ed Davids (Executive Sec)
🖥 www.twentschegolfclub.nl

## Veluwse (1957)
Nr 57, 7346 AC Hoog Soeren
☎ (055) 519 1275
🖥 (055) 519 1126
✉ secretariaat@veluwsegolfclub.nl
🖥 www.veluwsegolfclub.nl

## Welderen (1994)
POB 114, 6660AC Elst
☎ (0481) 376591
🖥 (0481) 377055
✉ golfclub@welderen.nl
✍ E Kleyngeld (Sec)
🖥 www.golfclubwelderen.nl

# Eindhoven & South East

## Best G&CC (1988)
Golflaan 1, 5683 RZ Best
☎ (0499) 391443
🖥 (0499) 393221
✉ vereniging@bestgolf.nl
🖥 www.bestgolf.nl

## BurgGolf Gendersteyn Veldhoven (1994)
Locht 140, 5504 RP Veldhoven
☎ (040) 253 4444
🖥 (040) 254 9747
✉ gendersteyn@burggolf.nl
🖥 www.burggolf.nl

## Golfclub BurgGolf Wijchen (1985)
Public
Weg Door de Berendonck 40, 6603 LP Wijchen
☎ (024) 642 0039
🖥 (024) 641 1254
✉ wijchen@burggolf.nl
🖥 www.burggolf.nl

## Crossmoor G&CC (1986)
Laurabosweg 8, 6006 VR Weert
☎ (0495) 518438
🖥 (0495) 518709
✉ info@crossmoor.nl
🖥 www.crossmoor.nl

## De Dommel (1928)
Zegenwerp 12, 5271 NC St Michielsgestel
☎ (073) 551 9168
🖥 (073) 551 9441
✉ info@gcdedommel.nl
🖥 www.gcdedommel.nl

## Eindhovensche Golf (1930)
Eindhovenseweg 300, 5553 VB Valkenswaard
☎ (040) 201 4816
🖥 (040) 207 6177
✉ info@eindhovenschegolf.nl
✍ Mrs W M Otten
🖥 www.eindhovenschegolf.nl

## Geijsteren G&CC (1974)
Het Spekt 2, 5862 AZ Geijsteren
☎ (0478) 531809/532592
🖥 (0478) 532963
✉ secretariaat@golfclubgeijsteren.nl
🖥 www.golfclubgeijsteren.nl

## Havelte (1986)
Kolonieweg 2, 7970 AA Havelte
☎ (0521) 342200
🖥 (0521) 343152
✉ info@golfclubhavelte.nl
🖥 www.golfclubhavelte.nl

## Haviksoord (1976)
Maarheezerweg Nrd 11, 5595 XG Leende (NB)
☎ (040) 206 1818
🖥 (040) 206 2761
✉ info@haviksoord.nl
✍ A W (Tony) Jackson (Manager)
🖥 www.haviksoord.nl

## BurgGolf Herkenbosch (1991)
Stationsweg 100, 6075 CD Herkenbosch
☎ (0475) 529529
🖥 (0475) 533580
✉ herkenbosch@burggolf.nl
✍ M Hermans (Manager)
🖥 www.burggolfherkenbosch.nl

## Het Rijk van Nijmegen (1985)
Postweg 17, 6561 KJ Groesbeek
☎ (024) 397 6644
🖥 (024) 397 6942
✉ info@golfbaanhetrijkvannijmegen.nl
🖥 www.golfenophetrijk.nl

## De Peelse Golf (1991)
Maasduinenweg 1, 5977 NP Evertsoord-Sevenum
☎ (077) 467 8030
🖥 (077) 467 8031
✉ info@depeelsegolf.nl
🖥 www.depeelsegolf.nl

## De Schoot (1973)
Schootsedijk 18, 5491 TD Sint Oedenrode
☎ (04134) 73011
🖥 (04134) 71358
✉ info@golfbaandeschoot.nl
🖥 www.golfbaandeschoot.nl

## Tongelreep G&CC (1984)
Charles Roelslaan 15, 5644 HX Eindhoven
☎ (040) 252 0962
🖥 (040) 293 2238
✉ gcc@golfdetongelreep.nl
✍ H C Smits (Sec)
🖥 www.golfdetongelreep.nl

## Welschap (1993)
Welschapsedijk 164, 5657 BB Eindhoven
☎ (040) 251 5797
🖥 (040) 252 9297
✉ secretariaat@golfclubwelschap.nl
🖥 www.golfclubwelschap.nl

# Limburg Province

## Brunssummerheide (1985)
Rimburgerweg 50, Brunssum
☎ (045) 527 0968
🖥 (045) 527 3939
✉ secr@golfbrunssummerheide.nl
🖥 www.golfbrunssummerheide.nl

## Hoenshuis G&CC (1987)
Hoensweg 17, 6367 GN Voerendaal
☎ +31 (0) 45 575 33 00
🖥 +31 (0) 45 575 09 00
✉ info@hoenshuis.nl
✍ Francis van Eeghem
🖥 www.hoenshuis.nl

## De Zuid Limburgse G&CC
(1956)
*Aubelsweg 1, 6281 NC Gulpen-Wittem,
(GPS: Landsrade 1, 6271 NZ Gulpen-
Wittem)*
☎ **(043) 455 1397/1254**
🖳 (043) 455 1576
✉ secretariaat@zlgolf.nl
🖥 www.zlgolf.nl

## North

## BurgGolf St Nicolaasga
(1990)
*Legemeersterweg 16-18, 8527
DS Legemeer*
☎ **(0513) 499466**
🖳 (0513) 499777
✉ stnicolaasga@burggolf.nl
🖥 www.burggolf.nl

## Gelpenberg    (1970)
*Gebbeveenweg 1, 7854 TD Aalden*
☎ **(0591) 371929**
🖳 (0591) 372422
✉ info@dgcdegelpenberg.nl
🖥 www.dgcdegelpenberg.nl

## Holthuizen    (1985)
*Oosteinde 7a, 9301 ZP Roden*
☎ **(050) 501 5103**
✉ golfclub.holthuizen@planet.nl
🖥 www.gc-holthuizen.nl

## Lauswolt G&CC    (1964)
*Van Harinxmaweg 8A, PO Box 36, 9244
ZN Beetsterzwaag*
☎ **(0512) 383590**
🖳 (0512) 383739
✉ algemeen@golfclublauswolt.nl
🖥 www.golfclublauswolt.nl

## Noord-Nederlandse G&CC
(1950)
*Pollselaan 5, 9756 CJ Glimmen*
☎ **(050) 406 2004**
🖳 (050) 406 1922
✉ secretariaat@nngcc.nl
♟ The Secretary
🖥 www.nngcc.nl

## De Semslanden    (1986)
*Nieuwe Dijk 1, 9514 BX Gasselternijveen*
☎ **(0599) 564661/565531**
🖳 (0599) 565594
✉ semslanden@planet.nl
🖥 www.golfclubdesemslanden.nl

## Rotterdam & The Hague

## Broekpolder    (1981)
*Watersportweg 100, 3138 HD Vlaardingen*
☎ **(010) 249 5566**
🖳 (010) 249 5579
✉ secretariaat@golfclubbroekpolder
.nl
🖥 www.golfclubbroekpolder.nl

## Golf & Country Club Capelle a/d IJssel    (1977)
*Gravenweg 311, 2905 LB Capelle a/d IJssel*
☎ **(010) 442 2485**
🖳 (010) 284 0606
✉ info@golfclubcapelle.nl
🖥 www.golfclubcapelle.nl

## Cromstrijen    (1989)
*Veerweg 26, 3281 LX Numansdorp*
☎ **(0186) 654455**
🖳 (0186) 654681
✉ info@golfclubcromstrijen.nl
🖥 www.golfclubcromstrijen.nl

## De Hooge Bergsche    (1989)
*Rottebandreef 40, 2661 JK Bergschenhoek*
☎ **(010) 522 0052/522 0703**
🖳 (08) 422 32305
✉ secretariaat@hoogebergsche.nl
🖥 www.hoogebergsche.nl

## Koninklijke Haagsche G&CC
(1893)
*Groot Haesebroekeseweg 22, 2243
EC Wassenaar*
☎ **(070) 517 9607**
🖳 (070) 514 0171
✉ secretariaat@khgcc.nl
♟ H P Wirth (Mgr)
🖥 www.khgcc.nl

## Kralingen
*Kralingseweg 200, 3062 CG Rotterdam*
☎ **(010) 452 2283**
✉ secretaris@gckralingen.nl
🖥 www.gckralingen.nl

## Leidschendamse Leeuwenbergh    (1988)
*Elzenlaan 31, 2495 AZ Den Haag*
☎ **(070) 395 4556**
🖳 (070) 399 8615
✉ secretariaat@leeuwenbergh.nl
🖥 www.leeuwenbergh.nl

## De Merwelanden    (1985)
**Public**
*Golfbaan Crayestein, Baanhoekweg 50,
3313 LP Dordrecht*
☎ **(078) 621 1221**
🖳 (078) 616 1036

## Noordwijkse Golf Club
(1915)
*Randweg 25, PO Box 70, 2200
AB Noordwijk*
☎ **(0252) 373761**
🖳 (0252) 370044
✉ info@noordwijksegolfclub.nl
♟ N H Smittenaar
🖥 www.noordwijksegolfclub.nl

## Oude Maas    (1975)
*(Rhoon Golfcenter), Veerweg 2a, 3161
EX Rhoon*
☎ **(010) 501 5135**
🖳 (010) 501 5604
✉ golfclouboudemaas@kebelfoon.nl
🖥 www.golfclouboudemaas.nl

## Rijswijkse    (1987)
*Delftweg 59, 2289 AL Rijswijk*
☎ **(070) 395 4864**
🖳 (070) 399 5040
✉ secretariaat@rijswijksegolf.nl
🖥 www.rijswijksegolf.nl

## Wassenaarse Golfclub Rozenstein    (1984)
*Dr Mansveltkade 15, 2242 TZ Wassenaar*
☎ **+31 (070) 511 7846**
✉ secretariaat@rozenstein.nl
♟ Miss IP Slikker (Office Mgr)
🖥 www.rozenstein.nl

## Westerpark Zoetermeer
(1985)
*Heuvelweg 3, 2716 DZ Zoetermeer, Ogoo-
Burg Golf*
☎ **(0900) 28744653**
🖳 (079) 3203132
✉ zoetermeer@burggolf.nl
♟ Mr V Slooten
🖥 www.burggolf.nl

## Zeegersloot    (1984)
*Kromme Aarweg 5, PO Box 190, 2400 AD
Alphen a/d Rijn*
☎ **(0172) 474567**
🖳 (0172) 494660
✉ secretariaat@zeegersloot.nl
🖥 www.zeegersloot.nl

## Utrecht & Hilversum

## Almeerderhout    (1986)
*Watersnipweg 19-21, 1341 AA Almere*
☎ **(036) 521 9160**
🖳 (036) 521 9131
✉ secretariaat@almeerderhout.nl
🖥 www.almeerderhout.nl

## Anderstein    (1986)
*Woudenbergseweg 13a, 3953
ME Maarsbergen*
☎ **(0343) 431330**
🖳 (0343) 432062
✉ info@golfclubanderstein.nl
🖥 www.golfclubanderstein.nl

## De Batouwe    (1990)
*Oost Kanaalweg 1, 4011 LA Zoelen*
☎ **(0344) 624370**
✉ secretariaat@debatouwe.nl
♟ Mrs MWJ van de Pasch
🖥 www.debatouwe.nl

## Flevoland    (1979)
*Parlaan 2A, 8241 BG Lelystad*
☎ **(0320) 230077**
🖳 (0320) 230932
✉ info@golfflevo.nl
🖥 www.golfflevo.nl

## De Haar    (1974)
*PO Box 104, Parkweg 5, 3450 AC Vleuten*
☎ **(030) 677 2860**
🖳 (030) 677 3903
✉ gcdehaar@xs4all.nl
🖥 www.gcdehaar.nl

## Hilversumsche Golf Club
(1910)
*Soestdijkerstraatweg 172, 1213*
*XJ Hilversum*
☎ **(035) 685 70 60 choose 2**
✉ clubmanager
@hilversumschegolfclub.nl
🖉 Mrs M G van den Hengel-Smink
🖥 www.hilversumschegolfclub.nl

## De Hoge Kleij (1985)
*Loes van Overeemlaan 16, 3832*
*RZ Leusden*
☎ **(033) 461 6944**
📠 (033) 465 2921
✉ secretariaat@hogekleij.nl
🖥 www.hogekleij.nl

## Nieuwegeinse (1985)
*Postbus 486, 3437 AL Nieuwegein*
☎ **(030) 604 2192**
📠 (030) 636 9410

## Utrechtse Golf Club 'De Pan'
(1894)
*Amersfoortseweg 1, 3735 LJ Bosch en Duin*
☎ **(030) 696 9120**
📠 (030) 696 3769
✉ secretariaat@ugcdepan.nl
🖉 Secretary
🖥 www.ugcdepan.nl

## Zeewolde (1984)
*Golflaan 1, 3896 LL Zeewolde*
☎ **(036) 522 2103**
📠 (036) 522 4100
✉ secretariaat@golfclub-zeewolde.nl
🖉 B Beekmans (Mgr)
🖥 www.golfclub-zeewolde.nl

---

# Norway

## Arendal og Omegn (1986)
*Nes Verk, 4900 Tvedestrand*
☎ **37 19 90 30**
📠 37 16 02 11
✉ post@arendalgk.no
🖥 www.arendalgk.no

## Baerum GK (1972)
*Hellerudveien 26, 1350 Lommedalen*
☎ **67 87 67 00**
📠 67 87 67 20
✉ bmgk@bmgk.no
🖉 Brede Kristoffersen
🖥 www.bmgk.no

## Bergen Golf Clubb (1937)
*Ervikveien 120, 5106 Øvre Ervik*
☎ **55 19 91 80**
📠 55 19 91 81
✉ info@bgk.no
🖥 www.bgk.no

## Borre (1991)
*Semb Hovedgaard, 3186 Horten*
☎ **416 27000**
✉ borregb@online.no

🖉 Thomas Pedersen
🖥 www.borregolf.no

## Borregaard (1927)
*PO Box 348, 1702 Sarpsborg*
☎ **69 12 15 00**
📠 69 15 74 11
✉ post@borregaardgk.no
🖥 www.borregaardgk.no

## Drøbak (1988)
*Belsjøveien 50, 1440 Drøbak*
☎ **+47 64 98 96 50**
✉ dgko@drobakgolf.no
🖥 www.drobakgolf.no

## Elverum (1980)
*PO Box 71, 2401 Elverum*
☎ **62 41 35 88**
📠 62 41 55 13
✉ post@elverumgolf.no
🖥 www.elverumgolf.no

## Grenland (1976)
*Luksefjellvn 578, 3721 Skien*
☎ **35 50 62 70**
📠 35 59 06 10
✉ post@grenlandgolf.no
🖥 www.grenlandgolf.no

## Groruddalen (1988)
*Postboks 37, Stovner, 0913 Oslo*
☎ **22 79 05 60**
📠 22 79 05 79
✉ post@grorudgk.no
🖥 www.grorudgk.no

## Hemsedal (1994)
*3560 Hemsedal*
☎ **32 06 23 77**
📠 32 06 00 84

## Kjekstad (1976)
*PO Box 201, 3440 Royken*
☎ **31 29 79 90**
📠 31 29 79 99

## Kristiansand (2003)
*PO Box 6090 Søm, 4691*
*Kristiansand*
☎ **38 14 85 60**
📠 38 04 34 15
✉ post@kristiansandgk.no
🖥 www.kristiansandgk.no

## Larvik (1989)
*Fritzøe Gård, 3267 Larvik*
☎ **33 140 140**
📠 33 14 01 49
✉ klubben@larvikgolf.no
🖉 Horten Ertsas
🖥 www.larvikgolf.no

## Narvik (1992)
*8523 Elvegard*
☎ **76 95 12 01**
📠 76 95 12 06
✉ post@narvikgolf.no
🖥 www.narvikgolf.no
✉ admin@nesgolf.no
🖥 www.nesgolfklubb.no

## Onsøy (1987)
*Golfveien, 1626 Manstad*
☎ **+47 69 33 91 50**
📠 +47 69 33 91 51

## Oppegård (1985)
*Kongeveien 198, 1415 Oppegård*
☎ **66 81 59 90**
📠 66 81 59 91
✉ leder@opgk.no
🖥 www.opgk.no

## Oslo (1924)
*Bogstad, 0757 Oslo*
☎ **22 51 05 60**
📠 22 51 05 61
✉ post@oslogk.no
🖉 Niels Vik
🖥 www.oslogk.no

## Oustoen CC (1965)
*PO Box 100, 1330 Fornebu*
☎ **67 83 23 80/22 56 33 54**
📠 67 53 95 44/22 59 91 83
✉ occ@occ.no
🖥 www.occ.no

## Sorknes (1990)
*PB 100, 2451 Rena*
☎ **45 20 86 00**
✉ post@sorknesgk.no
🖉 Mr Ken Baareng/Mr Lasse
Bendixen
🖥 www.sorknesgk.no

## Stavanger (1956)
*Longebakke 45, 4042 Hafrsfjord*
☎ **519 39100**
📠 519 39110
✉ steinar@sgk.no
🖉 Steinar Fløisvik
🖥 www.sgk.no

## Trondheim (1950)
*PO Box 169, 7401 Trondheim*
☎ **73 53 18 85**
📠 73 52 75 05
🖥 www.golfklubben.no

## Tyrifjord (1982)
*Sturoya, 3531 Krokleiva*
☎ **32 16 13 60**
📠 32 16 13 40
🖥 www.tyrifjord-golfklubb.no

## Vestfold (1958)
*PO Box 64, 3108 Vear*
☎ **33 36 25 00**
📠 33 36 25 01
✉ vgk@vestfoldgolfklubb.no
🖉 Knut Gran
🖥 www.vgk.no

---

# Poland

## Amber Baltic (1993)
*Baltycka Street 13, 72-514 Kolczewo*
☎ **(091) 32 65 110/120**
📠 (091) 32 65 333
✉ abgc@abgc.pl
🖥 www.abgc.pl

# Portugal

## Algarve

### Clube de Golfe de Vale do Lobo    (1968)
Vale Do Lobo, 8135-864 Vale do Lobo
☎ +351 289 353 465
🖶 +351 289 353 003
✉ golf@vdl.pt
👤 Hemani Estevão (Golf Mgr)
🖥 www.valedolobo.com

### Floresta Parque    (1987)
Vale do Poço, Budens, 8650 Vila do Bispo
☎ (282) 690 054
🖶 (282) 695 157
✉ alan.hodsongolf@vigiasa.com
👤 Alan Hodson

### Oceânico Pinhal    (1976)
Apartado 970, 8126-912
Vilamoura, Algarve
☎ 00 351 289 310 333
🖶 00 351 282 313 759
🖥 www.oceanicogolf.com

### Oceânico Academy Course    (2008)
Apartado 970, 8126-912
Vilamoura, Algarve
☎ 00 351 289 310 333
🖶 00 351 282 313 759
🖥 www.oceanicogolf.com

### Oceânico Faldo Course    (2008)
Apartado 970, 8126-912
Vilamoura, Algarve
☎ 00 351 289 310 333
🖶 00 351 282 313 759
🖥 www.oceanicogolf.com

### Oceânico Laguna    (1990)
Apartado 970, 8126-912
Vilamoura, Algarve
☎ 00 351 289 310 333
🖶 00 351 282 313 759
🖥 www.oceanicogolf.com

### Oceânico Millennium    (2000)
Apartado 970, 8126-912
Vilamoura, Algarve
☎ 00 351 289 310 000
🖶 00 351 282 313 759
🖥 www.oceanicogolf.com

### Oceânico O'Connor Jnr    (2008)
Apartado 970, 8126-912
Vilamoura, Algarve
☎ 00 351 289 310 333
🖶 00 351 282 313 759
🖥 www.oceanicogolf.com

### Oceânico Old Course    (1969)
Apartado 970, 8126-912
Vilamoura, Algarve
☎ 00 351 289 310 333
🖶 00 351 282 313 759
🖥 www.oceanicogolf.com

### Oceânico Victoria    (2004)
Apartado 970, 8126-912
Vilamoura, Algarve
☎ 00 351 289 310 333
🖶 00 351 282 313 759
👤 Romeu Mendes Gonçalves
🖥 www.oceanicogolf.com

### Palmares    (1975)
Apartado 74, Meia Praia, 8601 901 Lagos
☎ +351 282 790500
🖶 +351 282 290509
✉ golf@palmaresgolf.com
🖥 www.palmaresgolf.com

### Penina    (1966)
PO Box 146, Penina, 8501-952 Portimào
☎ (351) 282 420223
🖶 (351) 282 420252
✉ golf.penina@lemeridien.com
🖥 www.lemeridien.com/peninagolf

### Pestana    (1991)
Apartado 1011, 8400-908 Carvoeiro Lga
☎ (0282) 340900
🖶 (0282) 340901
✉ info@pestanagolf.com
🖥 www.pestanagolf.com

### Pestana Alto Golf    (1991)
Quinta do Alto do Poço, 8501 906 Alvor
☎ (00351) 282 460870
🖶 (00351) 282 460879
✉ info@pestanagolf.com
🖥 www.pestanagolf.com

### Pine Cliffs G&CC    (1991)
Praia da Falesia, PO Box 644, 8200-909 Albufeira
☎ (+351) 289 500100
🖶 (+351) 289 501950
✉ sheraton.algarve@starwoodhotels.com

### Pinheiros Altos    (1992)
Quinta do Lago, 8135 Almancil
☎ (0289) 359910
🖶 (0289) 394392
✉ golf@pinheirosaltos.pt
👤 Christophe Rindlisbacher
🖥 www.pinheirosaltos.pt

### Quinta do Lago    (1974)
Quinta Do Lago, 8135-024 Almancil
☎ (+351) 289 390 700
🖶 (+351) 289 394 013
✉ geral@quintadolagogolf.com
👤 Patrick Murphy
🖥 www.quintadolagogolf.com

### Salgados
Apartado 2362, Vale do Rabelho, 8200 917 Albufeira
☎ (0289) 583030
🖶 (0289) 591112

### San Lorenzo    (1888)
Quinta do Lago, 8135 Almancil
☎ +351 289 396 522
🖶 +351 289 396 908
✉ sanlorenzo@jjwhotels.com
👤 António Rosa Santos (Mgr)
🖥 www.sanlorenzogolfcourse.com

### Vale de Milho    (1990)
Apartado 1273, Praia do Carvoeiro, 8401-911 Carvoeiro Lga
☎ (282) 358502
🖶 (282) 358497
✉ reservas@valedemilhogolf.com
👤 M Stilwell (President)
🖥 www.valedemilhogolf.com

### Clube de Golfe de Vale do Lobo    (1968)
Vale Do Lobo, 8135-864 Vale do Lobo
☎ +351 289 353 465
🖶 +351 289 353 003
✉ golf@vdl.pt
👤 Hernani Estevão (Golf Mgr)
🖥 www.valedolobo.com

### Vila Sol Spa & Golf Resort    (1991)
Alto do Semino, Morgadinhos, Vilamoura, 8125-307-Quarteira
☎ (+351) 289 320 370
🖶 (+351) 289 316499
✉ golfreservation@vilasol.pt
🖥 www.vilasol.pt

## Azores

### Batalha Golf Course    (1996)
Rua do Bom Jesus, Aflitos, 9545-234 Fenais da Luz (Açores)
☎ +351 296 498 599/560
🖶 +351 296 498 612
✉ info@azoresgolfislands.com
👤 Pilar Melo Antunes
🖥 www.azoresgolfislands.com

### Furnas Golf Course    (1936)
Achada das Furnas, 9675 Furnas
☎ (+351) 296 498 559/560
🖶 (+351) 296 498 612
✉ info@azoresgolfislands.com
👤 Pilar Melo Antunes
🖥 www.azoresgolfislands.com

### Terceira Island    (1954)
Caixa Postal 15, 9760 909 Praia da Victória (Açores)
☎ (0295) 902444
🖶 (0295) 902445

## Lisbon & Central Portugal

### Aroeira    (1972)
Herdade da Aroeira, 2820-567 Charneca da Caparica
☎ +351 (212) 979 110/1
🖶 +351 (212) 971 238
✉ golf.reservas@aroeira.com
👤 Carlos Fonseca (Golf Dir.)
🖥 www.aroeira.com

### Belas Clube de Campo    (1998)
Alameda do Aqueduto, Escritórios Belas Clube de Campo, 2605-193 Belas
☎ (00351) 21 962 6640
🖶 (00351) 21 962 6641
✉ golfe@planbelas.pt

  Salvador Leite de Castro (Sec)
  www.belasclubedecampo.pt

## Estoril   (1936)
Avenida da República, 2765-273 Estoril
☎ (351) 21466 0367
🖷 (351) 21468 2796
📧 geral@golfestoril.com
🖥 www.palacioestorilhotel.com

## Estoril-Sol Golf Academy
(1976)
Quinta do Outeira, Linhó, 2710 Sintra
☎ (01) 923 2461
🖷 (01) 923 2461

## Lisbon Sports Club   (1922)
Casal da Carregueira, 2605-213 Belas
☎ (21) 431 0077
🖷 (21) 431 2482
📧 geral@lisbonclub.com
🖥 www.lisbonclub.com

## Marvão   (1998)
Quinta do Prado, São Salvador da
Aramenha, 7330-328 Marvão
☎ (245) 993 755
🖷 (245) 993 805
  R Wilson (Dir)

## Golf do Montado   (1992)
Urbanização do Golf Montando, Lte no.1 -
Algeruz, 2950-051 Palmela
☎ (265) 708150
🖷 (265) 708159
📧 geral@montadoresort.com
🖥 www.montadoresort.com

## Oitavos Dunes   (2001)
Quinta da Marinha, Casa 25, 2750-
004 Cascais
☎ 351 21 486 06 00
🖷 351 21 486 06 09
📧 info@oitavosdunes.pt
🖥 www.oitavosdunes.com

## Penha Longa   (1992)
Estrada da Lagoa Azul, Linhó, 2714-
511 Sintra
☎ (021) 924 9011
🖷 (021) 924 9024
📧 reservas.golf@penhalonga.com
🖥 www.penhalonga.com

## Quinta da Beloura   (1994)
Estrada de Albarraque, 2710 692 Sintra
☎ (021) 910 6350
🖷 (021) 910 6359
📧 beloura.golfe@pestana.com
🖥 www.pestanagolf.com

## Quinta do Perú Golf &
Country Club   (1994)
Alameda da Serra 2, 2975-666 Quinta
do Conde
☎ (021) 213 4320
🖷 (021) 213 4321
📧 pedro@golfquintadoperu.com
  Pedro De Mello Breyner (Club
Mgr)
🖥 www.golfquintadoperu.com

## Tróia Golf Championship
Course   (1980)
7570-789 Carvalhal GDL
☎ (+351) 265 499 400
🖷 (+351) 265 499 469
📧 info@troiaresort.pt
🖥 www.troiagolf.com

## Vimeiro
Praia do Porto Novo, Vimeiro, 2560
Torres Vedras
☎ (061) 984157
🖷 (061) 984621

## Madeira

## Madeira   (1991)
Sto Antonio da Serra, 9200
Machico, Madeira
☎ (091) 552345/552356
🖷 (091) 552367

## Palheiro   (1993)
Rua do Balancal No.29, 9060-414
Funchal, Madeira
☎ (00351) 291 790 120
🖷 (00351) 291 792 456
📧 reservations.golf@palheiroestate
.com
🖥 www.palheiroestate.com

## North

## Amarante   (1997)
Quinta da Deveza, Fregim, 4600-
593 Amarante
☎ +351 255 44 60 60
🖷 +351 255 44 62 02
📧 sgagolfeamarante@oninet.pt
🖥 www.amarantegolfclube.com

## Golden Eagle   (1994)
E.N. 1, Km 63/64, Asseicera, 2040-481
Rio Maior
☎ +351 243 940040
🖷 +351 243 940049
📧 reservations@goldeneagle.pt
  David Ashington
🖥 www.goldeneagle.pt

## Miramar   (1932)
Av Sacadura Cabral, Miramar, 4405-013
Arcozelo V.N.Gaia
☎ (022) 762 2067
🖷 (022) 762 7859
📧 cgm@cgm.pt
  President Alvaro Teles De Meneses
🖥 www.cgm.pt

## Montebelo
Farminhão, 3510 Viseu
☎ (032) 856464
🖷 (032) 856401

## Oporto   (1890)
Sisto-Paramos, 4500 Espinho
☎ (022) 734 2008
🖷 (022) 734 6895
📧 ogc@oportogolfclub.com
🖥 www.oportogolfclub.com

## Ponte de Lima
Quinta de Pias, Fornelos, 4490 Ponte
de Lima
☎ (058) 43414
🖷 (058) 743424

## Praia d'el Rey G&CC   (1997)
Vale de Janelas, Apartado 2, 2510 Obidos
☎ (+351) 262 905005
🖷 (+351) 262 905009
📧 golf@praia-del-rey.com
🖥 www.praia-del-rey.com

## Golfe Quinta da Barca   (1997)
Barca do Lago, 4740-476 Esposende
☎ (+351) 2539 66723
🖷 (+351) 2539 969068
📧 info@golfebarca.com
🖥 www.golfebarca.com

## Vidago Palace Golf Course
(1936)
Parque de Vidago, Apartado 16, 5425-
307 Vidago
☎ 00351 276 990 980
🖷 00351 276 990 912
📧 golf@vidagopalace.com
  Santiago Villar (Asst Mgr)
🖥 www.vidagopalace.com

# Slovenia

## Bled G&CC   (1937)
Public
Kidriceva 10 c, 4260 Bled
☎ +386 (0)4 537 77711
🖷 +386 (0)4 537 77722
📧 info@golf.bled.si
🖥 www.golf.bled.si

## Castle Mokrice   (1992)
Terme Catez, Topliska Cesta 35,
8250 Brezice
☎ (00386) 7 457 4260
🖷 (00386) 7 495 7007
📧 golf@terme-catez.si
  Aleš Stopar
🖥 www.terme-catez.si

## Lipica   (1989)
Lipica 5, 66210 Sezana
☎ +386 (0)5 734 6373
🖷 +386 (0)5 739 1725
📧 golf@lipica.org
🖥 www.lipica.org

# Spain

## Alicante & Murcia

## Alicante   (1998)
Av. Locutor Vicente Hipolito 37, Playa San
Juan, 03540 Alicante
☎ (96) 515 37 94/515 20 43

☎ (96) 516 37 07
✉ clubgolf@alicantegolf.com
✍ Angel LLopes Molina (Mgr)
🖥 www.alicantegolf.org

**Altorreal**   (1994)
Urb Altorreal, 30500 Molina de
Segura (Murcia)
☎ **(968) 64 81 44**
🖥 (986) 64 82 48

**Bonalba**   (1993)
Partida de Bonalba, 03110
Mutxamiel (Alicante)
☎ **(96) 595 5955**
🖥 (96) 595 5985
✉ golfbonalba@golfbonalba.com
🖥 www.golfbonalba.com

**Don Cayo**   (1974)
Apartado 341, 03599 Altea La
Vieja (Alicante)
☎ **(96) 584 80 46**
🖥 (96) 584 65 19
✉ info@golfdoncayo.com
✍ Alexis Garca-Valdes (Mgr)
🖥 www.golfdoncayo.com

**Ifach**   (1974)
Crta Moraira-Calpe Km 3, Apdo 28, 03720
Benisa (Alicante)
☎ **(96) 649 71 14**
🖥 (96) 649 9908
✉ golfifach@gmail.com
✍ Gonzalo Gonzalez
⊕ 9 holes, 3 Par 4's - Par 60

**Jávea**   (1981)
Apartado 148, 03730 Jávea, (Alicante)
☎ **(96) 579 25 84**
🖥 (96) 646 05 54

**La Manga**   (1971)
Los Belones, 30385 Cartagena (Murcia)
☎ **(968) 175000 ext 1360**
🖥 (968) 175058
✉ golf@lamangaclub.es
🖥 www.lamangaclub.com

**La Marquesa**   (1989)
Ciudad Quesada II, 03170
Rojales, (Alicante)
☎ **(+34) 96 671 42 58**
🖥 (+34) 96 671 42 67
✉ info@lamarquesagolf.es
🖥 www.lamarquesagolf.es

**Las Ramblas**   (1991)
Crta Alicante-Cartagena Km48, 03189 Urb
Villamartin, Orihuela (Alicante)
☎ **(96) 677 4728**
🖥 (96) 677 4733
✉ golflasramblas@grupoquara.com
🖥 www.grupoquara.com

**Real Campoamor**   (1989)
Crta Cartagena-Alicante Km48, Apdo 17,
03189 Orihuela-Costa (Alicante)
☎ **(96) 532 13 66**
🖥 (96) 532 05 06
✉ golf@lomasdecampoamor.es
✍ Elena Gonzalez
🖥 www.lomasdecampoamor.com

**La Sella Golf**   (1991)
Ctra La Xara-Jesús Pobre, 03749 Jesús
Pobre (Alicante)
☎ **(96) 645 42 52/645 41 10**
🖥 (96) 645 42 01
✉ info@lasellagolf.com
🖥 www.lasellagolfresort.com

**Villamartin**   (1972)
Avenida Las Brisas No 8, Urb. Villamartin,
03189 Orihuela-Costa
☎ **(96) 676 51 70/(96) 676 51 04**
🖥 (96) 676 51 70
✉ golfvillamartin@grupoquara.com
✍ Juan Miguel Buendia (Manager)
🖥 www.grupoquara.com

## Almería

**Almerimar**   (1976)
Urb Almerimar, 04700 El Ejido (Almería)
☎ **(950) 48 02 34**
🖥 (950) 49 72 33

**El Cortijo Grande Golf Resort**
(1976)
Apdo 2, Cortijo Grande, 04639
Turre (Almería)
☎ **(950) 479176**
✉ info@cortijogrande.net
🖥 www.cortijogrande.net

**Playa Serena**   (1979)
Paseo del golf No.8, 04740 Roquetas de
Mar (Almería)
☎ **+34 (950) 33 30 55**
🖥 +34 (950) 33 30 55
✉ info@golfplayaserena.com
🖥 www.golfplayaserena.com

## Badajoz & West

**Norba**   (1988)
Apdo 880, 10080 Cáceres
☎ **(927) 23 14 41**
🖥 (927) 23 14 80

**Salamanca**   (1988)
Monte de Zarapicos, 37170
Zarapicos (Salamanca)
☎ **(923) 32 91 00**
🖥 (923) 32 91 05
✉ club@salamancagolf.com
🖥 www.salamancagolf.com

## Balearic Islands

**Canyamel**
Urb Canyamel, Crta de Cuevas, 07580
Capdepera, (Mallorca)
☎ **(971) 56 44 57**
🖥 (971) 56 53 80

**Capdepera**   (1989)
Apdo 6, 07580 Capdepera, Mallorca
☎ **(971) 56 58 75/56 58 57**
🖥 (971) 56 58 74

**Ibiza**   (1990)
Apdo 1270, 07840 Santa Eulalia, (Ibiza)
☎ **(971) 19 61 18**
🖥 (971) 19 60 51

**Mallorca Marriott Golf Son
Antem**   (1993)
Carretera Ma 19, Salida 20-07620
Llucmajor, Mallorca
☎ **(+34) 971 12 92 00**
🖥 (+34) 971 12 92 01
✉ mallorca.golfclub@vacationclub
.com
✍ Yago Gonzalez (Director)
🖥 www.sonantemgolf.com

**Pollensa**   (1986)
Ctra Palma-Pollensa Km 49.3, 07460
Pollensa, (Mallorca)
☎ **(0034) 971 533216**
🖥 (0034) 971 533265
✉ rec@golfpollensa.com
✍ Cesar Riera
🖥 www.golfpollensa.com

**Poniente**   (1978)
Costa de Calvia, 07181 Calvia (Mallorca)
☎ **(971) 13 01 48**
🖥 (971) 13 01 76
✉ golf@ponientegolf.com
✍ Mr Jose Jimenez (Mgr)
🖥 www.ponientegolf.com

**Pula Golf**   (1995)
Ctra. Son Servera-Capdepera, E-07550
Son Servera-Mallorca
☎ **(971) 81 70 34**
🖥 (971) 81 70 35
✉ reservas@pulagolf.com
✍ Rahel Wanke
🖥 www.pulagolf.com

**Real Golf Bendinat**   (1986)
C. Campoamor, 07181 Calviá, (Mallorca)
☎ **(971) 40 52 00**
🖥 (971) 70 07 86
✉ info@realgolfbendinat.com
✍ Alison Bradshaw
🖥 www.realgolfbendinat.com

**Santa Ponsa**   (1976)
Santa Ponsa, 07180 Calvia (Mallorca)
☎ **(971) 69 02 11**
🖥 (971) 69 33 64
✉ hotelgolfsponsa@infonegocio.com
🖥 www.hotelgolfsantaponsa.com

**Golf Son Parc Menorca**   (1977)
Urb. Son Parc s/n, ES Mercadal-
Menorca, Baleares
☎ **+34 (971)-188875/359059**
🖥 +34 (971)-359591
✉ info@menorcagolf.es
✍ Paola Ferroni (Local Mgr)
🖥 www.golfsonparc.com

**Son Servera**   (1967)
Costa de Los Pinos, 07759 Son
Servera, (Mallorca)
☎ **(971) 84 00 96**
🖥 (971) 84 01 60

**Son Vida** (1964)
*Urb Son Vida, 07013 Palma (Mallorca)*
☎ **(971) 79 12 10**
🖶 (971) 79 11 27

**Vall d'Or Golf** (1985)
*Apdo 23, 07660 Cala D'Or, (Mallorca)*
☎ **(971) 83 70 68/83 70 01**
🖶 (971) 83 72 99
✉ valldorgolf@valldorgolf.com
✍ Julia Jana Litten (Sec)/Israel
   Rodrigues Rojas (Mgr)
🖥 www.valldorgolf.com

## Barcelona & Cataluña

**Aro-Mas Nou** (1990)
*Apdo 429, 17250 Playa de Aro*
☎ **(972) 82 69 00**
🖶 (972) 82 69 06

**Bonmont Terres Noves** (1990)
*Urb Terres Noves, 43300
Montroig (Tarragona)*
☎ **(977) 81 81 40**
🖶 (977) 81 81 46
🖥 www.bonmont.com

**Caldes Internacional** (1992)
*Apdo 200, 08140 Caldes de
Montbui (Barcelona)*
☎ **(93) 865 38 28**

**Club de Golf Costa Dorada
Tarragona** (1983)
*Apartado 600, 43080 Tarragona*
☎ **(977) 65 3361/(977) 65 3605**
🖶 (977) 65 3028
✉ club@golfcostadoradatarragona
   .com
🖥 www.golfcostadoradatarragona
   .com

**Costa Brava** (1962)
*La Masia, 17246 Sta Cristina d'Aro
(Girona), Catalunya*
☎ **(972) 83 71 50**
🖶 (972) 83 72 72
✉ info@golfcostabrava.com
✍ Ma Victoria Figueras Garcia (Gen
   Mgr)
⊕ 27 Holes
🖥 www.golfcostabrava.com

**Empordà Golf Resort** (1990)
*Crta Torroella de Montgri, 17257
Gualta (Gerona)*
☎ **(972) 76 04 50/76 01 36**
🖶 (972) 75 71 00
✉ info@empordagolf.com
✍ Anna Gurana
🖥 www.empordagolf.com

**Fontanals de Cerdanya** (1994)
*Fontanals de Cerdanya, 17538
Soriguerola (Girona)*
☎ **(972) 14 43 74**

**Golf Girona** (1992)
*Urbanització Golf Girona s/n, 17481 Sant
Julia de Ramis, (Girona)*
☎ **(972) 17 16 41**

🖶 (972) 17 16 82
✉ golfgirona@golfgirona.com
🖥 www.golfgirona.com

**Llavaneras** (1945)
*Cami del Golf 45-51, 08392 San Andreu de
Llavaneras, (Barcelona)*
☎ **(93) 792 60 50**
🖶 (93) 795 25 58
✉ lucas.bueno@golfllavaneras.com
✍ Mr Lucas Bueno (Gen Mgr)
🖥 www.golfllavaneras.com

**Masia Bach** (1990)
*Ctra Martorell-Capellades, 08635 Sant
Esteve Sesrovires*
☎ **(93) 772 8800**
🖶 (93) 772 8810

**Osona Montanya** (1988)
*Masia L'Estanyol, 08553 El
Brull (Barcelona)*
☎ **(93) 884 01 70**
🖶 (93) 884 04 07

**Peralada Golf** (1993)
*La Garriga, 17491 Peralada, Girona*
☎ **+34 972 538 287**
🖶 +34 972 538 236
✉ casa.club@golfperalada.com
✍ Nuria Bech Diumenge (Mgr)
🖥 www.golfperalada.com

**Golf Platja de Pals** (1966)
Pay and play
*Ctra. Golf, Num. 64, Pals - Girona 17256*
☎ **(+34) 972 66 77 39**
🖶 (+34) 972 63 67 99
✉ recep@golfplatjadepals.com
✍ Alexandra Reig (Mgr)
🖥 www.golfplatjadepals.com

**Reus Aigüesverds** (1989)
*Crta de Cambrils, Mas Guardià, E-
43206 Reus-Tarragona*
☎ **(977) 75 27 25**
🖶 (977) 12 03 91
✉ info@golfreusaiguesverds.com
✍ J Mourges (Mgr)
🖥 www.golfreusaiguesverds.com

**Terramar** (1922)
*Apdo 6, 08870 Sitges*
☎ **(93) 894 05 80/894 20 43**
🖶 (93) 894 70 51
✉ reservas@golfterramar.com
🖥 www.golfterramar.com

**Torremirona** (1994)
*Ctra N-260 Km 46, 17744
Navata (Girona)*
☎ **(+34) 972 55 37 37**
🖶 (+34) 972 55 37 16
✉ golf@torremirona.com
🖥 www.torremirona.com

## Burgos & North

**Castillo de Gorraiz** (1993)
*Urb Castillo de Gorraiz, 31620 Valle de
Egues (Navarra)*
☎ **(948) 33 70 73**
🖶 (948) 33 73 15

✉ administracion@golfgorraiz.com
🖥 www.golfgorraiz.com

**Izki Golf** (1992)
*C/Arriba, S/N, 01119 Urturi (Alava)*
☎ **(945) 378262**
🖶 (945) 378266
✉ izkigolf@izkigolf.com
✍ (945) 378262
🖥 www.izkigolf.com

**Larrabea** (1989)
*Crta de Landa, 01170 Legutiano, (Alava)*
☎ **(945) 46 58 44/46 58 41**
🖶 (945) 46 57 25

**Lerma** (1991)
*Ctra Madrid-Burgos Km195, 09340
Lerma (Burgos)*
☎ **(947) 17 12 14/17 12 16**
🖶 (947) 17 12 16
✉ calidad@golflerma.com
🖥 www.golflerma.com

**La Llorea** (1994)
*Crta Nacional 632, Km 62,
33394 Gijòn/Xixòn*
☎ **(985) 10 30**
🖶 (985) 36 47 26
✉ administraciongolf.pdm@gijon.es
🖥 www.golfallorea.com

**Real Golf Castiello** (1958)
*Apdo Correos 161, 33200 Gijón*
☎ **(985) 36 63 13**
🖶 (985) 13 18 00
✉ administracion@castiello.com
🖥 www.castiello.com

**Real Golf Pedreña** (1928)
*Apartado 233, Santander*
☎ **(942) 50 00 01/50 02 66**
🖶 (942) 50 04 21

**Real San Sebastián** (1910)
*Chalet Borda Gain Jaizubia, 20280,
Hondarribia, (Guipúzcoa)*
☎ **0034 (943) 61 68 45**
🖶 0034 (943) 61 14 91
✉ rgcss@golfsansebastian.com
✍ Bertol Oria
🖥 www.golfsansebastian.com

**Real Golf Club De Zarauz**
(1916)
*Lauaxeta, 7, Zarauz, (Guipúzcoa)*
☎ **(943) 83 01 45**
🖶 (943) 13 15 68
✉ info@golfzarauz.com
✍ Beatriz Aseguinolaza
🖥 www.golfzarauz.com

**Ulzama** (1965)
*31779 Guerendiain (Navarra)*
☎ **(948) 30 51 62**
🖶 (948) 30 54 71

## Canary Islands

**Amarilla** (1988)
*Urb Amarilla Golf, San Miguel de Abona,
38630 Santa Cruz de Tenerife*
☎ **(922) 73 03 19**
🖶 (922) 73 00 85

---

*For key to symbols and European dialling codes see page 725*

## Costa Teguise   (1978)
*Avenida del Golf s/n, 35508 Costa Teguise*
- ☎ **(928) 59 05 12**
- 🖥 (928) 59 23 37
- ✉ info@lanzarote-golf.as
- 🖦 www.lanzarote-golf.com

## Maspalomas   (1968)
*Av de Neckerman, Maspalomas, 35100
Gran Canaria*
- ☎ **(928) 76 25 81/76 73 43**
- 🖥 (928) 76 82 45
- 🖦 www.maspalomasgolf.net

## Real Club de Golf de Tenerife
(1932)
*Campo de Golf No.1 38350,
Tacoronte, Tenerife*
- ☎ **(922) 63 66 07**
- 🖥 (922) 63 64 80
- ✉ info@rcgt.es
- ✍ Vidal Carralero Ceva (Mgr)
- 🖦 www.rcgt.es

## Real Golf Las Palmas   (1891)
*PO Box 93, 35380 Santa Brigida,
Gran Canaria*
- ☎ **(928) 35 10 50/35 01 04**
- 🖥 (928) 35 01 10
- ✉ rcglp@realclubdegolfdelaspalmas
  .com
- 🖦 www.realclubdegolfdelaspalmas
  .com

## Golf del Sur   (1987)
*San Miguel de Abona, 38620
Tenerife (Canarias)*
- ☎ **(922) 73 81 70**
- 🖥 (922) 78 82 72
- ✉ golfdelsur@golfdelsur.es
- 🖦 www.golfdelsur.es

## Córdoba

## Club de Campo de Córdoba
(1976)
*Apartado 436, 14080 Córdoba*
- ☎ **(957) 35 02 08**
- ✉ administracion@golfcordoba.com
- 🖦 www.golfcordoba.com

## Pozoblanco   (1984)
*Ctra. La Canaleja Km. 3,, 14400
Pozoblanco, Córdoba*
- ☎ **(957) 33 91 71**
- 🖥 (957) 34 48 46
- ✉ pozoblancogolf@gmail.com
- ✍ Hazel Madrigal López (PR)

## Galicia

## Aero Club de Santiago   (1976)
*General Pardiñas 34, Santiago de
Compostela (La Coruña)*
- ☎ **(981) 954 910**
- 🖥 (981) 590 636
- ✉ reception@aerosantiago.es
- 🖦 www.aerosantiago.es

## Aero Club de Vigo   (1951)
*Reconquista 7, 36201 Vigo*
- ☎ **(986) 48 66 45/48 75 09**

## La Toja   (1970)
*Isla de La Toja, El Grove, Pontevedra*
- ☎ **(986) 73 01 58/73 08 18**
- 🖥 (986) 73 31 22

## Ria de Vigo   (1993)
*San Lorenzo-Domaio, 36957
Moaña (Pontevedra)*
- ☎ **(986) 32 70 51**
- 🖥 (986) 32 70 53
- ✉ info@riadevigogolf.com
- ✍ Cholmin Kwon (Gen Mgr)
- 🖦 www.riadevigogolf.com

## Granada

## Granada
*Avda de los Corsarios, 18110 Las
Gabias (Granada)*
- ☎ **(958) 58 44 36**

## Madrid Region

## Barberán   (1967)
*Apartado 150.239, Cuatro Vientos,
28080 Madrid*
- ☎ **(91) 509 00 59/509 11 40**
- 🖥 (91) 706 2174

## La Dehesa   (1991)
*Avda. de la Universidad, 10, 28691
Villanueva La Cañada*
- ☎ **(91) 815 70 22**
- 🖥 (91) 815 54 68
- ✉ secretaria@golfladehesa.es
- 🖦 www.golfladehesa.es

## Herreria   (1966)
*PO Box 28200, San Lorenzo del
Escorial, (Madrid)*
- ☎ **(91) 890 51 11**
- 🖥 (91) 890 26 13
- ✉ infosugerencias@golflaherreria.es
- 🖦 www.golflaherreria.com

## Jarama R.A.C.E.   (1967)
*Urb Ciudalcampo, 28707 San Sebastian de
los Reyes, (Madrid)*
- ☎ **(91) 657 00 11**
- 🖥 (91) 657 04 62
- ✉ golf@race.es
- 🖦 www.race.es

## Lomas-Bosque   (1973)
*Urb El Bosque, 28670 Villaviciosa de
Odón, (Madrid)*
- ☎ **(91) 616 75 00**
- 🖥 (91) 616 73 93

## La Moraleja   (1976)
*La Moraleja, Alcobendas (Madrid)*
- ☎ **(91) 650 07 00**
- 🖥 (91) 650 43 31
- ✉ info@golflamoraleja.com
- 🖦 www.golflamoraleja.com

## Puerta de Hierro   (1895)
*Avda de Miraflores, Ciudad Puerta de
Hierro, 28035 Madrid*
- ☎ **(91) 316 1745**
- 🖥 (91) 373 8111
- ✉ lmalonso@rcphierro.com

## Los Retamares   (1991)
*Crta Algete-Alalpardo Km 2300, 28130
Valdeolmos (Madrid)*
- ☎ **(91) 620 25 40**

## Somosaguas   (1971)
*Avda de la Cabaña, 28223 Pozuelo de
Alarcón, (Madrid)*
- ☎ **(91) 352 16 47**
- 🖥 (91) 352 00 30

## Valdeláguila   (1975)
*Apdo 9, Alcalá de Henares, (Madrid)*
- ☎ **(91) 885 96 59**
- 🖥 (91) 885 96 59

## Villa de Madrid CC   (1932)
*Crta Castilla, 28040 Madrid*
- ☎ **(0034) 91 550 2010**
- 🖥 (0034) 91 550 2023
- ✉ deportes@clubvillademadrid.com
- 🖦 www.clubvillademadrid.com

## Malaga Region

## Alhaurín   (1994)
*Crta A-387 Km 3.4, Alhaurín el Grande-
Mijas*
- ☎ **+34 95 25 95 970**
- 🖥 +34 95 25 94 586
- ✉ reservasgolf@alhauringolf.com
- 🖦 www.alhauringolf.com

## Añoreta   (1989)
*Avenida del Golf, 29730 Rincón de la
Victoria, (Málaga)*
- ☎ **(952) 40 40 00**
- 🖥 (952) 40 40 50

## La Cala Resort   (1991)
*La Cala de Mijas, 29649 Mijas-
Costa (Málaga)*
- ☎ **(952) 66 90 00**
- 🖥 (952) 66 90 34
- ✉ golf@lacala.com
- 🖦 www.lacala.com

## Guadalhorce   (1988)
*Crtra de Cártama Km7, Apartado 48,
29590 Campanillas (Málaga)*
- ☎ **(952) 17 93 78**
- 🖥 (952) 17 93 72

## Lauro   (1992)
*Los Caracolillos, 29130 Alhaurín de la
Torre, (Málaga)*
- ☎ **(95) 241 2767/296 3091**
- 🖥 (95) 241 4757
- ✉ info@laurogolf.com
- 🖦 www.laurogolf.com

## Málaga Club de Campo   (1925)
*Parador de Golf, Apdo 324, 29080 Málaga*
- ☎ **(952) 38 12 55**
- 🖥 (952) 38 21 41

**Mijas Golf International**  (1976)
*Apartado 145, Fuengirola, Málaga*
☎ **(952) 47 68 43**
🖷 (952) 46 79 43
📧 info@mijasgolf.org
🖹 www.mijasgolf.org

**Miraflores**  (1989)
*Urb Riviera del Sol, 29647 Mijas-Costa*
☎ **+34 (952) 93 19 60**
🖷 +34 (952) 93 19 42

**Torrequebrada**  (1976)
**Public**
*Apdo 120, Crta de Cadiz Km 220,
29630 Benalmadena*
☎ **(95) 244 27 42**
🖷 (95) 256 11 21
📧 bookings@golftorrequebrada.com
🖹 www.golftorrequebrada.com

## Marbella & Estepona

**Alcaidesa Links**  (1992)
*CN-340 Km124.6, 11315 La Linea (Cádiz)*
☎ **(956) 79 10 40**
🖷 (956) 79 10 41

**Aloha**  (1975)
*Nueva Andalucía, 29660 Marbella*
☎ **(952) 81 37 50/90 70 85/86**
🖷 (952) 81 23 89
📧 office@clubdegolfaloha.com
🖹 www.clubdegolfaloha.com

**Los Arqueros Golf & Country
Club SA**  (1991)
*Crta de Ronda Km44.5, 29679
Benahavis (Málaga)*
☎ **+34 952 784600**
🖷 +34 952 786707
📧 admin.losarquerosgolf
@es.taylorwimpey.com
✍ Lidia Martin
🖹 www.losarquerosgolf.com

**Atalaya G&CC**  (1968)
*Crta Benahavis 7, 29688 Málaga*
☎ **(952) 88 28 12**
🖷 (952) 88 78 97

**Las Brisas**  (1968)
*Apdo 147, 29660 Nueva
Andalucía, (Málaga)*
☎ **(952) 81 08 75/81 30 21**
🖷 (952) 81 55 18
📧 info@realclubdegolflasbrisas.com
🖹 www.realclubdegolflasbrisas.com

**La Cañada**  (1982)
*Ctra Guadiaro Km 1, 11311
Guadiaro (Cádiz)*
☎ **(956) 79 41 00**
🖷 (956) 79 42 41

**Estepona**  (1989)
*Arroyo Vaquero, Apartado 532, 29680
Estepona (Málaga)*
☎ **(+34) 95 293 7605**
🖷 (+34) 95 293 7600
📧 information@esteponagolf.com
🖹 www.esteponagolf.com

**Guadalmina**  (1959)
*Guadalmina Alta, San Pedro de Alcántara,
29678 Marbella (Málaga)*
☎ **(952) 88 65 22**
🖷 (952) 88 34 83

**Marbella**  (1994)
*CN 340 Km 188, 29600
Marbella (Málaga)*
☎ **(952) 83 05 00**

**Los Naranjos**  (1977)
*Apdo 64, 29660 Nueva
Andalucía, Marbella*
☎ **(952) 81 52 06/81 24 28**
🖷 (952) 81 14 28

**El Paraiso**  (1973)
*Ctra Cádiz-Màlaga Km 167, 29680
Estepona (Málaga)*
☎ **(95) 288 38 35**
🖷 (95) 288 58 27
📧 info@elparaisogolfclub.com
🖹 www.elparaisogolfclub.com

**La Quinta G&CC**  (1989)
*Urb. La Quinta, Nueva Andalucía
29660, (Marbella-Málaga)*
☎ **+34 (952) 76 23 90**
🖷 +34 (952) 76 23 99
📧 reservas@laquintagolf.com
🖹 www.laquintagolf.com

**Santa María G&CC**  (1991)
*Urb. Elviria, Crta N340 Km 192, 29604
Marbella (Málaga)*
☎ **(952) 83 10 36**
🖷 (952) 83 47 97
📧 caddymaster@santamariagolfclub
.com
✍ Rosa Olmo
🖹 www.santamariagolfclub.com

**Sotogrande**  (1964)
*Paseo del Parque, s/n, 11310
Sotogrande, Cádiz*
☎ **+34 956 785014**
🖷 +34 956 795029
📧 info@golfsotogrande.com
🖹 www.golfsotogrande.com

**The San Roque Club**  (1990)
*CN 340 Km 127, San Roque, 11360 Cádiz*
☎ **(956) 61 30 30**
🖷 (956) 61 30 12
📧 info@sanroqueclub.com
✍ Guillermo Navarro
🖹 www.sanroqueclub.com

**Valderrama**  (1985)
*Avenida de los Cortjos S/N, 11310
Sotogrande (Cadiz)*
☎ **(956) 79 12 00**
🖷 (956) 79 60 28
📧 greenfees@valderrama.com
✍ Derek Brown
🖹 www.valderrama.com

**La Zagaleta**  (1994)
*Crta San Pedro-Ronda Km 9,
29679 Benahavis*
☎ **(95) 285 54 53**

## Seville & Gulf of Cádiz

**Isla Canela**  (1993)
*Crta de la Playa, 21400 Ayamonte (Huelva)*
☎ **(959) 47 72 63**
🖷 (959) 47 72 71
📧 golf@islacanela.es
🖹 www.islacanela.es

**Islantilla**  (1993)
*Paseo Barranco Del Moro, S/N, 21410 Isla
Cristina (Huelva)*
☎ **(959) 48 60 39/48 60 49**
🖷 (959) 48 61 04
📧 reservasgolf@islantillagolfresort.com
🖹 www.istantillagolfresort.com

**Montecastillo**  (1992)
*Carretera de Arcos, 11406 Jérez*
☎ **(956) 15 12 00**
🖷 (956) 15 12 09
📧 commercial@montecastillo.com
🖹 www.montecastillo.com

**Montenmedio G&CC**
(1996)
*N-340 KM 42,5, 11150 Vejer-
Barbate (Cádiz)*
☎ **(956) 45 50 04**
🖷 (956) 45 12 95
📧 info@montenmedio.es
✍ Miguel Marin (Mgr)
🖹 www.montenmedio.es

**Novo Sancti Petri**  (1990)
*Urb. Novo Sancti Petri, Playa de la Barrosa,
11139 Chiclana de la Frontera*
☎ **0034 (956) 49 40 05**
🖷 0034 (956) 49 43 50
📧 sales@golf-novosancti.es
✍ Mrs Claudia Kühleitner (Sales &
Marketing Mgr)
🖹 www.golf-novosancti.es

**Real Sevilla**  (1992)
*Autovía Sevilla-Utrera, 41089
Montequinto (Sevilla)*
☎ **(954) 12 43 01**
🖷 (954) 12 42 29
🖹 www.sevillagolf.com

**Vista Hermosa**  (1975)
*Apartado 77, Urb Vista Hermosa, 11500
Puerto de Santa Maria, Cádiz*
☎ **(956) 87 56 05**

**Zaudin**
*Crta Tomares-Mairena, 41940
Tomares (Sevilla)*
☎ **(954) 15 41 59**
🖷 (954) 15 33 44

## Valencia & Castellón

**Escorpión**  (1975)
*Apartado Correos 1, Betera (Valencia)*
☎ **(96) 160 12 11**
🖷 (96) 169 01 87
📧 escorpion@clubescorpion.com
🖹 www.clubescorpion.com

**Real Club De Golf Manises**
(1954)
*C/ Maestrat, 1, 46940 Manises (Valencia)*
☎ **+34 96 153 40 69**
🖬 +34 96 152 38 04
📧 info@clubgolfmanises.es
🖎 D. Juan Jose Penalba Belda (Mgr)
🖳 www.realclubgolfmanises.es

**Mediterraneo CC**    (1978)
*Urb La Coma, 12190 Borriol, (Castellón)*
☎ **(964) 32 1653 (bookings)**
🖬 (964) 65 77 34
📧 club@ccmediterraneo.com
🖳 www.ccmediterraneo.com

**Oliva Nova**    (1995)
*46780 Oliva (Valencia)*
☎ **(096) 285 76 66**
🖬 (096) 285 76 67
📧 golf@chg.es
🖳 www.olivanovagolf.com

**El Saler**    (1968)
*Avd. de los pinares 151, 46012 El Saler (Valencia)*
☎ **(96) 161 0384**
🖬 (96) 162 7366
📧 saler.golf@parador.es
🖳 www.parador.es

## Valladolid

**Entrepinos**    (1990)
*Avda del Golf 2, Urb Entrepinos, 47130 Simancas (Valladolid)*
☎ **(983) 59 05 11/59 05 61**
🖬 (983) 59 07 65
📧 golfentrepinos@golfentrepinos .com
🖎 Angel Santiago Calleja (Mgr)
🖳 www.golfentrepinos.com

## Zaragoza

**Club de Golf La Penaza**    (1973)
*Apartado 3039, Zaragoza*
☎ **(976) 34 28 00/34 22 48**
🖬 (976) 34 28 00
📧 administracion@golflapenaza.com
🖎 Pablo Menendez
🖳 www.golflapenaza.com

# Sweden

## East Central

**Ängsö**    (1979)
*Box 1007, 72126 Västerås*
☎ **(0171) 441012**
🖬 (0171) 441049
📧 kansli@angsogolf.org
🖳 www.angsogolf.org

**Arboga**
*PO Box 263, 732 25 Arboga*
☎ **(0589) 70100**

🖬 (0589) 701 90
📧 info@arbogagk.se
🖎 Gun Peterson
🖳 www.arbogagk.se

**Askersunds**    (1980)
*Kärravägen 30, 696 75 Ammeberg*
☎ **(0583) 34943**
🖬 (0583) 34945
📧 info@askersundsgolfklubb.se
🖳 www.askersundsgk.com

**Burvik**    (1990)
*Burvik, 740 12 Knutby*
☎ **(0174) 43060**
🖬 (0174) 43062
📧 info@burvik.se
🖳 www.burvik.se

**Edenhof**    (1991)
*740 22 Bälinge*
☎ **(018) 334185**
🖬 (018) 334186
📧 info@edenhof.se

**Enköping**    (1970)
*Box 2006, 745 02 Enköping*
☎ **(0171) 20830**
🖬 (0171) 20823
📧 info@enkopinggolf.se
🖳 www.enkopinggolf.se

**Eskilstuna**    (1951)
*Strängnäsvägen, 633 49 Eskilstuna*
☎ **(016) 142629**
🖬 (016) 148729
📧 info@eskilstunagk.se
🖳 www.eskilstunagk.se

**Fagersta**    (1970)
*Box 2051, 737 02 Fagersta*
☎ **(0223) 54060**
🖬 (0223) 54000

**Frösåker**    (1989)
*Frösåker Gård, Box 17015, 720 17 Västerås*
☎ **(021) 25401**
🖬 (021) 25485
📧 info@frosakergolf.se
🖳 www.fgcc.se

**Fullerö**    (1988)
*Jotsberga, 725 91 Västerås*
☎ **(021) 50262**
🖬 (021) 50431
📧 info@fullerogk.se
🖳 www.fullerogk.se

**Gripsholm**    (1991)
*Box 133, 647 23 Mariefred*
☎ **(0159) 350050**
🖬 (0159) 350059
🖳 www.golf.se/gripsholmsgk

**Grönlund**    (1989)
*PO Box 38, 740 10 Almunge*
☎ **(0174) 20670**
🖬 (0174) 20455
📧 info@gronlundgk.se
🖳 www.gronlundgk.se

**Gustavsvik**    (1988)
*Box 22033, 702 02 Örebro*
☎ **(019) 244486**

🖬 (019) 246490
📧 info@gvgk.se
🖳 www.gvgk.se

**Katrineholm**    (1959)
*Jättorp, 641 93 Katrineholm*
☎ **(0150) 39270**
🖬 (0150) 39011
📧 info@katrineholmsgolf.nu
🖎 Olof Pettersson (Mgr)
🖳 www.katrineholmsgolf.nu

**Köpings**    (1963)
*Box 278, 731 26 Köping*
☎ **(0221) 81090**
🖬 (0221) 81277
📧 info@kopingsgk.nu
🖳 www.kopingsgk.nu

**Kumla**    (1987)
*Box 46, 692 21 Kumla*
☎ **(019) 577370**
🖬 (019) 577373

**Linde**    (1984)
*Dalkarlshyttan, 711 31 Lindesberg*
☎ **(0581) 87050**
🖬 (0581) 87059
📧 info@lindesbergsgk.se
🖳 www.lindegk.com

**Nyköpings**    (1951)
*Árilla, 611 92 Nyköping*
☎ **(0155) 216617**
🖬 (0155) 97185
📧 info@nykopingsgk.se
🖎 Gary Cosford
🖳 www.nykopingsgk.se

**Örebro**    (1939)
*Lanna, 719 93 Vintrosa*
☎ **(019) 164070**
🖬 (019) 164075
🖳 www.golf.se/golfklubbar /orebrogk

**Roslagen**
*Box 110, 761 22 Norrtälje*
☎ **(0176) 237194**
🖬 (0176) 237103

**Sala**    (1970)
*Norby Fallet 100, 733 92 Sala*
☎ **(0224) 53077/53055/ 53064**
🖬 (0224) 53143
📧 info@salagk.nu
🖎 Hans Eljansbo
🖳 www.salagk.nu

**Sigtunabygden**    (1961)
*Box 89, 193 22 Sigtuna*
☎ **(08) 592 54012**
🖬 (08) 592 54167
📧 info@sigtunagk.com
🖳 www.sigtunagk.com

**Skepptuna**
*Skepptuna, 195 93 Märsta*
☎ **(08) 512 93069**
🖬 (08) 512 93163
🖳 www.skepptunagk.nu

**Södertälje**    (1952)
*Box 9074, 151 09 Södertälje*
☎ **(08) 550 91995**
⌨ (08) 550 62549

**Strängnäs**    (1968)
*Kilenlundavägen 3, 645 47 Strängnäs*
☎ **(0152) 14731**
⌨ (0152) 14716
✉ info@strangnasgk.se
🖳 www.strangnasgk.se

**Torshälla**    (1960)
*Box 128, 64422 Torshälla*
☎ **(016) 358722**
⌨ (016) 357491
✉ kansli@torshallagk.com
🖳 www.torshallagk.com

**Tortuna**
*Nicktuna, Tortuna, 725 96 Västerås*
☎ **(021) 65300**
⌨ (021) 65302
✉ kansli@tortunagk.com

**Upsala**    (1937)
*Hâmö Gård, Läby, 755 92 Uppsala*
☎ **(018) 460120**
⌨ (018) 461205
✉ info@upsalagk.se
🖳 www.upsalagk.se

**Vassunda**    (1989)
*Smedby Gård, 741 91 Knivsta*
☎ **+46 (0) 185 72040**
⌨ (018) 381416
✉ info@vagk@telia.com
🖳 www.vassundagolf.se

**Västerås**    (1931)
*Bjärby, 724 81 Västerås*
☎ **(021) 357543**
⌨ (021) 357573
✉ info@vasterasgk.se
🖳 www.vasterasgk.se

### Far North

**Funäsdalen**    (1972)
*Golfbanevägen 8, 840 96 Ljusnedal*
☎ **(0684) 21100**
⌨ (0684) 21142
✉ info@funasdalengolf.se
🖳 www.funasdalengolf.se

**Gällivare-Malmberget**    (1973)
*Box 35, 983 21 Malmberget*
☎ **(0970) 20770**
⌨ (0970) 20776
✉ gmgk@telia.com
🖳 www.gmgk.se

**Härnösand**    (1957)
*Box 52, 871 22 Härnösand*
☎ **(0611) 67000**
⌨ (0611) 66165
🖳 www.harnosand.gk.just.nu

**Kalix**    (1990)
*Nyborgsvägen 175, 95251 Kalix*
☎ **(0923) 15945/15935**
⌨ (0923) 77735

✉ info@kalixgolfklubb.se
🖳 www.kalixgolfklubb.se

**Luleå**    (1955)
*Golfbaneväg 80, 975 96 Luleå*
☎ **(0920) 256300**
⌨ (0920) 256362
✉ kansli@luleagolf.se
🖳 www.luleagolf.se

**Norrmjöle**    (1992)
*905 82 Umeå*
☎ **(090) 81581**
⌨ (090) 81565
✉ kansli@norrmjole-golf.se
🖳 www.norrmjole-golf.se

**Örnsköldsviks GK Puttom**
(1967)
*Ovansjö 232, 891 95 Arnäsvall*
☎ **(0660) 254001**
⌨ (0660) 254040
✉ kansli@puttom.se
🖳 www.puttom.se

**Östersund-Frösö**    (1947)
*Kungsgården 205, 832 96 Frösön*
☎ **(063) 576030**
⌨ (063) 43765
🖳 www.ofg.nu

**Piteå**    (1960)
*Nötöv 119, 941 41 Piteå*
☎ **(0911) 14990**
⌨ (0911) 14960

**Skellefteå**    (1967)
*Rönnbäcken, 931 92 Skellefteå*
☎ **(0910) 779333**
⌨ (0910) 779777
✉ info@skelleftegolf.nu
🖳 www.skelleftegolf.nu

**Sollefteå**    (1970)
*Box 213, 881 25 Sollefteå*
☎ **(0620) 21477/12670**
⌨ (0620) 21477/12670

**Sundsvall**    (1952)
*Golfvägen 5, 86234 Kvissleby*
☎ **+46 60 515175**
⌨ +46 60 515170
✉ kansli@sundsvallsgolfklubb.se
🖳 www.sundsvallsgolfklubb.se

**Timrå**
*Golfbanevägen 2, 860 32 Fagervik*
☎ **(060) 570153**
⌨ (060) 578136
✉ timragk@telia.com
🖳 www.timragk.se

**Umeå**    (1954)
*Enkan Ramborgs väg 10, 913
35 Holmsund*
☎ **(090) 58580/58585**
⌨ (090) 58589
✉ info@umgk.se
✍ Lena D Lindstrom (Club Manager)
🖳 www.umgk.se

### Gothenburg

**Albatross**    (1973)
*Lillhagsvägen, 422 50 Hisings-Backa*
☎ **(031) 551901/550500**
⌨ (031) 555900

**Chalmers**
*Härrydavägen 50, 438 91 Landvetter*
☎ **+46 (0) 31 91 84 30**
⌨ +46 (0) 31 91 63 38
✉ info@chgk.se
🖳 www.chgk.se

**Delsjö**    (1962)
*Kallebäck, 412 76 Göteborg*
☎ **(031) 406959**
⌨ (031) 703 0431
🖳 www.degk.se

**Forsgårdens**    (1982)
*Gamla Forsv 1, 434 47 Kungsbacka*
☎ **(0300) 566350**
⌨ (0300) 566351
✉ kansli@forsgarden.se
🖳 www.forsgarden.se

**Göteborg**    (1902)
*Box 2056, 436 02 Hovås*
☎ **(031) 282444**
⌨ (031) 685333

**Gullbringa G&CC**
(1968)
*Kulperödsvägen 6, 442 95 Hålta*
☎ **(0303) 227161**
⌨ (0303) 227778
✉ kansli@gullbringagolf.se
✍ A Joelsson-Soetting
🖳 www.gullbringagolf.se

**Kungälv-Kode GK**    (1990)
*Ö Knaverstad 140, 442 97 Kode*
☎ **+46 303 513 00**
⌨ +46 303 502 05
✉ info@kkgk.se
✍ Pär Svensson
🖳 www.kkgk.se

**Kungsbacka**    (1971)
*Hamravägen 15, 429 44 Särö*
☎ **(031) 938180**
⌨ (031) 938170
✉ info@kungsbackagk.se
✍ Andri Reumert
🖳 www.kungsbackagk.se

**Lysegårdens**    (1966)
*Box 532, 442 15 Kungälv*
☎ **(0303) 223426**
⌨ (0303) 223075
✉ info@lysegardensgk.se
🖳 www.lysegardensgk.se

**Mölndals**    (1979)
*Hällesåkersvägen 14, 437 91 Lindome*
☎ **(031) 993030**
⌨ (031) 994901
✉ molndalsgk@telia.com
✍ Lars-Erik Hagbert
🖳 www.molndalsgk.se

## Öijared    (1958)
*Öijaredsvägen 59, 448 92 Floda*
☎ **(0302) 37300**
📠 info@oijared.se
✍ Lars Brydolf (Man Dir)
🖥 www.oijared.se

## Partille    (1986)
*Golfrundan 5, 433 51 Öjersjö*
☎ **+46 31 987043**
📠 info@partillegk.se
✍ Patrik Skoog
🖥 www.partillegk.se

## Sjögärde
*43963 Frillesås*
☎ **+46 (0) 340 657865**
📠 +46 (0) 340 657861
📠 info@sjogarde.se
🖥 www.sjogarde.se

## Stenungsund    (1993)
*Lundby Pl 7480, 444 93 Spekeröd*
☎ **(0303) 778470**
📠 (0303) 778350
🖥 www.stenungsundgk.se

## Stora Lundby    (1983)
*Valters Väg 2, 443 71 Grabo*
☎ **(0302) 44200**
📠 (0302) 44125
🖥 www.storalundbygk.o.se

## Malmö & South Coast

## Abbekas    (1989)
*Kroppsmarksvagen, 274 56 Abbekas*
☎ **(0411) 533233**
📠 info@abbekasgk.se
🖥 www.abbekasgk.se

## Barsebäck G&CC    (1969)
*246 55 Löddeköpinge*
☎ **(046) 776230**
📠 (046) 772630
📠 bgcc@barseback-golf.se
🖥 www.barsebackresort.se

## Falsterbo    (1909)
*Fyrvägen 34, SE 239 40 Falsterbo*
☎ **+46 (0)40 470078**
📠 +46 (0)40 472722
📠 info@falsterbogk.se
✍ Sandra Tancred
🖥 www.falsterbogk.se

## Flommens    (1935)
*239 40 Falsterbo*
☎ **(040) 475016**
📠 (040) 473157
📠 reception@flommensgk.se
🖥 www.flommensgk.se

## Kävlinge    (1989)
*Box 138, 244 22 Kävlinge*
☎ **(046) 736270**
📠 (046) 728486
📠 kansli@kavlingegk.com
🖥 www.kavlingegk.com

## Ljunghusen    (1932)
*Kinellsvag, Ljunghusen, 236 42 Höllviken*
☎ **(040) 458000**
📠 (040) 454265
📠 info@ljgk.se
✍ Stig Persson
🖥 www.ljgk.se

## Lunds Akademiska    (1936)
*Kungsmarken, 225 92 Lund*
☎ **(046) 99005**
📠 (046) 99146
📠 info@lagk.se
🖥 www.lagk.se

## Malmö Burlöv    (1981)
*Segesvängen, 212 27 Malmö*
☎ **(040) 292535/292536**
📠 (040) 292228
📠 malmoburlovgk@telia.com
🖥 www.malmoburlovgk.com

## Örestads GK    (1986)
*Golfvägen, Habo Ljung, 234 22 Lomma*
☎ **(040) 410580**
📠 (040) 416320
📠 info@orestadsgk.com
✍ Niklas Karlsson
🖥 www.orestadsgk.com

## Österlen    (1945)
*Djupadal, 272 95 Simrishamn*
☎ **(0414) 412550**
📠 (0414) 412551
📠 info@osterlensgk.com
✍ Stefan Minell
🖥 www.osterlensgk.com

## Romeleåsen    (1969)
*Kvarnbrodda 1191, 247 96 Veberöd*
☎ **+46 46 820 12**
📠 +46 46 821 13
📠 info@ragk.se
✍ Stellan Ragnar
🖥 www.ragk.se

## Söderslätts    (1993)
*Ellaboda, Grevievägen 260-10, 235 94 Vellinge*
☎ **(040) 429680**
📠 (040) 429684
📠 soderslattsgk@sslgk.se
🖥 www.soderslattsgk.se

## Tegelberga    (1988)
*Alstad Pl 140, 231 96 Trelleborg*
☎ **(040) 485690**
📠 (040) 485691
🖥 www.golf.se/tegelbergagk

## Tomelilla    (1987)
*Ullstorp, 273 94 Tomelilla*
☎ **(0417) 19430**
📠 (0417) 13657
📠 info@tomelillagolf.se
🖥 www.tomelillagolf.se

## Trelleborg Golf Club    (1963)
*Kämpingevägen 19, 231 93 Trelleborg*
☎ **(0410) 330460**
📠 kansli@trelleborgsgk.se
✍ Helen Nilsson
🖥 www.trelleborgsgk.se

## Vellinge    (1991)
*Toftadals Gård, 235 41 Vellinge*
☎ **(040) 443255**
📠 (040) 443179
📠 info@vellingegk.se
🖥 www.vellingegk.se

## Ystad    (1930)
*Långrevsvägen, 270 22 Köpingebro*
☎ **(0411) 550350**
📠 (0411) 550392
📠 info@ystadgk.com
🖥 www.ystadgk.com

## North

## Alvkarleby
*Västanåvägen 5, 814 94 Alvkarleby*
☎ **(026) 72757**
📠 (026) 82307
📠 info@alvkarlebygk.com
🖥 www.alvkarlebygk.com

## Avesta    (1963)
*Friluftsvägen 10, 774 61 Avesta*
☎ **(0226) 55913/10866/12766**
📠 (0226) 12578
📠 info@avestagk.se
🖥 www.avestagk.se

## Bollnäs    (1963)
*Norrfly 1634, 823 91 Kilafors*
☎ **(0278) 650540**
📠 (0278) 651220
📠 info@bollnasgk.com
🖥 www.bollnasgk.com

## Dalsjö    (1989)
*Dalsjö 3, 781 94 Borlänge*
☎ **(0243) 220080**
📠 (0243) 220140
📠 info@dalsjogolf.se
🖥 www.dalsjogolf.se

## Falun-Borlänge    (1956)
*Storgarden 10, 791 93 Falun*
☎ **(023) 31015**
📠 (023) 31072
🖥 www.fbgu.se

## Hagge    (1963)
*Hagge, 771 90 Ludvika*
☎ **(0240) 28087/28513**
📠 (0240) 28515

## Hofors    (1965)
*Box 117, 813 22 Hofors*
☎ **(0290) 85125**
📠 (0290) 85101

## Högbo    (1962)
*Daniel Tilas Väg 4, 811 92 Sandviken*
☎ **(026) 215015**
📠 (026) 215322
📠 info@hogbogk.com
🖥 www.golf.se/hogbogk/

## Hudiksvall    (1964)
*Tjuvskär, 824 01 Hudiksvall*
☎ **+46 (0) 650 542080**
📠 +46 (0) 650 542089

**Ljusdal**   (1973)
*Svinhammarsv.2, 82735   Ljusdal*
☎ **(0651) 16883**
📠 (0651) 16883
✉ kansli@golfiljusdal.nu
🖥 www.golfiljusdal.nu

**Mora**   (1980)
*Box 264, 792 24 Mora*
☎ **(0250) 592990**
📠 (0250) 592995
✉ info@moragk.se
🖥 www.moragk.se

**Sälenfjallens**   (1991)
*Box 20, 780 67 Sälen*
☎ **(0280) 20670**
📠 (0280) 20671
✉ info@salenfjallensgk.se
✍ Ingemar Simonsson (Secretary)
🖥 www.salenfjallensgk.se

**Säter**   (1984)
*Box 89, 783 22 Säter*
☎ **(0225) 50030**
📠 (0225) 51424

**Snöå Golfklubb**   (1990)
*Snöå Bruk, S-780 51 Dala-Järna*
☎ **+46 281 24072**
📠 +46 281 24009
✉ snoa.gk@telia.com
✍ Kjell Redhe
🖥 www.snoagk.se

**Söderhamns GK**   (1961)
*835 Sofieholm, 826 91 Söderhamn*
☎ **+46 270 281 300**
📠 +46 270 281 003
✉ info@soderhamnsgk.com
✍ Hans Wirtavuori
🖥 www.soderhamnsgk.com

**Sollerö**   (1991)
*Levsnäs, 79290 Sollerön*
☎ **(0250) 22236**
📠 (0250) 22854

## Skane & South

**Allerum**   (1992)
*Tursköpsvägen 154, 260 35 Ödåkra*
☎ **(042) 93051**
📠 (042) 93045
✉ info@allerumgk.nu
🖥 www.allerum.nu

**Ängelholm**   (1973)
*Box 1117, 262 22 Ängelholm*
☎ **(0431) 430260/431460**
📠 (0431) 431568
🖥 www.golf.se/golfklubbar
/angelholmsgk

**Araslöv**
*Starvägen 1, 291 75 Färlöv*
☎ **(044) 71600**
📠 (044) 71575

**Båstad**   (1929)
*Box 1037, 269 21 Båstad*
☎ **(0431) 78370**

📠 (0431) 73331
✉ kansli@bgk.se
🖥 www.bgk.se

**Bedinge**   (1931)
*Golfbanevägen, 231 76 Beddingestrand*
☎ **(0410) 25514**
📠 (0410) 25411

**Bjäre**
*Salomonhög 3086, 269 93 Båstad*
☎ **(0431) 361053**
📠 (0431) 361764

**Bosjökloster**   (1974)
*243 95 Höör*
☎ **(0413) 25858**
📠 (0413) 25895

**Carlskrona**   (1949)
*PO Almö, 370 24 Nättraby*
☎ **(0457) 35123**
📠 (0457) 35090
🖥 www.carlskronagk.com

**Degeberga-Widtsköfle**
*Segholmsu.126, Box 71, 297 21 Degeberga*
☎ **(044) 355035**
📠 (044) 355075
✉ dwgk@telia.com
🖥 www.dwgolfklubb.com

**Eslöv**   (1966)
*Box 150, 241 22 Eslöv*
☎ **(0413) 55 75 70**
📠 (0413) 18613
✉ info@eslovsgk.se
🖥 www.eslovsgk.se

**Hässleholm**   (1978)
*Skyrup, 282 95 Tyringe*
☎ **(0451) 53111**
📠 (0451) 53138

**Helsingborg**   (1924)
*260 40 Viken*
☎ **(042) 236147**
✉ office@helsingborgsgk.com
🖥 www.helsingborgsgk.com

**Karlshamn**   (1962)
*Box 188, 374 23 Karlshamn*
☎ **(0454) 50085**
📠 (0454) 50160
✉ info@karlshamnsgk.com
✍ Eva Tigerman
🖥 www.karlshamnsgk.com

**Kristianstad GK**   (1924)
*Box 41, 296 21 Åhus*
☎ **(044) 247656**
📠 (044) 247635
✉ info@kristianstadsgk.com
✍ Mats Welff
🖥 www.kristianstadsgk.com

**Landskrona**   (1960)
*Erikstorp, 261 61 Landskrona*
☎ **(0418) 446260**
📠 (0418) 446262
✉ info@landskronagk.se
🖥 www.landskronagk.se

**Mölle**   (1943)
*263 77 Mölle, Italienska Vägen 215*
☎ **(042) 347520**
📠 (042) 347523
✉ info@mollegk.se
✍ Peter Tublén (Manager)
🖥 www.mollegk.se

**Örkelljunga**   (1989)
*Rya 472, 286 91 Örkelljunga*
☎ **(0435) 53690/53640**
📠 (0435) 53670
✉ annika.hansson@multisystem.se
🖥 www.woodlands.se

**Östra Göinge**   (1981)
*Riksvägen 12, 289 21 Knislinge*
☎ **(044) 60060**
📠 (044) 67862
✉ 04460060@telia.com
🖥 www.oggk.se

**Perstorp**   (1963)
*Gustavsborg 501, 284 91 Perstorp*
☎ **+46 (0) 435 35411**
📠 +46 (0) 435 35959
✉ kansli@ppgk.nu
🖥 www.ppgk.nu

**Ronneby**   (1963)
*Box 26, 372 21 Ronneby*
☎ **(0457) 10315**
📠 (0457) 10412
🖥 www.golf.se/ronnebygk

**Rya**   (1934)
*PL 5500, 255 92 Helsingborg*
☎ **(042) 220182**
📠 (042) 220394
✉ kansli@rya.nu
🖥 www.rya.nu

**St Arild**   (1987)
*Golfvagen 48, 260 41 Nyhamnsläge*
☎ **(042) 346860**
📠 (042) 346042
✉ kansliet@starild.se
🖥 www.starild.se

**Skepparslov**   (1984)
*Sätesvägen 14, 291 92 Kristianstad*
☎ **(044) 229508**
📠 (044) 229503
✉ kansli@skepparslovgk.se
✍ Ulla Johnsson
🖥 www.skepparslovsgk.se

**Söderåsen**   (1966)
*Box 41, 260 50 Billesholm*
☎ **(042) 73337**
📠 (042) 73963
✉ info@soderasensgk.se
🖥 www.soderasensgk.se

**Sölvesborg**
*Box 204, 294 25 Sölvesborg*
☎ **(0456) 70650**
📠 (0456) 70650
✉ info@solvesborgsgk.se
🖥 www.solvesborgsgk.se

**Svalöv**   (1989)
*Månstorp Pl 1365, 268 90 Svalöv*
☎ **(0418) 662462**

☐ (0418) 663284
✉ svagk@telia.com
🖥 www.svagk.se

## Torekov    (1924)
Råledsv 31, 260 93 Torekov
☎ (0431) 449840
☐ (0431) 364916
✉ info@togk.se
🖥 www.togk.se

## Trummenas    (1989)
373 02 Ramdala
☎ +46 (0) 455 360507
☐ +46 (0) 455 360571
✉ trummenas.gk@telia.com
🖥 www.trummenasgk.se

## Vasatorp    (1973)
P O Box 130 35, S-250 13 Helsingborg
☎ +46 42 23 50 58
☐ +46 42 23 51 35
✉ info@vasatorpsgk.se
✍ Joakim Soderstrom (Club Mgr)
🖥 www.vasatorpsgk.se

## South East

## Älmhult    (1975)
Pl 1215, 343 90 Älmhult
☎ (0476) 14135
☐ (0476) 16565

## Åtvidaberg    (1954)
Västantorp, 597 41 Åtvidaberg
☎ (0120) 35425
☐ (0120) 13502

## Ekerum Golf Resort    (1990)
387 92 Borgholm, Öland
☎ (0485) 80000
☐ (0485) 80010
✉ info@ekerum.com
🖥 www.ekerum.com

## Eksjö    (1938)
Skedhult, 575 96 Eksjö
☎ (0381) 13525
✉ kansli@eksjogk.se
✍ Peter Börjesson
🖥 www.eksjogk.se

## Emmaboda    (1976)
Kyrkogatan, 360 60 Vissefjärda
☎ (0471) 20505/20540
☐ (0471) 20440
✉ info@emmabodagk.se
🖥 www.emmabodagk.se

## Finspångs    (1965)
Viberga Gård, 612 92 Finspång
☎ (0122) 13940
☐ (0122) 18888
✉ info@finspangsgk.se
🖥 www.finspangsgk.se

## Gotska    (1986)
Annelund, 62141 Visby, Gotland
☎ (0498) 215545
☐ (0498) 256332
✉ info@gotskagk.se
🖥 www.gotskagk.se

## Grönhögen    (1996)
PL 1270, 380 65 Öland
☎ (0485) 665995
☐ (0485) 665999
🖥 www.gronhogen.se

## Gumbalde
Box 35, 620 13 Ståga, Gotland
☎ (0498) 482880
☐ (0498) 482884

## Hooks
560 13 Hok
☎ (0393) 21420
☐ (0393) 21379
🖥 www.hooksgk.com

## Jönköpings GK    (1936)
Kättilstorp, 556 27 Jönköping
☎ (036) 76567
☐ (036) 76511
✉ info@jonkopingsgk.se
🖥 www.jonkopingsgk.se

## Kalmar    (1947)
Box 278, 391 23 Kalmar
☎ (0480) 472111
☐ (0480) 472314
✉ reception@kalmargk.se
✍ Jimmy Grön
🖥 www.kalmargk.se

## Lagan    (1966)
Box 63, 340 14 Lagan
☎ (0372) 30450/35460
☐ (0372) 35307
✉ info@lagansgk.se
🖥 www.lagansgk.se

## Landeryds GK    (1987)
Bogestad Gård, 585 93 Linköping
☎ (+46) 133 62200
☐ (+46) 133 62208
✉ bjorn.sturehed@landerydsgolf.se
✍ Björn Sturehed
🖥 www.landerydsgolf.se

## Lidhems    (1988)
360 14 Väckelsång
☎ (0470) 33660
☐ (0470) 33761
🖥 www.golf.se/lidhemsgk

## Linköpings    (1945)
Universitets vägen 8, 583 30 Linköping
☎ (013) 262990
☐ (013) 140769
✉ info@linkopingsgk.se
✍ Steven McDaniel (Dir)
🖥 www.linkopingsgk.se

## Mjölby    (1986)
Blixberg, Miskarp, 595 92 Mjölby
☎ (0142) 12570
✉ kansli@mjolbygk.se
✍ Viktoria Schedin
🖥 www.mjolbygk.se

## Motala    (1956)
Tuddarp 58, 591 92 Motala
☎ (0141) 508 56
☐ (0141) 208990
✉ info@motalagk.se
🖥 www.motalagk.se

## Nässjö    (1988)
Box 5, 571 21 Nässjö
☎ (0380) 10022
☐ (0380) 12082

## Norrköping    (1928)
Alsatersvagen 40, 605 97 Norrköping
☎ (011) 158240
☐ (011) 158249
✉ info@ngk.nu
✍ Morgan Allard
🖥 www.ngk.nu

## Oskarshamn    (1972)
Box 148, 572 23 Oskarshamn
☎ (0491) 94033
☐ (0491) 94038

## Skinnarebo    (1990)
Skinnarebo, 555 93 Jönköping
☎ (036) 36 29 32
☐ (036) 362975
✉ skinnarebo.golf@telia.com
✍ Lisbeth Johansson
🖥 www.skinnarebo.se

## Tobo    (1971)
Fredensborg 133, 598 91 Vimmerby
☎ (0492) 30346
☐ (0492) 30871
✉ info@tobogk.com
🖥 www.tobogk.com

## Tranås    (1952)
Norrc byvagen 8, Norrabyvagen 8, 57343 Tranas
☎ (0140) 311661
☐ (0140) 16161
✉ info@tranasgk.se
🖥 www.tranasgk.se

## Vadstena    (1957)
Hagalund, Box 122, 592 23 Vadstena
☎ (0143) 12440
☐ (0143) 12709
✉ kansli@vadstenagk.nu
🖥 www.vadstenagk.nu

## Värnamo    (1962)
Näsbyholm 5, 331 96 VÄRNAMO
☎ (0370) 23991
☐ (0370) 23992
✉ info@varnamogk.se
✍ Pia Berglund
🖥 www.varnamogk.se

## Västervik    (1959)
Box 62, Ekhagen, 593 22 Västervik
☎ (0490) 32420
☐ (0490) 32421

## Växjö    (1959)
Box 227, 351 05 Växjö
☎ (0470) 21515
☐ (0470) 21557
🖥 www.vaxjogk.com

## Vetlanda    (1983)
Box 249, 574 23 Vetlanda
☎ (0383) 18310
☐ (0383) 19278

**Visby Golf Club** (1958)
*Västergarn Kronholmen 415, 622 30
Gotlands Tofta*
☎ +46 498 200930
📠 +46 498 200932
📧 info@visbygk.com
🖉 Matz Bengtsson (Gen Mgr)
🖳 www.visbygk.com

**Vreta Kloster**
*Box 144, 590 70 Ljungsbro*
☎ (013) 169700
📠 (013) 169707
📧 info@vkgk.se
🖳 www.vkgk.se

## South West

**Alingsås** (1985)
*Hjälmared 4050, 441 95 Alingsås*
☎ (0322) 52421

**Bäckavattnet** (1977)
*Marbäck, 305 94 Halmstad*
☎ (035) 162040
📠 (035) 162049
🖳 www.backavattnetsgk.com

**Billingens GK** (1949)
*St Kulhult, 540 17 Lerdala*
☎ +46 511 80291
📧 info@billingensgk.se
🖉 Anders Karisson
🖳 www.billingensgk.se

**Borås** (1933)
*Östra Vik, Kråkered, 504 95 Borås*
☎ (033) 250250
📠 (033) 250176

**Ekarnas** (1970)
*Balders Väg 12, 467 31 Grästorp*
☎ (0514) 12061
📠 (0514) 12062
📧 info@ekarnasgk.se
🖳 www.ekarnasgk.se

**Falkenberg** (1949)
*Golfvägen, 311 72 Falkenberg*
☎ (0346) 50287
📠 (0346) 50997
📧 info@falkenbergsgolfklubb.com
🖉 Lars Andersson (Sec)
🖳 www.falkenbergsgolfklubb.se

**Falköping** (1965)
*Box 99, 521 02 Falköping*
☎ (0515) 31270
📠 (0515) 31389
📧 info@falkopingsgk.com
🖉 Peter Fritzson
🖳 www.falkopingsgk.com

**Halmstad** (1930)
*302 73 Halmstad*
☎ +46 35 176800/176801
📠 +46 35 176820
📧 info@hgk.se
🖳 www.hgk.se

**Haverdals** (1988)
*Slingervägen 35, 30570 Haverdal*
☎ (035) 144990

📠 (035) 53890
📧 info@haverdalsgk.com
🖉 Ann Jacobsson
🖳 www.haverdalsgk.com

**Hökensås** (1962)
*PO Box 116, 544 22 Hjo*
☎ (0503) 16059
📠 (0503) 16156

**Holms** (1990)
*Nannarp, 305 92 Halmstad*
☎ (035) 38189
📠 (035) 38488
📧 info@holmsgk.se
🖳 www.holmsgk.se

**Hulta** (1972)
*Box 54, 517 22 Bollebygd*
☎ (033) 204340
📠 (033) 204345
📧 info@hultagk.se
🖉 David Kirkham
🖳 www.hultagk.se

**Laholms** (1964)
*Vallen 15, 31298 Vaxtorp*
☎ +46 430 30601
📠 +46 430 30891
📧 kansli@laholmsgk.se
🖳 www.laholmsgk.se

**Lidköping** (1967)
*Box 2029, 531 02 Lidköping*
☎ (0510) 546144
📠 (0510) 546495
🖳 www.lidkopingsgk.se

**Mariestads Golf Course** (1975)
*Gummerstadsvägen 45, 542 94 Mariestad*
☎ (0501) 17383
📧 info@mariestadsgk.se
🖳 www.mariestadsgk.se

**Marks** (1962)
*Brättingstorpsvägen 28, 511 58 Kinna*
☎ (0320) 14220
📠 (0320) 12516
📧 info@marksgk.se
🖳 www.marksgk.se

**Onsjö** (1974)
*Box 6331 A, 462 42 Vänersborg*
☎ (0521) 68870
📠 (0521) 17106
🖳 www.onsjogk.com

**Ringenäs** (1987)
*Strandlida, 305 91 Halmstad*
☎ (035) 161590
📠 (035) 161599
📧 ringenas.golf@telia.com
🖳 www.ringenasgolfbana.com

**Skogaby** (1988)
*312 93 Laholm*
☎ (0430) 60190
📠 (0430) 60225
📧 skogaby.gk@telia.com
🖳 www.skogabygk.se

**Sotenas Golfklubb** (1988)
*Pl Onna, 450 46 Hunnebostrand*
☎ (0523) 52302

📠 (0523) 52390
🖳 www.sotenasgolf.com

**Töreboda** (1965)
*Box 18, 545 21 Töreboda*
☎ (0506) 12305
📠 (0506) 12305

**Trollhättan** (1963)
*Stora Ekeskogen, 466 91 Sollebrunn*
☎ (0520) 441000
📠 (0520) 441049

**Ulricehamn** (1947)
*523 33 Ulricehamn*
☎ (0321) 27950
📠 (0321) 27959
📧 info@ulricehamnsgk.se
🖳 www.ulricehamnsgk.se

**Vara-Bjertorp** (1987)
*Bjertorp, 535 91 Kvänum*
☎ +46 (512) 20261
📠 +46 (512) 20259
📧 info@vara-bjertorpgk.se
🖉 Mr Christian Tiden
🖳 www.vara-bjertorpgk.se

**Varberg** (1950)
*432 77 Tvååker*
☎ +46 340 480380
📠 +46 340 44135
📧 info@varbergsgk.se
🖳 www.varbergsgk.se

**Vinberg** (1992)
*Sannagård, 311 95 Falkenberg*
☎ (0346) 19020
📠 (0346) 19042
📧 info@vinbergsgolfklubb.se
🖳 www.vinhergsgolfklubb.se

## Stockholm

**Botkyrka**
*Malmbro Gård, 147 91 Grödinge*
☎ (08) 530 29650
📠 (08) 530 29409
📧 botkyrkagk.se
🖳 www.golf.se/botkyrkagk

**Bro-Bålsta** (1978)
*Jurstagarosvagen 2, 197 91 Bro*
☎ (08) 582 41310
📠 (08) 582 40006
📧 reception.bbgk@telia.com
🖳 www.brobalstagk.se

**Djursholm** (1931)
*Hagbardsvägen 1, 182 63 Djursholm*
☎ (08) 5449 6451
📠 (08) 5449 6456
📧 info@dgk.nu
🖳 www.dgk.nu (Swedish only)

**Fågelbro G&CC** (1991)
*Fågelbro Säteri, Fågelbrovägen 11-15, 139 60 Värmdö*
☎ +46 (08) 571 41800
📠 +46 (08) 571 40671
📧 kansli@fagelbrogolf.se
🖉 Anders Green (Manager)
🖳 www.fagelbrogolf.se

**Haninge** (1983)
*Årsta Slott, 136 91 Haninge*
☎ **(08) 500 32850**
📞 (08) 500 32851
📧 info@haninggk.golf.se
🖳 www.haningegk.se

**Husby** (1992)
*Husby V.11, 136 91 Haninge*
☎ **(08) 500 32285**
📧 info@husbygolfbana.se
🖳 www.husbygc.se

**Huvudstadens**
*Lindö Park, 186 92 Vallentuna*
☎ **(08) 511 70055 (Bookings)**
📞 (08) 511 70613
📧 info@huvudstadensgolf.se
🖳 www.huvudstadensgolf.se

**Ingarö** (1962)
*Fågelviksvägen 1, 134 64 Ingarö*
☎ **(08) 556 50200**
📞 (08) 546 50299
📧 info@igk.se
🖳 www.igk.se

**Kungsängen** (1992)
*Box 133, 196 21 Kungsängen*
☎ **(08) 584 50730**
📞 (08) 581 71002
📧 info@kungsangengc.se
🖳 www.kungsangengc.se

**Lidingö** (1933)
*Box 1035, 181 21 Lidingö*
☎ **(08) 731 7900**
📞 (08) 731 7900
📧 kansli@lidingogk.se
🖳 www.lidingogk.se

**Lindö** (1978)
*186 92 Vallentuna*
☎ **(08) 514 30990**
📞 (08) 511 74122

**Nya Johannesberg G&CC**
(1990)
*762 95 Rimbo*
☎ **(08) 514 50000**
📞 (08) 512 92390
🖳 www.golf.se/golfklubbar
/johannesberggcc

**Nynäshamn** (1977)
*Korunda 40, 148 91 Ösmo*
☎ **(08) 524 30590/524 30599**
📞 (08) 524 30598
📧 kansli@nynashamnsgk.a.se
🖳 www.nynashamnsgk.a.se

**Österakers**
*Hagby 1, 184 92 Akersberga*
☎ **(08) 540 85165**
📞 (08) 540 66832
📧 kansli@ostgk.se
🖳 www.ostgk.se   www.hagbygolf.se

**Royal Drottningholm Golf
Club** (1958)
*Lovö Kyrkallé 1, 178 93 Drottningholm*
☎ **(08) 759 0085**

📞 (08) 759 0851
📧 info@kdrgk.se
✍ Stefan Andorff
🖳 www.kdrgk.se

**Saltsjöbaden** (1929)
*Box 51, 133 21 Saltsjöbaden*
☎ **+46 (0)8 717 0125**
📞 +46 (0)8 717 9713
📧 klubb@saltsjobadengk.se
🖳 www.saltsjobadengk.se

**Sollentuna** (1967)
*Skillingegården, 192 77 Sollentuna*
☎ **(08) 594 70995**
📞 (08) 594 70999
📧 intendent@sollentunagk.se
🖳 www.sollentunagk.se

**Stockholm** (1904)
*Kevingestrand 20, 182 57 Danderyd*
☎ **(08) 544 90710**
📞 (08) 544 90712

**Täby** (1968)
*Skålhamra Gård, 187 70 Täby*
☎ **(08) 510 23261**
📞 (08) 510 23441

**Ullna** (1981)
*Roslagsvagen 36, 184 94 Åkersberga*
☎ **(08) 514 41230**
📞 (08) 510 26068
📧 ullna@ullnagolf.se
🖳 www.ullnagolf.se

**Ulriksdal** (1965)
*Box 8088, 170 08 Solna*
☎ **(08) 855393**
📧 info@ulriksdalsgk.se
🖳 www.ulriksdalsgk.se

**Vallentuna** (1989)
*Box 266, 186 24 Vallentuna*
☎ **(08) 514 30560/1**
📞 (08) 514 30569
🖳 www.vallentunagk.nu

**Viksjö** (1969)
*Fjällens Gård, 175 45 Järfälla*
☎ **(08) 580 31300/31310**
📞 (08) 580 31340
🖳 www.golf.se/viksjogk

**Wäsby**
*Box 2017, 194 02 Upplands Väsby*
☎ **(08) 514 103 50**
📞 (08) 514 103 55

**Wermdö G&CC** (1966)
*Torpa, 139 40 Värmdö*
☎ **(08) 574 60700**
📞 (08) 574 60729
📧 wgcc@telia.com
🖳 www.wgcc.se

---

### West Central

**Arvika** (1974)
*Box 197, 671 25 Arvika*
☎ **(0570) 54133**
📞 (0570) 54233
🖳 www.arvikagk.nu

**Billerud** (1961)
*Valnäs, 660 40 Segmon*
☎ **(0555) 91313**
📞 (0555) 91306
📧 kansli@billerudsgk.se
🖳 www.billerudsgk.se

**Dagsholm** (1987)
*Box 23, Dagsholm 1, 458 21 Färgelanda*
☎ **(0528) 20385**
📞 (0528) 20045
📧 r_heyman@hotmail.com
✍ Robert Heyman
🖳 www.dagsholmgolf.se

**Eda** (1992)
*Noresund, 670 40 Åmotfors*
☎ **(0571) 34101**
📞 (0571) 34191
🖳 www.edagk.com

**Fjällbacka** (1965)
*450 71 Fjällbacka*
☎ **(0525) 31150**
📞 (0525) 32122

**Forsbacka** (1969)
*Box 137, 662 23 Åmål*
☎ **(0532) 61690**
📞 (0532) 61699
📧 forsbackagolf@telia.com
🖳 www.forsbackagk.se

**Hammarö** (1991)
*Barrstigen 103, 663 91 Hammarö*
☎ **(054) 522650**
📞 (054) 521863
📧 info@hammarogk.se
🖳 www.hammarogk.se

**Karlskoga** (1975)
*Bricketorp 647, 691 94 Karlskoga*
☎ **(0586) 728190**
📞 (0586) 728417

**Karlstad** (1957)
*Höja 510, 655 92 Karlstad*
☎ **(054) 866353**
📞 (054) 866478
📧 info@karlstadgk.se
🖳 www.karlstadgk.se

**Kristinehamn** (1974)
*Box 337, 681 26 Kristinehamn*
☎ **(0550) 82310**
📞 (0550) 19535
📧 kristinehamnsgk@telia.com
🖳 www.golf.se/golfklubbar
/kristinehamnsgk

**Lyckorna** (1967)
*Box 66, 459 22 Ljungskile*
☎ **(0522) 20176**
📞 (0522) 22304

**Orust** (1981)
*Morlanda 135, 474 93 Ellös*
☎ **+46 304 53170**
📞 +46 304 53174
📧 orustgk@telia.com
🖳 www.orustgk.se

**Saxå**   (1964)
*Saxån, 682 92 Filipstad*
☎ **(0590) 24070**
🖳 (0590) 24101

**Skaftö**   (1963)
*Stockeviksvägen 2, 450 34 Fiskebäckskil*
☎ **+0046 (523) 23211**
🖳 +0046 (523) 23215
📧 kansliet@skaftogk.se
🖳 www.skaftogk.se

**Strömstad**   (1967)
*Golfbanevägen, 452 90 Strömstad 1*
☎ **(0526) 61788**
🖳 (0526) 14766
🖳 www.golf.se/stromstadgk

**Sunne**   (1970)
*Box 108, 686 23 Sunne*
☎ **(0565) 14100/14210**
🖳 (0565) 14855
📧 info@sunnegk.se
🖳 www.sunnegk.se

**Torreby**   (1961)
*Torreby Slott, 455 93 Munkedal*
☎ **(0524) 21365/21109**
🖳 (0524) 21351

**Uddeholm**   (1965)
*Risäter 20, 683 93 Råda*
☎ **(0563) 60564**
🖳 (0563) 60017
📧 uddeholmsgk@telia.com
🖳 www.uddeholmsgk.com

---

# Switzerland

Bern

**Golf & Country Club**
**Blumisberg**   (1959)
*3184 Wünnewil*
☎ **(026) 496 34 38**
🖳 (026) 496 35 23
📧 secretariat@blumisberg.ch
✍ Heinz Reber (Club Mgr)
🖳 www.blumisberg.ch

**Les Bois**   (1988)
*Case Postale 26, 2336 Les Bois*
☎ **(032) 961 10 03**
🖳 (032) 961 10 17

**Neuchâtel**   (1925)
*Hameau de Voëns, 2072 Saint-Blaise,*
*Hameau de Voëns 13*
☎ **(032) 753 55 50**
🖳 (032) 753 29 40
📧 secretariat@golfdeneuchatel.ch
✍ Sabine Daverat Hasler
🖳 www.golfdeneuchatel.ch

**Payerne**   (1996)
**Public**
*Domaine des Invuardes, 1530 Payerne*
☎ **(026) 662 4220**

🖳 (026) 662 4221
📧 golf.payerne@vtx.ch
🖳 www.golfpayerne.ch

**Golf & Country Club**
**Wallenried**   (1994)
*Chemin du Golf 18, 1784 Wallenried*
☎ **(026) 684 84 80**
🖳 (026) 684 84 90
📧 info@golf-wallenried.ch
✍ Mario Rottaris
🖳 www.golf-wallenried.ch

**Wylihof**   (1994)
*4542 Luterbach*
☎ **(032) 682 28 28**
🖳 (032 682 65 17
📧 wylihof@golfclub.ch
🖳 www.golfclub.ch

---

## Bernese Oberland

**Interlaken-Unterseen**   (1964)
*Postfach 110, 3800 Interlaken*
☎ **(033) 823 60 16**
🖳 (033) 823 42 03
📧 info@interlakengolf.ch
✍ Mr Martin Gadient
🖳 www.interlakengolf.ch

**Riederalp**   (1987)
*3987 Riederalp*
☎ **+41 (0) 27 927 29 32**
🖳 +41 (0) 27 927 29 23
📧 info@golfclub-riederalp.ch
✍ Willy Kummer
🖳 www.golfclub-riederalp.ch

---

## Lake Geneva & South West

**Bonmont**   (1983)
*Château de Bonmont, 1275 Chéserex*
☎ **(022) 369 99 00**
🖳 (022) 369 99 09
📧 golfhotel@bonmont.com
🖳 www.bonmont.com

**Les Coullaux**   (1989)
*1846 Chessel*
☎ **(024) 481 22 46**
🖳 (024) 481 66 46
📧 secretariat@golflescoullaux.ch
🖳 www.golflescoullaux.ch

**Crans-sur-Sierre**   (1906)
*Rue du Prado 20, 3963 Crans-Montana*
☎ **(027) 485 97 97**
🖳 (026) 485 97 97
📧 info@golfcrans.ch
🖳 www.golfcrans.ch

**Domaine Impérial**   (1987)
*Villa Prangins, 1196 Gland*
☎ **+41 22 999 06 00**
🖳 +41 22 999 06 06
📧 info@golfdomaineimperial.com
🖳 www.golfdomaineimperial.com

**Geneva**   (1921)
*70 Route de la Capite, 1223 Cologny*
☎ **(+41) 22 707 48 00**
🖳 (+41) 22 707 48 20
📧 secretariat@golfgeneve.ch
✍ François Lautens

**Lausanne**   (1921)
*Route du Golf 3, 1000 Lausanne 25*
☎ **(021) 784 84 84**
🖳 (021) 784 84 80
📧 info@golflausanne.ch
✍ Pierre Rindlisbacher
🖳 www.golfsuisse.ch

**Golf Club Montreux**   (1900)
*54 Route d'Evian, 1860 Aigle*
☎ **(024) 466 46 16**
🖳 (024) 466 60 47
📧 secretariat@gcmontreux.ch
✍ Jacky Rey (Manager)
🖳 www.golfmontreux.ch
/www.swissgolfnetwork.ch

**Sion**   (2002)
*Rte Vissigen 150, 1950 Sion*
☎ **(+41) (0) 027 203 79 00**
🖳 (+41) (0) 027 203 79 01
📧 info@golfclubsion.ch
🖳 www.golfclubsion.ch

**Verbier**   (1970)
*1936 Verbier*
☎ **(027) 771 53 14**
🖳 (027) 771 60 93
📧 golf.club@verbier.ch
🖳 www.verbiergolf.com

**Villars**   (1922)
*CP 118, 1884 Villars*
☎ **(024) 495 42 14**
🖳 (024) 495 42 18
📧 info@golf-villars.ch
✍ Eric Krol (Mgr)
🖳 www.golf-villars.ch

---

## Lugano & Ticino

**Lugano**   (1923)
*6983 Magliaso*
☎ **(091) 606 15 57**
🖳 (091) 606 65 58
📧 info@golflugano.ch
✍ Massimo Casartelli (Mgr)
🖳 www.golflugano.ch

**Patriziale Ascona**   (1928)
*Via al Lido 81, 6612 Ascona*
☎ **(+41) 091 785 1177**
🖳 (+41) 091 785 1179
📧 info@golfascona.ch
✍ Reiner Horlacher (Mgr)
🖳 www.golfascona.ch

---

## St Moritz & Engadine

**Golf Club Arosa**   (1944)
*Postfach 95, 7050 Arosa*
☎ **(081) 377 42 42**

---

📞 (081) 377 46 77
📧 info@golfarosa.ch
👤 Christian Danuser
🖥 www.golfarosa.ch

**Bad Ragaz**   (1957)
*Hans Albrecht Strasse, 7310 Bad Ragaz*
☎ **(081) 303 37 17**
📞 (081) 303 37 27
📧 golfclub@resortragaz.ch
👤 Ralph Polligkeit (Mgr)
🖥 www.resortragaz.ch

**Davos**   (1929)
*Postfach, 7260 Davos Dorf*
☎ **(081) 46 56 34**
📞 (081) 46 25 55
📧 info@golfdavos.ch
🖥 www.golfdavos.ch

**Engadin**   (1893)
*7503 Samedan*
☎ **(081) 851 04 66**
📞 (081) 851 04 67
📧 samedan@engadin-golf.ch
🖥 www.engadin-golf.ch

**Lenzerheide**   (1950)
*7078 Lenzerheide*
☎ **(081) 385 13 13**
📞 (081) 385 13 19
📧 info@golf-lenzerheide.ch
🖥 www.golf-lenzerheide.ch

**Vulpera**   (1923)
*7552 Vulpera Spa*
☎ **(081) 864 96 88**
📞 (081) 864 96 89
📧 info@vulperagolf.ch
👤 Markus Vesti
🖥 www.swissgolfnetwork.ch-9holes-vulpera

## Zürich & North

**Breitenloo**   (1964)
*Golfstrasse 16, 8309 Oberwil b. Nürensdorf*
☎ **+41 (0) 44 836 40 80**
📞 +41 (0) 44 837 10 85
📧 sekretariat@golfbreitenloo.ch

**Bürgenstock Golf Club**   (1928)
*6363 Oboürgen*
☎ **(041) 610 2434**
📞 (041) 612 9901
📧 info@golfclub-buergenstock.ch
🖥 www.buergenstock.ch

**Dolder**   (1907)
*Kurhausstrasse 66, 8032 Zürich*
☎ **(01) 261 50 45**
📞 (01) 261 53 02

**Entfelden**   (1988)
*Muhenstrasse 52, 5036 Oberentfelden*
☎ **(062) 723 89 84**
📞 (062) 723 84 36

**Erlen**   (1994)
*Schlossgut Eppishausen, Schlossstr 7,
8586 Erlen*
☎ **(071) 648 29 30**
📞 (071) 648 29 40
📧 info@erlengolf.ch
👤 Christian Heller
🖥 www.erlengolf.ch

**Hittnau-Zürich G&CC**   (1964)
*8335 Hittnau*
☎ **(+41) 950 24 42**
📞 (+41) 951 01 66
📧 info@gcch.ch
🖥 www.gcch.ch

**Küssnacht**   (1994)
*Sekretariat/Grossarni, 6403 Küssnacht
am Rigi*
☎ **(041) 854 4020**
📞 (041) 854 4027
📧 gck@golfkuessnacht.ch
🖥 www.golfkuessnacht.ch

**Golf Kyburg**   (2004)
*CH-8310 Kemptthal, Zürich*
☎ **+41 52 355 06 06**
📞 +41 52 355 06 16
📧 info@golf-kyburg.ch
🖥 www.golf-kyburg.ch

**Lucerne**   (1903)
*Dietschiberg, 6006 Luzern*
☎ **(041) 420 97 87**
📞 (041) 420 82 48
📧 info@golfclubluzern.ch
🖥 www.golfclublucerne.ch

**Ostschweizerischer Golf Club**   (1948)
**Club**
*9246 Niederbüren, Golfstrasse 106*
☎ **(071) 422 18 56**
📞 (071) 422 18 25
📧 osgc@bluewin.ch
👤 Daniel Schweizer
🖥 www.osgc.ch

**Schinznach-Bad**   (1929)
*5116 Schinznach-Bad*
☎ **(056) 443 12 26**
📞 (056) 443 34 83
📧 golfclub.schinznach@bluewin.ch
🖥 www.swissgolfnetwork.ch

**Schönenberg G&CC**   (1967)
*8824 Schönenberg*
☎ **(044) 788 90 40**
📞 (044) 788 90 45

📧 info@golf-schoenenberg.ch
👤 Peter Aeschbach
🖥 www.golf-schoenenberg.ch

**Golf Sempachersee**   (1996)
*CH-6024 Hildisrieden, Lucerne*
☎ **+41 41 462 71 71**
📞 +41 41 462 71 72
📧 info@golf-sempachersee.ch
🖥 www.golf-sempachersee.ch

**Zürich-Zumikon**   (1929)
*Weid 9, 8126 Zumikon*
☎ **(0041) 43 288 1088**
📞 (0041) 43 288 1078
📧 gccz.zumikon@ggaweb.ch
👤 C R Vane Percy
🖥 www.golfsuisse.ch

---

# Turkey

**Gloria Golf**
*Acisu Mevkii PK27 Belek, Serik, Antalya*
☎ **(242) 715 15 20**
📞 (242) 715 15 25

**Kemer G&CC**
*Goturk Koyu Mevkii Kemerburgaz,
Eyup, Istanbul*
☎ **(212) 239 70 10**
📞 (212) 239 73 76

**Klassis G&CC**
*Silivri, Istanbul*
☎ **(212) 748 46 00**
📞 (212) 748 46 43

**National Golf Club, Antalya**
(1994)
*Belek Turizm Merkezi, 07500
Serik, Antalya*
☎ **(242) 725 46 20**
📞 (242) 725 46 23
📧 info@nationalturkey.com
🖥 www.nationalturkey.com

**Robinson Golf Club Nobilis**
(1998)
*Acisu Mevkii, Belek, 07500
Serik/Antalya, Antalya*
☎ **(+90) 242 7100362**
📞 (+90) 242 7100391
📧 golf.nobilis@robinson.de
🖥 www.robinson.de

**Tat Golf International**
*Belek International Golf, Kum Tepesi Belek,
07500 Serik, Antalya*
☎ **(242) 725 53 03**
📞 (242) 725 52 99

# Rest of the World – Region and Country Index

Golf is a global game and more and more golfers are travelling further and further on holiday and often to countries less well known as golfing destinations so, from the 2009 edition *The R&A Golfer's Handbook* has added as an additional service information on clubs from around the world to its existing directory of clubs in Great Britain, Ireland and Continental Europe. The selection is by no means comprehensive but the intention to continue to improve this section continues with many new entries including seven new countries. Those clubs listed have been chosen at random from various sources.

## North America
Canada 894
USA 884

## The Caribbean and Central America
Antigua 896
Aruba 896
Bahamas 896
Barbados 896
Bermuda 896
Cayman Islands 896
Cuba 896
Dominican Republic 896
Grenada 896
Jamaica 896
Martinque 896
Mexico 896
Puerto Rico 897
St Kitts & Nevis 897
St Lucia 897
St Maarten 897
St Vincent 897
Trinidad & Tobago 897
Turks & Caicos 897
US Virgin Islands 897

## South America
Argentina 897
Brazil 898
Chile 898
Costa Rica 898
Ecuador 898
French Guyana 898
Paraguay 899

Peru 899
Uruguay 899
Venezuela 899

## Africa
Algeria 899
Boswana 899
Cameroon 899
Egypt 899
Ghana 900
Kenya 900
Madagascar 900
Mauritius 900
Morocco 900
Namibia 901
Nigeria 901
Réunion 901
Senegal 901
Seychelles 901
South Africa 901
Swaziland 903
Tunisia 903
Uganda 903
Zambia 903
Zimbabwe 904

## Middle East
Bahrain 904
Israel 904
Kuwait 904
Oman 904
Qatar 904
Saudi Arabia 904
United Arab Emirates 904

## Asia
Bangladesh 905
Bhutan 905
Brunei 905
China 905
Chinese Tapei 907
Hong Kong 907
India 907
Indonesia 908
Japan 908
Korea 908
Laos 908
Macau 908
Malaysia 909
Maldives 910
Myanmar 910
Nepal 910
Pakistan 910
Philippines 911
Singapore 911
Sri Lanka 911
Thailand 911
Vietnam 911

## Australasia and the Pacific
Australia 912
Cook Islands 913
Fiji 913
Guam 913
New Zealand 913
Papua New Guinea 914
Samoa 914
Tonga 914
Vanuatu 914

---

## A truly world-wide sport

If anyone remains in any doubt that golf is truly a world-wide sport they should consider the following, proof that the human spirit and a passion for the game will prevail under the most daunting of conditions.

**Highest golf course** – La Paz Golf Club in Bolivia stands at 10,650 feet above sea level at its highest point. One of the greatest hazards is oxygen deficiency with the compensation that a ball will fly further and faster in the thin mountain air.

**Most remote golf course** – Royal Thimpu Golf Club in Bhutan, a county so remote that is has only recently seen the arrival of television and the motor vehicle, lies in the heart of the Himalayas surrounded by some of the world's highest mountains.

**Most southerly golf course** – Ushuaia Golf Club in Argentina sits at the southern tip of the South American continent close to windy Cape Horn.

**Most northerly golf course** – North Cape Golf Club in Norway lies within the Arctic Circle offering a 24-hour golfing day for several months of the year.

# North America

## Canada

### Alberta

**Banff Springs**
www.banffspringsgolfclub.com

**Jasper Park Lodge**  (1925)
www.fairmontgolf.com

**Kananaskis**  (1983)
www.kananaskisgolf.com

**Stewart Creek**  (2001)
www.tsmv.ca

**Wolf Creek**  (1984)
www.wolfcreekgolf.com

### Atlantic Canada

**Crowbush Cove**  (2000)
www.golflinkspei.com

**Dundarave**  (1999)
www.golflinkspei.com

**Fox Harb'r Resort**  (2001)
www.foxharbr.com

**Highlands Links**  (1939)
www.highlandslinksgolf.com

**Humber Valley**  (2006)
www.humbervalley.com

### British Columbia

**Bear Mountain**  (2005)
www.bearmountain.ca

**Chateau Whistler**  (1993)
www.fairmont.com/whistler

**Grey Wolf**  (1999)
www.greywolfgolf.com

**Predator Ridge**
predatorridge.com

**Tobiano**  (2007)
www.tobianogolf.com

### Ontario

**Deerhurst Highlands**  (1990)
www.deerhurstresort.com

**Eagles Nest**  (2004)
www.eaglesnestgolf.com

**Muskoka Bay**
www.muskokabayclub.com

**Rocky Crest**  (2000)
www.clublink.ca

**Taboo Resort**  (2002)
www.tabooresort.com

### Saskatchewan and Manitoba

**Cooke Municipal**  (1909)
www.cookegolf.com

**Dakota Dunes**  (2004)
www.dakotadunes.ca

**Falcon Lake**
www.falconlakegolfcourse.com

**Granite Hills**
www.granitehills.ca

**Waskesiu**
www.golfsask.com/waskesiu.htm

### Quebec

**Le Château Montebello**
chateaumontebello@fairmont.com

**Le Diable**  (1998)
www.golflediamant.com

**Le Geant at Mont Tremblant**  (1995)
www.tremblant.ca

**Le Maitre de Mont-Tremblant**  (2001)
www.clublink.ca

**Le Manoir Richelieu**
www.fairmont.com/richelieu/Recreation/Golf

## USA

### Alabama

**Kiva Dunes**
www.kivadunes.com

### Arizona

**The Boulders Resort**
www.theboulders.com

**Camelback Inn**
www.camelbackinn.com

**Fairmont Scottsdale**
www.fairmont.com

**Four Seasons Scottsdale**
www.fourseasons.com

**Loews Ventana Canyon Resort**
www.loewshotels.com

**The Phonician**
www.thephoenician.com

**The Lodge at Ventana Canyon**
www.thelodgeatventanacanyon.com

**Stone Canyon**
www.stonecanyon.com

**Westin Kierland Resort & Spa**
www.kierlandresort.com

### California

**The Breakers**
www.thebreakers.com

**Cordevalle**
www.cordevalle.com

**Four Seasons Aviara**
www.fourseasons.com

**Pebble Beach**
www.pebblebeach.com

**Las Quinta Resort**
www.laquintaresort.com

**The Resort at Pelican Hill**
www.pelicanhill.com

**The Ritz-Carlton, Half Moon Bay**
www.ritzcarlton.com

**Torrey Pines**
www.lodgetorreypines.com

**Westin Mission Hills**
www.westin.com

### Colorado

**The Broadmoor**
www.broadmoor.com

**The Lodge & Spa at Cordillera**
www.cordilleralodge.com

### Florida

**Bay Hill Club & Lodge**
www.bayhill.com

**Boca Raton**
www.bocaresort.com

**Grand Cypress Resort**
www.grandcypress.com

**Grande Lakes Orlando**
www.grandelakes.com

**PGA Village**
www.pgavillage.com

**The Ritz-Carlton, Naples**
📄 www.ritzcarlton.com

**Sandestin Resort**
📄 www.sandestin.com

**Sawgrass Marriott**
📄 www.sawgrassmarriott.com

**Walt Disney World Resort**
📄 www.disneyworld.com

## Georgia

**The Ritz-Carlton Lodge**
📄 www.ritzcarltonlodge.com

**Sea Island**
📄 www.seaisland.com

## Hawaii

**The Fairmont Orchid**
📄 www.fairmont.com

**Four Seasons (Hualalai, Lanai and Maui)**
📄 www.fourseasons.com

**Grand Hyatt Kauai**
📄 www.grandhyattkauai.com

**Grand Wailea**
📄 www.grandwailea.com

**Kauai Marriott**
📄 www.kauaimarriott.com

**Mauna Kea Beach Hotel**
📄 www.princeresortshawaii.com

**Mauna Lani Bay Hotel**
📄 www.maunalani.com

**The Ritz-Carlton, Kapalua**
📄 www.ritzcarlton.com

**Turtle Bay**
📄 www.turtlebayresort.com

## Idaho

**Coeur d'Alene**
📄 www.cdaresort.com

**Sun Valley**
📄 www.sunvalley.com

## Indiana

**French Lick Resort**
📄 www.frenchlick.com

## Michigan

**The Inn at Bay Harbor**
📄 www.innatbayharbor.com

**Grand Traverse Resort**
📄 www.grandtraverseresort.com

## Minnesota

**Giant's Ridge**
📄 www.giantsridge.com

**Grand View Lodge**
📄 www.grandviewlodge.com

## Nevada

**Wynn Las Vegas**
📄 www.wynnlasvegas.com

## New York State

**Turning Stone**
📄 www.turningstone.com

## North Carolina

**Pinehurst**
📄 www.pinehurst.com

**Pine Needles and Mid Pines**
📄 www.pineneedles-midpines.com

## Oregon

**Bandon Dunes**
📄 www.bandondunesgolf.com

**Sunriver Resort**
📄 www.sunriver-resort.com

## Pennsylvania

**Hershey Resorts**
📄 www.hersheypa.com

**Nemacolin Woodlands Resort**
📄 www.nemacolin.com

## South Carolina

**Kiawah Island**
📄 www.kiawahresort.com

**Sea Pines Resort**
📄 www.seapines.com

## Texas

**Barton Creek**
📄 www.bartoncreek.com

**Weston La Cantera Resort**
📄 www.westinlacantera.com

**The Woodlands Resort**
📄 www.woodlandsresort.com

## Vermont

**The Equinox**
📄 www.equinoxresort.com

## Virginia

**The Homestead**
📄 www.thehomestead.com

**Kingsmill Resort**
📄 www.kingsmill.com

**Williamsburg Inn**
📄 www.colonialwilliamsburgresort.com

## Washington

**Resort Seniahmoo**
📄 www.semiahmoo.com

## West Virginia

**The Greenbrier**
📄 www.greenbrier.com

## Wisconsin

**The American Club**
📄 www.destinationkohler.com

## Creepies and Crawlies

Players at the Stone Canyon Club in Arizona are advised not to try to recover balls that land beyond the fairway as the area is heavily populated by rattlesnakes, scorpions and tarantulas.

# The Caribbean and Central America

## Antigua

### Cedar Valley GC
PO Box 198, Cedar Valley, St. John's, Antigua
☎ +1 268 462 0161
✉ cedarvalleyg@candw.ag
▤ www.cedarvalleygolf.ag

### Jolly Harbour GC
PO Box 1793, St. John's, Antigua
☎ +1 268 462 7771
✉ golf@jollyharbourantigua.com
▤ www.jollyharbourantigua.com /golf.html

## Aruba

### Aruba GC
Golfweg z/n, PO Box 2280 San Nicolas, Aruba
☎ +1 297 842 006
✉ arubagolfclub@yahoo.com
▤ www.golfclubaruba.com

### Tierra del Sol Resort, Spa & CC
PO Box 1257, Malmokweg z/n, Aruba
☎ +1 297 60 978
✉ tdsteetime@setarnet.aw
▤ www.tierradelsol.com

## Bahamas

### One & Only Atlantis
☎ +1242 888 877 7525
▤ www.oneandonlyresorts.com

### Treasure Cay
▤ www.treasurecay.com

## Barbados

### Barbados GC
Barbados Golf Club
☎ +1 246 428 8463
✉ teetime@barbadosgolfclub.com
▤ www.barbadosgolfclub.com

### Sandy Lane GC
Sandy Lane Hotel, St. James
☎ +1 246 432 2829
✉ mail@sandylane.com
▤ www.sandylane.com/golf

## Bermuda

### Belmont Hills G&CC
97 Middle Road, Warwick Parish, WK 09
☎ +1 441 236 6400
✉ golf@belmonthills.com
▤ www.belmonthills.com

### St George's GC
1 Park Road, St George's Parish, GE 03
☎ +1 441 234 8067
✉ sggc@bermudagolf.bm
▤ www.stgeorgesgolf.bm

## Cayman Islands

### Hyatt Britannia Golf Course
PO Box 1588 George Town, Grand Cayman
☎ +1 345 949 8020
▤ grandcayman.hyatt.com

### The Links at SafeHaven
PO Box 1311 George Town, Grand Cayman
☎ +1 345 949 5988
▤ www.safehaven.ky/links.htm

## Cuba

### El Varadero GC
Villa Xanadú, Dupont de Nemours, Cuba
☎ +53 45 668482
✉ info@varaderogolfclub.com
▤ www.varaderogolfclub.com

## Dominican Republic

### Casa de Campo: Teeth of the Dog; The Links and Dye Fore
La Romana Province, PO Box 140, La Romana
☎ +1809 523 3333
✉ reserva@ccampo.com.do
▤ www.casadecampo.com.do

### Playa Grande Golf Course
Km 9 Carretera Rio San Juan-Cabrera, Maria Trinidad Sanchez Province, North Coast
☎ +1809 582 0860
✉ info@playagrande.com
▤ www.playagrande.com

## Grenada

### Grenada G&CC
St. George, Grenada
☎ +1 473 444 4128
✉ grenadagolfclub@spiceisle.com
▤ www.grenadagolfclub.com

## Jamaica

### Ironshore G&CC
▤ www.superclubs.com

### Caymanas G&CC
Caymanas Golf & Country Club
☎ +1 876 922 3388
✉ play@caymanasgolfclub.com
▤ www.caymanasgolfclub.com

## Martinique

### Golf de la Martinique
97229 Les Trois-Ilets
☎ +33 5 96 68 32 81
✉ info@golfmartinique.com
▤ www.golfmartinique.com

## Mexico

### Baja California

### Bajamar GC
4364 Bonita Road #299 Bonita, CA 91902-1421 Ensenada, Baja California
✉ www.bajamar.com
▤ info@bajamar.com

### Centre

### Club Campestre de Aguascalientes
A.C.Vista Hermosa s/n, Fracc. Campestre 20100, Aguascalientes, Ags.
☎ +52 449 914 1001
▤ www.campestreags.com

### Central Pacific Coast

### Tamarindo Golf Course
k.m. 7.5 Carretera Barra de Navidad, Puerto Vallarta, Cihuatlan, Jalisco MX 48970
☎ +52 315 351 5032
▤ www.ycwtamarindo.com

## North

### El Cid G&CC
*Av. Camaron Sabalo s/n, P.O. Box 813,*
*Mazatlan, Sinaloa, Mexico 82110*
☎ +52 669 913 3333
✉ reserve@elcid.com.mx
🖥 www.elcid.com

## South

### Club de Golf Acapulco
*Av. Costera Miguel Aleman s/n Fracc. Club*
*Deportivo, Acapulco*
☎ +52 744 484
✉ gclubgolf@prodigy.net.mx

## Puerto Rico

### Dorado Beach Resort & Club
*100 Dorado Beach Drive, Suite 1, Dorado,*
*Puerto Rico 00646*
☎ +1 787 796 1234
✉ jcolon@kempersports.com
🖥 www.doradobeachclubs.com

### Palmas del Mar CC
*PO Box 2020 , Humacao, Puerto Rico*
*00792*
☎ +1 787 285 2221
🖥 www.palmascountryclub.com

## St Kitts and Nevis

### Royal St Kitts GC
*PO Box 858 Basseterre, St. Kitts, WI*
☎ +1 869 466 2700
✉ info@royalstkittsgolfclub.com
🖥 www.royalstkittsgolfclub.com

## St Lucia

### St Lucia G&CC
*Cap Estates, PO Box 328, Gros Islet, WI*
☎ +1 758 450 8522
✉ golf@candw.lc
🖥 www.stluciagolf.com

## St Maarten

### Mullet Bay Resort
☎ +1 599 545 3069

## St Vincent

### Trump International GC
*Charles Town, Canouan Island, St. Vincent*
*& The Grenadines, WI*
☎ +1 784 458 8000
✉ canouan@raffles.com

## Trinidad and Tobago

### Mount Irvine Bay Hotel and GC
*PO Box 222 Scarborough, Tobago, WI*
☎ +54 11 4468 1737
✉ mtirvine@tstt.net.tt
🖥 www.mtirvine.com/golf/golf.asp

## Turks and Caicos

### The Provo G&CC
*PO Box 662, Providenciales, Turks & Caicos*
*Islands, WI*
☎ +1 649 946 5991
✉ provogolf@tciway.tc
🖥 www.provogolfclub.com

## US Virgin Islands

### Buccaneer Hotel Golf Course
*The Buccaneer, St Croix, US Virgin Islands*
☎ +1 340 712 2144
🖥 www.thebuccaneer.com/golf.htm

# South America

## Argentina

### Buenos Aires

### Buenos Aires GC
*Mayor Irusta 3777, (1661) Bella Vista,*
*Buenos Aires*
☎ +54 11 4468 1737
✉ info@bagolf.com.ar
🖥 www.bagolf.com.ar

### The Jockey Club
*Av. Marquez 1702, San Isidro, Buenos Aires*
☎ +54 4743 1001
✉ adm.golf@jockeyclub.org.ar

### Marayuí CC
*Chapadmalal, Buenos Aires Province, Costa*
*Atlantica*
☎ +54 0223 460 5163
🖥 www.marayui.com

### Olivos GC
*Ruta Panamericana Ramal Pilar Km 32, Ing.*
*Pablo.Nogués, CP 1613, Buenos Aires*
☎ +54 11 4463 1076
✉ secretaria@olivosgolf.com.ar

### Sierra de la Ventana GC
*Avda. del Golf 300 - Bo. Parque Golf , C.C.*
*N° 33 (8168) - Sierra de la Ventana*
☎ +54 0291 491 5113
✉ golfsventana@infovia.com.ar

### Córdoba

### Ascochinga GC
*Sierras Chicas, Córdoba*
☎ +54 3525 492015
🖥 www.ascochingagolf.com.ar

### La Cumbre GC
*Belgrano 1095, 5178 La Cumbre, Córdoba,*
*Sierras*
☎ +54 03548 452283
✉ lacumbregolf@arnet.com.ar
🖥 www.lacumbregolf.com.ar

### Jockey Club de Córdoba
*Ave. Valparaíso Km. 3 1/2, Córdoba*
☎ +54 03543 464 2283
✉ golf@jockeyclubcordoba.com.ar
🖥 www.jockeyclubcordoba.com.ar

### Mendoza Club de Campo
*Elpidio González y Tuyutí s/n 5503*
*Guaymallén, Mendoza*
☎ +54 0261 431 5967
✉ ccampomza@nysnet.com.ar
🖥 www.clubdecampomendoza.net.ar

### El Potrerillo de Larreta Resort & CC
*Road to Los Paredones Km 3 -CC195-*
*(5186), Alta Gracia, Córdoba*
☎ +54 03547 423804 425987
✉ golf@potrerillodelarreta.com
🖥 www.potrerillodelarreta.com

### Cuyo

### La Rioja GC
*Buenos Aires 148, La Rioja, Cuyo*
☎ +54 43822 426142

### Amancay GC
*Av. Roque Saenz Peña 8116 (Este), Alto de*
*Sierra, San Juan*
☎ +54 0264 425 3313
🖥 www.jockeyclubvt.com.ar

## San Luis GC
C.C.280, 5700 San Luis
☎ +54 02652 490013

### Norte

## La Esperanza GC
Salta 140, 4500 San Pedro, Jujuy
☎ +54 03884 420000

## Salta Polo Club
Av. Bolivia 2800, 4400 Salta, Prov. de Salta
☎ +54 0387 439 2001
🖳 www.saltagolfclub.com.ar

## Santiago del Estero GC
Nuñez del Prado s/n (C.C. 162), 4200
Santiago del Estero
☎ +54 0385 434 0186

## Jockey Club de Tucumán
Av.Solano Vera, Km.2 , CP 4107 Yerba
Buena, Tucumán
☎ +54 0381 425 1038
🖂 golfalpasumaj@jockeyclubtucuman.com
🖳 www.jockeyclubtucuman.com

### Parques Nacionales

## Golf Club Corrientes
Camino a Santa Ana KM. 1500, 3400
Corrientes, Litoral
☎ +54 03783 424372

## Tacurú Social Club
Ruta 12 km 7,5. Posadas, Misiones
☎ +54 03752 480524

## Jockey Club de Venado Tuerto
Castelli 657 Golf: Ruta 8 Km 372 , 2600
Venado Tuerto, Santa Fe
☎ +54 03462 421043
🖳 www.jockeyclubvt.com.ar

## Rosario GC
Morrison 9900, 2000 Rosario, Santa Fe
Province, Litoral
☎ +54 0341 451 3438
🖳 www.rosariogolfclub.com

### Patagonia

## Chapelco Golf and Resort
Route 234, Loma Atravesada de Taylor,
San Martín de los Andes, Neuquén,
Patagonia
☎ +54 2972 421785
🖂 reservasgolf@chapelcogolf.com
🖳 www.chapelcogolf.com

## Ruca Kuyen Golf & Resort
Cruz del Sur 203, B° Las Balsas, Ruca
Kuyen, Neuquén
☎ +54 2944 495099
🖂 info@rucakuyen.com.ar
🖳 www.rucakuyen.com.ar

## Llao-Llao Hotel and Resort
Av. Ezequiel Bustillo km. 25, Bariloche, Río
Negro Province, Patagonia
☎ +54 02944 448530
🖳 www.llaollao.com

## Ushuaia GC
Ruta 3 Camino a Lapataia, Tierra del
Fuego, Patagonia
☎ +54 2901 432946

### Brazil

### Rio de Janiero

## Búzios Golf Club & Resort
🖂 buziosgolf@mar.com.br

## Gavea Golf & Country Club
🖳 www.gaveagolf.com.br

## Hotel do Frade and Golf Resort
🖳 www.hoteldofrade.com.br

## Itanhangá Golf Club
🖳 www.itanhanga.com.br

### São Paulo

## Damha Golf Club
🖳 www.damha.com.br

## Guarapiranga G&CC
🖳 www.guarapirangagolfe.com.br

## Lago Azul GC
🖳 www.lagc.com.br

## Quinta da Baroneza Golfe Clube
🖳 www.qbgc.com.br

## São Fernando Golf Club
🖳 www.saofernando.com.br

## Terras da São José – Itú
🖳 www.tsjgolfeclube.com.br

## Vista Verde GC
🖳 www.vvgc.com.br

### Paraná (Curitiba City)

## Alphaville Graciosa Clube
🖳 www.clubealphaville.com.br

### Rio Grande do Sul

## Porto Alegre Country Club
🖳 www.pacc.com.br

### Bahia

## Commandatuba Ocean Course
🖳 www.transamerica.com.br

## Costa de Sauipe Golf Links
🖳 www.costadosauipe.com.br

## Iberostar Praia do Forte Golf Club
🖳 www.praiadofortegolfclub.com.br

## Terravista Golf Course
🖳 www.terravistagolf.com.br

### Chile

## Club de Golf Los Leones
Pte. Riesco 3700, Las Condes, Santiago
☎ +56 562 719 3200
🖂 clubgolf@entelchile.net
🖳 www.golflosleones.cl

### Costa Rica

## La Iguana Golf Course
Playa Herradura, Puntalenas, Costa Rica
☎ +506 2630 9028
🖂 maria.cano@marriott.com
🖳 www.golflaiguana.com

### Ecuador

## Quito Tenis y Golf Club
Urb. El Condado Av. A N73-154 y calle
B (Entrada de Socios), Quito 17012411
☎ +593 0224 91420
🖂 golf@qtgc.com
🖳 www.qtgc.com

### French Guyana

## Golf de l'Anse
Centre de Loisirs du Centre Spatial,
97310 Guyane
☎ +33 5 94 32 63 02
🖂 golf-anse@wanadoo.fr

## Paraquay

### Carlos Franco Country GC

Arroyos y Esteros
☎ +595 16 252123
✉ secretaria@carlosfrancogolf.com
🖥 www.carlosfrancogolf.com

### Paraná CC

Supercarretera a Itaipu, Hernandarias
☎ +595 61 570181
✉ secretaria@carlosfrancogolf.com
🖥 www.carlosfrancogolf.com

### Hotel Resort & Casino Yacht y Golf Club Paraguay

Av. del Yacht 11, Lambaré
☎ +595 21 906 121
🖥 www.hotelyacht.com.py

## Peru

### Amazon Golf Course

#185 Malecon Maldonado, City of Iquitos, North East Peru
☎ +51 965 943267
✉ michaelcollis@amazongolfcourse.com
🖥 www.amazongolfcourse.com

### Lima GC

Av. Camino Real 770, San Isidro, Lima 27
☎ +51 442 6006
✉ gerencia@limagolfclub.org.pe
🖥 www.limagolfclub.org.pe

### Los Andes GC

Carretera Central Km. 23, Hacienda Huampani, Chosica District, Lima
☎ +51 497 1066
✉ administracion@losandesgolfclub.org
🖥 www.losandesgolfclub.org

### Los Inkas GC

Av. El Golf Los Inkas s/n, Monterrico, Surco District, City of Lima
☎ +51 317 7770
✉ email@golflosinkas.com
🖥 www.losinkasgolfclub.com

## Uruguay

### Club del Lago Golf

Ruta 93 Km 116.500, (Departamento de Maldonado), Punta del Este
☎ +598 42 578423
✉ info@lagogolf.com
🖥 www.lagogolf.com

### Fray Bentos GC

Barrio Anglo, Fray Bentos , Ciudad de Fray Bentos, Rio Negro
☎ +598 56 22427

### Sheraton Colonia Golf & Spa Resort

Continuación de la Rambla de Las Américas S/N,Colonia Del Sacramento 70000
☎ +598 52 29000
✉ colonia.golf@arnet.com.ar

## Venezuela

### Cardon GC

Av. 1, Urb. Zarabón, Comunida Cardon, Punto Fijo, Edo. Falcón
☎ +58 0269 2483739
✉ cardongolfclub@hotmail.com

### La Cumaca GC

Sector La Cumaca, Carretera vía Pozo, Urb. Villas San Diego, Country Clu, San Diego, Edo. Carabobo
☎ +58 241 8910077
✉ info@golfclublacumaca.com
🖥 www.golfclublacumaca.com

### Junko GC

Urbanización Junko Country Club, Calle El Empalme, Kilómetro 19 Carretera El Junquito, Estado Vargas
☎ +58 212 412 1254
✉ junkogc@cantv.net
🖥 www.junkogolf.com

### San Luis CC

Carretera vieja Tocuyito, antes de la Hacienda San Luis, Valencia, Edo. Carabobo
☎ +58 0241 824 7878
✉ info@sanluiscc.com
🖥 www.sanluiscc.com

# Africa

## Algeria

### Algiers GC

Rue Ahmed Ouaked Dely-Ibrahim 16000
☎ +213 757 90

## Botswana

### Phakalane Golf Estate

*Golf Drive, Phakalane, Gaborone*
☎ +267 360 4000
🖥 http://golfestate.phakalane.com

## Cameroon

### Likomba GC

Tiko, South West Province Cameroon
☎ +237 3335 1173
🖥 www.golflikomba.com

## Egypt

### Cairo

### Dreamland Golf and Tennis Resort

6th of October City Road, Dreamland City, Cairo
☎ +20 11 400 577
✉ pyramidsgolf@hilton.com

### The Pyramids G&CC

Soleimania Golf Resort, Kilo 55 Cairo-Alexandria Desert Road 600955
☎ +20 49 600 953
✉ amers@gega.net

### Alexandria

### Sporting Club Golf Course Alexandria

☎ +20 3543 3627

### Hurghada

### Cascades Golf Resort & CC

48 km Safaga Road, Soma Bay, Red Sea
☎ +20 65 354 2333
✉ major@thecascades.com
🖥 www.residencedescascades.com

### The Links at Stella di Mare

Km 46, Suez–Hurgada Road, Ain Al Sokhna
☎ +20 212 4586
✉ golf@stelladimare.com
🖥 www.stelladimare.com

## Sharm el Sheikh

**Jolie Ville Golf & Resort**
Um Marikha Bay 46619, Sharm el Sheikh, South Sinai
☎ +20 2 269 01465
✉ monika.elbadramany@jolieville-hotels.com
🖥 www.jolieville-golf.com

## Luxor

**Royal Valley Golf Course**
29, El Rahala El Boghdady St., Golf Area, Heliopolis, Cairo
☎ +20 2 418 5234
✉ marketing@royalvalley.com

## Sinai Peninsular

**Taba Heights Golf Resort**
☎ +20 69 358 0073
✉ info@tabaheights.com
🖥 www.tabaheights.com

**Achimota GC**
PO Box AH8, Achimota. Accra
☎ +233 21 400220
🖥 www.achimotagolf.com

**Great Rift Valley Lodge & Golf Resort**
North Lake Road, Rift Valley
☎ +254 27 123129
🖥 www.heritage-eastafrica.com

**Karen CC**
Karen Rd, Nairobi, Kenya, PO Box 24817, Karen
☎ +254 2 882801
✉ golf@leisurelodgeresort.com
🖥 www.westerncapehotelandspa.co.za

**Kitale GC**
PO Box 30, Kitale
☎ +254 32 531338

**Leisure Lodge Beach & Golf Resort**
PO Box 84383, Mombasa
☎ +254 40 320 3624
✉ dippd@wchs.co.za
🖥 www.leisurelodgeresort.com

**Limuru CC**
PO Box 10, Limuru
☎ +254 667 3189

**Mombasa GC**
PO Box 90164, Mombasa
☎ +254 1 22853

**Muthaiga GC**
PO Box 41651, Nairobi,
☎ +254 2 762414
🖥 www.muthaigagolfclub.com

**Nakuru GC**
PO Box 652, Nakuru
☎ +254 37 40391

**Nyali G&CC**
Mombasa North Coast, PO Box 95678, Mombasa
☎ +254 11 47 1589

**Royal Nairobi GC**
P O Box 40221, Nairobi
☎ +254 2 725769
🖥 www.royalnairobigc.co.ke

**Sigona GC**
PO Box 40221, Kikuya
☎ +254 154 32144
🖥 www.sigonagolf.com

**Windsor G&CC**
Ridgeways Road, PO Box 45587, Nairobi
☎ +254 020 862300
✉ reservations@windsor.co.ke
🖥 www.windsorgolfresort.com

**Golf Club d'Antsirabe**
Ivohitra Golf Course , BP 142 Antsirabe
☎ +261 020 44 94 387
✉ contact@golfantsirabe.com
🖥 www.golfantsirabe.com

**Belle Mare Plage GC (The Legend, Lemuria Championship Golf Course and The Links)**
Poste de Flacq
☎ +230 402 2735
✉ info@bellemareplagehotel.com
🖥 www.bellemareplagehotel.com/golf

**Paradis Hotel & GC**
Le Morne Peninsula
☎ +230 401 5050
🖥 www.paradis-hotel.com

**Tamarina Golf Estate and Beach Club**
Tamarin Bay
☎ +230 401 300
🖥 www.tamarina.mu

**Le Touessrok**
Trou d'Eau
☎ +230 402 7400
🖥 www.letouessrokresort.com

## Agadir

**Agadir Royal GC**
Km12, Route Ait Melloul, Agadir
☎ +212 4824 8551
✉ royalgolfagadir@multimania.com

**Golf Club Med les Dunes**
Chemin Oued Souss, Agadir
☎ +212 4883 4690

## Benslimane

**Ben Slimane Royal Golf**
Avenue des F.A.R. BP 83 Ben Slimane, Morocco
☎ +212 332 8793

## Casablanca

**Anfa Royal GC**
Hippodrome d'Anfa, Casablanca
☎ +212 0522 351026

**Settat University Royal GC**
Km 2, Route de Casablanca, BP 575 Settat, Morocco
☎ +212 2340 0755

---

## Longest par 3

The 19th hole at Legend's Golf & Safari Resort in South Africa sits near the foot of a 1,400 foot cliff. The distance between the tee and the hole is 907 yards. The tee is so inaccessible it can only be reached by experienced rock climbers or by helicopter. Used only for play-offs, Padraig Harrington is believed to be the only person to make par at this hole.

## El Jadida

### El Jadida Royal Golf & Spa
Route de Casablanca km7, B.P 116 24000
El Jadida
☎ +212 523 37910
✉ H2960@accor.com
🖥 www.accorhotels.com

## Fez

### Fez Royal GC
Km 15, Route d'Imouzzer, Fez
☎ +212 5566 5210

## Meknès

### Meknès Royal GC
Jnan Al Bahraouia, Ville Ancienne, Meknès
☎ +212 5553 0753
✉ rgm@royalgolfmeknes.com
🖥 www.royalgolfmeknes.com

## Rabat

### Dar Es-Salam Royal Golf
KM 9, avenue Mohammed VI / route des
Zaers Souissi, Rabat
☎ +212 3775 5864
✉ golfdaressalam@menara.ma
🖥 www.royalgolfdaressalam.com

## Namibia

### Windhoek G&CC
Western Bypass, Windhoek
☎ +264 61 205 5223
🖥 www.wccgolf.com.na

## Nigeria

### Ikoyi Club
6 Ikoyi Club 1938 Road, Ikoyi. PO Box 239,
Lagos
☎ +234 269 5133
✉ info@ikoyiclub-1938.org
🖥 www.ikoyiclub-1938.org

### Le Méridien Ibom Hotel & Golf Resort
Nwaniba Road, PMB 1200, Uyo, Akwa
Ibom State
☎ +234 808 052 7411
✉ reservations.ibom@lemeridien.com
🖥 www.lemeridienibom.com

### MicCom Golf Hotels and Resort
Ibokun Road, Ada, Osun Estate
☎ +234 1497 5445
🖥 www.gmiccomgolfhotels.com

## Réunion

### Golf du Bassin Bleu
75 rue Mahatma Gandhi-Villéle, 97435
Saint Gilles les Hauts
☎ +33 262 70 30 00
🖥 www.bassinbleu.fr

## Senegal

### Le Golf du Méridien-Président
Les Almadies, BP 8181 Dakar
☎ +221 33 869 69 69
✉ resa.meridien@orange.sn

### Golf de Saly
BP 145, Nagaparou
☎ +221 33957 2488
🖥 www.golfsaly.com

## Seychelles

### Lemuria Resort Golf Course
Anse Kerlan, Ile de Praslin
☎ +248 281 281
✉ golf@lemuriaresort.com
🖥 www.lemuriaresort.com

## South Africa

### Eastern Cape

### East London
22 Gleneagles Road, Bunkers Hill, East London
☎ +27 43 735 1356
🖥 www.elgc.co.za

### Humewood GC
Marine Drive, Summerstrand, Port Elizabeth 6013
☎ +27 41 583 2137
✉ info@humewoodgolf.co.za
🖥 www.humewoodgolf.co.za

### St Francis Bay GC
Lyme Road South, PO Box 3, St Francis Bay 6312
☎ +27 42 294 0467
✉ info@stfrancisclub.co.za
🖥 www.stfrancisgolf.co.za

### Gauteng

### Blair Atholl
Centurion, Gauteng 2068
☎ +27 11 996 6300
🖥 www.blairatholl.co.za

### Blue Valley
54 Buely Avenue, Centurion
☎ +27 11 318 3410
🖥 www.bluevalley.co.za

### Bryanston
63 Bryanston Drive, Byranston 2021
☎ +27 11 706 1361
🖥 www.bryanstoncc.co.za

### Centurion
Centurion Drive, John Vorster Avenue, Centurion
☎ +27 12 665 0279
🖥 www.centurioncountryclub.co.za

### Dainfern
633 Gateside Avenue, Fourways 2021
☎ +27 11 875 0421
🖥 www.dainfern.co.za

### Glendower GC
Marais Road, Edenvale, Johannesburg 1610
☎ +27 11 453 1013
✉ glengolf@mweb.co.za
🖥 www.lglendower.co.za

### Hodderfontein
Golf Course Drive, Hodderfontein, Johannesburg
☎ +27 11 608 2033
🖥 www.mgclub.co.za

### Houghton GC
2nd Ave, PO Box 87240, Houghton 2041
☎ +27 11 728 7337
✉ hgcm@houghton.co.za
🖥 www.houghton.co.za

### Johannesberg (Woodmead)
Lincoln Street, Woodmead, Johannesberg 2128
☎ +27 11 202 1600
🖥 www.ccj.co.za

### Kyalami CC
Maple Road, Sunninghill 2157
☎ +27 11 702 1610
🖥 www.kyalamicountryclub.co.za

### Maccauvlei
Old Sasolburg Road, Vereeniging
☎ +27 16 421 3196

### Parkview
Emmarentia Avenue, Parkview 2122
☎ +27 11 646 5725
🖥 www.parkviewgolf.co.za

### Pretoria
241 Sydney Avenue, Waterkloof 0181
☎ +27 12 400 6241
🖥 www.ptacc.co.za

### Randpark (Randpark & Windsor Park)
Setpark Street, Randpark, Randburg 2194, Johannesberg
☎ +27 11 476 1691
🖥 www.randpark.co.za

## Roodepoort
*Hole In One Avenue, Ruimsig, Roodeport*
☎ +27 11 958 1905
🖥 www.roodepoortcc.co.za

## Royal Johannesberg (East & West)
*1 Fairway Avenue, Linksfield North, Johannesberg 2119*
☎ +27 11 640 3021
🖥 www.royaljk.za.com

## Silver Lakes
*263 La Quinta Street, Silver Lakes, Pretoria*
☎ +27 12 809 2110
🖥 www.silverlakes.co.za

## Wanderers
*PO Box 55005, Northlands, Johannesburg 2116*
☎ +27 11 447 3311
🖥 www.wanderersgolfclub.com

## KwaZulu-Natal

## Champagne Sports
*Winterton 3340*
☎ +27 36 468 8000
🖥 www.champagnesportsresort.com

## Durban CC
*PO Box 1504, Durban, 4000*
☎ +27 31 313 1777
📧 mail@dcclub.co.za
🖥 www.dcclub.co.za

## Mount Edgecombe CC
*PO Box 1800, Mount Edgecombe 4300*
☎ +27 31 595330
📧 reception@mountecc.co.za
🖥 www.mountedgecombe.com

## Prince's Grant Golf Estate
*Babu Bodasingh Ave, PO Box 4038, KwaDukuza/Stanger 4450*
☎ +27 32 482 0041
📧 pglodge@saol.com

## San Lameer
*Main Road, Lower South Coast, Southbroom 4277*
☎ +27 39 315 5141
🖥 www.sanlameer.co.za

## Selborne CC
*Old Main Road, PO Box 2, Pennington 4185*
☎ +27 39 688 1891
📧 golfbookings@selborne.com
🖥 www.selborne.com

## Southbroom GC
*301 Captain Smith Rd, PO Box 24, Southbroom 4277*
☎ +27 39 316 6051
📧 info@southbroomgolfclub.co.za
🖥 www.southbroomgolfclub.co.za

## Umdoni Park
*Minerva Road, Pennington 4184*
☎ +27 39 975 1615
🖥 www.umdonipark.com

## Zimbali
*Umhali 4390*
☎ +27 32 538 1041
🖥 www.zimbali.co.za

## Mpumalanga

## Leopard Creek CC
*PO Box 385, Malelane 1320*
☎ +27 13 790 3322
🖥 www.leopardcreek.co.za

## Limpopo

## Elements
*5 Autumn Street, Rivonia 2128*
☎ +27 14 736 6910
🖥 www.elementspgr.co.za

## Hans Merensky Estate
*PO Box 4, Phalaborwa 1390*
☎ +27 15 781 5309
📧 gitw@hansmerensky.com

## Legend
*Entabeni Safari Conservatory, Sterkrivier*
☎ +27 32 538 1205
🖥 www.legend-resort.com

## Zebula
*Bela Bela 0840*
☎ +27 14 734 7702
🖥 www.zebula.co.za

## North West

## Gary Player CC
*PO Box 6, Sun City 0316*
☎ +27 14 557 1245/6
📧 kpayet@sunint.co.za
🖥 www.sun-international.com

## Lost City GC
*PO Box 5, Sun City 0316*
☎ +27 14 557 3700
📧 kpayet@sunint.co.za
🖥 www.sun-international.com

## Pecanwood CC
*PO Box 638, Broederstroom 0240*
☎ +27 21 7821118
📧 craig@pecanwood.biz

## Northern Cape

## Sishen
*Kathu 8446, Northern Cape*
☎ +27 53 723 1501
🖥 www.sishengolfclub.co.za

## Western Cape

## Arabella GC
*PO Box 788, Kleinmond, 7195*
☎ +27 28 284 9383
📧 dippd@wchs.co.za
🖥 www.westerncapehotelandspa.co.za

## Atlantic Beach
*1 Fairway Drive, Melkbossstrand 7441*
☎ +27 21 553 2223
🖥 www.atlanticbeachgolfclub.co.za

## Clovelly CC
*PO Box 22119, Fish Hoek 7974*
☎ +27 21 782 1118
📧 bookings@clovelly.co.za
🖥 www.clovelly.co.za

## Devondale Golf Estate
*Bottelary Road, Koelenhof, Stellenbosch 7605*
☎ +21 865 2080
📧 info@devonvale.co.za
🖥 www.devondale.co.za

## Durbanville GC
*Sportsway, Durbanville 7550*
☎ +27 21 975 4834
📧 manager@durbanvillegc.co.za
🖥 www.durbanvillegolfclub.co.za

## Erinvale Golf & Country Club Estate
*Louresnford Road, PO Box 6188, Somerset West 7129*
☎ +27 21 847 1906
📧 pro-shop@erinvale.com
🖥 www.erinvalegolfclub.com

## Fancourt (The Links, Montagu and Outeniqua)
*Montagu Street, Blanco, PO Box 2266, George 6530*
☎ +27 44 804 0030
📧 golf@fancourt.co.za
🖥 www.fancourt.co.za

## George GC
*PO Box 81, George, 6530*
☎ +27 44 873 6116
📧 info@georgegolfclub.co.za
🖥 www.georgegolfclub.co.za

## Goose Valley GC
*PO Box 1320 Plettenberg Bay 6600*
☎ +27 44 533 5082
📧 bookings@goosevalleygolfclub.com
🖥 www.goosevalleygolfclub.com

---

# What's up Croc?

Players on the Lost City course at Sun City in South Africa are warned to be aware of the crocodiles who dwell in a pit near the 13th hole.

---

*For key to symbols see page 725*

## Hermanus GC
Main Road, PO Box 313, Hermanus 7200
☎ +27 28 312 1954
✉ bookings@hgc.co.za
🖥 www.hgc.co.za

## Metropolitan GC
Fritz Sonnenberg Rd, Mouille Point, Cape Town 8001
☎ +27 21 434 9582
✉ golfmix@mweb.co.za

## Mossel Bay
17th Avenue, Mossel Bay 6500
☎ +27 44 691 2379
🖥 www.mosselbaygolfclub.co.za

## Mowbray GC
Raapenberg Rd, Mowbray, Cape Town 7450
☎ +27 21 685 3018
✉ info@mowbraygolfclub.co.za
🖥 www.mowbraygolfclub.co.za

## Oubaii
Herold's Bay, Western Cape
☎ +27 44 851 0131
🖥 www.oubaai.co.za

## Paarl GC
Wemmershoek Rd, Paarl 7646
☎ +27 21 863 1140
✉ bookings@paarlgolfclub.co.za
🖥 www.paarlgolfclub.co.za

## Pearl Valley Golf Estate
PO Box 1, Paarl 7646
☎ +27 867 8000
✉ golf@pearlvalley.co.za
🖥 www.pearlvalleygolfestates.com

## Pezula
Lagoonview Drive, East Head, Knysna 6570
☎ +27 44 302 5332
🖥 www.pezula.com

## Pinnacle Point
1 Pinnacle Point Road, Mossel Bay 6506
☎ +27 44 693 3438
🖥 www.pinnaclepoint.co.za

## Plettenberg Bay
Plesang Valley Road, Plettenberg Bay 6600
☎ +27 44 533 2132
🖥 www.plettgolf.co.za

## Rondebosch GC
3 Klipfontein Road, PO Box 495, Rondebosch, Cape Town 7700
☎ +27 21 689 4176
✉ info@rgc.co.za

## Royal Cape GC
174 Ottery Road, PO Box 186, Ottery 7808, Wynberg, 7800
☎ +27 21 797 5246
✉ manager@royalcapegolf.co.za
🖥 www.royalcapegolf.co.za

## Simola
1 Old Cape Road, Knysna 6570
☎ +267 360 4000
🖥 www.simolaestate.co.za

## Steenberg
Tokal Road, Tokal 7495
☎ +27 21 713 2233
🖥 www.steenberggolfclub.co.za

## Stellenbosch GC
PO Box 1, Paarl 7646
☎ +27 21 867 8000
✉ golf@pearlvalley.co.za
🖥 www.pearlvalleygolfestates.com

## Westlake GC
Westlake Ave, Lakeside 7945
☎ +27 21 788 2530
✉ info@westlakegolfclub.co.za
🖥 www.westlakegolfclub.co.za

## De Zalze Winelands Golf Estate
PO Box 12706, Die Boord, Stellenbosch 7613
☎ +27 21 880 7300
✉ info@dezalzegolf.com
🖥 www.dezalzegolf.com

## Swaziland

## Royal Swazi Spa CC
Main Road, Mbabane
☎ +268 416 5000
🖥 www.suninternation.com/Destinations/Resorts/Golf/Pages/Golf.aspx

## Tunisia

## Djerba

## Djerba GC
Zone Touristique BP360, 4116 Midoun
☎ +216 75 745 055
✉ contact@djerbagolf.com
🖥 www.djerbagolf.com

## Hammamet

## Golf Citrus (Le Fôret and Les Oliviers)
Hammamet BP 132, 8050 Hammamet
☎ +216 72 226 500
✉ golf.citrus@planet.tn
🖥 www.golfcitrus.com

## Yasmine Golf Course
BP 61, 8050 Hammamet
☎ +216 72 227 001
✉ info@golfyasmine.com
🖥 www.golfyasmine.com

## Monastir

## Flamingo Golf Course
Route de Ouardanine, BP 40, Monastir Gare, 5079 Monastir
☎ +216 73 500 283
✉ booking@golfflamingo.com
🖥 www.golfflamingo.com

## Palm Links Golf Course
B.P: 216 Monastir République, 5060 Tunisie
☎ +216 73 521 910
✉ info@golf-palmlinks.com
🖥 www.golf-palmlinks.com

## Port el Kantaoui

## El Kantaoui Golf (Sea and Panorama)
Station Touristique, 4089 El Kantaoui BP 32 Port el Kantaoui
☎ +216 73 348 756
🖥 www.kantaouigolfcourse.com.tn

## The Résidence Golf Course
Boite Postale 697, 2070 La Marsa, Les Côtes de Carthage
☎ +216 71910 101
✉ info@theresidence.com
🖥 www.theresidence.com

## Tabarka

## Tabarka Golf Course
Rte Touristique El Morjènel, 8110 Tabarka
☎ +216 78 670 028
✉ info@tabarkagolf.com
🖥 www.tabarkagolf.com

## Tozeur

## Oasis Golf Tozeur
Société Golf Oasis BP 48, Poste Elchorfa, 2243 Tozeur
☎ +216 76 471 194
✉ reservation.golf@tozeuroasisgolf.com
🖥 www.tozeuroasisgolf.com

## Tunis/Carthage

## Golf de Carthage
Choutrana II, 2036 Soukra
☎ +216 71 765 700
✉ reservationgc@planet.tn
🖥 www.golfcarthage.com

## Uganda

## Entebbe Golf Club
P.O.Box 107, Entebbe
☎ +261 020 44 94 387

## Uganda GC
Kitante Road. Kampala, Uganda
☎ +261 236848

## Zambia

## Chainama Hills
P.O Box 31385 Lusaka
☎ +260 211 250916
✉ dngambi@yahoo.com

**Livingstone GC**
*Victoria Falls, Southern Province*
☎ +260 321 323052
✉ info@livingstonegolf.com
▤ www.livingstonegolf.com

**Mufulira GC**
*PO Box 40141 / 40700, Mufulira,*
*Copperbelt Province*
☎ +260 212 411131
✉ mufuliraclub@ovation.co.za
▤ www.mufulira.co.za

**Ndola GC**
*PO Box 71564, Ndola*
☎ +26 005 588 6678
▤ www.ndolagolfclub.com

## Zimbabwe

**Chapman GC**
*Samora Machel, Avenue East, Harare*
☎ +263 4 747 328
▤ www.chapmangolfclub.co.zw

# Middle East

## Bahrain

**Awali GC**
*PO Box 25413, Awali, Kingdom of Bahrain*
☎ +973 1775 6770
✉ secretary@awaligolfclub.com
▤ www.awaligolfclub.com
⊕ 18 hole sand course

**Bahrain GC**
✉ salem_1956@hotmail.com
⊕ 18 hole sand course

**The Royal GC**
*PO Box 39117, Riffa, Kingdom of Bahrain*
☎ +973 1775 0777
✉ info@theroyalgolfclub.com
▤ www.theroyalgolfclub.com

## Israel

**Caesarea G&CC**
*PO Box 4858, Caesarea 30889*
☎ +972 463 61173

**Gaash CC**
▤ www.gaashgolfclub.co.il

## Kuwait

**Sahara G&CC**
*PO Box 29930 Safat 13160*
☎ +965 4769408
✉ info@saharakuwait.com
▤ www.saharakuwait.com
⊕ Fully illuminated for night time golf

## Oman

**Muscat G&CC**
*PO Box 3358, CPO, Postal Code 111,*
*Sultanate of Oman*
☎ +968 24 510065
✉ info@muscatgolf.com
▤ www.muscatgolf.com

**The Wave GC**
*Madinat Al Sultan Qaboos, PO Box 87, PC*
*118, Sultanate of Oman*
☎ +968 245 34444
✉ customerservice@thewavemuscat
.com
▤ thewavemuscat.com

## Qatar

**Doha GC**
*PO Box 13530, Doha, State of Qatar*
✉ info@dohagolfclub.com

**Mesaieed GC**
*Umm Said, Mesaieed, State of Qatar*
☎ +974 476 0874
✉ mgc_golf@yahoo.co.uk

**Dukhan GC**
*PO Box 49776, Dubai, State of Qatar*
✉ qatargasgolfopen@qatargas.com.qa

## Saudi Arabia

**Arizona Golf Resort**
*PO Box 8080, Riyadh 11482*
☎ +966 1 248 4444
✉ management@agr.com.sa
▤ www.agr.com.sa

## United Arab Emirates

**Abu Dhabi Golf &**
**Equestrian Club**
*PO Box 33303*
☎ +971 244 59600

**Abu Dhabi GC**
*PO Box 51234*
▤ www.adgolfclub.com

**Al Badia GC**
*PO Box 49776, Dubai*
☎ +971 460 10101

**Al Ghazal GC**
*PO Box 3167*
☎ +971 257 58040
⊕ Sand course

**Al Hamra GC**
*PO Box 6617, Ras Al Khaimah*
▤ www.alhamragolf.com

**Arabian Ranches GC**
*PO Box 36700, Dubai*
▤ www.arabianranchesgolfdubai.com

**Dubai Creek Golf &**
**Yacht Club**
*PO Box 6302, Dubai*
▤ www.dubaigolf.com

**Emirates GC**
*PO Box 24040, Dubai*
▤ www.dubaigolf.com

**Jebel Ali Golf Resort &**
**Spa**
*PO Box 9255, Dubai*
▤ www.jebelalo-international.com

**Jumeirah Golf Estates**
*PO Box 262080, Dubai*
▤ www.jumeirahgolfestates.com

**Palm Sports Resort**
*PO Box 1671, Al Ain*
▤ www.palmsportsresort.com

**Sharjah Golf &**
**Shooting Club**
*PO Box 6, Sharjah*
▤ www.golfandshootingshj.com

**Sharjah Wanderers GC**
*PO Box 1767, Sharjah*
▤ www.sharjahgolf.com
⊕ 9 holes sand, 9 holes grass

**The Els Club**
*PO Box 111123, Dubai*
▤ www.elsclubdubai.com

**The Montgomerie**
**Dubai**
*PO Box 36700, Dubai*
▤ www.themontgomerie.com

# Tower Links GC
*PO Box 30888, Ras Al Khaimah*
☎ +971 722 79939

# Asia

## Army GC
*Dhaka Cantonment*
☎ 0181 921 2211 (mobile)

## Bhatiary G&CC
*C/o 24 Infantry Division, Chittagong Cantonment*
☎ +880 031 278 7423
✉ bhatiarygolf@yahoo.com

## BOF GC
*Bangladesh Ordnance Factories, Gazipur Cantonment, Gazipur*
☎ +880 920 4613

## Bogra GC
*C/o 11 Infantry Division, Bogra Cantonment*
☎ +880 051 82080

## Dhaka Club Limited
*Ramna, Dhaka-100*
☎ +880 861 9180
✉ dcl@bdonline.com

## Jessore G&CC
*C/o Headquarters 55 Infantry Division (Ordnance Br), Jessore Cantonment, Jessore*
☎ +880 0421 68675
✉ +880 0421 67450

## Kurmitola GC
*Dhaka Cantonment, Dhaka 1206*
☎ +880 875 2520
✉ kgcdhaka@hotmail.com

## Mainamati G&CC
*C/o 33 Infantry Division, Comilla Cantonment, Comilla*
☎ +880 081 76381
✉ mgcc18@yahoo.com

## Rangpur GC
*C/o66 Infantry Division, Rangpur Cantonment*
☎ +880 673000

## Savar GC
*9 Infantry Division, Savar Cantonment, Savar 01714171790 (XO)*
☎ +880 779 1839

## Shaheen G&CC
*BAF Base Zahurul Haque, Patanga, Chattigong*
☎ +880 031-250 2033
✉ sgccpbaf@gmail.com

## Royal Bhutan GC
*Chhopel Lam, Thimphu*
☎ +925 232 5429

## Pantai Mentiri GC
*Km 15½ Jalan Kota Batu, Brunei Darussalam*
☎ +673-279102
✉ infodesk@pantaimentirigolfclub.com
🖥 www.pantaimentirigolfclub.com

## Royal Brunei G&CC
*Jerudong Park, Jerudong BG3122, Brunei Darussalam*
☎ +673 261 1582

## Anhui

### Huangshan Pine G&CC
*No. 78, Longjing, Jichang Da Av., Tunxi District, Huangshan City, Anhui*
☎ +86 559 256 8399
✉ pine@chinahsgolf.com
🖥 www.chinahsgolf.com

## Beijing

### Beijing CBD International
*No.99, Gaobeidian RD, Chaoyang District, Beijing 100023*
☎ +86 10 673 84801
✉ hongshuasale@h-cgolf.com
🖥 www.h-cgolf.com

### Beijing Taiwei GC
*Xiangtang New Culture Town, Cuicun County, Chanping District, Beijing 102212*
☎ +86 10 6072 5599
🖥 www.taiweigolf.com

## Chongqing

### Chongqing International GC
*Huaxi Town, Banan District, Chongqing 400055*
☎ +86 23 6255 4816
✉ chongqinggolf@sina.com.cn

## Fujian

### Orient (Xiamen) G&CC
*Haicang Investment & Development Zone Xiamen, Fujian Province 528234*
☎ +86 592 653 1317
✉ xiamen@orientgolf.com

## Quanzhou GC
*Zimao Town, Jinjiang, Fujian Province 362213*
☎ +86 595 595 1988
✉ golf@pub1.qz.fj.cn
🖥 www.qzgolf.com

## Trans Strait GC
*New Village, Wenwusha Town, Changle, Fuzhou, Fujian Province, China 350207*
☎ +86 591 2878 9567
✉ tsgolfc@pub6.fz.fj.cn

## Guangdong

### Dongguan Hill View GC
*Ying Bin Da Dao, Dong Cheng District, Dongguan, Guangdong*
☎ +86 769 222 09980
✉ hillview@tom.com
🖥 www.hillview-golf.com

### Nanhai Peach Garden GC
*Peach Garden, Songgang, Nanhai District, Foshan City, Guangdong Province 528234*
☎ +86 757 852 31888
🖥 www.peachgardengolf.com

### Zhuhai Golden Gulf GC
*Jinwan Road, Golden Coast, Jinwan District, Zhuhai, Guangdong 519041*
☎ +86 756 761 4000
✉ goldengolf@zhggg.com
🖥 www.zhggg.com

## Guangxi

### Gentle Uptown GC
*Nanwu Road, Naning, Guangxi Province 530024*
☎ +86 771 580 5501
✉ shichangbu@gentlegolf.com
🖥 www.gentlegolf.com

### Li River G&CC
*Foreign Marina, Overseas Chinese Tourism District, Guilin, Guangxi Province 541008*
☎ +86 773 390 9080
✉ golf@chin-taiwan.com
🖥 www.royal.fide.com

## Guizhou

### Guiyang GC
*Sanyuan, Zha Zuo Town Guiyang, Guizhou Province 550201*
☎ +86 851 235 1888
✉ gygolfclub@163.com
🖥 www.guiyanggolf.com

## Heilongjiang

### Heilongjiang Harbin Baiyun GC
*Harbin, Heilongjiang Province*
☎ +86 451 600 5242

## Hainan

### Haikou Meishi Mayflower International GC
*88 West Binhai Road, Haikou City, Hainan Province 570311*
☎ +86 898 6871 8888
✉ websitesales@meishigolf.com
🖥 www.meishigolf.com

### Kangle Garden Spa & GC
*Xinglong Town, Wanning, Hainan Province 571533*
☎ +86 898 6256 8888
✉ golfclub@kangleresort.com
🖥 www.kangleresort.com

### Yalong Bay GC
*No.168 Qiong Dong Road, Dongshan Town, Qiongshan, Hainan Province 572016*
☎ +86 898 8856 5888
✉ welcome@yalongbaygolfclub.com
🖥 www.yalongbaygolfclub.com

## Hebei

### Grandeur South G&CC
*No.1 Yongle Road, ZhuoZhou, Hebei Province 072750*
☎ +86 10 8120 2880
✉ members@gsgcc.com
🖥 www.gsgcc.com

### Xin'ao Group Elephant Hotel
*Jinyuan Road, Economic & Technological Development Zone, Langfang City, Hebei Province 065001*
☎ +86 316 606 1188
✉ pyn-golf@163.com

## Henan

### Synear International GC
*No.86, South Bank of The Yellow River, Zhengzhou City, Henan Province 450004*
☎ +86 371 636 26699
🖥 www.syneargolf.com

## Hubei

### Orient (Wuhan) Golf Country Club
*Xingxing, Jiangti Hanyang District Wuhan, Hubei Province 430051*
☎ +86 27 8461 2270
✉ wuhan@orientgolf.com
🖥 www.orientgolf.com

## Hunan

### Changsha Qingzhuhu International GC
*Qingzhuhu, Kaifu District, Changsha City, Hunan Province 410152*
☎ +86 731 678 3999
✉ golf@hunangolf.com.cn
🖥 www.hunangolf.com.cn

### Hunan Dragon Lake International GC
*Guan Yin Yan Reservoir, Wangcheng District, Changsha, Hunan Province 410217*
☎ +86 731 838 8277
✉ longhu.hn@2118.com.cn
🖥 www.dragonlakegolf.com

## Jiangsu

### Gingko Lake International GC
*No.1, Gingko Lake, GuLi Town, Jiangning District, Nanjing, Jiangsu Province 211164*
☎ +86 25 8613 9988
✉ gingkolake@gingkolake.com
🖥 www.gingkolake.com

### Nanjing Harvard GC
*No. 176 Zhen Zhu Road, Pukhou District, Nanjing City, Jiangsu Province 210031*
☎ +86 25 5885 3333
✉ welcome@harvardgolf.com
🖥 www.harvardgolf.com

### Shanghai West Country GC
*128 Huanzhen W. Road, Zhouzhuang, Kunshan, Jiangsu 215325*
☎ +86 512 5720 3888
✉ golf@shanghaiwest.com
🖥 www.shanghaiwest.com

## Jiangxi

### Nanchang Mingya G&CC
*No. 601, South Lushan Dadao, Nanchang City, Jiangxi.Province 330013*
☎ +86 791 382 1600
✉ info@mingya.cn
🖥 www.mingya.cn/golf

## Jilin

### Changchun Jingyetan GC
*Ingyuetan National Forest Park, Changchun, Jilin Province 130117*
☎ +86 431 528 3815
✉ jingyuetangolf@163.com

## Liaoning

### Dalian Golden Pebble Beach GC
*Dalian Jinshi Tan State Tourist & Vacational Zone, Liaoning 116650*
☎ +86 411 8791 2343
✉ jinqiu@dalianjinshigolf.com
🖥 www.dalianjinshigolf.com

### Dandong Wulong International GC
*Lishugou Village, Loufang Town, Zhen An District, Dandong, Liaoning 118000*
☎ +86 415 417 1857
✉ golf@wl-golf.com
🖥 www.wl-golf.com

## Shanghai

### Grand Shanghai International G&CC
*Yang-Cheng Lake Tour & Holiday Zone, Ba Cheng Town, Kunshan Jiangsu Province 215347*
☎ +86 512 5789 1999
✉ uugsighr@public1.sz.js.cn
🖥 www.grandshanghaigolfresort.com

### Orient (Shanghai) G&CC
*High-Technology Garden, Songjiang District, Shanghai 201600*
☎ +86 21 5785 4698
✉ shanghai@orientgolf.com

### Shanghai Links GC
*No. 1600 Ling Bai Road, Pu Dong New District, Shanghai 201201*
☎ +86 21 5897 5899
🖥 www.thelinks.com.cn

## Shandong

### Guoke International GC
*Economic Development Area in Qihe, Shandong Province 528234*
☎ +86 534 8550 0299
🖥 www.gk-golf.com

### Nanshan International GC
*Nanshan Tourist Zone, Dongjiang Town, Longkou, Shandong Province 265718*
☎ +86 535 861 6818
✉ service@nanshangolf.com
🖥 www.nanshangolf.com

## Shaanxi

### Xi'an Yajian International GC
*Cao-Tang Tourist & Holiday Resort, Hu County, Xi'an, Shaanxi 710304*
☎ +86 29 8495 1236
✉ rivergolf@163.com

## Shenzhen

### Shenzhen Airport Golf Resort
*Near to Bao An Airport, Shenzhen 518128*
☎ +86 755 2777 9991
✉ airportgolf@sohu.com

### Shenzhen GC
*Shen Nan Road, Fu Tian Qu, Shenzen, Guangdong 518034*
☎ +86 755 330 8888

## Shenzhen Tycoon GC
*Jiu Wei, Xi Xiang Town, Boan District, Shenzhen, Guangdong 518126*
☎ +86 755 2748 3999
✉ member@hkcts.com
🖳 www.tycoongolf.com

### Sichuan

## Sichuan International GC
*Mu Ma Shan Development Zone, Shuangliu County, Chengdu, Sichuan 610026*
☎ +86 28 8578 5010
✉ sigc@sigc.com
🖳 www.sigc.com

### Tianjin

## Tianjin Fortune Lake GC
*Tuanbo Town, Jinghai County, Tianjin 300193*
☎ +86 22 6850 5299
✉ tj_golf@eyou.com

## Tianjin Warner International GC
*N° 1 Nanhai Road, Teda, Tianjin 300457*
☎ +86 22 2532 6009
✉ warner@warner-golf.com
🖳 www.warnergolfclub.com

### Xinjiang

## Xinjiang Urumqi Xuelianshan GC
*West Hot Spring Road, Shui Mo Gou District, Urumqi, Xinjiang Province 830017*
☎ +86 991 487 3888
🖳 www.j-golf.com

### Yunnan

## Kunming Country GC
*14km Anshi Highway, Kunming, Yunnan Province 650601*
☎ +86 871 742 6666
✉ fhy@public.km.yn.cn

## Lijiang Ancient Town International GC
*Huangshan Town, Yulong, Lijiang City, Yunnan Province 674100*
☎ +86 888 662 2700
✉ Lg3102331@vip.km169.net

### Zhejiang

## Huangzhou West Lake International CC
*No.200 Zhijiang Road, Zhejiang Province 310024*
☎ +86 571 8732 1700
✉ golf@westlakegolf.com
🖳 www.westlakegolf.com

## Orient (Wenzhou) Golf CC
*Yangyi West Suburbia Forest Park, Lucheng District, Wenzhou, Zhejiang Province 325000*
☎ +86 577 8881 7718
✉ wenzhou@orientgolf.com
🖳 www.orientgolf.com

Chinese Taipei

## Chang Hua GC
*101 Lane 2, Ta Pu Road, Changhua City, Taiwan*
☎ +886 4 7135799

## Lily G&CC
*55 Hu Tu Tuan, Kuan Hsi, Hsinchu County, Taiwan*
☎ +886 3 5875111

## National Garden GC
*1-1 Shihjhen Village, Yuanli Township, Miaoli County, Taiwan*
☎ +886 37 741166

## North Bay G&CC
*5 Tsau Pu Wei, Tsau-Li Village, Shimen Township, Taipei County, Taiwan*
☎ +886 2 26382930

## Sunrise G&CC
*256 Yang Sheng Road, Yang Mei, Taoyuan County, Taiwan*
☎ +886 3 4780099

## Taichung G&CC
*46 Tungshan Road, Hengshan Village, Taya, Taichung County, Taiwan*
☎ +886 4 25665130~2

## Taipei GC
*34-1, Chihtuchi, Kengtsu-Tsun, Luchu-Hsiang, Taoyuan County, Taiwan*
☎ +886 3 3241311-5

## Ta Shee G&CC
*168 Jih Hsin Road, Ta Hsi Township, Taoyuan County, Taiwan*
☎ +886 3 3875699

## Wu Fong G&CC
*668 Feng-Ku Road, Feng-ku Village, Wu Feng, Taichung County, Taiwan*
☎ +886 4 23301199

Hong Kong

## Clear Water Bay G&CC
☎ +852 2719 1595

## Discovery Bay GC
☎ +852 2987 7273

## Hong Kong GC, Deep Water Bay
☎ +852 2812 7070

## Hong Kong GC, Fanling
☎ +852 2670 1211

## The Jockey Club
☎ +852 2791 3388

## Shek O CC
☎ +852 2809 4458

## Sky City Eagles GC
☎ +852 3760 6688

India

## Agra GC
*Tay Road, Agra 282001 UP*
☎ +91 5622 226015

## Bangalore GC
*2 Stanley Road, High Grounds, Bangalore 560001*
☎ +91 80 228 1876
✉ bgc1876@bgl.vsnl.net.in

## Bombay Presidency GC
*Dr Choitram Gidwani Road, Chembur, Mumbai 400074*
☎ +91 22 550 5874

## Chandigarh GC
*Sector 6, Chandigarh*
☎ +91 17 274 0350
✉ cgc@chai91.net

## Cosmopolitan GC
*18 Golf Club Road, Tollygunge, Calcutta 700033 West Bengal*
☎ +91 33 473 1352

## Delhi GC
*Dr Zakhir Hussain Marg, New Delhi 10003*
☎ +91 11 243 6278
✉ delhigolf@aibn.on.ca

## DLF Club
*DLF City, Gurgaon, Haryana*
✉ karan@dlfmail.com

## Eagleton GC
*30th KM Bangalore-Mysore Highway, Bangalore*
✉ eagleton@bgol.vsnl.net.in

## Gaekwad Baroda GC
*Lukshimi Villas Estate Baroda, Gujarat 390001*
☎ +91 26 524 33599

## Madras Gymkhana GC
*Golf Annexe 334 Mount Road, Nandanam, Chennai 600035*
☎ +91 44 56881

## Motacamuna Gymkhana CC
*Finger Post PO, The Nilgirls, Tamilnadu 643006*
☎ +91 42 324 42254

## Poona GC
*Airport Road, Yerawada Pune 411006*
☎ +91 20 266 94131

## Royal Calcutta
*18 Golf Club Road, Tollygunge, Calcutta
700033 West Bengal*
☎ +91 33 473 1352
▤ www.royalcalcuttagolfclub.com

## Tollegunge GC
*120 Deshapran Sasmal Road, Calcutta*
☎ +91 33 473 4539

## Indonesia

## Bukit Darmo Golf
*Blok G-2, Jl Bukit Darmo, Surabaya 60226*
☎ +62-31-7325555
▤ www.bukitdarmogolf.com

## Nirwana Bali GC
*Jl. Raya Tanah Lot Kediri, Tabanan 82171,
Bali*
☎ +62 361 815 960
▤ www.nirwanabaligolf.com

## Satelindo Padang Golf
*Bukit Sentul, Bogor 16810, West Java*
☎ +62 21 879 60266
✉ marketing@golfsatelindo.com
▤ www.golfsatelindo.co.id

## Japan

## Abiko CC
*1110 Okahotto, Abiko-shi, Chiba Pref.
270-1137*
☎ +81 (0) 4 7182 0111
▤ www.abikogc.com

## Aichi CC
*20-1 Yamanonaka, Itaka-cho, Takabari,
Meito-ku, Nagoya-shi, Aichi Pref. 465-0067*
☎ +81 (0) 52 701 1161
▤ www.aichicc.jp/top.htm

## Hirono GC
*7-3 Hirono Shijimi-cho, Miki-Shi, Hyogo
Pref. 673-0541*
☎ +81 (0) 794 85 0123

## Hodogaya CC
*1324 Kamikawaicho, Asahi-ku, Yokohama-
shi, Kanagawa Pref. 241-0802*
☎ +81(0) 45 921 0115
▤ www.hodogaya-country-club.jp/

## Ibaraki CC
*25 Nakahozumi, Ibaraki-shi, Osaka Pref.
567-0034*
☎ +81 (0) 72 625 1661
▤ www.ibarakicc.or.jp/

## Kasumigaseki CC
*3398 Kasahata, Kawagoe-shi, Saitama Pref.
350-1175*
☎ +81 (0) 49 231 2181
▤ www.kasumigasekicc.or.jp/

## Kawana (Fuji)
*1459 Kawana, Ito City, Shizuoka, Chubu,
Honshu*
☎ +81 557 45 1111
▤ www.princehotels.co.jp/kawana/

## Kobe GC
*Ichigaya Rokkosancho, Nadaku Kobe-shi,
Hyogo Pref. 657-0101*
☎ +81 (0) 78 891 0364

## Koga GC
*1310-1 Shishi-bu, Koga-shi, Fukuoka Pref.
811-3105*
☎ +81 (0) 92 943 2261
▤ www.kogagc.co.jp/english/index.html

## Nagoya GC
*35-1 Dondoro, Wago, Togo-cho, Aichi-gun,
Aichi Pref. 470-0153*
☎ +81 (0) 52 801 1111
▤ www.nagoyagolfclub-wago.gr.jp/

## Naruo GC
*1-4 Kanagadani Nishiuneno, Kawanishi-shi,
Hyogo Pref. 666-0155*
☎ +81 (0) 72 794 1011
▤ www.naruogc.or.jp/

## Sagami CC
*4018 Shimotsuruma, Yamato-shi,
Kanagawa Pref. 242-0001*
☎ +81 (0) 46 274 3130
▤ www.h3.dion.ne.jp/~sagamicc/

## Takanodai CC
*1501 Yokodo-cho, Hanamigawa-ku, Chiba-
shi, Chiba Pref. 262-0001*
☎ +81 (0) 47 484 3151
▤ www.takanodaicc.or.jp/

## Tokyo GC
*1984 Kashiwabara, Sayama-shi, Saitama
Pref. 350-1335*
☎ +81 (0) 4 2953 9111

## Korea

## Chungcheong

## Cheonan Sangnok Resort Golf Course
*669-1 Jangsan-ri, Susin-myeon, Cheonan-si,
Chungcheongnam-do*
☎ +82 41 529 9075

## Gangwong

## Alps Golf Course
*107 Heul-ri, Ganseong-eup, Goseong-gun,
Gangwon-do*
☎ +82 33 681 5030
▤ www.alpsresort.co.kr

## Gyeonggi

## Sky 72 GC
*2029-1 Woonseo-Dong, Joong-Gu, Incheon*
☎ +82 32 743 9108
▤ www.sky72.com/en/index.jsp

## Songchoo CC
*San 23-1, BeeAhm-Lee, KwangJuk-Myon,
YangJu-si, Gyeonggi-Do*
☎ +82 31 871 9410
▤ www.songchoo.co.kr/e-htm

## Taeyoung CC
*San38 Jukrung-ri Wonsam-myun Yong-in-
shi, Kyuongki-do*
☎ +82 31 334 5051
▤ www.ty-cc.com/english/introd.jsp

## Gyeongsang

## Bomun CC
*180-7 Mulcheon-ri, Cheonbuk-myeon,
Gyeongju-si, Gyeongsangbuk-do*
☎ +82 54 745 1680 2

## Gageun GC
*111-1 Ma-dong, Gyeongju-si,
Gyeongsangbuk-do*
☎ +82 54 740 5161

## Mauna Ocean Golf
*Shindaeri San 140-1 Yangnammyon
Gyeongjusi, Gyeongsangbuk-do*
☎ +82 54 77 0900

## Jeju

## Chungmun Beach GC
*3125-1, Saekal-dong, Sogwipo, Cheju-Do*
☎ +82 64 735 7241

## Nine Bridge Golf Course
*Kwangpyong-ri, Anduk-myon, South Jeju-
gun, Jeju Island*
☎ +82 64 793 9999
▤ www.ninebridge.co.kr

## Jeolla

## Club 900
*San 15-1, Ssangok-ri, Dogok-myeon,
Hwasun-gun, Jeollanam-do*
☎ +82 61 371 0900

## Pusan

## Dong Nae CC
*San 128, Son-dong, Dongnae-gu, Pusan*
☎ +82 51 513 0101

## Seoul

## Namsungdae GC
*419 Jangji-dong, Songpa-gu, Seoul*
☎ +82 02 403 0071

## Laos

## Santisuk Lang Xang GC
*Km14 Thadeua Road, Ban Nahai,
Vientiane, Laos*
☎ +856 21 812 071

## Macao

## Macau G&CC
☎ +853 871188

# Malaysia

## Labuan

### Labuan GC
PO Box 276, 87008 Labuan, Labuan
☎ +60 87 412 810

## Sabah

### Borneo G&CC
Km 69, Papar-Beaufort Highway, 89700 Bongawan, Sabah
☎ +60 87 861 888
✉ reservation.bgcc@vhmis.com

### Karambunai Resorts GC
PO Box 270, Menggatal, 88450 Kota Kinabalu, Sabah
☎ +60 88 411 215
✉ salesmgrkrgc@borneo-resort.com
🖥 www.borneo-resort.com

### Shan-Shui Golf & Country Resort
PO Box 973, Mile 9, Jalan Apas, Tawau, 91008 Tawau, Sabah
☎ +60 89 916 888
✉ ssgolfcc@tm.net.my

### Sutera Harbour G&CC
1 Sutera Harbour Boulevard, 88100 Kota Kinabalu, Sabah
☎ +60 88 318 888
✉ sutera@suteraharbour.com.my
🖥 www.suteraharbour.com.my

## Sarawak

### Damai G&CC
Jalan Santubong, PO Box 203, 93862 Kuching, Sarawak
☎ +60 82 846 088
✉ dgcc@po.jaring.my
🖥 www.damaigolf.com

### Hornbill Golf & Jungle Club
Jalan Borneo Heights, Borneo Highlands Resort, 94200 Padawan, Sarawak
☎ +60 82 790 800
✉ enquiry@hornbillgolf.com
🖥 www.hornbillgolf.com

## Johor

### Bukit Banang G&CC
No. 1, Persiaran Gemilang, Bandar Banang Jaya, 83000 Batu Pahat, Johor
☎ +60 7 428 6001
✉ bbgcc@po.jaring.my
🖥 www.berjayaclubs.com/banang/index.cfm

### Daiman 18 Johor Bahru
No.18 Jalan Pesona, Taman Johor Jaya, 81100 Johor Bahru, Joho
☎ +60 7 353 3100
✉ daiman18@daiman.com.my
🖥 www.daiman.com.my

### Desaru G&CC
PO Box 26, Bandar Penawa, 81900 Kota Tinggi, Johor
☎ +60 7 8222 333
✉ golf@desaruresort.com
🖥 www.desaruresort.com

### Palm Resort G&CC
Jalan Persiaran Golf, Off Jalan Jumbo, 81250 Senai, Johor
☎ +60 7 5996 222
✉ marcomm@palmresort.com
🖥 www.palm-resort.com

### Palm Villa Golf & Country Resort
PTD 44500, Jalan Pindah Utama, Bandar Putra, PO Box 69, 81000 Kulai, Johor
☎ +60 7 599 9099
✉ Honorius@IOI.po.my

### Ponderosa G&CC
10-C Jalan Bumi Hijau 3, Taman Molek, 81100 Johor Bahru, Johor
☎ +60 7 354 9999
✉ pgcc@tm.net.my
🖥 www.ponderosagolf.com

### Royal Johor CC
3211 Jalan Larkin, 80200 Johor Bharu, Johor
☎ +60 7 2224 2098
✉ rjcc@tm.net.my
🖥 www.royaljohorcountryclub.com

### Sebana Cove
LB 505 Kota Tinggi PO, 81900 Kota Tinggi, Johor
☎ +60 7 826 6688
✉ sebanacove@pacific.net.sg
🖥 www.sebanacove.com

### Starhill G&CC
6.5 Km Jalan Maju Jaya, Kempas Lama, Skudai, 81300 Johor Baru, Johor
☎ +60 7 5566 325
🖥 www.starhillgolf.com.my

### Tanjong Puteri G&CC
Ptd 101446, Mukim Plentong, 81700 Pasir Gudang, Johor
☎ +60 7 2711 888
✉ tpgolf@tm.net.my

## Kedah

### Black Forest G&CC
Zon Bebas Cukai, 06050 Bukit Kayu Hitam, Kedah
☎ +60 4 9222 790
✉ blackforest@sriwani.com.my
🖥 www.blackforest.com.my

### Cinta Sayang G&CC
Jalan Persiaran Cinta Sayang, 0800 Sungai Petani, Kedah
☎ +60 4 4414 666
✉ cintasayang@cinta-sayang.com.my
🖥 www.cintasayangresort.com/cs_golf.html

### Datai Bay GC
Jalan Teluk Datai, PO Box 6, Kuah, 07000 Pulau Langkawi, Kedah
☎ +60 4 9592 700
🖥 www.dataigolf.com

### Gunung Raya Golf Resort
alan Air Hangat, Kisap, Kuah, 07000 Pulau Langkawi, Kedah
☎ +60 4 9668 148
✉ reservation@golfgr.com.my
🖥 www.golfgr.com.my

### Sungai Petani Club
23-C Jalan Sungai Layar, 08000 Sungai Petani, Kedah
☎ +60 4 422 4894
✉ info@slgcc.com.my
🖥 www.slgcc.com.my/intro.php

## Kelantan

### Kelantan G&CC
5488 Jalan Hospital, 15200 Kota Bahru, Kelantan
☎ +60 9 7482 102

## Kuala Lumpur

### Bukit Jalil Golf & Country Resort
Jalan 3/155B, 57000 Bukit Jalil, Kuala Lumpur
☎ +60 3 8994 1600
✉ bgrb@bukitjalil.com.my
🖥 www.berjayaclubs.com/jalil

### Golf Club Perkhidmatan Awam
Bukit Kiara, Off Jalan Damansara, 60000 Kuala Lumpur
☎ +60 3 7957 1958
✉ gmkgpa@kgpagolf.com
🖥 www.kgpagolf.com

### Kuala Lumpur G&CC
10, Jalan 1/70D, Off Jalan Bukit Kiara, 60000 Kuala Lumpur
☎ +60 3 2093 1111
✉ klgcc@simedarby.com
🖥 www.klgcc.com

## Melaka

### A'Famosa Golf Resort
Jalan Kemus, Simpang 4 78000 Alor Gajah, Melaka
☎ +60 6 5520 888
✉ enquiries@afamosa.com
🖥 www.afamosa.com

### Pandanusa GC
PT.30, Pulau Besar, Mukim Pernu, Melaka Tengah Melaka
☎ +60 6 281 5015
🖥 www.members.tripodasia.com.my/pulaubesar

## Negeri Sembilan

### Nilai Springs G&CC
PT 4770, Bandar Baru Nilai, PO Box 50,
71801 Nilai, Negeri Sembilan
☎ +60 6 8508 888
📧 nsgcc@pd.jaring.my
🖥 www.nilaispringsgcc.com.my/golfing

### Port Dickson G&CC
Batu 5 1/2, Jalan Pantai, 71050 Port
Dickson, Negeri Sembilan
☎ +60 6 647 3586
📧 pdgcc@po.jaring.my
🖥 www.pdgolf.com.my

### Royal Palm Springs GC
Bt.13 Km.21 Jalan Pantai, Mukim Pasir
Panjang, Negeri Sembilan
☎ +60 6 661 9599
📧 palmspringsresortcity
@tancoresorts.com
🖥 www.palmspringsresortcity.com
/rpsgc/index

## Pahang

### Astana G&CC
Sungai Lembing, Bandar Indera Mahkota,
25200 Kuantan, Pahang
☎ +60 9 5735 135
📧 astana@tm.net.my
🖥 www.astanagolf@150m.com

### Pantai Lagenda G&CC
Lot 877, Kampung Kuala Pahang, 26660
Pekan, Pahang
☎ +60 9 4251 658
📧 pigolf@tm.net.my

## Penang

### Bukit Jambul G&CC
No.2 Jalan Bukit Jambul, 11900 Bayan
Lepas
☎ +60 4 644 2255
📧 bcc@po.jaring.my
🖥 www.bjcc.com.my

### Bukit Jawi Golf Resort
No.691 Main Road, Sg. Bakap, S.P.S.,
14200 Penang
☎ +60 4 5820 759
🖥 www.bukitjawi.com.my

### Penang Golf Resort
Lot 1687 Jalan Bertam, Seberang Perai,
Utara
13200 Kepala Batas, Penang
☎ +60 4 5782 022
🖥 www.penanggolfresort.com.my

## Perak

### Clearwater Sanctuary Golf Resort
Lot 6019 Jalan Changkat Larang, 31000
Batu Gajah, Perak
☎ +60 5 3667 433
📧 cesgolf@po.jaring.my
🖥 www.cwsgolf.com.my

### Damai Laut G&CC
Hala Damai 2, Jalan Damai Laut , Off Jalan
Teluk Senanging
32200 Lumut, Perak
☎ +60 5 6183 333
📧 resvns_dlgcc@swissgarden.com
🖥 www.swissgarden.com/hotels/sgrdl

### Meru Valley G&CC
Jalan Bukit Meru, Off Jalan Jelapang,
30020 Ipoh, Perak
☎ +60 3 5293 300
📧 info@meruvalley.com.my
🖥 www.meruvalley.com.my

## Selangor

### Bangi Golf Resort
No.1 Persiaran Bandar, Bandar Baru Bangi
43650 Selangor
☎ +60 3 8925 3728
📧 bgr@po.jaring.my

### Golf Club Sultan Abdul Aziz Shah
No.1 Rumah Kelab 13/6, 40100 Shah
Alam, Selangor
☎ +60 3 5519 1512
📧 cecy@kgsaas.com.my
🖥 www.kgaas.com.my

### Kelab Golf Seri Selangor
Persiaran Damansara Indah, Off Prsn
Tropicana, Kota Damansara, 47410
Petaling Jaya, Selango
☎ +60 3 7806 1111
📧 mktg@seriselangor.com
🖥 seriselangor.com.my

### Kota Permai G&CC
No.1 Jalan 31/100A, Kota Kemuning
Section 31, 40460 Shah Alam, Selangor
Darul Ehsan
☎ +60 3 5122 3700
📧 kpgcc@kotapermai.com.my
🖥 www.kotapermai.com.my

### Palm Garden GC
IOI Resort, 62502 Putrajaya, Selangor
☎ +60 3 8948 7160
📧 pggc@tm.net.my
🖥 www.palmgarden.net.my

### Rahman Putra GC
Jalan BRP 2/1, Bukit Rahman Putra, 47000
Sungai Buloh, Selangor
☎ +60 3 6156 6870
📧 krpm@streamyx.com
🖥 www.krpm.com.my

## Terengganu

### Awana Kijal Golf, Beach & Spa Resort
Km.28, Jalan Kemaman-Dungun, 24100
Kijal, Kemaman Terengganu
☎ +60 9 8641 188
📧 awanakij@tm.net.my
🖥 www.awana.com.my

### Tasik Kenyir Golf Resort
Kg. Sg., Gawi, Mukim Telemong, 2300 Hulu
Teregganu Terengganu
☎ +60 9 666 8888
📧 resort@lakekenyir.com
🖥 www.lakekenyir.com

## Maldives

### Kuredu Island Resort
Faadhipolhu,, Lhaviyani Atoll
☎ +960 230337
📧 info@kuredu.com
🖥 www.kuredu.com

## Myanmar

### Aye Thar Yar Golf Course
Aye Thar Yar, Taunggyi, Shanstate
☎ +95 81 24245
📧 ayetharyargolfresort@mptmail.net.mm
🖥 www.ayetharyargolfresort.com

### Bagan Golf Course
Nyaung Oo Township, Mandalay Division
☎ +95 2 67247
📧 bagangolfresort@mptmail.net.mm

## Nepal

### Le Méridien Gokarna Forest Golf Resort & Spa
Rajnikunj Gokarna, Thali, PO Box 20498,
Kathhmandu
☎ +977 1 445 1212
📧 golf@lemeridien-kathmandu.com
🖥 www.gokarna.com

### Royal Nepal GC
Tilganga, Kathmandu
☎ +977 1 449 4247
📧 rngc@mail.com.np

## Pakistan

### Arabian Sea CC
Bin Qasim, Karachi
☎ +92 21 475 0408
📧 info@asccl.com
🖥 www.asccl.com

### Royal Palm G&CC
🖥 www.royalpalm.com

## Philippines

### Fairways and Bluewater Resort
*Newcoast, Balabag, Boracay Island, Province of Aklan*
☎ +63 36 288 5587
✉ info@fairwaysbluewater.com
🖥 www.FairwaysBluewater.com

### Eagle Ridge G&CC
*Barangay Javalera, Gen. Trias, Cavite*
☎ +63 46 419 2841
🖥 www.eagle-ridge.com.ph

## Singapore

### Raffles GC
*Raffles Country Club, 450 Jalan Ahmad Ibrahim, Singapore 639932*
☎ +65 6861 7649
✉ jacqueline@rcc.org.sg
🖥 www.rcc.org.sg

### Singapore Island CC
*Thomson Road, PO Box 50, Singapore 915702*
☎ +65 645 92222
✉ enquiry@sicc.org.sg
🖥 www.sicc.org.sg

## Sri Lanka

### Victoria Golf & Country Resort
*PO Box 7, Rajawela*
☎ +94 812 376 376
✉ enquiries@victoriagolf.lk
🖥 www.srilankagolf.com

### Waters Edge GC
*316 Ethul Kotte Road, Battaramulla*
☎ +94 112 863863
✉ we@watersedge.lk
🖥 www.watersedge.lk

## Thailand

### Central Region

### Green Valley CC
*92 Moo 3, Bang Na-Trat Road Km.15, Bang Chalong, Bang Phli, Samut Prakan 10540*
☎ +66 2312 5883
✉ info@greenvalleybangkok.com
🖥 www.greenvalleybangkok.com

### Lam Luk Ka CC
*29 Moo 7 Lamsai Lam Luk Ka Khlong 11, Patum Thani 12150*
☎ +66 2995 2300
✉ info@lamlukkagolf.net
🖥 www.lamlukkagolf.net

### Royal Bangkok Sport Club
*1 Henri Dunant Street, Bangkok 10330*
☎ +66 66 2255 1420
🖥 www.rbsc.org

### Eastern Region

### Eastern Star Country Club & Resort
*241/5 Moo 3, Pala Ban Chang District, Rayong 21130*
☎ +66 3863 0410
✉ info@easternstargolf.net
🖥 www.easternstargolf.net

### Laem Chabang International CC
*106/8 Moo 4, Ban Bung, Sri Racha, Chon Buri 20230*
☎ +66 3837 2273
🖥 reservation@laemchabanggolf.com
🖥 www.laemchabanggolf.com

### Soi Dao Highland Golf Club & Resort
*153/1 Moo 2, Thap Sai, Pong Nam Ron District, Chanthaburi 22140*
☎ +66 3932 0174
🖥 booking@soidaohighland.com
🖥 www.soidaohighland.com

### Northern Region

### Chiangmai Green Valley CC
*183/2 Chotana Road, Mae Sa, Mae Rim, Chiang Mai 50180*
☎ +66 5329 8249
✉ info@cm_golf.com
🖥 www.cm_golf.com

### Gassan Khuntan Golf & Resort
*222 Moo3 Thapladuk, Mae Tha, Lamphun, Thailand 51140*
☎ +66 53 507006
✉ info@gassangolf.com
🖥 www.gassangolf.com

### Santiburi CC
*12 Moo 3, Hua Doi-Sob Pau Road, Wiang Chai District, Chiang Rai 57210*
☎ +66 5366 2821
✉ cr_golfreservation@santiburi.com
🖥 santiburi.com /SantiburiGolfChiangRai

### North Eastern Region

### Forest Hills CC
*195 Moo 3, Mittraphap Road, Muak Lek District, Saraburi 18180*
☎ +66 3634 1911
✉ mail@sirjamesresort.com
🖥 www.sirjamesresort.com

### Mission Hills Golf Club Khao Yai
*151 Moo 5,Thumbol Mhoosee, Pakchong, Nakornratchasima 30130*
☎ +66 4429 7258
✉ missionhills_khaoyai@yahoo.com
🖥 www.golfmissionhills.com/miskao.html

### Suwan G&CC
*15/3 Moo 2, Sisatong, A. Nakornchaisri, Nakornpathom 73120*
☎ +66 343 39333
✉ reservation@suwangolf.com
🖥 www.suwangolf.com

### Southern Region

### Loch Palm GC
*38 Moo 5 Vichit Songkram Road, Kathu, Phuket 83120*
☎ +66 7632 1929
✉ info@lochpalm.com
🖥 www.lochpalm.com

### Phuket CC
*80/1 Vichit Songkram Road, Katu, Phuket 83120*
☎ +66 7632 1038
✉ info@phuketcountryclub.com
🖥 www.phuketcountryclub.com

### Santiburi Samui CC
*12/15 Moo 4, Bandonsai, Tambol Maenam, Amphur Ko Samui, Surat Thani 84330*
☎ +66 7742 5031
✉ infosb@santiburi.com
🖥 www.santiburi.com

### Western Region

### Best Ocean GC
*4/5 Moo 7 Rama2 Road, Khokkham, Samutsakorn 74000*
☎ +66 34 451143
🖥 www.bestoceangolf.com

### Mission Hills GC
*27/7 Moo 7, Pang Thru, Tha Muang, Kanchanaburi 71110Tengah Melaka*
☎ +66 3464 4147
✉ hills@ksc.th.com
🖥 golfmissionhills.com/miskan.html

### Sawang Resort GC
*99 Moo 2, Sapang, Khao Yoi District, Petchaburi 76140*
☎ +66 3256 2555
✉ info@sawangresortgolf.com
🖥 www.sawangresortgolf.com

## Vietnam

### King's Island GC
*Dong Mo, Son Tay Town, Ha Tay Province*
☎ +84 34 686555
✉ kings_island@fpt.vn
🖥 www.kingsislandgolf.com

**Ocean Dunes GC**
*1 Ton Duc Thang, Phan Thiet*
☎  +84 62 823366
✉  odgc@vietnamgolfresorts.com
🖥  www.vietnamgolfresorts.com
   /index.php?id=7

**Tam Dao Golf & Resort**
*Hop Chau Commune, Tam Dao District,*
*Vinh Phuc Province*
☎  +84 211 896554
✉  marketing@tamdaogolf.com
🖥  www.tamdaogolf.com

# Australasia and the Pacific

## Australia

### Australian Capital Territory

**Royal Canberra**
*Bentham St, Yarralumla, ACT 2600*
☎  +61 (02) 6282 7000
✉  admin@royalcanberra.com.au
🖥  www.royalcanberra.com.au

**Yowani Country Club**
*Northbourne Ave, Lyneham, ACT 2602*
☎  +61 (02)6241 2303
✉  golf@yowani.com.au

### New South Wales

**The Australian**
*53 Bannerman Crescent, Rosebery, NSW 2018*
☎  +61 (02) 9663 2273

**Barham**
*Moulamein Road, Barham, NSW 2732*
☎  +61 (03) 5453 2971
✉  Barham.services.club@clubarham.com.au

**Howlong**
*Golf Club Drive, Howlong, NSW 2643*
☎  +61 (02) 6026 5822
✉  enquiries@howlonggolf.com.au

**Kooindah Waters**
*Kooindah Boulevard, Wyong, NSW 2259*
☎  +61 (02) 4351 0700
✉  info@kooindahwatersgolf.com.au

**The Lakes**
*Corner King St. & Vernon Ave, Eastlakes, NSW 2018*
☎  +61 (02) 9669 1311

**New South Wales**
*Henry Head, Botany Bay National Park, La Perouse*
☎  + 61 (02) 9661 4455
✉  admin@nswgolfclub.com.au

**Royal Sydney**
*Kent Road, Rose Bay, NSW 2029*
☎  +61 (02) 8362 7000
✉  reception@rsgc.com.au
🖥  www.rsgc.com.au

**Twin Creeks**
*Twin Creeks Drive, Luddenham, NSW 2745*
☎  +61 (02) 9670 8877
✉  karinad@twincreeks.com.au

**The Vintage**
*Vintage Drive, Rothbury, NSW 2320*
☎  +61 (02) 4998 6789
✉  golf@thevintage.com.au

**Yarrawonga**
*Gulai Road, Mulwala, NSW 2647*
☎  +61 (03) 5744 3983
✉  stayandplay@yarragolf.com.au

### Northern Territory

**Alice Springs**
*Cromwell Drive, Alice Springs, NT 870*
☎  +61 (08) 8952 1921
✉  admin@asgc.com.au

**Darwin**
*Links Road, North Lakes, NT 812*
☎  +61 (08) 8927 1322

**Palmerston**
*Dwyer Circuit & University Avenue, Driver, NT 831*
☎  +61 (08) 8932 1324

### Queensland

**Brisbane**
*Tennyson Memorial Avenue, Yeerongpilly, QLD 4105*
☎  +61 (07) 3848 1008
✉  mail@brisbanegolfclub.com.au

**Brookwater**
*1 Tournament Drive, Brookwater, QLD 4300*
☎  +61 (07) 3814 5500
✉  golfshop@brookwatergolf.com

**The Colonial**
*Paradise Springs Avenue, Robina, QLD 4226*
☎  +61 (07) 5553 7008
✉  info@playmoregolf.com.au

**Glades**
*Glades Drive, Robina, QLD 4226*
☎  +61 (07) 5569 1900
✉  enquiries@theglades.com.au

**Indooroopilly**
*Meiers Road, Indooroopilly, QLD 4068*
☎  + 61 (07) 3721 2122
✉  admin@indooroopillygolf.com.au

## World's longest golf course?

While it cannot claim to be the world's longest golf course in terms of playable yardage, the Nullabor Links in Australia stretches 848 miles along the Eyre Highway which skirts the southern end of the Nullabor Plain linking South Australia and Western Australia. Golfers will stop in turn at one of 18 towns or service stations along the highway, each equipped with its own tee, fairway and green.

Opened in October 2009, the course covers a distance greater than the entire length of Britain with the distance between holes sometimes exceeding 50 miles.

In the arid conditions of the Nullabor Plain, the course features synthetic greens ... although the sand traps will be real enough, especially for golfers who hit a stray shot into the desert!

*For key to symbols see page 725*

## Links Hope Island
Hope Island Road, Hope Island, QLD 4212
☎ + 61 (07) 5530 9030
✉ golf@linkshopeisland.com.au

## Noosa Springs
Links Drive, Noosa Heads, QLD 4567
☎ + 61 (07) 5440 3333
✉ info@noosasprings.com.au

## Robina Woods
Ron Penhaligon Way, Robina, QLD 4226
☎ + 61 (07) 5553 7520
✉ info@playmoregolf.com.au

## Royal Queensland
Curtin Avenue West, Eagle Farm,
Brisbane, QLD 4009
☎ +61 (07) 3268 1127
✉ info@rqgolf.com.au
🖶 www.rqgolf.com.au

## South Australia

### Echunga
Cnr Hahndorf and Dolman Road, Echunga,
SA 5153
☎ +61 (08) 8388 8038
✉ info@echungagolf.com.au

### Grange
White Sands Drive Seaton, South Australia
☎ +61 (08) 8355 7100
✉ info@grangegolf.com.au

### Kooyonga
May Terrace, Lockleys, South Australia
☎ +61 (08) 8352 5444
✉ administrator@kooyongagolf.com.au

### Mount Lofty
35 Golf Links Road, Stirling, SA 5152
☎ +61 (08) 8339 1805
✉ admin@mountloftygolfclub.com.au

### Royal Adelaide
328 Tapleys Hill Road, Seaton, SA 5023
☎ +61 (08) 8356 5511
✉ ragc@royaladelaidegolf.com.au
🖶 www.royaladelaidegolf.com.au

### Tea Tree Gully
Hamilton Road, Fairview Park, SA 5126
☎ +61 (08) 8251 1465
✉ ttggc@internode.net.au

## Tasmania

### Barnbougle Dunes
426 Waterhouse Road, Bridport, Tasmania
7262
☎ +61 (03) 363 560 094
🖶 www.barnbougledunes.com

### Royal Hobart
81 Seven Mile Beach Road, Seven Mile
Beach, Hobart, Tasmania 7170
☎ +61 (03) 6248 6161
✉ admin@rhgc.com.au
🖶 www.rhgc.com.au

## Victoria

### Barwon Heads
Golf Links Road, Barwon Heads, VIC 3227
☎ +61 (03) 5255 6275
✉ golf@bhgc.com.au

### Clifton Springs
92-94 Clearwater Drive, Clifton Springs, VIC
3222
☎ +61 (03) 5253 1488
✉ csclubhouse@iprimus.com.au

### The Dunes
335 Browns Road, Rye, VIC 3941
☎ +61 (03) 5985 1334
✉ golf@thedunes.com.au

### Growling Frog
1910 Donnybrook Road, Yan Yean, VIC
3755
☎ +61 (03) 9716 3477
✉ info@growlingfroggolfcourse.com.au

### Huntingdale
Windsor Avenue, South Oakleigh, VIC 3167
☎ +61 (03) 9579 4622
✉ manager@huntingdalegolf.com.au

### Kingston Heath
Kingston Rd, Heatherton, Melbourne, VIC
3202
☎ +61 (03) 8558 2700
✉ info@kingstonheath.com.au

### Ocean Grove
Guthridge Street, Ocean Grove, VIC 3226
☎ +61 (03) 5256 2795
✉ info@oceangrovegc.com.au

### Metropolitan
Golf Road, Oakleigh South, VIC 3167
☎ +61 (03) 9579 3122
✉ admin@metropolitangolf.com.au

### Mornington
Tallis Drive, Mornington, VIC 3931
☎ +61 (03) 5975 2784
✉ manager@ morningtongolf.com.au

### Royal Melbourne
Cheltenham Road, Black Rock, VIC 3193
☎ +61 (03) 9598 6755
✉ rmgc@royalmelbourne.com.au
🖶 www.royalmelbourne.com.au

### Settlers Run
1 Settlers Run, Cranbourne South, VIC
3977
☎ +61 (03) 9785 6072
✉ info@settlersrun.com.au

### Victoria
Park Road, Cheltenham, VIC 3192
☎ +61 (03) 9584 1733
✉ info@victoriagolf.com.au

### Yarra Yarra
567 Warrigal Road East, Bentleigh East,
VIC 3165
☎ +61 (03) 9575 0595
✉ reception@yarrayarra.com.au

## Western Australia

### Joondalup
Country Club Bouvelard, Connolly, WA
6027
☎ +61 (08) 9400 8811
✉ proshop@joondalupresort.com.au

### Kennedy Bay
Port Kennedy Drive, Port Kennedy, WA
6172
☎ +61 (08) 9524 5991
✉ info@kennedybay.com.au

### Lake Karrinyup
North Beach Road, Karrinyup WA 6018
☎ +61 (08) 9422 8222
✉ info@lkcc.com.au

### Mount Lawley
Walter Road, Inglewood, WA 6052
☎ +61 (08) 9271 9622
✉ admin@mlgc.org

### The Vines Resort and Country Club
Verdellho Drive, The Vines, Perth, WA 6069
☎ +61 (08) 9297 3000
🖶 www.vines.com.au

## Cook Islands

### Rarotonga Golf Club
Rarotonga, Cook Islands
☎ +682 20621

## Fiji

### Fiji Golf Club
Suva Area, Viti Levu
☎ +679 382872

### Pacific Harbour
Suva Area, Viti Levu
☎ +679 450262

## Guam

### Guam International CC
495 Battulo Street, Dededo, Guam 96912
☎ +1 671 632 4422
✉ gicclub@netpci.com
🖶 www.giccguam.com

## New Zealand

### Cape Kidnappers
☎ +64 (06) 875 1900
🖶 www.capekidnappers.com

### Gisborne
☎ +64 (06) 867 9849
🖶 www.gisborne.nzgolf.net

## Gulf Harbour
☎ +64 (09) 424 0971
🖥 www.gulfharbour.nzgolf.net

## The Hills
🖥 www.thehills.co.nz

## Jack's Point
🖥 www.jackspoint.com

## Kauri Cliffs
🖥 www.kauricliffs.com

## Lake View
☎ +64 (07) 357 2343
🖥 www.lakeview.nzgolf.net

## Lakes Resort Pauanui
☎ +64 (07) 864 9999
🖥 www.lakesresort.com

## North Otoga
☎ +64 (03) 434 6169
🖥 www.northotago.nzgolf.net

## Palmerston North
☎ +64 (06) 351 0700
🖥 www.pngolf.co.nz

## Queens Park
☎ +64 (03) 218 8371
🖥 www.queenspark.nzgolf.net

## Sherwood Park
☎ +64 (09) 434 6900
🖥 www.sherwoodpark.nzgolf.net

## Waitangi
☎ +64 (09) 402 7713
📧 waitangigolf@xtra.co.nz

## Papua New Guinea

## Port Moresby GC
PO Box 17 Port Moresby
☎ +675 325 5367

## Samoa

## Penina Golf Course
77 Faleolo Strip, Mulifanua
📧 golfpenina@samoa.ws
🖥 www.peninaresortandgolfclub.com

*For key to symbols see page 725*

## Tonga

## Tonga GC
PO Box 2568, Nuku'alofa
☎ +676 24949

## Vanuatu

## Port Vila G&CC
Mele, Vanuatu, South Pacific
☎ +678 22564
📧 pvgcc@vanuatu.com.vu

## White Sands
PO Box 906, Port Vila, Vanuatu, South Pacific
☎ +678 22090
📧 whitesan@vanuatu.com.vu

---

# China National Rules School 2013

The 7th China National Rules School, organised by The R&A and run in conjunction with the China Golf Association (CGA), took place in Shenzhen from 6–8 November 2013 The School was held at the CTS Tycoon Golf Club, located just on the northern outskirts of Shenzhen, Guandong.

This was the fourth year that the instruction at the National Rules School was provided jointly by The R&A and CGA instructors. Grant Moir and Shona McRae of The R&A were joined by Chinese instructors, Taylor Li, Benny Xiao, Sherry Shao and Ricky Chen who all assisted with translation, presentations, practical demonstrations and role play sessions.

The programme was run on the same basis as previous years with over 500 delegates attending the Preliminary stage and from there 108 progressed to the Intermediate stage. Of the 108 delegates who attended the Intermediate stage, 59 qualified to attend the final stage, the National Rules School.

The School focuses on the role of a referee. Sessions on preparing local rules, conditions of competition, marking the course and giving rulings were carried out by the instructors. In addition, the delegates had the opportunity to be involved in practical demonstrations on the course.

A number of the delegates had previously attended a National Rules School and were returning this year to try again to achieve the top award, a National "A" certificate. To achieve this top award a delegate must first score at least 75% in the Rules Exam (which has 65% of its content in English), then score at least 11 out of 15 marks in the Refereeing Role Play Exam.

Out of the 59 delegates, 34 delegates scored 75% or better in the Rules Exam but only the top 30 qualify for the practical role play examination on the final day. This high standard of attainment reflects the continuing improvement in Rules knowledge amongst those studying golf in China.

The practical examination on the final day was conducted in English only. Of the 30 that qualified to take the Exam, 14 achieved the national "A" certification. The delight of those passing the national "A" certification was evident as these delegates will now go on to referee at national events across China, including professional Tour events.

# Index

Fishwick Hall, 758
Five Lakes Resort, 744
Five Nations CC, 844
Fjällbacka, 890
Flackwell Heath, 730
Flamborough Head, 791
Flamingo Golf Course, 903
Flanders Nippon Hasselt, 845
Fleetlands, 748
Fleetwood, 758
Flempton, 778
Flevoland, 876
Flixton, 764
Flommens, 886
Florentin-Gaillac, 860
Floresta Parque, 878
Föhr, 862
Föhrenwald, 842
Folgaria, 871
Folke Golf Club, 741
Fontainebleau, 854
Fontana, 842
Fontanals de Cerdanya, 881
Fontcaude, 855
Fontenailles, 854
Fontenelles, 855
Forest Hill, 761
Forest Hills, 746
Forest Hills CC, 911
Forest of Dean, 746
Forest of Galtres, 792
Forest Park, 792
Forest Pines Hotel & Golf Resort, 762
Golf Hotel Club de la Forêt d'Orient, 856
Forêt Verte, 856
Forfar, 815
Forges-les-Bains, 854
Formby, 765
Formby Hall Golf Resort & Spa, 765
Formby Ladies', 765
Forres, 829
Forrest Little, 804
Forrester Park, 744
Forsbacka, 890
Forsgårdens, 885
Fort Augustus, 825
Fort William, 825
Fortrose & Rosemarkie, 825
Fortwilliam, 800
Fosseway CC, 775
Fota Island Resort, 801
Foulford Inn, 830
Four Marks, 748
Fourqueux, 857
Four Seasons (Hualalai, Lanai and Maui), 895
Four Seasons Aviara, 894
Four Seasons Scottsdale, 894
Fox Harb'r Resort, 894
Foxbridge, 785
Foxhills, 780
Foyle, 808
Frame Trophy, 355
France, amateur golf, 449
Franciacorta, 870
Frankfield, 801
Frankfurter Golf Club, 861
Fränkische Schweiz, 865
Franklin Templeton Shootout, 189
Fraserburgh, 813
Frassanelle, 873
Fray Bentos GC, 899
Frederikssund, 847
Frégate, 858
Freiburg, 868
French Closed Amateur Championship, 315
French Closed Championship, 399
French Lick Resort, 895
French Mid-Amateur Championship, 315
French Open Stroke Play Championship, 315
Freshwater Bay, 753
La Freslonnière, 851
Frilford Heath, 773
Frinton, 744
Frodsham, 733
Frome, 775
Le Fronde, 872
Frösåker Golf & Country, 884
Frys.com Open, 188
Fulda Rhoen, 861
Fulford (York) Golf Club, 792
Fulford Heath, 790
Fullerö, 884
Fulneck, 796
Fulwell, 767
Funäsdalsfjällen, 885
Furesø, 847
Furnas Golf Course, 878
Furness, 737
Fürstlicher Golfclub Waldsee, 868
Golf Club Fürth e.V., 865
Furzeley, 748
Fynn Valley, 778
Fyvie, 814


## G


Gaash CC, 904
Gaekwad Baroda GC, 907
Gageun GC, 908
Gaichel, 873
Gainsborough, 762
Gairloch, 825
Galashiels, 818
Galgorm Castle, 799
Gällivare-Malmberget, 885
Galway, 806
Galway Bay Golf Resort, 806
Ganay, 852
Ganstead Park, 792
Ganton, 792
Gap-Bayard, 858
Gardagolf CC, 871
Gardengolf Metz, 856
Garesfield, 786
Garforth, 796
Garlenda, 871
Garmisch-Partenkirchen, 864
Garmouth & Kingston, 830
Garnant Park, 833
Garon Park Golf Complex, 744
Gary Player CC, 902
Gassan Khuntan Golf & Resort, 911
Gatehouse, 819
Gathurst, 758
Gatley, 733
Gatton Manor Hotel & Golf Club, 780
Gäuboden, 865
Gavea Golf & Country Club, 898
Gävle, 886
Gay Hill, 790
Le Geant at Mont Tremblant, 894
Gedney Hill, 762
Geijsteren G & CC, 875
Gelpenberg, 876
Geneva, 891
Gentle Uptown GC, 905
George GC, 902
Germany, amateur golf, 450
German International Amateur Championship, 315
German International Women's Amateur Championship, 399
German National Championship, 315
German Women's Championship, 399
Gerrards Cross, 730
Ghyll, 758
Giant's Ridge, 895
Giez, 859
Gifford, 827
Gifhorn, 863
Gigha, 816
Gilleleje, 847
Gillingham, 754
Gingko Lake International GC, 906
I Girasoli, 872
Girls Home Internationals, 464
Gisborne, 913
Golf Girona, 881
Girton, 731
Girvan, 817
Glades, 912
Glamorganshire, 838
Glasgow, 824
Glasgow GC Gailes Links, 817
Glasson Country House Hotel and Golf Club, 811
Glebe, 809
Gleddoch, 831
Glen (North Berwick), 827
Glen Gorse, 761
Glen of the Downs, 812
Glenbervie, 832
Glencorse, 828
Glencruitten, 816
Glencullen, 804
Glendower GC, 901
The Gleneagles Hotel, 830
Gleneagles Scottish PGA Championship, 236
Glengarriff, 801
Glenisla, 830
Glenlo Abbey, 806
Glenmalure, 812
Glenmuir PGA Professional Championship, 235
Glenrothes, 821
Gloria Golf, 892
Glossop & District, 738
The Gloucestershire, 746
Gloucester Golf & Country Club, 746
Glyfada Golf Club of Athens, 869
Glyn Abbey, 833
Glynhir, 833
Glynneath, 838
Goal Farm Par Three, 780
The Gog Magog, 731

## S

There are many people to thank for their help in the publication of *The R&A Golfer's Handbook* 2014 not least our printer Mick Card who, single-handedly, did so much work to ensure that this latest edition was delivered on time. His daughter Paula Taylor dealt as expertly with the clubs section of this latest edition.

Michael Aitken helped enormously with the editorial content and Who's Who and I am grateful to all the other top British journalists – Derek Lawrenson, James Corrigan, John Hopkins, Bill Elliott, Alistair Tait, Lewine Mair and Mark Garrod along with Peter Stone from Australia who found time to write or help with statistics for what is a unique annual golfing global record of amateur and professional golf.

Former Tour player and now top commentator Warren Humphreys allowed us to make use of his extensive on-line statistics and David Cannon and Rob Harborne of Getty Images provided invaluable help with the photographs.

Alan and Heather Elliott looked after the amateur results and the addresses and contact numbers of national and international associations while Vicky Lamb and Debbie Heggarty were tirelessly helpful and cheery in the office.

Professional advice and encouragement was provided readily by Michael Tate, Executive Director of Business Affairs for The R&A for which I was very grateful during some uncertain times.

I hope you enjoy this year's edition.

Renton Laidlaw, Editor
December 2013